The
CHELSEA HOUSE LIBRARY
of LITERARY CRITICISM

The
CHELSEA HOUSE LIBRARY
of LITERARY CRITICISM

TWENTIETH-CENTURY
AMERICAN LITERATURE

Volume 5

General Editor

HAROLD BLOOM

1987
Chelsea House Publishers
New York
New Haven   Philadelphia

MANAGING EDITOR
S. T. Joshi

ASSOCIATE EDITORS
Peter Cannon
Patrick Nielsen Hayden
Teresa Nielsen Hayden
Beth Heinsohn
Edith Jarolim

EDITORIAL COORDINATOR
Karyn Gullen Browne

EDITORIAL STAFF
Marie Claire Cebrian
Richard Fumosa
Anthony Guyda
Perry King

BIOGRAPHER
Anthony C. Coulter

PICTURE RESEARCH
Susan B. Hamburger

DESIGN
Susan Lusk

Printed and bound in the United States of
America.

Library of Congress Cataloging in Publication
Data

Twentieth-century American literature.
   (The Chelsea House library of literary
   criticism)
   Includes bibliographies and indexes.
   1. American literature—20th century—
History and criticism—Collected works.
2. Authors, American literature—20th
century—biography—Dictionaries. I. Bloom,
Harold. II. Series.
PS221.T834 1985   810'.9'005
84-27430
ISBN 0-87754-801-3 (v. 1)
ISBN 0-87754-805-6 (v. 5)
Acknowledgments for selections used in this
volume commence on page 3207

CONTENTS

The Index to this series, *Twentieth-Century American Literature*, appears in Volume 8.

ABBREVIATIONS

AQ	Arizona Quarterly	*NL*	New Leader
ArtN	Artnews	*NR*	New Republic
AS	American Scholar	*NS*	New Statesman
At	Atlantic	*Nwk*	Newsweek
BF	Book Forum	*NY*	New Yorker
Bkm	Bookman	*NYEP*	New York Evening Post
CC	Christian Century	*NYRB*	New York Review of Books
Cmty	Commentary	*NYT*	New York Times
CoL	Contemporary Literature	*NYTBR*	New York Times Book Review
Com	Commonweal	*Pai*	Paideuma
CQ	Critical Quarterly	*Parn*	Parnassus: Poetry in Review
CR	Chicago Review	*PR*	Partisan Review
Critn	Criterion	*QRL*	Quarterly Review of Literature
DelR	Delta Review	*Ren*	Renascence
EJ	English Journal	*Shen*	Shenandoah
Enc	Encounter	*SN*	Studies in the Novel
Expl	Explicator	*Spec*	Spectator
GR	Georgia Review	*SR*	Saturday Review
HC	Hollins Critic	*SSF*	Studies in Short Fiction
HdR	Hudson Review	*SwR*	Sewanee Review
IR	Iowa Review	*TLS*	Times Literary Supplement
KR	Kenyon Review	*TM*	Theatre Magazine
Lon	London Magazine	*TriQ*	TriQuarterly
LT	Listener	*VLS*	Voice Literary Supplement
MPS	Modern Poetry Studies	*VQR*	Virginia Quarterly Review
MQ	Mississippi Quarterly	*WLT*	World Literature Today
MR	Massachusetts Review	*WR*	Western Review
NeR	New Review	*YR*	Yale Review
NHQ	New Hungarian Quarterly		

ILLUSTRATIONS

JAMES MERRILL

1926–

James Ingram Merrill, poet, novelist, and playwright, was born in New York in 1926. He was educated at the Lawrenceville School in New Jersey and then at Amherst College in Massachusetts, from which he graduated in 1947. He has traveled widely, particularly in Greece and Italy, and has taught at several American universities. He has lived in Stonington, Connecticut, since 1956.

Merrill began writing poetry early; while he was still at Lawrenceville his father, as a surprise, arranged for the private publication of *Jim's Book*, a collection of stories and poems written when Merrill was a teenager. This was followed in 1946 by another privately printed book, *The Black Swan*, a collection of poems the best of which were reprinted in *First Poems*, published in 1951. This latter work was a widely reviewed and generally well received collection, although Louise Bogan attacked the poems for being "as frigid and dry as diagrams."

In 1956 Merrill published *The Immortal Husband*, a prose play based on the myth of Aurora and Tithonus, which was followed in 1957 by his first novel, *The Seraglio*, about an elderly businessman's involvement with women. His second collection of poems, *The Country of a Thousand Years of Peace*, was released in 1959; these poems had something of the same mannered diction that characterized much of his earlier work, but were more relaxed in tone.

Merrill's second play, *The Bait*, appeared in 1960, and in 1962 a further book of poems was published; this collection, *Water Street*, was followed in 1965 by a second novel, *The (Diblos) Notebook*, about a young American author trying to write a novel about his experiences in Greece. A fourth collection of poems, *Nights and Days* (1966), won the National Book Award. This was followed by several others, including *The Fire Screen* (1969), *Braving the Elements* (1972), and *The Yellow Pages* (1974).

In 1976, Merrill published the *Divine Comedies*, which won a Pulitzer Prize; the greater part of the *Divine Comedies* consists of a long narrative poem "The Book of Ephraim," which was eventually combined with *Mirabell* (1978) and *Scripts from the Pageant* (1980) to produce a trilogy released in one volume in 1982 as *The Changing Light at Sandover*. This fantastically long poetic opus, to which Merrill added a coda, is in excess of five hundred pages and was composed with the aid of a Ouija board. *From the First Nine Poems*, another collection, was released at the same time. Merrill's most recent work is *Late Settings*, published in 1985.

Merrill's mature poems have generally been praised for their mastery of varied forms and for their subtle use of rhythm.

Personal

JAMES MERRILL
Interview by Helen Vendler

New York Review of Books, May 3, 1979, pp. 12–13

Helen Vendler: When you called your last book *Divine Comedies*, did you mean by that allusion to Dante that you were planning a trilogy?

James Merrill: Not consciously. I'd convinced myself that "The Book of Ephraim" told everything I had to say about the "other world." Because of its length and looniness I'd taken to calling *it* the Divine Comedy—not of course a usable title, until David Jackson thought of making it plural. Dante, subtler as always, let posterity affix the adjective.

HV: In your new book [*Mirabell: Books of Number*], you say there will be one more volume in this vein; after that you will be permitted to return to your "chronicles of love and loss." These three books have all been based on Ouija-board material. Is there anything else that unites them, in general, and that separates them from your earlier poetry?

JM: Chiefly, I think, the—to me—unprecedented way in which the material came. Not through flashes of insight, wordplay, trains of thought. More like what a friend, or stranger, might say over a telephone. DJ and I never knew until it had been spelled out letter by letter. What I felt about the material became a natural part of the poem, corresponding to those earlier poems written "all by myself."

HV: In "The Book of Ephraim," the first book, we heard the voices of the dead; but in *Mirabell* nonhuman voices are added, telling a complicated tale of evolutionary history, molecular biology, and subatomic behavior. Would you like to talk about the books you read before creating your phantasmagoria of "science"? (You mention *The Lives of a Cell*, and looking at a model of the double helix.)

JM: They weren't many. The simplest science book is over my head. At college I'd seen my dead frog's limbs twitch under some applied stimulus or other—seen, but hadn't believed. Didn't dream of thinking beyond or around what I saw. Oh, I picked up a two-volume *Guide to Science* by Asimov—very useful, still, each time I forget how the carbon atom is put together, or need to shake my head over elemental tables. A book on the black holes. Arthur Young's *Reflexive Universe*—fascinating but too schematic to fit into *my* scheme. The most I could hope for was a sense of the vocabulary and some possible images.

HV: Do you think the vocabulary, models, and concepts of science—cloning, DNA, carbon bonds, the ozone layer, protons, etc.—offer real new resources to poetry? So far, poets haven't seemed inclined to see poetry and science as compatible, even though Wordsworth thought they should.

JM: The vocabulary can be perfectly ghastly ("polymerization," "kink instability") or unconsciously beautiful, like things a child says ("red shift," "spectral lines"). Knowing some Greek helped defuse forbidding words—not that I counted much on using them. You'll find only trace elements of this language in the poem. The images, the concepts? Professor Baird at Amherst gave a course in "Science and Literature" which showed how much the "ideas" depended on metaphor, ways of talking. And while Science may have grown more "imaginative"—or at least more "apocalyptic"—in the decades since I left school, how many writers in that, or any, field are really wise to the ways of the word? Lewis Thomas is an exception—if only he would give us more than snippets. I'd like to think the scientists need us—but do they? Did Newton need Blake?

HV: What would you especially like a reader to be caught up by in your trilogy? The density of your myths? The civilized love of conversation? The range in tone? The domesticity?

JM: For me the talk and the tone—alone with the elements of plot—are the candy coating. The pill itself is another matter. The reader who can't swallow it has my full sympathy. I've choked on it again and again.

HV: The new mythology you've invented via the Ouija board—including the new God Biology, a universal past including Atlantis, Centaurs, and Angels, an afterlife which includes reincarnation—how real does it all seem to you?

JM: Literally, not very—except in recurrent euphoric hours when it's altogether too beautiful not to be true. Imaginatively real? I would hope so, but in all modesty, for the imagination in question kept assuming proportions broader and grander than mine. Also at times sillier; Atlantis, UFOs? I climbed the wall trying to escape that sort of material. But the point remained, to be always of two minds.

HV: In the past, you've written fiction as well as lyrics. Does the trilogy satisfy your narrative impulse as much as your fiction did? Or more?

JM: Before trying a novel I wrote a couple of plays. (The Artists' Theater—John Myers and Herbert Machiz—put them on in the Fifties.) Behind them lay one of my earliest literary thrills: to open a little Samuel French booklet, some simpleminded "play for children," and find on the page a fiction made up of stage directions more suggestive than any rendered narrative scene, and of words set down to be spoken by a real, undreamed-of mouth—my own if I wished! The effect was somehow far more naked, far less quilted, than the nicely written stories I fell asleep to. Twenty years later, I confused an exercise in dramatic form with "writing for the theater"—that royal road to megalomania. But those two plays left me on fresh terms with language. I didn't always have to speak in my own voice.

HV: Does the quartet activating the poem—you and David Jackson at the Ouija board, W. H. Auden and Maria Mitsotaki on the other side—make up a family constellation? Why do you think the poem needed a ghostly father and ghostly mother?

JM: Strange about parents. We have such easy access to them and such daunting problems of communication. Over the Ouija board it was just the other way. A certain apparatus was needed to get in touch—but then! Affection, understanding, tact, surprises, laughter, tears. Why the *poem* needed Wyston and Maria I'm not sure. Without being Dante, can I think of them as Virgil and Beatrice?

HV: The intense affection that binds you to your familiar spirit Ephraim, to dead friends, and even to the inhuman Bat-Angel you talk to in the new book, seems the quality celebrated and even venerated in the poem. Do you see this as a change from your earlier poems about your family and about love?

JM: In life, there are no perfect affections. Estrangements among the living reek of unfinished business. Poems get written *to* the person no longer reachable. Yet, once dead, overnight the shrewish wife becomes "a saint," frustrations vanish at cockcrow, and from the once fallible human mouth come words of blessed reassurance. Your question looks down into smoking chasms and up into innocent blankness. Given the power—without being Orpheus, either—would I bring any of these figures back to earth?

HV: If it's true that every poem, besides saying something about life, says something about poetry, what is this new form saying about itself?

JM: Something possibly to do with the doubleness of its source, spelled out on every page by the interplay between the spirits' capitals and our own lower-case responses. Julian Jaynes's book on the "bicameral mind" came out last year. Don't ask me to paraphrase his thesis—but, reading Jaynes as I was finishing *Mirabell*, I rather goggled. Because the poem is set by and large in two adjacent rooms: a domed red one where we took down the messages, and a blue one, dominated by an outsize mirror, where we reflected upon them.

HV: The predecessors you have in mind seem to be Dante, Yeats, and Auden. Do you think of yourself as in any way distinctively American? Or of this poem as in any active relation to American literature and American culture?

JM: I feel American in Europe and exotic at home—and haven't we our own "expatriate" tradition for that? I was about to suggest—until I recalled *The Anathemata* and John Heath-Stubbs's wonderful *Artorius*—that the long, "impossible" poem was an American phenomenon in our day. The thought didn't comfort me. How many of us get out of our cars when we hit the badlands in the Cantos, or take that detour through downtown *Paterson*? In such a context, "foreignness" would be the storyteller's rather than the missionary's concern for his reader's soul.

HV: How did the poem get transcribed and composed? The work of transcription alone must have been enormous.

JM: The board goes along at a smart clip, perhaps 600 words an hour. Sometimes it was hard to reconstruct *our* words—"What was the question?" as Miss Stein put it. Then what to cut? What to paraphrase? What to add? Plus the danger of flatness when putting into verse a passage already coherent in prose. I could have left it in prose, but it would have been too sensational—like Castaneda, or Gwendolyn's diary [in *The Importance of Being Earnest*].

HV: Couldn't you have written without the help of the Ouija board, since it all comes out of your "word bank"? If not, why do you suppose the Ouija board is indispensable, in terms of the workings of your imagination?

JM: (a) It would seem not. (b) You could think of the board as a delaying mechanism. It spaces out, into time and language, what might have come to a saint or a lunatic in one blinding ZAP. Considering the amount of detail and my own limitations, it must have been the most workable method. And, as I have said, it's made me think twice about the imagination. If the spirits aren't external, how astonishing the mediums become! Victor Hugo said of *his* voices that they were like his own mental powers multiplied by five.

HV: Can you tell yet what the last book of the trilogy will be like? What the ending of the whole will be?

JM: Oh yes. Forgive me if I don't go into it here. It should be out next year; I'm calling it *Scripts for the Pageant*. Full of surprises—it had *us* on the edge of our chairs. Naturally it was all "down" before I began to write, so that there were no false starts or agonizing decisions. I woke up day after day beaming with anticipation.

HV: Does Auden like the lines you've written for him to speak?

JM: It's true, I've put *some* words into his mouth, but not those. Shall we say, I like the lines he's given me to write?

JAMES MERRILL
"Condemned to Write about Real Things"

New York Times Book Review, February 21, 1982, pp. 11, 33

Interior spaces, the shape and correlation of rooms in a house, have always appealed to me. Trying for a blank mind, I catch myself instead revisiting a childhood bedroom on Long Island. Recently, on giving up the house in Greece where I'd lived for much of the previous 15 years, it wasn't so much the fine view it commanded or the human comedies it has witnessed that I felt deprived of; rather, I missed the hairpin turn of the staircase underfoot, the height of our kitchen ceiling, the low door ducked through in order to enter a rooftop laundry room that had become my study. This fondness for given arrangements might explain how instinctively I took to quatrains, to octaves and sestets, when I began to write poems: "Stanza" is after all the Italian word for "room."

Foreign languages entered my life early in the person of my governess. Although we called her Mademoiselle she was not a spinster but a widow. Neither was she French, or even, as she led us to believe, Belgian, but part English and part, to her undying shame, Prussian. She had lived in Brussels at least, and her sister who now taught music in Pennsylvania, had been decorated for playing duets with the old Queen Mother of Belgium. Mademoiselle's maiden name was Fanning. This meant some distant kinship with the explorer who discovered—I can see her finger poised above the open atlas—*those* tiny Pacific islands, and whose house a block away from mine in Stonington, Conn., I would be able to point out to her when she spent a day with me 30 years later.

I worshiped this kind, sad woman: her sensible clothes, her carrot hair and watery eyes, the sunburnt triangle at her throat, the lavender wen on her wrist. She taught me to say the Ave Maria and to sing Carmen's "Habanera." I got by heart the brother heroically dead, the sister in Johnstown, the other sister in Copenhagen. I resolved as soon as I gew up to marry her daughter, Stella, at that age plain and rather disagreeable, who was boarded out to a refined Catholic family in East Hampton—the light of love suffused even *them*. I heard all there was to hear about Mademoiselle's previous charges and prayed every night to grieve her less than spoilt Constance M. or devilish Peter T. had done. While she talked a needle flashed—costumes for my marionettes. Stories that ten years later would have convulsed me I drank in solemnly. For instance: Having to relieve herself at a border checkpoint during the war, Mademoiselle had overlaid the *"infecté"* toilet seat with some family letters she happened to be carrying in her purse. In the course of the "formalities" her innocent buttocks were bared by a uniformed matron and found to be stenciled with suspicious mirror writing, which triggered a long and humiliating interrogation. "Figure-toi!" she exclaimed, gravely fixing me through her gold-rimmed spectacles. I could indeed imagine. I too was being imprinted, there and then.

By the time I was eight I had learned from her enough French and German to understand that English was merely one of many ways to express things. A single everyday object could be called *assiette* or *Teller* as well as *plate*—or were plates themselves subtly different in France and Germany? Mademoiselle's French and Latin prayers seemed to invoke absolutes beyond the ken of our Sunday school pageants. At the same time, I was discovering how the everyday sounds of English could mislead you by having more than one meaning. One afternoon at home I opened a random book and read: "Where is your husband, Alice?" "In the library, sampling the port." If samples were little squares of wallpaper or chintz, and ports were where ships dropped anchor, this hardly clarified the behavior of Alice's husband. Long after Mademoiselle's exegesis the phrase haunted me. Words weren't what they seemed. The mother tongue could inspire both fascination and distrust.

But back to those octaves and sestets. Words might frustrate me, forms never did, neither did meter. Children in my day were exposed to a good deal of competent verse. Every first grader at St. Bernard's memorized his hundred lines of Walter Scott and received an apple for so doing. Before graduation he would speak deathless poetry in the annual Shakespeare play. The masters somehow let meaning take care of itself, a chip borne along by the rhetorical surge. Accordingly frustration was reserved for the content, or lack of it, in what I'd begun to write at boarding school. Gerrish Thurber, the mild and merciful librarian who "advised" the young editors of the *Lawrenceville Lit*, read through my first submission and nodded, saying only, "We can always use a well-made sonnet." It took me a while to fathom what he hadn't said.

My classmate Frederick Beuchner wrote his poem first. In a flash I thought: I can do that too! And away we went. Luckily perhaps, since it allowed us to polish without much thought for what (if anything) we were communicating, our callowness led us to second-rate, *fin de siècle* stuff—Wilde, Hérédia, Alice Meynell. These writers didn't figure in the Lawrenceville curriculum, although they met its chief requirement by having died. The living poets (unlike Milton or Keats, on whom white-haired Mr. Raymond had given us the last sonorous word) were still scandalously eluding definition in the pages of anthologies never seen in the classroom. Would our style ever mature? Or rather, dripping and sugary, would it ever unripen? Long after Freddy had gone on to Blake and Whitman, I dawdled behind with Elinor Wylie and the gaudier bits in Baudelaire.

On the threshold of our senior year the *Lit's* graduating editor summoned his two least trustworthy successors. Sucking at a pipe, this man of 18 urged us to recant. "Write about *real things* for God's sake: blondes and pistons!"—fetishes no less conventional than the moonlit foliage, masquerades, mad crones and pet monkeys that clotted our own poems and stories. We left his room with scornful smiles.

The airs I was giving myself ran in the family. My father had offered his Aunt Grace the sum, unheard-of in those Depression years, of $5 a page for memoirs of her Mississippi girlhood. She couldn't do it; the truth froze her pen. Not that she stopped writing. One summer a flier came in the mail from a vanity press in New York, announcing Aunt Grace's novel, *Femme Fatale*, "set against the turbulent background of the French court, this tale of searing passion. . . ." My mother and I, alone that year and needing diversion, at once ordered our copy—several copies: Christmas was coming. Before it did, German troops overran a real France Aunt Grace wouldn't have crossed the street to see, and *Femme Fatale* was never published or our money refunded.

Like Aunt Grace, and like many adolescents, I needed to feel that I was fulfilling myself in the face of heartless indifference. In fact my mother was both proud and critical of my early writing. She had taken a summer course in the short story at Columbia, worked on the Jacksonville newspaper and edited until her marriage a weekly gazette of her own. Some satirical doggerel she dashed off about the preparations for my sister's wedding dazzled me, at nine, with its zany, end-stopping rhyming. My father, who could compose long lucid letters in his beautifully rounded hand and read with X-ray eyes the to me impenetrable editorials in *The Herald Tribune*, looked to literature for a good cry. His favorite author was J. M. Barrie—indeed, Alice and her port-sampling husband may be found in Barrie's play *Dear Brutus*. My father had a way of his own with rhyme. Here is how he acknowledged one of my letters when I first went abroad:

> Though we're apart.
> You're in my heart—
> I too love Chartres.

He was also a powerful and unpredictable man, never more so, in my young eyes, than when, pretending to want for his scrapbook the poems and stories I'd written up to then, he had a small edition of them handsomely produced during my senior year at Lawrenceville. *Jim's Book*, as he titled it, thrilled me for days, then mortified me for a quarter-century. I wouldn't put it past my father to have foreseen the furthest consequences of his brilliant, unsettling gesture, which, like the pat on a sleepwalker's back, looked like approbation but was aimed at waking me up.

It partly succeeded: I opened my eyes enough at least to see how much remained to be learned about writing. Presently I was at Amherst, reading Proust, Dante and *Faust* in their various originals, Jane Austen and Pope with Reuben Brower, Shakespeare and Darwin with Theodore Baird. Here also Kimon Friar put before me the living poets and gave the nine-day wonders that shot up like beanstalks from this richest of mulches their first and only detailed criticism. Many hands made light work. Four years after graduation my *First Poems* had appeared, I was living alone and unhappy in Rome and going to a psychiatrist for writer's block.

The doctor wanted to hear about my life. It had been flowing along unnoticed in my absorption with the images that came and went on its surface. Now its very droplets were being studied on a slide. "Real things"—was I condemned to write about them, after all?

Of course I had been doing nothing else. Symbolist pastiche or makeshift jotting, our words reveal more than we think. The diary kept during my first year away at school reports a Christmas-break visit to Silver Springs, Fla. I'd like to go back there one day and ride again in the glass-bottomed boat, peering down at the cold pastoral of swaying grasses and glinting schools. There would be much to say about "unconscious depths," about my zodiacal creature the Fish, above all about the heavy pane of glass that, like a kind of intelligence, protected me and my mother from that sunken world while revealing its secrets in magical detail. But in 1940 the artless diarist records only this: "Silver Springs—heavenly colors and swell fish."

Two banalities, each by itself bad enough, and hopelessly so in conjunction. Yet in their simple awfulness they broach the issue most crucial to this boy not quite fourteen. Two years earlier my parents have been divorced and Mademoiselle amicably sent packing: I am thought to need "a man's influence." We hear how children suffer under these circumstances. I am no exception, my grades plummet, I grow fat gorging on sweets. "Heavenly colors and swell fish." What is that phrase but an attempt to bring my parents together, to remarry on the page their characteristic inflections—the ladylike gush and the regular-guy terseness? In reality my parents have tones more personal and complex than these, but the time is still far off when I can dream of echoing them. To do so, I see in retrospect, will involve a search for magical places real or invented, like Silver Springs or Sandover, acoustical chambers so designed as to endow the weariest platitude with resonance and depth. By then, too, surrogate parents will enter the scene, figures more articulate than Mademoiselle but not unlike her, either, in the safe ease and mystery of their influence: Proust and Elizabeth Bishop; Maria and Auden in the Sandover books. The unities of home and world, and world and page, will be observed through the very act of transition from one to the other.

General

DAVID KALSTONE
From "James Merrill: Transparent Things"
Five Temperaments
1977, pp. 77–83

> Toy ukelele, terrorstruck
> Chord, the strings so taut, so few—
> Tingling I hugged my pillow. *Pluck*
> Some deep nerve went. I knew
>
> That life was fiction in disguise.
> ("Days of 1935")

A child's dream, gaily recalled in James Merrill's "Days of 1935," is one of the best introductions to his work. Not that the motto "Life was fiction in disguise" can be extracted harmlessly, like an infant tooth, from this poem, a modern ballad, both mysterious and disingenuous in tone. The ballad's neat appetite for experience almost shrugs away what others raise their voices to assert. Still the tantalizing proposition remains. Many of Merrill's poems, weightier than "Days of 1935," return to fictions believed in childhood, later fleshed out by life: "Lost in Translation," "Matinees," "Chimes for Yahya," "The Broken Home." It is one of the things which makes his writing about himself so different from Robert Lowell's. A continuing access to childhood memories and insights nourishes Merrill's verse; with Lowell, the memories are most often terrifying and unavailing.

In Merrill's "Days of 1935" a child dreams of being kidnapped by Floyd and Jean, a gunman and his gum-chewing moll, rough parodies of Bonnie and Clyde. Their peculiar combination of fairy-tale and silver-screen glamor makes the child hope that he will never be ransomed. More than that, the openly exotic and erotic ménage transforms his bed on the floor into a magic carpet.

> The rag rug, a rainbow threadbare,
> Was soft as down. For good or bad
> I felt her watching from her chair
> As no one ever had.

Someone watching him, someone to watch: he spends a whole day telling fairy tales to the astonished Jean, himself astonished. "I stared at her—*she* was the child!" With Floyd and Jean the whole forbidden parental world is exposed to eye and ear:

> One night I woke to hear the room
> Filled with crickets—no, bedsprings.

My eyes dilated in the gloom,
My ears made out things.
Jean: The kid, he's still awake . . .
Floyd: Time he learned . . . Oh baby . . .
    God . . .
Their prone tango, for my sake,
Grew intense and proud.
And one night—pure "Belshazzar's Feast"
When the slave-girl is found out—
She cowered, face a white blaze ("Beast!")
From his royal clout.

Fantasies fulfilled, a star-struck child learns what romance violence stands for, and makes the inevitable connections with the tensions behind the etched, hieratic world of his parents:

Photographs too. My mother gloved,
Hatted, bepearled, chin deep in fur.
Dad glowering—was it true he loved
Others beside her?

Eerie, speaking likenesses.
One positively heard her mild
Voice temper some slow burn of his,
"Not before the child."

The daytime world to which he eventually returns is two-dimensional, by comparison with his red-blooded imaginings. His parents' guests, in a series of brilliant puns, are rendered as cartoon cut-outs, devitalized:

Tel & Tel executives,
Heads of Cellophane or Tin,
With their animated wives
Are due on the 6:10.

The energy to see them this way comes from the boy's own discovered vitality, his storytelling powers. The child sees sparks fly across the gap between truth and fiction: his invented kidnappers expose his parents to him in new ways, and allow him, later on in the poem, a glimpse into the indulgences and inhibitions put upon his own erotic life.

Part of the pleasure here lies in reclaiming banner headlines of the 1930s and film fantasies of the 1960s for the psychic life from which they spring. In the ballad form, the secrets of childhood, dreams of conquest and revenge, unfold with the ease and inevitability of nursery rhymes. And through fiction his parents become available to him in ways never possible in life.

That Merrill is writing a kind of autobiography in verse—however different from Lowell's or from so-called "confessional" poetry—becomes clearer with each of his books. "The Book of Ephraim" in *Divine Comedies* is only the most explicit and extended of these efforts. Yet it is also clear that Merrill is not engaged in capturing the raw momentary feel of experience in the present tense (what Lowell claimed to be doing in his first *Notebook*). The poems perform that continuing revision of a poet's life through his work to which many autobiographical writers are committed. But, as "Days of 1935" suggests, Merrill's poems come close to day-to-day living by discovering the fantasies behind our civilized arrangements, our secret links to fiction.

Like Lowell, Merrill has absorbed into verse many of the resources of daily conversation and prose. Still, there is a special strangeness and sometimes strain to Merrill's colloquial style, a taut alertness to the meanings which lurk in apparently casual words and phrases. We may find this in all good poets, but Merrill raises it to a habit of vigilance, a quickened control and poise, sometimes bravado, which he clearly trusts as a source of power. When Merrill uses an idiom, he turns it over

curiously, as if prospecting for ore. So, for example, the dead metaphor "on the rocks" springs unexpectedly to life in this section from "The Broken Home," a poem which anticipates the family strains of "Days of 1935."

When my parents were younger this was a popular
    act:
A veiled woman would leap from an electric, wine-
    dark car
To the steps of no matter what—the Senate or the
    Ritz Bar—
And bodily, at newsreel speed, attack
No matter whom—Al Smith or José Maria Sert
Or Clemenceau—veins standing out on her throat
As she yelled *War mongerer! Pig! Give us the vote!*,
And would have to be hauled away in her hobble
    skirt.

What had the man done? Oh, made history.
Her business (he had implied) was giving birth,
Tending the house, mending the socks.

Always the same old story—
Father Time and Mother Earth,
A marriage on the rocks.

All conversational ease and, at the end, outrageous humor, Merrill's wit allows us momentary relaxation and then plants its sting. This newsreel is one of the central panels of an often saddened and erotically charged work. The cartoon suffragettes and their male oppressors prove more than quaint in the context of a long poem whose speaker is exorcizing the ghosts of a broken home. Behind the gossip columnist's phrase ("on the rocks": shipwreck dismissed as if it were a cocktail) lies a buried colloquial truth about the tensions eternally repeated in a worldly marriage, Father Time and Mother Earth, re-enacted erosions and cross-purposes. Beneath amused glimpses of 1920s bravado, the verse penetrates to parents' energies (both envied and resented) that shape and cripple a child's.

How intensely people used to feel!
Like metal poured at the close of a proletarian novel,
Refined and glowing from the crucible,
I see those two hearts, I'm afraid,
Still. Cool here in the graveyard of good and evil,
They are even so to be honored and obeyed.

Merrill's absorption of prose rhythms and colloquial idioms has something of the structuralist's curiosity behind it, an interest in casual observations which both veil and betray buried feelings. In "Up and Down" Mother and son are alone in a bank vault to inspect her safe-deposit box: "She opens it. Security. Will. Deed." The puns are telling. The wit is there to reveal patterns that vein a life: a precarious and double use of ordinary speech much like the quality Merrill admires in the poetry of the contemporary Italian Montale, some of whose work he has translated. He speaks of Montale's

emotional refinement, gloomy and strongly curbed. It's surprisingly permeable by quite ordinary objects—ladles, hens, pianos, half-read letters. To me he's *the* twentieth-century nature poet. Any word can lead you from the kitchen-garden into really inhuman depths. . . . The two natures were always one, but it takes an extraordinary poet to make us feel that, feel it in our spines.[1]

With this in mind we can begin to understand Merrill's peculiarities as an autobiographical writer: his sense of the dual accountability of poetry to the "two natures," to daily life and to the "really inhuman depths."

Merrill's best poetry from *Water Street* (1962) on is autobiographical in more than accidental and local detail. Figures and places recur. The mother of "Up and Down" is the mother recalled in "The Broken Home" and "Lost in Translation." Kyria Kleo, the Greek maid, returns in "After the Fire" after her introduction in "Days of 1964." "Days of 1935" playfully refers us to "Days of 1971." But the place of narrative detail in Merrill's work is like the timely progress of a love affair behind a sonnet sequence. It is not so much what happens that counts, or the exterior order of events, the frame-by-frame record. It is the cumulative power of specific entrances and exits, the psychic resonance which key figures, places and objects come to possess. The figures who appear and re-appear in Merrill's poems have more substance than the legendary heroines who were muses to the sonneteers, but they also have the same mesmerizing force, as he considers and reconsiders their shaping impact on his life. To reread Merrill's books since *Water Street* is to discover him preparing a stage whose objects and cast of characters become increasingly luminous. They become charged with symbolic meaning and release symbolic reverberations from otherwise ordinary narrative event.

Take this playful insight into the psychopathology of everyday life, "The Midnight Snack," one of the "Five Old Favorites" in *Water Street*:

When I was little and he was riled
It never entered my father's head
Not to flare up, roar and turn red.
Mother kept cool and smiled.

Now every night I tiptoe straight
Through my darkened kitchen for
The refrigerator door—
It opens, the inviolate!

Illumined as in dreams I take
A glass of milk, a piece of cake,
Then stealthily retire,

Mindful of how the gas-stove's black—
Browed pilot eye's blue fire
Burns into my turned back.

The casual tone, the deft rhyming, the detachment of the sonnet, the triviality of the ostensible subject, all play against the real feeling—one small exploration of stolen pleasure in the presence of inhibition. The trick is in the handling of objects, allowing an apparently easy concentration to awaken the presences he feels in such a scene. It is all over before we have time to sort out our sense that wires have been crossed: the association of cold with nourishment and mother; of warmth with anger and father. Merrill hasn't had to resort to that psychic underlining. "You hardly ever need to *state* your feelings. The point is to feel and keep the eyes open. Then what you feel is expressed, is mimed back at you by the scene. A room, a landscape. I'd go a step further. We don't *know* what we feel until we see it distanced by this kind of translation."[2]

Much of Merrill's interest in narrative and everyday experience has been aimed at discovering the charges with which certain objects have become invested for him. He seems in his developed poetry to be asking the Freudian or the Proustian question: what animates certain scenes—and not others—for us? Over the years Merrill's poems have used the objects and stages of daily life, the arrangements of civilized behavior, almost as if he expected to waken sleeping presences and take by surprise the myths he lives by. It is not for nothing that he admires Joyce and Cocteau: "Joyce teaches us to immerse the mythical elements in a well-known setting; Cocteau teaches us to immerse them in a contemporary spoken idiom."[3]

Notes

1. "An Interview with James Merrill," *Contemporary Literature* IX (Winter 1968), p. 5. The interviewer is Donald Sheehan.

2. "The Poet: Private," *Saturday Review/The Arts* (December 2, 1972), p. 45. The interviewer is David Kalstone.
3. *Contemporary Literature*, p. 8.

JUDITH MOFFETT
"Sound without Sense: Willful Obscurity in Poetry"

New England Review, Winter 1980, pp. 294–312

I want to make some general points about poetry which is obscure by the wish and design of the poet, the sort of obscurity resulting from the poet's deliberate choice not to speak his mind, or express his feelings, or describe his experience, plainly. This is, of course, a different case from the obscurity resulting from a poet's inability to express himself clearly, or laziness, or the genuine absence of paraphrasable "content" from his concept of the poem he sets out to write (or discovers he has written).

The issues raised by willful obscurity forced themselves on my attention at an early stage of drafting a critical study of James Merrill's poetry. I was wholeheartedly devoted to most of it. The purposeful obfuscations in some of the rest distressed and affronted me, but why? I was at first far from clear or confident about this: perhaps the reaction was too possessive? Eventually, I decided not. Reluctant as I felt to disapprove seriously of Merrill's poetry in any way at all, my thinking at the time convinced me, and frequent rethinking has not dissuaded me, of the rightness of objecting to those of his poems *meant* to conceal—*meant* neither partially nor wholly to reveal—their meaning, while at the same time revealing that meaning had in fact been built into them.

This essay attempts to explain why that sort of concealment seems to me to be a very bad thing. Though I illustrate it with examples drawn from Merrill's work, I hope the conclusions apply equally to obscurity, when consciously cultivated (or unnecessarily and hence irresponsibly tolerated, for that matter), in anyone's.

Whenever I'm asked to suggest one of James Merrill's books to someone interested in getting to know his work, I mention *Water Street* (1962) or *Nights and Days* (the 1967 National Book Award winner), supposing that the two volumes before *Water Street* would strike most people initially as too ornate and unfeeling and those following *Nights and Days* as too formidable by reason of the poems' density and length. Certainly his Ouija Trilogy is no place to begin! The middle pair seem likeliest to please with the least effort and coaching, the books uninitiates will be least inclined to put down before giving themselves a fair chance to fall under Merrill's spell. And in some ways these two continue to be the most appealing of his books, the most accessible and likable, if not the most ambitious, remarkable, or all-round admirable. *Nights and Days* particularly contains passages beautiful beyond belief; and while masks as subject-matter are central to it, no attempt worth mentioning has been made to armor the poetry heavily in the manner of its presentation. In both decoration concedes to decorum, manner to manners; discretion and courteous reticence enclose / shield / conceal only the source of the emotion Merrill no longer cares to dissociate himself from. And, along with *Divine Comedies* (1976), these two are also the books most consistently courteous to the reader.

But with *The Fire Screen* (1969) and *Braving the Elements* (1972) we are back in deep water. It was usually possible to work out meanings for the difficult poems in the first books, but too often they didn't seem interesting enough to repay the effort. By contrast, many of the difficult later poems of Merrill's first, or pre-Ouija, period obviously *are* interesting—but there may be no way to find out what they mean. The reader no longer confronts a novice poet's impregnable surfaces but a mature artist's dim labyrinthine interiors which appear to lead nowhere and within which one cannot hope to meet the Minotaur. This intention *not* to communicate, occasionally indulged in *The Fire Screen*, is given way to altogether in *Braving the Elements* for some ten of its 73 pages. More problematically, while Merrill has abjured his bejeweling tendencies and fought successfully to overcome them, he has defended the interior obscurity. Here are parts of two poems, one from each book, to keep in mind while considering his apologia:

NIKE

The lie shone in her face before she spoke it.
Moon-battered, cloud-torn peaks, mills, multitudes
Implied. A floating sphere
Her casuist had at most to suck his pen,
Write of *Unrivalled by truth's own*
For it to dawn upon me. Near the gate
A lone iris was panting, purple-tongued.
I thought of my village, of tonight's *Nabucco*
She would attend, according to the lie,
Bemedalled at the royal right elbow. High
Already on entr'act Kummel, hearing as always
Through her ears the sad waltz of the slaves,
I held my breath in pity for the lie
Which nobody would believe unless I did.
Mines (unexploded from the last one) lent
Drama to its rainbow surface tension.
Noon struck. Far off, a cataract's white thread
Kept measuring the slow drop into the gorge.
I thought of his forge and crutch who hobbled
At her prayer earthward. What he touched bloomed.
. . .

(*The Fire Screen*, p. 27)

18 WEST 11TH STREET

In what at least
Seemed anger the Aquarians in the basement
Had been perfecting a device

For making sense to us
If only briefly and on pain
Of incommunication ever after.

Now look who's here. Our prodigal
Sunset. Just passing through from Isfahan.
Filled by him the glass.

Disorients. The swallow-flights
Go word by numbskull word
—Rebellion . . . Pentagon . . . Black Studies—

Crashing into irreality,
Plumage and parasites
Plus who knows what of the reptilian,

Till wit turns on the artificial lights
Or heaven changes. The maid,
Silent, pale as any victim,

Comes in, identifies;
Yet brings new silver, gives rise to the joint,
The presidency's ritual eclipse.
. . .

(*Braving the Elements*, p. 24)

It's common knowledge that Hemingway believed "you could omit anything if you knew that you omitted and the omitted part would strengthen the story and make people feel more than they understood." In stories like "Big Two-Hearted River" that idea worked well; but everything depends on what's omitted, and how much, and even why. When Hemingway did it, he was practicing an aesthetic theory. In Merrill's case,

too, Mallarmé and the French Impressionists provided a precedent; yet it's impossible not to speculate that inclination preceded theory and weighted the conclusions in his case— that things omitted are likely to be things Merrill didn't want known, that aesthetic reasons provided a rationale for personal ones. However sincerely and genuinely Merrill believed in the validity of what he was doing, the effect of his study of Mallarmé would almost certainly have been to confirm rather than to convert.

Poems like the two quoted from above are essentially unintelligible in themselves. All reference points a reader might make use of have been kept, or left, out. The result, but for a sense of the shaping intelligence behind even the darkest view, is like listening to obscenities or importunings being muttered in a language one doesn't understand, or to glossolalia at a Pentecostal meeting: highly emotional gibberish meaningful perhaps to the gibberer (and his interpreters?) but to nobody else. But even these differ from Merrill's practice in their intention. The muttering and the speaking in tongues are open to anyone who hath an ear to hear; they conceal not by their nature or the wish of the speaker but by limitations in the listener. Italian certainly can be learned, the Holy Ghost can probably be experienced; whoever wants to enough can, with effort and time, fit himself to understand. Merrill has written many poems of this sort, including some I would count among his finest work of all. But "Nike" and "18 West 11th Street" belong to an order of poem which is secretive by nature: they have been purposely written in such a way that they cannot, without external assistance, be understood.

It's important to distinguish between this sort of purposeful obscurity and the obscurity of John Ashbery, whose poetry typically appears to be a form of musical composition in which words have the function of notes and convey texture and feeling, without shutting the reader out from some guessed-at dimension of meaning. Ashbery's poetry is often quite literally sound without sense; "Nike" and "18 West 11th Street" only seem to be. Merrill's poems actually *are* "about" something (the Greek coup plus a failing love affair, and a house destroyed by the explosion of a Weatherman bomb, respectively), and the reader can tell they're about something, but not *what* they're about. This has the effect, if surely not the purpose, of teasing, as Ashbery's work does not.

Merrill would not deny much of this, if any, but he has repeatedly rejected the idea that there's anything necessarily dissatisfying about sounds that make no sense. "When I was eleven years old," he has said (in an interview done in 1967 and published in *Contemporary Literature*, Winter 1968), "I began being taken to the opera in New York; and the sense of a feeling that could be expressed without any particular attention to the words must have excited me very much." He adds, "I daren't go into the effects Mrs. Wix would have pounced upon, of the opera on my moral sense. All those passions—illness, ecstasies, deceptions—induced for the pure sake of having something to sing beautifully about." The statement is paraphrased in the sixth sonnet of the sequence "Matinees":

When Jan Kiepura sang His Handsomeness
Of Mantua those high airs light as lust
Attuned one's bare throat to the dagger-thrust.
Living for them would have been death no less.

Or Lehmann's Marschallin!—heartbreak so shrewd,
So ostrich-plumed, one ached to disengage
Oneself from a last love, at center stage,
To the beloved's dazzled gratitude.

What havoc certain Saturday afternoons
Wrought upon a bright young person's morals
I now leave to the public to condemn.

> The point thereafter was to arrange for one's
> Own chills and fever, passions and betrayals,
> Chiefly in order to make song of them.
>
> *(The Fire Screen)*

Working against his own nature, or his own conditioning at least, Merrill had had a difficult time getting Art to imitate Life: "Emerge, O sunbursts, garlands, creatures, men, / Ever more lifelike, out of the white void!" (*Water Street*, p. 55). It follows, perhaps, that to let Life imitate Art would be to flow with the current, not struggle against it—particularly since Life (along with Truth and Reality and all such humorless absolutes) had always seemed artificial anyway and not to be taken at face value. Even the nine-year-old in "Days of 1935" knows "life was fiction in disguise."

The opera analogy is central to Merrill's defense of his deliberate obscurity. He extends the analogy, in the same interview, to French art songs, "where, once more, though most of the words were intelligible, they made no great demands on the intelligence. It was only the extreme beauty of the musical line that was spellbinding. . . . The point about music and song is that theirs is the sound of sheer feeling—as opposed to that of sense, of verbal sense." (He adds, almost as an afterthought: "To combine the two is always worth dreaming about.") A later interview (*Saturday Review*, December 2, 1972) pursues the issue of sound and sense. The poem in question is "Yánnina", published in *Braving the Elements*; Merrill says:

> I'd wanted to let the scene, the succession of scenes, convey not meaning so much as a sense of it, a sense that something both is, and isn't, being said. I hoped that a reader's own experience would remind him that some things can go without saying. I was trying for an intimacy of tone, not of content. People are always asking, Was it real? Did it happen? . . . As if a yes-or-no answer would settle the question. Was it really Yánnina I went to? Was my companion real or imaginary? I can only say yes *and* no to questions like that.

There are problems, however, in the way the theory has sometimes been put into practice. In general I think the success or failure of this "intimacy of tone, not of content"—not just in Merrill's but in all poetry—can be determined by how it measures up against the following principle: Give the reader enough intimacy of any kind—enough of oneself in whatever form—and he will acquiesce; give him too little and he will be resentful. The investment must be personal, the consequence interpersonal. A poet need not after all write Poe's hypothetical little book "My Heart Laid Bare," or be the Whitman of "Crossing Brooklyn Ferry"; he may make himself available in a qualified, limited way, on his own terms (and Merrill does, more often than not); but something of himself *must* be made available, the nervous impulse must spark across the synapse, however fantastically disguised.

It seems that if the music is beautiful enough, the one who listens to the opera or poem won't care greatly what was sung, or mind being moved in ways he can't explain, so long as he *is* moved. Or make the "poetic" elements less compelling and tell him more; again he's reached and affected, and all will be well. As Helen Vendler observed in a review of *Braving the Elements* (*New York Times Book Review*, September 24, 1972), "without once mentioning his personal griefs in the odes, Keats made us know them almost by heart"; to be inexplicit isn't necessarily to be hermetic. Stephen Spender, in a review of the same book (*New York Review of Books*, September 20, 1972)— the book in which Merrill has been most permissive with his urge toward interior darkness—wrote that "the subjects of his poems (which can be very obscure) are really only excuses for the very rich harvest of a purely poetic—imagistic, allusive, word-jocular—world," and any of that may do instead of sense *or* music. Experience repeatedly confirms Eliot's observation in his essay on Dante, that "genuine poetry can communicate before it is understood." The difficulty comes when neither music, nor material, nor verbal energy, nor anything else, does communicate adequately from writer to reader, where the reader cannot feel in any meaningful sense that who touches this book, touches a man.

Since the exquisite craftsman Merrill long since developed into can do anything he likes—is in that way incapable of finishing and publishing a "bad" poem, one that has eluded his own purpose for it—what sort of attitude toward the reader is implied in his publishing some poems not directed toward and therefore not available to that reader on *any* level, not even the most superficial, despite whatever amount of independent effort? To answer this, it will be helpful to consider the shape of Merrill's development from the secretive, insecure young author of *First Poems* to the much more relaxed and confident poet of the middle books, whose voice divided thereafter for a time both into unprecedented openness and into an obscurity so extreme as to reveal an apparent indifference to all but the *perfect* reader, and who found still later that the nature of his material (in the Trilogy) required him to speak plainly about matters theretofore carefully concealed.

Most reviewers responded to Merrill's first two books with conscientious respect for his obvious gifts, yet without liking. His difficulty continues to make him a poet many readers acquire a taste for slowly if at all. Merrill must have known for many years that he couldn't ever hope for a large *popular* following. What he was most interested in doing and did most brilliantly was too cerebral to have wide appeal, and in fact the cerebral elements, the complexities of theme and symbol, the word-play, waxed dazzlingly as the coldness and decorativeness waned. His sensibilities are too rarefied, his vocabulary too copious, and his intelligence too high and too evident; and besides all this he has been—as a "neo-formalist" and "academic" poet—out of step all along with the Projectivist, Subjectivist, and Expressionist drummers, the champions of organic form, to whose beat most of his contemporaries have marched. Popularity, even of the modest sort that modern poets have sometimes enjoyed, was out of the question, if achievement and recognition in learned quarters were not. A like realization aggravated from Alfred Steiglitz his famous remark that "art is for the few, and by the few."

Any lingering doubt on this point would have been disposed of by the *New York Times* editorial of January 16, 1973, provoked by his having been awarded the Bollingen Prize for his "wit and delight in language, his exceptional craft. . . ." The *Times* complained, not that Merrill was himself undeserving of the prize, but about the Yale Library's continuing, year after year, to reward the "fastidious":

"A WORLD WEST OF YALE"

The awarding of the Bollingen Prize for Poetry, one of the richest and most prestigious in the nation, to James Merrill underlines once again the tendency of the administrator of the prize, the Yale Library, to reward poetry that is literary, private, traditional. Two decades have passed since an exception was made in the case of William Carlos Williams in 1953.

Mr. Merrill is a poet of solid accomplishment and sure craftsmanship. The quarrel is not with him, but with the Library's insistence down the years that poetry is a hermetic cultivation of one's sensibility and a fastidious manipulation of received forms. The Bollingen people flinch from poetry that is raucous in character or that has an abrasive public sound, from poetry in the Whitman tradition or poetry that is experimental, from the poetry of black writers, much of it now very visible and vocal.

Perhaps the academic grip on the Bollingen ought to be loosened. This is a big and varied land, and there is a whole world west of New Haven that the Yale Library seems to know little about.

That this editorial should have appeared in the *Times*, both arbiter and mirror of educated public taste, is very telling. Richard Howard's rejoinder, published three days later, refuted the letter of the editorial point by point without trying to deny the spirit. It must stand as a hard fact of contemporary life in America that the academic poets may take the prizes but that most people around the country who read poetry, including the many members of the Associated Writing Programs in colleges and universities "west of Yale," like better the very sort this editorial accuses the Bollingen trustees of flinching from. "At its best," writes Louis Simpson in a review of *Divine Comedies*, also published in the *Times* (March 21, 1976), "[Merrill's] writing is exotic and picturesque. The tone of easy, intimate conversation is a stylistic achievement. It is hardly the poet's fault that there are few readers of this kind of poetry."

How has Merrill felt about it all? Would he have liked the larger audience he has declined to court? When David Kalstone put that question to him in a 1972 interview, the answer was:

> When I search my heart, no, not really. So why invite it, even supposing I could? Think what one has to *do* to get a mass audience. I'd rather have one perfect reader. Why dynamite the pond in order to catch that single silver carp? Better to find a bait that only the carp will take.

But "one perfect reader" is at the opposite extreme from "a mass audience"; the choice is not that simple. Merrill has owned that when young he cared very much what other people thought about him and spent a lot of time and energy trying to figure out what they wanted so he could supply it, or be it. Interviews done in 1967 and 1968 (in *Shenandoah*, Summer 1968 issue), five and four years respectively before the *Saturday Review* interview with David Kalstone, both indicate that he felt, then, a sense of responsibility and connectedness with an audience which is missing from the view quoted above. "I think one should try in what one does to charm the reader," he states in the latter, and in the former: "I see no point, often, in the kind of poem that makes every single touch, every syllable, count. It can be a joy to write, but not always to read. You can't forego the whole level of entertainment in art." (An odd and self-effacing thing for him to say, by the way, since a strength of so many—probably most—of his own poems from *The Country of a Thousand Years of Peace* forward, including some of the most successful, has been exactly that every syllable *does* count. Often, indeed, it's *why* they're such a joy to read—the dozenth time round, anyway.) The 1967 interview, in fact, praises Proust for a "real triumph of manners" in his

> extreme courtesy towards the reader, the voice explaining at once formally and intimately. Though it can be heard, of course, as megalomania, there is something wonderful in its desire to be understood, in its treatment of every phenomenon (whether the way someone pronounces a word, or the article of clothing worn, or the color of a flower) as having ultimate importance. Proust says to us in effect, "I will not patronize you by treating these delicate

matters with less than total, patient, sparkling seriousness."

Having been touched himself by these things in Proust, how account for the violence Merrill has done to them in a poem like "18 West 11th Street"? Though the question is in the strictest sense unfair, since "18 West 11th Street" is an extreme rather than a typical example of Merrill's late first-period obscurity and there *are* no other poems quite like it, it does illustrate in an exaggerated way the difficulties inherent generally in this sort of obscurity.

I suggest that at the time he approached "18 West 11th Street" (and the other opaque poems of *Braving the Elements*) Merrill was caught up in a private conflict: he felt the need to talk about something *in a poem*—the sort of need Wallace Stevens was thinking of when he wrote "It is quite possible to have a feeling about the world which creates a need that nothing satisfies except poetry . . ."—but was for his own reasons unwilling to make his meaning clear. He needed to talk, but wished not to be understood. In order to manage that it was necessary to break faith with the reader.

"The reader" I keep alluding to was never, for Merrill, "the general reader"—but neither, originally, was he "one perfect reader." He is a reader serious about poetry and willing to work at it, one who may care as much or more for sound than for sense without being indifferent to sense, and who appreciates Merrill's incomparable grace and wit, his incomparable sweetnesses of style. This reader's heart belongs more to Eliot than to Williams. He probably thinks of a poem as a made artifact, a *work* of art. And it's likely that he also finds himself, like Merrill, at least a bit out of step with the most popular cultural drummers of his, the present, time. Beauty in art, says the aesthetician Eliseo Vivas, is "a character of some things, and in them *present*; but present only in the thing for those endowed with the capacity and the training through which alone it can be perceived" ("The Esthetic Judgment," *Journal of Philosophy*, 1936). Merrill's "reader" views training as appropriate preparation for aesthetic experience.

But it seems that at some point Merrill began to act uncompromisingly on a statement his autobiographical character, Francis Tanning, had made many years before in his first novel, *The Seraglio*: "I refuse to wear myself out trying to meet other peoples' terms"—even "his" reader's generous terms. Several very obscure pieces in *Braving the Elements* ("Yam," "Komboloi," "Under Mars," "Electra," "Black Mesa," as well as "18 West 11th Street") read as though all effort to provide points of access or reference had been renounced. Moreover this group is set to a music too strange to carry the day on its own. These poems are quite incomprehensible except by grace of private knowledge. Yet, curiously, they seem racked by the denied wish to be understood; each might be a locked chest in which a fist pounds ceaselessly on the underside of its lid. But for this a reader might feel differently about them.

Even Vladimir Nabokov, who once referred to his own ideal readers as "little Nabokovs," never went so far. One is struck finally with a conviction that when all's said and done the New Critics had a point: it ought not to be necessary to tear the membrane of a poem in order to make any sense at all of it, or to flay it alive in order to make all of it make sense. A surface level of meaning at least should be accessible to the serious reader. If those of Merrill's reviewers and critics whose knowledge isn't restricted to the published work have sometimes been able to say more helpful things than others about his books, it's little wonder. Naturally such writers betray no confidences. But private knowledge has to make a difference in how they feel about the poems under review, or rather don't feel: they don't, for instance, feel abandoned.

2567

Helen Vendler, rejoicing that in a number of poems in *Braving the Elements* Merrill's "single best subject—love—has found a way of expressing itself masked and unmasked at once, instead of hiding almost mummified in swathings of secrecy," makes plain how frustrating she herself had found his earlier expression of, exactly, sound without sense (italics mine):

> Secrecy and obliquity were Merrill's worst obstacles in his early verses; *though his tone was usually clear, the occasion of the tone was impossibly veiled:* who are these people? what relation are they in? what has just happened to provoke this response? what is the outcome?—all these questions led to the murkiest answers, if to any answers at all.

The desire for connection, the wish to understand what one is reading, is simply human. To quicken a reader's interest in some poems only to snub him in others, when the snub is arbitrary and not demanded by the terms of the work, is, for a writer, self-defeating. That Merrill has himself not been immune to the allure of the concealed is clear enough from his own reassuring curiosity about things concealed from him. His second novel, *The (Diblos) Notebook*, is printed with false starts and deletions; its author stated in 1968:

> It's a technique I might have discovered much earlier from, say, that edition of Keats' letters where the deletions are legible; and, of course, from letters one receives oneself: the eye instantly flies to the crossed-out word. It seems to promise so much more than the words left exposed.

It should not surprise Merrill, then, if his serious readers, engaged by and interested in what they've been given, echo Walt Whitman's pleas to the enigmatic mockingbird: "O give me the clew! (it lurks in the night here somewhere,) / O if I am to have so much, let me have more!"

Merrill's snubs in such poems are the more frustrating because of what one knows about his method. Layer beneath layer of meaning can be excavated from a single careful phrase when one *has* been given the clew, hence the reader's conviction that layers of meaning are present, beneath the obscurity, of which he is being deprived by Merrill's indifference to communicating them—or, in some cases, by his intent that communication *not* take place. Ironically, the very elements Merrill asks Art to help him brave—"terror, anger, love"—in *Braving the Elements* ("Dreams about Clothes," p. 62) are the ones most carefully concealed within the dense middle pages of that book: braved, it may be, in life by the help of Art, but a knucklebone still buried deep in the art itself.

In a *PMLA* essay entitled "Risk and Redundancy," (March, 1975), Liane Norman digresses from her discussion of the risks a reader runs to make the point that "while linguistic failures are bound to occur, deliberate obscurity in either writing or speech is like lying. Both obscurity and falsehood work in significant ways to injure social cohesion, to reduce continuity and trust, to increase hostility and the likelihood of conflict, and generally to destroy the social state." She adds, "Unsuccessful communication, particularly when it is intentional, threatens the reciprocity upon which society depends." The social contract operates on the small scale as well as on the great in literature as in politics, and mistrust founded on deliberate obscurity injures the writer-reader relationship just as it injures relationships in the larger society. Offered a poem he cannot understand despite his best efforts, and which he suspects he isn't meant to understand—yet might if he knew more—how can the reader help but feel betrayed?

The question then arises: Why *publish* poems like "Yam" and "The Black Mesa"? Why not simply print them up on broadsides, as Vachel Lindsay used to do with his poems to be traded for bread, and circulate them by *samizdat* among friends?

In the spring of 1967, when I was James Merrill's graduate student at the University of Wisconsin, a discussion developed in class one day about the barrage of criticism being leveled at then-President Johnson. Someone objected to the fact that so few of LBJ's critics troubled to distinguish between his foreign policy and the man himself, pouring vitriol indiscriminately, on the bombing in Vietnam as on Johnson's Texas accent and general lack of couth. People were justified in damning a president *politically*, he insisted, but to ridicule his lack of personal polish was unfair.

Merrill disagreed. He said that those who seek political office knowingly do so at the cost of exposing every part of themselves to the merciless public eye, so that everything about a politician—his character and personality as much as his policies—is fair game.

I thought then, and I still think, that this put the case too strongly and perhaps too simplistically. But one might draw a useful analogy between politician and writer. Each can write his speeches or poems in perfect safety at home. Neither is forced into print or onto the soapbox. But once either seeks the attention of the public, it seems to me, that status changes. A web of subtle responsibilities springs into being. What each says in public becomes public business; each is accountable for his public words and acts; each owes his constituency a respect he dare not trespass against.

Moreover, both the politician and the poet are privy to conventions of accepted lies and tricks, others that are unacceptable. Politicians may trade favors without consulting or informing the voter, but may not insult the voter to his face by talking over his head (as Eugene McCarthy sometimes did). Poets may bend or alter facts to make them truer, but may not write *and then publish* something not meant to be understood. Neither can both relieve their minds by speaking out, and safeguard their sources by speaking cryptic nonsense. Life offers many pleasures of indulgence and many of abstinence, but in all spheres these tend to be mutually exclusive.

"I think I do meet *my* kind of reader halfway," Merrill has stated in response to a question of mine. "But yes, probably the burden is on him. Though mine is just as heavy. You can call it the Sleeping Beauty Complex; let him hack his way through thorns and I'll be his forever after." Given something to hack *with*, Merrill's faithful readers will not mind having to work for his meaning; but he must supply the broadsword, the scene must be complete: princess, castle, forest of thorns, and hacking-tool leaned against a stem somewhere, sunlight glinting on its blade.

Leon Edel, writing with profound sympathy of Henry James's failure as a dramatist, speaks of his compensating realization that "the greatest art is not that which creates a sensation or a success—as [James's] new friend Rudyard Kipling was doing at that moment—but that which, by some strange and divine process of human relation, inspires in others an interest, a depth of feeling, an attachment." Merrill's readers ask "Was it real? Did it happen?" because he too has so often succeeded, "by some strange and divine process of human relation," in making them care whether it happened or not. The intensity of the reader's wish to know is proportionate exactly to the degree that he has been made to care. And having inspired the interest, the depth of feeling, the attachment, an artist who—like the Nabokov of *Look at the Harlequins!*, like Merrill in part of *Braving the Elements*—turns *in his art* upon the readers in whom he has inspired those things, forgets or has failed to realize that the relationship of writer and reader is a relationship of peculiar intimacy, although carried on from his side in public, to which he has responsibilities not essentially different from those owed any private connection. Salinger's solution—to stop publishing, break off the relationship—is fairer than to rebuff his devotees *in* the work they come to with love and trust.

Merrill might argue, and not unreasonably, that in fifty years the political and personal resonances behind poems like "Nike" and "18 West 11th Street" will be known, readily available to anybody who wants to look up the references. Like all his work, these poems are written not for the moment only but for the permanent record; what isn't understood immediately will be clear enough in time. All right. Yet again the choice is not so simple: when a writer *need* not choose between present and eventual comprehensibility, why *should* he do so? An epigraph, or a note in the back of the book explaining the events behind "18 West 11th Street," would have obviated the difficulty both in 1972 and in 2022, and shut nobody out; one could then move past this initial roadblock to the questions of how well the method succeeds and how good the poem is. Why didn't Merrill provide one? What was to be gained by mystery, except a greater exclusiveness? In human terms, it seems to make no sense to say *Here is a house that people, not necessarily you, may enter someday*: this takes the reading public of the future into account, but what of the frustrated individual reader of the present moment?

Admittedly, the impenetrable poems even in *Braving the Elements*, where these are most numerous, fill only about one-seventh of the book. All the long pieces in the first half of *Divine Comedies* belong to the accessible-with-difficulty category in which his best work is included. Only the first 44 lines of Section I in "The Book of Ephraim" are as implacable as that implacable seventh of *Braving the Elements*, and these follow many pages of lucid narrative, and of discourse that can be worked out with a bit of effort. More important, their density seems differently motivated from that of *Braving the Elements*, though the consequence for the reader must still be exclusion. Both *Mirabell* and *Scripts for the Pageant*— Volumes II and III of the Trilogy—are, while extremely demanding, altogether free of willful obfuscation; on the contrary, Merrill's whole will seems bent on getting a message across—not that he makes concessions to readers in order to court them. And let it be said that at no time have his smoke screens had the effect of lies.

In Merrill's case, then, the willingness to attract and then abandon, draw the devoted reader on only to shrug him off when it becomes convenient, may well be gone for good. Yet it remains the single important fault I find with all the poetry of his first period: a fault not of ability but of attitude.

For this is consistently true: that whenever Merrill has chosen intimacy, of tone or content—when his presence is somehow palpable in his words—his readers respond with gratitude and trust, no matter what demands he may otherwise make of them. Again and again, the response of perceptive reviewers to *Divine Comedies* comes from a sense, precisely, of connectedness. Willard Spiegelman (*Southwest Review*, Summer 1976) sees that "the elegant *objets* and artifacts which used to be more in the foreground of Merrill's work have surrendered the center stage to the mature poet's humane worries. Cozy and intimate in tone, like Pope, Merrill transcends mere coterie verse." In Helen Vendler's view (*New York Review of Books*, March 18, 1976), the conversational tone "locates value in the human and everyday. . . ." William H. Pritchard (*Hudson Review*, Autumn 1976) articulates the essential point precisely: "Verse like this, in its assurance that there *is*

somebody speaking to us out of the life lived, the love spent (to borrow from an earlier Merrill poem), also preserves us from too much frustration at not following all the intricacies and privacies of 'JM's' conversations with the spirit world, with affable, familiar Ephraim." Given enough, in other words, we'll take a great deal more on faith—an idea also expressed, somewhat differently, by Clara Claiborne Park in a sensitive review in *The Nation* (February 12, 1977):

> The reader's attention to verse narrative required faith, faith that prolonged attention would pay off, that a tale would emerge which was intelligible, exciting, and significant. Dante, like all the great narrative poets, lets us know clearly where he starts from, whom he proceeds with, what goes on—basic clarities which sustain us to attempt the incidental riddles and enjoy them. Merrill, though he's no more than Dante an easy poet, gives us all the clues we need to follow him through a poem of many riddles and many settings.

Earlier, Helen Vendler had written crisply in her *Braving the Elements* review that "When content remains dim, euphonies are useless," one way of saying that to her mind, intimacy of tone, not content, is not enough intimacy. But Vendler's review passes over that volume's most obscure poems completely in her pleasure at a group of narratives she calls "Merrill's best new ventures . . . autobiographical without being 'confessional': they show none of that urgency to reveal the untellable or unspeakable that we associate with the poetry we call 'confessional.'" In "After the Fire," "Days of 1935," "Strato in Plaster," "Up and Down," and "Days of 1971," the need to write hasn't been forced to strike a bargain with the desire not to be understood, and the absence of conflict allows for clear, straightforward storytelling. Though there had been precedents in three previous books, at its appearance *Braving the Elements* contained the largest group of such poems, and the most richly textured.

Admirable as this lucid-narrative mode certainly is, to me Merrill seems at his best when he finds a balance between lucidity and obscurity. The privacy of his nature seems too central for his finest work to be that of such (relative) openness. Daniel Hoffman has written that Poe's art "conceals while it reveals, reveals while it conceals"; and Merrill's art also profits more from holding his impulse to communicate, and his counterimpulse to mask and veil, in the tense, graceful balance of acrobats. This synthesis shows to advantage in ambitious poems like "The Thousand and Second Night" and "From the Cupola" in *Nights and Days*, "In Nine Sleep Valley" in *Braving the Elements*, and perhaps most brilliantly in the long, reminiscent, personal narratives of *Divine Comedies*—poems capacious enough to allow much to be shared, much else withheld from open statement but so integrated with what *is* given, through symbol and theme, that knowns and unknowns are worked together and make their effects jointly. Merrill's own description, in the 1967 interview, of the knowns and unknowns in "From the Cupola" illuminates this method:

> In the poem there are, let's see, three stories going. There's the story of Eros and Psyche which is, if not known, at least knowable to any reader. Then there is the contemporary situation of a New England village Psyche and her two nasty sisters and somebody writing love letters to her. And finally there is what I begin by describing as an unknowable situation, something I'm going to keep quiet about. But, in a way, the New England village situation is transparent enough to let us see the story of Eros and Psyche on one side of the glass and, perhaps, to guess at, to triangulate the third story, the untold one.

Each of the long poems in *Divine Comedies*, Part I, displays the part-open, part-hidden, beautifully-integrated strategy which I believe to be Merrill's surest way to excellence. Readers of another trilogy, Tolkien's, may recall how Gandalf racked his brain to hit on the open-sesame of the Moria Gates,

and how all the time it was inscribed, in runes he was misreading, on the stone right under his nose. Merrill's richest poems are like those gates: rock-solid, closed tight upon the treasure, but with the password that will open all written, sometimes cryptically, but in plain sight, there in the stone.

Works

DAVID KALSTONE
From "James Merrill: Transparent Things"
Five Temperaments
1977, pp. 83–105

II

The conviction that "life was fiction in disguise" charges ⟨Merrill's⟩ poetry from the very start. Yet *First Poems* (1951) and *The Country of a Thousand Years of Peace* (1959) stand apart. These are books in which Merrill is continually interrogating presences as if they were on the edge of eternity. *First Poems* is a lonely and tantalizing collection, whose characteristic speaker is a solitary, often a child, attempting to decipher or translate elusive natural emblems: a shell, periwinkles, a peacock. These poems address themselves, frustrated and transfixed, to scenes on the brink of transformation: the secretive "Periwinkles" whose insides are "all pearled / With nourishment sucked out from the pulsing world"; or, in "Transfigured Bird," a child toying with the "eggshell of appearance" which, blown empty, "is void of all but pearl-on-pearl / Reflections." Many of these poems take up the matter of going beyond appearances so earnestly as to make *First Poems* seem "last" poems as well. Still, behind the conversational ease and realism of Merrill's subsequent books is the feeling which animates the very first poem of this one, "The Black Swan": the child's yearning to see the world symbolically. It haunts, informs and strengthens everything he writes.

By the time of *The Country of a Thousand Years of Peace*—eight years had passed since *First Poems*—the solitary speaker had become a world traveller. Yet that worldly grounding only licenses and confirms his questions about the solidity of appearances. He is less interested in what the traveller sees and more in his distanced way of seeing things. Japan, India, Holland, Greece: the journey only confirms him in the feelings of exile and strangeness expressed in *First Poems*. The "country of a thousand years of peace" is Switzerland, where the young Dutch poet, Hans Lodeizen (1924–50), a friend almost Merrill's own age, died of leukemia. Lodeizen is the "necessary angel" of the book, as he is to be again a tutelary figure in the later "Book of Ephraim." The title poem and the final dedicatory verse of *Country* are addressed to him, and the true country of both the title and the book is "that starry land / Under the world, which no one sees / Without a death."

It is in *Water Street* that Merrill commits himself to his brand of autobiography and, with a title as specific as his previous had been general, turns his poetry toward a "local habitation and a name." The occasion of the book is moving to a new house. The closing poem of the book, "A Tenancy," settles him in Stonington, Connecticut, on the village street of the title, in the house which is to be a central presence in his work. The move confirms him in poetic directions he had already begun to follow: "If I am host at last / It is of little more than my own past. / May others be at home in it." *Water Street* opens with "An Urban Convalescence," a poem which dismantles a life in New York City where life is continually dismantling itself. Merrill's move is inseparable from the desire

to stabilize memory, to draw poetry closer to autobiography, to explore his life, writing out of "the dull need to make some kind of house / Out of the life lived, out of the love spent."

The domesticating impulse closes both "An Urban Convalescence" and "A Tenancy" and effectively frames the book. Imagined as dwelling places, the poems are at once new creations and dedications to what is durable, salvageable from the past. They emerge as signs of Merrill's deep and nourishing debt to Proust, whose work he had admired since his undergraduate days and had now found a way to absorb. There is a poem "For Proust" in *Water Street*, but Proust's mark is everywhere in the poems about the continuing presence of childhood memories.

In "Scenes of Childhood" a motion-picture projector, more explicitly realistic and Freudian than Proust's magic lantern, has the same power to resuscitate a personal past. A son and his mother go through the obsessive psychic replays which home movies permit and symbolize. They watch the mother in younger days, her sisters with plucked brows, and then the son as a child of four. A man's shadow "mounts" the mother's dress. The child breaks into tears, becomes a little fury. "The man's shadow afflicts us both." As they try to slow down the film it jams.

> Our headstrong old projector
> Glares at the scene which promptly
> Catches fire.
>
> Puzzled, we watch ourselves
> Turn red and black, gone up
> In a puff of smoke . . .
>
>   . . . Alone
> I gradually fade and cool.

Old movies silently fan old Oedipal flames and become indistinguishable from inner experience. There are no distanced emblems to be interpreted here, as there were in Merrill's earlier poems. The poet is at once overheated projector and the childhood he projects, part of the flow of images ("Father already fading— / Who focused your life long / Through little frames"). The anguish revived by the experience in "Scenes of Childhood" is not clearly resolved or dispelled as it is to be in later poems, but the manner of the poem is important. In his first two books Merrill had imagined the riddling objects and landscapes of nature and his travels as teasing him, just on the edge of releasing hidden meanings. They were stable, static, as if seen on a photographic negative or on an etcher's plate ("images of images . . . insights of the mind in sleep"). In *Water Street* the optical image is extended to motion-picture films and refined to accommodate mysteries interior and fleeting, stored in memory, only to be glimpsed in motion and discovered by activating the charged details of our own lives.

It is here that the author of *Remembrance of Things Past* is most clearly Merrill's master. Proust writes in *Time Recaptured* of the power of memory—involuntary memory—to awaken the riddling presences of the world.

> But let a sound, a scent already heard and breathed
> in the past be heard and breathed anew, simulta-
> neously in the present and in the past, real without

being actual, ideal without being abstract, then instantly the permanent and characteristic essence hidden in things is freed and our true being which has for long seemed dead but was not so in other ways awakes and revives, thanks to this celestial nourishment.[1]

Merrill was to say of his own habits of composition: "When I don't like a poem I'm writing, I don't look any more into the human components. I look more to the *setting*—a room, the objects in it. I think that objects are very subtle reflectors."[2] The best poems in *Water Street* are about the conditions under which the past becomes truly available and nourishing. What landscapes, what objects will, in Wallace Stevens's word, "suffice"?

"An Urban Convalescence" begins with an illness and ends in a resolute separation from New York, a gesture fulfilled by the "Tenancy" on *Water Street* which closes the book. Out for a walk in Manhattan after a week in bed, the poet falls into dazed self-questioning. Demolitions are going on in his block: he wonders "what building stood here. Was there a building at all? . . . Wait. Yes. . . . Or am I confusing it . . . ?" Soon the subject becomes memory itself. A garland remembered from the lintel of a demolished New York doorway leads back to a cheap engraving of garlands in which he had wrapped a bouquet presented to a now-forgotten Paris romance:

> Wait. No. Her name, her features
> Lie toppled underneath the year's fashions.
> The words she must have spoken, setting her face
> To fluttering like a veil, I cannot hear now,
> Let alone understand.

Forgotten faces are like forgotten fashions ("fluttering like a veil") and like the demolitions which began the poem ("toppled underneath that year's fashions"). By this point objects and setting have become so naturally entangled with inner experience that every statement widens to include memory or forgetfulness. The garland whose roots he spoke of earlier and whose memory reawakened the bouquet of flowers and the Paris romance ends with a truncated echo in the pockmarked walls exposed by the demolitions. "Wires and pipes, snapped off at the roots, quiver. / Well, that is what life does." His surroundings epitomize his own sense of failed connections and disintegrated personality.

> So that I am ready on the stair,
> As it were, of where I lived,
> When the whole structure shudders at my tread
> And soundlessly collapses.

"An Urban Convalescence" is designed to act out a false start and implicitly to suggest a search for more revealing and durable images. What he appears to be learning to do is to disentangle his own needs and style from the clichés of the world of fashionable destruction—a clarification of feeling signalled in the crisp rhymed quatrains from this point to the end of the poem. It ends with the implied resolve to find new and resonant settings in his memory.

> back into my imagination
> The city glides, like cities seen from the air,
> Mere smoke and sparkle to the passenger
> Having in mind another destination
>
> Which now is not that honey-slow descent
> Of the Champs-Elysées, her hand in his,
> But the dull need to make some kind of house
> Out of the life lived, out of the love spent.

Much of the poem's feeling is gathered in the now charged associations of *house:* the perpetual dangers of exposure and change, of fashion and modishness; the sifting of memory for patterns which will truly suffice. "An Urban Convalescence" is just such a sifting of memory. Entangling inner and outer experience, it leads us to see the poem itself as potentially a "house," a set of arrangements for survival or, to use Merrill's later phrase, for "braving the elements." Poems were to make sense of the past as a shelter or a dwelling place for the present.

In future poems, other houses were to become charged conductors of meaning—shelters explored, destroyed, mended, invoked; reflectors for glimpsing the larger patterns of his life. Among them: "The Broken Home"; his childhood house. "18 West 11th St.," destroyed by Weathermen making bombs; the love-scarred Athens house of "After the Fire"; the slumbering house in "Under Libra"; Psyche's house in "From the Cupola"; the Stonington house with its stardeck in "The Book of Ephraim."

But Merrill had probably begun to prepare this stage as early as the mysterious piece which closes *First Poems*. Called simply "The House," it goes without grammatical break from title to opening lines:

> Whose west walls take the sunset like a blow
> Will have turned the other cheek by morning, though
> The long night falls between, as wise men know:
> Wherein the wind, that daily we forgot,
> Comes mixed with rain and, while we seek it not,
> Appears against our faces to have sought
> The contours of a listener in night air,
> His profile bent as from pale windows where
> Soberly once he learned what houses were.

A house "turns the other cheek." Wind takes—or makes—the shape of "a listener in night air," who seems like a solitary bending from pale windows. With no syntactical breaks—and a confusing fluency—the poem dissolves ordinary boundaries between interior and exterior landscapes, the idea of "house" rendered completely metaphorical, like an astrological house. Nor are *inside* and *outside* the "house" distinct locations. We experience the "house" almost as a transparency, a shelter improvised against a larger exposure: "Night is a cold house, a narrow doorway."

> I have entered, nevertheless,
> And seen the wet-faced sleepers the winds take
> To heart; have felt their dreadful profits break
> Beyond my seeing: at a glance they wake.

What one feels in that dreamlike situation is, as Merrill was later to identify it, "something like the sleeping furies at the beginning of 'The Eumenides'—only as embodiments of the suffering they bring. An early example of elements braved?"[3] The particular houses Merrill writes about in later poems—however real, solidly located and furnished—are also imagined as vulnerable houses of the spirit. They are never mere settings. In the details he uses to conjure them up, there are always reminders of the particular kinds of exposure and emergency against which these domestic arrangements have been contrived. It is not simply that they displace confining dwellings of the past—the broken parental home, the narrow apartments of false starts. The very act of choosing what spaces, attributes, solid elements of the house to invoke *becomes* the action of the poem. A transparency of setting characterizes Merrill's writing, bleaching out distracting, merely accidental details and fixing most of his houses as improvised houses of survival and desire.

But in *Water Street*, the most powerful poems are those stressing the exposures against which Merrill's dwellings were to be devised. "An Urban Convalescence" is the best known of these poems, but "Childlessness" is probably the most important. "Childlessness" draws together narrative impulse and symbolic framework so violently that it seems not to fuse but confound them. Here, in a phantasmagoric landscape, houses "look blindly on"; the one glimmering light is not the poet's own.

> The weather of this winter night, my dream-wife
> Ranting and raining, wakes me. Her cloak blown
>   back
> To show the lining's dull lead foil
> Sweeps along asphalt.

Richard Saez has spoken of Merrill's "wrested comparisons." No paraphrase could do justice to the uncomfortable marriage of poet and Nature which permeates this poem. Whether he is thinking of Nature as fostering the children he does not have or as infusing the visions of art, he remains battered between dream and nightmare. What is played out is a stormy version of the cool drama enacted much later with the mother in "Up and Down." In that later poem the mother gives her son an emerald his dead father had given her when their child was born.

> I do not tell her, it would sound theatrical,
> *Indeed this green room's mine, my very life.*
> *We are each other's; there will be no wife;*
> *The little feet that patter here are metrical.*
>
> But onto her worn knuckle slip the ring.
> Wear it for me, I silently entreat,
> Until—until the time comes. Our eyes meet.
> The world beneath the world is brightening.

This later poem includes self-mockery and self-possession; above all, it is secure about an unspoken understanding between mother and son. "Childlessness," written ten years earlier, is more distraught, less resolved. At its close, the dawn is 'A sky stained red, a world / Clad only in rags, threadbare."

> A world. The cloak thrown down for it to wear
> In token of past servitude
> Has fallen onto the shoulders of my parents
> Whom it is eating to the bone.

The poem, because of its fierce freedom to move from level to level, to be both household drama and natural perspective, can include matters of individual guilt and responsibility, but can also transcend them. It conflates a number of views of Nature's gifts. The cloak which at the end consumes his parents like the shirt of Nessus is, at the beginning, part of the description of the winter night and belongs to his "dream-wife," the wintry weather. At times experience is measured on a human scale: Nature is a fantasy mate, a figure at different points accusing (nothing is planted in his childless "garden"), absolving, nourishing and tempting. But the conceit, once seized, opens a world of more mysterious operations among presences which dwarf and outlive us. The poem moves through a section of rapid and dizzying transformations:

> I lie and think about the rain,
> How it has been drawn up from the impure ocean,
> From gardens lightly, deliberately tainted;
> How it falls back, time after time,
> Through poisons visible at sunset
> When the enchantress, masked as friend, unfurls
> Entire bolts of voluminous pistachio,
> Saffron, and rose.
> These, as I fall back to sleep,
> And other slow colors clothe me, glide
> To rest, then burst along my limbs like buds,
> Like bombs from the navigator's vantage,
> Waking me, lulling me. Later I am shown
> The erased metropolis reassembled

> On sampans, freighted each
> With toddlers, holy dolls, dead ancestors.
> One tiny monkey puzzles over fruit.

The transformations are hard to keep track of; the refusal to allow experience to settle is part of the poem's point. Nature's cloak and the consuming cloak at the end of the poem are closely related to the bolts of material in this passage. The exotic colors of sunset, distilled from the storm, first *clothe* the poet, then *burst* along his limbs like *buds*. The image is meant to counter an earlier one: that nothing is planted in his garden (no natural blooms, like children). Then the *buds* become *bombs*, and the reward for being on target is a curious miniaturization of the world. A bombed metropolis is reassembled on sampans, a decimating version of the powers of art. The dream ends, as a *stained* dawn replaces the exotic dyes of sunset. Unlike those tropical shades, dawn's colors do not clothe him. For hours he cannot *stand* (both "bear" and "rise") to *own* the threadbare world—or to face its alternative: the cloak, a token for his parents who performed the expected service to nature. Their reward is also what devours them.

This is one of Merrill's most exposed poems, anticipated in the closing lines of "An Urban Convalescence." It offers rapid and conflicting perspectives against which to view the particulars of human feeling. Childlessness, guilt and suffering are set within the framework of nature's ample violence, its mysterious ecology, its occasionally exalting cyclical promise and power. Merrill has discovered a stage which will accommodate surrealistic effects released by a familiar domestic situation. The effect is like an opening out of space, a large corrective for moments of individual exposure. Merrill forces leaps from the "kitchen garden" to "really inhuman depths," the poetic gift he admired in Montale. But he also seems uncomfortable with these accesses of power. In "Childlessness" the technique is abrupt and insistent, a prey sometimes to strained self-justification or exaggerated guilt. It finds no way to separate the bareness and power of his own life from the punishment of his parents. And so the poem never really settles; at the close it comes to rest rather than resolution. Shuttling, adjusting perspectives constantly as we must to read this poem, we hear a mixture of self-accusation, self-delight and defiance. In the final lines the parents, consumed to the bone, are introduced with a baffling combination of bitterness, contrition and fierce confrontation with the way of the world. What happens violently in "childlessness" happens with more meditative certainty later in his career.

III

In "Childlessness" and other poems from *Water Street* Merrill moves toward more overtly autobiographical work. *Nights and Days* (1966), the next book, is the classic Merrill volume—jaunty, penetrating and secure. It contains some of his best poems, though later works were to be richer, more searching, high-flying, even shocking and relaxed. But several of the poems in *Nights and Days* are paradigms of how he was going to use autobiographical details in his poetry. Or to reverse it, in Merrill's own words, how the poet was to become a man "choosing the words he lives by."

"Time" is a poem about that process. It begins with a dazzling ambitious sentence, full of the bravado of a talented young poet finding outrageous metaphors for Time:

> Ever that Everest
> Among concepts, as prize for fruitful
> Grapplings with which
> The solved cross-word puzzle has now and then
> Eclipsed Blake's "Sun-Flower"
> (Not that one wanted a letter changed in either)

And jazz believed at seventeen
So parodied the slopes
That one mistook the mountain for a cloud . . .

The verse paragraph is itself a kind of pastime with its outrageous etymology for Everest and its breathy syntax. The seductively liberated fantasy transforms games of Patience into

Fifty-two chromosomes permitting
Trillions of 'lives'—some few
Triumphant, the majority
Blocked, doomed, yet satisfying, too,
In that with each, before starting over,
You could inquire beneath
The snowfield, the vine-monogram, the pattern
Of winged cyclists, to where the flaw lay
Crocus-clean, a trail inching between
Sheer heights and drops, and reach what might have
        been.

He starts out as a plucky adventurer, sure about the larger human curiosity which card games (and poems!—Blake's "Sun-Flower") stand for and the kinds of fear they overcome. In the lost game of Patience, you can still peek at the blocked cards and get a God's-eye view of the pitfalls.

Against that bravado play the voices of everyday life, what is possible—voices of the son who postpones his life and the father who nags at him:

He grasped your pulse in his big gray-haired hand,
Crevasses opening, numb azure. *Wait*
He breathed and glittered: *You'll regret
You want to   Read my will first   Don't
Your old father   All he has   Be yours*

With the entrance of the father, the imagined adventures of the poem's opening turn into something more dangerous: "Crevasses opening." An emerging vision—still cards, still mountain-climbing—is more mysterious, tempered by the long littleness of life. The father fades into a figure like Father Time and also becomes a distant peak, his features "ice-crowned,—tanned—by what?— / Landmark." The son, a fitful dreamer "smoothing the foothills of the sheet," has a new image of his journey:

You take up your worn pack.

Above their gay crusaders' dress
The monarch's mouths are pinched and bleak.
Staggering forth in ranks of less and less
Related cards, condemned to the mystique

Of a redeeming One,
An Ace to lead them home, sword, stave, and axe,
Power, Riches, Love, a place to lay them down
In dreamless heaps, the reds, the blacks,

Old Adams and gray Eves
Escort you still.

Without dropping his original vocabulary of pastimes, Merrill is exposed to a widening vision of what pastimes really are, how they are linked to ambition and faith eroded by time. The technique here as elsewhere is one of bold transformations: the "worn pack" of eternal card games merges with the mountain climber's burdensome pack. Tested against the experience of the beleaguered, procrastinating son, the images of the opening reveal unexpected depth and dimension. It is as if a curtain rises for the mesmerized speaker. Or as if the blinding defensive component of wit had fallen away. The surface royalty of the cards drops off "in dreamless heaps, the reds, the blacks, / Old Adams and gray Eves." Once triumphant they are now "condemned to the mystique / Of a redeeming One."

What is particularly remarkable is the way the poem is pitched toward discovery and makes us go through the process. As in "Childlessness" (though with less anger) he sees his surroundings, his daily experience, in an ever deepening perspective, though this time one *shared* by demanding father and reluctant son. In the son's drifting vision, the father actually *becomes* the landscape, the "ice-crowned . . . / Landmark," at the end of his journey. Meditated long enough, a dramatic situation, a scene, a landscape, even an object become transparent, like the pack of cards melting into the tired traveller's "worn pack." Merrill is committed to such unfolding images and to the puns which reveal them. "Time" acts as a rebuke to the gamesman at the opening of the poem, dwarfs his defenses, offers him a glimpse of the deep corrective wisdom of language.

I have said that *Nights and Days* is the classic Merrill volume. From this point on he seems entirely secure about the relation of his poems to autobiography and memory, to social surface and colloquial language. The security is reflected in pieces which begin or end with explicit references to writing, several in this volume: "The Thousand and Second Night," "The Broken Home" and "From the Cupola." (In later volumes, poems like "Yánnina," "Under Libra" and "Lost in Translation.") The poet will be seen at his desk, looking back at an encounter or a crisis, or in the heat of events will glance forward to the time when he is alone and unpressured. Merrill is as committed as other writers included here to capturing the immediate feel of experience, but often insistent that writing is part of that experience. Or, to put it his way, "What you feel is expressed, is mimed back at you by the scene. A room, a landscape. I'd go a step further. We don't *know* what we feel until we see it distanced by this kind of translation." The "translation" of which he speaks marks him off from the authors of *Leaflets* and *Notebook*. One thinks of Adrienne Rich's burning impatience with the way writing fixes experience ("A language is the map of our failures"), her preference for the provisional, the ever more authentic, and the present tense. In *Notebook* Lowell wanted "the instant, sometimes changing to the lost." For Merrill there is the experience and the settling in of the experience; "the blackbird whistling / or just after," as Stevens puts it.

Merrill is suspicious of the straightforward first-person present indicative active: "this addictive, self-centered immediacy, harder to break oneself of than cigarettes."

That kind of talk . . . calls to mind a speaker
suspicious of words, in great boots, chain-smoking,
Getting It Down On Paper. He'll never notice
"Whose woods these are I think I know" gliding
backwards through the room, or "Longtemps je me
suis couché de bonne heure" plumping a cushion
invitingly at her side. . . . Think how often poems
in the first-person present begin with a veil drawn, a
sublimation of the active voice or the indicative
mood, as if some ritual effacement of the ego were
needed before one could go on. "I wonder, by my
troth, what thou and I . . ."; "Let us go then you
and I. . . ." The poet isn't always the hero of a
movie who *does* this, *does* that. He is a man choosing
the words he lives by.[4]

These words are from an interview which accompanied the first publication of "Yánnina," a poem which ends with the poet at his desk as an intense experience slowly takes form in his mind. The quote suggests the conviction with which Merrill accepts the notions of poetic closure and the composed self—notions which many writers of autobiographical verse would suspect as artificial, false to the provisional nature of things. In many of Merrill's poems, the closing is also the point at which the poem opens out, as "Time" unfolds a new perspective in which to view the poet's actions and anxieties.

Merrill prefers poems in the first-person present which begin "with a veil drawn" ("a sublimation of the active voice or the indicative mood . . . a ritual effacement of the ego"). That attitude helps explain the presence of a short poem as prologue to each of his later books. In particular, "Nightgown," "Log" and "Kimono" are small ritual prefaces,[5] overheard, propitiatory, modest, veiled overtures of poet to Muse. "Nightgown," the short invocation to *Nights and Days*, is typical of their modest tone and function:

> A cold so keen,
> My speech unfurls tonight
> As from the chattering teeth
> Of a sewing-machine.
>
> Whom words appear to warm,
> Dear heart, wear mine. Come forth
> Wound in their flimsy white
> And give it form.

Prompted by exposure, writing begins as a form of slender protection. However commonplace the material, however awkward the gestures (the chattering teeth), words not only *seem* to warm but, in a second sense of *appear*, their express purpose is to warm the heart. The homely effort lures out an informing spirit: a poem's emergence signalled in the rapid shift in the last two lines from the disparate plural of words to the singular white form, *their* to *it*. Everything happens as a trust in process; the poem, homespun nightgown, eventually becomes the dreamer's garb.

The warming lure of words is a recurring form of invocation for Merrill. He introduces it, for example, into the beginning of "The Broken Home," summoning a *tongue* of fire in his cool sunless room ("a brimming / Saucer of wax, marbly and dim— / I have lit what's left of my life"). In "From the Cupola" the fiery tongues are those of the senses, "a certain smouldering five / Deep in the ash of something I survive." In that case, as in "The Broken Home," the fuel for the poem is the self, and the speaker a survivor who is there not only to tell his story, record a shock, but also to show how recollection probes an experience to release its larger meaning.

Richard Saez, in a brilliant description of the effect of some of Merrill's long poems, notes that:

> Each poem begins after a physical or emotional crisis has enervated the poet, effecting something like Proust's intensified sensibility after an asthmatic attack. A delicate but incisive sensuous perception leads from the present to related scenes in the past. . . . Movement is more in the rhythm of ritual dance—measured, repeated steps with darkly significant variations—than narrative action . . . eroticism is closer to the core than to the surface. When the focus has narrowed sufficiently to burn through the poet's self-absorption, remaining under the thin gauze of ashes is the poem: a cooling artifice which coalesces and refigures the past.[6]

Saez has conflated two of Merrill's own metaphors for the effect of poems: from "Log," the gauze of ash which remains "after the fire"; and, from "Days of 1971," the description of a miniature glass horse from Venice. The latter is a token from a now fading love affair, unwrapped at the end of the trip that concludes things between the lovers:

> Two ounces of white heat
> Twirled and tweezered into shape,
>
> Ecco! another fanciful
> Little horse, still blushing, set to cool.

The feelings of a no-longer-driven lover are inseparable from, are indeed discovered in, an image which has to do with ending a love poem. The love token suggests a miniature Pegasus. The mixture of unfulfilled love and unfulfilled anger spills over into mixed feelings about the poem: a sense of rueful accomplishment, of embarrassed pleasure ("still blushing"), of diminution, life miniaturized and "set to cool."

In other poems—say, "The Broken Home"—the cooling less irritably refigures the past. I wouldn't say of such works, as Saez does, that "fire—in any of its many forms—is more the protagonist than the poet who observes and meditates." But certainly the repeated motifs of aroused flames and cooling attune us to an intensity of involvement seemingly at odds with the almost deadpan wit and surface detachment of many of the poems. As readers we have to be aware of the verbal "layers" of a Merrill poem: his way of shadowing plots beneath the narrative surface and suggesting the complex involvement of the ego in any given experience. While the civilized storyteller takes us into his confidence, adjustments of time, temperature, light and background call attention to his own emotional activity and psychic experience of the poem.

"The Broken Home" shows that double movement at its clearest. The home is the one he grew up in, but also one we are given to feel *he* breaks within the poem. We must watch two actions at the same time. In one, the poem seems like a series of slides of the past, each a sonnet long, presenting the characters of his Oedipal tale and encounters between them. In the other action, the present tense of the poem, we watch the poet lighting his scenes. Behind these surfaces, changes of timing, brightness and scale render the scenes as transparencies. Or, to put it another way, the changes in his writing, the heightened temperature of involvement, coax out an inner experience. It is as if a poem required a kind of scrim among its resources, before or behind which action may be seen in new configurations as new beams of light are introduced.

To be specific: "The Broken Home" opens in the present with a set of contrasts. The poet has seen the family upstairs posed in their window in static tableau and as if with an overlaid fire ("gleaming like fruit / With evening's mild gold leaf"). Against this, the poet's own solitary room on the floor below is sunless, cooler, but potentially alive with an inner turbulence. Countering the waxen still life above, his room is "a brimming / Saucer of wax, marbly and dim," capable of generating a series of images from the past of his own very different sense of family. "I have lit what's left of my life." The problem of "Childlessness" is here acted out in a more controlled manner. "Tell me, tongue of fire, / That you and I are as real / At least as the people upstairs." On the surface the approach is oblique, a series of sonnets. Each detaches itself from the one before, seems to force a new start, appears to approach but skirt danger: a satiric portrait of his father; the projection of his mother's feelings into a vignette of angry suffragettes; next, a central panel of the poem, an openly erotic scene when the child enters his mother's darkened bedroom, the scene ending in a terse cartoon ("The dog slumped to the floor. She reached for me. I fled").

But we are drawn as into a labyrinth, away from detached and generalizing pasts ("My father, who had flown in World War I, / Might have continued to invest his life / In cloud banks well above Wall Street and wife"). By the fifth sonnet the poem shades from an immediate past into an eternal present: "Tonight they have stepped out onto the gravel. / The party is over."

> A lead soldier guards my windowsill:
> Khaki rifle, uniform, and face.
> Something in me grows heavy, silvery, pliable.

How intensely people used to feel!
Like metal poured at the close of a proletarian novel,
Refined and glowing from the crucible,
I see those two hearts, I'm afraid,
Still. Cool here in the graveyard of good and evil,
They are even so to be honored and obeyed.

The images are radiant and confusing. They tap emotions which have as much to do with getting past his own witty defenses (that toy lead soldier is, among other things, a guard) as with the knotted explosive family triangle. In the poem's power to woo and summon taboos, there is a release full of contradictions of identity. It is the two hearts of the parents which are with prime authenticity "Like metal poured at the close of a proletarian novel." Or is the son, earlier like a melting lead soldier, "heavy, silvery, pliable," also passing through the crucible and, by virtue of the experience, able to "see those two hearts . . . still"? The enjambed syntax is part of enjambed feelings and allows both interpretations. What has been kept separate before is here interlocked, all and forever present "in the graveyard of good and evil."

The passage, like the most intense moments in poetry, won't hold still before the eye. Depending on your phrasing, "How intensely people used to feel" links forward and puts the parents at an envied anachronistic distance ("Like metal poured at the close of a proletarian novel"). Or the phrase links backward, identifying the son with his parents in a shared deep focus. Seeing double works here because the feelings which are almost fused have, in the earlier part of the poem, been held so long in provocative tension. To follow one set of flickering clues: the poet's room at the opening is sunless and cool. Despite his invoking a "tongue of fire," the following sonnets are oddly distanced. The father is remembered through "smoked glass" ("The soul eclipsed by twin black pupils, sex / And business"). His gravitational pull is resisted by wit. ("When he died / There were already several chilled wives / In sable orbit") The link of father with sun is taken up glancingly later on. In the sleeping mother's bedroom "Blinds beat sun from the bed." The room is held in hushed reserve for the invading child and "red, satyr-thighed / Michael, the Irish setter."

What has been kept apart in detached and taboo encounters falls together at last in the fifth sonnet. There the son is both victim and secret sharer of his parents' lives. In one instant he seems miniaturized, unmanned, a toy soldier melting in a pliable and eternal childhood. At another instant he holds the parents in dated and envied perspective. In a third light he is the capable poet, with them in a lengthening landscape and sharing the self-knowledge of their casual frank exchange:

It's the fall
Of 1931. They love each other still.
She: Charlie, I can't stand the pace.
He: Come on, honey—why you'll bury us all!

Behind the ordinary blunt incompatibility of what they say are shadows already introduced into the poem: his hurrying ambitions, her survivor's protests ("Father Time and Mother Earth, / A marriage on the rocks"). I also hear another echo, which places the scene in a long perspective of repeated follies, worldly callousness and pressured lives. Proust's Duke and Duchess de Guermantes are late for a dinner party. There is time for the Duchess to turn back and change her black shoes for red ones that match her gown, but no time to absorb their friend Swann's news that he has only a few months to live. The Duke's voice drifts cheerily across to the retreating figures of Swann and Marcel: "You're strong as the Pont Neuf. You'll live to bury us all."

"The Broken Home" ends with the home itself, its detailed memory present, but the "real" home receding into the past:

The real house became a boarding-school.
Under the ballroom ceiling's allegory
Someone at last may actually be allowed
To learn something; or, from my window, cool
With the unstiflement of the entire story,
Watch a red setter stretch and sink in cloud.

It takes a moment to realize that the sense of release at the end, "the unstiflement of the entire story," is hypothetical ("Someone at last *may* actually be allowed . . ."). The relief accords so well with our feeling of what the poem has accomplished and our sense that in the puns of the final lines Merrill is at last disengaging himself. The window cools. The satyr-thighed dog, now almost a dream, merges through a play on words with the setting sun, erotic associations subsumed in the pun. There is probably a play on "story" as well, which along with the audacious "red setter" signals that words can accomplish such changes in landscape and feeling that they connect us to a larger planetary orbit—fathers and "suns" and the deep erotic doom of marriages under the sign of Father Time and Mother Earth.

It may be a common—and mistrusted—device of poetic closure, Merrill's calling attention to the poet's role at the end of the poem. But in *Nights and Days*—and especially in the long major poems, "The Thousand and Second Night" and "From the Cupola"—attention to writing coincides with the notion of a house, a dwelling place, a point of repair at a particular moment, the desk, the typewriter. It is as if these poems fulfilled the promise of "An Urban Convalescence"— "To make some kind of house / Out of the life lived, out of the love spent." The conventional ending seems, as in Proust, newly discovered, a psychological necessity.

The very title of this volume refers to the interpenetration and inseparability of the days of raw experience and the nights of imaginative absorption and recall. It is in those late night moments that the poems discover the poet at his desk and perform the ritual separations of poet from his poem. Such episodes, though they occur elsewhere in Merrill's work, seem to have their authentic emotional center in *Nights and Days*. The close of "The Thousand and Second Night" was almost an emblem of what poetry had come to mean for Merrill. Scheherazade survives by telling her nightly tales, but yearns for "that cold fountain which the flesh / Knows not." The bondage and the pleasure of her stories are expressed in her marriage to the Sultan, the daytime spirit whose joys lie "along that stony path the senses pave." It is he to whom things happen, she who "embroiders" what they mean. In the tenderness of their addresses to one another, the book lays its true and inner counterpoise to the deadlocked male and female voices of "The Broken Home" and to the guilty son of "Childlessness."

And when the long adventure reached its end,
I saw the Sultan in a glass, grown old,
While she, his fair wife still, her tales all told,
Smiled at him fondly. "O my dearest friend,"
Said she, "and lord and master from the first,
Release me now. Your servant would refresh
Her soul in that cold fountain which the flesh
Knows not. Grant this, for I am faint with thirst."
And he: "But it is I who am your slave.
Free me, I pray, to go in search of joys
Unembroidered by your high, soft voice,
Along that stony path the senses pave."

They wept, then tenderly embraced and went
Their ways. She and her fictions soon were one.
He slept through moonset, woke in blinding sun,
Too late to question what the tale had meant.

The almost eternal twinning of the Sultan and
Scheherazade is one of the ways Merrill has of showing how
memory and autobiography ("real life") serve poetry's power to
reveal the myths we live by. ("Joyce teaches us to immerse the
mythical elements in a well-known setting; Cocteau teaches us
to immerse them in a contemporary spoken idiom.") The final
desire of the Sultan and Scheherazade to be apart answers to
another kind of understanding in *Nights and Days*. The poet
alone in his study (in "From the Cupola") sees in his typewriter
carriage a "shrunken amphitheater . . . to moon / Hugely
above." There is always the danger of being merely elegiac
about experience, of "smelling of the lamp." Having gained his
equilibrium in the method of memory in *Nights and Days*, he
seems ready to throw it all aside in *The Fire Screen*, the strange
off-key book he was to publish three years later.

Notes

1. Marcel Proust, *Remembrance of Things Past (Time Regained*, tr.
   Stephen Hudson: Chatto & Windus, 1931), XII, 218.
2. "An Interview with James Merrill," *Shenandoah* XIX (Summer
   1968), p. 9. The interviewer is Ashley Brown.
3. Letter to David Kalstone, no date.
4. "The Poet: Private," *Saturday Review/The Arts* (December 2,
   1972), p. 45. The interviewer is David Kalstone.
5. To *Nights and Days, Braving the Elements* and *Divine Comedies*,
   respectively.
6. Richard Sáez, "James Merrill's Oedipal Fire," *Parnassus: Poetry in
   Review* (Fall/Winter 1974), p. 172.

RICHARD SÁEZ
From "James Merrill's Oedipal Fire"

Parnassus: Poetry in Review, Fall–Winter 1974, pp. 159–84

When James Merrill's "18 West 11th Street" appeared in
the *New York Review of Books* in the Spring of 1972, it
must have puzzled readers. A hermetic poem by America's
most elegant and apolitical poet about a politically explosive
topic in the very politically committed review! The address is
the house accidentally blown up in March, 1971, by Weathermen who were using it as a headquarters for constructing anti-
personnel bombs: explosives with nails taped to their exterior so
as to score their points more piercingly. Amongst them was
Cathy Wilkerson, a daughter of the wealthy financier who
owned the elegant address. Unlike some of the others, she
escaped the blast. She was seen—bleeding and naked—fleeing
from the burning building, and her long-sought image haunted
the headlines for months. But why had Merrill—who has
disclaimed contemporary events and even the present tense as
too hot to be handled by lyrical poetry—written about the
house? In one of his most memorable and frequently anthologized earlier poems, "The Broken Home" (*Nights and
Days*, 1966), as he remembers painfully his traumas as the
child of a wealthy financier, he defends his apolitical work and
his commitment to writing only about his private past and the
creative act. That was, of course, the point about "18 West
11th Street." Cathy Wilkerson and James Merrill had more
than an address in common. Still, even for readers familiar
with the poet's work, the poem remained obscure.

Merrill read it for the first time in New York at the New
School during the summer of 1972. He prefaced his reading by
saying that although it was not his habit to write about
contemporary events, he felt entitled to write about the

demolished building since he had been born there. When one
got over the extraordinary circumstance of fate—to have
enmeshed one of America's most distinguished poets with one
of her most psychologically and politically dramatic events—
"18 West 11th Street" immediately lost some of its hermeti-
cism. Merrill had not sought the headlines; in bold type the
headlines had sought him. And he had not abandoned his
usual themes: the poem is about his past, and it contrasts his
own creative endeavors with the revolutionary activity of the
Weathermen. But at the end of the reading, much of the poem
remained veiled. One remembered from earlier poems a few
details which teased with the promise of some light: in "An
Urban Convalescence" (*Water Street*, 1962) the poet imagines
one of his former homes collapsing, and in "The Broken
Home" (*Nights and Days*, 1966), while meditating on his
mother, he depicts thirties suffragettes hurling invectives at
political leaders: "*War mongerer! Pig! Give us the vote.*" It was
apparent that "18 West 11th Street" should be read in the light
of the style, themes, and structures developed throughout
Merrill's poetic career.

With almost masochistic glee Paul Valéry lamented the
poet's lack of a musician's precision tools: "no tuning forks, no
metronomes, no inventors of scales or theoreticians of harmony." The poet must "borrow language" from which he
creates his own mode of expression. The studious craft of James
Merrill's mode is increasingly evident. Within the past two
years he has published his most perfectly achieved volume of
poems, *Braving the Elements* (1972); several subsequent poems
which indicate he has entered a mature and sustained phase of
his career; and *The Yellow Pages*(1974)—a volume of previously uncollected early and late poems (1947–1968) "thrust aside"
over the years in the compilation of his several published
volumes. In effect, by showing us the rejected poems—
"yellowed, brittle with reproach"—he has helped define his
achieved style. "18 West 11th Street" is written in a personal
idiom which shows Merrill's debt to the language of the French
symbolist and English metaphysical poets.

Both the poems of *The Yellow Pages* and those of even his
most recent volumes rely heavily on the traditional forms,
meter, and rhyme of English prosody. One of the elements
which makes the "selected" poems more successful is that
Merrill understands Mallarmé's lesson to Degas: "Poems are
made not with ideas but words." He has stated frequently
enough in interviews, novels, footnotes to his poems, and in
the poems themselves that for him word must *elicit* word.
Indeed, Merrill's poems move and fulfill themselves as the
words—chiseled and molded by the poet's extraordinary
intuition and feeling—evoke and whisper their hidden resources: feelings and states of being only suggested in the poem
but intuited precisely by the reader. Merrill would again agree
with Valéry that poetry becomes, "musicalized, resonant, and,
as it were, harmonically related." As we shall see in "18 West
11th Street" and some of the later poems, Merrill would also
agree with Pound in seeing some of these musicalized poems as
"a network of tentacular roots" which reach "down to the
deepest terrors and desires."

"Willowware Cup" (*Braving the Elements*) is a perfect
example of the style. The poem is a meditation on dimestore
"chinaware" from which Merrill wrests *crazingly* complex
associations. The words he uses to describe the cup evoke as
mysterious presences as any Yeats imagined to dwell in the
English language, and the parts are intricately blended in a way
to make incision or excerpts impossible:

Mass hysteria, wave after breaking wave
Blueblooded Cantonese upon these shores

Left the gene pool Lux-opaque and smoking
With dimestore mutants. One turned up today.
Plum in bloom, pagoda, bluebirds, plume of willow—
Almost the replica of a prewar pattern—
The same boat bearing the gnat-sized lovers away,
The old bridge now bent double where her father signals
Feebly, as from flypaper, minding less and less.
Two smaller retainers with lanterns light him home.
Is that a scroll he carries? He must by now be immensely
Wise, and have given up earthly attachments, and all that.
Soon, of these May mornings, rising in mist, he will ask
Only to blend—like ink in flesh, blue anchor
Needled upon drunkenness while its destroyer
Full steam departs, the stigma throbbing, intricate—
Only to blend into a crazing texture.
You are far away. The leaves tell what they tell.
But this lone, chipped vessel, if it fills,
Fills for you with something warm and clear.
Around its inner horizon the old odd designs
Crowd as before, and seem to concentrate on you.
They represent, I fancy, a version of heaven
In its day more trouble to mend than to replace:
Steep roofs aslant, minutely tiled;
Tilted honeycombs, thunderhead blue.

From the imitation pattern on the cup the poet *invents* a legend. His story of the lovers' departure from the father does not arise inevitably from the pattern, but as Merrill becomes lost in his revery, the words, rising like mist from earthly attachments, return him to the flesh: "like ink in flesh, blue anchor." The fading of the pattern on the cup modulates on the word "blend," through a counterpoint of "mist" and "steam," into a tattoo worn probably by a past lover: another scene of departure. Just as the destroyer of the tattoo has been anticipated in the initial evocation of mass violence, the poem is also conscious of earthly passionate fulfillment: "hysteria," "gene," "bloom," and "stigma" (in its botanical sense of the pollen-receiving pistil). Then all focuses on the friend, as distant now as prewar China. At this juncture of two literal levels of meaning, a point on which most of Merrill's poetry is balanced, the poem can speak about the original Chinese pattern *and* the friend: a paradisiacal bliss lost in the absence of cultivated uniqueness. Finally, the lost version of heaven is abstracted beyond plate and friend into pure design and color:

> Steep roofs aslant, minutely tiled;
> Tilted honeycombs, thunderhead blue.

The poem presents a metaphysical vision in which diverse physical realities are seen against—and, thereby, seen through—a disembodied pattern. The implied metaphor between a noumenal-phenomenal dichotomy and expensive china and its cheap imitation is purposefully bizarre, as is the relationship between the tattoo and the dinnerware pattern. But this wrested comparison is typical of Merrill (more usually present in puns like "crazing" or "stigma"). The violent yoking, as artfully intentional as the catachreses of seventeenth century metaphysical poetry, helps to reveal a reality far away from earthly attachments.

This metaphysical element, the triune legend of father and lovers, the *medium* of heat in "mists" and "steam," and the interplay between legend and pattern are aspects of Merrill's mature thematic concerns to which I shall return in discussing

"18 West 11th Street." Before leaving a consideration of his style, I would like to compare the subtle harmonies of "Willowware Cup" with an earlier poem collected for the first time in *The Yellow Pages*. "Early Settlers" (1958) describes the failure of a pioneer couple. In the final quatrains the couple are seen spent and withdrawn, warming their winter with a fire:

> Evenings, the air thins. One of them must kneel
> Fumbling the skein of fumes till a dead branch
> Puts brilliant leafage forth, whose buffets draw
> From their drawn skins the same loud, senseless pulse.
>
> A life is something not invented yet,
> A square of linen worked in colored wools
> To stand between its maker and that drumming,
> Twitching, gibbering source of light and pain
>
> They turn to, hand in hand, themselves becoming
> Gnarled, then ashen, upon some hearth not seen
> But tended in impassive silence by
> A leathery god or two, crouched there for warmth.

The metaphor of an individual life as a fire screen upon which the vital source of Life fulfills itself is the most compelling element in the poem. The further leap which turns the couple into a source of fuel for a celestial fire screen seems forced and artificial. As so frequently in *The Yellow Pages*, it is a leap performed by an acrobatic poetic fancy rather than an arabesque unfolding quite naturally from poised language. In a later poem, "Mornings in a New House" (*The Fire Screen*, 1969), Merrill returns to the image of a fire screen. But that poem should be seen as an aspect of his phenomenology of fire: not only the heat present in the "steam" and "mists" of "Willowware Cup" and the fire screens of these poems but also the fire which destroys 18 West 11th Street.

In his novel *The (Diblos) Notebook*, Merrill reflects a difficult aspect of his poetry by creating what he calls "a composite literary hero: Perseus, Oedipus, Odysseus, Joseph (Mann), Hamlet, Don Q., Shelley, Houdini"; the French phenomenologist of poetic symbols, Gaston Bachelard, has taught us (mostly in *The Psychoanalysis of Fire*) that a relationship is to be found between the Oedipus complex and the Prometheus complex in a passionate desire "to know as much as our fathers, more than our fathers." Bachelard associates the imagery of fire used to describe the aroused male principle and the sexual shapes of the alchemist's tools with the intuition of fire as "the desire to change, to speed up the passage of time, to bring all of life to its conclusion, to its hereafter." Merrill often presents his poetic activity as a way of speeding up life to its "hereafter" and fire as the medium of change. In the earliest volumes and in *The Yellow Pages*, Merrill characteristically reflects the symbol in aesthetic objects—the gilder's or the potter's art and the "thin gold mask" in "For Proust" (*Water Street*)—in order to distance and intensify the psychic-aesthetic process. "Poem of a Summer's End" (*Water Street*) presents two lovers traveling in Umbria who, at the end of a decade of love, are at the point of intimacy which is both fulfillment and point of departure in a tensionless knowledge of each other:

> Weaker each sunrise reddens that slow maze
> So freely entered. Now come days
> When lover and beloved know
> That love is what they are and where they go.
> Each learns to read at length the other's gaze.

It is a moment Merrill returns to frequently. In this poem it is manifested as an Umbrian façade fired for an instant by the setting sun:

The time for making love is done.
A far off, sulphur-pale façade
Gleams and goes out. It is as though by one
Flash of lightning all things made
Had glimpsed their maker's heart, read and obeyed.

The façade seems to be a flat plate glazed into aesthetic timelessness by a celestial furnace while it also leads into the church and the shrines with which the rest of the poem is concerned: the "hereafter" of the lovers' inward mirroring gaze also holds God's holy fire.

These images of love, knowledge, creativity, and fire grow variously in symbolic density throughout Merrill's poetry. As with the "mist" and "steam" of "Willowware Cup," he also decorously or humorously displaces fire in painted red nails or the inebriate flushes of Dionysus. In recent poems, he seems to prefer the later stages of bio-geological life processes: creativity is represented in precious gems, crystal prisms, geological rock, and metals cooled into luminosity. As so often in Merrill, one is reminded of Proust when he speaks of the mind as a mineral deposit of life containing a potential work of art. The cooling of his symbols may reflect Merrill's growing mastery, but the phenomenological force of fire remains. In so recent a poem as "After the Fire" (*Braving the Elements*), an ancient muse figure is described as an "oven-rosy witch" whose fire the poet embraces in the closing verse: "and I/ Am kneeling pressed to her old burning frame."

"Dream about Clothes" (*Braving the Elements*) is more illustrative of Merrill's "composite hero." There fire appears as the "dry hell / Of volatile synthetic solvents," and the literal clothes being taken to the dry cleaners are those of a man who resembles the poet's father as described in his biographical novel, *The Seraglio*:

In some, the man they made
Penetrates the sunlit fitting room,
Once more deciding among bolts of dark.
The tailor kneels to take his measure.
Soon a finished suit will be laid out
By his valet, for him to change into.
Change of clothes? The very clothes of change!
Unchecked blazers women flutter round,
Green coverts, midnight blues . . .
My left hand a pincushion, I dispose,
Til morning, of whole closets full of clues.

The oedipal hero of this dry nocturnal meditation asks:

What ought I in fact to do with them?
Give away suits worn six, eight times?
Take them to the shrink until they fit?

But in refurbishing the psychic clothes of the poem, the poet turns from the Freudian exorcism of his early novel to a more consuming passion in a final invocation to "Art":

Tell me something, Art.
You know what it's like
Awake in your dry hell
Of volatile synthetic solvents.
Won't you help us brave the elements
Once more, of terror, anger, love?

Perhaps Merrill's most revealing metamorphosis of Promethean fire is into the linguistic process of "Lost in Translation" (*The New Yorker*, 6 April 1974). Here he remembers piecing together a puzzle with his multilingual governess, which evokes the more recent memory of a German translation by Rilke of Valéry's "Palme." Although he cannot find the translation, he imagines what is lost and retained in it:

Yet I can't
Just be imagining. I've seen it. Know
How much of the sun-ripe original

Felicity Rilke made himself forego
(Who loved French words—verger, mûr, parfumer)
In order to render its underlying sense.

For a poem in which the piecing together of a puzzle at every juncture responds to the fitting of words into a poetic pattern, the progress from a meditation on what is lost in literary translation to the transformation of life into literature is quite natural: "But nothing's lost. Or else: all is translation/And every bit of us is lost in it."

"Lost in Translation" is about Merrill's poetry in even more telling ways. Like the *oeuvre* itself, the legend of the puzzle—seen through the almost predominant pattern of its design—represents an "Eternal Triangle": a page (whom the governess imagines to be a son) torn between service to his sire or his sire's wife. (It is no surprise when the page's missing feet are found under the table with the child's own.) And the shapes of the individual pieces of the puzzle have—like the symbolist's words—their own significance:

Many take
Shapes known already—the craftsman's repertoire
Nice in its limitation—from other puzzles:
Witch on broomstick, ostrich, hourglass,
Even (surely not just in retrospect)
An inchling, innocently branching palm.

But nowhere does Merrill speak quite so precisely about his own craft—the individual poems and the totality of his work—as in the description by a medium of a "hand-sawn" individual piece of the puzzle:

But hidden here is a freak fragment
Of a pattern complex in appearance only.
What it seems to show is superficial
Next to that long-term lamination
Of hazard and craft, the karma that has
Made it matter in the first place.
Plywood. Piece of a puzzle.

The puzzle exists in Merrill's poetry. The whole is composed of intricately related parts, and it rewards explication even though once it has been puzzled out there may be little to do but dismantle it like the puzzle in "Lost in Translation." Its emphasis on "lamination" and "craft" returns us to a discussion of the forms of his poetry.

James Merrill has evolved his phenomenology of fire within three quite distinct generic forms which he handles with equal mastery: long narratives in traditional ballad stanzas, emblematic lyrics, and multi-sectioned meditations on time and the aesthetic process—the genre to which "18 West 11th Street" belongs. Each form aims at aesthetic possession. The worlds of the long ballad narratives—the dwindling aristocracy of an eastern summer resort in "The Summer People" (*The Fire Screen*, 1969) and a child's wish-fulfillment dream of kidnap in "Days of 1935" (*Braving the Elements*)—are framed in mock-heroic caricature:

That summer was the model
For several in a row—
High-water marks of humor
And humankindness, no
Discord at cards, at picnics,
Charades or musicales.
Their faces bright with pleasure might
Not have displeased Frans Hals.
("The Summer People")

The brief lyrics hold the world in monadic emblems cut and polished so precisely as to reflect the lights of Merrill's entire work. (They are abstract enough to reflect as well any lights the readers might bring). Their monadic quality isolates much of Merrill's phenomenology of fire.

"Mornings in a New House" emblazons the oedipal fire in a lyric which is Yeatsian both in quality and psychological overtones. A man awakens in a house to find the fire lit; a frozen window thaws, screening the claws of brightness. The poem then turns inward to contemplate his and his mother's childhood:

> The worst is over. Now between
> His person and that tamed uprush
> (Which to recall alone can make him flush)
> Habit arranges the fire screen.
>
> Crewel-work. His mother as a child
> Stitched giant birds and flowery trees
> To dwarf a house, *her* mother's—see the chimney's
> Puff of dull yarn! Still vaguely chilled,
>
> Guessing how even then her eight
> Years had foreknown him, nursed him, all,
> Sewn his first dress, sung to him, let him fall,
> Howled when his face chipped like a plate,
>
> He stands there wondering until red
> Infraradiance, wave on wave,
> So enters each plume-petal's crazy weave,
> Each worsted brick of the homestead,
>
> That once more, deep indoors blood's drawn,
> The tiny needlewoman cries,
> And to some faintest creaking shut of eyes
> His pleasure and the doll's are one.

Unlike the metaphor in "Early Settlers," this fire screen could support many interpretations. Perhaps the most obvious is the theme we have been tracing: crafted poetry informs psychic fire for both poet and reader, simultaneously re-animating life and comfortably distancing from its consuming heat. A whole complex of tenses as well as tension is unraveled in the crewel-work of the mother, and oedipal and promethean fire fuse in the violent eroticism: the sheathing of claws, the chipped doll's face, the drawing of blood, the mother's cries and the erotically-toned climax of pleasure as mother, doll, and son seem to have become one. The distancing of time backward toward the doll makes consummation possible.

In "Emerald" the distancing of time and possession is forward, and the disquieting oedipal eroticism of "The Fire Screen" is chillingly pressed into the brilliant and exquisite world of precious stone. The poem describes the poet's visit to his mother after the death of her second husband. Together they visit the vault where her valuables are kept. She offers him an emerald ring given to her by his father on the date of his birth and suggests he take it for his future wife, but the poet refuses:

> I do not tell her, it would sound theatrical,
> *Indeed this green room's mine, my very life.*
> *We are each other's; there will be no wife;*
> *The little feet that patter here are metrical.*

The two are immersed in a green light, and the poet implores her to keep the ring. The poem also describes the poet's pleasure at surviving with his mother her two husbands: "We are alive." It is poignantly conscious of death in a description of the mother's precautions against skin cancer—"Malignant atomies which an electric needle/Unfreckles from her soft white skin each fall"—and her appearance in the vault rummaging amongst her husband's "Will" and "Deed" as a "girl-bride jeweled in his grave." In the vault she is alive: "Her face gone queerly lit, fair, young,/Like faces of our dear ones who have died." While "Above ground, who can remember /Her as she once was?" Beneath the pressure of earth, the

speeded life of cells and the fired poetic imagination work toward a harmonious radiance. The poem closes with a ritual gesture and a poetic promise:

> But onto her worn knuckle slip the ring.
> Wear it for me. I silently entreat,
> Until—until the time comes. Our eyes meet.
> The world beneath the world is brightening.

"Lorelei" *(The Fire Screen)* embraces both past and future and perfects Merrill's habit of distilling the people of different times and places into the golden mask of one persona.

> The stones of kind and friend
> Stretch off into a trembling, sweatlike haze.
> They may not after all be stepping-stones
> But you have followed them. Each strands you, then
> Does not. Not yet. Not here.
> Is it a crossing? Is there no way back?
> Soft gleams lap the base of the one behind you
> On which a black girl sings and combs her hair.
> It's she who some day (when your stone is in place)
> Will see that much further into the golden vagueness
> Forever about to clear. Love with his chisel
> Deepens the lines begun upon your face.

Family and friends are the two primary sources of Merrill's poetic characters. "Lorelei" visualizes their temporal passage as one blends into the next. The expressive ambiguity "strands"—isolates or entwines—encourages the sense of an infinite series of receding mirror images in which past is contained by present into future infinity.

We are closer to "18 West 11th Street" in Merrill's long discursive lyrics. These poems reveal his phenomenology of fire and coalesce his biographical and aesthetic themes. Like the odes of the Romantic poets, they share several thematic and stylistic traits which are consistent and strong enough to give them the character of a personal genre. Each poem begins after a physical or emotional crisis has enervated the poet, effecting something like Proust's intensified sensibility after an asthmatic attack. A delicate but incisive sensuous perception leads from the present to related scenes in the past. There is a sense, and frequently the specified presence, of a crowd (a silent chorus watching the scene); and just as the different places and times in these poems are distilled into their aesthetic moment and structure, the crowd is narrowed toward a solitude. Movement is more in the rhythm of ritual dance—measured, repeated steps with darkly significant variations—than narrative action; fire—in any of its many forms—is more the protagonist than the poet who observes and meditates; and eroticism is closer to the core than to the surface. When the focus has narrowed sufficiently to burn through the poet's self-absorption, remaining under the thin gauze of ashes is the poem: a cooling artifice which coalesces and refigures the past.

Merrill's gradual mastery of this genre accompanies the subtle refinement of the forms and music of his poems. Several of the long lyrics anticipate "18 West 11th Street" in presenting erotic trauma and violent conflict between generations. In one of the earliest, "An Urban Convalescence," the scene of a demolished building leads the poet to imagine the destruction of a former home. Through demonic, erotic, and subtle light imagery, the poet does to his home in verse what the Weathermen accomplished with their brutal weapons. "The Broken Home" *(Nights and Days)* is quite explicit in its erotic concerns. During an evening walk, the window-framed sight of parents and their child evokes the poet's own childhood. His memory explodes the golden and static renaissance portrait in the window into a darkly shaded canvas of manneristic tension.

The memory of his father is dissected and frozen in rigid meter and rhyme:

> My father, who had flown in World War I,
> Might have continued to invest his life
> In cloud banks well above Wall Street and wife.
> But the race was run below, and the point was to win.
>
> . . .
>
> Each thirteenth year he married. When he died
> There were already several chilled wives
> In sable orbit—rings, cars, permanent waves.
> We'd felt him warming up for a green bride.

In verses we have seen, the mother's alienation takes cover in the image of suffragettes attacking the public figures of male authority, but there is nothing displaced about the poet's description of his own childhood trauma of erotic revelation:

> One afternoon, red, satyr-thighed
> Michael, the Irish setter, head
> Passionately lowered, led
> The child I was to a shut door. Inside,
>
> Blinds beat sun from the bed.
> The green-gold room throbbed like a bruise.
> Under a sheet, clad in taboos
> Lay whom we sought, her hair undone, outspread,
>
> And of a blackness found, if ever now, in old
> Engravings where the acid bit.
> I must have needed to touch it
> Or the whiteness—was she dead?
>
> Her eyes flew open, startled strange and cold.
> The dog slumped to the floor. She reached for me. I
>   fled.

Variation in the meter, precipitousness in the flow from verse to verse, and a slightly looser rhyme allow the bite, the hurt, the passion of the experience to come through. Finally the poem cools in a familiar pattern: in the *presence* of the home the past is creatively restructured.

"The Friend of the Fourth Decade" emphasizes not so much the recapture of time through poetic distillation as its destruction and, for the first time, associates the process with guilt. Like the infinitely receding mirror image of "Lorelei" and the fire screen of "Mornings in a New House," "The Friend of the Fourth Decade" evolves from an emblematic image. In a baptism not of fire but of "holy water from the tap," poet and friend remove stamps from postcards which are left "rinsed of the word." Bereaved of individuality they become a visual metaphor for verse—anonymous 3 X 5 scenes. When the friend announces a trip and, later, sends a postcard from a country where "Individual and type are one," metaphor and reality have become one; the friend has joined the poet's collection of postcards. We witness the violence and guilt of this reduction to measured scenes in the "danger" of the country from which the friend writes.

> "Here," he wrote on the back,
> "individual and type are one.
> Do as I please, I *am* the simpleton
> Whose last exploit is to have been exploited
> Neck and crop.

Despite the guilt, typical of Merrill and the metaphysical tradition in which he writes, all of these poems conclude with a sense of resolution and even joy.

The intimation of psychic violence in the poetic activity of "The Friend of the Fourth Decade" is fully explored in the surprisingly narrative development of "18 West 11th Street." The poem begins with the children of the age of Aquarius "perfecting a device / . . . /Of incommunication" in the basement. Suddenly, to this scene of Merrill's childhood in a broken home, the "prodigal/Sunset" returns, in the present, Merrill's most uneasy tense. His presence has a disorienting effect, and the poem suddenly explodes into a series of invectives against the mindless and vain love-hate violence of the Weathermen. Having established—through a pun on "premises"—the identity of the setting as both the poet's childhood home and the scene of Weathermen violence, the poem moves into a complicated rhythmic alternation between invertible scenes of the son's volatile past and the present poetic oasis of debris. The poet's home is recalled as it was: the funereal floral pattern of a carpet which nightly collected the ashes of metropolitan smokers, an erotically-tuned piano and the framed scene of ghostly presences above it. As the spectre of the past rises from the ruins, one realizes it had foreshadowed the present. Then, the chords of the piano modulate into the salt chords of surf, and several verses recall the Caribbean home of the Wilkersons (where the parents were vacationing at the time of the explosion). Headlines of the blast return us to the scene of ruin in "the March dawn." In visually stunning images, Merrill evokes the extinguished ruins, the floodlights of the bomb squad, the fire hoses and the defoliated trees. Again a return to the past of a hermetic but haunting scene of departure: two men and a woman, deeply and tragically involved, reach toward and through each other. In the final return to the March, 1971 scene there is a new tone of transfixed, if not transpired, purgation in which Cathy Wilkerson (as she was reported to have done by neighbors) makes a ghostly appearance. ⟨. . .⟩

The characteristics shared by Merrill's metaphysical lyrics are refined and completed in "18 West 11th Street." Here past blends imperceptibly into the present within the texture of his verses. For example, the second transition from the demolished site to the past is accomplished by allowing the description of the bomb squad's "cold blue searching beams" to suggest a metaphor for introspection and memory. In the final transition from the tragically involved human triad to the scene of ruin, an outburst of anger is transformed by metaphoric language into the smouldering fire, and the scene is changed:

> Discolorations from within, dry film
> Run backwards, parching, scorching, to consume
> Whatever filled you to the brim,
>
> Fierce tongue, black
> Fumes massing forth once more on
> Waterstilts that fail them.

The ironically-voiced *lingo* of the Weathermen—"brother? Love?"—is echoed in the description of the remembered triad: "Feeling how you reached past B towards him,/Brothers in grievance?" And, finally, the Dionysiac madness of Cathy Wilkerson and her "light-besotted saboteurs" is, as we shall see, embodied in Merrill's own voice. Within this closely woven texture, a metaphysical relationship between the different generations residing on West 11th Street is revealed in three of the most archetypal human myths: the prodigal son, original sin, Oedipus. In a poem about the conflict of generations, "18 West 11th Street," like the House of Thebes, becomes an emblem for some unavoidable matrix of fate which involves both poet and revolutionary.

There is an eloquent counterpoint in the poem between radical vocabulary ("word by numbskull word/Rebellion . . . Pentagon . . . Black Studies") and poised poetic language. The initial stanzas tease the reader with the similarity between constructing a bomb and the poetic process: "perfecting a device/ . . . Of incommunication ever after." "Incommunication" simultaneously brings to mind the reticence of much of Merrill's poetry and the parental excommunication which the child of a wealthy financier who had chosen poetry or radicalism as his life style would suffer. The poem continues to allude to the poetic process in many ways: the sleeping tuner, the construing of chromatic muddles, the arsenal of home-made elegies, the diffused deed, the charred ice-sculpture garden, the drunken backdrop of debris, and the pigeon's throat lifting. They are all focused in the last stanza into the poet's most moving evocation of his career:

> Forty-odd years gone by
> Toy blocks. Church bells. Original vacancy.
> O deepening spring.

In selecting the adjective "Toy," Merrill explores and detonates the psychic resources of words. This affecting reference to his craft, this pun within an intimated rhyme deepens the generic resolution in *joy*. "Toy" embraces both childhood and the mature note of universal pathos and loss at the core of the poem.

And just as the initial despair of the long lyrics deepens in "18 West 11th Street" into an awareness of the unchanging condition of the divinely but vainly gifted poet (only a puddle reflecting the backdrop of debris is healed), the crowd here is initiated and shares the poet's vision. Having seen a recoiling evil freeze over burnt-out life (as it does at the nadir of Dante's *Inferno*) and heard the song of the siren, this crowd intensifies into a "Rigorously chosen" coven whose gaze can still burn through the hermetic freeze. It knows that the destroyer of the West 11th Street home is not the aesthetic fire which glazes *objets d'art* nor the incidental anger of a confused generation but is deeply rooted in the human condition. Adam happened to be the name Cathy Wilkerson was heard to mutter before her escape, but the "Original vacancy" of the poem's conclusion is not merely the scene of departure from the poet's childhood. It is man's timeless exclusion from his unforgotten home.

Both the prodigal son and original sin strike a note of paternal betrayal. But "18 West 11th Street" is written in triple time: tercets, musical triads, and human triolism and a triple "composite" myth. In the first meditation on the past, the "three legged . . . thing in a riddle" almost names Oedipus, and the image is set to the suggestive and erotic tune of a piano provocatively fingering itself. The second meditation on the past describes two men reaching through a woman toward each other. As an alternative to the distilling of private passion into polished poetic images and forms—which Merrill does so well—he also displaces it in highly-stylized literary personae. (Note also the Eros and Psyche mask of "From the Cupola" in *Nights and Days*.) One scene from his long narrative of a child's fantasy kidnap, "Days of 1935" (*Braving the Elements*), comes to mind in connection with the veiled triad of "18 West 11th Street." Floyd and Jean are the Bonnie and Clyde-like kidnappers. When the son and Floyd are sleeping on the floor together because Jean is ill, Floyd passionately embraces the boy in his sleep. Of course, on second thought the analogy fails, but it is accurate to see the two as highly stylized and extreme forms of an "Eternal Triangle." Finally, the most forceful oedipal element in "18 West 11th Street" is the entangled relationship between Cathy Wilkerson's radicalism and James Merrill's poetry. Antigone and Oedipus were both born into the House of Thebes, and Cathy Wilkerson's destruction of her paternal home and James Merrill's pained elegies for his are acts of fate as well as their active wills. What had "Seemed anger" in the second verse is reticulated with such a wealth of biographical, historical, psychological, and archetypal insights in the course of the poem as to be totally transformed. Indeed, in the concluding tercet nature itself is deflected from its amoral cyclical course to be glazed—not

with the gliding, yellowing dust of earlier and lesser achieved poems but—with a patina of human destiny: "O *deepening* Spring." It is this awareness in "18 West 11th Street" which combines the calorism of fire and the animism of poetry with a tragic intensity greater than any previous poem by Merrill.

Merrill and Cathy Wilkerson standing as they do in mirrors at the two ends of "18 West 11th Street" almost have the effect of bracing the poem within the closed series of infinitely receding mirror reflections presented in "Lorelei." But in "Having passed through the mirror" at the poem's conclusion, Cathy Wilkerson seems to symbolize the psychic effect of the explosion on James Merrill and his poetry. The constant rhythm behind the complex thematic developments in "18 West 11th Street" is percussive: disorientations, explosions, ruptures, shocks, and quakes. It is as if in shocking leafless the pattern-making linden opposite the house, the explosion has also shocked Merrill from the long, consecutive lines of his earlier poetry. His measures here are uneven and shorter; his thought more driving. Although these new elements are coerced by communion with "who knows what of the reptilian," disorientation is not decline in poetic merit. Rather, Merrill seems to have reached back through Cathy Wilkerson to Rimbaud for a final lesson from the symbolists: "the poet makes himself a *seer* by a long and reasoned derangement of all his senses."

"Yánnina" (*Saturday Review*, December 1972), a recent poem which associates the Turkish tyrant, Ali Pasha, with the poet's father ("Ali, my father—both are dead."), indicates Merrill may continue delineating father surrogates in his poetry. But the subtle tension of temporal sequence in "18 West 11th Street"—most evident in a cascade of participal phrases—promises some significant changes in the texture of his poetry. The facility with technique in his earlier volumes—some of the most perfectly measured meters, balanced rhymes, and syntaxed prosody in contemporary American poetry—has evolved into the expressive freedoms of occasional metrical irregularities, dissonant rhymes, and strained and elided syntax. But the irregularities are held in absolute if elliptical orbit by the ghost of an already-perfected classical style. The light of Apollonian fire has cooled, and the rhythm is more frenzied, more Dionysiac. In this most recent poetry rather than an extraterrestrial animus—the artifice of eternity—we hear more frequently the voice of the elements themselves: minerals, landscape, nature. In "Under Libra: Weights and Measures" (*Braving the Elements*), instead of past and present biographical time resolved into the poet's artifice, several characters evaporate off an indistinguishable southwestern landscape. Like a Cézanne painting, the legend is almost submerged in the texture of the canvas. "The Black Mesa" (*Braving the Elements*) is written in the voice of the plateau. In "McKane's Falls" (*Poetry*, September, 1973), the protagonists and landscape blend wittily and pictorially into each other. At its conclusion, the waterfall itself rather than the poet assumes the voice of the poem:

> Now you've seen through me, sang the cataract,
> A fraying force, but unafraid,
> Plunge through my bath of plus and minus both,
> Acid and base,
> The mind that mirrors and the hands that act.
> Enter this inmostspace
> Its lean illuminations decompose.

It is as if Merrill has found in nature a second informing vision for his world. In a footnote to "Mornings in a New House," Merrill lamented that he had not been led by words from the fire screen through the "screen of fire" to the scene on the inside baffle plate. His poetry seems now to have traveled that route and located itself dead center.

Phenomenologically, fire has rarely been considered a part of nature. Rather it is man's divinely inspired instrument for transforming nature to his own purposes. In nature itself, as in Merrill's later poetry, the heat of biological life is buried, pressured and frozen into mineral form. Were future semiologists to compare the "deep structure" shared by the progression of life from the flushed heat of living organisms to the cool brilliance of precious stones and the trajectory of aesthetic processes, James Merrill's poetry could well be their "mastermind."

When *Braving the Elements* won the Bollingen Poetry Prize for James Merrill, the New York *Times* published an ill-informed editorial criticizing the foundation for making the award in troubled times to a genteel and private poet. It is true Merrill has avoided confessional poetry and topical or fashionable subjects. But for readers who understand Merrill's highly-informed language, the poems of *Braving the Elements* deal more memorably and more incisively with liberation, radical violence, kidnapping, space travel, the assassination of political leaders, and the effect of mass-media on the English language than any poetry written in America today. More importantly, Merrill is the finest poet translating the tradition of French symbolism into the English language. On the European continent, the predominant force in contemporary poetry is still the symbolist movement. In the English-speaking world other currents have deflected that potent language because Yeats found few successors sufficiently gifted in the style. Merrill is fluent in it. And if we are to understand lyrical poetry in the etymological sense of rootedness in musical expression, Merrill is one of its few preeminent masters.

HELEN VENDLER
From "James Merrill" (1976/1979)
Part of Nature, Part of Us
1980, pp. 210–32

Divine Comedies

Since he published his *First Poems*, James Merrill's energies have been divided between successive books of increasingly brilliant lyric poems (the most recent, *Braving the Elements*, in 1972) and attempts in larger fictional forms—two plays (1955 and 1960) and two novels (1957 and 1965). The flashes and glimpses of "plot" in some of the lyrics—especially the longer poems—reminded Merrill's readers that he wanted more than the usual proportion of dailiness and detail in his lyrics, while preserving a language far from the plainness of journalistic poetry, a language full of arabesques, fancifulness, play of wit, and oblique metaphor. And yet the novels were not the solution, as Merrill himself apparently sensed.

In his new collection, where most of the poems have a narrative emphasis, Merrill succeeds in expressing his sensibility in a style deliberately invoking Scheherazade's tireless skein of talk: the long poem, "The Book of Ephraim," which takes up two-thirds of this volume, is described as "The Book of a Thousand and One Evenings." In explaining how he came to write this novelistic poem, Merrill recapitulates his struggle with fiction:

> I yearned for the kind of unseasoned telling found
> In legends, fairy tales, a tone licked clean
> Over the centuries by mild old tongues,
> Grandam to cub, serene, anonymous.
> Lacking that voice, the in its fashion brilliant

> Nouveau roman (including one I wrote)
> Struck me as an orphaned form.

He once more tried his hand at writing a novel, but it lost itself in "word-painting":

> The more I struggled to be plain, the more
> Mannerism hobbled me. What for?
> Since it had never truly fit, why wear
> The shoe of prose?

His narrative forms in verse allow Merrill the waywardness, the distractions, the eddies of thought impossible in legends or in the spare *nouveau roman*, and enable the creation of both the long tale and of a new sort of lyric, triumphantly present here in two faultless poems, sure to be anthologized, "Lost in Translation" and "Yánnina."

Divine Comedies marks a departure in Merrill's work. He has always been a poet of Eros, but in an unwritten novel, about "the incarnation and withdrawal of / A god," "the forces joined / By Eros" come briefly together and then disperse:

> Exeunt severally the forces joined
> By Eros—Eros in whose mouth the least
> Dull fact had shone of old, a wetted pebble.

And Merrill's servant in Greece, whose name (Kleo) he had never seen written, turns out to be named not Cleopatra, as he had thought, but Clio; she is not the presiding surrogate for Eros but the incarnation of the Muse of history, Merrill's new patroness:

> "Kleo" we still assume is the royal feline
> Who seduced Caesar, not the drab old muse
> Who did. Yet in the end it's Clio I compose
> A face to kiss, who clings to me in tears.
> What she has thought about us all God knows.

If the divinity of youth was Eros, the divinity of middle age is Clio; if the metaphor for being thirty was embrace, the metaphor for being fifty is companionship; and if the presence in the mind was once love, it is now death.

Quickened by the thought of death, which so resists the rational intelligence, the imaginations of poets react and react and react, pressing back (to use Stevens' phrase) with all the inventions, illusions, conjectures, wiles, seductions, and protests of which they are capable. Nothing so compels poets to complication: and if what they conjure up to talk to them from the dark is a voice recognizably their own but bearing a different name, they (and their readers) are peculiarly consoled by the reflected Word. So Milton found his own best voice speaking back at him under the names of Phoebus Apollo and St. Peter; so Dante fell into colloquy with his elder self, Vergil; so Yeats invented his "mysterious instructors" who dictated to him and his wife his elaborate system of history and the afterlife; and so James Merrill, in his divine comedies, communicates with an affable familiar ghost named Ephraim, first evoked at the Ouija board in Stonington twenty years ago, and a frequent visitor since.

In his 1970 volume, *The Country of a Thousand Years of Peace* (literally Switzerland, but since Merrill's friend Hans Lodeizen had died there, also metaphorically the country of the dead), Merrill published his first Ouija poem, in which a candid, if ineptly expressed, stanza offers the motive for listening to "voices from the other world":

> Once looked at lit
> By the cold reflections of the dead
> Risen extinct but irresistible,
> Our lives have never seemed more full, more real,
> Nor the full moon more quick to chill.

These lines give at least some notion of the origins of "The Book of Ephraim." It is a poem in twenty-six sections, each beginning with a different letter of the alphabet, from A to Z, exhausting the twenty-six capital letters of the Ouija board. And yet, for all its ninety pages, the Book is not finished, scarcely even begun, its dramatic personae—living, dead, and invented—hardly glimpsed, and only partially listed, its tale of an unfinished novel still untold, its gaily inventive theology linking this world to the otherworld barely delineated.

Merrill casually and mockingly praises his own "net of loose talk tightening to verse" through his surrogates among the dead. Ephraim ("A Greek Jew / Born AD 8 at XANTHOS"), who communicates of course in the caps of the Ouija board, tells Merrill,

> . . . POPE SAYS THAT WHILE BITS
> STILL WANT POLISHING THE WHOLES A RITZ
> BIG AS A DIAMOND.

Instead of Vergilian solemnity, this guide to the otherworld uses social chitchat:

> U ARE SO QUICK MES CHERS I FEEL WE HAVE
> SKIPPING THE DULL CLASSROOM DONE IT ALL
> AT THE SALON LEVEL.

For rationalists reading the poem, Merrill includes a good deal of self-protective irony, even incorporating in the tale a visit to his ex-shrink, who proclaims the evocation of Ephraim and the other Ouija "guests" from the other world a *folie à deux* between Merrill and his friend David Jackson. But once the "machinery"—not here the sylphs and nymphs of *The Rape of the Lock*, but the ghosts of dead friends and other revenants—is accepted as a mode of imagination, what then can be said of the import of this strange poem?

It is centrally a hymn to history and a meditation on memory—personal history and personal memory, which are, for this poet at least, the muse's materials. The host receives his visible and invisible guests, convinced that Heaven—the invisible sphere—is "the surround of the living," that the poet's paradise is nothing other than all those beings whom he has known and has imagined. Through Ephraim,

> We, all we knew, dreamed, felt and had forgotten,
> Flesh made word, became . . . a set of
> Quasi-grammatical constructions . . .
>   Hadn't—from books, from living—
> The profusion dawned on us, of "languages"
> Any one of which, to who could read it,
> Lit up the system it conceived?—bird-flight,
> Hallucinogen, chorale and horoscope:
> Each its own world, hypnotic, many-sided
> Facet of the universal gem.

These "facets of the universal gem" shine throughout "The Book of Ephraim," which aims at being a poem of a thousand and one reflecting surfaces. The irregularities and accidents of life are summed up in the fiction of reincarnation which animates the book's theology: people pass in and out of life as the bodies in which their spirits are incarnated die of heart attacks, in fires, or by less violent means; spirits get placed in unsuitable bodies; and in the crowded world of the afterlife a constant influx of souls makes for an agitated scene. Merrill's father, dead and between lives, gets through on the board:

> Then CEM gets through,
> High-spirited, incredulous—he'd tried
> The Board without success when Nana died.
> Are we in India? Some goddamn fool
> Hindoo is sending him to Sunday School.
> He loved his wives, his other children, me;
> Looks forward to his next life.

The next life of Charles Merrill, announces Ephraim, is in Kew:

> YR FATHER JM he goes on (we're back
> In the hotel room) WAS BORN YESTERDAY
> To a greengrocer: name, address in Kew
> Spelt out.

This social comedy between otherworld and this world is one tone of "The Book of Ephraim": another is reminiscence of a simpler ego:

> *Götterdämmerung.* From a long ago
> Matinee—the flooded Rhine, Valhalla
> In flames, my thirteenth birthday—one spark floating
> Through the darkened house had come to rest
> Upon a mind so pitifully green
> As only now, years later, to ignite . . .
> The heartstrings' leitmotif outsoared the fire.

Still another tone juxtaposes the eternal confrontation of youth and age, Eros and entropy, Prometheus and the eroding Parthenon:

> Leave to the sonneteer eternal youth.
> His views revised, an older man would say
> He was "content to live it all again."
> Let this year's girl meanwhile resume her pose,
> The failing sun its hellbent azimuth.
> Let stolen thunder dwindle out to sea.
> Dusk eat into the marble-pleated gown.

Merrill's company of the dead comes in late exchange for the abandoned dream of the immortal couple, echoed through the book in Wagnerian terms, in Tristan's *"höchste Lust,"* and in Brünnhilde's choice of love over Valhalla: *"Nie Liebe liesse ich nie, mir nähmen nie sie die Liebe."* These sublimities remain, icons unattainable but not disallowed, at the edges of this deliberately social and tempered poetry. Wanting consuming passions, Merrill says, he has found only refining ones.

Merrill's lines, in their exquisite tones, are often painful to read. Though they keep their beautiful poise on the brink of sense and feeling, and aim here at the autumnal, or the ironic, they keep echoes, undimmed, of the past: Merrill is not yet, and I think will never be, a poet free of sensuality, love, and youth, actual or remembered. Enshrined with Brünnhilde in the section (Q, of course) of Quotations in "The Book of Ephraim" is Spenser's transcendent dream of the Garden of Adonis, where in "immortal blis . . . Franckly each paramour his leman knowes," in an equable and unfallen counterpart of Wagner's doomed couples.

"The Book of Ephraim," for the most part, refuses the postures thought appropriate to age—stoicism, resignation, disbelief, patience, or cynicism. The mild conviviality of Merrill's unearthly symposium is boyish in its welcome to comedy, sympathy, and nostalgia at once; and the poet's naive enthusiasm for "learning" from Ephraim the ins and outs of behavior and fate in the otherworld is so different from Dante's and Yeats's gloomy reverence for their guides that we are moved to delight by the refraction of these "divine comedies" from their more religious antecedents.

On the other hand, "The Book of Ephraim" is not really a comic poem. When Merrill and Jackson protest Ephraim's offhand tone about death, and say "Must *everything* be witty?" Ephraim answers, in a phrase that could be applied to the whole poem,

> AH MY DEARS
> I AM NOT LAUGHING   I WILL SIMPLY NOT SHED TEARS.

If life is "a death's head to be faced," it is also, in this poem, the repository of counterpointed treasures.

The claim of this long poem to moral significance rests in the way it balances two entirely opposite truths about middle age. One is the truth of perceived fate, as it declares itself in the simplest of sentences: *This is who I am; This is where I live; This is the person I live with; My father is dead; I will not fall in love again.* The other is the truth of received experience, as it glitters in a cloud of witnesses—all the things seen, the people met, the places traveled to, the books read, the faces loved, the lines written, the events lived through, the events imagined, the past absorbed—the past not only of personal life but of cultural history as well. The glowing dialectic of restriction of present life and expansion of experienced soul animates these pages into a visionary balancing of scales, now one pan up, now the other. Merrill's imagination has always been mercurial, airy, and darting, but here the counterweight of death adds a constant pull toward grief.

"The Book of Ephraim" might seem to risk the accusation of triviality, in its apparent refusal to take large issues seriously:

Life like the periodical not yet
Defunct kept hitting the stands. We seldom failed
To leaf through each new issue—war, election,
Starlet; write, scratch out; eat steak au poivre,
Chat with Ephraim.

But under this briskness lies a wasting ennui:

The whole house needs repairs. Neither can bring
Himself to say so. Hardly lingering,
We've reached the point, where the tired Sound just
          washes
Up to, then avoids our feet.

In this repetitive routine, Merrill is free to admit all the flotsam and jetsam floating in his mind, and to let us judge that mind as we will.

Because Merrill is a poet whose devotion goes to the Absolute under the form of the Beautiful, his range, like that of the Beautiful itself, is diverse: the Good and the True do not really participate in a spectrum of more and less in quite the same way. From bibelots to Beatrice, from embroidery to altarpiece, goes the scale, and Merrill's tone modulates along with its object. Like Proust and Nabokov, two other sensibilities more attached to the Beautiful than to the Scientific, the Philosophical, the Ethical, or the Ideological, Merrill avoids being polemical or committed, in the ordinary sense of those words. By taking conversation—from lovers' exchange of vows to friends' sentences in intimacy—as the highest form of human expression (in contrast to the rhapsode's hymns, the orator's harangues, or the initiate's hermetic colloquies with the divine) Merrill becomes susceptible to charges of frivolity, at least from readers with a taste only for the solemn. But this espousal of the conversational as the ultimate in linguistic achievement is a moral choice, one which locates value in the human and everyday rather than in the transcendent.

It is no accident that Merrill appropriates for himself Keats's image of the chameleon poet, as delighted by an Iago as by an Imogen; he draws out a constantly changing veil of language like the endless scarves of silk from the illusionist's hands, now one color, now another, scattering light in rainbow transparency over and under his subject. And yet the severity of death fixes a new, unwavering color on the apparently boundless earlier sympathy with the attractions of experience:

Already I take up
Less emotional space than a snowdrop.
. . . Young chameleon, I used to
Ask how on earth one got sufficiently
Imbued with otherness. And now I see.

Though the other poems in this collection share the conversational immediacy of "The Book of Ephraim," they also, in their persistent elegiac tone, seem to be fragments from a

modern version of *The Prelude*. "Lost in Translation," of which the putative subject is Merrill's putting together, as a child, a complicated jigsaw puzzle with the aid of his governess, is really a gorgeous combination of Popean diversity of surface talk and Wordsworthian rumination on the past, and on the powers and lapses of memory. It is an easier poem than "Yánnina," an elegy for Merrill's father set in the Turkish town of Yánnina, once ruled by Ali Pasha, who becomes in the poem the surrogate for Charles Merrill. We see Ali flanked by "two loves, two versions of the Feminine": one the "pious matron" Frossíni, drowned at Ali's order for having refused compliance; the other Vassilikí, pictured with Ali sleeping in her lap. Byron (whose ottava rima Merrill here borrows and rings changes on) visited Ali, and found him "Very kind . . . indeed, a father." Merrill continues,

Funny, that is how I think of Ali.
On the one hand, the power and the gory
Details, pigeon-blood rages and retali-
Ations, gouts of fate that crust his story;
And on the other, charm, the whimsically
Meek brow, its motives all ab ulteriori,
The flower-blue gaze twining to choke proportion,
Having made one more pretty face's fortune . . .
Ali, my father—both are dead.

Around this center vacillate feelings about the Oriental multiplicity of Yánnina—its provincial promenade cluttered with sellers' booths, a magician's tent, loudspeaker music— and feelings about the two women, the wronged matron and the complaisant concubine. The scene on the promenade resembles the London Fair in *The Prelude*, but the human jumble of sight and sound, so inimical to the recoiling Wordsworthian sensibility which required solitude and massive forms, is the food of life to Merrill, who needs movement, color, the vulgar and the passionate together. As for the two women, one, the wronged Frossíni, has become a secular saint:

And in the dark gray water sleeps
One who said no to Ali. Kiosks all over town
Sell that postcard, "Kyra Frossíni's Drown,"
Showing her, eyeballs white as mothballs, trussed
Beneath the bulging moon of Ali's lust.
A devil (turban and moustache and sword)
Chucks the pious matron overboard.

Frossíni's fate is half farce, half martyrdom; and "her story's aftertaste / Varies according to the listener," especially when her garish memorial postcard is placed against the skillful, still preserved, painting of Ali and Vassilikí—"almost a love-death, höchste Lust!" In the end, though, both versions of the feminine—"one virginal and tense, brief as a bubble, / One flesh and bone"—go up in smoke, and the poem dips momentarily into ghoulish images of death:

Where giant spits revolving try their rusty treble,
Sheep's eyes pop, and death-wish ravens croak
. . . At the island monastery, eyes
Gouged long since to the gesso sockets will outstare
This or that old timer on his knees.

The empty sockets would seem to betoken the end of Ali and his women, and of the blushing girls and radiant young men courting on the promenade as well:

Where did it lead,
The race, the radiance? To oblivion
Dissembled by a sac of sparse black seed.

This is Merrill's most complicated retelling of his family history. But since living, of itself, perpetuates nothing, he turns, almost reluctantly, to his pain and his pen at home, far from Yánnina, and invites us to enter with him, in fantasy, the magician's tent on the promenade where a woman can be sawed into two, then miraculously healed, a reassuring myth to set over against Frossíni's fate:

A glittering death
Is hefted, swung. The victim smiles consent.
To a sharp intake of breath she comes apart . . .
Then to a general exhalation heals
Like anybody's life, bubble and smoke
In afterthought.

Afterthought may, in comparison to life, be only "bubble and smoke," but afterthought is also the domain of art, where a dreamy eternity envelops Ali. In afterthought, the "elements converge":

Glory of windless mornings that the barge
(Two barges, one reflected, a quicksilver joke)
Kept scissoring and mending as it steered
The old man outward and away,
Amber mouthpiece of a narghilé
Buried in his by then snow white beard.

In this universe, the poet's reflective mind meets and internalizes all the Oriental opulence of Ali and his town, the prudishness and pathos of Frossíni, the luxuriousness of Vassilikí, and the recurrent chorus of the courting couples on the promenade: "What shall the heart learn, that already knows / Its place by water, and its time by sun?" It also accepts the ghastly permanence of the dead bodies visible in the monastery underground burial-place, and the dying animals turning on spits. But it believes that in writing it can make "some inmost face to shine / Maned with light, ember and anodyne, / Deep in a desktop burnished to its grain." The lights have vanished along the lake in Yánnina, but

Weeks later, in this study gone opaque,
They are relit. See through me. See me through.

The pun, like most of Merrill's plays on words, is serious, and the elegy has gone as far as a poem can go in attempting to take into its stylized world of "bubble and smoke" the fleshly lusts of Ali and the theatrical immolation of Frossíni, the Vanity Fair of the world and the gruesome end of the sexual impulse. It is an odd, crowded, and baroque elegy, with a remarkable joining of filial and paternal spheres.

It remains to be seen how Merrill, whose inventiveness is to be trusted, will continue with such narrative poems and, perhaps, with more installments of "The Book of Ephraim." Mozart, according to Ephraim, has been currently reincarnated as a black rock star: it makes one want more news from that source.

Mirabell: Books of Number

James Merrill's *Mirabell: Books of Number,* which won the National Book Award for 1978, is the middle volume of a trilogy composed with the aid of a Ouija board. The Ouija board is a symbol system that offers potentially unlimited combinations of letters and numbers, affirmations and denials; it can stand, we might say, for language itself. The first installment of Merrill's trilogy, "The Book of Ephraim" (printed in *Divine Comedies,* in 1976), exhausted the letters of the board; it was composed in twenty-six sections labeled "A" through "Z." The current volume uses up the numbers of the board in ten books going from zero to nine. The final volume, to be called *Scripts for the Pageant,* is left with "Yes" and "No." The Ouija board is a shared system, used by the dead and the living, in which tradition, in the person of the dead, meets an individual talent—or, in this case, the joint talents of the poet and his friend David Jackson. Together, as JM and DJ, in their house at Stonington, where the action of *Mirabell* occurs, they

transcribe the rapid gestures of a blue-willow cup that they use instead of a planchette. The messages from "the other side," all in the uppercase of the board, are edited by Merrill—compressed, made intelligible, made into poetry. The books of the trilogy consist of board messages interspersed with commentary and colloquy by the poet.

The pages of the books are typographically unnerving, as blocks of otherworldly uppercase—looking, as a friend remarked, like a computer printout—alternate with blocks of mortal lowercase. The uppercase, in the board's peculiar spelling—"before" becomes "B4," "you" becomes "U"—is sometimes a ten-syllable line (when dead people talk), sometimes a fourteen-syllable line (when the spirits, who enact "a fall from metrical grace," take over). Human talk is always decasyllabic, in "this rough pentameter, our virtual birthright." From time to time, a lyric form, like a strain of music, appears. The talk of the dead and of the living alike tends to rhyme in couplets and quatrains, but that of the spirits does not rhyme. The spirits, who are here represented chiefly by one among them bearing the number 741, seem to be in part what Milton would have called the fallen angels, and at first conceived of as black batlike creatures. At the center of the third book, 741 metamorphoses into a peacock, and he is later given the name Mirabell, supposedly after the "strut and plumage" of Congreve's hero, but also after "Merrill." Mirabell, "a paragon of courtly gentleness," here replaces the earlier Ephraim as familiar spirit. Ephraim was chatty, conversational; he was comfortable in iambic pentameter, since he was human ("A Greek Jew / Born AD 8 at XANTHOS . . . / a favorite of TIBERIUS . . . Died / AD 36 on CAPRI throttled / By the imperial guard for having LOVED / THE MONSTER'S NEPHEW [sic] CALIGULA"). However, Ephraim spoke rather rarely, and his book is narrated mostly by Merrill. Mirabell, on the other hand, speaks in ungainly syllabics, and the poet's interpolated lines serve as connective tissue between Mirabell's speeches and the speeches of the dead. The dead, principally, are Wystan Auden and Maria Mitsotáki, a childless Greek friend of Merrill's, whom he celebrated in a lyric, "Words for Maria" (1969), and who died of cancer.

Mirabell is a poem about the dead in part because it is a poem of the single life and childlessness; since there is no question of posterity, life is composed of oneself and one's friends, the dead as much as the living. The four bound together round the Ouija board—JM, DJ, Wystan, Maria—are chosen for their lessons because of their childlessness. To Auden's question "Why the four of us?" Mirabell answers, "KEEP IN MIND THE CHILDLESSNESS WE SHARE   THIS TURNS US / OUTWARD TO THE LESSONS & THE MYSTERIES." The scale of the poem is both domestic and cosmic. The domestic life includes day-by-day details of life in Greece and in Stonington, the visits of friends, the deaths of parents, an operation. The cosmic life, presided over in Manichean fashion by two gods—Chaos, the god of feeling, and an inexorable "God B" (for "biology")—is evolutionary, hierarchical, mythological, and intermittently purposive. God B's successive projects have included Atlantis, the centaurs, and Eden; he "is not only history but earth itself." The literary tradition in which the poem falls includes all works written by men to whom the angels speak outright: Dante, the four Apostles, Buddha, Mohammed, and, in later days, Milton, Blake, Victor Hugo, and Yeats. Merrill himself diffidently admits to doubts about "all this / warmed up Milton, Dante, Genesis," fearing "Allegory in whose gloom the whole / Horror of Popthink fastens on the soul"; he worries about being "cast / Into this paper Hell out of Doré / or Disney." On the other hand, the quintet of Merrill, Jackson, Auden, Maria Mitsotáki, and Mirabell is said to be an example of the "vital groupings of five," who do "V work"—the work of mind and heart (primarily poetry and music)—encouraged, according to Mirabell, by loves that do not envisage the production of bodies:

> LOVE OF ONE MAN FOR ANOTHER OR LOVE BETWEEN
>   WOMEN
> IS A NEW DEVELOPMENT OF THE PAST 4000 YEARS
> ENCOURAGING SUCH MIND VALUES AS PRODUCE THE
>   BLOSSOMS
> OF POETRY & MUSIC, THOSE 2 PRINCIPAL LIGHTS OF
> GOD BIOLOGY. LESSER ARTS NEEDED NO EXEGETES:
> ARCHITECTURE SCULPTURE THE MOSAICS & PAINTINGS
>   THAT
> FLOWERD IN GREECE & PERSIA CELEBRATED THE
>   BODY.
> POETRY MUSIC SONG INDWELL & CELEBRATE THE
>   MIND . . .
> HEART IF U WILL.

Few painters or sculptors enter this life of the mind, Mirabell adds, since they, "LIKE ALL SO-CALLED NORMAL LOVERS," exist for no purpose other than to produce bodies. This Platonic myth is mocked by Mirabell's listeners: "Come now, admit that certain very great / Poets and musicians have been straight." But the claim, however whimsical, has been made, and the whole of Merrill's trilogy can be seen as substitution of the virtues of mind and heart—culminating in music and poetry—for the civic and familial and martial virtues usually espoused by the epic.

We might hesitate to think of *Mirabell* in epic terms, since it learns at least as much from Pope and Byron as from Dante. But in its encyclopedic instructions about the history of the cosmos and its cast of characters from Olympus (if we may so locate the spirits) and from Hades as well as from earth, its traits are epic ones. For all its rueful tone as it fears and doubts its own matter and method, it goes irrepressibly along, piecing together shards of myth from all cultures—Akhnaton rubs shoulders with Mohammed and centaurs, while Mother Nature, in conjunction with the Sultan God B, presides over all. The hymn to nature in the seventh book articulates the ebb and flow of loyalty—now to mind, now to nature—implicit in the whole poem. Fearful of the power of the senses, Merrill, like some modern metaphysical, asks what rational instruments they have robbed him of—"What have you done with / My books, my watch and compass, my slide-rule?"—but nature answers with her own fascination of texture, whether in constellations or in bodies, "those infinite / Spangled thinnesses whose weave gosling and cygnet / Have learned already in the shell."

When Merrill contemplates what he has done in writing this book, he complains to Auden that the result is maddening:

> It's all by someone else!
> In your voice, Wystan, or in Mirabell's.
> I want it mine, but cannot spare those twenty
> Years in a cool dark place that *Ephraim* took
> In order to be palatable wine.
> This book by contrast, immature, supine,
> Still kicks against its archetypal cradle.
> . . . I'd set
> My whole heart, after *Ephraim*, on returning
> To private life, to my own words. Instead,
> Here I go again, a vehicle
> In this cosmic carpool. Mirabell once said
> He taps my word banks. I'd be happier
> If *I* were tapping them. Or thought I were.

Auden replies in a magisterial defense of convention, tradition, and fable. On convention:

> THINK WHAT A MINOR
> PART THE SELF PLAYS IN A WORK OF ART
> COMPARED TO THOSE GREAT GIVENS   THE ROSE-
>   BRICK MANOR
> ALL TOPIARY FORMS & METRICAL
> MOAT ARIPPLE!

On tradition:

> AS FOR THE FAMILY ITSELF MY DEAR
> JUST GAPE UP AT THAT CORONETED FRIEZE:
> SWEET WILLIAMS & FATE-FLAVORED EMILIES
> THE DOUBTING THOMAS & THE DULCET ONE
> (HARDY MY BOY WHO ELSE? & CAMPION).

On the superiority of fable to facts:

> FACTS JM WERE ALL U KNEW TO WANT,
> WRETCHED RICKETY RECALCITRANT
> URCHINS   THE FEW WHO LIVE GROW UP TO BE
> IMPS OF THE ANTIMASQUE.

In fable, "A TABLE / IS SET & LAMPS LIT FOR THE FEASTING GODS." Auden concludes that, given time, facts themselves take on the livery of fable, and become material for art. The poem ends as Mirabell withdraws in favor of a stern-voiced archangel Michael, speaking in long, irregular lines: he will be the next instructor, an unfallen rather than a fallen one, as Merrill proceeds into the *Paradiso* of his "Divine Comedies."

"Ephraim" is, on the whole, a cheerful book, constructed around a mythology of reincarnation: most people live on, over and over, even if in someone else's body. In *Mirabell*, Merrill and Jackson discover that their dead companions Auden and Maria will not be reincarnated, but will dissolve into their elements, having first been stripped of their earthly connections. The end of the book celebrates "Maria's Himmelfahrt" and Auden's. Goodbyes are said, of a careful lightness:

> How
> We'll miss you! We'd imagined—I know   CIAO

JM had imagined a thousand and one nights of conversation with these indispensable voices. But the Ouija board meets the law of dissolution, and in the last episode Auden and Maria seem to have disappeared, leaving behind only a snapshot— "Young, windblown / Maria with dark glasses and Gitane"— and a book "by Wystan / Face up . . . all week / Open to Miranda's villanelle." *Mirabell* is a book of long farewell to the parental figures of Auden and Maria, a book that holds on to the dead as long as possible. They are the people who call JM and DJ "MES ENFANTS" (Maria, known as "Maman") or "MY BOYS" (Auden). When these voices fall silent, there will be no one to whom the poet is a child. Though Merrill's mother is alive, she is deliberately left out of the trilogy, as "Ephraim" explains:

> All of which lights up, as scholarship
> Now and then does, a matter hitherto
> Overpainted—the absence from these pages
> Of my own mother. Because of course she's here
> Throughout, the breath drawn after every line,
> Essential to its making as to mine.

The deaths of David Jackson's parents preface the appearance of Mirabell. In the usual biological cycle, parents die after their children have become parents; the internalizing of the parental role, it is believed, enables the parents to be absorbed into the filial psyche. In the childless world of *Mirabell*, the disappearance of parents, or parental friends, is the disappearance of the parental and therefore of the filial; JM and DJ can no longer be "boys," but must put on the mortality of the survivor. However much the sweetness of posthumous conversation with Auden and Maria may be prolonged—with analyses of their character, examples of their wit, descriptions of their lives—the end of the exchange is envisaged from Maria's first warning, at the end of Book 1: "I HAVE MORE TO LOSE." In Merrill's myth, Maria will become a plant, not a human being; the radiation she endured as a treatment for cancer reduced her human soul to the vegetative level. Auden will be "stripped, reduced to essences, joined to infinity," like one of his beloved minerals:

> What must at length be borne
> Is that the sacred bonds are chemical.

The "seminar" of the participants round the Ouija board is itself such a "stripping process," since Mirabell, Wystan, and Maria will gradually fade away. Merrill's work in creating the trilogy is a comparable "stripping":

> Art—
> The tale that all but shapes itself—survives
> By feeding on its personages' lives,
> The stripping process, sort of. What to say?
> Our lives led *to* this. It's the price we pay.

If the artist needs new resources in middle age, it is not because the old ones are exhausted. On the contrary, the old ones, accumulating exponentially, seem to forbid the acquisition of the new. At some point the writer begins his replay in slow motion of all the eclectic litter and learning that crowds his mind: unburdening himself, he discharges, in an art relatively random by contrast to that of his earlier years, portions of everything he knows. So the board throws up bits and pieces of Merrill's reading (as *A Vision* threw up Yeats's, as *History* threw up Lowell's), and one of the difficulties with the trilogy is that no one of us duplicates Merrill's reading bank, any more than we duplicate Blake's or Milton's. The jumble that is any fifty-year-old memory poses for a reader the problem of other minds; the encyclopedic modern poem, from the *Cantos* on, presses the question almost intolerably.

Though the allusive density of *Mirabell* makes the poem at first difficult, the test of such a poem is not in the first reading (though if there is not enough pleasure in that, the reader is lost for good), but in the reading that takes place once the scheme, the family relations, and the life histories in question have become natural and familiar. In this poem Merrill is enterprisingly (with some incidental wreckage) enlarging his theater of operations. He avoids for lines on end the effortless jeweled effects for which he has been known, and he has turned aside from lyrics of the personal life to narrative, to mythological and metaphysical "explanations" of a discursive order ruled not by "feeling" or by "beauty" but by "truth." He is writing in voices other than his own. These undertakings are not wholly new: Merrill said as far back as 1962: "If I am host at last / It is of little more than my own past. / May others be at home in it." But the past of the earlier volumes was on the whole a selective one, careful of its references, arranged in exquisite forms, and restricted to crises of feeling. Two poems in *Nights and Days*, of 1966, appear to anticipate the trilogy. In a sequence of reflections on love called "The Thousand and Second Night," "the rough pentameter / Quatrains give way, you will observe, to three / Interpolations, prose as well as verse," reflecting on "mind, body, and soul (or memory)." The second instance is the inquiry into the nature of Eros in a long sequence called "From the Cupola." The poet adapts the myth of Eros and Psyche, and is himself both Psyche's poet (like Keats) and Psyche herself, receiving letters from the unknown Eros. Two caricatured evil sisters mock Psyche's claim to an invisible lover, but Psyche's real anxiety derives not from their realist cynicism, but, rather, from her own distrust of love's distorting idealism. She is consoled by her poet in Audenesque cadences:

> Psyche, hush. This is me, James
> Writing lest he think
> Of the reasons why he writes—
> Boredom, fear, mixed vanities and shames;
> Also love.
> From my phosphorescent ink
> Trickle faint unworldly lights.

By the end of *Mirabell* the faint unworldly lights have brightened into the radiance of enlightenment. But in his pursuit of truth Merrill has by no means forgotten his earlier homage to the senses. The daily life described in *Mirabell*, which offers itself as one realized version of human existence, is attentive to the senses, to friendship, to domesticity, to art—all the elements found in Merrill's lyrics—as well as to the dead, for whom the poet has had to invent his trilogy. "The dead," "Ephraim" tells us, "are the surround of the living."

Merrill's argument for the senses denies the old propriety that would distinguish the aesthetic from the sensual. (In this, he resembles Keats rather than his other master, Auden.) A continuity between the aesthetic and the sensual is at the heart of Merrill's work, from the earliest lyrics on—as if it were inconceivable that a love of textures, shapes, lines, light, and color should not also be a love of faces and bodies, even if "one falls back, soiled, blurred." Merrill's primary intuition is that of the absolute ravishment of the senses. As they combine and mingle, the senses create, in the order of flesh, interrelations and reinforcings that are like the elements of an artwork. Yet Merrill's interest in the translation of the data of the senses into the nonpictorial forms of verse and music poses difficulties. Language cannot imitate reality in any easily describable way; and the well-known pitfalls of testifying in verse to the more sensuous of the world's pleasures—pitfalls that are clearest in early Keats and Hopkins—argue against a too literal rendering of sensuality. Language, an abstract medium, is always in allegorical relation to perception and sensation.

In arguing that the sensual and the spiritual are indivisible, Merrill places his trust in the affections as a middle term. Faithlessness and infidelities are acts not of the flesh but of the spirit, and they occur when affection doubts or betrays its own powers. The certain loss of all "sacred bonds" underlies Merrill's verse. But as disbelief and death depopulate his real and imagined worlds, Merrill compensates by a poetry of exuberant mythology and a symposium of incarnate and discarnate voices. The eclectic banquet of youth is replaced in middle age by a Proustian feast of memory. In the fiction of *Mirabell*, the blessings of conversation replace the blessings of sensuality. The audible conversation of tongues—life's addendum to the sensual conversation of bodies—gives way to the inaudible ghostly converse of the dead and the disembodied, as language, letter by letter, assembles itself through the Ouija board. As narrator of, and Prospero to, the whole pageant, Merrill, though fictionally the child of the "father of forms and matter of fact mother" on "the other side," is the adult progenitor of all that happens. The providential and parental figures of Mirabell, Auden, and Maria are only the creatures of his creation.

We might ask whether Merrill's case, at least in the trilogy, is too special to be susceptible of translation into our own terms. Does this flood of transcriptions from another world, this massive treatise on "science" and "history," imply anything for us? Merrill's implicit protest against the censorship of feeling by our relentless ironic intellectualizing of life (he speaks here for all reflective people) takes the form of a defiant mythology—though, in a charming revenge exacted by the time we live in, the mythology must couch itself in "scientific" terms. The mysterious instructors told Merrill to write "Poems of Science." He went home and waited, but nothing happened, since his "word bank" was unfurnished with material. He resorted to potted science (Isaac Asimov, Lewis Thomas) and to remembered childhood myths, inventing macrocosmic and subatomic perspectives from which nothing can be hidden to the enlightened eye. Merrill's mythology attempts to ask what work we can find for that part of the mind hitherto occupied in inventing religious systems. Unlike Robert Lowell, who considered the really interesting people in history to be the emperors, the kings, and the politicians, Merrill thinks that the most attractive souls are those who thought up Edens and afterlifes, saints and satyrs.

It is surprising that Merrill, a poet of infinite finish, should come down so decisively in favor of large mythological outlines and of expository theology. Or perhaps it is not so surprising. The epic poetic of the trilogy demands the large, and even the prosaic. Whereas the lyric is discontinuous, and rejects the narrativity that (however much it may be submerged) links the successive events of drama and fiction, the epic goes beyond narrativity to an encyclopedic account of all things in heaven and earth. The instructors promise to return Merrill to his "chronicles of love and loss" after the trilogy is done, but he will not be the same poet who set down the first lines of "The Book of Ephraim"—the stretching and straining of this large effort cannot be forgotten in a contraction to lyric shapes.

The lessons of *Mirabell* are the unpopular ones of middle age. Most people, the poem tells us, are unevolved, and remain in an animal unawareness, in which they grow, couple, reproduce themselves, and die. Some souls evolve beyond this—into thought, vision, and art. (They are the souls "cloned" in the "Research Lab" of the spirits and sent into the world to do the "V work" of civilization—creating religions, symphonies, temples, cultures, poems.) There is no permanent culture; ours is one of successive attempts by God B to order chaos. The achievements of mind always seem to excel their material origins: hence the myth of inspiring Muses, mysterious instructors, visions, and oracles. The honey of generation is an opiate; the childless have freer access to the spiritual life. Everyone dies. The conversation of friends is precious. As parents and friends die, we dwell more and more on the dead. Our minds become a repository of all we have read, learned, been brought up on. We begin to think in larger terms—about history, about the survival of the planet, about genius.

But it is not for these or other worthy observations in their bald sense that we prize *Mirabell*. It is, rather, for the intimate and solid circumstantiality in which those truths are based. We know the death of parents not propositionally but circumstantially, in the long, particular narration of the death of David Jackson's parents, in "stupor, fear, incontinence," and their burial in a "raw trench." We know the loss of friends as Merrill accustoms us, through a hundred and seventy-eight pages, to the tender and solicitous raillery of Auden and Maria, and then, once we look forward to hearing them indefinitely, strikes the knell of their disappearance. We come to prize even the most frail creations of culture as Merrill's myths link the oldest constructions, like Atlantis and Eden, named rather than evoked, to the creation, metamorphosis, and humanizing of the bat-peacock Mirabell. First an inhuman other, Mirabell becomes, through "this world of courtesy"—the board of communication—someone who can love ("I HAVE COME TO LOVE U"), someone self-conscious and aesthetically reflective.

In his becoming we see the coming-to-be of every conscious creature, through language and love:

B4 OUR MEETINGS I WAS NOTHING   NO TIME PASSD
    BUT NOW
YR TOUCH LIKE A LAMP HAS SHOWN ME TO MYSELF & I
    AM
ME: 741! I HAVE ENTERED A GREAT WORLD   I AM
    FILLED
WITH   IS IT MANNERS?

There are stretches of flats in the exposition of the mythology, yet its density shares with all systems—from Leviticus to *The Book of Mormon* and Melville's cetology—a sheer willingness to bore. The visionary mind has its own pedantries. Just as complicated poets, like Milton, have to learn to be simple, so Merrill, natively compact, has here decided to learn a discursive plainness.

Before the concluding speech of the archangel Michael, who announces the next act of the comedy, Merrill speaks in his own voice of the world's diversity, as he glances out to numberless brilliances of light over the water:

The message hardly needs decoding, so
Sheer the text, so innocent and fleet
These overlapping pandemonia:
Birdlife, leafplay, rockface, waterglow
Lending us their being, till the given
Moment comes to render what we owe.

Merrill has offered a self-definition through metaphor in the course of the poem: his metal is silver (Auden's is platinum), his element air, his mineral crystal, his color "cold lavender." In themselves, these specifications are definitive. By middle age, one knows what one is. If Merrill reminds us sometimes of Ariel, he is yet an Ariel making a deliberate gesture toward an enlarging of style in his refusal to be exclusively beautiful. By its admission of the learning, conversation, and random use of language that underlie the crystallizations of lyric, Merrill's poem pays homage to the riches of unordered literary experience:

MANS TERMITE PALACE BEEHIVE ANTHILL PYRAMID JM
IS LANGUAGE   USE IT   STIR THE THINKERS &
    DETER THE REST.

Language "of such a depth, shimmer, and force" is the "life raft" that carries the poet over the flood of sensation. *Mirabell* is more a diary, in fact, than a planned "system": each section encompasses whatever rises to the surface at a given moment of composition. The mind whose word banks and image banks are here tapped is not in any way a typical one. It is preternaturally knowing, and eclectically read; it strikes attitudes; it is fond but acutely critical; it likes puns perhaps more than it should; its relativism is both despairing and elated. It never lacks fit language—silky and astringent by turns, lustrous and decorative one moment, attenuated and scholastically drab the next, candid or esoteric as its author decides.

What is in the American mind these days—the detritus of past belief, a hodgepodge of Western science and culture, a firm belief in the worth of the private self and in the holiness of the heart's affections, a sense of time and space beyond the immediate—is here displayed for judgment. Somewhat less general in reference, perhaps, is Merrill's examination of what, as a personal aim, can replace self-reproduction in childbearing. Once the biological purpose of life is even theoretically put aside as a justification of living, we must (theological justification having been abandoned long since) advocate something like Merrill's civilizing "V work." The Arnoldian doctrine of the saving remnant seems in this poem to have a new defender; but Merrill dwells, as Arnold does not, on the parallel necessity of private affection. Love and civilization here go hand in hand, the work of art and science refining life in public as the bonds of affection refine life in private. *Mirabell* is Merrill's hymn to the spiritual evolution that seems possible, if precarious, now that biological evolution has invented man; its dark undersong is Hiroshima in the realm of science, and subhuman stupidity in the realm of the private life.

What Merrill once said of Eugenio Montale—that his emotional refinement is "surprisingly permeable by quite ordinary objects: ladles, hens, pianos, half-read letters"—is true of Merrill himself. The claim of ordinary objects and ordinary events on lyric is a mark of the democratic sense in every modern poet of quality—from the priestlike Eliot down through the alchemizing Merrill—that the things of the world can lend a myth (as Crane said of the Brooklyn Bridge) to God. The tendency of modern American lyric poets to reclaim whole tracts of language and experience ceded in the nineteenth century to novels or nonfictional prose continues in Merrill. It is this tendency that has caused us to outstrip our parent stock in England. If to play so free with tradition one poet needs the Ouija board, and another, like Ginsberg, needs visions, and another, like Eliot, needs Buddhism, those who are not poets can only conclude that the work of creation proceeds by its own means.

PETER SACKS

From "The Divine Translation: Elegiac Aspects of
The Changing Light at Sandover"
James Merrill: Essays in Criticism
eds. David Lehman and Charles Berger
1983, pp. 159–65, 180–85

BUT MORTALITY ALLOWS FOR THE DIVINE TRANSLATION
(Mirabell)

In a downcast century whose poems of major length—*The Waste Land, The Bridge, Paterson, The Cantos, History, The Dream Songs*—have almost all suffered from the very darkness and fragmentation they have tried to overcome, how is it that James Merrill has succeeded in writing a long poem (more than 15,000 lines) that is, above all, triumphantly consoling? Unquestionably, *The Changing Light at Sandover* does confront pain and sorrow, the death of friends and parents, the extinction of cultures, even the threat of global ruin. But Merrill's astonishing achievement is to have transfigured the experience of loss and fear to one of celebration and to have moved, in a series of arduous revelations, beyond the stances of resignation or fractured yearning to one of magnificent confidence. In doing so, he has become our greatest poet of serious and far-reaching solace, a poet whose inspired defense against a dark view of mortality and fate burns brightly, "the way good solace seethes."

That last phrase comes from Wallace Stevens's elegy "The Owl in the Sarcophagus," and I suggest that *one* among several ways to read Merrill's poem is an elegy writ very large, as a multiple elegy of epic proportions. While such an approach cannot exhaust the poem's totality, it may nonetheless offer a perspective on certain organizing themes and motifs of the work as well as on essential features of its narrative structure and momentum. So, too, such an approach brings us close to the sources of the poem's distinctive power of consolation.

An elegy is a poem of mourning and consolation, in which, to quote Merrill himself,

Those ghastly graveyard facts become a dance
Of slow acceptance; our own otherwise
Dumb grief is given words. DJ: Or lies?[1]

David Jackson's rejoinder, an instance of *The Changing Light's* persistent questioning of its own fabulous nature, points here to the fact that most elegies necessarily depend on "lies" or rather on certain kinds of almost mythological figuration. After all, an elegy seeks to create a believable fiction that returns the dead to us in some transfigured version of themselves, be it as a flower, a star, a reborn infant, or a genius of the shore. Each of these versions derives, however implicitly, from the figure of a renascent god, to whom the dead are figuratively assimilated and who represents some principle or project that employs rather than suffers the passage of time and that grandly includes death as a necessary element of its career. In a successful elegy, the living come to recognize their role within that overarching career, involving as it does a close alliance with the dead.

Borrowing a definition of heaven from WHA (Merrill's Auden), we may see the elegy itself as a "MACHINE WHICH MAKES THE DEAD AVAILABLE TO LIFE."[2] No less, perhaps, it makes the living available to death. To write or read such a poem is to enter the enlarged space that the dead apparently create for the living, a realm compounded of their mourned absence from this world, and of their new, imagined dwelling places.[3] Indeed, an elegy should work between those two regions, rather in the way Merrill conjures both "sides" of the mirror and the Ouija board. By virtue of imagination, memory, love, *devotion*, the living seem to look or listen, with refined senses, into a region in which figures for the dead continue to exist. And where else but within that region and within those moments of devotion should they also seem to encounter those other imaginary beings, which they assume to be divine—familiar spirits, angels, God? As Merrill has written in "A Dedication" for the dead Hans Lodeizen, "These are the moments, if ever, an angel steps / Into the mind."[4] In its course, therefore, an elegy has the effect not only of elevating the dead but also of raising the living, of orienting and refining them toward a compensatory gift of poetic power, of hitherto concealed knowledge, or of their portion of divinity.

By thus celebrating the dead, the living come to rehearse their own immortality. The motif of resurrection may, therefore, govern their *own* experience of almost alchemical refinement, of stripping to divine densities. Greatly elaborated, this is perhaps the essential theme of the trilogy. Merrill and Jackson are drawn, largely by their continuing devotion to the dead (Jackson has spoken of his parents, for example, as having been taken up "like bait, to focus attention away from the preoccupations of the day and onto the dictée from the other world")[5] into a region of consciousness in which they communicate not only with the dead but also with progressively higher attendant and supervisory powers, Ephraim, Mirabell, the Archangels. The series of communications is structured precisely as an ascent, a graduated course of lessons, in which the living, aided and protected by the affectionate mediations of the dead, learn increasingly about the nature and history of creation, the forces of chaos and evil, and particularly about the deathless "V WORK" that strives for survival and for the possibility of paradise on earth.

Among other things, V represents *vie*, life; also the number five, associated with the human senses and with the V work's immortal paragons, the Five, of whom more later; also, in the chiasmic emblem for man (S, p. 192), "TWO ARMS REACHING UP-WARD," stretching "TOWARD REASON AND LIGHT." The V work, strives to "make sense of things," a project of conversion, not merely cognition. Furthermore, in its accompanying work on the process of perfecting human life and on assuring the "march toward Paradise," the V work depends on a constant reincarnation and improvement of human souls. As such, it makes sense of death itself and provides precisely the kind of overarching and immortalizing "career" that any genuine consolation requires.

Now, these elements—devotion to the dead, initiatory instruction, sensory and visionary refinement, reincarnation and apotheosis—all relate to the original sources of elegy, the ritualistic celebrations of death and rebirth associated with such deities as Osiris, Adonis, Dionysus, Persephone. The ceremonious enactments, originally of martyrdom and vegetal return, in the course of history gradually took on more elevated reference, modulating through Orphic and Pythagorean interpretations to become ascetic rites of intellectual ascent, guaranteeing spiritual resurrection. As is well known, Plato inherited much of this legacy, revealed not only in elements of his beliefs but also in his dialectical rites of philosophical self-purification and of continuing spiritual elevation. It is interesting to notice how thoroughly Merrill celebrates not only the figure of Plato—one of the immortal Five and represented by the beloved Muse Maria Mitsotáki—but also Plato's Academy, the only Academy, as we are told in the closing moments of the poem. Have not all the lessons and "seminars" in Merrill's poem been activities of this Academy and of its antecedent cults of divine death and rebirth?

It is not surprising, therefore, to learn at the very outset of the poem, in section A of "The Book of Ephraim," that the poet

> had, from the start, a theme
> Whose steady light shone back, it seemed, from every
> Least detail exposed to it. I came
> To see it as an old, exalted one:
> The incarnation and withdrawal of
> A god.[6]

The entirety of *The Changing Light* reveals how fully this theme involves not only "incarnation and withdrawal" but also reincarnation, a sequence to which Merrill assimilates a series of deaths and rebirths, from the desperate immolation of Simpson at the outset to the epilogue's superb account of the rebirth of Robert Morse. Indeed, by concentrating on this elegiac structure of the poem, one recognizes most deeply the appropriateness and splendor of that exact trajectory, and one notices how many of the poem's concerns converge on that final reincarnation.

Before exploring how Merrill has extended and revised this traditional thematic development, we should remark on related innovative aspects of the poem, such as the means of its astonishing vividness and drama. Much of the drama, with its dazzling masques and pageantry, derives from the poem's already mentioned affinity to the ritual Mysteries of rebirth, with their unfolding arcana and their highly theatrical ceremonies of purification, of procreative renewal and spiritual ascent. The actual vividness of presentation, the manner in which we seem to see and hear the dead, to be among them and to witness their transfiguration—this is an achievement in many ways unmatched since Dante. In Merrill's case we owe that dramatic intensity largely to the media of the mirror and the Ouija board, the means by which Merrill and Jackson communicate visually and verbally with the spirit world. We may regard these as instruments, metonymic emblems perhaps, of the mind's eye and the inner ear. They are the tools of inspiration: through them, the material of visionary poetry

reaches the poet and his psychic comedium, who thus find their place among such inspired scribes as Homer, Dante, Milton, Blake, and Yeats.

More specifically, the mirror and board relate to distinctly elegiac aspects of Merrill's vision. Together they form the "fair field" of the following beautiful lines:

> WE MET ON THIS FAIR FIELD & SEEM BY ITS EASE TO BE
> IN CONVERSE   YET WE ARE ALL THE DEAD & YOU THE
>   LIVING
> THAT U DO NOT DOUBT US IS WONDER ENOUGH   THAT
>   OTHERS
> DO IS NONE
> . . .
>
>   FOR WHO LIVING
> WELCOMES THE DEAD?
>   (*M*, pp. 163–164)

The mirror has of course been a recurrent motif not only in Merrill's earlier poetry but in the work of poets ranging from Spenser to Auden. As such, it has represented the artistic or poetic realm of composition, reflection, and speculation. In *The Changing Light* the mirror in addition becomes not only the point of contact between the living and the dead but the threshold between them and the "glassy foyer" through which Mercury-Hermes, messenger of the gods and transporter of souls (*M*, p. 152), ushers his charges. As though by the alchemical refinement that the entire poem celebrates, that "foyer" is created by the element mercury, which transmutes the black backing of egoism ("the screen / Of self which forms between God and His creature") into a permeable medium through which we not only "look *beyond* ourselves" but also, as in the case of Robert Morse, penetrate to heaven and to continuing contact with our friends on earth:

>   NEXT I STEPPED BAREASS
> THRU SAND & WATER OF YR MIRROR GLASS
> & SURFACED WHERE 2 OLD & 3 NEW CHUMS
> WELCOMED ME, SKINS GLISTENING WITH LIGHT
> NO BRUSH COULD EVER RENDER
>   (*S*, p. 216)

Mercury is also quick- or living-silver; and silver, we discover, is Merrill's defining mineral (*M*, p. 48). We begin to surmise the connection between the divine messenger, the alchemical element, the means of communication between the living and the dead and, of course, the language of the scribe. In a sense, Mercury is poetic language. And thus it is that after conferring on poetic techniques, WHA and JM are approved by the Archangel Michael in these words:

> IS THAT NOT THE DEAREST OF OUR FATHER'S
>   HOPES?
> MAN USING HIS MOST DELICATE MACHINE, MINING
>   LEAD &
>   PRODUCING QUICKSILVER?
>   (*S*, p. 64)

The connection between the Ouija board and language is even more obvious, but once again the essentially elegiac and redemptive aspects are worth stressing. As with the mirror, such associations derive not only from the board's function in the poem but from the images carefully associated with it. For example, the letters of the board are arranged in an arc or "covenant / With whom it would concern" (*DC*, p. 49). The covenantal rainbow arc of course signifies literal survival and spiritual salvation; but to extend the association by pun and metaphor, the board is also referred to as the "ARK," "THE LIFE RAFT LANGUAGE" (*M*, p. 25). More fully:

> THE STAGE WE ARE ON IS LIKE ALL STAGES A HALF
>   ARC

THUS THE LEGEND OF NOAH   THIS HALF MOON SHIP
    BORE THE DUST
GOD B SAVED OVER FROM THE FALL & ITS PARTICLES
    WERE
FORMULAS ATOMIC STRUCTURES COMMUNICANTS
    OF LIFE
THAT WAS GOD B'S METHOD & WE, APPROACHING U
    HANDS CUPPD
WITH LESSONS, HELPD U TO CONSTRUCT A METHOD OF
    YR OWN.
2 BY 2 HAVE ENTERD YR MINDS & NOW YEARS
    LATER
THE COMMUNICATION IS AFLOAT OVER A DROWND
    WORLD.
WE ARE NOT ALAS TO BRING U TO OUR ARARAT   WE
ARE TO BRING U TO THE MEANINGS U NEED   MUCH AS
    THE ARK
BROUGHT NOAH TO THE PEAKS & SLOPES OF A NEW
    WORLD.

                   (M, p. 159)

In the arc or ark of a survivor's language, the residue of a fallen world enters for preservation and rebirth. Like the mirror, the board is thus not only a redemptive field on which losses are recouped (S, p. 53) but the great transporting vehicle of language itself. Yet further, the ark imagery summons up the repository for the holy text of the Torah as well as the sacred chest by which the ancient Hebrews used to represent the presence of God among them.

So, too, the board, like an elegy perhaps, provides an "anchor point of heaven," a point at which the dead can moor themselves to the devotion of the living, and vice versa. This image of mooring is crucial to the poem, for as we are told, it was precisely a hubristic breaking free from their stone anchorages that brought on the fall of the dark angels and the destruction of their world. Merrill's task is thus, in part, to renovate the earthly anchor points and to restore the cables that connect them with the heavenly world. And with this mention of anchoring stones and cables, it is intriguing that the very first Ouija board communicant to visit Jackson and Merrill, "before Ephraim, before Stonington," had the name Cabel (Caleb?) Stone. As Mirabell later explains (M, p. 171), this seventeenth-century New Englander acted as a preliminary testing voice. And although DJ and JM were not yet ready to have their raft made fast "TO THE SHORES OF THE DEAD," the glow of their communication was sufficient to ensure future contact and to set in motion "THE SELECTION & TRAINING OF THE COMMUNI-CANT." ⟨. . .⟩

Most elegies traditionally draw attention to themselves as performances. They do this both to emphasize that a ceremony of some kind is being successfully completed and to focus on the poetic powers (frequently defined or enlarged by the elegiac performance itself) of the survivor. Hence the motifs of tests or contests and rewards, to foreground the singers' skills and their effects within the originally eclogic elegies. And hence the rhetoric of performance in many later elegies: "Begin again . . . Yet once more . . . I come to pluck . . . Weep . . . Weep no more . . . Thus sang . . . Tomorrow to fresh woods . . ." Once again, *The Changing Light* is brilliant and ample in its relation to such conventions.

Throughout the poem, Merrill has found ways to set off the performance of the work. As already mentioned, its action is marked by a carefully designed yet exuberant proliferation of masques, fetes, galas, pageants, and lessons (complete with A's and A+'s). Similarly, the poem's very texture displays the author's virtuosity in a deliberately and intricately varied array of verse forms—couplets, sonnet sequences, and terza rima, to

name a few—while, as we have seen, the mirror and board are constantly under focus as the work's very "field" of activity. In addition, the poem is itself a continuing subject of its own narrative and commentary, from the opening lines discussing its "present form" to the final revelation of its ordained provenance. From the bright line of the January light falling on Merrill's page as he begins "Ephraim" to the shower of drops that pucker the onionskin manuscript of the epilogue, the poet thus invites an abiding attention to the grand unfolding as well as to the minute formal, even physical, characteristics of the written poem.

Each major section of *The Changing Light* begins with a remarked gesture of commencement: "Admittedly I err by undertaking / This . . . ; Oh very well, then. Let us broach . . . ; Yes, Cup Glides from Board. Sun dwindles into Sound. / DJ and I look at each other. Well? . . . A new day—world transfigured yet the same— / We're back at our old table." We see the effect not only of repeated self-presentation but of a work continually resumed, as in the "Begin again" refrains of early elegies. So, too, the endings of such sections share a sense of resolution, of the poet's having worked his way into the receiving and hallowing presence of the ageless woman of the world, or of Michael, or of God, or of the assembled hosts. It is on this last resolution that I would like to dwell—the development by which JM prepares to perform his poem to his extraordinary audience.

As early as in "Ephraim," the dead had expressed a fascinated approval of the poem thus far ("To my surprise, all burn / To read more of this poem . . . / POPE SAYS THAT WHILE BITS / STILL WANT POLISHING THE WHOLES A RITZ / BIG AS A DIAMOND" (DC, p. 116). Appropriately enough, it is RM ⟨Merrill's Robert Morse⟩, shortly before his own reincarnation, who becomes an agent of JM's final and most complete emergence as performer. For it is RM's hints about the poem's "revelations" that awaken the desire of the spirit world to hear the completed work actually read out loud. It is with great excitement and very high spirits that the poem moves toward this climatic debut. But there are important interruptions.

Almost immediately after the "launching" of the reborn RM, and amidst a flurry of further news regarding the careers of the reincarnated MM, WHA, and GK ⟨Merrill's Maria Mitsotáki, W. H. Auden, and George Cotzias⟩, news comes of the unexpected death of Mimí, wife of the novelist Vasili Vassilikos. Continually open to such "buffeting of losses," the poem "makes room" for this new grief:

We don't quite understand—it's not yet morning—
Vasili's voice, from Rome, expressionless:
"Instantaneous . . . no pain, no warning . . ."
Dead? *Mimí?* And dressed in the white dress.

From such fragmentary and literal snatches of bewilderment, the following ten lines enact the poem's inclusive ceremonies of containment, moving towards the language of artifice and toward the prosodic resolution of an adjusted yet recognizable sonnet form:

We reach her, but she's dazed by the prompt call
Or the ungodly hour: BUT WHERE AM I?
WHO'S THIS   VASILI ARE YOU HIDING   WHY?

So Ephraim guides her from our love, which hurts,
Back to her patron's dim confessional
Where (though harp and trumpet fill the air)
She must sit upright on a little bench
And not cry if her finery reverts
To homespun rags, and shake out her long hair,
And be a candle for the dawn to quench.[7]

Mimí is taken up by the poem's established elegiac machinery, as Mirabell explains that she had incarnated a talent or density whose cycles were more rapid than those of human life. The theme and figures, however modernized, are essentially those of the familiar vegetation myths: "A DYING AS THE SEED / CYCLE CLINGS TO A PERENNIAL TALENT FAR BRIEFER / THAN HUMAN LIFE CYCLES" (*CLS*, "Coda"). And as the heavenly guests gather to hear JM's reading, Mimí herself is found among them in a place of honor. She is introduced to the assembly and is praised by no less a figure than Mother Nature, who "drawing Mimí to her breast . . . dries her tears" ("And wipe the tears forever from his eyes").

Yet more important, in several respects, is the figure of the mourner, Vasili. Indeed, it is upon him that the supervisory powers of Nature have come to bear. She admits having contrived to include him in the earthly contingent of the audience—an audience, we are now reminded, whose primary need may after all be that of consolation and whose faculties are perhaps best refined by grief itself: "I HAD PLANNED: / TO DRAW TO OUR CRITIQUE A GREEK, A LIVING EAR / SHARPENED BY LOSS" (*CLS*, "Coda"). So it is that Vasili arrives at the house in Athens at the precise moment that JM is about to begin his performance:

> MAJESTY AND FRIENDS—when shatteringly
> The doorbell rings. Our doorbell here in Athens.
> We start up.

Once again, the world of the poem is jarred open to admit bereavement.

> David opens to a form
> Gaunt, bespectacled, begrimed, in black,
> But black worn days, nights, journeyed, sweated
> in—
> Vasili? Ah sweet Heaven, sit him down,
> Take his knapsack, offer food and brandy—.
> He shakes his head. Mimí. Mimí in Rome
> Buried near Shelley. He can't eat, can't sleep,
> Can't weep.

> (*CLS*, "Coda")

Vasili's grief seems thus to challenge the very work of mourning and consolation and threatens a more than momentary disruption of Merrill's poem ("live despair [takes precedence] / Over a poem or a parlor game"). And yet, of course, so much of this poem is addressed precisely to such as Vasili. "Merely to listen" will help "to keep his head / Above the sucking waves, merely to listen / A little while." The poem is testing and defining its particular strength, even as it seems to let us know, as Stevens's elegy had, that the consoling forms we are about to see are "visible to the eye that needs."

The physical scene for JM's reading is the house in Athens. But the heavenly audience is accommodated in a "celestial ballroom," which in turn resembles the ballroom of "the broken home" of JM's childhood, Sandover. By a magnificent coup de theatre, this is now a rejuvenated version, a reincarnation, of that original place: "How many years before your 'restoration' / Brought to light this foreign, youthful grace" (*CLS*, "Coda"). Restoration, bringing to light, revelation of youthfulness and grace—these are, of course, central projects of the poem at large. Had not Mirabell insisted that the scribe's task is precisely "TO RENOVATE THE HOUSE OF MAN" (*M*, p. 145)? And had not JM himself speculated:

> Who can compete
> With Nature? She's Mind's equal. Not a slave
> But mother, sister, bride. I think we're meant
> To save that marriage, be the kids who stay

> Together for their parents' sake. DJ:
> Who wrote "The Broken Home"? No accident!
> (*M*, p. 135)

No less a part of that project is the raising of an earthly object or locale to its celestial version, particularly a version that replaces a scene of loss, displacement, and isolation with one in which the poet is truly found and "made at home" among a dazzling audience of those whom he most loves and admires.

I have already mentioned how most elegies rehearse, for themselves, the immortality established for the figures they mourn. In a sense, JM himself is sharing, at the level of an aesthetic performance, the reception or assumption that the dead have enjoyed within his poem. Like them, like Lycidas, he enters among "the sweet Societies / That sing, and singing in their glory move." And yet, whereas Lycidas, for example, is "entertained" by such societies, it is JM alone who sings. Perhaps to enter most truly among the dead, to take one's place most forcefully within tradition, is to play host to them, to entertain them. As Mirabell said, "YET YOU HOUSE US FOR ALL THAT WE / DO LITTLE BUT TAKE UP YR ROOM" (*M*, p. 163).

Of course, Merrill does not let us forget that the actual realm that includes both the mundane and celestial ballrooms is the mirror, mercurial region of the poem itself. It is just outside the mirror frame that JM waits, in the wings, while the guests take their seats. And it is into the mirror that he begins to read. This climactic image of JM reading into the mirror-ballroom-universe may well remind us of the image of God B singing alone into galactic space. For each, as for any elegist, there is a peculiar blend of pathos and grandeur in this act of utterance, an act so precariously having to sustain itself, having even to create its addressee. Of all poets, the elegist most needs to imagine that he addresses more than himself. The very presence of the mirror here, serving once again as threshold and field of transformation, rather than as terminus or medium of self-reflection, may therefore serve to emphasize how Merrill's poem is precisely *not* one of sheer self-communion. God's highest sense was, we recall, "EXERCISED OUTWARDS." And it is that most poignant and most performative aspect of language that the poem has so thoroughly advanced.

Indeed, language itself has been a steady object as well as means of this poem's devotion. "THE REVEALED MONOTHEISM OF TODAY IS LANGUAGE" (*M*, p. 145). And is not Merrill's poem circling to begin its rites again? *The Changing Light*, as the great vehicle of language and the "recurrent muse," thus also finally takes its place among its objects of reincarnation. And as the poet steps forward to utter the last and first word of his great work, the circle, emblem of eternity, closes and reopens.

Finally, lest we think that Merrill has lapsed from his revisionary myth of evolutionary reincarnation to one of mere recurrence, we should recognize how differently we now reread the beginning word and its successors. Like everything else in the poem, the word "admittedly" returns with refined and augmented meaning: what appeared at first reading as a concession of error, is now, in the context of what follows, a vindicated and rechosen way of beginning, signifying also the great theme of admittance. Like the poem, the word has been reincarnated at a higher level of interpretation. The readers, too, begin now at a higher level, as members of an audience of which they had not heard before reading the poem. We, ourselves, have thus become admitted, or perhaps translated, to the celestial ballroom and its guests.

Among the concluding lines of his beautiful poem, "Lost in Translation," Merrill had written:

But nothing's lost. Or else: all is translation
And every bit of us is lost in it
(Or found— . . .)

(*DC*, p. 10)

Notes

1. *Scripts for the Pageant* (New York: Atheneum, 1980), p. 53. Hereafter cited as *S*.
2. *Mirabell: The Books of Number* (New York: Atheneum, 1978), p. 166. Hereafter cited as *M*.
3. Space that is referred to in the following lines:

AS, OH, TO MILTON THE DROWNED LYCIDAS,

SO SOC TO PLATO . . .
HIS WHOLE LIFE & DOOM
FURNISHED THE GOLDEN SCRIBE WITH 'LIVING ROOM'

(*S*, p. 191)

4. *The Country of a Thousand Years of Peace* (New York: Atheneum, 1959 [revised edition, 1970], p. 83.
5. J. D. McClatchy, "DJ: A Conversation with David Jackson," *Shenandoah* 30:4 (1979), p. 35.
6. *Divine Comedies* (New York: Atheneum, 1976), p. 47. Hereafter cited as *DC*.
7. *The Changing Light at Sandover* (New York: Atheneum, 1982), "Coda." Hereafter cited as *CLS*.

Thomas Merton

1915–1968

Thomas Merton was born in southern France near the Spanish border on January 31, 1915, to two artists (his mother was American and his father a New Zealander). Merton received his early education during travels with his father in France, England, and America after his mother's death. He wrote novels during his years at a lycée in France and later at Oakham in Rutland, England. He had one turbulent year at Cambridge following his father's death, after which he left England for good, coming to America to live with his mother's relatives in New York. In 1935 he entered Columbia University and soon joined the staff of *The Jester of Columbia*, contributing cartoons, poems, and editorials to it and other Columbia publications. He was part of the literary group on the campus that included Robert Giroux, Edward Rice, John Berryman, Ad Reinhardt, and professors Mark Van Doren, Joseph Wood Krutch, and Daniel C. Walsh.

After graduation in 1938 Merton stayed on at Columbia for graduate study and taught briefly at Columbia University Extension and St. Bonaventure College before entering the Abbey of Gethsemani near Louisville, Kentucky, in 1941. Merton's conversion to Catholicism came as a surprise to his friends who had not known of his private quest for spiritual value. Merton later described that conversion in *The Seven Storey Mountain*. Merton's Trappist vow of silence was relaxed to accommodate his writing even though it meant subjecting the material to the scrutiny of the abbey fathers before sending it out to publishers. His first published work was a book of poetry, *Thirty Poems* (1945). *Seven Storey Mountain*, published in 1948 to glowing reviews and advance praise from Graham Greene and Evelyn Waugh, quickly became a bestseller.

Merton lived at Gethsemani for the next twenty years, writing poetry and essays (mostly philosophical and theological) and corresponding with a wide range of people—writers, clerics, musicians, Zen masters, leading religious figures in the East. He was greatly interested in Zen Buddhism, seeking to integrate elements of Eastern contemplation and meditation into his practice of Catholicism. Merton began to travel extensively in the last five years of his life. It was during a long tour of Eastern and Southeastern Asia that he met his death. He died on December 9, 1968, in Bangkok of an accidental electrocution.

Personal

Q: Could you tell us about the Columbia College of that period? It seems to have been a heady time, an era of intellectual ferment. What was it like when Thomas Merton arrived on the scene?

A: I was in the class of 1936, one year ahead of Merton— and a whole year makes a big difference in college. In the 1930s the country was still in the midst of the Depression; the times were serious, and most students seemed to be serious about their goals. There were a lot of interesting undergraduates at Columbia College then, like John Latouche, who became famous in the musical theater; Ad Rinehardt, who became a famous painter; Herman Wouk, who became a famous writer; John Berryman, who became one of our best poets; James Weschler, Leonard Robinson, Robert Lax, Robert Paul Smith, Ed Rice, Ernest Kroll, Robert Gibney, and many

more—they all made their mark as writers or in the arts. Thomas Merton had come to Columbia from England; the first thing I noticed was his British accent, which he quickly lost. He seemed to be better educated, and much more widely read, than most of my classmates; his years at Clare College, Cambridge, had left their mark. Like the rest of this group, Tom naturally gravitated toward the classes taught by Mark Van Doren. I also heard he was interested in *Jester*, the undergraduate humor magazine, for which he was drawing cartoons.

Q: When did your first meeting with Merton occur?

A: I was editor of the literary magazine, the *Columbia Review*, with offices on the fourth floor of John Jay Hall. This blond, stocky young man walked in and introduced himself as Tom Merton. We talked a bit and I found that he was interested in jazz, Harlem, and the movies—especially the films of W. C. Fields, the Marx Brothers, Charlie Chaplin, and Preston Sturges, enthusiasms I shared. This was in 1935. He said he had written something for us. It was a documentary piece, inspired by something he'd witnessed a couple of days before—an accident that had shocked him very much because it resulted in a death. I remember one image, a pack of cigarettes in a pool of blood. And one of the key words was *meaningless*. I thought, "This man is a good writer, he has an eye for detail, for the apt image." But the piece was too long, verbose, and overwritten. I cut it, and he was a bit upset and protested. I said, "No, Tom, what remains is really the best part and we'll print it." I became his editor at that point, you see. This was one of his first published pieces, I think, unless he had published at Cambridge. ⟨. . .⟩

Q: Did you meet him after college, before he joined the Trappists?

A: In the summer of 1941 (he joined the monastery late that year), I encountered him on Fifth Avenue, of all places—in Scribner's Bookstore, one of the best bookstores in New York. He touched me on the arm, and I turned around and there was Tom Merton. I said, "Tom, what are you doing these days? I hope you're still writing." He said, "Well, I've just been to the *New Yorker* to see Bob Gerdy"—another classmate of ours who was on the staff of the magazine. I asked, "Are you going to write for the *New Yorker?*" He said that they wanted him to write about Gethsemani, and when I asked what it was, he replied, "It's a Trappist monastery in Kentucky, where I've been making retreats." I was stunned; this was an absolute revelation. He said, "Yes, Gerdy wants me to write about it." When I said it sounded fascinating, he replied, "But I couldn't think of writing about it." That told me everything. His true character was now clear. I wished him well, and we parted. I next heard about him from Mark Van Doren, who phoned to say, "Tom Merton has become a Trappist monk." Again I was stunned, but less so this time. Mark Van Doren said, "We'll never hear from him again. He's taken a vow of silence, he can't write to us nor we to him—he's leaving the world. I think he's an extraordinary young man, and I don't believe we'll ever hear another word from him." Mark said that Tom had left him his manuscript of thirty poems, which he was sending to Jay Laughlin at New Directions, who published it. Little did we know what other books would follow.

Q: Did you think his vocation was going to last?

A: The monastery? I think I did, yes. I really knew nothing about the monastic life. I thought it would be a hard life, ascetic, severe, cut off from everything. And I knew Tom was a communicator, a person who was very good with words, a writer. How would he fit his talent and ability to communicate into an isolated and cut-off kind of life? That was Mark Van Doren's concern too. We both thought of him as an artist, you see, which he was. As it turned out, the abbot who was then presiding at Gethsemani, Abbot Frederic Dunne, must have been a very wise man. It is he who ordered Merton to write his life story. Tom told me he did not really want to write *The Seven Storey Mountain.* He was obliged to write it. He was given an office and a typewriter, and he resisted, thinking, "I've left behind my past life to come here." Yet he was made to relive it. So in a way Abbot Dunne solved the problem Mark Van Doren and I had perceived. And the great success of the book embarrassed Thomas Merton. Of course he was widely criticized for writing it, not only by reviewers but by other religious who said he'd taken the vow of silence. Even I, as his publisher, got hate mail, letters saying things like "Why don't you shut up this talking Trappist?" I had a standard reply: "Writing is a form of contemplation." ⟨. . .⟩

Q: You said that Merton wouldn't write about Gethsemani for a magazine, and yet he became the most public of private men.

A: This was a paradox that worried him, and he often wondered whether he should be publishing books at all. He was very sensitive to criticism from fellow monks, fellow religious, and laity too. The other paradox was that he found himself to be in touch with more people after he got to Gethsemani than he'd ever been in his life. It was due to his books. He had correspondence with Boris Pasternak in Russia, with Dr. Suzuki the Zen Buddhist in Japan, and with leading theologians and writers all over the world. His letters should be published. Tom's other language, of course, was French. Once when I was at the abbey he was assigned as the interpreter for the abbot general. The Trappist Cistercian order originated in France, and the general was a Frenchman who did not speak a word of English. Tom not only wrote in French, but spoke fluent French. After all, he was born in France and had his early schooling there.

Q: What would you say happened to Thomas Merton over the years?

A: He grew up fast, like Huckleberry Finn. Of all the writers I've known—and I've known some very great ones, very complicated ones—no one had quite the speed of intellectual growth that Thomas Merton had. He just deepened and matured, and became more and more intense and marvelous as the years went by, in a way that is quite remarkable. This growth was implicit in him. Why does a particular plant develop so fast? Because it has the capacity to do so and is helped by its environment. He himself lived in the climate and in the atmosphere that fostered intellectual and spiritual growth. He had really found his vocation. I'm sometimes asked, "What would he have been like if he hadn't been a monk?" I don't know. He probably would have been good at almost anything he might have undertaken. But at the monastery he was able to mature and grow in the most remarkable way. It was absolutely the right soil, the right setting, the right place for him. It wasn't without its difficulties. One irony was that Merton did not receive a penny of his enormous royalties, which of course belonged to the community of monks and helped them to build daughter-houses elsewhere in the country. I remember that one such monastery in the West consisted at that time of a group of Quonset huts. But imagine yourself a writer, writing the best you can, and then turning in your manuscript to your fellow-monks who tell you what's wrong with it. This was before the publisher ever saw it, you understand. The censors went through it, and often they would pick out absurd points, all kinds of things that had nothing to do with writing but with—well, public relations. But Tom was good-natured and cheerful, and put up with it. He'd let off some steam in letters, saying, "They have to do it, I understand, it's part of my life here."—ROBERT GIROUX, Interview by Paul Wilkes, *Merton by Those Who Knew Him Best,* ed. Paul Wilkes, 1984, pp. 15–24

General

Merton is a modest, not altogether satisfactory minor writer. But he is also, as far as my experience goes, easily the most promising of our American Catholic poets and, possibly, the most consequential Catholic poet to write in English since the death of Francis Thompson. Why the last forty years of the Catholic literary revival, which have seen the prose of Chesterton, Dawson and Waugh, have produced nothing as lasting as the light verses of Belloc is no doubt due to complex, partially intangible, causes. We must take what comes. What

Merton writes is his own, subtle and intense. So small and genuine an achievement is worth consideration.

The purpose of this review is to point up what Merton has done; this involves an analysis of his limitations and faults. I shall quote to the extent of making a short anthology and hope that each quotation will be read over until it is understood. My comments are more or less footnotes.

THE FLIGHT INTO EGYPT

Through every precinct of the wintry city
Squadroned iron resounds upon the streets;
Herod's police
Make shudder the dark steps of the tenements
At the business about to be done.

Neither look back upon Thy starry country
Nor hear what rumors crowd across the dark
While blood runs down those holy walls,
Nor frame a childish blessing with Thy hand
Towards that fiery spiral of exulting souls!

Go, Child of God, upon the singing desert,
Where, with eyes of flame,
The roaming lion keeps Thy road from harm.

This is modern and traditional, graceful and quietly powerful. The first ten lines are probably the finest in the entire book. Note especially the stern imagery and rhetorical éclat of the first stanza; the subtle shift of rhythm in the second stanza, and the unity of symbol, meaning and sound in line 10. About the last three lines I am less certain. Too much depends on the word *singing* (presumably, the poet means that the desert is simple and alive, in contrast to the tortured, twisted fury of the town) which prepares for the sinless *flame* of the lion.

THE BLESSED VIRGIN MARY COMPARED TO A WINDOW

Because my will is simple as a window
And knows no pride of original earth,
It is my life to die, like glass, by light;
Slain in the strong rays of the bridegroom son.
. . .
For light, my lover, steals my life in secret.
I vanish into day, and leave no shadow
But the geometry of my cross,
Whose frame and structure are the strength
By which I die,
. . .
Because I die by brightness and the Holy Spirit
The Sun rejoices in your jail, my kneeling
Christian. . . .

At first glance this is merely a tour-de-force, in imitation of Donne's "Of My Name in the Window." Then one realizes how persistently and honestly the conceit has been elaborated, how right the tone is for Our Lady. The figure of the window-frame and its shadow is almost as good as its original. Donne's and Crashaw's contributions to the poem detract nothing from its sincerity and freshness. The extracts that I have quoted should have been the entire poem, for the rest, in spite of much incidental brilliance, is repetitive, loose, wordy.

One of Merton's faults is a contrivance that he may have learned from some of the less successful poems of Crashaw (e.g., "The Weeper"), the atomic conceit: each conceit is an entity and the whole poem is seldom much more than the sum of its parts, often it is considerably less. My quotations should have made it plain that Merton is not writing a seventeenth century pastiche; he is using the old devices as an artist, not as an antiquarian. At the same time he follows so closely on the heels of his predecessors that the capacity of his vision is narrowed. Much of the old immediacy, power and mass are

lost. In fact, Merton's poems, like Christina Rossetti's, are precariously unlocated in time or place. Nor is this much helped by a trick that he may have gotten from Edith Sitwell or Cummings, that is, using a sound word where one would expect a *light* word. Occasionally this yields most effective lines, as in a Crucifixion poem which opens with: "When Romans gambled in the clash of lancelight." (*Lancelight* is an alliterative, Hopkinsian compound that works; however, the last line of the same poem is ruined by Hopkins: "Reeks of the death-thirst man-life found in the forbidden apple.") Elsewhere, as in the *singing desert* of my first quotation, a mannerism is made to bear the burden of inspiration.

"Flight into Egypt" is in Merton's most original style; "A Window" is more derivative but hardly inferior. There is a third Merton who is glib, sentimental and romantic.

THE HOLY CHILD'S SONG

When My kind Father, kinder than the sun,
With looks and smiles bends down
And utters my bodily life,
My flesh obeying, praises Heaven like a smiling
cloud.
Then I am the gay wheatfields, the serious hills:
I fill the sky with words of light, and My incarnate
songs
Fly in and out the branches of My childish voice
Like thrushes in a tree.

These lines are clearly superior to Kilmer's unwittingly obscene "Tree," but thinness is not disguised by one or two apt words and an ordered irregularity of meter. A lofty subject and enthusiastic imagery are often imaginative narcotics.

A variation on the style of "The Flight into Egypt" appears in the nature poems:

When cold November sits among the reeds like an
unlucky fisher
And ducks drum up as sudden as the wind
Out of the rushy river,
We slowly come, robbed of our rod and gun,
Walking amid the stricken cages of the trees.

This is charming and the details are solid as the details of "The Holy Child's Song" should have been solid. Unfortunately here, as in most of the other nature poems, the fine opening is undeveloped. Instead the *cages* flounder on into an impossible devotional metaphor, upholstered with *keys*, *jails* and *jailers*.

FOR MY BROTHER: REPORTED MISSING IN ACTION, 1943

Sweet brother, if I do not sleep
My eyes are flowers for your tomb;
And if I cannot eat my bread,
My fasts shall live like willows where you died.
If in the heat I find no water for my thirst,
My thirst shall turn to springs for you, poor traveller.

Where, in what desolate and smoky country
Lies your poor body, lost and dead?
And in what landscape of disaster
Has your unhappy spirit lost its road?

Come, in my labor find a resting place
And in my sorrows lay your head;
Or rather take my life and blood
And buy yourself a better bed—
Or take my breath and take my death
And buy yourself a better rest.

When all the men of war are shot
And flags are fallen into dust,
Your cross and mine shall tell men still
Christ died on each, for both of us.

For in the wreckage of your April Christ lies slain
And Christ weeps in the ruins of my spring:
The money of whose tears shall fall
Into your weak and friendless hand,
And buy you back to your own land:
The silence of Whose tears shall fall
Like bells upon your alien tomb.
Hear them and come: they call you home.

To appreciate how this string of commonplace figures constantly keeps shifting and moving and never becomes insincere,
extravagant or dead, the reader should have tried his luck with
epitaphs and have failed—have failed and thought he succeeded. Comparison should be made with Crashaw's verses on
"A Man and His Wife Who Were Buried Together." There the
metaphors are worked out with logic and care and the meter is
much firmer; but Merton's poem has its own virtues and is not
overshadowed.—ROBERT LOWELL, "The Verses of Thomas
Merton," *Com*, June 22, 1945, pp. 240–42

My first contact with Tom, back in the early 1940s, came
through Mark Van Doren. Mark was one of the greatest
teachers of literature we have ever had in this country. He was
Tom's mentor at Columbia.

When Mark, for whom I had published some poems at
New Directions, told me he had received thirty poems from a
very promising young poet, one with deep spiritual feeling and
one whom he thought I would probably not find out about in
the normal course of business, I was interested. I liked those
early poems very much. There was a freshness there, a
liveliness, a verbal sprightliness that was attractive. They were
not like anything that any of the other New Directions poets
were writing. There was an almost ingenuous character to
them, which was appealing.

The Catholic message in those early poems was strong. I
mean, there were poems about the night the monastery barn
burned up and the portrait of the Virgin in the cloister
. . . At first, such subjects didn't interest me too much. What
I liked was Merton's imagery and the way he could take a
religious subject and carry it into real-life metaphors, so that I,
as a heretic, a benighted Calvinist, was able to get some
feeling, as I never had before, of what the Catholic faith was
about.

At that time this was the only kind of poetry that the abbot
wanted Fr. Louis ⟨Merton's monastic name⟩ to write. As
religious poetry, it didn't come close to George Herbert or
Hopkins; yet those poems have passionate, authentic feeling for
what he is writing about. The finest of *Thirty Poems* is the
poem written in memory of his brother, John Paul, who was
killed in the war. This is a very beautiful, very moving poem by
anyone's standard. Just to quote a few lines:

FOR MY BROTHER:
REPORTED MISSING IN ACTION, 1943

Sweet brother, if I do not sleep
My eyes are flowers for your tomb;
And if I cannot eat my bread,
My fasts shall live like willows where you died.
If in the heat I find no water for my thirst,
My thirst shall turn to springs for you, poor traveller.

As Merton matured in the 1950s and 1960s, becoming more
secular in his interests, he began to write a different kind of
poetry, which was more concerned with what was happening
outside the monastery, and inside himself. ⟨. . .⟩

One might say that *The Seven Storey Mountain* is in some
respects slightly undisciplined, perhaps even preachy at times.
But in his later books, particularly in the journals, Tom
controlled himself more and held to the track. He also gained

greatly in writing style. Merton was a natural, born writer. He
understood the possibilities of language. And he got better and
better as he went along.

Once you've been bitten by Merton, you will continue to
read him, and read everything you can. How he actually did it,
who knows? Can any of us really analyze the particular magic
of a great? Something was combusting inside Tom, and it came
out in fine language, clear thought, persuasive communication. He touched people's minds and hearts.

I think the books (still unpublished) that really give both
an insight into his writing and his search are Tom's private
journals. He was a prodigious worker, and a very fast writer,
and when I visited him I saw that he was working on two sets of
journals. One set was the journals that he soon made into
books. The other was the private journals, which he kept in big
black ledgers. These were his very personal thoughts, like a
diary, written just for his own dialogue with himself. The
quality of them was very free, very frank; quite often he was
talking to God, asking advice from God. Often he was worrying
about whether he was a good contemplative, whether he
was indulging egotism in writing worldly books; seeking from
God enlightenment on why he had never had a major
mystical experience. He directed us, his trustees, that these
journals should not be published until twenty-five years after
his death. ⟨. . .⟩

We ⟨. . .⟩ see a profound change in Merton's poetry
about 1963 when his book *Emblems of a Season of Fury* was
published. This was the first time he felt he could write secular
poetry about social and political themes and get away with it.
Here was a superb poem called "Chant to Be Used in
Processions around a Site with Furnaces." This is about the
German concentration camps of the Holocaust. It is done with
a wonderful kind of ingenuous irony, such as he later uses in
"Original Child Bomb," his dead-pan account of the Hiroshima bomb. In "[Chant to Be Used in Processions,"] Merton
uses Pound's "persona" mask technique, where he speaks
through the mouth of one of the Nazi executioners. The irony
is devastating when the SS officer urges the prisoners in the
camp to write home to their friends to invite them to come to
their "joke." This kind of black humor crops up continually in
his later work.

The poetry of Merton that I find the greatest, the most
liberated from convention, and the most extraordinary is the
first book of his long poem, *The Geography of Lograire*. This
was planned to be his "work in progress," his *Cantos*, his
Paterson. He told me he expected to be working on it for the
rest of his life.

The "geography" of the poem simply is that of Merton's
mind. He intended to make a personal epic of everything that
had gone on in the geography of his mind, everything he had
read, everything he remembered, but all distilled into compact, almost symbolic short poems. He only completed one
volume of *Lograire*, which he left with me before he went to
Asia and said, "If anything happens to me, I want you to
publish this." I composed the necessary notes on his sources
and brought it out about a year after his death.—JAMES
LAUGHLIN, "Merton the Writer," *Merton by Those Who Knew
Him Best*, ed. Paul Wilkes, 1984, pp. 4–11

J. M. CAMERON
From "High Spirits"

New York Review of Books, September 27, 1979, pp. 25–26

With the publication in 1948 of his immensely successful
autobiography *The Seven Storey Mountain*, a book

praised by all kinds of people for all kinds of reasons, Merton achieved a fame he never lost. It is hard to read it again, after many years, without feeling slightly embarrassed. It has a generous rush of high spirits. The early Merton is like a young horse galloping round a field: it is a wonderfully invigorating sight but it has a peculiar pathos for the observer, who knows the bit and bridle and the harness have already been prepared. He is very knowing—too knowing—about ideas and writers he has come across in his growing-up. He is especially absurd on D. H. Lawrence, whom he took to be a worshipper of what he calls "the sex instinct" and a proto-fascist. In his account of his conversion to Catholicism and his later conviction that he has a calling to the life of a Trappist monk he is inclined to turn what is in any case dramatic into melodrama, and there is a touch of morose pleasure in some of the accounts of his inner turmoils. Neither Catholicism nor the calling to so hard a form of the religious life as the Trappist ⟨. . .⟩ need be blamed for the slightly self-indulgent soliloquy Merton goes in for —nothing could be more inept than Bishop Sheen's comparison of *The Seven Storey Mountain* to Saint Augustine's *Confessions.*

His later life and writings make it plain that beneath what is too easy in the autobiography there is a sane, serious, humorous, acute, kind, brave man. The irony of his life is all-encompassing: his autobiography made him the darling of Catholic *bien pensants* in the United States and elsewhere, but as he moved toward opposition to the Vietnam war and to the strategy of nuclear deterrence such admiration fell away and his former admirers tried to bully his abbot into suppressing his writings.[1] He became a Trappist to pursue the contemplative life in the silence and obscurity of a monastic community and his abbot encouraged him in a life of writing and teaching and administration. He fled from the world and the world pursued him to his refuge. He sought to live out his life in one place under religious obedience and away from the technical wonders of modern society, and he survived to find his abbey made noisy by elaborate machines and was himself electrocuted in Bangkok (Karl Barth, far away in Switzerland, died on the same day) through the malfunctioning of a lamp.

There is probably a Merton archive somewhere and I know that doctoral dissertations are being written about him. This is understandable; Merton's career and ideas represent an important bridge-passage in the history of American Catholicism. He gave a name of some note to those who came out in public and at some personal cost against the war in Southeast Asia, and he helped to construct arguments in their defense. He, with the Berrigan brothers and many others, did for that generation what Dorothy Day and the *Catholic Worker* had done, though with much less attention from the organs of publicity and information, for an earlier generation. (Not that the *Catholic Worker* influence vanished in the Sixties. On the contrary: my guess is that the future historian will find the stature of Dorothy Day and her collaborators increasing all the time; hard thinking, good writing, an evident unity of thought and action, such things may have little immediate effect, at least as the world sees it; but they count for much over a long period.) There is, however, a marked inclination ⟨. . .⟩ to think more highly of Merton's work than it deserves. Most agree that he wrote too much and too variously;

> The monastic life is a life wholly contingent upon this tremendous existential silence of God which nobody has ever been able to explain, and which is, nevertheless, the heart of all that is real. . . . The monastic life is not dedicated to a sounding communication among men. It lives by a soundless communication in mystery between man

and God, between man and his brother, and between man and all created things.

> The value of the monks' Public Prayer is therefore not drawn so much from its sound as from the deep silence of God which enters into that sound and gives it actuality, value, meaning. The beauty of Gregorian chant, and that which distinguishes it from every other kind of music, lies in the fact that its measured sound, in itself beautiful, tends to lead the soul, by its beauty, into the infinitely more beautiful silence of God. Chant that does not have this effect, no matter how great its technical perfection, is practically without value. It is empty of the silence of wisdom, which is its substance and its life.

This is a representative piece of Merton's work as expositor and analyst.

One notices how overwritten it is. The monastic life is *"wholly centered,"* God's silence is *"tremendous"* and *"existential"*; *"all that is"* is made to decline into the commonplace by the addiction of *"real."* Just to remove these and other excessive bits of writing strengthens the tone of the passage and brings it closer to having the effect Merton is seeking. As a piece of argument the second paragraph is curious. That monks spend much of their days and nights making a joyful noise to the Lord, that the Psalms of David are the heart of their devotional life, these seem to offer a difficulty for the Merton thesis about the Divine silence and about the monk's dedication to silence. All is made to look all right: the "actuality" and beauty of this sound, and its value, which is made into something over and above actuality and beauty, come from God's silence which "enters into" the sound. There is a vague sense that a problem has been set and solved; it strikes me as simply fudge.

Christian theology is indeed involved in the paradox of a God who speaks, who communicates his Word, his *Logos,* to men, not in the form simply of sound but in the flesh and blood of a man, and who also remains hidden, both absolutely and as one who appears incognito, and who lies beyond all positive predications. This paradox can be stated, or celebrated, as by Max Picard in *Die Welt des Schweigens,*[2] or analyzed by philosophers, or dismissed as a surd in the enterprise of Christian theology. But it can't be made smooth in the way Merton puts it. What in the passage is uncommonly interesting is not so much the problem set by God's speaking and God's silence as the problem set by the extraordinary character of the music of the chant.

To Simone Weil the chant seemed an expression of God's glory and man's response to it; Eric Gill tells us that when he first heard the chant, sung by the monks of Mont César at Louvain, he "was so moved . . . as to be almost frightened."[3] It is plain that Merton too was moved. The most affecting thing in the autobiography I find to be his account of the first impression of the assemblage of monks engaged in chanting the Office, the *opus Dei,* in the abbey that was later to be his home. It is overwritten in the same way as the passage I have just noted (for example, he can't write that something pierced him to the heart and leave it at that; he has to add the banal "like a knife"), but through the excesses and banalities of the style something authentic reaches out to us.

No one with a rudimentary religious and musical culture can fail to be shaken by a great monastic choir's singing of the chant. Such a choir may take some finding today. Some religious communities have responded to the happenings of the period since the second Vatican Council with a combination of recklessness and Philistinism, discarding the chant along with other—as they suppose—lumber. They lie under the mistaken impression that this recommends them to the intelligent laity.

Merton wrote many poems. Much of the poetry is like the prose, easy—too easy—and fluent. ⟨. . .⟩ Of course, the content and the thought are often interesting; such a late volume as *Cables to the Ace* is the work of a man whose mind is always working. A lot of it is, if not straightforwardly didactic and hortatory, concerned to excite approvable attitudes in the reader. In some of the earlier poems there is an old-fashioned romantic air one can't but like, as in "Rievaulx: St. Ailred":

> Once when the white clouds praised you, Yorkshire,
> Flying before the sun, flying before the eastern wind,
> What greenness grew along the waters,
> Flowering in the valleys of the purple moor.
> . . . .
> The sun that plays in the amazing church
> Melts all the rigor of those cowls as grey as stone—
> Or in the evening gloom that clouds them through
>   these tintless panes,
> The choirs fall down in tidal waves
> And thunder on the darkened forms in a white surf of
>   *Glorias*. . . .

This is engaging, but embarrassing, like the kind of verse one wrote in adolescence. We note the same faults in the verse as in the prose: "the *amazing* church," "the eastern wind," "tintless panes." I don't know what goes on in "creative writing" courses in universities, but I imagine the students are taught not to fall into such traps as these. Strangely, some of the earlier poems don't have these faults, as, for example, the fine "Song from Our Lady of Cobre." ⟨. . .⟩ Merton greatly admired Hopkins. Perhaps if he had, like Hopkins, found the relation between the poet and the religious a torturing one he would have written less but better. Not that one would wish a man to have the kind of fortune that enables him to write "Carrion Comfort" or "I wake and feel the fell of dark, not day"; but this is the standard by which one who seeks to transform an intense life in religion into poetry must be judged.

Merton will be remembered for two things: his place, especially among Catholics, in the thinking about the morality of war and, more broadly, of the way modern industrial society is run; and his partially successful attempt to bring out, through study and personal encounter, what is common to Asian and Western monasticism and to Asian and Western forms of mysticism and the contemplative life. (Other monks, Aelred Graham and Bede Griffiths, for example, ought to be mentioned in this connection.)

Historically American Catholics have found themselves, rather curiously, among the most intensely patriotic of American groups, even where the military enterprise was morally suspect. It is as though they were always trying to disprove the thesis of many native Protestants, especially in the South, that Catholics were necessarily half-hearted citizens, their loyalty in the last resort going to a foreign potentate, and a wop potentate at that. In the demonology of Protestant nativism they were classed with blacks and Jews, not quite fully members of the American family, and nourished alarmingly by the prolific Irish, Slavs, and Latins, all groups that within the memory of many living Americans were regarded as less desirable immigrants than the English and Scottish, the Scandinavians, and the Germans. It was the strength of this feeling against Catholicism that wrecked the presidential hopes of Al Smith; most were surprised to find it so diminished during the presidential campaign of John F. Kennedy.

Perhaps the Kennedy years marked not only the end of the effectiveness of a certain kind of political anti-Catholicism but also the end of unquestioning loyalty to great national objectives on the part of Catholics. The nation now saw nuns and clergymen marching in Selma, Alabama; and among the

first burners of draft cards and participators in other symbolic acts of protest against the war in Vietnam were Catholics, lay and clerical. In these years Thomas Merton passed from the somewhat simple-minded political stance that shows itself in the autobiography to a more severe view of the fundamental character of Western society.

In *Loving and Living*, a useful selection from Merton's occasional writings, there is a brief section on war.

> War represents a vice that mankind would like to get rid of but which it cannot do without. Man is like an alcoholic who knows that drink will destroy him but who always has a reason for drinking. . . . The motive for which men are led to fight today is that war is necessary to destroy those who threaten our peace! It should be clear from this that war is, in fact, totally irrational, and that it proceeds to its violent ritual with the chanting of perfect nonsense.

This is to take war to be a symptom of a general pathological state in which men as such are immersed. Later, Merton goes on to take the bombing of Dresden as an example of a great atrocity, greater than the bombing of Hiroshima and Nagasaki; but in characterizing Dresden as an atrocity he relies on arguments—that it was not a military target, that it was unnecessary to victory in the war—that seem not to be compatible with his view of war as generally vicious. He cites John XXIII's *Pacem in Terris* and the declaration of the second Vatican Council that "any act of war aimed indiscriminately at the destruction of entire cities or extensive areas along with their population is a crime against God and man himself [and] merits unequivocal and unhesitating condemnation" and seems to understand that such statements call for rational moral judgments of this or that act of war; but he then goes on to argue that "to appeal against war to reason is to make an appeal that cannot have any serious effect on the war makers themselves."

This very pessimistic doctrine isn't, of course, without some support from history, but it is a debilitating doctrine, morally and intellectually, all the same. It robs of its interest, and of its value as a precedent, the growth of "selective" conscientious objection during the war in Vietnam, where some objectors were not absolute pacifists but found their conscientious judgments made it impossible for them to fight in that particular war. These judgments have been subsequently ratified by so large a consensus of thoughtful Americans of very different political standpoints that they can no longer be thought willful or eccentric.[4]

Merton does not always offer this despairing analysis. Sometimes he speaks of violence as rooted in a particular social structure; and he has a vision of clean, small, frugal, loving communities to replace the wastelands of urban society, and in this he is ⟨. . .⟩ close to Schumacher's *Small Is Beautiful*, a book he didn't live to read. And if we have to say that his philosophy of society was made up of scraps that didn't always compose a systematic whole, we have to add that in his eclecticism he responded in a human way, and without sentimentality, to the two vilest phenomena of his period: anti-Semitism and racial discrimination founded upon pigmentation. And, as Woodcock writes: "the Negroes were the Jews of Merton's life."[5] What he wrote prompted the admiration and liking of many black Americans, Eldridge Cleaver among them. He saw more clearly than many liberals that out of the civil rights struggle of the early Sixties would come a tougher kind of black leadership. He seems to have welcomed this and, like so many, didn't perceive that this leadership is honored and not insulted by a rigorous criticism of the confused formulations of "black consciousness," "black theology," and so on.

One of the most engaging features of Merton's mind and sensibility is his feeling for what is authentic and pure, even when it occurs outside the house of Latin Catholicism. He was attracted by the tradition of the Shakers, who, he said, "have been something of a sign, a mystery, a strange attempt at utter honesty which, in trying perhaps to be too ideally pure, was nevertheless pure—with moments of absurdity." Later, he extended his interests and sympathies to the great non-Christian religions, especially the Buddhist traditions, and especially to their expression in the forms of monasticism. This was his last great passion ⟨. . .⟩ and in a sense he can be said to have had a happy death, for when he encountered his bizarre death in Bangkok it was not before he had been able to utter his own word:

> The combination of the natural techniques and the graces and the other things that have been manifested in Asia and the Christian liberty of the Gospel should bring us all at last to that full and transcendent liberty which is beyond mere cultural

differences and mere externals—and mere this or that.

Thus he spoke on the day of his death; and so he speaks to us still ⟨. . .⟩ in his surviving work. That we still want to criticize his arguments and debate his conclusions is a sign that his strenuously lived life contains much to tease and captivate us.

Notes

1. They had some success. Merton was reduced to economizing his vow of obedience; he circulated what he was writing in duplicated typescript.
2. Zurich, 1948; *The World of Silence*, translated by Stanley Godman (Henry Regnery, 1961).
3. Eric Gill, *Autobiography* (Cape, 1940), p. 186.
4. See on this issue Michael Walzer, *Just and Unjust Wars* (Basic Books, 1977); and my review of Walzer in *The New York Review*, December 8, 1977.
5. George Woodcock, *Thomas Merton: Monk and Poet* (Farrar, Straus and Giroux, 1978).

W. S. MERWIN

1927–

William Stanley Merwin, poet, was born in New York City on September 30, 1927, and grew up in Union City, New Jersey, and in Scranton, Pennsylvania. He was educated at Princeton University, receiving his B.A. in English in 1947. He worked as a tutor in France, Portugal, and Majorca from 1949 to 1951, teaching Robert Grave's son in Majorca for part of that time. He was playwright-in-residence for the Poets' Theatre in Cambridge, Massachusetts, in 1956 and 1957, and in 1962 he worked as poetry editor for the *Nation*. In 1964 and 1965 he was an associate at the Théâtre de la Cité in Lyons, France.

Merwin's poetry has shown a development over time from the relatively formal and traditional early works to poems which are much more surreal and intense. He began his career with *A Mask for Janus* (1952), issued in the Yale Series of Younger Poets. This was followed by further collections, including *The Dancing Bears* (1954); *Green with Beasts* (1956); *The Drunk in the Furnace* (1960); *The Moving Target* (1963); *The Lice* (1967); *The Carrier of Ladders* (1970; Pulitzer Prize); *Writings to an Unfinished Accompaniment* (1973); and *The Compass Flower* (1977). *The Miner's Pale Children* (1970) and *Houses and Travellers* (1977) are collections of prose parables, and *Darkling Child* (1956; written with Dido Milroy), *Favor Island* (1957), and *The Gilded West* (1961) are all plays. From the beginning of his career Merwin has studied other literary traditions, and he has been much praised for his translations, which include *Poem of the Cid* (1959), *The Satires of Perseus* (1961), and *The Song of Roland* (1963). He has also published a volume of recollections, *Unframed Original* (1982).

General

Merwin's own political activities, and writings, have been directed towards specific ends: he represents no party but his own. From 1958 to 1962, he wrote regularly for *The Nation*, mainly reviews, and the few political pieces dealt with individual events—an anti-war demonstration, and the attempt made by a group of men to sail the trimaran "Everyman" to Christmas Island in the Pacific, so as to interfere with projected atomic bomb tests. These incidents engaged Merwin's sympathy and sense of outrage, and he wrote skillfully against arbitrary preemption of power by the government. His anger at the arrests by Salazar of the Angolan poet, Agostinho Neto, made him examine generally the cost to a writer of political activity:

The danger is that his gift itself, necessarily one of the genuinely private and integral things he lives for, may be deformed into a mere loudspeaker, losing the singularity that made it irreplaceable, the candor that made it unteachable and unpredictable. . . . In the long run his testimony will be partial at best. But its limits will have been those of his condition itself, and rooted, as that is, in death; he will have recognized the enemy. He will not have been another priest of ornaments.

"Rooted in death"—the paradoxical phrase seems to summarize the whole of Merwin's work, emerging most clearly in his stories. Merwin is not well known for his fiction, and he does not write ordinary realistic stories. His characters are placed in a dreamlike landscape where places and dates are never named, and therefore the stories have a strange flavor, something like Poe's tales, or Kafka's, with however less fictional point to them. They are mostly stories of quest, of pilgrimages over alien terrains in search of unattainable goals. They contain little personal drama or conflict between characters: what concerns Merwin is individual evolution, the effect of experience on a single person. Everywhere there is the treadmill feeling; in "The Church of Sounds" the central character, having lost sight of the girl who has infatuated him, acknowledges her loss with this phrase: "the true despair was gone; it was over, or it had not yet begun." In "The Museum", which is placed in a Southwestern, or Mexican, landscape, we are given a village barber who discovers a catacomb beneath an abandoned house which he turns into a museum. The barber becomes an important figure in the village, until the owners come and have the bones shipped off to the capital. After that, he decides to continue the museum, and fills the niches with stuffed animals. These will not turn to dust, nor will they be taken away.—FRANK MACSHANE, "A Portrait of W. S. Merwin," *Shen*, Winter 1970, pp. 8–9

Merwin's aspiration is to become an empty nobody, an impersonal, expertly trained thing—a tool, an instrument, a pure vehicle for the "one truth," the vision that suddenly fills the fertile, incubating emptiness: the state in which the spirit has completely freed itself from comforts, needs, habits, freed from a human personality, freed from the body's claims, freed from the demands of other beings, freed from the brand marks of colleagues, family, country:

> If it's invented it will be used
>
> maybe not for some time
>
> then all at once
> a hammer rises from under a lid
> and shakes off its cold family
>
> its one truth is stirring in its head
> order order saying . . .
>
> (From "Tool")

This is the state of uttermost self-purification, disaffiliation, dispossession that Merwin has cultivated with unwavering tenacity in his last four volumes of original poetry, and throughout his prodigious career as this country's foremost living translator of verse from other languages. It is a condition of maximum plasticity and availability, a priming and predisposing of the receptive ear to become a psychic medium for the poetry of foreign tongues, as well as for deep images springing from the subconscious mind, or from the racial preconscious: images germinating in the visionary dream-life which have the authority and unshakable finality about them of last basic necessities; images which are as indispensable to survival in worlds of the spirit stretching to its outer limits, on the verge of breaking into new uncharted territory, as the barest physical necessities—a little water, roots, scant body-covering—are crucial to survival in the desert.

Regrettably, he cannot sustain this level of peak accessibility, since the habits of our cumbersome sensory apparatus operate in most of our routine daily living at levels of imprecision and inefficiency far less sensitive, less in touch with the hidden spirit in words, images, or objects than is necessary to support the scrupulous fidelity to quantities, nuances, shades, hues, lusters—quieter brilliancies, faded grays, softer delicate radiances—that Merwin's spirit of aspiring perfectibility demands for his art. Hence, the disturbing perplexity, approaching a cosmic vertigo, of psychic states in which we have fallen hopelessly out of touch with the spirit centers, registered in poems like "Habits," "Something I've

Not Done."—LAURENCE LIEBERMAN, "W. S. Merwin: The Church of Ash" (1973), *Unassigned Frequencies*, 1977, p. 123

Works

I have read through *The Moving Target* twice now and I find I don't have any great enthusiasm for it. I will try to assess why.

Generally the poems in this volume use a personal referent of persistent vagueness: them, their prayers, their faces, their names. Even a specific location is difficult not so much to identify (that might be beside the point) but to grasp some ready and sure sense of: spirit (whose, what), Possessor (a god? which, who). "They have taken my legs leaving me the shoes." "Forerunner, I would like to say, silent pilot / Little dry death, future, / Your indirections are as strange to me / As my own." The last quotation is from the poem called "Sire." So one could make guesses. The poem "To My Brother Hanson" begins "My elder," and I suppose there is no trouble with that. But I don't want to imply I've searched for instances to back up my point; they are the general rule, found almost at random. Merwin addresses the omniscient a lot of the time and, since he is a precisionist the rest of the time, the question comes up and leads to another.

Why does the verse need to be so metaphorical? For all the use of the concrete, to my eye what remains is suggestion, in context surprisingly abstract. In the poem "Lemuel's Blessing" he is addressing Spirit:

> From the ruth of approval, with its nets, kennels, and
>   taxidermists;
> it would use my guts for its own rackets and
>   instruments, to play its own games and music;
> Teach me to recognise its platforms, which are
>   constructed like scaffolds;
>
> . . .
>
> I have hidden at wrong times for wrong reasons.
> I have been brought to bay. More than once.
> Another time, if I need it,
> Create a little wind like a cold finger between my
>   shoulders, then
> Let my nails pour out a torrent of aces like grain from
>   a threshing machine;

There is a strain toward the weight of the parabolic, but as of my point thus far, it comes out comparison and it is difficult for me to tell what is thrown beside what.

I have no trouble hearing that the language is elegant at times, fine at others, and most times boldly enigmatic. And capable of an unusually probable sound:

> AS BY WATER
>
> Oh
> Together
> Embracing departure
> We hoisted our love like a sail
> And like a sail and its reflection
> However
> We move and wherever
> We shall be divided as by water
> Forever forever
> Though
> Both sails shudder as they go
> And both prows lengthen the
>   same sorrow
> Till the other elements
> Extend between us also.

Merwin is as good a poet as any other I know of, he has had a long and thoughtful practice for a poet who is still young. But he finds himself in that same boat with other men who are looking for a likely place to get out. I prefer "The Drunk in the Furnace" to any poem in this collection and mostly because that poem was able to direct my attention to an act, and a fact, of greater importance than a centrifugal brooding of the poet's writing. I'm not asking him anything so cranky as to say what he means; still, mystical socialism is not as engaging as socialism, individualism is not as interesting as an individual. Merwin has spoken more intelligently in his essay, "A New Right Arm," where his Swiftian sense of things registered a problem common to all of us in a way I haven't ever seen it done. I still have the notion that in our time a poem ought to make something clear as well as be beautiful.—EDWARD DORN, "Some Questions of Precision," *Poetry*, June 1964, pp. 184–85

Merwin powerfully dramatizes states of disorientation, spiritual vertigo. The speaker in the poems (in *The Lice*) is lost in time, lost to himself. He exists in stark disrelation. The sensibility of the persona is desperately trying to catch up with experiences—of self and the world—that have long since passed him by. The possibility of an inner life of spirit continues, as before, but we are helpless to embrace it: "Not that heaven does not exist but / That it exists without us." The artist cannot save us, but he employs a heroic intelligence in the task of defining the exact conditions of our helplessness:

> I
> Am all that became of them
> Clearly all is lost
> The gods are what has failed to become of us
> Now it is over we do not speak
> Now the moment has gone it is dark
> What is man that he should be infinite
> The music of a deaf planet
> The one note
> Continues clearly this is
> The other world
> These strewn rocks belong to the wind
> If it could use them
>
>   (from "The Gods")

These poems speak to our sensibility from the corridors of sleep, and there are moments in the reading of them, or just after reading them, when we feel the odd wide-awakeness—the super-alertness—that we experience when a deep sleep is suddenly interrupted by a very disturbing dream and we spring upright in bed with an absurd sense of relief, in the certainty that all of our questions have been answered, even the ones we never knew enough to ask. This poetry, at its best—and at our best as readers—is able to meet us and engage our wills as never before in the thresholds between waking and sleeping, past and future, self and anti-self, men and gods, the living and the dead.

In "Is That What You Are," man's spiritual disorientation is queerly externalized: the spirits of the dead hover on the sill of man's consciousness, bewildered, waiting to be re-positioned in man's scheme of the universe. Now that man has lost his identity, they too have lost theirs; the dead stare at us across an abyss, and, by an ironic reversal of traditional roles, they pose unanswerable questions to us; and we can only stare back, a race of somnambulistic amnesiacs:

> New ghost is that what you are
> Standing on the stairs of water
> No longer surprised
> Hope and grief are still our wings
> Why we cannot fly

> What failure still keeps you
> Among us the unfinished . . .
> I did not think I had anything else to give

As this poem proceeds, the gap between the living man—who is in reality "the dying"—and the dead spirit, who clings helplessly to the living, narrows, and finally one cannot tell them apart. The twin conditions of death-in-life and life-in-death dramatized by Yeats in the Byzantium poems are viewed here in a strikingly new relation. Yeats had envisioned the passage of the living artist's spirit into the antiworld of the dead as being a gesture of great spiritual energy, a state from which the living spirit could return to this world enriched, spiritually nourished. In Merwin, the opposition between the spirits of the two worlds has grown feebler and feebler, since life and death have grown to resemble each other more and more. Loss of identity, in both cases, has resulted in loss of spiritual vitality, and both heaven and earth are moving toward extinction; like the American soldiers fighting in Vietnam, "Nothing they will come to is real / Nor for long."

The most remarkable poems in this book are the ones in which the speaker confronts a strange alien being—a god, an animal, a dead spirit. The persona is the last man: he embodies what is left of the spirit of natural life-giving beauty in man. He has long since written off the question of survival, of saving anything for the future, as hopeless ("Today belongs to few and tomorrow to no one"). All that remains to him is to grace the obsequies of our passage into extinction with a few words of dignity and bitter truth:

>   . . . there are
>   Occupations
> My blind neighbor has required of me
> A description of darkness
> And I begin I begin . . .

Merwin, in this book, is a soul surgeon performing radical operations on modern man's failing spirit. The patient is on the critical list and the prognosis is very poor. In the bleakest poems, the patient has already died. The poet performs a spiritual autopsy: the anatomical findings reveal that the corpse had died many times over before being declared officially dead.—LAURENCE LIEBERMAN, "W. S. Merwin and Anthony Hecht: Risks and Faiths" (1968), *Unassigned Frequencies*, 1977, pp. 257–597

The imaginative largess of this book of prose (*The Miner's Pale Children*) is astonishing. Clearly, the negative offers Merwin a mode of getting on with his undoing which is as prodigal as all our pieties about "creativity," about "affirmation": "he could hear the pain of disappearance itself," he says of one of his creatures, "of which night is one form and day another." King Lear was wrong—everything comes of nothing, or out of nothing. And by the agency of prose it goes on, leaving behind only history—which Merwin calls the form of despair reserved for the living—and darkness ahead. How well Merwin has listened to Beckett: "The voice must have come. Because it has gone." And how hard he has looked at Magritte: "An occasional glimpse through an open window of a fly on an empty table, or a plate standing on edge." Fragmentation and forgetting are the method this writer employs to use himself up, to exhaust himself in "a travail which in itself of course is a delivery from confinement." Forgetting, because we are fallen creatures, because, as he puts it, "there is no returning to the ungrieved world. Now that it no longer exists, it never existed." And fragmentation, because the process is linear, persistent, unending; as he says in "The Fragments," a perfectly named morsel, "parts of it keep appearing. I have begun to have glimpses of all that I am doing, crossing the place where they have all been satisfied, and still finding fragment after fragment."

In one of the great "Psalms" from *The Carrier of Ladders*, Merwin makes a discovery: "in front of me it is written / *This is the end of the past / Be happy.*" And in one of his fragments from *The Miner's Pale Children*, he glosses that discovery: "most of what we call our virtues have been made out of necessities by processes we later tried to forget." Poetry then is the felicity of a redeemed world, ungrieved, regenerate. And prose? A *fabula rasa*.

I have not attached the usual tags of praise and blame to these enterprises which are so complementary, so instinct with one another's energies. Merwin long ago reached what I should call his majority as a poet, and when a man travels this far—or craves so to travel: "if only we could set out now, just as we are, and leave ourselves"—it is impertinent to assign grades, to hand out marks. The interesting thing is not to say that Merwin is a wonderful poet, or a wonderful prose writer, for "how many things," as he says, "come to one name/hoping to be fed!" *One reaches for definitions and touches darkness.* Pertinent, I hope, is the application to Merwin of what he says of his man "In a Dark Square": "that though no one is listening, he repeats aloud to the darkness that he will continue to put all his faith in himself."—RICHARD HOWARD, "A Poetry of Darkness," *Nation*, Dec. 14, 1970, p. 635.

⟨. . . The⟩ poems in *The Lice*, even more than those in *The Moving Target*, convey the hush and chill of hostages of silence; more than any other American poetry, in their forms, they seem really to follow the mind's first unpurposive gathering of images and words before it is forced to move towards concepts, conclusions, public utterance. In their logical thrust they are *preconceptual*, eschewing (as Merwin always has) even the circumstantialities by means of which most modern American poetry is logically anchored in a kind of emotional cause-and-effect: "I was *here*, (and so) I came to feel. . . ." If absolute despair has no art, then there must be degrees; partial despair over an often unthinkable and unspeakable age must find its poetic voice in regions of the mind somewhere below the orderly circles of discursive thought. As Merwin has put it in the "Notes" just cited, "I imagine the writing of a poem, in whatever mode, still betrays the existence of hope, which is why poetry is more and more chary of the conscious mind in our age." What it more and more turns to, in Merwin's writing pre-eminently, is the preconceptual and intuitive mind.

⟨. . . The⟩ *syntax* of his verse is straightforward enough, and such a rationale operates most obviously in *The Lice* in the total abandonment of punctuation. The reader is thereby forced to attend to the semantic movements of the verse very closely and open-mindedly; without the formal syntactical signals of commas, periods, question-marks to simplify things for him, he generally has several possible meanings opening before him at once. He thus cannot extrapolate to likely conclusions about the gist of a sequence of lines (as we all do to some extent in reading conventional poetry); indeed, often Merwin's lineation is mischievous, deliberately setting cognitive traps for the reader, as in the following lines from "Fly." A tame pigeon having died following his efforts to get it to fly again, the speaker says

So that is what I am

Pondering his eye that could not

Conceive that I was a creature to run from

I who have always believed too much in words

As a sense unit complete in itself, the first line is a brutally

direct and exclusive identification of the speaker as the killer of a trusting animal: he is *that*; but when this sense in drawn into the succeeding lines, the initial recognition, without being denied or minimized, is tellingly developed in terms of the human paradox of being a "creature" and yet having the power to "ponder" and believe in words.

More generally, if Merwin is among those poets who in different ways are in pursuit of the truth to be gotten in catching "the very movement of the mind," then in *The Lice* he often seems to be after a particular preconceptual mode— that of the riddle. As Aristotle points out in the *Rhetoric*, riddles and metaphors have much in common. And, as with a metaphor, in attending to a posed riddle we are not interested so much in "solving" it as in fully imagining the unfamiliar, maybe impossible union of details, which, we take it on faith, will be revealed to us as something familiar, but now to be seen in a new light. "What small children die of old age and their parents are still young people?" The meaning and certainly the pleasure of the riddle don't lie, I submit, in getting the answer itself, "leaves of a tree," but rather in the "willing suspension of disbelief" which the riddle licenses, the opening of the imagination to the possibility of such illogical circumstances, and the skewed perception of familiar objects which follows. The riddling imagination in Merwin is rarely so playful or direct; but in his persistent abrupt personification of natural objects and forces, in his omission of logical connections and transitions (as well as punctuation), in the way his titles so often seem to stand to their poems as answers to riddles, and overall in the way the poems metaphorically occupy, tease, short-circuit the workaday mind and liberate the preconceptual faculties, he really does seem to be practicing, in the line of Verlaine and Dickinson, a poetry of riddle.—JAROLD RAMSEY, "The Continuities of W.S. Merwin: 'What Has Escaped Us We Bring with Us,'" *MR*, Summer 1973, pp. 572–74

RICHARD HOWARD
From "W. S. Merwin: 'We Survived
the Selves That We Remembered'"
Alone with America
1969, pp. 378–81

In 1967, four years after *The Moving Target*, Merwin brought out his sixth book, *The Lice*. The odd title is taken from Heraclitus' fragment about Homer and the boys' riddle: "what we have caught and killed we left behind but what has escaped we bring with us"—their lice. Homer's failure to guess the riddle proves, Heraclitus says, that all men are deceived by the appearances of things. Merwin is content to abide by this knowledge, or this ignorance: he will present the appearances of things and welcome the deceptions in an effort to defeat them by suggesting their thinness and incompletion; for these are all poems of a visionary reality, hallucinatory in their clarity of outline, their distinctness of detail:

It is cold here
In the steel grass
At the foot of the invisible statue
Made by the incurables and called
Justice

The poems are entirely unpunctuated, and the virtuosity of their accessibility is great, for the continuities are extended beyond those of the last book, the voice sustained for longer units of expression; but (in keeping with Merwin's habit of articulating each of his modes in pairs of books) the work, whether wisps of a couple of lines and a single image, or deliberations of several pages and almost novelistic detail, are of the same inner coherence, the same outer necessity as those in *The Moving Target* ("May I bow to Necessity," he prays in "Wish," in the new book, "not / to her hirelings"). All the poems appear to be written from one and the same place where the poet has holed up, observant but withdrawn, compassionate but hopeless, isolated yet the more concerned, at least in quantity of reference, by the events of a public world. "The Asians Dying," "For a Coming Extinction," "When the War Is Over" are some of the titles, and one poem ends:

> On the door it says what to do to survive
> But we were not born to survive
> Only to live

It is as though the poet had decided, or determined, his own fate, which is one of dispossession and the *aigre* wisdom to be derived from it: "Now all my teachers are dead except silence / I am trying to read what the five poplars are writing / on the void." And once these interior distances have been explored:

> I think all this is somewhere in myself
> The cold room unlit before dawn
> Containing a stillness such as attends death
> And from a corner the sounds of a small bird trying
> From time to time to fly a few beats in the dark
> You would say it was dying it is immortal

—Merwin is free ("I know I'm free / this is how I live / up here") to attend to his visionary task, his responsibility to others:

> I take no pride in circumstances but there are
> Occupations
> My blind neighbor has required of me
> A description of darkness
> And I begin I begin . . .

There is a cool radiance in these poems, as Merwin himself had put it: "a clarity at once simple and formal, excited and cool, a limpidity"

> Of frost stirring among its
> Stars like an animal asleep
> In the winter night

—a detachment from the glamor of language as the canonical order had wielded it, from the glare of reality as the discursive impulse had submitted to it, and even from the gleam of vision as the latest web of fragmentary correspondences had invoked it. Part of the weird effect is simply the result of loneliness ("I am strange here and often I am still trying / to finish something as the light is going") and of the fantasies to which the self in isolation, unmoderated by social tact, is subject:

> At times night occurs to me so that I think I have
> been
> Struck from behind I remain perfectly
> Still feigning death listening for the
> Assailant perhaps at last
> I even sleep a little for later I have moved . . .
> If I could be consistent even in destitution
> The world would be revealed . . .

But even when Merwin speaks as a prophet out of his solitude into that opposing solitude which is Other People, as in "A Scale in May":

> To succeed consider what is as though it were past
> Deem yourself inevitable and take credit for it
> If you find you no longer believe enlarge the temple

—even when he acknowledges Other Poets ("you who were haunted all your life by the best of you / hiding in your death"), there is a chill, almost a silence that lines his speech, and a difference about his notation of the world which I take as the final achievement of his vast mutations; it is the welcoming of

his destitution among men in this book (as in the last it was the encompassing of his death in a private history) that sounds the special note of *The Lice:*

> All morning with dry instruments
> The field repeats the sound
> Of rain
> From memory . . .
> It is August
> The flocks are beginning to form
> I will take with me the emptiness of my hands
> What you do not have you find everywhere

These lines are from a poem called "Provision," and if we recall that the word means, precisely, a looking ahead, a vision of the future, we can see that the poetry of this man has moved from preterition to presence to prophecy, and that it is, in its latest, mastered avatar, *provisional* in the proudest as well as the humblest sense, foreseeing and providing for its own metamorphosis; perhaps what I have called coolness and detachment is merely the effect of a poetry which has altogether committed itself to that encounter with identity we call, at our best, reality; for no poetry, where it is good, transcends anything or is about anything: it is itself, discovering its own purpose and naming its own meaning—its own provision, as Merwin provides it in "For the Anniversary of My Death":

> Every year without knowing it I have passed the day
> When the last fires will wave to me
> And the silence will set out
> Tireless traveller
> Like the beam of a lightless star
> Then I will no longer
> Find myself in life as in a strange garment
> Surprised at the earth
> And the love of one woman
> And the shamelessness of men
> As today writing after three days of rain
> Hearing the wren sing and the falling cease
> And bowing not knowing to what

JAMES ATLAS
From "Diminishing Returns: The Writings of W. S. Merwin"
American Poetry since 1960: Some Critical Perspectives
ed. Robert B. Shaw

1973, pp. 72–81

III

From the beginning, Merwin has demonstrated a concern with reticence, with not speaking; *A Mask for Janus*, published in the Yale Series of Younger Poets (1952), consisted of ballads in archaic diction, songs, and mythic parables. Auden, who was then editor of the Series, noted in his introduction "The historical experience which is latent" in Merwin's poems: "By translating these feelings into mythical terms, the poet is able to avoid what a direct treatment could scarcely have avoided, the use of names and events which will probably turn out not to have been the really significant ones." What Auden meant was that these poems had been composed in a language devoid of immediate social content, abstract and imprecise. Their ornate, peculiar diction, an absence of all qualities distinguishing the modern, a derivative, self-conscious voice: this was the result of Merwin's decision to "avoid what a direct treatment could scarcely have avoided," and it has plagued his writing ever since.

Even so, an intelligence comparable to that of Wallace Stevens, though lacking Stevens' enviable grace, was at work in such lines as these, from "Dictum: For a Masque of Deluge":

A falling frond may seem all trees. If so
We know the tone of falling. We shall find
Dictions for rising, words for departure;
And time will be sufficient before that revel
To teach an order and rehearse the days
Till the days are accomplished: so now the dove
Makes assignations with the olive tree,
Slurs with her voice the gestures of time:
The day foundering, the dropping sun
Heavy, the wind a low portent of rain.

Harvey Gross, alluding to Merwin's as "a representative first volume," observes in his *Sound and Form in Modern Poetry* that "the poets of the late forties and fifties have shown an almost religious devotion to iambic pentameter, intricate stanzas, and close formal arrangements."[1] Rhetorical and stylized, Merwin's earliest poems conformed to the procedures of the English poetic tradition, even borrowing inversions ("The frame that was my devotion / And my blessing was"), words ("in priestly winter bide"), and characters (huntsmen, lords, and kings); while almost no traces of this lyrical, delicate style remain in Merwin's later collections, there are undeniable resemblances between what he was writing then and a mode that owes less to some identifiable period than to the language of English literature.

The Dancing Bears, which appeared in 1954, elaborated on the techniques introduced in *A Mask for Janus*; while an extended line widened prosodic possibilities:

And there where the spume flies and the mews
        echoed and beckoned
The bowing drowned, because in her hands love and
        the one song
Leap and the long faith is born gladly, there through
        the waters
Of the dead . . .

still the long narrative poems, variations on old romantic tales, replete with castles and maidens, disclosed an odd self-conscious prose that should have been ironic. It was "On the Subject of Poetry" that Merwin showed a subtle control, revealing a failure of confidence in his own medium that becomes obsessive later on:

When I speak, father, it is the world
That I must mention. He does not move
His feet nor so much as raise his head
For fear he should disturb the sound he hears
Like a pain without a cry, where he listens.

What is referred to here is that indistinct, unknown persona destined to become the speaker in Merwin's prose poems: the poet, the poet's father, or simply a man:

I do not understand the world, father.
By the millpond at the end of the garden
There is a man who slouches listening
To the wheel revolving in the stream, only
There is no wheel to revolve.

There are two possible readings here; either the wheel revolves without the poet's intervention, or what he hears is imagined, not a thing that exists at all. Believing the world to be inaudible, conjecturing whether "the mind of heaven be a mind / of questions", Merwin selected as a subject the tentative properties of language, and all that followed was an affirmation of silence.

Richard Howard, in *Alone with America*, proposed that Merwin's work, which then consisted of six volumes, be classified in three consecutive categories, which seems a legitimate reading of their changes; in such a scheme the middle period, embracing *Green with Beasts* (1956) and *The Drunk in the Furnace* (1960), appears to have been the most expansive and accomplished. Part I of *Green with Beasts*, subtitled "Physiologus: Chapters for a Bestiary", contained several of the poems that were selected to represent him in Donald Hall's well-known anthologies; elaborate elegiac lines, intense and varied modalities of metre and caesura, a heightened and rhetorical resonance: in these poems about "Leviathan", "Two Horses", "Dog", "White goat, white ram" Merwin explored the capacities of the sustained and complex poem, not reticent about risking the temper of elevated speech. "Fog" imitated Pound's use of Anglo-Saxon rhythms in "The Sea-Farer", compressing language, exacting from it a conscious alliteration and assonance:

Ships were not named for haven but if we were
There will be time for it yet. Let us turn head,
Out oars, and pull for the open. Make we
For mid-sea, where the winds are and stars too.

while in "Birds Waking", the repetitive insistence of Hopkins could have been detected:

Oh let it be by this violence, then, let it be now,
Now when in their sleep, unhearing, unknowing,
Most faces must be closest to innocence,
When the light moves unhesitating to fill the sky
        with clearness
And no dissent could be heard above the din of its
        welcome,
Let the great globe well up and dissolve like its last
        birds,
With the bursting roar and uprush of song!

The sheer exuberance of orchestrated effects, emphatic and exaggerated, coupled with a loud, unashamed eloquence, claimed obvious rewards, among them the reconciliation within a single voice of traditional and modern utterance.

Idiosyncratic in his themes, concerned less with a private self than with ill-defined motifs that wavered between the pastoral and metaphysics, Merwin has mastered the techniques of writing and then amplified their truths. It was not until the publication of *The Drunk in the Furnace*, though, that his own temperament became visible, his Being-in-the-world; voyages at sea, motifs of loss, and the phenomenon of surviving death, witnessing that moment of collective disaster when "our cries were swallowed up and all hands lost," had become obsessive concerns. In several poems, such as "Bell Buoy", "Sea Monster", "Cape Dread", and "Sailor Ashore", the sea mirrors and exemplifies our own alien condition; its meanings are interpreted as allegorical; a ship leaving port "has put / All of disaster between us; a gulf / Beyond reckoning. It begins where we are." And the closing lines of "The Bones" recall Kafka's parable of "Infinite Hope", but not for us":

Shells were to shut out the sea,
The bones of birds were built for floating
On air and water, and those of fish devised
For their feeding depths, while a man's bones were
        framed
For what? For knowing the sands are here,
And coming to hear them a long time; for giving
Shapes to the sprawled sea, weight to its winds,
And wrecks to plead for its sands. These things are
        not
Limitless: we know there is somewhere
An end to them, though every way you look
They extend farther than a man can see.

Merwin's tacit longing is to live among whatever he names, entering the world again in some other, elemental form. His is the chore of "giving / Shapes" to things, altering their appearance, transmuting them, just as our presence in the natural world enacts a sea-change on what surrounds us.

In opposition to this eternal, devastating sea, imposing in its immense and silent depths, is urban life; this other solitude, arriving in pool halls, wretched hotels, and old men's homes, evades "the real dark" of existence, concealed in a vast, incomprehensible universe. Merwin's portrait of "The Gleaners" evokes a desolate image of the dying:

> They always gather on summer nights there
> On the corner under the buggy street-bulb,
> Chewing their dead stubs outside the peeling
>   Bar, those foreign old men,
> Till the last street-car has squealed and gone
> An hour since into the growing silence,
> Leaving only the bugs' sounds, and their own
>   breathing;
>   Sometimes then they hobble off.

The language of these poems is both specific and spare, cautious and intense; rejecting nostalgia, Merwin writes as if he were speaking, as if in chronicling our own decline he becomes ashamed. Terse rhythms and vague anxieties ("Do not look up. God is / On High. He can see you. You will die.") are buried in the rubble of an abandoned home where unsalvageable machines, "crutched in their last seizures," resemble

> the framed ancestors, trapped in their collars,
> Beetling out of oval clouds from the black
> Tops of the rooms, their unappeasable jowls
> By nothing but frayed, fading colors leashed
>   To the leaking walls.

The larger significance of Merwin's vision, embedded in tropes and metaphor, remained in these poems unstated but inescapable. In "Uncle Hess" and "Grandmother Watching at Her Window" the casual cadences of undisturbed, unconscious meditation created their own reflective silences, spaces in which regret was implied and imprecise; the poems were sure of themselves.

The Moving Target, which appeared three years later, announced Merwin's departure from the disciplined versification and controlled narrative style of his earlier collections. Sprawling, unrhymed lines, idiomatic speech and the notation of trivial thoughts, irrational similes ("I bring myself back from the streets that open like long / Silent laughs"): there was in these unusual poems an oratorical "I" whose abrasive complaints echoed Eliot's dramatic monologues:

> Sunday, a fine day, with my ears wiped and my collar
>   buttoned
> I went for a jaunt all the way out and back on
> A street car and under my hat with the dent settled
> In the right place I was thinking maybe—a thought
> Which I have noticed many times like a bold rat—
> I should have stayed making some of those good
>   women
> Happy, for a while at least, Vera with
> The eau-de-cologne and the small dog named Joy,
> Gladys with her earrings, cooking and watery arms,
>   the one
> With the limp and the fancy sheets, some of them
> Are still there I suppose, oh no,

Or the speaker's was a disembodied voice, addressing some unknown Other, or talking out loud; irrational comparisons, partial syllepses ("Night, I am / As old as pain and I have / No

other story."), and puns proliferated, while the repeated use of animism ("the horizon / Climbs down from its tree") imbued the poems with a Surrealist confusion. Cesare Pavese, discussing "Certain Poems Not Yet written", decided against the mode of composition he called "narrating images" because "nothing can distinguish the words which evoke an image from those which evoke an object."[2] It is this, and an absence of distinction between words and things, that lies behind *The Moving Target*, where Merwin's belief is the similitude, even synonymity, of image and object.

His departure from the discursive revelation of objects becomes more noticeable in the closing poems; interruptions of thought, intrusions of unconscious mind are more pronounced, until in "The Crossroads of the World etc." all punctuation has been omitted, except a question mark that ends the poem. After that, there is none in this volume, or in the two that have succeeded it. Line breaks appear to be random, the words themselves are arbitrary, verging on hysteria:

> These words start rising out of my wax shoes I
> Say we must tell him
> We must go up there we must go up there and You
> Are The Next we must tell him
> The persuaders say he would deafen us
> When we say No no one hears us

It is this mode that Merwin has chosen to write in since 1967, the disturbing implications of which deserve to be examined.

IV

The compulsion to discover or invent a language capable of articulating what has happened in our time becomes essential to poets whose political experience defines expression. T. W. Adorno's claim that no poetry could be written after Auschwitz has been disproven, at least in Eastern Europe, through the most arduous linguistic efforts; there, language survives as epitaph, the discrete conclusion of an active cultural life. Even so, such poets as the Polish Zbigniew Herbert and the Yugoslavian Vasko Popa have produced a provisional literature, while the Hungarian Ferenc Juhász has participated in the tradition of his poetic ancestors, Ady and Attila József. All of these, as well as the Latin American poets, regard dislocated syntax, automatic images, unconscious associations, in effect all those properties that describe the French Surrealists, as the discourse proper to their own experience. The poems that belong to them, produced in a climate of political repression or, worse, cultural disintegration, appropriate a language reflecting their own historical moment.

In America, poems of obvious political significance, or that have as their subject politics, remain conventional in their choices of language and style; Lowell's *Notebook* contains the journal, in blank verse sonnets, of an individual whose own temperament accommodates the collective maladies of an entire age. Bly, introducing a selection of *Forty Poems Touching on Recent American History*, wants to reconcile these tensions between the personal and the political, between the spirit and the rational:

> It's clear that many of the events that create our
> foreign relations and our domestic relations come
> from more or less hidden impulses in the American
> psyche. It's also clear that some sort of husk has
> grown around that psyche, so that in the Fifties we
> could not look into it or did not . . . But if that is
> so, then the poet's main job is to penetrate that husk
> around the American psyche, and since that psyche
> is inside *him* too, the writing of political poetry is like
> the writing of personal poetry, a sudden drive by the
> poet inward.[3]

What this involves, it seems, is a rejection of those poetic modes which bind the writer to surfaces, externals; in order to plunge inward, as Bly suggests, a mediation is required between two disparate sorts of discourse: the received language of literature and the language of unconscious thought.

This is where Merwin, in his later poetry, encounters an alarming contradiction; having learned the workings of what Roland Barthes describes as "a decorative and compromising instrument, a writing inherited from a previous and different History, for which he is not responsible and yet which is the only one he can use,"[4] Merwin still resists the real significance of what he practises; the disruption of language is no more than a device in *The Lice* (1967) and *The Carrier of Ladders* (1970). Monotonous, interminable, self-imitative, each poem exudes unbearable exhaustion; none supports a close analysis. Here is "The Night of the Shirts":

> Oh pile of white shirts who is coming
> to breathe in your shapes to carry your numbers
> to appear
> what hearts
> are moving toward their garments here
> their days
> what troubles beating between arms
> you look upward through
> each other saying nothing has happened
> and it has gone away and is sleeping
> having told the same story
> and we exist from within
> eyes of the gods
> you lie on your backs
> and the wounds are not made
> the blood has not heard
> the boat has not turned to stone
> and the dark wires to the bulb
> are full of the voices of the unborn

What is the purpose of asking all these questions? Is the line "to appear" essential, or just a repetition of the previous line? What motivates the metonymous "heart"? Where is "here"? How does "their days" relate to the stanza? What is "it"? What is "the same story"? How does it happen that "we exist from within / eyes of the gods"? What are "the wounds", what "the blood"? Where does "the boat" enter in, to what does it refer? What suggests that it should have "turned to stone"? The poem has no meaning, not even a style; it sounds like a poor translation. ⟨A⟩ *Time* article celebrated Merwin as belonging among "The Specials", a poet inaugurating "the transmutation of modern dilemmas into the no-man's-land myth, a landscape of the imagination that is universal and particular at the same time." Perhaps, but I suspect that what appealed to them was the neutral, insouciant voice at work in these poems; excessive transmutation of our "modern dilemmas" has caused us to misinterpret them; what there should be more of at this time are critiques, poems that situate us in the world, or elaborate on real conditions.

As a translator, Merwin has been able to capture the concrete and actual dilemmas of Nietzsche, Gottfried Keller, Esenin, and Mandelstam, their desperation, the disturbed and turbulent voice of exile; unlike Lowell's *Imitations*, Merwin's translations have remained close to the originals, aware of their linguistic complexities, their context, and the historical moment informing them. Even though he claims, in the Foreword to *Selected Translations*, to have forgotten most or all of the German, Italian, and Latin he learned in college, while the rest (Russian, Greek, Vietnamese, among several others) are either based on French and Spanish translations or else have relied on collaboration with various hands, these poems

are secure in English. At home in the complicated origins of modern French and Spanish poetry (*The Song of Roland*, Spanish ballads, and *The Poem of the Cid*, as well as the picaresque novel *Lazarillo del Tormes*, have been issued in his translations), Merwin possesses an educated ease when called upon to translate Jean Follain's *Transparence of the World* or the late Argentinian Antonio Porchia's *Voices*; Follain, in whose poems "each detail, seen as itself, is an evocation of the processions of an immeasurable continuum,"[5] resembles Merwin in this, that the world appears absent in duration, outside of time, "au soir de l'existence". Open lines disappear like roads trailing off in the distance; and what Merwin observed in Porchia's aphorisms, an exegesis of "particular, individual experience,"[6] is here as well. It is in Merwin's own poems that, despite such profitable influences, despite his belief in translation "as a means of continually sharpening a writer's awareness of the possibilities of his own language,"[7] a concision has been lost, a rigor abandoned; his translation of Nicanor Parra's "Memories of Youth" demonstrates the dialectic of Surrealism, a coherence which includes incoherence, irrational ideas appearing in a rational relation to the world, in opposition to themselves:

> Crossing the thresholds of private houses,
> With my sharp tongue I tried to get the spectators to
>   understand me,
> They went on reading the paper
> Or disappeared behind a taxi.
> Then where could I go!
> At that hour the shops were shut;
> I thought of a slice of onion I'd seen during dinner
> And of the abyss that separates us from the other
>   abysses.

With Parra, emotional crises arise out of a conflict among things, objects obscure the heart's isolation, an onion slice recalls him to his own abyss. Merwin, in refusing to mean, to be responsible to what he names, sacrifices what is of crucial significance in Surrealism, the dialectical tension between language and meaning.

V

Merwin's last volume, *The Miner's Pale Children*, exploited a genre that extends from Baudelaire through Rimbaud and Mallarmé to Francis Ponge in France, that shares affinities with Lichtenberg and imitates Kafka: the prose poem. These pieces, less fiction than parable, explore an odd region where events are unexplained, where animals talk among themselves, where hope has been "a calm lake in early spring, white because the sky above it was the color of milk." Like the fables of Donald Barthelme, or Beckett's *stories and texts for nothing*, Merwin's episodic, elusive stories exist in a dimension of the mysterious, spoken through some unidentified voice. The language is dense and detailed, but about nothing, or, to be more specific, about the problem of nothingness, as in "The Cheese Seller":

> Everything, they say, everything that ever exists
> even for a moment floats on the black lake, the black
> lake, and there at each moment what is reflected is its
> opposite what is reflected is. This is one of the basic
> truths, without which existence itself would be
> impossible.

What recurs is a motif of listening among the disconsolate, the mad:

> Earth has gone. We float in a small boat that
> was once green, at an immense height on the unlit
> sea. No, there is no height, for the depth of the water
> is infinite. Good-bye height, goodbye depth. The sea

is everywhere. It has no shores. Above us the air of this sea. The black space. The stars have all moved out of sight.

Ponge, during a conversation with Philippe Sollers, described his own writings, or texts, as materialistic, in that words become "une réalité concrète, comportant toute l'évidence et l'épaisseur des choses du monde extérieur."[8] This is close to what Merwin has achieved in these prose pieces, the lessons of which could be: to write is to determine the world's actual properties.

Notes

1. *Sound and Form in Modern Poetry* (Ann Arbor: The University of Michigan Press, 1964), p. 248.
2. Cesare Pavese, *A Mania for Solitude* (London: Peter Owen, 1969), p. 27.
3. *Forty Poems Touching on Recent American History* (Boston: Beacon Press, 1970), p. 10.
4. Roland Barthes, *Writing Degree Zero* (New York: Hill & Wang, 1968), p. 86.
5. Jean Follain, *Transparence of the World*, selected and translated with a Foreword by W. S. Merwin (New York: Atheneum, 1969), vii.
6. Antonio Porchia, *Voices*, translated by W. S. Merwin (Chicago: Big Table Publishing Company, 1969).
7. W. S. Merwin, *Selected Translations 1948–1968* (New York: Atheneum, 1969), viii.
8. *Entretiens de Francis Ponge avec Philippe Sollers* (Paris: Gallimard/ Seuil, 1970), p. 169.

ROBERT PETERS

From "The Great American Poetry Bake-Off: or, Why W. S. Merwin Wins All Those Prizes" (1977)
The Great American Poetry Bake-Off

1979, pp. 264–68

Merwin's *Ezy-Myth Mix Method*: At times Merwin's facility for making a poem sound like an overly literal translation from the ancient Ainu or Greek or Cherokee doesn't work. It's apt to be too self-conscious an act. When these poems do succeed, though, they carry a strange, wondrous authority; poet appears as shaman—myth-wisdom of the ages is his mantle; his events (cowrie shells) he sets in the mythic past where our origins are. He tells us how the gods began, when fire came into being, and religion. Writer as *vates*, a difficult role for a mid-twentieth century American poet to assume.

"Division" is a frustrating example of Merwin's Ezy-Myth-Mix method. At the outset the loquacious story-teller tone puts me off:

People are divided
because the finger god
named One
so he made for himself a brother like him . . .

First, this is rhythmic prose of no particular distinction set out to look like poetry. Second, to say "familiar ground" is not enough. All myths about gods must begin somewhere, and if god is creator he must create his selves from himself. No news here. Perhaps it's too easy. Yes, it is too easy. Think of God's surprise had that Otherself leaped out of his belly, or his balls, without any need for His will at all. Load on surprise, W. S.! God's first responses to his partner-twin are jealousy, fear, threat.

But why is he a "finger god?" Why not a toe god? an ear

god? a pancreas god? What was One doing with that finger? Did it smell good?

The appeal is easy. Poets are supposed to sound like this! We earn our keep by being myth people; and if we can sound like rewriters of Genesis, embellishing here and there, readers in the great cupcake audience are happy. For these poems comfort us in our accedia. We feel that we aren't so far after all from our primitive roots.

Merwin's god drops big god-tears on the sand. A twin is not enough. His pair of selves is still lonely. So he creates two more look-alikes—twins. Fearing they'll lose each other, Merwin's twins create hands to hold them fast, and arms to connect the hands. Their hearts, though, fail to merge them into a single identity, against possible loneliness. This conclusion is fine, and I am caught in its poignancy. Too bad the Chingachgook opening isn't more original. As the Shakers knew, there are gifts for being simple, and Merwin maintains a Biblical simplicity of diction and tone. In turning with the poem I feel Merwin's winsomeness. And I do prefer his over-simplifications and his attempts to come off *vatic* to much of the clever, self-conscious, solipsistic nose-picking poetry around today. My carping is because Merwin's achievement is important. A final note here: his device of starting numerous lines with *and*, an easy device, suggests a primitive narrative style. You might see the *ands* as raisins in the plum pudding. Generally, Merwin knows when to restrain the device. Technically, even when he masquerades prose as poetry, he is nearly always right. ⟨. . .⟩

His persons sound like brothers to Samuel Beckett's persons: Beckett's characters might easily speak Merwin's poems. They seem depersonalized in the way that Beckett's lines are depersonalized and chromed. There is also a spaced—in the sense of dope-spaced or stunned—quality behind many of these poems (and I'm not accusing Merwin of being a head—you can be of the devil's party without knowing it). The sense of persons wandering after some remote voice or light, some of them with bandaged physiogs . . . they sound like partially lobotomized, dispirited Dicks and Janes seeking for SPOT (an anagram for GOD). Appropriate here is Merwin's "Dogs." Note the "Happiness is a warm puppy" echoes. "Loneliness," Merwin writes,

. . . is someone else's dog
that you're keeping
then when the dog disappears
and the dog's absence
you are alone at last . . .
but at last it may be
that you are your own dog
hungry on the way
the one sound climbing a mountain
higher than time

If we are "the one sound" climbing the mountain (are we also the one hand clapping?), our lives are miniscule semi-existentialist acts. Our strain is not quite that of Sisyphus'; although climbing a mountain, packless, bookless, can be wearing. The need for struggle of some kind is implicit. Shelley's idea of Beauty, in its origins and combinations, is similar. Shelley took the image of a forest lake: bubbles begin at the bottom and work their effervescent way almost soundlessly to the surface. These bubbles escape, combine with other bubbles emanating from other lakes, and from all living matter, to form finally the Symphony of Life-sounds in the Universe. In their highest ascension these sounds reach the One, the All. Well, this may not be good science, but it did make for a considerable art. And it still does: I can think of no better way to conclude this essay than to quote from the final stanza of the final poem in Merwin's book. "Gift" moves from pure Shelleyan statement to a prayer uttered by the speaker (Merwin?) in his separateness. The Shelleyan symbols (and even the Shelleyan language) reveal Merwin's sources, and his place in a long and easy tradition. Here are the examples culled from "Gift": "shadowless mountain" is the Romantic mountain seen as the Ideal in full light; night; silence is the alembic for Romantic mystical awareness; the Eternal—the mountain is "no child of time"; the morning—Romantic symbol of refreshment. These, Merwin says, are the "gifts." And from whom do we receive them? In answer, Merwin supplies this closing, surprisingly pure Shelleyan prayer:

I call to it Nameless One O Invisible
Untouchable Free
I am nameless I am divided
I am invisible I am untouchable
and empty
nomad live with me
be my eyes
my tongue and my hands
my sleep and my rising
out of chaos
come and be given

I call this "writing" rather than poetry, and I call it "never-fail writing." It's easy in its borrowings, and its leavenings (*chaos, nomad*). It's a Can't-Fail Concoction.

LEONARD MICHAELS

1933–

Leonard Michaels was born on January 2, 1933, in New York City. He attended the High School for Music and Art in New York, and received his B.A. from New York University in 1956 and his doctorate from the University of Michigan in 1967. Since 1970 he has been Professor of English at the University of California, Berkeley.

Michaels has published two volumes of short stories, *Going Places* (1969) and *I Would Have Saved Them If I Could* (1975). He has said of his writing that "it is usually about urban types and the various kinds of psychological violence they inflict on one another." Not easy to pigeonhole, his fiction is terse, fragmented, vigorous; his plots irrational, with twists both tragic and comic. A consistency of viewpoint, as represented by his recurring protagonist Phillip Liebowitz, brings an overall coherence lacking in individual stories. A short novel, *The Men's Club* (1981), a kind of answer to feminism in which a number of men gather to form a consciousness-raising group, continues the themes of the earlier stories. Influences on Michaels include Kafka, Roth, Malamud, and Borges.

Michaels received a National Endowment for the Arts grant in 1967, a Guggenheim Fellowship in 1970, and an American Academy Award in 1971. His work has appeared in such publications as *TriQuarterly, American Review, New Republic,* and *Antaeus*. With Christopher Ricks he has edited an anthology of essays, *The State of the Language* (1980).

Personal

Mr. Michaels's latest work, *The Men's Club*, is about a group of men in early middle age who get together in a Berkeley house for a night and swap tales. The sexual athlete Liebowitz (the protagonist of *Going Places* and *I Would Have Saved Them If I Could*) has been replaced by men who are burdened with families, careers and domestic feelings. As the men relax into intimacy, they begin to reminisce about their wilder pasts while simultaneously vandalizing the house in which they hold their meeting. Are these men in some kind of midlife crisis, reverting to boyhood as a sign of nostalgia for their youth? Mr. Michaels grimaces at the question:

"I'm not sure what a midlife crisis is. Personally, I've lived in a state of crisis for about 20 years." The grimace turns to a smile.

"As for the men in my novel, they are not so much thinking about midlife crisis as about the fact that they have lived long enough to see that things tend to happen to them in a particular way, in a pattern that is deeply personal. Yet they ask: Could this be me? In the group, they say things about themselves they wouldn't have said otherwise, and they learn about themselves this way. But just as important, they listen to the others, and each of them learns how much he is like the others. ⟨. . .⟩

At 47, Leonard Michaels looks as if he has lived through a lot. His dark curly hair, tumbled about as if never quite controllable, has tinges of gray, and his face is olive-skinned and rough, with deep lines running from his nose to his thin mouth. When he is thinking or feels uncomfortable, he furrows his thick brows over deep-set eyes and appears either bored or in pain. Yet he has a street-corner grace. One can imagine him dribbling a basketball (a game he played with fanatical zeal as a youth in New York) with fierce concentration across a city parking lot, his thin frame effortlessly dodging and bending around an obstacle course of cars. He still takes possession of a chair with the cool easy confidence of an athlete. This afternoon, in his basement study, he seems equally confident talking about *The Men's Club*, his first published novel. He calls it a "descent into the human."

"By that I mean that the considerations of literary art in this book are supposed to seem minimal. Everything I talk about, I try to talk about in regard to human reality, which is a much sloppier thing than art. There are no questions of form in life itself. People do what they are compelled to do and react the way they must."

The desire to be guided by reality rather than a notion of art is what Mr. Michaels says finally enabled him to write a novel. He twice before tried novels, but because of the "severe" ideas he then held about a writer's obligation to art, neither came to fruition. The first, which he wrote as a graduate student, he incinerated. The second turned into the staccato series of short stories in his collection *I Would Have Saved Them If I Could.*

"My stories were very much intended to be true to a kind of musical destiny, almost like poems," he says, leaning dangerously far back in his chair and looking pensive. "There's a story called 'Hello Jack' which I'm very fond of because it's written in a kind of New York music. But I think I've gotten beyond that now. No reader can suppose that I was obsessed with the look and sounds of words in the novel the way I was in my stories. I was careful about that: I reread the novel many times and whenever I'd spot a passage that was too well written, I'd mess it up."

Nevertheless, Mr. Michaels has not relinquished his concern with rhythm in his writing. He calls himself a "very physical writer," who feels the beat of his language unconsciously ("If my nerves go wrong, the writing goes wrong"); yet he considers the beat essential. "The beat is supposed to give you the feeling of lived time, or the quality of the tension in these men during the long night they spend together," he says emphatically.—HELEN BENEDICT, "A Talk with Leonard Michaels," *NYTBR*, April 12, 1981, p. 30

Works

Leonard Michaels is a young writer whose work has appeared in many of the more important literary magazines—*New American Review, Partisan Review,* the *Paris Review,* and the *Evergreen Review* among others. *Going Places* is his first collection.

The key events in his stories—usually holocausts in the lives of his protagonists—are indistinguishable from the settings in which they occur. Settings are felt to be a physical extension of the agonized victims who inhabit them. I am constantly reminded by Michaels' emblematic stage sets that no other time and no other place could have fostered precisely the form or quality of torture that strikes the persona dumb, dead, or fiercely awake—excruciatingly alive for the first time: Beckman, mugged and beaten within a millimeter of his life on the back floor of his cab, "begging as they dragged him by his hair over the front seat and onto the floor in back where the mat reeked of whiskey, stale butts, the corruption of lungs, and a million yards of bowel"; Philip, the hilarious nude fugitive encountered at the subway change booth by the Negro attendant guarding the turnstile, "Hey, man, you naked? . . . You're naked. . . . Scat, mother, go home"; Isaac, the talmudic scholar, discovering his physical deformity—following a fall on the icy street—in a phone booth "like a coffin"; Melanie, raped by the Turk on the "cracking, desiccated leather" front seat of his old Chevrolet, later identifying her hideously diminished self with "an armless, naked manikin" in a store window, and worse yet, "a thalidomide baby, all torso and short-circuited"; the voluptuous Miss Abbe Carlyle, confronted and slowly seduced by the twenty Puerto Rican boys congregated into the shape of a great bird of prey on a banistered front stoop in Spanish Harlem. This is the most imposing and unforgettable emblematic setting in the collection: "Twenty were jammed together on the stoop; tiers of heads made one central head, and the wings rested along the banisters: a raggedy monster of boys studying her approach." These are not simply locales, settings—traditional background—ever. Life does not merely occur in these machines, edifices; life transfigures the forms that

enshrine its daily happening, the forms merging with the bodies they enclose, altering and entering into their life stream.

In "Going Places," the title story, Michaels realizes a totally plastic, epidermal style. Every sentence is charged with a tactility of phrasing that suggests oddly that words are somehow being alchemized into skin. It is a style that gives new significance, a new literalness, to the expression, *he put a skin on everything he said:* "His brows showed the puffed ridges of a pug's discolored, brutalized flesh where a billion capillaries had been mashed and meat-hammered to the consistency of stone. Ugly, but not meaningless . . . memento moris twisted into living flesh reflected in his rear-view mirror." In this description of cab-driver Beckman's face following his beating, physical violence of a kind that leaves the victim with permanent scars ("memento moris") is viewed as a necessary initiation rite, a first step in the painful never-ending quest for "absolute physical being." Beckman's tragedy unfolds as we slowly realize that his blessing is a curse in disguise. The self-discovery resulting from his being beaten nearly to death enables him to change his life radically for the better, from cabdriver to painter, but it leaves him with an irresistible urge to return to total physical risk—courting suicide—and perhaps to crucify himself into the truth.

In two of the stories, "Crossbones" and "Intimations," Michaels is perhaps inventing a new genre, which may stand in the same relation to the conventional story as does the story, say, to the novella. The short-short form appropriates the compression and density of lyric poetry and brings them into fiction. Only a couple of pages in length, these stories need to be reread many times, and gradually, they leave the reader feeling the sense of totally apprehending complex human alliances—or misalliances—ordinarily possible only in the longer forms. One gets a marvelous grasp of the total life-network of the characters in Michaels' short-shorts, as though the essence of the whole novel has been successfully encapsulated in a couple of pages. Michaels' most impressive device in these stories is the elaboration of a long sinuous "crocodilian" sentence which manipulates syntax to catapult words across gulfs of experience; not unusually, seven or eight transitions—in thought or action—are scaled within a single synchromeshed sentence, a sentence that can shift instantly from high gear to low without friction.

The weaker stories in this volume are the wacky sexual fantasies. In some of them Michaels resorts overmuch to clever stunts. The characters display gimmicky dialogue and quirky personality trappings—nervous tics, limps, mutilations, all manner of Freudian and Reichian hangups—but the varieties of gaminess don't conceal the hollow characterization or the frayed seams in a story's overextended structure. These erotic stories are often wildly funny, but the humor is pitched to a scale of laughter that approximates—in its zany crudeness—the cartoons and jokes one finds in *Playboy.*

In the better stories of this type, "City Boy" and "Fingers and Toes," Michaels succeeds in burlesqueing the stock responses of slick pornography and achieves erotic satire of unmistakable originality. His surrealistic scenes are always gorgeously physical. People who are essentially crippled and ineffectual in their daily lives are enabled to blossom into absurdly fulfilled beings in their (or the author's) fleshly fantasies.

Michaels' language is a created, a freshly discovered, idiom revealing the remarkable plasticity of people who are at once trapped—and fantastically bursting alive—in their bodies. The body is always discovered shockingly anew to be the most grotesquely beautiful and delicate of machines; the body, acted upon by the crowded machinery in close quarters of the overpopulated Manhattan, can re-enact through exquisite sexuality—and thereby translate into personality and spirit—the numbingly complex physical intensities and can transform into a reordering synthesis countless and unrememberable daily physical contortions in autos, elevators, and phone booths. Sexuality in the stories assimilates monstrous mental and physical violations of the partner, but transcends them all in a wisdom of the body which can never be learned in any other way, and which must seem—in the world of these stories—to be worth any price that must be paid.—LAURENCE LIEBERMAN, "Words into Skin," *At*, April 1969, pp. 131–32

In *Going Places*, Leonard Michaels has given us what must surely be one of the longest 192-page books of short stories ever written. And since this remark, intended as a compliment, may be open to misinterpretation, let me quickly add that the apparent extraordinary length of the volume is the result not of any actual *longueurs* in the work but of a narrative and stylistic density so marked that it causes whole worlds to form, pass through their cycles, and vanish away on a single page. Where, for example, most writers, dedicated to capturing the synaptic leap on paper—but worried, perhaps, about not being understood—work as hard to reproduce the nerve fibers as they do to depict the energy that passes between them, Michaels, in some sort of haunted hurry (going places?), concentrates entirely on rendering the electric charge as it jumps the gap. Thus, one of his pages is the equivalent of three of nearly anyone else's, and the unwary reader is likely to find himself wondering anxiously, after only half an hour or so of *Going Places*, whether he has not already sat up long past his bedtime.

The collection consists of thirteen stories, several of which, it may be worth noting, received prestigious awards when they first appeared in periodicals like the *Paris, Transatlantic*, and *Massachusetts* reviews. Taken together, the pieces present a sometimes surrealistic, frequently very funny vision of that particular brand of New York–Jewish hysteria about which one might have supposed very little new could be said. But Michaels brings to what is today familiar enough material (boy meets girl at a neighborhood orgy) a compression of language and an intensity of imagery which constitute the real excitement of this first book. Indeed, in his preoccupation with style, he perfectly epitomizes the modern writer of Charles Feidelson's definition, the writer who views "the task before him neither as the expression of his own feelings nor as the description of given things but rather as an adventure in discovery among the meaning of words."

Michaels' virtuoso style runs to dazzling cinematic jump cuts ("Isaac") and to flashbacks ("Sticks and Stones") so complex and intentionally confusing as to obliterate any sense the reader may desperately be trying to retain of "real" time. But these familiar devices for undercutting the illusion of process and causality in fiction are in these pieces entirely functional. That is, the writer is obviously committed on every level of his work to the vision of things which his structures imply: to a sense, for example, that the world is only to be experienced in discrete, timeless, essentially static moments of intense living, moments which owe little or nothing to past or future but which are, to insist on the metaphor, the veritable sparks in the act of jumping the gap. ⟨. . .⟩

In one way or another, nearly all the stories in this collection set out from the irony implicit in the title to show that, as D. H. Lawrence puts it, "the end cracks open with the beginning," and that therefore the notion of progress with which we customarily fill up the space between beginnings and ends is in large measure illusory. The point is made quite

explicitly in "City Boy," a tale which begins and ends with the same scene—a passionate romp on a living-room rug—and in which the author suggests the absurdity of the protagonist's progress from the first seduction to the last by having him accomplish it stark naked and walking on his hands. But other of the stories circle around the same idea. "Isaac" begins and ends with a fall. "Making Changes"—again, the title ironically promotes the possibility of process while the tale itself denies it—is a very funny account of its hero's quest for a girl who, it turns out, has all along been his companion in the quest. And in perhaps the most brilliant of the pieces in the collection, "Sticks and Stones," random, violent movement is gradually reduced to a fixed, timeless moment of pure motion just as the protagonist, a compulsive sprinter, gradually rarefies and *slows* to the fixed, timeless, Platonic pure form of the sprinter—"a head on legs. Running."

The stylistic intensity, then, which makes this short book seem so long is a natural—indeed, an essential—aspect of its theme. Perhaps *Going Places* is a remarkable first step in its author's quest for the ultimate page, the perfect paragraph which will somehow apocalyptically expand to occupy all time. Or perhaps Michaels will now turn to longer and more extensive fictional modes. In any case, in this brilliant first book he has surely fulfilled his own definition of success. He is not merely going places; he has already gotten there.—ELLIOT L. GILBERT, *KR*, Summer 1969, pp. 422–25

Leonard Michaels's second collection of stories begins hot and doesn't cool down. In story after story, he wields his prose like a weapon: part bludgeon, part scalpel, it flickers, dense and resilient. With insane precision, he drops stink bombs. With a poet's twist of language, he decomposes civility into its not-so-secret elements of sex, perverse daydreams, inventive resentment. Every normal act is pitted with an abyss from which comes laughter, ridicule, murder. The brute is not the guest in the basement any more, he is not the secret (Freudian) of our "delicate intentions." The brute is in the streets, and "delicate intentions" are dead. That could be the subtitle of Michaels's book: The Death of Delicate Intentions.

In Michaels's urban madhouse, love is a hand job in the subway; community a surreal orgy on Sutton Place. Culture becomes a pornographer's view of the Holocaust: Nietzsche, Hegel, and Borges facing the world from the position of an exquisite mouth in a blue movie, kneeling before a row of male organs, the universal face to face with the particular. All of this is embodied in excruciatingly precise, almost sculptural, prose. The brute may be a maze of sexual kinks, but he never abdicates his gift of statement. Flaubert is in hell, but he is Flaubert nonetheless. ⟨. . .⟩

I Would Have Saved Them If I Could is a medley of stories, some no more than a few lines long. In many of the short pieces, the narrative deflects into parable and illumination, resembling prose poems more than stories. There is a theatrical quality in many of these pieces, as of people talking to themselves. In Michaels's view, the mind in its natural state is not a surrealist but a gossip and a playwright mixed together. This piece is called "Like Irony."

He pried me open and disappeared inside, made me urinate, defecate, and screech, then slapped my dossier shut, stuck it in his cabinet, slammed drawer, swallowed key. "Well," he said, "how have you been?" I said, "Actually, that's what I'm here to find out." He said, "People have feelings. They do their best. Some of us say things to people—such as you—in a way that is like irony, but it isn't irony. It's good breeding, manners, tact—we have delicate intentions." I apologized. "So," he said, "tell me your plans." I said, "Now that I know?" "That's right," he said, "I'm delighted that you aren't very stupid."

Michaels's themes are not new, nor, in a way, is his tone. His hero is the schlemiel of Jewish fiction. His madcap sex is how sons, after Portnoy, indulge the memory of Jewish mothers. The mother herself is present in a series of shrapnel-like fragments:

> "Everything is fine," I said. My mother said, "I hope so." "It is, it is." My mother said, "I hope so." I said, "Everything is wonderful. Couldn't be better. How do you feel?" My mother said, "Like a knife is pulling out of my liver."

The Freudian paradigm of sex to the rescue and biology as salvation isn't exactly original material these days, nor is the anticultural mania which has supplied the animus of so much recent literature. But Michaels doesn't care about new ideas— or old ones, for that matter. Ideas, themes, and tones are digested by his extraordinary stylistic gift and emerge transformed, hardened into an extreme. Liebowitz—his schlemiel- —isn't only inept and defeated; he is predatory. He is a schlemiel with teeth, and a Charlie Chaplin toe of the shoe in the rear. He cancels the genre.

Michaels's characters drift between "small personal miseries and fantastic sex," but the fantasy debunks the sex, and also debunks the debunking, leaving orgasm to perform by itself as an orgy of the particular, a weird flower of language. The unidentified hand in the subway is "a soft inquisitive spider pinching the tongue of his zipper, dragging it toward the iron floor that boomed in the bones of his rooted feet." The Hassidic rabbi and his wife:

> Twirling and individual, he stepped away snapping fingers, going high and light on his toes. A short bearded man, balls afling, cock shuddering like a springboard. . . . She, on the other hand, was somewhat reserved. A shift in one lush hip, was total rumba.

At the thematic heart of the book is a sequence of essaylike fragments that form the strangest exercise in literary criticism I have ever read. It might be called literature read by the Holocaust. Borges, in love with paradox, according to Michaels, writes a story about a suspected Jew who experiences ecstasy while in jail awaiting his execution: the Gestapo, an organization of death, is responsible for the "secret miracle" of redemption through ecstasy. It turns out that Borges got this story not from any experience of "photographable reality" but from another story. Culture, for Michaels, is a daisy chain of such stories which recline high in the redemptive air, while, at a distance, visible if you look, "a suspected Jew of average height, with bad teeth, gray hair, nervous cough, tinted spectacles, delicate fingers, gentle musical voice—physically and exactly disintegrates . . . between a hard stone wall and the impact of specific bullets."

Borges's ennobling ecstasy is a paradox for onlookers. But the Holocaust, the trapped, crazed lives that people Michaels's stories, condemn the "onlookers" who prefer to lift experience into the perenity of cultural statement. For Michaels, perenity is obscenity. His characters, however ridiculous or defeated, live a dance of victory because, as one of them says, "I am not interested in being superior to my sensations."

As philosophies of culture go, this may be too simple. Yet, as a fictional theme, its very oversimplification becomes a strength, and a plea that reverberates in every story.

Although one senses the hovering of recent literary kin— Burroughs, Barthelme, perhaps Roth—these stories are more nearly poems, with a tightly reasoned quality that calls to mind more distant, stranger ancestors: Baudelaire's *Little Poems in Prose*, or Aloysius Bertrand's *Gaspard of the Night*, with an ingredient of Lenny Bruce diverting them into belly laughter.

I Would Have Saved Them If I Could must be read to be believed. It is surely one of the outstanding works of fiction of the year.—PAUL ZWEIG, "Delicate Intentions," *Harper's*, Sept. 1975, pp. 68–69

A little culture can be a dangerous thing: more of it, still more so. Reading this collection of stories ⟨*I Would Have Saved Them If I Could*⟩ prompts one to wish that Leonard Michaels had never heard of alienation, sentiment of being, nihilism; his fragile talent might then have flourished in comparative innocence. As it is, these stories are crusted with the junk of fashionable culture, both the fashionable culture of today and the fashionable culture of yesterday. There is Bellovian swagger without Bellow's rich complication; Rothian sexual assertiveness without Roth's sense of fun; and there is Mailer, and Malamud, and Borges, and Counter-Culture, all rendered "heavy" in the sense that young people use that term. Behind the influences, references, knowingness, and bravado, one glimpses a rather sweet sensibility with a small, damaged gift for narrative and notation.

Mr. Michaels writes two kinds of stories: "American-Jewish," flauntingly bold and inauthentic, and a Borges-like stringing together of two or three paragraph sketches, vignettes, and reflections, featuring Marx, Freud, Trotsky, Nietzsche, Byron, Hegel, Dostoevsky, and other star players. This latter group of pieces I found impossible and often incomprehensible: they strain, with painful eagerness, for gnomic profundity, fables encompassing the absurdity of existence, and philosophical gags. They are of the sort likely to be described as "wild, man." The level of wit is suggested by Mr. Michael's remark that Marx was "an alienated Jew assuming the voice of Hegelienated Jew." His profundity is suggested by an anecdote about a woman who worries that people are starving while she brushes her teeth and this upsets her morally. But "being moral is a luxury, isn't it? No, it's asking the question. That's why I spend my time stealing, fucking, and taking dope." Wisdom literature is a risky genre.

The straight stories focus on urban trauma and blithe depravity. A gang of Jewish boys peeks into a rabbi's apartment as he makes love to his delectable wife, and then one of the boys suffers the punishment of being shipped off to a summer camp. A man is stroked to ejaculation by a stranger in the subway, whether male, female, or questionable is not clear and it hardly matters—it's just handiwork. A young married couple profit financially by submitting to sexual use at a corrupt publisher's party.

In delivering these sorry anecdotes Mr. Michaels affects a minimal method—minimal narrative, minimal characterization, minimal detail. Bang, bang, hardly any emotional fuss, and we reach the end, like the man in the subway. What is absent from these stories—differentiated and precise responses, say, among the boys peeking at the rabbi, some firm if tacit valuation of what their conduct, indeed, their whole story, signifies—is nothing less, as I see it, than the traditional substance of literature.

That Mr. Michaels is, somewhere, sensitive to such a view of his stories is indicated by the one about the young couple at the publisher's party, where he makes some effort at complication, provides some detail regarding the flow of confused feelings and that makes it the one story in the book which approaches the possibilities of serious writing. But his work is mainly marked by a swaggering reductionism, a naïve faith in the value of notation on the fly. It may be said, by profound critics, that this is what our life has been reduced to in the Age of Etc. Etc., but I think it more likely that it's Mr. Michaels who is doing the reduction, out of some modish idea that relieves him of responsibility for regarding his characters as, perhaps, human beings.

With mini-narratives there go maxi-sentences. The light on a roof is "derealized in brilliance." An "ocular perversion" becomes "the general cleansing nihil of a view." A character "indulged in ambiance, in space like eons." Another one, excited at a party, remarks: "Teeth stabbed out of my ass to eat the chair." The same fellow watches has wife being fondled by that corrupt publisher: "wishy-washy figures of an erotic urn, evoking the prick of perpetuity." Best of all is the character who finds himself "seized in a confusion of vectors."

And that's where Mr. Michaels left me, smack in a confusion of vectors.—IRVING HOWE, "Vectors," *NYRB*, Nov. 13, 1975, p. 42

Leonard Michaels's somewhat controversial reputation as a writer of fiction—confined until now to a fairly highbrow readership—has been based on two collections of short stories: *Going Places* (1969) and the more ambitious *I Would Have Saved Them If I Could* (1975). These stories seem very much of their period: hip-urban-Jewish in sensibility, full of casual violence, nerve-scraping New York encounters and trivialized or debased sex, late-modernist in their fragmented plot-refusing structures, and excessively literary in their inspiration. What is most interesting about them is a stylistic quality, a mode of phrasing that seems perfectly contemporary while at the same time echoing—in its wry, unexpected and slightly skewed locutions—the voice of a chiding Jewish parent in the background. Though obviously the work of a bright and talented writer, many of the stories seem to have dated rather badly; their substance is too thin, their mode too nervously self-conscious, for them to have withstood successfully the erosion of certain attitudes and literary mannerisms that we associate with the late 1960's.

Mr. Michaels has now written a short, funny and discomforting novel that seems certain to attract a much wider audience than any of his previous work, an audience likely to include the readers of *Playboy* as well as of *Partisan Review*. I do not mean this comment disparagingly or condescendingly; *The Men's Club*, for all its accessibility, strikes me as decidedly superior in literary terms to the earlier stories. It is in fact based upon—and expanded from—a short story of the same title that appeared in *Esquire* in 1978, a story that has been converted, with a few minor stylistic changes, into the first chapter of the novel. Part of the book's appeal will no doubt stem from its extreme topicality, for *The Men's Club* might at first glance seem to be part of an anti-feminist backlash, to draw its energies from male fantasies of revenge against the whole monstrous regiment of women. As an ostensible *cri de coeur* from a small herd of male chauvinist pigs, it will thrive upon the outrage it provokes and the rueful yearnings it indulges. But *The Men's Club* is subtler in its implications than might appear in a superficial reading. ⟨. . .⟩

There is no need to overpraise *The Men's Club*. It is more novella than "important" novel. Only three of its characters are developed enough to be in any way memorable; the narrator in particular remains ghostly, his profession and participation never made credible. Toward the end, the satire of California encounter-group jargon becomes too broad ("I feel you're feeling anger. . . . What do you feel about that?") and blunts the wittiness that elsewhere prevails. But such weaknesses inflict little damage. *The Men's Club* is excellent comedy with

a mouth-puckering aftertaste, a book for head-shaking and long sighs of recognition as well as laughter. Its style is full of small verbal surprises that match the glancing quality of its insights. Evidently the shifting of his fictional scene from New York to the Bay Area has been good for Mr. Michaels's art. There is a new expansiveness, an ease, in the writing of *The Men's Club* that distinguishes it from the rather twitchy and abrasive quality of the short stories. Though the characters are mostly de-racinated Jews living a long way from Brooklyn, faint traces of a Yiddish-English background can still be heard in some of the inversions of their speech ("Many things about this woman I admired . . ."). The literary influences so evident in the stories have now been largely assimilated. Leonard Michaels has become his own man, with his own voice and a subject substantial enough to grant his talents the scope they have needed all along.—ROBERT TOWERS, "Men Talking about Women," *NYTBR*, April 12, 1981, pp. 1, 29

In Leonard Michaels' novella ⟨*The Men's Club*⟩, there are no whimpers, only feral roars. Literally. During a long tedious night, seven supposedly typical California males—a psycho-therapist, the host; a doctor; a professor, the narrator; an attorney; a basketball player; a real estate dealer; and a business man—swap tawdry tales of sexual misadventure, gorge them-selves on food and wine, and wreck the furniture. Afterwards, the assembled group, the "Men's Club," begins to howl, like wolves, first individually and then in a pack:

> We sounded lost, but I thought we'd found ourselves. I mean nothing psychological. No psycho-logic of the soul, only the mind, and this was mindless. The table's treasure lay spilled and glittering at our feet and we howled, getting better at it as the minutes passed, entering deeply into our sound, and I felt more and more separated from myself, closer to the others, until it seemed we were one in the rising howls, rising again and again, taking us up even as we sank toward primal dissolution, assenting to it with this music of common animality, like a church-ly chorus, singing of life and death.

This is their reaction to feelings of abandonment and domesti-cation. The women, now "liberated," have left them to their selves, unverified and tamed. At the very end, after the host's wife, Nancy, returns to her savaged house and spoils their song, they beat it in a pickup truck, heading from Berkeley to San Francisco for breakfast, passing around the sacramental joint, singing now of their host, the Jolly Good Fellow. Nancy is left in her room "smashing [a pot] against the floor, the noise changing as it smashed a rug, bare boards, a wall, and then came breaking glass. Then it stopped. We heard the sobbing." How satisfying for the Men's Club that image of the hysterical woman! In the truck the professor: " 'Where are we going?' I screamed. Not for answer; just to scream."

A question persists, after one finishes the book, of what response Mr. Michaels wants from the reader. The satire of his characters' California "life-style" is brutal, if a cartoon; their sexual bravado reveals them as timid and empty, incapable of affection; and their wolfish gluttony and vandalism show them in all their infantilism. Still, at the conclusion, the author appears to celebrate their release from their own meager individualities, the dissolution of their weak "feminine" egos (one character is described as having a hair style once worn by little girls; while another is said to have a "face of an infant surprised by senility"); and to affirm their achievement of a primitive bonding—or at least as near as one can get to such a relationship in Berkeley. But if Mr. Michaels' attitude is ambiguous, constituting the novella's major flaw, it confirms, at last, the men's attempt to slough off their ordinary selves and to return to a "real" masculinity.

The Men's Club is a book of desperation, if not of despair. It is also informed by disgust, designed to instill loathing in the reader for all forms of social life, including sexuality. Mr. Michaels' own desperation can be seen in his reluctance to assume a certain, moral perspective, in his failure to suggest that his characters have interior beings, and in his inability to differentiate among them. All too often the reader is thoroughly confused as to who is speaking or acting. They all merge, despite the fact of their various professions and backgrounds, into a single primal scream. Now, these techniques may be a part of the author's strategy, developed to imply the mindless and spiritless condition of the professional middle class. If so, they don't work. What is required in fiction, just as in any form of art or thought, is clarity, depth, and genuine seriousness. Mr. Michaels does identify a grave moral disorder in our culture. But it is an inadequate art that limits itself to a jeering shrug—or worse, to celebrating incoherence itself.—DAVID KUBAL, *HdR*, Autumn 1981, pp. 460–61

The Men's Club is a provocative title that seems to herald male chauvinism's answer to *The Women's Room* and novels of that genre; a firing of defensive salvoes, perhaps, or even a counterattack claiming that the problems caused by negative discrimination are nothing to those engendered by the positive variety. But in fact, for all its surface liveliness, Michaels's novel turns out to have little to add to the increasingly lacklustre debate on sexual politics; its effect is merely to corroborate traditional views of the male and female character (female-nurturing, male-aggressive), despite a hint of tables being turned (almost literally; a dresser is crashed to the floor by an irate wife) in the final pages.

Michaels writes a choppy, muscle-flexing prose, intending, perhaps, to express an ironical stance towards the Maileresque style of literary tough-talking. Having accustomed oneself to nouns lopped of their articles and full-stops like kicks in the shins, one must admit that such a style has the virtue of tightness and immediacy, and also that it modulates easily into dialogue, a useful facility in a novel whose action takes place in the context of a group discussion. ⟨. . .⟩

The symbolism of food dominates the book. Even the most sustained and pivotal of the sexual confessions is about a man's desertion of the woman he loves because she steals a forkful of his pudding. It is not easy to sympathize with his chagrin, particularly as the dish in question is strawberries under flaming chocolate, a concoction that sounds more like a metaphor than a dessert. The novel falls short of its ambitions for a similar reason; at crucial moments the action seems to be dictated by the manipulation of symbols rather than the compulsions of character.—CAROL RUMENS, "Off the Leash," *TLS*, Oct. 16, 1981, p. 1219

ANTHONY DeCURTIS
"Self under Siege: The Stories of Leonard Michaels"

Critique, Volume 21, No. 2 (1979), pp. 101–10

In his two collections of stories, *Going Places* (1969) and *I Would Have Saved Them If I Could* (1975), Leonard Michaels depicts the contemporary struggle to shape a sensibility sufficiently intelligent, flexible, detached, and controlled to negotiate the contemporary world. The characteristic setting for his stories is New York City—the modern urban landscape, violent, unpredictable, energetic, taxing—challenging and meaningful enough to be a "vale of soul-making," dangerous

and depersonalizing enough to be a hell. Michaels criticizes the modern tendency to perceive the problems of life in such an environment as intellectual puzzles, to be resolved by calling in reserves of greater and greater amounts of consciousness, but his criticism is not the silly, fashionable kind that derides all intellectual processes in the name of the emotional life betrayed. While some of his characters "suffer from too much consciousness . . . a sort of modern disease in which the operations of mind exceed the requirements of life,"[1] Michaels' positive characters are witty, smart individuals for whom thinking is an active, energetic process which culminates in actions in the world. By isolating the pitfall of being entrapped by mind to the point of emotional paralysis, of seeking in the mind for solutions which only action can bring, Michaels has defined a psychological dilemma central to contemporary American fiction.

The most pressing problem Michaels' characters face is maintaining their humanity in the brutalizing circumstances of contemporary life. Violence becomes the natural force in a world in which nothing is really natural. At once random and horrifyingly specific in its focus, violence represents a twofold threat. Its victims must resist turning themselves into unfeeling objects, able to cope because nothing can penetrate their guard, at the same time that they withstand the temptation to elevate themselves to the level of secular holy men, "seized" and purified by violence "as the spirit seizes the prophet." Similarly, the depersonalization of intimate relations poses a threat to anyone who wants to be more than another indistinct face in the mass: "it wasn't easy to think, to ignore the great pull of the worm bucket and pretend to individuation."[2] More generally, Michaels is concerned about the forces working in the twentieth century to annihilate any meaningful notion about the significance of the individual life.

Michaels' stories evoke a sense of how tenuous the props are which provide some semblance of continuity to modern lives. He describes an unnamed character in "Storytellers, Liars and Bores" as "A city girl, nine to five in an office. The days didn't return to her bound each to each by daisies. The weather report was her connection between Monday and Tuesday."[3] Phillip Liebowitz, the most important recurring figure in Michaels' work, "makes his head out of cigarettes and coffee" in the morning before boarding the "screaming iron box" that is the subway (S39). "Chewing gum, cigarettes, candy, drugs, alcohol, and taxicabs" carry the female character in "Naked" "from Monday to Friday" (S34). The kinds of relationships and work which provide more substantial links to one's days and weeks are difficult to locate and certainly to sustain. The tendency is to paste the fragments of one's life together and be like Beckman, the cabdriver in "Going Places," described as "waiting for change to come into his life as if it might hail him from a corner like another fare" (157).

The disruptiveness of modern life is a crucial theme in Michaels' stories, but too great an awareness of the problem debilitates some of his characters as much as no awareness of it at all dehumanizes others. Reading "avant-garde novels and philosophical commentaries on the modern predicament" does not help Melanie Green, the heroine of "Manikin," deal with the rape which shatters the protected, unsatisfying life she had led. She ends up perceiving herself as being like an "armless, naked manikin" in a store window and eventually commits suicide. Discussions about "the keystone of modernity," "what's modern," the loss of "connection with the elemental life" occur with some frequency in Michael's stories and are symptoms of the very problem they assume as their topic. That these conversations typically take place at parties, the inevitable setting in contemporary literature of interactions which are artificial and contrived with the pretense of being intimate and communal, further emphasizes their shallowness. The female speaker in "Being Moral" states the situation most concisely: "Being moral is a luxury, isn't it? No, it's asking the question" (S93). To be self-conscious about consciousness, a part of our humanity, after all, is to paralyze oneself both emotionally and morally. No human action of any meaning is possible in such a state.

The question of moral knowledge itself is not abstract nor philosophical for Michaels, but rather intuitive, emotional, and affective. His characters often allow themselves to be confused by their intellect, using it to fabricate issues which help them avoid, not confront, external reality. In Michaels' own view, the real judgments, the real decisions, regardless of how his characters choose to act in the world, are made "in the pits of their minds where there were neither words nor ideas but only raging morality" (G4). Michaels posits a psychic landscape, obscured in daily life by the fog of obsessive ratiocination, where "life is true and bleak, where all things move in pure, deep knowledge of right and wrong or else they die" (G4, 160). The farther his characters move from this environ, the more their actions become parodic of actual life, the more they are living in bad faith. Again, one should not confuse this notion with a shallow primitivism in which the problems of life dissolve if one merely has one's guts in the right place. In the "pits" of the *mind*, intellect and emotion can fuse, producing energetic, appropriate action, Morality in Michaels' stories is passionate, intelligent engagement with the world, not the measurement of one's doings against one or another internalized, external standard. The complexities of life in the twentieth century do not allow for the latter.

The images Michaels uses to evoke the psychic underworld which can give us "pure, deep knowledge of right and wrong" are those of darkness and blackness. The light of reason and logic does not provide the means by which the situations of life can be comprehended and seen as subject to our control. Genuine insight is the product of emotion and intellect, and itself produces movement. Attempting to come to grips with his relationship to his friend, Henry, in "Fingers and Toes," Phillip hits on a course of action: "The idea just came to me. I didn't struggle to establish thesis and antithesis. It came BOOMBA. Real ideas strike like eagles. A man who loves premises and conclusions loves a whore" (G108). The source for these "real ideas" is the darkness and blackness within ourselves, spaces to which we must have access while we take care not to determine too neatly what those spaces contain.

As a stylist, Michaels is most interested in condensed, compact expression. His desire for compression, which obviously does not allow for very much standard description, places rhetorical responsibility for communicating a story's meaning on its verbs. The emphasis on action and movement suggested by Michaels' striking verbs is reflected also in the title of some of his stories: "Making Changes" and "Going Places." While stagnation is deadening, motion makes us tap the sources for self-knowledge within the self. "Murderers," the first story in *I Would Have Saved Them If I Could*, begins with an illustration of the theme: "When my Uncle Moe dropped dead of a heart attack I became expert in the subway system. With a nickel I'd get to Queens, twist again toward the George Washington Bridge—beyond which was darkness. I wanted proximity to darkness, strangeness" (3). Motion in Michaels' stories differs from the movement suggested by, for example, Maria Wyeth's aimless freeway driving in Didion's *Play It as It Lays* or the repetitive "yo-yoing" in Pynchon's V. The "proximity to

darkness" which Phillip's subway riding entails provides him with a means of coming to terms with his Uncle Moe's death and the emotional constriction which is his immigrant family's legacy. In other contexts, Phillip runs "down the night" at the end of "Sticks and Stones" and swims the night like a fish, "from blackness to blackness to blackness to blackness," at the end of "Fingers and Toes." Both of these stories center on Phillip's relationship to his friend, Henry, and their mutual involvement with Marjorie, currently Henry's consort, formerly Phillip's lover. Phillip's plunging into the night is not a strategy of avoidance but a means of working out his problems physically as well as mentally, the two processes becoming one. As he remarks in "Sticks and Stones," "Trying to think, I ran the streets at night. My lungs were thrilled by darkness" (G45).

In story after story in which he appears, Phillip Liebowitz is concerned with maintaining his identity and not succumbing to the temptation to create an untrue self or to assume roles others thrust upon him. In amusing, significant ways, he reminds himself who he is, re-introduces himself to himself, sometimes in a casual, matter-of-fact manner, more often by defining himself in his own terms or in opposition to some false conception of himself: "I was a city boy. No innocent shitkicker from Jersey," he states in "City Boy"; "I was the A train, the Fifth Avenue bus. I could be a cop. My name was Phillip, my style New York City" (G19). More philosophically, in "Sticks and Stones" he comments, "I was neither Nietzsche, Don Juan, nor Chateaubriand. My name was Phillip" (G39). His battle to hold on to a coherent notion of himself in an environment that works to frustrate such efforts is an especially prominent theme in "Making Changes." Phillip meets a girl named Cecily at a party "clogged with bodies," into which she disappears, "virtually torn out of my hands." He wanders through the apartment searching for her, encountering a variety of vapid people, conversations, and situations. The orgy going full-steam is described by Phillip as "the worm bucket," suggesting the level of sexual communication taking place, while this bit of conversation between two characters named Cosmo and Tulip captures the party's intellectual tone:

"Sexual enlightenment, the keystone of modernity, I dare say, can hardly be considered an atavistic intellectual debauch, Cosmo."

"But the perversions . . ."

"To be sure, the perversions of which we are so richly conscious are the natural inclination, indeed the style, of civilized beings." (G78)

The mindlessness of the conversation and the sexual undifferentiation of the orgy are not the only threats to Phillip's desire for "individuation." Others at the party repeatedly address him either impersonally, metaphorically, or incorrectly. "Wait there, you. . . . What sort of pervert are you?" is Tulip's opening gambit when she first spots Phillip (78). As he enters a bathroom, "A naked man sitting pertly in the tub said, 'I'll bet you're Zeus. I'm Danae.' I shook my head, backed out muttering, 'I'm Phillip'" (81). Finally, as he attempts to leave the party, having located Cecily, Phillip encounters a "big man" at the door who says to him, " 'I'm glad you came tonight, Harold,' 'I'm glad you're glad,' I said. 'Name is Stanley'" (85). In the thickening "stew" of the party, personal definitions are in danger of becoming undone. Phillip must resist the false selves others project upon him and maintain a clear vision of himself.

Creating possibilities for personal relationships, making claims on another while recognizing that person's individuality and avoiding possessiveness, becomes the focal theme of "Making Changes" after Phillip and Cecily leave the party.

Having spent the night with him, Cecily is preparing to leave his apartment in the morning. He wants her to stay, but even as he asks her to, he alludes wittily, defensively, to the modern cultural assumptions which tend to make intimacy a virtual impossibility: "What can I say? I'm aware the couple is a lousy idea. I read books. I go to the flicks. I'm hip. I live in New York. But I want you to come back. Will you come back?" (89–90). By the end of the day and the story, they are reintroducing themselves to each other, names again becoming emblems for the self. Phillip asks her name: " 'Cecily,' she said. 'I'm Phillip,' I said, 'but you knew that. Cecily? Of course, Cecily' " (92).

Beckman, the central character in "Going Places," has more awesome threats than an orgiastic party posed to his identity. The story, perhaps Michaels' fiercest and best, dramatizes compellingly a number of his most crucial themes: impersonal violence working as a force against individuals in the modern world; the imperative to change one's life which unforeseen crisis brings; the chilling sense that, regardless of how one's life is changed, brute circumstance can destroy lives as readily as crazed human agents.

A New York cabdriver, Beckman is robbed and beaten nearly to death by "two figures," a man and a woman, who hail him "in misty dismal twilight." Beckman's assailants strike impersonally but specifically, like the Turkish student in "Manikin" who robs the University Hotel and bludgeons the night porter "so murderously he took it in a personal way." The crimes themselves recede into the background in both these instances, becoming merely occasions and excuses for the exercise of arbitrary violence against other human beings. While Beckman pleads, "shrieking, 'Take my money,' " the woman chants, " 'Hey, hey, Beckman' . . . with the flat exuberance and dull inertia of a work song, repeated without change in pitch or intensity while fists rocked his skull and Beckman thrashed in the darkness" (159). The woman sings her "work song" because violence is her job, her function, from which she is as numbingly detached as Beckman is from his driving. Her direct address to Beckman during the assault underscores Michaels' belief that the random, brutalizing events of the modern world, which seem to strike us arbitrarily, contain messages to us about our lives. As a cabdriver, Beckman had been drifting, living "a life made wretched by rattling kidneys, the stench of gasoline, of cigarettes, of perfume, and alcohol and vomit" (156). He was a chauffeur to

> surly toughs, drunken women, whoring soldiers, vagrant blacks and whites, all the streaming, fearsome, pathetic riffraff refuse of the city's dark going places, though places in hell, while he, Beckman, driver of the cab, went merely everyplace, stopped, parked, dropped his head against the seat and lay mindless, cramped, chilled in a camp sweater and mucky underwear, lay seized by the leather seat, debauched by the night's long, winding, resonant passage and the abuse of a thousand streets. Every-place Beckman, anyplace Beckman, he went no-place. (156)

His close brush with death brings him up against the corrosive facts of his life, and to this degree, "the punches and kicks were heralds, however brutal, bearing oracles of his genius, the bludgeoning shapers of himself if properly understood" (159). His beating, "precisely what he deserved," provides him with the impetus to seize control of his life rather than continue "waiting for change to come into his life as if it might hail him from a corner like another fare," or like the "two figures" who hailed him "in misty dismal twilight" (157). His ability to comprehend the implications of what happened puts him in a position where he can reconstruct his life and

allow himself the satisfactions that a sane human situation can provide. Despite the elevated language and allusions which express the message communicated to him by his misfortune, Beckman understands that he is not a saint of some kind but is now at least able to locate a middle-ground in which human choice is possible. His is not "a shaman's face," and he is "no prophet, but neither a bag scrunched into leather, glass, and steel, commanded by anyone to stop, go, ache, count change out of nasty fingers, breathe gas and hear youth ticked away in nickels" (161).

Michaels understands that the modern world is bleaker, crueler, less predictable than current apostles of self-discovery would have us believe. Our options are only rarely determined by the extent of our self-knowledge. Neither a "prophet" nor an inanimate object, his mind, as well as his motives, focused in ways "entirely unlike the vague motions it had been given to while drifting through the dark streets of the city," Beckman lands a job with a paint contractor (156–57). The solidity of his new prospects is suggested by their seeming to him as "real as the hard, substantial hand which had enveloped and strongly shaken his hand" at the end of his job interview (155). On his first day at the job, Beckman crawls down a pipe high above an enormous factory to deliver a can of paint to one of his fellow-workers. He loses his balance momentarily, glances down to feel what the narrator earlier had termed the "proximity of annihilation," "the thrill of imminent nothing," and clings desperately to the pipe, willing or able neither to "let go nor drag toward the painter" (166). As Beckman clutches the pipe, his life only as secure as his grip, Michaels evokes through imagery ("sweat," "spit," "steel") and analogy not only Beck-man hanging on for his life in the factory, but his earlier descriptions of Beckman driving, living, and finally under attack in his cab:

> Against his mouth he smelled, then tasted, steel as it turned rancid with sweat and spit. He felt water pour slowly, beyond his will, into his pants as it had when they hit him and hit him for no reason and he twisted and shrieked on the floor of his cab. He felt the impulse to move and did not want to look around into the vacuous air, nor to imagine the beating or the possibility that the tremor in his chin and lips would become a long, fine scream spinning out the thread of his life as he dropped toward the machines and the concrete floor. He felt the impulse to move and he could remember how motion felt gathering, droning in the motor of his cab, to move him through the dark avenues of the city. (165–66)

This portrait of Beckman grasping the pipe, squeezing "life against his chest," while the other painters shout, "Don't let go, Beckman," closes the last story of Michaels' first collection: "He did not let go. The tremor passed into muscle as rigid as the steel it squeezed" (166).

"Going Places," then, traces Beckman's movement from aimless drifting to near death to self-awareness to a new sense of life's possibilities and leaves him struggling for his life in the final "place" to which he goes, hanging high above a factory's concrete floor. Catastrophes survived (and even learned from) provide no certainty for the future. Michaels develops this theme throughout his work but its clearest expression occurs in "The Subject at the Vanishing Point," a vignette in *I Would Have Saved Them If I Could*. The narrator's grandfather is prepared to leave Poland but is prevented from going when a pogrom begins. He is in danger outside his neighborhood but is saved because "Suddenly—for good or ill isn't known— somebody flung him into a cellar" (115–16). He returns home; everyone celebrates his survival, "But it was too late to get a visa," and he is forced to stay in Poland. Then, Michaels writes, "The Nazis came with the meaning of history—what flings you into a cellar saves you for bullets." For the person caught up in the circumstances of history as well as for isolated individuals like Beckman, the imminence of one's death is all that can provide either historical or personal meaning to one's life. In a world "incessantly created of incessant death," the process of self-creation is linked to the "proximity of darkness," "the proximity of annihilation." If one can be saved only "for bullets," what modes of action are available in the modern world? Like Beckman, we can embrace life—cold, unyielding, and dangerous as it is—and "not let go." In the midst of our energetic but ultimate impotence, we can be compassionate: "I would have saved them if I could" (127).

Michaels derived the title for his second collection of stories from a remark in a letter by Lord Byron describing the guillotining in Rome of three criminals. A portion of the letter, "Lord Byron's Letter," is presented as a vignette. Despite its author and date, the letter stands as a central document about the modern perception of and response to horror. In Michaels' excerpt, Byron's remarks begin as casual, observant, and informative:

> The day before I left Rome I saw three robbers guillotined. The ceremony—including the *masqued* priests; the half-naked executioners; the bandaged criminals; the black Christ and his banner; the scaffold; the soldiery; the slow procession, and the quick rattle and heavy fall of the axe; the splash of blood, and the ghastliness of the exposed heads—is altogether more impressive than the vulgar and ungentlemanly "new drop" and dog-like agony of infliction upon the sufferers of the English sentence. (125–26)

Byron goes on the compare the various responses of the three men to their imminent beheading and speculates further about the relative merits of guillotining in contrast with other means of execution: "It is better than the oriental way, and (I should think) than the axe of our ancestors. The pain seems little, and yet the effect to the spectator, and the preparation to the criminal, is very striking and chilling."

Byron's rendering of his own reactions to the criminals'

deaths thrusts home the full implications of his epistolary narrative, and Michaels' appropriation of it, for the reader of contemporary fiction or, indeed, for anyone who lives in the contemporary world. Commenting on the effects of the executions on himself, Byron states:

> The first turned me quite hot and thirsty, and made me shake so that I could hardly hold the opera-glass (I was close, but was determined to see, as one should see every thing, once, with attention); the second and third (which shows how dreadfully soon things grow indifferent), I am ashamed to say, had no effect on me as a horror, though I would have saved them if I could. (126–27)

In much contemporary fiction, characters participate in the emotions Lord Byron describes. They, too, are connoisseurs of the grotesque; they hunger for experience, to see and do it all and intensely, but are finally left jaded and unsatisfied; they are initially appalled by their violent, horrific world, but ultimately confused about how to come to terms with it. Does the notion of shock lose its currency when one is shocked at every moment and when shock is compromised by fascination? Indifference seems at times to be the necessary strategy of a survivor in an environment in which brutality is the stuff of everyday, but the lingering sense of guilt and shame it entails intimates that such indifference may be morally indistinguishable from cowardice. Finally, the combination of positive intentions and powerlessness is deadly, because the real presence of either raises suspicions about the authenticity of the other. The ungenuine life beckons like a desert mirage when reality is emotionally and morally undifferentiated. Leonard Michaels' stories effectively dramatize the ennobling power of resistance to that false appeal.

Notes

1. Leonard Michaels, in an unpublished interview.
2. Leonard Michaels, *Going Places* (1969; rpt. New York: Plume/New American Library, 1969), p. 83. Subsequent references are to this edition, cited when necessary as G.
3. Leonard Michaels, *I Would Have Saved Them If I Could* (1975); rpt. New York: Bantam Books, 1977), p. 51. Subsequent references are to this edition, cited when necessary as S.

JOSEPHINE MILES

1911–

Josephine Miles was born in Chicago, Illinois, on June 11, 1911. She received her Ph.D. from the University of California in 1938, and taught there from 1940 until 1979, when she retired as a University Professor. Her prolific and successful career as both poet and literary critic is even more remarkable in light of the fact that she has suffered from crippling arthritis since early childhood.

Miles has published seven volumes of criticism (including *Eras and Modes in English Poetry*, 1957, 2nd ed. 1964; *Style and Proportion*, 1967; and *Poetry and Change*, 1974) and several textbooks. From early on her criticism has been based upon a careful, scientific tabulation of American and British writers' use of different word types. The astute application of these findings have won her such prestigious awards for scholarship as the American Association of University Women fellowship (1939), Guggenheim fellowship (1948), and American Council of Learned Societies fellowship (1965).

Miles's first book of poetry, *Lines at Intersection*, came out in 1939, and her *Collected Poems* appeared in 1983. In the years in between she published twelve volumes of verse: *Poems on Several*

Thomas Merton

James Merrill

Edna St. Vincent Millay

ARTHUR MILLER

JOAQUIN MILLER

HENRY MILLER

Occasions, 1941; *Local Measures*, 1946; *After This Sea*, 1947; *Prefabrications*, 1955; *Poems, 1930–60*, 1960; *Civil Poems*, 1966; *Kinds of Affection*, 1967; *Fields of Learning*, 1968; *Saving the Bay*, 1969; *American Poems*, 1970; *To All Appearances*, 1974; and *Coming to Terms*, 1979. Her well-crafted poetry has been praised for its intelligence and humor; it is characterized by its use of the vernacular and its attention to the details of American life. In recognition of her poetry she has received, among others, the Shelley Award (1935), a National Endowment for the Arts grant (1967), the James Russell Lowell Prize (1975) and the Lenore Marshall Prize (1984). In 1978 she became the thirty-seventh poet to be awarded the fellowship of the Academy of American Poets.

Works

Some poets sing, others talk, but a good poet of either kind develops a recognizable, individual voice. Josephine Miles is a talking poet, and one who employs a variety of idioms: she can talk like a Professor of English, which she is, or like a small-town neighbor, which she also is, or like a taxi-driver or a real-estate salesman or a radio announcer—all of whom she most emphatically is not. Yet the sensitive reader will come to perceive behind all the different syntaxes and vocabularies, the tones of the same authentic voice.

Perhaps it is rather the viewpoint that we recognize: that of someone who looks at the world directly, always wondering, sometimes troubled, never afraid. Even in Miss Miles' satirical poems we are never allowed to forget human decency:

> But we didn't know what to give Oedipus; he had
> everything.
> Even in his loss, he had more than average.
> So we gave him a traveling case, fitted, which we
> personally
> Should have liked to receive.

The gesture was inadequate but well-meant, like most of our responses to life.

Sometimes Miss Miles can make very moving poetry out of inadequacy, as in "Height":

> Shoulder to head is the height of my life to me.
> My level eye
> Looks to his rib as his long and level eye
> Looks to the sky.

Or again in the second of "Four Songs":

> Unreasonable happiness troubles me.
> I look at my round face
> And I see, unreasonable happiness
> Is my disgrace.

"Unreasonable Happiness" might serve as an alternative title for the whole volume, which takes such keen pleasure in the human condition while remaining conscious of all its shortcomings.

And then again, Miss Miles often shows us that our responses are not quite so inadequate as we may think; she finds in everyday phrases a poetry that we had overlooked. The newsboy crying "*Herald*, sir?" is himself a herald announcing the new day and perhaps even some new light. A piece of market jargon, "cotton gray goods quiet and firmer," is seen as a line of poetry, charged with metaphor. There is poetry even in the misleading claims of advertisers, and pathos in their injunction by the Federal Trade Commission:

> They say La Jac Brite Pink Skin Bleach avails not,
> They say its Orange Beauty Glow does not glow,
> Nor the face grow five shades lighter nor the heart
> Five shades lighter. They say no.

Though all things human leave Miss Miles a shade disappointed, the American landscape never lets her down, whether it be her own California in "After This, Sea" or the exotic remainder of the country in "Brooklyn, Iowa and West."

Even a motel or a trailer court can fashion security for her once she is on the road:

> It was the tent and citadel of the many stars
> It was the rampart of the loud highway
> And we slept there, waking
> Into the thunder and silence of the unfolding
> Durable journey.

This is Walt Whitman's America, but the people who inhabit it do not always reassure her as they did Whitman. They do not always compare well with the men Michelangelo painted or carved; too often they have

> Smooth faces, smooth smooth faces
> Good mood good personality faces
>
> . . .
>
> Round bland planned personality faces.

But if Miss Miles is critical, she is also compassionate, toward Americans and toward all men. As her sedate voice talks on, in deceptively simple words, we see the world as it is, in all its beauty and irony, taking shape before our eyes.

> Men have their alien sons and love them,
> The dear fist clenched in theirs,
> The foreign taste fed at their table
>
> . . .
>
> But they hate the foreign, though an open
> Five-fingered hand like theirs,
> The gall taste deep as another nation,
> The ugly accent in an alien name.
> Hate all but him, dear father, and dear son.

—Vivian Mercier, "A Talking Poet," *Com*, Feb. 10, 1961, p. 511

Josephine Miles's new and selected poems show a quirky commenting mind still finding things of interest in the American scene, reliving in verse the Berkeley riots:

> Gassed going between classes
> Students said little,
> Huddled their books and ran.
> As helicopter crews waved down low at them
> They were silent
> Yelled and were silent.
> Now the trees speak, not running or reading
> But with cast leaves tallying
> The cost of a gas deterrent.
> My throat alive still cries
> But how to tell without dying
> Is not told by the dying trees.

There is a need for more poems of this sort, poems, so to speak, of the day's news, now largely a preserve of interested propagandists. But Miles can also be metaphysical, as in her fine poem on teaching, "Paths," about "going out into the fields of learning":

> Ant labors, hopper leaps away; too early for the bee,
> The spider's silk hypotheses unfold
> Tenacious, tenable.

"The spider's silk hypotheses" is worthy of Emily Dickinson, whose voice, in its dryer tone, has entered Miles's voice as well;

but Miles is more humane than Dickinson in her parables, of which my favorite is about the drowning man (in a poem called "Family") who hollers "help," caught in the undertow, while his unconscious family reply blandly:

> Hello, they will say,
> Come back here for some potato salad.
> It is then that a seventeen year old cub
> Cruising in a helicopter from Antigua
> A jackstraw expert speaking only Swedish
> And remote from this area as a camel, says
> Look down there, there is somebody drowning.
> And it is you. You say, yes, yes.
> And he throws you a line.
> This is what is called the brotherhood of man.

For all its comedy and factuality (two qualities present in all Miles's verse) the poem has the ring of moral truth, told by the survivor. Abstract help, when family is of no use at all, has rescued most of us at some time or other: in its stern impersonality, that help seems more sacred than any sponsored by blood ties. Miles has strict expectations of the world, a comic sense of her own unrealistic hopes, a stern judgment of her own failings, and an observant birdlike interest in classes of people unlike herself. She lacks the sweeter side of verse (or when it comes, it has an uncertainty about it) but her enterprise and sense of art are sure. Her early poem about poetry shares the satisfaction of the reader in the well-made thing, but ends in the uncertainty of the author as he looks for that satisfying shape:

> Familiar to our readers
> In all its special vein
> Is the form of the tale in the author's careful
>   form . . .
> The palpitant unfoldment
> And dear and sudden end,
> The shape of the tale in the author's burning hope
> Familiar to our readers,
> But not the blind
> Looking around of the mind for the shape.

Not enough of that "blind looking around" survives in Miles's poems, I think: they are almost too well-wrought, without yet having the inevitability of the best-wrought, but they never lack intelligence or feeling.—HELEN VENDLER, "A Quarter of Poetry," *NYTBR*, April 6, 1975, pp. 32–33

⟨. . .⟩ a poet who has changed very little in the years between her first book, *Lines at Intersection* (1939), and *To All Appearances: Poems New and Selected* (1974) is Josephine Miles. Like the friend of a friend she describes in her poem, "Friend," her work is "A singular complex of idiosyncratic qualities." Her outward consistencies are stanzaic, rhyming, and tonal; her usual poem is in quatrains, her diction colloquial, her attitude to life unsentimental yet perceptive and tender. The wit in her poems is not mere wordplay but the inevitable outcome of a view of life that juxtaposes contraries in recognition of their contradictory resemblances. She can be wryly metaphysical, as in "Monkeys"; comment on cultural disparities ("Savages"); make pleasurable lyrics from the contemplation of life in its daily purposelessness ("Belief," "Ride") or as seen under the sign of an ancient determinism ("Oedipus"):

> The gang wanted to give Oedipus Rex a going away
>   present.
> He had been a good hard-working father and king.
> And besides it is the custom in this country
> To give gifts on departure.

> But we didn't know what to give Oedipus; he had
>   everything.
> Even in his loss, he had more than average.
> So we gave him a travelling case, fitted, which we
>   personally
> Should have liked to receive.

Miles, who has published several distinguished studies of the language of poetry, is a celebrant of the quotidian. Her idiosyncracies seem an unexpected blend of the wit, moral steadfastness, and verbal inventiveness of Emily Dickinson and the contemporary British poet Stevie Smith; but nobody before her or since has made a style quite like hers, which can with such insouciance celebrate the most commonplace event, as she does in "Sale":

> Went into a shoestore to buy a pair of shoes,
> There was a shoe salesman humming the blues
> Under his breath . . .

who, on hearing her say "please I need a triple-A," immediately "plucked from the mezzanine the very shoe."

> Skill of the blessed, that at their command
> Blue and breathless comes to hand
> To send, from whatever preoccupation, feet
> Implacably shod into the perfect street.

The poems of Josephine Miles often seem similarly plucked by an unfailing skill from the mezzanine of alternative choices.—DANIEL HOFFMAN, "Poetry: Dissidents from Schools," *Harvard Guide to Contemporary Writing*, ed. Daniel Hoffman, 1979, pp. 593–94

Josephine Miles's *Collected Poems, 1930–83* draws on the author's eleven published volumes and adds to them old and new poems that were previously uncollected.

Some 250 pages of poetry, this selection from five decades of productivity is unusually meritorious—"one of the finest and solidest bodies of poetry to be found in this country," A. R. Ammons has commented. He joins a long and distinguished line of Miles's appreciators. In a review of her *Local Measures* for *The Nation* in 1946, Dudley Fitts spoke of this poet's remarkable virtuosity: "The arrangement of rhyme and assonance, the answering of stanza to stanza—everything is elaborately and even intensely worked out." You see what Fitts meant in a poem such as "So Graven," a bravura metrical performance in only six lines. An example: the "simplicity" of line one is, simply, two iambs; but in the last line of the poem, its position and the addition of "has" make it scan as an iamb plus an anapest. The agent of metamorphosis seems to be the "particular jig" of line four, whose bouncing scansion the later phrase duplicates, all in order to have "simplicity" reflect "unresolved event [that] moves in the mind."

Finally it is those unresolved events of the mind, the enigma of right thought and action, that most engage Miles; and her ideal mountain is less Parnassus than Sinai, which gave us the "great tablets [that] shatter down in deed." A concern for the unresolved also struck Randall Jarrell, another commentator on Miles's work. In *Poetry and the Age* he describes her techniques as "relishingly idiosyncratic," "just a little off" and "carefully awkward." Accurate assessment; and an important step for anyone learning to read this poet is to acquire a taste for her imbalances and "off" constructions— that is, to know them well enough to distinguish between the effective askew and the *in*effective. Sometimes, on purpose, it doesn't "work"; and then sometimes *still* doesn't. I can speak, though, as a reader to whom this poetry was almost entirely unknown before this year: it rewards rereading and study. Miles's American dialect is recognizable as a variant of daily speech, but it's not Williams's nor Frost's nor Bishop's. Less difficult than, say, conversational Portuguese, still you don't grasp it at first try. Then, like all acquired tastes, it takes on special flavor.

A certain self-effacement was the keynote of her early work; few autobiographical inferences can be drawn from it. Beginning in the 1960s, though, readers were allowed to see Josephine Miles in her role as a teacher and scholar of literature. (She has taught at the University of California at Berkeley since the 1940s and has published many studies of poetry, in particular, of poetic diction.) It also became apparent that she suffered from a lifelong physical handicap which severely limited her mobility. Knowing that helps us understand the importance for her of two ethical stances, pride and reason, which have been scanted in modern poetry. Without them, we can suppose, she wouldn't have accomplished what she has. She also expects to find pride and reason in those around her. She has an acute sense of how those qualities help constitute the social fabric on which we all depend, though we may be less conscious of it than she. Hence, one volume called *Civil Poems* (from which "Civilian" is taken). Violence and violent unreason she shows as failures in the social contract, occasions for shame. But she is not unaware of the coercive aspect of a poetry that chastises. Can one persuade without using a whip?

Those concerns stand silently behind the poems that deal with Berkeley activism during the Vietnam era and contribute to the moral anguish in them. Imperceptive observers of those times saw no middle term between, say, drug-addicted radicals and storm troopers in sworn fealty to S. I. Hayakawa. But there was a moderate, nonviolent current of opinion opposed to the war in Southeast Asia; Miles belonged to it. She saw the immorality of that way, but she also saw the consequences of losing a reasonable dialogue between opposing camps, the cost of suspending regular pedagogic relationship and the perils of violence on both sides. Some of the tears in Miles's poems of the 1960s are the tears of tragedy and others are the result of generous sprayings of Mace. The poems that she composed out of a divided sense of right are among her most disturbing, powered by the fuel of disappointment and anger.

Her most recent poems show her still searching, still breaking ground. *Coming to Terms* (1979) is remarkable for the directness of its autobiographical particularity. "Doll," an achingly literal account of the onset of her illness, shows Miles at her narrative best; the forty-two lines of the poem contain in germ the matter for a novella. The shorter poems on the same subject—"Parent," "Album" and "Mark"—are equally telling. And when the poet, in "Mark," can invoke "blessed necessity," I think we must pay more heed to the phrase than we usually do when it is proposed by more advantaged speakers. The poem's concluding two lines are an extra stroke of wise genius, bringing us back to our own helplessness before others' misfortunes and our almost comic efforts to help them bear it, to be Job's comforters.

I can concur with Helen Vendler in finding the "ring of moral truth" in Miles's poetry, a poetry based on "strict expectations of the world" and "a stern judgment of her own failings." Also, with Denis Donoghue when he says: "The poems of Josephine Miles offer evidence that contemporary poetry houses intelligence, magnanimity, humor and excursive power." Hers is a diverse achievement, original and singular.
—ALFRED CORN, "The Lenore Marshall Prize," *Nation*, Oct. 20, 1984, pp. 388–89

DENIS DONOGHUE
"The Habits of the Poet"

Times Literary Supplement, April 25, 1975, pp. 442–43

Josephine Miles's first book of poems, *Lines at Intersection*, was published in 1939, her first critical study, *Wordsworth and the Vocabulary of Emotion*, in 1942. It has been her enterprise since that time to study the vocabulary of English and American poetry in the conviction that "a history of values resides in the history of poetic recurrences and repetitions". Her terms of scholarly reference are continuity, change, proportion, recurrence, order, context, and pattern. She thinks of style as "a persisting complex of interrelated habits founded on values", and of mode as a part of style, "a complex of habits specifically in the use of language". These terms are most formidably deployed in her *Eras and Modes in English Poetry* (1957). In the meantime Miss Miles has been extending her survey to include English and American prose. She has been reading the poets again, sometimes with a concordance at hand, and noting not only the proportion of verbs, nouns, and adjectives, but the action of connectives in particular and syntax in general. *Poetry and Change* is a progress report on these matters, and *To All Appearances* a selection of her own work in poetry.

Miss Miles's study of vocabulary is based upon a distinction between three types of sentence structure: clausal, phrasal, and balanced. The clausal type is discursive: it emphasizes compound or serial predicates, subordinate verbs in relative and adverbial clauses, it concentrates upon the materials of controlled process in thought and speech as distinguished from the data of sense and status. This mode charts the movement of a mind thinking, and it uses therefore more verbs than adjectives, a vocabulary more conceptual than sensory, and in verse a stanzaic structure rather than an internal organization of sound. The phrasal type is a cumulative way of speaking: it features action suspended in a frame of description, its terms are sensuous and spiritual, it uses many adjectives and nouns, and often turns verbs into participles. Motion is observed in process and seen as qualitative rather than as active. In verse this type favours inner consonance rather than rhyme. The balanced type seeks a judicious correlation of clausal and phrasal elements. Miss Miles sometimes refers to the three modes as predicative, adjectival, and classical.

The main tradition of English poetry, according to these terms, is based upon the clausal mode which Miss Miles finds at work in Chaucer, Wyatt, Donne, Jonson, Herbert, in its early phase, and later in Coleridge, Byron, Landor, Browning, Hardy, Frost, and Auden. This tradition uses substantives (nouns and adjectives) in proportion to predicates (verbs) in a ratio of two to one. In the phrasal mode, the poets beginning with Spenser, Quarles, Crashaw, and Milton use rather a ratio of three to one, and even, for Thomson, Akenside, the Wartons, an extreme of four to one. The phrasal tradition is maintained by Blake, Keats, Tennyson, Whitman, and many American poets including Hart Crane. This mode accommodates much of the feeling which we describe as Whig, Protestant, enthusiastic, or sublime. Miss Miles finds the balanced mode in Dryden, Marvell, Goldsmith, Crabbe, Wordsworth, Hopkins, Stevens, Eliot, and Yeats: its great master is Wordsworth, whose special concern is with "the process of the reception and interpretation of sensation by feeling, in verbs of perception, in adjectives of size, scope, age, and affection, and in nouns of bodily and emotional sense half combined with concept and atmosphere."

The evidence for this version of English and American

poetic history is a series of word counts and factor analyses given and elucidated in several of Miss Miles's books; notably *The Continuity of Poetic Language* (1951), *Eras and Modes* (1957), *Renaissance, Eighteenth Century and Modern Language in English Poetry* (1960). So far as vocabulary and diction are in question, the evidence seems entirely convincing: it is hardly decent to comment on the evidence at all, of course, since it could only be refuted by someone who has done the same statistical analyses and reached different conclusions. In certain cases the evidence has to be modified. Miss Miles's own revision of her chapter on Blake, for instance, has had the benefit of the *Concordance*, and the result in *Poetry and Change* is a poetic situation slightly different in focus from the version in *Eras and Modes*. The difference does not undermine the earlier version, in fact it confirms the general conclusions which Miss Miles derived from a smaller sample of Blake's vocabulary.

In some cases Miss Miles's conclusions seem rudimentary when a full account of the matter is available. Her survey of Thomson's major vocabulary is helpful as far as it goes, but that is not very far by comparison with the detailed analysis offered in Ralph Cohen's *The Unfolding of "The Seasons"* (1970). Professor Cohen shows that Thomson's cardinal words are deployed in cadences and rhythms which transform them: a study of the individual words is misleading if it does not register the forces which render their meanings suggestible rather than rigid, in keeping with the movement of the seasons themselves. The poem deals with its vocabulary by involving, compromising, and incriminating its major terms in ways which a factor analysis cannot hope to describe. This makes a problem for Miss Miles's techniques. She can only deal with words on the understanding that they are simple and singleminded rather than complex, in the sense of William Empson's *The Structure of Complex Words*. Words like "wit", "sense", "fool" and so forth must be content with the same consideration which Miss Miles gives to "air", "cloud", "day", and "flood". Her work is a relief map of an enormous area in the poetry of Britain and America, with occasional investigations of the terrain in detail. As a critic, she loves to do close work upon texts that interest her, especially upon representative bodies of poetry from Donne to A. R. Ammons. But she is a maker of maps, too, and must keep her promises to that enterprise. It is more important to her work that it be reliable in general than impeccable in every detail.

If Miss Miles's maps are reliable, they offer a formidable challenge to our general understanding of literary history. Her study of poetic vocabulary tells us that we have exaggerated the differences between one poet and another in this respect. Blake is brought much closer to Thomson, Akenside, Collins, Young, and Gray than our standard sense of his work allows. Hopkins and Swinburne are nearer kin than we have supposed. We have made too much of the influence of genre, if Miss Miles is right in her conclusion that vocabulary is not radically affected by this consideration. We have been excessively intimidated by revolutions in poetry: revolutions appear much less dramatic when they are understood not as eruptions of violence but as points in a curve of feeling. If we take a long view of poetry from Chaucer to Ammons we see that there is a natural law sustaining common usage and the common stock of words. "The chief vocabulary of English poetry at any one time", Miss Miles argues, "reveals persistent strands, recent losses, incipient gains". A study of continuity and change in vocabulary points to "the cultural and professional determinations within which individual poets freely work". When change comes, it rarely comes from the major poets:

Usually the innovators, those who first emphasize terms which later are emphasized by many more, are what we think of as minor poets. They have some axe to grind, and they are better at the grinding than at the poetry as a whole. So-called major poets, on the other hand, tend to use most fully the emphases already accepted and available to them in the poetry of their time.

These conclusions, documented mainly in *Eras and Modes* and *Poetry and Change*, endorse Eliot's sense of the relation between tradition and the individual talent, and more particularly the rebuke Eliot administered to those readers who dwell with satisfaction upon the poet's difference from his immediate predecessors. "Whereas if we approach a poet without this prejudice", Eliot argued, "we shall often find that not only the best, but the most individual parts of his work may be those in which the dead poets, his ancestors, assert their immortality most vigorously". Or, in Miss Miles's version, "those most concious of moving ahead are most deeply involved in the past". It is unnecessary to remark that neither Eliot nor Miss Miles proposes merely to follow an antique drum.

The conclusions reached in *Poetry and Change* and, I think, in Eliot's "Tradition and the Individual Talent" are based upon an understanding of poetry primarily in terms of vocabulary and diction. On this showing, there is far more continuity than change. But I wonder what conclusions would offer themselves if the understanding of poetry were to proceed upon a different basis. The following proposition may be considered: that poets differ least in their vocabulary, most in their syntax. I accept Miss Miles's evidence that Hopkins and Swinburne are kin in vocabulary, but I maintain that syntax divides them again. Blake may receive his major words from Spenser, Sylvester, Crashaw, Milton, Vaughan, Thomson, and Gray, but he does not sound like any of these, his syntax makes him different. Miss Miles's three modes are three different structures of syntax, but she has studied the verbs, nouns, and adjectives as constituents of diction rather than as vectors of syntax. Her dominant concern is with the family likeness between one word and another, within the broad categories of subject and predicate.

In *Style and Proportion* (1967) she turned her attention to connectives, and this direction has resulted in new perceptions, especially in the chapter on Blake where his connectives are shown as certifying a Bacherlardian poetry of space rather than of time. But I think Miss Miles would agree that her study of poetic syntax has not yet gone as far as her account of poetic diction, and that her main interest until recently has been in the frequencies of reference and recurrence displayed by a poet's vocabulary, his congenial repertoire. It is useful to know from *Eras and Modes* that "sweet" is a major adjective common to Hopkins and Swinburne, but there is more to be done before we can distinguish in any productive way between Swinburne's

Laurel is green for a season, and love is sweet for a day;
But love grows bitter with treason, and laurel outlives not May.

and Hopkins's

Let me though see no more of him, and not disappointment
Those sweet hopes quell whose least me quickening lift.

Pope and Thomson often use the imperative "see", but the results are significantly different: a full description would concern itself with syntax, metre, and tone as well as diction. Meanwhile, we have in *Poetry and Change* Miss Miles's recent essays in the cartography of English and American literature, with close work attending upon Donne, Milton, Blake, eighteenth-century prose, Victorian prose (Darwin, mostly), E. A. Robinson and the contemporary poetic scene.

Miss Miles writes of these matters with impeccable grace. If she has an axe to grind, I cannot hear the noise. She attends upon her three modes with such generosity in each case that I have to invoke her own poems as evidence that she favours the clausal or predicative mode when it comes to a choice between her first two, and would favour the balanced mode if she could have one of the three for the asking. I infer that if she could have her wish as a poet she would begin like Donne with the poetry of a thinking process and achieve at length the structures of deliberation which she admires in Wordsworth. She admires "simple pattern" in preference to "prying arabesques", and aspires to "the strong predication of human standards and relationships in colloquial verse". In *Eras and Modes* she quotes from Wordsworth's "Essay on Epitaphs" a passage which seems to attend upon her own poems:

> Language, if it does not uphold, and feed, and leave
> in quiet, like the power of gravitation or the air we
> breathe, is a counter-spirit, unremittingly and noise-
> lessly at work, to subvert, to lay waste, to vitiate, and
> to dissolve.

Speaking of the contemporary situation in poetry, she says that "we are turning away from comparison and contrast on qualitative bases toward the synapses of juxtaposition, Charles Olson's sparks of energy jumping across chasms of disrelation", but I do not think she is content with that programme. If poetry is moving away from "values of immediacy and impact", there is evidence that she would urge a further move into "human validation". She wonders "how our system's civilization will make its way into value; how laws, plans, committees, bureaucracies, machines, will find some human validation". The wonder is Wordsworthian, too, and Miss Miles might have quoted that passage in which Wordsworth promises that, when science is ready to put on a form of flesh and blood, the poem "will lend his divine spirit to aid the transfiguration". Miss Miles's poems are keen to take part in any action which will help to transform systems into values. I assume that this is what she means when she describes "a language for thought to come to life in".

Many of her themes are domestic properties, for if thought is to come alive it ought to come on ordinary days, not just on exceptional occasions. Miss Miles has a famous poem on the assassination of President Kennedy, and a poem just as fine on the Berkeley student revolt, but normally she writes of summer, domesticity, death, love, community, becoming, friendship, change, "the beatitude of place", light, and the moon. There are also poems about smog, polo, sombreros, private property, fortune, ideas, distance, number, and the universal sources of doubt and amazement. She loves to find "inevitability sprung from the improbable" and "volition moving in the paths of chance". Just as she is concerned with the ways in which vocabularies come and go, she is devoted to the human situation in which "gardens of time happen, come into bloom, fade, happen again". Born in Chicago, she went west as a young girl and stayed there, but I cannot find a Californian element in her sensibility or anything in her language which would make her kin to the most celebrated Bay or Beat poets. Her poetry is American in its circumstance, but English and strongly predicative in its means. The tradition of the sublime which she has named as the dominant mode in American poetry I cannot hear in her poetry at all; she favours stanzaic forms, conceptual terms, rational limits, and does most of her work with verbs. In "Purchase of a Blue, Green, or Orange Ode" she teases the sublimists who live over the Pindaric mountain, a nice place to visit but you wouldn't want to stay there. She would prefer to live at sea-level and spend quiet time thinking of Sisyphus, giving him his measure of sympathy and then sparing a thought for the stone.

To All Appearances is a good place to start for one who has not read Miss Miles's poems, because it includes her selections from *Lines at Intersection* (1939), *Poems on Several Occasions* (1941), *Local Measures* (1946), *Prefabrications* (1957), *Poems 1930–1960* (1960), *Kinds of Affection* (1967), and thirty new poems which are some of her best. In *Eras and Modes* she chooses Wordsworth to illustrate the mind's excursive power, and speaks of his "encouragement of the tendency of perceptions to generalize themselves". I would place beside that praise Johnson's reference, in his *Life of Pope*, to "an intelligence perpetually on the wing, excursive, vigorous, and diligent". This is the way Miss Miles's mind moves, and therefore the way her poems move us. You will enjoy the poem "If You Will" if you like to see and hear what can be done by setting two people talking. Two poems, "Witness" and "Dolor", show what happens when a predicatively inclined mind goes on the wing between "tell" and "tally". "Players" plays a witty game of love, and "Toward I" picks up the pieces when the kissing has to stop. I assume that "Enlightenment" is an attempt to turn systems into values, since the excursion of mind is propelled by the incursion of statistical data, and there is much commuting between the illumination of candles. Some of Miss Miles's poems are so patient and selfless in their manner that the reader can easily miss their power and find himself on the next page before they have made their mark, as I missed a beautiful poem, "For Futures", until something later in the book reminded me of it and I went back:

> When the lights come on at five o'clock on street
> corners
> That is Evolution by the bureau of power,
> That is a fine mechanic dealing in futures:
> For the sky is wide and warm upon that hour,
> But like the eyes that burned once at sea bottom,
> Widening in the gloom, prepared for light,
> The ornamental standards, the glazed globes softly
> Perceive far off how probable is night.

There are twenty poems in *To All Appearances* which I would choose as evidence if challenged to show that contemporary poetry houses intelligence, magnanimity, humour, and excursive power. And, of these twenty, at least six go straight into my ideal anthology. The six are "If You Will", "Toward I", "For Futures", "Midweek", "Belief", and "Reason", the last a very funny poem ending "*Reason, Reason, is my middle name*".

EDNA ST. VINCENT MILLAY

1892–1950

Edna St. Vincent Millay was born in Rockland, Maine, on February 22, 1892. The appearance of her poem "Renascence" in a literary anthology in 1912 attracted considerable critical acclaim and paved the way to a scholarship at Vassar College which she entered in 1913. While in college she continued to write and publish poetry and also wrote and acted in plays. Her first book, *Renascence and Other Poems*, was published in 1917. After graduation Millay moved with her sister to Greenwich Village to work as an actress. She quickly became a celebrity among Village bohemian society. A *Few Figs from Thistles* and *Aria de Capo* were published in 1920, after which she traveled in Europe for two years. She received the Pulitzer Prize for poetry in 1923 upon her return to the United States, and married Eugen Jan Boissevain. Soon after they bought a house in upstate New York, Steepletop, which was to be their home for the rest of their lives. Miss Millay's work received many awards, honors, and high popular regard in the next ten years. She was considered a leading American lyrical poet. *The Harp-Weaver and Other Poems* (1923) and *The Buck in the Snow* (1928) were published at this time. The thirties brought critical reappraisal for Millay—some wondered at her continuing preference for traditional forms and subject matter. *Conversation at Midnight* (1936) was a departure from her previous work and was widely regarded as a mistake, while *Wine from These Grapes* (1934) received some praise.

America's entry into World War II moved Millay to write propaganda poetry, much of which was published in *Make Bright the Arrows*. The critics honored her sincerity of interest but could not quite forgive the bad verse. After the publication of *Collected Sonnets* (1941) and *Collected Lyrics* (1943) the critics began to lose interest in Millay.

A nervous breakdown in 1944 rendered Millay unable to write for two years. Her husband died in 1949 and Millay followed soon after in 1950. The poetry she wrote in the last four years of her life was published posthumously in *Mine the Harvest* (1954) and *Collected Poems* (1956).

Edna Millay's new book, *Huntsman, What Quarry?*, is "the first book since the publication of *The Buck in the Snow*," her publishers say, "in which [she] has brought together a new group of her lyrical poems." This statement seems to pass over the appearance, in 1934, of *Wine from These Grapes*, a collection of lyrics and sonnets which showed signs of Miss Millay's successful passage from the emotions and point of view of a rebellious girl to those of a maturely contemplative woman. The present book, although it bears marks of the poet's magnanimity of nature and her basic poetic gifts, is a strange mixture of maturity and unresolved youth. What further complicates its expression is the influence of the hampering and sometimes destructive role of the unofficial feminine laureate which Miss Millay has had to play for so long to her American public.

It is a dangerous lot, that of the charming, romantic public poet, especially if it falls to a woman. The temptation to repeat effects continually reappears; there are "occasional poems," which it seems necessary to write; and it is almost impossible for the poetess, once laurelled, to take off the crown for good or to reject the values and taste of those who tender it. Certainly Miss Millay has never completely granted the demands of groups whose favorite she has remained for so long. But it is difficult to see why she still writes certain kinds of poems. The delightful ballad, peppered with colorful place names; the poems built on picturesque and faintly feudal situations (the hunter and the acorn-gathering girl; the princess and the handsome groom); and the numerous poems which describe pride trampled, though never actually defeated, by an unworthy object of affection—a time and place exist for these, but it is not in the middle of a career. It is difficult to say what a woman poet should concern herself with as she grows older, because woman poets who have produced an impressively bulky body of work are few. But is there any reason to believe that a woman's spiritual fibre is less sturdy than a man's? Is it not possible for a woman to come to terms with herself, if not with the world; to withdraw more and more, as time goes on, her own personality from her productions; to stop childish fears of death and eschew charming rebellions against facts? Certainly some fragments of Sappho are more "mature" than others. And Christina Rossetti, who lived an anonymous life and somewhat resembled, according to the cruel wit of Max Beerbohm, "a pew-opener," explored regions which Miss Millay has not yet entered. And there is the case of Emily Dickinson.

Miss Millay has always fought, and is still fighting, injustice. She is still subject to moods of self-disgust as well as to moods of mutiny against mankind's infringements on its own human decency. Once or twice she contemplates a truce which "slackens the mind's allegiance to despair." And twice—in the poem just quoted and in the recessively titled "The Princess Recalls Her One Adventure"—she writes as beautiful lyrics as she has ever written. But what has happened to the kind of development announced in *Wine from These Grapes*, the most kindly disposed reader cannot say. If Miss Millay should give up for good the idea that "wisdom" and "peace" are stuffy concepts, perhaps that development might be renewed.
—LOUISE BOGAN, "Unofficial Feminine Laureate" (1939), *Selected Criticism*, 1955, pp. 154–56

One cannot really write about Edna Millay without bringing into the foreground of the picture her intoxicating effect on people, because this so much created the atmosphere in which she lived and composed. The spell that she exercised on many, of the most various professions and temperaments, of all ages and both sexes, was at that time exactly that which Vincent Sheean imagines she cast on the birds. I should say here that I do not believe that my estimate of Edna Millay's work has ever been much affected by my personal emotions about her. I admired her poetry before I knew her, and my most exalted feeling for her did not, I think, ever prevent me from recognizing or criticizing what was weak or second-rate in her work. Today, thirty years later, though I see her in a different "context," my opinion has hardly changed. Let me register this unfashionable opinion here, and explain that Edna Millay seems to me one of the only poets writing in English in our time who have attained to anything like the stature of great literary figures in an age in which prose has predominated. It is hard to know how to compare her to Eliot or Auden or Yeats—it would be even harder to compare her to Pound. There is always a certain incommensurability between men and women writers. But she does have it in common with the first three of these that, in giving supreme expression to profoundly felt personal experience, she was able to identify herself with more general human experience and stand forth as a spokesman for the human spirit, announcing its predicaments, its vicissitudes, but, as a master of human expression, by the splendor of expression itself, putting herself beyond common embarrassments, common oppressions and panics. This is man who surveys himself and the world in which he moves, not the beast that scurries and suffers; and the name of the poet comes no longer to indicate a mere individual with a birthplace and a legal residence, but to figure as one of the pseudonyms assumed by that spirit itself.

This spirit so made itself felt, in all one's relations with Edna, that it towered above the clever college girl, the Greenwich Village gamine and, later, the neurotic invalid. There was something of awful drama about everything one did with Edna, and yet something that steadied one, too. Those who fell in love with the woman did not, I think, seriously quarrel with her or find themselves at one another's throats and they were not, except in very small ways, demoralized or led to commit excesses, because the other thing was always there, and her genius, for those who could value it, was not something that one could be jealous of. Her poetry, you soon found out, was her real overmastering passion. She gave it to all the world, but she also gave it to you. As in "The Poet and His Book"—at that time, one of my favorites of her poems—with its homely but magical images, its urgent and hurried movement—she addressed herself, not to her lover, by whom, except momentarily, she had never had the illusion that she lived or died, but to everyone whose pulse could throb quicker at catching the beat of her poetry. This made it possible during the first days we knew her for John and me to see a good deal of her together on the basis of our common love of poetry. Our parties were in the nature of a sojourn in Pieria—to which, in one of her sonnets, she complains that an unworthy lover is trying to keep her from returning—where it was most delightful to feel at home. I remember particularly an April night in 1920, when we called on Richard Bennett, the actor, who had been brought by Hardwicke Nevin to the Provincetown Players, in the cheerful little house halfway downtown where he lived with his attractive wife and his so soon to be attractive daughters. I sat on the floor with Edna, which seemed to me very Bohemian. On some other occasion, we all undertook to write portraits in verse of ourselves. John's under the title "Self-Portrait," appeared in *Vanity Fair*, and we wanted to publish Edna's, but one of her sisters intervened and persuaded her that it wouldn't do. There was also a trip on a Fifth Avenue bus—we were going to the Claremont for dinner, I think—in the course of which Edna recited to us a sonnet she had just written: *Here is a wound that never will heal, I know.* For me, then rolling up Fifth Avenue, this poem plucked the strings of chagrin, for not only did it refer to some other man, someone I did not know,

but it suggested that Edna could not be consoled, that such grief was in the nature of things.

I used to take her to plays, concerts and operas. We saw Bernard Shaw's *Heartbreak House* together, when it was first done in New York, in the November of 1920. I had not liked it much when I read it and had told her that it was a dreary piece on the model of *Misalliance*. But the play absorbed and excited her, as it gradually did me, and I saw that I had been quite wrong: *Heartbreak House* was, on the contrary, the first piece of Shaw's in which he had fully realized the possibilities of the country-house conversation with which he had been experimenting in *Getting Married* and *Misalliance*. At the end of the second act, Edna became very tense and was rather upset by the scene in which Ariadne—who had just said, "I get my whole life messed up with people falling in love with me"—plays cat-and-mouse with the jealous Randell; and when the curtain went down on it, she said: "I hate women who do that, you know." She must have had, in the course of those crowded years, a good many Randells on her hands, but her method of dealing with them was different from that of Bernard Shaw's aggressive Ariadne. She was capable of being mockingly or sternly sharp with an admirer who proved a nuisance, but she did not like to torture people or to play them off against one another. With the dignity of her genius went, not, as is sometimes the case, a coldness or a hatefulness or a touchiness in intimate human relations, but an invincible magnanimity, and the effects of her transitory feminine malice would be cancelled by an impartiality which was amiably humorous or sympathetic. It is characteristic of her that, in her sonnet "On Hearing a Symphony of Beethoven," she should write of the effect of the music,

> The spiteful and the stingy and the rude
> Sleep like the scullions in the fairy-tale.

Spitefulness and stinginess and rudeness were among the qualities she most disliked and of which she was least willing to be guilty.

Between John Bishop and me relations were, nevertheless, by this time, becoming a little strained. Frank Crowninshield was complaining that it was difficult to have both his assistants in love with one of his most brilliant contributors. There was a time when, from the point of view of taking her out, I was more or less monopolizing Edna, and John, who, between the office and his perfectionist concentration on his poetry—which he recited in the bathroom in the morning and to which he returned at night—had collapsed and come down with the flu. I went to see him, and afterwards told Edna—no doubt with a touch of smugness—that I thought he was suffering, also, from his frustrated passion for her. The result of this—which I saw with mixed feelings—was that she paid him a visit at once and did her best to redress the balance. I knew that he had some pretty good poetry to read her, and this did not improve the situation.

But her relations with us and with her other admirers had, as I say, a disarming impartiality. Though she reacted to the traits of the men she knew—a face or a voice or a manner—or to their special qualifications—what they sang or had read or collected—with the same intensely perceptive interest that she brought to anything else—a bird or a shell or a weed—that had attracted her burning attention; though she was quick to feel weakness or strength—she did not, however, give the impression that personality much mattered for her or that, aside from her mother and sisters, her personal relations were important except as subjects for poems; and when she came to write about her lovers, she gave them so little individuality that it was usually, in any given case, impossible to tell which man she was writing about. What interests her is seldom the people themselves, but her own emotions about them; and the sonnets that she published in sequences differed basically from Mrs. Browning's in that they dealt with a miscellany of men without—since they are all about *her*—the reader's feeling the slightest discontinuity. In all this, she was not egotistic in any boring or ridiculous or oppressive way, because it was not the personal, but the impersonal Edna Millay—that is, the poet— that preoccupied her so incessantly. But she was sometimes rather a strain, because nothing could be casual for her; I do not think I ever saw her relaxed, even when she was tired or ill. I used to suppose that this strain of being with her must be due to my own anxieties, but I later discovered that others who had never been emotionally involved with her were affected in the same way. She could be very amusing in company, but the wit of her conversation was as sharp as the pathos of her poetry. She was not at all a social person. She did not gossip; did not like to talk current events; did not like to talk personalities. It was partly that she was really noble, partly that she was rather neurotic, and the two things (bound up together) made it difficult for her to meet the world easily. When Mr. Sheean met her, late in her life, she at first, he tells us, seemed tongue-tied; then puzzled him extremely by thanking him, as if it had happened yesterday, for his having, in some official connection about which he had completely forgotten, sent her some flowers five years before; then analyzed, with a closeness he could hardly follow, a poem by Gerard Manley Hopkins, the sense of which she insisted, with bitterness and an "animation" that brought out "her very extraordinary beauty—not the beauty of every day but apart," had been spoiled by Hopkins' editor Robert Bridges' having put in a comma in the wrong place. But although Edna sometimes fatigued one, she was never, as even the most gifted sometimes are, tyrannical, fatuous or vain. She was either like the most condensed literature or music, the demands of which one cannot meet protractedly, or like a serious nervous case—though this side of her was more in evidence later—whom one finds that one cannot soothe.—EDMUND WILSON, "Edna St. Vincent Millay," *The Shores of Light*, 1952, pp. 751–57

⟨. . .⟩ early insulation from the Millay cult, both personal and literary, enables me to speak of her more judiciously, perhaps, than some of her later critics have. Winfield Townley Scott, discussing her *Collected Poems*, in the *Saturday Review*, confessed to having outgrown poems which once had him "babbling in the streets by night." And John Ciardi, in an essay in the same magazine at the time of her death, described how in adolescence "we were moved, we were filled, we were taken" by verses which now seem no more important than our first cigarette. "One finds himself less inclined to criticism than nostalgia. At least it will be so for all of us who were very young and very merry and aren't exactly that any more, but who once long ago opened those little black books with their titles pasted on the binding, and suddenly found the wind blowing through everybody's hair and a wonderful girl running to us through the wind." John Crowe Ransom, though not so nostalgic about his youth, seems equally filled with pride in the fact that he is grown up, and adds to it a boastfulness about things "intellectual" and "male" so reiterate as almost to cause the reader to blush.

I approach the question of Edna's character and her poems without any of these obsessions. That she was a rage in the teens escaped me, as I have said. That her "reading appearances were triumphs"—though not "of trailing gowns and far-flung gestures," as Ciardi asserts, for there were no gestures and the gowns hung straight down and stopped at the

floor—also left me unmoved, for I did not entirely like the way she read her poems. They are melodic and she read them so slowly that for me the melody was lost. I also find it possible to be a man without inferring that women are thereby proven inferior. And as to the "lack of intellectual interest" which, according to Ransom, sums up her limitations—"it is that which the male reader misses in her poetry"—it was certainly not true of her nature, and I find it less true of what she wrote than of most lyric poetry. I agreed with Thomas Hardy when he said that, next to our skyscrapers, the poetry of Edna St. Vincent Millay was the thing he admired most in America. And I do not think anything has happened among us to alter that judgment. ⟨. . .⟩

I have to say then ⟨. . .⟩ that Edna had as clear, hard, alert and logical a mind as I have encountered in man or woman. She surprised me continually too with her large and accurate knowledge about many things—about nature, about language, about everything relating to her art. She had in these fields the instincts and discipline of a scholar. Far from being "indifferent to intellectuality," to quote another of John Crowe Ransom's naïvely revealing phrases, she was, for my taste, a little too austerely addicted to mental as well as moral discipline. She had a trace of the schoolmarm about her. It was this quality—surprisingly associated with her boldness in the enjoyment of sensual pleasures—that made it impossible for me to fulfill my dream of falling in love with her. ⟨. . .⟩

A ⟨. . .⟩ deeply self-damaging result of the puritanical streak in Edna was her disastrously conscientious attempt, in the crises of World War II, to write popular propaganda in the form of poetry. She gave all that she received for this poetry, and the manuscripts of it, to buy ambulances for the Red Cross. She was tremendously sincere—sincere enough, had it occurred to her, to go to work in a munitions factory, or wrap packages, or knit socks for the soldiers. That would have been a better gift to the war effort than bad poetry. But it would not have been the sacrifice of self that New England's rigid moralism demands. Edna may have imagined her name to be so renowned that her poetry, diluted to newspaper copy, would be an important help in "rousing the country," but I find this hard to believe. Her statement, "I have one thing to give in the service of my country, my reputation as a poet," strikes me as one of the most aberrant products of the modern brain-disease of propaganda. It was righteousness on the rampage, the sense of duty gone mad. And it ended, naturally, in a nervous breakdown.

"For five years," she wrote, explaining her illness to Edmund Wilson, "I had been writing almost nothing but propaganda. And I can tell you from my own experience that there is nothing on this earth which can so much get on the nerves of a good poet as the writing of bad poetry."

In sending us her beautifully titled book, *Make Bright the Arrows*, she wrote on the fly-leaf an inscription that was painful to read: "To Max and Eliena, who will not like the many bad lines contained in this book, but who will like the thing it wants so much to help to do, and who will like the reaffirmation of my constant affection and love. . . ." Many American writers—most of them—have at times diluted the purity of their art in order to make money; Edna's sin, we can say at least, was of a nobler-seeming kind. But it was a sin no less. She acknowledged later that this debauch of self-sacrifice had been a mistake, and regretted it sadly. But then it was too late. She never recaptured her lost self. She never wrote a great poem after that. . . .

Now I feel that I have to qualify what I have been saying, or define it more carefully. When I spoke of a certain asperity—or did I decide upon the word austerity?—in Edna's assertion of what she believed to be right or true, I did not mean to disparage her noble conception of the poet's role. She believed with Shelley that the poet should take his stand on the side of liberty and justice in the social and political struggles of his day, and of all days. She was greatly and courageously earnest in this—enough so to travel to Boston and risk imprisonment and the loss of her then monumental popularity by marching in the "mob protest" against the execution of Sacco and Vanzetti in 1927. Her presence in that hazardous and disreputable action is perhaps a better answer than I have made to those extremely literary critics who dismiss her as a bohemian play-girl and reduce her role in American literature to "adolescent self-discovery." None of them, I am sure, can boast of having shown up at Beacon Hill on that heroic occasion, or ever demonstrated their boasted "maturity" in an equivalent fashion. Delicate as her verse was, and lyric rather than dramatic, Edna Millay stands beside the poets to whom you raise your eyes after reading their books—poets who were minds and muscles in the world and not mere versifiers.

Perhaps it was inevitable that a combination of lyric waywardness with such a moral code should express itself sometimes in austere or puritanical forms that held me a little at a distance. Perhaps it was my own softy-ness, my wish at all costs to have things run smoothly, rather than any excessive sharpness of edges in Edna, that I was depicting with that word austerity. At any rate, it is not her consecration to the struggle against Nazism that I have been meaning to criticize, only her terrible mistake—worse than austere, fanatical—of sacrificing to it the integrity of her art.—MAX EASTMAN, "My Friendship with Edna Millay," *Great Companions*, 1959, pp. 79–83, 98–101

WINFIELD TOWNLEY SCOTT
"Millay Collected"

Poetry, March 1944, pp. 334–42

And all this time
Death beating the door in.

The truth is that Edna Millay's poetry has been damned with too much praise. If her work had bloomed quietly for twenty-five years in the nourishing privacy of a handful of devoted followers, there might be flourishing now a widespread cult of happy admiration for at least a dozen fine poems that bear a personality at its best expression and that would be, of course, untrammeled by common fame and the fame of a hundred lesser poems in the same books. The sort of development that occurred in the career of Lizette Woodworth Reese, for example; and heaven knows how many more. To be sure, qualities in the work itself are basic to any explanation of Miss Millay's popularity; nevertheless, the praise became so extravagant that it assured a reaction which has begun to look like an almost equally extravagant, or faddish reaction.

No doubt there were always dissenters. My supposition is, however, that the first considerable critical examination of Miss Millay's work was Horace Gregory's brilliant review of *Wine from These Grapes* in the *New York Herald Tribune Books* in 1934. I have purposely not looked it up, but my recollection of the review is of how penetratingly it related Miss Millay's entire work and the mood of the postwar undergraduate, and of how judiciously it assessed the character and limitations of that work. In the decade since, criticism has lost the judiciousness and cast away the penetration. A new attitude toward Edna St. Vincent Millay has pretty thoroughly been adopted by the literati, and if her popular audience is still not only faithful but large, she has—so far as I can determine—failed to excite any recent collegiate intelligentsia. The greatest insult you can offer any young woman poet in this country is to warn her that she may be the Edna Millay of her generation; which, being interpreted, means that she is in danger of glibness and of popularity.

Now if under the praise and the dispraise there are reasons for both to be found in Miss Millay's poetry, the fact remains that the adulation and the abuse have little to do with the worth of that poetry, since both have been excessive. They do merit preliminary mention because they make so difficult an attempt to write of a body of poetry that is neither the most unworthy nor the greatest since Sappho's. The attempt is particularly worth while just now (after all, you can't be sure that a new postwar generation will not rediscover Millay!) because of the one-volume publication of Miss Millay's *Collected Lyrics*.

I think we may begin by being pretty sure that in this book and in the *Collected Sonnets* published in the same handsome format in 1941, we have the work on which Miss Millay's eventual reputation must rest. Her poetic plays all seem too literary to be durable; *Conversation at Midnight* is an obvious tour de force of a poet whose talent is pre-eminently lyric; and as for her political verse, a somewhat hysterical emotionalism runs merely thin in *Make Bright the Arrows* and overflows embarrassingly in *The Murder of Lidice*. Anticipating time, we may as well forget these other books. So my text is a simple one (and except for the fury and the furor about Miss Millay would be ridiculous): that in this *Collected Lyrics* and its predecessor, the *Collected Sonnets*, there are some very poor poems and some very able poems.

It is sometimes not at all difficult to spot the poorer poems, but sometimes it is because the reader, soon aware that Miss Millay is repetitious in her moods and subjects, must try to determine what poem really sums up and surpasses half a dozen others that are very much like it. Again: this is what time will do in its inexorable reaping, and no contemporary can perfectly anticipate the process.

All her poems may be said to be variations on a theme announced by Housman: "Let us endure awhile and see injustice done." Occasionally this injustice is political and social in the sense uppermost in Housman's line; but generally with Miss Millay it is personal, and at her best it is always personal. Here are some of the things she has said so often in her verse:

This is a lovely world, almost unbearably beautiful as a work of nature; but the poet is usually, in this expression, writing from some particular point on earth which is markedly less desirable than another she is recalling, and therefore she writes in sorrow. Sorrow in general is a constant mood with her, and its most typical expression is through sorrow in love. Though her love poetry has ranged from the flip to the marmoreal, from the casual to the frenzied, it has elaborated at both extremes and all the way between that love is (1) fickle and (2) irresistible. A very short poem called "Being Young and Green" sums up (though I don't cite it as a superior poem) this whole conclusion:

Being young and green, I said in love's despite:
Never in the world will I to living wight
Give over, air my mind
To anyone,
Hang out its ancient secrets in the strong wind
To be shredded and faded . . .
Oh, me, invaded
And sacked by the wind and the sun!

Miss Millay's explanation for this sweet disaster is stated as well as anywhere in her verse in the concluding couplet of one of her early sonnets:

Pity me that the heart is slow to learn
What the swift mind beholds at every turn.

From her poem "Mariposa" the conviction that

Whether I be false or true,
Death comes in a day or two.

was lightened and extenuated through the famous *A Few Figs From Thistles*, and this theme runs with its own small variations through her work, the impudence changing to bitterness and sometimes, as in that unfortunate sonnet beginning "I too beneath your moon, almighty Sex," to wholly humorless arrogance.

As deliberately as anywhere in her work, I suppose, Miss Millay seeks to objectify her conclusions in the eighteen sonnets called *Epitaph on the Race of Man*. I like a couple of these as well as anything Edna Millay has ever written, but as a whole it is a sequence that suffers from repetitiousness and from the later grand manner of the poet. No one can sound so profound as Miss Millay at her falsest! However, as I understand them, these sonnets portray man's victories over his environment and conclude that his tragedy lies in his inevitable defeat by himself. It is a great theme, and sometimes Miss Millay handles it with great beauty and genuine (not bogus) dignity. Two of the sonnets are certainly among her best: the much admired "See where Capella with her golden kids" and the not enough admired "Observe how Myanoshita cracked in two." (By the way, if the reader will look at that sonnet and then at the two immediately following he will see what I mean by the repetitiousness: how immediately the poet says over again, not once but twice, what she has just said and has said better.)

Her poems say a hundred times that life is sad. At least as often, her poems say that death is the bitterest pill of all; and they fight against it, wail upon it, and defy death. This, when you come to think of it, adds up to a lot of troubled emotion. Maybe if Miss Millay had ever made up her mind, we should have had less poetry from her, and that would be unfortunate; nonetheless, by these conflicting emotions she has remained in an intellectual jam. There is obvious sentimentality in this contradiction; it afflicts a great deal of her verse and explains, I think, why the verse leaves us dissatisfied. Here too I suspect we come closest to the reason for Miss Millay's attractiveness for the undergraduate, or adolescent, mind.

(I seem to be saying unkind things, but I honestly want—as I implied heretofore—to try to cut down to what is firmest in this poetry.)

In other words, the mood of self-pity is exceptionally attractive to the young, and Miss Millay's verse has employed that mood (or vice versa) many, many times. The popularity of her poetry, of course, stems very largely from what we may call its familiarity: simple forms in rhyme and stanza, resemblances (whether or not fortunate) to poetry already well known, occasionally skillful reworkings of particular styles all the way from the Elizabethan to that of Robinson Jeffers. At her best, Miss Millay brings vigor and freshness to traditional forms and stamps them with a new personality more positively than any of her contemporaries has ever done. Thus, though you may feel "The Ballad of the Harp Weaver" is a shade literary, a shade too conscious of what it is doing, I think you must conclude that it is a strong and moving hymn to imagination and unselfish love. And with such a poem as "The Poet and His Book" I think we must give over all reservations; its power and feeling are genuine and are expressed with real passion. In that

poem, certainly one of her best, what might be called self-pity surpasses itself by an acceptance of physical death and by sounding the very human desire for a kind of immortality. And in such smaller poems as "Travel" ("The railroad track is miles away"); "Eel-Grass"; "Recuerdo" ("We were very tired, we were very merry"); and "Feast" ("I drank at every vine") her various romantic attitudes find their summation in memorable lyrics.

Undoubtedly the many influences on Miss Millay's poetry will sometime be studied. Among them will be found an astonishing variety. The Marlowe ranting of those early poems, "Interim" and "The Suicide," seems to shove over at times even for Miltonics and a quieting note from George Herbert. The medieval gimcrackery of the imagery in so many of the *Fatal Interview* sonnets will bear examination for what it shows of the literary assuming itself to be literature. There are a surprising number of ventures into free verse, and surely Elinor Wylie is present in "Moriturus":

If I could have
Two things in one:
The peace of the grave,
And the light of the sun;

and so on. Miss Millay's admiration for Jeffers is well known and it shows itself frequently in her later work; most notably in "Apostrophe to Man" since there it is not only Jeffers' style but Jeffers' thought, and in such a poem as "Modern Declaration," which, by the way, has as a preface to a declaration of constant love these very appealing lines:

I, having loved ever since I was a child a few things,
    never having wavered
In these affections; never through shyness in the
    houses of the rich or in the presence of
    clergymen having denied these loves;
Never when worked upon by cynics like chiroprac-
    tors having grunted or clicked a vertebra to the
    discredit of these loves;
Never when anxious to land a job having diminished
    them by a conniving smile; or when befuddled
    by drink
Jeered at them through heartache or lazily fondled
    the fingers of their alert enemies;

Quite aside from the style of that, I think we should observe, as to the sense of it, that it is true. Edna Millay has pursued her art according to lights that have varied in her career, but according to those lights with integrity. This is not a small matter.

Where her poetry has, so to speak, gone wrong is where she has mistaken attitudes for convictions, or mere moods for profound truths (as we all do). Thus, you get the absurd blather, "O world, I cannot hold thee close enough!", in "God's World," and the astounding insistence on so desiring the seashore that she is crying aloud for death by drowning. This is the common error of requiring an emotion to bear (if I may paraphrase Miss Wylie, who was talking of something else) a little more than it can bear. And along with such sentimentality in Miss Millay's work there has been a rapid loss of humor in its largest or smallest sense and a consequent gain in a grand manner that not only permits medieval impedimenta as aforesaid but even allows such solemn absurdities as celebrating the cleaning of a canary's cage and that thoughtful dinosaur that

    . . . held aside her heavy tail
And took the seed; and heard the seed confined
Roar in the womb;

These elements were always in Miss Millay's poetry. The

humorless dullness of her early "Ode to Silence" is a pertinent example. The disproportionate overloading of an emotion was done full-length in "The Blue Flag in the Bog." But the simpler elements have persisted, too, and it is those we come back to.

If the poet would go "screaming to God for death by drowning," she would all the same on another occasion—in the poem called "Exiled"—express the same nostalgia with control:

> I am too long away from water.
> I have a need of water near.

And we believe it. And I should like especially to note her marked ability of observation by several small and scattered examples among many:

> . . . the redness
> Of little leaves opening stickily.

Again:

> There rings a hammering all day,
> And shingles lie about the doors;
> In orchards near and far away
> The grey woodpecker taps and bores;
> And men are merry at their chores,
> And children earnest at their play.

There the wonderful word is "shingles." And again:

> Near some naked blackberry hoops
> Dim with purple chalk.

And once more:

> Now comes night, smelling of box and privet
> And the rain falls fine.

There is in the poem "Renascence" a simplicity which is at times girlish; legitimately so, of course. It holds the seed of Edna Millay's best poetry. In her subsequent work this girlishness sometimes became unpleasantly coy and mawkish, as for instance in the poem called "The Little Hill." On the other hand, in "Elaine" and "A Visit to the Asylum," bathos, however perilously, is really escaped; something pathetic and moving takes place; and again in such a small but specific and affecting poem as "Chorus" with its elegiac

> She will dance no more
> In her narrow shoes;
> Sweep her narrow shoes
> From the closet floor.

To the poems and two *Epitaph* sonnets I have mentioned with praise I should want to add, in any attempted Millay canon, six other sonnets: the two fairly early ones beginning, respectively "What lips my lips have kissed, and where, and why" and "Grow not too high, grow not too far from home"— the first because it seems to me the most memorable summary of her oft-repeated early love poetry, and the second because it is her own best statement of her own best art—and four from the *Fatal Interview* sequence: "Not in a silver casket cool with pearls," "I dreamed I moved among the Elysian fields," "Love is not all; it is not meat nor drink," and "Oh, sleep forever in the Latmian cave." These largely escape the copybook influences and the inflated manner of so much of the rest, and though they move on a sedate plane they do so with immaculate dignity. In those instances, at least, Miss Millay has controlled even in the grand manner a basic simplicity. Perhaps they are her best work. In any case they belong with the completely realized poetry of our times.

ARTHUR MILLER

1915–

Arthur Miller was born on October 17, 1915, to Isadore and Augusta Miller, a well-to-do Jewish couple. The first fourteen years of his life were spent in upscale Harlem; then, when the stock market crash of 1929 and subsequent Great Depression nearly ruined his father, a manufacturer of ladies' coats, Miller moved with his family to Brooklyn. He was an indifferent student, and when on graduating from high school he found that his grades were not good enough to get him into college—which, at any rate, he could not afford—he took a series of odd jobs, then worked for a year as a shipping clerk in an automobile parts warehouse. During this time he first began to read literature extensively. In 1934 Miller was accepted at the University of Michigan, where he enrolled as a journalism student and began to write plays.

His first two dramas, *Honors at Dawn* (1936) and *No Villain* (1937), both won minor awards, which encouraged him to pursue his ambitions as a playwright. By the time he graduated in 1938 he had completed one more play, as well as discovering the works of Henrik Ibsen; these became a lasting influence on his own writing. In 1938 he wrote a leftist comedy, *Listen My Children*, for the Federal Theatre Project. This was followed by four or five other plays, none of them ever produced, all of which he found unsatisfactory. It was not until 1944 that he wrote *The Man Who Had All the Luck*, the first notable play of his mature period, and a qualified success in its author's eyes as well. This was followed by a nonfiction book, *Situation Normal* (1944), based on interviews with American servicemen, and by *Focus* (1945), a novel about anti-Semitism.

Miller began to receive increasing critical notice with the production of his play *All My Sons* (1947), an Ibsenesque drama centered on the revelation of a small manufacturer's having supplied defective equipment under a government contract during the war. It was the next play that secured his reputation; *Death of a Salesman* (1949), the story of a failed traveling salesman and his two sons, became an instant classic of the American theater, and was awarded a Pulitzer Prize. His next work,

The Crucible (1953), which dealt with the Salem witch trials of 1692, was also well received, as well as attracting critical attention of another sort. Miller's history of affiliation with leftist organizations brought him under the eye of Senator Joseph McCarthy and the House Un-American Activities Committee (HUAC) during their investigations of alleged Communist infiltration of American institutions. Miller freely testified before the committee in his own behalf, but refused their requests that he name others who had been similarly involved. In the political climate of the time *The Crucible* was, perhaps understandably, read by many as a commentary on the McCarthyites' activities. Though HUAC found him an insufficiently friendly witness Miller's career survived the experience, and his *A View from the Bridge*, presented on a double bill with his short play *A Memory of Two Mondays* in 1955, brought him a second Pulitzer Prize.

It was also during this same period that Miller was divorced from his wife of many years, Mary Grace Slattery Miller, who had supported him and their two children during his unremunerative early writing career. In 1956 he married the actress Marilyn Monroe, and his screenplay for the 1961 film *The Misfits*, directed by John Huston and starring Clark Gable and Marilyn Monroe, was originally conceived as a vehicle for her. After a few years the second marriage ended in divorce as well, and in 1962 Miller married photographer Inge Morath, with whom he later collaborated on several books, writing text to accompany her pictures.

In 1964 Miller's *After the Fall*, a semi-autobiographical, almost novelistic play whose action spans several decades, was produced to mixed notices; some critics panned it as self-indulgent, while others have praised its complex exploration of character and moral issues. It was followed by *Incident at Vichy* (1965), a short play about Nazism and anti-Semitism in Vichy France, and by *The Price* (1968) and *The American Clock* (1979), both of which returned to Miller's earlier themes of domestic life and family conflicts. Besides his plays, Miller's other works include *I Don't Need You Anymore* (1967), a collection of short stories; *In Russia* (1969) and *In the Country* (1977), both with Inge Morath; an adaptation of Ibsen's play *An Enemy of the People*, first produced in that version in 1951; and *The Theater Essays of Arthur Miller* (1978), a volume of his previously uncollected short essays and criticism.

Personal

When Arthur Miller, author of *Death of a Salesman*, was indicted for contempt of Congress this February, the American liberal public was not aroused. The Civil Liberties Union in New York has about thirty such cases in its files; none of them, including the Miller case, has awakened much interest. This may be attributed to apathy ("People feel that this subject has had it," Mr. Miller says) or, in this particular instance, to a sense that nothing bad can really happen to the husband of Marilyn Monroe. ⟨. . .⟩ even assuming the worst, a long time would have to pass before Mr. Miller would be behind bars; the slow workings of American justice make such a prospect seem unreal and, considering the persons, positively fantastic. Off the screen, it is hard to summon up a vision of Miss Monroe talking to Mr. Miller (wearing convict garb) across a prison partition while stony guards look on. We have seen this scene too often in the movies to accept it in real life; the plot, too, is familiar; the husband is doing time for having refused to inform on his buddies. Mr. Miller's last play, *A View from the Bridge*, was about an informer.

Yet this is precisely the issue which the courts will consider: the refusal to play the informer before a Congressional Committee. Called before the House Un-American Activities Committee last June, Mr. Miller declined to name the names of persons he had seen at Communist-sponsored meetings, although he testified freely about his own past association with Communist-front groups. He was not the first witness to find himself impaled on a dilemma, that is, to be willing to talk about himself and unwilling to talk about others. But he was almost the only prominent figure heard by the committee who did not either tell all or take refuge in the Fifth Amendment, which protects a witness against self-incrimination. Against the ritual reply droned out so often during these past years—"I decline to answer on the ground that it might tend to incriminate me"—Mr. Miller's forthrightness struck a note of decided nonconformity.

Regardless of the legalities, in the eyes of the public, every witness who invoked the Fifth Amendment appeared to be guilty, and this fact was traded on by Senator McCarthy and other Congressional investigators, who delighted in confronting America with a parade of witnesses who, one after another, invoked the Fifth Amendment and were handed down from the witness-stand with an air of crisp satisfaction, just as though they had confessed to a long bill of dark particulars. Some of these witnesses, like Mr. Miller, had never been Communists; others had broken, years before, with the Party. But to the ordinary newspaper reader, every witness who used the Fifth Amendment was a dyed-in-the-wool member of what was felt to be a Communist conspiracy to keep the truth from him personally. The right to know took on the character of a basic democratic right which was being trampled upon by these silent witnesses with impunity. It was the public's right to know and Congress's right to ask that Mr. Miller challenged on June 21, in his testimony before the Un-American Activities Committee. Or, to be more exact, he conceded the committee's right to ask him any questions about himself (a right I am not sure the comittee really possessed), but denied its right to extract from him, under threat of contempt proceedings, the names of other people he had known in the Communist movement.

⟨. . .⟩ It is clear from his testimony that Mr. Miller and his questioners were utterly at cross purposes. He supposed, to judge from his attitude, that these Congressmen he was facing were authentically seeking knowledge and he sought earnestly to explain his views to them, rather in the manner of an author discussing his work at a writers' forum. He brought in Socrates and the Spanish Civil War and how it had felt to be a Jew in Brooklyn witnessing anti-Semitism during the early Hitler years. To the Congressmen, all this was a matter of total indifference. For them, the whole hearing hinged on a single point: was the witness willing to name others or not? That was the litmus test. Mr. Miller kept trying to explain to them what kind of man he was, but the Congressmen knew that they would learn what kind of man he was, very simply, when he let them know whether he would play the informer or not. And, in a sense, they were right. This really was the issue, and all the rest was cat-and-mouse play.

In the phrase, *play the informer*, lies the curious and twisted significance of these hearings. For the committee's purpose, it was not necessary that Mr. Miller *be* an informer; he was merely being asked to *act* like one, to define himself as the kind of person who would interpose no obstacle between them and their right to know. The two persons he was required to identify as Communists (for that was what the questions amounted to) had already been named as Communists by other witnesses, dozens of other witnesses, no doubt. That was how the committee had their names. The committee was not seeking information from Mr. Miller; it was applying a loyalty test. And for Mr. Miller it was not in reality a question of betraying specific people (who had already been denounced, so that his testimony could hardly have done them further harm), but of accepting the *principle* of betrayal as a norm of good citizenship.—MARY McCARTHY, "Naming Names: The Arthur Miller Case," *Enc*, May 1957, pp. 23–25

We are, I believe, at the end of a period. Certain things have been repeated sufficiently for one to speak of limitations which have to be recognized if our theater is not to become absurd, repetitious, and decayed.

Now one can no sooner speak of limitations than the question of standards arises. What seems like a limitation to one man may be an area as wide as the world to another. My standard, my viewpoint, whether it appears arbitrary, or true and inevitable, did not spring out of my head unshaped by any outside force. I began writing plays in the midst of what Allan Seager, an English teacher friend of mine at Michigan, calls one of the two genuinely national catastrophes in American history—the Great Depression of the thirties. The other was the Civil War. It is almost bad manners to talk about depression these days, but through no fault or effort of mine it was the ground upon which I learned to stand.

There are a thousand things to say about that time but maybe one will be evocative enough. Until 1929 I thought things were pretty solid. Specifically, I thought—like most Americans—that somebody was in charge. I didn't know exactly who it was, but it was probably a businessman, and he was a realist, a no-nonsense fellow, practical, honest, responsible. In 1929 he jumped out of the window. It was bewildering. His banks closed and refused to open again, and I had twelve dollars in one of them. More precisely, I happened to have withdrawn my twelve dollars to buy a racing bike a friend of mine was bored with, and the next day the Bank of the United States closed. I rode by and saw the crowds of people standing at the brass gates. Their money was inside! And they couldn't get it. And they would never get it. As for me, I felt I had the thing licked.

But about a week later I went into the house to get a glass of milk and when I came out my bike was gone. Stolen. It must have taught me a lesson. Nobody could escape that disaster.

I did not read many books in those days. The depression was my book. Years later I could put together what in those days were only feelings, sensations, impressions. There was the sense that everything had dried up. Some plague of invisible grasshoppers was eating money before you could get your hands on it. You had to be a Ph.D. to get a job in Macy's. Lawyers were selling ties. Everybody was trying to sell something to everybody else. A past president of the Stock Exchange was sent to jail for misappropriating trust funds. They were looking for runaway financiers all over Europe and South America. Practically everything that had been said and done up to 1929 turned out to be a fake. It turns out that there had never been anybody in charge.

What the time gave me, I think now, was a sense of an invisible world. A reality had been secretly accumulating its climax according to its hidden laws to explode illusion at the proper time. In that sense 1929 was our Greek year. The gods had spoken, the gods, whose wisdom had been set aside or distorted by a civilization that was to go onward and upward on speculation, gambling, graft, and the dog eating the dog. Before the crash I thought "Society" meant the rich people in the Social Register. After the crash it meant the constant visits of strange men who knocked on our door pleading for a chance to wash the windows, and some of them fainted on the back porch from hunger. In Brooklyn, New York. In the light of weekday afternoons.

I read books after I was seventeen, but already, for good or ill, I was not patient with every kind of literature. I did not believe, even then, that you could tell about a man without telling about the world he was living in, what he did for a living, what he was like not only at home or in bed but on the job. I remember now reading novels and wondering, What do these people do for a living? When do they work? I remember asking the same questions about the few plays I saw. The hidden laws of fate lurked not only in the characters of people, but equally if not more imperiously in the world beyond the family parlor. Out there were the big gods, the ones whose disfavor could turn a proud and prosperous and dignified man into a frightened shell of a man whatever he thought of himself, and whatever he decided or didn't decide to do.

So that by force of circumstance I came early and unawares to be fascinated by sheer process itself. How things connected. How the native personality of a man was changed by his world, and the harder question, how he could in turn change his world. It was not academic. It was not even a literary or a dramatic question at first. It was the practical problem of what to believe in order to proceed with life. For instance, should one admire success—for there were successful people even then. Or should one always see through it as an illusion which only existed to be blown up, and its owner destroyed and humiliated? Was success immoral?—when everybody else in the neighborhood not only had no Buick but no breakfast? What to believe?

An adolescent must feel he is on the side of justice. That is how human indignation is constantly renewed. But how hard it was to feel justly, let alone to think justly. There were people in the neighborhood saying that it had all happened because the workers had not gotten paid enough to buy what they had produced, and that the solution was to have Socialism, which would not steal their wages any more the way the bosses did and brought on this depression. It was a wonderful thought with which I nearly drove my grandfather crazy. The trouble with it was that he and my father and most of the men I loved would have to be destroyed.

Enough of that. I am getting at only one thought. You can't understand anything unless you understand its relations to its context. It was necessary to feel beyond the edges of things. That much, for good or ill, the Great Depression taught me. It made me impatient with anything, including art, which pretends that it can exist for its own sake and still be of any prophetic importance. A thing becomes beautiful to me as it becomes internally and externally organic. It becomes beautiful because it promises to remove some of my helplessness before the chaos of experience. I think one of the reasons I became a playwright was that in dramatic form everything must be openly organic, deeply organized, articulated from a living center. I used long ago to keep a book in which I would talk to myself. One of the aphorisms I wrote was, "The structure of a play is always the story of how the birds came home to roost." The hidden will be unveiled: the inner laws of reality will announce themselves; I was defining my impression of 1929 as well as dramatic structure.—ARTHUR MILLER, "The Shadows of the Gods" (1958), *The Theater Essays of Arthur Miller*, ed. Robert A. Martin, 1978, pp. 176–79

He was so little the intellectual that he was still signing up for popular-front causes during the late 1940's when most American writers had long ago seen that the Communist party was a sell and the Soviet Union an illusion. Most of the writers and intellectuals—Edmund Wilson, Ernest Hemingway, Sidney Hook, Dwight Macdonald, James T. Farrell, Ignazio Silone, Richard Wright, John Dos Passos—who had been attracted by the Communist program during the 1930's turned away from it by 1939 when Stalin and Hitler jointly attacked Poland and when the Soviets invaded Finland a year later. But it is in 1939 that we find Miller joining a Marxist study course in Brooklyn, and in 1940 he signed an application for Communist party membership!

Whatever fragments of influence the Communist party still exerted over American writers fairly well vanished after World War II when the Soviet *coup* in Czechoslovakia disabused them of their faith in Soviet promises of workers' democracy. But in 1947, 1948, 1949, we still find Miller sponsoring a World Youth Festival in Prague, a World Congress for Peace in Paris, a Peace Conference at the Waldorf-Astoria in New York, and a ragbag of other fronts. (It was the Waldorf conference, which was attacked by liberal and leftist intellectuals like Mary McCarthy, Dwight Macdonald, Robert Lowell, and Norman Mailer, that really did the fellow travelers in.) Miller drifted out of the front organizations after 1950. But he remained a silent apostate. As late as 1955, Howard Fast was writing an article in the *Daily Worker* entitled, "I Propose Arthur Miller as the American Dramatist of the Day." Fast eventually packed it in after the Khrushchev speech attacking Stalin, and he wrote a book about his disillusionment. Miller had had it some time before, but in all of his non-dramatic writing, there is no *intellectual* analysis of Marxism, Leninism, Stalinism, the nature of bureaucracy in the Soviet Union, the anti-Semitism there, the anti-cosmopolitanism, the cultural terror. He seems to have had no awareness of the critical writing on the Soviet Union, the Moscow purge trials, and the Spanish Civil War that had been done by André Gide, Max Eastman, Victor Serge, George Orwell, Hemingway, James Farrell, Sidney Hook, Edmund Wilson.

Miller was essentially what we used to call, in the 1930's, an "innocent." Now, there is nothing terribly sinister about his getting mixed up with a pack of frowzy fronts in the late 1940's. But it indicates either mental apathy about, or a studied lack of interest in, the history of one's time and its chief intellectual crises. It was not until 1957 when the USSR invited Miller to write an essay for a Dostoevski centenary in Moscow that he finally attacked Soviet censorship and the politicalization of the arts. But this was, for "America's foremost representative of the mind," rather late in the game. ⟨. . .⟩

Instead of regarding the match between Miller and Monroe as peculiar, one might say that it was almost inevitable. What was more logical than for Marilyn to fall in love with the country's leading unhappily married non-homosexual playwright? After all, actress and playwright make as compatible a coupling as any other combination. Eugene O'Neill, Sidney Howard, Charles MacArthur, Clifford Odets, William Saroyan, Maxwell Anderson, Hartley Manners, Robert E. Sherwood, Elmer Rice, George S. Kaufman, Moss Hart, are among those who have been or are married to actresses.

Devious psychological explanations are plentiful to justify Miller's love for Marilyn. One theory asserts that he was drawn to the "All-American sex symbol" to restore himself in the eyes of the American people after the humiliations he had suffered from investigating committees and red-baiting groups. A satirist in *Punch*, identified only as B.A.Y., celebrated the Miller-Monroe nuptials with a poem called "Epithalamic Blues":

> Arthur was a writer, he had Left Wing traits;
> He wrote *Death of a Salesman* and wowed them in the States.
> So then he wrote another piece, obliquely named *The Crucible*,
> And, politically speaking, it was almost unproducible.
> Arthur sought a passport from his Uncle Sam,
> And when he couldn't get it, he sure was in a jam—
> But he knew
> What to do
> And so
> He hauled off and married
> Marilyn Monroe.
> Yeah, he hauled off and married Marilyn Monroe!
> Her fans stayed as faithful as before, or more so,
> But turned their attention to her head from her torso,
> While in every milk-bar and sports arcade
> The hepcats sang this serenade:
> "I'm just crazy over Mrs. Arthur Miller!
> Mrs. Arthur Miller's my number one thriller.
> With her new-style dumb-intellectual blend
> She can show you how Timon is a girl's best friend.
> . . .
> "If her countrymen forget her real talent when she's dead
> You can wager they'll remember her for something else instead
> For she's made a public hero of a one-time Red—
> Mrs. Miller, the queen of them all!"
> —MAURICE ZOLOTOW, "Re-enter Mr. Miller," *Marilyn Monroe*, 1960, pp. 256–58

Works

A great deal has been said and written about what *Death of a Salesman* is supposed to signify, both psychologically and from the socio-political viewpoints. For instance, in one periodical of the far Right it was called a "time bomb expertly placed under the edifice of Americanism," while the *Daily Worker* reviewer thought it entirely decadent. In Catholic Spain it ran longer than any modern play and it has been refused production in Russia but not, from time to time, in certain satellite countries, depending on the direction and velocity of the wind. The Spanish press, thoroughly controlled by Catholic orthodoxy, regarded the play as commendable proof of the spirit's death where there is no God. In America, even as it was being cannonaded as a piece of Communist propaganda, two of the largest manufacturing corporations in the country invited me to address their sales organizations in conventions assembled, while the road company was here and there picketed by the Catholic War Veterans and the American Legion. It made only a fair impression in London, but in the area of the Norwegian Arctic Circle fishermen whose only contact with civilization was the radio and the occasional visit of the government boat insisted on seeing it night after night—

the same few people—believing it to be some kind of religious rite. One organization of salesmen raised me up nearly to patron-sainthood, and another, a national sales managers' group, complained that the difficulty of recruiting salesmen was directly traceable to the play. When the movie was made, the producing company got so frightened it produced a sort of trailer to be shown before the picture, a documentary short film which demonstrated how exceptional Willy Loman was; how necessary selling is to the economy; how secure the salesman's life really is; how idiotic, in short, was the feature film they had just spent more than a million dollars to produce. Fright does odd things to people.

On the psychological front the play spawned a small hill of doctoral theses explaining its Freudian symbolism, and there were innumerable letters asking if I was aware that the fountain pen which Biff steals is a phallic symbol. Some, on the other hand, felt it was merely a fountain pen and dismissed the whole play. I received visits from men over sixty from as far away as California who had come across the country to have me write the stories of their lives, because the story of Willy Loman was exactly like theirs. The letters from women made it clear that the central character of the play was Linda; sons saw the entire action revolving around Biff or Happy, and fathers wanted advice, in effect, on how to avoid parricide. Probably the most succinct reaction to the play was voiced by a man who, on leaving the theater, said, "I always said that New England territory was no damned good." This, at least, was a fact. ⟨. . .⟩

The play was always heroic to me, and in later years the academy's charge that Willy lacked the "stature" for the tragic hero seemed incredible to me. I had not understood that these matters are measured by Greco-Elizabethan paragraphs which hold no mention of insurance payments, front porches, refrigerator fan belts, steering knuckles, Chevrolets, and visions seen not through the portals of Delphi but in the blue flame of the hot-water heater. How could "Tragedy" make people weep, of all things?

I set out not to "write a tragedy" in this play, but to show the truth as I saw it. However, some of the attacks upon it as a pseudo-tragedy contain ideas so misleading, and in some cases so laughable, that it might be in place here to deal with a few of them.

Aristotle having spoken of a fall from the heights, it goes without saying that someone of the common mould cannot be a fit tragic hero. It is now many centuries since Aristotle lived. There is no more reason for falling down in a faint before his *Poetics* than before Euclid's geometry, which has been amended numerous times by men with new insights; nor, for that matter, would I choose to have my illnesses diagnosed by Hippocrates rather than the most ordinary graduate of an American medical school, despite the Greek's genius. Things do change, and even a genius is limited by his time and the nature of his society.

I would deny, on grounds of simple logic, this one of Aristotle's contentions if only because he lived in a slave society. When a vast number of people are divested of alternatives, as slaves are, it is rather inevitable that one will not be able to imagine drama, let alone tragedy, as being possible for any but the higher ranks of society. There is a legitimate question of stature here, but none of rank, which is so often confused with it. So long as the hero may be said to have had alternatives of a magnitude to have materially changed the course of his life, it seems to me that in this respect at least, he cannot be debarred from the heroic role.—ARTHUR MILLER, "Introduction to *The Collected Plays*" (1957), *The Theater*

Essays of Arthur Miller, ed. Robert A. Martin, 1978, pp. 140–45

In writing *Salesman*, Miller, first of all, accomplished something significant to the drama anthologists: he had tidied up a seventy-five-year cycle in the theatre. Titles like *From* Ghosts *to* Death of a Salesman, as John Gassner's latest collection is called, mean to suggest more, I think, than a simple bracketing of a group of recent plays. Gassner, in fact, has shown that Miller has taken the theatre back to Ibsen while at the same time assimilating most of the major technical influences that have arisen since that time. Moreover, the ghosts of paternal sin that trouble Oswald Alving are very much the same as those that plague Biff Loman, but Miller makes the whole cycle glitter by showing off the enriched post-Ibsen heritage in projecting them. "Here [in *Salesman*]" Gassner writes, ". . . the expressionistic and realistic styles exist in a fused state."

In the process of describing the cycle, the epicycle—the literary history of Arthur Miller—has, however, been largely ignored. The reason for this is implied almost in passing, again by Gassner: "[Miller] had been working steadily toward excellence and had already distinguished himself with much thoughtful writing in his thirty-three years." In other words, if a *Death of a Salesman* was going to be written at that moment, what more natural, he seems to say, than that it should come from this seasoned professional, this winner of a Critics' Circle Award, this published novelist, this keen social conscience who was never associated with the "private sensibility" drama most of his fellow playwrights were producing? The same lack of real interest in Miller was shared by the play's less friendly critics, who levied various reasonable, but impersonal complaints. Some dwelt, for example, on Willy Loman's failure as a tragic hero (a contention denied by some of the play's supporters). Others thought that the dialogue was "bad poetry." Eric Bentley said that the play was "vague" with a "blurring of outlines."

So, in general, *Salesman* was treated like a new baby whose arrival is not completely expected but is totally appropriate just the same because it is the product of an ideal marriage between a healthy, if nondescript, playwright and a dramatic tradition that has proved beautifully fertile after all. This fertility preoccupied most of the offspring's strongest admirers. Those less impressed carped about the shape of Baby's fingernails perhaps, but showed no great interest as to what it was in Miller's genes that made them that way. Father was only Father, too much respected maybe, but also too much taken for granted. The reason for restoring Miller's parental rights, thus, is not that he has been resentful of the dandling wayfarers' attentions to his progeny, but that it has become almost impossible by now to determine how much of the play is Miller, how much is that of the "can-a-little-man-be-a-tragic-hero?" scholar, and how much belongs to that almost legendary businessman who weeps in the orchestra because Willy Loman reminds him so much either of his Uncle George or of his own secret self.—WILLIAM WIEGAND, "Arthur Miller and the Man Who Knows," WR, Winter 1957, pp. 85–86

He is, basically, a political, or "socially conscious" writer. He is a distinguished survivor of the Thirties, and his values derive mostly from that decade. He is not much of a hand at exploring or exploiting his own consciousness. He is not inward. He writes at times with what may be a matchless power in the American theatre today, but not with a style of his own, and those who see his plays can leave them with little or no sense of the author as a character. He is not, in fact, much concerned with individuality of any sort. This is not an adverse judgment;

it is a distinction, or an attempt at one. What interests Miller and what he can often convey with force is the crushing impact of society upon its members. His human beings are always on the anvil, awaiting the hammer, and the act that landed him in his present trouble was an attempt to shield two or three of them from the blow. (It was, of course, a symbolic act, a gesture, for Miller knew very well that the committee knew all about the men he was asked to identify. He could not really shield; he could only assert the shielding principle.) What he was protecting was, in any case, a self-esteem that rested upon a social rule or principle or ethic.

One could almost say that Miller's sense of himself *is* the principle that holds "informing" to be the ultimate in human wickedness. It is certainly a recurrent theme in his writing. In *The Crucible*, his play about the Salem witchcraft trials, his own case is so strikingly paralleled as to lend color—though doubtless not truth—to the view that his performance in Washington was a case of life paying art the sincere flattery of imitation. To save his life, John Proctor, the hero, makes a compromise with the truth. He confesses, falsely, to having trafficked with Satan. "Did you see the Devil?" the prosecutor asks him. "I did," Proctor says. He recognizes the character of his act, but this affects him little. "Good, then—it is evil, and I do it," he says to his wife, who is shocked. He has reasoned that a few more years on earth are worth this betrayal of his sense of himself. (It is not to be concluded that Proctor's concession to the mad conformity of the time parallels Miller's testimony, for Proctor had never in fact seen the devil, whereas Miller had in fact seen Communists.) The prosecutor will not let him off with mere self-incrimination. He wants names; the names of those Proctor has seen with the Devil. Proctor refuses; does not balk at a self-serving lie, but a self-serving lie that involves others will not cross his lips. "I speak my own sins," he says, either metaphorically or hypocritically, since the sins in question are a fiction. "I cannot judge another. I have no tongue for it." He is hanged, a martyr.

⟨. . .⟩ Today, in most Western countries, ethics derive mainly from society and almost all values are social. What we do to and with ourselves is thought to be our own affair and thus not, in most circumstances, a matter that involves morality at all. People will be found to say that suicide, for a man or woman with few obligations to others, should not be judged harshly, while the old sanctions on murder remain. Masochism is in one moral category, sadism in another. Masturbation receives a tolerance that fornication does not quite receive. A man's person and his "sense of himself" are disposable assets, provided he chooses to see them that way; sin is only possible when we involve others. Thus, Arthur Miller's John Proctor was a modern man when, after lying about his relations with the Devil, he said, "God in heaven, what is John Proctor, what is John Proctor? I think it is honest, I think so. I am no saint." It is doubtful if anyone in the 17th Century could have spoken that way. The real John Proctor surely thought he had an immortal soul, and if he had used the word "honest" at all, it would not have been in the sophisticated way in which Miller had him use it. He might have weakened sufficiently to lie about himself and the Devil, but he would surely not have said it was "honest" to do so or reasoned that it didn't really matter because he was only a speck of dust. He was speaking for the social ethic which is Arthur Miller's—and he resisted just where Miller did, at "informing."—RICHARD ROVERE, "Arthur Miller's Conscience," NR, June 17, 1957, pp. 13–14

Miller's play ⟨*After the Fall*⟩ stands or falls on the authenticity of its moral seriousness, and on its being about "big" issues.

But, unfortunately, Miller chose as the method of his play the garrulous monologue of the psychoanalytic confessional, and falteringly designated the audience as the Great Listener. "The action of the play takes place in the mind and memory of Quentin, a contemporary man." The Everymanish hero (remember Willy Loman) and the timeless, placeless interior setting give the show away: whatever stirring public issues *After the Fall* may confront, they are treated as the furniture of a mind. That places an awful burden on Miller's "Quentin, a contemporary man," who must literally hold the world in his head. To pull that one off, it has to be a very good head, a very interesting and intelligent one. And the head of Miller's hero isn't any of these things. Contemporary man (as Miller represents him) seems stuck in an ungainly project of self-exoneration. Self-exoneration, of course, implies self-exposure; and there is a lot of that in *After the Fall*. Many people are willing to give Miller a good deal of credit for the daring of his self-exposure—as husband, lover, political man, and artist. But self-exposure is commendable in art only when it is of a quality and complexity that allows other people to learn about themselves from it. In this play, Miller's self-exposure is mere self-indulgence.

After the Fall does not present an action, but ideas about action. Its psychological ideas owe more to Franzblau than to Freud. (Quentin's mother wanted him to have beautiful penmanship, to take revenge through her son upon her successful but virtually illiterate businessman husband.) As for its political ideas, where politics has not yet been softened up by psychiatric charity, Miller still writes on the level of a left-wing newspaper cartoon. To pass muster at all, Quentin's young German girl friend—this in the mid-1950s—has to turn out to have been a courier for the 20th of July officers' plot; "they were all hanged." Quentin's political bravery is demonstrated by his triumphantly interrupting the harangue of the chairman of the House Committee on Un-American Activities to ask, "How many Negroes do you allow to vote in your patriotic district?" This intellectual weak-mindedness of *After the Fall* leads, as it always does, to moral dishonesty. *After the Fall* claims to be nothing less than modern man taking inventory of his humanity—asking where he is guilty, where innocent, where responsible. What I find objectionable is not the peculiar conjunction of issues, apparently the exemplary issues of the mid-20th century (Communism, Marilyn Monroe, the Nazi extermination camps), which Quentin, this writer *manqué* pretending throughout the play to be a lawyer, has recapitulated in his own person. I object to the fact that in *After the Fall* all these issues are on the same level—not unexpectedly, since they are all in the mind of Quentin. The shapely corpse of Maggie-Marilyn Monroe sprawls on the stage throughout long stretches of the play in which she has no part. In the same spirit a raggedy oblong made of plaster and barbed wire—it represents the concentration camps, I hasten to explain—remains suspended high at the back of the stage, occasionally lit by a spot when Quentin's monologue swings back to Nazis, etc. *After the Fall*'s quasi-psychiatric approach to guilt and responsibility elevates personal tragedies, and demeans public ones—to the same dead level. Somehow—staggering impertinence!—it all seems pretty much the same: whether Quentin is responsible for the deterioration and suicide of Maggie, and whether he (modern man) is responsible for the unimaginable atrocities of the concentration camps.

Putting the story inside Quentin's head has, in effect, allowed Miller to short-circuit any serious exploration of his material, though he obviously thought this device would "deepen" his story. Real events become the ornaments and intermittent fevers of consciousness. The play is peculiarly loose-jointed, repetitive, indirect. The "scenes" go on and off—jumping back and forth, to and from Quentin's first marriage, his second marriage (to Maggie), his indecisive courtship of his German wife-to-be, his childhood, the quarrels of his hysterical, oppressive parents, his agonizing decision to defend an ex-Communist law-school teacher and friend against a friend who has "named names." All "scenes" are fragments, pushed out of Quentin's mind when they become too painful. Only deaths, inevitably offstage, seem to move Quentin's life along: the Jews (the word "Jews" is never mentioned) died long ago; his mother dies; Maggie kills herself with an overdose of barbiturates; the law professor throws himself under a subway train. Throughout the play, Quentin seems much more a sufferer than an active agent in his own life—yet this is precisely what Miller never acknowledges, never lets Quentin see as his problem. Instead, he continually exonerates Quentin (and, by implication, the audience) in the most conventional way. For all troubling decisions, and all excruciating memories, Miller issues Quentin the same moral solvent, the same consolation. I (we) am (are) *both* guilty and innocent, both responsible and not responsible. Maggie was right when she denounced Quentin as cold and unforgiving; but Quentin was justified in giving up on the insatiable, deranged, self-destructive Maggie. The professor who refused to "name names" before the House Un-American Activities Committee was right; but the colleague who did testify cooperatively had a certain nobility, too. And (choicest of all), as Quentin realizes while touring Dachau with his Good German girl friend, any one of us could have been a victim there; but we could as well have been one of the murderers, too.

⟨. . .⟩ But perhaps the most appalling combination of reality and play lies in the fact that *After the Fall* is directed by Elia Kazan, well known to be the model for the colleague who named names before the Committee. As I recalled the story of the turbulent relations between Miller and Kazan, I felt the same queasiness as when I first saw *Sunset Boulevard*, with its dizzying parody of and daring references to the real career and former relationships of Gloria Swanson, the old movie queen making a comeback, and Erich Von Stroheim, the forgotten great director. Whatever bravery *After the Fall* possesses is neither intellectual nor moral; it is the bravery of a species of personal perversity. But it is far inferior to *Sunset Boulevard*: it does not acknowledge its morbidity, its qualities of personal exorcism. *After the Fall* insists, as it were, to the bitter end, on being serious, on dealing with big social and moral themes; and as such, it must be judged sadly wanting, in both intelligence and moral honesty.—SUSAN SONTAG, "Going to Theater, etc." (1964), *Against Interpretation*, 1966, pp. 140–44

After the Fall (1964) is unprecedented in dramatic literature as a personal confessional monologue which is its own subject, framework and form. It is the drama of a dramatist, the dramatization of the creative process of play-writing with the artist explaining what and why he must, here and now, write out of his system, and why; it is the only way he can find himself and make a fresh start. Both his identities are present: the old one which had wandered away in the maze of his fate and the new one which is at long last ready to clarify his position with painful lucidity. In the end, strengthened by all the learning experiences, a newly-born third identity of the writer leaves the stage.

The play is a kind of intellectual striptease. It is ruthless, very nearly exhibitionistic, in its sincerity and its attempts to

penetrate into the depths of hidden causes through persistent questioning. Quentin would like to know to what extent he is responsible for what has happened. Two broken marriages; two women who succeed in accusing him of the same charges; it is justifiable to pose this question in contemplating the responsibility of a third. Yet Maggie had taken her own life and he had not prevented it. It was through selfishness that he continued to live. He is compelled to give an account of his childhood: he is responsible to his parents, even to the girl with whom he was involved in a fleeting affair. He could not even save his best friend. He is unable to work, he cannot find peace. And, culminating this quasi-cosmic sense of responsibility, his new love, a European woman, inadvertently reminds him that he is a Jew and as such is also responsible for the most hideous tragedy in history, a tragedy which could not be forestalled by the united military strength of the Allied powers. "Nobody is innocent who is still alive!"

All this is presented by means of formal and creative techniques, first applied in *Death of a Salesman*, which follow the inner logic of self-examination unbound by time or spatial requirements. In *Death of a Salesman* the superposition of the past on the present was designed to project Willy Loman's painfully primitive reasoning and self-deception; in *After the Fall* we meet a creative intellectual, morally, socially and psychologically sensitive to the extreme; we witness the inner twistings and turnings of an intelligent mind guided by the artist personally. The fact that almost the entire play remains on an exclusively personal level of self-confession (although movingly authentic) is not a dramatic miscarriage but intentionally meant to be no more. Who better has the right to a public self-examination than a world famous playwright who has for years been in the spotlight both in his own right and that of his movie star wife? And what other way is there to free the dramatist from his spiritual demons other than by a public exorcism? Miller, who had always jealously separated the personal motives of his life from his work, could not undertake the almost impossible task of objectivizing purely personal raw material: so he used the most personal form to give vent to all that was in him.—MIKLÓS VAJDA, "Arthur Miller—Moralist as Playwright," *NHQ*, Summer 1975, pp. 176–77

DAVID LEVIN

From "Salem Witchcraft in Recent Fiction and Drama"

New England Quarterly, December 1955, pp. 537–42

In the last six years American publishers have issued one history, an anthology of trial documents, two novels, and two plays about the Salem witchcraft trials. The subject is especially interesting today because of a few parallels to McCarthyism and because of our interest in abnormal psychology, which has drawn some writers to study the adolescent girls whose fits and accusations led twenty people to the gallows. Since the Salem episode has become a symbol of the bigot's tyranny—a symbol so completely accepted that a prominent Washington correspondent of the New York *Times* and a comic-strip writer for the San Francisco *Chronicle* can both refer, without being corrected, to the witches whom Cotton Mather burned in Salem—the four recent novels and plays raise some interesting questions about the aims and techniques of historical fiction and drama. ⟨. . .⟩

The subject, of course, is adaptable to the stage, and Arthur Miller has taken advantage of its dramatic opportunities. One could transcribe verbatim the examination of any of a dozen defendants, and if played with moderate skill the scene would amuse, anger, and terrify an audience. The magistrates' persistent cross-examination, the afflicted girls' screams and fits (which Mr. Miller certainly underplays), the defendant's helplessness in the face of what seems to us a ludicrously closed logical system (*Examiner:* Why do you hurt these girls? *Defendant:* I don't. *Judge:* If you don't, who does?), the appearance of her "specter" on the beam or in the magistrate's lap at the very time when she is declaring her innocence, her evasive answers, her contradictions, and her collapse into confession—these are almost unbearable to watch.

The Crucible dramatizes brilliantly the dilemma of an innocent man who must confess falsely if he wants to live and who finally gains the courage to insist on his innocence—and hang. To increase the impact of this final choice, Mr. Miller has filled his play with ironies. John Proctor, the fated hero, has been guilty of adultery but is too proud to confess or entirely to repent. In order to save his wife from execution by showing that her leading accuser is "a whore," he has at last brought himself to confess his adultery before the Deputy-Governor of Massachusetts Bay; but his wife, who "has never told a lie" and who has punished him severely for his infidelity, now lies to protect his name. Denying that he had been unfaithful, she convinces the court that he has lied to save her life. In the end, Proctor, reconciled with his wife and determined to live, can have his freedom if he will confess to witchcraft, a crime he has not committed.

This battery of ironies is directed against the basic objective of the play: absolute morality. In the twentieth century as well as the seventeenth, Mr. Miller insists in his preface, this construction of human pride makes devils of the opponents of orthodoxy and destroys individual freedom. Using the Salem episode to show that it also blinds people to truth, he has his characters turn the truth upside down. At the beginning of the play, the Reverend John Hale announces fatuously that he can distinguish precisely between diabolical and merely sinful actions; in the last act the remorseful Hale is trying desperately to persuade innocent convicts to confess falsely in order to avoid execution. The orthodox court, moreover, will not believe that Abigail Williams, who has falsely confessed to witchcraft, falsely denied adultery, and falsely cried out upon "witches," is "a whore"; but it is convinced that Proctor, who has told the truth about both his adultery and his innocence of witchcraft, is a witch.

What Mr. Miller considers the essential nature of the episode appears quite clearly in his play. The helplessness of an innocent defendant, the court's insistence on leaping to dubious conclusions, the jeopardy of any ordinary person who presumes to question the court's methods, the heroism of a defendant who cleaves to truth at the cost of his life, the ease with which vengeful motives can be served by a government's attempt to fight the Devil, and the disastrous aid which a self-serving confession gives injustice by encouraging the court's belief in the genuineness of the conspiracy—all this makes the play almost oppressively instructive, especially when one is watching rather than reading it. When one remembers the "invisible" nature of the crimes charged, the use of confessed conspirators against defendants who refuse to confess, the punishment of those only who insist on their innocence, then the analogy to McCarthyism seems quite valid.

But Mr. Miller's pedagogical intention leads him into historical and, I believe, aesthetic error. Representative of the historical distortion is his decision to have the Deputy-Governor declare the court in session in a waiting room in order to force a petitioner to implicate an innocent man or be held in contempt of court. Obviously suggested by the techniques of Senator McCarthy, this action is unfair to the

Puritan Judge. And it is only the least of a number of such libels. In the Salem of 1692 there were indictments and juries; in *The Crucible* there are none. Mr. Miller's audience sees in detail the small mind and grandiose vanity of Samuel Parris, the selfish motives of the afflicted girls, the greed of Thomas Putnam; but it does not learn that a doubtful judge left the court after the first verdict, that there was a recess of nearly three weeks during which the government anxiously sought procedural advice from the colony's leading ministers, or that the ministers' "Return," though equivocal, hit squarely on the very logical fallacies in the court's procedure which *The Crucible* so clearly reveals. In 1692 there was a three-month delay between the first accusations and the first trial. Each defendant was examined first, later indicted, and then tried. In *The Crucible* the first "witch" is condemned to death just eight days after the first accusations, when only fourteen people are in jail. Whatever its eventual justice, a government which adheres to trial by jury and delays three months while 150 people are in jail is quite different from a government which allows four judges to condemn a woman to death within a week of her accusation.

Since Mr. Miller calls his play an attack on black-or-white thinking, it is unfortunate that the play itself aligns a group of heroes against a group of villains. In his "Note on Historical Accuracy," Mr. Miller remarks scrupulously that he has changed the age of Abigail Williams from eleven to seventeen in order to make her eligible for adultery. But this apparently minor change alters the entire historical situation. For Mr. Miller's Abigail is a vicious wench who not only exploits her chance to supplant Elizabeth Proctor when the time comes, nor only maintains a tyrannical discipline among the afflicted girls, but also sets the entire cycle of accusations in motion for selfish reasons. Although Mr. Miller's preface to the book suggests other psychological and historical reasons for the "delusion" and even admits that there were some witches in Salem Village, his portrayal of Parris, Abigail, and the Putnams tells his theater audience that a vain minister, a vicious girl, and an arrogant landgrabber deliberately encouraged judicial murder and that a declining "theocracy" supported the scheme in order to remain in power. One might fairly infer from the play itself that if Abigail had never lain with Proctor nobody would have been executed.

There can be no doubt that "vengeance" was, as Mr. Miller's Proctor says, "walking Salem," but it is equally certain that many honest people were confused and terrified. Underplaying this kind of evidence, Mr. Miller consistently develops historically documented selfish motives and logical errors to grotesque extremes. Every character who confesses in *The Crucible* does so only to save his skin. Every accuser is motivated by envy or vengeance, or is prompted by some other selfishly motivated person. And the sole example of ordinary trial procedure is an examination in which the judges condemn a woman because they regard her inability to recite her commandments as "hard proof" of her guilt.

The skeptical defendant's plight is naturally moving, but making the "witch-hunters" convincing is not so simple a task. Mr. Miller fails to do them justice, and this failure not only violates the "essential nature" of the episode but also weakens the impact of his lesson on the audience. The witch-hunters of *The Crucible* are so foolish, their logic so extremely burlesqued, their motives so badly temporal, that one may easily underestimate the terrible implications of their mistakes. Stupid or vicious men's errors can be appalling; but the lesson would be even more appalling if one realized that intelligent men, who tried to be fair and saw the dangers in some of their methods, reached the same conclusions and enforced the same penalties.

The central fault is Mr. Miller's failure to present an intelligent minister who recognizes at once the obvious questions which troubled real Puritan ministers from the time the court was appointed. Cocksure in the first act and morally befuddled in the last, Mr. Miller's John Hale is in both these attitudes a sorry representative of the Puritan ministry. "Specter evidence," the major issue of 1692, is neither mentioned nor debated in *The Crucible*. Preferring to use Hale as a caricature of orthodoxy in his first act, Mr. Miller does not answer the question which a dramatist might devote his skills to answering: What made a minister who saw the dangers, who wanted to protect the innocent and convict the guilty, side with the court?

Even though the dramatist must oversimplify history, the fact that dramatic exposition may be tedious does not excuse *The Crucible's* inadequacies; Mr. Miller finds plenty of time for exposition in the first act and in the later speeches of Hale and the Deputy-Governor. The fault lies in Mr. Miller's understanding of the period; its consequences damage his play as "essential" history, as moral instruction, and as art.

HENRY POPKIN
"Arthur Miller: The Strange Encounter"
Sewanee Review, Winter 1960, pp. 34–60

Arthur Miller's regular practice in his plays is to confront the dead level of banality with the heights and depths of guilt and to draw from this strange encounter a liberal parable of hidden evil and social responsibility. Each of his mature full-length plays (*All My Sons, Death of a Salesman, The Crucible,* and *A View from the Bridge*) exhibits the same basic pattern; each one matches ordinary, uncomprehending people with extraordinary demands and accusations. The characters are like the man in the old Jewish story who asks the price of bacon and then shudders at the sound of thunder out of the heavens; he protests meekly that he was only asking the price. Thunder sounds abruptly for Miller's people, too. From day to day they live their placid, apparently meaningless lives, and suddenly the eternal intrudes, thunder sounds, the trumpet blows, and these startled mediocrities are whisked off to the bar of justice. In the midst of banality, guilt appears: "You killed twenty-one fliers. You lived your life by false standards. You betrayed your wife and thereby caused her to be charged with witchcraft. You have condemned a family to starve." The little man protests: "What is the cosmos doing in my tacky living room? Must I decide the fate of the world? Am I my brother's keeper?" The crime is betrayal, the verdict is guilty, and the sentence is death. Punishment is imposed, directly or indirectly, by the victim himself. In Miller's first Broadway play, *The Man Who Had All the Luck*, betrayal and guilt are present, but retribution is nowhere to be found. The chief character spends most of his time feverishly searching for it. Miller's novel, *Focus*, has two crimes—being anti-Semitic and being Jewish; the chief character atones for the first by confessing to the second, of which he is not guilty.

At the center of each play is the tension between little people and big issues, and each play confirms our belief that little people cannot live up to big standards. Miller always goes to some pains to make his people sufficiently small. The banality is deliberate and dramatically effective; it belongs to the characters and not to Miller himself. His best-known hero, Willy Loman of *Death of a Salesman*, is even labelled a little man by his name: he is society's low man. Ideally, the little man are stripped of concreteness, intelligence, and literacy. If farmer John Proctor of *The Crucible* seems to be a superior human specimen, he is benefiting from the enchantment lent by a distance of three centuries. Joe Keller of *All My Sons* is a manufacturer, but a special point is made of his ignorance, so much so that we may doubt even the presence of the crude intelligence that made him a success in the first place. He wonders at his son's interest in the Sunday book section, asks if books come out every week, "brooches" subjects, and amiably parades his illiteracy. Willy Loman, the archetypal salesman, and Eddie Carbone, the longshoreman of *A View from the Bridge*, are equally inarticulate; disaster renders them speechless. Their plain talk is matched by their plain appearance. Most of the men and woman of Miller's plays are not beautiful, nor have they ever been. To name the actors who created the roles is to read the catalogue of honest careworn plainness: Lee J. Cobb, Ed Begley, Mildred Dunnock, J. Carroll Naish, Eileen Heckart. Even the younger leading men tend to be rugged and weatherbeaten: Arthur Kennedy, Van Heflin. To be exceptional is more dangerous than to be honestly homely: Happy, in *Death of a Salesman*, is, like Narcissus, seduced by his own beauty, and Rodolpho, in *A View from the Bridge*, is inevitably a victim of jealousy. If Abigail, of *The Crucible*, is "strikingly beautiful," she is also the devil incarnate.

In their language, their culture, their incapacity for comprehending their fates, these people may well possess as little imagination as any characters ever brought on the stage. By way of contrast, Odets gives his characters colorful language, and some of them have cultural aspirations. Even Hauptmann's proletarians aspire to change their lives, and Gorki's derelicts at least have interesting vices. But Miller's people inhabit the dead center of dullness as they sit and wait for the voice of doom. Or if they don't sit, they go about the daily round of their lives—washing cars, eating late snacks, playing football, picking up girls, going to movies, as if destiny would never come calling. And incidentally, we may wonder how unspeakably banal their whole lives would be if it were not for that timely trump of doom. In the shadow of crisis, they reminisce about the past, when life was happier without being essentially different. *All My Sons* contains some happy recollection of the prewar past suitably summarized by the play's heroine: "Gosh, those dear dead days beyond recall." (Much of *Death of a Salesman* is devoted to recreating the happy past, when Willy's sales were bigger, when Biff stole footballs instead of suits, when trees grew in the Lomans' section of Brooklyn.) Miller's short play, *A Memory of Two Mondays*, is an extended reminiscence of an uneventful past in which life is colored by a vague, unexpressed good fellowship and crises occur only in the lives of others. Miller has described it as "a kind of letter to that sub-culture where the sinews of the economy are rooted, that darkest Africa of our society." He adds that it conveys "the need for a little poetry in life." But *Memory of Two Mondays* is no more prosaic or sub-cultural than the other plays. True, one character points up the sub-culture by reading *War and Peace*, but the real difference is in the atmosphere of friendliness unspoiled by pressures from outside. Hitler is just a name in the newspaper, Roosevelt inspires hope as well as hostility, and, best of all, no one is capable of malice or of zeal for personal success.

Except for the boy who reads Tolstoy, none of Miller's characters, not even a "good" one, is capable of the sort of cultural reference that used to dot Odets' plays of middle-class life; Marx, Rouault, Verdi are names all equally unknown here. The only significant objectives are to earn a living and to kill time between working hours. The need to kill time may inspire some gala celebrations which are rather telling in their flatness. Willy Loman's wife tells him his sons are "gonna blow him to a big meal." This phrase is so catchy that she says it twice. Of course, going out for a big meal is also Joe Keller's idea of a bacchanalian revel. But the favorite activity is sitting home and putting strains on the family tie. Son accuses father, uncle desires niece—but they have little identity *beyond* the family tie.

The families of *All My Sons* and *Death of a Salesman* do not belong to any discernible ethnic group. They are deliberately made the washed out, colorless representatives of society in general. Miller himself was apparently endeavoring to assert the nonsectarian universality of *Death of a Salesman* in his remarks to the press when Thomas Mitchell succeeded Lee J. Cobb in the role of Willy Loman. Finding himself impressed with Mitchell's performance, Miller remarked that he did not realize he had written a play about an Irish family. Did he think he had written a family with any kind of ethnic identification? Ostensibly, not at all. Still, in an ingenious *Commentary* article of a few years ago, George Ross made a good case for the underlying Jewish elements in *Death of a Salesman*. One recognizes a possibly Jewish problem in the anger of the father whose authority is threatened and in the exaggerated Americanism that might logically belong to a second-generation family. Joe Keller has a son named Chris; that seems to de-Semitize the rather similar family in *All My Sons*. And yet, in Miller's earliest plays (extant but unpublished and never professionally produced), the families which encounter comparable problems are frankly Jewish. Miller's first Broadway play, *The Man Who Had All the Luck*, is transitional in this respect. It has an all-American setting, a small midwestern town, but in the published version (in *Cross-Section 1944*) the hero is named David Frieber. By the time the play was produced, he had become the brother of another character and had thus acquired the name of Beeves. In the novel *Focus*, published the following year, an anti-Semite gets accustomed to being taken for a Jew and finally identifies himself with the Jews. The character bears a suitably ambiguous name, Newman—as ambiguous as Miller's. Like Laura Hobson's *Gentleman's Agreement* (published soon after), *Focus* carries an odd implication—that Jewish identity is external, that it can be put on at will, that all that is essential to it exists only in the eye of the beholder. On the dust-wrapper, Miller seems to be playing his character's game in reverse; here he is quoted as telling how he was taken for "an Italian, a Pole, an Irishman," even a Jew. This account is in keeping with the implications of the novel and the plays: *anyone* is in danger of being taken for a Jew. True, the novel has a Jewish shopkeeper named Finkelstein, but, when ethnic identification is applied to *you* (Miller, Newman, Keller, Loman), it is a curious error. *You* don't belong to any group except the amorphous majority, and that makes *your* problem universal. But, as the characterizations in *Focus*, *All My Sons*, and *Death of a Salesman* reach for universality, they run the risk of being so general that they are, in some respects, nebulous.

Keller and Loman are made as general as possible so that they may play the role of Everyman in their dramatic parables. Eddie Carbone, of *A View from the Bridge*, is at least a cousin of Everyman; he is an Italo-American longshoreman, and his ancestry is significantly Sicilian. The Greek associations of Sicily encourage Miller to call the play a tragedy and even to employ a chorus. Also Eddie Carbone speaks verse of a sort; Eric Bentley wrote that when the printed version revealed "that a lot of dialogue was in verse, you could have knocked me over with a feather." Miller retreated to prose when *A View from the*

Bridge reappeared in the *Collected Plays*. But he had written in his preface to the earlier text: "Verse reaches always toward the general statement . . . it is the most public of public speech." He found a corresponding wideness of reference in the kind of play he was writing, "social drama," a genre which he takes to include Greek tragedy: "To put it simply, even oversimply, a drama rises in stature and intensity in proportion to the weight of its application to all men." In this play, as in his other serious dramas, Miller had written a parable which was intended to apply to everyone. Joe Keller is every man facing a responsibility to his nation in wartime. Willy Loman is every low man in our economic order. *The Crucible*, written at a time when many spoke of witch hunts directed against political heresy, was obviously designed to display a political parallel to our time in the Salem witch trials. And *A View from the Bridge* is Greek, poetic, and therefore all the more public in its object lesson on the folly of betrayal. The plays are dramatic parables or fables; their characters are as typical as the prodigal son or Aesop's lambs and wolves. They are as unattached and as nonsectarian as the medieval Everyman, and that is why they cannot be individuals.

But where ethnic associations may be vague, the characters' occupations are loaded with symbolic usefulness. Joe Keller must be engaged in war work, and it must be possible for his son in the air force to make use of the products he manufactures; the son's suicide is a public acknowledgment of guilt. There can be no more suitable emblem of our commercial society than the salesman Willy Loman, especially since we are never told what he sells. In a sense, he sells himself, but the product wears out. The waterfront is a suitable setting for *A View from the Bridge* because it had recently been the scene of a film in which Elia Kazan had apparently justified betrayal, in certain circumstances; with the evident intention of replying to Kazan, Miller returned to the waterfront.

Whatever else these plays may be, then, they are instructive. They argue cases; they prove points. Each play is constructed to expose a pattern of guilt, to find out who is guilty and to impose the penalty of death. The plot drives us from one to another of the devastating points which the prosecutor-dramatist makes against his characters. The purpose of *All My Sons* was, according to Miller, "to bring a man into the direct path of the consequences he had wrought." Up to the time of the play's action, Joe Keller has avoided consequences by avoiding the discovery of his guilt. By the end of the second act, his guilt is established with the help of a clue that any respectable mystery writer would be ashamed to use. Keller had pretended illness on the day his company approved some cracked cylinder heads for the air force. He gives himself away by inadvertently referring to his unfailing good health. The case is nearly complete, but Keller still refuses to take personal responsibility. In the last act, his son produces a letter—what is so telling as documentary evidence?—in which another son reveals that he committed suicide because of his father's misdeeds. Keller quits arguing and shoots himself, just in time to prevent his son from turning him over to the authorities. The case is, as they say in the law courts, proven, and it is as airtight a case as any stage detective could hope for. But like all the proofs offered by stage detectives, it proves a *fact*. Miller's goal is to demonstrate an *idea*, but his method is too rigid for exposition; it is suitable only to proof, and that implies simplicity on the part of the idea, the characters, or the author. The idea in *All My Sons* is the most elementary conception of social responsibility; as for the characters, Miller has informed us that he knows "how rarely the great issues penetrate such environments." Two simplicities collide—the idea and the man—and we recognize that on this dramatic railroad, Miller has constructed only one track.

Death of a Salesman is a play of a looser sort but is also to a degree constructed as a investigation—a word which, by the way, Miller applies particularly to *The Man Who Had All the Luck*. Willy Loman hunts the secret of his failure; he wants to know the right path. His mistake is that there is no right path; there is, however, a wrong path, and Willy has travelled on it for most of his life. He asks his brother Ben and his neighbor Charley for the secret; they can not tell him, and he cannot guess that it does not exist. He stumbles upon telltale clues and significant discoveries, but he manages to ignore most of them. It is his son Biff who plays detective more successfully. Present events make Biff see his lies about the past; he perceives the hollowness of the dream of success from the start. The real hostage of success, Willy Loman, remains unaltered. But once more, the terms of the courtroom apply to this play. Willy's offences against his wife, against his sons, against society are exposed so that sentence can be passed. Miller himself describes Willy as a man who "has broken a law" in which he deeply believes. This time, however, it is the play's purpose to show that the law requiring success is not or should not be valid.

The Crucible, too, turns upon a law which we should not respect: "Thou shalt not permit a witch to live." It takes the form of an investigation, for it begins with the arrival of the great investigator of witches. Our pursuit of the facts takes us over two paths; while the witch-hunters make their efforts to measure the extent of witchcraft in the community, we follow John Proctor's attempt to weigh the guilt in his infidelity to his wife. The question of Proctor's guilt peters out since his guilt is nothing beside the community's. The issues are made a good deal simpler than those of the earlier plays. In our eyes, the community condemns itself, totally and without qualification, as it builds its airtight case against John Proctor. Contrasting his crime with the court's, the defendant justifiably thinks better of himself: "Now I do think I see some shred of goodness in John Proctor."

The play sustains considerable dramatic interest as the witch-hunters descend upon the Proctors, but it surely falls short in the realm of ideas—and especially by pressing so hard to make a particular judgment prevail. The actions of the witch-hunters are evidently to be attributed to the invincible evil of their characters. Notes to the printed version qualify this interpretation by strengthening the hints that these villains are motivated by greed, but Miller himself states that he did too much to mitigate the evil of the judge. At the same time, we require Proctor to be a model of good. Since we regard his adultery as a sin against his wife alone, he expiates it easily enough by sacrificing his life for hers. But Miller unintentionally reminds us how hard he is working to set up this adequate expiation for Proctor. Only Proctor and his wife are taken seriously. Abigail, who corrupted Proctor and now accuses his wife of witchcraft, could have been no more than seventeen when Proctor was her lover. She tells him he "put knowledge in her heart," and she continues to protest her love to him. But she is totally vile, she seduced him, he feels no obligation toward her, and evidently we are to regard her becoming a prostitute as a fitting result of her total depravity. Surely she needs more careful attention, and so does Proctor's responsibility toward her. Something is seriously at fault here. Miller no doubt began with the intention of creating an ulterior motive for the charges of witchcraft and also with the purpose of giving Proctor a less than mortal sin to expiate. But, giving his closest attention only to Proctor and to the main issue of the play, he lost sight of Abigail as a participant in a human relationship.

A View from the Bridge also has at its core the proving of a case. Eddie Carbone desperately endeavors to conceal from himself and from the world his incestuous passion for his niece. He bitterly resents Rodolpho, the young man she favors, but he feels obliged to make his hatred publicly acceptable by proving Rodolpho to be a homosexual. He seizes Rodolpho and kisses him, then goes to a lawyer to offer this incident as proof that "the guy ain't right." Ultimately, Eddie uses the assumption of homosexuality and opportunism to justify him in turning Rodolpho and his brother in to the immigration authorities. To his death, he continues to plead his case, protesting the pure motives behind his treacherous action. But, obviously, we must conclude that informers, like the accusers of witches, must themselves be brought to judgment and that a verdict must be returned against them. Miller is more compassionate toward this informer, who is proved to be merely sick and not, like Abigail in *The Crucible*, totally depraved.

Each of the full-length plays, then, argues a case in public; structure and content are determined by rules of evidence appropriate to the theater. The characters themselves remind us that the case is fought in open court and not in the judge's chambers. Each protagonist fights for his good name, for the respect of his community, for a public verdict that will exonerate him. If Joe Keller, of *All My Sons*, fights the idea that he owes anything to society, he is won over by his sons. One has killed himself because he joins in the public condemnation which his father has ignored. The other son lives by his star, "the star of one's honesty"—a fitting symbol for the character the world attributes to him. Joe recognizes, as his sons have done, that he cannot live for his family alone, that he and his family belongs to the world, and therefore he commits suicide because he cannot live without his good name.

Willy Loman also plays to an audience; he is a salesman who is required to be approved, to be well liked. His life, however, suggests the public role he really plays:

> His name was never in the paper. He's not the finest character that ever lived. But he's a human being, and a terrible thing is happening to him. So attention must be paid. He's not to be allowed to fall into his grave like an old dog.

As the drama progresses, Willy's faltering claim on the respect and affection of others is matched by his new role as a horrible example, a public instance of the man for whom society has no further use.

John Proctor and Eddie Carbone die for their good name and make no bones about it. Proctor refuses to put his name to the lies he has told to save his life. He will lie privately, but he will die rather than compromise his public integrity: "How may I live without a name? I have given you my soul; leave me my name!" In a much worse cause, Eddie Carbone demands his good name from the man he has ruined: "I want my name! . . . Marco's got my name—and you can run and tell him, kid, that he's gonna give it back to me in front of this neighborhood, or we have it out." These are no private dramas; each frustrated, ruined hero compels attention, demands that some meaning be found in his catastrophe. Rightly or wrongly, he wants respect for his good name, even in defeat. For Eddie Carbone, it should be added that, although the action of the play indicates a self-created disaster, Eddie's wife tried to mitigate his guilt: "Whatever happened we all done it." This is no more than a plea for pity; it's too bad about Eddie, but, like Willy Loman, he has to be held responsible for what he does. And yet responsibility is somehow divided, not just in the sense that "we all done it." Guilt lies finally at the door of a more selective group of culprits, the secret rulers who exercise authority among us.

Whatever personal contribution Miller's heroes may make to their misfortunes, the main burden of guilt is usually borne by the dominant forces in their society. Miller begins by indicting parents. The revolt of a son against a father is at the center of both *All My Sons* and *Death of a Salesman*; in each play, a son painfully discovers his father's weakness and dishonesty. In his lecture before the New Dramatists Committee, "The Shadow of the Gods" (*Harper's Magazine*, August 1958), Miller identifies this conflict with parental authority as the starting point of lives as individuals:

> Be it Tolstoy, Dostoevski, Hemingway, you, or I, we are formed in this world when we are sons and daughters and the first truths we know throw us into conflict with our fathers and mothers.

But he speaks also of the need to discover that "the parent, powerful as he appears, is not the source of injustice but its deputy," and to extend dramatic conflict to "that realm where the father is after all the not final authority . . . when we see beyond parents, who are, after all, but the shadows of the gods." Above and beyond the parents are the "hidden forces" against which the ultimate accusations must be directed. The sinister hidden forces palpably contribute to the weakness of the corrupt parents in the early plays; they are present in the callous business world which creates the ideology of Joe Keller and Willy Loman. In *The Crucible*, the hidden, evil forces are visible in the courts; in *A View from the Bridge*, they manifest themselves in the heartless immigration authorities and in Eddie's desperate passion for his niece. Invariably, a large share of the blame falls upon the people in power, father's surrogates. Authority, the government, the courts, the community's official values all conspire to crush Miller's lonely, hapless tragic hero.

But if Miller's hero is lonely, he is still not altogether alone. Good as well as evil has hidden forces on its side. In *All My Sons*, the cynicism at the top is being publicly challenged by the united devotion of a nation at war, but, in the other plays, the forces of good form a sort of secret underground, a real community whose values are worth sharing. The good which this decent underground embodies is deep and instinctive; it rarely finds any verbal expression. In fact, if we do not look sharply, we may not find the hidden forces of good at all. The good people have no theories, no ideologies, except for their goodness. Their practice and their faith are the same—doing good. Their virtue needs no legal or official sanction, and, in practice, it may defy the official world.

The good society is present in the neighbors of whom we often hear in *All My Sons*. They help out when they are needed—"the day you were born and the water got shut off. People were carrying basins from a block away—a stranger would have thought the whole neighborhood was on fire!" But they also express their collective disapproval of the man who manufactured faulty equipment for the air corps—even when the courts exonerate him. We see this society more plainly in *Death of a Salesman* in the form of those inveterate good neighbors, Charley and his son Bernard. They are inexplicably—that is to say, naturally—plain, honest, and kind. Charley prospers in business without being hoodwinked by the ideology of salesmanship. Bernard wins glory by pleading before the Supreme Court, but he does this without any pushing from his father. Willy marvels, "You never took any

interest in him," and Charley tells him, "My salvation is that I never took any interest in anything." How do they get this way? How do they manage to be so decent and so happy? Apparently they do it by following the natural bent of their virtue, by not listening to the voices of greed, of selfishness, of private ambition. When necessary, they break the rules to do good. Bernard helps Willy's son Biff to cheat on his exams. As he later admits to Willy, he loved Biff, although Biff always took advantage of him. Charley aids in another deceit; when Willy is put on straight commission, Charley gives him fifty dollars each week so that Willy can pretend to his wife to be earning money. The purity of these good deeds is further indicated by Willy's failure ever to say even a moderately friendly word to Charley. Obviously, good deeds are not to be explained or to be measured by simpleton standards of law, honesty, or reciprocation. In the authorities defied here—the teachers who give exams to Biff, the company which withholds a salary from Willy—we have a foretaste of the wicked authority which governs Salem in *The Crucible* and the hard-hearted bureau of immigration in *A View from the Bridge*. Defying such authority is a prerequisite for a clear conscience.

The Crucible, too, has its kernel of good people who oppose the witch trials but become the victims of the courts. They are paragons of virtue. Even the visiting investigator of witches remarks, of the most improbable defendant: "If Rebecca Nurse be tainted, then nothing's left to stop the whole green world from burning." No merely personal resentment could turn their accusers against them; the principal motive is greed. The parson wants gold candlesticks and better living arrangements; a fellow conspirator grabs other men's lands. If the play itself leaves any doubt on this matter, Miller removes it in his notes. A final note gives us the consoling knowledge that the subterranean good society won out in the next century: "To all intents and purposes, the power of the theocracy in Massachusetts was broken."

The good society is equally strong and silent in *A View from the Bridge*. Informers may be technically obedient to the law, but good people ostracize them. We hear first of a neighbor who betrayed his uncle and was brutally beaten by his family: "You'll never see him no more, a guy do a thing like that? How's he gonna show his face?" This is Eddie Carbone's fate: no neighbor will speak to him, and the cousin whom he has betrayed, the honest and sober Marco, justly kills him.

The line between good and evil, between the good society and the oppressors, is always clearly drawn in Miller's plays. Biff Loman may not perceive the distinction soon enough, and Willy Loman may never see it, but *we* are never permitted any doubts. Miller's bold certainty is best illustrated by his comments on *The Crucible*. Charged with making his witchhunters too wicked, Miller replied that he did not make them wicked enough: "I believe now, as I did not conceive then, that there are people dedicated to evil in the world. . . . Evil is not a mistake but a fact in itself." Like the young man in Shaw's *Major Barbara*, Miller is sure he knows "the difference between right and wrong," and he permits his heroes—Chris Keller, Biff Loman, and John Proctor—to stand at last foursquare for righteousness. Even when he adapted Ibsen's *An Enemy of the People*, Miller permitted his hero no shillyshallying as he approached the firm distinctions between right and wrong. The play's Dr. Stockmann is, as Ibsen himself said, "muddle-headed." Leaping rapidly from one attitude to another, he briefly adopts the view that breeding can produce superior individuals. In the next act, he has flown off in the opposite direction and has decided to educate the town's riffraff, and he has thus exhibited his mercurial temperament.

But Miller would not permit him to be quite so mercurial. His free-wheeling cerebration was evidently rather appalling to a dramatist who knows exactly how far "good" characters may stray from the cause of right. Consequently, Miller omits the references to the importance of breeding. Explaining the change in his preface, Miller consistently fails to distinguish between Ibsen and Dr. Stockmann; he considers a "good" character to be a spokesman for the author, with no serious deviation. Apart from his consistent identification of the character with the author, Miller stumbles into some strange self-contradictions. First he assures us that Ibsen did not really believe in the efficacy of breeding: "That Ibsen never really believed that idea in the first place is amply proved." Then he tells us that Ibsen would never have adopted his heresy *in our time*—"In the light of genocide . . . it is inconceivable that Ibsen would insist today" on this odious theory. The implication now seems to be that Ibsen believed in Dr. Stockmann's heresy but would have rejected it in our century because of its sinister associations: "It is impossible, therefore, to set him beside Hitler." And remember, all this is about Ibsen, not Dr. Stockmann. There could be no clearer demonstration of Miller's insistence that a play is a parable of right and wrong, a parable in which no blurring of distinctions is permitted.

Miller's ideas and his technique are best illustrated in his most successful play, *Death of a Salesman*. This play exhibits all the most characteristic traits, in their plainest, most emphatic form. Plainness is achieved because Miller makes a principle out of his usual vagueness. The principle is Expressionism. The vague, typical hero becomes the embodiment of typicality, Willy the low man, who carries his status in his name. His friends Charley and Bernard—the only other family we see—have no last name at all, and neither does Willy's employer. Furthermore, the salesman is, as we have observed, the most representative member of our commercial society; in a sense, when the salesman dies, this society dies. Every strand of evidence, in and out of the play, points to the symbolic reading of the salesman's role. Replying to the many salesmen who thought they saw their own story writ large in the play, Miller has insisted: "I have and had not the slightest interest in the selling profession." The mystery of the salesman's product is preserved for symbolic reasons. Miller tantalizes us with references to stores in Boston and to Willy's eye for color, but, in response to questions, he invariably answered that the product Willy was selling was himself. Preserving the mystery keeps Willy the archetypal salesman of our time.

The details of Willy's origin are equally vague—or universal. Even if we recognize some of the stresses of Jewish family life, what is more highly visible is Miller's determined effort to iron out these specific elements, to make the family Everyfamily or Anyfamily. The Anyfamily quality is reflected in Miller's delight with Thomas Mitchell's Irish Willy Loman, and it is manifest also in his obvious intention of making the Loman family history recapitulate the history of the nation. Willy's father used to set out across the continent from Boston; Willy remembers sitting under a covered wagon in South Dakota while his brother Ben went on to look for their father in Alaska. Somehow, this sounds like an improbable origin for Willy Loman, salesman, of Brooklyn. The point is, I think, that Willy is not the product just of this family but of the adventurous American past. The colorful background helps to make Brooklyn's hapless Willy as commonplace as he is required to be. The shabbiness of Willy's life is made abundantly clear when his colorful brother stops off on his way to the gold fields and asks, "chuckling," "So this is Brooklyn,

eh?" The very presence of the daring entrepreneur is enough to show up the salesman who has been playing it safe all his life.

Willy is much more emphatically a representative figure, an American Everyman, than any of Miller's other characters; accordingly, his problems are much less personal dilemmas than they are public issues. Willy is a useful instrument for Miller's social criticism. This quality of his is the first trait by which we identify this play as an example of Expressionism. Certainly this concern with large social issues is the key to Miller's definition of Expressionism in his Harvard lecture ("The Family in Modern Drama," *Atlantic Monthly*, April 1956): "It is a form . . . which manifestly seeks to dramatize the conflict of either social, religious, or moral forces *per se*." In his most recent article, Miller finds that the Greeks and the Expressionists are alike in their effort "to present the hidden forces."

The hallmarks of Expressionism are its employment of symbolic characters—The Man, the Woman, the Nameless One (all three in Ernst Toller's *Man and the Masses*), Elmer Rice's Mr. Zero, Miller's Loman—and its presentation of dream states in which hidden forces of every variety become plainly visible. It was against the pioneer Expressionist, August Strindberg, that Zola lodged the complaint that he did not know the last names of the characters in *The Father*; the characters of this play are like Miller's Charley and Bernard in this respect, but no one complained about Miller's rootless figures. Perhaps the audience took it for granted that their name was Everyman. Certainly the acquired taste for Expressionism has made headway since the first American experiments in the 1920's. This dramatic *genre* had been in vogue among *avant garde* audiences for half a century before Miller adopted it. What is new is its presence in a popular success of fabulous proportions. If Strindberg won the connoisseur's attention with *The Dream Play*, O'Neill with *The Hairy Ape*, and Elmer Rice with *The Adding Machine*, what popular fame these writers earned rested on other plays. But with *Death of a Salesman*, Expressionism descended, in a slightly watered-down form, to the mass audience.

The Everyman element is obvious enough. To locate the dream-elements of the play also requires no great effort. Willy Loman's dreams occupy half the play; they are the dreams of all the world, the dreams of a happy, hopeful past and the inescapable dream of past guilt. The recollections are not straight flashbacks in the manner of the films, but they are distorted, speeded up, heightened by repetition and selection. The accompanying music and the distinctive lighting of the original production compelled us to set these remembrances apart from objective reality. Further testimony of unreality is to be found in one figure who appears in them but seems to have no existence in the real world—Uncle Ben, the embodiment of the American will to succeed. He is the fantastically rich relative who shuttles between the outposts of imperialism, Alaska and Africa. Long ago, he set out for Alaska to dig gold; he found himself on the way to Africa instead, and so he made his fortune in diamonds. When Willy last sees him, he is heading for Alaska. During the dream sequences, Willy seems unable to tell truth from fantasy, the present from the past. He loses himself in his recollections, interrupting a conversation with his neighbor Charley to address the absent Ben, losing all sense of the present in a men's room while he recalls his past exposure by his son. Willy is sick; his mental breakdown is certified by the hold his recollections have on him and by the great amount of obvious distortion in them. He has symptoms of schizophrenia, but his sickness is not his alone. His identification with Everyman assures us that, as in other

Expressionist plays, we are examining the malady not of an individual but of society.

Willy is drab and average; the surest guarantee of his drabness is in his commitment to the standard ideals, the standard commercial products, and even the standard language. His fidelity to the great American dream of success is at the very heart of the play. He believes in this dream in its simplest, its final form. Years ago, Horatio Alger preached that success was the reward of virtue, while Herbert Spencer and his American disciples preached that it was the reward of strength; Willy's brother Ben would seem to belong to the Spencerian or Social Darwinist school of success through strength. But Willy himself subscribes to a different and later form of the dream; he believes, with Dale Carnegie, that success is the reward of making friends and influencing people—being impressive, being persuasive, being well liked. One becomes successful by being confident, by thinking of success, and therefore success is all Willy knows, all he believes. The cultural heroes whose names are heard in Willy's household are without exception figures from the world of well publicized triumphs. Where Odets dots his dialogue with references to exponents of high art, low art, mass culture, the world of wealth, the world of politics, Miller has only these comparable references—B. F. Goodrich, Edison, Red Grange, and J. P. Morgan (the last of them cited to Willy by his neighbor). Like certain characters in Saul Bellow's recent fiction, Willy feels that successful men possess a secret which could be passed on to him; in vain he asks his brother Ben and his friend Charley to tell him the secret. Ben replies: "William, when I walked into the jungle, I was seventeen. When I walked out I was twenty-one. And, by God, I was rich!" That is to say, the riddle remains a riddle.

Willy Loman's catastrophe is one of the poignant and inevitable misfortunes of our society and our time. The various formulations of the idea of success, whether created by Horatio Alger or Herbert Spencer or Dale Carnegie, have contributed to the state of mind that makes failure a crime. Success is a requirement that Americans make of life. Because it seems magical and inexplicable, as it is to Willy, it can be considered the due of every free citizen, even those with no notable or measurable talents. One citizen is as good as any other, and he cannot be proved to be a natural-born failure any more than he can be stripped of his civil rights. The citizen may justly and perhaps even logically ask—If Edison, Goodrich, and Red Grange can make it, why not me, why not Willy Loman? In effect, this is the question Willy asks his brother Ben. It is unanswerable; the consequent disappointment that Willy feels is one of the great American exasperations. He postpones his anguish by transferring his ambitions to his sons, and so the play's free use of time permits us to observe aspiration and failure in both generations. The problems, the exasperation, and the pathos of this family were sufficiently serious and important to make *Death of a Salesman* a moving play and a spectacular success. As a resourceful and understanding treatment of a critical human problem, this play makes an unmistakable claim upon us. But to examine it as closely as it deserves is to discover that Willy transfers his qualities and his characteristic confusions to the play itself. This is a very subjective play; it seldom takes us outside the ideas, the aspirations, even the vocabulary of the doomed salesman.

Willy's language reflects his resoluteness in the pursuit of success. It is devoid of words for anything but the necessities of life and the ingredients or symbols of success. This world is full of aspirin, arch supports, saccharin (all the wrong cures for what ails Willy), Studebakers, Chevrolets, shaving lotion, refrigerators, silk stockings, washing machines. It is the only play I know that could stock a mail-order catalog. Everything but these commonplace objects is washed out of the characters' speech. In moments of excitement, they do not rise above "Knock him dead, boy," or "I'm gonna knock Howard for a loop," or "Knock 'em dead." In a context like this, phrases like "twist of mockery" or "masterful man" sound poetic, but the true fabric of language here is woven of the most ordinary stuff. Some dubious rhetoric is permitted on the few occasions when it is necessary to point a moral. This function is usually Linda's, but, at Willy's funeral, it comes to be shared by Charley, who speaks a eulogy not for Willy but, with striking appropriateness, for his calling: "A salesman is got to dream, boy. It comes with the territory." Buried under platitudes, Willy is allowed no more individuality in death than he has exhibited in life.

Willy is called to account by the crises of the play. He is weighed, and so are his values. There is some doubt as to just what tale the scales tell. Miller himself has made a recent contribution to this ambiguity. In a symposium on *Death of a Salesman* (in *Tulane Drama Review*, Summer 1958), he replies to a critic who finds Willy "vicious": "The trouble with Willy Loman is that he has tremendously powerful ideals. . . . The fact is he has values." Two pages later, he speaks of his play as "showing what happens when there are no values"; he explains: "I was trying in *Salesman*, in this respect, to set forth what happens when a man does not have a grip on the forces of life and has no sense of values which will lead him to that kind of grip." As the editor of the symposium observed, "Mr. Miller seemed to contradict himself." At least, Miller is very certain that values are involved. Miller himself is hammering out some values in the play, dramatizing them, recommending them to us. He seems to say: what Willy believes in is false, but it is a system of values nevertheless. On the one hand, the whole play is devoted to exposing Willy's errors. On the other hand, Willy has been so consistent and so conscientious in living by his false values that, at his funeral, his neighbor Charley (whom we are expected to take seriously) romanticizes the salesman's calling in the speech beginning: "Nobody dast blame this man." Although the values are real to Willy, they are so false that Miller can tell us in the symposium, right after he has insisted on their existence, that they do not exist. This confusion is abetted by the greater clarity of the rejected values which are embodied in the dream of success. The false dream is fully and vividly sketched; positive values seem rather dim and conventional.

Prominent among the bad values is, as we have seen, the idea of personal success in a competitive society—not only the great American dream but also the great American subject. Miller makes the conventional equation between commercial competition and personal combat. Brother Ben has one lesson for Willy's boy: "Never fight fair with a stranger, boy. You'll never get out of the jungle that way." He illustrates his lesson by tripping Biff and menacing him with his umbrella. This view of our society is common enough in criticisms from the left; it is present in Odets' *Golden Boy*, in which the prizefighter here differs only by combatting his opponents more directly than the rest of us. But Miller's favorite indictment is a variation on Proudhon's "Property is theft." Miller revises this to read "Competition is theft." Biff is the particular exponent here; imbued by his father with the spirit of competition, he steals a football, a carton of basketballs, a suit, and, less deliberately, a fountain pen. The equation between competition and theft is made automatically by a waiter when Happy tells him he and his brother are going into business together: "Great! That's the best for you. Because a family business, you know what I mean?—that's the best . . . 'Cause what's the difference? Somebody steals? It's in the family."

Happy shows his competitiveness in another way. His "over-developed sense of competition" leads him into many sexual adventures. He is thus an authentic product of our competitive system. Stealing enters the picture because Happy shows a special interest in the fiancées of his company's executives; he has seduced three of them. Sex is in itself an evil, a false value, in this play, as it is elsewhere in Miller. In *The Crucible*, John Proctor's affair with his beautiful teen-age servant is the source of his undoing. In *A View from the Bridge*, Eddie Carbone is ruined by his incestuous passion for his young niece. The wife in each play is a fine woman who is not in the least sexually interesting. The same is true of Linda Loman, to whom Willy is unfaithful. Biff's discovery of this infidelity marks the crucial turning point in the relationship between father and son; thereafter Biff no longer believes in Willy. Significantly, Willy recalls the exposure—and it is played out for us—just as his sons desert him for two floozies they have picked up in a restaurant. These two exposures of illicit sex, one in the past and one in the present, double their force by coming at just the same moment in the play. Small wonder that Willy has earlier warned Biff to be cautious with girls. On the whole, Miller's implicit indictment of sex as a wicked influence is remarkably consistent and emphatic. We may suitably apply to Miller his own words, from the notes of *The Crucible*: "Our opposites are always clothed in sexual sin."

But Miller does more than criticize illicit sexual activity; he makes it both the root and symptom of his heroes' disorders in these three plays. Eric Bentley has suggested that, in *Death of a Salesman* and *The Crucible*, sex serves to mask social criticism and to offer an alternative explanation of the heroes' disasters. Thus, we have a double accusation. Willy and his son Happy are brought to account for their faulty social philosophy and also for their philandering. In the profoundest sense, Willy is destroyed by his false ideals. But the greatest single disaster in the play's present events may well be his sons' flight with the floozies while he is in the men's room. Sex has undone him, and society has undone him: you take your choice. This double interpretation is accurate, but it does not prevent Miller from doing something else—from dramatizing, with telling consistency, a Puritanical, repressive attitude toward sex.

What is bad in society, illicit sex for instance, is directly and plainly shown. The positive values, if any exist, are dimly and imperfectly seen. The muscular, proletarian life is recommended as a healthy alternative to commercialism. Willy is most himself when he works with his hands, putting up ceilings, "making the stoop; finishing the cellar; putting on the new porch." At the funeral, Biff underscores the thematic use to which Miller puts Willy's neglected talents: "You know, Charley, there's more to him in that front stoop than in all the sales he ever made." Biff himself has the good sense to turn his back on a life of making sales and to work with his hands as a cowboy. He tells Happy, "We should be mixing cement on some open plain, or—or carpenters." The naturalness of such activity as this is associated with nature itself. We can be sure the Lomans are on the right track when they add to their manual dexterity a love of nature. Biff rhapsodizes about the inspiring "sight of a mare and a new colt" and about spring in Texas. When Willy loses his grip on himself, his salesman personality becomes submerged, and he can release his latent love of nature. He guiltily recalls that, driving along in a sort of trance, he found time to admire the scenery: "You can imagine, me looking at scenery, on the road every week of my

life." Later, he complains that brick buildings have blocked him in, and he fondly recalls the elm trees, lilacs, wisteria, and daffodils of the past. When he finally cracks under the double strain of present disappointment and unhappy recollections of the past, he dashes to a hardware store and buys seeds which he begins planting at night by flashlight.

These bits of talk and action which recommend nature and manual labor to us are brief and not entirely coherent, but they form the main repository of Miller's positive values. Their brevity and incoherence imply that Miller finds it difficult to come out for the good, in any form. The leftist dramatists of the thirties spoke more boldly of the good life and of the way to attain it. In the forties the proletarian mystique was less accessible; however, its previous authority in drama and other writing had helped to create an aura of vague proletarian *bonhomie*, based on instinctive faith in manual labor and the simple things. The "positive" references of *Death of a Salesman* reinterpret the proletarian mystique but in a hesitant and tentative fashion. Miller barely *tells* us what the good is, but he is able to *show* us the bad.

The political vagueness of *Death of a Salesman* had much to do with political circumstances in the world outside. The play was written in a period of popular-front progressivism; three months before its opening Henry Wallace wound up his Presidential campaign. Wallace's Progressive faith united many who were destined to take divergent political directions; the Progressive Presidential candidate himself now supports a Republican President. Basic differences were obliterated by a unifying emphasis on grass roots and on simple, direct human relationship. Vice-Presidential candidate Glen Taylor twanged his guitar, and hootenanies responded throughout the land. A favorite campaign song described the leading candidate as "friendly Henry Wallace." Wallace once observed that the main issue of the campaign was whether he would be permitted to play tennis in public with his friend the Negro singer Paul Robeson. Asked if he were supported by Communists, he would characteristically answer a question with a question: "What is a Communist?" The great distance between the Wallace movement and the seats of power, a distance reflected by Wallace's small vote in 1948, suggested to his followers that the good folk at the grass roots had gone underground, that being good was a surreptitious and sometimes illegal activity. Real, serious threats to civil liberty were already apparent in the beginnings of black-listing and of political prosecutions: ten Hollywood screen workers had been called before a congressional committee, and the leaders of the Communist Party were indicted. At just this time, radical toughness was replaced by the simplicity of Wallace's "What is a Communist?" and by the *bonhomie* which had been the chief stock in trade of the newspaper *PM* (by then defunct).

I consider the Wallace campaign to have been not an influence on *Death of a Salesman* but a parallel development, another instance of the decline of the revolutionary mystique into a combination of conventional proletarian gestures and vague belief in friendly good folks at the grass roots. Another parallel instance of submerged rebellion occurs in a play which opened two weeks after *Death of a Salesman*, Clifford Odets' *The Big Knife*, in which the hero's radical activities seem summarized by his statement: "I believe in FDR." In these post-Wallace plays, social criticism is put in such general terms that John Mason Brown, reviewing *Death of a Salesman*, was able to say of Miller: "He has the wisdom and the insight not to blame the 'System.'" But he does blame the "System." The trouble is that criticisms of the "System" were being muted and transposed that year.

Responding to the political climate, Miller's plays have moved steadily inward. Although each play has probed the impact of large, bewildering issues upon a simple man, the large issues have become increasingly dim. Some of the haziness is intrinsic, but some of it is induced by the simple man's mounting personal problems. In *All My Sons*, the issue is no less than the war itself. The play shares the weakness of its chief character, who finds it hard to make the war's values immediate and meaningful. *Death of a Salesman* strikes a balance between the social problem of the shattered myth of success and Willy Loman's sex and family problems. *The Crucible* shows us witch hunts, but the obvious contemporary reference is masked by the historical setting and by the very distinctive seventeenth-century speech; what remains is the tension between the incalculable malice of private individuals and the conscience of a guilt-ridden husband. With *A View from the Bridge*, Miller's focus moves still further within. Eddie Carbone is not only troubled and guilty; he is sick, and his symptoms resemble those that Tennessee Williams, the most typically "internal" of contemporary American dramatists, had made the common substance of Broadway drama—incestuous inclinations, psychotic sexual jealousy, frenzied hostility to homosexuality, and possibly incipient homosexuality. If these symptoms are present, it is less important that the immigration service also has its shortcomings; the play's main topic has become Eddie's troubles.

In the vagueness of Willy's identity and his occupation, in the mysterious success of Uncle Ben, in the inexplicable virtue of the good neighbors, in the incomprehensible magnetism of Willy's proletarian tendencies, we have not only the studied ambiguity of Miller's method but also the quality of the radical political climate. In more ways than the dramatist may know, his plays speak for the spirit of the time.

PAUL WEST
"Arthur Miller & the Human Mice"
Hibbert Journal, January 1963, pp. 84–86

Arthur Miller's long and disputatious introduction to his *Collected Plays* develops from his assertion on the first page that "the drama and its production must represent a well-defined expression of profound social needs". But not only is his drama's role social; so is its subject. He is concerned with "the kind of commitment" a man "makes to life or refuses to make", but also with "that moment when . . . a man differentiates himself from every other man". Commitment cramps the individual; differentiation fulfils. Miller ignores—is bound to ignore—those commitments (St-Exupéry, T. E. Lawrence, Hemingway) that fulfil; the usual concept of the hero interests him little. Even the dedicated self-sacrifice of war comes outside his elected scope. His usual hero (better called protagonist) is more of an Everyman than a *Führer* or Aristotelian high-ranker. The good man misguided is his main idea; his examples are Joe Keller in *All My Sons*, Willy Loman in *Death of a Salesman*, Bert in *A Memory of Two Mondays*, and Eddie in *A View from the Bridge*.

These characters are obscure and unknown. But they have more impact upon, and derive more from, society than they realise. Miller's one personage of near-heroic dimensions is John Proctor, the sane dissentient of *The Crucible*; but this voice crying in the social wilderness is that of the inspired loser. The plays give us, in laboratory conditions worthy of a Conrad, the psychology of unheroic economic man hovering between isolation and community, between selfishness and dedication.

Miller's philosophy is simple and three-fold: a man must fulfil his obligations to his fellows without losing either his all to society or his sense of his own uniqueness.

In other words, Arthur Miller's plays are meant to alert us to the facts of community, pride and spiritual sanctity. As Kenneth says in *A Memory of Two Mondays*, "Oh, the damn mice. But they've got to live too, I suppose". And the human mice, the Willy Lomans, have to live too. How they do it, in their unimportant and perhaps mediocre way, is just as important to Miller as why they cannot do otherwise. His plays are lyrics on the loneliness of being commonplace in a commonplace world; their irony is that the company of one's peers brings no esteem.

These are Christian plays; their concern (this word recurs in any discussion of Miller) is with sympathetic sanity, with being "present" to other lives. One must be vehement, but proportionately so. Miller is a John Proctor, agonising over his own crucible. An almost theological care for the meaning of the individual's life accompanies his intuition of the part of daily charity. The plays give us the sociology of ordinariness, the theology of the individual; and two in particular, *Death of a Salesman* and *The Crucible*, bring to mind another American writer, Mark Twain. The whole trend of Miller's thought is to resume the hampered decency of Huck Finn in terms of such a concept as Camus's *l'homme révolté*. Between Puritan survivals and democratic lip-service, Miller plays Camus to North America. The two have the same obsessions: the sacredness of the individual conscience; the need to be critical of the social machine; the absurdity of life without spiritual identity; the nihilism of state ambition; the need for syndicalism and *mesure*—the two traditions that German ideology and Christian otherworldliness have almost effaced.

Miller's most shattering play is *The Crucible*. Its point is blatant: if you take a man's conscience out of his own hands, you at once deprive him of identity and of pride. We must not sell our souls to society, but we must not, cannot, separate ourselves either. We should be able to think for ourselves, express what we think, or keep it quiet. We are entitled to be fairly reported, to be protected against false informers and wild assertion. The human community in Salem, Massachusetts, failed in its responsibility to its members; so also, says Miller in his introduction, did America fail its citizens during the McCarthy purge. Of his early response to McCarthyism he writes: "It was as though the whole country had been born anew, without a memory even of certain elemental decencies which, a year or two earlier, no one would have imagined could be altered, let alone forgotten". He goes on to say how he studied the record of the Salem trial: "After days of study it became quite incredible how Rebecca Nurse, a pious and universally respected woman of great age, was literally taken by force from her sickbed and ferociously cross-examined . . . There was a sadism here that was breath-taking".

He then talks of social guilt as allied to religious mania, and explains such manifestations in terms of absolute evil: "I believe now, as I did not conceive then, that there are people dedicated to evil, . . that without their perverse example we should not know the good". *The Crucible* shows the burning-away of human decency—of humanity its very self. "It is a tough play", says Miller; "my criticism of it now would be that it is not tough enough". It is a play about depravity. No one is capable of guessing at the innermost mind of another. To guess at it in order to do him some good is tricky enough, and presumptuous. To guess at it in order to jail him or to get him hanged is monstrous.

We are shown a progress of the human soul. An action

that begins with hysterical accusations eventually breaks into an awful calm in which some one can get up and say: "We've hanged a dozen people already; now, of course, we might seem to be wrong; but it would not be fair to the hanged if we spared the rest of the condemned". Institutions, says Miller, easily become dehumanised; we acquire habits, and soon the habits acquire us. What is most frightening and sickening in this play is the spectacle of once reasonable human beings in the act of rationalising their loss of charity, their discarding of good sense. Excess, as Camus has said, maintains its place in man's heart; murder and loneliness often go together. Everyman must strive to avoid the indifference which habit brings. A constant and fresh response to other lives is the only way to justify pride in being human.

Miller's other plays, less ferocious in their dialectic, propose the tragedy of modern man in terms of Christian existentialism. In such a dialectic, the corner grocer is as fit a figure for tragedy as the President of the United States; provided, of course, says Miller, that "the grocer's career engages the issues of, for instance, the survival of the race, the relationship of man to God—the questions, in short, whose answers define humanity and the right way to live so that the world is a home, instead of a battleground or a fog in which disembodied spirits pass each other in an endless twilight". Aristotle is dispatched with a quick rattle of historical fact; and we are given the rationale of a drama that pursues "the image of private man in a world full of strangers". The pursuit is very thorough, and the capture is distressing.

The story of *All My Sons* (1947) is simple enough. A young man discovers that his father has produced faulty aeroplane parts during the war. It is likely that as a result twenty-two pilots were killed. The trouble with Joe Keller, the father, is that he can't in any way see that he is obliged to his fellow men; he has no sense of human responsibility. His personality, says Miller, is divorced from the things he does. *Death of a Salesman* (1949) shows Willy Loman being crushed by the society to which he has sold himself. Where Joe Keller is apart, Willy Loman is too far in. The one is not for sale; the other is sold up. In *The Crucible* (1952) John Proctor defies a society which has given itself over to evil.

A Memory of Two Mondays (1955) is a pathetic and deceptively simple comedy; it is also Miller's favourite play. A boy works among people for a couple of years—shares their troubles, their tools, their moments of joy. When the time comes for him to go, he looks to them for a sign that he has been appreciated. No sign is forthcoming. He slips back into the human sea. In this instance, society has let down the individual—not destroyed him, but interrupted his faith. The antithesis to this apathy is shown in *A View from the Bridge* (1955): Eddie betrays the social code of a group of Italian immigrants, and dies for doing so.

Society is Miller's white whale. Some yield to it; others fight it or pretend it doesn't exist; others trust it, and are let down. There seem to be no guarantees built into the human contract; community, like faith, is a risk and a venture. It is said that Miller lacks an attitude of life. It is true that his characters rarely philosophise for him and that he is not easy to label. But his introduction alters all that. His philosophy is as clear as Christianity, and he no more needs a label than Camus does. Consider his statement about Willy Loman and the pathos of the stereotyped life: "He's not the finest character who ever lived. But he's a human being, and a terrible thing is happening to him. So attention must be paid. He's not to be allowed to fall into his grave like an old dog. Attention, attention must be finally paid to such a person."

The stress is on "finally". After all our evasions, we come back to the condition that includes most of us. Compassion is Miller's remedy, commonsense his curb. These are not spectacular ideas; the spectacle is on the stage. Surely there is not a great deal more to be said about the loneliness and self-searching so common in the lives of those not usually thought introspective. Miller's is the drama of human worry. It is intended to restore us to a sense of human and humane responsibility. And it is necessary to pursue that restoration until it brings us to an unsimulated responsiveness to all kinds of beings—especially the undistinguished and the mice.

PHILIP RAHV
From "Arthur Miller and the Fallacy of Profundity" (1964)
Literature and the Sixth Sense
1969, pp. 385–90

In his second play, *Incident at Vichy*, at the Repertory Theater of Lincoln Center, Arthur Miller recovers somewhat, even if only to a limited extent, from the disaster of *After the Fall*, a piece so pretentious and defensive that virtually nothing good can be said about it. In an openly subjective or confessional mood, bringing his own life behavior into question, Miller is more pitiable than ingratiating. In this new play, however, what is perceptible is not callow subjectivity but an overstrain of intellectual capacity. ⟨. . .⟩

The play is basically a discussion piece. The scene is a detention room at Vichy in the fall of 1942, where a number of "suspects" rounded up by the Nazis with the help of the French police are awaiting an interrogation presided over by a German "professor" of racial science—an interrogation from which the Jews among the "suspects," who are in the majority, are never to return. For the hour and a half that it lasts (there are no intermissions) it does generate an unquestionable dramatic tension not to be explained away by reference to the appalling historical experience it invokes. Recalling the gruesome suffering inflicted by the Nazis does not in itself create dramatic order and consequence—only the dramatist's integrative hand can accomplish that. The part that is best conceived and that does provide a certain meager element of plot is that of the non-Nazi German major who enacts his revulsion at what his superiors are making him do at the same time that he accepts it as a decree of our modern historical fate; and the performances, the parts of the Jewish psychoanalyst, of the sensitive and humane Austrian prince caught in the dragnet, of the German major, and of the actor still full of consoling illusions of what the future holds for him, are not only credible but sometimes even better than that.

What *au fond* I find objectionable, in a dramaturgical as well as in a plain logical sense, is the surprise ending of the play (welcomed by not a few reviewers as giving it "a jolt it badly needs," as one of them put it), in which at the very last moment the Austrian prince, a liberal of refined sensibilities, is released by the interrogators only to hand over his exit-permit to the doomed Jewish psychoanalyst. This Myshkin-like act of self-sacrifice seems to me to belie the entire portentous dialectic of guilt, responsibility, the horror of Nazism as the horror of human nature, etc., which Miller develops throughout the production. It is an ending dramatically unearned, so to speak, because on the symbolical plane at least it contradicts the entire emphasis of the ideas that preceded it. It is a melodramatic contrivance pure and simple, a sheer *coup de théâtre*. It may give the audience a lift, but it drops the play's intellectual baggage with a heavy thud. After all, liberalism, especially the aestheticized type of liberalism represented by the prince, has been belabored throughout, and here all of a sudden he gives his own life to save another man's, who is a stranger at that; nothing whatever in the play has prepared us for this exhibition of saintliness. Thus the author has it both ways: he condemns human nature ("We're all scum") at the same time that he appears to exonerate it in the way he brings his action to a close. Everything is indeed possible in life, but in dramatic art what is required is the seeming inevitability of an end, however tragic, which is truly a conclusion vindicating the organizing principle of the work as a whole.

I prefer to think that it is not theatrical opportunism but sheer intellectual confusion which brought Miller, who is one of our few authentic playwrights, to close his piece with such a patently arbitrary ending. The confusion is in his ideas, which have that stylish "profundity," masking a retreat from socio-political realities, that has been for many years now so much in vogue among our intellectuals. The collapse of Marxism has left them high and dry in an ideological sense, and they have long been looking for "profundities," from whatever source, to cover their nakedness; and the "profundities" they have gone in for, ostensibly explaining totalitarianism in all its varieties, have led in the long run to little more than idle theorizing and moralistic attitudinizing. The aim is somehow to replace at all costs the concrete analysis of historical forces in their specific social and political manifestations, for such analysis seems to many people nowadays to be so very stale and boring compared to the *divertissement* of "deep" thoughts, which commit them to nothing but more thoughts. Hence the attempt to understand Nazism—as for instance by resorting to individual psychology (e.g., Hannah Arendt trying to understand Eichmann's character) or to notions of human nature in general or Evil capitalized—has resulted in nothing so far but outright mystification.

What the Nazis did is in fact no mystery. It is implicitly or explicitly contained in their program, which they openly proclaimed long before coming to power; nor did they do anything which had not been done before throughout history; think of the Turks slaughtering the Armenians or of the Church-inspired Western crusaders slaughtering not only the Moslems but the Greek Orthodox Christians as well, to cite but two examples out of an innumerable array. The difference is that the Hitlerites commanded technological means permitting them to commit atrocities on a scale hitherto unknown. There is nothing "new" in terror; what is new is the means at the disposal of the terrorists. In the Nazi experience the point for us does not lie so much in what the Nazis did—what they did cannot be undone—but in the question of how they managed to take power in the first place without being forced to fight for it; only by examining the latter question can some useful lessons for the future be drawn. Hitler's greatest success was in sparing himself civil war while nevertheless grabbing the state power. And the blame for that is to be laid at the door of German big business no less than that of German small business, also of the German military, also of the Communists, ruinously manipulated by Stalin, also of the Social Democrats, in part immobilized by their Communist rivals and in part by their inherent lack of militancy. Nor can one absolve from blame the German intellectuals who, for the most part, instead of thinking and acting politically, were engaged as usual in misinterpreting life and history with their seductive abstractions and profundities. (There is an extremely revealing picture of that type of intellectuality, which is by no means a German monopoly, in Thomas Mann's *Dr. Faustus*, a picture far more

interesting and historically instructive than his so much more talked about invocation in that novel of its hero's Satan-inspired aesthetics.)

Now Arthur Miller appears to have absorbed quite a few of the mystifications with which some of our intellectuals have been at once perplexing and diverting themselves. Thus in his play the Austrian prince, who in this instance is clearly speaking for the author, says: "Many times I used to ask my friends: To be a good German why must you despise everything that is not German? Until I realized the answer. They do these things not because they are Germans but because they are nothing. It is the hallmark of the age—the less you exist the more important it is to make a clear impression." On the surface this may sound profound and, to be sure, it has the modish "existentialist" ring; but does it actually explain the German contempt for other nations? No human beings are "nothing," and to equate "good German" with "nothing" is a pointless piece of cleverness. The German contempt that Miller refers to is at bottom far from mysterious. It was a willed contempt functionally serving as the rationalization, politically and culturally, of their urge to exterminate other peoples in order to make *Lebensraum* for themselves. They thought it was a practical urge, but it turned out to be wholly impractical. German imperialism, in its first nationalistic as in its second totalitarian edition, was a historical phenomenon much too belated to realize its aims; and its worked-up claims of superiority, like its frightful ruthlessness, was an essential part of what one might call its character-armor. Why mystify ourselves with the metaphysics of "nothingness" when the explanation is really so much simpler?

Nor am I impressed by Miller's notion of anti-Semitism as his psychoanalyst voices it: "And Jews is only the name we give to that stranger, that agony we cannot feel, that death we look at like a cold abstraction. Each man has his Jew; it is the other. And the Jews have their Jews." But gentiles are drawn to anti-Semitism not because otherness as such repels them but for simpler reasons, such as the tempting contradiction in their image of the Jews. On the one hand they seem to them to be "pushy" and all too prosperous while on the other hand they seem so very helpless. It is this particular combination which invites the blows. And if Miller merely means to say that everyone wants to find someone he can look down upon or who might serve him as a scapegoat, that is the sheerest cliché. Again, the psychoanalyst says to the prince: "It's not your guilt I want, it's your responsibility." This too sounds deep, but what does it mean? Guilt feelings are essential if our conscience is to be stirred, and without pangs of conscience there can be no taking of responsibility. The thesis of the play, insofar as it has any coherent thesis at all, is that each of us is responsible for all, that whatever evil we do, however small, contributes to the greater evil that destroys humanity. Actually, this is one of Dostoevsky's ideas, which is scarcely convincing even in this context. It is a Christian thought put to false uses. He used it as apologetics for the absolutist Czarist regime, its state-dominated Church and other malign forces holding down the Russian people in ignorance and misery. Responsibility cannot be other than specific: if all are responsible none are responsible. It is simply not true that we are all responsible for the Nazi horrors, and to universalize in this fashion the German guilt is to transfer it to human nature in general and thus vaporize it. The argument from human nature in general is insubstantial because it is so exceedingly vague, explaining everything and nothing at the same time.

Miller is no ideologue, no thinker, but he has written some good things. Apart from *Death of a Salesman*, about which I have mixed feelings, I think his best play is A *View from the Bridge*, a simple but trenchant dramatic poem. *The Crucible*, too, is a fine work, once we disregard the analogies with McCarthyism, an entirely different phenomenon from the Salem witch trials, analogies that are not really in the text which I have recently read, but in the mind of the audience that first saw it produced. Now *Incident at Vichy* has been criticized by reviewers, though for reasons that seem to me somewhat external. Its actual ideas have not been examined in detail but mostly sneered at for not being deep enough. The trouble with these ideas, however, is precisely their apparent depth—depth without content.

LESLIE EPSTEIN
From "The Unhappiness of Arthur Miller"
Triquarterly, Spring 1965, pp. 165–73

I

I don't know of anyone with a serious concern for the theater who was not disappointed by *After the Fall*. At the same time, no critic has taken the time to give the play more than the back of his hand. Expectations have burst like balloons, and the loosened gas has been sour and petulant, as if Miller owed us a masterpiece, a measure of greatness beyond his scope, all the tokens of an absent lover returned to home. In this atmosphere of querulousness and hurt feelings ("I always felt he was a minor talent") the play has been snubbed as a *succés de scandale*, or written off as *too* autobiographical ("a thinly disguised confessional"—Brustein), and generally dismissed without examination.

The reasons for the failure of *After the Fall* are difficult and intriguing enough to deserve better treatment. First off, that issue of issues—the personal nature of the play. Somewhere in the web of sticky commentaries Miller has spun about this work there is this fly of a claim: that *After the Fall* is no more autobiographical than any of his other plays. In one sense, of course, this is true. It means that you don't make something from nothing, that literature is pretty exactly balanced by experience, that every play bears equally the weight of a personality. It is what Ibsen had in mind when he said, "All that I have written these ten years I have lived through spiritually."

On the other hand, Miller has lived through the events of *After the Fall* in something more than a spiritual sense. In another of the commentaries (this time in the *Saturday Evening Post*) Miller suggests that some people "will call it a play 'about' Puritanism, or 'about' incest, or 'about' the transformation of guilt into responsibility, or whatever." In fact, most people have taken it to be a play 'about' Arthur Miller and Marilyn Monroe, and their instinct is sharper than his speculation. I believe that the mere fact that the action of the play is drawn from preserved events and untransformed experience in no way disqualifies it as serious drama or high art. The finest American play is more intensely and painfully autobiographical than *After the Fall*: and if O'Neil's Mother had been, say, Greta Garbo, *Long Day's Journey into Night* would be a *succés de scandale* too. Ibsen's finest plays are intimate and introspective, the daily agonies of human contact, lived through as much at Gossensass in the Austrian Tyrol as in the spirit. Moreover, *After the Fall* is best where it is most personal, where the experience has been least rearranged: Mickey deciding to testify before a congressional committee, Holga realizing that after only two weeks she is boring Quentin, most of Maggie's dialogue ("I wish I knew some-

thing") and much of her action. These scenes—enough to make the reputation of a lesser playwright—ring true: they have the minimal virtue of honesty, the honesty of memory undistorted by afterthought. *After the Fall*, then, is not marred because its recollection is too exact; it is precisely because it too often blurs, dissolves into compulsive ratiocination and a sea of second thoughts that the play is so complete a failure.

To put it another way, Miller's play is destroyed not by his memory but by his understanding. The event is never allowed to speak for itself, stand by itself. Recollection is so often only an excuse for reflection that whatever conflict the play has is soon lost, and as the emphasis shifts from action to analysis, we move out of the realm of the dramatic altogether. This need not happen if Quentin, like Hamlet, could succeed in making something of his thoughts. Miller—quite consciously I'm convinced—has modeled his hero on Shakespeare's, whose enterprises also lost "the name of action."

While the comparison is ludicrous certainly ("I can't make a decision anymore" for ". . . the native hue of resolution/Is sicklied o'er with the pale cast of thought"), the likeness is worth nothing: both men so naive as to be stunned by the discovery of evil, both neurotic enough to continually confuse their own guilt with the world's, both seeking to excoriate their moral quality ("Not to see one's own evil—there's power! And rightness too! So kill conscience. Kill it."—"Thus conscience does make cowards of us all."), yet both think so precisely on the event that neither notices he is killing everyone about him. Despite what these heroes share, despite the fact that each appropriates to his mind the dramatic conflict of his play, *Hamlet* succeeds, *After the Fall* falls to shambles. There are dozens of reasons for this, but the most crucial is that Hamlet makes something of his thought: like a dry bulb blossoming, ratiocination bursts to realization. No sea-changes for Quentin, though. His drama ends, not with silence, but with question marks (ten of them in his last speech alone). Sure, there is a ham-handed echo of Elsinor ("Is the knowing all?"), but the rising inflection is the give-away. Quentin leaves as he entered—confused, conflicted, entirely self-deceived.

Another way of putting this is that in the course of his drama Hamlet becomes a protagonist while Quentin remains an antagonist. *The Murder of Gonzago*, like every play-within-a-play, is a kind of dream, from which King Claudius wakes screaming. For Hamlet, however, staging and rewriting is symbolic action, standing for and *clearing the way for* the real movement he is not yet ready to make. More than any other single act, it prepares for the transformation of thought to understanding. Quentin's one action is to walk into the Listener's office and stage a psycho-analytic session, a session in which he struggles against, interrupts, diverts, and finally denies the force of the action his own memories initiate.

What is *After the Fall*, then, but that tired old expression-istic horse, the Dream Play, with the analysis of the dream thrown in as a gesture to the times: a free-association play, if you will? There is nothing inherently wrong with this form; it fails so abjectly here, I think, for one reason: Miller's desire to understand and judge himself is matched only by his desire to deceive and forgive himself. To this last end, the one character who could force Quentin into self-confrontation, the Listener, is washed out of the play. His absence leaves Quentin free to present his conflict to his own specifications and resolve it to his own satisfaction, with the inevitable result that his undiscovered impulse screens him ever more effectively from self knowledge and judgment.

And ultimately *this* is what is wrong with *After the Fall*—it lacks courage. I am not saying it was not a painful play to write—clearly it was. It is just that Miller has shied from the greater pain of a more searching analysis, so that what is presented as a personal examination becomes a plea for exoneration. Miller works this sleight of hand in two ways: first he expands his own bad conscience until it becomes, and is lost in, the guilt of the world; second, he falsifies—just barely—his relationship to those around him.

The most repugnant example of Miller's first technique is his use of the concentration camp tower. Every time Quentin experiences aggression, either within himself or inflicted from without, the top of the tower lights up, indicating a hit, while Miller delivers the score:

> *No one* they didn't kill can be innocent again . . .
>
> *We are* very dangerous.
>
> Why is the *world* so treacherous?

On the great pin-ball machine of guilt, the crime of any one man rings a tiny, peccadillo bell ("The sickness is much larger than my skull.").

Of the many evasions performed on the second level, the most significant is Miller's self-characterization as a lawyer. This transformation allows him to separate his professional and personal lives, or, where they necessarily touch (his work for Maggie), to assert he did no damage. For an artist, of course, the private life and the professional life are one; and it is just this issue, Quentin's effect *as an artist* upon those he cares for, that Miller is most anxious to avoid.

Yet how many questions are answered, how many pieces fall into place, if we consider Quentin a playwright and not a lawyer. Of what is Quentin guilty? Of using other people, he finally tells Maggie. But as her lawyer and even as her husband he has used her well. Eliot might apply the criterion of the objective correlative more happily to *After the Fall* than to Hamlet. Quentin's sense of culpability is wildly disproportionate to any defect in his actions or character. But if Quentin is an artist, a playwright, his guilt is accounted for and even compounded. As an artist Quentin does use the people around him; in a sense he kills them, reduces them to material, to stone. In the play, Quentin cannot understand why he affects people like Medusa, why there is a chill in his presence, why women, especially, feel unconnected, unrelated to him ("I don't exist"), yet at the same time manipulated, deployed, and soon exhausted ("I'm boring you"): not only used, but used up. If he knew he were a playwright—that his personal relations and his professional interests are inseparable and that the link between them is discontent; if he knew that misery had, for a writer, a practical value ("All happy families are alike . . ."); if he knew, in short, that to fulfill himself he must cause pain to others, he might begin to understand why he is ashamed.

As it is, Quentin does not do all that badly. Groping through self-inflicted amnesia, he fingers themes, attitudes, symbols which bring him near comprehension. For example, Quentin is needled by the idea of Power, a word he murmurs again and again—in capital P's—to the Listener, who does not reply. Because the dialogue does not develop, Quentin fails to realize that the sense of power which both attracts and afflicts him is creative energy. This is clearest in the scenes with Felice. At one point, he actually does shape her (nothing more than approving a nose-job, I am pained to say), as if she were clay. The resulting sense of Power is both ecstatic ("she let me change her!") and excruciating. That Quentin's guilt is focused on his capacities as a creator is demonstrated by the penance he exacts from himself—his arms stretched in simulated crucifixion. He also plays God with Maggie ("you like gave me my feelings"), reforming her, fixing her, making her and, to the

extent that he cast her in his own image ("I'm an artist"), helping to destroy her.

For Quentin is a destroyer as well as a creator, and it is about the exposition of this destructiveness that Miller remains most reticent. Quentin's devastative and creative capacities are integral. Denied professional status, he is nevertheless a kind of seer, a bringer of truth: the pattern of his vision and his message is invariably dissolution ("whatever I look at, I seem to see its death"). This is the truth he feels compelled to inflict: he tells his Father of his wife's death, lets Lou see how he feels about defending him (thus easing Lou's suicide), kills his first marriage by compulsively dragging his motives about the house, and takes refuge from his second in honesty ("covered with truth like slime"), when love was deeded to avoid disaster. Quentin is a species of murderer, and it is in order to extenuate this clear fact, in order to reduce the charge from killer to accomplice, that Miller erects the superstructure of social circumstance, the winking tower, the disguises in identity.

Quentin is no more sure of himself as a bringer of truth than as a possessor of power. He distrusts every motive except one: his striving, his suffering for truth ("The truth saves, always remember that."). At the same time, he recognizes—in a fair sample of Miller's style—that "the truth, after all, may merely be murderous. The truth killed Lou; destroyed Mickey. Then what else is there? A workable lie?" Quentin's ambivalence about his own role and capacities is symptomatic of his inability (and Miller's) to recognize himself as an artist and accept the fact that life and art cannot be reconciled without pain. Miller, like many artists, suffers from what Otto Rank (in *Life and Creation*) calls the "feeling of guilt arising from the creative process itself." Such an artist is the one person exempt from Freud's diagnosis for happiness: his work either brings suffering on himself or inflicts it on those he loves. He cannot create without destroying; every new work requires, in a not altogether symbolic way, a new death. Rank's comment on Ibsen is equally applicable here:

> He needs, as it were, for each work that he builds, a sacrifice which is buried alive to ensure a permanent existence to the structure, but also to save the artist from having to give himself.

For a time, Arthur Miller avoided confronting this aspect of himself by splitting into a person and an artist: that is, he simply stopped writing. *After the Fall* does not heal this schism. It is no less an evasion, no more courageous than withdrawal. Perhaps it had to be written before Miller could become whole. But I doubt it. Rank points out that those sensibilities which feel the conflict between life and art with special intensity often resolve it by adopting a muse. In this way, the artist tries to repay a loved one with his work for the harm he has caused her in life. It is always a poor resort, here no less than elsewhere. It is unlikely that the exorcism of a ghastly muse will ease the author's conscience or bring peace to Marilyn Monroe (since "the artist seldom gives himself . . . the truly womanly woman often refuses to accept"— Rank). If anything, this play is liable to increase Miller's difficulties. Here and there in the commentaries he stressed the fact that *After the Fall* was a special kind of play, or rather not a play at all, but an event, a happening, a becoming, a process. This is half modish cant and half wishful thinking, yet there is an odd sense in which this baroque concept is true. If Quentin-Miller's guilt springs, as I believe, from the way in which creative activity uses and manipulates and eventually objectifies people, then *After the Fall* is a "happening" indeed: for in the very act of writing this play about his wife, his family, his associates, his friends, Miller has set the process through its motion and wound himself more tightly in the shame he has found he cannot endure.

II

I have mentioned Ibsen a number of times. More than any other modern writer, he succeeded in facing and dramatizing the theme that *After the Fall* skirts and evades. In the introduction to his own collected works, Miller records his admiration for the way in which Ibsen's work dramatizes the past as present experience—which is exactly what he attempts, and fails, to do in this play. And in his adaptation of *Enemy of the People*, Miller cut Dr. Stockmann's "undemocratic" speeches about the inability of the masses to govern themselves and the necessity for strong leaders to do it instead. Ibsen doesn't really mean it, is the excuse, "he could not have lived a day under an authoritarian regime of any kind." These alterations are a paradigm of the failure of courage that marks *After the Fall*. Ibsen *does* mean it. That the minority is always right, the majority wrong, is his "fundamental principle in every context and situation." But this minority must be understood in an artistic as well as a political context; for by it Ibsen means, "the minority which forges ahead in territory which the majority has not yet reached. I believe he is right who is most closely attuned to the future."[1] Miller cannot help but be comforting: the bringer of truth must believe in those he brings it to, ultimately there must be some understanding between the leader and the led, the artist and his public. Yet by this point in his career (1882), Ibsen had realized the hopelessness of reconciliation: "the strongest man in the world is he who stands most alone."

Within a decade he would also understand—and dramatize—that the conflict always ends in death. In doing so, Ibsen took his place within a tradition—call it the tradition of introspective drama—which stretches from Aeschylus to Bergman (*Through a Glass Darkly*) and Fellini (*8½*), and whose chief concern is the creative personality's encounter with his immediate society and his immediate society's encounter with him. The full range of impact was found by the Greeks—from the pain the truth-bringer suffers (*Prometheus Bound*) to the suffering he causes about him (*The Bacchae*). As Edmund Wilson has observed (*The Wound and the Bow*), *Philoctetes* sets the theme: human suffering is intrinsic to superhuman power; they are an ensemble: the bowman cannot be separated from his bow, the artist from his art, nor Philoctetes from his stinking foot. The artist and his society are inextricable—mutually exploitative, mutually dehumanizing, equally guilty, inflicting and undergoing each other.

Ibsen joined the tradition early and never left it. The architects and sculptors of his last plays are Peer Gynt grown old—Peer Gynt who used up, destroyed the people he loved, always promising to pay it all back in a year or two with his art. Ibsen lived long enough to discover the debt is irredeemable, that the dead children, the model turned to stone, can be paid back only in kind—through the death of the artist who made them. There is not time, nor is this the place, to examine Ibsen's last plays in detail. Still, I do want to show how Ibsen broke through the round of continual reproach and enforced inactivity that characterize Arthur Miller's work and life at present—how, in *The Master Builder* and to an even greater extent in his masterpiece, *When We Dead Awaken*, he faced that "guilt arising from the creative process itself" and worried it out, with real courage, to its only conclusion.

The Master Builder and *When We Dead Awaken* have a lot in common. Rubek, the hero of the latter play, is a great artist and, like Solness, one whose masterpiece lies behind him. For Rubek it was his sculpture, "The Day of Resurrec-

tion," and for Solness it was the church tower at Lysorges. Each man realized himself as an artist the day he completed his masterpiece—yet since that day the creative energy of both men has waned. Rubek turns out portrait busts and Solness designs commercial housing tracts. Both men are unhappy in their personal lives, especially with their wives. Each feels a vague unease, an anxiety, a sense of unspecified guilt. Suddenly into each old man's life the woman who had inspired his masterpiece returns. The sculptor, like the architect, follows his muse in a steep climb toward both artistic fulfillment, the consummation of love, and death. *The Master Builder* is superior in one important respect—the climb and fall from the church tower is more integrally related to Solness' work as an artist and is a finer symbol of sexual climax than Rubek's climb up the mountain and the subsequent avalanche. In every other respect—the economy of speech and action, the bitter relation of artist to wife, and especially the portrait of the muse (free from the irrelevant troll finery which weakens Hilde in the more famous play)—*When We Dead Awaken* is the finer work.

Rubek has two women in his life, his muse and the Frau Professor. He acquired his wife ("and to cap it all, you could afford to buy me"), along with a villa on the Taunitzer See and a mansion in the capital, only after he had completed his great work and his powers had begun to subside. He has become so bored with her and her lack of sensibility ("you were not exactly made to climb mountains") that he can barely suppress his hostility, his hidden wishing for a separation, a disaster, something . . .

The other woman, Irene, had served as the inspiration and the model for his masterpiece. In using her for the subject of his art, however, he has somehow destroyed her soul, turned her from a living person into an object, a statue, a stone. He did this by denying her *as a woman* ("to the muse . . . the artist seldom gives himself . . ."). Rubek's attempt to justify his action

> if I touched you, if I desired you sensually, my vision would be profaned so that I would never be able to achieve what I was striving after. And I still think there is some truth in that

is rejected by Irene (". . . and this the truly womanly woman refuses to accept."). Yet because, at one point in the past, she *had* accepted her de-humanization ("defeminization"—Rank), she has lost her soul and died as a woman. She realized this at the time the statue was made, and had tried to substitute an aesthetic function for a human one: she called "The Day of Resurrection" her child, the offspring of her artistic union with Rubek. Now, condemned to live the role she once freely accepted (she is the "naked statue" in a burlesque review), she is unable to bear real children—they are aborted as they are conceived.

Rubek, of course, is aware of all this, yet remains so much the artist, so little the man, that his remorse and guilt can be expressed only in terms of rearrangements in his work:

> I have portrayed myself in this group. In the foreground, beside a spring, as it might be here, there sits a man weighed down by guilt; he cannot free himself from the earth's crust. I call him remorse—remorse for a forfeited life . . . He must stay for ever in his Hell.

His situation is precisely that of Solness in *The Master Builder*. Solness' wife, Aline, like Irene, was a woman who could bear children:

> Aline had a talent for building, too . . . The souls of children. So that they might grow into something noble, harmonious, and beautiful.

These children, like those which Irene regularly miscarries, were sacrificed in fire:

> So that I should have nothing to bind me. No love or happiness or anything, you see. I was to be a Master Builder.

And once again, this sacrifice of life to art leads to guilt, unease, remorse:

> I must sit here and expiate! Pay for it. Not with money. But with human happiness . . . And not only with my happiness, but with the happiness of others, too. You see, Hilde! That's the price that my success as an artist has cost me—and others. And every day of my life I have to sit here and see that price being paid for me—day after day after day!

It was this price that Miller found himself unwilling to pay. The portrait of Rubek is all the more compelling because for a moment he falters and looks for a way out. Perhaps the muse, the Frau Professor, and the artist can live together in the villa (as Solness hoped to live with his wife and Hilde, as Miller is determined to live with his memories *and* Holga at the end of *After the Fall*). But the end of the play, in which Rubek's wife goes down the mountain (to life, to a man who uses his knife more sensually than her husband) as he ascends it, symbolizes the incompatibility of love and work, except in death.

No playwright since Euripides has examined so closely as Ibsen the relation of sexual energy to creativity. The draining away of the artistic impulse after marriage and its re-awakening by the muse is part of a delicate study of the dynamics of sublimation. What is most interesting is Ibsen's statement that the consummation of one's work necessarily means the consummation of one's life, and that a man is allowed this experience only once. From the context of Rubek's and Irene's conversations about climbing the mountain there can be no doubt that it represents for each of them a sexual union—his delayed acceptance of her as a woman. But it also represents a vision, an action of the spirit. His last act, then, his last work, since the avalanche, like Solness' fall from the tower, is fatal. Behind the destruction of family life and the dehumanization that lie in the wake of artistic activity, there is a grander tragedy, the final union of art and life, their fulfillment in death.

Lieben und Arbeiten, in Tod—anyone unwilling to accept the adjustment of the formula must disconnect his personal and his professional life, must disengage his experience from his activity—must cease writing altogether (Rimbaud), or write badly. Miller—his experience so painful, his talents so considerable—seems to have combined both alternatives. Perhaps in America, where the pressures on privacy are immense, he had no other course. He is still a young man, though—and so many of the plays of the most intricate introspection *(The Bacchae, The Tempest, When We Dead Awaken)* are last works, artifacts of old age. Arthur Miller has the time, still, to join the tradition.

III

He does not do so, however, in his next demi-play, *Incident at Vichy*, which I have just seen in a heavy-handed production at the Washington Square ANTA Theater. The weight of what has been said about this play (most pointedly, Philip Rahv in *The New York Review of Books*) falls most heavily on Miller's *Profundity*. The failure of *Vichy* is seen primarily as one of intelligence. I think this kind of judgment, at best, beside the point. It is not Miller's job—or any other playwright's—to masticate ideas. Will it make any difference to the success of a drama if Hanna Arendt's thoughts are served half-baked or toasted through? (Aristophanes misrepresented Scholasticism and Socrates in a wonderful play, *The Clouds*;

Seneca knew and dramatized Stoic thinking perfectly in a series of unproduceable and now unreadable dramas.) It is of course unfortunate that Miller wants to Think Big—in both *After the Fall* and *Incident at Vichy* he does tend to stumble over ideas. But this happens because in both plays Miller's *dramatic* intelligence is overwhelmed, not by thought, but by a sense of guilt he is unable to approach or represent through an action. The real point to make about Miller is not that he has abrogated the functions of philosophers, but that he has become so paralyzed that the philosophers have had to take over dramatic activity for him.

I said that *After the Fall* was destroyed by a failure of understanding and a lack of courage. I meant self-understanding, and the courage to face fully whatever pain the action implies. *Incident at Vichy* suffers the same disease. More precisely, Miller is again unable to locate and assign guilt, so that he is disqualified from rendering a judgment. We find ourselves on familiar and soggy ground: a play of prosecution ends in extenuation, accusation becomes amelioration, and we end in a mass of sweet and sticky evasion.

Who is guilty in this play? A number of Jews are forced to sit in a room, waiting to be identified and transported to Auschwitz. A Sophist of Aristophanes could see that the responsibility for this monstrous situation lies with its contrivors—the Nazis and their willing mechanics. Miller does not avoid what is so evident, and *Incident at Vichy* is best where it examines, occasionally, the sources of the German Atavism:

> That is their power. To do the inconceivable. . . . they are nothing. It is the hallmark of the age—the less you exist the more important it is to make a clear impression.

Thus the playwright, with the gaze of Seneca, blames the Germans, just as Quentin-Miller has blamed himself. But he does not judge. In the same way that Quentin's crimes were dissolved into the sins of the world, so the guilt of the Nazis fades away in the general culpability of mankind. Morality—the assignment of good and evil—is lost in ballooning collaboration. Judgment stretches, disappears like a dark spot on the surface of expanding rubber.

Guilt is classless—

> The aristocracy nods while its servants "adore Hitler" and the workers vote him into power.

It is nationless—

> Strange; if I did not know that some of them in there were French, I'd have said they laugh like Germans.

or

> The Russians condemn the middle class, the English have condemned the Indians, Africans, and anybody else they could lay their hands on, The French, The Italians—every nation has condemned somebody because of his race . . .

It is without race—

> I have never analyzed a gentile who did not have, somewhere hidden in his mind, a dislike if not a hatred for the Jews.

and

> The Jews have their Jews.

Which is to say, it is without meaning. We end with this kind of exchange:

> —Are you telling me all those people are dead? Is that really conceivable to you? War is war, but you still keep a certain sense of proportion. I mean Germans are still *people*.

—I don't speak this way because they're
    German.
(. . .) Excuse me, no. It's exactly because
    they are people that I speak this way.

So everyone, the French policemen, the frightened
waiters, the vulgar masses, the refined patrons of art, everyone
from the SS thug who cracks th heads of the Jews who are half
convinced of their inferiority anyway—they are all collaborators, all the willing mechanics of the machine. It is not
surprising that the sounding-board for guilt in *After the Fall*
and *Vichy* should be a psychiatrist. What you have to do, you
see, is get beneath the surface, beneath consciousness, penetrate the defenses; then you Understand All. Which leads to
Forgiving All. Or Condemning All. It doesn't really matter
which. Like *The Deputy*, another play which points its fingers
everywhere, *Incident at Vichy* will be popular in Germany. A
free wallow, with no extra indictments drawn up.

I want to make this point again. Miller is not wrong,
obviously, when he says that everyone is guilty. His mistake—
and it is a horrible one—is to let the insight blind him to the
distinctions, the different degrees, of guilt. To desire a crime,
to hate, to "have one's Jew" is one thing. To throw millions of
people into ovens is another. The supposition that in any real
sense they are the same is moral nihilism. Miller hurls this
whitewash ("your own complicity with this—your own humanity") over each action in the play. Wishes equal acts and
compulsion becomes collaboration, until no one is culpable
because everyone is guilty. Ultimately, Miller is again unable
to face whatever guilt is in himself. "There but for the grace of
God go I," he says sadly, and no judgment is made.

It is a particular shame because it is the dramatist's task to
make distinctions that are finer, more exact than philosophers
can measure. Jews hide in an apartment house. One family
closes its doors to them, another points them out to the
Gestapo, and a third bangs its shutters when they are led away.
These are three situations essentially separate. To reply, "I have
never analyzed a gentile who did not hate jews," is not a
judgment, it is a shrug. Compare it with the moral toughness
of—alas for the drama!—Karl Jaspers brave little book: *The
Question of German Guilt:*

> The categorical judgment of a people is always
> unjust. It presupposes a false substantialization and
> results in the debasement of the human being as an
> individual . . .
>
> To pronounce a group [for instance, mankind?]
> criminally, morally or metaphysically guilty is an
> error akin to the laziness and arrogance of average,
> uncritical thinking.

The German Government has not yet drawn up the lists,
assessed precise degrees of responsibility. Like Miller, it prefers
monuments and universal flagellation. Meanwhile, Jaspers has
made the distinctions. He has written the drama.

Arthur Miller has written something else. Uninterested in
"The human being as an individual" he presents us with
Incident at Vichy, a kind of medieval Morality Play, like
Everyman, in which characterization is replaced by attitude
and type. For example, those who wait to be examined are all
men, just like the cast of *Everyman*. Is this because women
can't be forced to prove their identities by opening their flies, or
is it because men make the best stereotypes? There is no
attempt to portray an individual (except for the German Major,
significantly). Instead, a medieval character chart is unrolled:
The Supercilious Actor, the Deceived Aristocrat, the Communist Worker Whose Faith is in History, the Old Jew, etc.
With such types, one cannot fashion even a Morality: there is
no sense of evil, no confrontation, struggle, no feeling of
destiny—only the declaration of a common circumstance
(almost happenstance) as one by one each attitude is cut down
with all the force, the fatality, of an ax chopping balsa.

Next to this, *Everyman* is a complex triumph. Its terror, at
least, is consistent. Beauty, Five Wits, Strength, Discretion,
"all at last do Everyman forsake," as useless to him as forged
passports to Miller's Jews. The last we see of Everyman, he and
Good Deeds "follow Death into the Grave." We are assured he
will soon rise and be welcomed as a Spouse to Jesu, but that in
no way mitigates the brutality of a world in which accomplishment and grace are futile.

Miller postulates a similar world, one of agression and
suffering, where not even Good Deeds holds one's hand at the
grave:

> —it can never be a lesson, it can never have a
>   meaning. And that is why it will be repeated
>   again and again forever.
> —Because it cannot be shared?
> —Yes. Because it cannot be shared. It is total
>   absolute waste.

Then his nerve fails him. As if to disprove his play's thesis, he
offers us a Good Gentile, the Baron, who hands his exit permit
to the remaining Jew, and thereby *does* share the fate of the
condemned. Taubman loved it—the American theater had not
Turned Its Back on Hope. Why be surprised or disappointed?
Or course the gift of the permit is gratuitous, unmotivated,
phony— a high-school gesture, not an act. But this what one
should expect. Wet-eyed sentimentality is the other side of the
coin of total accusation, Understanding All, the grace of God.
Unable to judge men, Miller offers his handerchief. It is the
Enemy of the People adaptation all over again. Heal the
differences among us; every man a member of the majority.
Compassion is a moral emotion; that is such a simple thing to
say. It seems to have eluded Miller's grasp.

It is decades since the Jews were murdered. It is an event
that only begins to be speakable. We, the world, have been in a
stage of shock for twenty years. No one has forgotten—there is
no danger, really, of that. It is just that it has been impossible to
remember. With few exceptions, such as Jaspers, it is now, only
now, here and there, in fragments, uncontrollably, that the
counter-attack begins. *Incident at Vichy*, though it has some
decent things to say about other matters (and though it contains
one genuinely dramatic moment: when the Old Jew's bundle to
which he clung tenaciously throughout the play is finally
ripped from him, it splits—and the air is filled with feathers,
only feathers) it has no part to play in the revulsion, the recoil,
the understanding or the judgment which must come.

Notes

1. Micheal Meyer's edition of *Enemy of the People*.

STEPHEN FENDER
"Precision and Pseudo Precision in *The Crucible*"
Journal of American Studies, April 1967, pp. 87–98

I

Writing almost four years after *The Crucible* was first
performed, Arthur Miller seemed uncertain how to
describe the ethics of the society he had tried to reproduce in
the play. He notes, for example, that the Puritans' 'religious
belief did nothing to temper [their] cruelty' but instead 'served
to raise this swirling and ludicrous mysticism to a level of high
moral debate'. 'It is no mean irony', Miller continues, 'that the

theocratic persecution should seek out the most religious people for its victims.'[1]

On the other hand—and in the same essay—Miller claims that he chose Salem for the play's setting precisely because it provided people 'of higher self-awareness than the contemporary scene affords', so that by opposing the articulate John Proctor to an equally articulate society he could dramatize his theme of the danger of 'handing over of conscience to another' (pp. 44–5).

But Miller's audience did not always appear to understand the theme, and the play's reception was mixed. The author has his own idea of what went wrong:

> I believe that the very moral awareness of the play and its characters—which are historically correct—was repulsive to the audience. For a variety of reasons I think that the Anglo-Saxon audience cannot believe the reality of characters who live by principles and know very much about their own characters and situations, and who say what they know [pp. 44–5].

Most Miller scholars have more or less accepted his account of the play as the story of John Proctor at odds with a monolithic society. Arthur Hunt, for example, writes that the play 'comments on modern fragmentation by withdrawing to the vantage point of a community which is whole and self aware'.[2] In an extremely interesting article on Miller, John Prudhoe interprets Proctor's stance against Salem as the 'most "modern" moment in The Crucible' because in it the hero works out his own solution 'unaided by confortable slogans, the weight of opinion of those around him or a coherently worked-out philosophy'. Proctor's thought is free of the traditional beliefs of Salem and of the 'surprisingly articulate' speech in which the town expresses its values. Proctor's plea for his 'name' at the end of the play 'is the cry of a man who has rejected the world in which he lives and hence can no longer use the language of that world'.[3]

This essay attempts to support Prudhoe's reading of The Crucible as a dramatic contest of language, but to question the assumption that he shares with Miller himself and with other critics of Miller that the Puritans in the play have a consistent moral outlook. Indeed, if one examines the language, both of real Puritans and of the characters in The Crucible, it becomes clear that it is the speech of a society totally without referents. Salem confronts Proctor not with a monolithic ethic (however misguided) but with the total absence of any ethic. The townspeople are certain of their moral standards only on the level of abstraction; on the level of the facts of human behaviour they share no criteria for judgement, and it is this lack which makes them victims—as well as protagonists—of the witch hunt. Their language reflects this complete disjunction between their theory and the facts of human action. Proctor finally demolishes their phoney language and painfully reconstructs a halting, but integral way of speaking in which words are once again related to their lexis. But the effect of this achievement is not to break away from the ethic of Salem; rather it is to construct the first consistent moral system in the play, a system in which fact and theory can at last coalesce. Proctor serves himself by recovering his 'name'; he serves Salem by giving it a viable language.

II

In the Introduction to the Collected Plays Miller writes that what struck him most forcefully when he examined the records of the Salem trials was the 'absolute dedication to evil displayed by the judges' (p. 43). What is more obvious to the audience of The Crucible is the extent to which Miller—always

sensitive to the spoken word—has picked up and transmitted the language of these verbatim reports, and not only the language but the entire Puritan 'system' of ethics which that language embodies.

The ethics of a society as nearly theocratic as that of the American Puritans owed much to the society's doctrine of salvation. American Puritans called themselves 'Covenanters' and thought of themselves as having achieved a compromise between the Calvinist theory of predestination and the Arminian stress on works as efficacious for salvation. Calvinism taught that before the Creation a certain, immutable number of men were elected to salvation, and the rest left to eternal damnation. Because nothing in the subsequent lives of men could affect their predestined fate, good works were inefficacious to salvation. The obvious practical application was that no one need bother about his conduct; though behaviour might or might not be an indication of one's predetermined state, it had no formal effect on it.

Covenantal theology tried to soften this demoralizing theory by developing the doctrine of the two Convenants. God was said to have offered man two Covenants: the first, the Covenant of Works, made with Adam, offered everlasting life in return for obedience to the Laws; after Adam had broken this agreement and his sin had been imputed to all mankind, God in his mercy offered another Covenant, first to Abraham, then through Moses to the Israelites, finally through Christ to Christians. This Covenant of Grace offered life in return for a more passive obedience: faith in, and imitation of God. Man must still keep the law to the best of his ability, but, by the new Covenant of Grace, he will be judged by the spirit, not by the letter, of the law.[4] It is doubtful, however, whether the doctrine of the covenants really altered much the basic tenets—and the practical effects—of the notion of predestination. Works might be interpreted as efficacious for salvation, but still only if they proceeded from a state of grace. Man's role was passive; once he had been involved in the Covenant of Grace, he could perform works fruitful to his salvation, but God withheld or extended the initial, 'triggering' grace at his pleasure. There could be no question of a man 'earning' grace by his works.

This, then, was predestination all over again.[5] The Puritan theologian, John Preston, writes: '*All men are divided into these two rankes, either they are good or bad, either they are polluted or cleane, either they are such as sacrifice or such as sacrifice not:* There is no middle sort of men in the world; . . .'[6]

How can one tell if he is among the elect?

> First; *the tree must be good*, as you have it in *Math.* 7. 16. 17. That is, a man then is said to be a good man, when there is good sap in him . . . when there are some supernaturall graces wrought in him. . . . Secondly; consider whether thou *bring forth good fruit*, that is, not onely whether thou doest good actions, but whether they flow from thee, whether they grow in thine heart as naturally, as fruit growes on the tree, that flowes from the sap within . . . and the meaning of the *holy Ghost* is therefore to show, that then a man is good, when his heart is fitted to good workes, when he knowes how to go about them, whereas another bungles them, and knowes not how to doe them . . .[7]

Preston's stress on man's passivity is unmistakable. Man is capable of efficacious works only after he has been touched by God's grace; they must flow 'naturally' from him; he cannot begin the process himself. But how is a man to know if his works—by any objective test 'good'—really and essentially proceed from a state of grace? The Westminster Confession, the articles of faith for the American Covenanters as well as for the Scottish Presbyterians, is even more uncompromising in refusing to answer the question:

> Good works are only such as God hath commanded in his holy word, and not such as, without the warrant thereof, are devised by men out of blind zeal, and upon any pretence of good intention [ch. XVI, i]. Works done by unregenerate men, although, for the matter of them, they may be things which God commands, and of good use both to themselves and others; yet, because they proceed not from an heart purified by faith; nor are done in a right manner, according to the word; nor to a right end, the glory of God; they are therefore sinful, and cannot please God, or make a man meet to receive grace from God [ch. XVI, vii].

It is possible to make too little of the Covenantal theologians' attempt to compromise with Calvinism; after all, though they confused Calvinism's brutal logic, they also made it more human and (dare one say it?) more Christian. Nevertheless, the central doctrine of predestination was left intact. Works are no longer exclusively inefficacious; now some good works are more equal than others. But we are still denied objective criteria for determining which is which. This fact, combined with the notion that, as Preston says, all men are 'good or bad' and 'there is no middle sort of men in the world' is the theory behind perhaps the biggest single effect of the Reformation on practical morality. For better or worse, as two American critics have noted, Puritan predestination breaks down the whole structure of Aristotelian–Scholastic ethics, sweeping away any idea of *degrees* of good and evil. H. W. Schneider makes this point in *The Puritan Mind*:[8]

> No one can live long in a Holy Commonwealth without becoming sensitive, irritable, losing his sense of values and ultimately his balance. All acts are either acts of God or of the Devil; all issues are matters of religious faith; all conflicts are holy wars . . . no matter how harmless a fool might be, he was intolerable if he did not fit into the Covenant of Grace; no matter how slight an offence might be, it was a sin against Almighty God and hence infinite.

And Yvor Winters applies this point to *The Scarlet Letter*, another literary re-creation of American Puritan society:

> Objective evidence . . . took the place of inner assurance, and the behaviour of the individual took on symbolic value. That is, any sin was evidence of damnation; or, in other words, any sin represented all sin. When Hester Prynne committed adultery, she committed an act as purely representative of complete corruption as the act of Faustus in signing a contract with Satan. This view of the matter is certainly not Catholic and is little short of appalling.[9]

The Roman Catholic doctrine of salvation was and is a rational system, depending on man's free will to do good and evil—actively and consciously. Sins are either venial or mortal. Everywhere the idea of degree prevails; the sinner can neutralize his transgressions by greater or smaller acts of penance, depending on the degree of sin committed. One spends a greater or lesser time in purgatory, according to one's degree of perfection. The practical psychological effect of this system is that by it man is taught to deal with his acts severally, to analyse the details of his behaviour and experience one by one and to weigh one against the other. On the other hand, the Calvinists, and even the Covenantal Puritans, were taught to think of their behaviour (and the behaviour of their neighbours) as evidence only, not as conscious acts causing salvation

or damnation. As evidence of total salvation or total damnation, their several acts were unimportant in themselves; there was less stress on evaluating each act and more on merely identifying it as evidence of grace or damnation.

In the light of these ideas, it is interesting to read, for example, through 'Concerning an History of some *Criminals* executed in *New England* for Capital Crimes . . .', originally written by 'one of the *New English Ministers* . . . in hopes that the horrible sight would cause that worst Enemy to fly before it', and reprinted in Cotton Mather's history of New England.[10] Mather includes the accounts of the trials and the confessions of the convicted in an appendix to his chapter '. . . Discoveries and Demonstrations of the Divine Providence in Remarkable Mercies and Judgements on Many Particular Persons . . . of *New England* . . .', remarking that, in the account of executed criminals, 'the *remarkable judgements of God* were wonderfully Exemplify'd' (book IV, p. 37). This statement itself is important. The sins of the criminals (in these cases, their crimes, though the distinction between sin and crime is rather vague in Puritan New England) are not acts leading to their damnation; they are evidence of divine judgement already determined.

The various accounts are written in such a way as to support the construction Mather puts on them. What is particularly interesting is the nature of the criminals' confessions, the way in which they deal with their experience, and the writer's remarks on their behaviour. For instance, James Morgan was a 'passionate fellow' who 'swore he would run a Spit into a man's Bowels' and '. . . was as good as his word' (book VI, p. 40). He was hanged in Boston in 1686. His confession recounts a number of his sins:

> I have been a great Sinner, guilty of Sabbath-breaking, of Lying, and of uncleanness; but there are especially two Sins whereby I have offended the Great God; one is that Sin of Drunkenness, which has caused me to commit many other Sins; for when in Drink, I have been often guilty of Cursing and Swearing, and Quarrelling, and striking others. But the Sin which lies most heavy upon my Conscience, is that I have despised the word of God, and many a time refused to hear it preached [book VI, p. 40].

It is too harsh, perhaps, to expect a man about to be hanged to analyse his behaviour with any great precision, but one cannot help noticing the curious confusion of values by which drunkenness and refusing to hear the word of God become major sins and murder is not mentioned. Later in his confession, when he does deal with the act that brought him to the gallows, Morgan treats it not as a sin, but as a crime, of civil importance only:

> I own the Sentence which the Honour'd Court has pass'd upon me, to be Exceeding Just; inasmuch as (though I had no former Grudge and Malice against the man whom I have kill'd, yet) my Passion at the time of the Fact, was so outragious, as that it hurried me on to the doing of that which makes me now justly proceeded against as a Murderer [Ibid].

And even here he (or whoever is helping him formulate his confession) speaks as though he were the passive agent in the act of murder. What counts is not the act itself (even the name of 'murder' is carefully circumvented by the periphrastic 'that which makes me now justly proceeded against as a Murderer'), but some 'cause proportionate' which the murderer is powerless to resist: drunkenness and 'Passion'. One recalls Preston insisting that good works must flow from within 'as the fruit growes on the tree'. Presumably this applies also to 'bad' works;

either way the need for human responsibility seems to be diminished.

It is worth looking at one more excerpt from this grisly catalogue, a sermon preached at the hanging in 1698 of a 'miserable Young Woman' who had murdered her illegitimate child. The minister makes only a passing reference to her 'crime' and, surprisingly, to her adultery: 'Thus the *God*, whose Eyes are like a Flame of Fire, is now casting her into a Bed of burning Tribulation: and, ah, Lord, where wilt thou cast those that have committed Adultery with her, except they repent!' (book VI, p. 48). The minister is really interested, for the most part, in her other sins:

> Since her Imprisonment, she hath declared, that she believes, God hath left her unto this undoing Wickedness, partly for her staying so prophanely at home, sometimes on *Lords Days*, when she should have been hearing the Word of Christ, and much more for her not minding that Word, when she heard it.
>
> And she has confessed, That she was much given to Rash Wishes, in her mad passions, particularly using often that ill Form of speaking, *I'll be hang'd*, if a thing be not thus or so; and, *I'll be hang'd*, if I do not this or that: Which Evil now, to see it, coming upon her, it amazes her! But this *Chief Sin* of which this *Chief of Sinners* now cries out, is, her undutiful Carriage towards her Parents. Her Language and her Carriage towards her Parents, was indeed such that they hardly durst speak to her; but when they durst, they often told her, It would come to this [book VI, p. 49].

Every aspect of this nasty document is important—the gallows humour, the language, the preacher's total confusion of values. In this strange system ignoring the Sabbath and insulting one's parents become as serious as adultery and murder. The girl's parents could see—where we cannot—that she was unregenerate and thus capable of *anything*. They knew it would come to this because she had been 'undutiful' at home. They knew that unless she finally showed evidence of being among the saved (through confessing and repenting) she was surely among the damned. One piece of evidence was as good as another.

III

Orwell said that if a politician wished to control a democratic country he had to begin by controlling its language—that, to put it simply, a man who wanted to persuade people to do things they didn't want to do might profitably begin by calling those things by different names.[11] Advertising, too, depends on distorting the conventional meanings of words, or even on coining deliberately imprecise phrases. Patent medicines are said to cure 'tired blood' or 'night starvation' because these terms are imprecise enough to include a wide spectrum of ailments and thus promote a wide sale. Jonson anticipated this trick when he made Volpone, as mountebank, advertise his elixir as a specific for *tremor-cordia* and retired nerves.

But, as any literary critic knows, language can be distorted less consciously and less maliciously by people who are merely uncertain of their attitude towards whatever they are using words to describe. It seems likely that the vague and ultimately meaningless language which the preacher brings to bear on the 'miserable young woman's' sin ('Tribulation', 'Wickedness', 'prophanely', 'Rash Wishes') results from his own uncertainty about the comparative value of various human acts. This uncertainty may also account for the dubious taste of the

passage, since what we call 'bad taste' is nothing more than a dislocation between a fact and the level of language used to describe that fact.

So, far from having a 'higher self-awareness', as Miller thought, the American Puritans were undecided about how much importance to give to specific human acts: good works may or may not proceed from a state of grace; all that was certain was that nothing was what it seemed; the concrete fact had no assured validity. But what Miller has caught so successfully, despite his theory, is the peculiar way in which the Puritans spoke whenever they talked about sin. One can say even more than that: Miller has, in fact, made the fullest dramatic use of the language, using its peculiarities to limit the characters speaking it and even making it part of the play's subject.

The language plays its part, for example, in establishing the rather complex ironic structure in the scene in which the Reverend Hale first appears. Betty is lying ill, and Parris, secretly fearing that she might be affected by witchcraft, has called in an expert in detecting witchcraft. The situation itself is ironic; it is a measure of his own confusion about Betty that Parris must call in an expert with weighty volumes under his arm to tell him what to think about his daughter's exhaustion and shock. The audience also suspects that Parris depends on Hale's authority as a compensation for being unable to deal with Abigail. Another aspect of the irony is that the audience knows the expert's opinion will change nothing; the Putnams and the other townspeople—even Parris himself—have now convinced themselves that witchcraft is to blame. Finally, of course, the audience has already been given enough evidence—in the hasty conference between Abigail, Betty and Mary Warren and in Abigail's plea to Proctor—that Hale's knowledge of witchcraft is irrelevant to the situation.

In the light of all this confusion, it is interesting to examine in some detail Hale's first extended speech:

> *Putman:* She cannot bear to hear the Lord's name, Mr Hale; that's a sure sign of witchcraft afloat.
> *Hale, holding up his hands:* No, no. Now let me instruct you. We cannot look to superstition in this. The Devil is precise; the marks of his presence are definite as stone, and I must tell you all that I shall not proceed unless you are prepared to believe me if I should find no bruise of hell upon her.

We miss the point if we see this scene as the opposition of the frightened, confused townspeople on the one hand, and the sane, certain, rational expert on the other. Hale's precision is pseudo precision: the speech is ironic because the audience knows that Hale's distinction between 'superstition' and real witchcraft is less clear than he supposes. His simile to illustrate the Devil's precision supports this reading: 'definite as stone'; it looks precise, possibly because it is a 'hard' image, but stone is actually an imprecise image for 'definite' because stone seldom appears clearly differentiated from other material, either in nature or in artifact.

Hale's pseudo precision is established beyond doubt a few lines further on in the scene:

> *Hale, with a tasty love of intellectual pursuit:* Here is all the invisible world, caught, defined, and calculated. In these books the Devil stands stripped of all his brute disguises. Here are all your familiar spirits—your incubi and succubi; your witches that go by land, by air, and by sea; your wizards of the night and of the day. Have no fear now—we shall find him out if he has come among us, and I mean to crush him utterly if he has shown his face!

At first sight this list—with its division of material into various categories—has all the exactness of the encyclopaedia, but at second sight we are not convinced that the categories are well chosen. (Why, for example, should witches be arranged according to how they travel?) A modern audience is uncertain about what all the terms means (just what is the difference between incubi and succubi?).

The audience familiar with Jonson may experience a tinge of *déjà vu* at this point. What we are hearing is a kind of conflation of *Volpone* and *The Alchemist*, Tribulation Wholesome acting the mountebank. In fact, the speech is a wild flight of jargon, quite unrelated to the situation with which Hale has been asked to deal, and if the audience has held out any hope for Hale's ability to recall the community to sanity, they must abandon that hope at this point. It is quite obvious that Hale, in his own unique way, is divorced from reality. The others see evidence of witchcraft in the illness of a hysterical girl, and the witch hunt will express their repressed envy, libido and land lust. Hale, too, sees witchcraft behind the events in Salem. He will use the witch hunt to express his manic expertise.

What makes Hale so vulnerable to the witch hunt is not—as with the other townspeople—his repressed emotions, but his love of abstraction. Hale, like any other educated Puritan, discounts the obvious. The concrete fact is not to be trusted. Thus at his first entrance, he recognizes Rebecca Nurse without having been introduced to her because she looks 'as such a good soul should'. But later, when he begins to apply his theories to the problem of Salem, he tells the Proctors 'it is possible' that Rebecca is a witch. Proctor answers: 'But it's hard to think so pious a woman be secretly a Devil's bitch after seventy year of such good prayer.' 'Aye,' replies Hale, 'but the Devil is a wily one, you cannot deny it.' His search for the form behind the shadow finally leads him to an almost comical reversal of cause and effect:

> I cannot think God be provoked so grandly by such a petty cause. The jails are packed—our greatest judges sit in Salem now—and hangin's promised. Man, we must look to cause proportionate. Was there murder done, perhaps, and never brought to light? Abomination? Some secret blasphemy that stinks to heaven? Think on cause, and let you help me to discover it.

When the facts become unimportant (and in this case the fact is Hale's 'petty cause'—Abigail's alleged jealousy of Elizabeth Proctor), the choice of words becomes unimportant also: 'abomination' and 'secret blasphemy' mean little to us because Hale himself is unsure of what he means by them.

Danforth, too, has his pseudo precision:

> . . . you must understand, sir, that a person is either with this court or he must be counted against it, there be no road between. This is a sharp time, now, a precise time—we no longer live in the dusky afternoon when evil mixed itself with good and befuddled the world. Now, by God's grace, the shining sun is up, and them that fear not light will surely praise it. I hope you will be one of those.

This reminds us of Hale's catalogue of witches, of John Preston's statement that '. . . *all men are divided into these two rankes, either they are good or bad*'; Miller has made good ironic use of the Puritan habit of constructing false disjunctions. Danforth's formulation looks precise, but misses the point because it establishes a false criterion of guilt (whether the accused approves of the court). So not only is it untrue to say that one is either with the court or 'must be counted against it'; it is irrelevant. The trial has now reached its final stage in its

retreat from the realities of the situation: it began unrealistically enough by examining the causes for the presence of something which had yet to be proved: then it began to take account of the wrong evidence, to listen to the wrong people; finally it becomes completely self-enclosed, and self-justifying, asking not whether the accused is guilty of being a witch but whether he or she supports the court.

In its withdrawal from reality the court takes advantage of the semantic uncertainty of the Salem townspeople, and, in so doing, makes them even more uncertain. Act Three opens with the sounds of Hathorne examining Martha Corey off-stage:

> *Hathorne's Voice:* Now, Martha Corey, there is abundant evidence in our hands to show that you have given yourself to the reading of fortunes. Do you deny it?
> *Martha Corey's Voice:* I am innocent to a witch. I know not what a witch is.
> *Hathorne's Voice:* How do you know, then, that you are not a witch?

Later, when even Hale begins to doubt the wisdom of the court, he tells Danforth: 'We cannot blink it more. There is a prodigious fear of this court in the country—' And Danforth answers: 'Then there is a prodigious guilt in the country.' Terms are now quite rootless; the parallelism of the syntax suggests that 'fear' and 'guilt' are interchangeable.

How can the honest man combat this utter confusion of language and of the values which language transmits? One solution is simply to reject the slippery terminology and revert to a more primitive way of speaking:

> *Danforth, turning to Giles:* Mr Putnam states your charge is a lie. What say you to that?
> *Giles, furious, his fists clenched:* A fart on Thomas Putnam, that is what I say to that!

This is one of the funniest moments in the play because it is true *discordia concors*. The audience senses the discrepancy (to say the least) between Giles's level of speech and the rhetoric of the court, but it also appreciates the desperate need to break away from the court's dubious terminology.

John Proctor's attack on the court's language is more serious, and more complex. He first meets it straightforwardly, trying to reverse the distorted meanings of the words it uses, or at least to restore the proper words to their proper places. When Cheever visits his house to tell him Elizabeth has been accused, Proctor says: 'Is the accuser always holy now? Were they born this morning as clean as God's fingers? I'll tell you what's walking Salem—vengeance is walking Salem. We are what we always were in Salem but now the little crazy children are jangling the keys of the kingdom, and common vengeance writes the law!' Although Proctor is talking here to Cheever, he is also trying to put right a false formulation that Hale has made earlier in the scene, a characteristically imprecise use of a concrete image as an abstraction: 'the Devil is alive in Salem'. Proctor is trying to reassert the authority of the proper word. 'We are what we always were'; only the words to describe us have changed.

But Proctor, of course, has his own guilt. Already he has been unable to say the word 'adultery' when asked to recite the commandments. Finally when he faces his guilt—and tries to make the community accept it—in court, his formulation is painfully inarticulate: 'It is a whore!' The statement contrasts powerfully with the smooth, meaningless language of his wife's accusers. At the end of the scene, when even his painful confession has failed to move them, he indicts them in *their* language, as though as a last resort he is trying to turn their own weapons upon them: 'A fire, a fire is burning! I hear the boot of Lucifer, I see his filthy face! And it is my face, and yours, Danforth!'

Even if Miller's stage direction didn't call for Proctor to 'laugh insanely' at this point, we could not accept this as the right solution; turnabout may be fair play, but in choosing to use their language, even against them, Proctor cannot escape its imprecision. There is, after all, some distinction between him and Danforth, and, in the terms of this play, this difference can only be asserted by a total rejection of Danforth's language. This rejection comes—by implication, at least—when Proctor makes his genuine sacrifice at the end of the play, when he reclaims his 'name': 'Because it is my name! Because I cannot have another in my life! Because I am not worth the dust on the feet of them that hang! How may I live without my name? I have given you my soul; leave me my name.' It is as though in regaining his name he finally ends the confusion about names which has been the town's sickness.

Proctor must indeed cast off the terminology of Salem. But what he is rejecting is not a monolithic system, not a 'coherently worked-out philosophy'. Salem speech is 'articulate' in only a very limited sense of the word; 'voluble' or 'smooth' would apply more aptly. One needs to make this point because our response to the play is more complex than it would be if Proctor were a modern existential hero working out his own solution in opposition to the conventions of society. Salem has no conventions. Its evil is not positive. Its ethics are wrong; they are non-existent. What makes the progress of the witch-hunt so terrifying for the audience is the realization that the trial has no programme. If Proctor and the others were being tested—and found wanting—according to a wrong-headed but consistent set of values, our reaction to the play would be quite different. What terrifies us is that we never know from what direction the next attack will come, and we are struck more by what Miller, in his introduction to the Collected Plays, calls 'the swirling and ludicrous mysticism [elevated] to a level of high moral debate' of the characters than we are by their 'moral awareness'. John Proctor acts not as a rebel but as the restorer of what the audience take to be normal human values. What Miller actually achieved in The Crucible is far more important than what he apparently feels guilty for not having achieved.

Notes

1. Introduction to *Collected Plays* (London, 1958), pp. 45–6. Subsequent references to this edition will appear in the text.
2. "Realism and Intelligence: Some Notes on Arthur Miller", *Encore*, 7 (1960), 15.
3. *English Studies*, 43 (1962), 430.
4. The doctrine was first popularized by William Perkins, Fellow of Christ's College, Cambridge, from 1584 to 1594; by his student, the Calvinist moral theologian William Ames; and by John Preston, the brilliant Fellow of Queen's College and later Master of Emmanuel. The works of all three men were widely read and admired in New England. One of the clearest of the early and basic statements of the Covenantal doctrine of salvation is Preston's *The New Covenant or the Saints Portion* (London, 1629), a collection of sermons edited by Richard Sibbes and John Davenport.
5. For a fuller discussion of the extent to which Covenantal theology modified the Calvinist doctrine of salvation, see Perry Miller, *The New England Mind* (New York, 1939). Professor Miller argues that the modification was considerable: '. . . by conceiving of grace as a readiness of God to join in covenant with any man who will not resist Him, the theory declared in effect that God has taken the initiative, that man can have only himself to blame if he does not accede to the divine proposal' (p. 395). For reasons given above and later in the paper, I should like to suggest that, essentially, or at least practically, the Covenantal Puritans retained the doctrine of the inefficacy of works.

6. Preston, vol. III, p. 23.
7. Preston, vol. III, pp. 26–8.
8. San Francisco (1930), pp. 51–2.
9. "Maule's Curse", in *In Defense of Reason* (Denver, 1947), p. 159.
10. *Magnalia Christi Americana* (London, 1702), book VI, pp. 37–49. Subsequent references in the text.
11. "Politics and the English Language", *Horizon* (April, 1946), pp. 252–65.

ARTHUR K. OBERG
"*Death of a Salesman* and Arthur Miller's Search for Style"

Criticism, Fall 1967, pp. 303–11

Arthur Miller's place in the contemporary theatre is based so exclusively upon the kind of social or public play he writes that the distinction of his language has been given small attention. When a play like *Death of a Salesman* has been considered for its speech, it has been dismissed as "bad poetry."[1] Although both Miller and Tennessee Williams have had plays directed and staged by Elia Kazan, critics tend to maximize the essential difference of their writing. In the established image, Miller's art is masculine and craggy; Williams', poetic and delicate. Such generalizations are not unjustifiable, but they obscure problems that Miller and Williams share and have attempted to solve in their respective dramas. For all of Miller's obverse comments on poetic poetry or the mood play,[2] his entire dramatic career has been an effort to get beyond a limited realism and a confining prose. Like Williams, he is in search of a style that will allow for an unusually expressive speech. And his use of a narrator in *A View from the Bridge* and his breakdown of time and space sequences in *Death of a Salesman* and *After the Fall* have been attempts at creating occasions when such language may be possible.

Miller's own comments and writings on the drama can be blamed for many of the unfavorable considerations that his dramatic prose has evoked. Miller is too harsh in insisting upon the differences between drama and literature. In realizing that a play is more than a verbal art, Miller in the "Introduction" to his *Collected Plays* makes his point at the expense of undercutting what importance a text does and can possess.[3] There is an uncritical and confused use of words such as "poetic" and "social" that conceals how much concern with a distinctive language Miller's plays reveal. A distrust of poetic poetry by Miller is understandable in view of the abortive verse play revival and the suspicion of audiences toward emotion and poetry, a suspicion evidenced by a drift toward "*indiscriminate* understatement"[4] in the theatre. But Miller's recorded devaluation of the language of a play is at strange odds with his continued excursions into finding an adequate stage speech in his work.

What the body of Miller's plays confirms is a situation that O'Neill found in the theatre many years ago and that continues to perplex the American dramatist—a lack of an established and available idiom. An interest in and employment of dialects—whether Irish, tough, sex, or alcoholic conversation[5]—became O'Neill's response to this situation. It recurs with slight variation in Miller's archaic Puritan speech in *The Crucible* and in his varieties of American localese in other plays. We are given dialogue that is different from what we are accustomed to hear, but always sufficiently recognizable for comprehension. Slices of life are presented that alternately provide us with the pleasure of hearing familiar speech and unfamiliar (or, to its users, *more* familiar) vernacular. Whereas

Shakespeare's use of dialect only pointed to the presence of some standard stage speech in the background, its use by O'Neill and Miller indicates the contemporary absence of an established idiom. Back in 1923 Ezra Pound objected to dialects as "a usual form of evasion in modern drama";[6] but such a judgment ignores considerations of their decorum for particular plays and of the competence with which they are employed. And the continuing use, for example, of Southern speech and slangy colloquialism in the American drama reveals both partial solutions and impasses unsolved.

Miller comes to a theatre whose audiences are daily glutted with words from the commercial media. He accepts the embarrassment of audiences before emotive writing while affirming the right of the theatre to make people both think and feel. Although poets and poetry are joked about in several of his plays, language is undercut only so that it may be possible at all. Like Shaw or Arnold Wesker or Jack Richardson, Miller presents the poet as dolt or dreamer.[7] And, like them, he then goes on to use words as if he had forgotten the difficulties involved. In the face of the absurd impossibility of finding even adequate words, Miller drives on to accomplish what would seem not allowed.

If the situation in the American theatre is as complex and discouraging as has been indicated—the lack of an established idiom, the suspicions of an audience toward poetry and emotion—Miller's various attempts toward solving the problems of text take on new meaning. They suggest as extensive an experiment as Eliot's with the verse line. Although Miller's revision of A *View from the Bridge* ended his one attempt at using a verse line in the theatre, each of his plays and non-dramatic works relates to a lifetime search for a distinctive style. Miller's approximations of Western speech in *The Misfits* and of seventeenth century speech in *The Crucible* solved this problem only for these particular works. Like Eliot after *Murder in the Cathedral*, Miller uncovers in his dramatic career an effort to forge a speech that would generally serve for whatever play he might happen to write. In *Death of a Salesman* and the plays that follow—with the exception of *The Crucible* whose style becomes an interruption, usable for one play—Miller picks up where the dialogue of *All My Sons* left off.

From Miller's earliest plays to *Incident at Vichy* there is a distinctive speech which, regardless of ostensible setting or background of characters, is based upon a New York idiom that often has recognizably Jewish inflection (e.g. the rising rhythms of "Does it take more guts to stand here the rest of my life ringing up a zero?").[8] Miller has an ear for speech that can be heard in any of the New York boroughs, for rhythms that have filtered down into Gentile conversation many miles from the city. Beginning with a particular speech, Miller arrives at something that approaches an American idiom to the extent that it exposes a colloquialism characterized by unusual image, spurious lyricism, and close-ended cliché. One has the impression of characters cheering themselves up with speech that is counterpointed by what we already know as audience about them. For Miller, it is a conscious selection from the speech that he has known and heard from childhood through which he exposes such discrepancies, particularly rents in the American dream. And it is in *Death of a Salesman* that he perfects this idiom to allow for a more successful revelation of complex character than in any other play he wrote.

The language of *Death of a Salesman* has characteristics that link it with all of Miller's work. Miller has a talent for using words and phrases as leitmotifs ("He's liked, but he's not—well liked"), for writing what approaches but is less obvious and

shorter than set speech. Linda and Willy's occasional soliloquy-like musings relate to the kind of patterned speech that typifies Miller's earlier and later plays:

> The cats in that alley are practical, the bums who ran away when we were fighting were practical. Only the dead ones weren't practical. But now I'm practical, and I spit on myself. I'm going away. I'm going now.[9]

> No, no. Now let me instruct you. We cannot look to superstition in this. The Devil is precise; the marks of his presence are definite as stone, and I must tell you all that I shall not proceed unless you are prepared to believe me if I should find no bruise of hell upon her.[10]

Similarly, prominent striking images ("He was so humiliated he nearly limped when he came in" [p. 211]; "All the talk that went across those two beds, huh? Our whole lives" [p. 137]), recall the earmarks of other plays, dialogue that hesitates between mixed metaphor and metaphysical conceit:

> Frank is right—every man does have a star. The star of one's honesty.[11]

> This society will not be a bag to swing around your head, Mr. Putnam.[12]

> Quentin, don't hold the future like a vase—touch now, touch me! I'm here, and it's now![13]

> You'd better ram a viewpoint up your spine or you'll break in half.[14]

Miller here reveals three things: a knack of linking an abstract and a concrete in metaphor, a pressing of metaphor to visual incongruity or cartoon-like animation, and a preference for letting an audience bear away one or two vivid images in contrast to the *copia* of a playwright like Christopher Fry. While implicit attitudes toward kinds of rhetoric possible within a contemporary play would further link *Death of a Salesman* with the body of Miller's work, it is the particular density of a familiar Miller rhetoric that gives *Death of a Salesman* a feel that none of his other plays achieves. And the density is dictated by the enclosed situation in which the main character is found.

When Miller undertook in *Death of a Salesman* to present the plight of Willy Loman, he offered a reexamination of radical aspects of the American dream. The Lomans, never a family of adults, gradually and painfully attest to discrepancies in the American success myth, discrepancies that their lives from time to time can no longer hide. What Willy and his sons and what Charley and Bernard indicate in their respective failures and successes is the presence of arbitrary gods. Willy clings to them as he is beaten by them, and Miller's "requiem" confirms them as a part of the territory. For Loman, they are both equipment for living and vestments of death. As the play moves through its rhythms of euphoric elation and relentless despair, Miller employs a speech that would uphold these values by embedding them in outworn, formulated clichés commonly negatively phrased: "Never fight fair with a stranger, boy," "nobody's worth nothin' dead," "No man only needs a little salary." But elsewhere there is language that draws near to "something of a poetic tinge," "a great air of something like poetry," "a kind of poetry":[15]

> The world is an oyster, but you don't crack it open on a mattress! (p. 152).

> When a deposit bottle is broken you don't get your nickel back (p. 154).

> Everybody likes a kidder, but nobody lends him money (p. 168).

But even when Miller attempts to revitalize language we detect one and the same process here going on—the reduction of living to a set of adages, whether familiar or not.

There are two actions concurrently running in *Death of a Salesman* and related to this reduction of living to cliché. One is a process of exposing and opening up, showing differences in the characters' ideals and lives; the other, an undermining of their clichéd and commonplace lives. The first movement is most obviously reflected in images of stripping down that recur in the play. When Willy protests that "you can't eat the orange and throw the peel away—a man is not a piece of fruit!" (p. 181), he ironically confirms Linda's early adage that "life is a casting off" (p. 133). In context, Linda's words sounded only like readily available consolation, but the brute honesty behind them becomes clear in the remark of Loman's uttered later in the play. Willy's and Linda's lines, when played against one another from such a distance, force an honesty that much of their talk would hide.

Further dislocations in the American dream become prominent in Miller's reconsideration of the ideals of athletic prowess, male friendship, popularity, unpopular success. A society that jointly praises the democratic ideal and the exceptional individual is seen to be schizoid in its confusion of opportunity, talent, and abstract right. Against the process of exposing these often contradictory ideals, Miller sets the weight of the entire clichéd speech of the play. What the characters say is an effort in conservation, an upholding of a societal structure that has made it less and less likely for the small man to succeed. Social and economic statement is involved, but Miller goes beyond this statement in presenting Loman as a man not only trapped by his culture, but growing ineffectual and old. Willy and his sons have reached a time in life when they can live neither together nor apart. Although Willy's feelings of loss and impermanence are intensified and partly caused by his lack of success, his predicament has more complex origins. Willy is a man of slipping powers, locked in the past. Pathetically, in the face of declining earning power and approaching death, he would keep what he does not have and provide for what is not allowed.

The passages of *Death of a Salesman* using intentionally spurious, lyrical metaphor and suggestive of the kind of counterpointing found in Chekhov and O'Neill provide their own charm and force:

> That's why I thank Almighty God you're both built like Adonises (p. 146).

> Like a young god. Hercules—something like that. And the sun, the sun all around him. Remember how he waved to me? (p. 171)

> Miss Forsythe, you've just seen a prince walk by. A fine, troubled prince. A hardworking, unappreciated prince. A pal, you understand? A good companion. Always for his boys (p. 204).

Such princely metaphor arises in moments of euphoria and functions much like the pal or buddy talk of Willy and his sons or like the diminutive language which ironically becomes *more* sentimental in seeking to reduce the sentimentality involved:

> A small man can be just as exhausted as a great man (p. 163).

> Be loving to him. Because he's only a little boat looking for a harbor (p. 176).

Yet, for all this recognizably stylized speech which is reminiscent of other of Miller's plays, it is finally the fragmented wisdom of cliché, shored against Willy's ruin, that defines the language of the play. Miller relentlessly pins down by means of New York dialect, and with a talent akin to Pinter's, the shrinkage and simplification of living made

possible by cliché. The Lomans in *Death of a Salesman* use formulated wisdom to hold off the night when they will have to acknowledge what they evade, unhappiness and failure. In contrast, Charley and his son use this wisdom to reflect the constricted perspective and unrestricted ambition often necessary in the pursuit of success. "The sky's the limit." "If at first you don't succeed. . . ." "One must go in to fetch a diamond out." "The only thing you got in this world is what you can sell." In their clichés, Miller's characters reveal both partial, pragmatically Puritan truths and denials of what an audience sees before their eyes—that all Americans cannot and do not succeed, that men do sometimes cry, that having sons is no guarantee of masculinity or success. Although Willy repeats that "the woods are burning," he refuses to locate what he only vaguely feels and knows. With the exception of those moments when honesty is pleaded for, Willy maintains and is maintained by speech that attempts to supply hope for a situation that excludes it.

Behind the reduction of living to a set of recurrent adages, we hear the helplessness, hopelessness, and frustration of words that can neither cheer Loman up nor improve his predicament. These time-worn phrases became useless and superfluous a long time ago. But they continue to be repeated, and almost religiously, by the characters in the play. Like a charm, they are an evasion and fear of redefining and delineating what has occurred. In the familiarly colloquial and deceptively self-sufficient clichés of the American dream, all is caught and held. The rhythms of the play, recognizably those of lower middle-class New York, could be heard across the country, with variations only in inflection and phrasing and specific cliché. In these rhythms Miller gives expression to a specifically American process or tendency to talk against facts of loneliness and loss, the fact of time-space breaking down under the pressures of memory and madness. He gives voice to rents in the American dream.

Unlike the plays of O'Neill or Williams where much of the power derives from "the cost to the dramatist of what he handled,"[16] *Death of a Salesman* relies upon a greater distancing and objectivity of the playwright. Whatever "otiose breast-beating"[17] occurs is either so subordinated to the play's elusive reticence or so much of an expression of a kind of emotional cliché that the impression is one of a succession of pre-verbalized states that were reinforced in the theatre by the poetic lighting, music, and staging of Kazan. As Willy and the other characters aspire toward greater truthfulness, they are held back by a stylized, cliché-riddled language that encourages evasion as it seeks to bring back a time when Thomas Edison and B. F. Goodrich and J. P. Morgan were still possible. That *Death of a Salesman* is both a document and requiem to this time explains the play's language, if it also provides a circular defense for that style.

However suitable the density of cliché finally is for Miller's purposes in *Death of a Salesman*, we are left with the general impression of a text that is undistinguished and flat. Arguments offered earlier for an intentionally spurious lyricism or for an unusual turn of cliché relate to moments in the play that are too few to absolve the longer stretches of Miller's prose. The play's text, although far from "bad poetry," tellingly moves toward the status of poetry without ever getting there.[18] Although the reasons given for this situation go a long way to explain the quality of the text, to let the case rest on the attitudes of the audience either toward poetry or toward emotion explains one matter only to ignore the power that the play continues to elicit on the stage. That the distinction of the play is not primarily verbal returns us to our earlier considerations of the achievement of *Death of a Salesman* as one of style—style as rhythm, rhythm as style.

As we noted, Miller in *Death of a Salesman* uses a stylistically clichéd language, based on the inflection of a New York Jewish speech and rising to a peculiarly American idiom, to reveal the disparities between Willy's pipe dreams and what has occurred; alternating rhythms of elation and despair dramatically and artistically realize what life less coherently and concentratedly presents. As a result, the strength of the speech of the Lomans resides in its pressing toward what it must never become. Never a poetry of full light, it is a prose characterized by clichés that guy rhythm as they create a style. Here, the distinctiveness of the play lies. In looking beyond the clichéd words of *Death of a Salesman* to the rhythms of the speech and to what the clichés would hide, we draw near to the kind of appreciation that vaudeville, another popular art, must exact—when what is central are not the words spoken but the "bounce" of the music hall line.

Notes

1. Eric Bentley, *In Search of Theater* (New York, 1957), p. 82.
2. Arthur Miller, "Introduction," *Collected Plays* (New York: The Viking Press, 1957), p. 12; "The Family in Modern Drama," *Atlantic Monthly*, CXCVII (April 1956), 40.
3. Miller, "Introduction," pp. 3–5.
4. Louis MacNeice, "Introductory Note" to *Sunbeams in His Hat, The Dark Tower and Other Radio Scripts* (London, 1947), p. 70. American Group Theatre in the thirties and Actor's Studio today, assuming that acting neither begins nor ends in speech, testify to the fact that even acting has been influenced by this drift toward understatement; on the assumptions of method acting see Eric Bentley, *The Dramatic Event* (New York, 1954), p. 173.
5. Bentley, *The Dramatic Event*, p. 32; *In Search of Theater*, pp. 225, 232; Kenneth Tynan, *Curtains* (New York, 1961), p. 203.
6. Ezra Pound, February 1923 Paris Letter, *The Dial*, March 1923, 277.
7. An interesting consideration of Shaw's Octavius and Marchbanks as "unintentionally sentimental" is given by Kenneth Muir, "Verse and Prose," *Contemporary Theatre* ("Stratford-Upon-Avon Studies" 4) (London, 1962), p. 103.
8. Arthur Miller, *Death of a Salesman, Collected Plays*, p. 212. Quotations from *Death of a Salesman* are hereafter given in the text and are taken from this edition.
9. Arthur Miller, *All My Sons, Collected Plays*, p. 123.
10. Arthur Miller, *The Crucible, Collected Plays*, p. 252.
11. Miller, *All My Sons, Collected Plays*, p. 118.
12. Miller, *The Crucible, Collected Plays*, p. 244.
13. Arthur Miller, *After the Fall* (New York, 1964), p. 100.
14. Arthur Miller, *Incident at Vichy* (New York, 1965), p. 31.
15. George Jean Nathan, Eleanor Clark, Harold Clurman, "Reviews of *Death of a Salesman*," *Two Modern American Tragedies: Reviews and Criticism of* Death of a Salesman *and* A Streetcar Named Desire, ed. John D. Hurrell (New York, 1961), pp. 57, 64, 66.
16. Stark Young, *Immortal Shadows* (New York, 1948), p. 65.
17. Tynan, *Curtains*, p. 260.
18. See the critical consensus in note 15.

THOMAS E. PORTER
"Acres of Diamonds: *Death of a Salesman*"
Myth and Modern American Drama
1969, pp. 127–52

The most salient quality of Arthur Miller's tragedy of the common man *Death of a Salesman* is its Americanism. This quality in the play is demonstrated by the contrasting reactions of American and English reviewers. The English took the hero at face value and found little of interest in his person or his plight:

There is almost nothing to be said for Loman who lies to himself as to others, has no creed or philosophy of life beyond that of making money by making buddies, and cannot even be faithful to his helpful and long-suffering wife.[1]

Brooks Atkinson, on the other hand, thought Willy "a good man who represents the homely, decent, kindly virtues of a middle-class society."[2] The Englishman treats Willy without regard for his American context, the New York reviewer sees him as the representative of a large segment of American society. When the literary critics measure the play against Greek and Elizabethan drama, they agree with the English evaluation; the hero seems inadequate. His lack of stature, his narrow view of reality, his obvious character defects diminish the scope of action and the possibilities of universal application.[3] Against a large historical perspective and without the American context, the salesman is a "small man" who fails to cope with his environment. But for better or worse, Miller's hero is not simply an individual who has determined on an objective and who strives desperately to attain it; he is also representative of an American type, the Salesman, who has accepted an ideal shaped for him and pressed on him by forces in his culture. This ideal is the matrix from which Willy emerges and by which his destiny is determined. It is peculiarly American in origin and development—seed, flower and fruit. For Arthur Miller's salesman is a personification of the success myth; he is committed to its objectives and defined by its characteristics. *Salesman* deals with the Horatio Alger ideal, the rags-to-riches romance of the American dream.

The success myth is not concealed beneath the facade of the action; it is used consciously by the playwright in depicting the plot-situation, in drawing the hero, in arranging the events of the action. Thoughtful American reviewers and critics got the point:

Success is a requirement Americans make of life. Because it seems magical, and inexplicable, as it is to Willy, it can be considered the due of every free citizen, even those with no notable or measurable talents. . . . The citizen may justly and perhaps even logically ask—if Edison, Goodrich, and Red Grange can make it, why not me, why not Willy Loman?[4]

Willy's quest for the secret of success is central to the drama. By choosing this focus for his play, Miller is drawing on the popular mind and a popular formula from which he shapes his dramatic form.

The attitudes which the myth expresses have a long history in American culture. The success myth, as Max Weber has demonstrated, has roots in seventeenth-century bourgeois England; it came to this continent with the founding fathers and was later popularized by the efforts of Ben Franklin, its outstanding exemplar. The "land of opportunity" offered enough verification of the basic tenets of the doctrine to assure its triumph in the popular mind. Virgin land, undeveloped resources, the possibility of industrial progress, all allowed scope for enterprise and imagination. No man lacked an enterprise to turn his hand to. The successful man became the idol of the public; the road to success was pointed out from the pulpit, in the marketplace, by the family fireside. From Franklin through the nineteenth century and well into the twentieth, the success myth, and all the possible variations on it, did not lack prophets and interpreters.

The success ideology developed a basic outline in the early Colonial period and its essential shape has not changed appreciably since. The Franklin image of the hard-working, early-rising, self-disciplined, ambitious adventurer engaged the public imagination in 1758 when *Poor Richard* included Father Abraham Weatherwise's monologue on "The Way to Wealth."[5] The proverbs from the 1758 *Poor Richard* passed into the texture of the American language: "Early to bed . . . Never leave till tomorrow that which you can do today." Emerson's doctrine of self-reliance fitted neatly into this pattern; the great lecturer subscribed to the theory that the thirst for wealth and the drive to power were essential to the growth of civilization.[6] . . . It suffices to recall that material success was taken to be the tangible sign of God's blessing and the reward of virtue.

In the latter half of the nineteenth century the alliance between religion and business took a curious turn. Business no longer received the benediction of religion, rather religion was described in terms of business. The servant became the master in that strange cultural reversal that has been described by Will Herberg. "Organized" religion passed into the hands of the corporation; the culture began to control the religious concepts. Clergymen found no disparity between the acquisition of riches and Christianity; indeed, they were delighted to find they went hand in hand. Russell H. Conwell, a Baptist preacher and the founder of Temple University in Philadelphia, traveled over the country, preaching this gospel. His celebrated lecture *Acres of Diamonds* was delivered in large cities and at whistle-stops, 5,124 times between 1870 and 1915. The central illustration in *Acres* is the story of the Arab who journeyed the world over in search of diamonds, while his successor on the farm found acres of diamonds in his own backyard. The industrious, the honest, the determined man can mine diamonds at home, in the city, wherever he is; this is Conwell's message.

> The men and women sitting here, who found it difficult perhaps to buy a ticket to this lecture or gathering to-night, have within their reach "acres of diamonds," opportunities to get largely wealthy. Never in the history of the world did a poor man without capital have such an opportunity to get rich quickly and honestly as he has now in our city.[7]

Conwell is content to show that religion and business are not opposed, that religion encourages men to get rich. Ten years later Bruce Barton reduced this kind of argument to an absurdity in his life of Jesus, *The Man Nobody Knows*. The Savior, Barton proclaimed, is an epitome of success, the greatest corporate leader and the most successful advertising man the world has ever seen. He is a man of great personal magnetism, possessed of all the qualities that mark the successful executive. The wheel comes full circle when Jesus becomes a Nazarene Carnegie, and Christianity is defined in terms of United States Steel.

Today, the author whose name is most closely linked with the dream of success is Horatio Alger, another clergyman, who embodied the myth in his novels. Alger caught the quintessence of the dream and developed a formula in which to express it. The ragged urchin, bootblack or newspaper boy of humble origin capitalizes on his opportunities and, by "pluck and luck," rises to the top of the economic heap. Alger made this formula an American byword.

> Like many simple formulations which nevertheless convey a heavy intellectual and emotional charge to vast numbers of people, the Alger hero represents a triumphant combination—and reduction to the lowest common denominator—of the most widely accepted concepts in nineteenth-century American society. The belief in the potential greatness of the common man, the glorification of individual effort

and accomplishment, the equation of the pursuit of money with the pursuit of happiness and of business success with spiritual grace: simply to mention these concepts is to comprehend the brilliance of Alger's synthesis.[8]

Alger converted the attitude that canonized the successful businessman into a popular literary formula, the rags-to-riches romance. His heroes, often with a boost from Fortune in their background (Tom the Bootblack is really the disinherited son of a successful businessman), rise to the top by seizing opportunity by the forelock, by being industrious, thrifty, devout (but not pious), commonsensical. They are likeable chaps with a ready quip and a vigorous sense of humor. They have little trouble getting employment and, once in the shop, there is no stopping them. "Ragged Dick" and "Tom the Bootblack" have that aura around them; success is natural to personalities of their stripe. In Alger as for preachers like Conwell, the key to success is not genius or gentle breeding, but "character."

> At best, successful methods were merely by-products of successful character. The businessman who had the right personal qualities would have little difficulty in developing the necessary managerial skills, but the possession of no amount of skill could compensate for lack of character or other essential personal traits.[9]

All success literature, of which Alger's was the fictional apotheosis, assumed that the individual could pull himself up by his bootstraps. "The Creator made man a success-machine . . . and failure is as abnormal to him as discord to harmony."[10] The Alger hero had character; luck and pluck brought him inevitably from rags to riches.

Between 1868 and 1929 Alger's books sold ten million copies, and the people who did not read the books could hardly have been able to escape the aura of the name. With the boom of the 1920s authors like Babson and Marsden and Bruce Barton kept the success doctrine before the eyes of the public. Whether they advocated success as the reward of virtue or as the result of strength or as the consequent of personality, their position was essentially the same. The secret lies inside the individual character. The emphasis can shift from one personal quality to another, but there is never any doubt where the quality is found. Moreover, if Christianity can be defined by business concepts, "virtue" can easily be reduced to "personality." The "miracles" of Jesus, according to Barton, reside in his personal magnetism. Thus, before the god Opportunity, all are equal. Those mysterious internal qualities of character—"virtue," "personality,"—become the charismatic gifts that are prayed for by the true believer and, when found, are acknowledged as the work of the Spirit. This myth, deep-seated in the American consciousness, provides the raw material for *Death of a Salesman*.

The success myth, in the hands of the playwright, becomes the model for the events of the plot, the situation and the character of the hero, but Miller uses this model in order to subvert it. His play is an anti-myth, the rags-to-riches formula in reverse so that it becomes the story of a failure in terms of success, or better, the story of the failure of the success myth. The events of the play are a mirror-image of the hero's progress. Willy Loman's history begins at the end of the line; instead of the young, determined bootblack an exhausted salesman enters, carrying, along with his sample cases, sixty years of uphill struggle. The subsequent events show him failing to overcome each obstacle, just as he has failed to achieve the phantom success he has pursued his life long. He returns from a trip without making a single sale, he braces the boss for a New York job and a salary raise (like the Alger hero) and is fired for his pains; his "boys," now well out of boyhood, make the big play for high stakes according to their father's teaching and fail. Willy finishes by facing the harsh fact that his whole life has been a lie. The triumphal ascent of the Alger hero is reversed in every particular. The rags-to-riches dream never materializes, and the salesman never escapes his rags. The race with the junkyard finds Willy an also-ran. In the collapse of the salesman, Miller attempts to illustrate the collapse of the myth.

Death of a Salesman encompasses two dimensions—the dream-world of the success myth with its merging of past triumphs, indications of glory to come, glimmering possibilities; and the actual world of the small, brick-enclosed house in Brooklyn. To achieve this merger, Miller uses an expressionistic setting, a skeletonized house which symbolizes the encroachment of urban economics on the family. The "one-dimensional" roof is surrounded on all sides by a "solid vault of apartment houses." The walls of the Loman home are cut away to permit free passage to the personae in dream and reminiscence sequences. This device, along with changes in lighting, allows for a condensation of time so that the life of the family can be encompassed by the action. "An air of the dream clings to the place, a dream rising out of reality."[11] The expressionistic technique—the use of typical personae, a symbolic setting, mobility in time—follows on the mythic focus of the playwright's vision. Miller himself is conscious of the possibilities of this technique and its significance; he defines expressionism: "The stage is stripped of knickknacks; instead it reveals symbolic *designs* which function as overt pointers toward the moral to be drawn from the action."[12] The freedom which this technique supplies allows the playwright to express the salesman's dream and his experiences in the context of the dream. The flashbacks in the course of the action can be considered hallucinatory, and the salesman can be played as mentally unbalanced, but such an interpretation takes actuality as the norm and loses sight of the mythical dimension.[13] Any attempt to decide which elements of the play are "real" and which "unreal" is as futile as trying to sort out the "historical" elements in any myth. The mythical attitude and Willy's experiences form one texture; they are the warp and woof of the salesman's world.

The typical characteristics of the Willy Loman persona establish him in the tradition of the mythical hero, or in *Salesman*, in the tradition of the anti-hero. The name is descriptive; Willy is "low man" on the economic and social totem-pole. Linda, his wife, who sees him clearly and sympathetically, calls him "a small man." He is a white-collar worker who works on salary and/or commission for a company, his economic future at the mercy of his employer. He does not show any marked intellectual capacity or training, and his wisdom, expressed in platitudes, is garnered from common-sense authorities. When he is away from home, his moral life functions according to the "traveling salesman" tradition, not excluding the clandestine affair or the blue joke. He does not, however, consider himself dissolute; according to his lights, he is honest enough. For better or worse, the salesman is intended to represent the average lower-middle-class American.

The antecedents of the salesman are also typical. For a man who resides in Brooklyn, the family background which Miller gives his hero stretches the imagination. In a sequence with Ben, Willy remembers his father, a man with a big beard who played the flute. His father, too, was a traveling salesman:

> *Ben:* Father was a very great and very wild-hearted man. We would start in Boston, and he'd toss the whole family into the wagon and then he'd drive the team right across the country; through

Ohio and Indiana, Michigan, Illinois and all the Western states. And we'd stop in the towns and sell the flutes that he'd made on the way. Great inventor, Father. With one gadget he made more than a man like you could make in a lifetime. (*Salesman*, p. 49.)

The father disappeared one day when Willy was a baby, following the Yukon gold-strike. He lived many years in Alaska, and Willy had a yearning to join him there. (*Salesman*, p. 85.) This is the stock from which Willy and his boys are sprung, American stock with a penchant for traveling and selling. This background fits an idealized model rather than any plausible or realistic family tree.[14] As typical character, the salesman has a typical background; he envisions his origin in terms of the American experience. It is one version of the idealized experience of the race.

Willy's status in society, his family background are typical; even more of a type is Willy's identity as Salesman. He is a product of a producer-consumer society in which the go-between is a pivotal figure. Society has labeled him, and Willy has accepted the label; society has offered Willy a set of values and an objective, and Willy has committed himself to those values and that objective. In so accepting, Willy becomes THE Salesman. He cannot define himself in any other terms. So he insists in his debate with Charley that "he has a job," that he is the "New England man," even after he has been fired. His adherence to the cult of personality, of being "well liked," is a reflection of his identity; before he can sell anything and if he can sell nothing else, he must sell himself, his own personality. He has been shaped by a society that believed steadily and optimistically in the myth of success, and he has become the agent and the representative of that society.

This image of the Salesman includes the image of an older, freer America. Before the frontier closed down and the apartments closed in, before business became an impersonal, corporate endeavor, opportunity knocked incessantly. For Willy (and for the audience), the achievement possible in this earlier society is typified by Uncle Ben, the shadowy figure who appears out of nowhere, to the accompaniment of flute music, on his way to new capitalistic triumphs. Whether Ben is a projection of Willy's imagination or a real figure out of the family history is irrelevant; his function in the action does not depend on his "reality." He comes from an idealized past; he is the robber baron, the captain of industry. Ben carries with him the aura of success, and when he visits, it is only for a few minutes between expeditions. There are diamond mines in Africa, timberlands in Alaska, and mysterious appointments in Ketchikan which demand his attention. Ben's methods are illustrated in a sparring match with Biff. He is physically strong—Biff can hit him in the stomach with impunity. He is ruthless—the sparring ends abruptly when Ben suddenly trips the boy and poises the point of his umbrella over Biff's eye. "Never fight fair with a stranger, boy. You'll never get out of the jungle that way." (*Salesman*, p. 49.) This is the code of the self-made man.

Ben possesses the precious secret to success. It is summarized in his ritual chant, the formula which sums up his accomplishment: "When I was seventeen I walked into the jungle and when I was twenty-one I walked out. And by God I was rich." (*Salesman*, p. 48.) What happened in the jungle is never explained. It is the mystery of success, the Eleusinian rite known only to initiates. Uncle Ben is the older version of the Salesman, the ruthless capitalist whose adventurous strength ripped riches from the frontier. To Willy, Uncle Ben is the palpable proof of his doctrine.

While the shadowy figure of Ben establishes the general

truth that any man can succeed, Willy does not accept (or perhaps has no chance to accept) Ben's method. Ben represents the robber baron who travels out to unknown frontiers and ruthlessly carves out an empire. As Ben's method has faded with the passing of the empire builders and with the advent of the big corporations, Willy decides to rely on personality:

> It's not what you do, Ben. It's who you know and the smile on your face! It's contacts, Ben, contacts! The whole wealth of Alaska passes over the lunch table at the Commodore Hotel, and that's the wonder, the wonder of this country, that a man can end with diamonds here on the basis of being well-liked. (*Salesman*, p. 86.)

This quality cannot be held in the hand like Ben's timber, but on the other hand, Ben's own formula—his inner strength and ruthlessness—is also mysterious. Willy accepts the Dale Carnegie approach to success; winning friends and influencing people become his pick and shovel to dig diamonds as industriously as Ben ever did. But Willy does not go off to Africa or Alaska, nor is his confidence in a transcendentally virtuous life. His faith in personality conceals the secret in an imponderable and makes that faith untestable by any pragmatic standard. The dream of success, in the eyes of the playwright, is the more destructive because, though indemonstrable, it has a myth-like capacity for inspiring a transcendent belief.

There are, however, certain tangible signs which characterize the personality likely to succeed. Willy discovers them in his sons. The boys are physically strong, well-built, attractive. Biff is a football hero, the captain of the high-school team; Happy, if not gifted with Biff's athletic ability, has a pleasant personality and basks in Biff's reflected glory. Against this picture of the glowing athlete and the hale fellow, Bernard, the neighbor's boy, wears glasses, studies hard, and is not well-liked. If physical prowess and a moderate anti-intellectualism seemed to have little to do with success, the propagators of the success ideology saw an intimate connection:

> Statistics show that executives are physically stronger and larger of stature than their subordinates. For example, college presidents, as a class, are taller and heavier than the college professors. Bank presidents are physically stronger than the clerks. Railway presidents are larger and physically stronger than the employees. . . . Physical welfare is the second qualification for winning the race of making good.[15]

Biff does not have to work hard at his studies; books are not necessary for advancement. Bernard, whose scholastic efforts are the object of mild derision, supplies Biff with answers and this is only right, the homage due the personable and popular. When, in spite of Bernard's help, Biff fails in math, Willy blames the teacher. Willy shows a typical ambivalence toward education. On the one hand, attendance at college confers prestige, especially when coupled with an athletic career; on the other, education does not really make an appreciable difference in the struggle to succeed. Some self-help advocates maintained that college was actually harmful to a young man's chances. It undermined those rugged personal qualities demanded by a career by an overemphasis on the development of the mind, it fostered an interest in impractical humanistic matters, it devoured the best years of a man's life.[16] The salesman finds in his sons those qualities which point toward success. As high-school boys, they are leaders, popular with the crowd, athletic and handsome. Their present status as philandering clerk and wandering farmhand cannot erase the glory of their past potential as Willy experienced it. "A star like that, magnificent, can never really fade away." (*Salesman*, p. 68.)

Willy's commitment to the success ideology directed the education of his sons. Even if success passes him by, he can still look forward to a vindication of his life in them. They have been instructed in the clichés of both the "virtue" and the "personality" school. Industry is important; whatever else can be said about Biff, he is a "hard worker." One of Willy's fondest reminiscences is the high sheen the boys kept on the red Chevvy. If Biff "gets tired" hanging around, he can paint a new ceiling in the living room. Willy's aphorisms emphasize the importance of industry and perseverance: "Never leave a job till you're finished." "The world is an oyster, but you don't crack it open on a mattress." But personality has its privileges and Willy can wink at the boys' faults in the name of personality. Biff has been a thief from his high-school days; he steals a football from the locker-room and lumber from a local construction job. Willy laughs at both thefts because they reveal the power of personality and a fearless competitiveness like Ben's. "Coach will probably congratulate you on your initiative. . . . That's because he likes you. If somebody else took the ball there'd be an uproar." (*Salesman*, p. 30.) When Charley warns Willy that the watchman will catch the boys at their thieving, Willy avers that, though he gave them hell, the boys are "a couple of fearless characters." When Charley responds that the jails are full of fearless characters, Ben adds that the Stock Exchange is also. The boys have been brought up to respect the success ideology; their success will be the salesman's vindication.

In the chronological present of the play Willy's fortunes are at low ebb. His faith in the myth is tested by harsh realities which he alternately faces and flees. He fights to hold on to his identity. This means holding on to his faith, and, in the name of faith, Willy lies constantly: about the gross sales he has made, about the reaction of businessmen to his personality, about his boys' success and importance, about his own prospects. These lies echo, not the drab reality about him, but the shining hope he has. From the observer's point of view established in the play through Charley and Linda, they are pathetic efforts to protect his identity. Willy is unfaithful to his long-suffering wife, but this infidelity is an assuagement of his loneliness on the road, a restorative to his flagging spirits, and a provision against the rebuffs of the day. When he momentarily faces reality—his inability to drive to Boston, the mounting bills and the dwindling income—he has to flee to the past and to project the future. The salesman cannot abandon the myth without reducing himself to zero. Thus he must hope.

Perpetual optimism, then, is not so much a piece of transparent self-deception as it is a necessary quality of his personality. It can be associated with the kind of wishful hoping that underlies the entire American business operation, an indefatigable spirit of the-impossible-takes-a-little-longer.

> Basically this optimism represents no precise philosophical position at all, but rather a studiously cultivated sense of euphoria. It is an emotional attitude marked by a tendency to emphasize the brighter side of things. . . . It is an effusive and expansive attitude. In the business world one of its typical manifestations is the conviction that there is no assignable limit to business opportunities, that markets need not remain static but are constantly open to further development, even with territory geographically limited. It is somewhat beside the point to ask if Americans believe in this optimism. It is not a thing you believe in. It is in the air. It is felt. It has its effect, whether you elect to believe in it or not.[17]

Miller has not left this optimism hanging in the air; he weaves it into his hero's personality. Happy's diagnosis is accurate:

"Dad is never so happy as when he's looking forward to something!" (*Salesman*, p. 105.) When Willy is lost, disturbed, hanging on the ropes, he demands that this hope be fed: "The gist of it is I haven't got a story [*read*: 'lie'] left in my head, Biff. So don't give me a lecture about facts and aspects. I am not interested. Now what've you got to say?" (*Salesman*, p. 107.) Willy must have hope because it sustains him; when identity is at stake, there are matters more important than facts and aspects.

The plot structure of *Salesman* dramatizes the failure of the myth by depicting the past and present failures of the salesman. Events in the chronological present are germinations of seeds sown in the past; both present and past are inextricably bound together in Willy's consciousness:

> *Linda*: And Willy—if it's warm Sunday we'll drive in the country. And we'll open the windshield and take lunch.
> *Willy*: No, the windshields don't open on the new cars.
> *Linda*: But you opened it today.
> *Willy*: Me? I didn't. (He stops.) Now isn't that peculiar! Isn't that a remarkable—(He breaks off in amazement and fright as the flute is heard distantly.) . . . I was thinking of the Chevvy. (Slight pause.) Nineteen twenty-eight . . . when I had that red Chevvy—(Breaks off.) That funny? I coulda sworn I was driving that Chevvy today. (*Salesman*, p. 19.)

Miller builds up a sense of fate in his drama by showing the impingement of the unalterable past upon the present. Willy's whole life has been shaped by his commitment to the success ideology, his dream based on the Alger myth; his present plight is shown to be the inevitable consequence of this commitment.

> What is perhaps less frequently stressed is the bearing of the past-present relationship on the metaphysical content of tragedy. It is probably true to say that the greater proportion of the 'past' that is allowed to impinge upon, or to modify, the present, the easier it is to give the impression of a rigid or semi-rigid structure enclosing the action, and the larger the apparent content of determinism.[18]

Just as the hero's commitment comes to him as a heritage of the American past, so his sorry situation at sixty comes of his early life. Except for the deceptive expanse of time, there is no real difference in the salesman's life then and now.

The events of the first act—past and present—contrapose optimism and harsh reality. In the chronological present Willy is a tired drummer and his boys are mediocre also-rans, a clerk and a farmhand, both over thirty. Biff and Happy are lost and confused by their failure to get ahead, and Willy is at the end of his rope because he can't even drive a car any more. Willy's return home after the abortive trip is contrasted with his return in the "good old days." Then he came home to the security of his boys' adulation, bringing with him the glamor of the traveler and his own ebullient interpretation of the trip. He is proud of his boys and their potential sustains him.

> *Willy*: Bernard can get the best marks in school, y'understand, but when he gets out in the business world, y'understand, you are going to be five times ahead of him. That's why I thank Almighty God you're both built like Adonises. Because the man who makes an appearance in the business world, the man who creates personal interest, is the man who gets ahead. Be liked and you will never want. (*Salesman*, p. 33.)

Willy "knocked 'em cold in Providence, slaughtered 'em in Boston." The patois of the rugged sportsman, of the prize ring, flavors Willy's speech and plants the image of the ideal career in his sons. It is reflected in the chronological present by Happy's wildly impractical scheme to recoup the Loman fortune. On the basis of the idea, they lay "big plans":

> *Happy*: Wait a minute! I got an idea. I got a feasible idea. Come here, Biff, let's talk this over now, let's talk some sense here. . . . You and I, Biff—we have a line, the Loman line. We train a couple of weeks, and put on a couple of exhibitions, see? . . . We play each other. It's a million dollars' worth of publicity. Two brothers, see? The Loman Brothers. Displays in the Royal Palms—all the hotels. And banners over the ring and the basketball court: "Loman Brothers." Baby, we could sell sporting goods!
> *Willy*: That is a one-million-dollar idea! (*Salesman*, p. 63.)

This scheme is generated out of the heart of the myth. "Loman Brothers" has, for Willy and the boys, the ring of personality and solidarity and achievement. It would not entail entering the impersonal arena of the office; the "boys" would be "out playin' ball again." With no regular hours to cramp their freedom and no fierce outside competition, there would be "the old honor and comradeship." Sportsmanship, clean living, economic freedom would blend in a million-dollar enterprise, the ideal life crowned with financial achievement. Only the glowing pair who ran to carry their father's valises and to listen to his prideful predictions would consider such a scheme "talking sense." It is significant that Happy makes the proposal; he is Willy's double without Willy's excuse, a liar and a philanderer. The flashback sequence explains the optimism the "big plan" generates.

Willy's reminiscences also cast another shadow over the present prospect. His version of the sales trip to young Biff and Hap is contrasted with the version he gives Linda. Bills have piled up and if business "don't pick up I don't know what I'm gonna do!" Willy confesses to his wife that people laugh at him, that he is not noticed, that he talks too much and laughs too loudly so that people don't respect him. (*Salesman*, pp. 36–37.) On the road, alone and assailed with doubts, without his wife and his sons to bolster his ego, he turns to the Woman. She picked Willy out, she likes him, he makes her laugh. Willy's problems are no different in the present, except that the financial crisis looms larger and the philandering has passed over to Happy. But in the first act all difficulties, past and present, are smoothed over by a pervading optimism.

Under the spell of the dream, Biff determines to see Bill Oliver, a former employer, and ask for financial backing. Family legend has refined his theft of basketballs from the firm out of existence and converted his position from shipping clerk into salesman. This prospect raises Willy's hopes; the dream can convert the possibility into triumphant actuality. "I see great things for you kids, I think your troubles are over." Given this incentive, the salesman determines to ask for a place in New York for himself, for an office job that would take him off the road. Personality yet may carry the day.

At the outset of the second act the hopes of the evening carry over to the following morning. The boys have departed "nice and early"; "early to rise" and "the early bird" are good omens. As he considers the actual burdens of the moment, however, Willy's spirits begin to slide. His description of the consumer's fate has a symbolic reference to his own life.

> Whoever heard of a Hastings refrigerator? Once in my life I would like to own something outright before it's broken! I'm always in a race with the junkyard! I

just finished paying for the car and it's on its last legs. The refrigerator consumes belts like a goddam maniac. They time those things. They time them so when you've finally paid for them, they're used up. (*Salesman*, p. 73.)

Earlier, it was made clear that Willy bought this brand because the company displayed the largest ads and, from the day of installation, the box chewed up belts. The battle of the Hastings (with Willy on the Anglo-Saxon side) was lost from the start. This discussion is a forecast of Willy's fate in the coming interview. The morning hope is somewhat revived when Linda gives him something to look forward to: the boys are going to "blow him to a big dinner." In anticipation of a victory celebration, the salesman goes off to his job interview with renewed confidence.

The interview incidents are central to the movement of the second act. They contrast with the typical interview of the Alger formula. For the Alger hero, this is the first rung on the ladder of success. The young bootblack or newsboy immediately engages the prospective employer's attention and impresses him with his intelligence, sensible adjustment to circumstances, industry, self-confidence, and honesty. Willy and Biff fail to impress on all points. Willy's employer, some years the salesman's junior—"I named him Howard"—has not the time to listen to Willy's reminiscences. He is preoccupied with industry's newest gadget, a wire recorder. The impersonal business world no longer has any room for personality among the machines. In a reversal of the Alger formula, the salesman's rambling convinces Howard that the company has no more use for him. He has outlived his limited usefulness, and the upshot is that Willy is summarily fired. Biff's interview is even more disastrous. He cannot even get inside the office, and far from demonstrating his honesty, he steals Oliver's fountain pen for no reason he can fathom. In terms of structure, the interview episodes, one witnessed and the other reported, are dramatizations of the failure of the myth as Willy understood it and preached it to his sons.

Their respective experiences produce different reactions in father and son. It is the pressure of past experience that is invoked to explain the difference. Willy cannot understand his defeat even when Charley, the good neighbor, spells it out for him:

When're you gonna realize that them things don't mean anything? You named him Howard, but you can't sell that. The only thing you got in this world is what you can sell. And the funny thing is that you're a salesman, and you don't know that. (*Salesman*, p. 97.)

At this late date, there is no chance that the salesman will be able to distinguish the marketable from the mythical. Moreover, he still preserves the hope of Biff's success and the prospect of the big dinner. To a man a little less the salesman than Willy, his chance meeting with Bernard, Charley's son and the high-school follower, would raise a rash of doubts. But Willy can only, in desperation, ask Bernard, who is off to try a case before the Supreme Court, about the secret of success. The lawyer does not volunteer any advice except not to worry about it. "Sometimes, Willy, it's better for a man just to walk away." (*Salesman*, p. 95.) Willy cannot walk away; he affirms his faith in his sons.

The meeting in the restaurant is an ironic reversal of the "victory" banquet. Biff's experience, as he relates it to Happy, has convinced him that his whole life has been "a ridiculous lie." He is determined to get the facts out in the open, but habit is not so easily broken. The salesman refuses to listen to "facts

and aspects"; he *will* have a celebration of the glorious future. When it becomes clear that Biff will not cooperate in the lie and that Willy cannot face the truth, the Loman boys react according to the pattern. They run away from the failure their father has become and from their own failure. They leave the old man babbling in the rest room and go off with two prostitutes. Happy is responding to his training when he denies his father before one of the floozies:

Letta: Don't you want to tell your father—
Happy: No, that's not my father. He's just a guy. Come on, we'll catch Biff, and, honey, we're going to paint this town. (*Salesman*, pp. 115–16.)

Happy cannot hear the cock crow; this unhappy wandering old man is not *his* father. Willy's own teaching and example flow back on his own head.

Bracketed within the restaurant sequence are two crucial past events, also the fruit of teaching and example. Biff's failure with Oliver is related to his failure in math and his flight to Boston. Relying on personality, Biff had mimicked the effeminate instructor to his face and had cut the class for football practice. In spite of Bernard's help on the exam, he lacked four points of passing, and the instructor refuses to make a concession. When the boy runs to seek his father's help, he finds the Woman in Willy's hotel room. His idol crumbles; his father is "a phoney little fake." The traveling-salesman joke becomes a traumatic experience for the boy, driving his disillusion deep and preparing him for his present insight. Biff sees the affair as a betrayal of Linda, the family and the home. The image of the husband and father is broken when Willy gives the Woman "Mama's Stockings." But Willy does not understand Biff's reaction; what he does on the road has no connection with his home-life. Thus all he feels is the weight of his son's disapproval. Biff has ruined his life "for spite." Willy's firing, Biff's panic at Oliver's, are linked with Biff's high-school failure and Willy's inability to cope with his boy's disillusion in the Boston hotel room.

The climactic scene in the second act is the confrontation of father and son. Because he suspects the truth, Willy is unwilling to face Biff or Linda. But this time Biff is not to be put off: "The man don't know who we are! The man is gonna know! (To Willy) We never told the truth for ten minutes in this house." Willy is no longer Salesman, no longer Father; Willy is "the man." The identity supplied by economic and familial society is stripped away and the issue is joined at rock bottom.

I am not a leader of men, Willy, and neither are you. You were never anything but a hard-working drummer who landed in the ash can like all the rest of them. I'm one dollar an hour, Willy! . . . Do you gather my meaning? I'm not bringing home any prizes any more, and you're going to stop waiting for me to bring them home. (*Salesman*, p. 132.)

But facts fall before faith and the salesman cannot admit such heresy. Willy knows who he is: "I am not a dime a dozen. I am Willy Loman, and you are Biff Loman." He simply cannot comprehend and, when Biff breaks down and sobs on his father's shoulder, Biff's emotional rapport destroys his point. There is the sudden revelation that Biff likes him; this the salesman can understand. The removal of Biff's disapproval rekindles the salesman's optimism—"that boy—that boy is going to be magnificent." In spite of all the explanations and because of the sudden emotional reunion, the myth endures. Whatever his failures on the road and in the office, Willy turns out to be "well-liked" by his alienated son.

With this realization and the resurgence of the myth, Brother Ben reappears. Ben's advice is now *ad hoc* and in the tradition of *Acres of Diamonds*: "It does take a great kind of man to crack the jungle. . . . The jungle is dark but full of diamonds. . . . One must go in to fetch a diamond out." (*Salesman*, pp. 133–134.) Ben's promise is the promise of all the self-help prophets of the nineteenth century. The salesman wanted to find his success in Brooklyn. Ben offers him his chance. There are "acres of diamonds" in his backyard. To achieve that success which thus far eluded him, Willy drives his car into the wall. In terms of the myth, his motivation is no different now than it was when he drove off to New England. His boy likes him and deserves the twenty thousand insurance money, the capital which will finally put him on the road to success. The success ideology is stronger than the reality, and he goes to his death with his goal sparkling before him.

The "success" structure in the play, as the critic immediately recognizes, is not the whole *Salesman* story. As the English critic sees Willy as a detestable little man, the American sees him as a pathetic figure who suffers deeply. The pathetic quality is produced by the playwright's emphasis on the culture that shaped the salesman's personality.[19] The pressures of economic growth in urban society created the salesman mystique and these same forces punish the unsuccessful inexorably. The 1929 crash impressed Miller greatly:

> The hidden laws of fate lurked not only in the characters of people, but equally if not more imperiously in the world beyond the family parlor. Out there were the big gods, the ones whose disfavor could turn a proud and prosperous and dignified man into a frightened shell of a man whatever he thought of himself, and whatever he decided or didn't decide to do.[20]

These powers were economic crisis and political imperatives at whose mercy man found himself. The myth holds them at bay, overcomes them, puts the successful man out of their reach. As anti-hero, the salesman (and his family) is at their mercy. Time-installment buying, the enclosure of the house by apartments, the impersonal attitude of the executive illustrate these external forces. If these "hidden gods" decide to doom a generation, they can grind exceeding small. When the stock market crashed, once safe and happy millionaires left by the window. The common man does not control such a phenomenon, and the success myth does not take such catastrophes into account. Willy's faith in the myth leaves him vulnerable to the big gods.[21] No version of the success myth really equips anyone to deal with these forces.

One solution to coping with this impersonal culture is a concomitant impersonality in dealing with it. Miller dramatizes this reaction in his depiction of the good neighbors, Charley and Bernard. Charley is a successful businessman in a minor way; Bernard, the bespectacled tag-along, is a successful lawyer. Out of the goodness of his heart, Charley supports Willy and Linda by "loaning" the salesman fifty dollars a week. He drops by to play cards with Willy and generally tolerates his blustering irritability. He offers Willy a steady job. He is the lone unrelated mourner at the funeral. Out of the salesman's own mouth, the bitter truth is that Charley is the only friend he has. The good neighbor has no theory about success, no magic formula but unconcern: "My salvation is that I never took any interest in anything." (*Salesman*, p. 96.) He never preached at his son or exhibited any interest in success or money. Without preaching, Charles goes about doing good. It is not clear where all the virtue this good neighbor displays springs from. He is the good Samaritan for whose conduct no explanation need be

given. More significantly, though Charley makes no concessions to the cult of success in his actions or his manner, he knows the rules: "The only thing you got in this world is what you can sell."

Bernard is the opposite number to Biff and Happy. He, too, is a good neighbor. Though his boyhood relations with the Lomans kept him a subordinate, he holds no grudge, is still sincerely interested in Biff and respectful with Willy. Bernard has followed his father's example, if not his counsel.

> Bernard: Goodby, Willy, and don't worry about it.
> You know, "If at first you don't succeed . . ."
> Willy: Yes, I believe in that.
> Bernard: But sometimes, Willy, it's better for a man
> just to walk away. (*Salesman*, p. 95.)

The successful lawyer has no other word for Willy, except perhaps a footnote to the success formula; he points out that Biff never prepared himself for anything. Charley and Bernard really have no alternate faith to offer Willy. They show a distrust of the big gods and treat them gingerly. Otherwise, they are good people who sympathize with the Lomans' plight, who understand their aspirations without emulating them, who put friendship above the law. They bear witness to the vacuity of success worship, but provide no faith with which to replace it.

This is not to say that Miller suggests no alternative. On the one hand, he suggests a family solidarity centering around the wife and mother; on the other hand, he tentatively offers a retreat from the competitive business world to an agrarian, manual-labor society. Linda is the heart of the family. She is wise, warm, sympathetic. She knows her husband's faults and her sons' characters. For all her frank appraisals, she loves them. She is contrasted with the promiscuous sex symbolized by the Woman and the prostitutes. They operate in the world outside as part of the impersonal forces that corrupt. Happy equates his promiscuity with taking manufacturers' bribes, and Willy's Boston woman can "put him right through to the buyers." Linda holds the family together—she keeps the accounts, encourages her husband, tries to protect him from heartbreak. She becomes the personification of Family, that social unity in which the individual has a real identity.

> The concepts of Father and Mother and so on were received by us unawares before the time we were conscious of ourselves as selves. In contrast, the concepts of Friend, Teacher, Employee, Boss, Colleague, Supervisor, and the many other social relations come to us long after we have gained consciousness of ourselves, and are therefore outside ourselves. They are thus in an objective rather than a subjective category. In any case what we feel is always more "real" to us than what we know, and we feel the family relationship while we only know the social one.[22]

If Willy is not totally unsympathetic (and he is not), much of the goodness in him is demonstrated in his devotion to his wife, according to his lights. Though he is often masterful and curt, he is still deeply concerned about her: "I was fired, and I'm looking for a little good news to tell your mother, because the woman has waited and the woman has suffered." (*Salesman*, p. 125.) Biff is attached to his mother, and Happy's hopelessness is most graphic in his failure to be honest with, or concerned about, his family. The family's devotion to one another, even though misguided, represents a recognizable American ideal.

Linda, for all her warmth and goodness, goes along with her husband and sons in the best success-manual tradition. She tries to protect them from the forces outside and fails. The memory of her suffering and her fidelity does not keep Willy and Happy from sex or Biff from wandering. Miller's irony goes still deeper. While Linda is a mirror of goodness and the source of the family's sense of identity, she is no protection—by her silence and her support, she unwittingly cooperates with the destructive myth. Linda follows the rules laid down by the self-help advocates. She is a good home manager, she understands and encourages her husband, she keeps her house neat and is a good mother. Babson recommends a good wife as a major factor in working toward success: "A good wife and well-kept house and some healthy children are of the utmost importance in enabling one to develop the six 'I's' of success and to live the normal, wholesome, upright life."[23] Linda stays in her place, never questioning out loud her husband's objectives and doing her part to help him achieve them.

As another possible alternative to the success myth, Miller proposes a return to a non-competitive occupation in an agrarian or trade-oriented society. In the context of *Death of a Salesman* he makes this offer, not explicitly as a universal panacea, but in terms of the Lomans' problem. The good days of hope and promise in the play are connected with a warm sun and clusters of trees in the neighborhood, fresh air and gardening. The reminiscence sequences are marked by this scenic change: "The apartment houses are fading out and the entire house and surroundings become covered with leaves." (*Salesman*, p. 27.) The neighborhood once bloomed with lilac, wisteria, peonies and daffodils, but now it is "bricks and windows, windows and bricks," and over-population. Willy is a talented workman; he has practically rebuilt the house: "All the cement, the lumber, the reconstruction I put in this house! There ain't a crack to be found in it any more." (*Salesman*, p. 74.) Biff, who understands this strength in his father, has actually escaped to the West. His ambition to succeed conflicts with the satisfaction he finds on the farm:

> This farm I work on, it's spring there now, see? And they've got about fifteen new colts. There's nothing more inspiring or—beautiful than the sight of a mare and a new colt. And it's cool there now, see? Texas is cool now and it's spring. (*Salesman*, p. 22.)

Biff suspects that perhaps the Lomans have been miscast in their salesman role:

> They've laughed at Dad for years, and you know why? Because we don't belong in this nuthouse of a city! We should be mixing cement on some open plain, or—or carpenters. A carpenter is allowed to whistle! (*Salesman*, p. 61.)

So when Biff comes to realize who he is, his insight flashes out of the contrast between the office and the open sky. The things he loves in the world are "the work and the food and time to sit and smoke." And his obituary for his father is a memorial to the good days when Willy was working on the house: "There's more of him in that front stoop than in all the sales he ever made." (*Salesman*, p. 138.) Charley agrees that Willy was "a happy man with a bunch of cement." In a freer, older society, the doomed salesman might have been a happy man.

The pathos of this situation—the square peg in a round hole—is dramatized in the garden scene. After the ordeal in the office and the restaurant, Willy feels the impulse to plant as an imperative; "I've got to get some seeds, right away. . . . I don't have a thing in the ground." (*Salesman*, p. 122.) He then begins to plant his garden in the barren patch beside the house by flashlight. All the contradictions in the salesman's life come into focus. His instinct to plant, to put something that will grow in the ground, is ineffectual—he must work by artificial light, surrounded by apartment houses, in the hard-packed dirt. The seeds will not grow; Willy, who was going to mine diamonds in Brooklyn, reverts to hoeing and planting, but the urbanization of his world has already defeated him. As he

plants, he talks "business" with Ben. His suicide will bring twenty thousand "on the barrelhead." This insurance money is the diamond he sees shining in the dark. (*Salesman*, p. 126.) All the forces that conspired to make—and break—Willy Loman are gathered here. His instinct to produce from the earth, the happy farmer he might have been, is frustrated by the society that has boxed him in. The dream of diamonds and his idealization of Ben have "rung up a zero"; the only way he can make his life pay off is by self-destruction.

Taken at the level of parable, the play presents the failure of the success myth by destroying the Horatio Alger image of the rags-to-riches triumph of the common man. This view of the play considers Willy as Salesman, Linda as Family, Ben as Success, and the moral of the play is the fall of the Golden Calf.[24] But Miller has not written a morality play in *Salesman*, nor does he make the mistake of preaching. The audience says, "That's the way middle-class America lives and thinks"; it also says: "I know a man just like that." The Willy Lomans who see the play do not recognize themselves and respond to Willy's collapse with the now legendary remark: "That New England territory was no damned good!" Wrapped in the trappings of instruction is the deep personal anguish of a contemporary American that audiences can recognize.

Willy the Salesman represents all those Americans caught in the mesh of the myth and the moral pressures it generates. As a type, he is a product of social and economic forces outside himself. But in his struggle with those forces, Willy is also a suffering human being. He battles to retain his faith, is shaken by doubts about his ability to live according to his belief, humiliates himself to discover the secret that lies at its heart. His blind commitment to his ideal is whole-hearted, and if Willy the Salesman is necessarily destroyed by that commitment, the audience feels that Willy the person is worth saving.

Thus, when he goes to his death without knowing why he has lived or why he is dying, he fulfills the destiny of the type, but as an individual who has suffered, he remains unfulfilled. The Salesman can neither suffer nor be converted (he would then cease to be Salesman), but the family man—the husband and father and friend—does suffer and, by virtue of it, can change. If Willy were only an abstract set of stereotyped characteristics, a figure in a Morality play, there would be little sympathy for his plight. In the "Requiem" epilogue, the various aspects of Willy's character come in for comment. Biff's epitaph considers what Willy might have been, the happy carpenter, the outdoorsman. Charley, on the other hand, reads the apologia for the Salesman:

> Nobody dast blame this man. You don't understand: Willy was a salesman. And for the salesman, there is no rock bottom to life. He don't put a bolt to a nut, he don't tell you the law or give you medicine. He's a man way out there in the blue, riding on a smile and a shoeshine. And when they start not smiling back— that's an earthquake. And then you get yourself a couple of spots on your hat, and you're finished. Nobody dast blame this man. A salesman is got to dream, boy. It comes with the territory. (*Salesman*, p. 138.)

This speech defends Willy in the context of myth and moral, but as a justification of his uncomprehending self-destruction, it fails to consider the individual who suffered through his life and rang up a zero at the end. Linda, the long-suffering, says the last word for the husband and the father:

> Willy, dear, I can't cry, Why did you do it? I search and I search and I search, and I can't understand it, Willy. I made the last payment on the house today. Today, dear. And there'll be nobody home. . . . We're free and clear. . . . We're free. (*Salesman*, p. 139.)

Linda cannot understand the mystery as Willy could not understand it. Suffering and sacrifice, for the family, have led to the "freedom" of an empty house and the grave.

Miller, who set out to write the tragedy of the common man, is finally trapped both by the myth he is denouncing and by the dramatic form he has chosen. The salesman's version of the success myth—the cult of personality—is shown to be a tissue of false values that lead only to frustration. Miller dramatizes the problem of guilt and the reality of Willy's suffering because of his values, but, try as he may, he can neither bring Willy to an insight by which he understands his failure nor find a societal strategy that can absolve him of it. The traditional tragic pattern of action demands an epiphany, a purgation and a renewal that does not cancel the suffering of the protagonist, but that does make sense of it. Miller recognizes this demand of the form and struggles to fulfill it; in the end the myth defeats him.

At the level of dianoia, the conscious treatment of values, Miller tries to find a replacement for the success myth and fails:

> This confusion [about "true" and "false" values] is abetted by the greater clarity of the rejected values which are embodied in the dream of success. The false dream is fully and vividly sketched; positive values seem rather dim and conventional.[25]

The false values, tightly woven into Willy's personality, are clearly destructive. But when Biff, the man who "knows who he is," advocates a return to the farm, it becomes clear how meager are the resources of the culture for coping with Willy's problem. The return to a pre-Alger agrarian way of life is an example of nostalgia for the garden; turning back the clock is no solution for a million city-dwelling Willy Lomans who left the farm to seek their fortunes. Charley's detachment from the myth does not supply a positive answer either. For Charley, whether he cares about it or not, *is* a success; he owns his small business and supports Willy. If the successful must protect the failures, then Willy's values are not altogether false, and the common man who cannot get along with the myth cannot get along without it either.

Society cannot absolve Willy; it can only understand and sympathize. Understanding and sympathy are not enough; Willy still goes to his "freedom" in the grave uncomprehending. At the level of dramatic action, there is no epiphany in which suffering leads to insight, that moment of revelation when the hero sees himself and his situation clearly, understands what he has lost, and finds the path to regeneration. Willy has suffered, but, because he is the Salesman, his suffering does not bring him to understanding. Miller recognizes this difficulty also and tries to circumvent it by promoting Biff to hero, by giving him the insight of which Willy was incapable. Nonetheless, it is Willy's fate that concerns us. He must go to his death hapless and deluded, but his end leaves the play without the final stage which the conventional tragic structure demands. Like the detective-hero, the salesman cannot acknowledge his mistake without also destroying his identity.

In *Death of a Salesman* Miller taps a popular formula for the structure of his drama. Although the Dale Carnegie approach, the cult of personality, is on the wane in the present generation, the drive for success is very much alive. Willy's plight, grounded in the excesses of a previous generation but fostered by attitudes still shared by the present generation, draws from the audience both recognition of the illusion and sympathy for the visionary. Willy's suffering is real and deep. America cannot accept the success myth—"Horatio Alger" is now a term of derision—but there is no real substitute for it.

Because Miller has built his play around an American dream, he strikes deep into the consciousness of the audience. The contemporary American, because he cannot solve the dilemma either, becomes involved in the sufferings of Willy the person as he watches the death of Willy the Salesman.

Notes

1. Ivor Brown, "As London Sees Willy Loman," New York *Times* (August 28, 1949), Book Section, p. 59.
2. "Death of a Salesman," New York *Times* (February 11, 1949), p. 27.
3. See R. B. Sewall, *The Vision of Tragedy* (New Haven, 1959), pp. 130, 167; H. J. Mueller, *The Spirit of Tragedy* (New York, 1956), pp. 316–17; T. R. Henn, *The Harvest of Tragedy* (London, 1956), p. 268.
4. Henry Popkin, "The Strange Encounter," *Sewanee Review*, LXVIII (Winter, 1960), 53.
5. The enormous success of this tract and its perennial appeal are attested by its frequent republication. In 1826 Simon Ide republished the essay along with Franklin's "Advice to Young Tradesmen." Much later, in 1921, Roger Babson's *Making Good in Business* reiterated the major points of Franklin's essay as part of Babson's advice to the success-seeker.
6. Ralph Waldo Emerson, *The Conduct of Life* (Boston, 1904), p. 95.
7. *Acres of Diamonds* (New York, 1915), p. 18.
8. Kenneth S. Lynn, *The Dream of Success* (Boston, 1955), pp. 6–7.
9. Irwin G. Wyllie, *The Self-Made Man in America* (New Brunswick, N.J., 1954), p. 27.
10. Orison Marsden, *Entering Business* (New York, 1903), p. 27.
11. Arthur Miller, *Death of a Salesman* (New York, 1949), p. 11. Subsequent references to this edition are marked *Salesman*.
12. Arthur Miller, "The Family in Modern Drama," *Atlantic Monthly*, CXCVII (April, 1956), 37.
13. See John Gassner, *Form and Idea in Modern Theatre* (New York, 1956), p. 13.
14. There have been attempts to give Willy a specific ethnic heritage. After seeing Thomas Mitchell do Willy, Miller himself commented that he did not realize he had written a play about an Irish family. (Popkin, "Strange Encounter," *Sewanee Review*, LXVIII, 35.) George Ross reviewed a Yiddish production, pointing out underlying Jewish elements in the play. He felt that Miller had "censored out" the specifically Jewish in favor of an anonymous Americanism. ("*Death of a Salesman* in the Original," *Commentary*, XI [1951], 184–86.) This controversy underscores the point—relating the Lomans to any ethnic background destroys Miller's perspective.
15. Roger Babson, *Making Good in Business* (New York, 1921), pp. 98–9.
16. Wyllie, *Self-Made Man in America*, p. 107.
17. W. J. Ong, *Frontiers in American Catholicism* (New York, 1957), p. 31.
18. Henn, *Harvest of Tragedy*, p. 29.
19. "Pathetic" is used here, not in the sentimental, nice-doggy sense, but in the root meaning. Willy is acted upon by outside forces, he suffers the incursion of societal pressures. As he is shaped by these forces, he is "pathetic."
20. "Shadows of the Gods," *Harper's Magazine*, CCXVII (August, 1958), 36.
21. Willy has an unhappy penchant for falling into their hands. He owns and operates a Hastings refrigerator and a Studebaker car.
22. Miller, "The Family in Modern Drama," *Atlantic Monthly*, CXCVII, 39–40.
23. *Making Good in Business*, p. 73.
24. Miller emphasizes this view. He is convinced that drama can instruct, that its power to move an audience can be reformatory: "There lies in the dramatic form the ultimate possibility of raising the truth-consciousness of mankind to a level of intensity as to transform those who observe it." ("The Family in Modern Drama," *Atlantic Monthly*, CXCVII, 41.)
25. Popkin, "Strange Encounter," *Sewanee Review*, LXIII, 55.

HENRY MILLER

1891–1980

Henry Miller, novelist and essayist, was born in Manhattan, the son of a middle-class tailor of German origin, on December 26, 1891. He attended elementary and high school in Brooklyn, where his family moved when he was one, but chose not to go to college, educating himself instead through wide reading and travel. In 1924 he left his job with Western Union to devote himself to writing, and in 1930 he moved to France.

Although Miller had written many stories and two novels in the 1920s and 1930s, his first published book, *The Tropic of Cancer*, appeared in Paris only in 1934; it is a novel, based on his experiences, about the life of an American artist in Paris, and was banned for decades in the United States and Britain (as were several of his other works) for its explicitly sexual passages. *Black Spring* (France, 1936; U.S., 1963), a collection of autobiographical essays, was followed by *The Tropic of Capricorn* (France, 1939; U.S., 1962), which draws on his adolescence in New York. Other writings from this period include *Aller Retour New York* (1935), a letter describing a trip to New York; *Max and the White Phagocytes* (1938), about an unusual friend; *The Cosmological Eye* (1939), a collection of fiction and essays; and *The Wisdom of the Heart* (1941), also fiction and essays.

In 1939 Miller made a trip to Greece which inspired *The Colossus of Maroussi* (1941); in 1940, with the onset of the war in Europe, he returned to the United States. *Sunday after the War*, a series of sketches, was published in 1944, and was followed by *The Air-Conditioned Nightmare* (1945), an account of a cross-country tour of the United States made by Miller and his friend, the American artist Abe Rattner, in 1940–41; this in turn was followed by a sequel, *Remember to Remember* (1947).

In 1944 Miller settled in Big Sur, near Carmel, on the California coast, where he worked on the autobiographical *Rosy Crucifixion* trilogy, consisting of *Sexus* (1949), *Plexus* (1953), and *Nexus* (1960), which, in a semi-fictional form, describes his life up until his decision to leave for France. In addition to this work, he published *The Smile at the Foot of the Ladder* (1948), a piece of fiction; *The Books in my Life* (1952), about books which had been of particular significance to him; *Nights of Love and Laughter* (1955), a collection of stories; *The Time of the Assassins* (1956), a study of Rimbaud; *Big Sur and the Oranges of Hieronymous Bosch* (1957), about his life in California; *To Paint Is to Love Again* (1960), which contains reproductions of his art; *Stand Still Like a Hummingbird* (1962), a collection of essays; *Just Wild about Harry* (1963), a play; and *My Life and Times* (1971), a series of tape-recorded interviews.

Living in California, Miller gradually became accepted as a major literary figure, and was an important influence on the Beats. He engaged, however, in constant battles with censors; the publication in the United States of *The Tropic of Cancer* (1961) and *The Tropic of Capricorn* (1962) provoked a series of obscenity trials which eventually concluded with a favorable ruling. In 1976 an anthology of Miller's writing selected by Norman Mailer appeared as *Genius and Lust*, with a lengthy introductory essay by Mailer. Many volumes of his correspondence, with Michael Fraenkel, Lawrence Durrell, Anaïs Nin, and others, have also been published. Miller died in 1980.

⟨. . .⟩ the one curious novel which has been published in Paris within the last year or so is not French at all; it is a novel in English by an American, Henry Miller. To this author stars, asterisks, and dashes are unknown, and those words, mostly of four letters, which print usually eschews, bestrew his every page. The language, admittedly, is essential to the narrative. In this novel, *Tropic of Cancer*, there are both words and deeds. It is a monotonous record of untidiness, insolvency, pimping, drunkenness, venereal disease, and the most sordid of sexual cravings and satisfactions. Yet the narrative of trivial squalor will suddenly be abandoned for a serious disquisition on, for instance, the painting of Matisse. The astounding thing is that the novel has qualities almost as great as its defects. There is no plot, but there is a pattern. The wearisome iteration of certain words is accompanied by a marked distinction in the writing. Above all, there is dynamism. The coarse language is essential because the novel is an expression of despair and disgust at human life. Only in an afternoon's communion with suburban nature does the wretched narrator come in the end to find a passing peace. The implication here is shallow. It remains that

Mr. Miller does produce a memorable and eddying effect by expressing nausea at the assumed conditions of human existence with the never-flagging gusto appropriate to *joie de vivre*. To this extent the despair of *Tropic of Cancer* echoes the despair of Falstaff.—MONTGOMERY BELGION, "French Chronicle," *Critn*, Oct. 1935, p. 86

When Henry Miller's *Tropic of Cancer* appeared a year ago I approached it with caution because, like a lot of other people, I did not wish to seem or to be impressed by mere obscenity. But I realise now, from the intensity with which it has stayed in my mind, that I underpraised it, and I would like to mention it again before dealing with his new novel, *Black Spring*.

The interest of *Tropic of Cancer* was that it cast a kind of bridge across the frightful gulf which exists, in fiction, between the intellectual and the man-in-the-street. English fiction on its higher levels is for the most part written by literary gents about literary gents for literary gents; on its lower levels it is generally the most putrid "escape" stuff—old maids' fantasies about Ian Hay male virgins, or little fat men's visions of themselves as Chicago gangsters. Books about ordinary people behaving in an ordinary manner are extremely rare, because they can only be written by someone who is capable of standing both inside and outside the ordinary man, as Joyce for instance stands inside and outside Bloom; but this involves admitting that you yourself *are* an ordinary person for nine-tenths of the time, which is exactly what no intellectual ever wants to do. *Tropic of Cancer* was a smaller book than *Ulysses*. It was not primarily a work of art and it made no attempt to analyse different states of consciousness. But in one way it bridged the gap between the thinking and the unthinking man more successfully than *Ulysses*, in that it was not complicated by feelings of horror and repentance. The average sensual man was not used as a kind of confession-box like Eliot's Sweeney, but taken for granted. The book's standpoint was really that of Whitman, but without Whitman's American puritanism (which escapes notice because disguised as a kind of nudist uplift) or his American bumptiousness. It was a notable effort to get the thinking man down from his chilly perch of superiority and back into contact with the man-in-the-street; it was only incidentally a pity, perhaps, that the street in question should be the Rue de la Harpe.

Black Spring is a book of different scope. It no longer deals with recognisable events of ordinary life, or rather it uses them only as nuclei round which spins a kind of Mickey Mouse universe where things do not have to happen according to the ordinary laws of space and time. Each chapter or each passage starts off with a fragment of reality which is so to speak blown out into a balloon of fantasy. I take one example more or less at random:

> . . . Men and women promenading on the sidewalks: curious beasts, half-human, half-celluloid. Walking up and down the Avenue half-crazed, their teeth polished, their eyes glazed. The women in beautiful garbs, each one equipped with a cold-storage smile. . . . Smiling through life with that demented, glazed look in the eyes, the flags unfurled, the sex flowing sweetly through the sewers. I had a gat with me and when we got to Forty-Second Street I opened fire. Nobody paid any attention. I mowed them down right and left, but the crowd got no thinner. The living walked over the dead, smiling all the while to advertise their beautiful white teeth.

You see here how something that is or might be a description of ordinary reality slides away into pure dream. There is no need to get bogged up in metaphysical discussions about the meaning of "reality". The point is that words are here being used to invade what is really the province of the film. A Mickey Mouse film breaks the rules of common sense more violently than any book ever written, yet because it is seen it is perfectly intelligible. Try to describe it in words and you will fail; worse, nobody will listen to you. The truth is that the written word loses its power if it departs too far, or rather if it stays away too long, from the ordinary world where two and two make four. A tendency to put his day-dreams on paper was apparent in Henry Miller's earlier book, and I think he has been led further in that direction by the remarkable power over words which enables him to slide from reality to fantasy and from urinals to angels without the smallest appearance of effort or incongruity. From a technical point of view this book is an advance on the other. At worst his prose can be flat and full of rhymes, like the passage I quoted above, but at its best it is astonishing. As usual I cannot quote any of the best passages, because of the unprintable words, but if you can get hold of a copy, have a look at the passage between pages 50 and 64, for instance. It is the kind of prose which, when I read it, makes me feel that I should like to fire a salute of twenty-one guns.

I advise anyone who can get hold of this book to read it, and if you happen to have a copy of the first edition, hold it tight, for it may be worth money some day. But I still prefer the earlier book, and I wish that Mr Miller would chronicle some more of the adventures of his disreputable friends, for which task he seems so admirably suited.—GEORGE ORWELL, Review of *Black Spring* (1936), *Collected Essays, Journalism and Letters*, Volume 1, eds. Sonia Orwell, Ian Angus, 1968, pp. 230–32

The Tropic of Cancer, by Henry Miller, was published in Paris four years ago, but nobody, so far as I know, has ever reviewed it in the United States, and it seems to me to deserve some notice.

Every phase of literary opinion is responsible for its critical injustices. During the twenties, this book would have been discussed in the *Little Review*, the *Dial* and *Broom*. Today the conventional critics are evidently too much shocked by it to be able to bring themselves to deal with it—though their neglect of it cannot wholly have been determined by the reflex reactions of squeamishness. A book bound in paper and published in Paris has no chance against a book bound in cloth and brought out by a New York publisher, who will buy space to announce its appearance. The conservative literary reviews have not been so easily outraged that they would not give respectful attention to John O'Hara's *Butterfield 8* or squander space on the inferior Hemingway of *To Have and Have Not*. As for the Left-Wingers, they have ignored *The Tropic of Cancer* on the ground that it is merely a product of the decadent expatriate culture and can be of no interest to the socially minded and forward-looking present.

Expatriate Mr. Miller certainly is: he is the spokesman, par excellence, for the Left Bank; but he has produced the most remarkable book which, as far as my reading goes, has come from it in many years. *The Tropic of Cancer* is a good piece of writing; and it has also a sort of historical importance. It is the epitaph for the whole generation of American writers and artists that migrated to Paris after the war. The theme of *The Tropic of Cancer* is the lives of a group of Americans who have all more or less come to Paris with the intention of occupying themselves with literature but who have actually subsided easily into an existence almost exclusively preoccupied with drinking and fornication, varied occasionally by the reading of a book or a visit to a picture exhibition—an existence for which they muster the resources by such expedients as pimping for travellers, playing gigolo to rich old ladies and sponging on one another. The tone of the book is undoubtedly low; *The Tropic of Cancer*, in fact, from the point of view both of its happenings and of the language in which they are conveyed, is the lowest book of any real literary merit that I ever remember to have read; it makes Defoe's *Newgate Calendar* look like Plutarch. But if you can stand it, it is sometimes quite funny; for Mr. Miller has discovered and exploits a new field of the picaresque.

The disreputable adventures of Mr. Miller's rogues are varied from time to time with phosphorescent flights of reverie devoted to the ecstasies of art or the doom of European civilization. These passages, though old-fashioned and rhetorical in a vein of late romantic fantasy reminiscent of *Les Chants de Maldoror*, have a youthful and even ingenuous sound in queer contrast to the cynicism of the story. And there is a strange amenity of temper and style which bathes the whole composition even when it is disgusting or tiresome. It has frequently been characteristic of the American writers in Paris that they have treated pretentious subjects with incompetent style and sordid feeling. Mr. Miller has done the opposite: he has treated an ignoble subject with a sure hand at color and rhythm. He is not self-conscious and not amateurish. And he has somehow managed to be low without being really sordid.

The last episode of *The Tropic of Cancer* has a deadly ironic value. A friend of the narrator called Fillmore, who is unique among these cadgers and spongers in enjoying a small regular income, becomes entangled in an affair with a French girl, who is pregnant and declares him responsible. Poor Fillmore first drinks himself into an insane asylum; then, emerging, falls straight into the clutches of the girl and her peasant family. They reduce him to utter abjection: he is to marry her, set her father up in business. The girl quarrels with him every night over dinner. The narrator suggests to Fillmore that he run away and go back home. For the latter, the glamor is all off Paris: he has been up against the French as they really are (in general these émigrés see nobody but one another); he realizes at last that the French regard Americans as romantic idiots; and he is weepily homesick for America. He allows himself to be sent off on a train, leaving the narrator a sum of money to provide for the girl's accouchement.

But as soon as Fillmore is gone, the helpful hero, left to himself, with the money for the girl in his pocket, decides that good old Paris, after all, is a wonderful place to be. "Certainly never before," he thinks, "had I had so much in my fist at one time. It was a treat to break a thousand-franc note. I held it up to the light to look at the beautiful watermark. Beautiful money! One of the few things the French make on a grand scale. Artistically done, too, as if they cherished a deep affection even for the symbol." Ginette need never know about it; and, after all, suppose her pregnancy was all a bluff. He goes for a drive in the Bois. Does he want to take the money, he asks himself, and return to America too? It is the first opportunity he has had. No: a great peace comes over him now. He knows that for half an hour he has money to throw away. He buys himself an excellent dinner and muses on the Seine in the setting sun. He feels it flowing quietly through him: "its past, its ancient soil, the changing climate." It is only when they are looked at close-to that human beings repel one by their ugliness; they become negligible when one can put them at a distance. A deep feeling of well-being fills him.

In retelling this incident from *The Tropic of Cancer*, have I made it more comic than it is meant to be? Perhaps: because Mr. Miller evidently attaches some importance to the vaporings of his hero on the banks of the Seine. But he presents him as he really lives, and not merely in his vaporings or his poses. He gives us the genuine American bum come to lead the beautiful life in Paris; and he lays him away forever in his dope of Pernod and dreams.—EDMUND WILSON, "Twilight of the Expatriates" (1938), *The Shores of Light*, 1952, pp. 705–8

Henry Miller, a surrealist writer living in Paris, was born in Brooklyn and still seems sore about it. The worst parts of *The Cosmological Eye* are cosmological eyewash, consisting of various and sundry bellyaches, very much dated attacks on American philistinism, and boyish anarchist howls. The rest of this collection of his sketches, stories, and essays indicates a vigorous if morbid imagination and considerable skill with words, though I cannot quite subscribe to the enthusiasm of his literary backer, Mr. James Laughlin, who writes about Miller as if he were a second Joyce. Mr. Miller is a sort of surly Saroyan. His I-am-God attitudes are childish and may be discounted, but stories like "Max" (an X-ray of suffering) and "The Tailor Shop" (low-life horrors, powerfully exploited) are not in the least childish and are well worth shivering at. Those who have an affection for vanguard writers and are not afraid of a little sewerage should look up Mr. Miller and his Dali dialogues.—CLIFTON FADIMAN, NY, Nov. 18, 1939, p. 105

Mr. Henry Miller is a difficult writer to assess. His novels are not novels; they are formless, sprawling, autobiographical slices of life, stamped with vitriol, coloured drably in black and white; above all they are iconoclastic, nihilistic, and always subjective.

It is difficult to see how he is compared with Proust and Lawrence, since Mr. Miller has created no memorable character worthy of such a comparison: all he has given—flaunted, rather,—is his own character in various stages of indiscreet exposure. His work is filled with his own personal prejudices; it is so uneven that you would say it was written under the compelling pressure of an obsession or drug. Yet he is sincere—he is no cheap jack peddling obscene pictures for profit (in fact few writers could have had a greater raw deal financially), and he believes in himself and his theories with an ardour that is sometimes depressing. At moments the *longueurs*, the shrill prophetic cries against a "doomed" world, give way to passages of frenzied brilliance, particularly in his early novels—the two *Tropics* and *Black Spring*—and it is then that he discovers something unique to say.

One explanation of his unequal work is probably to be found in his method. One gets the impression of a writer unused to planning or discipline of thought; once he is seized by his emotion it gains absolute control and swamps his intelligence. Things that normally would be pruned or cut out in that awful moment, the morning after the emotion has subsided, are allowed to remain under the assumption that what is conceived with passion must be treated as vision or revelation.

His latest work shows that his emotion gains control more often. In ⟨*Murder the Murderer* and *Sunday after the War*⟩ Mr. Miller becomes the denunciatory orator so determined to reform us that he forgets many of his arguments have been used too frequently before.

> The vast majority of mankind is either ignorant, or deluded, or both.
> The great sin, I think you will agree, is ignorance.
> The truth is that nobody is really fond of war, not even the military minded.
> We learn through suffering.

How many times, at Hyde Park Corner, or in the Army, have these things been thrown at our heads?

Murder the Murderer contains gems of this kind on every page. It is a flimsy publication produced by a new and apparently ambitious publisher, and consists of two private letters, the first written in 1941 and the second in 1944; and both are extracts from a book Mr. Miller is writing on America called *The Air-Conditioned Nightmare*. The strange title, by the way, is only matched by the crimson print, which is something of a nightmare for tired eyes.

Reading other people's letters is often a dull business, particularly if they are self-consciously written for publication, and these two epistles are heavy going. Fortunately for Mr. Miller the censor did not see these letters (they were never posted) because large fragments might have been objected to. Mr. Miller tells us that at the blackest period of the war he was in favour of allowing Hitler to conquer the world, on the strange assumption that once the Dictator gained his objective he would find it too much for him, and Nazism would collapse. This idea is inspired by Mr. Miller's admiration for the Indian theory of non-resistance, and his answer to those people who quite naturally demanded what he would do under the German regime, was simply that his books would receive no worse treatment under the Nazis than they had already suffered under the British and Americans. Pacifism has found many reasons for its existence, but surely never before has it been avowedly based on the sales of an author's books!

Sunday after the War has the advantage, at least, of being printed in conventional black print; again we are given a collection of fragments (this habit is almost becoming a disease) on Art, D. H. Lawrence and life. Two of these pieces were apparently commissioned but never published until they saw the light of day in this collection. There is a highly unpleasant description of a meeting with his family called "Reunion in Brooklyn," two letters to Anaïs Nin, and several more chunks of autobiography.

The emphasis this time is not on war, but on Mr. Miller's attitude towards humanity. He tells us that he has never been able to accept the modern way of life; and rather than compromise and become a slave to a system he thinks poison, he would rather go into the wilderness to seek voluntary isolation. It is difficult to do this in these days without a private income; and poverty has had a worse effect on him than a more ordinary way of life might have had. His isolation has only been a physical one, for intellectually he has never ceased living in and attacking the life he tried to renounce.

He tells the world that it is dying of too much sex, cinemas, radios, drugs, and other stimulants; though after reading the three fragments called *The Rosy Crucifixion* one might be forgiven for thinking that it is Mr. Miller who has had a surfeit, and not the world.

He is also tormented by the thought of women and their power over men. Emotion must be avoided like 'flu. The only trouble about this is that to make oneself proof against feeling is to leave one only a sterile world in which to live. It leaves a vacuum inside one, and makes all things meaningless such as, for example, Mr. Miller's liaisons with women. The episode where he seduces a waitress against a radiator is typical enough. A few words to start with; a little functional agitation, then an abrupt farewell, and Mr. Miller remains detached and not a little bitter. Where does all this lead, except to a literary and emotional graveyard?

But it is not until he gets on to the subject of cinemas in his "Preface to *Hollywood Hallucination*" that he lets off his really big guns. The most interesting part, factually speaking, is the new material he quotes from the Production Code on which the making of American films is based. It gives a strange insight into the minds of the American people.

> Revenge in modern times shall not be justified.
> In general, passion should be so treated that these
> scenes do not stimulate the lower and baser instincts.

In these two books Mr. Miller is often stimulating through his use of shock tactics, but taken in larger doses he palls and irritates. He has given us some of his worst faults with little of the redeeming brilliance of the earlier novels.—Robin King, "Potted Miller," NS, Feb. 1, 1947, pp. 100–101

It would be invidious to make extravagant claims for the genius of an author the greater part of whose best work is not available to his countrymen. This task were better left to the critics of a future age who will be able to discuss it with the impartiality it deserves. But one thing is certain: both America and England will one day be forced to come to terms with him on his own ground. Yet perhaps when this time comes—when he can be studied in the light of his intentions—even the moralists of letters (it is too much to hope that our puritan cultures will ever cease to bring forth moralists) may discover that, in an inverted sort of way, Miller is really on the side of the angels; and that his work, regarded in its totality (as he wishes it to be) is simply one of the great liberating confessions of our age, and offers its

readers the chance of being purged "by pity and by terror" in the Aristotelian way. It offers catharsis. . . .

But my job would be best done if I could succeed in situating him in the literature of our time—for he does not fit easily into any of the text-book categories. Indeed he is rather a visionary than merely a writer. I suspect that his final place will be among those towering anomalies of authorship like Whitman or Blake who have left us, not simply works of art, but a corpus of ideas which motivate and influence a whole cultural pattern.

Miller has elected to shame the devil and tell the truth, and his work is one of the bravest, richest and most consistent ventures in this domain since Jean-Jacques Rousseau. By its very nature such a task must transgress the narrow limits of what ordinary people regard as permissible; canons of taste, conventional ideas of beauty and propriety, they must be renovated in the light of his central objective—the search for truth. Often the result is shocking, terrifying; but then truth has always been a fierce oracle rather than a bleat or a whimper. But no one, I think, could read (as I have just done) through the whole length and breadth of his work without wonder and amazement—and finally without gratitude for what he has undertaken on behalf of us all. It isn't pretty, a lot of it, but then neither is real life. It goes right to the bone. It is absolutely veridic and unflinching in its intellectual bravery. It is significant, too, to mention that among the first few great men of the day to acknowledge Miller's greatness was a philosopher, Count Keyserling. I still remember the expression of amazed delight on the face of the author of *Tropic of Cancer* when he unfolded the telegram and read the message: "I salute a great free spirit."

To grasp the intention is everything. "I am *against* pornography and *for* obscenity," writes Miller; and again in another place: "My books are not about sex but about self-liberation"; and yet again: "The full and joyful acceptance of the worst in oneself is the only sure way of transforming it." These statements deserve the reader's fullest attention. ⟨. . .⟩

At peace with his neighbor, reconciled to friend and foe alike, and secure in the knowledge of his fame, he awaits the verdict of the young Americans of the future—not just the writers, but the ordinary folk as well, artisans, laborers and carpenters who buy their fifteen thousand copies of Whitman every year. . . .

What will they make of this great tortured confession which spans the whole range between marvelous comedy and grim tragedy? It is exciting to imagine. I am not gifted with second sight unfortunately but I imagine that they will realize that Miller has been honest on behalf of us all, so to speak, and that everything which he describes as true of himself is true of every man-jack of us, particularly what is self-indulgent, perverse or even downright horrible; particularly what is silly no less than noble or grand. What he has tried to do is to accept and so transform the warring elements in the secret life of man, and his work is a record of the battle at every stage. That is really the central message of Miller. Great vagabond of literature that he is, he will not want for readers among our grandchildren.—Lawrence Durrell, "Introduction" to *The Henry Miller Reader*, 1959, pp. ix–xi

More than thirty years after the publication of his first major work, Henry Miller's literary reputation remains uncertain and insecure. Those who acknowledged his ability early did so cautiously, recognizing that his work defied precise definition and description. To what extent was he writing autobiography? Or novel? Was his Paris world a Bohemian underground or an inner landscape to which the psychoanalyst rather than the literary critic had greater access? Even sympathetic critics found the word *literature* unsatisfactory when it was used to describe Miller's work.

His importance was more readily acknowledged in France, where, after all, his books were available. In 1947 one French study of modern American literature included a chapter on Henry Miller, prophesying that America would eventually recognize and accept him as an important writer. The same critic also realized that Miller's offensive realism should be explained by the anagogic pattern: his search for the absolute requires that he must first loathe and denounce before he acquires the power to move toward God or the absolute. His is the traditional path of the visionary and mystic, whatever apparently strange roads he insists on traveling.

Such recognition of Miller's importance and thematic concerns does not appear in American literary histories, however. If his work is mentioned at all, it is with an uneasy reluctance to accept him as a significant contributor to American literature. Critics often find it difficult to separate his work from his life, moreover, and both from an "offensive irrelevance" to the times through which he lived, despite his recent and flourishing popularity. Although Leslie Fiedler ⟨in *Waiting for the End*⟩ finds it astonishing that Miller could turn his back on human misery during the period of the Great Depression, he does find in his work a significant relevance to the present: "Miller is the laureate or, better, the prophet of the new personalism, and hence the first important self-consciously anti-tragic writer in America." Fiedler still sees Miller's fiction, however, as autobiographical in a narrow sense, and the precise nature of Miller's prophecy goes unexamined.

The first difficulty one has in evaluating Henry Miller is recognizing the nature of his vision. Tolerant readers can identify the street-corner prophet immediately and acknowledge his insistence that our civilization is a nightmare to be denounced. Yet he says nothing that is new or surprising on this subject. Those who recognize the religious intensity and consistency of his prophetic proclamations about the self, however, are often unwilling to acknowledge that such visions are substantial and universal. Like Kingsley Widmer, they see only adolescent posturing, although they recognize the vitality and sincerity that emerge from what they call formlessness and bad taste. In reviews of Miller's works helpless paradoxes emerge: Miller is a "basement" transcendentalist who writes "wearisome surrealism," "acres of plain careless" prose, and yet is our greatest existentialist and the "presiding genius at the *Götterdämmerung* of American transcendentalism."

Certainly before we praise or condemn Miller, we must clearly recognize the nature of his vision. The extreme and contradictory responses to his work suggest that this recognition has not yet occurred. ⟨. . .⟩

Miller belongs properly among those writers whose work Jung characterizes as *visionary*. Jung distinguishes between two modes of artistic creation, the *visionary* and the *psychological*. *Psychological* works of literature are those in which the writer's fictional world is easily recognized by what we call "consciousness," even though the reader may be forced to become fully aware of what he does not wish to confront. But the nature of a *visionary* work is different, and Jung's description of it ⟨in *Modern Man in Search of a Soul*⟩ reminds us of Miller's fiction:

> It arises from timeless depths; it is foreign and cold, many-sided, demonic and grotesque. A grimly ridiculous sample of the eternal chaos—a *crimen laesae majestatis humanae*, to use Nietzsche's words

—it bursts asunder our human standards of value and of aesthetic form. The disturbing vision of monstrous and meaningless happenings that in every way exceed the grasp of human feeling and comprehension makes quite other demands upon the powers of the artist than do the experiences of the foreground of life. . . . But the primordial experiences rend from top to bottom the curtain upon which is painted the picture of an ordered world, and allow a glimpse into the unfathomed abyss of what has not yet become.

Jung goes on to describe the usual reaction provoked by such visionary works:

> We are astonished, taken aback, confused, put on our guard or even disgusted—and we demand commentaries and explanations. We are reminded of nothing in everyday, human life, but rather of dreams, night-time fears and the dark recesses of the mind that we sometimes see with misgiving. The reading public for the most part repudiates this kind of writing—unless, indeed, it is coarsely sensational—and even the literary critic feels embarrassed by it.

Such visions may lead us to conclude that a highly personal experience lies behind the literary form, reducing the work itself to a problem in pathology. Jung argues, however, that the work of the visionary artist should be considered "the symbolic expression" of something imperfectly known. It is the world that seers, prophets, and enlighteners have been acquainted with throughout man's history, and it should be studied in its own right.

Visionary art lends itself successfully to archetypal criticism. A close scrutiny of the images in Henry Miller's fiction, for example, will reveal unmistakably the outlines and forms of these archetypes. In fact, those very episodes in which the images seem especially incongruous and the symbols hopelessly obscure, actually reveal the symbolic action central to the significance of Miller's early fiction.

One is able to discern not only the archetypal images but certain processes or patterns which define the self Miller is exploring and the nature of the struggle in which his narrative *I* is engaged. Behind what is apparently an account of amorous adventures—ludicrous, monstrous, and grotesque—is a struggle of the *I* as consciousness seeking to establish its independence from the unconscious, symbolized by the Archetypal Feminine and manifested in the female figures of Miller's world as well as in myriad non-human forms.

These images of the Archetypal Feminine are among the most significant of those which fill the pages Miller writes. His prose is characteristically highly textured in the sense that few passages appear in which there is not a proliferation of images. Jung has pointed out that the archetype itself can never be described, since it is a "form" of the unconscious, but that the images which fill out this form are the means by which the archetype "appears" to consciousness and is experienced by it. This process, which Jung designates a "symbolic process," is an "experience in images and of images." The images of the Archetypal Feminine which the *I* experiences in Miller represent only one aspect of the transpersonal unconscious Jung postulates. Yet, because the unconscious is frequently experienced as feminine, it is as a manifestation of the feminine that Miller's narrator usually encounters the unconscious as something threatening or promising, the source both of creative power and castrating dominance.—JANE A. NELSON, "Introduction" to *Form and Image in Henry Miller*, 1970, pp. 11–14

There is a poem entitled "Shitty" by Kingsley Amis in D. J. Enright's *Oxford Book of Contemporary Verse*. Reading it, I was instantly put in mind of Henry Miller, because it is not shocking but bright and funny, less a tone of voice than a startling gesture, the respectable writer clearing his throat and going *ptooey* while you watch. I think we are shockproof as far as coarse language is concerned; now, what alarms us, and rightly, is squalid action, the aristocrat and the boy scout, the traitorous don, the cabinet ministers wheeling and dealing in slag-heaps and ennobling shifty little asset-strippers. Next to these men's deeds, what is Miller's grunting? Anyway, he made it possible—he among others—for us to say exactly what we mean in our own words, and it is enjoyable to hear Mr Amis, grumpily profane, expressing common sentiments in direct language.

When Henry Miller stopped shocking people with his gonadal glow he was no longer taken seriously. But that was a long time coming. *Tropic of Cancer* was published in France in 1934, yet it was almost another thirty years before it was freely available in America and England. The illicitness contributed to his legend and he was forgiven his flatulence. A loophole in French law meant that books in English were not subject to censorship, and Miller's books could be regularly published under the Obelisk Press imprint alongside epics of coprophilia by "Akbar del Piombo."

Miller was a late bloomer—forty-two when his first book appeared—though he claimed that in the 1920s he hawked his prose-poems like Fuller brushes from door to door in his Brooklyn neighborhood. He loved this starving-artist image of himself, the romance of penury and neglect, writing against the odds, whistling in the dark, with his flat cap yanked over his eyes and (he says) muttering "Fuck you, Jack" to curious bystanders.

Anyone who has read Orwell's essay "Inside the Whale" knows how profoundly Miller affected and liberated at least one English temper. He was Orwell's opposite—reckless, amoral, loud, boastful, mendacious, and wholly contemptuous of politics. Orwell praised Miller's vigor and imagination, Miller returned the compliment by saying (in *The Paris Review*), "Though he was a wonderful chap . . . in the end I thought him stupid . . . a foolish idealist. A man of principle, as we say. Men of principle bore me . . ." What was Miller's philosophy? "One has to be a lowbrow," he said, "a bit of a murderer . . . ready and willing to see people sacrificed, slaughtered for the sake of an idea, whether a good one or bad one."

Typically, he talked through his hat, and apart from the most dubious generalities, didn't have an idea in his head. He claimed to be on the side of joy, freedom, criminality, insanity, ecstasy; he wasn't particular, but neither was Whitman, whom he much resembled. His writing was wild talk, scatological rather than sexual ("I am for obscenity and against pornography"). He was a shouter—a boomer, as they say Down South—and there are not many of those who achieve much in literature. His look, that of a Chinese sage, was misleading. Underneath was a hobo, the sort who sits stinking and dozing in public libraries, who screams abuse (some of it quite original) when he is told to move on, and who cherishes views such as "Civilization is the arteriosclerosis of culture."

He is the only hero in his books. Gore Vidal remarked (in a review of *Black Spring*) on how people are constantly saying, "You're wonderful, Henry!" and "How do you do it, Henry?" and never once does someone say, "Did anyone ever tell you you're full of shit, Henry?" Rumbustiousness was his watchword and his ego was all that mattered. From *Tropic of Cancer*

to the *Rosy Crucifixion* trilogy it is all Henry Miller, calling attention to himself. He attempted to write about Greece in *The Colossus of Maroussi*, but his cacophonous meditation obscures the ruins. His unfinished book on D. H. Lawrence was crowded with Miller on Life and Sex. In the early forties he applied for a Guggenheim fellowship to write a book about America. He was turned down for the fellowship but wrote the book all the same—*The Air-Conditioned Nightmare*, cross-country in a purring old car: Miller at large. By then he had just about stopped writing sentences such as "O glabrous world, O glab and glairy—under what moon do you lie cold and gleaming" and turned his attention to American bread, which he found disgusting and full of chemicals.

At the end of that trip he settled in what is certainly one of the most beautiful parts of America, the California promontory known as Big Sur, and wrote *Remember to Remember*, *The Books in my Life*, and his memoirs of the 'twenties, *Sexus*, *Plexus* and *Nexus*.

In his later years he moved to Los Angeles and found fulfillment playing table tennis with naked Japanese girls, which was one of his versions of paradise. I suspected he was gaga when he championed Erica Jong as a great writer. His judgement had not always been so bad. His literary friendships—Lawrence Durrell, Alfred Perlès—were wide-ranging and generous; he was besieged by would-be writers hoping for his bear hug.

I first read him in school, the smuggled *Tropics* and then *The Henry Miller Reader*. I was shocked and uplifted by what seemed to me great comedy and the rough and tumble of exuberant language. I had never read anything so deflating to pompousness, so manic or irreverent. It loosened something in my adolescent soul and helped me begin to write. I did not know that it was mostly fakery, using words for their sound alone, posturing and booming. It was a tonic, and it was only later that I discovered its ingredients to be piss and vinegar.

Earlier this year, a biography of Miller described that wonderful, hilarious life he claimed he had led to be totally imaginary. His life had been rather dull, he had been henpecked, he always did the washing-up. But this makes him, for me, a better writer—perhaps one of our more imaginative novelists instead of a noisy memoirist.

We are lucky to live in an age when books are seldom suppressed or banned—I speak of Britain and America, not Singapore or Paraguay or Iran. For this alone, our debt to Henry Miller is considerable. Walt Whitman wrote, "Unscrew the locks from the doors. Unscrew the doors themselves from their jambs!" Miller was not a very subtle carpenter. He kicked that door down, and allowed many writers to pass through.
—PAUL THEROUX, "Henry Miller 1891–1980" (1980), *Sunrise with Seamonsters*, 1985, pp. 215–17

HERBERT J. MULLER
"The World of Henry Miller"

Kenyon Review, Summer 1940, pp. 312–18

"Perhaps in reading this," writes Henry Miller in *Tropic of Capricorn*, "one has still the impression of chaos but this is written from a live center." The impression of chaos is plain enough. The latest chapter of his spiritual autobiography[1] is an extraordinary jumble of narrative, treatise, fantasy, satire, goat song, manifesto, and myth, pitched in every key from the obscene to the mystical; it is even fiercer than *Tropic of Cancer* in its defiance of the properties of art and life. "What is chaotic," Mr. Miller explains, "is merely peripheral, the tangential shreds . . . of a world which no longer concerns me"; but this is the world of social relationships and practical dealings that is the whole concern of most men. Nevertheless there is indeed something very live here: a remarkable personality, a remarkable talent. There is also a center, with significant lines of reference. Mr. Miller is not merely an original; his bearings as well as his gifts make it important to locate him.

The subtitle of *Tropic of Capricorn* gives the obvious clue—"On the Ovarian Trolley." The trolley is headed for the "ovarian world," the "super-infantile realm" where one may become attuned to the "life rhythm" and experience again the "irresponsibility of the anarchic man," a "New World" that is yet "a far older world than any we have known"—the world, in short, of D. H. Lawrence. Mr. Miller takes his place in the widespread revolt against intellect. "There's no improving the mind," he insists. "Look to your heart and gizzard." And he might well have added another organ. Though he does not so clearly as Lawrence exalt sex as the chief means to the good natural life, it is one of his main topics, and supplies the occasion and the vocabulary for a still more vehement protest against the convention that allows the unmentionable to be mentioned only in *de luxe* editions. "They [the rest of the world] are having sexual intercourse, God bless them"; Mr. Miller feels alone in the land of four-letter words. And the reviewer, who must paraphrase, feels like a sissy.

Mr. Miller's world also contains, however, elements not to be found in Lawrence: daredevil adventure, lusty laughter, exuberant fancy, extravagant caprice—a wild gaiety and gusto that temper his bitterness. He is in many ways a more natural and more attractive primitive than Lawrence. At the same time, his love of grotesquerie has been intensified by his defiant, rebellious attitudes; and so it finally carried him all the way into Surrealism and Dada. He was delighted by the incidental swagger of Dada, the freakish pranks and the play with such "startlingly marvelous phrases" as "doubt's duck with the vermouth lips." He also committed himself to the fundamental negations: the principle of scorning all principles, the logic of being illogical, the value of turning all accepted values inside out. Indeed, he is still more thoroughgoing in his anarchism. In "An Open Letter to Surrealists Everywhere" he objects even to Surreal*ism* (as no doubt he would to anar*chism*); any organized faith or creed is a sign of "impotency," all imitation is suicide. That a society of anarchic individuals is a contradiction in terms does not bother him. He insists that civilization is hell-bent anyway, and the sooner it gets there the better.

Now, it is at once hard and easy to attack Mr. Miller's position. It is hard because one cannot really get at him at all. He begins by rejecting all the principles and values to which one ordinarily appeals; opposition is absolute all along the line, every irresistible assertion collides with an immovable negation. It is nevertheless easy to point out fundamental inconsistencies in his attitudes, contradictions of fact—the practical futility of his whole effort to deny the consequences of having a mind and being a member of society. Mr. Miller's ideal man can exist only in the womb. He declares that he became sane when he finally saw through the bugaboo of Knowledge; the sane man has "very little brain because there is very little baggage to carry about." In fact, he himself has very considerable brains, constantly exercises them, and carries about an unusual erudition—intellectuals may often find it hard to keep up with him. Briefly, there is a great deal of romantic nonsense in Mr. Miller.

It is also, I believe, most dangerous nonsense. Today he may regard the war as the final proof of the hopelessness and

horror of civilization, but he may also have some misgivings about the glory of primitive instinct and unreason. He thrusts his ideas upon us so insistently, at any rate, that he lays himself wide open to the "ideological" criticism in which contemporaries specialize. Yet he is primarily an artist, not a social philosopher, and the immediate issue for criticism is what his attitudes do to his work as an artist. He has an ultra-romantic passion for utter freedom. Only when free, he remarks in "Hamlet," can the artist be *possessed*. Once possessed, however, the artist would seem to be no longer free; and I should say that the ideas that possess Mr. Miller are cause and effect of the most serious faults of his work.

Like Carlyle, he believes that the ideal is silence (he prefers music above all other arts "because it tends toward silence"); like Carlyle, he is forever talking and at the top of his voice. Often, moreover, he talks like a boastful youngster. "I know how to avoid work," he asserts, "how to avoid entangling relationships, how to avoid pity, sympathy, bravery, and all the other pitfalls." The idea is that the artist, as the most superior of anarchic individuals, must at all costs guard against attachments—to people and sentiments as well as to principles, traditions, ideas. Actually, of course, he cannot cut out all the fatal attachments—if he could, nothing would be left of the Self he prizes. Thus he also announces that below the belt all men are brothers, often exhibits decent, humane sentiments, even becomes banal in expressions of gratitude ("If it hadn't been for Fillmore I don't know where I should be today—dead, most likely."). His rebellion against society is finally in the name of a richer humanity. But meanwhile his autobiography is often simply unpleasant. In the latest installment he relates still more ostentatiously how he sponged on his friends, seduced their wives or sisters, lied, betrayed, stole.

Mr. Miller's ardent admirers seem to regard this extravagance as the proof of his originality, sincerity, depth, power. Similarly they applaud this disorder; in the introduction to *Tropic of Cancer* Anaïs Nin invites critics to strangle themselves with this "bundle of shreds and fibres." But Mr. Miller will be no better off for their strangling. The serious trouble with him is that his innumerable contradictions are all shapes of a deep confusion, the chaos is *not* merely peripheral. The world that supposedly no longer concerns him is in fact very much with him, and his efforts to be thoroughly consistent only emphasize the fundamental inconsistency. The result of this inner turmoil is not merely considerable waste motion and emotion but an aggravation of his natural tendency to excess. He makes a virtue of all his vices, a cult of anarchy. Now his remarkable talents merely fizz and sputter, now they explode all over the place.

More specifically, the issues raised by Mr. Miller's art center in his intoxicated hymn to life, Life! LIFE. Intellect, science, society, civilization, ninety-nine percent of what passes for art and literature—he hates them all as monstrous perversions of REALITY. Despite the capitals (his own), the meaning is a little vague. He has himself asked the pertinent question in his objection to Freudian adjustments to reality: *what* reality? *whose* reality? Nevertheless his passion for taking life straight explains his distinctive habits as a writer. He insists upon writing nothing but autobiography in the first person; fiction, invention presumably might be artificial or literary. He makes a necessity of the "divine jumble" he adores; to straighten things out is to tamper with life and gain nothing. For the same reason he is brutally outspoken, draws no lines, rejects all formal discipline, refuses to tidy up after a job. "The violence and obscenity are left unadulterated," Anaïs Nin explains, "as manifestation of the mystery and pain which ever accompanies the act of creation." The obscenity, unfortunately, is bound to get more attention than it deserves; I should say only that it is usually hearty and healthy, often a source of rich humor, never merely pornographic, but also at times unnecessary, forced to the point of nastiness. But the important issue is the whole attitude toward art and life; and the serious objection is that rawness is not the necessary sign of power, or violence of depth, or labor pains of sincerity, or messiness of mystery, or nakedness of truth—that, finally, there is no such thing in art as the whole truth and nothing but the truth. Despite his exaggerated indifference to Literature and fear of Art, Mr. Miller is a highly self-conscious writer of literature, and some of his virtuoso Surrealist performances even suggest artiness.

All this is indeed easy to say. Yet it is therefore too easy to overlook the value of Mr. Miller's attitudes. For those who cherish reason and reasonableness, his protest against modern society is not impertinent or merely quixotic. If his medicine would kill the patient, he is nevertheless attacking a real disease; his criticism of Proust and Joyce in "The Universe of Death," for example, reveals acute powers of diagnosis. Like Lawrence, at any rate, he forces us back to fundamentals, makes us clarify the premises of our faiths. But our immediate concern is again the individualized work of art, not the generalized philosophical or sociological footnote; and for the artist his attitudes have especial pertinence and value. The source of his limitations is as plainly the source of his strength.

However dangerous its implications, Mr. Miller's thought is from this point of view not perverse. It has been thoroughly earned, not merely learned; it is the product of his deepest experience. All the writers who have "influenced" him did not so much point out new directions as make him conscious of where he had already gone by virtue of his own peculiar genius. If his reaction against his society has carried him too far, the impulse was nevertheless his deepest needs as an artist and a man. His hymn to Life is accordingly whole-hearted through all its inconsistencies. At a time when there is so much worried rationalization, unhappy second thought, half-hearted faith, underlying fear of life or of death, he arrives through his negations at an impassioned Yea-saying: "The first word any man writes when he has found himself, his own rhythm, which is the life rhythm, is Yes!" One may disagree with the particular terms of Mr. Miller's Yes, as one may with Milton's argument for justifying the ways of God to man, or not know just what he means by Life in the abstract; but there is no questioning his imaginative and emotional power, or the flesh and blood of the life he creates. Few writers today seem so intensely alive.

As an artist he chiefly reminds me of Thomas Wolfe. Although the mighty America that struck Wolfe with awe is the epitome of all that Mr. Miller loathes—it is a huge cesspool, a slaughter-house, a monstrous death machine, and various unprintable metaphors—they are both American to the core, Mr. Miller never more plainly than in the furious energy and extravagance of his attacks upon his country. He is incidentally much like Wolfe in his original characterization, with its often grotesque detail; striking examples are "The Tailor Shop" from *Black Spring*, and the magnificent passages in *Tropic of Capricorn* dealing with his experience as personnel director of Western Union. In general he has the same immense appetite for experience, the feeling of wonder and awe, the teeming memory and blazing imagination, the gift of headlong eloquence. He also has much the same faults of fantastic excess; his picture of the true artist, who must "tear his hair with the effort to comprehend," "bellow like a crazed beast," "stand up on the high place with gibberish in his mouth and rip out his

entrails," is Eugene Gant to the life. And they both write autobiography, the endless story of this very romantic artist, and write his emotions twice their size.

This comparison also throws into relief, however, some significant differences. I doubt that Mr. Miller will ever achieve the resonance of Wolfe's greatest scenes; I also doubt that he will ever lapse into anything as banal as *The Web and the Rock*. He has broader interests, more sophistication, a much more varied background of experience, but above all greater intellectual powers than Wolfe had, and therefore greater possibilities of self-discipline, detachment, and command. Although he is as egocentric, he knows his ego better; unlike Eugene Gant or George Webber, his hero emerges as a definite personality. And he is more apt to grow. I say this even though *Tropic of Capricorn*, Mr. Miller's latest work, is by all odds his most violent and obscene. Here the flood of his emotion is canalized by more specific ideas about what he hates in modern civilization and what the good life should be; hence it might at first rage all the more. But for the same reason his subsequent work may be more measured and restrained.

Notes

1. The works on which this study is based are *Tropic of Cancer* (1934), *Black Spring* (1936), *Max and the White Phagocytes* (1938), and *Tropic of Capricorn* (1939), all published by the Obelisk Press, Paris. *The Cosmological Eye* (1939), published by New Directions, Norfolk, Connecticut, is a collection of pieces—necessarily somewhat expurgated—taken mostly from *Max and the White Phagocytes*.

KENNETH REXROTH
From "The Neglected Henry Miller"
Nation, November 5, 1955, pp. 385–87

Henry Miller is a really popular writer, a writer of, for, and by real people. In other countries he is read, not just by highbrows, or by the wider public that reads novels, but by the people who, in the United States, read comic books. In the United States he has been kept away from a popular public and his great novels have been banned. Only highbrows who could import them from France have read him.

I once crossed the Atlantic with a cabin mate, a French-African Negro, only partially literate, who was able to talk for hours on the comparative merits of *Black Spring* and the *Tropic of Cancer* and the *Tropic of Capricorn*. When he found out I came from California and knew Miller, he started treating me as if I were an archangel newly descended, and never tired of questions about Le Beeg Sur and Les Camarades du M'sieu Millaire. Miners in the Pyrenees, gondoliers in Venice, and certainly every *poule* in Paris, when they hear you're from California, ask, first thing, "Do you know M'sieu Millaire?" This doesn't mean he isn't read by the intellectuals. In fact I should say he has become part of the standard repertory of reading matter everywhere but in England and in the United States. If you have read Balzac, or Baudelaire, or Goethe, you are also expected to have read Miller. He is certainly one of the most widely read American writers, along with Upton Sinclair, Jack London, Fenimore Cooper and Caldwell.

This is the way it should be. Nothing was sadder than the "proletarian novelist" of a few years back. Nobody read him but other Greenwich Village esthetes like himself. The people Henry Miller writes about read him. They read him because he gives them something they cannot find elsewhere in print. It may not be precisely the real world, but it is nearer to it than most other writing, and it is certainly nearer than most so-called realistic writing. ⟨. . .⟩

It is hard to tell sometimes when Miller is being ironic and when he is being naive. He is the master of a deadpan style, just as he has a public personality that alternates between quiet gentleness, "like a dentist," he describes it, and a sort of deadpan buffoonery. This has led some critics to consider him a "modern primitive" like Rousseau.

Miller is a very unliterary writer. He writes as if he had just invented the alphabet. When he writes about a book, he writes as if he were the first and only man who had ever read it—and furthermore as if it wasn't a book but a piece of living meat whacked off Balzac or Rimbaud or whoever.

Miller has preserved an innocence of the practice of Literature almost unique. Likewise he has preserved an innocence of heart. But he is not unsophisticated. In the first place, he writes a muscular, active prose which is always under control. True, he often rambles and gets windy, but only because he likes to ramble and hear his head roar. When he wants to tell you something straight from the shoulder, he makes you reel.

Now the writer most like Miller in some ways, is the eighteenth-century *naif*, Restif de la Bretonne. If you want the common man of the eighteenth century, with his heart laid bare, you will find him in Restif. But you will also find thousands of pages of sheer boredom, and hundreds of pages of quite looney and obviously invented pornography. Miller too is liable at times to go off the deep end about the lost continent of Mu or astrology or the "occult," but it is for a different reason. If the whole shebang is a lie anyway, certainly the amusing lies, the lies of the charlatans who have never been able to get the guillotine in their hands, are better than the official lie, the deadly one.

In all literature there aren't many people like Miller. The only ones I can think of are Petronius, Casanova, and Restif. Their books give an overwhelming feeling of being true, completely uncooked. They are all intensely masculine writers. They all are great comic writers. They all convey, powerfully, a sense of the utter tragedy of life. I can think of no more chilling passages in literature than the tolling of the bell from the very beginning of Casanova's *Memoirs*, the comments and asides of the aged man, writing of his splendid youth, an old, sick, friendless pauper, in a draughty castle in the backwoods of Bohemia. And last, and most important, they were all what the English call spivs. Courtier of Nero or Parisian typesetter, they were absolutely uninvolved. They just didn't give a damn whether school kept or not.

Miller has often been compared with Céline, but I don't think the comparison is apposite. Céline is a man with a thesis. Furthermore, he is a litterateur. In *Journey to the End of the Night* he set out to write the epic of a Robinson Crusoe of the modern soul, the utterly alienated man. He did it, very successfully. Céline and his friends stumble through the fog, over the muddy ruts with the body of Robinson in a denouement as monumental as the *Nibelungenlied*. But it is all a work of art. I have been in the neighborhoods Céline described. They simply aren't that awful. I am sure on internal evidence of the story itself, that his family wasn't that bad. Céline makes a sociological judgment on Robinson. Miller *is* Robinson, and on the whole, he finds it a bearable role, even enjoyable in its way.

Henry Miller is often spoken of as a religious writer. To some this just seems silly, because Miller is not especially profound. People expect religion to come to them served in miracle, mystery, and authority, as Dostoevsky said. Blake

dressed his message up in sonorous and mysterious language, but the message itself is simple enough. D. H. Lawrence likewise. You could write it all on a postage stamp. "*Mene, mene, tekel, upharsin.* Your official reality is a lie. We must love one another or die." I suppose any writer who transcends conventional literature is religious in so far as he does transcend it. That is why you can never actually base an educational system on the Hundred Best Books. A hundred of the truest insights into life as it is would destroy any educational system, and society along with it.

Certainly Miller is almost completely untouched by what is called religion in England and America and Northern Europe. He is completely pagan. This is why his book on Greece, *The Colossus of Maroussi*, is a book of self-discovery as well as a very true interpretation of Greece. It is thoroughly classic. Although he never mentions Homer and dismisses the Parthenon, he did discover the life of Greece, the common, real life of the peasants and fishermen, going on, just as it has gone on, ever since the Doric invasions.

His absolute freedom from the Christian or Jewish anguish of conscience, the sense of guilt, implication, and compromise, makes Miller humane, but it effectively keeps him from being humanitarian. He might cry over a pet dog who had been run over, or even punch the guilty driver in the nose. He might have assassinated Hitler if he had the chance. He would never join the Society for the Prevention of Cruelty to Animals or the Friends' Service Committee. He is not involved in the guilt, and so in no way is he involved in the penitence. This comes out in everything he writes, and it offends lots of people. Others may go to bull fights and write novels preaching the brotherhood of man. Miller doesn't go to the bull fights in the first place. So, although he often raves, he never preaches. People have been taught to expect preaching, and of course they are offended if they don't find it.

Fifty per cent of the people in this country don't vote. They simply don't want to be implicated in organized society. With, in most cases, a kind of animal instinct, they know that they cannot do anything about it, that the participation offered them is really a hoax. It is for these people, the submerged 50 per cent, that Miller speaks. As the newspapers never tire of pointing out, this is a very American attitude. Miller says, "I am a patriot—of the Fourteenth Ward of Brooklyn, where I was raised." Life has never lost that simplicity and immediacy. Politics is the deal in the saloon back room. Law is the cop on the beat, shaking down whores and helping himself to apples. Religion is Father Maguire and Rabbi Goldstein, and their actual congregations. Civilization is the telegraph company.

So there isn't any social message in Miller, except an absolute one. When you get through reading James Farrell or Nelson Algren, you have a nasty suspicion that the message of the author is, "More playgrounds and properly guided social activities will reduce crime and vice." There is nothing especially frightful about Miller's Brooklyn; like Farrell's South Side, it is just life in the lower middle-class and upper working-class section of a big American city. It certainly isn't what queasy reviewers call "the slums." It's just the life the reviewers themselves led before they became reviewers. What outrages them is that Miller accepts it, just like the people who still live there. Accepting it—how he can write about it! He can bring back the whole prewar America, the bunny hug, tunes from *The Pink Lady*, Battling Nelson, Dempsey the Nonpareil, Pop Anson and Pearl White, a little boy rushing the growler with a bucket of suds and a sack of six-inch pretzels in the smoky twilight of a Brooklyn Sunday evening.

I think that is what Miller found in Paris. Not the City of

Art, Letters, and Fashion—but prewar-Brooklyn. It is certainly what I like best about Paris and it is what I get out of Miller's writing about Paris. He doesn't write about the Latin Quarter, but about the dim-lit streets and dusty squares which lie between the Latin Quarter and the Jardin des Plantes, where men sit drinking beer in their shirt sleeves in front of dirty little bars in the smoky Sunday twilight. But he writes very convincingly about that most Brooklyn-like of all the quarters of Paris, the district near the Military Academy, across the river from the Eiffel Tower, where the subway becomes an elevated, tall tenements mingle with small bankrupt factories, and people sit on the doorsteps fanning themselves in the Brooklyn-like summer heat, and sleep and couple on the summer roofs.

In the same way his intellectuals in Paris are assimilated to Brooklyn. They may talk about Nietzche and Dostoevsky, but they talk like hall-room boys, rooming together, working at odd jobs, picking up girls in dance halls and parks. "Batching" is the word. Over the most impassioned arguments and the bawdiest conversations lingers an odor of unwashed socks. The light is the light of Welsbach mantels on detachable cuffs and unmade beds. Of course that is the way they really talked and still do, for that matter.

There is a rank old-fashioned masculinity about this world which shocks the tender-minded and deluded. It is far removed from the Momism of the contemporary young American male. This is why Miller is accused of writing about all women as though they were whores, never treating them as real persons, as equals. This is why he is said to lack any sense of familial love. On the whole, I think this is true. Most of the sexual encounters in the *Tropics* and the *Rosy Crucifixion* are comic accidents, as impersonal as a pratfall. The woman never emerges at all. He characteristically writes of his wives as bad boys talk of their school teachers. When he takes his sexual relations seriously, the woman becomes an erotic giantess, a perambulating orgy.

Although Miller writes a lot about his kinship with D. H. Lawrence, he has very little of Lawrence's abiding sense of the erotic couple, of man and woman as the two equal parts of a polarity which takes up all of life. This again is Brooklyn, presuffragette Brooklyn. And I must admit that it is true, at least for almost everybody. A real wedding of equals, a truly sacramental marriage in which every bit of both personalities, and all the world with them, is transmuted and glorified, may exist. In fact, some people may have a sort of talent for it, but it certainly isn't very common. I don't see why Miller should be blamed if he has never found it. Hardly anybody ever does, and those who do usually lose it in some sordid fashion. This, of course, is the point, the message if you want a message, of all his encounters in parks and telephone booths and brothels. Better this than the lie. Better the Flesh than the World and the Devil. And this is why these passages are not pornography, but comic like *King Lear* and tragic like *Don Quixote*.

At least once, Miller makes up for this lack. The tale of the Cosmodemonic Telegraph Company is a perfect portrait of our insane and evil society. It says the same thing others have said, writing on primitive accumulation or on the condition of the working class, and it says it far more convincingly. This is human self-alienation at its uttermost, and not just theoretically, or even realistically. It is an orgy of human self-alienation, a cesspool of it, and Miller rubs your nose in it. Unless you are a prig and a rascal, when you get through, you know once and for all what is the matter.

Once Miller used to have pinned on his bedroom door a scrap of paper, written on it "*S'agapo*"—"I love you" in Greek. In "The Alcoholic Veteran" he says: "The human heart cannot be broken."

LESLIE A. FIEDLER
From "The Beginning of the Thirties: Depression, Return, and Rebirth"
Waiting for the End
1964, pp. 37–45

The Thirties ⟨. . .⟩ was the period in which Henry Miller produced his most valuable work, though the Thirties themselves did not know what to do with his untidy dithyrambics or how to judge his half-comic, half-earnest prophetic stance. The critics of the era, as a matter of fact, left him to be explicated by a frenetic knot of his friends (Lawrence Durrell, Alfred Perlès, Michael Fraenkel), through whose adulatory obfuscations we have been forced ever since to beat our way in search of Miller's real import. It is hard to remember that *Tropic of Cancer* (1934) and *Tropic of Capricorn* (1939) are genuine Depression novels, for they have long seemed to us forbidden books in the sense in which *Fanny Hill* was until only yesterday forbidden, rather than subversive books in the sense in which some readers once fondly believed *Grapes of Wrath* to be subversive, dirty rather than revolutionary. Moreover, they are the novels of an expatriate, celebrations of the illusion of freedom from Puritanism possible only to Americans abroad; yet they were produced at a moment when theoretically all American writers had turned their backs on such illusions in favor of home, responsibility and social progress.

To make matters even more difficult, the sentimentality of the two *Tropics* (and, in so far as they are not farcical, they are sentimental) was attached to certain quasi-mystical doctrines out of Krishnamurti, Nostradamus, Mme. Blavatsky and John Cowper Powys, rather than to the teachings of Marxism-Leninism, which lent to the more fashionable sentimentalities of the age an air of *Realpolitik*. And the style of Miller's books—his particular ideal of bad writing as an earnest of sincerity—was, in its pursuit of the garrulous and the centrifugal, quite different from the dogmatic and straightforward meagerness to which bad proletarian novels aspired. The anti-structure of his books, too, seemed unsympathetic to readers accustomed to the highly structured class-struggle novel, rigid, almost, as the Western story, because, like that popular genre, it denied personal expression in favor of ritual and cliché. In place of the mythos of the proletarian romance (the conflict of forces, the eruption of violence, the inevitable defeat of the preferred cause, and the conversion in the midst of defeat), Miller provided only erotic daydreams, broken by shrill exhortations to freedom, freedom not from economic exploitation but from conventional morality and from politics itself. Finally, however, it was his euphoria, his unrelenting hilarity, which baffled an era that could never manage to embody in its literature the optimism appropriate to its hope of social revolution. Over and over, but always in vain, the Marxist critics scolded the self-declared Marxist novelists for being unable to imagine in their fiction even minimal happy endings. ⟨. . .⟩

In a late book, full of tenderness toward himself and his own youth, Miller has listed Céline's *Journey to the End of the Night* among "The Hundred Books Which Have Influenced Me the Most"; but it seems difficult to believe that Miller ever really understood the rage and terror of Céline as well, say, as he understood the blander vision of the writers he lists just before and after the French novelist: Lewis Carroll and Benvenuto Cellini. Clown and cocksman, finally cocksman-clown, Miller is too *funny*, both intentionally and by mistake, to be ranked with a true descendant of the Marquis de Sade. To Miller, sex is not an instrument of power and degradation but a howling joke, and the most comic of all created things is the female sex organ as observed by his own oddly objective, though properly concupiscent, eye. Even now, however, in the moment of recognition and triumph, when Miller has come to play the Old Man to many in the generation of the Sixties, and his best books are printed for the first time in his own country, the real meaning of his work is scanted by the enlightened prigs, to whom his present vogue is largely an occasion for self-congratulation and is overlooked by the religioid Beats, to whom his muddled "serious" pronouncements seem to qualify him as prophet-in-chief to the modern world.

In any event, Henry Miller is just now coming into his own, making the difficult transition from a cult favorite, smuggled past customs into the land of his birth, to a popular author, displayed on newsstands in airports and supermarkets. Miller, however, has not merely survived long enough to be admired for certain older books which seemed in their own time offensively irrelevant, but to feel obliged to write new ones, in particular the trilogy *The Rosy Crucifixion*, which he speaks of as the last, the ultimate as well as the final, work of his life. He has felt obliged, that is to say, to be reborn as most Thirties writers have not—the luckiest among them managing to die, in one sense or another, the unluckier continuing to repeat themselves with diminishing vigor and conviction (like James T. Farrell). And in this sense, he is a fascinating case.

A comparison of *Plexus*, his last published major work, and *Tropic of Cancer*, the first of his books to appear, is especially illuminating in this regard. *Plexus*, which came out in 1953, is the second volume of *The Rosy Crucifixion*, of which the first, *Sexus*, was published in 1949, and the third, *Nexus*, is presumably still in progress. Like his first book, however, which was printed in France in 1934, the last deals with the only subject that has ever interested Miller, i.e., himself, retelling, with only the merest pretense at order, a series of events from his life already twice told or a score of time foreshadowed elsewhere, and rehashing notions, picked up in his early reading, about the lost continent of Mu, metempsychosis, and other vaguely mystical matters for which he has always had an unfortunate affinity. The mask of the narrator remains still the same, despite the passage of twenty years (but Miller as a writer was never young, being nearly forty-five when *Cancer* appeared): the mask of a half-American, a Noble Savage who is not also a Puritan, a citizen of the United States without guilt, or any commitment, however diminished, to diligence, industry, frugality, or duty.

Even more astonishingly, readers of *Plexus* will discover once more an American novelist who despises whisky (peace to Fitzgerald, Hemingway, and Faulkner) though he affects a taste for wine and adores good food despite the notorious fact that good meals are as rare in American books as satisfactory love affairs. And they will find, too, one who lived through the Thirties without acquiring the slightest interest in politics or social justice or, indeed, in people in groups larger than two or three. Others have meaning for Miller only as they impinge directly on him, hurting or sustaining him; he finds it difficult to imagine them as real to each other, even in pairs, much less in communities or nations, except in the moment of copulation. Miller has, it is true, an extraordinary ability to re-create, in fiction, his friends and enemies joyous in bed, but he is an idiot when he tries to imagine them miserable in society. "For the world in general," Miller has written in a memoir of his friend Alfred Perlès, "the ten years preceding the war [World War II] were not particularly joyful times. The continuous

succession of economic and political crises which characterized the decade proved nerve-racking to most people. But, as we often used to say: 'Bad times are good times for us.'"

The indifference of Miller to any *angst* except his personal one, his actual relish of the world's misery, seems the more incredible when we realize that the time on which he is commenting, the time, indeed, during which he found his authentic voice and style, was the period of the great Depression and of the terror of Between-the-Wars. It is an era which produced many brands of apocalyptic hysteria, but none so eccentric or so heartless as Miller's. That hysteria he is in the habit of presenting to us in the guise of joy; but it seems rather to be a symptom of the strange failure of the tragic sense, a way of apprehending experience as rich as it was black, which characterizes American literature from the time of Melville and Hawthorne to that of Hemingway and Faulkner, however desperately and vestigially in the latter. In this regard, perhaps, the work of Miller must be considered prophetic—a preparation for an age of maximum consumption and relative plenty, in which the tragic sense would become as obsolete as the maxims of *Poor Richard's Almanac*.

Miller represents, then, the moment at which a specially American way of coming to terms with human misery and evil, a way rooted in dying Puritanism and accompanied by obsessive guilt, particularly in regard to indolence and copulation, was being destroyed forever. In a sense, the concern with social justice, which so possessed those writers who were looking out at America at the moment Miller, in Paris, had turned his back on his country, seems a last effort to maintain and justify the long concern of our literature with "the blackness of darkness." But that concern, however little we knew it, was already doomed even in the Thirties, on the one hand by the attenuation of traditional guilts, and on the other by the replacement of a metaphysical or ethical view of man, a cosmic or social approach, by a personal one, self-congratulation or self-pity.

Miller is the laureate or, better, the prophet of the new personalism, and hence the first important self-consciously anti-tragic writer in America. It is a little misleading, all the same, to speak of him as a comic writer without further qualification, though he is howlingly funny, both intentionally (in the perhaps one-quarter of his books where he is at his best) and unintentionally (in the three-quarters where his self-awareness breaks down or his naïve susceptibility to pseudo-philosophy and mantic posturing takes over). What is funny in him, however, is rooted neither in social satire, whether directed against the deviant individual, like, say, Pope's, or a whole society, like G. B. Shaw's, nor in a vision of the total absurdity of mankind, like Chaucer's or, more recently, Samuel Beckett's. Miller's is the humor of mocking gossip, rooted in the kind of betrayal of friends (as his life-long friend, Alfred Perlès, somewhere suggested) in which many men and most women delight to indulge in private, but which committed to cold, public print scandalizes and disturbs us, as all revelations of the self we fear others see and hope they do not scandalize and disturb us.

In this sense we can identify Miller's humor as a function of the *persona*, the mask of the "Happy Rock" called Henry Miller, created by the form he loves best: transmogrified autobiography—not autobiography objectified by form and distance into proper fiction, but autobiography made truer to itself than mere fact by the skill of an inspired and malicious liar. The essential aim of that liar, as well as of the humor he makes his chief weapon, is to put down all the rest of the world and to glorify himself, without, however, denying that that self is a feckless, conscienceless sponger and deadbeat. In the very moment that Miller tells us how he rewarded by sleeping with their wives those who sponsored, clothed, fed, and subsidized him, he is further rewarding them by making a comic tale of that betrayal or by drawing comic portraits of the sex organs of those wives, thus compounding the initial treachery.

The man who disavows duty, work, and conscience—those moral burdens which our earlier writers chafed against without daring to slough—who really acts as if the world owes him a living, is likely to be loaded down with a new burden in place of the old, the burden of obligation and gratitude, unless he can laugh his benefactors to scorn. It is this desperate laughter, the last weapon against the last temptation to duty, the temptation to say thanks to those who sponsor a dutiless life, which rings through Miller's work. But even the desperation behind the laughter does not finally succeed in depressing him (though he confesses it overtly from time to time and betrays it unawares even more often) because he is convinced he is immortal, does not believe he will ever die, even now when he has passed his seventieth year.

How strange, for a grown man, this illusion which ordinarily sustains only the young! But it is characteristic of Miller to have begun to be young at forty-five, to have made the young man's move into exile precisely when writers like Fitzgerald (actually five years his junior) had begun the retreat toward maturity and despair, and it is typical of him, too, to be working at it still, or again, beyond the full span of three score years and ten. But it is this which makes him characteristically American as well as characteristically himself, for all of his rejection of Calvinism, guilt, and tragedy, and despite his preference for sex over whisky. He is not, however, an American in the line of Hawthorne, Melville, and Faulkner in this regard, but rather a late link in the chain that begins with Benjamin Franklin and passes through Emerson to Mary Baker Eddy: the line of self-congratulatory post-Christians who manufactured homegrown religions (often with hints of the mysterious East) to express their assurance that tragedy was an illusion and death was not real.

If, in his latest book, Miller sounds more like Franklin than Rousseau or even Whitman, this is not only because his personal success, his recent happy marriage (on the fourth try), and his first real relationship with children of his own have overtaken him late in life, at the moment he has returned to America, but also because America has at this moment returned to prosperity. From post–World-War-II America, Miller has returned, in *Plexus*, to the America of Post World War I, from one era of plenty to another, as well as from his old age to his youth. What has been dropped out is the middle of his life, the misery of his middle age memorialized in *Tropic of Cancer*, and the unnoticed years of the Depression, which coincided with that middle age. It is with nostalgia that he turns back to that earlier time, a nostalgia for old books, old buddies, and old loves. And though at the center of *Plexus* is the love affair with, and the marriage to, "Mona," Miller's second wife, it is only the best years of their relationship which he records.

He cannot stay away from the memory of her, even from the anticipation of her betrayal of him, any more than he can stay away from the Jews, to whom he has always been bound by a ferocious ambivalence; but this time everything is mitigated and blurred, rendered as a series of crucifixions not so much rosy in themselves as seen through rose-colored glasses. Even the pseudo-avant-garde style of *Cancer* has peeled away, that violence of image and language bred of an anguish near madness, as well as of Miller's attempts to please his improb-

able Muse, the much-overrated Anaïs Nin. This very joyousness of Miller, once frantic and subversive, his contemptuous negation of a prevailing melancholy ("No, this is a prolonged insult, a gob of spit in the face of Art, a kick in the pants to God, Man, Destiny, Love, Beauty . . . what you will. I am going to sing for you, a little off key perhaps, but I will sing. I will sing while you croak, I will dance over your dirty corpse . . ."), has become now mere smugness and cliché ("The first few months . . . it was just ducky. No other word for it. . . . We lived exclusively for each other—in a warm, downy nest . . ."), the banal nostalgia of an old man proud that he has lived so long, pleased with his still youthful vigor, and astonished that his published visions of failure and apocalypse have brought him success and peace.

STEVEN FOSTER
"A Critical Appraisal of Henry Miller's *Tropic of Cancer*"

Twentieth Century Literature, January 1964, pp. 196–208

There is a legend and an accepted mode of interpretation which surrounds and nearly suffocates Henry Miller. His work has not yet been released to the world of responsible criticism mainly because the ragged apostles who hold tightly to his coattails are unwilling to view their prophet as anything less than a prophet, and his highly personal idiom as anything less than Biblical utterance. Contrast this attitude with its opposite—that of the cautious critic who, though he could bring a wealth of experience and an objective perspective to the task, is reluctant to criticize Miller for fear of overexerting himself, or of dallying with a bomb that might be a dud. The works of Miller, especially the two *Tropics*, thus hang between life and death, between total acceptance and timid rejection. Either way it is unfortunate; although the quality of the author's message is mixed, many of his words have a relevant ring to them. A work like *Tropic of Cancer* must be given a life of its own.

Annette Kar Baxter has called the novel "surrealist autobiography."[1] Although convenient tags are rarely exact, this one provides access to an analysis of structure, and so is useful. After a fashion the novel does seem to fit the category; certainly Miller is writing about himself, and in a grotesque manner which cannot but invite questions as to the reality of his self-image. But the reader is continually aware of the surrealist technique in the novel; it constitutes a paradox not easily solved. The stylistic grotesqueries of Nathanael West, Breton, Eluard, Sartre (in his fits of nausea) and of Miller first of all plunge the reader into a world that is intensely personal. Reality must reluctantly bend itself, become absorbed and distorted, by the impish imagination of the artist. The product of surrealist process must always be recognized for what it is—the unique world of a particular man. But just as significant, the man has lost his own identity. Having created this fantastic museum of the unconscious, he cannot keep from wandering about, touching this or that transformed object with awe. In effect, there is a double change: nature is denied and the artist, the instrument of denial, finds that somewhere along the way he lost his own identity as well. The novel lies before him with the personal vision of a man whom he hardly understands. Not only are objective nature and inner vision disparate; the artist has also become alienated from his deeper self.

By writing in this manner Henry Miller has subjected the world to his own individualistic viewpoint. He has written something perhaps closer to biography instead, of a man other than himself, a man lost in the multifarious forms of his own creation. What the fictional Miller expresses is not always what the true Miller might desire. The two are distinct from each other and must be explained, not as an organic unit, but as separate identities sometimes speaking at cross purposes. At any rate, *Tropic of Cancer* is most conveniently a novel, "autobiographical" only in the hair-splitting sense; its hero is essentially fictitious, at least foreign to the man who created him. And if we are to regard the novel as Karl Shapiro would have us, as autobiographical "in the way *Leaves of Grass* is autobiographical,"[2] the conclusion would be much the same. Whitman's cosmic "new Adam" in "Song of Myself" certainly cannot be linked with his shy, unsuccessful creator.

In matters of style Miller can be justly identified with both Whitman and Melville. Their structures are essentially formless; they are "portmanteau" writers, "discursive, rambling and prolix":[3] vulnerable in matters of form because their visions are either too profound to be complete or left purposefully unfinished. *Tropic of Cancer* is large enough to include art theory, apocalyptic vision, Proustian memoir, "mysticism," and philosophy of history—all invested with a tentative quality. Apparently Miller expects the reader to supply his own conclusions, or at least to round things out and link fragmentary elements together. Miller is not a logician; in fact he shies away from any such formality. The effect is something like being met by a shot-gun blast in total darkness—every pellet hurts and seems effective, but there is neither rhyme nor reason to the whole painful pattern.

The random motion of *Tropic of Cancer* is rooted in the language of the novel. "Word drunk," elated by the possibilities of words and images, the author manipulates the language as an addict might use heroin: to kick himself free from the prosaic, to savor but never swallow. The images are strange but never fully explored. Again, it would seem that the primary interest in word usage is suggestivity, not satiation. Even in the Whitmanesque catalogues which appear every now and then like open man-holes, Miller seems to admit that though he could go on indefinitely to describe, time is limiting; "so here's a sample." His characterizations are rarely rounded because the imagery never quite comes to terms with demanded reality. The tendency to suggest, to make lop-sided and incomplete, is both the charm and fault of, for instance, this sketch of an Indian friend of the hero's:

> . . . but what with the murky light, the blotchy print, the tattered cover, the jigjagged page, the fumbling fingers, the fox-trotting fleas, the lie-a-bed lice, the scum on his tongue, the drop in his eye, the lump in his throat, the drink in his pottle . . . the grief from his breath, the fog of his brain-fag, the gush of his fundament, the fire in his gorge, the tickle of his tail, the rats in his garret, the hullabaloo and dust in his ears . . . he was hard-set to memorize more than a word a week.[4]

With a few slightly altered clichés, he has managed to set comprehension on edge. There is an impact to the catalogue, but it teases without fulfilling. Even in moments of verbal mastery, as in the following description of Tania, the words are brilliant and exciting, but rarely do they coalesce into a satisfactory picture:

> . . . *les voies urinaires*, Café de la Liberté, Place des Vosges, bright neckties on the Boulevard Montparnasse, dark bathrooms, Porto Sec, Abdullah cigarettes, the adagio sonata *Pathétique*, aural amplificators, anecdotal seances, burnt sienna breast, heavy garters, what time is it, golden pheasants stuffed with chestnuts, taffeta fingers, vaporish twilights turning to ilex, acromegaly, cancer and delirium, warm veils, poker chips, carpets of blood and soft thighs. (4)

Later on Tania is to become a symbol of universal fertility, but one never gets to know her; like the other characters in the novel, except perhaps for Miller's "id," Van Norden, she emerges into the world of living beings hampered by the author's habit of glancing and caressing with his words, but never perceiving in depth.

The usual procedure thus far has been to say that both the real and the fictional Miller are one and that they regard society in a most unique way, "the viewpoint of a man," says George Orwell, "who believes the world process to be outside his control and who in any case hardly wishes to control it."[5] Not only has Miller detached himself from people; he has withdrawn into a tomb: "Short of being dead, it is the final, unsurpassable stage of irresponsibility. . . . In Miller's case the whale happens to be transparent . . . he has performed the essential Jonah act of allowing himself to be swallowed, remaining passive, accepting."[6] David Littlejohn of Harvard seems to concur with Orwell: "In an age of pervasive and overwhelming social integration, Miller has achieved the all-but-impossible stance of total detachment. He is an Individualist so extreme as to seem at times prehistoric. He is above or below, or beyond or apart—uninvolved—in all our most intimate social concerns."[7]

There is a real danger involved in mixing the two Millers: the man and his fictional mask. The message conveyed by the novel is *not* one of detachment or withdrawal. The protagonist is *not* a "passive" observer, nor does he wish to remove himself to safety apart from "social integration." Perhaps this confusion of spokesmen stems from Miller's legendary stance of expatriation, many novelists of the twenties and thirties having been involved in such activity at one time or another. The expatriate attitude as characterized by Stephen Dedalus trudging off to Paris to "forge in the smithy of my soul the uncreated conscience of my race," is an exciting one, but lends itself too foolishly to biographical interpretation. To say that Miller's disengagement from a hateful society is the theoretical basis for his essential utterances in fiction amounts to folly, and implementing such theory in *Tropic of Cancer* means reaching for nonexistent clues. In this novel we are working with the fictional mask of Miller, and we will soon discover that his attitudes and activities are unique in their own right, demanding their own special pattern of criticism. The novel should be treated with the same methods as Sartre's *La Nausée*, whose hero Antoine Roquentin keeps a literary diary instead of writing a novel, is involved in somewhat similar problems, and has, strikingly, the same oblique resemblance to his creator.

Nietzsche has defined man as "an assemblage of atoms absolutely dependent, in his movements, on all the forces of the universe, their distribution and their modifications—and at the same time unpredictable like every atom, a being in himself."[8] The fictional Henry Miller, the hero of *Tropic of Cancer*, is the center and soul of the novel. He stands alone and apart, it is true, from character and event, but no more so than any modern being who feels himself to be unnaturally isolated and fights to return to the human community. The horde of moth-like characters wound around in his halo, the Miller world of action and desire—all are necessary components of his existence. And although one of his fundamental attitudes is to change his world, to recreate "the conscience of his race," this character constantly affirms his need, even more than his disgust, for other people.

Much has been made of Miller's so-called "Patagonian"

insights, the apparent ability to view the world with a "pre-civilized vision," separating the self from the society in order to be at the bottom looking up, investing the outside world with clothing stunning in its "primordial strangeness."[9] This idea appears frequently and might be considered a type of withdrawal. The desire is to be a child again, to enter the universe as if possessed by a primitive wonder, with every feeler extended: "I have been ejected from world like a cartridge. . . . I can feel the city palpitating, as if it were a heart just removed from a warm body" (57). The basic needs are hunger and sex, hunger above all: "my life is nothing but a big intestine. I not only think about food all day, but I dream about it at night" (63). The attitude most often takes a hedonistic turn: "The word must become flesh; the soul thirsts. On whatever crumb my eye fastens, I will pounce and devour. If to live is the paramount thing, then I will live, even if I must become a cannibal. . . . Physically I am alive. Morally I am free. . . . I go forth to fatten myself" (90). The Patagonian is capable of the extremes of behavior and emotion, has a zest for adventure and a child-like trust in human nature. Contrasted yet identified with this pre-civilized, amoral stance is the wish to dissolve everything but the soul and revert to the womb, not a death-wish, and certainly not a return to passivity and peace as Orwell and Littlejohn interpret it. At the beginning of the novel the hero writes to Tania:

> When into the womb of time everything is again withdrawn chaos will be restored and chaos is the score upon which reality is written. You, Tania, are my chaos. It is why I sing. It is not even I . . . I am still alive, kicking in your womb, a reality to write upon. (2)

It would appear that the Patagonian attitude is deliberately cultivated not so much to evade modern society as to afford possibilities to act upon reality; and the passionate desire to return to the safety of the womb is not a return to safety at all, but instead an embracing of "chaos." And we shall not go far before we discover that the Patagonian, the "womb-wish," Tania, "chaos," and the "reality to write upon" all comprise a loosely-tied bundle which signifies not passivity or escape, but an aesthetic theory of artistic creation. The fictional Miller removes and assumes the posture of a primitive simply to get a better perspective on reality and then to act creatively upon his discoveries. Returning to the womb is part of this active participation in life. The Patagonian viewpoint acts as stimulus; the frightful journey to the womb is the response.

Implicit in the fictional Miller's picaresque activity is a longing to find himself, to wed his ideology to action and thus fulfill himself. Women serve as possible objects of fulfillment. Early in the novel he laments that there is "No one to whom I can communicate even a fraction of my feelings" (6). He explains why Irène and Llona, two of his more intimate acquaintances, are unable to succor him: one would rather have letters than sex; the other is too selfish and "international" (6). Like a lead soldier he marches through a series of mindless copulations with the hope that someone will rise from the dark future to give him identity. He seems resigned to frustration. His tenderly regarded American wife Mona visits him in Paris and spends what promises to be a blissful night, but in the early morning light he watches her hair come "alive": "I pull back the sheet—more of them. They are swarming over the pillow" (18). Not only do lice breed frustration, but whores of various sorts keep falling asleep on him, or demand too much money, or try to tell him they love him. Even Germaine, the best of all trollops, with whom "everything clicked again," (40) bothered him not because she was "a whore all the way through" who

"put her heart and soul into her work" (43) but because she smelled badly of "weak coffee, cognac, apèritifs, Pernods and all the other stuff she guzzled between times . . ." (42). His escapades in the realm of women and sex, however, are only symptoms of a deeper world sorrow. He is a hopeful gambler playing a cosmic slot-machine, detesting the hard fact that the chips will rarely if ever fall his way, but futilely reaffirming his rights, like Dimitri in *Brothers Karamazov* or Willy Loman in *Death of a Salesman*, to play at this particular rigged game even if it is liable to mean total loss.

A friend of his named Papini, a kind of universal genius, is considered a "marvelous failure." The reason is that he refuses to have anything to do with friends who flock around him for bits of wisdom. "Don't bother me!" he says, and means it. "I need to be alone. I need to ponder my shame and my despair in seclusion; I need the sunshine and the paving stones of the streets without companions, without conversation, face to face with myself, with only the music of my heart for company" (59). Papini shuns the game in which the hero is so desolately involved. Miller needs people, their presence, their smells and attitudes, to give him meaning. And if he must have whores, he must also find his type of love in them. In the novel's most poignant lament the hero discovers he has an "insane desire to throttle all the birds in creation" every time he passes the concierge's window (219). There is so little genuine affection that it simply cannot be wasted on trifles: "At the bottom of every frozen heart there is a drop or two of love—just enough to feed the birds" (219). When love wanes and people begin to isolate themselves from each other and the world, the inanity of Papini's "Don't bother me!" is a horrible declaration of self-destruction.

As he watches a sea of Paris faces revolve around him the Miller of the novel jolts himself into an awareness of his own projected role as conciliator and finds himself wanting. His job as a proofreader represents an isolation perhaps even more effective than Papini's. He sarcastically reviews the universal significance of his "vocation":

> The world can blow up—I'll be here just the same to put in a comma or a semicolon. I may even touch a little overtime, for with an event like that there's bound to be a final extra. . . . On Sundays he steps down from his pedestal and shows his ass to the faithful. . . . The rest of the week he remains in the frozen winter marshes, an absolute, an impeccable absolute, with only a vaccination mark to distinguish him from the immense void. (133)

Besides, he has "adjusted" himself to the role without undue struggle. And this is perhaps far more frustrating than walking unfulfilled from a Paris brothel:

> And what is more strange is that the absence of any relationship between ideas and living causes us no anguish, no discomfort. We have become so adjusted that, if tomorrow we were ordered to walk on our hands, we would do so without the slightest protest. Provided, of course, that the paper came out as usual. (138)

From out of the numbness and lethargy of a society-imposed isolation, the fictional Miller desires to rise and walk. His artistic rebellion is based on the age-old desire to find self-purpose: "Ideas have to be wedded to action. . . . If it were only for the sake of an idea . . . Columbus would have foundered in the Sargasso Sea" (219). The statement of artistic purpose made by the author-hero as he begins his novel can hardly be interpreted as less than a desire to communicate and change, whatever the consequence:

This is not a book, in the ordinary sense of the word.
No, this is a prolonged insult, a gob of spit in the face
of Art, a kick in the pants to God, Man, Destiny,
Time, Love, Beauty . . . what you will. I am going
to sing for you, a little off key perhaps, but I will sing,
I will sing while you croak, I will dance over your
dirty corpse. . . . (2)

Lost in the gallery on the Rue de Séze, "surrounded by
the men and women of Matisse," the fictional Miller begins to
analyze and construct his role as artist and participant. Above
all, Matisse was impressively human, an artist "who has the
courage to sacrifice an harmonious line in order to detect the
rhythm and murmur of the blood" (147). Because he took part
actively in life, embracing both the filth and glory, he was
given a prophet's mantle, the ability to see behind reality to a
different reality, to foretell from present events an apocalypse
and a "revolution":

Behind the minutiae, the chaos, the mockery of life,
he detects the invisible pattern; he announces his
discoveries in the metaphysical pigment of space.
. . . Even as the world goes to smash there is one
man who remains at the core, who becomes more
solidly fixed and anchored, more centrifugal as the
process of dissolution quickens. (147)

The novel's hero longs for this touch of humanity. He wants to
place himself at dead center and reach out with his hands. He
cares not that the world shatters around him, for he, like
Matisse, must learn to propagate himself in the very midst of
confusion. "Even as the world falls apart the Paris that belongs
to Matisse shudders with bright gasping orgasms, the air itself is
steady with a stagnant sperm, the trees tangled like hair.
. . . The wheel is falling apart, but the revolution is intact"
(150).

Firmly associated with the Matisse vision is Van Norden's
hilarious episode with the whore and fifteen francs. While
Miller watches, his friend determinedly copulates for the sake
of a contract: "Without a spark of passion," says Miller, they are
"grinding and grinding away for no reason except the fifteen
francs. . . . And these two are like a machine which has
slipped its cogs. It needs the touch of a human hand to set it
right. It needs a mechanic" (130). The world with its
proofreaders, newspapers, insignificant lives and deaths, is
nothing more than a malfunctioning mechanism. It needs a
mechanic, a "primal cause," a Matisse or a Miller to set it
right. The world lacks the proper revolution, the correct
human action. "Somebody has to put his hand into the
machine and let it be wrenched off if the cogs are to mesh
again . . . Otherwise this show'll go on forever. There's no
way out of the mess" (131). Perhaps the heart of the novel
comprises the meditative acts of the hero-artist as he assumes
the role of the world's "mechanic"—the man who shoves his
arm into the machinery to be deified as a kind of glorified
"medicine man" holding the cure-all in his mangled right
hand.

As Stephen Dedalus comments in *Ulysses*, "there can be
no reconciliation if there has not been a sundering." The
fictional Miller must first break with the world before it breaks
him, and become, if it is possible, creatively nihilistic. As
Zarathustra commands: "He who must be a creator in good
and evil—verily, he must first be a destroyer, and break value
to pieces." Miller looks forward to this cataclysmic moment of
iconoclasm in several strongly flavored apocalyptic passages.
"Everything is slowly dribbling back to the sewer. For about an
hour there is a deathlike calm during which the vomit is
mopped up. Suddenly the trees begin to screech. . . . The
day is sneaking in like a leper" (145). The present world must

come to an end. Sartre strikes a similar pose in *La Nausée*
when the hero asks: "What if something were to happen? What
if something suddenly started throbbing?" The violence and
horror of a world gone mad with newly-created things like
"stone-eye, great three-cornered arm, toe-crutch, spider
jaw,"[10] although revolting, could be the foundation for a new
belief in personal existence. But the "existential hope," which
at times pokes its little head into *Tropic of Cancer*, offers in fact
very little hope. There is nothing but a sense of desolate waiting
for something that might be revolutionary, but probably is not.
Things and people wait to be recognized, used, enjoyed—yet
there seems to be no really new experience just around the
corner. Only objects are left, man-made signs which, in the
absence of humanity, have become objects. Still, with "tragic
optimism" the hero stoically anticipates the moment when all
will be derelict, when the present world as he knows it will be
dissolved by the powers of his own inner vision. As yet, "Not
one man . . . has been crazy enough to put a bomb up the
asshole of creation and set it off . . . it needs the *coup de
grâce*, it needs to be blown to smithereens" (24). Miller is the
man with the dynamite. When he dies to the world it will
succumb to his heroics and die with him. But his ambition
seems always stronger than his capabilities for action; his
idealism is continually smothered by a false bravado.

With Nietzschean blatancy the hero prepares to destroy
the existing order by creating his own "ready-made inferno."
He will torture himself in order to be liberated, "to emerge
clean of the past, a bright, gory sun-god cast up on an alien
shore" (164). Set free from his moorings, he will become a
Patagonian. Finding in this role a sense of identity, he is
prepared then to dissolve himself and the world with him. His
destiny lies in a womb of confusion, Tania's womb wherein
reality can be transcribed.

The fabulous Van Norden, the lonely, neurotic, "cunt-
happy" character who is symbolized by a phallic broomstick
and characterized by the desire to "wash all the dirt out of his
belly," (97) provides the key to the fictional Miller's projected
activity. The only completely realized minor figure in the
novel, Van Norden stands out because he is a prototype of the
protagonist, cut from the heart of the Miller hero's unconscious
life. As such he functions as a microscope through which we
discover new regions of motivation in the hero himself. Van
Norden is on a quest; he wants to "forget himself," to "give his
soul away" (117). His means are his sexual desires; his ends are
the various "cunts" who daily troop to and from his room. The
never-ending search amounts to a kind of death-wish, a desire
to lose or immolate himself in copulation. And though he is
able to forget himself momentarily in orgasm, he has not found
a whore capable or wistful enough to keep his soul once she has
taken it. So he continues to try out different women. "Don't
make me out to be a cunt-chaser," he complains, "it's too
simple" (119). And what complicates matters is that the essence
of Van Norden's search, the sexual sacrifice, can be reduced to
this remark made after using a flashlight on a whore one night:
"Jesus, it looked ghastly . . . It's an illusion. You get all
burned up about nothing" (126). Because Van Norden is
mostly a bundle of mindless emotions, he is not capable of
finding any meaning in this "ghastliness." Miller the intellec-
tualizer uses the same sexual organs to formulate his artistic
approach to the world.

The core of the novel is what might be called the GREAT
VISION—a long surrealist monologue which typically begins
when the fictional Miller happens to fix his gaze on a whore's
vagina. "A glance at that dark, unstitched wound and a deep
fissure in my brain opens up: all the images and memories

. . . break forth pell-mell like ants pouring out of a crack in the sidewalk" (222). The old has been destroyed, the new about to be built, and the creative artistic experience is symbolized by an act of copulation. Tania is recalled; the desire to find a home in chaos assumes meaning. In his vision Miller conjures up "the great sprawling mothers of Picasso" and "Molly Bloom lying on a dirty mattress" (223). These women are manifestations of old mother earth herself: "Great whore and mother of man with gin in her veins. Mother of all harlots, spider rolling us in your logarithmic grave, insatiable one, fiend whose laughter rives me!" (223). He discovers that he can identify with nature's creative processes:

> The earth is not an arid plateau of health and comfort, but a great sprawling female with velvet torso that swells and heaves with ocean billows; she squirms beneath the diadem of sweat and anguish. Naked and sexed she rolls among the clouds in the violet light of stars. (226).

He fancies himself as her lover: "I belong to the earth! I say that lying on my pillow and I can feel the horns sprouting from my temples" (229). His own new creation will be a progeny of mother earth. Her womb contains all the pain, the power, the incipient creativity to start a new world the other side of doomsday.

Miller's new relation to the world, his artistic attitude, is likened thus to sexual intercourse. "When I look down into that crack I see an equation sign, the world at balance, a world reduced to zero and no trace of remainder" (223). The artist must tip the scales in his favor by working with the "crater," the "festering obscene horror . . . the great yawning gulf of nothingness which the creative spirits and mothers of the race carry between their legs" (225). Having annihilated the world and himself, the artist can begin to create from the chaos he has begun to live within. In this confusion, this "horror," there is a pure remnant of reality, of Being, which not only is useful, but the soil for a new art:

> . . . a man who is intent on creation always dives beneath, to the open wound, to the festering obscene horror. He hitches his dynamo to the tenderest parts; if only blood and pus gush forth, it is something. The dry fucked-out crater is obscene. More obscene than anything is inertia. More blasphemous than the bloodiest oath is paralysis. If there is only a gaping wound left then it must gush forth though it produce nothing but toads and bats and homunculi. (225)

The "tropics of cancer," the syphilis and contamination, the "obscene horror," form a world where the fictional Miller has decided to live. There can be no doubt that this unsettling existence is similar to certain affective states (nausea, ennui, dread, joy), common to such existentialists as Sartre, Marcel, Kierkegaard, Nietzsche: the types of existence which attempt to reveal Being by wiping away the familiar face of things to get at the well-springs of creative energy.

But the end finds the hero peacefully musing on the "strange fauna and flora" of human activity (287). His quest has not been capped by a final dramatic discovery of his birthright. Probably more than anything else, the novel amounts to a gigantic wistful vision. The hero continues to work at insignificant jobs. But now he possesses a new symbol of civilization's decadence—money, (284) and this perhaps is the reason for a rather unconvincing hopeful attitude at the end. The existential readjustment to life is at best partial and continuous, and the fictional Miller is not quite secure in his "cancer and delirium."

Henry Miller has never been sensitive to traditional ethical standards. The fictional character in *Tropic of Cancer* is no less amoral. The problems of obscenity, pornography, the apparent destruction of tenderly-held ideals are baggage which he sheds on his journey back to the womb. It is necessary to bring all recorded history to naught if the artist is to begin anew with only a painful residue as a source for new morality. Like the "Superman" he must place himself beyond good or evil. Starting with a quotation from ancient Hindu scripture, "Evil does not exist,"[11] Miller scraps morality, not because standards of conduct continuously re-form and are only relative, but because the principles upon which ethics depend are essentially fictitious. His optimism, with its denial of evil even in the midst of evil, invites a certain amount of amazement. There is no aggressive attempt to establish or disestablish a personal standard. Miller writes as if codes did not exist, and for him they do not. The reader is pulled *in media res* into the Miller world, and chances are he is likely to lose himself because he cannot decide how he arrived in the first place or understand exactly where he is. The revolutionary call-to-arms, "Everything we are taught is false. Change your life!"[12] was made some time before the novel began and brashly excludes any theodicy. It is often a bit difficult to get into marching step with a man who is so self-satisfied with his own amorality that he neglects to tell us how and why he came to be so smug. Contrasted to the "unbearable disgust"[13] of a novelist like Céline, Miller's lack of ethics reads like a fairy tale. It is promising, exciting, but we wish there had been more of a struggle, even a twinge of agony. At least Céline begins with a thesis (the pointlessness of purpose) and recognizes the presence of something which is his enemy, allowing the reader to find a wall to back up against.

The real question is not one of accepting the pornography of the novel as being a part of this amoral stance, but that of understanding the reasons why such literature came to be written. The quarrel must ultimately be with the premise that evil is non-existent, and that all malevolence in the world can be negated without even a sign of hostility. Miller's pornography shocks us out of our Puritan skins mostly because it is just there, like a sore thumb which has never been wounded. We anticipate at least some Lawrentian suggestivity. But no, most of the fictional Miller's sexual escapades are either burlesque exaggeration or enervating through minute detail. He does not believe in Utopias; he is always hearing the toilet flush or the springs squeak, or wondering how he can cheat his whore and still have fun. There are no illusions; if good and evil do not exist, then there is no mystery involved in the sex act. Shapiro's characterization of Miller as "Gandhi with a penis"[14] is unfair to the amoral stance. The Miller-hero is a man without a touch of holiness, his friends just friends, his whores only women with gold teeth and a bottomless pocketbook.

There is no escaping moments of a mystical nature in the novel. This phenomenon is partly produced by the surrealist method of denying external reality to the senses. But surrealism amounts largely to technique and is not necessarily a yearning for the Absolute. When the style has been accounted for there still remain several visions where the fictional hero seems to lose himself by detaching from the outside world to flow with some inner stream of consciousness. While attending a concert the hero feels himself slipping away: "I have lost all sense of time and place. After what seems like an eternity there follows an interval of semiconsciousness balanced by such a calm that I feel a great lake inside me, a lake of iridescent sheen" (68). Again, a little farther on: "For the fraction of a second perhaps I experienced that utter clarity . . . In that moment I lost completely the illusion of time and space: the world unfurled its drama simultaneously along a meridian which had no axis. In this sort of hair-trigger eternity I felt that everything was justified" (88). If the philosophical Miller has counterparts in Nietzsche and the other existentialists, he has his mystical parallel in Walt Whitman, a poet who should never be called a mystic. Both Miller and Whitman try, in their rough way, to approximate the mystical experience, but they actually accomplish what Henri Bergson would call the "intuitive perception of inner duration."[15] Partly introspective, "inner duration" is reached and appropriated when the artist pierces the shifting but solid forms of the outer world and perceives the eternal movement of things within himself. Time and space take on new meaning and different motion; the past accumulates and swells into the future as an organism completely different in origin from the ordinary "time by the clock."[16] The "hair-trigger eternity" and the "meridian with no axis" cannot be lumped into mysticism. It is simply a perception by "intuition" of life in its subtle and penetrating flow from a vantagepoint somewhere beneath conscious states of mind.[17] One easily finds a model in Proust (whom Miller certainly read) who used his memory to kick himself into the world of "inner duration."

There are three types of comedy in the novel; one springs from the painful situations of modern life, another from a "particularizing" sense of humor. The third, which is so evident that it hardly needs mentioning, hearkens back to the burlesque tradition of Rabelais and Boccaccio. This last is happily evident in such scenes as those of the Indian visiting a Paris brothel (82f), Van Norden's sexual distractions in a restaurant (91f), the fifteen francs adventure (127f), the farcical weekend at Le Havre (180f), and the doomed attempt to rescue Macha, the Russian "countess," from the "clap" (208f).

Much of the laughter in *Tropic of Cancer* is partly hysterical, rather similar to the work of Nathanael West where we learn to laugh in spite of ourselves. But unlike the quixotic *Miss Lonelyhearts*, Miller's humor imposes from within, from the hero himself who is perfectly capable of laughing at himself, albeit a little desperately. Although ludicrous, *Tropic of Cancer* is not essentially comic, nor for that matter is *Miss Lonelyhearts*; both contain a core of tragic unfulfillment with a thick frosting of comedy. The announcement of artistic purpose at the start: "a gob of spit in the face of Art, a kick in the pants to God, etc.," is an attitude assumed by the fictional Miller whenever he is thwarted by the absurdities of society. This laughter is the kind of false joke one would make if he kept losing money in the slot machine. Because the chips obstinately refuse to fall his way, he passes off his frustration in pained laughter. Very seldom will a job, a friendship, a concert, a spring day, a barroom brawl, leave him happy. The comedy is ignited by incongruity; when things absurdly refuse to conform to your own sense of identity, exercise your will, fill out your sense of purpose by using the laughter medicine. The misfortunes of others, even their deaths, can be made a joke if there is the slightest hint of the ridiculous in their suffering, or the barest clue that these misfortunes might threaten you. On the death of an inconsequential proofreader named Peckover: "It's no use trying to invest the end with a little dignity—you have to be a liar and a hypocrite to discover anything tragic in their going. We laughed all night about it" (125). The better the disease or disaster, the louder the bravado:

> Everyone has his private tragedy. It's in the blood now—misfortune, ennui, grief, suicide. The atmosphere is saturated with disaster, frustration, futility. . . . However, the effect on me is exhilarating. Instead of being discouraged or depressed, I enjoy it. . . . I want the whole world to be out of whack, I want everyone to scratch himself to death. (11)

Two of his best friends, Fillmore and Van Norden, having lived awhile in misery, are dismissed at the novel's end with bursts of self-conscious laughter at what they have become. Fleeing from bedlam and a possessive wife, Fillmore hops a freighter for America (279). Van Norden, reduced to a bundle of nerves and inactivity by his "cunts," has carefully decided to take up masturbation (263).

In the second type of comedy the surrealist technique propels the fancy into realms of the ridiculous. Often a simple trifle—a tree, a waiter, a package, a room, a shop window—will call to mind a marvelous string of associations. "Everything interests me profoundly," says the hero, and he demonstrates in front of a "physical culture establishment."

> There are photographs showing specimens of manhood 'before and after.' All frogs . . . a frog should have just a wee bit of a paunch, like the baron de Charlus. He should wear a beard and a pince-nez, but he should never be photographed in the nude. . . . in the breast pocket of his sack coat there should be a white handkerchief protruding about three-quarters of an inch above the vent. . . . He should wear pajamas on going to bed. (66)

Rather than using humorous particularities to accent universal questions, Miller laughs at an advertisement and refuses to give it any more significance than it deserves. His comedy and point of view in such instances cannot be more realistic and essentially sane.

The Miller-hero examines the novel in retrospect as he prepares to bring it to a close:

> My idea briefly has been to present a resurrection of the emotions, to depict the conduct of a human being in the stratosphere of ideas, that is, in the grip of delirium. To paint a pre-Socratic being, a creature part goat, part Titan. In short, to erect a world on the basis of the *omphalos*, not on an abstract idea nailed to a cross. (220)

While it helps to keep the Patagonian dangling from the world's navel, it would seem that Miller has failed, at least in part, to give his literary aborigine enough reasons or veins to stay fictionally alive. The idea of artistic "sundering" and "reconciliation," the main theme of the novel, hearkens back at least as far as New Testament theology. Nietzsche may have given these doctrines a radical form (and Miller hardly improves on him), but his Superman nevertheless is built with the same abstractions. Miller's creature who is "part goat, part Titan" is barely acceptable except as an unattainable ideal. When he begins to debate his high calling as an artist and creator the umbilical hooked to reality melts into airy nothing. The paramount fault in characterization is the inability of two opposites, the man and the philosopher, to complement each other. They cannot be reconciled except by unnatural force. The resplendent visions present a man who doesn't think like a "creature," but as a Christ, and his desperate willingness to crucify himself and die to the world's ills for the sake of a new art, a new world, is just as abstract and ultimately unreal as the visions wherein he makes these resolutions. The disillusioned rogue who makes his way from bed to bed is better off and more real when he forgets to take flights into the spirit realm. Although the whole novel is an attempt to wed the "bright, gory sun god" to the "goat," the philosopher to the "satyr," the union is unconvincing, at best metaphorical. The fictional Miller lives best as a bachelor "goat." As Littlejohn remarks, "Miller the doom-shouting apocalyptic critic, Miller the archromantic prophet can be somewhat less than convincing."[18]

As for obscenity and pornography, contemporary art is

constantly inviting us to applaud the destruction of values which we often cherish, while the positive cause, for the sake of which the dismantlings are made, is rarely clarified. The sacrifices are liable to appear as demolition without motive. *Tropic of Cancer* hardly presents us with enough of a cause. Sometimes, though we might enjoy identifying with Miller, we are hard put to comprehend exactly why we should. The most naïve of questions can also be the most devastating when asked of this particular novel: Why does the hero want to be the way he is or say the things he says? The answer might be that Miller's work always projects itself into a twilight zone where no values are fixed. Born in anxiety, perhaps it is the function of the novel to transmit this anxiety to the reader, so that his encounter with the work amounts to a genuine existential predicament. Like Kierkegaard's God, *Tropic of Cancer* attacks and repels us with its aggressive absurdity.

At one point the hero writes: "There is only one thing that interests me vitally now, and that is the recording of all that which is omitted in books" (10). Miller, it is true, has kicked down certain ethical barriers in an attempt to bring into the open the most private experiences. But it is possible that these traditionally deleted "elements in the air which give direction and motivation to our lives" (10) have been left out of the canon for valid artistic reasons, or possibly because they are forever locked in confusion and contradiction. Henry Miller's cause has not been made clear enough to merit spontaneous applause. He must give sharper definition to his vision, clarity to his motives, consistency to his characters. A writer cannot construct two heroes and then attempt to pass them off as one in an "autobiographical" novel without inviting critical attacks on his own self-image. Formless and crude as the novel may be, however, it is the work of a healthy artist. And what it lacks above all is a basic responsibility, not to other artists or to society, but to art itself.

Notes

1. Annette Kar Baxter, *Henry Miller, Expatriate* (Pittsburgh, 1961), p. 8. Miss Baxter has culled a very fine Miller bibliography up to 1961.
2. Karl Shapiro, Introduction to *Tropic of Cancer* (New York, 1961), p. vi.
3. Lawrence Durrell, "Studies in Genius: VIII—Henry Miller," *Horizon*, XX (July, 1949), p. 56.
4. Henry Miller, *Tropic of Cancer* (New York, Grove Press, 1961), p. 82. The pages from which all further quotations are drawn are indicated in the text.
5. George Orwell, *Inside the Whale and Other Essays* (London, 1940), p. 174.
6. Ibid.
7. David Littlejohn, "The Tropics of Miller," *The New Republic*, 146 (March 5, 1962), p. 31.
8. Quoted by James Boyer May, Preface to *Henry Miller: His World of Urania* by Sydney Omarr (London, 1960), p. 9. I have been unable to find the original source of this definition.
9. Littlejohn, p. 31.
10. Jean Paul Sartre, *Nausea*, Transl. Lloyd Alexander (Norfolk, 1959), pp. 212–13.
11. Shapiro, p. xiv.
12. Ibid., p, xxiii.
13. A label used by Shapiro (p. x) in paraphrasing Orwell which is certainly not an apt one; "unbearable disillusionment" would be better, at least in terms of Céline's *Voyage au Bout de la Nuit*.
14. Shapiro, p. xiv.
15. Henri Bergson, *An Introduction to Metaphysics*, Transl. T. E. Hulme (London, 1912), p. 1.
16. This is a phrase of Eddington's against which Bergson places his concept of "inner duration." For a perceptive discussion of the matter see Albert William Levi, *Philosophy and the Modern World* (Indiana, 1959), p. 63f. Both *Tropics* traffic in concepts of time.

Miller's relationship to Bergson, I would think, is a fruitful area for examination.
17. Bergson, p. 65f.
18. Littlejohn, p. 31.

EDWARD B. MITCHELL
"Artists and Artists:
The 'Aesthetics' of Henry Miller"

Texas Studies in Literature and Language, Spring 1966, pp. 103–15

It is a commonplace of literary criticism that Plato felt it incumbent to cast the artist out of the Republic because the artist created imitations, because his work, thrice removed from reality, could not conceivably lead to knowledge of the eternal forms. What is less frequently noticed, however, is that this argument forms only half of Plato's objection to artists and to poetry, and in many respects not the most important half. As Plato goes on to explain to Glaucon, the poets, especially the dramatic poets, are dangerous to the Republic because they appeal to the emotions and the passions, and thus, as Plato puts it in the Cornford translation, "one who lends an ear to it [poetry] should rather beware of endangering the order established in his soul. . . ."[1] The artist must be expelled from the Republic because he destroys the carefully erected Platonic psychology wherein the reason, in league with the spirited element of the soul, controls the emotions. The banishment of the artist is the price of the Republic because the artist overturns the psychology of which the Republic itself is only an analogy "writ large."

It is interesting to place Henry Miller in this particular context because, unlikely as it might appear, Plato's and Miller's views of the nature of the poet, and his role *vis à vis* society, are almost identical. The only difference between them is that Miller argues against the banishment of the artist. While Plato argues for rule by philosophers, Miller insists on rule by artists, for it is his conviction that "the true leaders of the world are the men of imagination, the seers. To unite man with man and peoples with peoples is not the work of politicians or of social reformers; men are united only through illumination. The true poet is an awakener; he does not promise bread and jobs. . . . All ideas of government fail insofar as they exclude the poet and the seer who are one."[2] Whereas Plato would expel the artist from the Republic because he appeals to the irrational and imaginative faculties in man, Miller would call back the artist precisely because this *is* his function, and because, in Miller's view, no republic can operate in any meaningful way without him.

In order to understand why Miller does not share the Platonic conclusion regarding the necessary destiny of the artist, we will need to give some detailed attention to the notion of "the poet and the seer who are one." In so doing, however, it will be well to bear in mind that while Miller has written at some length on major literary figures, including Lawrence, Rimbaud, Proust, Joyce, Balzac, and Whitman, not to mention a considerable list of lesser-known figures, his criticism usually reveals more of his own position than that of the artist being examined. As Miller puts it, "no matter how much I dwell on the works of others I come back inevitably to the one and only book, the book of myself."[3]

Thus when, in *The Cosmological Eye*, Miller turns his attention to Proust and Joyce, he finds both of them wanting, which is not to say that they fail in what they set out to do, but that their work manifests an orientation sharply different from his own. It is that difference which is instructive. In Proust Miller finds "the full flower of psychologism—confession, self-analysis, arrest of living, making of art the final justification, but thereby divorcing art from life. An intestinal conflict in which the artist is immolated. . . . A worship of art for its own sake—not for man. Art, in other words, regarded as a means of salvation, as a redemption from suffering, as a compensation for the terror of living. Art as a *substitute* for life."[4] As Miller sees it, Proust, who thought himself to be making a book of his life, actually succeeded in revealing the plight of the modern man for whom there is no faith, no meaning, no life. Through his microscopic reflections and analyses, Proust immures himself in his art, for him "life was not a living, but a feasting upon sunken treasures, a life of retrospect."[5] In the work of Joyce, Miller finds the process of "soul deterioration" carried to even greater lengths, for "if Proust may be said to have provided the tomb of art, in Joyce we can witness the full process of decomposition."[6] *Ulysses*, then, is a paean to the atomization of man. In Miller's opinion, both Proust and Joyce are offering a picture of the world-as-disease, but Joyce's work is even more of a tomb than Proust's, because "through his chaos and obscenity, his obsessions and complexes, his perpetual, frantic search for God, Joyce reveals the desperate plight of the modern man who, lashing about in his steel and concrete cage, admits finally that there is no way out."[7]

The focal point for the preceding is actually a three-way comparison of Lawrence, Proust, and Joyce which was to form part of a projected, but never completed, book on Lawrence, of whom Miller says:

> Despite all that may be said against him, as an artist, or as a man, he still remains the most alive, the most vitalizing of recent writers. Proust had to die in order even to commence his great work; Joyce, though still alive, seems even more dead than Proust ever was. Lawrence on the other hand, is still with us: his death, in fact, is a mockery of the living. Lawrence killed himself in the effort to burst the bonds of living death. There is evidence for believing, if we study for example such a work as *The Man Who Died*, that had it been given him to enjoy the normal span of life he would have arrived at a state of wisdom, a mystic way of life, in which the artist and the human being would have been reconciled.[8]

Here we find, in contradistinction to "living death," that "mystic way of life" which is Miller's doctrine of acceptance under another name, this time found manifest in, or perhaps projected upon, the figure of Lawrence. And although, in Miller's opinion, Lawrence never successfully effected the reconciliation between the artist and the human being, still "it is against the stagnant flux in which we are now drifting that Lawrence appears brilliantly alive. Proust and Joyce needless to say, appear more representative: they *reflect* the times. We see in them no revolt: it is surrender, suicide, and the more poignant since it springs from creative sources."[9] In short, the difference Miller finds between Lawrence, on the one hand, and Proust and Joyce, on the other, is a qualitative difference, whereas the difference between Joyce and Proust is largely one of degree. In Miller's view, Lawrence was struggling to reassert the aristocracy of the individual, and to relate the individual to the cosmic processes surrounding and sustaining him. Lawrence's work, although not completely realized, was a hymn of affirmation, whereas in Proust and Joyce, Miller finds the keening accompanying a burial. Proust, defeated by reality, withdraws and makes of art a substitute for life, he lives only in the remembrance of things past. Joyce, for his part, hurls

himself into the abyss of the night mind and through a chronicle of dirty Dublin reveals the defeat of man in a war of attrition.

Whatever the excesses of such an interpretation, Miller's central point is still discernible. Although he finds much of the "poet" in Proust and Joyce, he finds none of the "seer." For Miller, the only adequate definition of artist is "the poet and the seer who are one." But such a definition clearly implies that Miller holds an unusual view both of what art is and what it does. This is in fact the case; and one conviction, which he repeats throughout his work, is particularly relevant here. He repeatedly insists that art, as that term is generally understood, must be transcended: "I believe that one has to pass beyond the sphere and influence of art. Art is only a means to life, the life more abundant. It is not in itself the life more abundant. It merely points the way, something which is overlooked not only by the public, but very often by the artist himself. In becoming an end it defeats itself."[10] In Miller's view there are two possible defeats involved here. First, the artist himself may be defeated if he makes of his art a substitute for life, if he becomes totally immured in his own realm of symbol and fantasy. Secondly, the purpose of art is defeated if the audience accepts any work of art as a fulfillment, as a final statement, rather than as an appeal to a greater liberation of the imaginative faculties, a fuller, richer, more meaningful means of viewing the world. And both of these possible defeats are related in that art, in two different ways, has become an end in itself.

Proust and Joyce, then, have permitted art to become an end in itself. However, Miller insists that not only is this unnecessary, it is in fact the mark of those who are not truly artists. The true artist, the poet-seer, is one who views art as a means for attaining a particular end:

> Strange as it may seem today to say, the aim of life is to live, and to live means to be aware, joyously, drunkenly, serenely, divinely *aware*. In this state of god-like awareness one sings; in this realm the world exists as poem. . . . This is the sublime, the a-moral state of the artist, he who lives only in the moment, the visionary moment of utter, far-seeing lucidity. Such clear, icy sanity that it seems like madness. By the force and power of the artist's vision the static, synthetic whole which is called the world is destroyed. The artist gives back to us a vital, singing universe, alive in all its parts.[11]

Miller goes on to assert that "when he [the poet-seer] succeeds in establishing this criterion of passionate experience . . . then, and only then, is he asserting his humanness. Then only does he live out his pattern as Man."[12] Rather obviously, Miller's definition of the artist is basically charismatic; and we find here also his characteristic insistence that being "aware" is the criterion of being human. Furthermore, he asserts that "the artist's dream of the impossible, the miraculous, is simply the resultant of his inability to adapt himself to reality."[13] We need to be aware, however, that the "reality" Miller means here is what he considers the insane reality of the unartistic everyday world, the misconception of reality that is "the static, synthetic whole which is called the world." In other words, we have here a statement very much like Blake's when he said that he did not see the sun, but rather a bright golden guinea. This part of Miller's view, then, is semiorthodox: the poet-seer lives out his humanness only when he images forth his experience of reality which is his vision.

But some of Miller's statements on the artist-art relationship are highly unorthodox. On the one hand they amount to an oblique reference to what the seer sees; on the other hand they entail an examination of the kind of art produced by those who are not seers. At one point, Miller elaborates an expanded image of what he calls the tree of life and death, which he sees as a combined artistic-historical metaphor. Employing the terms of the metaphor, Miller asserts that the creative individual gives ever greater expression to his life instincts until at the last limits of creativeness he is suddenly faced with the incontestable fact of his human limitations, his human finitude. The tree of life now becomes the tree of death. The creative individual now returns to the roots of his being and finds that rather than attempt to transcend death he must accept and incorporate it. In the process of facing this mystery of life and death, the individual is awakened to a totality larger than himself—he perceives the underlying unity of life. As Miller puts it:

> It is this acceptance of the laws of one's being which preserves the vital instincts of life, even in death. In the rush upward the "individual" aspect of one's being was the imperative, the only obsession. But at the summit, when the limits have been felt and perceived, there unfolds the grand perspective and one recognizes the similitude of surrounding beings, the interrelationship of all forms and laws of being—the *organic* relatedness, the wholeness, the oneness of life.[14]

What the artist as archetype becomes is a seer. And if we work through the enigmatic metaphor Miller chooses as his vehicle of expression, we find that what the seer sees is a vision very much like Miller's own, for the creative individual accepts the laws of being with his realization of the "organic relatedness, the wholeness, the oneness of life."

The true artist comes to accept and convert his human limitations because, in Miller's view, the struggle between his creative instincts and his eventual death, the starkest reminder of his human finitude, catapults him into an intuitive awareness of a transcendent and overriding unity. Paradoxically, the acceptance of death frees him to live. To attempt to glean any more meaning from Miller's metaphor in context is perhaps impossible; but more importantly, it is unnecessary. Miller is less interested in what the artist-seer sees than in the fact that he *does* see, because, as we shall note shortly, Miller insists that the artist-seer's vision is necessarily never wholly translatable. What Miller turns to instead is a consideration of the kind of art produced by those who are not seers. Here he finds that what such art reflects finally is the frustration of the would-be artist who can neither deny nor accept his human finitude: ". . . by living into his art he adopts for his world an intermediary realm in which he is all-powerful, a world which he dominates and rules. This intermediary realm of art, this world in which he moves as hero, was made realizable only out of the deepest sense of frustration."[15] Unaware of the transcendent unity and ultimate purposefulness which pervades the shifting temporality, but spurred by his creative impulses, the artist retreats into his art; and Miller concludes that "his whole art is the pathetic and heroic effort to deny his human defeat. He works out, in his art, an unreal triumph—since it is neither a triumph over life nor over death. It is a triumph over an imaginary world which he himself created."[16] In short, Miller is convinced that in the type of art which forms his standard of judgment, which is to say the art of the seer, there is an element of truth not to be found on any other level than the level of vision. The world reflected in the art of the seer is not "an imaginary world he has created," but the world of reality to which he has awakened.

However, when Miller has separated the sheep from the goats on this fundamental level, when he finds that "vision" is the standard of judgment for art, as "seer" is the quality which forms the standard of judgment for the artist, he is still faced with the fact that for the artist *qua* artist, whether seer or not, there is a sense in which he must "live into his art." The artist must, by the very nature of his creative act, turn upon himself; he must draw upon his own memory, thought, experience, he must withdraw from life and project himself into the work growing under his hands. Miller concedes this necessity and phrases it this way: "In order to accomplish his purpose, however, the artist is obliged to retire, to withdraw from life, utilizing just enough of experience to present the flavor of the *real* struggle. If he chooses to *live* he defeats his own nature. He *must* live vicariously."[17] Here, it would appear, Miller has involved himself in a fundamental contradiction. If the artist chooses simply to live, rather than create, he denies his nature as artist. On the other hand, so long as he creates works of art, he withdraws from life, he does not live according to the dictates of his awareness, rather he lives vicariously. Yet it is exactly vicarious living which is anathema to Miller.

Yet this difficulty, encountered by the artist-seer in relation to his art, forms only one half of the problem. From Miller's point of view the relationship of the audience to art can entail a danger of equal magnitude. In the attempt to come to grips with the vision of the seer imaged in the work of art, the audience may take the work as a fulfillment, a final statement, thus making of the artist's effort a lie which enchants and enslaves rather than an intimation which incites and liberates. Miller is speaking to this point when he says:

> Unconsciously I think that every great artist is trying with might and main to destroy art. By that I mean that he is desperately striving to break down this wall between himself and the rest of humanity. Not for the sake of the brotherhood of man . . . but in the hope of debouching into some more quick and vivid realm of human experience. He is not struggling to isolate himself from his fellow-men, since it is his very isolation which drives him to create, but rather to emancipate himself from false relations with his fellow-men, from false relations with nature and with all the objects which surround him. Art is only one of the manifestations of the creative spirit. What every great artist is manifesting in his work is a desire to lead a richer life; his work itself is only a description, an intimation, as it were, of those possibilities. The worst sin that can be committed against the artist is to take him at his word, to see in his work a fulfillment instead of an horizon.[18]

If what the work of all great artists manifests is a desire to "lead a richer life," then by implication what such artists desire for their audience is that they may go and do likewise. Miller states as much when he says that "what he [the artist-seer] clamors for, avowedly or unavowedly, is a new deal—in other words, *freedom*. His idea of freedom is life lived imaginatively."[19] Thus the greatest sin that could be committed against the artist is to take him "at his word," to find in his work a final answer, a fulfillment, a plan to be adopted, rather than an intimation of possibility. Art, in Miller's opinion, should serve to awaken the audience, it should instill in the perceiver a sense that at bottom art is aimed at "making poetry, or if you will, of making life a poem. It has to do with the adoption of a creative attitude toward life."[20]

The question remains, however, if the audience is to take a creative attitude toward life, *what* is it that the audience is to create? The blunt, and perhaps unsatisfying, answer is that Miller does not say, or at least he never makes an explicit answer. There is, however, a reason why Miller does not, indeed cannot, answer this question, and part of that reason is that he sees the aim of art as one of abolishing the audience altogether. For Miller, the intent of all true art is to make artists of the audience. But in order to understand why and how Miller sees this as coming about, we shall have to return to the relationship of the artist to his art, which is finally the cornerstone of Miller's "aesthetics."

The situation then is this: if the artist does not, in Miller's case for example, write, then he is denying his nature as artist. If he does write, he is not living according to his awareness, but he is living vicariously. In *Sexus* Miller makes the effort to come to terms with this problem; and we might note, parenthetically, that *The Rosy Crucifixion* is a trilogy which in one sense begins with the question of how and why to write, which in the course of the novels becomes transmuted into the larger question of why and how to become an artist on another level. After once again restating the problem, Miller says:

> No man ever puts down what he intended to say: the original creation, which is taking place all the time, whether one writes or doesn't write, belongs to the primal flux: it has no dimensions, no form, no time element. In this preliminary state, which is creation and not birth, what disappears suffers no destruction; something which was already there, something imperishable, like memory, or matter, or God, is summoned and in it one flings himself like a twig into a torrent. Words, sentences, ideas, no matter how subtle or ingenious, the maddest flights of poetry, the most profound dreams, the most hallucinating visions, are but crude hieroglyphs chiselled in pain and sorrow to commemorate an event which is untransmissible. In an intelligently ordered world there would be no need to make the unreasonable attempt of putting such miraculous happenings down.[21]

The real value of art, for Miller, is the "original creation," and the essential benefit of art therefore is bestowed upon the artist. However, Miller insists that

> It is only in the measure that he [the artist-seer] is aware of more life, the life abundant, that he may be said to live in his work. If there is no realization there is no purpose or advantage in substituting the imaginative life for the purely adventurous one of reality. Every one who lifts himself above the activities of the daily round does so not only in the hope of enlarging his field of experience, or even of enriching it, but of quickening it.[22]

If the artist is not aware, and if he does not see the preliminary act, the creation before writing, as the real value of art, then, at least as far as Miller is concerned, he is likely to be writing from no better motive than power, fame, success. But when the preliminary act of creation is seen to be the unique value of art, then the artist realizes that "the process in which he is involved has to do with another dimension of life, that by identifying himself with this process he *augments* life."[23]

The word *augment* is central here. In Miller's view the artist-seer does not alter life, in the sense that one builds a machine, or discovers a drug, or invents a process; rather, he realizes that through his art, at least the preliminary part, he is putting himself in unison with life. And, although no artist can put down exactly what he intended to say, he still augments life both for himself in the period of creation, as well as for others in the imaging forth of his vision which is aimed at enlarging, enriching, and quickening the experience of life. Miller, then, is not so much attempting to escape between the horns of his dilemma as he is attempting to transcend it, for he is convinced that "an author hopes that in giving himself to the world he will

enrich and augment life, not deny and denigrate it. If he believed in direct intervention, he would be a healer and not a writer. If he believed that he had the power to eliminate evil and sorrow, he would be a saint, not a spinner of words. Art *is* a healing process, as Nietzsche pointed out. But mainly for those who practice it."[24] But practice is the important point. If the artist is aware of "original creation," if he comes to realize the value of the eternal process into which he can fling himself like a twig into a torrent, with or without writing, if he does succeed in penetrating into some more quick and vivid realm of human experience, then he need not fear denying his nature as artist, be he writer, painter, sculptor. In short, a man cannot do nothing. For Miller, it is not a question of whether one is a writer, but whether one is an Artist, and the capital A is intentional. For if a man is aware, then he is an Artist; and if he happens also to be an artist, which is to say, in Miller's case, a writer, then he can fulfill his nature as artist because his art will be both an expression of, and his living out, his awareness.

Because the essential value of art, in Miller's opinion, accrues to the artist before words are set to paper, a finished work, a book, an artifact, is limited in its effect upon the audience. As Miller puts it, "a great work of art, if it accomplishes anything, serves to remind us, or let us say to set us to dreaming, of all that is fluid and intangible—which is to say, *the universe*."[25] The value of art for the reader or viewer is a by-product of the intrinsic value received by the artist; and thus the extrinsic value of a work of art is the chance of setting more people to dreaming. Still, what the artist-seer really desires is a world in which there would be no necessity for treating in "crude hieroglyphs" events which are not finally and wholly transmissible. The attaining of this condition is, however, an individual process; if art helps to forward this process, it can do so only to the extent that it awakens the audience, that it liberates the imaginative faculties of the audience and makes it aware of its own potential Artistry.

What the artist-seer desires is to emancipate the creative spirit of the audience. It is in this sense that the artist is trying to destroy art, for the essential effect of art is to awaken the audience; the artist's intent is to make Artists, though not necessarily artists, of the audience. Miller denies that he is interested in a cult of artists; rather, he is interested in fostering the faculty of vision in every man because he is certain that art, when properly understood, is the province of all men. Miller makes this point when he asserts:

> . . . art is only a stepping-stone to reality; it is the vestibule in which we undergo the rites of initiation. Man's task is to make of himself a work of art. The creations which man makes manifest have no validity in themselves; they serve to awaken, that is all. And that, of course, is a great deal. But it is not the all. Once awakened, everything will reveal itself to man as creation. Once the blinders have been removed and the fetters unshackled, man will have no need to recreate through the elect cult of genius. Genius will be the norm.[26]

"Genius is the norm" once man becomes aware; and we might note that this phrase becomes Miller's variation on Wordsworth's definition of the poet. We recall that Wordsworth describes the poet as a man like other men, only possessing a more lively sensibility, more enthusiasm, more tenderness— one who differs from his fellow man in degree, not in kind. While Wordsworth maintains that the poet is like other men, Miller insists that other men are like his conception of the poet; and if art has any purpose, it is to make the audience aware of that underlying similarity; if it has any power, it is the power to awaken the perceiver, to break down the "false relations" which exist between the artist and his fellow man.

We might note also that Miller's comments are not drawn entirely from, nor applied exclusively to, the realm of art *qua* art. At least once, in an essay titled "Artist and Public," Miller has taken up the question of the role of art on a more "practical" level. After discussing a plan for the maintenance of struggling artists, and while elaborating on a means for bringing contemporary art to the attention of all, Miller notes that "what is demanded of a society, what gives it life, is the ability to inspire a greater measure of enthusiasm, a greater measure of freedom."[27] A Utopia, even of art, is a dream, and dreams invariably outstrip accomplished actuality, which is what makes the imaginative dream of the artist-seer the *sine qua non* of a creative society. The important point for Miller is that "people have to be encouraged to make things themselves, in their own fashion, according to their own limited aesthetic instincts."[28] In this sense the comparative degree is essential to Miller's point of view—the measure of the artist-seer's achievement is itself measurable in terms of a greater enthusiasm and a greater freedom. The role of art is one of inspiring not awe or appreciation, but creativity: "the only tenable attitude towards art is to foster the artist in every human being, see to it that everything one handles, sees or hears is imbued with art."[29]

Obviously, this is neither balanced social philosophy nor unbiased literary criticism. Indeed, the point is that it is not. As we noted earlier, Miller's treatment of other artists tends to reveal much more about Miller than about the artist under discussion. For Miller, the experience of awakening is central and the chief characteristic of that experience is an intuitive insight into an inclusive, transcendent unity which resolves contradictions; and the experience of that insight, that awakening, comes with an emotional intensity producing a complete certainty of conviction. Thus the experience upon which the "aesthetics" is based goes far to explain the exhortative cast of the prose. Moreover, the seer who is also a writer must employ language, but language is by and large what Miller has called a "grammar of thought,"[30] and since what the artist-seer has to communicate is not thought, which is to say that his vision is not logical, inferential, and discursive, he is driven to paradox or symbology or both.

Thus, on the one hand, Miller appears to be using reason against rationalism: the value of irrationalism is presented in a semirational manner. On the other hand, he tends to see relationships and to use terms anagogically. The creativity of the artist is an anagoge to that larger creativity, which we might call a mode of reality as process. Furthermore, the anagogic use of terms and relationships has a double effect. First, once Miller establishes certain terms, for example creativity, artist, awakening, acceptance, for use in this way, he tends to reiterate them and the repetition adds to the reader's sense of exhortation. Secondly, the exhortation is annoyingly unprogrammatic, the anagoges appear to lead nowhere. Just as one cannot prescribe what form the creativity of the artist shall take, so one cannot prescribe what form the creativity of the seer shall take. Or to put it another way, what one does is dependent upon what one is, and what one is is dependent upon one's awareness or the lack of it, and for the acquisition of awareness there is no program.

What a position such as Miller's amounts to, in effect, is a denial of significant difference on any but the most fundamental level. The word *significant* is important because Miller admits differences and indulges in them to the point of contradiction—he simply denies that such differences are significant. To put it affirmatively, Miller asserts that contraries

are not mutually exclusive, but rather aspects of a unity which when perceived resolves contradictions. But the lack of perception, the failure to be aware, is significant; and what this means, on the level of art, is the denial that Proust and Joyce, for example, have a vision. Rather than seeing in the work of Joyce and Proust a manifestation of a vision different from his own, Miller simply sees their art as a manifestation of a lack of vision. The point is, however, that this appears to be the inevitable outcome of the positive advocacy of the notion of awareness. The fact that Miller has in a sense only one string to his critical, as well as aesthetic, lyre is directly traceable to his insistence on the notion of "the poet and the seer who are one." Yet, Miller's aesthetic position does reveal an internal consistency and interrelationship of its own; and it is a consistency which permits Miller a complicated, if not complex, solution to his artist-seer dilemma, while offering only an irritatingly singleminded criterion for the judgment of art. Furthermore, it is the kind of consistency which allows Miller to find that the social function of the artist is of the highest importance for the same reason that Plato found it keenly disturbing, while still permitting Miller to insist that the artist-seer has no program to offer his fellow man.

But in spite of the nonrational, intuitional nature of Miller's position, in spite of the fact that he insists that "we can never explain except in terms of new conundrums [because] what belongs to realm of the spirit, or the eternal, evades all explanation," Miller still does not feel that he is unique, that he is isolated. On the contrary, it is the very notion of awareness which establishes for him the real nature of tradition because

> . . . it reveals the genuine role of the poet and the true nature of tradition. Of what use the poet unless he attains to a new vision of life, unless he is willing to sacrifice his life in attesting the truth and the splendor of his vision? It is the fashion to speak of these demonic beings, these visionaries, as Romantics, to stress their subjectivity and to regard them as breaks, interruptions, stopgaps in the great stream of tradition, as though they were madmen whirling about the pivot of self. Nothing could be more untrue. It is precisely these innovators who form the links in the great chain of creative literature. One must indeed begin at the horizons where they expire—"hold the gain," as Rimbaud puts it—and not sit down comfortably in the ruins and piece together a puzzle of shards.[31]

In the ranks of these visionaries Miller places, again at the expense of differences, such figures as Gerald de Nerval, Dostoyevsky, Whitman, Strindberg, Nietzsche, Baudelaire, Hamsun, Rimbaud, Blake, and Lautréamont, among others.[32] What Miller finds these figures to have in common is that, rather than shore fragments against their ruins, they have attained to a new vision of life. For all their differences, they manifest the underlying and unifying quality of the "seer." And even more importantly, Miller finds that these visionaries are united in the common cause of making themselves unnecessary. Their interest is to liberate the creative spirit, to bequeath the power of vision; and to Miller's lights this is a continuous possibility because a vision is realized the moment one begins to live by it.

Notes

1. F. M. Cornford, trans., *The Republic of Plato* (Oxford, 1957), p. 340.
2. Henry Miller, *Sunday after the War* (Norfolk, Connecticut, 1961), p. 59.
3. Miller, *The Books in My Life* (Norfolk, Connecticut, 1952), p. 98.

4. Miller, *The Cosmological Eye* (Norfolk, Connecticut, 1961), pp. 109–110. This is the American reprint of the earlier *Max and the White Phagocytes* excluding the essay "The Eye of Paris," and including, from *Black Spring*, "Jabberwhorl Cronstadt," "Into the Night Life," "The Tailor Shop," and three other essays: "Peace! It's Wonderful!," "The Brooklyn Bridge," and "Autobiographical Note."
5. Miller, *The Cosmological Eye*, p. 126.
6. Ibid., p. 110.
7. Ibid.
8. Ibid., p. 108.
9. Ibid., p. 109.
10. Miller, *The Wisdom of the Heart* (Norfolk, Connecticut, 1960), p. 24.
11. Ibid., pp. 2–3.
12. Ibid., p. 3.
13. Ibid., p. 4.
14. Ibid., p. 10.
15. Ibid., p. 7.
16. Ibid.
17. Ibid., p. 8.
18. Miller, *The Cosmological Eye*, pp. 167–168.
19. Miller, *Stand Still Like the Hummingbird* (Norfolk, Connecticut, 1962), p. 60.
20. Miller, *The Cosmological Eye*, p. 152.
21. Miller, *Sexus* (Paris, 1962), p. 27.
22. Ibid., p. 269.
23. Ibid.
24. Miller, *Big Sur and the Oranges of Hieronymus Bosch* (Norfolk, Connecticut, 1957), p. 400.
25. Miller, *Sexus*, p. 27.
26. Miller, *Sunday after the War*, pp. 155–156.
27. Miller, *Remember to Remember* (Norfolk, Connecticut, 1960), p. 414.
28. Ibid., p. 413.
29. Ibid., p. 415.
30. Miller, *The Wisdom of the Heart*, p. 4.
31. Miller, *The Time of the Assassins* (Norfolk, Connecticut, 1946), p. 87.
32. See the "coda" to *Time of the Assassins*, pp. 159–163.

JOHN WILLIAMS
From "Henry Miller: The Success of Failure"

Virginia Quarterly Review, Spring 1968, pp. 225–45

On July 4, 1845, Henry David Thoreau, who had been living in Boston, moved a few personal belongings into a hut on the edge of Walden Pond, a small lake near Concord, Massachusetts, the place of his birth. He was twenty-eight years of age. As he tells us in *Walden*, he had tried a number of things before he made his escape into what he thought of as the wilderness. He had gone to Harvard and graduated; he had taught school for a brief time in his home town of Concord, and was by his own admission an unsuccessful teacher; he had thought of going into trade, and had worked briefly for his father, a small businessman who manufactured pencils; he had lectured before cultural groups in Concord, apparently without great success; he had written a few essays for the *Dial*; in exchange for room and board, he had performed odd jobs for Ralph Waldo Emerson; and he had been a tutor in the New York home of Emerson's brother William. Until his decision to abandon the "civilized pursuits" to which he was born, his was the ordinary life that any moderately intelligent young man, of no means but with some culture, education, and talent, might lead, given the conditions of his time and place. "The mass of men lead lives of quiet desperation. What is called resignation is confirmed desperation. From the desperate city you go into

the desperate country, and have to console yourself with the bravery of minks and muskrats. . . ."

Three generations later, in the year 1930, another Henry—Henry Miller, of New York City, the son of a lower-middle-class German-American family—sailed to Europe, where he had spent the year before as a tourist. He left behind him a first wife and a child, a second wife, and his other few worldly possessions. As we know from his many writings—the *Tropic of Cancer* and *Tropic of Capricorn*, the five volumes that now constitute *The Rosy Crucifixion*, and scattered essays and narratives in dozens of books—he had tried many things before finally making his escape from America. For two months he had attended the City College of New York, and failed to complete the semester; he had worked at a variety of clerical jobs, and in his father's tailor shop; he had been for three years a messenger employment manager for Western Union; and for about ten years, intermittently, had tried unsuccessfully to become a commercial writer of articles, stories, and novels. He was, in other words, a member of a vast underground of lower-middle-class Americans who wander beneath the surface or on the periphery of our increasingly complex society, unseen by the very society that dominates their lives; men who exist marginally upon our culture, who for one reason or another have been unable to find a place in the social order that strives to give their lives substance or meaning.

He was, in short, a failure; and in *Tropic of Capricorn*, the volume dealing with his pre-Paris years in New York, he announces that failure: "I couldn't waste time being a teacher, a lawyer, a physician, a politician or anything else that society had to offer. It was easier to accept menial jobs because it left my mind free. . . . The stabbing horror of life is not contained in calamities and disasters, because these things wake one up and one gets very familiar and intimate with them. . . . You know with a most disturbing certitude that what governs life is not money, not politics, not religion, not training, not race, not language, not customs, but something else, something you're trying to throttle all the time and which is really throttling you, because otherwise you wouldn't be terrified all of a sudden and wonder how you were going to escape. . . . One can starve to death—it is much better. Every man who voluntarily starves to death jams another cog in the automatic process. I would rather see a man take a gun and kill his neighbor, in order to get the food he needs, than keep up the automatic process by pretending that he has to earn a living."

One should recognize immediately that this is not the prose of prophecy or apocalypse, as it has often been taken; it is, in its peculiar tone of despair and in its very rhythm, the prose of the Depression. In a recent essay, "The American Left," Daniel Aaron quotes an anonymous letter published at the bottom of the Depression by one of the displaced; it might almost have been written by Miller himself.

"I wrote letters, I tramped hundreds of blocks to answer ads, I tried for jobs as teamster, clothing model, wringer man, floor-walker, garbage collector, truck driver. I wrote a Civil Service examination. I made ten dollars painting the ceiling of a barber shop. I managed an interview with my former superintendent, but he didn't remember me very well. I lived on a loaf of bread for ten days and then my money was all gone. . . . If it were necessary—if there were a famine, if I were a genius, an explorer, a martyr—I could endure cold and hunger, even degradation and insults, without a murmur. . . . But it is all so unnecessary, there is so little for me to look forward to, that I am beginning to think that it isn't so worthwhile to keep straight. The best I could look for, as a reward for going through another winter, or three, or five, like the last two, would be a job somewhere, sometime. And then could I feel secure? Another depression might catch me with no more resources than I had this time."

That Miller was not in this country during the worst of the great Depression does not matter; the "depressions" out of which both these passages spring are ones that are endemically American, always with us to one degree or another, in one way or another; they are more than political or economic; and the historical depression out of which the anonymous letter was written was only an intense symptom of a process that is implicit in our values and which has been with us nearly from the beginning of our country.

At the center of American life there is a polarity that I shall specify as the polarity of success and failure. This polarity has been generally recognized before, yet it is one whose precise identity cannot be seen except in a specific context of American history and culture.

The question of success and failure lies at the center of Thoreau's *Walden*, and it lies at the center of much of Miller's work, especially his "autobiographical romances"—the *Tropic of Cancer* and *Tropic of Capricorn*, *Black Spring*, and *The Rosy Crucifixion*. And the many statements of the two men upon the nature of success and failure are remarkably similar. Thoreau writes, "I would rather sit on a pumpkin and have it all to myself, than be crowded on a velvet cushion. I would rather ride on earth in an ox cart with a free circulation, than go to heaven in the fancy car of an excursion train and breathe *malaria* all the way." In the opening section of *Tropic of Capricorn*, Miller writes, "Everybody around me was a failure, or if not a failure, ridiculous. Especially the successful ones. . . . I think of all the streets in America combined as forming a huge cesspool, a cesspool of the spirit in which everything is sucked down and drained away. . . . The whole continent is a nightmare producing the greatest misery of the greatest number. I was one, a single entity in the midst of the greatest jamboree of wealth and happiness . . . but I never met a man who was truly wealthy or truly happy. At least I knew that I was unhappy, unwealthy, out of whack and out of step. That was my only solace, my only joy." ⟨. . .⟩

Almost from the beginning, in America, the question of success and failure has been a religious question; and it remains so, to some extent, even in the twentieth century. Thus Miller's rejection of the standard American attitudes toward success is actually a rejection of a lingering Calvinist ethic that still works beneath the surface of our culture, though his rejection is not, as we shall see, as unequivocal as one might expect.

The popular view of Miller is that of the American who has rid himself of all that is most American; who has brought into American literature the invigorating strain of European modernism; who has rescued American literature from provincialism and brought the genuine avant-garde to our own traditional shores. In some respects Miller seems to share this attitude about his own work and to encourage it in others. Except for his repeated admirations of Whitman, Emerson, and Thoreau, his literary praise has always been for the figures of another culture: he has at one time or another admired and acknowledged indebtedness to such men as Dostoevsky, Van Gogh, Nostradamus, Dante, Nijinski, Elie Faure, Rimbaud, Nietzsche, H. Rider Haggard, D. H. Lawrence, the Oriental mystical writers, as well as to such modern avant-gardists as André Breton, Blaise Cendrars, Céline, Ionesco, Anaïs Nin, and a variety of lesser Dadaists and Surrealists. And nearly all of his writings make some gestures toward the European "modernism" of the twenties: the highly charged but never quite believable dreams, the long metaphoric flights that

are simply extreme exaggerations of present reality, the passages of induced hallucination, the occasional excursions in automatic writing, and the literary affectations of madness.

But these are only gestures, and perhaps small debts, and one will not find the significance of Miller's work in them; for Miller is a writer who is essentially American, and American in a particular sense of that word.

If it appears perverse to suggest that in many ways Miller represents a nineteenth- and twentieth-century transformation of American Puritanism, it does so, I suspect, largely because of the celebrated question of his obscenity. One might wish to say that the issue of obscenity is in no way fundamental to Miller's work; and though one can almost say that, one cannot quite. For if Miller's use of obscenity is the most overt sign of his apparent rejection of the Puritan ethic, it is at the same time the covert revelation of the incompleteness of that rejection.

It should be clear to any serious student of American Puritanism that first the avoidance and then the symbolizing of sexual matters is one of the more obvious symptoms of the Puritan dilemma; and like many symptoms, it disguises more than it reveals. For obscenity and sexuality, in themselves, have little to do with the essential dilemma of American Puritanism; and when the more naïve among us wish to reject what we think of as the Puritan ethic, we turn immediately to the no doubt pleasant task of rejecting the Puritan sexual ethic—as if the taking of morphine might heal the wound.

In some ways Miller's obscenity is the most nearly innocent aspect of his art. The words he uses—the so-called Anglo-Saxon or four-letter words—we all know, else we would not be shocked by them. It is not a moral question, but a social one. If we are shocked by Miller's language, we are shocked not because our morality has been threatened but because our social standing has been; we are forced to confront and to admit the vital existence of one whose social standing appears lower than our own—one who would use such language, and so affront polite society. Thus snobbery subsumes morality, taboo overrides reason, and we are revealed to ourselves in all our cultural primitivism. We are made uncomfortable.

But though the language Miller uses is probably the basis for the widespread censorship of his books in this country, there are other pornographic techniques in Miller that are equally useful to his intention. Aside from the words, the sexuality and scatology found in Miller are of two sorts. First is that which is found with some frequency in the rather long, arty, and often irrelevant surrealistic fantasies that interrupt the narratives and expositions. By and large, such passages are so badly done that we have a hard time taking them seriously. Second, and more characteristic, are the sexual exploits that Miller attributes to himself in the autobiographical romances. And even these passages are strangely innocent; for they have that pathetic braggadocio and exaggeration of the lower-middle-class masculine world of the deprived adolescent (ugly, relentlessly shy, or merely poor) who finds himself outside the easy security of the promises of his society, and thus is committed to longing, talk, and the compensations of imagining.

When Miller is not indulging himself in quasi-surrealist nightmare sequences, or in the half-fantasies of symptomatic longing, his attitudes toward sex are almost embarrassingly moral, though not necessarily conventional. In the more straightforward narrative sections of the *Tropics*, he reveals himself to be, if not altogether proper in sexual matters, at least not the monster that we might expect from the more literary passages; and when he speaks "seriously" of sex, in his rôle as latter-day sage, in his essays upon the subject, and especially in a work that remained until a few years ago unpublished in this country, *The World of Sex*, his thinking is approximately as bold as that of a university-educated marriage counselor or sociologist—though the language in which he specifies this thinking is not likely to be found in either. Like Lawrence, he sees the rôle of sex as essentially religious, and he speaks sentimentally of its "mystery."

I do not wish to imply that Miller is a Puritan manqué, the archetypal American Calvinist in an outrageous disguise. I am, rather, suggesting that the dilemmas and polarities that have characterized American Puritanism are remarkably similar to the dilemmas and polarities that lie at the center of Henry Miller's most important and characteristic work. ⟨. . .⟩

For the ten years preceding 1930, Henry Miller had engaged in the pursuits that he must have hoped would lead him to success, and he had failed. It was only when he rejected the approval of his neighbors and his country, and when he renounced the possible value of his works, that he came to feel himself free. In one of his essays of the Paris period, entitled "Peace! It's Wonderful!," Miller writes: "Night after night without money, without friends, without a language I had walked these streets in despair and anguish. . . . In any case, the important thing is that in [Paris] I touched bottom. Like it or not, I was obliged to create a new life for myself. . . . In this life I am God, and like God I am indifferent to my own fate. . . . Just as a piece of matter detaches itself from the sun to live as a wholly new creation so I have come to feel about my detachment from America. And like all the other suns of the universe I had to nourish myself from *within*. I speak in cosmological terms because it seems to me that is the only possible way to think if one is truly alive. I think this way also because it is just the opposite of the way I thought a few years back when I had what is called hopes. Hope is a bad thing. It means that you are not what you want to be."

This is the Calvinist formula in its nineteenth-century transformation, a transformation made possible by a weakening both of a specific sense of sin and by the inevitable deterioration of dogma. "God" or "Christ" becomes the "self," the "natural" or "social" world becomes "America," and "heaven" becomes the "universe." But the habit of mind is clear beyond the transformation, and it is Calvinist. Emerson, Whitman, and Thoreau had wrought the transformation, and Henry Miller inherited it.

The notion of rebirth is central to Miller's thought, and it usually is tied, directly or indirectly, to the escape from America to Paris, from hope to unhope, from success to failure. For Miller does not consider that his writing is in any sense of the word a "good work," whereby he hopes to earn the approval of his neighbors. In the first page of what is probably his best single book, *Tropic of Cancer*, he announces his rejection of literature. "I have no money, no resources, no hopes. I am the happiest man alive. A year ago, six months ago, I thought that I was an artist. I no longer think about it. I *am*. Everything that was literature has fallen from me. There are no more books to be written, thank God.

"This then? This is not a book. This is libel, slander, defamation of character. This is not a book. . . . This is a prolonged insult, a gob of spit in the face of Art, a kick in the pants to God, Man, Destiny, Time, Love, Beauty . . . what you will."

It is, in other words, aimed precisely and destructively at all that we think of as Literature. In the biographical note at the end of *The Cosmological Eye*, the first book of Henry Miller to be published in the United States, he declares: "I use destruction creatively . . . but aiming always towards a real, inner harmony, an inner peace—and silence. . . . Ninety-

nine percent of what is written—and this goes for all our art products—should be destroyed. I want to be read by less and less people; I have no interest in the life of the masses, nor in the intentions of the existing governments of the world. I hope and believe that the whole civilized world will be wiped out in the next hundred years or so. I believe that man can exist, and in an infinitely better, larger way, without 'civilization.' "

Art, then, exists, not for its own sake, nor for ours, but for Miller's; and if the man who is Henry Miller has failed to the world, he may yet have succeeded to himself, who has become the object of his faith.

I am not the first to remark that, as pure theology, American Calvinism is a mess, a maze of contradictions, a chaos of impossibly opposed forces, a jungle of unresolved conflicts. In these respects, it resembles Miller's work, about which we could say many of the same things. I shall not attempt to resolve the illogicalities, to reconcile the opposing forces, or even to diminish the conflicts. The most I can hope to do is to offer some basis for understanding the conflicts, and perhaps thereby to suggest the significance and value that such an understanding may offer us.

One of the great conflicts in American Puritanism was between a mystical view of experience and a practical one. We find both impulses existing side by side in the early Puritan— one part of him is drawn toward the mystical being of God, and the other toward what is clearly a projection of God's strange will, the world itself. The Puritan conflict between idealism and realism is perhaps only another aspect of this earlier polarity, but it does have a peripheral identity in itself; in the Puritan ethic, that which exists in nature tends to be in conflict with that which exists in God's mind—hence our half-conscious aversion to sexuality, to bodily matters, to spontaneity, and to those shapes of flux and change that we must observe in natural processes. Yet the American Puritan found himself confronted with a natural world that he had to take with the utmost seriousness, if he was to survive; and in America, at least, the reconciliation of God and Nature has been an uneasy one.

And so has been the reconciliation of the conflict between aggressiveness and submission. Aggressiveness is supposed to be an almost exclusively American characteristic; and yet along with that aggressiveness, so often noted by foreign visitors, there is a deep strain of submissiveness that disguises itself in a number of ways. We may not willingly submit to fate, or even to simple fact; but we will almost without question submit to our neighbors' opinions of us. This, of course, is only a reflection of another pattern of aggression and submission; the Puritan had, by dogma, to submit to God's will; but, if he were to survive, he could not submit to the world—to nature, to the hostile environment that surrounded him; and, finally, in the historical evolution of Puritanism, he found himself in the curious position of becoming aggressive in the acquisition of worldly goods, the worldly goods being God's outward manifestation of inward Grace, and hence the sign of the aggressor's submission to God's will.

We need only to read in Cotton Mather's *Diaries* to find a recurring conflict between what might be called the apocalyptic vision and the practical vision, and between the impulse toward contemplative self-revelation and externalized activity. Certainly in a world view that is as rigidly deterministic as the American Calvinist's, the impulse toward the apocalyptic vision is inevitable; for if the course of the world is determined by God's will, and if that will is immutable, then one can predict events and make prophecies; for everything observable is a part of a meaning, and may be interpreted; a mouse gnawing through a Bible is a portent of whatever Mather can make of it, and the simple incompetence of a servant affords a prophetic view of things to come in the world at large.

But perhaps more important for our purposes is the Puritan conflict between self-examination, self-appraisal, and introspection on the one hand, and toward practical, externalized activity and an examination of the world on the other. Such a conflict sprang out of a psychological necessity imposed by the tenets of Puritanism itself; for if man's fate, his election or damnation, heaven or hell, was wholly at the mercy of God's whim, or his arbitrary will, and if the only evidence of that fate were those hints that God might place before the consciousness of man himself, then man inevitably would find one of his major occupations in constantly examining the state of his own soul, and at the same time examining those manifestations of the external world which impinged upon him and offered some hints as to his salvation or lack of it. Thus the external world, to the Puritan, was in one respect intimately linked to man's own internal being, and he tended to see the external world in terms of himself.

This view of the self and the world is everywhere observable in Henry Miller's work. It is not too much to say that virtually everything worthwhile and genuine in Miller is involved with Miller himself. George Orwell, an early admirer, praised Miller extravagantly for his social criticism, especially in the early *Tropics*; but what Orwell failed to understand, or at least to mention, was that Miller's social criticism was vital and worthwhile only when Miller himself was personally involved in the conditions of which he was writing. When he writes abstractly against social conditions in which he is not involved immediately and directly—as, for example, when he writes about war, which he is against—his remarks have all the depth and intensity of those we might find in a Sunday supplement article, or in a *Time* magazine essay. Unless his own person is immediately concerned, he is likely to be trite, unimaginative, verbose, or excruciatingly literary.

Everyone who has read the *Tropic* trilogy, and especially the *Tropic of Capricorn*, has no doubt remarked the almost mechanical alternation of method—the rather long, naturalistic passages interspersed with equally long passages of self-revelation and self-exploration. Narrative and introspection, scene and revery; this is the structure, insofar as the books have a very definable structure. And part of the point I am trying to make about this structure is that the two modes are never really integrated; they remain in tense opposition, no doubt because the impulses remain in some opposition within Miller himself.

If one is still unsure of this matter, one has only to read Miller's so-called travel book on Greece, *The Colossus of Maroussi*; it is one of the most extraordinary travel books ever written, surpassing even Lawrence's study of *Etruscan Places* for its egoism and self-concern. Though passages of self-revelation and description are alternated, we soon become painfully aware that Miller is really concerned only with himself, and Greece is important insofar as that country and its landscape are capable of eliciting responses from him upon love, death, sex, the peasant, war, life, literature, time, poverty, America, or whatever else Miller might have within him, needing release.

And there are dozens of other confusions, or conflicts, or polarities in Miller's work that have been noted, and condemned or justified, by nearly everyone who has read him. The most vulgar, low, and colloquial language that we can imagine exists immediately alongside the most intellectual and literary language that we can also imagine; I take it that this is, among other things, a reflection of that conflict between idealism and realism that I mentioned earlier. Apocalyptic vision, nightmare, and phantasy exist immediately alongside passages of the utmost practicality and naturalism; this, I take it, is a reflection of that Puritan conflict between mysticism and practicality. And passages of the utmost sentimentality jostle passages of utter cynicism: Miller is almost endearingly American in his view that all prostitutes—at least all French prostitutes—have hearts of gold, and he is capable of rhapsodizing for pages upon their essential virtues; and at the same time he is capable of describing with relish his bilking them of their earnings and of viewing their degradation with pitiless and sometimes eager enjoyment.

Like the Puritan, he feels himself to be an alienated being, a man on the outside, looking for a way in. As the Puritan made a kind of occupation out of self-examination and an elaborate questioning of his relationship to God, so Miller's whole work is an occupation of self-examination and elaborate questioning of his relation to—what? Miller cannot say, and neither can we. But we can say this: whereas the Puritan, in his effort to allay that deepening sense of alienation, moved closer and closer to the world as it was, and felt less and less the theological impossibility of doing so, Miller has seemed to move farther and farther away from the world and its dictates and its demands—has moved deeper and deeper into himself, into his own impulses, his own wishes, and his own visions. He has moved aggressively upon the world, in what he has called an act of creative destruction, so that he might become more submissive to the dictates of himself.

It is customary in a paper such as this, which attempts a general survey of the work of a man, to arrive at a simple critical judgment of the value of that man's work. I must confess an inability to arrive at such a simple judgment, and I make the confession with a little chagrin, though I must admit that the chagrin is tinged with irony. For it is a judgment that should be easy, one way or the other. After all, several things are unequivocal and clear. Miller is, and has been for several years, one of the most extravagantly praised (and damned) of all modern writers: for Lawrence Durrell, "American literature today begins and ends with the meaning of what Miller has done"; for Karl Shapiro "Miller is the greatest living writer"; and for Kenneth Rexroth he is to be "ranked with Balzac, Goethe, and Baudelaire."

But beyond this praise it is clear that Miller as a writer is guilty of virtually every major fault that it is possible for a writer to be guilty of. Stylistically, his work is a botch: he is incredibly prolix and repetitive, and many of his best effects are lost in jungles of approximate language; he is capable of an elephantine diction that sometimes makes Theodore Dreiser seem almost Flaubertian; the so-called "experimental" passages in his works often appear to be the kind of parodies, intentional or accidental, that the editors of a popular magazine might make upon some of the lesser Dadaists and Surrealists that in the twenties appeared in *transition* magazine; and he is capable of sentimentalities that would make a virginal New England school-teacher of a certain age blush with shame. He has almost no sense of structure, in either his longer or his shorter works: his work suffers from literary giantism, or disproportion, and one often has the dark suspicion that a passage is long or short, according to whether or not Miller might have been interrupted while writing it; and his solutions to structural problems are naïve to an extreme degree. Apparently conscious of the disorganization that dominates his work, he evokes the metaphor of a river, declaring that he "loves everything that flows," and attempts to justify his garrulous prose by that sentiment. He is incapable of constructing a dramatic scene, and he has no sense of character—except his own—and no ability to transmit the sense of another human being—except himself—to his reader. He is at his worst when he is most serious—that is, when he wishes his "ideas" to be taken seriously,—ideas which are, beneath the sometimes outrageous verbiage, so commonplace and old-fashioned as to be almost bewildering. And of the various costumes he wears—that of the innocent pornographer, the American abroad, the raucous prophet, the apocalyptic comedian, the outsider, the rebel, and the clown—none seems to fit him really closely. It is as if he had picked each of them up at some vast metaphysical rummage sale to wear as his mood suits him.

But after all this has been duly noted, and after we have read Miller, none of it seems really to matter; for cautious as we may be, we are left with the disturbing suspicion that we have been in the presence of an authentic genius, though a genius unlike any we have encountered in literature before. For in one respect, at least, we must take Miller at his word: he is not engaged in the act of writing literature. His work is, indeed, at bottom anti-literary, and anti-literary in a profound way that the Dadaists—those cultivated, highly educated, most humorous nihilists—could never have understood.

Miller's task has been, quite simply, to reveal himself, and to reveal himself as immediately and fully as his time and energy will allow him to do. Himself is the only subject he has ever had, and most of the time he has had the wit to know this, and not to pretend otherwise, at least to himself. He is not a novelist, and could never have been; for a good novelist must, perhaps, be offensively egoistic—that is to say, filled with pride and perhaps irrationally convinced of his own powers; but he cannot be egoistic—that is to say, so obsessed with the exclusive sense of his own identity that other identities have little reality, except insofar as they impinge upon him. And Miller is so consumed with a sense of his own identity that the question of his powers, or even the usual pride in his literary abilities, never really occurs to him. Nor, given his egoism, could he have been a philosopher, a social critic, an essayist—in short, he could not have been a writer, in the ordinary sense of that word.

Thus, seen in terms of its subject, the formlessness of his work begins to take on a new significance, so that the question of justification hardly arises. In a very real sense Miller is not engaged in writing books, or essays, or stories, or romances, or autobiographies, or whatever—he is engaged in writing, or revealing, himself, just as he is, or just as he thinks he is, at a given moment. And in Miller's view, to commit that self to a given literary form would be to betray it most profoundly; for finally he is not concerned that we see what he, Miller, *thinks* is true about himself; he wants us to see the thing itself.

And out of Miller's colossal, almost heroic egoism, the subject, Miller, is shown to us, not as a symbol of anything, not as a kind of everyman, but simply as itself. Miller never allows the integrity of his subject to be vitiated by lowering it to the level of myth or symbol; had he done so, it is likely that his work would have been without value to us.

It remains for me to suggest something of the nature of that character, that presence which constitutes the real subject of all that Miller has written; for it is in the nature of the subject that the significance of Miller lies.

I have said that at the center of Miller's work, and hence at the center of Miller himself, lies a set of polarities that curiously resemble the polarities found embedded in historical American Puritanism; but in saying that, I was not attempting to do anything very special, nor to imply any "mythic" quality to Miller's work. For the Puritan dilemma lies very near the

center of the American experience, particularly at the center of what we might call uninformed American experience. And the polarities that we see in Miller are versions of the polarities that we encounter every day, in ourselves and in the life around us.

Miller's character is extraordinary in only one respect: and that is that it is so ordinary. This darling of the avant-garde, this prototype of the twentieth-century rebel, this almost legendary man, this candidate for the Nobel Prize—he is the most ordinary figure that we can readily imagine. Except for the fact that we have him on paper, we have seen him everywhere in America, if we have cared to look: the son of lower-middle-class immigrant parents, who for the first forty years of his life lived a lower-middle-class life, on the periphery of a middle-class society, with the usual ambivalent attitudes toward middle-class values and aspirations—a man indifferently educated, whose reading is scattered and eccentric and not really very wide—a man who had that most common of aspirations, to be a successful writer (what more middle-class ambition can there be?), and who, like most who have that aspiration, failed—and a man, finally, who, confronted with the failure that his life had become, found within himself a deep and compelling reservoir of indifference to all that he had been taught that mattered. We see such men around us every day—men who finally have been forced to the great freedom of genuinely not giving a damn; and we look at them with our ambivalence of contempt and envy.

But within the ordinariness that is the character of Henry Miller, what a vast humanity, finally, we find; and what a vast generosity of spirit. With the compulsive honesty that is possible only to the heroic egoist, Miller shows us this fleck of humanity in the chaotic arena of kindness and cruelty, sentimentality and cynicism, pretension and simplicity, tenderness and obscenity, suffering and ecstasy, hypocrisy and sincerity, falsity and truth, that is, humanity itself. And if finally we are shocked by Miller we are shocked because we see, in unflinching and crude and graphic terms, written upon the page, beyond our evasion, simply ourselves, our selves that we hide from others and too often from ourselves; we see what we have made of ourselves, out of our time and circumstance; our real shock comes from nothing other than a glimpse of our persistent, affirmative, essentially amoral, and unhomogenized humanity.

In what we may think of as a typically American way, with what we may even call Yankee ingenuity, Henry Miller has made a success of his failure. The ten years of his life in America before he went to Europe, ten years when his sense of worldly failure steadily increased into his saving despair, and the ten years he spent in Europe as an itinerant menial, beggar, and hack writer,—these years are the vital center of his work, and hence of his life. He made of these years of failure his great success, which is his work, which is himself. And he has shown us the degree to which a man can be free, even in the prison of his ideas and attitudes, his time and circumstance.

As has Thoreau, whose name I evoked at the beginning of this essay. But the parallels I have drawn between certain aspects of the thought of the two men obviously break down; and the dissimilarities in the later stages of both their careers are perhaps even more enlightening than the early resemblances. Miller left Europe and returned to the United States in the winter of 1940; Thoreau left Walden Pond and returned to Concord in the summer of 1847. For both men, the times away from their homes were the climactic periods of their literary lives, and their significant and vital work comes out of those times of exile.

But the end of Thoreau's life was dramatically unlike these

late years of Miller's life. During his last two years, Thoreau was ill with tuberculosis, and he spent much of this time preparing a last group of essays for publication in *The Atlantic Monthly*. He did not live to see them appear there, but had he done so, he would have noted no untoward response to their publication. His first book—*A Week on the Concord and Merrimac*—was a failure from the beginning, and even *Walden* found but a very small body of readers during Thoreau's lifetime; most of his poems were not published, and those few that were went unnoticed; and his other essays were read as fugitive pieces in magazines. Thoreau died with the kind of worldly failure that he had, out of principle, courted for nearly all his life.

For the last several years, Henry Miller has been living in California. He is now a famous writer; he is moderately wealthy, sought after, widely admired and read; there is even a Henry Miller Society. Recently he was made a member of the American Institute of Arts and Letters, an eminently distinguished affair, our nearest equivalent to the Académie Française; I understand that he was pleased by his election. Miller has been living in a large modern house near Los Angeles; the house is most comfortably furnished, and like many southern California homes it has a large swimming pool on the spacious grounds. In his new prosperity, Miller has written almost nothing. But he is comfortable now, and I suppose at last he has earned his ironic success, which a few years ago he might have thought of as his damnation.

PETER L. HAYS
"The Danger of Henry Miller"

Arizona Quarterly, Autumn 1971, pp. 251–58

I do not mean to disparage Miller's great energy and obvious lust both for life and for telling of the life he has lived. Both the energy and the lust are evident in his impressively long bibliography. He is a moving storyteller, a painter with words as well as with water colors, and a modern-day Boswell of flamboyant, if gutter-dwelling, personalities. And he rightfully and brilliantly indicts an America and a world bent on destroying itself through pollution of air, water, land, gut, mind, and senses. But there my admiration of him ceases.

For Miller is not an artist. He never knows when to stop. He suffers from logorrhea, writing on and on about a scene with gusto, detailing sights, sounds, smells (especially smells), using many long words found only in dictionaries and more than a few that did not use to be in order to capture the essence of a scene, which he has the talent to do. But after he's captured the feeling of moment he goes on and on speaking until the very sound of his written voice obtrudes and drives the sense of scene away to leave only the sense of that irrepressible voice. For example:

> Walking toward Montparnasse I decided to let myself drift with the tide, to make not the least resistance to fate, no matter in what form it presented itself. Nothing that had happened to me thus far had been sufficient to destroy me; nothing had been destroyed except my illusions. I myself was intact. The world was intact. Tomorrow there might be a revolution, a plague, an earthquake; tomorrow there might not be left a single soul to whom one could turn for sympathy, for aid, for faith. It seemed to me that the great calamity had already manifested itself, that I could be no more truly alone than at this very moment. I made up my mind that I would hold on to nothing, that I would expect nothing, that hence-

forth I would live as an animal, a beast of prey, a rover, a plunderer. Even if war were declared, and it were my lot to go, I would grab the bayonet and plunge it, plunge it up to the hilt. And if rape were the order of the day then rape I would, and with a vengeance. At this very moment, in the quiet dawn of a new day, was not the earth giddy with crime and distress? Had one single element of man's nature been altered, vitally, fundamentally altered, by the incessant march of history? By what he calls the better part of his nature, man has been betrayed, that is all. At the extreme limits of his spiritual being man finds himself again naked as a savage. When he finds God, as it were, he has been picked clean: he is a skeleton. One must burrow into life again in order to put on flesh. The word must become flesh; the soul thirsts. On whatever crumb my eye fastens, I will pounce and devour. If to live is a paramount thing, then I will live, even if I must become a cannibal. Heretofore I have been trying to save my precious hide, trying to preserve the few pieces of meat that hid my bones. I am done with that. I have reached the limits of endurance. My back is to the wall; I can retreat no further. As far as history goes I am dead. If there is something beyond I shall have to bounce back. I have found God, but he is insufficient. I am only spiritually dead. Physically I am alive. Morally I am free. The world which I have departed is a menagerie. The dawn is breaking on a new world, a jungle world in which the lean spirits roam with sharp claws. If I am a hyena I am a lean and hungry one: I go forth to fatten myself. (pp. 97–98)[1]

There are many strong images in that passage, too many. They flood the mind and inundate the memory until no one stands out to leave a lasting impression. It's verbal overkill.

Nor is that the end. Having overwritten a scene in one book, obviously to his dissatisfaction, too, Miller returns to it in another book. And so *Quiet Days of Clichy* repeats episodes from *Tropic of Cancer*, and *Tropic of Capricorn* is regurgitated *ad infinitum* and *ad nauseam* in *The Rosy Crucifixion*. He admits freely, of course, that all of his writing is more or less autobiographical.

Miller himself boasts of his antiart: "This," he says on the second page of *Cancer*, "is not a book, in the ordinary sense of the word. No, this is a prolonged insult, a gob of spit in the face of Art. . . ." Nine pages later he continues this assault on form: "I have made a silent compact with myself not to change a line of what I write. I am not interested in perfecting my thoughts, nor my actions." Now we know that the first part, at least, is untrue—that he did rewrite *Cancer* three times in the two years between his first presentation of it to Jack Kahane of the Obelisk Press in Paris and its ultimate publication; perhaps that is why *Cancer* reads better still than many of his subsequent books. But it's easy enough to believe because certainly all of his "novels" and most of his essays appear to be the words-turned-to-print of a fiery monologist, such as he describes George Katsimbalis to be. They all ramble hither, thither, and yon. Although the *Tropics* have symbolic underpinnings, these are not apparent. *Cancer*, for instance, as the name implies, is supposed to depict the corruption abounding in the world: "No matter where you go, no matter what you touch, there is cancer and syphilis. It is written in the sky; it flames and dances, like an evil portent. It has eaten into our souls and we are nothing but a dead thing like the moon" (p. 185). But such simple statements are few and usually lost in the rush of sensation, are contradicted by their opposites: sentences that capture life, feeling, activity. There certainly is both symbolic and actual death all around, but we cannot become very concerned with it when Miller barges through it, barely acknowledging the existent pathos in his enormous gusto for life. His Whitmanesque acceptance and his emphasis on the comic or the mystic make the tragic seem negligible, insufficient—certainly not the center of attention, *Cancer's* title notwithstanding.

Miller's books start in hectic *medias res* and end, except for flights of expectable but not really prepared-for mystic affirmation, the same way. There is no pattern, no order, no real conclusion; in *Cancer*, what does the ominous hint about Collins mean; does Fillmore ever get to New York, sane; what happens to Ginette; does Miller keep the money that Fillmore gave him for her? These questions would perhaps be impertinent if Miller hadn't the skill he has of bringing these characters and their problems to life on the page. We're not all as dead as he sometimes accuses us of being, and he creates in us empathy for these characters which goes frustrated, sympathy that gets short shrift, as when he says of Max (of *Max and the White Phagocytes*): "I have no idea [what became of him]. I presume he was killed by the Germans when they overran France."[2]

Yet Miller berates Boris for not helping Max in his usual passionate language that urges us, as well, to help.

> Die, die, die a thousand deaths—but don't refuse to recognize the living man. . . . It's flesh and blood, Boris. *Flesh and blood.* He's screaming and you pretend not to hear. . . . You are dead before living flesh. Dead before your own flesh and blood. You will gain nothing, neither in the spirit nor in the flesh, if you do not recognize Max your true brother. . . . We need a breath of life. We need hope, courage, illusion. We need a penny's worth of human sympathy.[3]

But Miller's own sympathy seems to extend only to bestowing some cast-off clothing and then dropping Max in life, preferring to recreate him in writing and pleading there for more human feeling, as he does through all his writing. And this same self-contradictoriness pervades his works.

He sings of life, praising it, wallowing in it, while constantly depicting its dregs, filth, dirt, despair, and disease. His energy does convince me, or at least underscores my own sense of life's possibilities, but he rubs my face in the dirt so much while saying it that the message remains somewhat overpowered by the stench in my nostrils and the bad taste left in my mouth. There are also the wonderful grotesques he introduces us to, moving them on stage at random, then off again. Which brings me back to what I said before—Miller is not an artist, for an artist deals with form, selection, and order, and Miller does not. At least an artist does by the old-fashioned, square esthetic standards that I learned and teach to my students. And they are standards which I persist in clinging to, for reason.

Now granted, the autobiographical novel may be more veridical; it may better capture the haphazard, disorganized, random pattern of life than a plotted novel would, for certainly most lives are more nearly defined by Brownian movement than by neatly balanced Mondrian designs. And current film directors are conveying this to us by their modern techniques. But when Miller says, "The terrible emphasis today upon plot, action, character, analysis, etc.—all this false emphasis which characterizes the literature and drama of today—simply reveals the lack of these elements in our own life,"[4] he's right. If I want absurdity in action, I can read about Viet Nam, slashed funds for education, urban crises, racial prejudice, and governmental programs to correct these. I can look around me and see

random motion, disorder, violence, and the lack of compassion which Miller decried. And it's for those very reasons that I seek order in art, balance there if nowhere else, man as artistic, if not artist-as-man, giving something a definite and satisfying shape. Which Miller does not. And, of course, I do not simply wish that all literature be Pollyannaish in nature, but I do wish that what Miller wrote was more like literature. Whole chunks of his books could be omitted, for the segments present are discontinuous and are not linked at all by causality and only vaguely by chronology. He wants to recreate life as he lived it, with no moral judgments. I disagree: I think an author should indicate, if only by negation, how life should be lived. And I think that writers should shape their material. Writers as diverse as Keats, Wallace Stevens, and Hemingway wrestled with the problem of passion and form. Even someone as hedonistic in his poetry as E. E. Cummings is far from formless, and, in fact, depends upon our knowledge of standard forms and plays against them for the effects that he gets.

Miller despises forms. He's an anarchist, and not just in literature, which is why I consider his philosophy dangerous. Not his preoccupation with sex. Certainly sex is an important if not central element of life, as Freud said, and as Lawrence and Miller have campaigned to allow authors to say. And while we can't hold these individuals responsible for the freedoms they initiated, from *Peyton Place* to *Portnoy's Complaint*, had their messages been heeded and sex been accorded its natural, not illicit or sordid, place in our existence, the hang-ups described by more modern writers might not exist. Moreover I agree with Miller that what he writes is obscene, but not pornographic: he graphically describes sexual intercourse and the evacuation of excrement, but his purpose is not to excite or titillate. Once the shock is over—and it was only a shock when Miller was hard to obtain, no longer—Miller is not that exciting. The *Tropics* are not books one (or at least I) cannot put down; the discontinuous segments even invite such a reading. In fact, such passages as that where Miller watches a whore trying to earn fifteen francs from Van Norden, is not at all prurient: it's terribly sad and depressing.

> As I watch Van Norden tackle her, it seems to me that I'm looking at a machine whose cogs have slipped. Left to themselves, they could go on this way forever, grinding and slipping, without ever anything happening. Until a hand shuts the motor off. The sight of them coupled like a pair of goats without the least spark of passion, grinding and grinding away for no reason except the fifteen francs, washes away every bit of feeling I have except the inhuman one of satisfying my curiosity. The girl is lying on the edge of the bed and Van Norden is bent over her like a satyr with his two feet solidly planted on the floor. I am sitting on a chair behind him, watching their movements with a cool, scientific detachment; it doesn't matter to me if it should last forever. It's like watching one of those crazy machines which throw the newspaper out, millions and billions and trillions of them with their meaningless headlines. The machine seems more sensible, crazy as it is, and more fascinating to watch, than the human beings and the events which produced it. (pp. 143–144)

No, the sexual portions of Miller do not disturb me as much as his anarchy does, his celebration of life, energy, passion, ecstasy, and his condemnation of anything that restricts free enjoyment. He almost worships passionate, powerful speakers, men like Katsimbalis, but unfortunately demagogues, manipulators of emotion from Hitler to George Wallace frequently speak with more passion than more quiet, reasonable men like Adlai Stevenson or Eugene McCarthy. Miller worships energy, explosions of energy, that result in ecstasies of sadism, and the only things created are more pain and confusion. We have only to look about us to see examples of explosions of energy which create more tension than they release, and other anarchists who envision a perfect future after the destruction of the present, but whose immediate plans and actions go no further than the destruction of the present.

Miller is the prophet of the Apocalypse, to which we may well be headed: he describes the causes of our self-destruction well, and I agree with him about them. But I neither agree that we ought to rejoice at our world's collapse, bad as it is, nor do I believe as he does that it will be replaced, if there is a planet left on which to replace anything, by something better, finer, and true. That's why I'm frightened by such statements as "Until this colossal, senseless machine which we have made of America is scrapped there can be no hope." In *Cancer*, Miller says:

> Today I awoke from a sound sleep with curses of joy on my lips, with gibberish on my tongue, repeating to myself like a litany—"Fay ce que vouldras! . . . fay ce que vouldras!" Do anything, but let it produce joy. Do anything, but let it yield ecstasy. So much crowds into my head when I say this to myself: images, gay ones, terrible ones, maddening ones, the wolf and the goat, the spider, the crab, syphilis with her wings outstretched and the door of the womb always on the latch, always open, ready like the tomb. Lust, crime, holiness: the lives of my adored ones, the failures of my adored ones, the words they left behind them, the words they left unfinished; the good they dragged after them and the evil, the sorrow, the discord, the rancor, the strife they created, but above all, *the ecstasy!* (p. 252)

> It may be that we are doomed, that there is no hope for us, *any of us,* but if that is so then let us set up a last agonizing, bloodcurdling howl, a screech of defiance, a war whoop! Away with lamentation! Away with elegies and dirges! Away with biographies and histories, and libraries and museums! Let the dead eat the dead. Let us living ones dance about the rim of the crater, a last expiring dance. But a dance! (p. 257)

I am afraid of such a *danse macabre*. I fear the worshipers of energy uncontrolled, of enjoyment without restriction, of anarchy. Perhaps if more of the right people showed some impetus, I would be less fearful. But as Yeats said: "The best lack all conviction, while the worst are full of passionate intensity."

Miller admired Nietzsche, but probably the equally apocalyptic *Zarathustra*, rather than *The Birth of Tragedy*. There Miller would have found the Dionysian qualities he loves. But he would have been reminded that Dionysian energy led not only to creation, but to orgies of dismemberment, guilt, insanity, and death. The art of which Nietzsche spoke blended this Dionysian force with Apollonian control, which gave it shape, which gave it form—the qualities which Miller's writing and thought drastically lack.

In *Cancer* again he says that he is not attracted to men who express themselves perfectly; rather, "Show me a man who overelaborates and I will show you a great man!" (p. 253). A neat pat on the back for his own logorrhea. In *The Time of the Assassins*, he says, "I call that man poet who is capable of profoundly altering the world"—which makes the greatest poets of this century Josef Stalin and Adolf Hitler. He is a pacifist, but he is for violence. In his own words he is antiart; in

Ihab Hassan's terms, antiform. He is a revolutionary who sees the task of the artist—he uses the term though he denies art—as the need "to overthrow existing values, 'to make of the chaos about him an order which is his own, to sow strife and ferment so that by the emotional release those who are dead may be restored to life . . .'" (p. 253).

That's not for me. Without more assurance that the new world will be at least as good as this one, I'd "rather bear those ills we have than fly to others that we know not of." This world does need its "existing values" overturned, but I'm not sure that the order or disorder which an anarchist would fashion as his own would be any better. The examples of emotional release I have seen most recently are more likely to kill than restore the spiritually dead to life. It is undoubtedly Philistine of me to demand order in art and desire it in life, while Miller passionately rejects it. Certainly, our views on art are incompatible. And while our existing forms and conventions may be wretched, infuriating, and demeaning, it has taken man millions of years painfully to fashion these, and I am not yet ready to cast them completely aside, without a more convincing argument than that provided in the writing of Henry Miller.

Notes

1. All quotations from Henry Miller, *Tropic of Cancer* (New York: Grove Press, 1961), are included in the text.
2. Lawrence Durrell, ed., *The Henry Miller Reader* (New York: New Directions, 1959), p. 134. These words occur in Miller's headnote to his story of "Max."
3. Ibid., pp. 154–155.
4. As quoted by George Wickes in his Minnesota pamphlet, *Henry Miller* (Minneapolis: University of Minnesota Press, 1966), p. 12.

NORMAN MAILER
From "Henry Miller: Genius and Lust, Narcissism"
American Review, April 1976, pp. 2–37

I. Genius

Henry Miller ⟨. . .⟩ exists in the same relation to legend that antimatter shows to matter. His life is antipathetic to the idea of legend itself. Where he is complex, he is too complex—we do not feel the resonance of slowly dissolving mystery but the madness of too many knots; where he is simple, he is not attractive—his air is harsh. If he had remained the protagonist by which he first presented himself in *Tropic of Cancer*—the man with iron in his phallus, acid in his mind, and some kind of incomparable relentless freedom in his heart, that paradox of tough misery and keen happiness, that connoisseur of the spectrum of odors between good sewers and bad sewers, that noble rat gnawing on existence and impossible to kill, then he could indeed have been a legend, a species of Parisian Bogart or American Belmondo. Everybody would have wanted to meet this poet-gangster, barbarian-genius. He would have been the American and heterosexual equivalent of Jean Genet.

In fact, he could never have been too near to the character he made of himself in *Tropic of Cancer*. One part never fits. It is obvious he must be more charming than he pretends—how else account for all the free dinners he is invited to, the people he lives on, the whores who love him? There has to be something splendid about him. He may even seem angelic to his friends or, perish the word, vulnerable. Anaïs Nin, when describing the apartment in Clichy that Miller kept with Alfred Perlès, made, we remember, the point that Miller was tidying the joint. "Henry keeps house like a Dutch housekeeper. He is very neat and clean. No dirty dishes about. It is all monastic, really, with no trimmings, no decoration."[1]

These few details are enough to suggest *Tropic of Cancer* is a fiction more than a fact. Which, of course, is not to take away a particle of its worth. Perhaps it becomes even more valuable. After all, we do not write to recapture an experience, we write to come as close to it as we can. Sometimes we are not very close, and yet, paradoxically, are nearer than if we were. Not nearer necessarily to the reality of what happened, but to the mysterious reality of what can happen on a page. Oil paints do not create clouds but the image of clouds; a page of manuscript can only evoke that special kind of reality which lives on the skin of the writing paper, a rainbow on a soap bubble. Miller is forever accused of caricature by people who knew his characters, and any good reader knows enough about personality to sense how much he must be leaving out of his people. Yet, what a cumulative reality they give us. His characters make up a Paris more real than its paving stones until a reluctant wonder bursts upon us—no French writer no matter how great, not Rabelais, nor Proust, not de Maupassant, Hugo, Huysmans, Zola, or even Balzac, not even Céline, has made Paris more vivid to us. Whenever before has a foreigner described a country better than its native writers? For in *Tropic of Cancer* Miller succeeded in performing one high literary act: he created a tone in prose which caught the tone of a period and a place. If that main character in *Tropic of Cancer* named Henry Miller never existed in life, it hardly matters—he is the voice of a spirit which existed at that time. The spirits of literature may be the nearest we come to historical truth.

For that matter, the great confessions of literature are apart from their authors. Augustine recollecting his sins is not the sinner but the pieties. Julien Sorel is not Stendhal, nor the Seducer a copy of Kierkegaard. *On the Road* is close to Jack Kerouac, yet he gives a happier Kerouac than the one who died too soon. Proust was not his own narrator, even as homosexuality is not like to heterosexuality but another land, and if we take *The Sun Also Rises* as the purest example of a book whose innovation in style became the precise air of a time and a place, then even there we come slowly to the realization that Hemingway at the time he wrote it was not the equal of Jake Barnes—he had created a consciousness wiser, drier, purer, more classic, more sophisticated, and more judicial than his own. He was still naïve in relation to his creation.

The difference between Hemingway and Miller is that Hemingway set out thereafter to grow into Jake Barnes and locked himself for better and worse, for enormous fame and eventual destruction, into that character who embodied the spirit of an age. Whereas Miller, eight years older than Hemingway but arriving at publication eight years later, and so 16 years older in 1934 than Hemingway was in 1926, chose to go in the opposite direction. He proceeded to move away from the first Henry Miller he had created. He was not a character but a soul—he would be various.

He was. Not just a *débrouillard*, but a poet; not just a splenetic vision but a prophet; no mere caricaturist, rather a Daumier of the written line; and finally not just master of one style but the prodigy of a dozen. Miller had only to keep writing *Tropic of Cancer* over and over, and refining his own personality to become less and less separate from his book, and he could have entered the American life of legend. There were obstacles in his way, of course, and the first was that he was not publishable in America—the growth of his legend would have taken longer. But he had something to offer which went beyond Hemingway.

The cruelest criticism ever delivered of Henry James is that he had a style so hermetic his pen would have been paralyzed if one of his characters had ever entered a town house, removed his hat, and found crap on his head (a matter, parenthetically, of small moment to Tolstoy let us say, or Dostoyevsky, or Stendhal). Hemingway would have been bothered more than he liked. Miller would have loved it. How did his host react to the shit? How did our host's wife? My God, the way she smacked her nostrils over the impact, you can be sure her thighs were in a lather.

In fact, Hemingway would have hated such a scene. He was trying to create a world where mood—which Hemingway saw as the staff of life—could be cultivated by the scrupulosity of the attention you paid to keeping mood aloft through the excellence of your gravity, courage, and diction.

The eye of every dream Hemingway ever had must have looked down the long vista of his future suicide—so he had a legitimate fear of chaos. He never wrote about the river—he contented himself, better, he created a quintessentially American aesthetic, by writing about the camp he set up each night by the side of the river—that was the night we made camp at the foot of the cliffs just after the place where the rapids were bad.

Miller is the other half of literature. He is without fear of his end, a literary athlete at ease in earth, air, or water. I am the river, he is always ready to say, I am the rapids and the placids, I'm the froth and the scum and twigs—what a roar as I go over the falls. Who gives a fart? Let others camp where they may. I am the river and there is nothing I can't join.

Whereas, Hemingway's world was doomed to collapse so soon as the forces of the century pushed life into a technological tunnel; mood to Hemingway being a royal grace, could not survive grinding gears, surrealist manners—here's shit in your hat!—and electric machines which offered static, but Miller took off at the place where Hemingway ended. In *Tropic of Cancer*, he was saying—and it is the force of the book—I am obliged to live in that place where mood is in the meat grinder, so I know more about it. I know all of the spectrum which runs from good mood to bad mood, and can tell you that a stinking mood is better than no mood. Life has also been designed to run in the stink.

Miller bounces in the stink. We read *Tropic of Cancer*, that book of horrors, and feel happy. It is because there is honor in the horror, and metaphor in the hideous. How, we cannot even begin to say. Maybe it is that mood is vastly more various, self-regenerative, hearty, and sly than Hemingway ever guessed. Maybe mood is not a lavender lady, but a barmaid with full visions of heaven in the full corruption of her beer breath, and an old drunk's vomit is a clarion call to some mutants of the cosmos just now squeezing around the bend. It is as if without courage, or militancy, or the serious cultivation of strength, without stoicism or good taste or even a nose for the nicety of good guts under terrible pressure, Miller is still living closer to death than Hemingway, certainly he is closer if the sewer is nearer to our end than the wound.

History proved to be on Miller's side. Twentieth-century life was leaving the world of individual effort, liquor, and tragic wounds for the big-city garbage can of bruises, migraines, static, mood chemicals, amnesia, absurd relations, and cancer. Down in the sewers of existence where the cancer was being cooked, Miller was cavorting. Look, he was forever saying, you do not have to die of this crud. You can breathe it, eat it, suck it, fuck it, and still bounce up for the next day. There is something inestimable in us if we can stand the smell.

Considering where the world was going—right into the World-Wide Sewer of the Concentration Camps—Miller had a message which gave more life than Hemingway's. "One reason why I have stressed so much the immoral, the wicked, the ugly, the cruel in my work is because I wanted others to know how valuable these are, how equally if not more important than the good things . . . I was getting the poison out of my system. Curiously enough, this poison had a tonic effect for others. It was as if I had given them some kind of immunity."[2]

The legend, however, was never to develop. With his fingers and his nose and his toenails, he had gotten into the excrements of cancerland—he had to do no more than stay there, a dry sardonic demon, tough as nails, bright as radium. But he had had a life after all before this, tragic, twisted, near to atrophied in some of its vital parts, he was closer to the crud himself than he ever allowed. So he had to write himself out of his own dungeons and did in all the work which would follow *Tropic of Cancer*, and some of the secrets of his unique, mysterious, and absolutely special personality are in his later work—a vital search. We would all know more if we could find him.

II. Lust

Miller is not a writer whose life lends itself to clear and separated aesthetic periods, for it is characteristic of him to write in two directions at once. Even *Tropic of Cancer*, which is able to give the best impression of a single-minded intent, still presents its contrast of styles.

Nonetheless, there is some pattern to his life. Miller has his obsessions, and they are intense enough for him to spend a good part of his aesthetic career working them out. If there is a gauge which separates the artist from everybody else who works at being one, it is that the artist has risen precisely from therapy to art. He is no longer fixed at relieving one or another obsessional pressure on the ego by the act of expressing himself. The artist's ultimate interest is to put something together which is independent of the ego; such work can make you feel that you are traveling through that fine and supple mood we may as well call the truth. *Death in Venice* or *Daisy Miller* has that quality, and *The Red Pony* by Steinbeck. *Breakfast at Tiffany's* by Truman Capote will offer it and Katherine Anne Porter's *Noon Wine*. There are a hundred or rather a thousand such pieces of literature and they are art. It is not to say that they are the greatest achievements of writing itself—nothing of Dostoevsky, for example, could fit such a category of art; indeed it may be said that all of Dostoevsky is therapy, except that he elevated the struggle from his ego to his soul, and so we can all partake of the therapy. Forever beyond art, happily, is genius.

On this herculean scale of measure, if considerably below Dostoevsky, can Miller be found. His life impinges on his work ceaselessly, indeed his relation to the problems of his own life is so unremitting yet so scatterbrained that it is as if life is the only true spouse Henry Miller ever had. A crazy spouse, of course, a confirmed nitwit in her lack of stability. He can never feel calm enough to live in the world of art. In this sense, everything Miller writes is therapy. No American author, not even Thomas Wolfe, emits so intense a message that the man will go mad if he stops writing, that his overcharged brain will simply burst. It is as if Miller was never able to afford the luxury of art—rather he had to drain the throttled heats of the ego each day. Yet his literary act takes on such intensity that we are compelled to awe as we read him. Awe can be a proper accompaniment to great art.

Never pausing to take a breath, it is as if Miller creates art as a species of spin-off from the more fundamental endeavor which is to maintain some kind of relation between his mind and the theater beyond his mind which pretended to call itself reality.

That he was successful is part of his greatness. Most souls who go in for literary self-expression to relieve their suffering end on a treadmill. As they relieve themselves so do they repel readers. Excrement is excrement even when its name is therapy. But Miller brought it off. His product transcended itself and became literary flesh. What he did was therapy in that he had to do it, but it rose above every limitation. Maybe it is because he kept one literary grace—he never justified himself (which is the predictable weakness of all therapy), rather he depended on a rigorous even delighted honesty in portraying his faults, in writing without shit, which is to say writing with the closest examination of each turd. Miller was a true American spirit. He knew that when you have a nation of transplants and weeds the best is always next to the worst, and right after shit comes Shinola. It was all equal to him because he understood that it was never equal—in the midst of heaven a rent, and out of the slime comes a pearl; he is a demon at writing about bad fucks with all the gusto others give to good ones, no fuck is in vain—the air may prove most transcendent at the edge of the spew, or if not, then the nausea it produces can let the mind clear out its vertigo. So he dived into the sordid, and portrayed men and women as they had hardly been painted before. In *Sexus* we will be treated to a girl having her period in the middle of an orgy, cock, balls, knees, thighs, cunt, and belly basted with blood, then soap and towels, a round of good-byes—a phrase or two later he is off on the beginning of a ten-page description of how he makes love to his wife which goes through many a mood; he will go right down to the depths, no cellar has maggots or rats big enough to frighten him, he can even write about the whipped-out flayed heel-ground butt of his own desire for a whore, about fucking when too exhausted to fuck, and come up with a major metaphor.[3]

If some ultimate simplicity saved him, some writer's instinct to know that no account of an unpleasant event could survive its evasions—few authors have the courage to work with that!—it is just as well to recognize that Miller was not necessarily born with such simplicity but achieved it out of his own literary struggles and was forever losing it and regaining it and finally forged his escape from his life by daring to live at the deepest level of honesty he could endure in his life. This is not to say that he was always more honest than anyone else—his evasions also stand out—but it is not how absolutely honest we are, so much as the torture we are willing to bear in the attempt to be honest, which works as the lever of such literary deliverance. It is possible a coward attempting to be brave can light more iridescence in the cosmos than a brave man fulfilling a routine demand on his courage. The point is that Miller came out of a background which gave no medals for honesty, the parents from whom he emerged were at odds with each other, and his Brooklyn milieu, first Williamsburg then Bushwick at the turn of the century, was closed to the idea of literature itself.

⟨. . .⟩ Never have literature and sex lived in such symbiotic relation before—it is as if every curving stroke of his phallus is laying a future paragraph of phrases on his brain. He is the Grand Speleologist of the Vagina—out of the sensations of those caverns will he rediscover every item in the world. He may be the only writer in existence about whom we might as well suppose that without his prodigies of sex, he might have been able to produce no prodigies of literature. And without the successful practice of his literature we can wonder if his sexual vitality would have remained so long undiminished.

For Henry Miller had not set out to navigate through the world, but through himself, Henry Miller, with his brain and his balls and his daily life at the Cosmodemonic (read Western Union) telegraph office. One sloughed one's work and followed the line of one's sexual impulse without a backward look at what might be remotely desirable for society. One set out to feed one's cock (as Renaissance man had set out to feed his brain) and the new effort was pioneer. Never before had a future literary man given that much attention to the vagaries and outright contradictions of a stiff prick without a modicum of conscience; no one had ever dared to assume that such a life might be as happy and amusing as the next, or that the paganism of a big-city fucker could have its own balance, and such a man might be therefore equipped to explore the sexual mysteries with his phallus as a searchlight; yes, all sexual experience was valid if one looked at it clearly, and no fuck was in vain.

Some, nonetheless, came close. Once he began to write, he would work the way he fucked, and like many another self-educated author, would rush to grab at every great and obscure literary name he had read as if they were all pieces of flesh on the great body of culture, or ineluctable wrinkles in the cuneiform labyrinth of the Great Twat of Knowledge. The titles of other books ululate through his work like oscillating hairs of the labia majora. His cock seems covered with vibrations from a thousand cunts, and depression deep as the blackest chancres of the most venereal bogs will ride at times through his philosophy. He is even ready to believe that "the whole world, known and unknown, is out of kilter, screaming in pain and madness." That is his depression; be certain he will rise from it. He gets, after all, the livid ache of the groin, nine-tenths cramp, one-tenth sugar, the phallus *über alles* of the insatiable hard-on. One crazy fuck begets another—that is the message, over and over. One is connecting into the electrical system of a world which runs cock-cunt-cock-cunt like the poles in a wiring circuit for a solder-it-yourself super-heterodyne. Tapped into pain and madness, he is also part of the supersending-and-receiving apparatus of all that palpitating noumenal world he senses just the other side of the wall of the cunt. No philosopher, he comes near to visions and bounces off them, buggers his own ideas, an indefatigable stud of a mind which will fuck everything before it, callipygous tissue, old cored apples, used Kotex, armpits, bananas floating in grease. To enter Miller's mind is to write like him.

Sometimes, his writing even has the form of a fuck. All the roar of passion, the flaming poetry, the passing crazy wit, and not an instant of intellectual precision, no products of Mind but insights instead which smack the brain like a bouncy tit which plops full of fucky happy presence over your nostrils. Of course you can lose such insights as fast as you get them, the fuck is rolling down the river, and who looks back, ah, what tingles in the nose at rocks to come. Yes, one does well to recognize that the experience which makes his literature is precisely his sexual vigor, and he is next to no author without it. With it, he will spend a considerable part of his literary life exploring the vast watershed of sex from that relatively uncharted side which goes by the name of lust. It could be said that other writers from Casanova to Frank Harris had already made the same exploration, and they did, more or less. Less! It was with none of Miller's prodigious and poetic talent. That made it epic work for any man. Over the centuries, most poets have spent their lives on the familiar side of the watershed; they wrote of love. For lust is a world with vertiginous falls. It takes over the instinct to create life and converts it to a force. Curious force. Lust has all the attributes of junk. It dominates the

mind, appropriates loyalties, generalizes character, leaches character out, rides on the fuel of any emotional gas—hatred, affection, curiosity, even boredom—yet lust can alter on the instant to love. Indeed, the more intense lust becomes, the more it is out of focus—the line of the ridge between lust and love is exactly where the light is blinding, and the ground remains unknown. Henry, a hairy prospector, red eye full of lust, wandering those ridge lines during the early years of his literary life, got to know the mosquitoes in every swamp and could call to the ozones of cosmic lust on many a cloud-covered precipice. If cunts are only boscage and fodder for that lust they are also—it is the private little knowledge of lust—an indispensable step closer to the beyond. So, old Henry the ram, admits, "perhaps a cunt, smelly though it may be, is one of the prime symbols for the connection between all things."

He has slipped the clue across. Here is a clue to the lust that drives a man to scour his balls and freak his back until he is ready to pass out from the drubbing he has given his organs. It is a clue which all but says that somewhere in the insane passions of all men is a huge desire to drive forward into the seat of creation, and sink your cock to the hilt, sink it into as many hilts as will hold it. Since man is alienated from the nature which brought him forth, he must, if necessary, come close to blowing his head off in order to possess it. "Perhaps a cunt, smelly though it may be, is one of the prime symbols for the connection between all things." It is the horror of lust, and yet its justification, that wild as a blind maniac it still drives toward the creation. So Miller captured something in the sexuality of men as it had never been seen before, precisely that it was man's sense of awe before woman, his dread of her position one step closer to eternity (for in that step were her powers) which made men detest women, revile them, humiliate them, defecate symbolically upon them, do everything to reduce them so that one might dare to enter them and take pleasure of them. "His shit don't smell like ice cream either," says a private of a general in a novel, and it is the cry of an enlisted man whose ego needs equality to breathe. So do men look to destroy every quality in a woman which will give her the powers of a male, for she is in their eyes already armed with the power that she brought them forth, and that is a power beyond measure—the earliest etchings of memory go back to that woman between whose legs they were conceived, nurtured, and near strangled in the hours of birth. And if women were also born of woman, that could only compound the awe, for out of that process by which they had come in, so would something of the same come out of them; they were installed in the boxes-within-boxes of the universe, and man was only a box, all detached. So it is not unnatural that men, perhaps a majority of men, go through the years of their sex with women in some contract with lust which will enable them to be as fierce as their female when she is awash in the great ocean of the fuck. As it can appear to the man, great forces beyond his measure are calling to the woman then.

That was what Miller saw, and it is what he brought back to us: that there were mysteries in trying to explain the extraordinary fascination of an act we can abuse, debase, inundate, and drool upon, yet the act repeats an interest. It draws us toward obsession. It is the mirror of how we approach God through our imperfections, *Hot*, full of the shittiest lust. In all of his faceless characterless pullulating broads, in all those cunts which undulate with the movements of eels, in all those clearly described broths of soup and grease and marrow and wine which are all he will give us of them—their cunts are always closer to us than their faces—in all the indignities of position, the humiliation of situation, and the endless presentations of women as pure artifacts of farce, their asses all up in the air, still he screams his barbaric yawp of utter adoration for the power and the glory and the grandeur of the female in the universe, and it is his genius to show us that this power is ready to survive any context or any abuse.

III. Narcissism

The gusto of Miller's relation to sex is so outside the clam-like formulations of conventional psychoanalysis that it is probably incumbent to make a pass at the psychology of his sexual patterns. Some possible psychology, at any rate. Who can conceive today of a man without a psychology? On the other hand, let it be done in modesty. To analyze the sexuality of another person, any other person, is unattractive; it is not even a question of taste but philosophy. The implicit assumption is that the person who performs the analysis is sexually superior to the subject. One is equal at such times to a writer for *Time* who assigns objectivity to himself.

To analyze anyone's sexuality assumes we know what sex is about; even the assumption is offensive. But to suggest we know the psychological patterns of a great writer is doubly irritating. As soon talk about the real secret in the reflexes of a great athlete. Nonetheless, by the style of this apology, it is obvious some attempt is going to be made. There is a modern vanity which thrusts us into the dissection of our betters. Besides, in the case of Henry Miller, a species of cop-out exists. To the degree we come to know Miller's psychic apparatus, we can claim sympathy with the difficulty of what he managed to achieve.

Told often enough by the victim, Miller comes from a mother from whom he admits to receiving no love. In his childhood, he is, so far as his parents have influence, hermetically sealed against sexuality. Whatever sex is, it is on the other side of the wall. His first and fundamental relation to a woman is detestation. A grand beginning! To it he adds the formative logic of an eight-year-old. ⟨. . .⟩

June (Mona) has been met in a dancehall in 1923. She is to prove the love of his life. In writing about that love, he begins an infatuation with the number seven equal to Mann's in *The Magic Mountain*. He speaks of the first seven days of their meeting, and the seven years of their relation (which came to an end of sorts in 1930 when he went off to Europe alone—although they were to live together on and off for another few years). He must bring himself up to the point of trying to write about her at least seven times. In *Tropic of Cancer* he is about to begin more than once, and *Tropic of Capricorn* could be described as a book written entirely around the difficulty of trying to write about her. Forget the number seven—it will still take six years from the time of their divorce in 1934 before he can undertake to describe their affair and marriage in anything like novelistic fashion, and *The Rosy Crucifixion*, which just about covers the day-to-day movement of their five years of excursions and capers together in New York is a novel of 1,600 pages. If the first book, *Sexus*, was begun in 1940 it was not finished until 1945, and *Plexus* took from 1947 to 1949. *Nexus*, the final volume, was not even started until 1952 nor done until '59. He has spent close to twenty years on his magnum opus! Of course, he has written other books in the same time, *The Air-Conditioned Nightmare*, *The Time of the Assassins*, *The Books in My Life*, *Big Sur and The Oranges of Hieronymus Bosch*, plus some smaller works, but in comparison to the prodigies of talent he exhibited in the '30s with *Tropic of Cancer*, *Black Spring* and *Tropic of Capricorn*, he is something like half the writer stretched out to twice the length.

He is also, of course, now old for a writer. His work on

The Rosy Crucifixion corresponds almost exactly to his fifties and his sixties. He is not far from 70 when he is done, yet the mysteries of his relation with Mona have so beguiled him that he spent 36 obsessive years living with her and writing about her and never succeeds, never quite, in making her real to us, as novelistically real as Anna Karenina or Emma Bovary. She hovers in that space between the actual and the fictional where everything is just out of focus. Indeed Anaïs Nin in one page of her diary succeeds in making Mona as vivid as Miller ever can. (Yet, no more real.)

Henry came to Louveciennes with June.

As June walked toward me from the darkness of the garden into the light of the door, I saw for the first time the most beautiful woman on earth. A startlingly white face, burning dark eyes, a face so alive I felt it would consume itself before my eyes. Years ago I tried to imagine a true beauty; I created in my mind an image of just such a woman. I had never seen her until last night. Yet I knew long ago the phosphorescent color of her skin, her huntress profile, the evenness of her teeth. She is bizarre, fantastic, nervous, like someone in a high fever. Her beauty drowned me. As I sat before her, I felt I would do anything she asked of me. Henry suddenly faded. She was color and brilliance and strangeness. By the end of the evening I had extricated myself from her power. She killed my admiration by her talk. Her talk. The enormous ego, false, weak, posturing. She lacks the courage of her personality, which is sensual, heavy with experience. Her role alone preoccupies her. She invents drama in which she always stars. I am sure she creates genuine dramas, genuine chaos and whirlpools of feelings, but I feel that her share in it is a pose. That night, in spite of my response to her, she sought to be whatever she felt I wanted her to be. She is an actress every moment. I cannot grasp the core of June. Everything Henry had said about her is true.

By the end of the evening I felt as Henry did, fascinated with her face and body which promises so much, but hating her invented self which hides the true one. (*The Diary of Anaïs Nin, Vol. I*, p. 20)

Curious! If we fix on Miller's mind rather than June's beauty, Nin could be giving a description of his talent: *startling, burning, phosphorescent, bizarre, fantastic, nervous, in high fever*, full of *color, brilliance* and *strangeness* but possessed of an *enormous ego, false, weak, posturing* and finally *lacking the courage of its personality*, leaving behind *chaos* and *whirlpools of feeling*. Yet it may be all a *pose*. One *cannot grasp the core* of Henry Miller, and one can come near to *hating* (his) *invented self which hides the true one*.

It works: If one is to judge Miller's talent by the vices of his mind, the result is not unequal to the flaws in June's beauty. No wonder they have seven years together. It is a relation which proves obsessive but constantly changeable; fixed in compulsion yet stripped of roots; emotional as blood and yet as insecure as emotion itself. She will take him a long way in seven good and bad years from the cold mean calculating street-fucker, the hard-nosed Brooklyn hard-on by which he was still picturing himself when they met. He is one stud who has met more than his equal. She is more enterprising than he, wiser about the world, more subtly aggressive, a better hustler. Before a year is out, she has convinced him to quit work and try to write while she will make their living. If ever there is an inner movement in his life, it is here, indeed we are witness to his first metamorphosis. He shifts from an intelligent and second-rate promoter of bad debts, and some riotous Brooklyn nights, to a faithful and tortured young writer helplessly in love with a Junoesque woman whose maddening lack of center leads him into an intuition of his own lack of identity. He comes to discover all those modern themes which revolve around the discovery of oneself. Soon he will dive into the pit of recognizing that there may not be a geological fundament in the psyche one can call identity. Like June, he will have to re-create himself each morning, and soon realizes he has been doing it all his life. He has never looked back in moral guilt because whatever act he committed yesterday, and it could have been atrocious, heinous, or incommensurately disloyal to what he thought he believed or loved, it hardly mattered. He could look yesterday's act in the eye because the man who did it was no longer himself. In the act of doing it, he became another man, free to go in another direction. It can be 180° away from yesterday's attempt. Tomorrow he may be close again to the man he was day before yesterday, but never the same. He has passed from the sublimation of murder (by way of a sullen intent cock) to the liberation of the self from every cancer-habit of the past. Since he has a life full of adventure, debts, mishaps, and constant oncoming lack of funds, since June brings in their living as irregularly as changes in the weather, so there is no nicety to his liberation; no, Miller's psychic life is equal to a scatback scampering upfield on a punt return. He can lose ten yards as easily as gain them. And his head is forever ringing from the last concussion.

His confusion, however, is great; his passivity feels pervasive. He has changed from a stand-up hallway-fucker to a somewhat indolent husband-pimp. His wife is having the adventures, and he is home doing the writing, sometimes the cooking. He is in the untidy situation of a man who lives with a Brooklyn moral code for sex, "If she won't screw, she's frigid; if she does, she's a whore," yet the wife is a consummate liar, and makes money off men to the tune of $100 bills dropped in from the sky, never tells him how, a woman even more changeable than himself and vastly more bisexual—their love will crash finally when she brings home a girl to live with them, and becomes hooked on the girl. Sixteen hundred pages of *The Rosy Crucifixion* will founder on Miller's inability to penetrate these depths, or even come near them. He was brought up by a moral code which taught that love was attached to the living room; one's family was one's house. The living room carpet was one's rock. Now he floats in a fluid as limitless as amniotic fluid. He has no limbs and his feet are over his head, his eyes smell sounds and his nose hears colors, he is living with a woman even more incredible than himself. All the while he is becoming an artist. He is moving away from the use of himself as a skilled and stealthy sex murderer who can instill small deaths into every hot and humping fornication. Now, he is emerging as a narcissist at loose in the uncategorizability of his own experience.

It is too simple to think of the narcissist as someone in love with himself. One can detest oneself intimately and still be a narcissist. What characterizes narcissism is the fundamental relation. It is with oneself. The same dialectic of love and hate that mates feel for one another is experienced within the self. But then a special kind of insanity calls to the narcissist. The inner dialogue hardly ever ceases. The two halves of themselves exist like separate animals forever scrutinizing each other.

So two narcissists in love are the opposite of two mates who may feel a bond powerful as the valence holding the atoms of a molecule together. Narcissists, in contrast, are linked up into themselves. They do not join each other so much as approach one another like crystals brought into juxtaposition.

They have a passionate affair to the degree each allows the other to resonate more fully than when alone. Two narcissists might live together for 50 years in every appearance of matrimonial solidity (although it probably helps if money is present) but essentially, no matter how considerate they may be of one another, the courtesies come more from a decision to be good to the other than issuing from a love which will go forth whether one wills it or not. The narcissistic relation insists that the other continue to be good for one's own resonance. In the profoundest sense, one narcissist is never ready to die for the other. It is not love we may encounter so much as fine tuning. Small wonder that the coming together of narcissists is the natural matrimony of the Technological Century. Small wonder that Henry Miller, the last great American pioneer, is first to boff and bang his way across this last psychological frontier, there first with the most. No love in literature is so long recounted as his 1,600-page affair and marriage and separation from his Mona. *The Rosy Crucifixion* becomes one of the greatest failures in the history of the novel, a literary cake large as the Himalayas which fails to rise. And across half at least of its 1,600 pages are peaks and avenues and haunches and battlements and *arêtes* and basins and summits and valleys of writing so good one shakes one's head. Pity the poor aspiring mediocrity of a writer who reads Miller without protection—he will never write another word if he has any decency left. Pity for that matter the good writer. At times Miller is too good.

Yet *The Rosy Crucifixion* is one of the monumental failures of world literature. For in those 1,600 pages, Miller knocks on the door of ultimate meaning and it never opens a crack. By the end he is where he was at the beginning, at least so far as sexual satori is concerned. I-got-laid-and-it-was-wondrous is the opening theme of the book, and by the end not one new philosophical connection has been laid onto that first lay. Miller and the reader know no more of the intimate wonders beneath the first wonder after the book is done.

An obvious critical impulse is to decide the work is too long. But on examination it cannot be cut. Rather, as it stands, it is too fragmentary. Perhaps it should be a novel of 4,000 pages. What Miller has bogged into (precisely because he is the first American to make the attempt) is the uncharted negotiations of the psyche when two narcissists take the vow of love. Yet it is finally his own novelistic terrain. Since he has always eschewed politics as a literary subject (he merely issues calumnies against it), since he therefore has also eschewed the incomparably finicky and invaluable literary task of trying to place people in society, he never really writes about society except through metaphor. Since he is a great writer, his metaphors occasionally produce the whole and entire machine of society until it passes over one's brain like an incubus. He does this with his vision of the Cosmodemonic Telegraph Company and the unforgettable metaphor in *Tropic of Cancer* when Miller and Van Norden are exhaustedly fucking a worn-out whore like men standing up in the trenches.

His preference, however, is to create his literary world through the visions of dreams and the tides of whatever myths he finds appropriate to his use. Since that has to be a perfumed and farty literary game unless there is real novelistic meat on each mythic tendon, Miller naturally goes to sex for his meat. He is not a social writer, but a sexual writer. Even Lawrence never let go of the idea that through sex he could still delineate society; Miller, however, went further. Sex, he assumed, was a natural literary field for the novel, as clear and free and open to a land-grab as any social panorama. One could capture the sex-life of two people in all its profundity and have quite as much to say about the cosmos as any literary plot laid out the other way with its bankers and beggars, ladies and whores, clerks and killers. The real novel, went Miller's assumption, could short-circuit society. Give us the cosmos head on. Give it to us by way of a cunt impaled on a cock.

That is a herculean assumption. Because you need the phallus of Hercules to bring it off (and conceivably the brain of Einstein). A writer works with what he is given, and in Miller's case, for cosmic blast-off, he had a narcissistic cunt on a narcissistic cock and 36 years of bewilderment from the day of meeting his love to the hour he finished writing of her. She was so *changeable* went his everlasting lament.

It is hard enough for a man twisting a pencil through the traps and loops of his handwriting to get a character onto an empty page, but to create someone who shifts all the time! As soon teach one's spine to wind like a snake. The narcissist is always playing roles, and if there is any character harder for an author to create than that writer greater than himself, it may be a great actor. We do not even begin to comprehend the psychology of actors. ⟨. . .⟩

To the degree, however, that narcissism is an affliction of the talented, the stakes are not small, and the victims are playing their own serious game in the midst of the scenarios. If one can only break out of the penitentiary of self-absorption, there are artistic wonders, conceivably, to achieve. Indeed, for a narcissist to stay in love with someone else for a long period is to speak of the fine art of the beloved. They can tune, after all, the unspeakably complex machine of oneself.

Miller may have been playing, therefore, for the highest stakes we can conceive. He had the energy, the vision, the talent, and the outrageous individuality to have some chance of becoming the greatest writer in America's history, a figure equal to Shakespeare. (For Americans.) Of course, to invoke such contrasts is to mock them. A writer cannot live too seriously with the idea that he will or will not beat Tolstoy—he has rather some sense of a huge and not impossible literary destiny in the reverberations of his own ambition; he feels his talent, perhaps, as a trust; so he sees his loves as evil when they balk him. He is living, after all, with his own secret plot. He knows that a writer of the largest dimension can alter the nerves and marrow of a nation; no one, in fact, can measure what collective loss of inner life would have come to English people if Shakespeare had failed to write.

In those seven years with June, Miller was shaping the talent with which he would go out into the world. It is part of the total ambiguity with which he has surrounded himself (despite the ten thousand intimate details he offers of his life) that we do not know by the end of *The Rosy Crucifixion* whether she breathed a greater life into his talent or exploited him. We do not know if Mona was a Great Ice Lady who chilled a part of him forever, or a beautiful much-abused piece of earth-mother. We do not know if Miller could have become something like an American Shakespeare capable of writing about tyrants and tycoons (instead, repetitively, of his own liberation) if he had never met Mona, whether, that is, she left him frozen in obsession, and *The Rosy Crucifixion* could have become the most important American novel ever written if not for her; or—we are left wide open—the contrary is the true possibility and he might never have written at all if he had not met her, certainly never become a writer of the major dimension he achieved. All we know is that after seven years of living with her, he went off to Paris alone and learned to live by himself.

Notes

1. *The Diary of Anaïs Nin (Vol. I)* (New York: The Swallow Press and Harcourt, Brace & World, Inc., 1966), p. 62.

2. Jonathan Cott. "Reflections of a Cosmic Tourist." *Rolling Stone*, February 27, 1975, pp. 38–46, 57.
3. This passage and a few others in this section have been adapted from the chapter on Henry Miller in *The Prisoner of Sex*, Little, Brown, 1971.

MARY ALLEN
"Henry Miller: Yea-Sayer"

Tennessee Studies in Literature, 1978, pp. 100–110

When Melville praised Hawthorne for saying "No! in thunder. . . . For all men who say *yes*, lie,"[1] he spoke for the majority of American writers from his time to our own. Whether the view be based on a Puritan concept of sin and the distrust of pleasure, the crumbling of value systems before or after the wars, or on the more current visions of absurdity, our major tendency has been despairing, self-critical, and frequently cynical. Not that literature has ever told as much of pleasure as of pain. But American fiction, in particular, and increasingly so with increasing affluence, has, in novels as various as *Moby-Dick* and *The Great Gatsby*, turned on a soul sickness so severe—whether in response to cosmic or societal patterns—that the possibility of warm human responses is practically nonexistent.

While the classic fiction of America is rich with metaphysical and moral concerns, our failures scream out to us in the literature from its beginnings, with the world of Huck Finn as deeply flawed as that of *One Flew Over the Cuckoo's Nest*, where the society is a huge combine imprisoning and castrating its men. Whether the attack is against America directly, which is so often the case, or whether the literature simply springs from the place, it shows a life where little love and delight can occur. Independence and courage continue to be the favored values, but freedom leads only to frenzied activity and loneliness; energy results in violence. And the ugly ironies of our racial situation continue to supply ample material for self-castigation.

The diminutive line of yea-sayers in our classic repertoire—led by Emerson, Thoreau, and Whitman—petered out after the lush but often inflated rhetoric of Thomas Wolfe and, as Terry Southern points out, nearly became extinct with "one last overdose of *schmalz*"[2] by such a writer as William Saroyan. But there is one yea-sayer America has yet to meet head-on—Mr. Henry Miller, who believes that the first word a man must write when he finds the "life rhythm, is Yes! Everything he writes thereafter is Yes, Yes, Yes—Yes in a thousand million ways. No dynamo, no matter how huge—not even a dynamo of a hundred million dead souls—can combat one man saying Yes!"[3]

The name Henry Miller has raised many objections, the first and most dramatic being the obscenity charges: this is the man who writes the dirty books. But now that the pornography issue has lost its fire, and the censorship trials of his books are forgotten, perhaps we can see what else Miller says. His obscenity (rather than pornography, if that term refers to literature intended for erotic arousal) cannot shock as it once did, although it may offend some readers enough to drive them away. As Miller lards his writing with crude detail, we recognize the art of the child determined to do what is naughty. And he was very naughty in the thirties.

But Miller was never a man to thrive merely on the act of rebellion or on any masochistic impulse. Nor is he a satirist, whose primary concern is flaw. While he writes convincingly of pain and anger, he is one of the few who also record joyous feelings, in a time when it is not a convention to do so. Critic that he is, Miller is more original in his appreciations and in his honesty in expressing them. *Tropic of Cancer*, his best work, is an incredible song of joy—for freedom to curse, to make love, to eat, drink, beg, and ramble about Paris, unattached. Sadly, for some readers the book's obscenity obscures its real theme, which Miller says is liberty. Whether he is driving across the deserts of America or saying goodnight to a prostitute in Paris, Miller is lighthearted when he feels free. Not since *Walden* has there been such a clear-headed savoring of freedom, which is usually most poignantly shown by those deprived of it.

An important early attack on Miller is in George Orwell's generally appreciative "Inside the Whale." While recognizing Miller as a descendant of Whitman in the admirable tradition of acceptance, Orwell maintains, in 1940, that for anyone to say "I accept" is to say that he accepts "concentration camps, rubber truncheons, Hitler, Stalin, bombs . . . and political murders. . . . And on the whole this is Henry Miller's attitude."[4] Orwell was "intrigued" by this man who showed no interest in the Spanish war and wanted only to stay in Paris having a good time. But as the polemicists of the period were to become disillusioned in their approach (W. H. Auden, as the most obvious example) and as the taste for propaganda waned, criticism of the apolitical Miller lost its force. And while it was Orwell who made that attack most persuasively, it was he who pointed out a crucial and astonishing aspect of *Tropic of Cancer*: "The thing has become so unusual as to seem almost anomalous, but it is the book of a man who is happy."[5]

Some readers have objected to Miller, the persona of *Tropic of Cancer*, on other ethical grounds. He doesn't care what happens to people, although he may be extravagantly generous at times. Women are so obviously used only for sex that the fact hardly bears mentioning. Always ready to thrive on another's misfortune, Miller rushes out to get the job of the pathetic Peckover, a proofreader, when he is killed in a fall down the elevator shaft. And *Tropic of Cancer* closes on an idyllic note of contentment that comes after a meal he buys with the money his friend asked him to deliver to a girl. If one is looking for an exemplar of Christian virtues, Mr. Miller is clearly not the man to read.

But as one who honestly and refreshingly admits that our joys are not necessarily related to other people or to generous impulses (although we humanitarians may not easily admit the fact), Miller has few equals. He tells of the supreme pleasure that comes from one's own inventiveness—which for the writer will be a solitary exercise. Beginning with the knowledge that freedom and love have never gotten on well together, Miller is one of the few writers who dares to opt for freedom. He is never trapped, as someone like Hemingway was, in an attempt to live up to humanistic values that he does not believe in. Such an attempt fails for Hemingway in *For Whom the Bell Tolls*, for example, where he tries to make romantic and Christian love his themes, while his real instinct is for a violent test of courage for the individual man, an antisocial act. Miller eliminates the possibility of such a problem by stripping away any pretensions to the heroic on the first page of his book. And the poverty and passivity that follow become the luxuries that make freedom possible.

A further objection to Miller's writing is that it is repetitious and boring. Sometimes it is. But that does not negate the inspiring single song of *Tropic of Cancer*, with its opening section like nothing in our literature:

> This then? This is not a book. This is libel, slander, defamation of character. This is not a book, in the ordinary sense of the word. No, this is a

prolonged insult, a gob of spit in the face of Art, a kick in the pants to God, Man, Destiny, Time, Love, Beauty . . . what you will. I am going to sing for you, a little off key perhaps, but I will sing. I will sing while you croak, I will dance over your dirty corpse. . . .

> To sing you must first open your mouth. You must have a pair of lungs, and a little knowledge of music. It is not necessary to have an accordion, or a guitar. The essential thing is to *want* to sing. This then is a song. I am singing.[6]

What clod would be bored by this? And if Miller can free himself of the conventions of the novel as he writes, why shouldn't his readers be as free in their reading, tasting a book wherever and for only as long as they please? Miller wisely advises that "a book should be sought after even if it has only *one* great page in it: we must search for fragments, splinters, toenails, anything that has ore in it, anything that is capable of resuscitating the body and soul" (232). And one page of *Tropic of Cancer* has more exuberance in it than the whole of most other books.

As if these various objections to Henry Miller were not enough to damn him to oblivion, there is one more, which may be the subtlest and the most important of all: his *optimism*. It is simply not fashionable to be an optimist. And the more possessions we have, the easier it is to be glibly pessimistic. From comfortable circumstances we speak with authority of despair—that is, after making the necessary call to the TV repairman. Meanwhile, back in the fiction, we hold American technology and bureaucracy responsible for the death of the soul, considering anyone capable of being happy in this time and place an idiot.

Miller himself is known to some mainly as a critic of America, which is his approach in *The Air-Conditioned Nightmare*, where he repeats the worn attacks we have heard for years. In his unoriginal shouting Miller is not at his best. But what becomes fascinating about this book is the way his natural urge to rejoice prevails, as what begins as a diatribe on America's ugliness and sterility turns into a paean to unusual people and places. In spite of all he finds to attack, and the desire to make that attack, Miller naturally goes from a haughty antagonism to a song of wonder for America's loveliness. The Frenchman J. Rives Childs appreciates, as American critics have failed to do, that this work is to be cherished "not only for his tribute to France but also for his eloquent testimony regarding . . . the South. . . . one of the keenest appreciations of the South ever written and that is saying a great deal."[7] Miller is awed, too, by the American West. The Grand Canyon is "so grandiose, so sublime, so illusory, that when you come upon it for the first time you break down and weep with joy . . . it is one of the few spots on this earth which not only come up to all expectation but surpass it."[8] Out of bleakness Miller discovers the miracles that make a posture of despair untrue for him. And it is this capacity for wonder that shows him at his best.

Miller first rejoices in *Tropic of Cancer* for the act of creation, his writing. In the spirit of Genesis, he contradicts the notion, assumed in the modern period, that the artist's work is agony. "Divine creation, on the other hand, bears no such connotation. We do not think of sweat and tears in connection with the creation of the universe; we think of joy and light, and above all of play."[9] The theme of artist as sufferer is the focus of Edmund Wilson's well-known *The Wound and the Bow*, which examines the myth of the warrior Philoctetes, who is bitten by a snake on his way to fight and exiled because his wound produces such a horrible smell. Isolated on an island for ten years with the wound that will not heal, he is forced to become reflective, and in doing so he develops superior mental powers. As a result of energies stimulated by his suffering, Philoctetes comes to represent "the conception of superior strength as inseparable from disability."[10] Wilson points out that André Gide, in his *Philoctète*, is even more emphatic on this point, giving an implication "which must occur to the modern reader: the idea that genius and disease, like strength and mutilation, may be inextricably bound up together."[11] This concept has become so well established that in this century, with terrifying accuracy, it has been possible to predict the suicides of particular authors; the gruesome trend continues, perpetuating the image of artist as madman and martyr. Miller asks us to contradict this view, suggesting that although "we haven't had any healthy artists for centuries, . . . that's no reason why we can't."[12]

Perhaps Miller's hopefulness for the creator comes from the high-spirited painters he knew in Paris. Always a lover of clowns (he once wanted to be one), Miller was enchanted by the happy and comic creations of these artists:

> How grateful I am to have lived with these figures of Seurat. . . . They dwell in sunlight, in a harmony of form and rhythm which is sheer melody. And so with the clowns of Rouault, the angels of Chagall, the ladder and the moon of Mirò, his whole menagerie, in fact. So with Max Jacob, who never ceased to be a clown, even after he had found God. In word, in image, in act, all these blessed souls who kept me company have testified to the eternal reality of their vision. Their everyday world will one day become ours. It is ours now, in fact, only we are too impoverished to claim it for our own.[13]

Unlike most accounts of the act of writing, which is seen as the painful task of recording rotten truth, Miller sides with the painter for his appreciative art: "Whether you paint flowers, stars, horses or angels you acquire respect and admiration for all the elements which go to make up our universe. You don't call flowers friends and stars enemies, or horses Communists and angels Fascists. You accept them for what they are and you praise God that they are what they are."[14]

Miller loves this world, and Paris is very much the part of it that provides such pleasure in *Tropic of Cancer*. Like the writers of the twenties, he went there to escape; but for him it was more than a retreat where one could hide to write ugly things about America. He revels in an alternative life. For him in Paris, in spring,

> . . . the humblest mortal alive must feel that he dwells in paradise. But it was not only this—it was the intimacy with which his eyes rested upon the scene. It was *his* Paris. A man does not need to be rich, nor even a citizen, to feel this way about Paris. Paris is filled with poor people—the proudest and filthiest lot of beggars that ever walked the earth, it seems to me. And yet they give the illusion of being at home. It is that which distinguishes the Parisian from all other metropolitan souls. (61)

If the earlier expatriates enjoyed Paris as Miller did, the fiction of the period does not show it. Ironically, it is in the bleak thirties that Henry Miller comes like a wonderful joke, hedonistically proving that life can be fun.

Miller refers to Paris as a whore, which for him is a term of praise. His admiration of prostitutes is not merely for their humanity but because of their rare ability to live without security, to be free. He says of a favorite whore: "She would produce no children, contribute nothing to the welfare of the community, leave no mark upon the world in going. But

wherever she went she would make life easier, more attractive, more fragrant. And that is no little thing."[15]

Sex and food are on the same plane in *Tropic of Cancer*, but dinner has the edge. The protagonist is always hungry, always on the prowl for a free meal. "The mere thought of a meal—*another* meal—rejuvenates me. A meal!" (45). Miller acknowledges simply a preoccupation with food—how the idea of dinner keeps an afternoon alive. Although he is extremely hungry, his obsession with the next meal is amusingly normal. And that feast on a crust of bread is no mock heroic venture in this book. Unlike most food in literature, which is there to symbolize fastidiousness or excess, Miller's is real, tasty, life-giving food.

Despite the preoccupation with food and drink in *Tropic of Cancer*, we are spared the lethargy of overindulgence. The protagonist is unusually alert. As unlike Thoreau as Miller is, in obvious respects, *Walden* and *Tropic of Cancer* are similarly awake and clear-headed. *Cancer's* author might even qualify by Thoreau's standards as the one in a million who is "awake enough for effective intellectual exertion," even, perhaps, as the one in a hundred million awake enough for "a poetic or divine life."[16] A lean and hungry feeling pervades these two remarkable books, which show, as few books have, how a healthy attitude can change the world.

Miller rejoices in his robust physical health, which he equates with a happy mental condition. "Walking along the Champs-Elysées I keep thinking of my really superb health. When I say 'health' I mean optimism, to be truthful. Incurably optimistic!" (45). We so rarely hear anyone mention good health that Miller's account of the normal comes as a pleasant shock. And how quaint it is to meet gratitude.

Miller is ripely along in life by the time of *Tropic of Cancer*, and much of its wisdom springs from that fact. Perhaps like pity and compassion, appreciation is a sensation that comes late to us, only when we have worn out the melancholy ravings of youth and begin to understand that we will die. America's own youth and its preoccupation with the young, so often given as reasons for cultural deficiencies, may well be related to the failure to produce warmth in our literature. Miller agrees that " 'life begins at forty.' For the majority of men it is so, for it is only in middle age that the continuity of life, which death promises, begins to make itself felt and understood."[17] Miller was in his forties when he did his first successful writing, after following the styles of others and working for years at jobs he hated. He was also breaking from marriage, in which he never felt free. Although in *Tropic of Cancer* the protagonist claims to love his wife Mona (as he prowls happily after women in Paris), when she arrives his male freedom is curtailed by female demands, in traditional American fashion. Like the great adventurer Don Quixote, the protagonist of *Tropic of Cancer* must be without a family if he is to be about his creations. For both of these free souls, with maturity comes a tender appreciation for the gifts of food and drink, and one more chance to go down the road.

The most exhilarating discovery in *Tropic of Cancer* is the bliss of life without illusions, a theme Miller sings from the first page: "I have no money, no resources, no hopes. I am the happiest man alive" (1). And with nothing owned or expected, ah, no responsibility either. Acceptance of the world *as is* becomes Miller's key to satisfaction. And if a passive approach does nothing to improve a political or social situation (an aggressive approach is not effective either), Miller believes it *is* the way of individual creativity and the "law of love, which is based on absolute tolerance, the law which suffers or permits things to be as they are. Real love is never perplexed, never qualifies, never rejects, never demands."[18]

The startling thing in Miller is not his subject matter but his attitude toward it. As Orwell notes, his topics are as distasteful as anything in Céline's *Journey to the End of Night*, to which *Tropic of Cancer* has been compared. But the books have little else in common. Miller not only accepts but *embraces* his smelly world, while Céline's spirit is the expected one of disgust. Miller's is a form of Faustian heaven, where being alive is everything. However filthy Paris may be, it is never dead. Its energies, however, are not directed as they would be in America toward achievement and progress. "Over there you think of nothing but becoming President of the United States some day. Potentially every man is Presidential timber. Here it's different. Here every man is potentially a zero. If you become something or somebody it is an accident, a miracle. . . . But it's just because the chances are all against you, just because there is so little hope, that life is sweet over here" (135).

The zero approach, like Miller's attitude toward hunger and freedom generally, suggests a clean and exciting space that allows for life-giving movement. The creator must ensure himself of this freedom by constantly unloading baggage—patients, friends, admirers, possessions—in order to keep himself, as the Chinese say, " 'alive-and-empty.' "[19] While literature often enough attempts to persuade us to abandon our illusions for the sake of truth or self-preservation, Miller's purpose in doing so is that we might love life more. He asks that we change the nature of desire itself: "the monstrous thing is not that men have created roses out of this dung heap, but that, for some reason or other, they should want roses" (88).

In *The Smile at the Foot of the Ladder* Miller allegorizes this concept in a tale about Auguste, the clown, whose job is to lie at the foot of a ladder feigning ecstasy in order to make people laugh. His only delight in the role is the crowd's applause, and he is distraught when he loses the job. Then one night he dreams of falling to earth from a high ladder and landing on the ground as himself. In this he realizes the miracle of being alive and that the potential for joy exists only at the bottom of the ladder. Miller's philosophy of acceptance, "the gift of surrender," is epitomized by the clown, who makes the gesture symbolically. And "it is for us to make it real."[20]

In spite of the plethora of prophets of doom, joyful emotions must hide out in American hearts. Our literature is incomplete and frequently dishonest for so seldom illuminating them. The protagonist of *Tropic of Cancer*, wearied by the conventional pose of despair, proclaims that "everywhere I go people are making a mess of their lives. Everyone has his private tragedy. It's in the blood now—misfortune, ennui, grief, suicide. The atmosphere is saturated with disaster, frustration, futility" (11). Miller's emphasis here is noticeably on what people do to themselves, not on misfortunes that come from outside them. But his urge to accept responsibility for suffering is almost as unfashionable as the suggestion that happiness is possible.

According to Jacques Barzun, the "condition" of despair came into fashion early in the twentieth century and has altered little since then. As a result, writers for a long time have merely imitated an attitude that came about under very different circumstances from their own; they draw from the poison in the air without ever experiencing the particular destruction described. And they never let out the secret that they are sometimes happy. Barzun laments that critics, whose job is to give us new ideas, echo the writers of fiction in their message of hate against the world that has been in vogue for decades now, as they fall into "the dullest of conformities, the conformity of Dissent."[21]

One more reason why literature remains set in its grim track is certainly the mysterious difficulty of making the good dramatic. We expect noble characters to be dull and villains to be vital. In the words of Yeats, "the best lack all conviction, while the worst / Are full of passionate intensity." [22] Dostoevsky struggled to create saints who were dramatic, but Prince Mishkin and Alyosha never succeed as the devilish father Karamazov and the misery-loving Marmeladov do. As Miller says, "the literature of flight, of escape, of a neurosis is so brilliant that it almost makes one doubt the efficacy of health."[23] The subtlety of a quality such as kindness may make it difficult to portray dramatically. But what of the brilliantly fine moments of life, which are as earth-shaking as pain can be? Miller is daring enough to try for them.

American literature's failure to present warm emotions may be irrevocably shaped by the Puritan influence that gave us our first chilling classic, *The Scarlet Letter*. But whether the notion that pleasure is sinful be cause or symptom of a psychological condition, our literature is well established in terms of Freud's unpleasure principle. People often are uncomfortable with happiness. Miller dramatizes this truth in a scene in *Sexus* where a man stands up in a restaurant proclaiming that on his wedding anniversary he is still in love and would like everyone to share his happiness. But instead of joining him in celebration, the other diners refuse to admit what they see. Miller is not first noted for his psychological depth, but he shows considerable insight here into the phenomenon that people lack the honesty and the courage to be happy, and that they are uncomfortable with the happiness of others. Laugh and the world does not laugh with you.

In "The Fate of Pleasure" Lionel Trilling marks the demise of pleasure as a literary subject with the romantic poets of the late eighteenth century. Wordsworth's "Preface," with its often-quoted "emotion recollected in tranquillity," also refers to the "grand elementary principle of pleasure," a concept which has been ignored. Trilling suggests that it was with Keats, who showed pleasure at its most sensual level, that the idea of pleasure came into the sincerest doubt. And since then, with our increasing access to luxuries, we have become increasingly suspicious of their effect upon us and so have made "destruction of what is considered the specious good" a standard subject of modern fiction.[24] Presumably the attack is made against the ugliness and dehumanizing qualities of technology, but actually the belief is that the values of pleasure embraced by the bourgeois world hamper our individuality. To yield to pleasure in our time is to consent to the conditional nature of man (and thus not to be free), which is just what Dostoevsky's underground man refused to do, not merely because he envied what society had, which he did, but because he insisted on being unlike everyone else, no matter how disgusting and self-destructive he had to be. It is this factor, suggests Trilling, that puts Dostoevsky, rather than the sunshine-seeking Nietzsche, to whom he is sometimes compared, at the spiritual center of our time.[25]

Some of the prophesies of the yea-saying Miller are eerily coming true. In 1944 he predicted that the East and the West would meet in a "series of deathlike embraces" which would lead to a new coming together with the East. He also foresaw a great emancipation of women, suggesting that the "next great impersonation of the future" would be a woman.[26] His most extreme and optimistic statement is that there would be an "epoch of the threshold," a time in which man and artist would not be separate, and all people would live more creatively.[27]

Miller's most ambitious hopes may never be realized, but they do remind us that civilization does not necessarily decline and that in spite of inhumanity and suffering, now, as always, joy exists. If one of literature's first functions is to record the extraordinary, then the subject of happiness might now be approached as an *unusual* topic. As it becomes more difficult to arouse an audience by demonstrating life's horrors, the writer might startle his readers with the revelation that life is still a miracle. Sometime joy might knock you off your feet. And there may be peace. As Miller says at the end of his great book,

> After everything had quietly sifted through my head a great peace came over me. Here, where the river gently winds through the girdle of hills, lies a soil so saturated with the past that however far back the mind roams one can never detach it from its human background. Christ, before my eyes there shimmered such a golden peace that only a neurotic could dream of turning his head away. (286)

It is a stingy lie to hold back praise. Say it. The end is not yet.

Notes

1. Herman Melville, Letter to Nathaniel Hawthorne, in *The Portable Melville*, ed. Jay Leyda (New York: Viking, 1952), p. 428.
2. "Miller: Only the Beginning," *The Nation* (Nov. 18, 1961), p. 399.
3. *Tropic of Capricorn* (New York: Grove Press, 1961), p. 290.
4. *A Collection of Essays* (New York: Harcourt Brace, 1946), p. 218.
5. Ibid., p. 217.
6. (New York: Grove Press, 1961), pp. 1–2. Further page references to this edition are included in the text.
7. "Collecting Henry Miller: or, What Henry Miller Means to Me," in *Collector's Quest: The Correspondence of Henry Miller and J. Rives Childs, 1947–1965*, ed. Richard Clement Wood (Charlottesville: Univ. Press of Virginia, 1968), p. 181.
8. (New York: New Directions, 1945), p. 240.
9. Henry Miller, "Of Art and the Future," in *The Henry Miller Reader*, ed. Lawrence Durrell (New York: New Directions, 1959), p. 237.
10. (New York: Oxford Univ. Press, 1965), p. 235.
11. Ibid., p. 237.
12. *Henry Miller: Letters to Anaïs Nin*, ed. Gunther Stuhlmann (New York: Putnam, 1965), p. 190.
13. *The Smile at the Foot of the Ladder* (New York: New Directions, 1948), pp. 48–49.
14. *Stand Still Like the Hummingbird* (New York: New Directions, 1962), p. 40.
15. *Quiet Days in Clichy* (New York: Grove Press, 1965), p. 61.
16. *Walden* (New York: Random House, 1950), p. 81.
17. "The Wisdom of the Heart," *The Henry Miller Reader*, p. 259.
18. Ibid., p. 264.
19. Ibid., p. 260.
20. *The Smile at the Foot of the Ladder*, p. 47.
21. *The Energies of Art* (New York: Harper, 1956), p. 16.
22. "The Second Coming," *The Collected Poems of W.B. Yeats* (New York: Macmillan, 1965), p. 185.
23. "The Universe of Death," *The Henry Miller Reader*, p. 206.
24. *Beyond Culture* (New York: Viking, 1965), p. 76.
25. Ibid., p. 77.
26. "Of Art and the Future," pp. 232, 241.
27. Ibid., p. 232.

Joaquin Miller
Cincinnatus Hiner Miller

1837–1913

Joaquin Miller was born Cincinnatus Hiner Miller on September 8, 1837, near Liberty, Indiana. In 1852 Miller's family headed west in the gold rush, settling in Oregon. Miller attended the West Point School in Oregon and engaged in various skirmishes with the Indians (in one of which he was nearly fatally wounded) before heading to the California gold fields. A brief enrollment at Columbia College in Eugene, Oregon, ended when the school burned down in 1858, and Miller resumed life as an itinerant miner in Idaho and Montana. Returning to Eugene in 1862, Miller married Theresa Dyer and became editor of the pro-slavery Eugene City *Democrat-Register*.

Miller practiced law from 1864 to 1869, moving his family, now increased with two sons, to Canyon City. His first volume of poems, *Specimens*, had been published to mixed reviews in 1868; after unsuccessfully trying to curry Bret Harte's favor in San Francisco, Miller left for England to seek literary fame. *Songs of the Sierras* was published in 1871 to enthusiastic notices, and Miller was praised by W. M. Rossetti, Swinburne, Tennyson, and others. The novel *Life among the Modocs* (1873) ensured his reputation.

After lengthy stays on the Continent Miller returned to America, settling in New York. He had divorced his wife Theresa in 1869, and in 1879 married Abigail Leland, who gave birth to his beloved daughter Juanita. After living for four years in a log-cabin in Washington, D.C., Miller in 1887 bought some property in San Francisco and built his estate, The Hights, living there for the rest of his life. He became a leading member of the San Francisco *literati*, which included Ambrose Bierce, his longtime friend Ina Coolbrith, and George Sterling. In 1893 his Utopian novel *The Building of the City Beautiful* was highly received. Miller's collected poems were issued in six volumes in 1909–10. Joaquin Miller died on February 17, 1913.

Miller's pseudonymous first name was derived from Joaquin Murietta, a California bandit who was responsible for many murders and thefts during the gold rush.

Personal

As far asunder as the poles and the antithesis of Oscar Wilde was the next poet to dedicate a verse to me. He was Joaquin Miller, the poet of the Sierras, a child of nature and perhaps the most picturesque personality of the literary world. It was at Lord Houghton's house in Arlington Street, London, that I happened upon the famous Californian. ⟨. . .⟩

Often after this we met. He became a lion of the literary world; his poems were on every table. Rossetti, Swinburne, Tennyson, were among his admirers. He had lived a life of adventure, too, beginning by running away from school to mine for gold. He had been adopted by Indians, been imprisoned for some imaginary offence, had escaped from jail through the aid of an Indian girl, swam a river with her to freedom, and married her—all before he was twenty! At least, that was the story which was circulated in London, and which added piquancy to the interest created by his virile personality.

Ten years ago, and within a week of his death, I was so anxious to see him again that I motored over with some mutual friends to his home in the Piedmont Hills at the back of Oakland, California, where I was playing at the time. After a lovely drive, we gradually ascended the foot-hills of the Sierras until we reached a simple gate and entered his property, "The Hights." Winding up the beautifully wooded slopes—every tree planted by his own hand, he told me—we came abruptly upon his house, a wooden bungalow overgrown with vines. Although he knew I was coming, my visit was conditional on his being well enough to receive visitors, and I felt suddenly reluctant to intrude on the sick man, and afraid I might be unwelcome!

However, as the car stopped at the foot of an impossibly steep incline some yards below the hut, the door was thrown open and Mrs. Miller and her daughter came forward to meet us. We were at once taken into the living-room, which was large and occupied the centre of the ground floor, and there lay the great nature poet. His gaunt, thin form reposed in a tent-like bed, covered with a patchwork quilt, and with buffalo robes thrown over that. His white hair flowed on to the pillow, and his beard, grown very long, gave him a truly patriarchal appearance. A small uncurtained window on the farther side of the bed allowed the strong sunlight to outline Miller's fine features. He clasped my hand, looked in my face for what seemed to be an age before he spoke, and at last he said:

"The same eyes, the same blue eyes! Where did you get those big blue eyes?"

Then he motioned me to sit near him. I told him how glad I was to be allowed to see him, and he answered:

"Who would refuse to see Lillie Langtry? When you reach heaven St. Peter will open the gates wide." (I am not so optimistic.)

The walls of the room were literally papered with photographs and woodcuts of famous people he had known, many of which he requested Mrs. Miller to take down to show me at close quarters. Among these was a little faded picture of his friend Tennyson.

In due time his wife arranged a tea-table in the room of the dying man. The daughter, Juanita, soft-footed in moccasins, presided, and tempted me with epicurean and original dishes. There were pickled peaches, hot cakes, fresh goose livers, salted fish, and many other excellent things. The poet sipped a little honey.

The afternoon meal over, we went out and strolled through the property until, farther up the mountain side, we came upon a lane embowered in greenery, consecrated by a bishop, and through which Joaquin Miller desired his body to be carried to the funeral pyre, built with his own hands on a rocky promontory, and intended for his cremation. It is gruesome to describe, but, in reality, it was a beautiful idea to wish to sink into nothingness in view of the mighty Pacific, and to have his ashes float on the winds that blow through the Golden Gate.—LILLIE LANGTRY, *The Days I Knew*, 1925, pp. 94–98

⟨. . .⟩ I had an amusing experience with Joaquin Miller, who, when in the height of his fame, and always dressed as a cowboy, had made an immense sensation in the East and in London. He was now living in retirement on a hill across the bay, facing San Francisco. Quite recently he had written a poem on the passing of Tennyson, which I cut out of the local paper and sent to the New York *Critic*. I still think it one of the most beautiful tributes to a great man ever written. I summoned my courage and wrote him a letter expressing my enthusiasm; he replied with apparent gratification, and I invited him to call on me. An afternoon was appointed. When Hannah had ushered him into the parlor she came back to me with her face very red from suppressed mirth. "Oh, ma'am!" she giggled. "But he's a sight! All the children on the sidewalk were hooting at him, and he's dyed his hair!"

I went into the parlor. He had struck an attitude, and gazed at me silently as I entered. In truth he was a singular figure, and I didn't wonder that he had made a sensation in London, for the English like Americans to be as different from themselves as possible. He wore a black broadcloth suit, the trousers tucked into boots—with high heels!—that reached almost to his waist. His shirt had no collar but his neck was encircled by a lace scarf. On his head was a sombrero, which he removed with a sweeping bow as I entered, and I saw that his long hair, touching his shoulders, was gray on top, and ended in a series of stiff "rat tails" that were dyed a bright orange.

I told him how glad I was to see him, and we sat down. Still he had not uttered a word. An American woman is always willing to bear the burden of conversation, and I rattled on, although growing disconcerted by his persistent silence and his round unwinking stare. Finally I said tartly: "Have you lost your voice? Suppose *you* say something for a change." He fetched a sigh that might have come from the soles of his cowboy boots, and then his voice rumbled forth heavy-laden with tragedy. "What a pity!" he groaned. "What a pity we are both blondes! O-h-h-h, I would like to go up and take God by the beard!" And he raised his arm and waggled it as if in performance of the act. I repressed the obvious retort, and five minutes later he shot out without a word of farewell. But I was quite satisfied. It was my first experience with a genius; and no lion I have ever met has roared more accommodatingly. —GERTRUDE ATHERTON, *Adventures of a Novelist*, 1932, pp. 112–14

General

⟨*Songs of the Sierras*⟩ is a truly remarkable book. To glance through its pages is to observe a number of picturesque things picturesquely put, expressed in a vivid flowing form and melodious words, and indicating strange, outlandish, and romantic experiences. The reader requires no great persuasion to leave off mere skimming and set-to at regular perusal; and, when he does so, he finds the pleasurable impression confirmed and intensified.

⟨. . .⟩ The reader will hardly need ⟨. . .⟩ to be told that Byron is the poet whose spirit most visibly sways and overshadows that of Joaquin Miller. The latter is indeed a writer of original mind and style; and there is a weighty difference between a Californian who has really engaged in, or at least had lifelong cognizance of, all sorts of wild semi-civilized adventure, and a noble lord to whom the like range of experience forms the distraction of a season or the zest of a tour. Still, the poetic analogy is strikingly visible, and has a very mixed influence upon Mr. Miller's work. On one side, taking interest as he does, like Byron, in adventurous picturesque personages, with the virtues and vices of the life of defiance, full of passion and resource (for Mr. Miller has the art of making us respect the intellectual calibre of all his characters, whatever they may do, and however closely they may approximate to savages), he is lifted at once above the mild and mediocre or the merely photographic levels of work: on the other hand, he exhibits life not only under the rudimentary and incomplete conditions which his subject-matter suggests, but with an effect of abortiveness and gloom due partly, no doubt, to the Byronic tradition, and so extreme as to be almost morbid. His interest in life seems to be very much that of a gambler, who plays a stake, conscious that the chances are against him; or, one might rather say, of a man who watches a game played with loaded dice, and who sees his friends ruined by an undenounceable conspiracy. In "Ina," for instance, gratuitous misery is poured forth, as from a bucket, with a liberally cruel hand. It is intensely unsatisfactory to be told of a lovely, girlish, and wealthy widow, steeped in amorous grace, constancy, and spirit, making love to the hot-blooded youth who has adored her all his life, and whom she has confessedly adored—only to be repulsed with a stolid obtuse *morgue*, and then to wrap herself round in her dignity, and close the last avenue to a right mutual understanding. We see Love assassinated before our eyes by two lovers, who can find no better employment than persistently carving the death's-head and marrow-bones over his headstone. In this tale the very *motif* has a twist of dislocation: in some others, as our summary will have shown, the conception, though mainly monotonous, is interesting in a high degree, but the poet shows little gift for constructing a story. In "Arizonian," for example—an excellent and truly engrossing poem—the reader is unable to credit the central fact; namely, that the gold-washer, having for twenty-one years lost sight of his early love so entirely as not to know that she has been married for a long series of years, travels in good faith to search her out and wed her, and accepts at first sight her daughter as being her authentic self. It might perhaps be added, without cynicism, that the daughter, who so absolutely realizes to the many-laboured gold-washer the person of his long-lost love, should really have stood to his feelings in that relation; and that his natural and compensatory course would have been to court her on the spot.

Excitement and ambition may be called the twin geniuses of Mr. Miller's poetical character. Everything is to him both vital and suggestive; and some curious specimens might be culled of the fervid interfusion of external nature and the human soul in his descriptive passages. The great factors of the natural world—the sea, the mountains, the sun, moon, and stars—become personalities, animated with an intense life and a dominant possession. He loves the beasts and birds, and finds them kin to him: a snake has its claim of blood-relationship. At times he runs riot in overcharged fancies, which in "Ina" especially, recall something of the manner of Alexander Smith, whether in characterizing the objects of nature, or in the frenzied aspirations of the human spirit. It should be understood, however, that the only poet to whom he bears a considerable or essential analogy is Byron. In "Arizonian" indeed the resemblance of diction and versification is rather to Browning, and some passages might seem to be directly

founded on the "Flight of the Duchess": but I learn that this resemblance is merely fortuitous. As such, it is an interesting reciprocal confirmation of the value of the peculiarities of narrative form belonging to both poems. At times also there is a recognizable ring of Swinburne, especially as regards alliteration, and a vigorous elastic assonance, not only in the syllables but in the collocation of words and phrases.

There is little space, and not much occasion, for dwelling on verbal or other minute defects. The swing and melody of the verse are abundant: yet many faulty lines or rhymes, with some decided perversities in this way, could be cited; along with platitudes of phrase, or odd and inadmissible words. All these are minor matters. Mr. Miller has realized his poetic identity under very exceptional conditions, highly favourable to spirit and originality, but the contrary so far as nitid completion or the accepted rules of composition are concerned. He is a poet, and an admirable poet. His first works prove it to demonstration, and superabundantly; and no doubt his future writings will reinforce the proof with some added maturity and charm. He is not the sort of man to be abashed or hurt by criticism. Let me add that the less attention he pays to objections, even if well-founded, and the more he continues to write out of the fulness of his own natural gifts, the better it will probably be for both himself and his readers. America may be proud of him.—W. M. ROSSETTI, *Academy*, June 15, 1871, pp. 301–3

Well, Joaquin Miller is a *good* poet,—a very extraordinary poet,—one of the most original poets of the century,—perhaps the very greatest of all American poets. At least, such is our opinion. We are quite prepared for criticisms. We are willing to acknowledge that many of Miller's literary faults are serious ones; we can grant that his work is rough and lacks scholarly polish,—that it is replete with redundancies and repetitions,—that it is sometimes disfigured by affectations,—that it is not dignified by obedience to the canons of artistic construction,—that some of it is almost incomprehensible,—that more of it is open to ridicule,—that, as a whole, in point of finish it cannot be compared with the work of other really great poets of our day. Miller has never served, and never cared to serve a slow apprenticeship at the grand old trade of metre-smiths and verse-jewelers;—he may be regarded merely as a dealer in virgin ore, a speculator in uncut stones of price. Nevertheless we do not hesitate to affirm that there is a richness in his ores,—that there is such a largeness and a lustre in his jewels,—that none of the literary goldsmiths and lapidaries of to-day can afford to ignore him. Men who affect never to have read Miller, or to despise his products, steal his fancies and spoil them in the stealing. Men who have really never had one of his books in their hands, quote him without knowing it. Fragments of pyrites may be found among his samples of gold,—flints may be discovered among his emeralds; but the gold and the jewels have such luminosity and such purity that the literary world would be foolish not to forget and to forgive the adulteration. Miller has been parodied, but it required no ordinary verse maker to parody him,—and no vapid poet, no singer not possessing strong originality, can be successfully parodied at all. Above everything else Miller has originality,—strong, Homeric originality,—the originality of that born genius whose impression is ineffaceable. Here and there the influence of other poets may be traced in his work; but the savage splendor of his own thought shines out with such dazzling that one instantly feels the American superior to his European teacher. What poet, ancient or modern, wrote more puissant lines than these:—

> . . . I saw the lightning's gleaming rod
> Reach forth, and write upon the sky
> The awful autograph of God. . . .

All the poetry of the Orient furnishes nothing finer;—the Japanese singer who described the Creator as a mighty artist, painting with Light for a brush spoke more feebly.

⟨. . .⟩ Miller is essentially a poet of nature,—a wild and untrained singer if critics so please; but a singer of might, a speaker of immense force, like those Indian orators whom he himself describes as "hurling thought like cannon-shot." He has traveled much, and sung in many parts of the world; and he revealed himself not less great when he chanted of Italy than when he sang of the far West. ⟨. . .⟩

Miller is often diffuse, rambling;—the "Isles of the Amazons," and even the marvelous "Ship in the Desert,"—offer remarkable instances of this fault. Yet in spite of this occasional and seemingly purposeless diffuseness, there are few living poets so capable of compressing large ideas into a limited space, or of creating so majestic and impressive a picture with equally few strokes of the brush. As an instance, we might cite the magnificent prelude to "The Tale of the Tall Alcalde":—

> Thou Italy of the Occident!
> Land of flowers and summer climes,
> Of holy priests and horrid crimes;
> Land of the cactus and sweet cocoa!—
> Richer than all the Orient
> In gold and glory, in want and woe,
> In self-denial, in days misspent,
> In truth and treason, in gold and guilt,
> In ivied ruins and altars low,
> In battered walls and blood misspilt,—
> Glorious, gory Mexico!

⟨. . .⟩ For a time misfortune silenced his muse. But that muse has uttered some of the grandest thoughts and pictured some of the most impressive things belonging to the literature of the nineteenth century. There are passages in Miller's work that deserve to live as long as English is spoken, and that probably will live, metamorphosed, in the languages of other peoples.—LAFCADIO HEARN, "Joaquin Miller" (1886), *Essays on American Literature*, ed. Sanki Ichikawa, 1929, pp. 203–9

It cannot, of course, be said that Joaquin Miller is a great poet. But that he did excellent service in the cause of American poetry cannot be denied. He was by no means a poor technician, and it is only in his careless moments that he fails to write musical verse. He was as capable in the meters which he set for himself as his predecessors, and few American poets have surpassed him in the use of iambic tetrameter.

His imagination was capable of extraordinary flights, sustained flights; and he painted his West in such colors that the men of his day were lured to that region to see for themselves what the poet had described so lavishly. With his legends and lore and his own inventions in the subject matter of poetry he contributed to the culture of the West. Unlike Bret Harte, who brought to the West an Easterner's culture and point of view, Joaquin Miller was of the West, and his culture, such as it is, was developed there. He grew up in actual contact with frontiersmen, and he helped them to interpret their life and their world. *Songs of the Sierras* and *A Song of Creation* are at least preludes to the unwritten Western epics. Finally, Miller wrote "on the spot"—if not quite literally, almost so—and his songs have the indigenous qualities that go with firsthand inspiration. With reference to his diction, while it lacks something of the present tendency toward highly individualized language, for Miller was at his most conventional in this respect, it is a diction that wears well and that bears the stamp of his personality. He is distinctly an American poet.

Too suggestive of a defunct Byronism, too indulgent of the melodramatic, too luxuriant in its descriptive passages, the poetry of Joaquin Miller, despite its limitations, is amazingly alive at times and occasionally beautiful. A few of Miller's poems, no doubt, are permanent additions to American literature.—MARTIN SEVERIN PETERSON, "Literary Technique," *Joaquin Miller: Literary Frontiersman*, 1937, pp. 177–78

AMBROSE BIERCE
San Francisco Examiner, January 30, 1898

The Whitaker & Ray Company, San Francisco, successors to the late and deeply unlamented Bancroft Company, have published *The Complete Poetical Works of Joaquin Miller*. This title is a little misleading. The book does not contain all, nor nearly all the works, more or less poetical, that Mr. Miller has acknowledged as his very own, but only such as he seems to care for now; and many of these have been abbreviated and otherwise revised with an unsparing hand. Nor are the book's contents altogether poetical; besides the preface and appendix there are prose notes to many of the longer poems, making altogether a considerable body of matter, mostly biographical, largely irrelevant, sometimes false, and frequently silly. The book would have been better without it. In truth, Mr. Miller cannot be trusted to write prose, nor to write of himself, which means about the same thing; for the moment he unfixes his eyes from the summit of Parnassus the charms of his own picturesque personality lure him from the path of truth into the confusing byways, conducting into the Land That Is Not—whereof he is king, parliament and people. He may be described as the St. Simeon Stylites of literature, perched atop of his capital I, and occasionally removing his rapt regard from his own toes to burst into song of the outlying universe.

In the prose part of Mr. Miller's book the reader will catch a new note—that of penitence. It is, however, the penitence which finds expression in denial of sin. A weaker manifestation of this feeling once led him to "hurl back the allegation" that he had stolen a horse, affirming that it was a mule: he is now willing to forget the mule.

Seriously, it is rather late for Joaquin to complain of the "fearfully coarse insults and falsehoods" that pursued him, "simply because" he had "at such cost" glorified his mountain environment. The insults and falsehoods may be granted—what writer of distinction escapes them? But the provocation is insufficiently stated. Indubitably they had their origin in his own affectations—in his identification of himself with his heroes—in his weakness for incredible and untrue narratives of his personal adventures and travels—in the transparent cloud of mystery with which he has always loved to envelop a really commonplace early life. Even now in his age, when from a failing memory of his famous arrow wound he sometimes limps with the wrong leg, he is obviously reluctant to surrender his lifelong claim to the laurels of the bandit Joaquin Murietta, and altogether indisposed to forego his new and remarkable pretensions to classical education. As to his claim to fellowship and companionship with the distinguished men of two worlds, it is the breath of his nostrils and the soul of his heart; he affirms it with a diligence that is proof against fatigue, or irrelevance which, like death, hath all seasons for its own. If sometimes he errs as to the true titles of his illustrious, and now mostly deceased, intimates (as in the instance of the French Prince Imperial whom he calls "Prince Napoleon") the fault is perhaps not entirely his. Like the man who bewailed his marriage to a widow these personages were possibly guilty of "contributory negligence." They should have been thoughtful enough to "define their positions" to the slack attention of that careless Western observer.

All this may seem out of place and ungracious; and if these remarks were intended as grave criticism of "poetical works" it certainly would be. But such is not the case. Mr. Miller has chosen to "mix with his sacred flame the flame profane" of a monstrous and insistent personal vanity to which everything is fuel, and the turbid light of it invites objection. It is hardly too much to say that every line of the prose in this book is both needless and foolish.

In nothing is Mr. Miller more foolish than in his convictions about his art—which to him is not an art, but merely the spontaneous utterance of a born singer's untrained emotions. As an example of the insupportable stuff that a really great poet can write when, destitute of intellect and real training, he abandons the domain of feeling for that of thought, take this from the conclusion of his preface—an instruction to poets. "Finally, use the briefest little bits of baby Saxony words at hand. The world is waiting for ideas, not words. . . . We have not time for words. A man who uses a great big-sounding word when a short one will do is to that extent a robber of time. A jewel that depends greatly on its setting is not a great jewel. When the Messiah of American literature comes he will come singing, so far as may be, in words of a single syllable."

Mr. Miller himself is not a master of condensation; prolixity is his "besetting sin," as in "The Sea of Fire," where he requires no fewer than one hundred and fifteen lines to relate the landing of a ship in fair weather with nothing to prevent; but in this prose passage he has managed to pack a remarkable number of schoolboy errors into a very small space. Many words of one syllable are strong and sweet, but a number of them together are feeble, dull, unmelodious. In poetry, especially, they are to be avoided. Some red idiot of the wild has written one entire poem in monosyllables, and every few years it makes the circuit of the newspapers as a glittering example of what can be done in that way. I have no doubt that it had much to do with the genesis of Mr. Miller's theory—and no doubt, either, that if he had happened to write it himself he would incontinently have chucked it into the cuspidor where it belongs. A line of verse in monosyllables is painful, two are insupportable, and three would make a boy strike his father.

Our words of one syllable are commonly Saxon words, that is to say, the words of a primitive people without a wide range of thought, feeling, and sentiment. One can express in them only what their inventors had to express; the richer thoughts and higher emotions must clothe themselves in the words of peoples to whom they are known—in the ductile derivatives of the Norman-French, the Greek, and the incomparable Latin. It is to the unlearned only that our brief, bald Saxon words seem the only natural, graphic, and sufficient ones.

"We have not time for words," quoth he! As if poetry were a thing to be devoured along with the breakfast egg of the business man with one eye on the page and the other on the clock. Mr. Miller is justly wroth when a money-grubbing wretch inquires if the planting of olive trees will pay, and here he would himself go pruning away the rich exuberances of our noble tongue in the interest of the car-chasers and the quick-lunchers who hoard their minutes as a miser his coins.

Begging Mr. Miller's pardon, thought and emotion in poetry are jewels that depend very much indeed on their setting. If they did not, his distinction as a poet would be less than it is by much, for his charm does not inhere in the greatness and sweetness of his thoughts, but in the felicity of their expression—not so much in what he has to say as in how he says it. It is very rare indeed that he justifies his declaration that he is "of the kings of thought," but his poetry is none the worse for that; for philosophy is one thing and poetry another. The two may acceptably go together, or remain apart; but certainly the jewel, if present, has an added value if well set. Least of all poets of his rank can Mr. Miller afford to extol matter over manner. It is commonly said, and doubtless believed, that biography is a great help to the understanding of literature—that one may profitably go to an author's life for light upon his work. This is one of those popular errors which certainly low intelligences sedulously promote; for they thrive by writing about writers and find their account in dignifying a vulgar and impudent curiosity regarding an author's personal affairs as an enlightened interest in literature. The truth is that nothing is more false and misleading than biography—except autobiography. When the "subject" is an author it operates to prevent, or rather to postpone, a clear judgment of his work and rank. As a rule there is no relation between the character and the work of a man strong enough and wise enough to write what is worth considering; the apparent relation is almost wholly the work of the biographers, who, knowing little of the character (and who really does know much of the character of another?), base their account of it upon what they find, or think they find, in the work. As an author's own account of himself, it is like anybody's account of himself—altogether untrustworthy, with an added incredibility from his knowledge of the credibility of his readers, who from a distinguished author will accept anything with the unquestioning faith of a pet pig at the feeding trough. Among the several reasons why in literary matters the judgment of posterity is better than that of an author's contemporaries, the chief is that posterity knows less about his life and character, and is in a position to consider his work on its merits without prepossession or prejudice, just as if it had fallen down from the clouds, or grown up from the ground, without human agency. And that is the way that all must eventually be judged, excepting those few unfortunates whose biographies (or autobiographies) are themselves works of permanent literary vitality. It is not likely that Doctor Johnson will ever be granted the justice of a hearing before his judges without that smirking Boswell being present to darken counsel. None of the poems in Mr. Miller's book needed any "sidelights" thrown upon it, biographical or other. A poem that does would better not have been written—it is not literature. These prose commentaries and narratives are not only "impertinent," but as the obvious expression of a deplorable personal vanity, offensive. Worst of all, they are largely untrue, as I am in a position to affirm, for I have Mr. Miller's true history pigeonholed, along with that of another Pacific Coast celebrity. The sooner his prose vagaries are forgotten the better it will be for his reputation as a poet, and he could not very well have better advice than to be told to publish another and final edition of his *Complete Poetical Works* without a line of prose to discredit it. In impugning Mr. Miller's veracity, or, rather, in plainly declaring that he has none, I should be sorry to be understood as attributing a graver moral delinquency than he really has. He cannot, or will not, tell the truth, but never tells a malicious or thrifty falsehood. From his incursions into the realm of romance he returns with clean and empty hands. Excepting for his vanity and inveracity he is an honorable and high-minded man. That he is a poet of high rank is so well understood that I have no intention of reviewing here those of his poems which, by preserving them in this book, he declares to be his own choice from among the much more that he has written and published. Despite his prolixity, his tiresome repetitions, his frequent hyperbole, and more frequent unnaturalness; despite, too, the general thinness of his thought,

Mr. Miller has, in my judgment, the greatest natural gift of song of any American except Poe. That he lacks the moral sanity and intellectual training to make the most of it is a misfortune that lacks little of the character of a national calamity.

VAN WYCK BROOKS
"The Byron of the Sierras"
Sketches in Criticism
1932, pp. 236–40

Joaquin Miller's handwriting is—or used to be, in the days when there were more to care about it—a byword among autograph-collectors. When I was a boy one of my friends wrote to the poet asking for his signature. He replied with not one signature but twenty: scraps of verse he had written, portraits of himself clipped from newspapers, "sentiments" scrawled on bits of paper and signed with Indian hieroglyphics. A bountiful harvest indeed for one stilted boyish note to have reaped! What did it matter that, turn it about as we might, we could scarcely decipher a word of all this extravagant script the poet had showered upon us?

We were grateful to the kindly poet; we were also duly impressed. This handwriting was appropriately barbaric; but not until years later did I discover that there was a motive in its illegibility. I then learned from another poet who had had commercial dealings with the old man that in epistolary discussions of the problems of real estate Joaquin Miller's handwriting became, and consistently remained, very legible indeed. But what literary man is without his vanity? If the democratic American bard forgoes the privilege of shocking the grocers, who is to judge him harshly for wishing to impress schoolboys? One is only amused to note that for ways that are dark, or dusky, the Christian pioneer is quite as peculiar as the Heathen Chinee. These apostles of the simple life, these lovers of nature and scorners of civilization, and all its duplicity and complexity—how far from simple they often are themselves! Truly, as Henry Adams said, "Simplicity is the most deceitful mistress that ever betrayed man."

Certainly Joaquin Miller was far from simple. If the evidence of his autograph is insufficient, glance at his photograph. The long white beard, the high boots, that aspect of the *muzhik* philosopher, are plainly reminiscent of Tolstoy; but the boots are patent-leather boots, such as Buffalo Bill might have worn at a presidential reception, and there is something that suggests the gentleman-gambler of the old mining-camps in the carefully curled moustache that adorns the prophet's beard. As one studies this theatrical apparition, one becomes more and more fascinated; the word "pose" of which people used to be so lavish entirely fails to quiet one's curiosity. If the face is the portrait of the soul, then there was never a more singular revelation of conflicting attitudes, of incompatible desires. This man, we say to ourselves, has fed on the dream of Tolstoy, and there we have the communist Joaquin Miller who wrote *The Building of the City Beautiful*. But the moustache seems to add: "Do not take this communism too seriously. I wish to keep on terms with a society where the real-estate agent is the leading citizen." And the patent-leather boots chime in: "I've been a cowboy. I've been a woolly desperado. Fifty cents admission." If you are under fifteen, the photograph impresses you as much as the autograph. If you are over thirty, you feel, first the absurdity, and then the pathos of it.

For what a drama that career was! One may not greatly admire *The Songs of the Sierras*: they are somewhat coarse and gaudy. Besides, they are too evidently derivative. In essence, Joaquin Miller's Sierras are merely a literary reflection of Byron's Alps; the rhythms are Byron's, too, and would this Western poet ever have conceived his brigands and filibusters if Byron had not given him the models in his Giaours and his Corsairs? These flowers of Byron are gaudy enough indeed, sunflowers at best, if not actual interlopers in the garden of poetry; and in Joaquin Miller the selfsame seeds grew up outside the garden altogether. But whoever denied the presence in that work of a certain exuberant force, a richness of temperament, that energy, in short (however unmodulated and uncontrolled), of which Matthew Arnold said that poetry is "mainly an affair"? It was the want of art, of the disciplined feeling which lies behind art, that left this work not poetry but journalism; but the energy was there, the germ was there, and what became of that? Glance once more at our poet's photograph. A part of the secret, perhaps, may be divined in this face and figure.

What one sees, written as it were all over it, is the word environment. Here is the professional Californian; and here is something else, something very like a mountebank. And if one knows how the pioneers regarded the poet as a type, how instinctively they despised him as a drone and a molly-coddle, one can understand these two aspects of Joaquin Miller. He was obliged to make amends for being a poet by showing that the poet had a pragmatic value in the pioneer scheme of things. There one has the professional Californian, the walking advertisement of California, in all its aboriginal pictur-esqueness. And what is the natural impulse of a man who feels his rôle despised but to play that part melodramatically, as a sort of protest? There one has the mountebank. Between these two lines of activity, what energy was there left for the poet, the poet who dreamed of a communistic Utopia, to invest in his own personal development? What at first had been a spontane-ous expression became, when he returned to California from his triumphs in London, a factitious glorification of pioneering in the abstract. No one who has read his '49 needs to be told to what depths of artistic infamy he was willing to descend in order to keep the name of a local patriot. No one who remembers the assiduous dithyrambs, in prose and verse alike, on the subject of Californian scenery, which he pumped out of himself for a generation, will mistake the note of the press-agent or doubt that Joaquin Miller was an "asset" of the State of his adoption. There was the pragmatic value of the poet in the pioneer scheme of things! And our Byron of the Sierras was compelled to prove it, as the price of his survival. He was so much the pioneer himself, so unconscious indeed, that he probably never felt it as a violation of his own proper freedom. Yet this alone was enough to kill the poet in him.

And that other activity? That hardest of hard work, that posing, as people used to call it, which is, in reality, the counterbalancing of one's feeling of inferiority by extravagant assertions of oneself? We all remember the story of his début in London, the story of that dinner in the midst of which he drew from his pocket two cigars and, thrusting them both into his mouth at once, exclaimed, with a great burst of fire and smoke, "That's the way we do it in the States!" It is a sort of courage of despair that leads a human being to behave in that fashion: one feels impelled to do something a little *outré*, if one finds oneself at too great a disadvantage. And Joaquin Miller, because he was a poet, felt himself at an equal disadvantage in his own little pioneer world. Was it not because of this that he, Cincinnatus Hiner Miller, like the savage who eats his enemy's heart in order to absorb his enemy's virtue, assumed the name of Joaquin Murietta, well knowing that a bandit's name commands respect? And with what a halo of adventurous prowess he surrounded his boyhood in that fabulous autobiography which contains, one is told, not a syllable of truth! Without this history and this mystery and the legend of all these

exploits, what would a rhymester's life and fame have been worth among all those rowdy seekers of gold? In the light of this, one can understand our poet's theatricality and those unceasing efforts to cover himself with the lustre of romance—the photographs, and the autographs, and the Indian hieroglyphics.

STEVEN MILLHAUSER

1943–

Steven Millhauser was born on August 3, 1943, in New York City. He received his B.A. from Columbia College in 1965 and pursued graduate study at Brown University from 1968 to 1971.

Millhauser's first novel, *Edwin Mullhouse: The Life and Death of an American Writer, 1943–1954, by Jeffrey Cartwright*, was published in 1972. A mock biography told from the viewpoint of its subject's slightly older closest friend, *Edwin Mullhouse* succeeds both as a parody of literary biography and as an affecting, unsentimental evocation of childhood. In 1975 it received the Prix Medicis Étranger from France.

His second novel, *Portrait of a Romantic* (1977), focusses on early adolescence, taking the form of a reminiscence by twenty-nine-year-old Arthur Grumm of his life from ages twelve to fifteen. Grumm in his youth was caught between two friends, one his "double" the other his "triple," representing respectively the extremes of realism and romanticism in approaching life.

Millhauser has published short stories in the *New Yorker, Grand Street, Antaeus, Twilight Zone*, and other magazines. A collection of his stories, *In the Penny Arcade*, appeared in 1986. While his brilliance has always been recognized by discerning critics, Millhauser—perhaps in part because he prefers not to push for publicity—has yet to gain the broad acceptance that his work merits.

Like great actors in mediocre plays, there are some writers whose talent seems larger than the vehicles they have chosen to contain it. A case in point is this first novel by Steven Millhauser, a remarkably well-written and sometimes funny account of the hitherto unrecognized genius Edwin Mullhouse, novelist *(Cartoons)* at ten, mysteriously dead at eleven. Supposedly written by Edwin's Boswell and best friend, Jeffrey Cartwright, the narrative takes us from Edwin's first gurgles to his creative Later Years and, as such, is a devilish satire on those exhaustive biographies that weigh down shelves with their bulky worthiness and unrelieved tedium. The tone is sly and articulate, as if written by one of Salinger's Glass children, and though the initial idea is admittedly small and even fey, Millhauser makes the most (if not too much) of it, detailing for us the most ordinary of childhoods through Jeffrey's pompous New Crit perspective. (The two boys react to each other like a sinister Holmes and Watson—Edwin makes fun of Jeffrey, whom he rightly sees as a drip, and Jeffrey's underlying resentment and disapproval occasionally come to the narrative surface with quiet hilarity.) We are provided with baby footprints, a chronology of Edwin's learning to talk and walk, the momentous glimpses of his first comic book and Viewmaster, and his doomed second-grade passion for the disturbing Rose Dorn ("There was something wrong with her, we all knew that; she was like a page on which a waterdrop has dried, leaving a faint ripple").

This kind of elaborate literary conceit, of course, is beloved by academics because it presupposes not only a familiarity with existing literature but a conscious limiting of scope to emphasize verbal dexterity (something Nabokov used to more comic effect in *Pale Fire*). Millhauser takes some sideswipes at this approach and has some fun dropping

pseudopedantic clues. But given his own material, it is all pretty much a case of biting the hand that feeds. The danger in this kind of cerebral writing is an absence of emotion, and Millhauser, alas, runs the familiar gamut from A to B. Certainly he can't be faulted for his fluency and sense of prose style—he can write like a streak—but even the dazzling eventually wearies. Such a lot of cleverness! Detail after detail, send-up after send-up, are piled one on top of another, rococo, style, until the structure becomes top-heavy and collapses—a 300-page game. What begins as a satire on exhaustive biographies becomes, itself, an exhausting satire.

The trouble is that such jokes (especially at this length) are self-defeating. To write about an uninteresting childhood in all its minutiae is to make the account itself uninteresting and boring. Beyond the initial joke, who could possibly *care* about these children? This novel has some of the most beautiful pointless prose in recent fiction. Moreover, the other level on which the book operates—that of a commentary on, and remembrance of, childhood—is licked before it starts by the distance a satirical style imposes. Millhauser plays his nostalgic cards well—scarcely a detail is left out, from root-beer barrels and Mary Janes to penny-filled plastic containers for the March of Dimes—but they hang there in decorative isolation, like a list of Golden Oldies, because there is nothing to pin them on, no internal life in the book to connect with. At times one gets the impression of Millhauser playing hide-and-seek with his own talent, trapped by cleverness and by irony that turns on itself endlessly. And it is all too bad because, despite its length and fundamental triviality, this is the work of a very gifted young writer. No doubt one's disappointment is partly the result of the inflated expectations these very gifts arouse. But it is disappointing all the same. Young Edwin Mullhouse ends his *Cartoons* with a Looney Tunes "That's All, Folks!" But for a talent like Millhauser's, this cleverly executed number is not nearly enough.—JOSEPH KANON, "Satire and Sensibility," *SR*, Sept. 30, 1972, pp. 73–74

Portrait of a Romantic is about 30,000 words too long, and most of them are adjectives; massed battalions of them, lovingly marshalled in pages of relentlessly detailed description for what is, at a second glance, disarmingly slight tale.

The romantic in question is the prosaically named Arthur Grumm and the novel concerns itself with the first year or so of his adolescence and his relationships with three friends in an anonymous American suburb some time—I would guess—in the 1950s. The friends slot themselves easily into prototypical roles. There's William, an earnest swot, secretary of the mineralogy club; Philip, a languid, chain-smoking sophisticate, reader of Poe and Stevenson; and Eleanor, the romantic heroine—mercurial, mysteriously ill and wan, raven-haired, etc. Such narrative drive as there is laboriously works its way around to dangerous games of Russian roulette with a loaded pistol that finally put paid to the pragmatic William who has, by the end of the novel, fatally caught the romantic malaise that so virulently infects the others.

This romanticism is of the most lush and hackneyed sort. Millhauser regularly breaks into flights of purplish descriptive fancy and makes lavish use of clichés which one might have thought long gone; this results in sentences like: "I was pierced with a painful sweetness, a rapturous sorrow, a mild tranquillity, a serene despair. O restless listless yearning-unyearning, drowsy delirium, fevered oblivion . . ." The suspension dots are his, another literary tic which, along with plangent cries of "O!", is generously strewn about the pages.

For a while one hopes that this might be some elaborate ironic ploy, a sustained parody of a genre, but that can not be admitted in the end. Millhauser's endless reiteration of lyrical, moody description effectively blankets the novel beneath a fog of sub-Keatsian excess. His characters are damagingly one-sided too, as if seen through the soft-focus gaze of some benign Victorian cleric. He seems to have forgotten that only one lens of the adolescent's visionary spectacles is rose-tinted; the other is shaded muddy brown, and is frequently flawed or cracked to the detriment of the world upon which it unflinchingly peers.

The darker side of adolescence, the paranoia, the guilt, the grime, the unswerving pursuit of taboo subjects, the spots and pimples and everything else produced by the inevitable hormone-shake are absent, making the portrayal of these years curiously inert. For Millhauser's children the most innocuous covert acts—brief glimpses of nude adults, tremulous pubertal exhibitionism—merit no real curiosity or illicit glee, only swoonings and hot flushes and pages of intense pulse-taking analysis.

American writing of the past fifty years has dominated the field of the fictional presentation of adolescence and has honourably established a tradition of acute and wry observation. One thinks particularly of Hemingway's Nick Adams, Fitzgerald's Basil Duke Lee and of course of Salinger's Holden Caulfield. And although it is possible to perceive—with some effort—that Steven Millhauser has a real affection for his adolescents and sometimes writes knowingly and poignantly about them, Arthur Grumm, on this showing, is some distance away from joining that select band.—WILLIAM BOYD, "Adolescent Agonies," *TLS*, July 28, 1978, p. 872

Every generation has its writers who, while generally unknown, manage to maintain a small but fiercely loyal following, particularly among other writers. The shelf life of a work of fiction, no matter how much hoopla it engenders, is sadly short these days, and ends usually in the graveyard of remainderism; but some books persist through sheer force of will and word of mouth, and their authors' reputations build up invisibly. One such book is Steven Millhauser's astonishing novel *Edwin Mullhouse* (published originally by Knopf in 1972, and just reissued by Penguin Books). I cherish it so much I give it as a gift. Millhauser's fans are legion, constituting a cult that doesn't know itself; when I ask other writers, "Do you by any chance know a novel called *Edwin Mullhouse?*" I'm often greeted by flushed cheeks, shrieks of delight, cries of "Yes, yes, it's my very favorite book! But I thought no one had ever read it but me."

Edwin Mullhouse (the full title of the novel is *Edwin Mullhouse: The Life and Death of an American Writer 1943–1954 by Jeffrey Cartwright*) is an exploration of the world of childhood built upon an ingenious conceit: though the concerns of Edwin, Jeffrey, and their friends are the concerns of children, their voices and minds are those of adults. Edwin, deemed America's "most gifted writer" by his best friend and next-door neighbor, Jeffrey, is the author of a novel, *Cartoons*. In an almost Mishima-like act of planned suicide, Edwin has shot himself on the eve of his eleventh birthday, and Jeffrey has taken upon himself the task of writing his biography—a project whose difficulties he summarizes in a "Preface to the First Edition": "I feel that grateful thanks are due to myself, without whose kind encouragement and constant interest I could never have completed my task; to myself, for my valuable assistance in a number of points; to myself, for doing all the dirty work; and above all to myself, whose patience, understanding, and usefulness as a key eyewitness can never be adequately repaid." Jeffrey's voice is dry, ironic, and highly cynical, and he is given to long Fieldingesque ruminations on the art of the "lowly biographer" as opposed to that of the novelist. Like his creator, he is dedicated to detail and offers us a scrupulous accounting of Edwin's life and career that includes a record of his earliest sounds, drawings of his baby feet and hands, and modest interpretive analyses of Edwin's very earliest writings, declaring at one point, "It would be absurd to pretend to see the future author of *Cartoons* in the early word-lists (tip, top, tap, pit, pot, pat, spit, spot, spat), and yet the student of Edwin's work cannot help being struck by this intimation of the later wordplay."

As much as *Edwin Mullhouse* is a cunning parody of biography, it is also a deeply affecting, richly evocative novel in its own right, a novel that declares its importance in spite of the literal smallness of its subjects. Millhauser's writing is dazzling, perhaps most so in the descriptive set pieces he creates, scenes that evoke with heart-stopping exactitude the moments of Edwin's life—cold winter evenings gathered with his family in front of a living-room fire, fifth-grade playground violences, long Sunday afternoons of board games—as well as astonishing lists and summations, fictions within the fiction that give the reader a Borgesian shudder. Jeffrey scrupulously notes every book Edwin owns at the age of three (they include *Ha Ha the Hee Haw and the Moo Moo Who Said Meeow* and *The Immortal Moment: A Survey of English Literature from Beowulf to Joyce*), and offers the text of a particularly influential book, *The Lonely Island*, in its forty-four-line entirety; he lists the cartoons Edwin saw at kiddie matinees every Saturday; he gives summaries of every story Edwin ever wrote, as well as a detailed exegesis of his brilliant novel. And in his accounting of the antics and doings of Edwin's other friends, from the ridiculous Billy Duda to the tragic Arnold Hasselstrom, Jeffrey (and behind him, Millhauser) offers a portrait of American childhood so true and tender it's hard not to feel a deep recognition, as if what you're reading is your own biography. The book has heart as well as fierce intelligence, and that combination, to my mind, signifies greatness.

Since writing *Edwin Mullhouse* in 1972, Millhauser has published only one other novel, *Portrait of a Romantic*, which almost no one seems to have read and which remains, sadly, out of print. In addition, stories have appeared occasionally in literary magazines, among them *Grand Street*, *Antaeus*, and *The New Yorker*. Now, almost ten years since the publication of that last novel, Knopf has brought out *In the Penny Arcade*, a collection whose very existence is cause for celebration. Once again, the subject of most of these stories is childhood, and while some—the title story and "The Sledding Party," for instance—seem less stories than beautifully realized frozen scenes requiring a novelistic context to bring out their sense, others are masterful and complete in their own right. Of particular note is "A Protest Against the Sun," in which an adolescent girl, at the beach with her beloved parents on a blazing-hot summer day, finds herself enraged by the mysterious presence of a bundled and winterized young man marching along the shore. Millhauser's Vermeerian gift for the tableau-vivant rendering of detail is given full reign in the odd and beautiful "Cathay," less a story than a catalog of wonders from a mysterious kingdom dedicated to the creation of complex miniatures—to precision and order. One catalog entry, entitled "Yearning," reads in its entirety as follows: "There are fifty-four Steps of Love, of which the fifth is Yearning. There are seventeen degrees of yearning, through all of which the lover must pass before reaching the Sixth Step, which is Restlessness."

But the masterpiece of the collection is its opening novella, "August Eschenburg." A deeply moving meditation on artistic motive, August's story is also a fascinating account of the nineteenth-century rage for automatons—little clockwork men and women programmed to act out human behavior. August is an artist of automata, dedicated to the goal of exactly replicating human movement, while erasing all hints of prior programming; a clockwork Pygmalion, he wants to create an utterly convincing illusion of life. The flourishing and corruption of August's art—and August himself—as he moves toward and finally away from this goal, makes for a story that is as compelling as it is wise, for the issues Millhauser confronts here are difficult ones. Are the facts of any life "the secret signs of a destiny, as intimate and precise as the watermark on a postage stamp?" he ruminates at the end of the novella. "Or were they merely accidents, chosen by memory among the many accidents that constitute a life?" This is the fine, perplexing question with which Millhauser leaves us. We can only hope the next ten years bring a larger burst of writings than the last from this supremely gifted and underappreciated writer.—DAVID LEAVITT, "The Unsung Voices," *Esquire*, Feb. 1986, pp. 117–18

TIMOTHY DOW ADAMS
From "The Mock-Biography of Edwin Mullhouse"

Biography, Summer 1982, pp. 205–14

"Even biographers are subject to those little distresses of the nervous system that so engage our sympathy when the nervous system happens to belong to an immortal genius." (Jeffrey Cartwright)

Steven Millhauser's first novel, *Edwin Mullhouse: The Life and Death of An American writer, 1943–1954 by Jeffrey Cartwright*, is an interesting and valuable book for a con-

sideration of the complexities of the art of biography, especially the relationship between the biographer and subject. Millhauser's novel is the biography of Edwin Mullhouse (who wrote his only novel, *Cartoons*, at the age of eleven) written by his eleven-and-a-half year old friend, Jeffrey Cartwright. Because the biographer, Jeffrey, is a fictional character who narrates the story from his point of view, the reader is given direct access into the biographer's mind at work, and the novel becomes not only Jeffrey's biography of Edwin, but also Jeffrey's autobiographical account of his childhood with Edwin, his decision to become Edwin's biographer, and his struggles to impose order on Edwin's life. Jeffrey is Edwin's constant companion from an early age: "Ten years later as we sat talking late into the night, gathering material for his autobiography, I asked Edwin (half in jest) if he remembered our first meeting, and he replied (half in jest) that he remembered it very well indeed: 'a vague sensation of someone bending too close to me.' He smiled, and I instantly moved away, and I was never able to ascertain whether or not he did in truth remember; but I record this snippet of midnight conversation in support of the very real possibility that I was Edwin's first memory."[1]

During his short eleven-year life-span, Edwin is constantly watched by Jeffrey, only six months his elder. Because he is Edwin's next door neighbor (like Kinbote in *Pale Fire*), Jeffrey is in an ideal situation to satisfy his inherent urge to write Edwin's life. "Compared to Jeffrey's zealous sense of purpose, his industrious concentration on his subject's infinite variety and plenitude of sameness," writes Pearl Bell, "James Boswell seems inattentive, Richard Ellman's *Joyce* slipshod, Leon Edel's *James* cursory."[2] ⟨. . .⟩

Like most mock-biographies *Edwin Mullhouse* has a false air of nonfiction about it. An introductory note, written by a fictional character named Walter Logan White, includes a reference to a "definitive article in the *Journal of American Letters*, XXII (1966), 22–43, which compares Jeffrey's very American life of Edwin with Boswell's very British life of Johnson" (p. 6). Jeffrey Cartwright's satiric preface mocks the usual "smug adult" prefaces by stating that the youthful author is "not thankful to Dr. and Mrs. Mullhouse for moving away with the remains" or to "Aunt Gladys for mislaying eleven chapters" and that he "has never received any encouragement at all from anyone about anything" (p. 9). The eleven year old biographer concludes his bitter preface by remarking: "I feel that grateful thanks are due to myself . . . for my valuable assistance in a number of points; to myself, for doing all the dirty work; and above all to myself, whose patience, understanding, and usefulness as a key eye-witness can never be adequately repaid, and who in a typical burst of scrupulousness wish to point out that the 'remains' mentioned above are, of course, literary remains" (p. 9).

Following the fictional introduction and the mock-preface, comes a chronological table which lists such important events in Edwin's life as the first day of kindergarten, and which divides his life into the early, pre-literate period; the middle, literate period; and the late, literary period.

Jeffrey Cartwright is a classic unreliable narrator who constantly intrudes into his autobiography by calling attention to himself, his own wonderous memory, and his devotion to biography. He explains that he first met Edwin, the potential subject of his biography, at the age of six months and three days, when Edwin was only eight days old. With his "half-year old heart . . . hammering away" he remarks on his already "extraordinary, truly inspired memory" (p. 23), and states that "it is with no desire of thrusting myself forward, but only of presenting the pertinent details of a noteworthy occasion, that I thus intrude my personal history into these pages" (p. 23).

With all the seriousness of the most scholarly biographer, the year old Jeffrey begins to collect and record the early conversation of Edwin. Jeffrey analyzes pre-baby talk as thought it contained the seeds of Edwin's future literary genius:

> By six months (I was a year old and walking) Edwin had achieved more elaborate combinations:
>
> kakooka
> pshhh
> dam dam dam
> chfff (an early version of Jeffrey?)
> keeee (accompanied by a grin and
> flapping hands)
> kfffk
> dknnnnz
> shksp-p-p-p
> kaloo
> kalay
> aaaaaeeeeee (singing)

Some of his bolder adventures in the realm of sound were later suppressed by the polite requirements of civilized noise. I refer not so much to his intricate belches and exquisite winds as to his astonishing salivary achievements. How I long to convey to the adult reader his breathtaking combinations of the buzz and drool, his dribbles and drizzles, his bubbles and burbles—whole salivary sonatas enhanced by gushing crescendos and hissing fortissimi, gurgling glissandi and trickling pianissimi, streaming prestissimos, spouting arpeggios, those slurps and slops, those drips and drops, those spluttering splattering splurts of sputum and drippy splish-splashings of melodious spittle. Adult speech, Edwin used to say, is ridiculously exclusive.

The questing biographer gazes with fondness upon this slightly damp picture of brighteyed baby Edwin sporting among sounds, a happy porpoise, untouched by purpose, diving blissfully in the moneybins of language like a latter-day Scrooge McDuck. Surely Edwin's later and highly sophisticated delight in language may be traced back to these early months, when sound was not yet a substitute for things but rather a thing itself, the gayest of his toys: a toy that could be rolled and bounced and licked and swallowed and twisted into a thousand delightful shapes. In general, language for little Edwin combined the virtues of rubber dogs, rattles, and breasts. (pp. 27–28)

Raw material for Jeffrey's biography includes sketches of Edwin's hand and foot, traced from prints taken at age six-and-a-half months, and a chronology of "First Steps," "Some Things I Said And Did," and "My Baby Hair," taken from *My Story: A Baby Record*" (p. 32). Edwin's early droolings gave way to phonetic imitations of Shakespeare, Chaucer, and Dickens, authors who were read aloud to the child:

> "A bee a noppity: assa question!"
> "It wuzza besta time, it wuzza wussa time, it wuzza age a whiz, it wuzza age a foo!"
> "Wanna opril wishes sure as soda!" (p. 47)

At first Jeffrey tries to tell Edwin's life-story chronologically: "God pity the poor novelist. Standing on his omniscient cliff, with painful ingenuity he must contrive to drop bits of important information into the swift current of his all-powerful plot, where they are swept along like so many popsicle sticks. . . . The modest biographer, fortunately, is under no such obligation. Calmly and methodically . . . in a way impossible for the harried novelist who is always trying to do a hundred things at once, he can simply say what he has to say, ticking off each item with his right hand on the successively

raised fingers of his left" (p. 64). But soon, realizing that biography shares many characteristics with novels, he begins to use flashbacks and flashforwards, remarking that "memory and chronology simply do not make good bedfellows" (p. 50). He announces a plan to "abandon the madness of chronology altogether and simply follow my whims" but decides he must get his biography back under control. Using his usual images of childhood, Jeffrey declares that writing a biography "does not resemble the making of a jig-saw puzzle . . . but one of those connect-the-dot pictures that lead you in a series of invariable steps from a seeming chaos of numbers to a sudden recognition of the still incompleted pattern of the final closing of the gap, when number 63 is at last joined by number 1 and you see before you a flower, a kitten, a weeping clown" (p. 51).

His brief desire to break with chronological order for a moment over, Jeffrey continues his chronicle of the budding American novelist. Like most biographers he is fond of frequent catalogues which list the raw material of his subject's life. In a parody of children's book titles, Jeffrey lists such "literary influences" on young Edwin at the age of three as "The Hippopota Mister and The Hippopota Miss," "Ho Hum and Heave Ho," Willy of Chile," "The Little Pretzel Who Had No Salt," and "Donald Dandelion and Oopsy Daisy" (p. 52). Jeffrey begins to give samples of Edwin's early writings, including his first grade valentine poem to Rose Dorn, about which Jeffrey writes, "If I include this poem in my biography, it is evidence not of his artistry but of his misery" (p. 172). Edwin's valentine includes such verses as:

> Rose Dorn, Rose Dorn,
> I am forlorn.
> My heart is torn
> By Rose, Rose Dorn
> (p. 172)

and

> Roses are Rose,
> Violets are violet.
> I love your nose,
> And I love your eyelid.
> (p. 173)

Edwin's early poems gave way to short stories (Edwin and Jeffrey are now in the second grade) which Jeffrey numbers and categorizes and summarizes. Story number 16 concerns "the letter *l*, who is sad because he is the thinnest letter in the alphabet. One day he is chased home from school by *o*. His father, *L*, finding him in tears, explains to him that letters are not important by themselves but only as parts of words. He is part of 'elephant,' 'eagle,' and 'whale,' while *o* is part of 'worm,' 'hog,' and 'toad'" (p. 201). This childish *Story of O* is followed by number 31, "a story about the death of a crayon called Green who gets smaller and smaller until he disappears. In the usual happy ending, we learn that Green lives on in the drawings of the boy who caused his death" (p. 203). Of Edwin's masterpiece, *Cartoons*, which he writes in the fifth grade, we learn little except that its style is based on the comic book and the animated cartoon and that it ends with the classic cartoon closing, "That's All Folks! (p. 279)."

Soon the desire to alter chronology begins to dominate Jeffrey's biographical integrity. He rationalizes the necessity for order and pattern by arguing that "biography provides an illusion of completeness, a vast pattern of details organized by an omniscient biographer whose occasional assertions of ignorance or uncertainty deceive us no more than the polite protestations of a hostess who, during the sixth course of an elaborate feast, assures us that really, it was no trouble at all" (p. 111). Jeffrey begins to justify his frequent lapses from accuracy by arguing that "the fatal flaw of all biography, according to its enemies, is its helpless conformity to the laws of fiction" which hold "that all the details of the hero's life are necessarily related to . . . a central image" which is probably not true at all to the life of "the hero himself, sporting in his meadow outside the future cage of his biography" (pp. 110–111). Roy Pascal comments on this tendency of the autobiographer/biographer to leave incorrect facts in his work, even when he knows that they are false: "On the one side are the truths of fact, on the other the truths of the writer's feelings . . . and we often find open admissions in autobiography of the conflict between the two truths. What is interesting is . . . that so many authors felt that their false impression was as important as the truth, and that the autobiographer has to tell us as much what the writer is as what the facts are."[3]

Jeffrey begins to abandon all pretense at objectivity and accuracy and openly admits to deviating from the facts, and even justifies his departures from truth by claiming that "the false fusion of memory may reveal truths beyond chronology, and the fearless biographer, in his tireless search for the past, must be willing to heed the kind of evidence contradicted by clocks" (p. 185). His willingness to twist the facts is typical of what Stanley Weintraub calls the biographer's "perennial paradox" in his introduction to *Biography and Truth*:

> The biographer perennially faces two paradoxes: the facts do not always add up to truth, and invention, which frequently furnishes tantalizing material for the biographer, often has its own kind of truth. . . .
>
> Perhaps the problem is that the writer of a "life" must aim at several kinds of truth, and biographers—who are often the best critics of biographical writing—will be debating the value of the unprofitable fact versus the telling invention as long as people remain interested in reading about other people.[4]

Jeffrey's increasing difficulty at keeping to the facts concerns him greatly "lest biography degenerate into fiction" (p. 184), until he becomes obsessed with forcing Edwin's life to fit into his pre-conceived pattern. As Leon Edel writes, "there must be, I take it, a strong and compelling element in a biographer's attraction to his subject which pushes him on his difficult and often obsessive task, and it is mixed up in different degrees with all sorts of drives: a boundless curiosity, not unmixed I suppose with elements of *voyeurism*; a drive to power, common I suppose to most professions; a need for omniscience."[5] Jeffrey's drive for power and omniscience causes him to worry about the difficulty of completing a biography while his subject's life continues to run on: "Even then I suppose I perceived dimly that the design was marred somewhat by Edwin's indefinitely continued existence, but at the time I was less concerned with hazy future than with the luminous past" (p. 260).

But Edwin's continued existence threatens to throw Jeffrey's biography out of proportion and he reveals with grim overtones, "I, for one, can testify that even a modest biographer may be driven to strange devices for the sake of his throbbing book" (p. 271). Finally what once was a slight worry, keeping chronology straight, has developed into a grim desire on the part of the biographer for the death of his subject so that he can complete his biography: "The three-part division of his life had already established itself in my mind, and it was emphatically clear to me that we had passed the middle of Part Three and were mere chapters, mere pages, from the tragic end. He had written his book: now he must bow and depart; all else was in a manner superfluous" (p. 295).

In the story's shocking denouement, Jeffrey and Edwin plan what Edwin thinks is only a childish game of biography in which Edwin pretends to kill himself at the exact hour, and minute—eleven years later—that he was born, to give his life a perfect symmetry. Although Edwin thinks it is only a game, Jeffrey—whose biographical impulse has driven him mad—is perfectly serious:

> And calmly raising the gun to his right temple, Edwin whispered: "Bang, I'm dead," and fell backward on the bed with his eyes shut, clutching the silent gun. A moment later his eyes opened and he said: "Now what?" In a split second I was leaning over him, gripping his gun-gripping hand; and I remember thinking, quite lucidly in the midst of a dreamy numbness, that the entry under "I Am Born" in *MY STORY: A BABY RECORD* allowed a certain leeway in the matter of seconds. (p. 316)

When Jacques Barzun remarked that "Every biography is something like a detective story,"[6] he could hardly have imagined the grisly ending of *Edwin Mullhouse*, in which the biographer murders his own subject for artistic effect and a smooth ending. To add further to the terror of Jeffrey's act, once he finishes his biography of the late Edwin Mullhouse, he notices that a new family has moved into the old Mullhouse home and that their youngest son, little Paul Hooper, "is really an interesting little fellow and I expect to be seeing more of him in the near future" (p. 320). Jeffrey has picked the subject for his next biography, and poor dead Edwin is forgotten, his mock-suicide note revealing ironically his ultimate fate: "I aspire to the condition of fiction" (p. 311). Edwin Mullhouse has become fiction in the form of Steven Millhauser's mock-biography. The biographer has literally "taken" his subject's life.

Notes

1. *Edwin Mullhouse: The Life and Death of An American Writer, 1943–1954 by Jeffrey Cartwright* (New York: Popular Library, 1972), pp. 24–25. Parenthetical references are to this text.
2. "It's a Wise Child," rev. of *Edwin Mullhouse, New Leader* (October 16, 1972), p. 15.
3. *Design and Truth in Autobiography* (Cambridge: Harvard Univ. Press, 1960), p. 68.
4. "Introduction," *Biography and Truth* (New York: Bobbs-Merrill, 1967), p. 5.
5. "The Biographer and Psycho-Analysis," in *Biography as an Art*, ed. James L. Clifford (New York: Oxford Univ. Press, 1962), p. 229.
6. "Truth in Biography: Berlioz," in Clifford, p. 155.

N. SCOTT MOMADAY

1934–

Navarre Scott Momaday was born in Lawton, Oklahoma, on February 17, 1934. An American Indian (Kiowa), he is vitally concerned in all his work with the art, history, and culture of his people.

In Momaday's first book, the novel *House Made of Dawn* (1968), Abel, a young Kiowa veteran of World War II, leaves the reservation for the demi-monde of Los Angeles, later returning to die tragically, unable to reconcile the opposing Anglo and Indian cultures. Cited in *Library Journal* as strong in "imagery, descriptive detail and evocation of the natural world," *House Made of Dawn* won the Pulitzer Prize in 1969. Praised as a poet early in his career by Yvor Winters, Momaday has published two collections of poetry, *Angle of Geese and Other Poems* (1974) and *The Gourd Dancer* (1976). Other works include *The Way to Rainy Mountain* (1969), an account from three different perspectives of the migration of the Kiowas from the headwaters of the Yellowstone River to Oklahoma three hundred years ago, and *The Names: A Memoir* (1976).

Momaday received his undergraduate degree from the University of New Mexico in 1958 and his doctorate from Stanford University in 1963. Since 1973, after holding positions at the University of California, Santa Barbara, and the University of California, Berkeley, he has been Professor of English at Stanford University. Momaday received a Guggenheim grant in 1966, an American Academy award in 1970, and a Western Heritage Award in 1974.

This first novel ⟨*House Made of Dawn*⟩, as subtly wrought as a piece of Navajo silverware, is the work of a young Kiowa Indian who teaches English and writes poetry at the University of California in Santa Barbara. That creates a difficulty for a reviewer right away. American Indians do not write novels and poetry as a rule, or teach English in top-ranking universities either. But we cannot be patronizing. N. Scott Momaday's book is superb in its own right.

It is the old story of the problem of mixing Indians and Anglos. But there is a quality of revelation here as the author presents the heartbreaking effort of his hero to live in two worlds. Have you ever been to the Rio Grande country of New Mexico and wandered through the adobe Pueblo village there? It is a frustrating experience. The long-haired Indians with their blankets and headbands are not hostile—just indifferent. One returns to the comfort of Santa Fe feeling vaguely discontented and wondering why everything Anglo seems callow and obvious compared with this ancient culture that doesn't even bother to pave the streets.

Young Abel comes back to San Ysidro to resume the ancient ways of his beloved long-haired grandfather, Francisco. Abel is full of fears that he has relaxed his hold on these ways, after living like an Anglo in the Army. He is our tortured guide as we see his Indian world of pollen and rain, of houses made of dawn, of feasts and rituals to placate the gods, of orchards and patches of melons and grapes and squash, of beautiful colors and marvelous foods such as piki, posole, loaves of sotobalau, roasted mutton and fried bread. It is a wantless "world of wonder and exhilarating vastness."

The task of seeing it is made easier for us by the grandfather, who symbolizes the long and static continuity of Pueblo tradition. He shows us the richness of the Indian mixture through New Mexico's ages. The Jemez of San Ysidro have Navajo and Sia and Domingo and Isleta relatives—even a strain of Bahkyush, who fled from the East long ago, bringing to San Ysidro the finest of rain makers and eagle hunters. The Mexican priest, Father Olguin, is also a symbol of tradition. He is devoting his life to understanding these poetic people, just as other Catholic priests did in 17th-century New Mexico. He can smile as they smiled when he notes how they rank his

shrine of Our Lady of the Angels second in spiritual importance to the adjoining kiva.

Abel's troubles begin at once. He has a brief and lyrical love affair with a white woman from California seeking some sort of truth at San Ysidro. Then he runs afoul of Anglo jurisprudence, which has no laws covering Pueblo ethics. He is paroled to a Los Angeles relocation center and copes for a time with that society, neither Anglo nor Indian. He attends peyote sessions; he tries to emulate his Navajo roommate, who almost accepts the glaring lights and treadmill jobs, the ugliness of the city and the Anglo yearning to own a Cadillac. Abel cannot "almost" cope. Because of his contempt, a sadistic cop beats him nearly to death. But he gets home in time to carry on tradition for his dying grandfather.

There is plenty of haze in the telling of this tale—but that is one reason why it rings so true. The mysteries of cultures different from our own cannot be explained in a short novel, even by an artist as talented as Mr. Momaday.—MARSHALL SPRAGUE, "Anglos and Indians," *NYTBR*, June 9, 1968, p. 5

House Made of Dawn (something broken-backed about that title to begin with) is the story of a young American-Indian war veteran who returns to the reservation after World War II and attempts to cope with the conflicts of his mixed heritage. Abel is a moody sort and gets off to a bad start by murdering a mysterious albino who seems to personify evil in Abel's befuddled brain. A subsequent attempt at coping with modern life in the Indian community of Los Angeles is almost as spectacular a failure, and he returns once more to the wide open spaces of the reservation and a mystic acceptance of his Indian-ness.

Mr. Momaday writes in a lyric vein that borrows heavily from some of the slacker rhythms of the King James Bible, with echoes of those mannerisms that Hemingway indulged to convey the manly and the sincere: "You can hear the drums a long way on the land at night and you don't know where they are until you see the fires, because the drums are all around on the land, going on and on for miles, and then come over a hill and suddenly there they are, the fires and the drums, and still they sound far away." Like the example of Mr. Momaday's style that the publishers offer on the jacket, it makes you itch for a blue pencil to knock out all the interstitial words that maintain the soporific flow. It is a style that gets in the way of the content. Mr. Momaday observes and renders accurately, but the material seems to have sunken slightly beneath the surface of the beautiful prose.

Mr. Momaday's characters, too, are all bemisted by words, although they seem interesting when they occasionally shine through. His hero does not come through at all, but the incidental characters manage to assert themselves with an intermittent vividness that suggests a much more exciting novel behind that unfortunate veil of literature in front of them. —WILLIAM JAMES SMITH, *Com*, Sept. 20, 1968, p. 636

Interest in the American Indian is at a new high, and studies are appearing in various forms. Only an occasional work, however, illuminates the Indian as a person rather than a statistic in history. Even among the university presses—which, we are inclined to believe, are in a better position than commercial publishers to do so—there is considerable variety in the methods of studying and understanding the Indian. Pulitzer Prize-winner Scott Momaday, himself a Kiowa, evokes the spirit of his people and their land ⟨in *The Way to Rainy Mountain*⟩, and does so in prose that is often close to poetry. ⟨. . .⟩

The land was considerably more intimate to the Indian than it is now to most technology-oriented whites. Momaday suggests that "Once in his life a man ought to concentrate his mind upon the remembered earth. . . . He ought to give himself up to a particular landscape in his experience, to look at it from as many angles as he can, to wonder about it, to dwell upon it." At the very least he can do this through memory, through the imagination.

Momaday's subject matter is ostensibly the migration made by the Kiowa 300 years ago from the headwaters of the Yellowstone River to the southern Plains. (Rainy Mountain is in Oklahoma.) During the trek the Kiowa acquired horses and were suddenly "free of the ground." They became a lordly society of sun priests, fighters, hunters, and thieves, maintaining this position for 100 years, to the mid-nineteenth century. The story itself is impelling, but it is Momaday's method of presentation that makes it meaningful.

Each set of facing pages contains three paragraphs, in three different kinds of type. The first paragraph is the telling of legend, timeless; the second is the telling of history, largely from the nineteenth century; the third paragraph is the author's contemporary impression or comment from having heard the legends, read the history, and traveled the same route taken by his forefathers centuries before.

Toward the end of *Rainy Mountain* one section consolidates the three parts in a non-distinguishable group so that the three "voices" are the same. Legend, history, and contemporary experience come together, as they should, in a personal reality. The three's becoming one reflects a basic method and concern in Western American literature; thus it is no surprise that Momaday stresses three things in particular throughout the book (in addition to his three voices): a time that is gone forever, a landscape that is incomparable, and a human spirit which endures. —JOHN R. MILTON, *SR*, June 21, 1969, p. 51

It must be admitted that American Indians as a group have yet to make any substantial impact upon our national literature; their languages and cultures are so alien to European-Americans that art too credibly reflecting the literary forms or, indeed, the reality of Indian perceptions, is apt to be rejected as esoteric. One critic, William James Smith in *Commonweal*, recently attacked the lack of clarity, and of economy, in N. Scott Momaday's 1969 Pulitzer Prize novel, *House Made of*

Dawn, the story of a young Indian's attempt to live in two cultures, in two worlds. But Marshall Sprague better understood the Kiowa author's purpose:

> There is plenty of haze in the telling of this tale—but that is one reason why it rings so true. The mysteries of cultures different from our own cannot be explained in a short novel, even by an artist as talented as Mr. Momaday.

Few first novels have shown so clearly the technical competence demonstrated by Momaday's, for the author served a long apprenticeship, publishing both verse and fiction in various literary journals. His style manages to be both impressionistic and precise, a unique combination of Hemingway-clauses strung into Faulkner-sentences; and it works:

> You can hear the drums a long way on the land at night, and you don't know where they are until you see the fires, because the drums are all around on the land, going on and on for miles, and then you come over a hill and suddenly there they are, the fires and the drums, and they still sound far away.

To what extent does *House Made of Dawn* reflect Momaday's ancestral literary heritage? Very little on the surface, but profoundly in terms of tone and emphasis; as *Library Journal* noted, the novel is strong in "imagery, descriptive detail and evocation of the natural world, this book will tax readers used to definite plot lines and vivid characterization." Momaday has developed a unique fictive voice.

The Kiowa author's sudden prominence should hasten the day when Indian writers as a group forsake blatant protest and employ more imaginative—and probably more persuasive—forms; the pressure of their plight has tended to force Indian writers into desperate excoriations of conditions. Like Afro-American writers who have found that subtlety is often a more effective social weapon than shrill anger, native American artists are beginning to discover their own most moving modes of expression.

Because poetry has traditionally played so prominent a role in Indian life, it may be the area of greatest potential contribution to our national literature by Indian writers. Momaday's exquisite use of language in his fiction is the product of his considerable practice with poetry; he is, in fact, probably the most highly regarded American Indian poet now writing. —GERALD W. HASLAM, "Poets of the Cosmos: American Indian Literature," *Forgotten Pages of American Literature*, 1970, pp. 23–25

In *The Gourd Dancer* N. Scott Momaday writes in the iambic tradition, in short-line free verse, and (of Indian lore or inventions) in paragraph-poetry. He is a good poet in all three modes. His best iambic lines are good examples of the "spiritual control" his mentor Yvor Winters admired in closely varied meter: "No imprecisions of commingled shade,/No shimmering deception of the sun"; "Mere hunger cannot urge him [the pit viper] from this drowse"; "in the windless noon's hot glare"; "And death this cold, black density of stone"; "The polar currents close,/And stiffen, and remain." His best short-line free verse has comparable force, and it shares the primary theme—the radical unintelligibility of nature—as though one tried by sheer force of gaze to stare down nature, to will it to be comprehensible, then to record its unyielding.

His iambic and free-verse poems, good as they are, display too much their rigored tooling—and too much their sources: Yvor Winters, Wallace Stevens (as Winters interpreted him), Edgar Bowers. Nor is nature as incomprehensible as Momaday suggests. It permits us to live here, against what would be, were our existence an accident, fantastically astronomical odds; it is knowable, say, by science and by the logistics of woodcraft; it is often very beautiful, which declares to us the fact of beauty.

Momaday's best poems are, in my judgment, the Indian poems in paragraphs, which have a wonderful freshness of rhythmical movement, an exact rightness as celebration of courage and labor and of mysterious beauty in the world: such poems as "The Fear of Botalee," "The Story of a Well-Made Shield," "The Stalker," and, best of all, the magnificent "The Colors of Night" and "The Horse That Died of Shame."
—PAUL RAMSEY, "Faith and Form: Some American Poetry of 1976," *SwR*, Summer 1977, p. 535

N. Scott Momaday's *House Made of Dawn* is replete with symbolic provocatives that have elicited widely varied critical responses. The most significant of these is the set piece beginning scene, in which Abel runs alone in the dawn. The scene proves to be a backdrop for the entire novel, as we gradually learn that Abel, like his grandfather before him, must get back to a natural relationship with the physical universe. The book is punctuated with Francisco's recollections of his ceremonial runs, and on his deathbed the last memory he recalls for his grieving grandson is the time he finally overcame the physical torment of overexertion and "ran beyond his pain." (*House Made of Dawn*, p. 188) The account is of course an all-important legacy for Abel, because he has been struggling for years to overcome personal torments both physical and mental in a modern world that will not allow him to be himself. When Francisco dies, Abel at last knows what he must do, and after he prepares his grandfather for burial and notifies the priest, he goes out in the dawn to run the ceremonial race. He goes, like his grandfather before him, to run the race which Momaday has called "an expression of the soul in the ancient terms of sheer physical exertion."

What follows is apparently a race with other ceremonial runners, during which Abel manages, like his grandfather before him, to run past his pain. I say "apparently," because I want to suggest a more intense interpretation of Momaday's dramatic conclusion. What Abel must accomplish, if he *is* to succeed in overcoming his physical and mental limitations, is surely what Father Olguin, testifying at the murder trials earlier, had called "an act of imagination so compelling as to be inconceivable to us." (p. 94) I therefore suggest that Francisco's death is *not* after all exactly coincidental with the tribe's ritualistic run, and that Abel accomplishes the ultimate "act of imagination" by going alone into the dawn and *imagining* the other runners. This reading eradicates any traces of contrivance, and it gives the ending a lyric intensity. It enables me to see a man imagining so powerfully that he "came among" those he imagined, and "huddled in the cold together" with them before the race began (p. 190). Finally, I see him running after the others, drawn on by the sight of their "slim black bodies" ahead of him, "gliding away without sound." (p. 191) He falls in agony, but he rises, and at last he is "alone and running on," past the need for the other runners, and finally past the pain. I am at once reader and participant, then, and imagining Abel so strongly that I am with him as he runs away. —CHARLES WOODARD, *Expl*, Winter 1978, pp. 27–28

N. Scott Momaday's novel *House Made of Dawn* ⟨(New York: Harper and Row, 1968)⟩ is replete with ambiguities. At least two of these center on the novel's beginning scene, which in this circular narrative is also its conclusion. The novel opens with the protagonist Abel, a young Native American from Jemez Pueblo who has been exposed to white culture after serving in World War II, running in a ritual race at the Pueblo. He participates in this ritual, elsewhere called a "running after evil" (p. 96), after years of estrangement from his native culture

and several futile attempts to come to terms with evil on an individual basis, a technique more characteristic of white than Jemez culture. Abel's participation in the race occurs immediately after he has prepared the body of his grandfather Francisco for burial according to Jemez custom. His adherence to the Jemez pre-funerary rites and his running in the ritual race apparently signal Abel's reintegration into the Pueblo way of life.

One ambiguity about the race relates to its implied outcome. Most critics seem to hold that Abel has indeed effectively recommitted himself to Jemez culture and will henceforth flourish at the Pueblo instead of floundering under white influence as he has done since returning from the war. However, Charles R. Larson has suggested that the race is suicidal, that Abel runs toward an inevitable death. Larson enumerates several points to support his position, especially the state of Abel's health at the time. He has been out of a Los Angeles hospital under treatment for a severe beating for only a week and has been drunk on at least two occasions since his release. He is hardly in condition for the intense physical exertion of long-distance running. Although the ambiguity of the race's outcome can fuel plenty of critical debates, I am more interested here in a second ambiguity.

Writing in *The Explicator*, Charles Woodard has contended that Abel *imagines* the other runners in the race. If I read Woodard correctly, Abel himself is actually running, but not in the ritual race that he imagines. According to Woodard, his perspective on the novel's beginning/ending accomplishes two things. First, it removes "any traces of contrivance" (p. 28) from the death of Francisco. Woodard sees too much coincidence in the old man's dying immediately before "the tribe's ritualistic run" (p. 28), an event Francisco repeatedly remembers from youthful participation throughout the novel and which, in fact, constitutes his last recorded memory before death. Moreover, interpreting the race as imaginary reinforces what Woodard sees as a major theme in the novel, the power of the imagination. (This is indeed an important idea in much of Momaday's poetry and nonfiction as well.) By describing Abel's participation in the race as an imaginary act, Woodard asserts, the novelist augments the reader's own imaginative participation in the literary experience.

Woodard's view may seem plausible at first glance, but I believe that he is incorrect—that Momaday means for the race to be taken as "real"—for two reasons. For one thing, an examination of the Jemez ritual calendar demonstrates that the race occurs at an appropriate time. Francisco had died sometime early on February 28. Abel prepares the body in the proper manner and then begins the race at dawn of that same day. Surely, Momaday had a clear purpose, that of relating the events in his narrative to the ritual calendar, when he chose to date the novel's occurrences. The February date is consistent with what Momaday has written about the customary life of Jemez in an essay for *Ramparts*: "The first race each year comes in February, and then the dawn is clear and cold, and the runners breathe steam. It is a long race, and it is neither won nor lost. It is an expression of the soul in the ancient terms of sheer physical exertion." It is perhaps also supportive of the reality of the race that Momaday came to use some of the imagery and concepts from this brief, nonfictional description in his account of Abel's experience.

Another argument in favor of the race's reality is that it does occur in such close juxtaposition with Francisco's death. In a novel such as *House Made of Dawn*, this kind of coincidence is contrived, but reflective of the deepest reality. For Momaday is clearly myth-making in the novel, identifying his narrative with the stories orally recounted for generations at Jemez. For example, the novel begins and ends with the formulaic Jemez words which are used in oral performances of myths and folktales. The novel also depicts its characters in mythic terms, associating Abel with the Bear's Son, hero of an internationally told folktale type (pp. 169–170), and his adversaries with serpents (pp. 129, 136). Furthermore, the novel continually reminds the reader of the pervasive presence of myth and ritual by descriptions and allusions to such aspects of Jemez life. And *House Made of Dawn* (the title comes from a Navajo healing chant) particularly singles out Francisco as the perpetuator of the mythic and ritualistic. It is highly appropriate—not contrived in the least within the context of such a mythic novel—that Francisco's life end shortly before the ritual race, in which he distinguished himself as a young man, begins.

Does reading the race as real rather than imaginary detract from the novel's theme? Not unless that theme relates solely to the power of the imagination. I agree with Woodard that such a theme operates in the novel, but I believe more importance is assigned to the idea of restoration of the individual to the traditional culture and his recognition that it provides better survival mechanisms for the Native American than does the way of life of the white man. Nor do I think that the other ambiguity about the race, whether or not it will lead to Abel's death, is a matter of great concern. Alive or dead at the end of the race, he will again be a part of Jemez tradition, purged of the contamination of the white world.—WILLIAM M. CLE-MENTS, *Expl*, Winter 1983, pp. 60–62

WILLIAM BLOODWORTH
From "Neihardt, Momaday, and the Art of Indian Autobiography"
Where the West Begins
eds. Arthur R. Huseboe and William Geyer
1978, pp. 156–60

In the autobiographical writings of N. Scott Momaday we have Indian autobiography that differs radically from that of *Black Elk Speaks* and from most other collected life histories of native Americans. The source of this difference is Momaday's own life, that of an unusually successful and well-assimilated Indian. Momaday was born on ancestral grounds in Oklahoma in 1934 (where his name was recorded on the Kiowa Indian Census Roll as Number 2035) and spent much of his early childhood there. However, his Kiowa father and his part-Cherokee mother, having made successful careers for themselves in art and education, taught Momaday English as his "native" language and later sent him off to Eastern schools. He was particularly influenced by his mother's love of English literature: "I have seen Grendel's shadow on the walls of Canyon de Chelly, and once, having led the sun around Hoskinini Mesa, I saw Copperfield at Oljeto Trading post."[1] Capitalizing on such advantages, Momaday has become a literary scholar, a professor at the University of California at Berkeley, a Pulitzer Prize winning novelist (with *House Made of Dawn* in 1968), and a widely-recognized poet. Although this kind of academic and literary achievement may disqualify Momaday as a genuine representative of traditional tribal Indian culture, it also indicates the unusual literary talent that Momaday brings to the practice of autobiography. Separated as he is by time, circumstance, and good fortune from "pure" Indian life, Momaday pays scant attention to mysticism or visionary experience. Instead, in both *The Way to Rainy*

Mountain and *The Names* his writing involves a highly personal and often poetic articulation of remembered myths, legends, and family stories.

The Way to Rainy Mountain is not explicitly autobiographical. Yet it represents Momaday's attempt to fuse his personal and ancestral pasts into an imaginative whole. To do this Momaday makes use of three kinds of material: the first is Kiowa verbal tradition as expressed in myths and legends, the second is factual history, and the third is Momaday's own poetic response to remembered expressions and facts of Kiowa culture. *The Way to Rainy Mountain* contains twenty-four numbered sections, and each section contains three items— one from myth or legend, one from history, and one from personal reflection. The sections themselves are divided into three groups: "The Setting Out," "The Going On," and "The Closing In." This progression follows Kiowa history from the tribe's seventeenth-century origins in the Northern Rockies to their nineteenth-century conquest of the Southern Plains to their eventual life on the Oklahoma reservation near Rainy Mountain in the Wichita Range. Momaday's method is clear in section I. The first item of the section relates the Kiowa coming-out myth, in which "the Kiowas came one by one into the world through a hollow log."[2] The second item shifts to history and offers a straightforward explanation of how the original names of the tribe meant "coming out." The final item tells of Momaday's own perceptions when he retraced the migration of his people and "came out" of the Rocky Mountain forests onto the expansive landscape of the High Plains:

> I could see the still, sunlit plain below, reaching
> away out of sight. At first there is no discrimination
> in the eye, nothing but the land itself, whole and
> impenetrable. But then smallest things begin to stand
> out of the depths—herds and rivers and groves—and
> each of these has perfect being in terms of distance
> and of silence and of age. Yes, I thought, now I see
> the earth as it really is; never will I see things as I saw
> them yesterday or the day before (p. 17).

Just as the emergence of the Kiowas from the mountains forever changed their culture, Momaday's imagination produces a permanent change in his attitudes.

In the freedom of its poetic associations, *The Way to Rainy Mountain* can be a difficult book to appreciate on first reading. "My major feelings are those of being cheated. I want to know a great deal more about the Kiowas," one of my students once wrote, with some justification, in an informal paper on Momaday's book. *The Way to Rainy Mountain* is an extremely personal statement, and at times even a sentimental one. It is a literary attempt by Momaday to discover and explore his Kiowa roots. In *The Names*, his later and more explicitly autobiographical book, he refers to what his mother did in her childhood and adolescence when she began to think of herself as an Indian despite the fact that her actual Indian blood was only that of a Cherokee great-grandmother: "That dim native heritage became a fascination and a cause for her. . . . She imagined who she was. This act of the imagination was, I believe, among the most important events of my mother's early life, as later the same essential act was to be among the most important of my own life" (p. 25). *The Way to Rainy Mountain* is the "essential act," or a large part thereof, which Momaday equates with his mother's effort at assuming an Indian identity, and the emphasis on personal imagination in the book is unmistakable. In section XXIV he offers a rationale for what he has been doing throughout his pages:

Once in his life a man ought to concentrate his mind upon the remembered earth, I believe. He ought to give himself up to a particular landscape in his experience, to look at it from as many angles as he can, to wonder about it, to dwell upon it. He ought to imagine that he touches it with his hands at every season and listens to the sounds that are made upon it. He ought to imagine the creatures there and all the faintest motions of the wind. He ought to recollect the glare of noon and all the colors of the dawn and dusk (p. 83).

Momaday uses the verb *imagine* or its equivalents throughout this passage because, as he explains in his prologue, "The imaginative experience and the historical express equally the traditions of man's reality" (p. 4).

For Momaday in *The Way to Rainy Mountain* there are two kinds of imaginative experience. One is that embodied in the rich verbal tradition of his Kiowa ancestors, the tradition by which they "dared to imagine and determine who they were" (p. 4). The other is Momaday's own imagination which works *through* the verbal tradition of his people to recover and re-establish who he is.

In *The Names*, Momaday's most recent book, he also relies on the Kiowa verbal tradition for material and form, but in a less noticeable way. Primarily he models—or at least claims to model—his book on the way oral stories were told:

In general my narrative is an autobiographical account. Specifically it is an act of the imagination. When I turn my mind to my early life, it is the imaginative part of it that comes first and irresistibly into reach, and of that part I take hold. This is one way to tell a story. In this instance it is my own way, and it is the way of my people. When Pohd-lohk told a story he began by being quiet. Then he said *Ah-keah-de*, "They were camping," and he said it every time. I have tried to write in the same spirit. Imagine: They were camping (prefatory note, n.p.).

Yet the book, complete with sepia-tone photographs of relatives and Momaday himself, looks like a typical autobiography and, in many places, reads like one. It involves a certain amount of celebration of self which reflects a compromise between the form of written autobiography and the nature of Indian culture. In spite of these things, however, the emphasis in the book is less on the individual whose autobiography it is than on the traditions and people that gave him existence and meaning.

This emphasis is implied in the title of the book and in the more or less central episode of Momaday's own naming. He was given the Kiowa name of Tsoai-talee ("Rock-Tree Boy") by his step great-grandfather, Pohd-lohk. *Tsoai* means "Rock-Tree" and refers specifically to the Devil's Tower in Wyoming, a geological formation of sacred significance in Kiowa mythology:

He took up the child in his hands and held it high, and he cradled it in his arms, singing to it and rocking it to and fro. With the others he passed the time of day, exchanged customary talk, scattered small exclamations on the air: Yes, yes. Quite so. So it is with us. But with the child he was deliberate, intent. And after a time all the other voices fell away, and his own grew up in their wake. It became monotonous and incessant, like a long running of the wind. The whole of the afternoon was caught up in it and carried along. Pohd-lohk spoke, as if telling a story, of the coming-out people, of their long journey. He spoke of how it was that everything began, of Tsoai, and of the stars falling or holding fast

in strange patterns on the sky. And in this, at last, Pohd-lohk affirmed the whole life of the child in a name, saying: Now you are, Tsoai-talee (pp. 56–57).

Pohd-lohk, Momaday says earlier, "believed that a man's life proceeds from his name, in the way that a river proceeds from its source" (prefatory note). In *The Names* Momaday returns to his source through attention to his name, to the names of those he knew in childhood, white as well as red, and to the lives of those who bore the names. Significantly, the final passage of the book, in Momaday's always vivid and powerful prose, is an imagined return "with the eyes of my own mind" to the coming-out place of the Kiowas: "And then there were meadows full of wildflowers, and a mist roiled upon them, the slow, rolling spill of the mountain clouds. And in one of these, in a pool of slow light, I touched the fallen tree, the hollow log there in the thin crust of the ice" (p. 167).

The Names abounds with scenes of childhood and adolescent imagination which chart the inner process of an Indian boy growing up in a largely white world. For instance, Momaday tells of his formative preadolescent years in Hobbs, New Mexico, during World War II, a period when he constantly imagined himself as a fighter pilot in the Pacific Theatre or as a football star on the local gridiron; he also devotes many pages to his adolescent years at the Jemez Pueblo where his mother and father ran the Jemez Day School for the Bureau of Indian Affairs. But consistently he draws attention to his Kiowa roots, the "old, sacred world" from which he had come. His pages are filled with references not only to the people whom he knew or had imagined, but also to the storytelling tradition passed on to him by his step great-grandfather and his father. While his mother read or made up stories for him, his father told "the old Kiowa tales." These were many times more exciting than anything I found at school; they, more than the grammars and arithmetics, nourished the life of my mind" (p. 88). Actually, the tales nourished his imagination, it seems, and Momaday's early acquaintance with the Kiowa way of imagining who they were—through storytelling and naming—was the source of his own literary ambitions.

Notes

1. N. Scott Momaday, *The Names* (New York: Harper and Row, 1976), p. 60. Other references to this book are noted parenthetically.
2. N. Scott Momaday, *The Way to Rainy Mountain* (Albuquerque: Univ. of New Mexico Press, 1969), p. 16. This book is also available in a paperback edition published by Ballantine Books. Other references are noted parenthetically.

ALAN VELIE
"Cain and Abel in N. Scott Momaday's *House Made of Dawn*"

Journal of the West, April 1978, pp. 55–62

The most common view of readers of N. Scott Momaday's *House Made of Dawn*—at least if my students of the last six years, both white and Indian, are any indication—is that Abel, the Indian protagonist, is a noble red victim of the barbaric forces of white America. This impression is based on several things. First, Momaday is himself an Indian, and so readers often expect him to blame Abel's failures on racial injustice. Secondly, Abel's name is an obvious allusion to the Bible's first victim. When I ask my students who is the Cain that destroys Abel, they always answer, "white society." Last, if least, there is the inevitable comparison with Ira Hayes, the

Pima Indian who helped raise the flag on Iwo Jima, an act memorialized in the famous Marine Corps statue. After the war, when Hayes returned to the reservation, he became an alcoholic, and died from exposure while drunk. His death received a good deal of attention from the press, and Hayes' story served on the basis of the film "The Outsider." Tony Curtis, a non-Indian from the Bronx, played Hayes in accordance with the Hollywood stereotype of the Indian as victim. The point of the movie was that it is a pity that Indians can die for their country, but can't live in it with dignity.

However, whatever the reasons for the reader to believe that Abel is simply a victim of white society, the conclusion is incorrect, far too simplistic. Momaday presents a highly complex portrait of Abel, and does not rely on Hollywood clichés, or those of students.

First of all, although there is a general similarity in the situation of Abel and Ira Hayes—both Indian veterans from the southwest who cannot adjust to life in postwar America, and so turn to alcohol—the resemblance may simply be coincidental. Momaday has said that his chief models in creating Abel were Indians he knew at Jemez, New Mexico, the "Walatowa" of *House Made of Dawn*. In an interview in November 1974 Momaday told Charles Woodard,[1] an Oklahoma University graduate student, "I knew an Abel at Jemez who was a close neighbor . . . I was thinking of him; he's one of the people who adds to the composite Abel."

No doubt Momaday had heard of Hayes, and may possibly have had him in mind to some extent, but it must be realized that there is an enormous difference between Momaday's complex character and the stereotype into which Hollywood turned Hayes. To those who read press accounts of Hayes' death, or saw "The Outsider," Hayes was a hero during the war, and a victim of white injustice afterwards. In the normal way these terms are used, Abel was neither. In a very curious sense he may have been both, to some ambiguous extent, but in ways so different from Hayes there is really no basis for comparison.

The only glimpse we get of Abel's combat experience is the curious scene in which Abel gives an enemy tank the finger. His fellow soldiers find this bizarre, not heroic. The gesture, totally inexplicable in terms of modern warfare, seems a rough equivalent of the old Plains Indian custom of counting coups. Plains warriors considered it more glorious to ride up to an armed enemy and touch him harmlessly with a stick, than to shoot and kill him from a distance. This gesture, which showed the enemy you scorned his ability to harm you, seems to be what Abel has in mind, though Momaday never says so. This is not to imply that Abel, a Navajo/Tanoan, would have known about or have consciously thought about coups, but that he is displaying the same attitude towards the enemy. Momaday, a Kiowa, would certainly have known about counting coups.

The matter of Abel as victim of white injustice brings us to the next point, the significance of his name. Momaday told Woodard, "I know about Abel and the Bible and that certainly was in my mind, but I don't think I chose the name on that account." This seems a slight evasion. Momaday may have chosen the name because he knew an Abel, but he doesn't give Abel a surname, and a man as sensitive to symbolic meaning as Momaday could not have failed to realize that his readers would have imagined a link between a character named Abel and the Bible's first victim. The question is, who victimizes Abel? In these secular times, even in the Bible Belt, where I teach, students have forgotten the Bible. Cain was Abel's brother, not some hostile outsider. In *House Made of Dawn*

two of the men who do the worst damage to Abel are his brother Indians, John Tosamah, the Kiowa "Priest of the Sun," who ridicules Abel until he drives him to drink (admittedly it was a short drive) and Juan Teyes Fragua, the Tanoan albino who humiliates Abel, and whom Abel murders, as a result spending seven years in jail. Abel's third tormentor, the sadistic policeman Martinez, is either a Chicano or an Indian with a Spanish surname—at any rate, not a WASP. He appears to be a free lance grafter, and not in any very direct sense a representative of the white society the students have indicted.

The albino is a very curious figure. From Fray Nicolas's letter of January 5, 1875 (p. 49)[2] we know that at the time he and Abel participate in the festival of Santiago, Fragua is 70 years old, although apparently still remarkably athletic. In some mysterious way the albino is evil. In the scene in which the albino watches, or spies on Francisco, (pp. 63, 64) Francisco senses the presence of evil, although he sees no one. The scene is ambiguous, but it is evident that Momaday wants the reader to apprehend the albino as evil, possibly to recognize him as a witch. H.S. McAllister argues that the albino is linked through witchcraft and possession with Fray Nicolas and the Bahkyush witch Nicolas *teah-whau*. The three are, in McAllister's words, "three manifestations of a single person."[3] I find this thesis farfetched, or at least in excess of the evidence McAllister has marshalled, but according to Momaday himself, the albino is a witch. Momaday told Woodard about the passage in question: "He (the albino) is manifesting the evil of his presence. Witchcraft and the excitement of it is part of that too." Abel is aware that the albino is evil, but his decision to kill him seems to spring from a specific incident, the beating at the festival of Santiago.

One of the rituals accompanying the celebration of the patron saint of Walatowa involves burying a rooster to its neck, and having horsemen ride by, trying to pull the rooster out of the ground. The one who succeeds chooses a victim, and beats him with the rooster until the bird is a bloody pulp. The albino pulls the rooster out of the ground, and chooses Abel to beat. Abel is furious at this humiliation, and determines to kill the albino. Momaday refers to this gory ritual as a game, and it is a game in the sense that it is an activity done for entertainment, and governed by a well defined set of arbitrary rules. If Abel decides to play the game, he should be aware of the risks, and willing to suffer the consequences. His anger and decision to kill the albino are wrong. It is as if a black halfback considers it a racial incident when he is tackled by a white linebacker, and wants to fight him. A man who doesn't want to be knocked down shouldn't play football, and a man who doesn't want to be beaten with a rooster should avoid rituals in which that is the practice. Nonetheless, Abel doesn't see it that way. He kills the albino.

In understanding the albino we must recognize that there is a symbolic dimension to his character. The conjunction of whiteness and evil inevitably suggest Melville's *Moby-Dick*. In chapter 42, "The Whiteness of the Whale," Melville describes how white not only symbolizes purity and goodness to men, but also may transmit the spectral qualities of terror and evil. As Melville puts it, White is "the intensifying agent in things the most appalling to mankind."[4] Melville particularly mentions the albino man who "so peculiarly repels and often shocks the eye, as that sometimes he is loathed by his own kith and kin."[5]

Momaday told Woodard of his special interest in Melville, whom he includes in his courses in anti-romantic American literature at Stanford. In his interview with Woodard he confirms the influence of Melville in the depiction of the albino.[6]

One of the most interesting things about the albino is that throughout *House Made of Dawn* Momaday refers to him as the "white man." We must remember that we are dealing with symbolism here, not allegory. The albino does not stand for Caucasian American like Bunyan's Mr. Wordly Wiseman stands for earthly knowledge. Primarily, Juan Reyes Fragua is a Tonoan Indian who interacts with other characters on a purely realistic level. However, there is an additional symbolic and ironic sense in which the "white man" represents white society. Perhaps this is most strongly felt in the scene in which Abel murders the albino. Although Momaday is describing a stabbing, the terms he uses are obviously sexual:

> The white man raised his arms, as if to embrace him . . . Then he closed his hands on Abel and drew him close. Abel heard the strange excitement of the white man's breath, and the quick, uneven blowing at his ear, and felt the blue shivering lips upon him, felt even the scales of the lips and hot slippery point of the tongue, writhing. (p. 78)

What is happening here is that on a literal level Abel kills the albino, and on the symbolic level the white man rapes Abel.

What exactly this means in terms of the novel is impossible to pin down. As Momaday told Woodard about Fragua: "There is a kind of ambiguity that is creative in the albino—the white man, the albino, that equation, whatever it is."

Abel's other "brother" is Tosamah, the enigmatic Priest of the Sun who suspiciously resembles Momaday in a number of respects. First of all, Tosamah is the only Kiowa in *House Made of Dawn*. Momaday's father is Kiowa, and his mother is Cherokee. As he makes clear in *The Way to Rainy Mountain*, Momaday considers himself a Kiowa, and although today he lives in Palo Alto, California, he returns to Oklahoma every year to participate in the Kiowa powwows on July Fourth and Veterans Day.

Secondly, Momaday's description of Tosamah— "big, lithe as a cat, narrow eyed" (p. 85)—fits Momaday himself. More importantly, Momaday has Tosamah express some of his most deeply felt ideas about the sacred nature of the word and the power of language in the sermon Tosamah delivers to his parishioners (p. 85ff). Finally, and most remarkable, when Tosamah tells his life story, it is Momaday's story that he tells. The chapter headed "January 27" of the "The Priest of the Sun" section is the Introduction to the *The Way to Rainy Mountain*, the book in which Momaday mixes Kiowa history and legends with incidents from his own life and that of his forebears.

If Tosamah is the character in *House Made of Dawn* who most closely resembles Momaday, how do we account for the fact that Tosamah despises Abel? Tosamah says that the whites

> deloused him (Abel) and gave him a lot of free haircuts and let him fight on their side. But was he grateful? Hell, no, man. He was too damn dumb to be civilized . . . He turned out to be a real primitive sonuvabitch, and the first time he got hold of a knife he kills a man. That must have embarrassed the hell out of them. (p. 135)

Obviously Tosamah is being ironic about the generosity of the whites—"they let him fight on their side"—but he means what he says about Abel—that he is "too damn dumb to be civilized," and a "real primitive sonuvabitch." Tosamah doesn't see anything noble in Abel's savagery. He is ashamed that Abel, a member of the same ethnic group, has made a spectacle of himself. Abel has "embarrassed the hell out of" Tosamah by fulfilling the white stereotype of the Indian— primitive, violent, superstitious, backward.

Tosamah is so scornful of Abel that he baits him until he breaks Abel's spirit. As a result of Tosamah's taunting Abel gets violently drunk, loses his job, and with it his hopes for a new life in California. Tosamah never shows any compassion or understanding of Abel; to Tosamah Abel is simply an object of derision. Momaday's attitude towards Abel is obviously more sympathetic than Tosamah's, but it is hard to avoid the conclusion that Tosamah does not reflect one side of Momaday.

Although Momaday is Indian—not ⅛ something, but Indian on both sides, and a participating member of the Kiowa tribe—during his youth he was an outsider to the Indians he lived among. When Momaday was one his family left western Oklahoma, the home of the Kiowas, and moved to the southwest where his mother and father worked for the Indian Service. He spent the longest time at Jemez, New Mexico, where his father was principal of the day school and his mother the only other teacher. So, during the time he was growing up, Momaday was a Kiowa among Navajos and Pueblos. Momaday has written at length in *The Names* about his affection for the Navajo and Jemez, but he makes it clear that he and his family were outsiders:

> And throughout the year (at Jemez) there were ceremonies of many kinds, and some of them were secret dances, and on these holiest days guards were posted on the roads and no one permitted to enter the village. My parents and I kept then to ourselves, to our reservation of the day school.[7]

In understanding his attitude towards Abel, his childhood fantasies are of interest. In *The Names* he recounts that as a child in Oklahoma he spent hours stalking and killing an ugly Indian named "Big Knife" or "Knife Thrower."[8] and in a work he wrote entitled "The Strange and True Story of My Life with Bill the Kid,"[9] he relates:

> Riding is an exercise of the mind. I dreamed a good deal on the back of my horse, going out into the hills alone. Desperadoes were everywhere in the brush. More than once I came on roving bands of hostile Indians and had, on the spur of the moment, to put down an uprising. Now and then I found a wagon train in trouble, and always among the settlers there was a lovely young girl from Charleston or Philadelphia who needed simply and more than anything else in the world to be saved. I saved her.

Obviously in his fantasy life Momaday considered himself if not white, at least different from the Indians. In his fantasies Momaday rode with Billy the Kid, and the Indians he encountered were "hostile." Perhaps this explains some of the hostility that Tosamah, Momaday's stand-in, feels for Abel.

But Tosamah is only one side of Momaday, and he is a caricature at that. Momaday gives him the middle name of Big Bluff, and Tosamah, in fact, sounds very much like the Kiowa word for "woman of the house," to·so·a·mah. Momaday says Tosamah has the voice of a "great dog" (p. 85), and there are deflating comic touches in his sermon:

> May the great Spirit—can we knock off the talking there—be with you always. (p. 86)

In short, Tosamah reflects one side of Momaday, but Momaday treats his character with irony, and Tosamah is clearly more of a caricature of Momaday than a self portrait.

To return to the subject of injustice and prejudice, Abel's problems stem more from intolerance on the part of Indians than whites. I do not mean a few individuals like Tosomah and the albino, but the whole Tanoan community of Walatowa.

Abel's mother and grandfather Francisco were Tanoans, but Abel was considered an outsider because of his illegitimacy:

> He did not know who his father was. His father was a Navajo, they said, or a Sia, or an Isleta, an outsider anyway, which made him and his mother and Vidal somehow foreign and strange. (p. 15)

Abel's mother and brother die during his childhood, and Abel is alone in a hostile world save for his grandfather. Obviously Abel is not living successfully within the framework of the Indian cultural tradition before he goes to live in the white world, although this impression is fostered by the back cover of the New American Library edition—the one the students use. It reads:

> His name was Abel, and he lived in two worlds. One was that of his fathers, wedding him to the rhythm of the seasons, the harsh beauty of the land, the ecstasy of the drug called peyote. The other was the world of the twentieth century, goading him into a compulsive cycle of sexual exploits, dissipation, and disgust.

Abel's chief problem before he goes to war, and immediately after he returns, is that he is *not* living in the world of his fathers. He doesn't know who his father is, and he doesn't know who he is.

Abel's problem is most acute just after he returns from the war. He finds that he is totally alienated from his grandfather. His frustration is that he is completely inarticulate. Language, the power of the word, is extremely important to Momaday, and he makes it clear that Abel's problem is that because he cannot express himself, he is emotionally stifled and repressed, and so potentially violent.

> His return to the town had been a failure, for all his looking forward. He had tried in the days that followed to speak to his grandfather, but he could not say the things he wanted; he had tried to pray, to sing, to enter the old rhythm of the tongue, but he was no longer attuned to it . . . Had he been able to say . . . anything of his own language . . . (it) would have once again shown him who to himself; but he was dumb.

A short time later Momaday describes Abel's walk into the hills:

> He was alone, and he wanted to make a song out of the colored canyon, the way the women of Torreon made songs upon their looms out of colored yarn, but he had not got the right words together. It would have been a creation song; he would have sung lowly of the first world, of fire and flood, and of the emergence of dawn from the hills. (p. 57)

The song Abel is looking for is the Navajo hymn "House made of dawn . . ." which he later learns from his roommate Benally.

Abel remains inarticulate and emotionally repressed throughout his years in jail, and during his relocation in Los Angeles where, as Momaday points out symbolically with the scene of the grunions (p. 83), he is like a fish out of water. Abel achieves emotional release with the death of his grandfather. When Francisco dies, Abel buries him in the prescribed Tanoan fashion. For the first time since his disastrous participation in the rooster ceremony, Abel takes part in a Tanoan ritual. The act symbolizes his entry into the culture of his fathers. Immediately after preparing his grandfather for burial, Abel goes to run in the race for good hunting and harvests. His grandfather had won the ritual/contest more than half a century earlier, in what had been the climactic point of his life:

> Some years afterward, when he was no longer young and his leg had been stiffened by disease, he made a pencil drawing on the first page of a ledger book which he kept with his store of prayer feathers in the rafters of his room. It was the likeness of a straight black man running in the snow. (p. 12)

One cannot help thinking of the contrast with A. E. Housman's runner who dies shortly after winning his race.[10] Francisco survives to join the "rout/Of lads that wore their honors out,/ Runners whom renown outran."

As the novel ends, Abel smears his arms and chest with ashes as the ritual prescribes, and joins the runners, though unlike Francisco he runs behind them. As he runs he sings the song he had longed to sing: "House made of pollen, house made of dawn."

This is a happy ending, or as happy an ending as the novel will allow. Abel has entered into the ceremonial life of his people, and he has regained his voice. The fact that he is running is symbolic of his emotional and spiritual health, despite the fact that his legs buckle and he falls. For him to win the race would be impossibly hokey—a totally discordant note of contrived cheerfulness.

Abel doesn't win this race, nor does Momaday imply that he will in the future. Yet by the simple fact of entering the race Abel establishes that despite the onslaughts of the Cains who have attacked him, he has survived.

Notes

1. Woodard is now a professor of English at South Dakota State University. The interview has not been published.
2. All quotes from *House Made of Dawn* are taken from the New American Library edition, New York, 1969.
3. *American Indian Quarterly*, Volume 2, Number 1, Spring 1975, pp. 14–22.
4. Houghton Mifflin edition (Boston, 1956) p. 163.
5. Ibid., p. 160.
6. Woodard: "Is there anything Melvillian about him? The ambiguity of his color?" Momaday: "Yes. I don't know how far I would go with that, but yes, I certainly had that in mind when I was writing."
7. New York, 1976, p. 147.
8. Ibid., p. 76.
9. Parts of the work have been published in the Sante Fe *New Mexican*, but the work as a whole has not yet been published.
10. "To an Athlete Dying Young."

BAINE KERR
"The Novel as Sacred Text: N. Scott Momaday's Myth-Making Ethic"
Southwest Review, Spring 1978, pp. 172–79

Recently I sat through a noisy, irreconcilable argument between two Anglos about Indians. An Irish lawyer for the Navajos from Chinle, Arizona, accused an anthropologist friend of blind sacrilege in the Southwest. The anthropologist, who was not present, was defended as an ally of Indians and preserver of culture. The specific issue concerned the unearthing of Anasazi pueblos and especially gravesites in New Mexico's Chaco Canyon, and the withering fear of the Navajo crews once within the Old Ones' middens. The most unholy of trespasses, the lawyer called it, and one likely to bring charges that the crew were *brujos*. Help the Indians, he said, but don't transgress the sacred charnel.

The larger issue, of course, is the dilemma not only of anthropologists but of any investigator, interpreter, even traveler, and perhaps especially writer, dealing with another people.

To what degree is it possible to shed one's civilization and descend (to use William Carlos Williams's phrase, applied to Sam Houston) into a different culture? To what degree is it possible to bring forth honestly and intact the findings of the descent? Should the transcultural leap be attempted at all? Is it sacrilege, another form of feckless Anglo plunder? Can the imagination ever really presume to transcend cultural borders?

Near the end of N. Scott Momaday's *House Made of Dawn* the old man, Francisco, in the fever of dying, recalls a solitary bear hunt from his youth. A preliminary and, it seems, self-imposed ritual to the hunt was a visit to a cave of the Old Ones. He climbed the face of a cliff where the "ancient handholds were worn away to shadows . . . pressing with no force at all his whole mind and weight upon the sheer ascent." He entered a cave, stood among mounded dead embers, earthen bowls, a black metate, charred corn cobs. An eagle rushed across the mouth of the cave, struck a rodent, and rose, and Francisco, we assume, went on. The bear hunt which follows is a central tale in the novel, in the same way that Francisco, the protagonist's grandfather, is a central cohering character. The hunt was an occasion of great, self-conscious manliness, carried off through conscientious application of racial skills and virtues, and accorded, in the pueblo, well-earned esteem. But most interesting, I think, is the quiet trespass in the Anasazi cave—a terrifying sin of commission, according to the lawyer. A sacrilege, and therefore the height of bravery.

Francisco works as a structuring principle in *House Made of Dawn*. His lime-twig trap, his hope to snare the sacred, frames the eighty pages and thirteen days of Part One. His inexpressible grief sets the tone that broods behind every page. Until the last part, Francisco is inarticulate and peripheral, a still point against whom the story's violence brushes and whom it then leaves alone. But in this book peripheries are profound, delineating limbuses. Francisco—heroic, crippled, resonant with the old ways, impotent in the new—acts as a lodestone to the novel's conflicting energies. His incantatory dying delirium in Spanish fixes Momaday's symbolic compass: Porcingula, the white devil, the black runners. The commotions of the narrative gather and cool around the old man, and around his dying the book shapes its proportions. Francisco becomes at the end the lens for the single sharp image the novel has been struggling to focus on: Abel's convalescent, redemptive participation in the running. The direction, the structure of *House Made of Dawn* is toward proportion, toward a falling into place. The novel resolves into Francisco's recollections and is driven by tensions revealed to be his: sacrilege and sacredness, fear and courage.

It is a brave book. Momaday's ambition is enormous and untried; he is attempting to transliterate Indian culture, myth, and sensibility into an alien art form, without loss. He may in fact be seeking to make the modern Anglo novel a vehicle for a sacred text.

In the effort massive obstacles are met by author and reader, and one should perhaps catalog Momaday's literary offenses. Style must be attended to, as it demands attention. The first paragraph—six quite short sentences—is a composite of quiet, weak constructions: only one active verb (grazed), eight uses of the verb *to be* (primarily in the verbals *there was* or *it was*), *and* repeated nine times. Repetition, polysyndeton, and *there* as subject continue to deaden the narrative's force well into the book. Happily, the style crisps a good deal after the first twenty-eight pages, when the story finally begins. But what are we to do with, for example, "There is a town and there are ruins of other towns," or "The rooms were small and

bare, and the walls were bare and clean and white"? The reader (this reader, at any rate) is tempted to shelve the book instantly; it seems spackled with pretentious, demipoetic cheap shots intended to solemnify, without justification, simple declarative statements.

The language in the first part vacillates between lugubrious flatness of this sort and fascinating thought, as in "the eagle ranges far and wide over the land, farther than any other creature, and all things there are related simply by having existence in the perfect vision of a bird," or precision of imagery:

> She could see only the flashes of lightning and the awful grey slant of the flood, pale and impenetrable, splintering upon itself and cleaving her vision like pain. The first fast wave of the storm passed with scarcely any abatement of sound; the troughs at the eaves filled and flowed, and the thick ropes of water hung down among the hollyhocks and mint and ate away at the earth at their roots; the glaze of rainwater rose up among the clean white stones and ran in panels on the road; and across the road the rumble and rush of the river.

But, whether fascinating or irritating, the language, especially in Part One, *is* disconcerting. We have all been told that when language distracts from character or story or sense the author is sliding into unforgivable error. It is the sin of poets writing fiction, and unacceptable in a conventional novel.

Even more blameworthy, or brave, is Momaday's mutilation of narrative. The story does not begin until page 29, when Abel meets Angela Grace St. John (a rather heavy-handedly significant series of names). No writer, we feel, can expect his audience to dally undirected that long. Moreover, once the story begins, it diffuses, delays, fades in and out. We muddle back and forth from ceremony, through seemingly arbitrarily introduced material such as an antique diary; to beautifully evoked place information and history (pp. 54–56); to ceremony again; through powerful but incompletely explained passion in the priest and white Angela; to Abel's surreal and inscrutable murder of the albino; then back to the old man, his lime-twig, and his inchoate loneliness. And that is Part One—a staggeringly difficult interrupted narrative.

But the fact is that it works. Something is going on here. Momaday, one realizes, is adhering to the perception of one of his characters, Father Olguin, of "an instinctive demand upon all histories to be fabulous." Halfway through the novel one forgets aggravations and begins to hope that he can pull it off.

The plot of *House Made of Dawn* actually seems propelled by withheld information, that besetting literary error. We know virtually nothing of Abel's brother Vidal until a flashback on page 109, and never learn about his death, clearly a crucial tragedy for the family. The critical character of Francisco builds only in slow accretions, not complete until a few pages before the end when we discover that he was "sired by the old consumptive priest." That bit of suppressed information cannot be excused. We cannot be expected to recognize the meaning of the old priest's diary, 138 pages back, only then. And the revelation of Francisco's cross-cultural mestizo blood, his sacrilegious parturition, is too vital to have been procrastinated.

But Momaday very effectively adumbrates the identity of Porcingula. She is characterized partially, vaguely, and as different figures in different places; she emerges as a fleshed-out, dramatic character only at the end—here again providing a gloss to the old priest's diary. But the author is not confused or contemptuously confusing us with this masquerade. Porcingula *is* many things: the totem of the Bahkyush; a Christian saint

(Maria de los Angeles); a whore; Francisco's lover; and, in remote yet richly possible connections, Pony, Angela, and most importantly Tai-me, Momaday's heartfelt creation deity. Porcingula is a spirit drifting through the book, and, by its end, credible in any guise. The same holds for the novel's figures of evil. Not conventional three dimensional villains, they remain shadowy and unknown—as evil is to Indians—and should not be expounded. We don't need to know who the albino was or what became of Martinez the _culebra_, the bad cop. In this sense of the art's springing from within Indian experience, the distractions of language are likewise appropriate. Image _can be_ more important than story or sense because in Momaday's, the Pueblos,' the Kiowas' social reality, image _is_.

But Momaday has to give a little. Part One—the story of Abel's return from the war, his brief affair with Angela St. John, his weird murder of the ophidian albino—might stand alone as a portrait of reservation life and anxiety, but as narrative it remains a farrago riddled with half-developed possibilities. Consequently the book is structured in form, not function, as is Nabokov's _Pale Fire:_ introductory poetics followed by commentary. Parts Two, Three, and Four are each dominated by a new voice supplanting Momaday's coy omniscience in Part One, supplying fact and context which the novel could not have done without.

The first of these voices is "Big Bluff" Tosamah, the prolix, brilliant "Priest of the Sun." Tosamah, in his two magnificent "sermons," is really an incarnation of the author, Momaday's mouthpiece, giving us what we've been denied: interpretation of Indian consciousness, expatiation on themes. In the first sermon, "The Gospel According to St. John," Tosamah perceives the Book of John as an overwrought creation myth, applies the lightning bolt concept of the Word to the Kiowa myth of Tai-me, and apotheosizes the Indian gift of the human need for a felt awe of creation: "There was only the dark infinity in which nothing was. And something happened. At the distance of a star something happened, and everything began. The Word did not come into being, but _it was_. It did not break up the silence, but _it was older than the silence and the silence was made of it._"

At the same time the sermon precisely elucidates aspects of Part One. St. John refers specifically back to Angela St. John, her half-understood awareness of the need "To see nothing, slowly and by degrees." Angela, like John, did glimpse _it_, "the last reality," but, we may assume, also like John "had to account for it . . . not in terms of his imagination but only in terms of his prejudice." Tosamah is providing an exegesis of Part One, formulating what Angela's and Anglos' limitations are, what Abel and Indians are losing, and buttressing Momaday's themes of the importance of myth ("the oldest and best idea man has of himself") and mystical vision.

The point is that Momaday had to root his story in sense and significance here, had to help us mystified Anglos out. Tosamah is an intriguing, well-crafted interlocutor, but also a slightly caricatured self-portrait—like Momaday a Kiowa, a man of words, an interpreter of Indian sensibility. "He doesn't understand," we are informed later through Ben Benally, "he's educated." It is as if, by speaking through the voluble megaphone of Tosamah, Momaday is apologizing for having to stoop to _words_ to convey the obvious. To be sure, it is an oblique approach to a necessary literary office—the clear explication of mythic and intellectual context—but right on the mark.

Tosamah's next sermon leaves the web of the novel entirely and expands a personal journey into an elegaic history of the Kiowa. This is so much the author speaking, and speaking, he must have felt, correctly, so well, that Momaday lifted this chapter straight (except for a few inexplicable alterations and deletions) into his next book, titled, as is the sermon, _The Way to Rainy Mountain_. This monumental instance of self-plagiarism illustrates, I suppose, that Momaday fears no literary taboo. Unfortunately, _The Way to Rainy Mountain_ does not much profit from a reworking and distension of Tosamah's sermon and Tai-me story.

The book recounts the Kiowa's pilgrimage in a conversation of sorts between three distinct voices seriatim: a teller of legends, a historian/anthropologist, and the first-person author connecting memory to myth. Each of the three interpreters is a representative facet of Momaday's imagination, and their counterpoint is a self-conscious exercise in salvaging both the letter and spirit of the Kiowa's epic quest. Momaday is indulging his ethic of myth-making, is gunning for the sacred text. He was more on target in _House Made of Dawn_.

Both books develop from within the culture, but the perspective of _The Way to Rainy Mountain_ is wholly locked inside Indian sensibility, focusing on itself. The novelist's hand is not in evidence contriving character or tale. It appears that the more successful _House Made of Dawn_ owes its strength partly to the distancing and emotional content that a novel can bear. Momaday's ambition—the transfiguration of culture through art—seems to require a fictional imagination.

Ben Benally, the interpretative voice following Tosamah in _House Made of Dawn_, was, like Tosamah, pressed again into service in _The Way to Rainy Mountain_, though not identified by name. Here Benally's conversational argot records antique times and tales: "You know, everything had to begin, and this is how it was." In _House Made of Dawn_, however, Benally complements Tosamah's exposition of history, myth, and theme by setting forth contemporary Indian ways. For example, speaking directly to the reader, he explains, "You know, you have to change. That's the only way you can live in a place like this [Los Angeles]." Once more Momaday is responding to the need to inform, to keep us with him, and the response is excellent. Benally's sane, quiet voice applies a leavening perspective to the book's turbid events. With him Momaday has begun fashioning the proportions vented in the voice of the third and last interpreter to speak—Francisco.

Abel's grandfather acts as the alembic that transmutes the novel's confusions; his retrospection marks off the book's boundaries, points of reference, and focal themes: the great organic calendar of the black mesa—the house of the sun (which locates the title—as a central Rosetta stone integrating the ceremonies rendered in Part One, and the source place by which Abel and Vidal could "reckon where they were, where all things were, in time." The summoning of the highest of Indian graces and abilities in Francisco's initiatory bear hunt. His passion for the wild witch spirit Porcingula; his fear and loss with their stillborn child. His participation in ritual, "his perfect act" in drumming for the dancers, which determined his stature and enabled him to heal. Then, his running "beyond pain" in the race of the dead.

The dawn runners, the runners after evil, compose the central, framing image of the novel: "They were whole and indispensable in what they did; everything in creation referred to them. Because of them, perspective, proportion, design in the universe." Similarly, the method of the last part, "The Dawn Runner," is to arrange perspective, proportion, design in the novel. Francisco's voice, which had "failed each day only to rise up again in the dawn," parallels the running. His memories, "whole and clear and growing like the dawn," infuse the book with sense and order. And his death urges Abel's stumbling regeneration through joining the race at dawn.

In Los Angeles Benally and Abel dreamt of a "plan" to go home together and ride out to the hills alone: "We were going to get drunk for the last time, and we were going to sing the old songs." Their plan, in other words, was to hold a valedictory for their heritage. But Momaday eschews this highly exploitable scene and leaves us with Abel running, an image that argues perfectly against a valediction for the Indians. "All of his [Abel's] being was concentrated in the sheer motion of running on, and he was past caring about the pain . . . he could see at last without having to think." In this ability is Abel's survival and that of his people.

The novel concerns survival, not salvation, enduring rather than Faulkner's sense of prevailing. The dawn runners physically manifest *the* Indian strength—they abide, "and in this there is a resistance and an overcoming, a long outwaiting." And Momaday is proposing not only a qualified hope for cultural continuity, but a holy endurance. The running is a sacred rite and an act of courage, thus a warding off of fear and evil, the specters (consolidated in such demons as Martinez and wine) that gnaw at Indian probity throughout the book. The race at dawn is additionally a sacrament of creation. As such it outlines the novel's purpose and achievement.

House *Made* of *Dawn*. Its subject is creation myth, the antithesis of Benally's "plan." The book's metaphysics build from a sequence of creation schemata: the diaspora of the Bahkyush, the feast of Santiago, St. John's Word, Tai-me, Benally's songs, his grandfather's story of the Bear Maiden. The book *is* a creation myth—rife with fabulous imagery, ending with Abel's rebirth in the old ways at the old man's death—but

an ironic one, suffused with violence and telling a story of culture loss. Sacrilege repeatedly undercuts sacredness. Father Olguin constantly faces the corruption of his faith, from Angela's mockery, from the perverse vision of a Pueblo Christ child. The vitality of ceremony is juxtaposed to the helplessness of drunks. The peyote service is sullied, almost bathetic. But sacrilege impels sacredness here, as fear does courage, and loss survival. The series of myths, each variously imperfect, each with common corruptions and shared strengths, overlap, blend, and fuse as this novel.

The word *Zei-dl-bei* or "frightful," Momaday tells us in *The Way to Rainy Mountain*, was his grandmother's response to evil. "It was not an exclamation so much, I think, as it was a warding off, an exertion of language upon ignorance and disorder." Language, then, can be a fundamental cultural defense. And as the expression of the imagination, language defines culture. Culture, Momaday writes, "has old and essential being in language." A people come of age by "daring to imagine who they are." Such mythifying, "peculiarly the right and responsibility of the imagination," is clearly Momaday's literary ethic and the one process on which he places a sort of moral value. The imagination that transfigures reality is the source of cultural identity.

Momaday has ur-Anglo Angela St. John compose a creation myth honoring Abel, her Indian lover. It is her son's favorite story—a young Indian brave, noble and wise, born of a bear and a maiden. Her tale astounds Ben Benally: Angela has become a myth-maker, has transcended cultural boundaries with her imagination, has preserved what was holy in Abel. Likewise Momaday is a preserver of holiness in *House Made of Dawn*. He has transported his heritage across the border; in a narrative and style true to their own laws, he has mythified Indian consciousness into a modern novel.

MARIANNE MOORE

1887–1972

Marianne Craig Moore, poet, was born the second child of Mary and John Milton Moore on November 15, 1887, in Kirkwood, a suburb of St. Louis, Missouri. Shortly before her birth her father suffered a nervous breakdown and went home to his parents in Ohio; consequently Mrs. Moore had returned to the home of her own father, the Reverend John Riddle Warner, for whom she acted as a housekeeper. When Warner died in 1894 the family moved to Carlisle, Pennsylvania. Between 1896 and 1905 Moore was educated at the Metzger Institute, which later became part of Dickinson College, in Carlisle. Between 1905 and 1909, when she received her B.A., she was a student at Bryn Mawr College in Pennsylvania; her first published poetry appeared in Bryn Mawr's *Tipyn O'Bob* and *The Lantern*. She then entered Carlisle Commercial College in 1909; after completing her business training in 1910, she made her first visit to England and Paris with her mother and, on her return, began teaching commercial subjects at the United States Industrial Indian School in Carlisle.

Marianne Moore's first professional publication, the poem "To the Soul of Progress," appeared in *The Egoist* (London) in 1915; a number of other poems were published in that year in *Poetry* (Chicago) and *Others* (New York), and she began to win a reputation as one of the "new" poets. In 1916 she moved with her mother to Chatham, New Jersey, to keep house for her brother John, a Presbyterian minister. When her brother joined the navy in 1918 Moore and her mother moved to Manhattan where they lived together for eleven years. In the year or two following her arrival Moore worked as a secretary in a girls' school and as a private tutor. In 1921 her first book, *Poems*, was published in London by the Egoist Press, and in that year her poems began to appear in *The Dial*, then the leading U.S. journal of literature and the arts. Between 1921 and 1925 Moore was

MARIANNE MOORE

N. SCOTT MOMADAY

STEVEN MILLHAUSER

WILLARD MOTLEY

WRIGHT MORRIS

TONI MORRISON

employed as an assistant at the Hudson Park branch of the New York Public Library; in 1925, after her book of poems *Observations* (1924) had won the Dial Award, she became an acting editor of *The Dial*. In 1929 *The Dial* ceased publication, and she and her mother moved to Brooklyn, where she devoted her time fully to writing and to criticism, contributing to many journals and "little" magazines in the U.S. and Britain. *Selected Poems*, with an introduction by T. S. Eliot, was published in 1935, followed by, among others, *The Pangolin and Other Verse* (1936) and *Collected Poems* (1951), the latter winning not only the Pulitzer Prize but also the Bollingen Prize, the National Book Award, and the Gold Medal for Poetry from the National Institute of Arts and Letters. Her translation of *The Fables of La Fontaine*, published in 1954, was awarded the Croix de Chevalier des Arts et Lettres. A collection of critical essays, *Predilections* (1955), was followed by various books of poems, including *Like a Bulwark* (1956), *O to Be a Dragon* (1959), *The Arctic Ox* (1964), and *Tell Me, Tell Me* (1966). In 1967 her *Complete Poems* were published; they appeared again in a final and definitive version in 1982, after Moore's death in 1972.

Marianne Moore was showered with awards and honorary degrees during her own lifetime. Her early work was well known in Britain, and was generally admired by the avant-garde, including I. A. Richards, Ezra Pound, and T. S. Eliot. Her poems are urbane and conversational; her imagery is precise and her subject matter has been called uniquely American.

MARIANNE MOORE
Letter to Ezra Pound (January 9, 1919)
Ezra Pound: Perspectives, ed. Noel Stock
1965, pp. 116–20

Dear Mr. Pound:
In your letter of December 16th, I have a great deal to thank you for. My contemporaries are welcome to anything they have come upon first and I do not resent unfriendly criticism, much less that which is friendly.

I am glad to give you personal data and hope that the bare facts that I have to offer, may not cause work that I may do from time to time, utterly to fail in interest. Even if they should, it is but fair that those who speak out, should not lie in ambush. I was born in 1887 and brought up in the home of my grandfather, a clergyman of the Presbyterian church. I am Irish by descent, possibly Scotch also, but purely Celtic, was graduated from Bryn Mawr in 1909 and taught shorthand, typewriting and commercial law at the government Indian School in Carlisle, Pennsylvania, from 1911 until 1915. In 1916, my mother and I left our home in Carlisle to be with my brother—also a clergyman—in Chatham, New Jersey—but since the war, Chaplain of the battleship Rhode Island and by reason of my brother's entering the navy, my mother and I are living at present in New York, in a small apartment. Black Earth, the poem to which I think you refer, was written about an elephant that I have, named Melancthon; and contrary to your impression, I am altogether a blond and have red hair.

The first writing I did was a short story published in 1907 by the Bryn Mawr undergraduate monthly and during 1908 and nine, I assisted with the editing of the magazine and contributed verse to it.

Any verse that I have written, has been an arrangement of stanzas, each stanza being an exact duplicate of every other stanza. I have occasionally been at pains to make an arrangement of lines and rhymes that I liked, repeat itself, but the form of the original stanza of anything I have written has been a matter of expediency, hit upon as being approximately suitable to the subject. The resemblance of my progress to your beginnings is an accident so far as I can see. I have taken great pleasure in both your prose and your verse, but it is what my mother terms the saucy parts, which have most fixed my attention. In 1911, my mother and I were some months in England and happening into Elkin Mathews's shop, were shown photographs of you which we were much pleased to see. I like a fight but I admit that I have at times objected to your promptness with the cudgels. I say this merely to be honest. I have no Greek, unless a love for it may be taken as a knowledge of it and I have not read very voraciously in French; I do not know Ghil and La Forgue and know of no tangible French influence on my work. Gordon Craig, Henry James, Blake, the minor prophets and Hardy, are so far as I know, the direct influences bearing on my work.

I do not appear. Originally, my work was refused by the *Atlantic Monthly* and other magazines and recently I have not offered it. My first work to appear outside of college was a poem, which one of three, I do not recall—published by the *Egoist* in 1915 and shortly afterward, four or five poems of mine were published by *Poetry*, a fact which pleased me at the time, but one's feeling changes and not long ago when Miss Monroe invited me to contribute, I was not willing to. Alfred Kreymborg has been hospitable and does not now shut the door to me and Miss Anderson has been most kind in sending me copies of a number of *The Little Review* in which some lines of mine have appeared with which I am wholly dissatisfied. Moreover, I am not heartily in sympathy with the *Little Review* though I have supported other magazines for which less could be said. I grow less and less desirous of being published, produce less and have a strong feeling for letting alone what little I do produce. My work jerks and rears and I cannot get up enthusiasm for embalming what I myself accept conditionally.

Anything that is a stumbling block to my reader, is a matter of regret to me and punctuation ought to be exact. Under ordinary circumstances, it is as great a hardship to me to be obliged to alter punctuation as to alter words, though I will admit that at times I am heady and irresponsible.

I like New York, the little quiet part of it in which my mother and I live. I like to see the tops of the masts from our door and to go to the wharf and look at the craft on the river.

I do not feel that anything phenomenal is to be expected of New York and I sometimes feel as if there are too many captains in one boat, but on the whole, the amount of steady co-operation that is to be counted on in the interest of getting things launched, is an amazement to me. I am interested to know of your having had a hand in the publishing of T. S. Eliot. I like his work. Over here, it strikes me that there is more evidence of power among painters and sculptors than among writers.

I am glad to have you send the prose to the *Egoist* and to have you keep the two poems that you have, for your quarterly. As soon as I have it, I shall send you something new. Perhaps you would be interested in seeing a poem which I have just given to one of our new magazines here, a proposed experiment under the direction of Maxwell Bodenheim, and a poem of mine which appeared in the Bryn Mawr college *Lantern* last year?

To capitalize the first word of every line, is rather slavish and I have substituted small letters for capitals in the enclosed versions of the two poems you have.

I fully agree with you in what you say about the need of being more than defensible when giving offense. I have made

> You are right, that swiftmoving sternly
> Intentioned swaybacked baboon is nothing to you
>   and the chimpanzee?

to read

> You are right about it; that wary,
> Presumptuous young baboon is nothing to you and
>   the chimpanzee?

For

> And the description is finished. Of the jaguar with
>   the pneumatic Feet,

read

> What is there to look at? And of the leopard, spotted
>   underneath and on its toes:

Leopards are not spotted underneath, but in old illuminations they are, and on Indian printed muslins, and I like the idea that they are.

its-self may read its self

and I have made

> The little dish, dirt brown, mulberry
> White, powder blue or oceanic green—is half
>   human and any
>   Thing peacock is "divine."

to read

> the little dishes, brown, mulberry
> or sea green are half human and waiving the matter
>   of artistry,
>   anything which can not be reproduced, is "divine."

Confusion is created by introducing contradictory references to lizards; I have therefore left out stanzas seven and eight and I have made other alterations.

In "A Graveyard," I have made *is* to end the line as you suggest and for the sake of symmetry, have altered the arrangement of lines in the preceding stanzas. I realize that by writing consciousness and volition, emphasis is obtained which is sacrificed by retaining the order which I have, and I am willing to make the change, though I prefer the original order.

WILLIAM CARLOS WILLIAMS
"Marianne Moore" (1925)
Selected Essays
1954, pp. 121–31

The best work is always neglected and there is no critic among the older men who has cared to champion the newer names from outside the battle. The established critic will not read. So it is that the present writers must turn interpreters of their own work. Even those who enjoy modern work are not always intelligent, but often seem at a loss to know the white marks from the black. But modernism is distressing to many who would at least, due to the necessary appearance of disorder in all immediacy, be led to appreciation through crtitical study.

If one come with Miss Moore's work to some wary friend and say, "Everything is worthless but the best and this is the best," adding, "only with difficulty discerned" will he see anything, if he be at all well read, but destruction? From my experience he will be shocked and bewildered. He will perceive absolutely nothing except that his whole preconceived scheme of values has been ruined. And this is exactly what he should see, a break through all preconception of poetic form and mood and pace, a flaw, a crack in the bowl. It is this that one means when he says destruction and creation are simultaneous. But this is not easy to accept. Miss Moore, using the same material as all others before her, comes at it so effectively at a new angle as to throw out of fashion the classical conventional poetry to which one is used and puts her own and that about her in its place. The old stops are discarded. This must antagonize many. Furthermore, there is a multiplication, a quickening, a burrowing through, a blasting aside, a dynamization, a flight over—it is modern, but the critic must show that this is only to reveal an essential poetry through the mass, as always, and with superlative effect in this case.

A course in mathematics would not be wasted on a poet, or a reader of poetry, if he remember no more from it than the geometric principle of the intersection of loci: from all angles lines converging and crossing establish points. He might carry it further and say in his imagination that apprehension perforates at places, through to understanding—as white is at the intersection of blue and green and yellow and red. It is this white light that is the background of all good work. Aware of this, one may read the Greeks or the Elizabethans or Sidney Lanier even Robert Bridges, and preserve interest, poise and enjoyment. He may visit Virginia or China, and when friends, eager to please, playfully lead him about for pockets of local color—he may go. Local color is not, as the parodists, the localists believe, an object of art. It is merely a variant serving to locate acme point of white penetration. The intensification of desire toward this purity is the modern variant. It is that which interests me most and seems most solid among the qualities I witness in my contemporaries; it is a quality present in much or even all that Miss Moore does.

Poems, like painting, can be interesting because of the subject with which they deal. The baby glove of a Pharaoh can be so presented as to bring tears to the eyes. And it need not be bad work because it has to do with a favorite cat dead. Poetry, rare and never willingly recognized, only its accidental colors make it tolerable to most. If it be of a red coloration, those who like red will follow and be led restfully astray. So it is with hymns, battle songs, love ditties, elegies. Humanity sees itself in them, it is familiar, the good placed attractively and the bad thrown into a counter light. This is inevitable. But in any anthology it will be found that men have been hard put to it at all times to tell which is poetry and which the impost. This is hard. The difficult thing to realize is that the thrust must go through to the white, at least somewhere.

Good modern work, far from being the fragmentary, neurotic thing its disunderstanders think it, is nothing more than work compelled by these conditions. It is a multiplication of impulses that by their several flights, crossing at all eccentric angles, might enlighten. As a phrase, in its slightest beginning, it is more a disc pierced here and there by light; it is really distressingly broken up. But so does any attack seem at the moment of engagement, multiple units crazy except when viewed as a whole.

Surely there is no poetry so active as that of today, so unbound, so dangerous to the mass of mediocrity, if one should understand it, so fleet, hard to capture, so delightful to pursue. It is clarifying in its movements as a wild animal whose walk corrects that of men. Who shall separate the good Whitman from the bad, the dreadful New England maunderers from the others, put air under and around the living and leave the dead to fall dead? Who? None but poems, such as Miss Moore's, their cleanliness, lack of cement, clarity, gentleness. It grows impossible for the eye to rest long upon the object of the drawing. Here is an escape from the old dilemma. The unessential is put rapidly aside as the eye searches between for illumination. Miss Moore undertakes in her work to separate the poetry from the subject entirely—like all the moderns. In this she has been rarely successful and this is important.

Unlike the painters the poet has not resorted to distortions or the abstract in form. Miss Moore accomplishes a like result by rapidity of movement. A poem such as "Marriage" is an anthology of transit. It is a pleasure that can be held firm only by moving rapidly from one thing to the next. It gives the impression of a passage through. There is a distaste for lingering, as in Emily Dickinson. As in Emily Dickinson there is too a fastidious precision of thought where unrhymes fill the purpose better than rhymes. There is a swiftness impaling beauty, but no impatience as in so much present-day trouble with verse. It is a rapidity too swift for touch, a seraphic quality, one might have said yesterday. There is, however, no breast that warms the bars of heaven: it is at most a swiftness that passes without repugnance from thing to thing.

The only help I ever got from Miss Moore toward the understanding of her verse was that she despised connectives. Any other assistance would have been an impoliteness, since she has always been sure of herself if not of others. The complete poem is there waiting: all the wit, the color, the constructive ability (not a particularly strong point that, however). And the quality of satisfaction gathered from reading her is that one may seek long in those exciting mazes sure of coming out at the right door in the end. There is nothing missing but the connectives.

The thought is compact, accurate and accurately planted. In fact, the garden, since it is a garden more than a statue, is found to be curiously of porcelain. It is the mythical, indestructible garden of pleasure, perhaps greatly pressed for space today, but there and intact, nevertheless.

I don't know where, except in modern poetry, this quality of the brittle, highly set-off porcelain garden exists and nowhere in modern work better than with Miss Moore. It is this chief beauty of today, this hard crest to nature, that makes the best present work with its "unnatural" appearance seem so thoroughly gratuitous, so difficult to explain, and so doubly a treasure of seclusion. It is the white of a clarity beyond the facts.

There is in the newer work a perfectly definite handling of the materials with a given intention to relate them in a certain way—a handling that is intensely, intentionally selective. There is a definite place where the matters of the day may meet if they choose or not, but if they assemble it must be there. There is no compromise. Miss Moore never falls from the place inhabited by poems. It is hard to give an illustration of this from her work because it is everywhere. One must be careful, though, not to understand this as a mystical support, a danger we are skirting safely, I hope, in our time.

Poe in his most-read first essay quotes Nathaniel Willis' poem "The Two Women," admiringly and in full, and one senses at once the reason: there is a quality to the feeling there that affected Poe tremendously. This mystical quality that endeared Poe to Father Tabb, the poet-priest, still seems to many the essence of poetry itself. It would be idle to name many who have been happily mystical and remained good poets: Poe, Blake, Francis Thompson, et cetera.

But what I wish to point is that there need be no stilled and archaic heaven, no ducking under religiosities to have poetry and to have it stand in its place beyond "nature." Poems have a separate existence uncompelled by nature or the supernatural. There is a "special" place which poems, as all works of art, must occupy, but it is quite definitely the same as that where bricks or colored threads are handled.

In painting, Ingres realized the essentiality of drawing and each perfect part seemed to float free from his work, by itself. There is much in this that applies beautifully to Miss Moore. It is perfect drawing that attains to a separate existence which might, if it please, be called mystical, but is in fact no more than the practicability of design.

To Miss Moore an apple remains an apple whether it be in Eden or the fruit bowl where it curls. But that would be hard to prove——

"dazzled by the apple."

The apple is left there, suspended. One is not made to feel that as an apple it has anything particularly to do with poetry or that as such it needs special treatment; one goes on. Because of this, the direct object does seem unaffected. It seems as free from the smears of mystery, as pliant, as "natural" as Venus on the wave. Because of this, her work is never indecorous as where nature is itself concerned. These are great virtues.

Without effort Miss Moore encounters the affairs which concern her as one would naturally in reading or upon a walk outdoors. She is not a Swinburne stumbling to music, but one always finds her moving forward ably, in thought, unimpeded by a rhythm. Her own rhythm is particularly revealing. It does not interfere with her progress; it is the movement of the animal, it does not put itself first and ask the other to follow.

Nor is "thought" the thing that she contends with. Miss Moore uses the thought most interestingly and wonderfully to my mind. I don't know but that this technical excellence is one of the greatest pleasures I get from her. She occupies the thought to its end, and goes on—without connectives. To me this is thrilling. The essence is not broken, nothing is injured. It is a kind hand to a merciless mind at home in the thought as in the cruder image. In the best modern verse, room has been made for the best of modern thought and Miss Moore thinks straight.

Only the most modern work has attempted to do without *ex machina* props of all sorts, without rhyme, assonance, the feudal master beat, the excuse of "nature," of the spirit, mysticism, religiosity, "love," "humor," "death." Work such as Miss Moore's holds its bloom today not by using slang, not by its moral abandon or puritanical steadfastness, but by the aesthetic pleasure engendered where pure craftsmanship joins hard surfaces skilfully.

Poetry has taken many disguises which by cross reading or intense penetration it is possible to go through to the core. Through intersection of loci their multiplicity may become revelatory. The significance of much reading being that this "thing" grow clearer, remain fresh, be more present to the mind. To read more thoroughly than this is idleness; a common classroom absurdity.

One may agree tentatively with Glenway Wescott, that there is a division taking place in America between a proletarian art, full of sincerities, on the one side and an aristocratic and ritualistic art on the other. One may agree, but it is necessary to scrutinize such a statement carefully.

There cannot be two arts of poetry really. There is weight and there is disencumberedness. There can be no schism, except that which has always existed between art and its approaches. There cannot be a proletarian art—even among savages. There is a proletarian taste. To have achieved an organization even of that is to have escaped it.

And to organize into a pattern is also, true enough, to "approach the conditions of a ritual." But here I would again go slow. I see only escape from the conditions of ritual in Miss Moore's work: a rush through wind if not toward some patent "end" at least away from pursuit, a pursuit perhaps by ritual. If from such a flight a ritual results it is more the care of those who follow than of the one who leads. "Ritual," too often to suit my ear, connotes a stereotyped mode of procedure from which pleasure has passed, whereas the poetry to which my attention clings, if it ever knew those conditions, is distinguished only as it leaves them behind.

It is at least amusing, in this connection, to quote from *Others,* Volume 1, Number 5, November 1915—quoted in turn from J. B. Kerfoot in *Life:* "Perhaps you are unfamiliar with this 'new poetry' that is called 'revolutionary.' It is the expression of democracy of feeling rebeling against an aristocracy of form."

As if a death mask ever could replace
Life's faulty excellence!

There are two elements essential to Miss Moore's scheme of composition, the hard and unaffected concept of the apple itself as an idea, then its edge-to-edge contact with the things which surround it—the coil of a snake, leaves at various depths, or as it may be; and without connectives unless it be poetry, the inevitable connective, if you will.

Marriage, through which thought does not penetrate, appeared to Miss Moore a legitimate object for art, an art that would not halt from using thought about it, however, as it might want to. Against marriage, "this institution, perhaps one should say enterprise"—Miss Moore launched her thought not to have it appear arsenaled as in a textbook on psychology, but to stay among apples and giraffes in a poem. The interstices for the light and not the interstitial web of the thought concerned her, or so it seems to me. Thus the material is as the handling: the thought, the word, the rhythm—all in the style. The effect is in the penetration of the light itself, how much, how little; the appearance of the luminous background.

Of marriage there is no solution in the poem and no attempt to make marriage beautiful or otherwise by "poetic" treatment. There is beauty and it is thoughtless, as marriage or a cave inhabited by the sounds and colors of waves, as in the time of prismatic color, as England with its baby rivers, as G. B. Shaw, or chanticleer, or a fish, or an elephant with its strictly practical appendages. All these things are inescapably caught in the beauty of Miss Moore's passage through them; they all have at least edges. This too is a quality that greatly pleases me: definite objects which give a clear contour to her force. Is it a flight, a symphony, a ghost, a mathematic? The usual evasion is to call them poems.

Miss Moore gets great pleasure from wiping soiled words or cutting them clean out, removing the aureoles that have been pasted about them or taking them bodily from greasy contexts. For the compositions which Miss Moore intends, each word should first stand crystal clear with no attachments; not even an aroma. As a cross light upon this, Miss Moore's personal dislike for flowers that have both a satisfying appearance and an odor of perfume is worth noticing. With Miss Moore a word is a word most when it is separated out by science, treated with acid to remove the smudges, washed, dried and placed right side up on a clean surface. Now one may say that this is a word. Now it may be used, and how?

It may be used not to smear it again with thinking (the attachments of thought) but in such a way that it will remain

scrupulously itself, clean perfect, unnicked beside other words in parade. There must be edges. This casts some light I think on the simplicity of design in much of Miss Moore's work. There must be recognizable edges against the ground which cannot, as she might desire it, be left entirely white. Prose would be all black, a complete black painted or etched over, but solid.

There is almost no overlaying at all. The effect is of every object sufficiently uncovered to be easily recognizable. This simplicity, with the light coming through from between the perfectly plain masses, is however extremely bewildering to one who has been accustomed to look upon the usual "poem," the commonplace opaque board covered with vain curlicues. They forget, those who would read Miss Moore aright, that white circular discs grouped closely edge to edge upon a dark table make black six-pointed stars.

The "useful result" is an accuracy to which this simplicity of design greatly adds. The effect is for the effect to remain "true"; nothing loses its identity because of the composition, but the parts in their assembly remain quite as "natural" as before they were gathered. There is no "sentiment"; the softening effect of word upon word is nil; everything is in the style. To make this ten times evident is Miss Moore's constant care. There seems to be almost too great a wish to be transparent and it is here if anywhere that Miss Moore's later work will show a change, I think.

The general effect is of a rise through the humanities, the sciences, without evading "thought," through anything (if not everything) of the best of modern life; taking whatever there is as it comes, using it and leaving it drained of its pleasure, but otherwise undamaged. Miss Moore does not compromise science with poetry. In this again, she is ably modern.

And from this clarity, this acid cleansing, this unblinking willingness, her poems result, a true modern crystallization, the fine essence of today which I have spoken of as the porcelain garden.

Or one will think a little of primitive masonry, the units unglued and as in the greatest early constructions unstandardized.

In such work as "Critics and Connoisseurs," and "Poetry," Miss Moore succeeds in having the "thing" which is her concern move freely, unencumbered by the images or the difficulties of thought. In such work there is no "suggestiveness," no tiresome "subtlety" of trend to be heavily followed, no painstaking refinement of sentiment. There is surely a choice evident in all her work, a very definite quality of choice in her material, a thinness perhaps, but a very welcome and no little surprising absence of moral tone. The choice being entirely natural and completely arbitrary is not in the least offensive, in fact it has been turned curiously to advantage throughout.

From what I have read it was in "Critics and Connoisseurs" that the successful method used later began first to appear: If a thought presents itself the force moves through it easily and completely: so the thought also has revealed the "thing"—that is all. The thought is used exactly as the apple, it is the same insoluble block. In Miss Moore's work the purely stated idea has an edge exactly like a fruit or a tree or a serpent.

To use anything: rhyme, thought, color, apple, verb—so as to illumine it, is the modern prerogative; a stintless inclusion. It is Miss Moore's success.

The diction, the phrase construction, is unaffected. To use a "poetic" inversion of language, or even such a special posture of speech, still discernible in Miss Moore's earlier work, is to confess an inability to have penetrated with poetry some crevice of understanding; that special things and special places are reserved for art, that it is unable, that it requires fostering. This is unbearable.

Poetry is not limited in that way. It need not say either

Bound without
Boundless within.

It has as little to do with the soul as with ermine robes or graveyards. It is not noble, sad, funny. It is poetry. It is free. It is escapeless. It goes where it will. It is in danger; escapes if it can.

This is new! The quality is not new, but the freedom is new, the unbridled leap.

The dangers are thereby multiplied—but the clarity increased. Nothing but the perfect and the clear.

T. S. ELIOT
From "Introduction"
Selected Poems
1935, pp. x–xiv

The first aspect in which Miss Moore's poetry is likely to strike the reader is that of minute detail rather than that of emotional unity. The gift for detailed observation, for finding the exact words for some experience of the eye, is liable to disperse the attention of the relaxed reader. The minutiae may even irritate the unwary, or arouse in them only the pleasurable astonishment evoked by the carved ivory ball with eleven other balls inside it, the full-rigged ship in a bottle, the skeleton of the crucifix-fish. The bewilderment consequent upon trying to follow so alert an eye, so quick a process of association, may produce the effect of some 'metaphysical' poetry. To the moderately intellectual the poems may appear to be intellectual exercises; only to those whose intellection moves more easily will they immediately appear to have emotional value. But the detail has always its service to perform to the whole. The similes are there for use; as the mussel-shell 'opening and shutting itself like an injured fan' (where *injured* has an ambiguity good enough for Mr. Empson), the waves 'as formal as the scales on a fish'. They make us see the object more clearly, though we may not understand immediately why our attention has been called to this object, and though we may not immediately grasp its association with a number of other objects. So, in her amused and affectionate attention to animals—from the domestic cat, or 'to popularize the mule', to the most exotic strangers from the tropics, she succeeds at once in startling us into an unusual awareness of visual patterns, with something like the fascination of a high-powered microscope.

Miss Moore's poetry, or most of it, might be classified as 'descriptive' rather than 'lyrical' or 'dramatic'. Descriptive poetry is supposed to be dated to a period, and to be condemned thereby; but it is really one of the permanent modes of expression. In the eighteenth century—or say a period which includes *Cooper's Hill*, *Windsor Forest*, and Gray's *Elegy*—the scene described is a point of departure for meditations on one thing or another. The poetry of the Romantic Age, from Byron at his worst to Wordsworth at his best, wavers between the reflective and the evocative; but the description, the picture set before you, is always there for the same purpose. The aim of 'imagism', so far as I understand it, or so far as it had any, was to induce a peculiar concentration upon something visual, and to set in motion an expanding succession of concentric feelings. Some of Miss Moore's poems—for instance with animal or bird subjects—have a very wide spread of association. It would be difficult to say what is

the 'subject-matter' of 'The Jerboa'. For a mind of such agility, and for a sensibility so reticent, the minor subject, such as a pleasant little sand-coloured skipping animal, may be the best release for the major emotions. Only the pedantic literalist could consider the subject-matter to be trivial; the triviality is in himself. We all have to choose whatever subject-matter allows us the most powerful and most secret release; and that is a personal affair.

The result is often something that the majority will call frigid; for to feel things in one's own way, however intensely, is likely to look like frigidity to those who can only feel in accepted ways.

The deepest feeling always shows itself in silence;
not in silence, but restraint.

It shows itself in a control which makes possible the fusion of the ironic-conversational and the high-rhetorical, as

I recall their magnificence, now not more magnificent
than it is dim. It is difficult to recall the ornament,
    speech, and precise manner of what one might
        call the minor acquaintances twenty
            years back.

. . .

strict with tension, malignant
in its power over us and deeper
    than the sea when it proffers flattery in exchange
        for hemp,
rye, flax, horses, platinum, timber and fur.

As one would expect from the kind of activity which I have been trying to indicate, Miss Moore's versification is anything but 'free'. Many of the poems are in exact, and sometimes complicated formal patterns, and move with the elegance of a minuet. ('Elegance', indeed, is one of her certain attributes.) Some of the poems (e.g. 'Marriage', 'An Octopus') are unrhymed; in others (e.g. 'Sea Unicorns and Land Unicorns') rhyme or assonance is introduced irregularly; in a number of the poems rhyme is part of a regular pattern interwoven with unrhymed endings. Miss Moore's use of rhyme is in itself a definite innovation in metric.

In the conventional forms of rhyme the stress given by the rhyme tends to fall in the same place as the stress given by the sense. The extreme case, at its best, is the pentameter couplet of Pope. Poets before and after Pope have given variety, sometimes at the expense of smoothness, by deliberately separating the stresses, from time to time; but this separation—often effected simply by longer periods or more involved syntax—can hardly be considered as more than a deviation from the norm for the purpose of avoiding monotony. The tendency of some of the best contemporary poetry is of course to dispense with rhyme altogether; but some of those who do use it have used it here and there to make a pattern directly in contrast with the sense and rhythm pattern, to give a greater intricacy. Some of the internal rhyming of Hopkins is to the point. (Genuine or auditory internal rhyme must not be confused with false or visual internal rhyme. If a poem reads just as well when cut up so that all the rhymes fall at the end of lines, then the internal rhyme is false and only a typographical caprice, as in Oscar Wilde's 'Sphynx'.) This rhyme, which forms a pattern *against* the metric and sense pattern of the poem, may be either heavy or light—that is to say, either *heavier* or *lighter* than the other pattern. The two kinds, heavy and light, have doubtless different uses which remain to be explored. Of the *light* rhyme Miss Moore is the greatest living master; and indeed she is the first, so far as I know, who has investigated its possibilities. It will be observed that the effect sometimes requires giving a word a slightly more analytical pronunciation, or stressing a syllable more than ordinarily:

> al-
> ways has been—at the antipodes from the init-
> ial great truths. 'Part of it was crawling, part of it
> was about to crawl, the rest
> was torpid in its lair.' In the short-legged, fit-
> ful advance. . . .

It is sometimes obtained by the use of articles as rhyme words:

> an
> injured fan.
> The barnacles which encrust the side
> of the wave, cannot hide . . .
> the
> turquoise sea
> of bodies. The water drives a wedge . . .

In a good deal of what is sometimes (with an unconscious theological innuendo) called 'modernist' verse one finds either an excess or a defect of technical attention. The former appears in an emphasis upon words rather than things, and the latter in an emphasis upon things and an indifference to words. In either case, the poem is formless, just as the most accomplished sonnet, if it is an attempt to express matter unsuitable for sonnet form, is formless. But a precise fitness of form and matter mean also a balance between them: thus the form, the pattern movement, has a solemnity of its own (e.g. Shakespeare's songs), however light and gay the human emotion concerned; and a gaiety of its own, however serious or tragic the emotion. The choruses of Sophocles, as well as the songs of Shakespeare, have another concern besides the human action of which they are spectators, and without this other concern there is not poetry. And on the other hand, if you aim only at the poetry in poetry, there is no poetry either.

My conviction, for what it is worth, has remained unchanged for the last fourteen years: that Miss Moore's poems form part of the small body of durable poetry written in our time; of that small body of writings, among what passes for poetry, in which an original sensibility and alert intelligence and deep feeling have been engaged in maintaining the life of the English language.

CLEANTH BROOKS
"Miss Marianne Moore's Zoo"

Quarterly Review of Literature, 1948, pp. 178–83

Several years ago there appeared in one of the learned journals a solemn study on animals in modern poetry. The scholar duly numbered the antelopes that appear in modern poetry, the raccoons and the spiders, and even tallied the occurrences of fabulous monsters like the unicorn. The poetry of Marianne Moore, I believe, was included in the tabulation, and Miss Moore's poetry was certainly capable of furnishing more animals than any three of the other poets combined.

Though I think that we shall learn very little from tables of statistics on her animals, I do think that her preoccupation with animals is significant. It obviously testifies to a vivid and exact perception of the world about her, for this exactness of perceptions informs, not merely her descriptions of the mocking-bird or the octopus, but also her descriptions of the crape myrtle tree or a paper-weight or a quartz clock. But I think that Miss Moore's preoccupation with her beasts tells us much more than that she is an accurate observer.

I am interested primarily in what it has to tell us about the poems themselves. How does this concrete and vivid description function in the poems? The primary function, I believe, is that of a device of indirection—that of a frame of reference which allows the poet to say what she has to say about her world. To state the matter thus, however, may seem to be at once vague and pretentious in accounting for the fact that Miss Moore has given us so varied and charming a natural history. Yet, this seems, on the whole, the soundest account of the general function which Miss Moore's birds and beasts perform in her poetry: they provide the perspective through which to see our (and her) finally human world. Birds and beasts have, of course, performed such general functions in literature from the time of Aesop down to the time of Walt Disney. Miss Moore's use of them is a variant of this general function, for all that Miss Moore's variant is peculiarly her own.

It is, however, so peculiarly her own that the superficial reader may easily be baffled. Miss Moore's descriptions will seem to him a long way from Pope's:

> The bright-eyed perch with fins of Tyrian dye,
> The silver eel, in shining volumes roll'd,
> The yellow carp, in scales bedropped with gold.

It will even seem a long way from Smart's

> Strong is the lion—like a coal
> His eye-ball—like a bastion's mole
> His chest against the foes. . . .

Confronted with, and perhaps overpowered by, the complex and edged detail with which the "vehicle" is treated, the reader may conclude that there is no "tenor" at all—that he is dealing, not with a metaphor, but with a thing presented, almost scientifically, for its own sake.

Yet, of all men, it is the poet for whom man must be the measure of all things. In Marianne Moore's poetry, man is the measure ultimately. Her beasts give her, as they have given other poets, a way of breaking out of the conventionally human world—or, to put it more accurately, a way of penetrating into her human world, as it were, from the outside. All of which means that Miss Moore's animals are not conceived of clinically and scientifically even though they are not treated romantically or sentimentally. The latter point is to be emphasized. For Miss Moore's animals do not become easy caricatures of human types that we know. The poet does not patronize them. Not even the more furry, tiny ones ever become cute. Instead, she accords them their dignity; she accepts them with full seriousness, and they become the instruments by which man is judged and known.

Consider, for example, her poem "Elephants." The great beast does not become a semi-humorous type of the placid fat man. Nor does he become an allegorical symbol of certain virtues in a kind of modern bestiary. Furthermore, he does not become a sort of marvel, a blood-sweating behemoth in a romantic dithyramb upon the wonders of the world. We have the feeling that he is being accepted for himself and that he is realized for us, perhaps for the first time, in his qualities:

> Uplifted and waved until immobilized
> wistarialike, the opposing opposed
> mouse-gray twined proboscises' trunk formed by two
> trunks, fights itself to a spiral inter-nosed
> deadlock of dyke-enforced massiveness.

The qualities are given human references—how else could it be?—the author is not an elephant, but a human being:

> His straight trunk seems to say: when
> what we hoped for came to nothing, we revived.
> As loss could not ever alter Socrates'
> tranquillity, the elephant has contrived
> equanimity.

Yet we do not have the sense of a conscious and patronizing transference, or a kind of moral allegorizing. The animal has not been used as a kind of comfortable stalking horse from which to dart out observations on the human situation. Socrates' tranquillity gains almost as much from the comparison as the elephant's equanimity gains from the comparison to Socrates.

The poet can even risk an explicit "moral," as she does at the end of the poem:

> Who rides on a tiger can never dismount;
> asleep on an elephant, that is repose.

She can risk the moral because she does not treat her animals solemnly. She is willing to be whimsical, and even witty. She is constantly alive to the humorous collocations which the shapes and habits of her creatures set up. But the whimsy, when it occurs, is never a sniggering human-being-before-the-monkey-house kind of humor. It is as solid as that displayed by Alice toward the birds and beasts of Wonderland, and as little romantic.

In this connection, what I am tempted to call the gnomic quality of Miss Moore's poetry may properly come up for comment. Like the medieval bestiaries, or like Aesop's fables, her poems are strewn with gnomic utterances: "Art is unfortunate," "punctuality is not a crime," "love is the only fortress strong enough to trust to." Some are proverbial, or seem proverbial—though Miss Moore has usually provided a context which will whet the proverb to a fresh edge. Others are not proverbial at all, but are statements of fact, or the poet's own generalizations on facts. And here again the high level of concrete observation, the absence of cuteness, the refusal to talk down—all these qualities give a resonance to the brief generalizations that allows them to be taken as "true" and appropriate, or else as justified whimsies. Indeed, one of the perpetual tasks of the poet, it seems to me, is so to weight whimsies that they jar the reader with their unexpected solidity, or so to utter truisms that they take on the freshness of whimsy. (The careful reader will not be confused, and he will be forced to explore and construct his own judgment. The careless reader will have to be disregarded anyway.)

Thus far I have illustrated Miss Moore's treatment of animals principally from her poem "Elephants," and this poem may be felt by the reader to constitute a special case. For he may feel with Cicero (I avail myself of Miss Moore's note) that the elephant is "somehow allied with man" as the other beasts are not. But Miss Moore's general purpose is served also by the butterfly or the buffalo or the paper nautilus. For contrast is of the essence of this poet's method, and dissimilarity—even grotesque difference—is a principal device of hers for controlling tone. She states the matter neatly enough in her 'Pangolin':

> Among animals, *one* has a sense of
>   humor.
> Humor saves a few steps, it saves years.

Serious and careful observations which achieve point and definition in terms of minute perceptions, but observations whose intrinsic seriousness is given stability by a sense of humor—this is Marianne Moore's poetry. Among animals one does have a sense of humor, and the poet invites the reader to take advantage of this fact to the end that she may be as serious as she pleases. If one could define the special blend of seriousness and humor, one would be on the way to characterizing the special tone of which she is mistress. If one could state accurately the role which her beasts play in developing this tone, he would be able to generalize upon the essential role which they perform in her poetry. But if it is difficult to generalize, none can at least offer illustrations.

First, for an easy case, "The Wood-weasel," which, unlike most of her poems, almost flattens into mere playfulness. In the poem the Wood-weasel "emerges daintily," but, having given him the benefit of such an entrance, the poet reveals him under his baser name as the skunk. But she proceeds to validate him in his skunkhood: "well-cuttlefish-inked wool," "noble little warrior," "He is his own protection from the moth," etc. Having rehabilitated him, not by disguising him or fumigating him, but by making us *see* him, she concludes:

> Only
> Wood-weasels shall associate with me.

Ordinary weasels, presumably including the human weasels, need not apply.

But the staple of Miss Moore's poetry has to be represented by a poem like "The Pangolin" or "He 'Digesteth Harde Yron'" or "The Jerboa." Of the last poem Mr. Eliot has remarked that it "would be difficult to say what is the 'subject-matter.' . . . For a mind of such agility, and for a sensibility so reticent, the minor subject, such as a pleasant little sand-coloured skipping animal, may be the best release for the major emotions." The warning against concluding that the poem is trivial because it lacks an *obvious* subject matter is quite proper. But if the reader persists in demanding a "subject matter," we do not have to let the question go by default. We can break "The Jerboa" down to its skeleton, if it be required: "The Jerboa" is a vertebrate, not a jellyfish. There are the sectional headings, "Too Much" and "Abundance" to serve as pointers. There is the sense in which the jerboa is the least of the Pharaoh's animal subjects, "a small desert rat / and not famous"; the sense in which, like the Pharaoh, it is the master of its desert world; the sense in which it is superior to the Pharaoh, who needs the Nile—the jerboa "lives without water"; but there is also in the poem the dignity and beauty of the Pharaoh's world realized for us lest we vulgarize the contrasts between man and rat; there is the interest of the Pharaoh and his people in "small things" to lead up to, and perhaps to justify, the minute examination of the jerboa which the poem makes; there is the detailed description itself in which the jerboa is "Seen by / daylight"—"silvered to steel by the force / of the large desert moon—asleep," "the nose nested in fur" or in flight, making "fern-seed / foot-prints with kangaroo speed"—description which affirms the right of the jerboa to be used in the contrast and which at the same time warns us against reducing it to a mere term in the contrast. There is, above all, the constant pressure of the poet's own intelligence to prevent us turning this detail into preciousness or that observation into solemn moralization.

The poem "says" something, says a great deal. But it says that something so richly, so fully, that all attempted summaries become falsifications of what is said, and it says it with such complete control of the nuances that what is said can be only fumblingly approximated in a paraphrase. To be unparaphraseable is to be at the other extreme from saying "nothing."

HUGH KENNER
"Supreme in Her Abnormality"

Poetry, September 1954, pp. 356–63

Miss Moore's solid achievement is to have brought over a number of the 241 poems (in *The Fables of La Fontaine*) virtually intact, and (by dint of persevering with the least tractable) to have discovered the principles of a badly needed idiom, urbane without slickness and brisk without imprecision. Since Chaucer's fell into disuse, English verse, constantly allured by the sonorous and catachrestic, hasn't had a reliable *natural* idiom that can imitate the speech of civilized men and still handle deftly subjects more complex than the ones whose emotions pertain, like Wordsworth's, to hypnotic obviousness; hence nothing existed for a La Fontaine to be translated into. Pope's ease (as distinguished from his wit) is slippery, treacherous even in his own hands; Dryden's direct-ness clangs on iron stilts; and the "naturalness" of various minor 18th century compoundings—tinctured by ballads and diluted by preoccupations with nerveless diction—offers no equivalent at all for La Fontaine's hard neatness. Miss Moore's best work demonstrates that a specialization of one language may be the best possible parallel for the simplicities of another; the very artlessness with which she can employ a Latinate diction without sounding as though she had read Vergil ("Clemency may be our best resource" for "Plus fait douceur que violence") helps to keep her least natural locutions in touch with speech.

Her artlessness isn't at all like La Fontaine's transparency; it resembles the "unconscious fastidiousness" which she once illustrated, in *Critics and Connoisseurs*, by adducing "childish . . . determination to make a pup eat his meat from the plate." Her air of plunging without premeditation into tor-tuousness which she subdues *ambulando* is sometimes annoy-ing, but it confers virtue too, complicating the plain sense enough to fend off *simplesse*. La Fontaine's curiously *pastoral* urbanity (not the least like Pope's), his devaluing of lions and busy kings, his citation of self-sufficient foxes or asses wise too late, and his implicit appeal to the wisdom of a Greek slave who perceived a wealth of analogies between the courtly world and the animal kingdom because he stood outside both of them, present the translator with problems perhaps greater than those posed by his intricate rhythms and rhymes. Previous translators, assuming that the transparent sense will look after itself, have been misled into foisting on their author a world of simple follies from which one can detach oneself by an act as facile as walking out of the zoo, in order to live by a few *simpliste* maxims. His situations are casually taken for granted:

> Maître corbeau, sur un arbre perché,
>   Tenait en son bec un fromage;
> Maître renard, par l'odeur alléché,
>   Lui tint à peu prés ce langage:

A crow with some cheese, and a fox attracted by the smell; nothing more casual (assuming that foxes like cheese). The fox has a few conventional phrases:

>   "Hé bonjour, Monsieur du Corbeau.
> Que vous êtes joli! que vous me semblez beau!
>   Sans mentir, si votre ramage
>   Se rapporte à votre plumage,
> Vous êtes le phénix des hôtes de ces bois."

Perceiving however that the French neatness would make for empty English, Miss Moore with incomparable deftness complicates the diction very considerably:

>   On his airy perch among the branches
>   Master Crow was holding cheese in
> his beak.
>   Master Fox, whose pose suggested fragrances,
>   Said in language which of course I
> cannot speak,
>   "Aha, superb Sir Ebony, well met.
> How black! who else boasts your metallic jet!
>   If your warbling were unique,
>   Rest assured, as you are sleek,
> One would say that our wood had hatched nightin-
> gales."

The "airy perch," the pose suggesting fragrances, "Sir Ebony," the "metallic jet," the "warbling," the sleekness and the nightingales we owe to Miss Moore; La Fontaine by contrast sketches his situation with a few swift platitudes. What has happened, however, is not simply the interposition of a more crinkly language; the tone, and so our relationship to the fable, is newly complicated. "À peu près ce langage" is one of La Fontaine's negligent gestures of paraphrase; he wasn't there at the time (as he frequently tells us in other fables), but feels it safe from general knowledge of flatterers to assume that the sense was about as follows. Miss Moore's deliciously practical "language which of course I cannot speak" effects at a stroke however the complete separation of this incident from its human analogies: this is fox- and crow-talk. Hence the "Sir Ebony," the "metallic jet," and the rest of the specificities; hence too the pervading *strangeness* of idiom, which she isn't at all at pains to mitigate. In the authoress of "The Jerboa" and "The Pangolin" this strangeness may be idiosyncrasy, but here idiosyncrasy is as good as principle. La Fontaine's crow, responding to the fox's flattery, "pour montrer sa belle voix, ouvre un large bec." He reminds us of a man. But in Miss Moore's version,

>   All aglow, Master Crow tried to run a few scales,
>   Risking trills and intervals,
> Dropping the prize as his huge beak sang false.

Exquisitely absurd, because he is unambiguously a crow; and his corvine ungainliness gives the twentieth-century fable an edge the seventeenth-century ones acquire, in a different language, by different and more insinuating means.

That a Marianne Moore crow even in a translation should be unmistakably a crow, not a symbol, is what we should expect from the use to which she puts the celebrated animals in her poems. Her characteristic beast is the only thing of its kind, prized for its uniqueness (thus in "Four Quartz Crystal Clocks": "an aye-aye is not / an angwantíbo, potto, or loris"); her "zebras, supreme in their abnormality" and "elephants with their fog-coloured skin" don't impress us as members of the animal kingdom but as grotesque individualities; while the indubitably human cat in the same poem ("The Monkeys") who speaks the astringent moral isn't "people" but a well-remembered person. When she uses an elephant to voice her characteristic theme in "Melancthon":

> Openly, yes,
> with the naturalness
>   of the hippopotamus or the alligator
>   when it climbs out on the bank to experience
>   the
> sun, I do these
> things which I do, which please
>   no one but myself. . . .

it isn't the elephant's abstract ponderosity that recommends it to her as a persona: rather, the gesture it performs by existing at all

>   (for the
> patina of circumstance can but enrich what was
> there to begin with)

allies itself with her own temperamental taut self-sufficiency, mutating primness into resilience.

The uncompromising inhabitants of Miss Moore's zoo, cross-bred with the citizens of the urbane La Fontaine's hierarchic animal kingdom, lend to an enterprise endangered by obviousness a jaunty manner of speaking that always arrests and often wholly entrances the modern reader:

> A mite of a rat was mocking an elephant
> As it moved slowly by, majestically aslant,
>   Valued from antiquity,

> Towering in draped solemnity
> While bearing along in majesty
> A queen of the Levant—
> With her dog, her cat, and sycophant,
> Her parakeet, monkey, anything she might want—
>   On their way to relics they wished to
>   see. . . .

Every word has its presence, and the tone is inimitable. Some of the beginnings (less often the endings) are less happy:

> When warm spring winds make the grass green
> And animals break from winter captivity,
> A certain wolf, like other creatures grown lean,
>   Was looking about for what food there might be.
> As said, a wolf, after a winter that has been hard
> Came on a horse turned out to grass. . . .

This isn't the way to begin this story, though it is a desperate attempt to include all the words that are in the French. La Fontaine, however, arranges them differently; he begins with the wolf ("Un certain loup dans la saison / Que les tièdes zéphyrs ont l'herbe rajeunie . . .") and the "Un loup, dis-je" five lines later is accompanied by a discreet cough as he realizes that he has been drawn into digressive poetizing about the spring. Miss Moore, on the other hand, began with the spring, then got round to the wolf, and looks excessively awkward when two lines later she has to pretend that she is remembering with a start a subject only just introduced. Given her opening, omission of the "As said, a wolf" clause would make infinitely better sense; it is probably a sound rule in translating to omit what won't function in your new poem. Whether her native stubbornness interfered, or a failure to comprehend La Fontaine's delicate gesture involved itself with a determination to render his faults word for word as well as his beauties, there is no guessing. There is a third possibility. From an exceedingly odd foreword to the volume we learn of a condition—presumably the publishers'—"that Professor Harry Levin examine the work to ensure a sound equivalent to the French;" further that after Mr. Levin's "scholastic intensities of supervision" Mr. Monroe Engel of The Viking Press "ameliorated" persisting ungainlinesses"; finally that "as consulting editor at the Press Malcolm Cowley pronounced certain portions of the text 'rather far from the French'; he has contributed lines in addition to pedagogy." With such a committee at work, one may trust that every word of the French has gotten represented somewhere. It is perhaps surprising that Miss Moore was able to get away with inserting "Aha, superb Sir Ebony"—though no one's vigilance prevented "Le fantôme brilliant attire une alouette" from getting rendered by ". . . allured by his bright mirroring *of her* a lark" (p. 131). Surely it was the sun's reflection, not her own, that attracted her?

It is only her habitual nonchalance that prompts enquiry into Miss Moore's poetic lapses; their magnitude is seldom sufficient to damage even single poems, and the enterprise as a whole succeeds astonishingly. As often as not they occur where oddness of expression (for the sake of tone) complicates the sense beyond easy decipherment:

> Where in spring find the flowers gardens bore,
> Like Flora's own in bloom at his door?

seems an unnecessarily tortuous way of saying that Flora's choicest gifts grew in this man's garden. When Miss Moore gets preoccupied (understandably) with tucking all the words into the given rhythms and rhyme-schemes she frequently produces what may be the neatest solution to this particular cross-word puzzle but is not the best way of conveying the subject at hand in English.

It is often, however, the best way of creating a climate of mind, not heretofore available in English, in which the wit of the Fables can thrive. All convincing translation remains miraculous, but the normal excellence of this one is surprisingly sustained: the work of a deliberate and indefatigable intelligence, which earns its reward when the translator's special diction, personal and by existing literary standards impure, re-creates the French aplomb with an absoluteness no careful reader is going to ascribe to luck.

HOWARD NEMEROV
From "A Few Bricks from Babel"
Sewanee Review, Winter 1954, pp. 655–63

Offhand I would probably have shared what seems a widespread impression that Marianne Moore was admirably qualified, not only by talent but by sympathy as well, to translate the *Fables* of La Fontaine; this impression appears to have been based on a very rapid summing-up of both poets: "Ah, yes—animals." But there is, I find, a great distance between a Moore jerboa and a La Fontaine rat, and because I enjoy some of Miss Moore's poetry a good deal I am sorry to have to say that the results of this cooperation strike me not as merely inadequate or mediocre but as in a positive way terrible. My fine critical hindsight tells me now, what it didn't warn me of beforehand, that Miss Moore has never been a fabulist at all, that her animals never acted out her moralities; that their function was ever to provide a minutely detailed, finely perceived symbolic knot to be a center for the pattern of her recondite meditations; that what she shares with La Fontaine is a shrewdness and delicacy of the moral judgment, but that the two poets' ways of getting there—their *fables*, in fact—are so different as to be opposed. I still feel, with somewhat less conviction than before, that Miss Moore might have got a happier result by setting herself to *tell* La Fontaine's stories in English, for it seems that a critical factor in the failure of these translations may have been an uncertainty about the ideal degree of her dependence on the French: as poems to be read in English, they are irritatingly awkward, elliptical, complicated, and very jittery as to the meter; as renderings of the French they vacillate between pedantic strictness and strange liberty.

I began with the intention of reading the volume through without reference to the original—since if the poems could not be read as English it did not seem to matter how accurate they might be as translations—but was at once pulled up by the dedication to the Dauphin, of which Miss Moore has printed the French on the facing page. Inescapably, "Je chante les héros dont Ésope est le père" had come out as "I sing when Aesop's wand animates my lyre." There is nothing necessarily wrong with this: it is precisely the *unnecessary* distance from the original which is odd. And in the last couplet, where La Fontaine's sentiment is rigorously conventional—"Et, si de t'agréer je n'emporte le prix/J'aurai du moins l'honneur de l'avoir entrepris"—Miss Moore has written something much more friendly: "And if I have failed to give you real delight,/My reward must be that I had hoped I might." I read on according to intention but with an occasional uneasy sense of missing things; and presently began turning to the French simply to make certain here and there of what was being said. For example, in the fable about belling the rat (II,2) the rats hold their meeting while the cat goes courting:

> Now as he climbed, or creeps lengthened his
>   loin
> In his renegade quest for some tabby he'd court,

Through the witches' sabbath in which they'd con-
    sort,
Surviving rats had seen fit to convene
In a corner to discuss their lot.

I was struck, or maybe stricken is a better word, by "creeps lengthened his loin." Application to La Fontaine revealed what was behind all this:

Or un jour qu'au haut et au loin
Le galant alla chercher femme,
Pendant tout le sabbat qu'il fit avec sa dame,
Le demeurant des Rats tint chapitre en un coin
Sur la nécessité présente.

It is easy to see how *"loin"* became "loin," though not so easy to see why, or what has been gained except a false rime to "convene." But a number of other difficulties come up as a result of this investigation. Granting the necessity of lengthening the first two octosyllabic lines to ten syllables and twelve, is there any other justification for "renegade quest"? Even if the cat has earlier been called "un diable," why should the sabbath be a "witches' sabbath," when the meaning is simply that the rats got a rest? Why confuse the issue with "they," which grammatically seems to want to mean the rats (since "consort" doesn't have to have a sexual meaning)? And why, having expanded the mere suggestion of "au haut et au loin" to the monstrous "as he climbed, or creeps lengthened his loin," does Miss Moore then economize by cutting out La Fontaine's thematic figure—whereby in the moral the rats become "chapitres de moines . . . chapitres de chanoines"—and give us "had seen fit to convene" for "tint chapitre en un coin"? So that she can go on to translate "doyen" once as "doyen" and then later on as "dean"?

Perhaps these are quibbles; I'm sorry if so. And I would give them up instantly if it seemed that the sacrifice of simplicity, accuracy and sense had resulted in some clear gain in the English version; but it was the oddity of the English which in the first place drew my notice. And while the first line of that passage is outstandingly exceptionally silly, the general nature of the faults it indicates can be illustrated by numerous examples, of which I shall give a few.

Miss Moore habitually invents metaphors for her poet. La Fontaine talks of people pretending to sophistication and travel, who, "caquetants au plus dru,/Parlent de tout, et n'ont rien vu," for which Miss Moore supplies, "Boasting he's seen this spot and that,/Whereas his alps have all been flat." Gratuitous, probably harmless in this instance, but at least irrelevant and probably destructive when "Les petits, en toute affaire,/Esquivent fort aisément" becomes "modesty any-where,/Glides in as when silk is sewn." Even when the figure itself is clever, particularly when it is clever, it is disturbing to feel the immediate suspicion that La Fontaine wrote something different.

Miss Moore tends to extremes of latinity, sometimes I suspect because she will do anything for a rime, often a false rime. If a falcon says to a capon, "Ton peu d'entendement/Me rend tout étonné," Miss Moore writes, "Wretched phenome-non/Of limitation. Dullard, what do you know?" La Fontaine begins to consider the head and tail of the serpent with: "Le serpent a deux parties/Du genre humaine ennemies," and Miss Moore brings out, "A serpent has mobility/Which can shatter intrepidity."

The general objection, of which the two foregoing objections are specific instances, is that Miss Moore is so often found going the long way around, making complexities out of simplicities, loading lines with detail until they are corrupted in sense or measure, and writing, in consequence, absurdly

bad English. "Une Huitre, que le flot y venoit d'apporter" (to the beach, that is) appears in translation as "an oyster amid what rollers scatter."

It is not much of a compliment to say that there are better things in this translation than these examples suggest; there would have to be. But I give the examples because they seem to me to typify the faults in Miss Moore's practice. Even when things are going well so far as the translation is concerned, the tone and texture of the language remain very uncertain; just as we think we begin to hear in English the modesty and humorous dignity of the fabulist, along comes some monstrous circumlocution or complicated syntactical maneuver to ensure the fall of the rime. And meanwhile the meter is, to say the least of it, very strange; it is syllabic, I think, and Miss Moore in her Foreword mentions "my effort to approximate the original rhythms of the Fables," but what emerges in English is frequently a kind of gallop now and again flattened by a reduction to prose. The following passage seems a fair sample:

Then he burned bones when they found a roadstead,
Soiling Jove's nostrils with the noisomeness engen-
    dered,
And said, "There, Sire; accept the homage I've
    tendered—
Ox perfume to be savored by almighty Jupiter.
These fumes discharge my debt; I am from now on a
    free man."

I am sorry to be unable to like these translations better than I do; the labor of their preparation must have been long and hard, and the quality of Miss Moore's original talent justified very high expectations. The difficulties of the matter seem to have been faced up to, but rather added to than overcome by the translator's own predilections and powers. One final quotation will perhaps serve as a summary of what appears to me to have gone wrong, as a suggestion, too, that somewhere near a poem of La Fontaine there exists, potential-ly, a poem of Marianne Moore, but that the two have not come into phase. The Epilogue of Book Six begins thus:

Bornons ici cette carrière:
Les longs ouvrages me font peur.
Loin d'épuiser une matière,
On n'en doit prendre que la fleur.
Our peregrination must end there.
One's skin creeps when poets persevere.
Don't press pith from core to perimeter;
Take the flower of the subject, the thing that is rare.

This passage was translated by Elizur Wright in 1841 as follows:

Here check we our career.
Long books I greatly fear.
I would not quite exhaust my stuff;
The flower of subjects is enough.

The general question raised by this comparison is as much concerned with what translators try to do as with what they actually get done; whatever we think of Elizur Wright's version—I hold it to be very fine—we must agree that it shows a detailed deference to the meaning of the original *and* an idea, perhaps a very simple idea, of what English verse is. Now the famous revolution in modern poetry, accompanied by a special uprising in the translation business, destroyed at least the security of that idea of English verse if not the idea itself; but this revolution, product of a few great talents, itself produced no idea of English verse but only the examples of the few great talents, with the stern recommendation: Go thou and do otherwise. It did produce some general notions, what Mr. Pound called his "results," and Miss Moore declares that "the practice of Ezra Pound has been for me a governing principle," but it is doubtful that these general notions, in so complex an affair as translation, ever did more than prescribe avoidances; and a principle cannot substitute for a habit of mind and ear, nor for ease and fluency in the measure or the idiom.

I have observed, too, that modern translations are praised precisely because they are modern translations. Since Mr. Eliot's celebrated remark about Gilbert Murray all those scholarly gentlemen who "did" (often indeed in both senses) "the classics" have been held mightily in disrepute, while recent translators are flattered by critics and publishers (and sometimes preen themselves prefatorily) on writing their versions in "modern, idiomatic English," "the speech of living English, the language a poet would choose for his own work today." But this sort of judgment seems to put an undue strain on the qualities of "living English," and one thinks mournfully of the ghosts of Golding, Chapman, Pope, who never had a chance.

For the translator's problem, a special and poignant case of the artistic problem generally, is that of making flat maps of a round world; some distortion is inevitable. Bearings and distances become accurate at the expense of sizes and shapes, and the end result will never *look* much like the real thing but the hope is that real navigation will be possible with its aid.

CHARLES TOMLINSON
"Abundance, Not Too Much: The Poetry of Marianne Moore"
Sewanee Review, Autumn 1957, pp. 677–87

The appearance of a new volume by Miss Moore offers the pleasantly appropriate occasion for looking back over the continuity of her poetic achievement. In her recent *Like a Bulwark* there are no startlingly new departures. What one has, rather, is a reperusal of themes that have always interested her, consolidated by a lifetime's sharpening of her collage technique. The consolidation is at once evident in the four best pieces in this short volume, "Tom Fool at Jamaica," "Then the Ermine," "The Sycamore," and "Apparition of Splendor". In two of her new pieces, "The Staff of Aesculapius" and "Blessed Is the Man," Miss Moore's attempt to use the apparently intractable ("business documents and/school-books; all these phenomena are important" as she once wrote in *Poetry*) does not quite achieve her object. The attempt, as always, is interesting, but the details of plastic surgery in the first poem and the eloquence of President Eisenhower's ghost-writer in the second, defeat her indefatigable will to experiment. "Logic and 'The Magic Flute,'" a piece on the first telecolor transmission of that opera, is closer to success, but it remains, I feel, an experiment as earlier grapplings with the intractable do not (one thinks, for example, of "Four Quartz Crystal Clocks" and "People's Surroundings"). The dexterity and intelligence of other poems in *Like a Bulwark* are nimble variants of that keyboard, that system of transitions between fact and moral fantasy which characterizes Miss Moore, with its counterpoint which can encompass and utilize every combination between those chosen limits.

The system of transitions was established in the themes of Miss Moore's earliest poetry. Her symbolical use of animals is the perfect expression of a spontaneous but orderly mind. The orderliness manifests itself in the precise style of writing, the spontaneity in this fantasy where questions of conduct and manners are referred to the animal world. Miss Moore's fantasy is a controlled fantasy, a high seriousness that refuses to be

merely solemn. In "Black Earth," for instance, the monologue of the elephant presents us with the discussion of the relationship between "external poise" and "spiritual poise." It is a poem which is so central to what Miss Moore has to say that I will deal with it first as an introduction to the themes of her work. "Black Earth" is a poem about spontaneity and about that richness and depth of individuality, "spiritual poise," which occurs when past experience combines with the influx of fresh feeling. It opens with the elephant's declaration of its habits and its nature:

> Openly, yes,
> with the naturalness
>   of the hippopotamus or the alligator
>   when it climbs out on the bank to experience
>   the
> sun, I do these
> things which I do, which please
>   no one but myself . . .

This is the first half of the declaration. Spontaneity is measured against the touchstone of the hippopotamus which is natural and spacious, the alligator which is natural but may bite, against the act of emerging from water into sunshine. Its element is the sun. It pleases no one but its possessor, for its expression shocks the prude and embarrasses the self-conscious. Even the encrusted layers of old experience, of old knowledge, of habit which might have deadened, are enlivened once more; the entire self is brought into play:

> . . . Now I breathe and now I am submerged;
> the blemishes stand up and shout when
>   the object
>   in view was a
>   renaissance; . . .

The elephant shifts its considerations to another point of view in order to reflect upon those layers of personality which have been deposited, as it were, by circumstance rather than *given*. What relation do they bear to the source of individuality? What part do they play in "natural," spontaneous action, in *living?*—

> . . . shall I say
> the contrary? The sediment of the river which
> encrusts my joints, makes me very grey, but I
>   am used
> to it, it may
> remain there; do away
>   with it and I am myself done away with, for the
>   patina of circumstance can but enrich what
>   was
> there to begin
> with . . .

The "patina of circumstance" teaches us to cope with future circumstances; protects one in difficult experiences because of the knowledge it enables one to carry about; teaches one how to behave in the future, because the deposit is a valuable memory of how one behaved or how one erred in the past. This "patina" becomes part of one's growing self, part of one's manner of thinking. The elephant's skin is implicitly made to symbolize the protective power of both personal insights and traditional wisdom. It complements spontaneity.

> . . . This elephant-skin
>   which I inhabit, fibred over like the shell of
>   the cocoanut, this piece of black glass through
>   which no light
> can filter—cut
> into checkers by rut

> upon rut of unpreventable experience—
> it is a manual for the peanut-tongued and
>   the
>
> hairy-toed . . .

The elephant-skin, "cut into checkers by rut upon rut" and equated with "black earth," is thus a kind of double image. It embodies the idea of an enriching element of adult wisdom going side by side with natural spontaneity and then is *itself* compared to the earth cut into checkers. This gives the adult wisdom an earthy quality and also makes one see the elephant-skin more vividly, so that the thing symbolized and the physical presence of the symbol both gain in intensity. "The peanut-tongued and the hairy-toed," the monkeys in the human-animal jungle, require a "manual" because they "do . . . things which [they do], which please no one but [themselves]," but, unlike the elephant, possess no power complementary to their spontaneity and sense of freedom, no "patina of circumstance." They are ignoble savages, men who have remained children in mentality and outlook. Possessing no richness of experience they have not discovered the real art of living and the really adult balance of spontaneity and—in no limiting sense—formality. They do not, to paraphrase, understand what civilization is, or should be; for social conduct—the fusion of experience and spontaneity—remains unknown to them.

> . . . Black
> but beautiful, my back
>   is full of the history of power. Of power? What
>   is powerful and what is not? My soul shall never
> be cut into
> by a wooden spear; through-
>   out childhood to the present time, the unity of
>   life and death has been expressed by the circum-
>   ference
> described by my
> trunk; nevertheless I
>   perceive feats of strength to be inexplicable after
>   all; and I am on my guard; external poise, it
> has its centre
> well nurtured—we know
>   where—in pride; but spiritual poise, it has its
>   centre where?
>   My ears are sensitized to more than the sound of
> the wind. I see
> and I hear, unlike the
>   wandlike body of which one hears so much,
>   which was
>   made
>   to see and not to see; to hear and not to
>   hear; . . .

In this passage the poet goes on to assess the nature of power, by which she means not something bullying but something unashamed of itself, something positively human, evolved out of experience ("throughout childhood to the present time") and with its source deep in the individual and the individual's spontaneity. "Power" takes its origin from "spiritual poise," it has its mystery ("I perceive feats of strength to be inexplicable after all . . .") and also its dangers—it may well be confused with its antithesis "pride," "external poise." The elephant has "spiritual poise," "power" (positive and fully adult) and is thus superior to "the peanut-tongued and the hairy-toed," the uncivilized apes, and superior also to their antithesis in false refinement, "the wandlike body," which might be anything between a nineteenth-century poet's conception of what a woman ought to be like and the corsetted

modern version in Mayfair or Park Avenue. The elephant is not intimidated by "beauty"; spontaneity, earthiness, a touch of mystery, contribute more readily to a conception of what is fully human than sensitive nerves, fragile prettiness and the world of glassy egotism and over-refinement in which these exist. Accordingly, the elephant rejects that wandlike body as being over-refined and yet not refined enough in a fully human, unneurotic way: it is

> that tree-trunk without
> roots, accustomed to shout
>   its own thoughts to itself like a shell, maintained
>   intact
>   by who knows what strange pressure of the
>   atmosphere;
> that
> spiritual
> brother to the coral-
>   plant, absorbed into which, the equable sap-
>   phire
>   light
>   becomes a nebulous green . . .

The wandlike body is a denial of human individuality, a simplification of a human being to fit aesthetic preconceptions. Extended indefinitely it would produce a universe of rootless neurotics and egotists incapable of the life of community and relationship:

> . . . The I of each is to
> the I of each
> a kind of fretful speech
>   which sets a limit on itself; . . .

The poem concludes with a final definition of what the elephant, seen in its full symbolical context, represents in terms of stability, spontaneousness, balance, as against that world of false refinements, of "phenomena/which vacillate like a/translucence of the atmosphere." Beauty is more than skin deep or it does not exist. The mysterious power of the elephant, its stability (with a "beautiful element of unreason under it") which can withstand the shocks of experience ("it/has looked at electricity and at the earth-/quake and is still/here; . . .") reveals the ephemeral titillations of "fashion," "society," "the poetic" for what they are worth:

>   . . . the elephant is
> black earth preceded by a tendril? Compared with
>   those
> phenomena
> which vacillate like a
>   translucence of the atmosphere, the elephant is
>   that on which darts cannot strike decisively
>   the first
> time, a substance
> needful as an instance
>   of the indestructibility of matter; it
>   has looked at electricity and at the earth-
> quake and is still
> here; the name means thick. Will
>   depth be depth, thick skin be thick, to one
>   who can see no
>   beautiful element of unreason under it?

An important corollary derived from the "social" implications of "Black Earth" appears in "Silence." The first poem contains a conception of civilized values; the second a specific comment on the qualities to be desired in guest and host:

> My father used to say,
> "Superior people never make long visits,
> Have to be shown Longfellow's grave

Or the glass flowers at Harvard."
. . . Nor was he insincere in saying, "Make my
    house your inn."
Inns are not residences.

The relationship between host and guest is an important one and its quality the test of how much real "civilization" has gone their making "Self-reliant like the cat" and "The deepest feeling always shows itself in silence;/not in silence, but restraint" emphasize once more a fusion of spontaneous resource and formality (again, I wish to use the word positively) resulting in positive social conduct. Thus, "Silence" causes one to return to "Black Earth" and vice versa, because both contain a clue to the alternative to false relationships and to that balance of personality which makes any relationship possible.

An objective symbol of the values proposed in these two poems is to be found in the description Miss Moore gives us of the little town in "The Steeple Jack." It is the symbol of a social and also a natural mean. The town makes no attempt to "impress"; it possesses "spiritual poise";

    . . . The church portico has four fluted
        columns, each a single piece of stone, made
    modester by white-wash. This would be a fit haven
        for
    waifs, children, animals, prisoners,
    . . .
    It could scarcely be dangerous to be living
        in a town like this, of simple people
    Who have a steeple-jack placing danger-signs by the
        church
    when he is gilding the solid-
        pointed star, which on a steeple
    stands for hope.

Nature is present in "the sweet sea air," the "water etched/with waves as formal as the scales on a fish," in the sea-gulls, the lobsters, the storm that "bends the salt/mask grass, disturbs stars in the sky and the/star on the steeple," in "the trumpet vine,"

    fox-glove, giant snap-dragon, a salpiglossis that has
        spots and stripes; morning-glories; gourds,
            or moon-vines trained on fishing-twine
    at the back door

But, to use the subtitles of "The Jerboa," it is natural "Abundance," not "Too much":

    . . . There are no banyans, frangipani, nor
        jack-fruit trees; nor an exotic serpent
    life. Ring lizard and snake-skin for the foot, or
        crocodile;
    but here they've cats, not cobras, to
        keep down the rats. The diffident
    little newt
    with white pin-dots on black horizontal spaced-
        out bands lives here; yet there is nothing that
    ambition can buy or take away.[1]

In this setting "the hero, the student,/the steeple-jack, each in his way,/is at home." The student perceives the presence of the human mean beside the natural in "an elegance of which/the source is not bravado" that characterizes the architecture of the town, "the antique/sugar-bowl-shaped summer house of interlacing slats," the church spire, and its portico "made modester by white-wash." The harmony of civilization and nature in the scene is made doubly telling by the intermingling of human and natural attributes in each others' own sphere: the waves are "formal," the pitch of the

church spire is "not true" as though it had grown there rather than been built.

I have written of only three pieces in any detail, all from *Selected Poems* (1935). It would be possible to go on to examine many more, but my aim has been merely to establish the touchstone against which the reader can judge the poems in the subsequent volumes and observe their essential continuity of theme and method. The fundamental concerns do not change. Indeed, one might say that in the interaction of order and spontaneity Miss Moore had found the theme on which to variate in all that follows and that the degree of her success has lain in the observance of the limits of her method. The temptation to "improve" on it appears, however marginally, in *What Are Years* (1941) and more noticeably in *Nevertheless* (1944). The successes among the later poems—and I think, among others, of such pre-eminent pieces as "Virginia Britannia," "The Pangolin," "Elephants," and "His Shield"—result from a delicate and subtle balance within such artistic limits as I have attempted to outline in my account of the three earlier pieces. When the spontaneity is consciously worked, as in certain of the later poems, there is a resultant lack of significance in the order, in the form, of what is offered:

        is some such word
            as the chord
                Brahms had heard
                from a bird,
        sung down near the root of the throat;
        it's the little downy woodpecker
                    spiralling a tree—
                    up up up like mercury . . .

The effect here (in "Propriety," which provides a fairly representative example) is to simplify and to sentimentalize. Stylistically it represents a kind of self-parody:

        . . . Brahms and Bach,
            no; Bach and Brahms. To thank Bach
        for his song
        first, is wrong.
            Pardon me; . . .

The order and the spontaneity no longer coalesce, no longer fuse: the order becomes merely typographical dexterity and the spontaneity the exploitation of a willed simplicity. "Propriety" illustrates a loss of stylistic decorum within Miss Moore's chosen limits. Two other much longer poems, "In Distrust of Merits" and "Keeping Their World Large" show what happens when she ventures outside of them. Both attempt to deal with the theme of war and both fail because the feeling is no longer contained. Her characteristic achievements derive from an impersonality in the means of the poetry which, in fact, permits the fusion of both personal and impersonal in their most significant form. There occurs no invitation to "feeling" because the means do not admit of such. In her two wartime pieces, however, the means admit of little else:

        They're fighting, fighting, fighting the blind
            man who thinks he sees,—
        who cannot see that the enslaver is
        enslaved; the hater, harmed. O shining O
            firm star, O tumultuous
                ocean lashed till small things go
            as they will, the mountainous
                wave makes us who look, know
    depth.

It is precisely in the avoidance of an over-elaboration of the rhetorical machinery, as here, and of that inviting coyness of diction as in "Propriety," that makes her latest volume, *Like a Bulwark*, so refreshing. But this is to put the matter negatively. The verse of "Tom Fool at Jamaica" will establish the point in positive terms:

> Look at Jonah embarking from Joppa, deterred by
>   the whale; hard going for a statesman whom nothing
>   could detain,
>   although one who would not rather die than
>   repent.
>   Be infallible at your peril, for your system will
>   fail,
>   and select as a model the schoolboy in Spain
>   who at the age of six, portrayed a mule and a
>   jockey
>   who had pulled up for a snail.

There Miss Moore is, to my ear, playing a quite new tune— one that owes something to the metric of her La Fontaine translations, but is rhythmically more stable. Tone and typography determine each other:

> "There is a submerged magnificence, as Victor Hugo
>   said." *Sentir avec ardeur*; that's it; magnetized by
>   feeling. . . .

The pause between the great man and the verb of his pronouncement registers exactly the degree of seriousness which we are to accord it, just as the quick snippet from the Marquise de Boufflers and "that's it" which follows, point the joke with a calculated note of impatience. And again, later in the poem, with similar ease, Miss Moore turns the tone lightly and dexterously against herself:

> Tom Fool is "a handy horse," with a chiseled foot.
>   You've the beat
> of a dancer to a measure or harmonious rush
> of a porpoise at the prow where the racers all win
>   easily—
> like centaurs' legs in tune, as when kettledrums
>   compete;
> nose rigid and suede nostrils spread, a light left
>   hand on the rein, till
>   well—this is rhapsody.

Spontaneity and order, the theme which underlies the early "Black Earth" and "The Steeple-Jack," is enunciated here in scherzo movement. In "The Sycamore," the keenness of a wondering humility, which is the outcome of Miss Moore's resolution of the claims of these opposites, appears in her evocation of the tiny insect over against the gigantic tree:

> Worthy of Imami,
>   the Persian—clinging to a stiffer stalk
>   was a little dry
>   thing from the grass,
>   in the shape of a Maltese cross,
>   retiringly formal
>   as if to say: "And there was I
>   like a field-mouse at Versailles."

The moral correlative of that balance appears in descriptive exactness, as in the picture of the porcupine as "the double-embattled thistle of jet." Moral awareness speaks through the natural scene and the natural scene is recreated through moral awareness:

> as when the lightning shines
>   on thistlefine spears, among
>   prongs in lanes above lanes of a shorter prong,
> "with the forest for nurse," also dark
>   at the base—where needle-debris
> springs and shows no footmark;
>   . . .
> Maine should be pleased that its animal
>   is not a waverer, and rather

> than fight, lets the primed quill fall.
>   Shallow oppressor, intruder,
>   insister you have found a resister.

In a poem like this ("Apparition of Splendor") one feels that Miss Moore is exploiting her best minor vein. She doesn't try for the world-shattering immensities of "In Distrust of Merits" and "Keeping Their World Large," and she is consequently able to achieve something far stabler and more profound. For she is working within the acknowledged limits which have contained her real vitality from her earliest verse onwards, a vitality which I have attempted to define in her own phrase— "abundance, not too much."

Notes

1. The flower-fruit-animal passages are regrettably omitted from *Collected Poems* (1951).

HUGH KENNER
From "Disliking It"
A Homemade World
1975, pp. 88–118

At various times in her lifetime we discern Miss Moore being a librarian, an editor, a teacher of typewriting: locating fragments already printed; picking and choosing; making, letter by letter, neat pages. So one might itemize her poetic procedure.

Her poems are not for the voice; she sensed this in reading them badly. In response to a question, she once said that she wrote them for people to look at. Moreover, one cannot imagine them handwritten. As Ruskin's tree, on the page, exists in tension between arboreal process and the mind's serial inventory of arms, shields, tables, hands and hills, so Miss Moore's cats, her fish, her pangolins and ostriches exist on the page in tension between the mechanisms of print and the presence of a person behind those mechanisms. Handwriting flows with the voice, and here the voice is as synthetic as the cat, not something an elocutionist can modulate. The words on these pages are little regular blocks, set apart by spaces, and referrable less to the voice than to the click of the keys and the ratcheting of the carriage.

The stanzas lie on the page, one below another, in little intricate grids of visual symmetry, the left margin indented according to complex rules which govern the setting of tabulator stops. The lines obey no rhythmic system the ear can apprehend. We learn that there is a system not by listening but by counting syllables, and we find that the words are fixed within a grid of numerical rules. Thus "The Fish" has twenty-seven syllables per stanza, arranged in five lines on a three-part scheme of indentation, the syllables apportioned among the lines 1, 3, 9, 6, 8. (In the last line of stanza one, "opening" has two syllables.) And since a mosaic has no point of beginning, the poem is generated from somewhere just outside its own rigidly plotted field: generated less by ichthyological reality than by two words: "The Fish," which are part of the first sentence but not part of the symmetrical pattern, being in fact the poem's title. Therefore:

THE FISH

> wade
> through black jade.
>   Of the crow-blue mussel-shells, one keeps
>   adjusting the ash-heaps;
>   opening and shutting itself like
> an
> injured fan.

To begin this sentence we read the title, and to end it we read three words (four syllables) of the next stanza: for the single stanza is a patterned zone specified within, but not coterminous with, the articulation of the sentences. The single stanza exhibits an archaic disregard of the mere things human desire does with sentences. The voice shaping sentences is anxious to be understood; these stanzas are cut and laminated in severe corrective to that anxiety, posing against it their authority of number (1, 3, 9, 6, 8) and typography. They even evade the sounds of speech with their rhymes, not performing, however, the traditional offices of rhymes, not miming a symmetry, clinching an epigram or caressing a melodic fluid, but cutting, cutting, cutting, with implacable arbitrariness: "like / an / injured fan."

It is a poem to see with the eye, conceived in a typewriter upon an 8½" × 11" sheet of paper. If metric is a system of emphases, centered in human comfort, human hope, syllable count is a system of zoning, implied by the *objectivity* of the words, which lie side by side for their syllables to be counted. If the stanzas of "Go, lovely rose" are primarily audible, created by the symmetries of the uttering voice, the stanzas of "The Fish" are primarily visible, created by an arrangement of words in typographic space, the poem made for us to look at. Miss Moore could even revise a poem from beginning to end without changing a word in it. The first three times "The Fish" appeared in print its stanzaic system grouped the syllables not 1, 3, 9, 6, 8 but 1, 3, 8, 1, 6, 8, and in six lines, not five:

THE FISH

wade
through black jade.
　　Of the crow-blue mussel-shells, one
　　keeps
　　　adjusting the ash heaps;
　　opening and shutting itself like
an
　injured fan.

What readers have been looking at since 1930 is a revised version. The poem was twelve years old when the author made this change, and, despite the mechanical ease of retyping, it is not a trivial change, since it affects the system by which pattern intersects utterance, alters the points at which the intersections occur, provides a new grid of impediments to the over-anxious voice, and modifies, moreover, the intrusiveness of the system itself: the new version actually relents a little its self-sufficient arbitrariness, and consigns more leisurely fish to only half as many winking little quick monosyllabic turns. We can nearly say that we have a *new* poem, arrived at in public and without changing a word, by applying a system of transformations to an existing poem. We may remember Charles Ives's statement that American music is *already written* (he had no need to invent tunes), and his "What has music to do with *sound?*", as who should ask, what has poetry to do with people's anxiety to make themselves understood?

It contains, of course, the rituals generated by that anxiety, as music contains sound. Marianne Moore's poems deal with those rituals as music dealt with them before the clavichord's mathematic was supplanted by the throb of the violin. She will not imitate the rising throbbing curve of emotion, but impede it and quick-freeze it. One impediment is the grid of counted formalisms. Another is the heavy system of nouns:

THE FISH

wade
through black jade. . . .

The black jade got onto the page by the same processes as Ruskin's arms, shields and hills, but without the syntactic lubricants that slide us past a comparison. Simile becomes optical pun, and we have to concentrate on visual likeness amid assault from the strangeness of everything else. "Black jade" (for water) is an optical pun. So are the "ash-heaps" of the "crow-blue mussel-shells." Optical precision brought these ash-heaps and crows into the poem; a moment later it will bring a fan, to swell the bizarre submarine population, and before the poem is over we shall have taken stock of spun glass, turquoise, stars, pink rice-grains, green lilies, toadstools, an iron wedge, a cornice. Each of these optical puns a moment's thought will resolve, yet each such moment interrupts the attention (which does not expect such objects underwater) and interrupts also the expectations of the English sentence, which has two uses for nouns, as doer and as thing done to, "*John* threw the *ball*," and can cope with the odd noun used otherwise ("The dog *treed* the cat"), but loses mobility beneath such a rain of nouns as this poem pours through it, until we are apt to find something odd about so orthodox a usage as "move themselves with *spotlight* swiftness." The sentences are formally impeccable, but their impeccability takes some searching out, interrupted as it so constantly is by its intersections with a different system entirely for displaying nouns.

Just as idiosyncratically the poems deal with quotations. These lie on the page with as arbitrary a look as the nouns wear, set off by quotation marks, yet seldom (never?) familiar quotations: not allusions therefore but found objects, slivers of excellence incorporated into the *assemblage*. One function of the notes to these quotations is to persuade us that they are genuine found objects, not discoveries fabricated by setting quotations marks around phrases of the poet's own devising. The notes are not, like the notes to *The Waste Land*, part of our education; we are not meant to look up the sources; a note to the notes asks that we "take probity on faith" and disregard them. And it is probity, of course, that these poems most obviously enact, creating, within rigorous homemade rules, a crystalline structure, bristling with internal geometry, which (1) exhibits patent optical symmetries; (2) reassures us, if we take the trouble to trace out its syntax, by fulfilling any syntactic law we care to apply; (3) maneuvers through this system, with a maximum of surface discontinuity, some dozens of surprising words and phrases, treated as objects, laid end to end; and (4) justifies each of these objects by a triumphant hidden congruity. The poem is a system, not an utterance, though one can trace an utterance through it.

A thing made, then, not a thing said; and when Williams in the 1920's was working out this distinction, and denominating "the Imagination" as the zone where the poem existed, he had almost no examples to go on but Marianne Moore's. It is hardly too much to say that he arrived at *Spring and All*, and so at the assurances of his own triumphant career, by pondering her 1921 *Poems* (London: the Egoist Press; the selection was made by "H.D." and [by Mrs. Robert McAlmon, better known as] Bryher). "Marianne's words remain separate," he wrote in *Spring and All*, "each unwilling to group with the others except as they move in one direction." That was something to ponder: they were not caught up in the momentum of a *saying*. And though he admitted that "Her work puzzles me. It is not easy to quote convincingly," still it helped him define his distinction of

prose: statement of facts concerning emotions, intellectual states, data of all sorts . . .

and

poetry: new form dealt with as a reality in itself.

For "the form of poetry is related to the movements of the imagination revealed in words."

The line-ending that does not coincide with a rhetorical pause helps establish the autonomy of the words, "each unwilling to group with the others." They are superbly indifferent, as they move along, to the urgencies of *saying*. And if Williams does not count syllables, or seldom, he divides lines—we have seen him at it—where the voice would not divide them. He does so, that is, after his Jacob's wrestle with the poems of Marianne Moore. In the 1916 "Tract" we find rhetorical line-divisions, later (in the 1917 *All Que Quiere!*) modified into a system of medial spaces:

> I will teach you   my townspeople
> how to perform   a funeral—
> for you have it   over a troop
> of artists—
> unless one should   scour the world—
> you have the ground sense necessary. . . .

But post-Moore ("At the Faucet of June," 1923) we find,

> The sunlight in a
> yellow plaque upon the
> varnished floor
> is full of a song
> inflated to
> fifty pounds pressure
> at the faucet of
> June that rings
> the triangle of the air
> pulling at the
> anemones in
> Persephone's cow pasture— . . .

which neither observes the voice's way of pausing nor has anything particularly sensible to offer us upon the plane of *saying*.

The poem is *other* than an utterance: other than what the poet "has to say." Williams often contrived, as Miss Moore did not, that this fact should be underlined by leading the syntactic line through nonsense, while the Imagination reaped its harvest of strange groupings. Miss Moore preferred to double the otherness by setting within the poem some autonomous envelope of energies, a fish, a cat, a ballplayer, to which the poem could conform its oddly depersonalized system of analogies. This autonomous thing she always represents as fulfilling the laws of its being by minding its own business, which is not ours. It also fulfills laws of the poem's being, serving frequently as a point of departure, left behind. Thus the poem headed "An Octopus" is really "about" a glacier, a glacier that not only exists but behaves, and in a way meant to earn our approbation:

AN OCTOPUS

of ice. Deceptively reserved and flat,
it lies 'in grandeur and in mass'
beneath a sea of shifting snow-dunes;
dots of cyclamen-red and maroon on its clearly
    defined
    pseudo-podia
made of glass that will bend—a much needed
    invention—
comprising twenty-eight ice-fields from fifty to five
    hundred feet thick,
of unimagined delicacy.
'Picking periwinkles from the cracks'
or killing prey with the concentric crushing rigor of
    the python,
it hovers forward 'spider-fashion
on its arms' misleadingly like lace;

its 'ghostly pallor changing
    to the green metallic tinge of an anemone-starred
        pool'. . . .

The icy octopus has by this time torn up and carried toward us not only the normal detritus of the landscape but five separate quotations, being in this respect as "deceptively reserved" as the poet. And the poem continues to edge forward glacially, picking up and shifting periwinkles, pythons, spiders, lace, anemones. In fact, by the time it has drawn toward its close (having incorporated *inter alia* the Greek language, Henry James, and numerous citations from the National Parks Rules and Regulations) it appears to be discussing its own decorum as much as that of the glacier-octopus:

Relentless accuracy is the nature of this octopus
with its capacity for fact.
'Creeping slowly as with meditated stealth,
    its arms seeming to approach from all directions' . . .

It resembles, in its "capacity for fact," the capacity of the imaginary garden, in the celebrated example, for real toads. Marianne Moore's subjects—her fields of preoccupation, rather—have these two notable characteristics among others, that they are self-sufficient systems of energy, and that they can appropriate, without hostility, almost anything that comes near. They affirm, without saying anything, that "In This Age of Hard Trying, Nonchalance is Good," and that "There is a great amount of poetry in unconscious / fastidiousness." They are frequently animals; they feed and sleep and hunt and play; they are graceful without taking pride in their grace. They exemplify the qualities of the poems in which they are found.

Yes, they do; yes, it is striking, this pervasive singleness (though never obvious: nothing is *obvious* here). The singleness helps explain why she was able to make a revolutionary discovery, perhaps without ever knowing what it was. She resembles Columbus, whose mind was on something other than opening new worlds, and died supposing he had shown how to sail to China. For the language flattened, the language *exhibited*, the language staunchly condensing information while frisking in enjoyment of its release from the obligation to do no more than inform: these are the elements of a twentieth-century American poetic, a pivotal discovery of our age. And it seems to have been Marianne Moore's discovery, for Williams, who also discovered it and extended it beyond the reach of her temperament, seems to have discovered it with the aid of her poems. A woman who was never convinced she was writing poems ("I would hardly call it a poem," she said of "Marriage," and "What I write . . . could only be called poetry because there is no other category in which to put it"); she and a frantically busy physician who kept a typewriter screwed to a hinged leaf of his consulting-room desk, to be banged up into typing position between patients: not "poets," not professionals of the word, save for their passion: they were the inventors of an American poetry. The fact is instructive.

Extracting its instruction, we may begin with her avowed hostility to the poetic. We had better not dismiss this as whimsy; it was heuristic.

"I, too, dislike it," she wrote of something called "Poetry." ("I, too"? In alliance with whom? The public? Well, sensible people, presumably.)

I, too, dislike it.
    Reading it, however, with a perfect contempt for
        it, one discovers in
    it, after all, a place for the genuine.

That is all she finally chose to say about "Poetry," on an otherwise blank page of her 1967 *Complete Poems*, though—sensing perhaps that some buyers might otherwise feel cheated

—she offered the "original version" as a two-page footnote. (Had a longish poem ever before been a footnote to a three-line excerpt from itself? She didn't care. The only tradition she acknowledged was that of rectitude. That's instructive, too.)

It wasn't merely her octogenarian conscience that suffered these drastic fits of rectitude. "Poetry" has a long history of being fussed with, and as long ago as 1924, when the author was a merry-eyed 37, a convulsive revision deprived it of fully seventy percent of its words, including the famous ones that stipulate "imaginary gardens with real toads in them." She also expelled "the immovable critic twinkling his skin like a horse that feels a flea," and the counted-syllable grid, and the five-stanza layout. By 1932 a new upheaval had restored the stanzas, but only three of them, arranged on a different grid. The critic was also back, but now "twitching" his skin, and "flea" had been escalated to "fly," but "Poetry" was still gardenless and toadless. Two years later the poem looked pretty much as it had originally, toads, five stanzas and all, with "twitching" retained but "fly" once more "flea," the syllable count of unprecedented elasticity and about midway a whole line missing. This is the so-called "original version" of the 1967 footnote, appended to the most calamitous reworking of all, in which toads, gardens, critic and just about everything else—the baseball fan, the statistician, the bat, even plural elephants—went down the tubes. It's hard not to conclude that her asserted dislike of poetry, nearly the one stable element amid all these upheavals, extended to dislike of words she'd written at 32 and subsequently could neither subdue nor bring herself to discard. However they plagued her, they said something she wanted to say.

She did indeed dislike poetry, she used emphatically to insist. One time, citing

No man may him hyde
From Deth holow-eyed,

she made a little inventory of dislikes:

I dislike the reversed order of words; don't like to be impeded by an unnecessary capital at the beginning of every line; I don't like, here, the meaning; the cadence coming close to being the sole reason for all that follows, the accent on "holow" rather than on "eyed," so firmly placed that the most willful reader cannot misplace it. . . .

This is to reject, well, very much. If more careful in its discriminations than Williams' shoving aside of "Europe—the past," it has a comparable thrust. Nevertheless, reading poetry without enchantment, "one discovers in it, after all, a place for the genuine": a place, as she went on to say in 1919, for "real toads." That's what poetry is, a place; not a deed but a location. "A kind of collection of flies in amber," Miss Moore was to call her own poetry, "if not a cabinet of fossils."

This attitude rejects historical nostalgia. When Dr. Johnson wrote their Lives, "the Poets" were all nearly contemporaneous: men alive so recently that everyone understood the world nearly as they did. We may guess that Miss Moore would have been at home in that climate, when a poem collected concentrations of acknowledged wisdom, and felicities of expression were prized and borrowed. Expulsion from such a paradise occurred, however, soon afterward, when historical consciousness was engrossing poets and poetry began to feed on its own past, finding delicious succulence in words like "faery":

. . . The same that oft-times hath
Charm'd magic casements, opening on the foam
Of perilous seas, in faery lands forlorn.

Keat's poem calls itself an "Ode," an historical ritual. By mid-century it seemed part of the office of art to incorporate the contemporary into history. Into an evocation of romantic departure, already ritualized by 1866, the young Mallarmé inserted the word "Steamer" (an English word, moreover):

Je partirai! Steamer balançant ta mâture,
Lève l'ancre pour une exotique nature!

At just about the same time, Manet painted two Parisian dandies, one of them his own brother and both in the studio dress of that day, at the center of an iconography paraphrased from Giorgione. When the fuss had died down after several decades, it became clear that *Le Déjeuner sur l'herbe* was a bland incorporation of the Present into Art History, into the artifice of eternity. Its visual idiom, quoting Giorgione, declines to view a bohemian picnic as if through contemporary eyes. In much the same way Eliot, quoting the idiom of Tennyson, declines to render Prufrock's social malaise empirically—

There will be time to murder and create,
And time for all the works and days of hands
That lift and drop a question on your plate . . .

—moving his subject into the domain occupied by "Poetry," by verbal rituals historically sanctioned. We can tell that "Prufrock" sounds like Poetry before we can tell what realities it engages with. And Eliot's work infuriated Williams (though not Miss Moore, who admired its aplomb).

Miss Moore's modest effort was not to deflect "poetry" or to destroy it, but to ignore it: that is to say, ignore its rituals. She made up difficult rules of her own, some of which as they evolved remained in force (end-stopped lines for choice, and after 1929, rhyme), while others—the specific syllable grid, the density and audibility of the rhymes—hold good only for the duration of the poem in hand. It's a homemade art, like the sampler wrought in cross-stitch. Sometimes it will allow the conjunction between rule and theme to appear almost naïvely, as though a principle known to Homer or Donne had just been improvised. A rapid alternation of sounds in "Light Is Speech" was suggested by the winking of a lighthouse—[1]

One can say more of sunlight
than of speech; but speech
and light, each
aiding each . . .

and the assertion that the Jerboa moves

By fifths and sevenths,
in leaps of two lengths

is encompassed in a stanza that opens with five syllables per line and closes with seven. But the primary function of rule is not to look jauntily appropriate but to intercept the flow of phrasing, and make us pause, pause, pause, on the single words:

By fifths and sevenths,
in leaps of two lengths,
like the uneven notes
of the Bedouin flute, it stops its gleaming
on little wheel-castors, and makes fern-seed
foot-prints with kangaroo speed.
Its leaps should be set
to the flageolet;
pillar body erect
on a three-cornered smooth-working Chippendale
claw—propped on hind legs, and tail as third
toe,
between leaps to its burrow.

—as usual a thick system of seeming nouns, many of which turn out to be adjectival, each one an act of attention, and the Gestalt *exhibited* with superb indifference to literary history.

The single words are stripped of history, "pillar" of classical associations, "Chippendale" of antique ones. Word by word, we must take the point, and let historical overtones go. One cannot call the verse formless; one cannot succumb, either, to unreflective ritual enjoyment, caressed by sounds. Attention, attention, that is the injunction, as it was Thoreau's injunction. Averting attention we can follow nothing, neither the structure of a sentence nor the applicability of a phrase. Through cluttered tidiness, the reader must move like a cat.

And feeding into this verse, nourishing it, tumbles a richness of found phrases: not, however, the "pleasing wraiths of former masteries" that Dr. Williams discerned enhancing the words of traditional poetry, but simply the accuracies of people who have observed something interesting. Thus "New York" gleaned a comparison of the fawn's spots to satin needlework from the *Literary Digest*, a snobbish vaunt from a book about *The Psychology of Dress*, and a terminal phrase, "accessibility to experience," from James. The effect of such a procedure is to democratize "tradition" very considerably; anyone may enrich tradition if he will just keep his mind on his subject. Leafing the Notes, one is struck by the near absence of phrases gleaned from poets, by the scarcity in general of "literary" names, and by the high concentration of magazine writers. The *Illustrated London News* is much drawn on; writers were likely to suit Marianne Moore's purposes when they had pictures nearby to keep them honest. The notes to "Nine Nectarines" preserve a citation from an auction catalogue (though, oddly enough, the part of the poem to which it refers was deleted before 1951) and the notes to "Four Quartz Crystal Clocks" call a Bell Telephone technical leaflet to our attention: such writings bespeak a minute obligation to fact.

She chose all the snippets for a single reason: she admired the phrasing. Her longest poem, "Marriage," she later described simply as "statements that took my fancy which I tried to arrange plausibly." In *Observations*, extending this principle, she even supplied an amusing Index to the things the poems try to arrange plausibly; among the C's we find,

> chipmunk, nine-striped, 85
> CHOOSING, PICKING AND, 55, 97
> Christ on Parnassus, 102
> chrysalis, 57, 98
> cigars, 57
> circular traditions, 75, 102
> circus, 107
> clay pots, 28
> coach, gilt, 65; wheel yellow, 35
> cockatrices, 71, 101
> cockroaches, 57
> coffin, 79, 104
> Coliseum, 63

She even gleaned found objects from the likes of editorial pages, addressing a Rose through polysyllabic clichés:

> You do not seem to realize that beauty is a liability
>   rather than
>   an asset—that in view of the fact that spirit creates
>   form we
>   are justified in supposing
>   that you must have brains. . . .

This brought to Eliot's delighted mind the vision of "a whole people playing uncomfortably at clenches and clevelandisms," but Miss Moore, whose conscience was her admirers' despair, later disliked the poem (perhaps as disrespectful to its materials?) and banished it.

That suppressed poem ("Roses Only") chattered with the voices of others, molded into a single voice which became the poet's somewhat alarming, notably tart *persona*. It is yet one

more instructive episode: speech not her own became a means of satire, and was itself satirized. She was uncomfortable with satire, and the poem, which dates from 1917, was deleted from every collection after 1935. In what continued to be reprinted we hear one voice only, hers, sharp and economical at first, in later years fussily generous. Such a sequence as

> . . . Émile Littré,
> philology's determined,
> ardent eight-volume
>   Hippocrates-charmed
> editor. A
> man on fire, a scientist of
> freedoms, was firm Maximilien
> Paul Émile Littré. . . .

tells us remarkably little while nodding its head in vehement approbation. And it takes up one fifth of its poem. (The note is more economical: "Littré [1801–81] devoted the years 1839–62 to translating and editing Hippocrates.") Contrast the speed, eighteen years earlier, of the lines on Adam—

> Unnerved by the nightingale
> and dazzled by the apple,
> impelled by 'the illusion of a fire
> effectual to extinguish fire',
> compared with which
> the shining of the earth
> is but deformity—a fire
> 'as high as deep
> as bright as broad
> as long as life itself',
> he stumbles over marriage,
> 'a very trivial object indeed'
> to have destroyed the attitude
> in which he stood—
> the ease of the philosopher
> unfathered by a woman. . . .

—and consider the damage done to the poetry by a sensed obligation to be respectful.

Like Stevens', hers is a poetry for one voice; like Stevens', it works by surface complication, with little variety of feeling. Unlike Stevens', it has no traffic—has never had any at all—with the cadences of the Grand Style, with Tradition, but works by a principle exclusively its own, the witty transit through minute predilections. Unlike Stevens' poetry, finally, hers deteriorates, as it were, through insufficient grasp of its own principles. Having been held together by a temperament, it grows dilute as the temperament grows more accommodating. And yet it is a turning point, as Stevens' is not. When American verse was looking for a way to cope with the perceived world's multifarious otherness, it was Marianne Moore's best work that was decisive.

Causing her best poems to enact with such rigor the moral virtues they celebrate, Miss Moore skirted the tradition of the dandy, whose life was a controlled thing and whose norms of conduct were stylistic. Dandyism's principal modern celebrant was Ernest Hemingway, whose bullfights and lion-hunts were aesthetic gestures and whose descriptions of clear water running over stones were moral achievements. It was Hemingway in our time who fulfilled most dramatically Ruskin's precept that to see something, and tell what one saw in a plain way, is "poetry, prophecy and religion all in one," though the second term would have made Hemingway uneasy. We may see in his career one apotheosis to which the discipline of describing natural objects was tending during many decades.

But Hemingway's conception of style as the criterion of life contains one element totally alien to any poetic effect of Marianne Moore's: *self-appreciation*. To take satisfaction in one's achievements, and to undertake like achievements in quest of more of that satisfaction—this is the dual temptation by which such a poetic is beset; and the theme of many poems of Miss Moore is precisely the duty to resist it. Her black elephant utters an opening vaunt not immune from self-congratulation:

> Openly, yes
>   with the naturalness
>   of the hippopotamus or the alligator
>   when it climbs out on the bank to experience the
>
> sun, I do these
>   things which I do, which please
>   no one but myself . . .

but midway through the poem a crucial discrimination is made:

> . . . nevertheless I
>   perceive feats of strength to be inexplicable after
>   all; and I am on my guard; external poise, it
>
> has its centre
> well nurtured—we know
>   where—in pride; but spiritual poise, it has its
>   centre where?

To offer behavior which is "inexplicable after all" is to take no credit for it. The "beautiful element of unreason" has its uses. Another poem recommends "unconscious fastidiousness," and having surveyed with some astringency the behavior of a swan and of an ant, asks,

>   . . . What is
> there in being able
>   to say that one has dominated the stream in an
>   attitude of
>   self-defence;
>   in proving that one has had the experience
>   of carrying a stick?

—For that matter, of fighting a bull? To "prove that one has had the experience" of playing with a cat, or seeing a fish, or pretending to be an elephant, is just what a poetic of visual experience is likely to find itself engaged upon, even as Ruskin tended to be intent on proving that he alone had ever really seen a fir tree. In the same way, much fine photography stirs feelings closer to envy than to delight: "The man who held the camera was *here*," it tends to say, "and moreover at this unique moment; do you not wish you had been here, too?"

Some of the formal obstacles Marianne Moore laid across the assertions of her sentences were to help her avoid seeming to imply that a cat or a fish has never really been looked at before. Their presence raises, however, a further problem: how to avoid asserting that one has had the dexterity to overcome formal obstacles. It is here that her preoccupation with otherness helps.

For those autonomous envelopes of energy she so admired are *other*, as Nature for Wordsworth never was. Where Hemingway imitated bullfighters, she was content to admire ballplayers. Her cats, pangolins, jerboas, elephants are not beings she half-perceives and half-creates. Their accomplishments are wholly their own. It is not the poet who notes that the jerboa is sand-colored, but the jerboa that "honours the sand by assuming its colour." Similarly, it is the jerboa that has discovered a flute rhythm for itself, "by fifths and sevenths, / in leaps of two lengths," and to play the flageolet in its presence is not our ingenuity but our obligation. "Its leaps should be set /

to the flageolet." So when, as normally, we find that the poem is itself enacting the virtues it discerns in its subject, we are not to say that it is commenting on its own aesthetic, as in Hemingway's celebrations of the way one works close to the bull; rather that its aesthetic is an offering to the virtuosity of the brisk little creature that changes pace so deftly, and direction so deftly, and keeps intent, and keeps alert, and both offers and refrains from flaunting its agility.

This works best with animals, because they don't know their own virtuosity, and with athletes because at decisive moments they haven't time for self-appreciation, there being a ball to catch that won't wait. ("I could of caught it with a pair of pliers," said the exuberant outfielder, but that was afterward.) That is why Miss Moore's best poems are unpeopled save by glimpsed exemplars of verbal or synaptic dexterity. It is also why, as she admitted to her system other people's values, a poetic misfortune for which her sense of wartime obligations may be in part blamed, she relaxed and blurred her normal deftness and neatness, aware of the inappropriateness of seeming crisp. To be crisp even in praise of people's excellence is to make oneself a little the proprietor of their virtue; one senses that she sensed that to be improper.

At her best, she was other from us, and her subjects other from her, and saying with the elephant, "I do these / things which I do, which please / no one but myself," she was fulfilling a nature of her own. For the unclubbable cat she had offered this defense:

> As for the disposition
> invariably to affront, an animal with claws wants to
>   have to use
>   them; that eel-like extension of trunk into tail is
>   not an
>   accident. To
> leap, to lengthen out, divide the air—to purloin,
>   to pursue.
>   To tell the hen: fly over the fence, go in the
>   wrong way in
>   your perturbation—this is life; to do less
>   would be
>   nothing but dishonesty.

And a being with an eye wants to have to use it, and a being with a typewriter, and a being with a memory. So by a long way round, by way of a poetic that dislocates, seemingly, each nuance of normal utterance, this rendition of the experience of the eye came to seem natural after all, an instance of commendable behavior. It was a limited, remarkable achievement. It imitates without congratulating itself on having thought to imitate, or on having found the means. It compels our minds to move across an opaque and resistant surface, that of the printed language, in emulation of the eye's experience moving across the contours of a pangolin's armor; and it impedes the facilities of the conclusion drawn, the thing said, the instance appropriated into a moral system, on the principle that while psychic experience flows naturally into utterance, optical experience must be carefully anatomized before we can too readily allow it to be psychic. For the supreme insult—this is its final claim—the supreme insult to that which is other than we, that which, perceived by the eye, is *therefore* other: the supreme insult we can offer to the other is to have, on too little acquaintance, something to say "about" it.

Notes

1. According to a reminiscence of the late Lester Littlefield's.

CHRISTOPHER MORLEY

1890–1957

Christopher Darlington Morley was born May 5, 1890, in Haverford, Pennsylvania. After a brief time with his family in Baltimore, Morley returned to Haverford and the Quaker men's college for undergraduate study. Upon graduation in 1910 Morley traveled to Oxford as a Rhodes scholar. While studying modern history at New College he wrote his first book, a volume of poetry called *The Eighth Sin*, in 1912. In 1913 he was back in the United States and working for Doubleday. His first novel, *Parnassus on Wheels*, was published 1917. After four years in New York he moved with his wife and family to Philadelphia where he was first an editor for the *Ladies' Home Journal* and then a columnist for the *Phildelphia Evening Public Ledger*. 1918 saw the publication of *Shandygaff*, the first of his sixteen books of essays. In 1920 the Morleys moved to Roslyn, New York, on Long Island. By 1924 he was a contributing editor of the *Saturday Review of Literature* and a columnist for the *New York Evening Post*, as well as author of two more novels, *Where the Blue Begins* (1922) and *Thunder on the Left* (1925). He produced a series of popular melodramas in Hoboken, New Jersey, from 1928 to 1930, stopping only with the discovery of his partner's unscrupulous business management. In the late thirties Morley undertook the editing of the eleventh (1937) and twelfth (1948) editions of Bartlett's *Familiar Quotations*. His bestselling novel *Kitty Foyle* came out in 1941.

By the time of his death on March 28, 1957, in Roslyn, Morley had written eighteen novels, sixteen books of essays, sixteen volumes of poetry, and four plays, and had contributed to more than twenty other books. A well-known literary celebrity for the better part of three decades, Morley was treated as a writer of popular entertainment, garnering more attention from readers than from critics.

There is not much of him that I can set down here. Journalist, essayist, novelist, poet, and playwright, like his own Paumanok, he is constantly evasive, and the smoke of his writing has drifted over the pages of too many different kinds of books. Years ago, in the *Freeman*, Robert Hillyer wrote an essay on "The Decline of Gusto." In Christopher Morley gusto has never declined. Because of that he is often called an Elizabethan born out of his century—an easy phrase of throttled meaning. I suppose there is no writer of our day who is more vividly entangled with the present. If he has been in love with London, with seashells in Normandy, the prose of neglected Gissings, and all Old World exuberance, he has never forgotten that his pulse is measured to the rhythm of New York, that jungle "thick with beauty and terror," whose impatient heart he has sweated to understand. His surrender to Walt Whitman makes him more of a modern than most of us. His very language, even in its immaculate moments, is the language of a stylist whose corporate indebtedness includes *Variety* as well as Conrad and Sir Thomas Browne. In the wide range of his talent you may find the work of many Morleys, but in none of it can you testify to a spirit unexultant. This would not be remarkable in a humorist; but Morley's humor is only an affidavit of his gusto, and therefore but a fraction of the man. It is true that anxiety for expression sometimes leads him into the immensest trivialities, when, as Dr. Canby has said, "he sweeps the whole scenery to his eager breast." It is also true that these Andesan fires have tempered his greatest passages of prose. A journalist habit, begun on the *Philadelphia Public Ledger* and continued over two successive carpets of "The Bowling Green," has induced him to assemble in the questionable permanence of books virtually everything he has ever written. Nearly thirty volumes in a decade and a half is too much for any writer. Were it already compiled, *The Best of Morley*, like Mr. Lucas' little anthology, *The Best of Lamb*, would cruelly prove the point; but the best of Morley is still to be written, and final deductions have no office here.

It was Christopher Morley who remarked that H. M. Tomlinson is a cross between Confucius and Puck. He might have said it of himself, for in him the philosopher and jester are Estaban and Manuel. They, indeed, might have been the two for whom "Duets in a Hot Bath" were written. When the philosopher is strongest, Morley is most powerful, writing the essay or the novel with the utmost command. When the jester stands ascendant, he is openly the journalist, gravid always with consecutive thought, but subject in long interludes to whimsy and a certain (not always uncharming) sentimentality. The struggle, of course, has always been for the philosopher. Morley eight years ago was invariably the journalist. He was never the constant Max Beerbohm. Even in James Joyce there has not been a more important change of style than in his between the Philadelphia years and the Burgundian period of the "Green." The man in F.P.A.'s column who parodied him a while ago would never have attempted it in 1920. Yet no other contemporary has so graciously conducted his education in public. To read Morley is not only a liberal schooling in the rudiments of enthusiasm but an introduction to unselfish catholicity in taste.

These are general notions and marginalia on the hem of all his books. The difficulty with Morley is that he has dropped potato eyes in every furrow, no matter how sterile the soil. Of his own work he is singularly incapable of differentiation. *Thunder on the Left*, which first ran in *Harper's Magazine*, was followed by relatively futile stories called "The Arrow" and "Pleased to Meet You." The titles alone give the matter away. How could anyone subscribe to such fervently buoyant ideas as *Granules from an Hour Glass*, *Where the Blue Begins*, *Parnassus on Wheels*, "Jamie Comes to Hy-Brasil," *Thunder on the Left*, and then underwrite a *Pleased to Meet You* or a plain *Mince Pie*? For Morley has every discipline but the discipline of suppression. I shall not argue that this is entirely a fault. Like Hernani (in this one respect) he can say *Je suis une force qui va*. It is possible that the same gusto which has bent him to the novel plays an equal part in the manufacture of pot-boilers. If it does, then he is steadily perfecting himself where many writers are merely wasting their time. George Borrow was such a man, and his patient elaboration of English criminal cases is not known to have dulled his pen. But the casual reader, the taster of letters, does not always know this. The "works" of Morley, in the expensive and premature Haverford edition, if opened severally and at the wrong places, can put their author under a cloud of bias. What are the novels of Gissing compared with *The Private Papers of Henry Ryecroft* and *By the Ionian Sea?* What are Morley's poems and *Tales from a Roll-top Desk* compared with the early chapters of *Thunder on the Left*, with *Inward Ho!* and the flower of his essays?

As an essayist he is still far more popular than any American in his field. Where other collections sell in the hundreds, his reach the fortunate goal of thousands. Yet it was not essays that opened the way for a national appreciation. His first and firmest admirers were won through the charm and originality of *Parnassus on Wheels* and *The Haunted Bookshop*. Both had champions. People took them up. Why not? Morley is the born bibliophile, and all the affection and kindling of a young man in the pursuit of reading he poured into these boyishly ebullient novels. In them he might pass for a modern Richard de Bury. They are Morley, Jr., at his best; and writing conjugal with the very handling of books.

That was at the turn of the twenties, with the wine of Oxford still in his veins, and the philosopher as yet a little boy. Succeeding to the business of columnist he indulged, as he still indulges, his delight in literary discovery and experience. It was here that he became the writer's writer and spokesman in behalf of neglected or undiscovered genius. For years he labored valiantly to promote the popularity of Conrad, William McFee, H. M. Tomlinson, C. E. Montague, and many others. There was nothing personal in it. He did the same thing for Whitman, O. Henry, De Quincey, Lamb, and Keats. His loves and advocacies were multitude. One strained even through the mind like beans in a sieve. Enthusiasm became a disease. If it was not for men and books it was for places; if it was not for places, it was for talk and friendship. A series of volumes testify to the period: *Shandygaff, Mince Pie, Pipefuls, Travels in Philadelphia, Plum Pudding, Religio Journalistici, The Power of Sympathy.* With them Puck did not die; but the philosopher went into long trousers.

It was *Where the Blue Begins*, published in 1923, that brought him numerically his first popular success. As a novel it combines a curious array of elemental and spiritual ideas. People have objected to its canine symbolism, but that is of secondary importance. The important thing was in the proof clearly that Morley had attained the dimensions of a novelist. Roger Mifflin (of *Parnassus*) amounted to character, but Mr. Gissing became at once a real person. He was a singular emancipate, a fellow of universal appeal, the ghost of our waking selves living out the adventures in freedom the very thought of which we all but stifle. After that, in 1926, came *Thunder on the Left*, which critics and readers alike laid immediately upon the altars of discussion. In part its popularity and success—over the number who dispraised it—rode on the sales of *Where the Blue Begins*. Yet it was, and is, a deeply more significant book. Its early chapters and the handling of the children are superb. As a story it outruns itself: something, it may be, beyond the author's own understanding; but the mechanics are sound, and the grasp, the theater, of it argues only the pen of a craftsman. Pages of its prose, lucid and

punctual but rarely overfine, are the essence of good writing. ⟨. . .⟩

With the tightening of his mood to that novel, what must have been a by-product at the time developed into a book of still better coin. I mean, of course, *The Romany Stain*. A slice of this was written on a long sojourn in France; and looking through the files of the *Saturday Review of Literature* I recall again the exquisite pleasure so many of these papers gave me as they were printed from week to week. Some of them belong, surely, in the company of noble letters, American or British. The highest praise I can summon now is that they should be read again.—DAVID McCORD, "Christopher Morley," *EJ*, Jan. 1930, pp. 1–5

In *Kitty Foyle*, Christopher Morley, if only once over lightly, does for the Philadelphia Main Line what Mr. Marquand in *Wickford Point* did for the phosphorescent relicts of Boston Brahminism. Though it crumples a bit toward the end and betrays the flaw of all Morley novels (too much Morley, not enough novel), I think it's pretty successful. What Rittenhouse Square and the Assembly will think of it is another (Philadelphia) story, but it's probable that they're so busy being descendants they're hardly apt to notice Mr. Morley's amiable jibes. Somehow one doubts that they'll be greatly pained. It's a little unrewarding to twit a fellow about his laziness when he's suffering from *encephalitis lethargica*.

Mr. Morley's critique of what his heroine neatly terms Sankatown is reflected through the stream of consciousness of Kitty Foyle. Kitty is of healthy, lower-class, humorous Irish-American stock. Her father is a former night watchman. From him, Kitty inherits a wide-open heart, a capacity for making something out of herself, a salty tongue, and a ribald imagination. She talks a sound vernacular, tart, natural, and American as apple pie. I don't see how any male reviewer can categorically affirm that Mr. Morley has succeeded in getting inside a girl's mind and staying there for 340 pages; all I can say is that it sounds plausible, and if Mr. Morley's feminine readers give him the O.K., I guess it should be clear enough that he's pulled off something of a brilliant stunt.

The Kitty I like best is the one who exchanges wisecracks with her priceless old father and her brothers, the one who sets awagging the tongue of the delicious Myrtle (colored help), the one who recalls her summers as a long-legged kid in the town of Manito, Illinois. The Midwestern chapters particularly exude a fine Tarkington, almost a Mark Twain, aroma: Mr. Morley has a way with juveniles, and his girls are even more convincing than his boys.

The big thing in Kitty's life is Wyn Strafford, a Philadelphia gentleman. A Philadelphia gentleman is not made quickly; it takes at least seven generations of pleasant dullness. Kitty falls for Wyn—it's all very O. Henry, but Mr. Morley is full of novel twists—has a glorious affair with him, but is in the end defeated by the code to which Wyn, who hasn't enough courage to thumb his nose at it, must submit. Wyn marries, you will not be surprised to know, a nice girl of his own set, whose veneer will not wear off, as it goes all the way through.

The love affair is well rendered, with a tender touch, half poetic, half realistic, but the best stuff has to do with Kitty herself and her white-collar-girl slant. She sounds real, if a trifle too clever. Wyn, however, is attractive only because Mr. Morley has put his own good things in his character's mouth. "Everybody has a Public Relations counsel—except the Public," says Wyn, but it still sounds like Morley to me. The last word on him is uttered by Kitty's sensible Midwestern girl friend Molly, who asks, "Is that boy an American?" It's a legitimate query, for, unless Mr. Morley's dope on the

Philadelphia Old Cricketing Families is sheer caricature, they ought to be investigated by the Dies Committee.

Those who have been afraid of Mr. Morley because they figure his whimsy will come off on them should not on that account steer clear of *Kitty Foyle*. It has the Morley touch, all right, but the fancifulness is restrained, and somehow the book seems pretty close to certain realities of the twenties and early thirties. Mr. Morley has an eye for the little things that make up the flavor of a period, and there are enough of them in the book to add up to something reasonably big and true.

Guess that's about all except for two minor matters. The first has to do with the jacket of *Kitty Foyle*, which is, unlike most jackets, beautifully and originally designed. The second concerns the time when Wyn Strafford and his fine-fathered friends try to start an imitation in Philadelphia of the magazine you are now reading and, in preparation for it, visit these very premises. "I was relieved," reports Kitty, "one day when Wyn told me he'd been to the office of *The New Yorker* and said they were a weird-looking crew." Go Climb a Family Tree, Mr. Wyn Strafford.—CLIFTON FADIMAN, "Kit Morley and His Philadelphians," NY, Oct. 28, 1939, p. 77

JON BRACKER
From "Introduction"
Bright Cages
1965, pp. 13–34

Although well known as the author of *Parnassus on Wheels*, *Where the Blue Begins*, *Thunder on the Left*, and *Kitty Foyle*, Christopher Morley thought of himself as essentially a poet and wanted to be remembered as such. Late in his career he confided, "I have never been completely happy except when writing verse. I've the horridest feeling that after it's too late for me, someone will say, 'He wrote poetry.'" When given the opportunity in 1942 of making a selection of his writing for Whit Burnett's anthology, *This Is My Best*, Morley contributed four poems, remarking, "I hope it will not startle you if I say I think I should prefer to enter your caravan as a poet rather than in other possible disguises. . . . poetry was and remains my first love."

Morley's first book, *The Eighth Sin*, appeared in 1912 when he was twenty-two years old, and his last, *Gentlemen's Relish*, was published in 1955, two years before his death; both were volumes of verse. Enough poems for sixteen additional collections were written during a remarkably productive career. The selection of poems in *Bright Cages*, however, was made from twenty-two books, all but one of them out of print, because the best of Morley's verse spilled over into two novels, a collection of essays, and an early autobiography. ⟨. . .⟩

It would be unjust to condemn Morley's juvenilia for being no more than competent and engaging light verse not particularly different from that produced by fellow Oxford students, for the poet himself was aware of their slightness and later included only one poem from the volume in his first retrospective collection. He was to write of *The Eighth Sin*, "The perpetrator, if he thinks of it at all, thinks of it fondly as a boy's straggling nosegay, somewhat wilted in a hot eager hand, clumsily tied together with honest love."

The New York City which attracted Morley on his return from Oxford was an exciting place to seek a career. The second sight which impressed him on arrival (the first had been the starry ceiling of Grand Central Station) was the gold statue of Diana on the old Madison Square Garden, a shining silhouette against the sky; she became for Morley a symbol of this stimulating phase of his life, a symbol he used more than once in his poetry. ⟨. . .⟩

The details of the lifelong affair are recorded in Morley's poetry: the panorama of faces in the subway, the sounds at night of traffic in the streets, the tiny fluffs of milkweed blown into the city on an October day; these are the pictures Morley drew, partly recreated from notes taken on the spot, partly the products of happy memories. One of his longer efforts, the excellent "Ballad of New York, New York," captures much of the essence of "the Town so big men name her twice, / Like so: N'Yawk, N'Yawk"; Morley was proud of the poem, which he worked out over a period of ten months, and believed that in it were "a few of those lightning strokes of phrase and purview that lift feet over hedges." If he had written nothing else than this poem, which is already being quoted in print and is making its way into anthologies, Christopher Morley would have earned the right to be called a poet. ⟨. . .⟩

In 1917 Morley moved his family to Philadelphia, where he became briefly, as he put it, "one of the little group of wilful men who edit the *Ladies' Home Journal*." The next year he was conducting a daily column for the *Philadelphia Evening Public Ledger*; there in a rolltop desk was born the first of his "translations from the Chinese," which are not translations at all, but original poems, often with an Oriental flavor, which sometimes deal with Oriental subjects. First, as "Synthetic Poems," they were Morley's mild burlesque of the then new imagism. But Morley "also had a feeling that free verse, then mainly employed as the vehicle of a rather gaudy impressionism or of mere eccentricity, might prove a viable medium for humorous, ironic, and satiric brevities. . . ."

The Oriental aspect was added to the "translations" after Morley read in the fall of 1918 the just-published first of Arthur Waley's important translations, *170 Chinese Poems*, and learned "that the ancient Chinese poets themselves were both wise and humorous." Enjoying a vogue in America, Oriental verse influenced poets whose work was known to Morley: Witter Bynner (*The Beloved Stranger*, 1919) and Amy Lowell (*Fir-Flower Tablets*, 1921). A *History of Japanese Poetry* by Curtis Hidden Page—the recipient of Morley's poem entitled "To C.H.P."—was published in 1923. "To paraphrase the old English song," Morley wrote, "it was 'Loud sing Hokku' all across the map."

Returning to the New York scene in 1920, Morley found "a landscape bizarre enough to move him deeply" and the first of the poems actually printed as "translations from the Chinese" appeared. In the beginning the verses were attributed to such pseudo-poets as "No Sho," "O B'Oi," "Po Lil Chile," and "P'Ur Fish," but, as their creator later described the process, "little by little my Chinese sages began to coalesce and assume a voice of their own. I became not their creator but their stenographer. I began to feel a certain respect and affection for the 'Old Mandarin' who was dimly emerging as their Oriental spokesman. I began to realize that the mind speaks many languages, and some of its sudden intuitions and exclamations are truly as enigmatic to us as Chinese writing. . . ." As the "Old Mandarin" took shape, Morley's verses became more poetic. Their creator no longer felt a need to apologize humorously for his lack of knowledge of Chinese, based largely as it was on the reading of laundry slips, which caused him when in doubt as to the exact meaning of a phrase always to translate it as "a bowl of jade filled with the milk of moonlight."

Although Morley thought of the "translations" as a whole as essentially American in tone, it is interesting to consider the comments of Pearl Buck, whose qualifications as an American novelist of Chinese life make her a critic worth listening to. She wrote to Morley in 1932:

> Of course, as you know, I have considered your poems in the mandarin mood quite matchless, and I have never understood how it was an American or even an Occidental could write them. After I met you, however, I divined in you a certain quality of the mandarin, and then came to the conclusion that either you had once been a mandarin in some previous life, or that the mandarin quality, which I consider invaluable because it is both precious and rare, is more universal than I thought. The explanation depends on whether one is Oriental or Occidental at bottom; you may choose the one you like better.

There is a universal quality to the "translations," yet it is also true that, in the later poems, the "Old Mandarin" came to sound a great deal like Morley, or the "Old Man" as he was known to family and intimate friends. Indeed, Louis Greenfield, Morley's office manager for a number of years, writes that the poet was actually called the "Old Mandarin" by close associates; in any case, both the fictional character and his creator were occasionally referred to by the abbreviation "O.M."

Morley had hoped that someday the "translations," which appeared over a period of thirty-five years and were sometimes published along with his regular poems, might be separately collected; the best of them appear together in *Bright Cages* in a division of their own. Now one can see why as early as 1927 Leonard Bacon, the distinguished writer of light verse, claimed that "if Mr. Morley had never done anything other than *Translations from the Chinese* he would still be a notable figure. . . . Few poets restore more generously the mystery that our own clumsy hands have rubbed from the butterfly wings of the familiar."

In 1920 Morley moved his family to a large house in Roslyn, Long Island; he called the rambling structure "Green Escape" and lived there until his death thirty-seven years later. Soon after the move, a change could be perceived in Morley's writings. He became less the journalist—for he had produced many essays and much popular fiction since his return from Oxford—and more the creative writer, less the versifier and more the poet. It was the writing, in 1921, of an unmarketable short story, "Referred to the Author," Morley maintained, that marked the dividing line if one were to be drawn. The next year saw the publication of his first important novel, the allegorical *Where the Blue Begins*, which was prefaced with a lyric in which Morley expressed his determination to break through the elements which held him pent and to "make his furious sonnet." More and more he wanted to be able to give up the hack work which had been necessary, and to get on to the projects which could engage his heart as well as his head. The little collection of fervently philosophical essays, *Inward Ho!*, which came out in 1923, further indicated Morley's new and serious concerns. In 1923 also he left the *New York Evening Post*, for which he had conducted a weekly column for three years. The poem "Grub Street Recessional" is Morley's verse farewell to the newspaper world, as *Religio Journalistici* (1924) is his prose goodbye. Although that year he became a contributing editor of *The Saturday Review of Literature* and wrote for the magazine once a week for fourteen years, Morley now only commuted to Manhattan for part of the week and was able to do a portion of his writing at home. As the sale of his prose works increased and his reputation grew, Morley became financially somewhat less dependent on pleasing an audience, particularly in poetry, which he wrote now more from private desire than public demand. ⟨. . .⟩

Life in Roslyn not only gave Morley material for a number of his finest poems, but also provided the setting for his last novel, the partially autobiographical *The Man Who Made Friends with Himself*. Richard Tolman, a literary agent who is the main character of the novel, expresses in verse his and Morley's enthusiasm for existence:

> The least last latest trivial thing
> Is what empowers me to sing:
> The labile sweetness of the rose,
> Or peonies, pepper to the nose;
> How, on your memory, imprint
> The sharpness of my backyard mint?

This was the problem that Morley set himself to solve: the communication of universal sensations. In *John Mistletoe* he had said:

> One of the things I shall miss most when I am dead
> Will be walking with naked feet on bare floors
> In summer nights, when the hardwood boards
> Are deliciously tepid to the palms of the feet.
> For if you love life you should love it all over
> And even feet have their privileges.

Knowing that after he was gone no one would notice things just as he had, Morley left us in poetry a legacy of his loves.

It is tempting to try to divide a man's career into neat compartments, each one exhibiting greater virtues until one can crown the person an indisputably major figure. "Juvenilia" is the easiest label to make stick, and "early work" is not hard to apply, but after that the going gets rougher and the man's writing will not always fall into three groups to be called "mature," "more mature," and "most mature." Having said this, one still feels that in the case of Morley the publication of the large retrospective collected *Poems* of 1929 marks a division worth noting. In the volume Morley collected all of the poetry he wished to preserve; he omitted all of *The Eighth Sin* and a number of poems from the other early volumes. A few new poems, among them two charming lyrics, were added.

Included in the *Poems* was the unusual long poem, *Toulemonde*, which had been published separately the previous year. In this work Morley took as his theme the meaning of a man's life; it was a theme he was to return to more than once, and particularly in the adventures of Richard Tolman, whose name is an adaptation of "Toulemonde," or "everybody." The form, however, of blank verse varied with interludes of song, was not entirely successful and although Morley felt a strong affection for the poem and returned to the theme in later shorter "Toulemonde" poems, most reviewers agreed that the volume was not one of his best.

If during the early '20's Morley showed an increased concentration on the problems of the art of writing, he was faced in the early '30's—his forties—with problems in the art of living. His recent two year fling at play producing in Hoboken had ended in financial difficulties and the shock of discovering the dishonesty of a trusted associate. Morley began to take stock of himself and the more bohemian aspects of his theatrical experience lost some of their allure. He had a "concern"—in the Quaker sense—to tell of an examined life and did so in *John Mistletoe*, his reflective, poetic autobiography, which was published in 1931. Succeeding years showed a somewhat mellowed man.

After the juvenilia of 1912 and the early celebrations of domesticity of 1914–29, a third period of Morley's verse is represented in *The Middle Kingdom*, *Spirit Level*, *Poetry Package*, and *The Ballad of New York, New York, and Other Poems*; the poems in these collections were written in the years 1929–50. In them Morley's individual voice is heard more clearly than in preceding collections. Here are the poetic milestones of the passage of time. One of the most successful is "Ammonoosuc," a ballad which describes a deeply felt experience in Morley's life, a return to nature which rejuvenated the poet and committed him to rededication. Of the poem William Rose Benét wrote, "Emerson is one of my gods as a poet, and I get the same feeling when I read:

> Where her crystal overran it
> I lay down in channeled granite;
> Braced against the pushing planet
> I bathed in Ammonoosuc.

The last two lines Emerson would have wished to write." Another moving experience, the marriage of his daughter Louise, is the subject of "For a Daughter's Wedding." Also among the poems of this period is the tender description of Morley's fifteen year-old spaniel, through which Corky may well join the company of Cowper's Beau and Elizabeth Barrett Browning's Flush. Realizing that he, too, was advancing in years, Morley wrote his fortunately premature "Nightsong of Lord Culverin on the Drawbridge of Castle Querulous," the lovely last lines of which call for no editorial comment:

> Soft airs, wing-beetles, crowd about!
> Good night, my lovers. My lamp is out.

Some of the best poems of Morley's middle period appeared in *Poetry Package*, a book which has a curious publishing history. Thirty-six years earlier Morley had bought a magazine on the train which brought him to New York City; in it an advertisement for William Rose Benét's *Merchants from Cathay* caught his eye. "Would it ever be possible," he mused, "for me also to get some poems printed, and even maybe to meet, just once and a while, men of printed poems and musical names . . ." Morley and Benét did meet and become close friends in the early '20's. Now, in 1949, another advertisement caught Morley's eye. A large New York department store was offering, among other books in a "Sale of the Unsalable," a book of poems by Benét and one by himself together as a "Poetry Package" for a dollar. At Morley's suggestion, then, the two poets selected the best poems from among their most recent and had them published by Louis Greenfield in an attractive paperbound volume. The co-authors of *Poetry Package* were only identified by their initials on the cover and title page; inside, the poems were attributed to "D.D." and "P.C.," which only initiates would recognize as "Dove Dulcet" and "Pigeon Cove," pseudonyms under which Morley and Benét, respectively, had published verse. The introduction, signed only "Cuckoo," was actually by the respected critic Chauncey Brewster Tinker; the motif was further carried out by a cover caricature of the poets as birds, Benét a pigeon operating a typewriter with one toe, and Morley a bearded and bespectacled dove writing with a quill pen. When the book came out, Morley told an interviewer that it had been published in memory of another collaboration, the *Lyrical Ballads* of Wordsworth and Coleridge.

Like Thomas Hardy, whose poetry he admired, Morley wrote some of his finest poems toward the end of a long writing career. Writing of Hardy, Morley could have been speaking of himself:

> Someone is sure to reiterate the old legend that it was pique or deep indignation at fool criticisms that turned Hardy from the novel to poetry. That seems to me inconceivable. A man of his vitality and toughness writes as and how he pleases; and the sequence of a man's work obeys laws deeper than publicity. He turned to poetry, one may guess, because he could better express in that measure what he wanted to say.

After completing *The Man Who Made Friends with Himself,* Morley wrote to friends that "I have a sudden horrid feeling, probably glandular, that I am grown up; therefore I now devote myself to the only perfect excitement I have ever had, writing verse." He was not displeased with past performances and for Christmas, 1951, sent to friends a privately printed pamphlet, *A Pride of Sonnets,* which contained nineteen previously published poems. Among them was the charming "Charles and Mary," which Walter de la Mare had chosen as one of twenty-four sonnets, some of them by such masters as Shelley, Keats, and Wordsworth, for "Sweet as Roses, A Little Treasury of Sonnets," which appeared in *The Saturday Book* for 1950. The sonnet form was a favorite of Morley's; his success with the conventional structure is shown in the sixteen examples in *Bright Cages.*

The fourth and final division in Morley's career as a poet is that of the poems produced after a stroke suffered in 1951 temporarily paralyzed his right arm and hand. Painfully he taught himself to type again (Morley had given up writing with a fountain pen in the late '30's, in an attempt to simplify his style). In his slow recovery from illness, Morley discovered that "when a word makes its way safely and scribably from skull to fingers . . . I probably really mean or want it." Enough poems were written for a final collection, *Gentlemen's Relish,* before a second stroke two years before his death in 1957 made both speech and writing impossible.

The approach of death can be seen in several poems in the volume, but the book itself is full of life. "Elected Silence: Three Sonnets," for example, in which Morley pays tribute to the memory of William Rose Benét, who had died in 1950, is refreshingly free from elegiac formality. Another individual treatment of the theme of death is the witty "Morning After," in which, asked by St. Peter what he would most enjoy in Heaven, the poet answers: "To learn again how words, well shuffled, / Can sort miraculously into rhyme; / Or better still, read as for the first time / One of the Adventures of Sherlock Holmes." Morley thought of himself, with some reason, as a forgotten man in his last years, but the once popular poet was not bitter towards a fickle public. He felt that he had written well and was content. As he expressed it in verse:

> All passion spent, and all publicity,
> My telephone not numbered in the book,
> Nowhere will you find a happier man.
> All birds are redbreast in the setting sun.

As to the technical aspects of the poetry, one wonders just what service would be performed the reader were we to approach Morley's verse with the various tools of the critic—to count the number of syllables and ascertain the stresses, noting the sequence of feminine and masculine rhymes both internal and external, carefully paying attention to the distinctions between a rondeau and a rondel, a ballad and a ballade, and finally to correctly label the various specimens like so many butterflies preserved in an exhibit case. It is well, perhaps, to note that Morley successfully essayed a number of complicated French verse forms in addition to being adept at the more usual English ones, to remark that on occasion he wrote *vers libre* but that, except for the "translations from the Chinese," he was basically an old-fashioned poet for whom rhyme was important. If one were to read some of Morley's favorite poets— Austin Dobson, Sir William Watson, and Robert Louis Stevenson, as well as Keats, Shelley, and Wordsworth—one might better assess what he attempted, but it may well be better simply to read and enjoy each poem separately.

One thinks wryly of the teacher who told his students, "Go home and appreciate these poems by Monday." But even such a respected writer as T. S. Eliot has defined the critic he was most grateful to as "the one who can make me look at something I have never looked at before, or looked at only with eyes clouded by prejudice, set me face to face with it, and then leave me alone with it. From that point, I must rely upon my own sensibility, intelligence and capacity for wisdom."

Perhaps the editor might remark that the "Wooing Song for Sir Toby" was written to supplement the action of Shakespeare's *Twelfth Night*, in which Morley felt that Sir Toby and Maria marry too precipitately; it may be helpful for the reader to know, too, that the Sir Kenelm mentioned in the poems is Sir Kenelm Digby, the seventeenth century English naval commander, diplomat, and author. Further interest may be derived from the poems if one is reminded, when reading "Oh to Be in 'Bartlett' Now That April's Here," that Morley edited two versions of *Familiar Quotations*; when reading "Portrait of a Mathematician," that Morley's father was a noted geometer; and that the Chateau de Missery of the poem was an estate on the Cote d'Or at which Morley was once a guest. But

basically such information is small beer; if the lines are good it cannot make them better and if they are bad, it cannot help at all. Morley's poetry, it need only be noted, exhibits symbolism without recourse to private mythology, knowledge without offensive pedantry, and complexity with neither wilful obscurity nor any of the seven types of ambiguity discovered by William Empson and embraced so ardently by the gradgrind mind. No, Christopher Morley's poetry is too honest and too human and communicates too directly with the reader for an explicator to feel very much at home. As Morley's "Old Mandarin" put it:

> I am weary
> Of critical theory.
> I'm empiric
> About a lyric.
> Either it sings
> Like a happy peasant,
> Or—one of those things—
> It just doesn't.

WRIGHT MORRIS

1910–

Wright Morris, novelist and photographer, was born on January 6, 1910, in Central City, Nebraska. His mother having died a few days after his birth, he was brought up by his father, who moved to Omaha in 1919 and five years later settled in Chicago. In 1930 Morris entered Pomona College in Claremont, California. In 1933 he left Pomona for a year of travel in Europe, and on returning to California married Mary Ellen Finfrock. Between 1944 and 1958 he lived in suburban Philadelphia, and in 1961 he divorced his first wife and married Josephine Kantor. The following year he began teaching in the Creative Writing Department of San Francisco State University, where he remained until his retirement in 1975. He has also taught at Princeton, the University of Nebraska, and Amherst.

Wright Morris has published some twenty novels, beginning with *My Uncle Dudley* (1942), based on his travels across America. His other novels, which are largely concerned with the American experience, alienation, and the idea of the "American Dream," are *The Man Who Was There* (1945); *The World in the Attic* (1949); *Man and Boy* (1951); *The Works of Love* (1952); *The Deep Sleep* (1953); *The Huge Season* (1954); *The Field of Vision* (1956, National Book Award); *Love among the Cannibals* (1957); *Ceremony in Lone Tree* (1960); *What a Way to Go* (1962); *Cause for Wonder* (1963); *One Day* (1965); *In Orbit* (1967); *Fire Sermon* (1971); *A Life* (1973); *Here Is Einbaum* (1973); *The Fork River Space Project* (1977), and *Plains Song: For Female Voices* (1980). Morris's stories are collected in *Real Losses, Imaginary Gains* (1976). He is also an accomplished photographer, and has published several books in which text and photographs are combined: *The Inhabitants* (1946); *The Home Place* (1948): *God's Country and My People* (1968); *Love Affair* (1972), and *Photographs and Words* (1982). He has written a critical study of American literature, *The Territory Ahead* (1958), as well as several books of essays on that subject: *A Bill of Rites, a Bill of Wrongs, a Bill of Goods* (1968), *About Fiction* (1975), and *Earthy Delights, Unearthy Adornments* (1978). *Will's Boy*, published in 1981, is an autobiographical book about his youth.

Personal

For some time, as part of *The Territory Ahead*, I had been pondering Norman Rockwell's America. His portraits of the presidential candidates Eisenhower and Stevenson, widely displayed in a series of posters, had aroused renewed interest in his work. My own taste and sentiments had been shaped by Rockwell quite beyond my grasp or the telling of it, and this knowledge gave edge and persistence to my reactions. What a bill of goods he had sold me—and I had bought! That barefoot boy with cheek of tan, his feet sticky with roofing tar, his face

smeared with the pie still cooling at the pantry window, had also leaped from the bridge into the quicksand, and turned from there to try his hand at walking on water.

No cliché has been evaded; every cliché alters the actual image of the past in the interests of the sentiments of the present. To what end? Had the actual past been so bad that the memory of it had been suppressed? To what end would one diminish the truly memorable moment in the interests of a sham sentimentality? Was it a failure of nerve (a fashionable phrase at the time) or of memory itself? Was it feebleness of taste, or intelligence, that would lead us to prefer the spurious to the genuine? Calendar pictures of romantically nuzzling horses (a movie innovation) to the realities of the farmyard? Americans who had searing memories of poverty and hardship, of sickness and death, of real losses without imaginary gains, had put it all behind them with the first calendar pictures of mixed litters of kittens and puppies, steamboats rounding the bend, and amber waving fields of grain. On the graves of what had been both forgotten and suppressed, Rockwell assembled a fiction that was pleasant to remember, and made us all feel good. Including myself. My *Boys' Life* mind had been honed and buffed by the *Saturday Evening Post* covers that celebrated so much I seemed to have forgotten. What access did I have to the real past? Where might it be said to be located? It was my first dim perception that *history* was not a volume of authorized texts, to which, in time of doubt, I would always have access, but rather a landscape of immense and cloudy horizons peopled with figures of my own imagination. The past to which I had access was a film that flickered on my own eyeballs. I might buff it up, and add to or subtract from it (as I had just done in *The Field of Vision*), but I would never find it on those maps nailed to the walls of railroad stations. Norman Rockwell had his version—the gentle, white-haired old lady (a negotiable image, in the absence of an icon) and the decent small boy, "snapped" at the moment of prayerful silence as they say grace in a "rough" railroad café—and I would eventually prove to have mine if I insisted on writing about it. At the extremities of our lives, youth and age, we had established two durable fictions, but even as I prepared to mock them, I was aware they were receding. I, too, was receding, unobserved by myself, on a belt of time external to my perceptions, about which I sometimes felt quite superior. Hadn't I learned, as a fiction writer, how to run it both forward and reverse? The flashback, that bit of craft cunning, permitted me to conjure up a time of my own, all the while concealing from myself the time in which I was captive. I would get a glimpse of a larger time in those first photographs from space, where planet earth, a sort of timepiece, ticked away like a pocket watch. I would never long be free, however, of the tricks time would play on such an observer as myself, able to stop time in such a way the blur in the film indicated its passage, a happening to which I bore elaborate witness.

This elusive, ineluctable time had become a common-place property of fiction. Katherine Anne Porter's story "Old Mortality" closes with Miranda's reflections on her entrapment in time past, but her high hopes for time future.

> . . . I can't live in their world any longer, she told herself, listening to the voices back of her. Let them tell their stories to each other. Let them go on explaining how things happened. I don't care. At least I can know the truth about what happens to me, she assured herself silently, making a promise to herself, in her hopefulness, her ignorance.

As a young, and not so young, man, I felt that the conjunction of time and place—in particular, place—that left on me such a memorable impression was a property of the place and the time rather than of an event that took place within me. I also felt that such impressions of time and place were commonplace. Anyone (I felt) with a past would share them. The passage of time, indeed, had given rise to these impressions.

After a lifetime of being time's fool, and observing my own peculiar behavior, I conclude that my response to the time-place syndrome is not as widespread as I had imagined. Ingredients are present in nostalgia, but they are like shavings that have not taken fire. I know these feelings, and I feel such ties, but that is not what I am describing. Many, if not all, writers share it, since it is part of their purpose to recover losses, but the parallel I feel to be more exact is what many feel for "holy" places. That is my feeling, once I allow for a profoundly different orientation. Had I been bred or trained to religious observance, or sentiments, I would have been more than open to religious vibrations, to unearthly perceptions, to "seeing" the appropriate manifestations. Rather than merely open, I would have been eager. Between me and these "places" there is a pact that is earthly enough, in its origins, but with a bit of cultivation gives off its palpable aura. Henry James has captured both its earthly and its unearthly trappings.

> To be at all critically, or as we have been fond of calling it, analytically minded—over and beyond an inherent love of the general many-colored picture of things—is to be subject to the superstition that objects and places, coherently grouped, disposed for human use and addressed to it, must have a sense of their own, a mystic meaning proper to themselves to give out: to give out, that is, to the participant at once so interested and so detached as to be moved to a report of the matter.

That remarkably accommodates the sensations I have been evoking, and a lifetime of considering their complexity. I would add to this the exposed but uncritical soul of the child—or any person, such as myself, who accepted the world before he analyzed it, and accumulated a large, ticking store of impressions saturated with their own mystic meaning to give out. I became, as if on a higher order, the participant so interested and so detached that I was moved to a report on the matter.

On such a participant as myself, actual events, casual or dramatic, are of relative unimportance. They might be likened to the blurs in a photograph, indicating time's passage. If my training had been religious, my participation would surely have spoken of "voices," of visitations, of materializations, and called on the resources of the "séance" to give substance to my sensations. The space beneath the porch, or some other concealment, provides the child with his own magical trappings, and I am impressed—as a restless analyst—with how closely they resemble the more orthodox holy places. In Chicago, grown too large for concealment, I attributed qualities to everything at hand, and to routines that empha-sized recurrence. The streetcar ride from the Loop: the platform of this car became for me a "place" of ritual observation, with the smell of the track sand as incense, and the view down the streets to the east, the vista over the lake, a prospect of life enhancement. Chicago, indeed, mystically collaborated with a naive but highly conscious young man whose inner voices required a cultivation of more outward forms. I was perhaps overripe for the picking, the quick transplant to Eden, the California oasis that mingled the groves of academe with those of lemons and oranges. In such wise I was approaching that moment, as a participant, when the mystic meanings to which I had been exposed, and it was proper of things to give out, would begin to elicit from me a lifelong response.

This clarified for me why, on my return from Europe, and before I had written a line of fiction, I found myself evoking in words these epiphanal images from my boyhood, those objects and places, coherently grouped, disposed for human use and addressed to it. In terms of what was given, I had been destined to be such a participant.—WRIGHT MORRIS, *A Cloak of Light: Writing My Life*, 1985, pp. 223–27

General

After more than twenty-five years of sustained productivity, during which he has published nineteen books—many of them distinguished—Wright Morris seems to have become arrested permanently on the brink of major reputation. The obvious injustice of this has troubled his admirers for a very long time and caused them to insist, as each new book of his appears, that surely this one will bring him the kind of general recognition he so clearly deserves. Yet when the publication furor dies away and critics have written their usually laudatory reviews, Morris seems to be more firmly established than ever in his position as the least well-known and most widely unappreciated important writer alive in this country.

As a result, the effort to obtain justice for Morris has now reached the proportions of a literary Dreyfus case, and this new work ⟨*Wright Morris: A Reader*⟩ is the most vigorous and convincing example of it we have had to date. Presented in the form of a "reader" and containing excellent selections from Morris's best fiction and nonfiction, it is introduced by Granville Hicks quite explicitly as a major appeal to the court of public recognition.

The book thus raises once again the question which any serious estimate of Morris must finally attempt to engage: just why it is that, in spite of the impressive achievement which these selections everywhere illustrate, Morris has so far been unable to win the literary status and readership he would seem by now to have earned. In seeking an answer we need to consider both the kind of writer he is and the nature of his fictional world. And we also need to understand some of the ways in which Morris is strikingly unlike many of his contemporaries who have succeeded where he has failed. In particular, it should be said in his defense that he has had to make his way entirely on his merits as an artist, and without benefit of the support and publicity that so often come to writers in our time for reasons that have little or nothing to do with the actual quality of their work.

Unlike Saul Bellow, for example, Morris has never been the darling of any influential literary establishment. He has never been recognized as expressing in his work ideas or experiences which a particular community of intellectuals might identify with or have strong extra-literary interests in promoting. He has therefore lacked a coterie of publicists who could advertise him in the right magazines, inflate him into a fashion, and, as Mailer once said, "relax the bite of the snob to the point where he or she can open the mouth and sup upon the message." It is extremely doubtful if an establishment any longer exists that would be able or willing to support a writer whose fictional interests are generally American rather than oriented specifically to a minority group, and whose best novels are not about the urban East but the rural and small-town life of the Midwest, a kind of life which, except in Morris's fiction, seems in the last thirty years to have lost the authority it once had as a metaphor of widely typical American experience.

Morris also does not write about social problems as such but rather about people who, insofar as they relate to society at all, have spiritual roots in the frontier past or are burdened by a nostalgic obsession with society as it was when they were young, and whose problem is most often their inability to feel, the old-fashioned dilemma of the frigid Anglo-Saxon puritan which so fascinated Sherwood Anderson and Sinclair Lewis—writers, incidentally, whom Morris in some ways resembles far more closely than he does any of his contemporaries. This is to say that Morris has never been a social observer or reporter of the contemporary scene in the sense, for example, that Mailer has been. He appears to be altogether lacking in political

consciousness and the instincts of the journalist, and on the few occasions when he has tried to be topical—as in *Ceremony in Lone Tree*, which is enacted against the background of an atomic bomb test, or in *One Day*, a novel built around the assassination of John F. Kennedy—he seems awkward and out of depth.

Morris, finally, is not a modish or eccentric writer in the manner of Nabokov, Pynchon, or John Barth. He has a strong and individual style, but he would never attract attention because of the bizarre nature of his language or the grotesqueries he uses it to describe. In fact, it is one of his basic working premises that literary style should be heard but not seen, should serve no purpose other than to advance, as inconspicuously as possible, the story it is designed to tell. His novels are similarly self-contained and self-effacing. They are not really about anything except themselves. They are finely textured, discrete images of reality which do not depend for their meaning on social externals any more than they depend for their evocative power on the embellishments of style.

They do, however, depend, as any fiction must, upon materials which are derived, however obliquely, from actual experience, and which Morris has spent his whole career struggling to put to creative use. Morris, in fact, has always been peculiarly conscious of the recalcitrance of his particular materials. He has spoken again and again of the great labor required of any writer who tries to process the overly abundant raw experience of American life and give it the shape and significance of serious art. But while one recognizes that this has been a perennial problem for our writers—as painful for Henry James who solved it as for Thomas Wolfe who did not—one also senses that it is a special problem for Morris. For he, far more than most contemporary writers, has been troubled by the fact that his given materials, the materials of what he calls the "plains imagination," are by their very nature singularly hard to dramatize, and have been so thoroughly processed by distinguished predecessors such as Anderson and Lewis, that they are buried now under thick layers of cliché. His task, therefore, has been to try to exhume them, endow them with the authenticity of his individual vision, and give them freshness and relevance to the contemporary moment.

The result is that very often in his fiction one is aware of a marked disparity between the high intensity of Morris's art and the low artistic potential of his materials, a quality of strain which frequently takes the form of a willed inwardness, a specious complexity, a reaching after mythic and symbolic significance which the materials cannot always support. In Faulkner—to take an extreme and probably unfair example—one feels that the experience is literally there out of which he fashions his fantastically elaborate fictive designs. Faulkner appears to be dealing with family relations and dynastic histories that were, or might have been, as complicated and bizarre in actual life as they are in his fiction. And the past which figures so prominently in both his novels and Morris's continues to exist for Faulkner in the form of lovingly preserved ceremonies, in tribal rites and atrocities whose effects are still alive and charge the present with tragic meaning. But for Morris the problem is that the past is at best a fading phantom or a literary cliché—the cliché of the frontier—and it is incessantly being torn down, plowed under, and left behind to make way for progress, the movement of the frontier westward into the trackless present. His people remember not a coherent and recapturable history but disparate fragments of lost experience—an event recalled from childhood, a house that is no longer there, a vanished love affair, a stillborn ambition. These are the limited *givens* on which Morris's imagination is obliged to work, and to use one of his favorite phrases, it is cause for wonder that he has made as much of them as he has.

This is not quite to suggest that if Morris had had access to more promising material he might become a Nebraska Faulkner. But it is possible that he has been as much the victim of his particular kind of experience as Hemingway was the victim of his style and Henry James of his endlessly refracting sensibility. His experience has obviously not made him into the writer he has become, but it has helped to create his particular limitations and perhaps part of his particular inaccessibility to the general reader. Nevertheless, its lack of promise as material is indicative of just how fine his imagination has been to extract from it the meaning and vitality it is revealed to have in his best work. There is excellence in that work, a very great deal of excellence, certainly more than enough to entitle him to the major reputation he should have had years ago.—JOHN W. ALDRIDGE, "Wright Morris's Reputation" (1970), *The Devil in the Fire*, 1972, pp. 257–60

Works

NOVELS

When you settle into middle age you discover a new and peculiar pleasure which arises from the fact that now most of the books are being written by your contemporaries. Whether any of the creative writers among them use the past as intricately as Henry James or as majestically as Mark Twain is beside the particular point that it is now frequently *your* past which you keep coming upon. And one or another novelist, apparently by no more than coincidence of birth, will seem startlingly to have your experience of time and place, your sense of seasons and landscape and neighborhood—even though in literal fact his areas of the country, his sources from travel or whatever, are not yours, and even though you may feel that what you know is but part of so much that he seems to know. Thus Wright Morris has for years, so to speak, been writing my novels for me. I daresay he has many readers who feel the same way.

For one thing—but it is basic to his work—Morris is so simply and naturally an American novelist. Aside from contemporaries who don't much use the home place we have some who use it a shade too thoughtfully: their bones of theory show through. Not Morris—he is marvelously observant, and he knows the look of American town and people as he knows his own skin. He can by one detail take you instantly where he wants you, as for example "grass"—"McKee had sat on the porch, which was so close to the ground grass grew through the cracks in it. . . ." He can with quick strokes show a specific character in instantly recognizable images, thus the same McKee—"A simple frame-house sort of life with an upstairs and a downstairs, and a kitchen where he lived, a parlor where he didn't, a stove where the children could dress on winter mornings, a porch where time could be passed summer evenings, an attic for the preservation of the past, a basement for tinkering with the future, and a bedroom for making such connections as the nature of the house would stand." And his prose is American: often inaccurate by the schoolbook but never by the ear, and it can range from daily illiteracy to an unforced lyric beauty.

This passionate possession of American detail makes *The Field of Vision* repeatedly exciting, as it has Morris's earlier novels. Again, too, he uses the segmented structure of storytelling; we are passed back and forth among the characters, each "a circle overlapped by countless other circles." The levels of action are intricate. The "action" of the novel consists of a few hours watching bullfights in Mexico. The bulk of

narrative is made, though, of the intertwined pasts of these people; incidents echo and re-echo in their minds and in Morris's theme.

That bullring circle and the failure or success of the heroic matadors make a symbolic image of the theme. For central to *The Field of Vision* is the exceptional man, Boyd: a hero in his youth, a ridiculous failure now, but he has influenced all the lives that touched his—given McKee and the others a difference. In tiny ways McKee emulates his friend. Mrs. McKee—one of Morris's chill women—has never gotten over the kiss Boyd gave her. McKee's children are his own but they look like Boyd. Yet more bizarre symbols of individuality are Paul Kahler, the man who has become a woman, and old Scanlon who dreams his father's memories of westward trek and frontier days. All this, then: a serious comedy of the impingement of lives, a drama of "seem" and "be," of the endless variants of reality. I'm afraid it is too fantastically and wilfully contrived to be as impressive in total as it is in a hundred moments. What Morris knows is surer than what he thinks. I would guess, however gratuitously, that what his comic-nostalgic vision wants is a little less smartness and a little more sadness.—WINFIELD TOWNLEY SCOTT, "Ring around a Hero," *SR*, Oct. 6, 1956, pp. 24, 46

In *Ceremony at Lone Tree* Wright Morris has expanded and deepened the fictional world whose truth was revealed, at the bull-ring, to the characters of his earlier *The Field of Vision*. The present novel takes place about two and a half years later, and the ceremony in question is the ninetieth birthday of the old man, Scanlon, in a ghost-town in Nebraska, attended by his family from all over the state. The occasion is eased ⟨. . .⟩ into general significance by virtue of the complex relationships of all the book's characters to the past. By the time that Gordon Boyd, the American hero *manqué* of both this and the earlier book, can say that "The past is dead, long live the past," both past and present have become thoroughly realized in concrete and symbolic terms. An atom bomb test, sharp reports of shooting, outbreaks of senseless teen-age violence ironically contrasted with the bow-and-arrow hunting of one of the more childish adults, all serve to fill in the sketched outlines of a contemporary moment, caught in the process of observing its own recession into the past while a part of the past is itself becoming myth.

Boyd's lifelong friend and admirer, McKee, the old man, his daughters and grandchildren all play different roles in this ceremony of history. Mr. Morris represents these by means of a narrative device he has employed consistently in his novels since *Man and Boy* in 1951; each chapter is given over to a particular character, not to his interior monologue, as in *As I Lay Dying*, but rather to the character himself as a dominating presence and focus of interest. In all the sections, we continue to see things through Mr. Morris' eyes, and the language remains, with occasional lapses, a neutral one. But in no one of them have we access to the mind of anyone but the "owner" of the chapter. What the author's perception notices is, as always, quite accurate, and he contrives to see the facts of midwestern American life with all of the clarity, if no longer with the ruthlessness, of what Lionel Trilling has called the "urban intelligence," that distinguished his camera's eye in *The Home Place*. He continues also to evidence his fine sensitivity to the nuances of an eternal war in America between men and women, a war about which he has written with as much detachment as James Thurber has scrutinized it with brilliant nervousness.

There can be no doubt, I think, that Wright Morris is one of our best novelists. He has always seemed to me to have been weighed down a little with an overpowering sense of a novelistic tradition in America with which he has had to come to terms. In his very considerable body of work he appears time and again to be insisting that it is never local or regional fiction, but rather something more universal, that he is producing. By bringing the characters of *The Field of Vision* together in a Mexican bull-ring, he was perhaps dramatically making just such an insistence. In *The Huge Season*, this half-allusion to Hemingway's post–World War I Europe is paralleled by a rewrite of a party scene in *The Great Gatsby*. In *Ceremony at Lone Tree* he has perhaps begun to break new ground, if only in that he has been able to widen his range without importing into his narrow world cosmopolitan symbols like bull-fighting and Swiss psychiatrists. This is a more successful book than the frequently tiresome and exasperating *The Field of Vision*. There is a central event here toward which all the action and digression alike move with great force, while the "mythical" events of the earlier novel, such as Gordon Boyd's squirting pop at a bull, his childhood feats in connection with Ty Cobb and walking on water and the kiss he gave Lois McKee, are all buried amid fragments of cross-perspective and personal insight. The characters who intrude upon the family scene in this book remain to illuminate it. But most important of all, the elements of symbolic theme which appear throughout the story, such as whistling sounds, a loaded revolver, a flaw in a glass pane (an "eye in the glass"), are all employed with brilliance and economy to pull together various scattered events into a dense moment in the history of a few people, of Nebraska, and of the Western World.—JOHN HOLLANDER, YR, Sept. 1960, pp. 155–56

In *In Orbit*, in and of itself, the relationships between events, people, and things are as close and complex, as similar and different, as the suggested quality inherent in all of Morris' work. The words are there, the always interesting and well-realized characters are there, but the *design* is crucially important and superbly achieved. Every *thing* comes to work for the design. For as widely different and separate as the characters are, and quite unbeknownst to each other, they keep seeing and feeling and experiencing the same things, and not just in "fact" but in imagination. They make the same metaphors and similes, same and different. They live through the same weather, one and all. Their separation from each other, the fragmentary character of their individual lives, is heightened by a virtuoso exercise in rapidly shifting point of view. The principal characters all see different things and reflect upon them and are forever unable, it would seem, to communicate these things and reflections to each other. Yet they all *share* a common experience, in general and in close detail. All things, all events, become symbols then, by a process of cumulative association. One thinks, for analogy, of Malcolm Lowry's *Under the Volcano*. And then one realizes that Morris has achieved a similar effect in a very short novel.

There is a difference. He carries it a step beyond; he wants something else. Lowry did it in terms of a single tortured consciousness known in depth. Morris does the same thing using half a dozen points of view, all seen briefly, swiftly. Ordinarily, and we all know it, this method is used to demonstrate what we cannot know. The cliché of the method is that the reports of many witnesses establish that there is no design, no "truth." Yet each of these witnesses does in fact and within the context and confines of his or her very specific limitations, faults, and hangups, see the same thing without knowing it. Who knows it, then? The reader does. The reader has all the pieces. The reader is therefore privileged to be aware of the outlines of the design, though the Design it reflects, the

Creation, remains enigmatic, beyond simple answers. It is a glimpse of the working out of that ineffable design in time, a flashing view of what was once called Providence. Chance is terribly urgent, but Chance [like Dame Fortune of old] is part of the Design. When all things come together, as they do, we the readers discover that the characters are not so different as they dream they are and they wish to be. In a profound sense, in spite of rape, stabbing, violence, and a terrible twister, *In Orbit* is a human comedy. A black comedy? Not quite. It's more like the boy, Jubal Gainer himself, with his madras face. He didn't *mean* anything. But—"As luck would have it"—fleeing the draft, his past, lunging into an unknown future on a stolen motorcycle, he happened to hit the town of Pickett and to run out of gas, happened to run into enough eccentrics and mischief to last a man a lifetime, happened to get lifted into literal orbit by a twister he didn't see coming from behind him, and in the end is back on the road, gassed up, and rolling . . . well, *somewhere*. Looking much as he did before; *described* in fact in the same terms and with the same analogies. With a difference.

> On his chest J. S. Bach dries in a manner that enlarges his forehead, curves his lips in a smile. Is that for what looms up ahead, or lies behind? This boy is like a driver who has gone too deep and too long without air. If the army is no place for a growing boy, neither is the world. . . . There is no place to hide. But perhaps the important detail escapes you. He is in motion. Now you see him, now you don't. If you pin him down in time he is lost in space. Somewhere between where he is from and where he is going he wheels in an unpredictable orbit. He is as free, and as captive, as the wind in his face.

Morris has created, with elegant precision, control, and condensation, a comedy of doom and destiny. The wounds of comedy are real enough, but laughter helps to ease the pain. Nobody we have around could have done this book. It took a lifetime and twenty-five years of professional writing to do it. *In Orbit* makes the image-makers look like what they are—bush league. It makes the novel seem brand new again. It ought to make those who are trying to write novels and those who are trying to read them happy. Like Jubal we've got something to look forward to. Unlike Jubal we know that whatever it is it will be good. Meanwhile here in *In Orbit* we have as much of the magic, as much of the joy of art as we could ask for.—GEORGE GARRETT, "Morris the Magician: A Look at *In Orbit*," HC, June 1967, pp. 11–12

ESSAYS AND CRITICISM

Beginning in 1942 with *My Uncle Dudley*, Wright Morris has published nine novels, as well as two books made up of photographs and text. His recent years have been particularly fruitful: *Man and Boy* in 1951, *The Works of Love* in 1952, *The Deep Sleep* in 1953, *The Huge Season* in 1954, *The Field of Vision* in 1956, and last year *Love among the Cannibals*. Serious, talented, and versatile, he has produced more good work in the Fifties than any other writer I can think of.

Although he is anything but a dilettante, Morris has many interests, and whatever interests him interests him intensely. He has tried to be, in Henry James's phrase, "one on whom nothing is lost." Although one might not guess it from his novels, which are not in the least bookish, he has read much and read thoughtfully. *The Territory Ahead* is a report on some of that reading, with particular reference to the aims, possibilities, and perils of the writer in America.

Morris begins with the observation, frequently made, that American writers have a way of not fulfilling their promise, and he looks about for explanations. He finds two. In the first place, he maintains, American writers, with only a few exceptions, with only one really notable exception, have fled from the present. Flight may take any one of several directions, but in America the writer usually flees into the past.

Nostalgia is what our writers most often feel, and although it has given us great books, it is not the kind of emotion, the kind of attitude, on which literary careers are built. Then, in the second place, he argues that most writers share the general American preference for facts, for raw material, and are comparatively indifferent to the techniques by which raw material may be processed. Morris seems to recognize more exceptions to this generalization than to the other but here again his great exception is Henry James.

As he proceeds with his examination of particular writers and their books, Morris sometimes bases his argument on one of his theories and sometimes on the other, and his analyses are not always easy to follow. I am not sure whether he holds that the two theories are related in some significant way or are quite independent so that either fallacy or both may be operative. The truth is, indeed, that the book rests on a series of perceptions rather than on rigorous logic, but these perceptions are so acute that the reader doesn't worry much about the absence of a completely coherent esthetic theory.

What Morris does first is to look at four of the acknowledged masterpieces of the nineteenth century, books for which he himself has great admiration: *Walden, Leaves of Grass, Moby-Dick,* and *Huckleberry Finn.* Each of them he regards as both representative and exceptional. Thoreau fled to the woods, Whitman took to the open road, Melville sailed on the high seas, and Mark Twain embarked on the river. Furthermore, all four of these men, Morris insists, are preoccupied with facts, Thoreau and Whitman most obviously so but the others too. He makes the additional point that each of them was isolated, even Whitman, who wrote so much of comradeship but wrote best about himself. In spite of all this, each was able, for reasons Morris sets forth, to write a great book. None, however, was capable of growth. "Not knowing what he was doing," he writes, "never having truly known, Twain soon gave it up."

In a middle section Morris discusses Henry James as a writer who did know what he was doing, and then, surprisingly but aptly, talks about an illustrator, Norman Rockwell, as a master of the cliché. Now he is ready to turn to four contemporary writers: Hemingway, Wolfe, Fitzgerald, and Faulkner. Wolfe he despises, pities, and blames for a great deal of what is wrong with contemporary fiction; the other three he admires. But if he thinks that Hemingway has triumphed through his perfecting of a style, that Fitzgerald transformed nostalgia into a virtue, that Faulkner achieved greatness in the expression of rage, he sees in each qualities that have prevented growth.

Henry James has already emerged as the hero of the book. In addition to the chapter I have mentioned, there is a chapter on one book, *The American Scene,* and here Morris lets himself go. Writing some fifty years ago, he says, James saw more than the most perceptive observers see today: "The American novelist, midcentury, will read this book with fear and trembling, since it puts in question the very reason for his existence—his contemporaneity. Having climbed to some pinnacle, or dived to some depth, he turns to see that James, like Kilroy, was already there."

Morris quotes wonderful passages to support his argument, and he sums up: "It was James's distinction in *The American Scene* to have been the first to view that scene from the *present,* free from visions of the future and crippling commitments to the past. It is this *presentness* that resulted in impressions consistently prophetic."

Morris's enthusiasm for James is very great, and yet he has revealed in the earlier chapter that he does have misgivings. There is some validity, he grants, in "the charge that James lacked raw material." "His passion was his craft, but out of craft one cannot conjure up *the* grand passion. It is here that life exercises its precedence over art." And again: "In James we have the artist who apprehended much of life without the crippling effects of having lived it. . . . He remains free to generalize; too free for the novelist."

It seems to me that Morris never quite comes to terms with these objections he has raised. But if he is not perfectly clear about James, he is clear about his own position. The concluding section of the book begins: "If I have emphasized technique, the primacy of technique, over such things as experience and raw material, it is because the primacy of life—in the American scene—is obvious. . . . But there is no substitute for the material itself—the *life* in literature." Thereupon he transfers the argument overseas, preferring the life in D. H. Lawrence to the technique of the later Joyce and thus taking issue with T. S. Eliot.

Morris doesn't really make his point about Lawrence any more than he really solves the question of James. He is less than just to Melville, and perhaps to Hemingway and Faulkner as well. In part the disappointments I feel result from the brevity with which Morris has chosen to treat his subjects, but that isn't the heart of the matter. His mind lends itself to tangents, rather than, as he says James's did, to parentheses, and he can sometimes be led into outer space by a figure of speech. But he is not merely right in his general emphasis; his sensitivity is unfailing.

It its faults were ten times as great as I think they are, *The Territory Ahead* would still be a rich and rewarding book.
—GRANVILLE HICKS, "Wright Morris as Critic," *SR,* Oct. 25, 1958, p. 14

Is it a measure of the sickness of our age that essays which take our temperature and find it feverish can seem so lacking in fresh insight? Do we nod because the patient needs no doctor to tell him where he hurts, or because the malady has weakened our capacity for feeling the shock of truth? Perhaps the patient is already dead. One of Wright Morris' better essays in *A Bill of Rites, a Bill of Wrongs, a Bill of Goods* is called "Reflections on the Death of the Reader." The reader is dead, says Morris, because he concerns himself with tracking reputations in the *New York Review of Books* instead of reading the books that journal is supposed to review. Having the dope—knowing Pritchett on Bellow, Mailer on McCarthy—is more important than the experience of reading imaginative literature, because the world cries out for communicable data. What happens, Morris asks, to Keats's belief in the holiness of the heart's affections and the truth of the imagination when the heart becomes an interchangeable part?

Wright Morris, after fourteen novels, all worthwhile, some of them excellent, tries to tell us how we are, not in fiction but in fact. If the death of the reader has stifled Morris' imagination, the loss is serious, all the more because Morris is a better diagnostician when he lies like a poet than when he tells the truths of the social scientist.

In his novels, Morris likes to take a small observed object, idea or phrase and let the imagination play with it. In *Love among the Cannibals,* the gorgeous Greek kicks off her shoes before getting into bed, and Morris' metaphysical imagination turns the simple gesture into a metaphor for the novel's central act, "bolting." A garish American convertible stripped of everything portable by cheerful Mexican thieves tells us something about the metaphorical stripping the hero of the novel is undergoing, and also something about parking a convertible in Acapulco. But while there are vivid bits of observation in *A Bill of Rites*, most of the time the object observed is one with which we are all too familiar. A sightseeing old lady overtipping a waiter is (as Morris himself says) a character from one of his novels come to life, and she tells us far more about growing old gracelessly than does the *Dear Abby* letter about drinking senior citizens he quotes in the essay, "Going Crazy in Miami." But more commonly, Morris finds himself trying to freshen Los Angeles, the ears of Mr. Johnson's beagles, or the resonant voice of the Senate Minority Leader reciting the Pledge of Allegiance on the Red Skelton show. He cites these in an essay called "Mom & Pop Art" to argue that the banalities of real life outdo the banalities of Pop art at their own game. But most of his book tries to turn phenomena equally prevalent and equally fatuous into metaphors for the Modern Condition. What, one asks, can such things stand for either sillier or (alas) more significant than themselves?

A world so bizarre that art can hardly imagine what to do with it is Morris' major subject in his book. He gazes upon the Vietnamese War, the space program, Haight-Ashbury, television commercials, Mr. McLuhan, Mr. Warhol, and to nobody's surprise he discovers selfishness, mindlessness and hopelessness. What can a man do? He can rage. A book written in anger is likely to suffer from the defects of anger—petulance, repetition, disorganization. These are certainly the vices of *A Bill of Rites*. An epigraph tells us, in Henry James's words, that the case was "magnificent for pitiless ferocity." But ferocity must exclude self-pity along with pity for abuses, and Morris hasn't done so. Morris also quotes T. S. Eliot on "The conscious inpotence of rage / At human folly." Conscious impotence may be the only stance available to a serious writer today, but Morris' rage doesn't make for orderly social criticism.

"Of our rapidly diminishing natural resources one remains inexhaustible," says Morris: "our genius for coining the memorable word or phrase for things we do not like." Indeed, the rage of this gifted writer occasionally produces a passage of lively railing. "The American novel and the American adolescent," he says, "seems to emerge equally from the nursery and the attic." Marshall McLuhan "runs a rake through the bins of history and hastily assembles his own collage." The hucksters of the New Sensibility "specialize in gorging and upchucking. . . . It has been found that the mind can be emptied as easily, and to better effect, than the stomach." Of the inevitable day when the acidhead hippie passes 30 and ceases to be trustworthy: "It is interesting to speculate what will happen when he tunes in on his first dry martini, and experiences the strange, rocky euphoria of the cocktail hour. That will be new. . . . The full circle of this syndrome will be complete when the alcoholic hippy, put into dry dock, is treated with LSD to put him back on his feet." One hundred seventy pages of such writing is too much.

Before he became an autobiographical symbol, Norman Podhoretz wrote a famous essay in which he announced that one traditional function of the novel, "bringing the news" about the current scene, had now been assumed by essays and magazine articles. Morris makes that claim seem even more tenuous than it is. His novel, *In Orbit*, describes the coincidental joint passage through a freshwater college town of a motorcycle-riding young draft dodger and a tornado. As a

commentary on the strange spinnings of men and events as they orbit from where they were to where they are going, the novel is to *A Bill of Rites* as dinner at Julia Child's is to potluck at a diner. There are good jokes in the book—the helmeted and goggled cyclist is described as "a spaceman" by the half-witted farm lady he tries to rape—but the jokes also give the reader some cause for reflection about the problems of making sense of someone young, free and aimless. Reading *In Orbit* serves as a fresh reminder of what we have known all along: that the discipline of form gives to an artist's perceptions a fullness far exceeding anything available to a purveyor of information. Wright Morris implies this very point in *A Bill of Rites, a Bill of Wrongs, a Bill of Goods*: he ought to have acted accordingly. We readers may be weakening, but reports of our death are greatly exaggerated.—PETER BEREK, "Bills Past Due," *Nation*, April 8, 1968, pp. 478–79

ALAN TRACHTENBERG
"The Craft of Vision"

Critique, Winter 1961–62, pp. 41–55

Again, the mind must think of itself, of the conditions of its existence (which are also conditions of growth), of the dangers menacing its virtues, its forces and its possessions, its liberty, its development, its depth. (PAUL VALERY)

The American literary inheritance has not been a comfortable one for modern writers. Often a burden with its preponderance of metaphysical themes, its shadowy people, and its eccentric styles, the native tradition has amounted to a free and robust language, and nothing more. For Wright Morris, however, that tradition is a good deal more than a down-to-earth sentence style. Morris has tried to make his literary past usable by inventing new forms for the old themes of innocence and corruption. His craft is his response to tradition. In Morris's view, expressed in *The Territory Ahead*, American literature has been dominated by the notion that the "raw material" of experience is more important than technique or the way in which that material is processed "for human consumption." Even though writers like Whitman and Mark Twain achieved their best work through a first-rate technique, they always preferred the "facts" of actuality to the "mind" of technique. This split between mind and fact, Morris points out, is based on the American version of primitivism, the belief that nature is real and purifying while society is artificial and corrupting. Starting with Emerson and Thoreau, Americans have behaved as though nature has its own pristine order which society (the world of Huck Finn's Aunt Sally) gets in the way of; reality, therefore, always lies somewhere else, where life is raw and unprocessed. Our culture has tended to place its hopes in "the territory ahead," which, as Mark Twain demonstrates, lies behind us in the pastoral idyll of childhood. The most American trait of our literature, Morris believes, is a lament for the loss of innocence and harmony, the "naturalness" of the past. Scratch beneath the hard-boiled and sophisticated disguises of Hemingway, Fitzgerald, and Faulkner, and you will find the Big Two-Hearted River, the green world in the eyes of Dutch sailors, and the freshly-cut clearing in the woods.

For Wright Morris, the pastoral dream-lament has lost its integrity. Huck Finn has been copyrighted into a pastel dream by Norman Rockwell. The "raw material myth" has become a soft-focus vision, tinted with nostalgia which the writer, and every man, must resist. The antidote to the American Dream that selfhood lies waiting fully formed in a "territory ahead" is hard and clear vision. As a writer, Morris has made vision a dominant theme. The craft of vision, at the same time, is his technique.

Morris's technique, I want to show, owes a great deal to the art of photography. Morris was a photographer before he became a novelist and, in an original way, remains a photographer in his novels. To call his works "photographic," however, is misleading. He is not mainly a pictorialist, although physical description of a high order is a mark of his style. Rather, photography has given Morris a rich sense of the technical and symbolic possibilities of sight in fiction. Throughout his work we find references to photographs and pictures and to images of lenses and sight; see, for example, the opening sections of *The Works of Love, The Deep Sleep, The Huge Season,* and *Ceremony in Lone Tree.* Two of his most interesting books, in fact, join picture and text in imaginative ways. But the clearest evidence of a creative incorporation of the lessons of one art form to the requirements of another is *The Field of Vision,* the National Book Award winner in 1957. In this novel, vision defines both theme and technique, and to understand their complexities we must first learn what vision in the photographic sense has meant to Wright Morris.

I

Photography has been a significant educator of artists for almost a hundred years. Perhaps most obvious and somewhat over-emphasized has been its influence against naturalism in painting. "If the camera can see the real world better than I can," we suppose Picasso to have thought, "then why should I compete?" But the important movements in painting since impressionism have not been simply anti-photographic; they have been instead concerted efforts to represent more of the world than had been seen through traditional conventions. With Cézanne, sight itself became a new order of conception as well as perception, of mind as well as eye. In the movement toward a reconstruction of the visual field according to its hard-rock components, the camera was an important ally; it helped defeat the old conventions, not by capturing them, but by showing, scientifically and mechanically, their inadequacies. First of all, through its ability to record the world of appearances more accurately than the hand, the camera gave painters a useful instrument for studying the details of form. Then too, and more important, the camera showed that the process of vision itself is more complex, more analytical, than the academic conventions had allowed. It showed that the eye does not merely record, but that it creates. Vision begins in the head.

For literature, the lessons were not as plain and dramatic. The wealth of detail in naturalistic and impressionistic prose is mistakenly called photographic, on the assumption that the details reconstruct themselves in the reader's mind to form a picture as accurate as a photograph. But this is a misuse of the adjective "photographic." If photography is a process of creation as well as selection, then the finished print of a serious artist is an accurate record *only* of the maker's vision, not of an honorific reality which awaits, fully composed, before the eye. The print, as Alfred Stieglitz more than anyone else convinced his fellow artists, is as much a contrived artifact, a created thing, as a cubist painting or a poet's metaphor (Picasso, in fact, recognized that he and Stieglitz were working in the same spirit). Writers like Dos Passos in his "camera eye" reveries and his montage technique, and Hart Crane in his visionary metaphors, are closer to a literary use of photography than naturalists like Farrell. But few writers so far have incorporated photography into their work with as much careful thought as Wright Morris.

Curiously enough, Morris's uses of photography are illuminated by his literary debt to Henry James. James is for Morris the only American writer who remained undamaged by the "raw material myth." If Norman Rockwell is the technician of latter-day pastoralism, creating the sweet illusion that our culture still has its young innocence, then Henry James, the "restless analyst" of *The American Scene,* is the technician with an alternative. James was the sole American writer able to face the present moment without "the consolations of the past, without recourse to the endless vistas of optimism." Morris simplifies James a good deal to make him useful, and what he admires, it seems to me, is less a philosophical outlook (James indeed had his own consolations) and more the craft which James founds on the "faculty of attention." This faculty for James is the ability to confront our immediate experience, in art or life, with all our capacities intact; attention is the way we make our experiences vibrant with meaning. This is the faculty which made James such a keen *observer* and which is displayed nowhere with more acumen and poise than in *The American Scene.* From that book of unparalleled insight into American manners and scenes, Morris has taken this passage as a classic formulation of the Jamesian point of view he wishes to adopt:

> To be at all critically, or as we have been fond of calling it, analytically minded—over and beyond an inherent love of the many-colored picture of things—is to be subject to the superstition that objects and places, coherently grouped, disposed for human use and addressed to it, must have a sense of their own, a mystic meaning proper to themselves to give out: to give out, that is, to the participant at once so interested and so detached as to be moved to a report of the matter. (New York, 1907, 263)

Here James describes a point of view toward "objects and places" which anyone familiar with the art of photography will recognize. Here is a point of view—an esthetic—we find in the memorable prints of Stieglitz, Paul Strand, Edward Weston, Walker Evans, and Morris as well. The "straight photography" of these artists is based precisely on James' "superstition" that, first of all, the objects which occur in the field of vision contain their own life, their own "sense," which has only to be *seen* to be known; second, that the camera is an excellent instrument for *seeing* in this sense of knowing (which makes the act of sight an act of participation); and third, that through the camera, what is seen can be kept at enough distance from the personality of the seer, to permit a "report of the matter." In photography, the enforced objectivity makes possible the passionate subjectivity of vision we feel in the prints of masters. The artist in photography gives us not copies of a real world, but the world *as it is seen* by the artist; the seeing makes the world real. In the hands of a "restless analyst," the camera transforms the idle sensations of sight into the "mystic meaning" of vision. The effect that one gets from the pictures of, say, Walker Evans (who collaborated with James Agee in *Let Us Now Praise Famous Men*) is a sudden arrestment of time, a jolting of the mind into a state of attention. He forces us to look and to see as we have never done before, and what he shows us in the faces and textures of his rural and city scenes is a "mystic meaning" almost too much to bear. Does any man have the right to look so closely? We ask this, not because privacy has been invaded (it has not; his portraits are posed, not "candid"), but because our own flabbiness of vision has been provoked and challenged. We are forced to experience a report of things with a sense of their own. Evans's pictures, and Morris's, are not invitations; they are imperatives.

In what was, I suspect, an effort to discover what lessons his photography had for his fiction, Wright Morris produced two unique books about fifteen years ago. *The Inhabitants* (1946) and *The Home Place* (1948) combine, each in its own way, words and pictures. These books are based on the photographic outlook toward the world which I have just described. In neither book are the pictures illustrations of the text, although they appear to be so in *The Home Place*. This is a short novel about the return of a Nebraskan to his childhood home after a thirty year absence. *The World in the Attic* (1949) continues this story, whose point is that "home is where you hang your childhood." (67) In *The Home Place*, the pictures are a dimension of the action separate from, but equivalent to the events of the narrative. If the theme of the book is the return of a "rural expatriate" and his efforts to revive the past, then the pictures pursue this theme on the level of graphic reminiscence. The pictures of farm equipment, corners of rooms, sewing baskets, old chairs and stoves and shoes and newspaper clippings, beds and shaving mugs and lace curtains are all rich with associations, and together they reconstruct a "home place" on the visual level just as the hero tries to reconstruct it for himself on an emotional level. The narrative is in the first person, and the hero says, "I'm trying to get my bearings. I'm trying to feel at home out here." Each picture is a phase of past experience rediscovered; the entire sequence comprises a visual metaphor of the hero's emotional life.

One weakness of this book is that the pictures, which are all direct and straightforward, with an occasional close-up, compete with the narrative for our attention. Seeing them on alternate pages of the text, we cannot always experience them and the narrative simultaneously. This is avoided in *The Inhabitants*, a more successful and, for his fiction, more useful synthesis. This book has an entirely different principle. The work is structured on three separate levels, a brief monologue of an "I" who meditates on the theme of what an "Inhabitant" is, a sequence of pictures of vacant houses, and a short prose "voice" with each picture. The theme of the book is that objects and people have their own "look" about them, which comes from something that "inhabits" them. This something is, in James' words, their "mystic meaning," the "sense" they give out to the interested yet detached participant. The pictures of vacant houses are the "look;" the prose voice, sometimes third person, sometimes first person, sometimes dialogue, is a verbal translation of what "inhabits" the house. It belongs to the picture. "An Inhabitant is what you can't take away from a house. You can take away everything else—in fact, the more you take away the better you can see what this thing is." (2) The first person monologue, which announces the theme and pursues it through the book, referring to people and places he has known across America (mainly rural America), is the argument of the book. A section of the monologue (sometimes a sentence, sometimes more) and the prose voice (entirely separate from the monologue) face each picture. All three levels, then, are available at once to the reader.

This triangular structure creates a rich complexity in the book and looks forward to the narrative devices Morris has developed in his fiction of the last ten years. The monologue provides a narrative frame in the present tense (it is not an action, but an address to the reader, conveying a dramatic immediacy); the voices are taken as moments in the past stirred up by the pictures, which are in a present simultaneous with the monologue. Each picture and voice, meanwhile, is a separate moment of consciousness, in which a mind (the voice) confronts its own experience in the form of a visual equivalent. The voices, which, taken in their entirety, are disconnected, do not comment upon the pictures, nor explain them, nor are they in any obvious way related to the pictures. Rather, the voices emerge from the pictures metaphorically as vernacular translations. At the same time, the entire sequence of picture and voice comprises the consciousness of the "I" of the book; it is that upon which he meditates. In other words, the "I" (whom the reader both watches and joins) perceives his own mind by perceiving the picture and the voice, and the entire sequence, all at once. In *The Field of Vision*, the "I" has disappeared, or more accurately, it has been transformed into the implicit continuity of the work; while the voices, each confronting its own past and present experience, carry the entire narrative. Each voice is a segment of the entire action, which the reader reconstructs in his own mind's eye.

II

In *The Field of Vision*, Wright Morris assembles his characters at a bullfight in Mexico. There is a family group, consisting of eighty-seven year old Tom Scanlon, his middle-aged daughter Lois and her husband Walter McKee, and their young grandchild, Gordon McKee. Also at the bullfight is the McKees' old friend, Gordon Boyd, an ex-playwright who has been living precariously for several years. He is accompanied by two exotics, a Dr. Leopold Lehmann, Boyd's analyst, and the ambiguous Paula Kahler, another patient of Dr. Lehmann. The entire novel takes place during the two and a half hours of the bullfight. The characters are spectators, relatively stationary; the real action of the novel takes place in the consciousness of each character. Varieties of sight, including blindness, provide the major symbols of this highly symbolic work. Morris shows that each character, looking at the events of the bullfight, sees only himself. However, because they are unable to focus beyond the narrow rim of their own pasts, they do not really see themselves. Unable to see each other and to see themselves in the eyes of each other, they are figuratively blind. Their limited vision expresses their limited self-knowledge.

Morris exploits the symbolic suggestions of sight by means of a complex narrative form. The book is divided into twenty-four sections, each given over to an account of a single character's mind as it confronts the action occurring in the present (the bullfight). Morris lets us see the immediate action through the minds of his five sentient characters (Paula Kahler and Gordon McKee are presented only through the eyes of the others); from their references and cross-references to the events in the bull ring, the reader, functioning like an eye assembling particles of light into a coherent picture, can reconstruct a whole event which obeys the unity of time. The bulls come in, the ceremony begins, a man on horseback moves toward the center of the ring, then backs off, a boy from the stands suddenly springs into the ring and is gored by a bull, Mrs. McKee faints and Mr. McKee takes her to their car outside, Boyd squirts pop at a bull, and so on. The reader does not perceive these actions in a sequential form; rather, the action occurs as events of consciousness in the minds of the characters. The reader, in other words, perceives the character as he receives the event through the web of associations that comprise his mental life. These associations return to various moments in the past, both the immediate past of the day before, sightseeing in Mexico, or the distant past of childhood. The time dimension of the novel is even further complicated by the presence of four generations, from Tom Scanlon to his great-grandson, Gordon Boyd. Also, Mr. and Mrs. McKee and Gordon Boyd share several experiences in childhood and young adulthood, and these experiences form yet another level of narrative.

Morris's use of several intersecting *personae* differs from the interior monologue technique in that each mind is presented in the third person. This consistent third person point of view keeps the reader at enough distance, we might say photographic distance, from the character so that he can see the character in several contexts at once, the contexts of the immediate action, of memory, and of the entire community of consciousness. The reader, then, is simultaneously aware of past and present, individual and community. He has the materials for an act of consciousness of his own, which is the perception of the "mystic meaning" in the groups of minds "disposed for human use" before him.

Some readers may find this method of structuring a novel especially trying since no single character serves as a central focal point. But Morris has tried to convert this difficulty into an advantage. The journey into the past becomes not only a psychic one, but a communal one as well. Through several novels in the fifties, Morris has been breaking away from the familiar disconnected hero who has made both the picaresque and stream of consciousness techniques so popular in recent fiction. In this novel, Gordon Boyd does have the lineaments of such a hero, and he does in fact become the character we care most about; however, his life in the novel is inseparable from the community of consciousness which creates a web of connection between him and the world. It is quite obvious that Morris intends to bring the dangling American hero back into a society, not to give him a comfortable social role to play but, instead, to confront him with his image in the minds of others, and by so doing, to teach him something about the nature of the mind itself.

III

As an epigraph to *The Field of Vision*,[1] Wright Morris quotes Satan's famous lines,

    A mind is its own place, and in itself
    Can make a Heav'n of Hell, a Hell of Heav'n.

Although this is a vain boast on the part of the fallen Lucifer, there is a great deal of "romantic agony" in these lines. The rebellious hero who cuts himself off from the source of his being, full of pride in his self-sufficiency and blindly confident of his powers to create a world in his own image—this is the familiar romantic hero of western culture. For Milton, of course, the fierce pride and unremitting egotism is an unerring measure of Satan's damnation. But in spite of the inevitable self-destruction of this hero-figure, his appeal persists. We find him throughout American literature, on the high seas and the open roads, as well as in the tailored estates of Long Island. Throughout Morris's work we find heroes of this sort whose huge capacities seem to bestow life upon their captivated followers; the others in their worlds are either witnesses or victims. In *The Field of Vision*, Gordon Boyd is such a hero; or at least he was. His heroics as a youth have left him stifled and empty as a man. As a boy, he had his earliest glory by ripping Ty Cobb's pocket from his pants after a game. Twenty-five years later, the pocket is still with him, now a rag he cannot lose, "the portable raft on which he floated anchored to his childhood." (61) As a young man, he stole a kiss from Lois Scanlon, while Walter McKee, her fiance who had not yet kissed her, stood by, smiling helplessly. Then Boyd dashed off with Walter to an old sandpit, boasting that he could do the impossible and walk on water. "Right up till he failed, till he dropped out of sight, McKee had almost believed it himself." (9) Neither Boyd nor McKee nor Lois has ever quite recovered, each in his own way, from Boyd's heroics. Even after years of not seeing Boyd, Mrs. McKee at the bullfight "didn't trust her own senses, and the ground kept shifting beneath her feet" (31) in his presence. But Boyd, alone of the three, struggles to

release the hold of the past. In this novel, he succeeds as far as divesting himself of his personal myths, and touches "bottom." In *Ceremony in Lone Tree*, a sequel to *The Field of Vision*, he and the McKees, after a series of subtle re-enactments of the past, reach a certain harmony and peace.

What Boyd learns during the course of the bullfight is the necessity of "transformation." The world is not what it *seems*; sight is only the beginning of vision.

> What had *he* seen? How long would it take him to puzzle it out? He was now a jigsaw loose in its box, the bullfight one of the scarlet pieces, but he would not know its meaning until the pattern appeared. And that he would not *find*. No, not anywhere, since it did not exist. The pattern—what pattern it had— he would have to create. Make it out of something that looked for all the world like something else. . . . Its called for transformation. Out of so many given things, one thing that hadn't been given. His own life. An endless sequence of changes, a tireless shifting of the pieces, selecting some, discarding others, until the pattern—the imagined thing— began to emerge. Death would fix the outlines. Frame the picture as no man would ever see it himself. (138)

Boyd's search for "his own life" begins when he realizes that having failed to do the impossible, to "walk on water," no other heroics remained. He says of himself, "Profession: hero. Situation: unemployed." Boyd found himself something like Huck Finn, who is left at the end with the spurious Tom Sawyer clichés of heroism on one hand, and "the territory ahead" on the other. Boyd had chosen as new territory the field of failure. When he came to Dr. Lehmann, he was a "dedicated no-man, one who had turned to failure as a field that offered real opportunity for success." (61) Lehmann recalls a prologue to one of Boyd's unproduced plays, in which

> Boyd advised his public that he *hoped* to fail, since there was no longer anything of interest to be gained in success. He went on to speak of culture as a series of acceptable clichés. A photographer's salon where ready-made frames, hung on walls of rustically historical gardens, lacked only the faces of succeed- ing generations in the ready-made holes. This hand- me-down world defined the realm of the possible. The impossible—become a cliché itself—had been ruled out. This left the artist—Boyd himself, that is—with only one suitable subject and life itself with only one ironic result. This was Failure. (62–63)

Through failure Boyd had hoped to reach his true self. He lived in poverty, unkempt and disheveled. But through Lehmann he discovered, sometime before the events of the book, that this too was a cliché, the reverse side of the Norman Rockwell coin. "The cliché of failure, like that of success, hung on the walls of the room he decayed in, and through the hole in the ready- made frame he popped his own head." (63) Because of his "armor of clichés," Boyd had actually failed to fail; he had failed, that is, "to touch the floating bottom of himself." He had come to Mexico with Lehmann to observe, and maybe write about, one who had indeed failed, had touched bottom, and who came up radically transformed and radically crippled. I am referring to Lehmann's other patient, Paula Kahler, the man who had willed himself into a woman.

Through Paula Kahler, the Tiresias-sphinx who poses the riddle of life but can tell no answer, and through Tom Scanlon, Wright Morris portrays the wider dimensions of Boyd's prob- lem. Both had succeeded in transforming themselves, yet at the sacrifice of their ability to live fully. The ultimate self-awareness, which is self-creation, leaves its scars. In each, the mind has become so much "its own place," that it has closed the world out. Both are blind to the events of the world and of the bullfight; their sight turns only inward. Their blindness, then, is metaphoric. In Tom Scanlon, the paradox of transformation, being both self-creation and self-destruction, is particularized as American; in Paula Kahler, it is universalized. Scanlon, an old Nebraskan plainsman, lives only in a fantasy world of the frontier past. "When the century turned and faced east, he stood his ground. He faced the west." (38) Paula Kahler has gone even further; she has eliminated the past and all time. She lives completely in a sightless present. Also, both characters "died" sometime in the past—Scanlon in a recurring fantasy in which he sees himself lying dead on the western desert and Kahler in a serious illness ("She had been sick to the death—she had died, that is—and passed over to the other side. From there all things looked the same." 100–101) In their recreated worlds, sight in the usual sense is unnecessary. Paula Kahler sits wide-eyed and sees nothing; her head lolls to the side. Scanlon, in fact, "didn't know he was so blind until they came for him. In Lone Tree, where nothing had changed, he saw things in their places without the need to look at them. They were in their places without the need to look at them." (45)

In Scanlon's fantasies, Wright Morris recreates his own version of the American frontier experience. The divestment of civilization on the journey across the desert is a bizarre event; it is a symbolic journey through the inferno of self-discovery. According to the familiar legend, the inessentials are stripped away. But the legend is transformed in the imagination of Tom Scanlon who, although he re-enacts in his dreams the crossing of the desert, had never been west of Lone Tree, Nebraska. And by making the crossing an imagined act, Morris is able to suggest its symbolic scope. Here is Scanlon's imagination working:

> The wagons were like ants in the neck of a bottle, and all along the trail, wherever you looked, they were busy putting something down, or picking something up. Everybody seemed to have a lot more than they needed, and right beside the trail, where you could reach out and touch them, were sacks of beans and sugar, and slabs of bacon stacked like cords of wood. Back on the plains people would trouble to hide it, thinking they would come back for it later, but there in the canyon they just dumped it beside the trail. Anything that was heavy, that would lighten the wagon, they dumped out first. Some had brought along every fool thing they owned, rocking chairs, tables, and barrels of dishes, and others had big framed pictures they would like for setting up house. Some had brought along books, trunks of fine linen, all the tools they might need for building a home, and you could see what a man valued most in his life from where he put it down. Towards the last you began to see people, friends who had sworn they would never part, or relations who had got too old, or too weak, left to shift for themselves. They weighed too much. So they were just dumped like everything else. (85)

To see how accurately Morris has gotten to the heart of the frontier journey, compare this passage, with its grotesque humor, to the stagecoach scene early in Mark Twain's *Roughing It.* In both cases, the dumping of books and the paraphernalia of civilization is a necessary ritual. But Morris shows, more than Mark Twain, the ambiguous implications of the ritual. Here, the discarding of civilization means the

discarding of people, of community. Tom Scanlon's imagined pioneers are unaware of what they are up to. "No matter where it was people had been, or where it was they thought they were going, they wanted it to be the same as wherever they were from." (85–86) What was dumped by one party was picked up by another, so that people would see, "ahead on the trail, what they had put down themselves a day's ride back." But no one stopped to pick up people.

In Scanlon's fantasy, the crossing of the desert is a journey through the hell in which a man must lose himself in order to find himself. Out there, while he is desperately searching for water in the hot sands, Scanlon stumbles on a dead body—his own. It does not surprise him. "There were two men within him, and he knew for sure that one of them had died." (167) And it was the better man of the two who had died, he believes, leaving the other man to spend out his days dreaming of the first death. Scanlon, unlike his fellow pioneers, had touched bottom on his imaginary frontier and never recovered. But although the old plainsman had sacrificed the present to his fantasy of the past, his lesson is clear: the shortest way to heaven is straight through hell, and "the thing about Hell was that you had to go in, if what you wanted was out." (168) Paula Kahler, whose disconnection from actuality is more extreme than Scanlon's, makes this lesson universal and at the same time shows with what expense the knowledge is bought. Unable to endure the world, Paul Kahler merely changed his nature, making himself Paula and closing his mind into itself. The peace he—or she—finds is the peace of catatonic insanity. In her death-like sleep, she cries out "Help!" Her transformation has taken place outside the community of men; by recreating her self so totally, she has destroyed herself. Her loss is a warning against so thorough a change. As Lehmann, who hears her cry and devotes himself to her, remarks, "There was no mind if the lines to the past were destroyed. If the mind, that is, was nothing but itself." (182)

During the course of the bullfight, which intrudes upon the characters as reenactments of past events or as metaphors of present conditions, the McKees, solid and average citizens of Nebraska, do nothing more than suffer in their own narrow visions. Happily married in appearances, they are ironically the least connected of the entire group. They fail to see each other. The book ends as McKee's wife gazes at him through the car window with what he misunderstands as her "serene blue eyes." He senses, however, that they are "ice-blue." But his sight ends with that perception. McKee, with his unseeing eyes, is a foil for Boyd; as McKee fails to see himself in his wife's eyes, Boyd, looking into the eyes of McKee's grandson, suddenly "detected a change in himself." This change is the critical psychological event of the novel. The boy's gaze takes Boyd back to a moment in his recent past, when, watching the "passionate lives" of scampering children in a New York playground, he dozed off on a bench.

> When he awoke the bullring was empty, the swings and teeter-totters idle, but a small child leaned against the heavy wire fence, her eyes to one of the holes. So absorbed with what she saw, or what she thought she saw, she gazed into Boyd's face as if he were blind. As if she could see into his eyes, but he could not see out of them. He felt himself—some self—in the midst of a wakeful dream. Had he dozed off with his own eyes wide open, seeing nothing? Had this child stood there for some time, gazing in? This child—for that was all she was, a soiled faced, staring little monkey—seemed to have seen in him what Boyd could not see himself (176)

The child, Boyd feels, "had run up the blind on his true *self*," and he is unable to move or to close his eyes. He thinks he is mad or, perhaps, sane for the first time in his life. "Able to see, at that moment, from the other side. Behind appearances, such as the one he made himself." This is Boyd's moment of truth: by smiting his sight the innocent child, in short, has restored his vision. In this moment, the unity of Morris's theme and technique is perfectly clear. The act of seeing, with both passionate interest and detachment, is the appropriate symbol for the act of knowing.

Vision, Boyd has learned, is an austere form of consciousness. To see the real self through the veil of clichés requires the flexing of muscles flabby with habit. But the mind, Morris shows, is a perilous place. In striving to know itself, it runs the risk of knowing nothing else. Blindness, as for Paula Kahler, is the consequence of a too subjective sight. There is no way of avoiding the risk. Tiresias must lose his eyes to gain his sight. Americans, as a rule, have supposed that the gain can be made without the loss. Like his master, Henry James, Morris is an exception to the rule. For him, the gain of truth is

the loss of illusion—and painful. That gain, for Boyd as for Strether, is the perception of oneself as a figure in a landscape with a "mystic meaning" all its own. Integrity of mind depends upon this vision of one's place in the composition.

Morris deserves our attention because he has thought deeply about man's dilemma in a New World which has promised the end of all dilemmas. In spite of its minor failings, such as an excessive symbolic contrivance, *The Field of Vision*—and this seems to me to be the highest praise—occasions serious thought by Americans about themselves as human beings. Morris's craft of vision focuses upon the community of men in America searching for a way to convert the loss of pastoral innocence into a gain of personal integrity. Vision itself is both the instrument and the substance of this transformation.

Notes

1. All page references to *The Field of Vision* are to the Signet edition, New York, 1957.

Toni Morrison

1931–

Novelist Toni Morrison was born Chloe Anthony Wofford, on February 18, 1931, and grew up in Lorain, Ohio, the second of four children of George Wofford, a shipyard welder, and his wife Ramah Willis Wofford. After attending Lorain High School she went to Howard University, where she majored in English and minored in classics. She joined the Howard University Players, and in the summer toured the South with a student-faculty repertory troupe.

After earning an M.A. at Cornell in 1955 Morrison taught for two years at Texas Southern University, and then in 1957 took a teaching position at Howard, where she married Harold Morrison, a Jamaican architect. In 1964 she divorced Morrison and returned with her two sons to Lorain; a year and a half later she became an editor for a textbook subsidiary of Random House in Syracuse. By 1970 she had moved to an editorial position at Random House in New York, where she eventually became a senior editor. In the early 1970s she began to write a series of articles, most of which appeared in the *New York Times Book Review*. She has taught Afro-American literature and creative writing at the State University of New York, Purchase, Yale University, and Bard College.

Toni Morrison began to write when she returned to Howard in 1957, and since then she has published several novels in which the problems of Black women in the north are a major theme. Her books have a fabulistic quality, and she has at times been directly inspired by Afro-American folktales. Her novels are *The Bluest Eye* (1970); *Sula* (1974); *The Song of Solomon* (1977); and *Tar Baby* (1981).

Personal

Morrison, like many of the powerful women in her fiction, has capacities that strike her friends as otherworldly. "I have a sense of Toni as a mythic character—as somehow larger than life," says novelist Mary Gordon. "I once dreamed that she bought a huge old Victorian mansion. It would one day be beautiful, but now it was a wreck, with cobwebs, broken windows, mice, rats and vermin everywhere. I asked her how she was going to deal with all that mess. She simply said, 'No problem,' and waved her arms in the air. Immediately the rats and roaches disappeared and the house was beautiful."

To Toni Morrison, however, there is no magic in writing, editing, teaching and raising two boys alone. Interviewed at home—a lovely, four-story former boathouse on the Hudson River north of Manhattan—she finishes fixing breakfast for 19-

year-old Harold, then looks out of her bright kitchen window over the frozen expanse of river and muses: "Sure it's hard, but you do what you have to do. You *make* time; I don't go to theater or operas or dinners. But I think women dwell quite a bit on the duress under which they work, on how hard it is just to do it at all. We are traditionally rather proud of ourselves for having slipped creative work in there between the domestic chores and obligations. I'm not sure we deserve such big A-pluses for all that." She comes from a long line of people who did what they had to do to survive. It is their stories she tells in her novels—tales of the suffering and richness, the eloquence and tragedies of the black American experience. She saw a great deal of that pain and that strength in her own family's past.

Born in Lorain, Ohio, in 1931, she was christened Chloe

Anthony Wofford. Her mother's family had migrated north from Greenville, Ala., around 1910. "They had lost their land, like a lot of black people at the turn of the century, and they were sharecroppers, which meant they were never able to get out of debt. My grandfather had left Greenville for Birmingham to earn money playing the violin. He sent money back, but my grandmother began to get nervous, all alone in Greenville, because her daughters were reaching puberty and that was a dangerous business in the South, in the country, because white boys began to circle. So my grandmother decided to leave. She sent her husband an oral message: 'We're heading north on the midnight train. If you ever want to see us again, you'll be on that train.'

"She didn't know if he got the message, but with $18 to her name she packed up her six or seven children and got them all to the train in Birmingham. It was the first city my mother had ever seen—she still remembers, 'We had *white* bread!' My grandfather was nowhere in sight. As the train left the station the children began to cry—then about an hour later, he showed up. He'd been there all along, hiding, for fear somebody would recognize him and stop them for owing money."

They traveled to Kentucky, where her grandfather worked in a coal mine. "My grandmother did washing, and my mother and her sister went to a little one-room school. One day the teacher, who was about 16 and white, was doing long division and having trouble explaining it. Since my mother and her sister already knew long division, they explained it to the teacher and the class. They came home all excited and proud of themselves, crowing, 'Mama, guess what we did? We taught the teacher long division!' My grandmother just said to her husband, 'Come on, Johnny, we have to move'."

They continued north, settling in the steel-mill town of Lorain on Lake Erie. The story of Morrison's father is "different but the same." "My father was a racist," she declares with a smile that does nothing to detract from the seriousness of what she is saying. "As a child in Georgia, he received shocking impressions of adult white people, and for the rest of his life felt he was justified in despising all whites, and that they were not justified in despising him." Did his racial attitudes cause his children to distrust whites? "Not when we were little," says Morrison. "I knew he was wrong. I went to school with white children—they were my friends. There was no awe, no fear. Only later, when things got . . . sexual . . . did I see how clear the lines really were. But when I was in first grade nobody thought I was inferior. I was the only black in the class and the only child who could read!"

Her father did provide her with a strong sense of her own value on her own terms. At 13, she cleaned house for a white family after school. One day she complained to her father because the work was hard and the woman was mean. He said: "Girl, you don't live there. You live *here*. So you go do your work, get your money and come on home."

All her early life she absorbed the black lore, music, language, myths and rituals that give her prose its special flavor and tone. "We were intimate with the supernatural," she recalls. Her parents told thrillingly terrifying ghost stories. Her mother sang constantly. Her grandmother kept a dream book and played the numbers off it, decoding dream symbols to determine what number to bet on. Morrison's world, like the world of her novels, was filled with signs, visitations, ways of knowing that reached beyond the five senses.

As a studious adolescent, she read the great Russian novels, *Madame Bovary*, Jane Austen. "Those books were not written for a little black girl in Lorain, Ohio, but they were so

magnificently done that I got them anyway—they spoke directly to me out of their own specificity. I wasn't thinking of writing then—I wanted to be a dancer like Maria Tallchief—but when I wrote my first novel years later, I wanted to capture that same specificity about the nature and feeling of the culture I grew up in."—JEAN STROUSE, "Toni Morrison's Black Magic," *Nwk*, March 30, 1981, pp. 53–54

Works

Shoemakers' children go barefoot, we are told. And physicians must be reminded to heal themselves. What happens to editors who write novels? The question is not academic, as Toni Morrison is an editor with a New York publishing firm, and ⟨*The Bluest Eye*⟩ is her first novel. She reveals herself, when she shucks the fuzziness born of flights of poetic imagery, as a writer of considerable power and tenderness, someone who can cast back to the living, bleeding heart of childhood and capture it on paper. But Miss Morrison has gotten lost in her construction.

The title pinpoints the focus of her book. Pecola Breedlove, in her first year of womanhood, is black, ugly and poor, living in a store front, sharing a bedroom with her brother, her crippled mother and her drunken father. Pregnant by her father, she goes to Soaphead Church, a man who believes himself possessed of holy powers. What she wants are blue eyes.

In this scene, in which a young black on the verge of madness seeks beauty and happiness in a wish for white girl's eyes, the author makes her most telling statement on the tragic effect of race prejudice on children. But the scene occurs late in the novel—far too late to achieve the impact it might have had in a different construction. For most of the way, Pecola yields center stage to Frieda and Claudia—who, aside from knowing her, and perhaps offering contrast, by themselves being black and poor (though from a happier home), serve little purpose beyond distraction.

Claudia tells the story part way into each of the four seasonal divisions of the book. From her, the narratives branch out to assorted portraits and events throughout the black community of Lorain, Ohio, with Pecola, whose story this eventually is, too often playing a secondary role until the novel zeroes in on her for the ending. Her mental breakdown, when it comes, has only the impact of reportage.

Miss Morrison never bores as she wanders around town. There are vivid scenes: Pecola's first "ministratin'"; a "pretty milk-brown lady" driving Pecola from her home for the killing of a cat, by the woman's own son; the young Cholly Breedlove (later to be Pecola's father) caught during the sex act by white men and being forced to continue for their amusement. Given a scene that demands a writer's best, Miss Morrison responds with control and talent. Yet there are moments when the mind stops and questions. The novel begins: "Nuns go by as quiet as lust . . ." (How quiet is lust? Is it always?) Or: ". . . he will not unrazor his lips until spring." Does that mean he will not shave around his mouth all winter? And just what is "an ivory sleep"?

With the flaws and virtues tallied, I found myself still in favor of *The Bluest Eye*. There are many novelists willing to report the ugliness of the world as ugly. The writer who can reveal the beauty and the hope beneath the surface is a writer to seek out and to encourage.—HASKEL FRANKEL, *NYTBR*, Nov. 1, 1970, pp. 46–47

It is true that Morrison operates within many of the racial commonplaces. First in *The Bluest Eye* (1970), now in *Sula*, she has staked out an area of the Midwest made familiar to us by Sherwood Anderson, the small Ohio town governed by a rigid moral prudery that dampens spontaneity and twists natural appetites. She focuses on the black sections of those towns and, to the middle-class hypocrisy attacked by Anderson, she adds the racial prejudice of the whites. But this is the weakest strain in her novels, for it is virtually impossible to do anything fresh with a vein that has been mined to exhaustion. We begin to fidget when we see her stacking the deck against such easy marks as the black bourgeoisie and reaching for the heartstrings when describing the humiliation of some proud black soldiers on a Jim Crow railroad car.

Her originality and power emerge in characters like Sula, that we have seldom seen before and that do not fit the familiar black images. One-legged Eva Peace, Sula's grandmother, burns her son to death when she feels he is trying "to crawl back into my womb." Sula's mother, Hannah, entertains men without discrimination in the pantry of Eva's home. Sula's friend Nel realizes that she experienced a thrill of pleasure when she watched Sula's victim drown. Against the background of the respectability of black Medallion, Ohio, these acts and emotions appear as the thrust of some powerful new force, loosening the foundations of the old stereotypes and conventional manners.

Writers like Toni Morrison, like Ed Bullins and Alice Walker, are slowly, subtly making our old buildings unsafe. There is something ominous in the chilling detachment with which they view their characters. It is not that their viewpoint is amoral—we are asked for judgment. It's that the characters we judge lie so far outside the guidelines by which we have always made our judgments.

For example, Morrison at first seems to combine the aims of the Black Freedom Movement and women's liberation. Sula and Nel discover when they are 11 years old "that they were neither white nor male, and that all freedom and triumph was forbidden to them." When they grow up, Nel slips on the collar of convention. She marries, has two children, becomes tied to her "nest," a slave to racism and sexism. Sula goes to the big city, gets herself an education, and returns a "liberated" woman with a strange mixture of cynicism and innocence: "She lived out her days exploring her own thoughts and emotions, giving them full rein, feeling no obligation to please anybody unless their pleasure pleased her . . . hers was an experimental life."

But the perspective Morrison gives us upon these two black women is not pure black freedom or pure women's liberation. We may wish that Nel had absorbed some of Sula's independence of mind and willingness to take risks, and had not plunged so completely into the humdrum atmosphere of conventional family life, with all its sexist and racial overtones. Yet we cannot approve the freedom that licenses Sula casually to steal Nel's husband and condemn her childhood friend to a ruined life, while she just as casually abandons him. That is not freedom but selfishness, and it is immoral, however contemptuous we may be of the pitifully conventional virtues of married life, or however much we may feel that marriage oppresses women. Besides, the freedom that Sula achieves is as much a prison as it is liberation. Totally free, she becomes obsessed with herself, unable to love, uncontained by the normal rules and boundaries we have come to associate with human beings.

Morrison does not accept—nor does she expect us to accept—the unqualified tenets of either of the two current freedom movements. There is more to both society and the individual, and she subjects each of these to a merciless analysis. The result is that neither lends itself to a clear moral judgment. For all her selfishness and cruelty, Sula's presence elicits the best in people, diluting their usual meanness and small-spiritedness. Indeed, with Sula's death the "Bottom" dies, its black people rushing headlessly in a comi-tragedy of communal suicide.

The feeling I get from this, however, is not so much that of the familiar literary viewpoint of moral complexity as that of a calm sardonic irony over the impossibility of ever sorting out the good from the bad. This feeling gives *Sula* a portentousness that makes it perhaps an inadvertent prophet, whose prophecy is that all our old assumptions about morality are disintegrating before a peculiarly black assault against them. It is as if Morrison, and other young black writers with her, are saying, like Sula, "If we can do this to ourselves, you can imagine what we can do to you."—JERRY H. BRYANT, "Something Ominous Here," *Nation*, July 6, 1974, pp. 23–24

Toni Morrison's first two books—*The Bluest Eye* with the purity of its terrors and *Sula* with its dense poetry and the depth of its probing into a small circle of lives—were strong novels. Yet, firm as they both were in achievement and promise, they didn't fully forecast her new book, *Song of Solomon*. Here the depths of the younger work are still evident, but now they thrust outward, into wider fields, for longer intervals, encompassing many more lives. The result is a long prose tale that surveys nearly a century of American history as it impinges upon a single family. In short, this is a full novel—rich, slow enough to impress itself upon us like a love affair or a sickness—not the two-hour penny dreadful which is again in vogue nor one of the airless cat's cradles custom-woven for the delight and job-assistance of graduate students of all ages.

Song of Solomon isn't, however, cast in the basically realistic mode of most family novels. In fact, its negotiations with fantasy, fable, song and allegory are so organic, continuous and unpredictable as to make any summary of its plot sound absurd; but absurdity is neither Morrison's strategy nor purpose. The purpose seems to be communication of painfully discovered and powerfully held convictions about the possibility of transcendence within human life, on the time-scale of a single life. The strategies are multiple and depend upon the actions of a large cast of black Americans, most of them related by blood. But after the loving, comical and demanding polyphony of the early chapters (set in Michigan in the early 1930's), the theme begins to settle on one character and to develop around and out of him.

His name is Macon Dead, called "Milkman" because his mother nursed him well past infancy. He is the son of an upper middle-class Northern black mother and a father with obscure working-class Southern origins. These origins, which Milkman's father is intent on concealing, fuel him in a merciless drive toward money and safety—over and past the happiness of wife and daughters and son. So the son grows up into chaos and genuine danger—the homicidal intentions of a woman he spurned after years of love, and an accidental involvement with a secret ring of lifelong acquaintances who are sworn to avenge white violence, eye for eye.

Near midpoint in the book—when we may begin to wonder if the spectacle of Milkman's apparently thwarted life is sufficient to hold our attention much longer—there is an abrupt shift. Through his involvement with his father's sister, the bizarre and anarchic Pilate (whose dedication to life and feeling is directly opposed to her brother's methodical acquisition of things), and with Guitar, one of the black avengers, Milkman is flung out of his private maelstrom. He is forced to discover, explore, comprehend and accept a world more dangerous than the Blood Bank (the ghetto neighborhood of idle eccentrics, whores, bullies and lunatics, which he visited as a boy). But this world is also rewarding, as it opens into the larger, freer sphere of time and human contingency and reveals the possibility of knowing one's origins and of realizing the potential found in the lives, failures and victories of one's ancestors.

Although it begins as a hungry hunt for a cache of gold that his father and Pilate left in a cave in Virginia, Milkman's search is finally a search for family history. As he travels through Pennsylvania and Virginia, acquiring the jagged pieces of a story that he slowly assembles into a long pattern of courage and literal transcendence of tragedy, he is strengthened to face the mortal threat that rises from his own careless past to meet him at the end.

The end is unresolved. Does Milkman survive to use his new knowledge, or does he die at the hands of a hateful friend? The hint is that he lives—in which case Toni Morrison has her next novel ready and waiting: Milkman's real manhood, the means he invents for transmitting or squandering the legacy he has discovered.

But that very uncertainty is one more sign of the book's larger truthfulness (no big, good novel has ever really ended; and none can, until it authoritatively describes the extinction from the universe of all human life); and while there are problems (occasional abortive pursuits of a character who vanishes, occasional luxuriant pauses on detail and the understandable but weakening omission of active white characters), *Song of Solomon* easily lifts above them on the wide slow wings of human sympathy, well-informed wit and the rare plain power to speak wisdom to other human beings. A long story, then, and better than good. Toni Morrison has earned attention and praise. Few Americans know, and can say, more than she has in this wise and spacious novel.—REYNOLDS PRICE, "Black Family Chronicle," *NYTBR*, Sept. 11, 1977, pp. 1, 48

Storytelling can disclose the order of the world or, if necessary, invent an order the world lacks. In her previous fiction, Toni Morrison has revealed the structure of rural black communities, small worlds coherent and vital in themselves but precariously isolated within a hostile white culture. More often than not, these communities in isolation have included the supernatural as well as the realistic. In *The Bluest Eye* there is a misanthropic fortuneteller; in *Sula*, symbolic repetitions and predictive dreams; in *Song of Solomon*, fulfilled prophecies and outright magic. Like Isaac Bashevis Singer, who also writes about communities isolated and beset, Morrison seeks to preserve the experienced richness of communal life against an outer world that denies its value. Again like Singer, Morrison turns to a heritage of folklore, not only to disclose patterns of living but also to close wounds. The supernatural events of her fiction represent the strivings of a culture denied, a leap beyond walls of oppressive circumstance. And in that imaginative leap, Morrison seeks to release bonds and to redefine boundaries.

Although *Tar Baby* contains magical presences and ends with intimations of the supernatural, it differs from Morrison's previous work. Here, the small black communities that nourish her mythology are peripheral, displaced by locations that represent the dominant culture: a Caribbean island retreat and New York City. Instead of folk-speech, she gives us speeches; rather than experiencing a heritage, her characters discuss it; rather than expressing communal possibility, they quarrel over the value of racial identity. *Tar Baby* is, in effect, a novel of ideas set in the white world. ⟨. . .⟩

Morrison's concerns in *Tar Baby* are race, class, culture and the effects of late capitalism—heavy freight for any narrative. Indeed, their mass may account for the structural braces discernible in the novel: paired conversations and contrapuntal scenes, an allegory of names and places, and a particularly insistent use of color symbolism. After all, she is attempting to stabilize complex visions of society—that is, to examine competitive ideas in what is essentially a novel of ideas.

Undoubtedly, *Tar Baby* is successful as such, but, like most works in that genre, it remains teasingly deficient as a novel of character. Because the primary function of Morrison's characters is to voice representative opinions, they arrive on stage vocal and highly conscious, their histories symbolically indicated or merely sketched. Her brief sketches, however, are clearly the work of an artist who can, when she chooses, model the mind in depth and detail. In acquainting us with Jadine, for instance, Morrison tunnels the experience of a 12-year-old observing the patient surrender of a bitch in heat. Although Morrison uses this incident to explain Jadine's initial fear of Son Green, the rich psychology it suggests flashes by us too quickly and is subsequently abandoned. Morrison simply shifts her attention away from the character's evolution, onto the character's ideas.

This is, of course, a storyteller's prerogative, but novelist Toni Morrison is capable of focusing on both. More to the point, she has a rare gift for characterization; George Eliot comes to mind as a comparison. Like Eliot, she can compel her readers to learn about themselves by experiencing, through her characters, states of mind that they would ordinarily disavow. In her first novel, *The Bluest Eye*, emotion, personal history and social forces produce in Cholly Breedlove a momentary compulsion of character. In that moment, his love for his daughter becomes rape—an aberration dismissed by his community as mindlessly random, but transformed through Morrison's art into a coherent, explicable and desperately human act.

If, in *Tar Baby*, she presses her audience to redefine their thinking, she has elsewhere shown herself capable of forcing them, against the grain of experience, to redefine themselves.—BRINA KAPLAN, "A Fierce Conflict of Colors," *Nation*, May 2, 1981, pp. 529, 534

THOMAS LeCLAIR

From "'The Language Must Not Sweat': A Conversation with Toni Morrison"

New Republic, March 21, 1981, pp. 26–29

*L*eClair: How do you conceive of your function as a writer?

Morrison: I write what I have recently begun to call village literature, fiction that is really for the village, for the tribe. Peasant literature for *my* people, which is necessary and legitimate but which also allows me to get in touch with all sorts of people. I think long and carefully about what my novels ought to do. They should clarify the roles that have become obscured; they ought to identify those things in the past that are useful and those things that are not; and they ought to give nourishment. I agree with John Berger that peasants don't write novels because they don't need them. They have a portrait of themselves from gossip, tales, music, and some celebrations. That is enough. The middle class at the beginning of the industrial revolution needed a portrait of itself because the old portrait didn't work for this new class. Their roles were different; their lives in the city were new. The novel served this function then, and it still does. It tells about the city values, the urban values. Now my people, we "peasants," have come to the city, that is to say, we live with its values. There is a confrontation between old values of the tribes and new urban values. It's confusing. There has to be a mode to do what the music did for blacks, what we used to be able to do with each other in private and in that civilization that existed underneath the white civilization. I think this accounts for the address of my books. I am not explaining anything to anybody. My work bears witness and suggests who the outlaws were, who survived under what circumstances and why, what was legal in the community as opposed to what was legal outside it. All that is in the fabric of the story in order to do what the music used to do. The music kept us alive, but it's not enough anymore. My people are being devoured. Whenever I feel uneasy about my writing, I think: what would be the response of the people in the book if they read the book? That's my way of staying on track. Those are the people for whom I write.

As a reader I'm fascinated by literary books, but the books I wanted to write could not be only, even merely, literary or I would defeat my purposes, defeat my audience. That's why I don't like to have someone call my books "poetic," because it has the connotation of luxuriating richness. I wanted to restore the language that black people spoke to its original power. That calls for a language that is rich but not ornate.

LeClair: What do you mean by "address"?

Morrison: I stand with the reader, hold his hand, and tell him a very simple story about complicated people. I like to work with, to fret, the cliché, which is a cliché because the experience expressed in it is important: a young man seeks his fortune; a pair of friends, one good, one bad; the perfectly innocent victim. We know thousands of these in literature. I like to dust off these clichés, dust off the language, make them mean whatever they may have meant originally. My genuine criticism of most contemporary books is that they're not *about* anything. Most of the books that are about something—the books that mean something—treat old ideas, old situations.

LeClair: Does this mean working with folklore and myth?

Morrison: I think the myths are misunderstood now because we are not talking to each other the way I was spoken to when I was growing up in a very small town. You knew everything in that little microcosm. But we don't live where we were born. I had to leave my town to do my work here; it was a sacrifice. There is a certain sense of family I don't have. So the myths get forgotten. Or they may not have been looked at carefully. Let me give you an example: the flying myth in *Song of Solomon*. If it means Icarus to some readers, fine; I want to take credit for that. But my meaning is specific: it is about black people who could fly. That was always part of the folklore of my life; flying was one of our gifts. I don't care how silly it may seem. It is everywhere—people used to talk about it, it's in the spirituals and gospels. Perhaps it was wishful thinking—escape, death, and all that. But suppose it wasn't. What might it mean? I tried to find out in *Song of Solomon*.

In the book I've just completed, *Tar Baby*, I use that old story because, despite its funny, happy ending, it used to frighten me. The story has a tar baby in it which is used by a white man to catch a rabbit. "Tar baby" is also a name, like nigger, that white people call black children, black girls, as I recall. Tar seemed to me to be an odd thing to be in a Western story, and I found that there is a tar lady in African mythology. I started thinking about tar. At one time, a tar pit was a holy place, at least an important place, because tar was used to build things. It came naturally out of the earth; it held together things like Moses's little boat and the pyramids. For me, the tar baby came to mean the black woman who can hold things together.

The story was a point of departure to history and prophecy. That's what I mean by dusting off the myth, looking closely at it to see what it might conceal. . . . ⟨. . .⟩

LeClair: As an editor, you look for quality in others' work. What do you think is distinctive about your fiction? What makes it good?

Morrison: The language, only the language. The language must be careful and must appear effortless. It must not sweat. It must suggest and be provocative at the same time. It is the thing that black people love so much—the saying of words, holding them on the tongue, experimenting with them, playing with them. It's a love, a passion. Its function is like a preacher's: to make you stand up out of your seat, make you lose yourself and hear yourself. The worst of all possible things that could happen would be to lose that language. There are certain things I cannot say without recourse to my language. It's terrible to think that a child with five different present tenses comes to school to be faced with those books that are less than his own language. And then to be told things about his language, which is him, that are sometimes permanently damaging. He may never know the etymology of Africanisms in his language, not even know that "hip" is a real word or that "the dozens" meant something. This is a really cruel fallout of racism. I know the standard English. I want to use it to help restore the other language, the lingua franca.

The part of the writing process that I fret is getting the sound without some mechanics that would direct the reader's attention to the sound. One way is not to use adverbs to describe how someone says something. I try to work the dialogue down so the reader has to hear it. When Eva in *Sula* sets her son on fire, her daughter runs upstairs to tell her, and Eva says "Is?" you can hear every grandmother say "Is?" and you know: a) she knows what she's been told; b) she is not going to do anything about it; and c) she will not have any more conversation. That sound is important to me.

LeClair: Not all readers are going to catch that.

Morrison: If I say "Quiet is as kept," that is a piece of information which means exactly what it says, but to black people it means a big lie is about to be told. Or someone is going to tell some graveyard information, who's sleeping with whom. Black readers will chuckle. There is a level of appreciation that might be available only to people who understand the context of the language. The analogy that occurs to me is jazz: it is open on the one hand and both complicated and inaccessible on the other. I never asked Tolstoy to write for me, a little colored girl in Lorain, Ohio. I never asked Joyce not to mention Catholicism or the world of Dublin. Never. And I don't know why I should be asked to explain your life to you. We have splendid writers to do that, but I am not one of them. It is that business of being universal, a word hopelessly stripped of meaning for me. Faulkner wrote what I suppose could be called regional literature and had it published all over the world. It is good—and universal—because it is specifically about a particular world. That's what I wish to do. If I tried to write a universal novel, it would be water. Behind this question is the suggestion that to write for black people is somehow to diminish the writing. From my perspective, there are only black people. When I say "people," that's what I mean. Lots of books written by black people about black people have had this "universality" as a burden. They were writing for some readers other than me.

LeClair: One of the complaints about your fiction in both the black and white press is that you write about eccentrics, people who aren't representative.

Morrison: This kind of sociological judgment is pervasive

and pernicious. "Novel A is better than B or C because A is more like most black people really are." Unforgivable. I am enchanted, personally, with people who are extraordinary because in them I can find what is applicable to the ordinary. There are books by black writers about ordinary black life. I don't write them. Black readers often ask me, "Why are your books so melancholy, so sad? Why don't you ever write about something that works, about relationships that are healthy?" There is a comic mode, meaning the union of the sexes, that I don't write. I write what I suppose could be called the tragic mode in which there is some catharsis and revelation. There's a whole lot of space in between, but my inclination is in the tragic direction. Maybe it's a consequence of my being a classics minor.

Related, I think, is the question of nostalgia. The danger of writing about the past, as I have done, is romanticizing it. I don't think I do that, but I do feel that people were more interesting then than they are now. It seems to me there were more excesses in women and men, and people accepted them as they don't now. In the black community where I grew up, there were eccentricity and freedom, less conformity in individual habits—but close conformity in terms of the survival of the village, of the tribe. Before sociological microscopes were placed on us, people did anything and nobody was run out of town. I mean, the community in *Sula* let her stay. They wouldn't wash or bury her. They protected themselves from her, but she was part of the community. The detritus of white people, the rejects from the respectable white world, which appears in *Sula* was in our neighborhood. In my family, there were some really interesting people who were willing to be whatever they were. People permitted it, perhaps because in the outer world the eccentrics had to be a little servant person or low-level factory worker. They had an enormous span of emotions and activities, and they are the people I remember when I go to write. When I go to colleges, the students say "Who are these people?" Maybe it's because now everybody seems to be trying to be "right."

LeClair: Naming is an important theme in *Song of Solomon*. Would you discuss its significance?

Morrison: I never knew the real names of my father's friends. Still don't. They used other names. A part of that had to do with cultural orphanage, part of it with the rejection of the name given to them under circumstances not of their choosing. If you come from Africa, your name is gone. It is particularly problematic because it is not just *your* name but your family, your tribe. When you die, how can you connect with your ancestors if you have lost your name? That's a huge psychological scar. The best thing you can do is take another name which is yours because it reflects something about you or your own choice. Most of the names in *Song of Solomon* are real, the names of musicians for example. I used the biblical names to show the impact of the Bible on the lives of black people, their awe of and respect for it coupled with their ability to distort it for their own purposes. I also used some pre-Christian names to give the sense of a mixture of cosmologies. Milkman Dead has to learn the meaning of his own name and the names of things. In African languages there is no word for yam, but there is a word for every variety of yam. Each thing is separate and different; once you have named it, you have power. Milkman has to experience the elements. He goes into the earth and later walks its surface. He twice enters water. And he flies in the air. When he walks the earth, he feels a part of it, and that is his coming of age, the beginning of his ability to connect with the past and perceive the world as alive.

LeClair: You mentioned the importance of sound before.

Your work also seems to me to be strongly visual and concerned with vision, with seeing.

Morrison: There are times in my writing when I cannot move ahead even though I know exactly what will happen in the plot and what the dialogue is because I don't have the scene, the metaphor to begin with. Once I can see the scene, it all happens. In *Sula*, Eva is waiting for her long lost husband to come back. She's not sure how she's going to feel, but when he leaves he toots the horn on his pear-green Model-T Ford. It goes "ooogah, ooogah," and Eva knows she hates him. My editor said the car didn't exist at the time, and I had a lot of trouble rewriting the scene because I had to have the color and the sound. Finally, I had a woman in a green dress laughing in a big-city laugh, an alien sound in that small-town street, that stood for the "ooogah" I couldn't use. In larger terms, I thought of *Sula* as a cracked mirror, fragments and pieces we have to see independently and put together. In *Bluest Eye* I used the primer story, with its picture of a happy family, as a frame acknowledging the outer civilization. The primer with white children was the way life was presented to the black people. As the novel proceeded I wanted that primer version broken up and confused, which explains the typographical running together of the words.

LeClair: Did your using the primer come out of the work you were doing on textbooks?

Morrison: No. I was thinking that nobody treated these people seriously in literature and that "these people" who were not treated seriously were me. The interest in vision, in seeing, is a fact of black life. As slaves and ex-slaves, black people were manageable and findable, as no other slave society would be, because they were black. So there is an enormous impact from the simple division of color—more than sex, age, or anything else. The complaint is not being seen for what one is. That is the reason why my hatred of white people is justified and their hatred for me is not. There is a fascinating book called *Drylongso* which collects the talk of black people. They say almost to a man that you never tell a white person the truth. He doesn't want to hear it. Their conviction is they are neither seen nor listened to. They also perceive themselves as morally superior people because they do *see*. This helps explain why the theme of the mask is so important in black literature and why I worked so heavily with it in *Tar Baby*.

JOHN IRVING
"Morrison's Black Fable"

New York Times Book Review, March 29, 1981, pp. 1, 30–31

A novelist's vice usually resembles his virtue, for what he does best he also tends to do to excess: if he's good at being lyrical, he's too lyrical; if a cruel fate or accident seems to attend each character's childhood, that doom announces itself like a gun going off too long before the bullet's arrival. Our best and most ambitious writers indulge their vices as freely as their virtues; they are unafraid of them and think it small-minded to exercise restraint.

Thomas Hardy, for instance, much maligned for the preachy element in his prose—his instructions to mankind that intrude upon his narrative like a voice over a loudspeaker in the midst of some public crisis—chooses not to describe Tess d'Urberville's deflowering as if it affected only one victim; instead he addresses a larger injustice, which may be what many readers dislike in Hardy—especially today—but this is also what makes Hardy Hardy.

The more ambitious a novelist is, the more willing he is to elevate his characters to the level of myth—to give their births,

their relationships, their deaths, even their names, the resonance of legend. Dickens conveys such an ambition in his titles
(*Bleak House, Great Expectations, Hard Times*) and of course
in his characters' names (Lady Dedlock, Mr. Jaggers, Gradgrind). The 19th-century novel is rich with such risk, such
mischief.

Toni Morrison seems to be returning such risk and
mischief to the contemporary American novel, and never more
extravagantly than in *Tar Baby,* her fourth and most ambitious
book. In *Song of Solomon* (1977) she gave us a hospital called
Mercy Hospital, popularly called "No Mercy." That novel
began with a life insurance agent leaping off the hospital roof in
an attempt to fly to the other side of Lake Superior: "I will take
off from Mercy and fly away on my own wings. Please forgive
me. I loved you all." Toni Morrison loves them all, too—all
her characters, in all her books. She mythologizes her
characters almost as they're conceived, at least as soon as
they're born, but she has the good novelist's sense of detail that
makes these mythic people live. The boy born in the hospital
on the day the life insurance agent fails to fly is named
Milkman; he's the first black baby born at "No Mercy"; his aunt
is named Pilate, and she's born without a navel.

Miss Morrison has been up to this kind of dramatic
exaggeration for some time. In *Sula* (1974) she managed to
turn a poor black part of Ohio into a fairy tale (in a town called
Medallion, the black people live in a place called the Bottom
and celebrate National Suicide Day). The main character,
Sula Peace, is such an upsetting heroine that her return to the
town of Medallion is "accompanied by a plague of robins."

Now, in *Tar Baby,* Miss Morrison gives us a candy
manufacturer named Valerian Street, a white man, who
marries a woman he sees riding a winter carnival float holding
the paw of a polar bear: She is Miss Maine, in fact, and is
called the Principal Beauty of Maine. Valerian Street's best
friend is a French dentist named Michelin. Valerian's own
name was once used for a kind of candy that failed because
nobody bought it but blacks in the South.

Despite this failure, Valerian Street is a wealthy man.
When we meet him he is trying to live out his last years on a
Caribbean island called Isle des Chevaliers. He is still attracted
to Northern flowers, however, and indulges himself with a
greenhouse in which he plays music to those species that don't
grow in the tropics.

Miss Morrison makes greater mischief with Valerian's
paradise than simply poking fun at his flowers. He lives
oblivious to a story within his own family—a story too good for
me to spoil for the reader (and too awful for the frail Miss
Maine to cope with). The family's loyal black cook, Ondine,
will reveal the tale; she and her husband, Sydney, the butler,
have devoted most of their lives to serving Valerian Street.
They are the white man's dream of "good Negroes," which
means they love their master's child as if he were their own,
they keep their place, they grow quietly and uncomplainingly
old.

They also provide Miss Morrison with an opportunity to
exercise her considerable gift for dialogue; this old couple's
conversation is sparkling and through it the reader learns the
circumstances of Valerian's retirement to the Caribbean. It is
both his and his wife's sorrow that their only son won't share
this paradise (the mystery of the novel, and it's a gruesome
mystery, is why the son, Michael, stays away). Valerian escapes
from his disappointment to his greenhouse: "When he knew
for certain that Michael would always be a stranger to him, he
built the greenhouse as a place of controlled ever-flowering life
to greet death in."

In *Tar Baby* Toni Morrison lavishes her strongest prose on
descriptions of nature: "Bees have no sting on Isle des
Chevaliers, nor honey. They are fat and lazy, curious about
nothing. Especially at noon. At noon parrots sleep and
diamondbacks work down the trees toward the cooler undergrowth. At noon the water in the mouths of orchids left there
by the breakfast rain is warm. Children stick their fingers in
them and scream as though scalded."

At times this effort to see the world from nature's point of
view seems precious, even cute ("Margaret was not dreaming
nor was she quite asleep, although the moon looking at her
face believed she was"), but the richness of the best of these
passages (a description of the death of a river, for example)
makes Miss Morrison's excesses tolerable.

Less tolerable, however, is her excessive use of dialogue:
too much of the story is told through dialogue—and not only
through the old couple's conversations. Their niece, Jadine, a
super-educated, super-beautiful young woman, a Paris model
who "made those white girls disappear. Just disappear right off
the page," has a love affair with an escaped criminal, a poor,
uneducated north Florida black. This affair is the book's erotic
and dramatic center. Jadine and her lover Son (his father was
called Old Man) passionately and violently debate the best way
for blacks to be independent of the white man's world. Their
arguments are lengthy and become tedious, but they vividly
expose the novel's racial tensions.

Jadine was educated on money given her by her aunt's and
uncle's employer; her friendship with Mrs. Street is severely
tested by Son's intrusion (he jumps ship and swims ashore on
Isle des Chevaliers, hiding in the Street family's bedrooms for
four days, sneaking food, before he is caught). Son's presence
reveals the racism in both the whites and blacks in Street's
household; he is—in the black's own words—"just a swamp
nigger."

What's so powerful, and subtle, about Miss Morrison's
presentation of the tension between blacks and whites is that
she conveys it almost entirely through the suspicions and
prejudices of her black characters. It is the white world that has
created this, and in the constant warring between Sydney,
Ondine and Jadine, and between Jadine and Son, Miss
Morrison uncovers all the stereotypical racial fears felt by
whites and blacks alike. Like any ambitious writer, she's
unafraid to employ these stereotypes—she embraces the
representative quality of her characters without embarrassment, then proceeds to make them individuals too.

Jadine takes Son to New York City, but after his
immersion in Caribbean life he sees black Americans with the
keen perspective of a foreigner: "The black girls in New York
City were crying and their men were looking neither to the
right nor to the left. Not because they were heedless, or intent
on what was before them, but they did not wish to see the
crying, crying girls split into two parts by their tight jeans,
screaming at the top of their high, high heels, straining against
the pull of their braids and the fluorescent combs holding their
hair."

Son then takes Jadine back to his north Florida home,
where the "real" blacks live, but Jadine is bored and repulsed.
In the end she returns to Paris, possibly to have a rich white
man's child, while Son searches for her on Isle des Chevaliers—an almost atavistic figure returning to the swamp, losing
himself in a powerfully superstitious island culture, radically
different from the culture of black America.

Tar Baby is, of course, a black novel, a novel deeply
perceptive of the black's desire to create a mythology of his own
to replace the stereotypes and myths the white man has

constructed for him. It is also a book about a woman's anger at—and her denial of—her need for an impossible man, and in this regard it is a woman's novel too. Leaving Son behind her, Jadine bravely concludes: "A grown woman did not need safety or its dreams. She *was* the safety she longed for." Yet Toni Morrison's greatest accomplishment is that she has raised her novel above the social realism that too many black novels and women's novels are trapped in. She has succeeded in writing about race and women symbolically.

This movement from realism to myth can be seen at its best, for example, in a crucial fight between Jadine and Son: "She looked at him and when he saw the sheen gone from her minky eyes and her wonderful mouth fat with disgust, he tore open his shirt, saying, 'I got a story for you.'

"'Get out of my face.'

"'You'll like it. It's short and to the point.'

"'Don't touch me. Don't you touch me.'

"'Once upon a time there was a farmer—a white farmer . . .'

"'Quit! Leave me *alone*.'

"'And he had this . . . farm. And a rabbit. A rabbit came along and ate a couple of his . . . ow . . . cabbages.'

"'You better kill me. Because if you don't, when you're through, I'm going to kill you.'

"'Just a few cabbages, you know what I mean?'

"'I am going to kill you. *Kill* you.'

"'So he got this great idea about how to get him. How to, to trap . . . this rabbit. And you know what he did? He made him a tar baby. He made it, you hear me? He made it!'

"'As sure as I live,' she said, 'I'm going to kill you.'

"But she didn't. After he banged the bedroom door, she lay in wrinkled sheets, slippery, gutted, not thinking of killing him."

Alongside the ferocity of this battle, Valerian Street's greenhouse and the problems besetting his wife (the "Bride of the Polar Bear") seem trivial in the extreme, but Miss Morrison never withholds her sympathy from her minor characters. If the excesses of the book's dialogue and lyricism are acceptable vices of ambition, the precision of Miss Morrison's minor characters and scenes reveals her craftsmanship. When she abandons that precision, it doesn't seem a lapse in her artistry so much as a way of announcing her more visceral intentions.

Some readers will find the overlapping narrative structure an irritation; this is one of the problems with Miss Morrison's dependence on dialogue to advance and fill in the story. Some readers may resist the movement toward myth in the book's deliberately symbolic ending—and some complaints, some wish to know more concretely what happens, may be justified. Will Son ever connect with Jadine again? Will Jadine allow herself to be bought by the safe, white world of Paris? And will Sydney and Ondine, despite the indignities they have been forced to suffer, continue to serve the Streets, who—at the novel's end—are devastated by the revelation of their family's inner violence?

But Toni Morrison is less interested in the final details of her characters' lives than she is interested in demonstrating the vast discrepancies between the places black people end up and the places they seek. Son chooses to lose himself in the rain forest, "where the champion daisy trees still grow," rather than give himself up to a black world that has been corrupted by whites. Son invents his own life from scratch; his almost fatal love for Jadine has only momentarily distracted him from this goal.

Thomas Hardy would have appreciated Miss Morrison's old-fashioned authorial intrusions, her wise counsel to her

readers. It is an earned moment when Miss Morrison gives Valerian Street the following revelation or benediction:

"At some point in life the world's beauty becomes enough. You don't need to photograph, paint or even remember it. It is enough. No record of it needs to be kept and you don't need someone to share it with or tell it to. When that happens—that letting go—you let go because you can. The world will always be there—while you sleep it will be there—when you wake it will be there as well. So you can sleep and there is reason to wake. A dead hydrangea is as intricate and lovely as one in bloom. Bleak sky is as seductive as sunshine, miniature orange trees without blossom or fruit are not defective; they are that. So the windows of the greenhouse can be opened and the weather let in. The latch on the door can be left unhooked, the muslin removed, for the soldier ants are beautiful too and whatever they do will be part of it."

Although Valerian has been largely innocent of the crimes in this novel visited upon blacks and whites, Miss Morrison concludes: "An innocent man is a sin before God. Inhuman and therefore unworthy. No man should live without absorbing the sins of his kind, the foul air of his innocence, even if it did wilt rows of angel trumpets and cause them to fall from their vines."

This judgment is as sympathetic as it is severe. Thomas Hardy, full of his own instructions to damaged mankind, would have loved this book.

BARBARA CHRISTIAN
From "The Concept of Class in the Novels of Toni Morrison"
Black Feminist Criticism: Perspectives on Black Women Writers
1985, pp. 73–80

In the contemporary period, black women novelists have continued to analyze the relationship between class, race, and gender. One of our finest novelists, Toni Morrison, has illuminated in her four novels, *The Bluest Eye, Sula, Song of Solomon,* and *Tar Baby,* the definition of woman in relation to race and class assumptions.

The Bluest Eye is about a black girl's desire for the bluest eyes, the symbol for her of what it means to be beautiful and therefore worthy in our society. At the center of the novel is Pecola Breedlove, who comes from a family that is poor and virtually cut off from the normal life of a community. The Breedloves despise themselves because they believe in their own unworthiness, which is translated into ugliness for the women of that family. Associated with their condition is funk, violence, ugliness, and poverty, symbolized by their storefront house. In contrast, Pecola's mother, Pauline, works as a domestic in a beautiful house that is a reflection of the ideal woman. She is, in effect, a black mammy to the wealthy blonde girl-doll who lives in the beautiful house. In a pivotal section of the novel, Pauline expels her "ugly," "poor," daughter Pecola from this house because she drops a hot pan of blueberry pie and dirties the floor. Instead of comforting her daughter, who has been burnt, Pauline rushes to console the girl-doll who is upset by the accident. This scene is beautifully constructed to contrast the extremes of class positions in terms of what is desirable. For Pauline hates the ugliness of her house, her daughter, her family, herself and blames her sense of unworthiness on being black and poor. Instead, she aspires to the polished copper and sheen of the kitchen she works in where everyone is clean, well-behaved, and pretty. For her, any violation of that paradise by anyone, even her daughter, is paramount to a crime. The mother's own internalization of the desirable woman as beautiful, well-taken-care-of, cuddled, results in her rejection of her own daughter, who by virtue of her blackness and her poverty cannot possibly obtain such a standard.

Between the bottom, Pecola and her storefront house, and the top, the little girl-doll in her perfect home, Morrison presents us women situated on different points along the scale. Their positions are generally symbolized by the order of their homes and their shade of skin color. Just below the girl-doll is Maureen Peal, the light-skinned dream girl with green eyes who lives in a fine house, wears immaculate clothes, and is seen by everyone around her as a princess. Geraldine is slightly darker than Maureen. Because she is precariously on the edge of bright skin, she hates any element of funk, which she associates with blackness, and she rigidly maintains her prissy home. She also expels Pecola from her house, for this black girl with her nappy hair represents to Geraldine both racial and class deterioration. In the novel, both Maureen and Geraldine are also associated with a fear of sex. Maureen is clearly interested in learning about "it." But since that would violate the status of her position, she tries to learn about "it" from Pecola, who, because she is black, must know about such nastiness. Geraldine is so afraid of funk creeping into her pseudo-white middle-class life that she is frigid in much the same way southern ladies were supposed to be.

Freida and Claudia McTeer's mother is just one level above the Breedloves, at least economically. Somehow she has managed to hold onto her self-respect, despite her love of Shirley Temple dolls, "good hair," and bright skin. Her home is not a storefront, though stuffed newspapers in the cracks are necessary to keep out the cold. Instead, there is a hard, firm love that permeates her home. She and her women friends form their own community as they waver precariously on the edge, between Mrs. Breedlove's total alienation from any community and their desire not to work and to own a neat home like Geraldine.

Morrison comments on these various positions throughout the novel by using a device that underlines the pervasiveness of normative class distinctions. The words from the Dick and Jane primer are juxtaposed to appropriate sections in the novel. The primer tells us what the society says the ideal family should be like and is based on a middle-class ideal where the father works, the mother stays home, the children are happy, clean, and well-behaved, and even the dog and cat are well-groomed, friendly, socialized. There are no messy emotions, no unsatisfied needs, no funk.

The Bluest Eye, at core, is about the contradiction fostered by racism, sexism, and class distinctions that assails the black girls of this book. These contradictions are too intense for Pecola to sustain her sense of worth. As a result, she descends into madness. The other girls, Claudia and Frieda, barely manage to survive. Claudia, the narrator of this story, summarizes Pecola's tragedy in this way:

> All of our waste which we dumped on her and which she absorbed. And all of our beauty, which was hers first and which she gave to us. All of us—all who knew her—felt so wholesome after we cleaned ourselves on her. We were so beautiful when we stood astride her ugliness. Her simplicity decorated us, her guilt sanctified us, her pain made us glow with health, her awkwardness made us think we had a sense of humor. Her inarticulateness made us believe we were eloquent. Her poverty kept us

generous. Even her waking dreams we used—to silence our own nightmares. And she let us, and thereby deserved our contempt. We honed our egos on her, padded our characters with her frailty, and yawned in the fantasy of our strength.[1]

At the crux of the novel is society's need for a pariah, the need of its members to have someone to look down upon and therefore enhance one's constantly threatened sense of worth. Beyond the economic basis, one of the major psychological effects of class distinction is a need for a sense of superiority. Morrison's first novel succinctly expresses the vulnerability of poor black girls and how easily they can become the pariahs, which the structure of our society must have.

Morrison's second novel, *Sula*, pushes the idea of the black woman as pariah even further. Although she constructs the hierarchy of class relations in *Sula* quite differently from *The Bluest Eye*, the concept of class and its relation to sex and race is still very much a part of the novel. On an obvious level, Nel's mother, Helen Wright, could be called the image of the lady in the novel. She is presented in the hypocritical contours of this image. What is more interesting to me, however, is the complex way in which Morrison shows us how woman as helpmate, mother, and housekeeper is connected to the sense of failure black men often feel in a world that denies them status. Jude marries Nel in the novel because of his sense of this failure, his need to feel himself a man after being denied a job building the River Road:

> The more he thought about marriage, the more attractive it became. Whatever his fortune, whatever the cut of his garment, there would always be the hem—the tuck and fold that hid his raveling edges; a someone sweet, industrious and loyal to shore him up. And in return he would shelter her, love her, grow old with her. Without that someone he was a waiter hanging around a kitchen like a woman. With her he was head of a household pinned to an unsatisfactory job out of necessity. The two of them together would make one Jude.[2]

The standard of womanhood that Nel represents in the novel, at least during her marriage to Jude, is not the pure image of the ideal southern lady. Rather it is the variant that is based on the status of black men, on the status, in fact, of working-class men in the society. This role is seen by Nel's community as *good*, while Sula is seen as *evil*. For Sula not only refuses that role, she steps outside the caste of woman, beyond any class definition within that caste, when she insists on making herself. She does not work, but neither is she taken care of; she is freely sexual, but is not really that interested in men as men; she is interested neither in being beautiful nor becoming a mother. She defines herself outside of the sex, class, race definitions of the society. That she becomes a pariah in her community has much to do with her resistance to any clearly recognizable definition of a woman that the Bottom can tolerate.

In *Sula*, Morrison captures most profoundly the way concepts of good and evil are related to societal definitions of woman. For the Bottom, that definition has much to do with the status of black people within the larger society, which ironically is the basis for the adventure and rebellion that Sula represents. As important, the Bottom characterizes all its women as a class, though not in terms of dependent beautiful ornaments. Because of this black community's vulnerability, the distinguishing characteristics of the class of woman is that she make others, that she insure the continuity of the community by bearing children and by supporting the beleaguered men either sexually, emotionally, or financially. Such a position can result in the strength of an Eva, the rebellion of a Sula, or the stolid endurance of a Nel. But in the end none of these positions, it seems to me, results in self-fulfillment.

Morrison's third novel, *Song of Solomon*, does not primarily focus on the concept of woman, for its protagonists are men. Yet class in relation to race becomes even more focal in this novel than in her first two. For though Milkman's quest for his identity is the dominant thread of the novel, the major obstacle he must overcome is the deadening effects of his father's need to own as much property as possible in order to protect himself against racism. And Milkman is accidentally propelled on his search for himself as a result of his desire for gold. That journey leads him back through his personal past to a racial history that had been vehemently opposed to materialism and greed. It is a history that was created from the suffering imposed upon his people by the greed of others.

Although Morrison does not focus primarily on the relationship of gender to class in *Song of Solomon*, she does integrate that concern into her major theme. There are two important women in Milkman's life: his mother, Ruth, and his aunt, Pilate. As the daughter of the only black doctor in town, Ruth is bred to an upper middle-class existence. She is presented in the novel as the underside of the ideal southern lady image. She is totally cut off from life—benevolently imprisoned by her father who tries to make her into his girl-doll, spitefully contained by her husband who marries her because of her class position, then despised by him for her inherent weakness. Ruth's life is one of uneventful waste, interrupted only by the birth of her son, who she tries to keep a baby as long as possible. After he is grown, the only sign of life in her world is the watermark on her impressive dining room table, for her sole achievement had been the elaborate centerpieces she arranges for it. Ruth is symbolic of the terror that awaits those women who become the emblem of a man's wealth and class position.

While Ruth is the quintessence of the ideal southern lady image carried to a grotesque extreme, Pilate is the woman without a navel, the woman completely outside societal structures. She is the guide in the novel to essences beyond outward appearance or material things. As Ruth is a society lady, so Pilate is totally outside society as symbolized by her house outside the town, which is not even wired for electricity. Yet Pilate is also the embodiment of the tradition of her family and is the pilot for Milkman in his necessary journey to the past. Morrison compares and contrasts these two women in this marvelous passage:

> They were so different, these two women. One black, the other lemony. One corseted, the other buck naked under her dress. One well read but ill traveled. The other had read only a geography book, but had been from one end of the country to another. One wholly dependent on money for life, the other indifferent to it. But those were the meaningless things. Their similarities were profound. Both were vitally interested in Macon Dead's son, and both had close and supportive posthumous communication with their fathers.[3]

They come together in this novel, the upper middle-class lady and the conjure woman, to save Milkman, in a sense the symbol of their continuity. That both these women are nurturers is, I believe, important, especially when one juxtaposes them with Sula. In *Song of Solomon* and in her latest novel, *Tar Baby*, Morrison seems to modify the image of Sula as an ideal. Sula was so powerful a character that she ignited the imagination of many readers, who reversed the Bottom's judgement, transforming her from the evil witch into a totally

positive ideal. But though Sula is a product of her community, she has no concern for it. And Morrison has her die for lack, it seems, of a community. The distinction that Morrison makes in *Song of Solomon* between class and community and between autonomy and self-absorption is represented, I think, by the towering figure of Pilate, who is totally beyond class distinctions and yet is the embodiment of the spirit of her community. In having Ruth and Pilate come together, Morrison may be suggesting that the effect of class distinctions, the fragmentation of community, may be able to be overcome by women in their overriding concern for the living.

Pilate, however, is rooted in the past. Although she is still effective in the present, she leaves us no future. One cannot pretend that electricity does not exist and that the world is a village. Missing from Pilate's character is a sense of contemporary life. Cut off from men, her daughter Reba becomes obsessed with them and her granddaughter Hagar is finally killed by her insatiable desire for Milkman. Ironically, her community, made up solely of women, becomes psychically dependent on men, because it does not know them. Pilate, then, is so apart from the everyday world that her way cannot be the basis for transforming it. As heroic as she is, Pilate belongs to another time.

In *Tar Baby*, Morrison adds the quality of contemporaneity to her characterization of an independent black woman. And in the love story of Jadine and Son, she develops her most compelling relationship between a man and a woman. But Jadine is presented in the novel as essentially classbound. Her desire to "make it" in the world binds her not just to whites, but to upper-class whites. Her values are not so much that of the ideal southern lady as they are of the white male world. She does not wish to be the lady dependent on the husband's wealth and status. She wants parity, but it must be parity in a world of material gain. In no way is she a nurturer, not even to her aunt and uncle, who made her access to wealth possible by becoming life-long servants to the rich Valerian.

To Jadine, independence for a woman means looking out for herself—she is not concerned with any community or with justice for anyone. In developing a Jadine, who uses her belief in herself as a woman as a rationale for "making it," Morrison may be suggesting not only that class concerns are now more critical than racial bonds, but that women, in their search for autonomy, may be taking on patriarchal values. Jadine is a feminist in appearance without any of the concern for social justice that the concept should embody.

In contrast to Jadine, Son, her lover, is a man totally outside of society, a runaway criminal. Like Pilate, he resists the materialism of the society. Like Pilate, he has no future, for he really lives in Eloe, a country of the past. More importantly, he refuses to contend with the social forces that deprive him of fulfillment. His solution is to retreat, run, opt out. Although he feels an intense racial identity, he does not join with others to change anything. He is not so much beyond class as much as he is perceived as part of an under class—totally alienated from the world he moves in. He finally moves into the realm of myth.

Both Jadine and Son are at a dead end. In going to Paris, Jadine will probably marry a wealthy Parisian, repeating the pattern of some of her foremothers, except that they were *forced* by circumstances to enter the more dominant race and class through their use of their sexuality. As independent as she might seem, then, her need for material well-being makes her dependent on the class of the wealthy and powerful. Son, on the other hand, simply leaves this world for another, affecting nothing for anyone.

Whatever the flaws of *Tar Baby*, it is Morrison's most recent example of how she consistently creates a world of characters, each of whom represents a specific social value. In all her books, the particular concept that is foremost in her mind is divided into different aspects that her characters embody. In *The Bluest Eye*, the idea of physical beauty is looked at in terms of its impact on black girls and women along class lines and skin shade. In *Sula*, the idea of woman is represented by the many female archetypes that the world has invented, from the domineering Eva through the handmaiden Nel to the witch Sula. In *Song of Solomon*, she investigates the meaning of black racial identity, how that common history is responsible for people as diverse as the rebellious Guitar, the materialistic Macon, and the spiritual Pilate. And in *Tar Baby*, where the relationship between class and race is pivotal,

Morrison introduces white characters, the wealthy Valerian and his wife, as well as non-American blacks, Gideon and Therese, who are practically serfs in their Caribbean home. As Morrison creates a body of work, her analysis of our society through the creation of these diverse characters asks basic questions about whether sex, race, or class are separate entities, at least in America. Or whether, like the images of a kaleidoscope, these elements are so organically connected that one must understand their interrelationship in spite of their ever-shifting appearance.

Notes

1. Toni Morrison, *The Bluest Eye* (New York: Holt, Rinehart & Winston, 1970), p. 163.
2. Toni Morrison, *Sula* (New York: Knopf, 1974), p. 82.
3. Toni Morrison, *Song of Solomon* (New York: Knopf, 1977), p. 139.

WILLARD MOTLEY

1909–1965

Willard Francis Motley was born on July 14, 1909, in Englewood, a middle-class white suburb of Chicago. The Motleys were the only black family in the neighborhood. After graduating from high school in 1929 Motley began traveling around the United States writing short stories and working at a variety of jobs: migratory laborer, ranch hand, cook, shipping clerk, photographer, radio scriptwriter, newspaper editor. He submitted his stories to a number of magazines and newspapers between 1930 and 1935; all were rejected. Subsequent travels in the west provided more experience and material, including a month-long jail sentence in Wyoming for vagrancy. He returned to Chicago in 1939 and took a slum apartment at Fourteenth and Union. Using material from his travels he wrote nonfiction articles for auto-touring magazines. He began work on his novel *Knock on Any Door* in 1940. Published in 1947, this highly naturalistic work about a poor Italian family living in the slums of Chicago met with overwhelmingly positive critical response. It was eventually made into a movie starring Humphrey Bogart. After the publication of *We Fished All Night* in 1951 Motley moved to Mexico.

The sequel to *Knock on Any Door* was *Let No Man Write My Epitaph*, published in 1958. Critical reception was unenthusiastic. Motley's last novel, *Let Noon Be Fair*, was published a year after his death in Mexico from intestinal gangrene on March 4, 1965.

Personal

I never knew Willard Motley in any real sense; I met him only once and he wrote to me from Mexico only once, asking me to meet him at his mother's house on the west side of Chicago to talk and have beer, during that summer of 1960 when he was planning to come home.

We didn't meet that way, though. It was a very uncomfortable meeting, unpleasant for everybody in the room—Archibald Motley, Hugh Grayson, Willard and myself. We were all standing, suddenly, in the kitchen of the Motley home. (I had gotten to know Archibald fairly well earlier, first because we both had paintings in Gayles Gallery, and second because I had talked with him several times to get information on his career, in order to build a magazine article, which was accepted by *Black Orpheus*, in Nigeria, but never published.)

Relatively speaking, Willard Motley had been somewhat important to me. His books, *Knock on Any Door* and *We Fished All Night* (not so much *Let No Man Write My Epitaph*, though I read it half-heartedly), had a strange impact on me. When I was in high school and had read everything by Richard Wright, I turned to other black writers, among them Willard Motley. A kind of ghost among Negro writers, he was. In those

first two big, raw, clumsy books, I found something vital and real. They were valid for me—though Motley was hardly considered a respected and "serious" writer by most black and white critics. But I could look at the *bulk* of his work and, from a writer's point of view, get inspiration. *All that work!* God it was amazing! I used to open them and read at random. He really knew a lot about the social habits of Italians, Poles, Jews, and the bums of West Madison Street.

But then he lived a long time among those poor Italians, Poles, Jews, and bums. Archibald, his brother, a big, impressive man with skin the color of peach, with eyes like two soft lights, a goat's T of hair on his chin, stood up from where we were sitting at the dining room table and demonstrated for me how carefully he had to walk across the floor boards in Willard's basement apartment, during Willard's West Madison Street days, because mud was oozing up between the boards onto Archibald's shoes. Willard Motley actually lived in *that* kind of poverty while writing *Knock on Any Door*. He *chose* to live that way. The manuscript was finally shipped off in a crate—it was that big—only to be rejected for being too long and too crude. Archibald said his younger brother had baffled them all when he moved out of the comfort of the family home to live in such squalor. But Archibald came to understand very soon that it was something that "Brother" *had* to do.

I remember the nervous pitch of Willard Motley's thin, soft voice; the almost effeminate way his mouth formed words, which reminded me also of Truman Capote's mouth forming sounds. Norman Ross was interviewing Motley once on his VIP show, and the novelist couldn't seem to get his voice above a whisper. Ross asked, "Why do you write about people around West Madison Street rather than about Negroes?" (i.e., as other Negro writers do). Motley said softly, "I find the plight of the people on West Madison Street *more* urgent." I almost fell off my chair. There he was, sitting there in his white silky-looking suit, like a butterscotch-colored South American tobacco-inspector, saying some shit like *that*! I turned to Grayson, who was also watching it, and I couldn't see his face, only the interior of his mouth—he was laughing so hard. Even my wife, in the kitchen making coffee, fell out.

As I say, I saw nothing in *Let No Man Write My Epitaph* and didn't even bother to try to read *Let Noon Be Fair*. Even if the latter is in some way worth reading or is good or is better than anything he wrote prior to it, I probably will never know . . . I mean, by the time the novel came out, which was, I think, after his death in 1965 or 1966, I was no longer interested in Willard Motley. I wasn't impressed by all that work anymore. I was moving on. Besides, I was turning away from fiction in those days toward psychology, anthropology, history, etc.

Another thing. The name Richard Wright was a very evil word—or so I gathered—in the Motley home. Archibald was quick to let me know that! The verbal energy with which he put down *Black Boy* and *Native Son* almost turned the pages of my notebook!

Willard Motley died still being put to the side by critics who studied Negro fiction. In any evaluation of American Negro literature he is to be considered. Usually, however, he is treated with as much disrespect as is Frank Yerby. But unlike Richard Wright or William Demby, both excellent craftsmen, Yerby and Motley turned out the kind of lusty or sensational material that brought to them considerable wealth. (And Yerby, of course, is still at it.)—CLARENCE MAJOR, "Willard Motley: Vague Ghost after the Father," *The Dark and Feeling*, 1974, pp. 95–97

Works

Let it be stated at once: an extraordinary and powerful new naturalistic talent herewith makes its debut in American letters. But let it be added immediately: Chicago's Mr. Motley has a deal of graduate work to do in literature's school of realism before attaining all the honors of his craft.

His resemblance to Farrell, and especially to Dreiser, is striking. Indeed he has clearly played the sedulous ape to the latter; not a few readers will catch echoes in his book of *An American Tragedy*. And, though he lacks that master's qualities of cosmic brooding and massive eloquence, he has something of his rugged narrative drive, his cumulative emotional power and his kindling sense of compassion. Dreiser would have been proud of his disciple.

The critical, however, will regret the oversedulousness of Mr. Motley's apings: the Dreiserian windiness of his style, the Farrell-like accent on verbal shock and the naturalist's blurry gift for adding detail and subtracting impact. Mr. Motley is not subtle. He writes like a whole glee club of sob-sisters. And in the continuous din of his wailings and shriekings—his book is a sordid sequence of heartbreak in Chicago's slums: suicides, desertions, lost loves, lost ladies, alcoholism, broken mothers, broken homes, murders—the still small voice of critical reason may easily be overwhelmed.

For example, the oversigned expects to be a dissenting minority in his contention that *Knock on Any Door* badly confuses, even partly confutes, its own central point. This is an old thesis of naturalism—namely, that environment conditions the man. Given slums, poverty, police viciousness, political corruption, parental neglect and church failure, therefore, and we may expect, in due course, to be given crime as well. In general this is true, although in practice the theory often finds itself confronted by the mysterious fact of man himself. Thus, men from the best-regulated families may become criminals as men from the worst possible homes and slums may turn out to be socially useful citizens.

In the case at hand (and it is a dramatized slice of sociology), Nick Romano is introduced to us as an altar-boy who goes wrong at about the same time that his family suffers a reverse of fortune. He is taken to live in a slum. He is brutally beaten by a well-meaning but stupid father. He takes to the street and the street takes to him; at first, young corner toughs, later professional delinquents, hoboes, prostitutes, jackrollers, panhandlers, gamblers, homosexuals. Reform school helps the process of deterioration, jail speeds it, police sadism brings it to climax in a suspensive duel to the death.

But Nick is not entirely friendless or without guides. His mother, although ineffectual, loves him. His brother tries to interest him in Hull House. A professional sociologist gives him sound advice over the years. Two decent girls fall in love with him; one marries him to escape the bitterness of her own domestic hell (her story is told in a clumsy interpolation) only to find herself in an even worse emotional inferno.

How does handsome Nick react? Conscious of what reform school did to him, conscious of his wicked ways, he is still enamored of easy money and easy sex. He deliberately rejects conscience, boasts of his creed—"live fast, die young, and have a good-looking corpse"—achieves all three objectives. The case of Nick Romano, in short, is too complicated merely for sociology. Psychiatry must be called in, too. One may admit and deplore the effects of a physical slum. What of the ego of a man wallowing in its own spiritual slum?

Mr. Motley's Chicago Bowery comes to murky life. His poolroom people have animation. But his novel is distorted to fit a thesis; his protagonist is too complex for his role. A less intelligent Nick might have served admirably to illustrate the destructive influence of environment. The Nick here so brilliantly realized is a *willing* victim of circumstance and so belongs to Freud as well as to the social scientists.

And yet, *Knock on Any Door* achieves a powerful, although rude, vitality. It will absorb the individual reader as it will challenge society to mend its body and soul. Motley is one of the finds of the year.—CHARLES LEE, "Disciple of Dreiser," NYTBR, May 4, 1947, p. 3

Knock on Any Door is the counterpart among the city novels of violence of the forties to Dreiser's *An American Tragedy*. Like the earlier novel, it makes a dramatic statement of the premise that individual crime is rooted in social conditions, and that individual guilt, therefore, constitutes a public accusation. Although Dreiser's novel indicts society as a whole for its economic inequality and materialism, and Motley's novel deals more specifically with poverty and the slums, both generalize the significance of their particular dramatic situation by stressing its typicality and inevitability to the times. In both novels the main action consists less of what the protagonist does, as an individualized being, than of what society does to him through its combined and pervasive forces. Thus Clyde

Griffiths and Nick Romano are registers of their environments; and they are doomed because they accept uncritically and unconditionally standards and goals of the world in which they live. Without premeditation—without any real awareness of what is happening to them—they both turn into destructive agents: this is the consequence of their compliance. And yet they themselves are also the pitiable victims of uncontrolled destructive forces.

Characteristically, *Knock on Any Door* is a much more violent novel than *An American Tragedy*. Motley presents the violence of the back alley and the city's lower depths. There is criminal assault, jack-rolling, and murder. There is the degradation of self-prostitution and suicide. And most condemnable, there is the brutality of organized authority, which subjects the children in reformatories and the underworld captives in prisons to sadistic beatings with hose, blackjack, and fists and to merciless grillings undertaken with a heartless scientific precision.

Yet even though the structure of *Knock on Any Door* includes a pattern of violence (in *An American Tragedy* even the murder is nonviolent), the novel is simpler than its prototype. In order to stress the sociological thesis, it has reduced character, situation, and setting to skeletal essentials. Thus, Nick is a stereotype of the juvenile driven to delinquency through bad influence. He lacks the individuality that Clyde had by virtue of his peculiar romantic and sensuous temperament, the special endowment of all Dreiser's protagonists. Nick is first a perfectly unequivocal "good boy," devout, happy with his family, school, and priest, tenderhearted and innocent—not at all like the malcontented, rather neurotic Clyde. Also, the influences that change Nick are much more specific, and hence more simplified, than those that act on Clyde. First it is poverty, with its consequences of bad environment and bad companions, and then the brutality of the reformatory that turn Nick against the social order. The action of these influences is concentrated, so that Nick suffers under their impact in intense and unforgettable moments, as when his friend Tommy dies in the reformatory or when he returns to the raucous, dirty, evil slum that is his home. While the influences that act upon Clyde are cumulative, they are diffused through a life's experience, short though it was; and they have the apparent aimlessness which they have often in life. It is only when we see and appreciate their cumulative effect in *An American Tragedy* that we are horrified by the undercurrent of destructive forces in the modern urban world. Even the tone of *Knock on Any Door* has been reduced to one single expression, whereas in Dreiser's novel, there are the nuances of pity, anger, irony, despair, pathos—and horror. Nick kills out of his obsessive hatred of the law, because of what it has come to symbolize to him. Clyde's crime comes about through a series of involuted acts, and even the crime itself has its complexities, as Clyde finds himself curiously more a witness to the murder than its perpetrator. Finally, the range of Nick's reactions is limited, and it fits a strict stereotyped pattern of the sociological case history. Clyde may experience mainly the emotions of a "moral coward"—regret, fear, yearning, anxiety—but his emotional pattern is always complex because he is caught in conflict and indecision; and he never is as unequivocally good or bad as Nick. The secondary characters in *Knock on Any Door* are also reduced to a sociological stereotype: the bad companion, the pure young wife, the not-understanding father, the hard-working brother, the socially conscious writer (who comments upon the action), and the brutal policeman.

Whatever effect of richness the novel has is achieved mainly through setting. Since environment plays the role of antagonist, it is fully realized as a dramatic entity. The style, however, is as bleak as the story. Short declarative sentences carry the main burden of the narrative; and while these may be a fitting vehicle for expressing Nick's limited thought and sensibility, they tend to become monotonous. There is the recurrent imagery of a small trapped animal, which comes to symbolize the trapped child Nick, as well as all of the innocent children caught and brutalized by the slums. Nick is always to remember the wounded mouse he had once rescued from a tormenting cat, and the dead dog lying in the street: these images merge with that of himself as he is finally caught and trapped and prepared for death in a prison cell.

Structurally, the novel follows a unilateral pattern of social causation; and the theme is that of social guilt. This theme is made explicit by the defense attorney who presents the theory that the "real" Nick Romano is not guilty of murder: ". . . he is guilty of having been reared in desperate poverty in the slums of a big city. He is guilty of having had the wrong environment and the wrong companions. He is guilty of the poolrooms and the taverns whose doors were open to him from the time he was fifteen. He is guilty of learning about sex on street corners. . . . He is guilty of learning police procedure by having been picked up and beaten by the police whenever they chose. He is guilty of the foul treatment of a reform school. . . ." The defense ends with the dramatic accusation against society, the murderer of the "real" Nick Romano, the saintly child at the church altar. " 'Nick Romano was murdered seven years ago! . . . Society . . . murdered!—Nick Romano! . . . We brutalized and murdered him and we made this rendezvous with him seven years ago. . . .' " The opening and closing epigraphs to the novel sustain this conclusion. Motley here makes his social point explicitly: one can knock on any door in the city's back alley and find a Nick Romano, perverted, brutalized, made murderous by hatred and frustration.—BLANCHE HOUSMAN GELFANT, " 'What of the Back Yard, and the Alley?,' " *The American City Novel*, 1954, pp. 248–52

N. JILL WEYANT
From "Willard Motley's Pivotal Novel: *Let No Man Write My Epitaph*"

Black American Literature Forum, Summer 1977, pp. 56–61

Often dismissed from serious critical consideration because of its crude style and sensational subject matter, Willard Motley's third novel, *Let No Man Write My Epitaph* (1957), should perhaps be reexamined before it is rejected altogether. There are several practical reasons why *Epitaph* is the weakest of Motley's four published novels. The fact that it is a sequel to Motley's astoundingly successful *Knock on Any Door* (1947) perhaps condemned *Epitaph* to the region of the second rate from the outset (are sequels ever as good as their originals?). Furthermore, the decision to write a sequel to *Knock* was dictated in large part by Motley's desperate financial situation in 1952 when *Epitaph* was begun. Frankly, *Epitaph* was written to make money, and Motley's poverty may help account for *Epitaph*'s tone, which is noticeably more bitter than in the other novels, the focus on then-explosive social problems like the heroin trade and miscegenation, and the undisguised plagiarism from *Knock*, the novel that brought wealth to its publisher but not to its author. And, with his melodramatic approach and stereotyped characters, including the arch-villain Frank Ramponi, Motley seems to be appealing to society's least common denominator and to be lowering the intellectual level of the novel, possibly hoping that this too might sell the book.

However, there are more complex psychological reasons why *Epitaph* is one of the most confused and confusing novels ever written. If carefully examined in light of Motley's personal development as revealed in his manuscripts and private papers,[1] *Epitaph* reflects a transitional stage in Motley's thinking from racial naïveté to an acute awareness of racism, or, to use more familiar terms, from innocence to experience. In many ways, Motley seems to be a case of delayed development, going through this initiation much later in his life than most other post-Renaissance Black writers (aged 40 when he began this novel, Motley was no adolescent when he underwent racial maturation) and much, much later than might be expected in light of the direction pointed early in the '40s by the ascendence of Richard Wright. The confusion in *Epitaph* might reflect Motley's state of mind at this time, but more important in a critical sense, *Epitaph* manifests Black pride and Black consciousness in Motley *for the first time* in print and shows him pivoting from writing novels of white life with only an occasional Black character (*Knock*; *We Fished All Night*, 1951) to a more fully developed examination of racial exploitation (culminating in the Mexican novel *Let Noon Be Fair*, 1966). In *Epitaph* Motley alternates between white characters—Nick Romano's son Nick, Jr., and brother Louie—and Black characters. The long sections on the suffering of the Black community represent Motley's delayed acceptance of his own racial identity as well as his arrival at a truer understanding of racial relations in racist America. This understanding is absolutely crucial to Motley's literary development, for without it, he would have been doomed to remain a second-rate novelist lacking depth, to continue to move in circles groping to recapture the almost accidental success of his admittedly powerful but thematically and structurally simplistic first novel *Knock*. *We Fished* and *Epitaph* were literary regressions for Motley, but his last novel *Noon*, written after the transition I see in *Epitaph*, seems to be a step forward in structure and theme that might have been improved on in other novels, had he lived to write on.[2]

I

Motley's muted but nevertheless demonstrable manifestation of racial awareness in *Epitaph* is at first surprising because, as we know from his personal papers, he was always rather isolated from other Black artists as well as from the Black community. Yet, though he had lived a sheltered, bourgeois life in a white neighborhood, his novels reflect the changing racial temper of the times. *Knock* and *We Fished* were written in the spirit of conciliation of the late '40s. But *Epitaph* reflects the emerging '50s and '60s push for Civil Rights signalled by Brown vs. the Board of Education (1954), even though *Epitaph* was written in Mexico by a man who had expatriated in 1951! To me, this suggests that Motley underwent an archetypal initiatory experience regarding race, that the sincere idealism manifest in *Knock* was replaced by a more realistic appraisal of America's racial milieu, and that the confusion and bitterness which attended this shift are reflected in *Epitaph*. I apply the word *archetypal* because all his life and especially after his move to Mexico, Motley was isolated from the Black community, from Black myth and folklore, and from Black culture as well as from the company of Black artists. Despite Motley's personal background, unique in the history of Black American writers, he followed, both privately and professionally, the development of most other Black American literary artists in such a way as to suggest participation in Jung's unconscious memory of the race, the collective unconscious.

According to Lindsay Patterson, the awakening to the meaning of racism is the Black man's fall from Eden:

> I mean by lost innocence that specific moment when a Black discovers he is a "nigger" and his mentality shifts gears and begins that long, uphill climb to bring psychological order out of chaos. It is not a moment, however, easily detected. All of Black literature is more or less unconsciously preoccupied with precisely pinpointing and defining it.[3]

Indeed, Motley had written a piece with the significant title "I Discover I'm a Negro" (in Motley mss., NIU[4]), and though the essay deals not with race *per se* but with Motley as a conscientious objector in World War II, the title indicates that this initiatory experience may have been ready to emerge in his consciousness. While a moment such as this cannot be pinpointed in Motley's work or in his private papers, he had been struggling with the problem of his racial identity since at least his high-school diaries, in which he refers to his Blackness as his "affliction." A reading of *Epitaph* makes a student of Motley feel that his long racial identity crisis had been passed by the time he wrote the novel and that he was now trying to deal with it. The chaotic structure and clumsiness of *Epitaph*, far beneath the quality of the first two novels, may reflect the psychological chaos Patterson mentions as part of the Black man's discovery that he is automatically stigmatized, even if he has espoused the "right," i.e., pro-white, attitudes as Motley had. That the book is badly flawed, in fact, the worst of the four novels Motley published, tends to support the notion of its being conceived by someone in a confused, embittered state of mind.

II

In order to write a sequel to Nick Romano's story, Motley had to have a new Nick. Nick's kid brother Louie seemed a natural, and Motley did use him, but Motley also needed a new crusade. In his first novel, *Knock*, Motley had shown the general debilitating effects of a bad environment; his second novel, *We Fished*, showed the corruption and graft (in the form of Chicago's notorious political machine) which had created and perpetuated that bad environment. His third novel, then, was to take a look at one specific kind of exploitation, the drug traffic. None of the original Romano family seemed to be likely victims of drug addiction, so Motley apparently turned to Nellie, the only one of Nick's many sexual conquests shown in any detail, to be cast as the mother of the new Nick and a person with the potential for addiction. Nellie's movements in the world of addicts could be used to show the human suffering in the drug world. Nick, Sr.'s benefactor, Grant Holloway, could also be resurrected to provide documentary information on the drug culture ⟨. . .⟩

After we witness Nellie's degradation due to drugs and her son's addiction and cure, the last section of the novel, *Let No Man Write Their Epitaph*, gives us a variation of the book's title. In this section, after recalling Nick's execution, Motley shifts to the only three characters who have hope for the future: Louie Romano; his fiancée, Judy, a mulatto; and Nick, Jr. They are hanging in the balance and could go toward happiness or toward ruin. The ending verse shows the interrelatedness of all things, especially a cataclysmic event like Nick, Sr.'s death, the ripples from which have spread to all the characters in the book:

> A tree falls.
> A leaf flutters down.
> No life is lived in vain.
> No voice is lost to an ear.
> Nellie? Nick the father? Nick the son?
> Let no man write their epitaph.[5]

Motley here admonishes the reader not to give Louie, Judy, and Nick a fatal shove in the wrong direction by making them the victims of the kind of prejudicial judgment which led to the tragic fate of Nick Romano, Sr. Since epitaph writers are by definition judges, Motley makes the point that no one can judge anyone else because there is no way to know all the circumstances behind an action. The last line in the passage is a plea which echoes, with a slightly different connotation, the novel's title. By changing "their epitaph" to "my epitaph," Motley widens his comment by speaking for himself as author as well as for all people. All of us are potential victims of mistaken prejudice or of misunderstanding. By not passing judgment on others, we may benefit by not having judgments passed against us. In the verse, Motley comments on his characters, but in his title, he makes a universal plea on behalf of us all.

In the novel, the Black characters are more disadvantaged than the other Americans because their epitaph—or fate—is stamped on their hands and faces. No matter where they move or how they "improve" themselves, they will not be able to change the basic attribute of skin color that makes them the victims of caste, a designation that goes far deeper than class. Motley, for the first time in his published full-length fiction, takes a close look at Black culture, showing its unique qualities in an affirmative light while delineating the basic character of the Blacks as good, despite their ill treatment. All of Motley's evil characters—Officer Riley in *Knock*, The Power in *We Fished*, and The Wolf in *Epitaph*—belong to the white race, while Motley depicts members of the Black race as virtuous. In Motley's work, as in the writings of so many other Black writers, white is the color of evil.

III

There are several elements in *Epitaph* which suggest a shift in Motley's thinking. First, he inserts a Black contest in which characters compete to see who is the Blackest, with the winner, Extra Black Johnson, gaining status because of his dark color. This is indeed a departure from Motley's inability to admit in his diary that he is Black (calling his Blackness his "affliction") and his desire to pass for Mexican on a trip to the West Coast in the '30s. Secondly, he delineates the strength of Black people in his portrayal of various character types, such as Big Florabelle, the un-Jemima-like earth mother; Fran, the beautiful Black woman used as chattel by white men; and Judy, the tragic mulatto whose misfortune is to fall in love with white Louie in a racist society.

In addition to the individual portraits, Motley gives a group picture of the Black community as fun-loving, creative, and good-hearted, despite the private tragedies in which they all must participate. They are a strong people who can endure great privation and should be admired, not pitied, for it. Names like Seldom Seen and Raggedy Bob, songs by Ruth Brown, and solidarity and warmth are prevalent throughout the Black sections of the book. It is an incredible performance by a "raceless" writer. Far from denying the Black race, Motley's book celebrates its tribulations and joys. The novel asks how any group of people with so many problems can go through life so gracefully. ⟨. . .⟩

Motley's concept of a bad environment is very concrete, and this too corresponds to the custom of other Black writers. When the heroes of contemporary white American fiction—the Alexander Portnoys and the Holden Caulfields—claim to be disadvantaged in middle-class homes and prep schools, we know they are talking rather neurotically about psychological or imagined disadvantages. The milieu faced by a Motley protagonist has very physical dangers which make those in a

Roth or Salinger novel look paltry. Death lurks everywhere, in gang warfare, in attacks by hustlers like The Wolf, in overdoses. The dregs of society reside in Motley's ghettoes, among them jack rollers, sexual hustlers male and female, drunks, drug dealers, and addicts. There are few jobs for these people and those available pay poorly. These neighborhoods are victims of the greatest political graft. Residents of Motley's novels have compelling physical reasons for their shortcomings. They do not rationalize their imperfections to a psychiatrist; they live them and live with them. They have fallen from society's grace without having committed any apparent sin. This view of environment is very similar to the view held by Richard Wright and Chester Himes that no matter how much a Black man may imagine that he is being persecuted, he probably is not far from the literal truth. There may be no such thing as paranoia in Black literature. The unfortunate result of this life situation for Blacks is that if a case of psychotic illness does occur, it cannot easily be detected until it is so acute that cure is impossible. James Baldwin theorizes that this is precisely what happened to his father, whose paranoia was so much like his usual distrusting, suspicious nature that no one supposed him ill until he refused to eat, fearing his family was trying to poison him. Treatment at this point did no good.[6]

V

The criticism of *Epitaph* shows the carelessness with which well-meaning critics have approached Motley. He has not been read closely or accurately. If he is going to receive negative criticism, it seems only fair that that criticism be based on the facts. And, I feel Motley's reputation will benefit from more careful readings which will reveal heretofore unacknowledged strengths. The published articles on *Epitaph* contain basic errors. Alfred Weissgärber thinks that *Epitaph* is Motley's second novel and that *We Fished* is his third.[7] John Bayliss, in "Nick Romano: Father and Son," refers to Nick, Sr., as Nellie's "dead husband" when, of course, it is crucial to know that Nick and Nellie were never married.[8] We might be able to overlook mistakes such as these if critical interpretations of Motley were clearly the result of consideration of his real strengths. However, since there is no accurate critical evaluation of his literary skills, these trivial mistakes, showing evidence of careless reading, become emblematic of the superficial way critics have approached Motley. Though Motley is sometimes melodramatic and sometimes filled with affectation, his writing in *Epitaph* suggests that he turned away from the "racelessness" for which he had been attacked and toward an attempt to understand and express the plight of those who are victims of prejudice, including racial prejudice. This is a step forward for a Black artist who rather myopically had claimed that there were no differences between the races in America.

Motley's *Epitaph*, though artistically weak, is an important document in the archives of Black American literature because of its graphic demonstration on several levels of the damaging effects of racism on the writer and his work. Dictated in large part by the negative sanctions of racism, Motley's career before *Epitaph* had been a hoop-jumping attempt to please white readers and white publishers, and the results were the suppression of racial reality and economic exploitation damaging to Motley's psyche and financial position. Having, in *Knock*, authored a runaway best seller made into a movie starring Humphrey Bogart, Motley should have been set for life in terms of prestige and prosperity, but, because he was Black, he was left in obscurity and poverty soon after the dust settled from the explosive appearance of *Knock* on the literary scene. Before *Epitaph* there had been a disjunctive separation between Motley's method of stark realism and his idealistic hope, expressed as literary theme, that exposure of injustice would bring reform. Motley had to be freed of his illusions in order to liberate his fictional talents, and *Epitaph* is the sign that that exorcism was taking place. Though he resisted acknowledging the profound effects of racism more than most Black writers, Motley came to realize, and belatedly to express, what has now become commonplace: that despite one's best and strongest efforts to transcend racism, it will persist in dictating the limits of one's existence. As uncomplimentary and unbelievable as it sounds, Motley had tried throughout his adolescence, his youth, and into middle age, to deny his race and to dissociate himself from it in order to please white America and win its approval. That Motley, light in color, genteel in manner, thrown into white society at an early age, and reared in an extremely racist milieu, desired to be assimilated into American society and to deny his race is, I think, understandable. That he was able to throw off his background and embrace his race, despite his isolation from it, is, I think, remarkable. *Let No Man Write My Epitaph* is, then, the product of one man's struggle with economic and psychological racial exploitation, and is a kind of crossing the racial bar prerequisite to Motley's full development of theme and method. In this novel, Motley's Black consciousness seems to have been raised so that he could aim his protest at racial exploitation directly. His next and last novel *Let Noon Be Fair* does just that.

Notes

1. From Motley's diaries, begun in his freshman year in high school, we learn that his family was the only Black family in a then all-white neighborhood in Chicago's Englewood district (near Hyde Park), that his high-school chums were all white, that he fantasized about white teen-age girls in solitude rather than dating the Black girls accessible to him. We also learn that the Motley family was middle class and that this status provided Motley with an excuse for dissociating himself from the Black masses whom all his white friends hated. In an effort to make himself acceptable to his racist white friends, Motley developed his habit of down-playing his own race, an attitude summarized by his favorite motto, "My race is the human race," which continued to be his slogan until after the publication of *Knock on Any Door*; indeed the writing of *Knock* with its cast of white characters was an attempt to prove this saying true. In the diaries, we see Motley's performance in high school sports as his effort to win white approval and to overcome the limitations of being Black in racist South-side Chicago. Later, we

see his writing become a substitute for the approval and acceptance which participation in sports once brought him. Through the usual circumstances of his background, Motley became in his circle, a kind of token Negro, accepted as an exception to the usual stereotyped "nigger," and perhaps understandably in the climate of the time, he preferred to be tolerated by whites rather than wholeheartedly accepted by Blacks. Very conscious of being an example for integration, Motley began his writing career fully deserving of the "raceless" label later pejoratively applied to him by Robert Bone and other critics, for Motley attempted to show the irrelevance of race to life and to literature, in the latter case specifically by writing about white characters in his first two novels.

2. For a study of the structure and theme of *Noon*, see N. Jill Weyant, "Lyrical Experimentation in Willard Motley's Mexican Novel: *Let Noon Be Fair*," *Negro American Literature Forum*, 10 (1976), 95–99.

3. Lindsay Patterson, "Introduction," in *Black Theater* (New York: New American Library, 1971), pp. ix–x.

4. The Motley papers are on loan to Northern Illinois University. NIU has been given permission to make facsimiles of the mss., and the collection is now being catalogued by Craig S. Abbott who plans to publish a descriptive bibliography of the complete holdings. These papers cover the years from about 1924, when Motley was a high-school freshman, to about 1951, when he moved to Mexico after having published his first two novels. A general overview of this collection was published by Jerome Klinkowitz and James Giles in 1972 ("The Emergence of Willard Motley in Black American Literature," *Negro American Literature Forum*, 6 [1972], 31–34). The NIU mss. include extensive correspondence to and from Motley; 28 volumes of diaries; tss. and mss. of unpublished short fiction, essays, and drama; mss., tss., and composition notes for two of his novels, *Knock* and *We Fished*; a ts. of his last novel *Noon*; and a ts. of a full-length non-fiction work on Mexico, *My House is Your House*. The collection also contains a great deal of memorabilia—such as Christmas cards, photos, a sugar cube, etc.—of no apparent literary value but of some biographical importance. And, there is a history of the Motley family from slavery times until about 1950 on wire tapes.

5. Willard Motley, *Let No Man Write My Epitaph* (New York: Random House, 1958), p. 467. Future references will be to this edition by page number in the text.

6. As Baldwin says, "We had not known that he was being eaten up by paranoia. . . . His illness was beyond all hope of healing before anyone realized that he was ill" (*Notes of a Native Son* [New York: Bantam, 1964], p. 74).

7. Alfred Weissgärber, "Willard Motley and the Sociological Novel," *Studi Americani*, 7 (1961), 307.

8. John F. Bayliss, "Nick Romano: Father and Son," *Negro American Literature Forum*, 3 (1969), 21.

LEWIS MUMFORD

1895–

Lewis Mumford was born on October 19, 1895, in Flushing, New York, and grew up on the West Side of Manhattan. In 1909 he entered Stuyvesant High School, where he planned to study engineering; by the time he left three years later he had decided to become a writer instead. Over the next several years he studied at the City College of New York and, simultaneously, took a variety of classes at Columbia University, New York University, and the New School for Social Research; while doing this he satisfied his remaining curiosity about the way urban systems worked by serving as an investigator in the garment industry, a lab helper in the Bureau of Standards, and a U.S. Navy radio operator. In 1919 he left his various colleges without taking a degree, despite having accumulated the required credits, and accepted a position as editor of the *Dial*.

In 1920, after a half-year as a lecturer and editor in England, Mumford returned to the United States to concentrate on writing. In 1923 he published his first major book, *The Story of Utopias*; since then he has published more than thirty other major works on art, literature, social policy, and architecture. These include *Sticks and Stones: A Study of American Architecture and Civilisation* (1924), *The Golden Day: A Study of American Culture and Experience* (1926), *Herman Melville* (1929), *The Brown Decades: A Study of the Arts in America, 1865–1895* (1931), *The Culture of Cities* (1938), *The Human Prospect* (1955), *The City in History* (1961), *The Myth of the Machine* (volume 1, 1967; volume 2, 1970), and *The Urban Prospect* (1968). Although fewer than half of his books have concentrated on architecture and urban planning, it is in these fields that he has left his greatest mark, to the extent that he has found it often necessary to defend himself against charges that he is a trained architect: "I like to remind people that a person who investigates crime is not necessarily a criminal."

After many years spent as a professor and visiting lecturer at Columbia University, Dartmouth College, M.I.T., and other schools, Mumford lives today in upstate New York. In 1979 he published an autobiographical work, *My Works and Days: A Personal Chronicle, 1895–1975*.

This book, it seems to me, is chiefly a personal essay—a confession by a significant man. You will find, here, excellent pages on the "romanticism" of the pioneer, on the genius of Emerson, on the limitations of Dewey and Santayana. You will find other pages less adequate: as the discussions of Whitman, Melville, Poe and Dreiser. What interests me most in *The Golden Day* is not its assemblage of interpretations, but its focus.

This focus is external. Mr. Mumford is outside his own book. He depicts superbly the Platonic, pagan and mystical glories which in America's Golden Day were called Emerson, Thoreau, Whitman. But they are experientially remote from Mr. Mumford: as remote as Dante and Aquinas. Ideally, of course, we share all greatness and find its recognition in our souls. Yet those medieval worlds were not actually ours: their source, their form and their behavior differ. Mr. Mumford depicts, also, and with no less eloquence, the horrors of the American scene: the barbaric frontier, the Protestant decadence, the tyranny of the machine and of the job, the fallacies of materialism, utilitarianism, experimentalism, pragmatism. But he is outside the experience of these also. When he praises the age of Emerson, there is an aloofness of elegy. When he exhorts the young men, his contemporaries: "Allons. The road is before us!" there is an aloofness of rhetoric. What is the matter with Mr. Mumford?

The matter is that he has considered us, rather than experienced us. He has gone deep to behold our past greatness, our present miseries; but not deep enough to establish the vital connection between them, and between them and himself. America is an organic subject. Mr. Mumford, for all his studies in causation, treats as a series of isolate manifestations, "good" or "bad," "tasteful" or "disgusting," what are really acts of a single spiritual Organism, yet immature, yet basally "in the making." The Golden Day whereof the author so wistfully sings was not a day at all: it was not even a dawn: it was, if you insist on solar terms, *a* dusk of Europe. But only in its ideologies and cultural forms! More accurately, it was a moment in the American childhood when the spirit spoke lyrically, before the whelming demands of body—of nutrition and of growth—plunged America more fully into chaos. The fact that this age was not a Day is plain in its shimmering, surface passage over the American mind: and in the sequence when America transformed the idealism of its transcendentalists and poets into immediate adolescent matters of expansion and of self-indulgence. Mr. Mumford makes Emerson the hero of this "day." Yet if ever a man was a congeries of lovely echoes, of wistful longings, of fleeting and unfleshed intuitions, Emerson was he! His intimations of immortality were almost literally those which the great Wordsworth beheld on the visage of a babe! Emerson *was* such an intimation on America's huge child face. He was our first, unfleshed, undifferentiate glimpse of manhood—of a manhood still very far ahead.

In Whitman this intimation is no longer the tremorous glimpse so well symbolized in Emerson's frail and evanescent prose. It is a roar of adolescence: a true hunger call: no more. Now, note Mr. Mumford's basic misunderstanding of Poe and Melville. These men were the first to try to *flesh* what we might style the Emersonian intuition in American life. Mr. Mumford calls them figures of the twilight. And yet, from the standpoint of a study of the American Organism, they are more advanced than such more successful artists as Whitman and Thoreau. Poe's mystical attitude toward the mechanism and applied science, his marvelous attempt to add a dimensional sense to the inherited experience of life; and Melville's tragic effort to wed God and whaling—these are the first organic *acts* after the childhood intimations of the men whom Mr. Mumford esteems as makers of our Noon. And the author fails to recognize them, because he has no organic experience in America to guide him. He is in love with the gesture, the dream, the childhood faëry of our past: yet he rejects the *body*—our present interim of the Machine and of the romanticisms of the Machine—whereby alone this promise from our past may be organized into a living future.

Therefore, finally, his book brings the flavor of a plaint: his envoi is wistful and vague, his call to future action has no ring. For American future spiritual action must rise organically from the facts of our hideous present, since these facts are an insuperable sequence from our past ideals. Mr. Mumford, in this book, is a man sincerely, prophetically in love with the sweet spirit of childhood; yet turning from the physical, often bestial process whereby alone the child can grow in order to express that spirit. When the child America lisps purities half understood, Mr. Mumford blesses. But when the child America gulps food, wallows in mud, slugs and robs comrades, adventures, bullies, cheats—Mr. Mumford merely scolds.
—WALDO FRANK, "Dusk and Dawn" (1926), *In the American Jungle*, 1937, pp. 174–77

JAMES T. FARRELL
From "The Faith of Lewis Mumford" (1940/1945)
The League of Frightened Philistines
1945, pp. 109–10, 122–27

Lewis Mumford's master has been Patrick Geddes, a town planner, nature lover, an educator, a man of good will, and sponsor of "the scientific doctrine of civism." Geddes styled himself an "ideopraxist," that is, a practical idealist. He acknowledged his intellectual debt to nineteenth-century French feudal thinkers; in fact, he defended De Maistre, De Bonald, and Le Play from the charge of being reactionary. In essence a reformist, he had grandiose dreams of a new age of regional culture, beautiful cities, and a happy humanity, which, he argued, would pay dividends to the capitalists and to society as a whole. This new age was more than a dream to him, for he saw concrete proofs of it in the life of his time. Mumford and Geddes have dreamed the same dreams.

In 1915, when Europe was being torn apart in a bloody carnage, Patrick Geddes, in *Cities in Evolution*, wrote about "the nobler cities of a not necessarily distant future" and proclaimed "the neotechnic order so plainly arising in other lands—Norway being the best example, as having no paleo-technic development." He found real evidence of the new era, "Eutopia," in the Kaiser's Germany. Mumford saw the same "Eutopia" in the Germany of the Weimar Republic.

Lewis Mumford was in Germany in 1932, precisely at the time when Germany was being split asunder by the threat of civil war. During this period the Nazis were invading working-class districts of German cities and there were frequent weekend riots. National Socialism was already in power in Prussia and Thuringia. The Weimar Republic was a vanishing shadow, which Brüning's decree laws had been unable to save. Germany's reformist holiday was over. Returning to America, Mumford wrote an article, "Notes on Germany," for *The New Republic* (October 26, 1932). What did he see in the Germany of 1932? He discovered that the German people were enjoying excellent health and that "the cult of the sun was the symbol of an almost religious revival that had taken place in Germany since the war." He lauded the civic improvement and the growth of interest in sports and physical culture. Even a National Socialist had, in his pre-Nazi days, written a book about naked women that "gave a deep impulse both to the culture of the body and its comely development." He stated that "the new Germany" had "utilized all the latent good of the old Germany." ⟨. . .⟩

Mumford's conception of society as an organism provides the rationale for his ideas of social reform. Social problems are viewed as analogous to physical and/or mental illness. A social disease is the result of the mal-functioning of a member. If a part is out of gear, the whole is affected. The classes and social groups are all functions of one another.[1] Any function that is working anarchistically is destroying social integration. It focuses the problem of integration. The concept of the reform flowing from these assumptions is that of adaptation. Adaptation is the typical reformist's concept of social change. Society, the social and economic structure of society, is given. There must be adaptation to that which is given. The same concept can be described by the word *reintegration*. The ailing member must be restored to its proper function in the organism. The split-off part must again be put back into the whole. Thus is social harmony attained. The functional conception of society is substituted for the class conception. The assumption that society is an organism removes the hypothesis of economic determinism from its central position as a primary premise in the analysis of history and of social problems. Instead of looking on society as a structure organized in terms of productive relationships and economic interests, you see society as a whole. The community has precedence over the class. Here we have a secularized modern version of De Maistre's ideal of the harmonious society: in place of God, vague ethical notions are substituted.

Now, Mumford goes a step further in confusion. Now, we must begin making ourselves "organic" in order to make society "organic." And this means we must "think" like Mumford.

This spirit pervades Mumford's ideas of social reforms. He has postulated a "system" termed "basic communism." "A normalized mode of consumption is the basis of a rationalized mode of production," he says in *Technics and Civilization*. "Basic Communism" proposes a normalized basis of consumption for the entire community, which would set the groundwork for the planning of production. Thus does he offer a solution for the problems generated by the functioning of capitalist economy—scarcity, unemployment, crises. The fundamental problem posed by a capitalist economy is seen as that of establishing a higher standard of consumption rather than one concerning a change in ownership of the means of production. "The problem presses for solution; but in one sense it has already been solved." How? For almost a century, widows, orphans, and others have been living well from insurance payments and stock dividends. This *rentier* class has produced "a Milton, a Shelley, a Darwin, a Ruskin . . ." If this plan is extended to the whole of society, so that all become one *rentier* class, the problem will be solved by the productive system. Society will pay everyone a kind of alimony. A basic income will be normalized. Production will be planned to satisfy the wants purchasable with this income. Competition for more goods will be centered around getting more than is procurable with the basic income. Thus will end the deadly "peaceful warfare" of competition. Everyone will be integrated into the harmonious community. Mumford does not specify how this plan is to be put into operation but says that it would be a tremendous human gain if it were. ⟨. . .⟩

The role that Marxists ⟨. . .⟩ have given to political action in social change, Mumford attributes to an unspecified process of evolution. Instead of men and political parties and classes acting to effect change, changes have just been taking place of themselves. This "post-Marxian" view is, to Mumford, superior to Marxian eschatology. However, Mumford is himself an eschatologist. Mumford will have no traffic with the Marxian concept of the withering away of the state. But what he has actually believed in and has promulgated amounts to nothing less than the prediction that capitalism, itself, is withering away. Herein we see why Mumford has been so quixotic concerning the study of the means necessary to achieve his ends. The reason he has been so cavalier about the crucial question of *political power* is now laid bare.

Mumford has written grandiose and well-intentioned plans for a better society. He tells us that these plans must be put into effect. He advocates no concrete political action. Rather, he proposes that the best minds get together and plot the next step for the evolution of the progressive tendency. Such attitudes are at the root of his reformism. This was embodied in his book, *The Culture of Cities*. Reviewers hailed this work as a major contribution to knowledge; it can be more precisely described as the classic of settlement house culture. Mumford and Geddes both have been the prophets of this kind of social reform. It is thus that, in *The Culture of Cities*, he expresses regret because society has neglected to provide adequate meeting halls for the workers, as if that would have been an important contribution to the solution of those political problems that the worker must face. Similarly, Patrick Geddes once applauded the Boy Scout movement, both as the solution of the problem of the wayward boy and as a means of increasing a love of nature among boys. It is in these features of both Mumford and Geddes that we can most clearly discern the influence of Le Play. Given to regrets about the past, Mumford has lamented that the influence of Le Play has not been strongly felt. The basis of that lament was almost removed.

Press dispatches informed us that De Maistre was revived in Petain's France as a leading ideologist. Le Play might have been similarly resurrected. His ideas were made to order for Marshal Petain. The Hero of Verdun tried to substitute for the great words of the French Revolution—Liberty, Fraternity, Equality—those of *work, family, nation.* The trinity of Le Play was *place, work, people* (or *folk*).

Herein we see some of the involutions and implications of Mumford's faith in the organic. To repeat, these are primarily based on a secularization of the Catholic conception of the unity of society in God. And they serve the role of masking the class character of society. The "organic" here is a fog, a mist, a camouflage, concealing the naked and brutal facts of societies, past and present.

Notes

1. This explains why Mumford's thinking has led him so close to contemporary Catholic thinkers, who favor the corporate state, as well as to contemporary totalitarian thinkers. The idea of the corporate state of the Papal encyclicals is, and must be, based on the hypothesis that society is an organism. The corporations then represent the various members of the organism: they are functions of one another. Mumford is also close to the Austrian economist, Othmar Spann, who has helped break the ideological ground for fascism. His system of "universalism" is totalitarianism. He conceives society as an organism. The society that fits best into his system is that of the Middle Ages; it is his ideal society. Like Mumford, Spann criticizes bourgeois economists for having atomized economics. He substitutes the conception of functions for that of causal relationships. Like Mumford, he stresses the necessity of seeing events and phenomena as qualities rather than as quantities, as if these categories were strictly polar opposites. In his system of universalism, he establishes a hierarchy of functions; Mumford implicitly also has the idea of a hierarchy of functions as the means for distributing consumer goods and for organizing the flow of social energies. For a while Spann was in favor with the Nazis and was invited to Berlin not long after Hitler came to power. However, he fell into disfavor.

ROGER STARR
From "Mumford's Utopia"
Commentary, June 1976, pp. 59–62

Mumford's ideas have been effectual primarily in the fields of architecture and city and town planning, where he has attracted the most public attention. Yet despite having won gold medals from both the Royal Institute of British Architects and the British Town Planning Institute, he is neither architect nor planner. Nor, since he has never held governmental office, has he had the chance to impose his ideas on even a single city, as many other non-architects and non-planners have managed to do, Robert Moses and Edward Logue coming to mind at once.

Mumford's influence on his time, then, has been largely indirect, exerted through the impact of his writing on those with immediate responsibility for shaping the urban world, or, perhaps more relevantly, on the educated public whose ideas define the area within which planners and developers may act. Here again, Mumford presents something of an anomaly. For those writings of his which specifically discuss architecture, structures, and the nature of government sponsorship of buildings are the aspect of his work that he himself holds in the lowest esteem, as compared with his "serious" books on art and social history, technological development, and literary activity.

Nevertheless, it seems likely that many who revere

Mumford do so not on the basis of those "profound" and on the whole boring works, but because of the practical criticism which he himself takes most lightly, and which he has chosen to omit entirely from his current book ⟨*Findings and Keepings*⟩, as well as from its immediate predecessor, *Interpretations and Forecasts, 1922–1972.* (That volume pointedly was described on its jacket as containing all of Mumford's "essential thought.") What Mumford does publish in these volumes is difficult to read, which is probably a good thing for his public esteem. For the direction of Mumford's "essential thought" runs counter to the goal which most of his admiring readers cherish (and mistakenly think, from reading his practical criticism, that *he* cherishes)—the survival of the cities in something like their present form, with their major shortcomings removed and their beauties emphasized.

Mumford's practical criticism consists mainly of essays on architecture and related problems of urban design and planning which have appeared over the years in the *New Yorker.* Whatever Mumford's opinion of them, they are deservedly popular as architectural criticism, combining basic affection for their subject with sensible judgments about specific characteristics and managing to convey the experience of a building to even the least well-prepared reader. A brief review of how Mumford operates in this area might begin with his scrutiny of the contemporary use of glass as the exterior surface for high-rise office buildings. Glass, in Mumford's view, is used perversely for such a purpose, and represents the triumph of technological abandon over good sense. He admits that a building clad in glass offers a previously unobtainable range of architectural effects—no one has written more glowingly than Mumford about the glass walls of the UN Secretariat building in New York—but he insists that the several consequent costs overwhelm them. In an essay entitled "The Case against Modern Architecture," Mumford explains that the interior space of a glass-walled building is inevitably irrational. The transparency seems to promise contact with sunlight and fresh air, but it produces quite the opposite effect: layers of hermetically sealed cubes. Mumford also complains about the lack of walls against which to arrange furniture and the lack of privacy which the glass imposes.[1]

Yet for all that Mumford seems to be talking about a technological issue in his discussion of glass walls, what he really objects to is the office buildings clothed by those walls. Indeed, his dislike of modern office buildings antedates by far the advent of the glass wall. As early as 1924, when he published *Sticks and Stones* (described by him as a study of American architecture and civilization), Mumford was hurling invectives at the "skyscrapers" which were then attracting European attention as glorious examples of the same naive American culture which had already produced Negro spirituals and hot dogs. As with his complaint about glass, Mumford's criticism of skyscrapers was ostensibly founded on the objective shortcomings of these big buildings: their inhuman scale, their heavy shadows, their siting difficulties which made it impossible for observers on the ground to perceive their dramatic perpendiculars without interference from other structures, and, finally, their disruption of the harmony and integrity of all other adjacent buildings.

In both of these cases, the fundamental reason for Mumford's antipathy lay not in anything having to do with matters of technology or form; it was a question of function. The truth is that Mumford does not like office buildings because he does not like offices, and he dislikes offices because he dislikes the people who work there, and he dislikes office people because he dislikes the kind of work they do, or the life that they represent to him. That life, in a word, is not "organic." ⟨. . .⟩

The central problems in Mumford's thought can perhaps be summarized in his attitude toward the Brooklyn Bridge, a structure whose beauty has repeatedly engaged his imagination and inspired his awe. He has written enthusiastically about the thrilling curves of the four great suspension cables and the roadway itself, and about the unique emphasis, in this bridge, on the suspending elements in contrast with the roadway. For Mumford, this equalizing tension between suspending and suspended elements dramatizes, above all, the conquest of gravity through pure imagination. Yet in his play about the bridge which appears in *Findings and Keepings*, the vast powers of mind which went into solving the technical problems presented by the bridge's construction are set in gloomy contrast to its builders' ignorance and conceptual poverty when it came to questions of value or the philosophical *meaning* of technology. Thus, the character in the play who seems most closely to represent the author's point of view chides the bridge's visionary builders for their avoidance of questions of final value which, he says, must come before the achievement of technics.

It is tempting to argue this question with Mumford; the question, that is, of whether the conscious goals of society, its basic conceptions, shape its technology, or whether the technology shapes the articulation of its goals. But no one living in the city of the Brooklyn Bridge today would accord an urgent priority to this ponderous discussion. The simple fact is that no matter how evil the Paleotechnic era may now appear to Mumford, *it* is what made the bridge possible. One cannot disengage from the incidental horrors of the Paleotechnic era the wrought-iron wires (the first used in construction) and the compressed-air submarine caissons (powered by steam engines) in which the foundation diggers worked. The urban social environment is what made possible the human coordination, assembled the resources, and provided the nourishment to keep the labor force working through the twelve years during which the bridge was built. Finally, the continued survival today of that glorious artifact—the bridge itself—depends on the grubby business of keeping its cables and girders painted, and this humble maintenance procedure in turn depends on the wealth of the municipality, and this in turn depends on a continuing balance between the wealth of the city and its expenses.

The trouble with Mumford's work is that it is in the end self-defeating. Failing to distinguish immediate necessities, and refusing to answer present questions in a search for more "profound" answers, it sows a fatal confusion between the needs of this world and the illusory possibilities of recapturing or bringing to birth a Golden Age.

Notes

1. To these criticisms, two new ones might be added. Glass-sheathed buildings offer a potential fire hazard because the unopenable windows make ventilation dependent on a system of mechanical blowers and ducts, extraordinarily well adapted to spreading smoke throughout a building while shielding its source. Secondly, though designers have become very imaginative in curving the walls of glass sheathing, technicians have so far been less successful in calculating how the panes are to be kept in place. Falling glass sheets have become a deadly menace in several cities.

JOHN L. HESS
"A Mumford Chronicle"

Hudson Review, Spring 1980, pp. 126–30

The notion that History is shaped by great minds is not flattering to them, for if it were true, then genius would bear the blame for "the crimes, follies and misfortunes of mankind." It seems more plausible that History chooses for its standard-bearers those thinkers who appear to justify turns it has already taken. Thus John Maynard Keynes has dominated the dismal science for nearly half a century ("We are all Keynesians now," President Nixon exclaimed), but the fiddling with the currency that is now identified with Keynes preceded his ideological triumph, and one still would be hard put to cite a single government that has actually practiced his teaching. Thus also it is evident that Henry Ford, a man of limited intellectual depth, had vastly greater influence on our society than did Lewis Mumford. But how much finer a world would we live in had it been the other way around! That gloomy reflection strikes one again and again in reading almost everything written by Mumford over the last half century and more. Are we now obsessed with the rot of our cities, the cancer of our suburbs, the dreariness of our buildings, the pollution of our environment? Mumford had warned us, elegantly, logically, passionately and in good time. We heard him, and went on with our folly. Yet to read Mumford is, in the end, uplifting. The problems he has posed are still with us, and his answers are as fresh and valid as ever. Further, it is life-enhancing to meet a man of letters, a Renaissance master of our own time, a disappointed but ever hopeful utopian who could write to a lover (in 1930): "Damn utopias! Life is better than utopia!"

My Works and Days: A Personal Chronicle is Mumford's twenty-seventh book, a cornucopia of diary notes and letters and poems, including an early poetic memoir. It no doubt was drawn from materials the author used in writing his autobiography—a work he describes as being as candid as Rousseau's, and which he has therefore withheld from publication but may soon release. This one, then, must hold us, and whet our appetite. Another aim of the author, and a pardonable one, is to demonstrate that he was not "only" an urbanist and critic of architecture, as readers of *The New Yorker* and of many of his books remember him, but also a critic and historian of American art and letters, of morals and civilization. And if *The New Yorker* was the platform that gave him his widest audience, it should be noted in passing that his intellectual growth began and flourished in "little magazines" of the 1920s, notably the *Dial*, the *Sociological Review* of London, and the *American Caravan*.

Mumford was born in New York on October 19, 1895, to a cultivated family of modest circumstances. A bookish boy, he attended City College and Columbia but left before graduation, and although he later taught for many years at Stanford, the University of Pennsylvania, and M.I.T., his approach to academe was always quizzical; it never met his Attic standards. He grew up in an age when the foundations of the arts and sciences were being shattered by explosive discoveries: atomic radiation, the theory of relativity, cubism, Freudianism, Bloomsday. The temper of the times identified progress with change and change with rejection of the past, but somehow, Mumford escaped both the optimism of the technocrats and the nihilism nurtured by the bloodbath of World War I. In a juvenile note at age twenty he wrote, "The greatest task of the Superman is to prevent the human race from committing suicide." Young Mumford fell under the spell of Patrick

Geddes, the British utopian and "urban ecologist" whom the writer forever would call "my master." Geddes in turn hailed from Victorian humanists like Ebenezer Howard, William Morris, and John Ruskin, who fought the ravages of nineteenth-century industrialization. Geddes, Mumford reminds us, "distrusted sweeping innovations and clean slates." The phrase is, of course, aimed at the hubris of the opposing, and victorious, school led by Le Corbusier, whose famous plan to raze Paris and replace it by an airy forest of high-rise slabs on stilts has been in part realized at La Défense outside Paris, in Brasilia and in many other modernist failures. In *The New Yorker* in 1957, Mumford penned a devastating critique of Le Corbusier's much emulated "masterpiece," the fearfully costly and foolishly designed Unity House at Marseilles, an uncomfortable luxury dwelling subsidized by the state. He said Le Corbusier's plans for Paris "unconsciously symbolize the inflation of money, the deflation of human hopes, and what one must perhaps call the 'normalization of the irrational.'"

> This last is a characteristic of an age that is busily engaged in the exploitation of atomic energy without first pausing to find a safe way to dispose of its lethal peacetime by-products: an age that in order to insure abundant crops is recklessly poisoning with deadly insecticides and pesticides those who consume the food that has been "scientifically" so saved.

Note (I digress, but to read Mumford is to cover the whole sweep of our contemporary experience) that the foregoing appeared six years before Rachel Carson's *The Silent Spring*, which awoke the country to the ravages of DDT. And the reference to nuclear wastes was made twenty-two years before the subject reached the national consciousness in the wake of the accident at Three Mile Island. Nor was this Mumford's first attack on atomic folly. That came with Hiroshima. Mumford had shortly before lost his only son in combat, and a loving souvenir of the child forms a chapter of *My Works and Days*. But a diary note says the news of the annihilation of a Japanese city gave the father an "almost physical nausea." He penned an essay for *The Saturday Review* headed: "Gentlemen: You Are Mad!"

It goes almost without saying that Mumford was an early and eloquent foe of our Vietnam war. He includes here a thunderous open letter to President Johnson in 1965, and the vibrant peace appeal that was his own inaugural address that year as president of the American Academy of Arts and Letters. Like his master Geddes, he was something of a socialist, but in letters as early as 1930, he observed that Marx, "a grand fellow," had failed to apply his analysis to life under a socialist society, and he expressed fear that a revolution would turn into the tyranny that it fought. He went on to campaign for collective security against Hitlerism, and in 1940 he resigned as a contributing editor of *The New Republic* because of the magazine's neutralist stance. A realist about Stalin, he was also, during the war, remarkably reserved in his private comments on Roosevelt and Churchill.

Like his mentor Geddes and unlike Jane Jacobs, Mumford was a believer in planning—indeed, he was a founder of the Regional Planning Association—and he is honored in Britain as one of those who inspired the postwar New Towns movement. Where Geddes and Mumford differed from the prevailing school was in thinking small. They based their prescriptions on the needs of man, for company, for solitude, for exchange, for air. Thus vest-pocket parks and low elevations, not high rises; thus intimate and balanced new towns, not sprawling suburbs. Thus railroads and parkways *between* cities, not, for God's sake, slashing *through* cities. I find myself

flouting Mumford's wish that he be portrayed as far more than a specialist on habitat, because I dipped into this book, as a reader will, while observing the urgent business of the world. As I watched, I was repeatedly reminded that Mumford had said it long before. Do Senators and soldiers calmly debate the mathematics of mutual destruction? Mumford told them thirty-three years ago that they were mad. Do journalists discover that we need electric cars but must improve the batteries? Mumford told them so at least twenty-two years ago. Does the Government persist in spending far more on superhighways than on public transportation, and do the civic fathers of New York prefer a fearfully costly new road to equivalent funds for transit? More than two decades ago, fighting one of the highway projects that would ravage his birthplace, Mumford wrote: "The first lesson we have to learn is that a city exists, not for the constant passage of motorcars, but for the care and culture of men." Does the Government order that thermostats be set at less comfortable levels to save fuel? Mumford long ago denounced the fearful waste of energy in the glass slabs that are still rising everywhere, emulating Mies van der Rohe's "elegant monuments of nothingness."

> The best contributions to metropolitan architecture today have the exquisite appropriateness of a fine meal bestowed upon a prisoner who is to be executed next morning. As with so many other irrational phenomena of our day, like the building of bigger and better nuclear bombs or of wilder and more whimsical counterfeits of motorcars, people have come to regard the pathological as normal, and the more senseless a proposal is in terms of vital human needs, the more likely they are to give hundreds of millions of dollars for its execution.

He explains why:

> Unfortunately, there is a huge vested interest in raising hell with nature, and there is very little money—in fact, none at all—in letting well enough alone.

That 1959 essay ends:

> If the process goes on, we will wake up one morning to discover that our city has become as helpless and useless as a stranded whale, unable either to swim back to the sea or crawl forward on land. That will be the end—and no jet planes or moon rockets will save us.

I read that passage on the tenth anniversary of man's landing on the moon. On television, Isaac Asimov was saying that civilization would have to colonize space, if it were to survive at all—implying that the earth was no longer a viable habitat. But Mumford is not so despairing. In a 1960 essay he wrote:

> Once we accept the challenge of creating an environment so rich in human resources that no one would willingly leave it even temporarily on an astronautic vacation, we shall alter the whole pattern of human settlement. Ebenezer Howard's dream of garden cities will widen into the prospect of a garden civilization.

The *Times* of London once called him "the Cassandra of modern technology." But the picture that emerges from *My Works and Days* is that of a rich and happy life. As a man of letters, a colleague of Van Wyck Brooks in the revival of pride in nineteenth-century American writing. As a fortunate monogamist, despite tantalizing hints of episodes of romantic pluralism. As a critic friendly to the new art between the wars, to Fernand Leger and Georgia O'Keeffe, but revolted by "the infantilism of Pop Art and the mindless evacuations of the pop artists."

In the great periods [he wrote wistfully to Brooks], more was expected of the people than we expect today: they were expected to make more of an effort to reach the highest level, and evidently had enough of an inward life to respect it and reach it. Perhaps the gap was already widening in Shakespeare's time; but the man in the street nevertheless stayed through the whole performance, even if he didn't understand it completely, instead of demanding that all of it be on the level of the clowns; and this was true in Pepys' time, or in Haydn's, when the chambermaids or the serfs could share the same music, and like it.

Mumford is not anti-modern. He is, on the contrary, enthusiastic about the possibilities of new technology, as exemplified in much of the work of Frank Lloyd Wright (though not the Guggenheim Museum). He is not against functionalism, but he denies the functionalism of Le Corbusier and the Bauhaus. They, he charges, forgot that the function of architecture was to serve man. Speaking of Unity House, he said:

The irrational and the extravagant, the morbidly monumental and the empty formalistic are more in keeping with the tone and temper of this age than buildings that are conceived in human and sensible terms. Architecture is thus in the same state as literature or painting—or politics or motorcars.

As with the rest of us, gloom pervades his recent observation of the passing scene—with all the more reason in that he warned us, time and again. But he loves life too much to despair totally, or to leave it without a smile. On receiving the National Book Award in 1972, he said, "I would die happy if I knew that on my tombstone could be written these words: 'This man was an absolute fool. None of the disastrous things that he reluctantly predicted ever came to pass.'"

There is, unfortunately, no danger that that epitaph will be carved. Disasters that he predicted have come to pass and no doubt will recur. But at least he told us why they were happening, and what must be done to ward them off. Perhaps, if enough of us will listen, there is still time for us to save ourselves.

VLADIMIR NABOKOV

1899–1977

Vladimir Vladimirovich Nabokov, novelist and man of letters, was born in St. Petersburg (Leningrad) on April 23, 1899. The son of a leading member of the liberal Cadet party and of the Kerensky government, Nabokov perforce left Russia in 1919. He attended Trinity College, Cambridge (B.A. 1922), where he studied French and Russian literature, and then lived in Berlin (1923–37) and Paris (1937–40), writing mainly in Russian under the pseudonym "Sirin."

In 1940 Nabokov and his wife and young son moved to the United States; from then on all his novels were written in English, and in 1945 he became an American citizen. Nabokov taught at Wellesley College (1941–48) and was then made a professor of Russian literature at Cornell University (1948–59) until earnings from his writings—in particular *Lolita*—enabled him to retire. In 1959 he moved to Montreux, Switzerland, where he was able to concentrate on his writing and pursue his interest in the study of butterflies. He died in Switzerland in 1977.

Nabokov's first published works were two collections of poetry, *Poems* (1916) and *Two Paths* (1918), which appeared while he was still living in Russia. While at Cambridge he continued to write verse, mostly in Russian but some in English, the Russian poems appearing in *The Rudder*, the leading emigré newspaper in Berlin.

In 1923 two further collections of poems were issued, *The Cluster* and *The Empyrean Path*, followed in 1924 by the publication of Nabokov's first short story; from that point on he worked mainly in prose. His first novel, *Mary* (Germany, 1926; published in the United States in 1970), is about a young Czarist officer living in exile in Berlin who experiences his first love affair; it was followed by a second, *King, Queen, Knave* (Germany, 1928; United States, 1968), a highly stylized account of a young man's affair with his married aunt.

The novel which firmly established Nabokov's reputation as the best of the Russian emigré writers was *The Defense* (Germany, 1930; U.S., 1964), about a chess master who acts as if his own life were a chess game. This was quickly followed by a novella and four novels: *The Eye* (Germany, 1930; U.S., 1965); *Glory* (France, 1932; in London, as *Camera Obscura*, 1936; U.S., 1938); *Despair* (Germany, 1936; U.S., 1966); and *Invitation to a Beheading* (France, 1938; U.S., 1959); these last two were the first to have a worldwide impact. *The Gift* (France, 1937; U.S., 1963) is a pseudo-autobiography about a Russian expatriate in Berlin after World War I, and has often been considered Nabokov's best Russian novel. It was followed by two plays, *The Event* (1938) and *The Waltz Invention* (1938).

Nabokov's first novels in English were *The Real Life of Sebastian Knight* (1941) and *Bend Sinister* (1947); generally these are not considered to rank with his best Russian works. His next novel, however, was more successful, and won something of a *succès de scandale*; this was *Lolita* (1955), the story of Humbert Humbert, a middle-aged emigré, and his sexual obsession with a teenage girl. After this appeared several other novels: *Pnin* (1957), about a Russian teaching at an upstate New York College; *Pale Fire* (1962), a technically elaborate work about an exiled king in a New England college town; and three novels which received rather mixed reviews: *Ada* (1969), *Transparent Things* (1972), and *Look at the Harlequins!* (1974).

Nabokov's stories have been gathered into several collections, and some of his verse appears in *Poems* (1959) and *Poems and Problems* (1971). His major critical works are *Nikolai Gogol* (1944), a book-length study of that writer, and a four-volume commentary on his own translation of Pushkin's *Eugene Onegin*, published in 1964 and revised in 1977. *Conclusive Evidence* (1951; revised as *Speak, Memory*, 1966) and *Strong Opinions* (1973) contain, respectively, autobiographical sketches and his collected answers to journalists' questions.

Personal

On February 17, 1968, Martin Esslin came to see me at my hotel in Montreux with the object of conducting an interview for *The New York Times Book Review*. The following letter awaited him downstairs.

"Welcome! I have devoted a lot of pleasurable time to answering in writing the questions sent to me by your London office. I have done so in a concise, stylish, printable form. Could I please ask you to have my answers appear in *The New York Times Book Review* the way they are prepared here? (Except that you may want to interrupt the longer answers by several inserted questions). That convenient method has been used to mutual satisfaction in interviews with *Playboy, The Paris Review, Wisconsin Studies, Le Monde, La Tribune de Genève*, etc. Furthermore, I like to see the proofs for checking last-minute misprints or possible little flaws of fact (dates, places). Being an unusually muddled speaker (a poor relative of the writer) I would like the stuff I prepared in typescript to be presented as direct speech on my part, whilst other statements which I may stammer out in the course of our chats, and the gist of which you might want to incorporate in The Profile, should be used, please, obliquely or paraphrastically, without any quotes. Naturally, it is for you to decide whether the background material should be kept separate in its published form from the question-and-answer section.

I am leaving the attached material with the concierge because I think you might want to peruse it before we meet. I am very much looking forward to seeing you. Please give me a ring when you are ready."

The text given below is that of the typescript. The interview appeared in *The New York Times Book Review* on May 12, 1968.

How does VN live and relax?

A very old Russian friend of ours, now dwelling in Paris, remarked recently when she was here, that one night, forty years ago, in the course of a little quiz at one of her literary parties in Berlin, I, being asked where I would like to live, answered, "In a large comfortable hotel." That is exactly what my wife and I are doing now. About every other year she and I fly (she) or sail (she and I), back to our country of adoption but I must confess that I am a very sluggish traveler unless butterfly hunting is involved. For that purpose we usually go to Italy where my son and translator (from Russian into English) lives; the knowledge of Italian he has acquired in the course of his main career (opera singing) assists him, incidentally, in checking some of the Italian translations of my stuff. My own Italian is limited to *"avanti"* and *"prego"*.

After waking up between six and seven in the morning, I write till ten-thirty, generally at a lectern which faces a bright corner of the room instead of the bright audiences of my professorial days. The first half-hour of relaxation is breakfast with my wife, around eight-thirty, and the creaming of our mail. One kind of letter that goes into the wastepaper basket at

once, with its enclosed stamped envelope and my picture, is the one from the person who tells me he has a large collection of autographs (Somerset Maugham, Abu Abdul, Karen Korona, Charles Dodgson, Jr., etc.) and would like to add my name, which he misspells. Around eleven, I soak for twenty minutes in a hot bath, with a sponge on my head and a wordsman's worry in it, encroaching, alas, upon the nirvana. A stroll with my wife along the lake is followed by a frugal lunch and a two-hour nap after which I resume my work until dinner at seven. An American friend gave us a Scrabble set in Cyrillic alphabet, manufactured in Newtown, Conn.; so we play Russian *skrebl* for an hour or two after dinner. Then I read in bed—periodicals or one of the novels that proud publishers optimistically send me. Between eleven and midnight begins my usual fight with insomnia. Such are my habits in the cold season. Summers I spend in the pursuit of lepidoptera on flowery slopes and mountain screes; and, of course, after my daily hike of fifteen miles or more, I sleep even worse than in winter. My last resort in this business of relaxation is the composing of chess problems. The recent publication of two of them (in *The Sunday Times* and *The Evening News* of London) gave me more pleasure, I think, than the printing of my first poems half a century ago in St. Petersburg.

VN's social circle?

The tufted ducks and crested grebes of Geneva Lake. Some of the nice people in my new novel. My sister Elena in Geneva. A few friends in Lausanne and Vevey. A steady stream of brilliant American intellectuals visiting me in the riparian solitude of a beautifully reflected sunset. A Mr. Van Veen who travels down from his mountain chalet every other day to meet a dark lady, whose name I cannot divulge, on a street corner that I glimpse from my mammoth-tusk tower. Who else? A Mr. Vivian Badlook.

VN's feelings about his work?

My feelings about my work are, on the whole, not unfriendly. Boundless modesty and what people call "humility" are virtues scarcely conducive to one's complacently dwelling upon one's own work—particularly when one lacks them. I see it segmented into four stages. First comes meditation (including the accumulation of seemingly haphazard notes, the secret arrowheads of research); then the actual writing, and rewriting, on special index cards that my stationer orders for me: "special" because those you buy here come lined on both sides, and if, in the process of writing, a blast of inspiration sweeps a card onto the floor, and you pick it up without looking, and go on writing, it may happen—it has happened—that you fill in its underside, numbering it, say, 107, and then cannot find your 103 which hides on the side, used before. When the fair copy on cards is ready, my wife reads it, checking it for legibility and spelling, and has it transferred onto pages by a typist who knows English; the reading of galleys is a further part of that third stage. After the book is out, foreign rights come into play. I am trilingual, in the proper sense of writing, and not only speaking, three languages (in that sense practically all the writers I personally know or knew in America, including a babel of paraphrasts, are strictly monolinguists). *Lolita* I have translated myself in Russian (recently published in New York by Phaedra, Inc.); but otherwise I am able to control and correct only the French translations of my novels. That process entails a good deal of wrestling with booboos and boners, but on the other hand allows me to reach my fourth, and final, stage—that of rereading my own book a few months after the original printing. What judgment do I then pronounce? Am I still satisfied with my work? Does the afterglow of achievement correspond to the foreglow of conception? It should and it does.—VLADIMIR NABOKOV, *Strong Opinions*, 1973, pp. 108–11

'To borrow and to borrow and to borrow . . . as the Bard said, with that cold in his head,' hack writer Quilty tells Humbert, who has tracked him down to his baroque Pavor [Latin: 'fear'] Manor, where he kills Quilty for his abuses of language as well as for his misuse of Lolita. Nabokov in conversation toyed with language continuously; and, though he worked slowly and carefully on his prose, his written puns must have come to him quickly and easily. Two examples: when my wife and I visited Montreux in 1970 Nabokov was most interested to know if my classes at Northwestern University had been disrupted by demonstrations. No, nothing very dramatic, I replied, apart from one male student who expressed his disapproval of the war in Vietnam by calling me a eunuch. 'Oh, no, Alfred, you misunderstood him,' Nabokov said quickly. 'He called you "a unique".' 'My classroom problems are not political,' I continued. I told him about a nun who sat in the back row of one of my lecture courses, and who one day complained after class that a couple near her were always spooning. 'Sister,' I had said, 'in these troubled times we should be grateful if that's all they were doing'; and I related this to Nabokov rather smugly, proud of what I deemed to be my quick wit. 'Ohhh,' moaned Nabokov, mourning my lost opportunity, clapping his hand to his head in mock anguish. 'You should have said, "Sister, be grateful that they were not forking."'

The brilliance of at least the latter pun reinforces one's sense of that aura of invincibility and absolute authority which Nabokov projected so successfully in his many prefaces, interviews and letters to the editor (see his *Strong Opinions*, 1973). Yet the protective coloration of that persona (personae?), characterized by some as 'cold', 'arrogant', or 'imperial', is in a way unfortunate, inasmuch as it allowed no hint of the gentleness and sweetness that Nabokov, ensconced in Montreux, extended to casual visitors, friends, and, of course, to his family. Sympathetic readers of Nabokov should not find this surprising, given the authenticity of the filial love and tenderness expressed in so many of his works: *The Gift* (1938), *Speak, Memory*, and *Pale Fire* (1962), where John Shade observes that his homely and gentle daughter, Hazel, subsequently a suicide, had been cast in the school play not as a fairy or elf but 'as Mother Time,/A bent charwoman with slop pail and broom,/And like a fool I sobbed in the men's room'. Or the awkward overtures made by Pnin (1957) to his surrogate son, Victor (the gift of a football to an unathletic boy); the anguish of widower Adam Krug in *Bend Sinister* (1947), when he learns that his young son has been murdered by the State; the anxieties of the Russian widow who has not been told yet that her son has died in 'Breaking the News' (1935), the émigré precursor of 'Signs and Symbols' (1948), whose desperately hopeful parents refuse to read the deathly coded messages

alluded to in the story's title; or the grief of the father for his dead son in 'Christmas' (1924), a very early tale arrayed in that concluding volume, *Details of a Sunset*.

How fitting that Nabokov, whose love for his father shines from so many pages, should have as *his* principal translator his own son, Dmitri (nine books in English, *Transparent Things* into Italian). And 'translation' may well be the central metaphor for what happens in every act of human speech, in every (imperfect?) attempt to communicate and interpret the word and the world. The fantastic verbal games of *Pale Fire* certainly suggest as much, as did Nabokov's almost fanatical devotion to his theory and practice of absolutely literal and utilitarian verse translation, 'beauty' sacrificed to accuracy, his only formal religious belief. By the time the novel's title passage from *Timon of Athens* (Act IV, Scene 3) has been translated from English to Zemblan and reversed into English again, the sun and the moon have exchanged genders, Shakespeare's phrase 'pale fire' has disappeared altogether, and we are indeed in the dark ('I live like Timon in his cave,' says Kinbote), asked to confront and contemplate the mysteries of identity and communication and perception. The brilliant fun—pointless or off-putting to lazy, complacent readers—here adumbrates fundamental concerns.

Because of the intensity of his love for his wife and his father, whose liberal ideals he shared, the author of *Pale Fire* could himself translate experience poorly. As jurist, editor and journalist, V. D. Nabokov was a notably active foe of anti-Semitism. It was nevertheless unusual for someone in his 'set' to marry a Jewish woman, as his son did in Germany in 1925. Young Nabokov was thus at least doubly sensitive to the perniciousness of anti-Semitism. He would tolerate neither insults nor the blandest of innuendoes. Subtle protests are scattered throughout his American works. The class list of forty names at Lo's school, an American archetype memorized by Humbert and interpolated in his text, includes 'Flashman, Irving'. Humbert offers brief comments on several of the children, concluding with 'Irving, for whom I am sorry.' Why is he sorry for him? 'Poor Irving,' answered Nabokov, 'he is the only Jew among all those Gentiles.'—ALFRED APPEL, JR., "Remembering Nabokov," *Vladimir Nabokov: A Tribute*, ed. Peter Quennell, 1980, pp. 21–23

General

This is Nabokov's moment; Nabokov just now is king over that battered mass society called contemporary fiction. And he is king not only because of *Ada*—truly royal pleasures!—but also because he does not belong to any country but his own. *We* call him "king"—he sees nothing in political relationships, not even the mythical ones to which his genius lends itself. Ours is an age so dominated by politics, historical "necessity," the seeming total reality of social and racial conflict, that Nabokov stands out just now because he has no country but himself. He is the only refugee who could have turned statelessness into absolute strength. The penniless have-not fleeing the Crimea in 1919 has turned out to be, in his blessedly unconventional, unyielding terms, the true possesser. The torments of so many decent and even talented Soviet writers in the Hell of total obedience contrast so ironically with the freedom of our *barín*—the last and by no means the smallest of the aristocrats who made Russian literature *international*. And Nabokov's imaginary realm puts his own readers to shame, for *they* are still in bondage to actual states and cruel political abstractions.

Is Fiction the only true freedom? Who lives by a "fiction"—the slaves of political "reality" or the stateless exile luxuriating in his own imagination? And where, in this ever crueler treadmill of "progress," are *we* to find the comfort of being at home with ourselves except by escaping from fictions into Fiction? Ours is a tragic generation, for at our best we want to raise everybody, yet never has this essentially religious idea been so violated by the arrogant exclusions of politics as well as by the aggressiveness of political language.

So we who are not Nabokov, who must perhaps remain in bondage to all those "realities" that genius is right to scorn, must first of all salute him for being *free*. In an age of total propaganda for the total state, of a coercion that rests on forms of power that require another kind of genius even to understand, in the age of "society" incarnate and of its only possible hero, The Totally Obedient Man, Nabokov the Russian-American lives in Switzerland, writes in his own delightful space-time, and so ends by receiving our astonishment even more than our homage.—ALFRED KAZIN, *TriQ*, Winter 1970, pp. 364–65

Vladimir Nabokov's most recent novel, on one of its last pages, invites us, "Imagine me, an old gentleman, a distinguished author, gliding rapidly on my back, in the wake of my outstretched dead feet, first through that gap in the granite, then over a pinewood, then along misty water meadows, and then simply between marges of mist, on and on, imagine that sight!" This man had imagined death so often, from Luzhin the chessmaster's fall into a chasm of "dark and pale squares . . . at the instant when icy air gushed into his mouth" to Cincinnatus C.'s false beheading ("A spinning wind was picking up and whirling: dust, rags, chips of painted wood, bits of gilded plaster, pasteboard bricks, posters; an arid gloom fleeted") and to the reported demise of Mrs. Richard F. Schiller, née Dolores Haze, yclept Lolita, while "giving birth to a stillborn girl, on Christmas Day 1952, in Gray Star," and on to the death by gunshot of the poet John Shade and by "time-and-pain" of Van Veen—Nabokov had imagined death so often, so colorfully and variously and searchingly, that we felt him to be exempt, having already passed through, into that Switzerland he inhabited as a chocolate-box province of immortality, the last and most playful of his exiles. His death, at the ripe age of seventy-eight, comes too soon, too coarsely—an ugly footnote to a shimmering text, reality's thumbprint on the rainbow.

Posterity's judgment can sort out the best: in English, *Lolita*, perhaps, and, in Russian, *The Gift*. What matters now is that the least of his writings offered a bygone sort of delight: a sorcerer's scintillant dignity made of every sentence a potentially magic occasion. He wanted the reader to share his extraordinary intimations; this generosity gave even his scholarly dissertations and diatribes a certain spaciousness, a giddying other dimension. He lived in the world, and more peripatetically and traumatically than many of us, yet in his art declined to submit to the world; rather, he asked that the world submit to the curious, spotty evidence of its own mimetics, its streaks of insane tenderness, its infinitely ingenious interior markings. Few minds so scientific have deigned to serve the gods of fancy; with his passion for precision and for the complex design, he mounted for display the crudest, most futile lurchings of the human heart—lust, terror, nostalgia. The violence and violent comedy of his novels strike us, in the main, as merely descriptive, the way the violences of geology are. He saw from a higher altitude, from the top of the continents he had had to put behind him.

Though some of his asides sounded arrogant, and even peevish, his life in its actions demonstrated immense resilience and a robust optimism. Few men who have lost so much have complained so little. He brought to America the body of a forty-one-year-old man of genius in his native language, but offered no excuse of exhaustion; the same active mind that entertained his insomnia with the invention of chess puzzles now turned to inventing himself anew, as an American writer. That he succeeded, and taught us new ways to use our language and to experience our milieu, is perhaps less remarkable than his willingness to try, when a hundred college Slavic Languages Departments held shelter against the raging of the strange democratic culture whose uncodified quirks swarmed about him. On page 53 of *Lolita*, as Humbert Humbert's love-fever comes to a boil, there is a sudden list of forty names, beginning

Angel, Grace
Austin, Floyd
Beale, Jack

and ending

Williams, Ralph
Windmuller, Louise.

It is, the author explains, "a poem, a poem, forsooth!" It is one of Lolita's class lists; it is, with the odd chiming of its relentless alphabetization of fuzzy, budding souls, the class list all Americans have been part of. We have sat in those classes, Nabokov had not; yet it was he who put one into literature, along with so many other comic, correct details of his adopted "lovely, trustful, dreamy, enormous country." His patriotism won him few friends in our literary establishment, but it gave his American novels the fervor of the explicit. His most gracious compliment to the United States was to merge it, in *Ada*, with the Russia of his memory to make one paradisiacal Antiterra.

His prose was festive, though his characters were doomed. Now he has joined them, in that state he so often imagined—sometimes as the blackest of blacknesses and at other times as a transformation as harmless and amusing as that from chrysalis to butterfly. In his youthful novella *The Eye*, the hero shoots himself and reports, "Some time later, if one can speak here of time at all, it became clear that after death human thought lives on by momentum." Nabokov's momentum originated at the beginning of the century and should continue to its end and beyond. Gentleman, aesthete, metaphysician, wit: the words to describe him have an old-fashioned ring. The power of the imagination is not apt soon to find another champion of such vigor. He was one of the last delegates from the nineteenth century; he takes with him the secret of an undiscourageable creativity, he leaves behind a resplendent oeuvre.—JOHN UPDIKE, "Notes and Comment," *NY*, July 18, 1977, pp. 21–22

Works

NOVELS ORIGINALLY IN RUSSIAN

In *Mashenka*, the first novel written by Nabokov, in 1925, the central concern is the expected arrival in Berlin of a girl named Mashenka who has been allowed to leave the Soviet Union. This is simply a variation on the themes of memory and return, with the difference that in *Mashenka* the past is traveling to Berlin. The epigraph to the novel is from Chapter One of *Eugene Onegin*: "*Remembering romances of former years,/ remembering former love.*"

The novel is built on the simple and time-honored principle of the Grand Hotel grouping: a number of people living in a single hotel, rooming-house, or dormitory and the—always—complex web of relationships that develops between them.

⟨. . .⟩ because of ⟨its⟩ carefully measured and conveyed

sense of tempo, *Mashenka* may be profitably compared with Hemingway's first short novel *The Sun Also Rises*—which also was published in 1926—particularly in its scenes of quiet stress and oblique intercourse. One Russian critic spoke of the clearly discernible stylistic influence of Bunin, which is, up to a point, true, and one may note as well a certain similarity to Chekhov (the dramatist, not the short-story writer). But such imaginary echoes are merely the analogies inevitably suggested by a work of art that speaks in its own distinct voice, and their application to the novel is in the end the best confirmation of *Mashenka's* originality. Although it is no more a "slice of life" than is *The Sun Also Rises*, *Mashenka* is one of the best portraits of Russian émigré life in Berlin in the 1920's. The sole estimate of *Mashenka* as a major work of art at the time of its appearance, however, was made by the critic A. S. Izgoev, who wrote: "This is a page not only in the biography of a young author, but also in the history of Russian literature, and not merely its émigré branch. *Mashenka* has about it something of the national self-awareness of the Russian intelligentsia." Unfortunately, Izgoev spoils the prophetic thrill of early recognition by going on to discuss the novel in relation to two of Nabokov's favorite authors: Chernyshevsky and Turgenev.—ANDREW FIELD, *Nabokov: His Life in Art*, 1967, pp. 125–29

Korol, Dama, Valet ⟨King, Queen, Knave⟩ was first published in Berlin in 1928. The author's son Dmitri Nabokov has now turned a somewhat revised version of the original into American English.

Half-way through the novel, the narrator ascribes to one of the characters a certain habit of perception. Dreyer's interest in any object, 'animated or not, whose distinctive features he had immediately grasped, or thought he had grasped, gloated over and filed away, would wane with its every subsequent reappearance.' A film of familiarity would settle upon it. 'The bright perception became the habitual abstraction.' At the end of the paragraph this pattern is translated into aesthetic terms, the translator adding his own irony. 'Thus an experienced artist sees only that which is in keeping with his initial concept.' Ironic or not, the generalisation applies to this novel. 'Of all my novels this bright brute is the gayest,' Mr Nabokov writes in a new introduction. The initial concept, it appears, was to write a farce, using material which other writers have been accustomed to treat as tragic. The aim is disengagement, entertaining certain impressions while curbing their importunity. Characters become monsters without losing their banality. Dangerous to themselves, they remain farcical to others.

The pantomime is conducted with the connivance of King Dreyer, Queen Martha and Knave Franz, 'those three court cards, all hearts'. The game consists of miming the procedures of the Love Story (*Anna Karenina*), the Psychological Story (*Madame Bovary*), the Murder Story (any one) and the Bedroom Comedy (any one). 'She was no Emma, and no Anna,' the narrator says of Queen Martha. If a mock-heroic poem bows with elaborate deference to heroic values now, alas, irrelevant, Mr Nabokov's novel performs the same oblique service toward feelings from which he proposes to release himself. These feelings may be consulted in other books. In this novel Mr Nabokov releases himself from the humiliating clamour of well-rounded characters by confining himself to two dimensions: by intention, these court cards are deprived of depth, since depth is the cause of mess.

At one point Dreyer muses about his relation to the world, meaning his relation to certain animate or inanimate objects called Erica, Martha and so on. 'The world stands like a dog, pleading to be played with.' But Dreyer, no longer young, is not prepared to learn new tricks of affection. The reader, in turn, is discouraged from the indulgence of similar banalities, dabbling in a greasy world. He is to look at the world as if its appearances were to be improved by distance and abstraction. 'Nearsightedness is chaste'—a motto for this novel, given in a remarkable scene where the Knave breaks his spectacles and defends himself from the prostitute world. Restored to clear sight, Franz takes his place in the farce, ready for adultery. Martha is already dressed for such occasions. Dreyer, a wealthy salesman dazzled by erotic puppets, is waiting in the wings, horns ready.

The brute is bright, but not as gay as *Lolita*, as funny as *Pnin*, as brilliant as *The Gift*. There are moments in which it seems to aspire to the condition of *Kind Hearts and Coronets*, but the debonair effects are not continuous, effort keeps breaking in. It is common to say that Mr Nabokov's novels are best understood by taking them as dream plays, figments, mirror images. Perhaps the present novel should be read as a form of literary criticism, since the incidents assume the presence of similar incidents in other books, standing between this new fiction and the begging world. Mr Nabokov's book applies the force of practical criticism to the analysis of bourgeois passion. If anything survives the translation into farce, it may be allowed to pass.—DENIS DONOGHUE, *LT*, Oct. 10, 1968, p. 480

For some years now, Vladimir Nabokov has been presenting the pleasant spectacle of a writer expanding at both ends—frontally, from the brow of the present, with each new novel in English, while one by one his Russian novels, in filial translations edited paternally, emerge from behind the hill of the past. In *Glory*, or *Podvig* (The Exploit), as it once was, the final one of these, it is strange, and oddly warming, to find the experienced ironist in one of his first bouts with his own talent and its lifelong preoccupations. With emotion still limpidly trying on its first masks, memory with its jointures melting but still plain, and people still somewhat conventionally islanded in their own solitudes, not yet so clearly caught in the necromancer's palm.

Martin Edelweiss, a half-Swiss Russian boy, closer to his endearingly freckled, tennis-playing, Anglophiliac mother than to the father, from whom she is separated, leaves Yalta with her at the time of the Revolution, after the death of the father and the exhaustion of their means. On their journey to Switzerland and Uncle Henry—a cousin who will support them and eventually marry his mother—Martin has the "classical" first episode with a woman. Sent to Cambridge, he has the classical university experience as seen through the eyes of young novelists of any nationality, is spurned in love, embarks on his kind of Wanderjahr and vanishes, too quickly for the book's duration, into a fantasy-deed which hovers between his wonderlands and his realities. "Even *le sport* is not all," he says, explaining it to a Frenchman in a train. "There are besides—how shall I say?—glory, love, tenderness for the soil, a thousand rather mysterious feelings." For which disappearance the young writer of 1930 has not prepared us as clearly—or even as obscurely—as he thinks.

Yet in this flat summary—recourse of reviewers and rightful cause of rage for all novelists worthy of the name—we have said little of what the book is, then and now. Martin's Cambridge already has an émigré solitude poking out of its casements, toward other books. We almost recognize the family Milanov, whose parlor travels with them from London back to Berlin; their Sonya, who elliptically escapes other lovers as well as Martin but shares with him the dreamland of Zoor; her father hiding his own exploits behind his newspaper articles but trailing the whole flexion of émigré life behind him;

Archibald Moon, silly savant of a Russian language more correct than the native Martin's—and of plumper boys; and even Budnov, that "other" writer, whom Nabokov must twit for merely daring to be. In a scenery already on the way to the familiar mnemonics of travels-between and juxtapoise, all are already here—though in a book truncated in its own effects.

This is the young Nabokov's novel, but by the hazards of life and publication it can never be that for us. As with the young jacket-picture of the author at 34, with its gosling neck, high forehead and lips pursed in proud promise, we know what this book will be like when "it" is old. When it will be rewritten by a stout, longer-nosed balletomane of butterflies, in the style of a prince with the irony to know he is a giraffe. Like Gide, James, and dozens of others (who against howls from Montreux we hasten to say the work of Nabokov in no other way resembles)—like Shakespeare and Chekhov as a matter of fact—he is a very homogeneous writer, in whose pages the same experience, imaginary or life-cognate, is transubstantiated over and over.—HORTENSE CALISHER, *NYTBR*, Jan. 9, 1972, p. 1

Laughter in the Dark and *Lolita* differ tremendously in nearly all respects, not least in the degree of self-awareness of their chief characters, the suggestively named Albinus and the self-designated "Humbert Humbert." Yet Albinus and Humbert stand closer together in a crucially important respect than any other two characters in Nabokov. Both are possessed by a thirst for the infinite, suffer from the metaphysical obsession traditionally named the "desire and pursuit of the whole." Further, both have received a true intuition that the route to the infinite is through attachment to an adorable image or eidolon, yet both blunder, perversely and fatally, by haplessly confounding the image with its illusory reflection or echo in the flesh of a child-woman. The consequence is that they fall, into an enslavement entailing their torture and mockery by demonic men, artists themselves, who as film makers are in the business of degrading images, who as nemeses raised by the obsessions of their victims have (and delight in) the task of punishing Albinus and Humbert for their idolatrous passions.

Literally, "camera obscura" means "dark chamber." More comprehensively, a camera obscura is any dark chamber including photographic cameras, darkened cinema palaces, a prison cell, and, for Nabokov, the cranial cell behind the eyes wherein imprisoned consciousness languishes, with a lens or opening through which an image may be projected in "natural" colors onto a receptive surface. Nabokov's choice of the camera obscura as a guiding metaphor in his account of Albinus' dismal fate becomes perfectly logical and appropriate, given his powerfully visual imagination, his notion of images as windows and apertures, his notion of man as a prisoner languishing within walls of time and contingency, and his conviction that imagination is the faculty of consciousness which attempts to spy beyond the prison walls through image making. Albinus, an art dealer and connoisseur, sins through the eyes, by entering a darkened motion picture house and glimpsing there something deeply illicit and corrupt which he mistakes for a vision of human felicity. He is led on and on into deeper and darker mistaking until he receives the appropriate punishment for his misuse of the faculty of vision. Physically blinded, morally degraded, mocked, confined, and at last murdered by his vicious young mistress, he is the object of that awful laughter in the dark made mention of in the American translation's title.

Laughter in the Dark makes darkly ironic play with the "optical" themes of art connoisseurship, painting and caricature, film making, life modeling, and film stardom in conjunction with a melodramatic plot recalling the famous German film *Die Blaue Engel* to suggest that, whereas true art is a way of seeing truly in darkness, attachment to false images leads only to a deeper benightedness and closer confinement. ⟨. . .⟩

Much of *Laughter in the Dark* is composed in Nabokov's sprightliest and most playful vein. But to complain of the author's apparent callousness to the sufferings of his central character is to miss the important point. Albinus' "passion for art" which betrays him into a realm of sexual and social pathology really does contain "immortal longings" with which the author has complete sympathy. But the author understands, as Albinus does not, that the beguiling images and forms beckoning in the murk of human reality are for seeing and not for possessing—an insight available to the true artist though not to the connoisseur with his checkbook and collections. "Albinus' speciality had been his passion for art; his most brilliant discovery had been Margot. But now . . . it was as though she had returned to the darkness of the little cinema from which he had once withdrawn her." On his way into the Argus Cinema Albinus had noticed a poster showing "a man looking up at a window framing a child in a nightshirt." This representation, which will reappear as an imagistic theme in *Lolita*, scrupulously balances an idea of aspiration toward something purely beautiful with the pathology of voyeurism and sexual perversion. It is also a warning which Albinus cannot read or heed because he is so mad for form that he will not distinguish between form and its replica or model: "Now, the vision of the promised kiss filled him with such ecstasy that it seemed hardly possible it could be still further intensified. And yet beyond it, down a vista of mirrors, there was still to be reached the dim white form of her body, that very form which art students had sketched so conscientiously and so badly."—JULIAN MOYNAHAN, *Vladimir Nabokov*, 1971, pp. 25–31

NOVELS WRITTEN IN ENGLISH

The Real Life of Sebastian Knight is the life story of a fictitious English novelist of note; a story told by his half-brother, and told with a brilliancy, a delicacy and a grave and exquisitely venomous humor which make it a delight to read. The imaginary Sebastian and the author of the book share the same father (for argument's sake, at least), a Russian officer of the old regime: "a fine soldier, a warm-hearted, humorous, high-spirited man." Sebastian's mother was a beautiful English lady who, on page nine of the book, leaves "husband and child as suddenly as a raindrop starts to slide tipwards down a syringa leaf." From her, Sebastian inherits his "strange, almost romantic passion for sleeping-cars and Great European Express Trains . . . and the long sad sigh of brakes at dimly surmised stations. . . ." The book follows Sebastian with poetic passion through his childhood in Russia, his education at Oxford, his love-affairs, his literary career. To state that the facts of Sebastian Knight's life seem oddly similar to those of Vladimir Nabokov's, and that it might be possible to conceive of this book as a private individual's exposé of his public self, would be simplifying a matter which implies, but scarcely lends itself to, simplification. It is a far profounder and more symbolic issue which brings us to the startling and dramatic end.

In a note which accompanies the book, James Laughlin tells us that Nabokov has twenty volumes to his credit; and with that admirable determination to give us the artist complete, Laughlin adds that New Directions will publish the other volumes as rapidly as they can be done into English. It would therefore scarcely suggest limitation in the nature of the present work itself if one should judge this single book as a fragment of a still undistinguishable whole. *The Real Life of Sebastian Knight* is an illuminating if restricted glimpse of a construction which has not yet been revealed to us in its entirety.—KAY BOYLE, "The New Novels," *NR*, Jan. 26, 1942, p. 124

⟨Humbert Humbert in *Lolita*⟩ is, like his creator's novels, morally isolated in the interests of bliss. And although the treatment of "normal" relationships is disgusted or farcical, this isolation is unavoidably tragic. Nabokov's genre is, in fact, tragic farce. There is here a slight resemblance to Graham Greene, who also has the power to see through a joke into an abyss; but a much stronger resemblance to Sterne.

In *Bend Sinister* this is very strong, partly because of a coincidence of theme; for *Bend Sinister* treats, as Sterne did, of a "clash between the world of learning and that of human affairs" (Douglas Jefferson). The hero is a famous philosopher called Adam Krug, a somewhat Nabokov-like man with an easy conviction of his own superior powers. This survives his grief at the death of his wife and blinds him to danger threatening himself and his young son; for the new régime, the dictatorship of the Average Man, is the instrument of a wretched fellow he had bullied at school; and since the policy and the personnel of the Government are alike contemptible he cannot take them seriously. His son becomes the victim of cruelty as careless as it is frightful, his friends are removed by stupid and dirty police; finding himself once more in the school-yard with his old enemy Paduk, the head of the state, he tries and (unlike Humbert) fails to murder the lout who has broken his life and his mind. He is a tragic Shandy; the fate of his son is a consequence of an obsession with intellect, the habit of expecting matters to fall out in accordance with intelligent prediction, just as his father's preoccupation with book-learning, and the obsessive researches of Uncle Toby, brought disaster to Tristram. The difference between Sterne's comedy and Nabokov's tragedy is simply that the hard facts upon which the Shandys bruise themselves are orderly and to be respected; whereas Krug's victors are aimless and banal, and their policy the corruption of a philosophy.

This material difference does not detract from the impressive linguistic and formal resemblances between Nabokov and Sterne. Both, for example, use scientific language for farce:

The strong, compact, dusky forehead had that peculiar hermetic aspect (a bank safe? a prison wall?) which the brows of thinkers possess. The brain consisted of water, various chemical compounds, and a group of highly specialised fats. The pale steely eyes were half-closed in their squarish orbits under the shaggy eyebrows which had protected them once from the poisonous droppings of extinct birds—Schneider's hypothesis. The ears were of goodly size with hair inside. Two deep folds of flesh diverged from the nose along the large cheeks. The morning had been shaveless. He wore a badly-creased dark suit and a bow tie, always the same, hyssop violet with (pure white in the type here, Isabella) interneural macules and a crippled left hindwing. *Etc.*

My father, who dipped into all kinds of books, upon looking into *Lithopaedus Senonensis de Partu difficili*, published by *Adrianus Smelvgot*, had found out, that the lax and pliable state of a child's head in parturition, the bones of the cranium having no sutures at that time, was such,—that by force of the woman's efforts, which, in strong labour-pains, was equal, upon an average, to the weight of 470 pounds averdupois acting perpendicularly upon it;—it so happened, that in 49 instances out of 50, the said

head was compressed and moulded into the shape of an oblong conical piece of dough, such as a pastry-cook generally rolls up in order to make a pye of.—Good God! cried my father, what havock and destruction must this make in the infinitely fine and tender texture of the cerebellum!—Or if there is such a juice as *Borri* pretends,—is it not enough to make the clearest liquid in the world both feculent and mothery?

Sterne adds a note correcting this: *Lithopaedus* alludes to a petrified child and has been mistaken for an author's name by a pardonable error, the word being so similar to the right name, *Trinecavellius.*

Shandy is reading about normal childbirth, Krug is not only a philosopher but a man. This fantastic relation with the obvious comes out also in Sterne's ubiquitous Latin and the invented Slavonic language which erupts all over Nabokov's text as a farcical acknowledgment of the need for verisimilitude, though it is also an indulgence of superior linguistic powers. In the same way both writers have the power to produce photographic realism to a point so far beyond the normal that it looks almost mad. In the dark Krug sees a lantern move "knight-wise, to check him"; the rear lamps of bicycles are "anal rubies"; "Krug, a hunchback for the nonce, inserted his latchkey"; "at the dry-leaf touch of Gleeman's hand, the cat rose like boiling milk." And so forth.

Nabokov plays the devil with his narrative, just in the Sterne manner. Little notes are addressed to the author himself. "Describe the bedroom. . . . Last chance of describing the bedroom." The author intervenes out of pity: "it was then that I felt a pang of pity for Adam and slid towards him along an inclined beam of pale light—causing instantaneous madness." He introduces long digressions, including a long one on *Hamlet* which undoubtedly attempts to overgo the Scylla and Charybdis episode in *Ulysses.*

⟨. . .⟩ Merely to write centrifugally, to torment the narrative line, to destroy the illusion by inconsistencies of presentation, all this is within the scope of any rudimentary, slightly sophisticated talent. It might be done by anyone who thinks, as many do, that the structure of a work of art is the business not of the artist but of the observer.

But this is not Nabokov's way. *Bend Sinister* is not finally wanton, any more than Sterne was. There is a pretty rigorous subordination of all these stunts and rhetorical exercises to the shape of the whole.—FRANK KERMODE, "Aesthetic Bliss," *Enc*, June 1960, pp. 83–84

The work under review ⟨*Pnin*⟩ is very very clearly supposed to be funny. The action—various small-scale misadventures of a White Russian scholar in the American university world—is a thin trickle between prodigious banks of whimsical commentary and ejaculatory, parenthesis-ridden description: on every page there are little fire-work displays about Pnin's trouble with his radiator, Pnin under his sunlamp, Pnin's difficulties with English, Pnin bathing, Pnin learning to drive, Pnin's 'sparse auburn beard (today only white bristles would sprout if he did not shave—poor Pnin, poor albino porcupine!).'

Yes, it *must* be funny! And it must be brilliantly satirical too, by virtue of being set on the campus, and having professors' wives in it. And it must be rather profound, somehow, because there are lots of literary and artistic allusions. And sad, because we aren't allowed to forget for a moment that Pnin is a permanent exile from Mother Russia. And, finally, it establishes itself as belonging to a tradition . . . the little man . . . innocence . . . beset by circumstances, but . . . eyes of a child . . . tender . . . rich humanity . . . pathos . . . clown. . . .

That this limp, tasteless salad of Joyce, Chaplin, Mary MacCarthy and of course Nabokov (who should know better) has had delighted noises made over it by Edmund Wilson, Randall Jarrell and Graham Greene is a mystery of some dimensions. The last-named whose comment in its entirety reads: 'It is hilariously funny and of a sadness . . .' was presumably overcome by emotion before he could finish. The Wilson view that Nabokov is 'probably' like Gogol is also arresting. It just goes to show, doesn't it?—KINGSLEY AMIS, "Russian Salad," *Spec*, Sept 27, 1957, p. 403

Pnin is the most gently and sadly comic of all of Nabokov's books, and Timofey Pnin is the most winning of all his eccentric characters. This is, in large part, a formal matter. In Nabokov's other novels the humor—and Nabokov has never written a novel that is not in some degree funny—derives from the highly developed self-irony of the narrator (Humbert Humbert is the best instance of this, and, in quite a different way, John Shade is another) or else its source is a radical disparity of norms in which either the character (the chess master Luzhin in *The Defense*) or the society (*Invitation to a Beheading*) must be adjudged "mad." In *Pnin* the humor is not a vital function of Timofey Pnin's personal misfortunes (that is, the humor is not a *device* of the novel; one can rather easily mentally transpose the dour personality of Luzhin into the narrative in place of Pnin, and it would remain essentially the same novel, but Pnin could never play the part of Luzhin). Neither madness nor self-irony play any role in *Pnin*. Pnin does have a delightful donnish sense of humor, but his conscious wit is minor indeed in comparison to the hilarious eccentricity of which he is quite unaware and which has made him an academic legend and source of cocktail-party hilarity at Waindell. The humor in *Pnin* comes to us directly (or, as seen from a different vantage point, indirectly) from a discreetly omniscient narrator. In this, the novels closest to *Pnin* are *Mashenka* and *The Gift*, but neither of these novels allows humor anywhere near the scope and prominence that it has in *Pnin*.—ANDREW FIELD, *Nabokov: His Life in Art*, 1967, pp. 130–31

On the surface it appears that the perfect novelist to strike off unlimited sparks would be Nabokov, and one needs to go through the new short novel ⟨*Transparent Things*⟩ twice before things begin to fall into place. Not that having them fall in place makes everything transparently clear: John Updike, in his *New Yorker* review, allows to not understanding it (though he doesn't blame the book for this) and I don't claim to be a better reader of Nabokov than Updike. But for all the admiration and loving care he has directed toward the explicating and appreciating of the Master's novels, Updike sounds a bit uneasy this time. Rightly so, for *Transparent Things* carries further into compressed and urgent stylistic parody the main tendencies of Nabokov's last novel, *Ada*; while by the same token it makes seem more remote, since it is discontinuous with, the attractive imaginative generosity animating his best novels: *Lolita*, *Pnin*, *Pale Fire*. This generosity was surely fed by Nabokov's fascination with America (a love-affair, it has been called) and the marvelous small-town landscapes—dotted with dotty, middle Americans—of *Pnin* and *Lolita* are given glory through the stolid single-mindedness of Timofey or the obsessed impatience of Humbert; while *Pale Fire* always struck me as split between the rich comedy of Kinbote stalking Shade in New Wye and the tedious fantasies about what did or didn't happen in mythical Zembla. These novels were unabashedly fictions, as self-consciously and ingeniously parodic as anyone could wish, but they also existed at the level of comic realism. With *Ada*, and now *Transparent Things*, that level is at the

vanishing point. The erotic flights in *Lolita* were surely Nabokovian but also seemed truly to emanate from an imagined not-so-humble Humbert. But in *Ada* we got this, as Van is set upon by Lucette and Ada: "Lucette's dewy little contributions augmented rather than dampened Van's invariable reaction to the only and main girl's lightest touch, actual or imagined. Ada, her silky mane sweeping over his nipples and navel, seemed to enjoy doing everything to jolt my present pencil . . ." See, I'm a writer, these are my imagined creations, look what I can make them do.

I could not finish *Ada*, and though no such problem occurred with *Transparent Things* the final result was no happier. The hero, "Hugh Person" (you, person) is constantly played with and harassed by the brilliant word-man who conducts, with side excursions into various transparencies, the narration. As always there is fine Nabokovian contempt at the expense of new fashions, as when Hugh attends an avant garde play craftily titled *Cunning Stunts*:

> In matters of art, "avant garde" means little more than conforming to some daring philistine fashion, so, when the curtain opened, Hugh was not surprised to be regaled with the sight of a naked hermit sitting on a cracked toilet in the middle of an empty stage. Julia giggled, preparing for a delectable evening. Hugh was moved to enfold in his shy paw the childish hand that had accidentally touched his kneecap.

The hermit on the toilet is vintage Nabokov, but has nothing at all to do with Hugh, while the "shy paw" is a stage prop left over from *Lolita* that sounds authentic when Humbert speaks of it but just feels embarrassing and patronizing here. Nabokov is interested in the transparencies of history, of memory, of love, and above all else of language; but as far as this novel goes his interest in character, in human beings, is imperiously disdainful or frothily indulgent. What are we to do with a "hero" whose toleration of his wife's sexual preferences is described in this manner:

> Our Person's capacity to condone all this . . . endears him to us, but also provokes limpid mirth, alas, at times. For example, he told himself that she refused to strip because she was shy of her tiny pouting breasts and the scar of a ski accident along her thigh. Silly Person!
> Was she faithful to him throughout the months of their marriage spent in frail, lax, merry America? During their first and last winter there she went a few times to ski without him, at Aval Quebec, or Chute, Colorado. . . . although actually, as we know, she had enjoyed full conjunction with only a dozen crack lovers in the course of three trips.

Of course we don't know, and do we care a bit? But with Lolita we did care; "frail, lax, merry America" was something more than a happy *trouvaille*, just as the fates of poor Luzhin (*The Defence*) or mad Kinbote (*Pale Fire*) endeared them to us as something more, though never independent of, their creator's splendid use of language. *Transparent Things* is too transparently a fiction, all made up: the reader feels lonely and hopeless because there's nothing for him to care about except Nabokov brilliantly all alone with his magic.—WILLIAM H. PRITCHARD, "Long Novels and Short Stories," *HdR*, Spring 1973, pp. 227–28

OTHER WORKS

This four-volume presentation of one of the world's most attractive poems ⟨*Eugene Onegin*⟩ contains much material which will primarily interest the Pushkinist. The sound and penetrating Appendix on prosody deserves a wider readership—if only because nowadays there is a mass of writing about all aspects of poetry except the one thing which actually defines it as poetry rather than prose, its technique and metric. (It might be supplemented by lines 30–38 of Nabokov's own poem *An Evening of Russian Poetry*.) The long Commentary which fills out half of this bulky production is full of insights too: for example on "the aphoristic style which was Pushkin's intrinsic concession to the eighteenth century". It is also a regular rodeo of hobbyhorses. Nabokov scoffs at Virgil, *Hudibras*, Swift, Shchedrin, Béranger. He thinks Coleridge's "The Pains of Sleep" a great poem. He urges the abolition of the Cyrillic alphabet. He sneers at other translations. Odd stuff, but at least individual. As with Yvor Winters preferring Bridges to Hopkins, agreeing or not we must respect this more than a thousand acceptances by rote of current, and probably ephemeral, orthodoxy. Meanwhile, we can note in passing, from Nabokov's extreme rudeness to previous translators, that he would hardly expect any hostile criticisms of himself to be too muted.

In an age of "re-creations"—parasites sucking a little vitality from some great host—it is good to find Nabokov defining true translation as "rendering, as closely as the associative and syntactical capacities of another language allow, the exact contextual meaning of the original". He adds that, whatever the ideal situation, it is impossible to translate a poem like *Eugene Onegin* truly with the retention of its rhymes. But here we begin to get into difficulties. There is, of course, a great deal to be said for a straight prose translation. Still, if we miss the versification of the poem we miss a very great deal indeed—particularly as Pushkin, like Racine in a different mode, depends a lot on an inevitably felicitous handling of what appear on analysis to be ordinary phrases and stylized properties.

But let us have prose, if we must. Unfortunately Nabokov does not go the full length. He takes the view that something can be retained: the iambic rhythm. This turns out to be pointless, as it results in a totally different form and style—a blank verse varying from four syllables to twelve or more. Moreover, he has retained a single "poetic" device, and one which only falls naturally in a highly formal verse structure and even then is something to be cautious with—inversion.

So we get (a fair example):

> Having decided to detest
> the coquette, boiling Lenski did not wish
> to see before the duel Olga.
> The sun, his watch he kept consulting . . .

In fact, the approach produces awkwardness and insipidity. This is a pity, for Nabokov's own attempts at metrical paraphrase are rather effective (see vol. 2, page 120).

There is a more essential blemish yet—an unsuitable vocabulary. Nabokov speaks admirably in the Commentary of the twin errors of "impoverishing or enriching the sense". He himself has not been able to resist the temptation. We get "pacific sites" for a Russian "peaceful places", and so on. Worse still, this tendency leads to a liberal scattering of inappropriately stilted or antiquated words: buttsome, vernant, strangeling, youthhood, infantine, joyance, vacillant, half-wise, lightsome, moveless, plangorous, varivoiced, familistic, yearnsome, juventy, monocratically, prevene, volation. Almost invariably rendering something quite ordinary in Russian, these may remind us of Auden's complaint, about an Anglo-Icelandic Dictionary, that it was "full of non-existent words". In fact a few are strictly non-existent (not even in the big OED): others are "obsolete, chiefly Scotch", or to be found

only in the OED word-cemetery, not even making the very tolerant "Shorter" OED. Even those that do get that far will mostly be recognized as full of "ancientry" (another Nabokov word)—the equivalents of the "blithesome and cumberless" which made Hogg's notorious lines such a laughing-stock.

Moreover, we get "mollitude" for luxury; "sauvage" for *dik*, wild; "campestral" for the simple *polevoy*; "Adrian" for Adriatic; "the fairs" for "the fair ones"; "ananas" for pineapple; "Tsargrad" for Constantinople; "Eol" for Aeolus. For *loshadka* Nabokov objects to Oliver Elton's "old mare", but he himself gives us "naggy". There is inappropriate slang (e.g. "tosh", first quoted by the OED from 1872). And so on.

It is sad to knock any attempt to bring Pushkin before us. There are long passages without these faults. Nevertheless, on the whole this is too much a transposition into Nabokovese, rather than a translation into English. It gives the impression of a foreigner who has not quite learnt the language with the extreme perfection required, perhaps, only at this extravagant periphery of idiom. Under control, Nabokov could have given us a good, undecorated prose translation—even, with great toil, a fine verse one. Meanwhile, the reader with no Russian will probably find one or other of the despised verse renderings (Elton's advisedly) still the best available, with all the faults that Nabokov rightly points out in them.—ROBERT CONQUEST, "Nabokov's *Eugene Onegin*," *Poetry*, June 1965, pp. 236–38

Vladimir Nabokov has prepared a new edition of his autobiography, originally published in 1951, in this country as *Conclusive Evidence*, in England as *Speak, Memory*. The present version is called *Speak, Memory: An Autobiography Revisited*. Nabokov has added from twenty-five to fifty pages, mostly concerned with his forebears, especially his father, whom he describes vividly and with affection. A few passages have been expanded, and there has been some stylistic revision, but the book has not been changed in any fundamental way.

What we have is what we had before—an extraordinary evocation of the life of the Russian upper class before World War I. The Nabokovs were people of social rank, considerable wealth, cosmopolitan culture, and liberal political views. The wealth and leisure they enjoyed were not abused but, by and large, served both conscience and intelligence. Young Nabokov received the education of a poet rather than the education of an autocrat, but he was bound to be an autocratic poet.

Most of the book describes Nabokov's life before the Bolshevik Revolution, which took place in his eighteenth year. The family escaped from Petrograd to the Crimea, but soon was forced to migrate to England and the Continent. Nabokov writes a little about his years at Cambridge University, and then briefly tells what it was like to be an exile and a writer in Western Europe from 1922 to 1940. It was in the latter year that he and his wife and their child fled to the United States, and it is with their departure that the book ends.

Although Nabokov wrote ten or a dozen books in Russian during his European exile, he barely touches on his literary career. He does say things, however, that bear directly or indirectly on problems raised by his novels and short stories. "In the course of my twenty years of exile," he observes, "I devoted a prodigious amount of time to the composing of chess problems. A certain position is elaborated on the board, and the problem to be solved is how to mate Black in a given number of moves, generally two or three. It is a beautiful, complex, and sterile art related to the ordinary form of the game only insofar as the properties of a sphere are made use of both by a juggler in weaving a new act and by a tennis player in winning a tournament."

After describing the fascination that the construction of such problems had for him, he continues, "Deceit, to the point of diabolism, and originality, verging upon the grotesque, were my notions of strategy." And lest the reader should fail to see that what Vladimir Nabokov says about his chess problems is applicable to his fiction, he declares: "It should be understood that competition in chess problems is not really between White and Black but between the composer and the hypothetical solver (just as in a first-rate work of fiction the real clash is not between the characters but between the author and the world), so that a great part of the problem's value is due to the number of 'tries'—delusive opening moves, false scents, specious lines of play, astutely and lovingly prepared to lead the would-be solver astray."

Nabokov thus admits that each of his novels is a game in which he tries to mislead his reader and prove his superiority over him, and this is exactly what certain critics have charged. ⟨. . .⟩

Nabokov's Quartet spans, as the author points out, "four decades of literary life." "An Affair of Honor," the earliest story, shows that even as a young man Nabokov knew how to bring a trick off. Although the author warns against calling "The Visit to the Museum" Kafkaesque or Freudian, it is an allegory of some sort. "The Vane Sister," the only one of the stories originally written in English, is another sort of game, and amusing enough, although one would be likely to miss the ultimate joke if the author's preface didn't offer a clue. Nabokov has written better stories than these, but they do suggest how persistently and in how many ways he has invited the reader to a contest of wits.—GRANVILLE HICKS, "All about Vladimir," *SR*, Jan. 7, 1967, pp. 27–28

With ⟨his⟩ constant and pervasive interest in the artificially produced illusion of reality and in the genuinely experienced reality of illusion, it would seem inevitable for Nabokov to become interested in drama as a literary form. Indeed, throughout his European period, when he wrote in Russian only, Nabokov repeatedly attempted the dramatic genre. His three brief verse plays, published in Berlin in 1923 and 1924 (*Death, The Grandfather*, and *The* [North] *Pole*), are not yet mature Nabokov. Reading these plays, one is struck by the testimony they offer to the autobiographical significance of those passages in *The Gift* that describe the hero's literary apprenticeship to Pushkin. The particular brand of iambic pentameter, the general diction, and occasionally even the sentence structure of Pushkin's "little tragedy," *Mozart and Salieri*, are effectively copied in Nabokov's three little plays, which could perhaps be more aptly characterized as narrative poems in dramatic form. Also evident is their stylistic relationship to the most neglected of Pushkin's verse narratives, *Angelo* (Pushkin's version of Shakespeare's *Measure for Measure*), which the hero of *The Gift* is also said to have studied. The most obviously Nabokovian of these early plays, *Death*, uses a situation that was later to reappear in a pivotal passage in *The Eye*: an unsuccessful would-be suicide believes himself dead and takes his continuing life for a posthumous experience. Not much can be said of Nabokov's five-act play *The Man from the U.S.S.R.* (1927), since only its first act has been published. It is apparently a spy thriller with a film actress for a heroine and it seems to have been performed by an émigré company in Berlin soon after its writing.

The most interesting and significant work to date of Nabokov the playwright was all done in a single year. It consists of the two full-length plays, *The Event (Sobytie)* and *The Waltz Invention (Izobretenie Val'sa)*, both written in 1938 and published the same year in the Paris émigré journal *Russkie*

Zapiski. (The Waltz Invention is now also available in English, in a somewhat revised version.) These two plays, written after such mature novels as *The Exploit (Podvig), Despair*, and *The Gift*, benefit from Nabokov's literary mastery at its most original and inventive. Both plays are firmly connected with Nabokov's central preoccupation with creative imagination. Like the novels, they are also "portraits of an artist as something else." *The Event* can be described as a portrait of an artist as a coward, and *The Waltz Invention* as a portrait of an artist as a madman-politician. These descriptions are of course schematic, aimed at pointing out the basic similarity of the two plays to Nabokov's novels; there are many additional aspects of these plays that such a scheme could not even begin to indicate. ⟨. . .⟩

Vladimir Nabokov has not returned to the drama since his two important plays of 1938. The contrast between these two works is all too evident, yet both clearly fit within the rest of his work and contribute to our understanding of Nabokov's depth and scope. A parallel from another art would be offered by Maurice Ravel's two masterpieces in piano concerto form, both written within the same year (1929–1930). The Piano Concerto in G is witty and sparkling; the Concerto in D for the Left Hand Alone is brooding and introspective. Vastly different from each other in conception, execution, and mood, the two concerti are major and typical works of Ravel. *The Event* and *The Waltz Invention* are also major and typical Nabokov in their exploration of his basic themes and in their relevance to his fundamental concepts of life and art.—SIMON KARLINSKY, "Illusion, Reality, and Parody in Nabokov's Plays," *CoL*, Spring 1967, pp. 268–69, 279

VLADISLAV KHODASEVICH
From "On Sirin" (1937)
tr. Michael H. Walker
eds. Simon Karlinsky and Robert P. Hughes
TriQuarterly, Winter 1970, pp. 96–101

A rt cannot be reduced to form, but without form it has no existence and, consequently, no meaning. Therefore the analysis of a work of art is unthinkable without an analysis of form.

Analysis of form would be a proper way of beginning every judgment about an author, every account of him. But formal analysis is so cumbersome and complicated that, in speaking of Sirin, I should not venture to suggest that you enter into that region with me. Besides, even I have not produced a true and sufficiently complete analysis of Sirin's form, real work in criticism under present conditions being impossible. All the same, I have made certain observations—and I shall permit myself to share the results.

Under thorough scrutiny Sirin proves for the most part to be an artist of form, of the writer's device, and not only in that well-known and universally recognized sense in which the formal aspect of his writing is distinguished by exceptional diversity, complexity, brilliance and novelty. All this is recognized and known precisely because it catches everyone's eye. But it catches the eye because Sirin not only does not mask, does not hide his devices, as is most frequently done by others (and in which, for example, Dostoevsky attained startling perfection) but, on the contrary, because Sirin himself places them in full view like a magician who, having amazed his audience, reveals on the very spot the laboratory of his miracles. This, it seems to me, is the key to all of Sirin. His works are populated not only with the characters, but with an infinite number of devices which, like elves or gnomes, scurry back and forth among the characters and perform an enormous amount of work. They saw and carve and nail and paint, in front of the audience, setting up and clearing away those stage sets amid which the play is performed. They construct the world of the book and they function as indispensably important characters. Sirin does not hide them because one of his major tasks is just that—to show how the devices live and work.

Sirin has a novel built entirely on the play of autonomous devices. *Invitation to a Beheading* is nothing more than a chain of arabesques, patterns and images, subordinated not to an ideological, but only to a stylistic unity (which, by the way, constitutes one of the "ideas" of the work). In *Invitation to a Beheading* there is no real life, as there are no real characters with the exception of Cincinnatus. All else is merely the play of the stagehand elves, the play of devices and images that fill the creative consciousness or, rather, the creative delirium of Cincinnatus. With the termination of their playing the story comes to an abrupt end. Cincinnatus is not beheaded and is not not-beheaded, since through the length of the entire story we see him in an imaginary world where no real events of any kind are possible. In the concluding lines, the two-dimensional painted world of Cincinnatus caves in over the collapsed backdrop: "Cincinnatus made his way," says Sirin, "amidst the dust, and falling things, and the flapping scenery, in that direction where, to judge by the voices, stood beings akin to him." Here, of course, is depicted the return of the artist from creative work to reality. If you wish, the beheading is carried out at that moment, but not the same one nor in the same sense as that expected by the hero and the reader: with the return into the world of "beings akin to him," the existence of Cincinnatus the artist is cut off.

Peculiar to Sirin is the realization, or perhaps only a deeply felt conviction, that the world of literary creativity, the true world of the artist, conjured through the action of images and devices out of apparent simulacra of the real world, consists in fact of a completely different material—so different that the passage from one world into the other, in whichever direction it is accomplished, is akin to death. And it is portrayed by Sirin in the form of death. If Cincinnatus dies, passing from the creative world into the real one, then conversely, the hero of the story "Terra Incognita" dies at that instant when he finally plunges completely into the world of imagination. And although the transitions are accomplished in diametrically opposed directions, both are equally depicted by Sirin in the form of a disintegration of the stage set. Both worlds, in their relationship one to the other, are for Sirin illusory.

In exactly the same way the butterfly dealer, Pilgram, in the story "The Aurelian," is dead for his wife, for his customers, for the whole world, at that moment when he finally sets out for Spain—a country not coincident with the real Spain, because it has been created by his fancy. In exactly the same way Luzhin dies at that moment when, throwing himself out of the window onto the pale and dark squares of a Berlin courtyard, he once and for all slips out of reality and plunges into the world of his chess creation—there where there are no wife, no acquaintances, no apartment, but where there are only the pure, abstract relationships of creative devices.

If "The Aurelian," "Terra Incognita" and *Invitation to a Beheading* are wholly devoted to the theme of the interrelationship of worlds, then *The Defense* is the first work in which Sirin rose to the full stature of his talent (because here, perhaps for the first time, he found the basic themes of his work)—then *The Defense*, belonging as it does to the same cycle, at the same

time contains a transition to the second series of Sirin's writings, where the author poses different problems for himself—invariably, however, connected with the theme of a creative work and the creative personality. These problems are of a somewhat more limited—one could even say professional—character. In Luzhin's person the very horror of such professionalism is shown; it is shown that a permanent residence in the creative world, if the artist is a man of talent and not of genius, will, as it were, suck out his human blood, turning him into an automaton which is not adapted to reality and which perishes from contact with it.

The Eye depicts a charlatan of the arts, an impostor—a man without gift and by nature a stranger to creative work, but endeavoring to pass for an artist. Several mistakes committed by him are his ruin, although he of course does not die, but only changes his profession, for he, after all, has never been in the world of creative work and there is in his story no passage from one world into the other. However, in *The Eye* the theme is already set forth and it becomes central in *Despair*, one of Sirin's best novels. Here are shown the sufferings of a genuine, self-critical artist. He perishes because of a single mistake, because of a single slip allowed in a work which devoured all of his creative ability. In the process of creation he allowed for the possibility that the public, humanity, might not be able to understand and value his creation—and he was ready to suffer proudly from lack of recognition. His despair is brought about by the fact that he himself turns out to be guilty of his downfall, because he is only a man of talent and not of genius.

The life of the artist and the life of a device in the consciousness of the artist—this is Sirin's theme, revealing itself to some degree or other in almost every one of his writings, beginning with *The Defense*. However, the artist (and more concretely speaking, the writer) is never shown by him directly, but always behind a mask: a chess-player, a businessman, etc. The reasons for this are, I believe, manifold. Foremost among them is that here, too, we have to do with a device, though quite an ordinary one. Russian formalists call it "making it strange." It consists in showing the object in unexpected surroundings, which place it in a new position, reveal new aspects of it, and force a more direct perception of it. But there are also other reasons. Had he represented his heroes directly as writers, Sirin would have had, in depicting their creative work, to place a novel inside a story or a story within a story, which would excessively complicate the plot and necessitate on the part of the reader a certain knowledge of the writer's craft. The very same would come about, but with some other difficulties, if Sirin had made them painters, sculptors or actors. He deprives them of professional artistic attributes, but Luzhin works on his chess problems and Hermann on plotting a crime in exactly the same manner that an artist works on his creations. Finally, one should take into consideration the fact that, except for the hero of *The Eye*, all of Sirin's heroes are genuine, inspired artists. Among them, Luzhin and Hermann, as I mentioned, are only gifted men and not genuises, but even they cannot be denied a deep artistic nature. Cincinnatus, Pilgram and the nameless hero of "Terra Incognita" do not possess those detrimental traits with which Luzhin and Hermann are marked. Consequently, all of them, being shown without masks as undisguised artists, would become (expressed in the language of teachers of literature) positive types, which, as is known, creates exceptional and, in the present instance, unwarranted difficulties for the author. Moreover, in such a case it would be too difficult for the author to deliver them from that pompous and sugary tone which almost inevitably accompanies literary portrayals of true artists. Only the hero of

The Eye could have been made a man of letters by Sirin while avoiding these difficulties, for the simple reason that that hero is a fake writer. However, I think—I am even almost convinced—that Sirin, who has at his disposal a wide range of caustic observations, will some day give himself rein and favor us with a merciless satiric portrayal of a writer. Such a portrayal would be a natural development in the unfolding of the basic theme with which he is obsessed.

F. W. DUPEE
"Nabokov: The Prose and Poetry of It All"

New York Review of Books, December 12, 1963, pp. 10–12

Readers of *Lolita* may recall that Humbert Humbert, who delivers himself of the contents of the book while in confinement awaiting trial for murder, is something of a poet. "You can always count on a murderer for a fancy prose style," he says, and you can count on this particular murderer for scattered flights of verse as well. His are "occasional poems" in the most invidious sense possible. Humbert's muse materializes only intermittently, and when she does it is in response to situations of a kind that do not, as a rule, give rise to *la poésie pure*—or whatever we may call the opposite of occasional poetry.

Hoping, for example, to calm his restless Lolita he improvises a bit of what he tells her is "nonsense verse."

The Squirl and his Squirrel, the Rabs and their
    Rabbits
Have certain obscure and peculiar habits.
Male humming birds make the most exquisite
    rockets.
The snake when he walks holds his hands in his
    pockets.

"Nonsense is correct," Lolita says mockingly, perhaps guessing that Humbert's weakness for nymphets like herself lends the poem a certain "obscure and peculiar" sense which she would prefer to ignore. As a poet, Humbert succeeds no better with Rita, a temporary replacement for Lolita, and one who knows her time is short. He tries to stop her accusing sobs by extemporizing some verses about a certain "blue hotel" they have just motored past. "Why blue when it is white, why blue for heaven's sake?" she protests and starts crying again. Humbert's lengthiest effort is a ballad, full of literary allusions, *double-entendres*, and straight French, which he writes to console himself for the loss of Lolita. One stanza reads:

Happy, happy is gnarled McFate
Touring the States with a child wife,
Plowing his Molly in every State
Among the protected wild life.

Humbert, like other of Nabokov's creatures, foreign or nutty or both, has a peculiar flair for knowing what is going on in the American literary world. He knows, for example, that "light verse" has been made respectable by Mr. W. H. Auden, whose own fine efforts in that form have rarely excelled Humbert's McFate ballad. He knows, too, that poetry of *any* weight lends itself nicely to depth analysis. His own analyst, Humbert says of his ballad: "It is really a maniac's masterpiece. The stark, stiff, lurid rhymes correspond very exactly to certain perspectiveless and terrible landscapes and figures . . . as drawn by psycho-paths in tests devised by astute trainers." He is aware, too, of that specialty of American poetics, the belief that poetry inheres in phenomena themselves rather than in the poet and that to compose a poem one need only catalogue phenomena

in sufficiently impressive numbers. So he pounces upon a mimeographed list of the names of Lolita's classmates, sur-names and first names intriguingly reversed for the purpose of alphabetization (e.g., FANTAZIA, STELLA; FLASHMAN, IRVING; HAZE, DOLORES). "A poem, a poem, forsooth!" he exclaims, and goes on to imagine the occupants of the classroom: "Adorable Stella, who has let strangers touch her; Irving, for whom I am sorry, etc." Nor does Humbert's muse desert him on the ultimate occasion. When, gun in hand, he delivers sentence on his rival Clare Quilty prior to shooting him dead, he does so in the accents of a certain poem, well known to the literary world, about sin, penitence, and death:

Because you took advantage of a sinner
because you took advantage
because you took
because you took advantage of my disadvantage . . .

"That's damned good," says Quilty, providing Humbert with an approving, if captive, audience at last.

For Humbert, the uses of poetry are rather low. He might even be said to prostitute his muse. The uses of poetry for Mr. Nabokov are high, though not so high as to rule out the efforts of those who are compelled into song by mixed motives, including lust, revenge, and the hope of a check from *The New Yorker*. Like that other master of prose, James Joyce, Mr. Nabokov aspired in youth to be a poet. More than Joyce did, he has continued to write verse and to fill his novels with reflections on poetry. The reflections are often of major importance; the verse—the verse in English at least—is minor, as minor as verse could be and still remain interesting. His forthcoming translation of Pushkin's *Eugene Onegin* will conceivably stand as his main poetic achievement. For years he has been going on about Pushkin ("the gold reserve of our literature"), meanwhile preparing us for the *magnum opus* by translating other Russian poets. He brings to poetry and the informal criticism of poetry the same spirit of connoisseurship that enlivens his work as a whole—an impassioned connois-seurship that unites the naturalist in him with the literary artist in him and does duty, it would seem, for ideology. He has a mind too rich to be impoverished by ideas. His "commitment" (in the starkly fashionable sense) is to perceptions, discrimina-tions, prejudices, and to the purveying, as he says, of "aesthetic bliss." Before 1940, when he came to live in the United States and started publishing in English, he contributed a number of poems to Russian *émigré* periodicals in Europe. Between 1943 and 1957 he wrote the fourteen poems which, described as "his complete poetic works in English," were collected in a miniature volume succinctly entitled *Poems* (1959). *Pale Fire*, his most recent novel in English (1962), consists of a long poem, or quasi-poem, ostensibly written by an American poet, and of lengthy notes ostensibly supplied by a European-born editor.

The last novel Mr. Nabokov wrote in Russian has lately come out in English—authentic Nabokovian English. *The Gift* is a delightful novel. It is also invaluable for what it tells us about its author's relation to the twin disciplines of poetry and prose, in the past as, I venture, at present. With *The Gift* as a main text, let me inquire into those relations, to the extent that I can do so in short space and with no knowledge of Russian.

The Gift has been widely and pleasantly reviewed during the months since it appeared. So far as I am aware, however, no one has pointed out that the book is a sort of hail and farewell to the poetic muse considered as a full-time compan-ion. A young poet formidably named Fyodor Godunov-Cherdyntsev is the hero. (One of *The Gift's* best reviewers, Mr. Stanley Edgar Hyman, tells us this was Nabokov's own pen name as a poet—he signed his novels V. Sirin.) An *émigré* Russian who has forfeited much to the Bolsheviks—a country estate, a St. Petersburg town house, probably a father, possibly a future as a native writer, Fyodor lives an exile's desultory life in Berlin. There he moves from furnished room to furnished room, gives stupid Germans reluctant Russian lessons, composes verses, imagines the fine reviews his recently published book of poems will get, recalls his Russian childhood, mingles diffidently with his quarrelsome fellow exiles, loses his keys, gets his clothes stolen at the Grünewald swimming lake. His life is almost as unreal as the phenomenon we find him scrutinizing on the novel's first page: a moving van with "the name of the moving company in yard-high blue letters, each of which (including a square dot) was shaded laterally with black paint—a dishonest attempt to climb into the next dimension." Fyodor seeks to climb into the next dimension, the heaven of aesthetic bliss, by the frail but not dishonest ladder of poetry alone. True, he has a distinct "gift" for it, a charming craze for words, and a capacity for hallucination that verges on secular mysticism. The first chapter of *The Gift* is, among other things, a little anthology of his poems. They are about incidents remembered from his childhood in Russia.

> My ball has rolled under Nurse's commode.
> On the floor a candle
> Tugs at the ends of the shadows
> This way and that, but the ball is gone . . .

Knocked from its hiding place by a poker, the ball *"Crosses the whole room and promptly goes under/The impregnable sofa."* The long line nicely reproduces the effect of the ball's trip across the room. And the ball stays lost.

As the novel unfolds, we see Fyodor's situation—which resembles the ball's—reflected back at him in various ways by the plight of other *émigrés* around him in Berlin. There is the tragedy (or tragic farce) of the young poet Yasha, a recent suicide, whose hopeless attachment to a German youth of the blond and blue-eyed type forms, incidentally, a grim parody of a familiar Thomas Mann theme. There is the pure farce of Mr. Busch, a Latvian with pretensions to poetic drama. Before an audience choking with stifled laughter, he reads his "new, philosophical tragedy." It is *Faust* out of *Brand* out of Busch, and includes the following conversation in a "Street of Sin":

> *First Prostitute:* All is water. That is what my client Phales[1] says.
> *Second Prostitute:* All is air, young Anaximines told me.
> *Third Prostitute:* All is number. My bald Pythagoras cannot be wrong.
> *Fourth Prostitute:* Heracles caresses me whispering "All is fire."
> *Lone Companion* (enters): All is fate.

"There is no great poetry without parody," Fyodor explains; and in *The Gift* the parodies tend to be better than the poems. So Fyodor begins to feel that he will eventually want "to speak in quite another way, not in miniature verse with charms and chimes, but in very, very different manly words." Indeed, during an imaginary conversation with an older poet he respects, Fyodor hears the man say: "By the way, I've read your very remarkable volume of poems. Actually, of course, they are but models of your future novels." Fyodor then stops trying to recapture his childhood. Instead, he undertakes to reconstruct, first the final days of his beloved father, a celebrated naturalist who has vanished on a scientific expedition to Asia, the victim of an accident or of the Bolsheviks; second, the life of Chernyshevski, the celebrated social critic of

the 1860's, father of Russian utilitarianism, Lenin's mentor. For these projects, Fyodor abandons verse, wooing instead "the Muse of Russian prose-rhythms." His assault on Chernyshevski's crude version of the liberal imagination strangely foreshadows the assault that Proust, at the start of *his* career as a serious writer, made for somewhat similar reasons on Sainte-Beuve. But *Contre Sainte-Beuve* (which, incidentally, is of recent discovery and could not therefore have been in Mr. Nabokov's mind during the years 1935–37 when *The Gift* was written) is the tirade of a tyro compared to Nabokov-Fyodor's explosive yet touching portrait of Chernyshevski, whose dreadful sufferings as a man effectively belied his doctrinaire optimism as a philosopher. Rejected by a publisher as "a syringe of sulphuric acid," the Chernyshevski portrait is really part of Fyodor's attempt to contemplate Russian history without nostalgia—that nostalgia of the exile which, in Nabokov's view, so often ends in the exile's paranoia. "Why," he asks, "had everything in Russia become so shoddy, so crabbed and gray, how could she have become so befooled and befuddled? Or had the old 'urge toward the light' concealed a fatal flaw, which in the course of progress toward the objective had grown more and more evident, until it was revealed that this 'light' was burning in the window of a prison overseer, and that was all?"

But Fyodor's attempt to climb into the next dimension depends on other things than writing. He must unite himself, with a pretty, intelligent, hard-working girl who loves him and his poems, her name being Zina Mertz. Zina embodies, along with a poetic sensibility, the advantages—figuratively speaking—of good prose. Is this putting it too neatly? I think not. The novel itself has a rather pat way of making its points, a somewhat mechanical way of contriving its games of reality and appearance. After all, *The Gift* is a comparatively early work. In most respects, though, the mature Nabokov is already in command. Fyodor and Zina meet in a setting that is prosaic with a vengeance. It is one of those superlatively dreary interiors, epitomized by the communal bathroom and the communal bar of soap with the single hair in it, which Nabokov loves to swoop down on, whether in Berlin or the U.S.A., from the high wire of fantasy. This feeling for the commonplace at its commonest shows that his affinity with Joyce equals his affinity (more obvious in *The Gift*) with Proust. Fyodor writes a poem addressed to Zina but printed as prose. "Look at that street—it runs to China straight, and yonder star above the Volga glows!" Thus, in a fashion, the man and the woman, the exile and his homeland, the poet and the prose writer are all momentarily united.

Need we conclude that Mr. Nabokov himself has "sacrificed" poetry to prose? I doubt it. The English poems, all but two of them first printed in *The New Yorker*, are, it is true, of a kind often called, with a certain condescension, "lapidary." Nevertheless, as Mr. Nathaniel Reicheck has suggested, "the poet goes beyond the limits of his art [the "light verse" art] without violating its canon. This enlargement of a traditional form is made possible by his campaign to re-design the English language. His prosody is a unique and subtle parody of the original." This, again, may be overstating things, but not by much. The English poems do have a peculiar miniature excellence: perfect lucidity, precise wit, the glow of a lighted candle cupped in an expert hand against the windy verse roundabout. "A Literary Dinner" turns on a misunderstanding such as might occur between an American hostess whose enunciation was unclear and a foreign guest whose ear was imperfectly tuned to slurred English. "I want you, she murmured, to eat Dr. James." And so, amid dull talk at the table, he does eat Dr. James.

> All was good and well-cooked, but the tastiest part
> was his nut-flavored, crisp cerebellum. The heart
> resembled a shiny brown date,
> and I stowed all his studs on the edge of my plate.

Such a *nice* foreign guest, obliging, hungry, and neat. For wit mingled with lyrical delight, "An Evening of Russian Poetry" comes closest to being "great"—besides being a helpful treatise on versification. Referring to the Russian poets' "passion for expansion," the lecturer goes on to exemplify it in several asides, by turns paranoiac and nostalgic in mood.

> My back is Argus-eyed. I live in danger.
> False shadows turn to track me as I pass
>
> . . .
>
> Beyond the seas where I have lost a sceptre
> I hear the neighing of my dappled nouns,
> soft participles coming down the steps,
> treading on leaves, trailing their rustling gowns,
> and liquid verbs in *ahla* and in *ili*,
> Aonian grottoes, nights in the Altai,
> black pools of sound with 'L's' for water lilies.
> The empty glass I touched is tinkling still,
> but now 'tis covered by a hand and dies . . .

While writing his English verses Nabokov was elaborating the English prose which, somewhat subdued in *Sebastian Knight*, sometimes out of hand in *Bend Sinister*, would culminate in the controlled sinuosities of *Lolita*, the almost paranoid eloquence of *Pale Fire*. Kinbote's eloquence, I mean, for the point of the novel, rhetorically speaking, seems to lie in the contrast between the inflamed yet often beautiful writing of Kinbote's editorial notes and the paler fires, the intermittent beauties, of John Shade's poem. Mary McCarthy has said much about the book in her superb analysis and panegyric in *The New Republic*. One need only add a few words on Shade's poem itself. Distressed by his daughter's suicide, the father tries to convey his grief, his thoughts on death in general, in a kind of Popian four-part epistle constructed of the appropriate couplets. But he cannot rise either to Pope's scarifying realism or to the dashing architectonics of Pope's verse. Shade starts to quote the great lines from the *Essay on Man*:

> See the blind beggar dance, the cripple sing,
> The sot a hero, lunatic a king.

But he breaks the lines midway, explaining that "they smack of their heartless age." Shade's poem has an inner subject that goes unperceived by either Shade or his editor, who imagines the poem is about him, and *his* "lost sceptre," *his* living "in danger." The inner subject is the blindness of Shade's grief, his helplessness before the extremities of passion and death, the spiritual deformity which was his daughter's sole inheritance from him but which the singing cripple of Pope's lines and the crippled Pope himself do not share. So the poem maunders along, lovely in spots, penetrating in other spots, now elegiac, now cheery. It clothes itself in a simulacrum of Popian couplets without attaining to the hard antitheses, the decisive pauses, which are the prosodic mirror of Pope's tougher mind.

John Shade is a kindly, even affectionate, portrait of the American poet-in-residence. Like Robert Frost he maintains a stoic patience and a well-ordered life in the face of domestic disaster. As with lesser specimens of the type his muse is so thoroughly "in residence," so domesticated, that he is impelled, on one hand into academic verse, on the other into drink. Indeed, he could do with some of Kinbote's madness and passion, just as Kinbote could do with a lot of Shade's common sense. But the exchange of qualities does not take place. Instead, Shade gets the bullet intended for Kinbote—or, more accurately, for Kinbote's landlord. In *Pale Fire*, as so often in our author's work, it takes two men to make a proper Nabokovian man—two men who, however, rarely succeed in uniting. With a writer, if he is a genius, the duality may be made to work for him, just as the Siamese twins in the story, "Scenes from the Life of a Double Monster," are finally put to work by Uncle Novus. Nabokov has done the same with the poet and novelist in him, made of them a team. Thus he has been able to perfect an English prose medium whose flexibility is adapted to the astonishing range, the endless contradictions, of his nature, of Nature itself. Some of those future novels of which Fyodor's poems were the models have, we know, already come into being. After the translation of Pushkin's novel in verse, others may follow.

Notes

1. It is Busch's fault, not the proofreader's, that Thales becomes Phales, Anaximenes becomes Anaximines, and Heraclitus becomes Heracles. [F.W.D.]

ROBERT ALTER
"Nabokov's Ardor"

Commentary, August 1969, pp. 47–50

V ladimir Nabokov possesses what is probably the most finely cultivated sense of form of any living writer, and so there is a satisfying justness in the fact that not only his individual works but also the sequence of his books should evince a formal harmony. In his 1956 afterword to *Lolita*, Nabokov warned that any assessment of his writing was bound to be out of focus without an awareness of his Russian work; since then, the translation or reissue in English of seven of his nine Russian novels has in fact demonstrated that *Lolita*, far from being a brilliant sport, was merely the most radiant and engaging in a line of books that for three decades had explored the paradoxical untertwinings of imagination and reality, the artist and his world, through athletically allusive, involuted, and parodistic fictional forms. These same concerns were then given even more original and intricate formal expression in *Pale Fire*, while a new central emphasis in *Lolita* on the quest for a paradisiac past (Humbert Humbert's golden "princedom by the sea") appeared in oblique refraction through Kinbote's longing for his lost kingdom. Now, in his seventieth year, at an age when most novelists one can think of are already gone sadly to seed, Nabokov has produced a major work that in a purely formal sense culminates most of what he has attempted in over forty years of active writing. *Ada* is the fullest realization of the program for the novel articulated in 1941 in Nabokov's first English book, *The Real Life of Sebastian Knight*; as Sebastian Knight aspired to do, the author of *Ada* "use[s] parody as a kind of springboard for leaping into the highest region of serious emotion," and thus succeeds in illuminating in new depth and breadth the relation between art, reality, and the evanescent ever-never presence of time past.

Because parody is intrinsic to Nabokov's method, and because he more often parodies plot, situation, and motif than style and narrative technique, a plot-summary of any of his novels is bound to be thoroughly misleading. (To mislead the unsuspecting, of course, is precisely what Nabokov intends: thus, the four concluding paragraphs of *Ada* are a pitchman's synopsis of the book, the prose of the novel followed by what the narrator, tongue in cheek, calls "the poetry of its blurb.") *Ada*, which is surely one of the sunniest works of fiction written in this century, sounds, to judge by the initial outlines of its plot, like a dark drama of fatal, incestuous passion. Van Veen, the retrospective nonagenarian narrator, has an ecstatic affair at the age of fourteen with twelve-year-old Ada, ostensibly his cousin, later discovered to be his sister. The two are irresistibly drawn to each other by their inner nature but are separated by social taboo and the course of outward events. In the two decades from early adolescence to mature adulthood, the lovers enjoy four fleeting periods of illicit ardor together, but each time the subsequent separation is longer, and while Van seeks the simulacrum of his Ada in a thousand whores and mistresses, both he and she are physically thickened and coarsened by the passing years, until at last they come together in late middle age, all passion not spent but certainly muted. In the background, moreover, of their partings and joinings, as the third, unequal angle of a thoroughly incestuous triangle, is the pathetic figure of Lucette, their mutual half-sister, who loves Van relentlessly body and soul, loves Ada, periodically, in a more strictly bodily sense, and finally destroys herself when she is rejected by Van.

All this may sound like rather lurid stuff, especially when one adds that there is a much higher degree of descriptive specification about sexual matters here than anywhere else in Nabokov's fiction. The actual tenor of the novel, of course, is precisely the opposite of what this summary suggests. On a stylistic level, the seeming paradox is easy enough to explain: Nabokov's intricately wrought, elaborately figurative style, with its painterly effects and its perspectivist mirror-games, transmutes objects of description, even the most pungently physical objects, into magical *objets d'art*. When, for example, the narrator, in a spectacular set-piece, describes all three siblings in bed together (surely a parody of the *ménage à trois* grapplings that are stock scenes of pornographic literature), he invites us to view the action as though it were reflected in the ceiling mirror of a fancy brothel, and then proceeds to convert the rampant eroticism into a formal contrasting and blending of colors and movements. Physical details are not spared—"the detail is all," Van Veen had affirmed earlier about the reality of all experience and memory—but, to cite a strategic instance, the exposed sexual fluff of redheaded Lucette and black-haired Ada becomes here a new-fledged firebird and an enchanting blue raven, varicolored birds of paradise in a poet's Wonderland.

When we move from effects of style to the larger narrative patterns of the novel, it is difficult to make full sense of the incestuous complications without attention to the ubiquitous use of literary allusion. In order to talk about the allusions, something first must be said about the setting. The principal action of *Ada* takes place in the late 19th and early 20th centuries of a world alternately referred to as Antiterra and Daemonia, which has the same geography as our world but a teasingly different though parallel history. The area we call Russia having been conquered some centuries earlier by the Tartars, America has been settled by Russian as well as English and French colonists, and so Nabokov's own three native languages and literary traditions are able to flourish side by side, as complementary parts of a single national culture. From a terrestrial viewpoint (Terra the Fair, by the way, is a supposedly celestial place believed in mainly by the deranged on Antiterra), historical periods as well as cultural boundaries have been hybridized—the Daemonian 19th century combines the quiet country houses of Chekhov and Jane Austen with telephones, airplanes, skyscrapers; a mock-Maupassant figure is contemporaneous with the author of a *Lolita*-like novel masquerading (anagrammatically) as J. L. Borges. This device of a fictional antiworld gives Nabokov a free hand to combine and permute the materials of culture and history in

piquant and suggestive ways, though perhaps it also sometimes tempts him into self-indulgence, so that one begins to feel he is playing his games of anagrams, trilingual puns, coded hints, and conflated allusions for their own sake, not because they have any imaginative necessity in a larger design. (It must be admitted, though, that many of the incidental games, especially those involving literary figures, are so delightful in themselves that one would hesitate to give them up. My own favorite is the treatment of T. S. Eliot, who appears as a truncated version of his own ape-necked Sweeney, "solemn Kithar Sween, a banker who at sixty-five had become an *avant-garde* author; . . . had produced *The Waistline*, a satire in free verse on Anglo-American feeding habits"; and who is seen, in most poetic justice for a versifier of anti-Semitic innuendos, in the company of "old Eliot," a Jewish real-estate man.)

The most important advantage, in any case, that Nabokov gains through the freedom he allows himself to shuttle across temporal and cultural boundaries is that he is able to compress into the life-space of his protagonist a parodistic review of the development of the novel. The story begins in the classic age of the novel, and, really, everything that happens occurs in purely novelistic time and novelistic space. Ardis Manor, where young Van Veen will meet Ada, is glimpsed for the first time, characteristically, in the following fashion: "At the next turning, the romantic mansion appeared on the gentle eminence of old novels." The narrative is frequently punctuated with such notations to remind us that everything is taking place against a background of jaded literary conventions, as the view shifts quickly, and not necessarily chronologically, from Romantic *récit* to Jane Austen, Turgenev, Dickens, Flaubert, Tolstoy, Dostoevsky, the pornographic novel, the Gothic novel, Joyce, Proust, and Nabokov beyond them. The "plot," in fact, is from one point of view comprised of a string of stock scenes from the traditional novel—the young man's return to the ancestral manor, the festive picnic, the formal dinner, a midnight blaze on the old estate, the distraught hero's flight at dawn from hearth and home as the result of a misunderstanding, the duel, the hero's profligacy in the great metropolis, and so forth.

Though the technique of allusion is common to all of Nabokov's novels, there is a special thematic justification for this recapitulation in parody of the history of a genre, for what Van Veen's story represents is a reversal of the major thematic movement of the novel as a genre. The novel characteristically has concerned itself with lost illusions—the phrase, of course, was used as a title by Balzac—from the quixotic knight who finally abandons his pursuit of a Golden Age, a broken man renouncing his chivalric vision and dying; to Flaubert's Emma, spitting out her daydreams of a blue Beyond in the last hideous retches of an arsenic suicide; to Anna Karenina—the first sentence of her story is quoted, in reverse, in the first sentence of *Ada*—ending her tortured love under the wheels of a locomotive. What "happy endings" one finds in the classic novel are generally a matter of mere acquiescence to convention (Dickens) or sober accommodation of the protagonists to society (Jane Austen, George Eliot). *Ada*, in direct contrast, is an attempt to return to paradise, to establish, in fact, the luminous vision of youth and love's first fulfillment as the most intensely, perdurably *real* experience we know. It bears affinities to both Molly Bloom's great lyric recall of first flowering love at the end of *Ulysses* and to Proust's triumph over time through art in the last volume of his novel, but it is a more concerted frontal attack on Eden than either.

Two key allusions are especially helpful in understanding what Nabokov is up to with his incestuous lovers. One is simple, a mere negative parallel to serve as a foil; the other is complex, being a kind of imaginative model for the whole book and ramifying into other, related allusions. Several passing references are made to Chateaubriand; Ada jokingly calls Van her "René"; and the first half of the novel's title, *Ada or Ardor*, looks suspiciously like a parody of that most Romantic title, *René ou les effets des passions*. René, like Van is a singular man with an artist's soul who enjoys the rare delights of bucolic ambles with his dear sister until the incestuous nature of her attachment to him forces them to separate. So much for the parallels; all the rest is pointed contrast. *René* is a book suffused with Romantic *mal de siècle*, and René and Amélie, unlike the Veen siblings, are anything but "children of Venus"; the paradisial fulfillment of premoral desire is quite unthinkable for René and his sister, so that the very existence of such desire drives Amélie into a convent and ultimately leads to martyrs' deaths for both of them. In *Ada*, one can see from the sunlit river Ladore near the Ardis estate a view of Bryant's Castle (Gallicized, *Château-Briand*), "remote and romantically black on its oak-timbered hill." The chief quality of Van Veen's world, by contrast, is brightness and intimate closeness, social and sexual, tactile and visual; and its oak trees, as we shall see, are part of a landscape very different from the dark romantic wood. René actively longs for death, even before the revelation of his sister's passion; he sees in it a hazy, alluring *ailleurs*, as though the concrete objects of this world could not conceivably satisfy the needs of his own swoon of infinite desire. Nabokov's hero and heroine, on the other hand, delight in the concrete particulars of this world, observe and recall them with tender meticulous care, and they both passionately love existence in this world, each being the other's ultimate point of anchorage in it, Van's male V or arrowhead (*ardis* in Greek) perfectly fitting into its inverted and crossed female mirror-image, the A of his sister-soul (ideogrammatists take note, Freudians beware).

The mirror play of Van's and Ada's initials—underscored at one point when Nabokov finds dramatic occasion to print the A upside-down—suggests that the two are perfect lovers because ultimately they are complementary halves of one self. Indeed, Van's book is really "written" by the two of them, one imagination called "Vaniada" expressing itself in two antiphonal voices. The birthmark on the back of Van's right hand reappears in exactly the corresponding spot on Ada's left hand, for both physically and psychically the lovers are really the two halves of that androgynous pristine human zestfully described by Aristophanes in Plato's *Symposium*. According to rabbinic legend, Adam in the Garden before the creation of Eve was androgynous, and it is clear that Nabokov, like the rabbis, has conjoined the Greek and the Hebrew myths, creating in his deliciously intertwined sister and brother an image of prelapsarian, unfragmented man.

A major clue to Nabokov's intention in this respect is the repeated allusion, especially in the Ardis section of the novel, to one of the most splendidly realized experiences of paradise in English poetry, Marvell's "The Garden." Adolescent Ada tries to translate the poem into French (in her version, an oak tree stands prominently at the beginning of the second line); after the lovers' first separation, the poem, most appropriately, serves as a code-key for the letters in cipher that they exchange. The second stanza of the poem, not quoted in the novel, begins as follows: "Fair quiet, have I found thee here,/And Innocence thy Sister dear!/Mistaken long, I sought you then/In busie Companies of Men." The lines are, of course, applicable point for point to the novel, a kind of adumbration of its plot, though both "sister" and "innocence" are given rather different

meanings. Marvell's poem is a vision of bliss beyond the raging of physical passion; the solitary garden-dweller, however, does revel in the pleasures of the senses, luscious fruit dropping from the trees to delight his palate, while his mind withdraws into the happiness of self-contemplation where it—like the author of *Ada?*—"creates, transcending these,/Far other Worlds, and other Seas." In *Ada's* ardisiac setting, luscious fruit also comes falling from the branches, when the tree-climbing young Ada slips and ends up straddling an astonished Van from the front, thus offering him an unexpectedly intimate first kiss, since, as we are told several times, she wears no underpants. In a moment Ada will claim that this is the Tree of Knowledge, brought to the Ardis estate from Eden National Park, but her slip from its branches clearly enacts a Happy Fall, for in this garden, as in Marvell's, no fatal sin is really possible. Marvell's poem also gives us a comic image of a Fall with no evil consequences: "Stumbling on Melons, as I pass,/ Insnar'd with Flow'rs, I fall on Grass." The interlaced limbs of ardently tumbling Van and Ada are similarly assimilated to the premoral world of vegetation, likened to tendril climbers; and Van, rushing away from a last embrace of Ada at the moment of their first separation, is actually described "stumbling on melons," an allusion which would seem to promise that he will eventually return to his Ada-Ardis-Eden.

It is the concluding stanza, however, of Marvell's "Garden" that offers the most suggestive model for what Nabokov seeks to achieve in *Ada*. After the garden-dweller's soul, whetting and combing its silver wings among the branches, has experienced ecstasy, the poet glances backward at the first Adam's paradise and then returns us to the "real" world of time, but it is a time now transfigured by art, nature ordered by "the skilful Gardner" in a floral sundial to measure time. The industrious bee, then, no less than man, "computes its time" (in 17th-century pronunciation, a pun on "thyme" and thus a truly Nabokovian wordplay) with herbs and flowers; time the eroder has been alchemized in this artful re-creation of paradise into a golden translucence, delighting palate and eye. Nabokov means to create just such an inter-involvement of art and pleasure transcending time, or rather capturing its elusive living "texture," as Van Veen calls it, and this, finally, is the dramatic function of the novel's unflagging emphasis on erotic experience. The point is made clearer in the novel by still another allusion. Marvell's "Garden" modulates into several other poems in the course of the narrative, but the most significant is Baudelaire's *Invitation au voyage*, which is burlesqued in the novel with an oak tree inserted in the second and third line, to establish the cross-link with Marvell. The Baudelaire poem is also a ravishing dream of a perfect world, a world saturated with both generally sensual and specifically erotic delight, but realized, as such bliss can only be realized, through the beautiful ordering of art. Against the background of the novel, the famous opening lines of the poem become an evocation of Ardis, Van addressing Ada: "*Mon enfant, ma soeur,/Songe à la douceur/D'aller là-bas vivre ensemble!/Aimer à loisir/Aimer et mourir/Au pays qui te ressemble!*" ("My child, my sister,/ Think of the delight/ Of going there to live together!/ To love at ease/ To love and die/ In the land that resembles you!") It is noteworthy that fragments of these lines are bandied about by Ada at the point in the narrative when their first sexual intimacy is recollected; significantly, this is the one moment in the novel when Ada actually says to Van that they are not two different people.

Baudelaire's poem, then, suggests what is also clear in the novel in other ways, that *Ada* is formed on the paradox of rendering the perfect state of nature through a perfect state of art, self-conscious, allusive, and exquisitely ordered. In this respect, Nabokov also follows the model of Milton (who is burlesqued in tetrameters at one point) in the fourth book of *Paradise Lost*, where prelapsarian Eden is described through the most finely ostentatious artifice—a natural garden full of sapphire founts, sands of gold, burnished fruit, crystal-mirror brooks, in which the preceding literary tradition of envisioned paradises is incorporated through the cunning strategy of negation ("Not that fair field/Of Enna . . . ," and so forth). It may be that *Ada* pays a price as a novel for being an extended poetic vision of Eden: Van and Ada sometimes seem to be more voices and images in a lyric poem than novelistic characters; the excess of perfection they must sustain makes them less interesting individually, less humanly engaging, than many of Nabokov's previous protagonists. In compensation, the expression in *Ada* of a lover's consummated delight in life and beauty is an achievement that has very few equals in the history of the novel. Let me offer a brief representative instance, in which the lovers' present is juxtaposed with their ardisiac past:

> Her plump, stickily glistening lips smiled.
> (When I kiss you *here*, he said to her years later,
> I always remember that blue morning on the balcony
> when you were eating a *tartine au miel*; so much
> better in French.)
> The classical beauty of clover honey, smooth,
> pale, translucent, freely flowing from the spoon and
> soaking my love's bread and butter in liquid brass.
> The crumb steeped in nectar.

The honeyed bread-slice here is very much a Nabokovian equivalent of Proust's *petite madeleine* and of that more erotic tidbit, the ambrosial seedcake which Molly Bloom puts from her mouth into her young lover Leopold's. Through its sweetness past and present fuse, or, to speak more precisely, they fuse through its sweetness minutely observed and recollected, then distilled into the lucid order of a poem that moves in alliterative music through a poised choreography of dactyls and trochees to the culminating metaphorical paradox of the honey as liquid brass and the final substitution of nectar for the honey, now become "literally" food for the gods.

At several points in the novel the narrator takes pains to inform us that Ada in Russian means "hell." The point, I would assume, is that Ada and Van in their Eden are in a state before the knowledge of good and evil, when heaven and hell cannot be distinguished. This also suggests, however, that there could be an ambiguous underside of evil in the edenic fulfillment offered Van by his sister-soul, and the suicide to which the two of them inadvertently drive Lucette may indicate that a paradisiac love can have evil consequences when it impinges on the lives of others outside the Garden. In any case, the ultimate sense of the novel is of all threats of evil, including the evil of the corrosive passage of time, finally transcended by the twinned power of art and love. One last clue encodes this idea as a signature of affirmation at the end of the novel. Moving around mysteriously in the background of the concluding section is an unexplained figure named Ronald Oranger. Since he marries the typist responsible for Van's manuscript, and since he and his wife, according to a prefatory note, are the only significant persons mentioned in the book still alive when it is published, one may assume that his is the final responsibility for the text of *Ada*, he the presiding spirit at the end. All we really know about him is his name, which means "orange tree" in French. No orange trees are explicitly mentioned in Marvell's "Garden," though they are spectacularly present in "Bermudas," another remarkable poem by Marvell about a garden-paradise. In any event, "Ronald

Oranger" has an anagrammatic look, and could be rearranged as a reversal of the book's title, "angel nor ardor"—which is to say, the fixative force of art, working through the imagination of love, has extracted heaven from hell, Eden from Ada, has established a perfected state that originates in the carnal passions but goes quite beyond them. Fortunately, the code-games and allusions in *Ada* are merely pointers to the peculiar nature of the novel's imaginative richness, which does not finally depend on the clues. Few books written in our lifetime afford so much pleasure. Perhaps the parody-blurb at the end is not so wrong in proffering the novel as a voluminous bag of rare delights: Nabokov's garden abounds with the pleasurable visions whose artful design I have tried to sketch out here, and, as the blurb justifiably concludes, with "much, much more."

TONY TANNER
From "On Lexical Playfields"
City of Words: American Fiction 1950–1970
1971, pp. 33–39

Nabokov and Borges are two writers whose work is exerting a strong influence on the American fiction of the present. Whether or not Nabokov's American passport makes him an American writer is a piece of taxonomy which is of very little interest—it is probably better to say that he is a Russian writer who spent long years in Europe before continuing his exile in America. Clearly his experience of America helped to influence the final form of two of his major works, while his latest novel he describes as 'set in a dream America'. But scholars such as Andrew Field have shown that the seeds of his 'American' novels were sown and growing before he emigrated there, and it is what might be called the *example* of Nabokov that I wish to comment on here. In an interview he stated his opinion that 'Average reality begins to rot and stink as soon as the act of individual creation ceases to animate a subjectively perceived texture.'[1] These creative acts effectively maintain reality, just as—it is his comparison—electricity binds the earth together. The desire to 'animate a subjectively perceived texture' is visibly at work in many contemporary American novels and among other things it leads to ⟨. . .⟩ foregrounding. ⟨. . .⟩ A book like *Pale Fire* is nearly all foreground. Something of this is implicit in Nabokov's comment in the same interview that

> one of the functions of all my novels is to prove that
> the novel in general does not exist. The book I make
> is a subjective and specific affair. I have no purpose at
> all when composing the stuff except to compose it. I
> work hard, I work long, on a body of words until it
> grants me complete possession and pleasure.

Not until it mirrors some pre-selected area of external reality. This is rather like James's 'fun', but taken further. For in *Pale Fire* we cannot even be sure of what is notionally real and what is illusion or sport. Lewis Carroll is one of Nabokov's favourite writers, but we do see Alice before she passes through the mirror or falls down the hole; a boundary between differing worlds is visibly crossed. Whereas in *Pale Fire* we don't know whether mad Kinbote 'exists' and Shade is his fantasy; or whether Shade is indeed a poet and Kinbote a projection of his subconscious. We have only documents: a Foreword, a poem, a commentary, an index. Were they all written by Kinbote, by Shade? All we can be sure of is that they were all written by Nabokov.

In a sense this is a banal truth about all novels, that they are the fictions of the author. But there are certain conventions for establishing the status of the referents in the book. When James says London, or Joyce says Dublin, we permit ourselves to draw on our associations from more orthodox geographies. But when Nabokov says America and Zembla and puts them together in the same frame as though belonging to the same dimensions—cohabiting on one plane—then our reading of the signs is necessarily more confused, the old associations are unsettled, and normal confidences as to the location of the 'real' are shaken. The old geographies no longer obtain. This of course is exactly what he intends and I think we can imagine the kind of delight it might give to American writers who have a suspicion of old maps. It certainly gave pleasure to Mary McCarthy, who wrote a very persuasive and appreciative eulogy on the book when it appeared.[2] She appreciated the novel just because it was such a beautiful game: 'a novel on several levels is revealed, and these "levels" are not the customary "levels of meaning" of modernist criticism but planes in fictive space . . . Each plane or level in its shadow box proves to be a false bottom; there is an infinite regression, for the book is a book of mirrors.' She concluded with the assertion that the book is 'one of the very great works of art of this century.'

I am not maintaining that all American novelists responded with this degree of enthusiasm to *Pale Fire*, but McCarthy's pleasure at Nabokov's subversion of 'customary levels of meaning' and the expertise with which he conducts his games in 'fictive space' seems to be indicative of a dissatisfaction with the norms and procedures of the more conventional novel shared by many of her contemporaries. Among other things *Pale Fire* is an exhibition of the kind of freedom from inherited formulae and prescriptions which many American writers are seeking. In a book of mirrors every statement is dubious since we cannot establish the degree of refraction or indeed the reliability of the source, but Kinbote perhaps speaks for his author when he insists 'that "reality" is neither the subject nor the object of true art which creates its own special reality having nothing to do with the average "reality" perceived by the communal eye.' This is of course a king talking, whether a genuine or a fantastical one does not matter, and he reveals at the very least a regal contempt for the 'communal' models of reality.

Nabokov's work is full of individuals who experience intense isolation of consciousness. No matter what is the particular occasion of their alienation or self-imposed sever-ance from the commonalty, they are all types of the artist, created by the man who said, 'the type of artist who is always in exile even though he may never have left the ancestral hall or the paternal parish is a well-known biographical figure with whom I feel some affinity.' There is obviously a good deal of aristocratic disdain here for the mass of ordinary people labouring heavily in more clogged and constricting versions of reality. But it is equally clear that a large number of American writers feel a great dismay or repugnance at the idea that the reality they live in should be determined by the surrounding masses and their media. Nabokov's apparently effortless ges-tures of self-liberation through the sheer activity of writing—he is a veritable Houdini in slipping out of the bonds of the established genres—could well make him an attractive, even heroic example to many of them. For it is not uncommon for an American writer to feel 'always in exile' while still at home. There is a minor figure mentioned in *Pale Fire* who, we are told, one day 'thought he was God and began redirecting the trains'. He is called a lunatic but Shade defends him as a fellow poet and rejects the former term. '"That is the wrong word," he said. "One should not apply it to a person who deliberately

peels off a drab and unhappy past and replaces it with a brilliant invention."' For those seeking to 'invent' themselves rather than be content to become the third persons of other people's definitions, there is much solace to be found in this authorita-tive defender of 'brilliant invention'.

The insistence throughout his work is that there is no such thing as life or reality, there is only your life and what you make of it, your reality and how you shape it. Of course a majority of the people may accept the conditions and terms of reality as it is already defined for them. In some senses they may have to. Nabokov tells us that the first inspiration for *Lolita* was a story about an ape who after months of coaxing produced the first drawing by an animal; 'this sketch showed the bars of the poor creature's cage.' It is obviously a pregnant and pathetic story for a writer whose work is full of prisons of all kinds, political and psychological, social and personal—the lonely motel room, the claustrophobia of an obsession. Alfred Appel is right to say that 'his characters continually confront mirrors where they had hoped to find windows, and the attempt to transcend solipsism is one of Nabokov's major themes.'[3] But in addition his characters might find bars where they had looked for windows, and like the poor ape take these as the necessary limits of reality. Both Humbert and Kinbote are effectively in prisons while they are writing their stories or notes, but they do not limit themselves to describing the bars of the cage. If anything their bars are all but banished by the almost compulsive resourcefulness of their styles. There is a literary, as well as a metaphysical, moral in this and my contention is that American writers have not been slow to see it.

There are already many admirable critics and exegetes of Nabokov's work, such as Andrew Field, Alfred Appel, Carl Proffer, and Mary McCarthy herself. For any adequate treatment of Nabokov's work, they should be consulted. My only purpose here is to make a few points about *Pale Fire* which are relevant to the context of this study. One of the readings which the novel allows (to put it no more strongly) is that Kinbote is Shade's creation, his fantasy life, the other half of the dour New England poet who projects himself in the poem; the mad notes being, as it were, the complement of those rational and balanced Pope-like couplets. An important clue here could be Nabokov's statement in the same interview that 'John Shade in *Pale Fire* leads an intense inner existence' and in the Notes we do read of a character who reminds one 'of a slow speaking ventriloquist who is interrupted by his garrulous doll'. This fits rather well the terseness of Shade's poem, and the intrusive volubility of Kinbote's notes, thrusting in Zemb-lan material on the smallest pretext or no pretext at all. If we take Kinbote as someone—something—living in unwilling exile in a rather unspecific sense, something suppressed and all but totally excluded from those places into which he wishes most to be accepted, then I think it is quite possible to see him as incorporating the fantasy life of John Shade. Which is the 'real life' of John Shade, the factual or the fantastic? Nabokov's fiction is certainly not going to decide. It is quite possible that Shade has found release for his fantasy life in an imaginary world which he has constructed around the 'Zembla' he came across in Pope's poetry. In another interview Nabokov said that 'a sad and distant kingdom seems to have haunted my poetry and fiction since the twenties. It is not associated with my personal past.'[4] It seems appropriate in all sorts of ways that the last entry in the index, which is the last line in *Pale Fire*, should simply be: 'Zembla, a distant northern land.' In differing ways that land is Kinbote's, Shade's and Nabokov's.

The least contentious or digressive of Kinbote's notes is his comment on lines 557–8, 'the loveliest couplet in this canto'. The couplet reads:

How to locate in blackness, with a gasp,
Terra the Fair, an orbicle of jasp.

The Russian *zemlya* apparently means land, terra; and Terra the Fair could be earth or Zembla, any world you can locate which will, to go on to line 559, help you 'keep sane in spiral types of space'. It would seem that on this sentiment Shade and Kinbote are at one; as though Pope and the mad king had found a point of concurrence in Shade's poem. *Pale Fire* is Nabokov's 'orbicle' in which different orders of reality can be brought together in new relationships by the 'combinational magic' of the author. The idea of usually separate realms merging, communicating or interpenetrating is kept alive in various ways throughout the book, and crucial motifs throughout are those of the mirror and the window, the obvious meeting points of different 'spaces' or worlds. Most critics have pointed out that the first lines of Shade's poem

I was the shadow of the waxwing slain
By the false azure in the windowpane;

point directly to the possible confusion of realms—seeing an extension of ordinary reality in what is in fact a reflection—which is at the heart of the book. In one sense it is Nabokov's delight to conflate these realms; but there is also the warning of the bird which is dead because of its inability to perceive where one world gives way to another. This should perhaps remind us that the book is among other things a murder story, and that the physical Shade is unmistakably dead at the end, even if the royal creation of his fantasy lives on in desperate disguises.

There are several ominous breakages which seem to presage the fatal intersection of the poem and the bullet—a stained-glass window broken by a football, a TV screen smashed by a thunderbolt. The way these hard, mindless facts shatter the fragile panes of fancy simply through the force of their propulsion is an apt prefiguration of the movement of Gradus towards the last line of Shade's poem. Gradus is represented as a creature of a lower order, a 'dummy', a 'clockwork man'. He comes from that group called the Shadows dedicated to destroying the king, one of whose members 'had lost a leg in trying to make anti-matter'. Such people exist only to further the work of negation. And clearly Gradus is representative of all that is utterly inimical and hostile to art and imagination. It is worth noting that when Nabokov/Kinbote is describing the behaviour of Gradus he does so in a style which is minutely factual and detailed. By itemizing his meals, his newspaper, his bowel movements, Nabokov emphasizes the utter physicality of the man—a thing among things—and it seems clear that Nabokov is at the same time offering a low parody of realism and naturalism, as though to demonstrate that such a style is only appropriate for creatures immersed so deeply and mindlessly in the realm of fact.

The exact identity or status of Gradus/Grey I am not attempting to decide; in a book of mirrors it is proper that it should remain ambiguous. But his role in Nabokov's overall pattern is hinted at in a couple of clues which can point us to Nabokov's own attitude towards literature. Early on in his search Gradus, not for the first time, goes astray. 'In the vicinity of Lex he lost his way among tortuous lanes.' When he is finally searching for his prey on the campus it happens again, this time in the library. A library is very exactly a lexical town and what we notice here is that Gradus gets completely lost every time he approaches the realm of words and books. Shade and Kinbote on the contrary are very much at home on what Kinbote aptly calls 'lexical playfields'. To make the point even clearer, Kinbote tells us that Shade had a great fondness for 'all sorts of word games and especially for so-called word golf', and

that he himself has done 'hate-love in three, lass-male in four, and live-dead in five'. On lexical playfields man enjoys a flexibility, indeed a mastery, that he cannot hope to gain in the world of material fact. The rigid categories and concepts of life and death, the great mysteries of sexual differences and emotional opposites become plastic and malleable—the deft player can turn them into their opposites. This is the artist's temporary triumph over the brute materiality and momentum incorporate in Gradus. On lexical playfields a man can be a king, even if he is a king in hiding, while Gradus is doomed for ever to get lost as he approaches the city of Lex.

Card games and chess games of course proliferate in Nabokov's work, and so does another game—literary parody ('parody is a game' he said in the second interview referred to). This game, like many games, is also a form of defence; it is a way of distancing an influence and reducing its potency. Proust said that a writer might parody another writer to become free of his spell and thus able to write his own novels. Just so we could see Nabokov keeping at bay, for example, Poe and Dostoevsky, in *Lolita*. This is of particular relevance to young writers who, with all the writers in world literature ready to impress forms on their creative minds, have found a special value in parody as a way of writing which liberates itself from the style it seems to be emulating. The game, then, is the thing: ' "Oh, my Lolita, I have only words to play with!" ' cries Humbert, but we have seen that for Nabokov that is how the game has to be played. One of the things that all games have in common is that they occupy a distinct symbolic space which is organized by fixed rules which do not apply outside the playfield. Clearly there is some very radical urge for stability, for known and familiarized territory, in the human instinct to invent games. Kinbote at one point talks of 'the fanning out of additional squares which a chess knight (that skip-space piece), standing on a marginal field, "feels" in phantom extensions beyond the board, but which have no effect whatever on his real moves, on the real play.' It is the space around the board which stimulates the sense of the need for marked squares and rules governing lines of motion.

In Shade's poem he says that the I.P.H. (Institution for Preparation for the Hereafter) among other things prepared one for possibly unpleasant surprises after death.

What if you are tossed
Into a boundless void, your bearings lost,
Your spirit stripped and utterly alone,
Your task unfinished, your despair unknown . . .

Then it is that the I.P.H. taught you 'how to locate in blackness' that 'orbicle of jasp', and 'How to keep sane in spiral types of space.' The orbicle, the chessboard, the card game, the novel—these are all ways ultimately of keeping sane in space, of establishing some known and organized terra firma which can support and sustain you in the 'boundless void'. There has always been a highly developed awareness of 'space' in American writing, and the compulsion to erect a verbal world, map out a lexical playfield, to triumph over vertigo, diffusion, and victimization, which the perpetual exile Nabokov exhibits, has certainly had its effect on a generation of American writers who are not unfamiliar with those feelings in their own country.

Notes

1. This interview appeared in the *Listener*, October 10th, 1968.
2. Mary McCarthy's article appeared in *Encounter*, October 1962.
3. 'Lolita: The Springboard of Parody' by Alfred Appel, Jr., *Wisconsin Studies in Contemporary Literature*, ii 1967.
4. 'An Interview with Vladimir Nabokov', *Wisconsin Studies in Contemporary Literature*, ii 1967.

EDMUND WHITE
"The Esthetics of Bliss"

Saturday Review, January 6, 1973, pp. 33–34

The great irony is that Nabokov should be both Russian and American. The two cultures are equally avid of message, equally insistent upon confessional sincerity, equally leery of disinterested pleasure—and Nabokov is precisely that writer who has announced that he entertains no general ideas, who regards the diary as the lowest form of writing, who subscribes solely to the esthetics of bliss. And yet a closer look reveals he's had his fun with both sets of dour compatriots; he is the flinty antagonist, his brilliance the light sparked from friction. He plays games with our expectations, now frustrating them, now fulfilling them, now forcing them to change; if you're not already one, you must become a bit of a prig in order to experience the thrill of having Nabokov scandalize you in all the right places. Nabokov *needs* you to believe in the suburban pieties (progressive education, sentimental leftism, psychoanalysis, Thomas Mann), just as his parodic style requires that you be familiar with mystery stories, case reports, scholarly monographs, utopian novels, fairy tales.

His superb disdain, of course, will not be imitated; who else could burn with such fine, old-fashioned indignation against "tension-releasing" group therapy, symbol-hunting criticism, Marxist doubletalk? *Our* nerveless method of dealing with dogmatism and vulgarity is to be in sly, weary collusion with it (Andy Warhol, that terminally American figure, once said his work was "a way of liking things"). Although passivity masked as irony might seem objectionable to Nabokov, he cannot object to our ignoring his morals and studying his manners; when he talks about books, he always restricts himself to an appreciation of technique: he deals in glittering particularities.

When looked at line by line, as one looks at poetry, Nabokov's is a technique of precision. In *Transparent Things* we have these distinctions: "A bunch of bellflowers and bluebonnets (their different shades having a lovers' quarrel) had been placed, either by the assistant manager, who respected sentiment, or by Person himself, in a vase on the commode next to Person's shed tie, which was of a third shade of blue but of another material (sericanette)." In every book the exact word is found, the imprecise locution rejected. When Humbert Humbert says goodbye to Lolita for the last time, he reports: "I was surprised (this a rhetorical figure, I was not) that the sight of the old car in which she had ridden as a child and nymphet, left her so very indifferent."

What's remarkable is that this precision doesn't isolate the sentence and turn it into a free-standing paragraph, as precision quite literally makes paragraphs out of virtually every sentence in a Firbank or Kawabata novel. But then, unlike those two monks of natural and social detail, Nabokov is possessed of the very worldly compulsion to tell a story, and that compulsion links his sentences rhythmically and psychologically.

The most distinctive aspect of the Nabokovian sentence is its length, its flexibility, its comprehensive and rapid notation of complex sensations and thoughts. Nabokov has reminded his fellow authors that in a single sentence an image of innocent delight can be turned, through a Gogolian simile, into the last rites for a dying civilization. I'm talking about the close of the first chapter of *Speak, Memory*. Nabokov's father is being tossed in the air by local peasants, while young Vladimir watches from an upper window: "Thrice, to the mighty heave-ho of his invisible tossers, he would fly up in this fashion, and the second time he would go higher than the first and then

there he would be, on his last and loftiest flight, reclining, as if for good, against the cobalt blue of the summer noon, like one of those paradisiac personages who comfortably soar, with such a wealth of folds in their garments, on the vaulted ceiling of a church while below, one by one, the wax tapers in mortal hands light up to make a swarm of minute flames in the mist of incense, and the priest chants of eternal repose, and funeral lilies conceal the face of whoever lies there, among the swimming lights, in the open coffin." That sentence, when we first read it, was good, black caviar to convalescents fed on *style blanc*.

A novel is not a poem, however, or, in the case of Nabokov, not just a poem. Through hundreds of pages the novelist must decide: how many times he should return to the hero's clumsiness in order to imprint it on the reader's mind; whether Suspense, that tease, should shed six or seven veils during her dance; whether the sweet nothings his lovers say should be quoted in all their banality or paraphrased from the more flattering distance of indirect discourse.

A whole book would be necessary to evaluate Nabokov's skill in wielding fictional structures. Let one lone example, lightly sketched in, suffice. In *Pale Fire* Nabokov is faced with the special problem of how to maintain our interest in Kinbote, the lunatic commentator and repellent character. The austere Beckett, I suppose, would not have worried whether we were or were not interested in Kinbote. A hack would have made Kinbote "psychotic" and depended on our compassion for the sick to do the trick. But Nabokov introduces us to a new sensation—admiration for, even collaboration with, Kinbote's insane exegesis even as we loathe or laugh at the exegete. How does the writer make us both a judge of, and an accessory to, the crime? By placing us at the exact center of an expanding system, by showing us how that system elaborates itself, by making us participants in a project as risky and speculative as writing a novel or living. We are all living life as if it were a novel that will one day surrender a meaning or, at least, assume significant form; how willing we are to help Kinbote impress *his* version of himself on the resistant text of experience.

Poetic precision and a large grasp of fictional structures, then, make Nabokov's writing exemplary. May the example be well taken! On the map of contemporary American literature he is due N.—magnetic, cold, giving a sense of direction to smaller craft. He certainly provides an admirable contrast to another widely imitated American writer, Norman Mailer. Mailer is our D. H. Lawrence. He is as turbulent, as concerned with sex and power and the unconscious, as messianic. Like Lawrence, he runs the risk (to borrow, out of context, a phrase from Richard Poirier) of confusing his body with the body politic. Small occurrences (a hangover, a headache), which would seem meaningless to any less acute observer, take on vast significance for him. If an elephant does a good handstand at a demonstration for Nixon, Mailer is quite capable of finding in the animal's cleverness a sign that Nixon's people may be "in command of small subtleties"—though Mailer reserves judgment and, quite seriously, enters this datum into the "first freshets of his brooding." Nabokov could never seem as relevant to young, or as ludicrous to mature, minds.

Nor could Nabokov ever write, as Mailer wrote in *An American Dream*, a sentence of this sort: "The only true journey of knowledge is from the depth of one being to the heart of another and I was nothing but open raw depths at that instant alone on the balcony, looking down on Sutton Place, the spirits of the food and drink I had ingested wrenched out of my belly and upper gut, leaving me in raw Being, there were

2802

clefts and rents which cut like geological faults right through all the lead and concrete and kapok and leather of my ego, that mutilated piece of insulation, I could feel my Being, ridiculous enough, what! I could feel lights shifting inside myself, drifting like vapors over the broken rocks of my ego while a forest of small nerves jumped up, foul in their odor, smelling for all the world like the rotten, carious shudder of a decayed tooth."

If Nabokov were not with us, would Americans have thought *that* was the way to do it? Without Nabokov, would we still be cultists of tough-guy sincerity? Would we ever have known that an artist can be as convincing as a polemicist? Americans have seldom felt at ease with literary art. They have wanted it to be uplifting or "activist." They have expected books to be thermometers, taking the temperature of the *Zeitgeist*—or at least battle reports from the front lines of a beleaguered ego. Without Nabokov, we might have gone on thinking *Ars gratia artis* meant Oscar Wilde; how useful to know it can also mean ardor, grace, *Ada*.

GARRY WILLS
"The Devil and Lolita"

New York Review of Books, February 21, 1974, pp. 4–6

It begins when a match is struck on a darkened hotel porch, and a soft voice rasps "th' equivocations of the fiend."

"Where the devil did you get her?"

"I beg your pardon?"

"I said: the weather is getting better."

"Seems so."

"Who's the lassie?"

"My daughter."

"You lie—she's not."

"I beg your pardon?"

"I said: July was hot. Where's her mother?"

"Dead."

Humbert Humbert knew, without knowing it, that McFate would speak in time—"Aubrey McFate," the obscure thwarter hovering somewhere. Even when this private devil acquires a face (and endless cars), there is nothing to call him, for a long time, but McFate. Only when clues jumble near each other for a long time do they, clair-obscurely, finally spell out in patches this devil's name: Clare Quilty.

Nabokov's *Lolita* is (at last estimate) two thousand or so things—prominent among the rest, a detective story. (McFate is sometimes called Lieutenant Trapp.) As in *Crime and Punishment*, the detective is also the criminal; but Dostoyevsky makes Raskolnikov play this double role, back and forth, through a policeman essentially outside the crime: he must stalk the man who stalks him. Humbert and Quilty, by contrast, track in on each other as mutual accuser-criminals, growing toward each other's destruction, Humbert in terror and Quilty with a leer. Not only Humbert, but Lolita herself, is possessed by Quilty, who can only be exorcised at last by murder. This detective story does not solve a crime, but *is* solved *by* one.

It is also, of course, a love story, as many have realized. All the clinical talk of girls half-nymphed into womanhood—time's mermaids, amphibious, belonging fully to neither world—is in the long run misleading. Lolita does not fulfill Humbert's obsession with nymphets; she destroys it. His concern had been for a type, cocooned outside of time in a frozen moment of becoming. The mounted butterfly cannot decay, because it cannot (any longer) live. Humbert, with a

thousand such butterfly slides to view, in his poise of remote satisfaction, meets Lolita at just her moment of chrysalis—loss and descent from nymphethood—and he follows her down. The two years of his life with her, and the two years after, are all post-nymphet years. He sees her last in a splayed and cowlike pregnancy, and never loved her more. By his own fastidious measure, cultivated half a lifeless lifetime, she represents his fall from an aesthetic state of grace. He dies into time with every sag of her flesh. Having flirted with her in his Eden of the mind, he loves her outside the fiery gates—now his and her flesh darken together back toward earth. He is redeemed by his fall, made capable of loving. And so capable of damning her.

> She was only the faint violet whiff and dead leaf echo of the nymphet I had rolled myself upon with such cries in the past; an echo on the brink of a russet ravine, with a far wood under a white sky, and brown leaves choking the brook, and one last cricket in the crisp weeds . . . but thank God it was not that echo alone that I worshiped. What I used to pamper among the tangled vines of my heart, *mon grand pêché radieux*, had dwindled to its essence: sterile and selfish vice, all *that* I canceled and cursed.

Lolita is an even rarer thing than an honest love story. It is our best modern hate story. Unrequited love is, from the outset, half made up of hate. Self-hate for loving—or else, on the other side, for not loving; a shared intimacy of detesting, uncontrollable as love itself. To be the unwilling object of another's love is embarrassing, oddly debilitating. What should be a reciprocal relationship is both interrupted and uninterruptible; an intensely "personing" energy pounds at the unresponding object, thrusting an Other in on a violated Self. It gives the loved an unwanted responsibility for the lover, victimizing the loved as an unwilling victor.

It is common to say that we become, in some measure, those we love. It is a circularly weird fact that we become, will we or not, those who love us. The very lack of reciprocation forges a bond. After all, no one cares as much for anyone as does that person's lover—except each of us caring for himself. No matter what the diversion or barriers between a cold loved person and the lover, they agree on one crucial point—both *do* love the same person. There is a union achieved by reason of a common object, which is the one kind of union lacking in the true reciprocity of love, where the lovers have different objects—A's being B, and B's being A. In the case of the loved unlover (who is an unmoved mover), the secret tie lies in a barren uniformity under all the reversals: both A and B love A, and only A. Set apart in all things else, on this point they are undivided—and what was put apart in heaven cannot be sundered on earth. The broken circuit pours all its electrocuting force into the point of rupture, which is a unifying focus. Bound, by division.

This is the bond Humbert and Lolita share, wedded by her unresponsiveness. She accepts that burden, and even appeals to it, later, asking for financial support as a dark marriage right. But as they both loved the same object ("Lo"), they are also linked, in a camaraderie of plague victims, by hating the same object: the Humbert mirrored back on Humbert in her own revulsion or coarsening. Eve cannot hate the serpent near as well as the serpent does. The love that freed Humbert from Eden—and now binds him—crippled and distorted her. There is nothing crueler than love. He needs her, and diminishes her by the need; and despises himself for doing so. He preys on what he admires, destroying it with admiration. He is her tempter, but also—quite sincerely, as he assures Quilty at the end—her father. Both God and Satan to her, creating and undoing her. Romantic agony over his own deterioration he could stand, and even prettify. But love breaks him out from all such excuses into a larger prison—hers, the one he forged for her in darkness. His hell is the fact that he damned her. Listening from a hill to the play of children, he muses:

> One could hear now and then, as if released, an almost articulate spurt of vivid laughter, or the crack of a bat, or the clatter of a toy wagon, but it was all really too far for the eye to distinguish any movement in the lightly etched streets. I stood listening to that musical vibration from my lofty slope, to those flashes of separate cries with a kind of demure murmur for background, and then I knew that the hopelessly poignant thing was not Lolita's absence from my side, but the absence of her voice from that concord.

Love destroys. We all seduce and abuse one child, the one we once loved best, the one we were born as; and we mistreat all others in obscure revenge for what was done to us (mainly by us). Of course, Lolita's fall—like Margaret's—was "the blight she was born for." It is, always, Margaret we mourn for. But woe to him by whom the scandal comes into the world. Humbert, fallen, can pay that price—this constitutes his superiority to the prelapsarian dandy of the book's first pages. But he "rose" to moral responsibility by making her fall with him.

Why is Quilty needed? Humbert is quite sufficient to his own dis-Edening. We all glide as our own serpent into our own garden. Why blame this on any other? Humbert mirrors the answer back on Humbert: the hate in him mocking his love, growing with it, inseparable—until he kills it, hating his hatred out of existence, destroying himself for love. The intertwinedness of love and hate at their height does not correspond, as we dimly experience that clash, to neat metaphysical defenses of "all being as good." By this account of things, evil is nonbeing (*a defectus entis*)—not something positive itself, but the failure of all being that is limited, the brink, the fall-off into nonbeing, the point where good ceases to be good because it ceases to be anything at all.

Whether that argument makes sense to philosophers, I do not know. But it hardly matters to the rest of us, persons involved in stories—it is the very essence of our grasp upon ourselves that we figure in various plots. And in stories, for many and deepest reasons, evil is always a villain. Evil comes at us personified because we grasp it in ourselves as a *person's* act. We are at our worst, not where we tend not to be at all, but at the very peak of our powers. We get into "towering" rages, and are "beside ourselves" with an overflow of destructive indignation. We become something *more* just as we are making others less—Humberts feeding on our own Lolitas, our loved things marred. Evil is what Milton called it, "Heav'n ruining from Heav'n," the highest things in us deliberately reaching down.

There is a Humbertian irony in the fact that William Blatty, author of *The Exorcist*, chose Teilhard de Chardin as his model for the book's saint, for the practiced wrestler with embodied fiends. Teilhard, that anthropological mystic, believed in the *defectus entis* approach to evil. For him, evil was the mere lag that any temporal evolution must entail—and since evolution moves away from inert matter and on toward universal personhood, he must deny the existence of a Lucifer whose fall predates man's rise. (What was there, before the omega-ing of man and time, to "fall," or to fall *from*?) Evil is, for him, the blind backward tug and brute reluctance of that marble from which evolution is sculpting the person. It is

literally "low life," falling away from the evolutionary mainstream toward no-life.

But everyone knows the devil is a toff. He is not low on the scale of being, but intimidatingly high—in art as well as doctrine; and, most important of all, in us. There is something in man that promotes treason at the top of his best efforts, that turns back and betrays—and *grows* by betraying, displaying new human powers. It is no good to talk, in this area, of man's mere encasement in the flesh, or the world's solicitings. Lucifer rebels in the clouds, and falls from them, in regions where mere hatred becomes selfless, rapt by an ideal of undoing.

> And the barest branch is beautiful
> One moment, when it breaks.

God, as Chesterton wrote, made the world and saw that it was good—mud and sky and flesh. But hell is all a work of the spirit. It is terrifyingly high, not low, on the evolutionary scale.

Real hatred, the staggering mysterious thing, has a kind of purity to it. Men surpass themselves, reach out, open windows of transcendence, by hatred as easily as love. All men are the same to Moby Dick. Only Ahab seeks the one thing consecrated by his hatred. Nature, red in tooth and claw, ravages mildly, with impartial voraciousness. Man alone reaches that height from which the real fall comes—the odd selflessness of hatred, trying to reverse creation. And as unrequited love intrudes without mercy on a man, so does apparently motiveless outside hate. The nut mail arrives, signaling one's importance to a stranger, the heat of a total person radiated toward one in reverse devotion. It is like being cared for by a very solicitous nurse from hell. Love tries to absorb the other, and so does hate. The unwilling recipient of this attention has obviously inflicted an agony he was unaware of, just like the loved person who cannot respond.

In this way does the cool, intelligent malice of Quilty dog and disanimate Humbert till he turns at bay to hunt down his hunter. Everything doubled and palindromic in Humbert Humbert—the father who cradles, and rapist who tore—adds up to the need for exorcizing Quilty. In the hall of mirrors that is man, we always mean more (or less) than we mean to mean; and are more or less than we aimed to be, minute by minute. And each of our other selves—greater or lesser—born out of the shadowy "real" self, nags at and haunts us. That must explain Plato's strong appeal to artists—the creative *idea* of oneself, pitted against the idea's mere reflection, so much less than we fantasied. Yet where did the "greater" fantasy come from but this "lesser" actuality? An "ought" echoes mockingly our "is," yet *is* the is, or comes from it. The prelapsarian I judges the fallen I—by permission of the fallen I's mind and struggle to be truly "I" and a soul. We fell before we were.

Yet that "I" which is before the world began can tower into dark majesty as well as primordial light. Quilty has not descended into the flesh by loving Lolita. He represents the pure butterfly-collecting Humbert of the book's first pages, living on untouched, playing in lepidopteral heaven—until boredom begins to twist the colored slides new perverse ways. Quilty uses and moves on, laughing. Of course, his amusements become more recondite, as his final temptations to Humbert indicate: he would have his chum with a gun join him in connoisseurship of "a young lady with three breasts, one a dandy." He barely remembers the girl who gave Humbert a soul to be damned. He remains a Humbert not yet fallen down toward love, a truly angelic mocker.

And Lolita is still fascinated by that "higher" Humbert, to which the lower one introduced her, seducing her—as it turns out—for another. *His* other. So Quilty must be destroyed, to rescue her. In the novel's mythic scheme, we never question the necessity of killing Quilty. Devils must be exorcised, destroyed even when this is self-destruction. Humbert therefore kills, like Ahab, trammeled up in his own act: "I rolled over him. We rolled over me. They rolled over him. We rolled over us."

This fierce exorcism over, Humbert rests in his own hell. Destroying his image, he has stepped through the mirror, gone where his *simius Dei* dwelt, whence he looks out now, suspended in an eternity of upside-down, the last Orwellian state:

> The road stretched across open country, and it occurred to me—not by way of protest, not as a symbol, or anything like that, but merely as a novel experience—that since I had disregarded all laws of humanity, I might as well disregard the rules of traffic. So I crossed to the left side of the highway and checked the feeling, and the feeling was good. It was a pleasant diaphragmal melting, with elements of diffused tactility, all this enhanced by the thought that nothing could be nearer to the elimination of basic physical laws than deliberately driving on the wrong side of the road. In a way, it was a very spiritual itch. Gently, dreamily, not exceeding twenty miles an hour, I drove on that queer mirror side

The "wrong side" is now his natural condition. He has achieved his hell through love, and the entire book, written in retrospect, is a set of love letters from hell. Hell, that is, is not an absence of love (*defectus amoris*), but a conscious love that tortures itself for what it has done to the beloved:

> Unless it can be proven to me—to me as I am now, today, with my heart and my beard, and my putrefaction—that in the infinite run it does not matter a jot that a North American girl-child named Dolores Haze had been deprived of her childhood by a maniac, unless that can be proven (and if it can, then life is a joke), I see nothing for the treatment of my misery, but the melancholy and very local palliative of articulate art.

So the hellish letters get written. By killing his devil-image in the mirror, Humbert has achieved his self-abdication, and can rest in hell.

Admittedly, Quilty is a fantasy within a fiction, Humbert Humbert's endless humbertizing, the shadow of a shadow. Mere symbol. But to call the devil a symbol is not to answer much. A symbol of what? Is it a necessary symbol? Does it say something for which we have no better sign or language? Why do men resort to this symbol again and again, in fresh circumstances? Literature is haunted by the evil *Doppelgänger*—the huge dim image reflected back on man as he both stretches himself out and diminishes himself in the endless tug and self-rendings of trapped hate and love. *Why, that is, does man so often come, at his best moments of discernment, to understand himself as an angel looking at the devil in a mirror?*

Lolita would not be the masterpiece it is without Quilty. The devil is, at least, necessary in that sense. Humbert, however complexified internally, needs his "outside" devil to become himself—by destroying himself. There is no question, here, of shifting blame onto another. We come to be, after all, in and through others. The serpent is in Eden for the same reason that Adam and Eve are—they must have a dialogue to have a seduction; man falls as part of a story, and drops into history.

And if calling the devil a mere symbol does not truly lay that ghost whose strength has always been precisely as a symbol, what are we to make of the dismissal of our devils as mere "personifications"? What else can persons do but "per-sonify" themselves and others, in the dialogue that gives them a story—i.e., a self? The mind—incapable of parthenogenesis, of *being* by simply thinking, of impregnating itself with an idea—*does* achieve mutual autogenesis with other minds, which mate themselves into existence, becoming their own and each other's offspring. Each mind is, at its least, two "generations" parenting and childed, simultaneously, in and on others. What will the offspring be? That depends on the entanglements of love and hate. Lolita, blossoming and blighted through Humbert, will reciprocally blight him in his blessed fall.

All our children are, in some measure, Rosemary's babies—and are ourselves. We play Laius to our own Oedipus. The mind "personifies" itself in others. "Selves." Throws off lesser or larger images of what *it* is—an image. Who is not a "personification"? We day by day create and uncreate each other in each other, suffering the gain-loss of our love-hates in endless chain reactions. We angel or ape on each other in half-conscious passing fits of mental coition, dealing and receiving life or death in a word or smile, filling the air with angels or devils that are our mental progeny; then driving off the devils, or beckoning them back. We all live by a mutual rescue, and die by a suicide pact. That is our shared original—and terminal—sin. History is a dialogue, of man with man, man with himself, each man with his own serpent. And as heart speaks to heart, our serpents, too, are whispering together.

Hell is others? Yes. And so is heaven. Just as hell is self, and so is heaven. We damn and redeem each other in a dialectic, by inextricable bindings and loosings. Others touch us, and strength flows from us, to help or hurt; cripple, or cure cripples, as we pass; exorcise, or possess. We blunder on, angeling in ape-form, falling from our angelhood just at the instant when we, at last, perceive it, living our death as we undo our lives. There is a doubleness to all we do, the balancing fall into love and rise into hate, the hovering and cloudy battle done over our heads by our best and worst at their alien height within us.

Is this devil enough, powers and principalities enough to prey in and on us; and, through us, in and on others? Perhaps—perhaps that is why we want to disentangle ourselves from such disturbing thoughts, and those works of art which lift us up where great men battle darkness. Better, it seems, to breathe free under a spiritless sky and in a dry vista. But at times that rasp and whisper can still be heard, behind us. Is it a person, an image, a symbol? Oneself, or a part of oneself—or that self "personed" in others? Part of me? Then *which* part? That which went out and reached others, mingled with them, grew large and came back at me as alien, unwanted? The corruption I bred absent-mindedly in others—the child come home for revenge on its parent? A person, a necessary aspect of personality; an inter-person, a "personing" where our spirit touches others?

One of these, or all of them? Whatever. It is Quilty. Deliver us from Him.

RICHARD POIRIER

New York Times Book Review, October 13, 1974, pp. 2–4

After Joyce with his "portrait" of Stephen, after Proust with his "remembrance" of Marcel, there are few reasons to be surprised, and many reasons to be disappointed, by the complicated interplay between Vladimir Nabokov and the narrator of ⟨*Look at the Harlequins!*⟩, his 37th book. Vadim Vadimovitch is a Russian emigré writer and a mirror image or "double" of Nabokov as man and writer; but unlike Proust or

Joyce, Nabokov never uses this version of himself as a way of questioning the authenticity of his own identity. The fictional self never challenges the "real" or authorial self. Nabokov and his works hover on the margins of the text, so to speak, as a static reality against which Vadim is to be measured. So that while the style of the novel is characteristically brilliant when it comes to erotic comedy or setting a scene or sketching in minor figures, it is deficient in another and far more important way. It lacks the dramatic intensifications, the exploratory feeling that in Joyce and Proust—and in our own time very often in Mailer—is a consequence of their wonderfully vital, vulnerable, intimidated (and not simply intimidating) relationship to fictional copies of themselves.

Vadim is allowed to do nothing that will surprise Nabokov, to test nothing that Nabokov hasn't already tested. For all his famous confidence in the power of fiction to create reality, even while conceding the arbitrariness of the methods for doing so, Nabokov is here, with an arrogance nearly charming in its absoluteness, loath to surrender much if any of *his* constituted self, as our greatest master of prose, to a mere fictional aspirant.

The puzzles and teasers in the book are fun to figure out when they are broadly parodistic, and altogether less so (though in these instances the vanity of discovery might pass for fun) when they require a detailed knowledge of the whole of Nabokov's *oeuvre* and the byways of his literary career. In either case the puzzles are without the resonance of personal drama that continues to move us in Proust or Joyce after all the exegesis is finished and that was also powerfully at work in *Lolita* and *Pale Fire*.

Vadim tells his story chronologically, beginning with his coming down from Trinity College, Cambridge, in 1922 (Nabokov came down from the same place in 1923), but in the last chapter we learn that he has been narrating from the perspective of his 71st year, a recent, near-fatal illness, and his acquisition of what sounds like the best and truest love of his life—she is 28 and identified only as the "you" to whom he gradually comes to address his narrative. With several outright admissions of the artificial form which the very act of writing is giving to his life, Vadim recounts his romantic, marital and literary career, especially the wooing of four wives in which his literary fame is used as an inducement.

The first is Iris, herself a would-be writer of detective stories, who is murdered in Paris. The second is Annette, a comically miserable match, with whom he emigrates to the United States, specifically to Quirn University (much like the Cornell where Nabokov taught) and begets a daughter named Bel—a model for a Lolita figure who will appear in Vadim's equivalent novel (entitled *A Kingdom by the Sea*). Sometimes mistakenly called Annabel (perhaps to remind us that Humbert's lost love was named, after Poe, Annabel Lee), she goes cross country with Vadim, once she is an accredited nymphet, on a motel-visiting trip. Vadim's third wife is Louise, rich widow of one of his colleagues at Quirn. The fourth is "you," who seems at last to bring him both some measure of personal happiness and a new artistic promise.

This, Vadim's 13th book—six others in Russian and six in English are listed at the front—is intended, he tells us, as an "oblique autobiography . . . dealing with the mirages of romantic literary matters." Insofar as it is an "autobiography" of Nabokov as well as of Vadim, the details connecting the two must therefore themselves be full of "obliquity." Even as we're told that Vadim's first wife, Iris, is the source of his pen name, V. Irisin, we are doubtless expected to know that, spelt backwards, Iris is the pen name used by Nabokov until 1940,

Sirin—almost but not quite. Her name falls just one letter short of being directly wedded to the Big N. This little anagrammatic game is but one clue that Vadim, like Nabokov, is a novelist for whom loving and writing are somehow composed of the same letters, of similar words.

Look at the Harlequins! is a novel in which Nabokov, acting as some kind of Prince of Letters, imagines what it might have been like if the kiss of love had transformed him only halfway from a frog. The works credited to Vadim, and the summaries of them, are meant to be recognized as tawdry versions of Nabokov's, and most of the romances and marriages credited to him are equally tawdry, worthy of a hero in a novel by Philip Roth. Vadim aspires, in love and art, to a position Nabokov has attained, but he is not passably successful in love till the very end. Even then his subsequent way of telling his story is an indication that he has yet to gain the assurance, personal and literary, exhibited by his master. There may even be ominous significance to the few passing allusions in the novel to the Othello-Desdemona relationship.

When Vadim characterizes his novel as "a story of love and prose," it draws attention to the evidence in the prose itself of the failure of love, thus far, to infuse him with the literary power he covets. There is as yet no Véra, Nabokov's wife for close to 50 years, to whom this and a good many of his other books are dedicated. "You" is only the promise that someone like Véra has entered late into Vadim's life, a presence of truth. As she opens a door to his hospital room near the end, "I emitted a bellow of joy and Reality entered." In theory, for both Vadim and Nabokov, "love and prose" ideally create Reality in forms that can dispense with many of the details of life, render them "nonessential." And yet, even with "you" at his side, Vadim can allude to details "too trivial to record" while proceeding nonetheless to record them, along with bracketed dates after names and the translation of foreign words like "aber (but)." Stylistic parody of this kind abounds in the book and, as is often the case even in Joyce, it serves not to develop or complicate the point it's making but only to illustrate it, to reiterate, in this instance, the character of Vadim as a failed Nabokov.

Vadim can be said to suffer in search of his better self even to the point of translating into an affliction some of the Nabokovian stand-bys about the problematic relation between time and space (as in the treatise on "The Texture of Time" in *Ada*). It is consistent with the connection in Vadim's and in Nabokov's mind of "love" with the writing of "prose," of the erotic with the literary career, that Vadim should feel obliged to explain to each of his prospective wives symptoms of a "mental flaw" which the reader may recognize as being, for Nabokov, a central justification for the kind of superior fiction he writes. Vadim is worried that his anxieties about the relation of time and space will lead to madness and disqualify him as both a writer and a husband.

Only vaguely and with "you" can Vadim begin to see in his "mental flaw" not the threat of insanity but a condition and potential opportunity for the practice of art, past, present and future. He is suggesting that he now sees that his perplexities about time and space belong to the working tradition of art (and maybe physics), that someone else will carry on the work, and just before this scene he has been drowsily groping, with comical confusions of spelling and sound, toward identification with the man, Nabokov, who has been conspicuously perpetuating that tradition.

Precedents in other novels by Nabokov, such as *The Gift* or *Bend Sinister*, where he is a spectral presence or even a direct intruder into the drama of the artist as lover/writer, only point to the unprecedented extent to which this latest book depends on Nabokov's use of himself as a double to the main character. *Look at the Harlequins!* nearly sinks under the weight of self-referential parodies and allusions. The complex interaction between Nabokov and Vadim, who admits to "impersonating somebody living as a real being beyond the constellation of my tears and asterisks . . . incomparably greater, healthier, and crueler than your obedient servant," can only be located by those willing to become "little Nabokovs," as the author once referred to his ideal readers. But aspirants to the title will fail if they depend for their nurturing only on this particular book; they will need to have been reared on all the others, as if the *oeuvre* were Nature itself.

And why not? Because, I suppose, there is a difference between any work that asks a reader to recognize some blurred similarities between the characters in it and figures outside it who belong to the great myths of our culture, ancient or modern—between, that is, a novel by Melville or Joyce, Faulkner or Pynchon—and a work like this one which almost exclusively refers us back into the confines of the writer's own life and literary career. Of course, objections on principle can, at many points, give way to pleasure when the allusiveness explains and redeems itself. But as a general rule the interplay depends upon a heady assumption about the Nabokoviana the reader knows or might possibly even care to know.

For example, when Vadim gets outraged at a Parisian bookseller named Osip Oksman, or Oks for short, because he compliments him for having written *Camera Obscura*, it is perhaps not unreasonable to suppose that we can get the joke: Vadim's bibliography lists *Camera Lucida* (with an English title of *Slaughter in the Sun*) while it is of course Nabokov who wrote *Camera Obscura* (English title: *Laughter in the Dark*). Presumably, however, we are also supposed to recognize, and for reasons that have to do only with some quite minor aspect of Nabokov's career, that the brief portrait of Oksman is a glancing blow at a Russian emigré book-store proprietor named Nicholas Otsup who edited a magazine in the early thirties called *Numbers*, not *Prime Numbers*, as Vadim reports, in which Nabokov was attacked.

Look at the Harlequins! is finally an altogether coterie book, and while initially it may seem more available than *Ada*, it proves, after any but the most superficial reading, resolutely presumptuous about the commitment expected from its readers. The profusion of abstruse literary jokes and esoteric coinages—such as one that refers us back to a volume of Verlaine called *Mes Hôpitaux* in order to understand Vadim's allusion to *Mes Moteaux*—makes us wonder if perhaps his deformations of Nabokov are not in themselves a series of jokes intended to make him the equivalent and not merely the inferior impersonator of Nabokov.

Nabokov, one has been made aware, is supposed to be the greatest "harlequin" of them all; and when Vadim was a boy his aunt would tell him to "Stop moping! Look at the harlequins!" "What harlequins? Where?" "Oh, everywhere. All around you. Trees are harlequins, words are harlequins. So are situations and sums. put two things together—jokes, images—and you get a triple harlequin. Come on! Play! Invent the world! Invent reality!" It is as if Vadim and Nabokov were to be allowed to compete within the covers of the book for the privilege of "inventing" the true Nabokov.

However, feats of allusiveness do not translate themselves into the kind of internal, autobiographical drama which they momentarily promise. And the reason, I suspect, is precisely the enormous aloofness implicit in all of Nabokov about his own powers of superior invention and the power of literature

itself. His parodies have unmistakable brilliance, but they presuppose a reader who is at once uniquely erudite and yet capable of mistaking literature for life to a degree hardly possible in anyone minimally educated.

Behind the often delightful invitation to play of mind there lurks a persistent didacticism. In correcting any mistaken ideas we may have about fiction and reality, Nabokov means to demonstrate that if fiction is not Reality, then neither is so-called "reality" outside of fiction. Reality, as he is fond of saying, always belongs in quotation marks. The ground thereby claimed by Nabokov's own fictional enterprise is, to say the very least, exorbitant—and he chooses to govern it all by himself.

As we've seen in the past ten years, any number of little Nabokovs will be ready to make such an investment in a book of this kind that they end up admiring it as their own handiwork, their own "invention." To some extent this is always and quite properly the case. But the kind of exegetical efforts we are invited to make here need to be distinguished from those we are willing to make while reading Melville or Joyce or Pynchon. At their many puzzling moments those writers direct the attention of the reader not principally to their own literary texts and lives but to the life and texts of the existent world, with all its inheritances, in which they live and write. Theirs seems to me an altogether more exciting and important venture than Nabokov's, even if he has sometimes been called—and sometimes deserves to be called—our greatest living writer.

He stands on the periphery of the great tradition of American literature since Hawthorne and Melville, and of 20th-century literature since Joyce, in that he is, despite his terror of solipsism, its most awesome practitioner. He is not sufficiently vulnerable to—and his style is only infrequently enriched by—the power of the social and literary institutions by which man continues to invent himself.

In his splendid disdain for the power of most other fictions, except for some exclusively literary ones (as note his notorious contempt for Freud), Nabokov has at last proposed in his novel that he himself exists as an institution and that he is not only a product of artistic invention but, taken all together, the exemplification of it. It is therefore interesting to wonder, even while acknowledging the genius displayed in *Lolita* and *Pale Fire*, whether Nabokov's great admiration for Joyce would at this point be reciprocated by a writer who left us such decisive parodies and implicit critiques of Walter Pater. Pater, in his disposition if not in the range of his mind or energy, seems to me the most direct antecedent to the Nabokov who wrote this book.

CAROL T. WILLIAMS
"Nabokov's Dozen Short Stories: His World in Microcosm"

Studies in Short Fiction, Summer 1975, pp. 213–22

Out of print in paperback for several years, the short story collection *Nabokov's Dozen* has recently been reissued—a welcome edition[1] for both the Nabokov and the general literature teacher. The former can welcome the *Dozen* for accessible entry into Nabokov's world, and the latter for both excellence in the short story form and insight into human nature and "our times." Nabokov's is a baker's dozen of thirteen stories dating from the 1930's through the early 1950's, which, whether they focus on individual misfit-heroes or mirror the crazed, cracked world of this century, are pieces in the pattern of their author's fictional world.

Nabokov scholarship reiterates that he is the "conjurer," whose omnipresent mirror reflects not-quite-opposites because it is rippled—his definition of art is "the necessary ripple."[2] This ambiguous image—the Nabokov story—is of the imaginative human being's ennobling, destructive quest to unite this world with another, ideal "state of being where art (curiosity, tenderness, kindness, ecstasy) is the norm."[3] It is not that his malcontent/aspirers would "escape into aesthetics,"[4] but that they would apply to this world the rules of the other. They would create and immortalize. For this audacity they pay—Nabokov's biographer, Andrew Field, is wrong: his "real artist" cannot "move freely between the two spheres" and "return unharmed and exhilarated" from his vision of Eternity.[5] His overreachers bridge the abyss between this world and another state of being where "'the only real number is one,'"[6] but they can neither share what they know nor, ironically, can they escape into *this* world. The special Nabokov fillip is his own omnipresence in his irony: as creator of this fiction, he too is a visionary. When Humbert tells Lolita that "the only immortality" they may share is "the refuge of art," we cannot miss the irony that both share the refuge of Nabokov's art. He has created them, "captured them in print"; and thus they both must die, just as the butterflies of Nabokov the lepidopterist must be killed if their beauty is to be preserved.

All of the stories in *Nabokov's Dozen* are about this quest to unify the two worlds of the mundane and the ecstatic. (*Ecstasy*, with its paradoxical connotations of lunacy and transcendent joy, is the perfect word for Nabokov's realm of art, the mad, paradisial mortal approximation of ideal "bliss.") All thirteen, like all his novels, end with the failure of the quest; but all are rich with the beauty encountered along the way to the inevitable falling short. "The only son of a great khan lost his way during a hunt (thus begin the best fairy tales and thus end the best lives)," says Nabokov.[7] No matter if they focus on the individual "Lance" (a properly "mod" form of "Lancelot"), or on this "era of Identification and Tabulation" ("Time and Ebb," p. 129), the subject and pattern are the same: a dialectic between two states of being, and a synthesis—properly Hegelian—in which neither the thetic nor the antithetic "arc" is eliminated, but "spirals" are *aufgehoben*: *put aside*, in the paradoxical sense of both *cast away* and *preserved* in artistic resolution.[8]

A *Dozen* story that illuminates Nabokov's "dialectic" clearly is "Conversation Piece, 1945" (or "Double Talk," its original title). The narrator is typically Nabokovian: a Russian émigré, unnamed (because the unnamed is the unknown), and seemingly an elitist, ineffectual intellectual. Like Hermann, the narrator of *Despair* (1937), he believes he has a "disreputable" double, but his obsession with this invisible *semblable* seems unrelated to the subject: an encounter in the present, 1945, in a genteel Boston home with a Fascist apologist whom the narrator tries stammeringly to best. Yet the denouement suggests that "Dr. Shoe" is in fact one of the double's "intrusions" into the narrator's life, not by "chance" as he says but because (like the double in *Despair*), "Dr. Shoe" is the narrator's *doppelgänger*, his darkly unwelcome antithetical side. At the end, as usual in his short stories, Nabokov reveals the antithetical spiral. A disarming "all that remains to be told" is followed by a letter, our first word from the scorned double: "'Esteemed Sir, . . . You have been pursuing me all my life,'" with "'depraved, decadent writings'" and now "'you have the arrogance to impersonate me and to appear in a drunken condition at the house of a highly respected person. . . . I suggest that by way of indemnity. . . .'" And the

narrator concludes, 'The sum he demanded was really a modest one.'

Here he disappears—an example of Nabokov's aloof rhetoric because now we are full of questions. If he can be blackmailed, who has intruded on whom? Is he Nabokov's ironic self-portrait? (Nabokov often characterizes himself as "decadent" in the eyes of the Bolsheviks, from whom his family fled in 1919.) And if the narrator was drunk, can we believe his characterization of "Dr. Shoe"? Perhaps he is the Fascist. Whom can we believe? What is real? And with this question we see the political "arc" of the tale. Here too it reflects *Despair* and foreshadows Nabokov's best political story *Bend Sinister*, in its exposure of the murderous fallacy of *oneness* on earth: ". . . history had never yet known . . . such faith in the impending sameness of us all. . . . Communism shall indeed create a beautifully square world of identical brawny fellows."[9] Unity in this world means totalitarianism; the Jews, Dr. Shoe tells the (receptive) Bostonians, "'forced [World War II] upon two nations that have so many things in common'" (p. 106).

"Cloud, Castle, Lake" (1937, in Russian) also condemns Nazi Germany, our whole civilization of "Identification and Tabulation" as well, and specifically, the masses, those "bouquets of stupidity" (*Despair*) that beleaguer the imaginative man. The narrator is again insubstantial: "I cannot remember his name at the moment. I think it was Vasili Ivanovich." And again he is "my representative." He is another intellectual Russian émigré, this time, again like Nabokov, in Berlin in "1936 or 1937." He has won a pleasure trip with a group of Germans who reveal themselves as gross bullies easily led by their "leader" (sent by the "Bureau of Pleasantrips") to harass Vasili because he would rather be alone and finally, rather leave the "communal journey" for a "dream" he "discover[s]" on the group's hearty, mass tramp: an "ancient black castle" beside a "pure, blue lake," in the exact middle of which a "large cloud was reflected in its entirety." It is a dream for Vasili (in the artistic form of a living painting) because the "inexpressible and unique harmoniousness of its three principle parts . . . was something so unique, and so familiar, and so long-promised, and it so *understood* the beholder" that he longs to stay there forever (p. 96).

Vasili is Nabokov's typical Lancelot, questing perfection because he sees it, and sees it in disparate, mundane "details," when they converge and hence transcend their insignificance. On "the configuration of some entirely insignificant objects—a smear on the platform, a cherry stone, a cigarette butt," he would grieve the loss of the dream in life, what Nabokov's *semblable* Borges, in "The Immortal" calls the "preciously precarious": "Never, never would he remember these three little things here in that particular interrelation, this pattern, which he now could see with such deathless precision" (p. 93). What Vasili cannot do that Nabokov can is accept the loss. As the Germans drag him away from his dream, he cries, "'Oh, but this is nothing less than an invitation to a beheading. . . .'" (p. 98). Cincinnatus C., protagonist of the Nabokov novel *Invitation to a Beheading* (1935) is another visionary imprisoned in the "'dark dungeon of the "here"'" because he had "'discovered the little crack in life where it broke off'" from "'something . . . genuinely alive.'"[10] To signify the false unity of the German group in "Cloud," Nabokov doubles their names (cf. Humbert) and their appearances and then pronounces their destiny and that of his dreamer: "all gradually melted together, merging together, forming one collective, wobbly, many-handed being, from which one could not escape" (p. 94).

In another *Dozen* tale, "Scenes From the Life of a Double Monster" (1950), this monstrous truth about mortal unity is embodied in absolute form. Human that the narrator Floyd is, he cannot recognize the intimations of ideal unity in his Siamese twinship with Lloyd: ". . . the interrupted gesture of one twin would be swallowed and dissolved in the enriched ripple of the other's completed action. I say *enriched* because the ghost of the unpicked flower somehow seemed to be also there, pulsating between the fingers that closed upon the fruit" (p. 137). If even Siamese twins cannot appreciate what it means to be "enriched"—to be "swallowed and dissolved," but also "somehow . . . there, pulsating," what chance have Nabokov's lovers?

"First Love" (1948) illuminates how memory functions in artistic creation. Early in the tale the memorist (apparently Nabokov himself, for he calls this "true" autobiography) describes childhood dreams of a "glass marble" (p. 45). At the end, describing his farewell to Colette in a Paris park (they are both ten), he reflects the marble again, unifying the story and irradiating its meaning:

> . . . and [Colette] was off, tap-tapping her glinting hoop through light and shade, around and around a fountain choked with dead leaves near which I stood. The leaves mingle in my memory with . . . some detail in her attire (perhaps a ribbon on her Scottish cap . . .) that reminded me then of the rainbow spiral in a glass marble. I still seem to be holding that wisp of iridescence, not knowing exactly where to fit it, while she runs with her hoop ever faster around me and finally dissolves among the slender shadows cast on the graveled path by the interlaced arches of its low looped fence.

As we visualize all these arcs—the hoop, the arches of the looped fence, the fountain, and especially the marble—we may see this first love as a "spiral" enclosed, but within glass and "rainbow" color. In *Speak, Memory* (pp. 204–205), Nabokov describes his own life as "a colored spiral in a small ball of glass," with his years in Russia (1899–1919) the "thetic arc"; the "voluntary exile" in France, Germany and England (1919–1940) the "obvious antithesis"; and the years in his "adopted country," the "beginning of a synthetic envelopment." "Mademoiselle O" ("true" enough to be a chapter in *Speak, Memory* as well as a *Dozen* tale) is another reflection of her author's dialectic. Nabokov's governess is alien in two worlds: her homeland Switzerland and Russia, in which she was merely hired help and which she loved only in memory after she had left. Nabokov compares her to an "uncouth" swan trying to hoist itself into a boat, "dodo-like" but "strange[ly] significan[t]," and recalling "*Cynge*" of one of his favorites, Baudelaire: "*Comme les exilés, ridicule et sublime.*" Like "First Love" and all Nabokov's fiction, "Mademoiselle O" seems basically about its author's lost homeland.

"Spring in Fialta" (1938) is one of Nabokov's most delicate configurations of the details of a hopelessly imperfect human love. "Spring in Fialta is cloudy and dull," Victor begins. Yet at the end of his narrative of the fifteen years of Nina's and his sporadic meetings, he is telling us that as she left him in Fialta, "suddenly I understood something I had been seeing without understanding," and at this moment, Fialta becomes "saturated with sunshine." What is clarified for Victor (or V.; V. Nabokov's "representatives" are often called V.) is an "insignificant" detail: "why a piece of tin foil had sparkled so on a pavement." He had seen it earlier, irrelevantly. Listening to complaints about the weather from Nina's husband, touching her elbow immediately after the surprise chancing upon her, why should he notice a "bit of tin foil"? And why, after she leaves, is it part of his sudden understanding?

Why except that just before her leaving, for the first time in their "supposedly frivolous" affair, "apprehensive" about a "rational interpretation of my existence" (p. 23), he has said he loves her. A rational interpretation of his marriage and his "carefree" affair requires that he tabulate, or "pin" Nina. And for this, of course, she must die. V's synthetic passage, all one sentence, flows from "saturated with sunshine" into a "dissolve" of meaning, a literal translation of the film maker's dissolve from one scene to another.[11] ". . . and now it was sun-pervaded throughout, and this brimming white radiance grew broader and broader, all dissolved in it, vanished, all passed, and I stood on the station platform of Mlech with a freshly bought newspaper, which told me that . . . Nina . . . had turned out after all to be mortal." Nabokov's lovers—mortals who would become one—can never live in this world. But why Nina's death instead of Victor's? (Why Lolita's before Humbert's?) After all, it was V. who suggested the fatal "state of being." Of course the answer is that it is *beauty* that must be immortalized, and the artist must live to do the pinning.

The "V." who controls "'That in Aleppo Once . . .'" (1943) is a Russian émigré writer in New York and a collector of "lichens," i.e., another Nabokov. He is only the recipient of the nameless narrator's letter, and the letter is the story; but at its end, in the synthetic moment, the narrator turns control of his story's title over to V., and in this choice lies V. Nabokov's message. As always, in "'Aleppo'" we cannot know what is real or who tells the truth. All we can know is that to label is to possess, and to possess is to kill love—a banal message, enriched by the "intricate route." The narrator of "'Aleppo'" and his wife (also unnamed) are separated while fleeing the Nazis in France in 1940. Now he writes to convince V. that his wife "never existed," that she is only a "character in . . . one of your stories" (pp. 114–115). He says that after he found her in Nice, she confessed that she had deceived him, but then denied it: "'You will think me crazy. . . . Perhaps I live several lives at once. Perhaps I wanted to test you. Perhaps this bench is a dream'" (p. 12). Her contradictory confessions unnerve him, and he tortures them both by questing obsessively for The Truth. After their visas appear, she again disappears and, finally giving up, he sails alone. But on the fourth day out another passenger says he saw his wife a few days before the sailing, walking "aimlessly" and saying "I would presently join her."

"It was at that moment," he writes V., "that I suddenly knew for certain she had never existed at all," and safe now in America, he longs for "real" life. And then a haunting sentence and incisive finish: "Somewhere, somehow, I have made some fatal mistake. . . . It may all end in *Aleppo* if I am not careful. Spare me, V.: you would load your dice with an unbearable implication if you took that for a title" And of course V. Nabokov does take his title from Othello's final speech before killing himself, the lines in which the Moor justifies himself as a hero that in Aleppo once, smote thus the circumcised dog who had beat a Venetian (V. ii. 352–356). To Nabokov's mind, Othello has no reason to murder the Moslem (he writes his "'Aleppo'" about Europe in 1943). Nor has he reason to pursue the truth about Desdemona, his possession— no reason, that is, but human nature. Pathetic Othello, and pathetic nameless refugee in real life, fatally tormented by a vision of the perfectly "rational," and skewered by the final unbearable implication of his creator.

Two of Nabokov's most subtle miniatures of human impenetrability in the *Dozen* have as their protagonists old people who appear to be insensitive under the blows of this world's inexplicable and inexorable laws and orders. In addition, "Signs and Symbols" (1948) defines the Nabokov dreamer in *extremis*: mad. This is the old couple's son, not an actor in the story but the object of its focus, as of his parents. Incarcerated in a mental hospital, a victim of " 'referential mania,' " he "imagines that everything happening around him is a veiled reference" to himself. Other people he excludes from the "conspiracy—because he considers himself to be so much more intelligent than other men." But all of "phenomenal nature shadows him," and he must "devote every minute and module of life to the decoding of the undulation of things" (p. 54).

Like Nabokov's other victims of " 'referential mania' "— Humbert, Kinbote (*Pale Fire*), Cincinnatus, and particularly Luzhin, his chess master (*The Defense*), the young man would "tear a hole in his world and escape." (Note the self-directed irony in these creations of a writer devoted to the "decoding of the undulation of things.") The story takes place on a day when he has again tried suicide. Bringing his birthday present to the asylum "for the fourth time," the parents are delayed by some of fate's mundane signs and symbols: rain, a stalled subway train and a bus that is late and "crammed with garrulous high-school children." The "camera" narrator records details similar to the bit of tin foil in "Fialta"—an "unfledged bird . . . helplessly twitching in a puddle" by the bus stop, for example (p. 53). The old couple may not notice these details—unlike Nabokov's "representatives," his "V.'s," a camera cannot look into minds—but they imprint themselves on our developing picture of their world.

At the asylum they respond to the "brightly explained" news about their son just as they responded to the delays en route and, we are sure, to every one of the griefs of their years. They are mute, silent in the way of those permanently defeated. But after they return home, "he kept clearing his throat in a special resonant way he had when he was upset" (ibid.), and "she felt the mounting pressure of tears," and finally, "past midnight," " 'No doctors, no doctors,' he moaned. . . . 'We must get him out of there quick. Otherwise we'll be responsible. Responsible!' " (p. 57).

Just then, "the telephone rang." Of course we expect that the boy has killed himself. But instead: " 'Can I speak to Charlie,' said a girl's dull little voice." The husband resumes his "excited monologue" on how they will care for their son at home. "The telephone rang again." *This* is the asylum; the first call, we say, represented the delusive moment of hope conventional to ironic tragedy. But no. "The same toneless anxious young voice asked for Charlie." The old man explains: " 'You are turning the letter O instead of the zero.' " Then, "flushed and excited," they sit down to an "unexpected festive midnight tea," and as with "clumsy moist lips" he spelled out the "eloquent labels" on the boy's birthday jellies ("apricot, grape . . ."), Nabokov concludes: "He had got to crab apple, when the telephone rang again."

Is it the young girl? That is, does the drab mundane world of disordered buses harass the old couple once again? Or this time is it the bright voice from the asylum? The "Lady and Tiger" ostentatiousness of Nabokov's trick forces us to fit it into the story, and then we see its irony: who the next caller is is irrelevant, for alive or dead, the young man cannot live in this world. Earlier in the story his mother told us this when she

thought of the endless waves of pain that for some reason or other she and her husband had to endure; of the invisible giants hurting her boy in some unimaginable fashion; of the incalculable amount of tenderness contained in the world; of the fate of this tenderness, which is either crushed, or wasted, or

transformed into madness; of neglected children humming to themselves in unswept corners; or beautiful weeds that cannot hide from the farmer and helplessly have to watch the shadow of his simian stoop leave mangled flowers in its wake, as the monstrous darkness approaches (p. 56).

It is Nabokov's typical irony that such sensitivity is part of a drab, nameless woman—one of the beautiful, vulnerable weeds in a world apparently "brightly explained" but in reality, "simian." And if she is beautiful, what of that "anxious" young voice without a face, a name, a character, that entered the world of Nabokov's story by chance? How lovely she might be.

In "The Aurelian," too (1931, in Russian), a Nabokov artist, alien in this world, is camouflaged with its dull trappings. He looks like a "churlish" German shopkeeper, but actually "Pilgram belonged, or rather was meant to belong (something—the place, the time, the man—had been ill chosen), to a special breed of dreamers, such dreamers as used to be called in the old days, 'Aurelians'—perhaps on account of those chrysalids, those 'jewels of nature,' which they loved to find hanging on fences above the dusty nettles of country lanes" (p. 79). Something—the place, the time, the man—had been ill-chosen: like Nabokov's other voyeurs in this world, Paul Pilgram is fated to duplicity.

Pilgram's obsession, unknown even to his wife, is "*himself* to net the rarest butterflies of distant countries" (p. 81); and finally, although he knows it is "madness" to leave Eleanor to their debts, he sneaks off. As he leaves, he perceives his happiness "leaning toward him like a mountain" (p. 88). We have read of the stroke that cancelled one of his earlier dreams: "(like a mountain falling upon him . . .)" (p. 78). So we know what the recurrence of the mountain image means and are insulted by the conclusion, in which Pilgram's death is loudly announced. But like the end of "Signs and Symbols," the obituary is only apparently Nabokov's rhetoric of disdain. His persona, unmasking at the end as always, judges that Eleanor's discovery of the body is "irrelevant" because she has already found Pilgram's note: " 'Off to Spain. . . .' " The death of his body is irrelevant because the note reveals his other, real life, and that revelation, which makes a whole of Pilgram's life, makes his death in this world inevitable. After death, Nabokov's narrator gives Pilgram his dream: "one can hardly doubt that he saw all the glorious bugs he had longed to see." (p. 89) But *bugs* counters the glory of this dream, just as earlier the narrator had described it with phrases like "the furious throbbing of wings" (p. 81) and "the black pin upon which [a] silky little creature was crucified" (p. 82). At the end, Pilgram is not only a drab shopkeeper and an exotic "aurelian"; when the two converge, we see a complex, enigmatic, very real synthesis of lover and crucifier.

Perhaps the most provocative exploration in *Nabokov's Dozen* of the play between our urge toward ideal bliss and our mortal fear of "slipping into a different dimension,"[12] is the short story of the modern knight of the grail, the astronaut "Lance." Written in 1952, it was a prescient, and is a haunting judgment on our attempt to master space. Typically, however, Nabokov denies it social import: "Not for me are the artificial little satellites that the earth is promised; . . . set up by terrestrial nations in a frenzy of competitive confusion, . . . and savagely flapping flags" (p. 161). And typically he deceives us. (His interest in this world is clearest in the *Dozen* in "Time and Ebb" [1944], the 21st-century memoir of a ninety year-old who characterizes the 20th century as "atavistically prone to endow the community with qualities and rights which they refused to the individual" [p 126]).

Thus carefully cut off from the science fiction "business"

(p. 161), Nabokov's tale of "Emery L. Boke, more or less remote descendant of mine who is to be a member of the first interplanetary expedition," is told by a Nabokov representative who is "fifty and terrified" (pp. 162–3). The unimaginative and the terrified still exist in Lance's era. When he returns from his adventure in space, his parents tell him that Chilla, his beloved chinchilla, is "'with child.'" But Lance is indifferent. His parents leave the hospital room where he is being kept from human "'contacts,'" and in the elevator they join others from a world Lance has left forever. The story concludes: "Going back [into space] in November (Lancelin). Going down (the old Bokes). There are, in that elevator, two smiling women and, the object of their bright sympathy, a girl with a baby, besides the gray-haired, bent, sullen elevator man, who stands with his back to everybody."

Nabokov's persona, although terrified, is different from Lance's parents or the sullen elevator operator. He understands that Lance is not "the ordinary hairless ape, who takes everything in his stride," but rather, "the man of imagination and science, whose courage is infinite because his curiosity surpasses his courage. . . . He is the ancient *curieux*, but of a hardier build, with a ruddier heart" (p. 170). The narrator grasps Lance's "main problem," also our haunting question: "Will the mind of the explorer survive the shock" of the "atavistic moment" in which he leaves this world? (p. 169). "Deep in the human mind, the concept of dying is synonymous with that of leaving the earth. To escape its gravity means to transcend the grave, and a man upon finding himself on another planet has really no way of proving to himself that he is not dead—that the naive old myth has not come true." (p. 170). And really, Lance has not survived. (Have our real astronauts?) Like all of Nabokov's dreamers, he has not returned unharmed from another sphere. On earth he can only talk about his experience, especially his partner Denny, who did die in space. He is eager to return. And also, the narrator notes, he has a nosebleed.

Thus, silently, the narrator unmasks. Through this mere detail, a nosebleed, he recalls a reminiscence of his own earlier in the story. Then, in what had seemed a digression from Lance's story, he had recounted his "vaguely recurrent" childhood dream of a nosebleed he ignored in his anxiety to shovel into a little pail the "mass of something— . . . oppressively and quite meaninglessly shaped," which infuriated him because he could not "walk around the view to meet it on equal terms." The elements in his dream were not conventionally mythic; his quest was only to see a shadow's face, only to know the unknown. In other words, it was only the most atavistic myth of all. And, he says, perhaps when "Lance and his companions reached their planet, [they] felt something akin to my dream" (p. 171).

Thus Nabokov's "Dozen" are like all his fictions: "'web[s] of sense'" (as John Shade describes life in his poem, "Pale Fire"[13]), composed of startling configurations of images, dialectical in structure, and each a slowly unfolding pattern of paradoxical truths concluding with a synthesis that reveals final

truth—to be unknowable. The message camouflaged by Nabokov's art is Keat's principle of *"Negative Capability"*: "When a man is capable of being in uncertainties, mysteries, doubts, without any irritable reaching after fact and reason."[14] To be known—to be "captured in print"—is to be immortalized, but it is also to be mortally dead. To know, transcendentally, is to be God, but also doomed in this world. That is the artist Nabokov's essential, ironically autobiographical conundrum. He is generally called precious, an elitist. But insofar as we are all *curieux* like Lance, all lovers like V., and all prisoners like Vasili Ivanovich—insofar as we dream—then we can see that it is finally for this world and not another that Nabokov creates.

Notes

1. Vladimir Nabokov, *Nabokov's Dozen* (New York: Bard Avon Books, 1973). Originally published in 1958 by Doubleday & Co., and in paperback by Popular Library in 1959 under the title *Spring in Fialta*. All references are to the new edition and are in the text.
2. *Nikolai Gogol* (Norfolk, Conn.: New Directions, 1944), p. 145.
3. Nabokov, "On a Book Entitled *Lolita*," *Lolita* (New York: G. P. Putnam's Sons, 1955), pp. 316–317.
4. Page Stegner, *Escape into Aesthetics* (New York: The Dial Press, 1966).
5. *Nabokov: His Life in Art* (Boston: Little, Brown and Co., 1967), pp. 238, 180.
6. Nabokov, *The Real Life of Sebastian Knight* (Norfolk, Conn.: New Directions, 1959), p. 105.
7. *The Gift*, tr. Michael Scammel in collaboration with the author (New York: G. P. Putnam's Sons, 1963), pp. 145–146.
8. Nabokov on "Hegel's triadic series [that] expressed . . . the essential spirality of all things in their relation to time," is in his memoir, *Speak, Memory*, Universal Library (New York: Grosset and Dunlap, 1960), p. 204
9. *Despair*. Tr. by the author (London: John Long Ltd., 1937), pp. 31–32.
10. Tr. Dmitri Nabokov in collaboration with the author (New York: G. P. Putnam's Sons, 1959), pp. 93, 205.
11. More is needed on Nabokov's use of film though Alfred Appel's new work *Dark Cinema*, is a good start. ("First Love" [1948] also ends as Colette "dissolves among the . . . shadows"). One of Nabokov's cinematic devices is the visual motif—as in "Fialta," the bit of tin foil, and also the violet, associated with Nina, and the train, a favorite Nabokov image, associated with our "intricate route" through life. The reason why cinema fascinates Nabokov is revealed in "The Assistant Producer" (1943; *Nabokov's Dozen*), in which the Russian émigrés hired as extras by a German film company are described as "totally unreal people [hired] to represent 'real' audiences in pictures. The dovetailing of one phantasm into another produced upon a sensitive person the impression of living in a Hall of Mirrors, or rather a prison of mirrors, and not ever knowing which was the glass and which was yourself." (p. 66). For an artist who would suggest the slipperiness of reality, the world of film is an ideal metaphor.
12. *The Gift*, p. 309.
13. Nabokov, *Pale Fire* (New York: G. P. Putnam's Sons, 1962), p. 63.
14. Letter to George and Thomas Keats (21 December 1817), *Selected Letters of John Keats*, ed. Robert Pack (New York: New American Library, 1974), p. 55.

OGDEN NASH

1902–1971

Ogden Nash, author of light verse, was born on August 19, 1902, in Rye, New York. The son of a businessman, he was raised in Savannah, Georgia, and several other East Coast cities. After attending St. George's School in Newport, Rhode Island, Nash entered Harvard in 1920, but by 1921 he had dropped out because of financial difficulties. In 1925, after working at various jobs, he joined the advertising department of Doubleday, Page, which in 1927 became Doubleday, Doran. During these years Nash wrote serious poetry during his free time but, unsatisfied with the results, he soon began to restrict himself to light verse.

Nash's first book, written with Joseph Alger and illustrated by Christopher Rule, was a children's story called *The Cricket of Carador* (1925). While still working at Doubleday, Doran, Nash collaborated with Christopher Morley, Cleon Throckmorton, and others on *Born in a Beer Garden* (1931), which contains his first published piece of comic writing. This was followed later that year by *Hard Lines*, in which one can already see all the essential characteristics of Nash's verse writing: the rhymes which rely on an odd misspelling or a strange pronunciation, the purposely awkward rhythms, and the whimsical mangling of commonplace constructions. The book sold extremely well, and Nash soon quit his job in advertising, worked on the staff of the *New Yorker* for three months in 1932, and then became a freelance writer.

Nash's first collection of verse was followed by many others, beginning with *Free Wheeling* (1931), *Happy Days* (1933), and *The Primrose Path* (1935). Having married Frances Rider Leonard in 1931, and having become the father of two small girls, Nash published *The Bad Parents' Garden of Verse* in 1936; this was followed by *I'm a Stranger Here Myself* (1938); *The Face Is Familiar* (1940); *Good Intentions* (1942); *Many Long Years Ago* (1945); and *Versus* (1949).

Between 1936 and 1942 Nash worked as a script-writer, and while in Hollywood he met S. J. Perelman, with whom he collaborated on the musical *One Touch of Venus*, for which Kurt Weill wrote the score. First produced on Broadway in 1943, this musical proved a tremendous success. Nash also wrote for radio and television, and himself appeared regularly on several radio programs.

In the 1950s and 1960s Nash gave more and more attention to writing children's verse while continuing to write his verse for adults, producing such works as *Parents Keep Out* (1951), *The Christmas That Almost Wasn't* (1957), *Custard the Dragon* (1959), *Girls Are Silly* (1962), and several others. The books of verse written for adults include *Family Reunions* (1950), *The Private Dining Room* (1953), *You Can't Get There from Here* (1957), and *Everyone But Thee and Me* (1962). Ogden Nash died on May 19, 1971.

Personal

I first met Ogden Nash at the beginning of 1927, when I joined him in the advertising department of Doubleday. For two years we commuted together; we took the 7:49 train from Penn Station and faced each other all day across two desks at Garden City. After we became well acquainted, he got into the habit of occasionally tossing me a bit of folded yellow paper that, being opened, was found to contain a verse of the kind that was to make him famous. Some of them appeared in his first book, *Hard Lines*.

We were young together, both in our early twenties. It was the era of the ignoble experiment, and we ignored the law in each other's society more than once. We used to go to Yankee Stadium to see Babe Ruth in his greatest year and the Yankees in theirs. In May we drove to Mineola and saw *The Spirit of St. Louis* a few days before her pilot took off for Paris. During the Presidential campaign of 1928 both of us were enthusiastically for Al Smith, and, as I recall, we were as much surprised as disappointed when Hoover swamped him.

Ogden was invariably entertaining to be with, as spontaneous in conversation as in those verses that I was not bright enough to recognize as more than unconsidered trifles; nor did I guess where his inexhaustible spontaneity was leading him. Between verses and asking me questions like "Do you remember the names of Happy Hooligan's nephews?" (I did and do), he was a first-class copywriter. I remember a headline he wrote

for an ad when *The Plutocrat* by Booth Tarkington was riding high on the best-seller lists: "First in New York, First in Chicago, and First in the Hearts of His Countrymen." One of the Doubleday vice presidents, a benign elderly gentleman, was a bit scandalized. Ogden could have had a successful career in advertising, but his celebrated first published poem made it clear that he did not want to sit in an office at 244 Madison Avenue or anywhere else.

Ogden Nash was not the only writer who could make frivolity immortal. But he was unique—not at all like Gilbert or Lear or Lewis Carroll, still less like his immediate predecessors in America: Dorothy Parker, Margaret Fishback, F. P. A. By the same token, he was and remains inimitable—easy to imitate badly, impossible to imitate well. He was quite aware of this, though at the same time he was an objective and infallible critic of his own stuff. To his friends he would speak his mind, but never with the intention of being overheard. He was incapable of hurting the feelings of a fellow creature. In the forty-four years of our friendship I never saw him lose his temper, or even give a sign that he had a temper to lose. He was a gentleman.

An opinionated gentleman, to be sure. His opinions were the essence of his verse; so were his extremely acute observations. He was by no means all frivolity. As a close friend of mine, who I think did not know him, wrote me when he died, "Something important has gone . . . that special under-

LEWIS MUMFORD

OGDEN NASH

VLADIMIR NABOKOV

ANAÏS NIN

GEORGE JEAN NATHAN

ROBERT NATHAN

HOWARD NEMEROV

standing of what we are." Ogden Nash was a sane man, in a world considerably less sane than he was. He should have died hereafter—surely he had in him ten more good years to combine the separate springs of wit and humor into the single stream whose rapids he had such fun riding.

In recent years I saw less of him, since we lived over a hundred miles apart, but we never lost touch. Occasionally we would meet for lunch in New York, or something would come up that led to a brisk correspondence. Still, we were young together. In one of his early poems, a serious one called "The Old Man," he wrote, "The old men know when an old man dies." As far as I am concerned, Ogden was always young, and always will be.—GEORGE STEVENS, "Ogden Nash: A Memoir," *SR*, June 19, 1971, p. 19

Works

Ogden Nash has been both overpraised and underrated; his stock has gone up and down and up again, his highs are often confused with his lows. Nevertheless, in a rapidly changing world and a nervously fluctuating market, he has always had more orders than he could fill. Although highly salable, his work is interesting to brows of all altitudes; it is intelligent and always unpredictable. Nash is, therefore, something of a phenomenon as poet and producer, and he merits a more detailed stock-taking than he has received.

There are, first of all, Nash's two most obvious characteristics. Both of them are curiosities in technique: the long, asymmetrical lines, and the elaborately inexact rhymes. One or two fanatical source-hunters have found the origin of Nash's lengthy eccentricities in Gilbert's "Lost Mr. Blake." But an unprejudiced comparison will show that the two styles have nothing in common. Apart from the almost opposite idioms, Gilbert's lines are consistently long and fairly regular, while Nash's line-lengths vary from two to sixty-two syllables. Nash's unmatched and unscannable lines are his own, a distinct technical departure. Nevertheless, I do not think they are particularly effective. Their charm is the frail charm of the unexpected; with each repetition the surprise is a little less surprising—so much so that when Nash, after hundreds of purposefully shapeless verses, printed a few poems in traditional meters, his readers were really surprised. In ⟨*I'm a Stranger Here Myself*⟩, as in the preceding *The Bad Parents' Garden of Verse*, the keenest as well as the most comical verses are those in which the rhythm is regular and the lines quite orthodox in shape. I would be disposed to put the "invention" of the irregular line on the debit side.

The rhymes are another matter. Here the reader is constantly and incredibly assaulted by a shock which is partly esthetic and partly galvanic. A rhyming word is usually a preparation for another rhyming word; Nash delights the reader with the pleasure of inexactitude, with words that rhyme reluctantly, with words that nearly-but-do-not-quite rhyme, with words that never before had any relation with each other and which never again will be on rhyming terms. These distortions are at their best when they are their worst. What reader can fail to be startled when confronted with a poem that begins:

> Oh, sometimes I sit around and think, what would
>   you do if you were up a dark alley and there was
>   Caesar Borgia,
> And he was coming torgia,
> And brandished a poisoned poniard,
> And looked at you like an angry fox looking at the
>   plumpest rooster in a boniard?

Such rhymes are as delightful as they are astonishing; they are like apparently improvised speeches in which the errors are more lively—and more likable—than the prepared accuracies. I should say that Nash's calculated recklessness in rhyme belongs definitely on the credit side.

Nash has been applauded for his industry and his verbal ingenuities. Both are virtues, but they become vices with Nash. For one thing, he writes too much. At first his work seems amazing; then it becomes amusing; after too many repetitions of the same effects, it descends to the mechanical. The present volume contains almost three hundred pages: were it half as long it would be twice as good. Productiveness not only compels Nash to pad but to pretend. He has to pretend to be funnier than he really is or to be funny when he wants to be serious, or to give a "snap" to a title which might better have been casual or non-commital. I feel he is working too hard when he forces himself to such titles as "To Bargain, Toboggan To-Whoo!" "Boop-Boop-Adieup, Little Group!" "Man Bites Dog Days," "Where There's a Will, There's Velleity," "Little Miss Muffet Sat on a Prophet," "Barmaids Are Diviner Than Mermaids." Working overtime and straining too often put much of Nash's output on the debit side.

But the rest of Nash belongs on the sunny side of the ledger. His verse always makes good reading; often it is the best light verse written in America today. The territory might be extended to include England, for, with the possible exception of A. P. Herbert, there is no one here or abroad who can surpass the straight-faced absurdity of "Adventures of Isabel," the sensible nonsense of "Curl Up and Diet," the clipped but devastating disposals of "Fellow Creatures." Nash's *The Bad Parents' Garden of Verse*, and in particular *The Tale of Custard the Dragon*, proved he could be as nimble and original as A. A. Milne; page after page in ⟨*I'm a Stranger Here Myself*⟩ proves he can take the leap from childlike fancy to social satire in one effortless stride. It is hard for me to understand why no musician, manager, or theatrical producer has made Nash supply book and lyrics for a series of native comic operas, especially since there seems to be an almost hopeless search for librettists with imagination.

It is in this realm, the realm of incalculable imagination, that Nash is happiest and at his highest. Time and again he begins inconsequentially, with a wisp of an idea, or with no thought at all. Once upon a time, he mumbles to himself, there was a man named Mr. Strawbridge. Strawbridge rhymes with drawbridge and so the poem not only is about Mr. Strawbridge who wanted a drawbridge, but about what kind of drawbridge would please him best. He wanted it because he wanted to interfere with traffic; on his house he had a veranda built (rhyming with Vanderbilt) so that he could look at the Atlantic Ocean.

> But he said sometimes on Sundays and holidays he
>   couldn't see the Atlantic for the motorists.
> And he said he'd rather see the former than the latter
>   even though they were handsome and respect-
>   able Kiwanians and Lions and Rotarists.

And so the poem goes wildly on from one mad fantasy to another—and all because the name of Strawbridge popped into Nash's oddly proportioned mind.

Nonsense and criticism elbow each other in Nash; he is a crazy story-teller one moment, a satirist the next, a wit who takes to clowning to correct pretense and expose hypocrisy. Playfully but incisively he makes his summaries with the deceptive calm of the following "tribute":

> How courteous is the Japanese;
> He always says, "Excuse it, please."
> He climbs into his neighbor's garden,

And smiles, and says, "I beg your pardon";
He bows and grins a friendly grin,
And calls his hungry family in;
He grins, and bows a friendly bow:
"So sorry, this my garden now."

Such moments occur frequently enough to lift Nash above his own pleasant insanities; they are funny, but they are wryly, seriously humorous. Some day the committee which gratifyingly awarded a Pulitzer Prize to Morrie Ryskind, George S. Kaufman, and the Gershwins for "Of Thee I Sing" will give Nash that honor for adding a new approach, a new style, and a new meaning to American social verse. This will be as much a surprise to the committee as it will be to Mr. Nash.—LOUIS UNTERMEYER, "Inventory of Nash: 1938," *SR*, June 4, 1938, pp. 6–7

Many long years ago it was, indeed—fifteen, I believe—that Ogden Nash's first published writing appeared in *The New Yorker*. It was the immortal lyric entitled "Spring Comes to Murray Hill," which contained the couplet:

The Pilgrims settled Massachusetts in 1620 when
      they landed on a stone hummock.
Maybe if they were here now they would settle my
      stomach.

The depression had produced a poet. Since then Ogden Nash has been, at one time or another, a magazine editor, Hollywood writer and musical-show librettist, but students yet unborn will find him listed in their History of English Literature as a poet.

Nash is the laureate of a generation which had to develop its own wry, none-too-joyful humor as the alternative to simply lying down on the floor and screaming. His ragged verse is remarkably like Ring Lardner's unpruned prose in effect—a catalogue of the annoying trifles that constitute our contemporary civilization, set down with a friendly leer. Lardner wrote about prohibition, golf, the stock market, Americans traveling abroad, million-dollar prizefights and similar nostalgic nuisances; Nash runs the gamut from the depression to Hitler, touching upon such disparate subjects as detective stories, crooners, the theatre-ticket shortage, Father's Day, knitting, colds, fruit salad, bankers, the circus, rain, strong drink, marriage and children's parties.

Many Long Years Ago is a sort of retrospective volume, representing Nash's published work to date. Any but the most well-read and retentive-minded Nash fan would find it difficult to separate the early verse from the recent. Both rejoice the innocent reader's heart with their leisurely tempo and indifference to formal scansion and their miraculous quasi-rhymes. Further, Nash is one of the rare people who can make a pun and make you like it. He can write sentimental rhymes about his children and make you like those, too. In short, he can do almost anything in the poet line, and he has been doing it for fifteen years.

A hair-spring sense of outrage is Nash's most valuable bit of professional equipment. He can be as angry at marshmallow or whipped cream on a salad as at an absconding banker, and as mad at the absconding banker as at Hitler. He is an urbane and articulate Donald Duck, an Alexander Pope with a hangover, a Rabelais whom you could introduce to your sister.—RUSSELL MALONEY, "Ogden Nash Nosegay," *NYTBR*, Oct. 14, 1945, p. 4

LOUIS HASLEY
"The Golden Trashery of Ogden Nashery"
Arizona Quarterly, Autumn 1971, pp. 241–50

A well of poor English undefiled. A fountain of fizz, fun, and frolic. A Christmas tree under a colored light wheel. Plus gentle admonitions about the *p*'s and *q*'s of this world. . . .

In undertaking to write about the poems of Ogden Nash, I think one may be excused, if not exonerated, for thus trying to seize in metaphor some breath of the poet's spirit. For in the world of humorous literature he is *sui generis*, almost without lineage; certainly we have little critical tradition to account for how he came to be. That is, if you take the world of literature to exclude the writers of bad verse, including "the sweet singer of Michigan," Julia Moore, whose verses inspired his artfully distorted syntax, gnarled rhythms, and mangled rhymes. Not since Lewis Carroll, I suppose, has any versifier gathered such a universal readership among both ordinary and discriminating readers. And probably no poet has had so many imitators.

I have been able to locate only a few of the poems of Julia Moore, but from them I can readily see that her flights were homely sentimental effusions notable for irregularities of rhythm, cliché expressions, awkward inversions, and inept rhymes. While Nash has sidestepped the homespun and the sentimental, he uses the same devices as Julia Moore, the good-humorous effect resulting principally from exaggeration. In his work, the irregularities are wild, the clichés are altered, the inversions are extreme; and the rhymes, elaborately contrived, often become outrageous word distortions. Bonus additions are redundancy and vernacular grammar. All these devices characteristically appear under a carefully assumed naïveté of expression and even manage at times to have an integral appropriateness.

O Duty,
Why hast thou not the visage of a sweetie or a cutie?
Why displayest thou the countenance of the kind of
      conscientious organizing spinster
That the minute you see her you are aginster?
Why glitter thy spectacles so ominously?
Why art thou clad so abominously?
Why art thou so different from Venus
And why do thou and I have so few interests
      mutually in common between us? . . .
                              ("Kind of an Ode to Duty")

Merely to mention, however, the characteristic Nash techniques as outlined above is narrowly misleading; for he shows impressive resourcefulness in avoiding stereotype. On some occasions he writes in conventional modes, which means dropping the playful and the lightly satirical to write the pure lyric or to add a didactic note to the prevailing humorous tenor of his verse.

Ogden Nash is thoroughly imbued with American life, liberty, and the pursuit of happiness. His verse tells us that he has an unflagging love of the American way of comfortable living. He sees from a reasonably high and cushy middle-class perch. We are not fooled when we observe in his poems a criticism of the people who enjoy a high standard of living. The genial cynicism is such that it shows both a self-awareness and an engagingly candid self-indulgence. He is an amiable bystander who would be unhappy if the passing parade yielded no foibles for him to toy with. Of course no reader is asking that he don sackcloth and ashes, and he is not about to do so.

Born in the New York suburb of Rye in 1902, Ogden Nash has lived in Baltimore, in New Hampshire, and in what has been his permanent residence for many years, Manhattan. He attended St. Georges School, Newport, Rhode Island, and was a Harvard dropout after one year. Followed a brief stretch of school teaching and another, in New York, trying to sell bonds. (He says he sold only one bond—and that to his godmother—but that he saw a lot of good movies.) After eight more years in advertising and editorial work, including three months on the staff of the *New Yorker*, he gave up formal employment; married, in 1931, Frances Rider Leonard; and in the same year published his first two volumes of verse. They were not only immediately popular but achieved critical praise, launching Nash on a productive career of uninterrupted prestige that earned him membership in the Academy of Arts and Sciences and the National Institute of Arts and Letters. Besides writing his many hundreds of poems, he collaborated with Kurt Weill and S. J. Perelman on a successful musical comedy, *One Touch of Venus* (1943). He has done some lecturing and given readings of his poems and was a regular member of the popular television program "Masquerade Party." He has two daughters, both writers, one of whom is also an illustrator.

The late Thomas Sugrue called Nash "the little man's laureate," not in the sense of championing underdog causes, but as dealing with universal themes at an easily accessible level. Anyone who has been in love, or yearned to be; who has lived with parents, or spouse, or children; who has had some smattering of parties, dinners, or almost any kind of social life; or who has been fascinated by language will catch the bright gleam of his own thoughts and experiences in Nash's verse.

What may at first seem a serious limitation in range is the absence of some aspects of American life. Aside from a few dozen short, conventional, humorous poems, describing such members of the animal kingdom as pig, rabbit, oyster, phoenix, grasshopper, and smelt, there is little reflection of Nature—no rural life, no landscape, no world of mountains, rivers, forests. Nash stays near the drugstore, the theater, and the night club; that is, his world is that of the representative humorist in this mid-half of the twentieth century. That world is the life of the city, of structured society, ritual entertainment, and organized leisure. So that in terms of contemporary American life, which is predominantly urban, the exclusions seem now of little moment, except for the grimmer aspects represented by war, industrialism, and social injustice, subjects which are left to the Black Humorists for whatever drops of humor can be wrung out of the dark cloth of our time.

> The country was made first,
> Yes, but people lived in it and rehearsed,
> And when they finally got civilization down,
> Why, they moved to town.
>
> ("The City")

Food, taxis, cocktails, language, love, the common cold, the theater, travel, conscience, money, birthdays, card games, weather, football, matrimony—these topics and others, take his exuberant fancy. But the exuberance is seldom bubbly. More characteristically it is introspective, taking the form of a psychological process which is based on close observation of some subject that is commonly considered unimportant. Though it is marked by surface nonsense, it may be interpenetrated by a satiric common sense. Yet there is a range from poems expressing a serious, if covert, theme, to other poems that are arbitrarily, coyly playful—mere play—poems that make no attempt to reflect life or its texture, but accomplish only a momentary, sensuous tickle or tease, as in the expert limerick "Requiem" (don't ask why the title):

> There was a young belle of old Natchez
> Whose garments were always in patchez.
>   When comment arose
>   On the state of her clothes,
> She drawled, When Ah itchez, Ah scratchez!

In a serious assessment of a poet with an overgenerous spirit of fun, the question of how much the content weighs in judging quality must be faced. No precise rule can be laid down; only a rough guide that goes something like this: the lighter the content, the greater the burden carried by the form. Language being an intellectual vehicle of meaning, we readily conclude that the poem must have *some* content, cannot be mere gibberish. It may, however, briefly forego discursive content if it can supply a psychological reflection of mood, which is itself a kind of content, even if it is expressed surrealistically. Moreover, a subject matter is not in itself necessarily heavy or light. Nuclear physics can be treated lightly, humorously; humor can be treated heavily, philosophically. What matters in determining lightness or heaviness is the poet's attitude and the details in which his attitude is embodied.

The practice of literary criticism yields supporting evidence for the relative importance of content. The "heavier" critics rarely undertake to deal with light verse poets. They may even demand a view of reality unmarked by humor. One remembers Matthew Arnold's refusal to give the highest rank to that great poet-humorist, Chaucer, because of a lack of "high seriousness." Of course, other critics do not give the same overwhelming importance to content; different schools of criticism place different values on the proper proportions of substance and form. But *no* literary critic will denominate as literature "The Ballad of Beautiful Words," a mere series of discrete words without predication and arranged in rhymed stanzas. For years this affront to literature was proudly printed periodically in a large metropolitan newspaper. As a "poem," it possessed only form in the shape of technique, or device, and was entirely without substance.

Of course there are no scales on which to weigh content. How account for—*can* we account for—the rather high place in literature of Lewis Carroll's *Alice in Wonderland?* Right off, assuming its highly skillful form, it won't do to maintain that it is the political and social allegory of Victorian England that satisfies the requirement of content; for such allegory has become a labored irrelevancy and is largely inaccessible to today's reader. What then? Not realism, for the story is a dream. But precisely so. Dreams are a part of life, a significant part whether or not we can determine accurately their meanings. The haunting lunacy of Alice's dream is disquietingly and amusedly seen as reflective of our own psychological processes, a lunacy and inconsecutiveness by no means confined to dreams.

The relevance of this reasoning to the poems of Ogden Nash should be clear. Its application is not always complimentary; certainly it is not always derogatory.

First of all, he is a very prolific poet. He has kept the presses warm with volume after volume. Every so often he publishes a selected volume which omits many previously published poems. Despite the selectivity, he could well afford to be much more selective. Many of the poems, even of those that survive the winnowing, evidence hasty composition and lax standards. One can only conclude that Nash sometimes scamps the arduous polishing needed to create a fully satisfying poetic experience. Not infrequently the reader perceives, not that the basic technique should have been different, but that Nash has not used well his own technique. The confident reader (brash, if you prefer) may feel that he knows how Nash should have said it to achieve a surer result.

This is particularly true of occasional rhymes which, instead of being expertly awkward, are awkwardly awkward. There exists a strong imperative for exact rhymes in light verse, and the lighter the verse the stronger the imperative. Not that Nash's rhymes must be conventionally exact. They should be *un*conventionally exact; and he should not allow the Eastern provincialism of pronouncing *Canada* to rhyme with *janitor*, a kind of offense of which he is guilty more than a few times. Where his poems betray such weaknesses of form, the literary needle registering the charge scarcely quivers.

If it were always so, this essay would not have been written. For Nash at his best is good indeed. He has adroitly blended the rhythms of prose and the varying line lengths of free verse with end-rhyming that is customarily alien to free verse. When not metrical, each couplet, often each line, moves like a prose sentence to a strong pause or full stop at the end. The often grotesque rhymes, the prose rhythms, and the widely varying line lengths blend to form a caricature of conventional versification.

Some indefatigable counter has declared that the number of syllables per line in Nash varies from two to sixty-two. The vast majority of his rhymes occur in couplets. Of course many poems follow regular metrics and regular stanza forms in almost every variety, more than a few of them parodying the tone and cadence of established works of literature. Something of this is suggested through titles, such as "Tarkington, Thou Should'st Be Living in This Hour," "Correction: *Eve* Delved and *Adam* Span," and "All, All Are Gone, the Old Familiar Quotations," as well as in clichés, whether oral or written, as in "A Dog's Best Friend Is His Illiteracy" and "You Bet Travel Is Broadening."

Amidst the elaborately artificial naïveté so much employed by Nash, his use of clichés cannot escape attention. Probably no other writer of literary stature has employed so many. If the unsophisticated reader is uneasy about this because he has been taught to avoid clichés, let him become enlightened as to their use in humor. They have been tellingly used by James Thurber, Robert Benchley, and probably every modern humorist you can name, including Frank Sullivan, whose fictional character, Doctor Arbuthnot, is a cliché expert, a collector of clichés. Nash himself (in a letter to me dated September 25, 1958) has put his finger precisely on the explanation for the effective use of clichés. "The trick is," he wrote, "that it must be somebody else's cliché and not the author's own." What that means is that the author keeps the cliché he uses from being considered naturally his own by a satirical, sophisticated context, or by an artful alteration in its phrasing. In one delightful poem of twenty-four lines, "The Visit," he manages seventeen clichés, a few of which are found in these lines:

She welcomes him with pretty impatience
And a cry of Greetings and salutations!

. . .

Snug as a bug, the cup he waits
That cheers but not inebriates.

. . .

And now he whispers, a bit pajamaly,
That he's fed to the teeth with his whole fam damily,
Perhaps she'll forgive an old man's crotchet
And visit Bermuda on his yachat.

There is a considerable amount of mild didacticism in Nash's verse. Some part of it rises to the level of social criticism. A gift for epigrammatic summation is suggested by these lines:

It is easier for one parent to support seven children
    than for seven children to support one parent.
Women would rather be right than reasonable.
Never befriend the oppressed unless you are prepared
    to take on the oppressor.
Frankness consists in having your back bitten right to
    your face.

In such poems as reveal an unfaltering finesse there is usually a sufficient insight into individual thought or behavior patterns, or into social mores, to satisfy the reader who asks for a worthy, memorable, and enduring experience. The fact that Nash is one of the most quotable of poets supports the judgment that he is frequently master of harmoniously effective combinations of language and meaning.

Not surprisingly, the meaning is often only adequate and the pleasure lies in the language. Tortured rhymes of great ingenuity abound (Buddha, shouldha; *savoir-faire*, back of a chair; house the pup in, to dress up in; waiter, potater). So, too, examples of tortured grammar and word order (let one suffice): "The driest point in America is not Death Valley, but a man with lots of important work on his desk's throat." Puns are scarce, but other forms of wordplay are frequent if not constant. ("Today I am a swashbuckler, would anybody like to buckle any swashes?" "Ye clergymen, draw near and clerge. . . ." "Who wants my jellyfish/I'm not sellyfish!") Because his own practice has the special purpose of humor, it is not inconsistent of him to satirize the popular substitution of *like* for *as*: "Like the hart panteth for the water brooks, I pant for the revival of Shakespeare's *Like You Like It*." Nonsense neologisms are found in "Your Lead, Partner, I Hope We've Read the Same Book," in which he tells of inventing Amaturo, a card game:

The deck has seven morkels
Of eleven guzzards each,
The game runs counterclockwise,
With an extra kleg for dreech,
And if you're caught with a gruice,
The score reverts to deuce.

Nonsense coinages nevertheless are rare in Nash. So, too, is fantasy:

And as for being lazy, I know one robin that held
    down two jobs at once just so his younger
    brother (their parents had passed away unin-
    sured) could get to be a transport pilot,
But if you mentioned it he was modest as a buttercup
    or a vilot. . . .

Almost all of Nash's devices reveal some form of deliberate naïveté and therefore the reader appeal is, at least in good part, a flattering feeling of superiority. Such a device is circularity.

My attention has recently focussed
Upon the seventeen-year locust.
This is the year
When the seventeen-year locusts are here,
Which is the chief reason my attention has been
    focussed
Upon the seventeen-year locust.

How much of "the real Ogden Nash" is revealed in his poems? In the use of point of view, he tends to identify with the "I" or the poet speaking in the poem. He is capable, however, of writing on both sides of a quarrel in different poems, as in those dealing with the battle of the sexes. For example, contrary to custom, he takes the point of view of the woman in "The Trouble with Women Is Men." And in "If Fun Is Fun, Isn't That Enough?" he argues that no humorist is totally trustworthy.

They'll sell their birthright every time
To make a point or turn a rhyme.
This motto, child, is my bequest:
There's many a false word spoken in jest.

One feels sure, however, that when Nash is not writing as a humorist, he is writing out of honest attitudes and convictions. The occasional "straight" poem from his pen can be an unadulterated joy. "Listen" (beginning "There is a knocking in the skull") is a metaphysical poem worthy of Emily Dickinson. "A Lady Thinks She Is Thirty" is a pure lyric holding strains of seventeenth-century love poetry. The tightly held compassion in the six-line "Old Men" bursts forth in the closing couplet:

People watch with unshocked eyes;
But the old men know when an old man dies.

In "A Carol for Children" we catch a glimpse of an underlying religious reverence. It is a rare and sober note in Nash that reveals a sense of nostalgia for a time when faith was strong:

Two ultimate laws alone we know,
The ledger and the sword—
So far away, so long ago,
We lost the infant Lord.

From even a mere dozen of Nash's poems chosen at random, a reader could hardly fail to observe that, while Nash sees and enjoys the misfortunes, the ineptitudes, and the chicanery of men, he is not greatly exercised by the debit side of existence. In short, he is an optimist. Not a cheap one, but a cheerful one. While he is no professional celebrant of our country right or wrong, the detached and optimistic observer shows clear in the following lines from "Look What You Did, Christopher!":

The American people,
With grins jocose,
Always survive the fatal dose.
And though our systems are slightly wobbly,
We'll fool the doctor this time, probly.

Reviewing Nash's first volume of verse in the *Saturday Review of Literature* in 1931, William Rose Benét declared that it was "about as good a picture of his life and times as others have spent volumes on." Now, umpteen volumes later, the picture has taken on additional richness and detail and continues to delight as well as to provide some confections for reflection. The well-read will be rewarded by many allusions to song and character and story worked deftly into the fabric of the poetic experience. Varying elements of didacticism, never heavy, often merely playful, tease the ruminative mind. In his meanings, he seldom has depth, though there is more than the casual reader might think—more than a little of it social criticism. In his form and technique he has made a contribution to humorous literature—not momentous, perhaps, only ineradicable. Too much of him read at a sitting can indeed cloy. But read a little at a time, he provides unique and continuing delectation.

Grace. Gaiety. Charm. The artfully, quaintly naïve. Bounce. The puckish. The fantastic. The frivolous. These furnish some of the pleasures we get from what one of his inspired book blurbs called "The Golden Trashery of Ogden Nashery."

GEORGE JEAN NATHAN

1882–1958

George Jean Nathan was born on February 14, 1882, in Fort Wayne, Indiana. When he was six his family moved to Cleveland, where he was educated by private tutors and took frequent trips to Europe before entering Cornell University in 1900. Nathan edited several school publications at Cornell, graduating with a B.A. in 1904. After a year spent at the University of Bologna in Italy, Nathan became, through family influence, a reporter and drama critic for the *New York Herald*; from here he became associated with many newspapers and magazines in New York, until in 1908 he became drama critic and, in 1914, co-editor with H. L. Mencken of the *Smart Set*. Mencken and Nathan gave that magazine its distinctive air of sophistication and iconoclasm, and Nathan became the most respected and feared drama critic in the country; his incisive and oftentimes vicious reviews appeared in journals throughout America, and were also published in many foreign periodicals. Through the *Smart Set* Nathan discovered Eugene O'Neill and F. Scott Fitzgerald, and promoted the dramatic careers of Lord Dunsany, Theodore Dreiser, James Branch Cabell, James Joyce, Aldous Huxley, and many other writers.

In 1923 Mencken and Nathan founded the *American Mercury*, but two years later Nathan left the magazine and in 1932, with O'Neill, Cabell, and Ernest Boyd, founded the *American Spectator*. Nathan later served as president of the New York Drama Circle Critics. George Jean Nathan died on April 8, 1958.

Nathan collaborated with Mencken on several volumes, including *Europe after 8:15* (1914), the play *Heliogabalus* (1920), and *The American Credo* (1920). Among Nathan's own works are *The World in Falseface* (1923), *Materia Critica* (1924), *The Autobiography of an Attitude* (1925), *Passing Judgments* (1934), and many others. *The Intimate Notebooks of George Jean Nathan* were published in 1932.

Personal

What is my own philosophy of life? It is, in simple, merely this: to forget the miseries of the past and remember only its charm, to live the present to the limit of its utmost possibilities, and to view the future as one who has traveled romantically in a colorful far country views the skyline of his nearing homeland—with a sense of great content and slightly sad resignation.

The older I grow, the more I am persuaded that hedonism is the only sound and practical doctrine of faith for the intelligent man. I doubt, indeed, if there ever has lived an intelligent man whose end in life was not the achievement of a large and selfish pleasure. This latter is often shrewdly swathed in the deceptive silks of altruism or what not, but brush the silks aside and the truth of self-gratification is visible in all its nudity. Mohammed's altruism was as completely hedonistic as Charlemagne's frank hedonism. The greater the idealist, the greater the hedonist behind the whiskers.

Altruism, it seems to me, is the highest flowering of selfishness. In the heart of the greatest altruist one will always find the largest mirror. The history of altruism is a long series of self-engraved, adulatory epitaphs.

I find, upon honest reflection, that I am uplifted not by my virtues, but by my vices. They cheer me, make me happy and contented, make life seem worth while when my day's work is done, send the blood of tonic joy shooting through my veins, banish blueness and self-doubt and worry and despond.

I am not what is generally known as the popular type of man. That is, I am not the sort of man who is liked by the majority of persons with whom he comes into contact. I have a number of very good friends, among both men and women; but, aside from these, the general run of people whose paths cross my own are of as little personal interest to me as I am, assuredly, to them. I am not interesting to these persons because I prefer their disinterest, and am at no pains to conceal it. I know and always feel that it would be the simplest thing in the world to provoke their interest, at least to a degree—a technic grantedly not occult—but I am not able to persuade myself that their interest in me, the one way or the other, is worth concerning myself with. If I like a person, he or she knows it; I show my interest at once. If I don't care for a person, he or she knows it just as quickly; the lack of interest on my part is at once obvious.

All this makes for unpopularity. To be popular, one must show interest in persons and things that do not interest one and simultaneously conceal the interest that one has in persons and things that do interest one. One must always side with the prejudices and emotions of the person one happens to be with, however idiotic. One must laugh when one doesn't feel like it; be quiet when one would be gay. One must tell old women one loves them, and young women one doesn't. One must be humorous but never witty, interested but never enthusiastic, complacently bored but never tired. When one is with one's intellectual inferiors, one must agreeably reduce one's self not to the level of these others, but below that level, that they may have the comfortable feeling of being at complete conversational ease. One must be privy to the trick of flattering another person's vanity by contradicting what he says and then allowing him to convince one that he is right. One must pretend to take lightly what one feels about most profoundly. One may be original in manner, but never in thought.

I am able to negotiate all these things, but I decline to do so. Among the many millions of persons in this fair land, there are not more than a dozen at the very outside, who, known to me personally, interest me personally in the slightest. The rest, so far as I am concerned, can go chase themselves.—GEORGE JEAN NATHAN, "Personal Attitude," *The Autobiography of an Attitude*, 1925, pp. 6–9

Not long ago I visited Nathan when he had a spell of illness. He has lived in the same hotel since 1906, when he began writing dramatic criticism, and in the very same apartment for the past twenty-eight years. It looks like an ancient and honorable and wonderful second-hand bookstore. Books and pictures are all over—piled high on chairs and on the floor. There are busts of Nathan himself serving as doorstops, there are plaques on the walls, some probably dating back to his fencing days at Cornell, others gifts from cultural and not-so-cultural organizations. There is a huge papier-mâché Indian head, standing on a table, close by a group of wineglasses that he must have got two or three decades ago. Hard by a window is a heavy and wonderfully large writing table, piled with papers and pens and pencilled notes. (Nathan writes all his things in longhand and then has the script typed by a professional typist.)

Not used to illness, Nathan felt talkative and I kept my silence most of the time. He talked about F. Scott Fitzgerald (why in his opinion *The Great Gatsby* was an inferior book), Sean O'Casey ("Did you notice the violinist in his eyes?"), television and particularly the current queens in the field ("They have voices like cash-registers or calliopes—and imagine the romantic appeal of a girl selling an automatic washing-machine!"), radio breakfast-programs ("The husbands should get annual Nobel Prizes for Christian kindness"), what veils do to dancing girls that tights can never do, the very sad state of quality periodical journalism in the United States and the reasons for this, the last letter he received from Bernard Shaw ("That really made me feel good!"), how he met a female author whom he discovered on the *Smart Set* years ago ("She can't write any more, but she still has ink on her fingers, and I wonder how it got there"), a practical joke with embarrassing results that he and Mencken had played on one of their more gullible publishers some twenty years ago, why freckle-faced girls should be taken more seriously than they have been, how wonderful some of O'Casey's unproduced plays are and how sad it is that New York producers have not yet taken them up, the virtues of both vegetarianism and meat-eating, the continuing inferiority of the works of Clifford Odets, the last tragic days of Ernest Boyd ("Remember the article he wrote for the *American Spectator* in which he said that adultery is preferable to multiple matrimony?"), a good nerve tonic, the ravages of neuralgia (which has troubled him for forty years), the prospects for the Yankees next season (Nathan has just become a convert to the cause of this American League club), the immeasurable superiority of the writer's life to that of any other on the globe, the charm of some of the early short stories of Edith Wharton and Willa Cather, Somerset Maugham as a writer and as a man, Nathan's and Mencken's difficulties in escaping the non-literary demands of the illiterate females who vainly yearned to appear in the *Smart Set* ("With the most insistent ones we used to make dates at certain trees in Central Park and never show up"), James Boswell's strange combination of lechery and piety, Roxy's degrading influence on American entertainment, how to judge a girl's mind ("Ask her how she would get to the Grand Central Station; if her answer is fifty per cent correct, she is intelligent enough"), and several other subjects.

When I left him I felt refreshed. He has the true artist's magnificent irrepressibility of spirit. He has added an engaging liveliness to the American scene. He has been a definite force in our cultural life. He will be remembered and he will be read, I believe, for a long time.—CHARLES ANGOFF, "Introduction" to *The World of George Jean Nathan*, 1952, pp. xxvii–xxviii

General

To a man so fertile in ideas and so facile in putting them into words there is a constant temptation to make experiments, to plunge into strange waters, to seek self-expression in ever-widening circles. And yet, at the brink of forty years, Nathan remains faithful to the theater; of his half dozen books, only one does not deal with it, and that one is a very small one. In four or five years he has scarcely written of aught else. I doubt that anything properly describable as enthusiasm is at the bottom of this assiduity; perhaps the right word is curiosity. He is interested mainly, not in the staple fare of the playhouse, but in what might be called its fancy goods—in its endless stream of new men, its restless innovations, the radical overhauling that it has been undergoing in our time. I do not recall, in any of his books or articles, a single paragraph appraising the classics of the stage, or more than a brief note or two on their interpretation. His attention is always turned in a quite opposite direction. He is intensely interested in novelty of whatever sort, if it be only free from sham. Such experimentalists as Max Reinhardt, George Bernard Shaw, Sasha Guitry and the daring nobodies of the Grand Guignol, such divergent originals as Dunsany, Ziegfeld, George M. Cohan and Schnitzler, have enlisted his eager partisanship. He saw something new to our theater in the farces of Hopwood before any one else saw it; he was quick to welcome the novel points of view of Eleanor Gates and Clare Kummer; he at once rescued what was sound in the Little Theatre movement from what was mere attitudinizing and pseudo-intellectuality. In the view of Broadway, an exigent and even malignant fellow, wielding a pen dipped in *aqua fortis*, he is actually amiable to the last degree, and constantly announces pearls in the fodder of the swine. Is the new play in Forty-second Street a serious work of art, as the press-agents and the newspaper reviewers say? Then so are your grandmother's false teeth! Is Maeterlinck a Great Thinker? Then so is Dr. Frank Crane! Is Belasco a profound artist? Then so is the man who designs the ceilings of hotel dining rooms! But let us not weep too soon. In the play around the corner there is a clever scene. Next door, amid sickening dullness, there are two buffoons who could be worse: one clouts the other with a *Blutwurst* filled with mayonnaise. And a block away there is a girl in the second row with a very charming twist of the *vastus medialis*. Let us sniff the roses and forget the thorns!

What this attitude chiefly wars with, even above cheapness, meretriciousness and banality, is the fatuous effort to turn the theater, a place of amusement, into a sort of outhouse to the academic grove—the Maeterlinck-Brieux-Barker complex. No critic in America, and none in England save perhaps Walkley, has combated this movement more vigorously than Nathan. He is under no illusion as to the functions and limitations of the stage. He knows, with Victor Hugo, that the best it can do, in the domain of ideas, is to "turn thoughts into food for the crowd," and he knows that only the simplest and shakiest ideas may undergo that transformation. Coming upon the scene at the height of the Ibsen mania of half a generation ago, he ranged himself against its windy pretenses from the start. He saw at once the high merit of Ibsen as a dramatic craftsman and welcomed him as a reformer of dramatic technique, but he also saw how platitudinous was the ideational content of his plays and announced the fact in terms

highly offensive to the Ibsenites. . . . But the Ibsenites have vanished and Nathan remains. He has survived, too, the Brieux hubbub. He has lived to preach the funeral sermon of the Belasco legend. He has himself sworded Maeterlinck and Granville Barker. He has done frightful execution upon many a poor mime. And meanwhile, breasting the murky tide of professorial buncombe, of solemn pontificating, of Richard-Burtonism, Clayton-Hamiltonism and other such decaying forms of William-Winterism, he has rescued dramatic criticism among us from its exile with theology, embalming and obstetrics, and given it a place among what Nietzsche called the gay sciences, along with war, fiddle-playing and laparotomy. He has made it amusing, stimulating, challenging, even, at times, a bit startling. And to the business, artfully concealed, he has brought a sound and thorough acquaintance with the heavy work of the pioneers, Lessing, Schlegel, Hazlitt, Lewes et al.—and an even wider acquaintance, lavishly displayed, with every nook and corner of the current theatrical scene across the water. And to discharge this extraordinarily copious mass of information he has hauled and battered the English language into new and often astounding forms, and when English has failed he has helped it out with French, German, Italian, American, Swedish, Russian, Turkish, Latin, Sanskrit and Old Church Slavic, and with algebraic symbols, chemical formulæ, musical notation and the signs of the Zodiac. . . .

This manner, of course, is not without its perils. A man so inordinately articulate is bound to succumb, now and then, to the seductions of mere virtuosity. The average writer, and particularly the average critic of the drama, does well if he gets a single new and racy phrase into an essay; Nathan does well if he dilutes his inventions with enough commonplaces to enable the average reader to understand his discourse at all. He carries the avoidance of the *cliché* to the length of an *idée fixe*. It would be difficult, in all his books, to find a dozen of the usual rubber stamps of criticism; I daresay it would kill him, or, at all events, bring him down with cholera morbus, to discover that he had called a play "convincing" or found "authority" in the snorting of an English actor-manager. At best, this incessant flight from the obvious makes for a piquant and arresting style, a procession of fantastic and often highly pungent neologisms—in brief, for Nathanism. At worst, it becomes artificiality, pedantry, obscurity. I cite an example from an essay on Eleanor Gates' *The Poor Little Rich Girl*, prefaced to the printed play:

> As against the not unhollow symbolic strut and gasconade of such over-pæaned pieces as, let us for example say, *The Blue Bird* of Maeterlinck, so simple and unaffected a bit of stage writing as this—of school dramatic intrinsically the same—cajoles the more honest heart and satisfies more plausibly and fully those of us whose thumbs are ever being pulled professionally for a native stage less smeared with the snobberies of empty, albeit high-sounding, nomenclatures from overseas.

Fancy that, Hedda!—and in praise of a "simple and unaffected bit of stage writing"! I denounced it at the time, *circa* 1916, and perhaps with some effect. At all events, I seem to notice a gradual disentanglement of the parts of speech. The old florid invention is still there; one encounters startling coinages in even the most casual of reviews; the thing still flashes and glitters; the tune is yet upon the E string. But underneath I hear a more sober rhythm than of old. The fellow, in fact, takes on a sedater habit, both in style and in point of view. Without abandoning anything essential, without making the slightest concession to the orthodox opinion that he so magnificently disdains, he yet begins to yield to the middle years. The mere shocking of the stupid is no longer as charming as it used to be. What he now offers is rather more *gemütlich*; sometimes it even verges upon the instructive. . . . But I doubt that Nathan will ever become a professor, even if he enjoys the hideously prolonged senility of a William Winter. He will be full of surprises to the end. With his last gasp he will make a phrase to flabbergast a dolt.—H. L. MENCKEN, "George Jean Nathan," *Prejudices: First Series,* 1919, pp. 217–23

As critic of critics, Mr. Nathan performs a service for the reviewers of local theatrical entertainment which is not available to other gazetteers. Most newspaper men go on their way without any salutary criticism from without. Save for the periodic and little-noted judgments handed down by the School of Journalism at Columbia, no one says "well done" or "pretty rotten" to the newspaper man. Within his own fold, the rare word of commendation or the absence of reproof from the terrifying managing editor is, except for his conscience, his only guide. It is curious that no such non-professional review as *The Literary Digest* has ever undertaken a steady running criticism of the journalistic achievements of each passing week.

But the dramatic critics have their George Jean Nathan, who whacks and trounces and jibes the local Hazlittry with great gusto in his own private and personal *Smart Set.* Their ignorance, bred by decades of low entertainment, is quite general and familiar. But, as targets, none of them is beneath Nathan. Not even the docile and nervous little fellows who write sweet nothings about plays and players with one eye on the clock and the other on the advertising manager. Not even the late William Winter, whose colossal unfamiliarity with the modern drama, what it had done, and what it was trying to do, ever afforded a fine opening for the witty and inexhaustible Nathan. Winter comes in for a parting shot in *Comedians All.*

With Winter gone, Nathan finds a tempting mark in the venerable J. Ranken Towse of *The New York Evening Post,* whose wistful feeling that nothing has ever seemed quite so good as the otherwise forgotten efforts of one Samuel Phelps at Sadler's Wells in Mr. Towse's salad days, lays him wide open to the nimbler and more widely cultured chronicler of *The Smart Set.* Then he also engages in several lively brushes with the sages of Morningside Heights—Brander Matthews and Clayton Hamilton. Sage brushes, Mr. Nathan would doubtless call them, for he will have his little joke, even if it's a bad one, which it by no means always is. Dr. Matthews did, in his chatter about stage conventions, inattentively expose a peculiarly tempting and accessible reach of pedagogical trouser to the Nathan slapstick, to borrow a familiar and somewhat overworked Nathanism. These are only the more palpable hits. No one 'scapes whipping.

Many popular misconceptions and dislikes begotten by the Nathan mannerisms (for he is as manneristic as Louis Mann or Madge Kennedy) should not betray his not inconsiderable public from profiting by the soundness of much that he writes. For instance, there is no reason why the puzzling, nay, the unaccountable, note of self-importance which, appearing in his chapter "The Foremost American Producer," stands out even in a book not notable for a lack of complacency, should be allowed to vitiate the worth of a really sensitive and discerning essay on the priceless Arthur Hopkins.

Nor should it be thought that the array of and sometimes facetiously imaginary information on the theatre in other lands with which Nathan is wont to obliterate his neighbors, is just that *Smart Set* jackanapes showing off again, as his irritated victims are likely to believe. It is true that he labors to make his fellow-babblers believe that no one who has not seen all the productions up some side street in Odessa or Osaka is a poor

creature, unfit to analyze the art of Eva Tanguay. It is true that no local farce is too paltry to inspire him to some windy dissertations on certain Swedish and Bulgarian prototypes. But this is not prompted by an itch for self-display, as is popularly believed. It is simply the output of a naturally punditical mind, whose true professorial quality is never quite concealed by his sedulous jocosity.

Then it is all wrong to laugh at Nathan's judgments in the matter of actors. His periodic approvals and disapprovals are forever being misread by his followers as facetious and greeted with what must be disconcerting hilarity. This is as cruel an injustice as it would have been to have laughed at the untrained Trilby's first croaking of "Ben Bolt" in the studio in the Rue Notre Dame des Champs. In matters of acting Nathan is incurably tone-deaf. He probably knows more about modern dramatic literature than any one now writing regularly on that subject in England or America, but he knows nothing at all about the player's art. He really thinks Mrs. Fiske is a muddleheaded, ineloquent, third-rate actress and that Margaret Illington is the greatest comedienne of her time. He honestly does, and it isn't fair to laugh.—ALEXANDER WOOLLCOTT, "Mr. Nathan's Criticisms of Dramatic Criticism," *NYTBR,* Oct. 26, 1919, p. 598

George Jean Nathan doesn't give a damn for the rest of us. With a disarming frankness, he admits his selfishness and his total engrossment in his personal pleasure. Whether he is contemplating life or art, he is governed by the subjective aestheticism that was modish in the 1920's. Most of his stock opinions are equally typical of the period when he and H. L. Mencken shocked the bourgeoisie every month in the *American Mercury.* Thus, he is impatient at the intrusion of any moral issue into the judgement of art—or of life. He has only disdain for most of his fellow-Americans, especially those who live in rural areas, but he has high praise for the few who maintain an "articulate metropolitan and world-balanced note," the world's elite, among whom he numbers himself. He is convinced that all women are, or ought to be, playthings, that intellectual women are either pitiful or vicious, and that marriage is a trap. Without any qualifications, he despises politics and politicians; this attitude is, in particular, a legitimate offspring of the Harding-Coolidge era. He has an especial aversion to reform and reformers; so thoroughly has he persuaded himself that any kind of social reform is undesirable that he was able to write, in the dark year of 1931: "The world, as I see it, is sufficiently gay, beautiful, and happy as it stands." A year later, he referred to Dreiser's membership on "committees protesting the lynching of Negro Lotharios." At least, Mr. Nathan's cynicism deserves credit on the score of honesty. His colleagues on the New York *Journal-American* claim lofty reasons for supporting callous doctrines.

The real oddity of Mr. Nathan's case is that, granted all his quirks, he is still one of the very few drama critics who are worth reading. Although Charles Angoff's new sampling of Mr. Nathan's writings (*The World of George Jean Nathan*) insufficiently represents the drama criticism, there is enough to remind us what this critic excels at—the diagnosis of various kinds of badness in the theatre. The author, like his readers, obviously gets the most fun out of his unfavorable reviews. Mr. Nathan exhibits considerable critical sense even when he is discussing plays that he likes, but here his remarks sometimes become perfunctory; he evidently lives by his belief that no favorable review can have anything very new in it. What is most curious in his criticism is his marked preference for authors whose social views are the opposite of his own. First among contemporary dramatists he ranks the arch-reformer

Shaw, and his favorites among the Americans are the sympathetic, sometimes sentimental, O'Neill and Saroyan. Such preferences testify to Mr. Nathan's critical independence; when he is in the theatre he is free even of many of his private crotchets. This independence is often disparaged on the grounds that his interest in the theatre, unlike Shaw's, is isolated from all of society, from the great world outside. —HENRY POPKIN, "Candor with Indifference," NR, June 9, 1952, p. 21

JOHN MASON BROWN
"George Jean Nathan"
Upstage: The American Theatre in Performance
1930, pp. 233–42

Though George Jean Nathan has two hands and a use for each of them, they both serve but a single purpose. Nor is one of them ever allowed to be uninformed as to the other's doings. With one—his right no doubt because it is farthest from his heart—he writes dramatic criticism, the most topical, topsy-turvy, intelligent, high-brow, low-brow, penetrating, bladder-bursting dramatic criticism that has come out of America. And with the other—the one nearest his heart of course—he directs at the theatre, at life in general and the contemporary scene as he sees it, a nose-thumbing of such unwearied endurance and Gargantuan proportions that it would long ago have sprained the wrist of Atlas, had he tried, as Mr. Nathan has succeeded in doing, to maintain the gesture for twenty years or more.

With both hands, however, he strikes an attitude, a mucker pose such as could be struck only by a man who had never outgrown the decision, made in his cradle, to be the *enfant terrible* of the American theatre for forty-eight hours out of every twenty-four. And it is that attitude—of being above illusions or emotions, and ag'in in the government, ag'in everything, in fact—of which he has been the gleeful biographer in each of his many books, and in every article printed under his name.

This George Jean Nathan, who lived so long on the printed page as the Pythias to H. L. Mencken's Damon, is proudly, stridently immodest about everything on earth except that other Nathan who may be hiding behind the falseface, or who may exist in spite of the Nathan myth which is the result of such successful, though unresting, labor. This Mr. Nathan of the public prints talks about himself with the same insistency, though without the same excuse, as does the other and now gray-bearded George, who was once a dramatic critic before he took to writing plays and prefaces. Sometimes this Mr. Nathan speaks out frankly, with a modesty covered by his own and no other patent. "I am, alas," he boasts, "the kind of ignoble fellow who laughs at Rabelais, a certain pamphlet of Mark Twain's, the unexpurgated Swift, Walt Whitman's last words, General Grant's bed-time stories and *Reigen*." Having picked a company of fitting peers, he concludes, "I am, therefore, doomed to meet Abraham Lincoln in hell." Sometimes, in self-definition, if not in self-defense, he tries his hand at an epigram which shows that, in book form, he is still pursued by the "dull devil" of the *Smart Set*. "There are two kinds of dramatic critics," he writes, using both his hands but closing both eyes, "destructive and constructive. I am destructive. There are two kinds of gun: Krupp and pop."

Often, however, Mr. Nathan prefers to explain himself by an implication which is so thinly veiled that it would send honest shudders up and down the spine of his old enemy, Anthony Comstock. "In every thoroughly charming and effective person," he says, keeping the thumb to his nose, but managing at the same time, as it can be done, to point his little finger at himself, "one finds a suggestion and a trace, however small, of the gutter. . . . In the soul of every fetching man" (the same gesture can be used here again) "there is a streak of ingratiating commonness." At other times, even when he is explaining his mountebankery, Mr. Nathan grabs the iron crown out of his readers' hands and claps it resolutely on his own head. "When we denounce a man for mountebankery," he warns us—because at this point Mr. Nathan seems anxious to admit us to the plural pronoun—"we often overlook the fact that a touch of charlatanism is necessary to any honest, sincere, and first-rate man in the Republic, if he is to get his message, whatever it may be, across to the millions of boobs and blockheads who hem him in on all sides. There are men who are born frauds: there are others who have fraudulence thrust upon them. The former are not worth tobacco juice; the latter are often deserving of the highest and most intelligently critical praise."

The George Jean Nathan of the printed page, in spite of the gutter qualities he affects, and the commonness he assumes, that is not always "ingratiating," is worth decidedly more than "tobacco juice." He is, in truth—even if he had not told us so himself—"deserving of the highest and most intelligently critical praise." Charlatan he is, of course. But behind his mountebankery, his eagerness to don cap and bells, lie the sharpest, most all-seeing eyes and the most generally informed and alert brains, to say nothing of the most vigorously outspoken sentences that have yet been brought to the American theatre's dramatic criticism. Of all American dramatic critics, he has the highest visibility and the lowest gullibility. It is because of these finer qualities with which he is abundantly endowed that the methods and the bad manners of the mountebank acquire a special interest.

Whether you happen to have read him in the *Smart Set* or in *Punch*, in *Judge*, *The American Mercury*, or *The New Freeman*; or in any of those books of his which have been more annual than Christmas since 1914, those vigorous scissors-and-paste collections of his essays, such as *The Popular Theatre*, *The Theatre, the Drama, and the Girls*, *The World in Falseface*, *Materia Critica* or *The House of Satan*, you will find that this Mr. Nathan of the public prints employs a vocabulary which is most decidedly his own. The style of Alexander Woollcott may be—and is—personal, repertorial and thoroughly alive. But it is coldly academic beside Mr. Nathan's, forced to play the part of Thorvaldsen to his Brancusi, and Rameau to his Gershwin. Mr. Nathan has not only mastered the language of the *Handbooks of Composition*, he has invented a jargon of his own. His sentences bristle with such Nathanisms as flapdoodle, jerkwater salons, spank-spots, six-day sock-wearers, flubdub, wish-jags, guffaw-sesame, schnitzels of buncombe, hornswoggle, the barrack of balderdash, pfui opus, hick-pricker, Rialtors, dooflickus, the cowhouse of art, The Adventures of Phallus in Wonderland, yokel-yankers, boobletariat, and a thousand others of the same kind which even Isaac Goldberg, the official and it should be added extremely readable biographer of Nathan, has tired of before listing to their full extent.

When his verbal inventions fail him, this Mr. Nathan has other rabbits in his hat. Turning to Geneva, he borrows words from the tongues of every member of the League of Nations with which he glibly sprinkles his paragraphs. Or he delights in prefacing the names of the people he is ridiculing with such weighty titles as Doctor, "la," Herr, Professor, and Reverend, and thus covers his ridicule with a double insurance. On subjects which in other hands would be an excuse for much pontifical piety and blighting erudition, he loves to jerk his readers back to an earth-earthy earth by sudden anatomical references—dubbed "phallic fooleries" by Mr. Goldberg—that are as completely unexpected as they are exuberantly sophomoric.

Another of Mr. Nathan's favorite devices is his use of fact-crammed catalogues. He does not make his facts the slaves of gossip as Mr. Woollcott is inclined to do. Nor does he dodge them to blow diaphanous æsthetic bubbles as Mr. Young occasionally does. Instead he recruits them, and parades them with a belligerent interest in the idea under whose banner they are made to serve. When, for example, in *The Popular Theatre* (and Mr. Nathan hates the popular theatre), he considers the personnel of a first-night audience in New York, he puts his facts to a favorite and jocular use. "It is probably," he says in a typical passage written in 1918 which is equally true for 1930, "an eminently safe wager that, when the curtain lifts on the average Broadway *première*, there are not, at the very most, ten persons in the entire audience who know that Rüderer is not a brand of champagne, that Anatole France is not a French adaptation of Schnitzler, and that Richard Strauss is not the junior partner of Abraham Strauss' department store in Brooklyn. And, in the entire audience, there are in all probability not more than two or three, at the outside, who are able clearly to distinguish between Verdun and Verdi, or J. S. Bach of Thuringia and J. S. Bache of the Wall Street firm of J. S. Bache & Co."

He does the same thing—and with every good reason—when he turns the white heat of his contempt on such a treacly play of A. A. Milne's as *Michael and Mary*. "A. A. Milne, the Chelsea Pollyanna, the chain candy-stores of English literature and the Happiness Boys of the London drama, is with us again in an exhibit called *Michael and Mary*. Attending it is much like going to a marshmallow roast with Dr. Frank Crane's ghost, Jane Cowl, J. M. Barrie's boyhood Sunday-school superintendent, the Messrs. Page and Shaw, the man who first thought of putting cream in the Alexander cocktail, Ada Mae Weeks and Ethelbert Nevin. It is the *Nachtasyl* of over-sweetened sentimentality, the *King Lear* of virtuous pap, the *Old Oaken Bucket* of the grease-paint E-string. It is so good, so pure, so moral, so upright, so tender, and so damned noble that it hurts."

The articles and the books of this Mr. Nathan abound with such illustrations, are in fact so over-rich in them, that they become fatiguing and dull Mr. Nathan's style so that too much of him cannot be read at one sitting. His writings abound, too, in short, pithy sentences that frequently achieve a blinding brilliancy, but that just as frequently are the smart-alec epigrams that a grade school boy might be proud of if he had just read Oscar Wilde for the first time. They range from "An artist of the violin may have a face like a dollar watch and a figure like a boardwalk rolling chair, but the difference between him and the actor is that he merely has to *play* the violin; he does not have to look like it," to such a superb description of Sir James Barrie as "the triumph of sugar over diabetes." And, in *Land of the Pilgrim's Pride*, they descend to such childishness as, "Nothing is so ruinous to an artist as love of money. Nothing is so ruinous to a business man as love of art."

But all of them—the epigrams that sparkle as well as those that come out flat on the brush, the illustrations, the mock-serious titles, the facts, and the "phallic fooleries"—are but tricks in the repertory of that Mr. Nathan, whose genius for low-comedy, farce and slap-stick, has made him seem the leading red-nosed comico of American criticism, even while he is its most rational and illusionless practitioner. They are what he himself would doubtless call "yokel-yankers for the boobletariat," the weapons he employs to fight off dullness, to escape the ordinary critical jargon which he despises, and to demonstrate his sainted "indifference" and superior callousness. They are, too, the means by which he asserts his he-mannishness aggressively. And his maleness is as important a part of his writing as is his superior callousness. It is that which makes him contemptuous of both sentiment and sentimentality in any form. It is that, too, which makes him happiest when he stands alone and defies the pack. And it is also that, no doubt, which makes him delight in disliking such a play as *Journey's End*, and in describing it as "The Bachelors' Cotillion Club goes to War," "Some excellent Pinero actors go to war against the Hun" and "All quaint on the Western Front."

Even while he is resorting to the hokum of his own devising, however, Mr. Nathan is engaged in a furious crusade against every other kind of hokum he may encounter in the world around him, fighting it ceaselessly with a candor and an honesty that—while they may be expressed as but parts of his attitude—no other critic has exhibited.

Naturally enough, the negative talents of Mr. Nathan are at their best when they encounter sham. He not only slays dragons well, but he enjoys slaying them so much that his pleasure is contagious. He spares nothing. The playwright, the actor, the manager, the public, the critics, even his own person, are all crowded into a tumbril and sent mockingly to the guillotine. The religious play, the mystery play, the farce, the pseudo-intellectual drama, the sex play and all their kind, are spoofed by him with an unerring malice and a delicious common sense. Though the taste of his methods may exceed the limits of questionability, the taste and the learning behind his bad manners can seldom be doubted.

Long before the names of many of the now well-known continentals were familiar to Broadway, Mr. Nathan was writing of them. In the midst of his ribald horse-play, he has for years quoted from critical forebears, the very existence of whom had not been suspected by the dramatic critics reared in the police courts. For years, too, he has raised his rapier, his broad-sword or his fool's stick, against pretensions and fought for honesty. He hates the critics who, in order to pass as learned æsthetes, pretend to prefer Olga Nethersole to Ann Pennington. "He"—Mr. Nathan it can be presumed because he is writing of "discerning critics"—"wants horse-play, belly-laughter, pretty girls, ingenious scenery, imported ladies of joy and eminent home talent, insane melodrama, lovely limbs, lively tunes, gaudy colors, loud humours, farce, flippancy, fol-de-rol."

The reason is that, as he has come to see it, "the place of the theatre in the community is infinitely less the place of the university, the studio and the art gallery than the place of the circus, the rathskeller, and the harem. . . . The theatre," as he defines it, "is simply, plainly—and in the soundest critical definition—a place where a well-educated, well-bred, well-fed man may find something to divert him pleasantly for a couple of hours." That is the theatre of George Jean Nathan, the theatre where Florenz Ziegfeld is honored with Shakespeare and George M. Cohan with Duse, the theatre of the passing show and a ready anxiety to applaud merit wherever merit may be found and regardless of its pretensions. It is the theatre of a man who is so free of the pretensions usual to his own profession that he can say, "When I write that I enjoy the comedy of Shakespeare more than the comedy of Harry Watson, Jr., I lie."

But there is more to Mr. Nathan than that. He has, in fact, more sides to him than an Elizabethan tragedy has subplots. His power for destruction, even his honesty, do not cover him. They may explain the Nathan who is a hedonist trumpeting his hedonism, the Nathan who lives untouched by anything in a world apart, the Nathan who says, "I do not care who writes the laws of a country so long as I may listen to its songs," the Nathan who does "not care a tinker's damn whether Germany invades Belgium or Belgium, Germany," or who boasts that "on the day during the world war when the most critical battle was being fought, I sat in my still, sunlit, cozy library, composing a chapter on æsthetics for a new book on the drama."

That is the Nathan of the attitude, who is honest to that attitude. But it does not explain the Nathan who strikes the attitude. It does not explain the Nathan who took the trouble to write that chapter on æsthetics, or who in writing it stooped to the most obvious saw-dust tricks, in order to win the attention and approval of those very boobs he sincerely despises. It has nothing to say about the Nathan who aided Eugene O'Neill in getting *Beyond the Horizon* produced and who has been his champion again and again; the Nathan who has won the friendship of Gordon Craig; who has written some of the most illuminating paragraphs on criticism, acting, direction and playwriting which modern criticism has produced; the Nathan who has raised his voice shrilly against the movies; or the Nathan who so won the admiration of A. B. Walkley and other critics the world over that the covers of his books are decked out with "Nathan bibliographies," "library references," and con-gratulatory notices from each member of the British Empire to show that the sun never sets on George Jean Nathan.

The reason is, of course, that George Jean Nathan contains more persons within himself than his name does parts. He is a paradox of paradoxes. There is a false Nathan and a true Nathan as surely as there was a false Armistice Day and a true one, but he celebrates them both conjointly. He says serious things, but he says them so that no one can suspect their seriousness, or, what would be even worse, accuse him of having been serious about them. He says unmentionable things out loud in a country which, since it was first visited by the Pilgrim Fathers, has preferred to have them whispered in corners. And he laughs instead of chants, as we like our critics to do. He laughs, not because he does not love, but because he believes that "beauty makes idiots sad as it makes wise men merry."

This kaleidoscopic Mr. Nathan is assuredly one of the wise men. No one can question that. But he has stubbornly refused to grow up to his wisdom. Instead he has chosen to be a naughty boy, telling people who have long since stopped believing, that there is no Santa Claus, and telling them when he has much more to say. The pity is that this Mr. Nathan seems to feel that his first allegiance is to the attitude rather than to the Nathan who strikes it. The pity is, too, that the most penetrating of our critics and the one whose intellect is both the most aloof and the most vigorous, should delight in a mucker pose, which tends to make him seem at times not only every other inch a gentleman—as someone once said of Michael Arlen—but every other inch a critic, too.

ROBERT NATHAN

1894–1985

Robert Nathan, prolific novelist, poet, and playwright, was born January 2, 1894, in New York City. A direct descendant of Rabbi Gersham Seixes, one of the eighteenth-century incorporators of Columbia College, he was also a nephew of Annie (Nathan) Meyer, founder of Barnard College. After graduation from Phillips Exeter Academy he entered Harvard, where he became editor of *Harvard Monthly*. In 1915 he left Harvard without a degree to get married.

Nathan's first book, *Peter Kindred* (imprinted 1919 but not published until early 1920), was a *Bildungsroman* of the sort that the sad young men of the lost generation identified with in the years after World War I. *Autumn* (1921), his first fable in fantasy, established the pattern of short, ironic novel that he was to write for the rest of his career. He had his first commercial success with *One More Spring* (1933), a Depression novel, which was made into a motion picture. *Portrait of Jennie* (1940), probably his best-known work of fiction, was also adapted for the cinema. His last novel, *Heaven and Hell and the Megas Factor*, appeared in 1975.

Nathan was one of the charter members of the New York branch of P.E.N., and later served as its president. Elected to the National Institute of Arts and Letters in 1935, he was a Chancellor of the Academy of American Poets. He was married six times. A man of feeling, Nathan best deserves to be recognized for his power to evoke in his work the sentiment of love: the love between man and woman, the love of man for mankind, and the love that opens the way to God. He died on May 25, 1985, in Los Angeles, California.

EDITH McEWEN DORIAN
From "While a Little Dog Dances—
Robert Nathan: Novelist of Simplicity"

Sewanee Review, April–June 1933, pp. 129–40

Since 1919 when Robert Nathan published his first book, he has put into the pages of ten novels a shrewd and penetrating criticism of America's dominant middle class ideals. Like others of the younger American intellectuals whose work began to make itself felt in the nineteen twenties, Nathan has been concerned for a civilization subservient to the materialistic ideals of the machine age. He has shown scant sympathy for the destruction of beauty at the dictates of the acquisitive instinct. He has shown even less for the repressive forms of a middle class Puritanism only half-alive but still warping the herd mind and negating tolerance. "Where am I now?" asks the angel in *The Bishop's Wife*. "In a land where those who do not enjoy anything, make laws to deprive others of their pleasures; where God and prosperity are worshipped as one, and men taught to hate before they are taught to love." Yet equally Nathan dislikes the sentimentality of the "folksy village" school with its evasion of fundamental truths and its degeneration of intellectual fiber into fact-fearing optimism. A note of disillusion runs through his books. "Life," decides Margaret Bade in *Autumn*, "is so much spilled milk," and Farmer Barly in the same volume has learned that "people are queer crotchets." Nathan's villages are narrow, hard, gossipy places where human life may be bleak and frustrated. But though the note of disillusion persists it is tempered by the conviction that love and beauty lie close at hand, that man may yet work out his own salvation. For there is no cynicism about Robert Nathan. Interested in life, unafraid of its implications, he wisely concludes that it is a simpler thing than man has made it. Love, beauty, simple, natural happiness he finds eminently desirable qualities in a complex world of misunderstanding. He stresses them unwearyingly.

The material with which he chooses to work is adapted with adroit simplicity to his themes. There is little of the heroic about his figures; he has no more use for the hero and heroine as such than had William Dean Howells. He has never been concerned either with the favorite American motif: the triumphant career of the self-made man who starts from scratch and ends in Congress. Rather his characters are homely men and women in their daily lives,—a puppet-master at work on his marionettes, an itinerant fiddler doing chores for a winter's board, children playing in the park, the owner of a carousel replacing his animals with up-to-date aeroplanes, a bishop campaigning for a towering new cathedral, a school teacher weary from a long struggle with the village school. Nothing much happens in his tales; his men and women love and marry, work at their appointed tasks, live their uneventful outer lives; his plots are made of the little strands of everyday living. But with no other material could Nathan so adequately emphasize the futility of man's materialistic aspirations, or so happily make his plea for the creative spirit and for simple, natural happiness. The creative spirit, indeed, he takes seriously whether it express itself in superb acting, or in scraping a fiddle while a little dog dances. For the artist, he feels, has learned to take care of himself, to make use of human emotions, of love, of joy, of sorrow, for the advantages of his art. The artist is the courageous individualist. As Anton Pembauer of *The Orchid* sturdily puts it: "Consider: with what does he come forward, to wring a living from the world? He is no soldier, with cannon and a uniform, or a rich man with iron and steel. His weapon is a little catgut, or a bit of lead no longer than his finger. To get along with a tool like that, one must have courage, and above all, common sense." And the reward? It cannot be measured by applause, by what the world calls success. "The reward is in the art itself, or it is nowhere." Robert Nathan's creative artists may not, in accordance with Cabell's economist theory, exact immortality from the brief loan of their bodies while the rest of us ride thriftily toward oblivion, but they do manage to discover vestiges of love and beauty in a workaday world.

On the whole, Nathan prefers the fantasy to any other form, but his fantasies, it must be remembered, are more than graceful pages of romanticism; they are the sincerely thoughtful commentaries of a keen observer. His is emphatically not the shoddy romanticism which spills over into half-baked truths and hasty generalities hidden under a welter of colorful words. He knows surely and certainly what he wants to say, and knowing that, proceeds to say it with delightful irony through the wisdom of barnyard fowls, if such wisdom suits his purpose. In fact, a sensitive adaptation of narrative treatment to theme has marked Nathan's work. He has, moreover, the poet's and the musician's ear for subtle cadences, for rhythm in a sentence. His style is peculiarly his own. Never "precious" or artificial, it combines beauty of phrase with a racy, ironical humor. Robert Nathan is at once too well-endowed with humor and too thorough a craftsman to mar his work by over-emphasis; he never forgets the power of entrained simplicity.

In his earliest work, *Peter Kindred*, published in 1919, Nathan seems to have felt the influence of the muckraking movement, then in its decline, but still magnetic to any young intellectual with a problem to present. Certainly the book, in form at least, is not entirely typical of its author. Already, however, he was viewing with disturbed eyes the civilization that the machine age had developed, and was championing an unhampered creative individualism. His two boys, each embodying the opposite quality of a dual personality, develop against a background of Exeter and Harvard. David, the romantic dreamer and musician, finds Harvard a place into which he does not fit. He fades from the tale, but Peter goes successfully on, up-to-date in every way, even to eugenics. The book is interesting, but perhaps not wholly disciplined in ideals of craftsmanship.

When *Autumn* appeared two years later, it struck a new note, and marked the beginning of Nathan's success. In some ways, the book, underneath its romance, is not far removed from *Winesburg, Ohio*. For *Autumn*, like *Winesburg*, is full of grotesques, stifled, cramped, petty, unsatisfied. And like *Winesburg*'s people, these people, too, have been taught to care only for the "stuffs of life." In both books, people are, as Anderson phrases it, tricked by life, made fools of. But the tone of the two is different: *Winesburg* is almost mechanically deterministic: *Autumn*, profoundly ironic. Throughout Nathan's tale, things are seen through the eyes of Mr. Jeminy, the village schoolmaster, disciple of Boethius and St. Francis. "Love, peace, the quiet of the heart, the work of one's hands," are the world's treasure to Mr. Jeminy, and he is troubled over a people interested only in the philosophy of plus and minus. He would like to teach his pupils to be happy, to convince them that "happiness is not in owning much, but in owning little: love and liberty, the work of one's hands, fellowship and peace." "These things have no value," he admits; "they are not to be bought; but they alone are worth having." Hillsboro naturally finds Mr. Jeminy queer and impractical; his housekeeper occasionally finds him shocking, especially in his friendship for the Widow Wicket, who as "the earthly remains of a sinner," obviously had no right to enjoy herself. For a period after he loses his place as schoolmaster, Mr. Jeminy finds peace away from his village. With Margaret and Aaron Bade on their farm, he regains faith in himself, but his life with them is particularly an evasion of reality. He is drawn back into the world again when he learns that his dying housekeeper is calling for him. He is still fumbling for an answer to life, however, as he gazes at her body: "Do you see, at last, the meaning of the spectacle you have just quitted? . . . . You are free to ask God to explain it to you; you can say, 'I saw armies with banners, and scholars with their books.' Perhaps he will tell you the meaning of it. But for us, who remain, it has no meaning. Well, we say, this is life. We laugh, applaud, talk together, and think about ourselves. And one by one we slip away, no wiser than before." In the last analysis, then, the book is an indictment of materialism, and of a Puritanical morality that unites to destroy natural happiness and the simple joy of life itself. For none of these people in Hillsboro is really happy or content; each one is dreaming of strange adventures, of new experiences. The characterizations—even thumb-nail sketches—all contrive to emphasize the irony of these inarticulate lives. Especially effective are the glimpses of Miss Beal, the village dressmaker, and of Mrs. Grumble, Jeminy's housekeeper. Anna Barly and the Widow Wicket are handled with a more poignant truth. The chapter, School Lets Out, is, incidentally, one of the most quietly wise that Nathan has yet produced. ⟨. . .⟩

His books have made no bid for popular approval, have followed no current literary fashion. But he has written steadily at the dictates of his own artistic conscience. He sees life whole: its meanness, cruelty and tragedy, but its generosity, love and devotion as well. For mere efficiency and respectability he has no sympathy, but he champions even the shiftless if within them he finds the qualities of love and simplicity which give depth and warmth to human existence. Profundity is beyond him perhaps; wisdom is not. With kindly understanding he gets to the souls of his creations. And in the slightest of stories, he can charm by his tenderness, his humor, the limpid simplicity of his prose.

STEPHEN VINCENT BENÉT
From "The World of Robert Nathan"
The Barly Fields by Robert Nathan

1938, pp. v–xii

Every writer worth his salt makes a world of his own, and, in spite of the excellent adage—"Write about what you know about"—the world that he makes is not always the world directly in front of his eyes. For realism, as realism, only goes so far. Otherwise, you could assemble a novel as you assemble a Ford car—and that has been done, as well, and we know those novels. They are admirable books, full of fresh, contemporary problems and temporary life. They deal, in a clear-eyed way, with marriage and divorce, they describe the problems of the dried-fish industry in unflinching detail, they do everything in the world but interest you ten years later. It does not matter, for there are always more of them. And, meanwhile, some small work of the imagination lives forever.

Perhaps it is as good a test of Mr. Nathan's abilities as any that the five short novels collected in ⟨*The Barly Fields*⟩ should show so little age. I wonder of how many contemporary novelists that might be said. It even seems a little unfair, at times. For, while novel after novel that was gripping and devastating and searched the American scene has walked with firm steps and electrically-lighted eyes, wired for sound, direct

from its publisher's announcements into oblivion, Mr. Aristotle and Papa Jonas, Mrs. Heavenstreet and the dog Musket have remained very much as they were—living creatures, with foolish hearts and the breath of life. They never pretended to be more, and the life within them has remained. The streets around the Square have altered their look somewhat but the afternoon light still falls in yellow, dusty bars and Mr. Aristotle's tragedy is still a tragedy though it is played by a puppet. The great cock-fight between Bartholomew and the Malay cross is as good as ever it was and the seasons in Barly have not changed. That is something to have done—it is so that work lasts out its year and takes on another life.

It is curious to look back at the beginnings. The required project for young novelists of the Twenties was a school-and-college novel—it changes with each generation. There were a number of them by various hands—through Yale, Harvard, Princeton, Chicago and other leading American universities, the hero took his way, full of irony and pity and very much bothered by life. Among them was one called *Peter Kindred*. It was not a successful book, though it had two things which distinguished it among its fellows—a grave sobriety of style and a remarkable paucity of big adjectives. But, as far as plot was concerned, it followed the accepted pattern of adolescence, college and first love. It was easy to see how the author was going to turn out.

He had been born and brought up in New York City—obviously, his next book would be a serious, realistic study of Manhattan and the younger generation. Eventually he might branch out into the other boroughs—perhaps even as far as Long Island. But it didn't happen like that. The next published book was a pastoral called *Autumn*, concerned with a country schoolmaster and bearing about as much relation to the literary movements and fashions of its time as Blake's *Songs of Innocence* bore to the movements and fashions of his. There was only one thing about it. A good many other people could have written most of our second novels. But nobody but Robert Nathan could have written *Autumn*—or could write it still.

For here was a kind of writing of which there is never much in any one time—a style at once delicate, economical and unobtrusively firm, sharp enough to cut but without rancor, and clear as water or air. And with it went an airy mockery, and the imagination of the heart. With it also went a sensitive love of life and a deep hatred of all those who would maim and distort it for any end, which, perhaps, have not been sufficiently assessed by Mr. Nathan's critics. For, while Mr. Nathan writes well, he does not write with a sugar-stick, and Metabel's horror in the church is a true horror.

Then there is the melancholy—not an inky cloak but the shadow of a summer cloud—and the humor that illuminates without destroying. The angel, in *The Bishop's Wife*, has a difficult time on earth, Mr. Lewis-Levy, in *There Is Another Heaven*, an equally difficult one in the Protestant Heaven to which he has been consigned. Even Musket, the dog, does not find all things arranged to his taste, in spite of his artistic reputation. Nevertheless, they live, with enthusiasm mixed with surprise—they are apt to fall down but they are apt to get up again. Let me quote once to give you a taste of the quality. "The love of man and woman is a different thing entirely. It is full of pain, and human hunger; in the unending desert of eternity, it is an illusion of comfort, it is a mirage of consolation. It is also, in addition, an irresistible impulse of a purely animal nature. I know nothing about it myself, but I have studied the poets."

That is George Herman Wutheridge, Professor of Semitic Languages, speaking, in *The Bishop's Wife*. It is very easy to read—it is very hard to write, in its sly balance. For you did not expect exactly what you have received, and, by the last sentence, you are gently let down a step that you did not know was there. That is part of Mr. Nathan's method—if you can call good writing a method.

It is this mingling of imagination and reality—of reality seen in the mirror of imagination—that gives Mr. Nathan his unique position in our letters. For, even when his tales are most frankly fables, they never lose touch with humanity. Witness the extraordinary depictions of children, from Amy May Holly in *The Puppet Master* to the two little boys known merely as Potter and Johnson in *The Bishop's Wife*. They are real children, with all the small barbarisms and touching grace of childhood. They are ruthless, self-absorbed and perfectly enchanting. They live in their own world, and partly in ours. No one has done them better, in our time. Here is one brief incident at a Christmas party.

"Juliet's face quivered. She approached her mother with her head bent and put her arms about her knees. 'I haven't any clown.' She said in a trembling voice 'I love a clown. You gave my clown to Potter. It's my tree. It's my party. You gave him my lovely clown.'

"She began to weep. 'I haven't any party suit.' She sobbed 'I haven't any nice new party suit.'

"Potter paid no attention to her. 'Here I go jumping,' he remarked, throwing the doll into the air, 'and here I fall down, bang.'"

Those are only a few sentences, but, with them, the ghosts of a thousand children's parties rise. Nor is Mr. Nathan any the less accurate, when he is touching a deeper problem—when Mr. Cohen, the millionaire, gives Michael, the archangel-deacon, his own reasons for remaining a Jew.

"No, my friend; if I do not turn Christian, like so many others, it is not because of the religious practises. It is because I do not want my grandchildren to hate the Jews. There is too much hate in the world as it is; in this country it flourishes like the weed. Here even the poets hate one another. Very well, I stay a Jew, I do not go over on the side of the haters. I do not buy my way up, so that I too, can spit down on my people. Do you think I love the Jews so much? How can I tell, when I am one? But I am sick of those who hate them, because I am sick of hate. What we need is more politeness in the world. Let people shake hands and say, Come in.

"Do you think it is a pleasure to be kept out of everything? . . ."

That was written in 1928—it is part of Mr. Nathan's curious timelessness that it should be so applicable today. But what does make these books so timeless? I wish I knew. Of the five books collected ⟨in *The Barly Fields*⟩, two are laid in a country village, two in the city of New York and one in Heaven. The chief characters include a dog, an angel, a famous actress, a bishop, a rooster, a little green man and a woodcutter. They deal with happy love and unhappy, with the small and greater sorrows of the flesh and spirit, with youth and age and the deceptions of Time. They do not inform you, except about human nature, and they are neither pretentious nor obscure. Moreover, they are written with loveliness.

Yet, in spite of these grave defects, one reads and keeps on reading, remembers and turns back to quote. It may be the fiddler of Barly who has just been rebuked for idleness by the Reverend Dr. Flood.

"Left to himself, the fiddler gazed after the retreating figure of Dr. Flood with a smile.

"'Come' he said to himself 'there is always the host and the guest, wherever you go. Some people do not like to be the guests; they are only happy if they are hosts. They want to be at home, and make the arrangements. Well, well, my dear fellow, come in; here is a harp and a crown. When you were alive, you never gave me any trouble. Now I will do as much for you. There is no wine here, and the women have wings, but no legs. You have nothing to do but be happy and enjoy yourself in a nice way.'" ⟨. . .⟩

It may be Bartholomew, the rooster, before his fight. "He opened his eyes again because, after all, that was more manly. But the first things he saw were his own spurs, of shining steel, thin and sharp, curved like a scimitar. There is death, he said to himself, and held them up, one by one to look at."

But whatever it is—from young lovers straying the grass of a summer meadow to a man perplexed on the banks of Jordan—a dog or a cricket—an angel or creatures less divine—it is life that has touched us, with true fantasy, lightly as the touch of a leaf, but memorably. A humorous and wise observer has been at our side. He cannot command every instrument—that is true enough. But the note of his own is true, unforced and searching—you will not find many like it—and it lingers in the mind.

It is not the province of this foreword to discuss Mr. Nathan's poetry, though I could wish that it were. But he was a poet, I think, before he was a prose-writer, and the discipline of poetry shows in his work. As for his literary ancestors—perhaps there was Anatole France, at the beginning; but I should put him nearer Hans Christian Andersen on one side and Nathaniel Hawthorne on the other. The Puritan horror of Hawthorne is absent from his work and the spirit is gentler and more gently mocking. But it is hard to find any other American work but the work of the Hawthorne of *Twice Told Tales* with which this work may be compared. And, as I say, I know of no contemporary work that is like it at all.

For it is work of complete integrity that has finally won its way to a wide public, not by fulfilling one set of fashionable requirements or another, but because the writer wrote with skill, beauty and understanding, and wrote as he chose, of the things that pleased him best. To see such work succeed is heartening—it is more important than movements and groups and trends. We can always have those, and they are very entertaining, but we cannot always have the clean line drawn and the true thing said. And when it is said with wit, imagination and sensitive reality, we may count ourselves lucky.

HERBERT FEIS
"Speaking of Books: Robert Nathan, Storyteller"
New York Times Book Review, December 19, 1965, p. 2

Robert Nathan wrote his first novel almost 50 years ago—*Peter Kindred*—a rather artless story of a shy and lonely youth at Exeter and Harvard. It was submerged in the acclaim of Scott Fitzgerald's more glittering and effective novel, *This Side of Paradise*. Ever since, every year or so, another volume of verse or fiction (more than 40 now) has come out of his study, denoting his continuous devotion to his craft. Affianced readers await each one.

I have heard it asked, as it was by a reviewer of his latest book, "What does it all add up to?" The answer for those of us who hail his books is simple: It adds up to "enjoyment"—enjoyment of his ironic portrayal of human frolics and follies, of his shrewd wit, his fancy and even his pervasive gloominess.

I have also heard it asked, "What is he trying to do?" That I cannot say with satisfying assurance, and I do not know whether he could. But I should think that he was trying to communicate his sense of the strangeness and wonder of daily existence and of the curious happenings that befall all of us, and to console himself and us for the brevity of life and the elusiveness of joy. By enveloping raw realities in a transparent gauze of imagination and tinting them with irony, he relieves their hurt. He applies the salve of tragi-comedy to our experiences.

Nathan's awareness of the deep differences between his writings and of those who are now attracting far greater attention is made plain in a note written in response to a letter about his latest book—*The Mallot Diaries*—a tale of the archeological discovery of a surviving small tribe of Neanderthal people in the Sierra Madre Mountains and adventures among them. "If I had described some strange new way of copulation indulged in by the Neanderthals—with explicit directions—I would be acclaimed a major prophet, like Jeremiah, or Henry Miller. I have aimed all my life at the wrong targets; at Anatole France instead of Norman Mailer; at James Stephens instead of James Baldwin, or Retchy (*there's a vomit for you!*)"

His conception of his favored way of telling a tale is conveyed in one comment found in *The Puppet Master*. "The artist is not a pedant. He should speak only to suggest. That is why puppets are a great art, they suggest with the utmost economy, and in a severe manner, the noblest virtues and the most terrible passions."

The philosophy he has tried to adopt may be discerned in another passage pondering the tasks and opportunity of all artists, "to keep the blood moving, to keep the cold at bay— what else is there for man to do in the world? Let him build cities, pray to God, write histories, and compose for orchestras—the dark and the cold lie waiting, ready to flow over him without a sound. Life is all that he has; it is momentary, it is so small that all the world with its entire history seems no larger than a drop of water; yet in its warmth lies joy and grief, out of which beauty grows, and lasts forever."

To this conception, his poetic style and his envelopment of the human scene by a gently woven tapestry of nature is well adapted. Yet through the lilt of his prose, precision of expression and his sardonic wit peer out clearly. Between their many displays it is hard to choose one or two as illustrations and reminders. One, contained in a letter written long ago, still tickles my memory. "When I write that I have a fever, a throat, and a nurse, and that I am in bed with two of them, it might suggest to you that my nurse was ugly, or that I was feeling weak—at any rate that I was in bed with my fever and my throat, and that the nurse has been left outside—and not that I was mortally ill with two nurses."

For original wit, two brief comments may serve to exemplify hundreds of others. From one of his books—which one I have at the moment forgotten—"Just imagine if the young men of the future were to be men of good will. That would be a great joke on their parents." And from *Sir Henry*, the tale of a reluctant knight seeking to serve and please two ladies, on encountering a dragon: "There was a dragon. He— or she (it is always a question with dragons)—had its den or lair about a mile downstream in a darksome thicket of trees, and near a deep pool, good for fishing and swimming. But it was, for all practical purposes, a private pool; for no one—and nothing—care to go swimming with a dragon."

He often expresses so much in very few words that the depth and originality of his insight may not be appreciated. So many of his pithy comments rush to the tip of my pencil that I find it hard to quote only a few. One from *So Love Returns:*

"After all, age is not only a pattern of wrinkles. It is a quality of love; it is a weariness of heart." Another, from *Winter in April*: "There is such a thing as too much history and we are having it." Another from *One More Spring*, a tale of the Depression: "As for science, it must be remembered that Mr. Oskar was only a small dealer in antiques, whose business had been ruined. It made no difference to him that the physicists had decided that space was curved, and that the universe was exploding like a balloon." Can more of the truth be caught in a smaller pitcher?

Then there is the pervasive quality of tranquillity which his books convey. This may indicate a tendency to derive greater enjoyment from the later remembrance of an experience than was ever derived from the experience itself. He shares with his readers the pleasure of possessing a round-trip ticket to yesterday.

The wry humor of many of his books plays particularly around women. And why should it not, for it has been nurtured by unusual chances of observation during six marriages, all grave and affectionate encounters and all subject to the twists and turns of the spirit.

An unusual characteristic of his writing is his absorption in the idea of time as a fourth or fifth dimension. Of this he makes glowing use—in some of his best tales—causing past, present and future, alike in their illusionary effect, to glide into one another. This imparts reality to the imaginative conception of the eternity of sentiments.

Even those of his readers who are beguiled by these gifts have often been aware of what seemed to them faults and limitations in the tales he tells. In some of his books he has allowed the great theme that he has chosen—a theme appropriate to tragic novelists like Dostoyevsky or a ponderous historian—to shrink down into the trivial dimensions of personal foibles or a minor love story. When this happens, his characters, faced by most serious actual situations, dwindle from figures to figurines.

Sometimes also crises of character elude him and us, as he skims over them with some bright but obscure and inadequate remark. Once when I was annoyed by this, I recalled the surmise of Joseph Wood Krutch, that when Gilbert (of Gilbert and Sullivan) was confused about morals and manners, he took refuge in wit. Anent which Nathan might well ask all of us, "Who is not often confused? What better refuge?"

Others may find that the talk between animals and children in some of his books unintentionally turns into a patter indicative of childishness in the author. Lastly, there are those who have become weary of his work because they think he reverts too often to the same themes. But they are too jaded and over-demanding. There have been ups and downs in the merit of those many books he has written over the years, but enough variety of theme and mood to keep our enjoyment fresh and praise well earned.

He has now been writing long enough for the youngest generation—the grandchildren of those who read his earliest books—to begin to respond to his wry and dreamy tales when they are tired of the all-too-familiar dreadful realities. Should this occur, it would be a fitting conjunction with the revolution in the age of the main characters in his books; for those written while he was young are mainly concerned with aged or aging persons; those written as he has grown older are primarily concerned with younger men and women.

Even when Nathan disappoints, he leaves us regretful, not scornful. For the steady procession of his tales has provided us with enchanting and memorable company. Long before *Lolita*, in several of his novels he revealed to us the affections evoked by the Lolitas; but his adolescent maidens left their aging admirers and mentors bemused and not besmirched. In *A Portrait of Jennie* he has added to the small number of women that remain in our memories eternally lovely and faithful. In *One More Spring* he has uncovered the consolation that may be found during trials of poverty and depression in human companionship and kindliness. In *Sir Henry* he leaves

us smiling at the difficult tests to which a gallant man is put to prove himself glorious in the eyes of a woman, be she romantic or practical.

He transmutes rasping realities into comforting allegorical tales in which all of us figure, as children of various ages. We wait eagerly for his next tale, for the enjoyment each gives is so lovely and lasting.

HOWARD NEMEROV

1920–

Howard Nemerov was born on March 1, 1920, in New York City, and graduated from Harvard University in 1941. After serving as a pilot with the Canadian and American army air forces during World War II, he began a teaching career during which he has taught at Hamilton College, Bennington College, Brandeis University, and Washington University in St. Louis. In 1947 his first book of poetry, *The Image and the Law*, appeared in the Yale Younger Poets series; since then he has published many collections of verse, including *Guide to the Ruins* (1950), *The Salt Garden* (1955), *The Blue Swallows* (1967), *The Western Approaches* (1975), *Sentences* (1980), and *Inside the Onion* (1984). Although Nemerov is less known as a novelist than as a poet, his three novels *The Melodramatists* (1949), *Federigo: Or the Power of Love* (1954), and *The Homecoming Game* (1957) have nonetheless attracted increasing critical attention over the years, as has his quasi-autobiographical essay *Journal of the Fictive Life* (1965). In addition he has contributed a considerable quantity of criticism and essays to various periodicals and collections, some of which may be found in *Figures of Thought: Speculations on the Meaning of Poetry and Other Essays* (1978).

One of today's more honored poets, Nemerov has received many awards, including the 1955 *Kenyon Review* fellowship in fiction, the 1959 Harriet Monroe Memorial Prize, and the first Theodore Roethke Memorial Award in 1968 for *The Blue Swallows*. In 1978 *The Collected Poems of Howard Nemerov*, published the previous year, won both the Pulitzer Prize and the National Book Award. In 1964 Nemerov was the Consultant in Poetry for the Library of Congress.

Nemerov lives in St. Louis, Missouri, with the former Margaret Russell, his wife since 1944; they have three children.

Being largely under the sway of Wallace Stevens, Mr. Nemerov has appropriated not only the basic dichotomy of that poet but also his special tactics of treating ideas and perceptions severally and oppositionally. About half of his pieces ⟨in *The Image and the Law*⟩ deal with "images," while the other half are concerned with the "law," i.e., the normative function of the mind. I can discern no methodological connection between the two sets, not even the dialectical one of active contrasts moving toward some kind of synthesis. Not a few of the "images"—that is, the strictly descriptive or anecdotal pieces— are quite good in their whimsical way; though rarely witty they have to their credit a certain mordancy, acumen, and lightness of touch. Stylistically they hover between Stevens and K. Rexroth, with occasional sallies—no spoils resulting—into Empson's domain. When Mr. Nemerov deals with ideas he is as a rule less satisfactory; partly through simple lack of style— his identification with Rexroth becomes intolerable at times, especially in his most ambitious attempt, *The Frozen City*, which despite several impressive lines is a towering monument to bathos, cf. "Moving, I saw / The murderer staring at his knife, / Unable to understand, and a banker / Regarding a dollar bill with fixed / Incomprehension," etc.—partly through conceptual confusion, as in "The Place of Value," where a plea for relevance is made in the most irrelevant terms: the neurotic individual versus the healthy statistician, fortuitous

versus expiatory death, etc. Yet, oddly enough, it is in this category that we must look for Nemerov's best poems: "Warning: Children at Play," "An Old Photograph" and, particularly, "Lot's Wife"—poems which suggest that ideation may after all be this poet's forte and that, by turning division of mind and eye into collaboration, he may yet achieve a fine body of poetry.—F. C. GOLFFING, "Question of Strategy," *Poetry*, Sept. 1947, pp. 96–97

Standing and thinking on the shore of the wide world has long been a favorite situation of the poet. With sand between his toes (the atoms of Democritus? Heaven in a grain?), he gazes out to the swaying unsyllabled sea, and back toward his rocky, babel-tongued city. Birds and stars wheel over him; pods and shards, fishbones and bugs turn up under his feet. Clearly, it is all a Great Writing, in which the poet on the shore is a character attempting to read the sentence in which he appears.

Once, writes Nemerov, villainous William of Occam exploded the dream that we could confidently assign the authorship of the Great Writing. And yet science, social science, and philosophy go on confidently assigning. "Nature," they cry; "Man," they cry; "God," they cry—physics in one tongue, theology in another. What Occam in fact pointed out was that what a thing is in itself in no way depends on how we think of it. But it is by thought embodied in language, and by language embodied in institution, that we construct the civilization in which we live, the human world which so often appears to be simply the Self writ large. The poet's job, strangely enough, is to 'unwrite' by going back to the beginning; to make such speech as we have faithful to 'things as they are' rather than to our arrangements of them; to make language live by confronting things with the 'innocent' mind of an Adam, by naming them to themselves afresh through the powers of that mind which is somehow continuous with them. Nemerov is not alone in observing how many of our languages are dead. Since the medieval synthesis

> It's taken that long for the mind
> To waken, yawn, and stretch, to see
> With opened eyes, emptied of speech
> The real world where the spelling mind
> Imposes with its grammar book
> Unreal relations on the blue
> Swallows.

Nemerov, then, does not seek to impose a vision upon the world so much as to listen to what it says. He works in closer relationship with literal meaning than is presently fashionable; consequently his worst fault (he says so himself) is sententiousness, but his corresponding virtue is a clarity whose object is not to diminish the mystery of the world but to allow it to appear without the interposition of a peculiar individuality, or of fancy-work or arabesque. He is, as much as any modern can be, a romantic poet; he is a religious poet without religion; a prophet, especially in the polemical and ironic mode, without portfolio. When he writes about history, as Stanley Hyman has said, his theme is "history from the point of view of the losers." Thus when he wants to write about Moses, he does so from the point of view of Pharoah after the Red Sea debacle; and instead of writing about Perseus, he presents the nitwitted predecessors of that hero, who approached Medusa without a mirror and were turned to stone. To judge by his later poems, being turned to stone is the least agreeable and most probable fate for human beings and their institutions together.—JULIA RANDALL, "Genius of the Shore: The Poetry of Howard Nemerov," *HC*, June 1969, pp. 1–2

⟨. . . A⟩ book that agitates and soothes in equal measure, a little-known, undoubtedly undersold book, is *Journal of the Fictive Life*, by Howard Nemerov, published in 1965 by Rutgers University Press. It is an honest, unabashed account of a painfully dry period in the life of a writer. Nemerov seeks to batter his way out of the enclosure by investigating his own creative process, keeping notes during one summer. He details particularly the conflict between the poet and the novelist trapped in his own being, the struggle to let the novelist out. This series of reflections caught and held me fast. *Charming! true!* I have added in the margin alongside: "For a Jewish Puritan of the middle class, the novel is serious, the novel is work, the novel is conscientious application—why, the novel is practically the retail business all over again." Later, *The languor of the first sentence!* stands outside a paragraph on the terror of beginning. "What a great weight one adds to the heart by simply saying, 'It was a fine morning in summer,'" Nemerov has written.

It fascinates, this dichotomy between poet and novelist. Nemerov moves back into his own history, seizes on his dreams, invents others when he cannot drag specifically dreamt ones into the light and attempts to discover, through self-analysis, the sources of his blocks as well as his creativity. *The danger,* I find inked between two paragraphs, *is that the self-analysand tortures his material to fit his scheme.* Other objections are sprinkled in the margins, so that the book in my hand has become a dialogue.

How fitting it seems to reread this book in summer, some twelve years from the season of its actual composition. I am chewing gristle just now to get to the bone of a novel I want to write. *Journal of the Fictive Life* comes through to me this time almost as an exhortation to leave off complaining and begin. "I have tried to keep this inquisition reasonable in tone," Nemerov says toward the end, "certainly not to hoke it up by getting rhapsodic, or by the usual literary claim that all this showed great courage on my part, and therefore must be very grand literature."

Is it too much to claim that home-making women, by virtue of their early encounters with solitude, boredom, and frustration (for instance, three children serially contract chicken pox in November), have an extra modicum of insight into the writer's encounters? Probably. At least I ought to try not to hoke it up. I ought to remember Yeats's disclaimer, in the introduction of his *Essays*, of any connection between the poet and "The bundle of accident and incoherence that sits down to breakfast."

Or, as Nemerov has analyzed the creative process, "No matter how often and how far you digress, no matter how many clever improvisations you make . . ., so long as you keep patiently bringing yourself back."—MAXINE KUMIN, "On Howard Nemerov's *Journal of the Fictive Life*" (1975), *To Make a Prairie*, 1979, pp. 70–71

RAYMOND SMITH
From "Nemerov and Nature: 'The Stillness in Moving Things'"
Southern Review, January 1974, pp. 166–69

The Ulysses myth is only one of the myths used by Nemerov to develop his poem (⟨"Runes"⟩). The thirteenth stanza is developed in terms of Joseph Conrad's *Heart of Darkness*, with the poet amplifying the idea of a "commonwealth" of blood and death. The complementary fifth and eleventh stanzas examine the universe through the views of the Old and New Testaments, treating the theme of atonement first in Hebraic terms, then Christian. There are two movements, or rhythms, to the poem, the more superficial and conventional one in terms of the rhythm of the seasons, with the poem moving from late summer through autumn and winter to spring. The second rhythm, supported by the structure of the work itself, is a movement inward to the center of the poem—to the very "pit" of death—than an outward movement to the conclusion. The exact center of the poem, both structurally and thematically, is stanza eight, developed in terms of the dominant image, running water—in this case, falling water, dark water. The spirit flows along culverts, through swamps to the pit. Like Ulysses and Mrs. Mandrill, it enters nature:

> To fall with the weight of things down on the one
> Still ebbing stream, to go on to the end
> With the convict hunted through the swamp all
>   night.
> The dog's corpse in the ditch, to come at last
> Into the pit where zero's eye is closed.

Hints of renewal earlier in the stanza—in seeds and hibernating animals—prepare for the ultimate ambiguity of absolute zero. In its circular form the zero is a symbol of life; in its lack of substance, an image of nullity. Zero is personified as if it were some kind of god, lying here in the middle of Nemerov's universe, being at once the beginning and the end, the alpha and omega, of the thing and/or the idea of the thing.

As close to zero as one can get in the world of this poem

without becoming a hunted convict or a dog's corpse is to be a member of contemporary society which Nemerov sees, as T. S. Eliot does, as existing in a "dehydrated age." The stanzas immediately preceding and following the journey into the pit both deal with this age. The speaker's voice in these sections is satiric, as Nemerov's usually is when he deals with contemporary matters. This satire can be deliberately jarring as it is in the image of sterility that concludes stanza seven, where the Muse, "in her transparent raincoat, resembles a condom." In stanza nine, moral-imaginative dehydration is depicted in terms of the vulgarization, the commercialization of Christianity, with reference to men

> . . . who bottle holy water
> In plastic tears, and bury mustard seeds
> In lucite lockets, and for safety sell
> To be planted on the dashboard of your car
> The statues, in durable celluloid,
> Of Mary and St. Christopher, who both
> With humble power in the world's floodwaters
> Carried their heavy Savior and their Lord.

The pervading travel motif, the central images of seed and water, all take on a new dimension here. Water and the mustard seed of parable are frozen in plastic, reduced to good luck charms, symbols taken literally by dry imaginations; the heroic bearers of Christ through the "world's floodwaters" have been reduced to celluloid statues—"durable" things in this world of flux, making safe this journey by car.

The poem concludes on a lyric note, with the theme expressed again in images of moving water. The running water is a hieroglyph; contained therein is the secret—of life, of the universe. The stanza opens on an April world of light and movement, though there are slightly jarring notes in the lyric flow: the "freshets" limp as well as leap, the field is "tilted," the millpond "green, grave and opaque."

> To watch water, to watch running water
> Is to know a secret, seeing the twisted rope
> Of runnels on the hillside, the small freshets
> Leaping and limping down the tilted field
> In April's light, the green, grave and opaque
> Swirl in the millpond where the current slides
> To be combed and carded silver at the fall;
> It is a secret. Or it is not to know
> The secret, but to have it in your keeping,
> A locked box, Bluebeard's room, the deathless thing
> Which it is death to open. Knowing the secret,
> Keeping the secret—herringbones of light
> Ebbing on beaches, the huge artillery
> Of tides—it is not knowing, it is not keeping,
> But being the secret hidden from yourself.

We move with the running water down to the sea, where the herringbone pattern on the sand, the ebbing light and water, all suggest the secret, the death locked up in all life, which we will only fully realize, or know, at our own death. Running contrary to this falling, ebbing movement is the overall structural flow of the poem that follows the progress of the seasons into spring, coloring this stanza with the durability of April's green. Nevertheless, as with much of Nemerov's poetry, the emphasis is on the running down—on death. This is the "stillness in moving things," his runic message.

This is the answer he has in "The Blue Swallows" for those, like himself, who persist in seeing a more mystical meaning in nature, who try to read the message of the darting birds, "seeing the swallows' tails as nibs / Dipped in invisible ink, writing. . . ." Like the medieval nominalist William of Occam, whom he mentions, he proceeds to separate the idea from the thing, pointing out the subjectivity of the "spelling

mind." Having disabused us, he shows us a "new thing." And this is the fact that "even the water / Flowing away beneath those birds / Will fail to reflect their flying forms." The flow of life continues while individual forms perish. There is a "stillness in moving things." But "The Blue Swallows" does not end on this note. Rejecting the naming of things for the things themselves, the poet goes on to forge a new union between consciousness and nature in the striking image that ends the poem:

> O swallows, swallows, poems are not
> The point. Finding again the world,
> That is the point, where loveliness
> Adorns intelligible things
> Because the mind's eye lit the sun.

Poetry is rejected for the world—the world perceived, and perceived with love. This "loveliness" of things is an important aspect of Nemerov's view of nature. Seldom made explicit, it is usually in the background, evident in his description of nature, in the images of poems like "Runes" and "The Blue Swallows." Nature's beauty, then, must be taken into account together with the running down of things. Nemerov is somewhat like the little boy in "The View from the Attic Window," who "cried because life is hopeless and beautiful." In "The Blue Swallows," though not in the same sense as in "Sunday Morning," "Death is the mother of beauty."

There is still the dichotomy between the individual consciousness and nature in the universe of Howard Nemerov. Man is ultimately outside of nature. The relationship between the two is almost antithetical to that developed in the poetry of James Dickey. For Nemerov, nature is more the object of contemplation than celebration; human reason is superior to natural instinct; nature is more emblematic than mythic. His New England forest is "unmitigated by myth" ("Deep Woods," *The Salt Garden*). It is this alienation from nature that may help to account for the essential pessimism, the resignation, the passivity in much of his poetry. Nature, even though running down, will go on, but the "mind's eye," outside nature, will close.

MARY KINZIE
"The Judge Is Rue"
Poetry, September 1981, pp. 344–50

The last poem in Howard Nemerov's new *Sentences* is called "Because You Asked About the Line Between Prose and Poetry." It is about rain gradually turning into snow, but still acting like rain (only somehow lighter and thicker), until—there is suddenly snow flying instead of rain falling. The poem rhymes as a quatrain and a couplet and is composed in Howard Nemerov's own pentameter, an organism we recognize by the off-handed inversions of sentence order that sound at once decorous and colloquial; by that studied freedom of address and careful familiarity with old puns ("clearly flew"); and by the chill, dry precision of analogy ("gradient . . . aslant . . . random"). To these idiosyncratic marks of character, Nemerov adds the unassuming realism of the plot: you recognize only much later the poet's providence in having put something dark, living, and winged into the background.

> Sparrows were feeding in a freezing drizzle
> That while you watched turned into pieces of snow
> Riding a gradient invisible
> From silver aslant to random, white, and slow.
> There came a moment that you couldn't tell.
> And then they clearly flew instead of fell.

Formally, the poem is masterful, reassuring in its regularities, disturbing in its hints of chaos—those twin impulses that make up at least the necessary conditions of great verse. In Nemerov's rhymed poems, there is more activity in the final feet than in his unrhymed; the hints of chaos in "Because You Asked . . ." are whispered by the rhyme-dissonances between "drizzle" (the end of the fifth-foot amphibrach) and "invisible" (whose four syllables make up the two regular iambs of the fourth and fifth feet, with no supernumerary unstressed syllable at the end). Although DRIZ- rhymes with -VIS-, and although both DRIZZLE and INVISIBLE have final Ls, these rhyming sounds fall in different metrical places. We swallow the last two syllables of INVISIBLE—naturally, because the main accent falls on -VIS-, and in Nemerov's lines, because we are half-consciously trying to make the metrically nonparallel words match.

This rhyming on words that are, so to speak, cross-woven metrically, and the swallowing of certain lines (which necessitates the elongation of others) are parts of a larger design in which are also woven sentence and pause. For as the words unfold forward within the abstract metrical frame, they also pick up unaligned threads of grammatical periods and endings, which then hitch back across those lines, and even back across whole stanzas. If the metaphor of fabric-weaving applies to the making of verses, we must imagine either the warp as regular and the shuttle as uneven, or the warp as erratic and the voice of the shuttle as constant. The process in either case must accommodate both glide and tug, both smooth progress and lurching regress. The subject of the sentence that forms the quatrain of Nemerov's poem is "Sparrows," but the burden of the quatrain's theme is the "drizzle" that turns (for two-and-a-half lines) to "pieces of snow." A further twist is that, while "drizzle" is technically in command of the syntax for only one-half line, it is still continuing to fall through the ensuing transformations.

Because poetry moves backwards and forwards at once, the bit of cloth you wind up with is irregular, full of holes, yet also peculiarly complete, like a cat's cradle held on one hand by an adult and on the other by a child. Even the "symmetry" of the Popean couplet depends on radical asymmetries in the puns and in their disposition among parts of speech and in non-matching metrical places. In Nemerov's poem the adjectives "aslant" and "slow" do not inhabit the same semantic realm; yet for the moment of their expression, they are parallel in their doubleness: both render both shape *and* speed. Indirectly, "silver aslant" shows us rain razoring down quickly, while "random, white, and slow" suggests how the snow is starting to coast lethargically, scoot sideways, move any way but straight down.

Even so bald a device as the choice of poly- over monosyllabic words in a metrical line is an indispensable means of varying speed, sentence structure, and texture. Compare the second line, "That while you watched turned into pieces of snow," with its commanding monosyllables, and the rhopalic series of polysyllables in the third line, "Riding a gradient invisible," which is softer, more rapid (because of weak secondary stresses on the last two words), more abstract, and syntactically unfinished.

In support of diction, syntax, and meter, Nemerov also employs a hovering effect, based sometimes on ambiguity, and sometimes on error. For example, I might revise his final couplet to expose the grammatical clumsiness of the final line:

There came a moment when you scarcely knew.
And then instead of fell they clearly flew.

But in Nemerov's couplet, with its authoritative rhyme, the ungrammatical use of "fell" is largely concealed, perceived by us only as a dull after-throb. In addition to softening the awkwardness in the last line, Nemerov also invigorates the meanings in the penultimate. By using "that" instead of "when," he divides the reference between time and quality: (1) There came a moment during which you could not tell which was which; (2) There came a moment that you couldn't tell about. Of course the poem is about not being able to pinpoint delicate change: but it is also about not being able to describe how something got itself changed from rain into snow, prose into poetry, while watcher and writer know very well what the final state has come to: "And then they clearly flew."

What clearly flew? Clearly, the pieces of snow, now soft and crowded flakes. But in the poem's updrafts are also borne aloft those feeding sparrows—not literally, rather as part of the suggestive warrant for any kind of flight. In other words (the words of the title), so is the poem launched. Not going straight to its goal—not falling like rain—a poem imperceptibly thickens itself out of the visible stream of prose. It crosses a line, before which it was transparent, following which it is opaque, by being *in lines*, displaying the words it holds in common with prose so that these are increasingly bracketed, thereby more choice, but also more free.

That poetry holds words in common with prose is a truth for which Howard Nemerov gives especially profound warrant in his poetry (which now numbers roughly 600 pages). He is a master of blank verse in the brief lyric and the middle-length poem, and has molded the unrhymed iambic pentameter line into some of the subtlest formal bodies we have. His forbear in this is Frost, but Nemerov is less heavily stressed and less the rural *poseur*. Not that Nemerov lacks his poses; on the contrary, he can be most irritating in his roles as watcher-of-broadcasts, man-walking-dog, suburban-stroller, visitor-of-parks. He lets the bourgeois into his satiric poetry, but also in his lyrics, he lets in (in less censored or censorious fashion) the world of solitary privilege. The finest poem in *Sentences*, "By Al Lebowitz's Pool," provides a protected bell jar for Nemerov's meditations on time, light, youth, distance, and correspondence. It is a superior poem, but also one that depends on our *liking* the moneyed reserve of the middle classes.

Al Lebowitz's pool, however, does not represent class so much as reflect season. The owner himself barely appears. The poet observes the untouchable and undesired daughters swerving like fish through the water, on which surface, on other days, float only beach balloons or a wasp. The summer wanes. The speaker usually has a drink in hand. Idly, the poet roves among these details, which seem to provide at last, in each of the poem's five sections, the hypnagogic abstraction necessary for elegy. After a late summer storm,

> The banked furnace of the sun
> With reliquary heat returns in splendor
> Diminished some with time, but splendid still.
> Beside the pool we drink, talk, and are still,
> These times of kindness mortality allows.

In such seamless weavings of the poetic tradition with his own personal tone ("With reliquary heat," "The banked furnace"), Nemerov proves that the line between poetry and prose must be crossed not only by the word but by the heart. He is a poet who, like all of us, lives in the prosaic; and he acknowledges it in order to mine it.

But in contrast to other masters of the typical like Frost, Auden, and Cunningham, Nemerov is not, even in his sublime poems, always able to decide what he should do with the prosaic side of feeling. His worldly poses are often double-jointed—excuses for personal pathos where we expect the satirist's probity. His jokes frequently protest their humor. Since his first poems, *The Image and the Law* (1947), his books have been marred by gnomes too glib and constructed to be true. He tries to be playful, but sounds grim. And when he wants that grimness to be prophetic, he sounds inward and crotchety. He wants to be "bitter" as Yeats was, but has not Yeats's stake in the culture (perhaps no American has this), nor Yeats's obsessive delusions. Nemerov's temperament and language are not suited to displays of *saeva indignatio*, although his temperament is also such as to think it is. I do not think we hear in Nemerov that harsh transport of which J. V. Cunningham wrote in 1947 when he characterized the poetic gift:

> These the assizes: here the charge, denial,
> Proof and disproof: the poem is the trial.
> Experience is defendant, and the jury
> Peers of tradition, and the judge is fury.

I suspect that Howard Nemerov desires to be viewed as a poet who can range, with indulgence, majesty, or fury, over a broad geography of subjects and moods. This is not the case. His best mood, the one that brings out the tenderest and most credible language, is that mood of pitying praise in the presence of natural law and intellectual construct. In another age, Nemerov would have been bard to the Royal Society or an enclave of Thomists. He was framed to celebrate the edifice of mind from a gargoyle's niche; he depends, that is, on a tradition of shared intellectual achievement to which he can pay orthogonal homage in the form of tears. For that is the heart of his lyricism: astrophysics, syllogism, fluid geometry, and Zeno's paradox fleshed, formal, and full of rue:

> Intent upon the target eye
> The arrow pierced a garden air
> Fragrant with flowers yellow and blue
> It flew beside a shining hedge
> And over cobwebs jeweled with dew,
> It passed above a still black pool
> With a fountain for a heart
> Lifting its silver droplets up
> So slowly (and the flight so swift)
> They stood in air before they fell
> Tap tap upon the dark dripstone.
> Always, while burrowing in the brain,
> Always, and while the victim fell,
> The hastening arrow held that still
> Moment along its shining shaft.
> Its feathers whistled that still air.
>   ("In Zeno's World")

This lovely lyric is written in the same loose tetrameters Nemerov used for "The Blue Swallows" in 1967, another poem about "finding again the world" by a conscious application of the mind's eye to what is (therefore) "intelligible." In the protected garden of the mind, Nemerov has made a perfect gazebo.

In another poem, the cerebral and the emotional mingle with more homely point. A little aircraft is guided down by crossing needles, course, and height

> Till finally it's funneled in and down
> Over the beacons along a narrowing beam,
> Perfectly trusting a wisdom not its own,
> That breaking out of cloud it may be come
> Back to this world and to be born again,
> Into the valley of the flarepath, fallen home.
>   ("The Little Aircraft")

The final consonants in these lines, from the m/n family, form a second kind of instrument panel, guiding the plane, by dark longing moans, down to its home.

During a solar eclipse, the poet considers how the life of one man may be charted even to its end against the rare punctuations by the moon's darkened disc across the second great wanderer among the worlds:

> A man may see, as I have done, but four,
> In childhood two, a third in youth, and this
> In likelihood my last. We stand bemused
> While grass and rock darken, and stillness grows,
> Until the sun and moon slide out of phase
> And light returns us to the common life
> That is so long to do and so soon done.
>   ("During a Solar Eclipse")

The final monosyllabic line is a tour de force of plain-style pathos. Monosyllables serve a different function in "Insomnia I," that of blunt, noncommittal background for two more elaborate styles. If unable to sleep, you should, says Nemerov, go downstairs, have a bit to drink, read a mystery.

> Then, when you know who done it, turn out the
>   light,
> And quietly in darkness, in moonlight, or snowlight
> Reflective, listen to the whistling earth
> In its backspin trajectory around the sun
> That makes the planets sometimes retrograde
> And brings the cold forgiveness of the dawn
> Whose light extinguishes all stars but one.

Nemerov attaches a drag-line to the music of the spheres—the rationalist terminology of Miltonic syntax and Latinate jargon, a vocabulary cancelled by the glistening Anglo-Saxon gray of the phrase "cold forgiveness of the dawn" and by the uncodifiable undersong of the "whistling earth."

A final example of Nemerov's pathos-of-the-intellect, "The Makers." The first poets, those nameless makers of the consciousness of interval, who made poetry and language possible, are those who felt (as immediately as the odor of a rose) that the ability to form and distinguish vowels and consonants was what made it possible to make metaphors.

> They were the first great listeners, attuned
> To interval, relationship, and scale,
> The first to say above, beneath, beyond,
> Conjurors with love, death, sleep, with bread and
>   wine,
> Who having uttered vanished from the world
> Leaving no memory but the marvelous
> Magical elements, the breathing shapes
> And stops of breath we build our Babels of.

This is blank verse both cerebral and melodious, yet what moves us is not that balance, but the frailty of fame and the doomed circularity of poetic endeavor. The breathing shapes and stops, the vowels and consonants, are the foundations of shifting Babels whose magic is ephemeral. Like "The Makers," all of Nemerov's best poems are strangely sad. Encumbered with habitual self, they rise to plateaus of nostalgic obedience to the world, on which a natural, rich simplicity is flexed by mutability:

> . . . if these moments could not pass away
> They could not be, all dapple and delight.

Sentences is a disappointing and self-indulgent volume on the whole, but has some landmark poems. In these serious poems, not only has Nemerov continued to accommodate himself to the literary tradition without falling back on parody; he has also in this handful of poems extended the resources of blank verse beyond what any modern practitioner, himself included, has managed to do. This extension comprises more than a mere prosodic advance; it is a rhetorical and imaginative advance. "By Al Lebowitz's Pool," "The Makers," "Monet," and "A Christmas Storm," for example, are dazzling in their very naturalness, especially when we take into account that the last two are single, elaborated sentences, each of which encourages all the digressive ribbons and falls of thought, as the poet draws them back into coherent movements of syntax and line. No one since Frost has done as much to move blank verse forward from where Wordsworth and Coleridge had left it. The long sentence that falls variously from clause to clause and line to line in the last verse paragraph of "By Al Lebowitz's Pool" reminds us of the feats of the Romantics, but on a scale at once more thematically restricted and more spiritually daring:

> Enchanted afternoon, immune from time,
> Illusion's privilege gives me the idea that I
> Am not so much writing this verse as reading it

> Up out of water and light and shadow and leaf
> Doing the dance of their various dependencies—
> As if I might daydream my way again
> Into the world and be at one with it—
> While the shadows of harder, more unyielding things
> Edge steadily and stealthily around the pool
> To translate the revolving of the world
> About itself, the spinning ambit of the seasons
> In the simple if adamant equation of time
> Around the analemma of the sun.

This final verse paragraph, by turns reserved and gorgeous, yielding and severe, also convinces me that even a limitation, if acknowledged and persisted in, can approach transcendence.

ANAÏS NIN

1903–1977

Anaïs Nin was born on February 21, 1903, in Neuilly, France, outside Paris. Her mother, Rosa Culmell Nin, was a singer, and her father, Joaquin, was a concert pianist and composer. Nin spent her first eleven years in France, but after her father left her mother, her mother took her and her two brothers to live in New York City. Nin entered the public school system in New York, but by 1918 she had dropped out, after which she educated herself in the public libraries. About five years later, at the age of twenty-one, she married Hugh Guiler, who as Ian Hugo became known as a filmmaker, engraver, and illustrator of Nin's books. Sometime shortly afterwards she moved to Paris, where she remained until the outbreak of World War II.

Anaïs Nin's lifetime friendship with Henry Miller began in Paris in the 1930s. She assisted him in publishing his first book, *Tropic of Cancer* (1934), and he in turn worked on Nin's *House of Incest*, and dedicated his novel *Black Spring* to her. Two other important acquaintances, whose influence may be perceived throughout her work, were the psychiatrists René Allendy and Otto Rank. She also became part of a literary and artistic circle which included Lawrence Durrell, Antonin Artaud, Alfred Perlès, and Michael Fraenkel.

Back in the U.S., where she spent most of the rest of her life, Nin met and became friends with the young Gore Vidal. He was later to write about her in his *roman à clef, Two Sisters* (1970). She established the Gemor Press in New York in order to make her own works available, since few publishers showed any interest in her writing. In fact it was not until 1961 that all her fiction became available. Although she had had a small following for over thirty years, it was only after the publication of her diaries, beginning with the release of the first volume in 1966, that she became popularly known. In the years that followed she frequently appeared as a lecturer and wrote introductions to books by other authors. Nin died in Los Angeles on January 14, 1977.

Anaïs Nin's principal works include fiction, literary criticism, and her diaries. Her first book, *D. H. Lawrence, An Unprofessional Study* (1932), was a critical work, and was followed by, among other things, *The House of Incest* (1936), which is a surrealistic prose-poem; *The Winter of Artifice* (1939), a collection of three novelettes; *Under a Glass Bell* (1944), and *This Hunger* (1945), both collections of short stories; *Ladders to Fire* (1946), Nin's first novel; *The Four-Chambered Heart* (1950), her third novel; *A Spy in the House of Love* (1954), her most popular novel; and *Collages* (1964), a loosely structured novel in the form of a series of sketches. Nin's most ambitions work was *Cities of the Interior*, a continuous novel in five parts published irregularly between 1946 and 1961. *Delta of Venus* (1977) is a selection of erotica written during the 1940s. Her *Diary* appeared in six volumes (1966–76) and was followed by *Linotte* (1978), which is a further diary, kept between the ages of eleven and seventeen. Critical works include *On Writing* (1947), *The Novel of the Future* (1968), and *A Woman Speaks* (1975).

The unpublished diary of Anaïs Nin has long been a legend of the literary world, but a project to have it published by subscription seems never to have come to anything, and the books that she has brought out, rather fragmentary examples of a kind of autobiographical fantasy, have been a little disappointing. She has now, however, published a small volume called *Under a Glass Bell*, which gives a better impression of her talent.

The pieces in this collection belong to a peculiar genre sometimes cultivated by the late Virginia Woolf. They are half short stories, half dreams, and they mix a sometimes exquisite poetry with a homely realistic observation. They take place in a special world, a world of feminine perception and fancy, which is all the more curious and charming for being innocently international. Miss Nin is the daughter of a Spanish musician, but has spent much of her life in France and in the United States. She writes English, but mostly about Paris, though you occasionally find yourself in other countries. There are passages in her prose which may perhaps suffer a little from an hallucinatory vein of writing which the Surrealists have overdone: a mere reeling-out of images, each of which is designed to be surprising but which, strung together, simply fatigue. In Miss Nin's case, however, the imagery does convey something and is always appropriate. The spun glass is also alive: it is the abode of a secret creature. Half woman, half childlike spirit, she shops, employs servants, wears dresses, suffers the pains of childbirth, yet is likely at any moment to be volatilized into a superterrestial being who feels things that we cannot feel.

But perhaps the main thing to say is that Miss Nin is a very good artist, as perhaps none of the literary Surrealists is. "The Mouse," "Under a Glass Bell," "Rag Time," and "Birth" are really beautiful little pieces. "These stories," says Miss Nin in a foreword, "represent the moment when many like myself had found only one answer to the suffering of the world: to dream, to tell fairy tales, to elaborate and to follow the Labyrinth of fantasy. All this I see now was the passive poet's only answer to the torments he witnessed. . . . I am in the difficult position of presenting stories which are dreams and of having to say: but now, although I give you these, I am awake!" Yet this poet has no need to apologize: her dreams reflect the torment, too.

The book has been printed by Miss Nin herself and is distributed through the Gotham Book Mart, 51 West Forty-Seventh Street. It is well worth the trouble of sending for.
—EDMUND WILSON, NY, April 1, 1944, pp. 81–82

There is no proper relation between the stories of Peter Taylor and Anaïs Nin and yet, forced to read the collections together, I could not help but shudder at the odd hostility between the two generations, the unnatural reversal of temperaments which makes the older writer seem promiscuously immature and the younger one prematurely middle-aged. Anaïs Nin, who has been publishing since 1930, persists in an ostentatious and desperate youth, an agitated and sometimes admirable truancy; Taylor, appearing in book form for the first time, is even now a kind of A student, modest, corrigible, and traditional. There is a toll to be paid by both sides. Taylor has more talent than ambition; he is too serene, too precocious. In his stories one longs, now and then, for harshness, indiscretion, that large, early ugliness a young writer can well afford, a battle with the inexpressible. In Anaïs Nin the attraction to the inexpressible is fatal and no writer I can think of has more passionately embraced thin air. Still, she has nerve and goes on her way with a fierce foolishness that is not without beauty as an act, though it is too bad her performance is never equal to her intentions. I suppose it is true that nothing is so boring as intransigence that does not lead to art superior or even equal to that which is dramatically snubbed. The dreary, sour side of programmatic purity—egotism, piety, boastfulness—annihilates what was meant to be joyful and releasing and leaves only the vanity, like that outrageous pride one sees on the faces of the more interesting American derelicts, those who know they can, if they pull themselves together, still go into the family business.

No doubt this middle-class bum is vanishing; martyrdom and the illusion of righteous protest are just as "dated" on the Bowery as elsewhere. In the same way Anaïs Nin, one of our most self-consciously uncompromising writers, seems old-

fashioned. She is vague, dreamy, mercilessly pretentious; the sickly child of distinguished parents—the avant-garde of the twenties—and unfortunately a great bore. Nevertheless, her weakness has its highest appeal when placed beside the competence, caution, and gentility of most of the serious young writers of the moment. ⟨. . .⟩

Anaïs Nin ⟨. . .⟩ shuns the real world as if it had a bad reputation. This elegant snobbishness seems not designed to get her on in good society, but to allow her to sneak away to the psychological underworld revealed in the following, frightening images. "I walked pinned to a spider web of fantasies spun during the night, obstinately followed during the day. This spider web was broken by a foghorn, and by the chiming of the hours. . . . I sank into a labyrinth of silence. My feet were covered with fur, my hand with leather, my legs wrapped in accordion-pleated cotton, tied with silken whips. Reindeer fur on my breast."

A few of the short pieces in *Under a Glass Bell* are quite effective, but in all of them there is too much straining for the exotic and a pathological appetite for mystification. Miss Nin likes abstractions ("The unveiling of a woman is a delicate matter. It will not happen overnight. We are all afraid of what we shall find.") and falls without warning into an ecstasy which reminds me of nothing so much as those smalltown spiritualists who spoil their productions by undramatic impatience and go into a trance before they have taken off their hats.

The subject matter of these stories is usually the eternal feminine. On the surface there is the hint that great secrets are being revealed for the first time and yet, as the atmosphere of revelation thickens, the language becomes increasingly indirect and unsuggestive. It seems to be characteristic of women writers to "unveil" by pulling out every old veil in the trunk. The more they know about themselves and their sex the more they are, unconsciously I believe, determined to keep the faith. They set out grimly to make a speech, weaken, and end by doing a pantomime with gestures, moods, and rhythms, a sort of modern dance, which gives the illusion of having opened the bedroom door without involving the performer in a recognizable scandal. It is not the discretion that is out of place, but the implication that an innocent tea party has really been a brawl. As Jung observed, men worship Circe, a clear and realistic figure, while the women set out grandly after the Flying Dutchman. This hapless journey through space soon becomes dull, in spite of the quick, nervous energy women writers put into it. Facts, drama, and temptation are replaced by the rhetoric of enormous emotion; the scenery of passion, the garden of love, are wonderfully rendered in the elaborate, elusive style for which women are famous. It is only in the end, after the clever spell is broken, that we realize Adam and Eve have been omitted. Or were they present in disguise, perhaps speaking to us as a tree and a brook?

All of these hesitations in the woman writer's treatment of love and sexual emotion are particularly important in Anaïs Nin's work, because sex is the true object of her considerable literary devotions. And she is thoroughly feminine in that this subject, certain to assure a man's income for life, has not only made her work commercially unprofitable, but almost unreadable. The contemplation of passion and the soul of a woman leads her not to the rocks, but high up in the stratosphere, so high the mind cannot follow her curious flight.

Another bedeviling aspect of Anaïs Nin's work is the problem of the fabulous diary. This diary, unpublished so far as I know, is said to be at present in its sixty-fifth volume. At least Henry Miller has read it and his opinion goes, "When given to the world it will take its place beside the revelations of St.

Augustine, Petronius, Rousseau, Proust, and others." I would not mention this private, buried work if its contents were not so often necessary to the understanding of Miss Nin's fiction. One story begins, "I was eleven years old when I walked into the labyrinth of my diary," and another ends, "The little donkey—my diary burdened with my past—with small faltering steps is walking to the market. . . ." We are told nothing about the diary, but asked to feel, by some mysterious projection, its significance and power as a dominating theme. And then, in a really extraordinary way, the undivulged contents of the diary seem to contain the meaning of a long novelette, *Winter of Artifice*, reprinted in this new collection. The tone of this story is heavy, urgent, and ominous; there is not a moment of humor, not a word of relief from its underwater agony. In it you learn vaguely that a girl has loved her father too well, though in just what way is ambiguous, but she has loved him so terribly she must be psychoanalyzed. "Her father's jealousy began with the reading of her diary." No doubt the diary fully explains the relationship and gives adequate motivation for the anguish echoed here. As it is, however, *Winter of Artifice* can only be read as a Greek chorus chanting about the most miserable of women and apparently unaware that the tragedy has been withheld from the audience.—ELIZABETH HARDWICK, *PR*, June 1948, pp. 705–8

Diary-keeping belongs to a curious and special order of literature; it is the imagination held at bay by the self—the individual so preoccupied with personal experience that he must re-rehearse it compulsively on a sheet of paper. It is inevitably an act of self-absorption; in the process it becomes also an act of self-revelation—in spite of all that it attempts to conceal. Its interest for the reader resides in its offering glimpses into private worlds—worlds to which we do not otherwise have access.

Anaïs Nin's diary, kept with consistency (and almost, one might say, addiction) over many years, is thus primarily a document rather than an act of creation, a record of self-contemplation in many mirrors—public rather than private mirrors. She began keeping it as a child. Her father, the Spanish composer Joaquín Nin, had left her Danish mother, and the latter took her children to America. To fill the absence of her father, the young Anaïs began to write down all that happened to her, in the hope that some day she might show it to him. She wrote her diaries wherever she went, carrying them with her as a musician carries his instrument. Her voluminous notebooks of the self thus fulfill many purposes. They were, for Miss Nin, a way of giving herself concrete proof of her own existence. The diary also became, as it were, her father; and we catch in these pages the straight, questioning look of a little girl interrogating life and trying to be well-behaved and dutiful. But there is something more complicated as well: the diary is that of a daughter, living or imagining a life that would be pleasing to the absent parent.

That life is divided (in the more adult years of 1931 to 1934 here published) between bourgeois respectability and a king of anarchistic Bohemia. Miss Nin lived on the edge of Paris, at Louveciennes in the *paysages* exquisitely preserved for us by Pissaro's canvasses. To her orderly home came the literary anarchists of the Depression era, and especially Henry Miller. Thus we have in these pages the double image of an intellectual bluestocking who can also be a haunter of bistros and visitor of brothels. Miss Nin disciplined, logical, a *"petite fille littéraire,"* as one called her, meticulous in thought and dainty in word, self-questioning, busy discovering for herself the discovered world. When she is reflective and philosophical, she is an earnest, papa-pleasing little girl; when she looks up

from the pages of her writing, she sees the world as a sensitive observer; when she allows herself to feel rather than reflect, her pages take on the color of life rather than of literature. To the critical reader, seeking a self-portrait between these lines, Miss Nin appears above all as a troubled pre-adolescent pursuing a dream of reuniting her parents and recovering her father; and this is why so much of this journal is devoted to her attempts to make peace between substitute figures, Henry Miller and his estranged wife.

The present excerpts are important above all for the subjective, and probably refracted, "portraits" of Miss Nin's psychoanalysts. Readers will be particularly interested in her account of her analytic sessions with Otto Rank, Freud's brilliant if erratic disciple. Through the blur of Miss Nin we glimpse Rank expertly unveiling to her the defenses she has created in her life by her diary-keeping, not least the ways in which the diaries prevent her from developing as an artist by making her an annotator rather than a creator. Miss Nin gives the impression that she conducted the sessions as if she were the analyst. By her account both her French analyst René Allendy, and the Viennese Rank become fathers and lovers; the symbolic house of incest (the title of her first novel) is recurrently revived.

Henry Miller, with understandable partiality and consistent exuberance, has described Miss Nin's diaries as destined to take their place beside the confessions of St. Augustine, Petronius, Abelard, Rousseau, and Proust. Whether this is true of the millions of unpublished words we cannot say; but the present "sampling" offers a modulated and lowpitched portrait of the early Depression years in Paris after most American expatriates had fled. The myth of D. H. Lawrence prevailed; and life in the Villa Seurat had not yet become the Miller-Durrell legend. Miss Nin is a child of the Lawrentian revolt and of the Surealists, the phase of the movement which looked inwardly into the distortions of the dream. Literary history will probably place her with that last backwater of Romanticism before World War II.

Her diary contributes much to that history, and one hopes for more of the 150 volumes. But they should be quarried, it might be suggested, with caution, lest they become like Frankenstein monsters, too large for Miss Nin's own childlike, lotus-flower essence.—LEON EDEL, "Life without Father," *SR*, May 7, 1966, p. 91

HENRY MILLER
From "Un Etre Etoilique"

Criterion, October 1937, pp. 33–43

As I write these lines Anaïs Nin has begun the fiftieth volume of her diary, the record of a twenty-year struggle towards self-realization. Still a young woman, she has produced on the side, in the midst of an intensely active life, a monumental confession which when given to the world will take its place beside the revelations of St. Augustine, Petronius, Abelard, Rousseau, Proust, and others.

Of the twenty years recorded half the time was spent in America, half in Europe. The diary is full of voyages; in fact, like life itself it might be regarded as nothing but voyage. The epic quality of it, however, is eclipsed by the metaphysical. The diary is not a journey towards the heart of darkness, in the stern Conradian sense of destiny, not a *voyage au bout de la nuit*, as with Céline, nor even a voyage to the moon in the psychological sense of escape. It is much more like a mythological voyage towards the source and fountain head of life—I might say an *astrologic* voyage of metamorphosis.

The importance of such a work for our time hardly needs to be stressed. More and more, as our era draws to a close, are we made aware of the tremendous significance of the human document. Our literature, unable any longer to express itself through dying forms, has become almost exclusively biographical. The artist is retreating behind the dead forms to rediscover in himself the eternal source of creation. Our age, intensely productive, yet thoroughly un-vital, un-creative, is obsessed with a lust for investigating the mysteries of the personality. We turn instinctively towards those documents—fragments, notes, autobiographies, diaries—which appease our hunger for more life because, avoiding the circuitous expression of art, they seem to put us directly in contact with that which we are seeking. I say they 'seem to', because there are no short cuts such as we imagine, because the most direct expression, the most permanent and the most effective is always that of art. Even in the most naked confessions there exists the same ellipsis of art. The diary is an art form just as much as the novel or the play. The diary simply requires a greater canvas; it is a chronological tapestry which, in its ensemble, or at whatever point it is abandoned, reveals a form and language as exacting as other literary forms. A work like *Faust*, indeed, reveals more discrepancies, irrelevancies and enigmatic stumbling-blocks than a diary such as Amiel's, for example. The former represents an artificial mode of synchronization; the latter has an organic integration which even the interruption of death does not disturb.

The chief concern of the diarist is not with truth, though it may seem to be, any more than the chief concern of the conscious artist is with beauty. Beauty and truth are the by-products in a quest for something beyond either of these. But just as we are impressed by the beauty of a work of art, so we are impressed by the truth and sincerity of a diary. We have the illusion, in reading the pages of an intimate journal, that we are face to face with the soul of its author. This is the illusory quality of the diary, its art quality, so to speak, just as beauty is the illusory element in the accepted work of art. The diary has to be read differently from the novel, but the goal is the same: self-realization. The diary, by its very nature, is quotidian and organic, whereas the novel is timeless and conventional. We know more, or seem to know more, immediately about the author of a diary than we do about the author of a novel. But as to what we *really* know of either it is hard to say. For the diary is not a transcript of life itself any more than the novel is. It is a medium of expression in which truth rather than art predominates. But it is not *truth*. It is not for the simple reason that the very problem, the obsession, so to say, is truth. We should look to the diary, therefore, not for the truth about things, but as an expression of this struggle to be free of the obsession for truth.

It is this factor, so important to grasp, which explains the tortuous, repetitive quality of every diary. Each day the battle is begun afresh; as we read we seem to be treading a mystic maze in which the author becomes more and more deeply lost. The mirror of the author's own experiences becomes the well of truth in which offtimes he is drowned. In every diary we assist at the birth of Narcissus, and sometimes the death, too. This death, when it occurs, is of two kinds, as in life. In the one case it may lead to dissolution, in the other to re-birth. In the last volume of Proust's great work the nature of this re-birth is magnificently elaborated in the author's disquisitions on the metaphysical nature of art. For it is in *Le Temps retrouvé* that the great fresco wheels into another dimension and thus acquires its true symbolic significance. The analysis which had

been going on throughout the preceding volumes reaches its climax finally in a vision of the whole; it is almost like the sewing up of a wound. It emphasizes what Nietzsche pointed out long ago as 'the healing quality of art'. The purely personal, Narcissistic element is resolved into the universal; the seemingly interminable confession restores the narrator to the stream of human activity through the realization that life itself is an art. This realization is brought about, as Proust so well points out, through obeying the still small voice within. It is the very opposite of the Socratic method, the absurdity of which Nietzsche exposed so witheringly. The mania for analysis leads finally to its opposite, and the sufferer passes on beyond his problems into a new realm of reality. The therapeutic aspect of art is then, in this higher state of consciousness, seen to be the religious or metaphysical element. The work which was begun as a refuge and escape from the terrors of reality leads the author back into life, not *adapted* to the reality about, but *superior* to it, as one capable of recreating it in accordance with his own needs. He sees that it was not life but himself from which he had been fleeing, and that the life which had heretofore been insupportable was merely the projection of his own phantasies. It is true that the new life is also a projection of the individual's own phantasies, but they are invested now with the sense of real power; they spring not from dissociation but from integration. The whole past life resumes its place in the balance and creates a vital, stable equilibrium which would never have resulted without the pain and the suffering. It is in this sense that the endless turning about in a cage which characterized the author's thinking, the endless fresco which seems never to be brought to a conclusion, the ceaseless fragmentation and analysis which goes on night and day, is like a gyration which through sheer centrifugal force lifts the sufferer out of his obsessions and frees him for the rhythm and movement of life by joining him to the great universal stream in which all of us have our being.

A book is a part of life, a manifestation of life, just as much as a tree or a horse or a star. It obeys its own rhythms, its own laws, whether it be a novel, a play, or a diary. The deep, hidden rhythm of life is always there—that of the pulse, the heart beat. Even in the seemingly stagnant waters of the journal this flux and reflux is evident. It is there in the whole of the work as much as in each fragment. Looked at in its entirety, especially for example in such a work as that of Anaïs Nin, this cosmic pulsation corresponds to the death and re-birth of the individual. Life assumes the aspect of a labyrinth into which the seeker is plunged. She goes in unconsciously to slay her old self. One might say, as in this case, that the disintegration of the self had come about through a shock. It would not matter much what had produced the disintegration; the important thing is that at a given moment she passed into a state of twoness. The old self, which had been attached to the father who abandoned her and the loss of whom created an insoluble conflict in her, found itself confronted with a nascent other self which seems to lead her further and further into darkness and confusion. The diary, which is the story of her retreat from the world into the chaos of regeneration, pictures the labyrinthine struggle waged by these conflicting selves. Sinking into the obscure regions of her soul she seems to draw the world down over her head, and with it the people she meets and the relationships engendered by her meetings. The illusion of submergence, of darkness and stagnation, is brought about by the ceaseless observation and analysis which goes on in the pages of the diary. The hatches are down, the sky shut out. Everything—nature, human beings, events, relationships—is brought below to be dissected and digested. It is a devouring process in which the ego becomes a stupendous red maw. The language itself is clear, painfully clear. It is the scorching light of the intellect locked away in a cave. Nothing which this mind comes in contact with is allowed to go undigested. The result is harrowing and hallucinating. We move with the author through her labyrinthine world like a knife making an incision into the flesh. It is a surgical operation upon a world of flesh and blood, a Caesarian operation performed by the embryo with its own private scissors and cleaver.

Let me make a parenthetical remark here. *This diary is written absolutely without malice.* The psychologist may remark of this that the pain inflicted upon her by the loss of her father was so great as to render her incapable of causing pain to others. In a sense this is true, but it is a limited view of the matter. My own feeling is rather that we have in this diary the direct, naked thrust which is of the essence of the great tragic dramas of the Greeks. Racine, Corneille, Molière may indulge in malice—not the Greek dramatists. The difference lies in the attitude towards Fate. The warfare is not with men, but with the gods. Similarly, in the case of Anaïs Nin's journal: the war is with herself, with God as the sole witness. The diary was written not for the eyes of others, but for the eye of God. She has no malice any more than she has the desire to cheat or to lie. To lie in a diary is the height of absurdity. One would have to be really insane to do that. Her concern is not with others, except as they may reveal to her something about herself. Though the way is tortuous the direction is always the same, always inward, further inward, towards the heart of the self. Every encounter is a preparation for the final encounter, the confrontation with the real Self. To indulge in malice would be to swerve from the ordained path, to waste a precious moment in the pursuit of her ideal. She moves onward inexorably, as the gods move in the Greek dramas, on towards the realization of her destiny.

There is a very significant fact attached to the origin of this diary, and that is that it was begun in artistic fashion. By that I do not mean that it was done with the skill of an artist, with the conscious use of a technique; no, but it was begun as something to be read by some one else, as something to influence some one else. In that sense as an artist. Begun during the voyage to a foreign land, the diary is a silent communion with the father who has deserted her, a gift which she intends to send him from their new home, a gift of love which she hopes will re-unite them. Two days later the war breaks out. By what seems almost like a conspiracy of fate the father and child are kept apart for many years. In the legends which treat of this theme it happens, as in this case, that the meeting takes place when the daughter has come of age.

And so, in the very beginning of her diary, the child behaves precisely like the artist who, through the medium of his expression, sets about to conquer the world which has denied him. Thinking originally to woo and enchant the father by the testimony of her grief, thwarted in all her attempts to recover him, she begins little by little to regard the separation as a punishment for her own inadequacy. The difference which had marked her out as a child, and which had already brought down upon her the father's ire, becomes more accentuated. The diary becomes the confession of her inability to make herself worthy of this lost father who has become for her the very paragon of perfection.

In the very earliest pages of the diary this conflict between the old, inadequate self which was attached to the father and the budding, unknown self which she was creating manifests itself. It is a struggle between the real and the ideal, the annihilating struggle which for most people is carried on

fruitlessly to the end of their lives and the significance of which they never learn. Scarcely two years after the diary is begun comes the following passage:

> Quand aucun bruit ne se fait entendre, quand la nuit a recouvert de son sombre paletot la grande ville dont elle me cache l'éclat trompeur, alors il me semble entendre une voix mystérieuse qui me parle; je suppose qu'elle vient de moi-même car elle pense comme moi. . . . Il me semble que je cherche quelque chose, je ne sais pas quoi, mais quand mon esprit libre dégage des griffes pussantes de cet ennemi mortel, le Monde, il me semble que je trouve ce que je voulais. Serait-ce l'oubli? le silence? Je ne sais, mais cette même voix, quand je crois être seule, me parle. Je ne puis comprendre ce qu'elle dit mais je me dis que l'on ne peut jamais être seule et oubliée dans le monde. Car je nomme cette viox: Mon Génie, mauvais ou bon, je ne puis savoir. . . .

Even more striking is a passage in the same volume which begins: 'Dans ma vie terrestre rien n'est changé. . . .' After recounting the petty incidents which go to make up her earthly life, she adds, *but*:

> Dans la vie que je mène dans l'infini cela est différent. Là, tout est bonheur et douceur, car c'est un rêve. Là, il n'y a pas d'école aux sombres classes, mais il y a Dieu. Là, il n'y a pas de chaise vide dans la famille, qui est toujours au complet. Là, il n'y a pas de bruit, mais de la solitude qui donne la paix. Là, il n'y a pas d'inquiétude pour l'avenir, car c'est un autre rêve. Là, il n'y a pas de larmes, car c'est un sourire. Voilà l'infini où je vis, *car je vis deux fois.* Quand je mourrai sur la terre, il arrivera, comme il arrive à deux lumières allumées à la fois, quand l'une s'eteint l'autre se rallume, et cela avec plus de force. Je m'éteindrai sur la terre, mais je me rallumerai dans l'infini. . . .

She speaks of herself mockingly at times as '*une étoilique*'—a word which she has invented, and why not, since as she says, we have the word *lunatique*. Why not '*étoilique*'? 'Today', she writes, 'I described very poorly *le pays des merveilles où mon esprit était*. Je volais dans ce pays lointain où rien n'est impossible. Hier je suis revenue, à la réalité, à la tristesse. Il me semble que je tombais d'une grande splendeur à une triste misère.'

One thinks inevitably of the manifestoes of the Surrealists, of their unquenchable thirst for the marvellous, and that phrase of Breton's, so significant of the dreamer, the visionary: 'we should conduct ourselves as though we were really *in the world!*' It may seem absurd to couple the utterances of the Surrealists with the writings of a child of thirteen, but there is a great deal which they have in common, and there is also a point of departure which is even more important. The pursuit of the marvellous is at bottom nothing but the sure instinct of the poet speaking, and it manifests itself everywhere in all epochs, in all conditions of life, in all forms of expression. But this marvellous pursuit of the marvellous, if not understood, can also act as a thwarting force, can become a thing of evil, crushing the individual in the toils of the Absolute. It can become as negative and destructive a force as the yearning for God. When I said a while back that the child had begun her great work in the spirit of an artist I was trying to emphasize the fact that, like the artist, the problem which beset her was to conquer the world. In the process of making herself fit to meet her father again (because to her the world was personified in the Father) she was unwittingly making herself an artist, that is, a self-dependent creature for whom a father would no longer be necessary. When she does encounter him again, after a lapse of almost twenty years, she is a full-fledged being, a creature fashioned after her own image. The meeting serves to make her realize that she has emancipated herself; more indeed, for to her amazement and dismay she also realizes that she has no more need of the one she was seeking. The significance of her heroic struggle with herself now reveals itself symbolically. That which was beyond her, which had dominated and tortured her, which *possessed* her, one might say, no longer exists. She is de-possessed and free at last to live her own life.

Throughout the diary the amazing thing is this intuitive awareness of the symbolic nature of her role. It is this which illuminates the most trivial remarks, the most trivial incidents she records. In reality there is nothing trivial throughout the whole record; everything is saturated with a purpose and significance which gradually becomes clear as the confession progresses. Similarly there is nothing chaotic about the work, although at first glance it may give that impression. The fifty volumes are crammed with human figures, incidents, voyages, books read and commented upon, reveries, metaphysical speculations, the dramas in which she is enveloped, her daily work, her preoccupation with the welfare of others, in short, with a thousand and one things which go to make up her life. It is a great pageant of the times patiently and humbly delineated by one who considered herself as nothing, by one who had almost completely effaced herself in the effort to arrive at a true understanding of life. It is in this sense again that the human document rivals the work of art, or in times such as ours, *replaces* the work of art. For, in a profound sense, this *is* the work of art which never gets written—because the artist whose task it is to create it never gets born. We have here, instead of the consciously or technically finished work (which to-day seems to us more than ever empty and illusory), the unfinished symphony which achieves consummation because each line is pregnant with a soul struggle. The conflict with the world takes place within. It matters little, for the artist's purpose, whether the world be the size of a pinhead or an incommensurable universe. *But there must be a world!* And this world, whether real or imaginary, can only be created out of despair and anguish. For the artist there is no other world. Even if it be unrecognizable, this world which is created out of sorrow and deprivation is true and vital, and eventually it expropriates the 'other' world in which the ordinary mortal lives and dies. It is the world in which the artist has his being, and it is in the revelation of his undying self that art takes its stance. Once this is apprehended there can be no question of monotony or fatigue, of chaos or irrelevance. We move amid boundless horizons in a perpetual state of awe and humility. We enter, with the author, into unknown worlds, and we share with the latter all the pain, beauty, terror and illumination which exploration entails.

Of the truly great authors no one has ever complained that they over-elaborated. On the contrary, we usually bemoan the fact that there is nothing further left us to read. And so we turn back to what we have and we re-read, and as we re-read we discover marvels which previously we had ignored. We go back to them again and again, as to inexhaustible wells of wisdom and delight. Almost invariably, it is curious to note, these authors of whom I speak are observed to be precisely those who have given us *more* than the others. They claim us precisely because we sense in them an unquenchable flame. Nothing they wrote seems to us insignificant—not even their notes, their jottings, not even the designs which they scribbled unconsciously in the margins of their copy books. Whereas

with the meagre spirits everything seems superfluous, themselves as well as the works they have given us.

At the bottom of this relentless spirit of elaboration is care—*Sorgen*. The diarist in particular is obsessed with the notion that everything must be preserved. And this again is born out of a sense of destiny. Not only, as with the ordinary artist, is there the tyrannical desire to immortalize one's self, but there is also the idea of immortalizing the world in which the diarist lives and has his being. Everything must be recorded because everything must be preserved. In the diary of Anaïs Nin there is a kind of desperation, almost like that of a shipwrecked sailor thrown up on a desert island. From the flotsam and jetsam of her wrecked life the author struggles to create anew. It is a heart-breaking effort to recover a lost world. It is not, as some might imagine, a deliberate retreat from the world; it is an involuntary separation from the world! Everyone experiences this feeling in more or less degree. Everyone, whether consciously or unconsciously, is trying to recover the luxurious, effortless sense of security which he knew in the womb. Those who are able to realize themselves do actually achieve this state; not by a blind, unconscious yearning for the uterine condition, but by transforming the world in which they live into a veritable womb. It is this which seems to have terrified Aldous Huxley, for example, when standing before El Greco's painting, 'The Dream of Philip the 2nd'. Mr. Huxley was terified by the prospect of a world converted into a fish-gut. But El Greco must have been supremely happy inside his fish-gut world, and the proof of his contentment, his ease, his satisfaction, is the world-feeling which his pictures create in the mind of the spectator. Standing before his paintings one realizes that *this is a world!* One realizes also that it is a world dominated by vision. It is no longer a man looking *at* the world, but a man inside his own world ceaselessly reconstructing it in terms of the light within. That it is a world englobed, that El Greco seems to Aldous Huxley, for example, much like a Jonah in the belly of the whale, is precisely the comforting thing about El Greco's vision. The lack of a boundless infinity, which seems so to disturb Mr. Huxley, is on the contrary a most beneficent state of affairs. Everyone who has assisted at the creation of a world, any one who has made a world of his own, realizes that it is precisely the fact that his world has definite limits which is what is good about it. One has first to lose himself to discover the world of his own, the world which, because it is rigidly limited, permits the only true condition of freedom.

GORE VIDAL

From *Two Sisters: A Memoir in the Form of a Novel*
1970, pp. 3–13

Despite my protests, Marietta revealed her breasts.

"You would never know—well, *you* would, but no one else—that I shall be fifty-two years old this November. Sagittarius, what else? That's why we get on so well. Cancer always does with Sagittarius."

"Libra." As I gazed without lust at those familiar not altogether fallen breasts, they suddenly resembled scales, my birth sign made absurdly flesh.

"They still look awfully nice. But I think you'd better cover up." I indicated the building opposite. The sight of her had frozen two plasterers at their work: the scales had become the minatory eyes of Medusa.

"You were always such a prude." With a brisk shake, reminiscent of her old friend Isadora Duncan, she returned the relics of our past association to her blouse. Released from Marietta's spell, one workman dropped a bucket and looked to heaven for a sign while the other, eyes shut, gripped his genitals—in Italy a common gesture and not, as foreigners think, a sign of lewdness or lice but a way of touching base in order to ward off the evil eye.

Marietta often has that effect on men. It is no accident that her favorite adjective is *ensorcelled*. She cannot write a book without it. Unfortunately I cannot read a book that contains it (excepting always the handsome prose of Anaïs Nin). This had made for a degree of coolness between us since Marietta wants to be not only a love goddess (a legend in her own time, as the reviewers say—as, in fact, she herself has so often noted in the five volumes of memoirs she has to date given us) but an artist of the first rank, heiress to Sappho, George Sand, Virginia Woolf, a colossa of literature whose shadow falling across the waste land of twentieth century art makes sickly pale those contemporaries who must dwell forever in her shade, particularly Mary McCarthy, Carson McCullers and Marietta's near-contemporary Katherine Anne Porter.

Marietta Donegal is sixty-eight not fifty-two; yet in her way she is still beautiful, preserved by an insatiable appetite for glory and sex. Alone among the women of our time, Marietta has managed to domesticate Sophocles' cruel and insane master. At eighty she will be making love and writing about it in that long autobiography which begins with our century and will, I am certain, last well into the next for like it or not, we live in *her* age—was she not the mistress of D. H. Lawrence (two volumes hardly described the three—or was it four?—times she bedded that ensorcelled genius) as well as the beloved inspiration—and brutal seducer—of so many other writers, painters, sculptors and even one President, though whether it was sunrise or sunset at Campobello has never been entirely clear (out of admiration for Eleanor Roosevelt she has yet to give us the entire story). She is unique in all but talent.

"I could hardly believe it when I heard you'd written *Myra Breckinridge*. It was so out of character."

After a quarter century of publication, I have learned never to discuss my work with other writers. It excites them too much. I shifted Marietta's attention to Nabokov's *Ada* which had just been published. I half expected her to tell me that she had been his muse, too, but apparently they had not met. I was not surprised to learn that his current vogue distressed her, as it does us all (writers are by nature envious, and easily undone: is there *no* justice?), even though the success of men writers usually does not upset her quite as much as that of women. Shortly after an entire issue of *Horizon* had been devoted to Mary McCarthy's "The Oasis," the two girls met by accident at Martha's Vineyard. With a terribly cry, Marietta fainted from rage.

"I was so upset by what Nabokov said about you in *Time*."

"I'm afraid I don't read *Time*."

This is not true. I am addicted to *Time*'s political "reporting" in which one can follow from week to week the fictional adventures of actual people. Instead of decently ending, the novel seems to have got a new lease upon our attention in the form of the weekly "news" magazine.

"Nabokov attacked everyone. Tolstoi. You. Mailer."

"Ah, that old world charm . . ."

"Charm! I find it disgusting."

"But normal. Writers like to attack their betters."

This was a mistake. Inadvertently, I had left an opening which she was capable of filling; happily, Czarist Russia's gift to our poor letters continued to distract her. "He attacked *Portnoy's Complaint* . . ."

"That was unkind. I should have thought the man who celebrated pedophilia would regard masturbation with a tolerant eye."

". . . and said that even *you* were more interesting than Philip Roth."

"That was perceptive."

"But you know what he *meant*."

"I still enjoy his books. Oh, perhaps not as much as he does. That would be impossible but . . ."

"How easily taken in Americans are! They are mad for foreigners who make fun of them."

"Don't worry. No one will ever read *Ada*."

"It is already a best seller."

"And has taken its historic place beside *By Love Possessed*, *Ship of Fools*, and *The Confessions of Nat Turner*. Books that defy one to read them, in just the way the Sunday *New York Times* does. They are ceremonial artifacts to be displayed but not used." I was launched upon a favorite theme. Also, in the back of my mind, the perfect analogy to Nabokov had suddenly surfaced. James Branch Cabell. I began to compose a blurb. "Not since Cabell's *Jurgen* has there been a novel so certain to delight the truly refined reader as Nabokov's *Ada*."

But Marietta was on her own tack. "*The Heart's Archery* hasn't sold twenty thousand copies since March."

"The what?"

Marietta's eyes became hard malachite. The voice dropped an octave. "My last book of memoirs. I sent it to you. You never answered."

"I never got it." This was true. "There is no such thing as a mail service in Rome. Do you know how many sacks of mail there are at San Silvestro?"

The subject did not intrigue her. "You're in the book, you know." She sounded threatening. "That party in Los Angeles. Isherwood's in it, too."

Marietta was one of the first to realize that in an age of total publicity personality is all that matters. And if one has "mattered" in the world, by middle age one is sure to have figured in a dozen novels, a hundred memoirs, a thousand newspaper stories. I have already made a number of appearances under my own name in Marietta's memoirs where, inevitably, I say something disagreeable which she gets slightly wrong. Yet, sexually, she is surprisingly coy. Her lovers—if alive—are only embedded, as it were, in her fiction. The three months we lived together in 1947 (I twenty-two, she forty-seven) formed the central motif to one of her most Lorenzian novels in which I appear as a faun-faced poet, so overwhelmed by her autumnal beauty and ripe wisdom as to contract an acute case of priapism. At least that is Marietta's version. My recollection is that I was tired a good deal of the time (I was coming down with hepatitis) but enjoyed being with her at the Hôtel de l'Université in Paris for a summer (in 1947 it was always summer) because she had a gift for intimacy. She was—is?—one of those rare women with whom one likes to talk after the act. *Post coitum Marietta* I once called her. I don't think she was pleased.

As we sat on my terrace overlooking all of Rome to the west of the Largo Argentina, a fine if jumbled view of golden buildings, one twisted tower (Borromini's St. Ivo), the green Gianicolo and a dozen domes, the nearest Sant' Andrea della Valle (*Tosca* Act One), the farthest St. Peter's like a gray-ridged skull, Marietta discussed the latest details of her literary career. I shall not record what she said since she is bound to confide it to us in Volume Six of her memoirs.

At first I could not figure out what she wanted. True, she still expects me to compose a full-scale critique of her work in which, once and for all, her quality is established. For twenty years we have played this game, she cajoling, threatening, weeping. I backing and filling, evading the dread commitment. I had assumed when she rang me this morning to say she was in Rome and needed my advice that, once again, I would be asked, first, to write about her at length or, failing that, to praise in a line or two the . . . what was the title? *The Heart's Archery*. But the expected request was not made. She had something else on her mind.

"Eric Van Damm. You remember him, don't you? From Paris."

A long shut door swings open to reveal high summer— yes, it was always summer twenty years ago. I am standing in a room at the Hôtel de l'Université as Eric, tall, slender, blond, quite naked, takes apart for the hundredth time his German movie camera. That moment has remained as vivid to me as Henry James's recollection after a half century of a boy cousin being sketched in the nude at Newport before his life was "cut short, in a cavalry clash, by one of the Confederate bullets of 1863." ⟨. . .⟩

Now Marietta wants to know what I had thought of him. I answer, truthfully, that although I have a sensuous memory of him I do not, strictly speaking, *think* of him. I don't tell her that what I best recall are long legs covered with golden hair. To be candid with Marietta means to be fixed for all time in the distorting aspic of her prose.

"I loved him." Marietta can say that sort of thing in a most winning way; it is only when she writes that she loses.

"Is he still in California?" The last I had heard of Eric he was making documentaries for television.

Marietta gave me a long look, then she said, very carefully, "If you had read *The Heart's Archery*, which I'm sure you got, you would have known that Eric is dead . . ."

Saw the long legs reduced to bone; saw the blue eyes glaze, and fall back into the skull, saw the skull without skin, lips, smile. Yet it is summer in Rome as I write these lines.

"How?"

But Marietta is an artist first, a messenger second. "I've known for some time that you take no interest in my work. Or anything outside yourself . . ."

Some minutes later when she had exhausted herself if not the subject, I learned that Eric had fallen off a roof while filming a riot in Berkeley.

"Such a ridiculous way to die." Marietta was blunt, having no more fear of death than of life.

"Anyway, I have something of his which I want to show you." She opened her handbag and removed a scruffy red notebook of the sort French children use in school, and a manuscript.

"He left these by mistake in Paris, for that sister of his . . ."

That sister of his! Erika had been a perfect feminine version of Eric's own perfect youth. Fantasies of the two of them (they were twins, she dark, he fair) have figured, I am certain, in a thousand erotic dreams for they were rare beings, and quite unknowable. Each made love with the same sort of kind good humor, yet neither seemed entirely present in the act. I looked at the notebook hopefully. Was I about to find out why?

"I was quite upset that summer, as you remember."

I do not but said I did.

"It was understood that he stay in my room at the Hôtel de l'Université until I got back from Turkey. Well, when I came back he had left with what's her name, the bad actress . . . ?"

Memory stirred. "Didn't you use that in your novel, *The Archaic Smile?*"

Marietta looked at me like a child given a present. She was, for an instant, a girl again. "Yes! Yes! Oh, you did read *Smile!* It won the Prix d'Avignon, you know, in French. Yes, I wrote all about Eric and me, and his disappearing, and then running into him years later in Monterey as though nothing had happened. Yes, I wrote it all, just the way it was . . ."

"You never invent, do you?" I could not resist the comment.

"Why should I? The only thing that matters is the life. What *really* happened. You make up everything, don't you?"

"Oh, yes. Everything. Even you."

But she was not listening.

"Now. I want your professional advice. I read somewhere that you were doing the film of *Myra Breckinridge*."

"Not exactly. Someone named Zanuck is doing it. He is very talented. But I am doing a screenplay of *Julian*."

"Strange the way you've always been drawn to history. I hate the past. You're very like Eric, you know, he liked classical history, too. This . . ." She held up the script. ". . . takes place in the third century B.C." I felt a premonitory weariness at the thought of Eric as guide to that lost world.

Then Marietta was all business. She wants to sell the script to a movie producer. With Eric dead, she would be able to keep the money from the sale and buy the Positano villa which, until now, she only rents. "I think I should ask a hundred thousand dollars for it, don't you?"

I tried to explain to her that it was most unlikely that anyone would want to make a film based on a twenty-year-old screenplay by an unknown writer, but Marietta was confident. "That sort of thing is extremely popular, now. Look at Fellini and *Satyricon*. The timing couldn't be better. And with you knowing all these film people . . . well, I'm sure you'll find somebody who'll buy it. You are such a friend, really!"

"What is the notebook?"

Marietta frowned. "Very odd. I don't think you'll like it. After all, you're in it. We all are."

"A diary?"

"No. Just . . . well, you'll see. Eric was not what he seemed."

I realized at the moment that I did not want to read either notebook or script. Most people—and all women—are eager to read other people's mail, eavesdrop upon other people's conversations, to find out just what it is that others say of them. I am the opposite. I have no desire to know the worst or for that matter the best, unlike Marietta who reads everything written about her. From Kyoto to Spokane, book reviewers have been astonished to receive long letters from Marietta, analyzing what they have said of her and though no praise has ever been quite sufficient (I compared her once to Katherine Mansfield; she did not speak to me for a year), Marietta is a master of "enscorcelling" those who write book chat for the press, turning to them that legendary Aphrodite face which D. H. Lawrence had on three—no, three and a half—occasions scratched with his bronze fox beard. The reviewer has not been born who can entirely resist the full panoply of such all-conquering charm; as a result, her pen pals now range across the earth and her fame increases with each passing year for, truth to tell, Marietta is an astonishingly good writer of the sacred monster sort and the decades in which she was regarded as something of a joke ("Claire Clairmont without the wit," Cyril Connolly was supposed to have said) made her not only bitter but strong and infinitely cunning in exhibiting both self and work as one until, just as the postwar period became prewar (circa 1965), she was able to enter her kingdom for she is exactly what the times require: a writer who is neither more nor less than what he writes. Entirely lacking in the creative imagination, Marietta Donegal is triumphant, though not as rich as she would like to be.

LYNN SUKENICK
"The *Diaries* of Anaïs Nin"
Shenandoah, Spring 1976, pp. 96–103

Autobiographical forms raise critical questions which are different from the questions raised by novels and poetry. Because novels and poetry do not purport to be records of fact they do not move us to check veracity: they stand or fall by their convincingness, which need not be a matter of strict mimesis but of truth of feeling, rightness of form, and richness of language. A serious work of autobiography also bases much of its success on these elements but inevitably forces the reader to consider additional criteria, the most prominent of which is— is it true?

Perhaps it would be more accurate to say, does it *seem* true, for we infrequently turn to other accounts for verification of a diary or a memoir unless we are scholars: we rely on the veracious tone, the probability, common sense, and proportion of a work for our satisfaction. In certain instances scholarship or common knowledge confirms an author's reputation as a liar, as in the case of Cellini, whose autobiography we enjoy as the brilliant self-revelation of a braggart, as vivid and undeceptive as a braggart in the flesh.

The diaries of Anaïs Nin, although revised and intensely compressed, and revised—as Nin has said—by the novelist, are, by their nature, a species of autobiography. Although their excellence has caused them to be ranked with works of imagination, a rank accorded few autobiographies in spite of the current popularity of the genre, they are not novels—one has only to put them next to her novels to feel that—and to ignore that fact is to miss out on the special reading experience which they seem to inspire. Nin's diaries are books of wisdom which have elevated their author to the status of a sage and have had a healing effect on many of her readers, an effect which would be altered if the books were semi-fiction, although, clearly, works of fiction can function as books of wisdom. It is unlikely that anyone has bent to kiss her hem as did one adoring reader of George Eliot, but Nin has evoked in her readers a response similar to the tenacious adulation that surrounded Eliot in her later years, and has joined the company of those great teachers—Eliot, Wordsworth, and the savage but salutary D. H. Lawrence—who had a visionary sense of the healing power of feeling. "The effect of her being on those around her was incalculably diffusive," says George Eliot of Dorothea Brooke, and it is not less true of the Nin who emerges in these diaries, a woman who teaches not through precept but through influence. The diaries, depicting Nin's influence on those around her, also teach us, her readers, how to be influenced, how to be susceptible.

Nin's power to stir us and change our lives is not in direct proportion to the quantity of information in the diaries, not a direct function of how much she tells us. Although Nin places her deepest expectations in the personal and private sphere, the diaries are not confessional works. Nin was a practicing Catholic until her teens and therefore familiar with the ritual of confession; she was a student of psychoanalysis and herself an analyst, accustomed to the recuperative monologues of the analysand, but her diaries are not confessional in the most common sense of the word. She does not seek to unburden herself of material as if that material is an impediment to her freedom, nor does she pay guilty attention to the more ignoble details of her life as if to absolve herself by virtue of her typicality or detestability. If anything, she is herself the priest or lay confessor, confessing to herself by means of the diary, but also, by means of the diary, absolving herself from raw experience by transmuting it into form—not just any form, but conscious and lucid writing which expresses control even when she is discussing her weaknesses.

In certain respects the diaries are as elusive as the father they are written to—the absence of Nin's husband in these pages, for instance, necessarily leaves a fissure which would make all other relationships undergo a geological shift—and Nin's omissions have been a focus for criticism of her work, some readers asserting that she appears to have led a life less conditioned by circumstance than the diaries reveal, thus giving us a falsely reassuring picture of human abilities (insofar as she comes to stand for human abilities). This is a criticism that becomes more important as her diaries tend to become more and more models of a life and books of wisdom, for if we look to Peter Pan to teach us to fly but do not see the hook and wire holding him to the ceiling we are in trouble, though he may temporarily increase our optimism.

If Nin does omit crucial elements which would change the tone and nature of the diaries as they now stand she is also persuasive in making us comprehend that these elements are not as crucial as the principles of realism have led us to think. For our idea of what a "life" is, based on only relative tenets of Western perception, economy, and chronology, does not necessarily match the shape or proportion with which Nin lives hers, and it is her great strength that she has resisted the habituating sets that conquer and form most of us, her vision changing our notions of the plausible and possible. Just as certain yogis dispel our assumption that we need continuous breath to stay alive, so Nin persuades us that it is not impractical to be guided by dreams, not impossible to defy gravity for a few minutes longer than we think. It is important to note that the characters in Nin's novels also have lives which are, in ordinary terms, unconditioned, possessing an anonymity and inconsistency at odds with the crystallized characterization handed down from the nineteenth-century novel, lives which are not Nin's own but which she sees in a similar way.

For Nin, realism is a form of defeat. She craves the idyllic, the supreme version, and her drive toward the perfect, the harmonized, the Utopian, and her impulse to make things as intense, prolific, and beautiful as possible, is a central feature of the diaries. Transforming her optimism into an esthetic, she believes that the role of the artist is to transform ugliness into beauty, in life as well as in writing. Taking her father's desire to be thought perfect and generously inverting it, she wants others to think they are perfect. And if she makes myth of herself and writes herself large, it is not as a narcissist but out of a desire to transform her life by means of discipline and optimism into the most lovely and elevated existence possible.

The supreme version can be a fiction, however, and we do not want diaries to be fiction, nor, for that matter, do we want novels to be fairy-tale. Nin's passion for harmony expresses itself in her distaste for harsh contradiction or polemic. She does not hold the belief that exigence and contradiction are necessary for genuine selfhood. For Nin, logic and argument, all the voices of the head as opposed to the heart, are only translations from an original emotional reality. Feeling and intellect are not different ends of a continuum but exist on separate planes, and she rejects the quality of negation in modernist literature which comes from the hegemony of intellect, for it is the intellect that doubts; the body, the feelings, are usually sure. "The highest goodness is like water," says Lao Tzu. "Water is beneficent to all things but does not contend." Just so with Nin: in both diaries and fiction she emphasizes synthesis over antithesis, maintaining a tone that holds everything in the same plane, neutralizing the distinction between figure and ground, muting conflicts in interpretation. Her style determines that people tend to read her either very loyally—moved by faith to relate, unite, and connect rather than to dispute—or not at all.

Nin's occasional neglect of sincerity and candor in the diaries—the lies she tells to others to make improvements or not to hurt, to maintain harmony and dissolve disruption—is directly related to her desire for perfection. She realizes it as a weakness—this tendency to invent or conceal—and she presents her weakness openly, not only in her own person but in figures who reflect and enlarge the problem, living it out to an extreme degree. Lying—her father's, June's—is a deep concern in Diary I, and is a theme that develops richness in *Spy in the House of Love*, where Nin attempts to find relief from it once and for all, creating a final punctuation in the person of the Lie Detector.

Nin's belief in transmutation and alchemy inspires her to alter the surface and style of things and to take adornment seriously, embracing as a pleasure what many people use only as a strategy of defense. She alters her costume to transform the occasion, dressing like a warrior to resist Artaud, acknowledging the power of the material realm and putting it to magical use. This passion for adornment is intimately linked to the possibilities of impersonation, for though Nin shows us how impersonation may whittle away selfhood she also makes clear that it can be a temporary but releasing expression of unlived life, truer than rigidly held consistency. If young Werther expressed his sincerity by an unchanging mode of dress, mistakenly clinging to romantic simplicity, Nin (who associates romanticism with neurosis perhaps because of this pretense of divided consciousness to innocent unity) dons masks and costumes in order to celebrate the complexity of identity, the unlimited truths of personality. She has a sane longing to be whole but does not pretend, sentimentally, to a wholeness she hasn't earned or an innocence that would simplify her life without being true to it.

"Give a man a mask and he will tell you the truth." Oscar Wilde's dictum suggests that protected by a mask we are more willing, unwittingly perhaps, to be and reveal ourselves. The artist creating his/her own environment goes even further, including the mask as part of the revelation rather than hiding behind it, aware that the creation of a compelling mask expresses degrees of inventiveness and levels of aspiration which are as much a part of the self as ordinary guise. Although Nin escapes the mechanical and hypocritical impersonations of social existence in the diary, her pursuit of "transmutation" continues there, and the diary itself becomes both an active force in transforming her life (as when she draws portraits of people and shows them their portraits) as well as a distilled account of her experience. Notable for a grace and certainty of style, Nin's diary is utterly distinct from the current outpourings of confessional journalism, undigested notation encouraged by the general abolition of etiquette and the preeminence of therapies which encourage and value the public revelation of personal material. She does not give herself away in her writings but serves us by remaining intact even after we have devoured her work.

Perfection of, attention to style is suspect in autobiography, for we tend to feel, almost superstitiously—Romanti-

cally—that the genuine self—naked, chaotic—cannot be contained by language, and that inadequacy of language or stress of expression pays homage to the large undefinable self. Kerouac's rough work clothes and associative prose seem more authentic at first glance than Henry Adams' balanced and dressed up coat and tie sentences. Yet Adams' prim, if profound, accuracy is as revealing of personality as Kerouac's often evasive casualness. Nin's distilled style is a part of the personality being revealed by it. She has a sense of style—in dress, in personal relations, in her self-discipline—which makes transmutation of the raw into the fine a natural and constant process in her life. Stylization is not only a task of the social self, as it is for most people; it is, for Nin, instinctive and intimate. The diary is edited to make it a manageable length and to prevent injury to the living; it is also highly appropriate to Nin's stance that the diary emerges first as a distilled version of the original, for her life itself is a highly distilled version of what, with less will and vision, it might have been.

The advocates of spontaneity, from Rousseau on, have regarded artifice as an offense against sincerity and the spirit of democracy (for a doctrine of equality gives value to and an opportunity for candor). A sisterly relation with the reader is desired, a certain obligation to be no better than the reader. But Nin, by aiming high and extracting noble qualities from her experience, improves herself and shows others the way. Nin's distilled style allows us more space for ourselves than the confessional outpourings which make accomplices of us. Her diary, perfected and sometimes reticent, becomes a mirror into which we can look and, often, find ourselves clearly expressed. Her polished surface reflects the reader.

Nin's relation to the reader is not unlike her relationships to real people in the diaries, where her personal allure is clearly an overpowering factor in her experience. Her diaries are seductive rather than confessional, extending to the reader a subliminal invitation to fall in love—with her, *and* with the world—and she instinctively knows, having been traditionally feminine in many respects, the importance of concealment to the arousal of desire. Yet she is fascinated by veils actual and symbolic not out of conquetry, or modesty, but out of an appreciation of tact, subtlety, and the more enduring connections these approaches inspire.

Nin's tact, discretion, gentleness and sympathy are crucial to all of her relationships as they are portrayed in the diary, at times, in her own opinion, to excess. Virginia Woolf has stated that sympathy was a concern of laggards and losers, and certainly in the era of modernism it has seemed minor, mediocre, and peripheral. But Nin insists on it—"What makes us human is empathy, sympathy," she says—and she is willing to cry out, "This hurts people!" the kind of objection ordinarily made only by unpublished mothers. The most remarkable thing about Nin is how she revives the wisdom of sympathy in an age which tends to be embarrassed by it.

The spareness and omissions of Nin's diaries result partly from her wanting to ignore—in Virginia Woolf's phrase—the "appalling narrative business of the realist," just as her strategy as a novelist is to wean us from simple curiosity and a hunger for ordinary narrative. But it is more than likely that sympathy and discretion are as responsible as formal considerations for the withholding of information in the diaries. Nin's unwillingness to injure coincides with her doctrine of omission and extends the portrait of her as a woman of sympathy. There is in fact a substitution of sympathy for confessional sincerity in the diaries. Nin relates how she sometimes conceals things from others in order not to hurt them, offering warm comfort instead of cold fact. She writes in the diary to compose herself, literally, to offset her empathic merging with others. Yet even this private act, now made public, offers comfort, now to her readers, who receive insights into and a blueprint for the opening of the heart, solicitude and creative energy. The apex of Nin's tact is that she creates an atmosphere of intimacy at the same time that she refrains from a policy of open disclosure. We feel, somehow, that the diaries reach into our lives, that they are intimate about *us*, intimating to us our own latent potential, the latent life force in us.

Nin's wisdom fits nicely into the American credo of "Make thyself" and many of her readers have saved and changed themselves through the inspiration of her work. There is a certain innocence and pragmatism about this reception of her diaries which should be distinguished from the character of Nin herself. She is sophisticated, European, not an innocent, though some skeptics might see her sympathetic nature as innocent. Her naturalness is real but hard won against the cold artifice of her father and her warmer inclinations to masks and perfections. She is not broad and candid by nature but tactful, oblique, delicate. It is this complexity—this chord—her given nature and her growth out of it—that makes her diaries interesting. Her openness is earned and the self she discovers and enriches is all the more authentic for being complex and struggled for.

Only an honest person should tell the truth. Candor does not guarantee integrity of spirit or freedom from self-deception. The indirect autobiographer, humbly aware of this, may have a greater respect for the integrity of the self than the most ardent confessor. The mode or attitude of sincerity does not insure honesty; to behave as if you are telling everything does not mean that you are, and may indeed be a way of disarming reader (and writer) from probing deeper. Discretion is, in effect, an open refusal of information less misleading at times than the confession which accidentally or deliberately conceals.

These are important issues, for there are readers who depend on Nin's diaries to be sincere, straightforward exposition and are then disappointed (or elated) to discover a more complex mix of modes and motives. Others relinquish all the claims and expectations we bring to autobiography and call these novels. But the diaries, however, unconfessional, contain a wisdom in their obliquity and omissions. Nin teaches us to get rid of the dross of our lives, to pursue essence and ignore the masses of ordinary detail we have been trained to think of as necessary or authenticating. She compels us to believe that the supreme version is worth having, and she revives without apology and with panache the importance of sympathy and aspiration.

JOYCE CAROL OATES

1938–

Joyce Carol Oates, novelist, short-story writer, and critic, was born on June 16, 1938, the eldest of three children of Catholic, working-class parents. Until she was seventeen she lived in rural Erie County, outside of Lockport in western New York State. She attended primary school at a nearby one-room schoolhouse, junior high school in Lockport, and high school in Buffalo. At the age of seventeen she entered Syracuse University as a scholarship student, and in 1960 graduated as class valedictorian with a B.A. in English and a minor in philosophy. While in college she won the first of many awards, first prize in *Mademoiselle*'s college fiction contest for her story "In the Old World."

In 1960 Oates attended the University of Wisconsin in Madison, completing an M.A. in English in 1961. While still at school she met Raymond J. Smith, whom she married soon afterwards. When her husband got a teaching job in Beaumont, Texas, she moved there with him and began a Ph.D. in English at Rice University, which she shortly abandoned in order to become a professional writer. In 1962 the Smiths moved to Detroit, where Oates took a job as an English instructor at the University of Detroit. In 1967 she joined her husband at the University of Windsor in Ontario, Canada, where she remained for many years. She is presently teaching at Princeton University in New Jersey.

Joyce Carol Oates has written a great deal. Her novels, many of which are violent, are, she claims, an attempt to transcend the ego-consciousness of modern culture. They are more or less naturalistic in style, although they have overtones of the neo-gothic, and include *A Garden of Earthly Delights* (1967), *Expensive People* (1968), *them* (1969, National Book Award), *Wonderland* (1971), and *A Bloodsmoor Romance* (1982). She has also written numerous short stories and has published essays and works of literary criticism.

Personal

Joe David Bellamy: What are your writing habits? What times of day do you like to write? How many pages do you average— if there is an average? How do you manage to write so much? Is this simply natural facility, or have you cultivated it in some unusual way?

Joyce Carol Oates: I don't have any formal writing habits.

Most of the time I do nothing, and the fact of time passing so relentlessly is a source of anguish to me. There are not enough hours in the day. Yet I waste most of my time, in daydreaming, in drawing faces on pieces of paper (I have a compulsion to draw faces; I've drawn several million faces in my life, and I'm doomed to carry this peculiar habit with me to the grave). We live on the Detroit River, and I spend a lot of time looking at the river. Everything is flowing away, flowing by. When I'm with people I often fall into a kind of waking sleep, a daydreaming about the people, the strangers, who are to be the "characters" in a story or a novel I will be writing. I can't do much about this habit. At times my head seems crowded; there is a kind of pressure inside it, almost a frightening physical sense of confusion, fullness, dizziness. Strange people appear in my thoughts, and define themselves slowly to me: first their faces, then their personalities and quirks and personal histories, then their relationships with other people, who very slowly appear; and a kind of "plot" then becomes clear to me, as I figure out how all these people came together and what they are doing. I can see them at times very closely, and indeed I "am" them—my personality merges with theirs. At other times I can see them from a distance; the general shape of their lives, which will be transformed into a novel, becomes clear to me; so I try to put this all together, working very slowly, never hurrying the process. I can't hurry it any more than I can prevent it. When the story is more or less coherent and has emerged from the underground, then I can begin to write quite quickly—I must have done forty or fifty pages a day in *Expensive People*, though not every day. Most of the time only fifteen to twenty pages a day. In *Wonderland* (published in October, 1971) I did about the same number of pages on certain days; in fact last summer, working in a kind of trance, elated and exhausted, for many hours at a time. I wasn't creating a story but simply recording it, remembering it. This is true for all of my writing; I have never "made up" a story while sitting at the typewriter. ⟨. . .⟩

Bellamy: What is your concept of characterization? Or what are your ideas about characterization? This is overly general perhaps (and maybe less coherent than one might hope for). How about this: Do you think "hardened" character such as the kind in Victorian novels is real or valid?

Oates: Your questions about characterization are quite coherent questions, yet I can't answer them because—as you might gather from what I have already said—I don't write the way other people evidently write, or at least I can't make sense of what they say about their writing. My "characters" really dictate themselves to me. I am not free of them, really, and I can't force them into situations they haven't themselves willed. They have the autonomy of characters in a dream. In fact, when I glance through what I have tried to say to you, it occurs to me that I am really transcribing dreams, giving them a certain civilized, extended shape, clearing a few things up, adding daytime details, subtracting fantastic details, and so on, in order to make the story or the novel a work of art. Private dreams have no interest for other people; the dream must be made public, by using one's wit.

People say that I write a great deal, and they are usually curious about when I "find time." But the odd thing is that I waste most of my time. I don't think I am especially productive, but perhaps other writers are less productive. In the past, however, writers like Henry James, Edith Wharton, Dickens (of course), and so on and so forth, wrote a great deal, wrote innumerable volumes, because they were professional writers and writers write. Today, it seems something of an oddity that a writer actually writes, and some writers or critics who don't spend much time writing seem to resent more productive writers. Someone said that John Updike publishes books as often as John O'Hara did, but thankfully his books weren't quite as long as O'Hara's. . . . This is an attitude I can't understand. Any book by Updike is a happy event. The more, the better. If any critic imagines that he is tired of

Updike, then he should not read the next Updike novel and he certainly should not review it.

. . . I don't know that the above will strike you as good enough, or that I have answered your questions. I know one thing, though: I would never have thought of some of these things in a person-to-person interview. The whole *social* aspect of such interviewing gets in the way of ideas.

You are kind in the many things you say about my writing and about me (you probably do know me quite well, because I've told you things that acquaintances and social friends of mine would never be told, not in dozens of years)—it may be that I am mysterious, in a way; certainly there are things about myself that don't make sense to me and are therefore mysterious, to me; but the main thing about me is that I am enormously interested in other people, other lives, and that with the least provocation (a few hints of your personal life, let's say, your appearance, your house and setting), I could "go into" your personality and try to imagine it, try to find a way of dramatizing it. I am fascinated by people I meet, or don't meet, people I only correspond with, or read about; and I hope my interest in them isn't vampiristic, because I don't want to take life from them, but only to honor the life in them, to give some permanent form to their personalities. It seems to me that there are so many people who are inarticulate, but who suffer and doubt and love, nobly, who need to be immortalized or at least explained.

Here in Windsor, life is filling up with people: parents coming to visit, trunks to be packed, last-minute arrangements to be made, a dozen, a hundred chores, such as what to serve for dinner tonight. But thank God for trivial events! They keep us from spinning completely off into the dark, into the abstract universe.

I hope these answers make some kind of sense to you. Much of this I haven't thought out, until now; it sounds bizarre but is very honest.—JOYCE CAROL OATES, Interview by Joe David Bellamy, *At*, Feb. 1972, pp. 63–67

General

So the days pass, and I ask myself whether one is not hypnotised, as a child by a silver globe, by life; and whether this is living. (Virginia Woolf *Diary*, 28 November 1928)

A "sense of fright, of something deeply wrong." In Joyce Carol Oates's most notable novel, *them*, this seemed to express itself as a particular sensitivity to individual lives helplessly flying off the wheel of American gigantism. While writing *them* (a novel which ends with the 1967 eruption of Detroit's Blacks) she said that Detroit was "all melodrama." There a man can get shot by the brother of the woman he is lying next to in bed, and the body will be disposed of by a friendly policeman. The brother himself pops up later in the sister's life not as a "murderer," but as a genially obtuse and merely wistful fellow. Nothing of this is satirized or moralized as once it would have been. It is what happens every day now; there are too many people for murders to count. There are too many murderers about for the murderer to take murder that seriously.

Joyce Carol Oates seemed, more than most women writers, entirely open to *social* turmoil, to the frighteningly undirected and misapplied force of the American powerhouse. She plainly had an instinct for the social menace packed up in Detroit, waiting to explode, that at the end of the nineteenth century Dreiser felt about Chicago and Stephen Crane about New York. The sheer rich chaos of American life, to say nothing of its staggering armies of poor, outraged, by no means peaceful people, pressed upon her. It is rare to find a woman writer so externally unconcerned with form. After teaching at the University of Detroit from 1962 to 1967, she remarked that Detroit is a city "so transparent, you can hear it ticking." What one woman critic, in a general attack on Oates, called "Violence in the Head," could also be taken as her inability to blink social violence as the language in which a great many "lower-class" Americans naturally deal with each other.

Joyce Carol Oates is, however, a "social novelist" of a peculiar kind. She is concerned not with demonstrating power relationships, but with the struggle of people nowadays to express their fate in terms that are cruelly changeable. Reading her, one sees the real tragedy of so many Americans today, unable to find a language for what is happening to them. The drama of society was once seen by American social novelists as the shifting line between the individual and the mass into which he was helplessly falling. It has now become the free-floating mythology about "them" which each person carries around with him, an idea of causation unconnected to cause. There is no longer a fixed point within people's thinking. In the American social novels earlier in the century, the novelist was a pathfinder and the characters were betrayed as blind helpless victims of their fate, like Hurstwood in *Sister Carrie* or virtually everybody in Dos Passos's *U.S.A.* Joyce Carol Oates is not particularly ahead of the people she writes about. Since her prime concern is to see people in the terms they present to themselves, she is able to present consciousness as a person, a crazily unaccountable thing. The human mind, as she says in the title of a recent novel, is simply "wonderland." And the significance of that "wonderland" to the social melodrama that is America today is that they collide but do not connect.

Praising Harriette Arnow's strong, little-known novel about Southern mountain folk, *The Dollmaker*, Joyce Oates said:

> It seems to me that the greatest works of literature deal with the human soul caught in the stampede of time, unable to gauge the profundity of what passes over it, like the characters of Yeats who live through terrifying events but who cannot understand them; in this way history passes over most of us. Society is caught in a convulsion, whether of growth or of death, and ordinary people are destroyed. They do not, however, understand that they are "destroyed."

This view of literature as silent tragedy is a central description of what interests Joyce Oates in the writing of fiction. Her own characters move through a world that seems to be wholly physical and even full of global eruption, yet the violence, as Elizabeth Dalton said, is in their own heads—and is no less real for that. They touch us by frightening us, like disembodied souls calling to us from the other world. They live through terrifying events but cannot understand them. This is what makes Oates a new element in our fiction, involuntarily disturbing.

She does not understand why she is disturbing. She takes the convulsion of society for granted, and so a writer born in 1938 regularly "returns" to the 1930s in her work. *A Garden of Earthly Delights* begins with the birth on the highway of a migrant worker's child after the truck transporting the workers has been in a collision. Obviously she is unlike many women writers in her feeling for the pressure, mass, density of violence in American experience not always shared by the professional middle class. "The greatest realities," she has said, "are physical and economic; all the subtleties of life come afterward." Yet the central thing in her work is the teeming private consciousness, a "wonderland" that to her is reality in action—but without definition and without boundary.

Joyce Oates is peculiarly and painfully open to other minds, so possessed by them that in an author's note to *them* she says of the student who became the "Maureen Wendall" of the novel, "Her various problems and complexities overwhelmed me. . . . My initial feeling about her life was, 'This must be fiction, this can't be real!' My more permanent feeling was, 'This is the only kind of fiction that is real.'" Her ability to get occupied by another consciousness makes even *them*, her best novel to date, a sometimes impenetrably voluminous history of emotions, emotions, emotions. You feel that you are turning thousands of pages, that her world is as harshly overpopulated as a sleepless mind, that you cannot make out the individual features of anyone within this clamor of everyone's existence.

This is obviously related to the ease with which Joyce Oates transfers the many situations in her head straight onto paper. I sense an extraordinary and tumultuous amount of purely mental existence locked up behind her schoolgirl's face. She once told an interviewer that she is always writing about "love . . . and it takes many different forms, many different social levels. . . . I think I write about love in an unconscious way. I look back upon the novels I've written, and I say, yes, this was my subject. But at the time I'm writing I'm not really conscious of that. I'm writing about a certain person who does this and that and comes to a certain end." She herself is the most unyielding lover in her books, as witness the force with which she follows so many people through every trace of their feeling, thinking, moving. She is obsessive in her patience with the sheer factuality of contemporary existence. This evident love for the scene we Americans make, for the incredible profusion of life in America, also troubles Joyce Carol Oates. Every writer knows himself to be a little crazy, but her feeling of her own absurdity is probably intensified by the dreamlike ease with which her works are produced. It must indeed trouble her that this looks like glibness, when in point of fact her dogged feeling that she writes out of love is based on the fact that she is utterly hypnotized, positively drugged, by other people's experiences. The social violence so marked in her work is like the sheer density of detail—this and this and this is what is happening to people. She is attached to life by well-founded apprehension that nothing lasts, nothing is safe, nothing is all around us. In *them* Maureen Wendall thinks:

> Maybe the book with her money in it, and the money so greedily saved, and the idea of the money, maybe these things weren't real either. What would happen if everything broke into pieces? It was queer how you felt, instinctively, that a certain space of time was real and not a dream, and you gave your life to it, all your energy and faith, believing it to be real. But how could you tell what would last and what wouldn't? Marriages ended. Love ended. Money could be stolen, found out and taken . . . or it might disappear by itself, like that secretary's notebook. Objects disappeared, slipped through cracks, devoured, kicked aside, knocked under the bed or into the trash, lost. Her clearest memory of the men she'd been with was their moving away from her. They were all body then, completed.

The details in Oates's fiction follow each other with a humble truthfulness that make you wonder where she is taking you, that is sometimes disorienting, for she is all attention to the unconscious reactions of her characters. She needs a lot of space, which is why her short stories tend to read like scenarios for novels. The amount of *listening* this involves is certainly singular. My deepest feeling about her is that her mind is unbelievably crowded with psychic existences, with such a mass of stories that she lives by being wholly submissive to "them." She is too attentive to their mysterious clamor to *want* to be an artist, to make the right and well-fitting structure. Much of her fiction seems written to relieve her mind of the people who haunt it, not to create something that will live.

So many inroads on the suddenly frightening American situation is indeed a problem in our fiction just now; the age of high and proud art has yielded to the climate of crisis. Joyce Oates's many stories resemble a card index of situations; they are not the deeply plotted stories that we return to as perfect little dramas; her novels, though they involve the reader through the author's intense connection with her material, tend as incident to fade out of our minds. Too much happens. Indeed, hers are altogether strange books, haunting rather than "successful," because the mind behind them is primarily concerned with a kind of Darwinian struggle for existence between minds, with the truth of some limitless human struggle. We miss the perfectly suggestive shapes that modern art and fiction have taught us to venerate. Oates is another Cassandra bewitched by her private oracle. But it is not disaster that is most on her mind; it is the recognition of each person as the center of the coming disturbance. And this disturbance, as Pascal said of his God, has its center everywhere and its circumference nowhere.

So her characters are opaque, ungiving, uncharming; they have the taciturn qualities that come with the kind of people they are—heavy, hallucinated, outside the chatty middle class. Society speaks in them, but *they* are not articulate. They do not yet feel themselves to be emancipated persons. They are caught up in the social convulsion and move unheedingly, compulsively, blindly, through the paces assigned to them by the power god.

That is exactly what Oates's work expresses just now: a sense that American life is taking some of us by the throat. "Too much" is happening; many will disappear. Above all, and most ominously, hers is a world in which our own people, and not just peasants in Vietnam, get "wasted." There is a constant sense of drift, deterioration, the end of things, that contrasts violently with the era of "high art" and the once-fond belief in immortality through art. Oates is someone plainly caught up in this "avalanche" of time.—ALFRED KAZIN, "Cassandras," *Bright Book of Life*, 1973, pp. 198–205

Works

In 1963, prospects for the future of the short story were brightened by Vanguard's willingness, perhaps eagerness, to introduce Joyce Carol Oates with fourteen short stories, *By the North Gate*. Despite the success of Philip Roth's *Goodbye, Columbus*, such collections, particularly by new writers, promise only a meagre return. But few recent first novels manifest a talent as forceful, controlled, and promising as Miss Oates's. Only four of the stories had appeared previously: "The White Mist of Winter" was included among both the *O. Henry* and the *Best American* short stories of 1963. Since many of the new stories are superior to some of the earlier ones, it is clear that Vanguard did not put together a collection on slim pretenses. One encouragement may have been the pattern of relatedness in character, theme, technique, locale, raw material detail, mood, and atmosphere which unifies the collection.

Although an aura of the late thirties and of the forties suffuses the events—that was the period of Miss Oates's childhood—a talent for objectivity sustains a distance between the author and her painfully observed raw material. In a time when many young writers greet their contemporaries on the me-rack of subjectivity, this writer utilizes the third person, central intelligence and, on occasion, the omniscient-point-of-

view technique. And although most of the stories are set in rural upstate New York near Lake Erie in fictional Eden County and a powerful sense of place is evoked, these are not regional stories. In this collection, an ability to conceptualize is in control, and a vision begins to take shape. But the farm and small town social context, and the family unit, though conceived in terms of generations coeval, are not depicted through the kind of historical continuity that is characteristic of Southern fiction. There is no history beyond the immediate family. The universal family and society of man is projected with an almost pure radiance in the violent light of a dismal rural landscape, devoid of the pastoral, observed in extremes of summer heat, autumnal decay, and winter snow.

The organization of the collection is expressive, opening and closing with stories about old men who refuse to believe at the end of life that irrational violence and hatred are dominant forces in human nature, until each is disillusioned by a direct encounter. Expressing the attitude of many Oates characters, the grandfather's son in "Swamps" whines that he is "sick of this life." But the old man tells his grandson, "You pay him no mind. This-here is a damn good world, a *god*-damned good world, it's all you got an' you better pay attention to it." In his refusal to allow a pregnant woman to commit suicide, the grandfather celebrates birth. But when the mother slays her baby and wounds the grandfather, he spends his last days whining, "They robbed me." In "By the North Gate," old Revere's affirmation of life is betrayed by unprovoked violence, also.

In each story some form of sudden, irrevocable, senseless violence focuses a crucial moment in the lives of the characters. Usually, a knife is the ritualistic, ceremonial instrument of violence. In her depiction of complex motivations toward violence, Miss Oates often subjects her main character to the revelation that men are brutal but pitiable. However, her compassion does not dim the harsh glare she casts upon the violence in human nature.

Most devastatingly affected are the sensitive female characters, possibly various masks for the author. In a world of violence and evil, these girls live on the verge of self-annihilation. Best of these stories is "Pastoral Blood." Deliberately exposing her beautiful body to violence, Grace forces male complicity in her attempted suicide. Dressed with intentional cheapness, she picks up a man, who becomes desperately concerned for her, and lures other men, creating a situation of drunken violence in which men fight over her like animals. In a resolution of ironic grace, she is returned to the family and fiancé whose blandness had defined her desire to cease "being." A convincing impression of the interior paralysis induced by the suicidal impulse is conveyed.

Using expressionistic, lyrical, and realistic techniques in three other, less successful, stories—"Images," "Sweet Love Remembered," "The Legacy"—Miss Oates discovers theme through a penetrating examination of character. The recurrent character, realizing that it is her capacity for vision rather than violence that estranges her from her family and others, sees her own responsibility and claims a disproportionate and unbearable guilt. Haunted by this vision of human separateness, she suffers the impossibility of identifying deeply with others and of achieving a reciprocal love. Although the point-of-view character, Leo, a young English instructor, is a male, "The Expense of Spirit" belongs to this group. It is as though the girl were drawn out of Eden into the intellectual reality of the university (which Miss Oates knows well), a society even more desperately devoid of love. The smug witticisms, the nauseating fun and games in which the guests at a party indulge are dehumanizing, as an innocent freshman co-ed, whose beauty attracts the violent attentions of a white man and a black man, discovers.

The violent male, sometimes a brother to the female figure, also recurs. Probably Miss Oates's most successful story is "The Fine White Mist of Winter." Driving to the sheriff's office with a captive Negro, Deputy Rafe Murray waits out a violent snowstorm in a lonely filling station. There he encounters two Negroes who talk in sly riddles about him and his captive. Convinced that the Negroes intend to free the prisoner, and sensitive of his image as a young, self-confident deputy, Rafe experiences a fear possibly greater than that which the fugitive feels. But at the height of the tension, the two Negroes reveal that it has all been a joke to win the sheriff's favor. As though it were inconceivable that Negroes would conspire to free one of their own, they had assumed that Rafe caught on to the mockery immediately. Ironically, they insist that this proud Negro be made to endure the same humiliations and torture that they, literally, have suffered. Isolated from the world, and from the others, in the fine white mist of winter, Rafe witnesses the spectacle of degraded men divesting themselves of their humanity, and he is profoundly changed. Few characters in a short story have had their very beings so thoroughly shocked by a single, double-edged, experience.

"In the Old World," a somewhat similar story, is stunningly ironic and perhaps more complex, though not quite as fascinating. Swan, a rural white boy, has cut a Negro boy's eye out with a knife. An innate sense of decency compels him to seek an explanation and a punishment for his crime. His father having failed him, he goes to the jail in town where he encounters an even grayer vagueness. The development is handled with remarkable restraint and an expressive ambiguity.

Three stories of imminent death, "Boys at a Picnic," "An Encounter with the Blind," and "The Edge of the World" project male violence. In the best of these, "The Edge of the World," Shell, a young motorcyclist, ceremoniously and fearfully enters a test of courage, to which Jan, an elderly ex-racer, has challenged him. Ignorant of the nature of the test as the story ends, Shell does feel clearly a sudden isolation from his comrades and a rigid reluctance to die. The superbly observed details of the junkyard create an atomosphere in which the reader feels an unbearable sense of impending ritualistic death.

In a Kafka-esque manner, "The Census Taker" provides another haunting impression of the isolation that exists among the people of Eden County. "Ceremonies," one of the best stories, emphasizes the function of ritual, convention, and ceremony in Miss Oates's stories. A funeral ceremony occasions a communal "we" point of view in the recounting of a local legend. The wildly beautiful and willful Elizabeth is one of the author's several memorable characters.

In *By the North Gate*, she showed that she has a remarkable facility for embodying in her characters and developing in their predicaments her ironic themes. Most striking was her ability to convey a sense of the very substance of the reality she perceives. But because she had not yet achieved a style as commanding as her themes and raw material, I was perplexed by her sometimes serious immaturity. While she usually avoided rhetorical excess and strove for precision and accuracy, passages erupted that were contrived, awkward, and overblown.—DAVID MADDEN, "The Violent World of Joyce Carol Oates," *The Poetic Image in 6 Genres*, 1969, pp. 27–31

In the last several years, Joyce Carol Oates has made a great impression. She has received many awards, including a Guggenheim Fellowship, a number of short-story prizes, and now the National Book Award for fiction. And indeed, her achievements are impressive. At the age of thirty-two Miss Oates has published six books—four novels and two volumes of stories; her latest novel, *them*, is being hailed as a masterpiece. All of her books treat insanity, sexual obsession, and violent death. We admire writers who deal with violence, perhaps because they attempt to confront the chaos that surrounds us and yet defies our comprehension—or perhaps because they have the courage to pursue their own imaginings to ultimate conclusions.

Miss Oates's work presents a mixture of two styles—one of them a large, earnest naturalism from which come detailed scenes of rural and urban desolation, the other a tendency to push beyond these life scenes toward transcendent meaning, an urge that expresses itself in the eruption of hallucinatory violence. In the first collection of stories, *By the North Gate* (1963), an old man delivers the baby of a wild, crazy slut and then is hit over the head and left for dead by the girl, who also drowns her child. In another story, another old man finds the dead body of his faithful dog with its belly slashed open by boys for a joke. In a third, three teenage boys on a killing spree rob and strike a girl with a heart condition, frightening her to death. And there are two stories of humiliation and horror inflicted upon Negroes.

The second collection, *Upon the Sweeping Floor* (1966), raises the ante even higher. In seven of the eleven stories there is at least one death, and in an eighth someone is hit by a car. A story called "What Death with Love Should Have to Do" is rather typical of the subjects the writer favors: there a girl tries to produce a miscarriage by riding on the back of her boyfriend's motorcycle in a race and bleeds to death. This plot also crystallizes the motif of sex and death, a sort of *lumpen liebestod*, that reappears in the novels.

There is an authentic feeling in these stories for the physical ambience of poverty, for the grease stains, the stale smells, the small pathetic decorative objects of plastic. One atmosphere that is particularly well evoked is the sleazy, dangerous world of small-town, lower-class teenagers that seem always hovering on the edge of violence. What seems less authentic, however, is the violence itself, and the rather programmatic way it is used to resolve every situation. In style, the stories are quite literary, with a kind of writers-workshop correctness of structure and development that makes the violence seem all the more deliberate and unreal, as though it derived from literary models rather than from experience. In the subject matter and the oppressive air that hangs over it there are intimations of Steinbeck and the early Faulkner; there is also an attempt to exploit a residual Catholicism to give violence a religious meaning, suggesting the influence of Flannery O'Connor. The allusions to the Chruch remain merely decorative, however; there is no genuine religious vision here as there is in O'Connor.

Miss Oates's first novel, *With Shuddering Fall* (1964), has the authentically bleak setting of the stories, and the same obsession with an idealized and literary violence. Karen, a beautiful seventeen-year-old girl, runs away from her respectable Catholic family with a racing driver, a brutal demon-lover type who hits her father on the head with a rifle butt, takes Karen's virginity in some unspecified but degrading way, later has intercourse with her so violently that she has a miscarriage, and finally, driven wild by their hopeless passion, smashes his car into a wall. Karen then runs bleeding into the street, where a race riot touched off by her lover's death is in progress. After a few months in a mental hospital, Karen is received back into her family; the book ends with Karen at Mass, praying for forgiveness. The rather correct structure of the stories gives way here, and through the transparent implausibility of the plot there looms a sado-masochistic fantasy which endows the heroine with tremendous power.

The figure of the girl whose beauty and sensuality bring about the eruption of madness and violence appears again in A *Garden of Earthly Delights* (1966). The heroine, Clara Walpole, the child of migrant farm workers, runs away from her family with a man who gets her pregnant and then abandons her. She becomes the mistress and finally the wife of a wealthy older man, and her son by her first lover grows up in this man's house, through Clara's manipulation gradually displacing his stepbrothers. At last, just as the son is on the point of realizing Clara's dreams by taking over his stepfather's business, in a frenzy of guilt and self-hatred he shoots the old man and himself. Clara, like Karen, winds up in a mental hospital. Of all Joyce Carol Oates's books, this is probably the best. The early part, dealing with the brutal and pitiful lives of the migrant workers, is convincing and often moving. The novel does suffer, however, from the banality of its conception; the story of Clara's rise and fall recalls too many popular novels and movies about the girl who schemes her way to the top and is then struck by retribution.

Expensive People (1968), which appeared two years after A *Garden of Earthly Delights*, extrapolates the mother-son theme from the earlier novel and transposes it to a new setting: the ambitious mother and the tormented son are now in sterile, affluent suburbia. Written in the first person by the son after he has murdered his mother, the novel tries unsuccessfully for an effect of black humor and biting satire. The mother is named Nada, the boy's elegant private school is Johns Behemoth, and the parents have friends called Maxwell Voyd, Harrison Vemeer, etc. The other attempts at satiric exaggeration are similarly heavy-handed and without humor. The writer of this sort of thing must have a certain degree of sophisticated complicity with the milieu he is satirizing; Joyce Carol Oates is simply too heavy and earnest a writer to carry it off. The book provides an experience rather like seeing the side of a barn hit over and over again with a baseball bat.

The new novel, *them*, is a larger, richer, and more carefully conceived work, covering the lives of two generations of a Detroit slum family and derived from the history of a student in an English class taught by the author at the University of Detroit, a girl called Maureen Wendall in the novel. The story begins in the depression with Loretta, Maureen's mother, but it is principally concerned with two of her children, Jules and Maureen, who grow up in the chaos of Loretta's life in Detroit. At sixteen Maureen begins prostituting herself and is found out by her stepfather, who beats her severely. After the beating Maureen withdraws into a catatonic state, from which she emerges after more than a year, to return to school, to take a course from Joyce Carol Oates, and, ultimately, through her strange helplessness and vacancy, to seduce a married professor into leaving his wife for her. Her brother, Jules, has many bizarre and violent adventures, the strangest of them his obsessive affair with a girl named Nadine, who shoots him in the chest, nearly killing him. At the end of the novel, Jules gets caught up in the Detroit riots and kills a policeman.

In the preface, the author says that she became fascinated with the Wendalls "because their world was so remote from me." Yet although the urban setting of *them* is new, its themes are familiar from Joyce Carol Oates's earlier work. In *them* the girl who uses her sexuality to destroy and is in turn destroyed is

split into two characters: Maureen, the passive victim who invites violation, and Nadine, her cold, sadistic counterpart. Like Karen and Clara in the earlier novels, Maureen becomes mentally ill. Even the race riot at the end of the book recalls the first novel.

But *them* is much richer in disaster than anything else the author has written. The calamities suffered by Maureen and Jules are only slightly more horrible than the regular tenor of their family's existence—a daily round of illness and death, quarrels, beatings, drunkenness, arrests, madness, and murder. The author writes in the preface: "Nothing in the novel has been exaggerated in order to increase the possibility of drama— indeed, the various sordid and shocking events of slum life, detailed in other naturalistic works, have been understated here, mainly because of my fear that too much reality would become unbearable." The problem, however, is rather the reverse: nothing even threatens to become unbearable. The dosage of violence is so high and so regular that the reader becomes immune to it, and none of it seems to matter much.

One reason for the oddly bland effect of all the horror is the lack of structure and internal impetus in the narrative. Events do not build toward a climax, or accumulate tension and meaning, or illuminate each other, but seem simply to happen in the random and insignificant way of real life. There is no particular reason why Maureen and her sister Betty should kick their grandmother down the porch stairs before Maureen's stepfather beats her up, or after Jules gets cracked over the head by a policeman's gun butt. It could just as easily have been the other way around, and the reader comes to feel rather lost in a succession of lurid and dreary events that might have come from the pages of the *Daily News*.

Moreover, the style reflects a certain attitude toward the characters that deprives their misfortunes of context and significance. About her father, Maureen's and Jules's grand- father, Loretta thinks, "He had made thousands of dollars in a single month with his construction crew and then lost it all in a way Loretta could never figure out and didn't care much about—because to her and to the other women in the family it was lost and that was that—an incontestable and somehow respectable fact!" And later, "Loretta's father kept drinking and finally he was a kind of aged youngish man of the type Loretta often saw on Sunday mornings, sleeping in the doorways of churches or closed shops. That was that. A change, a different man. A new man." The assumption here is that people like "them," the Wendalls of the world, do not respond to misfortune as you or I or the author would, that it is as natural to them as the air they breathe. The style, with its rather thin, flat, "that was that" quality, is an attempt to avoid imposing on the character an alien sensibility, a capacity for grief or indignation she would not possess. Yet the result is only that things happen, and it is hard to care much about the people they happen to. ⟨. . .⟩

The reader is told that the author did a great deal of research for this novel, and that it is based mainly on the recollections of the real Maureen Wendall. The book even contains two letters beginning "Dear Miss Oates" and signed "Maureen Wendall." There is a lot of documentation of the day-to-day life of a lower-class family: jobs, houses, schools, conversations, clothes, hairdos. It all has some interest—we like knowing about other people's lives; but ultimately, like much naturalistic detail, it seems to pile up in excess of the power of the novel's conception to unify and animate it. The descriptions of Jules's day at the parochial school or of Maureen getting her hair set with rollers and spray just lie there inertly, slices of life, with the tedious and undifferentiated quality of our own least significant daily experience.

"What is form?" Maureen asks in a letter. "Why is it better than the way life happens, by itself?" The order of this novel is supposedly that of Maureen's story, of the way life happens by itself to people like "them." The author writes in the preface, "This is the only kind of fiction that is real." And indeed, at the end the characters do emerge into the reality of recent history, to take their places before the television cameras. But it is just at this point that the novel is at its most literary, that we become most aware of an author manipulating the material through style, trying to make of the facts of these people's lives a metaphor for her own vision of experience. Just before he kills the policeman, Jules is described riding through the burning streets of Detroit with a gun in his hands:

Jules felt blood running down his face. Blood. He thought of blood. He thought of two girls in his childhood, twins, who had been stabbed to death along a city block, one of them struck down in front of her house and the other chased and stabbed so that blood ran in thin streams along the sidewalk, and the next morning everyone had come out to look at the blood . . . the Hecht twins . . . blood. Jules's own blood, pounding in his ears. In the frenzied pounding of his blood he felt something heavy emerging, a solid, violent certainty. . . .

The theme of blood is established by the obtrusive device of the flashback to childhood, and sustained by insistent repetition. The reader feels a point being made about the steady violence of American life, and the point plainly comes from the author, not from Jules. Beneath this didactic surface, there is no identification with Jules, no deeply felt experience, no real pity or terror.

It is hard to know what the author means when she says, "This is the only kind of fiction that is real." *them* is a novel; its materials come from life, but they have been reworked by the mind of the author until they resemble her other books as much as their real life source. Even the letters from Maureen have plainly been edited or rewritten (or else she did not deserve that F she claims the author gave her). The failures of the novel are failures of literary intelligence, of structure and style. And as in much of Joyce Carol Oates's other work, the violence is mainly violence in the head.—ELIZABETH DALTON, "Violence in the Head," *Cmty*, June 1970, pp. 75–77

Wonderland comes close to fulfilling what Oates has called her "laughably Balzacian ambition to get the whole world into a book." Paradoxically, it may also seem her least "realistic" novel, because its perspective is largely that of characters who, in a more sophisticated way than any in the earlier works, substitute self-created hermetic worlds for formless, accident-prone reality. Doctors and scientists, they are too "civilized" to indulge in the violence of a Shar, too strong-willed to lapse into the somnolence of a Howard Wendall, too ambitious to settle for those "tidy rooms in Bedlam" furnished by a Clara or Maureen. Yet these very qualities give birth to wonderlands more remote from mundane reality than anything their predecessors could conceive, to hospitals and laboratories where human personality can be scientifically controlled.

The novel begins in familiar Oatesean fashion: during the thirties, in a town ominously named Yewville, with a violent response to biological accident. Jesse Harte's father, maddened by his wife's latest pregnancy, slaughters the entire family except Jesse, who escapes. Bereft of parents, and thereafter of a grandfather who rejects him, Jesse feels that he no longer exists, that he has been excluded from the human family and

denied the past upon which identity depends. To remain sane he must repress the image of the slaughter and renounce everything "dragging Jesse back to Jesse's . . . childhood," including the self his father had tried to murder, his grandfather repudiated. He must find new parents, a new home, a new self. That Oates considers this to be figuratively true of all young Americans is implied by the title of the first book: "Variations on an American Hymn"; but in Jesse's case the process of "inventing himself" continues beyond boyhood.

After Dr. Pedersen adopts him, Jesse establishes a pattern he will follow from then on. Modeling himself on a surrogate father, he seeks his identity within a family. *"Let me be like them, let them love me, let everybody know that I am one of them,"* he prays, so that he can know "precisely who he was." Like them, he voraciously consumes food and information as urged by the Doctor, who thinks to control everything and everyone by engorging them. Pedersen's other children defeat him by retreating into their own wonderlands, Hilda's built with mathematical, Frederick's with musical symbols, while his wife periodically escapes into disorderly drunkenness. Hence, Pedersen's hopes focus on Jesse, whom he tries to mold into the " 'complete form of the self I have imagined for him.' " But in spite of the boy's willingness to be formed, his compassion for Mrs. Pedersen leads him inadvertently to oppose her husband, to be repudiated, and to be told once again that he does "not exist."

Pedersen continues to exist for Jesse, however. Although he changes his name for the second time, this time to Vogel, Jesse retains his stepfather's ideals. He too becomes a doctor. Believing that man's fate is ultimate perfection, he too wants to " 'organize the future' " not only for himself, his family, and his patients but even to the extent of saving " 'everyone from dying.' " Dr. Perrault is simply a less Dickensian Pedersen, and by imitating him, Jesse turns himself into a " 'copy of a copy of a human being.' " A machine operating on patients whom he views as machines, Perrault considers the distressingly unstable human personality an enemy, and while insisting that one person cannot own another, his actions reflect the contrary assumption. Science in general and Perrault's aims in particular appeal to Jesse for obvious reasons. "Isn't the great lesson of science *control*," he thinks. "*Control*. That was all he wanted."

What distinguishes Jesse from his surrogate fathers is that he seems less concerned with control of others than with control of himself, less intent on ridding others of personality than on destroying his own. He "did not want a personality," because personality is based on memory and Jesse's memory is full of monsters too horrible to contemplate. Now even as a scientist, Jesse suspects that the past is ineradicable, arguing in a medical journal that earliest memories are most staunchly retained and collecting news clippings asociated with his own buried life. Still, he tries to believe that he need remember only "as far back as he wanted to remember—that is, as far back as he had been Jesse Vogel"—thereby purging himself of a personality he dreads. In performing brain surgery, he is then vicariously trying to remove the "poisonous little beads" from his own head. The result is not health but fragmentation.

Because salvation as Jesse conceives it also demands freedom from emotional involvement, he withdraws into the laboratory, the operating room, the study, where he can disregard his patients' "personal history" and love them only in the abstract. Trick Monk is quite correct in saying that Jesse " 'aspires to a condition of personal bloodlessness.' " Monk's friendship must be abjured, in fact, not only because he would emotionally involve himself with Jesse but because he is a " 'kind of equivalent' " of the "other Jesses . . . sinister and unkillable" who must be kept buried. A doctor turned poet, Monk addresses his *Poems without People* to Jesse, who, in his way, also constructs "poems" devoid of disturbing human presences. The difference between them is that Monk knows his wonderland is imaginary and affirms personalities by pretending to exclude them.

Oates has said that "without personality there cannot be art," for without it we cannot imagine the existence of others or create the metaphors needed to understand ourselves. Jesse's memory, one of the bases of personality, is too mutilated even to understand literary plot, the "necessary pattern . . . that demanded completion." He believes that all stories, like his own life, are "fragments from shattered wholes" and not, in any case, "'believable' in the way his medical texts were believable." Thus he would like to replace "trivial human language," another basis of personality, with the language of the surgeon's hands, the psyche, container of all time, with the "inviolable . . . timelessness" of the operating room. Neither replacement is possible. Like Maureen (Wendall in *them*), the other Jesse struggles to find the "exact words that would explain his life" and waits "for someone else—a woman, perhaps—to draw these sacred words out of him, to . . . redeem him as Jesse."

His wife cannot help him. Recognizing that Jesse is a "'jumble of men'" who, seeking integration, wants to *be* his wife and children, she also realizes that her own identity is too shaky, her own head too filled with unformed words to elicit any from him. The only woman who might have succeeded is Reva. As her name implies, she is more dream than reality, more *anima* than a simple, separate person. This is why Jesse thinks he has known her before, why her name is "made up," and why he feels that by possessing her he would "penetrate . . . all parts of himself." Reva herself believes that together they could complete a plot and bring about a new start. But Jesse cannot afford union with Reva, for that would mean acknowledging Jesse Harte and "slaughtering" his family. Instead, he mutilates himself once again. It is indeed "The Finite Passing of an Infinite Passion": the sacrifice of an integrated passional self to the gods of his domestic and scientific wonderlands.

Both fail him. He gives a scientific name to a patient's uncontrollable mental disorder but senses that it should be called *The Tragedy of Joseph Ross.* After his daughters are born, he thinks that finally "his life was in his control" but soon learns that he can control neither his children nor his emotions toward them. Shelley disobeys his command, an echo of Dr. Pedersen's, that she "'speak only in complete sentences'" and is frightened by *Alice in Wonderland* because she sees herself diminished and dragged through the air by her father. The Kennedy assassination disturbs them both—Jesse because it was a death he could not prevent, Shelley because her father cannot alleviate her terror. Moreover, when she runs from home, she not only repeats Mrs. Pedersen's flight but seeks in drugs what the latter sought in alcohol, Jesse in his work: darkness without memory, the destruction of personality.

Jesse is condemned to relive his past in another way. He is now the pursuer rather than the pursued, acting out the role of Pedersen in trying to repossess the rebellious object of his possession and swearing that "'Nobody is going to die tonight.'" To Noel, her presumed saviour, Shelley even echoes Mrs. Pedersen's words to Jesse—"'he gets into my head'"— and is similarly reclaimed by her would-be owner. Actually, she had achieved no more freedom than the Doctor's wife. Haunted by thoughts of her father, she needs Noel as Mrs. Pedersen needed Jesse. In treating Shelley as his property, Noel

is a surrogate father; in proclaiming that passion is fate, he is the other Jesse. The combination is irresistible to Shelley, representative of a "Dreaming America" desiring both autonomy and communion, self-assertion and loss of self, the restoration of the past and freedom from it.

The period when Jesse was a member of a family has been temporarily recaptured, but so has the past he hoped to escape. Shelley has in her way dissolved the family; Jesse is now tempted to repeat his father's violence by slaughtering his wife, his children, humanity itself as exemplified by a youthful Chicago mob. Hating its "formlessness," he wants to "destroy them all. . . . So much garbage in the world," he thinks, "And most of it human!" Although he resists that temptation, the ending to the novel is hardly happy. Jesse has not only failed to "catch up with his own consciousness"; he has failed to discover the wonderland of controlled order that he has envisioned for so long. Like Oates's other novels, *Wonderland* begins in violence and ends not with the restoration of order characteristic of tragedy but with the exhaustion born of defeat. In her world, the only order is that of art, the only one in control the artist herself.—ROBERT H. FOSSUM, "Only Control: The Novels of Joyce Carol Oates," *SN*, Summer 1975, pp. 293–97

Bellefleur is the most ambitious book to come so far from that alarming phenomenon Joyce Carol Oates. However one may carp, the novel is proof, if any seems needed, that she is one of the great writers of our time. *Bellefleur* is a symbolic summation of all this novelist has been doing for 20-some years, a magnificent piece of daring, a tour de force of imagination and intellect.

In *Bellefleur* Miss Oates makes a heroic attempt to transmute the almost inherently goofy tradition of the gothic (ghosts, shape-shifters, vampires and all that) into serious art. If any writer can bring it off (some will claim it's already been done), Joyce Carol Oates seems the writer to do it. One thinks of the astonishing, utterly convincing scene in her novel *The Assassins* where Stephen Petrie, a child sitting at his desk in school, has his terrifying out-of-the-body experience, and the scenes in which Hugh, his artist brother, has his brushes with the Angel of Death; one thinks of the psychic business in *Childwold*, the ominous rappings of tyrannical spirit in *Wonderland*, the horror-ridden, love-redeemed world of William James and his circle in *Night-side*; above all one thinks of *Son of the Morning*, Miss Oates's magnificently convincing study of a snake-handler and miracle-worker, Nathan Vickery.

What we learn, reading *Bellefleur*, is that Joyce Carol Oates is essentially a realist. She can write persuasively of out-of-the-body experiences because she believes in them. But she does not really believe in a brutal half-wit boy who can turn into a dog, a man who is really a bear, vampires or mountain gnomes. (In one scene members of the Bellefleur family come across some gnomes escaped from Washington Irving, thunderously bowling on a mountain meadow. One of the gnomes gets captured and, though his whole race is inexplicably mean, turns into a devoted servant of the novel's heroine, Leah. Why? Who knows? The world is mysterious.)

Miss Oates believes in these legendary characters only as symbols; and the problem is that they are not symbols of the same class as those she has been using for years, the symbols provided by the world as it is when it is viewed (as Miss Oates always views it) as a Christian Platonist's "vast array of emblems." The only really frightening scenes in *Bellefleur* deal with real-world atrocities—a boy's stoning of another boy, for instance, or the murder of a family by a bunch of drunken thugs—and these scenes in fact come nowhere near the horror of scenes in earlier novels by Miss Oates, such as the murder of Yvonne in *The Assassins*. What drives Miss Oates's fiction is her phobias: that is, her fear that normal life may suddenly turn monstrous. Abandoning verisimilitude for a different mode (the willing suspension of disbelief), she loses her ability to startle us with sudden nightmare.

Still, the tale is sometimes thrilling. The opening chapter (strongly recalling that wonderful collection of ghost stories, *Night-side*) has prowling spirits, a weird storm, a glorious scary castle in the Adirondacks, all presented in an absolutely masterly, chilling style; but the chapter's crowning moment comes when a frightening, vicious, rat-like thing, which none of the frightened occupants can identify, is allowed out of the rain (screaming) into the house and, when seen in the morning, turns out to be a mysteriously beautiful cat. The transformation startles us, catches us completely by surprise (classic Oates), fills us with awe and vague dread, prompting the question we so often ask when reading her: *What in heaven's name is the universe up to now?*

I cannot summarize the plot of *Bellefleur*; for one thing, it's too complex—an awesome construction, in itself a work of genius—and for another, plot surprises are part of the novel's glory. Suffice it to say that this is the saga of the weird, sometimes immensely rich Bellefleur family over several generations, a story focused mainly on Gideon Bellefleur and his power-mad, somewhat psychic, very beautiful wife Leah, their three children (one of them extremely psychic) and the servants and relatives, living and dead, who inhabit the castle and its environs. It's a story of the world's changeableness, of time and eternity, space and soul, pride and physicality versus love.

Much as one admires the ambition of *Bellefleur*, the novel is slightly marred by it: It too noticeably labors after greatness. The book has most of the familiar Oates weaknesses: the panting, melodramatic style she too often allows herself; the heavy, heavy symbolism; and occasional esthetic miscalculations that perhaps come from thinking too subtly, forgetting that first of all a story must be a completely persuasive lie. In *Bellefleur*, the artifice undermines emotional power, makes the book cartoonish. ⟨. . .⟩

Whatever its faults, *Bellefleur* is simply brilliant. What do we ask of a book except that it be wonderful to read? An interesting story with profound implications? The whole religious-philosophical view of Joyce Carol Oates is here cleanly and dramatically stated. She has been saying for years, in book after book (stories, poems, a play and literary criticism) that the world is Platonic. We are the expression of one life force, but once individuated we no longer know it, so that we recoil in horror from the expression of the same force in other living beings. "Don't *touch* me," Gideon Bellefleur keeps saying, as Yvonne Petrie said in *The Assassins*, Laney said in *Childwold* and a host of other characters said elsewhere. Blinded to our oneness, we all become assassins, vampires, ghosts. We are all unreflectable nonimages in mirrors, creatures of time, and time is an illusion; we are all sexual maniacs, lovers engaged in a violent struggle to become totally one with those we love (copulation and murder are all but indistinguishable); we are all crazily in love with the past—first our own Edenic childhood, second the whole past of the world. So Leah, in *Bellefleur*, strives to reconquer the whole immense original Bellefleur estate—and ends up dead, not even buried, burnt up with the house after the plane crash.

Bellefleur is a medieval allegory of *caritas versus cupiditatem*, love and selflessness versus pride and selfishness. The central symbol of the novel is change, baffling complexity, mystery. One character makes "crazy quilts" in which only she can see the pattern. Another has been trying all his life to map the Bellefleur holdings, but everything keeps changing—rivers change their courses, mountains shrink. Time is crazy. In fact what is known in Shakespeare criticism as "sliding time" becomes a calculated madness in *Bellefleur*. Chapters leap backward and forward through the years—and that's the least of it. Our main dramatic focus, though she's a minor character, is the psychic child Germaine Bellefleur, whom we follow from birth to the age of 4. But *in the same time* her father passes through 20 or 30 years, and the setting passes through something like a thousand years, with hints of a time-span even greater. People regularly get taller or shorter, depending on . . . whatever. The holy mountain in the Adirondacks to which Jedediah goes to find God is at first 10,000 feet high but by the end of the novel only 3,000 feet high.

Joyce Carol Oates has always been, for those who look closely, a religious novelist, but this is the most openly religious of her books—not that she argues any one sectarian point of view. Here as in several of her earlier works the Angel of Death is an important figure, but here for the first time the Angel of Life (not simply resignation) is the winner. In the novel's final chapters Gideon Bellefleur turns his back on all he has been since birth, a sensualist; starves himself until we see him as a death figure; finally becomes his family's Angel of Death.

But there's one further chapter, set far in the past, entitled "The Angel." Whereas Gideon's flight and kamikaze self-destruction as he crashes his plane into his ancestral home are presented in mystical metaphors (the rise into spiritual air, and so on), the final chapter is utterly physical. An Indian boy, a friend of the family, comes to Jedediah on his mountain and tells him to return to the world. With no belief in God and no interest in the worldly, Jedediah returns to the woman he once loved and becomes the father of those who will figure in this novel, becomes the instrument of the blind life force that, accidentally, indifferently, makes everything of value, makes everything beautiful by the simple virtue of its momentary existence. Thanks to Jedediah, God goes on senselessly humming, discovering Himself. That is, in Miss Oates's version, the reason we have to live and the reason life, however dangerous, can be a joy, once we understand our situation: We are God's body.

Joyce Carol Oates is a "popular" novelist because her stories are suspenseful (and the suspense is never fake; the horror will really come, as well as, sometimes, the triumph), because her sex scenes are steamy and because when she describes a place you think you're there. Pseudo-intellectuals seem to hate that popularity and complain, besides, that she "writes too much." (For pseudo-intellectuals there are always too many books.) To real intellectuals Miss Oates's work tends to be appealing, partly because her vision is huge, well-informed and sound, and partly because they too like suspense, brilliant descriptions and sex. Though *Bellefleur* is not her best book, in my opinion it's a wonderful book all the same. By one two-page thunderstorm she makes the rest of us novelists wonder why we left the farm. How strange the play of light and shadow in her graveyards! How splendid the Bellefleurs' decaying mansion! How convincing and individual the characters are—and so many of them! In one psychic moment, when the not-yet-2-year-old Germaine cries "Bird—bird—bird!" and points at the window a moment before a bird crashes into it, breaking its neck, we're forced to ask again how anyone can possibly write such books, such absolutely convincing scenes, rousing in us, again and again, the familiar Oates effect, the point of all her art: joyful terror gradually ebbing toward wonder.—JOHN GARDNER, "The Strange Real World," *NYTBR*, July 20, 1980, pp. 1, 21

JOANNNE V. CREIGHTON
From "Joyce Carol Oates's Craftsmanship in *The Wheel of Love*"

Studies in Short Fiction, Fall 1978, pp. 375–84

The *Wheel of Love* is most frequently mentioned as Joyce Carol Oates's best short story collection; indeed, this volume, which includes many prize-winners, contains some extremely fine stories. It also contains some less successful ones, and as such it offers the opportunity to examine the artistic vicissitudes of this prolific and versatile writer. The volume, like so many of Oates's collections, has thematic unity: focusing exclusively on the emotional complexity of human relationships, the collection offers a rich—if distressing—view of the mysterious, volatile, and disorienting power of love. But the very obsessiveness of this thematic emphasis may contribute to the reader's disaffection with Oates. The reader is overcome with fatigue, bombarded as he is with repeated instances of unrelieved emotional misery. Moreover, he is likely to lose sight of the well-realized story in the chaff of the less luminous ones.

In this collection sexual love is invariably a compulsive, essentially joyless, terrifying, painful and unwelcome experience. Commonly, Oates depicts a character seeking release from the "strain and risk"[1] of love. The woman of "Unmailed, Unwritten Letters" imagines her lover's violent death and listlessly attempts to effect her own by pressing her wrist against the jagged and rusty edge of a tin can. "I Was in Love" begins: "I was in love with a man I couldn't marry, so one of us had to die—I lay awake, my eyes twitching in the dark, trying to understand which one of us should die" (p. 337). Nadia of "Wheel of Love" commits suicide, trapped in the claustrophobia of her husband's love. Nina of "The Heavy Sorrow of the Body" finds an equally extreme expedient: she takes on the identity of a male, since "men had a kind of anonymity she desired; they were negations most of them. . . . She wanted to draw into herself the terrible experiences of her life—the violence of her love for men, the violence of her fear of them—and, in herself, bring them to nothing" (p. 290). The woman of "I Was in Love" articulates the disorienting power of love: "Before falling in love, I was defined. Now I am undefined, weeds are growing between my ribs" (p. 341), while the woman of "Unmailed, Unwritten Letters" underscores the pain of lovemaking: "A woman in the act of love feels no joy but only terror, a parody of labor, giving birth. Torture. Heartbeat racing at 160, 180 beats a minute, where is the joy in this, what is this deception, this joke" (pp. 63–64).

But these women, caught in the maelstrom of love, are at least capable of feeling. *The Wheel of Love* is populated with innumerable men and women who have sealed themselves off from physical and emotional experience. Oates often employs clerics such as Sister Irene of "In the Region of Ice" and Father Rollins of "Shame" to depict the emotional sterility that sometimes accompanies the protective sanctuary of the celibate life. Sister Irene, safe behind her double screen of nun and professor, is terrified by the personal appeal made to her by a brilliant, disturbed student, and her retreat from such involvement contributes to his decision to commit suicide. Father Rollins can respond to the frankness of the aggrieved widow of a friend only with hollow religious platitudes. Other men and women of the volume do not need the garb of the religious life to exclude physicality from life. For example, Pauline of "Bodies," a talented sculptress interested only in "heads," is coolly aloof from "bodies," from the physical and emotional bonds among people, until an emotionally disturbed young man forces her into a relationship by the violent expedient of slashing his throat before her on the street.

Sometimes the fragile shell of immunity from emotional relationships is in danger of cracking. Pauline becomes crazed after the young man attempts suicide in front of her and thinks that the blood which splashes on her causes a grotesque pregnancy. But many of the characters face no dramatic crisis, but rather the quietly suppressed hysteria of unrelieved selflessness. These emotionally sterile individuals sometimes imitate the seeming normality of others. Dorie, the impressionable young college girl of "Accomplished Desires," infatuated with her professor, his wife, and their life, succeeds in literally moving in and supplanting the wife after she conveniently commits suicide, but despite her "accomplished desires" Dorie is unable to overcome her daydreaming vacuousness: "she was this girl sitting at a battered desk in someone's attic, and no one else, no other person . . . she was herself and that was a fact, a final fact she would never overcome" (p. 130). Sissie of "Four Summers" has so memorized an identity that she is safe in her anonymous sameness: "I am pretty, but my secret is that I am pretty like everyone is. My husband loves me for this but doesn't know it. I have a pink mouth and plucked darkened eyebrows and soft bangs over my forehead; I know everything, I have no need to learn from anyone else now. I am one of those girls younger girls study closely, to learn from" (p. 198). But like Dorie's, Sissie's selflessness is felt despite the success of her assumed identity: "I let my hand fall onto my stomach to remind myself that I am in love: with this baby, with Jessie, with everything. I am in love with our house and our life and the future and even this moment—right now—that I am struggling to live through" (p. 201). David of "Convalescing," anxious to be judged normal, tries to anticipate the expected responses to a public opinion questionnaire and clings to his vivacious wife for the strength and identity he personally lacks.

Clearly, most characters in this volume are too weak to stand the "strain and risk" of love, and even if they can, the momentary highs of sexual ecstasy or felt love are inevitably accompanied by prolonged lows. Either the loved one dies ("The Wheel of Love," "What Is the Connection Between Man and Woman?") and the bereaved husband or wife is inconsolable in his grief, or the lovers seek death to be relieved from the burden and pain of powerful feelings ("Unmailed, Unwritten Letters," "I Was in Love"), or the lovers are punished for their happiness by the resentment of others (the woman's son attempts death in "I Was in Love" after her rendezvous with her lover; the husband in "Convalescing" is involved in a serious auto accident after hearing of his wife's affair). Furthermore, a number of Oatesian characters are so entangled in filial relationships that they are incapable of healthy love relationships outside of the family. Often a child is inhibited by the strength and vibrancy of the parents. The problems of Marion of "You" are compounded by the fact that she shares the meager love, attention and cast-off boyfriends of her voluptuous movie-star mother with another slender twin. Similarly, the acne-faced adolescent of "Boy and Girl" is diminished by his father's success and good looks and by his mother's disappointment in him, a mother "who had been destined for a life of luncheons and dinners and the fulfillment of a good marriage and the enjoyment of a successful son" (p. 259). Sometimes the child is alienated by the world of his parents as is the girl of "How I Contemplated the World from the Detroit House of Correction"; but despite her rebellion, which includes stealing and living with a junkie, she is, in the end, overpowered by her influential, affluent parents and returned to the sterile sanctuary of their world. Several of the characters are locked into a role of responsibility for an aged parent ("The Assailant," "Demons," "Matter and Energy"), to be freed only when a lover acts out a Freudian drama and literally assaults the tyrannizing father, as do the lovers in both "The Assailant" and "Demons."

Feeling themselves to be unworthy of love or unable to risk it, or unable to experience it, or unhappy within it, jointly the characters of the collection offer a dismal view of the human being's incapacity to enjoy a healthy and wholesome emotional life. The pervasive low resiliency of the characters may fatigue and depress the reader as well; and from the volume as a whole, one may be left with an overwhelming sense of pessimism about the potentiality for fulfilling human relationships. Indeed, I think readers are put off by what strikes them at first reading as a repetitive sameness; and they are less disposed to observe the unique craftsmanship of the individual stories and the richness and complexity with which similar themes are treated in the better stories. In other words, the thematic unity of the volume invites a faulty generalization which obscures rather than enhances the artistry of the separate stories. Oates is not writing about Human Nature; she is rather fashioning incidents which depict the problems and limitations of individual human beings. She excels in her ability to individuate and to specify; she is less successful when she attempts to draw generalized human types and situations.

The least successful kind of story, in my opinion, is usually unrelieved interior monologue, often in first person, in which an emotionally distraught person dwells obsessively upon his unhappiness. Although the technique is innovative, the cleverness of conception does not compensate for the monotony of content. One such story, a favorite of Oates herself, is "Unmailed, Unwritten Letters." In this story a young woman caught miserably in the throes of love composes letters to her lover, his child, her husband, and her parents as a kind of self-therapy to cope with feelings that cannot be openly expressed to these people. The device of such "unmailed, unwritten letters" serves to introduce specific information into the story—such as the attempts of her lover's ten-year-old daughter to upset her with gifts signed with fictitious names—and to recapitulate pertinent background about her marriage and her affair, while it simultaneously records the immediate responses of the woman to the people and events which shape her life. Moreover, the final eight pages of the story, in the guise of an extended imaginary letter to her husband, re-create in detail the last hours of her most recent rendezvous with her lover; here Oates is attempting to compensate for the disadvantages of the epistolary technique—which tends towards summary and generalization rather than dramatized, specifically rendered scenes—by the compulsive need of this woman to "tell it all." The letter begins:

> My dear husband,
> I want to tell you everything. I am in a motel room, I've just taken a bath. How can I keep a straight face telling you this? Sat in the bathtub for an hour, not asleep, the water was very hot . . . (p. 60).

Later, after her lover leaves, the moment-by-moment commentary relentlessly continues:

> My knees are trembling. There is an ocean of cars here at Metropolitan Airport. Families stride

happily to cars, get in, drive away. I wander around, staring. I must find my husband's car in order to get home. . . . I check my purse again, panicked. No, I haven't lost the keys. I take the keys out of my purse to look at them. The key to the ignition, to the trunk, to the front door of the house. All there. I look around slyly and see, or think I see, a man watching me. He moves behind a car. He is walking away. My body still throbs from the love of another man, I can't concentrate on a stranger, I lose interest and forget what I am afraid of . . . (p. 67).

The staccato-like report of this driven woman is monotonous and annoying. I suppose it is psychologically valid that she attempts to contain her near-hysteria within the short sentences of her exhaustively thorough confession, but the story does not build in dramatic intensity through the bombardment of every detail of action and feeling. This compulsive writer of imaginary letters does not have the restraint and skill of a short story craftsman.

A more conventional story, "I Was in Love," is a tedious account of the state of high tension, guilt, and suppressed hysteria of a woman who is having an adulterous affair. The story reaches a contrived climax by the attempted, perhaps successful, suicide of her son, who jumps out of the car in protest over the look of sexual satiety his mother is unable to remove from her face. Oates has attempted to prepare for this event by the child's unrest earlier. But nonetheless how is the reader to take this climactic conclusion? Surely, one rejects simplistic morals such as adulteress gets her just deserts, or sins of parent are revisted upon child; for the woman repeatedly claims that she cannot really help her condition and gets very little pleasure out of it. The message that love is burdensome, inconvenient, and disruptive is blatantly clear; but Oates fails to place this observation within a larger context, fails to raise our perception above this hysterical woman's complaint. Should one accept this woman's misery as the inevitable consequence of love, or does Oates mean to isolate specific traits of this woman which create her suffering? Oates has failed to give her story a meaningful shape. Like the woman herself, the reader achieves no perspective on her situation; there's no illumination, no epiphany, no climax beyond the contrived death of her son.

Some stories fail for just the opposite reason: the specific situation rendered fails to support the ponderous generalization affixed to it. Such a story is "What Is the Connection Between Men and Women?," a rhetorical question that is not, in my reading, satisfactorily answered in the story. This story, told in third person, is punctuated by italicized questions posed apparently by the omniscient narrator to heighten the restless insomnia and the mounting tension of an aggrieved widow who is the focus of the story. Again Oates employs an unconventional technique and again it fails to redeem the content. A man with a striking resemblance to the widow's husband follows her, telephones her, and apparently pursues her to the door of her apartment. At the end of the story, "She reaches up to slide the little bolt back and everything comes open, comes apart" (p. 383). Here is the climactic epiphany in which the disparate pieces of the story come together? Perhaps, but what has happened? Has her husband revisited her from the grave? Has she been engaged in a compelling fantasy dream which "comes apart" when she opens the door? Is a stranger about to assault her sexually? At the alleged moment of illumination, all remains dark. What *is* the connection between men and women? Surely the story doesn't show or tell. At the very most it attempts to show the connection between an intensely overwrought woman and an enigmatic pursuer, but it is impossible to conclude that their "connection," whatever it is, exemplifies *the* connection between men and women. This woman is not Women even though the narrator would make her so. *"How does it feel to be a woman?"* Surely not like this, the "answer" to the ponderous question: "Eyeballs: dense white balls of matter. Skin: stretched tight and hot across the bones" (p. 382). The universal quality of this woman and this man is as invalid as the conclusion of the story is nonluminous.

If Joyce Carol Oates wrote only stories like these three or like others one could name, such as "Matter and Energy," "The Assailant," and "An Interior Monolgue," her work would be disappointing. But fortunately Oates has written many perfect or near-perfect stories which bear only a thematic resemblance to these ill-conceived ones. Paradoxically, Oates is at her best when she is most conventional, when she relies on her impressive skill as an omniscient third-person narrator who selects and refines details in such a way that a story is rendered with dramatic immediacy and intensity. Oates's most successful vantage point is at a distance from her characters where she dispassionately sketches with deft strokes their interior and exterior lives, places them in vividly specific contexts, and clinically records the mounting tension and conflicts of the story. Two of the most memorable stories of this collection, "In the Region of Ice" and "Where Are You Going, Where Have You Been?," display Oates's scalpel-like control of her metier. Both stories begin with a sketch of the central character which does not so much describe the woman as it suggests through a few descriptive details qualities of disposition which will function importantly in the story: the imposing illusion of intelligence, seriousness, and restraint of Sister Irene; the shallow, adolescent narcissism of Connie. Oates introduces early in each story the man who will generate the tension. Sister Irene is challenged in class by the probing query of a visiting student; Connie notices at a shopping plaza the man who later shows up at her place.

At the same time Oates brilliantly re-creates the plastic world of shopping centers and fly-specked drive-in restaurants which serve as the adolescent haven and stalking ground in "Where Are You Going." Connie and her carbon-copy friends languidly stroll "in their shorts and flat ballerina slippers that always scuffed on the sidewalk, with charm bracelets jingling on their thin wrists: they would lean together to whisper and laugh secretly if someone passed who amused or interested them" (p. 30). Connie, bathed in "trashy daydreams" and in the sentimental lyrics of popular songs and prompted by vague stirrings of sexual consciousness, experiments with sexual provocation tried on like cheap makeup, when she is outside the suspicious eye of her mother: "She wore a pull-over jersey blouse that looked one way when she was at home and another way when she was away from home. Everything about her had two sides to it, one for home and one for anywhere that was not home" (p. 30).

The story is enriched by the very ordinariness of Connie and her friends and their dreamy infatuation with the sleazy and experimental no man's land of adolescence. Connie's encounter with Arnold Friend is not just a unique instance of how one girl's experimental flirtation jettisons her too rapidly into the world of experience, not just one girl's perception of the deception of appearances and the terrible reality of evil, but a particularly vivid instance of a universal experience: the loss of innocence. Indeed, Oates plays up the representational quality of the experience by inviting the reader to see Arnold Friend as the Arch Friend, the Devil in disguise.[2] The tension of the story is incrementally heightened through Connie's

gradual awakening to the nature and intent of her visitor. At first puzzled and flattered by his attention, she is coolly and coyly flirtatious. But she observes without registering the significance some anomalies such as the year-old slang expression on Friend's car and his failure to "come together" into a credible image in spite of his mod gear and his popularized, predictable speech and manner. Then, shockingly, Friend's much older self begins to emerge through his painted lashes, black wig, reflecting sunglasses, and cosmetically tanned face—with its tell-tale aging throat inadvertently exposed. Connie's terror reaches such a height that she is immobilized, screaming hopelessly into the dial tone of the telephone. At the end of the story, she is moved off unresistingly by her creepy seducer, whose formulaic sing-song words, "My sweet little blue-eyed girl"—probably taken from a popular song— complete the mockery of brown-eyed Connie's dream world.

While Connie is hopelessly led off into the world of experience, Sister Irene successfully retreats into the region of ice, a protective state of innocent noninvolvement, but not without irreparable damage to both Allen Weinstein, the brilliant and disturbed student who appeals to her for emotional and intellectual communion, and herself. A much different kind of story, "In the Region of Ice" is developed not through the rich and suggestive descriptive detail of "Where Are You Going" but through an exact recording of Sister Irene's feelings toward Weinstein. She is stimulated by his presence in class, hurt when he is absent, simultaneously responsive to and chilled by his appeals for sympathy, hurt and confused when he appears indifferent, protective when he seems vulnerable. But most dominant is her terror at becoming involved: "She was terrified at what he was trying to do—he was trying to force her into a human relationship" (p. 18). But against her will she is drawn to him, and ironically she, a nun, feels that for the first time "she was being forced into the role of a Christian, and what did that mean?" (p. 19).

In response to his letter sent from a mental sanitorium, she appeals to his parents to bring him home, an extraordinary gesture of concern from this restrained and inhibited woman. But later, when Weinstein again visits her at her office and appeals to her for a personal relationship, she backs out of involvement: "'I want something real and not this phony Christian love garbage—it's all in the books, it isn't personal— I want something real—look . . .' He tried to take her hand again, and this time she jerked away. She got to her feet. 'Mr. Weinstein,' she said 'please—'" (p. 27). Resuming the mask of nun and professor, she retreats in terror of the personal relationship. He drops out of her life; she returns to the regularity and anonymity of her teaching career. Later, hearing of his suicide, "she could not really regret Weinstein's suffering and death; she had only one life and had already given it to someone else. He had come too late to her" (pp. 27–28). Presumably the someone else is God to whom she has made her religious vows, but those vows did not include a negation of all human relationships. Obviously, she is retreating conveniently behind her sisterhood, restricted not by her vocation, but by her emotional timidity and frigidity. She questions the limitations of her identity: "She was only one person, she thought, walking down the corridor in a dream. Was she safe in this single person or was she trapped?" (p. 28)—but her inability to feel anything, even guilt, prevents her from knowing the answer. Yes, she is trapped, as emotionally deadened as Weinstein's drowned corpse. One sympathizes with her terror of the feelings that she has wrestled with and finally suppressed, especially since she has felt the impropriety of such feelings with her professional and religious roles, but clearly she has failed both Weinstein and herself in this choice of the "region of ice."

What makes "In the Region of Ice" and "Where Are You Going" so memorable is not only the precise rendering of the central character's evolving response to the male intruder in her world, but also the richness and clarity of thematic statement in each story. Unlike the lesser stories—where the reader is frequently unable to rise above the tortuous responses of the characters themselves—"In the Region of Ice" and "Where Are You Going" do give the reader perspective on the protagonists' predicaments. Sister Irene is one of many frigid, inhibited women in Oates's fiction, but unlike many of them, she is portrayed as a person at least partially responsible for her own limitations. Offered the chance for redemption, for human communion, she chooses to remain isolated and alone. One should, of course, not underestimate the difficulty of the situation for her—this anguish is what makes the story so richly complex—but the reader does not go away from the story as he does from the lesser ones with an overwhelming sense of hopelessness about the potentiality of all human relationships. This particular one fails because Sister Irene lacks the courage to participate in it, not because all relationships are doomed to be ineffectual and miserable. Because the reader understands her personal failure as she does not, he is not locked in the same hopelessness as she is.

Similarly, "Where Are You Going" is more than a tale of the inevitable seduction of a young girl like Connie. Oates captures so well the vacuousness, cheapness, and narcissism of life for Connie and her friends who have nothing better to do than to stroll up and down a shopping center plaza looking for excitement. That this fictional scene is in fact a mirror-image of reality for many young teenagers does not mean that the adolescent world is inevitably as Oates creates it. The implications of the title are that Connie has not been asked "where are you going, where have you been?" with any rigor by her nagging mother and her indifferent father. Left to her own amusements, she plays dangerously with a sexuality she poorly understands, since she unconsciously invites her seduction out of a misguided desire for attention. Again, the reader rises above the character's predicament and as such is illuminated rather than simply depressed at the conclusion of the story. Oates has given her story a meaningful shape as well as a vivid rendering.

These two stories are not unique achievements in this volume or in Oates's cannon. Repeatedly, she demonstrates her skill as a short story craftsman. Other stories which I find particularly successful in this collection are: "Accomplished Desires," "Convalescing," and "You," and to mention a few in other volumes: "First Views of the Enemy," "Stigmata," "By the North Gate," "Pastoral Blood," "Magna Mater," "Waiting," and "Upon the Sweeping Flood."

Joyce Carol Oates is a writer of psychological realism; the drama of her work is played out within the psyches and upon the emotions of her characters. Indeed, Oates claims, "All my writing is about the mystery of human emotions."[3] But the successful story must not leave the reader mystified as well. To be sure, the writer need not be an all-knowing seer who applies platitudinous morals to his stories, but he must give each story a discernible shape and significance. Oates has written some stories where the reader cannot rise above the emotional duress of the characters, stories, often in first person, of unrelieved and tedious delineation of misery better told to a psychiatrist than to the reader. Occasionally Oates makes first-person narration work. She even experiments successfully with sec-

ond-person; "You" is an effectively crafted account of a daughter's obsession with "You," her mother. But she is more often successful with the built-in restraints of third-person narration. This angle of vision allows her to set up character and scene dispassionately. The carefully chosen details, the directly rendered action, the heightening tension, and the coolly incisive authorial descriptions of feelings replace the unrelieved harangue of an emotionally distraught character and contribute to a sense of distance and perspective.

Finally, I might also note that, while for many readers Oates focuses too frequently upon the bizarre, the bloody, and the insane, often her most successful stories have to do with ordinary people, people like the majority of us who live out our lives with a minimum of violence and hysteria, people who have achieved some modicum of adjustment to life. She is devastating at showing just what adjustments entail, such as the selfishness and terror behind the affluent respectability of the mother in "First Views of the Enemy"; the sexual insecurity and dependence upon male approval behind the professional competence of Nora, the university professor of "Magna Mater"; the invitation to sexual assault behind the adolescent flirtation of Connie; the horror of emotional commitment behind the religious vows of Sister Irene. She creates these vivid portraits with the precision and craftsmanship that will secure her position among America's major short story writers.

Notes

1. Joyce Carol Oates, *The Wheel of Love* (1970; rpt. Greenwich, Conn.: Fawcett, 1972), p. 57. Hereafter cited by page number in the text.
2. This point is convincingly developed in Joyce W. Wegs, "'Don't You Know Who I Am?' The Grotesque in Oates's 'Where Are You Going, Where Have You Been?'," *The Journal of Narrative Technique,* 5 (January 1975), 66–72.
3. This quote appears on a front page of several of the paperback editions of Oates's works.

MARY KATHRYN GRANT
From "The Tragic Vision"
The Tragic Vision of Joyce Carol Oates
1978, pp. 117–31

If we had immortal life (but we don't), it'd be reasonable to do as we do now: spend our time killing one another . . . (John Cage, "DIARY: How to Improve the World [You Will Only Make Matters Worse] Continued 1969 [Part V]" Liberations)

One of Joyce Carol Oates's persistent concerns is to make the tragic vision real to the twentieth century. She seeks through her works to awaken contemporary society to its own destruction, to deepen the consciousness of her readers to the tragic dimensions of life. This task demands that her own perceptions of the times be sharply defined, that she confront—because resolution is impossible—the ambiguities of the day without trying to answer them, and that in so doing she offer to her readers something more than the sensationalism of the daily news.

From Oates's fiction—particularly those places where she indulges in authorial intrusion or philosophizing about art and writing—and from her essays, it is possible to cull a theory of art. She has stated often that art, particularly great art, is necessarily flawed—not because the artist's vision is inadequate, but because his vision is too adequate. The artist recognizes, as others before her noted, "Life is a mystery to be lived, not a problem to be solved." Life is a riddle: unsolvable but not inscrutable. Oates likens this paradox to a Zen koan which is an experience and not a puzzle. To solve the koan is to solve the vexing problem of existence itself[1]. It is to this relentless scrutiny that Oates addresses herself. Her theory of art might well be formulated: *human life is an inescapable tragedy which, unless and until it is so recognized, can never be transcended.* Her entire body of writings is thus directed at the recognition of this tragedy. In Oates's world the greatest mistake is not to succumb to the tragic but to fail to recognize it.

This tragic mystery of life cannot be solved, and it is futile to try, but it must be explored. Oates often refers to Franz Kafka to whom she has a certain indebtedness. Frequently a character will quote Kafka, as in the case of Sylvia, who reminds her estranged husband of his earlier fondness for two lines from Kafka's diaries, " 'What an effort to keep alive! Erecting a monument does not require the expenditure of so much strength' "[2]. Merely remaining alive is a victory. Where Kafka, however, does not believe in tragedy, Oates does. She is firmly rooted in the tradition of tragedy, in a belief in the self which struggles to achieve personality and identity and to transcend.

Without attempting the impossible—the formulation of a precise, simple, clear definition of tragedy—it is nevertheless possible to discuss the tragic dimensions of Oates's works as well as to describe the tragic vision which informs them. Certainly none of her characters are "tragic heroes" in the traditional or classical sense of the concept. Hers are the tragic tales of ordinary men and women who suffer, are exploited, and are destroyed, often without knowing it. Their significance lies only in their ability to survive, to "get through," to cope with the limitations of the human world. For Oates, the subject matter of tragedy has always been this heroic, but failed, striving against inexorable powers.

Her narratives reveal the petty lives and struggles of unheroic human beings. Writing on the drama of the absurd, Oates expresses a fundamental difficulty with which she grapples in her writings: "how to create tragedy, which is predicated upon the uniqueness of human beings, in a leveled world in which all are equal and all are perhaps without value"[3]. This dilemma persistently plagues her works. In the fictive world which she has created, her characters are all equal—all are victims. How much she posits value in them as human beings is difficult to say; certainly the characters recognize little value in one another, and society, as depicted in the novels, seems not genuinely to value human life generally nor the individual particularly. Where one expects to find sympathy and concern, one finds only rebuff and humiliation. In school, children are belittled and berated for their ignorance and illiteracy[4]. Social agencies are dehumanizing, as Grandma Wendall experiences when she visits the clinic in Detroit (*them* 103–7). The church women who call on the Walpoles are repulsed by what they see; Clara astutely observes the "strange discrepancy between their mouths, which were smiling, and their eyes, which looked frightened . . ." (GED 91). Not even Jack Morrissey's adolescent discovery of "superior people"[5] repudiates the fundamental equality, characteristic of Oates's "leveled" world.

Suffering and poverty—both economic and psychological—bring her characters to the same level and raise the issue of their personal value and worth. Oates's tragedies deal with ordinary people who are struggling to make sense of their lives and who work at defining themselves. It is they who endure the "ceaseless struggle with the fabric of the universe . . . a constant, daily heart-breaking struggle over money, waged against every other ant-like inhabitant of the city, the stakes

indefinable beyond next month's payment of rent or payment on the car."[6]

Tragic literature deals with the deepest questions of human existence and the meaning of life, of the presence or possibility of order in the shaping of reality. To date, Joyce Carol Oates's major works have raised and wrestled with these questions. Oates knows—as we all do—that there are no final solutions; the important thing is to pursue the right questions and to continue the searching. All of her works are attempts to answer the question Maureen Wendall asks of her fictional teacher, Joyce Carol Oates: "How can I live my life if the world is like this?" (*them* 330). Because this is an imperfect world, because a feeling of impotence leads a person to violence, because the need for community is so frequently thwarted and unfulfilled, because this is a tragically diminished urban world, we all ask Maureen's question. The tragic vision which informs Oates's works reflects her perceptions of the twentieth century—and it yields the hope of a hope.

Oates repeatedly searches for the meaning and purpose of art. In her prefatory comments in *Scenes from American Life*, she identifies three types of art: "works of art that explain nothing that dispel order and sanity; works of art that contradict our experience . . . ; works of art that refuse to make sense. . . ."[7] But, art, for Oates, must be purposeful, born from an irresistible necessity to create, to transform, and to reveal. The interaction, the exchange between the artist together with his art and the personality who receives the art, is sacred. Nowhere does she write more strongly and emphatically about this relationship and the consequent responsibility of the artist than in *New Heaven and New Earth*. If art indeed can refuse to make sense, can explain nothing, can contradict experience, it must do so as an effort to illumine human experience and to give some shaping order to the terrifying tragedy of our time. "When exceptional individuals integrate the warring elements of our culture in themselves," she writes, "and experience in themselves the evidently 'tragic' personality of the epoch, we have great art." The "serious artist insists upon the sanctity of the world" and does not shrink from presenting his tragic vision in his art. He does so "to force up into consciousness the most perverse and terrifying possibilities of the epoch, so that they can be dealt with and not simply feared. . . ." Such is his mission as artist. He may be dismissed, or "denounced as vicious and disgusting," when in reality he is "in the service of [his] epoch" (NHNE 6, 7).

The artist then must in some way be immune to negative or unfavorable criticism because he creates out of an intense inner conviction that his vision ought to be shared, and that it can affect another's perceptions. Oates repeatedly refutes the assumption that art should please. She questions whether we should even want to be pleased. "It is only through disruption and confusion that we grow," she contends, "jarred out of ourselves by the collision of someone else's private world [the artist's] with our own."[8]

Much of Oates's fiction has been criticized for being vicious or disgusting—but such negative reaction does not deter her from continuing to write out of her tragic vision, spurred on, no doubt, by her own sense of what her responsibility as an artist is and of the power of art. She implicitly likens herself to Franz Kafka when she quotes in the epigraph to *New Heaven and New Earth*, "Evil does not exist; once you have crossed the threshold, all is good. Once in another world, you must hold your tongue."[9] After this, there can only be affirmation, an affirmation which yields to "only existence."

Only then does one hold one's tongue. But for Oates the visionary of our time cannot escape his mission to attempt to analyze and to record the tragedy of the epoch—even though his art may be "disturbing, vicious and disgusting." He must speak. "Such artists," she continues, "are passionate believers in the authenticity of their visions . . ." (NHNE 6).

The paradise / hell paradox only obfuscates the power of great art to reveal what is truly tragic, to awaken the consciousness of others to inexplicable mysteries of human life. Evil does exist in Oates's fictive world, personal evil and guilt, malevolent forces in the world which threaten to "unhinge the universe"[10]. It is Oates's firm conviction that that evil can and should be exorcised.

By continually focusing her works on small, miserable, and unhappy people, Oates forces her reader to examine these lives in detail, from every conceivable point of view. With the persistence of an air hammer she drives home her theme: that human life can be redeemed.

Oates's fiction is imbued with the "tragic sense of life" of which Miguel de Unamuno writes, a sense which "carries with it a whole conception of life itself and of the universe . . . [which] does not so much flow from ideas as determine them . . ."[11] Hers is a vision of both the sensible world and the ideal world, the "child of hunger" and the "child of love" of the Spanish philosopher.[12] Her fiction emphasizes most explicitly the world of hunger, yet it nevertheless yields the possibility of the ideal of love. With keen insight, she shares the tragic awareness of Unamuno that if "the problem of life, the problem of bread, were once solved, the earth would be turned into a hell by the emergence in a more violent form of the struggle for survival."[13] Once the tragic cycle has begun, there is no stopping it. The continuous and growing pressure to survive, to climb, to surpass metastasizes, killing off all other human aspirations and ambitions and tragically strangling any possibility of self-fulfillment and community.

The capstone of modern tragedy is the "lamentable loss of connection between men," according to Raymond Williams in his analysis of modern tragic literature.[14] Oates focuses not only on the loss itself but also on the effect it has on the person. Pushed to the furthest limits of human endurance, Oates's characters cling to the hope that so long as they can connect with someone else, so long as they can dial a number, they can live. Terrifying as this loss of connection is, there remains the undying hope of restoring a sense of connectedness.

While it is not the only profound and reasoned sense of life, the tragic vision is the "antithesis of popular vision, or lack of vision, in its comprehension of complexity, incongruity and paradox."[15] A tragic vision need not be despairing; though it cannot be naïvely optimistic, it can, in fact, be affirmative and celebrate life. The most profound tragedy reveals, according to Richard Sewall, "a full if fleeting vision, through the temporary disorder, of an ordered universe." Sewall goes on to explore the essence of that tragic vision, which is

in its first phase primal, or primitive, in that it calls up out of the depths the first (and the last) of all questions, the question of existence: What does it mean to be. It recalls the original terror, harking back to a world that antedates the conceptions of philosophy, the consolations of later religions, and whatever constructions the human mind has devised to persuade itself that the universe is secure. It recalls the original un-reason, the terror of the irrational. It sees man as questioner, naked, unaccommodated, alone, facing the mysterious, demonic forces in his own nature and outside, and the irreducible facts of suffering and death. Thus it is not for those who cannot live with unsolved questions and unresolved doubts, whose bent of mind would reduce the fact of

evil into something else or resolve it into some larger whole.[16]

It is man, the unaccommodated, lonely searcher who is at the heart of Oates's tragedies: man asking if the world is like this, how he can live his life.

In the face of what is "questionable and terrible," the "tragic artist is no pessimist—he says *yea* to everything,"[17] according to Friedrich Nietzsche. This close affinity between the tragic vision and affirmation is emphatically reiterated in Nietzsche's essays, as it is persuasively demonstrated in Oates's fiction. The philosopher promises the "advent of a tragic age, during [which will flower] the highest art in the saying of yea to life, 'tragedy' . . ."[18] Consequently, to the tragic artist, the question of how man can live in this world never implies the alternative of not living but seeks to know the manner in which he may survive and one day transcend.

Sewall observes that no civilization, no matter how advanced or superior a culture it enjoys, is immune from this questioning. The original terror may return at any time, and the old formulations cannot dispel it. There is never a time impervious to the sudden jarring loose again of the questions of human destiny and ultimate justice.[19] The tragic vision must necessarily be tailored to the historical and existential situation, but its essence is unchanging. Man returns again and again to the same questions of the meaning and purpose of the universe and of his individual existence.

A tragic vision is incisive; it cuts through to the very life. Without resolving the ambiguities of life, without minimizing the pain, it offers a vision of man—alone and lonely, struggling both to be free and to be himself, bent on creating his world. It does not shrink from the harsh reality of the human situation, but it searches out the contours and dimensions of that reality to discover its meaning, its order. The tragic vision is a testimony to the fact that man spends a good part of his life waiting, "thinking, remembering, dreaming, waiting for something to come . . . and give a shape to so much pain" (*them* 341). The man with tragic vision has an "attitude of attentiveness to the contingencies and sufferings that it is the lot of man to endure," and he is "engaged by a dream of some brave new world or country of the spirit wherein the brokenness of man may be repaired and healed."[20]

Any complete vision of the tragic must necessarily face the problem of evil. It must not, as Sewall warns, magnify evil into something greater than it really is, nor can it reduce it to something else. Evil in Joyce Carol Oates's world is that tragically created by human beings. It is born out of feelings of self-worthlessness, of powerlessness, of hatred, of selfishness. Not an impersonal, malevolent force, evil is rather created by characters often incapable of fully realizing what it is they are doing.[21] It may be the product of blind emotion, but it is always the creation of man. The focus of Oates's novels, however, is on the social effects or consequences of evil—from Karen Herz's willful complicity in the death of Shar Rule through Elena Howe's skillful manipulation of Jack Morrissey away from his wife and their adopted child. The emphasis is not on what prompts or motivates the evil but on the effect it has on the lives of others.

Oates does not search out the root of evil in the human heart. Her novels deal with the surfaces of the lives of her characters, because that is all they can comprehend. Only the occasional glimpses she gives of the corrosive sense of impotence suggest a possible source of evil. Nowhere does she analyze those drives and forces within man that lead him to execute evil. The evil on which she focuses the attention of her novels is the evil of society, and since society is man, it is the evil of man's own making. Her novels depict evil; they do not try to discover its causes.

Of central concern in her tragic vision is the destruction of simple people and the sad fact of their not realizing and consequently of their not being able to resist this destruction. What most frequently destroys them is, tragically, their own lack of self-identity and self-fulfillment. When she discusses the thesis of Wendell Berry's "A Place on Earth," Oates comes close to articulating the thrust behind all her works. "The earth and human relationships are our only hope," she muses. But "to be 'saved' in this culture one must sell oneself as shrewdly as possible. One's fate depends not upon his sacred relationship with the land, but his secular deceptive relationship with society."[22] Something is wrong, deeply wrong: the simple and the poor suffer the most because in their simplicity they fail to see their destruction, and in their poverty, they are powerless, even if they could see, to change radically the way things are.

But Oates is committed in her fiction to the raising of the consciousness of those who are being destroyed. Her writings are part of her attempt to awaken in them an awareness of the tragic dimensions of their lives. She promises, moreover, to move from an extreme concentration on the nightmare quality of modern life to a more optimistic, affirmative stance. Through her writings, she hopes, eventually, to offer a vision of transcendence. More than merely "getting through," more than just holding together the thousand pieces of one's life, her promised vision will point the way, for those who possess a tragic vision, toward finding a shape for so much pain.

The tragic vision that informs and quickens Oates's fiction eschews simple answers and glib solutions. It is hard, unflinching, and at times, incredible. But as she explains in the introduction to *them*, she intends to deal with a fiction that seemingly cannot be real. But ultimately it is the "only kind of fiction that is real." In fact, she admits she has understated some of the facts because she feared "that too much reality would become unbearable."

Confronted with their tragic lot in life, Oates's characters flirt with a metaphysic of luck. Having long ago realized their impotence to change their fate, they surrender to it, reserving only the faint hope that one day their luck might change. The power of this hope in luck is nowhere more poignantly dramatized than in the gesture of Loretta, who, fleeing the scene of the murder of her young lover, stops to pick up a penny for good luck (*them* 41). When it would appear that nothing worse could possibly happen, at least one can simply or naïvely hope that one's luck might change. Without this kind of optimism, it might not be possible to survive at all. Loretta figuratively picks up pennies for "good luck" throughout her life, for had she not this simple hope, she could not go on. Although Oates herself condemns a facile optimism, she at the same time acquiesces in the belief that survival is possible only for those who do hope. Literature is "wonderfully optimistic," she hyperbolically exclaims in an interview, "because it so often demonstrates how human beings get through things, maneuver themselves through chaos, and then *write about it*."[23] Oates is consistent and successful in portraying the lives of little people who, when confronted with the almost overwhelming demands of life, tentatively attach their hopes to a dream of "better luck."

Because of this hope, nihilism has no place in Oates's fictive world. "Nothing can come from nothing," she affirms; "nihilism is overcome by the breaking-down of the dikes between human beings, the flowing of passion . . ." (EOI 6). In commenting on Herman Melville's *The Confidence Man*, she maintains that the "disintegration into nihilism must be

resisted." Man is delicately poised between confidence and despair, "between the illusory contentment of charity and the confrontation of truth that will not be comforted—that is, despair" (EOI 80). Although it has often been regarded as a critical deficiency in Oates's writings, her characters rarely despair. They may have nervous breakdowns, they may withdraw into silence, they may escape by drinking or by running away—but not one of the central characters of her major works, no matter how extreme his straits may be, despairs. This may be a fault or weakness in the works, but it is nevertheless consistent with Oates's strong belief that not only survival, but also transcendence, is possible. She denounces those works of literature in which death is the way of transcendence. In her own writings, this stance, directly opposed to nihilism, is easily discernible, although at times it is also less than convincing. Writing of Eugene Ionesco's art, she laments that it is the "tragic expression of those who cannot transcend the crippling biological, social, and accidental banality of their lives. The only 'transcending' is death, but this is surely a parody of what man has always meant by the transcending of his mortal life" (EOI 227). Firm and inflexible is her belief in the power of human beings to endure; intolerant is she of those artists whose vision is nihilistic and nonaffirming.

Never, however, in all her fiction does Oates reveal what inner power or strength enables her characters to get through. We see only persons buffeted and beset by the most unspeakable trials and sufferings and successfully maneuvering themselves through the chaos. But the vexing question remains: what enabled them to endure? We see them only from the outside, and while we may applaud their endurance, we are nevertheless perplexed by not knowing how they accomplished it. ⟨. . .⟩

Oates is very much concerned with the question of the presence or possibility of tragedy in this age. While she acknowledges the provocative theses of Joseph Wood Krutch, George Steiner, and Leon Abel, who argue the death of tragedy and the impossibility of tragedy in the Western world, she quietly continues to speak of modern tragedies and to search for viable forms of tragic literature in the twentieth century.

Acknowledging that a traditional concept of tragedy, a concept which required a God, is dead, Oates presses on toward a new basis of tragedy. "The art of tragedy," she writes, "grows out of a break between self and community, a sense of isolation" (EOI 3). Her search for new forms for tragic literature leads her to ask what tragedy has been dealing with all along, to which she responds, "has it not been the limitations of the human world? . . . If communal belief in God has diminished so that, as writers, we can no longer presume upon it, then a redefinition of God in terms of the furthest reaches of man's hallucinations can provide us with a new basis for tragedy. The abyss will always open for us, though it begins as a pencil mark, the parody of a crack; the shapes of human beasts—centaurs and satyrs and their remarkable companions—will always be returning with nostalgia to our great cities" (EOI 8). Modern tragedy is thus shaped by the dissolution of community, the death of God, and the transformation of the domestic landscape into wilderness.

Tragic literature is in some elusive way related to the effort of forging communal bonds. The power of an extraordinary work of literature lies "in its insistence on the barrenness of life, even a life lived in intimacy with other human beings, bound together by ties of real love and suffering."[24] If tragedy grows out of the failure to establish community, it must necessarily touch on the fundamental urge of men to become related to one another through the bonds of community. "Suffering," she notes, "does not draw us into brotherhood." And tragedy which, according to William Butler Yeats, seems to tear down the "'dykes that separate man from man,'" Oates sees as an "aesthetic rather than humanistic" experience (EOI 156).[25] Tragedy, for Joyce Carol Oates, is in part an expression of the failure to answer the inexorable need to create community.

Notes

1. Joyce Carol Oates, *New Heaven, New Earth* (New York: Vanguard Press, 1974), pp. 267–68. Hereafter cited as NHNE.
2. Oates, *Marriages and Infidelities* (New York: Vanguard Press, 1972), p. 123. Hereafter cited as MI.
3. Oates, *The Edge of Impossibility: Tragic Forms in Literature* (New York: Vanguard Press, 1972), p. 124. Hereafter cited as EOI.
4. Oates, *A Garden of Earthly Delights* (New York: Vanguard Press, 1967), pp. 42–50. Hereafter cited as GED. *them* (New York: Vanguard Press, 1969), p. 74. Hereafter cited as *them*.
5. Oates, *Do with Me What You Will* (New York: Vanguard Press, 1973), p. 198. Hereafter cited as DWM.
6. Oates, "An American Tragedy," *New York Times Book Review*, 24 Jan. 1971, p. 12.
7. Oates, ed., *Scenes from American Life* (New York: Random House, 1973), p. vii.
8. Ibid., p. viii.
9. Franz Kafka, *Diaries*, quoted in Joyce Carol Oates, *New Heaven and New Earth* (New York: Vanguard Press, 1974), epigraph.
10. Oates, *Angel Fire* (Baton Rouge: Louisiana State University Press, 1973), p. 46. Hereafter cited as AF.
11. Miguel de Unamuno, *The Tragic Sense of Life* (London: Macmillan, 1926), p. 17.
12. Ibid., pp. 25–27.
13. Ibid., p. 55.
14. Raymond Williams, *Modern Tragedy* (Stanford: Stanford University Press, 1966), p. 13.
15. Herbert Muller, *The Spirit of Tragedy* (New York: Knopf, 1956), p. 3.
16. Richard B. Sewall, *The Vision of Tragedy* (New Haven: Yale University Press, 1959), pp. 1, 4–5.
17. Friedrich Nietzsche, "Why I Write Such Excellent Books," *Complete Works*, XVII (New York: Macmillan, 1924), p. 73.
18. Nietzsche, "'Reason' in Philosophy," Ibid., XVI, p. 23.
19. Sewall, p. 7.
20. Nathan Scott, *The Tragic Vision and the Christian Faith* (New York: Association Press, 1957), pp. x, xi.
21. See Paul Ricoeur, *The Symbolism of Evil* (New York: Harper and Row, 1967), pp. 232–78.
22. Oates, "An American Tragedy," p. 2.
23. "Transformations of Self: An Interview with Joyce Carol Oates," *Ohio Review*, 15, (Fall 1973): 55.
24. Oates, "An American Tragedy," p. 2.
25. Cited in Joyce Carol Oates, *The Edge of Impossibility: Tragic Forms in Literature* (New York: Vanguard Press, 1974). See also Williams, pp. 37–45.

EDWIN O'CONNOR

1918–1968

Edwin Greene O'Connor was born in Providence, Rhode Island, on July 29, 1918, to a second-generation Irish-American family, and grew up in nearby Woonsocket. After studying classics at the LaSalle Academy, a Catholic parochial school in Providence, in 1935 he entered the University of Notre Dame. O'Connor flourished in Notre Dame's atmosphere, which combined a pragmatic and somewhat conservative approach to academic subjects with vigorous Catholic idealism, and his years there remained a strong influence on him for the rest of his life. By his senior year he had decided to become a writer, but on the advice of his department head, who told him to find a salaried job which would leave him time to write, he worked from 1940 to 1942 as a radio announcer for stations in Rhode Island, Connecticut, Florida, and upstate New York.

After the United States entered World War II in late 1941, O'Connor tried to enlist in the Army, but was turned down because of his poor vision. A few months later he enlisted in the Coast Guard, in which he served for three years. Among his posts was the Public Information Office in Boston, where he first became acquainted with the indigenous Irish-American city politicians who figure prominently in his novels. After the war ended O'Connor remained in Boston doing radio work, but quit after a year to concentrate on his writing. In 1946 the *Atlantic* began to publish essays and stories by him, and in 1949 he moved to 11 Marlborough Street, across the street from that magazine's offices, and solidified what was to be a long, unofficial association with it, a friendship unaffected even by their rejection of his first novel and assorted short stories and articles.

O'Connor's first published novel, *The Oracle* (1950), was a satirical farce about a radio commentator; it was neither a critical nor a commercial success, and O'Connor waited five years before trying another. His second novel, *The Last Hurrah* (1956), was prompted by two factors: The Atlantic Monthly Press was offering a prize of $5,000 for the best new novel, and O'Connor had become increasingly interested in big-city machine politics as a reflection of the Irish experience in America. The book won the Atlantic Monthly Press prize, sold more than a million copies, was made into a film in 1958, and has been called the best American novel about urban politics. Despite strong sentiment in its favor, however, it failed to win the Pulitzer Prize, as the committee was deadlocked that year and awarded no prize.

In 1957 O'Connor published a blackly humorous cautionary tale for children, *Benjy: A Ferocious Fairy Tale*. In 1961 he published another novel about Bostonian Irish Catholics, *The*

Edge of Sadness, dealing with the loss of faith and redemption of an alcoholic parish priest. It received the Pulitzer Prize in 1962, and remained O'Connor's own favorite among his works. That same year he married Veniette Caswell Weil, to whom he remained devoted until his death. His next work, *I Was Dancing*, was originally written as a play, but when the production was delayed he turned it into a novel; in 1964 the novel was published and the play was finally produced. *All in the Family* (1966) is the last and most ambitious of his political novels, and deals with the third-generation urban Irish who were O'Connor's own contemporaries.

O'Connor's last work was a play, *The Traveler from Brazil*. He was working on two further novels when he died of a cerebral hemorrhage on March 23, 1968. A collection, *The Best and the Last of Edwin O'Connor*, was posthumously published in 1970.

The *Saturday Review* reports that when a Boston newspaper sent *The Last Hurrah* to James M. Curley, former Mayor of Boston, and asked him to review it, Mr. Curley replied that after reading the book, he had referred it to his attorneys and was contemplating legal action. As one of the characters in the book would say: "Amazing. Marvelous."

This is the story of the final effort of a 72-year-old politician, Frank Skeffington, to be elected Mayor of Boston for the umpteenth time. The campaign is observed largely through the eyes of Skeffington's nephew. In the course of it, by mingling with the crowd and listening to his uncle's reminiscences, the nephew (like the reader) learns much about the social and political mores of the present older generation of the "Boston Irish"—the grandsons of the refugees from the potato famine of a century ago.

At least one reviewer has hailed this book as the great American political novel; another, lately arrived from England, calls it "truly subversive." Both opinions are unduly intemperate, though some possible justification may be found for each of them.

If this is a political novel, it's also a historical one, or so the author seems to think. His message is that the old days of political machines, of bosses like Frank Skeffington, have passed, their stock in trade having been appropriated by the welfare state. So, quite naturally, Skeffington's only real expressions of hatred are reserved for Franklin D. Roosevelt; so, inevitably, the old machine, built on personal contacts and loyalties, goes down to defeat. Now in this there is considerable truth—but it is also true that personal favors, personal likes and dislikes, personal *concern* (or the appearance of it) for the problems of people in trouble, will continue to influence elections as long as democracy endures. I would urge young political scientists and aspiring politicians to read this book, not merely as a tale of the benighted past, but as a revelation of some enduring aspects of political life.—THOMAS H. ELIOT, "Robin Hood in Boston," *NR*, March 12, 1956, p. 28

Most of 〈O'Connor's〉 humor is backward-looking—the old people's dinner-table talk in *The Edge of Sadness*, for instance—reminiscence or survival of a generation in which character had such free play that what now seems wildly exaggerated or eccentric was nothing out of the ordinary. How much of the comedy in *The Last Hurrah* is actually in Skeffington's recollections; how much more of it is exemplified in characters like Ditto Boland or Cuke Gillen, who, blessedly all unwitting, are on the verge of extinction. The young are seldom funny: indeed, the younger, distinctly the unfunnier. One could cite, to be sure, the boobish "reform" candidate, Kevin McCluskey, with his telegenic family and his rented telegenic dog, but McCluskey is not funny as an individual and there is nothing very merry about what he fronts for. The only real exception is Father Danowski, the baroque Polish curate in *The Edge of Sadness*. He is funny enough. And he is treated with the underlying tenderness otherwise reserved for the old

folks. But then, though he is little more than a boy, he belongs as a Polish-American to a generation roughly equivalent to that of the narrator's Irish-American father—a fact which I am not certain occurred to his author.

In most ways Ed O'Connor was a present-minded man. He was urbane, well informed, concerned with politics as a citizen, full of the sense of how much needs desperately to be done here and now, and always very interested in the young. He was impatient with sentimental, unhistorical praise of the good old days. Like Goldsmith, whom he admired, he was a very sane writer, well aware of abnormality and viciousness but dealing by preference with that smaller, more ordinary range of aberrations which we count as reasonably normal human conduct. I think that one of his fundamental assumptions was that the human mixture in every age and clime had about the same general proportions of decent men and rogues and fools. But he did not assume that every age or every phase of society inhibited or, alternatively, called forth and rewarded the same qualities and responses. Some were definitely more inclined toward evil than others. Some were relatively good—like the society we both had known as boys.

It was not only his humor that was backward-looking. He looked back, too, for his standards of normality. Or he seemed to. In his books the basic recurrent pattern is of something coming unexpectedly to an end, generally something complicated and of long standing. To the casual eye it has appeared sound, but now as it starts to come apart the observer (the narrator) realizes that actually the signs of approaching dissolution have been all about and unmistakable, most noticeably a blind, self-satisfied irrelevance to present conditions. If the observer then turns to what is now not so much beginning as emerging, already largely developed, from under the wreckage, he is likely to feel no more than a very wary hope. The newly emergent may offer fresh promise, but it is a promise strictly limited by the weaknesses of this fallen flesh. After all, the old, too, was once new and shiny and full of ruthless vitality, and blindly, self-satisfiedly unaware that no generation escapes the consequences of original sin.

You may wonder, where is the hope or normality in that? Well, it is not either in the new, which has not yet life's lessons, or in the old, which by this time has forgotten them. The normality he was looking for was the mature complexity of the ordinary; and you look for that somewhere in the middle of the process. He and I first knew the Irish-American process toward the end of its heyday. Our parents knew it in its prime. When we had grown up we knew that that phase of society, though it looked eternal to us as boys, was transitional in the extreme, and could not have lasted long under any circumstances. It had come into being about the turn of the century when a modest prosperity had become general among the Irish, most of whom by then had been born and educated here. Many symptoms signaled its rapid demise—the rise of the funeral home and the destruction of the wake; the death of the old people, the last links with that vanished mid-nineteenth-century Ireland from which we were all originally recruited; the disappearance of the genial, uncomplimentary nicknames; and finally, the lack of any continuing force, like discrimination, or afterward the resentment of remembered discrimination, strong enough to hold the society together from without or within. Whatever happened, there came a time when nobody felt very Irish anymore, or had much reason to. By the late 1940s that society was practically all gone. The people were still there; their lives were, if anything, more complicated than ever; but not in terms of the familiar, habitual complexity that was so harmless and satisfying and whose passing he regretted.—JOHN V. KELLEHER, "Edwin O'Connor and the Irish-American Process," At, June 1968, pp. 50–51

I had been rather astonished by the success of his second novel, *The Last Hurrah*, ⟨. . .⟩ and, with the exception of the unsatisfactory interludes of the diabolic fairy tale *Benjy* and the adapted play *I Was Dancing*, his later books were also best-sellers. These, *The Edge of Sadness* and *All in the Family*, were occupied, like *The Last Hurrah*, with the Irish Catholic world of Boston, which had never before been exploited with this seriousness, intelligence and intimate knowledge. *The Last Hurrah* had dealt with the old-fashioned Irish political boss, frankly corrupt and feudally benevolent; *The Edge of Sadness* dealt with the priesthood and, in one of its most effective scenes, pitted the sophisticated and snobbish Boston priest against the sincere ascetic who has chosen to mortify himself by devotion to an illiterate and discouraging parish; his last novel *All in the Family* represents the Kennedy generation which stands somewhere between the old Irish world of Boston and the new world of cocktails and enlightenment. In all this, there is no attempt whatever to fall into the once accepted clichés and represent the Irish Americans as lovable or humorously happy-go-lucky or, except in a satiric fashion, to touch the chords of *Mother Machree*. O'Connor gives us rather the brutal and quarrelsome and histrionic sides of the Irish, and his attitude toward them, though friendly, is sometimes extremely acid. He specialized in hypocritical, tyrannical and completely self-centered old men—old Carmody in *The Edge of Sadness*, who exhibits a scene of contrition on what is supposed to be his deathbed but repudiates it when he recovers—and vituperative and wrangling old women, such as the sister in *I Was Dancing*. He composed so many conversations in which the parties were slanging and scoring off one another that I was interested to hear him say, after his first visit to Ireland, that he could not stand the literary life of the pubs—Ed did not drink at all—on account of its malignant backbiting. I was amused by his relations with Mayor Curley, who had more or less inspired Frank Skeffington, the boss politician of *The Last Hurrah*. A Boston paper sent the book to Curley, inviting him to review it. Curley looked at it and wrote the editor that he was putting the matter in the hands of his lawyer. When, however, the author by chance met the Mayor for the first time, the latter said, "What I liked best was where I say on my deathbed that if I had my life over, I'd do it all over again." It was *The Last Hurrah*, apparently, that stimulated Curley later to write an account of his life. He there confessed to misdeeds that profoundly shocked Ed: Ed could never have invented such unscrupulous wickedness as Curley's public support of the Ku Klux Klan, let alone a public official who was shameless enough to tell about them.—EDMUND WILSON, "'Baldini': A Memoir and a Collaboration," *The Best and the Last of Edwin O'Connor*, ed. Arthur Schlesinger, Jr., 1970, pp. 344–45

HOWARD MUMFORD JONES
"Politics, Mr. O'Connor, and the Family Novel"
Atlantic, October 1966, pp. 117–20

In *All in the Family*, his latest novel, Edwin O'Connor returns to that nameless metropolis and that imaginary commonwealth (any resemblance to any other commonwealth is purely coincidental) he has visited two or three times before. It was there that Waltzing Daniel Considine (*I Was Dancing*) finally surrendered his bedroom in his son's house and retired to an old-age home. There, in *The Last Hurrah*, defeated for re-election as mayor, the great Frank Skeffington took to his bed and died, a lonely combination of charlatanism and genius, understood only partially by his nephew, Adam Caulfield. And there in *The Edge of Sadness*, Father Hugh Kennedy fell into alcoholism, was cured, comforted the dying Charles Carmody, another lonely old Irishman, refused a better parish, and stuck to St. Paul's in the slums and to his Polish associate, Father Danowski.

These lives are all in the past. The new novel is, so to speak, in the present tense. Money talks powerfully in the living generation of Irish leaders in that anonymous city, and most of the money seems to belong to Jimmy Kinsella, whose language is not cultivated, though he sees to it that his three sons go to the right schools and acquire cultivation. One of them is James, who becomes a priest and fades genteelly out of the book. Charles is elected governor, largely through the influence of his father's money. Phil, a temperamental idealist, for a time goes along. But Phil grows more and more uneasy as campaign promises are left persistently unfulfilled and as he watches the soft corruption of ambition deaden his brother's zeal for modernizing the state government. Coming to believe that both the honor of the family and the welfare of the commonwealth are at stake, he ultimately launches an attack on his brother, which Charles stops cold with one of the nastiest and most ruthless devices I ever learned of in public life or the political novel.

This story encloses, and is enclosed by, another one. The novel is told through the eyes of a cousin of the three boys, Jack Kinsella, a professional writer who has experienced disaster in his branch of the family. When he was a lad, his charming mother and his smaller brother were mysteriously drowned in an ice-cold lake—an opening episode told with haunting poignancy. Tortured by self-accusation concerning his own negligence (if there was any), the father takes Jack to Ireland to revisit the scenes of his courtship and honeymoon. There for the first time Jack meets and lives with Uncle Jimmy's tribe, who are temporarily domiciled on an Irish estate. Later, his father having died, Jack marries; and for no apparent cause his wife (was it impulse? was it passion?) runs off with a lover. By and by she asks to return, comes back, and creates a problem of readjustment. The narrative about Uncle Jimmy and Charles and Phil is seen across the temperament and the troubles of Jack Kinsella, and comes in two unequal portions: the experiences of boyhood and the immediacy of adult reporting.

The boyhood portion, told through a Proustian feat of memory, is narrated with wonderful skill as the adult looks over the shoulder of the lad he once was and remembers how the world looked. There is nothing in the Irish part of the book that is obvious preparation for Charles's election, and one hunts about to see why this prologue to the main action exists. I think the answer is twofold: aside from the education of Jack through sorrow, we get these glimpses into the boyhood life of the three Kinsella lads in something like the natural environment of an Irish family. But the section also hints that the dislocation of Irish family life in America may be the remote cause of the final disaster.

The manager of a Dublin hotel, Mr. Guilfoyle, makes both young Jack and the reader subtly aware of the increasing distance between traditional Ireland and life in America. Moreover, the residence of Uncle Jimmy and his family in Ireland is but temporary and seems to have small relation to Irish life around them. During the visit Jack's father impresses upon his son the difference between the Old World and the New:

I heard about my great-grandfather (my father's grandfather) [says Jack] who had been born not far from where we were driving now in a cottage with a dirt floor and a roof made of straw, and who had come to America as a very young man and had got a job putting down railroad tracks; about his son, my grandfather, who had left school before finishing and had run away to sea, and then, a few years later, had come back home wearing a very handsome suit and with more money than an ordinary sailor could have hoped for.

This money forms the basis of the Kinsella millions in the United States.

O'Connor has an enchanted ear for varieties of human speech, and his ear does not fail him in *All in the Family*, except, I think, in the case of Uncle Jimmy, who talks a stage slang that reads as if it came out of O. Henry. But the pace of Jack's boyhood memories and of the conversations therein is finely controlled; and in the rest of the novel even the long monologues are a delight to the ear and to the critical intelligence. It is true that aside from Uncle Jimmy we are listening in on more cultivated circles than in *The Last Hurrah*, so that some of the pungency of that amazing book is lost. But the conversations and the speeches move, they express, they delineate, they demonstrate the Irish capacity for word-spinning, they vividly render individuals and individual idiosyncrasies. History, somebody said, does not exist until it is read. The same thing is true of fiction. O'Connor's power in recording speech is so compelling that the reader wants to turn the page to see who is talking next.

O'Connor is sometimes regarded as a political novelist. The standard political novel commonly has some public issue at its center, as in the parliamentary novels of Trollope, and the fortunes of the characters are involved in the fortunes of the issue. The political novel is a major branch of American fiction, going back to Brackenridge's *Modern Chivalry* and coming down to books by authors like Faulkner and Robert Penn Warren.

In this country the political novel has undergone at least three major transformations. As written by Brackenridge and James Fenimore Cooper it commonly illustrated the ignorance and venality of the mass of voters, who need to be guided by enlightened and responsible gentlemen. After Lincoln, a second type appears. In the second type the citizenry has right instincts but is misled by venal politicians, a corrupt church, and cynical capitalists. *The Gilded Age*, a bad novel but a brilliant document, is a naïve example of this type. In the later development of the second type in the muckraking era, a young man, often a lawyer of Lincolnesque temperament, exposes political corruption, rallies the people around him, and is elected to the governorship or to Congress, where he triumphantly routs the devil and all his works. Paul Leicester Ford's *The Honorable Peter Stirling*, Booth Tarkington's *The Gentleman from Indiana*, and Winston Churchill's *Coniston* are of this order.

In the third and latest phase of the type, the voter virtually disappears or is dimly seen at the periphery of the book as an undistinguishable gray mass. The novel concentrates on the workings of the political scene as viewed from within, and more particularly upon the psychological quirks of the chief protagonist and his drive for power. The psychology of the politician is, then, the theme; civic responsibility is either taken for granted or ignored. *All the King's Men* is of this order; so is *Advise and Consent*. Not the intellectual issues that are part of statesmanship, but sentiment for the poor and a determination to win are central. The writers have an air of having gone to school to Lincoln Steffens, who, muckraker though he was, concluded that political bosses were intricate mixtures of good and evil desires, and likewise men with greater insight into human woe than was true of reformers. *The Last Hurrah* is a political novel of this third type. Skeffington is a complicated personality whom we see across a variety of temperaments and through a mixture of emotions ranging from hatred to adoration: the result is a composite photograph that takes on a three-dimensional reality. *All in the Family* is a political novel in one sense, since it explores the psychology of politicians and reformers, but its strength lies elsewhere.

Though a recurrent theme in O'Connor's fiction is the life of the Irish in America, as a novelist he refuses to be typed. No two books by him are of the same construction. *The Oracle*, with which he began, was a merely competent, machine-made exposure of hypocrisy in a radio commentator. *I Was Dancing* and *Benjy*, that "ferocious fairy tale" (which is among his triumphs), are short stories in novel form, each in a style appropriate to its special theme and each a straight-line narrative. Beginning with *The Last Hurrah*, O'Connor started a series of experiments in narrative by indirection. Thus Skeffington is first presented sketchily and in the raw; his figure takes on bulk and humanity as we view him through the eyes of innumerable persons and learn things about his biography in episodes that often begin as if they were irrelevant. In *The Edge of Sadness* O'Connor shifted to first-person narrative, making Father Hugh the chronicler of his own dishonor and his own recovery—a difficult technical task—and endowing him with extraordinary sensitivity and a tenacious memory. Through his sensitivity a complicated family story—or rather two of them—is slowly revealed.

The indirect method is pushed to its limits in *All in the Family*. The first section has no apparent relation to the main narrative. There is a huge gap in time: we drop Jack as a boy and take him up as an adult. Jack tells the story, but he is naturally preoccupied with his personal bewilderment and his domestic problem. Moreover, he and his wife absent themselves from America while important events build up about the Kinsella family in the United States. As a political novel, necessary scenes are omitted because Jack cannot be present at them. We have to take for granted, for instance, the crucial change in Charles Kinsella's outlook after his election; we are not prepared for Phil's extraordinary outburst of jealousy and civic virtue; nor are we present during a long and lonely night when Phil tries to make up his mind about meeting Charles's trick attack. We are present at the crucial scene between the two brothers mainly because Uncle Jimmy calls a family council into which Jack and his wife wander almost by accident. If the novel is a political novel, the technique is awkward.

But is it a political novel? I think politics is the occasion, not the theme, of the story. That theme is one recurrent in O'Connor's books, and concerns not the state but the family. Thus in *I Was Dancing*, the problem is that of family responsibility for the aged, especially as they grow cantankerous. *Benjy* is a Swiftian satire on children's books, sentimental motherhood, and the Century of the Child, and shows what happens when the husband is displaced from his proper role as a father. The great disappointment of Frank Skeffington is not his defeat but the inadequacy of his shallow son; that is why he calls in Adam Caulfield as a son substitute. The intricate design of *The Edge of Sadness* pivots on a problem of family disruption: in this book as in the others the patriarchal role is eaten into by modernity. American life is, it appears, the enemy of the traditional family pattern, and no amount of verbal concealment by brilliant Irish talk hides the fact that among the American Irish neither the church, nor respect for the old, nor patriarchal authority, nor the power of money, nor the clan spirit can withstand the constant erosion of traditional family ways by arrant American individualism.

In the new book the conflict between Charles and Phil, the temperamental gulf between tough-minded Uncle Jimmy and his sensitive nephew Jack Kinsella point once more to the survival of a family in modern America. O'Connor puts the case without riding a thesis. It is perhaps significant that in the last pages of the story Jack and his wife go back to Ireland, where it is revealed that the wife is pregnant; and if they return to America it may be to illustrate that, the ancient Irish clan being out of date, some other basis for a family in America may become possible.

From time to time academic quarterlies, writers' conferences, lecturers in the colleges, and highbrow writers of fiction anxiously announce that the novel is dying. The novels that form the basis of these gloomy forecasts are usually intricate exercises in the subconscious mind, tales in which no action is what it purports to be, no motive is rational, and no character is prepared to accept any responsibility for the society into which he was born. These themes have enlarged the scope of fiction, but only by a narrow strip and along a dead-end road. They offer too few permutations and combinations. They do not accept the long line of narrative achievement from Fielding through Scott and Dickens to, if you like, writers like Edwin O'Connor.

Yet the principal duty of the novelist is to get himself read, as the principal duty of the playwright is to get himself acted before a considerable audience. Otherwise his support becomes artificial—fellowships, grants-in-aid, publishers' advances, and writers' conferences. But in accepting these well-meant yet adventitious supports, the novelist loses living touch with a potential public in a manner that would have horrified Dickens and puzzled Henry James. Meanwhile, the great undifferentiated public goes on happily reading detective stories and science fiction, two branches of narrative excessively ignored by "literary" criticism, though they keep the central virtue of the novel, which is expectancy. O'Connor has this virtue. His reader is kept in a continual stream of expectation. When the American novel gets over its extralegal love affair with sex and psychiatry and heads back to the main line of fiction, it will perhaps discover that writers like O'Connor are the proper heirs of the great tradition. A storyteller's holiday is a contradiction in terms.

ARTHUR SCHLESINGER, JR.
From "Introduction"
The Best and the Last of Edwin O'Connor
1970, pp. 9–14, 28–30

III

What interested him was politics as a distillate of the Irish-American experience. He was well aware that the life of the Irish in America was entering a new phase. "As I began thinking," he told Lewis Nichols, "it seemed to me that [the older day] was a wonderful time, the time of the eccentric in politics. It was both wonderful and not fully appreciated, mostly misunderstood." This taste for the eccentric found rich sustenance in Boston. Here, like a geologist inspecting a cliff, he could see every stratum of the Irish-American experience. The city of John Boyle O'Reilly and John L. Sullivan, of Martin Lomasney and Honey Fitz and James Michael Curley, of Knocko McCormack and the Honorable Frankie Kelly, of Maurice Tobin and Joe Casey and Jack Kennedy, was a mine of lore and anecdote. Someone had better get it all down, Ed must have thought, before the antic wild men of the old time gave way entirely to the new generation. ⟨. . .⟩

Politics thus became a vehicle through which he could explore the Irish-American peresonality. And he had another objective. As he had pondered the question of Irish-American fiction, "I began to say to myself, 'Where the hell is the humor?' It was sullen stuff, depressed. Now the Irish writers— O'Casey, Joyce—they have humor, but the Irish-Americans never seemed to capture it." Certainly the old, free humor had been a casualty of the Irish-American search for lace curtains and respectability. Ed's friend John V. Kelleher, professor of Irish literature and history at Harvard, has reminded us of "the public humorlessness that settled down over the American Irish about the turn of the century when the Irish societies drove the Irish comedians off the stage." "Irish-Americans can be very funny people," Ed thought, "but no one seemed to set it down. I thought I'd try." Yet his ambitions were more complex. He hated being taken as a professional Irishman and especially as a professional Irish entertainer. He once said to a friend, "I would like to do for the Irish in America what Faulkner did for the South." ⟨. . .⟩

IV

The Last Hurrah portrays the evolution of Irish America through an account of the rise and fall of Frank Skeffington, twice governor of an eastern state, now mayor of its largest city. The book begins with Skeffington's decision on his seventy-second birthday to run for re-election. He summons his cohorts, lays on the style of campaign that had so often carried him to victory, battles his political enemies in the Irish community, feuds with the Cardinal, negotiates with the Italians, inveighs against the Yankees, gives speeches, attends wakes, goes down to unexpected and disastrous defeat, dies.

Skeffington, a subtle, cynical, generous, vengeful, witty, resourceful, high-spirited man drawn with Dickensian lavishness and exuberance, dominates the book. But the Irish supporting cast is brilliantly perceived and differentiated, and the Yankees and the Italians, though cast in more conventional molds, are serviceable. The characters reveal themselves above all through talk; and the talk is magnificent. As the panorama unfolds, a larger picture emerges. Skeffington, the "tribal chieftain," has lived beyond his time. He has accumulated too many enemies among the Irish. The Italians are escaping from political peonage and becoming claimants for power in their own right. The Yankees have waited a generation for revenge. The outs have found a new Irishman, young, bland and meaningless—"nut-boy McCluskey," as Charlie Hennessey calls him—who sweeps through to triumph. In the end, O'Connor, speaking through the character of Jack Mangan, offered his own explanation for Skeffington's downfall:

> What really did the job, sport, wasn't McCluskey, or Garvey, or Cass or Amos Force. . . . You can forget all of us. All you have to remember is one name: Roosevelt. . . . He's the man, sport, who really put the skids under your uncle, and he did it years ago. It's just that it took until now to catch up with him. . . .
>
> He destroyed the old-time boss. He destroyed him by taking away his source of power. He made the kind of politician your uncle was an anachronism, sport. All over the country the bosses have been dying for the last twenty years, thanks to Roosevelt. . . . The old boss was strong simply because he held all the cards. If anybody wanted anything—jobs, favors, cash—he could only go to the boss, the local leader. What Roosevelt did was to take the handouts out of the local hands. A few little things like Social Security, Unemployment Insurance, and the like—that's what shifted the gears, sport. No need now to depend on the boss for everything; the Federal Government was getting into the act. Otherwise known as a social revolution.
>
> So you can see what that would do in the long run. The old-timers would still string along with the boss, of course, because that's the way they always did things. But what about the kids coming along? . . . To begin with, they were one step further away from the old country; he didn't have the old emotional appeal for them. You know, the racial-spokesman kind of thing. For another, a lot of them had been educated away from home. . . . It was a new era, sport, and your uncle belonged to the old.

It was not only the end of the old-time political boss; it also, O'Connor suggested, marked the exhaustion of the distinctively Irish impulse in the Irish-American community. Skeffington and his generation had been an embattled group within American society, united by external ethnic and religious hostility, cherishing their own tradition and identity, advancing to the fight under weird native war cries. Theirs had been the generation that battered down the gates of the old establishment. In many respects they won their fight. The new generation proceeded to rush through the opening—and lost its Irishness along the way. Acceptance was turning the sons and grandsons of Erin into Americans quite as commonplace and tepid as any other Americans. Respectability had become a curse. "Where there had been a Skeffington," muses the old Yankee Nathaniel Gardiner (a character suggested by Henry Lee Shattuck), "there was now a McCluskey. The old buccaneer, for all his faults, had at least been a capable, vivid, unforgettable personality; he had been succeeded by the spearhead of a generation of ciphers." ⟨. . .⟩

The critical notes, such as they were, were drowned out in a general crescendo of applause. The Book-of-the-Month Club took the book; it became a quick best-seller and by 1969 had sold over a million copies in the United States alone. The name of Skeffington has passed into the speech, and *The Last Hurrah* is properly regarded as the best American novel about urban politics. Nor is its appeal confined to Americans. In 1961 Prime Minister Nehru, going away for a brief vacation, asked J. K. Galbraith, then American Ambassador to India, for some books to take with him. Galbraith gave him, among others, *The Last Hurrah*. "He called me on his return," Galbraith later wrote, "to express his intense delight and to say it was the best political novel he had ever read. Some in this country have suggested that Ed O'Connor's special talent was Boston and its ethnic groups. There could be no better demonstration that his was a universal sense of the problems of political organization and leadership than this reaction of an experienced politician like Nehru." ⟨. . .⟩

XI

"It would seem," Lionel Trilling has written, "that Americans have a kind of resistance to looking closely at society. They appear to believe that to touch accurately on the matter of class, to take full note of snobbery, is somehow to demean themselves. . . . Consider that Henry James is, among a large part of our reading public, still held to be at fault for noticing society as much as he did." Explaining the American resistance to the novel of manners by an obsession with a generalized conception of "reality," Trilling insisted that the power to create character derived from intense and special concern with manners.

> It is inescapably true that in the novel manners make men. It does not matter in what sense the word manners is taken—it is equally true of the sense which so much interested Proust, or of the sense which interested Dickens or, indeed, of the sense which interested Homer. The Duchesse de Guermantes . . . Mr. Pickwick and Sam Weller, Priam and Achilles—they exist by reason of their observed manners. So true is this, indeed, so creative is the novelist's awareness of manners, that we may say that it is a function of his love.

As a consequence of the American commitment to generalized reality, "our social sympathies have indeed broadened, but in proportion as they have done so we have lost something of our power of love, for our novels can never create characters who truly exist."

O'Connor was in this sense a novelist of manners, and he manifested his "power of love" in the surging abundance and vitality of his creations. The people in his novels are rich and unforgettable; they stride out of the pages in exuberant life; they inhabit one's memory long after the incidents in which they were involved fade away. They disclose themselves in their cascade of talk—their fears, vanities, pretensions, evasions. O'Connor loved Irish talk—and recognized its perils. Thus Father John Carmody in *The Edge of Sadness* on the conversation at his father's table:

> They all have that special, dreadful kind of talk that doesn't exist anywhere but here. It's not conversation. It's not anything. Just a suffocating cloud of words that keeps on growing and growing and coming and coming. Like a fog. . . . I simply like talk to have some point. And this had none. It never does. In the first place because no one is talking *to* anyone. They're just *talking*. And secondly, because in all rational talk, no matter how much you digress, you usually come back to the main road once in a while. But in my father's house no one comes back to the main road for the simple reason that there *is* no main road. Everybody there deals exclusively in detours. . . .
>
> Just as you think that maybe this time there just might be a possibility of some sort of logical progression you suddenly find yourself trapped in the middle of some lunatic story about a man named Danny McGee who always slept in a maple tree or Little

Philsy Kerrigan who once saved up a trunkful of
doughnuts. And there you are. God knows how you
got there, but there you are and there you stay.

Sometimes O'Connor had to struggle to bring his gift of
mimicry under control. He did so with increasing success as his
work ripened.

It was sometimes observed, and I think justly, that he was
an heir of James and Howells, or that he was doing for the
Massachusetts Irish what Marquand had done for the Massachusetts Yankees. (But he distinguished himself from Marquand, observing once, "The trouble with Marquand is that he
got to like the people he wrote about.") He caught and
transfixed the Irish-American community in its ordeal of
acculturation, chronicling the modes by which Micks turned
into WASPs and suggesting the losses and gains in the process.

Committed neither to the past nor the future, he accepted
change as the law of life. He left behind an ironic chronicle of
a vital part of American society—a chronicle that, along with
the more somber and desperate early work of James T. Farrell
(and Chicago was a more somber and desperate city than
Boston), future historians must consult to understand a way of
living that will have ceased to exist. The fact that Ed's work
came to fruition in the brief but brilliant age of the Kennedys
validated, for the time being at least, his equability as against
Jim Farrell's despair. And in the end, as his friend Daniel
Aaron has acutely commented, he was no more an "ethnic"
writer than Saul Bellow or Ralph Ellison. He had no minority
hang-ups, and the lucidity with which he perceived the world
about which he wrote made that world a universal human
experience.

FLANNERY O'CONNOR

1925–1964

Flannery O'Connor, novelist and short-story writer, was born in Savannah, Georgia, on March 25,
1925. Her family moved to Milledgeville, Georgia, when her father became ill with lupus, a
degenerative disease that finally killed him when O'Connor was sixteen. She attended Peabody
High School and Georgia State College for Women in Milledgeville, and then spent three years in
graduate studies at the University of Iowa, followed by two more years at the Universities of New
York and Connecticut. When she herself began to develop lupus she returned to Milledgeville, and
with her mother moved to a farm about six miles outside of town. Here, except for occasional visits
to the University of Georgia, she remained for the rest of her life. She died on August 3, 1964.

O'Connor's fiction is set in the rural South, and is written, according to O'Connor, "from the
standpoint of Christian orthodoxy"; it is often violent and grotesque, full of concrete images of sin,
suffering, and redemption.

During her relatively short life O'Connor wrote two novels and many short stories and articles.
Her novels are *Wise Blood* (1952) and *The Violent Bear It Away* (1960). Her short stories were first
published in *A Good Man Is Hard to Find* (1956) and *Everything That Rises Must Converge* (1965),
and then in *Collected Stories* (1971). O'Connor's articles and book reviews, which reflect her broad
philosophical interests, were published in various academic, literary, and religious journals.
Mystery and Manners (1969) is a selection of her occasional prose, edited by Sally and Robert
Fitzgerald.

BARNABAS DAVIS

"Flannery O'Connor: Christian Belief in Recent Fiction"

Listening, August 1965, pp. 5–21

T he short stories and two novels of the late Flannery
O'Connor will be supplying the theology-literature discussion now beginning in earnest,[1] with valuable source
material for some time to come. Besides her fiction Miss
O'Connor's legacy includes perceptive essays and some interview pieces.

Flannery O'Connor was intent on making her Christian
faith relevant to modern life and insisted that she could do this
as an artist. "I think there is a danger," she told an interviewer
in 1963, "in talking about the Catholic writer as if his religion
blotted out or stood in opposition to his personality."[2] It is
perhaps chiefly for her efforts in relating Christian faith and
true art in our times that Miss O'Connor must be held in honor
by us all. Her opinions on religious belief and its relationship to
literature can be validly extended from her own Catholic

viewpoint to a more general Christian attitude; in fact, the
ecumenic core of her work has already been explored.[3]

Whatever value may eventually be placed upon her
contributions to a genuine Christian literature, there can be no
doubt that she geared her creativity to respond to a dire
contemporary plea. The distinguished Protestant thinker Amos
Wilder, himself deeply concerned with the issue, has echoed
Miss O'Connor's opinion that modern man feels himself under
constraints whose authority he does not recognize, caught in
social patterns which dwarf him and breed hostile frustration. Dr.
Wilder has further stated his belief that literature "often uncovers
these tangibles more discerningly than moral theology."[4]

At any rate, the theological dimension of fiction is
receiving increased attention today and presents those working
in this area with a medley of specialized problems. On the
Continent, Christian thinkers such as Denis de Rougemont
and the late Gerardus van der Leeuw have taken the major
initiative. But literary criticism is admittedly a difficult business
and it is no easy matter to say of any piece of fiction: this is
Christian.

This difficulty derives from the inner logic of the encounter between art and religion. Because a Christian vision in fictional art must play through the ambiguities of human lives and motivations while trying to untangle the interconnections of good and evil, it can never be a cliché-ridden interpretation of life. Literary art—and Dr. Wilder would surely agree—is no simple form of Christian catechresis. What the Christian writer faces today is a problem of balance. "Religious" or moralizing fiction leans to the obvious rather than offering a reflection of reality's complexity; on the other hand, the purely "secular" approach to a Christian message can easily obscure supernatural implications. The Christian writer must struggle to avoid sermonizing in his art while yet making his meaning clear, his religious *Weltanschauung* present to his reader.

We may further explore the same idea. An exclusively moralistic novel or short story will be artless literature and hence not literature at all. In this case the moral perspective will call everything to serve itself; its creator will likely as not insist that literature must influence behavior in some rather direct fashion. But by oversimplifying the human situation, fiction of this sort stands opposed to a truly Christic viewpoint. It can only result in a misreading of the world, the nature of man and of God.

How then is the Christian artist to achieve a mean that is not compromise? Flannery O'Connor's insight into this problem has made her contribution to the contemporary discussion perhaps more lasting than her fiction itself. She clearly saw that careful artistic exaggeration serving religious belief need not be equated with the distortion of natural realities.

A Georgian Sophocles

Mary Flannery O'Connor died at her home in peaceful Milledgeville, Georgia, during the summer of 1964. Not yet forty years of age, she was already assured a place among southern Catholic writers. Miss O'Connor's literary concerns will now and again remind us of the best in French Catholic fiction—of Bloy, of Mauriac. Yet what she was able to distill from experience in her native Georgia and from her Christianity marks her work as essentially American. Thomas Merton, himself a Southerner by choice, has eulogized Flannery O'Connor (her first name was dropped when she began to write in 1946) in a singular tribute: "When I read Flannery I don't think of Hemingway, or Katherine Anne Porter, or Sartre, but rather of someone like Sophocles. What more can you say for a writer?"[5]

Miss O'Connor has left us a novella "The Lame Shall Enter First" (*Sewanee Review*, Summer, 1962) and two novels, *Wise Blood* (Harcourt, 1952) and *The Violent Bear It Away* (Farrar, Straus, 1960). Like the writers of the Catholic revival in France and England, she is deeply concerned with the tangible reality of sin, with the blight a guilt-encrusted conscience can bring to human existence and with a certain mysterious communication of guilt from one generation to another. Among her recurrent themes is that parents who are docile to grace and God-fearing, no matter how ignorant and shiftless, will generally produce children psychologically and morally healthy. But the children of the proud and contemptuous, regardless of what natural gifts they may possess, are likely to grow up in some way warped. Biblical in its roots, this was precisely the central motif of "Greenleaf" which first appeared in the *Kenyon Review* (Summer, 1957) and was winner in the O. Henry Contest that year.

Her first collection of stories, *A Good Man Is Hard to Find* (Harcourt), had been published in 1955; her remaining stories, originally contributions to the magazines of the *haute*

monde, were anthologized this past spring by her friend Robert Fitzgerald under the title *Everything That Rises Must Converge* (Farrar, Straus).

A few years before her death—Miss O'Connor had suffered from a rheumatic disease which made her a semi-invalid for the last thirteen years of her life—Evelyn Waugh observed about her writing, "If this is the unaided work of a young lady it is a remarkable product."[6] Mr. Waugh's slight brow-lifting is hardly surprising. Surely Flannery O'Connor possessed a vision for fiction unexpected in a woman frail in health, raised and educated—except for a short time at the University of Iowa—in a small southern town. At first acquaintance her approach to the novel and short story seems Poe-like, her writing shot through with the macabre and the cruel. There is Johnson, a club-foot juvenile delinquent with a 140 I.Q. in "The Lame Shall Enter First;" in *The Violent Bear It Away* we meet the child idiot, Bishop; and a central character in "The Life You Save May Be Your Own" is the pitiable deaf-mute Lucynell Crater. Even taken as a whole, Miss O'Connor's work delineates a world full of physical ills and moral freaks: a homicidal maniac, dubbed simply The Misfit, in "A Good Man Is Hard to Find;" a nymphomaniac in "The Comforts of Home;" a hermaphrodite in "A Temple of the Holy Ghost;" and a young atheistic spinster equipped with a Ph.D. and a wooden leg in "Good Country People."[7]

On no account is Flannery O'Connor easy reading, unless one wishes to caricature her as merely the author of a type of sophisticated horror story. Unfortunately, this has been the attitude of critics who dismissed her as a purveyor of the "gratuitously grotesque" or of "sardonic brutality," as one *Time* reviewer described her work.[8] But the reader willing to reflect on what she has really written for us and on how she conceived her role as creative artist will soon discern that her considerable talent was well used. Flannery O'Connor's fiction has intention and her artistic vision has a precise focus.

This perspective was articulated near the end of her short career. "I see from the stand-point of Christian orthodoxy," she reflected.

> This means that for me the meaning of life is centered in our Redemption by Christ. . . . I don't think that this is a position that can be taken half way or one that is particularly easy in these times to make transparent in fiction.[9]

Given a charge frequently brought against her work, this last remark is especially significant. Her fiction, it was said, contained little attempt at intelligibility; rather what was in evidence was an effort to shock by presenting ugly and incongruous aspects of life.[10] But it can be seriously questioned whether the obvious is ever a literary artist's real message for the reader. It would certainly seem that most often this is merely a vehicle for the author's message. Then too, some have chosen to overlook the fact that Flannery O'Connor was not writing for the Christian audience; indeed, her first contribution to a publication under Catholic auspices came only after her reputation had been established through journals such as *Harper's* and *Esquire*. Certainly only a formidable Christianity would brave the sullenness of the secular arena and Miss O'Connor's was not found wanting.[11]

The Christian as Artist

Flannery O'Connor was firmly convinced that the fiction writer with Christian concerns finds deformities in modern life which are grossly repugnant to the believer. When these incongruities are in actual fact moral aberrations, then, she believed, they should appear as such to an audience used to accepting them as commonplace. If the literary artist and his readership hold the same attitudes toward ethical values, she argued, the artist will have little trouble communicating; he may then employ a normal tone of voice, so to speak. Obviously, contemporary America did not share Miss O'Connor's vibrant faith in Christ: in this estrangement situation, she felt a different tack required. It was from this perspective that her technique evolved; she reasoned that "you have to make your vision apparent by shock, and for the almost blind you draw large and startling pictures."[12]

The Christian writer in our day, then, will have sharp instinct for the depraved, for those sectors of our world that are decadent. Flannery O'Connor found the forum of the perverse and unacceptable the most advantageous site for discussing the differences between her own beliefs and those of her readers. "Redemption is meaningless unless there is a cause for it in the actual life we lead," she insisted at a symposium on American fiction, "and for the last two centuries there has been operating in our culture the secular belief that there is no such cause."[13] If her sometimes violent efforts to point up that neglected cause startle us, Miss O'Connor never laid claim to originality in her insight. This general posture with regard to Christian belief conceives the Incarnation as erupting in human history precisely for our redemption; had man not sinned, the Word would not have become one of us, flesh of our flesh.[14]

It is really not so surprising that Miss O'Connor grasped the intrinsic connection between Christ and man's perversion through sin. What tends to startle us is that she was able to express this relationship in artistically valid terms while still quite young; no doubt it was this accomplishment that won her Mr. Waugh's measured admiration. Man is viewed in her work at the extreme limits of his condition, in a predicament where he is fallen in nature but redeemed through grace by Christ—if he will only accept that Christ-life when proffered him.

As in Miss O'Connor's first novel, *Wise Blood*, the portrayal of this struggle is usually carried out in rural Protestant America by characters such as Hazel Motes. Although a deeply sincere individual, Motes loses his faith in Jesus as Saviour during military service; now he preaches a new redemption with his own Church of Christ without Christ. His salvation has come through technology; he preaches a redemption to be found in the good life of modern convenience from the car he uses as a pulpit. Motes is modern man exposed in full absurdity as he seeks a brand of Christianity which will not involve commitment. If he is an uncomfortable refraction from the prism of our age, it is not one of complete tragedy. Miss O'Connor was an artist rather than a cartoonist and she sketches into Motes's character the very real generosity and potential of his non-fiction counterpart. When he eventually loses his "pulpit," Hazel realizes God does not wish to speak to man through this kind of Christ-less Christianity. With Old Testament severity, Motes impulsively blinds himself with quicklime in a gesture of self-punishment.

Wise Blood does not contrive a plot to "get across" a religious message; even without the supernatural dimension the story is an integral piece of fictional art. And yet the higher meaning is almost unavoidable: sin is the real cause of Motes's blindness, a self-inflicted punishment for his enormous crime of substituting for Christ. Ultimately all the moral and physical deformities of Miss O'Connor's characters dramatize this theme of sin for sin.

Fiction's Theological Dimension

We may well ask, however, whether this perception of sin, the product of the writer's religious orientation, is a legitimate subject for artistic treatment. Indeed, what is the relationship between faith and art? Does a fiction writer's faith intrude into and vitiate his creative ability and must this invasion be fought off?

A few years back, author Philip Wylie claimed yes; it was his opinion that a devout Catholic, one "sold on the authority of his Church, is also brainwashed whether he realizes it or not." Miss O'Connor took wide exception to this remark in an article in the Catholic weekly, *America*.[15] She replied to those who thought that she could not be an authentic artist because of her Catholicism. It was, she said, "because I am a Catholic (that) I cannot afford to be less than an artist." In her mind the real limitations a writer must impose on his work grow out of the demands of the material itself, and these strictures are far more exacting than any a religious belief might impose. As a literary artist she claimed her Christianity added to her status rather than diluted her creativity.

She was willing to concede, of course, that faith adds a dimension to a writer's view of reality which many readers will not bring themselves to acknowledge. But, she insisted, as long as they can acknowledge what *is* present to be an accurate reflection of reality, no valid claim of a denial of artistic freedom can be placed. Miss O'Connor's polite rebuttal went on to point out that a dimension missing in an art work is one thing, while a dimension added is quite another; the art product should be judged objectively by the truthfulness and completeness at the literal level of its portrayal of reality. It may not be written off simply because it offers more than the natural level, for this would not damage nor interfere with an accurate portrayal of the real.

Hence, if the Christian artist wishes to integrate a supernatural leitmotif into his work this must be done— indeed, can only be done—by describing what he sees from where he is. In the young Southerner's mind two corollaries followed from this position. Whenever religious belief is introduced into fiction:

a) all "sentimentality" or saccharized compassion must be eliminated. If man, personally wounded by the sin of Adam as religious ancestor or representative of the human race, is healed by the redemptive act of Christ, then our daily task becomes a striving to participate in that act, a struggle to receive specifically Christian grace.[16] But when sentimentality is introduced into novels or other art forms there also comes the tendency to skip over this process of growth through grace, making for an early arrival at a false state of innocence. In Miss O'Connor's theory of Christian fiction, sentimentality will make the paths of a sin-scarred human nature naively smooth.[17]

b) the pornographic is gross artistic error. For Miss O'Connor this follows from the first corollary, because the obscene is essentially sentimental. Obscenity cannot help but blur the affinity of sex with its natural purposes. Pornography disconnects sex from its meaning in life by presenting it as an experience for its own sake. She would define pornography as the representation, with the artist's approval, of misoriented sexual activity. In the final analysis, such a depiction of sex must falsify fiction: it is the author remaking reality to his own design. Nevertheless, Miss O'Connor was insistent that physical debilities and moral perversions are actually part of our *Sitz-im-Leben*, and the artist may not legitimately unmake the situation in which we find ourselves; he may not "cover up" for life.

In her view, then, the fiction writer lacks license to distort reality; he may exaggerate certain aspects of it, as for example in making his religious vision apparent, but only within clearly recognizable boundaries. Her own Christianity obliged her to draw from this basic theorem her two corollaries, the one regarding undue sentiment, the other the application of sentiment to sex, which results in the obscene.

Both these principles, her refusal to divinize man's life with sugary compassion and her refusal to animalize his sexuality by separating it from its transcendent purposes, are exemplified in Miss O'Connor's story "Good Country People."[18] Here the girl Hulga, spiteful at man and God for the loss of her leg, studies for a doctorate degree so that she can express her hatred in an articulate atheism. When an itinerant salesman takes an interest in her, Hulga decides—perhaps incited by his product, the Bible—to lure him into a barnloft and seduce him. Thus in one action she hopes to tear down the images of both God and man, to "get even" for the wooden stump on which she must walk out her life. The author, who spent her own last years on crutches, sketches Hulga's frustration at her plight without any salve of sympathy. "This is life," the story seems to say; "let's not put drops in our eyes."

The scene in the barn when the girl finally confronts the salesman well illustrates Flannery O'Connor's handling of the illicit sex situation; it is so brutally drawn that all possibility of obscenity, as discussed above, is eliminated. The young salesman proves to be even more of a nihilist than Hulga when he opens his literally hollow Bible, takes out whiskey and contraceptives, and finally runs out with her wooden leg in his valise. The discovery that there could be perversion deeper than her own threatens to unhinge Hulga's atheism. No reader can escape the author's view that the two characters are abnormal members of the human family. It is difficult to avoid an inkling of that extra Christian dividend Miss O'Connor felt was legitimate in fiction, in this case her belief that a crime against another person is a crime against God, and that, far from injuring God, sin can be the occasion of man's conversion to the Creator as the source of all his actions. In this light we can easily perceive the immoral and yet human nature of the story's action.

As fine an example of her technique as "Good Country People" may be, it is not typical of Flannery O'Connor's art. We have seen that her avowed focus for literature was not man's fallen nature but his redemption by the death of Christ. These are, of course, allied notions for the theologian. It is to be expected that sin and redemption should give mutual emphasis in Christian fiction, each theme employed to sharpen understanding of the other.

Fiction and the Sacramental Life

The theologian is constantly aware that he cannot discuss one Christian doctrine to the exclusion of another. The beliefs of Christianity are integral, forming one whole. The writer who professes Christianity must accept a similar handicap. In each piece of fiction, he must hold out to the reader some aspect of his Christian vision and yet realize that he may be misunderstood.

An interview with C. Ross Mullins about a year before her death found Miss O'Connor speaking very openly about her specific preoccupations as a Christian artist. This openness, however, was demanded by the reception her work was still receiving in some quarters.[19] She spoke at this time of a paradox she had uncovered; the fiction writer not only reveals but also obscures the realities he knows best, those very insights about which he feels most deeply. Her own concerns, as she was then able to elaborate them, centered around the themes of grace and free will, of death and the diabolical. Hers were the problems of mankind and of divine faith seen with a biblical mentality. Miss O'Connor naturally realized that her Catholic readers were not yet likely to understand her meaning. But this did not particularly bother her:

The fact that Catholics don't see religion through the Bible is a deficiency in Catholics. And I don't think the novelist can discard the instruments he has to plumb meaning just because Catholics are not used to them. You don't write only for now.[20]

The influence of Vatican II and the direction it was bringing to the Biblical renewal prompted her to suggest to Mullins that Scripture themes were going to mean a great deal to Catholic fiction in the future. "Maybe in fifty years or a hundred Catholics will be reading the Bible," she wistfully prophesied; "I can wait that long to have my fiction understood."[21]

It was not only her Biblical motifs which puzzled some Catholics, but also the fact that all Flannery O'Connor's "real" believers are Protestant fundamentalists. Her standard lecture to college groups during the limited traveling she was able to do was called "The Catholic Novelist in the Protestant South." In the people of rural America, close at once to the earth and to the inspiration of the Scriptures, the Georgia writer found something rare and virginal on which to exercise her own religious faith and on which to build her art.

If the religious outlook of her characters strikes us as unique because it is seen through the eyes of a Catholic writer, then so also is the Southland they inhabit. It is not recognizably Margaret Mitchell's Magnolia South nor Faulkner's Yoknapatawpha County. It is rather a southern Catholic's rural Georgia, an untraveled country in the world of fiction. Still, Miss O'Connor's stories are not parochial nor her meaning confined by its atmosphere; because her vision is Christian it is unfettered and universal. She told us as much when she created characters who are for the most part displaced persons, living on the land but not possessing it. Robert Fitzgerald, in an astute commentary on Miss O'Connor's art, has pointed out that her people are not so much social or political as religious refugees; her stories imply again and again that their characters are fugitives from the Christian life rather than from any civilian community.[22]

In "The River" we have several O'Connor themes and techniques brought together: the absence of all mellowing sentiment, the mystery of human motivation which can never quite remove itself from the realm of grace, and the repeated suggestion that if there is exaltation in Christ's victory on the Cross, there is human tragedy there, too, and we must not expect any different an experience in our lives. Again all this is accomplished without sermonizing.

The story is about Harry, five-year-old son of pagan and hence, as we might expect, dissipated parents. The boy is consigned to a maid's care and taken to a river-side prayer meeting, allowing his parents time to recover from hangovers. With this good Christian woman Harry listens to the traveling preacher who stands knee-deep in a red mud stream seeking converts for Christ. The crowd on the shore includes the healthy and the ill, believers and scoffers; it is a crowd not unlike those of the New Testament. The youthful faith-healer, like all Miss O'Connor's false prophets, preaches a redemption for the flesh:

> Listen you people! There ain't but one river and that's the River of Life, made out of Jesus' Blood. That's the river you have to lay your pain in . . . it's the River full of pain itself, pain itself you hear, moving toward the kingdom of Christ to be washed away, slow, you people, slow as this here old red water river round my feet.[23]

Harry is among those who go forward for baptism. Wet and exhausted from the experience, he returns home to the existence of an unwanted, unloved child.

Even if the healer's sacramental action has no effect on the boy's condition in life, the message of salvation in Christ, once conveyed by the preacher, takes root in Harry's soul. The next morning he steals off again to the river. This time he knows he has no need for clerical ministrations; he will baptize himself by plunging in, going on until he really *does* find the Kingdom of Christ in that Red Sea of mud. But Harry, the rejected one, the outcast of his people, has been followed to the river by a certain Mr. Paradise, who has a hunk of candy and immoral intentions. Both wade into the water, one seeking Christ there, the other sin. The swiftly moving current catches Harry "like a long, gentle hand,"[24] pulling him down in a baptism which saves him from Paradise and for Christ.

Here we have physical violence touching a five-year-old boy to keep him from the touch of moral violence; there is sadness in "The River" but there is also exaltation. It is the hand of God to which Harry falls willing victim and "since he was moving quickly and knew he was getting somewhere, all his fury and his fear left him."[25] When the evil Mr. Paradise leaps from that same saving water "like some ancient water monster," defeated in his clever temptation of a Holy Innocent, Harry has literally, albeit unconsciously, put Satan behind him.[26]

What did Miss O'Connor hope all this brutality would accomplish artistically? When discussing her last novel *The Violent Bear It Away*, which also centered around the essential sacrament of Christian life, she recalled her pledge to shout at the deaf. It was still her feeling that:

> When I write a novel in which the central action is baptism, I have to assume that for the general reader or the general run of readers, baptism is a meaningless rite, and I have to arrange the action so that this baptism carries enough awe and terror to jar the reader into some kind of emotional recognition of its significance. I have to make him feel, viscerally if no other way, that something is going on here that counts.[27]

The Violent has its title from St. Matthew's Gospel (11:12); the general theme is Christianity afloat on the sea of our age. More specifically, this is a portrayal of the individual vocation of the Christian and the demands his faith makes upon him. Miss O'Connor relates the tale of a boy, his uncle and his granduncle. No supernatural "intrusion" distorts the narration of events or the characterizations into a fictional sermon. But this book, as we have seen, should be considered in the theological dimension which the author intended. *The Violent* concerns "the conflict between an attraction for the holy and the disbelief that we breathe in with the air of the times."[28]

Mason Tarwater and his grandnephew live together on a dilapidated farm in backwoods Georgia. Mason is keeping the fourteen-year-old boy in a state of rural Christian insulation from his nephew Rayber, a big city school teacher for whom "reason" has replaced religion. Rayber is now an agnostic; for the old man, this simply means that his nephew's intellect is demoniac. On the other hand, the elderly Tarwater considers himself a prophet—at one with the great names of the Old Testament—and believes with the wisdom within him that young Tarwater has also been called to the prophetic ministry.[29] Old Tarwater dies, having apparently succeeded in raising the boy "to expect the Lord's call . . . and to be prepared for the day he would hear it."[30]

But not quite. Young Tarwater, now the novel's central figure, is still unwilling to accept the ecclesial mission his granduncle assigned him: the baptism of Rayber's idiot son, Bishop. The boy fights against his vocation, fearing that he in turn might inherit the old man's life desire "to hasten to the banks of the Galilee to eat the loaves and the fishes that the Lord had multiplied."[31] He is afraid of having naught besides, afraid that if he should take the mantle of minister then "nothing would heal or fill his stomach but the bread of life."[32] Young Tarwater flees to the city and Uncle Rayber.

The uncle is anxious to convert the boy from that brand of primitive "Christian" independence, irrational and unscientific, which the old man in the backwoods had tried to instill. Tarwater is fast becoming the victim of a guilt complex, Rayber feels, because he is failing the prophet's command by not baptizing pathetic little Bishop. Rayber believes that the same modern science which has diagnosed his son's ailment is the lone force with the possibility of curing him.

But gradually, as Rayber waits for the boy to come around to his own agnostic, scientistic view of life, Tarwater begins sensing the basic sterility of science as a religious faith. Torn within himself, Tarwater cannot ignore the prophet's mantle which looms above him nor forget his vocation as baptizer. And so they struggle, Rayber fighting for Tarwater's mind while the confused Tarwater, in a sense against his own will, fights for an opportunity to bring the idiot and the salvific water together. The explosive climax of *The Violent* finds Rayber finally managing to destroy the boy's Christian faith and Tarwater, discarding his mantle, drowning Bishop in a gesture of despair, all the while speaking the sacred words of the baptismal formula. Coming from his mouth, the words of eternal life astonish even the unfrocked baptist.

Life Held Fast in Christ

We immediately note the similarities between this final novel and "The River:" the baptized does not have the use of reason, the circumstances insert a non-voluntary element into the reception of the sacrament, and another's sin—in the short story, Mr. Paradise's, and in the novel, Tarwater's—is somehow the cause of a human soul's salvation. All this poses at least two serious problems: Did Miss O'Connor's artistic imagination eventually fail her and, more importantly, did she have a sound theology behind her Christian vision?

It is commonly supposed that the plot resolution using death as an essential component indicates an amateur writer, and often enough this is true with the novice author struggling for drama. Its treatment frequently rings false precisely because so little can be done with it; death is one of nature's mysteries.

The Christian, however, sees death as the path into true, eternal life. For Flannery O'Connor, then, this was not a theme to be explored early in her career and then left behind in favor of the more comprehensible aspects of life. Given her outlook, death was not a theme that could be sufficiently examined and settled once and for all, any more than the faith of an individual Christian could be given a thorough and definitive sounding. Death intrigued her and she was frank about it: "Death has always been brother to my imagination. I can't imagine a story that doesn't properly end in it or in its foreshadowing."[33] This confession reveals Miss O'Connor's affinity with those modern theologians who see death as the highpoint of Christian life.[34]

In returning to the baptism-through-death theme in her last novel the Georgia writer answers the charge that her theology is not orthodox. This answer proved insufficient for at least one of her commentators. Writing a year after *The Violent* appeared, Robert Bowen challenged the theological implications of her work. He labeled her fiction anti-Catholic, deterministic and a unique example of a "thorough point-by-point dramatic argument against Free Will, Redemption and Divine Justice."[35]

Specifically, Bowen objects to the circumstances of Bishop's baptism. The idiot lacks both ability to reason and the consent necessary for belief. Yet we are asked to accept his entry into the Kingdom through Tarwater's action, even in the face of the latter's renunciation of faith and of his sacerdotal function. The drowning, in Bowen's view, is a sacrilege rather than a sacrament, more like a death-through-baptism than the reverse.

But is it?

This depends on what aspect of Christian belief the author emphasizes. It seems to the present writer that Miss O'Connor is here proclaiming the complete gratuity of man's salvation, that "the Spirit blows where it will." If we were to insist on an explicit portrayal here of the part the human will plays in salvation, i.e., on the doctrine that man is not saved without his own cooperation, then we would find Miss O'Connor's last novel unsatisfactory.

"The River" is theologically accurate even though Harry's baptism was caused by the diabolical Mr. Paradise frightening the boy into deep water and evil is never the direct cause of good. The Georgia writer was rather showing evil as an indirect cause of good, i.e. that God can bring good out of evil. The child, after all, is drowned and saved not by Paradise but by the "gentle hand" of water. Further, it seems legitimate to read the boy's death as a kind of baptism of desire or even of blood. He wades beyond his depth in panicky defense of his moral and physical integrity, seeking a supernatural embrace alone.

Such interpretations of Miss O'Connor's fiction are possible without reading into it notions which are not there. Of course, if we demand in fiction an ideal that escapes even the systematic theologian (who also uses art to set forth his thought for others) then less favorable verdicts are also possible. No finite mind, novelist's or theologian's, can completely encompass the mystery of Christianity. The theologian can show us how God is perfectly just and how He is perfectly merciful. But it is quite beyond his ability to explain how God is both in regard to an individual soul. So, too, the novelist with his characters.

Miss O'Connor emphasizes now one truth of the Christian faith, now another. What Bowen has called for would require the presence of every Christian belief in every work of Christian art. In the concrete situation, this is an impossible demand. Since fiction attempts to represent the existential situation, this would tax the fiction writer with containing the mystery of Christianity within a particular character or his actions. In ultimate terms, this demand would burden the artist who wishes to portray the Christus with encompassing the God-Man, *the* Mystery of Christianity, in a single piece of art. In short, this denies the limitations of the finite order.

What is possible for the artist, and what Miss O'Connor gives us, are sectional representations of reality perceived by the Christian. Each of her stories is a reflection of the real world seen through a Christic looking glass which never distorts that world but exaggerates details the secularist eye might not see.

One perceptive commentator has said that all of Miss O'Connor's fiction reflects the action of redemptive grace at work in the soul of man and his response to its influence.[36] Flannery O'Connor on one occasion defined this action as one "by which charity grows invisibly among us, entwining the living and the dead . . . [and] called by the Church the Communion of Saints."[37] For her the channels of this grace could be conveyed through fiction as "lines that join the most diverse lives and that hold us fast in Christ."[38]

Notes

1. Representative works in this interdisciplinary field would be: Cleanth Brooks, *The Hidden God: Studies in Hemingway, Faulkner, Yeats, Eliot and Warren* (New Haven: Yale University Press, 1963); Abbe Charles Moeller, *Littérature du XXe siècle et christianisme* I-IV (Tournai: Casterman, 1953–1960); a broad bibliography is contained in Nathan A. Scott, Jr., ed., *The New Orpheus: Essays toward a Christian Poetic* (New York: Sheed and Ward, 1964).
2. C. Ross Mullins, Jr., "Flannery O'Connor: An Interview," *Jubilee*, XI (June, 1963), 34.
3. Sr. Mariella Gable, "Ecumenic Core in Flannery O'Connor's Fiction," *The American Benedictine Review*, XV (June, 1964).
4. Amos N. Wilder, *Theology and Modern Literature* (Cambridge: Harvard University Press, 1958), p. 115.
5. Thomas Merton, "Flannery O'Connor," *Jubilee*, XII (Nov., 1964), 53.
6. Cited by James Greene, "The Comic and the Sad," *The Commonweal*, LXII (1955), 404.
7. These stories were collected in Miss O'Connor's *A Good Man Is Hard to Find* (New York: Harcourt, Brace & Co., 1955) together with the early novella "The Lame Shall Enter First."
8. Miss O'Connor was given membership in the "cult of the Gratuitous Grotesque" by William Esty, "In America, Intellectual Bomb Shelters," *The Commonweal*, LXVII (1958), 588. The anonymous *Time* reviewer was unable to decide whether or not he approved of the sardonic brutality he attributed to the Georgia writer. Cf. discussion by Robert McCown, S.J., "Flannery O'Connor and the Reality of Sin," *The Catholic World*, CLXXXVIII (1959), 286.
9. Flannery O'Connor, "The Fiction Writer and His Country," in Granville Hicks, ed., *The Living Novel* (New York: Macmillan, 1957), p. 162.
10. For example, Esty irritably remarks: "All these overingenious horrifics are presumably meant to speak to us of the Essential Nature of Our Time, but when the very real and cruel grotesquerie of our world is converted into clever gimmicks for *Partisan Review*, we may be forgiven for reacting with the self-same disgust as the little old lady from Dubuque." (loc. cit.)
11. At the time of her death Miss O'Connor was again working on what she hoped would grow into a novel. Tentatively called *Why Do the Heathens Rage?*, a portion of it appeared in *Esquire*, LX (July, 1963), 60f. Her stories had also been published in *Kenyon Review*, *Sewanee Review* and, as Esty implied supra, *Partisan Review*.
12. Hicks, p. 163.
13. Ibid., p. 162.
14. In his *Summa*, Aquinas discusses the implications of this opinion, stating his own belief that it is more in accord with Scripture to hold that Christ became man so that He might die a man's death as the remedy for sin. From the context it is clear that St. Thomas sees Christ as *the* remedy and that although sin was indeed the occasion for the Incarnation, it need not have been, if we consider the absolute power of God. Cf. *Summa Theol.*, III, q. 1, a. 3.
15. Flannery O'Connor, "The Church and the Fiction Writer," *America*, XCVI (March, 1957), 733ff.
16. For a systematic theologian's view on the same point, cf. Edward Schillebeeckx, O.P., *Christ the Sacrament of the Encounter with God* (New York: Sheed and Ward, 1963), p. 59.
17. "When fiction is made according to its nature, it should reinforce our sense of the supernatural by grounding it in concrete observable reality. . . . To look at the worst will be for him [the writer] no more than an act of trust in God." ("The Church and the Fiction Writer," 734.)
18. Esty castigates this story in particular, even while admitting that the respected critic Allen Tate felt "Good Country People" best exemplified Miss O'Connor's deep Christian concerns. (loc. cit.)
19. Cf. Robert Bowen, "Hope versus Despair in the Gothic Novel," *Renascence*, XIII (Spring, 1961). For a strong defense of Miss O'Connor's theology see Sumner Ferris, "The Outside and the Inside," *Critique*, III (Spring, 1960).
20. Joel Wells, "Conversation with Flannery O'Connor," *Critic*, XXI (Aug.-Sept., 1962), 5.

21. Ibid.
22. Robert Fitzgerald, "The Countryside and the True Country," *Sewanee Review*, LXX (Summer, 1962), 394: "The stories not only imply, they as good as state again and again, that estrangement from Christian plentitude is estrangement from the true country of man."
23. Flannery O'Connor, "The River," collected in *A Good Man Is Hard to Find*, p. 8.
24. Ibid., p. 87.
25. Ibid.
26. To John Hawkes, who made a study of "Flannery O'Connor's Devil" in *Sewanee Review* (Summer, 1962) Miss O'Connor wrote: "I want to be certain that the devil gets identified as the devil and not as this or that psychological tendency." Cf. Gable, op. cit., p. 132 fn. This identification has apparently been accomplished here by connecting Mr. Paradise with the water monsters of the creation myths preceding Genesis, and hence more proximately with the serpent in the Garden whose name he bears. Cf. also the Epistle of St. James (4:7) for a possible Biblical parallel to the story.
27. Mullins, loc. cit.
28. Ibid.
29. It is perhaps important for us to understand that, for Miss O'Connor, old Tarwater really does have wisdom because he has religious faith. Wisdom in the sense the Bible presents it in the sapiential literature is nothing other than an abiding fear of the Lord. This approval of a theme strong in southern Fundamentalism confuses some of her Catholic readers, but the author always insisted: "I'm not interested in sects as sects; I'm concerned with the religious individual, the backwoods prophet." Quoted by Granville Hicks, "A Writer at Home with Her Heritage," *Saturday Review*, XLV (May 12, 1962), 22.
30. *The Violent Bear It Away*, p. 5.
31. Ibid., p. 21.
32. Ibid.
33. Mullins, op. cit., 35.
34. Cf. for instance, Claude Geffré, O.P., "La Mort comme necessité et comme liberté," *La Vie Spirituelle*, CVIII (Aug.-Sept., 1963).
35. Bowen, (loc. cit.), 147.
36. Sr. Bertrande Meyer, D.C., "Four Stories of Flannery O'Connor," *Thought*, XXXVII (Sept., 1962). Our attention is here called to Miss O'Connor's "choice of ordinary, often poor and deprived people with a defective sense of spiritual purpose as prototypes for this action." (426)
37. Flannery O'Connor, "Mary Ann," *Jubilee*, IV (May, 1961), 35.
38. Ibid.

WALTER SULLIVAN

From "Flannery O'Connor, Sin, and Grace: *Everything That Rises Must Converge*"

Hollins Critic, September 1965, pp. 1–10

The stories in *Everything That Rises Must Converge* are the last fruits of Flannery O'Connor's particular genius; and though one or two of them display an uncertainty that must have been the result of her deteriorating health, they are for the most part successful extensions of her earlier fiction. God-ridden and violent—six of the nine end in something like mayhem—they work their own small counter reformation in a faithless world. Flannery O'Connor's limitations were numerous and her range was narrow: she repeated herself frequently and she ignored an impressively large spectrum of human experience. But what she did well, she did with exquisite competence: her ear for dialogue, her eye for human gestures were as good as anybody's ever were: and her vision was as clear and direct and as annoyingly precious as that of an Old Testament prophet or one of the more irascible Christian saints.

Her concern was solely with the vulgarities of this world and the perfections of the other—perfections that had to be taken on faith, for the postulations and descriptions of them in her work are at best somewhat tawdry. She wrote of man separated from the true source of his being, lost, he thinks and often hopes, to God; and of a God whose habits are strange beyond knowing, but Who gets His way in the end. That she was a Southerner and wrote about the South may have been a fortunate coincidence. The South furnished her the kind of flagrant images her theme and her style demanded, and Southern dialogue augmented and perhaps even sharpened her wit. But the South as locale and source was quite peripheral. She once wrote Robert Fitzgerald, "I would like to go to California for about two minutes to further these researches [into the ways of the vulgar]. . . . Did you see that picture of Roy Rogers' horse attending a church service in Pasadena?" Had she been born in Brooklyn or Los Angeles, the surface agonies of her work would have been altered: perhaps they would have been weakened: but the essential delineations of her fiction, the mythic impulse itself would, I believe, have been essentially unchanged.

As a novelist, she was not successful. She could never fill a booklength canvas: the colors thinned out, the relationships weakened, the images became, before the denouement, rigid and brittle. The weakness obviously was not in her theme, which was big enough to fill the world, powerful enough to shape some of the greatest of all literary careers in the past, and in our own time those of Eliot and Mauriac and Graham Greene and William Golding. What went wrong was technical. Flannery O'Connor used to be fond of saying that the way she wrote a story was "to follow the scent like an old hound dog." At first glance, one might conclude that her novels were written with too little forethought. *Wise Blood* is full of loose ends: the theme dribbles away through the holes in the structure. According to Fitzgerald, the idea for having Hazel Motes blind himself came to O'Connor when, stuck at the crucial point in her manuscript, she read *Oedipus* for the first time. Then the earlier parts of the novel had to be reworked to prepare for the ending.

But a lot of novels get written and rewritten this way. And some novels of real power have ends as loose as that left by Enoch Emery who is last seen disappearing into the night in his ape's suit. Except for Haze, all the characters fade off—Hawkes and Sabbath and Hoover Shoates. The landlady fills the void in the last chapter. But what Motes means to do, and what O'Connor meant for us to understand concerning what he does, seem clear enough. Driven by the Christ he cannot escape from, the "ragged figure" who "moves from tree to tree in the back of his mind," and motions "him to turn around and come off into the dark where he was not sure of his footing," he murders his double, the false prophet of his own false religion and therefore kills that part of himself. Then by blinding himself, he exhibits the strength of belief that Hawkes was unable to muster; he redeems Hawkes' failure and turns his vision totally inward away from this world, toward the Christ who exists in the inner darkness.

A better case can be made for *The Violent Bear It Away*. The beginning is extraordinarily powerful: the old man dies at the breakfast table, the boy abandons the partially dug grave, gets drunk and burns the house down. The lines of the conflict are clearly drawn between the scientific attitude—which is to say, the new gnosticism—of Rayber and the gift of Christian grace which Tarwater has not been able to escape. That Tarwater is a reluctant vessel enhances the drama of the novel: he does the work of God in spite of himself and a part of the resolution of the story in his understanding of his role and his acceptance of it. Having been abused by a homosexual, he has a vision of a burning bush, and a message comes to him: GO WARN THE CHILDREN OF GOD OF THE TERRIBLE SPEED OF MERCY. And in the final scene he is moving toward the darkened city where the "children of God" lie sleeping.

The characters here are fewer than in *Wise Blood*, which is in itself a kind of virtue: every novelist needs to learn what he can do without. The plot is rounded off neatly. The old man has been buried by some Negroes. The feeble-minded child has been baptized and drowned. The prophet's will has been done: Rayber is defeated. The scent has been true and truly followed and all ought to be well, but the novel remains, for me at least, unsatisfactory. The difficulty does not lie in faulty concept or structure: the scenes balance out nicely and the pace is sure. The trouble, I think, is with the characters: brilliantly drawn and fascinating and symbolically significant as they are, they will not hold up through a long piece of fiction. They are too thin, in the final analysis, and too much alike.

Yet, the characters, the clothes they wear, the gestures they make, the lines they speak, the thoughts they think are what make Flannery O'Connor's work so magnificently vivid and so totally memorable. The dialogue ranges from the outrageous to the absolutely predictable, the latter done so well that it never fails to delight. For example, in "The Life You Save May Be Your Own," Mr. Shiftlet says, "There's one of these here doctors in Atlanta that's taken a knife and cut the human heart—the human heart . . . out of a man's chest and held it in his hand . . . and studied it like it was a day old chicken, and lady . . . he don't know no more about it than you or me."

Or take this passage from "The Displaced Person."

> "They came from over the water," Mrs. Short-ley said with a wave of her arm. "They're what is called Displaced Persons."
>
> "Displaced Persons," he said. "Well now. I declare. What do that mean?"
>
> "It means they ain't where they were born at and there's nowhere for them to go—like if you was run out of here and wouldn't nobody have you."
>
> "It seems like they here, though," the old man said in a reflective voice. "If they here, they some-where."
>
> "Sho is," the other agreed. "They here."

The illogic of Negro thinking always irked Mrs. Shortley. "They ain't where they belong to be at," she said.

Again in "The Life You Save," Shiftlet offers the old woman a stick of chewing gum, "but she only raised her upper lip to indicate she had no teeth." In *The Violent Bear It Away*, Tarwater makes a face suitable for an idiot to fool the truant officer, the old man lies down in his coffin to try it out—his fat stomach protrudes over the top—and the wire to Rayber's hearing aid characterizes the quality of his intelligence. All this is very fine, supported as it is with O'Connor's keen sense of the world in its various aspects: the buildings and sidewalks and trolley cars of the city, the fields and trees and clouds—many clouds—and barns and houses and pigs and cows and peacocks. Her people function richly as images and frequently they evolve into symbols.

In "A Good Man Is Hard to Find," the Misfit represents the plight of man from the beginning of Christian history to the modern age, and he sets forth the dilemma with such blunt clarity that it cannot be misread. Jesus was truly God or he was not: between being God and not being God there is no middle ground. If He were, then He must be followed. If He were not,

then all men are free to work out their own destinies and the terms of their own happiness for themselves. The Misfit is aware of his own helplessness. Life is a mystery to him: the ways of fate are inscrutable: he denies flatly that he is a good man, and he expects neither human charity nor the mercy of God. He know only that he does not know, and his awareness is the beginning of all wisdom, the first step toward faith.

It is an awareness that the grandmother and the other characters in the story do not share. "You're a good man!" she says to Red Sammy Butts, owner of the roadside restaurant, and he readily agrees. But he is not: nor is she a good woman: nor are Bailey or his wife or his children good. Their belief in their own virtue is a sign of their moral blindness. In pride they have separated themselves from God, putting their trust in modern technology: in paved roads and automobiles (Red Sammy gave two men credit because they were driving a Chrysler); in advertising messages along the highway and tapdancing lessons for children and in motels and pampered cats. "A Good Man Is Hard to Find" makes clear—as does *Wise Blood*—that the characters in Flannery O'Connor's work may not be distinguished as good or bad, or as guilty or innocent. All are guilty; all are evil. The distinctions are between those who know of God's mercy and those who do not, between those who think they can save themselves, either for this life or for the next, and those who are driven, in spite of their own failings, to do God's purpose. In the general retreat from piety, man and the conditions under which he lives have been perverted.

It was Flannery O'Connor's contention that the strange characters who populate her world are essentially no different from you and me. That they are drawn more extravagantly, she would admit, but she claimed that this was necessary because of our depravity: for the morally blind, the message of redemption must be writ large. This is not to say that she conceived of her art as a didactic enterprise: but rather that like all writers of all persuasions, she wrote out of her own ontological view which remained orthodox and Catholic, while the society in which she lived and for which she wrote became more profane and more heretical every day. She could no sooner have stopped writing about God than Camus could have ceased being an existentialist. She was committed and she had to shout to be heard.

But in writing, as in all other human endeavors, one pays his money and makes his choice. He gives up something to get something, and to get the outrageously drawn, spiritually tormented character, it is necessary to sacrifice the subtlety that long fiction demands. Complex characterization is the *sine qua non* of the novel: the characters must not only have epiphanies: they must change and develop in terms of what they have done and seen. It was the nature of Flannery O'Connor's fictional vision that discovery on the part of her people was all. When one has witnessed the flaming bush or the tongues of fire or the descending dove, the change is final and absolute and whatever happens thereafter is anticlimax. This is why the characters in O'Connor's novels fade and become static and often bore us with their sameness before we are done with the book. But fulfilling their proper roles—that is of revelation, discovery—in the short stories, they are not boring and they do what they were conceived to do.

In the society which is defined by the grandmother and the Misfit, the central conflict is between those who are driven by God and those who believe in their own self-sufficiency. This idea was put forth in *Wise Blood*, but the struggle took place too much inside the mind of Motes, and O'Connor's efforts at finding images for her values were not entirely successful. In the heavily ironic "Good Country People," the conflict is between two of the godless. Hulga, the Ph.D. in philosophy, is deprived of her wooden leg by Pointer, the Bible salesman, when she will not submit to his advances. But more than this, she is robbed forever of her belief in the final efficacy of the rational process. This issue is fully joined, as I indicated earlier, in *The Violent Bear It Away*: Rayber believes in the social sciences, their theories, their statistics. To him, all mysticism is superstition, nothing is finally unexplainable, and man is the product of his environment. That the latter may not be quite true is made clear from the outset by the presence of Rayber's idiot son. But Rayber sees Bishop as the kind of mistake of nature that will ultimately be eradicated in the course of scientific advancement. All things will sooner or later be subject to the control of man. Tarwater, the unwilling instrument of grace, represents the super-rational quality of the Christian impulse. Determined not to do what his uncle, the prophet, had set for him to do, he does so anyway. Every step he takes away from the task of baptising Bishop takes him closer to that very act. All his bad temper, his country cunning and his determination to be and to act to suit himself avail no more than Rayber's educated scheming. God snatches whom He will and sets His will in motion. ⟨. . .⟩

Jacques Maritain says, in *Art and Scholasticism*, "A reign of the heart which is not first of all a reign of truth, a revival of Christianity which is not first of all theological, disguises suicide as love." This is to say, in a more complex and sophisticated fashion, that the road to hell is paved with good intentions. And who in Flannery O'Connor's work is without his good intentions? Only those who are conscious of their own evil. Only those who are driven by the grace of God. Julian in the title story of *Everything That Rises* is charity itself in his view toward the world at large; but his mother, in whose house he lives, is the object of his scorn and hatred. He despises her for her stupidity which is real and for her narrowness: she is against integration. On the bus, Julian sits beside Negroes and makes conversation with them, not because he loves his fellow man, but to annoy his mother. Later, she patronizingly offers a penny to a little Negro boy, is knocked down by the boy's mother and Julian is delighted. But like Sheppard, he too in the end is forced to see his own guilt. ⟨. . .⟩

Of the nineteen stories by Flannery O'Connor so far published—I am told that at least one has not yet been printed—nine end in the violent deaths of one or more persons. Three others end in or present near the end physical assaults that result in a greater or less degree of bodily injury. Of the remaining seven, one ends in arson, another in the theft of a wooden leg, another in car theft and wife abandonment. The other four leave their characters considerably shaken but in reasonable case. Each of the novels contains a murder and taken together, they portray a wide range of lesser offences, including sexual immorality, ordinary and otherwise, voyeurism, mummy stealing, self-mutilation, assault with a deadly weapon, moonshining, vandalism and police brutality. All this, performed by characters who are for the most part neither bright nor beautiful, is the stuff of Flannery O'Connor's comic view.

Her apparent preoccupation with death and violence, her laughter at the bloated and sinful ignorance of mankind informed her continuing argument with the majority view. Believing as she did in a hereafter, she did not think, as most of us do, that death is the worst thing that can happen to a human being. I do not mean that she held life cheap, but rather that she saw it in its grandest perspective. Nor did she conceive of earthly happiness and comfort as the ends of man. The old lady

in "The Comforts of Home" brings a whore into the house with her own son because she believes that nobody deserves punishment. This is the other kind of sentimental, self-serving charity, the obverse of that practiced by Sheppard and Asbury. Both kinds result from a misunderstanding of ultimate truth. But so much of even the apparent worst of O'Connor is funny, because, as Kierkegaard made clear, under the omniscience of God, the position of all men is ironic: measured against eternity, the world is but a dream.

In her work the strain of hope is strong. "Revelation" stands not necessarily as the best story she ever wrote, but as a kind of final statement, a rounding off of her fiction taken as a whole. O'Connor's version of the ship of mankind is a doctor's office and here sits Mrs. Turpin surrounded by the various types of humanity; the old and the young, the white and, briefly, the black, the educated and the uneducated, trash and aristocrat and good country people. Mrs. Turpin's thoughts are mostly on differences, on how, if Jesus has asked her to choose, she would have come to earth as a Negro of the right sort before she would have come as a trashy white person. The conversation is of human distinctions and of the race question, and from the beginning a silent girl with a bad complexion and a Wellesley degree regards her with loathing from behind a book. Finally, while Mrs. Turpin is in the act of thanking Jesus for making her who she is and putting her where she is, the girl attacks her and calls her an old wart hog from hell.

Mrs. Turpin's satisfaction with herself is broken: for her the scuffle in the doctor's office has shaken the scheme of things: her concept of herself and her relationships with both God and man have been called into question. She has a vision at the end.

> She saw the streak as a vast swinging bridge extended upward from the earth through a field of living fire. Upon it a vast horde of souls were rumbling toward heaven. There were whole companies of white trash, clean for the first time in their lives, and bands of black niggers in white robes, and battalions of freaks and lunatics shouting and clapping and leaping like frogs. And bringing up the end of the procession was a tribe of people whom she recognized at once as those who, like herself and Claud, had always had a little of everything and the God-given wit to use it right. . . . They were marching behind the others with great dignity, accountable as they had always been for good order and common sense and respectable behavior. They alone were on key. Yet she could see by their shocked and altered faces that even their virtues were being burned away.

So no one escapes the need for grace: even the virtues of this world, being worldly, are corrupt. But it is easy to guess what Mrs. Turpin sees. Passing before her is that gallery of rogues and lunatics who are the *personae* of Flannery O'Connor's work—all of them loved from the beginning, and all of them saved now by God's mercy, terrible and sure.

ROBERT DRAKE

From "'The Bleeding Stinking Mad Shadow of Jesus' in the Fiction of Flannery O'Connor"

Comparative Literature Studies, 1966, pp. 183–96

The fiction of the late Flannery O'Connor poses a unique problem. Unlike some contemporary Christian writers, she makes no concessions to the non-Christian world: on the whole, she refuses to make her ideology palatable to non-Christian readers by suggesting any philosophical frame of reference other than that of Christian orthodoxy. And today this is an extremely big risk to take: such a theme and such methods inevitably deny the Christian writer many readers. Significantly, many of those same readers find Dante and Milton as rewarding as ever. But one suspects that they may be reading *Paradise Lost* and the *Divine Comedy* simply as "poetry" and discounting what they believe to be the theological residuum as "history"—interesting but no longer relevant in these enlightened times.

This approach, however, is almost impossible with Miss O'Connor. For one thing, she is only recently dead: in a sense, she has not yet passed into history. The settings of her novels and stories are thoroughly contemporary; and, more significantly, her overriding strategy is always to shock, embarrass, even outrage rationalist readers—and perhaps most especially those like the sort mentioned above who think Dante and Milton are great poets as long as one does not have to take their theology seriously. Such readers, significantly, are very quick to defend the King James Bible against the encroachments of modern translations—not on any theological grounds but rather as a literary masterpiece in danger of competition from cheap imitations. T. S. Eliot has pointed out that such a defense assumes of course that the theological content is dead: it is just the literature they are interested in.

But Miss O'Connor really seems to believe all that stuff, and she cannot be written off for a long time as "history." The theology is simply there—as such—and must be reckoned with. In her case the theology is perhaps even more obtrusive than it is in a writer like Eliot, many of whose poems seem "patient of" a Christian interpretation but not exclusively so. Furthermore, she often seems to regard her function as prophetic or evangelistic and makes no bones about it: she has, in a sense, come to call the wicked to repentance—and none more so than the modern intellectuals who have no use for Christianity, the Church, or its traditional doctrines. And this may be what does limit her audience: she makes a crucial problem of belief. And the fact that she is writing in what has been called the post-Christian world (as Dante or even Milton were not) may force her to adopt a kind of shock tactics.

But by no means is this to say that Miss O'Connor was writing programmatic or propagandistic fiction: if she had been, she would not have written nearly so well. She was not writing just tracts for the times; though, in the broadest sense, her fiction is that too. It is to say, however, that her vision of man in this world was uncompromisingly Christian: she saw all of life in Christian terms; she thought the Gospels were really true; and she accepted the historic teachings of the Church. And this intellectual and philosophical position informed everything she wrote. She was not trying to "sell" Christianity; she was—as indeed any writer is—trying to "sell" her particular perception of life in this world as valid.

Though born and bred a Roman Catholic, Miss O'Connor rarely wrote about her fellow communicants, largely, one suspects, for geographical and historical reasons. As an almost lifelong resident of rural Georgia, she inevitably knew more—and perhaps more about—Protestants, particularly those in the fundamentalist and pentecostal sects. But there was nothing narrow or sectarian in her theology: she was Catholic in the oldest and widest sense of the term. Indeed, one suspects that Miss O'Connor's hot-gospelers and the Church of Rome have much more in common than not, though of course many of her fictional characters do look on the Pope as the Whore of Babylon.

Certainly, it does not seem true, as has been once or twice suggested, that she was a sophisticated Roman making sport with the eccentricities and grotesqueries of her good Southern Baptist brethren. Such a charge is wide of the mark. If anything, Miss O'Connor seems to take a grim, ironic pleasure in siding with the Southern fundamentalists against the modern, willful intellectuals or the genteel, self-sufficient schemers who are her greatest villains. The Southern Baptists or the Holy Rollers may be violent or grotesque or at times even ridiculous; but, she implies, they are a whole lot nearer the truth than the more "enlightened" but godless intellectuals or even the respectable do-gooders and church-goers who look on the Church as some sort of glorified social service institution while preferring to ignore its pricklier doctrines.

In the light of these observations, then, Miss O'Connor's major theme should come as no surprise to us. It is that the Christian religion is a very shocking, indeed a scandalous business ("bidness" some of her characters would say) and that its Savior is an offense and a stumbling block, even a "bleeding stinking mad" grotesque to many. He "upsets the balance around here"; He "puts the bottom rail on top"; He makes the first last and the last first. In short, He revolutionizes the whole Creation and turns the whole world upside down, to the scandal of those who believe that two plus two always equals four (and, with craft, possibly five) or those who believe that they do not need any outside help (a savior) because they are doing all right by themselves. And this Christ comes not lamb-like and meek, as a rule, but comes in terrifying glory, riding the whirlwind: He is more like Eliot's "Christ the tiger" than gentle Jesus meek and mild. There is nothing sweet or sentimental about Him, and He terrifies before He can bless.

This theme, along with several related sub-themes, constitutes the principal burden of Miss O'Connor's work; and, even when it is not obvious, it is usually lurking in the background (like her Christ), ready to spring out to confront her rationalists and do-gooders (and the reader) with its grisly imperative: "Choose you this day whom ye will serve." And it is impossible, implies Miss O'Connor, to blink the issue: there is no place for Laodiceans in her world. For this reason her fiction, though carefully ordered, even sedate and regular in its narrative progressions, has often the urgent intensity, the ordered ferocity of a dramatic but sober evangelistic sermon. And one feels that, in her continuing insistence on the immediacy and importance of the four last things, she recaptures (as indeed the fundamentalist sects try to do) something of the atmosphere of the Primitive Church.

Indeed, the world of Miss O'Connor's fiction seems to wait hourly for Judgment Day—or some new revelation or perhaps a transfiguration, in any case, some sign that the Almighty is still "in charge here." Exactly *what* the event will be is not so important as that her world is subject to the continuous supervision of the Management, who makes itself known sometimes quietly and sedately but, more often here, in a "purifying terror."

With such considerations in mind, it is well now to proceed to an examination of Miss O'Connor's fiction, both thematically and structurally, to see for ourselves this apocalyptic writer at work and to note the strategies she employed (or was forced to employ) to embody her disturbing visions for a largely indifferent or even hostile public.

Except for some fugitive stories and critical essays, Miss O'Connor's work consists of four published volumes: her first novel, *Wise Blood* (1952); her first collection of stories, *A Good Man Is Hard to Find* (1956); a second novel, *The Violent Bear It Away* (1960); and a posthumous collection of stories,

Everything That Rises Must Converge (1965). Though she seems to have wanted to write more novels, her real *forte* was the short story—and for reasons which are perhaps not difficult to ascertain. The violent but fiercely controlled intensity with which she wrote is extremely difficult to sustain for the length of a novel, and the ironic reversals on which so many of her plots turn seem to demand the shorter form. Her prose style is lean and spare, her narrative method swift and sinewy—perfectly adapted to her highly compressed story form. Full-scale portraiture and character development have little place in such fiction, and indeed what seems to be the principal flaw in her novels is that they are just too spare: too much of the canvas remains empty after the bold outline has been violently brushed on.

Wise Blood, her first novel, is perhaps the least successful of Miss O'Connor's more ambitious works. And the reason may be that her shattering perceptions about fallen man have not sufficiently coalesced into a strong thematic design. Her familiar themes, her trade-mark characters are here aplenty; and the whole fabric of the novel pulsates with frenzied energy. But it might be that Miss O'Connor was trying too hard to say too much too soon.

Hazel Motes, a name that already establishes her flair for the grotesque and perhaps the allegorical, is the protagonist here. He returns southward after a hitch in the service to become a sort of anti-evangelist, to preach the "Church Without Christ." "I'm going to preach there was no Fall because there was nothing to fall from and no Redemption because there was no Fall and no Judgment because there wasn't the first two. Nothing matters but that Jesus was a liar," he proclaims. And indeed, the case for that side of the argument cannot be better stated. And Haze, as he is sometimes called, has not side-stepped the issue: this day he has chosen.

The novel is full of other characters not so bold—or so honest—as Haze: people who feel the need of some kind of "outside help," some sort of savior; but who are not willing to decide for Christ. Among them are the familiar O'Connor characters—rural Southerners uprooted from their traditional environment and set down, to their confusion, in the anonymity of the city to face the modern world.

Asa Hawks is a disgraced evangelist. He once promised to blind himself in public to prove his faith, but his nerve failed and he spends his time now hiding as a "blind" man behind dark glasses with his red-hot up-to-date daughter, Sabbath Lily Hawks, acting as his guide. She had once written an advice columnist about how far to go in sexual matters, only to receive the following reply: "Light necking is acceptable, but I think your real problem is one of adjustment to the modern world. Perhaps you ought to re-examine your religious values to see if they meet your needs in Life. A religious experience can be a beautiful addition to living if you put it in the proper perspective and do not let it warf [sic] you." Sabbath Lily Hawks, like many of Miss O'Connor's characters, perhaps has counted the cost of the Christian choice and finds it too high. All things in moderation indeed. . . .

Another contemporary attitude toward the Christian religion is well realized in a man calling himself Onnie Jay Holy (his real name is Hoover Shoats), who tries to horn in on what he thinks is Hazel Motes' racket. Holy has been a radio evangelist in his time—on a program called "Soulsease, a quarter hour of Mood, Melody, and Mentality," and his brand of the Gospel is based "on your own personal interpretation of the Bible." But Hazel, with his perverse honesty, is not having anything to do with such money-changers in the temple. He

continues to plump for Anti-Christ: he does not think Jesus is a medicine which can be taken as needed, certainly not a commodity to be purveyed. "Blasphemy is the way to the truth," he continues to proclaim.

The most puzzling of Hazel's opponents may be Enoch Emery, who has come from the farm to the city and taken a job as guard in the city museum. Enoch asserts that he has "wise blood" that tells him what is important and when things are going to happen. And this wise blood urges him to show to Hazel his secret savior—a dwarf-like mummy in the museum. "See theter notice," he tells Haze; "it says he was once as tall as you or me. Some A-rabs did it to him in six months." And this grotesque *memento mori* Enoch later steals from the museum; and, after setting it up in his room like a god in a tabernacle, he takes it to Hazel as perhaps the man who really knows what it is all about.

Later Enoch, still in search of some identity in the depersonalizing city, shakes hands with Gonga the Gorilla at a movie theater (the first hand he has shaken since coming to the city) and resolves to steal the gorilla suit because apparently he thinks it will give him some sort of identity. And the gorilla suit supplants the mummy as his savior. "No gorilla in existence, whether in the jungles of Africa or California, or in New York City in the finest apartment in the world, was happier at that moment than this one, whose god had finally rewarded it."

And perhaps Hazel himself has a savior: his beat-up old "rat-colored" Essex car, which becomes his soul's retreat and his means of escape from whatever situation displeases him. "Nobody with a good car needs to be justified," he says. But Hazel has been fighting all his life to avoid the Savior preached by his evangelist grandfather, the Jesus "moving from tree to tree in the back of his mind, a wild ragged figure motioning him to turn around and come off into the dark where he was not sure of his footing, where he might be walking on the water and not know it and then suddenly know it and drown." And like many other modern, Hazel had then begun to have the "deep black wordless conviction in him that the way to avoid Jesus was to avoid sin." He thought he could manage all right by himself too.

But when Hazel has violently disposed of one of the "false" prophets who give him his competition and then lost his old Essex, he undergoes some kind of fierce conversion and (like Oedipus?) blinds himself, perhaps in remorse. When his landlady, who "was not religious or morbid, for which every day she thanked her stars," says she is as good "not believing in Jesus as many a one that does," Hazel replies, "You're better. If you believed in Jesus, you wouldn't be so good." Indeed not. Christian belief would bring conviction of sin and perhaps a healthy distrust of good works. Later he shuts her up with "Mind your own business. You can't see," as presumably he now does in blindness. And like some early Christian ascetic, he wears barbed wire beneath his shirt—presumably the modern Southern equivalent of a hair shirt.

Though *Wise Blood* is uneven and sometimes not sufficiently "rendered" or even coherent, Miss O'Connor's major themes are already emerging. Man cannot justify himself; he cannot find salvation in any of the modern saviors, whether sex or technology or consumer goods; and Christ, when accepted, is sometimes a terrible Savior indeed—scandalous to the "enlightened" but stern and all-demanding to the converted. Attempts to escape Him or deny Him make man at once warped and ridiculous. Yet it is often those whom the upright and wholesome regard as grotesque and morbid who become chosen vessels indeed. And this is the scandal of the Gospels:

the real grotesques are the self-justified; the apparent grotesques may be the blessed.

It should never be forgotten, of course, that always in Miss O'Connor's fiction behind the grotesque lies the ultimate concept of straightness or "ought-ness," without which the grotesque is meaningless: we cannot know that anything is crooked unless we know that something else is straight. ⟨. . .⟩

Miss O'Connor's themes and her presentation of them, though unique in contemporary American fiction, would seem inevitably to deny her the widest audience, even among the most genuinely sophisticated readers. Often, with the best will in the world, such readers will simply not be able to accept her uncompromising theological frame of reference: some tension in that quarter seems unavoidable. Nevertheless, whether or not they can accept her particular interpretation, many readers would agree that Miss O'Connor's diagnosis of the human condition is pretty accurate. For all its darkness and terror, her Georgia is no foreign country; and we are none of us strangers there.

REBECCA R. BUTLER
"What's So Funny about Flannery O'Connor?" (1979)

Flannery O'Connor Bulletin, Autumn 1980, pp. 30–40

When Flannery O'Connor was asked why the story about the grisly family murder, "A Good Man Is Hard to Find," appeared to be her favorite, she corrected that impression: She chose that story for her public reading engagements, she explained, not because of a special preference for it, but because, she said, it was the only one she could get through out loud without laughing.[1]

Now, if any of you have ever studied or taught that particular O'Connor short story, you may agree with the author that it is entirely possible to read right through it without once being incapacitated by laughter. I know myself that I can keep a perfectly straight face as I read of the children and their mother being marched off into the woods at gunpoint, followed by the sounds of shots. And when the grandmother calls out to the Misfit, " 'You're one of my own children!' " and he shoots her three times in the chest, I don't even smile. On the other hand, I think it would take some practice for me to maintain a deadpan throughout the grandmother's story of her youthful suitor, Mr. Edgar Atkins Teagarden from Jasper, Georgia, whose love-token, a watermelon carved with his initials, E. A. T., and left on the front porch, was eaten by an evidently literate "nigger boy." Similarly, the repartee between the grandmother and her saucy granddaughter, June Star, and the entire episode at Red Sammy Butts' barbecue house do give rise to laughter. To explain just how and why this story, which ends with the grandmother dead in a pool of her own blood, can be called comic is risky. E. B. White gives this warning to would-be analysts of comedy: "Humor can be dissected," he wrote, "as a frog can, but the thing dies in the process and the innards are discouraging to any but the pure scientific mind."[2] O'Connor herself used the same image in voicing a similar complaint about the fate of her stories: "Every time a story of mine appears in a freshman anthology," she said, "I have a vision of it, with its little organs laid open, like a frog in a bottle."[3] So it seems that, as an investigator of the comic, I face two alternatives: to step aside now or to proceed with caution. I will take the second route, using as my guide Louis Rubin, himself a masterful analyst of the American comic tradition who, in his Preface to *The Comic Imagination in American Literature*, acknowledged that "writing *about* humor and

humorists" is necessarily "an awkward business" which always risks making the analyst look ridiculous.[4] But he went right ahead and wrote, adhering to the principle that understanding heightens enjoyment.

Despite O'Connor's implication that many of her stories were too funny for her to read before an audience, some critics have failed to see the humor in the O'Connor canon. In the first place, of course, some commentators were interested in other aspects of the work than the humorous. For a while, the words most frequently used to describe her writing belonged to one of two groups: Such words as *prophecy*, *vision*, *spiritual quest*, *redemptive grace*, *vocation*, and *sacrament* belong to one group, and to the other such words as *perverse*, *demonic*, *grotesque*, *insane*, *hostile*, and *obsessive*. In other words, most of the early criticism has emphasized the religious dimension or the psychological dimension of the work, sometimes both. An articulate appreciation of the comic dimension was slower in coming. When Martha Stephens published a study of the tone of the fiction, entitled *The Question of Flannery O'Connor*, she sparked just such an articulate assessment. In her book Stephens goes so far as to say that O'Connor was not truly a comic writer, that her novels "are not *comic novels* in any accepted sense of the term."[5] In fact, Stephens accepts only "a few stories" as belonging within the category of comedy. This thorough analysis of the fiction in terms of the deep ambivalence it seems to elicit from most readers does address intelligently some of the crucial and most complex issues of O'Connor's method, but, like so many less persuasive commentators before her, Stephens fails to maintain the double vision that O'Connor used in blending the laughable and the serious in her tales. There is an assumption, more or less obviously at work, for instance, that overt references to religion, violence, or death automatically shift the tone to the somber or horrific end of the scale. According to this same frame of reference, O'Connor's personal religious views, as they are discovered in the fiction, are so repugnant and oppressive with their contempt for ordinary human life, that they mar the entire work. As evidence of this contempt, Stephens cites the physical descriptions of characters, their ugliness, their animalistic features.

It was to this one-sided reading of such conventional comic techniques as exaggeration and caricature as indications that "human life is a sordid, almost unrelievedly hideous affair,"[6] that Carter Martin seemed to be addressing his analysis of "Comedy and Humor in Flannery O'Connor's Fiction."[7] Equally pertinent was Louis Rubin's contribution to the O'Connor Symposium in Milledgeville in 1977, "Flannery O'Connor's Company of Southerners; or, 'The Artificial Nigger' Read as Fiction Rather Than Theology."[8] Martin indicates a corrective direction by reviewing the broad contours of Western comedy from Aristophanes to Jonson to Bergson; what he calls the "comic-cosmic" view of man, that more inclusive view, is certainly the one that O'Connor found most workable and is the context into which her work fits most comfortably. And, in particular, it fits into the American version of that view, as Rubin indicates by reminding us of the wealth of comic writers and characters who belong to the Middle Georgia region where Flannery attended high school and did her mature writing. Uncle Remus, Simon Suggs, Polly Peachblossom, Major Jones, Johnson Jones Hooper all lived in or hailed from this special region. And a comparison of O'Connor's comic characterizations and themes with those of Joel Chandler Harris or Augustus Baldwin Longstreet shows that, no more than they was she ridiculing, disdaining, or demeaning these poor rural folk nor their lives. The conventions of the tradition can be understood through a meaningful perspective.

It is not unusual to be tone-deaf when encountering a new style. My own students, I know, are sometimes unable to see anything comic in Manley Pointer's theft and desertion of Joy-Hulga in "Good Country People," nor do they always laugh at Mrs. Crater's sly campaign to marry her not-entirely-eligible only daughter, Lucynell, to Mr. Shiftlet. For critics to be so unappreciative, however, is disappointing. The students, after all, know little of the stylistics of comedy, and they are only beginning to develop their imaginative "ears." For the benefit of the student or any reader new to O'Connor's fiction, a relatively brief tuning-up period is in order. First on the checklist are titles: occasionally the title will sound a bit peculiar or zany itself, like "The Artificial Nigger" or "You Can't Be Any Poorer Than Dead." More often the title gains comic momentum as it recurs in the story, the way "A Good Man Is Hard to Find," a familiar song title, does as it reappears as a hackneyed expression in Red Sammy Butt's conversation, and is repeated with a twist by the Misfit who, by his own admission is not a good man, but would like to be able to verify the reported goodness of Jesus. "The Life You Save May Be Your Own" was actually the winning slogan in a contest sponsored by the Department of Public Safety during the early 1950's when highway deaths were on the rise. The phrase is particularly appropriate for Mr. Shiftlet, being, as it is, a direct descendant of Simon Suggs' motto: "It is good to be shifty in a new country." The second benchmark, applicable in any comic work, is the name of any character or place. Why name a con artist Manley Pointer, or Hoover Shoats for that matter, if your aim is a primarily sober one? And we have already mentioned Red Sammy Butts, an ideal name for a buffoon-host. Although all of O'Connor's names are actually well-known in certain Southern regions, usually they are uncommon; they seem to be chosen for their suggestiveness or their sound effect: Hooten, Parrum, Turpin, Cheatham, Godhigh, Farebrother, Ham, Block, Fox, Pitts. Place names work in a similar fashion: Taulkinham, Eastrod, Toombsboro, Timberboro, Partridge. And there are the ladies with three names, for some reason always good for a laugh: Sally Poker Sash, Lucynell Crater, Sarah Ruth Cates. In "The Displaced Person," Mrs. McIntyre's litany of worthless tenants suggests a recital of the plagues of Egypt: there were the Shortleys, Ringfields, Collinses, Garrits, Jarrells, Perkinses, Pinkins, and Herrins. From the same story, the unpronounceable Guizac is rendered "Gobblehook" by Mrs. Shortley, who also says that she'd as soon call a child Bollweevil as Sledgewig. Such films as "The Displaced Person," televised by the Public Broadcasting System as part of its American Short Story series, demonstrate a third way to overcome quickly the handicap of "wooden ear" which can strike any of us upon encountering a new writer. Because a dramatization allows us to see and hear the characters in action, the imaginative ear does not have to bear the burden of interpretation alone. Furthermore, I have seen illuminating dramatizations of "A Good Man Is Hard to Find," "A View of the Woods," and "Revelation." The rhythm and lilt of O'Connor's dialogue, for instance, can enter through the ear rather than be interpreted on the silent page. This can be especially important to a reader who is not native to the South. Perhaps you remember this little speech by Mr. Shortley, the dairyman whose position is threatened by a new tenant, a refugee from Poland, Mr. Guizac:

"All men was created free and equal," he said to Mrs. McIntyre, "and I risked my life and limb to prove it. Gone over there and fought and bled and died and come back over here and find out who's got my job—just exactly who I been fighting. It was a hand-grenade come that near to killing me and I seen who throwed it—little man with eye-glasses just like his. Might have bought them at the same store. Small world," and he gave a bitter little laugh. He had the power of making other people see his logic. He talked a good deal to the Negroes.

Comic dialogue is, of course, O'Connor's specialty, and one to which we will return.

Now there's one other element of O'Connor's fiction that perhaps cannot be analyzed and explained as readily as the first three items or our checklist, but it cannot be ignored, and that is the sense of threat, of danger, of violence that, in some form, permeates all of her stories. It is a commonplace, of course, that all accomplished comedy contains or rests upon some deeply serious or horrifyingly repugnant reality. While the underlying seriousness of O'Connor's humour is relatively obvious, a simple definition will not do it justice. I am not convinced that this Southern woman, for example, was evangelizing through her fiction. I have found a comment by E. B. White on this topic that sounds so much like something she would have written that I will let it serve. White does not agree with those who say that the humorist is fundamentally a very sad person. ". . . [I]t would be more accurate, I think," he writes, "to say that there is a deep vein of melancholy running through everyone's life and that the humorist, more sensible of it than some others, compensates for it actively and positively. Humorists fatten on trouble. They have always made trouble pay. They struggle along with a good will and endure pain cheerfully, knowing how well it will serve them in the sweet by and by."[9] And serve it does! It serves as an antidote to that mind-dulling sentimentality O'Connor attacked at every opportunity. Again and again in her occasional prose we find this word, *sentimentality*, used as a scourge against mindless Catholic readers, mindless critics, mindless writers. A similar favorite phrase was "hazy compassion," and she described one of her reader's affection for the Misfit as "sentimental." In her resistance to heart-warming and uplifting characterization, O'Connor is adhering to one of Comedy's oldest purposes—that of dispelling illusion. Sentimentality, as represented by the Grandmother and quite a number of upright matrons, is a self-deceit that O'Connor shock tactics are designed to expose. A sentimental comedy, of course, would contain no murders, no abandonments, no strokes, no handicaps nor illnesses of a disfiguring nature. No wooden legs, no coffins too small for the body, no cans of peanut brittle filled with teeth-fracturing springs, no women pregnant in iron lungs, no wheel chair veterans left in the sun beside the Coke machine. The "paraphernalia of suffering," as Nathanael West called it, serves as unlikely fodder for this "realist of distances," as O'Connor called herself.

Once the checklist has done its work and the newcomer is well-launched on O'Connor's comic seas, he is ready for more detailed study which could follow any of several approaches. Careful reading of a critical theorist like Northrop Frye, for instance, yields a systematic framework on which to test and measure individual stories and characters. Frye discusses the importance in Shakespearean comedy of the term "grace," a word central to O'Connor's fiction, and he explains why a religious outlook requires the comic mode. Even such a theorist as Freud, who would seem to be an unsuitable companion for O'Connor, produces a characteristically economic definition of the comical as "an unintentional discovery in social relations" that seems to match ideally with her own description of the "totally unexpected" action that serves as the pivot for each of her stories. Manley Pointer's theft of Joy-Hulga's wooden leg is just such an unexpected, unintentional discovery, not only for the reader, according to O'Connor, but for the author as well. The denouement occurred to her only lines before she wrote it! Other similar comic surprises may be profitably compared with O'Connor's from the works of Mark Twain, Eudora Welty, William Faulkner, and Nathanael West.

Consideration of the principles that unify the comic imagination in American letters should be particularly fruitful approaches to this twentieth-century Georgian. What Rubin calls "the Great American Joke" is certainly one that O'Connor was in on. America is a country that cherishes its ideals, but carefully avoids any institution that has traditionally embodied them—thus, no aristocracy, no monarchy, no state church. Ideals without institutions is the Great American Joke that allows for the triumph of the banal—from Mark Twain's Emmeline Grangerford to Nathanael West's Miss Lonelyhearts to Joseph Heller's Bob Slocum. For O'Connor, the Great American Joke paved the way for numberless religious eccentrics, probably best explored in *Wise Blood*, and for an equal number of abstracted or sentimental idealists, often her matrons, but drawn in greater detail as Rayber the pedant in *The Violent Bear It Away*. Probably more accessible for most readers is a conflict that is very much alive in virtually all American comic writing, and that is what Rubin has identified as the incompatibility of the vulgar and the genteel viewpoints within a single society. "Each persists in making the other look ridiculous," according to Rubin, "and usually that is what is funny."[10] *Huckleberry Finn* is the most widely known, extended example of this clash of cultural modes, and contains some of the most memorable examples of the language that embodies this clash, the vernacular and the refined. O'Connor fits squarely in this tradition, as her dialogue attests. Ripely vernacular, the exchanges between the landed and the servant classes, for example, demonstrate just how incompatible but how interdependent the two verbal styles are. Listen to Mrs. Hopewell, the eternal optimist, and her hired hand, Mrs. Freeman:

> When Mrs. Hopewell said to Mrs. Freeman that life was like that, Mrs. Freeman would say, "I always said so myself."
>
> She was quicker than Mr. Freeman. When Mrs. Hopewell said to her after they had been on the place a while, "You know, you're the wheel behind the wheel," and winked, Mrs. Freeman said, "I know it. I've always been quick. It's some that are quicker than others."
>
> "Everybody is different," Mrs. Hopewell said.
> "Yes, most people is," Mrs. Freeman said.
> "It takes all kinds to make the world."
> "I always said it did myself."
>
> The girl was used to this kind of dialogue for breakfast and more of it for dinner; sometimes they had it for supper too.

When the property-owning Mrs. Cope urges A Higher View in the story, "A Circle in the Fire," her tenant, Mrs. Pritchard, parries with sour logic.

> "Every day I say a prayer of Thanksgiving. Think of all we have," she said, and sighed, "We have everything."
>
> Mrs. Pritchard studied the woods. "All I got is four abscess teeth," she remarked.

This verbal dueling is a hallmark of O'Connor's humor, and it illustrates her use of that distinctive American juxtaposition of vernacular and refined speech, each working to make the other

sound laughable. Whether it takes on the tone and force of a Punch and Judy routine or the subtle shrewdness of a horse swap, every conversation in every story is essentially an argument, a contest between rival wills; and for this reason, the dialogue is a good place to take the pulse of her fiction and to discover, first, how alive, indeed, it is, and second, how completely it depends upon the tensions of unresolved opposition. Returning to the question of what place the shocking, the ugly, the violent can have in a work of comedy, in O'Connor's comedy, at least, it provides the frame, the context within which the laughable can be appreciated to full advantage. To return once more to the story, "A Good Man Is Hard to Find," and the question of why and how that story can be called comic, it may now be clearer that the violence of that story is never completely without a humorous coloring. The early dialogue among the Grandmother and June Star and Bailey becomes more than trivial bickering. It now becomes intensely significant that the Grandmother has dressed so that anyone coming upon her body after a highway accident could see at once that she was a lady. The violence supercharges, in a manner of speaking, the comedy, and this is explicitly illustrated in the Misfit's parting tribute: "'She would of been a good woman . . . if it had been somebody there to shoot her every minute of her life.'"

O'Connor accepted philosophically the fact that some of her readers failed to see her humor. About her audience she wrote: "You discover your audience at the same time and in the same way that you discover your subject; but it is an added blow."[11]

Notes

1. Flannery O'Connor in a conversation with Robert Drake, August, 1963.
2. "Some Remarks on Humor," in *The Second Tree from the Corner* (1954), rpt. in *The Comic in Theory and Practice*, eds. John J. Enck, Elizabeth T. Fortner, Alvin Whitley (New York: Appleton-Century-Crofts, 1960), p. 102.
3. Flannery O'Connor, "On Her Own Work," in *Mystery and Manners*, eds. Sally and Robert Fitzgerald (New York: Farrar, Straus and Giroux, 1957), p. 108.
4. Louis D. Rubin, ed., *The Comic Imagination in American Literature* (New Brunswick, N.J.: Rutgers Univ. Press, 1973), x.
5. (Baton Rouge: LSU Press, 1973), pp. 14, 18.
6. *The Flannery O'Connor Bulletin*, IV (1975), 1–12.
7. *The Flannery O'Connor Bulletin*, VI (1977), 47–71.
8. "Some Remarks on Humor," p. 102.
9. Rubin, "Introduction," pp. 8–13.
10. Rubin, "The Barber Kept On Shaving," p. 385.
11. *Mystery and Manners*, p. 118.

CLARA CLAIBORNE PARK
From "Crippled Laughter:
Toward Understanding Flannery O'Connor"

American Scholar, Spring 1982, pp. 249–57

Once upon a time a grandmother, her son, his wife, and three children were driving to Florida through a locality where a dangerous criminal had escaped from prison. After their car was disabled on a lonely road they encountered the criminal, known as the Misfit, and two henchmen. When the grandmother allowed him to see that he had been recognized, he ordered the shooting of the entire family except the old lady. A brief conversation ensued between them, in which the Misfit showed himself to be a man of fastidious manners, deep feeling, and highly developed religious consciousness. The grandmother expressed her sympathy for his evident pain; he then shot her in the chest.

Once there was a girl with a philosophy Ph.D., a weak heart, and an artificial leg, who because of frail health lived with her good-hearted but conventional mother on a back-country road, compensating for her dependence and isolation by making herself as unattractive as possible and asserting her intellectual superiority as unpleasantly as she knew how. She had fantasies of seducing a young Bible salesman, the first man who had ever seemed attracted to her, but his attraction was in fact to her wooden leg, which he made off with, leaving her humiliated and desolate, marooned in a hayloft.

I

"I am certainly glad you like the stories," wrote Flannery O'Connor to Robie Macauley soon after the publication of *A Good Man Is Hard to Find*, "because now I feel it's not so bad that I like them so much. The truth is I like them better than anybody and I read them over and over and laugh and laugh." Let us begin with that laughter; it is the most obvious way into the thicket of paradoxes that is O'Connor's writing.

Master of a prose whose directness and precision give almost physical pleasure, unusually aware of her relationship to her readers, Flannery O'Connor was consciously committed to communication. "One never writes for a subtle reader," she wrote to a friend. "Or if you do, you shouldn't." "Unless the novelist has gone completely out of his mind," she told a Georgia audience, "his aim is still communication, and communication suggests talking inside a community." Yet she submitted her readers to tests they failed repeatedly, which indeed they were bound to fail. She was committed to a Southern fiction. Yet her stories left Southern readers indifferent, while feeding every Northern stereotype of Southern degeneracy and fanaticism. She was committed to a Catholic fiction. Yet Catholic readers could not recognize sainthood in the backwoods Protestants she put forward as prophets, or the operation of grace in the violence she thought necessary to counter the sentimentality of the religious—nor could Catholic or Protestant understand, in the harsh universe she presented as Christian, the invisibility of hope. She was committed to the standards of the sophisticated Northern literary establishment which made her reputation and to which she sold her stories. Yet its secular liberalism could be depended on to reverse good guys and bad, and to see nihilism and absurdity in fictions expressly framed to deny them; "The Misfits, Shiftlets, Manley Pointers," one critic wrote, "are O'Connor's God." She embraced the neo-critical orthodoxy of the self-sufficiency of the work. Yet in letters, lectures, and public readings she was indefatigable in supplying friends and strangers with explanations the stories were to have made unnecessary.

The inability to laugh as loud as the author is only the first indication of the reader's failure. The stories invite us to misevaluate character and event as grossly as any freshman encountering, in the introductory anthology, the obligatory O'Connor story. Her own critical writings, collected as *Mystery and Manners*, are substantially concerned with setting the reader straight, and misunderstanding is a continuing theme of the extraordinary letters collected by Sally Fitzgerald as *The Habit of Being*. Throughout O'Connor's career, expert readers, writers, and friends missed the point or, worse, mistook it. In 1955 she wrote:

I spent the weekend in Connecticut with Caroline [Mrs. Allen Tate]. . . . The chief guests were dear old Malcolm Cowley and dear old Van Wyke Brooks [*sic*]. Dear old Van Wyke insisted that I read a

story. . . . I read "A Good Man Is Hard to Find," and Mr. Brooks later remarked . . . that it was a shame someone with so much talent should look upon life as a horror story. Malcolm was very polite and asked me if I had a wooden leg.

Three years later she complains to another correspondent:

All my stories are about the action of grace on a character who is not very willing to support it, but most people think of these stories as hard, hopeless, brutal, etc.

And in 1963, a few months before her death:

I heard from C. Carver [for years her preferred editor]. . . . She thought ["Revelation"] one of my most powerful stories and probably my *blackest*. Found Ruby evil. . . . I've really been battling this problem all my writing days.

When stories so artfully crafted (and assiduously revised) consistently require the ministrations of their author, something has gone wrong. We who have been trained to luxuriate in ambiguity will scarcely reject a fiction of paradox. The Comic and the Terrible can be opposite sides of the same coin, as O'Connor claimed they were, and that "grace comes somehow violent" has been the burden of tragedy since the *Agamemnon*. But we must distinguish between the paradoxes that express real complexities, the mysteries of this world or another, and those unresolved discords that announce the artist's and the reader's linked failure.

It is not that the explanations O'Connor provided to so many audiences and correspondents are unconvincing. On the contrary, they are extraordinarily successful in saving the fictional phenomena. The cannily placed Christian symbols become transparent in their strong light, and black hats so readily distinguishable from white that we wonder how we ever confused them. Once we have read the letters, it is no longer possible to make the Misfit into a Christ symbol or the grandmother into a witch (as Andrew Lytle did) or to recoil from the bloodstained prophets of *Wise Blood* and *The Violent Bear It Away*. Characters are saved, or identified as devilish; and when we return to the stories, we must agree that the clues are there.

Yet the explanations, in the very elegance of their economy, expose a central miscalculation. Fiction, O'Connor cautioned, has no instant answers: it should leave us, "like Job, with a renewed sense of mystery." But this is exactly what the explanations do not do. Instead of renewing mystery they relocate it, transferring it from the characters and events of the story of the realm of theology. Perhaps this is the proper place for it. Yet the stories seem to shrink under these anagogical readings—a word she does not hesitate to borrow from Saint Thomas. What remains after explication is not the rich tangle of human reality but clear exemplars of the central Christian mystery of redemption through the acceptance of violence and pain. Again a paradox: no author warns more explicitly against "the tendency . . . towards the abstract, and therefore toward allegory, thinness." "When you can state the theme of a story, when you can separate it from the story itself, then you can be sure the story is not a very good one. The meaning of a story has to be embodied in it . . . not abstract meaning but experienced meaning." Yet her explanations *require* us to allegorize, and once we learn to bridge the gap between the midcentury modernity of her fictional method and her Catholic value system, mystery flies heavenward. As incursions of grace through arson and through murder and through sudden stroke become familiar to the point of predictability, all moral ambiguity evaporates, leaving the stories that puzzled us all too clear.

Certainly O'Connor was not well served by her literary mentors. Her letters are laced with references to the rules of the neo-critical neoclassicism she learned in Paul Engle's class at Iowa. Caroline Tate never let her forget them; and for all her originality, she was not ready to let them go, as if, in her isolation, they were a lifeline to the world outside. They sustained her literary practice as her Catholic orthodoxy sustained her moral life, guiding revision after revision, digested again and again for the young writers to whom she was so generous with encouragement. Careful about that omniscient narrator. Watch out for the point of view. "If you violate the point of view you destroy the sense of reality and louse yourself up generally." "The omniscient narrator is not supposed to use colloquial expressions." "When you present a situation you have to let it speak entirely for itself." "A story is not an essay." "Show these things and you don't have to say them." But sometimes you do. In stories stiff with craft, the readers still went wrong. Principles elicited from Joyce and James were not adequate to carry a burden of conviction more like Dostoevski's. O'Connor was out for bigger epiphanies, and both her readers and her art might have been better served by fictions looser and more baggy, by some of the explicitness, adaptiveness, and stylistic generosity of her letters. She herself perceived it; there was not much she did not perceive. "I did fail myself," she wrote of "The Displaced Person." "Understatement is not enough."

Taught by Brooks and Warren, she placed a heavy burden on symbols. "Read 'The Dead,'" she advised. "See how he makes the snow work in that story." In "The Enduring Chill" a young know-it-all returning home near death from a disease he refuses to have treated is humbled when it is identified as merely undulant fever; the "shock of self-knowledge" that ensues, she explains, "clears the way for the Holy Ghost." The operation of the third person of the Trinity is to be recognized not in any change that takes place in the boy, but in a bird-shaped water stain on his bedroom ceiling. The wooden leg of poor Hulga who has rejected Joy and embraced ugliness of body and spirit symbolizes "a wooden part of her soul": "When the Bible salesman steals it, the reader realizes that he has taken away part of the girl's personality and has revealed her deeper affliction to her for the first time." O'Connor maintains a double standard of symbolism that takes some getting used to. She laughs loud and often at readers who "try to make everything a symbol." The questioner who hankered to know "the significance of the Misfit's hat" was told it was to cover his head. Freudian symbolism is impatiently dismissed; church steeples are emphatically *not* phallic, and Oedipus is visible in the bushes only to Northern sophisticates. "The Freudian techniques can be applied to anything at all with equally ridiculous results," she wrote to William Sessions. "Lord, Billy, recover your simplicity. You ain't in Manhattan." Religious symbols, however, lurk in the most realistic imagery. In "A View of the Woods," "the woods, if anything, are the Christ symbol. They are bathed in a red light, and they in the end escape the old man's vision and march off over the hills." It is not by accident that to Joy-Hulga's nearsighted vision the departing Bible salesman appears to be walking on water.

By the time we have read a few more such explications (and there is one for almost every story), we have learned our lesson: "to be on the lookout for such things as the action of grace in the Grandmother's soul, and not for the dead bodies." But as O'Connor told an audience of writers, "a story is good when you continue to see more and more in it." If we allow such explanations to carry full conviction, we are in danger of seeing less and less.

Nevertheless, we go on reading the stories, as inadequately, most of us, as most readers have read them in the more than quarter century since they first began to appear, horrified still when we should laugh, dissatisfied alike with our readings and with explanations which for all their elegance fail to resolve the dissonances which assault us. "John Hawkes has a theory that my fiction is the voice of the devil," O'Connor wrote Cecil Dawkins the year before she died, conceding that for one story at least ("The Lame Shall Enter First") it was "a good insight." It is a stunning concession, and an unsettling one. We can trust neither the tale nor the teller. For most readers, the stories do not and cannot resolve as she would have them, but retain the murky hostility and anger out of which they grew.

Our task as readers would be easier if her explanations had remained inaccessible. Without the preservative of print, authorial intentions known by hearsay, if at all, could conveniently be forgotten. But the explanations are there, in all the clarity of their exposition and the intensity of their conviction. And discordant as they are with the actual experience of the fiction, they draw us beyond it into a lived experience in which we see not less and less but more and more. The value of the occasional writings, and above all of the letters, is not that they unlock the stories—though they do that—but that they introduce us to the extraordinary human being whose darker voice the stories were. For the richest discordancy of all is left to us to resolve—that between the luminous warmth of the letters and the fiction's merciless laughter.

⟨. . .⟩ The facts of her life are now well known: that her mortal illness struck her when she was scarcely into adulthood; that, separating her from her contemporaries and her intellectual peers, it brought her home to live with her mother on a dairy farm four miles outside a small town in Georgia; that it took fifteen more years to kill her. From these years the nearly six hundred pages of published letters are only a selection; she wrote many more. She wrote to friend and stranger; she made strangers friends. The letters poured through the Milledgeville post office, scarcely a day without one. Out of the airless isolation of a small Southern town, out of weakness, pain, and loss, out of progressive crippling and disfigurement, the voice reaches, amazing by the strength with which she says what is hers to say and the delicacy with which she fashions it to the interests, the needs, the emotional and intellectual and spiritual readiness of each correspondent, reaching out to the life from which she had been excluded in a daily manifestation of the Christian charity she could not practice directly. They can be read in, read through, read again. Trivial and profound, they envelop us in an atmosphere of responsiveness, encouragement, and affection. "If you believe in the divinity of Christ," she writes, "you have to cherish the world at the same time as you struggle to endure it." The world, in the fiction, is scarcely endurable; we who cannot laugh at its dark mayhem enter it armored and withdraw as soon as we can. It is in the letters that she cherished it. ⟨. . .⟩

But the letters frustrate quotation: one never wants to break off. These we *can* "read over and laugh and laugh," at one-legged peacocks and one-eyed swans, at the unwieldy packaging of the books that were always passing between her and her friends in the mail, at the customs of the natives ("My standard is, When in Rome, do as you done in Milledgeville"), at her illness. About that she joked continually, lest by any chance she should invite what she least wanted, could least afford to accept: that pity which threatened as nothing else could her Stoic fortitude and her Christian patience.

These jokes tell us more about the stories than any explication. "The only way you can help a person on crutches is when going down the steps, to hold on to her belt in the back. Then if she falls, you got her. For my part I am always glad to have the door held open, but that's all." Such hard-won equilibrium was re-won daily:

> An old lady got on the elevator behind me and as soon as I turned around she fixed me with a moist gleaming eye and said in a loud voice, "Bless you, darling!" I felt exactly like the Misfit and I gave her a weakly lethal look, whereupon greatly encouraged, she grabbed my arm and whispered (very loud) in my ear, "Remember what they said to John at the gate, darling!" It was not my floor but I got off and I suppose the old lady was astounded at how quick I could get away on crutches. I have a one-legged friend and I asked her what they said to John at the gate. She said she reckoned they said, "The lame shall enter first." This may be because the lame will be able to knock everybody else aside with their crutches.

If that passage reflects back on "A Good Man Is Hard to Find," it also looks forward to "The Lame Shall Enter First," in which the lame character is a devil of cruelty and resentment, and the one who offers sympathy a fool. At the close of "A Good Man," the Misfit remarks of the murdered grandmother that "she would of been a good woman if it had been somebody there to shoot her every minute of her life." The Misfit took on the job for the grandmother, but it is the author who takes care of the reader. Any time we begin to feel sympathy, she shoots us.

Only to the two correspondents to whom she was closest, Maryat Lee and the anonymous "A.," both fellow Southerners, both working at writing, did she, at rare intervals, risk speaking of what illness and exile meant to her, and then only after she had managed to wring out the necessary acceptance. To A.:

> I have never been anywhere but sick. In a sense sickness is a place, more instructive than a long trip to Europe, and it's always a place where there's no company, where nobody can follow. Sickness before death is a very appropriate thing and I think those who don't have it miss one of God's mercies.
>
> Needing people badly and not getting them may turn you in a creative direction. [My father] wanted them and got them. I wanted them and didn't. We are all rather blessed in our deprivations if we let ourselves be, I suppose.

To Maryat Lee, who was considering leaving New York:

> So it may be the South. You get no condolences from me. This is a Return I have faced and when I faced it I was roped and tied and resigned the way it is necessary to be resigned to death, and largely because I thought it would be the end of any creation, any writing, any work from me. And as I told you by the fence, it was only the beginning.

Roped and tied and resigned as to death, no condolences asked or given. "In my own stories I have found that violence is strangely capable of returning my characters to reality and preparing them to accept their moment of grace. Their heads are so hard that almost nothing else will do the work." Dear old Malcolm was not without perspicacity when he asked if she had a wooden leg. To her, too, violence had been done.

To profit fully from the immense body of writing that Flannery O'Connor produced in her years in the country of the sick we must put the letters first. I do not mean merely to read them first, although there is every reason not to postpone the pleasure, but to *put* them first. To understand the whole that is more than the sum of its parts, let us take the letters as primary and the fiction as a gloss upon them, the black repository of all that the letters do not say, of the rebellion and disappointment and anger which the letters show so thoroughly surmounted that we might almost believe they were never felt.

Such a reading will show why she could give pity no place even in a Christian fiction, why she jeered even at compassion, its more expansive synonym. "It's considered an absolute necessity these days for writers to have compassion. Compassion is a word that sounds good in anybody's mouth and which no book jacket can do without." Within pity lay self-pity, everywhere in ambush.

Her gift, she was sure, was for the grotesque, for freakish characters maimed in body and soul, though "not . . . any more freakish than ordinary fallen man is." Sternly she told her audiences how to read: "When the grotesque is used in a legitimate way, the intellectual and moral judgments implicit in it will have the ascendancy over feeling." She embraced her limitations with excruciating self-knowledge: "The writer cannot choose what he is able to make live, and as far as he is concerned, a living deformed character is acceptable and a dead one is not." She could tell A. what was none of Malcolm Cowley's business: "My disposition is a combination of Nelson's [in "The Artificial Nigger"] and Hulga's." Presented with the emotional detachment that for her was "legitimate," her grotesques require from the reader an answering detachment— not compassion, but acquiescence in her own authorial judgment, even if it calls upon us to join in the immemorial laughter elicited by kicking a cripple. Though our bemused emotions may refuse to respond to her comic exigencies, we realize that the author has a right to laugh; Jews laugh at Jewish jokes and even originate them. "His prophet-freak is an image of himself."

Of us too, perhaps. We are all freaks, we say easily, and (as she wrote in another letter) we are all the poor. But it is an elevated perspective indeed from which some are not poorer than ourselves, and entitled to our compassion; few of us have earned it, and secular liberals need not apologize for their halting practice of what is, after all, a Christian virtue. In any case, as we read letters and stories together—what she typed out in ease and intimacy and what she crafted with cunning— we open ourselves to something tougher and more challenging than that "hazy compassion" she contemptuously dismissed as a threat to judgment: to understanding and admiration of a choice that, while it fatally weakened the art she pursued in the only pride she allowed herself, exalted the meaning of that for which she took no credit, the life she lived. If we are to understand what she meant by grace, we need both stories and letters, both tale and teller, for it is in the letters, not the fiction, that grace is enacted.

Such a deliberate confusing of life and work, certainly, makes the experience of fiction—the most impure of the arts, O'Connor called it, and the most human—more impure and more human still. Characteristically, she tried to fend off such a reading, writing A. that "of course I have thrown you off . . . by informing you that Hulga is like me. . . . You cannot read a story from what you get out of a letter. Nor, I repeat, can you . . . read the author by the story. You may but you shouldn't—See T. S. Eliot." By her harsh standards she was right. For if we read like this, intellectual and moral judgments lose their ascendancy, elbowed out of the way by feeling, and we find ourselves gripped by emotions not often elicited by the printed text, by love for its author, and gratitude not for what she created but for what she was. In a final paradox, it may be just such sloppy, intrusive emotions that transport us back to the cool realms of criticism and allow us to grope our way further into the literary puzzle we began with: how so accomplished an artist consistently failed to convey to her fallen readers the meanings she intended.

The reader who makes his way beyond horror and blind pity is most likely to perceive the pervasive theme of O'Connor's fiction, not as the operation of grace but as the humiliation of the proud. The old man of "The Artificial Nigger" sets out to teach his cocky grandson a lesson; he gets a devastating comeuppance. More commonly the pattern of pride is a middle-aged woman; usually she runs a dairy farm, like the woman Flannery O'Connor knew best. Strong and narrow, widowed or dominating a weak husband, Mrs. McIntyre of "The Displaced Person," Mrs. May of "Greenleaf," and Ruby Turpin of "Revelation" are complacently sure of their superiority and competence. Violently these are wrenched from them, by death or the next thing to it. It is a revealing pattern, the more so as we read the letters and see how the stories have darkened foibles treated in the letters as material for comedy and not for horror. But still more revealing is the complementary pattern of pride that occurs first alongside the other, then gradually takes over, the festering pride of that train of grown-up children, living in sullen dependence on mothers now seen through their conventionality as hardworking and loyal patterns of unthanked love. The children are called girls and boys even into their thirties, not merely by their mothers, but by that omniscient narrator, even, in her letters and lectures, by O'Connor herself. The theme becomes obsessive; Joy-Hulga is joined in the second collection not only by Asbury but by Tom in "The Comforts of Home," Mary Grace in "Revelation," Julian in the title story, "Everything That Rises Must Converge." In "The Partridge Festival" there are two of them. Sore, hostile, and condescending, they are literally and figuratively ugly, ugly in the particular sense that every Southern child learns as soon as it can speak. "How come you be so ugly sometimes?" asks the cook in one of the few stories where the child actually is a child, "A Temple of the Holy Ghost." "God could strike you deaf dumb and blind . . . and then you wouldn't be as smart as you is." The child replies, "I would still be smarter than some." The Negro hired hands ask the same question about Asbury: "How come he talks so ugly about his ma?" Hulga has embraced ugliness as Asbury embraces illness, compounding pride and despair, deadliest sins of all, as she stumps around in a grotesque sweatshirt and insists that her mother must take her "LIKE I AM." The letters here tell us more than we have any business knowing; it is with a sense of unpardonable eavesdropping that we read Flannery's account to A. of her own shirt, embossed with a bulldog "with the word GEORGIA over him," which she wore "all the time, it being my policy in life at that time to create an unfavorable impression." We learn from Robert Giroux that she chose to paint her self-portrait at her ugliest, face swollen from cortisone and hair fallen out from fever. The pain we feel as we look at the jacket photo for *The Habit of Being* is less for a young woman's crutches and disfigured face than for the gallant self-discipline behind the prim smile, the neat dark dress, the pearls, the pumps she had learned to wear to please her mother. "A Temple of the Holy Ghost" is a story more positive than most; in it the child, listening to the "Tantum Ergo" in the school chapel, is freed for a time from her "ugly thoughts," and prays "Hep me not to be so mean," "Hep me not to talk like I do." That prayer, too, is not easy to overhear. It is the prayer of a fiction that asserts grace but enacts pride, ugliness, and rebellion in order to castigate them—a penitential fiction. The prophet of *Wise Blood* bound his body with barbed wire and blinded himself with lye.

Is this, as Josephine Hendin claims, "an art as emotionally flat as Robbe-Grillet"? As we have seen, O'Connor asks us not to sympathize but to judge. So sparely conceived a fiction might indeed seem preventive of the sentimentality she found so inimical personally and artistically. But though the buttoned-down techniques of the Joycean short story may enforce more objectivity than we wish to feel, the problem lies beyond technique, in a definition of sentimentality that seems to widen to include feeling itself. "I come from a family," she wrote A., "where the only emotion respectable to show is irritation. In some this tendency produces hives, in others literature, in me both." Feeling was suspect in religion too. When a friend who accompanied her to Mass said afterward that "he hadn't felt any warmth in it," she wrote her longtime correspondent, Father McCown, "They look for that and we never think about it." When A. left the church, it only confirmed O'Connor's sense of the fragility of a faith which "must always be emotionally involved." Faith, she wrote to another friend, is not "a big electric blanket." But the readers and reviewers who wanted something "more affirmative" were not necessarily looking for an emotional bath in "pious pap," "that large body of pious trash for which we [Catholics] have long been famous." What is in question is not the right she defended to A., the artist's right "to select a negative aspect of the world to portray." But she was not a Céline or a Genet; her subject matter was not theirs. When what is to be communicated is a vision of grace, a little affirmation may be in order. That suffering can hammer understanding into hard heads is not a controversial discovery but a common experience, and one not limited to Christians. But grace is not only violent—even in the Christian exemplar the violence of crucifixion is preceded, as it is followed, by demonstrations of love.

"You can safely ignore the reader's taste, but you can't ignore his nature. . . . Your problem is going to be difficult in direct proportion as your beliefs depart from his." Indeed. She persuaded herself that she wrote violently because "violent literary means" were needed to communicate her vision to a "hostile audience" that "does not believe in evil"; the discordancies and distortions of the grotesque, she claimed, were what would make people see.

> When you can assume that your audience holds the same beliefs you do, . . . you can use normal means of talking to it; when you have to assume it does not, then you have to make your vision apparent by shock—to the hard of hearing you shout, and for the almost blind you draw large and startling figures.

But the means she chose to bridge the gap between her readers and herself only made it wider. It was to A. that she identified the real question: "not is this negative or positive, but is it believable." The repetitive mayhem of her fiction does not invite belief but parody.

O'Connor was on stronger ground when she argued, not from her readers' limitations, but from her own. The negative she knew she could make live: "Anybody who has survived his childhood has enough information about life to last him the rest of his days." She doubted her capacity to vivify the positive; she was only beginning to try. "The meaning of a story has to be embodied in it." When a writer is, as she said, "only really interested in a fiction of miracles," the miracles must be credible; they must be enacted within the fiction. The reader needs more than a water stain in the shape of the Holy Ghost to make us believe in sullen Asbury's redemption. We may, conceivably, be saved through sacraments, but not through literary symbols.

II

Asbury's train stopped so that he would get off exactly where his mother was standing. . . . Her thin spectacled face below him was bright with a wide smile that disappeared as she caught sight of him bracing himself behind the conductor. The smile vanished so suddenly, the shocked look that replaced it was so complete, that he realized for the first time that he must look as ill as he was.

"The meaning of a story is not abstract meaning but experienced meaning." It was hard experience that had taught O'Connor that violence can "return . . . characters to reality and prepare them to accept their moment of grace," that it can prepare them to forgive the ugliness of others and combat their own. Such experience was hinted to a few but confided to none; it existed in a privacy as complete as that in which poor Hulga cherished the stump of the leg she had seen blown off at ten years old. Roped and tied and resigned in the way it is necessary to be resigned to death, Flannery O'Connor had experienced the change that comes to Asbury, that is in preparation for Hulga—accepted and enacted the inner turning that is the root meaning of the word *conversion*. She could put it into symbols, but as yet she could not acknowledge the pain and loss and open it to compassion; even in her fiction she was not ready to share it. She would take her ugly characters up to the moment of grace, even, on occasion, allow them a vision. But she herself had gone beyond symbols into a world of believable, daily action. The stories never carry us there.

So little love shows in them that it is easy to conclude that she does not care about her characters. Those who knew her knew better. She loved her grotesques, though she refused them her pity; perhaps she refused it because she loved them. "Maryat's niece asked her why I had made Mary Grace so ugly. 'Because Flannery loves her,' said Maryat. Very perceptive girl." The letters show her thinking about her characters long after they had reached what is for most authors the remoteness of print, inventing new adventures for Enoch of *Wise Blood*, weighing the possibilities of salvation for the Misfit, sketching a Christian future for Asbury or the young prophet of *The Violent Bear It Away*. We learn to know them better there than in the stories themselves, where we never enter their minds in full sympathy, and at crucial points do not enter them at all. "Who do you think you understand?" she challenged A. "If anybody, you delude yourself. I love many people, understand none of them." We may take this as a statement of humility—or, like her other proclamations of limitation, of pride. "LIKE I AM." Whichever it is, it is a dangerous claim for a novelist. If grace operates at all, it operates inwardly. To make her chosen subject believable, she would have had to dare her way into more understanding than she was yet ready to admit, and find the artistic means to carry her readers with her. Without it, it is the violence she made live, and not the kingdom of heaven she believed it could bear away.

ANDRÉ BLEIKASTEN
"Writing on the Flesh:
Tattoos and Taboos in 'Parker's Back'"

Southern Literary Journal, Spring 1982, pp. 8–18

. . . son discours n'égalerait jamais en éloquence celui que sa chair, organe de sa vie et réceptacle de sa sensibilité, aurait tenu si, se faisant l'objet d'une sorte de damasquinage, il avait à ce grimoire naturel, son organisme humain, surimposé un autre grimoire plein à craquer de signes et n'admettant aucun point mort. (Michel Leiris, *Le ruban au cou d'Olympia*)

Flannery O'Connor's novels and stories are not all of equal merit, yet each of them has its moments of eerie intensity, each of them at some point verges on what Freud, in one of his essays, termed "the uncanny," *das Unheimliche*—that disquieting strangeness apt to arise at every turn out of the most intimately familiar, and through which our everyday sense of reality is made to yield to the troubling awareness of the world's otherness. Much of the impact and lasting resonance of O'Connor's work proceeds from its ability to *bewilder* the reader, to take him out of his depths and jolt him into a fictional environment which is both homely *(heimisch, heimlich)* and uncannily estranged.

"Parker's Back" is a case in point: homely, indeed, in its rural setting and characters, homely too in its action—a domestic tragicomedy pitting wife against husband—yet at the same time wildly extravagant, throbbing with violence, ablaze with madness and terror, *unheimlich*. The story has fascinated me for years, and I can think of no other in the O'Connor canon that holds one as firmly and as persistently in its spell. As a short story, it is perhaps not to be counted among her finest achievements. Yet, to me at least, it is one of her most enigmatic and most gripping texts, the more so as it was her last, written in a hospital, a few weeks before her death.[1]

What is it that makes "Parker's Back" so uniquely intriguing? Not its manner, assuredly, nor its subject. In most respects it is a very typical O'Connor story, a story about sin and salvation, taking, or, rather, catapulting, its protagonist, as in nearly all of her later stories ("Greenleaf," "The Enduring Chill," and "Revelation" at once come to mind), from numbness and self-complacency to painful spiritual awareness. What we have here is another narrative of *conversion*, and once again conversion is achieved most unexpectedly through the sudden and brutal action of grace. "Parker's Back" belongs with O'Connor's most explicitly religious stories. The Old Testament names of the two central characters, the harsh fundamentalism of Parker's wife, the "burning bush" experience undergone by Parker in the farming accident, and the Byzantine Christ tattooed on his back are as many signposts, clearly pointing to the religious issues at stake in the text, and fastidious readers might well wince at the bluntness of its symbolism and at the unambiguousness of its intended message. O'Connor obviously wanted the story to be read in religious terms, as that of a Christian *malgré lui*, and so sought to reduce ambiguity to a minimum, instead of resorting to the more risky procedures of indirection she had adopted in most of her earlier fiction.

Whether she succeeded is of course open to question. She has indeed succeeded insofar as she has persuaded most critics to follow up her clues: nearly all readings of "Parker's Back" are merely elaborations of the religious meaning intended by its author. Yet, as in all truly literary texts, there are meanings in excess of the one we are asked to accept as valid and final by the writer, and I can see no point in endlessly embroidering the pattern of interpretation which O'Connor wanted to impose on her audience. Not that the pattern can be entirely eluded, for even if we deny her a privileged status as interpreter of her work, even if we refuse to be bullied into submission to authorial authority, we cannot disregard the apologetic intentions encoded in her texts. They are unmistakably there, and no honest reading of her fiction can leave them out of account. Other avenues of inquiry and interpretation, however, are not only possible, but legitimate, and some of them are well worth exploring. So far, O'Connor's novels and stories have been read predominantly in analogical and anagogical terms, along the orthodox guidelines she so diligently supplied in her public statements. As a result, a good deal of O'Connor criticism strikes one as heavily redundant and, in the last resort, fussily futile. To refresh our perception and appreciation of her work, what is probably needed now is a freer, less timorous and less pious approach, focusing on the multiple meanings produced by the interplay of signifiers rather than on a unique, unequivocal transcendental signified equated with ultimate truth.

Let us not be intimidated, then, by O'Connor's theological asumptions and the deferential glosses of her exegetes, and let's try to reread her strange fictions as if we read them for the first time, in full response to their strangeness and wonder. What is it that startles and shocks us in reading a story like "Parker's Back"? Obviously, its most arresting feature, the one most likely to disturb a modern reader, is Parker's *tattooing*. The more surprising it is that in most discussions of the story it should have been given so little consideration. To be sure, all commentators refer to it, vaguely puzzled and perhaps even a bit disgusted (tattooing, in our "civilized" countries, has come to be considered an "unnatural" practice, associated with either savagery or deviant behavior), yet, in their eagerness to convert it at once into a secular metaphor for Parker's supposed spiritual quest, they tend to overlook its complex and shifting implications in the story of his development.

Parker's obsession with tattoos, we are told, begins when he is fourteen (in many cultures the canonical age for initiation) and sees a cricus performer tattooed from head to foot, "flexing his muscles so that the arabesque of men and beasts and flowers on his skin appeared to have a subtle motion of its own."[2] The youth is at once fascinated by the spectacle and undergoes a kind of illumination, after which the course of his existence will take a radically different turn:

> Parker had never before felt the least motion of wonder in himself. Until he saw the man at the fair, it did not enter his head that there was anything out of the ordinary about the fact that he existed. Even then it did not enter his head, but a peculiar unease settled in him. It was as if a blind boy had been turned so gently in a different direction that he did not know his destination had been changed. (p. 513)

O'Connor here emphasizes—rather heavily, as she is often prone to do—the turning-point the experience at the country fair represents in Parker's destiny, and the reader is clearly "programmed" to see it not only as the beginning of a new life of "unease" and unrest, but also as a prefiguration of Parker's later conversion. One might see it too, however, less spiritually and more psychologically, as the beginning of an "identity crisis," a period of psychic disturbance taking Parker to the verge of madness. And what seems to be at stake in this crisis is above all his *body*.

No sooner has Parker seen the tattooed man than he identifies with him. Yet, strictly speaking, there is no identification with a person (the man is watched from a distance, and will never be more to him than a remembered object of vision). What enthralls Parker is a body or, more precisely, a body *image*, the seductive spectacle of a pattern engraved on a human skin. The word "pattern" could not be more apropos, referring as it does to either an ornamental design or a model worthy of imitation. To Parker it is clearly both. Henceforth he will not rest until he has equalled his model, driven on by the compulsion to collect tattoos on his own body, to have his whole skin covered with them, to become in turn a pattern

made flesh. Each new tattoo, however, only leads to further frustration:

> Parker would be satisfied with each tattoo about a month, then something about it that had attracted him would wear off. Whenever a decent-sized mirror was available, he would get in front of it and study his overall look. The effect was not of one intricate arabesque of colors but of something haphazard and botched. (p. 514)

At this point, anyone familiar with Jacques Lacan's writings will be reminded of that decisive moment in the constitution of the ego which he designates by the name of "mirror stage" (*stade du miroir*).[3] According to Lacan, that moment normally occurs between six and eighteen months, when the child comes to recognize his or her own image in the mirror, and thereby anticipates his future acquisition and mastery of the bodily integrity which he still lacks. What Parker goes through during his encounter with the tattooed man is like a replay of that infantile experience: it is the unexpected meeting of a mirror self, the discovery of an ideal double. The man, as Parker sees him, is "one intricate arabesque of colors"; he has managed, that is, to achieve unity, integrity, and harmony, by making his body into an artifact, a work of art, and so comes quite naturally to serve as paradigm to Parker's own imaginarily anticipated metamorphosis. A boy, up to then, "whose mouth habitually hung open" (p. 513), he could hardly be credited with a self of his own. The sight of the tattooed man startles him out of his drooling stupor into awareness of a body not yet totally his, a body to be appropriated and made whole and beautiful. An "awakening" has indeed occurred, but not in any spiritual sense, as Parker's exclusive concern, once he has had his "revelation," is the individuation of his body through systematic adornment of his skin. His enthrallment with the tattooed man points to nothing else but his late awakening to the exorbitant demands of narcissism.

By tattooing his skin, Parker, one might argue, attempts to phallicize his body, to turn it into a living fetish. Significantly enough, most of his tattoos are either pictures of wild animals (eagles, falcons, tigers, panthers, serpents) or conventional symbols of love (hearts pierced with arrows, a royal couple), not to mention the "obscenities" scribbled on his belly (cf. p. 514). They are all indecent, of course, not least the heart with his mother's name, for, even though Parker hardly cares about what they represent, they all illustrate his narcissistic fantasies and attest to his desire for sexual daring, sexual potency, and unrestrained sexual gratification. One might add that they even seem to make some of his secret wishes come true. After being tattooed, Parker sets out to assert his manhood according to established norms of manliness. He begins, that is, "to drink beer and get in fights" (p. 513), and, what is more, his self-fetishization transforms him into a successful seducer: "He found out that the tattoos were attractive to the kind of girls he liked but who had never liked him before" (p. 513). In his amorous career at least, the investment he has made in his body seems to pay off rather nicely.

Parker's tattooing, then, has most remarkable effects in his life, altering as it does his relationship to himself as well as to others. Yet, as we have already noted, far from dispelling what O'Connor calls his "dissatisfaction" (p. 514), each new tattoo only makes it more acute. The more tattoos on his skin, the deeper his internal disorder and distress. As might be expected, the narcissistic attempt to transfigure his body ends in a shambles. In looking at himself in the mirror, Parker realizes with dismay that the tattoos fail to cohere, and that their overall effect is "of something haphazard and botched" (p. 514). And, if his long overdue "mirror-stage" proves a total mess, his series of cheap sexual triumphs comes likewise to a sorry end when he meets his wife-to-be, Sarah Ruth Cates.

His encounter with her marks the second turning-point in his destiny, and what follows it is his daily confrontation with someone who, in all conceivable respects, is his very opposite. Daughter of a "Straight Gospel preacher" (p. 517), Sarah Ruth is a fanatical fundamentalist. She finds Parker's cursing outrageous, his tattoos repulsive, and when he makes advances towards her, she knocks him down straightaway. Later, in a hilariously ironical (in)version of Eve's temptation of Adam, he tries to win her over by offering her an apple: Sarah eats it with unruffled composure, as primly proof to sin as ever. Why a man like Parker should court and marry a woman like Sarah Ruth is the more perplexing as the latter, apart from being a redoubtable shrew, is "plain, plain" (p. 510), the sort of sallow, dried-up country girl whom under normal circumstances he would not have looked at twice. To Parker himself the implausible choice is an endless source of gloomy wonder and speculation. What drew him and still draws him to Sarah Ruth has assuredly little to do with ordinary sexual attraction; it has much to do, however, with her *otherness*—not, this time, the alluring otherness of a gaudy *doppelgänger*, but the radical otherness of the Law, whose fiercely uncompromising representative she turns out to be. Parker "had planned never to get himself tied up legally" (p. 511); Sarah Ruth destroys his dream of carefree philandering by insisting on lawful marriage. It is she, too, who coaxes him into owning his Christian name, Obadiah Elihue, which he had been concealing behind noncommittal initials, and so brings him to acknowledge his identity as shaped by language and lineage. True, there is much more at issue in his Old Testament name,[4] but, before searching for scriptural parallels, one would perhaps do well to recognize that Sarah Ruth's immediate function in the story is to discipline the unruly male, to cure him of his extravagant fantasies and make him conform to the accepted standards of a cultural order, and that, in this role, she performs a socializing (or "civilizing") task often assigned to woman in American fiction. To point out these secular implications of "Parker's Back" is not to belittle its religious significance, but rather to emphasize the interrelatedness of the sacred and the profane in its densely woven texture. While "Parker's Back" is clearly another O'Connor story about the bizarre and brutal workings of divine grace, it is also a grimly humorous folk tale about a boy's blundering search for selfhood and about the taming of a husband by a shrew, and it is all the better for being both.[5]

On the other hand, even if one chooses to follow the author's suggestion to read her stories as religious fables, there is no valid reason to forever harp on the same themes. If sin and salvation are indeed central issues in "Parker's Back," there is at least one other theme just as worthy of consideration: the theme of the *image*, and more specifically the question of the legitimacy—or illegitimacy—of representing the sacred. Parker and Sarah Ruth disagree on practically everything, but it is precisely on this point that their antagonism appears to be the sharpest. Whereas Parker pays allegiance to the image from first to last, Sarah Ruth remains throughout a consistent and militant iconoclast. As such, she is true not only to her fundamentalist faith, but to a fundamental and millenary religious tradition. In sharp contrast to pagan polytheism, monotheistic religions, from Judaism to Islam, have always been prone to condemn representations of God and have always been suspicious about images and icons at large. In the Bible, we might recall, one of the prerequisites of God's covenant with the Hebrew people in observance of the taboo

on representation: "Thou shalt not make thee any graven image, or any likeness of anything that is in heaven above, or that is in the earth beneath, or that is in the waters beneath the earth."[6] It was a common accusation brought against the Jews and early Christians alike that they had neither altars, nor temples, nor any visible aids to devotion, and this charge was never denied. True, Christianity was later to give rise to a luxuriant proliferation of sacred images, yet it is probably not fortuitous that two of the most critical periods in the history of Christendom have been marked by fierce controversies about the legitimacy of their use: the iconoclastic movement, the "quarrel over images,"[7] is the most dramatic episode in the history of the Byzantine Empire, and in 16th century Europe, during the Reformation, the issue was likewise a matter of hot dispute between Catholics and Protestants. These historical reminders are only meant to suggest that Sarah Ruth's position is by no means eccentric, and that it will not do to dismiss her off-handedly as the mouthpiece of benighted bigotry. A heartless fanatic she may well be, and, insofar as she implicitly denies the mystery of Incarnation, her Christianity itself becomes extremely questionable. Yet she also stands, albeit, as a caricature, for one of Christianity's essential dimensions, for what we might call its Judaic heritage. In objecting to the Christ figure tattooed on Parker's back and telling him that "He's a spirit. No man shall see his face" (p. 529), she voices not only the letter but also the spirit of the biblical tradition. Hers is the invisible and unrepresentable Lord of the Hebrew people, hers the stern Law engraved on Moses' tables, hers the religion of the Book and the Word and the Name, the religion of the Father.

What Sarah Ruth represents is precisely what Parker lacks and what he must submit to in order to become a true Christian. For, at the outset, Parker, although he appears to be the more *naturally* religious of the two, or at least the one more responsive to mystery, is indeed a pagan idolater wandering in a deceptive world of fantasies and fetishes. It takes Sarah Ruth's ruse to make him acknowledge his *calling*, that is to say, to make him admit that he is being called—no more free to call himself, to name himself than to sign his body. And it takes her "icepick" eyes to pierce and disrupt his fantasy world, and to prepare him for the "all-demanding" eyes of Christ.

That, to please his wife, he should have "the haloed head of a flat stern *Byzantine* Christ" (p. 522; italics added) etched on his back, is of course highly significant and shows quite clearly how much he has been influenced by her and how close he has come to acceptance of her purely transcendent God. Of all representations of Christ, none have been more immune to the blandishments of human, all too human beauty and more suggestive of divine otherness than the glorious, hieratic, full-front Pantocrators of the Byzantine artists. For the latter, the challenge had been to find a way to represent Christ without exposing themselves to the charge of impiety. As Jean Paris notes, their solution of the problem was "as simple as it was prodigious: they inverted the relationship of seeing to seen; they imposed God, no longer as an object to be contemplated, but as a subject contemplating us."[8] It is precisely such an inversion that occurs after Parker's final tattooing: ". . . even though he could not summon up the exact look of those eyes, he could still feel their penetration. He felt as though, under their gaze, he was transparent as the wing of a fly" (p. 524). Unlike Parker's former tattoos, the last one is no longer an adornment to be exhibited and looked at, and since it has been engraved on his back, it takes two mirrors for him to see it at all—to see it staring at him: "The eyes in the reflected face continued to look at him—still, straight, all-demanding, enclosed in silence" (pp. 525–26). The eyes of the Byzantine Christ are "eyes to be obeyed" (p. 527): inscribed on Parker's skin, fixed on it almost like grafted organs, they betoken the final dis-owning, the final ex-propriation of his body, the ultimate dispossession of his self through absolute surrender to the Law. Like Hazel Motes and young Tarwater, Obadiah Elihue Parker is ready, at long last, to become one of God's prophets and martyrs.

When Parker returns home and whispers his full name through the keyhole to get admittance from Sarah Ruth, he experiences a short moment of radiant stillness and harmony, as he feels "the light pouring through him, turning his spider web soul into a perfect arabesque of colors, a garden of trees and birds and beasts" (p. 528). The intimation is that his desire for patterned wholeness has eventually fulfilled itself, not, as he first expected, through a transformation of his body, but through a transfiguration of his soul. Yet the story does not end in beatitude, and in the closing scene we see poor Parker thrown out of his own house and thrashed by Sarah Ruth: "There he was—who called himself Obadiah Elihue—leaning against the tree, crying like a baby" (p. 530). Reborn, perhaps, but rather than accession to a new and higher identity, the last glimpse we get of Parker evokes regression to the utter helplessness of the newborn child, and if we try to imagine his future, we can think of nothing but further confusion, further humiliation, further suffering, in a grotesque *imitatio Christi* most likely to end in another crucifixion.[9]

The half-comic, half-pathetic ending of "Parker's Back" may well leave the reader puzzling whether, after all, he has not been treated to a stark and savage travesty à la Nathanael West, rather than to an edifying religious fable. For all overt symbols and authorial intrusions, ambiguity doggedly persists to the story's very end, and the contradictions and tensions that give it life are not dissolved. Perhaps they also remained unresolved in the author, and it is indeed tempting to read O'Connor's text as well as an almost autobiographical parable, in which are raised in analogical fashion some of the questions she had herself to face as artist and believer. Was the image, the representation of the sacred not also *her* problem? The writer deals in words, not in images, yet good writers have always been credited with "imagination," and whoever writes fiction attempts to make words into images, to move from the abstract mediacy of language to the vivid immediacy of the actual, and to render, as Joseph Conrad put it, "the highest kind of justice to the visible universe."[10] As to O'Connor, she wanted moreover to render the highest kind of justice to the invisible universe, to reconcile, as the Byzantine artists had done, the aesthetic with the religious. Yet, alert as she was to all manifestations of evil, she must have sensed from the outset that artistic activity is never quite innocent, that it is always potentially guilty, especially when it takes over and turns into an exclusive passion. Art springs from a refusal of life *as given*. And so does tattooing, which is perhaps one of the most elementary and most archaic forms taken by the aesthetic impulse. The urge to adorn one's body reflects dissatisfaction with one's body in its natural state, as a mere given, a random and transient fragment of the world. As we have pointed out, Parker's tattooing rage, at least in its early phase, has no other source: he rejects his given body, even as he rejects his given name, because he wishes to become the sovereign shaper of his own gorgeous self. This wish is surely also the artist's, the writer's, and Parker, therefore, should be seen, not only as one of O'Connor's preacher figures, but also as an artist figure, and probably even as a comically distorted projection of the writer. Which is to say that tattooing in "Parker's Back" is as well a

metaphor of writing, a metaphor the more relevant as its tenor and vehicle are indeed homologous: as tattooing is to the flesh, writing is to the blank page, to the ground of writing, and in both cases the move is from blankness to inscription, from undifferentiated and senseless matter to an "arabesque" of signs expanding into a unique individual blazon, a signature that cannot be mistaken for any other. Writing, in the last resort, is perhaps little more than an elaborate and displaced form of tattooing, a sublimation of the tattooed body into the *corpus*, tomb and temple of the written self.

This it certainly also was for Flannery O'Connor. As any true writer, she did her best to recover through her writing a unity and permanence of being she was unable to achieve in life. Hers was, as we know, a short one, soon ravaged by disease and overshadowed by the certainty of an untimely death. At twenty-five she knew that she would not live long, but long enough to suffer, long enough to witness her physical deterioration and watch the progress of her illness to its fatal end. How bravely she put up with her fate is evidenced by her letters, none of which shows the slightest trace of self-pity. What her letters also attest to is that her courage was sustained throughout by her faith and her work. To wonder which was the more important to her would be idle speculation, yet the extraordinary energy and stubbornness with which she clung to writing, and did so to the very last, leave no doubt about the impassioned intensity of her devotion to art. Writing was her "no" to despair, her "no" to death, the erasure of her diseased, disfigured and slowly dying body and the production, in its stead, of a "well-wrought urn" that would endure. Or, to reuse the central metaphor of "Parker's Back," she added tattoo after tattoo, hoping that in the end they would cohere into a beautiful design. And where Parker, her ultimate fictional double, her brother in suffering, failed, she did indeed succeed. Her grotesques and arabesques have not paled. They are as fresh, as mysterious, and as compelling as ever, and insofar as the reader is *impressed*, he becomes in turn the writer's posthumous second skin.

Notes

1. See Caroline Gordon, "An American Girl," in *The Added Dimension: The Art and Mind of Flannery O'Connor*, ed. Melvin J. Friedman and Lewis A. Lawson (New York: Fordham University Press, 1966), pp. 135–36.
2. "Parker's Back," in *The Complete Stories* (New York: Farrar, Straus and Giroux, 1971), p. 513. Subsequent page references will be found in parentheses in the text.
3. See "Le stade du miroir comme formateur de la fonction du Je," in *Ecrits* (Paris: Seuil, 1966), pp. 93–100.
4. For a lengthy discussion of Parker's biblical name, see Leon V. Driskell and Joan T. Brittain, *The Eternal Crossroads: The Art of Flannery O'Connor* (The University Press of Kentucky, 1971), pp. 115–23.
5. The only critic to comment on this combination is Martha Stephens, in *The Question of Flannery O'Connor* (Baton Rouge: Louisiana State University Press, 1973), pp. 189–96.
6. Deuteronomy, 5:8. See also Exodus, 20:4. Tattooing is explicitly proscribed in Leviticus 19:28.
7. The phrase is common among French and German historians of the period. See, for example, Louis Bréhier, *La Querelle des images* (Paris, 1904).
8. *L'Espace et le regard* (Paris: Seuil, 1965), p. 154. My translation.
9. The Christlike character of Parker's suffering is suggested through similes, as in the following sentence: "Parker fell back against the door as if he had pinned there by a lance" (p. 528).
10. Flannery O'Connor quotes this statement from Conrad's preface to *The Nigger of the "Narcissus"* in one of her letters. See *The Habit of Being*, ed. Sally Fitzgerald (New York: Farrar, Straus and Giroux, 1979), p. 128.

MADISON JONES
"A Good Man's Predicament"

Southern Review, October 1984, pp. 836–41

Flannery O'Connor's "A Good Man Is Hard to Find" has been for the past decade or more a subject of virtually countless critical readings. Any brilliant work of fiction resists a single interpretation acceptable to everyone, but judging by the variousness and irreconcilability of so many readings of "A Good Man" one might conclude, as R. V. Cassill does, that like the work of Kafka the story "may not be susceptible to exhaustive rational analysis." The suggestion, I believe, would be quite apt if applied to a good many O'Connor stories. Not this one, however. If there are in fact authorial lapses, moments when the reader's gaze is led a little awry, they are simply that, lapses, instances of O'Connor nodding.

Much has been made of O'Connor's use of the grotesque, and the vacationing family in "A Good Man" is a case in point. The family members are portrayed almost exclusively in terms of their vices, so much so, it would seem, as to put them at risk of losing entirely not only the reader's sympathy but even his recognition of them as representatively human—a result certain to drain the story of most of its meaning and power. Such is not the result, however. What otherwise must prompt severity in the reader's response is mitigated here by laughter, the transforming element through which human evil is seen in the more tolerable aspect of folly. The author laughs and so do we, and the moral grossness of the family becomes funny to us. This is what engages and sustains our interest in them and, through the effect of distance that humor creates, makes possible our perception of their representative character.

What we see portrayed is increasingly recognizable. Here embodied in this family are standard evils of our culture. Indeed the term "family" is itself a misnomer, for there is no uniting bond. It is each for himself, without respect, without manners. The children, uncorrected, crudely insult their grandmother, and the grandmother for her own selfish ends uses the children against her surly son. The practice of deceit and the mouthing of pietisms are constants in her life, and her praise of the past when good men were easy to find degrades that past by the banality of her memories. Even such memories as she has are not to be depended on; in fact, it is one of her "mis-rememberings" that leads the family to disaster.

But this portrait of unrelieved vulgarity is extended, and by more than implication only, to suggest the world at large. This is the function of the interlude at Red Sammy's barbecue joint where the child June Star does her tap routine and Red Sammy bullies his wife and engages with the grandmother in self-congratulatory conversation about the awfulness of the times and how hard it is to find a "good" man these days. It is hard indeed. In a world unleavened by any presence of the spiritual—a world portrayed, incidentally, in scores of contemporary TV sitcoms—where is a good man to be found? Nowhere, is the answer, though in one way the Misfit himself comes closest to earning the description.

The Misfit is introduced at the very beginning of the story by the grandmother who is using the threat of him, an escape convict and killer, as a means of getting her own way with her son Bailey. After this the Misfit waits unmentioned in the wings until the portrait of this representative family is complete. His physical entrance into the story, a hardly acceptable coincidence in terms of purely realistic fiction, is in O'Connor's spiritual economy—which determines her technique—like a step in a train of logic. Inert until now, he is nevertheless the conclusion always implicit in the life of the family. Now events produce him in all his terror.

The Misfit comes on the scene of the family's accident in a car that looks like a hearse. The description of his person, generally that of the sinister red-neck of folklore, focuses on a single feature: the silver-rimmed spectacles that give him a scholarly look. This is a clue and a rather pointed one. A scholar is someone who seeks to know the nature of reality and a scholar is what the Misfit was born to be. As the Misfit tells the grandmother:

> "My daddy said I was a different breed of dog from my brothers and sisters. 'You know,' Daddy said, 'it's some can live their whole life without asking about it and it's others has to know why it is, and this boy is one of the latters. He's going to be into everything!'"

And in the course of his life he has been into everything:

> "I was a gospel singer for a while," the Misfit said. "I been most everything. Been in the arm service, both land and sea, at home and abroad, been twict married, been an undertaker, been with the railroads, plowed Mother Earth, been in a tornado, seen a man burnt alive oncet," . . . "I even seen a woman flogged," he said.

Life and death, land and sea, war and peace, he has seen it all. And his conclusion, based on his exhaustive experience of the world, is that we are indeed in the "terrible predicament" against which Bailey, who is about to be murdered for no cause, hysterically cries out. "Nobody realizes what this is," Bailey says, but he is wrong. The Misfit knows what it is: a universal condition of meaningless suffering, of punishment that has no intelligible relationship to wrongs done by the victim.

> "I call myself the Misfit," he said, "because I can't make what all I done wrong fit what all I gone through in punishment." . . . "Does it seem right to you, lady, that one is punished a heap and another ain't punished at all?" . . . "No, lady," . . . "I found out the crime don't matter. You can do one thing or you can do another, kill a man or take a tire off his car, because sooner or later you're going to forget what it was you done and just be punished for it."

Now the Misfit signs everything and keeps a copy. That way:

> "you'll know what you done and you can hold up the crime to the punishment and see do they match and in the end you'll have something to prove you ain't been treated right."

The Misfit, of course, makes reference here to one significant experience not included in the catalogue previously quoted, but this experience was probably the crucial one. He was sent to the penitentiary for a crime—killing his father—of which he has no memory. In fact he is certain that he did not do it. But they had the papers on him. So, without any consciousness of the crime for which he was being punished, he was "buried alive," as he says. And his description of his confinement, with walls every way he turned, makes an effective image of the Misfit's vision of the world.

The penitentiary experience, however, has a further important thematic significance. It is the very figure of a cardinal doctrine of Christianity, that of Original Sin. Man, conscious or not of the reason, suffers the consequences of Adam's Fall. Guilt is inherited, implicit in a nature severed from God's sustaining grace and submitted to the rule of a Prince who is Darkness. Hence a world deprived of moral order, where irrational suffering prevails: the world that the

Misfit so clearly sees with the help of his scholarly glasses. Here, he believes, are the facts, the irremediable facts, of the human condition.

What the Misfit cannot see, or cannot believe in, is any hope of redress for the human condition. He may be haunted, at times tormented, by a vision of Christ raising the dead, but he cannot believe it: he was not there. All that he can believe, really believe, is what his eyes show him: this world without meaning or justice, this prison house where we are confined. Seeing this, what response is fitting? Says the Misfit:

> "then it's nothing for you to do but enjoy the few minutes you got left the best way you can—by killing somebody or burning down his house or doing some other meanness to him. No pleasure but meanness,"
> he said and his voice had become almost a snarl.

It is like the response of Satan himself, as Milton envisions it:

> Save what is in destroying; other joy
> To me is lost.

But release for hate of an unjust creation is at best an illusory pleasure. "It's no real pleasure in life," the Misfit says, after the carnage is complete.

What has driven the Misfit to his homicidal condition is his powerful but frustrated instinct for meaning and justice. It may be inferred that this same instinct is what has produced his tormenting thoughts about Christ raising the dead, making justice where there is none. If only he could have been there when it happened, then he could have believed.

> "I wisht I could have been there," he said, hitting the ground with his fist. "It ain't right I wasn't there because if I had of been there I would of known. Listen lady," he said in a high voice, "if I had of been there I would have known and I wouldn't be like I am now."

It is torment to think of what might have been, that under other circumstances he would have been able to believe and so escape from the self he has become. In light of this it is possible to read the Misfit's obscure statement that Jesus "thowed everything off balance," as meaning this: that it would have been better, for the world's peace and his own, if no haunting doubt about the awful inevitability of man's condition ever had been introduced. In any case it could only be that doubt has made its contribution to the blighting of the Misfit's soul.

But doubts like this are not enough to alter the Misfit's vision. In the modern manner he believes what he can see with his eyes only, and his eyes have a terrible rigor. It is this rigor that puts him at such a distance from the grandmother who is one of the multitude "that can live their whole life without asking about it," that spend their lives immersed in a world of platitudes which they have never once stopped to scrutinize. This, his distinction from the vulgarians whom the grandmother represents, his honesty, is the source of the Misfit's pride. It is why, when the grandmother calls him a "good" man, he answers: "Nome, I ain't a good man," . . . "but I ain't the worst in the world neither." And it is sufficient reason for the violent response that causes him so suddenly and unexpectedly to shoot the grandmother. Here is what happens, beginning with the grandmother's murmured words to the Misfit:

> "Why, you're one of my babies. You're one of my own children." She reached out and touched him on the shoulder. The Misfit sprang back as if a snake had bitten him and shot her three times through the chest.

Given the Misfit's image of himself, her words and her touching, blessing him, amount to intolerable insult, for hereby she includes him among the world's family of vulgarians. One of her children, her kind, indeed!

This reason for the Misfit's action is, I believe, quite sufficient to explain it, even though Flannery O'Connor, discussing the story in *Mystery and Manners*, implies a different explanation. The grandmother's words to the Misfit and her touching him, O'Connor says, are a gesture representing the intrusion of a moment of grace. So moved, the grandmother recognizes her responsibility for this man and the deep kinship between them. O'Connor goes on to say that perhaps in time to come the Misfit's memory of the grandmother's gesture will become painful enough to turn him into the prophet he was meant to be. Seen this way, through the author's eyes, we must infer an explanation other than my own for the Misfit's action. This explanation would envision the Misfit's sudden violence as caused by his dimayed recognition of the presence in the grandmother of a phenomenon impossible to reconcile with his own view of what is real. Thus the Misfit's act can be seen as a striking out in defense of a version of reality to whose logic he has so appallingly committed himself.

Faced with mutually exclusive interpretations of a fictional event, a reader must accept the evidence of the text in preference to the testimonial of the author. And where the text offers a realistic explanation as opposed to one based on the supernatural, a reader must find the former the more persuasive. *If* the two are in fact mutually exclusive. And *if*, of course, it is true that the acceptability of the author's explanation does in fact depend upon the reader's belief in the supernatural. As to this second condition, it is a measure of O'Connor's great gift that the story offers a collateral basis for understanding grace that is naturalistic in character. This grace may be spelled in lower case letters but the fictional consequence is the same. For sudden insight is quite within the purview of rationalistic psychology, provided only that there are intelligible grounds for it. And such grounds are present in the story. They are implicit in the logic that connects the grandmother and the Misfit, that makes of the Misfit "one of my own children." In the hysteria caused by the imminence of her death, which strips her of those banalities by which she has lived, the grandmother quite believably discovers this connection. And so with the terms of the Misfit's sudden violence. His own tormenting doubt, figured in those preceding moments when he cries out and hits the ground, has prepared him. Supernatural grace or not, the Misfit in this moment sees it as such, and strikes.

These two, the author's and my own, are quite different explanations of the Misfit's sudden violence. Either, I believe, is reasonable, though surely the nod should go to the one that more enriches the story's theme. *If* the two are mutually exclusive. I believe, however, that they are not. Such a mixture of motives, in which self-doubt and offended pride both participate, should put no strain on the reader's imagination. And seen together each one may give additional dimension to the story.

"A Good Man Is Hard to Find" is perhaps Flannery O'Connor's finest story—coherent, powerfully dramatic, relentless, and unique. In essence it is a devastating sermon against the faithlessness of modern generations, man bereft of the spirit. This condition, portrayed in the grossness of the vacationing family, barely relieved by the pious and sentimental prattle of the grandmother, produces its own terror. The Misfit enters, not by coincidence but by the logic implicit in lives made grotesque when vision has departed. He, O'Connor tells us, is the fierce avenger our souls beget upon our innocent nihilism.

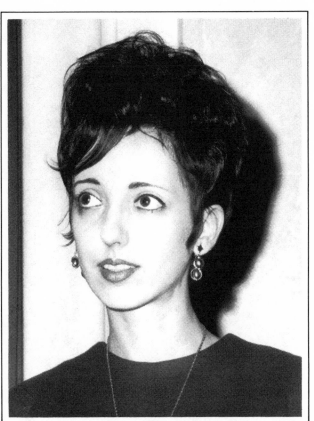

JOYCE CAROL OATES

EDWIN O'CONNOR

FLANNERY O'CONNOR

FRANK O'HARA

TILLIE OLSEN

CLIFFORD ODETS

CLIFFORD ODETS

1906–1963

Clifford Odets, playwright, scriptwriter, and director, was born on July 18, 1906, in Philadelphia. At the age of six he moved with his family to the Bronx section of New York City. In 1923 he left high school to work as an actor and joined the Group Theatre in 1930. Creative directors Harold Clurman, Cheryl Crawford, and Lee Strasberg envisioned Group Theatre as a place for actors to train and their plays a means by which to change society. They felt that good and decent people were being held back by the "system" and encouraged action as a response to the crippling economic depression. Odets acted in a few productions before submitting his play, *Waiting for Lefty*, for Clurman's consideration. The play made its debut in early 1935 and was hailed as a triumph. *Awake and Sing!*, already in rehearsals, opened shortly thereafter, to very favorable reviews. Odets's next play, *Paradise Lost*, was deemed a disappointment and closed after seventy-three performances in the autumn of 1935.

Odets accepted an offer to write scripts for Paramount Studios and moved to Hollywood at the beginning of 1936. Even though several of his scripts were produced he took credit for *The General Died at Dawn* (1936) alone, because it was the only one not substantially rewritten by other studio writers.

Odets returned to New York in 1937 for the opening of *Golden Boy*, the greatest commercial success of his career. After *Clash by Night* (1941) the Group Theatre disbanded and Odets returned to Hollywood. He continued to write for the New York stage while writing and directing films. *The Big Knife* (1948) was followed by *The Country Girl* in 1950 and *The Flowering Peach* in 1954. Some of his films include *Humoresque* (1946) and *The Sweet Smell of Success* (1957). Several of his plays were made into films without his participation.

In 1952 he was brought before the U.S. House of Representatives Committee on Un-American Activities. He and many in the Group Theatre had been members of the Communist Party in 1934. In acknowledging the influence of leftist ideology on his early works, he explained that the rhetoric of the Communist Party had served as inspiration for his revolution of the spirit. He was, in fact, a cardholding member for only eight months.

In 1961 he was honored with the Drama Award from the American Academy of Arts and Letters. He died in Hollywood on August 14, 1963.

Personal

In my disconsolate meanderings from place to place I found Clifford Odets constantly by my side. I cannot remember how this came about, for, as I have said, his personality, though peculiar enough, had not strongly impressed itself on my consciousness. We began to see each other nightly, and with hungry hearts wandered aimlessly through sad centers of impoverished night life. We would drop in at some cheap restaurant and over a meager meal make dreams of both our past and future. We would see a movie on a side street, pick up more friends, who, whether working or not, seemed equally at odds with the now consumptive city. We listened to queer conversations on street corners, visited byways we had never suspected before. There grew between us a feeling akin to that which is supposed to exist between hoboes in their jungles, and we were strangely attracted to people and places that might be described as hangdog, ratty, and low.

At no other time before or since did either of us visit so many burlesque houses. The shows had no sex lure for us; they had the appeal of a lurid dejection. Somehow we felt close to the down-in-the-mouth comedians and oddly tender about the bruised beauties of the chorus. (One night we saw a girl we knew in a naked tableau of indescribable drabness. The night we happened into the middle of the show was the first night of her new work. She had never had such a job before, but now it seemed the only thing available to her.) Most of the jokes, aside from the usual rancid ones, concerned the low estate into which the world had fallen. An empty pocket, for instance, was called a Hoover dollar. There was more social significance buried in this grime than in all of Burns Mantle's collection.

We heard that a special showing of a picture based on Hauptmann's *Weavers* was being given at the old Proctor's on Broadway and Twenty-eighth Street. When we arrived at the theatre, we were overcome by an atmosphere of neglect, of damp, of cavernous emptiness. Only a few hollow-eyed people composed the audience.

When we had seen the film and were ready to leave, a man, in a navy-blue flannel shirt with a suit and face that matched it, came out and addressed the audience with a simple conviction that must have been hard to maintain under the circumstances. He was a radical of some kind—the real article, not its phony counterpart—and he urged strong political action against the terror of the crisis, the unemployment, hunger, destitution of the day. Odets applauded with sudden spontaneity,—as if unprepared to do so and himself surprised that he had. I was no less surprised, but did not question him. I understood that his applause was not so much a matter of intellectual approval as almost a physical movement of union with the speaker who had uttered words that needed to be spoken one way or another.

On this same platform, where I had once seen Stella Adler in a dramatization of Feuchtwanger's *Power*, in another two years *Waiting for Lefty* would be presented at a benefit for the taxi-drivers' union.

After these excursions into dubious places of amusement Odets and I penetrated the mysterious night that separates Times Square from Greenwich Village. There was a very popular meeting-place in that year of the hunger and bonus marches: Stewart's Cafeteria on Sheridan Square, where the Greenwich Village Theatre, in which I had made my stage debut, had once stood. At midnight it had the festive air of Madison Square Garden on the occasion of a big fight. Here the poor and jolly have-beens, ne'er-do-wells, names-to-be, the intellectual, the bohemian, the lazy, neurotic, confused and unfortunate, the radicals, mystics, thugs, drabs, and sweet young people without a base, collected noisily to make a very stirring music of their discord and hope.

Though this cafeteria must have represented a high degree of affluence to the really hungry, it struck me as a sort of singing Hooverville. For, strangely enough, this incubator of the depression, with many marks of waste and decay upon it, was in point of fact a place rank with promise. Some of the old Village (1915–25) was going to pot here, but also something new, not wholly aware of itself, and to this day still immature, was in an early state of gestation. 〈. . .〉

Odets knew many of the people here. In some respects he was like them. Before the formation of the Group and during its first winter he had lived in a dismal hotel west of Columbus Circle, and here he had cultivated a little horror and more love for the atmosphere of dejection and defeat. It was as if he wanted to be one with the semi-derelicts who were moldering in this pesthouse. Now that he was moving from the Fifty-seventh Street Group apartment down to the Village, he came upon an environment that corresponded in poverty with that which he had already known, but the difference was that in the first instance there was a feeling of permanent breakdown, while here, despite much looseness, there was a seeking for the future and some hope for it. Odets seemed to share a peculiar sense of gloomy fatality, one might almost say an appetite for the broken and rundown, together with a bursting love for the beauty immanent in people, a burning belief in the day when this beauty would actually shape the external world. These two apparently contradictory impulses kept him in a perpetual boil that to the indifferent eye might look like either a stiff passivity or a hectic fever. 〈. . .〉

Odets, I repeat, was very sympathetic to 〈. . .〉 those failures in whom he could discern former power, and those whose potentiality he felt threatened by unfavorable circumstances. Later he would say that he had written his first plays because he had seen his schoolmates, whom he had always thought cheerful good fellows, turn into either tasteless messes of nameless beef, or become thin, wan, sick ciphers. He wanted to explain what had happened to them, and, through them, to express his love, his fears, his hope for the world. In this way, instead of wallowing in his unhappiness, he would make it a positive force.

Here at the Stewart's Cafeteria, Odets began to tell me a little about the play he was writing; he sought my opinion of such new projects as the Theatre Collective and the Theatre Union, and probed the content of my mind and the secrets of my soul. Neither of these was very secret. And apropos of one of my problems he ventured the opinion that "no Adler could ever be made a Group person"! He knew that I was disconsolate, frustrated, stewing in creative juices. This and funny habits I had, idiosyncrasies and gestures of helplessness or naïveté, seemed to endear me to him.

One absurdity we developed together: the poorer we both got, the more solace we seemed to take in smoking cigars. Together with a sandwich, coffee, and pie at the cafeteria, we rarely failed to order two small Coronas. I like chewing the thick weed, and the cigar's red band under the electric light in the tobacco rack seemed to beckon me with an undercover hint

of well-being. I puffed like a kid, not a capitalist, and it made Odets laugh. He was younger than I, but he treated me as if he were an affectionate older brother. I liked him too perhaps because he listened to me so understandingly and responded warmly to my moods, but if I had been asked about him, I believe I should have confessed that I liked him for being so physical a person. He reacted to everything, not with words or articulate knowledge, but with his body. His senses were extraordinarily alive, though he was not professionally "sensitive." To be near him was like being near a stove on which a whole range of savory foods was standing ready to be served.

The strength I drew from this period of apparently aimless ambling through the dark of depressed areas in place and spirit was crystallized for me one day when I was struck as if by the miracle of conversion with the feeling that no matter how bitter things became for me, personally, professionally, economically, I would never allow myself to be destroyed from within; it would never get me down; I would sustain all kinds of disappointment and distress without ceasing to believe, to hope, to love. I would never yield to the temptation of pessimism, to the ease of despair or withdrawal. It was as if I took an inner vow

> never to allow gradually the traffic to smother
> With noise and fog the flowing of the spirit.

I believed, as some ancient had said: "It is not within thy power to finish the task, nor is it thy liberty to abandon it." From this inexorable maxim I drew an abiding joy. In this sense I swore fealty to myself.

Thus that historically cruel winter of 1932–3, which chilled so many of us like a world's end, became for me a time of renewed faith, because I appeared to be withstanding a sort of test. In our exchange Clifford Odets and I contributed much to each other, but we both received most of our nurture at this time from the world around us, even as it was reflected in such humble, none too glamorous haunts as I have described.
—HAROLD CLURMAN, "The Winter of Our Discontent," *The Fervent Years*, 1945, pp. 114–20

When Clifford Odets died last month, the gist of the newspaper comment was that he had failed on Broadway.

In the long run, that is true. After the sensational success of *Waiting for Lefty*, *Awake and Sing!*, *Golden Boy* and other stinging plays in the nineteen-thirties, he lost the Broadway rhythm. During the last 20 years he produced only three plays *The Big Knife* (1949), *The Country Girl* (1950) and *The Flowering Peach* (1954); and only *The Country Girl* was a success.

But as a friend of Odets's (if I can regard as a friend a man I met only two or three times) I felt dissatisfied with the negative tone of the comment. It implied that it was Odets's duty to succeed. There seemed to be an assumption that a man who had bowled Broadway over a quarter of a century ago was under moral obligation to keep on pushing the Sisyphean stone to the top of the hill for the rest of his life.

That would be a harsh attitude to take toward an enthusiastic, generous, humane person who never did harm to anyone. On the contrary, he wanted everyone he knew to share the pleasures he discovered for himself as he drifted through life. He indulged his succession of enthusiasms with an obsessive innocence that dissipated his energies as a playwright but increased his areas of awareness.

First, it was music. As soon as *Awake and Sing!* relieved him of poverty, he discovered the world of classical music. He listened to records hour after hour; he read and talked about music constantly. His colleagues wished he would get on with his career. Then, it was art. He collected Klee as if he had discovered Klee. He started painting by himself and took himself seriously as an artist.

Then, it was stamp-collecting. There was a time when, if you walked east from Eighth Avenue on 43d Street, you could see one of America's foremost dramatists sitting by the window of a second-story stamp salesroom, gazing through a magnifying glass at rare and beautiful stamps that possibly could make his fortune. Again, he became an instant expert. A diffuse person, Odets gave himself to the things that interested him with boyish fanaticism. No doubt he would have enjoyed having a succession of hits on Broadway. But he was not sulking.

After Marilyn Monroe died in August, 1962, Odets joined a panel of her friends on a television program to discuss this bewildering catastrophe. Using the vocabulary of astronomy, he said that she was like one of the stars that are bound to a dark companion. The dark companion of her private miseries finally extinguished the star that the public knew.

Odets's figure of speech was notable on two counts. It illustrated his rare gift in the use of language. It also showed the range of his perceptions. There was nothing hackneyed about his style or his thinking.

He, too, had a dark companion. It consisted in the waywardness with which he indulged himself in hobbies. Having a vivid private life, he did not need continual reassurance from the public. Although he was always full of ideas for plays and blandly convinced of his own genius, he was unable to accept the harsh disciplines of writing and staging plays on Broadway.

When *The Flowering Peach* was on the road, Odets agreed with his producer, Robert Whitehead, that the last act needed rewriting. After postponing the chore for weeks he promised Mr. Whitehead one afternoon that he would stay in his hotel room in Washington until he had finished it. But he didn't. Odets slipped out and spent the afternoon listening to one of the McCarthy committee hearings in the capital. The rewriting was never done and *The Flowering Peach* was not a box-office success.

But his charming play had enough merit to induce the Pulitzer drama jury to recommend it for the prize which, in fact, went to *Firolello!* Odets's dark companion was his naiveté about practical affairs. Call him inconsistent, vain and foolish. But don't dismiss this talented writer as unworthy of Broadway's respect. He did not fail as a person.—BROOKS ATKINSON, *NYT*, Sept. 3, 1963, p. 30

Works

A new production by the Group Theater supplies the answer to a question I asked in this column three weeks ago. Mr. Clifford Odets, the talented author of *Awake and Sing!*, has come out for the revolution and thrown in his artistic lot with those who use the theater for direct propaganda. The earlier play, it seems, was written some three years ago before his convictions had crystallized, and it owes to that fact a certain contemplative and brooding quality. The new ones—there are two on a double bill at the Longacre—waste no time on what the author now doubtless regards as side issues, and they hammer away with an unrelenting insistency upon a single theme: Workers of the World Unite!

Waiting for Lefty, a brief sketch suggested by the recent strike of taxi drivers, is incomparably the better of the two, and whatever else one may say of it, there is no denying its effectiveness as a tour de force. It begins *in media res* on the platform at a strikers' meeting, and "plants" interrupting from the audience create the illusion that the meeting is actually taking place at the very moment of representation. Brief flashbacks reveal crucial moments in the lives of the drivers, but the scene really remains in the hall itself, and the piece ends when the strike is voted. The pace is swift, the characterization is for the most part crisp, and the points are made, one after another, with bold simplicity. What Mr. Odets is trying to do could hardly be done more economically or more effectively.

Cold analysis, to be sure, clearly reveals the fact that such simplicity must be paid for at a certain price. The villains are mere caricatures and even the very human heroes occasionally freeze into stained-glass attitudes, as, for example, a certain lady secretary in one of the flashbacks does when she suddenly stops in her tracks to pay a glowing tribute to *The Communist Manifesto* and to urge its perusal upon all and sundry. No one, however, expects subtleties from a soap-box, and the interesting fact is that Mr. Odets has invented a form which turns out to be a very effective dramatic equivalent of soap-box oratory.

Innumerable other "proletarian" dramatists have tried to do the same thing with far less success. Some of them have got bogged in futuristic symbolism which could not conceivably do more than bewilder "the worker"; others have stuck close to the usual form of the drama without realizing that this form was developed for other uses and that their attempt to employ it for directly hortatory purposes can only end in what appears to be more than exceedingly crude dramaturgy. Mr. Odets, on the other hand, has made a clean sweep of the conventional form along with the conventional intentions. He boldly accepts as his scene the very platform he intends to use, and from it permits his characters to deliver speeches which are far more convincing there than they would be if elaborately worked into a conventional dramatic story. Like many of his fellows he has evidently decided that art is a weapon, but unlike many who proclaim the doctrine, he has the full courage of his conviction. To others he leaves the somewhat nervous determination to prove that direct exhortation can somehow be made compatible with "art" and that "revolutionary" plays can be two things at once. The result of his downrightness is to succeed where most of the others have failed. He does not ask to be judged by any standards except those which one would apply to the agitator, but by those standards his success is very nearly complete.

Waiting for Lefty is played upon what is practically a bare stage. It could be acted in any union hall by amateur actors, and the fact accords well with the intention of a play which would be wholly in place as part of the campaign laid out by any strike committee. Indeed, it is somewhat out of place anywhere else for the simple reason that its appeal to action is too direct not to seem almost absurd when addressed to an audience most of whose members are not, after all, actually faced with the problem which is put up to them in so completely concrete a form. The play might, on the other hand, actually turn the tide at a strikers' meeting, and that is more than can be said of most plays whose avowed intention is to promote the class war.

As for the other piece, *Till the Day I Die*, there is much less to be said in its favor. The hero is a young German whose loyalty to the Communist Party survives the tortures applied by fiendish storm troopers, but a note on the program suggests the reason why the play lacks the air of reality. It was "suggested by a letter from Germany printed in the *New Masses*," and obviously the author had too little to go on. However much *Waiting for Lefty* may owe to a Marxian formula, both the characters and the situation come within the range of the author's experience and there is a basis of concrete reality. *Till the Day I Die* is founded upon nothing except the printed word, and the characters are mere men of wax. In so far as we believe it at all, we do so only because we have been told that such things do happen. There is little in the play itself to carry conviction, and neither its hero nor its villains seem very much more real than those of the simplest and most old-fashioned melodramas. The acting in the two pieces is as different as they are themselves. Mr. Odets's Germans strike attitudes and declaim. His strikers are so real—perhaps so actual would be better—that when the play is over one expects to find their cabs outside.—JOSEPH WOOD KRUTCH, "Mr. Odets Speaks His Mind," *Nation*, April 10, 1935, pp. 427–28

Awake and Sing!, which had been in rehearsal about ten days when *Lefty* was first presented, opened on February 19, 1935. It was accorded a very favorable but not sensational newspaper reception. In the *New York Times* Brooks Atkinson, after calling Odets the Group's "most congenial playwright," went on to say: "Although he is very much awake, he does not sing with the ease and clarity of a man who has mastered his score. Although his dialogue has uncommon strength, his drama in the first two acts is wanting in the ordinary fluidity of a play. . . . To this student of the arts *Awake and Sing!* is inexplicably deficient in plain theatre emotion."

Awake and Sing! was written out of the distress of the 1932 depression (not to mention Odets's whole youth). It was completed in 1933 and belatedly produced in 1935. Yet only when it was revived in 1939 did the same reviewer say: "When Clifford Odets's *Awake and Sing!* burst in the face of an unsuspecting public four years ago, some of the misanthropes complained that it was praised too highly. Misanthropes are always wrong. For it is plain after a glimpse of the revival last evening that *Awake and Sing!* cannot be praised too highly. . . . When it was first produced, it seemed febrile as a whole and dogmatic in conclusion. It does not seem so now; it seems thoroughly normal, reasonable, true."

Now when no one ever mentions the possibility or desirability of a repertory theatre, it might be pointed out that there can hardly be any true theatre culture without it, since most judgments in the theatre are as spotty and short-sighted as those Mr. Atkinson confessed. Indeed, the judgment of any work of art on the basis of a single hasty contact would be as frivolous as most theatre opinion. And, since I have paused to make the point, I might add that only by constant repetition through the seasons did the plays of Chekhov become box-office in Russia. ⟨. . .⟩

But the talk of Chekhov's influence on Odets's work was a minor note in the reception of his plays. Far more common was the bugaboo of Marxism or Communism. They constituted the specter that haunted the thirties. Rumor on these subjects was so prevalent that it reached even the daily theatrical columns. One reviewer, for example, spoke of "the simplicity of his [Odets's] communist panaceas." He preferred *Awake and Sing!* to *Lefty* because in the latter "one finds Mr. Odets working now as a party member." ⟨. . .⟩

Perhaps Odets privately harbored the belief that socialism offers the only solution for our social-economic problems. Perhaps his desire to share a comradely closeness to his fellowmen might attract him to those who hoped to bring about a socialist society, but he must also have suspected that temperamentally he might prove a trial to any well-knit party. Instead of being an adherent of a fixed program, a disciplined devotee of a set strategy or system, Odets possessed a talent that always had an ambiguous character. If because of all this the regular press was misled into chatter about his "Marxism" while the Left press was frankly perplexed and troubled by him,

it may also be guessed that Odets too was pretty much in the dark on this score.

On the one hand, Odets felt himself very close to the people—the great majority of Americans—even in his bent for the "good old theatre"; on the other hand, his heart was always with the rebels. But who precisely were the rebels, and what did they demand of him? Those he knew were a small minority, and they marked out a line for him that he could not altogether accept. After the first flurry of Odets's success had passed, everyone discovered a "change" in him. The conventional reviewers were glad; the Left was disconcerted. But, in the sense they had in mind, both were wrong—Odets had not changed.

Perhaps the truth is that the vast majority, to which Odets felt he belonged as much as to any rebellious few, had not yet created for itself a cultural clarity or form, not to speak of other kinds of clarity or form—had not, for example, yet made for itself a theatre in which he could function freely. Perhaps the "few" who often criticized him more harshly than anyone else did not know how much they had in common with those they professed to scorn.

Whatever later wisdom might declare, Odets in the spring of 1935 was the man of the hour. Theatrically speaking, the climax of the Odets vogue came with the production of *Lefty* as a regular show on Broadway.

Since *Lefty* was only an hour long, we had to have a companion piece to go with it. Odets himself supplied this by dramatizing a short story purporting to be a letter from Nazi Germany he had read in the *New Masses*. The play, written to order, was finished in less than a week. Cheryl Crawford directed it, and the setting was designed by an unofficial Group apprentice, Paul Morison, who had performed similar services for us at Green Mansions.

This twin bill opened at the Longacre Theatre on March 26, 1935 at a price range from fifty cents to a dollar and a half—something of an innovation on Broadway.

In order not to disturb the casting of *Awake and Sing!*, all the actors not engaged in that play took over the production of *Lefty* and *Till the Day I Die*, which, incidentally, was one of the first serious anti-Nazi plays to reach the New York stage. ⟨. . .⟩

The new play was respectfully received though the *New York Times* reviewer thought: "If you want to register an emotional protest against Nazi polity, Mr. Odets requires that you join the Communist brethren"—a rather peculiar interpretation of a play that at most called for a united front against Nazism. But the plea for such a front in those days was chiefly associated with Communists.

The play actually was a rather old-fashioned piece of theatre in a style that derived from the swell of Odets's sentiment, an unavowed inclination toward romantic drama, and a feeling for social currents. It was a little artificial, yet not without some qualities of youthful sweetness and idealism.

Awake and Sing! never made much money. Odets believed the failure of *Awake and Sing!* to become a box-office smash was due to the Group's lack of business ability. He was wrong; the play attracted an important but small part of the theatre-going public: those who bought the cheaper tickets. *Lefty* and *Till the Day I Die* were seen by a devoted and intelligent public still too small (and poor), alas, to furnish box-office comfort.

Yet, except for their bewildered backers, the plays were an enormous success. They were the talk of the town, the thing-to-see for all who wished to remain abreast of the times. —HAROLD CLURMAN, "Awake and Sing!," *The Fervent Years*, 1945, pp. 149–53

It seems to me the first thing about Mr. Odets' new play that we should mention is a certain quality in the dialogue. He has a sense of character drawing that exhibits the courage of outline. An unusual number of the characters in *Golden Boy* are set beside one another with the right bold theatre instinct, a perception of the fact, unknown to most playwrights nowadays, that character in fiction and character on stage are two different matters—see the fuzzy nonsense in most British plays that come to Broadway. He has an intuition of emotional impacts that make real theatre instead of mere description. The story in *Golden Boy* wanders for a few moments at the start but goes straight on after that. The numbers of motifs in personality, reactions, inheritance, hurts, secrecies, hopes, happiness, fate, bodily conditions, and so forth may seem crowded in at times, to lack a steady, or mature, distribution and proportion, but the direction is a good one nevertheless, it makes for abundance, it interweaves elements that promise a living fabric. His conception of the scenes, where to emphasize, where bring down the curtain, has grown neater and sharper. And the insistence, more or less adolescent, that once three things in our faces is warmed now into both better persuasion and better taste.

The point I wanted to stress as where his theatre gift most appears is in the dialogue's avoidance of the explicit. The explicit, always to be found in poor writers trying for the serious, is the surest sign of lack of talent. To write in terms of what is not said, of combinations elusive in detail, perhaps, insignificant, of a hidden stream of sequences, and a resulting air of spontaneity and true pressure—that is quite another matter. In this respect Mr. Odets is the most promising writer our theatre can show. The effect very often, and always the promise, of such a manner of dialogue is glowing, impressive and worthy of the response and applause that the audience gives it.—Stark Young, NR, Nov. 17, 1937, p. 45

Hollywood has been generally blamed for Clifford Odets's failure to live up to the promise of *Awake and Sing!* and *Waiting for Lefty*. But the faults of *Clash by Night* aren't the faults of Hollywood; indeed, Mr. Odets might to advantage have borrowed more liberally from the movies' adroitness for plot mechanics and episodic elaboration, particularly in his static second act. No: *Clash by Night* suffers principally from a lack of direction arising from the want of any adequate frame of reference.

Odets's frame of reference in 1935 was the class struggle. What has lasted over into 1942 is principally a humanitarian intuition of the individual's private separation, which is valid background for pathos but not for tragedy. Here is a triangle of the bored wife, the insentient husband and the handsome lodger: surely no novelty in the theater and demanding the justification of a fresh approach. Or at least a special quality of perception and analysis. It is disappointing to report that Odets has given it neither. Nor has he given the familiar situation stature by relating it to any moral or social standard. Infidelity is meaningless outside the moral arena; tragedy requires a villain, whether it be a person or a society. Odets no longer indiscriminately blames Society, and doesn't recognize the Devil. He succeeds in interesting us in his characters' temperaments, but never in their tragedy.

Before he lets us down, however, Odets gives us three scenes out of his top drawer. Here he shows himself again a master of vivid colloquial dialogue—occasionally over-stylized so that single phrases stand out in epigrammatic isolation, but the stylization is in general a benefit; "lifelike" dialogue is a far more subtle affair than mere stenographic naturalism.—David Burnham, *Com*, Jan. 16, 1942, pp. 319–20

Clifford Odets was a brash and talented young man when—to adopt his own point of view—he "sold himself to the movies." He emerges now still brash and still talented but hardly improved. He is as indignant as he must always have assumed that he would be, and *The Big Knife* (National Theater) is an exposure of the movie capital which must take its place beside the exposures of the advertising business written by bright young advertising men and the exposures of the publishing business written by bright young publishers. Since understatement was never his besetting sin, this is, not unexpectedly, a very Hollywoodish version of Hollywood. All the emotions represented in gorgeous technicolor.

Most of us think of Hollywood as a place where mediocrity is overpaid—in money and in fame; but to Mr. Odets it is, instead, a place where genius is prevented from expressing itself. His hero is a fabulously successful young leading man of the films whose better self we are expected to take on faith while he, languishing under a fourteen-year contract assuring him several dollars, laments that he cannot get away from it all into some world where he can indulge his natural integrity. The fact that this hero is played—and played very well—by John Garfield, who is in real life himself a fabulously successful young leading man of the films, seems to put him also in the ambiguous position of the author and to make the whole production appear a rather remarkably vivid example of what might be called biting the hand that overfeeds you. What, one is always tempted to ask, prevents this hero from getting away from it all? And the action of the play is really one long effort to convince us that he can't.

It seems that before the first curtain rises he had been on a drunken spree with an extra-girl and had had the misfortune to run down a child in the street. It seems further that he had agreed to the studio's scheme under which a publicity man is persuaded to pretend that it was really he who was driving what I am afraid we must call "The death car." Now, whenever the star gets restless, the studio threatens to expose him—though it is a little difficult to understand how it could do that without also exposing itself. And even if we are willing to assume, as apparently we are expected to do, that the drunken spree and refusal to take the consequences are somehow not the fault of the hero but the fault of Hollywood, it is still rather hard to see how a simple walking away would cost him anything except the millions which he professes to despise. At one point in the action he remarks, very sagely indeed, that "there is nothing so habit-forming as money"; and if Mr. Odets had not been so anxious to shift all the guilt from his hero to "the industry," he might have written a very interesting play on just that theme. Its moral would be that you cannot eat your cake if you insist on having it too. And that is the moral which, despite all the playwright's efforts to distract attention from it, keeps shouting itself out from almost every scene.

If Mr. Odets were not a man of considerable talent, the subject would hardly be worth discussing. But he is a man of considerable talent with a real gift for words, which he all too often misuses, and a real gift for writing effective scenes. As in the old days, he can still strike out a bitter wisecrack and still invent the seemingly irrelevant remark which, like the irrelevant remarks in his professed master, Chekhov, is not really irrelevant. He can also, as is here illustrated by the role of the movie magnate, well played by J. Edward Bromberg, sketch out a grand melodramatic villain. But the tendency to blame everything on some system or other becomes obviously absurd when Hollywood and the California climate have become responsible for everything which he used to blame on capitalism. Even the doves are in conspiracy against him, and when, at one curtain, the hero is expressing his exasperation by cooing into the telephone, one is tempted to protest: The fault, dear Brutus, is not in the bougainvillea or the mile-high malteds, but in ourselves, that we are thus and so.

At one point in the play our hero remarks that "when people say, 'Be yourself,' they don't really mean, 'Be yourself'; what they really mean is, 'Be like me.'" That is Odets at his best. But when, almost at the very end, this same hero utters his final complaint, "I have always wanted a world which would bring out the best in me," that is so completely Odets at his worst as to sound almost like satire. The desire for exculpation is all too plain. Something, alas, is always preventing Odets from being what he ought to be. Sometimes it is the Hollywood system; sometimes it is just "the system." And that makes it rather too much like a woman who might say, "I always wanted a world in which I could be chaste; but the men just will go on asking me."—JOSEPH WOOD KRUTCH, *Nation*, March 19, 1949, pp. 340–41

No one interested in the theatre can fail to take an almost personal satisfaction in the success which, with *The Country Girl*, has again come to Clifford Odets, and come because of his having deserved it. Success is a strange matter, as Mr. Odets is in a better position to know than most. He achieved it early—and with a bang. He was twenty-nine when *Waiting for Lefty* exploded like a bomb behind New York's footlights and when in *Awake and Sing!* he wrote one of the richest, warmest, and most probing dramas an American has written in our time. This was in 1935, a year which theatrically must be described as an Odets year. During this same season *Till the Day I Die* and *Paradise Lost* also reached production, and playgoers experienced the exhilaration which comes from realizing that a new, fine, and magnificently vigorous talent has emerged.

Mr. Odets's career can be said to have got off to a poor start if for no other reason than that it started off too well. It did not work up to a climax; it began with one. It commenced, so to speak, with the fifth act—a process which, however heady and exciting, is not in accordance with the safer canons of dramatic practice. The challenge with which it confronted Mr. Odets was cruel. In the years following his initial triumph he was bound to be penalized by his own achievement. He had to live up to himself, and so great was the hope his admirers had invested in him that this amounted to his having to live down his own reputation. This is why Mr. Odets must know, as few do, how bitter the sweet fruits of success can become.

Trigorin in *The Sea Gull* was aware of one of the most poignant aspects of literary endeavor: the realization that what one has written is neither what one wanted to write nor so good as what others have written on the same subject. When a novel of his was printed, Trigorin said the public read it but always with the comment, "Yes, charming, clever. Charming but nothing like Tolstoy. A very fine thing, but Turgenev's *Fathers and Sons* is finer." Trigorin's lament was that, when he was dead, they would be saying at his grave, "Here lies Trigorin, a delightful writer but not so good as Turgenev."

Since 1935 Mr. Odets has suffered a sadder fate than Trigorin's. Instead of being compared unfavorably with his betters, he has been compared unfavorably with Odets. From *Golden Boy* (1937) to *The Big Knife* (1949) there was a marked falling off. Slow as it was, it was steady and disheartening. Although proofs of the old Odets magic were to be found in such new plays as *Rocket to the Moon*, *Night Music*, and *Clash by Night*, these proofs gradually became rarer and rarer.

Indeed, there were many of us who, two seasons back when we saw *The Big Knife*, became truly concerned about Mr. Odets. It seemed as if his talent had slowly dried up. He

was scolded, of course, as if the fault were his. When writers who have pleased us by writing well disappoint us by writing badly, their fate is to be treated as if they wrote badly on purpose. One of the more ridiculous aspects of criticism is the regularity with which it finds people who cannot write telling people who can that they should have written better. Unquestionably they are writing as well as their gifts permit them to *at that time*. All of us are apt to forget that authors cannot subpoena genius and that a writer's talent may leave him as unpredictably as a singer's voice. This is what appears to have happened to Mr. Odets. This is why, too, it is agreeable to be able to report that in *The Country Girl* the stream which had thinned to a trickle is flowing once more.

Although *The Country Girl* is not Mr. Odets's best play, it has some of his best writing in it. Moreover, it discloses a new and unexpected Odets. This in itself is reassuring and welcome. Mr. Odets has usually been associated with dramas of social significance if not of social protest. His favorite theme song, sung in anger or with enormous vitality, has been "Awake and sing, ye that dwell in the dust." His characters have shared "a fundamental activity: a struggle for life amidst petty conditions." His explanation of their personal frailties used to be the over-simple one that they were victims of The System.

It is interesting to see in *The Country Girl* that Mr. Odets can write from affection with the same intensity and insight with which he first wrote from indignation. This time he is making no plea, addressing no mass meeting, and leaving The System not only unblamed but unmentioned. The theatre, which he loves as warmly as he hates Hollywood, is his background, and people are his concern. He is telling the story, a messageless one, of how a devoted wife struggles to keep her actor-husband sober so that he can make a comeback in the leading part a trusting producer is convinced he can play. The director falls in love with the wife after having at first misunderstood her. At the end, however, hers is Candida's choice of the man who has the greater need of her because he is the weaker.

Plainly such a theme in such a setting is neither new nor earth-shaking. As Sidney Howard pointed out long ago, the age and service-stripes of a story have little to do with eligibility. The point is that Mr. Odets makes the story his own. He gives it the benefit of his high-voltage feeling and phrasing. He allows us to see far beneath the surface of his characters into what is the mainspring of their frustrations or their actions. With skill and subtlety he misleads us at the outset into accepting as true the lies the actor has told about his wife in order to excuse his own weaknesses. Then, little by little, Mr. Odets enables us to see her as she is. His scenes race forward with the drive of his earliest works. His gift for deriving tension from small things is as effective as it used to be in developing large climaxes.

The originality which sharpens his writing is equally present in his direction. The sense of hard-pressed poverty, of abandoned hope, and of squandered talents which he establishes is admirably visualized in Boris Aronson's sordid dressing-room and pathetic boarding-house backgrounds. ⟨. . .⟩

When *The Big Knife* opened two seasons ago, I was forced to confess, "Few scripts have made me more uncomfortably aware of the inner despair of the authors; few have left me more apprehensive about their writers' immediate future." *The Country Girl* makes such apprehension groundless. After a stormy and troubled period Mr. Odets has refound himself and his talent. This should mean a great deal to our theatre which stands desperately in need of all that is energizing and distinguished in his gifts.—JOHN MASON BROWN, "The Man Who Came Back," *SR*, Dec. 9, 1950, pp. 26–27

Mr. Odets' new play is a beautiful one. His finest, in fact. *The Flowering Peach* he calls it. It opened at the Belasco last evening with a tender, lovely, humorous performance.

Imagine the fable of Noah's voyage told in terms of a temperamental though closely united Jewish family and there you have the plan of *The Flowering Peach*. Years ago Mr. Odets came into the theatre with another play about a Jewish family. In *Awake and Sing!* the members of the family were temperamental and united, too.

The tone of *The Flowering Peach* shows how far Mr. Odets has traveled since the cocksure days of *Awake and Sing!* The brassy, ricocheting dialogue has matured into humorous, modest talk about great subjects that neither Mr. Odets nor the rest of us are likely to solve. For the new play is the story of mankind living out its destiny under the benevolent eye of God.

There were giants on the earth in those days of the Deluge. In spirit Noah was the greatest. It is Mr. Odets' mood not to put him on a pedestal but to characterize him as the worried head of a family of ordinary individuals—a peevish though loving hero who feels himself close to God. As Noah, Menasha Skulnik, previously celebrated as a low comedian, gives a memorable performance in terms of comedy, temper, pettiness and devotion. Call it a masterpiece of character acting and you cannot be far from the truth.

No doubt, the first half of *The Flowering Peach* is the more endearing. The second half is a little repetitious and garrulous. But no matter, really, for the story of how Noah persuades his skeptical family that God has given all of them a mission, how they bicker, yet do the job obediently, how God helps them solve the most prodigious problems, how they scamper into the ark when the rains fall—all this, told with sympathetic humor in the form of a folk fable, ought to be enough to delight and move any theatregoer.

In the second act the voyage concludes triumphantly with the grounding of the ark, the flowering of the peach and the departure of the family in their several ways to replenish and fructify the earth. It is a triumphant conclusion, but after a long series of quarrels and sorrows that symbolize the eternal questing of God's children. ⟨. . .⟩

If you listen closely you can probably discover a message of hope for the sullen world of today. But Mr. Odets is not setting himself up as an oracle. He does not pretend to have the magic formula. Contemplating the long history of the race in terms of some disarming people, he is facing the world with respect and humility. *The Flowering Peach* is his testament to the endurance and native wisdom of mankind.—BROOKS ATKINSON, *NYT*, Dec. 29, 1954, p. 20

MICHAEL J. MENDELSOHN
From "The Dramatist in Hollywood"
Clifford Odets: Humane Dramatist
1969, pp. 83–97

Soon after *The Flowering Peach* closed, Odets settled in California, with all evidence pointing to an indefinite stay. His remarks on this situation in 1961 sounded almost wistful:

> Well, in some ways it would be much better for me [if there were no film industry], because I might have been more productive in the serious aspects of my work instead of the mere craft aspects. So, in some ways it would have been better, in some ways worse, because I have never made a living out of the theatre.

I think I might have been better off if there had been no movies to go to. . . . I would have scrounged around this way and that way, gotten out from under this big tent and pitched smaller tents in many a wild and strange terrain. And good would have come out of it, more good than has come out of my present way of life. I'm almost certain of that. (Interview)

Odets' motion picture career can be roughly divided into three periods. The first was 1936–38; the second, 1943–47; and the third, 1955–61. Odets had his name finally attached to only seven produced films, but he estimated the output of those years variously from fifteen or twenty scripts to "dozens." The disparity is explained by the Hollywood practice of script-doctoring. In his most specific statement on the matter, Odets told an interviewer for the *Times* (Aug. 27, 1944) that though he had written many scripts, he had taken credit only for *The General Died at Dawn*. " 'The others were rewritten for me, after I left town, by four or five hacks to each script,' he says, 'and rather than share credit for what they churned out between gin-rummy games, I decided to pass up fame and keep my self-respect.' "

The seven film scripts that bear his name (with dates of New York release) are:

1. *The General Died at Dawn*, Paramount, 1936. Adapted from a novel by Charles G. Booth.
2. *None But the Lonely Heart*, RKO, 1944. Adapted from a novel by Richard Llewellyn.
3. *Deadline at Dawn*, RKO, 1946. Adapted from a novel by William Irish.
4. *Humoresque*, Warner Brothers, 1946. Adapted from a novel by Fannie Hurst.
5. *The Sweet Smell of Success*, United Artists, 1957. Adapted from a short story by Ernest Lehman.
6. *The Story on Page One*, 20th Century Fox, 1960.
7. *Wild in the Country*, 20th Century Fox, 1961. Adapted from a novel by J. R. Salamanca.

Odets also directed two of these films, *None But the Lonely Heart* and *The Story on Page One*. Four of Odets' own plays found their way onto the screen: *Golden Boy* in 1939, *Clash By Night* in 1952, *The Country Girl* in 1954, and *The Big Knife* in 1955; however, Odets did not participate in the filming of any of them. It is common knowledge in Hollywood that among the films which Odets had a hand in without final credit were *Rhapsody in Blue* (a Gershwin biography), and a controversial treatment of the Spanish Civil War, *Blockade* (1938). The script for *Blockade* in the Academy of Motion Picture Arts Library in Beverly Hills shows Odets and John Howard Lawson as co-authors; when the picture reached the screen, however, only Lawson was credited.

While there is no certainty that a Hollywood contract automatically carries an attached rider demanding a debasement of artistic standards, many Broadway people have treated the idea as axiomatic. Playwright William Gibson, who has faced the same problem, commented informally on this point. Asked if Odets compromised artistic integrity in some way by working in Hollywood, Gibson generalized in his response:

> He sells time, and that is the only thing which cannot be replenished. Whether there is any kind of damage to one's standards by working in movies, I do not know. I think that we too glibly assume that there is, but I'm not altogether persuaded that that is a fact. But you cannot write a movie and a play at the same time.

The attitude of a great number of theatre people toward

abandonment of Broadway in the mid-Thirties is nicely summed up in an incident related by Clurman. Describing a brief visit with ex-Group member Franchot Tone, he writes:

> In the afternoon we would chat, mostly about the theatre, play badminton, swim in the pool, dine, and see a picture in the projection-room, right off the pool. It was quite a pleasant routine that we followed almost every time we visited them. Once, while I lay afloat in the pool, basking lazily in the Sunday sun, Franchot observed me with friendly malice and remarked: "The life of a prostitute is pretty comfortable, isn't it?"[1]

In fairness to Odets' detractors, it must be admitted that it was mainly Odets' own frequent idealistic expressions on the subject of the betterment of mankind that invited the quizzical looks and open ridicule when he left New York and began to write film scripts. The mixed feelings evidenced by Franchot Tone soon appeared in Odets as well.

During its palmy days, the film industry in the United States was inclined to hire writers at a furious rate. Any author who managed to produce a best-selling novel or a highly successful play soon found Hollywood agents on the telephone attempting to lure him out of the East. Once he succumbed to the lure, he often found himself ensconced in a neat office, with a dictaphone, a secretary, and some sharp pencils, but with rather little to do.

So it was that Odets, suddenly a famous young writer in the spring of 1935, received his first tentative overtures from the film world. Within a year, his reputation only slightly damaged by the poor reception of *Paradise Lost*, he was working for Paramount Studios at $2500 per week and apparently enjoying the sudden change in atmosphere immensely. An interviewer for the New York *Times* (May 3, 1936) captured some early impressions:

> Some of his friends have spoken with feeling about his desertion of the cause for Hollywood gold. "They call me a rat," he says. But he rather enjoys the situation and is militant in his declaration that the movies will never "get" him. He laughs about his $2500 salary and refers to it as one of the contradictions of capitalism.

The same interview records his earliest rationalization of the process: "If every playwright could spend two or three months in Hollywood each year, he would make enough to go back home and write the kind of plays he wants to write." ⟨. . .⟩

Of all his film work, *None But the Lonely Heart* stands as the most artistically satisfying both to Odets and the critics. In spite of a tendency to play up the more obvious sentiment, Odets infused the script with a sincere compassion for Ernie Mott, his mother, and the other stifled London slum dwellers. Odets' solid theatrical background also helped him in this, his first directing experience. James Agee, then writing for *Nation*, praised the direction highly, adding,

> I base my confidence in him chiefly on the genuine things about his faith in and love for people, which are as urgent and evident here as his sentimentalities; . . . I was impressed . . . because Odets was more interested in filling his people with life and grace than in explaining them, arguing over them, or using them as boxing-gloves.[2]

In *Humoresque* on the other hand, the sentimentality got the upper hand, though the script was rescued occasionally by a sharp Odets line. The climax of the film is reached in a grand Hollywood cliché. The unsympathetic heroine, rather than continue to ruin the life of the budding young violinist,

commits suicide by walking out into the sea, accompanied on the sound track by the crashing chords of Wagner's "Liebestod." While some of the troubles with this script obviously stem from the novel itself (by Fannie Hurst), Odets and Zachary Gold, his collaborator on the project, must share the responsibility.

None of the other Odets films is of more than routine interest, but one of them should be considered in detail along with his plays. *The Story on Page One* is the sole identifiable example of an original Odets film story; furthermore, Odets directed the film. Therefore, this motion picture is unquestionably the purest finished product of any task Odets attempted in Hollywood. The entire work, from its conception as a story idea to its actual filming, may safely be credited to Odets.

It is unfortunate, then, that the net result of a tremendous amount of effort on the part of the author-director is not more satisfying. *The Story on Page One* is a rather ordinary courtroom melodrama, not even saved by any suspense in connection with the crime. True to the tradition of the long-lasting *Perry Mason* television series, the defense is clever, vigorous, occasionally taken by surprise by a prosecution maneuver, but never in doubt of ultimate victory; the prosecution team is clearly the villain of the piece. Viewers conditioned by several years of watching the unconquerable Mr. Mason on television would easily forecast the jury's verdict. Odets' script does not even have the merit of saving the unraveling until the end; the viewers are let in on the entire story almost from the beginning. ⟨. . .⟩

Seeking a new outlet for his talent and his energy, Odets began a final and very brief phase of his career early in 1963. Even while working on a libretto for a musical adaptation of *Golden Boy*,[3] Odets allied himself with actor Richard Boone and in a flurry of new publicity began preparations for a new television series for the fall. In his last byline, Odets provided a typically flamboyant and exuberant account of how he became editor in chief for *The Richard Boone Show*:

> To begin with, Jean [Renoir] said one night, over a poignantly delicate bottle of 1953 Chateau Lascombes: "TV, I don't think you understand, my dear Cliff, is, for a writer of your popular inclination, the medium of the future. It is fast, to the point, without frills, wide open for any technical innovations; and the audience is always waiting for you with open arms!" He had made a provocative point.
>
> Only some few weeks later I found myself sitting (sans wine) with Dick Boone, a kindly, bluff acting man, who can be fearfully direct when rough-house or persuasion are needed. (Incidentally, Dick often reminds me of John Steinbeck, another friend; they seem cut exactly from the same textured tweed.)
>
> Dick was talking about doing a television show together and I was playing the reluctant bride. It was only when he said, "But I don't think you understand. Don't you realize that together, with a hand-picked company of players, that we probably can make the first real theatre on TV?"—It was only then, according to Dick's later version, that I "jumped over the table!" (Los Angeles *Times*, Aug. 1, 1963)

When this article appeared, Odets was already in Cedars of Lebanon Hospital; he was dead in two weeks.

His work for the new television series excited Odets tremendously. He had an office at M.G.M. Studios, where the programs were taped, and he plunged himself into his work with renewed vitality until his death. Odets completed three scripts, "Big Mitch," "The Mafia Man," and "The Affair."

"Big Mitch," drafted during April 1963 and revised during May, was presented on NBC on December 10, 1963. It was Odets' first and best work for television. Considering the fact that the playwright was working within a totally new framework, with less than an hour to develop his characters and situation, Odets showed many expert touches in this play. Mitch is a fine character, a little like Willy Loman, a little more like O'Casey's Cap'n Boyle. He is not exactly lazy, but he is unwilling easily to demean himself by taking work below his imagined "station." ⟨. . .⟩

The best scenes in "Big Mitch" are reminiscent of Odets' early work in *Awake and Sing!* As Mitch and his little crony from next door sit around the house hopelessly watching afternoon television, the dialogue accurately captures the sterility of their existence. Just as the Berger family members seek an escape from their drudgery in the glamor of films, so Mitch and Happy Felcher gaze with vacant eyes and unthinking admiration on the little screen that brings some magic into their homes. Once Mitch rouses himself to a significant, bitter comment about his own life as he watches an afternoon movie on his television set:

Movie stars, they come and go. It's styles—cycles. I hope they made hay an' put it away. Because, brother, when you go out of style and don't have it, you are just a whisper in the world.

Hampered by a lack of time in which to give his audience the necessary background for his intriguing central character— all we know is that Mitch's father was once Mayor of Glendale—Odets nevertheless brings alive a small and poignant situation.

"The Mafia Man," presented January 7, 1964, is thinner stuff. Merely an exercise in suspense melodrama, "The Mafia Man" is unlike anything else Odets ever wrote. Even the incredible murder at the end of *Clash by Night* is better conceived and better managed than the two that occur in this script. ⟨. . .⟩

Odets' final play for the television series reached the stage of a rough draft. Set in a Maine summer resort and a New York apartment, "The Affair" concerns a difficult marital crisis in the lives of two mixed-up, somewhat neurotic people. George Meyers, a jealous attorney, suspects his wife of having an affair with an artist; she actually is having an affair—but with a different man. When George and Ellie return to New York they have a couple of stormy emotional scenes and reveal that the main problem in their marriage stems from the death of their infant son, Bobby. Ellie had turned to a psychoanalyst at the time, leaving George nothing on which to release his own profound grief. The climactic scene, during which George and Ellie discuss their emotional reaction to the death of their child, shows power and insight even in unpolished draft.

"The Affair" is similar in many ways to the early Odets play *Rocket to the Moon*, the most noticeable likeness resting with the emotional reaction to the death of a child. The psychological insights displayed in the draft of this drama suggest that, had Odets lived to polish it as he wished, this would have been his finest television script.

On the basis of these three short scripts, each very different from the other, it is difficult to make any general appraisal of Odets' work in this new medium. He entered it as he entered his film work, cheerfully confident that he could reach new and wider audiences. He tended to separate his playwriting from his film and television writing, though he frequently asserted that he was not ashamed of anything he wrote. To the end of his life he was filled with grandiose plans; something big was always in the immediate offing. Much as he

wished to outgrow his reputation as the playwright of the Thirties, Odets was never granted more. He was left behind the times. Like his almost pitiful television character, Mitch, Odets watched the world pass him by. Hollywood was never the answer. He became an onlooker rather than a participant. Like Mitch he issued manifestoes concerning what he was going to do tomorrow; like Mitch he faced a terrible prospect: "When you go out of style . . . you are just a whisper in the world."

Notes

1. Harold Clurman, *The Fervent Years* (New York: Knopf, 1945), p. 187.
2. James Agee, *Agee on Film* (New York: McDowell, Oblensky, 1958), p. 128.
3. In the fall of 1962, Odets wrote to me about some of the problems he was encountering in transforming *Golden Boy* into a musical. Of course, since the play was being written for Sammy Davis, Jr., there was the added element of the interracial relationships. But Odets was proceeding in his customary exhuberant manner even though musicals were a totally new form for him. He claimed to be finding the experience enjoyable. With a script thoroughly reworked after Odets' death by his friend William Gibson, the musical finally reached Broadway in the fall of 1964 and had a long, successful run. Gibson's introduction to the paperback edition of the musical version is a touching tribute to Odets.

HAROLD CLURMAN
"Will They *Awake and Sing* in 1970?" (1970)
The Divine Pastime
1974, pp. 232–37

R eading the announcement of the off-Broadway revival of Clifford Odets' *Awake and Sing!* caused me to speculate on what the reaction to it today might be. Much, of course, depends on the quality of its staging. Still, I could anticipate that many might find it "dated"—always an easy out for the careless spectator. After all, the play was first presented in New York on February 19, 1935.

All plays are dated. They are products of their time. Do we complain of *The Importance of Being Earnest* because its idiom is not Osborne's? Even those dramatists who aim at timelessness—Samuel Beckett, for instance—are representative of a period. *Waiting for Godot* could not have been written in 1912 any more than we can imagine plays like those of Congreve being written in Shakespeare's day.

The dramatist's datedness applies chiefly to the historical circumstances of his writing: what was going on in the world at the time he set about doing his work. He employs the speech of his environment, uses the techniques which he has inherited from the past and adds something of the present which (at best) points to the future. What is permanent in his creation is that element which his fellow countrymen still find nourishing to their inner health and pleasure in later days.

The thirties, of which Odets' plays are the outstanding dramatic expression, are chiefly remembered as the time of the great Depression. We are now presumably living in a period of affluence. There was much talk in those "ancient" times of rescuing the suffering working class, supporting the rising trade unions, and some even espoused socialism of one kind or another. Today many are convinced that the unions are not only greedily monopolistic but often reactionary, the working class by no means underprivileged, and "socialism" a dirty word.

Still, Secretary of the Interior, Walter J. Hickel, in his letter to President Nixon was able to say "What is happening today is not unrelated to what happened in the thirties."

Secretary Hickel was not simply referring to the rash of "confrontations" which now afflict the nation. There is a considerable difference in meaning between the call to strike which ends Odets' first flaming outcry, *Waiting for Lefty*, and the demands of organized labor today. But the references to unemployment, starvation, breadlines, evictions, and the need for workers to realize their power, which resound in lyric exuberance or melancholy plea in Odets' early plays, are not what is essential in his basic message or to his intrinsic value for us at present. The correspondence between the upheavals of the thirties and those of the present, suggested by Secretary Hickel, lies in a sense of something fundamentally wrong in our society that statements of benevolent intention or minor reforms will neither satisfy nor mend.

Odets was never a political playwright, nor even a "revolutionary" one in the limited sense attached to that epithet then or now. His was a rebellion against our materialism, our subservience to the idol of Success as the supreme good. Odets' denunciation of this blight was not that of a sociological preacher. He knew its corrosive properties because they dwelt within *him*, and he hated them because they were crippling him and, at last, literally killed him.

There was a tormenting duality in Odets, as there is in most important artists, a duality which makes them dramatic. It is from the conflict within themselves (of different kinds within different artists) that they create. Where the duality is resolved or kept in balance, the result is benign; where the duality is finally insuperable, the artist's career is fatally damaged.

The duality in Odets consists of his being an impassioned idealist and, at the same time, a creature constantly lured by the trappings of the bitch goddess (Success) whose seductions he knew were lethal. If we examine Odets' history (his twelve plays and his Hollywood activities) we perceive the drama of defeat issuing from a foundation of the noblest aspirations. This drama is an American tragedy. It is related to what O'Neill had in mind when planning his never completed nine-play cycle, the theme of which he declared was to be centered in the challenge of "What shall it profit a man if he gain the whole world and lose his own soul?"

There was in Odets an inextinguishable, characteristically native, optimism. All but one of his plays end on an "up-beat" even when the curtain rings down on a death. His plays point to that future which would unify all men in mutual understanding and reconstructive effort. Odets' favorite author in his youth was the Victor Hugo of *Les Misérables* with its compassion for the downtrodden; later he turned to Walt Whitman with his dream of a truly democratic America peopled by sound individuals. "Life should have some dignity" old Jacob says in *Awake and Sing!*, and the play's prophetic title is indicative of Odets' mood in this, his purest play. And to attain that dignity, Jacob adds, we must "go out and fight so life shouldn't be printed on dollar bills." To which his grandson's ultimate response is "Let me die like a dog, if I can't get more from life [than that which the Depression has produced]. . . . I want the whole city to hear it, fresh blood, arms. We got 'em. We're glad we're living."

This is not only youthful high-heartedness but a declaration of the activism (the meaning of "Strike!" in *Lefty*) emblematic of Odets and the thirties in their early stages. Jacob, who constantly cites Marx but who has not read him, describes himself as a man "with good ideas, but only in the head. . . . That is why I tell you—*do!* Do what is in your heart and you carry in yourself a revolution." All of Odets' first

"heroes" are determined to "change the world," to make America yield the fruits of its promise.

But Ralphie, the twenty-two-year-old grandson, also hankers for his "name in the papers" just as Joe Bonaparte in *Golden Boy* yearns for "fame and fortune," which leads him to give up his musical talent to battle for more visible benefits. For the poor boy (Bonaparte-Odets) the booty of the battle is expressed in the purchase of an expensive car. This is a naïvely romantic image which signifies that American materialism is not only a monetary matter but manifests itself in the impulse to parade the success with which one's efforts have been crowned. Odets was nothing if not a romantic.

Right after *Awake and Sing!* opened to generally enthusiastic notices, Odets bought an elaborate record player. (He had a genuine love of music.) When, after *Golden Boy*, his greatest commercial success, he signed to write screenplays for Paramount Pictures, he bought a Cadillac. Later, after *The Flowering Peach*, he bought a Lincoln Continental. When he undertook to write a picture for Elvis Presley, he rationalized the act, as he did his contract to supervise an undistinguished television series. When hard times ensued for him again—after 1955, Odets always lived beyond his means—he shied from dining at prominent restaurants for fear of the pity or patronizing attitude with which he imagined his colleagues might greet him.

The golden boy destroys his talent. Odets understood the pattern of the confused idealist intuitively and objectively. When he came to write about Hollywood in *The Big Knife*, his knowledge had become unmistakably subjective but shamefaced. (When, on reading the script, I objected that the movie star Charles Castle's desire to escape Hollywood was not convincingly plotted, Odets exclaimed "But he really loves Hollywood!" which was a splendid insight but was suppressed in the actual telling of the play's story.) "I wanted to be two other guys," Castle says when he has just been told point blank by the play's only uncontaminated character, "You've sold out." And in *The Flowering Peach*, Odets' swan song, old Noah, wearied of his virtues, decides to settle down with his complacently rich son, rather than with the socially rebellious one, because it's "more comfortable" that way.

Nothing is more typical of the struggle within Odets' soul than his testimony at the hearing before the House Committee on Un-American Activities in 1952. He did not wish to present an abject figure; indeed he intended to be defiant. Though he had long since abandoned his association with the Communist Party, he did not want to disavow the humanistic impulse which had led him to join it. Yet he acquiesced in the Committee's bidding by inculpating his closest colleagues in the theatre, while he tried to suggest that he still believed that there were some good arguments for socialism. The Committee did not thank him for his cooperation and he, later, wept because he had not been more courageous.

Odets once declared that he experienced in his flesh and bones every desire and emotion that the ordinary man feels, even when he (Odets) found them reprehensible. This consanguinity with the small fry in the American ferment gives Odets' work an authenticity which is not present to the same degree in any other playwright. Through this closeness to his people there arises in his best writing a warm intimacy, a special tenderness—"tenement tenderness" I once called it—which makes his use of the word "love" more than the fatuous slogan it tends to become. His actual love scenes are among the best in our theatre.

Odets' plays are rich with vividly defined characters. They are brimful with the juices of life. The fever of his writing directly communicates the turbulence of his spirit. His dialogue pulsates with the beat and whirl of the city. While his language is a compound of New York dialects, one cannot say that it is "dated" because no one ever really spoke exactly as Odets' characters do any more than the Elizabethans spoke as Shakespeare wrote.

Odets had a wonderful ear. His language is a personal poetry wrought from phrases, jokes, popular word-coinage and songs heard in the street and in homes, things he read in newspaper captions as well as in the funnies, remarks picked up from desultory companions and relatives. These have all been recast in the fire of his imagination and transfigured into a beautifully original rhetoric. *Awake and Sing!* was not understood when it was produced in Israel because it is much less Jewish than thoroughly "United States." His writing is full of salty humor and melody. It makes us aware that even his most impatient outbursts were part of his exultation in the hope for a better life, a saner world.

This brings us back to our point of departure. Odets *is* still pertinent. For though our present economic and social problems are not precisely what they were in the thirties (except for our intensified sense of possible annihilation) the basic disturbances in the whole fabric of our living are due to a lack of truly generative ideals—practical ideals—not mere alterations in nomenclature. We want something to transform the conduct of our lives day by day.

The alarming "wildness" of our youth is a symptom of our failure to make our deeds correspond to our professions of faith. We know that the negatives of "anti-Communism" will not help, nor will or should our young be content with the solace of comparison with other people who "don't have it as good" as we do. We know that we must act so that we radically affect our physical environment, our economic and political structures, our buildings, the aspect of our streets, our manners, our educational institutions, our arts, our entire comportment.

Even when they don't rightly understand it, know how to organize it, and are often corrupted by some of the diseases which afflict their elders, there is a revolution going on in the hearts of the young which must either lead to the "new world" invoked in *Awake and Sing!* or to a veritable hell of destructiveness (to the self and to others) which is always the consequence of idealism betrayed.

This is the crux of Odets' dramatic statement and what in its totality it portends.

FRANK O'HARA

1926–1966

Frank O'Hara, poet, playwright, and art critic, was born in Baltimore on June 27, 1926. In 1927 his family moved to Grafton, Massachusetts, and between 1933 and 1944 he attended parochial schools nearby. While growing up O'Hara was a serious music student with intentions of becoming a concert pianist; after serving in the navy during World War II, he entered Harvard in 1946 to pursue his musical studies. He soon, however, changed his major to English, and made up his mind to become a writer; his first published works, poems and stories, appeared in the *Havard Advocate*. He received his B.A. in 1950, and then entered the Graduate School of the University of Michigan, from which he received an M.A. in 1951.

While still living in Cambridge O'Hara became acquainted with the poets John Ashbery and V. R. "Bunny" Lang. During visits to New York he met Kenneth Koch and James Schuyler, as well as many painters, including Larry Rivers, Fairfield Porter, Willem de Kooning, Franz Kline, and Jackson Pollock. When he settled in New York O'Hara began to gravitate towards the art world, and became known as something of a "poet among painters." In 1951 he worked at the Museum of Modern Art as a clerk in the information and sales desk; he returned in 1955 and by 1960 had become an assistant curator. Between 1953 and 1955 he was an editorial associate of *Art News*, for which he wrote reviews and occasional articles, and in 1961 he served as art editor of the quarterly *Kulchur*.

O'Hara was a leading member of the so-called New York School of poets. His collections of poetry include A *City Winter* (1952), *Meditations in an Emergency* (1957), *Second Avenue* (1960), *Odes* (1960), *Lunch Poems* (1964), and *Selected Poems* (1973, National Book Award). *Collected Poems*, edited by Donald Allen, was published in 1971. *Selected Plays* (1978) collects his theatre pieces, some of which were first performed by the Living Theatre. *Jackson Pollock* (1959) is a full-length exhibition catalogue, and *Art Chronicles* (1975) is a collection of his criticism. *Standing Still and Walking in New York* (1975) and *Early Writing* (1977) gather essays and notes. O'Hara died on June 25, 1966.

Personal

Frank O'Hara was born in Maryland, but grew up in Grafton and Worcester, Massachusetts; he had a Yankee way of speaking, nasal, yet not unmusical. He attended a Jesuit high school, which he hated, studied the piano privately and, in the Second World War, served in the Pacific as a Radarman 3rd class. On completion of his service, he returned home, intending to go to the New England Conservatory, but his family demurred, and he entered Harvard instead. He majored first in music, then switched to English, but he never quite forgave his family the loss of the chance to study with his idol, the composer and pianist Rachmaninoff. In his posthumously published *Collected Poems*, there are several apostrophizing the musician on his birthday: especially fine the one beginning, "Quick! another poem before I go off my head . . ."

After Harvard he went to Ann Arbor, where he received an Avery Hopwood Award for an unpublished manuscript of poems, and worked on a novel, never completed. Then to New York, where he resumed Harvard friendships, particularly those with the poet and critic John Ashbery, and with Larry Rivers, Jane Freilicher and (another Harvard poet) Kenneth Koch. One of the most lasting of the friendships formed then was with the imaginative John Bernard Myers, art dealer (Tibor de Nagy Gallery, where many of Frank's painter friends first exhibited) and art world force.

I first met Frank at a party at John Myers' after a Larry Rivers opening; de Kooning and Nell Blaine were there, arguing about whether it is deleterious for an artist to do commercial work. I was most impressed by the company I was suddenly keeping. A very young-looking man came up and introduced himself (I had already read a poem by Frank in *Accent*, the exquisitely witty "Three Penny Opera," written either at Harvard or at Michigan). He asked me if I had read Janet Flanner that week in the *New Yorker*, who had just disclosed the scandal of Gide's wife burning all his letters to her. "I never liked Gide," Frank said, "but I didn't realize he was a *complete* shit." This was rich stuff, and we talked a long time; or rather, as was so often the case, he talked and I listened. His conversation was self-propelling and one idea, or anecdote, or *bon mot* was fuel to his own fire, inspiring him verbally to blaze ahead, that curious voice rising and falling, full of invisible italics, the strong pianist's hands gesturing with the invariable cigarette.

Frank told me he had taken a job at the Museum of Modern Art, working in the lobby at the front desk, in order to see Alfred Barr's monumental retrospective of Matisse. Frank had idols (many) and if Matisse was one, so was Alfred Barr, and remained so during all Frank's years of association with the museum. The first time I dropped by to see him, I found him in the admissions booth, waiting to sell tickets to visitors and, meanwhile, writing a poem on a yellow lined pad (one called "It's the Blue!"). He also had beside him a translation of André Breton's *Young Cherry Trees Secured against Hares* (although he made translations from the French—Reverdy, Baudelaire—his French was really nothing much). Soon we were sharing an apartment on East 49th Street, a cold water flat five flights up with splendid views.

Frank O'Hara was the most elegant person I ever met, and I don't mean in the sense of dressy, for which he never had either the time or the money. He was of medium height, lithe and slender (to quote Elaine de Kooning, when she painted him, "hipless as a snake"), with a massive Irish head, hair receding from a widow's peak and a broken, Napoleonic nose: broken in what childhood scuffle, I forget. He walked lightly on the balls of his feet, like a dancer or someone about to dive into waves. How he loved to swim! In the heaviest surf on the south shore of Long Island, often to the alarm of his friends, and even at night during an electric storm. His manners were impeccable, except sometimes late at night when he was drunk and would turn waspish. That was both unpleasant and alarming, since he would say whatever came into his head, giving his victim a devastating character analysis, as with a scalpel.

Frank's friends! They came from all the arts, in troops. As John Ashbery has written in his introduction to *The Collected Poems* (nearly seven hundred pages of them): "The nightmares, delights and paradoxes of life in this city went into Frank's style,

as did the many passionate friendships he kept going simultaneously (to the point where it was almost impossible for anyone to see him alone—there were so many people whose love demanded attention, and there was so little time and so many other things to do, like work and, when there was a free moment, poetry)."

Then there were the events. Frank was in love with all the arts: painting and music and poetry, almost all movies, the opera and, particularly, the ballet. Then there were the parties and dinners and old movies on late night TV. When did the poems get written?

One Saturday noon I was having coffee with Frank and Joe LeSeure (the writer with whom Frank shared various apartments over the years), and Joe and I began to twit him about his ability to write a poem any time, any place. Frank gave us a look—both hot and cold—got up, went into his bedroom and wrote "Sleeping on the Wing," a beauty, in a matter of minutes.

Then, his book *Lunch Poems* is literally that. In 1955, Frank became a permanent member of the International Program at the Museum of Modern Art at the behest of the then-director, Porter A. McCray. I later wended my way into the same department and had ample opportunity to observe Frank in action. He would steam in, good and late and smelling strongly of the night before (in his later years, his breakfast included vodka in the orange juice, to kill the hangover and get him started). He read his mail, the circulating folders, made and received phone calls (Frank suffered a chronic case of "black ear": I once called him at the museum and the operator said, "Good God!"; but she put me through). Then it was time for lunch, usually taken at Larré's with friends. When he got back to his office, he rolled a sheet of paper into his typewriter and wrote a poem, then got down to serious business. Of course this didn't happen every day, but often, very often.

It has been suggested that the museum took too much of so gifted a poet's time. Not really: Frank needed a job, and he was in love with the museum and brooked no criticism of it. At times, of course, he became impatient with the endless and often seemingly petty paperwork connected with assembling an exhibition, and I have seen him come from an acquisitions meeting with smoke coming out of his ears (he never divulged a word of what passed at these highly confidential affairs). But Frank had a rare gift of empathy for the art of any artist he worked with; he understood both intention and significance. And he was highly organized, with a phenomenal memory. When I say "he got down to work," I mean it: he worked, and he worked really hard.—James Schuyler, "Frank O'Hara: Poet among Painters," *Art N*, May 1974, pp. 44–45

General

Frank O'Hara's charms are inseparable from his overproduction—the offhand remark, the fleeting notation of a landscape, the Christmas or birthday verse, the impromptu souvenir of a party—these are his common forms, as though he roamed through life snapping Polaroid pictures, pulling them out of his camera and throwing them in a desk drawer sixty seconds later. And here they are—some over-exposed, some underdeveloped, some blurred, some unfocused, and yet any number of them succeeding in fixing the brilliance of some long-forgotten lunch, or the curve of a body in a single gesture, or a snowstorm, or a childhood movie. If these poems are photographic in their immediacy, they resemble too the rapid unfinished sketches done by an artist to keep his hand in or to remind him of some perishable composition of the earth. If there were a movie equivalent to a sketch, some of these poems would be better called verbal movies—the "I-do-this, I-do-that" poems, as O'Hara himself called them.

The generic form of O'Hara's poems is conversation, the generic punctuation the exclamation point, the generic population O'Hara's friends, the generic landscape Manhattan and Fire Island, the generic mythology the flora and fauna of art shows, radio shows, and movie shows. Sureness and insouciance mark O'Hara's lines. But two aspects of his work tended to do O'Hara in: his radical incapacity for abstraction (like Byron, when he thinks he is a child) and his lack of a comfortable form (he veered wildly from long to short, with no particular reason in many cases for either choice). The longest poems end up simply messy, endless secretions, with a nugget of poetry here and there, slices of life arbitrarily beginning, and ending for no particular reason. "Dear Diary," says O'Hara, and after that anything goes. The perfect freedom any diarist enjoys—to put anything down that happened on a certain day only because at the head of the page there is that hungry date saying June 13, 1960—is what O'Hara claims for himself in the long poems. Beside these poems, even Ginsberg looks formal. The theoretical question O'Hara forces on us is a radical one: Why should poetry be confined in a limited or closed form? Our minds ramble on; why not our poems? Ramblings are not, to say the least, the native form of poets with metaphysical minds, but O'Hara, in his fundamental prescinding from the metaphysical, believes neither in problems nor in solutions, nor even in the path from one to the other. He believes in colloquies, observations, memories, impressions, and variations—all things with no beginnings and no endings, things we tune in on and then tune out of. Turn on the oscilloscope, attach the leads to the tuner, take gauge readings—these are the O'Hara processes. In one sense, there is no reason why a poem of this sort should ever stop. The inherent limitation seems not to be a formal one within the poem, but an external one: the limited attention span of the poet or his reader. We can attend to life in this hyperattentive way for only a short time, and then our energy flags, so that like overexcited electrons we subside back into our low-energy orbits. The poet's language weakens, our response sags, and the poem loses us. And yet O'Hara was stubborn enough to wish, like Emily in *Our Town*, that life could always be lived on the very edge of loss, so that every instant would seem wistfully precious. Therefore the attitude of perpetual wonder, perpetual exclamation, perpetual naiveté. O'Hara had enough of all these qualities by nature (judging from their consistent presence from the earliest poems to the latest) so that this poise at the brink of life was no pose, but it does make me wonder how he would have endured that jadedness of age that, in their different ways, all old poets confront.

Some of O'Hara's poems are already deservedly famous, for the best reason in the world: nobody else has done anything like them in English. One reading of "Blocks" guarantees that the stunning last half will never be forgotten:

O boy, their childhood was like so many oatmeal
    cookies.
I need you, you need me, yum, yum. Anon it
    became suddenly
like someone always losing something and never
    knowing what.
Always so. They were so fond of eating bread and
    butter and
sugar, they were slobs, the mice used to lick the
    floorboards
after they went to bed, rolling their light tails against
the rattling marbles of granulation. Vivo! the dex-
    trose

those children consumed, lavished, smoked, in their
    knobby
candy bars. Such pimples! such hardons! such
    moody loves.
And thus they grew like giggling fir trees.

The intense appeal of these lines comes from their having suppressed nothing of adolescence: the persistence of the childish in candy bars and giggles; the startling new growth "like fir trees"; the incongruous nursery scene of the mice in the children's bedroom eating their bedtime snack while the children suddenly discover themselves having hardons and pimples; the sudden flash of the personal ("I need you, you need me") combined painfully with its psychic results ("like someone always losing something . . . such moody loves"). Almost all other poems about adolescence have concealed one or the other of these facets of the state, whether out of shame or aesthetics one scarcely knows. An aesthetic that permits the coexistence of moody loves, hardons, mice, and candy bars has a good chance of being a new source of truth.—HELEN VENDLER, "The Virtue of the Alterable," *Parn*, Fall–Winter 1972, pp. 5–7

Frank O'Hara's *Collected Poems*, as profuse in their inventiveness as they are pervasive in their influence, demand that we attempt to judge their place in American poetry. It is not only because these poems skirt the edges of such contiguous but opposing aesthetic qualities as artless simplicity and dazzling elaboration that they are hard to judge. These poems outline their own territory by operating with a high degree of consciousness about themselves as literature, and simultaneously flouting the notions of decorum and propriety. Just when they seem placed, or placeable, in some historical or theoretical classification, they are off again saying such classifications don't matter, and it's clearly wrong-headed of people to ask any poem to maintain an attitude long enough to be labelled. For all we can say about them, they yet remain chastely irreducible, as if they wanted nothing so much as to beggar commentary. But if we read them in bulk, we are left with the peculiar sensation we've been listening to a manic waif, someone for whom any audience becomes the most charitable therapy, for as soon as the poems stop talking, stop chatting, their speaker will fall dead. The chatter registers the *frisson*, the stimulation, but it also hints at the shiver of fear, the *gouffre*. Like all great improvisational artists, O'Hara thrives in the realm of nostalgia, a looking back that can never for a moment become true regret. Like the Steinberg drawing of the hand holding the quill pen which has just completed the profile of its own face, O'Hara's poetry startles as does any utterance clearly self-begot.

Self-begot in more than one sense, for these are the most autobiographical poems we have; they make "confessional" poetry seem alexandrine or allegorical by comparison. The friends, the places, the objects, the very reverie: they are all his and all there for us to rummage through. Just by writing them down, just by taking note of them, O'Hara won for his personal ephemera another status. "Save him from the malevolent eyes of / spiders but do not throw him to the swans," he begs in "Words to Frank O'Hara's Angel," wanting neither gothic terror nor fruity sublimation. This poem ends with a simple, a necessary plea: "Protect his tongue." His tongue assumes the duties of his soul, of course, the principle of his individuation. An ordinary biography of O'Hara would be a distraction when looking at the poems. Yet reading the poems in an autobiographical, chronological order, we're struck by an early despair, the hint of a habit of mind that could have been crucial in the determination of the poetry's final texture. Frank O'Hara may well have despaired of ever escaping himself.—CHARLES MOLESWORTH, "'The Clear Architecture of the Nerves': The Poetry of Frank O'Hara," *IR*, Summer–Fall, 1975, pp. 61–62

JOHN ASHBERY
From "Introduction"
The Collected Poems of Frank O'Hara, ed. Donald Allen
1971, pp. vii–ix

For his poetry is anything but literary. It is part of a modern tradition which is anti-literary and anti-artistic, and which goes back to Apollinaire and the Dadaists, to the collages of Picasso and Braque with their perishable newspaper clippings, to Satie's *musique d'ameublement* which was not meant to be listened to. At Harvard he majored in music and did some composing, and although he wrote poetry too, he was more influenced by contemporary music and art than by what had been going on in American poetry. The poetry that meant the most to him when he began writing was either French— Rimbaud, Mallarmé, the Surrealists: poets who speak the language of every day into the reader's dream—or Russian— Pasternak and especially Mayakovsky, from whom he picked up what James Schuyler has called the "intimate yell." So it was not surprising that his work should have initially proved so puzzling to readers—it ignored the rules for modern American poetry that had been gradually drawn up from Pound and Eliot down to the academic establishment of the 1940s. To ignore the rules is always a provocation, and since the poetry itself was crammed with provocative sentiments, it was met with the friendly silence reserved for the thoroughly unacceptable guest.

It is true that much of Frank's early work was not only provocative but provoking. One frequently feels that the poet is trying on various pairs of brass knuckles until he finds the one which fits comfortably. It is not just that it is often aggressive in tone—it simply doesn't care. A poet who in the academic atmosphere of the late 1940s could begin a poem

> At night Chinamen jump
> On Asia with a thump

was amusing himself, another highly suspect activity. But these poems, so "French" in the pejorative sense the word so often had in America, were essential in the early, muscle-flexing period of his work. Just as he was constantly interested in a variety of people, in several branches of the arts at once and in an assortment of writers of whom one had never heard (Beckett, Firbank, Jean Rhys and Flann O'Brien were among the then almost unknown writers he was reading when I first met him in 1949), so he was constantly experimenting in his poetry in different ways without particularly caring whether the result looked like a finished poem.

The first four or five years of Frank O'Hara's writing— from about 1947 to 1952—were a period of testing, of trying to put together a tradition to build on where none had existed. Except for some rather pale Surrealist poetry written in England and America during the 1930s, and an occasional maverick poet like John Wheelwright or Laura Riding; except for Hart Crane in his vatic moments and the more abandoned side of Dylan Thomas and the early Auden, there was nothing like a basis for the kind of freedom of expression that Frank instinctively needed. One had to look to France, and even there the freedom was as often as not an encouraging sentiment expressed in poetry ("*Il faut être absolument moderne, plonger au fond du gouffre*") than as a program actually carried out in search of new poetic forms. Even French Surrealist poetry can

be cold and classical, and Breton's call for *liberté totale* stopped short of manipulating the grammar and syntax of the sacrosanct French language.

So it was natural for Frank to turn to other branches of the arts, closer to home, where a profounder kind of experimentation was taking place. One of these was American painting, which was just then in what is now called the "heroic period" of Abstract Expressionism. This art absorbed Frank to such a degree, both as a critic for *Art News* and a curator at the Museum of Modern Art, and as a friend of the protagonists, that it could be said to have taken over his life. In return it gave him a conception of art as process which, if not exactly new (it was close to Gertrude Stein's definition of creative thinking, which applied both to her own work and to Picasso's: "Real thinking is conceptions aiming again and again always getting fuller, that is the difference between creative thinking and theorising"[1]), still had never before been applied in America with such dramatic results. Frank O'Hara's concept of the poem as the chronicle of the creative act that produces it was strengthened by his intimate experience of Pollock's, Kline's and de Kooning's great paintings of the late 40s and early 50s, and of the imaginative realism of painters like Jane Freilicher and Larry Rivers.[2]

Frank also listened constantly to music, not only to composers of the recent past as diverse as Rachmaninoff and Schönberg (his elegies to both of them are in this volume) but to contemporary avant-garde composers such as Cage and Feldman. We were both tremendously impressed by David Tudor's performance at a concert on New Year's Day 1952 of John Cage's "Music of Changes," a piano work lasting over an hour and consisting, as I recall, entirely of isolated, autonomous tone-clusters struck seemingly at random all over the keyboard. It was aleatory music, written by throwing coins in a method adapted from the *I Ching*. The actual mechanics of the method escaped me then as it does now; what mattered was that chance elements could combine to produce so beautiful and cogent a work. It was a further, perhaps for us ultimate proof not so much of "Anything goes" but "Anything can come out."

This climate—Picasso and French poetry, de Kooning and Guston, Cage and Feldman, Rachmaninoff, Schubert, Sibelius and Krenek—just about any music, in fact—encouraged Frank's poetry and provided him with a sort of reservoir of inspiration: words and colors that could be borrowed freely from everywhere to build up big, airy structures unlike anything previous in American poetry and indeed unlike poetry, more like the inspired ramblings of a mind open to the point of distraction. The result has been a truly viable freedom of poetic expression which, together with other attempts at technical (Charles Olson) and psychological (Allen Ginsberg) liberation, has opened up poetry for today's generation of young poets. In fact without the contribution of poets like these, and O'Hara in particular, there probably wouldn't be a young generation of poets committed to poetry as something living rather than an academic parlor game.

It is not surprising that there should be experiments which didn't work out among these early poems, considering they were part of an attempt to plot a not-yet-existent tradition with reference to what it was and what it wasn't. The posturing that mars "Oranges" and the obfuscation that makes reading "Second Avenue" such a difficult pleasure were useful because they eventually turned out to be unsatisfactory; it would not be necessary to try them again. That it was nevertheless worthwhile to do so once is proved in poems like "Easter"—an example of what I think of as Frank's "French Zen" period, where the same faults don't impair but rather make the poem—whose form is that of a bag into which anything is dumped and ends up belonging there.

What was needed was a vernacular corresponding to the creatively messy New York environment to ventilate the concentrated Surrealist imagery of poems like "Hatred," "Easter" and "Second Avenue." Though a conversational tone had existed in his poetry from the beginning, it had often seemed a borrowed one—sometimes with overtones of home-grown Surrealism, as in "Poem" ("The eager note on my door . . ."); sometimes veering into Parisian artiness ("Oh! kangaroos, sequins, chocolate sodas!/You really are beautiful!"). It was not yet a force that could penetrate the monolithic slipperiness of the long poems, breaking up their Surreal imagery and partially plowing it under to form in the process a new style incorporating the suggestions and temptations of every day as well as the dreams of the Surrealists. In the poems he was to write during the remainder of his life—from about 1954 to 1966, the year of his death—this vernacular took over, shaping his already considerable gifts toward a remarkable new poetry—both modest and monumental, with something basically usable about it—not only for poets in search of a voice of their own but for the reader who turns to poetry as a last resort in trying to juggle the contradictory components of modern life into something like a livable space.

That space, in Frank O'Hara's case, was not only the space of New York School painting but of New York itself, that kaleidoscopic lumber-room where laws of time and space are altered—where one can live a few yards away from a friend whom one never sees and whom one would travel miles to visit in the country. The nightmares, delights and paradoxes of life in this city went into Frank's style, as did the many passionate friendships he kept going simultaneously (to the point where it was almost impossible for anyone to see him alone—there were so many people whose love demanded attention, and there was so little time and so many other things to do, like work and, when there was a free moment, poetry). The term "New York School" applied to poetry isn't helpful, in characterizing a number of widely dissimilar poets whose work moreover has little to do with New York, which is, or used to be, merely a convenient place to live and meet people, rather than a specific place whose local color influences the literature produced there. But O'Hara is certainly a New York poet. The life of the city and of the millions of relationships that go to make it up hum through his poetry; a scent of garbage, patchouli and carbon monoxide drifts across it, making it the lovely, corrupt, wholesome place New York is.

Another way in which his work differs from that of other New York poets is that it is almost exclusively autobiographical. Even at its most abstract, or even when it seems to be telling someone else's story (see Donald Allen's footnote to the poem "Louise," whose title was suggested to Frank by a louse he says he "found on my own immaculate person") it is emerging out of his life. Yet there is little that is confessional about it—he does not linger over aspects of himself hoping that his self-absorption will make them seem exemplary. Rather he talks about himself because it is he who happens to be writing the poem, and in the end it is the poem that materializes as a sort of monumental backdrop against the random ruminations of a poet seemingly caught up in the business of a New York working day or another love affair. This is the tone in great poems like "In Memory of My Feelings," "For the Chinese New Year and for Bill Berkson"; this is the tone of the Odes, Lunch Poems and Love Poems (love is as important as lunch). Half on contemptuously familiar terms with poetry, half embarrassed or withdrawn before its strangeness, the work

seems entirely natural and available to the multitude of big and little phenomena which combine to make that almost unknowable substance that is our experience. This openness is the essence of Frank O'Hara's poetry, and it is why he is read by increasing numbers of those who, in Kenneth Koch's phrase, are "dying for the truth."

Notes

1. Quoted by Leon Katz in his text for the catalog of the show of the Stein collections, "Four Americans in Paris," Museum of Modern Art, New York, 1970.
2. James Schuyler takes issue with my estimate of the role of painting in Frank's work. He says in a letter to me, "I think you are hampered by a feeling of disapproval, or irritation (also felt by others—Schuyler, Koch . . .) for Frank's exaltation of the New York painters as the climax of human creativity, as something more important than his own work and talent. Perhaps the kindest (and it may even be true) way of seeing it would be along the lines of what Pasternak says about life creating incidents to divert our attention from it so that it can get on with the work it can only accomplish unobserved."

MARJORIE PERLOFF
From "New Thresholds, Old Anatomies: Contemporary Poetry and the Limits of Exegesis"

Iowa Review, Winter 1974, pp. 88–95

I have been arguing that the New Criticism with its sophisticated apparatus for the elucidation of metaliteral meanings cannot cope with the intentionally "literal" poetry of the present. This does not mean, however, that we should revert to the opposite extreme by simply accepting anything that calls itself New Poetry as the New Gospel, by assuming that if a poet announces he intends to do something, then surely he is doing it. This Intentionalist mode of criticism is, of course, even less effective than Symbolist exegesis. The Intentionalist, who is invariably an apologist for the poet or poets in question, assiduously collects, cites, paraphrases and explains the poet's own statements as to aim and methods, assuming that if, say, Williams declares his prosodic unit to be something called the "variable foot," then, by God, Williams' poetry must be written in variable feet, whatever those may be. The recent publication in book form of ten interviews with Robert Creeley, conducted over a ten-year period by ten different interviewers, exemplifies this solemn-eyed approach to contemporary poetry. Not only does Creeley inevitably repeat himself over and over again since the different interviewers naturally ask pretty much the same questions, but one begins to wonder where in Creeley's rather slim poetic output all those tremendous innovations and revolutionary devices, of which he so lucidly and charmingly speaks, could possibly be found.

How, then, to approach contemporary poetry? My own view is that we have much to learn from the Russian Formalists, themselves defenders of Futurist and Cubist poetry against what they considered to be, in the early 1920's, the outmoded literary school of Symbolism. In many circles Formalism, erroneously used as a synonym for the New Criticism, has become a dirty word for a reductionary approach to literature, a method that turns the poem into an autotelic object, a mere surface divorced from an informing consciousness, from the very life that nourished it. Yet Viktor Shklovsky, the first and probably the greatest of the Russian Formalists, defined art not as the creation of well-made objects but precisely in its intimate relation to life. Let me cite a passage from his famous 1917 essay "Art as Technique." For those of us who know no

Russian, the English translation, evidently a fairly free one, of this essay by Lee T. Lemon and Marion J. Reis should be compared to the French version by Tzvetan Todorov as well as to Gisela Drohla's excellent German translation, entitled "Kunst als Kunstgriff."[1] What follows is my own collation of these three:

> In order to restore to us the sensation of life, to make us feel things, to make the stone stony, there exists that which we call Art. The purpose of art is to impart to us the sensation of an object as it is *perceived* and not merely as it is *recognized*. To accomplish this purpose, art uses two techniques: the defamiliarization (*singularisation, verfremdung*) of things, and the distortion of form so as to make the act of perception more difficult and to prolong its duration. For the process of perception is an end in itself and must be prolonged. Art is a way of experiencing the coming into being (*devenir, Werden*) of an object; that which has already become what it is is not important for art.

This definition of art, which is the basis of Shklovsky's studies of the process of "making it strange" in specific poems and novels,[2] seems to me one of the real watersheds in literary theory. For Shklovsky understood, as have few modern theorists, that poetry can stand in direct relationship to life without existing primarily to make a cognitive statement, to convey a complex set of meanings subject to interpretation. The "purpose" of an image, says Shklovsky, "is not to make us perceive meaning, but to create a special perception of the object—*it creates a 'vision' of the object instead of serving as a means for knowing it.*" This insistence on the perceptual nature of art looks ahead to contemporary poetics, particularly to the aesthetic writings, however informal, of Frank O'Hara, whose own definition of poetry oddly echoes that of Shklovsky: "It may be that poetry makes life's nebulous events tangible to me and restores their detail; or conversely, that poetry brings forth the intangible quality of incidents which are all too concrete and circumstantial."[3]

O'Hara's own poetry seems so literal, matter-of-fact and trivial that it has baffled critics who accept Symbolism as the poetic norm. His work is best understood in the context of his role as Curator of the Museum of Modern Art and champion of Abstract Expressionist painting. In his essays on the great New York painters of the fifties and early sixties, O'Hara erodes the myth that nonfigurative painting is somehow bloodless and that formalist criticism is no more than a narrow-minded defense against painful social and political realities. On the contrary, O'Hara's poetry and prose testify to the truth that an overriding concern for formal aesthetic properties can go hand in hand with the expression of intense personal emotion.

For O'Hara, as for Shklovsky, the key to art is *attention*, the recovery of the sensation of life. From the painter Larry Rivers, for example, O'Hara says he learned "to be more keenly interested while I'm still alive. And perhaps this is the most important thing art can say."[4] He admires Jasper Johns, whose art expresses "a profound boredom . . . with the symbols of our over-symbolic society,"[5] and Claes Oldenburg, whose loving creation of giant baked potatoes and ketchup bottles "arouses the fondness one feels for a found object, challenging in intimacy as well as structure all the autobiographical associations that a found object embodies."[6] But O'Hara's predilection is not, as is often thought, for Pop Art, whose "smugness" and "crackerbarrel cheerfulness" he finds superficial and boring.[7] His favorite contemporary painter is Jackson Pollock, and his comments on Pollock's Action Painting shed much light on his own poetry.

Pollock's *Number 29*, a "painting-collage of oil, wire-mesh, pebbles and shells composed on glass," is, according to O'Hara, "unique in that it is a masterpiece seen front or back, and even more extraordinary in that it is the same masterpiece from opposite sites of viewing":

> What an amazing identity *Number 29* must have!—like that of a human being. . . . Its reversible textures . . . the tragedy of a linear violence which, in recognizing itself in its own mirror-self, sees elegance, the open nostalgia for brutality expressed in embracing the sharp edges and banal forms of wire and shells, the cruel acknowledgement of pebbles as elements of the dream, the drama of black mastering sensuality and color, the apparition of these forms in open space as if in air, all these qualities united in one work present the crisis of Pollock's originality. . . .[8]

The artist, in other words, enters his art directly; line, color, texture, object, spatial relationships can, without *representing* anything, enact the artist's inner violence, brutality, sensuality or elegance. And perhaps it is the new use of line that is the secret:

> In the past, an artist by means of scale could create a vast panorama on a few feet of canvas or wall, relating this scale both to the visual reality of known images . . . and to the setting. . . . Pollock, choosing to use no images with real visual equivalents . . . struck upon a use of scale which was to have a revolutionary effect on contemporary painting and sculpture. The scale of the painting became that of the painter's body, not the image of a body, and the setting for the scale, which would include all referents, would be the canvas surface itself. Upon this field, the physical energies of the artist operate in actual detail, in full scale. . . . It is the physical reality of the artist and his activity of expressing it, united to the spiritual reality of the artist in a oneness which has no need for the mediation of metaphor or symbol. It is Action Painting (pp. 28–29).

I cite these long statements because they point so graphically to what O'Hara does in his poetry. Here, for example, is "Essay on Style," written in 1961:

> Someone else's Leica sitting on the table
> the black kitchen table I am painting
> the floor yellow, Bill is painting it
> wouldn't you know my mother would call
> up
>   and complain?
>   my sister's pregnant and
> went to the country for the weekend without
> telling her
>   in point of fact why don't I
> go out to have dinner with her or "let her"
> come in? well if Mayor Wagner won't allow private
> cars on Manhattan because of the snow, I
> will probably never see her again
>   considering
> my growingly more perpetual state and how
> can one say that angel in the Frick's wings
> are "attached" if it's a real angel? now
> I was reflecting the other night meaning
> I was being reflected upon that Sheridan Square
> is remarkably beautiful sitting in JACK
> DELANEY'S looking out the big race-track window
> on the wet
>   drinking a cognac while Edwin
> read my new poem it occurred to me how impossible

it is to fool Edwin not that I don't know as
much as the next about obscurity in modern verse
but he
            always knows what it's about as well
as what it is do you think we can ever
strike *as* and *but*, too, out of the language
then we can attack *well* since it has no
application whatsoever neither as a state
of being or a rest for the mind no such
things available
                        where do you think I've
got to? the spectacle of a grown man
decorating
                a Christmas tree disgusts me that's
where
            that's one of the places yetbutaswell
I'm glad I went to that party for Ed Dorn
last night though he didn't show up do you think
,Bill, we can get rid of *though* also, and *also*?
maybe your
                lettrism is the only answer treating
the typewriter as an intimate organ why not?
nothing else is (intimate)
                    no I am not going
to have you "in" for dinner nor am I going "out"
I am going to eat alone for the rest of my life.
                                (CP, 393–394)

If we look for symbolic design in "Essay on Style," we are bound to be disappointed. For unlike those "sawdust restaurants with oyster shells" which so devastatingly symbolize the death-in-life of J. Alfred Prufrock, O'Hara's "JACK DE-LANEY'S" is just another bar; it refers to nothing outside itself. Again, unlike Frost's "blanker whiteness of benighted snow," the symbolic equivalent of the poet's own secret "desert places," or Stevens' Snow Man, who perceives the "Nothing that is not there and the nothing that is," O'Hara's snow is just that—a weather condition that mercifully prevents his mother from entering Manhattan. Indeed, the poem shifts ground constantly as if to insist that there is nothing *behind* the items presented. If the kitchen table is black and the floor yellow, this is not to suggest that there is an implicit conflict between, say, the black of death and the yellow of sunlight. The table could just as well be white and the floor blue. Similarly, the reference to the Leica as "someone else's" does not hint coyly at a relationship between poet and absent lover; the camera someone has left behind sits on the kitchen table for no better reason than that our apartments and lives are indeed cluttered with such paraphernalia.

Since O'Hara's images thus resist symbolic interpretation, we must make do with their literal meanings. But how do we proceed? Conventional explication would provide something like the following. "Essay on Style" is a stream-of-consciousness meditation on the relation of art to life. The scene is O'Hara's Village apartment, the time, the Christmas season during a snowstorm so heavy that Mayor Wagner has ordered private cars not to enter Manhattan until the streets have been cleared. Bill and Edwin are, respectively, Bill Berkson and Edwin Denby, both close friends and fellow New York poets. As Frank and Bill are busy painting, the phone rings. It is Frank's mother, complaining about the behavior of her pregnant daughter, his sister, and begging to see him. The snowstorm provides a convenient excuse and anyway Frank is preoccupied. He ponders various artistic problems he has been trying to solve: the fuzzy terminology used in describing kinds of sculpture, the similar futility of function words such as "but" and "also" in poetry. He recalls an evening discussing his poems with Edwin Denby over drinks at Jack Delaney's; he

thinks of last night's party for Ed Dorn, which Dorn himself didn't bother to attend, and of Bill's theory that typographical effects are central to the new poetry. Wholly engaged in these questions of aesthetic, the poet mentally rejects his mother's request and opts for total privacy.

The theme that seems to emerge from this running commentary is the artist's need to maintain his integrity, to concentrate on his craft, sidestepping the petty demands of his bourgeois family. A subsidiary and related theme is the need to "purify the language of the tribe," to create an art free from cliché and dead matter. Such statements may describe what the poem *says* but they give us little impression of the way it *works*. For the originality and distinction of "Essay on Style" depend upon what Shklovsky called "defamiliarization" or "making it strange"—the removal of objects from the "automatism of perception."[9] Not the meanings of individual words or word groups but the *structure* of these meanings should be our concern.

The poem's central structural principle, I would posit, is the comical non sequitur, the repeated raising of an expectation only to deflate it. Thus what begins as a still life ("Someone else's Leica sitting on the table") immediately gives way to an unrelated series of conversations, memories and incidents. Reading "Essay on Style" is like watching one of those film cartoons in which an object is initially presented only to fly apart, revealing a whole string of new objects we never knew were inside it. When our expectations are thus countered, we are forced to pause and concentrate on each item presented, to become *aware* of it. The kitchen table, for example, is at first a backdrop for the new camera; then it moves into the foreground with the yellow floor as new backdrop. Charles Olson's famous dictum in "Projective Verse" that "One perception must immediately and directly lead to a further perception" is perhaps the central norm that governs O'Hara's poetic structures.

Consider the syntax. "Essay on Style" avoids all commas, colons and periods; grammatically, it is one long run-on sentence. The emphasis, as in Pollock's paintings, is on process, but it is important to understand that process is not equivalent to progress. There can be here no question of a beginning, middle and end. Such systematic progression is impeded by various devices. We may note, to begin with, that the only form of punctuation used in the poem is the question mark, which occurs six times in fifty-one lines. The questions, being chiefly rhetorical, do not constitute sharp structural breaks; they serve, rather, as brief deflections from the forward movement, as gentle hesitations that make us pause to reconsider a given image. Linear progression is further resisted by what we might call the "floating clause" or phrase. In line 2, for example, "I am painting" refers either to "the black kitchen table" or "the floor yellow" or both. The same technique occurs in lines 8–10 where "in point of fact" can relate back to "telling her" or forward to "why don't I go out. . . ." Like the "reversible textures" O'Hara admires in Pollock's *Number 29*, these floating word groups, poised in midair, force us to look at them from both sides, to "read" them in a new way.

A related device is the incomplete declarative statement. "My sister's pregnant," the poet reports, comically paraphrasing his mother's telephone tirade, "and went to the country for the weekend without / telling her." Telling her what? That she was going to the country? That she was pregnant? Or a third revelation? Later in the poem, the speaker remembers looking out of the "big race-track window" of Jack Delaney's "on the wet." Wet what? It doesn't matter because the word "wet" quickly modulates into "cognac"—another wet substance.

O'Hara's conjunctions, for that matter, are usually pseudo-conjunctions, as if to suggest that we instinctively relate items that have no relationship. In the phrase cited above, "my sister's pregnant and / went to the country," we stop for a moment to puzzle out the connection between the two predicates only to realize that there is none. Similarly, in line 16, the poet's "growingly more perpetual state" (how can something "perpetual" be described as "growingly"?) suddenly gives way to the unrelated question about the Frick angel, the word "and" again acting as false connective.

The pronouns in "Essay on Style" have a similar indeterminacy. In line 3, the phrase "Bill is painting it" seems to refer to the floor, but "it" can also refer to the Leica on the kitchen table. The referents of given pronouns shift repeatedly so that the characters are viewed from different angles. Thus Bill is originally viewed in the third person, later becomes "you," and finally, in the last few lines of the poem, is replaced by another "you" who is the poet's mother. Such mistrust of pronouns, like the pointless use of conjunctions, is related to the poet's declared retraction of function words even as he uses them. The words, "well if Mayor Wagner won't allow private / cars on Manhattan" come back to haunt the speaker twenty lines later when he declares "then we can attack *well* since it has no / application whatsoever." This retraction process gradually speeds up, culminating in the question, "do you think / ,Bill, we can get rid of *though* also and *also*? Such acceleration (the first word takes twenty lines to retract, the last only two words) points to the poet's growing agitation.

O'Hara's verbal landscape is, then, characterized by incompletion, contradiction, indeterminacy. Repeatedly, the poet asks, "wouldn't you know?", "do you think?", "where do you think I've got to?", "do you think Bill?", "why not?" What starts out as a still life and a poem about painting turns into one about poetry: the typewriter supplants the camera. Nothing is what it seems to be: "how / can one say that angel in the Frick's wings / are 'attached' if it's a real angel?"; Ed Dorn doesn't attend his own party; grown men decorate Christmas trees; Jack Delaney's has a "race-track window"; when one reflects on something, one is really "being reflected upon."

Such willful confusion makes it impossible to take the poem as a serious rejection of petty family ties in the interests of art. For the poet is not making judgments about his querulous mother. Their conversation is not meant to shed light on his neurosis as it would in, say, a Lowell confessional poem. When the poet playfully puts the blame for not being able to see his mother on Mayor Wagner, he is merely striking a pose. In another mood, at another time, he might, after all, want to see her. Similarly, when O'Hara talks about cleaning up the language, he is not trying to tell us that art is superior to the messiness of life, a proposition he vigorously and continuously denied in his writings. If the intimacy of mothers palls, so, the comic non-sequiturs suggest, does the intimacy of the typewriter. Who is to say which one should be rejected first?

Helen Vendler has argued that one of O'Hara's real limitations is his "radical incapacity for abstraction."[10] But how can a poet who believes, as does O'Hara, that to prolong a sensation is to kill it, deal in abstractions? I would argue that, on the contrary, the avoidance of abstraction is central to O'Hara's poetic achievement. For, just as in Pollock's art "the scale of the painting becomes that of the painter's body, not the image of a body," so in O'Hara's poetry the "scale" becomes the poet's consciousness itself, not the ideas on which that consciousness meditates. "Essay on Style" enacts the poet's awareness that anything that inhibits the immediacy of response—whether his mother's phone call, or going to the same bar with the same friends, or the use of function words like "but" and "well"—destroys one's sense of immanent presence. Style, for O'Hara, is thus a matter of suppressing all the connectives that impede the natural flow of life, that freeze its momentum. Hence there can be no fixed meters, no counting of syllables, no regularity of cadence, no sound repetitions at set intervals. Just as the syntax must be as indeterminate as possible, so no two lines must have the same length or form. Thus the verse forms themselves enact the poet's basic distrust of stability, his commitment to change.

Notes

1. See Shklovsky, "Art as Techniques," in *Russian Formalist Criticism: Four Essays*, trans. and ed. Lee T. Lemon and Marion J. Reis (Lincoln, Nebraska: Univ. of Nebraska Press, 1965), p. 12; Tzvetan Todorov, "L'Art comme procédé," in *Théorie de la literature: Textes des Formalistes russes* (Paris: Éditions du Seuil, 1965), p. 83; "Kunst als Kunstgriff," *Theorie der Prosa*, ed. and trans. Gisela Drohla (Frankfurt, S. Fischer, 1966), p. 14. In "The Contribution of Formalism and Structuralism to the Theory of Fiction," *Novel*, 7 (Winter, 1973), 134–151, Robert Scholes points out that the cited passage is not very accurately translated. His own version of the last sentence is "Art is the meanings for experiencing the making of the thing, but the thing made is not important in art" (140).
2. See Lemon and Reis, pp. 3–5; Victor Erlich, *Russian Formalism: History and Doctrine* (The Hague: Mouton & Co., 1955), Chapter 10 passim.
3. Shklovsky, "Art as Technique," p. 18; O'Hara, "Statement for *The New American Poetry* (1960); rpt. in *The Collected Poems of Frank O'Hara*, ed. Donald Allen (New York: Alfred A. Knopf, 1971), p. 500. This text is subsequently designated as CP.
4. "Larry Rivers: A Memoir" (1965), CP, p. 515.
5. "Art Chronicle," *Kulchur*, 2 (Spring, 1962), 86.
6. Ibid., 85.
7. "Art Chronicle," *Kulchur*, 3 (Spring, 1963), 59.
8. *Jackson Pollock* (New York: George Braziller, 1959), pp. 26–27.
9. See Lemon and Reis, pp. 12–13.
10. "The Virtues of the Alterable" (review of the CP), *Parnassus*, 1 (Fall–Winter, 1972), 5.

MICHAEL DAVIDSON
From "Languages of Post-Modernism"
Chicago Review, Summer 1975, pp. 11–15

The artist in the period since World War II has, for the most part, been involved in a critique of language which has reverberations in the history of mimetic and representational forms.

The confluence of artists, dancers, poets and musicians at Black Mountain brought a wide variety of realizations of this "field" together. I am interested in possible ramifications of Olson's concerns with the physiological basis of the poem and his adherence to a personalized, "everyday" language in the painting and poetry of the post-abstract expressionist generation in New York. And I am interested in such extensions ("the languages of post-modernism") in terms of their use of the work of art structured *as* a language and as part of an ongoing critique of language itself.

The writing of the poets associated with the New York School extends notions of "everyday" speech in a direction which would seem the opposite of Black Mountain formalistic concerns. And yet, the work of Frank O'Hara, John Ashbery, James Schuyler, Kenneth Koch and others is certainly a "field" proposition in that what happens during a given moment structures the shape of the poem. The emphasis is less, however, on complex systems of notion, spacing, punctuation, etc., and more on the overall "feel" of a day's events.

Frank O'Hara's "Personist" manifesto puts it in a nutshell:

> You just go on your nerve. If someone's chasing you down the street with a knife you just run, you don't turn around and shout, "Give it up! I was a track star for Mineola Prep." (*The Collected Poems of Frank O'Hara*, p. 498.)

And later he describes the origins of "personism": "I was realizing that if I wanted to I could use the telephone instead of writing the poem." And this reevaluation should be seen in the context of developments in current philosophy of language which locates at the level of ordinary discourse a problematic of the sign with pertinence for contemporary art in general. To "do" one's art means to solve problems in a language which the art establishes as it is being created. Its grammar and lexicon emerge less as a result of a commitment to prior forms and more as a response to immediate necessity.

It is some such possibility which is opened up by notions of "field" verse as formulated by Charles Olson and other poets of the Black Mountain group during the early fifties. "Field" verse contains a conception of the poem as a place where things happen, an open area of possibility or, as Robert Duncan calls it, "a place of first permission." Olson derived the idea from his work in topology, quantum mechanics, his interest in the philosophy of Whitehead, and the linguistics of Sapir and Whorf. For these concerns, the field is a nexus, a convergence of separate points which, like beams in a holograph, come together to make an event. Perhaps the most useful statement of "field" in terms of writing is made by Robert Duncan:

> The poem is not a stream of consciousness, but an area of composition in which I work with whatever comes into it. Only words come into it. Sounds and ideas. The tone leading of vowels, the various percussions of consonants. The play of numbers in stresses and syllables. In which meanings and ideas, themes and things seen, arise. So that there is not only a melody of sounds but of images. Rimes, the reiteration of formulations in the design, even puns, lead into complexities of the field. But now the poet works with a sense of parts fitting in relation to a design that is larger than the poem. (*Bending the Bow*, p. vi.)

And perhaps the best commentary on New York poetry comes from O'Hara's art criticism and his introductions to the work of Pollock, Motherwell and others. In discussing the term "action painting" in relation to Jackson Pollock, he speaks as well for his own purposes as a poet:

> So difficult is the attainment that, when the state has finally been reached, it seems that a maximum of decisions has already been made in the process, that the artist has reached a limitless space of air and light in which the spirit can act freely and with unpremeditated knowledge. His action is immediately art, not through will, not through esthetic posture, but through a singleness of purpose which is the result of all the rejected qualifications and found convictions forced upon him by his strange ascent. (*Jackson Pollock*, p. 21)

Like Stein's attempt to approximate the activity of cubism, O'Hara's connection with the first generation abstract expressionists is significant for a view of his poetry. The blank canvas is a field of action and would be the record of a painter's activity much as Olson wanted to include the physical breath and metabolic ratios of the poet in his poem.

O'Hara's long poems have a kind of innocent aimlessness

to them—like letters of friends or conversations with oneself. "In Memory of My Feelings," to take a great example, is a meditation on the problem of one's masks, but O'Hara does not step outside of those masks and describe them. He adopts one after another, moving from scenes at a race track to a discourse on his family to an Arabian desert to the deck of the Prinz Eugen among German prisoners. The theme, if the poem has one, is stated towards the end:

> Grace
> to be born and live as variously as possible. The conception
> of the masque barely suggests the sordid identifications.
>
> (*The Collected Poems*, p. 256)

This variousness occurs in the poem as a series of images which change direction almost from line to line. If it is frustrating to read, it is because O'Hara so totally occupies the terms of the poem:

> My quietness has a man in it, he is transparent
> and he carries me quietly, like a gondola, through the streets.
> He has several likenesses, like stars and years, like numerals.
> My quietness has a number of naked selves,
> so many pistols I have borrowed to protect myselves
> from creatures who too readily recognize my weapons
> and have murder in their heart!

The poem's opening, quoted here, moves out gently like the gondola but quickly changes pace when the revery is seen to be mediated by self-protecting masks. We see the problem firsthand; the paranoia which demands "pistols" to "protect myselves" creates forms of itself and speaks from those centers of uncertainty.

As tempting as it might be to read a development of "personae," O'Hara speaks confidently in his own voice. The images which pass before us as we read through the poem do not reduce themselves to any given pattern. And despite the darkness of the opening lines, the poem is at turns playful, at times reflective. What he captures is the "scene" of his masks which, paradoxically, is the one aspect of his life that he cannot have:

> I could not change it into history
> and so remember it,
>   and I have lost what is always and everywhere
> present, the scene of my selves, the occasion of these ruses,
> which I myself and singly must now kill
>   and save the serpent in their midst.

The "scene" in which each mask is adopted is what the poem may contain, despite his denial. O'Hara wants to "bend the ear of the outer world" and tell us about the situation of masks and about the frustration of living after them. As a meditation on the failure of art in the face of personal despair, it is a powerful dialogue with the creating self as it throws off disguises.

Although the long, rambling poetry of "In Memory of My Feelings" is a customary mode, much of the New York writing is programmatically formal, at least in the sense that it investigates the limits of form. Attempts at writing sestinas, villanelles, epistolary novels, sonnets, collaborations, etc., are not uncommon. The basic form of the proposition "it is possible that . . . ." leads to a multiplicity of variations on the theme of classical forms. Most significant is a challenge to the idea that there are discrete differences between prose and poetry. The influence of the French prose poem and of Stein's attempt to create an "extended present" in prose are some of the sources for such experimentation.

ANTHONY LIBBY
From "O'Hara on the Silver Range"
Contemporary Literature, Spring 1976, pp. 247–53

The other hero of Action Painting's "heroic" days in New York, certainly O'Hara's hero, was Jackson Pollock. Dead now like O'Hara, killed under similar conditions and at a similar age, he is forever what Richard Howard said O'Hara will always retrospectively be: "the man who was to die at forty."[1] The enormous difference is that Pollock was always this, even alive; while O'Hara's death by dune-buggy was an accident freakish enough for black pop art, Pollock's crash, though now inevitably overromanticized, had the retrospective inevitability of the arrow striking the target. Properly the art created by Pollock's destructive energies fascinated the elegiast O'Hara, who once quoted Pasternak on another hero, Mayakovsky: "'In the poet who imagines himself the measure of life and pays for this with his life, the Romantic conception manifests itself brilliantly and irrefutably in his symbolism. . . . something inscrutable was incarnate [in his life] . . . demanding self-destruction and passing into myth.'"[2]

It is unusual that O'Hara, in a time of poetic preoccupation with personal or cultural death, shows little interest in death as a mystical or terrible condition, or as a metaphor for such conditions. What he sees is an accompanying luminosity, the radiance of the remembered dead, or the sense of life's present vitality that accompanies the memory of Pollock and others in "A Step Away from Them," or the sense of illumination that may accompany the experience of approaching death, moving into the final winter of annihilation. The brilliant early poem "On Looking at *La Grande Jatte*, the Czar Wept Anew" reminds us not only of the general color and sharpness of the early Stevens, but of various specific themes of "Sunday Morning." Here O'Hara opposes the seductively colorful Edenic vitality of the summer painting to death's imminent winter: "snow, the blinding bed, the gun" (*CP*, p. 63). In the Czar's final acceptance of death there is not only a self-affirming dignity, but the sense of an illumination that radically dims the tame visual treat offered by Seurat:

> his eyes widen with
> sleet, like a cloudburst fall the summer,
> the lake and the voices! He steps into
> the mirror, refusing to be anyone else,
> and his guests observe the waves break.
> (*CP*, p. 63)

Beauty flows not so much from dying as from confronting death. In "Study for Women on a Beach," a title also suggestive of painting, O'Hara again uses the sea as a traditional symbol of death; the women "see now tigers by the sea" and despite the summer landscape, "an icy combustion." But, more passive than the Czar, they cannot "fear death." Rather, as one says:

> caught up, gull
> on the dolorous possibilities of
> waves, I find my flesh more free.
> (*CP*, p. 128)

What most powerfully calls to O'Hara's imagination is not just the beauty or freedom attendant on ordinary confrontations with death, but the painful illumination suffered by the artist who ascends into realms of deadly force. The dream-ritual poem "The Hunter" describes an overbold explorer's death-defying foray after "the real chamois" in a turbulent and magic landscape where—as in the Czar's vision—autumn turns to winter as he climbs. Because of the autumn wind, the dropping leaves and more specifically the "dish / of pears" (*CP*, p. 167) which is his only weapon, the poem's initial stanza suggests the "Death is the mother of beauty" stanza in "Sunday Morning." But death is avoided here, for something mysteriously worse. After experiencing painful revelation—"The stars fell / one by one into his eyes and burnt"—and a sense of triumph—"I have come to rule!"—the explorer loses to the fauna:

> The chamois found him and they came
> in droves to humiliate him. Alone,
> in the clouds, he was humiliated.

Though presumably never humiliated by chamois, Pollock was such an explorer, taking extreme risks to capture a new world in the ritual of his painting, able to release and guide destructive energy in the service of extraordinary explosions of light. O'Hara, who met Pollock in 1952, the year before he wrote "The Hunter," was inevitably fascinated. O'Hara: "If Jackson Pollock tore the door off the men's room in the Cedar it was something he just did and was interesting, not an annoyance. You couldn't see into it anyway, and besides there was then a sense of genius. Or what Kline used to call 'the dream'" (*CP*, p. 512).

Like many early fifties O'Hara poems, Pollock's paintings of the early forties, still image-dominated, usually suggest primitive ritual. Speaking of *Bird*, Bryan Robertson writes, "There is a suggestion of a mandola [sic], or a cosmos, in this painting as in so many other paintings by Pollock, and intimations of a sacrificial or placatory ritual, as in *The Moon Woman Cuts the Circle*, of 1944–45." He goes on to emphasize "Pollock's intent if idiosyncratic insight into the ritual patterns of human behaviour, with their recurrent duality. . . . The double-edged nature of sexual union and death concerned him: the elements of victory and defeat implicit in both appear, formally transposed, in *Pasiphaë*, *Guardians of the Secret* and *Male and Female*. The idea of union and a quest or pursuit with a violent conclusion or catharsis is in all three paintings."[3] The frequent sexual preoccupations of O'Hara's poetry are perhaps even more evident than Pollock's; even the suddenly reversed "sacrifice" of "The Hunter" seems inspired by an embattled female elemental: "There were occasionally / rifts in the cloud where the face / of a woman appeared, frowning" (*CP*, p. 167).

But nowhere does early O'Hara come closer to early Pollock than in "Easter," O'Hara's wildly uneven high-velocity meditation on sex, death, sperm, shit, and the stars, which Kenneth Koch described as mainly "a procession of various bodily parts and other objects across a vast landscape" ("Notes," *CP*, p. 526). Especially suggestive of Pollock is the constant mutual interpenetration of savage bodies and primitive terrain ("the Sun sings in the stones of the savage / when the world booms its seven cunts"), which O'Hara uses to convey the sense of a rush of sexual creation and destruction both cosmic and immediately personal. Though somewhat more coherent in tone and general shape than "Second Avenue," "Easter" also creates a rapid blur of images, some of which are forced, self-conscious, or undigested; this too suggests the frequently crude early Pollock, whose overall control of his canvas was often tenuous.

But at its best, especially in the long stanza beginning "furious senses your lianas forest the virgin," "Easter" is comparable to the mature Pollock of *Easter and the Totem* (painted in 1953, the year after the poem was written). The painting juxtaposes a green, apparently female, stalk-like form (Easter?), budding and elegant, and a black-brown phallic totem, whose onlooking eyes and waiting mouth express both somber humor and malevolent threat; the two are accompanied by two smaller, mostly purple figures who seem either to suffer or cavort. In "Easter" O'Hara almost appears to continue the action implied by this scene:

> the princess in the clear heart of summer sucks her
>   flower
> and honey drowns her in a green valley
> she is privately caught in the breeze blown silence
> night without eyelids
> tied to the jet of my mysterious galley
> my cuckoo my boomerang
> I have sunk my tongue in the desperation of her
>   blood
> strangely her features are Easter
> . . .
> a rivulet of purple blood runs over the wise hands
> of sobbing infants. (*CP*, p. 99)

Even the sometimes camp humor of "Easter" has some analogue in the painting, though Pollock was usually far more grim than O'Hara. (Only in the 1943 *Search for a Symbol*, where gay shapes dance against a background of technicolor magenta, does he seem as lighthearted as O'Hara frequently was.)

Such precise though partial confluence of image and vision is perhaps less significant than the formal characteristics the two artists shared in their typically mature work. Both were strongly influenced by surrealism; as O'Hara writes in his monograph on Pollock, "The influence of Surrealism, though as a movement it provoked few masterpieces, has been considerable and seldom has been given its just due."[4] As Pollock left the "surrealism" of his early work for a more absolute abstraction, O'Hara moved away from the somewhat programmatic surrealism of "Easter" and "Second Avenue." Both tended to leave mythology behind for more personal rituals. Pollock, as some of his revolving-molecule paintings almost literally suggest, began to shatter the image as his scientific contemporaries were splitting the hydrogen atom, hoping to control the energies he released. The total openness of his "field" paintings, drip-paintings, in which the specific centers of interest are reduced or discarded so that the eye can only follow the track of the painter's erratically inspired hand, suggests the shape of O'Hara's final poetry. Richard Howard calls "In Memory of My Feelings" (1956), "one of the first of his overall poems, where the energy is distributed in a pattern of looping enunciations, without linear impulse or accumulated tension, but rather with the obsessive ubiquity of a Pollock drip-painting."[5]

Even those O'Hara poems which accept linear progression often follow Pollock in abandoning ordinary visual imagery. For instance, the extreme vividness of "The Day Lady Died" depends not so much on visualization as evocation; a precise state of consciousness is delineated largely through the abstract color of proper names. The poem's final image—"she whispered a song along the keyboard" (*CP*, p. 325)—is enormously effective, in part because it is almost the poem's only image. Appropriately, "Why I Am Not a Painter"—which in fact suggests that he is—contains no visual images at all, though it describes the development of a painting. As in Pollock, what replaces image is not so much plot, though the poem does tell a story and imply an argument, as the movement of the individual line, frequently circling back on itself to create the

duration as well as the depth and texture of a particular experience:

> "Sit down and have a drink" he
> says. I drink; we drink. I look
> up. "You have SARDINES in it."
> "Yes, it needed something there."
> "Oh." I go and the days go by
> and I drop in again. The painting
> is going on, and I go, and the days
> go by. I drop in. The painting is
> finished. "Where's SARDINES?"
>   (*CP*, pp. 261—62)

The meaning of "abstract" varies almost as much as the meaning of "imagination." Though abstracted from image, "Why I Am Not a Painter" clearly represents a sequence of acts and ideas. "Ode on Causality" (in one version entitled "Ode at the Grave of Jackson Pollock") involves some more literal attempts to abstract both from visual shape and from explicable meaning:

> seizing a grave by throat
> which is the look of earth, its ambiguity of light and
>   sound
> the thickness in a look of lust, the air within the eye
> the gasp of a moving hand as maps change and faces
>   become vacant
> it's noble to refuse to be added up or divided, finality
>   of kings
>
>   (*CP*, p. 302)

Here, or in "All that shining fierce turned green and covered the bays with grass," the images seem caught in the process of dissolution into pure sensation and color. Of course, as in most of Pollock, the image never entirely departs; as Bryan Robertson writes, "Throughout Pollock's work we find this struggle between image and non-image."[6] Paintings like *Eyes in the Heat I* deliberately exploit this tension, and even such relentless abstraction as the late masterpiece *Blue Poles*, which seems all texture, forms endless near-images as we watch its depths change. Conversely, in "To the Film Industry in Crisis," which seems so dominated by realistic images as to suggest a movie montage more than abstract painting, O'Hara deliberately runs images together to form lines of tone or color; not so much pictures of individuals as the sense of a phase-shifting moon emerges from:

> Mae West in a furry sled
> her bordello radiance and bland remarks, Rudolph
>   Valentino of the moon,
> its crushing passions, and moonlike, too, the gentle
>   Norma Shearer

Similarly, not movie magazine photos but a swelling (and squirming) line of motion dominates:

> Gloria Swanson reclining,
> and Jean Harlow reclining and wiggling, and Alice
>   Faye reclining
> and wiggling and singing
>
>   (*CP*, p. 232)

What really dominates "Film Industry" and most of the later poetry is the play of O'Hara's personality. From "Personism," more definitions of "abstraction": "Abstraction (in poetry, not in painting) involves personal removal by the poet. . . . Personism, a movement which I recently founded and which nobody knows about, interests me a great deal, being so totally opposed to this kind of abstract removal that it is verging on a true abstraction for the first time, really, in the history of poetry. Personism is to Wallace Stevens what *la poésie pure* was to Béranger" (*CP*, pp. 498–99). Experimentally, let us be serious about this. Abstraction (in painting, not in poetry) has involved an increasingly more conspicuous entrance of the artist into his painting, until Pollock—as everyone including Pollock and O'Hara has pointed out—was physically and psychologically as much "in" the painting as anyone could possibly get. After him, American artists had nowhere to go but back out again, to "emotional disengagement, formal rigor, and anonymity of authorship."[7] But O'Hara followed the last of the full-tilt romantics away from the abstraction of personal removal to the abstraction of personism.

He did not, perhaps, adventure so far as Pollock, return with such treasures, or lose his life in the quest, though he lost it just the same. Yet if by some incalculable calculus O'Hara was not as "great" as the genius Pollock, if he lacked the impossible consistency of Pollock's intensity, he was often capable of a similar richness. As O'Hara's rather labored mythic explications of early Pollocks in *Jackson Pollock* suggest by their inadequacy—and as various critics have recently argued—Pollock's greatness lies not in his exploration of the mythology of the unconscious, not in any systematic interpretation of the world, but in his pure lyric ability to capture and extend immediate sensation. "Undoubtedly," as has been argued by Hunter and Jacobs, "Abstract Expressionism will one

day be remembered best for its specific contributions to an evolving visual language rather than for its ideas or intellectual ambience."[8] In such final triumphs as *Scent* or *Ocean Greyness* Pollock paints nothing but the magic complexities of the most elementary sensations, working in what O'Hara called "the state of spiritual clarity. . . . This is not a mystical state, but . . . the artist has reached a limitless space of air and light in which the spirit can act freely and with unpremeditated knowledge."[9] Beyond the charming play of personality, O'Hara's presentation of his experience in his richest poems derives its depth and significance from such spiritual clarity.

Notes

1. Richard Howard, "Frank O'Hara," in *Alone with America* (New York: Atheneum, 1969), p. 397.
2. *The Collected Poems of Frank O'Hara*, ed. Donald Allen (New York: Alfred A. Knopf, 1971, p. 503; hereafter cited as *CP*.
3. Bryan Robertson, *Jackson Pollock* (London: Thames and Hudson, 1960), p. 138.
4. Frank O'Hara, *Jackson Pollock* (New York: Braziller, 1959), p. 15.
5. Howard, p. 402.
6. Robertson, p. 52
7. Sam Hunter and John Jacobs, *American Art of the Twentieth Century* (New York: Abrams-Prentice-Hall, 1973), p. 372.
8. Hunter and Jacobs, p. 262.
9. O'Hara, *Pollock*, p. 21.

JOHN O'HARA

1905–1970

John Henry O'Hara, novelist and short-story writer, was born in Pottsville, Pennsylvania, on January 31, 1905, the eldest of eight children of a prominent physician. Despite his parents' strong Catholic values, O'Hara was an unruly child and was kicked out of several preparatory schools. He had intended to go on to Yale, but was unable to afford to do so after his father died intestate in 1925. He became a journalist instead, but was fired from one newspaper or magazine after another. Despite this O'Hara was able to sell many short stories to the *New Yorker* from 1928 onwards; forty years later he had published over two hundred, more than any other author, and had strongly contributed to the *New Yorker*'s characteristic tone.

O'Hara's first book was the novel *Appointment in Samarra* (1934), which was quite successful and led to his employment by Paramount Studios as a screenwriter. After leaving Paramount O'Hara worked with a number of other major film studios until the 1950s. In addition he also wrote the libretto for Rogers and Hart's musical adaptation of his *Pal Joey* stories, which opened to acclaim on Broadway in 1940.

O'Hara's fiction is characterized by a sharp, satiric tone and an acute eye for social behavior; he has been praised by critic Malcolm Bradbury as "the best modern case of the writer as social historian." His novels and short stories have frequently not been well received by critics, but they have almost always been popular. They include, among many others, *The Doctor's Son* (1935), a collection of short stories from the *New Yorker*; the above-mentioned *Pal Joey* (1940); and his novels *Butterfield 8* (1935) and *A Rage to Live* (1949). O'Hara died on April 11, 1970.

Mr. O'Hara's first book ⟨*Appointment in Samarra*⟩ is highly readable and grossly entertaining; and it has the advantage of belonging to the most popular of present schools of the novel, the school which includes Hemingway more or less complete and such recent books as *The Postman Always Rings Twice* and *Brain Guy*; it is the school which gives provisionally permanent expression to the attitude which produces a weekly *New Yorker* and a monthly *Esquire*. Thus the dedication is to F.P.A., and the title—which means an appointment with

inescapable and sudden death—is explained in an epigraph drawn from an unpublished play of Somerset Maugham's.

Because the school, not only is the content of its productions but also in its public relations, is, so to speak, becoming tough and domineering in terms of its positive but limited virtues, Mr. O'Hara's book deserves examination at a certain length. It is a segmentary novel, occupying Christmas Eve, Christmas, and the day after Christmas, 1930, in the city of Gibbsville, Pennsylvania, with various cut-backs and two postscripts. It contains a telescopic history of Gibbsville and exhibits a segmentary view, as a segmentary novel should, of many of its citizens, most often in a sexual or alcoholic but always evidently normal posture: all these in terms of the characterization above.

The protagonist is Julian English, aged thirty, of the aristocracy, who loves his wife but drinks too much. On Christmas Eve he throws a highball in the face of Harry Reilly, who is self-made Irish Catholic, and a bore, and to whom Julian owes $20,000. This occurs at the Lantenengo Country Club. On Christmas night he gets drunk, and because his wife refuses to keep a date with him in their parked car, he takes the mistress of Gibbsville's leading bootlegger out of a roadhouse into somebody else's parked car. This occurs in front of his wife, some of his friends, and one of his employees. The day after Christmas is a bad day for Julian, with his servants, his wife, and at his office. So he beats up a one-armed friend and a Polack lawyer or two at the Gibbsville Club. This happens in front of the club steward. Then he drives round the country to cool off, back to town, and finds his wife coming out of her mother's house. When he tells her the latest she tells him she is through and calls off the big party they were to have given that night. Julian goes home, sets to work on the liquor for the party and on the female society reporter who calls for the guest list. Then, at the safety point of alcoholic stupor, he kills himself in his garage by carbon-monoxide poisoning.

The book also contains the life histories of Julian, his wife Caroline, his father the doctor, Al Grecco the bootlegger's runner; short sketches of Harry Reilly, Monsignor Creeden, Ed Charney the big shot, Luther Fliegler the normal American salesman; and thumbnail sketches or characteristic anecdotes of a score of others. Luther Fliegler, the normal man, opens and closes the book and is the only chorus for its climax. He is, I think, the author's only ironic representation, but he has no integral part in the action. Al Grecco, whose history is given at the next greatest length to that of Julian, has no integral part either; although, like Fliegler, he is apparently to suffer because of Julian's actions. Fliegler and Grecco are not so much subordinate as parallel characters. The quality of agency so far as the main story goes is reserved to Julian alone. The other characters are interesting as lookers-on and innocent by-standers, affected or injured by Julian's private and inexplicable explosion.

It is characteristic of this school of writing that its crucial gesture is inexplicable. The man kills himself without having once, before that day, thought of death as a solution, and without ever having felt death's lag or its magnetism. We are told only, early in the book, that his grandfather killed himself after having embezzled considerably. Julian is in debt, but not, with his family resources, inextricably. He kills himself, apparently, because his wife does not immediately forgive his drunken stupidity. He kills himself, so far as I can see, either pointlessly or out of back-handed good-will, out of gruff, tough, sentimental loyalty to a code itself pointless.

Part of this pointlessness is due to the segmentary character of the novel. The different groups of characters in the book, their motives and objects, are segments fitted one after another. They do not grow together, nor, I think, are they meant to. They achieve a kind of specious unity by being printed in sequence and by interrupting each other, and they further comprise a patchwork background. It is true that both Fliegler and Al Grecco act in some part as mirrors or reflectors in which we get images of Julian as a real guy, but they are not otherwise even apparently made to work into the main action. However interesting they may be in themselves, and they are

interesting, as agents of this novel they are incredibly wasteful and meretricious. In short, although the book is dramatic in the sense that it is exciting, is vivid and written at high speed, is accurate and often penetrating, it is not a well-designed drama, in the sense that its parts do not supplement, bind, and enforce each other. Much of it might exactly as well be in some other novel.

But the book would no doubt repeat that it meant to be pointless and fragmentary. That is the way things are thought to happen ever since Hergesheimer became Hemingway: they are poignantly pointless to the point of sentimentality. Only, to make a book, they have to be tough and exciting about liquor and women. With these stipulations, we have the kind of craft which makes a good detective story good reading: a craft of particulars, and surfaces, and anecdotes, covering a highly artificial convention of reality: an exciting craft to appreciate while the story lasts.

In other words, however immediate and however great the claim to reality, to authority, such a book makes, we are actually reading a romance, which can have as its best merit that it entertains and thrills. The romance I mean is that defined by Henry James as experience liberated, cut loose from our sense of the way things ordinarily happen. The only fault with this sort of writing is that it pretends not to cut loose where it cuts the sharpest: where it makes a morality of pointlessness, and an action out of intoxication.

It may be, of course, that Mr. O'Hara is right. Certainly his first novel has the vigor of conception, the ear for speech, and the eye for effect that make good writing; and he has, more valuable, the facility for the immediate aspects of character. The fault of romanticism I find may be merely a failure to combine his merits with the persuasive force of style. The pointlessness may be right, at least in the legitimate field of sex and liquor. But it is certainly not a new vocation.—R. P. BLACKMUR, "A Morality of Pointlessness," *Nation*, Aug. 22, 1934, pp. 220–21

O'Hara has been affected by both Hemingway and Fitzgerald, though the influence is not particularly literary. According to a passage in his writing which may be taken as autobiographical, he read them at that impressionable age when all reading tends to become an imaginary extension of experience. His world, as we see it in his novels, is that of the Younger Generation, no longer so young, but still sustaining a fiction of youth. It has been supplemented by those who were boys and girls when the soldier's pole had fallen and who, at bars, are level now with men.

It is a world of country clubs and speakeasies, manufactured in Detroit, where in the 1920's the frontier took its last stand and for a time paid tremendous dividends, for though there was less of nature to exploit, there was more of humankind. It runs, this world, as it has been said the motors of the future will do, on alcohol. We are in the prosperity of Mr. Coolidge, the depression of Mr. Hoover.

Here are the loves of Fitzgerald turned into quick adulteries on the seats of parked cars or in the apartments of Park Avenue, the freedoms that have run to perversions, lost happinesses, and lives mechanized out of all meaning. That consciousness of death which pervades so much of Hemingway's writing has here become that *goût du suicide* which gave a special savor to the decade. It is fitting that the Appointment in Samarra should be kept in a garage: Death could not come more appropriately than in the fumes of a running motor. In Hemingway, the emotions that are not there are a silence underlying all sound, a lack which, once felt, constantly gives poignancy to the whole. But in the world of John O'Hara, these emotions are not even missed. His plots have a mechanical perfection, which well they may, for nothing from within moves these people. They merely react, like Behaviorists' dogs, to certain stimuli; they have appetites, they come into heat, they suffer from sex as from a last disagreement of nature. One imagines their emotional connections as having been put through by the telephone operator of Butterfield-8. It is a mere matter of putting in and taking out plugs. The rest is conversation. For when, as in ⟨*Butterfield 8*⟩, O'Hara would give us a human emotion, the episode falls flat; any affair which involves love is nothing more than a schoolboy recollection. It does not, in this world cannot, exist.—JOHN PEALE BISHOP, "The Missing All," *VQR*, Winter 1937, pp. 120–21

John O'Hara ⟨like James M. Cain⟩ derives from Hemingway, and his short stories sound superficially like Hemingway's. His longer stories, like Cain's, have it in common with Hemingway that the heroes and heroines are doomed. But O'Hara's main interest in life is of an entirely different kind from Hemingway's, and his writing really belongs to a different category of fiction.

O'Hara is not a poet like Hemingway, but primarily a social commentator; and in this field of social habits and manners, ways of talking and writing letters and dressing, he has done work that is original and interesting. It is essentially the same kind of thing that Henry James and his followers developed, but the center of attention has shifted. The older novelist dealt almost exclusively with a well-to-do upper stratum, and the chief contrast he had to depict was between the American upper classes and the European upper classes, or between the established and cultivated people and the vulgar *nouveaux riches*. John O'Hara subjects to a Proustian scrutiny the tight-knotted social web of a large Pennsylvania town, the potpourri of New York night-life in the twenties, the nondescript fringes of Hollywood. In all this he has explored for the first time from his peculiar semi-snobbish point of view a good deal of interesting territory: the relations between Catholics and Protestants, the relations between college men and non-college men, the relations between the underworld and "legitimate" business, the ratings of café society; and to read him on a fashionable bar or the Gibbsville country club is to be shown on the screen of a fluoroscope gradations of social prestige of which one had not before been aware. There is no longer any hierarchy here, of either cultivation or wealth: the people are all being shuffled about, hardly knowing what they are or where they are headed, but each is clutching some family tradition, some membership in a select organization, some personal association with the famous, from which he tries to derive distinction. But in the meantime, they mostly go under. They are snubbed, they are humiliated, they fail. The cruel side of social snobbery is really Mr. O'Hara's main theme. Only rarely, as in the excellent story called *Price's Always Open*, do the forces of democracy strike back.

This social surface, then, Mr. O'Hara analyzes with delicacy, and usually with remarkable accuracy. His grasp of what lies underneath it is not, however, so sure. His point of view toward his principal characters tends to be rather clinical; but even where his diagnosis is clear, we do not share the experience of the sufferer. The girl in *Butterfield 8* is a straight case of a Freudian complex, somewhat aggravated by social maladjustment; but we don't really know her well. Julian English of *Appointment in Samarra* is apparently the victim of a bad heredity worked upon by demoralizing influences; yet the emotions that drive him to suicide are never really shown. The whole book is in the nature of an explanation of why Julian

threw the highball in the face of the Irish climber; yet the explanation doesn't convince us that the inevitable end for Julian would be the suicide to which his creator brings him. As for Mr. O'Hara's latest novel, *Hope of Heaven*, a story of Hollywood, I have not been able to fathom it at all—though here, too, there seems to be discernible a Freudian behavior-pattern. One wonders whether the personality of the script-writer who is telling the story is intended to play some role of which he himself is unaware, in connection with the conduct of the other characters, or whether the author himself does not quite know what he is doing.

One gets the impression—confirmed by a statement which Mr. O'Hara is reported to have made—that he improvises more or less and never reworks or revises. His longer stories always sound like drafts which ought to be trimmed and tightened up—which might be turned into very fine little novels, but which, as it is, remain rather diffuse and rather blurred as to their general intention. What is the relevance to the story, for example, of the newspaperwoman in *Appointment in Samarra*, whose career is described on such a scale? The account of her beginnings is amusing, but the part she plays in the drama doesn't seem to warrant this full-length introduction. What is the point of the newspaper reporter who suddenly gets into the picture, and more or less between us and it, at the end of *Butterfield 8*? What on earth is the justification—aside from establishing the atmosphere for a drama of general crookedness—of the long story about the man who stole the traveler's checks at the beginning of *Hope of Heaven*? If Mr. O'Hara has definite ideas about the meaning of these characters in his scheme, I can't see that he has brought it out. He seems merely to be indulging his whims. He happens, however, to be gifted with a clean, quick and sure style, which by itself gives an impression of restraint; and the unfaltering neatness of his writing carries him over a good deal of thin ice. But he appears, in perfecting this style, to have been following, from the point of view of architecture, a line of least resistance. Each of his novels has been less successful, less ambitious and less well-disciplined than the one that went before; but while the long stories have been deteriorating, the short stories have been improving: in the most successful of them he has achieved his characteristic effects as he has hardly been able to do in his novels. The best of his work, in my opinion, consists of *Appointment in Samarra*, the admirable long short story called *The Doctor's Son* in the collection of that name, and the short pieces of *Files on Parade* (though there are also a few memorable ones in the early volume—such as *Ella and the Chinee*).

As for *Pal Joey*, his last-published book, it is funny, well-phrased, well-observed; but, heel for heel, Pal Joey is a comedown after Julian English. *Appointment in Samarra* is a memorable picture both of a provincial snob, a disorganized drinking-man of the twenties, and of the complexities of the social organism in which he flourished and perished. But Pal Joey is merely an amoeba of the night-life of the jitter-bug era; and he is a little amoeba-monster. It is not that one objects to O'Hara's creating a monster—*Pal Joey* is successful as satire precisely because the author is not afraid to go the whole hog; but that he seems to represent a contraction of John O'Hara's interests.

The truth is perhaps that O'Hara has never really had his bearings since he dropped Gibbsville, Pa. He was all awash in *Butterfield 8* in the night-life of New York—though he still kept some capacity for judgment; and in *Hope of Heaven* he showed serious signs of suffering from Hollywood light-headedness. He partly retrieved himself by becoming the outstanding master of the *New Yorker* short-story-sketch; but we expected, and still expect, more of him.—EDMUND WILSON, "The Boys in the Back Room" (1940–41), *Classics and Commercials*, 1950, pp. 22–26

John O'Hara ⟨. . .⟩ certainly belongs in *The New Yorker* and ⟨. . .⟩ in his fiction accomplishes what most of the other *New Yorker* authors merely seem to parody; compared with O'Hara, most of the others often seem like girls trying to play baseball. But O'Hara is the real McCoy. He has a rich gift for social observation, for knowing how people are, what they are because of their background, and he has an acute, accurate ear which makes it possible for his characters to possess reality when they converse. But best of all, O'Hara is a snob (in the fundamental attitudes with which he regards his characters); he is as sensitive to social distinctions as any *arriviste* ever was, and his snob-sensitivity provides him with inexhaustible energy for the transformation of observation into fiction. It was probably neither accident nor intention which made O'Hara call the scapegoat hero of his first novel, Julian English; for English is an Anglo-Saxon, he resents the Irish, he belongs to what is supposed to be the upper class, and the tragic action which leads to his suicide is his throwing a drink in the face of a man with the choice name of Harry Reilly. It might as well have been Murphy, O'Mara, or Parnell. So too in the story by O'Hara in ⟨*55 Short Stories from* The New Yorker⟩, the hero is named Francis Townsend, he comes of a good family and a rich one, he smokes cigars in an Irish bar "as though William Howard Taft or Harry Truman had just asked his advice on whom to appoint to the Court of St. James"; and he certainly is the end of the town or at least that part of the town, since he is drinking himself to death, having been told that he could not hope to practice medicine because his mother and father had gone insane. An author like O'Hara is perfect in *The New Yorker* because *The New Yorker* is in the most thorough-going way devoted to a sense of the social milieu, the hopes, resentments, frustations, and fears which the American scene creates or compels. And if there is a persistent nastiness and contempt for human beings in much of O'Hara's writing, that is valuable too, because many people feel like that without admitting it. O'Hara's explicitness is desirable, just as candor is more desirable than hypocrisy, although one might well prefer the compassion of Dostoevsky, or at least Scott Fitzgerald, but let us not be Utopian, difficult to satisfy, and worst of all, *highbrow*.—DELMORE SCHWARTZ, "Smile and Grin, Relax and Collapse," *PR*, March 1950, pp. 294–95

O'Hara nursed his grudges with the acumen of a Balzac hero. The more he published and the richer he became, the more he identified himself with the lonely grandeur of the underrated. He published so many books that he virtually ran out of titles—his short story collections were getting called *Assembly, The O'Hara Generation,—And Other Stories*. By the time he died in the spring of 1970, he had published more than thirty books, over two hundred and fifty short stories, and he was full of riches—his own riches and the lore of the American rich. He now helped them to find names for their racehorses. He was a conspicuous and angry success who in print enumerated the number of cars in his garage with as much passion as he did the number of stories he had written. He even had the square body, totally wary face and somehow arranged look of propriety that used to be the mark of American managers of industry who had made their way up—seemingly with the force of their faces. But O'Hara in his riches revealed the same inability to tolerate the existence of other American novelists that the Anglos, Irish and Polish had felt about each other in O'Hara's tight and venomous corner of the coal country. So much rancor was now

said to be old-fashioned. But O'Hara kept an unrelenting fist on the most trivial signs of social differentiation in an America now much more fluid and hedonistic in the ever-spreading middle class. O'Hara's earliest images of how people succeed in society made up his capital as a writer; he was never able to understand to what extent many younger writers, especially those also writing for *The New Yorker*, took for granted the prodigious enriching of all sorts of uninteresting people in the United States. Least of all was he interested in the churchless individual seeking a "religious" life, as were Salinger and Updike. O'Hara, fantastically overspecialized in the social signs, as fanatical about keeping up the class struggle as a nineteenth-century coal baron, finally the prisoner of his own professional pride, took the easy way out of so much social change; he wrote the same kind of story over and over. It was easy because he was concerned with minute social antagonisms; the time remained America's Iron Age.

O'Hara was able to write so much because he finally indulged *himself* in mapping out social roles. For a moment he even became for some critics documentation of *their* heightened concern with social differences. He once wrote, with his usual bristle, that the emergence of the United States in the first half of the twentieth century was the greatest possible subject for a novelist. But this "emergence" meant, for O'Hara, not a sense of America the superpower at mid-century, but external evidences of the struggle for existence—the struggle between random samples of humanity in America totally preoccupied with their material progress. O'Hara was a novelist of manners crushingly interested *only* in manners, a documentarian whose characters were equivalents for the same social process. But he was never as monotonous as he might have been—he was merely discouraging. He had an old-fashioned avidity for what he never ceased to think of as (especially woman's) Dirty Little Secret.

O'Hara's world is one of total ambitiousness (an abstract idea) humanized only by extreme lust. The lust is as predictable as the ambitiousness, but shameful. O'Hara's respect for the American game that produces only winners and losers is so great that the people in his later novels are entirely exchangeable; they seem to get their characters only from their competence in the social process. The lust, the dirty little secret—always treated as one of those sneakinesses that explains the ascendency of certain people—is the most glaring example of the scarcity of motive that dominates O'Hara's mind. O'Hara finds human beings as easy to explain as the profit-and-loss system for which they live; thus they repeat themselves to the point of reproducing themselves from novel to novel as they did from story to story. What does make O'Hara's world exciting is the terror of social displacement never far from the surface. We have reason to identify with that terror; America is a rich country in which many people feel poor. The social soil is still too thin to hold anything of people but their ambition. O'Hara's corner of America seems more "lived in" than most, but it is not human personality that makes it interesting, it is O'Hara's personal excitement, the outsider concentrating on every detail of the world in which he is making his way up. O'Hara's is one old-fashioned class saga in which the *value* of position or great wealth is never doubted. The contention for it is everything. "Society" always comes out on top. Never again, in the work of an American novelist, would there be so much faith in the Establishment.

In February 1968 O'Hara wrote in the preface to *And Other Stories* that although he loved to write short stories and did them easily, ". . . the writing of short stories is becoming an expensive luxury at my age. No one writes them any better than I do, but in energy and time they have become costly because the energy and time come from sources that I must budget for a long novel. . . ." The overgrown novels that O'Hara now published were in fact pointlessly extended biographies of American careers. The only real interest of these absurdly swollen histories was his command of any immediate social situation. The short story was indeed his form, his imaginative model. O'Hara had begun as a reporter probably because he was a natural writer of "pieces." He became a prodigiously expert and expectable writer of stories out of the particular sense of social differences and the pride in his sense of fact that for him were synonymous with the practice of fiction. But he could think of fiction as endless stories, could collect them into book after book because, though this society stirred in O'Hara a fear like Kafka's, O'Hara devoutly believed in the American system itself, never questioned its reality to his characters, and thought of his many casualties as inevitable. As he said, "the development of the United States in the first half of the 20th century is the most important subject for a novelist."—ALFRED KAZIN, "Professional Observors: Cozzens to Updike," *Bright Book of Life*, 1973, pp. 105–9

LIONEL TRILLING

"Introduction"

Selected Short Stories of John O'Hara

1956, pp. vii–xiii

The thing that we all know about John O'Hara's fiction—whatever else we may know—is that it is preeminent for its social verisimilitude. The work of no other American writer tells us so precisely, and with such a sense of the importance of the communication, how people look and how they want to look, where they buy their clothes and where they wish they could buy their clothes, how they speak and how they think they ought to speak. It is thus that they protect themselves with irony; it is thus that they try to wound with sarcasm; thus they mispronounce the weighty word they have somewhere read, thus they retrieve or obscure the error when once they have become aware of it. This is how they talk to the waiter.

But of course it isn't "they" who talk to the waiter. It is a particular person from a particular state and a certain town in that state, who was brought up in a certain part of the town which had well-defined feelings about all the other parts of town; he went to a certain college which favored certain manners, tones, affectations, and virtues. It is all this, and ever so much more, that makes a particular man speak to a waiter in the way he does, and O'Hara is aware of every one of the determining circumstances.

In the man's mode of address to the waiter there is, to be sure, something that is generally or "typically" American. But O'Hara's peculiar gift is his brilliant awareness of the differences within the national sameness. It is commonly said that American life is being smoothed out to a kind of factory uniformity, that easy and rapid communication and an omnipresent popular culture have erased our particularities of difference. Perhaps this process actually is in train, but it is not so far advanced as people like to say it is, and O'Hara directs his exacerbated social awareness upon what differences among us do still remain.

The passionate commitment to verisimilitude which is so salient a characteristic of O'Hara's work is a very important trait in a writer. It is a good deal more important than we sometimes remember. "In this book a number of dialects are used, to wit: the Missouri Negro dialect; the extremest form of the back-

woods Southwestern dialect; the ordinary 'Pike County' dialect; and four modified varieties of this last. The shadings have not been done in a hap-hazard fashion, or by guesswork; but painstakingly, and with the trustworthy guidance and support of personal familiarity with the several forms of speech." Mark Twain's anxious pedantic pride in the accuracy of the dialects of *Huckleberry Finn*—what part can it possibly have played in creating the wonderfulness of the book? What can it possibly have to do with the *truth* of the book? The relation between accuracy of detail and the truth and beauty of any book would be difficult, and perhaps impossible, to demonstrate. Yet we know with all our feelings that the writer who deals with facts must be in a conscientious relation to them; he must know that things are *so* and not some other way; he must feel the necessity of showing them to be as they really are.

This commitment to fact—to mere fact, as we sometimes say—is not of equal importance for all writers. But for some writers it is of the very essence of their art, however far beyond the literary fact their art may reach. This may be said of writers of quite diverse kinds. Without his devotion to the literal fact, Kipling would be nothing; the same is true of Hemingway. It is no less true of Flaubert. Melville could not have ventured the sublimities of *Moby Dick* had he not based them on the hard facts of the whaling business; whatever the heights of meaning to which Proust and Joyce may soar, they take off from a preoccupation with literal reality.

I speak of the specifically literary importance of detail and verisimilitude because I detect a tendency of our critical theory to belittle it; and also because I detect a tendency in some of the judgments that have been made of O'Hara to suggest that his devotion to the detail of social life is gratuitous and excessive. I think that there are occasions when it can indeed be said of O'Hara that he is excessive in the accumulation of the minutiae of social observation. His novel A *Rage to Live* is an example of this. In this work (which certainly has much to recommend it to our interest) the passion for accuracy is out of control, and we feel that we miss the people for their gestures and intonations, and the enumeration of the elaborate gear of their lives, and the record of their snobberies, taboos, and rituals. But if O'Hara's use of detail can sometimes be excessive, it is never gratuitous. It is always at the service of O'Hara's sense of the startling anomaly of man's life in society, his consciousness of social life as an absurd and inescapable fate, as the degrading condition to which the human spirit submits if it is to exist at all.

O'Hara has no lack of responsiveness to the elemental in human nature. Quite the contrary indeed—there are few contemporary writers who undertake to tell us so much about the primal facts of existence. But his characteristic way of representing the elemental is through its modification by social circumstance. What, we might ask, have death and snobbery to do with each other? In "Summer's Day," one of O'Hara's most striking stories, they are brought together in a very brilliant way. The elemental datum of the story is bereavement: an aging man has lost his only child, a daughter; she has committed suicide. But the story proceeds on a series of small observations which include the protocol of an exclusive beach club and the question of who is sitting on whose bench; the social position of Catholics; the importance of election to a Yale senior society; the kind of epicene gossip that well-brought-up adolescents might take pleasure in. And the elemental fact which we confront when the story comes to its end is a good deal more elemental than what we blandly call bereavement, it yields an emotion much more terrible than grief—the father's knowledge that he has reached the end of manhood and that nothingness of life has overtaken him.

I have alluded to the objection that is sometimes made to O'Hara's degree of preoccupation with the social distinctions among people and with the details of behavior and taste that spring from and indicate these differences. The principle behind the objection is, I suppose, that these differences do not really matter, or at any rate that they ought not to matter. And perhaps especially that they ought not to matter at a time when all decent people are concerned to wipe out distinctions that lead to privilege, or to lack of privilege, or to conflict. The implication is that the awareness of the differences, and the belief that they have an effect on personality and behavior, constitute an enforcement of their existence; if we didn't think they were significant, they wouldn't exist and make trouble. It is not hard to have sympathy with this attitude, and certainly it proposes the right rule for personal conduct and for political conduct. But the good writer has a more complicated time of it than the good man and the good citizen. He has to serve not only the ideal but also the reality. He will be happy to say—and no one is happier to say it than O'Hara—that a man's a man for a' that, and a' that. But then he will have to go on to say that a Catholic's a Catholic, and a Jew's a Jew, and a Protestant's a Protestant, for a' that, and a' that. Not to mention an Irish Catholic, an Italian Catholic, a German Catholic; not to mention a Lithuanian Jew and a German Jew; and an Episcopalian and a Methodist, and a New York Episcopalian and a Boston Episcopalian, and a Northern and a Southern Methodist. And none of these people, if they tell the truth, will say anything else than that being of one group or another has made some difference to them down to the very roots of their being. The difference is not equivalent to their total humanity, but it is never trivial. It cannot be trivial, for its determinants are not trivial—religion is not trivial, national or ethnic tradition is not trivial, class is not trivial, the family is not trivial.

The differences among us have mixed moral results, good ones as well as bad ones. At the moment we are rather more conscious of the bad results than of the good. We ought not be concerned with our particularity, we ought not be proud of it, we ought not be resentful when it does not get its due share of consideration, we ought not "over-compensate," we ought not be self-protective, we ought not worry about prestige, we ought not think in competitive terms, we ought not fret about status. We ought not, but alas we do. This is the social fact and O'Hara is faithful to it.

When once we have conceived the idea of a general essential humanity, nothing can seem more irrational than the distinctions which people make among themselves. They are absurd, and the society which makes up the sum of the distinctions, and has the duty of controlling them and of adjusting them to each other, shares their absurdity. Like most writers who effectively represent society in the full detail of its irrational existence, O'Hara is half in love with the absurdity. The other half of his feeling is fear. I suppose there are no two writers who at first glance must seem more unlike and less likely to sustain comparison than O'Hara and Kafka. Yet there is a recurrent imagination in O'Hara that brings him very close to the author of *The Trial*. It is the imagination of society as some strange sentient organism which acts by laws of its own being which are not to be understood; one does not know what will set into motion its dull implacable hostility, some small thing, not very wrong, not wrong at all; once it begins to move, no one can stand against it. It is this terrible imagination of society which is the theme of O'Hara's first novel, the

remarkable *Appointment in Samarra*; it recurs frequently in the short stories, in, for example, "Where's the Game?," "Do You Like It Here?," "Other Women's Households," "A Respectable Place." This element of almost metaphysical fear in O'Hara's view of society is indeed impressive, and it is important to take account of it in any general view of his achievement. But it must not be thought to be more of a warrant of his seriousness than is his love of the absurdity of society for its own sake, his wonder at the variety which human pretensions can take, and his delight in its comicality.

NORMAN PODHORETZ
From "John O'Hara and Mary McCarthy" (1956)
Doings and Undoings
1964, pp. 76–80

O' Hara is a realist; that is, he considers his principal duty to be the creation of a plausible likeness of the world. His care and skill in achieving accuracy of detail are truly astonishing, so much so that if a vivid surface were all that mattered O'Hara would be a very great novelist. But his details are more than merely accurate. He is endowed with the kind of shrewdness that can derive the world from a brand label, and the whole universe from a fraternity pin. Sharing O'Hara's angle of vision, one begins to believe that to learn where a man was born, educated, and buys his clothes is to know virtually all there is to know about him.

The brilliant surface makes O'Hara's world immediately recognizable. The moment you step into it, you feel at home and at the same time excited by all the bustle around you. O'Hara's prose style, casual and tweedy in texture, contributes to the relaxed, informal atmosphere of the visit. Only after you have been there for a while, when you pause and reflect, do you realize what a strange place you have come to.

The name of the place is often Gibbsville, Pennsylvania, though at times it has been New York or Hollywood or another Pennsylvania town. It is a place in which the social has superseded all other considerations. The nature of Gibbsville was most purely bodied forth in O'Hara's first novel, *Appointment in Samarra*, a book which seems to me a minor classic of our time. Julian English, the hero, in a fit of drunken petulance throws a highball into the face of an influential Gibbsvillian, and the insult sets off a chain of events that leads within three days to the break-up of Julian's marriage and his suicide. It speaks for O'Hara's integrity of conception that he makes this fantastically disproportionate sequence credible, convincing, and even inevitable. And fantastic the story is: no other word will do. A breach of the peace at a country club followed by a few tactless moves (most crucial of which is Julian's flirtation with another woman)—and an apparently happy life is cut off.

Of course there is a history behind Julian's disaster. Though he is of good family, a perfectly respectable businessman, and a member of the best circles in town, he has always been a "bad boy." But all this seems to mean is that he committed a few harmless pranks as a child, and as a young man proved unable to behave himself quite properly when drinking. The fact remains that in Gibbsville tactlessness is deemed a mortal offense: the real horror of Julian's death is that no one complains of its madness. In Gibbsville, people would no more question the supremacy of the social values than most us would question the laws of gravity. The social values are all they have. With no inner resources to sustain them against the decrees of the country club, an infringement of the rules leaves them helpless and submissive, meekly awaiting punishment, and convinced that they deserve whatever they get.

To put all this another way, O'Hara appears to conceive that a man is exhaustively defined by his observable behavior— by what is usually called his manners—and beyond that, by his sexual habits. There is nothing else, either implied or specified. But it must be understood that O'Hara is not a "novelist of manners" in the sense in which literary critics have used that term. Manners in O'Hara refer to nothing outside themselves or deeper than themselves. They are neither an index of sensibility nor the expression of moral impulses: O'Hara is no disciple of Henry James. Nor does he share in the same tradition as Fitzgerald. Like most 19th-century novelists of high life, Fitzgerald attributed a spiritual value to money and social position. "The really rich," he said, "are different from us"—and he meant that they were more beautiful, more interesting, *better* (though he would have been hard pressed to define how they were better). Other novelists who have dealt with the rich have presented them sometimes as better, sometimes as worse than the rest of us—but always as different, and always the difference had a meaning. What is curious about O'Hara's preoccupation with the rich is that despite his meticulous care in describing the way they live and think, he draws no conclusions from class. Which is to say that he is not a snob. The rich appear to him most representative of the human condition, because their lives are frankly, clearly, and fully implicated in the life of society.

O'Hara's concern with sex, and with erratic sexual tastes in particular, sometimes seems gratuitous, as, for example, when he devotes several pages to a description of the bedding down of two peripheral characters. Love-making of all varieties goes on in his books; an O'Hara character is bound to have a very positive sexual personality, especially the women. But mere prurience does not account for these erotic passages—or at least not all of them. In the world of O'Hara, sex is the one area of a man's life in which he can achieve a certain individuality of expression. Everything else belonging to him, defining him, identifying him, comes from environment and returns to it, bit by bit throughout the years. We have no privacy, no inner life, no unique irreducible qualities—no mystery. Except, that is, in the bedroom, the domain of the unpredictable, the individual.

But O'Hara has grown older—he is over fifty now—and he no longer feels satisfied with his original account of life. *Ten North Frederick*, his latest novel, is the most comprehensive picture he has yet given us of Gibbsville. It covers three generations and various social strata of the town, concentrating on the life span of Joe Chapin, Gibbsville's leading citizen, and his wife Edith. The book ends with the following passage:

> There is here, in the biography of Joe Chapin, nothing that could not have been seen or heard by the people whose lives were touched by Joe Chapin's life. . . . Ten years after Joe Chapin's death, the people who remember him slightly or well have to go by what he said and did and looked like, and only rarely by what he did not say or do. Somewhere, finally, after his death, he was placed in the great past, where only what he is known to have said and done can contradict all that he did not say, did not do. And then, when that time was reached when he was placed in the great past, he went out of the lives of all the rest of us, who are awaiting our turn.

The mystery of life has finally caught up with O'Hara in the fact of death, and *Ten North Frederick* is his attempt to reinterpret the universe in the light of that fact. The tone is less jaunty, less smart-alecky than in his previous work; it conveys

an impression of a man in quest of answers rather than of a shrewd bird in the know. But it is in the nature of O'Hara's special genius that it should be helpless before questions of meaning, that it should penetrate only so far and no further. The world as he sees it, as he cannot help seeing it, contains no mysteries; at most, it accommodates a paradox or two. His angle of vision is not a matter of choice, but the way he responds to experience, and consequently not to be modified by additions but only by a radical revision.

Ten North Frederick is still written from the same vantage point as *Appointment in Samarra*, except that O'Hara tries to introduce another dimension by acknowledging that a man's life is more than his observable behavior. But on this subject O'Hara has little to say, and the mere presence of the acknowledgment is enough to make the old O'Hara who survives in *Ten North Frederick* less convincing. The drama below the surface in the history of Joe and Edith Chapin is crudely imagined. Joe is animated by the secret ambition to become President of the United States, and when this ambition falls flat his apparently enviable life turns into an insipid affair, ending in alcoholism and moral collapse. Edith is driven by the desire to "own" another human being, and O'Hara gives us to understand that this evil wish poisons her husband's soul. O'Hara never shows the inner struggle between Joe and Edith; it is mentioned many times but remains an unrealized idea. Actually, what comes through as the cause of Joe Chapin's failure is precisely the same error that destroyed Julian English—a tactless move. Joe attempts to further his political career without consulting Mike Slattery, the local boss, and O'Hara is very good when he portrays the disastrous consequences of this offense against the system. For the rest, all the talk about the Joe Chapin-nobody-knew and the "real" Edith Chapin strikes us as a propitiatory gesture toward the gods O'Hara once slighted and whose sovereignty he is now ready to proclaim.

ALFRED KAZIN
From "The Great American Bore" (1958)
Contemporaries
1958, pp. 161–68

John O'Hara's latest novel, *From the Terrace*, is almost nine hundred pages long, costs almost seven dollars, and is such a mercilessly repetitive and meaninglessly detailed documentary of upper-middle-class life in the first half of the American Century that it was sold to the movies long before publication and will undoubtedly become a best seller. It is the kind of book that Hollywood producers can pick and choose from without ever troubling with the author's point of view; and for the same reason it will be read by a great many people who derive cultural prestige by buying a "big" book. Also, it has more scenes directly describing sexual intercourse than any other recent "big" American novel, and some of the details are even more flavorsome and unexpected than the descriptions of sex in Mr. O'Hara's own *A Rage to Live*, James Gould Cozzens's *By Love Possessed*, James Jones's *From Here to Eternity*, and Vladimir Nabokov's *Lolita*.

From the Terrace is a book that makes no great demand on anyone's mental faculties, for the narrative (which even has footnotes!) is so loose and so full of extraneous information that one can nod over dozens of pages without losing the thread. There is no plot, no dramatic unity of any kind to enforce suspense or even tension. The book is simply the biography of a Pennsylvania steel manufacturer's son, Alfred Eaton, who becomes an investment banker and an Assistant Secretary of the Navy in 1943. He could be James V. Forrestal or Robert Lovett or any comparable figure of his period; one derives the same pleasure from the story of Alfred Eaton that one gets from any solidly documented biography—except that biographies deal with people who are real to begin with, which this character is not, and that in biographies there is usually no occasion to itemize every sex experience a man may have in some sixty years of living.

Why are such books called novels? *From the Terrace* has no story except in the external sense, no dramatic situation apart from the historical circumstances, which everyone already knows. There are several minor characters who appear only as names, and there are others—no less minor in their effect though they often reappear in the book—for whose conduct there is not the slightest explanation. The book is simply a large piece of American history in our time, ripped out of the reference books, and it is only because Mr. O'Hara is relentless in his determination to get on paper everything he knows—or can find out—about the upper middle class in this country that the book exists at all.

Mr. O'Hara's mimetic talent for fiction, which is considerable, has never been accompanied by a point of view that is anything but surly. So long as he wrote in his early novels as a social sorehead from the wrong side of the tracks in Pottsville, Pennsylvania, his fiction still had wit and organization. But for some time now Mr. O'Hara has been as vain and oracular as any Broadway celebrity in "21," and with the disappearance from his fiction of any real point of view, his books have become overgrown and meaningless in the vanity of their documentation, to the point where someone whose talent was always for the ironic social fact, for the thrust and bite of the short story, no longer knows how to keep a book under control. He pointlessly brings in characters from his other books; he even coyly refers to himself, in a way that makes us realize that he has substituted his own creative vanity for an imagined subject. But he can do this because the form of the "big" novel, the "great American novel," is one that Americans identify with their history. ⟨. . .⟩

The increasing tendency of American writers to tell us everything about each sexual encounter springs from the same naïve belief that a novel exists in order to disgorge information; the naïveté, the utterly vulgar naïveté, lies in the belief that sex is a wholly physical activity which can be described in the same terms that we might use to describe a fight or a dance. The late Dr. Kinsey sincerely believed that statistics on the number of ejaculations men have a week tells us something about sex in America. He was no less naïve, however, than John O'Hara, who can never describe an encounter between lovers without telling us what each partner wore, how much each disrobed, what happened where, and exactly how long it took. Sex, as everyone who has read O'Hara's other novels knows, is a subject whose external—and therefore standard—manifestations have unbelievable interest for him; it is not unfair to suggest that the emotional resonance is so powerful because sex still seems evil and even outrageous to him. In his recent novels it is always the female of the species who is rapacious, who despises love as "sentimental" in favor of raw sex. Mr. O'Hara goes to great trouble in this book to note exactly what debutantes might have worn at a Long Island dance in 1921, and he even lists in a footnote the subjects necessary for entrance to the Princeton class of 1915. But he will not bother to get the psychology of individuals down right, and if his women characters often sound suspiciously like Broadway males at Toots Shor's, even when they are supposed to be

Southern ladies, it is because the real uselessness of this kind of novel, either as literature or as social reportage, is that it is based on general types, not on individuals at all.

The persistent weakness of all American sociological thinking is that it is precise and statistical to an extreme without ever clearly defining the object of its interest. Much of this sort of writing rests on social envy, on the outsider's feeling that he can nail something down by being entirely factual; it is based, like so many stories in *Time*, on adoration of the American as success. What O'Hara, too, is concerned with is not the true novelist's question—*Who* is this human being?—but the typical American competitive question—*How* did he get this way? Just as the story of a celebrity in *Time* finds it necessary to first-name or nickname the subject in order to bring him down to our level, so the reportorial "big" novel functions by denying the humanity of the hero, which is inevitably what happens when you begin with the type and have to work up to the individual. O'Hara certainly does want to work forward; he is a writer who is obstinate rather than crude, and no one can miss the enormous effort he has put out in an attempt to make us realize the individual "psychology" of Alfred Eaton. (The formula for this: his father preferred a younger brother to Alfred, and Alfred slowly takes on the coldness and inner weakness of his father. But this is not made clear until the end, and is explicitly stated rather than dramatically visible.) But an artist does not try to reach an individual by way of a type: one realizes the type in the individual.

O'Hara is so full of his hard-won knowledge as a social observer that he simply runs off the track half of the time trying to pin down the exact emphasis of speech, the actual food eaten, the courses taken at Princeton. He cannot describe the sex life of a married couple without psychologizing crudely in terms that have only the most general application; hence these pearls of wisdom: "What had happened to her was that she unconsciously abandoned the public virginity and, again unconsciously, began to function as a woman." He describes the difficult relationship between the two brothers in terms that sound as if he had been reading Dr. Spock: "If William slapped Alfred or otherwise punished him, the difference in age was always mentioned while William himself was being punished; and each time that that occurred the age separation contributed to a strengthening of the separation that was already there because of, among other considerations, the two distinct personalities." This is from a novel!

O'Hara's knowingness belongs to the television era, the celebrity-on-the-quiz show, the age of Gunther. But in his case, as always, the unforgivingness of the lower-class man deprived of access to the prep school and to Princeton has been rendered not only pedantic but meaningless by his admiration for everything in this class, from the Racquet Club tie and bar to the line of roll-top desks that the partners occupy at a famous private bank.

Nine hundred pages! Nine hundred pages of characters who appear for a paragraph and are forgotten; nine hundred pages of rapacious females who talk about sex like college sophomores discovering that "sex is nothing but sensation anyway." Nine hundred pages of detail about rich men's stables, what workmen ate for lunch in a Pennsylvania steel mill in 1900, of careful notations about lemon phosphates and who was mad at whom and who slept with whom, and what people ate at a prep-school lunch in the 1920s ("Excellent potato salad, excellent baked ham, excellent summer sausage . . . choice of milk, tea, or coffee"). Nine hundred pages—to tell us that in the early 1920s it was still called "the Martini cocktail," not a Martini, and that in this same period collegians at a dance would tuck their black ties under their collars, that "almost every young man thus attired wore a gold watch chain from which depended a collegiate charm, and the majority parted their hair in the middle."

What is all this information for? Why does O'Hara pour it on so? The answer is that "intensity" and "sincerity"—the cardinal American virtues when you are trying to sell something—take, when it comes to novels, the form of massive blockbusters, of stampeding you with information. It is true, as Mr. O'Hara has said in a recent interview, that the first half of this century was the most exciting time in the world's history. But what exactly do we learn of this period from his novel that we did not know before? We never know exactly why one leading character in the book turns homosexual, or why a big Texas oil man, after being sentimentally and almost fulsomely admired for his kindness to the hero, is shown up as a monster. But we are deluged, suffocated, drowned in facts, facts, facts, until the American need to have news of ourselves finally turns into the same obscene narcissism as the mirror on the bedroom ceiling and the same meaningless technical efficiency as the great American science of duplicating and spreading and illustrating information.

The dream of the "great American novel"—that in it we would find the ultimate figure in the carpet, the secret theme of American life—has turned in books like these into a mechanical intensity of accumulation, and it is about time that someone pointed out that the great sex thrill for which so many people turn to these books has finally, as in American psychology generally, become a department of human activity as humdrum as the parent-teachers' association. In such books the collapse of the novel as a form, of plot as a device for bringing out the unexpected drama of life, of character as a response to a situation, has made for a final irony. Where once the "great American novel" sought to uncover the essence of American life, there must, by now, be a book of this kind for each period, class, race, and stratum in American life. In this accumulation of brute fact, novelists like John O'Hara have finally succeeded in making America seem as unremarkable as themselves.

LOUIS AUCHINCLOSS
From "The Novel of Manners Today:
Marquand and O'Hara" (1960)
Reflections of a Jacobite
1961, pp. 148–55

Every sociologist comments on our enormous suburban white-collar population and its habit of classifying the different strata of which it is composed by such artificial standards as number of automobiles or television sets. I do not deny that people can care passionately for such things or that their caring is a proper subject for a novelist, but it is thinner material than what the Victorian writers had to deal with. Today snobbishness is more between groups than classes, more between cliques than between rich and poor. Surely the resentment aroused is of a different degree. Surely there is a difference between the feelings of the man who has not been asked to dinner and those of the man who has been thrown down the front stairs. What I find out of proportion in the novels of John O'Hara is the significance which he attaches to the former.

In the strange, angry world that he describes, the characters behave with a uniform violence, speak with a uniform crudeness and make no appreciable effort to control

lusts which they regard as ungovernable. The most casual meeting between a major and minor character will result either in an ugly flare-up or a sexual connection, or both. It is impossible for an O'Hara hero to order a meal in a restaurant or to take a taxi ride without having a brusque interchange with the waiter or driver. Even the characters from whom one might expect some degree of reticence—the rich dowagers, for example—will discuss sex on the frankest basis with the first person to bring the subject up. And in Gibbsville or Fort Penn the first person to bring it up is the first person one meets. A great deal is said about each character's exact social position, perhaps because it is so difficult to determine it from his habits and conversation. Everyone, apparently, does *everything*, and everyone knows that everyone else is doing it. But that does not mean that the shibboleths of an older society are dead. Far from it. The code of an earlier culture, though only dimly remembered, is superstitiously venerated. O'Hara's men and women dance around the Victorian traditions of class distinction and sexual restraint like savages around a cross left by murdered missionaries and now adorned with shrunken heads. The hatred of the immigrant who coughed his lungs out in a coal mine is kept alive in the hatred of the rich Irishman who can't get into the Lantenengo Country Club. And although the O'Hara hero knows that sexual liberty is now the rule, he clings to a dusky little hope that the magic of the marriage vow will somehow safeguard his spouse. Thus Robert Millhouser in *Ourselves to Know*, a man versed in the ways of prostitutes, who has married a nymphomaniac half his age with full notice of her vicious propensities, shoots her dead without a qualm when he discovers that she has been unfaithful to him.

From time to time there emerges from the jungle a superman or superwoman, the darling of the author, to dominate the scene, such as Grace Caldwell Tate in *A Rage to Live* and Alfred Eaton in *From the Terrace*. They differ from their contemporaries in that they have a little more of everything—more sex appeal, more brains, more money, more social position. But, above all, they have more defiance. They look the universe in the eye and spit. They are defeated in the end of their chronicles, but only by accumulated envy; they have not been able to learn that the other beasts in the jungle cannot endure the sight of so many advantages. Grace Tate might have been able to live in Fort Penn with a husband, but as a beautiful widow she is hounded out of town as an unmated lioness is hounded out of the pride by the others of her sex. And Alfred Eaton, for all his brilliant capabilities, is condemned to a life of idleness because he is too plain spoken. The *hubris* of O'Hara's superpeople is not that they have offended the gods. They have offended the grubby little people who share their faults but resent their success.

If O'Hara were consciously trying to describe the chaos of a society where each individual flouts the moral code, yet applies it with brutal bigotry to his neighbor, and where the inhabitants of every town play at being masters and serfs like boys and girls in a school play dressed up in wigs and hoops, he might be a more important novelist than he is. Surely it is a damning picture of the contemporary world. But my complaint is that what he seems to be doing, underneath all the violence and bluster, is to be writing an old-fashioned novel of manners where the most important item about any character is the social niche in which he was born. Each hero must start the race of life with a particular ribbon pinned to his lapel, and he will never be able to take it off, whether he be proud of it or ashamed. To O'Hara, in other words, it really seems to matter if he belongs or does not belong to the Lantenengo Country Club.

If background is everything, background must be described in detail, and O'Hara's descriptions amount almost to inventories. A friend of mine, who was brought up in a Pennsylvania town similar to Gibbsville, assures me that these descriptions are remarkably accurate. But I question their significance. When I learn that Mary Eaton's father wore "pince-nez spectacles with small lenses, a blue and white polka dot bow-tie and a Tau Beta Pi key on his watch chain," that his "tan kid oxfords were polished and he had on black silk socks with a thin white stripe," I do not immediately realize that he is half business man, half professor. I can think of too many lawyers and judges and doctors who might be guilty of the same combination. Nor do I really see the difference in Fort Penn between those who say "The Tates" and those who say "Sidney and Grace." Nor do I really believe that Mary Eaton's Rowland blood would make her "automatically acceptable" to anybody. When Grace Tate tells Roger Bannon that it would take her a lifetime to explain the difference between him and the men at the Fort Penn Club, I wonder if at the end of the lifetime he would know. But she teaches him more than she thinks with a single word:

> "A lady? What do you know about a lady? Where would you ever learn about a lady? Have you ever seen one? You contemptible son of a bitch, you wouldn't know a lady if you saw one."
>
> "Yes, I would. You're a lady, and probably you're acting like one."
>
> "Oh, balls."

When he takes for his hero a Gibbsville aristocrat of the old school, O'Hara, like Marquand with George Apley, writes his most successful novel of manners. Joe Chapin, in *Ten North Frederick*, is a man who has been brought up with high ideals (though this is largely blamed on a passionately possessive mother), and he is unique among O'Hara characters in that he seeks to live according to his own somewhat fuzzy conception of the old moral code. He is faithful to his wife, conscientious and high-minded in the practice of law and active in civic affairs. The tragic flaw in his character is his irrational belief that he is destined to become the President of the United States. Many men have been so obsessed but few can have suffered from Joe's peculiar delusion that he could attain his objective by the simple expedient of attending meetings of bar associations. The other characters are puzzled as to what Joe is up to, and, indeed, it takes all the genius of Mike Slattery to guess it from the nature of Joe's activity. When Joe, in his late fifties, finally decides that the time is ripe to throw his hat in the ring, he offers Mike a hundred thousand dollars for the nomination of lieutenant-governor. Mike quietly pockets the money for the party, and Joe is left to drink himself to death. It is difficult to be sympathetic with a man so deluded, and it is not clear that Joe's ideals at the end are any higher than Mike Slattery's, but the contrast between the two men is always interesting. We see Joe against a background of privilege and Mike against its opposite; we see the even greater disparity between their wives; we see Joe fumble, outmaneuvered, and fall into the clutches of his wily and contemptuously pitying opponent, and we learn more about the forces of society that has placed the two in conflict than in a whole volume about polka-dot ties and fraternity pins.

When I turn, on the other hand, to the defeat of Julian English in *Appointment in Samarra*, I can understand it only in terms of a compulsion to suicide. Taken as such, the novel is certainly a powerful description of self-destruction, possibly one of the most powerful ever written. But again I am troubled with the nagging suspicion that this may not be what the author

intends. Is Julian meant to be destroyed by himself or by Gibbsville? Does his instinct to antagonize lead him surely to the most dangerous persons, or is their envy of his looks, his breeding, his easy manner and apparent success what makes them hunt him down? Had Julian lived elsewhere than in Gibbsville, that lumberyard of chips on the shoulder, would he have survived? But I suppose such speculations are idle. Julian belongs to Gibbsville, and it is never difficult to find enough hate in Gibbsville with which to destroy oneself. From one end of town to the other the populace fairly throbs with hurt feelings. Al Grecco provides its motto as he drives through Lantenengo Street early Christmas morning and lowers the car window to shout out at the darkened homes:

"Merry Christmas, you stuck-up bastards! Merry Christmas from Al Grecco!"

Perhaps it is the motto of O'Hara himself and of the contemporary novel of manners.

GORE VIDAL
"John O'Hara" (1964)
Homage to Daniel Shays
1972, pp. 164–73

In 1938, writing to a friend, George Santayana described his first (and presumably last) encounter with the writing of Somerset Maugham. "I could read these [stories], enticed by the familiarity he shows with Spain, and with Spanish Americans, in whose moral complexion I feel a certain interest; but on the whole I felt . . . wonder at anybody wishing to write such stories. They are not pleasing, they are not pertinent to one's real interests, they are not true; they are simply graphic or plausible, like a bit of a dream that one might drop into in an afternoon nap. Why record it? I suppose it is to make money, because writing stories is a profession . . ." In just such a way, the Greek philosophers condemned the novels of the Milesian school. Unpleasing, impertinent, untruthful—what else can one say about these fictions except to speculate idly on why grown men see fit to write them. Money? There seems nothing more to be said.

Yet there is at least one good reason for a serious consideration of popular writing. "When you are criticizing the Philosophy of an epoch," wrote Alfred Whitehead in *Adventures of Ideas*, "do not chiefly direct your attention to those intellectual positions which its exponents feel it necessary to defend. There will be some fundamental assumption which adherents of all the various systems within the epoch unconsciously presuppose." Writers of fiction, even more than systematic philosophers, tend to reveal unconscious presuppositions. One might even say that those writers who are the most popular are the ones who share the largest number of common assumptions with their audience, subliminally reflecting prejudices and aspirations so obvious that they are never stated and, never stated, never precisely understood or even recognized. John O'Hara is an excellent example of this kind of writer, and useful to any examination of what we are.

Over the last three decades, Mr. O'Hara has published close to thirty volumes of stories, plays, essays and novels. Since 1955 he has had a remarkable burst of activity: twelve books. His most recent novel, *Elizabeth Appleton*, was written in 1960 but kept off the market until 1963 in order that five other books might be published. His latest collection of short stories, *The Hat on the Bed*, is currently a best seller and apparently gives pleasure to the public. In many ways, Mr. O'Hara's writing is precisely the sort Santayana condemned:

graphic and plausible, impertinent and untrue. But one must disagree with Santayana as to *why* this sort of work is done (an irrelevant speculation, in any case). Money is hardly the motive. No man who devotes a lifetime to writing can ever be entirely cynical, if only because no one could sustain for a lifetime the pose of being other than himself. Either the self changes or the writing changes. One cannot have it both ways. Mr. O'Hara uses himself quite as fully and obsessively as William Faulkner. The difference between them lies in capacity, and the specific use each makes of a common obsession to tell what it is like to be alive. But where Faulkner re-created his society through a gifted imagination, Mr. O'Hara merely reflects that society, making him, of the two, rather the more interesting for our immediate purpose, which is to examine through certain popular works the way we live now.

Mr. O'Hara's work is in the naturalistic tradition. "I want to get it all down on paper while I can. The U. S. in this century, what I know, and it is my business to write about it to the best of my ability with the sometimes special knowledge that I have." He also wants "to record the way people talked and thought and felt, and to do it with complete honesty and variety." In this, he echoes Sinclair Lewis, Emile Zola, and (rather dangerously) the brothers Goncourt.

The Hat on the Bed is a collection of twenty-four short stories. They are much like Mr. O'Hara's other short stories, although admirers seem to prefer them to earlier collections. Right off, one is aware of a passionate interest in social distinctions. Invariably we are told not only what university a character attended but also what prep school. Clothes, houses, luggage (by Vuitton), prestigious restaurants are all carefully noted, as well as brand names. With the zest of an Internal Revenue man examining deductions for entertainment, the author investigates the subtle difference between the spending of old middle-class money and that of new middle-class money. Of course social distinctions have always been an important aspect of the traditional novel, but what disturbs one in reading Mr. O'Hara is that he does so little with these details once he has noted them. If a writer chooses to tell us that someone went to St. Paul's and to Yale and played squash, then surely there is something about St. Paul's and Yale and squash which would make him into a certain kind of person so that, given a few more details, the reader is then able to make up his mind as to just what that triad of experience means, and why it is different from Exeter-Harvard-lacrosse. But Mr. O'Hara is content merely to list schools and sports and the makes of cars and the labels on clothes. He fails to do his own job in his own terms, which is to show us *why* a character who went to Andover is not like one who went to Groton, and how the two schools, in some way, contributed to the difference. It would seem that Mr. O'Hara is excited by fashionable schools in much the same way that Balzac was by money, and perhaps for the same reason, a cruel deprivation. Ernest Hemingway (whose malice was always profound) once announced that he intended to take up a collection to send John O'Hara through Yale. In his own defense, Mr. O'Hara has said that his generation did care passionately about colleges. Granting him this, one must then note that the children and grandchildren of his contemporaries do not care in the *same* way, a fact he seems unaware of.

The technique of the short stories does not vary much. The prose is plain and rather garrulous; the dialogue tends to run on, and he writes most of his stories and novels in dialogue because not only is that the easiest kind of writing to read but the easiest to do. In a short story like "The Mayor" one sees his technique at its barest. Two characters meet after three pages of

setting up the scene (describing a hangout for the town's politicians and setting up the personality of the mayor, who often drops in). Then two characters start to talk about a third character (the mayor) and his relationship with a fourth, and after some four pages of dialogue—and one small uninteresting revelation—the story is over. It has been, in Santayana's image, a daydream. One has learned nothing, felt nothing. Why record it?

Another short story, "How Can I Tell You?" is purest reverie. Once upon a time there was a car salesman who by all worldly standards is a success; he even gets on well with his wife. All things conspire to make him happy. But he suffers from accidie. The story begins *in medias res*. He is making an important sale. The woman buying the car talks to him at great length about this and that. Nothing particularly relevant to the story is said. The dialogue wanders aimlessly in imitation of actual speech as it sounds to Mr. O'Hara's ear, which is good but unselective, with a tendency to use arcane slang ("plenty of glue") and phonetic spellings ("wuddia"). Yet despite this long conversation, the two characters remain vague and undefined. Incidentally, Mr. O'Hara almost never gives a physical description of his characters, a startling continence for a naturalistic writer, and more to be admired than not.

The woman departs. The salesman goes to a bar, where the bartender immediately senses that "You got sumpn eatin' you, boy." The salesman then goes home. He looks at his sleeping wife, who wakes up and wants to know if something is wrong. "How the hell can I tell you when I don't know myself?" he says. She goes back to sleep. He takes down his gun. He seems about to kill himself when his wife joins him and says, "Don't. Please?" and he says, "I won't." And there the story ends. What has gone wrong is that one could not care less about this Richard Cory (at least we were told that the original was full of light and that people envied him), because Mr. O'Hara's creation has neither face nor history. What the author has shown us is not a character but an event, and though a certain kind of writing can be most successful dealing only with events, this particular story required character shown from the inside, not a situation described from the outside and through dialogue.

Elizabeth Appleton, O'Hara's latest novel, takes place in a Pennsylvania university town. Will the dean, Elizabeth's husband, be made president of the college? He is a popular choice, and in line for the post. Elizabeth has been a conscientious faculty wife, in spite of being "aristocratic" (her family used to go to Southampton in the summer). Elizabeth also has money, a fact which her patrician good taste insists she hide from her husband's world. But hidden or not, for those who know true quality Elizabeth is the real thing. She even inspires the reverence of a former New York policeman who happens to be sitting next to her during a plane trip. There has been bad weather. Danger. Each is brave. The danger passes. Then they talk of . . . what else do Mr. O'Hara's people talk of in a pinch? Schools. "You're a New York girl, even if you did get on at Pittsburgh." Elizabeth allows that this is so. Then with that uncanny shrewdness the lower orders often demonstrate when they are in the presence of their betters, the flatfoot asks, "Did you ever go to Miss Spence's Finishing School? I used to help them cross the street when I was in that precinct." No Franklin High School for him. "I went to Miss Chapin's," says Elizabeth quietly, as if declaring, very simply, that she is a Plantagenet. Needless to say, the fuzz knows all about Chapin, too. He is even more overcome when he learns her maiden name. He knows exactly who her father was. He even recalls her family house "on the north side of Fifty-Sixth between

Madison and Park. Iron grillwork on the ground floor windows. . . . Those were the good days, Mrs. Appleton, no matter what they say," he declares in an ecstasy of social inferiority.

Like so many of O'Hara's novels, the book seems improvised. The situation is a simple one. Appleton is expected to become Spring Valley's next president. He wants the job, or nearly (readers of the late John P. Marquand will recognize with delight that hesitancy and melancholy which inevitably attend success in middle age. Is this all there is to it? Where are my dreams, my hopes, my love?). Elizabeth wants the promotion, partly for her husband's sake, partly because she is guilty because *she has had an affair*. It is over now, of course. Her lover has taken to drink. But with the aid of flashbacks we can savor the quality of their passion, which turns out to have been mostly talk. Sometimes they talked about schools, sometimes about games; occasionally they discussed the guilt each feels toward her husband, and the possibility of their own marriage one day. But aside from talk nothing happens. In fact, there is almost no action in Mr. O'Hara's recent work. Everything of consequence takes place offstage, to be reported later in conversation—perhaps his only resemblance to classical literature.

To be effective, naturalistic detail must be not only accurate but relevant. Each small fact must be fitted to the overall pattern as tightly as mosaic. This is a tiresomely obvious thing to say, but repetition does not seem to spoil the novelty of it as criticism. Unfortunately Mr. O'Hara does not relate things one to the other, he simply puts down the names of schools, resorts, restaurants, hotels for the simple pleasure of recording them (and perhaps, magically, possessing them in the act of naming). If he can come up with the name of an actual entertainer who performed in a real club of a known city in a particular year, he seems to feel that his work as recorder has been justified. This love of minutiae for their own sake can be as fatal to the serious novelist as it is necessary to the success of the popular writer . . . which brings us to the audience and its unconscious presuppositions.

Right off, one is struck by the collective narcissism of those whose tastes create the best-seller lists. Until our day, popular writers wrote of kings and queens, of exotic countries and extreme situations, of worlds totally unlike the common experience. No longer. Today's reader wants to look at himself, to find out who *he* is, with an occasional glimpse of his next-door neighbor. This self-absorption is also reflected in the ubiquitous national polls which fascinate newspaper readers and in those magazine articles that address themselves with such success to the second person singular. Certainly, fiction is, to a point, an extension of actual life, an alternative world in which a reader may find out things he did not know before and live in imagination a life he may not live in fact. But I suggest that never before has the alternative world been so close to the actual one as it is today in the novels of John O'Hara and his fellow commercialites. Journalism and popular fiction have merged, and the graphic and the plausible have become an end in themselves. The contemporary public plainly prefers mirrors to windows.

The second unconscious presupposition Mr. O'Hara reveals is the matter of boredom. Most of the people he describes are bored to death with their lives and one another. Yet they never question this boredom, nor does their author show any great awareness of it. He just puts it all down. Like his peers, he reflects the *taedium vitae* without seeming to notice it. Yet it lurks continually beneath the surface, much the way a fear of syphilis haunted popular writing in the

nineteenth century. One can read O'Hara by the yard without encountering a single character capable of taking pleasure in anything. His creatures are joyless. Neither art nor mind ever impinges on their garrulous self-absorption. If they read books, the books are by writers like Mr. O'Hara, locked with them in a terrible self-regard. Strangely enough, they show little true curiosity about other people, which is odd since the convention of each story is almost always someone telling someone else about so-and-so. They want to hear gossip but only in a desultory, time-passing way.

Finally, there is the matter of death. A recent survey among young people showed that since almost none believed in the continuation of personality after death, each felt, quite logically, that if this life is all there is, to lose it is the worst that can happen to anyone. Consequently, none was able to think of a single "idea," political or moral, whose defense might justify no longer existing. To me this is the central underlying assumption of our society and one which makes us different from our predecessors. As a result, much of the popular writers' glumness reflects the unease of a first generation set free from an attitude toward death which was as comforting as it was constraining. Curiously enough, this awareness is responsible for one of Mr. O'Hara's few entirely successful works, the short story "The Trip," from *Assembly*.

An elderly New York clubman is looking forward to a boat trip to England, the scene of many pleasures in his youth (the Kit Kat Club with the Prince of Wales at the drums, etc.). He discusses the trip with his bridge partners, a contented foursome of old men, their pleasant lives shadowed only by the knowledge of death. An original member of the foursome died some years earlier, and there had been some criticism of him because he had collapsed "and died while playing a hand. The criticism was mild enough, but it was voiced, one player to another; it was simply that Charley had been told by his doctor not to play bridge, but he had insisted on playing, with the inevitable, extremely disturbing result." But there were those who said how much better it was that Charley was able to die among friends rather than in public, with "policemen going through his pockets to find some identification. Taxi drivers pointing to him. Look, a dead man." Skillfully O'Hara weaves his nightmare. Shortly before the ship is to sail for England, one of the foursome misses the afternoon game. Then it is learned that he has died in a taxicab. Once again the "inevitable, extremely disturbing" thing has happened. The trip is called off because "I'd be such a damn nuisance if I checked out in a London cab." This particular story is beautifully made, and completely effective. Yet Boccaccio would have found it unfathomable: isn't death everywhere? and shouldn't we crowd all the pleasure that we can into the moment and hope for grace? But in Mr. O'Hara's contemporary mirror, there is neither grace nor God nor—one suspects—much pleasure in living.

Why our proud Affluency is the way it is does not concern us here. Enough to say that Mr. O'Hara, for all his faults, is a reliable witness to our self-regard, boredom, and terror of not being. Nor is he without literary virtues. For one thing, he possesses that rare thing, the narrative gift. For another, he has complete integrity. What he says he sees, he sees. Though his concern with sex used to trouble many of the Good Gray Geese of the press, it is a legitimate concern. Also, his treatment of sexual matters is seldom irrelevant, though touchingly old-fashioned by today's standards, proving once again how dangerous it is for a writer to rely too heavily on contemporary sexual mores for his effects. When those mores change, the moments of high drama become absurd. "Would you marry me if I weren't a virgin?" asks a girl in one of the early books. "I don't know. I honestly don't know," is the man's agonized response, neither suspecting that even as they suffer, in literature's womb Genet and Nabokov, William Burroughs and Mary McCarthy are stirring to be born. But despite Mr. O'Hara's passionate desire to show things as they are, he is necessarily limited by the things he must look at. Lacking a moral imagination and not interested in the exercise of mind or in the exploration of what really goes on beneath that Harris tweed suit from J. Press, he is doomed to go on being a writer of gossip who is read with the same mechanical attention any newspaper column of familiar or near-familiar names and places is apt to evoke. His work, finally, cannot be taken seriously as literature, but as an unconscious record of the superstitions and assumptions of his time, his writing is "pertinent" in Santayana's sense, and even "true."

SCOTT DONALDSON
"Appointment with the Dentist: O'Hara's Naturalistic Novel"

Modern Fiction Studies, Winter 1968–69, pp. 435–42

Appointment in Samarra, John O'Hara's first and best novel, achieved an immediate popular success in the depression year of 1934, but the critics were less enthusiastic in their response. R. P. Blackmur, for example, argued that the book's hero, Julian English, had no adequate justification for committing suicide; his death was morally pointless.[1] Henry Seidel Canby was disturbed by the "thoroughgoing vulgarity" of the novel; the characters had "no values" and writing about them, no matter how well, was "only craftsmanship."[2] Similarly, another reviewer concluded that the book amounted to "a skillful bit of writing about perfectly worthless people."[3] Each of these readings suggests the frustrated moralist waiting in vain for useful generalizations about the shallowness of Gibbsville society; in vain, because O'Hara is too good a naturalist to let the didactic compromise the descriptive.

The reviews also reveal the kind of frustration suffered when reading mystery stories with loose ends. Where is the motive for this self-murder? Why does Julian English take his own life? This frustration, however, can be relieved. O'Hara supplies the answer through action and dialogue, not through intrusive commentary. Julian English's death is made inevitable by the kind of world he lives in *and* its psychological effect upon him. As O'Hara wrote of the novel, "what I really mean when I say it's true is that the psychological patterns were real."[4]

The title, of course, reinforces the idea of inevitability. According to the legend, a servant encounters the figure of Death in the marketplace at Bagdad, and flies in panic to Samarra. Death then meets the servant's master and explains how surprised he was to see the servant in Bagdad, since he had an appointment with him that evening in Samarra. The application of this legend to Gibbsville, Pennsylvania, O'Hara's home stamping grounds, begins on Christmas eve, 1930, when Julian English, 30, old-family, handsome, married to the beautiful Caroline, throws a drink in the face of Harry Reilly, an up-and-coming Irishman who has lent Julian $20,000 for his Cadillac agency. This seemingly trivial incident leads in the next two days to a chain reaction of socially unacceptable behavior, including an overt public attempt to seduce the mistress of the local bootlegger, a fight with another old-family type who's lost an arm in the war, and a private and unsuccessful crack at seducing the Gibbsville *Standard's*

society columnist. Then, his marriage and business on the rocks, Julian gets roaring drunk, turns on his Cadillac's motor with the garage doors locked, and climbs inside to die. Throughout, O'Hara alternates straightforward development of the plot with flashbacks into the family history and youth not only of Julian English but of several others, including some minor characters. Blackmur objected to this "segmentary" attention to the background of such minor characters as Irma Fleigler and Al Grecco; although interesting in themselves, he maintained that "as agents of this novel they are incredibly wasteful and meretricious."[5]

These characters actually perform a critical function, however: they help to define the importance of social class in Gibbsville, an importance which is immediately and powerfully evoked in the first chapter of the book. *Appointment in Samarra* begins in the bedroom of Luther and Irma Fliegler, a middle-class couple (he works for Julian's auto company) who are admirably adjusted to each other, sexually. They are happier than any other married people in the novel, but there is a worm even in this apple, as we discover when O'Hara takes us inside the mind of Irma Fliegler. Irma is old family too, and pleased to be living on Lantenengo Street, where she knows she belongs, but not so pleased at having the Brombergs for neighbors, because the Brombergs definitely do not belong and might be followed by "a whole colony of Jews." The Flieglers do not yet belong to the Lantenengo Country Club, but may join next year, she reflects. Irma is proper, stuffy, and fond of euphemisms, the very model of an upwardly mobile middle class wife.[6]

The first chapter ends with the bootlegger's assistant, Al Grecco, driving into town with a carload of liquor for the party which Julian and Caroline English have scheduled for the day after Christmas. It is a working day for Al, who on remembering it is Christmas opens the windows of the car and hollers at the darkened homes of Lantenengo Street: "Merry Christmas, you stuck-up bastards! Merry Christmas from Al Grecco!" (20). Al Grecco, Italian-American, ex-fighter and ex-con, is making good money, but he's never going to make it to Lantenengo Street, much less to the Lantenengo Country Club, still less to the smoking room of the L.C.C., still less to the Gibbsville Club, and least of all to the board of the Gibbsville Assembly. Al considers himself superior to Jews, but his status is underlined when Mrs. Grady, Julian's cook, calls him a "dago wop" (146).

In the first chapter, then, O'Hara carefully constructs a ladder of social position in Gibbsville, and places Julian English at the top of the ladder. English is introduced, in the middle section of the chapter, as he is partying in the smoking room of the country club among some twenty others who are the spenders, drinkers, and socially secure. His social position seems unassailable, but one of the things O'Hara is saying in this book is that such a position, however solid it may seem, is necessarily precarious and depends on adherence to certain unwritten but nonetheless inviolable rules of behavior. Julian has done nothing in particular to deserve his status; it is the joint product of his and his wife's family background. As a consequence, he is constantly trying to prove himself, to deserve the social superiority conferred upon him. He sets out to prove his worth in those activities where he excels: as a drinker, as a clubman, and above all as a lover. Ironically, these attempts to prove his superiority lead to his social downfall— for Julian, a fate worse than death.

Julian throws the drink at Harry Reilly partly because he is drunk, but still more because Harry Reilly is the kind of story-telling Irishman who signals the end of a story by slapping his knee and roaring at his own punch line. Reilly's presence in the inner circle of the smoking room crowd, though not yet of the Gibbsville Assembly, represents a kind of challenge to Julian's pre-eminent social position. "Reilly had gone pretty far in his social climbing" (12), Julian reflects before the incident; afterwards, when Caroline and others chide him for his action, he feels that most of them "would agree that Reilly was a terrible person, a climber, a nouveau riche in Gibbsville where fifty thousand dollars was a sizable fortune" (71). Still later, beginning to understand his motivation for throwing the drink, Julian recalls that it was Harry's ubiquity, his constant presence in those situations reserved for the best of Gibbsville society, that annoyed him: "You went to the Gibbsville Club for lunch; Harry was there. You went to the country club to play squash on Whit Hofman's private court, and Harry was around. You went to the Saturday night drinking parties, and there was Harry! inescapable, everywhere. Carter Davis was there, too, and so was Whit; so was Froggy Ogden. But they were different. The bad new never had worn off Harry Reilly" (148). What right had Harry Reilly, "bad new" and Irish to boot, to associate with the good old families?

Even more than Irma Fliegler, who longs for the day she will join the country club, and Al Grecco, who takes the outcast's revenge by accumulating money, Julian English's actions are dictated by his social position—and the way he feels about it. *Appointment in Samarra* is a naturalistic novel in several ways. There is the lavish attention to surface details, the breaking of the Howellsian taboo against sex, and the physical violence associated with naturalism. Most conspicuously of all, because it is spelled out in the epigraph and title, there is the theme of determinism. Heredity is hinted at as a possible explanation for Julian's suicide; his grandfather, after embezzling some money, had taken his own life, and Julian's father, a basically incompetent and over-enthusiastic surgeon, privately attributes his son's demise to the bad seed having skipped a generation. But if hereditary influences have in fact contributed to Julian's tragic end, O'Hara implicitly argues, these influences have stemmed from the stern and unloving figure of Dr. Billy English, not from grandfather. In any case, it is not heredity but the social environment—the "rigidity of social class lines," as one critic puts it—which acts as the most powerful deterministic agent.[7] It is difficult to climb up the status ladder (although Harry Reilly is making the climb, and so, less sensationally, are the Fliaglers); one must climb carefully, one rung at a time. Having reached the top rung, it is still more difficult to maintain one's position, especially since others are jostling the ladder. When you lose your place, you are liable to slip all the way to the bottom.

Julian English is terribly jealous of his place on the ladder, willing to share it with only a few others, and eager to demonstrate his right to pre-eminence. In short, he is a howling snob. His very name underlines his status. The surname is English, WASP. The middle name is McHenry, and he likes his monograms to read J. McH. E., a fact that only Caroline knows. The elegant given name contracts, in the speech of his wife and close friends, to "Ju," and he is most uncomfortable when someone who does not know him really well, such as the dentist Ted Newton, uses his nickname (13). The reason is transparently clear; Jews are barred from the higher status levels of Gibbsville, just as they are barred from membership at the Lantenengo Country Club. Julian functions as a self-appointed gatekeeper for all his clubs; whenever he is challenged, he responds by bringing up the question of membership. Bobby Herrmann undertakes the job of kidding Julian about the drink-throwing episode, and Julian retaliates

weakly with the membership gambit: "Who is this man? Did he come here with a member?" (61). Later, when he is brutally criticized at the Gibbsville Club by Froggy Ogden, who has the distinction of having fought and lost an arm in the war, Julian tries to avoid fisticuffs until a Polish lawyer intervenes on Froggy's behalf. Once again, Julian's immediate response is to ask whether the lawyer is "by any chance a member of this club" (153). The question is only seemingly irrelevant; if lawyers named Luck, or "Lukashinsky, if I know anything," are allowed to join the Gibbsville Club, Julian's pride in the exclusivity of his status is wounded. He'd be a hard man on the membership committee.

Similarly, Julian English behaves very badly indeed at the first hint of any presumption on the part of the hired help. He is a regular guy to the gangster Ed Charney, who regards "the English" as "copacetic" (16). Ed is a source of liquor supply, and a Cadillac customer as well. But Al Grecco, who works for Ed, is another matter, as Julian drunkenly makes clear: "Just call me Mr. English, Al. You call me Mr. English and I'll call you Al. The hell with this formality. We've known each other all our lives" (113). The next morning, hung over, he argues with Mrs. Grady, the cook, because he is annoyed by her contemptuous manner: "There it was again: servants, cops, waiters in restaurants, ushers in theaters—he could hate them more than persons who threatened him with real harm. He hated himself for his outbursts against them, but why in the name of God, when they had so little to do, couldn't they do it right and move on out of his life?" (128).

Such attitudes reveal a deep-seated, basic insecurity; so do Julian's dealings with Lute Fliegler and Mary Klein, his best salesman and secretary at the Gibbsville-Cadillac Motor Car Company. Lute quite cogently and dispassionately spells out for his boss the probable consequences of the drink-throwing incident (they'll lose a sale or two they can ill afford to lose to the Buick dealer), and Julian listens without rancor. Although a Pennsylvania Dutchman, Lute Fliegler is, for Julian, "one of the swellest guys that ever lived." He has a theory to explain that anomaly, however; maybe "Lute's mother had had a quick one with an Irishman or a Scotsman." Mary Klein is Pennsylvania Dutch too, plain, solid, respectable, Lutheran middle class Pennsylvania Dutch. Though she is Julian's employee, she also plays another role by giving her boss the kind of approval he requires. Thus Julian comes to the office with his hangover and jots down some figures on a pad, looking very busy and hoping "he was making a good impression on Mary Klein" (141).

The pattern that emerges is that of a desperately insecure man, trying to live up to a social position he knows he has not earned. Julian can stand only so much rejection by others, since he knows such rejection will mean loss of his social status. One way he has always been able to satisfy the idea of himself as a superior person (an idea which society imposes on him and he unquestioningly accepts) is through the conquest of women. Even as a young boy he had been able to "get away with murder" where women were concerned. Irma Fliegler, who taught him in Sunday School, never reported him when he sneaked out to go to the ball game instead. Irma, he realizes, would make the ideal confidant as his troubles multiply; Julian wishes he could tell her all, but she is also the wife of one of his employees and he "must not forget that" (131). Mary Manners, a beautiful Polish girl, fell in love with Julian and did whatever he asked her to do. Snobbishly, the one thing he could not ask her to do was to marry him. There were others, too; Julian had either had an affair, or been on the brink of an affair, with almost every female member of the country club crowd. In most of these relationships, Julian placed himself in the role of the bad boy who misbehaves *in order to* be forgiven. (In boyhood, he had stolen a flashlight at the dime store: his father, sensitive to family history, concluded that Julian was a thief and never forgave him.) Thus when Caroline goes to bed with him on Christmas afternoon, the act represents for Julian a form of forgiveness for throwing the drink at Harry Reilly. When, later that night, she declines to meet him at the car for another sexual engagement, Julian immaturely decides to be as bad as possible: it is then that he gets roaring drunk and takes Ed Charney's mistress out to the car in her stead.

When Caroline breaks their midnight date in the car, Julian's uneasy accommodation to Gibbsville society starts to come apart at the seams. Harry Reilly won't talk to him or accept his apology. Froggy Ogden reveals that he had never liked him, partly because of his success with the Polish girl and with Caroline. The news takes him back to childhood, to horrible Saturday mornings at the dentist's, when the rest of the kids were playing but he had to face something painful (152). Still greater pain lies in store when he returns from the fight at the Gibbsville Club and discovers that Caroline will no longer take his side without question. Julian does not tell her the details of his get-together with "Captain Ogden, the war hero," but he does make an appeal: "This is a pretty good time for you to stick by me. . . . Blind, without knowing, you could stick by me. That's what you'd do if you were a real wife, but, what the hell" (165).

The final blow comes when the society columnist, Alice Cartwright, refuses his attentions. Julian attempts to seduce her in his own home, when she comes calling to check on the guest list for the party Caroline has called off. Miss Cartwright, who is no beauty and no virgin, admits to a yen for Julian, but turns him down because he's "married to a swell girl." He foresees one rejection after another—"all the pretty girls in Gibbsville, trying to make him believe they all loved Caroline." He also envisions his own precipitous plunge down the status ladder in attempts to assert the sexual superiority that is slipping away with his youth:

> Thirty years old. "She's only twenty, and he's thirty. She's only twenty-two, and he's thirty." She's only eighteen, and he's thirty and been married once, you know. You wouldn't call him young. He's at least thirty. No, let's not have him. He's one of the older guys. Wish Julian English would act his age. He's always cutting in. His own crowd won't have him. I should think he'd resign from the club. Listen, if you don't tell him you want him to stop dancing with you, then I will. No thanks, Julian, I'd rather walk. No thanks, Mr. English, I haven't much farther to go. Listen, English, I want you to get this straight.

Julian, I've been a friend of your family's for a good many years. Julian, I wish you wouldn't call me so much. My father gets furious. You better leave me out at the corner, becuss if my old man. Listen, you, leave my sister alone. Oh, hello, sweetie, you want to wait for Ann she's busy now be down a little while. (177–178)

Only after he traces out this depressing future does Julian decide to get really drunk for the last time and to take his life. His cigarette burns the phonograph and he considers a lie (Julian has always lied, fixed tickets, sought the easy way out) to explain the burn before realizing, for the first time, that "it would not make any difference." The burn will not matter when he is dead (179).

Why does Julian English kill himself? After the fight at the Gibbsville Club, he drove out of town to escape, but "something . . . pulled him back. You did not really get away from whatever it was he was going back to, and whatever it was, he had to face it" (156). The something which pulls him back to disaster is not an incomprehensible and foreordained fate. Julian is controlled by the interaction between society and himself. Society has given him a certain elevated stature. He wants to live up to this position, which has been imposed upon him by the accident of birth. But he also feels guilty because he has done nothing to earn his place on the status ladder, and insecure because others are climbing up to threaten his position. Rudeness to the lower classes serves to reinforce his pride of place, and sexual prowess provides him with a pleasing sense of control over others, but he still remains insecure. When the servants start talking back and when his sexual powers begin to flag, he realizes that society has decided against him. Julian's tragedy is that he accepts society's judgment as both inevitable and final. Society's standards are his own; rejected by others, he rejects his own existence rather than take the slide down the status ladder. Caroline, who had always loved him but comes to understand him only in death, concludes that "God help us all but he was right. It was *time* for him to die" (188). All that remained for him was one horrible endless Saturday morning in the dentist's chair.

Notes

1. R. P. Blackmur, "A Morality of Pointlessness," *Nation*, CXXXIX (August 22, 1934), 220.
2. Henry Seidel Canby, "Mr. O'Hara and the Vulgar School," *Saturday Review of Literature*, XI (August 18, 1934), 55.
3. Herschel Brickell, New York *Post* (August 18, 1934), 34.
4. John O'Hara, *Appointment in Samarra* (New York, 1953), foreword.
5. Blackmur, 220.
6. John O'Hara, *Appointment in Samarra* (New York, 1945), pp. 6–8. Subsequent page references within the text are to this edition.
7. E. Russell Carson, *The Fiction of John O'Hara* (Pittsburgh, 1961), p. 3.

TILLIE OLSEN

1913–

Tillie Olsen, novelist and essayist, was born in Nebraska on January 14, 1913, the second of six children. Her parents, Samuel and Ida Lerner, were Jewish immigrants who had fled Russia after the 1905 revolution; her father, a manual laborer, later became state secretary of the Nebraska Socialist party. Olsen left high school without graduating, and worked in factories and warehouses. She joined the Young Communist League, and was arrested in the early 1930s for trying to organize Kansas City packinghouse workers. By 1933 she had moved to California, where she settled permanently. As a union worker she took part in the San Francisco Warehouse Strike of 1934, and spent some more time in jail. In 1936 she married Jack Olsen, a printer; to help support their three daughters Olsen worked as, among other things, a waitress, launderess, and secretary.

In 1956, a year after enrolling in a San Francisco State University creative-writing course, Olsen won a Stanford University fellowship. With the aid of several subsequent grants she embarked on a career as a writer and teacher. *Tell Me a Riddle*, her first book, was published in 1961, and the title story of this collection received the O. Henry Award for the best short story of that year. Between 1969 and 1972 Olsen taught at three universities: Amherst, the University of Massachusetts, and Stanford. After a year as a writer-in-residence at M.I.T. (1973) she returned to the University of Massachusetts (1973–74) as a visiting professor.

Olsen's writing has been influenced by her feminist concerns and by her working-class background; her major theme has been the waste of human potential that results from poverty, sexism, and racial prejudice. In addition to her collection of stories she has published *Yonnondio* (1974), a novel about life in the 1930s, and *Silences* (1975), a collection of essays.

Personal

"I could never have been eligible for inclusion in *The God That Failed*," Tillie Olsen told me, "because for me it never was a God and it never failed. I was an atheist's daughter from the beginning." There also never was a time when she didn't have a first hand knowledge of oppression and of revolutionary tradition. Her parents had participated in the 1905 democratic upheavals against the Czar in Russia. When these were suppressed, they emigrated to this country. They settled first on a farm in Nebraska, but soon moved to the city of Omaha, where her father became the state secretary of the Socialist Party. Tillie Olsen was born in 1912 or 1913 and was exposed early to the language of the great socialist orators, some of whom would stay at her house when they came to attend meetings in town. She remembers how she sat on Eugene Victor Deb's lap and was one of three little girls chosen to give him red roses when he spoke at the town hall. She remembers how he said that "human capacity and human activity were like a great symphony with each person playing his own instrument." When guests would come to their house, the children would have to sleep on chairs, two, three, four or even five chairs—depending upon how old the children were at the time—lined up next to one another. Old copies of *The Comrade,* a magazine which reprinted democratic and revolutionary art and classics from around the world as well as literature from the Native American populist and socialist movements came to her house. It was through Upton Sinclair's *Cry For Justice*, most of which was taken from *The Comrade*, that Tillie Olsen had her first exposure to contemporary European literature and art in reproduction. "It was a rich childhood from the standpoint of ideas," Tillie Olsen told me. But economic struggle was constant. There was never a time when she was not doing something "to help the family out economically." When she was ten, she used to work after school shelling peanuts. And since she was the second oldest of six children, she was always taking care of someone younger. She remembers from an extremely early age that sense of never having enough time which has haunted her for most of her life, that sense of most women and her own mother feeling starved for time. It was only because she was sick a great deal—she had all of the childhood diseases, even scarlet fever—that she had any time at all to read and write. She used to hate winter because she always had a running nose, one of the many things that made her feel self-conscious when, one of the few out of her neighborhood, she "crossed the tracks" to attend Omaha's only academic High School. There a beloved teacher introduced her to Shakespeare and Edna St. Vincent Millay and to the prose rhythms in Sir Thomas Browne, De Quincy and Coleridge, who made sure that she was present when Carl Sandburg came to town to read and play on his guitar. She later wrote parodies of Sandburg's poetry which she gave to the teacher as new poems of Sandburg. She wanted this erudite person to be her friend and tried too hard. Eventually the teacher hit her in the forehead with a book over a misunderstanding around the meaning of Hamlet's talking to his dead father. Although Central High School stimulated her intellectually, she felt that it crucified her socially, setting up "hidden injuries of class."

As a child she stuttered. Therefore she kept quiet and listened a great deal. She loved to listen to the language of those around her, the speech of the powerful socialist orators who had such a profound influence on her own use of language, revealing to her early how language was able to affect and move people, the language of the immigrants who did not yet know all of the words they needed in order to express themselves, who had to somehow make do with the words they did know, stretching them, the language of the working people. "The people of the packing house strike were not masters of language," she told me, "but when they would get up to speak, they would speak with such beauty . . . the sodders, the sod farmers used the language of the prairie when it was all grass and no trees, wind . . ." She was also deeply affected by the language of her black neighbors and school mates, the language that she returns to in "Oh Yes," with its rhythms that she could not fully enter, yet longed for. "Very early that chasm between us began, which books opened up for me," she told. She spoke to me movingly about how she watched the "lessening" of human beings with whom she lived in an everyday way, her school mates, her neighbors, those in her family, of how even very early she sensed that harming and impairing of capacity happening in herself as well.

Very early books became a passion. She remembers the Kansas published Haldeman Julius 5¢ Blue Books designed to be small enough to be buttoned into a working man's shirt pocket, which seemed to reprint everything one might want to read. Millions were published in the twenties. Then there was Harriet Monroe and *Poetry Magazine*. Again with her sense of urgency about time, she taught herself to become a speed reader. She kept pushing herself at this task, until she was able to read a book in fifteen minutes. Then she decided that she would read every book in the fiction, poetry and biography section of the Omaha public library, beginning with the As. She would pick up a book and read a couple of pages and, if she didn't like it, she would move on to the next. The librarian, she later found out, was Willa Cather's niece. They had a rather ambivalent relationship, Tillie Olsen remembers, but she was allowed to have adult reading privileges early. And even though she often neglected to bring books back on time, or, eating an apple right down to the core, she would let seeds drop on the pages, those reading privileges were never rescinded. It was during those years that she also "made a few literary friends." She met John Neihardt, the poet laureate of Nebraska who wrote *Black Elk Speaks*. But most of her life was centered about the purely practical necessities of survival. In 1931, at the age of eighteen, she joined the Young Communist League. This too she sees as a primarily practical decision. "I was one of millions of kids who had the problem of survival," she told me. "I couldn't live on my family. Probably between 1934 and 1936 or '37, a million joined the party."

"In the very early days of the Depression," she went on, "in 1931 and '32 and '33, when a third of the nation was ill-housed, ill-clothed, ill-nourished, there were a million people riding the box cars, most of them young, the homeless youth. Nobody wrote an 'on the road' for our generation. The family behind us cooked and killed their dog to eat. Those were the Hoover years of no welfare, do nothingism and denial, when there were long, long lines and apples, everything that people know about now in that shadowy mythical way . . ." She stopped.

Yonnondio was to be that "on the road" for the thirties that nobody ever wrote, as well as a kind of portrait of the artist as a young woman for that particular generation. Tillie Olsen first began to write it in late February of 1932 when she was nineteen years old, "to show what a criminal system this was, and what this did to human beings." Begun at the same time Tillie Olsen's first baby was born, she describes it as having come out of the colleges of motherhood, of everyday work, of human struggle bursting the thick wall of self, as it went on." Deliberately she had chosen to focus on the family because she felt that it was only there that one could really see how social forces and social circumstances limit and shape what one can do. She spoke of how seldom one finds in literature "that realistic knowledge of what happens in human beings, what it is that really shapes or misshapes human beings in our society."—ERIKA DUNCAN, "Coming of Age in the Thirties: A Portrait of Tillie Olsen," *BF*, 1982, pp. 209–11

Works

TELL ME A RIDDLE

Tillie Olsen uses the minutiae of obscure lives to pose and reflect on major metaphysical questions. Such abstract questioning, as has been noted, is rare in women's writing of this period. When it occurs it is apt to be associated with the socialist or anarchist doctrines that were very much a part of working-class life among immigrants. Olsen goes far beyond ideology, however. What meaning can be found in life at the end of life? she asks, in the prose of *Tell Me a Riddle* (1961), as Yeats asked in his poems of old age. Here, these are questions put in a female voice, questions that value the high creeds of revolutionary self-sacrifice in terms of "one pound soupmeat, one soupbone . . . bread, day old" and "cheap thread." These cares are what an old woman remembers in her mortal agony, and they overwhelm memories of dedication to the Movement, marriage, children born and laboriously raised. Love, anger, frustration, hope, the fellowship that endured poverty—all fall away before the inescapable chores of living, relieved only by a sudden echo from music heard in childhood. To her husband the old woman becomes an astonishing, disturbing stranger: "It seemed to him that for seventy years she had hidden a tape recorder, infinitely microscopic, within her, that it had coiled infinite mile on mile, trapping every song, every melody, every word read, heard and spoken—and that maliciously she was playing back only what said nothing of him, of the children, of their intimate life together." He is right. What she had hoped for was a patch of life of her own, completely to herself; and then death intervened.

The full weight of consciousness is present and expressed in the simple events of life for Olsen's women. "I stand here ironing," begins a woman in the story of this title (in *Tell Me a Riddle*) and weighing out the inescapable failure of her care for her oldest child, raised without her father, passed to a neighbor in order that the mother could earn enough to keep them both, a little girl who had to be good and was; of whom too much was demanded. Reflection can find no cure, no solution, only note again how childhood loneliness was matched with adult anguish and balanced against what the other children needed, "that terrible balancing of hurts and needs I had to do . . . and did so badly, those earlier years." Awareness of what we owe each other and cannot give, of what humanity might become if love could be unrestricted, shapes this story, though "I will never total it all now," the mother tells herself. "My wisdom came too late . . . Let her be. So all that is in her will not bloom—but in how many does it? There is still enough left to live by. Only help her to believe—help make it so there is cause for her to believe that she is more than this dress on the ironing board, helpless before the iron."
—ELIZABETH JANEWAY, "Women's Literature," *Harvard Guide to Contemporary American Writing*, ed. Daniel Hoffman, 1979, pp. 364–65

Her first book, the short stories collected in *Tell Me a Riddle*, was published when she was 50. Besides "I Stand Here Ironing" it contains three other fictional pieces of extraordinary intensity. "Hey, Sailor, What Ship?" is a character sketch of a seaman defeated by loss of belief in himself and his work, ruining his life and health with drink. The daughter of old friends he visits is now ashamed of one she used to show off to her friends. Yet love and loyalty warm even Whitey's bleak future. When the daughter first sees him sitting on the sofa with her parents, she thinks:

Never saw so many peaceful wrecks in my life . . . That's what I want to be when I grow up, just a peaceful wreck holding hands with other peaceful wrecks.

(As I grow older, I have come to see this as no mean ambition in life.)

"Oh, Yes!" is an introduction to racism and the class system as experienced by two young girls, one black, one white, who have been close friends but are now parted involuntarily into separate worlds. The initiation begins with the white girl's attendance at a black religious service, where the intense emotionalism causes her to faint. It continues by means of a rigid high school tracking system until the white girl asks: "Oh why is it like it is? And why do I have to care?" The mothers are as involved as the girls, and at the end the white mother muses silently: "Caring asks doing. It is a long baptism into the seas of humankind, my daughter. Better immersion than to live untouched. . . . Yet how will you sustain?"

The great title story of the volume, "Tell Me a Riddle," while it recounts the quarrel between an aged grandfather (who wants to retire to the Happy Haven, play cards and watch TV) and an obdurate grandmother, eventually seen to have cancer (who wants silence, selfness, and reconnection with the revolutionary humanist ideals of their Russian youth), also conveys the larger dimensions of America's own loss of contact with its idealistic, hardworking, communal roots. Before her death, the old woman awakens these memories in the old man:

> "Aaah, children. . . . how we believed, how we belonged." And he yearned to pack for each of the children, the grandchildren, for everyone, *that joyous certainty, that sense of mattering, of moving and being moved, of being one and indivisible with the great of the past, with all that freed, ennobled.* Package it, stand on corners, in front of stadiums and on crowded beaches, knock on doors, give it as fabled gift.

⟨. . .⟩ "Tell Me a Riddle" was about her own mother and dedicated to her, Olsen said, in a clear, mid-western, ladylike voice that quavered slightly. Like the grandmother in the story, her mother had been part of a movement to effect change in the Russia of 1905 before she came to this country. Since in that repressive regime religion had allied itself with power, in the name of human possibility and freedom she had become an incorruptible atheist. All her life she had been silent, hardworking, yet—like so many mothers—wise, loving and creative.

Just before her death, Tillie Olsen's mother had a dream in which someone knocked on her bedroom door. She smelled a marvelous smell, heard a neighing sound, and saw three wise men in gold, blue and crimson robes, embroidered as in her old village. "We've come to talk to you," the first one said. When she replied, "I'm not a believer," he assured her, "We don't want to talk about that. We want to talk about wisdom."

"Come in," her mother said. Then she saw that country. ⟨. . .⟩ They were worn out, but they had come to worship a universal human infant who was going to be crucified into sex, race and class divisions. In her dream, Tillie Olsen's mother joined them in this worship.

This memory, linked with personal inspiration, is undoubtedly close to the source of Olsen's vocation as storyteller of the silent, hardworking men and women who find their voice in her fiction. Its vision is the root of its force. Olsen's art helps us to make sense out of the pain and defeat that life inflicts on ordinary people by pointing to the dignity and wonder still present there. On fire as she is with this sense of human possibility, her stories call out to their readers to be responsible for serving this potentiality in every person they

encounter in the tarnished yet real miracle of everyday existence. Heir to a vital prophetic tradition of humanism, Tillie Olsen expends her energies to pass that tradition on to us. In reading her stories, we encounter the ambivalence of the human condition itself.—SALLY CUNNEEN, "Tillie Olsen: Storyteller of Working America," *CC*, May 21, 1980, pp. 572–74

YONNONDIO

A great many American novels have concerned themselves with poverty and the Depression, but most of them have been very quickly smothered in that sentimental form known as 'documentary.' *Yonnondio* is written by a young girl who could never have heard of such a thing, since the book has that quality of innocence which comes from wonder rather than from knowledge: "'I am Maizie Holbrook,' she said softly, 'I am a knowen thing. I can diaper a baby. I can tell ghost stories. I know words and words'." Maizie is the child of one of those families which were slowly beaten into shape during the 'thirties when "words and words" were the merest palliative in the struggle to live. But Maizie's mother, a beautifully achieved character known as Anna, wants an "edjication" for her children and the whole family go on a long desolate wandering through America: they become tenant-farmers until their debts overtake them, and then they move into one of those restless American cities which were at that moment testing their strength. It is here that Tillie Olsen leaves them, to a fate which was not worth having.

It is a conventional story, as stories go, but the plot is in fact the least important element of the novel. This is not because it is incomplete (the book has only recently been recovered in a less than perfect form), but because the narrative is consumed by the effects of Miss Olsen's prose. A pattern of images is cast over the writing from the opening chapters, and there is a characteristic attention to description rather than analysis—it is a matter of dialogue rather than character, of situations rather than incidents. *Yonnondio* is a romantic novel, in the sense that Man and Nature are seen in a close and often destructive relationship, and its language becomes the space between them—instinctive with life, both mortal and at the same time capable of expressing certain permanent truths.

It is out of the mouths of children that this will come most naturally and there are some marvellously childish moments in this book. A young girl dreams of things which will not come:

> Luxuriously on her rug, pretend silk slinking and slithering on her body, turbanned, puffing her long pretend cigarette: Say vamp me, vamp me. I'm Nazimova. Take me to the roadhouse, I want to make whoopee. Hotcha. Never never never. O my gigolo, my gigolo. A moment of ecstacy, a lifetime of regret.

And the spell is broken by younger children who sing of things which certainly will come:

> Mother, Mother I am sick
> Call the doctor quick, quick, quick.
> Doctor, Doctor, will I die?
> Yes. You will. And so shall I.

Yonnondio is one of the most powerful statements to have emerged from the American 'thirties; a young woman has pulled out of that uneasy time a living document which is full of the wear and tear of the period, and she has done so without doctrinaire blues, and without falling into the trap of a sentimentality which is, at bottom, self-pity.—PETER ACKROYD, "The Living Image," *Spec*, Dec. 14, 1972, pp. 767–68

Suppose that we could recover the literary texts that have been lost, censored, and suppressed. Suppose, too, that we could figure out why they had been erased from consciousness while other texts had come down to us as cultural legacies. Our discoveries might add up to a new literary and social history, an analogy to the way in which the concept of the black hole has given astrophysicists the premise for a new cosmology.

Tillie Olsen's novel, *Yonnondio*, is a recovered text. She began the book in 1932. She was then 19 years old. A chapter was published and praised in 1934. Two or three years later she abandoned the project and, for a long time, writing itself. Her silence was less the result of a romantic rendezvous with the abyss at the edge of language than of acute self-doubt, the responsibilities of raising four children, the need to hold a full-time job, the demands of community tasks, and the moral pressure of radical politics. Such a constellation of causes is more apt to affect the writer who is a woman than the writer who is a man.

Nearly forty years later, her reputation as a writer finally established through a collection of stories, *Tell Me a Riddle*, Olsen was going through some old papers. Among them she found the chaotic, disheveled, unfinished manuscript that she had thought she had lost and that she has now reconstructed.

Ostensibly, the action of *Yonnondio* occurs in the early 1920s. It concerns the Holbrook family: Jim, the physically powerful father; Anna, the once energetic and idealistic mother; the five children they have, within eight years, conceived in genuine passion and she has borne in some pain. The Holbrooks represent the people from whose toil a Tom Buchanan profits sufficiently to buy a Daisy a string of pearls and himself a string of polo ponies. Jim works in a mine, on a tenant farm, on a sewer construction crew, in a hellish meat-packing plant. Anna struggles with the children in the houses in which Jim settles them. When she can, she takes in laundry.

The Holbrooks are vital and decent. Their children, for whom they are ambitious, justify their struggle to realize the American dream. Capable of love in the present, they wish to exercise that love for the sake of the future. Like Whitman at his most cheerful, Olsen believes that human nature, if permitted to express itself freely and spontaneously, will be good. (She takes her novel's title from a Whitman poem.) Physical nature is the most fertile setting for such expression, although moments of human community, a family singing or a picnic, can suggest a harmonious balance among people, animals, plants, earth, water, fire, air. The Holbrooks are happiest on the farm, which they lose. The industries Olsen despises most—mining, early agri-business, slaughterhouses—spoil both human and physical nature for financial gain.

The "overwhelming, hostile forces" of modern capitalism bar the Holbrooks from their Eden. The modesty, the simplicity of their hopes help to make their failure poignantly grievous. Anna wants nothing more than:

> School for the kids, Jim working near her, on the earth, lovely things to keep, brass lamps, bright tablecloths, vines over the doors, and roses twining.

Eventually, an angry, frustrated Jim will brutalize his wife and children; an exhausted Anna will also turn on the children, will lapse into a psychic coma; a sensitive little girl will escape from an urban slum into a memory of the farm so enveloping that she veers toward schizophrenia. Anna, who has nearly died during a pregnancy terminated by a miscarriage, weeps on the back porch of a rickety house, which the stink of garbage and packing plants commands:

> The children. What's going to happen with them? How we going to look out for them in this damn world? Oh Jim, the children. Seems like we cant [*sic*] do nothing for them.

As Jim comforts her, he silently makes "old vows again, vows that life will never let him keep."

Olsen's compelling gift is her ability to render lyrically the rhythms of consciousness of victims. Imaginative, affectionate, they are also alert to the sensual promise of their surroundings. Harsh familial, social, political and economic conditions first cramp, then maim, and then seek to destroy them. The fevers of poverty, dread and futility inflame their sensibilities. They risk reduction to defensive fantasy, pain, madness or cruelty. They remain, if in shadow, heroes and heroic.

Olsen assumes that such victims cannot often speak for themselves. Their dumbness is no fault of their own. Her self-imposed task is to become their voice as well as their witness, their text as well as their mourner. She signifies her respect for their dignity in the exactitude and scrupulous effort of her work. She sardonically tells her reader that the received categories of culture, such as classicism and romanticism, also fit the citizens of a Wyoming town as they wait to hear how many men have died in a mine explosion that official cowardice, incompetence and corruption have caused. If she were to take part in that theological quarrel over whether an artist's primary commitment is to craft or to social change, she might say that an artist can work for change through writing about the oppressed with all the craft and tools at hand. She also comments on the economic basis of high culture. She writes of an adolescent boy forced into the mines:

> Earth take your dreams that a few may languidly lie on couches and trill "How exquisite" to paid dreamers.

Olsen's politics and anger are a part of a particular decade: her subtitle, "From the Thirties," is seriously meant. She notes that *Yonnondio* "bespeaks the consciousness and roots of that decade, if not its events." An anachronism or two betrays the gap between narrative setting and actual reference. Despite her nostalgia for rural ritual, she refuses to offer an exclusive vision of bucolic joy. She wants unions and solidarity among all workers, no matter what their race or ethnic heritage. In an apostrophe to a rebellious young worker which approaches polemic, she writes:

> I'm sorry . . . as hell we weren't stronger and could get to you in time and show you that kind of individual revolt was no good, kid, no good at all, you had to bide your time and take it till there were enough of you to fight it all together on the job . . . till the day millions of fists clamped in yours, and you could wipe out the whole thing, the whole goddam thing, and a human could be a human for the first time on earth.

—CATHERINE STIMPSON, "Three Women Work
It Out," *Nation*, Nov. 30, 1974, pp. 565–66

SILENCES

Tillie Olsen's is a unique voice. Few writers have gained such wide respect based on such a small body of published work: one book of short stories, *Tell Me a Riddle*, and the unfinished novel, *Yonnondio: From the Thirties*. Among women writers in the United States, "respect" is too pale a word: "reverence" is more like it. This is presumably because women writers, even more than their male counterparts, recognize what a heroic feat it is to have held down a job, raised four children and still somehow managed to become and to remain a writer. The exactions of this multiple identity cost Tillie Olsen 20 years of her writing life. The applause that greets her is not only for the quality of her artistic performance but, as at a grueling obstacle race, for the near miracle of her survival.

Tillie Olsen's third book, *Silences*, is about this obstacle course, this ordeal, not only as she herself experienced it but as many writers have experienced it, in many forms. It begins with an account, first drafted in 1962, of her own long, circumstantially enforced silence. She did not write for a very simple reason: A day has 24 hours. For 20 years she had no time, no energy and none of the money that would have bought both. It may be comforting to believe that garrets are good for geniuses, that artists are made in Heaven and God will take care of them; but if you believe, as Tillie Olsen does, that writers are nurtured on Earth and nobody necessarily takes care of them, society cannot be absolved from the responsibility for what it produces or fails to produce in the way of literature.

Though Tillie Olsen begins with her own experience, she rapidly proceeds to that of others. The second part of the book is a grab bag of excerpts from the diaries, journals, letters and concealed autobiographical work of a wide range of writers, past and present, male and female. They are used to demonstrate, first, the ideal conditions for creation as perceived by the writers themselves, and second, almost every imaginable impediment to that creation. The financial and cultural pressures that gagged Melville, the religious agonies of Hopkins, the bitterness of Thomas Hardy after the vicious reception of "Jude the Obscure," Willa Cather's feeling of nullity in the face of the suave Eastern establishment; political, cultural, sexist and sexual censorship; the denial of a voice to a race, a class, a sex, by the denial of its access to literature; breakdowns, abdications, addictions; all are cited. Reading this section may be hazardous if you are actually writing a book. It's like walking along a sidewalk only to be shown suddenly that your sidewalk isn't a sidewalk but a tightrope over Niagara Falls. How have you managed to do it at all? "Chancy luck," Tillie Olsen replies, and in view of the evidence she musters, she's probably—for all writers not white, male, rich and from a dominant culture—quite right.

Tillie Olsen's special concern is with how her general observations on silencings apply, more heavily and with additions, to women. Here, the obstacles may seem to be internal: the crippling effects of upbringing, the burdens of motherhood, the lack of confidence that may prevent women from writing at all; and, if they do write, their own male-determined view of women, the fear of competing, the fear of success. We've heard a lot of this before, but it's invigorating to see its first expressions by women coming new to the problems: Virginia Woolf worrying about her childlessness, Katherine Mansfield having to cope with all the domestic arrangements while John Middleton Murry nagged her about tea. And, in contrast, quotations from men whose wives dedicated their lives to sharpening pencils and filling the inkwell for them. As Tillie Olsen points out, almost all of the women in the 19th century who wrote were childless or had servants. Her study of Rebecca Harding Davis, author of the remarkable *Life in the Iron Mills*, is a telling example of what happened to one writer who made the switch from solitude to child-rearing.

In construction, *Silences* is a scrapbook, a patchwork quilt: bits and pieces joined to form a powerful whole. And, despite the condensed and fragmentary quality of this book, the whole is powerful. Even the stylistic breathlessness—the elliptical prose, the footnotes blooming on every page as if the author, reading her own manuscript, belatedly thought of a dozen other things too important to leave out—is reminiscent of a biblical messenger, sole survivor of a relentless and obliterating catastrophe, a witness: "I only am escaped alone to tell thee."

The tone is right: The catastrophes do occur, daily, though they may not be seen as such. What Tillie Olsen has to say about them is of primary importance to those who want to understand how art is generated or subverted and to those trying to create it themselves.

The true measure of a book's success, for the reader, is the number of people she wants to give it to. My own list is already long.—MARGARET ATWOOD, "Obstacle Course," *NYTBR*, July 30, 1979, pp. 1, 27

JOANNE S. FRYE
" 'I Stand Here Ironing':
Motherhood as Experience and Metaphor"

Studies in Short Fiction, Summer 1971, pp. 287–92

Motherhood as literary metaphor has long been a cliché for the creative process: the artist gives birth to a work of art which takes on a life of its own. Motherhood as literary experience has only rarely existed at all, except as perceived by a resentful or adoring son who is working through his own identity in separation from the power of a nurturant and/or threatening past. The uniqueness of Tillie Olsen's "I Stand Here Ironing" lies in its fusion of motherhood as both metaphor and experience: it shows us motherhood bared, stripped of romantic distortion, and reinfused with the power of genuine metaphorical insight into the problems of selfhood in the modern world.

The story seems at first to be a simple meditation of a mother reconstructing her daughter's past in an attempt to explain present behavior. In its pretense of silent dialogue with the school's guidance counselor—a mental occupation to accompany the physical occupation of ironing—it creates the impression of literal transcription of a mother's thought processes in the isolation of performing household tasks: "I stand here ironing, and what you asked me moves tormented back and forth with the iron."[1] Indeed, this surface level provides the narrative thread for our insights into both Emily and her mother. The mother's first person narrative moves chronologically through a personal past which is gauged and anchored by occasional intrusions of the present: "I put the iron down" (p. 12); "Ronnie is calling. He is wet and I change him" (p. 17); "She is coming. She runs up the stairs two at a time with her light graceful step, and I know she is happy tonight. Whatever it was that occasioned your call did not happen today" (p. 19).

As we read the story, then, we are drawn through a knowledge of the present reality and into participation in the narrative process of reconstructing and visualizing the past. With the narrator, we construct an image of the mother's own development: her difficulties as a young mother alone with her daughter and barely surviving during the early years of the depression; her painful months of enforced separation from her daughter; her gradual and partial relaxation in response to a new husband and a new family as more children follow; her increasingly complex anxieties about her first child; and finally her sense of family equilibrium which surrounds but does not quite encompass the early memories of herself and Emily in the grips of survival needs. We construct, too, an image of the stressful growth of the daughter from infancy through a troubled, lonely childhood, an alienating relationship to schools and friends, and an unsettled adolescence—and finally into the present nineteen-year-old, who "needs help," as the counselor insists, but who has also found a strong inner resource in her talent for mime and in her own sense of self.

The story is very fundamentally structured through the mother's present selfhood. It is her reality with which we are centrally concerned, her perception of the process of individuation to which the story gives us access. Her concerns with sorting through Emily's past are her concerns with defining the patterns of motherhood and of the limitations on her capacity to care for and support the growth of another human being. As she rethinks the past, she frames her perceptions through such interjections as "I did not know then what I know now" (p. 11) and "What in me demanded that goodness in her?" (p. 12)—gauges taken from the present self to try to assess her own past behavior. But throughout, she is assessing the larger pattern of interaction between her own needs and constraints and her daughter's needs and constraints. When she defines the hostilities between Emily and her sister Susan—"that terrible balancing of hurts and needs" (p. 16)—she asserts her own recognition not only of an extreme sibling rivalry but also of the inevitable conflict in the separate self-definitions of parent and child. Gauging the hurts and needs of one human being against the hurts and needs of another: this is the pattern of parenthood. But more, it is the pattern of a responsible self living in relationship.

The story's immediate reality continually opens onto such larger patterns of human awareness. Ostensibly an answer to the school counselor, the mother's interior monologue becomes a meditation on human existence, on the interplay among external contingencies, individual needs, and individual responsibilities. The narrative structure creates a powerful sense of immediacy and an unfamiliar literary experience. But it also generates a unique capacity for metaphorical insight into the knowledge that each individual—like both the mother and the daughter—can act only from the context of immediate personal limitations but must nonetheless act through a sense of individual responsibility.

The narrator sets the context for this general concern by first defining the separateness of mother and daughter: "You think because I am her mother I have a key, or that in some way you could use me as a key? She has lived for nineteen years. There is all that life that has happened outside of me, beyond me" (p. 9). Almost defensively, she cites too the difficulties of finding time and being always—as mothers are—susceptible to interruption. But in identifying an even greater difficulty in the focus of her parental responsibility, she highlights the thematic concern with guilt and responsibility: "Or I will become engulfed with all I did or did not do, with what should have been and what cannot be helped" (p. 9). She is, in other words, setting out to assess her own responsibility, her own failure, and finally her need to reaffirm her own autonomy as a separate human being who cannot be defined solely through her parental role.

When she identifies the patterns of isolation and alienation between herself and her daughter, she is further probing the awareness of her own separateness and the implicit separation between any two selfhoods. The convalescent home to which she sent Emily as a child is premised on establishing an "invisible wall" between visiting parents and their children on the balconies above (p. 14). But, in fact, that wall is only an extreme instance of an inevitable separateness, of all the life that is lived "outside of me, beyond me" (p. 9). Even in her memory of deeply caring conversations with her daughter, the mother can only claim to provide an occasional external eye, a person who can begin to narrate for the daughter the continuity of the daughter's own past and emergent selfhood but who must stand outside that selfhood separated by her own experiences and her own needs.

In Emily's concern with her physical appearance we can see, distilled, the limitations of a parent's capacity to foster a child's growth in selfhood and finally of the possibilities of any full bridging of human separateness. Emily insists on being told "over and over how beautiful she had been—and would be, I would tell her—and was now, to the seeing eye. But the seeing eyes were few or non-existent. Including mine" (p. 10). The particular poignancy in Emily's own circumstances and needs does not lessen the power of the general insight: a human being cannot rely on the perpetual presence of external seeing eyes to validate her own authenticity as a separate self. Emily, feeling her isolation, and Emily's mother, feeling helpless to overcome her daughter's painful alienation, together give us a powerful lens on the vulnerability to external perceptions of selfhood: "the unsureness, the having to be conscious of words before you speak, the constant caring—what are they thinking of me? . . ." (p. 17) Consequently, Emily's achievement of external validation as a gifted performer of pantomime cannot be expected to overcome her isolation: "Now suddenly she was Somebody, and as imprisoned in her difference as she had been in anonymity" (p. 19). And in watching her daughter's moving performance, the mother herself had confronted a new consciousness of separateness as she lost her sense of recognition for her own daughter: "Was this Emily?" (p. 19).

One of the central defining premises for the working out of separate personal identity for both mother and daughter is the power of cultural circumstances. The narrative is laced with references to the depression, the war, the survival needs which dictate unsatisfactory child care arrangements and equally unsatisfactory work circumstances. Even the dictates of pediatric treatises on breast-feeding by the decree of the clock (p. 10) become a part of the general cultural pressure which operates to define and limit the power of individual choice. Over and over, we are told of the limitations on choice—"it was the only way" (p. 11); "They persuaded me" (p. 13)—and verbs of necessity recur for descriptions of both the mother's and Emily's behavior. In the attempt at summing up, the mother concludes: "She kept too much in herself, her life was such she had to keep too much in herself. My wisdom came too late. She has much to her and probably little will come of it. She is a child of her age, of depression, of war, of fear" (p. 20).

In such statements as "my wisdom came too late," the story verges on becoming an analysis of parental guilt. But though the mother expresses frequent regret for her own past limitations and failings, she is not at all insisting on guilty self-laceration. Rather she is searching for an honest assessment of past behavior and its consequences and for an accurate understanding of the role of cultural necessity which nonetheless allows for individual responsibility. She recognizes that there are some questions "for which there is no answer" (p. 16) and some causal relationships which cannot be deciphered: "Why do I put that first? I do not even know if it matters, or if it explains anything" (p. 10). At the same time, she insists upon the power and significance of her own actions within those limiting circumstances: that, of course, is the premise for the whole narrative reconstruction of the past through the self-awareness founded in present knowledge.

This claim to her own self-validation remains primarily a general premise of the story rather than a specific claim at points within the narrative. Her actual absolution—to the extent that she is seeking absolution from parental guilt—does not come in the particular recognition of past success or failure. Rather it comes in the growing emphasis upon Emily's separateness and Emily's right to make her own imprint upon the world in which she lives. The narrative's first interruption by immediate maternal necessity—the crying of the younger brother with wet diapers—marks the beginning of a clearer resistance to the forces of external necessities through this acceptance of Emily's separate selfhood. As Ronnie says "Shoogily," the family word for comfort which originated with Emily, the mother recognizes the impact of Emily's presence and personhood: "In this and other ways she leaves her seal" (p. 18). The narrative then moves quickly into the identification of Emily's own special talent in pantomime and the balancing of external necessity, parental responsibility, and the assumption of Emily's own ultimate self-responsibility: "You ought to do something about her with a gift like that—but without money or knowing how, what does one do? We have left it all to her, and the gift has as often eddied inside, clogged and clotted, as been used and growing" (p. 19). Consequently, the second interruption—in Emily's own return from school—reaches toward the story's tenuous resolution in relinquishing the claim to controlling her daughter's destiny; the mother returns to her private monologue/dialogue, thinking: "She is so lovely. Why did you want me to come in at all? Why were you so concerned? She will find her way" (p. 20).

The tension in Emily's personality—which has continually been defined as light and glimmering yet rigid and withheld—comes to a final focus in the self-mocking humor of her allusion to the most powerful cultural constraint on human behavior: nothing individual matters because "in a couple years we'll all be atom-dead" (p. 20). But Emily does not, in fact, succumb to that despairing view; rather she is asserting her own right to choice as she lightly claims her wish to sleep late in the morning. Though the mother feels more heavily the horror of this judgment, she feels its weight most clearly in relation to the complexity of individual personhood and responsibility: "because I have been dredging the past, and all that compounds a human being is so heavy and meaningful in me, I cannot endure it tonight" (p. 20). And when she goes on from her despairing inability to "total it all" to the story's conclusion, she recenters her thoughts on the tenuous balance between the powerful cultural constraints and the need to affirm the autonomy of the self in the face of those constraints: "Let her be. So all that is in her will not bloom—but in how many does it? There is still enough left to live by. Only help her to know—help make it so there is cause for her to know—that she is more than this dress on the ironing board, helpless before the iron" (p. 21).

Her efforts, then, "to gather together, to try and make coherent" (p. 18) are both inevitably doomed to failure and finally successful. There cannot be—either for parent or for story-teller—a final coherence, a final access to defined personality, or a full sense of individual control. There is only the enriched understanding of the separateness of all people—even parents from children—and the necessity to perceive and foster the value of each person's autonomous selfhood. Though that selfhood is always limited by the forces of external constraints, it is nonetheless defined and activated by the recognition of the "seal" each person sets on surrounding people and the acceptance of responsibility for one's own actions and capacities. At best, we can share in the efforts to resist the fatalism of life lived helplessly "before the iron"—never denying the power of the iron but never yielding to the iron in final helplessness either. We must trust the power of each to "find her way" even in the face of powerful external constraints on individual control.

The metaphor of the iron and the rhythm of the ironing establish a tightly coherent framework for the narrative probing of a mother-daughter relationship. But the fuller metaphorical structure of the story lies in the expansion of the metaphorical power of that relationship itself. Without ever relinquishing the immediate reality of motherhood and the probing of parental responsibility, Tillie Olsen has taken that reality and developed its peculiar complexity into a powerful and complex statement on the experience of responsible selfhood in the modern world. In doing so she has neither trivialized nor romanticized the experience of motherhood; she has indicated the wealth of experience yet to be explored in the narrative possibilities of experiences, like motherhood, which have rarely been granted serious literary consideration.

Notes

1. Tillie Olsen, "I Stand Here Ironing," in *Tell Me a Riddle* (New York: Dell, 1976), p. 9. Subsequent references will be indicated within the text.

ROBERT COLES
"Tell Me a Riddle by Tillie Olsen"
New Republic, December 6, 1975, pp. 29–30

In the prelude to *Middlemarch* (only three paragraphs long, but in them one of the most powerful and satisfactory statements about the predicament of women in our society) George Eliot refers to "blundering lives," to "a life of mistakes," to "a tragic failure which found no sacred poet and sank unwept into oblivion." She had in mind both masses of women and particular women, all of whom have suffered by virtue of what she describes as "meanness of opportunity," the general kind so many men and women alike faced in the 19th century, and the special kind women had to endure then, and still now. The novel is a masterful psychological presentation and analysis of rural, middle-class, early 19th-century England, but also, for the most part, a chronicle of loss, sadness, disappointment and failure. Characters endowed with intelligence and ambition, one after the other, fall upon bad times—not poverty, but the consequences of fate, that is, the world's accidents, incidents and circumstances which, in sum, exert their enormous, tellingly destructive influence. The novel falls just short of tragedy: a village, a county, all of England's rising bourgeoisie had at least another half century or so to go. Yet, the story is littered with unfulfilled dreams.

So with Tillie Olsen's *Tell Me a Riddle*—four short stories which lack Eliot's extended, intricate dedication to character portrayal of the workings of historical change, but in which sensibility, point of view, and mood are spiritual kin of *Middlemarch*. The first, and briefest, "I Stand Here Ironing," introduces the reader to a woman who has known and suffered from the "meanness of opportunity" George Eliot mentions, a 20th-century American version of it. The title reveals the scene, tells of all the action to come—a mother reflecting upon the hard, curbed, sad life of her 19-year-old daughter, born in the Great Depression of the early 1930s. A social worker or guidance counselor or psychologist or psychiatrist (who knows which, and who cares—a substantial number of them all sound drearily alike) has told the mother that the young woman, her oldest child, "needs help." The mother is skeptical, and quietly, thoughtfully scornful. Not "defensive" or "guilty," not lacking in a capacity for psychological introspection, either—as might be said of her by the person who wants her to come in for one of those self-conscious "talks" that have become so much a part of so many lives in recent years—but determined to hold on to her dignity, to her right as an intelligent woman, however hard-pressed by life, to comprehend what it is that has happened to herself and her children, and just as important, to resist the interfering, gratuitous, self-serving or wrong-headed interpretations of others. "Let her be," the mother says to herself—a remark meant, also, for the one who, with the barely concealed arrogance and condescension of the clinic, had called and said, "I wish you would manage the time to come in and talk with me about your daughter." The story is a mother's effort to understand for herself how her daughter came to be the person she is, and to do so by taking account of the overwhelming (social, economic, cultural) reality of a certain kind of life—a reality which generates, rather than merely influences, currents in the mind's life. Put differently, the story is an interior monologue devoted to the exterior—the insistent, enduring, molding press of the things of this world upon our dreams, nightmares, hesitations and aspirations.

"She was a miracle to me," the mother remembers. When the baby was eight months old there was a sudden change: "I had to leave her daytimes with the woman downstairs for whom she was no miracle at all, for I worked or looked for work." The father, desperate for lack of a job, humiliated and beaten, said good-bye. The mother was only 19, as old as the daughter she is now thinking about as she does her ironing. The story moves on from there—a chronicle, related in one heartbreaking incident after another, of a girl's growing up under the adversity of the depression years. A chronicle, too, of a mother's attempt to keep her own head above water (she remarried, had more children, pursued work to the best of her ability, tried to do right by her children and new husband). And a chronicle of a particular child's suffering: nurseries where she was ignored at best; schools where the teachers were callous or mean; clinics where arbitrariness and bureaucratic self-importance determined the way she was treated, the recommendations made to her mother; a convalescent home whose horrors, covered by a veneer of sugary sentiment Charles Dickens would have known how to document. And in the family: a fight for herself, her rights and her terrain, in the face of the children born later to her mother—an especially hard and bitter fight because there were so few victories possible in a family so impoverished and vulnerable.

But the child did not grow to be a mere victim of the kind so many of us these days are rather eager to recognize—a hopeless tangle of psychopathology. The growing child, even in her troubled moments, revealed herself to be persistent, demanding, observant. In the complaints we make, in the "symptoms" we develop, we reveal our strengths as well as our weaknesses. The hurt child could summon her intelligence, exercise her will, smile and make others smile: "The control, the command, the convulsing and deadly clowning, the spell, then the roaring, stamping audience, unwilling to let this rare and precious laughter out of their lives." And at times her mother could observe, "She is so lovely"; and immediately wonder why they in the clinic were so anxious to talk about the daughter's "problems."

"Let her be," the mother says, not defiantly and not out of escapist ignorance. "So all that is in her will not bloom," she continues, "but in how many does it? There is still enough left to live by." And in case the people at the unnamed clinic already have in response their various "interpretations," their "insight," the mother has a quiet request to make—that the young lady be accorded respect, be allowed her dignity, be regarded as and told she is "more than this dress on the ironing board, helpless before the iron."

That is all; the last words of the story bring the reader back to the first words, but not in a forced or contrived way—the all too clever and tidy work of a "literary" writer of short stories who has learned in school about rising action and falling action, and "structure," and the need for "impact" or "coherence." A working woman is making the best of *her* situation, even as she expects her daughter to do so. A mother shakes her fist at the universe, not excitedly, and with no great expectation of triumph, but out of a determination to assert her worth, her capabilities, however injured or curbed, her ability to see, to comprehend, to imagine; and too, her daughter's—everyone's.

The other stories reveal the same struggle for personal dignity, against the same high, almost impossible odds. They are each sad stories, yet leavened with humor, and made compelling, even entertaining (despite the subject matter) by the writer's wonderful, eye-opening ability to make her fine social awareness, her strongly-felt political passions, her abiding interest in, and her fighter's anger at the condition of her sex here and in other countries, mere instruments in a commitment to the integrity of the private psychological reverie, really—the idiosyncratic as well as representative ideas and emotions of the men, women and children she chooses to portray, and wants desperately (the heart of her effort, the basis perhaps of her special appeal) to uphold and make the rest of us (companions of hers, thereby) also uphold.

The last story, whose title the author has given to the collection as a whole, is the longest and is, again, all too easily given a summary—the way an aging couple, once poor and active in radical politics, now reasonably well-off, come to terms with death. The author allows herself a bit more leeway than she has before; the story has sustained, compelling dialogue, a more relaxed pace of development, a thread of humor and sarcasm that offset the grief and heartache. The husband and wife, 47 years married, have developed their own ways with each other. He is alternately teasing and encouraging. Most of all he wants to forget the past and make the best of everything. She is suspicious, silent, quite unwilling to gloss over a lifetime's trials and sorrows. There are marvelous exchanges, as he coaxes her, and in the course of the story, calls her a succession of bitter-sweet names that provide the story continuity: Mrs. Word-Miser, Mrs. Take It Easy, Mrs. Telepathy, Mrs. In a Hurry, Mrs. Excited Over Nothing. She parries his thrusts, lets him plan, and involve her in his hopes for a new life. They will move to one of those "havens" for the elderly. But in the clutch she says no; she is tired, she will not go along with him. She seems to know that she is sick, will soon die. She has a critical detachment about her (with respect to him, their children and grandchildren, never mind the world at large) that contrasts with the immediacy and warmth of his response to people, places, things. A husband and wife in America—old, full of memories, scarred by a life that was not easy, either materially or psychologically, and now compelled to face their last challenge together. Tell me a riddle, the grandchildren ask; the grandmother cannot, will not. How can she when she has learned, decade after decade, that life itself, hers and maybe everyone's, is a bundle of riddles? The grandmother can only have silent reveries, occasions for the author to turn into a haunting, brooding poet. And the grandfather's bravado soon enough gives way, as he struggles to face death, his wife's and his own—that final riddle which no one, of whatever disposition or station in life, manages to avoid or figure out.

Since the collection *Tell Me a Riddle* was published, 15 years ago, Tillie Olsen has not come out with more short stories. She was 47 when *Tell Me a Riddle* was published, is now in her 60s. Her own life is well worth knowing; she worked for years in factories, was the Nebraska-born daughter of a Socialist organizer, married a union man, a printer, and fought alongside him in a long series of working-class struggles during the 1930s and 1940s. She also brought up four children, and being poor and a conscientious political activist, had little or no spare time for the writing which she yet craved to do. She has written about herself, and much more, in two essays, "Silences: When Writers Don't Write," and "Women Who Are Writers in Our Century: One Out of Twelve." She is, has been for decades, a feminist—unyielding and strong-minded, but never hysterical or shrill. Her essays reveal her to be brilliant, forceful and broadly educated, if without degrees to wave around. She has also published (1974) the novel *Yonnondio*, about working-class life in the 1930s—its terrible, lacerating reality. And she has written a long biographical interpretation to accompany a reissue by the Feminist Press of Rebecca Harding Davis' *Life in the Iron Mills*, originally issued in 1861.

At times she has allowed herself, in a confessional vein not unlike that of "I Stand Here Ironing," a moment of regret, if not self-pity: if only there had been more time, an easier life—hence more stories, novels, essays written. Proud and stoic, though, she pulls back immediately; that is how it goes— and besides, for others, for the overwhelming majority of the world's people, in the past and now, too, there has been *no* spare time, no chance for anything like writing, like constructing stories and in them giving expression to ideas and ideals. She need not, however, have one moment of regret. Others have produced more, but she has never once faltered. It is as if she had no time for failure, either. Everything she has written has become almost immediately a classic—the short stories especially, but also her two essays, her comment on the life and writing of Rebecca Harding Davis, her recent novel. She has been spared celebrity, but hers is a singular talent that will not let go of one; a talent that prompts tears, offers the artist's compassion and forgiveness, but makes plain how fierce the various struggles must continue to be.

CHARLES OLSON

1910–1970

Charles Olson, poet and literary theorist, was born on December 27, 1910, in Worcester, Massachusetts, but while still quite young he moved to Gloucester, on the Massachusetts coast. After high school he studied at Wesleyan and Yale, and then went on to Harvard, from which he received a Ph.D. in American Studies. He held various jobs at different times, sailing on a fishing boat, serving as a mailman, and teaching briefly at Clark University and at Harvard. He also worked for the Office of War Information and, during Roosevelt's campaign for a fourth term, for the Democratic National Committee.

The first work of Olson's to be published was an essay entitled "Lear and Moby Dick" (1938), but the book which established his reputation was *Call Me Ishmael*, a study of Melville which appeared in 1947. From 1948 until its collapse in 1956, Olson taught at Black Mountain College in North Carolina, and between 1951 and 1956 he also served as rector of the College. At Black Mountain, in addition to writing poetry and theoretical works, Olson collaborated with Merce Cunningham on a number of dance dramas, and also participated in early "happenings" with Cage, Rauschenberg, Cunningham and others. His principal students and followers were Robert Creeley, Robert Duncan, and Denise Levertov, and with them he worked on publishing the *Black Mountain Review*, which has been credited with creating a new poetic style. After the demise of Black Mountain College Olson was long associated with the Department of Further Studies at New York State University in Buffalo. He died on January 10, 1970.

Olson's shorter poems printed in *In Cold Hell, in Thicket* (1953) and *The Distances* (1960) are collected in *Archeologist of Morning* (1970). *The Maximus Poems* (1–10, 1953; 11–22, 1956; combined, 1960), *Maximus IV, V, VI* (1968), and *The Maximus Poems, Volume Three* (1975) form one long organic work. Other non-poetic works include *Projective Verse* (1959), an influential theory of poetics; *Mayan Letters* (1953) written to Creeley from Mexico; *A Bibliography on America for Ed Dorn* (1964); *Human Universe* (1965), essays; *Letters for "Origin"* (1969), written to Cid Corman; *Causal Mythology* (1969); *Poetry and Truth* (1971); and a collection of verse plays entitled *The Fiery Hunt* (1978). *Selected Writings*, edited by Creeley, appeared in 1966.

Personal

I want to tell you about Mr. Olson. He is . . . gosh, words fail me . . . about ten steps higher than stupendous. He is about six feet eight or nine and has shoulders like an ox. He must weigh about two hundred and sixty or seventy. He eats, well, let me tell you about last night's meal when I went in and sat by him after everybody else was through and he was talking to one of the students.

On the table was a plate that had about five hot dogs on it.

Another plate had about ten buns, another had heaping piles of tomatoes and lettuce, and then there was another that was stacked high with potatoe chips and oh so many more food.

When I left, everything was gone except a few pieces of casual leftover lettuce bits. He thrust his face within about six inches of the girl who he was talking to (hey, I'm fifteen minutes overdue for lunch, I gotta scram, finish later . . .) (Sorry kiddo, I have nearly a half hour more to write, I thought lunch was at 12:15, it ain't, it's at 12:45)

Anyhow, Olso picks up a hot dog, breaks it in half, smears one end in a mess of mustard on his plate, takes a bun rips it in two and then into quarters and then into very small bits. He takes a gargantuan bite of the hot dog, crams a bit of bun in, reaches across the table, grabs a slice of nice red tomatoe, pushes this in his mouth, still clutching the outer edge of the tomatoe, bites down on it and his paw returns with a little pale red dripping of what was once a tomatoe. Then he scrapes up a few fingers full of potatoe chips and he squeezes these in his mouth. Then another bite of the hot dog, etc . . . All this time telling about Howard Fast, Saroyon, Ezra Pound, T.S. Eliot, Thomas Wolfe . . . etc . . . and smoking a cigarette and drinking a glass of milk!

Well, that's Olson. He doesn't like Thomas Wolfe, Saroyon, Scholem Asch, Irving Stone, and I am very disappointed for I thought sure, just one would suit his taste. I asked him the other night,

"Mr. Olson, how do you like Wolfe."

"No good, bad on public morals."

"Saroyan?"

"No good."

"Scholem Asch?"

"No good."

"Why?" He saw the questioned and puzzled look on my face and he said, "Every dog has his own fleas."

Then he turned and walked away laughing very loud.

He read us something of Carlos Williams who was writing about Ezra Pound, and when he hit something funny, he (Olson) would begin to wheeze, and then out he would come with this great torrent of laughter, mounting higher and higher and louder and louder till crescendo. A roar like a lion. Believe me Ca and Bill, that man is huge, like a giant, and he is as wonderful as he is big.

When he said to me about every dog having it's own fleas he bent over and rested his elbow on my shoulder, inhaled a tremendous drag on his cigarette, winked at me and said, "Every dog has his own fleas."—FIELDING DAWSON, "A Letter from Black Mountain (July 12, 1949)," *Olson*, Fall 1974, pp. 5–6

Perhaps it should be *scholar*, Olson the Scholar, but I share Auden's preference for Chaucer's word. A clerk, glad learner and teacher, loving guardian of the language, defender of words and of all good things made of words; Olson was such a clerk.

I guess I was the first recipient of his teaching. The subject, Melville. Always Melville. Clerk Charlie at midnight, in Paul Bunyan's bathrobe, his great eyes gleaming, his hair crazy like a fright wig, pacing the room in a rapt adagio, Melville in his hand, Melville on his lips. The Melville in his hand was his first and favorite *Moby-Dick*, the little, green, back-broken, dog-eared, all-underlined Modern Library edition, the pigmy not the giant, unillustrated by Rockwell Kent, annotated only with Charlie's scrawled marginalia. (What became of it? There would be a treasure!) The room? Well, it might be here at college, or his room in Gloucester, or my room in Mountainville, or, later, his or my room at Harvard. And the words? Almost any words out of the Pequod's long voyage. But the ones I remember best, in his voice, his ringing voice, are the ones that begin,

> Winding down from within the very heart of this
> spiked Hotel de Cluny where we here stand,

and end,

> Question that proud, sad king! A family likeness! aye,
> he did beget ye, ye young exiled royalties; and from
> your grim sire only will the old State-secret come.

Then hand and book and eyes and hair would soar and wave, the blue bathrobe would cut a caper, and Charlie would holler, "That's prose, Finch! Prose is the stuff! Match that in poetry. See, you can't do it! Yah, yah, you can't do it!"

Out of such glad fury came Charlie's clerkship on Melville's *Moby-Dick*. And now, out of his clerkship comes a dream of another kind of Academia from the kind we know.

Imagine it with me. A place where the writing of learned articles and scholarly books is, if not forbidden, deeply, darkly frowned upon. Unbecoming conduct for a teacher. Publication gone underground. Quarterlies run off in boarded basements on hand presses, circulated furtively in satchels. A place where the mere rumor of a monograph would be enough to block promotion. "Poor Tweedledum, four of his things in *PMLA*, they say. He'll never make Associate. Better try coaching." Or—"Poor Tweedledee, he committed a bibliography! Wait till the deans get wind of that! Hell to pay."

A nightmare? Maybe, but a nightmare with fringe benefits, for in such a place no one would mine his dissertation for those two dreary articles that may spell a raise. No one would haunt the stacks padding out his one tiny perception about—say—"Leda and the Swan" with feathery footnotes. No one would feel obliged to publish, laboriously, lovelessly, just not to die. So in such a place only the irresistible articles would get themselves written, only the irrepressible books.

The point of my dream is simply this. In such an Academia, *Call Me Ishmael* would still have been written. Charlie would still have brooded on the *Essex* disaster, and sought out Melville's Shakespeare set, and deciphered the hand-written riddle on the last flyleaf of the last volume, and shown us *Moby-Dick* reilluminated in the light of *Lear* and *Hamlet*.

Call Me Ishmael was not written for a promotion, or a raise, or a job, or not to die. It was written on demand, its own demand. Charlie's love of Melville had to find expression in such a book. His joy in *Moby-Dick* would stay bottled up no longer. It dictated the wild rhetoric, animated the ballet-like form. The book happened like a sneeze. The book came prancing.

Once Charlie took me to see Melville's eyes. We went together to the gracious Cambridge home of Eleanor Metcalf, Melville's granddaughter, where graciously she showed us the Eaton portrait, hanging in her front parlor. Charlie had warned me about the eyes, lidded, gentle, mysterious, and steely with "the fine, hammered steel of woe." "You can't escape them, Finch, so don't try. Wherever you go, they'll follow you." He was right.

And now there is another pair of eyes, clerk's eyes, dancer's eyes, looking this way.—JOHN FINCH, "Dancer and Clerk," *MR*, Winter 1971, pp. 38–40

Friendships came easy for you. Rapport was instantaneous, whether because of your size, which never failed to impress a newcomer, or the sheer charm and blarney of your speech. You had a way of convincing people immediately that you were interested in them.

To young poets, who felt they belonged to an "underground" that opposed a literary "establishment," you appealed inevitably as a great guru of myth and mysticism and as the leading "underground" poet. It mattered little that you claimed to detest mysticism and guru gimmickry. Or that you saw yourself as the main line of American poetry after Pound and Williams. You *were* the establishment.

To graduate students, numbed by years of professional pedantry and aching with the academic blues, you were the paragon of the antiacademic. A common Olson complaint, on the other hand, as you would pore over your dozens of Cambridge Ancient History pamphlets, was that academics and graduate students today weren't academic enough. They didn't know enough. They didn't read enough.

To housewives, faculty wives, student wives, lady poets, and lonely hearts everywhere, you presented yourself as a teddy bear with a heart of gold, to be hugged and nurtured, loved and fed.

To truck drivers and fishermen, waitresses and cleaning women, you were unfailingly an equal, a *compadre*, a man who would listen patiently to their own hard stories and who had a few of your own, who knew hard work and poverty firsthand and didn't have to patronize grief when he saw it. You valued their ability to get something done with their hands, though your own world—poetry!—was as far removed from theirs as the imagination could reach.

But you talked. And how you talked! You knew the words that everyone wanted to hear and had to hear. Who can say what you really were: a father in heaven? an honest-to-god prehistoric poet in the flesh in plastic fantastic America? a man who had all the answers? or should have? Whatever it was, you cherished the role. In fact, you insisted on it.

Once you told us how a former student of yours had come to Gloucester to see you, bringing his wife along, and how he started arguing with you about some point or other in one of your books.

"I had to put him down," you said, "and I hated to do it in front of his wife, but what does he expect when he comes down to lock horns with the big bull?"—CHARLES BOER, *Charles Olson in Connecticut*, 1975, pp. 69–70

General

Charles Olson ⟨. . .⟩ exists in the world of factions—of manifestoes and extravagant gestures. He appears to be influenced by such rebels against orthodoxy as Pound and the Rimbaud of *Les Illuminations*. So far so good, I suppose: Pound and Rimbaud were geniuses who succeeded, against all probability, in expanding the boundaries of poetry. In Olson, however, the habit of scholarly detail inherited from Pound clutters the imagination, and the habit of recklessness in the imagination (inherited maybe from Rimbaud) cancels out any possible consistency or relevance in the scholarly details. These twin disasters come about, I suspect, because he has little interest in the sensible world except as a handle on which to hang bits of poetry. The result is to be seen in the description of some motorcyclists on a beach in the poem with the attractive title "The Lordly and Isolate Satyrs."

> Wow, did you ever see even in a museum
> such a collection of boddisatvahs, the way
> they came to their stop, each of them
> as though it was a rudder
> the way they have to sit above it
> and come to a stop on it, the monumental solidity
> of themselves, the Easter Island
> they make of the beach, the Red-headed Men
> These are the Androgynes,
> the Fathers behind the father, the Great Halves

And in the whole poem there is little description of them, evocation of them, as they are: they continually are described in terms of what they are not. The things they are not (Androgynes, etc.) are evoked, it seems, purely at random: the poem consists merely of a gigantic list of associations accumulated at whim. If we want the explanation of his technique, we may find it in his essay on "Projective Verse," printed in *The New American Poetry 1945–1960* (Grove Press),

which though it has been very influential, it would not be unfair to describe as the worst prose published since *Democratic Vistas*. This passage opens with the statement of a rule:

ONE PERCEPTION MUST IMMEDIATELY AND DIRECTLY LEAD TO A FURTHER PERCEPTION. It means exactly what it says, is a matter of, at *all* points (even, I should say, of our management of daily reality as of the daily work) get on with it, keep moving, keep in, speed, the nerves, their speed, the perceptions, theirs, the acts, the split second acts, the whole business, keep it moving as fast as you can, citizen. And if you also set up as a poet, USE USE USE the process at all points, in any given poem always, always one perception must must must MOVE, INSTANTER, ON ANOTHER.

The description of this psychological process was first made several hundreds of years ago, and the recommendation of it as a specifically poetic process was made at least as early as the start of the nineteenth century, but it is the complete lack of qualification, the absolutism of his demand, that distinguishes Olson's enunciation of it as a rule for writing poetry. And there is a clear connection between what he is saying with this shrill jargon and what he is doing in the passage about the motorcyclists. "Put down anything so long as you keep writing" would be a fair enough paraphrase. The result is *The Distances*, which consists of performances as flat and inept as the feeble rhymes that are printed daily in the New York *Herald Tribune*.—THOM GUNN, "Outside Faction," YR, Summer 1961, pp. 595–96

Ann Charters's book ⟨*Olson/Melville: A Study in Affinity*⟩ is valuable to those readers who have but a slight acquaintance with Olson's work, and none at all with the commentary on it by such men as Edward Dorn, Robert Duncan, and Robert Creeley. But it is one of those books that rise and fall in interest, the heights being excerpts from the work of the subject himself, and the depths, sadly, being the critic's own commentary. But I see Mrs. Charters struggling with this complicated man, and deciding to make one facet of his work crystalline; it is a primer, really, but it should get the reader away from it as fast as possible to the work itself. I don't want to draw up a catalogue of things that Mrs. Charters presents, but it is worth noting that certain of Olson's conceptions are traceable to the scholastic philosophers' conception of *quidditas*, the "whatness" of things. Mrs. Charters is wide-eyed about this, as if it is a strange idea. She says that Olson's "concerns are those of a philosopher", which is not true. She speaks of Olson's methodology as one that juxtaposes facts and parts to "create a multi-layered texture as complex in its intuited interactions as the experience of life itself", which, while so, is a structural device employed by much classical modern literature. She will say: "Olson's similes, like Melville's, are Homeric—hyperbole, larger than life." There is nothing larger than life for Olson, nor Melville, nor Homer. And, "Olson is a visionary, and the characteristic of a visionary is that he sharply limits what he sees. In the last two sections of *Call Me Ishmael*, Olson focuses only on the tragic aspects of Melville's life." Melville *had* a tragic life. And there is more. But, as I said, Mrs. Charters points out those works of Olson's that are important not only to an understanding of his view of Melville, they are important to an understanding of Olson. The most valuable part of the book is the postscript, which is a lecture given by Olson at Black Mountain in 1956. From that lecture, let me take a rubric, if you will, for a few notes on *Maximus IV, V, VI*.

"One can define an act of art as a vector which, having become private and thus acquired vision, ploughs the vision back by way of primordial things. Only thus can it have consequence." And, later, he says, "the objective immortality of actual occasions requires the primordial permanence of form, whereby the creative advance ever re-establishes itself endowed with initial creation of the history of one's self." Now let me jump over to "Causal Mythology," a lecture given at Berkeley in 1965. "The Earth, then, is conceivably a knowable, a seizable, a single, and *your* thing." And, "As I said, I have arrived at a point where I really have no more than to feed on myself." And in "Billy the Kid," an essay which appears in *Human Universe*, this: "What strikes one about the history of sd States both as it has been converted into story and as there are those who are always looking for it to reappear as art—what has hit me is, that it does stay, unrelieved. And thus loses what it was before it damn well was history, what urgency or laziness or misery it was to those who said and did what they did. Any transposition which doesn't have in it an expenditure at least the equal of what was spent, diminishes what was spent. And this is loss, loss in the present, which is the only place where history has context." So, presented with these brief quotes, we get a sense of the plan of Olson's *Maximus*. A remedy whereby the past may be "relieved"; the poet must push and tear, thus, at Gloucester, as *polis*, so that it give up to him its unrelieved past. (1) Gloucester is not in Europe, it is not of that historical past, and the poet is in Gloucester—it is his city. (2) Its shaping force and reason for being is ocean (*Okeanos*) and the fruits thereof. And the dangers. The sense of the sea: people who are born and raised on the coast have a totally different sense of the world than those who are born inland—believe it. See, throughout *Maximus*, Olson's clear writing on storms through which men sail. Here, read *3rd letter on Georges, unwritten*. (3) The materials of Gloucester's history are freed by the intercession of the poet, who orders, *not* by his ego, but by the sense of himself in this city, part of its continuing process, history here, not as a sense of time past, but as present to us as time in space: "the objective immortality of actual occasions", that is, the past is *here*, "in the present, the only place where history has context".

Thus, Olson, telling you for himself, in "Letter 27":

> An American
> is a complex of occasions,
> themselves a geometry
> of spatial nature.
>
>   I have this sense,
> that I am one
> with my skin
>
>   Plus this—plus this:
> that forever in the geography
> which leans in
> on me I compell
> backwards I compell Gloucester
> to yield, to
> change
>   Polis
> is this

—stating the three concerns of this major undertaking.

So we see that the simple allusions to *The Cantos* and *Paterson* are not precise, are, in fact, incorrect. Pound insists on time to yield to him, he walks through time, he goes back into it; Williams takes Paterson as a repository of American corruption, the breaking down of the sweet gifts of nature by the Puritan ethic, linked with the commercial, but finds his hope in art. (But in *Paterson 5*, however, goes out of Paterson to find it.) While Olson has attempted in this poem to replace the ego as the force which drives into history with the poetic

intelligence as receptacle, into which history flows and is carried by the vector of art, into the present. So Olson's care for Herodotus as against Thucydides. The former acting on history, finding out, his self *in* it; and the latter, the camera or tape recorder, "just the facts, ma'am", which are *just* the facts, that is, what is *not* recorded also *happened*. And stays unrelieved. Which the poet relieves by the word, an entity, the absolute key, that is, if it cannot be said, it is not. Olson writes, "one can't do anything right without the right words to go with it."

Now let me end this by, perhaps, getting myself in trouble. Olson holds the most delicate balance, the poem teeters, always, that is: I see Olson as a lyric poet, in both senses of that term. But a lyric poet who selected the long poem in which to make his most important statement. But on the one hand, his "lyrics", his songs, are a falling backward, as another poet once termed it; and in those pieces of *Maximus* I see Olson's ego come clear, wrench itself loose from that denial of ego so otherwise apparent here. On the other hand, we see the lyrical voice, the man himself speaking, not *into* history, but as a part of historical incident, reacting to the incidents also around him. What I am trying to get at here is that Olson, along with the other achievements of his career, has given us a new sense of the lyric, that is, that it is possible for a man to say "I" in his poem and have that "I" considered as part of the space and time of history: the "I" carries the event into the present and is a strangely natural "I": it is a rock, or it can range about freely as the seas. But I also love the contradictory—if it be so—song we are given as gift. We are dealing here with a very remarkable artist, and with a sensibility that makes the process of the poem inestimably richer.—GILBERT SORRENTINO, "Black Mountaineering," *Poetry*, May 1970, pp. 117–20

In the tradition of western culture it is assumed that one speaks of knowledge or, in art, radiance when one is satisfied that the multiplicity of the thing is understood in terms of a single principle, a logos or theme. Otherwise, one is "incoherent." The same term is used for intellectual and artistic failure as for madness. Consequently, it is necessary to limit the perspective or, as Olson would have said early in his career, close the field. Information, bound by unifying disciplines, and works of art, themselves seamless self-enclosing forms, become inert, unless reference is made to totalizing chains of larger abstract unities which reach finally to some absolute, the Beautiful and the Good, the unmoved mover, God, or some surrogate absolute, the state or culture itself.

During the nineteenth century the development of technology allowed an opportunity finally to put theory into practice. The industrial revolution was a test not only of the scientific information which had accrued but also habits of mind which organized knowledge in a hierarchy of increasingly inclusive timeless forms. In practice, these beautifully coherent theoretical precepts resulted in cruel, destructive chaos. The eternal verities—necessarily true in logical space—served to make life in time even more treacherous than before, and, as they worked out so badly applied to practical life, people began with good reason to doubt their value, if not their absolute truth.

Olson's perception of this problem was not unique. He was anticipated by Melville, Nietzsche, Charles Sanders Peirce, Rimbaud, Oswald Spengler, Whitehead, Jung, and others. His work is addressed to the central cultural and intellectual problem of the past century. What does one *do* with the massive accumulation of information when the structure which seemed the source of its ultimate meaning and use suddenly collapses? Piecemeal repair of the structure is impossible. It is an all or nothing situation: the structure depends upon its absolute coherence. The liberal response, therefore, is disallowed on logical grounds. At best, it results in drift, in vagueness of thought and indecisiveness in action. When Olson was beginning his career the options were clearly determined: there was a choice between totalitarianism (in thought, in the broadest cultural sense) or radical reform of the institutions of artistic and intellectual production. These were the terms in which the *political* situation presented itself to Olson. The lack of political vitality was only a symptom.

In his radical vision Olson undertakes to demonstrate how fact relates immediately to fact and how factual complexes relate immediately to life, without resort to abstract forms. He takes unity to be the final, achieved condition, when everything is counted, not something which is assumed at the outset.

The process of the *Maximus* is the enumeration of emergent forms. In "I, Maximus of Gloucester, to You" he disallows allegiance to any absolute but the immediate present. With that entry into time, the logical unity produces a duality, and the duality produces a trinity. These three—space, fact, and stance, as Olson initially calls them—discover an identity with the mother, the father, and the son, the figures of the family drama. Olson's account of the family, however, though it derives from Freud, is not Freudian. Three is no more final than two. Freud's narrative of repressive fathers, fickle mothers, and murderous sons allows for individual adjustment to the chaos of the family and to the chaos of a social, temporal order which cannot reconcile itself with the timeless structure of the knowledge which it uses. In *Maximus* the son does not *replace* the father, he becomes a citizen. In the poem in which the circle—father to father—begins to close, Maximus literally, typographically, breaks out, and he prays, "rest Beloved Father as Your Son/goes forth to create Paradise/Upon this earth" (*Maximus* III, 121; see text for typography). The three generates a four, a political reality.

At this point the *Maximus*, which is a creation from an almost endless array of voices, can no longer contain the process in a single voice. The relevant information no longer bears on a single person. The world of the poem is no longer specific to the poem. It becomes the task of others. In "Letter 6" Maximus says,

> so few
> have the polis
> in their eye
>   . . .
> so few need to
> to make the many
> share (to have it,
> too)

The few who make the city do not share a program or a belief, only a sharpness of eye which keeps them so close to the physical demands of their lives and jobs that a shared place appears, so

> that one suddenly is walking
> in Tartarian-Erojan, Geaan-Ouranian
> time and life love space
>   time & exact
> analogy time & intellect   time & mind   time &
>   time
> spirit
>   the initiation
> of another kind of nation.
>   (*Maximus* III, 228)

—Don Byrd, "The New Democracy," *Charles Olson's* Maximus, 1980, pp. 196–98

ROBERT DUNCAN
"Notes on Poetics
Regarding Olson's *Maximus*"
Black Mountain Review, Spring 1956, pp. 201–11

I

> The mind, Ferrini,
> is as much of a labor
> as to lift an arm
> flawlessly
>   (*Letter 5*, p. 22)

No more difficult than walking, this leisurely and exact talking; if "leisure" be seen as an "increment of association" (which term I get out of Pound): no effort as great as the million-year gain incorporated by the child in his upright simple complexity (control and coordination) of walking.

In American poetry the striding syllables show an aesthetic based on energies

> Bulkeley, Hunt, Willard, Hosmer, Meriam, Flint,
> possessd the land which renderd to their toil
> hay, corn, roots, hemp, flax, apples, wool and wood.
>   (Emerson, *Hamatraya*)

John Dewey in *Art as Experience* points to the difference "between the art product (statue, painting or whatever), and the *work* of art." Again, he writes: "Order, rhythm and balance simply means that energies significant for experience are acting at their best." I point to Emerson or to Dewey to show that in American philosophy there are foreshadowings or forelightings of *Maximus*. In this aesthetic, conception cannot be abstracted from doing; beauty is related to the beauty of an archer hitting the mark. Referrd to its source in the act, the intellect actually manifest as energy, as presence in doing, is the measure of our arêté (as vision, claritas, light, illumination, was the measure of Medieval arêté).

Pose the visual spirit of Italian 14th century painting. And then the muscular spirit of American 20th century painting. In *Maximus*, Olson points to Marsden Hartley: "to get that rock in paint"—a getting, a taking grasp, a hand that is the eye. "But what he did with that bald jaw of stone." "Did with" not "saw in." And here Olson comes to the hand—Hartley's hand, Jake's hand: "a man's hands, / as his eyes."

American 20th century painting: the difference between energy referrd to (seen) as in the Vorticist and Futurist work—particularly Wyndham Lewis and Boccioni—and

                energy

embodied in the painting (felt), which is now muscular as well as visual, containd as well as apparent: the work of Hofmann, Pollock, Kline—and most importantly (for this is the work that has given me my clues) in San Francisco of Still, Corbett, Bischoff (in his nonobjective period), Hassel Smith, Diebenkorn, Abend, Roeber, Lili Fenichel, Jacobs, Collins, Brockway, Sonia Getchtoff . . .

II

Starting with the image, and so with Ezra Pound (but I mean this as beyond imagism—the vision he makes clear in the Cavalcanti piece) embodied in the language, a speech in which the eye works, and moving by means of the embodying in the language of the "act" toward the act—in taking hold. "I grasp what you mean." Hence, the *Cantos* are central, as active; and the *Waste Land* or *Four Quartets*, beside the point, as dramatic.

Pound circa 1928 in *How to Read* lists three "kinds of poetry." It is in the description of the third mode, *logopoeia,* that I find suggestions of what I am talking about. Indicating the first two for the purposes of my task here: *melopoeia* (summd up by Dante in *De Vulgari Eloquentia*) represents the gain of hearing, the physiological mastery ear-wise in the poem. By Dante's time a comprehensive explication could be made—the chips were down. (Edith Sitwell's notes on tone bear the relation to Dante's that the delights of antiquarian lore bear to the original necessity.) The sound now coheres (and so, sound is "sound"; the quality of a thing earliest is told by its "ringing true".).

phanopoeia ("a casting of images upon the visual imagination"—why does Pound make it remote this way, almost passive, ¿a wraith of Plato in his neo-Platonic sourcer?) was initiated in Dante's gaining sight of the "psychological" universe and moves toward some point of summing up beyond the *Imagist Manifesto*. The chips are not down; but we have the responsibility of seeing. The discipline of the eye, clarity, is acknowledged measure. A poet who cant hear and who cant in addition see is now obviously deficient (tho they exist & thrive all about us, and greatest poets, like Milton and Joyce, have "lost sight" of the target.) It is in point here to remind any reader who may be partisan to my argument that I am sketching out "a" way of poetry, not "the" way of poetry; and that terms—"responsibility", "gain", "deficiency"—are all terms along the way.

The hand is intimate to the measurings of the eye. Michael McClure in an early poem refers to the hand: "Opposable, . . . in the way, . . . dumb" and again, "this eye my thumb." A rule of thumb. McClure refers to the role of the hand in perception; the hand & eye estimate, and we feel what we see.

Metrics as it is still incoherent depends on accent. The consciousness, not yet having the "feel" of it, must have the boldest tum-te-tum to proceed by. For the inexpert there must be reference to a "ruler" in time. Hence the convention. Metrics, as it coheres, is actual—the sense of language in terms of weights and durations (by which we cohere in moving). This is a dance in whose measured steps time emerges, as space emerges from the dance of the dody. The ear is intimate to muscular equilibrium. The line endures. It "feels right".

logopoeia—"the dance of the intellect among words", Pound writes. He describes this new mode (outside of this reference to the "dance") in terms of *placement and displacement*; as if he were attempting to convey or define the dance *as it is seen* (a series of photographd positions of the body playing upon one's visual expectations). "It is the latest come, and perhaps most tricky and undependable mode." Of course, tricky and undependable to the eye (seen as an aesthetics of arrangements); as we find it difficult to translate our image in the mirror (the body seen) into the language of movement. It may now be suggested that one may lose sight of the target in order to gain insight of the target. ¿The eye retraind in the dark?

The significance of the mode lies for Pound in the meaning level. "It employs words not only for their direct meaning, but it takes count in a special way of habits of usage, of the context we *expect* to find with the word, its usual concomitants, of its known acceptances, and of ironical play." Its manifestation is verbal.

THE RISK: to suggest that the conquest of babble by the ear—to distinguish and organize, to make significant, to relate as experience, to name—is the origin of speech and emotion. Speech at this level articulates internal sensations. "The inner voice." The recurrence of vowels and consonants, the tonal

structure, is related to heart and alimentary tract in its rhythmic organization; it is expressive. It is "moving"—melopoeia is the passionate system of the poem. The conquest of passion by the eye, *phanopoeia* is at once and in the same a physiological gain, a focussing, and a gain in meanings. To "see" is to reform all speech. Significances are shiftings and transformings possible in the relationship of eye and brain. The reality of what is witnessd disciplines the speech, and it is only by poetry, by the making-up of the real through language (I mean by poetry here all made-up things—language thus is as a man makes his way as well as as a man makes his speech, drawings, objects, governments, story) that one can witness. Meanings and functions are intimately related, if not merely different aspects of the same event. Now: Mr. Pound's *logopoeia* seems to be not only a verbal manifestation by a physiological manifestation. Ambiguities, word-play, ironies, disassocations appear as we watch the meanings; but it is the action of the language, the muscular correlation of the now differentiated parts of the poem, that so expresses itself. The point: just as the ear and eye have been incorporated in the act of making in language, the locomotor muscular-nervous system is being calld into the adventure. The disciplines of the ear and the eye are primary—soundings and focussings—in order to be prepared in this work. The disciplines of movement, of those potentialities of the language analogous to the acts of "muscle control and use" are the task at hand.

/ I owe as much to Louis Zukofsky's work on Shakespeare as I owe to *Maximus*. Many of my ideas here spring from "Bottom's Dream" which appeard in *New Directions 14*, from subsequent talks with Zukofsky and from his manuscripts as yet unpublishd from which for an all too brief session he read to me. If the reader would understand what might be implied in "To see is to re-form all speech", he would do well to read "Bottom's Dream", and to follow Zukofsky's work as it may at last find the light of day.

RECAPITULATION. The coming into life of the child: first, that the breath-blood circulation be gaind, an interjection! the levels of the passions and inspiration in phrases; second, that focus be gaind, a substantive, the level of vision; and third, the complex of muscular gains that are included in taking hold and balancing, verbs, but more, the movement of the language, the level of the ear, the hand, and the foot. All these incorporated in measure.

III

how to dance
sitting down
(*Tyrian Businesses*, p. 34)

There is reference everywhere in *Maximus* to the exercise of poetry. "By ear, he sd." This is the beginning point (as the discrimination of speech). But, if the muscular realization of language is the latest mode of poetry, the beginning point was muscular too, localized in the discharge of energy expressd in the gaining, first, breath, and then, tongue. The gift of spirit and of tongues.

Joyce after addressing his energies to clarity (*Portrait of the Artist*), goes on to the conquest of locomotor writing (*Ulysses*) which remains, like the *Cantos*, Marianne Moore's or William Carlos William's opera, a masterpiece of this mode. If we are seriously involved, we must go to school to these.

Finnegans Wake returns (turns back) to the beginnings, not only in reference (intestinal alimentary mythic meaning levels) but in mimesis, as a thing done (the alimentary babbling speech; the gobbling, the breaking down into). Here meanings are being churnd up, digested back into the original chaos of noises, decomposed. Certainly the masterpiece of a psychoanalytical period. In *logopoeia* meanings then may be puddled as is Joyce, or they can be playd as in H.D.'s war trilogy by a sleight-of-mind. The one poses uniquely the proposition of letting go, back to the visceral process.

Olson insists upon the active. Homo maximus wrests his life from the underworld as the Gloucester fisherman wrests his from the sea.

> the underpart is, though stemmed, uncertain
> is, as sex is, as moneys are, facts
> to be dealt with as the sea is . . .
> be played by, said he coldly,
> the ear.

We are perhaps as deraild by the excitements of Freudian psychology as the Middle Ages were by the excitements of Aristotelian logic—with psychoanalysts as counterparts of scholastics, with infantology replacing angelology, and the phantasmogoria of metapsychology in place of the phantasmogoria of metaphysics.

> There are so many, children
> who want to go back, who want to lie down
> in Tiamat.
> You can tell them this: the land-spout's
> put all the dispers
> up in trees.

Not a digression: but to indicate that the "taking hold" of the *Maximus* poems is pitted against "letting go", is a conquest of Tiamat. The emergence from vitality of faculties. Joyce retreats from his faculties to his mere vitalities.

/ But the conversion of passions, the "use" of internal organs is not simply a turning back; it is parallel here again to the development of the individual. He discovers his "self"; that is, he achieves tone or arêté—on the most common level, he is toilet traind, he governs his emotions, he withholds or releases tears at will, etc. Seen in this light, *Finnegan* represents not a "letting go" as I first saw it, but an integrating process: the will to let go or to use or to retain is achieved. Joyce is no longer prey of his emotions but preys upon his emotions. Seen thus, graspd thus, felt thus, Joyce sets his faculties at work upon his vitalities. What is in point is that he "lives off nature" and thus provides a contrary that might make clear the moral structure of *Maximus*. "ya, selva oscura". Joyce plays with his self. Olson, addressing himself to *homo maximus*, outraged by "those who use words cheap, who use us cheap", cries "that you should not be played with."

Against Tiamat:

> The carpenter is much on my mind:
> I think he was the first Maximus.
>
> Anyway, he was the first to make things,
> not just live off nature . . .
>
> for example, necessities the practice of the self,
> that matter, that wood.

————: Maximus is a *makaris*; is then Olson, or his measure. Now I may be understood perhaps in saying that "The Songs of Maximus" (Letter 4) ring true, are clearly seen, take hold, measure up.

> No eyes or ears left
> to do their own doings

is a protest that rises from the, is rooted in, keen sense of what eye and ear need be. Sights and soundings, "the attention, and / the care".

It is enough. Enough surely. The reader can put it all together: the "by ear", "be played by . . . / the ear", "she looks / as the best of my people look / in one direction", "the

hands he'd purposely allowed to freeze to the oars", "eyed (with a like eye)", "look right straight down into yr pages", "polis is / eyes", "that those who are sharp haven't got that way / by pushing their limits", "his eyes / as a gull's are", "by gift? bah by love of self? try it by god? ask / the bean sandwich", "As hands are put to the eyes' commands", "a man's hands, / as his eyes, / can get sores)", "(each finger) their own lives' acts", "to have a heart",

> And I feel that way,
> that the likeness is to nature's
> not to these tempestuous
> events.

The major address of the poem is to what the act need be—to
> falicity
> resulting from life of activity in accordance with

On the level of reference, the gain from Whitman's address to his cosmic body to Olson's address to "The waist of a lion / for a man to move properly" is immense.

M. L. ROSENTHAL
"Olson/His Poetry"

Massachusetts Review, Winter 1971, pp. 45–57

How shall we think of Charles Olson's poetry? He made a very brave run, and did some brilliant things, and pushed into some difficult problems. *Was* he a "lance," a "metal hot from boiling water," compounded of "jewels and miracles," as he calls himself in the first of *The Maximus Poems*? For that matter, *was* Walt Whitman a "kosmos"? Yes, if you allow them their magic, let them earn it by listening to what their poems tell you. I should like to suggest some of the issues that Olson gets us into, for the whole question of his success has to do with the way they are built into the poems, the way the poems find a language and a system for them.

The leading issue—but it is involved with a complex of others—is that of the identity created in the speaking voice of the poems. Any poem, necessarily, has its voice, its guiding sensibility. But Olson makes this identity a major theme and a center of poetic method. In "Maximus to Gloucester: Letter 27" (published in the 1968 volume *Maximus Poems* IV, v VI), he tries to locate the time-context and cultural context of the identity being developed, starting with his own childhood memories that include a grotesque incident in the life of his parents. The process, he says, is

> the generation of those facts
> which are my words, it is coming
> from all that I no longer am, yet am,
> the slow westward motion of
> more than I am. . . .

And:

> An American
>
> is a complex of occasions
>
> themselves a geometry
>
> of spatial nature.
>
> I have this sense,
>
> that I am one
>
> with my skin

Plus this—plus this:

that forever the geography

which leans in

on me I compell

backwards I compell Gloucester

to yield, to

change

      Polis

is this

We can see the connection between Olson's sense here of the speaking self as embodied history and culture and something very similar in works as disparate otherwise as *Song of Myself*, the *Cantos*, *The Bridge*, *Four Quartets*, and *Paterson*. Olson comes closest to the last of these in the way he converts an affirmation into its personal idiom. His syntactic compression projects a resistance and a reciprocal outward pressure of the private self, which is also being molded by "the slow westward motion" of a more inclusive identity. The slightly involved elliptical thought-movement becomes his fingerprint.

Now this is all a rather difficult tack to sustain. Olson was using the still unclarified form of the poetic sequence, for which he was heavily dependent on the models I have named. These sequences combine narrative, lyric, and expository elements in possibly overloaded structures, and most of them use a good many documentary passages as well. Again, they all develop principles of overall movement and patterning, if not of dynamic progression, with various hesitations, interferences, or repetitions. But Olson wants more than the others to get the whole range of tones, intensities, and materials back into his own skin, as he suggests in the passage just quoted. American meanings, and the local data of Gloucester, Massachusetts, are going to be *compelled*, made to yield, to this purpose.[1] It is a confusing task for a poet to keep this sort of intention clear over the long haul, and impossible to make one's own idiom stand entirely clear of one's models. Olson, however, with his rugged and sophisticated intelligence, his humor, his curmudgeonly independence, and his language of inwardness and modesty, helped us all to see what was at stake poetically.

In a curious way, Laura Riding's experience illuminates his problem. Despite obvious differences, her aim was critically comparable to Olson's. She viewed her poems, she said, as "a long exploration of the possibility of using words in poetry with the true voice and the true mind of oneself." After 1938, she changed her view, not of poetry's aims but of its capacities. "I began to see poetry differently, even to see it as a harmful ingredient of our linguistic life. . . . As I reflected on my past poetic activity, I perceived that, in casting my voice and my mind in the poetic mold of speech, I had shut out the realization of the very thing I sought. The equivalence between poetry and truth that I had tried to establish was inconsistent with the relation they have to each other as—the one—*art* and—the other—*the reality*. I came close to achieving, in my poems, trueness of intonation and direct presence of mind in word. But what I achieved in this direction was ever sucked into the whorl of poetic artifice, with its overpowering necessities of patterned rhythm and harmonic sound-play, which work distortions upon the natural proprieties of tone and word."

Miss Riding characterized her own work—all this in a special statement for the BBC some years ago—as "poetry *in extremis*, poetry caught in and confronted with its factitious

nature as a mode of linguistic expression." She had learned, she said, "that poets, to be poets, must function as if they were people . . . on the inside track of linguistic expression, people endowed with the highest language-powers." This assumption she found erroneous, for it "blocks the discovery that everyone is on this inside track" and the poet's very successes "leave ordinary speech, and its literary counterpart, prose, sunk in their essential monotony and uninspiringness." She concluded that "the only style that can yield a natural and happy use of words is the style of truth, a rule of trueness of voice and mind sustained in every morsel of one's speech," and that "for the practice of the style of truth to become a thing of the present, poetry must become a thing of the past."

The history of modern poetry, beginning at least as far back as Blake and the *Lyrical Ballads*, is the history of this struggle, or attempted mutual assimilation, or overlapping, of modes. American poetry has added to it the straining for a language at once indigenous and not provincial—dominating motifs of *Paterson* and of *In the American Grain*, to cite the most obvious instance, that of Williams. The American as what Olson calls "a complex of occasions," his private self "the slow westward motion of/more than I am," comes up against the "despair" of which Williams spoke, the sense of making "poetry *in extremis*" that Laura Riding felt, the "barbaric glass" of impersonal reality that Stevens nevertheless looked through (though this last example may be changing the subject slightly). Of course, Laura Riding was wrong in thinking that she had come to a dead end in her own efforts. As Spender says, her poems show "intense personal seriousness, an anguish of being," and embody "the pain of being a woman of genius." I would add that the anguish and pain could not be resolved through poetry, but only realized; and that even if this one poet felt she had reached her limits, this was clearly no proof for others. Olson seems to have felt the issue less as a personal crisis than as a challenge to reorientation organically related to nineteenth-century findings in science and to the character of American local and national experience. There are certainly moments of anguish and pain in his poetry, but they do not involve despair for the art, unless the call for reorientation of method be thought the positive side of despair. The program, however, is no more despairing than Mallarmé's comment on what happened to French poetry after Hugo. "Poetry," he wrote, had "waited patiently and respectfully until this giant (whose ever more grasping, ever firmer blacksmith's hand was coming to be the definition of verse) had disappeared; then it broke up. The entire language was fitted out for prosody, and therein it rediscovered its vital sense of pause. Now it could fly off, freely scattering its numberless and irreducible elements. Or we might well compare it to the multiple sounds issuing from a purely verbal orchestration."[2]

The great issue of form with which Olson contends is implicit in that conception of an "entire language fitted out for prosody" and then suddenly broken up into "numberless and irreducible elements." His greatest immediate predecessors had been forced to let their sense of form make way for another sense—that of the process creating an *illusion* of form. Their insistence was nevertheless on the ultimate, if possibly desolate, expectation of humanized form that would dominate mere process. They felt, and both resisted and yielded to, the great, new pull toward the void: reality abandoned by the human imagination. And yet we always have an instinctive confidence in the congruence, or at least reciprocity, of the objective and subjective, external reality and our inner selves. It is what makes the recordings of whale-songs that I heard recently so absorbing. Not only do whales sing, but each has his own characteristic song, which can be heard for hundreds of miles at sufficient depth. The songs are strange, something like electronic music. We recognize that strange musicality, for the referent, present in the very sound, is a living being whose every note is counterpointed by the wash and roar of the sea: a perfect reciprocity by the very nature of things. The strangeness, the idiosyncratic curve of sound expressing the whole of a vibrant, massive being in its own—but still destructive—element, is its idiom. Old wooden sailing ships used to transmit the sound, and the sailors thought they heard sirens or mermaids. "I await a thing unknown," says the heroine in Mallarmé's *Hérodiade*. Process and expectation do not require the actual realization of humanized form to suggest its presence; their reciprocity suggests it. This is what is really meant by open form. It is the reason that all form in poetry, poetry that *counts*, is ultimately open, dependent on arbitrary juxtapositions that create a tentative balance only.

Once we accept—and, more important, *absorb*—this principle, it is possible to move with greater ease within a centrifugal structure like *The Maximus Poems* and to take it on its own terms. I have had occasion elsewhere to argue that the basic method of these poems is not really new, that there is virtually nothing in it for which we cannot find certain predecessors. "The real change," I have suggested, "lies in their focusing on the inwardness of the caught moment of consciousness as it flickers across the surface of deep awareness. This focusing, however, is crucial to the new thinking about form." It is not that the struggle for form has been abandoned, but that the greater emphasis on process—as opposed to older efforts at integration in terms of revised definitions of the possibilities of traditional form—"has altered the conception of form itself."[3]

An anonymous recent reviewer of *The Maximus Poems* in the *Times Literary Supplement* (13 November 1970) thinks to denigrate the poems by saying that they are derivatively modeled on the great earlier sequences of the century, that their syntax is awkwardly idiosyncratic, and that they allude to obscure colonial American history and contain obscure documentary snatches. Furthermore, the reviewer charges that "in accordance with his literary programme, Olson leaps in mid-line from the poet's surroundings while writing to the memories his impressions provoke, or from minute autobiography to extracts from historical documents, or from economic theory to invective against America." Again, Olson's "language is deliberately flat, slangy, anti-poetic. But the surface of toughness dissolves in the few lyric passages, which could not be softer or more conventional." I quote from this review simply to show how little many people have learned after a half-century or more of the modern sequence. Only the comment on the "few" lyric passages (there are in fact many lyric passages) calls for anything like refutation. The rest of the critique explodes the same kind of little paper percussion-caps that have been used against most of the great earlier American poets of the Pound-generation. The only difference is that the names of those poets, once the intended victims of the same toy pistols, are now being used as caps themselves.

"The unhappy few," says this reviewer, "who listen for lines that engrave themselves on the tablets of memory, for rhythmic subtlety or the undeniably right choice of words, for grace of sound or felicity of perception, for a fresh, true insight into the human condition—in other words, for significant art—will feel generally thwarted." This writer reminds me of those British critics—and a fair number of American ones—who for years never could catch the quick music of Williams because of the way he tasted the beauty of everyday speech and

related it to the more familiar poetic values. I suspect that the unknown reviewer would consider a passage like the following one non-lyrical and infelicitous. It is "Song 3" of "The Songs of Maximus."

This morning of the small snow
I count the blessings, the leak in the faucet
which makes of the sink time, the drop
of the water on water as sweet
as the Seth Thomas
in the old kitchen
my father stood in his drawers to wind (always
he forgot the 30th day, as I don't want to remember
the rent

a house these days
so much somebody else's,
especially,
Congoleum's
      Or the plumbing,
that it doesn't work, this I like, have even used paper
      clips
as well as string to hold the ball up And flush it
with my hand
            But that the car doesn't, that no moving
      thing moves
without that song I'd void my ear of, the
      musickracket
of all ownership . . .
            Holes
in my shoes, that's all right, my fly
gaping, me out
at the elbows, the blessing
                  that difficulties are once more
      "In the midst of plenty, walk
as close to
bare
            In the face of sweetness,
piss
            In the time of goodness,
go side, go
smashing, beat them, go as
(as near as you can
tear
In the land of plenty, have
nothing to do with it
                  take the way of
the lowest,
including
your legs, go
contrary, go
sing

This song is one of many nearly invisible lyric passages in the sequence. There are things in it I would criticize, rhythmic effects I would not care to try for myself. But the conformation of diction, rhythm, sentence-movement—that is, its *music*—is absolutely inseparable from the speaking self of the poem: his tone, his sense of life, his posture that is as natural to him as that of Yeats when he writes: "Others, because you did not keep/That deep-sworn vow, have been friends of mine." Yeats's understatement, his beautifully subdued internal rhyme ("you did not *keep* that *deep*-sworn vow"), his colloquial edge are not actually far removed from the effects of Olson's poem. Here too we have some exquisite echoings of sound, and a powerful emotion at first held in check by a certain minimizing effect—in the word "small," in the attention to minutiae ("the leak in the faucet," the domestic detail, the water-drops):

> This morning of the small snow
> I count the blessings, the leak in the faucet
> which makes of the sink time, the drop
> of water on water. . . .

Both poems, too, move later into violently emotional, even melodramatic statement, though Olson's goes through more phases—from a slightly wry ecstasy to comic play to sheer anger and then song. But to look solely at Olson's poem now: the details of his idyllic dream are of a sufficiently simple, sufficiently physical and laborious existence. He wilfully rejects the pressure of an abstract, organizing force in our economic life that drains men of significant personality, experience, and memory all at once, bribing them with conveniences. Behind the song lies an informed neo-primitivism, unreconciled to modern states and economies. The *argument* may in itself be oversimplified; the speaking personality is nevertheless alive, humorously cross-grained, and deliberately using the vernacular to sustain an image of itself without romantic clichés. Isn't this, in what is after all a minor passage, just such a "fresh, true insight into the human condition" as the *TLS* reviewer requires, with considerable "grace of sound" in its own terms— "Holes / in my shoes, that's all right, my fly / gaping, me out / at the elbows, the blessing / the difficulties are once more." Among other things, this is high-spirited modern pastoral.

One more point concerning this song. Its intimacy, its sheer vulnerability, is the best clue to Olson's talent—partly, no doubt, because when he gives the game away, almost mumbling to himself at times (showing us the view from the peacock's back, as it were), we still receive enough evidence in the long run of artistic and intellectual rigor. Passages like "Song 3," their musicality and formal modulations always playing on the ear, are spotted throughout his work. They provide perfectly clear points of reference to his strong but self-correcting dominating sensibility.

At any rate, within this context of ultimate rigor and highly developed sensibility, Olson's way of letting go, tuning in on himself without inhibition, serves to give a special kind of subjective body to his work. It seems to me that he has influenced some poets to think that this is the whole of the real thing, the only honest, candid, immediate thing in poetry; that the whole process consists in catching some fleeting memory, in mid-sentence, the grammar turned awry perhaps because it is really a note of association caught in midstream:

> after the passage-way of the toilets
> and the whores
>
>   (as that movie-house,
> Boston, you buy your ticket
> but you don't enter, you find yourself
> in an alleyway. . . .

On the other hand, a serious poet like LeRoi Jones has learned to use Olson's sort of inwardness of speech brilliantly:

> I am inside someone
> who hates me. I look
> out from his eyes. Smell
> what fouled tunes come in
> to his breath. Love his
> wretched women.
>   ("An Agony. As Now.")

Jones, like Olson, deploys such effects to feed the language of literal awareness and free association into firmly realized structures. In *The Maximus Poems*, passages like these go side by side with a myriad other kinds. Sometimes they are extremely concentrated and organized lyrical moments, such as that which begins "Tyrian Businesses":

> The waist of a lion,
> for a man to move properly
> And for a woman,
> who should move lazily,
> the weight of breasts
> This is the exercise for the morning

The narrative passages, historical, personal, and fantasied, have a lyrical dimension too. They not only give clarity of reference and description to a good part of the sequence, but often are a kind of primitive story-telling, touched with pure imagination:

> She sat down and sang a song, a great foam
> or froth rose to the surface and in it appeared the back
>   and tail
> of a great serpent, an immense beast. The woman
> who had taken off her clothes, embraced
> the creature, which twined around her, winding
>   inside
> her arms and legs, until her body was one mass
> of his. . . .

But this is not the occasion for an exhaustive account of the various types of poetic effect that Olson balances off against one another, or for extended analysis of even one passage. My aim, rather has been to suggest the character and elements of the process in this loosely articulated structure. The character, the bearing, and the affect of Olson's verse, its human involvement with the issues of poetry *in extremis*, makes it a telling witness to that continuing pressure which has extended the limits of the poetic almost unrecognizably in our century. It is a curious gathering, the congregation of American poets of our moment, trying in their separate yet related ways to see their own inner selves, and the volatile historical situation, and the crisis of art, in the same single organic vision. They must define the very landscape of their lives, the very language they are to use, the very sense of personality. Here is Lowell, whose frenzied sense of his own suffering is meant to be the key to reality for all of us. Not far off is the late Sylvia Plath, who marked out a pure, all but obscene curve of death, naked and beautiful—that was a kind of suicide of poetry. And Jarrell, who kept reaching for a lost individual possibility, buried somewhere perhaps still in the neglected common life. But the list need not be further proliferated here and now. Charles Olson, who snapped his sentences open like twigs as he wrote, and whose mind moved outward in a series of intersecting ripples pushing against his syntax, sought to mobilize all that he could of language and local human reality and the most cherished memories of tradition against the new "pejorocracy." He was conceivably the unacknowledged leader of all these unacknowledged legislators. Poetic leadership, I suppose, consists not in directives and programs but in accurate perceptions—

> It is undone business
> I speak of, this morning,
> with the sea
> stretching out
> from my feet

And, finally:

> I set out now
> in a box upon the sea.

Notes

1. It is to emphasize this intention—to *will* its success, I think—that he doubles the *l* at the end of "compel" in this passage.
2. "Crisis in Poetry," in *Selected Prose Poems, Essays, and Letters,* translated by Bradford Cook (Baltimore: Johns Hopkins Press, 1956), pp. 34ff.

3. "Dynamics of Form and Motive in Some Representative Twentieth-Century Lyric Poems," *ELH*, 37 (March, 1970), pp. 136–151.

J. B. PHILIP
"Charles Olson Reconsidered"

Journal of American Studies, December 1971, pp. 293–305

I

My major concern in this essay is with the poetry and prose of Charles Olson. However, I wish to approach his work by way of comments passed upon it by both Gabriel Pearson and Martin Dodsworth in a recent critical anthology, edited by the latter, and entitled *The Survival of Poetry*.[1] In the course of an essay on Robert Lowell, Mr Pearson mounts an attack on what he takes to be Olson's characteristic position, and many of the points that he makes are echoed by the editor in his introductory remarks. It will be my concern to show that neither of these critics deals justly with the scope of Olson's work, or with the vision of man in America that we find in it. Attention in England had been focused almost exclusively on the manifesto 'Projective Verse'.[2] However, we now have enough texts available to us to be able to set that single work in a wider context, and this is the task that must be achieved if Olson's work is not to suffer the premature dismissal that these critics seem eager to mete out to it. In his essay, 'The Black Mountain Poets', in the same book, Donald Davie begins this work, but there is much more to be done.

At the heart of Gabriel Pearson's attack lies his belief that Olson's work is the expression of a deep-seated evasion of the facts of American history and society. Olson, he suggests, misleads men into a fascination with their own physiology, or with the details of their immediate experience. To do this is already to distract them from those processes of confrontation with the past by which men learn most accurately of their situation. Moreover, the object of Olson's search, an Adamic innocence on which to reground human experience, in itself constitutes a disastrous refusal of the power of history. Pearson sums up what he believes to be Olson's position in the following sentence.

> The past can always be encountered without guilt, since the present determines the past, never issues from it. And the present can be made perpetually anew, in each poem, in each act. Hence the curious innocent cheerfulness, the ontological optimism, the essential refusal of evil that we find in all these poets . . . (p. 78).

The pursuit of such innocence is seen not only as simpleminded, but also as vicious in so far as it constitutes a more or less conscious attempt to disguise the real issues of American history. As such it is seen as co-operating with other and more familiar American myths.

> The dream of innocence permits technological man to unknow, positively to unwill, and so carry on—in deliberate innocence—performing his deed, freed from the traditional sanctities and controls. To return poetry to some base in the physiology of the breath is the equivalent of other forms of sanctioning myth— the myth of the frontier, the myth of economic self-help, the myth of the westward movement of civilization—that underwrote the exploitation and devastation of the continent . . . (p. 77).

For Mr Pearson, then, this habit of evasion is one that has its roots deep in the American character. He suggests, moreover, that it is one to which, more often than it should, American poetry has given a voice. In his essay he is concerned to attack not only Olson's work, but also that tradition out of which he sees it as coming. Thus he speaks of 'the tradition that stems from Whitman', and again of the 'Whitman tradition' that 'eschews history and literature in favour of geography and the specificity of speech' (p. 57). It is Whitman, then, who is primarily accused, but besides Olson, both William Carlos Williams and Ezra Pound are named as twentieth-century inheritors of his spirit. What characterizes them as a group is the fact that they have all used their art to provide 'poetic versions of the propaganda of good news' (p. 78). It is in contrast to these vices that he seeks to suggest the virtues of Robert Lowell. It is Lowell who has resisted and defused the myths, who has faced with greater honesty the facts of American life, and who has used his art to make public the essential processes of historical confrontation.

Mr Pearson's views on Whitman are justifiable, but the same cannot be said for his advancement of such simple lines of inheritance. There is obviously much more to be said about the relationships of Pound and Williams to Whitman, and of these two writers to each other. However, our concern here is with Charles Olson, and it is clear that, in his case also, what Mr Pearson has to say constitutes a simplification of the facts. In defining Olson as the most recent representative of the Whitman tradition, he perhaps overlooked the following passage from *Call Me Ishmael*.

> Whitman we have called our greatest voice because he gave us hope. Melville is the truer man. He lived intensely his people's wrong, their guilt. But he remembered the first dream. The *White Whale* is more accurate than *Leaves of Grass*. Because it is America, all of her space, the malice, the root.[3]

Olson here rejects Whitman, and does so precisely on the basis of his too great optimism, his inability to deliver anything except 'the good news'. Moreover it is clear that Olson is not deluded concerning the forces that have directed the advance of America, nor does he seek to disguise them. Melville is applauded for his recognition of 'the malice, the root', and his attempt, in *Moby-Dick*, to clarify 'his people's wrong, their guilt'.

II

Confrontation with the American past, far from being neglected in Olson's work, in fact constitutes an essential aspect of it. Many of the *Maximus Poems* are devoted to the process of understanding the network of misappropriation and exploitation that surrounds the one place, Gloucester. Olson goes to work on the records and attempts to apportion blame to the particular acts of particular men. Moreover, the constant awareness of the nature of this past affects not only the content but also the characteristic emotional tone of the poems. The following passage from 'Capt. Christopher Levett (of York)' should make this clear:

> About seven years
> and you can carry cinders
> in your hand for what
>
> America was worth. May she be damned
> for what she did so soon
> to what was such a newing
> that we, who out the side
> of her come (have cut ourselves
>
> out of her drugstore flattened—hillside gut
> like Wash-Ching-Geka cut
> the Winnebago nation out
> of elephant—'the fish,
> sd Levett, which we there saw,

> some with wings, others with manes
> ears, heads, who chased
> one another with open mouths
> like stone Horses in a parcke'—
> We gave the gain. We know
> what Levett Smith or Conant
> didn't, that no one
> knew better
> than to cash in on it. Out,
> is the cry of a coat of wonder[4]

We find here a summary of that sense of history of which the details are given in the particular accusations of other poems. The direction of the nation's advance is implicit in the development of even the earliest settlements. Olson outlines the claiming of power over the resources of Gloucester by the Plymouth colony, and describes it as 'nascent capitalism', as 'ownership getting in to, the community'.[5] What characterizes such acts and others like them is a deafness to the 'newing', the refreshment of individual and social values offered by the new environment, to which others, such as the three men mentioned here, are seen as more responsive. What triumphs instead is the determination simply to 'cash in on it'. For Olson, contemporary America is little more than the product of such energies reproduced on a vast scale. In an apt image, the 'drugstore flattened-hillside', he characterizes the landscape of this present; it is for him a panorama of the devastation of natural resources and the enslavement of a people through induced and obsessive consumption. The despair and frustration occasioned by participation in such a world finds its expression in the figure of containment within the elephant. However, if we consider this image, it becomes clear that despair is not the only emotion that it is supposed to convey. For what is envisaged is the possibility of cutting a way out of the elephant, that is to say of letting the light in upon the accretions of guilt and exploitation, of understanding the forces that have shaped American reality. This process, at root a critical one, is obviously seen by Olson as the beginning of other, more positive, ventures. By the use of his image he associates it with the activities of the energetic culture-hero who is the subject of the Winnebago legend. What he looks forward to is the re-ordering of American values. However it is clear that he believes that the human agencies that will be able to achieve this will be those that have been disciplined by their spell inside the elephant, and their struggle to admit light to that darkness. It is there that an essential discrimination is learnt, and essential energies generated. What he sees as emerging from this confrontation with the past is a determination for change, but one that is based upon a wariness concerning human nature and the blindness and excesses of which it is capable:

> We have the gain. We know
> what Levett Smith Conant
> didn't, that no one
> knew better
> than to cash in on it . . .

If that is the stance that he commends to his fellow Americans, it is also the stance out of which he himself most often writes. Here again we must take issue with Mr Pearson. Believing that Olson's major concern is to evade the consequences of history, he suggests that his usual tone is one of 'curious innocent cheerfulness', or 'ontological optimism'. In fact his characteristic stance is very different. The quality that he seeks to promote is, to use the word that he himself uses most often to describe it, not an innocence, but an 'humilitas'. Thus in the second half of the essay 'Projective Verse' he looks

forward to the moment when man will achieve 'an humilitas sufficient to make him of use'.[6] In a recently reprinted text, *The Special View of History*, we find a passage that throws considerable light on the precise meanings that this word carries for him. Speaking of the situation of the contemporary American, he suggests the following as essential attributes:

> (1) the constant of despair for any man, therefore his need for courage; and (2) the immediate rejoining of the struggle—to close the gap, to seek to make the thing from (the act, or say, the love of another) the equal of what one knows.
>
> Let me reverse that a minute, simply that I have found out that most moderns know nothing because they don't know that both of these two results of discrimination hold for any of us; despair, and faith. For there is a counter that includes them both, and the Latins called it 'humilitas', but the word is an old Indo-European root meaning arrogance, actually (from rogo, to ask a question to or of something, to make a demand which has to be answered).[7]

It is clear then that for Olson this 'humilitas' is a strangely mixed quality, one that includes both despair and hope. It is clear also that it is a stance that corresponds closely to his sense of the past, his acknowledgement of the disasters of American history, but his belief that there is a way through and beyond these events. It is interesting that for corroboration of this attitude, and for vindication of it as an inherited American position, he turns once again to Melville. The following is a passage from *Call Me Ishmael* where Olson is describing the role of Ishmael in *Moby-Dick*.

> He is a chorus through whom Ahab's tragedy is seen, by whom what is black and what is white magic is made clear. Like a Catskill eagle Ishmael is able to dive down into the blackest gorges and soar out into the light again . . . He cries forth the glory of the crew's humanity. Ishmael tells *their* story and *their* tragedy as well as Ahab's and thus creates the Moby-Dick universe in which the Ahab world is, by the necessity of life—or the Declaration of Independence—*included*.[8]

It would be as true to say of Olson's work that the 'Ahab world is included', that is to say that a faith in man is announced, and the possibility of change glimpsed beyond the facts of American history and society. However, to say that it is included is not to say, as Mr Pearson would have it, that it is ignored. The positive forces upon which Olson puts his trust are deeply implicated in the facing of the negative facts; the powers of integration can only be awoken by taking the full force of the disintegration. We might further make the claim that this attitude represents a fuller and more interesting response to the conditions of American life than does the bleaker despair of Robert Lowell. The latter owes its being more to a literary inheritance from T. S. Eliot and lacks the obstinacies and contradictions of the lived situation than we find in Olson.

III

Another of the aspects of Olson's work that both these critics are led to question is his concern with the processes and details of the natural world. It is to these, they suggest, and to the problems of man's relationship to them, that he escapes away from the responsibilities of American life. Thus Mr Pearson claims that what he seeks to achieve is a 'return to the *plenum*, to become an open, undetermined, blessedly irresponsible thing, a sheer utterance, like the projectivist poem object, to re-enter the wilderness . . .' (p. 85). For Mr Dodsworth also Olson's interest in the natural world is essentially escapist. 'Olson posits an ideal natural expressiveness arising from a poet's properly establishing his relation to the world of objects around him, and this should be the compensatory quality for the lack of faith in any community . . .' (p. 6). To test the validity of these claims it will be worth considering the poem 'Maximus to Gloucester, Letter 27'. It will be necessary to quote at some length:

> I come back to the geography of it,
> the land falling off to the left
> where my father shot his scabby golf
> and the rest of us played baseball
> into the summer darkness until no flies
> could be seen and we came home
> to our various piazzas where the women
> buzzed
>
> To the left the land fell to the city,
> to the right, it fell to the sea
>
> I was so young my first memory
> is of a tent spread to feed lobsters
> to Rexall conventioneers, and my father,
> a man for kicks, came out of the tent roaring
> with a bread-knife in his teeth to take care of
> a druggist they'd told him had made a pass at
> my mother, she laughing, so sure, as round
> as her face, Hines pink and apple,
> under one of those frame hats women then
>
> This, is no bare incoming
> of novel abstract form, this
>
> is no welter or the forms
> of those events, this,
>
> Greeks, is the stopping
> of the battle
>
>   It is the imposing
> of all those antecedent predecessions, the precessions
> of me, the generation of those facts
> which are my words, it is coming
>
> from all that I no longer am, yet am,
> the slow westward motion of
>
> more than I am
>
> There is no strict personal order
> for my inheritance.
>
>   No Greek will be able
> to discriminate my body.
>   An American
> is a complex of occasions,
> themselves a geometry
> of spatial nature.[9]

It is clear that this is a poem in which Olson expresses to the full his delight in the natural world. We notice the accuracy of the remembered perceptions: 'and the rest of us played baseball /into the summer darkness until no flies/could be seen . . .' We notice also the way in which the human events are encompassed and given shape by a familiar ever-present landscape: 'to the left the land fell to the city/to the right, it fell to the sea'. However, it is clear also that this turning to the natural world is seen by Olson not as an evasion of his identity as an American, but rather as a confirmation of it. In the middle section of this passage he says that his sense of these particular occasions is only part of a wider process of perception; that beneath and beyond the single events there is a greater object of contemplation, that is to say, 'the slow westward motion of/more than I am'. Olson is here endeavouring to convey his full sense of life as it exists on the American continent. The phrase suggests the human exploration and

settlement of the land, but it also carries hints of movement of a more fundamental kind, that is to say, the immensely slow westward drifting of the continent itself. This is a fact that holds particular fascination for Olson, perhaps because it suggests an unstillness at the heart of the most apparently solid realities. By referring to this fundamental process, Olson manages to suggest all those other natural processes that supersede upon it and that make up the varied life of the continent. In his view, an American who is really in search of his 'inheritance' cannot avoid a confrontation with this natural order. Moreover the vast dimensions of space and time that it encompasses work to reduce the scale of that human history of which his own life is a part. It is these changes of perspective that interest Olson. He sees them as working to develop in man a new sense of the natural world, but also as affecting personality in more complex ways. Along with a new sense of the size of nature comes a new sense of the size of man. The world is discovered to be 'more than I am'; human existence begins to take on the quality of participation in a wider community of life. This affects an individual's attitude both to himself and to the society of which he is a part. Olson finds the evidence for these changes in the lives of those Americans towards whom he directs our attention. It is in this light that we should read what he has said about such early writers as John Smith and John Josselyn, about Melville, about the geographer Carl Sauer, about the lives of the Gloucester fishermen.

What Olson is attempting to show in this poem is that a sense of the dramatic meeting of man and land does in fact constitute an important common ground within the American sensibility. The poem's casual opening makes its effect by suggesting that, for the American, even the simplest and most personal movements of mind are saturated by a particular kind of 'geographical' awareness. It is this awareness which he concentrates upon in the rest of the poem, suggesting the roots of it in the American past, and its continuing presence as a latent, but significant, force. However, it is clear that he wishes us to take the analysis a stage further. He suggests that the effort to define and advance this sense of the world will necessarily involve a clash with other values, with, as he puts it in this poem, 'the Greeks'. What he means by this we can see by referring to one of the many other passages in his work where he mounts a similar attack. This is from the essay 'Human Universe':

> We stay unaware how two means of discourse the Greeks appear to have invented hugely intermit out participation in our experience, and so prevent discovery. They are what followed from Socrates' readiness to generalise, his willingness (from his own bias) to make a universe out of discourse instead of letting it rest in its most serviceable place . . . With Aristotle, the two great means appear: logic and classification. And it is they that have so fastened themselves on habits of thought that action is interfered with, absolutely interfered with, I should say.[10]

Olson quarrels with these structures of thought primarily because he believes that they have brought about distortions in man's conception of his active role in the world. By placing an emphasis on the capacity of the single man to order and control his environment they have underlain and fostered the aggressive individualism of the Western world that finds its culmination in the American advance. Olson elsewhere describes this force as 'the egocentric concept, a man himself as, and only contemporary to himself, the PROOF of anything, himself responsible only to himself by the exhibition of his energy, AHAB, end'.[11] The American condition thus begins to appear to him as a drama of opposing forces; as at once the culmination of old energies and the possible beginning of new ones. We can see the way in which these arguments get into the poem above. What is deplored is the determination of the individual to prosecute a 'battle' against the world that is going on outside him, to treat it as mere material to be reduced to a 'strict personal order'. Olson suggests as a feature of the American experience the existence of a significant counter-energy, a new excitement at the processes of the physical world, and a new sense of 'participation' in them. He says that the natural context of his own life is so close and living a thing to him that he thinks of it as he does of his own 'body'. What he is concerned to explore in his work are the changes of individual and social attitude that flow from this experience, and the confrontations that are demanded with habitual Western values.

We can see then how the argument opens out. But we should not forget that the whole process has its roots in the natural movement of Olson's mind back to those incidents of his youth. It is this that opens the door to the wider processes of perception and the investigation of them. The poem in fact reproduces on a small scale the movement of the whole of his art. He is concerned to speculate about the American condition, but to do so from the basis of a firm understanding of that condition as it exists in the minds and hearts of particular men and women. That is why the *Maximus Poems*, though wide in their scope, return always to details of the lives of himself, his family and the past and present inhabitants of Gloucester. He is concerned with the natural world, but that concern is not an instant invention of his to evade American realities. He discovers it within the structure of his own life; it comes to him as a responsibility, as an 'inheritance'. He attempts to understand the roots of it in the American past, and the use of it in the present as a countering force to the energies that have predominated in the shaping of American reality. What he urges upon his audience is not a wholesale rejection of all their contacts, but rather a careful review of each individual life and the context and history out of which it comes. To characterize him as a Pied Piper is to underestimate both his own activities and those that he asks of the reader.

IV

For Martin Dodsworth, Olson's major fault is the evasion not so much of American history, but rather of the society that immediately confronts him. Thus he speaks of 'the kind of total repudiation of existing society that we find in Olson', and suggests that Olson never attempts a 'direct confrontation with the issue: what sort of society do we actually have?' Moreover, referring specifically to the *Maximus Poems*, he suggests that when Olson 'has to speak of the present society of Gloucester, he can do little but turn from it in revulsion' (pp. 26, 27, 29). Such criticisms are hardly a fair representation of the facts. It is clear first of all from many passages in his work that Olson is vitally concerned with the experience of community. Take, for instance, this passage from A *Special View of History* where he is outlining the major dilemmas facing contemporary Americans.

> There are two estrangements the permanent one, from that which is slipping by in the grass without moving a leaf of grass's top; but this other one, the contingent, of touch on all sides—of the company of the living, that they are distracted and dispersed . . . Man has the context of his own species for his self or he is a pseudo creature, of two kinds, Nature's, or the machine's.[12]

The experience of community, of 'the company of the living',

is here held up as an essential aspect of the well-being of man; moreover the effort to redefine and advance it is seen as being as important as that other task of the development of attention to the natural world, to 'that which is slipping by in the grass'.

This concern with community in fact pervades the *Maximus Poems* and provides one of their central themes. The town of Gloucester is explored *as a community*, for the kinds of corporate life that are present or latent within it. Mr Dodsworth is of course right to suggest that there are aspects of the place from which Olson turns 'in revulsion'. However, it is also clear that there are other elements of the life of the city that give him grounds for considerable hope. Gloucester is a place where 'polis/still thrives',[13] and of whose inhabitants he can say:

> so few
> have the polis
> in their eye
>   The brillian Portuguese owners,
>   they do. They pour the money back
>   into engines, into their ships,
>   whole families do, put it back
>   in. They are but extensions of their own
>   careers
>   as mastheadsmen—[14]

The city is in fact a battleground, an arena in which, as he writes the poems, the issues of community are being fought out. What he is particularly concerned about is the increasing invasion of all aspects of life by centralized commercial interests. He deplores the way in which the local dimension has been lost as the values of the individual have become subject to manipulation on an ever grander scale. He attacks the images and slogans of advertising as the means by which this introjection is achieved, by which the man engaged with local realities is transformed into the standardized consumer:

>   colored pictures
>   of all things to eat: dirty
>   postcards
>   And words, words, words,
>   all over everything
>   No eyes or ears left
>   to do their own doings (all
>   invaded, appropriated, outraged, all senses
>   including the mind, that worker on what is[15]

Along with this manipulation of values goes a centralization of economic power that Olson also deplores: 'The ships, even the wharves, absentee-owned . . .'[16]

Thus Gloucester has been colonized by the world of the spectacle, but Olson is firm in his conviction that there are significant pockets of resistance. Most of what he has to say in this direction concerns the notion of 'polis', and if we look again at the passage about the Portuguese owners, we can see something of what he means. What Olson particularly admires about these men is the fact that they have not allowed the purely commercial aspects of their operation, the making of profit, to overrule all other concerns. Fishing for them remains fishing; it is the actual contact with the natural world that still absorbs their energies and their resources, 'they are but extensions of their own careers/as mastheadsmen'. Moreover this excitement is seen as not only a personal matter, but also as bonding 'whole families' together; out of the sense of a shared drama there issues a particular kind of social cohesion. Olson sees their lives as a network of related energies. The process of fishing, the learning of the details of species and of territory, generates in them an 'attention' to the context in which they live; to all the other life going on around them. This in its turn sets going a similarly detailed sense of the human life around them, a particular 'care'[17] for the quality and management of their community. We can see, then, something of what Olson means when he speaks of the experience of community as one of 'touch all round', of life lived amidst 'the company of the living'. Of course his work poses questions that it does not answer. We are left to speculate upon the political and economic decentralization necessarily implied. But his concern is not to argue tactics so much as to bear witness to the living processes of one place; the existence of a community, the erosion of it, the continuing hunger and estrangement. We should notice finally the way in which, at the beginning of the *Maximus Poems*, he specifically commits the act of writing to this task. He attacks the magazine *Four Winds*, published in Gloucester, for the vagueness of its political and literary themes. Instead he demands that the writer should submit himself to the exactitude of local concerns, should work for the definition and defence of a 'place we can meet'. As he says to Ferrini, the editor of the magazine:

> It's no use,
> There is no place we can meet.
> You have left Gloucester.
> You are not there, you are anywhere
> where there are little magazines
> will publish you[18]

V

In this essay I have not attempted a total explication of Olson's work. There is much more investigation to be done, of the texts themselves, of the sources that Olson uses in the establishment of his own positions, and of the contacts with other American writers, notably Edward Dahlberg and Waldo Frank, that nourished him early in his career. What I hope to have been able to suggest is that at the heart of his work there lies an interesting and vivid analysis of the American condition, and one that has not yet received just treatment in the hands of critics in this country. As I suggested at the beginning, the cause for this failure of vision seems to lie in a mis-reading of the 'Projective Verse' manifesto in relation to the rest of his work. It is certainly true that in that essay Olson asks for a new attention to the on-going details of experience, and proffers the poem as a means of achieving this. However, in the light of the rest of his work it is clear that he does so not in search of any immediately available 'innocence'. What he is looking for is a method of revealing the detailed structure of a life in such a way as to understand the forces that act upon it, and the context, or lack of context, amidst which it proceeds. The poem is thus best seen as the central act within a wider critical process. Moreover it is the whole process that he seeks to convey to the reader. On several occasions he refers enthusiastically to Herodotus' definition of history as '. . . a verb, to find out for yourself: istorin, which makes anyone's acts a finding out for him or her self . . .'[19] It is such active processes of enquiry that his own work consistently urges upon us.

Notes

1. *The Survival of Poetry, A Contemporary Survey*, edited by Martin Dodsworth (London: Faber and Faber, 1970). All further references to this volume are given as page numbers in the text.
2. Reprinted in *Human Universe & Other Essays* (New York: Grove Press Inc., 1967).
3. *Call Me Ishmael* (London: Cape Editions, Jonathan Cape, 1967), p. 19. Published in the U.S. by Grove Press, 1959.
4. *The Maximus Poems* (New York: Jargon/Corinth Books, 1960), p. 135. Published in England by Cape Goliard.
5. *The Maximus Poems*, p. 101.
6. *Human Universe & Other Essays*, p. 60.
7. *The Special View of History* (Berkeley: Oyez Press, 1970), p. 30.
8. *Call Me Ishmael*, p. 57.
9. *Maximus Poems IV, V, VI*, (London: Cape Goliard Press, 1968), p. 14. Reprinted by permission of the Estate of Charles Olson, the publishers, and Grossman Publishers, New York.
10. *Human Universe & Other Essays*, p. 4. Olson's views on the Greek philosophers owe much to his close reading of the work of A. N. Whitehead, particularly *Process and Reality*.
11. *Human Universe & Other Essays*, p. 20.
12. *The Special View of History*, p. 25.
13. *The Maximus Poems*, p. 22.
14. *The Maximus Poems*, p. 28.
15. *The Maximus Poems*, p. 13.
16. *The Maximus Poems*, p. 10.
17. See Olson's use of these particular words in *The Maximus Poems*, p. 28.
18. *The Maximus Poems*, p. 25.
19. *The Maximus Poems, IV, V, VI*, p. 79.

L. S. DEMBO
"Charles Olson and the Moral History of Cape Ann"
Criticism, Spring 1972, pp. 165–74

Robert Creeley has argued that were the *Maximus Poems*, Charles Olson's major work, merely "social criticism," they would not be very interesting.[1] The same could be said, of course, for Pound's *Cantos* and Williams' *Paterson*; all three poems seek to express new forms of poetic perception and language. Yet it is equally true that social criticism, set in the context of a moral vision of history, is responsible for what thematic coherence these poems have. Olson, with his contrast between *polis*, the ideal society, and *pejorocracy*, the debased world of materialism, is akin to Pound, with his vision of the ideal City or Culture in opposition to the conditions that exist under the pervasive influence of "usury" and other forms of exploitation. In his localism, in which the poet's psychological and spiritual state is closely related to the moral state of a particular place, Olson is akin to Williams. The *Maximus Poems* are unified by a specific reading of the history of Gloucester and Cape Ann, a history that in its stylized consideration of men and events aims not simply at the disclosure of what happened, but at the revelation of moral truth.

Thus, in Olson's portrayal of the founding of Gloucester—as early as the "fishing stage" incident, a confrontation between Dorchester fishermen and Puritan settlers over a wharf or "stage" used to dry fish (c. 1626)—the conflict between the values of polis and pejorocracy is discernible. The fishermen had taken possession of a stage that the Puritans had constructed but failed to use—"hadn't yet got to / fishing that season (stayed in bed)." When the latter returned, led by Miles Standish, they were challenged by the fishermen who were prepared to defend their drying catch. With "3 Plymouth vessels / on station," however, the Dorchestermen had no choice but to yield.[2] Olson concludes:

> They should raise a monument
> to a fisherman crouched down
> behind a hogshead, protecting
> his dried fish
>
> (114)

The fishermen are engaged in commerce, but the commerce is sound, a contrast to modern credit practices, with "each man and woman / and child living off / things paid on / 33 years schedule" (113). A diatribe against installment buying is wholly consistent with Olson's basically ascetic values and with his insistence on the distinction between true and false plenty.

Thus, the episode and others like it contain, for Olson, profound economic and ethical implications. It

> is more than the fight of one colony with another, it
> is the whole engagement against (1) mercantilism
> . . . and (2) against nascent capitalism except as it
> stays the individual adventurer and the worker on
> share—against all sliding statism, ownership, getting
> into, the community as, Chamber of Commerce, or
> theocracy; or City Manager. (101)

The original party of fourteen men is idealized by Olson chiefly because it was constituted by fishermen *per se*, "artisans" rather than exploiters. Their motive was "the adventure / of the new frontier / (not boom, / or gold, / the lucky strike, / but work" (104); even though their whole enterprise failed, or perhaps because it failed, these men were heroic. Olson seems to share Williams' vision of America as a vast new world demanding a totally new point of view: a "nakedness" of perception to correspond to a naked land:

> He left him naked,
> the man said, and
> nakedness
> is what one means
>
> that all start up
> to the eye and soul
> as though it had never
> happened before
>   (107)

John White, the original advocate of a settlement in America for Dorchester fishermen, had seen the land in his "mind's eye," but "fourteen men / of whom we know eleven," had seen it directly: "twenty-two eyes / and the snow flew / where gulls now paper / the skies" (108).

The Puritans did not see with such eyes because they were too concerned with twisting "back to Convenantal / truth" the "things / of this world (new / world" (130). Or worse, they were corrupted by the values of pejorocracy—"Wow sd Pilgrimes ONE HALF MILLION BUCKS in five years from / FURS at the same time FISH pulling all of Spain's bullion out of" (109). (This latter allusion is to the profitable trade with Spanish America.) The supplanting by John Endecott of Roger Conant, who, disaffected from the colony at New Plymouth, had been appointed "governor" of the Gloucester party by the Dorcester Company, indicates, for Olson, the general triumph of Puritanism over the more "authentic" values. Olson makes much of the fact that the house Conant built, a symbol of his solidity, was removed to Salem, when the plantation was resettled, and appropriated by Endecott for his mansion, "the frame of it was that sound" (45). The moral here is that

> the newness
> the first men knew was almost
> from the start dirtied
> by second comers
>   (135)

The obscure poem, "Stiffening, in the Master Founders' Wills," records the failure of the Puritan mind to cope with "American space." "Descartes, age 34, dates Boston's / settling," the piece begins, and the implication is that Cartesian rationalism and the desire for "proportion" underlay the thought and action of the "master founder," John Winthrop. An enemy to "enthusiasm," religious or otherwise, Winthrop experienced the difficulty of realizing his values in the face of the "desperate densenesses" of human nature and the conditions in which "things / are knots where instance / hides order,

and a man / does not run as sheep" (128). His struggle with the Antinomian enthusiast, Anne Hutchinson, who emphasized the absolute irrelevance of good works to grace and insisted on revelation as the only mode of recognizing one's own salvation, was characteristic and, indeed, symbolic. Winthrop was bested in court by Anne Hutchinson's arguments and he succeeded in having her expelled from the colony virtually by court fiat alone.

Olson depicts Winthrop as "a single man in this wilderness" aware that "a thing surely wasn't / how he'd done it [in] East Anglia" and that space, in America, did not have his name written on it, as it did, in England, for Shakespeare, who

> when young,
> by fields from Shottery home
> from her bed (Mistress Hathaway's)
> saw William written
> in Cassiopeia overhead[3]
>   (129)

The truth is that "American space / was 1630 still sailors' / apprehension not / Boston's leader's."

Puritan rationalism (or legalism) could not prevent the emergence of purely materialistic values. As a matter of fact, it was, in a sense, conducive to it. "Not savages but thought / has invaded / the proposition," Olson asserts, and he goes on to indicate the replacement of intrinsically valued agricultural pursuits by the desire for commercial gain—"Canaan / was Cane's, and / all was faulting, / stiffening in the master / founders wills." Thus, the "things of this world" began to dominate and men's souls began to "dry." The Puritan, to whom "outward was inward act," saw his religious and ethical fervor cooling into the "mettlesomeness" of the merchant:

> Sailors,
> come ashore / tell
> the tailor's sewing's
> in a different
> light. But it's still
> sewing—
>   (131–32)

Maximus sees in it only the origins of modern corruption. Neither the original Puritan values ("the soul's / desire to be blind, in service / or in ecstasy") nor the modern idealization of plenty, with its neglect of all spiritual values, is the essence of polis, and the poet-prophet can only pick "a private way / among debris / of common / wealths." He can do no more than reassert his own ideal that "the soul / be naked / at the end / of time": true commonwealth, polis, is a "public fact" that is merely an extension of personal "nakedness."

Juxtaposed with Winthrop is Captain Christopher Levett, who established a fishing plantation at Monhegan Island, Maine. Associating him with Roger Conant, emblemized by his solidly constructed house, Olson finds characteristic virtues in Levett. Whereas Puritanism developed into the pejorocracy prevalent in modern America, men like Levett are at the basis of polis:

> A man
> who speaks as Levett does
> of what he's done
> ("I have obtained a place
> of habitation in New—
> England, where I have built
> a house, and fortified it. . . .
>
>   . . .
> speaks (as he does of each
> new thing he saw and did
> in these new parts). . . .
>   (134)

It was precisely the "newness" that was "dirtied by second comers," dirt in this sense including the "dirtiness of goodness" and overabundance. When Cartesian "thought / . . . invaded / the proposition," the ideal of appropriate speech, such as Levett's, the nominalist principle that there "may be no more names than there are objects" or "more verbs then there are actions" was violated and the true response to the new world was lost.

For Olson the chief figure in the line that Levett continued was John Smith, "the stater of quantity and precision," who "changed / everything: he pointed / out / Cape Ann, / named her / so it's stuck," and "planted / fisheries / so they've stayed put, / on this coast, from Pemaquid / to Cape Cod" (124). These achievements are related to his ability to respond appropriately: "the eye he had / for what New England offered, / what we are other than / theocratic" (50). Just as Olson cites various passages from the writings of Levett to reveal the man's character in his simple description of things in the New World, so he quotes from Smith's *Sea-Grammar*, a sailor's manual and lexicon, and, indirectly, from A *Description of New England*. Smith was a "sea-mark" (the title of a poem used as an epigraph to *Advertisements for the Unexperienced Planters of New England*), a wrecked ship that warns approaching vessels of shoals (69–70) and for Olson the symbolism is clear. Like other such men, "Smith also got shoved aside," to the peril of the whole continent. There is more than literal fact in the statement that Smith was "refused / as a navigator by / the Pilgrims, Standish / chosen instead" (69).

In a series of enigmatic passages in "Some Good News" Smith seems to acquire metaphysical as well as ethical dimensions. He remains for Olson a sign that is not easily comprehended ("too early yet / to be understood") and he appears to be associated with Maximus as the Man in the Word or the Figure of Outward. The shoals that he marks stand for the conditions of the New World, no less than Georges Bank, north of Gloucester:

> shifty new
> land, [that] sucks
> down, into the terrible
> inert of nature (the Divine
> Inert. . . .
>
>   (122)

"Divine Inert" appears in *Moby-Dick*, and Olson seems to be elaborating Melville's meaning. Discussing Ahab's use of theatrical devices to enhance his power, Melville said that only "true princes of the Empire" (God's chosen) kept themselves from "the world's hustings" (the theatricality of electioneering), left the highest honors to active but inferior men, and remained among "the hidden handful of the Divine Inert."[4]

Olson's ideal is the quiet man of inner passivity who faces terror calmly. Smith, like Maximus, is the spokesman for explorers and fishermen,

> the literary man
> of these men
> of the West,
> who knew private
> passivity as these
> quartermasters knew
> supplies. . . .

His message is that "it has to be" (the terrible faced with passivity?) if "princes / of the husting / are to issue from / the collapse / of the previous soul." Olson has distorted Melville's image here and one can only speculate on the meanings. The previous or European soul collapses upon encountering the dangers of the New World; from its demise there issues, ideally,

the prince of the husting or representative of the new society. Smith is himself, perhaps, one such prince since he not only endured much and saw with correct vision, but as a sea mark is a passive and misunderstood spokesmen or petitioner. In any event we learn that he

> as Sam Grant after,
> was futile
> until the place
> and time burned
> with the same heat as
> the man. . . .
>
>   (123)

Smith's kind of vision is part of a tradition that goes back to the early explorers of the North Atlantic coast—such as the Portuguese Juan de la Cosa, before whom "nobody / could have / a mappemunde," Verrazano, and Cabot, among others. In the poem to which de la Cosa lends his name, the new world again appears as a terrible force, half natural, half mythic, "swimming . . . out of the mists / . . . out of mermaids & Monsters"—again a manifestation of the "Divine Inert." The poem emphasizes the cost in lives for its discovery and exploration, as well as for its development. De La Cosa's descriptions are in the same direct language as are those of Smith; his distinction as a map-maker, also shared by Smith, is characteristic of his stature. At one point in the work Maximus himself is identified with Marinus of Tyre, another map-maker, and Olson goes so far as to present graphically surveyors' notes of crucial property in the early history of Gloucester (145).

Map-making is closely associated in Olson's vision with ideal language: "metric . . . is mapping," he tells us in a "footnote" on certain Indian languages, "and so . . . congruent means of making a statement" (144). Behind this association is the idea that languages like Yana and Hopi are "peculiarly adjusted to the topological as a prime and libidinal character of a man, and therefore of all his proximities." Actually, "topological" refers to the study of surfaces, specifically the geometrical properties that remain constant despite distortions of shape; here it seems to mean the qualities of human character defined by a given place (*topos*). The topological *is* the prime and libidinal character of a man, and thus Maximus is concerned with himself *as* Gloucester ("myself as here-a-bouts"). To make a map of one's locality is, in a sense, to measure ones own "surfaces" or forces ("measure me, measure my forces"), an activity that is precisely equivalent to writing poetry. Hopi language represents an extreme of nominalization, since it destroys syntax and "spatializes" or renders as a substantive temporal action:

> I, as Mr. Foster, went
> to Gloucester, thus:
> "And past-I-go
> Gloucester-insides
> being Fosterwise of
> Charley-once-boy
> insides"
>
>   (144)

However nonsensical this rendition of the famous jingle, it does seem to suggest an indissoluble relation between man and place, Gloucester, Foster, Maximus, and Charles Olson (as a boy?) being intermingled.

In the moral history of Cape Ann, and of New England in general, certain figures, for various reasons, are singled out as pejoracrats: Sir Richard Hawkins, son of the explorer, engaged in the slave trade (62 ff.); Nathaniel Bowditch, navigator and later president of Harvard, represents the

> movement of NE monies
> away from primary production & trade
> to the several cankers of profit-making
> which have, like Agyasta, made America great.
>
> (72)

Stephen Higgenson, who, in a letter to John Adams ascribes the decline in prosperity of the Cape Ann fishing communities to lack of "industry and frugality," is, to Olson, typical of the commercial mentality and "an example of how wrong you can be and still / run this country" (75).

Pacing off the property divisions around the old Meeting House Green while part of it is being excavated for a new highway, Maximus contemplates fragmentarily the early settlers and their commercial ambitions, the influence of the sea, mythic as well as economic, on Gloucester, and the geology of the Cape. Robert Duncan has related that Olson was very much interested in physical morphology, in the idea "that the universe puts its stamp on everything and that it's one universe. . . . he became very excited when the one continent theory came up again—the idea that one continent separated into a number of continents and is in the process of congealing again into a single continent."[5] Duncan believes that the theory can be used to explain the *Maximus Poems* in general, which move from "a oneness back to a oneness, but so slowly and so far beyond its own lifetime that it cannot conceivably be composed." Actually, the idea is no less applicable to Olson's vision of history. The epigraph to *Maximus* reads "All my life I've heard / one makes many" and later we are told "That we grow up many / And the single / is not easily / known" (52). In the "geology of history," form is created, disintegrates, and reestablishes itself in endless process: men shift as ice does. Thus even while presenting a diagram of the Meeting House Green properties, Olson begins to question its changes ("did Eveleth go to the present Marsh St?," "What did Bruen want? He had already shifted from Piscataqua / to Plymouth, then to Gloucester and now to New London. . . .") Commerce moves northwest in the same fashion as ice moving south. (". . . the commerce of NW shifting / man—it ends . . . in the ice.") But despite all the commercial activity and migration that mark the history of Gloucester, there is "then to now nothing / new, in the meaning." Pejorocracy remains the one form behind the many.

Yet it is perhaps the idea of a truly unitary universe that underlies Maximus' reflections. Commercial activities, the acquisition and exchange of property, the fishing trade,—indeed the whole of life in Gloucester in the seventeenth and twentieth centuries—along with personal reminiscences coalesce in Maximus' imagination. "Interfused / with the rubbish / of creation," he is the multiplicity of Gloucester—the stench of the fish-processing industries as well as the fragrance of the tansy. The identity of early settlers, manipulators or not, like Sylvester Eveleth, holds the key to Maximus' own ("I take my air / where Eveleth walked / out the west / on these hills"). And in calling upon the bulldozer working at the excavation for the new highway to "clean the earth / of sentimental / drifty dirty / lazy man" he is speaking of a part of himself.

Maximus had written: "Because of the agora [marketplace] America is, was, from the start, the moral struggle." When the Greek navigator, Pytheas, had explored Ultima Thule (possibly the New World in Olson's account), he found that earth, air, and water had fused into a single substance or "sludge" that made navigation impossible. The modern poet finds himself in the same geological-moral morass:

> Am in the mud
> Off Five Pound Island
> is the grease-pit
> of State Pier.
>
> (150)

He argues that "the present / is worse give nothing now your credence / start all over."

His own method of starting over—facing again the Inert of history as the first settlers faced that of the continent—is to invoke the aid of the historian, Frances Rose-Troup, who, in Olson's mind, clearly understood the origins of Gloucester ("she put you back on the launching platform"). Olson approves of the historian precisely because he sees nominalist virtues in her:

> It looks as though Miss Rose-Troup connects back to
>   Champlain[;]
> the number of wigwams show Freshwater Cove
>   above Cressy's
> in Tolmans field near Half Moon or possibly the old
>   Steep
> Bank where Kent Circle maybe it's Apple Row or
>   Agamenticus Height
>
> (151)

If my addition of the semi-colon does not represent a misreading, the sense here would seem to be that Rose-Troup is in the tradition of Champlain, who in turn is a "Map-Maker" of the order of Juan de la Cosa. The poet's reflections on this point conclude with his presenting a chart of the depths of the approach to Gloucester harbor, with the notation "[their ship]" marked just outside "Ten Pound Island." The reference is perhaps to the Dorchester fishing vessel that landed the fourteen men with whom the history of Gloucester as a settlement begins. And once again the poem has returned us to the irreducible nominalist equation. The graphic notations of Maximus pacing out the properties surrounding the Meeting House Green, made amidst the intrusions of technology, has its origins in the old chart; both are symbols of an ideal that mark the beginning and the climax of the moral deterioration of a continent. The annual ceremony in Gloucester of casting flowers out to sea in honor of the dead is for Maximus one of the recurrent signs of hope. But there can be no ultimate fulfillment. As in *The Cantos* the onslaught of the forces of pejorocracy is as permanent as the course of history, and the poet must invariably ask,

> . . . the [Route] 128 bridge
> now brings in
> what,
> to Main Street?
>
> (160)

Notes

1. *Yugen* 8 (Fall 1962), 53.
2. *The Maximus Poems* (New York: Jargon/Corinth Books, 1960), pp. 112–13. All citations are to this volume. A second volume, *Maximus Poems IV, V, VI* (Cape Goliard/Grossman) appeared in 1968. The basic historical views I wish to discuss are laid down in the first volume; the second is chiefly concerned with the mythic dimension of Olson's vision.
3. Cf. Olson's remarks: "The greatest poet of mars in the language . . . is William Shakespeare. I discovered that in wyoming, lower case w, last year. No Cassiopeia in the air overhead. No J O Joyce in—anywhere. No juice. No Zeus. No Joyce, no Zeus, no—" (*Charles Olson Reading at Berkeley*, Coyote, 1966, p. 22).
4. *Moby-Dick*, second to last paragraph of ch. 33. I am indebted to Professor Merton Sealts, Jr. for this reference. The Melville passage, itself obscure, is explained by Charles Fiedelson, Jr., in his edition of the novel (Bobbs-Merrill, 1964), pp. 198–99.
5. In a taped, unpublished conversation, April, 1967.

PAUL A. BOVÉ
From "The Particularities of Tradition:
History and Locale in *The Maximus Poems*"
Destructive Poetics:
Heidegger and Modern American Poetry
1980, pp. 235–51

J. B. Philip's refutation of Pearson and Dodsworth is a useful corrective to those who see Olson falling into some naive theory of original beginnings. Philip's essay, "Charles Olson Reconsidered," establishes, by a close analysis of "Maximus to Gloucester, Letter 27," that Olson's poetry is crucially involved both with society and the past: "What [Olson] is looking for is a method of revealing the detailed structure of a life in such a way as to understand the forces that act upon it, and the context, or lack of context, amidst which it proceeds. The poem is thus best seen as the central act within a wider critical process."[1] Yet Philip, too, insists that Olson is trying to project a new society, a new tradition which, free of the excesses and evils of the old, will function as the new center that is needed to replace the disintegrated past. Such readings of Olson are too comforting and too comfortable. They simplify Olson's work and, in their own ways, reify the process of his poetry into a new canon, a new, "better" artifact. Even so, Philip's analysis of Olson's involvement with society and history is obviously closer to Olson than any of the critics who charge Olson with egotism and eccentricity.

In *The Maximus Poems*, according to Philip, the process of criticizing the commercial, discursive, and exploitative American society "is obviously seen by Olson as the beginning of other, more positive ventures. . . . What he looks forward to is the reordering of American values." This reform will only be brought about by those who have come to know the "darkness" of contemporary society by living in it and by trying to bring "light" to it: "It is there [in the darkness of that society] that an essential discrimination is learnt, and essential energies generated." From a confrontation with the darkness, Philip asserts, will emerge a "determination for change."[2] Despite his sense of the pressures of change in Olson, Philip describes the poetry in an un-destroyed language filled with metaphysical metaphors of dualism and transcendence: light and dark. Although Philip's insight into Olson's work is restricted by this critical language, his refutation of Pearson's and Dodsworth's claims makes it unnecessary to prove that Olson attacks the "pejorocracy" of Modern society and that he does examine his own relation to the past to find some alternative to the accepted "tradition." It is necessary, though, to go beyond Philip to examine what Olson finds to condemn in society and what he finds to praise in the past. Most importantly, it must be argued that Olson is perhaps the most radically interpretive poet of this century. That is, Olson insists upon a relation to the past and a "method" of encountering the past and nature which over-throws entirely the notion of "tradition" and its concomitant ideas of *stasis*, continuity, and "objective" criticism.

The earliest letters of *The Maximus Poems* are predominantly concerned with a presentation and destruction of society and the "tradition" upon which it rests. "The Songs of Maximus" and "Letter 3" are both of primary interest because of their concentration upon the misuse of language and the abuse of literature in the "pejorocracy." "The Songs of Maximus" seem to be more interesting as poetry, however, because of the clearer sense of movement in their lines and because of their fuller analyses of the failures of twentieth-century mass culture. "Letter 3" is marred by the rather

generalized usage of the tansy flower as an alternative to the crassness of the language abusers of Gloucester. Further, "Letter 3" is given over to prose statement so entirely that it seems to violate Olson's own maxim that the line must conform to breath.

Both of these poems begin with a sense of the obscuring of things in the world by language. "Song 1" of "The Songs of Maximus" is perhaps the most complex statement criticizing the "pejorocracy":

> colored pictures
> of all things to eat: dirty
> postcards
>   And words, words, words
> all over everything
>   No eyes or ears left
> to do their own doings (all
> invaded, appropriated, outraged, all senses
> including the mind, that worker on what is
>   And that other
>   sense
> made to give even the most wretched, or any of us,
>   wretched,
> that consolation (greased
>   lulled
> even the street-cars
> song
>
>   (*MxP*, 13)

In typical Olson fashion, this poem begins in the middle of things, in the process of thinking about, of writing the poem. It avoids the full sentence of conventional verse as well as the end stop line. Like Williams' and Pound's line, Olson's runs over to maintain the sense of movement that the end-stop violates and to draw attention, visually and aurally, to those "unimportant" items of poetry which the iambic pentameter line normally obscures, e.g., "all" and "is." Drawing attention to "words" in such a way seems to contradict the main complaint of the poem that there are already too many words. But this seeming contradiction opens the poem up in an important way and insists upon an interpretation of that phrase "And words, words, words / all over everything."

The Olsonian line draws attention to words as words precisely because the "pejorocracy" does not realize that all it sees and hears in its encounter with the world are "words." In existential language, one could say that the "they," the "crowd," substitutes inauthentically, like the ironic New Critics, a world of words for the actuality in which we live as free human beings. Indeed, Olson himself in "Human Universe," points out that, as a result of our history, of what we have chosen as our "tradition" (perhaps because of what has chosen us), we live in a "universe of discourse" (*SW*, 54). In other words, things can be hidden by words. The potential of words themselves to disclose is covered-up. The existence of beings in the world is obscured. Language is used inauthentically to present or maintain preformed, a prioristic versions of the objects in the world. The crowd in the "pejorocracy" deals with words in place of things, and, in fact, with a world of words and not with a "real" world at all.

It is not coincidental that the poem, which is essentially an attack on the misuse of language, opens up with a mention of pictures and advertising. Ads are "dirty postcards" because they seduce the populace into the falsely comforting, consuming, exploiting mentality of its society. More importantly, however, Olson's initial emphasis on "vision" in this poem on language is an attack on the reduction of language to "picture." In other words, in the context of Modern poetry's insistence upon the primacy of the visual image in verbal art, these opening lines are a critique of the ironic or image-making imagination. Even more broadly, as Sartre suggests in *Nausea* about the symbolists' use of language, the opening of this poem points out that the ironic, iconic, spatial use of language to project images is ultimately no different from the commercialized exploitation of language in ads and of nature in industry. In an intriguing reversal of Stephen Dedalus' assertion that imagistic language is not pornographic, Olson suggests that, like ads, images and symbols are pornographic because seductive. They turn the mind and the senses away from the dreadful world of objects and death toward a world of words. As Olson says in "Song 3" of "The Songs of Maximus," "the blessing / that difficulties are once more" (*MxP*, 14). In other words, when the world is replaced by words—commercial or imagistic—"difficulty," which is the basic state of living in the world as one object among others, is obscured, and with it man's primary sense of his place in creation.

The anti-imagistic reading of the first lines is supported by the speaker's claim that eyes do not function in their own way any longer in our society. Language as discourse and as image displaces the immediate sensual perception of objects, which Heidegger calls *noein*, as the way to knowledge. The eyes only "see through" a web of words or they only see a series of images, constructed by others, interfering with the natural vision of things. The eye is potentially phenomenologically reduced; that is, the eye is capable of seeing the world free of the conceptions which discursive language imposes upon it and uninhibited by the intrusion of a verbally created, yet visually interfering, aesthetic artifact. In the "pejorocracy," however, the natural function of the eye is interrupted and a conscious, often violent process of stripping away the intruding "words" must take place before the eyes can function in their own way.

Of course, Walt Whitman makes precisely the same point in *Leaves of Grass* when he asserts that each and every American poet must see things for himself. Whitman welcomes poets who are not his imitators, but who will attend to the world more carefully than he has and, therefore, surpass him. Pound and Williams insist upon similar phenomenologically reductive maxims: "Make it new!" and "No ideas but in things." Of course, Husserl's initial definition of phenomenology makes the same assertion: "Zu den Sachen Selbst," and even Heidegger, despite his hermeneutical emphasis, insists, in his own definition of phenomenology, upon allowing a thing to manifest itself from itself and in itself.

Olson, like these various phenomenologically oriented writers, does not insist that a poet see a thing in a *certain* way, but, rather, that he simply see. However, just how difficult it is to see becomes clear not only in *The Maximus Poems*, but in *The Special View of History*, where Olson explains that the "difficulty" of seeing results from the accumulation of a fraudulent scheme in the West for the last two thousand years. Olson discovers that seeing for oneself is authentic "history." Claiming the Greek historian Herodotus for his model, Olson says: "By history I mean to know, to really know" (*SVH*, 21). "History" is opposed to "discourse," which Socrates and the Greek philosophers invented. For Herodotus, according to Olson, "*historin* . . . appears to mean 'finding out for oneself,' instead of depending on hearsay" (*SVH*, 21). "Hearsay" is not merely the idle talk of the crowd in the "pejorocracy" but, as Olson makes clear in "Human Universe," it is an abuse of language which defines our entire tradition and, thus, inhibits our seeing:

We stay unaware how two means of discourse the Greeks appear to have invented hugely intermit our participation in our experience, and so prevent discovery. They are what followed from Socrates' readiness to generalize, his willingness (from his own bias) to make a "universe" out of discourse. . . . With Aristotle, the two great means appear: logic and classification. And it is they that have so fastened themselves on habits of thought that action is interfered with, absolutely interfered with, I should say. (*SW*, 54–55)

Olson explains that the "universe" of discourse "is one of the first false faces of the law which I shall want to try to strike away" (*SW*, 54). Like Heidegger, he is aware of the violence needed to break down the traditional wall of habit which inhibits discovery. Olson's "goal" is to "dis-close"; like Heidegger, he tries to reveal what the discursive covers-over.

The tradition impedes the proper functioning of the human organism by cutting it off from the world. It is through the circuit of world-senses-imagination that creativity proceeds, that dis-coveries are made. Language as discourse and image disrupts this circuit at every point. It obscures the world by representing it in concepts and pictures; it frustrates the senses by denying them contact with objects in the world; and it rapes and coerces the mind:

. . . all
invaded, appropriated, outraged, all senses
including the mind, that worker on what is

The mind and the senses are "greased / lulled" by the veneer of words. They are made incapable of creative discovery. Man's potential for self-generation and action in the world is cut off: "And that other sense / made to give even the most wretched, or any of us, wretched / that consolation. . . ." The combination of the sexual connotation of the world "outraged" and the suggested loss of potency in this last passage indicates the sterility and inactivity of the word-world of the pejorocracy.

When the circuit of world-senses-mind-action is complete, however, the poet can "disclose values" (*SW*, 63) which his community "could make use of" (*SW*, 63). Art created in the completion of this circuit is "kinetic," directly opposed to the static art of Stephen Dedalus and the New Critics. As such, kinetic art is an alternative to traditional metaphysics, which, according to Olson, is always "descriptive," i.e., "distanced" and "disinterested." Art is unique, different from metaphysics (and from the critical-poetic tradition defined by its language) because kinetic art alone can "get what you are after—so far as a human being goes, his life" (*SW*, 61). The New Criticism, of course, emphasizes an art which is not *interested* in life or the World but only in the Word. Such poetry cannot "get life." As Whitman's *Leaves of Grass* makes clear, only a poetry of process can re-produce a man and make him aware of his basically active, i.e., temporal, nature.

Olson argues that "There is only one thing you can do about the kinetic, reenact it." Throughout *The Maximus Poems*, he reproduces the actions of men, of lives—his own and those of others, like John Smith. By doing so he gets through the veil of words, and images to the things themselves and thus breaks through to the beginning of the circuit of creativity:

art is the only twin life has—its only valid metaphysic. Art does not seek to describe but to enact. And if man is once more to possess intent in his life, and to take up the responsibility implicit in his life, he has to comprehend his own process as intact, from outside, by way of his skin, in, and by his own powers of conversion, out again. (*SW*, 61)

Man is to "re-gain" or "re-veal" his potential to act from "intent" and not from habit or "tradition." But Modern society, based on a metaphysics of static description—through concept and image—lulls the mind of man into a state of ease in which his ability to act "intentionally" is abrogated. (I will return to a discussion of intent in a later treatment of Olson's notion of "care.")

Olson is clearly aware of what is lost in Modern society, but is not as clearly certain of how to go about getting back the potentialities of acting in the world with conscious intent:

> And I am asked—ask myself (I, too, covered
> with the gurry of it) where
> shall we go from here, what can we do
> when even the public conveyances
> sing?
>   how can we go anywhere,
> even cross-town
>   how get out of anywhere . . .
>   (*MxP*, 13)

"Song 2" of "The Songs of Maximus" poses precisely the question of direction: which way to go to find an alternative, an "anywhere" that is free of "the bodies / all buried / in shallow graves?" (*MxP*, 13).

As Olson quickly discovers, the *public* ways out are themselves taken over by the false singing of the electrically produced song of the trolley cars. The poet is "covered" with the rottenness of the "pejorocracy" and needs to find a nonpublic, non-traditional way to go. For Whitman, the road to travel was easily found, since in America there was still quite a "newing." But one hundred years later, Whitman's heir, who wants desperately to travel, to begin making the connections with the world which will trigger the "circuit" of creation, must first un-earth a way to go.

"Song 3" suggests the two most important ways which Olson discovers. He goes back into himself, his family, his locale, and its history by first attending with some care to the specifics of the world around him:

> This morning of the small snow
> I count the blessings, the leak in the faucet
> which makes the sink time, the drop
> of the water on water as sweet
> as the Seth Thomas
> in the old kitchen
> my father stood in his drawers to wind (always
> he forgot the 30th day, as I don't want to remember
> the rent
>   (*MxP*, 14)

Rather obviously, this song connects the specific initial encounter with an insignificant object in the world with a memory which it triggers. The circuit begins in this moment. The poet accepts the "energy," the emotional value of the falling water. The immediate data of the snow and water enter through the senses and encounter the poet's "inner energy . . . his dreams, for example, his thoughts, . . . his desires, sins, hopes, fears, faiths, loves" (*SW*, 60). The particulars of "external reality" contact the "inner energy" so proximally that the degree to which man and nature are one emerges quite clearly.

The "mind" immediately works upon "what is," the "inner" and "outer," the "one," and transforms the act of the moment into the language of the moment. In "Human Universe," Olson insists upon writing a poetry in which the language is "the act of the instant" and not "language as the act of thought about the instant" (*SW*, 54). The latter is at best discourse or the "suck of symbol" (*SW*, 61). Olson hopes to differentiate his poetry from Wordsworth's poetic intent to write

from "emotion recollected in tranquility."[3] He wants to get the event down quickly before any of its energy is lost. His poems are like the Maya he admires so much: "O, they were hot for the world they lived in, these Maya, hot to get it down the way it was—the way it is, my fellow citizens" (*SW*, 66).

Olson's poems do not work reflexively, that is, they are not the records of events "recollected" and "described" in a later moment. The temporal-spatial distance from the initial energy of the moment's encounter and thought which is necessary for such tranquil "recollection" is the basis of the aesthetic distance which breaks the circuit Olson considers the basis of creativity. Delay cuts the poet off from the world and his sensual impressions of it and, thus, separates the mind from "what is." The imagination in recollection works only on what is contained in memory, "purified" of its immediacy, and, thus, "cool." The heat of the moment of discovery and encounter provides the violent energy needed to break down the hardened tradition which threatens to enclose all experience within its autotelically determined frame. The passage of time eases the strain on the poet's imagination in the process of experience and, after the experience is *all over*, when it is *completed*, and *finished*, when it can be *seen all at once* from the vantage point of the knowledge of the "end," it is more amenable to traditional forms and concepts. Recollection allows for an easier time of covering-up the discovery of the moment. In the moment of discovery, when all is *not clear* to the poet, when his knowledge is "incomplete," the authentic poet of process, must be prepared to remain in doubt and uncertainty. He must possess "Negative Capability."[4]

Keats, of course, is a major source of Olson's awareness of the nature of the tradition as cover-up. Along with Heraclitus, whose fragments pepper Olson's work, Keats articulates the dissatisfaction of the poet of immediate process with the intellectual coercers of the "tradition," with those whose will to know is so powerful that, like Coleridge, they will let go the insight of the moment because of their "irritable reaching after fact and reason." In Olson's poems we can see the condemnation of those poets who create in recollection and those who do not possess negative capability. To create a poem about the act of the moment, by means of the greater "knowledge" provided by the awareness of the "whole" experience, is to coerce language and experience into forms which are not "true" to the "way it is." Olson sees a deep contradiction between the truth of the experience of the moment and any record or description of that event made afterwards. Olson realizes that truth is discovery, is what occurs in the process of opening-up the world in immediate experience. Language which in the moment reenacts the discovery is thus "truer" than language which records after the immediacy of the discovery cools. Olson's poems are ongoing disclosures with sudden changes in direction, abrupt discontinuities, frequent repetitions, and fragmented linguistic structures. As Olson argues in "Projective Verse," every kinetic poem must move unceasingly from one perception to the next without concern for logic or preconceived order. The only guideline is to "get down" the experience as it is and while it is "hot":

> ONE PERCEPTION MUST IMMEDIATELY AND DIRECTLY LEAD TO A FURTHER PERCEPTION. It means exactly what it says, is a matter of, at *all* points (even, I should say, of our management of daily reality as of the daily work) get on with it, keep moving, keep in, speed, the nerves, their speed, the perceptions, theirs, the acts, the split second acts, the whole business, keep it moving as fast as you can, citizen. And if you also set up as a poet, USE USE USE the process at all points, in any

given poem always, always one perception must must must MOVE, INSTANTER, ON ANOTHER! (SW, 17)

The opening of "Song 3" of "The Songs of Maximus" is an example of the discontinuous nature of Olson's poetry of discovery. It begins the poem's movement, as Heidegger might say, along-a-way. There is a complete break with the language and problems of "Song 2." The "snow" and the "faucet" present themselves and they are immediately recorded. The poet breaks away from his meditation upon the weaknesses of the society and its language and is drawn to a world of things. These objects in turn spontaneously trigger the memory and love of Olson's "inner energy." And the circuit of action begins. In this moment, the poet has found his way. Yet, clearly, he does not know where he is going along this route. Following the presentation of the sink and clock whose measure and time contrast to the music and song of the pejorocracy, the poet's reverie of his father is itself disrupted. The path leads him to his childhood house, and lets him double back somewhat upon his earlier theme, the artificiality of our culture: the house in which there was love and energy now belongs to "Congoleum."

"Song 3" moves back to previous themes and images, but always by going forward to new ex-posures, new dis-coveries. Although Olson's poems often turn a quick look backward, they do not gather the past into themselves as they progress toward a future goal. A New Critical poem accretes meaning from interconnected patterns. The projective poem often changes direction with each discovery the poet makes on the way. But it never means a halt in the progress, an arrival at some end. Like Whitman, who, after his amazing poetic victory in the face of death in "Out of the Cradle," Olson never comes to a standstill; he never rests at a given point. His poems cannot stop in this way because they move to no *telos*; indeed, Olson's poems, as "reenactments" of life reveal that there is no end, no goal, no *telos*.

Following the brief "aside" on the "house," "Song 3" picks up on the fact that the dripping faucet does not work, does not do its job. At this point, the poem looks backward, but records the discovery of the poet who suddenly "sees" the potential significance of these mechanical failures:

> Or the plumbing,
> that it doesn't work, this I like, have even used paper
>   clips
> as well as string to hold the ball up And flush it
> with my hand
>   But that the car doesn't, that no moving
>   thing moves
> without that song I'd void my ear of, the music-
>   kracket
> of all ownership . . .
>
>   (MxP, 14)

Olson resists immediately transforming these details into any abstract assertion. The sudden shift of the poet's attention to the plumbing is an example of how his poems move rapidly from one perception to another. The abrupt turn to the broken car keeps the poem and poet, as well as the eye and mind of the reader, constantly in motion. Appropriately, the broken-down toilet is presented in fragments of sentences and images. No particular detail gains any privileged significance of symbol or allegory. Each part remains what it is, no more and no less. The "heat" of the immediate perception is transmitted by the fragmentary and hurried language which insistently violates the sentence and the formality of a "completed" thought. But quite typically, the abrupt transformation from the broken toilet to the malfunctioning car triggers the ideas of motion and noise.

These notions, combined with the fact that the car is a means of conveyance, return the poem termporarily to the theme of the first two songs: the corruption of language in a commercial society. Language and capitalism are once again explicitly connected. The poet has found new evidence of this particular corruption. He has paradoxically "discovered" something he "already" "knew." Attention to detail, following the way wherever it leads him, brings Olson to the personal uncovering of evidence of the pejorocracy in one of the most common assumptions of our culture: the right to private ownership.

Yet, the poem does not pause over this "discovery," this concrete repetition of something already abstractly known. Despite the increase in awareness which comes with this passage, the poem is immediately diverted to a new perception:

> Holes
> in my shoes, that's all right, my fly
> gaping, me out
> at the elbows, the blessing
>   that difficulties are once more
>   (MxP, 14)

In *Being and Time*, Martin Heidegger argues that not until instruments begin to fail as such do we become aware of their independent existence and being. Analogously, as I have argued in chapter two, not until the "tradition" no longer works does it become evident that the "tradition" actually obscures rather than reveals. Olson in "Song 3" senses or dis-covers the same phenomenon. The smooth working of the "pejorocracy" lulls and greases the mind and senses so that the poet is not even aware that there are normal mental and sensual functions which are being denied him. But when the society and its support, its ground, that is, "tradition," begins to disintegrate, then its pernicious cover-up becomes clear.

The singing car and trolley of this poem indicate how completely the "pejorocracy" corrupts motion and direction. The electronic and mechnical Sirens obscure the risks and particularities—as well as the potential rewards—of traveling along a road marked by difficulties. Olson would "void [his] ear" of all this racket, all its noise and exploitation. And he finds as an alternative to this commercialization and ownership a poorer way. The closest details of his dress reveal to him how in his own being as a poet who refuses to submit to the "plentitude" of society he has an alternative present at hand. Like Lear who must strip off the trappings of his kingly role to see what lies closest to him—Cordelia's love and Goneril's hate—Olson must recognize in his own unaccommodated state "the blessing / that difficulties are once more."

The way which must be taken to find that "anywhere" that has no shallow graves appears to be the poet's denial of any compromise with the crowd that surrounds him. Constant attention to his own position in the world and the details about him keep the poet on the path to some renewed dis-covery. The intrusion of the break-downs of the system makes him aware of its ontological and poetic inadequacies. But only his vigilance, his own refusal to seek accommodation, provides the necessary disruption which keeps the poet on the way. "Difficulties" cannot be smoothed over. They draw the poet back to himself and his world. Most importantly, they compel the mind and senses to confront phenomena which have not *already* been digested and articulated in the language of the "they." Thus, difficulties are the means to dis-covery. They reveal the precariousness of man in the world and deny him the fiction of ease and comfort.

Following this discovery, Olson allows himself to summarize the value of his "vision." Yet even the seemingly "abstract" section of this poem grows out of a very specific and—to the poem and poet—new concrete detail. The general statements which "end" "Song 3" emerge from Olson's memory of and reading in *Gammer Gurton's Needle* and Ezra Pound's *Cantos:*[5]

> "In the midst of plenty, walk
> as close to
> bare
>   In the face of sweetness,
> piss
>   In the time of goodness,
> go side, go
> smashing, beat them, go as
> (as near as you can
>
> tear
>
> In the land of plenty, have
> nothing to do with it
>   take the way of
> the lowest,
> including
> your legs, go
> contrary, go
> sing

(MxP, 14–15)

The poem moves toward this articulation of a recurring theme. The "discovery" of the way of detail, of failed instruments, and of the importance of difficulties reaches its fullest statement and its most general significance in this passage.

"Song 3" moves from one detail and perception relentlessly to another. On the way, the poet opens up the existence and being of these things, not in their instrumentality, but in their thingness. At each encounter, the themes are basically the same; but they are repeated with an increase in the poet's awareness at each point. In the immediate elements of his life and history, the poet finds "evidence" for what is "really" true. As I have pointed out in chapter three about Kierkegaard's theory of the stages, temporal repetition—as opposed to New Critical "recollection"—always exposes greater degrees of awareness. Each "stage" of a repetition brings the poet closer to "voiding" himself of the "musickracket" of the "pejorocracy."

Basically, in poems like "Song 3," the poet's confrontation with details and particulars strips off layers of verbal interference maintained by both the tradition and our society. As a result of each "un-layering," the poet "sees" various things directly. In the larger context of *The Maximus Poems*, Olson destroys the images, concepts, and preconceptions which intrude between man and world and, thus, the poems allow the unity of man and nature to become apparent. Almost any Olson poem exemplifies his linguistic breakdown of the traditional privilege accorded the completed sentence. Further, most of his poems refuse to employ the "image" in the ironic senses of Modern literature and criticism. Most importantly, in Olson's *Maximus Poems*, as in "Song 3," things are not apprehended spatially, all at once, to provide static relief from change. Rather they insist upon process as *the* defining characteristic of life. They impose upon their readers the primordiality of time. By refusing to be completed, by breaking open the completed sentence, by denying creation via "recollection," they escape the "tradition," which reduces art to the formal completion of life and life's defense against disorder.

Olson's implicit attack on "recollection" results from his awareness of the fictional nature of the "tradition's" version of itself, of its "history." To give itself certainty and validity, the "tradition" assumes that its own "history" of itself is privileged. Yet, Olson is aware that it is impossible "to know what happened, even to oneself" (*SVH*, 19). In language reminis-

cent of Wallace Stevens, he writes: "At no point outside a fiction can one be sure" (*SVH*, 19). Like Kierkegaard, Olson knows that memory, "recollection," always lies because it oversimplifies. To order the past into comprehensible and understandable structures, the memory selectively removes from consciousness both points of ambiguity and any painful contradictions. "Recollection" explains the events "leading up to" the present, the "end," in order to make sense of their order and to clarify how "history" brings us to "where we are." Again, like both Stevens and Kierkegaard, Olson realizes that the attempt by "historians" to order the past is an aesthetic impulse, a desire to find a "certainty" which the events themselves in their unformed immediacy do not possess.

Thus, *The Maximus Poems*, quite consciously, disrupt the continuity of poetic "tradition," insofar as it is defined by "recollection" and "closed form." Like "The Songs of Maximus," *The Maximus Poems* undercut the "tradition's" claim to certainty not only by suggesting its "fictional" and therefore unprivileged, blinded nature, but by suggesting alternatives which the "tradition" omits in order to make itself work. It is in the latter that Olson differentiates himself from Wallace Stevens. Stevens feels we have no choice but to believe in a fiction since *everything* is a "fiction" and, to quote Heidegger's "What Is Metaphysics," "nothing else."[6] Olson, however, is similar to Heidegger in a different way. While, like Stevens, he disputes the "tradition's" distinction between "history" and "fiction," he agrees with Heidegger, and prefigures de Man, in claiming that there are mystified and demystified stances toward the world: "In other words there are TWO stances. Always are. It isn't a question of fiction versus knowing. 'Lies' are necessary in both—that is the HI-Magination" (*SVH*, 19). The "tradition" is mystified in its claim that its "history" of itself is "certain" and privileged. Olson, however, is "demystified" in realizing that there is truth and error in all "historical" claims.

Notes

I use the following abbreviations: *The Maximus Poems* (New York: Jargon/Corinth Books, 1960), *MxP*; *The Special View of History*, ed. Ann Charters (Berkeley: Oyez, 1970), *SVH*; *Selected Writings of Charles Olson*, ed. Robert Creeley (New York: New Directions, 1966), *SW*.

1. *Journal of American Studies* 5 (1971), pp. 304–5.
2. Philips, p. 296.
3. This famous phrase of Wordsworth's comes, of course, from the "Preface to the *Lyrical Ballads*": "I have said that poetry is the spontaneous overflow of powerful feelings; it takes its origin from emotion recollected in tranquility." While the first half of this quotation seems to contradict the second and to suggest that Olson misunderstands Wordsworth, the full development of this idea makes clear that Wordsworth understood the newly generated emotion to be free of all unsettling and painful elements: "all these [rhyme, meter, ordinary language] imperceptibly make up a complex feeling of delight, which is of the most important use in tempering the painful feeling always found intermingled with powerful descriptions of the deeper passions." *Poetical Works*, ed. Thomas Hutchinson, rvsd. Ernest de Sélincourt (New York: Oxford University Press, 1969), p. 740.
4. *The Letters of John Keats*, ed. Hyder Edward Rollins (Cambridge: Harvard University Press, 1958), vol. 1, p. 193.
5. C.F. Butterick, "An Annotated Guide to *The Maximus Poems* of Charles Olson," unpublished dissertation (1970), p. 13. See also, Butterick, A *Guide to the Maximus Poems of Charles Olson* (Berkeley: University of California Press, 1978). Since this expanded version of Butterick's dissertation appeared after I completed this chapter, I continue to refer to the original dissertation. The arrangement of Butterick's text facilitates any cross-reference between the two versions.
6. *Existence and Being*, trans. Werner Brock (Chicago: Henry Regnery, 1949), pp. 327–29.

EUGENE O'NEILL

1888–1953

Eugene Gladstone O'Neill, dramatist, was born in New York City on October 16, 1888. His father, James O'Neill, was a popular romantic actor, who exposed his son to the theatre at a very early age. O'Neill entered Princeton in 1906, after attending a Catholic boarding school and a preparatory school in Connecticut, but within a year he had flunked out and had taken up an adventurous life, working variously as a seaman, gold prospector, journalist, and actor.

O'Neill wrote his first play *The Web* in the winter of 1913–14 and by 1916 he had become associated with the Provincetown Players, who in the following three years produced many of his plays, including *Bound East for Cardiff* (1916) and *The Moon of the Caribbees* (1918). His first great success came in 1920 with the Broadway production of *Beyond the Horizon*, which won O'Neill a Pulitzer Prize. He followed this with several other naturalistic tragedies with American settings; these were not tragedies of destiny or fate, but of personal psychology. They include *Chris Christopherson* (1920), rewritten as *Anna Christie* (1921; Pulitzer Prize); *Diff'rent* (1920); *Gold* (1921); *The Straw* (1921); and *The First Man* (1922). O'Neill also created two experiments in symbolic expressionism: *The Emperor Jones* (1920) and *The Hairy Ape* (1922). After *The Hairy Ape* he returned to a naturalistic approach with *All God's Chillun Got Wings* (1924) and *Desire under the Elms* (1924).

The political *Fountain* (1925) was followed by *The Great God Brown* (1926), in which masks are worn; *Lazarus Laughed* (1927), featuring choral chanting; *Marco Millions* (1928); *Strange Interlude* (1928, Pulitzer Prize), in which O'Neill experimented with a stream-of-consciousness technique; and *Dynamo* (1929). *Mourning Becomes Electra*, an adaptation of Aeschylus' theme, followed in 1931. *Ah, Wilderness!* (1933), a light comedy, and *Days without End* (1934) were the last plays to be produced for many years, although O'Neill worked on several others, including *The Iceman Cometh* (1946). In 1936 he was awarded the Nobel Prize.

O'Neill's masterpiece *A Long Day's Journey into Night*, a semi-autobiographical family tragedy, was written in 1940–41, and posthumously produced in 1956. *A Moon for the Misbegotten*, his last play, was written by 1943 and produced in 1947. After O'Neill's death in 1953 a number of other plays were posthumously produced; *Hughie*, a one-act character study, was acted in 1958, and two plays from a projected eleven-play cycle, *A Tale of Possessors Self-Dispossessed*, were also produced: *A Touch of the Poet* (published 1957, acted 1958) and its sequel *More Stately Mansions* (1964). His *Poems* were collected in 1980.

In creating a drama which attempted to confront powerful social and moral issues realistically and with force, O'Neill, despite his debt to Strindberg and Ibsen and his somewhat simplistic use of the ideas of Freud, Jung, and others, made an original contribution to the American stage, and has generally been considered his country's greatest playwright.

Personal

I was looking at Eugene O'Neill's face today while I sat there with him in the apartment on Grove Street that belonged to Eleanor Fitzgerald. She was the manager and practical mind and inexhaustible friend of the Provincetown Playhouse, and had telephoned me that O'Neill had not been well and had asked her to tell me that he wished I would come and see him.

A handsome face on which for the moment there was a certain shade of brutality, which seemed to change immediately into a kind of delicate and fierce withdrawal—or shall I say a proud shadow?—and also a kind of covered entreaty. The mouth was both sensuous and hard; but when he smiled the effect was boyish and fresh—a stretch of white teeth—curiously candid and shy at the same time—the sudden engaging air of a child. As was usual in his case I felt vaguely an emotion of pity and defense. Though there was nothing particularly to defend him against, I wanted to defend him, to take his part.

I dwell on this for the simple reason that the more I have thought of the matter the more assured I am that some such similar feeling is behind what many of those who champion Eugene O'Neill's work bring to him. Among his plays at times the story limps, or the texture of the style is flat and barren, or

the thought is creaking; but at the heart of it we sense a pressure, a spasm of desire and sanity or torment and madness that leaves us defending the play, swearing by the author, going to his aid with whatever glamor or common sense we can muster; and meanwhile with a half-subconscious admission, deep down in ourselves, that, even if awkwardly, he can feel compassion where we feel only some tragic situation.

You heard of harsh times with him, violent even, especially when he was drinking. As to this drinking of Eugene O'Neill's there were plainly earlier years when he seemed to have gone to it with a vengeance, and in these later years there had been scenes, ructions, ferocities not easy to forget; but it happened that I never saw him in the worst of such spells, and the time came presently when he was not drinking at all, strictly nothing.

I have sometimes on second thought wondered whether he was dramatic enough, shrewd enough as regards his own legend to let it stand his being a drunk, a wild drunk, just as he let stand the legend of a poor young artist, though he spent a good deal of money in his time. (His father had something of a fortune, and his brother, who was said to have died of drink, must have left him something.)

As to shrewdness, I remember once at dinner with Robert

Edmond Jones, the leading stage designer of his time, that I said something in praise of shrewdness. Bobby went straight into a horror at the mere thought, a good Puritan conscience objecting. On a higher plane, if you like, it reminded me of the good man who said he was going to Boston to get drunk, and oh, how he dreaded it! But what I said was that to be shrewd did not mean that you had to be crooked; the highest use of shrewdness was, if you believed in something, to use the very best of your brains in its behalf. But that semi-dishonest Puritan morality of Bobby's refused to yield an inch. Later on I told Gene about this conversation—it had been a strangely long argument, futile on my part. All he said, drily, was, "If you want to know how shrewd Bobby is ask him to tell you how to put something over."

There was always a kind of sweetness or young quality in Eugene O'Neill's relation to me, though far back of it I could feel at times a core of resentment at the world as people live it, a touch even of hate. But this I got from the plays perhaps, rather than from himself directly. It belonged to some crisis in his mind or to some play he was working at rather than to his habitual temper. A certain sense of helplessness had something to do with it, I thought. He had to summon his fiercer will, had to violate himself as it were, in order to create that effect of emotional power that the best remembered passages in his plays afford.

More than any other of our playwrights he was concerned, as he said himself, not with plays about man's relation to man, but with man's relation to something larger than man and beyond him. On the one hand it could be said of Eugene O'Neill, as Gide said of himself, that the idea of death followed his thought as the shadow follows the body. In various plays, on the other hand, there seems to be a debate as to whether this suffering and aspiration toward something larger than man and beyond him is justified or whether it is merely his own desire and rage. Vergil in the *Aeneid* has a like thought when Nisus, the young soldier, says to his friend Euryalus: "Do the gods put this ardor into our hearts, or does his own fierce longing become to each man a god?"—STARK YOUNG, "Eugene O'Neill: Notes from a Critic's Diary" (1923), *Harper's*, June 1957, pp. 66–67

I have been reading his plays in advance manuscript form for, now, something like sixteen years and, sometimes, long before they have seen the light of theatrical performance, have expressed my favorable or unfavorable opinion of them to him. He has sulked on occasion, has even called me a damned fool, when we have differed, but it has meant no more to him than it has to me when, for instance, upon reading the advance manuscript of one of my recent books, he has expressed a very decidedly unfavorable opinion of it and I, in turn, have called him a damned fool. We are, I suppose, friends for better or worse, till the water-wagon or continued bad work in the case of either doth us part, and that—disturbing as it may be to some—is that.

When I started to confect this chapter on him, I had an inclination to give it the title, "The New O'Neill." I refrained for the reason that, though the O'Neill of today is a considerably changed man from the O'Neill I have known in past years, no man ever really changes so greatly as to warrant any such absurd politico-journalistic caption. Yet that there has been a change in the old O'Neill is unmistakable.

When I first knew him, back in the earlier Nineteen Hundreds, he exuded all the gay warmth of an Arctic winter. To say that he was a melancholy, even a morbid, fellow is to put it mildly. Life to him in those days—and not only life but his stock-taking of his own soul—was indistinguishable from a serial story consisting entirely of bites from mad dogs, fatal cancers and undertakers disappointed in love. His look suggested a man who was just about to guzzle a vase of $C_{33}H_{45}No_{12}$, and his conversation suggested a man who *had* guzzled it. In addition, he was chronically so nervous and physically so restive that he generally gave one the impression, what with his constant sharp, jerky glances to the left and right, that he was imminently on the worried look-out for the police. When he took hold of a highball glass, his hand shook so that he sounded like a Swiss bell ringer. In the last four years he has regained a calm and tranquillity of such proportions that their very *adagissimo* induces in one all the nervousness and restiveness that used to be his. Nothing any longer disturbs or remotely agitates him. He is at peace with himself and with the world.

One of the greatest recent changes that has come over him, however, is a recapture of the humor that was in him in those distant days before even he began to write, in the days that I have described in the volume called *The Intimate Notebooks of George Jean Nathan*, when, at the dives known as Jimmy the Priest's and the Hell Hole, where he made his residence, he was part and parcel of such low buffoonery as has seldom been chronicled in the biography of *homo literarum Americanus*. There was a long period when humor and the O'Neill drama were strangers—the period when he himself was in the spiritual, mental and physical dumps—although even then, despite the seeming skepticism of his critics, there were occasional fleeting symptoms of that grim humor which was in him in the old, previous days and which was struggling pathetically and often baffled to come again to the surface. But the new O'Neill humor is not a grim humor; it is a kindly and gentle and often very tender humor, wholly unlike any that has fitfully edged its way into even those of his plays that have not been abruptly catalogued by his critics as "morbid," "gloomy," "lugubrious," or what not. Much of his prospective work must surely testify to the fact. ⟨. . .⟩

O'Neill is the hardest worker that I have ever known, and, in the roster of my writing acquaintances, I have known a number of pretty hard workers. There isn't a minute of the day that his thoughts are not in some way or another on his work. Even when sound asleep, his wife informs me, he will once in a while grunt and be heard to mumble something about Greek masks, Freudian psychology, or Philip Moeller. Not so long ago, swimming with him after two hours in what seemed to me to be waters still at least sixty dreadful miles from the safe Georgia shore, and with both our stomachs full of wet salt, he turned over on his back for a moment, ejected a good part of the Atlantic Ocean from his mouth and told me that he had just been thinking it over and had decided to change one of the lines in his second act. I have eaten, drunk, walked, motored, bicycled, slept, bathed, shaved, edited, run, worked, played, even sung with him, and it has been a rare occasion, take my word for it, when he has not interrupted whatever we were doing to venture this or that observation on this or that manuscript he was then busied upon. He may be reading the morning newspaper, or studying the Washington financial letter service to which he subscribes, or lying half-asleep on the beach, or fishing for pompano, or gobbling a great bowl of chop suey, or hugging his wife, or openly envying some new-fangled sport shirt you may happen to be wearing, or making a wry face over Dreiser's poetry, or doing anything else under God's sun, but you may be sure that what he is thinking about all the time and turning over in his mind is something concerned with his playwriting.

A dozen times a day he will stop in the middle of a

sentence and, without a word of apology or explanation, depart, head dejected, to his writing room to make note of a line or an idea that has just occurred to him. He has, at the present moment, notebooks full of enough dramatic themes, dialogue and what not to fill all the theatres in New York for the next twenty years, with sufficient material left over to fill most of those in London, Paris, and Stockholm. I not long ago asked him about two or three rather fully developed ideas for plays that he had told me of a few years before at LaPlessis, in France, where he was then living. "Oh, I don't think I'll ever do anything about them," he allowed. "I've got a couple of dozen or so new ones I begin to like better."

O'Neill's chief professional concern in more recent years has been the problem of casting his plays to his own satisfaction. The dearth of good actors, principally in the male department, causes him no end of anxiety. So much, indeed, that not long ago he confided to me that his ambition, once he gets enough money to be safe, is not to permit his future plays to be produced but simply to publish them, uncorrupted by careless and obfuscating acting, in book form. "You can say what you want to about the theatre back in my old man's time," he held forth; "you can laugh at all those tin-pot plays and all that, but, by God, you've got to admit that the old man and all the rest of those old boys were *actors!*"—GEORGE JEAN NATHAN, "O'Neill," *Passing Judgments*, 1935, pp. 114–20

I first met Eugene O'Neill at Provincetown in the summer of 1917. He lived on the edge of the ocean in an abandoned Coast Guard Station, which was formerly the home of the famous Mabel Dodge, and to reach his home it was necessary to trudge for about three miles across the sand dunes. Rumor had it that Robert Edmond Jones had decorated the house in the gay blue-and-white color scheme which it then wore, and the large room which formerly contained the coast guard lifeboat was now the living room.

On the beach just below the house was the wreck of a large schooner, and O'Neill, costumed in a bathing suit, took me onto the beach where, somewhat superfluously, I emptied the sand out of my shoes. The resounding surf, the background of the wrecked sailing ship, and the lithe, muscular body of O'Neill, his dark Irish eyes set deep in his sun-tanned face, made an appropriate O'Neill setting for my first meeting with our foremost playwright, with whose destiny my own was later linked for so many years. We talked over the production of *In the Zone* by the Washington Square Players, after which he invited me to join him in a swim. This I refused, being no swimmer in a high surf (or even in a low one), whereupon O'Neill plunged in and displayed his prowess with a swift overarm stroke of which he was very proud. Like Bernard Shaw, O'Neill's favorite sport is swimming; indeed it is the only form of athletics in which he has indulged during the time I have known him. My last view of him, as I bade him farewell at this first meeting, was his silhouette at the side of the house, the ocean behind him and the wind blowing his hair awry. It was also my last view of the old Coast Guard Station, for the restless Atlantic swallowed it up a few years later and not a trace now remains but the endless ocean and the lonely dunes.

Ever since I read O'Neill's first volume of one-act plays, I regarded him as our outstanding American dramatist. In the days of the Washington Square Players I helped bring about the rapprochement between that organization and O'Neill, which resulted in our producing his *In the Zone* which was later booked in vaudeville by Al Lewis and Max Gordon. O'Neill once expressed the opinion that the Provincetown players were artists while the Washington Square Players were an "uptown" commercial theatre and not worthy to be regarded as competi-

tion. We in turn regarded the Provincetown Players as "amateurs" in everything except their playwrights, O'Neill and Susan Glaspell.

I was determined to bring the Theatre Guild and Eugene O'Neill together, but all my early attempts ended in failure. 'Gene, on his side, wanted to work with the Guild.

One day in 1919 not long after *John Ferguson* had opened, as I was standing in the Garrick Theatre lobby, Agnes O'Neill, then 'Gene's wife, came in with a manuscript of his new play, *The Straw*. "'Gene wants you to have this," she said to me. As I left the lobby, one of the Guild directors asked if he could read the play over the week end. A few days later I asked for it. "I returned it to O'Neill," he said. "It's all about consumptives. I decided we'd never do it." I was furious. I tried to get the play back, but it had already been sent to another management. ⟨. . .⟩

Later on, O'Neill, Robert Edmond Jones and Kenneth MacGowan formed a producing firm which had considerable success and which produced O'Neill's *Welded*, *All God's Chillun Got Wings*, *Desire under the Elms* and *The Fountain*. O'Neill went to live in Bermuda and came to New York from time to time.

In the spring of 1927 I suffered from a severe cold and was advised by my doctor to take a couple of weeks off to recuperate. By this time the producing firm with which O'Neill had associated himself had dissolved, and O'Neill spent most of his time in Bermuda. I had a hunch that a visit to Bermuda might not only restore me to health but also enable me to restore the personal relation which had formerly existed between O'Neill and myself, and which had very naturally become cloudy for the reasons I have explained above. My hunch turned out to be correct.

O'Neill welcomed me warmly and we had some talks about the possibility of the Guild producing *Marco Millions*. From that he went on to discuss the future of the American theatre, and what he hoped to contribute toward it. Walking up and down the sandy beach near his white-roofed coral house which had been built by a Seventeenth-Century privateer, and stood at the edge of the sea, 'Gene explained that he was experimenting with ways and means to break down "realism" in the theatre, and had just finished a play in which the characters not only talked to one another but also spoke their thoughts in a form of aside which he thought the audience would accept. The idea fascinated me and I asked him if I might read the play, which he informed me was called *Strange Interlude*. He also told me that it would take six hours to play it. In view of our experience with *Back to Methuselah*, this did not daunt me.

A few days later I was invited to O'Neill's home for a swim and dinner afterward, and I spent the evening with him discussing the theme of the play. He told me that he had already promised it to a well-known American actress who was his first choice, but that if I liked the play and she did not, I might have it for the Guild. Meanwhile, I could read it and let him know what I thought of it. He then handed me the first six acts of the manuscript, which I still possess. It was half again as thick as an ordinary play, for not only was it a double-length play, but so long that nearly forty pages were subsequently cut out of it. Clutching the precious manuscript to my bosom I returned in the horse cab which had been ordered for me (there were no automobiles in Bermuda at the time) and drove along the shore road in a gale which at times seemed so strong that I feared horse cab, *Strange Interlude* and myself would all be blown together into the sea.

I went to bed intending to read at least part of the play

before I fell asleep; the storm outside grew more and more violent as the play grew more and more exciting. The tropical thunder and lightning, and the fierce howling of the gale which began to assume hurricane proportions, failed to interrupt me. All night long I read and read, and at four o'clock in the morning, my eyes strained and throbbing, I finished the sixth act. Before I went to sleep I examined my feelings about the play as far as I had read. I judged it one of the greatest plays of all time.

The storm died down during the night, and the next morning was bright and clear; as soon as I was awake I telephoned 'Gene and told him how enthusiastic I was about the play. He invited me over to his home again. This time he definitely promised me that if the actress to whom he had offered the play did not care to do it (and he thought there were certain reasons why she might not), the Theatre Guild could have it. Then he gave me a breath-taking exhibition of his overarm stroke which I photographed with my cine-kodak. 'Gene at this time was about thirty-eight years old, and at the height of his mental and physical powers. He was built like an athlete, his deep black eyes set in a sunburnt Irish face, as handsome as one could hope to see anywhere, and the skin of his lean body was the color and texture of mahogany with underlying muscles of whipcord. At no time before or since have I seen him in such good health. I luckily recorded his appearance at the time with my movie camera.

After my return to New York, I wrote 'Gene telling him I had stirred up some interest in *Marco Millions* and asking him to send us a copy of *Strange Interlude*. On the arrival of the manuscript, I circulated it among my fellow directors. To my horror, they did not all share my enthusiasm. One of them even went so far as to say that if all the asides were taken out, the play would be greatly improved. I wanted to choke him, but restrained myself. ⟨. . .⟩

O'Neill, after condensing both *Marco Millions* and *Strange Interlude*, came to New York, and he stayed at our home on Eleventh Street. He was with us for about two weeks, and we went into all phases of the two plays. He saw very few friends while with us but he finally consented to our giving a small party for him. "The reason I avoid parties is because I'm extremely bashful," he told me. "In my younger days I used to drink in order to get up the nerve to meet people. Since I've quit drinking, it's become worse. When I once started, I was like a sailor on shore leave—a holdover from my seafaring days." He told me in Bermuda that he had entirely sworn off drinking, and gave as one reason the effect of alcohol on the brain as explained to him by a doctor friend. "It's just like turning the albumen in your brain into the white of a poached egg!" This vivid and horrible picture made me a hesitant drinker for the many years which have intervened.

During all the time I knew O'Neill, and this goes back to when we were both in our twenties, I never saw him drink any kind of liquor. However, he assured me that he was, in his youth, a notoriously stalwart drinker, and he, in my opinion, built this up into the proportions of a legend. He told the story that at one time he was seated in the Provincetown Playhouse watching one of his plays when a young woman in the seat in front of him remarked to her escort, "Do you know that Eugene O'Neill, the author of this play, is a terrible drunkard?" "No," replied the young man. "Yes, and not only does he drink to excess, but he takes drugs, too." This was too much for 'Gene. "Excuse me, Miss," he said to the young lady, "you are wrong there. I do *not* take drugs!"—LAWRENCE LANGNER, "O'Neill and *Strange Interlude*," *The Magic Curtain*, 1951, pp. 228–35

General

Within little more than a week two plays by Eugene O'Neill have been produced in New York. Both plays are said to have been rewritten from earlier versions. But criticism has nothing to do with that, since it is in their present form that Mr. O'Neill has chosen to give his works to the world. The production of both plays is far more than adequate. In *Anna Christie* (Vanderbilt Theater) the central part is played by Miss Pauline Lord, an unequal but fascinating artist and personality, with haunting subtlety and quiet power; in *The Straw* (Greenwich Village Theater) Mr. Otto Kruger does the best work he has ever done and illustrates the old truth that the test of an actor is the human verisimilitude of his part. Under these circumstances we have an unusual opportunity for the inquiring into the somewhat vexed question of the quality and character of Mr. O'Neill's talent and work.

A group of critics and a group of friends will not allow that any such question exists. A more disinterested vision cannot overlook that goading of the imagination in *Emperor Jones* which Gilpin's acting concealed, the strange psychological leaps in *Diff'rent*, the creaking structure and the cheaply romantic devices of *Gold*. Even in *Beyond the Horizon* there were moments when action and passion were deflected for the sake of a theatric pattern. And the same vital weakness once more disfigures *Anna Christie*. The standard reply begins with the question: "But who else in America has . . . ?" Very well. It is precisely because Mr. O'Neill is a man of high talent and high intellectual integrity that an easy acceptance of very imperfect work is neither a compliment to him nor a service.

His experience of life has been very intense but apparently rather narrow. Upon this experience he has reflected profoundly in the mass but impatiently in detail. His types and motives are recurrent. The seafaring men hover a little on the fringes of life. They are never quite central in significance and the edge of that significance is often dulled by a touch of the fantastic. His women, up to Anna Christie, are romantically and conventionally seen through common fallacies of their changeableness, innocence, and inner dependence. He has kept personally aloof from the theater but family tradition and, it may be, managerial pressure have kept him painfully aware of its supposed exigencies. The superior inner logic of *The Straw* may be attributed to the fact that he wrote the play in five scenes and dispensed with the conventional division into acts. It is clear, at all events, that he conceives his actions both powerfully and philosophically. The moment he begins to write, however, he abandons the leadership of his conception. Somewhere his plays begin to break. There are strange gaps, twists, insufficiencies. He grasps after straws: lover and father of a woman sign up, by coincidence, for the same ship to the same port; a woman is convinced she loves one brother and suddenly discovers that her choice is wrong; an acute and poetic young journalist doesn't see that a very naive and sincere girl has set her whole heart on him (she gives the audience every evidence of her feeling; he stands beside her and watches her and sees nothing; a revolver is flashed for no reason except to heighten the theatric momentum); an obliging storm casts upon a barge a man who, starved in an open boat for three days, recognizes at once in the barge-master's daughter the fated passion of his life. Synopses of O'Neill's plays would need constantly to use such phrases as: "But just at that moment . . . but he (or she) did not realize." Coincidence and cross-purposes prolong his actions, not the iron march of events or the unanswerable necessities of the soul.

Yet he knows that march of events and those necessities. When her wretched, fuddled old father begs for her forgiveness

Anna Christie replies: "Don't bawl about it. There ain't nothing to forgive anyway. It ain't your fault and it ain't mine and it ain't his neither. We're all poor nuts. And things happen. And we just get mixed in wrong, that's all." In that speech and in that moment the essentials of human tragedy are faultlessly set forth. And, indeed, the entire fable of *Anna Christie* was calculated to set them forth; the father's fear and hatred of the sea, his belief that inland good people would guard his child, the poor girl's tragic and ironic history, and its gradual revelation to him. But the incidents used to convey that revelation are gross and palpable devices of the theater from which flash forth, lonely and estranged, the genuinely noble moments that were inherent in the original conception. At the end of the third act Anna Christie speaks the words I have quoted; at the end of the fourth we are asked to envisage her idyllically in a cottage, a lamp in the window, waiting until her father and her husband return from their long voyage which is to bring them forgetfulness of their misery and of her shame. In *The Straw* the action is kept tighter and its development follows a purer line. As always in O'Neill's plays individual characters—here old Carmody and Mrs. Brennan—are superbly done. He has this mark of the creative dramatist, that his minor characters are often as memorable as any. But again the line of action has its terrible wavering and almost breach in the plain debatableness, to put it mildly, of Stephen Murray's utter ignorance of Eileen's feelings toward him. And the line snaps off and does not reach its culminating point when Stephen discovers, too late, that he loved Eileen all the time. In a word, Mr. O'Neill is austere in conception and atmosphere, not in the development of his fables. He interferes with fate. He helps it out. He must learn to be more passive and vigilant. He must keep closer to the humble truth. In it are power, greatness, permanence. He does not need storms, pistols, misunderstandings, coincidences. He, of all our dramatists, can afford to forego them. When he does he will write not memorable fragments but a memorable play.—LUDWIG LEWISOHN, "Eugene O'Neill," *Nation*, Nov. 30, 1921, p. 626

Eugene O'Neill is the one dramatic genius that America has produced. He has spun all of his plays out of his own bowels, lifting them up into the light of eternal cosmic and human laws. From *Bound East for Cardiff* to that superb fantasy of ironic humor and ironic wisdom, *Marco Millions*, one may trace the evolution of the soul of O'Neill, if one has the clairvoyant and imaginative eye.

America is not so badly off when such men as O'Neill, Cabell, Jeffers, Mencken and Gershwin, in utterly different fields, smash their way to a hearing through a dense army of embattled and goose-stepping morons and create audiences of their own. They brought mountains to Mahomet.

Marco Millions is the roots of O'Neill become a gorgeous flower. The black in O'Neill's soul has become gold. Social venom is transmuted into the ironic laughter of the mournful gods. Impotent melancholy bursts into the flame of philosophic wisdom. "Caliban" has become "Hamlet"; "Yank, the Hairy Ape," has become "Kublai Khan," epicurean pessimist.

I glance at the roots of O'Neill and his powerful, vital, pessimistic dramas. He was baptized in the same physical and spiritual hells as Gorky, Dostoievsky, Strindberg and Poe. Beachcomber, adventurer, water-front bum, a "down-and-outer" with sailors and stevedores, a man fired from a hundred jobs, a nervous smash-up that landed him in a sanitarium; a man of melancholic, tragic temperament, having been at Gethsemane and having walked the fiery, alcoholic hells (a more tremendous feat than water-walking), Eugene O'Neill came out of the sanitarium like Lazarus newly risen.

Curious trick of Life! It bludgeons us so that we shall get up and spit back at it. The Eternal Thug pounds us to a pulp and then says whimsically, "Well, I see you're not dead. Get up! You win!" O'Neill got up, spat back at it—and won! When he came out of the sanitarium, he says:

"My mind got a chance to re-establish itself, to digest and evaluate the impressions of many past years, in which one experience had crowded on another with never a second's reflection. I really thought about my life for the first time, about past and future."

This was in 1913, when he was twenty-five. Before this he had not thought, he had not reflected; but the matrix of his plays was moulded. The bed had been made for the birth. He read Ibsen and Strindberg, masters of the Bitter Laugh. But, to me, Ibsen and Strindberg are negligible quantities in his work. O'Neill is too original, too thoroughly individualistic, too singular and too personal in his experiences and reactions to take his hat off to any "master."

What are the characteristics, the mental, moral and social ingredients of O'Neillism as I find them in his plays?

Man versus the Universe: All the characters in the O'Neill plays might be sculpt as the Laocoön. They struggle with the serpents of heredity and environment and are doomed. The universe conspires every moment against the individual. He is born to be toyed with, degraded, slaughtered.

There is no "redemption" anywhere, except perhaps in smug conformity and gold. For those who think, feel and revolt there is awaiting them a Caucasus or a Calvary. Prometheus, Christ and Laocoön are the everlasting symbols of Man.

Irony: Irony is the belly-guffaw of Rabelais frozen in the brain. Or maybe it is only a hard-boiled tear. The irony of O'Neill is the latter—a hard-boiled tear, for it is doubtful whether he is capable of a guffaw.

His is the irony of Strindberg, Ibsen, Octave Mirabeau and Ambrose Bierce. It is an irony implicit in the very nature of his characters—whether it is Yank, the Emperor Jones, Anna Christie or Marco Polo. Each one carries within himself the germ of his own buffoonery.

"Man is the only animal," says Cabell, "that plays the ape to his ideal." In O'Neill's plays we are all apes, trying to imitate ourselves, seen in the mirror of our brain-dreams. But the irony of O'Neill is not bitterly anti-human, as it is in Swift and sometimes in Bierce. At its heart is pity—or at least a vast sympathy—which is always superior to pity.

The Social Conventions: In O'Neill's dramas the conventions, customs and laws of society are everywhere the enemy of the human being. Only the strong, unscrupulous, daring Dionysiac being stands a chance of carrying away the gates of Gaza.

In the first seven years of his life O'Neill "bummed" it with his father, James O'Neill, from town to town, while the latter barnstormed in *Monte Cristo*. He thus began life outside of the conventions. He was the born wastrel, the dissenter, the outsider. But he has no illusions about the fate of the "enemies of society." You are either stoned to death or dragged back to conformity by the undertow in the blood.

The Hairy Ape, Diff'rent, All God's Chillun Got Wings and *Marco Millions* are the most drastic American satires on society of the age. How weak and tepid are *Elmer Gantry* and the infantile *An American Tragedy* of Dreiser alongside of them!

Amoralism: It is in vain that one looks through O'Neill's plays for a "message," and "ethic." He is always, even in some of his earlier unimportant plays, beyond good and evil. He is as inexorable as Sophocles, Thomas Hardy, Turgenev and Strindberg. His characters are chemical and psychological experiments, just as all of us are in the hands of the unseen Master of the Laboratory.

"I am not here to teach—I am here to reveal," might be the motto of the author of *Desire under the Elms*, as it has been of every artist worthy the name from Æschylus to Robinson Jeffers, another great American master of Tragic Beauty.

As to minute analyses of the plays, picking out "weak spots" and all that, I leave to critical gelders who know more about dramatic construction and destruction than I do. About "technique" I care nothing. All original men smash technique and make their own rules.

Some of O'Neill's plays I do not like, notably *The Straw* and *The Great God Brown*. But there are at least ten of his plays that are, to me, tremendous; which brings me to the point where I intended to start, to one of the finest fantastic and philosophical plays of any time, *Marco Millions*, a play which is not only a landmark in the American stage, but which is probably the turning point in the mental evolution of Eugene O'Neill.

In this, his latest play, O'Neill is poet, satirist and thinker. The poetry is inherent in the theme and the atmosphere, which is Oriental. The satire lies in the transposition of the soul of Babbitt into the body of Marco Polo, of Polo Brothers, commercial travelers, of Venice. It is a universalization of an American theme.

O'Neill's irony in this play is no longer bitter. It has become mellow, laughing—a noiseless laugh, it is true; the laugh of the brain, not of the mouth. For of Polo himself and his uncle and his father I will not tell you a line. But Marco is a man you know, that everybody knows, that Homer, Job and Cervantes knew; a man who is as eternal as stupidity, smugness and tabloid editorials. But you will not know him really until you either read or see *Marco Millions*.

And now the irony of the whole matter lies in the fact that he who has shown us in his dramas the hopelessness of the individual's struggle against the universe and society, he who has visioned for us the world as a place of forlorn defeat, has himself stormed and conquered life, a Laocoön who has strangled the serpents, a Prometheus who has shooed away the vultures.

As Cabell would say, that's the very cream (if not the box-office) of the jest!—BENJAMIN DE CASSERES, "Eugene O'Neill: From Cardiff to Xanadu," *TM*, Aug. 1927, pp. 10, 58

One great service was rendered to American literature by George Cram Cook. He founded the Provincetown Theatre, and discovered Eugene O'Neill: a wild boy who had run away from home, and shipped as a sailor, and lived a vagabond life in various ports of the world. He happened to be in Provincetown "with a trunkful of plays," when the little group of radicals were trying to start a proletarian drama. So he got a hearing, which the commercial theatre of Broadway would not have given him in a thousand years. And so the commercial theatre of Broadway has been mocked.

If you think that my understanding of proletarian art is Socialist lectures disguised as novels and soap-box orations preached from a stage, then let me hasten to say that these early plays of O'Neill are part of what I want and have got. Here is a man who writes about the sea, from the point of view of the wage-slaves of the sea, with full knowledge, insight, and pity; yet, so far as I can recall, there is not one word of direct propaganda, hardly even of indirect. Let a man show capitalism as it really is in any smallest corner—as O'Neill has done in *Bound East for Cardiff*—and the message of revolt rings from every sentence.

And then *The Emperor Jones*: the first O'Neill play to reach California, and so the first that I saw on the stage. A rigid Leninist would call that a reactionary play, because it suggests a permanent, hereditary inferiority of the black race. But it is a play so full of pity and terror, of truly magical entrance into the heart of savage humanity, that it operates to humble pride and break down barriers. I have put so much denunciation into this book, you may think me hard to please; so take note that I am ready to praise what I can, and not afraid to hail a masterpiece in my own day. *The Emperor Jones* is my idea of great drama and great poetry, a leap of the imagination and an enlargement of the possibilities of the theatre.

And then *The Hairy Ape*, which my friend Floyd Dell hailed as definitely reactionary. For my part, I am glad of small favors; I note a short scene in a headquarters of the I. W. W., in which these men behave exactly as they would have done in reality. Am I correct in saying that it is the first and only time this has happened in the acted theatre of America? If O'Neill had chosen one of these rebel workers for his hero, I would have been still more pleased, but the theatre public would have waited some years to hear of it. As the author of *Singing Jailbirds*, I do not speak at a guess!

Our great proletarian playwright has grown pessimistic, and is now groping in the fogs of metaphysics. I followed him for an uncomfortable evening in *The Great God Brown*, and when he was through I didn't know what he was driving at, and neither did he—I know it, because he was indiscreet enough to write a long statement on the program, trying to tell me. My counter-statement will be briefer, and nobody will have any doubt what I mean.

Pessimism is mental disease. It is that wherever and under whatever circumstances it appears, in art and philosophy, as in everyday life. It means illness in the person who voices it, and in the society which produces that person. If it continues unchecked in an individual, it is a symptom of his moral breakdown; if it prevails in the literature, art, drama, politics, or philosophy of a nation, it means that nation is in course of decay.

All truly great art is optimistic. The individual artist is happy in his creative work, and in its reception by his public; the public is active and sound, occupied in mastering life and expanding the social forces. It is only when those forces exhaust themselves, that the art public enjoys contemplating moral impotence, and that the individual artist does not know whether life is worth living.

The fact that practically all great art is tragic does not in any way change the above thesis. I have named the three great classic dramas, the *Prometheus Bound* of Aeschylus, the *Prometheus Unbound* of Shelley, and the *Samson Agonistes* of Milton. All three are tragic; but in each case the hero struggles in the cause of a new faith. And the same thing applies to *The Emperor Jones*, and *The Hairy Ape*; their individual protagonists go down to defeat, but they struggle for light, and this impulse is communicated to us.

Capitalist art, when produced by artists of sincerity and intelligence, is pessimistic, because capitalism is dying; it has no morals, and can have none, being the negation of morality in social affairs. Proletarian art is optimistic, because it is only by hope that the workers can act, or dream of acting. Proletarian art has a morality of brotherhood and service, because it is only by these qualities that the masses can achieve their freedom.

And in order to avoid cheap sneers and misunderstandings, let me add that there is a capitalist art of false optimism, based upon the master-class desire to keep the workers in ignorance as to their conditions and prospects. To unmask this art is the first task of the social rebel, and I have tried to do my share of this service.—UPTON SINCLAIR, "The Springs of Pessimism," *Money Writes!*, 1927, pp. 175–77

As "a bit of a poet" O'Neill sought "to transmute his personal and private agonies into something rich and strange, something universal and impersonal." He often achieved the strange, occasionally the rich, seldom the impersonal. As for the universal, he saw especially to that: the abiding theme of his plays was the struggle between life and death. Varied and modified by other themes—the conflict of love and hate, the clash of faith and skepticism, the confusion of illusion and reality—the major theme was metamorphosed into a compulsive preoccupation: the maintenance of an equilibrium between life-sickness and death-fear. Attributing the sickness to loss of faith, O'Neill was convinced that capitulation to disbelief could result only in death, that immersion in the "destructive element" would be suicidal. Accordingly he wrote plays of conversion wherein the ecstatic religiosity was contrived, histrionic in fervor, tentative in finality. In an effort to recover spiritual comfort, that of his early childhood or that of the race, he continued the "backward tendency" that had been revealed in the naturalistic dramas as an aspect of primitivism; for he never truly believed that religion was an illusion with a future.

Love O'Neill identified as the prime component of faith and found it equally elusive and illusory. He had his characters plead for love, profess it, pursue it, but seldom experience it in any but the most elemental way. Human relationships, individual as well as social, were almost invariably discordant. Suffering, among other things, from excessive self-consciousness, O'Neill's heroes, at odds with society, sought the remoteness of the cosmos, the privacy of the womb, the anonymity of the grave. In their neurotic self-obsession they remained indifferent to the suffering of other men while bravely avowing their love for Man. They strove to love much as they struggled to believe, reproaching themselves for their failure, exhausting themselves by their effort. The situation was always one in which both the intellect and the will were powerless; overwhelmed, the victim passed into a state of torpor from which he emerged only in the conversion plays. O'Neill's impotence in these matters caused him to overcompensate, to produce the strained effects which characterized so much of his work—the turgid style, the hysterical intensity.

Although he began his career at the start of the First World War and ended it at the conclusion of the Second, O'Neill paid little heed in his plays either to specific circumstances of world catastrophe or to significant occurrences of two intervening decades of turbulent peace. Sequestering himself, he distilled from modern life the futility, the emptiness, the chaos, and left out the particulars of external events. Yet, preoccupied though he was with the universal and the abstract, he continually revealed the thinly disguised particular and concrete facts of his personal history. A consideration of the details of his private life is far more illuminating than a study of contemporary political and social history. Even a moderately penetrating biography would reveal the extent to which O'Neill's early years—the religious apostasy, the resentment of the father, the deep devotion to the mother—conditioned his personality and motivated his experiences: the troubled conscience, the neurotic sensibility, the emotional and intellectual instability, the antithetical toughness and tenderness; and then the youthful self-imposed period of destitution, the drunkenness, the early sickness, the unhappy marriages, the pervasive life-sickness, the virtually medieval dread of death.

Frequently when the transmutation of personal and private agonies failed to result in something rich and strange it produced something crude and familiar. Such failure was most conspicuous, perhaps, after the attempted synthesis of religion and theatre had begun to disintegrate and as O'Neill attempted "to do big work" by digging "at the roots of the sickness of today." Then he appeared to display something more than a "backward tendency"—as if he were not merely drawn to his early past, but as if he had never really left it. For he seemed somehow under compulsion to repeat, to fulfill, the vapid philosophical and prophetic observation that he had made back in 1912 in the verse called "The Lay of the Singer's Fall":

> When Truth and Love and God are dead
> It is time, full time, to die!

Thus, while O'Neill advanced along technical lines, while he sharpened certain perceptions, while he probed more deeply into some conditions, he failed generally to move intellectually and emotionally beyond early manhood. What is more, language and imagery, appropriate to the content of 1912, continued to be appropriate one, two, and three decades later. O'Neill's style remained not only strained and turgid, but awkward, inarticulate, banal.

Whereas O'Neill thought that he was digging at the roots of the sickness of today, much of the time he was really digging at his own roots. Having conceived Man in his own image, he took for his tragic theme Man suffering, and sought the source of the suffering in such dark areas as existence itself, the ill-conceived universe, the stupidity of the human race. Yet, while keeping himself private he was, without knowing it, in the stream and, like the other great writers of the age, a victim of time out-of-joint. He reacted in his own way not only to the disjunction but to the dehumanization, the inwardness, the spiritual vacuity, the self-destructiveness of the world in which he lived and united with the others in presenting variations of the archetypal waste land image—with men dwelling in oases which they have themselves constructed out of mirages. For anyone dedicated to the writing of tragedy the implications of this world view have been especially disquieting. Faced with what has been called the dilemma of modern tragedy, he has been forced to choose honesty and reject sublimity. Unable to accept the assumption that God, Nature, a Moral Order confirm man "in his feeling that his passions and his opinions are important," the tragic writer has had to deny the Tragic Fallacy, one of the "mighty illusions by means of which human life has been given a value." O'Neill tried to supply what dramatic tragedy seems to demand: sublimity as well as honesty; struggle, triumph, and illumination to balance the suffering. But his conception of reality made transfiguration untenable, impelling him to seek release rather than reconciliation. And that outside the bounds of agonized living—in embryo or corpse. Himself a victim of the time, O'Neill struggled more heroically—with greater courage, strength, determination—than did most of his own protagonists. His example, his best plays, his powerful influence are a measure of his triumph.

Beside most of his fellow American playwrights he was uncommonly gifted, exciting, original, prolific. The most competent of them lacked his stature; his intensity, his power, his grandeur both true and false. None was so inordinately ambitious as he; none strove so prodigiously, displayed such firm integrity; none was so uncompromising; none exerted so much influence. For O'Neill imparted to a large American audience an awareness of problems—psychological, philosophical, religious—with which the commercial theatre had never dared concern itself. He incited and inspired other playwrights with examples, good and bad, of dramaturgy by which to guide their course. He discomfited the multitude of hacks in the American theatre, thereby doing a significant service for the serious dramatist. Greater than the sum of its parts, his total achievement was an impressive triumph and made him, in an important sense, the master as well as the victim of the time.—EDWIN A. ENGEL, "Conclusion," *The Haunted Heroes of Eugene O'Neill,* 1953, pp. 297–300

On November 28, 1963, the theatre world presumably commemorated the tenth anniversary of the death of Eugene G. O'Neill. In 1960, Harper's published *O'Neill* (943 pp., 70 photographs), by Albert and Barbara Gelb, surely the definitive work to date. The authors pronounce him "a consummate artist" and "the greatest American dramatist" of history. There is abundant evidence that O'Neill shared that opinion. Yet it is possible, though perhaps imprudent, to differ from this accolade. I can think of at least four of his contemporary playwrights: Maxwell Anderson, Sidney Howard, George Kelly, and Thornton P. Wilder, who equalled his list of box office successes and excelled him in depth and craftsmanship. None of them, it is true, prospected for gold, weathered tuberculosis, shipped as an able seaman, hobnobbed with hoodlums and derelicts, or had a famous actor for a father. Nor did any of them wash dirty linen in public.

Is a writer to be accredited with his ambitions, what he aspires to, what he envisions, or with what he achieves, what he successfully embodies in art? If the former, then O'Neill was a very great writer indeed. Galloping megalomania grew on him with the years. The maker of one-acters suddenly swelled to the genie who could say nothing in less than three evenings in the theatre and twelve or more acts. In his last years, plagued by ill health, he dreamed of a cycle of eleven plays to set forth the history of an American family over a period of 175 years (his own family, no doubt, the only family he seems ever to have known). Ambition, yes, in plenty. But, Browning to the contrary, I hold that a writer should be measured by solid achievement. O'Neill's reach exceeded his grasp by miles. Of his twenty-five long plays, one, *The Emperor Jones,* is a technical masterpiece but a clinical triumph, nothing more; the substance is small. The one play in which a great idea is greatly expressed, a social idea of universal interest, as old as humanity, is *The Hairy Ape,* which brings face to face the haves and have-nots, the overprivileged and underprivileged, the two nations of this planet and of history which are always with us. He never again successfully welded the *what* and the *how* of artistry.

O'Neill never mastered the first rule of all good writing: what *not to say.* He had a fatal facility in fluent, effortless dialogue which, as often as not, was static, doing nothing to advance the play toward its destined goal. Exhibit A is the great dramepic (to coin a term) in nine mortal acts covering a period of twenty-five years, *Strange Interlude.* Why he quit after nine acts is among the mysteries: the play's only structural principle being accretion, he might have gone soap opera and continued it indefinitely. Perhaps *Mourning Becomes Electra,* a marathon in two parts, twelve (fourteen?) acts, was nudging for his attention. No one more than fifteen, mentally, could possibly care what happened to, or became of, Nina Leeds, for the simple reason that Nina Leeds is not a person. Like so many denizens of the O'Neill jungle, she is merely an algebraic symbol in a long equation having to do with the Great Enigma, Life. O'Neill was not a thinker. Mere cerebration is not thought. A thinker is not merely a man who can ask questions, raise doubts, present problems. Ibsen could do that and, incidentally, produce very interesting plays in the process. A

thinker is one who can answer questions, resolve doubts, and solve problems. O'Neill once said, "Too many playwrites are writing about people when they should be writing about Life." That statement pinpoints the secret of his failure. It is precisely people that people come to the theatre to see, people like themselves with the same hopes, fears, woes, and problems. Picture these and Life will take care of itself.

Still, *Strange Interlude* is one of the four O'Neill plays that won Pulitzer Prizes. By this time it should be clearly apparent to even the most incorrigible celebrity cultist that the following question is quite debatable: does the Pulitzer Prize measure the man or does the man measure the Pulitzer Prize? Later O'Neill won the Nobel Prize. But so did Sinclair Lewis. And it might easily have been F. Scott Fitzgerald. Mauriac won it in France while Paul Claudel, who never won it, was still living. Teddy Roosevelt, the greatest Hotspur in our history, was awarded the Nobel Prize for peace.

O'Neill could be quite grandiloquent on the subject of tragedy, the part that it plays in life and how best to transfer it to the stage. He seemed to see little essential difference between Greek, Elizabethan, and modern drama. But there is a world of difference, all the difference between three entirely different *Zeitgeists,* three different religious philosophies: fatalism, libertarianism, and scientific environmentalism. As a matter of fact, no authentic tragedy has been possible on the Western stage since Elizabethan-Jacobean tragedy whimpered and died; there have been only the raw materials: misery, agony, despair. The religious outlook that wrought the miracle of the state of exaltation of spirit in the spectator of a Greek drama of Fate and Destiny or Elizabethan one of free will and personal responsibility, is non-existent today. In modern "tragedy" the wheel has come full circle in a fashion and we are back in the Greek milieu, where human beings are caught like flies in a web, innocent but penalized. Since Ibsen's impact, Character is Destiny, and character is the result of heredity, environment, and the circumstances of the moment, none of which is under our control. Though he may still pay lip-service to the Christian ethos, the dramatist, taught by science, tends to think in the terms of Darwin and Freud, evading, for the most part, all moral commitments. What difference does it make what we call the predetermining power so long as the predetermination is there? Yet, with these simple facts staring him in the face, O'Neill could still superimpose the machinery of the Agamemnon trilogy on the occupants of a New England farm and see no reason why it should not fit. This is *Mourning Becomes Electra,* the opus that sealed him "the greatest American dramatist." He strews the stage with murders, suicides, and madness. All this, he intimates, was fated. Lavinia (Electra) locks herself up to live with her ghosts and her guilt as a self-imposed punishment. Punishment for what—if it was all fated? But who cares? Lavinia, like Nina Leeds, is a robot.

That O'Neill swept away tradition and lifted the American stage to the plane of art is now established dogma. Whether he swept away tradition or not is unimportant. Tradition has been swept away so often. The Elizabethan theatre destroyed the innyard and the mystery play; the Restoration stage buried the Shakespearean drama under a cascade of sex and wit; the nineteenth century playhouse banished sex and wit and enthroned hokum; the modern dramaturgy restored sex—and not much else. We are required to believe that O'Neill made Tennessee Williams and William Inge possible. I can well believe that. He may also have made the Theatre of the Absurd: Ionesco, Genet, and Samuel Beckett, not merely possible, but inevitable. One thing only is certain: he was permitted to turn the American theatre into a private laboratory for personal experimentation, out of which came, eventually, such things as *The Great God Brown*, the O'Neill play invariably chosen for inclusion in anthologies of modern drama intended for the use of college students. And who knows what it means? O'Neill himself tried to explain the play and ended by striving, unsuccessfully, to explain his explanation. Only one thing is clear: Dion Anthony, the sensitive artist soul, and William Brown, the successful, crass money-getter, are natural enemies and Brown secretly envies Anthony. Was ever so little told to so many in so many words?

After bleeding through the saga-legend of O'Neill, it is very difficult to escape the conclusion that greatness was thrust on the man by those who had a vested interest in the commercial possibilities of the son of Monte Cristo: the producers, including the Theatre Guild, the publishers, Hollywood, and other such entrepreneurs. His fame was not based solely on the considered opinions of the best dramatic critics of his day: Brooks Atkinson, George Jean Nathan, and John Mason Brown. They often disliked his plays and said so, both publicly and privately. But once the public became aware that a new controversial dramatist had raised his head, the propaganda machine went into action. It became reactionary, even un-American, to question the greatness of the new product. What completed the victory was the utter sincerity and boundless self-belief with which O'Neill himself became convinced of the authenticity of his own genius and his mission to save the stagnant American theatre. He anathematized the commercial stage in unmeasured terms. But was there ever a theatre that was not commercial? If so, it didn't last long. The Provincetown Players did not remain pure idealists, nor was his final powerful sponsor, the Theatre Guild, completely altruistic.

A great drama is the work of a mind that sees life steadily and sees it whole, that sees people and things as in themselves they really are. Steadily? O'Neill changed his opinions and attitudes as he changed his hat. Whole? The only world he seems to have known or cared about was the underworld inhabited by sailors and prostitutes, derelicts and hoodlums, all with hearts of gold but no other worldly wealth. He was uncomfortable in contact with anyone he could not dominate: his father, his second wife, his daughter Oona.

The faithful point pridefully to the fact that, except Shakespeare and possibly Shaw, O'Neill has been more widely published and produced abroad than any other dramatist. This is to be expected. Jack London, the Socialist, is, or long was, Russia's favorite writer. Any American writer who pictures the seamy side of American capitalism is sure to be relished in lands that suffer, or think they suffer, from the American economic colossus.

O'Neill proved his genius by being pleased with nothing whatsoever. He was equally indignant with producers who accepted and producers who rejected his works. There were no good actors in America save John Barrymore, who was a genius, but who, somehow, shied away from all O'Neill plays. Time and again he complained after a performance, "But that isn't the play I wrote. They ruined it." When the one-actor, *In the Zone*, proved popular in vaudeville, it became "the worst thing I ever wrote." When *Lazarus Laughed* turned out to be unactable, it became "the best thing I ever did." His favorite theme was "the real me," which, it seems, nobody ever perceived.

The myth that he restored tragedy to American drama will die hard, no doubt. What he really restored was melodrama in false whiskers. (Melodrama is here not synonymous with bad drama. Melodrama may be good or bad. *Hamlet* is melodrama

raised to the highest level.) O'Neill's level is not high. His apprenticeship one-actors, which he tossed off like sparks from an anvil, were incredibly crude. He firmly believed that violence and abnormality were necessary and sufficient for high tragedy. The sea-change into something rich and strange so necessary to greatness is almost never present. The ease with which his defenders admit that he had every defect possible to a dramatist: unrealism of plot, weakness in characterization, limitless verbosity, tiresome repetitiousness, a strong tendency to preach, while blithely maintaining his greatness is a critical paradox hard to understand.

Ever since *The Emperor Jones*, an obviously psychological play, the Freudians have had a field day with O'Neill's works. They have seen O'Neill and his love-hate family complex in all of his characters, even the females: Lavinia, for instance, in *Mourning*. One young Western professor discovered nine to be the key to *Strange Interlude*: there were nine acts, nine months is the period for human gestation, and the heroine's name was Nina Leeds. Had O'Neill read Freud? O'Neill had not read Freud, he said most emphatically. He was quick to resent any implication that his greatness had any architects other than Nature and O'Neill. He confessed to only two admirations, Strindberg and Nietzsche, both of whom went insane.

It is a pleasure to recall his one lone comedy, the light-hearted satire on the popular morality of the late nineties, *Ah, Wilderness!* If some traveler from Antarctica should discover an unsigned copy of that play in the rubble after the next war, he will ascribe it to Booth Tarkington.—LOUIS F. DOYLE, "The Myth of Eugene O'Neill," *Ren*, Winter 1964, pp. 59–62, 81

O'Neill's world cannot be separated from the time of its birth. Young O'Neill was heralded as a revolutionary; his career coincides with an age of drama in which change has been the rule rather than the exception. Two central vectors in it are seen by Gassner: "A continuing tension between naturalism and a variety of alternatives of dramatic stylization has characterized the century's theatre." Taking some playwrights mentioned by Gassner and adding a few remarkable colleagues from several countries to their company, one might say that this tension has been felt almost universally. It is the fate of modern dramatists.

Since the 1860's, realism has been killed and resurrected half a dozen times. One of the most paradoxical features in this circular movement is that exactly those major playwrights who once killed this "out-dated" style have returned to it—and, vice versa, the very masters of realism have in one phase of their career or another given up realistic drama in favor of a more imaginative, more poetic theatre. Ibsen, of course, is a case in point; so is Strindberg. There is a long distance from the Shaw of *Mrs. Warren's Profession* to the author of *Back to Methuselah*—as long as from the Hauptmann of *Die Weber* to the poet of *Die versunkene Glocke*. On the other hand two young playwrights, Harold Pinter and Edward Albee, have shown a peculiar inclination to glide between the positions of realism and absurdism. Both realistic and theatrical elements have figured in the epic theatre of Bertolt Brecht, and in the grotesque and parodical world of Friedrich Dürrenmatt. Unable to choose between realism and theatricalism, most playwrights have taken both.

O'Neill was furthest away from realism in the twenties. After having escaped from the middle-class living room to the wide seas of his youth and into the sordid surroundings of his young manhood, he turned to stylistic experimentations. It had a marked effect on his later scenic images that he wrote several plays either under the influence of expressionism or as one of the pioneers of his style. The influence was doubtless more fruitful than were O'Neill's contacts with Macgowan's romantic ideals of an Imaginative Theatre. What he learned from his explorations of the European theatre was a liking for strong dynamics. He was encouraged to create sharply contrasting scenic images; Ibsenesque discussion plays were replaced by librettos for the theatre. He was not saved from errors; yet he had developed what might be called a massive belief in the interaction of scenic images when he selected the other road open to modern playwrights, "fluid and poetic drama without breaking the mold of effective realistic dramaturgy." O'Neill's late dynamic realism can be understood only as an outgrowth of his experimental period. Both phases can be connected with the drama created in his surroundings—and with his own person. O'Neill had lived, in an intensive manner, the rebellious years of an angry young man from the 1910's. Toward the end of his life he lived just as furiously the turning back of an old man, in remembrance of things past. All the time, he lived in his art. He was a true dramatist.

Another facet of O'Neill's relationship to his time is that he was a contemporary of the pioneers of stagecraft in this century. He had a fresh continent before him, even if Adolphe Appia and Gordon Craig were somewhat ahead in time; and he faced a frontier in the field of serious drama. As an actor's son, Eugene O'Neill knew that the written text was not all of the theatre. The ideas of contemporary renewers of the stage confirmed his faith in all kinds of scenic means of expression. He was at his worst when trying to create self-containing poetry; the beginnings of his success were in his interest in "what a modern theatre should be capable of."

O'Neill's masks and "thought asides" are indications of the revolutionary breakthrough of psychoanalysis. He did not only demonstrate Freudian lines of thought on the stage; he also overburdened these ideas, trying to find in them a solution to man's metaphysical dilemma. Yet he is also an exponent of a more sober application of these ideas: complexes, neuroses, or love-hate relations do not solve anything; they just exist. Psychoanalytic elements are, of course, possible building materials for works of art; what is doubtful is whether they can be emphasized as strongly as they were before World War II. *Long Day's Journey into Night*, O'Neill's posthumous masterpiece, definitely belongs in this and other respects to the postwar era.

Mennemeier has seen O'Neill as a forerunner of absurdism. One of the themes O'Neill shared with this school of playwriting is that of difficulties in communication. The enjoyment in happy phrasing, experienced by Shakespeare and other Elizabethans, has been replaced by a widespread distrust in the communicative value of language. Enlarging the sphere of discussion outside the theatre we might hint at modern philosophers, careful students of semantics; or at the lesson in the abuse of language taught by Hitler. Though absurdist playwrights were cautious, they kept on creating—for the theatre. Though O'Neill apparently had his misgivings about the possibility of true communication, he kept creating situations in which his characters grope for and occasionally achieve mutual understanding. The problem for O'Neill and the absurdists is the same; the artistic form given to it is different.

Eugene O'Neill's connections with his time emphasize the theatrical quality of his works. When attempting a critical evaluation of the method applied in this study, it is worth remembering that O'Neill is a playwright ideally suited for a scenic approach. He wrote his visions into precise stage directions; he grew up close to the stage; verbal skills were not one of his strong points. Charney, incidentally, mentions

O'Neill as an opposite to his own object of study: "It would be much simpler to discuss the presentational imagery of such dramatists as O'Neill or Ibsen, for their stage directions are much fuller than Shakespeare's and the theater for which they wrote much closer to us." In other words, the margin of speculation is bound to be wider when the distance in time and cultural climate grows between a present-day scholar and the object of his interest.

The central concepts employed in this study might be more applicable when dealing with the modern drama than when trying to extend the method to older plays. Yet there is help available from another branch of *Theaterwissenschaft*—from the history of the theatre. It remains to be seen whether mental reconstructions of past conditions in the theatre can offer a solid basis for a research concentrating on the scenic images of, say, a Renaissance playwright.

On the other hand, a portion of the criticism in the field of drama since Ibsen has a slightly anachronistic flavor, because the criteria applied are derived from studies in poetry or in older drama. It is not unusual to read complaints of the definite inferiority of the modern playwrights: why do they not write poetry on the level of Shakespeare? The basic answer is, of course, that they write for a different kind of theatre in which the development of stagecraft has made the functions of dialogue less prominent than before. A critical principle phrased by Peacock has not been acknowledged generally enough: "The intertexture of drama differing so markedly from that of poems, we judge its imaginative quality by different criteria. . . . The poetry of drama is not that of a romantic lyric or symbolist poem." It has been taken as something different in this study. If the central concepts developed will help to make the scenic approach to drama more legitimate, they will have served an essential purpose.

In my introduction the creative process of a playwright was supposed to be more mechanical than it actually is, in order to clarify the argument. It has been so throughout the study. Purely artistic solutions made by Eugene O'Neill have probably been described as having happened too consciously. This procedure has only served as a kind of shorthand. Some part of O'Neill's mind must have relied on the expressive power of his dialogue when he started writing *Long Day's Journey into Night*: and to that part has been given the name "he." The purpose here has been to show that these solutions were arrived at, not to set forth any theories as to how this happened, somewhere deep in the subconscious mind of a creative artist. This reservation is presented here and now, rather than having been interpolated every time there might have been reason for it.

Nor has it been my intention to write down laws to be followed by all future playwrights. If there are any elements pointing toward a general theory of drama, these are connected with three basic criteria. It seems to be worthwhile to examine whether a playwright uses his scenic means of expression in harmony with the themes of his play, with the style he has chosen, and with his personal qualities. The concepts utilized in this study do not presuppose any absolute standards within any of these dimensions.

The concept of "scenic image" has been used as a surgical knife: it has not been resorted to when it has been possible to characterize a play along more general lines. Admitting that it is questionable whether this instrument is of considerable value for a scholar studying older drama, and admitting that Eugene O'Neill has been an ideal patient, one finds it possible to look toward new vistas in the study of the modern drama. How do new findings along these lines change our total picture of a playwright? What is the relation between Bertolt Brecht's images and the formalistic machinery of his epic theatre? What could one find out about the position of the plays-within-plays on Jean Anouilh's stage? How does Friedrich Dürrenmatt construct his grotesque and parodical scenic images? There are a great many chapters to be written before a study of the relations between the modern playwright and his stage can be complete.—TIMO TIUSANEN, "Conclusion: O'Neill's Scenic Images," *O'Neill's Scenic Images,* 1968, pp. 343–48

Eugene O'Neill's playwriting career resembles a saint's legend. Having committed himself to drama at the age of twenty-four, by beginning to write plays while in a tuberculosis sanatorium, he never swerved—"an artist or nothing." Neither money nor fame seduced him; he neglected family and friends for his work; he allowed neither alcohol nor illness to prevent him from writing. He persevered monomaniacally, seeking to create great American tragedy. His strongest expression of disapproval was "easy." He never wooed Broadway, he suffered no play-doctors, and he rarely accepted suggestions from actors or directors. He received the Nobel Prize at approximately the time he was struck by a debilitating illness, but he kept on writing. Crippled beyond the possibility of creation, O'Neill had the courage to destroy all but one of the plays of the Cycle to which he had decided to dedicate his life. Astoundingly, he made these sacrifices though he lacked that basic gift of a major playwright—the ability to write dialogue that was both functional and distinctive.

O'Neill's early plays oscillate between the stilted rhetoric of melodrama and the ungrammatical colloquialism (including dialect) of the realistic novel. He was to continue using these two main idioms until his last plays. In both idioms O'Neill early began to use two techniques that have become synonymous with his name—verbal repetition and extended monologue (however often the latter might be interrupted by scenic directions). Moving from a realistic surface to his two Expressionist plays, *Emperor Jones* and *The Hairy Ape,* O'Neill combined these techniques—in different dialects—more effectively than in any of the pretentious and messianic plays of the following decade. Between 1924 and 1934 O'Neill wrote dramas based on black-white polarities: literally black and white in *All God's Chillun,* metaphorized into stones vs. gold in *Desire under the Elms,* theatricalized into opposing masks in *The Great God Brown,* experimentalized into normal speech vs. thought asides in *Strange Interlude,* abstracted into love vs. death in *Mourning Becomes Electra.* In spite of extravagant staging, these dramas revolve about a few simple ideas which are repeated in refrains, rather than translated into acton and character by means of dialogue.

After this decade of verbal stretch and strain, O'Neill is often said to have "returned" to realism, but we have too little evidence to be sure, since he destroyed so many manuscripts. *More Stately Mansions,* which he meant to destroy, bursts and languishes in the feverish idiom of the plays of the extravagant decade. And in spite of the new control, humor, and concreteness of the language of the "Irish" plays, *A Touch of the Poet* and *A Moon for the Misbegotten,* they are not major works. Finally, there are three masterpieces among O'Neill's forty-six published plays: *Hughie, The Iceman Cometh, Long Day's Journey into Night.* And even these last two have traces of what Hofmannsthal early designated as O'Neill's wet sponge tendency. Hofmannsthal also criticized O'Neill's characters as "not sufficiently fixed in the present because they are not sufficiently fixed in the past." Only at the end of his creative life was O'Neill able to fix his characters indelibly in our present by making them resonate through his own past.

Though he was just past fifty when he wrote his great works, the world's ills and his own had aged him and wisened him. What is miraculous is that he should have been able, exceptionally and extraordinarily, to express his new wisdom through the anxieties of his characters' credible speech.

But then saints' legends traditionally end in miracle. —RUBY COHN, "The Wet Sponge of Eugene O'Neill," *Dialogue in American Drama,* 1971, pp. 66–67

Even in the second half of the twentieth century, performances of O'Neill's work have continued to raise new questions concerning America's greatest dramatist, new world drama, and even modern drama as a whole. After his early successes he was recognized as a great talent, and it was assumed that he would go on to become a master. But his development as a dramatist was not dictated by any logic deducible from the development of modern drama. It was not merely a matter of a more mature craftsmanship or a greater consolidation of a philosophical *Weltanschauung.* Recent decades have seen many attempts to force the phenomenon of O'Neill into the framework of an unambiguous system of ideas like the ones to which Ibsen, Pirandello, and Brecht lend themselves. But any such attempt must confine itself to one single phase or aspect of his work. At various points in his career the "definitive" O'Neill seemed to have emerged, yet invariably within a short time the restless, insatiable experimenter was at work again. It is not simply a case of failing to reach a final judgment since, after all, in art there never can be a final judgment. With O'Neill, we have not even been able to bring into focus his fundamental idea or the essentials of his artistic position.

When we look at this dramatist's voluminous work within the context of contemporary ideologies, literary currents, and fashions, we recognize so much that is already familiar, so much that has already been more forcefully expressed and more meaningfully demonstrated that we have no recourse but to revise our impression of O'Neill as an elusive loner. Is his work then just a conglomerate of ideas adopted from other writers and held together by his instinctive theatrical sense? Could it be that his great achievement was not so much to have written timeless, enduring works as to have played a great historical role in breaking new ground for a decaying theatrical tradition of superficiality and commercialism? Did he break out the windows of an established American theater in order to let in the light of European drama? Many critics believe so. In 1932, the English critic and dramatist St. John Ervine said that O'Neill was merely America's Marlowe, preparing the way for its Shakespeare. Such facetious judgments, applicable only to some nonexistent figure, reveal the uncertainty of some critics, even those of the stature of St. John Ervine, in attempting to come to grips with the O'Neill phenomenon.

In relating O'Neill to his forerunners and contemporaries as well as to his literary trends abroad, some characteristics of O'Neill's work offer points of departure. Up to *Beyond the Horizon,* his early plays show the same painstaking, detailed realism of European naturalistic drama and the determinism and positivism of Zola. Even here the "pipe dream" theme, so close to Ibsen's "life-sustaining lie," which will recur again and again until the closing movements of *More Stately Mansions,* is already emerging. The programmatic suggestions O'Neill made to the Provincetown group show that even as a young man he believed the most effective contemporary dramatic styles to be those of Ibsen and Strindberg. The references in his Nobel Prize speech to Strindberg as the master of modern dramatists, the monologue technique in *Before Breakfast,* the love-hate relationship of the husband and wife in *Welded,* the mutual castigation of the Tyrones in *Long Day's Journey into*

Night—all this provided considerable justification for regarding O'Neill as a belated American Strindberg. But in the course of O'Neill's development, Strindbergian elements were no more lasting than naturalism, and they do not dominate his mature work.

Attempts to define his artistic personality rely to a surprising degree on simplistic generalizations which relegate him to a subsidiary, derivative position and reduce his dramaturgy to a convenient formula. He has been called, for example, the American Georg Kaiser. Unquestionably he did go through an Expressionistic phase, in which certain techniques and themes approximated those of the German Expressionists. Yet despite the numerous similarities between O'Neill and Kaiser, there remains an important distinction between these two playwrights: O'Neill was primarily concerned not with the rebirth of man through social revolution, but rather with the fate of individuals, whose existence and problems are not confined to any particular social structure. His heated reaction to criticism of *The Hairy Ape* as a play of social propaganda stressed a point that holds true for his work in general: he was not an exponent of George Bernard Shaw's sober brand of social propaganda or of the rhetorical social protest of many Expressionists. His work, written at a time when social criticism dominated the arts, shows an almost anachronistic indifference to such matters of intellectual fashion.

Yet to regard this as a virtue in itself would be to negate the element of socio-historical relevance which prevents art from floating in a timeless void. We have to admit that O'Neill as a thinker is often weak, unreliable and superficial. He has been called "a peddler of second-hand ideas," and even if this criticism overstresses the ideological content of his plays, there can be no doubt that he frequently faltered whenever he tried to be profoundly philosophical or "modern," whenever he entered the realm of abstract ideas. Along with James Joyce, Thomas Mann, and Hermann Broch, he participated in the rediscovery of myth initiated by T. S. Eliot, but his attempt to "psychologize" the Greek tragedians' concept of fate resulted in the Zolaesque determinism of *Mourning Becomes Electra*. Not only does his study of women in *Strange Interlude* exceed the limits of an individual psyche, but the play itself, with its somewhat awkward dramatization of the stream-of-consciousness technique, exceeds the limits of effective theater. Yet to dismiss O'Neill for his lack of skill in developing ideas presupposes that his plays are to be judged primarily as vehicles for ideas. Like Joyce, O'Neill has often been evaluated on this basis, but his best works are no more plays of ideas than are García Lorca's tragedies.

Few elements in O'Neill's dramatic style remain constant throughout his work. Early in his career he revealed his extraordinary gift for lending a dramatic, articulate force to slang, the speech of the inarticulate. His farmers, seamen, bums, and prostitutes, like the Irish peasants in J. M. Synge, speak a language of poetic musicality, full of unexpected naive, oblique images, which often fail to crystallize. One critic charged, with some justification, that O'Neill often confused the forcefulness of this language with the forcefulness of its expletives. In many of his plays he develops a consistency of tone, a musical unity. The tone of hauntedness that pervades *Long Day's Journey into Night* characterizes also *The Emperor Jones*, where it takes on an explicitly musical form, produced by the use of sound, especially drums. Most of the plays contain rhythmic repetitions of what might be called a refrain; in *Lazarus Laughed* the "musical" laughter of the liberated Lazarus serves this function. Besides this musical tendency to

dispense with words, O'Neill also displays an affinity for film techniques. The use of masks in *The Great God Brown*, for example, obviously owes much to careful study of the possibilities of the motion-picture camera. The cinematographic medium is far more suitable than the conventional stage for conveying the dramatic effect of all the differentiated crowd scenes in *Lazarus Laughed*. The same applies to the minute detail of O'Neill's stage directions, which only the camera could properly translate into visual terms.

One characteristic is consistently evident throughout O'Neill's career: an unusual technical flexibility, a readiness to experiment and take risks, which he never lost even in his later years. His plays explore the full range of dramatic expression, which continued to fascinate him as long as he lived. Parallel to this runs his experimentation with ideas. Many writers have left their mark, stylistic or philosophical, on his work; they include Spengler, Nietzsche, Marx, Freud, Aeschylus, Shakespeare, Ibsen, Strindberg, Gerhart Hauptmann, and Georg Kaiser. While O'Neill's work in its totality indicates chaos and helplessness, the individual plays show a tentative reaching out, quickly overcome, toward nihilism and Catholicism, determinism and the triumph of human freedom. This is what St. John Ervine meant when he said that O'Neill does not develop, he just expands. But it was precisely this infinite reluctance to declare or commit himself that constituted the artistic as well as the philosophical and religious freedom so indispensable to O'Neill. This predilection for epic completeness—or rather "all-embracingness"—is just as evident in the total *œuvre* as in the individual later plays and dramatic cycles, which can no longer be contained within conventional limits. It is a characteristic O'Neill shares with James Joyce, Hermann Broch, and Robert Musil. He was no more capable than the author of *Finnegans Wake* of complying with Ervine's demand that he adopt a final artistic position, formally and philosophically.

To look for O'Neill's enduring value in his flexibility and his adroit acrobatic (often superficial) handling of ideas—the sort of relative value that Joyce enjoys—may seem questionable. Nevertheless his great works are best approached, not by way of his technical experiments or his "ideas," but by insight into an experience of life almost untouched by ideas and mastered only through the imposition of artistic form. The quality of a play like *Long Day's Journey into Night* stemmed from personal suffering rather than from a dramatic idea. O'Neill's often unique experiments may prove to be dated, but his best plays, with their spontaneity and confessional intensity, are genuine and powerful expressions of the spiritual anguish, helplessness, lies, and mutual human destruction, which O'Neill knew only too well. They give us a glimpse of the man behind the experimenter, suffering and sacrificing himself to art. This is what distinguishes O'Neill from any fashions, trends, or movements to which he may have subscribed or with which he may have been identified.—HORST FRENZ, "Conclusion," *Eugene O'Neill*, tr. Helen Sebba, 1971, pp. 100–106

Works

The short play ⟨*The Emperor Jones*⟩—needing another one-act play to piece out an evening's entertainment—tells the story, in eight short scenes, of Brutus Jones's fall from 'emperor' of a West Indian island to a crawling savage, killed by his rebellious people. The first and last scenes are realistic; the middle six scenes are expressionistic; in the first and last scenes other characters appear and speak; in the middle scenes we hear the monologues of Jones and see the visions of his fearful mind. The blazing afternoon sunlight of the first scene reveals the white-walled and white-pillared chamber of Jones's palace; in the room's center is the Emperor's scarlet throne. (Here white and red predominate.) The dialogue between Jones—described as 'a tall, powerfully-built, full-blooded Negro of middle age', with eyes of 'cunning intelligence', wearing a colorful uniform with brass buttons and gold chevrons, carrying a holster with a 'pearl-handled revolver'—and the Cockney trader, pasty-faced, shifty-eyed, mean, cowardly, dangerous Smithers, reveals how Jones came to the island as a stowaway, how he exploited the 'bush niggers' with tricks he learned from the white men he met as a Pullman porter, that he has six bullets in his revolver, the last a silver bullet, and that the natives are now in revolt against him, signified by the faint sound of the tom-tom.

The 'nightfall' of the second scene finds Jones at the edge of the Great Forest through which he plans to escape from the natives. In this scene he talks to himself about 'the long journey' ahead of him, and sees creeping out of the forest the first of his nightmarish visions, 'the Little Formless Fears'. He fires his first shot at them, as the throb of the tom-tom quickens, and Jones plunges into the forest. The next scenes, lit by the beams of the moon, reveal to Jones's frightened imagination the black man whom he killed in a crap game, the white prison guard whom he also killed, a slave auction block where slaves are sold to Southern planters, a slave ship where wretched Negroes sway with the roll of the ship. In the last of the expressionistic scenes, Jones finds himself at 5 a.m. at the foot of 'a gigantic tree by the edge of a great river', near which 'a rough structure of boulders' resembles 'an altar'. He kneels before it 'as if in obedience to some obscure impulse', then he utters: 'What—what is I doin'? What is—dis place? Seems like—seems like I know dat tree—an' dem stones—an' de river. I remember—seems like I ben heah befo'. *(Tremblingly)* Oh, Gorry, I'se skeered in dis place! I'se skeered! Oh, Lawd, pertect dis sinner!' A Witch-Doctor appears; he dances and croons, completely hypnotizing Jones. A crocodile, emerging from the river, crawls toward Jones as Jones crawls toward it. Jones cries, 'Lawd, save me! Lawd Jesus, heah my prayer!' and as if 'in answer to his prayer', he realizes he has the silver bullet left in his revolver. He fires, and the crocodile sinks back into the river. The scene ends with Jones lying face to the ground, 'his arms outstretched, whimpering with fear', as the sound of the tom-tom 'fills the silence'. The play's last scene, realistic, outside of the forest at 'dawn', informs us that the natives have made silver bullets to kill Jones. Lem, the leader of the revolt, and Smithers talk, the tom-tom stops beating, and we learn that Jones is dead. His body is brought on stage, and Smithers, displaying grudging admiration, exclaims that Jones 'died in the 'eight o' style, any'ow!' because he was killed with silver bullets.

The play's middle expressionistic scenes produce a high pitch of emotion in Jones and in the audience. The terrible fear of Jones as he flees through the forest is visualized by the appearance of the ghosts of his personal past and his racial past. At the same time, the moonlight adds its eerie glow to Jones's hallucinations, and the sounds punctuate the increasing threat of his dark environment. The beating of the tom-tom—which starts at a 'normal pulse beat—72 to the minute' and gradually accelerates to the end of the play, ceasing only when Jones is dead—powerfully suggests Jones's panic. This incessant throbbing is augmented by the other sounds in the play—the wind moaning in the leaves, the Formless Fears laughing mockingly, the moans of the slaves in the ship, the Witch-Doctor's croon and howl, and especially the various sounds that come from Jones himself, from murmurs to wails. And each shot from the revolver, an obvious melodramatic gimmick which

O'Neill learned from his father's theatre, adds to the play's general atomosphere of suspense and fear. The play's remarkable intensity is the result of all of these theatrical effects working with the fast-paced monologues of a single character as he races through the nightmarish forest of one night. O'Neill, even at this early stage of his development, seems a master of manipulation. He effectively uses color and costume and light and sound and movement (including the pantomimic movements of 'automatons' and 'marionettes') to produce tension and excitement. He overwhelms his audience by theatrically dramatizing the nightmare world of a frightened guilty man. The expressionistic stage techniques work, drawing the audience *into* Jones's shattering experience.

If the play did just this, however, it would be merely a theatrical *tour de force*. That O'Neill allows the play's expressionism to inform an archetypal idea gives the play its high value. Jones's long night's journey, so vividly realized, is physical and psychological and racial and universal. It reveals the condition of that one black man, of all black men, and of all men. On the physical level, Jones has an arduous journey through a literal forest. He is a hot, tired, hungry Jones, whose feet hurt. As the play progresses, Jones strips his emperor's clothes and finally dies almost naked. Because he was lost, his physical journey ends where it began; he has come full circle. On the psychological level, Jones travels through the guilty moments of his personal past. He meets his general fears, then the black man he killed, then the white man he killed. Reliving these personal experiences brings him terror; the psychological stripping reveals the subconscious fears which haunt him.

At the same time, his personal memories are part of a larger pattern, so that his journey through the forest proceeds on a racial level as well. If we reverse the order of the expressionistic scenes, we discover the history of the black experience in America—from the jungle with its crocodile gods and witch-doctors, to the slave ships coming to the New World, to the slave markets in the South, to prison gangs, demeaning jobs, gambling, killing, and all the fears that stem from the foregoing. Seen in this way, the racial journey of the black man from the jungle to civilization is regressive; certainly, his soul was more pure in the beginning of that journey, and certainly, he has become the victim of the white man's greed and cruelty. The sickly and corrupt Smithers represents the civilized white man, an obvious contrast to the intelligent, self-reliant, grand Jones, who learned his exploitive habits from the white man and has come to understand the difference between little stealing and big stealing, offering the play's most effective social comment: 'You heah what I tells you, Smithers. Dere's little stealin' like you does, and dere's big stealin' like I does. For de little stealin' dey gits you in jail soon or late. For de big stealin' dey makes you Emperor and puts you in de Hall o' Fame when you croaks.' Jones travels back to his racial roots, and recognizes from whence he came—'seems like I ben heah befo'.' On the archetypal level, Jones's journey through his night mirrors that of all men. Beneath the veneer of civilization, under the 'robes and furred gowns' which 'hide all' (as King Lear, another self-stripper, would express it), lurk the primal urges, the Dionysian claims, the heart of darkness. Beneath 'the surface of the river . . . unruffled in the moonlight' lurk 'the forces of evil' which 'demand sacrifice', lurks the crocodile, as Scene Seven insists. Mankind is lost in the Forest, which explains the potency of that image, whether that forest be part of Dante's landscape, or related to Shakespeare's moon-drenched wood in *A Midsummer Night's Dream*, or inherited in Jung's collective unconscious. Like the sea of O'Neill's *Glencairn* plays, the forest makes its own dark claims. Brutus Jones feels the kind of terror we all feel when we are forced to plunge through the forest of our pasts, to confront our ghosts, to contemplate the mysterious forces 'behind life'. In short, a play that is theatrically exciting because of its bold expressionism and its basic appeal to the senses is at the same time thematically persuasive in asserting truths about the black man in particular and all men in general.—NORMAND BERLIN, "The Early Twenties," *Eugene O'Neill*, 1982, pp. 56–60

It is amusing to look back upon the emission of drool precipitated by the presentation of O'Neill's *All God's Chillun Got Wings*. Participants in the geyser of nonsense included everyone from Prof. Dr. Arthur Brisbane, of the Bibliothèque Hearst, to Colonel Billy Mayfield, of the Benevolent Protective Order of the Ku Klux Klan, Texas Lodge, from the dramatic critic of the Windgap, Pa., *International News-Herald* to the shepherd of the Baptist flock at Horsecough, Va., and from a member of the faculty of Princeton University to the owners, publishers, editors, and editorial writers of half the Southern newspapers. Black men protested in the press that the play was a libel on their race, since it showed an educated Negro taking for wife a drab of the streets. White men protested in turn that it was an insult to their race, since it showed a white woman, no matter what her morals, taking unto her bosom a coon. The heroic Colonel Mayfield, in an editorial in the *Fiery Cross*, demanded the immediate dispatch of the author on the ground that he was a Catholic and hence was doubtless trying to stir up the Negroes to arm, march on Washington, and burn down the Nordic White House. The always passionately sincere Brisbane, in an editorial in the Hearst journals, cried Look Out! There Will Be Race Riots! The New York moral morons were hot with indignation because O'Neill showed a white woman kissing a Negro's hand. Dramatic critics denounced the play vehemently on the ground that it was played by a real Negro and a white actress, which was awful. The American Legion, through certain of its mediums of expression published in the Middle West, announced flamingly that it considered the play subversive of 100 per cent American patriotism in that it sought to undo all the good that was accomplished by the Legion's winning of the late war. The lucid argument of the Legion was that a piece of writing that dealt with miscegenation and that was supposed to be authentically American was sure to alienate certain of our late allies in arms. It was the further belief of the Legion's spokesmen in the Middle West that there was German propaganda concealed in the enterprise. In all probability, observed the Legion's spokesmen, the producers of the play would be found to be either German or of German descent. The names of these producers, whom the Texas Chapter of the Ku Klux on the other hand insisted must be Jews, were clearly of a German-Yiddish flavor, to wit, Macgowan, O'Neill and Jones.

It has been some time since a play has succeeded in causing so much commotion. Why this particular play caused it, I can't make out, unless it is that the number of half-wits in America is increasing much faster than any of us has believed. There is absolutely nothing in the play that is in the slightest degree offensive to any human being above the mental level of a dog-show judge. The initial thread of theme is simply *Abie's Irish Rose* with Abie blacked up. And the final turn of theme is simply that of Wilson Barrett's *The Sign of the Cross* with the offstage howling of lions left out. *Uncle Tom's Cabin* has been played at different times by six companies with real Negroes in the role of Uncle Tom—two black prize-fighters (the famous Peter Jackson was one of them) are among those who have played the part—and no one, even south of the Mason-Dixon line, has so much as let out a whisper when these real Negroes

have fondled and kissed the white Little Evas. The late Bert Williams not only played in many sketches with white women, but cavorted gayly for years with white feminine flesh on our music show stage. And Belasco has lately and popularly in *Lulu Belle* mixed up blacks and white indiscriminately. In *All God's Chillun Got Wings*, there is no physical contact between the Negro and the white woman save in the matter of their hands. Once, true enough, after a scene of frenzied mental aberration, the white actress is called upon to kiss the Negro's hands "as a child might, tenderly and gratefully," but the intrinsic feeling and impression here are not far removed from the Uncle Tom–Little Eva kind of thing.

To object to the play because it treats of miscegenation is to object to the drama *Othello* ("Othello is made by Shakespeare in every respect a Negro"—August Wilhelm Schlegel), or to the opera *L'Africaine*, or to the Kipling story of "Georgie Porgie." To object to it because it shows a man and a woman of different color and of antagonistic race in the attitude of lovers is to object to Sheldon's *The Nigger*, De Mille's *Strongheart*, Selwyn's *The Arab* and the lately produced *White Cargo*, to mention but four out of any number of popular theatre plays that have gone their way unmolested, to say nothing of *Madame Butterfly*, *Lakme* and *Aïda*. To argue against it that, since it shows a white woman marrying a Negro, it therefore *ipso facto* places its mark of approval on such marriages is to argue that since *Tosca* shows a woman stabbing a chief of police to death it therefore *ipso facto* places its mark of approval on the universal murdering of policemen. The O'Neill play, it is quite true, shows a certain white woman and a certain Negro in the married relation, but it obviously has no more intention of generalizing from this single and isolated case than such a play as *The Bowery after Dark* which, following the line of profound logic that has been exercised in the case of the O'Neill play, would seek to prove that all Chinamen are bent upon getting white women into dark cellars for purposes of anatomical dirty work. *All God's Chillun Got Wings* is simply O'Neill's attempt to show what *would* happen psychologically *if* a white woman, whatever her station, *were* to marry a Negro. Plainly enough, in order to show what *would* happen, he has theatrically and dramatically to deduce his findings from the visualized situation. Otherwise, save he wished to resort to the bogus dream formula—which doubtless would have pacified the dolts who were so much worked up—he would have no play. How far he has succeeded in achieving his intention, the readers of the play may judge for themselves. It is my own belief that he has achieved the end he had in view. His play is unquestionably enfeebled by its sketchiness, by its perhaps too great economy of means, but it nonetheless presents its theme sincerely, intelligently, sympathetically and, it seems to me, dramatically. There is a measure of cloudiness in its final passages, yet this cloudiness is doubtless inherent in the very nature of the theme. The hoopdedoodle that was raised over that theme and over the theatrical presentation of the play expounding it must make any half-way intelligent Pullman porter shake his head sadly in pity for the mentality of a certain portion of the race that, by the grace of God, sits in the plush chairs.—GEORGE JEAN NATHAN, "The Play and the Playwright," *The House of Satan*, 1926, pp. 202–7

Despite the obvious differences between *All God's Chillun* and *Desire under the Elms*—in setting and dialect, especially—the two plays are linked. As heavily disguised re-enactments of critical family confrontations in O'Neill's adolescence and young adulthood, both plays anticipate the action of the last plays; and in their view of human kinship violently destroyed, they also anticipate the plays immediately to follow. O'Neill, beginning to reveal the longer-range effects of the deaths of his mother and brother, is beginning to find isolation to be man's natural destiny.

All four central figures of *Long Day's Journey* are represented in *Desire under the Elms*. It is easy enough to recognize in the darkly sensitive Eben one of the many anticipations of Edmund Tyrone, but it is not quite so easy to recognize Eben's rebellious and rambunctious brothers as an early variation of the Mephistophelean, alcoholic side of Jamie Tyrone in these plays. O'Neill's previous representations of his brother were in figures whose debauches are much subordinated to their protective qualities. Eben's brothers, on the other hand, are presented as ruthless competitors, hardly protective in any sense. Ten years older than Eben (Jamie is ten years older than Edmund), Simeon and Peter sell their birthright (the farm) much as the real Jamie sold his birthright (acting talent) for an illusion: "gold" for Simeon and Peter, the "good life" of the Broadway "sport" for Jamie. After years of submission, Simeon and Peter, like Jamie, finally defy a tyrant father, and in their defiance literally "whoop it up" like wild Indians, action which may stand for Jamie's irreverent, undisciplined behavior.

As Simeon and Peter anticipate Jamie Tyrone, Ephraim Cabot anticipates James Tyrone, Sr. Cut from the same cloth as the stubborn tyrants in O'Neill's early plays—Captain Keeney in *Ile*, Chris Christopherson in *Anna Christie*, or Isaiah Bartlett in *Gold*—Ephraim Cabot in his dogged commitment to his farm strongly parallels James Tyrone in his commitment to his play. And as with James, that commitment has brought frustration and hardship to those around him. As James justifies himself by lengthily telling of his early struggles, Ephraim lengthily and in similar tones (if not dialect) tells of his. Such matters are of course treated with understanding and even humor in *Long Day's Journey*. *Desire under the Elms* was written well before O'Neill had the distance and experience to treat these subjects in so detached a fashion. Nevertheless, both plays make us finally forgive and even admire their tyrannical fathers. What we admire in both the old men is their capacity to endure. James has a wife who is a seemingly incurable drug addict, Ephraim a wife who is guilty of infanticide. Both have the strength, never fully explored in either play, to survive the awesome emotional hardship each has to face. Stubborn tyrant, volatile fraud, abject confessor—these chief variations in all O'Neill's dramatic treatments of his father are linked by a consistent tone of forgiveness.

Far more complex than Ephraim, and more difficult to recognize as the representation of O'Neill's mother in *Desire under the Elms* is the figure of Abbie Cabot. To understand what Abbie represents in this play, one needs first to consider her image at the end, where she is forgiven, as Mary is forgiven in *Long Day's Journey*. Roger Asselineau has convincingly identified the play's conclusion as an attempt to create a kind of death-transcending kinship. It is an ending in which the lovers transcend the terrible event which has divided them. Abbie's murder of her baby has the same connotations as Mary's addiction. It creates in herself and others an aura of fear and disgust that go far beyond what one might associate with other "crimes." And thus the forgiveness must assume extraordinary proportions. *Desire under the Elms*, like *Long Day's Journey*, is an attempt to dramatize that extraordinary forgiveness, and thus Abbie's links with Mary are most recognizable at the conclusion of the play.

But kinship in death is a far cry from kinship in life. The kinship of Eben and Abbie at the play's conclusion is not one of this world. Eben's responses to Abbie, like Jim's toward Ella in

All God's Chillun, represent a determination to blot out the evil, to return to a state of innocence. In both plays, the world forces a united pair to know they must somehow leave it together if they are to remain united. This is hardly the kinship of the sea plays, or the kinship we will come to know in the later works. In fact, Abbie and Eben, like Ella and Jim, must look forward to a union that is essentially a union in withdrawal, and that is precisely the destiny figures like Simon Harford struggle against. Madness and the gallows in these plays are more an anticipation of Lavinia Mannon's or Deborah Harford's withdrawals than of the kinship in the Tyrone family or the love of Josie Hogan and Jim Tyrone. Instead of kinship, then, it might be more accurate to say that it is a morbid reconciliation that these plays yearn for.

But the figure the young hero must be reconciled with remains a figure representing O'Neill's mother. I have briefly suggested that Abbie Cabot at the end of the play suggests Mary Tyrone. The problem is to recognize her early in the play in that context. If Abbie is indeed a stand-in for O'Neill's mother in this play, she does not seem so at first, during her developing relationship with Eben. Rather, she *becomes* that figure rather abruptly as the play progresses.

O'Neill's mother died shortly before this play was conceived, and Eben's reactions before he meets Abbie unquestionably have to do with that event. Eben is fiercely loyal to the memory of his recently dead mother, who he feels was the only one who loved him. But his love for her is not simple or uncomplicated. O'Neill describes the two enormous elms on each side of the house as maternal symbols, but it is "a sinsiter maternity." The elms "appear to protect and at the same time subdue." There is "in their aspect, a crushing jealous absorption." Clearly, Eben's sinister domination by the memory of his dead mother is O'Neill's by the memory of his.

Abbie's appearance, then, must at first conflict with everything associated with Eben's mother. With her entrance, Eben's attention is drawn away from his dead mother's memory, much as he struggles to keep that memory alive. Abbie attracts him sexually, and she attracts him maternally. As she leads him on sexually, she also refers to herself as his "new Maw." In effect, Abbie at first replaces the town whore "Min," to whom all the Cabot men have gone periodically both for sex and motherly comfort. Eben struggles against Abbie, to be sure, but it is a losing struggle. Abbie easily dominates him erotically and less easily begins to dominate him maternally. In effect, Abbie in these early scenes is an Earth Mother, the first of many in O'Neill's plays—a woman who can fulfill a man's need for both sexual satisfaction and mothering without feeling or evoking guilt in the process. She comes as a new manifestation of "Min."

But it is the sex that from the start creates the play's complications. The living Abbie cannot in fact be the mythic Min. As soon as the burning, repressed sexuality bursts into open sexual encounter, guilt does set in, and the image of Abbie shifts inexorably from Earth Mother to real mother. From that point on, Abbie does more than replace Eben's "Maw." She becomes O'Neill's Maw—a figure torn between powerful possessiveness and haunting, decimating guilt. The scene (Part Two, scene 3) in which Abbie makes her transformation most apparent warrants closer analysis. After their lust has figuratively burned down the wall between their bedrooms, Abbie, instead of making love to Eben in his room, insists that they do so in the front parlor Eben so insistently associates with his dead mother. She does this, she feels, to drive home the domination she now feels she has over Eben and the entire household, but she does not realize the strange effect this determination will have. As soon as she enters the parlor O'Neill tells us that a "change has come over the woman. She looks awed and frightened now, ready to run away." This is certainly different from her assertiveness of the previous scene and parallels once more the descriptions of the many characters who anticipate Mary Tyrone. In the parlor, at Abbie's urging, Eben begins suddenly to be reconciled to the thought of his dead mother's acceptance of what is going on. Abbie works on him through the mutual resentment both have felt for the intransigent Ephraim.

> *Eben:* . . . . She was soft an' easy. He [Ephraim]
>   couldn't 'preciate her.
> *Abbie:* He can't 'preciate me!
> *Eben:* He murdered her with his hardness.
> *Abbie:* He's murderin' me! (I. 241–43)

What Abbie is doing here reflects the change O'Neill referred to. Abbie is getting Eben to identify with her response to her husband just as later Mary gets Edmund to feel sympathy for her treatment by the intransigent James. Mother wins son in opposition to father. But this is supposed to be a seduction scene—and so it is, in two ways. The seduction is both sexual and maternal. Abbie is possessed, says the horrified O'Neill, of a "horrible mixture of lust and mother love." Without abandoning her sexual drive, Abbie becomes in the special parlor belonging to Eben's dead mother (again recalling Mary's "spare room") a new manifestation of that mother. Abbie then commits a terrible crime in that parlor, as Mary commits a terrible crime in her spare room. She not only commits adultery, but in effect sleeps with her own son—and what follows is guilt upon guilt.

What one also comes to realize about *Desire under the Elms* is that none of the action which follows Abbie's seduction of Eben, even the horrifying murder of a helpless infant, has the force of that seduction scene. The dramatic energy of that scene feels completely spontaneous, while that of much which follows feels contrived. Only Ephraim's feverishly grotesque solo dance at the party for the new baby seems to emanate from the kind of authentic feeling that underlies the seduction. The party itself, with its gossipy neighbors and the sulky Eben refusing to attend, lacks the ironic impact O'Neill intended for it. This is probably true because the baby and everything surrounding it is a contrivance. The baby has no identity. It functions simply as a means by which Abbie and Eben "get back" at Ephraim—that is, the means by which mother and son "get back" at father—and its murder is the terrible crime for which Eden at first violently condemns and later forgives Abbie—that is, the terrible crime for which Edmund at first violently condemns but later forgives (or tries to forgive) his mother.—MICHAEL MANNHEIM, "*Desire under the Elms*," *Eugene O'Neill's Language of Kinship*, 1982, pp. 35–39

Praise the Phoenix Theatre for producing Eugene O'Neill's *The Great God Brown* anew. George Jean Nathan thought it O'Neill's best play, an opinion I do not share, but one step toward the making of a true theatre in our country is the production of old plays of merit.

It is not sufficient, though, that such plays be seen merely as new "shows"; they should be comprehended as part of a development in their author's work and as part of our own history. It is no longer of first importance that O'Neill used masks in this play, a device considered highly "experimental" in 1926, when the play was originally presented. What is important is the play's theme and the anguish O'Neill imbued it with. The theme is the practical man's envy of the artist and the artist's jealousy of the dominant practical man—a peculiarly American theme in the period of the play's conception.

O'Neill probed further than this bald statement might suggest. He saw the American businessman—for that is what Brown represents, though O'Neill made him an architect—becoming infected with the artist's yearnings and unable finally to realize himself either as one thing or another. Brown suffers some of the inner dissatisfactions which plague and impel the artist without possessing the artist's sensibility or skill. More strikingly, O'Neill portrays his artist, Dion Anthony, as a trammeled human being, really a half-artist with a gnawing sense of inadequacy in his philosophy, his personality and his adjustment to life. That is a crucial American tragedy: the incompleteness of American civilization as it focuses in the individual.

This sounds old-fashioned. Today, only a brief "moment" since the dilemma appeared poignant in the growing American consciousness, terms and circumstances have altered their outer form. The businessman of today is emotionally more complacent: if he appreciates the artist's function, collects paintings, attends concerts and reads certain books or book reviews, he expresses his disquiet otherwise than O'Neill's Brown. Similarly, the artist today seems to have taken his "proper" place in our society, so that with a little maneuvering, rationalization, psychoanalysis and publicity he can feel pretty much in the same boat as the Browns. The results is that they are both prepared to moan in monotonous chorus about taxes and the threat of atomic extinction.

The core of the matter, however, is not changed as much as we pretend; if we believe otherwise, that is chiefly because we rarely think of any "core" at all, except to indulge ourselves in a specious vocabulary of high-brow platitudes. O'Neill was no intellectual; if his play suffers in form and thought as well as in clarity, its impulse and source are nevertheless real and deep.

In O'Neill's work as a whole the theme of *The Great God Brown* recurs again and again in the most diverse guises; and if we refer even cursorily to O'Neill's life we become aware that the conflicts which made the theme urgent were rooted in his relationship to his father, his mother, his brother. A blood tie binds *Beyond the Horizon, Desire under the Elms, Marco Millions, Long Day's Journey into Night, A Touch of the Poet* into a single underlying meaning: the individual American has not reached fulfillment; he is not full grown; neither as a doer nor as a feeling person has he yet made peace with himself or with the world, and all the blather about the "American way of life" will not heal the sore.

Note too that O'Neill's artist, for all his mockery of Brown, is not presented as a "genius." It is always clear that O'Neill never thought of himself as a master in any way. He identified himself with derelicts and failures. He has no heroes; all his central figures yammer and yearn, curse and are as much lost as Yank the laborer in *The Hairy Ape*. Immature on the level of ultimate power, O'Neill is the dramatic poet of our own immaturity—which in his work is not merely an artistic or an intellectual flaw, but a lacerating wound.

You may be embarrassed by some of the awkwardness and feeble verbiage of *The Great God Brown*, particularly in the last act; and you can, if you wish, disparage O'Neill, in academic loftiness, by comparing his plays with the best work of the European playwrights of the past forty years. The fact remains that he is not only our most important dramatist, but one whose total product is, even in some of its faults, more truly relevant to the American people—whose "story" after all concerns the whole of modern society—than any other dramatist of this period anywhere.—HAROLD CLURMAN, "*The Great God Brown*, 1959" (1959), *The Naked Image*, 1966, pp. 98–100

In *Strange Interlude* he is still wearing the robes of the prophet; he appears to be suggesting to us that he is getting at something very secret and esoteric; we are going to be told something extremely important about life, and miraculously new. And precisely what this message is we never find out.

But, fortunately, there is much more than this. The play is really a novel for the stage—a novel (thanks largely to the use of the asides) pitched in the key of the interior monologue. We can, if we like, observe in this regard that the use of the aside is merely a return to the freer and larger liberalism of (for example) the Elizabethan stage—an outpouring, unchecked by niggling stage traditions, of life's prodigal and artless abundance. If the novelist may be permitted to sit, like a signalman in a trainyard signal box, somewhere behind the hero's frontal bone, watching the arrival and departure of every image or effect, why should not the dramatist be allowed a similar freedom? Shakespeare was not inhibited by the convention that we cannot know what a man is thinking—his Hamlets and Gertrudes and Claudiuses unpack their hearts with words to excellent effect. There is no good reason why Mr. O'Neill should not do likewise. The device seems new only because it has not recently been used and because he uses it wholesale.

Whether Mr. O'Neill uses it with entire success is another question. If one regards it simply as a technical device, then one may say that on the whole he does. Mr. O'Neill's instinct for the stage has always been almost uncannily sound, and the present instance is no exception. Many of the asides in the present play make pretty tough reading but prove actable to an astonishing degree. Asides which on the printed page sound flat or empty or grandiose or over-tense or maudlin megaphone over the footlights with instant effect. And there are many scenes in which the queer and delicious counterpoint provided by the contrast between two or more streams of consciousness, simultaneously going their own ways, is productive of the finest kind of dramatic value.

But on the psychological side, a side which is clearly just as important for Mr. O'Neill as it is for us, one is not quite so sure. If one takes *Strange Interlude* simply as a story and chiefly the life history of Nina, certainly one can extract an almost unflagging pleasure from it. But the minute one begins to analyze the characters who compose this story and to put together or take apart the psychological motives which supply the *donnée* of the action, one becomes slightly uneasy. One has always felt, a little, that Mr. O'Neill's sense of character was oddly deficient. He sees a shape, a guise, a color, an emotional tone, a *direction* (if one may apply such vague terms to the sense of character), but somehow or other he very nearly always just misses the last quintessence of what one calls individuality.

One cannot wholly, in this play, believe that Nina would have done what she did. Not that her actions are in any way impossible, but that she isn't, by Mr. O'Neill, quite made for us the sort of creature of whom we would have expected them. In the same way, Marsden remains unconvincing throughout, and so does Darrell, and so does Evans. They think, in their asides, the things which the *situation* would naturally and inevitably demand of them, but they do not think the things exactly, or richly, which their own inner *identities* would demand of them: they have not, in other words, that ultimate surplusage of sheer *being*, in their own rights, which a Shakespeare would have given us. One feels, rather, that Mr. O'Neill has come to them from outside, has made for us a set of admirably lifelike puppets and has urged them into a series of admirably plausible actions, but that there are very few moments when any of these people become subtly or power-

fully or aromatically *themselves* and, *ipso facto*, run away with the scene as a first-rate character creation ought to do.

And it is precisely in the asides that Mr. O'Neill had, of course, his golden opportunity to bring this about. Here, one would suppose, Nina or Evans could have come before us with naked and terrifying reality. But one has, on the whole, the feeling that Mr. O'Neill's poetic divination has not been quite equal to the task.

Perhaps, in *Strange Interlude*, he comes closer to this kind of divination than he has ever come before? . . . That is hard to say. One still feels a kind of hollow and melodramatic unreality in Mr. O'Neill's realism: an operatic largeness which is not quite life itself. And, nevertheless, it would be ungracious and dishonest not to admit that this play seemed to the present reviewer the finest play by an American which he ever saw on the stage—and the most moving.—CONRAD AIKEN, "O'Neill, Eugene" (1928), *A Reviewer's ABC*, 1958, pp. 316–18

What we have in *Mourning Becomes Electra* is a story far grimmer than *The Scarlet Letter*, which was a tale of a sin against conscience, where great lovers failing to reconcile their beliefs with their acts were forced into penance as the only resolution of the conflict. But the Mannons, New England shipbuilders, great people in their great house, sinned against their own nature. Scarlet in them became a duller crimson. Love was a guilty passion, and it broke through, was thwarted, was suppressed, according to opportunity, not conscience or even whole-hearted desire. The dead Mannons, Abe and David, had both loved Marie Brantôme, the servant in the house; Abe's wife loved David; David took Marie; Abe, the elder, drove him out and ruined him; Marie was deserted; David hung himself; the very house in which the brothers lived was torn down in a jealous fury; and the passions of this family, first suppressed and then exploding, passed into the family character, where they made a doom which is the subject of this play. The tensity of this earlier situation accentuated every psychological trait of a family already strongly marked by Puritan tenacity and animal passion, and this tensity became a trait so heritable that every one of the descendants, Marie's illegitimate child like the rest, shared it in common with an abnormal family resemblance. Lovers and enemies were fused into the Mannon type.

And this doom, which is reasonable only if you suppose that the affair of love and jealousy described above was a crisis of already determined character, became a psychological nightmare. Every Mannon in the play takes a double role, and every Mannon wears a mask-like face which hides a constant inner conflict. General Ezra, expected back from the war when the curtain rises, looks always like a statue on a memorial monument and yet rages with a purely sensual passion for a wife that he wishes to have as mistress. Lavinia, his daughter, is jealous of her mother and in love with her father. Orin, his son, is jealous of him and in love with his mother. Christine, the mother, is in love with her son, and when he is forced away from her into the war by a jealous father, takes on the mariner, Captain Brant, who is no other than the illegitimate son of Marie Brantôme and David Mannon. Orin, Brant, and Ezra are replicas in appearance. "Vinnie" is her mother over again, but soured and repressed. In this family there are two characters, one raging for love and life but held back and holding back, one freely moving toward desire (are they Abe and Marie Brantôme?), but these are mingled and blended until each individual is drawn and torn by conflicting temperaments.

And for three plays, each an act in a trilogy which is

inconclusive except as a whole, O'Neill debates the question as to whether happiness is right. Christine desires it and takes Brant as her lover. Ezra desires it, and humbles himself before Christine. She poisons him, and Vinnie, taking Electra's part and already jealous because of Brant, turns Orin (her Orestes) against his mother, drives him into murdering Brant, and Christine into suicide. Orin desires happiness and will marry the gentle Hazel; but Vinnie fears that he will reveal the family secrets, and when the price of his renunciation is set at the anesthetizing guilt of an incestuous relationship with herself, she helps him to self murder. Vinnie is still determined to escape into love and life, but in the complexity of her guilt finds that she cannot marry her simple lover Peter without poisoning his nature and his happiness. She goes back into the house of Mannon, the shutters are closed, and she puts on mourning for life.

Thus O'Neill offers three solutions for a life entanglement. First, a ruthless break through into satisfaction, which here is blocked by situations arising from the Mannon character. Second, a drowning of conscience in guilt so complete that character disintegrates. This the weak Orin finds possible, and the strong Vinnie impossible. Third, a return to stoicism, either the stoicism of death, or the stoicism of renunciation, each sterile. The last curtain falls on this solution.

These Mannons and the village dependents who serve as chorus are written up in the low tone and speak in the familiar language of the realistic drama, but all are symbols, and the tragic figures have the shadowy greatness of romantic heroes and heroines capable of anything. The Mannons and the Mannon wives are Byronic figures, each like the spectral troop in Beckford's *Vathek* hiding a burning heart, and masking the character which is the fatal family gift.

And one is forced to the rather astonishing conclusion for this day and generation that to the ultra-modern Mr. O'Neill (who in *Strange Interlude* introduced the populace to Freud), the American Puritan, with his conflicts between duty and desire, is still romantic. Like Hawthorne he veils and adumbrates his characters into shadowy and terrible greatness, like Hawthorne he sees no solution to the conflict and so wrecks his characters upon it as upon the rock of fate. Is this due to some racial compulsion, which we, in our light skepticism have overlooked, or has he wearied of the trivial interludes of modern love affairs and gone back to soul-searching Puritanism for a theme, precisely as the writers of movie scenarios yearn back to a long-vanished Wild West in seach of a virile story?

And indeed there are clear indications that Mr. O'Neill is riding his romance too hard in *Mourning Becomes Electra*. The old rigors, the old conflicts that inspired Hawthorne are no longer enough, they have no "kick" in them for O'Neill unless they are lifted from imagination into nightmare and lead to situations so sensational that it is horror rather than imaginative sympathy which they inspire. All, all the Mannons must be made incestuous in wish, because the last step in the suppression of desire by a code is a spiritual morbidity where the tortured soul can be satisfied only by what is forbidden in every man's taboo. All, all in their imaginations long for some "happy island" of the South Seas (and Lavinia goes to seek it) where they can lapse into primitivism with their beloveds and doff their karmas with their garments. The Puritan tradition of greed and suppression, duty and accomplishment, is driven into a baleful Purgatory with no way out but a return to savagery, or a final extinction of all that makes it human. This is the kind of alternative that Byron used to offer a shuddering Europe. It was excess then, it is excess now. The dramatist has

tortured his situation until it becomes an abnormality, and his tragedy suffers from the law of diminishing returns.—HENRY SEIDEL CANBY, "Scarlet Becomes Crimson" (1931), *Seven Years' Harvest*, 1936, pp. 140–43

Although Mr. O'Neill has been absent from the theatre for twelve years *The Iceman Cometh* is only seven years old. He wrote this bitter reverie in 1939, and it ranks toward the top of his collected works. It also returns us to a line of pure speculation that was broken when the war blew the world apart. Even if *The Iceman Cometh* had been written only a year ago, it is doubtful that the violence of the war would have affected it much. For of all the writers in the world Mr. O'Neill is the one most able to live his own life and do his own thinking by anatomizing his own soul.

Look back over his career that began thirty years ago in Provincetown and you realize that the affairs of the world have not influenced it much. He has never been a topical writer. Most of the human experience out of which he has written his long shelf of drama comes from the early period of his life that began in 1909, when he went gold-prospecting in Honduras, and that concluded three years later when his health failed and he went into a tuberculosis sanitarium. Those three years made a deep impression on him. He went to sea in a sailing vessel, found himself stranded on the beach in Buenos Aires, shipped to Africa and then home in a freighter and hung around Jimmy the Priest's broken-down saloon.

Dynamo, Strange Interlude, Mourning Becomes Electra, Lazarus Laughed and *Days without End* mark the period when Mr. O'Neill was more preoccupied with books than with experience, more with ideas than with human beings. *Ah, Wilderness!* was a holiday excursion back into the humors of his boyhood. But the bulk of his work derives from those three years when he was at loose ends. Since his eminence as a writer comes from his passionate, poetic wonder about the truth of the universe, the characters in his dramas are hardly more than illustrations for his ideas; he is not confined by their experience. But no group of characters has made such a deep impression on him as the battered men and blowzy women he knew in those squalid years when he was on the bum. Elemental people, they are good instruments for conveying the elemental quality of Mr. O'Neill's meditations on life.

The Iceman Cometh returns to the thick-fumed world of beer and whisky where the raw-mannered characters of SS *Glencairn* and *Anna Christie* dwelled a quarter of a century ago. Inside Harry Hope's grimy saloon Mr. O'Neill has assembled a group of fugitives from the bustling world of politics, labor insurgency, commerce, amusement and crime; and they represent men he knew in the days when he was sleeping in the backrooms and nibbling at the free lunch. Since he has not lost his capacity for drawing lucid characterizations or for writing stormy dialogue, his long portrait of a saloon full of charlatans is fascinating as a job of professional writing.

But the quality of an O'Neill play is always the malevolent rhythm of the things that are not spoken. In *The Iceman Cometh* he is again probing under the slag-heap of life into the black mysteries of the universe. Like a poet, Mr. O'Neill is forever trying to pluck out the heart of the mystery. During his bookish period, in *Lazarus Laughed* and *Days without End*, he came up with mystic confirmations of life; he accepted the universe. Now he is preoccupied with death. His befuddled characters are clinging to life by steeping their minds in pipe-dreams. To escape the curse of a guilty feeling they "hide behind lousy pipe-dreams about tomorrow." They justify their presence in a doss-house by inventing romantic legends about their past. Not one of them regards himself as a common bum.

A fanatical salesman tries to reform them by making them face the truth about themselves. He promises them peace if they will murder their gaudy illusions. But facing the truth terrifies them. Furthermore, it develops that the apostle of peace is fraudulent. He has already stepped into the edge of the shadow of death; he is a condemned man. In these circumstances, conversion to peace is nothing more than renunciation of life and acceptance of death. Having learned that much, Mr. O'Neill's rag-tag and bobtail joyfully return to their pipe-dreams, bottles and contentment.

Not the overtones, but the undertones capture the audience of an O'Neill play. For the surface dramatics are often cheap and commonplace. Read *The Iceman Cometh*. Like the gauche title, the dialogue often seems wooden, crude and unfinished, as if it were the work of an industrious apprentice. The play, which takes four hours in the theatre, seems verbose and torpid. Although the main theme is simple enough and reiterated about every five minutes ("damnable iteration," Falstaff would call it), the logic of the symbolism is difficult to work out. No one is quite sure that he understands the significance of every character and idea.

But put all this in the theatre and it suddenly becomes a living organism. The dialogue becomes vigorous speech; the drama that seems tediously wordy in the reading glows with promethean flame and the symbolism is no more than an unimportant after-thought. Although Mr. O'Neill is detached from the modern theatre, he is our most dramatic dramatist.
—BROOKS ATKINSON, "*The Iceman Cometh*" (1946), *Broadway Scrapbook*, 1947, pp. 241–43

The characters of *Long Day's Journey* are people to whom something once happened. It is worth saying this before remarking that for the rest of the play nothing happens. Mary, a convent-educated girl who might have become a nun, fell in love with a romantic actor. Tyrone, the actor, was once praised by Edwin Booth, but he sold his soul to a popular 'vehicle' and killed a notable talent. Jamie, a brilliant boy, was expelled from college. Edmund, the failed poet, once took to the sea and discovered its freedom. These events are now over; the pain and sweetness of their recollection remain, imprisoning their victims in corresponding images of value and desire. When Edmund is drunk he reverts to the sea, now inordinately heroic in his Conradian memory. In Shakespeare Tyrone finds the standard by which he condemns himself, the nobility which makes everything else seem sordid. Jamie's decadence is shamed in the sight of a greater decadence, in the poems of Baudelaire, Dowson, Wilde. Mary retreats to her father's house, a heaven-haven in memory. Nothing will happen; we are not watching *Ghosts* or *Hedda Gabler*. These people will not break away into freedom or romance, open wide the windows: there are no wild ducks. The Tyrones look back, or yearn back, to the first colours of life. Fate gave them the first line of their lives for nothing, but they have not carried on from there in the same glad spirit, they have not written their poems. So an action is begun, and the victims suffer its consequences. We know that under certain auspices it is possible to equate Action and Passion. Thomas's first speech in *Murder in the Cathedral* urges this equation:

> They know and do not know, what it is to act or
>   suffer.
> They know and do not know, that action is suffering
> And suffering is action. Neither does the agent suffer
> Nor the patient act. But both are fixed
> In an eternal action, an eternal patience
> To which all must consent that it may be willed
> And which all must suffer that they may will it,

> That the pattern may subsist, for the pattern is the
>   action
> And the suffering, that the wheel may turn and still
> Be forever still.

Thomas can transcend the dichotomy of action and passion by equating them, appealing to the higher term, the will of God, which reconciles them. But when the higher term is missing, or when the identification with the will of God is refused, the terms split apart. There is a passage in 'Little Gidding' which ponders this situation; when action and passion split apart, we are told, action becomes more motion:

> Where action were otherwise movement
> Of that which is only moved
> And has in it no source of movement—
> Driven by daemonic, chthonic
> Powers.

This is an accurate description of *Long Day's Journey*. For these characters there is no higher term to resolve or contain the passion: this is the degree of their exposure. They are driven by what O'Neill elsewhere calls 'the Force behind'. Mary can forget the present pain by remembering the pleasure of her childhood, but the cost is that she cannot remember anything else; her recession to childhood is thus 'fated': 'None of us can help the things life has done to us. They're done before you realise it, and once they're done they make you do other things until at last everything comes between you and what you'd like to be, and you've lost your true self for ever.'

It is hard to think of this play as a tragedy if we insist upon tragic heroes and roles which they assume with a more or less steady march into the future. Unless we are prepared to admit the tragic spirit when the motives are ambiguous and barely conscious, we must look for another name. But this is hardly necessary. Northrop Frye has been discussing Tragedy in terms which suit our present occasion. We come close to 'the heart of tragedy', he says, 'when the catastrophe is seen, not as a consequence of what one has done, but as the end of what one is'. Hence 'the Christian original sin, the medieval wheel of Fortune, the existentialist's "dread" are all attempts to express the tragic situation as primary and uncaused, as a condition and not an act, and such ideas bring us closer than Aristotle's flaw *(hamartia)* does to the unconscious crime of Oedipus, the unjust death of Cordelia, or the undeserved suffering of Job'. In O'Neill's play 'the Force behind' has so arranged things that the characters are what they are; and, being what they are, they are driven along those fateful lines. Harold Rosenberg distinguishes between a personality and an identity in terms which clarify *Long Day's Journey*. A character in a play has an identity when there is a role available to him and he is sufficient to take it up. He is a personality where no role is available or he is insufficient to it. We find this situation so often in daily life that we are not surprised to see it in the theatre. Hamlet at the beginning of the play is merely a personality: however richly endowed, he is insufficient to the only role he is offered, the Revenge Hero. Later, after his return from England, he becomes an identity; he is now sufficient to the role, and identified with it. In *Long Day's Journey* the tragic condition is the fact that no roles are available to these particular people. So, even if they have very few qualities, the qualities they have are in excess of their occasions; they are spiritually unemployed. The play is saved from tedium by the fact that we don't know, at any moment, whether the several uneasy factors given at the start will be kept apart and separately disposed, or whether they will be brought into sinister conjunction. 'And then life had me where it wanted me,' Tyrone says: the action of the play is the action of Fate in doing this, getting these people where it wants them.

This is where the idea of Original Sin is relevant. For the local ills of life O'Neill often implies specific cause; cause in heredity, childhood, society, and so forth. But there is a residue of pain and evil for which no historical cause can be assigned. It might be argued that O'Neill's presentation of this evil in social and biological terms is a secular version of the Christian belief in Original Sin. According to this belief we inherit a categorical guilt; in O'Neill's version we are never free from the evil of being born and the second evil of being the children of our parents. The argument might be extended. When O'Neill gave up his Catholicism, he did not shed the secular patterns of that faith. He could not be a Pelagian, denying Original Sin: he continued to believe in evil and guilt as categorical conditions. The Christian believes that Christ and the Church mediate between that guilt and his own soul; that Christ's sacrifice was accepted for that end. If you give up the Christian faith and yet retain belief in a secular version of it, you must find some other means, some mediation between yourself and the inherited guilt. There is no evidence that O'Neill solved this problem, and every evidence that it plagued him. The only way out was to assume an universal determinism and live under its shadow. ⟨. . .⟩

The figure the play makes in our minds ⟨. . .⟩ is a painful rhythm of loss and gain, the gain less than the loss, until in the end, it seems, the loss is irrevocable. Mary's regression to childhood, her slipping away from life, is the major cadence within which lesser cadences in the same form are defined. When she comes down the stairs carrying her wedding-gown and babbling of Sister Martha, the drunken Jamie says: 'The Mad Scene. Enter Ophelia!' This is the greatest regression, but the play is vivid with smaller versions; as when Edmund says, 'It felt damned peaceful to be nothing more than a ghost within a ghost.' If this rhythm seems relentless, it is because it is introduced at the start and played over and over again, with different materials, different combinations of feeling and sound. The climax is its musical conclusion. In that sense the principle of the cadence is inescapable, even though the precise form of its embodiment cannot, at any moment, be anticipated. It is as if the cadence were, like the guilt, categorical and we have merely to wait for each of its manifestations: but we do not know when any will come.

This is how O'Neill's theatre-poetry works; it is a matter of structure, rhythm, cadence, coming from life and flowing back into life again. It is not, in the first instance, a verbal matter. The easy thing to say of O'Neill is that he cannot write. He said it himself. Edmund, O'Neill's *persona* in *Long Day's Journey*, has a long drunken speech about his experiences at sea. The style is high, a hectic mixture of Conrad, O'Neill, and Melville. At the end, Tyrone, the silent audience, says: 'Yes, there's the makings of a poet in you all right.' And Edmund says, sardonically: 'The *makings* of a poet. No, I'm afraid I'm like the guy who is always panhandling for a smoke. He hasn't even got the makings. He's only got the habit. I couldn't touch what I tried to tell you just now. I just stammered. That's the best I'll ever do. I mean, if I live. Well, it will be faithful realism, at least. Stammering is the native eloquence of us fog people.' We take Edmund at his word; he is not a failed poet for nothing. And we accept the identification of Edmund and O'Neill. It is easy to agree that O'Neill lacks the finesse of words which we find in Yeats, Eliot, Mann, or—to shame him further—Shakespeare. There are many speeches in O'Neill's plays in which he tries to conceal the stammer by recourse to the high style and the high bravado. But *Long Day's Journey* is

a poetic play because of the coherence of its elements and the depth at which the coherence is achieved. The elements are not, in the first instance, verbal; they are movements of feeling, gestures, relationships, the things that Yeats called Life when he invoked two rival 'ways', the other being Words. It is the urgency and coherence of these elements that makes the play poetic. What we demand of the words is that they will not shame the feelings placed in their charge: everything else is a bonus. If Shakespeare writes like an angel and O'Neill stammers like poor Poll, this is a fair measure of the difference between them; but it should not blind us to the fact that O'Neill has something of that poetic and theatrical sense which prompted Shakespeare, in *Macbeth*, to bring in the Porter's scene immediately after the murder scene. If we put the two men irrevocably apart, it is only after putting them, in this respect, together. The impact of *Long Day's Journey* comes from finesse certainly not verbal but, to a high degree, formal, a finesse of structure; so that the excitement of waiting to see whether the ingredients are combined in an innocent or a catastrophic way goes along with a formal excitement; what Charles Morgan calls 'the suspense of form', the latency of form until the form is eventually fulfilled. The form, it is hardly necessary to remark, acknowledges a life which is neither formal nor linguistic.—DENIS DONOGHUE, "The Old Drama and the New," *The Ordinary Universe*, 1968, pp. 152–59

LIONEL TRILLING
"Eugene O'Neill"

New Republic, September 23, 1936, pp. 176–79

Whatever is unclear about Eugene O'Neill, one thing is certainly clear—his genius. We do not like the word nowadays, feeling that it is one of the blurb words of criticism. We demand that literature be a guide to life, and when we do that we put genius into a second place, for genius assures us of nothing but itself. Yet when we stress the actionable conclusions of an artist's work, we are too likely to forget the power of genius itself, quite apart from its conclusions. The spectacle of the human mind in action is vivifying; the explorer need discover nothing so long as he has adventured. Energy, scope, courage—these may be admirable in themselves. And in the end these are often what endure best. The ideas expressed by works of the imagination may be built into the social fabric and taken for granted; or they may be rejected; or they may be outgrown. But the force of their utterance comes to us over millennia. We do not read Sophocles or Aeschylus for the right answer; we read them for the force with which they represent life and attack its moral complexity. In O'Neill, despite the many failures of his art and thought, this force is inescapable.

But a writer's contemporary audience is inevitably more interested in the truth of his content than in the force of its expression; and O'Neill himself has always been ready to declare his own ideological preoccupation. His early admirers—and their lack of seriousness is a reproach to American criticism—were inclined to insist that O'Neill's content was unimportant as compared to his purely literary interest and that he injured his art when he tried to think. But the appearance of *Days without End* has made perfectly clear the existence of an organic and progressive unity of thought in all O'Neill's work and has brought it into the critical range of the two groups whose own thought is most sharply formulated, the Catholic and the Communist. Both discovered what O'Neill had frequently announced, the religious nature of all his effort.

Not only has O'Neill tried to encompass more of life than

most American writers of his time but, almost alone among them, he has persistently tried to *solve* it. When we understand this we understand that his stage devices are no fortuitous technique; his masks and abstractions, his double personalities, his drum beats and engine rhythms are the integral and necessary expression of his temper of mind and the task it set itself. Realism is uncongenial to that mind and that task and it is not in realistic plays like *Anna Christie* and *The Straw* but rather in such plays as *The Hairy Ape, Lazarus Laughed* and *The Great God Brown*, where he is explaining the world in parable, symbol and myth, that O'Neill is most creative. Not the minutiae of life, not its feel and color and smell, not its nuance and humor, but its "great inscrutable forces" are his interest. He is always moving toward the finality which philosophy sometimes, and religion always, promises. Life and death, good and evil, spirit and flesh, male and female, the all and the one, Anthony and Dionysius—O'Neill's is a world of these antithetical absolutes such as religion rather than philosophy conceives, a world of pluses and minuses; and his literary effort is an alegbraic attempt to solve the equations.

In one of O'Neill's earliest one-act plays, the now unprocurable *Fog*, a Poet, a Business Man and a Woman with a Dead Child, shipwrecked and adrift in an open boat, have made fast to an iceberg. When they hear the whistle of a steamer, the Business Man's impulse is to call for help, but the Poet prevents him lest the steamer is wrecked on the fog-hidden berg. But a searching party picks up the castaways and the rescuers explain that they had been guided to the spot by a child's cries; the Child, however, has been dead a whole day. This little play is a crude sketch of the moral world that O'Neill is to exploit. He is to give an ever increasing importance to the mystical implications of the Dead Child, but his earliest concern is with the struggle between the Poet and the Business Man.

It is, of course, a struggle as old as morality, especially interesting to Europe all through its industrial nineteenth century, and it was now engaging America in the second decade of its twentieth. A concious artistic movement had raised its head to declare irreconcilable strife between the creative and the possessive ideal. O'Neill was an integral part—indeed, he became the very symbol—of that Provincetown group which represented the growing rebellion of the American intellectual against a business civilization. In 1914 his revolt was simple and socialistic; in a poem in *The Call* he urged the workers of the world not to fight, asking them if they wished to "bleed and groan—for Guggenheim" and "give your lives—for Standard Oil." By 1917 his feeling against business had become symbolized and personal. "My soul is a submarine," he said in a poem in *The Masses*:

> My aspirations are torpedoes.
> I will hide unseen
> Beneath the surface of life
> Watching for ships,
> Dull, heavy-laden merchant ships,
> Rust-eaten, grimy galleons of commerce
> Wallowing with obese assurance,
> Too sluggish to fear or wonder,
> Mocked by the laughter of the waves
> And the spit of disdainful spray.
> I will destroy them
> Because the sea is beautiful.

The ships against which O'Neill directed his torpedoes were the cultural keels laid in the yards of American business and their hulls were first to be torn by artistic realism. Although we now see the often gross sentimentality of the S.S. *Glencairn*

plays and remember with O'Neill's own misgiving the vaudeville success of *In the Zone*, we cannot forget that, at the time, the showing of a forecastle on the American stage was indeed something of a torpedo. Not, it is true, into the sides of Guggenheim and Standard Oil, but of the little people who wallowed complacently in their wake.

But O'Neill, not content with staggering middle-class complacency by a representation of how the other half lives, undertook to scrutinize the moral life of the middle class and dramatized the actual struggle between Poet and Business Man. In his first long play, *Beyond the Horizon*, the dreamer destroys his life by sacrificing his dream to domesticity; and the practical creator, the farmer, destroys his by turning from wheat-raising to wheat-gambling. It is a conflict O'Neill is to exploit again and again. Sometimes, as in *Ile* or *Gold*, the lust for gain transcends itself and becomes almost a creative ideal, but always its sordid origin makes it destructive. To O'Neill the acquisitive man, kindly and insensitive, practical and immature, became a danger to life and one that he never left off attacking.

But it developed, strangely, that the American middle class had no strong objection to being attacked and torpedoed; it seemed willing to be sunk for the insurance that was paid in a new strange coin. The middle class found that it consisted of two halves, bourgeoisie and booboisie. The booboisie might remain on the ship but the bourgeoisie could, if it would, take refuge on the submarine. Mencken and Nathan, who sponsored the O'Neill torpedoes, never attacked the middle class but only its boobyhood. Boobish and sophisticated: these were the two categories of art; spiritual freedom could be bought at the price of finding *Jurgen* profound. And so, while the booboisie prosecuted *Desire under the Elms*, the bourgeoisie swelled the subscription lists of the Provincetown Playhouse and helped the Washington Square Players to grow into the Theatre Guild. An increasingly respectable audience awarded O'Neill no less than three Pulitzer prizes, the medal of the American Academy of Arts and Sciences and a Yale Doctorate of Letters.

O'Neill did not win his worldly success by the slightest compromise of sincerity. Indeed, his charm consisted in his very integrity and hieratic earnestness. His position changed, not absolutely, but relatively to his audience, which was now the literate middle class caught up with the intellectual middle class. O'Neill was no longer a submarine; he had become a physician of souls. Beneath his iconoclasm his audience sensed reassurance.

The middle class is now in such literary disrepute that a writer's ability to please it is taken as the visible mark of an internal rottenness. But the middle class is people; prick them and they bleed, and whoever speaks sincerely to and for flesh and blood deserves respect. O'Neill's force derives in large part from the force of the moral and psychical upheaval of the middle class; it wanted certain of its taboos broken and O'Neill broke them. He was the Dion Anthony to its William Brown; Brown loved Dion: his love was a way of repenting for his own spiritual clumsiness.

Whoever writes sincerely about the middle class must consider the nature and the danger of the morality of "ideals," those phosphorescent remnants of a dead religion with which the middle class meets the world. This has been Ibsen's great theme, and now O'Neill undertook to investigate for America the destructive power of the ideal—not merely the sordid ideal of the Business Man but even the "idealistic" ideal of the Poet. The Freudian psychology was being discussed and O'Neill dramatized its simpler aspects in *Diff'rent* to show the effects of the repression of life. Let the ideal of chastity repress the vital forces, he was saying, and from this fine girl you will get a filthy harridan. The modern life of false ideals crushes the affirmative and creative nature of man; Pan, forbidden the light and warmth of the sun, grows "sensitive and self-concious and proud and revengeful"—becomes the sneering Mephistophelean mask of Dion.

The important word is *self-concious*, for "ideals" are part of the "cheating gestures which constitute the vanity of personality." "Life is all right if you let it alone," says Cybel, the Earth Mother of *The Great God Brown*. But the poet of *Welded* cannot let it alone; he and his wife, the stage directions tell us, move in circles of light that represent "auras of egotism" and the high ideals of their marriage are but ways each ego uses to get possession of the other. O'Neill had his answer to this problem of the possessive, discrete personality. Egotism and idealism, he tells us, are twin evils growing from man's suspicion of his life and the remedy is the laughter of Lazarus—"a triumphant, blood-stirring call to that ultimate attainment in which all prepossession with self is lost in an ecstatic affirmation of Life." The ecstatic affirmation of Life, pure and simple, is salvation. In the face of death and pain, man must reply with the answer of Kublai Kaan in *Marco Millions*: "Be proud of life! Know in your heart that the living of life can be noble! Be exalted by life! Be inspired by death! Be humbly proud! Be proudly grateful!"

It may be that the individual life is not noble and that it is full of pain and defeat; it would seem that Eileen Carmody in *The Straw* and Anna Christie are betrayed by life. But no. The "straw" is the knowledge that life is a "hopeless hope"—but still a hope. And nothing matters if you can conceive the whole of life. "Fog, fog, fog all bloody time," is the chord of resolution of *Anna Christie*. "You can't see where you vas going, no. Only dat ole davil, sea—she knows." The individual does not know, but life—the sea—knows.

To affirm that life exists and is somehow good—this, then, became O'Neill's quasi-religious poetic function, nor is it difficult to see why the middle class welcomed it. "Brown will still need me," says Dion, "to reassure him he's alive." What to do with life O'Neill cannot say, but there it is. For Ponce de Leon it is the Fountain of Eternity, "the Eternal Becoming which is Beauty." There it is, somehow glorious, somehow meaningless. In the face of despair one remembers that "Always spring comes again bearing life! Always forever again. Spring again! Life again!" To this cycle, even to the personal annihilation in it, the individual must say "Yes." Man inhabits a naturalistic universe and his glory lies in his recognition of its nature and assenting to it; man's soul, no less than the stars and the dust, is part of the Whole and the free man loves the Whole and is willing to be absorbed by it. In short, O'Neill solves the problem of evil by making explicit what men have always found to be the essence of tragedy—the courageous affirmation of life in the face of individual defeat.

But neither a naturalistic view of the universe nor a rapt assent to life constitutes a complete philosophic answer. Naturalism is the noble and realistic attitude that prepares the way for an answer; the tragic affirmation is the emotional crown of a philosophy. Spinoza—with whom O'Neill at this stage of his thought has an obvious affinity—placed between the two an ethic that arranged human values and made the world possible to live in. But O'Neill, faced with a tragic universe, unable to go beyond the febrilely passionate declaration, "Life is," finds the world impossible to live in. The naturalistic universe becomes too heavy a burden for him; its spirituality vanishes; it becomes a universe of cruelly blind

matter. "Teach me to be resigned to be an atom," cries Darrell, the frustrated scientist of *Strange Interlude*, and for Nina life is but "a strange dark interlude in the electrical display of God the father"—who is a God deaf, dumb and blind. O'Neill, unable now merely to accept the tragic universe and unable to support it with man's whole strength—his intellect and emotion—prepares to support it with man's weakness: his blind faith.

For the non-Catholic reader O'Neill's explicitly religious solution is likely to be not only insupportable but incomprehensible. Neither St. Francis nor St. Thomas can tell us much about it; it is neither a mystical ecstasy not the reasoned proof of assumptions. But Pascal can tell us a great deal, for O'Neill's faith, like Pascal's, is a poetic utilitarianism: he needs it and *will* have it. O'Neill rejects naturalism and materialism as Pascal had rejected Descartes and all science. He too is frightened by "the eternal silence of the infinite spaces." Like Pascal, to whom the details of life and the variety and flux of the human mind were repugnant, O'Neill fells that life is empty—having emptied it—and can fill it only by faith in a loving God. The existence of such a God, Pascal knew, cannot be proved save by the heart's need, but this seemed sufficient and he stood ready to stupefy his reason to maintain his faith. O'Neill will do no less. It is perhaps the inevitable way of modern Catholicism in a hostile world.

O'Neill's rejection of materialism involved the familiar pulpit confusion of philosophical materialism with "crass" materialism, that is, with the preference of physical to moral well-being. It is therefore natural that *Dynamo*, the play in which he makes explicit his anti-materialism, should present characters who are mean and little—that, though it contains an Earth Mother, she is not the wise and tragic Cybel but the fat and silly Mrs. Fife, the bovine wife of the atheist dynamo-tender. She, like other characters in the play, allies herself with the Dynamo-God, embodiment both of the materialistic universe and of modern man's sense of his own power. But this new god can only frustrate the forces of life, however much it at first seems life's ally against the Protestant denials, and those who worship it become contemptible and murderous.

And the contempt for humanity which pervades *Dynamo* continues in *Mourning Becomes Electra*, creating, in a sense, the utter hopelessness of that tragedy. Aeschylus had ended his Atreus trilogy on a note of social reconciliation—after the bloody deeds and the awful pursuit of the Furies, society confers its forgiveness, the Furies are tamed to deities of hearth and field: "This day there is a new Order born"; but O'Neill's version has no touch of this resolution. There is no forgiveness in *Mourning Becomes Electra* because, while there is as yet no forgiving God in O'Neill's cosmos, there is no society either, only a vague chorus of contemptible townspeople. "There's no one left to punish me," says Lavinia. "I've got to punish myself."

It is the ultimate of individual arrogance, the final statement of a universe in which society has no part. For O'Neill, since as far back as *The Hairy Ape*, there has been only the individual and the universe. The social organism has meant nothing. His Mannons, unlike the Atreides, are not monarchs with a relation to the humanity about them, a humanity that can forgive because it can condemn. They act their crimes on the stage of the infinite. The mention of human law bringing them punishment is startlingly incongruous and it is inevitable that O'Neill, looking for a law, should turn to a divine law.

Forgiveness comes in *Ah, Wilderness!*, the satyr-play that follows the tragedy, and it is significant that O'Neill should have interrupted the composition of *Days without End* to write it. With the religious answer of the more serious play firm in his mind, with its establishment of the divine law, O'Neill can, for the first time, render the sense and feel of common life, can actually be humorous. Now the family is no longer destructively possessive as he has always represented it, but creatively sympathetic. The revolt of the young son—his devotion to rebels and hedonists, to Shaw, Ibsen and Swinburne—is but the mark of adolescence and in the warm round of forgiving life he will become wisely acquiescent to a world that is not in the least terrible.

But the idyllic life of Ah, Wilderness!, for all its warmth, is essentially ironical, almost cynical. For it is only when all magnitude has been removed from humanity by the religious answer and placed in the Church and its God that life can be seen as simple and good. The pluses and minuses of man must be made to cancel out as nearly as possible, the equation must be solved to equal nearly zero, before peace may be found. The hero of Days without End has lived for years in a torturing struggle with the rationalistic, questioning "half" of himself which has led him away from piety to atheism, thence to socialism, next to unchastity and finally to the oblique attempt to murder his beloved wife. It is not until he makes an act of submissive faith at the foot of the Cross and thus annihilates the doubting mind, the root of all evil, that he can find peace.

But the annihilation of the questioning mind also annihilates the multitudinous world. Days without End, perhaps O'Neill's weakest play, is cold and bleak; life is banished from it by the vision of the Life Eternal. Its religious content is expressed not so much by the hero's priestly uncle, wise, tolerant, humorous in the familiar literary convention of modern Catholicism, as by the hero's wife, a humorless, puritanical woman who lives on the pietistic-romantic love she bears her husband and on her sordid ideal of his absolute chastity. She is the very embodiment of all the warping, bullying idealism that O'Neill had once attacked. Now, however, he gives credence to this plaster saintliness, for it represents for him the spiritual life of absolutes. Now for the first time he is explicit in his rejection of all merely human bulwarks against the pain and confusion of life—finds in the attack upon capitalism almost an attack upon God, scorns socialism and is disgusted with the weakness of those who are disgusted with social individualism. The peace of the absolute can be bought only at the cost of blindness to the actual.

The philosophic position would seem to be a final one: O'Neill has crept into the dark womb of Mother Church and pulled the universe in with him. Perhaps the very violence of the gesture with which he has taken the position of passivity should remind us of his force and of what such force may yet do even in that static and simple dark. Yet it is scarcely a likely place for O'Neill to remember Dion Anthony's warning: "It isn't enough to be [life's] creature. You've got to create her or she requests you to destroy yourself."

BONAMY DOBRÉE
From "The Plays of Eugene O'Neill"
Southern Review, Winter 1937, pp. 435–44

It is not, perhaps, altogether fair for an Englishman to adjudge the work of a contemporary American playwright. It is not only that few of his plays have been acted in England, but that the whole atmosphere of response is different. A play, more than any other work of art, is a collaboration; it is, indeed, a mass collaboration, and unless the critic can sense the mass reactions, the instrument he can use is bound to be

one way or another unfit for its purpose. Yet the principles of the drama are eternal, the emotions of men throughout the world differ only in detail or stress, not in essentials; a judgment *sub specie aeternitatis* can be applied without more than the usual hazards. It is, admittedly, a severe test to apply to contemporary work, but it is one which Mr. O'Neill challenges, since his plays have far more than a local habitation.

Nothing can be more dangerous than to try to fit works of art into a preconceived pattern, a pattern, that is, constructed from previous things of the same kind, for it is precisely the business of a work of art to be different from other works of art. The wearisome criticism, "This is not a play," was one thrown at those of Ibsen and Tchekov alike. One would not go so far as this in talking of Mr. O'Neill's works, yet one may suggest that there is a certain lack of dramatic quality in a great deal of his work for the theater. That a work holds an audience is not enough to constitute it dramatic; it is the mood in which the audience is sent away that counts. We associate drama with a certain mood, a "full repose," to use the old phrase; something has happened to us, certain conflicts of emotion, emotions on all sorts of levels, the subconscious ones perhaps battling with the more purely mental ones; or on one level only, certain moralities being perhaps brought into opposition; and we go away from a play, or rise from its reading, with those conflicts resolved. It is a feeling familiar to all playgoers, and used to be called katharsis. It carries with it a sense of satisfaction; we have had an intellectual or emotional meal. But from most of Mr. O'Neill's plays we rise with a sense, rather, of dissatisfaction; we are puzzled, or we say, after considering the events put before us, "Well, what of it?"

This may be due to a failure on Mr. O'Neill's part to "generalize" his story or his characters enough; but it occurs to one after reading a number of his plays that what is wrong, what makes them, that is to say, fail to provide a sense of satisfaction, is mainly due to the fact that he seems to set before us stage novels rather than stage plays. The general run of novels—one must beware of making too broad statements on so varied a form—usually achieve much the same sort of effect, but it is less intense, and brought about by an accumulation of detail, a succession of small stimuli, a series of events. The method of the novel is less rapid, less violent, for it has a longer time to produce its effect in; it can, moreover, be far more comprehensive and diffuse. A drama is concentrated, and gets its effect by continual changes of speed and tension, especially of speed. The moment at which the speed changes, or the tension increases or relaxes, is the dramatic moment. The structure of a play, as of a novel, ultimately consists of the structure of emotions built up in ourselves; but since the drama is much shorter than the novel the structure has to be built up by different, possibly more violent means. The majority of Mr. O'Neill's plays seem to have the pace of the novel, the form, the slow steady development of the novel, far more than the varied rhythm of the drama. In the space allowed, Mr. O'Neill does not succeed in building up a structure of emotions which is in itself complete: the novelistic process has not had time to take effect; the dramatic impact is absent.

That two of his later dramas, *Strange Interlude* and *Mourning Becomes Electra,* are not open to this last charge is really an indication of the justice of what has been said. They are very long plays, twice the length at least of an ordinary play; the latter, moreover, is an adaptation of the *Oresteia,* which, as a drama, has withstood the ages, and so Mr. O'Neill reaps the benefit. It is more dramatic in form than the others. *Strange Interlude,* with its "internal" soliloquies, is essentially a novel—if "drama" really is "action." But what strikes one as being most significant is the length of time Mr. O'Neill requires to bring off his effect; and the suspicion that the above analysis is right is reinforced; he needs the time precisely because his dramas have the more leisurely, steady, almost uniform pace of the novel, rather than the more rapidly effective change of pace that characterizes plays as we have known them heretofore.

It may be that Mr. O'Neill himself feels this: his elaborate descriptions of his personages, not of their external characteristics but of their interior make-up, and in such a way as to be utterly unrealizable on the stage, seem to show that he does not think they explain themselves in action. How is the actor to portray the charactere of Michael in *Welded*, and how can the man be understood unless he does?

> One feels a perpetual strain about him, a passionate tension, a self-protecting and intellectually arrogant defiance of life and his own weakness, a deep need to love and to be loved, for a faith in which to relax.

That is a fairly simple example. The result is that this complex character, when his emotions are translated into action, seems simply a sentimental, uncontrolled neurotic. Given poets and a plenitude of words, benefits denied to the modern drama, such a character might be portrayed, a Hamlet say; but the form of modern drama does not allow for such complicated personalities, and they have to exist in the novel only. The dramatist has therefore to isolate simpler qualities, such as we get in Ibsen or Strindberg. Given the paucity of words of the modern drama, the only thing to do is strip character to a few bare essentials.

Mr. O'Neill, of course, cannot help being a child of his time, and the time is singularly unfortunate in some respects from the point of view of the writer of drama, especially for the kind of drama that it would appear Mr. O'Neill would wish to write, in which the motives of the characters are tangled. Recent theory, in which popular entertainers have made alliance with university professors (adversity does indeed make strange bedfellows), has lost sight of the fact that the ultimate technical material of which the drama is made is words, and again words (the action is the symbol of the idea): and it has yielded to a vicious notion that there is a thing called "good theater" which has nothing whatever to do with literary quality. They will accept any trick of scenery or costume, such things as Aristotle rightly said had nothing to do with the drama, but were part of the haberdasher's art, so long as they momentarily divert the audience—divert is the right word—and give as much importance to those as to the real matter in hand. The dramatist, of course, has every right to make full use of what aids various advances in the technique of carpentry and lighting can offer him, but increased facility in brute mechanism is not necessarily an advantage to the artist: it may be a trap. Mr. O'Neill, one feels, relies too much upon tricks, too little upon the quality of words, to do the work he wants done. He seems himself to have been carried away by the excitement of the new. We get separate rooms shown at the same time in *Desire under the Elms* and *Dynamo;* masks in *The Great God Brown* and *Lazarus Laughed;* accessory noises in *Bound East for Cardiff* and *The Emperor Jones:* and it is very doubtful if the means have really conduced to the end. The mask especially seems to have peculiar fascination for Mr. O'Neill, for even when masks are not worn, there is often a constant insistence on the mask-like qualities of the faces of his personages. He has, however, abandoned "noises off" as characters in his dramas; he has, perhaps, thrown aside actual masks, and the rest, we hope, will follow. One can admire and applaud his

experimental boldness, but one must insist that the things in which he has experimented are merely subsidiary, and a sign of weakness rather than of originality. The only originality that counts is that of the mind.

This brings us to what is, one need hardly say, the true subject matter of criticism, what the writer has to say, a matter inextricably bound up with the form. The form of the drama, as has already been suggested, is the structure of the emotions built up in the spectator. The sort of structure, the kind and quality of the emotions, are what constitute the individuality of a writer; they are the "what he has to say." And although one cannot but feel that much of Mr. O'Neill's work, interesting as it usually is, is largely unsatisfactory and fumbling in form, yet it is clear that he has something to say. But what that something is it is hard to discover. This is partly due, of course, to his virtues as an artist; he is not concerned with the discussion of the petty problems of today, still less with their solution, and his method of statement, like that of every great creative dramatic artist, is indirect. One feels very definitely that he is struggling to say something, that he has a vision, however obscured it may be, which seems to him of great and permanent importance in the understanding of humanity. It may be that his vision is nothing new, that it is the age-old sense of a fate stronger than man; he has, in fact, a sense of the tragic in life, the sense even that life is essentially and necessarily a tragedy, a struggle in which the gods are always stronger than man. This particular sense has, of course, nothing new about it, but it continually needs restating, reclothing in the psychological habiliments which, on the surface at least, vary in every age. Mankind may remain always fundamentally the same; what alters is the varying importance he gives to different emotions and desires, the stress he lays on the numerous facets of his nature.

Yet we are not conscious of this sense in all Mr. O'Neill's plays, especially the more realistic ones, such as *Straw*, which seems designed to show mainly the meanness of people. There is nothing to be done, we feel, by merely portraying the ruthless callousness of men and women, and the appeal to sympathy through the heroine's dying of consumption is no more than sentimental, as so much of Mr. O'Neill's work is— of which more later. Again, many of the shorter plays are nothing more than anecdotes, such as *Before Breakfast* or *The Dreamy Kid*, though the latter possibly contains the germ of an idea, an idea that Mr. O'Neill is fond of, namely, that through our emotions we create something that is stronger than ourselves. Mr. O'Neill, it would appear, is an unbeliever, who believes, however, as has been suggested by Dr. Pellizi, in evil. The same critic has also suggested that, as a relic of his Irish Catholic ancestry, besides hating puritanism he also believes in the miracle of grace, in some kind of redemption. Sometimes, indeed, a sentiment which might be taken to imply redemption intrudes, as when the father in *Desire under the Elms* momentarily admires his son for what, when we think about it for an instant, is a reaction as brutal as any of the others that urge this rustic hero to action. In *Mourning Becomes Electra* there is no redemption; there are the Choephoroi, certainly, but no Eumenides, the only major instance in which the modern writer departs from Aeschylus. There is, then, no necessity, no fate, against which Mr. O'Neill's people struggle outside what they themselves create, except possibly in *Bound East for Cardiff*, and we get this notion of the self-created fate as early as *The Emperor Jones;* the superstitious terrors which drive Jones to his doom are such as mankind has created (we meet this in a weaker form in *The Dreamy Kid*): in nearly all his plays it is the same notion which gives to them what form they have, and which, apparently, urged him to write.

To give this man-created fate validity, to make it strong enough to seem real, Mr. O'Neill found it necessary, it would appear, to make most of his people so odd as to be abnormal. The whole matter is perhaps most clearly revealed in *Dynamo*. There the "hero," Reuben, is clearly deranged. He is, to begin with, half-witted, or at least subnormal, and the loss of his faith in his father's peculiarly arid form of Christianity completely unhinges him. Only this can account for his making a god out of the dynamo, so completely that he feels bitterly that he has defiled the altar when he possesses the girl he loves in the engine-room; as a result he kills her and goes completely mad. That he should kill himself on the machine afterwards is not tragic; it is merely a very good thing. If the fate were not man-created it might be impressive, but it is not even that. The heroine in *All God's Chillun Got Wings* is again subnormal in intelligence and will. All the people in *Desire under the Elms* are half-witted; the drama deals entirely with the play of brute instinct, as though this, without its interplay with something implying different values, were of any interest whatever. The hero of *Diff'rent*, the heroine of *Strange Interlude*, are both psychologically abnormal, victims of fixations. ⟨. . .⟩

A further weakness is that Mr. O'Neill's notion of fate being what it is, one does not feel that the fate that encompasses his personages is compelling. Even in his version of the *Oresteia*, mercifully hard and unsentimental, there is no law compelling Orin (Orestes) to kill his father's murderer, his mother's lover. He does so because his sister—an Electra who serves her hatred, her Oedipus complex, rather than the gods, who are just—induces him to do so; and it must be remarked that this Orestes too is abnormal, not the normal, moral young man of Aeschylus, but one who is suffering from a head wound received in the Civil War. Thus there is nothing profoundly tragic about his murdering Brant. Brother and sister are pursued by the Furies, and the Furies win because their victims are profoundly neurotic. Yet *Mourning Becomes Electra* is by far Mr. O'Neill's best play simply because it exhibits throughout a certain hardness.

It may be argued, of course, that in representing his people as essentially immature, Mr. O'Neill is being true to life; it is recognized, I believe, by psychiatrists, that the great majority of human beings do not progress beyond the mental age of fourteen. But Mr. O'Neill seems to think that his people are grown up; he appears often to identify his thoughts and feelings with those of his characters, for they are not presented critically. However much he may advance in power, in skill, in the management of his craft, one feels that unless he grows out of emotions we associate with adolescence, and unless he achieves a philosophy, his work will not attain permanence, a permanence to which his other powers entitle him.

For he has great powers. He can handle a plot to give it momentary significance; his scenes are often very vivid. He fails in his use of the word, but not relatively to most other contemporary playwrights. He has psychological acumen; within his own limits he knows a great deal about the ways of men. His plays have enough in them to hold the attention; he has closely observed the externals of life; he frequently stimulates the hope that some attitude towards life may be forthcoming. He deals with truths, but they are the truths of the moment; they have no implication beyond themselves which the mind can comfortably accept. This judgment may seem harsh; but without feeling the intellectual climate of America in one's bones, it is the only one that can be passed.

LEON EDEL
"Eugene O'Neill: The Face and the Mask"
University of Toronto Quarterly, October 1937, pp. 18–34

When Mr. Eugene O'Neill last November received the Nobel prize for literature, he modestly remarked that it was "a symbol of the coming of age of the American theatre," thus dividing the honours with his contemporaries, many of whom no longer considered him artistically contemporaneous. For there has been in recent dramatic literature no more interesting example of an early flowering and—though the point is disputable—a premature fading: the explosion of a dynamic force that spent itself within its decade. There is ample justification for seeing the awarding of the Nobel prize a belated crowning of Eugene O'Neill's early promise rather than of his later and grosser success. The prize consecrates his historic position in the American theatre, but is capable of exaggerating his importance to the drama of the 1930's. In a word, if in O'Neill the American theatre came of age, it is going on to maturity in other hands.

This means that Mr. O'Neill has failed to go on, though perhaps only for the moment. He is still this side of fifty, and holds the promise of many plays to come. Bernard Shaw, at fifty, stood at the threshold of his dramatic career, and he had passed his seventieth birthday before he became a laureate of the Swedish Academy. The history of literature and the theatre is full of "later manners" and "final periods." Who knows but that O'Neill, despite the apparent finality of the body of his work, may have in reserve some later, some third period?

For such a period, if we are to take academic measurement of his work, would be his third. His first, roughly speaking, embodies the plays of outer, vivid action; his second, those of inner struggle; the first drawn from ready experience, fruit of a youth energetically lived, the second clearly testifying to subsequent introspection attendant upon success, leisure, and ease. These "periods" are by no means a water-tight classification. Among the early plays are works foreshadowing the later experiments, even as among the later plays there is an occasional return to the earlier material. *The Great God Brown*, produced by the Theatre Guild in 1925, can be taken as a rough boundary post planted on the roadway that leads from the O'Neill of the sea plays to the O'Neill of *Strange Interlude* and *Mourning Becomes Electra*. And like the characters of *The Great God Brown* who changed their masks when they changed personalities, O'Neill, the adventurer, has put on the mask of O'Neill, the successful Broadway playwright, reversing the situation in his own play, for Dion has thus put on the mask of Brown.

More than ten years have elapsed, and he has not removed it.

The Face

The story of O'Neill's early life is well known. He has recounted it himself, nor need one go to the various books that have been written about him to discover it. It leaps at you from the early plays, fruit of the years in which O'Neill tramped and sailed and drank, met men and women as fellow-workers, faced constantly the struggle for existence, and knew unemployment and its boon companions, sleeplessness and starvation.

The son of an actor, O'Neill had the theatre in his blood, and the lust of a wanderer, for his father had wandered up and down and across the United States playing a stage version of *The Count of Monte Cristo*. One can almost visualize Eugene, young and earnest, his chin firmly set, watching his father plunge his hands into the treasure and shout, "The world is mine!" and deciding then and there to seek out that world and its treasure. He found instead the loneliness of sky and sea, the foul smells and wretched food aboard cattle-boats, the griminess and sweat of the stoke-hole, the ever-present threat of starvation during weeks ashore and the squalor and despair of the waterfronts. In the mind of a boy not yet twenty, these experiences must have been extremely vivid: but they do not seem to have imprinted themselves indelibly on his mind. One experience was effaced by another: he remained, apparently, a spectator rather than a participant, too immature for profound reflection and too volatile for serious participation.

After some years of this varied hard living there came a breakdown and a sojourn in a sanatorium, during which, O'Neill tells us, he decided to write. He had ready experience to draw upon, and the dramatic form had ever been before him. And yet the period of apprenticeship was long. He fumbled at first, writing plays and destroying them. He read avidly, seeking to grasp the dramatic forms of his predecessors, Ibsen and Strindberg, and he taught himself German over the pages of Nietzsche. He studied at the Harvard Workshop under George Pierce Baker. O'Neill was no inspired dramatist whose flowing pen might straightway turn experience into drama. He approached his chosen field fully conscious of his intentions, and, with a world to write about, hesitated before giving it form.

I think there are other important reasons for O'Neill's long apprenticeship, aside from the fact that the drama itself, a cruel and exigent form, demands long preparation. First of all, O'Neill is not a born dramatist, still less a facile writer. He is essentially a man of the theatre, not of the library, and any examination of his plays, however cursory, reveals effort and strain in the writing. The stage directions abound in *clichés* and in careless use of words, and the speeches are often stock-in-trade dramatics. Another reason is that experiences for him seem to be isolated and lacking in depth, so that he is uncertain of his ideas, and reaches for them insecurely. An impressionable man, he did not synthetize all that happened to him into a profounder understanding of his fellow-men, into one vast fund of experience which could stand him in good stead through all the artifices of creation. Instead, he became a reporter-dramatist, as inconstant, unsearching, unquestioning as the day-to-day journalist. How else explain the fact that O'Neill exhausted his various adventures by writing a play about each, and then had no more to say about them? For you can match the plays of his first period unfailingly with his life, and see how he jumped from play to play as he did from adventure to adventure. He had known wanderlust, and tells of it in *Beyond the Horizon*. His sea experiences he recounts in the one-act sea plays. He prospects for gold, and writes a play called *Gold. The Hairy Ape* treats of the stoke-hole; *Anna Christie*, of the waterfront; *The First Man*, probably some acutely felt domestic experience; *The Straw*, life in a sanatorium. . . . O'Neill reported on his experiences faithfully and vividly, but with all the superficiality of the reporter.

In all these plays he eschews the drama of ideas; he prefers cold objectivity to passionate appeal. As a result his pictures have scenic interest, and dramatic consequence, but lack the alert and lively qualities which animate the social drama of the present day. Let it be remembered that the drama of O'Neill's first period is social drama, and O'Neill himself a vague representative of that equally vague wave of socialistic liberal sentiment that swept the United States in the years following the War. Here are the sailors, says O'Neill; what a tough life they lead; it's just one drunk after another in port, and you're lucky if the dame doesn't get the roll and you're not shanghaied on some long voyage round the Horn.

. . . This sailor life ain't much to cry about leavin' —just one ship after another, hard work, small pay, and bum grub; and when we get into port, just a drunk endin' up in a fight, and all your money gone, and then ship away again. Never meetin' no nice people; never gettin' outa sailor-town, hardly in any port; travelin' all over the world and never seein' none of it; without no one to care whether you're alive or dead. *(With a bitter smile)* There ain't much in all that that'd make yuh sorry to lose it.

Thus Yank, the dying seaman in *Bound East for Cardiff*, conveying Mr. O'Neill's picture of hopeless futile lives spent at odds with the sea and the world of ships; brawling and drunkenness, as in *The Moon of the Caribbees*; frustrated love and homesickness, as in *In the Zone*; pathetic struggle to leave the sea, as in the case of the shanghaied Swede in *The Long Voyage Home*.

The same hopelessness and futility in *Beyond the Horizon*, which shows the wanderlust O'Neill had experienced, tied down and unable to escape the confines of a New England farm; in *The Hairy Ape*, the perplexed and confused mind of a stoker caught in forces that are beyond his control; in *Desire under the Elms*, with its unpleasant story of New England farm-life, the transference of Tolstoy's *Power of Darkness* to an American environment.

Of all these plays, the *Emperor Jones* and *The Hairy Ape* illustrate the best and the worst in the young dramatist. *Emperor Jones*, a bold experiment, with its striking use of sound on the stage in the form of the beating tom-toms, its monologue structure and rapid scenic description of a state of mind, has become almost a classic in its own time. O'Neill made it almost entirely a dramatic picture of fear, primitive and unconfined. His use of the material, particularly his dramatization of the Emperor's stream of consciousness, showed him to be an unhesitating experimentalist, who could rely, when all else failed him, on his sense of the theatre. For *Emperor Jones* is essentially theatric; and it is O'Neill's "theatre" that is interesting rather than his drama.

The Hairy Ape could have been more successful still, for where O'Neill had dramatized a state of mind in *Emperor Jones*, he attempted in his picture of the ape-like stoker to dramatize a consciousness struggling to penetrate a world beyond its reach. This is a much vaster, infinitely richer, and more complex theme. The central idea was to show a worker, blind to all else but his own strength and his belief that it is he who provides the creative force and energy that "makes the world go round;" and by successive stages to portray his disillusionment and collapse when he discovers that he is merely the helpless instrument of other forces, and that it is their will that moves the world, for they control it. O'Neill made of this a gloomy picture of a child-man beating against a wall he cannot scale. As a pathetic study of an individual case, a weak man, weak in all but his physical strength, the play has many touching moments, but the drama is weakened by the very weakness of the central figure. A dramatist more aware than O'Neill of social conflict, would have selected an intelligence capable of perceiving the issues, at first dimly, and later more clearly, and would have thus built a stronger and truer play. Mr. O'Neill merely asks us to contemplate a pathetic case, and the pity aroused in us for this poor man can be no greater than for some powerful caged beast, roaring to be freed, but imprisoned for always. The stoker's monologue becomes monotonous and repetitive after its first fiery outbursts. What might have been a strong picture of valiant struggle and defeat—and therefore an inspiring picture—ends in the sad embrace in the zoo in which the ape-hero is symbolically crushed to death in the arms of his ape-ancestor. "Why not have the man kill the ghost, instead of the ghost the man?" was Shaw's advice to Henry James. One would like to apply it to this play in which O'Neill dismisses the most important question of this century with an indecisive shake of the head.

I will not dwell on the more "literary" efforts which also fall in the first period, such as *Marco Millions*, or *The Fountain*. Their hackneyed phrases sound strange to-day. The last stage direction in *The Fountain*, in which O'Neill talks of two strains of music blending and filling the air "in an all-comprehending hymn of the mystery of life," is characteristic. He was to write many speeches in an apparent search for the "mystery of life," remaining ever intensely mystified and disconcerted by it. Or he was to offer us, in *The Great God Brown*, such a specimen of "grim irony" as the curtain of act four, scene two, when the police captain asks for details concerning the strange death of Dion-Brown:

> Captain (*comes just into sight at left and speaks without looking at them, gruffly*): Well, what's his name?
> Cybel: Man.
> Captain (*taking a grimy notebook and an inch-long pencil from his pocket*): How d'yuh spell it?

For all its weaknesses, the first period of O'Neill's dramatic is a prolific, fruitful period. He brought truthful statement and robust dialogue into the American theatre and reflected faithfully a series of personal adventures that had been vividly if superficially experienced. Perhaps it was his background in the theatre that prevented him from participating more fully in that life of adventure in which he seems to have lived as a resolute observer. He went to sea, it must be remembered, after a brief taste of college life at Princeton. The immature freshman, adolescently emotional and sensitive, may have been, like his character Smitty, a perpetual outsider among the seamen. He may very well have seen his fellow-sailors, from the outset, as so many characters in a play. And this is important, for it explains to a degree the reportorial character of these plays.

O'Neill nevertheless opened new horizons for the American theatre during these years, assimilating ideas from the contemporary European theatre and adapting them easily to his needs. He borrowed freely from Strindberg; he flirted with the so-called "expressionistic" drama of the Germans; in fact, no experiment, no dramatic invention, seemed too bold or dangerous. He did not lack courage, or sincerity, and his sea plays, with *Beyond the Horizon*, *Emperor Jones*, *Anna Christie*, and *Desire under the Elms*, seem destined to hold the stage. Written with earnest conviction, one might almost say youthful fervour, original and inventive in their scenic content, these plays forecast the strong social drama of the 1930's. This is the great anomaly in O'Neill. Containing within him all the germs of a fine social dramatist, he did not allow them to take root and flourish. He showed the younger play-writing generation the way to a more living theatre of flesh-and-blood creatures talking their own sturdy language; he gave them a precedent for the unprecedented on the stage, for hardy experiment and the free play of all possible stage techniques. He showed the way to the socially-conscious theatre, and then retired himself to the drawing-room. In the 1920's he was, we might say, writing for the 1930's. In the 1930's he is most definitely a dramatist of the empty 1920's.

The Mask

I know that it is dangerous thus to check off decades, as if art is to be parcelled with the years like the newspapers. But if ever there was a period in English and American literature that marked itself with the stamp of the years—as much as the over-emphasized nineties—it was the 1920's. From the uncertainty of the War the young men and young women of that time found themselves suddenly moving into a broad era of noisy reconstruction and world boom, and, in the United States, of wild spendthrift prosperity. Early in the 1920's James Joyce had published *Ulysses*, and immediately a generation of Joyces sprang up, those who were influenced and those who imitated. In most he inspired a feeling of inferiority. They had all been such promising young men and young women and here had come this universe-embracing Irishman, with his vast Dublin panorama and his fatal brilliance. They thought themselves puny weaklings—and of course most of them were. T. S. Eliot wrote at the time: "I hold this book to be the most important expression which this age has found: it is a book to which we are all indebted, and from which none of us can escape . . . it has given me all the surprise, delight and terror that I can imagine. . . ." Such a blurby-sounding pronouncement from the meticulous author of a series of polished and important essays was typical and significant. Is it any wonder that the Left-Bankers struck attitudes, that *transition* came into being, that adolescent youths quoted from *Anna Livia Plurabelle*, and that the poem which had most influence during the period was called *The Waste Land*? Older writers who had shown promise even before the twenties underwent curious metamorphoses. Virginia Woolf changed her style overnight. Ezra Pound wrote exhortatory poetry, poems which invariably began "Let us . . ." do this and "Let us . . ." do that. But nothing was done. E. E. Cummings experimented with typographical effects, allowing his poems to be influenced by his unwillingness at times to use—either purposely or accidentally—the shift-key on his typewriter. Aldous Huxley admitted defeat, and portrayed it. John Middleton Murry published all the fragments left by Katherine Mansfield, although she had written in her journal that it would be terrible to die leaving odds and ends behind. H. L. Mencken, with a series of "phony" gestures and an assortment of foreign words that seemed to belie the adequacy of the American language, became the idol of the undergraduate. Those were the great days of the *American Mercury*: born and nurtured in the 1920's, it collapsed sadly in the alien thirties. D. H. Lawrence, he an early Georgian, burning in these later years with the fever of tuberculosis, wrote *Lady Chatterley's Lover*. The middle-aged "creative" generation now felt that all was futile; the younger accepted futility without even feeling it, and drowned its assumed drift in alcohol, for those were the prohibition years. James Branch Cabell wrote sentimental fables which his colleagues wisely labelled "escape literature." Ernest Hemingway reduced story-telling to a cross between the newspaper and the *Pilgrim's Progress*. Gertrude Stein's word-games had their greatest vogue; was it not she who spoke of those around her as a "lost generation"? Sherwood Anderson sat at the feet of Gertrude Stein. The life of Harry Crosby, Left-Bank dilettante who tore through the twenties in airplanes to end as a sordid suicide, expressed the emptiness of the years. Writers found it impossible to follow a consistent development; against the better dictates of instinct and art they changed "manner" with every book. Drama received its first attack from the talking pictures. Literary reputations were made one night and forgotten the next. Between the signing of the Treaty of Versailles and the stock-market crash in New York, art and literature steered a hazy, often alcoholic course, through outwardly serene years, and revealed with extraordinary sureness their hopeless drift.

The world crisis came as a rude and even beneficent awakening. Fascism followed with a ruthless disregard for all that the thinking world cherished. There now arose a younger generation of writers sharply conscious of struggle and crisis, unemployment and world economic disaster. But unlike O'Neill these younger men were not spectators. They had participated in the *débâcle*. Those who were in school and college during the last flurry of prosperity, now were jobless, faced with a hopeless future. A new awareness crept into the writing, as if a fog had lifted. In some cases it expressed ineffective disillusion; in many it was a forthright demand, an overwhelming question—"What are you going to do about it?" Journalism became eager and interrogatory. The social drama, dormant for years, awoke to new possibilities and literature roused itself from casual introspection and the stream of consciousness. . . . It was no longer sufficient to state a case, plumb a soul, dissect a mood. There was an honest, searching return to the great tradition of English and American literature that links the contemporary so-called "proletarian" novelist to Dickens and his predecessors, and the dramatist to the Elizabethans.

Where was O'Neill, the worker, the sailor, the tender of cattle, during these changing years? He who, after the War had given America a realistic and serious drama, who had sought sincerely, if not always effectively, to lift a challenging voice in the theatre, this man had long ago crawled into his ivory tower. His new series of plays represented elaborate and nearly always interesting experiments in form, but all the early inspiration was gone. Retired among his books he seemed to have forgotten—strangely enough completely forgotten—that *alter ego* who had wandered over the face of the earth before becoming a successful playwright. The early life and passion were burned out; the old atmosphere of futility remained, but it was synthetic futility. The dramatist had evolved into a puppet-master, manipulating his personages in a theatric vacuum. The direct inspiration from life was gone. Instead O'Neill played with abstruse ideas and fanciful themes inspired by an inner consciousness that was not adequate to the demands he made on it.

He wrote *Lazarus Laughed*, his first experiment with classical forms, and *The Great God Brown*, to which we have already alluded. He wrote *Dynamo*, an attempt to sing of the power of the machine and man's enslavement to it; but the song rang false, the machines being too great for his crude lyricism. He wrote *Ah, Wilderness!*, dimly reaching back into his own youth, attempting to recapture something of a boy's adolescent misgivings, but saw his boy with the eyes of a man, and resurrected only a sad caricature. Finally, he wrote *Days without End*, his most recent play, a return to his preoccupation with dual personality. But it did not enjoy a long run. The audiences of the thirties had become more difficult.

Standing out among these works are two plays which, because of their experimental form, their unusual length and content, deserve closer attention: *Strange Interlude* and *Mourning Becomes Electra*.

Strange Interlude was a brave attempt to give dramatic form to the Joycean stream of consciousness. O'Neill thus yielded to the most important literary obsession of the twenties. His experiment had this interest, that instead of resorting to the time-worn soliloquy or aside, which requires a very real intimacy between actor and audience, he invited his characters to murmur, *sotto voce*, their inward thoughts, as a corollary to their speeches. A soliloquy is spoken directly to the audience; these speeches are echoed thoughts which the audience is intended to overhear.

In this he really created nothing new. His Emperor Jones, or the stoker in *The Hairy Ape*, speaking their long monologues gave a much closer representation of the stream of consciousness than his characters in *Strange Interlude*. And where, in the earlier plays, the monologue served to advance the action, it tended to halt it in this play. The idea was foredoomed to failure, since objectivity is the essence of drama, and the whole art of the dramatist consists in peopling a stage and conveying thought through speech and conduct, thus evoking a representation of life. To introduce thought as a constant accompaniment to speech is to rob a drama of its fine economy, all its formal interest. The stream-of-consciousness speeches in *Strange Interlude* encumber the play with so much excess baggage. There might have been some saving grace for these speeches had O'Neill given them poetic value. Unfortunately, he is not a poet.

Moreover, Mr. O'Neill gave himself away in his plot. Instead of choosing characters from the world of his experience, instead of revealing the consciousness of sailors, or New England farmers, or waterfront prostitutes, he remained within the confines of his readings in psychology. *Strange Interlude* is just so many dramatized case-histories from Havelock Ellis or Sigmund Freud. Nine Leeds suffers from sexual frustration and accompanying forms of hysteria. There is a dramatized Oedipus complex, and a family with hereditary insanity. Characters, scenario, thought-stream, are lifted from contemporary explorations of the unconscious. And at all times the experiment is more important to O'Neill than the play. The effect is as elusive and unreal as the analytic fiction of which Arthur Christopher Benson said: "It is as though one wandered in tortuous passages, full of beautiful and curious things, without ever reaching the rooms of the house." However, Mr. O'Neill is not imaginative enough to fill his passages with the beautiful and the curious, nor poet enough to hold our interest by his use of words.

The Broadway success of *Strange Interlude* is best explained by the excellence of the Theatre Guild production, the interest awakened by the play's novelty, and the fact that while Broadway audiences can be exigent, they are also often gullible, and clever publicity can convince them that a pretentious effort is necessarily "profound," and a profound effort necessarily requires their attendance. The less critical movie audiences laughed outright as the characters in the film version of the play registered pained expressions while their spoken thoughts echoed through the talking-picture palaces. Nor can that laughter be ascribed to a movie audience's lack of appreciation of the finer dramatic art. As recently as this year, a correspondent of the *New York Times*, describing a performance of the play in, of all capitals, that which is likeliest to be most aware of the new psychology, Vienna, wrote: "While the work was well received as a whole, the audience that packed the theatre showed a tendency to take some of the most tragic moments humorously." *Strange Interlude* has, in fact, had little success abroad. In London it lasted only a few weeks.

Mourning Becomes Electra was quite another matter. Modelling his story of the New England Mannons on the *Oresteia* of Aeschylus, O'Neill wrote a clever melodrama, pitched on a plane of high hysteria, in which murder engenders murder, and suicide, suicide. During the long evening we must make acquaintance with four corpses.

The play is as long as its predecessor, but much more closely knit, being blessed with the classical framework of

Greek tragedy. It consists of three plays in one: *Homecoming*, in which a frustrated wife who has taken a lover, murders her husband on his return from war; *The Hunted*, in which the daughter pursues her mother for her crime and with the aid of her brother, murders the lover, driving the mother to suicide; *The Haunted*, in which the brother, now cut from his mother's apron-strings, seeks escape in suicide. The remaining Mannon, the stoical murderous Lavinia-Electra, returns to the New England house to live with the ghosts. A chorus of village rustics in homely language comments on these lurid episodes.

I remember distinctly the feeling of unreality and nightmare this play gave me when I first saw it in New York. One heaved a sigh of relief as suicide followed suicide, glad that the characters thus put themselves out of their misery. Later, when I had occasion to review the road-show in Montreal, I wrote under the immediate impression of seeing it for a second time: "Not without a certain presumptuousness Mr. O'Neill has turned to the *Oresteia* of Aeschylus and attempted to give us a modern tragedy that would have, he hoped, something of the sweep and grandeur of the Greek. It hasn't. In the Greek tragedy all is external and objective; the people are in the hands of a relentless fate that lifts them off their feet . . . and the audience experiences an inevitable catharsis. . . . But Mr. O'Neill turns the wrong end of the telescope to his audience and he turns it on to a petty business. The New England Mannons, all-subjective and internal, and each of them illustrating some psychological complex, haven't the stuff of great tragedy in them. They just suceed in being pathetic; until finally one is watching an Oedipus complex talking to an Electra complex and realizes that the play has come not from life but from the pages of a psychology textbook. . . . The people have nothing to recommend them; they do not seem to be worth, with their perpetual self-laceration, all the power the dramatist expends on them. One comes away feeling sorry, and that is all . . . And one feels that even O'Neill hasn't any pity for his people."

Yes, Mr. O'Neill in the 1920's was writing for the 1930's, and in the present decade he is most definitely a dramatist of the futile 1920's. He made his contribution to the American theatre early in his career; thereafter his genius ceased to function. The young men whose plays are finding audiences in New York to-day owe to him their use of realistic dialogue, their experimental approach to the theatre, their sincere desire to show in dramatic action sailors and stevedores, taxi-drivers and cotton-spinners—in fact the whole of the working world, instead of merely the world of the drawing-room which hitherto seemed to be regarded as the sole terrain of the playwright.

And they have gone far beyond O'Neill. Their characters ask for positive action and a solution to their wrongs: attacked, they strike back courageously; defeated, they are ready to fight beyond defeat. That is why *The Hairy Ape*, or any of O'Neill's sea plays, become merely negative pictures when placed beside *Let Freedom Ring*, *Stevedore*, *Black Pit*, or *Waiting for Lefty*. These plays are the works of more subtle and more understanding minds than Mr. O'Neill's, young men who have not merely been touched by the reality of things, but have been and are a part of that reality.

The author of *Mourning Becomes Electra* and *Strange Interlude* is young enough to change, shrewd enough a dramatist to be able, perhaps, in the not-too-distant future, to report on the new world that has come up around him. But I fear that at best it will be but a superior sort of dramatic reporting. The later O'Neill may very well remain a casual experimentalist, lost in a world in which art already seems to

count for so little beside the overshadowing moral destructiveness created by the existence of mighty armies, and the thought of their potential destructiveness when they will go to battle.

GILBERT NORWOOD
"The Art of Eugene O'Neill"
Dalhousie Review, July 1941, pp. 143–57

How many of us have discussed, in whimsical essays or casual talk or profound novels, the coming of the next world-teacher or consummate artist! And utterly as the imaginative prophet, the commonplace theorist and the rest of us have differed in all else, we have agreed in one particular: "Anyhow, when he *does* come, it will be in the most unlikely guise, place and conditions; all the great, the kings and awful ecclesiastics, men of deep learning, mellow wisdom and far-reaching experience, will fail to recognize him and will revile, persecute, perhaps even kill him." It was long a favourite daydream of my own that people would *really* be taken off their guard—that the wonderful new religious reformer would be an Archbishop of Canterbury, the world-shaking philosopher a dutiful fellow who had taken metaphysics in Chicago, getting maximum credits for Hegel or Descartes and a Ph.D on Some Aspects of Something-or-other. "What a delicious setback for our knowing little cynics!"

So engrossed was I in hugging this imagined triumph, this Paradise of the Embittered Professor, that quite a little time had elapsed before I realized that it had happened: the great new dramatist had emerged—and lo! he had taken Professor Baker's course in playwriting at Harvard! And he had *not* been rejected with amazed contempt by every manager and producer in Europe and America. He as, and is, acclaimed amid harp, sackbut, psaltery, dulcimer, and all kinds of music: no sooner had Mr. O'Neill exhibited a play as good as *Still Waters Run Deep* than the heavens were rent with American hosannas, and even the ranks of Bloomsbury could scarce forebear to cheer.

All this might have been foreseen. When Ibsen began his social dramas, our mandarins poured upon him a torrent of scared abuse: "this dirty old blackguard" is the tamest that I recall. Then it appeared that they were wrong: instructed opinion at length declared (of course by the time Ibsen lay at death's door) that he was at once a great ethical teacher and a superb dramatist. Meanwhile Shaw's stage-career had opened, and again the critics met defeat: he was universally extolled (of course by the time he was turning out deplorable senilities) as at once the finest wit and the most consummate playwright of the day. Taught at last by failure, the critics murmured: "Next time, we will *not* be caught napping. Let anyone bring out another play that we can't understand, or that is just the opposite of *Abie's Irish Rose*, and we shall be ready with the garlands and tomtoms." So it came about that ribbons were pinned upon threadbare melodrama, thinly disguised by Irish politics or what in Ireland passes for politics. So it is that a playwright—possessed, indeed, of the highest merit, who has nevertheless often written weakly or in falsetto, and whose variety in method and conception of his art renders him recalcitrant to every type of glib formula—so it is that Eugene O'Neill has been caparisoned by critics with all the conventional garnish of *Attitudes to Life*, *Dark Period*, *Temporary Loss of Direction* and the like, familiar to those who peruse literary manuals. In the hideous phrase of the film-papers, they have been grooming him for stardom. Most essays, known to me, dealing with O'Neill offer such neat illustration of the havoc wrought by mechanical manipulation of clichés and the worn counters of supercilious pseudo-psychology, that I am half tempted to turn aside and discourse upon it rather than upon these dramas themselves.

For I can think of no distinguished playwright on whom it is more difficult to buckle the usual harness of influences, attitudes and the rest; if we make the attempt, we must either falsify the plainest facts (as more than one has done) or pronounce him chaotic—which matters nothing, as it means only that our schemes fail to fit him. But naturally some of his works are better than others: a few so magnificent that O'Neill must be counted among the ten or twelve greatest dramatists; the others not indeed usually negligible, but seldom deserving emphatic eulogy. All that can legitimately be done by way of a scheme is to sort the plays roughly into five groups, the last of which falls into sub-divisions.

First comes a series of one-act plays, nearly all sea-pieces. They have small value, though the author probably found them useful as practice. *Bound East for Cardiff* is placed in the forecastle of a tramp steamer during fog, and centres round the death of a seaman—just a picture of rough sailor's life, regarded as powerful drama only because most of us have not worked our passage across the Atlantic, and would prefer not to try. *The Rope* has a good moment or two, but on the whole is as squalidly vapid as *Tobacco Road*, though it has the advantage in brevity. The end, where that frightful child flings the hoarded money into the sea, has power; but consider what assemblage of uncouth machinery is needed to secure it: the foolish business of the rope swinging in full view—for years, apparently; the child's habit of playing in this particular barn; careful emphasis on the fact that the sea is deep at the cliff's foot (no use trying to get the money back!); and the uncle who, with a froliscome abandon concealed by all uncles of my own experience, encourages the child earlier to throw a single dollar over the cliff—putting ideas into her head! Others among these one-act plays are affecting, *The Long Voyage Home* above all; concerning *Where the Cross Is Made* more shall be said later.

Those were all composed before 1920, in which year O'Neill reached the age of thirty-two. The four other kinds are chronologically jumbled; more disconcerting still, it might be debated concerning some whether they belong to this kind or to that.

One group I incline to call thesis-plays, by which I mean that O'Neill, having discovered some definite dogma about some definite factor in human life, writes a play to prove the dogma: a dangerous method, almost certain to result not in art but in stiffness and more or less open propagandism. Some plays of Brieux (for instance, *Les Avariés*) suggest a useful comparison: artistically almost piteous, they achieved a feat irrelevant though valuable—compelling the public to face certain dreadful results of vice. Now, in O'Neill the moral (as it used to be named) is not only present, of course, but fairly clear, though it does not shout at us with Brieux's ghastly explicitness; on the other hand, it has usually strength enough to produce the fault surely unavoidable in a thesis-play: to wit, that the characters move with stiff joints and are obviously saying less what human beings would say than what the author's formula dictates. In *Beyond the Horizon* all has been moulded to reveal the disasters wrought by book-fed, feckless romanticism: Robert is not a full character dramatically, but weak yearning for "over there" personified; and all the other people cluster round him, not living with any complete personality of their own, but acting as foils to Robert. The idea of *Diff'rent* is that one should not look for perfection in a husband. Emma throws over honest Caleb because of what

they used to call a peccadillo (now it is known as "refusing no form of experience"). As a result, she not only misses happiness but becomes revolting: the last act is downright hideous; and she hangs herself, and so does Caleb. *Dynamo*, as I understand it, means that if we are victims of a superstitious temperament, our emancipation from one stupid religion means only subservience to a new. Reuben's life is spoiled by his parents' coarse Puritanism and crass religiosity: he ends by thinking the dynamo at which he works is a goddess—a good instance of the falsetto mentioned earlier. By far the finest of this group (if in fact it belongs thereto) is *All God's Chillun Got Wings*, which demonstrates not merely the power of love, but the sovereignty of divine patience amid dread suffering. Its theme, abstractly stated, is America's colour-problem in its acutest form, mixed marriage; in the concrete, a particular pair of living people, Jim and Ella: and the two sides, general and particular, are held in admirable balance. In this technical respect, *All God's Chillun* is among O'Neill's best plays—you see a whole mixed community: in a different focus, you see the few individuals. After a rather amateurish opening, the work grows stronger and more certain, with utter sincerity of emotion. Utter sincerity of emotion!—there is one of the O'Neill marks: he never shirks a situation, however terrible. And by facing the fact, he obtains his appropriate reward, a far more piercing beauty. Here Ella, the white girl, and Jim, the young negro lawyer, after a trying period of love and doubt, at length marry. Ella is torn horribly between genuine strong affection and the unconquerable instinct which forces her to gasp at him in agonized hysteria, "Nigger! nigger!" That is already notable art. Further, this conflict unseats her reason, and then comes really noble drama—a climax heart-breakingly simple, far too simple for some critics—but natural, indeed necessary, for a beautiful, rather feminine, soul like Jim's. At the close Ella, now childish, asks him to play the old games with her, and he replies: "Honey, honey, I'll play right up to the gates of heaven with you!" . . .

The next kind of group I will call the spectacular, because, although one can with greater or less pains discover a thesis for each, the thesis or moral is in any case far less obvious than the picturization, a rather elaborate pageant marshalled round one figure. The clearest instance is the earliest, belonging to 1920—*The Emperor Jones*, which I think O'Neill's first unmistakable success, interesting for this reason only, that he has produced what is in strictness not a play but a succession of scenes threaded on to the same personality and using cinema-technique. This quality sets *The Emperor Jones* apart: nowhere else does the "legitimate" drama owe anything to the cinema, except in an experiment by Mr. Atkinson, the Australian playwright, whose *Nocturne*, however, merely combines actual film with actual stage-work. *The Hairy Ape* can best be appreciated as a lyric put into rudimentary dramatic form. Just as Browning made extremely vocal the barely human Caliban, so here the stoker Yank, hardly nearer to normal humanity, voices his sense that the only people on the liner who have meaning—who "belong," in his favourite phrase—are the stokers by whom the ship is driven, the passengers being mere baggage. We should be wrong to talk here about the dignity of labour: Yank has only feeling, not doctrine—the feeling that he is an organ in a vast animal. But of course if he is allotted speeches, they must have some degree of purely intellectual coherence—a great difficulty of elaborate lyric, in any hands. Even so, Yank is a splendid personification of what Whitman called the "barbaric yawp." Beside these great speeches are found scenes quite normal, and valueless except as breaking up, and thus emphasizing, the lyrical passages: for instance, the girl's only function is to startle and awaken Yank by the contrast of her white freshness amid the heat and glare of the furnaces.

The other three works belonging to this group, *The Fountain, Marco Millions, Lazarus Laughed*, are notable only for the variety and picturesqueness of their scenes. The first title alludes to a fabled spring in Cathay, by drinking from which a man may regain his youth. Don Leon seeks it and after many adventures (not all caused by his quest) dies without finding it. The whole plot—or, rather, story—embellished with Moorish arches and minstrels, dashing Spaniards, mantillas and moonlight, Eldorado, baking sunshine, *patios*, and of course Christopher Columbus—has for its essential thought nothing more novel or profound than an elderly soldier's painful realization that the youthful Beatriz does not even think of falling in love with him. *Marco Millions*, though utterly different on the surface, belongs to the same type of dramaturgy. In a procession of rich and exciting scenes we are shown Marco's travels as a merchant and his elevation to power under the Great Kaan, then his long voyage as he escorts the Princess Kukachin to her bridegroom; and his steady declension from an imaginative boy to a glib cunning moneygetter. The Princess falls in love with him, but he has eyes for nothing except gain. In an epilogue we learn (if we have not guessed it) that he is a satire on the contemporary American businessman; indeed, he literally walks out of the theatre and drives off in a motor-car: how this feat of realism is supposed to be carried through, I cannot well conceive. The whole piece suggests a diluted blend of *Hassan* and *Peer Gynt*. In *Lazarus Laughed*, again, we observe the same method: theatricality rather than drama—cunningly varied and exciting scenes, vehement language that conveys only the illusion of spiritual intensity. The whole pageant proclaims with (to tell truth) a noisy insistence that the good life consists in joy: "Laugh! laugh! laugh!" Incessantly it is said and sung that there is no death—we pass, in truth, over into God's laughter. Accordingly Lazarus, having received a revelation during his three days' sojourn beyond the grave, moves up and down the world laughing. We follow him through vivid scenes in Palestine and later in Italy, at the court of Tiberius, that admirable but grumpy potentate, here presented as a disconcerting mixture of Scott's Louis XI and the Fagin of *Oliver Twist*. Whatever happens, usually something sinister, Lazarus laughs in earth-shaking yet melodious paroxysms. The most horrible part of all, however, is that the merriment proves uncannily contagious. Centurions, peasants, the Prince Caligula, everyone, burst into fits of laughter—everyone, that is, except Lazarus's wife . . . ! *There* is the point at which a really alert playwright would begin; but O'Neill here is not alert, only riding a theatrical hobby-horse.

The next group can be given no more arresting label than "the more or less normal;" they reveal no marked peculiarity of underlying idea, characterization or plot-structure. They are *Anna Christie, The Straw, The First Man, Ah, Wilderness!*: the last alone of these need be discussed here. In this drama O'Neill's stage-technique is defter than anywhere else, even than in the masterpieces to which we shall come later.

The topic is adolescent love, which asks of the dramatist (as of ourselves in everyday life) beyond perhaps all other forms that love assumes, boundless caution, patience, understanding. One of the few real advances that we have made in the last generation or two concerns this delicate bloom that so often tinges the hesitant beginnings of maturity. At one time the fashion was to deride it, to dub it "calf-love" and try to ignore it, merely because so often short-lived—as if anything that stirs

and opens the soul were less lovely, less vital, because it faded soon. We think and feel differently now. But it has scarcely ever been well handled in literature, because those upon whom its spell descends are too young to command the skill in words, the insight of brain and heart alike, from which literature springs. It was revealed, though not quite directly, in Keats's *Endymion*; Edgar Allan Poe gave it more explicit and poignant expression, but by the very nature of the case in boyish manner. *Ah, Wilderness!*, written when O'Neill was in the middle forties, offers us a direct treatment, not glorious, not noble, yet instinct with charm, sincerity and perfect understanding. The hero, Richard Miller, is one of his two or three most completely projected characters: deeply in love, gawky, full of fits and starts, tinged with priggishness, crudely defiant, crudely weak, sound and generous at heart, inspired by poetry and all great ideas as well as by his own insurgent maturity, responsive on the instant to intelligent sympathy. His love takes on strength and direction—and, on the artistic side, dramatic effectiveness—from a squalid but in the upshot ennobling encounter with an entirely different kind of girl. The picture is (as it were) framed—given clearer meaning, still livelier attractiveness—by two other love-interests, excellently depicted in themselves and adroitly subordinated to the main theme: one of them is the relation between the lad's parents, which provides a most beautiful close to the whole play. Moreover, the modelling and the focussing of details show delightful mastery. For example, at the opening we have to meet no fewer than seven members of the family, *plus* a friend: they are introduced with notable skill, not in a bunch, but at neatly arranged yet brief and natural intervals.

There remains a final group, containing (among other works) those masterpieces to which have alluded more than once. In the works already discussed we have often noted talent, sometimes marked excellence; but no reason has yet been shown for assigning to O'Neill a place among the world's greatest playwrights. In one kind of power, to be next described, he attains a height never surpassed by any other dramatist, ancient or modern: power to depict the naked soul, its nature, its activities recondite and hitherto unguessed, to trace the finest quivering tendrils of thought, emotion, barely incipient tendency or strain. Here lies O'Neill's root interest, here rises his towering achievement.

It is no doubt true that all imaginative writers are concerned with apprehending and vividly portraying human nature; above all, the novelists and the playwrights. But it must further and in particular be observed, that however the English writers (let us say) may have differed, or however closely they may have equalled one another, in depth and clarity of their own insight, there has been an unmistaken increase of the psychological revelation that they offer their *public*. We see it most plainly in the novel, only less clearly in the drama. From the reader's or spectator's standpoint, earlier work deals more with the surface: we are shown what people do, say and suffer, but see comparatively little of action's hidden causes. As time goes on, artists render stratum transparent below stratum—not merely permitting us to guess, but displaying, and with ever more conscious elaboration, the shape and entanglement of the soul's very roots. The progression from Smollett through Thackeray and Meredith to Joyce is in this respect startling. It is hardly less so in dramatic art.

Where stands O'Neill? First, as to his status or merit, his work is at its best sublime, unsurpassed by Aeschylus, Shakespeare, Racine, Goethe or Ibsen—in this particular effect of exhibiting a naked soul with terrific power while maintaining a recognizable human individual. At times, indeed, he achieves the acme of psychological revelation: where he does *that*, he is far less excellent, just because the balance between outside and inside vanishes: and when that happens, plays or novels resemble those horrible clocks with no faces, which allow a full view of the brass intestines at their intricate but unlovely work. In brief, he sometimes "lets himself go", and becomes too exclusively the vivisector. This final group of O'Neill's works may therefore be divided into at least four different sub-species, different both in technique and in success.

The first intimation of his concern with such study occurs as early as the one-act play, *Where the Cross Is Made* (1918), a not particularly striking tale of a sea-captain who goes mad through his obsession with hidden treasure. Now, three years later O'Neill took this story up again and treated it with far more fulness and power in *Gold*, a play excellent both in adventure and in psychology. The last act is simply a revision of *Where the Cross Is Made*, and Capt. Bartlett's madness, with gleams of sanity, is magnificently done, pointing forward to the greatest scenes of the Electra dramas. Three years later again, in 1924, came *Welded*, concerning which the most conflicting opinions are possible: to dismiss it as crazy balderdash would be pardonable; to acclaim it as brilliantly acute and fearless, not less intelligible. The explanation is that O'Neill has made an unflinching attempt to state in full the spiritual, moral and intellectual quality of sexual love. This he has put into words— already a great enterprize. But far more, being a playwright, he has given those words to be *spoken* as dialogue between two married lovers, with another man and woman to extend and deepen the presentation. It is a play to read: to witness it would be horrible. There are things which may be said, but which should not be overheard; candid love-making is among them. Our earlier dramatists, above all in *Romeo and Juliet*, triumphantly avoid this fault by endowing their lovers with poetry. The real dialogue of such encounters it is indecency to record—a mistake committed by a very few novelists, by too many filmwriters, and here by O'Neill . . . unless . . . unless we take his play as a deliberate endeavour to extend the bounds of art, to force his *dramatis personae* upon an inhuman explicitness. On that view, he is not committing a vulgarity, but making a pardonable artistic error. He has not written thus again, but evolves new and very odd technique for such utterances. And even here we observe with interest that he is groping forward: in one place, he tells us, "they speak each ostensibly to the other, but showing by their tone it is a thinking aloud to oneself, and neither appears to hear what the other has said."

The method tentatively employed for a moment here, and much more fully in *Dynamo*, attains more complete function and far greater import in *Strange Interlude* (1928), where each person says not only what is meant to be heard by their companions, but also (in an aside, for the audience only) his private thoughts, or half-articulate feeling, on the same topic. A device familiar enough! But O'Neill has enlarged its use almost beyond recognition. Here for instance is a scrap of conversation between two jealous men.

Marsden: (Now I know! . . . absolutely! his face!
    . . . her voice! . . . they did love each other
    . . . they do now . . .) When did you get
    back from Europe?
Darrell: This morning on the *Olympia*. (Look out for
    this fellow . . . always had it in for me
    . . . like woman . . . smells out love . . .
    he suspected before . . . well, who gives a
    damn now? . . .)
Marsden: (What has brought him back? What a
    devilish cowardly trick to play on poor unsus-

pecting Sam! . . . But I'm not unsuspect-
    ing . . .) What brought you back so soon?
Darrell: My father died three weeks ago. I've had to
    come back about his estate. (Lie . . . Father's
    death just gave me an excuse to myself . . .)

(Let me interject that in one of these asides occurs perhaps the only passage of notable wit that O'Neill has hitherto given us. The rather finicking novelist Marsden mutters: "That is true! . . . I've never married the word to life! . . . I've been a timid bachelor of arts, not an artist!") This astonishing device is by no means the whole point of *Strange Interlude*, which could be performed without the vast array of asides and would be a first-rate piece, so given. But what shall we think of the device itself? Of course we must not condemn it out of hand as "unlike real life:" every kind of dramatic presentation is that, in one particular or another; not least our own convention of a room with the fourth wall removed. The only test is: does this device help to convey the dramatist's intention more complete-ly? Very well: these asides are a geniune and useful, though cumbrous, addition to stage-craft: any playwright who aims above knockabout farce or sword-and-cape stuff must hence-forth ask himself whether he had not better adopt this method. If he does decide for it, he must beware of two mistakes from which its originator has shown himself not completely im-mune. Firstly, it seems unwise to make the official dialogue as long as a normal play, and insert also a huge mass of surreptious talk: the audience must have its meals! Secondly, this development raises in its most urgent form a question that concerns the very basis of all art. In an artistic creation two parties, not one, are concerned: the creator and . . . let us say "the public," to include the person who examines statuary, listens to music and so forth. The public is not extraneous, but (in a sense important yet sometimes hard to define) actually contributes to the work of art. Now! Here is the problem: how great is the public's contribution to be, of filling in gaps, leaping to meet the artist half-way? The deepest difference between classical and non-classical literature is that the former leaves much more for the public to supply than does the latter. Nevertheless, all schools of all arts that ever existed leave a good deal for us to supply for ourselves: it is out of the question for them to do otherwise, else they would not be creating art-work at all. What would happen can be learnt from those cinema-films so common formerly, where, if one man tele-phones to another, you are shown the bell ringing in the other man's office. There lies the peril of the *Strange Interlude* method, that the public may have nothing to do save wait till it is over, if ever.

A play both vigorous and subtle is this, depicting the history of a woman's heart with utter sincerity—and by "sincerity" I *mean* sincerity, not that exclusive attention to the squalid which is all that the noble word "realism" is nowadays permitted to suggest. Nina is superbly portrayed as she gains strength, richness and elasticity of soul from her experience of youthful love, later marriage and the destruction of her unborn child, her amour, her second marriage. Her expansion offers an impressive contrast with the progressive hardening and stiffening of Lavinia in the Electra trilogy. Nowhere, perhaps, is O'Neill's realism so fine as in the scene where Nina reveals that she has at last reached full happiness by having three men attached to her—her husband, her lover and the fatherly friend who at the close marries her. She even insists that the baby belongs to all four of them. Candour indeed! I wish O'Neill had found space to show what Nina would feel if each of her three husbands took two other wives . . .

The innumerable asides, then, of *Strange Interlude* are one expedient plainly engendered by our author's passion to reveal the soul: another is even more celebrated, even more audacious—the use of masks. This technique has no resemblance to that of *Marco Millions* and *Lazarus Laughed*, where masks are employed for quite another purpose: namely, as in the ancient Greek drama, and especially the choruses thereof, where for the accidental and irrelevant variations of humanity is substituted a set of faces indicating qualities shared by a group. In *The Great God Brown* and *Days without End* their function is just the opposite: not to conceal individuality, but to display its depths, not by the mere wearing of masks but (at least in the former play) by their manipulation. *Days without End* uses a comparatively simple technique. The main character, John Loving, is presented by two beings: one—called John—the better self, wearing no mask; the other—called Loving—the evil self, who wears a sneering mask. Loving, though of course in physical fact present and visible as well as audible, is supposed invisible to the other people on the stage. Whenever John talks with anyone, especially his uncle, the sympathetic priest, his amiable remarks are interrupted or continued by Loving, much to the dismay of the other characters, who are puzzled by the sudden eruption of black-hearted and blasphemous utterances from the innocent John. Finally, the bad self is slain in a church through John's attainment of utter belief in Christ.

In *The Great God Brown* the four chief persons all have masks—or rather, when Dion Anthony dies, Billy Brown takes his mask and for a time pretends to be both men by rapidly running in and out of rooms, changing clothes and the like. When these people are alone and really themselves, they wear no masks; when confronting others, they usually present the mask which indicates the character wherewith society credits them. One result is that when any of these is alone, but is suddenly visited by someone, he must dive for the mask and put it on. Occasionally he is caught unawares. There occurs a gruesome scene where Margaret (maskless) faints in the presence of Dion (maskless). As their sons rush in, he puts on his mask hastily. They stare at the unrecognized woman on the bench:

> *Eldest:* We heard someone yell. It sounded like Mother.
> *Dion:* No. It was this lady—my wife.
> *Eldest:* But hasn't Mother come yet?
> *Dion:* Yes. Your Mother is here.

He then puts Margaret's mask on her face and stands back, whereupon the boys exclaim "Mother!" and run to her. The inner meaning of this drama as a nexus of symbolism has been described at some length by O'Neill himself in a letter to the press; but into that explanation I do not propose to enter, as it seems to me hopelessly confused and impossible to render lucidly by any such action and device as we find in the play itself. The employment of masks—and, further, a change of masks to indicate the ravages of experience—is a failure because unbearably grotesque. Nevertheless, O'Neill should be honoured as a splendidly original "man of the theatre" who labours to expand the resources of his art. He may yet, for he is little past fifty, evolve a great new technique of production.

At length we reach the two plays which are at once the finest ever composed in America and the finest composed anywhere since Ibsen, even that reservation being by no means beyond dispute.

Desire under the Elms unfortunately lay for some time under a censorial ban, which warps public opinion by arousing irrelevant condemnation or irrelevant praise. The marital complications result in no tinge of pornography: as in *Oedipus Tyrannus*, they are vital to the ideas and emotions that inspire and drive the three chief persons. Old Ephraim Cabot wishes at all costs to have a son who—unlike the three long ago born to him—shall prove a worthy heir to his monomania, a grim half-religious love for the farm. His third son, Eben, is determined to avenge his own mother upon his father—the mother whose life was crushed out by her husband's crabbed cruelty. Between them stands Abbie Putnam, the newly wedded third wife of Ephraim, and presently her child, supposed Ephraim's, but really the child of young Eben. This situation O'Neill handles with a subtle and magnificent mastery our sense of which will be deepened if we set beside this play another work which at least one critic (with whatever justification) has compared to it: *Les Fossiles*, by Francois de Curel. The French play is open to the reproach that I brought against several works of O'Neill, though its manner may rather suggest Pinero—unnatural, doctrinaire, simplification of psychology. The woman who corresponds to Abbie has, indeed, no particular character at all: at one point she actually uses as an argument *mon caractère indécis!* Such comparison brings out effectively the daemonic power wherewith O'Neill has projected his own heroine. But his artistic triumph lies mainly herein, that each of the three persons is ridden by a complication of emotions, which again cross and recross those cherished by the others. Old Ephraim passionately desires that the farm may find a master like himself; *but* he *also* longs for a son whom he can at last approve. Abbie rejoices to have the child, by whatever father, that so, after her years of wretchedness, she may root herself securely in the new-found home; *but* she *also* loves Eben for himself. Eben thirsts to injure his father through the new wife precisely because Eben's ill-used mother was the former wife; *but* he *also* adores Abbie in her own person. That is how great drama comes to birth: first in the conception of people vividly human, then in the orchestration of their conflicting passions, nobilities and sins.

It would be cumbrous, and therefore misleading, to work out on paper the marvellously deft and keen-sighted interlacement of character, the juxtaposition—nay, the interpenetration—of the basest and the noblest instincts. Let me rather add two notes. Many have been repelled by what they feel as a gritty, even squalid, realism: the work lacks any touch of soul-quieting beauty—a touch of lyrical quality, shall we say? That is not without truth, or relevance; but the dramatist has in fact given a hint of this: more than once the characters, cloddish as they mostly are, remark badly yet poignantly on the fairness of the landscape; and at the very close Eben and Abbie, as they walk forth hand-in-hand to their fate, pause to gaze with devout rapture at the sunrise. The other point concerns what has been so often discussed, the revelation of naked souls. Here the balance is beautifully preserved between the external and the internal: we are shown not merely the appearance and talk, not only the actions and purposes, but moreover (so far as seems possible) the complete soul of three human beings—agonized and terrible, yet in their hour, and by virtue of their humanity, sublime.

Mourning Becomes Electra, however, marks beyond question the greatest height to which O'Neill has yet risen; some will, indeed, find it difficult to believe, perhaps even to imagine, that he or anyone could produce work of more stupendous power. It is a trilogy, a sequence of plays closely related—*Homecoming, The Hunted, The Haunted*—based on the Greek tragedies which treat the story of Agamemnon's murder by his wife and her lover, and the consequent vengeance exacted by her children, Orestes and Electra. This affiliation is quite openly acknowledged, if only by the title, for no woman called Electra appears among O'Neill's *dramatis personae.* He has naturally used his materials with complete freedom, in external details great and small, and in psychology. For Agamemnon home from Troy he substitutes Brigadier-General Ezra Mannon back from the American Civil War; Aegisthus, the murderous lover, is modernized with fascinating skill. To Electra and Orestes—here Lavinia and her brother Orin—are added a subsidiary pair who contribute powerfully to the plot, Hazel and her brother Peter, who are to marry Orin and Lavinia, but who after dreadful encounters are forced to withdraw in perplexity and horror. The Greek chorus is practically expunged, and rightly. Though to the Aeschylean plays it makes contributions of immense value, such an element would be felt as hopelessly alien in a twentieth-century domestic drama; and O'Neill shrewdly contents himself with mere remnants of this form—at one point a group of half-drunken villagers, at another a few friends of the Mannon family, but (most interestingly of all) the old gardener Seth Backwith, by whose brief but timely entrances the tragedy is enriched and deepened.

In the whole range of dramatic literature there is perhaps no study more instructive and to certain temperaments more profoundly attractive than the changes which O'Neill has imposed on the characters of Aeschylus, their emotions and consequent acts. Orestes slays Aegisthus almost as a matter of course, with no misgiving at any time; but the causes that impel Orin to kill Brant are complex. His experience of bloodshed in the Civil War has given him a strange sense that he is fated to continue such deeds. His love for his mother, portrayed with a remorseless insight into deeps concealed and by him unguessed, leads him to kill not less through jealousy than in his father's quarrel. Only less frightful, if less at all, is this, that his mother uses his morbid loyalty and love in hopes to sunder him from Lavinia, with whom she rightly fears that he may form a league of vengeance. Again, this league is in Aeschylus simple and natural enough; in the modern work it leads, after the vengeance, to hideous intimacy of guilt made more unbearable yet by morbid entanglements of tortured love and mutual dread.

In Aeschylus, the central physical fact is that Orestes slays his mother with his own hand. Here the brother and sister, after Brant has been killed, announce the deed to their mother, and she kills herself. But the spiritual outcome is none the lighter: indeed her children's remorse brings an appalling climax. For the most impressive difference between the ancient and the modern work lies here. In Aeschylus, the matricide, having engendered an open quarrel between the deities of Heaven and of Hades, at length finds justification or solution in scenes which for religious profundity, wisdom and poetry may well be thought the noblest masterpiece even of Greek genius. O'Neill has conceived a finale utterly different. Orin, reeling through more and more dread agonies of frenzy, ferocity and remorse, at length destroys himself. Lavinia on her emotional side changes horribly into the semblance of her mother, while spiritually she hardens and stiffens into a creature whose very being is irremediable guilt, till at last she condemns herself to a lifelong imprisonment in the ancestral home, alone with the ghosts of her family. O'Neill has succeeded in depicting the very lineaments of damnation. Here, parting company with Aeschylus, he rises to the height of another supreme artist: Goethe, in *Iphigenie*, has essayed the same awful task; yet even he has not shown a loftier, more unflinching mastery.

But Goethe was a poet; so was Aeschylus. O'Neill is not. That difference places him far below them in power to exalt as well as to illumine. Nevertheless, he remains one of the world's finest playwrights, in the strictest sense of that word; of realists he is perhaps the very greatest.

JOHN GASSNER
From "O'Neill in Our Time"
The Theatre in Our Time
1954, pp. 252–56

Primary for O'Neill was a cosmic anguish. It was anguish over the inscrutability of fate and over the search for the faith he personally lost in abandoning Catholicism and that others had lost in abandoning the various religions into which they had been born. The twist of the tragic rack on which our Eugene O'Neill placed both his dreamers and his materialists—whether in *Beyond the Horizon, Desire under the Elms, The Great God Brown*, or *Days without End*—was loud in the theatres where his plays were performed. The rack could be love and life frustrated by possessiveness or twisted into hate by failure, lust, or environment. The rack upon which he stretched his characters could be past life and the sense of devouring fate—Chris Christopherson's "old davil sea" in *Anna Christie*. The torment could come from man's sense of being separated from nature and not yet attaining complete humanity, of not "belonging" in the universe, as in *The Hairy Ape*; or of not belonging to either the old supernatural god and the new scientific god represented by the machine, as in *Dynamo*; or of not belonging to oneself and of not quite belonging to any all-fulfilling love, as in *Strange Interlude*; or of wanting to belong, incestuously, to a forbidden object, as in *Mourning Becomes Electra*. Wherever the tension came from, the suffering blackened man's horizons in O'Neill's dramas while the worshippers of material comfort rode the crest of optimism under Presidents Harding, Coolidge, and Herbert Hoover.

O'Neill cast a weird shadow on the easeful life, on money-bought comfort and specious consolations. He stood stonily unreconciled in the land of plenty and promise. He was heroically saturnine. When he smiled for more than a fleeting moment in his plays, it was mainly to smile to scorn the American Babbitt he incarnated in a Venetian one, the Marco Polo of *Marco Millions*. Not until 1933, in recalling the beginning of our tragic century in *Ah, Wilderness!*, was his smile genial, steady and conciliatory to life and to a father-image. His major theme was man's disorientation, man's bedevilment from within and from without. O'Neill made himself the dramatist of ironic Fate and of the psychological tensions Freud's interpreters and misinterpreters were then communicating to us in books and lectures. And the young and the brave of the nineteen-twenties found exhilaration in his confronting the bitter "truth" for them so stalwartly—even if many of them were more inclined to make parlor palaver rather than drama out of it, unless they made melodrama out of it by drinking themselves into a frenzy during the years of the "noble experiment." The important point, of course, is that O'Neill made strong drama and exciting theatre out of this "truth." He took for his masters the Greek tragedians of fate, to whom he ultimately paid the tribute of imitation in *Mourning Becomes Electra*, and Strindberg, the Scandinavian dramatist of man's division and search for reunification, to whom he also paid the tribute of imitation in *Welded* and *Strange Interlude*.

O'Neill was not unaware of society and its effects, I hasten to add, although neither his anti-political nor his leftist critics have cared to concede this fact. Surely his ironic romance *Marco Millions* made an explicit reckoning of the era of

Prosperity and of the mounting stock-market. His "hairy ape," the stoker Yank, was Worker as well as Man. The society he presented in *The Hairy Ape* with the slumming heiress Mildred Douglas and the spats-wearing automatons of the Fifth Avenue Easter parade scene had what the leftists of the nineteen-thirties called "social significance." He also took sharp notice of racial discrimination and slum life in *All God's Chillun Got Wings*, of poverty and prostitution in *Anna Christie*, of grinding and narrowing impoverished farm life in *Beyond the Horizon*, and of the loneliness and sorry satisfactions of sea-faring men in the *S. S. Glencairn* one-act cycle. The tensions produced by New England patriarchal authority and the struggle for land figured in *Desire under the Elms*. Brahmin family pride, joy-denying puritanism, and mercantile possessiveness were the correlates of the love drama and incest tragedy of *Mourning Becomes Electra*. "Problem plays" alone found him indifferent.

Deny it who can! O'Neill, who contributed to the Socialist *Call* in his early days of journalism and who mingled with the political vanguard of liberals associated with the Provincetown Players, was a social critic of sorts. And more important to art is the fact that he rendered life and speech in his realistc plays authentically. He did not abandon colloquial dialogue until late in the nineteen-twenties, and then only for good reasons—and he returned to it in 1939 with the writing of *The Iceman Cometh*. He depicted environment scrupulously. And he was virtually the first serious American dramatist of any standing to bring characters from all walks of life on to the stage, noting their origins of race and background with sympathy and understanding. It would not be difficult to sustain the point that he gave us social pictures and socially conditioned, if not altogether socially determined, actions with greater credibility and vitality than most "social dramatists" of the nineteen-thirties and since then. He is, indeed, historically important as the first American to make naturalist art prevail on our stage.

Nevertheless, he was not a "naturalist," and struck out, in fact, against the belief that mere transcriptions of life were the province of art. He fused naturalistic detail with symbolist mood, suggestiveness, and symbol. And taking his cue from his admired Strindberg, he resorted to the "expressionist" dramatic style of distortion of action, speech, and scene, as in the weird calvary of his Emperor Jones through the jungle and in the Fifth Avenue scene of *The Hairy Ape*. Tireless in his search for theatrical means of projecting the inner life and the metaphysical idea, he used interior monologue—speech on different levels of consciousness—in *Strange Interlude*, and he experimented with masks as a method of dramatization—with partial success in *The Great God Brown* and with virtually none in *Lazarus Laughed*. He even employed monologue in one highly effective scene of so realistic a comedy as *Ah, Wilderness!*, and he split the protagonist of *Days without End* into two characters who had to be played by two actors. This constant, if not indeed always satisfactory, experimentation, is actually another important feature of O'Neill's work. It was his role to open all the stops of theatre art in America, and we have reason to be grateful to him.

The well-known restiveness of his personal life had its correlate in his restiveness as an artist which made him seek new forms of expression even after succeeding in one particular style; and the unpredictability of his style added to the excitement that his playwriting brought to an increasing number of playgoers. To contend that this tendency to shift the artistic base of his work prevented O'Neill from completely perfecting himself on one basis is legitimate. To protest that he should not have done so is absurd. He acted under creative, as

well as psychological, compulsion in the flux of his life and in the flux of the transitional civilization apparent in both drama and fiction after 1914. He entertained extremely high expectations for the theatre which the success of motion pictures and radio, as well as high production costs, had not yet dampened for the profession; and he had high, sometimes recklessly high, ambitions for himself as a dramatist. In *Strange Interlude* and *Mourning Becomes Electra*, as well as later in *The Iceman Cometh*, O'Neill even violated the sacred right of the playgoer to discharge his obligations to the stage in two hours and a half of theatre attendance. He resorted to epic dimensions, taking some risk of introducing elephantiasis into playwriting. *Strange Interlude* acquired some of the qualities of a large impressionist or expressionist novel. *Mourning Becomes Electra* brought back the spaciousness, if not the imaginativeness, of the Aeschylean trilogy.

He also aspired to the estate of a poetic dramatist, and he rightly sensed that his artistic necessity and the requirements of his matter and point of view would be unfulfilled unless he became one. Whether he succeeded is debatable. It is a strongly held opinion that he lacked "language" equal to the reach of his non-verbal powers. This was noted with particular justice in the case of *Mourning Becomes Electra*. Granted the validity of the charge, it is none the less possible and only right to modify and moderate it. As long as he wrote about common life—of sailors and farmers and social outcasts—he managed his language securely, often with strong effect, sometimes with poetic overtones appropriate to his subject. When he set out to be deliberately poetic, he failed—sometimes embarrassingly. When he turned to middle-class or upper-class society, he missed fire in those parts of his plays in which he tried to generalize a feeling or an idea. Yet it may be conceded that even then he could achieve a poetic effect of low degree through the full rhythms of his sentences, if not through cadences and imagery.

If my memory serves, he was once referred to as a "prose Shakespeare." His plight, apart from personal reasons of insufficient endowment and of insufficient control over slang and colloquialisms (as in the constant harping on "pipe-dreams" in *The Iceman*), was due to the modern division between prose and dramatic poetry—a large subject which cannot be explored here. If, because of his turbulence and reiterations of an idea, he also appeared to lack "taste," it is questionable whether he really lacked it. It is sufficiently present, for example, in *Ah, Wilderness!*; and it is difficult for me to believe that I am the only one who found an adequate substitute for it in *Desire under the Elms*, in my opinion his best play. He simply did not bother about "taste" or balance when the surge of conflict and anguish was strong. Those who press the charge of want of "poetry" in the man should be reminded, moreover, that they got his "poetry," as other modern playwrights have done, not from verbal beauty but from the breadth and reach of his imagination, mood, or feeling, and, especially, from his theatrical—at times exaggeratedly theatrical—sense. If he was not felicitous in creating verbal poetry, he often created a "poetry of theatre"—this in effects of which a few examples are the tom-toms in *Emperor Jones*, the firemen's forecastle and the Fifth Avenue nightmares of *The Hairy Ape*, the mask and transformation effects of *The Great God Brown*, the evocation of the farmhouse and land in *Desire under the Elms*, and the Greek colonnade, the chanty refrain, and Electra-Lavinia's tragic closing of the doors upon herself in *Mourning Becomes Electra*.

O'Neill did not become the full-fledged tragic poet he evidently aspired to be. And want of language was only one reason. Another was his tendency to set up abstract personalities and issues, as most conspicuously in *Dynamo* and *Lazarus Laughed*, or to schematize characters and deprive them of possible range—this in order to develop a psychological conception or an argument. This tendency can be found in *The Great God Brown* and even in *Strange Interlude* and *Mourning Becomes Electra*. Perhaps he took ideas *per se* with too much of the seriousness of those who have only recently discovered "ideas." He sometimes took these in too simplified a form, and in too rarefied a form for drama—an error not committed by Sophocles and Shakespeare, though committed by other dramatists of distinction such as Euripides and Shaw under the pressure of an "intellectual" climate. He also tended to give a passion a bear-hug instead of an austere embrace, which is the more usual way with master-tragedians. And one may reflect, finally, that he did push too furiously toward catastrophic consummations and drive his characters too hard toward their destiny, thereby eliciting the charge of writing melodrama rather than tragedy. On this score, however, it must be said that he had company among the late "minor Elizabethans," who also piled horror upon horror. He bore, in fact, a resemblance to them in his susceptibility to extremes of passion, will, and affliction, as we may note in John Webster's *The Duchess of Malfi* and John Ford's *'Tis Pity She's a Whore*.

I believe that O'Neill wrote tragedy of a naturalistic-poetic kind in *Desire under the Elms*, and that he approached, if he did not quite reach, the altitude of high tragedy in *Mourning Becomes Electra*. Generally, moreover, if he failed to write tragedy, as he plainly intended in much of his work, he achieved a noble tragic mood—and this in a context of exciting drama. I believe this will be found to be the case in such plays as *Beyond the Horizon, Anna Christie, The Hairy Ape, All God's Chillun Got Wings*, and *The Iceman Cometh*, regardless of what faults can be ascribed to them. And if the quality of his mind prevented him from securing a maximum of meaning from many of his plays, he at least secured a maximum of tension—which is or contains a meaning of some sort not lightly to be dismissed in the kind of theatre we have had since 1914. He was hardly ever as sharp as Strindberg in scoring his points, and he lacked the agility of a Pirandello in dealing with them. But he was virtually the only American playwright to confront ideas on more than an elementary level and to wrestle with them "tragically"—heroically. He often set loose a mighty smoke with his fire, and consequently the fire was obscured, especially when it was the fire of an idea. But the smoke came from dramatic heat, and it created an atmosphere of dramatic feeling and conception which few other American playwrights have been able, or have seemed disposed, to create.

NICOLA CHIAROMONTE
"Eugene O'Neill" (1958)
Sewanee Review, 1960, pp. 494–501

Everything is to be found in Eugene O'Neill's plays: naturalism, symbolism, expressionism, *intimisme*, decadence, pessimism, spiritualism, Freudianism, and all the rest of the *isms*, all singularly confused and singularly un-worked-out. It has often been said that the founder of American drama lacks any positive faith: and in particular that he was tormented all his life by the problem of God and of the *raison d'être*, a problem that he never succeeded even in stating, let alone in solving. It would be easier to say that he was unable to see it in theatrical terms, to make it the material for dramatic action.

But, in spite of all his weaknesses and exaggerations, his oppressive wordiness and the irrepressible bombast of his style, O'Neill remains the most original playwright after Pirandello. Tormented in mind and troubled by physical disabilities as he was, it cannot be said that he was unsuccessful as a writer. In the first place the circumstances in which he began to write for the theatre, in the America of the years immediately after the first world war, were particularly favorable for the expression of his talent: there was a readiness for theatrical experiment and for the fight against commercial theatre. Then, as happens in America, O'Neill had no sooner thrown down his challenge than fame clamorously befriended him. And his success brought a new freedom to the American stage (to playwrights, actors, and producers). He was followed by disciples and imitators: Clifford Odets, Tennessee Williams, and Arthur Miller owe to O'Neill the road along which they so rapidly sped towards success.

Everything can be found in O'Neill, but his main characteristic is an honesty, sincerity and integrity which can only be defined as "romantic." The use he makes of the stage is romantic, displaying, declaiming and proclaiming there his problems, or I should rather say dreams and nightmares of problems, including the most romantic of all, the dream he never fulfilled, of reaching the heights of tragedy. But romantic above all, romantic in an American way, is the stand he takes both as prosecution and defence, his deliberate pessimism, his malcontented and sullen pose as *poète maudit*. For, in the end, O'Neill's accusation against American morality, and life in general, is not in social terms. Soviet critics were right, after applauding him at first, to turn against him: he is not concerned with capitalism and the redemption of the oppressed. O'Neill is concerned with the fact that no individual can live his life in accordance with those rare and fleeting moments in which each man is aware that he contains the absolute: moments which can only be expressed in poetry, after which (as Edmund says in *Long Day's Journey into Night*) "God is dead," and the Catholic religion (Irish rather than Roman, in O'Neill's case) can no longer help him.

But life cannot be made up of poetry. Life is made up of the crushing determinism of its circumstances: a nightmare against which one rebels by crime, by suicide, by madness and by poetry. Only a Philistine can accept it as reasonable: a business man, hated by all, the Marco Polo of O'Neill's imagination, a being literally without a soul. There is no question of understanding it: one of the most meaningful symbols of O'Neill is the stoker in *Hairy Ape*, significantly called Yank, to whom the apparition of a woman in the hell of the engine room reveals his state as an outsider, and who dies torn to pieces by the gorilla from whom he had sought the company refused to him by man.

To the very end O'Neill proclaimed, with a conviction and obstinacy which exact respect, the tremendous sadness of the position of the man who cannot understand. And it was on this feeling that his nonconformity was based. When, in 1946, Henry Luce wanted to rope him in, as a national figure and a Nobel Prize-winner, in support of his project to improvise a Pantheon of Americanism, the writer, little tempted by the honor of figuring in miniature on the covers, of *Time*, replied that he held the belief that the United States, instead of being the most successful country in the world, was the biggest failure . . . having progressed so rapidly, it had had no time to put down real roots. Its main idea was still the everlasting game of trying to possess its own soul by laying hold on something external. Noble words, and words which place O'Neill in a worthier American tradition than the one which national conformity was trying to fabricate at the time; but also very romantic. O'Neill's own work seems to be a vainly repeated attempt at trying to possess his own soul by laying hold on something external.

Long Day's Journey into Night is one of those tortuous attempts. It forms part of a series of nine plays which he had planned to write as the "story of a family," and which, if he had been able to finish it, would have given us his full autobiography, but of which he completed only three. *Long Day's Journey into Night* is a continual beating on the bars of the prison in the knowledge that they can never give way, that one will never understand what is wrong with oneself or with others as long as one moves only between the poles of accusation and commiseration. The vicious circle becomes obsessive. The action lasts for one day, but it might have lasted for a century: it lasts in fact as long as the torments of hell. Everything depends on the extent to which you believe in hell, meaning in reality: in the reality of the miserliness of the old actor, James Tyrone, but also in his perfect good faith; in the reality of his wife's drug taking; of the hardness of the eldest son, Jim, with his wild life and his heart of gold; in the reality of the consumption of young Edmund, but still more in his lyrical desperation; in the reality, lastly, of the rancor and the affection of each for all and all for each. Each of these facts can be as final as the last judgment, or it can be as transitory as one circumstance among many; it depends on the importance we give them, or on the state of mind in which we consider them and suffer them. One thing is certain: for O'Neill the sufferings of these four persons linked together by the ties of biology and of affection, have an immeasurable importance: an importance at one and the same time infinitely small and infinitely great. What causes him pain, and what he rebels against, is that things should be like this, and not otherwise: the same motive underlies the sterile and formless suffering, which seeks relief in drink, drugs, dreams and aspirations toward poetry (more than in poetry itself, which is not a remedy). But, once they are caught in the web of circumstances, there is no escape: so Mary Tyrone, the young girl, was about to turn nun, to dedicate herself to God, and instead . . . instead she fell in love with James. And what is so terrible about this? James loves her, the children love her, even if she has become a slave to the drug. Yes, but *from a certain point of view* it is the fault of James' advice that Mary has become a morphine addict; while from another point of view it is nobody's fault, and would have been terrible in any case, just because of being forced to be what one is, instead of living purely the life of the soul, a life of dreams. The hellish torture for O'Neill's characters is solitude: each one, in solitude, struggles with himself, wounds others. And nobody understands why.

For three hours O'Neill compels us to take part in this monotonous and obstinate round of suffering; it would, we feel, be stupid, were it not for his sincerity. Up to a certain point it fascinates us. The trouble is that, after putting his case before us with extreme simplicity and force, when we have already understood and accepted his reasoning, he goes on trying to convince us, trying to explain to himself the reasons of his reasons, and trying to get to the bottom of his pain: but like all the torments of hell, it is bottomless. The play ends precisely at the moment when everything begins: at the moment when Mary, under the influence of the drug, tells how, instead of entering the convent, she fell in love with James.

A Moon for the Misbegotten was the last play written by O'Neill, the third of the series comprising *Long Day's Journey into Night* and *A Touch of the Poet*. The plot is concerned chiefly in extracting from Jim, the libertine son of the ham actor, James Tyrone, the confession of a sin which arouses more pity than horror, and in showing us how one day his restless and tormented soul found a brief respite in the arms of Josie Hogan, the daughter of one of his tenants, and a hardened sinner. The hellish sin which seems to Jim to eat out his very soul, is this: in the train on which he accompanied his mother's body to its final resting place, instead of weeping over and repenting for the suffering he had caused her by his abandoned and drunken life, he had passed the three nights which the journey lasted with a whore. This Jim must confess to Josie, whom he believes to be pure and a virgin, before he can enjoy the affection he feels for her, and which he knows she returns. But Josie, for her part, is simply out to get Jim to make love to her. From this (apart from a question of business between Jim and Josie's father, who wants to get the farm cheap, which adds to the general misunderstanding) springs the difficulty for the two to meet on the level of human beings and not of animals.

This gives rise to one of the most awkward and clumsy, and at the same time most extraordinarily touching scenes in modern drama; it lasts for half the second and the whole of the third act, and is played entirely (with a few brief interruptions) between Josie and Jim. I cannot remember any comparable passage in any work of literature: nowhere else is the almost insurmountable difficulty preventing two human creatures from communicating as such, expressed with like violence, with like torment, with a like rough, wordy and disorderly confusion, but with like moving authenticity. It is not a scene of passion or exaltation, but simply this: for an hour and a half Jim struggles like an enraged bull to break down the barrier of incommunicability, and Josie, who at first thought she knew what she wanted, is pulled down by him into the whirlpool. The whole, naturally, accompanied by glass after glass of whisky. At the end Jim succeeds in making his confession, Josie feels purified and the two fall asleep worn out in each other's arms, on the steps of the house in the light of the moon which shines for the misbegotten. In the morning they drink a last draught of whisky and say farewell. What has been has been. They go back to speaking the deaf and dumb language of everyday reality.

We are present not at a dialogue but at a struggle in the dark. We emerge exhausted and, if not moved, at least shaken. Theatre, novel, autobiography: there is some of everything in O'Neill, and a kind of mystic lament to boot.

But it is impossible to say what such a work means. It is only possible to affirm that it is sincere and true to life: it gives, in fact, such an impression of probability that we lose all sense that it is a play. But we lose at the same time the sense of artistic invention: we have only—it seems—to go to America, into the Connecticut countryside where O'Neill's plot is laid, to find ourselves in the thick of similar events. And, in the certainty that there have been similar cases in real life, the stage fiction becomes for us singularly pleonastic and redundant. It fixes in immutable words something—a day in the life of two people—which is essentially ambiguous and changeable, because its meaning depends on what had gone before, and on what was to happen after. It lifts out of reality that which can only be comprehensible and genuine in its real setting; it gives an excessive and incalculable importance to something of which only the final outcome can tell if it had any importance at all. The frenzy of confession to which the hero gives himself up under the influence of whisky may mean nothing at all. In such circumstances even the confession of the most terrible sins, even the most atrocious suffering, has no final value; it is necessary to wait and see what will happen once he has slept it off.

We are left with the torment. We are left with O'Neill's convulsive sincerity, with the need he felt to tell his story. Maurice Blanchot declares that modern literature took its name from Rousseau in that he invented sincerity. Urged on by the impulse to reveal himself to the full, to be absolutely transparent and to come to terms with himself, Rousseau, according to Blanchot, was forced to rebel against the very essence of literature, which is artifice; but he could only achieve this aim by writing, that is by existing passionately on the level of words, and words are artifice. Therefore by the very fact of expressing himself, Rousseau alienated that immediacy and truth at which he aimed; and to get back to them somehow he was forced to go on writing and confessing, and to shut himself up more and more in the solitude which he needed in order to write and confess the truth of his being. Hence his greatness, and his madness.

A similar line of thought can easily be applied to the works of O'Neill, or rather to the torment which gave birth to the plays of this singularly genuine and at the same time singularly wistful writer. While however Rousseau's madness fed on ideas and found outlet in ideas, O'Neill's debate ended in a cul de sac. We are left therefore with his bare sincerity, or rather with a continual alienation, a continual missing of the mark, which is ill concealed behind emphatic symbols and measureless ambitions, such as the ambition to go back to Greek tragedy. And the inner rage did nothing but feed on itself, without ever finding a convincing form of release. O'Neill never succeeded in uttering his confession, in identifying the man with the writer in significant speech. Yet throughout the whole of his work this has been his one aim: he wanted to achieve this in the most open and public form—the stage, which at the same time was the form least suited for this kind of inner struggle. If ever there was an unhappy writer it was O'Neill. I might add that he was unhappy as only an American would know how to be; this because for him to be unhappy was to be blameworthy, and there should be expiation for his guilt—while instead there is no atonement. Rousseau's solitude is in this way cruelly confirmed. O'Neill could not believe, as Rousseau believed, that *it was the fault of others*. In effect he no longer believes in anything, except in the sequence of cause and effect. The only way out lies in whisky or in art. But whisky is followed by the morning after, and art can only mirror the reality from which he seeks refuge in drink.

This is the vicious circle in which O'Neill is imprisoned: the cause of his over-emphasis, of his confusion, of the mixture of the genuine and the wistful which is to be found in all his plays. But from this springs also his truth. O'Neill is a realist in that he bears the brunt of the whole of reality, without understanding it. As an artist he is unhappy because not wishing only to describe but also to express his sufferings, he shuts himself up jealously with them, refusing to have recourse to reason and ideas, which hold out the only hope of solution, of catharsis. It is the moralist—not to say the puritan—in him which refuses to turn to intellect to find a way of escape. For this reason his plays, including this last, however rough and intemperate, always reach in the end the essential effect of drama: they lead us to reflect on the reason for the action. The kind of realism which rules on the Italian stage, instead, is entirely painless and problemless: it does not turn away from ideas distressed by moral scruples as to their integrity: the indifference is genuine.

EUGENE M. WAITH
"Eugene O'Neill: An Exercise in Unmasking"
Educational Theatre Journal, October 1961, pp. 182–91

Dramatic inventiveness is O'Neill's surest claim to fame.[1] I include in this term both the feeling for theatre which enabled him to hit upon highly effective devices for the staging of his plays, and another kind of imagination which enabled him to find situations corresponding to his various concepts of the human dilemma. The attempt to find answers to all the big questions in life produced some exquisitely painful prose in such plays as *Lazarus Laughed* and *The Fountain*, but it also determined the characteristic form of an O'Neill play. The answers themselves, unsatisfactory as they are, contribute importantly to the success of the best characterizations. I shall have very little to say about either the philosophical or psychological worth of O'Neill's insights. My concern is the way in which these insights are embodied in dramatic form, and here is where his remarkable inventiveness is to be seen. I shall concentrate on an aspect of his technique based on masks.

Masks were used in several O'Neill plays staged in the twenties: in *The Hairy Ape, The Ancient Mariner, All God's Chillun Got Wings, The Fountain, The Great God Brown, Marco Millions* and *Lazarus Laughed*. In 1932, two years before resuscitating the device in *Days without End*, O'Neill published his "Memoranda on Masks" in *The American Spectator*. Here he expressed his conviction that masks would be found to be the "freest solution" of the problem of expressing in drama "those profound hidden conflicts of the mind which the probings of psychology continue to disclose to us."[2] In an oracular style, probably influenced by *Thus Spake Zarathustra*, he gave his "Dogma for the new masked drama.—One's outer life passes in a solitude haunted by the masks of others; one's inner life passes in a solitude hounded by the masks of oneself." But the most significant of the "Memoranda" for the understanding of O'Neill's technique was the question, "For what, at bottom, is the new psychological insight into human cause and effects but a study in masks, an exercise in unmasking?" The mask was a way of getting at the inner reality of character. In fact, it may be said that for O'Neill it was *the* way, for even in the many plays where actual masks are not used, we find the same preoccupation with concealment and discovery. These plays too are studies in masks.

O'Neill was in good company. Some of the liveliest imaginations of an extraordinarily vital period of artistic activity were haunted (to use a word O'Neill liked) by the mask. The director, Kenneth Macgowan, collaborated with Herman Rosse on a book called *Masks and Demons*, illustrated with reproductions of masks from Greece, Japan, the Congo, and New Mexico. Macgowan suggested a kind of identity between the dramatic process and the uses of the mask in both primitive and civilized societies.[3] In psychology the conception of the mask was prominent. What was the "inferiority complex" but a mask for aggression? Finally, the mask was part of an exciting stylistic revolution in the arts. Macgowan devoted a chapter in *The Theatre of Tomorrow* to expressionism, in which, as he explained, a formal expression of the artist's emotion was substituted for realistic representation. Gordon Craig, who influenced both Macgowan and Robert Edmond Jones, gave tremendous importance to the mask.

When O'Neill joined in a triumvirate with Macgowan and Jones at the Provincetown Playhouse it was inevitable that he should experiment with masks. In *The Great God Brown,* he used them to bring out, among other things, the divided consciousness of his hero, Dion Anthony, whose name was intended to suggest Dionysus and St. Anthony. Not only does the mask of a mocking Pan conceal and protect the real face of a sensitive and spiritual artist, but the mask itself changes in time from Pan to Mephistopheles. O'Neill attempted to portray by means of the mask the complicated inner tensions of a personality and the development which those tensions produce. Problems of this sort always concerned him. Through his career he dramatized "the divided man," as John Gassner has said,[4] and when he did not use masks he often used analogous devices. The asides in *Strange Interlude* are a clear example.

But this rather obvious use of the mask was not the most important one to O'Neill. In a statement given to the New York *Evening Post* he explained that in writing *The Great God Brown* he meant the "background pattern of conflicting tides in the soul of Man" to be "mystically within and behind [the characters], giving them a significance beyond themselves. . . ."[5] Later, in the "Memoranda on Masks" he said he would like to make the masks in this play symbolize more definitely the abstract theme, rather than stress the superficial meaning that people wear masks before other people.[6] In this same article he referred to *Strange Interlude* as an attempt at the "new masked psychological drama . . . without masks," but considered that it was not wholly successful where it tried to probe deeply. Kenneth Macgowan had spoken repeatedly of the mysteriousness of masks.[7] O'Neill said in his statement about *The Great God Brown* that mystery—a meaning felt but not completely understood—was what he wanted to realize in the theatre. Here we encounter the extraordinary spiritual zeal which informed some of the theatrical activity of the twenties. In O'Neill's case the urge to invest the theatre with religious significance, though it led to the unmitigated disasters of *Lazarus Laughed* and *Days without End*, was elsewhere a source of power. He was never content to catch the surface of a character. He must always by some means suggest what lay beneath and beyond in the character's relations to his inmost self, to his family, to society, and finally to the source of all things, whether referred to as God or Life-with-a-capital-L. The title of his first Broadway play was emblematic: *Beyond the Horizon.*

O'Neill arranged Coleridge's *Ancient Mariner* for the Provincetown Players in their 1923/24 season.[8] In the playbill James Light, who made the masks, talked of the spiritual atmosphere in which the mask lives and of their hope that the masks would intensify the theme of the poem. Since the words are entirely Coleridge's, the dramatic version is an excellent example of ways in which the mask could be used as an auxiliary device. We can readily see what elements are intensified by it. Most conspicuous is the supernatural. The Ancient Mariner himself wears no mask, but as he begins his tale his shipmates appear, wearing the masks of drowned men, which are later changed for those of holy spirits and finally angels. Death wears the mask of a black skull, and the Woman's face, though unmasked, is heavily made up to resemble a white skull. A comparable use of the device is found in *The Great God Brown*, where both the mask and the real face of the hero suggest supernatural forces—mocking demon and ascetic saint—at war in the hero's soul. In the case of Cybel, the prostitute, the mask shows her profession, while her own face reveals the spiritual dimension of Earth Mother—a combination which was bound to appeal strongly in the twenties, being both shocking and religious. Cybel marked an important advance beyond La Dame aux Camélias, a harlot who was merely good-hearted.

Another element of Coleridge's poem which is intensified

by the masks is the contrast between the Mariner and the unthinking mass of mankind. The two wedding guests who go on to the wedding have mask-like faces; the bride and groom, glimpsed for a moment, look like dolls, and the others in the wedding party are seen once as dancing shadows on a windowblind. The third wedding-guest differs from the others in being "naturally alive—a human being," and thus the spell cast over him by the mariner makes clear the connection between genuine vitality and spiritual vision. Not to share in the dream or the intimation of what lies beyond the horizon is to be part of the faceless crowd of "men and bits of paper whirled by the cold wind" in a "twittering world," to borrow Eliot's words. This expressionistic use of masks to suggest the horror of the anonymous crowd is also found in other O'Neill plays. The Sunday morning crowd on Fifth Avenue in *The Hairy Ape* were given masks, and so were the crowds, Jewish, Greek, and Roman, in *Lazarus Laughed*.

Thus, in the plays of the mid-twenties O'Neill repeatedly used masks not only to present the divided man but to bring out some relationship between the individual and society or between the individual and the realm of the supernatural, and thus to give the characters "a significance beyond themselves." In *Lazarus Laughed* there was a fantastic proliferation of masks, which proved happily to be the flood tide of this phase of O'Neill's experimentation; for as he himself realized later, the device had overwhelmed the drama. The insistence on something beyond the surface was so great that the characters and their actions, instead of gaining an added dimension, lost all reality. One turns with relief back to the first O'Neill play to be produced, the one-act *Bound East for Cardiff*, a mainly realistic play, where the sense of something beyond is given by a simple device. The ship's foghorn, blown at regular intervals, accompanies the action of the play, which is nothing but the death of the injured seaman, Yank, in his bunk below deck. One is never allowed to forget the context in which this action is taking place.

Bound East for Cardiff is a beautiful illustration of another aspect of O'Neill's technique. In speaking of the new psychological insight in the "Memoranda" he used the phrase "an exercise in unmasking." The ship's whistle keeps reminding us of her slow progress through the fog while below deck in the forecastle, Yank is painfully approaching death. Most of the dialogue is his conversation with his mate, Driscoll, to whom, toward the end, he confides his longing to have a farm "way in the middle of the land," far from the sea. It is an unexpected revelation of his character and by its intimacy it brings Driscoll closer to him than ever before. Shortly afterward he dies. As he does so the whistle stops. The fog has lifted. The play is unassuming but powerful, and I believe that the movement of its action is the characteristic movement of an O'Neill play—a movement toward discovery or revelation or both—a kind of unmasking.

Toward the end of an O'Neill play there almost always comes a moment when the principal characters are for the first time fully revealed to the audience, and often it is only then that they fully understand themselves or their relationships to each other and to the world they live in. These recognition scenes are O'Neill's high points and in his best plays they are very moving. However, there are major differences to observe between these recognitions. In some of them there is a final heroic confrontation with the forces of life or destiny; in others, the hero in retreat reaches the final devastating acknowledgement of despair. O'Neill seems to have thought of his characters' coming to terms with life as movement forward or back. In the early versions of *Days without End* an antithesis is set up between "going back"—refusing in some way to accept the challenge of life—and going "on to Hercules," a curious phrase, intended at one time to be the title of the play, and meaning acceptance of life, even if life itself is meaningless, determination to create goals for oneself, a heroic gesture with overtones of romantic grandeur. Hercules here is the constellation, but suggests also the great hero's final transcendence of a fate which he accepts. In *Days without End* the choice between two opposite directions is explicit: in other plays it is implied. The backward movement of O'Neill characters is always flight from the problem posed by existence; forward movement is the heroic, sometimes ecstatic, acceptance of them. Both movements may be toward death, but death in significantly different forms.

None of his plays gave O'Neill more trouble than *Days without End*, which was after all a commercial and artistic failure of the first magnitude. His notes and several early versions, now in the O'Neill Collection at Yale, are most interesting, however. What they reveal has an important bearing on the rest of O'Neill's work. Though in each version there is a choice of a way forward and a way back (which, unlike the way up and the way down, are not at all the same), the specific courses of action to be chosen are altered in a most surprising way. The hero, John Loving, is plagued by his loss of faith (he was born a Catholic), and by the guilt he feels for his unfaithfulness to his wife. Initially O'Neill planned for him to commit suicide at the end in front of a statue of the Virgin—an end which was intended to suggest that mother-worship had turned to death-worship—a return to the protective womb of religion. Next O'Neill decided to make the play "less definitely Catholic," and in the first completed draft the wife dies and the hero curses God. In another version the hero is split in two: the mocking, Mephisthophelean part of him finds a death of denial, consistent with his life, while the other part finds faith, even though he also dies. Here the rediscovery of religion has a clearly positive value, even exceeding the value of heroic persistence in the face of meaninglessness—the "On to Hercules" attitude. The symbol of Christ on the cross is substituted for the statue of the Virgin. The religious solution is retained in the final version, though here the hero also achieves reintegration by imposing his will upon his alter ego, and is rewarded by the forgiveness and survival of his wife. The last scene again takes place at the foot of a crucifix, and the acceptance of Christianity is an assertion of life. The point, as this brief consideration of the earlier versions makes clear, is that he was looking for a dramatic solution which would show the *movement* of his hero from the crossroads where we first meet him. Which solution to the philosophical problems O'Neill himself might have chosen at this period of his life I would not presume to guess. He was obviously capable of imagining several.

The characteristic structure of an O'Neill play, then, is determined by a movement toward unmasking, which is often also a movement of the principal characters toward discovery of the stance they must take toward the fundamental problems of existence. In many of the early plays O'Neill chose an episodic form in which he could show the stages by which, in the course of time, the final discovery was reached. Later he reduced the compass of the time to one day, though contriving to retain the same emphasis on the experience of discovery. Even this one day is a journey. Before discussing in more detail *The Great God Brown*, *The Iceman Cometh*, and *Long Day's Journey into Night*, I shall give some clear-cut examples of the two sorts of character-development of which I have spoken, the movements backwards and forwards.

The Emperor Jones remains one of O'Neill's more impressive plays. When Brutus Jones, the former Pullman porter, who has made himself emperor of an island in the West Indies, is faced with rebellion, he starts immediately on an escape he has planned through the great forest to the coast, where he is to be met by a ship. But what was planned as an escape turns into a retreat from the symbols of civilized success which he has won for himself to fantasies of primitive terror which lie deep within him. The flight through the forest is a fine theatrical symbol for the psychological regression brought about by panic as Jones loses his way in the darkness and hears the drums of the rebelling natives. The use of the tom-tom, beating first at the rate of the normal pulse, and then gradually faster until it stops at the moment of Jones's death, is a theatrical device comparable in effectiveness to the whistle in *Bound East for Cardiff*.

One of the most brilliant revelation scenes in the plays of the early twenties is the final scene of *All God's Chillun Got Wings*, which has been excellently analyzed by Doris Falk[9] in the light of the psychological problems which are her main concern. Ella, the white girl married to an ambitious Negro, destroys an African mask, which has been established as a symbol of artistic achievement and religious mystery, but which she perversely takes as a symbol of degradation. A quarrel ensues, followed by reconciliation. Ella is a little girl again: "I'll just be your little girl, Jim—and you'll be my little boy—just as we used to be." Jim is seized by a kind of religious ecstasy. On his knees he prays to be made worthy of the child God has given him as a wife, and when she asks him to "come and play," he replies, "Honey, Honey, I'll play right up to the gates of Heaven with you!" What makes the scene particularly effective is his belief, at the very moment when all his hopes have been frustrated, that he has found happiness—that he too has wings. Utter defeat presents itself to him in the guise of victory.

The final moments of these plays reveal the principal characters reverted to savagery or childhood. I shall spend less time in illustrating the contrary movement toward a wider horizon—an acceptance of life which is not resignation. Juan Ponce de Leon, the hero of *The Fountain*, is described as half "ambitious thinker," half "romantic dreamer." The goal he sets himself when he goes on the expedition to find Cathay is glory for Spain and himself, but the self which sets this goal is only half the man, and the less important half. The repressed romantic dreamer is his true self. In an interview at this time O'Neill said that what he tried to put in his plays was an ennoblement of life, an exaltation, an urge toward life, which, he made clear, derived in some way from dreaming.[10] Juan's ambitious self is presented as a "bitter, mocking mask," and only at the end is the dreamer allowed to emerge. The expedition in search of Cathay turns into a spiritual quest, and at the moment when Juan's hopes of glory are defeated he is granted a mystical vision. Though he finds neither Cathay nor the Fountain of Eternal Youth, he comes at last to what seems to him the source of life. His voyage of discovery across unknown seas is the exact opposite of the flight of the Emperor Jones through the forest.

The relentless forward movement of *Lazarus Laughed* toward more and more exultant assertion of the value of life is part of what makes it the tedious play it is. There is no let-up in this yea-saying. Lazarus himself is a cross between Nietzsche's Zarathustra and Molly Bloom: his first word, like her last, is "Yes!" to be said, according to the stage-direction, "Suddenly in a deep voice—with a wonderful exultant acceptance in it." A far more convincing example of acceptance occurs in a far better play, *Desire under the Elms*, in which the two principal characters, Eben and Abbie, move through a sequence of false attitudes toward each other to true understanding and love. Like Juan in *The Fountain*, they have found more than they knew they were looking for.

The Great God Brown enjoyed a run of eight months in 1926 when it was first produced. When O'Neill was asked to choose a scene from one of his plays to be included in Whit Burnett's anthology, *This Is My Best*, published in 1942, he chose one from *The Great God Brown* and said: "I still consider this play one of the most interesting and moving I have written. It has its faults of course, but for me, at least, it does succeed in conveying a sense of the tragic mystery drama of Life revealed through the *lives* in the play." Though the faults of which O'Neill was aware are serious ones, it is, as he thought, one of his most interesting plays, and contains more penetrating analysis of character than many more competent pieces of dramaturgy with which it could be compared.

The central problem of the play is both subtle and complex: it is the deformation of a creative impulse in a hostile environment. The urge toward artistic creation is also the urge toward spiritual self-fulfillment, as in so many O'Neill plays, and therefore the artist (in this case an architect) is given the name Dion Anthony, whose religious implications I have already mentioned. The basic conflict in the play is between his aspirations, religious and artistic, and the doctrine of success as understood in a materialistic society. Dion's friend, Billy Brown, is the embodiment of worldly success, playing the role of the ant to Dion's grasshopper. The relationship, as Kenneth Tynan acutely observed in his review of the recent revival, seems to anticipate the mingled love and hate between the two brothers in *Long Day's Journey*. He might have added that in turn it was anticipated to some extent by the relationship between the two brothers in *Beyond the Horizon*, and by the two warring natures within Juan Ponce de Leon or Marco Polo. In none of these other plays, however, did O'Neill attempt to chart so precisely the interaction of the two temperaments.

Yet the two men have a remarkably large area of shared experience. Both love Margaret, Dion's wife; both patronize Cybel; both are architects, and both work in the same office. In fact Dion's designs are apparently passed off as Billy's. In Acts III and IV, after Dion's death, O'Neill uses Dion's mask to show how one character almost fuses with the other; for Billy inherits the mask. This symbolic action has been prepared for at the end of Act II by the revelation that Dion first assumed the mask as a child to protect himself from the cruelty of Billy, who envied his ability to draw and teased him by destroying his pictures. In a sense, Billy and Dion are complementary halves of one personality, for each in some way wishes to be the other. Their conflict is resolved only at the end of the play when Cybel, seeing Billy with Dion's mask, says, "You are Dion Brown!" It is Billy, no longer the great god of success, who finally has the mystic illumination which Dion Anthony sought.

In presenting the tortured progress of this divided personality, O'Neill used the mask to show both the reaction of one half to the other, and also the further division within each half. The gradual change of the mask from Pan to Mephistopheles shows the increasing bitterness of Dion's reaction to his alter ego, the complier with the world. Even the spiritual self hidden by the mask follows a parallel course toward the denial of life. Destructive demon is matched with ascetic saint. When Billy inherits the demonical mask, it initiates him into Dion's sufferings, but the final result is not the same. In the last scene,

where Billy is stripped bare and without the mask, he seems to have become the Dionysus which Dion potentially was. This dying god is the inner core of the composite character, whose complex reactions to environment have hitherto concealed the truth.

The complications are far too many (I have omitted several) and the dependence on the mask is far too great. Not only is it impossible in the theatre to see clearly the changes in the masks which O'Neill prescribes, but the conception is tiresomely schematic. However, the movement of the characters toward their final revelation is handled with greater finesse than in any of the earlier plays.

In two of the later plays, *The Iceman Cometh* and *Long Day's Journey into Night*, an equal complexity of movement is managed without the machinery of masks and without another encumbrance which handicaps many of the plays in the mid-twenties. In *The Fountain*, *The Great God Brown*, *Lazarus Laughed*, and one or two others, O'Neill tries unsuccessfully to elevate certain crucial moments by the use of a rhapsodic, pseudo-poetic prose. He seems to have been aware himself that he never carried it off, for in the "Memoranda on Masks" he has the interesting comment, à propos of a rejected plan to use masks in *Mourning Becomes Electra*: "Masks in that connection demand great language to speak—which let me out of it with a sickening bump!"[11] The connection he had in mind was with Greek tragedy, but more broadly it is true, whether or not he fully realized it, that he was unable to write in the formal style which his experiments in theatrical formalism demanded. In all of these plays an inadequacy of language hampers, to a greater or lesser degree, the success of his dramatic inventiveness. In the two late plays I have just mentioned the realistic style which he could handle well is perfectly suited to his conception and does not prevent him from achieving the effects he strove for in the more obviously contrived plays.

The effectiveness of *The Iceman Cometh* derives from the progressive stripping of the characters, brought about by their interaction. Again O'Neill plays two characters against each other, Parritt and Hickey, but this time, instead of being opposite, they are equivalents whose careers are counterpointed. Hickey suffers from guilt for the murder of his wife, Parritt from guilt for the betrayal of his mother. Between the two, so to speak, is the pivotal character of Larry, a former lover of Parritt's mother. These are the central characters.

The whole movement of the play, which occupies just under two day's time, is like the advance and retreat of a huge wave. The play opens in the torpor of a drunken sleep; as it gathers force the human derelicts in Harry Hope's bar are impelled toward action; at the end most of them are quickly slipping back into drunken stupor; only three of them have been flung free of the wave—Hickey, Parritt, and Larry. When Hickey urges everyone to give up pipe dreams he merely gives added impetus to Parritt's movement toward explanation and ultimately confession. At the same time he urges Larry to give up his pose of non-commitment and pass judgment on Parritt's betrayal. Hickey himself moves toward the shocking discovery that he has always hated his wife. Each of the three pushes the others toward a discarding of illusion which means the admission of failure in life. At the end one has committed suicide, one has given himself up to the police, and the third prays for death.

Long Day's Journey into Night is wave-like in quite a different way. Each of the principal characters, James and Mary Tyrone and their sons Jamie and Edmund, is borne toward his final destination by a series of impulsions, between which he may even seem to drift in the contrary direction. The rhythm of the play is one of movement regularly interrupted and regularly resumed. It is Mary's backward movement into drug-addiction which dominates the play, and the stages of her regress give the play its structure. The first act ends with Edmund's suspicion that she has begun again; the first scene of the second act with Tyrone's assurance that she has; the second scene with her plan to go to town for more "medicine." In the third act, which is mostly hers, the drug has already made her quite remote. It ends as she goes upstairs for more. At the end of the fourth act she has arrived at her destination—her girlhood in the convent. Her action precipitates a crisis in the family, which is augmented by news from the doctor that Edmund has tuberculosis. Reacting to these emotional stresses, each of the three men comes to a recognition of his aims and motives. For two of them, Tyrone and Jamie, this amounts to a confession of defeat as humiliating as Hickey's or Larry's. For Edmund alone the darkness of the night into which they are all travelling is relieved by sparks of remembered hope.

The fourth act is a series of "epiphanies," managed with superb control of the theatrical medium. It is night, and the fog which Mary loves because "it hides you from the world" has become a dense wall outside the living room where all the action takes place. The act begins with Tyrone and Edmund, the old actor with a miser's love of property and the young poet with tuberculosis. Depressed by the events of the day, and already partly drunk, they drink more and talk until they goad each other to a show-down. They quarrel over Tyrone's stinginess and his possible responsibility for Mary's drug-addiction. Occasionally arresting themselves, but always resuming the quarrel, they finally tell each other the truth. Edmund accuses his father of economizing even on the treatment of his tuberculosis. Tyrone defends himself by self-pitying reminiscences of his youth, and then admits what he has never admitted to anyone before, that he was corrupted by early success and prostituted his talent for financial gain. For the first time in the play his character is fully revealed, and as he voices his regret for the actor he might have been, we realize that his longing for his youth is no less poignant than his wife's.

His admission puts an end to the quarrel, for it elicits sympathy from his son, but it sets in motion another revelation. Moved by his father's memories, Edmund drunkenly describes some extraordinary experiences "all connected with the sea." They are not wrong turnings but moments of illumination when "the veil of things as they seem [is] drawn back by an unseen hand." Earlier in the evening Edmund has told of a walk he has just taken in the fog, trying to lose himself, and feeling like a ghost. As he now speaks of seeing beyond the veil, he also recalls that after the vision the veil always falls "and you are alone, lost in the fog again. . . ." He describes himself romantically as one who will always be a stranger, "a little in love with death." He is somewhat like his father in his self-dramatization and self-pity; somewhat like his mother in his almost voluptuous surrender to the fog; yet, unlike either of them, he is capable of extracting a significance from his experiences which seems to redeem life from utter meaninglessness. Even though he is "a little in love with death," he does not fall back on self-deception, like his father, nor refuse to live in the present, like his mother. There is still the hope of forward movement. His reminiscences not only reveal him but place him in relation to his parents.

When Jamie comes in, an equally remarkable and effective scene ensues, in which the pretenses of Edmund's ne'er-do-well brother are stripped off for the first time. Again we have the halting movement of a quarrel which seems at

moments about to end in reconciliation but then resumes. The jerkiness of the movement is accentuated by Jamie's nature, for he is one of O'Neill's divided characters, half mocking cynic, half good fellow. Jamie, like Hickey, conceals hate under the guise of love. He has pretended and partly believed himself that his kid-brother is his best pal, for whom he would do anything, but now with terrifying frankness he proclaims his jealousy and resentment of Edmund, whom he has tried to corrupt in order to keep him from succeeding. "The dead part of me," he says, "hopes you won't get well." Beneath Jamie's rather feckless charm lies a hatred of life so venomous that it would willingly destroy Edmund. This carefully concealed attitude is almost the exact opposite of the one revealed by Edmund to his father in recalling those times when he felt a part of "Life itself." For all his melancholy, Edmund has none of his brother's destructiveness. Rather, he is the creator.

The unmasking of Jamie, one of the most powerful episodes in the play, is almost the end. There remains only the final view of Mary, now thoroughly lost in the dream of her childhood. Her pathetic immaturity is the ultimate truth about her and her oddly remote chatter about the convent marks the end of her journey. In one sense she is a spokesman for the entire family. Each of them, in groping for the truth about himself, has turned back to some part of his past, and since the present which each of them faces is sad, there is special appropriateness in her last lines, which close the play: "Then in the spring something happened to me. Yes, I remember. I fell in love with James Tyrone and was so happy for a time."

This is O'Neill at his best. In these last plays he gave up his reliance on elaborate theatrical contrivance and attempted no forcing of his muse to rhapsodic heights. As a result his genuine gifts are seen to the best advantage. These plays are a kind of unmasking of their author.

Notes

1. This paper was given at the Seminar in Twentieth-Century Drama arranged by the English Graduate Club of Duke University, March 11–12, 1960. I am grateful to Mr. Donald Gallup, Curator of the Yale Collection of American Literature, for making available many items in the O'Neill Collection established by Mrs. Carlotta Monterey O'Neill, and for permission to publish information derived from them.
2. (Nov., 1932), p. 3.
3. (New York, 1923), pp. xii, 161, 163.
4. "Eugene O'Neill: The Course of a Modern Dramatist," *Critique*, I (1958), 10.
5. Quoted by Barrett Clark, *Eugene O'Neill: The Man and His Plays* (New York, 1933), p. 162.
6. *American Spectator* (Dec., 1932), p. 2.
7. *Masks and Demons*, p. 55.
8. This version was published for the first time by Mr. Donald Gallup in the *Yale Library Gazette*, XXXV (1960), 61–62.
9. *Eugene O'Neill and the Tragic Tension* (New Brunswick, 1958), pp. 87–90.
10. Mary B. Mullet, "The Extraordinary Story of Eugene O'Neill," *American Magazine* (Nov., 1922), p. 118.
11. *American Spectator* (Dec., 1932), p. 2.

JACKSON R. BRYER
"'Hell Is Other People':
Long Day's Journey into Night"
The Fifties: Fiction, Poetry, Drama
ed. Warren French
1970, pp. 161–70

In a tragedy, nothing is in doubt and everyone's destiny is known. That makes for tranquility. There is a sort of fellow-feeling among characters in a tragedy: he who kills is as innocent as he who gets killed: it's all a matter of what part you are playing. Tragedy is restful; and the reason is that hope, that foul, deceitful thing, has no part in it. There isn't any hope. You're trapped. The whole sky has fallen on you, and all you can do about it is to shout. (Jean Anouilh, *Antigone*)

One of the many ironies in the career of Eugene O'Neill is that, in 1931, when he deliberately tried to write a modern play which would approximate the Greek ideal of tragic drama, he produced *Mourning Becomes Electra*. This thirteen-act monstrosity is one of the great white elephants of our theater history. Not only does it lack the great dialogue of tragedy but it also fails because of its over-simplified view of characters entirely motivated by Freudian complexes which O'Neill substituted for the Greek idea of Fate. A decade later, however, when he simply sat down and wrote out the story which had been torturing him for years—that of his own family—O'Neill produced, in *Long Day's Journey into Night*, one of the very few modern plays which we can see as tragic.

To talk about any modern play as a tragedy is immediately to enter what are at best muddy waters. For decades critics have quarreled over what constitutes a "modern" tragedy. A few distinctions are clear, however. One is that the strictures which Aristotle supplied in classical times no longer apply. The assumption of the Greeks that theirs was a universe controlled by the gods has never been less warranted than today, when the very existence of any deity is questioned. And there is little or no agreement as to the nature and omnipotence of a God even when His existence is acknowledged. But to remove Fate as the major cause in tragedy is not to suggest that, in the modern theater, we have been unwilling to substitute other forces for this Greek idea. Not surprisingly, we seem to have supplied causes which result from universally held notions of our day, as the idea of Fate deriving from the gods was held by the Greeks. Because we live in a highly scientific age—and because the beginnings of modern drama parallel the dawn of that age—our causes, principally heredity and environment, are major determinants in the lives of individuals and, hence, we accept them as irreversible and uncontrollable forces in the lives of dramatic characters. Thus, Ibsen in *Ghosts* and Chekhov in *The Cherry Orchard* represent the two germinal strands of the modern theater, each writing plays of tragic proportions based primarily on heredity and environment, respectively.

But I would carry this one step further and suggest that for a modern play to be truly tragic we must have more than these uncontrollable forces operating on an individual. His demise must also be partially his own fault before a true ambivalence can exist. Again, the reason can be found in the assumptions of our society as opposed to the Greeks. We live in an essentially humanistic age. Because of this, while we accept the influence of heredity and environment, we do not see them as totally determining our lives. The Greeks, on the other hand, did see the gods in this way. We have a more sophisticated and complicated view of the causes for our actions and for the directions our lives take. To be convincingly tragic a modern play must reflect this more complex perspective. There are relatively few examples of American drama that meet this challenge; but where it is met we can see the attributes noted above. In Tennessee Williams' two great classics, *The Glass Menagerie* and *A Streetcar Named Desire*, and in Arthur Miller's *Death of a Salesman* and *The Crucible*, we see characters who are victims both of their backgrounds and environments and of characteristics within themselves.

Finally, it is possible to make some further observations about the nature of these characteristics which are partially responsible for the figurative or literal downfall of the tragic protagonist. In many cases, the character's flaw—to borrow from Aristotle—is often the quality which in another sense makes him exceptional. Laura's flaw in *The Glass Menagerie* is, at least to some extent, that she cannot exist in the real world (this is, in fact, the flaw of all three Wingfields); but is it not also her strength, the basis of her uniqueness? Similarly, in *The Crucible*, it is John Proctor's integrity and honesty which set him apart; but it is these very qualities which make him choose death instead of a false confession. Even in *Oedipus Rex*, if we discount for a moment the overall causative factor of Fate, Oedipus' outstanding quality is his inquiring mind which has enabled him to solve the riddle of the Sphinx; but it is the same spirit of inquiry which makes him continue to question Tiresias and thus bring about his tragedy. This, then, seems to be one of the paradoxes inherent in tragedy—that a man's weakness is also his strength and that this very quality which sets him apart from other men may cause his destruction—or at least be responsible for his unhappiness.

Long Day's Journey into Night exhibits most of these characteristics of modern tragedy; and it goes beyond other plays of the modern American theater in two major respects: first, it involves four tragic characters whose lives are inextricably bound but who are nonetheless decided individuals, complexly and completely depicted and explored; and second, rather than offering only heredity and environment as the partial—and uncontrollable—elements in the destinies of these figures, O'Neill offers a far more profound and abstract additional factor—love. Love binds together the four Tyrones; but love is also at the basis of their tragedy. Were there not love between the members of the family, Jamie and Edmund could leave, James could detach himself from his wife's illness and his sons' problems, and Mary could, in a sense, return to the safety of her girlhood. But, as in Sartre's *No Exit*, hell for the Tyrones is other people, each other.

All of them in the course of the play express, either explicitly or implicitly or both, a yearning for an isolated existence. The most overt examples of this are Edmund's speeches at the beginning of Act IV in which he admits that all he wants is "to be alone with myself in another world where truth is untrue and life can hide from itself." For him, the sea is the epitome of this condition and in his long reminiscence about his experiences at sea he expresses total satisfaction with an existence in which he was alone with nature, with "none of the crew in sight," a time when he belonged "to a fulfillment beyond men's lousy, pitiful, greedy fears and hopes and dreams."

Jamie's continual state of drunkenness is an expression of *his* longing for isolation; just as Mary's drug addiction implies the same sort of desire to escape the real world and envelop herself in a protective fog. James' escapes are more subtle. In one respect, his refuge is *The Count of Monte Cristo*, the "big money-maker" on which he has squandered his talents. It has enabled him to stop living creatively. His pose as a patrician land-owner also provides him with an escape from his true heritage as a shanty Irishman and makes it possible for him often to dissociate himself from his contemporaries.

But at the same time that the Tyrones seek escape, they see that it is impossible; they realize that they are hopelessly tied to one another for life. This realization, combined with the desire to escape, produces what is perhaps the major tension in the play, a tension which is expressed primarily in a continual series of expressions of love and hatred on the part of each character. Throughout the play, each Tyrone says and does many things deliberately to hurt another. They strike out at each other like the caged animals that they are; but, in virtually the next breath, they profess deep and genuine affection. This ambivalence provides *Long Day's Journey* with one of its most complex elements.

In Act IV, Jamie drunkenly admits to Edmund that he deliberately introduced him to the dissolute existence that he, Jamie, relishes because he "never wanted you to succeed and look even worse by comparison." He then blames Edmund's birth for Mary's dope addiction and, while he admits that it is not Edmund's fault, he declares, "God damn you, I can't help hating your guts—!" But, almost immediately, he adds, "But don't get the wrong idea, Kid. I love you more than I hate you." Similarly, in Act I, when all three Tyrones are concerned about the possible return of Mary's habit, it is Jamie, whose love for his mother is the cause of his hatred of Edmund, who deliberately lets slip the fact that Edmund's illness is more than a cold, a disclosure which he knows is likely to help drive her back to morphine. Later in the same act, Edmund, who is even closer to Mary than Jamie is, unnecessarily tells her that he heard her go into the spare room the night before, a sure indication that she is back on the drug.

Mary and James accuse one another continually, Mary blaming her husband for not providing a home for his family and for being a miser, James bitterly blaming her for ruining their happiness. Yet, at the end of their most heated exchange, early in Act II, Scene 2, Mary exclaims, "James! We've loved each other! We always will!" And, in Act II, Mary reminds Jamie that he should have more respect for his father: "You ought to be proud you're his son!" Both Mary and James also reminisce often about how happy they were with one another once; and they do so in terms that make it very clear that they still love each other a great deal.

Both sons lash out at their father throughout the play. Mary even at one point tells Edmund, "I never knew what rheumatism was before you were born!" Yet, despite all this rancor, there is abundant evidence of abiding affection. This is ironically and appropriately symbolized at the very end of the play when Mary, completely under the influence of morphine, drifts in dragging her wedding gown and wanders about the room reminiscing about her girlhood. The reverie concludes with her memory of senior year when she decided to be a nun; but then, she recalls, "in the spring something happened to me. . . . I fell in love with James Tyrone and was so happy for a time." This brief passage sums up all of one aspect of the tragedy. Mary's love for James, and all the Tyrones' love for each other, is both their great strength and the cause of their torture. If they did not love each other so much, they could not strike out so cruelly, they could not hate. Edmund's remark about Mary—"It's as if, in spite of loving us, she hated us!"—might well be changed to read because she loves us, she hates us, and then applied equally to all the relationships in this family. And, finally, each character's desire to escape the others, to find an isolation away from the complications of other people, is really no more nor less than a wish to evade one of the major responsibilities of the human condition, contact with other human beings and all the conflicting emotions and attitudes that these contacts produce. As Edmund says in Act IV—and as many an O'Neill protagonist could and does echo—"It was a great mistake, my being born a man. I would have been much more successful as a sea gull or a fish."

But there are other tragic aspects to *Long Day's Journey*. An important one is suggested by my earlier remarks about the forces operating on an individual in modern tragic drama. In O'Neill's play, each of the Tyrones is both responsible and not responsible for the part he is playing. The best example of this is James. The three members of his family accuse him of being miserly and there is ample confirmation of this charge, most especially in his efforts to send Edmund to an inexpensive sanitorium. But, in Act IV, James admits to Edmund that perhaps he is a "stinking old miser" and goes on to explain this trait by describing his childhood when he "learned the value of a dollar" working twelve hours a day in a machine shop, a "dirty barn of a place where rain dripped through the roof," for fifty cents a week. With this disclosure it becomes clear that James is not entirely to blame for his penurious ways. It is not his fault that he was brought up in a penniless and fatherless family. This background understandably has made him overly sensitive to the evils of the poorhouse. And yet we cannot totally excuse this quality in James because we feel that, once he became financially successful, he should have developed more generous instincts in accordance with normal familial devotion. Clearly, however, the responsibility for James' weakness is divided between forces in his background over which he had no control and present factors which he should be able to alter.

The same sort of divided responsibility can be seen in the three other characters. Jamie's drunken and dissolute ways are certainly his own fault to an extent, but they can also be traced to the family situation. His father introduced him to drink and brought him up in an atmosphere where he could meet the cheap tarts and low types with whom he now associates. Jamie's failures in life can also be linked partially to his father's refusal to allow him to be a success. This is perhaps because James realizes that he has sold his own talents for a sure financial return and he must therefore keep his son from being any more successful than he is. Jamie's problems are also further compounded by his relationships with his mother and his brother. He feels, with considerable justification, that Mary dotes on Edmund and ignores him. He also is, as he admits to Edmund in Act IV, extremely jealous of his brother and of the possibility that he will succeed and make him look worse by comparison.

Mary also is both victim and causative factor. She is guilty of forcing her family into an almost death-like inaction by her drug addiction; but when we look at her background and the cause of her illness, we find ample extenuating circumstances. She is, in many ways, still the shy convent girl who, as O'Neill stresses in his long stage direction introducing her, "has never lost" her "innate unworldly innocence." Because of this she is totally unable to cope with the cruel realities of the world around her. In this she shares more than a literal kinship with Edmund, who also cannot face the world because of a sensitive poetic nature. Both Mary and Edmund feel a tremendous lack of belonging, a loneliness. It is difficult to decide whether Mary's addiction, like Laura's limp in *The Glass Menagerie*, causes her isolation or whether the addiction is merely an overt manifestation of the isolation which is already there. Mary has not been at peace since she left her father's house to marry James. While it is true that James has never given her the house she so desperately wants, she would undoubtedly have been unable to cope with one had she been asked to do so. Mary's retreat into the past through drugs is her way of going back to what was for her an ideal world, an escape from a real world which she cannot handle. Her addiction is probably no more than a means towards an end which she would have reached—or tried to reach—through another method had morphine not been available. Thus, we cannot totally blame her problems on James and the "cheap quack doctor" who attended her at Edmund's birth. Nor can we blame Edmund's present illness for her reversion to dope. Mary's difficulties are far more deep-seated than this. Her protected childhood has made her constitutionally and emotionally unable to deal with life. On the other hand, Mary *is* guilty of refusing to face her problem. Unlike James, she will not admit either to herself or to her family that she cannot exist in the real world and hence she is torturing her husband and her sons. James can look objectively at his background and see it as a major influence upon his present personality; but Mary, while she can realize that the "past is the present" and "the future too," cannot act on that understanding.

As I've already said, Edmund is much like his mother—and this probably accounts for the fact that he understands her more fully than anyone else. He is the typical O'Neill protagonist who, he himself realizes, "never feels at home, who does not really want and is not really wanted, who can never belong, who must always be a little in love with death." Unlike his mother and like his father, Edmund does try to face up to his inadequacies and attempts to understand why he does not belong. Mary totally rejects life because she cannot understand it and does not want to try; Edmund accepts life, understanding that he can never really be a part of it. In his long soliloquy midway through Act IV, after he describes the ecstasy of life at sea, he tells how, after that moment, "the hand lets the veil fall and you are alone, lost in the fog again, and you stumble on toward nowhere, for no good reason." But Edmund too is both the victim and the originator of his troubles. His sensitive nature makes him unable to deal with most of the world around him, just as so many O'Neill characters from the Mayo brothers in *Beyond the Horizon* and Yank in *The Hairy Ape* down to the denizens of Harry Hope's bar in *The Iceman Cometh* cannot belong in the real world with which they are faced. But he is also a victim of that world which is so insensitive to him and to his special needs. He is a poet in a world which rejects its poets. And his understanding of this fact is revealed in Act IV, just as Jamie's and James' awareness are disclosed during this final explosive section of the play.

In fact, this last act serves to complicate our responses to these characters enormously in that their capacity to understand and articulate their own weaknesses makes them fit objects of our respect as well as our pity. Up to this point, we are quite ready to accept James as a miser who has repressed his family disastrously, Jamie as a wastrel who has been the major disappointment of his father's life, and Edmund as a foolish dreamer; for these are the pictures we get of them from the three other characters. But when, in Act IV, we hear their side of the story, we can no longer be content simply to dismiss them this easily. What we end up with is the sense of divided responsibility which I defined at the beginning of this essay. It is expressed overtly in *Long Day's Journey* through two brief passages. The first, appropriately enough spoken by Mary, expresses the forces over which she and her family have no control: "None of us can help the things life has done to us. They're done before you realize it, and once they're done they make you do other things until at last everything comes between you and what you'd like to be, and you've lost your true self forever." The second occurs when Edmund remarks to his father that life is "so damned crazy" and James corrects him: "There's nothing wrong with life. It's we who—*He quotes.* 'The fault, dear Brutus, is not in our stars, but in ourselves that we are underlings.'"

The consequence of this divided responsibility is that, as in any tragic play of the modern era, it is impossible to assign blame. Both controllable and uncontrollable forces operate on the lives of the Tyrones, with the added complication that the very family situation they live in is both a contributor to and a result of the tragic situation. Not only could each of these characters by himself be the subject of a tragic drama—as he could—but also a major share of the tragic element is attributable to their interrelationships. Unlike the Greeks who tended to center their tragedies on one flawed protagonist, O'Neill in *Long Day's Journey* (and, to a certain extent, other modern playwrights like Chekhov, Ibsen, and Williams), seem to see groups of individuals—most often families—caught in webs partially of their own devising but woven by outside forces as well.

The degree of struggle possible within these webs varies from play to play. In *Long Day's Journey* there seems to be very little. In the terms of the passages from *Antigone* quoted as the epigraph to this essay, there is definitely a "tranquility" here, a "fellow-feeling" among the four Tyrones, who are, in numerous ways, one character. They are certainly all subject to many of the same tensions and ambivalences. There is, as I've stressed, no easily assigned guilt or innocence; we certainly can find no villain or hero in this play. While there may be some hope for Edmund, it is primarily medically-based or founded quite irrelevantly on the assumption that he is Eugene O'Neill who, after all, did become a successful playwright. Far more germane is the obvious fact that Edmund will never "belong" in the real world any more than his mother will; he will always be "the stranger" that he realizes he is now. Without hope, as Anouilh notes, a tragic play like *Long Day's Journey* is "restful." The characters are "trapped," as the single set for the play and the fog continually rolling in explicitly indicate. There is a good deal of shouting in the play, but most of it is the ultimately ineffectual beating at the bars of four caged animals who have no other means of voicing their frustrations.

Just as in a later American play with which it shares many common elements, *Who's Afraid of Virginia Woolf?* nothing really happens in *Long Day's Journey.* There is very little action, in the conventional dramatic sense of the term; and none of the characters change at all. The reason for this is simple: nothing can happen to four figures in this situation. All we can do is contemplate them in their web and endeavor to understand them with the assistance of the skill of the playwright who unfolds their lives to us. Because no American playwright has depicted more complex and complete characters with more compassion and sheer dramatic power than Eugene O'Neill in *Long Day's Journey,* it deserves a place among the great plays written in any age in any language. It is a further measure of its magnitude that it is also one of the few American plays which meet most of the measures of modern tragedy. That it does so within the framework of a generally conventional realistic four-character domestic drama, rather than through a consciously super-imposed classical mold, merely makes O'Neill's achievement that much more remarkable.

ROGER ASSELINEAU
"Eugene O'Neill's Transcendental Phase"
The Transcendental Constant in American Literature
1980, pp. 115–23

Though to all appearances O'Neill was primarily a playwright and an experimenter with dramatic forms who never considered himself a thinker, he was in fact desperately trying to express "something" in all his plays. He chose drama as a medium, but, for all his interest in technique, he never considered it an end in itself, but rather a means to live by proxy a certain number of problems which obsessed him. In *Lazarus Laughed*, he speaks of men as "those haunted heroes." Actually this is less a definition of mankind than a description of himself. He composed plays because he had to write in order to liberate himself and exorcise ghosts. It was a compulsion. The result was plays because of his environment, because his father was an actor and he was an "enfant de la balle," but it might have been novels just as well, and he would probably have written better novels than plays, for he was constantly hampered by the limitations of the stage. In his case literary creation was not a gratuitous activity, but an intense imaginative experience, an *Erlebnis*. He lived it. It was a passionate answer to the problems which tormented him with excruciating strength. This is no mere figure of speech. He roamed the world for years in search of a solution, trying to find a remedy for his fundamental despair, giving up the comfort and security of family life and nearly losing his health and life in the process.

After his wandering years, his *Wanderjahre*, when his health broke down and he was obliged to bring his restless comings-and-goings to a close, he went on exploring the world in imagination, not as a dilettante or a tourist in the realms of thought, but as a passionate pilgrim in quest of a shrine at which to worship. Though brought up a Roman Catholic, he lost his faith as an adolescent. Yet his nature abhorred this spiritual vacuum and he ardently looked for a substitute ever after. His religious faith was killed by rationalism and scientific materialism, but the restlessness and violence of his quest for a personal religion sprang from no coldly rational intellect.

Each of his plays is thus not only an experiment in craftsmanship, but also an attempt to find God or at least some justification for the flagrant inconsistencies of the human condition. His interest was less in psychology than in metaphysics. He said so himself in a letter to Joseph Wood Krutch: "Most modern plays are concerned with the relation between man and man, but that does not interest me at all. I am interested only in the relation between man and God."[1]

In spite of its apparent dramatic directness, therefore, *Desire under the Elms* is essentially, like his other plays, a philosophical tragedy about man and God rather than a naturalistic chunk of life depicting the mores of a bunch of clumsy New England rustics.

Reduced to essentials in this very primitive setting, man appears primarily as an animal. The first specimens whom we have a chance to observe when the curtain rises, Eben and especially Simeon and Peter, look like oxen, eat, work, and behave like a team of oxen, and feel tied up to the other animals of the farm by bonds of brotherhood: ". . . the cows knows us. . . . An' the hosses, an' pigs, an' chickens. . . . They knows us like brothers—and likes us" (Part I, scene 4).[2] They obey their instincts blindly and think only of drinking, eating, and fornicating. Their lust is quite literally bestial, as shown by Eben's account of his visit to Min: "I begun t'beller like a calf an' cuss at the same time . . . an' she got scared, an' I just grabbed holt an' tuk her" (Part I, scene 3).[3] When Abbie courts Eben, the scene is not much different. She kisses him greedily and at first he submits dumbly, but soon, after returning her kisses, he hurls her away from him and, O'Neill tells us, "they stand speechless and breathless, panting like two animals" (Part II, scene 2).[4]

These inarticulate, animal-like creatures differ from their dumb brothers in only one respect (but it is hardly an improvement): they are possessed with the mania for owning things, whether gold or land. They all crave money or title deeds. In short, they bear a strong family likeness to Swift's

Yahoos. They have only one redeeming feature: an embryonic sense of beauty which makes them exclaim "purty" in a rather monotonous manner whenever they notice the beauty of their surroundings. The only exception is the sheriff, who at the very end of the play passes very matter-of-fact and anticlimactic comments on the salable value of the farm while Eben and Abbie admire the beauty of the sunrise.

Far from being a free agent, man is thus by and large the slave of his instincts, and O'Neill here revives the old Calvinistic dogma of predestination. As early as his very first play, *The Web*, of the transparent title, he attempted to show that man is caught in a web of circumstances, a web that is not of his own weaving. At the end of *The Web*, O'Neill tells us that Rose, the prostitute, "seems to be aware of something in the room which none of the others can see—perhaps the personification of the ironic life force that has crushed her."[5] In *Desire under the Elms*, Eben feels trapped in exactly the same way: "Each day," the stage directions inform us, "is a cage in which he finds himself trapped."[6] He is indeed trapped by circumstances—tied up to that bleak New England farm which he somehow considers part of his mother, and he is also psychologically trapped by an all-powerful mother complex which unknown to him determines his whole behavior toward his father as well as toward women in general. His temperament is wholly determined by his heredity: it is a combination of his mother's softness and lack of will, as his father again and again points out, and of his father's aggressiveness and obstinacy, as his two elder brothers repeatedly tell us: "he is a chip off the old block, the spitting image of his father. . . ."

As for Abbie, she is just as trapped as he is. When she enters the stage, we are warned that she has "the same unsettled, untamed, desperate quality which is so apparent in Eben."[7] And shortly afterward we learn that she "was a orphan early an' had t'wuk fur others in other folks' hums," and her first husband "turned out a drunken spreer" and got sick and died. She then felt free again only to discover that all she was free for was to work again "in other folks' hums, doin' other folks' wuk" till she had almost given up hope of ever doing her own work in her own home (Part I, scene 4).[8]

Ephraim Cabot himself, for all his will power and vigor, is caught in the same web as the others. His whole behavior is conditioned by his Puritan upbringing. He cannot think of anything but work, hard work on a barren New England farm. *Laborare est orare*, Carlyle claimed, "work is worship." Ephraim Cabot is a degenerate Puritan. Work has ceased to be a form of worship for him, yet he believes in its virtue and absolute value because he has been brought up that way. He once tried to escape his self-imposed serfdom. Like many other New Englanders, he went West and in the broad meadows of the central plains found black soil as rich as gold, without a stone. He had only to plough and sow and then sit and smoke his pipe and watch things grow. He could have become a rich man and led an easy and idle life, but he preferred to give it up and return to his New England farm and to hard work on a stony soil,[9] which proves the extraordinary strength of his Puritan compulsions. They practically deprived him of his freedom of choice.

So, at the start at least, the three major characters of *Desire under the Elms* are not free. They bear psychological or moral chains. Consequently, they cannot be held responsible for their actions, and Simeon with his pleasant shrewdness is perfectly aware of it. When Eben accuses his father of killing his "Maw," Simeon retorts: "No one never kills nobody. It's allus somethin' that's the murderer" (Part I, scene 2).[10] "Somethin'," that is to say one of those mysterious things which impel men to act this way or that, whether they like it or not, whether they are aware of it or not. This is a modified form of Puritan pessimism: all men are sinners in the clutches of Satan—or of God who is always "nagging his sheep to sin" (Part I, scene 4),[11] the better to punish them afterward, always ready to smite His undutiful sons with His worst curse.

How can a man save his soul under such circumstances? Though, theoretically, O'Neill's approach is strictly non-theological and he is not concerned with the problem of salvation, he is constantly obsessed with it all the same, and in this play, he gives it a Nietzschean answer: passion. Passion alone, he suggests, can enable man to transcend his animal nature. He repeatedly exalts the purity and transfiguring power of love. Eben's passion for Abbie, which at first is mere lust, soon becomes love—and there is a difference in kind between the two. The passage from lust to love is similar to the transmutation of lead into gold. Whereas lust, which is tied to the body, is finite and transient, love, which transcends the body, is infinite and eternal. Abbie kills her infant son to prove her love to Eben, and at the end of scene 3 of Part III proclaims that her love for Eben will never change, whatever he does to her. The play ends on an apotheosis of love. The two lovers stand "looking up raptly in attitudes strangely aloof and devout" at the "purty" rising sun, which contrasts with the pallid setting sun that lit up the opening of the play, at a time when everything took place on the plane of coarse material things and lust.

Man can thus be redeemed by a great passion and save his soul and attain grandeur. The farm under the elms, which looked so sordid when the curtain rose, witnesses a sublime *dénouement* and at the end almost becomes one of those places where the spirit bloweth.

The reason for this extraordinary change is that, in Hamlet's words:

There are more things in heaven and earth . . .
Than are dreamt of in all [our] philosophy,

as Cabot again feels, for all his hardness and insensitivity: "They's thin's pokin' about in the dark—in the corners" (Part II, scene 2).[12] "Even the music can't drive it out—somethin'. Ye kin feel it droppin' off the elums, climbin' up the roof, sneakin' down the chimney, pokin' in the corners. They's no peace in houses, they's no rest livin' with folks. Somethin's always livin' with ye" . . . (Part III, scene 2).[13]

What is that "somethin'" whose presence disturbs him? It is the "Desire" of the title—an irresistible life-force (somewhat similar to G. B. Shaw's), which flows through the elms and through old Cabot himself sometimes, as when it makes him leave his farm in spring and go in search of a new wife. But it is especially powerful in Eben and Abbie. It is that thing which makes Eben look like a wild animal in captivity when he enters the stage, and feel "inwardly unsubdued." It is quite impersonal, and Eben refers to it in the neuter: "I kin feel it growin' in me—growin' an' growin'—till it'll bust out" (Part I, scene 2).[14] It is the magnetic force which draws Eben to Abbie through walls and partitions (Part II, scene 2). It is Nature—and Abbie intones a hymn to her—or it—in her own inarticulate way when she presses Eben to yield to his passion: "Hain't the sun strong an' hot? Ye kin feel it burnin' into the earth—Nature—makin' thin's grow—bigger 'n' bigger—burnin' inside ye—makin' ye want t'grow—into somethin' else—till ye are jined with it—an' it's your 'n—but it owns ye—too—an' makes ye grow bigger—like a tree—like them elums" (Part II, scene 1).[15]

In short, the "Desire" which flows through the elms and drips from them and pervades everything under them is God—though the word is never used. It is not, however, the God of the Christians, but rather a dynamic, impersonal, pantheistic, or panpsychistic deity present in all things, whether animate or inanimate, breaking barriers between individuals as in the case of Eben and Abbie, dissolving their lonesomeness and making them feel one. In a way it is a pagan God, a Dionysian deity, for it partly manifests itself in the form of carnal desire. Under its influence, Eben and Cabot become inspired poets (in prose) and sing woman, the lovely incarnation of the soft and warm goddess of fertility and life: "She's like t'night, she's soft 'n' warm, her eyes kin wink like a star, her mouth's wa'm, her arms 're wa'm, she smells like a wa'm plowed field, she's purty" (Part I, scene 2).[16] "Yew air my Rose o' Sharon! Behold! yew air fair; yer eyes air doves; yer lips air like scarlet; yer two breasts air like two fawns; yer navel be like a round goblet; yer belly be like a heap o' wheat,' exclaims old Cabot, echoing chapters 4 and 7 of the Song of Solomon.[17]

The omnipresent God is fundamentally a cosmic sexual urge, spontaneous, beautiful, unselfish, and amoral. In this perspective the notion of sin becomes meaningless. "He was the child of our sin," says Eben of the baby, but Abbie proudly answers "as if defying God" (the God of the Christians): "I don't repent that sin. I ain't askin' God t'fergive that" (Part III, scene 4).[18] The two lovers have gone back to the Garden of Eden from which Adam and Eve were expelled. They have become "Children of Adam," to take up Walt Whitman's phrase.

The life-force, the desire which circulates through the elms as well as through the *dramatis personae*, is the very reverse of the God worshipped by Ephraim Cabot, which has the hardness and immobility of a stone—and the sterility of one (Part II, scene 2). His God is the God of repression and lonesomeness and hard work—the God humorously called up by Robert Frost in "Of the Stones of the Place," and to some extent a duplicate of Robinson Jeffers's anti-human God.

Abbie, on the contrary, recommends yielding to the life impulse, letting Nature speak at every hazard "without check with original energy."[19] It is against nature, it is impious, she claims, to resist its will: "It's agin nature, Eben. Ye been fightin' yer nature ever since the day I come" . . . (Part II, scene 1).[20] With her, Emerson's Nature has acquired sex.

This is a combination of Nietzsche's Dionysian philosophy and Freudianism, and in *Desire under the Elms* it leads—in spite of the Dostoevskian quality of the *Crime and Punishment* situation at the end of the play—to an optimistic conclusion: the couple Eben-Abbie is not crushed by adverse circumstances. They have fulfilled themselves, they have fully lived and, far from being driven to despair by their trials, they are full of a strange "hopeless hope" when the curtain falls.

In this play we thus witness the dramatic clash of two opposite philosophies: Old Cabot's Puritanism and Abbie's worship of Dionysius—a conflict between the stones of the former and the elms of the latter, which O'Neill himself seems to have experienced throughout his life. He obviously sympathized with warm uninhibited characters like Eben and Abbie in *Desire under the Elms* and with Marie Brantome and Christine in *Mourning Becomes Electra*, though he never was warm and uninhibited himself. In everyday life, except when he was under the influence of alcohol, he was to some extent closer to Cabot than to Eben. Other things being equal, he suffered from the same dichotomy as Dr. Jekyll. Two men were at war within him. He was both Billy Brown and Dion Anthony. But the twain never fused. He was probably thinking of his own predicament when he made Dion, "life's lover," complain in *The Great God Brown* "with a suffering bewilderment": "Why am I afraid to dance, I who love music and rhythm and grace and song and laughter? Why am I afraid to live, I who love life and the beauty of flesh and the living colors of the earth and sky and sea? Why am I afraid of love, I who love love? . . . Why must I be so ashamed of my strength, so proud of my weakness"? (Prologue).[21] He would have liked freely to worship "the Great God Pan,"[22] as Dion calls him; instead of that he had to bear "the intolerable malice of life."[23] He would have liked to laugh with Lazarus and shout like Lazarus's followers:

> There is only life
> There is only laughter
> (Act II, scene 1),[24]

but his ingrained masochistic Catholicism made laughter die on his lips. *Desire under the Elms* is the secret expression of his poignant nostalgia for a joy of life he was unable to experience.

However, his personal failure and his acute awareness of the cruelty of the human condition did not prevent him from concluding that life is a vivid and exciting experience well worth the trouble to the very end. And that is why Abbie and Eben do not commit suicide in the last act, and even Lavinia refuses to kill herself in *Mourning Becomes Electra*, thus breaking one of the most imperative laws of tragedy. O'Neill's ultimate attitude to life during this nostalgic period (1923 to 1926) is best expressed by the hero of *The Great God Brown*: "I've loved, lusted, won and lost, sung and wept" (Act II, scene 2).[25] And anyway, as O'Neill proclaimed in *Lazarus Laughed* in a conformity with Nietzsche's teachings: "Men are . . . unimportant . . . Man remains . . . For Man death is not." The same life-force flows through all men, and whatever their personal limitations may be, whether they are bums, drunken sailors, or New England farmers, it endows them all with tragic grandeur. All individuals are potentially as worthy of interest as the mighty kings and queens of Greek tragedies. *Desire under the Elms* is thus the quiet affirmation of the fundamental dignity of all men in a godless (?) universe—or at least in a universe deprived of the help and support of the personal God posited by Christianity.

Notes

1. Quoted by Joseph Wood Krutch in his introduction to the Modern Library Edition of O'Neill's *Nine Plays*, p. xvii.
2. Ibid., p. 152.
3. Ibid., p. 148.
4. Ibid., p. 174.
5. *Ten Lost Plays* (New York: Random House, 1964), p. 53.
6. *Nine Plays*, p. 137.
7. Ibid., p. 155.
8. Ibid., p. 160.
9. Ibid., p. 172.
10. Ibid., p. 141.
11. Ibid., p. 161.
12. Ibid., p. 174.
13. Ibid., p. 189.
14. Ibid., p. 144.
15. Ibid., p. 164.
16. Ibid., p. 145.
17. Ibid., p. 167.
18. Ibid., p. 203.
19. Walt Whitman, "Song of Myself," *Leaves of Grass*, sec. 1, ll. 1, 13.
20. *Nine Plays*, p. 164.
21. Ibid., p. 315.
22. Ibid., p. 318.
23. Ibid., p. 375.
24. Ibid., p. 418.
25. Ibid., p. 347.

JOHN ORLANDELLO
"Conclusion"
O'Neill on Film
1982, pp. 162–67

The translation of any work from one medium into another unavoidably seems to require that both artistically valid changes as well as damaging compromises be made. The fifty-year history of O'Neill's work on the screen suggests that changes made in structure or emphasis in the process of adaptation are often useful, but that compromises seldom, if ever, benefit the adaptation. Compromises, while sometimes necessary, more often tend to be merely expedient, or else are based on ephemeral considerations. Several of the O'Neill adaptations suffer from concessions to expediency, to formulas, or to public morals and from fear of the censor's shears. Often these varieties of compromise overlap in a single adaptation.

For example, *Summer Holiday* suffers from the expediency of using a screenplay that MGM had on hand from an earlier film version of O'Neill's play. The conventionalizing tendency of the earlier screenplay became magnified in the second screen version, and the central character became broadened into caricature. Another financial expediency was the casting, because of assumed box-office appeal, of Mickey Rooney, who was wrong for the role. Similarly, in *Strange Interlude* the casting of Norma Shearer and Clark Gable in the principal roles, ill-suited to them, was box office-minded. In neither case did the casting make the films commercially successful, and both were flawed artistically by having inappropriate stars. And *Strange Interlude* is the most damagingly flawed of the O'Neill adaptations by concessions to censorship. This play, which commingles passion and philosophy, is stripped of both, and the power of censorship is reflected in the cutting of all words ot do with passion as well as all references to God. All of the other adaptations of O'Neill managed to escape such bowdlerization, if not a certain toning down or prettifying of characters and actions in conventional ways, as in the 1930 version of *Anna Christie*, and both film versions of *Ah, Wilderness!*

Hollywood has consistently exhibited a bent for the formulaic, and one of the most enduring formulas is that of the "love story." Several of the O'Neill adaptations have had their dramatic and thematic proportions altered by an insistence on romance whether or not it is relevant to—or even used consistently throughout—the film. This tendency is clearly evidenced all the way from the 1930s to the 1950s, from *Anna Christie* to *Desire under the Elms*. The two versions of *Ah, Wilderness!* turn O'Neill's bittersweet comedy of family life into what is essentially a teenage love story, and the play must be restructured to accommodate the romance. In *Strange Interlude* a patently unromantic marriage based on self-sacrifice becomes a typically romantic affair. In *Desire under the Elms* a generally sordid and latently incestuous relationship is gratuitously and inconsistently treated in a visually conventional romantic way. The film version of *The Emperor Jones* introduces two female characters to allow romantic affairs and rivalries extraneous to the theme and the major actions of the work. And in the sound version of *Anna Christie* one inconsistent scene is added to enhance the romantic formula.

The preparation and, to a great extent, evaluation of stage to screen adaptation had been persistently influenced by another formula—the convention of opening up, or breaking out of the confines of limited stage or studio space. Compromises in this direction have lessened the effectiveness of several of the O'Neill adaptations, simply because they have been merely formulaic and not part of a larger reworking of the play for film. Quite frequently such alterations are connected to the reapportioning of the romantic elements in the transition from stage to screen. For example, the exterior scenes in *Desire under the Elms* and *Strange Interlude* are part of the inconsistent romantic qualities of the works. Both films have exterior scenes irrelevant to the themes and atmosphere of the whole film, and are presented in an unconvincing way. The tendency toward conventional opening up is seen also in *Mourning Becomes Electra*, which has generally opted to follow the theatrical and thematic form of the original. In all of these cases, if for somewhat different reasons, the exterior scenes merely underline the hybrid film/theater nature of the cinematic versions.

Other, more effective films, such as *The Long Voyage Home*, *Long Day's Journey into Night* and *The Iceman Cometh*, substantially avoid the merely formulaic, employing the device of opening up only as it is relevant to both the thematic core of the original work and its recreation on film. Ford's *The Long Voyage Home*, the most fully realized in atmosphere of the O'Neill adaptations, uses exterior scenes beautifully and consistently throughout, but only as part of a unified reworking of the original for film. The exterior sequences, apart from their technical competence and convincing realism, spring naturally from the work as the mere formulaically included scenes in other of the O'Neill adaptations do not. A masterful director such as Ford can also accept the essentially confined physical space of the original and use this to cinematic advantage. It is important to note in this regard that technical developments in the late 1930s made it possible to shoot confined physical space with greater visual interest, because of the increased depth of field possible and increased camera mobility. Ford and his technically innovative cameraman, Gregg Toland, use these possibilities to make the interior sequences as dynamic as the outdoor scenes. This point is relevant also to *Long Day's Journey* and *Iceman*, both of which essentially retain the confined physical space of the original, but rework compositional space into viable cinematic form. Neither film makes formulaic concessions to opening up, which would be thematically counterproductive, but neither film can be called simply a filmed stage play because of the significant and significating intervention of the camera between the work and the audience's experience of it. Ford, Lumet, and Frankenheimer have made cinematic form follow thematic function, and all three were both skillful and highly sympathetic to the O'Neill work in their direction of these adaptations.

John Ford was decidedly the best director to bring O'Neill to the screen. Very often the adapted works of O'Neill were entrusted to far less capable directors, notably Robert Z. Leonard, whose direction of *Strange Interlude* lacks force and significance; Dudley Murphy, who takes little advantage of the expressionist visual potential of *The Emperor Jones*; Delbert Mann, whose work on *Desire under the Elms* is often clumsy and inappropriate; and Dudley Nichols, who, while highly capable as a screenwriter and sympathetic to O'Neill's work, lacked imagination in his direction of *Mourning Becomes Electra*.

Other, more accomplished directors brought O'Neill to the screen with varying degrees of effectiveness, depending to a great extent on the stylistic suitability of the director to the adapted work. The style of the remarkable producer-director-editor Thomas Ince was well suited to the silent version of *Anna Christie*. Clarence Brown, the conventionally skillful

MGM director of many star vehicles for Greta Garbo and Joan Crawford in the 1930s, was not stylistically suited to the tone and atmosphere of *Anna Christie*. Brown's style, inclined to rather lush and romantic visual effects, seems much more appropriate to the nostalgic *Ah, Wilderness!* Rouben Mamoulian, an often extraordinary and innovative director, directs the musical numbers in *Summer Holiday* with far more skill than the dramatic scenes, and the work becomes uneven. And Sidney Lumet and John Frankenheimer, the highly capable recent directors of O'Neill on film, have done some of their finest screen work in adapting *Long Day's Journey* and *The Iceman Cometh* to the screen.

While directorial sureness is of foremost importance, much of the ultimate effect of a film necessarily relies on its performances. The indomitable and magnifying eye of the camera demands physical aptness as well as craft on the part of the performer. The intensified visual dynamics of film also demand uniformity of acting styles. The O'Neill adaptations have been variously enhanced by superb performances and diminished by ones that are either inadequate or inappropriate. The individual performances of, say, Greta Garbo or Paul Robeson have substantially contributed to the effectiveness of the O'Neill films in which they star. On the other hand, the inappropriateness of Mickey Rooney in *Summer Holiday* or Burl Ives in *Desire under the Elms* or Norma Shearer in *Strange Interlude* has had deleterious effects on both O'Neill's characterizations and the film adaptations. Perhaps even more crucial on film is the compatibility of the acting styles of an entire cast of a work. The film versions of *The Emperor Jones*, *Mourning Becomes Electra*, and, most noticeably, *Desire under the Elms* are flawed by the incongruous acting styles of the players. Both of the O'Neill adaptations directed by Clarence Brown are notable in their ensemble playing; a single dominant mood emerges from the acting in *Ah, Wilderness!*, and, to a lesser extent, in the sound version of *Anna Christie*, owing to the screen power of Garbo. *The Long Voyage Home* is greatly enhanced by the fine assortment of character actors whose performances are skillfully fused. The most remarkable ensemble playing, however, occurs in the last two O'Neill works brought to the screen—*Long Day's Journey* and *Iceman Cometh*. The meaning and emotional effect of both works stem from an intense interaction among the characters, and the individual performances and exceptional ensemble playing account for much of the artistic success of both adaptations. It should be noted in this connection that both Lumet and Frankenheimer had far greater autonomy in casting than did the directors working under the corporate structure of the studio system in the adaptations of O'Neill in the decades prior to the 1960s.

In all of O'Neill's major work the characters of the plays are profoundly affected by the atmosphere and environment in which they exist. The film medium has distinct advantages in the creation of atmosphere and expressive settings, and the most effective of the O'Neill works on the screen recreate O'Neill's dramatic milieu in striking cinematic form. This is often the result of the sympathetic and long-term alliance of director and cinematographer, as with John Ford and Gregg Toland in *The Long Voyage Home*. The collaboration resulted in the most compelling film translation of O'Neill's mystique of the sea. The sympathetic alliance of Clarence Brown and William Daniels, successful in many films of the late 1920s and 1930s, accounts for much of the vivid recreation of atmosphere in *Ah, Wilderness!* The combination of Sidney Lumet and his frequent cinematographer, Boris Kaufman, resulted in a superb film realization of the claustrophobic ambience essential to O'Neill's *Long Day's Journey into Night*. And most recently, the stifling atmosphere of O'Neill's lower depths was vividly given filmic form in the collaboration of John Frankenheimer and cinematographer Ralph Woolsey.

As suggested in the introduction to this study, a primary function of adapting a stage work to the screen is to revivify or recreate the essential atmosphere, mood, characters, and themes of the original work within the aesthetic dynamics of film. While all of the O'Neill films treat the original with some fidelity, some are faithful in outline rather than in essence, such as *Strange Interlude* or *Desire under the Elms*. Several others, while having striking moments and some superb performances, are flawed as film recreations of the original play because of the accentuation of elements only tenuously connected to essential considerations of characters and themes of the original, as discussed from various angles in the specific analyses of *Anna Christie* (1930), *The Emperor Jones, Ah, Wilderness!*, and *Summer Holiday*. While admirably retaining the essentials of theme, character, and mood, *Mourning Becomes Electra* would also be less than fully realized according to this idea of adaptation because it does not sufficiently recreate and revivify these elements into cinematic form. A variety of other considerations, of course, having to do with production and direction values, acting, screenplay, and cinematography also play important roles in any evaluation of these adaptations, as discussed above.

The most effective adaptations of O'Neill yet on film are, discernibly, Ford's *The Long Voyage Home* and Lumet's *Long Day's Journey into Night*. While the two films work in very different ways, both recreate and restore the essential core of the adapted works in striking cinematic form. Ford's *The Long Voyage Home*, in a wealth of atmospheric details, superb ensemble performance, and exceptional cinematography, captures in a kind of cinematic poetry all of the richness and diversity of O'Neill's imagery associated with the sea. Similarly, the fusing of superb visual details, ensemble playing, and cinematography in Lumet's *Long Day's Journey into Night* finds a visual language in shots and rhythms which revivifies O'Neill's language on the screen, and focuses the emotional core of the work. It is indeed remarkable that such disparate original works and stylistically different films should result in the most artistically successful screen translations of O'Neill's work.

Contrasts abound. The original short plays which make up *The Long Voyage Home* are slight compared to the *Long Day's Journey*—O'Neill's masterpiece. Ford's film relies to a great extent on the atmosphere of nature and natural forces—Lumet's film is almost totally confined within the walls of a house. Ford's film takes verbal and structural liberties with the original—Lumet's film follows the original script religiously. Contrasts could be extended into the realm of characterization, thematic differences, length of the works, verbal dynamics, and so forth, but the essential point is that superior adaptations can be made from widely ranging dramatic sources. What the two films do share is a probing and revitalizing treatment of the original material, which is actualized by skillful directorial control, uniformly excellent and suitable performers, and a visual style which finds precisely appropriate means of translating the dramatic, thematic, and emotional core of a stage work into masterful cinematic form.

Ideally, the process of stage-to-screen adaptation should be reciprocal—the film translation should not only shine with a light of its own, but should also help to illuminate the original work. Ford's *The Long Voyage Home* and Lumet's *Long Day's Journey into Night* certainly enhance our understanding of these works of O'Neill. Much the same can be said of Frankenheimer's trenchant version of *The Iceman Cometh*, and Nichol's intelligently compressed *Mourning Becomes Electra*. But the merger of O'Neill and Hollywood may perhaps be longest remembered for Lumet's *Long Day's Journey* and its illumination of the painful past that so influenced the career of Eugene O'Neill.

GEORGE OPPEN

1908–1984

George Oppen was born in New Rochelle, New York, on April 24, 1908. He is perhaps best known for his association in the early 1930s with the "Objectivist" poets, who included William Carlos Williams, Louis Zukofsky, Carl Rakosi, and Charles Reznikoff, although his poetry received some wide recognition in 1969 when he was awarded the Pulitzer Prize for the volume *Of Being Numerous*. Oppen's career is unusual in that he gave up writing poetry to devote himself to politics for over a quarter of a century: his first book, *A Discrete Series*, was published in 1934, his second, *The Materials*, in 1962.

Oppen and his wife Mary moved to France in 1929 and there established To Publishers press, which put out An *"Objectivists" Anthology*, edited by Louis Zukofsky, in 1932. Upon their return to New York in 1933, the Oppens founded the short-lived Objectivist Press, which published Oppen's first book of poetry. During the twenty-eight years between books, Oppen devoted himself to leftist politics, agitating for workers' rights. In 1950–59 the Oppens lived in Mexico, where Oppen operated a furniture factory and worked as a tool-and-die maker.

Soon after his return to the United States Oppen began writing poetry again. His work, later as earlier, is characterized by its spare, concise style. In the next decades he published *This in Which* (1965); *Alpine: Poems* (1969); *Seascape: Needle's Eye* (1972). His *Collected Poems* were first published in England (1973), and then two years later in the United States. His final volume was *Primitive* (1978); in 1980 he was given the American Academy and Institute of Arts and Letters Award. He died in California on July 7, 1984.

Personal

George Oppen is a man who came difficultly by knowledge—which makes his Jewishness a very different thing from that of ⟨Louis⟩ Zukofsky. I recognised the latter's as soon as we had entered his apartment. It had the same flavour that had given point and aliment to my adolescence, when the refugees from Hitler's Germany arrived in the English midlands. Here were people who had records of Bruckner and Brecht's Dreigroschenoper at a time when both were unknown to us. Among them I had heard Kant's categorical imperative explained as if it were a fact of daily life, had listened to a description of Thomas Mann glimpsed paring an apple 'with surgical intentness', had discovered that Heine, Kafka, Rilke could still exist among the coal dust and the fumes from pottery chimneys. In this Jewishness one experienced a familial sense at once secretive and hospitable, subtly tenser than one's own involvement in the painful day to day of family bathos, where lack of money and lack of imagination had produced a stale stoicism. That experience of an eagerly tense intellectuality returned as one met the Zukofskys. Not so, with the Oppens.

To gain their apartment in Henry Street, one passed the ground floor window where a pleasant-looking young man sat writing, as George later told me, pornographic fiction. The scarred hallway and stair led up to the top of the house and at the stairhead stood a man with a lined and weathered face like a Jewish sea-captain—a man who, as it transpired, owned a sailing boat but no car. This was George Oppen. Like Zukofsky he saw the humorous side of things, but he listened more. His speech was less fluent, more meditative; it was exact with a pondered exactness like his poetry.

We talked much of Mexico that evening—for we had been there earlier the same year—and of the Oppens' phase of exile in Mexico City and his joinery shop there. In his talk one warmed to a union of the passionate and the deliberate: there was accuracy and there was economy in this, and somehow, in one story he told us, he had managed to carry these to a point where they seemed like miracle or luck. Tired of the way Mexican drivers aimed their cars at you, George, crossing the Zocalo, had once refused to submit to this humiliation and, as the projectile approached, planted his fist square in the windshield: it was not the fist but the windshild that shattered. 'A stupid thing to do,' said George. The owner of the car got out, apparently for the show-down, but looking first at Oppen and then at the shivered glass, could find no way in which *machismo* could account for, admit or take action against such folly, shrugged, re-ascended and drove off. George has a genius for such inevitabilities. They need not always be the fruit of happy violence. In England, nine months after our meeting, the Oppens were at Ozleworth on an afternoon when the vicar called. Conversation turned on the New English Bible and I expended a good deal of wasted wrath on our pastor's admiration for this moribund document. He explained that in order to make sure that its idiom was truly current the committee had consulted a bishop's secretary. George was far more of a marksman than I with my incoherent rage. As the vicar was about to leave, George said with a sort of courteous finality, 'The next time you translate the Bible, call in a carpenter—and make sure he's a Jewish carpenter.' Later, walking down the nave of Wells Cathedral, he gave vent to another unexpected apophthegm: 'I guess I'm a Christian,' he said, 'but with all the heresies.'

The apartment in Henry Street was very much a presence in our conversation on that first encounter. As we sat eating, the evening moved into possession of the scene outside. High above Brooklyn, we watched the sun go down to the right of the Statue of Liberty, swiftly like a coin into a slot. Light shone from the Statue's torch and from the windows of Manhattan—these of a strange greenish hue as if an effect taken up from the water in the summer dusk. Across the bay the Staten Island ferry switched back and forth, a trail of lights above the milky turquoise it was travelling over. The television antennae on the near roofs of Brooklyn looked like ships' masts drawn up before the harbour below. This was a room and a view we were to revisit several times before the Oppens left for San Francisco in 1969 when Henry Street was threatened with demolition. The place seems a cell in a larger aggregate from which memory picks out the building in a street close by where Whitman printed *Leaves of Grass*, now a Puerto Rican restaurant; the commemorative plaque on its wall (stolen, sold and then recovered); what *The Materials* calls 'The absurd stone trimming of the building tops'; the site of the old Brooklyn Ferry and behind its dilapidated stakes the line of Brooklyn Bridge—Whitman superimposed on Hart Crane.—CHARLES TOMLINSON, "Objectivists: Zukofsky and Oppen, a Memoir," *Pai*, Winter 1978, pp. 439–40

General

George Oppen is a deceptively simple poet. To read his work, in some sense, is to be forced to learn it. Throughout his writing life he has devoted himself to the investigation of a few central questions, and all his work is of a piece—interconnected, issuing from a single source, each poem strengthened by the presence of the others. The language is almost naked, and the syntax seems to derive its logic as much from the silences around words as from the words themselves. There is little ease in Oppen, little to reassure us in his surfaces. Constantly struggling against the lure of facility, he will never use a word that has not first been won and absorbed through experience. For style in his work is as much a question of moral concern as anything that might be said within the poem.

Oppen's work begins at a point beyond the certainty of absolutes, beyond any pre-arranged or inherited system of values, and attempts to move toward some common ground of belief on which all men can stand. The locus is always the natural world, and the process is one that originates in the perception of objects, in the primal act of seeing:

> Impossible to doubt the world: it can be seen
> And because it is irrevocable
>
> It cannot be understood and I believe that fact is
>   lethal
>
>   (*Collected Poems*, p. 83)

Oppen is a man who is able to *look*, whole-heartedly and without distraction. As Carl Rakosi has written, Oppen "has a great eye, precise and irreducible. If you've never seen what it sees, it's because you haven't sat still long enough and looked as hard· as he has":

> There is no beauty in New England like the boats.
> Each itself, even the paint white
> Dipping to each wave each time
> At anchor, mast
> And rigging tightly part of it
> Fresh from the dry tools
> And the dry New England hands.
>
>   (*CP*, p. 40)

This notion of "each itself"—which is to say: "the thing in itself"—is central to Oppen's work. Again and again he poses awe of the physical world, a wonder in the sheer this-ness of things, against the confusion and brutality of the social world, as if seeking the basis for a new kind of language, a test, as he has said, of the word "humanity," in the simple fact of presence:

> . . . Nothing more
> But the sense
> Of where we are
> Who are most northerly. The marvel of the wave
> Even here is its noise seething
> In the world; I thought that even if there were
>   nothing
> The possibility of being would exist;
> I thought I had encountered
> Permanence; thought leaped on us in that sea
> For in that sea we breathe the open
> Miracle
> Of place, and speak
> If we would rescue
> Love to the ice-lit
> Upper World a substantial language
> Of clarity, and of respect.
>   (CP, p. 140)

As his work has developed over the years, Oppen's quest for this "substantial language/Of clarity, and of respect" has led him away from his early preoccupation with things and individual perceptions to larger questions of society and the possibility of community:

> Obsessed, bewildered
> By the shipwreck
> Of the singular
> We have chosen the meaning
> Of being numerous.
>   (CP, p. 151)

Oppen offers no solutions to the problems he raises, and his confrontation of the public and historical world seems to spring more from a feeling of isolation and loss than from a naive hope in the future: ". . . because we find the others/ Deserted like ourselves and therefore brothers" (CP, p. 33). There is a deep sense of solidarity in this statement, but it offers very little on which to base a society. Oppen, however, can assert not more than this without abandoning his convictions, and his refusal to overstep the limit of his own beliefs is both ruthless and salutary. If his work holds no ultimate promise of redemption, there is nevertheless a redemptive quality in this work precisely because it does not offer false hopes. What emerges from Oppen's poetry is above all the decency of the man himself—a human voice speaking outward from the deepest chasm of solitude. Oppen is a public poet, but in such a way that this term takes on a new definition, for his concern is less with event than with feeling, with concern itself and the obligation to see "That which one cannot/Not see" (CP, p. 176). His aim has never been to make pronouncements about the world, but, quite simply, to discover it. The sentence that occurs in one of his poems—"We want to be here" (CP, p. 143)—is to be read, therefore, not as a desire to be in a particular place, but as a fundamental article of faith. It is an acceding to that which cannot be known, and for Oppen it carries all the power and mystery of a theological premise.
—PAUL AUSTER, "A Few Words in Praise of George Oppen," *Pai*, Spring 1981, pp. 49–51

At long last, in his 68th year, George Oppen's work can be had in one volume ⟨*Collected Poems*⟩ instead of five-plus: 24 pages of new poems, annexed to a handsome resetting of the earlier books. Those were thin books, and participation in the bulk of a single volume now changes the import of every poem. The first sequence dates from 1934. All those years, academe (alas) is about to discover, an Oeuvre has been growing.

Alas, but why not? Academe is what takes care of Poetry for us, and we may as well not begrudge it something substantial, to vary its diet of flies. "The question is," Oppen wrote some 15 years back,

> How does one hold something
> In the mind which he intends
> To grasp and how does the salesman
> Hold a bauble he intends
> To sell? The question is
> When will there not be a hundred
> Poets who mistake that gesture
> For a style.

Salesmanship, that's what often passes for poetry. Berryman and Auden were past masters.

Oppen never insists, he takes note.

> . . . Crusoe
> We say was
> 'Rescued'.
> So we have chosen.

—have chosen, it grows clear, "the meaning of being numerous" rather than the politics of selfhood. He apprehends it as a precarious, perhaps revocable, choice, exhibiting itself in little more than our use of the word "rescued" when we talk of Crusoe.

That typifies Oppen's spare method, clean-cut silences framing the words. There was even a silence of over 25 years, given to political involvement ("the meaning of being numerous"), which he couldn't shirk but by which he refused to let poetry get contaminated. So he didn't make verbal gestures in New Masses, and his political friends weren't called on to respond to his being a poet because "I didn't tell them."

Still, the mind is one, and the man who spent money when he had it, 40-odd years ago, on publishing other poets (Williams, Pound, Zukofsky) is the same man who later kept going by manual craftsmanship (he has been among other things a tool and die maker, and a furniture designer in Mexico City), and the same who now fits a poem intricately together, testing each strut, each joint.

A chair is assembled, but you don't see that happen. You do see and hear a poem come into being—at one stage there's nothing there but the first word—and if what you behold isn't quite how it got written, part of its game is to behave as if that were so. In one important way a poem does resemble a chair. As the wood acquires its meaning from the craftsman (mahogany by itself is no more than a tree "characterized by monadelphous stamens"), so the poem, according to Oppen, isn't the sum of virtuous words but is what confers upon the words their virtue. (Who'd care about the word "nightingale" save for Keats?)

So the moments of tension occur when a new word offers its credentials.

> The steel worker on the girder
> Learned not to look down, and does his work
> And there are words we have learned
> Not to look at,
> Not to look for substance
> Below them. But we are on the verge
> Of vertigo

"There are words that mean nothing," this poem goes on to specify "But there is something to mean." That in turn gets specified:

> Not a declaration which is truth
> But a thing
> Which is.

Declarations consist of words, mere words. "A thing which is" attracts words by its obduracy, and if we aren't vigilant it will attract the wrong ones.

Nothing better characterizes Oppen than this wariness about the language itself, this distrust of inherent fluency. *The Materials* was the title of his second collection to imply unuttering things like rock and stem and iron:

> . . . streets boarded and vacant where no time will
> hatch
> Now chairs and walls,
> Floors, roofs, the joists and beams,
> The woodwork, window sills
> In sun in a great weight of brick.

It's dangerous to be fluent about slums and wreckage. In the title of his first collection Oppen concealed a similar mistrust. He called it *Discrete Series*, meaning not a series like 2, 4, 6, 8 . . . , which you can generate forever once you know the rule (just keep adding 2), but a series like 14, 23, 28, 33, 42, which Oppen once told a correspondent he wishes he'd had the wit to put on the flyleaf. It's "the names of the stations on the east side subway," and there's no way you can derive those numbers from one another. They derive from a reality prior to number, the street grid of Manhattan (inflected by geology and commerce and history), and each gives access to a whole life. In the same way the words in the ideal Oppen poem derive not from the neighboring words but from wordless obduracy.

Still, men need words (and need poets to monitor them).

> Fifty years
> Sidereal time
> Together, and among the others,
> The bequeathed pavements,
>   the inherited lit streets:
> Among them we were lucky
>   —strangest word.

Strange to the point of impiety, and yet accurate. And changed by this poem, "Blood From the Stone," the stone being planetary rock, which Oppen calls, with an exclamation point of amazement, "Mother/Nature!" Explanations of how we come to be here invoke evolutionary chance, one sense in which we are "lucky."

As Oppen's readers, for that matter, we're lucky too. So intent, so reluctant a poetry, it keeps hinting between the lines that it nearly didn't come into existence at all. Did life ever manage to come into being on Mars? Maybe we'll know next year, or never know. On Earth good poems seem to be quite as unlikely. Still some, like these, get written sometimes (and trees, Oppen reminds us, sometimes take root in pavements).—HUGH KENNER, *NYTBR*, Oct. 19, 1975, p. 5

WILLIAM CARLOS WILLIAMS
"The New Poetical Economy"

Poetry, July 1934, pp. 220–25

Mr. Oppen has given us thirty-seven pages of short poems (in *A Discrete Series*), well printed and well bound, around which several statements relative to modern verse forms may well be made.

The appearance of a book of poems, if it be a book of good poems, is an important event because of relationships the work it contains will have with thought and accomplishment in other contemporary reaches of the intelligence. This leads to a definition of the term "good." If the poems in the book constitute necessary corrections of or emendations to human conduct in their day, both as to thought and manner, then they

are good. But if these changes originated in the poems, causing thereby a direct liberation of the intelligence, then the book becomes of importance to the highest degree.

But this importance cannot be in what the poem says, since in that case the fact that it is a poem would be a redundancy. The importance lies in what the poem *is*. Its existence as a poem is of first importance, a technical matter, as with all facts, compelling the recognition of a mechanical structure. A poem which does not arouse respect for the technical requirements of its own mechanics may have anything you please painted all over it or on it in the way of meaning but it will for all that be as empty as a man made of wax or straw.

It is the acceptable fact of a poem as a mechanism that is the proof of its meaning and this is as technical a matter as in the case of any other machine. Without the poem being a workable mechanism in its own right, a mechanism which arises from, while at the same time it constitutes the meaning of, the poem as a whole, it will remain ineffective. And what it says regarding the use or worth of that particular piece of "propaganda" which it is detailing will never be convincing.

The preface seems to me irrelevant. Why mention something which the book is believed definitely not to resemble? "Discrete" in the sense used by Mr. Oppen, is, in all probability, meant merely to designate a series separate from other series. I feel that he is justified in so using the term. It has something of the implications about it of work in a laboratory when one is following what he believes to be a profitable lead along some one line of possible investigation.

This indicates what is probably the correct way to view the book as well as the best way to obtain pleasure from it. Very few people, not to say critics, see poetry in their day as a moment in the long-drawn periodic progress of an ever-changing activity toward occasional peaks of surpassing excellence. Yet these are the correct historic facts of the case. These high periods rest on the continuity of what has gone before. As a corollary, most critics fail to connect up the apparently dissociated work of the various men writing contemporaneously in a general scheme of understanding. Most commentators are, to be sure, incapable of doing so since they have no valid technical knowledge of the difficulties involved, what has to be destroyed since it is dead, and what saved and treasured. The dead, granted, was once alive but now it is dead and it stinks.

The term, technical excellence, has an unpoetic sound to most ears. But if an intelligence be deeply concerned with the bringing up of the body of poetry to a contemporary level equal with the excellences of other times, technique means everything. Surely an apprentice watching his master sees nothing prosaic about the details of technique. Nor would he find a narrow world because of the smallness of the aperture through which he views it, but through that pinhole, rather, a world enormous as his mind permits him to witness.

A friend sticks his head in at the door and says, "Why all the junk standing around?"

The one at work, startled perhaps, looks up puzzled and tries to comprehend the dullness of his friend.

Were there an accredited critic of any understanding about, he might be able to correlate the details of the situation, bringing a reasonable order into these affairs. But the only accredited critics are those who, seeking order, have proceeded to cut away all the material they do not understand in order to obtain it. Since man has two legs, then so also must the elephant. Cut off the ones that are redundant! Following this, logically, they describe a hollow tail and a tassel sticking out just above the mouth. This is my considered opinion of the position of the formerly alert critic, T. S. Eliot.

Then there are the people who do reviews for the newspapers. They haven't the vaguest notion why one word follows another, but deal directly with meanings themselves.

An imaginable new social order would require a skeleton of severe discipline for its realization and maintenance. Thus by a sharp restriction to essentials, the seriousness of a new order is bought to realization. Poetry might turn this condition to its own ends. Only by being an object sharply defined and without redundancy will its form project whatever meaning is required of it. It could well be, at the same time, first and last a poem facing as it must the dialectic necessities of its day. Oppen has carried this social necessity, so far as poetry may be concerned in it, over to an extreme.

Such an undertaking will be as well a criticism of the classics, a movement that seeks to be made up only of essentials and to discover what they are. The classics are for modern purposes just so much old coach.

And once again, for the glad, the young and the enthusiastic, let it be said that such a statement as the above has nothing to do with the abiding excellence of the classics but only with their availability as a means toward present ends. In the light of that objective, they are nostalgic obstacles.

Oppen has moved to present a clear outline for an understanding of what a new construction would require. His poems seek an irreducible minimum in the means for the achievement of their objective, no loose bolts or beams sticking out unattached at one end or put there to hold up a rococo cupid or a concrete saint, nor either to be a frame for a portrait of mother or a deceased wife.

The words are plain words; the metric is taken from speech; the colors, images, moods are not suburban, not peasant-restricted to serve as a pertinent example. A *Discrete Series*. This is the work of a "stinking" intellectual, if you please. That is, you should use the man as you would use any other mechanic—to serve a purpose for which training, his head, his general abilities fit him, to build with—that others may build after him.

Such service would be timely today since people are beginning to forget that poems are constructions. One no longer hears poems spoken of as good or bad; that is, whether or not they do or do not stand up and hold together. One is likely, rather, to hear of them now as "proletarian" or "fascist" or whatever it may be. The social school of criticism is getting to be almost as subversive to the intelligence as the religious school nearly succeeded in being in the recent past.

The mast
Inaudibly soars; bole-like, tapering
Sail flattens from it beneath the wind.
The limp water holds the boat's round sides. Sun
Slants dry light on the deck. Beneath us glide
Rocks, sand, and unrimmed holes.

Whether or not a poem of this sort, technically excellent, will be read over and over again, year after year, perhaps century after century, as, let us say, some of Dante's sonnets have been read over and over again by succeeding generations—seems to me to be beside the point. Or that such a test is the sole criterion of excellence in a poem—who shall say? I wish merely to affirm in my own right that unless a poem rests on the bedrock of a craftsmanlike economy of means, its value must remain of a secondary order, and that for this reason good work, such as that shown among Mr. Oppen's poems, should be praised.

MICHAEL ANDRÉ BERNSTEIN
"Reticence and Rhetoric:
The Poetry of George Oppen"
George Oppen: Man and Poet, ed. Burton Hatlen
1981, pp. 231–37

Mais Racine? . . . Lequel des deux prefereriez vous? ou qu'il eut été un bon homme . . . bon mari, bon pere, bon oncle, bon voisin, honnete commerçant, mais rien de plus; ou qu'il eut été fourbe, traitre, ambitieux, envieux, mechant; mais auteur d'*Andromaque*, de *Britannicus*, d'*Iphigenie*, de *Phèdre*, d'*Athalie*.[1]

So entirely has Diderot's preference become part of our pre-judgment about how to engage a work of art properly that it may almost stand as a kind of antonomasia for all the diverse arguments designed to secure the aesthetic as a category independent of other modes of cognition and other kinds of response. But in so unreflecting an acceptance of this division, salutary, perhaps even indispensable, though it undoubtedly is, we risk forgetting the whole complex network of historical forces within which the argument was initially articulated and the pressures that remain to contest it today. Still, to reopen the question, even in a discussion of George Oppen, is to risk both misunderstanding and a certain embarrassment. After all, no one can have much confidence in a criticism presumptuous enough to include, as one of its central exhibits, the reader's (inevitably distorted and partial) sense of an artist's "exemplary conduct" or "personal integrity." Even the more fashionable decision to limit the commentary to impulses and attitudes expressed purely within the work itself, categorically excluding any moralizing about the biography of its creator, does not provide a more secure foundation. Not only would this criticism still find itself subject to the same risks of arbitrariness, cultural blindness, etc., but (1) strictly speaking, it would have to be mute in the face of any art that does not articulate a recognizable ethics, and (2) it would have no means, short of a blanket condemnation or facile recuperation, to confront texts which deliberately assault our habitual assumptions about human notivation and desires (e.g., writers as diverse as Flaubert, Céline, Beckett, et. al., to say nothing of de Sade or William Burroughs).

And yet the impulse remains. Rightly so, as well, for our use of words like "sincerity" and "honesty" is not always a mere recitation of cant phrases best set aside when we talk seriously about art. Rather, these words define one kind of response, a reaction to something vital in an artist's work which it is simply fatuous to ignore.

Because the poetry of George Oppen raises all these issues with a quiet, unhectoring insistence unrivaled by any of his living peers except Basil Bunting, I can think of no honest way to avoid them here. And if I spoke earlier about a certain embarrassment, it is because I think the very language of modern criticism, for all its theoretical subtlety, has shown itself remarkably impoverished at registering the authority of a work compelling precisely because of its commitment to what one can only call the "common decencies" of a shared discourse and world. It is these very words, "sincerity," "honesty," and "clarity" that recur throughout Oppen's famous 1968 interview, always enunciated in consort with the strictest notion of the poem as an articulated, crafted ("objective," if you will) structure:

What I felt I was doing was beginning from imagism as a position of honesty. The first question at that time in poetry was simply the question of honesty, of sincerity. But I learned from Louis [Zukofsky], as against the romanticism or even the quaintness of the imagist position, the necessity for forming a poem properly, for achieving form. That's what "objectivist" really means.[2]

Or, in the words of one of his poems from the collection *Of Being Numerous* (1968):

Clarity, clarity, surely clarity is the most beautiful
    thing in the world,
A limited, limiting clarity
I have not and never did have any motive of poetry
But to achieve clarity.[3]

In a sense, the issue in both of these quotations is one of decorum in its full, classical sense: an obligation to find the particular words, tones, rhythms and shapes most suitable to the subject matter at hand. The best criticism of Oppen somehow must also show, in its own articulation, the imprint of such a decorum. Hence the exact justice of Hugh Kenner's comment about Oppen's many years of political exile and poetic silence: "Hugh Kenner interrupted my explanation to him of these years by saying, 'In brief, it took twenty-five years to write the next poem.' Which is the way to say it."[4]

Decorum may seem like an unusual term to apply to the work of a poet famous initially for having emerged as the printer of such iconoclastic volumes as Pound's *ABC of Reading* and An *"Objectivists" Anthology*, and as the author of the slim but technically adventurous collection, *Discrete Series* (1934). But neither this beginning, at the vanguard of experimental verse in the early 1930s, nor the subsequent decision to set aside his art for immediate political and social imperatives, qualifies the impression that Oppen has always written—and acted—out of a scrupulous respect for the tact his diverse tasks enjoined. Thus, although he was ready to make immense personal renunciations for his politics, he refused to write the kind of polemical, socialist poetry that filled American literary journals throughout the Depression. As he explained years later,

I didn't believe in political poetry or poetry as being politically efficacious. I don't even believe in the honesty of a man saying, "Well, I'm a poet and I will make my contribution to the cause by writing poems about it." . . . If you decide to do something politically, you do something that has political efficacy. And if you decide to write poetry, then you write poetry, not something that you hope, or can deceive yourself into believing, can save people who are suffering.[5]

In many ways this is an admirably lucid realization, but it is also more problematical than Oppen's admirers have been ready to acknowledge, and its ambiguity is centrally linked to the sustaining tensions at the core of the poetry itself. I doubt that Oppen means here exactly what W. H. Auden did in writing, "For poetry makes nothing happen" ("In Memory of W. B. Yeats"). Clearly our century alone has provided numerous examples of verse which are both politically committed and aesthetically satisfying (Pound, Brecht, Neruda, Mayakovsky, to name only some obvious examples). Instead, it seems to me that Oppen is, at least in part, speaking out of a recognition that his own individual skill as an artist depends upon establishing a poetic voice that renounces the conclusive, the unwavering certainties any immediately exhortative verse must be able to summon. In fact, much of Oppen's writing is balanced within a seemingly contradictory epistemology whose distinct impulses provide the poem with its characteristic

energy and tone. On the one hand, Oppen is committed to a view of consciousness as inherently inter-subjective, as bound up, from the outset, with the existence of the world and its other inhabitants. The very first poem in *Discrete Series* already announces a decision to see, as sharply as possible, the multiplicity "Of the world, weather-swept, with which/one shares the century" (*CP*, p. 3), and all of the subsequent volumes remain faithful to that first urging. The lures of preciosity or pure self-reflexivity which have, for the past fifty years, compromised a great deal of the best American poetry held no fascination for a writer convinced—and able to state with such calm assurance—that

The self is no mystery, the mystery is
That there is something for us to stand on.
We want to be here.
The act of being, the act of being
More than oneself.
                                    (*CP*, p. 143)

Because Oppen is certain that "it is the/real/That we confront" ("Route," *CP*, p. 196), rather than some solipsistic "dream," an abiding attentiveness to the physical details of the world, its natural and man-made variety, marks his verse at both the lexical and the thematic level. So well-known is Oppen's reputation as a complex, "experimental" poet that the verse's sheer sensual delight in light and water, in sexuality and landscape, is often overlooked. But his writing is a store-house of gatherings from different domains of experience, ranging in one typical piece from

And every crevice of the city leaking
Rubble: concrete, conduit, pipe, a crumbling
Rubble of our roots

to a vision of

Earth, water, the tremendous
Surface, the heart thundering
Absolute desire.
                                    (*CP*, p. 21)

On the other hand, balanced against this confidence there tugs an equally strong sense of the limitations in any one man's mind or language, limitations that severely restrict how much of that larger world he can honestly (again, the unavoidable word) grasp. Thus, the superficial paradox of the Marxist poet who has never written a party strophe, and thus, also, the more important paradox of the poet committed to the world beyond his own artistic compatriots announcing with wry dignity

One imagines himself
addressing his peers
I suppose. Surely
that might be the definition
of 'seriousness'? I would like,
as you see,
to convince
myself
that my pleasure in your response
is not
plain vanity
but the pleasure of being heard,
the pleasure
of companionship, which seems
more honorable.
                                    (*CP*, p. 142)

Indeed, many of Oppen's most touching poems enact their openness towards others not by moving such large counters as "class conflict" or "historical inevitability," but rather by commemorating the field of personal loves and friendships that have given shape to his emotional life. The splendid pieces to

Mary Oppen—splendid in their gentleness and humanity—seem to me to stand, along with Williams' poems to Flossie and Zukofsky's to Celia, as among the best love poetry American verse has given us in this century:

> To find now depth, not time, since we cannot, but
>   depth
>
> To come out safe,   to end well
> We have begun to say good bye
> To each other
> And cannot say it
>
> (CP, p. 220)

At the same time, however, I think that it is Oppen's resistance to the rhetoric of assertion, a rhetoric one aspect of his epistemology could easily have encouraged, that enabled him to fashion a new and quite different rhetoric, one which succeeded in making notions like "honesty," "sincerity," and "clarity" not only components of the work's intended effect, but also constituent thematic and stylistic elements of its very structure as an utterance. The "difficulty" of some of Oppen's verse (usually a question of punctuation and transitions rather than of complex imagery) is one attempt—not always his most convincing—to create this new rhetoric in which language both seeks to engage "Not the symbol but the scene this pavement leads/To . . ." ("Route," CP, p. 192) and yet stay aware of its status as only the articulation of one man writing from the particularities of his time and perception.[6]

In 1965, Frank O'Hara perceptively defined one of the principal dangers attendant upon any poetics which seeks to make out of its very fidelity to a modest, unassertive tone, a new claim to authority.

> But of course . . . you have another element which is making *control* practically the subject matter of the poem. That is your *control* of the language, your *control* of the experiences and your *control* of your thought. . . . the amazing thing is that where they've pared down the diction so that the experience presumably will come through as strongly as possible, it's the experience of their paring it down that comes through more strongly and not the experience that is the subject.[7]

Although both Robert Creeley and Denise Levertov, the two poets to whom O'Hara was referring in the interview, clearly have managed to rise above such limitations in their best work, there is all too much evidence that many of their less talented imitators have not. (The charge also seems to hold more for younger writers intent upon aping Creeley than for those who have taken Levertov's quite different poetics as a primary model.) Similarly, however, poems by some of George Oppen's disciples reveal a tendency towards the same kind of misdirection of attention that O'Hara criticized. But in their case, I think one can more readily indicate just how carelessly they

have read their master. For ultimately, the honesty about which I have been writing is not at all the result of the poet's "paring down" of his diction, nor of his substituting a virtuoso's "control" for the integrity of his subject. Oppen's strength has little to do with the creation of any simplistic "anti-poetical" strategy. Rather, it emerges out of a precarious intersection of urges and in the rigorous fidelity to an epistemology in which one is always both alone and numerous, confined within one's language and open to the world with which those words retain an indissoluble bond. Balanced between the many and the one, the intimate and the panoramic, a rhetoric and its reticences are simultaneously crafted giving Oppen's *Collected Poems* their particular and hard-won "sincerity." And perhaps only someone who has disciplined himself so strenuously within this double duty can, at the end, maintain the tentative, secular decorum of his poetic line and still sustain a tone of celebration:

> We stared at the end
> Into each other's eyes   Where
> She said hushed
>
> Were the adults   We dreamed to each other
> Miracle of the children
> The brilliant children   Miracle
> Of their brilliance   Miracle
> of
>
> (CP, p. 229)

Notes

1. Denis Diderot, *Le Neveu de Rameau*, ed. Jean Fabre (Genève: Librairie Droz, 1963), pp. 11–12. ("But what about Racine? Which of the two would you prefer? That he would have been a good man, a good husband, good father, good uncle, good neighbour, trustworthy businessman, but nothing more; or that he would have been a swindler, a traitor, a careerist, envious and evil, but the author of *Andromaque, Britannicus, Iphigénie, Phèdre,* and *Athalie?*") The peculiarities of spelling and accentuation in the French are those of Diderot himself as established in Fabre's brilliant edition of *Le Neveu*.
2. George Oppen Interview in *Contemporary Literature*, 10:2 (Spring, 1969), 159–177. The passage quoted is on p. 160.
3. George Oppen, *The Collected Poems of George Oppen* (New York: New Directions, 1975), p. 185. All references are to this edition and are acknowledged directly after the quotation in the text as *CP*.
4. Oppen Interview, op. cit., p. 174.
5. Oppen Interview, op. cit., p. 174.
6. For a more detailed discussion of the attack upon rhetoric as inherently "anti-poetical," and a defense of the rhetorical element in Pound, Williams, and Olson, see the author's *The Tale of the Tribe: Ezra Pound and the Modern Verse Epic*, Princeton: Princeton U. Press, 1980, esp. Chapter Ten, "The Old Measure Of Care."
7. Frank O'Hara's Interview with Edward Lucie-Smith, in Donald Allen (ed.), *Standing Still and Walking in New York*, Bolinas: Grey Fox Press, 1975, pp. 3–26. The passage quoted is from p. 23.

CYNTHIA OZICK

1928–

Cynthia Ozick, novelist, short-story writer, and essayist, was born in New York City on April 17, 1928. Her father, William Ozick, owned a drugstore in the Bronx. Ozick was educated at New York University (B.A., 1949) and at Ohio State University (M.A., 1950). While in school she read heavily, Henry James being a particular favorite. Ozick began to write after college, and spent seven years on a long philosophical novel she never finished, although two excerpts have appeared: "The Butterfly and the Traffic Light," which can be found in *The Pagan Rabbi and Other Stories* (1971), and "The Sense of Europe," published in *Prairie Schooner* in 1956. Between 1952 and 1953 Ozick worked as an advertising copywriter at Filene's Department Store in Boston. In 1952 she married Bernard Hallote; they have one daughter.

In the early 1950s Ozick began an intensive study of the literature, history, and philosophy of Judaism, and since then her writing has been centrally concerned with religious issues. Her first novel, written between the ages of twenty-nine and thirty-six, appeared in 1966 as *Trust*, and received generally favorable reviews. In this novel, as in many stories that followed, the essential conflict is between the pagan—the idolatrous worship of nature or art—and the sacred, that is, Judaism.

Although Ozick has written a second novel, *The Cannibal Galaxy* (1983), and published dozens of essays, she is best known for her three collections of fiction: *The Pagan Rabbi and Other Stories*; *Bloodshed and Three Novellas* (1976); and *Levitation: Five Fictions* (1982). A *Treasury of Yiddish Poetry* (1969) is a collection of her translations edited by Irving Howe and Eliezer Greenberg.

General

Some writers are so enthralled by ideas (one thinks of Doris Lessing) that their characters become debaters, and their fables approach allegory. Other writers are pretty but dumb; their prose may beautifully render the physical world but it is contentedly mindless, as though to entertain an idea were a gaffe in literary propriety, a descent into the essayistic. Miss Ozick falls between these two extremes. Ideas interest her, but only as they force decisions, determine actions, lead to self-deception and ruin or spawn strange feats.

In her celebrated (and very funny) novella "Puttermesser and Xanthippe," in *Levitation: Five Fictions*, a lawyer working for New York City, Ruth Puttermesser, becomes obsessed with a vision of a better community. This idea eventually leads her, almost unconsciously, to create a golem, a big and steadily-getting-bigger demon-servant named Xanthippe, who reforms New York—and then destroys it with her rampant sexual appetites. But this horrible outcome derives from Puttermesser's initial utopian idea:

"Every day, inside the wide bleak corridors of the Municipal Building, Puttermesser dreamed an ideal Civil Service: devotion to polity, the citizen's sweet love of the citizenry, the light rule of reason and common sense, the City as a miniature country crowded with patriots—not fools and jingoists, but patriots true and serene; humorous affection for the idiosyncrasies of one's distinctive little homeland, each borough itself another little homeland, joy in the Bronx, elation in Queens, O happy Richmond! Children on roller skates, and over the Brooklyn Bridge the long patchwork-colored line of joggers, breathing hard above the homeland-hugging green waters."

This passage reveals the Gogolian side of Miss Ozick's style: her robust zest for details that never sink a sentence but rather spurt out of it, her vivid rendering of an inspired but cracked dream that issues forth from the brain of a minor functionary, a sleight-of-hand within a single paragraph that transforms naturalistic detail ("wide bleak corridors") into an imagined glimpse of the sublime ("homeland-hugging green waters") and a seemingly childlike but actually artful snatching after expression that makes the syntax hard to diagram but thrilling to read ("joy in the Bronx"). Here one detects all the energy and drive of Miss Ozick's style and the tricky transitions it can negotiate from one level of narrative reality to another. ⟨. . .⟩

Precisely on account of her style, Miss Ozick strikes me as the best American writer to have emerged in recent years. Her artistic strength derives from her moral energy, for Miss Ozick is not an esthete. Judaism has given to her what Catholicism gave to Flannery O'Connor—authority, penetration and indignation.—EDMUND WHITE, "Images of a Mind Thinking," *NYTBR*, Sept. 11, 1983, pp. 3, 46–47

Works

TRUST

Cynthia Ozick's *Trust* is that extraordinary literary entity, a first novel that is a genuine novel, wholly self-contained and produced by a rich, creative imagination, not an imitation of someone else's work or thinly disguised autobiography. Moreover, it stands boldly apart from the two types of serious fiction that have dominated the postwar years in America: the activist-existential novel of Saul Bellow, William Styron and Walker Percy; and the realistic novel of information, the novel of "what it was like," of J. D. Salinger, Reynolds Price and John Updike. The tradition of narrative to which *Trust* returns, I think, is that of James, Conrad and Lawrence. It is the tradition that explores and reveals the inward man.

Trust deals with events in the life of Allegra Vand, a very rich, very spoiled, twice-married women who has "alertness without form, energy without a cause." She had recklessly flirted with communism and free-love in the thirties, and at the time of the novel, 1957, wishes to regularize her affairs so that her present husband may be appointed to an ambassadorship. Part of the necessary tidying up includes a forced meeting between a daughter and her actual father, Allegra's one-time lover from the thirties.

These events, interesting in themselves, exist to reveal the sensibility of the narrator, Allegra's daughter. She is never given a name. Hers is the only voice we hear directly, whether scene and event occur in New York in the summer of 1957, or whether they occur in Germany after World War II when she was 10, or in England just before the war.

The narrator begins at the moment of her graduation from college, when she finds herself simmering in envy over the coming marriages of her acquaintances. She longs to play some simple, easy feminine role herself. But she faces the fact that she is both appallingly intellectual and an emotional recluse. She has cultivated her wit, but has been unable to define her role as a woman. As she prepares to confront her father, we are made aware that the mother's wish to protect her own reputation has stunted and twisted the daughter's emotional life. We also learn that Enoch Vand, who married Allegra for her money and is an adjunct to her self-esteem, has always refused to acknowledge his stepdaughter as anything but a minor curiosity. Thus the daughter, at the age of 22, is eager for the prerequisites that should be hers as a woman, but is floundering badly in their pursuit.

The main body of the novel, then, is a revelation of the narrator's inner, turbulent, psychic drama, which ends with her reprieve. Her father has performed this small but believable miracle, naturally and inadvertently, by being for her what he has been for her mother and for all of his women: the sly, sexually provocative male animal.

There is an occasional, irritating marring of the novel's carefully wrought prose. In the midst of setting forth perceptions and emotional states delicately balanced, Miss Ozick sometimes gives us weedy passages of exposition that must be got through. These may serve as verbal equivalents of the narrator's feelings, but for me they impede communication. Take, for instance, the description of a thunderstorm which occurs when the narrator is in a state of erotic excitement. The storm "sailed like a woman in long silky hems across a brush-hard lawn; at uneven intervals she stoops and we hear the burred movement of her gloves across the ears of the grass—all that is left of the thunder is this sly caress, and all that is left of the lightning are those erratic senile imbecile winks and licks."

If the flow of images occasionally gets out of hand, this is at worst only a minor blemish. In ordering the difficult interplay of elements, characters observed simultaneously by the narrator and by the reader in somewhat different ways, the author is wholly successful. More important, she succeeds because her protagonist insists upon coming to terms with the recalcitrant sexual elements in her life and, by fictional extension, in ours. Because *Trust* is the product of a highly perceptive intelligence, one responds to its substance from the deepest recesses of self-knowledge.—DAVID L. STEVENSON, "Daughter's Reprieve," *NYTBR*, July 17, 1966, p. 29

It's hard to say what Cynthia Ozick's subject is, or if there is one. *Trust* is strikingly assured and yet insubstantial, as if it lacked a sufficient reason for being what it is. It's a novel of manner: illustrating the luxuriance manner can attain when exploited for its own sake, and the variety of manner at the disposal of a striving young novelist.

The debt is mainly to the high art and oblique characterisation of 60 years ago. Allegra Vand is fairly established as a wealthy New York horror; but other figures we have to grope after: 'his nature was metaphoric, which is another way of saying he was adaptable, and took his resurrections lightly.' Some sort of moral game is being played at the same level of abstraction: the girl who narrates (name unknown), Allegra's daughter by a temporary lover, is a pawn of the Vands, whose eyes are on an ambassadorship. The spectacle is one of an acquisitive society with much of the surface of a fine society; the talk extravagantly witty, motives rarely what they seem. It's set up with some brilliance, but only for the purpose of demolition. Edith Wharton had the same way of knocking down her own elaborate social constructions, and already it looked an artificial exercise. Miss Ozick does it for effect at a still greater remove from reality.

The narrator is a grave girl, in the distinguished line of American heroines whose trust is abused. But if she has a cool, discriminating manner, she also has another that wanders off allusively: 'even redemption, that suspect covenant, can be revised by the bitter and loveless Christ to whom alone nothing, not even life, is irretrievable,' etc. Her quest for self-discovery (unlike her observation of her mother) is largely conducted in the second manner; and not surprisingly it's far from clear, after 560 pages, where the quest has led. It provides, however, a vision of a kind: the girl's discovery of her real father (in a ruined mansion on an island) and an act of sex in which she feels she has 'witnessed the very style of her own creation'. This grandiose passage, with its swooning poetry and Gibbonian inflections, is in the novel's black manner. It suggests a Djuna Barnes of enormous proportions—and correspondingly hollow.—ROBERT TAUBMAN, "Allegra's Daughter," *NS*, Jan. 20, 1967, pp. 85–86

THE PAGAN RABBI

The seven stories in *The Pagan Rabbi*, Miss Ozick's first book since her remarkable novel *Trust* (1966), are of a piece, variegated but not different because energized by common obsessions. Miss Ozick breaks up familiar experiences and reconstructs them in such surprising ways that common passions—the wish to escape and transmogrify flesh, the exaltation of fantasy into a life-saving reality, the overlapping estrangement of Jew and Gentile (taking different cultural forms, but departing from the same quality of desperation) transcend towards new truths, revelations.

The short story is an excruciatingly demanding medium. One, at the most two, preoccupations can be handled within its compass. The gift of compressing and conducting obsession into single themes, allowing principal characters to be consumed by their idée fixe and retain credibility is exceptionally difficult. Most contemporary writers of the short story strive for the beautiful mood, the language elegant and lovely and precise, and one is left with a perfect sense of crushed flowers and mottled leaves, little definitions and small dreams. Or else, with the so-called "Jewish" writers, the reader receives sociologies rather than visions, for most Jewish writers use Jewish information like a duelist his poniard, good for little jabs and quick flight.

Cynthia Ozick comes forward in this masterful collection, not as a Jewish writer, but as a Jewish visionary—something more. All of her characters are, to begin with, distraught, distended by the world, trapped by misunderstanding, incommunicativeness, loneliness, exhaustion. But their distraction is only a starting-point. The stories are never simply descriptive or evocative. Isaac Kornfeld, the pagan rabbi, who surrenders to his lust for a mythological dryad he has conjured and in his passion to enforce upon her pure spirit the vividness of his flesh, loses her and in grief is hung (hangs himself) by his trailing prayer shawl. The great public scholar of the Law, husband of Sheindel who has survived the death camps, father of children, an upright and grave young scholar has pressed beyond the restricted order of the Jewish security system of girdles and fences and wandering free has found only madness and death. "The Dock Witch," another mythological extrusion, is the Gentile counterpoint to "The Pagan Rabbi," for the young shipping executive from Ohio, obsessed with the sea and the ships that bear people away from their flat worlds encounters an omnipresent sea nymph, aged, ageless Undine, who is all immediacy of flesh and sensational violence and through his love and terror loses all contact with ordinary days. One death, two transfigurations.

"Envy; or Yiddish in America," one of the funniest stories ever written—funny, mordant, miserable—chronicles the infinite frustrations and bitterness of a Yiddish writer who is dying with his language. Offsetting Edelshtein of "Envy" is "Virility," a story narrated by a desiccated *Wasp* journalist named Edmund Gate who is depredated by a greenhorn who pilfers his name (he is born Elia Gatoff from Glusk-, Russia, via Liverpool, to New York). Young Elia/Edmund insists upon becoming an English poet and despite no talent manages—and that is the mystery of the story—to become the most celebrated poet of his day, vaunted for his masculinity, his energy, his potency. Edelshtein collapses under the weight of his frustration before universal anti-Semitism and Edmund Gate, the bogus, is last seen by Edmund Gate, the real, masqueraded as a quasi-transvestite, his virility hopelessly compromised by the revelation that his masculine power was all copped from his old Jewish aunt who stayed behind in Liverpool.

Cynthia Ozick is always refining and winnowing obsessions and for the projection and substantiation of obsessions, thought is indispensable. A writer has to mind the language when obsession is at stake. It isn't enough to record the experience, because the experience is not given. It is wrested free from the encumbrance of normal perception and wrenched apart, examined like the entrails of a haruspex, and sewn up again differently. For this work all of the literature, philosophic, moral, mythological, and all of the language, its unfamiliar words and its delicious words have to be used. And Cynthia Ozick does all this, the language textured by a network of associations, reminiscences, allusions to the vast intellectual tradition of the West which has tried to crack the hard nut of thought with its bare teeth.

If the modalities and forms of her obsession shift there is a constancy in the recurring theme of reconciliation (or reconcilement as she calls it in "The Doctor's Wife" and "The Butterfly and the Traffic Light"). But reconciliation which entails mutual compassion and reconcilement which is the accommodation of self to societies and histories never comes off. All the stories end with a kind of bleakness and disturbing obduracy. Perhaps the only one which suggests an ultimate nobility without a scream, the questing Rabbi Isaac Kornfeld in the title story, concludes in apotheosis. In all of Miss Ozick's stories there is the effort to call out over the horizon of human existence to the nameless one. The nameless one does not answer. He doesn't recognize his name. And we don't know the right one.—ARTHUR A. COHEN, *Com*, Sept. 3, 1971, pp. 461–62

The characters in Cynthia Ozick's first collection of stories, *The Pagan Rabbi*, are uncommon, and though there is a category of fiction known as "the American Jewish novel", Mrs Ozick's Jewish characters would not be at ease in the company of the people who appear in the work of Malamud, Bellow, Roth and Co. This is to her credit, and it might go some way toward reviving what must be by now a flagging interest in a literary form made up exclusively of extended ethnic jokes and backhanded compliments. She writes of people and situations

who are rarely if ever seen in American novels, and one is interested to know whether her own novel *Trust* had the same imaginative daring.

Isaac Kornfeld, the pagan rabbi of the title story, has hanged himself in a New York park. The narrator, his old friend, visits Kornfeld's widow, who produces her dead husband's notebook. She is upset—understandably: it emerges from the gouts of script on the pages that Kornfeld has been communing with nature—or rather, Nature—and, more than that, has had a number of nocturnal meetings with a charming little dryad. The rabbi is torn between scripture and sensuality, and his body, made light and airy under Pan's influence, regards his soul (personified by a dusty old man with his nose stuck in a book) as something futile. It can be seen as a serious philosophic effort, but ultimately it fails, partly because it depends so much upon classical fantasy, and mainly because it is insufficiently dramatized and unpersuasive as a story. "The Dock-Witch" has the same result: a beautiful idea which an excess of fantasy deflates.

In this one the narrator works for a shipping line; he meets and eventually spends the night with Undine (or Sylvia), a vulgar middle-aged sprite who at one point walks around the wharf area naked and carrying a lyre. When one has decided, hearing Undine claim that she sings in Phoenician, that the joke has gone far enough and is even becoming just the teeniest bit preposterous, one reads on to find Undine transformed into a wooden century-old figurehead on a sailing ship. Explanation? Well, the narrator might be crazy—craziness could account for Kornfeld's visitations, and craziness could explain the narrative careering out of control in "The Doctor's Wife." But this doesn't explain everything, nor do the heavily symbolic names. Though these stories are marvellously written, they shift their points of view so often they never arrive at a point of resolution.

Yet two of the stories are excellent in all ways. The first of these, "Envy; or, Yiddish in America", is a portrait of Edelshtein, a Yiddish poet whose special curse is to remain without a translator in a country where the only glory is in being translated into English. He is tenacious in his struggle to be recognised, but he is unknown and unwanted: people giggle and mutter at his lectures and are bewildered by his recitations. "He was a rabbi who survived his whole congregation," and he is, credibly, the supreme Yiddishist, the last Jew. Mrs Ozick is at her best in describing Edelshtein's maniacal, self-consuming envy for Yankel Ostrover (who bears a passing resemblance to I. B. Singer), a short story writer who, ably translated from Yiddish to English, has won the admiration of everyone. Ostrover has a fleeting affair with Mireleh, Edelshtein's wife, and in spite of the fact that Edelshtein loathes Ostrover, he

> noticed with self-curiosity that he felt no jealousy whatever, but he thought himself obliged to throw a kitchen chair at Ostrover. Ostrover had very fine teeth, his own; the chair knocked off half a lateral incisor, and Edelshtein wept at the flaw. Immediately he led Ostrover to a dentist around the corner.

At one of Ostrover's hugely successful readings Edelshtein meets Hannah, and later in an epistolary dialogue with the young girl sums up his dilemma, which is the dilemma of "Jewish writing." He tries to persuade Hannah to be his translator and implies that in doing so she will redeem her generation. Hannah refuses for the understandable reason that she doesn't like the old man very much. Edelshtein's delirium at the end is amply justified, but not a wholly satisfactory conclusion to what is otherwise a wonderful and pointed tale. "Virility", her other superb story—this one about an internationally acclaimed poet who is a determined plagiarist (but with a twist: like turning Nabokov's story "A Forgotten Poet" inside-out)—confirms Mrs Ozick's skill and shows her to be a vigorous, sly and accomplished writer, who deserves a very wide audience.—PAUL THEROUX, "Miseries and Splendours of the Short Story," *Enc*, Sept. 1972, pp. 72–73

BLOODSHED

The struggle against the assaults and seductions of the Gentile world continues to absorb Cynthia Ozick in her latest collection of fiction, *Bloodshed and Three Novellas*. Three of the four novellas here are directly about that confrontation, and though free of the actual "bloodshed" promised by the book's title, do throb with ominous intensity.

The first story, "A Mercenary," introduces Lushinski, a Polish Jew by birth, now a citizen and the UN representative of a tiny African nation, and a permanent resident of New York. Lushinski's prodigious services and warm attachments to other cultures, African and American, are stimulated by the stark fear of his own Jewish identity, but his mistress, whom he calls a German countess, and his UN assistant, a true African by the name of Morris Ngambe, have little difficulty penetrating the ironic mask of the intellectual and exposing the vulnerable Jew, the potential victim, beneath. In the title story, "Bloodshed," a Jewish fund-raiser visits his distant relative in a newly established hasidic community outside New York. Suspicious of fraudulence in others, he is forced, during the course of an interview with the *rebbe*, to acknowledge his own deceit and his own demonic capacities. "An Education," the earliest and the least successful of the four novellas, is a heavily ironic treatment of a prize student who tries, and fails, to understand life by the same ideal systems of grammar and definition that can be used in Latin declension. In the last novella, "Usurpation," the protagonist-narrator is a Jewish writer identifiable with the author herself. With disturbing unreserve, the writer-narrator covets, appropriates, and then corrupts the work of others in her own need to make a perfect story and to win the "magic crown" of fame and immortality.

The unsettling effect of both action and style in this last story is deliberate. The novella blurs the normal lines of demarcation between fact and fiction: the narrator tells us that she attended a public reading by a famous author and heard him read a story that she felt to be "hers"; then gives us the plot of a recently published story by Bernard Malamud that the knowledgeable reader would recognize as *his*; then changes the ending of the Malamud story and proceeds to find the "real persons" on whom the story was presumably based, as well as the unpublished manuscripts of its main character. In questionable taste, Miss Ozick also incorporates into her novella another story, which she uses as a literary foil, an actual work that she had seen in manuscript (it was subsequently published in *Response* magazine) by a young writer with a less secure reputation than Malamud's. On this story too she builds her own, in a candid act of plagiarism.

The novella, which freely reworks and passes comment on the works of other writers, is intended to undermine the act of fiction as process and as product. To deflate the mystique of the artist, Miss Ozick presents "herself" as a selfish and somewhat nasty finagler. In place of the grand notions of creativity, she gives us the petty emotions and treacherous techniques, the false bottoms and promises that produce the illusion of fictional magic.

But this act, the "Usurpation" of "Other Peoples' Stories," to use the double title of the novella, is only the lower manifestation of a higher, more significant act of false appropriation to which Miss Ozick wishes to draw attention. The thoroughly Jewish concern of this work is the writing of fiction itself, in Miss Ozick's view an inheritance from the Gentiles and by nature an idolatrous activity. Art—in the Western tradition of truth to fiction as its own end—is against the Second Commandment, she says, and anti-Jewish in its very impulse. As a Jewish artist, Miss Ozick undertakes to subvert the aesthetic ideal by demonstrating its corrupting and arrogant presumption to truth. Thus, the Hebrew poet Saul Tchernikhowsky, one of those who worshipped at the shrine of pagan freedom and natural beauty, finds himself, at the end of the novella, caged in Paradise before a motto that teaches: "All that is not Law is levity." Like the pious widow who hardened her heart against the pagan rabbi, the Jewish artist must refuse and denounce the allure of art.

It is not unusual in modern fiction for a story or novel to question its premises without giving them up. *Bloodshed*, however, commits an act of self-destruction. Like a prizefighter who cannot stop punching at the signal of the bell, Miss Ozick adds a preface to her four novellas to push her meaning home. It is she herself who "explains" her final story, reducing it like a tendentious reviewer to a moral function:

> "Usurpation" is a story written against story-writing; against the Muse-goddesses; against Apollo. It is against magic and mystification, against sham and "miracle," and, going deeper into the dark, against idolatry. It is an invention directed against inventing—the point being that the story-making faculty itself can be a corridor to the corruptions and abominations of idol-worship, of the adoration of magical event.

The preface tells us when the stories were written, why they have been included here, what they are about. This is not footnoting, like Eliot's notes to "The Waste Land" to which the author ingenuously compares it, but self-justification and special pleading.

The preface betrays the insecurities of both the artist and the Jew. Though she admires the transforming, magical kind of art, Miss Ozick is, in fact, an intellectual writer whose works are the fictional realization of ideas. Her reader is expected, at the conclusion of her stories, to have an insight, to understand the point of events rather than to respond to their affective power. Miss Ozick has publicly regretted this quality of hers, and accused herself of lacking what George Eliot calls "truth of feeling." It is true that, marvelously imaginative as she is with words and ideas, Miss Ozick is not on the whole successful at creating autonomous characters whose destiny will tantalize or move the reader.

Because she is a Jewish writer who prides herself on the "centrally Jewish" quality of her work, Miss Ozick has hit a curious snag here. The writer who can achieve "truth of feeling" produces universal art whatever the ethnic stuff of his subject, but a writer of ideas requires a community of knowledge and shared cultural assumptions. In her preface, Miss Ozick says she has to explain the meaning of "Usurpation" because a certain non-Jewish critic had failed to understand it. This failure she attributes not to the story's possible artistic shortcomings, but to its Jewish specificity, which puts it outside the critic's cultural range: "I had written 'Usurpation' in the language of a civilization that cannot understand its thesis." As the prophet of an indigenous Jewish culture in the English language, she might have been expected to hail the critic's failure to understand as a milestone—an authentic breakthrough in the creation of a distinctive Jewish literature. Instead, determined to have both the cake and the eating of it, she anxiously becomes her own translator, explaining Tchernikhowsky, Torah, the large ideas as well as the factual underpinnings of her work. If her kind of art is not inherently universal, she is apparently prepared to provide "art with an explanation" in order to spread the splendor wide.—Ruth R. Wisse, "American Jewish Writing, Act II," *Cmty*, June 1976, pp. 42–43

LEVITATION

"You have no feelings", one character accuses another in one of Cynthia Ozick's new stories, but the accusation is immediately modified: "he meant that she had the habit of flushing with ideas as if they were passions." And the whole book ⟨*Levitation*⟩ flushes likewise, with passionate learning and with passionate phrasing. Cynthia Ozick is a woman, and Jewish; and a New Yorker; these conditions in combination might be expected to produce a narrow art, if any at all. And certainly there are few men in these stories, fewer gentiles, and hardly a single out-of-towner, but the result is anything but narrow; the absentees are hardly noticed.

Cynthia Ozick has the enviable knack of moving, with impressive speed, in opposite directions at the same time; her specialities are prose poetry, intellectual slapstick, meticulous detail, and wild rhetorical fantasy. The result at its best is an audacious and unorthodox balancing of forces, both within the story and within the sentence. Within the story, there is tension between a carefully rendered milieu and the wildly elaborated fantasy which arrives to transform it. Within the sentence, there is a running battle between a realism that describes things as they are, and a rhetoric that takes constant liberties with the appearances.

Consider for example the intricate beauty of this passage: ". . . the kitchen too seemed transformed—a floating corner of buoyancy and quicksilver: it was as if the table were in the middle of a Parisian concourse, streaming, gleaming; it had the look of a painting, both transient and eternal, a place where you sat for a minute to gossip, and also a place where the middle-aged Henry James came every day so that nothing in the large world would be lost on him." This grotesque splendour of evocation, an altogether satisfactory substitute for a physical description, is lavished on a small Manhattan kitchen in which an artificial human being has just cooked a soufflé for her creator, a civil servant called Ruth Puttermesser; the incongruity and the excess are perfectly calculated. The passage goes just too far enough.

The story of Puttermesser and her creature ("Puttermesser and Xanthippe") takes up over half the book and contains most of its high points; the fantastical elaboration, ballasted by an intimate knowledge of bureaucracy, of Puttermesser's rise to worldly power (Mayor of New York, inevitably, given the book's priorities) is oddly balanced by a matter-of-fact account of her progressive gum disease.

The pair of sketches entitled "From a Refugee's Notebook" are by far the weakest in the volume. The first portentously analyses the décor of Freud's house in Vienna; the second is a surprisingly leaden fantasy about a craze, on the planet Acirema (which no doubt should be read backwards), for Sewing Harems: groups of women who can be hired to sew themselves together. These fragments contain the ingredients of Cynthia Ozick's successful fiction, but wilfully separate them into one piece of non-fiction and one aimless improvisation.

When the materials are properly combined, the results are formidable: the text flushes with the idea of Jewishness and the idea of New York. The sense of history and the sense of place become resources of fact and feeling for an entirely new enterprise, and the whole unlikely rocket takes off, trailing sparks and coloured rain. After a vivid and exhilarating flight, admittedly, all that comes clattering down through the trees is a scorched stick; but with very little more discipline and expertise Cynthia Ozick will produce fireworks that can carry passengers.—Adam Mars-Jones, "Fantastic Flushes," *TLS*, April 23, 1982, p. 456

THE CANNIBAL GALAXY

Because the literary weather in this country is generally inclement, a prudent writer wears two hats. From under the brim of one, Cynthia Ozick has launched tough-minded, humorless pronouncements: "Where writers are taken too seriously, watch out for something rotten, incomplete, unhealthy." When she dons the other, intricate and witty stories have emerged. At the risk of being thought rotten and unhealthy, I've been praising them for years. Ozick's first novel, *Trust*, was an exercise in Henry James. Three collections of short stories followed—*The Pagan Rabbi, Bloodshed* and *Levitation*—and it is on these that her reputation principally rests. Now after 17 years she returns to the novel form. James's mannerisms have been abandoned, but a vestige remains: the clash of the old world with the new.

The hero of *The Cannibal Galaxy*, Joseph Brill, is the principal of an ambitious, dismal, private elementary school somewhere in Middle America. Brill is a French Jew, a refugee from the Holocaust. It is his conceit that a school might develop what he calls a "Dual Curriculum": half Talmudic studies, half European culture. Such an education would embrace a passion for the ideal and a passion for sardonic detail: "Two such separated tonalities . . . could between them describe the true map of life." Brill is a bachelor, a failed astronomer, "a melancholic, a counter of losses. . . . used to consorting with the Middle." His students are middling and so is his faculty, which is given to assigning long lists for memorization. Ozick picks him up at age 58, confronting the mother of a dull student. The mother, Hester Lilt, is European, too, a formidable philosopher: "an imagistic linguistic logician." Ozick has modeled her, I suspect, on Hannah Arendt. Brill is at first sycophantic, but Lilt rebukes him: she's too good for a man who quit trying to be great too soon. She taunts him by sending him her writings—until Brill unexpectedly discovers that the guiding principle behind her thinking is a sham.

I can't in fairness reveal more of the story, or even what the odd title of this novel means. Ozick writes so well that her plot assumes a secondary importance. On every page she displays intelligence, wit, energy and the promise of design. Her language is precise and highly figurative. A woman whom Ozick presents for no more than a paragraph in this novel dies of a heart attack, but that heart attack is hers alone: "her heart fanned, stirred, slowed, became as agitated as a cricket; then dropped into the cage of death." As for the mothers of Brill's students: "The unselfconscious inexorable secretion ran in all of them. From morning to night they were hurtled forward by the explosions of internal rivers, with their roar of force and pressure. The mothers were rafts on their own instinctual flood. Encirclement, preservation, defense, protection: that was the roar and force. That was why they lived, and how: to make a roiling moat around their offspring." That's grand stuff. Ozick's imagery may offend some of her women readers, but it's nonetheless tough-minded and in the highest sense comical. And so is her novel: tough, sad, funny, beautiful in its design.—Peter S. Prescott, "Vision and Design," *NwK*, Sept. 12, 1983, pp. 76, 78

SARAH BLACHER COHEN
From "Jewish Literary Comediennes"
Comic Relief:
Humor in Contemporary American Literature
1978, pp. 179–86

A Jewish writer not preoccupied with her characters' gender identity and more sure of her artistic identity is Cynthia Ozick. Finding the designation "woman writer" too confining and essentially discriminatory, she regards the entire range of human experience as the fit subject matter for her fiction. Exploring the consciousness of both male and female characters, she doesn't mind being considered a betrayer to the feminist cause or a trespasser in male territory. What does concern Cynthia Ozick is that her fiction retain an authentically Jewish nature. At the American-Israel Dialogue of 1970, she described the characteristics of a genuine Jewish literature in the American diaspora. Its language, though written in English, will be "New Yiddish." "Centrally Jewish in its concerns," the literature will be "liturgical in nature." By "liturgical" she does not mean "didactic or prescriptive," but "Aggadic, utterly freed to invention, discourse, parable, experiment, enlightenment, profundity, humanity." As for its potential for humor, this "New Yiddish" literature, Ozick claims, "will be capable of genuine comic perception in contrast to the grotesqueries of despair that pass for jokes [in the literature of] current Gnostics and aestheticians."[1]

Cynthia Ozick's "Envy; or, Yiddish in America,"[2] is an excellent illustration of this liturgical "New Yiddish," since it is a parabolic comedy in which morality and humor are inextricably linked. Edelshtein, the central figure of the story, is a sixty-seven-year-old Yiddish poet desperately striving for forty years to have his talents recognized in America. In one respect he is still the fearful little man of the *shtetl* who has a Chaplinesque sense of himself as the accidental and insignificant creature barely surviving in the hostile world. In another respect he has the hauteur of the high priest of Yiddish culture, censuring superficial Jewish-American writers and a slickly translated Yiddish author, Yankel Ostrover, who have made financial killings in the literary marketplace. Edelshtein's feelings of extreme inferiority and extreme superiority incur Ozick's humorous treatment. When he is the insecure *shtetl* figure, she compassionately views him as a saintly fool in his valiant efforts to keep Yiddish alive for American Jews. She sympathizes with him when at the first Yiddish word in one of his lectures, "the painted old ladies of the Reform Temples would begin to titter from shame, as at a stand-up television comedian" (p. 43). She acknowledges the ruefully comic incongruity of his mourning the death of Yiddish in synagogues which have become Cecil B. DeMille amusement parlors and fancy catering halls. Like other Jewish-American novelists, she ridicules the gastronomic Judaism and edifice complexes of *nouveau riche* American Jewry. But she also harshly mocks Edelshtein when he becomes the supercilious Yiddish purist. This is not to suggest that Ozick totally disagrees with his assessment of American Jewish literature. With the exception of Saul Bellow, whom she respects as the "most purely and profoundly ideational"[3] of the Jewish-American novelists, she generally shares Edelshtein's belief that they are largely ignorant of their Jewish heritage, yet reviewers praise them for their ethnic wit and perception. Indeed, much of the story's amusement stems from the fact that Edelshtein acts as the stringent literary critic who, often expressing Ozick's views, employs the quaint accent and syntax of Yiddishized English to

pronounce his unkind judgments. He deplores, for example, the cheap way Jewish-American novelists add Yiddish local color to their work: "Their Yiddish! One word here, one word there. *Shikseh* on one page, *putz* on the other, and that's the whole vocabulary. . . . They know ten words for, excuse me, penis, and when it comes to a word for learning they're impotent" (pp. 79–80). Edelshtein is just as merciless in his lampooning of Yankel Ostrover, the third-rate Yiddish writer who enjoys national and international acclaim because his modernist English translators freed him of the "prison of Yiddish" (p. 47). Edelshtein both ridicules Ostrover for his graceless Yiddish style and comically exaggerates the perversities of his characters' behavior: "boys copulating with hens, butchers who drank blood for strength behind the knife" (p. 47). Clearly Ostrover, whose fiction about imaginary Polish villages reeks of the occult and pornographic, is a caricature of Isaac Bashevis Singer. Since Ozick abhors the violations of taste committed by such a caricature, she has Edelshtein dwell upon what an obscene literary faker Ostrover is, thus exposing the idiocy of the literary establishment for considering Ostrover a universal genius.

What Ozick finds most objectionable and worthy of satire about Edelshtein is his hypocrisy. Much as he mocks Ostrover, he prefers to be like him. He, too, would like to escape from the "prison of Yiddish" (p. 47), if he could achieve fame. He pretends to lament the waning of Yiddish when he actually laments the waning of an audience to appreciate his creativity. His hypocrisy is attacked, however, not by the author but by a twenty-three-year-old Yiddish-reading woman whom Edelshtein implores to be his translator, though she is a devotee of Ostrover. Refusing to give life to Edelshtein's dying poems, she heartlessly lashes out at him: "You jealous old men from the ghetto. . . . You bore me to death. You hate magic, you hate imagination, you talk God and you hate God, you despise, you bore, you envy, you eat people up with your disgusting old age—cannibals, all you care about is your own youth, you're finished, give somebody else a turn!" (pp. 94, 97–98). We are not to side with the young woman, however. Her diatribe shows the limitations of American-born Jewish youth who would readily sacrifice the parochial for the universal and, in so doing, lose their claim to any distinctiveness. Because Yiddish is an indigenous part of Edelshtein, and because Christians and anti-Semitic Jews alike won't allow him to forget this fact, he can't give up Yiddish. Since he has the misfortune of living at a time when Yiddish "died a sudden and definite death, in a given decade, on a given piece of soil" (p. 42), Ozick sympathizes with his desire to communicate and be understood in an alien land. She can even forgive his envy of those who achieve a spurious kind of communication.

Satiric indictment and sympathetic acquittal of petty Yiddish writers is not Ozick's primary concern in "Envy." The story allows her to express her affection for Yiddish, the *mamaloshen*, the mother tongue, in which childhood endearments, *shtetl* solidarity, and a closeness with God are conveyed. Moreover, she laments the American Jews' abandonment of Yiddish for English, a language they consider more secular and thus more aesthetic. Abandonment of the Jewish sources for creativity in pursuit of more worldly fame is also the theme of "Virility,"[4] the next short story Ozick wrote after "Envy." On the surface, "Virility" appears to be a feminist comedy of literary manners revealing the double standard in the world of letters. Edmund Gate, born Elia Gatoff, has come to America from Czarist Russia via Liverpool to make his literary fortune. His first attempts at poetry are marred by contrived alliteration and polysyllabic diction. Though his work is continually rejected, he is a confident male and still believes in his talent. After several years of persistence, his poems miraculously improve and appear in the best magazines. Promoted by a married woman with whom he has had two illegitimate children, he publishes five volumes of poetry, each entitled *Virility.* The critics, more impressed with the title of the poetry than with its substance, single out what they consider its masculine virtues and overpraise them: "If Teddy Roosevelt's Rough Riders had been poets, they would have written poems like that. If Genghis Khan and Napoleon had been poets, they would have written poems like that. They were masculine . . . poems . . . [like] superbly controlled muscle . . ." (p. 257).

It turns out, however, that Edmund Gate is not the author of these poems. They have been written by Tante Rivka, his spinster aunt who cared for him in Liverpool. Soon after his arrival in America, he has been passing off as his own the eloquent poems she sent him in her letters. Three years after her death, he has nearly exhausted the supply of her poetry and faces artistic sterility. A Jamesian mentor convinces him to confess his plagiarism and do right by Tante Rivka. Her remaining poems, which were to comprise Gate's *Virility VI,* are published under her own name as *Flowers from Liverpool.* This collection contains Tante Rivka's finest poetry, yet the reviewers are unimpressed. Employing phallic criticism, they find her book to be "Thin feminine art," "Limited as all domestic verse must be. A spinster's one-dimensional vision" (p. 266). Yet Gate's poetry they acclaimed as "Seminal and hard," "Robust, lusty, male" (p. 254).

This flagrant example of male critical bias which Cynthia Ozick describes with bitter humor could be straight out of Victorian England. Elaine Showalter mentions a similar occurrence concerning the publication of George Eliot's *Adam Bede.* Since the book was thought to be too good for a woman's work, the critics hastily found the male whom they assumed to be the author, a clergyman named Joseph Liggins, who readily accepted credit for the book. When the real George Eliot could not abide the homage paid to the fraudulent author and revealed her identity, the reviews changed. "Where critics had previously seen the powerful mind of the male George Eliot . . . they now discovered feminine delicacy . . . a disturbing unladylike coarseness."[5]

"Virility," however, is not exclusively an attack upon male parasites and male supremacists. Ozick includes an element of the ludicrous within Edmund Gate's treachery for the purpose of jest and symbolic import. Since he has appropriated a woman's talents, Ozick has him fear he has acquired a female's gender as well. Clutching his genitals to confirm his sex, his last words to the narrator are: "I'm a man" (p. 266).

Gate's uneasiness about his anatomy is symptomatic of his uneasiness about being a Jew. He readily saps the creativity of Tante Rivka, Ozick's allegorical figure representing Judaism, but he is reluctant to acknowledge his indebtedness to her. Once in America he ceases to communicate with her and lets her starve to death. If he had provided nourishment for her, she would have survived many more years and prolonged Gate's poetic career. Instead, Tante Rivka, productive until the end, died with dignity, whereas Edmund Gate, disaffected Jew and poet manqué, committed suicide.

In a recent novella, "Usurpation (Other People's Stories),"[6] Cynthia Ozick mocks herself as author for pilfering other writers' fiction. That the novella's narrator-protagonist is a woman writer who has plagiarized from the works of male writers is not at issue. Her prime concern is not the invasion of the males' literary domain to redress the wrongs perpetrated against her sister writers. Rather, she is an asexual spinner of tales who jests about the snags in her narrative technique and the literary larceny she commits.

She informs us that at a public reading she heard a famous writer read a story which she had already composed in her own mind. That story is unmistakably Bernard Malamud's "Silver Crown." Filled with the same envy which Edelshtein had for the successful Ostrover, she is bent on winning her own fame. She rewrites the ending of Malamud's work by incorporating a story which she filches from a young writer, David Stern, and further modifies it by including a parable she has stolen from Agnon. Unlike Edmund Gate, she does not try to conceal that she is a literary purloiner. She openly admits her crimes, applauds herself for her cunning, and instructs neophyte writers to adopt her questionable practices.

One of the purposes of "Usurpation," other than providing the true confessions of a story thief, is to ridicule the writing of fiction itself. It is revealed not as a miraculous process whereby the finished product emerges fault-free from the divinely inspired head of the creator. Rather, it is shown to be a suspect art, relying on counterfeit experience, dubious techniques, and contrived language to achieve its lifelike effects. Ozick also mirthfully punctures the inflated positions of the writer. Her narrator-protagonist is a vain, short-tempered opportunist who values public renown over the perfection of her craft. For her, no edifying relationship exists between tradition and the individual talent. She is too busy exploiting the talent of others to appreciate tradition and to cultivate her own creativity.

Ozick disapproves of the art of fiction not only on aesthetic and ethical grounds. For the Jewish writer, fashioning a make-believe reality through words is an idolatrous act, in direct violation of the Second Commandment. Story-telling is too Christian an activity as well, since it reminds her of the "Eucharist, wherein the common bread of language assumes the form of a god."[7] But her greatest objection to story-telling is its usurpation, since the author appropriates from God the role of creator. To prevent readers from missing the theological meaning of "Usurpation," Ozick further explains it in a preface to the collection in which it appears: " 'Usurpation' is a story written against story-telling; against the Muse-goddesses; against Apollo. It is against magic and mystification, against sham and 'miracle,' and, going deeper into the dark, against idolatry. It is an invention directed against inventing—the point being that the story-making faculty itself can be a corridor to the corruptions and abominations of idol-worship, or the adoration of magical event."[8]

Ozick herself claims to "dread the cannibal touch of story-making," yet continues to "lust after stories."[9] Similarly, the narrator-protagonist of "Usurpation" is aware of the evil consequences of story-telling, yet continues to "moon after magical tales" (p. 131). When the ghost of the Jewish poet Tchernikhovsky asks her to choose between the "Creator or the creature. God or god. The Name of Names or Apollo" (p. 176), she unhesitatingly selects the pagan deity and becomes the prolific transmitter of pagan narratives: "Stories came from me then . . . none of them of my own making, all of them acquired, borrowed, given, taken, inherited, stolen, plagiarized, usurped, chronicles and sagas invented at the beginning of the world by the offspring of giants copulating with the daughters of men" (p. 177).

Ozick here suggests that as long as the Jewish storyteller writes in this world, where he is exposed to an alien culture and must employ a secular language, he will be an idolatrous fiction-monger. And if he chooses to write about the heathen rather than the holy in the next world, then the pagan inhabitants of Paradise, like Hitler in this world, will not allow him to forget that he is a Jew. He will be caged and instructed: "All that is not Law is levity" (p. 177).

Fortunately, Cynthia Ozick has not been caged, and she writes about levity and Law. Of the Jewish women writers discussed, she has shown the most *chutzpah.* She has not taken refuge in the hackneyed jokes of Jewish masochism or mocked things Jewish with a self-advertising bravado. Her humor does not confine itself to stereotypes, nor does she exploit ethnic externals for ready laughter. Steeped in the Jewish tradition and aware of its conflicting viewpoints, she deftly reveals its wry paradoxes. A comedienne of ideas, she transforms the farcical into the philosophical. But because of her wit and imagination, her "philosophical stories" do not "make excellent lullabies."[10] They keep her readers awake and amused.

Notes

1. Cynthia Ozick's address at the American-Israel Dialogue of 1970 was published as "America: Toward Yavneh," *Judaism,* 19 (Summer, 1970), 264–282. This quotation appears on pp. 279–280.
2. "Envy; or, Yiddish in America" was originally published in *Commentary,* 48 (November, 1969). It later appeared in Cynthia Ozick's collection, *The Pagan Rabbi and Other Stories* (New York: Alfred A. Knopf, 1971). Citations to "Envy" are from this collection.
3. "Ozick, "America: Toward Yavneh," p. 266.
4. "Virility" was originally published in *Anon,* February, 1971. It later appeared in *The Pagan Rabbi.* Citations are from this collection.
5. Elaine Showalter, "Women Writers and the Double Standard," in *Woman in Sexist Society,* ed. Vivian Gornick and Barbara K. Moran (New York: New American Library, 1972), p. 476.
6. "Usurpation" was originally published in *Esquire,* May, 1974. It later appeared in Cynthia Ozick's collection, *Bloodshed and Three Novellas* (New York: Alfred A. Knopf, 1976). Citations are from this collection.
7. Ozick, "Preface," *Bloodshed,* p. 11.
8. Ibid.
9. Ibid., p. 12.
10. Ozick, "Usurpation," p. 143.

KATHA POLLIT
"The Three Selves of Cynthia Ozick"

New York Times Book Review, May 23, 1983, pp. 7, 35

This ⟨*Art & Ardor*⟩ is not your typical collection of essays by an eminent middle-aged writer of fiction. You know the sort of book I mean—a graceful miscellany of book reviews, introductions and speeches, all wrapped up and offered to the public less as a book, really, than as a kind of laurel, a tribute to the author's literary importance. The magazine articles collected here do more than stand on their own. They jump up and down, they grab the reader by the shirt-front. We may be living in "an era when the notion of belles-lettres is profoundly dead," as Miss Ozick says in her foreword, but it's thriving in *Art & Ardor,* which is by turns quarrelsome, quirky, unfair, funny and brilliant.

Looked at one way, these essays, though originally published in magazines as divergent as *Ms.* and *Commentary,* are a unified and magisterial continuation of Miss Ozick's short stories by other means. Admirers of her three story collections (her one novel, *Trust,* is, sadly, out of print) will recognize at once her yeasty, extravagant prose, her intellectual preoccupations (jeremiads against violations of the Second Commandment, for instance—that's the one about worshiping idols) and

some of her characters too. The lecturer lovingly memorialized here in "Remembering Maurice Samuel" might have spoken at the 92d Street Y the night before Miss Ozick's Yankel Ostrover gave the reading that drove his fellow Yiddish writers wild with jealousy in her story "Envy: or, Yiddish in America." The critic Harold Bloom emerges from the drubbing he gets here in an essay titled "Literature as Idol" as the spiritual cousin of the fictional Isaac Kornfeld, Miss Ozick's pagan rabbi. And surely Ruth Puttermesser, a heroine of *Levitation,* who resented having "Miss" put in front of her name was standing over her author's shoulder in 1971 when she wrote her essay "Previsions of the Demise of the Dancing Dog," a furious, sane and still entirely timely feminist argument.

Looked at another way, though, *Art & Ardor* is the work not of one Cynthia Ozick but three: a rabbi, a feminist and a disciple of Henry James. Among them, this trio—old classmates, perhaps, or relatives, but hardly friends—have co-authored a fascinating and very odd anthology of essays about Judaism, women and literature.

As rabbi, Miss Ozick's chief target is idol worship, whose ramifications, she argues, include the Holocaust, Jewish assimilation and much modern literature, all of which are the result of substituting "aesthetic paganism" for moral seriousness. "When a Jew becomes a secular person he is no longer a Jew," she writes in "Toward a New Yiddish"; he's merely a neuter, an "envious ape" of gentile culture. It follows that Miss Ozick regards most of the writers we think of as Jewish—Proust, Kafka, Heine, not to mention Philip Roth and Norman Mailer—as Christians *manqués,* the main exception being Saul Bellow, for reasons I couldn't quite catch. (Actually, the writer who best fits Miss Ozick's criteria is Miss Ozick herself, whose fiction does indeed answer her call for "a new Yiddish," that is, a culturally Jewish-American literature informed by a "sacral imagination" and an engagement with history.) Since so few Jews can pass her entrance exam, the rabbi would like to fill up the ranks with honorary members like Dickens and George Eliot, on the grounds that the Victorian novel was "Judaized," that is, moral and realistic. The rabbi hates ancient Greece, John Updike's Bech books, "experimental fiction," "nonfiction novels" and much modern poetry. At her gloomiest, Miss Ozick wonders if "Jewish writer" is not a contradiction in terms.

The feminist Ozick, a more cheerful sort, takes on Anatomy as Destiny. "If anatomy were destiny, the wheel could not have been invented; we would have been limited by legs," she snaps in "The Hole/Birth Catalogue," a masterly demolition of Freud on women. She's outraged by sentimentalists who patronize women by comparing housekeeping or pregnancy to artistic creation: "It is insulting to a poet to compare his titanic and agonized strivings with the so-called 'creativity' of childbearing, where—consciously—nothing happens. One does not will the development of the fetus . . . the process itself is as involuntary, and unaware as the beating of one's own heart."

Miss Ozick reserves particular scorn for the "Ovarian Theory of Literature," whose proponents include feminist literary scholars, the author's own college students (who decided Flannery O'Connor was "sentimental" when they learned she was not a man) and most book reviewers: "I think I can say in good conscience that I have never—repeat, *never*—read a review of a novel or, especially, of a collection of poetry by a woman that did not include somewhere in its columns a gratuitous allusion to the writer's sex and its supposed effects," she wrote in 1971. The feminist makes short work of Elizabeth Hardwick's timid suggestion, made some two decades ago, that women's slighter musculature would forever ban them from the highest literary achievements. "The making of literature," Miss Ozick counters, "is, after all, as unknown a quantity as mind itself."

At this point, the Jamesian Ozick takes over. For her, the imagination is a holy mystery and the writing of fiction the only thing that matters. The Jamesian knows precisely what was wrong with R. W. B. Lewis's biography of Edith Wharton—it left out her life as a writer. She's devastating on Truman Capote's arch early novels—perhaps too devastating, for she denounces "Other Voices, Other Rooms" like someone going after a hummingbird with a chain saw. The Jamesian even knows that worshiping James is a trap: Art may be all that matters, but one can't be an artist if one lives as though that were true. As I'm trying to indicate, Cynthia Ozick has a complicated mind.

All three Ozicks love a good fight, which is one of the reasons *Art & Ardor* is so much fun to read. They share some less attractive qualities too—a tendency to seize irrelevant moral high ground, and to present Ozick as a beleaguered minority of one (to read her on other feminists, you'd thing she was the only woman writer who hasn't retired to a lesbian commune to write prose poems about the Great Mother). She draws wild inferences from ideas she opposes and then uses her extrapolations as a club. How could Harold Bloom possibly answer her charge that his theory of strong and weak poets is a covert defense of human sacrifice?

The problem is not that there is a polemic at the heart of most of these essays, but that Miss Ozick's true targets are not always fully acknowledged. Would she have slammed quite so hard into poor Mr. Capote had he not, as she reminds us in a casual aside, once complained of a "Jewish Mafia" in American letters? (Never mind for the moment that she doesn't think the writers he meant are truly Jewish, or that her own characterizations of them—"envious ape," for instance—echo traditional anti-Semitic slanders.) Perhaps, but she does favor hit-and-run tactics, as when she drops into a discussion of the late Israeli scholar Gershom Scholem the suggestion that "the seeds of the Inquisition somehow lie even in the Sermon on the Mount." They do? Where? If she wants to say that Christianity is innately murderous, let her stand her ground and produce her evidence, not deliver a one-liner and move on.

Miss Ozick is fond of grand pronouncements, and she delivers them with such confidence one might almost not notice that many of them are flatly invalid. "Homosexuality did not begin with Lytton Strachey, but homosexual manners did," she writes in "Morgan and Maurice: A Fairy Tale," eliminating Oscar Wilde and a century of dandyism with a stroke of the pen. Virginia Woolf, she tells us, shared her own contempt for "female separatism" in literature. In fact, Woolf was intrigued by the possibility that men and women wrote differently by nature, and even wrote some very silly paragraphs about Jane Austen's need to reshape the "heavy" male-invented sentence of her day. To help her praise moral fiction, she denies morality to poetry, dismissing it as a "decoration of the heart" and ultimately evil. Forget the religious, social, political and moral visions of Milton, Blake, Dickinson, Frost, Lowell.

We go in one paragraph from *Tintern Abbey* to the Hitler Youth.

Such sweeping overstatements may be pardoned as a byproduct of exuberance. A more serious difficulty, at least for me, was a growing sense that Cynthia Ozick's three selves were not very well acquainted with each other. How, I found myself wondering, does she square her commitment to sexual egalitarianism with her passionately traditional Judaism (for needless to say, she has nothing but contempt for Reform Judaism, the only branch that would let her be a rabbi for real). There are those who argue that Conservative and Orthodox Judaism offer separate but equal spheres for men and women, but I doubt that Miss Ozick is one of them, and anyway, separate but equal is not what she wants. Why is it incumbent upon Jews to write as Jews, even if they must first acquire a whole religious and historical education to do so (not to mention learn Hebrew) but anathema for women to write as women? And if biology is irrelevant to a writer's work, why does Miss Ozick discuss the childlessness of Woolf and Wharton at all, let alone bring in moralistic terms like "solipsistic"? She doesn't tell us which of the male writers she discusses were fathers (although we do learn which ones were homosexual). If it matters that Woolf and Wharton were free from household chores, it ought also to matter that John Updike and I.B. Singer are too. Contradictions and excluded middles of this sort are the reasons why my copy of *Art & Ardor* is as heavily scored with question marks and irritated cross-references as it is with passages underlined for saving.

Miss Ozick tells us that she culled these essays from over 100, and some of her choices could have been better. I wish, for instance, that she had dropped the second half of her Gershom Scholem essay, a worshipful profile that finds time to moon over Mrs. Scholem's cooking (the feminist must have been on vacation that day) and given us instead the hilarious "We Are the Crazy Ladies," which appeared in an early issue of *Ms*. Here we learn that although the imagination may be sexless, writers are not and that Miss Ozick, as much as those feminists she castigates, has had to contend with snubs and belittlements on account of her sex. Also left out is "Notes toward Finding the Right Question," from the lively Jewish feminist quarterly *Lilith*. This long and complex essay does not resolve the dichotomy between Miss Ozick's ideas about women and her strict interpretations of Judaism, but at least it gets the rabbi and the feminist talking to each other.

I suspect that Cynthia Ozick's three selves do not try harder to make peace with each other because they sense it can't be done. The secular drift she castigates as a religious Jew is, after all, exactly what gives her the freedom to reexamine traditional notions of women, and to posit the imagination as sovereign. All the same, it would be interesting to see what she would come up with if she set herself the task of synthesis. For now, though, it's enough that she has given us this wonderful, if sometimes frustrating book—among whose gems, I must not forget to mention, is a childhood memoir, "A Drugstore in Winter," that is as rich and dense as the best of her fiction. The book it so splendidly concludes deserves a wide readership among women and men, Jews and gentiles, lovers of fiction and lovers of ideas.

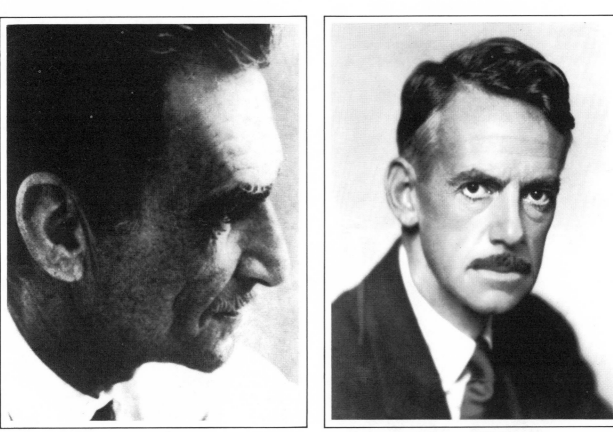

GEORGE OPPEN

EUGENE O'NEILL

THOMAS NELSON PAGE

THE BETTMANN ARCHIVE

WALKER PERCY

S. J. PERELMAN

DOROTHY PARKER

THOMAS NELSON PAGE

1853–1922

Thomas Nelson Page was born on April 23, 1853, in Oakland, Virginia. Raised by a strict religious family, Page had little formal education until he entered Washington and Lee College in Lexington, Virginia, in 1869; he left three years later without a degree. By 1873 he had acquired enough money to enter the law school at the University of Virginia, passing the bar examination in 1874. Moving to Richmond in 1876, Page practiced law for many years, teaming up in 1885 with his kinsman Thomas Nelson Carter. In 1886 he married Anne Seddon Bruce, but she died two years later.

Page's earliest writings were poems and stories sold to *Scribner's Monthly,* the *Century,* and other magazines. In 1887 the collection *In Ole Virginia* was published to high praise. In 1890 Page began to lecture widely on Southern topics; on a tour in Chicago he met Florence Lathrop Field, a wealthy widow; they married in 1893 and settled in Washington, D.C. From this date until his death Page led a very active life in the sophisticated society of the day. Page wrote prolifically, including the novels *Red Rock* (1898) and *Gordon Keith* (1903), several collections of essays and lectures, and a biography of Robert E. Lee. *The Novels, Stories, Sketches, and Poems of Thomas Nelson Page* (The Plantation Edition) was issued in eighteen volumes from 1908 to 1912.

In his later years Page became involved in political affairs. At the 1912 Democratic convention he initially opposed the nomination of Woodrow Wilson but later supported Wilson's candidacy for president; for his services Wilson appointed Page ambassador to Italy in 1913, a post he held until 1919. Under the management of Page and his wife the Italian Embassy became a supply base and hospital during World War I. Returning to Virginia in 1920, Page died at his home in Oakland on November 1, 1922. His incomplete novel *The Red Riders* was completed by his brother Rosewell and published in 1924.

Sarvent Marster! Is dis de co'te
  Whar my Marse Tom is 'bleeged to go,
Warin' short pants and his best coat—
  Lookin' mighty gran', I tell you so?
You'd know? 'Bassadur, he is—
  Bigger'n President, sho' it is!

Golly boy, is you de King
  Warin' all dat lace an' gol',
Powder'haid, an' big brass ring,
  And stuffed wid all de pride you'll hol'?
Well, I 'clar' ter Gord! A sarvin' man!
  And I done think you royal and gran'!

Yes, suh, I'se Unc' Gabe, Marse Page's man,
  I raise dat chile, an' hol' his han'
And tuk him to school, an' writ his books
  And brung him up to min' his looks.
Dey ain' nuffin' dat boy knows
  I ain' put on 'im wid his clo'es.

All de folkses he writ about
  Were 'zackly as I foun' 'em out;
Gordon Keith, Meh Lady, an' Marse Chan,
  Doctor Cary and dat nigger Sam,
Mistress Polly and Jacquelin Gray
  Were fren's o' mine, an' people say
Dat Marse Tom woundn' 'a' got to co'te
  Ef he didn't wrote 'em down jes ez I tho't.

Dar's de King? He sut'nly is quality!
  You tell dat King Marse Tom's as good ez he;
D' ain' nuffin' Ole Ferginyer, I know,
  Better'n our folks is—jes so!

An' w'en America wants her bes'
  Old Ferginyer leads all de res'—
De Presiden', Marse Tom an' me
  Is jes' a few of de quality.
Bow yo' haid, you onnery cuss—
  Dat's Marse Tom a'lookin' at us!

    —ROBERT BRIDGES, "Marse Tom at Co'te,"
      Bkm, Aug. 1913, p. 605

Beginning in 1887, with the sketches and stories of *In Ole Virginia,* he expressed the nostalgia of the Southerners for their lost regime, quite without bitterness towards the North but with little of the objectivity that might have preserved his work for another generation. He was so free from sectional bias that his later tales of the people of Maine might almost have been written by Sarah Orne Jewett, and there was a measure of realism in his stories of the South. He could make fun of the lover of freedom who would not admit that even freedom was as good as it had been "before the war," and he knew how to describe the Virginian who had eyes for a good horse, its muscles, knee-joints, sinews, teeth and gait. He was full of convincing lawyer-talk, like other Southern writers,—Richard Malcolm Johnston, for one example,—who presupposed one's interest in court-procedure; and the character in *Red Rock* at least were sufficiently alive and real,—"everybody's" Cousin Thomasia, the planter, the doctor. Another real character was the rascally overseer who takes over the old place and who pretends that his family, the Stills, are descended from Sir Richard Steele,—so close to the Virginia mind were the days of Queen Anne. Page sketched well the old plantations where harvest, corn-shucking and the holidays alone marked the passage of the quiet seasons, where a strange carriage or a single horseman on the road was an event, and he liked to revive family memories of the Negro cobbler in his tumble-down hut and "Cousin Fanny," who had always sided with the boys. It was she who had taught them their Latin, and after the war, with her old maid's temper, she refused to leave the plantation, ruined as it was. She pottered about on her ancient mare, prowling round the country, visiting disabled Negroes and poor people in the pines.

In all these ways the Virginian Page was a faithful historian of the pre-war South, whose hospitality especially he liked to picture, along with the courtly Negro servants, predestined servants as they appeared, who constantly talked of the quality they had known so well. Often the white folks were seen through their adoring eyes,—a fictional device that was natural enough but owing to which the old society was endowed in the reader's eyes with a preternatural glamour. Miss Charlotte and Marse Chan were notably larger than life when one saw them through the mist of an elderly Negro's devotion, and so was the plantation with the big gate and the carved stone pillars in the great days when there "warn no troubles nor nuttin'." The Negro in question, moreover, was inclined to draw a long bow about his own family connection before the war, how fine the carriages were and how grand was the house and how the darkies there were as thick as weeds. There was no one like an old retainer who had always worn a swallow-tail coat to pile up these effects of baronial splendour, while Page's own mind lent itself to similar illusions and simplifications, saturated as it was with the romantic reading of his childhood. One found too much that was vague and unreal in his portraits of elderly spinsters, merely to call upon whom was like reading Scott, or generals who suggested French field-marshals of the days that Froissart wrote about and who could not have surprised you if you had appeared in armour. But, like the "old gentleman with the black stock" whose metier was to bring lovers together, these characters delighted readers in the nineties and later. They pleased an age that had long forgotten Melville's *Moby-Dick* and was still charmed by Curtis's *Prue and I*.—VAN WYCK BROOKS, "The South," *The Confident Years: 1885–1915*, 1952, pp. 44–45

Thomas Nelson Page is considered one of the most eloquent defenders of the Plantation tradition, and his best known works are tributes to the Old South. The people and legends of Hanover County provide the inspiration for Page's fictional vindication of an aristorcratic society. His fond recollections of old-time Virginians sometimes lead him to depart from psychological realism in his portraits of chivalrous landowners and happy submissive slaves. Such men are spokesmen for a way of life and as individuals are less important than the ideal they represent. Because Page wants to demonstrate the ennobling aspect of a "superior" civilization, he may be guilty of exaggerating the virtues of Dr. Cary in *Red Rock* and of minimizing the reckless behavior of Rupert Gray and Steve Allen in the same novel. Page believes in an ordered society, roughly based on the principles of the Great Chain of Being, but modified by Christian charity and paternalism. He maintains that the harmony of civilization depends upon a stratified society whose leaders are guided by the twin virtues of duty and honor. Any disregard for order or careless evasion of duty threatens the social structure. Page feels that the New South along with the rest of America in the late nineteenth and early twentieth century has failed to provide an upper class worthy of emulation. Page's later novels, *Gordon Keith* and *John Marvel, Assistant*, contain satirical thrusts at American mores following the Civil War. This satirical fiction is not so memeorable as Page's short tales and romantic novels of the Old Dominion,

but it reveals passages of detached and ironical commentary seldom noted by critics. With considerable wit and candor Page ridicules high society in general, especially its rich women and fashionable clergymen.

These are curious subjects for Page to attack since he, himself, played a prominent role in American and European society, was married to an heiress, and had a brother who was an Episcopal clergyman. Still, there is no conflict between Page's personal life and the satirical portraits in his books. He does not condemn the economic system which permits the existence of a leisure class. He criticizes the abuse of leisure and the irresponsibility of socialites who place pleasure before duty. The Southern aristocrat was, according to Page, a talented and hard-working citizen. He was interested in politics and government, protected his family and his slaves, maintained civic order, and supervised the management of his properties. Page asserts that, in contrast, the guiding principle of American business magnates is the accumulation of wealth by any possible means.—KIMBALL KING, "Satirical Portraits by Thomas Nelson Page," *MQ*, Winter 1965–66, pp. 74–75

More than any other writer in late nineteenth-century American literature, Thomas Nelson Page is associated with the plantation tradition, with the recrudescence of an ideal way of life that vanished with the Civil War and Reconstruction. In his finest fiction he recalls a golden age, a time of stability when the South was agrarian and self-contained, and the ruler of the land was the great white planter. Page created a myth that embodied only those characteristics of ante-bellum life he wished to remember, but he projected that myth in forceful and compelling legends which persuaded a generation of readers of their author's accuracy, and which still linger in the popular mind, even though Page's fiction is rarely read today.

Page was a local color writer, with a limited though delicate and often impressive talent. His one contribution to American letters—the evocation of life in Virginia before the war—still remains as a standard of its kind. In its own time its influence on Southern writers was wide-spread and great. "It is hard to explain in simple terms," wrote Grace King in her memoirs, "what Thomas Nelson Page meant to us in the South at that time. He was the first Southern writer to appear in print as a Southerner, and his stories, short and simple, written in Negro dialect, and, I may say, Southern pronunciation, showed with ineffable grace that although we were so bereft, politically, we had now a chance in literature at least."

So typical a statement testifies to Page's historical and esthetic significance, the large and pervasive effect that he had on his contemporaries. Indeed few critics and scholars of his time—Northern as well as Southern—questioned Page's crucial role in American literary history; he was in many ways the literary spokesman of the South during the 1880's and 1890's. The early stories of *In Ole Virginia* (1887), the essays collected in *The Old South* (1892), *The Old Dominion* (1908), and *The Negro: The Southerner's Problem* (1904), represented for the general reader the traditional view of the conservative Southerner. As spokeman, Page attempted to reconcile the two sections in all that he wrote, claiming, in the preface to his collected works, that he had "never wittingly written a line which he did not hope might tend to bring about a better understanding between the North and the South, and finally lead to a more perfect Union."

For today's reader Page's significance is two-fold: first, as the creator of a collection of compelling stories that evoke the old South, that recreate in idealistic and sentimental though poignant terms plantation life as it might have been before the Civil War; and second, as the most lucid and impressive chronicler of a myth of heroism that champions the Southern gentleman, the Southern lady, and inevitably the Southern way of life. More representative perhaps than any post-bellum Southern author of the nineteenth century, Page preserved a plantation legend that, as Arlin Turner points out, "dominates Southern fiction half a century after it took shape in the 1880's" and still "is by no means dead." ⟨. . .⟩

Since his death Page has received less than ideal treatment by most critics; he has either been ignored or relegated to a footnote as one of the important local colorists. But his work deserves more extensive examination. Historically Page's fiction and essays reveal the typical attitudes of the nineteenth-century Southern conservative and offer a reasoned point of view that is still very real in American politics and life today.

Esthetically Page is of less significance. Most of his fiction is burdened by traditional sentimentality, by a rigid point of view that causes him to polarize the various character types in his work. "My design," he explained, "is to picture Life as it appeals to me and as it appears to me, and to show that whatever the hardships may be, it is after all worth living." Consequently, most of his heroes are heroic beyond belief and his villains are ludicrous contrasts, the stock types of popular Romance. In fiction like *Gordon Keith* and *John Marvel, Assistant*, where the locale is not the South and the subject is not the death of ante-bellum civilization, Page is as maudlin and predictable as most sentimental writers. In *Red Rock* and other works which deal with the post-bellum South and racial problems, he yields too easily to the formula of reconciliation; he converts his tales into tendentious propaganda that is often artistically inorganic. From all that he wrote—from the great number of essays and novels, stories and sketches, poems, plays, and addresses—there remain a few minor masterpieces: "Marse Chan," "Unc' Edinburg's Drowndin'," "Meh Lady," and "Ole 'Stracted." These poignant tales offer a unique and memorable vision of idealized plantation life in the ante-bellum South at the moment of its decline; as such they are "the epitaph of a civilization," and belong among the small but original achievements in American literature.—THEODORE L. GROSS, "Thomas Nelson Page: Creator of a Virginia Classic," GR, Fall 1966, pp. 338–39, 350–51

LUCINDA H. MACKETHAN
From "Thomas Nelson Page:
The Plantation as Arcady"

Virginia Quarterly Review, Spring 1978, pp. 317–32

II

The three aspects of the antebellum world which Page turned into staples of his Arcadia were the plantation locale itself with the great house at the center; the image of the Southern gentleman; and most important, the "old time" Negro, the slave or "servant" as Page calls him, through whose voice the Old South achieves mythic status. Taking up these points as they appear in Page's major works, we begin, as almost all of his descriptions of plantation life begin, with the planter's home, which was for Page the hub of the universe. It is of interest to note that most of Page's stories and novels, and the essays dealing with Southern culture as well, contain, near their beginning, a fairly thorough account of the home occupied by the hero or heroine, and at any time in the stories the threat of the loss of that home portends a tragedy of major proportions.

One of Page's most lyrical panegyrics to the Old South is entitled "Social Life in Old Virginia before the War." The

essay begins with a description of Oakland, his own boyhood home. With few alterations, Oakland could serve as the setting for almost all of Page's plantation stories. The striking quality of his description of the house is his orderly arrangement of the picturesque scene into a composite that contains all the elements which he cherished about the Old South. "Oakland" is notable for the plainness of its construction; there is a quaintness in its design, a "manliness" about its offices and quarters, a special dignity in the way it is set among historic oaks, and an ineffable grace showing through the orchards and gardens that flourish on the grounds. When Page called again on his memories of Oakland to provide the setting for *Two Little Confederates*, his description emphasized two qualities: an excellence based on simplicity and a beauty based on older and, by implication, surer standards: "It was not a handsome place, as modern ideas go, but down in Old Virginia, where the standard was different from the later one, it passed in the old times as one of the best plantations in all that region."

When we read any of Page's stories of the Old South, we are made aware that his locales are charged with special significance. Every story contains reference, often extended, to the homes of the leading characters. And it is through these descriptions that Page is establishing the credentials of his heroes—if they come from a fine plantation, they are almost invariably of high moral quality and deserve universal admiration. A study of the stories in Page's first volume, *In Ole Virginia*, reveals that the plantation homes described are uniformly designed to be outward and visible signs of the spirit of the people who settled the Southern region and created an aristocratic utopia out of a wilderness. In these early stories, the preservation of the old estates represents for those involved in it an effort to maintain the nation's only remaining stronghold of non-material values.

In Page's first story, "Marse Chan," the white narrator, a stranger to the Southern locale he is visiting, is struck immediately by the atmosphere surrounding the "once splendid mansions" which seem to him, in their "proud seclusion," to indicate that "Distance was nothing to this people; time was of no consequence to them. They desired but a level path in life, and that they had, though the way was longer, and the outer world strode by them as they dreamed." The outer world is always somewhere beyond the settings that Page uses for the stories in *In Ole Virginia*. The pertinent action in most of them takes place before the Civil War, so that the serenity of the scene is not disturbed, although the sense of impending destruction is always present. It is of this world that Page's most famous narrative spokesman, the venerable Unc' Sam of "Marse Chan," says: "Dem wuz good ole times, marster—de bes' Sam ever see!"

In the story "Meh Lady," the sense of place is the strong motivating force by which a young Virginia belle and her faithful retainers struggle to maintain a home constantly threatened by Yankees or carpetbaggers. To leave the plantation, it is implied, would be death. After the war Meh Lady's estate stands as a small, embattled island where the old values and sense of pride are being defended against the rude forces of change.

The story in *In Ole Virginia* which least meets with Page's idea of normal conditions of plantation life is "No Haid Pawn." The plantation with the weird name "No Haid Pawn" is the antithesis of Oakland and the estates described in Page's other stories. Page wants to show here what happens to the plantation ideal when unworthy beings attempt to imitate its concepts. No Haid Pawn was built by strangers to the area, men of Creole blood who "never made it their permanent home. Thus, no ties either of blood or friendship were formed with their neighbors, who were certainly open-hearted enough to overcome anything but the most persistent unneighborliness."

Because they are not Anglo-Saxons reared in the Virginia manner, the owners of No Haid Pawn build a mansion totally out of keeping with what was expected from the true plantation house. An unhealthy atmosphere surrounds the place from the very beginning, and eventually, in what was probably an attempt to copy the fate of Poe's House of Usher, Page allows nature to reclaim what the evil Creoles forfeited by their lack of morality and their disdain for the customs of the community. In this respect, the story offers some interesting parallels to Faulkner's treatment of "Sutpen's Hundred" in *Absalom, Absalom!* In "No Haid Pawn," Page experimented with a new kind of atmosphere and setting, yet he ended by re-emphasizing a cardinal principle applied to all his plantations; that is, the place reflects its owner and thus the *true* plantation will symbolize and proclaim the ethical superiority of its inhabitants.

Page's most successful novel, *Red Rock*, contains an interesting treatment of the kind of values that the plantation represented for him. "Red Rock" is the name of a Southern estate which, like Page's own Oakland, is full of the history, memories, and the pride of its owners. In *Red Rock*, Page tells the standard Southern version of Reconstruction as he chronicles his heroes' loss of their homes to scalawags and carpetbaggers. Thrown into a world in which money is the new standard of power and influence, the Southern gentry are almost completely helpless. Their plantations, Page would have us believe, were never operated for profit but only for the purpose of upholding the lifestyle of the gentlemen who maintained them. The plot of *Red Rock* tells how several old Virginia plantations were lost after the Civil War through the virtuous naïvety of their owners, and how eventually right conquers might, so that the plantations are restored to the only people who deserve them.

The real threat to Red Rock and other places like it is defined by Page's chief spokesman in the novel, Dr. Cary, who points out that the enemy is not just the Yankee. "We are at war now," Dr. Cary tells the townspeople, "with the greatest power on earth: the power of universal progress. It is not the North we shall have to fight, but the world." Dr. Cary announces the South's last stand but recognizes the battle is a hopeless one. "From having been one of the most quiet, peaceful and conservative corners of the universe," Red Rock's county becomes, at the mere rumor of hostilities, a scene of "almost metropolitan activity," and the old world can never be the same again. ⟨. . .⟩

IV

The Negros of *In Ole Virginia* are the most important figures that Page produced in his fiction. Not only are they more lifelike than the white heroes he created, but also they carry the chief responsibility for making and proving his arguments about the benevolence of race relations in the Old South. This is not to say that the Negro as Page presents him is not a stereotype, but only that Page, in conceptualizing the Old South darky, felt free to be more imaginative and less dogmatic than he was with his Old South gentlemen, and the result is that his black men usually have much greater appeal than his whites. Page lost some of his inhibitions when he used the voice of the Negro to tell his tales. They still preach his personal philosophy, but they do so in a way that enlarges and to some degree changes our vision of the world that he wanted us to see.

Sam, the old black freedman who was companion and

servant to Page's Marse Chan, expresses the crux of Southern race relations in refreshing terms; speaking to his master's dog, he says, "Yo' so sp'ilt yo' kyahn hardly walk. . . . Jus' like white folks—think 'cus you's white and I's black, I got to wait on yo' all de time." The old servant's pointed remark, however, is meant to be more of a joke on himself than a criticism of white attitudes, as his subsequent actions show. The dog is treated with all the respect and favor due a monarch, simply because he once belonged, as did Sam himself, to the beloved Marse Chan. The fact that Sam was, by the sheer fact of his black skin, a slave, does not bother him at all. Actually he longs pitifully for the time when "Niggers didn' hed nothin' 't all to do—jes' hed to 'ten to de feedin' an' cleanin' de hosses, an' doin' what marster tell 'em to do."

Page's fiction was designed to dramatize his racial views, and his stories became in fact his most effective tool for displaying what he felt was the true case concerning the relationship between whites and blacks which had once existed and could again exist in the South. Francis Pendleton Gaines points out that Page's Negroes feel a "not incongruous dignity" at being included as members of the plantation family. Page's argument was that the slave enjoyed a secure place in life and a certain sense of status through his bondage. Only by being a slave could he participate in the exclusive world of the planter, yet his gratitude for the opportunity was nevertheless unbounded.

Such is the case with Sam when he is given to his young master in "Marse Chan." Sam relates with pride what was for him the greatest moment in his life, when "ole marster" singled him out: "An den he sez: 'Now Sam, from dis time you belong to yo' young Marse Channin'; I want you to tek keer on im ez long ez he lives. You are to be his boy from dis time. . . .' And from dat time I was tooken in de house to be Marse Channin's body servant."

Page was trying to make the point in "Marse Chan" that it would have been better for Sam if slavery had never ended, but for the modern reader Sam's description of all the wonders of the old time cannot disguise the fact that his present misery is the direct result of his having been made, at birth, totally dependent on a way of life which could not save either him or itself from destruction. Of course, Sam sees nothing of this, and his account of his existence before the war is meant to be an uncritical defense of the old regime, one that would put to rout the image left by Harriet Beecher Stowe's Uncle Tom. This it managed to do more effectively than even Page could have hoped, as witnessed by the reported spectacle of the abolitionist, Thomas Wentworth Higginson, weeping over Sam's description of Marse Chan's untimely death.

There is more pathos in Marse Chan's death than simply the fact that it keeps him from being reconciled with his true love. He dies in a war that he opposed in order to defend a system already doomed. And in spite of his brotherly regard for Sam, and Sam's undying loyalty to him, he is unable to provide for his slave's future. The result is a pathetic figure whom Page devised in order to praise the Old South, but who also reveals, all unconsciously, the plantation's inherent weaknesses.

The situation of Unc' Billy in "Meh Lady" is not as pathetic as that of the other Negro narrators in *In Ole Virginia*. For him, the old world manages to be retained on his plantation through the auspices of a former Northern soldier (with Virginia ancestors, Page hastens to inform us) who returns after the war to win the hand of Meh Lady and restore her home to its elegance. Viewing the reconciled pair of lovers, who represented for Page's readers an idyllic reunion of North and South, Unc Billy sits with "de moon sort o' meltin' over de yard," and thinks "hit 'pear like de plantation 'live once mo', an' de ain' no mo scufflin', an' de ole times done come back agin."

It is fitting that, at the wedding of Meh Lady and her lover, Billy takes the responsibility unasked when the minister requests someone to give the bride away. His reasoning is simple and yet full of dignity: "an' I don' know huccome 'twuz, but I think 'bout Marse Jeems an' Mistis when he ax me dat, an' Marse Phil, whar all dead, an' all de scufflin' we done been th'oo, an' how de chile ain' got nobody to teck her part now 'sep' jes' me; an' . . . I 'bleeged to speak up, I jes' step for'ard an' say: 'Old Billy.'" Although Billy achieves a great deal of stature in this scene, his explantion nevertheless borders on being an apology for his presumption, and Page is quick to put him back in his place as simple darky.

There is one story in *In Ole Virginia* which differs from the rest in its focus and its message. Although not told from a Negro's point of view, the central character is a Negro whose tragic situation is not minimized by any of Page's usual propaganda of white benevolence. "Ole 'Stracted," in the story of that title, is a former slave who had been sold many years before to help to pay off his master's debts. His wife and child were sold elsewhere, and the old black man lives only to be reunited with his master, who had promised to buy him back with his family. Though he has no memory of anything that has happened to him since the sale, he has made his way back to his plantation, which is now in ruins and is owned by "po' white trash." The old man's only identity is bound up in his belief that his master is coming for him. Thus he spends his time dreaming "of a great plantation, and fine carriages and horses, and a house with his wife and the boy."

Ole 'Stracted's hopeless fantasy is matched by the far more compelling dream of a young neighbor who turns out to be the old black man's son. Ephraim is a freedman trying with dignity against impossible odds to make a good living for his wife and family. In spite of the new sort of potential here, there are still some of the standard biases. It is a poor white and certainly not a Southern gentleman who victimizes Ephraim, and Ole 'Stracted never considers freedom a favorable alternative to the idyllic conditions he knew as a slave—the point is never made that the plantation system was responsible for separating him from his family in the first place. But Ephraim is a different kind of Negro from those whom Page had treated sympathetically in his other stories.

Ephraim's dream, like his father's, is of a Southern Arcady, but his is based on a future which holds dignity and self-sufficiency for his family, while Ole 'Stracted's is based on his memories of a time when his master provided for him. Ephraim has a recurring vision "in which he saw corn stand so high and rank over his land that he could scarcely distinguish the stalk, and a stable and barn and a mule . . . and two cows which his wife would milk, and a green wagon driven by his boys . . ." (149–50), in which, in short, he would be a prosperous farmer sustaining himself and his family through his own labors on his own land.

This dream is a simple one which involves all of Ephraim's energy and keeps his hopes alive. It is one which Page lets us feel Ephraim has every right to realize, and this is what makes "Ole 'Stracted" so different from the other stories of his first collection. Page's usual attitude toward the freedman is one of scorn concerning the "new issue nigger" who does not have the proper respect for the old values. He frequently advised that the freedman should turn to his master for guidance and remain dependent on the white man until some vague future time when his race might finally "deserve" to govern themselves. In this one story, however, he seems to admit the justice of a plan whereby the Negro could take his life into his own hands through owning and working his land.

Page's story, despite the sympathy it gives to Ephraim's dream, finally demonstrates that the young freedman's hopes are as futile as his father's belief that his master will find him. Ephraim and his wife do not own their land, and never in a lifetime of sweating in the fields and taking in washing could they hope to earn enough to buy it. Everything they can possibly raise goes to pay their rent to the white man who lives on the hill. Page has sympathy, but in the story, as well as in the essays he devoted to solving the "Negro Question," he has few practical ideas as to how the Negro could maintain his self-respect and achieve his dreams in a white man's world. Yet Page evidently could not bear the indictment of the old world that his story implied, so he got himself off the hook through a fortuitous, if improbable, coincidence of the kind that he uses to resolve most of the potentially tragic situations in his works. The money that Ole 'Stracted has saved to buy back his wife and son goes at his death to Ephraim, who discovers just in time that the feeble-minded old man is his father. Thus he can buy his land and make his dream come true.

Page's conclusion is not a solution but an evasion of the implications of his story. The most disturbing element about "Ole 'Stracted" is that it appears in the same volume with "Marse Chan" and "Meh Lady," stories in which the Negroes themselves sing the praises of the system that causes all of the suffering in "Ole 'Stracted." Even Ole 'Stracted longs for the past, however; his energies have always been fixed on the idea that his master will save him, so he is incapable of doing anything to save himself.

The situation of the black man in Page's pastoral kingdom is ambiguous at best, though it was clearly the author's intention to depict plantation life as the ideal mode of existence for both master and slave. His black spokesmen are meant to illustrate that Negroes and whites, in the old and better world, were united in their pursuits and purposes. In taking this stand, Page carves an image of the white man as the hero of Arcady, dedicated to preserving a civilization perfect in its innocence and magnificent in its program for the good life. His Negroes, however, remain his most compelling creations, as characters lost in a new world and from their longings creating the myth of a world which fulfills their need for identity and purpose.

That Page never consciously explored the flaws of the Old South, that he failed to see the ambiguities of his own recreations of the plantation as an ideal world, is only too clear a fact. His intention was not to hide the sins of the past, for indeed, he was blind to them himself. What he hoped to accomplish was to challenge the practices of the present by comparing them in art to the customs of a simpler, more natural time. Thus his stories have the force of a pastoral rebuke, and they also have the even more compelling force of a dream. Page created out of his own deep convictions a romantic world whose charm at times overshadows the realist's demand for a counterbalancing acknowledgement of truths based purely on fact. We return from Page's fiction to the real world very much aware that his vision is marred, yet also aware that as dreams go, the one Page fashioned for the Old South was convincing enough to give force to a myth that has itself shaped many realities and outlasted many others.

GRACE PALEY

1922–

Grace Paley, short-story writer, was born in the Bronx, New York City, on December 11, 1922. The daughter of Isaac Goodside, a doctor, she was educated at city schools and colleges, attending Evander Childs High School and, in 1938 and 1939, Hunter College. Although she later took courses at New York University and studied poetry with W. H. Auden at the New School for Social Research, she did not ever earn a college degree, since she had little interest in formal academic study. In 1942, at the age of nineteen, she married Jess Paley, a motion-picture cameraman. They had two children and were divorced over twenty years later.

Paley began writing in the mid-1950s. Her stories, which are largely about New York life and have been praised for their humor and original style, have been published in three collections: *The Little Disturbances of Man* (1959), *Enormous Changes at the Last Minute* (1975), and *Later the Same Day* (1985). In addition, passages from an uncompleted novel appeared in little magazines in the 1960s. She has been accused of sacrificing her writing to her political activity; she is particularly involved in feminist and anti-war causes.

Paley has also been a teacher since the early 1960s, when she taught at Columbia and Syracuse Universities; presently she lives in Manhattan with her second husband Robert Nichols, and teaches at Sarah Lawrence in Bronxville, New York.

Personal

Q: Does your reading influence your writing a lot?

A: I used to read a lot more than I read. For years I was what was called a big reader. Now I read a lot less. I think that everything I ever read is very influential on my writing and by that I mean the stuff you read from a very early age. The poets I read had a strong influence on me. But I think when we talk about influences we omit some of the most important influences on our writing, and they're never discussed really, and they're not literary at all. It may be why I feel close to Russian writers. It's because that's the language of my father and mother. So one of the major influences on my writing, I feel, is the street in which I grew up. I was out in it all the time. And the language of my family which was English and Russian and some Yiddish running back and forth a lot at great speed, and the life they talked about, the life they led. That language that I heard, and the language of the street, of the kids and also of the grown ups, who hung out in the street a lot in those days, that was as great an influence on my writing as anything I've read. As for form, that's another thing. I'm just like anyone my age. I read a lot of Joyce when I was a kid and those stories probably had a lot to do with my first ideas of form. I read a lot of Chekhov. I think those old things have influence. I don't think that anything you read . . . now, can strongly influence you, it can superficially do so but not really deeply.

Q: Can you talk about the writing process in terms of your thinking? Do you "think on the page"? Do you do a lot of thinking about something before you begin to write? Or do you discover it as you write?

A: Well, I begin by writing something, and I just write it, and I may not even look at it for the next two years. So I have a lot of pages lying around. When I finish a story I start going through all my pages. I have all these pages. Some of them, I'm amazed to see, are part of what I'm thinking about. We have this one head, so everything is just in there all the time. You write a few pages and then you . . . go away. . . . Which is, again, the distractable way that I work and it's not to be construed as a decent or honourable way of doing things [*laughter*] but I do think about things a long long time. When I'm really into a story I work very very hard on it. People ask me, How do you know when it's at an end? I just thought last

week what was the answer: I know I'm at the end when I say to myself, How'm I going to end this thing? When I think I've finished it I then begin to go over it and I go over it for falsity mostly, and for lies. I just revise. I just think of it in those terms. I don't want anybody to think I just write when I feel like it, especially who are going to go into that line of work. You write also when you don't feel like it. It really is such hard work that if you are naturally lazy, like I am, you often feel like it, so you have to keep that in mind.

Q: What do you think are the most commonly encountered lies that come up in your work?

A: Wanting certain characters to be something, or pushing them around. You get stuck with your own examples of things. The example I always use is how I got stuck giving some guy the wrong job. I was working on this story for a very long time and I just couldn't move ahead on it, and the reason was I'd given him the wrong job. He really was a taxi-driver and I think I gave him some sort of administrative responsibility somewhere. [*Laughter*] It really was bad, but until I realized that . . . I'd call that a lie. I wanted him in an office, you know? But once I'd got him out of the office, because he didn't belong there, then a lot of other things changed. There are other kinds of lies too. There are lies of language where you exaggerate, or put in a lot of adjectives, or you try to be high styled, or you try to be up-to-the-minute with what's being done. Those are lies. You can go through a story again and again and again until you can't change it any more, and then at the end . . . don't think in terms, is this story good or bad, you know? Because you never will know. What you can think about is whether it's true as you can make it. And then even if you think it's bad, you're probably wrong. "Oh, this lousy story I just finished." But it's what I had to say, and it's what I said, and everything in it is truly invented and true . . . then you probably have a good story.

Q: Could you say something about humour in short stories?

A: The only thing I can say about humour is that if you're not funny you can't be. [*Laughter*] But did you want me to say something more serious about it? [*Laughter*] Humour I think by its very nature is out of place. I mean that. You have humour when you have great disparity.—GRACE PALEY,

Interview by Alan Burns, Charles Sugnet, *The Imagination on Trial*, 1971, pp. 130–32

Works

THE LITTLE DISTURBANCES OF MAN

The glad tidings from this reviewer's corner are of the appearance of a newcomer possessed of an all-too-infrequent literary virtue—the comic vision. Grace Paley is the writer, and heretofore, apparently, her light has been confined to some of the smaller quarterlies. Now, however, *The Little Disturbances of Man* brings together ten of her short stories, and a welcome event it is. While they may not, to be sure, fully satisfy confirmed plot-watchers, they are by no means simply "mood" stories—rather, they are marked throughout by a well-defined and artfully guileless form of narrative progression. But the heart of the matter in these tales is their serio-comic stance: character revealed through the wry devices that man contrives, consciously and unconsciously, to shore up his uncertain existence and, sometimes, to salvage laughter from lamentation.

In "The Loudest Voice," for example, the Paley approach is glimpsed in the reaction of a Jewish immigrant to his wife's horrified announcement that their child is to be in a Christmas—a *Christian*—play. "You're in America," the husband retorts. "In Palestine the Arabs would be eating you alive. Europe you had pogroms. Argentina is full of Indians. Here you got Christmas." Or in the lyrically risible opening of "The Contest"—"Up early or late, it never matters, the day gets away from me. Summer or winter, the shade of trees or their hard shadow, I never get into my Rice Krispies till noon."

The people in these tales exist on the far periphery of the Important world; and the themes are as the title states: the little disturbances of man—"little" vis-à-vis cosmic catastrophes, but major to the personal business of daily living. A middle-aging, sanguine-spirited "bachelor girl" recollects an amorous past on the eve of her marriage to a long-ago beau; a determined teen-ager cons a bemused young soldier into a thoroughly entangling alliance; a husband-abandoned wife and mother wait out the idolized prodigal's return, imperturbably confident; a pixilated youth who lives in a philodendron-decorated automobile and functions as a kind of curb-service problem consultant; a girl's long, frustrated need for love is examined from her own viewpoint—and from the viewpoint of the man she wants. These are a few of the characters who move through the oblique human comedy of Mrs. Paley's stories. Small-time people, in terms of the world worldly, they none the less reflect the perdurable instinct of most people everywhere to improvise ways and means of accepting the indifferent universe.—PATRICIA MacMANUS, "Laughter from Tears," *NYTBR*, Apr. 19, 1959, pp. 28–29

Grace Paley's collection of short stories, *The Little Disturbances of Man*, has recently been reissued by the Viking Press, nine years after its original hard cover publication by Doubleday, eight years after the Meridian reprint edition, and two or three years after it went out of print or otherwise became impossible to find, to the consternation, I imagine, of a few more readers than myself. I owned the book on three separate occasions and lent it away each time, was more pleased than not when it failed to come back twice, for I knew where it was, or where it wasn't—the temptation to spread the glad tidings is stronger with this book than with most, and in both instances, when I thought to check, it was far from the hands into which I'd placed it. The third time, when trips to several bookshops failed to turn it up, I felt less charitable; I felt, in fact, a sense of loss which was not even assuaged by occasional encounters with the author; with Grace Paley, as with no other writer I have known, such solace was at least a possibility, for her voice, manner, *style*, are hardly different in the flesh as on the page. This correspondence is so nearly perfect that when I met her accidentally during the march on the Pentagon last October, the woman I was with, who did not know her but had read her book, was able to identify Grace from a fragment, a most unliterary snatch of dialogue.

This is not so much a matter of language, which in her work has been justly praised as subtle, fanciful, energetic, wild, and undeniably unique, while in conversation she will come across as straight and true as your (good) mother or mine, but results rather from a rare identity of her mode of expression and her deepest concerns, or put the other way, from an absence of scrims, of "style" in its least happy sense—as a barrier between the way a writer lives in the world, and the way he puts it down. The ten stories in *The Little Disturbances of Man* explore the levels of feeling and turmoil beneath the "little disturbances" of our lives in a variety of ways, from many points of view. By turns, often at once, the stories give quirky, anguished, funny, loving, deep and antic glimpses into the hearts and lives of children, mothers, lovers, spouses divorced and abandoned, the ageing and the old, in a prose as resilient and unpredictable as one imagines the fate of her characters to be at any story's end, no matter how often one has read it.

Yet when I asked the author not long ago, in connection with the reissue of her book and the piece I might do about this glad event, to say a word about her fiction, or about the impulse which led her to write the kind of thing she does after her beginnings as a poet, she could say, "I felt bad about men and women," and with that profoundly simple remark, worthy of a number of the living, bleeding humans who inhabit her pages, she could illumine the connection I have been trying to describe: that she lived precisely where she worked, wrote out of the heart of her perplexity and sense of wonder at the countless ways we have for dealing with each other, her grief that it so often turns out so badly, joy all the greater because less often found.

It is a sticky painful way to write, and the very excellence of the result, the moving, honest, somehow *unbreakable* quality of her stories, seemed, to some, sufficient explanation of why, in the years following the book's first appearance, Grace Paley produced so little else. She was known to be "working on a novel," and, indeed, sections of it would appear in magazines from time to time—in the defunct *noble savage*, in the first issue of *New American Review*—but of shorter pieces there were few, and these very short, and rather playful. Those whose task this is began to mourn her as one of the mysterious casualties of the literary life—writers who give us a brilliant first work of fiction and then falter, or are heard from no more. (I have often wondered how that latter judgment, this side the grave, is ever arrived at. Even a writer like Anatole Broyard, whose story "What the Cystoscope Said" is as powerful today as when it first appeared in *discovery*, 14 years ago, but who has published, to my knowledge, only one much slighter story since, and has lately begun to turn up in the pages of various journals passing usually sour judgments on the work of others, even he, next week or year, can confound the gloomiest expectations.)

But during her literary lean years, Grace Paley's life was fat. She gave to the roles of wife and mother the profound, existential attention her readers would have been able to predict. She was among the earliest and fiercest agitators against the grisly treatment afforded inmates of Greenwich

Village's Women's House of Detention, her human and political involvement in this and other "community" matters widening along with the war in Vietnam to the point where she was and remains in the thick of resistance to that bizarre, bloody conflict, and to the Administration which continues to wage it. Operating out of the Greenwich Village Peace Center, she is an indefatigable pamphleteer and hander-out of leaflets, was among the signers of the Writers and Editors War Tax Protest, is an active member of both the local and national committees of *Resist*, in which connection she was arrested, not for the first time, during the pre-dawn gathering at the induction center on Whitehall Street last December, for voicing particularly vociferous objection to the tactics of the police, and she saved a few young heads from being broken in the process.

For the past several years she has been giving courses in the short story, at Columbia, at Syracuse, and at Sarah Lawrence (where she teaches still). Her classes at Columbia, when I was there, were always oversubscribed, her students full of praise of her and an eagerness to work. Whatever the often justifiable criticisms made of "creative writing" courses, it was easy to see that something was being transmitted during that particular once-weekly two-hour stretch which was not listed in the catelogue: that Grace Paley was able—probably, she had no choice—to gift her students with herself.

And what of her novel? The signs are that it will be along. Lately, in the midst of all busyness, she has begun to publish again. In the past several months, first-rate short fiction has appeared in the *Atlantic* and in *Esquire*, as well as the aforementioned excerpt from her novel in *New American Review*. One wants to exhort the pundits to fight back the crocodile tears, and have a little patience.

Meanwhile, as we wait, the Viking edition of *The Little Disturbances of Man* has come out to tide us over.—IVAN GOLD, "On Having Grace Paley Once More among Us," *Com*, Oct. 25, 1968, pp. 111–12

ENORMOUS CHANGES AT THE LAST MINUTE

When Grace Paley's first collection of stories, *The Little Disturbances of Man*, appeared in 1959, it was clear at once that a fresh writing talent had presented itself. While her subject matter—the frantic life of urban men and women, mostly Jews, in and around the West Village—was hardly new, her style was very much her own. She wrote like the ultimate *yenta*, Molly Goldberg raised to a fine art without losing her roots in oral speech, and the stories she told were splendidly suited to her style, being mostly tales of feminine woe of the kind that would set Molly Goldberg's tongue wagging—women abandoned by husbands, women caring for small kids in airless flats, and in the best of the tales in that first book, "Goodbye and Good Luck," a woman kept by a celebrated actor of the Yiddish theater. In this triumph of style, a conventional story of a young girl and an older man is turned into a comic routine with a happy ending.

But a comic routine isn't even a three-act Neil Simon play, and a virtuoso style has its own pitfalls, more obvious in Paley's new collection, *Enormous Changes at the Last Minute*, which reprints a generous selection of her work from the past 15 years. The setting is the same—the increasingly grimy and decaying streets of Manhattan and Brooklyn—and many of the same characters appear for a second turn, most notably Johnny Raftery and Ginny, and piecemeal Faith with her boys Richard and Tonto—while the style is, if anything, more dazzling than ever.

The question is: to what purpose so much bedazzlement?

And the answer, I think, is: to keep the stories from sinking into the quicksands of their own misery. For even with the glitter of its style, over which Paley skates like some Olympic champion of language, *Enormous Changes* is a book of losses and failures that add up to one of the most depressing works of fiction to be published in the last decade, hardly a time noted for the prevalence of upbeat writing.

First there's the setting. Paley knows what travel writers and eager young things don't want to see, that New York is a city of failures. Of course there are successful ones, more than a handful, dwellers in certain East Side blocks, luxury apartments and Fifth Avenue cooperatives, but they're the cream, 500,000 skimmed off the 6.5 million others huddled in cramped tenements, clustered in Lefrak City's human hive, or wiping the venetian blinds in antique brick semidetached houses clinging to the edges of the city in Canarsie or Staten Island.

These failures are Paley's people and the inhabitants of her stories, especially the mothers who sit lumpily on park benches so that their pasty-faced children will get as much of the sun as the smog-ridden parks can attract. And they are going nowhere but home to kitchens of sour milk and roaches, a fact they try to disguise with all the jauntiness they can muster, a true New York salesman's jauntiness, like the diamond pinky ring flashed to conceal the too-shiny suit and the shirt with a frayed collar.

But beneath that jauntiness, which is Paley's style, the stories sag into consistent failure. Poor blonde Faith, who moves easily from the first collection to the second and takes on a more detailed existence, finds no way out of her impasse as an aging divorcée with two sons growing up and away from her, sans career or even a job to lend her identity. A young friend of hers dies. Her childhood neighborhood has been taken over by blacks who consume even her memories. Ahead is only the old age of her parents.

Death and old age are, in fact, the leitmotifs of this collection, even when young people are featured. Paley can't imagine any public stage for them to act upon and she has lost confidence in the ability of private passions to assure happiness. Nor is it a dilemma imagined for the sake of plot—put 'em in a box and watch 'em get out again. Most of Paley's stories are too short for any plot. They're quick sketches, blackouts, comic monologues spoken in a theater bereft of audience by a voice increasingly desperate for coherence.

Finally though, there isn't any coherence, or nothing more substantial than the style, to which we return in the absence of anything else that will reward our attention. One of her characters exclaims, "Tragedy! . . . When will you look it in the face?" But it's not tragedy that weighs down these stories, it's no more than despair and repetition. Tragedy suggests depths and alternatives and is built into a world of choices. Paley's world, while a plausible look at the way we live now, is severely limited, the world as given, without any imagined alternatives, only endless vistas of crumbling buildings, bedrooms opening onto air shafts, and a phalanx of old people's homes rimming the boardwalk where young people frolicked so long ago that even the memory of such happy days can barely be clutched from the darkening air.—MICHELLE MURRAY, *NR*, March 16, 1974, p. 27

Enormous Changes at the Last Minute is not, as advertised by some reviewers, inferior to *The Little Disturbances of Man*. It is a different book by the same author (who, changed by life and time, is also a little different here), a continuation of the other, a further exploration. Where Grace Paley's first book, for all its originality and surprise, is a collection of by and large traditionally made stories, the second is made up of a number of seeming fragments, an indication not of haste ("art is too long and life is too short," the author modestly tells us), but of a distillation of materials, a more daring openness of form. Paley's titles, The Little *Disturbances of Man* (emphasis mine) and Enormous *Changes at the Last Minute*, playing off the first, refer to size in an exaggerated, essentially ironic way. The author's characterization of what she's about, an occasion for the literal-minded to complain she has not given us the major (meaning large) work we've been led to expect, is a little like Cordelia's representation of her love to her father. Paley is often at her best in *Enormous Changes*—her fiction at its most consequential—in the smallest space.

In *Enormous Changes*, as in the first collection, Paley writes about families, about lost and found love, about divorce, death, ongoing life—the most risky and important themes—in a style in which words count for much, sometimes for almost all. The stories—in some cases, the same stories—deal on the one hand with their own invention and, on the other, profoundly (and comically) with felt experience. In this sense, and in a wholly unschematic way, Paley combines what has been called the "tradition of new fiction" in America with the abiding concerns of the old.

Grace Paley's stories resist the intrusion of critical language about them, make it seem, no matter what, irrelevant and excessive. The stories are hard to write about because what they translate into has little relation, less than most explication, to what they are: themselves, transformed events of the imagination. The voice of Paley's fiction—quirky, tough, wise-ass, vulnerable, bruised into wisdom by the knocks of experience—is the triumph and defining characteristic of her art.

"An Interest in Life," probably the best piece in *The Little Disturbances of Man*, and one of the best American stories of the past twenty-five years, illustrates Paley's mode. A story initially about a husband's desertion of a wife and four children, it opens: "My husband gave me a broom one Christmas. This wasn't right. No one can tell me it was meant kindly." The matter-of-fact, ironic voice of the protagonist, Ginny, distances the reader from the conventions of her pathos, makes light of easy sentiment, only to bring us, unburdened by melodrama, to an awareness of the character as if someone known to us intimately for a long time. Ginny, in a desperate moment, writes out a list of her troubles to get on the radio show, "Strike it Rich." When she shows the list to John Raftery, a returned former suitor unhappily married to someone else, he points out to her that her troubles are insufficient, merely "the little disturbances of man." Paley's comic stories deal in exaggerated understatement, disguise their considerable ambition in the modesty of wit.

"Distance" in *Emormous Changes at the Last Minute* is a retelling of some of the materials of "An Interest in Life" through the self-justifying (also self-denying) point of view of Ginny's officious neighbor, Mrs. Raftery. "You would certainly be glad to meet me," Mrs. Raftery introduces herself, "I was the lady who appreciated youth." The victories Mrs. Raftery claims for herself are undermined by events, defeated by her own story. "Distance" begins in self-assertion and ends with the narrator's loneliness and mystification.

Time, or the shortness of time, is at issue in almost all of the stories in the new collection. "Debts" is about the obligations writers have, or that the narrator feels writers ought to have, to keep the people close to them alive by giving voice to their stories and the stories of their families. It is an impossible obligation—impossible like the "wants" of the story of that title—which the narrator tries hopelessly (and successfully) to fulfill.

In "Wants," the narrator returns two overdue books to the library—the books overdue for eighteen years—and meets a former husband; the meeting and conversation are like a creation of the narrator's imagination, a day dream or obsessive fantasy. What comes out of it for the woman is a catalogue of her failures—her best intentions, her "wants" defeated by fleeting time and the ordinary, quirky circumstances of a life. The occasion for "Wants" is metaphoric, its details hyperbolic, but the story touches us through its humanity and perception—Paley's vision like nothing else—as strongly as if it were taking place in that literary convention we call the "real world."

An improvisatory casualness is another of the disguises of Paley's fiction. A high degree of technical sophistication is its true condition. Paley's stories rarely insist on their own achievement, deny their own audacity, her craft to cover its own traces. To say that Paley is knowing as a writer is not to imply that her work relies in any way, obvious or subtle, on formula. Each of Paley's stories is a separate discovery, as if she begins again each time out to learn what it is to make a story.

Themes and characters move into one another from story to story. Life is too short, moving too quickly (all of us going in private directions) to do all the things one means to do. "Living" is about a missed connection, about the distraction of being caught up in one's own life. At the start, a friend, Ellen, calls Faith, the narrator of the story, to announce that she's dying. Faith reports, not altogether metaphorically, that she's dying too. Ellen dies; Faith recovers, her own dying (and living) precluding involvement in Ellen's. At the end, Faith comes to an abrupt realization of her friend's death and, correspondingly, the implications of her own survival. The economy of the story—it runs barely two and a half pages—makes it all the more powerful, avoiding, as Paley almost always does, easy emotional appeals or inflated sentiment.

"The Burdened Man" also deals with survival and renewal. A man, anxious about money, which is to say loss of self, becomes friends, outgrowth of a public fight, with a neighbor's wife. "Now," he decides, "it was time to consider different ways to begin to make love to her." He goes to the woman's house one Sunday and is confronted by her husband, a policeman, who shoots up the kitchen and wounds the burdened man. Passion and survival unburden the title character of his displaced obsessions. "Until old age startled him, he was hardly unhappy again."

These brief accounts of narratives do limited justice to the specialness of Paley's stories. Her sentences are small miracles of their own, risky, deceptively simple, capable of unexpected turns and flights. For example:

> He leaned over the rail and tried to hold her eyes. But that is hard to do for eyes are born dodgers and know a whole circumference of ways out of a bad spot.

> He had had a habit throughout the twenty-seven years of making a narrow remark which, like a plumber's snake, could work its way through the ear down the throat, halfway to my heart.

Paley is a major writer working in what passes in our time as a minor form. Her short fiction has continually deceived media, that system of mirrors that tends to discover the very things it advertises to itself, into taking it for less than it is. "A Conversation with My Father," my favorite of the second collection, concerns itself in part with the making of fiction. The narrator's father asks her why she doesn't write simple stories like de Maupassant or Chekhov. "Just recognizable people and then write down what happened to them next." To please her father, to prove the task hopeless, she offers him (and us) in abbreviated form a plain story, a self-fulfilling failure since the narrator holds that "Everyone, real or imagined, deserves the open destiny of life." The father complains that she leaves everything out, and Paley's narrator invents another, more elaborate version of the same story. The longer version is no closer to the kind of story the father wants, and he berates her for making jokes out of "Tragedy." "A Conversation with My Father" is by implication a self-criticism, a limiting and defining of mode, yet, symptomatic of Paley's best work, it illustrates by example the large and complex seriousness she affects (as if placating the gods) to deny herself. —JONATHAN BAUMBACH, "Life-Size," *PR*, 1975, pp. 303–6

LATER THE SAME DAY

In *Later the Same Day,* her third collection of stories, Grace Paley plunges us back into the lives of a group of Greenwich Village characters (in both senses) who entered literature in her 1959 collection, *The Little Disturbances of Man.* Here they all are: Faith, the protagonist or narrator of many of the stories; her neighbors; the local shopkeepers; Faith's pals from the antiwar movement, playground, and PTA; their children, lovers, ex-lovers, husbands, ex-husbands (who sometimes switch roles within the group), aging parents, and even a reappearing grandparent (whom the reader recognizes by the frozen herring he carries in his pocket). The settings too are familiar. By now some of the characters, most of them good leftists, have visited the People's Republic of China (the focus of two stories in this collection), and sometimes they go back to Brooklyn to relive the past or visit the Children of Judea Home for the Golden Ages, Coney Island Branch; but despite what Faith calls "my wide geographical love of mankind," we seldom see them north of 14th Street. There are newcomers to the scene—friends of the original crew, visitors from China, a younger playground crowd, shtetl ancestors—but they enter the book as naturally as new people enter our lives: they're political comrades, neighbors, relatives, friends of friends. All are rendered with that wildly comic Paley charm, her generous politics, her perfect ear-hand coordination. Again she tells her sad/funny stories and wry parables, in a wisecracking, ironic New York voice that sounds like no other—except, amazingly, Isaac Babel.

Going from *Little Disturbances* to *Later the Same Day* we hardly notice that time has passed. True, the kids we saw in the playground in earlier stories may have grown up, some swallowed by "history" (living underground, dead of an overdose, mad, gone to California, or off "in different boroughs trying to find the right tune for their lives"); the married couples memorialized by having sandwiches named after them at the Art Foods Deli may have gotten divorced; and some of the sandbox mothers of 20 years before are turning 50 or starting to die. But Paley can do for time what astrophysicists do for space: whether stretching or shrinking it, they deepen the mystery with every advance in describing it. As her narrator comments, "the brain at work pays no attention to time and speedily connects and chooses." Knowing this, Paley blithely sprinkles her stories with lines like, "Hello, my life, I said. We had once been married for twenty-seven years, so I felt justified" or, "What did you do today with your year off?" In a Paley story connections are forged—between generations, eras, cultures, continents—to show how different worlds are essentially the same; thus *Later the Same Day* might be 40 years later—as in the story "Ruthy and Edie," which begins when Ruthy and Edie are children, then halfway through rushes ahead to Ruthy's 50th birthday party—or it might be a century

earlier, when Faith's ancestors (activists like Faith and her friends) opposed the tyranny of the Tsar. With its vision of universal reconciliation, Paley's sensibility simply cannot be restricted by the ordinary boundaries of space or time.

Paley has sometimes been criticized for allowing her passionate commitment to politics to "interfere" with her art, but the two feed each other, are in fact one. Paley is as political as García Marquez or Camus. In story after story she demonstrates the inseparability of "private" and "public" passions—especially the passion to save the children, which she implicitly equates with saving the world. In Paley's universe children ("babies, those round, staring, day-in-day-out companions of her youth"), the ever-precarious next generation, are the raison d'être of political action. When Faith asks herself, recalling the PTA struggles of a bygone time, "Now what did we learn that year?" her answer is "The following: Though the world cannot be changed by talking to one child at a time, it may at least be known."—ALIX KATES SHULMAN, "The Children's Hour," *VLS*, June 1985, p. 9

MARIANNE DeKOVEN
"Mrs. Hegel-Shtein's Tears"
Partisan Review, 1981, pp. 217–23

In contemporary fiction, the impulse to recreate form is at loggerheads with the impulse to tell about everyday life. Grace Paley is a rare contemporary who feels both impulses, and in her work they cohere. It would be easy to read her stories without recognizing that they give two very different kinds of pleasure—the intellectual, aesthetic pleasure of inventive language and form, and the emotional, moral pleasure of deftly handled, poignant theme—without realizing that one was having the best of two historically sundered fictional modes.

Though Paley has published only two collections of stories, *The Little Disturbances of Man* and *Enormous Changes at the Last Minute,* she is nonetheless an important writer—important in the significance of the fictional possibilities she realizes rather than in the uniform merit of her published work. She is not always at her best. But when she is, Paley reconciles the demands of avant-garde or postmodern form for structural openness and the primacy of the surface with the seemingly incompatible demands of traditional realist material for orchestrated meaning and cathartic emotion.

"A Conversation with My Father," in *Enormous Changes,* makes of this seeming incompatibility an argument between father and daughter, from which emerges the statement, crucial to Paley's work, that traditional themes can no longer be treated *truthfully* by formally traditional fiction: formal inventiveness and structural open-endedness not only make fiction interesting, they make it "true-to-life." Paley's concern is not mimesis or verisimilitude, but rather the problem of creating a literary form which does not strike one as artificial; which is adequate to the complexity of what we know. Her narrator in "A Conversation with My Father" calls traditional plot "the absolute line between two points which I've always despised. Not for literary reasons, but because it takes away all hope. Everyone, real or invented, deserves the open destiny of life." Her father, arguing that plot is the truth of tragedy, wants her to write like Chekhov or Maupassant: "Tragedy! Plain tragedy! Historical tragedy! No hope. The end." Paley's narrator-surrogate, arguing for open-ended hope and change, clearly bests her father in the conversation. But in the story, Paley gives him the last word: the setting is his hospital room, and he speaks from what we may assume is his deathbed. His lecture on writing is "last-minute advice," and the closing speech, from father's pain to daughter's guilt, is his: "'How long will it be?' he asked. 'Tragedy! You too. When will you look it in the face?'"

The assertion of hope through change and open-endedness is therefore neither easy nor unambiguous. As the literary father sees, an inevitable component of optimistic belief in saving the situation through "enormous changes at the last minute" is evasion of genuine and unavoidable horror, the father's tragedy. As Faith herself says in "Living" (*Enormous Changes*), "You have to be cockeyed to love, and blind in order to look out the window at your own ice-cold street."

Paley herself, though endorsing in the structure of her fiction the narrator's point of view, is increasingly ambivalent about traditional storytelling. She discusses that ambivalence, which she divides in this story between the narrator and the father, in a "Symposium on Fiction" (reprinted in *Shenandoah* Vol. XXVII, No. 2, 3–31):

> When you talk about new forms or different forms, it seems to me this non-linearity has really run its course, played its game out. I understand it, it has been my way of working too. I haven't moved dead ahead except once in a while in that sense, and I wonder about our need for storytelling in its most simple linear sense of *what happened then, and then what happened, and what came next.* . . . People ought to live in mutual aid and concern, listening to one another's stories. That's what they ought to do. I'm not doing that, I'm very much a person in my time.

Though linear storytelling is attractive to Paley's moral-political sensibility, and she feels guilty that she doesn't write that way, the marrow of her fictions remains "enormous changes at the last minute." Her narrator in "A Conversation with My Father" claims that she does not hate plot "for literary reasons." But Paley's narrator is either misrepresenting or misunderstanding the "literary reasons" of Paley's fiction. Traditional plot does not necessarily preclude the possibility of hope; or, in cruder terms, the possibility of a happy ending. The narrator confuses the closure of traditional plot with the closure of despair, and once we acknowledge her mistake, we can go on to see her very "literary" reason for making it: it is the "enormous change" *as a phenomenon of literature* that is life-giving and hope-giving. In "Life" (the conversation between father and daughter), the father in his hospital room not only propounds but represents the tragic vision: he is dying testimony to the inevitability of what the narrator, meaning hopelessness, calls plot. In "Literature" (the story-within-a-story the narrator invents about a redeemed junkie), the narrator insists not so much on a happy ending for her character but on sudden and total change interrupting what would be a tragic trajectory toward doom in the kind of traditional fiction her father wants her to write. Life, unlike the narrator, has no pity: it is about to deprive her of her beloved father. The locus of the "open destiny of life," where hope and "enormous changes at the last minute" are possible, is fiction itself.

Paley places the tragic material which interests and moves her within an antitragic structure of sudden, abrupt transformations, "enormous changes," but the tragic material is nonetheless left intact. There is none of the hollow laughter, the mocking, alienated distance from pathos that is characteristic of serious modern fiction. But transformation undercuts tragic inevitability—fictional structure becomes tragedy's antidote rather than either its vehicle or its negation—and, equally important, as we will see, transformation undercuts the sentimentality that so easily trivializes pathos.

The people Paley's narrator in "A Conversation with My Father" would accuse of having merely "literary reasons" for rejecting traditional plot might explain the "enormous change" as an interesting substitute for outworn, tedious literary convention (linear plots are stale and boring), infusing new life into fiction. But Paley's structures are more than that. They are rooted not only in an assertion of openendedness and possibility, and in a nonlinear vision of life's events, but also, ultimately, in a profound commitment to freedom as a primary value (nonlinearity is not as alien to Paley's politics as it might appear). For many postmodernists, that freedom is problematic; tangled with fear of chaos on one hand and of authority on the other (see Tony Tanner's *City of Words*). But the freedom implied for Paley by "enormous changes," the freedom from inevitability or plot, is synonymous with hope; hence her larger assertion that open-endedness in fiction is the locus of "the open destiny of life," to which everyone is *"entitled"*—a strongly political statement. Paley's phrase "enormous changes at the last minute" is the speech of a hippy cabdriver-songwriter-motherlover who assures middle-aged Alexandra, childless, whom he fills with hope in the form of a baby, that his generation will save the world:

> The kids! The kids! Though terrible troubles hang over them, such as the absolute end of the known world quickly through detonation or slowly through the easygoing destruction of natural resources, they are still, even now, optimistic, humorous, and brave. In fact, they intend enormous changes at the last minute.

Tentatively and comically, Paley offers fiction's "enormous changes" as a warbling counternote to the tragic gong, even in twentieth century political life, that notoriously unredeemed domain.

The tragic subject matter of Paley's work reaches the reader emotionally as pathos, a tricky entity because it so easily becomes sentimental. However, pathos remains pathos in Paley's work: she jerks no tears but neither does she freeze them. Instead, she distracts the reader from pathos at dangerous moments, when sentimentality threatens, by calling attention to her wildly inventive, comic language and imagery. In those moments when her language takes on the burden of simultaneously communicating and distracting from pathos, Paley creates a unique and fascinating literary object.

In "Faith in the Afternoon" (*Enormous Changes*), Faith, recently abandoned by her husband, is visiting her parents in their old people's home. "The Children of Judea." Faith's mother belongs to the "Grandmothers' Wool Socks Association," governed by the formidable Mrs. Hegel-Shtein, who rolls noiselessly in and out of everyone's privacy "on oiled wheelchair wheels." Mrs. Hegel-Shtein is an ineluctable and pitiless purveyor of sad stories. She forces Faith's mother, who wants to spare her daughter more unhappiness, to discuss the tragic fates of various of Faith's childhood friends, beginning with Tess Slovinsky, whose first child was a "real monster," and:

> "[The second] was born full of allergies. It had rashes from orange juice. It choked from milk. Its eyes swoll up from going to the country. All right. Then her husband, Arnold Lever, a very pleasant boy, got a cancer. They chopped off a finger. It got worse. They chopped off a hand. It didn't help. Faithy, that was the end of a lovely boy. That's the letter I got this morning just before you came."
> Mrs. Darwin stopped. Then she looked up at Mrs. Hegel-Shtein and Faith. "He was an only son," she said. Mrs. Hegel-Shtein gasped. "You said an only son!"

Mrs. Hegel-Shtein is vulnerable to Arnold Lever's gruesome fate through her love of her own "only son," Archie. Faith's mother tells Arnold Lever's story from the great distance of the comic grotesque. He does not represent the kind of pathos Paley is interested in: his is sensational horror, not the unostentatious, commonplace pain of everyday life. Because she feels deeply Mrs. Hegel-Shtein's commonplace pain, Paley reaches a moment of potential sentimentality, her cue for magnificent writing: "On deep tracks, the tears rolled down her old cheeks. But she had smiled so peculiarly for seventy-seven years that they suddenly swerved wildly toward her ears and hung like glass from each lobe." The image of Mrs. Hegel-Shtein's tears swerving along deep tracks, formed by seventy-seven years of pecular smiling, to hang from her ear lobes like crystals, is so striking that it appropriates most of our attention as we read, preventing us from noticing particularly the pathos which we nonetheless feel. The fate of Mrs. Hegel-Shtein's tears is exactly the fate of our own. They fall, but they are "wildly" diverted along literally comic tracks to become something other than tears, something not at all commonplace; in fact, something transcendent: they crystallize into literary epiphany.

Pathos is neither transformed nor displaced by language: it remains intact, registered at a more or less subliminal level. But it combines with the startling, comic-bizarre language and imagery to make a profound literary moment which we experience simultaneously as a unity beyond both pathos and language, and also as a concatenation of the two separate elements, each maintaining its integrity.

For Paley, "life" need not be rescued from sordid insignificance by "literature." She does not translate or transform one into the other, but rather allows them to coexist in her work, partly separate, partly clashing, partly fused. We do not look *through* her images to find the meanings behind them; instead, the arresting, startling language and imagery comprise one element of the fiction, the feelings and meanings they communicate another. We receive them with different kinds of attention:

> "I was popular in certain circles," says Aunt Rose. "I wasn't no thinner then, only more stationary in the flesh. In time to come, Lillie, don't be surprised— change is a fact of God. From this no one is excused. Only a person like your mama stands on one foot, she don't notice how big her behind is getting and sings in the canary's ear for thirty years. Who's listening?"

That opening establishes the story's central contrast between Aunt Rose's painful, unconventional, but authentic life and her sister's conventional but empty life. While we focus on the excessive, absurd comic image of the fat woman standing on one foot singing in a canary's ear, and on the inventive language, we absorb, almost subliminally, the essential geography of a conventional thematic terrain.

But just as often as they function separately in Paley's work, prose surface and story come together in the peculiar way of Mrs. Hegel-Schtein's tears, in those moments when language must suddenly distract the reader from pathos, misleading us about the primary emotion of the fictional material. Again, in the best of those moments, surface and feeling register on the one hand separately, as strangely irreconcilable, and on the other harmoniously, as an irreducible literary epiphany.

Paley's work is honeycombed with such moments:

> Eddie looked up and saw his father. Their eyes met and because of irrevocable pain, held. That was

the moment (said Shmul, later on after that and other facts) that Eddie fell head-first into the black heart of a deep depression. This despair required all his personal attention for years.

> He had a habit throughout the twenty-seven years of making a narrow remark which, like a plumber's snake, could work its way through the ear down the throat, halfway to my heart. He would then disappear, leaving me choking with equipment.

> I own two small boys whose dependence on me takes up my lumpen time and my bourgeois feelings. . . . When I'm not furiously exhausted from my low-level job and that bedraggled soot-slimy house, I praise God for them. One Sunday morning, my neighbor, Mrs. Raftery, called the cops because it was 3 a.m. and I was vengefully singing a praising song.

> He took hold of me with his two arms as though in love and pressed his body hard against mine so that I could feel him for the last time and suffer my loss. Then he kissed me in a mean way to nearly split my lip. Then he winked and said, "That's all for now," and skipped off into the future, duffel bags full of rags.

> Air was filtering out of my two collapsing lungs. Water rose, bubbling to enter, and I would have died of instantaneous pneumonia—something I never have heard of—if my hand had not got hold of a glass ashtray and, entirely apart from my personal decision, flung it.

> After that, Alexandra hoped every day for her father's death, so that she could have a child without ruining his interesting life at the very end of it when ruin is absolutely retroactive.

At the heart of Paley's engagement with everyday life is her deep empathy with her characters. Even the deserters and betrayers she allows their "reasons," as she might say, and the rest she actively likes—a stance even more unusual in serious postmodern fiction than her assertions of hope in the face of our despair. It is not surprising that this uncommon empathy, which is really the condition of adherence to subjects of everyday life, is the province of a woman. Empathy and compassion are legacies of sexism that women do well to assert as privileged values rather than reject as stigmata of oppression. Uncomfortable as it makes her to write in such a predominantly male tradition, as a woman in the avant-garde, Paley is in an especially propitious position to unite interesting forms with important themes. She uses innovative form much as she uses innovative activism, to make new the endlessly dreary and shameful moral-political world we inhabit.

CLARA CLAIBORNE PARK
From "Faith, Grace, and Love"

Hudson Review, Autumn 1975, pp. 482–88

This ⟨. . .⟩ is Grace Paley's third book of stories, collected as *The Little Disturbances of Man, Enormous Changes at the Last Minute*, and now, *Later the Same Day* (each title a glowing marble in the water). They span thirty full years of her time of knowing and of paying attention, and of showing us how we too may attend and know. They comprise not quite 600 pages, neither large nor closely printed. You can read them all—and you have to, since increasingly no one of her stories wants to stand alone. It's ungrateful to deplore the fact that she's written so little, when we can sink so deep into what she has written, and stretch so wide, the depth of a poem, a novel's breadth.

Yet one could argue narrowness. Except for an excursion to China, another to Puerto Rico, and her friends' trip to visit Selena, New York is the only setting. But such a New York! Recognizably our own ("Look at this place, looks like a toxic waste dump. A war"), and yet:

> What a place in democratic time! One God, who was King of the Jews, who unravels the stars to this day with little hydrogen explosions, He can look down from his Holy Headquarters and see us all. . . . He sees south into Brooklyn how Prospect Park lies in its sand-rooted trees among Japanese gardens and police, and beyond us north to dangerous Central Park. Far north, the deer-eyed eland and kudu survive, grazing the open pits of the Bronx Zoo.
> *(Enormous Changes at the Last Minute)*

Thus some years ago Faith surveyed the city from her tree, fifteen feet up on a fine May morning. The cosmic vision in space and history (one God, who *was* King of the Jews, the final unraveling of the universe, this world itself from Africa and Japan to Brooklyn)—Paley opens it all up with the shimmer of an allusion. She can do it even from the confined locality of bed, where Faith, middle-aged now, would like to conceive another baby to renew the world, "to extract a new person from all-refusing Zeus and jealous Hera. My God, said Jack, you've never mentioned Greek gods in bed before. No occasion, I said."

Our world needs renewing; the planet "is dropping away from us in poisonous disgust," it has become noticeable that "life is short and sorrowful." For that reason the world must be praised; T. S. Eliot, who otherwise has nothing whatever in common with Paley, wrote of "having to construct something upon which to rejoice." Paley too knows which of the seven sins is deadliest: she and her characters are "ideologically, spiritually, and on puritanical principle against despair." It is all the more necessary, then, to praise "our own beloved city crowded with day and night workers, shoppers, walkers, the subway trains which many people fear but they're so handsomely lined with pink to dark brown faces, gold tans and yellows scattered amongst them," because "It's very important to emphasize what is good or beautiful so as not to have a gloomy face when you meet some youngster who has begun to guess." To guess that we age and it grows late; the dark strands that were always there in Paley's texture, that kept her love lyrics acridly unsentimental, now cluster as never before. But she will not forsake her station in democratic time, or be disloyal to the colors of her city.

Or to its voices. Paley has the gift of tongues which all-refusing Zeus so seldom vouchsafes to fiction writers. It is a gift, not an acquisition. Henry James and Virginia Woolf didn't have it and didn't want it. Chaucer had it, Forster had it, Joyce had it; so did Flannery O'Connor. Where it exists it is the manifest of a consciousness that thrives on human difference. Paley's ear is unerring for the speech of children, women, and men. She knows a three-year-old doesn't talk like a five-year-old or a fresh nine-year-old like a fresh adolescent. She won't pretend that social classes don't exist in America, or that they sound the same. Her city is loud with voices—Irish, Puerto Rican, black, Jewish, of all degrees of generationality, intellectuality, and education, a continuing festival of difference. Paley's New York is as wide as the world, but it is unshakeable in the specificity of its peopled streets and parks and schools, stores and subways and playgrounds. Not since Dublin has there been such a city. Reinhabiting these stories, I realize at length the uniqueness of this gradually accreting body of work,

a uniqueness much more than stylistic. For years now, while our most sophisticated literary voices have spoken for isolation, Paley, second to none in narrative sophistication, has been establishing a subject-matter of neighborhood, of affirmed community, the mingled James Joyce and Jane Jacobs of our time and place.

What community stretches out from is family and friends. Families are everybody's subject-matter. But I do not know another writer who writes so centrally about friendship. The story about Selena and Abby is called "Friends." Faith and Ann and Susan have taken the long train ride to be with Selena; she makes it easy for them to leave so they won't miss the return express. She even makes them sandwiches. They know they won't see her again. They talk about her on the train back. Can a story be about so little? But the story is full, crammed with characters, with names imagined into life in thickness and strength. Besides Faith and Ann and Susan and Selena and Abby, we have Max, Bob Simon and that great guy Bill Dalrymple (both killed in automobile accidents), Matthew, Jeannie, Mike, Al Lurie who was murdered on Sixth Street, the little kid Brenda who O.D.'d on the roof, Artie and Franky and the big surgeon David Clark—these in the first four pages of eighteen, and as many more to come. There are no stories of solitude; all are full of people and names. "Ruthy and Edie" is named from names; it is about a forty-year friendship and a birthday party shadowed by the intractability of politics, the absence of Ruthy's Rachel, who isn't there because history seized her "when her face was still round as an apple" and sent her off to follow her hard conscience. Who knows where she is, in Canada or Cuba? The years and places have been full of separations and losses, of discontinuities which neighborhood and friendship must hold together as best they may.

The thirty-year roll-call for these stories would do credit to an epic: Ginny, Mrs. Raftery and her John, darling Kitty Skazka, beautiful Anna Kraat, plain, nice Dottie Wasserman, Ellen who died in a story called "Living" though she was a mother and not old, Phillip Mazzano, Jack son of Jacob, Eddie the butcher, Orlando the grocer, Mrs. Finn, Frederick J. Lorenz, Mr. Wong, Joe Larsen, Faith's Chinese friend Xie Feng—I have scarcely begun. Some are one-time mentions, but most turn up from story to story, as people do turn up in New York, sometimes springing into individuality in a few lines of talk and narrative comment, sometimes with a story of their own. Earlier the same day, though the friends were there, it was parents and sex and children that held the world and the stories together. To some extent they still do, but when parents weaken and children depart and time makes the nuclear family less of a nucleus, Paley turns to friends. And we see that their recurrences have been stabilizing the stories all along, securing beneath the shifts and surprises of stylistic modernity a world almost Trollopian in its trustworthiness. Paley makes us experience it in separate bursts of meaning, but this thirty-year accretion has become a body of work for which the term "stories" can no longer be adequate. *Dubliners* too has a city for a subject, and in *Dubliners* too names recur. But Paley's human texture is thicker, and the Faith stories, growing in the loam of the stories about Ginny and Mrs. Raftery and Dottie Wasserman and Kitty, seem to call on us to call them a novel.

They behaved most traditionally like a novel in *Enormous Changes*, which, though Faith remained outside some of the most brilliant stories, gathered itself around her ironic consciousness and sturdy survivability. We could follow her emergence from "crummy days and crummy guys and no money and broke all the time and cockroaches and nothing to do on Sunday but take the kids to the park and row on that lousy lake" through the May sunshine of Washington Square to the freedom and "steamy energy of middle age." In "The Long-Distance Runner" she leaves her almost-grown boys to get by on "that rotten Celtic supper" Mrs. Raftery makes and jogs to her childhood neighborhood of Coney Island, now devastated but rich with the hopeful black children of the future, and learns from them "as though she was still a child what in the world is coming next." It is the book's last line.

Rereading the stories, it's easy to see that Paley has never encouraged us in the shallow notion that if things are going well for our heroine they are tipping toward sunshine for everybody. But we like thinking that, and though four of the stories in *Enormous Changes* dealt directly and piercingly with death, our minds gravitated to the title's assertion of continuing possibility, and the upbeat ending. In *Later the Same Day* things are still going well for Faith—she's with Jack still, the boys are doing ok, she even has a car. Eight of the seventeen stories, and three-quarters of the pages, belong to her in one way or another. But she is no longer the center. "I am trying to curb my cultivated individualism," she begins one story (in which only two proper names distinguish the speaker from Paley herself), individualism "which seemed for years so sweet. It was my own song in my own world, and of course it may not be useful in the hard time to come." It is that individualism that the new stories decisively curb. The reader's commitment to Faith, to her parents, to her children, now young men, need not dissipate, but it must expand, with Faith's, to a wider embrace. The new stories offer even more focuses of attention. Never conventionally organized, they are more discontinuous than ever. Form follows function. Paley has always despised plot, she has told us. And why? "Not for literary reasons, but because it takes all hope away," because it denies the possibility of those enormous changes, because "everyone, real or invented, deserves the open destiny of life." But the lack of plot no longer asks us to believe that everything is possible ("Oh, Pa," I said. "She could change [*Enormous Changes at the Last Minute*]). We owe it to the young and to ourselves not to put on a gloomy face, but this novel by accretion now makes another statement. It is, as Paley has said elsewhere, not the "I" but the "we" that is important.

Novel? Paley will not present it as such. Loose ends and inconsistencies are left from story to story and volume to volume as if to mock our conviction that her inventions are solider than our wraithlike lives. Why does Arthur Mazzano become Phillip, as he definitely does in Volume Three? Did Faith grow up in Coney Island or the Bronx? The stories are a web, a tapestry, something woven, or embroidered, or a patchwork—feminine handiwork anyway, extensive enough that irregularities don't matter and threads and bits and snippets in all colors can be greeted and made welcome.

The form for such an entertainment will not be linear. In the same story in which she repudiates individualism (in the most individual of voices) Faith—Paley—identifies the habit of beginning a story at the beginning as something men love and do. Middles, she implies, are for the untidy world of women, whose work and webs are never done. It is in middles that life is woven close. Paley's work will take its meanings, not from a beginning artificially charged with the significance of a climactic ending, but from the daily, seemingly inconsequential maintenance-work of the enduring and expanding middle. Paley was found some years ago with friends from the Women's Peace Center occluding entrance to the Pentagon with skeins of bright wool. Of course.

It is that sense of the web, of women's values, that infuses Faith's late-night rendition of the story of Sarah, who had a baby in old age—the story that, read "with interlinear intelligence," ends "with those three monotheistic horsemen . . . Christianity, Judaism, and Islam."

> Just the same, I said to softly snoring Jack, before all that popular badness wedged its way into the world, there *was first* the little baby Isaac . . . looking at Sarah just like all our own old babies—remember the way they practiced their five little senses. Oh, Jack, that Isaac, Sarah's boy—before he was old enough to be taken out by his father to get his throat cut, he must have just lain around smiling and making up diphthongs and listening, and the women sang songs to him and wrapped him up in such pretty rugs.

Such pretty woven rugs. By his father to get his throat cut. What more need be said about patriarchy than that?

The stories' feminist texture, then, is strengthening; in the very last one a Lesbian friend complains, "You've told everybody's story but mine," and Faith—Grace—implies a promise to work in that strand too. The mode of weaving, embroidery, patchwork, is inclusion, not exclusion. For that reason we should not see this as a woman-centered world where men enter only as neglectful dads and stuck-up though seductive studs. Some of the finest voices belong to men—the old father of "Faith in the Afternoon," brainy light still shining, who has here his own heart-rendingly beautiful story, "Dreamer in a Dead Language"; the black janitor who tells the terrible story of the rape and murder of "The Little Girl" (*Enormous Changes at the Last Minute*). And Jack speaks too, and Phillip and Joe and Nick and Mr. Wong and the rest of them, each with the uniqueness accorded him by his creator's affection and respect. Most remarkably, there is the story "Zagrowsky Tells," in which for the first time we see Faith not as observer but observed. Faith and her friends picketed Zagrowsky because "Zagrowsky Is a Racist," though he'd never refused to bring them penicillin up four flights of stairs when the kids were sick at midnight. How could they know they would precipitate the near destruction of a family, such terrible pain? Zagrowsky shows us another Faith, self-righteous, certain, unintentionally but willingly merciless. "Faith, I still can't figure out why you girls were so rotten to me." "But we were right." Zagrowsky names the condition: "This lady Queen of Right"—rightness, the occupational disease of people of good will trying to be responsibly active in this place in democratic time. Yet poor Iz *was* a racist; they *were* right, and his pathetic mad daughter has given him a dark brown grandson to prove the warmth of their rightness amid its chill, another child to renew the world, his cherished Emmanuel, "the smartest boy in kindergarten," his "little best friend."

The intractability of politics shadows this book as never before, not only the anxiety of annihilation, but the ugly ambiguities which did not arise when it was so simply right to oppose the war. "Why did China recognize Pinochet just about ten minutes after the coup in Chile?" "You three lead such adversarial lives," says Edie, who teaches children and has more direct interventions to perform. Politics units friends and divides them. There's the morning when the narrator (this time it really is Paley) sees "a fine-looking woman named Margaret, who hadn't spoken to me in two years."

> We'd had many years of political agreement before some matters relating to the Soviet Union separated us. In the angry months during which we were both right in many ways, she took away with her to her political position and daily friendship my own best friend, Louise—my lifelong park, P.T.A., and anti-war movement sister, Louise.

But the storyteller sees "Margaret's good face, and before I remembered our serious difference, I smiled." Margaret smiles back, and "so foolish is the true lover when responded to that I took her hand as we passed, bent to it, pressed it to my cheek, and touched it with my lips." Because friendship, finally, is what it's all about, and if politics doesn't know that, it doesn't know anything. The story opens *Later the Same Day*. It is called "Love."

These books will help to repudiate that new *trahison des clercs*, those high-rise theories that try to persuade us we're naive to think about people in stories as if they were real. To merge the real and the invented is one of Paley's most attractive games. In "Love," her husband insists that he used to go out with Dottie Wasserman, and when she tells him Dottie's a character in a book, "just plain invented in the late fifties,"

he pays no attention. That's how securely Paley's people are imagined into life, woven, confected out of love and memory, invented as "the life-long past is invented, which, as we know, thickens the present and gives all kinds of advice to the future."

You can read these stories over and over, until you know bits of them by heart, just like a poem. You can absorb the characters into your life, just like a novel. You can cry over them, as I did more than once, writing this review. For Christ's sake, you can even *study* them. Grace Paley is better than anybody we've got. She has been for years and years, and now, finally (a page in *Time*, two in *PW*, a film), it's plain for all to see. Philip Larkin thinks "a short story should be either a poem or a novel." I will call these stories both—heirlooms of our moment, beautiful, permanently made things.

DOROTHY PARKER

1893–1967

Dorothy Parker, poet, short-story writer, and critic, was born Dorothy Rothschild in West End, New Jersey, on August 22, 1893. Her mother, a Scottish Presbyterian, died in her infancy, and she was raised by her wealthy Jewish father and by her stepmother, another Scottish Presbyterian, who sent her to a Catholic convent school and to Miss Dana's School in Morristown, New Jersey, from which Parker graduated in 1911. Parker begun writing poetry in convent school and in 1915 one of her verses was accepted by *Vogue* magazine, for which magazine she was also hired to write captions for fashion illustrations. In 1917 she became drama critic for *Vanity Fair*, and in that year married Edwin Pond Parker II. Dorothy Parker, who was becoming famous for her quick wit and low wisecracks, became part of what came to be known as the Algonquin Round Table, a group of writers which included, at that time, Alexander Woollcott, Heywood Broun, Robert Benchley, and George S. Kaufman. After leaving *Vanity Fair* Parker had her poems, reviews, and short stories printed in a variety of journals, including most notably the *New Yorker*, with which she has been particularly identified. She was a newspaper correspondent in Spain during the Civil War in the 1930s, and later in Hollywood wrote scenarios and screenplays with her second husband Alan Campbell for many well-known films, including A *Star Is Born* (1937) and Hitchcock's *Saboteur* (1942). She died on June 7, 1967.

Dorothy Parker's first book of poetry appeared in 1926 as *Enough Rope*. This and the two volumes which followed, *Sunset Gun* (1928) and *Death and Taxes* (1931), were collected in *Not So Deep as a Well* (1936). Her short stories and sketches were published in *Laments for the Living* (1930) and *After Such Pleasures* (1933), and later collected in *Here Lies* (1939). *Close Harmony* (1929; written with Elmer Rice) and *Ladies of the Corridor* (1953; written with Armand d'Usseau) are both plays. In 1944 the Viking Portable Library issued a popular edition of her main works; it has remained in print, and a revised edition was issued in 1973.

If I should labor through daylight and dark,
  Consecrate, valorous, serious, true,
Then on the world I may blazon my mark;
  And what if I don't, and what if I do?

—DOROTHY PARKER, "Philosophy" (1926), *The Collected Poetry of Dorothy Parker*, 1936, p. 65

Rereading Dorothy Parker ⟨. . .⟩ has affected me, rather unexpectedly, with an attack of nostalgia. Her poems do seem a little dated. At their best, they are witty light verse, but when they try to be something more serious, they tend to become a kind of dilution of A. E. Housman and Edna Millay. Her prose, however, is still alive. It seems to me as sharp and funny as in the years when it was first coming out. If Ring Lardner outlasts our day, as I do not doubt he will, it is possible that Dorothy Parker will, too.

But the thing that I have particularly felt is the difference between the general tone, the psychological and literary atmosphere of the period—the twenties and the earlier thirties—when most of these pieces of Mrs. Parker's were written, and the atmosphere of the present time. It was suddenly brought home to me how much freer people were—in their emotion, in their ideas and in expressing themselves. ⟨. . .⟩

It is a relief and a reassurance, in reading her soliloquies and dialogues—her straight short stories, which are sometimes sentimental, do not always wear quite so well—to realize how recklessly clever it used to be possible for people to be, and how personal and how direct. All her books had funereal titles, but the eye was always wide open and the tongue always quick to retort. Even those titles were sardonic exclamations on the part of an individual at the idea of her own demise. The idea of the death of a society had not yet begun working on people to paralyze their response to experience.

⟨. . .⟩ It seems to me, though I shall name no names, that it has been one of the features of this later time that it produces imitation books. There are things of which one cannot really say that they are either good books or bad books; they are really not books at all. When one has bought them, one has only got paper and print. When one has bought Dorothy Parker, however, one has really got a book. She is not Emily Brontë or Jane Austen, but she has been at some pains to write well, and she has put into what she has written a voice, a state of mind, an era, a few moments of human experience that nobody else has conveyed.—EDMUND WILSON, "A Toast and a Tear for Dorothy Parker" (1944), *Classics and Commercials*, 1950, pp. 168–71

It is a little startling to realize that Dorothy Parker, even while she lives and continues to write (now and then), has achieved the kind of celebrity that belongs only to a few very great writers, like the contributors to the Bible, Shakespeare, and Alexander Pope. That is to say, Mrs. Parker is the sort of person who is always suspected of being the author of a famous, but elusive, quotation.

Whenever one is asked to identify a ringing line notable for its frightening sagacity, one automatically risks the guess that it must be from the Bible. When such a quotation bowls along competently in iambic pentameter, the ear whispers to the mind that surely this must be Shakespeare. If the point of a saying tinkles out its passage in a rhyming couplet, one draws a deep breath of relief and says, Alexander Pope. But if wisdom puts on a wry-lipped smile and expresses itself with a startling aptitude that rocks the mind momentarily out of its usual mood of somnolent acceptance, one blinks and says, Dorothy Parker.

There cannot be much doubt about it now. Dorothy Parker is one of the few writers of our time who is destined for immortality. It is nice for us who have always cherished her gift to know that in centuries to come she will represent the sad, cocky, impudent mood of our tragic era. Waking from our graves five hundred years from now, we shall be pleased to see Dorothy Parker strolling Olympus, perhaps in the company of Marguerite of Navarre and Madame de Sévigné. Proudly we shall say, "We knew her when she was just a quick-witted girl who kidded around with Robert Benchley and wrote pieces for the *New Yorker*.—JAMES GRAY, "A Dream of Unfair Women," *On Second Thought*, 1946, pp. 196–97

ALEXANDER WOOLLCOTT
From "Our Mrs. Parker" (1933)
While Rome Burns
1934, pp. 142–52

As we ⟨Alexander Woollcott and William Allen White Jr.⟩ loped up the aisle during the intermission rush for a dash of nicotine, I pointed out celebrities in the manner of a barker on a Chinatown bus. Young Bill seemed especially interested in the seamy lineaments of a fellow Harvard man named Robert Benchley, then, as now, functioning on what might be called the lunatic fringe of dramatic criticism. Seated beside him was a little and extraordinarily pretty woman with dark hair, a gentle, apologetic smile, and great reproachful eyes. "And that, I suppose," said the lad from Emporia, "would be Mrs. Benchley." "So I have always understood," I replied crossly, "but it *is* Mrs. Parker."

In the first part of this reply, I was in error. At the time I had not been one of their neighbors long enough to realize

that, in addition to such formidable obstacles as Mrs. Benchley, Mr. Parker, and the laws of the commonwealth, there was also a lack of romantic content in what was then, and ever since has been, a literary partnership seemingly indissoluble. At least it has had a good run. Mrs. Parker's latest and finest volume of poems carries on the flyleaf the simple dedication: "To Mr. Benchley," and even a dozen years ago, these two shared a microscopic office in the crumby old building which still houses the Metropolitan Opera.

There was just about room in it for their two typewriters, their two chairs, and a guest chair. When both were supposed to be at work, merely having the other one there to talk to provided a splendid excuse for not working at all. But when Benchley would be off on some mischief of his own, the guest chair became a problem. If it stood empty, Mrs. Parker would be alone with her thoughts and—good God!—might actually have to put some of them down on paper. And, as her desperate editors and publishers will tell you, there has been, since O. Henry's last carouse, no American writer so deeply averse to doing some actual writing. That empty guest chair afflicted her because the Parker-Benchley office was then so new a hideaway that not many of their friends had yet found a path to it, and even Mrs. Parker, having conscientiously chosen an obscure cubby-hole so that she might not be disturbed in her wrestling with *belles-lettres*, was becomingly reluctant to telephone around and suggest that everyone please hurry over and disturb her at once.

However, this irksome solitude did not last long. It was when the sign painter arrived to letter the names of these new tenants on the glass door that she hit upon a device which immediately assured her a steady stream of visitors, and gave her the agreeable illusion of presiding over as thronged a salon as even Madame Récamier knew. She merely bribed the sign painter to leave their names off the door entirely and print there instead the single word "Gentlemen."

Thus pleasantly distracted through the years, Mrs. Parker's published work does not bulk large. But most of it has been pure gold and the five winnowed volumes on her shelf—three of poetry, two of prose—are so potent a distillation of nectar and wormwood, of ambrosia and deadly nightshade, as might suggest to the rest of us that we all write far too much. ⟨. . .⟩

I think it not unlikely that the best of it will be conned a hundred years from now. If so, I can foresee the plight of some undergraduate in those days being maddened by an assignment to write a theme on what manner of woman this dead and gone Dorothy Parker really was. Was she a real woman at all? he will naturally want to know. And even if summoned from our tombs, we will not be sure how we should answer that question.

Indeed, I do not envy him his assignment, and in a sudden spasm of sympathy for him, herewith submit a few miscellaneous notes, though, mark you, he will rake these yellowing files in vain for any report on her most salient aspects. Being averse to painting the lily, I would scarcely attempt a complete likeness of Mrs. Parker when there is in existence, and open to the public, an incomparable portrait of her done by herself. From the nine matchless stanzas of "The Dark Girl's Rhyme"—one of them runs:

> There I was, that came of
>   Folk of mud and flame—
> I that had my name of
>   Them without a name—

to the mulish lyric which ends thus:

> But I, despite expert advice,
>   Keep doing things I think are nice,

And though to good I never come—
Inseparable my nose and thumb!

her every lyric line is autobiographical.

From the verses in *Enough Rope, Sunset Gun,* and *Death and Taxes*, the toiling student of the year 2033 will be able to gather, unaided by me, that she was, for instance, one who thought often and enthusiastically of death, and one whose most frequently and most intensely felt emotion was the pang of unrequited love. From the verses alone he might even construct, as the paleontologist constructs a dinosaur, a picture of our Mrs. Parker wringing her hands at sundown beside an open grave and looking pensively into the middle-distance at the receding figure of some golden lad—perhaps some personable longshoreman—disappearing over the hill with a doxy on his arm.

Our Twenty-First Century student may possibly be moved to say of her, deplorably enough, that, like Patience, our Mrs. Parker yearned her living, and he may even be astute enough to guess that the moment the aforesaid golden lad wrecked her favorite pose by showing some sign of interest, it would be the turn of the sorrowing lady herself to disappear in the other direction just as fast as she could travel. To this shrewd guess, I can only add for his information that it would be characteristic of the sorrowing lady to stoop first by that waiting grave, and with her finger trace her own epitaph: "Excuse my dust."

But if I may not here intrude upon the semiprivacy of Mrs. Parker's lyric lamentation, I can at least supply some of the data of her outward life and tell the hypothetical student how she appeared to a neighbor who has often passed the time of day with her across the garden wall and occasionally run into her at parties. Well, then, Dorothy Parker (née Rothschild) was born of a Scotch mother and a Jewish father. Her people were New Yorkers, but when she came into the world in August 1893, it was, to their considerable surprise and annoyance, a trifle ahead of schedule. It happened while they were staying at West End, which lies on the Jersey shore a pebble's throw from Long Branch, and it was the last time in her life when she wasn't late.

Her mother died when she was still a baby. On the general theory that it was a good school for manners, she was sent in time to a convent in New York, from which she was eventually packed off home by an indignant Mother Superior who took umbrage when her seemingly meek charge, in writing an essay on the miracle of the Immaculate Conception, referred to that sacred mystery as spontaneous combustion. When, at her father's death a few years later, she found herself penniless, she tried her hand at occasional verse, and both hands at playing the piano for a dancing school.

Then she got a job writing captions on a fashion magazine. She would write "Brevity Is the Soul of Lingerie" and things like that for ten dollars a week. As her room and breakfast cost eight dollars, that left an inconsiderable margin for the other meals, to say nothing of manicures, dentistry, gloves, furs, and traveling expenses. But just before hers could turn into an indignant O. Henry story, with General Kitchener's grieving picture turned to the wall and a porcine seducer waiting in the hall below, that old marplot, her employer, doubled her salary. In 1918, she was married to the late Edwin Parker, a Connecticut boy she had known all her life. She became Mrs. Parker a week before his division sailed for France. There were no children born of this marriage.

Shortly after the armistice, the waiting bride was made dramatic critic of *Vanity Fair*, from which post she was forcibly removed upon the bitter complaints of sundry wounded people of the theater, of whose shrieks, if memory serves, Billie Burke's

were the most penetrating. In protest against her suppression, and perhaps in dismay at the prospect of losing her company, her coworkers, Robert E. Sherwood and Robert Benchley, quit *Vanity Fair* at the same time in what is technically known as a body, the former to become editor of *Life*, and the latter its dramatic critic.

Since then Mrs. Parker has gone back to the aisle seats only when Mr. Benchley was out of town and someone was needed to substitute for him. It would be her idea of her duty to catch up the torch as it fell from his hand—and burn someone with it. I shall never forget the expression on the face of the manager who, having recklessly produced a play of Channing Pollock's called *The House Beautiful*, turned hopefully to Benchley's next *feuilleton*, rather counting on a kindly and even quotable tribute from that amiable creature. But it seems Benchley was away that week, and it was little Mrs. Parker who had covered the opening. I would not care to say what she had covered it with. The trick was done in a single sentence. *"The House Beautiful,"* she had said with simple dignity, "is the play lousy."

And more recently she achieved an equal compression in reporting on *The Lake*. Miss Hepburn, it seems, had run the whole gamut from A to B.

But for the most part, Mrs. Parker writes only when she feels like it or, rather, when she cannot think up a reason not to. Thus once I found her in hospital typing away lugubriously. She had given her address as Bed-pan Alley, and represented herself as writing her way out. There was the hospital bill to pay before she dared get well, and downtown an unpaid hotel bill was malignantly lying in wait for her. Indeed, at the preceding Yuletide, while the rest of us were all hanging up our stockings, she had contented herself with hanging up the hotel.

Tiptoeing now down the hospital corridor, I found her hard at work. Because of posterity and her creditors, I was loath to intrude, but she, being entranced at any interruption, greeted me from her cot of pain, waved me to a chair, offered me a cigarette, and rang a bell. I wondered if this could possibly be for drinks. "No," she said sadly, "it is supposed to fetch the night nurse, so I ring it whenever I want an hour of uninterrupted privacy."

Thus, by the pinch of want, are extracted from her the poems, the stories, and criticisms which have delighted everyone except those about whom they were written. There was, at one time, much talk of a novel to be called, I think, *The Events Leading Up to the Tragedy*, and indeed her publisher, having made a visit of investigation to the villa where she was staying at Antibes, reported happily that she had a great stack of manuscript already finished. He did say she was shy about letting him see it. This was because that stack of alleged manuscript consisted largely of undestroyed carbons of old articles of hers, padded out with letters from her many friends.

Then she once wrote a play with Elmer Rice. It was called *Close Harmony*, and thanks to a number of circumstances over most of which she had no control, it ran only four weeks. On the fourth Wednesday she wired Benchley: "CLOSE HARMONY DID A COOL NINETY DOLLARS AT THE MATINEE STOP ASK THE BOYS IN THE BACK ROOM WHAT THEY WILL HAVE."

The outward social manner of Dorothy Parker is one calculated to confuse the unwary and unnerve even those most addicted to the incomparable boon of her company. You see, she is so odd a blend of Little Nell and Lady Macbeth. It is not so much the familiar phenomenon of a hand of steel in a velvet glove as a lacy sleeve with a bottle of vitriol concealed in its folds. She has the gentlest, most disarming demeanor of anyone I know. Don't you remember sweet Alice, Ben Bolt?

Sweet Alice wept with delight, as I recall, when you gave her a smile, and if memory serves, trembled with fear at your frown. Well, compared with Dorothy Parker, Sweet Alice was a roughshod bully, trampling down all opposition. But Mrs. Parker carries—as everyone is uneasily aware—a dirk which knows no brother and mighty few sisters. "I was so terribly glad to see you," she murmurs to a departing guest. "Do let me call you up sometime, won't you, please?" And adds, when this dear chum is out of hearing, "That woman speaks eighteen languages, and can't say No in any of them." Then I remember her comment on one friend who had lamed herself while in London. It was Mrs. Parker who voiced the suspicion that this poor lady had injured herself while sliding down a barrister. And there was that wholesale libel on a Yale prom. If all the girls attending it were laid end to end, Mrs. Parker said, she wouldn't be at all surprised.

Mostly, as I now recall these cases of simple assault, they have been muttered out of the corner of her mouth while, to the onlooker out of hearing, she seemed all smiles and loving-kindness. For as she herself has said (when not quite up to par), a girl's best friend is her mutter. ⟨. . .⟩

It should be added that that inveterate dislike of her fellow creatures which characterizes so many of Mrs. Parker's utterances is confined to the human race. All other animals have her enthusiastic support. It is only fair to her eventual biographer to tip him off that there is also a strong tinge of autobiography in that sketch of hers about a lady growing tearful in a speak-easy because her elevator man would be stuffy if she should pick up a stray horse and try to bring him to her apartment.

⟨. . .⟩ Woodrow Wilson was, I think, the name of the dog at the end of her leash when I first knew her. This poor creature had a distressing malady. Mrs. Parker issued bulletins about his health—confidential bulletins, tinged with skepticism. He *said* he got it from a lamp post.

Of her birds, I remember only an untidy canary whom she named Onan for reasons which will not escape those who know their Scriptures. And then there were the two alligators which she found in her taxi, where someone had been shrewd enough to abandon them. Mrs. Parker brought them home and thoughtfully lodged them in the bathtub. When she returned to her flat that night, she found that her dusky handmaiden had quit, leaving a note on the table which read as follows: "I will not be back. I cannot work in a house where there are alligators. I would have told you this before, but I didn't suppose the question would ever come up."

Well, I had thought here to attempt, if not a portrait, then at least a dirty thumb-nail sketch, but I find I have done little more than run around in circles quoting Mrs. Parker. I know a good many circles where, by doing just that, one can gain quite a reputation as a wit. *One* can? Several can. Indeed, several I know do.

BRENDAN GILL

"Introduction"

The Portable Dorothy Parker

1973, pp. xiii–xxviii

I

There are writers who die to the world long before they are dead, and if this is sometimes by choice, more often it is a fate imposed on them by others and not easily dealt with. A writer enjoys a vogue, and, the vogue having passed, either he consents to endure the obscurity into which he has been thrust or he struggles against it in vain, with a bitterness that tends to increase as his powers diminish. No matter how well or badly he behaves, the result is the same. If the work is of a certain quality, it survives the passing of the vogue, but the maker of the work no longer effectually exists. Even though he goes on writing, he dwells in the limbo of the half-forgotten, and his obituary notices are read with a flippant, unthinking incredulity: who would have guessed that the tattered old teller of tales had had it in him to hang on so fiercely? What on earth had he been waiting for? Hoping for? Dreading?

A protracted life-in-death is all the more striking in the case of writers who make a reputation in youth and then live on into age. It is most striking of all in the case of young writers whose theme is the pleasingness of death, and for whom it amounts in the world's eyes to a betrayal of their theme when they are observed to cling far more tenaciously to life than their happier contemporaries have managed to do. Dorothy Parker's career was of this nature. She enjoyed an early vogue, which passed, leaving her work to be judged on its merits, and because the subject of so large a portion of her verses was the seductiveness of a neat, brisk doing away with herself, many people were astonished to read of her death, in 1967, from natural causes, as an old lady of seventy-three. Under the circumstances, it seemed to them a tardy end, and by an irony that had been one of Mrs. Parker's chief stocks in trade she would have been the first to agree with them. She had indeed taken an unconscionably long time to leave a world of which she had always claimed to hold a low opinion. Her husbands, her lovers, and most of her friends had preceded her; for a person who boasted of wooing death, she had proved the worst of teases—an elderly flirt of the sort that she herself at thirty would have savaged in a paragraph.

There had been, of course, more at stake for her than a reluctance to keep old promises made in poems. The gap between her life and her work had grown very wide. The fact was that as she put on years she seemed unable to make a favorite of either life or death; she refused to take sides. It was as if she had hung on not fiercely or grimly but because she lacked the tiny tremor of will required to give up. She had had fame, and for long periods in Hollywood a very large income. The world would have said that she had every opportunity to fulfill her talent, and now she lived alone, with a raspy little concierge of a dog, in a hotel room in Manhattan and waited for nothing and hoped for nothing and got through the day, often enough with a bottle. She had been tiresome when she drank in youth, and with age she could scarcely be expected to improve; the occasions for drink were not merry ones. There were besides, no suitable companions left to raise hell with—no incomparably joyous Benchleys to babble nonsense to, no Hemingways to hero-worship. Even if there had been, she would surely have found ways to alienate them. Early in life she had developed a strong bent for cutting ties with friends; to the born wisecracker, uttering the one funny word too many is the last appetite that fails.

Mrs. Parker had been a writer whose robust and acid lucidities had been much feared and admired, and it was sad that she should be making such a messy finish; she was never so muddled as not to see that and to make her apologies for it. By the standards of her prime, what she was engaged in committing—what, plainly, she was helpless not to commit—was an inexcusable social and aesthetic blunder: she was becoming the guest who is aware that he has outstayed his welcome and who yet makes no attempt to pack his things and go.

II

Readers coming to Mrs. Parker for the first time may find it as hard to understand the high place she held in the literary world of forty or fifty years ago as to understand the critical disregard into which she subsequently fell. The first precaution for such readers is to bear in mind the fact that the so-called world that gave her her reputation was really only a province, and, like all provinces, it considered itself much bigger and more important than it was. Its arbiters did well to praise Mrs. Parker, but she was a better writer than they took her for, and the difference between who she was and who they supposed she was held considerable risks for her. Not the least of these risks was the likelihood that when her champions came to be swept away into the dustbin, she, too, would be swept away. The small literary set that centered on New York in the twenties and thirties and that hailed Mrs. Parker as one of its leading lights was made up largely of second- and third-raters. Mrs. Parker perceived this in her middle years and passed judgment on her old colleagues with the acerbity of one who has been overpraised by people unfit to offer either praise or blame. She *was* one of their leading lights; to be that, she might have said, it would have sufficed to be a glowworm. She pointed out that the major American writers of the period had not been members of any set; they had lived and worked far from the coterie of self-promoters who gathered under the heading of the Algonquin Round Table. Hemingway, Faulkner, Lardner, Fitzgerald, Dos Passos, Cather, Crane, and O'Neill were not to be found cracking jokes and singing each other's praises or waspishly stinging each other into tantrums on West 44th Street. Some of Mrs. Parker's companions at the Algonquin were exceptionally attractive people (Robert Benchley, Robert E. Sherwood, Marc Connelly) and some of them were exceptionally unattractive (Alexander Woollcott, George S. Kaufman, Edna Ferber), but, companionship aside, by any reasonable historic measure, what a trifling harvest was to be gained from them! If a number of Mrs. Parker's short stories and poems will last and if some of Benchley's humorous pieces will also last, still, it is hard to think of works by other members of that well-touted little clique that are likely to survive the century.

Mrs. Parker's reputation suffered from the literary company she kept; it suffered also from the fact that the milieu that was her natural subject matter—the narrow sector of American society that could be summed up as Eastern, urban, intellectual, and middle class—underwent a sudden and overwhelming change during the Depression. The people Mrs. Parker had kept under close scrutiny and about whom she had written with authority seemed so remote from the realities of the post-Depression period as to be stamped, for a time, with a kind of retroactive invalidity. In the forties and fifties they simply did not matter any more, and the reading public was tempted to conclude, mistakenly, that they ought never to have mattered. Little by little over the years, the period and the people who gave it its character have recovered importance. By now we find it worth while to make an effort to apprehend them fairly, according to the tone and temper of their day, and in order to do so we turn with relish to Mrs. Parker.

No doubt it will strike young readers as odd, but the twenties in which Mrs. Parker began work were considered an era of extreme and perhaps dangerous permissiveness, especially in regard to the social experiments being carried out by women. Drinking, smoking, sniffing cocaine, bobbing one's hair, dancing the Charleston, necking, getting "caught"—it was hard to imagine that things could go much farther before civilization itself broke down. The young women who set the

pace were called sophisticated, though few of them were; their shocking motto was "Anything goes," and they meant it. New York was their noisy Sodom, and Mrs. Parker's verse gave glimpses of the license to be met with there and its heavy cost in terms of one's emotions. These verses, which became something of a national rage, were thought to be strong stuff: brusque, bitter, and unwomanly in their presumed cynicism. They gave the average reader an impression of going recklessly far in asserting a woman's equal rights inside a sexual relationship, including the right of infidelity. The verses do not seem brusque, bitter, and unwomanly today; moreover, the verses that at the time of their first publication appealed to readers as the real thing, full of a pain of loss splendidly borne, are the ones likeliest now to set our teeth on edge, as being tainted with a glib gallantry every bit as false as the revolting cuddly high spirits of Mrs. Parker's literary mortal enemy, A. A. Milne. Mrs. Parker was quoted incessantly by her admirers; the quotations were almost always from poems that current readers would regard as among her cleverest but least heartfelt:

> And let her loves, when she is dead,
>   Write this above her bones:
> "No more she lives to give us bread
>   Who asked her only stones."

> By the time you swear you're his,
>   Shivering and sighing,
> And he swears his passion is
>   Infinite, undying—
> Lady, make a note of this:
>   One of you is lying.

> Princes, never I'd give offense.
>   Won't you think of me tenderly?
> Here's my strength and my weakness, gents—
>   I loved them until they loved me.

> Razors pain you;
>   Rivers are damp;
> Acids stain you;
>   And drugs cause cramp.
> Guns aren't lawful;
>   Nooses give;
> Gas smells awful;
>   You might as well live.

The most popular woman poet of the twentieth century, prior to Mrs. Parker, was Edna St. Vincent Millay, who was often thought to have served as a literary model for her. It was not altogether so; for one thing, Miss Millay was a much more skillful prosodist than Mrs. Parker, with a mastery of many forms of verse that Mrs. Parker never attempted, and, for another, Miss Millay enjoyed a far wider range of expressible feelings, which she spent a lifetime of hard intellectual effort exploring. She struggled to achieve greatness, and if the effort failed, it produced a number of sufficiently remarkable volumes of poems. Mrs. Parker worked less hard and less steadily, and she flinched from thorough self-examination: the depths were there, and she would glance into them from time to time, but she was not prepared to descend into them and walk their bounds. Her true literary mentor was that forbidding male spinster, A. E. Housman, who with the help of high intelligence, classical learning, and an exquisite ear, contrived to turn a reiterated whining into superior poetry. One reads Housman today not for the sense but for the sound, wishing often that it were not necessary to understand his long-drawn-out adolescent howl and could listen, instead, to the matchless positioning of his syllables—"For this of old the trader/ Unpearled the Indian seas." Housman pretended to look into the depths, but they were other people's depths and not his. Such lines as his audacious mock-Roman "Life, to be sure, is nothing much to lose" often moved Mrs. Parker to strike just the wrong note of lofty, sentimental not-caring; her verses are also marred on occasions by "lads" if not "chaps," and she shares Housman's tendency to shower congratulations upon anyone who takes his life when young. (Like Mrs. Parker, Housman was to live into his seventies and die of natural causes. He believed in suicide, but with this proviso—that it was for others.) Mrs. Parker wrote what was essentially light verse; it was not Housman's perennial ruefulness that she ought to have imitated, but the witty aplomb of her contemporary, Ogden Nash. Along with, in her sunnier moods, Miss Millay, Nash broke up the old forms and fashioned new ones that accommodated to perfection the spoken language of the period. Nevertheless, Mrs. Parker was someone to be taken seriously. Edmund Wilson wrote at the time that he had been "sometimes accused of overrating the more popular irony of Mrs. Dorothy Parker. It is true that Mrs. Parker's epigrams have the accent of the Hotel Algonquin rather than that of the coffee houses of the eighteenth century. But I believe that, if we admire, as it is fashionable to do, the light verse of Prior and Gay, we should admire Mrs. Parker also. She writes well: her wit is the wit of her particular time and place, but it is often as cleanly economic at the same time that it is flatly brutal as the wit of the age of Pope; and, within its small scope, it is a criticism of life. It has its roots in contemporary reality, and that is what I am pleading for in poetry."

Wilson expressed that opinion of Mrs. Parker nearly fifty years ago; it continues to be a sound one, and the poems that we admire today are those that most ably sum up her particular time and place. It is a world that has grown very distant from ours, but because she was true to its nature it remains, with certain attendant risks, visitable. In 1944, in the course of reviewing the first edition of this book, Wilson wrote in *The New Yorker* that, while he found Mrs. Parker's poems a little dated, her prose seemed to him as sharp and funny as in the years when it was first coming out. Again, a sensible judgment, worth quoting after almost thirty years. If it is easier to visit the world of the twenties and thirties through Mrs. Parker's short stories and soliloquies than through her verse, it is also more rewarding; to a startling degree, they have a substance, a solidity, that the poems do little to prepare us for. Not the least hint of the Round Table is detectable in the stories—no sassy showing off, no making a leg at the reader. The author keeps her distance, and sometimes it is a distance great enough to remind one of Flaubert. She has written her tales with grave care and given them a surface as hard and smooth as stone, and there is no need for her to flutter about in the foreground and call attention to her cleverness. We perceive from one sentence to the next that we are in the hands of a skilled and confident guide and that each story can be marched through from beginning to end without our stumbling into uncertain or gratuitous asides. One has only to sample the superlatively self-assured opening sentences of two or three of the stories:

He was a very good-looking young man indeed, shaped to be annoyed.

If the Bains had striven for years, they could have been no more successful in making their living-room into a small but admirably complete museum of objects suggesting strain, discomfort, or the tomb.

The woman with the pink velvet poppies twined round the assisted gold of her hair . . .

The force of that "assisted," slipped so unobtrusively into the text, is like a hammer-blow. The opening paragraph of her late story, "The Lovely Leave," displays the Parker style at its simplest and best; not a word amiss:

Her husband had telephoned her by long distance to tell her about the leave. She had not expected the call, and she had no words arranged. She threw away whole seconds explaining her surprise at hearing him, and reporting that it was raining hard in New York, and asking was it terribly hot where he was. He had stopped her to say, look, he didn't have time to talk long; and he had told her quickly that his squadron was to be moved to another field the next week and on the way he would have twenty-four hours' leave. It was difficult for her to hear. Behind his voice came a jagged chorus of young male voices, all crying the syllable "Hey!"

At the time she was writing them, Mrs. Parker's soliloquies caused a great stir among her readers and especially among her fellow writers. These soliloquies were like star turns by an acrobat working up at the top of the tent without a net, and part of the pleasure they gave lay in the reader's wondering how she could possibly bring off a feat so difficult. Like most feats of this order, they were made to look easy by the person performing them—what did they consist of, after all, but an unidentified woman nattering away to herself as a succession of thoughts tumbled helter-skelter across her consciousness?—but it soon turned out that, simple as the principle of the feats was, mastery of it was next to impossible; Mrs. Parker had few imitators. One of the more celebrated of her soliloquies was "The Telephone Call," which began:

Please, God, let him telephone me now. Dear God, let him call me now. I won't ask anything else of You, truly I won't. It isn't very much to ask. It would be so little to You, God, such a little, little thing. Only let him telephone now. Please, God. Please, please, please.

Another was called "The Little Hours" and began:

Now what's this? What's the object of all this darkness all over me? They haven't gone and buried me alive while my back was turned, have they? Ah, now would you think they'd do a thing like that! Oh, no, I know what it is. I'm awake. That's it. I've waked up in the middle of the night. Well, isn't that nice. Isn't that simply ideal.

In Wilson's review of the first edition of the Portable, he drew a contrast between the twenties and the forties that was notably unfavorable to the latter:

The thing that I have particularly felt is the difference between the general tone, the psychological and literary atmosphere, of the period—the twenties and the earlier thirties—when most of these pieces of Mrs. Parker's were written, and the atmosphere of the present time. It was suddenly brought home to me how much freer people were—in their emotion, in their ideas, and in expressing themselves. In the twenties they could love, they could travel, they could stay up late at night, as extravagantly as they pleased; they could think or say or write whatever seemed to them amusing or interesting. There was a good deal of irresponsibility, and a lot of money and energy wasted, and the artistic activities of the time suffered from the general vices, but it was a much more favorable climate for writing than the period we are in now.

The passage was written during the Second World War, under circumstances grimmer than any we have known since in this country. For the young writers of the seventies the situation is not unlike the one that Wilson remembered the young writers of the twenties having enjoyed and—certainly in his own case and in that of Mrs. Parker—gained intellectual stimulus from. Writers today are free to love and travel and stay up late (a curious privilege for Wilson to have noted: neither in the forties nor at any other period in his long life did he feel obliged to go to bed early), and they are free to think or say or write whatever seems to them amusing or interesting. In the light of continued warfare abroad and continued social injustice at home, they cannot be as carefree in their emotions as Wilson hints that he and his contemporaries were—there are dark thoughts that no amount of love and travel will expunge—but money and energy are in ample supply, and the squandering of them is not always as irresponsible as it looks. We are indeed in possession of a favorable climate for writing, and this may be one of the reasons that many of us are more powerfully drawn to the twenties than the usual processes of nostalgia would account for. A very deep and wide gulf separates us from those years, but we do not feel in the least estranged from them, as we do from the forties and fifties—sharper than ever to us are the lineaments of the writers we admire as we look back upon them over half a century. It is not surprising that we choose for good companions Fitzgerald, Lardner, Hemingway, and the other boys in the back room, nor is it surprising that there should pop up among them, glass in hand, hat askew, her well-bred voice full of soft apologies, the droll, tiny figure of Mrs. Parker.

III

The essential facts of her life, long as it was, are quickly told; and this is a mercy, since few careers, after a brilliant start, can be seen to have so continuously and sadly extinguished themselves. She was born Dorothy Rothschild, in 1893, at her family's summer place in West End, New Jersey. Her mother, who died in Dorothy's infancy, was Scottish; her father, a well-to-do garment manufacturer, had no connection with the banking Rothschilds. She grew up in New York, intensely disliking her strict father and even stricter stepmother; she attended a Catholic convent school in Manhattan and Miss Dana's School in Morristown, New Jersey; and in 1916, having sold some verses to Frank Crowninshield, the editor of *Vogue*, she was given an editorial position on that magazine. Her task was to write captions for fashion photographs and drawings, and her salary was ten dollars a week. She became one of Crowninshield's innumerable platonic protégées, and within a year he offered her a far better position on another magazine of which he was the editor—the charming and elegant *Vanity Fair*. She was to become its drama critic, and since she appears to have manifested no previous interest in the theater, Crowninshield must have been following one of his celebrated canny whims. At about the same time, she married a good-looking young man from Hartford named Edwin Pond Parker II. They were divorced some years later, but she continued to use his name, which she preferred to her own. She felt a constant resentment at being Jewish; life might have pleased her better if it had been her mother who had been Jewish and her father Scottish, and she had been born a Marston.

On *Vanity Fair* she met Benchley and Sherwood, two other congenial unemployables whom Crowninshield had perceived literary virtues in, and her career as the wittiest member of the Algonquin Round Table was launched. She made wisecracks—often quite admirable wisecracks—as easily as most people say, "Is it hot enough for you?" or, "Please pass the bread." Having left *Vanity Fair*, she became one of the handful of writers who helped form the character of *The New Yorker*, founded by Harold Ross in 1925. Her short stories in the magazine, at first scarcely more than scraps of lacerating dialogue, led to the development of what was afterward assumed by critics to be a recognizable genre—*The New Yorker*

short story—though none of the writers of these stories, including Mrs. Parker, O'Hara, Fuchs, Cheever, and Salinger, would agree that the genre existed. (Mrs. Parker's work was to appear in the magazine at irregular intervals from 1926 until 1955.) She went abroad and met the Gerald Murphys and the Hemingways and the Fitzgeralds. She worked hard at her writing, and when her book of poems, *Enough Rope*, was published, it became a best seller. In the thirties she married an actor-writer named Alan Campbell, who was eleven years younger than she and bisexual; he had in common with her an ancestry half-Jewish and half-Scottish. Though it was probably the case that no man could have remained married to her for long, Camapbell was not only a devoted husband but also a capable manager of their professional and domestic affairs, and the marriage lasted longer than any of her friends had predicted. They went to Hollywood as a writing team, at a salary of something over five thousand dollars a week. They also bought a farm in Bucks County, Pennsylvania. To her delight, at the age of forty-two she became pregnant; she lost the baby in the third month. Back in Hollywood, she became an ever more ardent left-wing political activist, to the jeopardy of Campbell's and her screenwriting career. They worked on many movies, rarely to her satisfaction. During the Second World War Campbell, though well past draft age, volunteered for the Army and served overseas. They were divorced in 1947 and remarried in 1950; they separated two years later and then settled down to a marriage of sorts in 1956. Campbell died in 1963 in Hollywood, and Mrs. Parker—again, as nearly always, Mrs. Parker—returned to New York. Her last original writing of importance was a play, *The Ladies of the Corridor*, in which she collaborated with Arnaud d'Usseau. In his review of it in *The New Yorker*, Wolcott Gibbs described the play as an account of life in a residential hotel in the East Sixties "that is the last resort of those [women] who have lost their husbands, whose children have grown up and moved away, and who have nothing to do with their remaining years except go to the movies, attend to their little dogs, and discuss one another's affairs with intense and delighted malignance." Gibbs found a good deal to admire in the play. "Some familiarity with the past performances of both authors," he wrote, "leads me to conclude that Mrs. Parker, who is in the habit these days of irritably deprecating her reputation as a wit, is responsible not only for the precise and deadly wit that frequently punctuates the script but also for the acute understanding of human loneliness, cruelty, stupidity, and occasional glowing, unpredictable fortitude that gives the characters their intermittent flashes of absolute fidelity to life." Mrs. Parker had worked hard on the play; she hoped it would enjoy a big success and provide her, no matter how belatedly, with a fresh start in life. The majority of the reviews of the play proved unfavorable, and it closed after forty-five performances. Mrs. Parker said of it afterward, "It was the only thing I ever did that I was proud of."

IV

Mrs. Parker was given to making reckless remarks, and it may be that she made that particular reckless remark on other occasions in her life. It was not true, or was true only for as long as she needed it to be. Certainly she had been proud of many poems and many stories; certainly she had been proud when she was asked to assemble them for a Viking Portable. She was less proud of the screenwriting she had done, and rightly so, for in nearly every case it had been pawed over by others and disimproved in the traditional Hollywood fashion. She wrote a large number of book reviews, mostly for *The New Yorker* and *Esquire*, and although, at the time, she may have thought of them as fugitive journeyman pieces, she fussed over them with as much care as if they were fiction. She did not have, like Wilson, a natural gift for literary journalism—where he cast the widest possible net and hauled up, to the world's astonishment, an unprecedented variety of fascinating sea monsters, Mrs. Parker dealt with books and writers on a small scale, sometimes with a facetiousness bred of unease. Evidently she feared that the praise she bestowed in her reviews would give readers less pleasure than the malicious one-line dismissals for which she was famous ("Tonstant Weader fwowed up").

Astonishingly, in the light of her harum-scarum ways, a large body of work had been accumulated. The book reviews and play reviews and other journalism aside, there stood the volumes in their not unimpressive number, and glancing along the row one saw that, whether by chance or design, the titles amounted to a capsule autobiography. *Enough Rope, Sunset Gun, Laments for the Living, Death and Taxes, After Such Pleasures, Not So Deep as a Well, Here Lies*—with a single exception, the titles all speak directly or indirectly of death, and the exception is concerned with man's loss of something profoundly good: the contentment after making love that is more than satiety. Why cannot we as cocks and lions jocund be? Why cannot we turn away even at the moment of highest joy from the distress of our continuously prefigured death? Under whatever disguise, this was Mrs. Parker's theme, and she never feared to sound its heartbreaking note throughout fifty years of writing. She was one of the wittiest people in the world and one of the saddest; if even now we go on laughing at something she happened to say very late at night in some long-since-vanished bar, we do so at our peril. Man is the animal that knows he dies, and the death's head grinning in the mirror back of all those lighted bottles is our own. There is nothing good in life, Mrs. Parker said, that will not be taken away. One of the things she admired most in Hemingway was how he had struggled to face this problem both in his life and in his writing. He had been so sure in youth that he would not choose his father's way out of life, by suicide, and Mrs. Parker had been so sure in youth that she could find no other means of dealing with the pain of being; and so Hemingway had killed himself and she had lived on, and toward the end there were only ghosts in the corners of the hotel room, silently reproaching her for having had the cowardice to live. It was no use asking them when she had ever claimed to be brave. If, as she said, she had always been the greatest little hoper in the world, she had known that hope was a form of folly and had nothing to do with either courage or wisdom.

Hope it was that tutored me,
    And Love that taught me more;
And now I learn at Sorrow's knee
    The self-same lore.

People ought to be one of two things, young or old.
No; what's the use of fooling? People ought to be one
of two things, young or dead.

But she had been young, and it had not been satisfactory. It was precisely then, in the years, say, from sixteen to twenty-three, that she was confirmed in her bleak view of how things are. We know little about her during those years, except that she had left the school she disliked and the family she disliked and was making her own difficult way in the world. Delicate and bold and virginal in her teens, she must have been determined even then to be found worthy of heartrending misadventures. There are hints of them in the early poems—hints that, given a choice between happiness and unhappiness, she would be prompted by some devil in her to choose unhappiness. She had the imagination of disaster, as so many people do who have lost a mother in infancy, and she cultivated this form of imagination and made it flourish. Her knack for causing things to end badly amounted, in her friends' eyes, to genius, and one cannot help thinking with sympathy of the miserable days and nights through which she drove a succession of distracted lovers. Edna St. Vincent Millay's confident, "We were very young, we were very merry,/We went back and forth all night on the ferry" would not have served the purposes of little Dottie Rothschild, standing tiptoe on the brink of doom: "Lips that taste of tears, they say,/Are the best for kissing." The lines are from the first poem in her first book, and we are not surprised to see that the poem is entitled "Threnody." She began her career as a poet with a song of lamentation and she ended it with what she called a war song, in which she urged her soldier-husband to be unfaithful to her. The span of her work is narrow and what it embraces is often slight, but the author of it is perhaps luckier than she supposed herself to be: as a writer, she had not counted on surviving, and the continued interest in her work in schools and colleges, where she is being read by the great-grandchildren of her contemporaries, would startle and delight her. There were circumstances under which, with an effort, she could refrain from making wisecracks; though it is risky to assume that an occasion for paying homage to her would be among them, we do well to take that chance. Mrs. Parker had, after all, when she chose to display them, perfect manners. She would be eager to conceal from us, for our sakes, how much readier she was to accept abuse than praise. Greatly daring, we salute her.

KENNETH PATCHEN

1911–1972

Kenneth Patchen was born on December 13, 1911, in Niles, Ohio, and attended public school in nearby Warren. In 1928 he graduated from high school and went to work in the local steel mill. Over the next two years he studied at the University of Wisconsin and at Commonwealth College in Mena, Arkansas. From there he took to the road, traveling around the United States and Canada while supporting himself doing odd jobs, and eventually came to rest in New York where he briefly attended Columbia University. In 1933 he went to Boston, where he was befriended by Conrad Aiken and John Wheelwright; that same year he met and married Miriam Oikemus, a marriage which lasted the rest of his life. Returning to New York, the couple settled in Greenwich Village, where Patchen worked on the WPA's American Guide series, and began selling verse regularly to a variety of magazines.

In 1936 Patchen's first book of verse, *Before the Brave*, was published by Random House to generally favorable reviews. With a Guggenheim fellowship in hand, the Patchens moved west that year, where in Los Angeles in 1937 Patchen suffered the disabling back injury which would plague him for the rest of his life. For the next two decades the couple relocated frequently, as Patchen continued to publish collections of verse and illustration, and to suffer more and more from the effects of his injury. In 1950 Patchen underwent the first of several operations on his spine, an effort paid for by money raised through a series of benefits organized by a committee headed by T. S. Eliot, Thornton Wilder, W. H. Auden, and Archibald MacLeish. Like the later operations, the surgery was ultimately unsuccessful, though a similar procedure in 1956 had beneficial effects which lasted until they were undone by a "surgical mishap" in 1959.

Moving to Palo Alto, California, Patchen spent the late 1950s preoccupied with what became known as the "poetry-with-jazz" movement, reading with jazz groups in clubs and halls up and down the West Coast. Though his back disability eventually forced him to return to a more sedentary way of life, Patchen continued to write and publish volumes of poetry, prose, and painting until his death on January 8, 1972.

Patchen's works are many and varied; notable among them are *First Will and Testament* (1937), *The Journal of Albion Moonlight* (published by private subscription in 1941), *Memoirs of a Shy Pornographer* (1945), *Sleepers Awake* (1946), *Red Wine and Yellow Hair* (1949), *Poems of Humor and Protest* (1954), *Hallelujah Anyway* (1966), and *The Collected Poems of Kenneth Patchen* (1968). Also important are two recordings, *Kenneth Patchen Reads with the Chamber Jazz Sextet* (1957) and *Kenneth Patchen Reads with Jazz in Canada* (1959).

From the *Journal of Albion Moonlight* by Kenneth Patchen.

I have forgotten my mask and my face was in it.

Man has been corrupted by his symbols. Language has killed the animal.

We permit no one to enter the web of flesh where we have our home . . . We retreat more deeply into ourselves; with each advancing moment the self retreats from us.

What horror can be greater than an army of monstrous dogs led by a human intelligence.

I say I hate the poor for the humility which keeps their faces pressed to the mud.

I have spent two years becoming a saint. It was not easy because always the man I was got in the way. This man's name was Albion Moonlight. He was puzzled by my behavior. I feel that he is nearly dead now.

Beware Albion Moonlight . . . They are beginning to suspect the truth.

He describes the nightmare of the war. The nightmare of the fragmented self. All the voices of the subconscious speaking simultaneously. "I propose to make the future and the present and the past happen at once."

"How it is possible to act if there be no result whatsoever but murder?"

Patchen does not exist in human life, human emotions. His figures are those of a nightmare, mutilated and incomplete. He is not in the dream either because if he were he would reach a world of cosmic unity, the collective unconscious. He is a man who reads newspapers and has nightmares. A blind man in the world of man.

What he describes is an animal awakened to fear and danger and hunger and murder. *Albion Moonlight* is chaos. If in Patchen there is a quest for insight and awareness it is the fumbling one of a blind man touching everything in darkness. His assertions seem like orders to force the self to be born, but the self is shattered, drifting, floating. Each time he begins anew. But the personage dissolves into nothingness. He begins

again. He describes a hundred abortions of the self. Each day a birth, abortion, and murder. No flowering. A blind man caught up in the violence of action before he has found his soul, the metaphysical seeing-eye dog. He seeks the reality of other human beings, but must murder in order to approach it and possess it. Or he himself must be murdered. The dimension of feeling by which people truly possess each other never appears. The book is full of groans, cries, but they are all physical, animal. It is a drama of impotence and destruction. Albion Moonlight has a vision which dissolves him and he is born and dies many times but is never truly born or never truly dies. The figures are incomplete, maimed.

They are prompt to action and lacking in emotional dimensions. There is a confusion of languages, gutter jargon, literary, colloquial, inflated to achieve rhetorical grandeur, a Tower of Babel creating only chaos. Albion is lost in mass murders. He is in limbo, the space before birth, when the eyes are not yet open. A child is weeping. He is possessed and haunted. There are all the preparations for birth, the preparation for the poem, for the novel; they are announced, about to be written, but never take form. Albion Moonlight carries an umbilical cord which was never severed. The amniotic fluid poisons its fetus. Every word is like floating debris, which does not coalesce into a thought.

An eye looked over his shoulder and made a cruel judgment.

There are always dogs waiting. They smell death and decay. There is a recurrent nightmare of martyrdom, persecution, and punishment. Albion is persecuted by soldiers, by gangsters, by his friends. He is always trapped.

Close the covers of this book and I will go on talking. You will be told that what I write is confused, without order, and I will tell you that my book is not concerned with the problems of art but with the problems of this world, with the problem of life itself, yes, of life itself.

I give them a look at the naked, snarling animal.

Albion writes a journal. Then he vanishes. A hand is writing a novel and seeking to capture Albion. Men embrace women. Men are murdered. Men appear in a setting of war that is not a war. Albion dies many times. But he is not born.

He utters cries of affirmation to create himself: "I am tender, I am strong, I am. I am."

It is a nightmare of violence. Every act of love or desire is an act of murder. Every act of sex remains strangely unconsummated, a murder takes the place of it. What I see in this book, what cries behind windows, haunting every scene, sightless, voiceless, throughout the drama of violent acts, what is murdered each time anew, what passes from one man to another, is a soul dispossessed by violence, crying to be born, *a soul not yet born.*

But where is the whole vision which will catalyze this chaos and guide it to its birth? Is this the American nightmare: violence, castration, fragmentation?

Is it Albion or Patchen who is blind and touches the letters of the writing as if they were Braille, the raised letters which must be touched but cannot be allowed to penetrate the blood directly through human vision? Chaos is born out of the great fissures which happen in the telling of the story. There are pauses. Silences. Mysteries. Fissures. It is a quest in the darkness, a stuttering. What is he hiding from? What crime has he committed? Is it a story of atonement, punishment? The self has to begin each day anew to reassert its existence. Every phrase is a contradiction of the other phrase. If language has killed the animal, then how is it only the animal is present in the book? When the animal repossesses man he goes mad. Murder takes the place of the sexual communion. Sightless, voiceless, wordless, howling animal Albion Moonlight.

Patchen comes sometimes without warning. He rings the bell. I know his ring because it is so heavy. He stands mute at the door. He does not utter a greeting. He sits down. Or he goes to the icebox to look for a drink. He sees that I am working. There is a half-finished page in the typewriter. He envinces no curiosity. His flesh is heavy.

I attend to his comfort. "Do you want coffee? Do you want a sandwich?" I attempt to create a conversation. "What do you hear from Henry?" I give him my notes on *Albion Moonlight.* He does not understand them. He turns on the radio. At first I thought there was a softness in his animal eyes. I talked to them. But they revolve unseeing. He is inert. He has the paleness of the sick. I understand Artaud's madness but not Patchen's. I understand Artaud because he *felt*, and was artistically articulate. But there is another reason. Artaud's was a torment of the spirit, and Patchen's is a hell from which all spirit is absent.

In his madness, Artaud never became a snarling animal. Artaud's concerns were with expression. With creation in the midst of his own nightmare. Patchen says only: "I need fifteen dollars for my gas bill." I explained the reduction of my income, the writing I was doing for the collector, and my last money order sent to Henry. There is no human understanding or response. Only silence and sullenness. No possible friendship there.—ANAÏS NIN, *The Diary of Anaïs Nin 1939–1944* (entry for December 1940), ed. Gunther Stuhlmann, 1969, pp. 62–66

The first thing one would remark on meeting Kenneth Patchen is that he is the living symbol of protest. I remember distinctly my first impression of him when we met in New York: it was that of a powerful, sensitive being who moved on velvet pads. A sort of sincere assassin, I thought to myself, as we shook hands. This impression has never left me. True or not, I feel that it would give him supreme joy to destroy with his own hands all the tyrants and sadists of this earth together with the art, the institutions and all the machinery of everyday life which sustain and glorify them. He is a fizzing human bomb ever threatening to explode in our midst. Tender and ruthless at the same time, he has the faculty of estranging the very ones who wish to help him. He is inexorable: he has no manners, no tact, no grace. He gives no quarter. Like the gangster, he follows a code of his own. He gives you the chance to put up your hands before shooting you down. Most people, however, are too terrified to throw up their hands. They get mowed down.

This is the monstrous side of him, which makes him appear ruthless and rapacious. Within the snorting dragon, however, there is a gentle prince who suffers at the mention of the slightest cruelty or injustice. A tender soul, who soon learned to envelop himself in a mantle of fire in order to protect his sensitive skin. No American poet is as merciless in his invective as Patchen. There is almost an insanity to his fury and rebellion.

Like Gorky, Patchen began his career in the university of life early. The hours he sacrificed in the steel mills of Ohio, where he was born, served to fan his hatred for a society in which inequality, injustice and intolerance form the foundation of life. His years as a wanderer, during which he scattered his manuscripts like seed, corroborated the impressions gained at home, school and mill. Today he is practically an invalid, thanks to the system which puts the life of a machine above that of a human being. Suffering from arthritis of the spine, he is confined to bed most of the time. He lies on a huge bed in a doll's house near the river named after Henry Hudson, a sick giant consumed by the poisonous indifference of a world which has more use for mousetraps than for poets. He writes book after book, prose as well as poetry, never certain when "they" will come and dump him (with the bed) into the street. This has been going on now for over seven years, if I am not mistaken. If Patchen were to become well, able to use hands and feet freely, it is just possible that he would celebrate the occasion by pulling the house down about the ears of some unsuspecting victim of his scorn and contempt. He would do it slowly, deliberately, thoroughly. And in utter silence.

That is another quality of Patchen's which inspires dread on first meeting—his awesome silence. It seems to spring from his flesh, as though he had silenced the flesh. It is uncanny. Here is a man with the gift of tongues and he speaks not. Here is a man who drips words but he refuses to open his mouth. Here is a man dying to communicate, but instead of conversing with you he hands you a book or a manuscript to read. The silence which emanates from him is black. He puts one on tenterhooks. It breeds hysteria. Of course he is shy. And no matter how long he lives he will never become urbane. He is American through and through, and Americans, despite their talkiness, are fundamentally silent creatures. They talk in order to conceal their innate reticence. It is only in moments of deep intimacy that they break loose. Patchen is typical. When finally he does open his mouth it is to release a hot flood of words. His emotion tears loose in clots.

A voracious reader, he exposes himself to every influence, even the worst. Like Picasso, he makes use of everything. The innovator and initiator are strong in him. Rather than accept the collaboration of a second-rate artist, he will do the covers for a book himself, a different one for each copy. And how beautiful and original are these individual cover designs from the hand of a writer who makes no pretense of being a painter or illustrator! How interesting, too, are the typographical arrangements which he dictates for his books! How competent he can be when he has to be his own publisher! (See *The Journal of Albion Moonlight.*) From a sickbed the poet defies and surmounts all obstacles. He has only to pick up the telephone to throw an editorial staff into a panic. He has the will of a tyrant, the persistence of a bull. "This is the way I want it done!" he bellows. And by God it gets done that way. —HENRY MILLER, "Patchen: Man of Anger and Light" (1946), *Stand Still Like the Hummingbird*, 1962, pp. 27–29

Even in *First Will and Testament*, Kenneth Patchen had already taken a new turn, startling us by his audacious disdain of traditional methods of poetic composition. His spiritual kinship with the Surrealists is revealed in his ability to circumvent the guard of censorship and allow tabooed reports to trickle past the frontiers of censorship. He is drawn between two poles of creative desire: one leads him toward the creation of poetry that is hard, sensuous, direct, of the earth, earthy; the other prompts him to experiment with "metaphysical," dissociated, spiritualized images and lines distilled from the alembic of the unconscious, nebulous as mist, puzzling and "aberrational" as a Surrealist painting by Salvador Dali. More and more, Patchen is setting himself in opposition to the world of reality by seeking to escape from it. He has become, as in *The Teeth of the Lion*, an intrepid explorer of the underworld of the unconscious. Obsession with the cruelty and evil of contemporary life is in this volume masked beneath a surface of Surrealist imagery, but now and again the conscious hurt leaps forth in a piercing cry of horror. It is the madness and homicidal hatred of men which Patchen cannot bear, and this serves to explain "the neurosis of escape," "the Surrealist paranoia," from which he seems to suffer. He has reached the stage where his love of life, his worship of its overwhelming beauty, its infinite variety and profusion of forms, leaves him almost inarticulate, grasping for words that will shadow forth, however dimly, the mystery of this radiant super-reality, but unlike the professional Surrealists he is never irresponsible. His violent dissociations of ideas and "free" imagery are controlled by a prophetic ideal, a fundamental personal integrity. Where Freud found the death-wish implanted in human beings, the poet discovers it in the civilization of his time. *The Dark Kingdom*, for example, is the poetic, imaginative expression of Freud's essay, "Thoughts on War and Death," published during the height of the First World War. Patchen's poetry is an outpouring of horror and an outburst of compassion. Man must make his peace with death; the savior must be born anew.—CHARLES I. GLICKSBURG, "The World of Kenneth Patchen," *AQ*, Autumn 1951, pp. 264–65

Often at night, when I see that, indeed, the sky is a "deep throw of stars," I think of a poet named Kenneth Patchen, who once told me that it is. Because of this and a few other passages I remember years after first reading them, I have tried to keep track of Patchen, and have gone through most of his books (all, in fact, except *Sleepers Awake*, which I abandoned in despair). I have heard recently that he has joined the "San Francisco School," but in reality he was its only permanent member twenty years before the group was ever conceived in the impatient mind of Kenneth Rexroth, and is still, despite having produced a genuinely impassable mountain of tiresome, obvious, self-important, sprawling, sentimental, witless, preachy, tasteless, useless poems and books, the best poet that American literary expressionism can show. Occasionally, in fragments and odds and ends nobody wants to seek out any more, he is a writer of superb daring and invention, the author of a few passages which are, so far as I can tell, comparable to the most intuitively beautiful writing ever done. He is a poet not so much in form as in essence, a condition of which we should all be envious, and with which we should never be satisfied. To evoke the usual standards of formal art in Patchen's case is worse than meaningless. He cannot give anything through the traditional forms (those who suggest that

he ought at least to try should take a look at some of the rhymed poems in *Before the Brave*). I do not like to read most of Patchen's work, for it seems to me a cruel waste, but he somehow manages to make continuing claims on my attention that other more consistent poets do not. If there is such a thing as pure or crude imagination, Patchen has it, or has had it. With it he has made twenty-five years of Notes, in the form of scrappy, unsatisfactory, fragmentarily brilliant poems, for a single, unwritten cosmic Work, which bears, at least in some of its parts, analogies to the prophetic books of Blake. Yet the words, the phrases, and the lines that are supposed to make up the individual pieces almost never coalesce, themselves, into wholes, because Patchen looks upon language as patently unworthy of the Vision, and treats it with corresponding indifference and contempt. This is the reason he is not a good writer, or a good prophet, either: this, and the fact that his alternately raging and super-sentimental view of things is too violent, centerless, convulsive, and one-dimensional to be entirely convincing. But he has made and peopled a place that would never have had existence without him: the realm of the *Dark Kingdom*, where "all who have opposed in secret, are . . . provided with green crowns," and where the vague, powerful figures of fantasmagoric limbo, the dream people, and, above all, the mythic animals that only he sees, are sometimes as inconsolably troubling as the hallucinations of the madman or the alcoholic, and are occasionally, as if by accident, rendered in language that accords them the only kind of value possible to this kind of writing: makes them obsessive, unpardonable, and magnificent. It is wrong of us to wish that Patchen would "pull himself together." He has never been together. He cannot write poems, as the present book (*When We Were Here Together*) heartlessly demonstrates. But his authentic and terrible hallucinations infrequently come to great good among the words which they must use. We should leave it at that, and take what we can from him.—JAMES DICKEY, "Kenneth Patchen" (1958), *Babel to Byzantium*, 1968, pp. 71–72

WILLIAM CARLOS WILLIAMS
"A Counsel of Madness"

Fantasy, 1942, pp. 102–7

White moonlight, penetrating, distorting the mind is a symbol of madness. It denotes, negatively, also an absence of the sun. The sun does not touch the pages of Kenneth Patchen's *The Journal of Albion Moonlight*. So that what virtues are to be found here may be taken for madness. Could we interpret them we should know the cure. That is, I think, Patchen's intention, so, in reverse, to make the cure not only apparent but, by the horror of his picture, imperative.

By such exhibitions the paterfamilias of fifty years or more ago, showing the horrible effects of syphilis, would seek to drive his sons to chastity. The age is syphilitic, cancerous, even leprous in Patchen's opinion—show it then, in itself and in its effects, upon the body and upon the mind—that we may know ourselves and be made whole thereby. And of it all, says Patchen, perhaps the only really normal and good thing remaining is the sexual kiss of two bodies, full fledged.

In criticising such a book one should pay Patchen at least the compliment of being as low down as he is himself—and as outspoken. If he has attempted drastic strictures upon his age may we not demand of him by what authority he does so? Is his picture a true one? And does he prove himself sufficiently powerful as a writer to portray it? To scream violently against vile practices does not dispose of them. Furthermore, though this book is full of violent statement, is it violent, really? Violence overthrows. Does this succeed in overthrowing anything at all or is it not, lacking full ability, no more than a sign of the author's and our own defeat, hiding itself in noise? Shall not one say, finally, that this book is erotically and pornographically sound; if it lives at all it will be for no more than its lewdity that it does so? That is the danger.

Everything depends upon the writing, a dangerous genre: either to the minds of those who read it it will work toward the light or burrow in the mud. It can't be half good. It can't do both.

For myself I ask for no authorities, so likely to be gutted of any worth in our day, if not positively rotten. There is no authority evidenced in this but the man himself. If there are others like him, if we are not all somewhat as he is, provided he write truthfully and out of a gifted mind, he has a right to speak and needs no other authority. But if he belies himself and us, overpreens himself and makes use of devices that are shopworn and cheap, that's a different matter. We owe Patchen nothing as Patchen. But if he's a man and we feel a great fellowship with him, a deep sympathy, then we can tolerate his vagaries, his stupidities even, even his screaming. But if he shows that he enjoys that more than the cure. That would be bad.

For what we're after is a cure. That at its best is what the book's about. A man terribly bitten and seeking a cure, a cure for the bedeviled spirit of his day. Nor are we interested in a Punch and Judy morality with a lily-white soul wrapped in a sheet—or a fog, it doesn't matter which. We are ready and willing to accept a low down human spirit which if it didn't have a hip-joint we'd never be in a position to speak of it at all. We know and can feel for that raving reality, bedeviled by erotic dreams, which often enough is ourselves. This book is from the gutter.

The story is that oldest of all themes, the journey, evangelical in purpose, that is to say, with a purpose to save the world from impending doom. A message must be got through to Roivas, read the name backward.

May 2. It starts under a sky of stone, from the region about New York City, in a countryside where an angel lies in a "little thicket." "It couldn't have hurt much when they slit its throat."

There is a simple statement of faith at the beginning:

> He was the Word that spake it;
> He took the bread and brake it;
> And what the Word did make it,
> I do believe and take it.

He must get through a message to the people such as they are who have lost hope in the world.

It gets up to August 27. And that is all. It ends. It ends because it has never succeeded in starting. There is—after a hundred thousand words—nothing to be said.

Albion's heart is broken by the war in Europe. Surely his message has to do with that. That is the message. But it is not advice to go in or to stay out. It is order lost. For the war has been caused by humanity, thwarted not by lack of order but by too much. Murder is the desperate theme. Murder out of despair.

The chief defect of such a book lies in the very plan and method of it, one is locked up with the other.

Patchen slams his vivid impressions on the page and lets them go at that. He is investigating the deformities of truth which he perceives in and about him. Not idly. He is seeking, the book is seeking, if I am correct, a new order among the debris of a mind conditioned by old and persistent wreckage. Patchen is seeking a way through among the debris and, as he goes, seeks also to reveal his meaning by truthful statement—

under conditions of white moonlight. From that to reorder the universe.

There can be no checks, taboos or revisions permitted to such a plan since the only chance it has of laying down positive values comes from first impressions, and they distorted. What else, in the writing, could a man do or say other than to put down the moonlight delineaments of the landscape he is witnessing? Could any traveller through a jungle do more? Or less? All that we demand of him is that he do not see and put down what is not there. Also that he do not fail to put down what is there. It is, in fact, one mind, his tortured own, that Patchen is travelling through and attempting to reveal to us by its observed attributes. In treating of that there can be no deleting, no pruning no matter how the initiative may wander.

Where does the journey take place did I say? In America? Why not? One place is like another. In the mind? How? What is the mind? You can't separate it from the body or the land any more than you can separate America from the world. We are all one, we are all guilty. No accusation is here permitted—Moonlight himself must, is forced to, take part in the murder no matter how he would escape it. All he can do is take part *willingly*.

The journey does traverse the mind. Therefore it gets to Chicago, Arizona, Galen. The dream which is more solid than the earth. And out of the cauldron of thought the earth itself is reborn and we walk on it into the small towns of Texas and Missouri.

There can be no graph except the map you pick up at a gas station—but as we hold it the graph becomes vertical also and takes us up into the tips of the mountains of Galen. People expand and shrink to the varying proportions of those in *Alice in Wonderland*, and every day but—desperately. We are at war, we are insane.

Reality? Do we think that America is not reality or that human beings are excluded from it? Death Valley appears. It is the mind itself, where Jackeen lies murdered. By Moonlight himself. It rots and stinks and is arrested and hung up—while one foot drops off on the gallows and a geranium sprouts from its left ear with roots in the heart of that corpse. Who is doing the hanging? It is again—Moonlight. Moonlight. He himself must be identified with the foulest crimes he imagines. He must. He cannot separate himself and be alone. Such is his journey.

Naturally everything observed will not be significant or new and it is the business of the writer to be careful of that. Yet, I shouldn't wish to advise him—at the edge of the thicket may lie a discovery, no matter how small it will seem at the time, which holds that quality of coming out of foulness faultlessly clean, a new order of thought shucking off the old which may justify a thousand redundancies. That's the chance taken by such a method. Tortured and perverted as we may think it, the book represents the same outlook over the world as did the Vita Nuova—reversed.

It is a book come of desperation, the desperation of the thwarted and the young. Write and discover. Go, move, waggle your legs in more terrible jungles than any primitive continent could ever afford, the present day shambles of the Mind. Tortured as you may be, seek cleanliness, seek vigor, unafraid. Seek love! Such is the New Life dimly perceivable through the mediaeval horrors of Patchen's hell. This is the order he is seeking.

Oh, we had a call to "order" some years ago, dead now or nearly dead now, fortunately. Its warts, like the hair of corpses, continue a separate existence, in the academies, and breed others of the sort from year to year; but the body has hygienically rotted away. This is not what Patchen is thinking of. Such an "order" consisted mainly in amputating all the extravagances, all the unimaginable off-shoots of the living thing to make it conform to—those very restrictions from which, at its best, the present day is an almost miraculous escape. What they attempted was like that Nazi "order" now familiar in Europe which already in order to maintain itself has found it necessary to commit three hundred and fifty thousand murders among the cilivian population.

Whether or not this book is a good one (let's not talk prematurely of genius) I believe it to be a right one, a well directed one and a hopeful one. It is the sort of book that must be attempted from time to time, a book to violate all the taboos, a racial necessity as it is a paradisiacal one, a purge in the best sense—suggesting a return to health and to the craft itself after the little word-and-thought pansies have got through their nibbling. I don't say it's the best *sort* of book, as the world goes, but it is the sort of book some one should write in every generation, some one writer—let himself go! and drop it for at least twenty years thereafter.

Patchen lets himself go. Such a book will rest heavily on the character, ability and learning of the man who writes it. If it is a failure, not clear or powerful enough to deserve the concept of it I am suggesting, that is his hard luck. But the book should be written, a book that had better perhaps have been postponed to a maturer period of the man's career—but which had after all to be written *now*.

That's precisely it. Even though it acknowledge itself to be a foregone failure—the book must still have been made as it is, the work of a young man, a new man—finding himself unprepared, though vocal, in the world. He voices the world of the young—as he finds it, screaming against what we, older, have given him. This precisely is the book's prime validity.

Though Patchen is still young, still not ready, shall he be silent for that? That is the significance and reason for all his passion, that he is young, the seriousness and poignancy of it. And it does, whatever its failings, find a crack in the armament of the killing suppression which is driving the world to the only relief it knows, murder! today. It is itself evidence, as a thing in itself, of our perversity and failure.

We destroy because we cannot escape. Because we are confined. There is no opening for us from the desperate womb of our times. We cannot get out. Everywhere we turn, to Christ himself, we are met by a wall of "order," a murderous cross fire which is offered us by "learning" and the frightened conformists of our world.

For once a writer insists on the maddening facts of our plight in plain terms; we grow afraid, we dare not pretend that we know or can know anything, straight out, in our own right. We have to be "correctly" educated first. But here and there, confronting Christ with Hitler—you won't believe it can be done—there are passages in this book where the mind threatens to open and a vivid reality of the spirit to burst forth and bloom in terrifying destructfulness—the destroying of all that we think we know in our time. It threatens to break out through the writing into a fact of the spirit even though it may not often be quite powerful enough to do so. I cannot specify these knots of understanding, of candor that—are the book's high places. The feeling that is experienced at those best moments is of an impending purity that might be. This is the order that I speak of.

What might it not do to the world if ONCE a universal truth, order, of the sort glimpsed here could be made free. It is as if it were too bright and that that is the reason no one has yet glimpsed it. Too bright! Van Gogh went mad staring at the sun and the stars.

I say all this is approbation—but writing is also a craft and we have to look well at that in this book. Florid and uncontrolled as Patchen's imagination may be, his images foetid, the passions of his Honeys and Claras funnelled into the socket of sex, compressed as a bomb to explode in colored lights—the writing must not be florid in any loose sense. And I should say, tangential as the thought may be, the writing is, in general well muscled, the word often brilliantly clear.

Many devices are used at time successfully, but not always so. There are lapses, disheartening lapses, and though I have said that in this sort of writing a man cannot stop for corrections yet, as readers, we have a right to object.

However we face it, one must still hold to the writing. Writing is not an instrument. The best writing happens on the page. It is the proof, with that stamp of the man upon it signifying it alive to live on independent of him, a thing in itself. The Word. We are responsible finally to that.

The book's defects are glaring, conjoined, as I have said, inextricably with its virtues. It must have been written haphazard to unearth the good. Whether or not there is enough good to carry off the method will remain the question. Many will doubt it, find the book to be no more a journey than that taken by a dog trying to catch his own tail.

One of the chief weaknesses of the book is its total lack of humor. Certainly the style is green and needs seasoning—but having said that, one has begged the entire question— nevertheless it must be said. The book would benefit by revisions and rather severe cutting. Sometimes the effect is fat and soft, even spotted, when Patchen confuses his subject matter with the workmanship to bad effect. These things make it at times difficult for the reader to plow ahead. But if, in spite of that, he is willing to face and cross these sapless spaces he will come to patches of really astonishing observation, profound feeling and a strongly imaginative and just use of the word which, to me, give the book a highly distinctive character.

FREDERICK ECKMAN
"The Comic Apocalypse of Kenneth Patchen"
Poetry, September 1958, pp. 389–92

To begin with a familiar point of reference: Patchen seems to me more like Blake than any other contemporary poet. There is the same sense of deep isolation, partly self-willed, from the mass of humanity; of choking rage at shoddy secularity, orthodoxy, and materialism; of a tender, childlike wonder for the beautiful, pure, and innocent; of a desire for joy and freedom that leads at last into mystic contemplation. His poems, like Blake's, are of three kinds: lyrics of purity and gentleness; fierce satires directed at the modern world; poems of mystic prophecy. The principal difference appears to be one of tone: Patchen's world view, or vision of apocalypse, is frequently comic, while Blake's is never.

I would not push the comparison further, wishing only to note that after a century and a half Blake still remains an enigma to all but a handful of devoted students. Literary criticism, which as its natural function seeks to place every poet's work within a rational structure that includes the work of every other poet, will find Patchen as difficult to categorize as it has found Eliot easy. Most of the recorded attempts thus far— and they are pitifully few—accomplish nothing: dreamy praise by friends and disciples, careless dismissal by the orthodox.

But this is merely a book review, not a definitive essay. I generalize thus far only to make clear the present state of things, which is this: after twenty years and twenty-five books, who knows anything about Patchen? I speak here as a poet, rather testily challenging the self-avowed competence of modern literary criticism, and let the matter rest.

Selected Poems is a revised edition of the inexpensive New Classics volume issued a decade ago. Nearly sixty poems have been added, from four new titles. Patchen apart, the enlargement is a good idea, and I hope that the publisher will consider doing the same for the companion volumes by Pound, Williams, and Rukeyser. *Selected Poems* is a valuable book in two ways: as an excellent introduction to Patchen for those unfamiliar with his work, and as a convenient volume for the reader of modern poetry who cannot easily acquire or read through Patchen's long list of difficult-to-locate titles. The provenance of each poem is indicated in the table of contents, another convenient feature that the recent ruckus over Auden's *Collected Poems* makes us appreciate. Those who recall Patchen as the *enfant terrible* of late Depression days will be pleased to find "Street Corner College," "Do the Dead Know What Time It Is?", "The Origin of Baseball," "Fog", and "The Character of Love Seen as a Search for the Lost":

> You, the woman; I, the man; this, the world:
> And each is the work of all.
>
> There is the muffled step in the snow; the stranger;
> The crippled wren; the nun; the dancer; the Jesus-
>   wing
> Over the walkers in the village; and there are
> Many beautiful arms about us and the things we
>   know.

And those who have not seen the recent amusing *Hurrah for Anything* will enjoy such pieces, with Patchen's own fantastic illustrations, as this:

THE CARELESS LITTLE SPY

> There was a careless little spy
> Who carried the Secret Code in the same briefcase
> With the Master Plan and a wad of dancehall tickets;
> Which may explain why some very Big Wheels
> Are running about on their rims this morning.

When We Were Here Together is a beautiful book, inside and out. In an attractive octavo format, on fine paper with large, readable type, it is a volume typographically worthy of its contents, as so few books of contemporary poetry are. Unfortunately the publisher did not include a colophon to give his printer well-deserved credit. These are all lyric poems, ranging in tone from gentle through savage to weirdly comic. Nearly half of them are in a form which I take to be Patchen's own: eighteen lines, each with a fixed number of words (5, 4, 3, etc.) and a regular pattern of stanza divisions (4, 1, 4, etc.). Each poem has a three-word title, and each contains exactly seventy words. The intention is clearly toward a sonnet variation:

AN EASY DECISION

> I had finished my dinner
> Gone for a walk
> It was fine
> Out and I started whistling
> It wasn't long before
>
> I met a
>
> Man and his wife riding on
> A pony with seven
> Kids running along beside them
> I said hello and
> Went on
> Pretty soon I met another
> Couple
> This time with nineteen
> Kids and all of them

> Riding on
> A big smiling hippopotamus
> I invited them home

It might, if nothing else, be offered to refute the long-standing charge that Patchen's work is "formless"—whatever that means. But I for one would be content to let the poems stand on their other, non-prosodic, excellences.

Poemscapes is another title from the press of Jonathan Williams, who seems at present the only sustaining competitor of New Directions for publishing in quantity the best avant-garde poetry in the most original formats. This volume is made up, rather like a book of hours or a breviary, into fifty-two "poemscapes"—each consisting of four short prose poems. As with the sonnet-variations, there seems to be an imposition of form by word-count. I find these poems eloquent and beautiful, but difficult of immediate comprehension. Except that their imagery is more exotic and their pattern somewhat more formal, they remind me a great deal of Williams's *Kora in Hell*. The difference is that Williams had set about to solve a creative problem which he found essentially secular, where Patchen seems to be moving further and further away from things of this world and into purely mystical realms:

> Bloodred are the fishes that sleep in the grove. Bloodred are their dreaming faces, bloodred the leaflike scale on their little hands. Soon will the maidens come to wake them, the lilylike maidens . . .
>
> Milkwhite are the fishes that sleep in the grove. Milkwhite the dreamlike glow from their little breasts that are so cold. Soon will the masters come to wake them, the masters of the longlost. . . . O soon will the masters come in their snow-sheeted robes . . .
>
> Deathcolored are the fishes that sleep in the grove. Deathcolored the fishes . . .
>
> O the color of life itself are the fishes that sleep in the grove! Lifecolored are their slowly opening eyes, lifecolored the twiglike unfolding of their gentle hands! Soon they will come among us. (XVII)

As a concluding generalization, I note that Patchen's satire, a virtue of the early poems, seems to be absorbing itself into the larger pattern of his mature work; that his rollicking sense of the comic has mellowed into humor; that his intensely personal love lyrics are widening out into a gesture of compassion toward all things created. At times he seems almost saintly:

> Wide, wide in the rose's side
> Sleeps a child without sin,
> And any man who loves in this world
> Stands here on guard over him.

RAYMOND NELSON
From "Personalism"
Kenneth Patchen and American Mysticism
1984, pp. 50–63

Patchen's use of ⟨. . .⟩ moralistic literary personalism is seen best, even if with some difficulty, in *The Journal of Albion Moonlight*, in which the nature of moral consciousness and the release of its literary voice are central themes. Here Patchen (or, more exactly, his representative, Albion) repeatedly describes his method in explicitly personalistic terms. "My purpose?" he writes, "It is nothing remarkable: I wish to speak to you."[1] He elaborates this attitude in language that resembles his friend and colleague, Henry Miller's: "Men were made to talk to one another. You can't understand that. But I tell you that the writing of the future will be just this kind of writing—one man trying to tell another man of the events in *his own heart*. Writing will become speech" (200). He emphasizes the intensity of his efforts to make direct contact: "I think you will agree that I am alive in every part of this book; turn back twenty, thirty, one hundred pages—*I am back there*. That is why I hate the story; characters are not snakes that they can shed their skins on every page—there can be only one action: what a man is . . . ah! but I am in the room with you. I write this book *as an action*. Like knocking a man down" (261).

The Journal of Albion Moonlight opens with a series of entries by Albion, who is leading a band of pilgrims toward Galen, the home of Roivas (go ahead, read it it backward), and presumably a place of peace and fulfillment. Although the pilgrims have in a sense abandoned a civilization committed to war and subjected themselves to a nightmarish journey through madness in order to find some better world, they insist that they are not running away. Their pilgrimage is also a missionary venture into America, a last desperate attempt to reestablish innocence—"It was essential that we bring our message to the people who had lost hope in the world. . . . Our religion was life. Flowers, brooks, trees. . . . Now we are held here and the world will perish because no one is saying we love you, we believe in you" (17). The Albion of this early pilgrimage is a defensively tough character who is nevertheless determined to save humanity and is already making his first assaults on the literary culture he associates with the general failure of civilization. His circumstances reflect the plight of the transcendental artist: his journal is written in the service of humanity, but he is threatened with destruction by those who do not understand it.

In these opening pages Albion is also a visionary mystic who is capable from time to time of exultation in a "love for all beings." He experiences mystical identification with other persons, and even participates momentarily in a rapt union with the knowledge and nature of God. However, he is not entirely in control of his mystical faculty, so that the quality of his extensions of self is determined primarily by the nature of the being with which he identifies. Mystical identity depends heavily on perception, and at this point Albion's perception is largely conditioned by the terrifying forces of war and insanity.

Albion's early writing is as largely uncontrolled as his life itself. The journal in which this fragment of the story is told is, of course, a nonliterary mode; it is not given form by an intellect outside of its time and aware of overall causality, but simply follows day-to-day action indiscriminately. The significance of this choice of genres may be explained by Van Wyck Brooks, who for several years early in his career was preoccupied with the moral and spiritual dilemma posed by literary form. Brooks defined poetry in Emersonian terms as the primordial language of spirit ("For poetry was all written before time was," Emerson said). Form, Brooks thought, was a social institution that allowed people to communicate, but was subject to economic and political pressures, and thus stifled in rhetoric the primordial and spontaneous element of poetry. To put poetry into form, then, compromised poetry. The writer must incessantly struggle, to greater or lesser success, with that necessary compromise, but some advanced spirits—Brooks called them sufferers from the "malady of the ideal"—found themselves unable to make it:

A great vision shatters them. They become fragmentary. They can express themselves only in the intimacy of personal confessions, unrelated, of

which every sentence is warm, molten, malleable, without the alloy of rhetoric which gives form and currency to literary works. . . . In their hands the journal becomes a kind of vicarious work of art—the work of art perhaps of souls in harmony with the universal. It endeavors to record the soul's impressions immediately without the brokerage of form, to give an expression to intuitions having the spontaneity of the intuitions themselves.[2]

Brooks was referring specifically to several French journal-keepers, but his observation might illuminate as well the fondness of American mystical writers for the journal form and fictional adaptations of it. Notable examples include the voluminous journals and diaries of Emerson and Thoreau, Whitman's *Memoranda during the War*, Williams's *Kora in Hell* and "The Descent of Winter," Merton's fictional *My Argument with the Gestapo* and autobiographical *The Sign of Jonas*, and Steinbeck's *Log* from *Sea of Cortez*.

Late in his narrative, Albion Moonlight himself becomes a theoretician of the significance of the journal. The passage also defines his symbolic stature:

The journal, whether real or imaginary, must conform to only one law: it must be at any given moment what the journal-keeper wants it to be at any given moment. It is easily seen from this that time is of the greatest importance in the journal; indeed, there must be as many journals as there are days covered. The true journal can have no plan for the simple reason that no man can plan his days. Do you seriously doubt this? I did. I ventured forth early this summer with a definite project in my mind: it was my intention to set down the story of what happened to myself and to a little group of my friends—and I soon discovererd that what was happening to us was happening to everyone. . . .

It was too late to write a book; it was my duty to write all books. I could not write about a few people; it was my role to write about everyone. (305–6)

The journal, then records the daily circumstances of the pilgrims, and if the causality of their strange world is sometimes lacking (because Albion only partly understands it), the narrative is relatively uncomplicated and easily followed. It is the movement in time from one place to another toward Galen and Roivas, which are ostensibly positive although vague goals, and the demonic presences that haunt the expressionistic landscape represent the difficulties of the way. After fifty-seven pages, however, Albion begins a novel, the text of which alternates with the journal for nearly the remainder of the book and complicates matters considerably. The novel attempts to understand the events of the journal by fictionalizing them, and its themes, characters, and action are interwoven so tightly with those of the journal that it is impossible to distinguish between them with perfect clarity. Journal and novel, however, are parallel texts, and the particular concerns of the novel are epitomized in the pleadings of a wise hag whom Albion encounters during one of his mystical seizures of self: "I ask ye not to do murder, not to think evil, not to violate the girl-child in the thicket of thy despair" (113). The thematic concern with the violation of the girl-child in the novel parallels the concern with war, the historical obscenity, in the journal. The journal laments the general failure of mankind to find love and peace; the novel records the failure of the individual to respect innocence. In the novel, the meaning of the journey to Roivas (who assumes here overtones of evil) is echoed in the chase after Leah, Roivas's disturbingly beautiful daughter, whose many incarnations represent the idealization of the feminine principle, and whose appearances are marked by violent changes of tone. As a transcendental poet, Albion wants desperately to be able to portray tenderness and purity in both woman and the sexual relationship, but he is forced to record instead the details of an essentially sordid struggle for sexual priority. Passages shift within a sentence or so from lyrical delicacy to cynical lewdness, and Albion himself is transformed in as short a space from lover to rapist and murderer.

The violence of the novel is every bit as pervasive as that of the journal, and even more feverish. One nightmarish scene is definitive and recurs with compulsive regularity. In it, Albion hurriedly writes his fiction as he is on trial or about to be executed for a rape-murder which he both did and did not commit, which both did and did not happen. Albion is guilty of the crime because he shares as a man in all human guilt, but his judges (usually the other pilgrims) are not swayed by considerations of justice. They are determined to assassinate him solely because, as a poet, he sees through hypocrisy and deceit, and thus represents the destruction of the old world.

The narrative line of *The Journal of Albion Moonlight* breaks into more novels, journals, and abortive scraps of other forms than I have identified here, and it is of some importance to distinguish among them if the fiction is finally to make sense.[3] For our limited purposes, however, the original novel and journal will suffice, because the other formal digressions are basically elaborations upon them. The original journal, which runs from 2 May to 27 August, continues throughout the book, although it appears several times to have been abandoned and especially near the end is difficult to follow. The novel supplements the journal nearly to the conclusion of the narrative. In the journal the pilgrimage to Galen progresses (without any consistent geographical orientation) across America, and the American continent becomes the great battlefield of the war. The account of the pilgrimage also develops into an extended satire (interposed with descriptions of war, and lighter in tone) on the American scene. In a series of brief satirical sketches of small-town life in the United States, the pilgrims visit the likes of Buford, Mississippi; Decatur, Illinois; and Saginaw, Michigan.

As Albion grows accustomed to the dangers of the road, his mysticism becomes increasingly less determined by external forces and his literary inspiration increasingly dominant. Among the values metaphorically associated with Galen are absolute identity and true art, and Albion, closing in, becomes powerful enough to change the nature of even the reality he must survive. As the journey nears Galen, and Albion himself is more forcefully offered as the definitive basis of art, the texture of the narrative degenerates, and the journal and novel entries become increasingly difficult to pick out of the literary rubble which clutters every page. Albion's novel, a literary form, simply runs down and collapses into its component parts. The journal, as a nonliterary form, continues to the end. Both novel and journal, however, culminate in a death scene in which the worldly Albion, who shared in the guilt for the girl-child, is destroyed in order that his spiritual self may be released (250), and the narrative ends in a still ambiguous Galen, where Albion again displays the wisdom gleaned from his physical death. That his knowledge is neither comforting nor redeeming indicates the depth of Patchen's despondency during World War II.

Although it is the most reliable narrative element, the movement in time and space from the New York of 2 May to the Galen of 27 August provides no indisputable reality on which to build an interpretation. Near the end, a parallel entry for 2 May in "The Little Journal of Albion Moonlight" (there

has been one other variant entry for this first day of the pilgrimage) suddenly informs us that Albion has never left home. "There is more of the world here in this room with me than I can understand" (306), he tells the friends who would have been (and in the main narrative are) his companions on the way. The surprise is not meant to confuse or complicate the story line, but to return the fiction to its definitive vision of what is real—the author at his desk.

The Journal of Albion Moonlight is about itself, its growth, and its own authorial narrative consciousness. It systematically destroys the conventional responses readers bring to fiction in order that Albion Moonlight (who is simply the poetic aspect of Kenneth Patchen) may expose the reader to his moral perception without the intermediary stages of meaning fiction usually employs. His attacks on traditional literary form are meant to explode the audience-consciousness that distinguishes books from other realities and force us to accept him, rather than our usual authorities, as our guide. His role as Whitmanian poet-priest informs two characteristic passages from *The Journal*: "The great writer will take a heroic stand against literature: *by changing the nature of what is to be done,* he will be the first to do what the voice of dreaming does; he will heal the hurt where God's hand pressed too hard in His zeal to make us more than the animals" (308); and: "Thus, against murder, against hypocrisy, and for life, for all that is most beautiful and noble in man, for the immense joy of being alive, do I speak. I am an island in a cess-pool called History" (204). This purpose challenges the writer to create a new body of literary assumptions, which Patchen attempts to incorporate into the figure of Albion himself.

Albion Moonlight is the author of his various narratives at the same time that he is a character in them, and he is openly aware that he is a created literary character in a fiction (although both "character" and "fiction" are in a process of redefinition). Because he is his own creator, and because of a perverse convention he adopts for his narrative—"this novel is being written as it happens" (145)—he must continue writing to continue living; it is only through art that he can overcome the continual crises of his world. His life consists of creating fiction, and his consciousness is determined by the fiction he creates. He stays alive, he says, "to discover what takes place next in this book" (145). Not only does he create himself by art, he also determines to some degree the nature of the reality with which he must live. Reality in *The Journal of Albion Moonlight* consists of an interaction between what is external and the perceiver. It is not solipsistic, because what is perceived is largely occasioned by causes outside the narrator-author, and it is not entirely deterministic because the artist can summon the powers of the imagination and change reality by creating new perceptions of it. In other words, Albion is developing illuminated artistic models of truth from moment to moment; his book is exactly his consciousness. Unless he simply abandons the book, the reader is forced to experience what Albion experiences, to perceive with Albion's perception. By making his book into a person Albion attempts to prod the sensitive reader into a true (that is, innocent) perception, and thereby to expose him to the profound wrongness of things.

The emphasis on engaging the reader has other important literary consequences. Personalism holds at its core a fundamental experiential knowledge that cannot be taught. Because of the mystical attitude that recognizes truth only as it is apprehended by particular persons, each reader must, in a sense, re-create that knowledge by the activity of his own imagination. The poem inspired by that knowledge, then, becomes the ground on which the imaginations of poet and reader meet, and the reader becomes the necessary ally of the poet in realizing truth. Before the work of art is morally or aesthetically satisfactory—before it can fully exist—it must be re-created by the experience of individual readers. A model for this conspiracy of inspired imaginations, acting independently, spontaneously, and with only the tacit instruction provided by the common experience of the poem (which is a primary sense of the "this" of the first line below) might be found in the passage which culminates Whitman's long strategic approach to the reader in "Crossing Brooklyn Ferry":

> What is more subtle than this which ties me to the
>   woman or man that looks in my face?
> Which fuses me into you now, and pours my
>   meaning into you?
> We understand then do we not?
> What I promis'd without mentioning it, have you not
>   accepted?
> What the study could not teach—what the preaching
>   could not accomplish is accomplish'd, is it not?

The creative act demanded of the audience would ideally be as difficult as the poet's own. It thus demands a high degree of spiritual development, which is commonly attributed to a future that contemporaneous culture is in the process of preparing. Whitman, for instance, insisted in "An Old Man's Rejoinder" that "to have great heroic poetry we need great readers—a heroic appetite and audience." Henry Miller assumed a similarly lofty standard. He envisioned that art would cease to be a separate category of activity and, in its final phase, become life itself—"but for that to become possible man must become thoroughly religious, not a believer, but a prime mover, a god in fact and deed. He will become that inevitably."[4] More playful, but with a similar concern for the future of both his poem and the progress of his audience, is William Carlos Williams's dedication of the personalistic "January Morning,"[5] in which the final line is the kicker:

> All this—
>   was for you, old woman
> I wanted to write a poem
> that you could understand
> for what good is it to me
> if you can't understand it?
>   But you got to try hard—

Such personalistic aspirations to the reorientation or evolution of an audience have inspired a number of often negative literary methods which might seem perverse to one trained in more traditional disciplines. Most fundamentally, perhaps, the concept of meaning as an abstractable, verbalizable component of a poem or fiction is either redefined or dismissed by personalistic writers, who are unwilling to postulate a referent for meaning separable from the total experience of the work of art. Meaning, T. S. Eliot says in *The Use of Poetry and the Use of Criticism*, keeps the reader occupied while the poem works upon him.[6] The danger of that approach is that the meaning will be mistaken for the poem—as in Eliot's own work, which to his distress was often read as an inspired intellectual game in which an approved meaning rewarded the diligent researcher. Like the Zen Buddhists, who deliberately make their teaching meaningless, American mystical writers fear that meaning might be seized upon as a way of evading rather than discovering access to the full experience of the poem. In their most ambitious work, they attempt to keep the life of a poem or fiction beyond paraphrase and deny their audience any too easy thematic statement on which reaction might be wasted. Readers of "Song of Myself," *Spring and All*, *The Journal of Albion Moonlight*, or *Tropic of Capricorn* are

expected to be more than witnesses. They should consider themselves extensions of the action.

Patchen's typically uncompromising reliance upon the creativity of the reader sometimes develops an obscurity that is more apparent than real. His weaving of the reader into the texture of the poem and the resulting moral and artistic intensity are illustrated in one of his compassionate poems of psychological terror. "The Lute in the Attic" (*Collected Poems* 378) is a monologue addressed by an unidentified speaker to one William Brewster Hollins (Willy) concerning events of which the reader is ignorant. Because the speaker assumes a knowledge of these events in his or her allusive remarks, the reader, who has the poem only as a sort of overheard fragment, is immediately thrust into the center of its situation. With Willy, he is addressed as "you" and expected to react to the strange things of the past with which he is darkly confronted. He is told "things in confidence."

The story involves some crime Willy committed when young, after which he fled the community. Only the primordial nature of his sin—that it was violent and bloody and probably sexual—is made explicit, and the terror of it is dimly suggested by reference to its circumstances and effects: the seven fat ducks with their mouths full of blood, the insanities of Willy's father and Isalina, who lay naked with Willy a few hours before "it" happened, the suggestion that Sam Hanner's alcoholism was caused by watching "it." There is some hint also that Willy's crime betrayed kinship. He is called back to "stand here / By the fog-blunted house that is silent now," which, with other details, may suggest that the house was that of his family, whose generations were cut off by his act. Later, he is called to "Lie here at the side of your brother," as if justice demanded it. It is even conceivable that Isalina is his sister. With the allusion to the authority of "the Fathers" and the elemental imagery of water, vegetation, and animal life, the unknown event at the center of the poem takes on something of the quality of the earliest, most brutal mythological murders.

The mystery of "The Lute in the Attic" is intensified by the anonymity of the speaker, of whom we can definitely say only that he or she knows Willy intimately, has observed the consequences of his act and brooded about it for many years. The portentousness of his or her call to Willy, which, with a frightening calmness, is the characteristic tone of "The Lute in the Attic," is intensified by the peculiarly appropriate form the poem takes. The first and last of its five stanzas are parallel invocations, while the middle three are descriptive. The first stanza issues the opening call, and then establishes the fundamental situation in free verse lines of varying length, which fall into a loose parallelism as the shorter lines pick up and extend the basic image of the longer:

> The apples are red in Chandler's Valley
>   redder for what happened there
> And the ducks move like flocculent clocks
>   round and round, and round

The stanza then continues with another, more formal, invocation of Willy by his full name and a demand that he return to "the fog-blunted house" he has made sinister. The final two lines hint that he will be exposed to the full understanding and consequences of his crime when he again glimpses "these terrible ducks."

In the second, third, and fourth stanzas, the nature of Willy's act is suggested by its crippling effect upon witnesses. Here, evocations of intolerable emotion contrast eerily with the speaker's deliberate calmness, and suggest some only barely restrained insanity in the narrative voice. Then the final stanza, in which a resolution is at least made possible, parallels the first in form. It opens with the same line, proceeds to the same summons, repeats the formal invocation of "William Brewster Hollins" and, like the first stanza, gives the words "I call you back!" a line of their own, in contrast to the longer rhythmical unit of the other lines. The first stanza is also echoed in the demand that Willy return to the place he has fled—to lie by his brother "here in the rain and the dark beside the willows / Hearing the voices of lovers under the flowery hedge." Other patterns of repetition are completed by the image of the "seven lean ducks" which replaces the earlier "fat ducks," implying that some grisly retribution awaits Willy, and by the final two lines which, like those of the first stanza, hint at an inevitable horror—in death as in revenge: "And show you worse things than your father sees / And show you things far worse than your father sees, Willy." The repetition and balances by which the implied narrative is ended, coupled with the fact that the calling is done only in the opening and closing stanzas, lend a kind of chantlike and ritualistic quality to the poem. In fact, with their naked anger and anguish Patchen's verses seem akin to the primitive rituals humanity first erected against the moral chaos of its world.

This powerful sense of ritual and the emotion behind it remain unfocused while the speaker remains anonymous. Because whoever is narrating the poem is close to past events we need a firm identification in order to piece them together. Without an attribution we do not understand the significance of details, or know if the pain and anger of the poem are the active emotions of a victim or the resigned emotions of a witness. Perhaps the narrative voice is nothing more than that of a concerned observer, but its relationship to Willy seems more intimate than that, and Patchen probably intends that we involve ourselves by speculating about the matter. One possibility—and the choice is almost purely intuitional—is that the speaker is Willy's mother. She is the only important member of the family not mentioned in the poem, and an occasional phrase, such as "your father," may seem vaguely maternal. By identifying a mother who has survived a family atrocity and yearns for the return of her son so that her agony and his might be completed, we might be able to extend the implications of the poem's title. Of course the lute is primarily a symbol of the lyric art with which humanity has responded to the challenges of failure, death, and the unknown. But it could also be a physical object which has been put away and forgotten, and which, being turned up, triggers a stream of melancholy associations. If we assume that dramatic situation, the lute in the attic becomes as well a psychological metaphor for memory and conscience.

We might also argue that Willy's brother is the speaker. The call from the grave of a spirit that needs revenge before it can rest could explain the maniacal intensity of the poem, the "so much hate" of the final stanza, and the chilling vision of death in the concluding lines. The speaker *could* be the brother, and the identification would be appropriate, but there is no conclusive way to establish it. With all the evidence in, it might as well be a snoopy neighbor, or God, or Willy himself. It might even be Isalina—a narrative turnabout that would not be at all out of keeping with a schizophrenic vision Patchen ofen employs.

Patchen's failure to identify his narrative voice would be disastrous in a poem aimed at a statement of what events mean. As it stands on the page, however, "The Lute in the Attic" is a sort of raw material which has a meaning only when a reader engages it. We are not asked to decipher Patchen's words so much as to search out our own obscure voices and confess to ourselves our own unspeakable sin. Everyone is liable to the

primordial crime of blood and lust that is the subject of the poem, and Patchen's meaning involves the entire process of self-knowledge and purgation by which that crime is brought to consciousness. Because the meaning exists only in the individual it is not paraphrasable. To approximate it, we must remove ourselves so far from the language of the poem that our words cannot affect it. "Know thyself" might be a "meaning" of "The Lute in the Attic." "Be whole" might be another. The purpose of the poem recalls Albion Moonlight's vision of the artist as healer.

The demand "The Lute in the Attic" makes upon the creative reader may be seen more clearly in the earlier "Panel 19" of *Panels for the Walls of Heaven* (retitled "The Builders" in *Collected Poems*). An unsympathetic reader might accuse me of attempting to transmute failure into virtue in my discussion of "The Lute in the Attic," but "Panel 19" quite obviously demands that the reader bring creativity to it and is inchoate until he does. A series of surrealistic images of light, clouds, and mud opens the piece, which is narrated in the first person and defined almost entirely by the progress of a wall that is being built next to the narrator's home. The building of the wall is described in terms of sensual dissociation. At first, the narrator hears the pounding of nails and the grunting of men and horses, and is able to "smell the giant labor," without being able to see what is causing all the commotion. Later he sees the frenzied activity of both men and animals without hearing them. Although it is raining, proximity to the wall exposes him to great heat and, at one point, a mysterious concussion.

As the narrator describes the wall and its bewildering effects upon his senses, he is clearly living in a reality different than his wife's; she finds him dreaming, or sleepwalking, or rolling around in the mud. There are suggestions that he may be insane: he is convinced that his wife is conspiring to hurt him; he sees his dead brother in the fields and at work on the wall; he is led home by an invisible hand and voice. At the most intense moment of the narrative, he finds that his wife does not recognize his presence in the house and sees her weeping over a strange man in their bed. As the narrative ends, the wall is finished and, almost gratuitously, the narrator repeats in inverted order the images with which the poem had begun. Through all of this the narrative is alogical and apparently inconsistent. It seems like raw automatic writing until the reader brings to it an understanding of what has happened that simply is not part of the poem itself. We must recognize that the narrator dies in the course of his narrative but does not know it. In a sense, the reader must share the narrator's agony, experience death (as Patchen understood it during those grim years), and name it for himself. Unless he does so, the poem is stillborn.

The apparent obscurity of "Panel 19" represents the critical problem raised by personalism. That system of shared and shifting identities can be difficult because it results in literary practices with objectives and standards different from those of the traditionally oriented literature for which we have a critical vocabulary. The greatest weakness of the personalistic poem limits it to the weaknesses of its creator, because it cannot be polished to the same degree as the art object, which assumes its own existence after its maker's work is done. But the literature of personalism is strong in its potential for discovering more truth than its creator himself can know. It is not limited to perfection.

Notes

1. Kenneth Patchen, *The Journal of Albion Moonlight*, pp. 22. Further page references will be cited in the text. All editions of this book have the same pagination.

2. Van Wyck Brooks, *The Malady of the Ideal* (Philadelphia: University of Pennsylvania Press, 1947), pp. 34–36. For Brooks on the romantic dilemma of the conflict between poetry and form, see my *Van Wyck Brooks: A Writer's Life* (New York: Dutton, 1981), pp. 72–88.

3. A rough skeleton of the main forms and digressions in the narrative follows: pp. 1–57: the original journal; pp. 57–156: the original journal and the first of Albion's novels alternate with one another; p. 156: the second novel begins, and continues to p. 168 (it is also part of the first novel); pp. 160–63: a second journal, with parallel entries for 2 May–15 June (it is part of the second novel); p. 163: the third novel (a one-part fragment explicitly about the violation of the girl-child); p. 168: return to the first novel; p. 169: return to the first journal, which continues to p. 268; pp. 179–83: a double narrative of historical violence (the text) and the violation of the girl-child (the margin), both of which are set in a medieval age, and are more of Albion's fictions as part of the first journal; pp. 216–57: as part of his journal, Albion includes his "Notes," which are fragments of his experience and thinking which have not been worked into any of the novels or journals—this section becomes a kind of long Whitmanian poem interposed with scraps of nonfiction, catalogues, and some important narrative material, including (pp. 249–52) the account of Albion's death; p. 257: return to the first journal; p. 268: the first journal "ends" at 17 August (this is a red herring—the journal picks up again later); pp. 269–81: the "Notes" again; p. 281: the original novel again, a variant of chapter 14, and it is important to cross-reference it with the original (p. 140); pp. 282–95: the tables of contents of two novels, both part of the text of the first novel; pp. 304–6: "The Little Journal"—parallel entries for 2 and 3 May; and, p. 306 to end: the original journal. Richard Morgan has elaborated this outline in *"The Journal of Albion Moonlight: Its Form and Meaning,"* in *Kenneth Patchen: A Collection of Essays,* edited by Richard Morgan (New York: AMS Press, 1977), pp. 176–78.

4. Henry Miller, *The Wisdon of the Heart* (Norfolk, CT: New Directions, 1941), p. 24.

5. William Carlos Williams, *The Collected Earlier Poems* (New York: New Directions, 1951), p. 166.

6. T. S. Eliot, *The Use of Poetry and the Use of Criticism* (Cambridge: Harvard University Press, 1933), p. 144.

WALKER PERCY

1916–

Walker Percy, novelist and essayist, was born in Birmingham, Alabama, on May 28, 1916. When Percy was eleven his father committed suicide; two years later his mother was killed in a car crash. Percy and his two brothers were adopted by his father's cousin, William Alexander Percy, who was an acquaintance of such men as William Faulkner and who had himself written a minor classic entitled *Lanterns on the Levee* (1941). Percy's interests at first turned to the sciences and he received a B.A. in chemistry from the University of North Carolina in 1937 and an M.D. from Columbia University in 1941. In 1942, however, he became seriously ill with pulmonary tuberculosis while interning at Bellevue Hospital, and this put an end to his intentions to pursue a career in psychiatry; during the two years he spent as an invalid he converted to Roman Catholicism and decided to abandon medicine to pursue a writing career instead. In 1946 he married Mary Bernice Townshend, and today they have two daughters and live a private life at their home in Covington, Louisiana.

Percy is not a typical Southern writer in that he makes no special attempt in his fiction to evoke a Southern atmosphere. Frequently addressing philosophical questions in his writing, he has been influenced by French and Russian novelists, and by philosophers such as Kierkegaard, Heidegger, Sartre, and Camus. His first book, *The Moviegoer,* was published in 1961 and won a National Book Award. Four further novels have followed: *The Last Gentleman* (1966), *Love in the Ruins* (1971), *Lancelot* (1977), and *The Second Coming* (1980). *The Message in the Bottle* (1975) is a collection of essays on the philosophy of language. In his most recent work of nonfiction, *Lost in the Cosmos* (1983), Percy attacks the modern preoccupation with self-indulgent personal fulfillment.

Personal

Walker Percy stood on the sun-bleached pier at the edge of Bogue Falaya and pitched a wood chip into the bluegreen water. Tiny circles rippled through the surface, chasing larger ones, and the author spoke.

"It's a natural thing to go from thinking about persons in a psychiatric sense to presenting them as characters in fiction. Fiction becomes, in this light, more advantageous than expository writing."

The author of *The Moviegoer* and 1962 winner of the National Book Award was referring to his own writing, which will have its second example of the fiction form when his new novel, *The Last Gentleman,* appears this June.

Previous to the publication of his first book by Alfred A. Knopf, the nephew of beloved Mississippi author William Alexander Percy had specialized in articles following philosophical and psychiatric lines, in addition to literary criticism, in such periodicals as the *Partisan* and *Sewanee Review,* the *Journal of Psychiatry* and *Forum.*

His interest in psychiatry possibly stems from his medical degree (from Columbia) and current participation in a research project conducted with clinical tape recordings regarding schizophrenia, but it was not until he reached his middle-forties that Percy sought to translate these notions into fiction.

"I felt that it would be a fascinating idea to start out with a young man whose life was free of all ordinary worries, one with a good family, fair financial stability and things with which he should be aesthetically satisfied, but who, somehow, finds himself as one of the 'outsiders' about which existentialists talk," Percy said in reference to *The Moviegoer.*

The book was actually written twice, with the second version correcting weaknesses which became apparent especially in the last third of the book. Its author admits that he was not, and is not, completely satisfied with the novel as a whole, but looks more optimistically toward his upcoming product which features a displaced Southerner in New York. Eventually, the character is led through bouts with amnesia, and geographically South through Virginia, the Carolinas, Alabama and finally to Sante Fe, New Mexico. *The Last Gentleman* is written in the third person, while *Moviegoer* was presented in first person.

Percy is a writer who actually looks like a physician in collegiate clothes, his greying hair contrasting his sweater and sneakers. He spends about three hours in the morning at his typewriter, and sometimes a couple of hours in the afternoon. Most of his work is done in his handsome home on the banks of the Bogue in Covington, Louisiana. "The woman who built this house wanted a French chateau, but couldn't resist the Louisiana influence," he said as he shuffled through the leaves and into the screened porch to the rear of the house.

He took up a cup of strong coffee, prepared by the family maid, Ida Mae, who watched with caution the affectionate year-old German Shepherd, "Lady."

"I've heard," she remarked, "that those dogs can be mighty mean if you're not good to 'em. So I'm being specially friendly."

The work hours of Walker Percy, unlike many authors, are not filled with joy and rapturous thanksgiving at the completion of every paragraph. He writes and rewrites, over and over. On occasion, he has been known to junk as many as 200 or 300 pages once he realizes the story line is unacceptable.

"I usually am not acutely aware of the logic at the beginning, but as the work goes along, it becomes more apparent. By following a predestined plan with outlines, like some writers, I could foresee the action and likely it wouldn't go veering off on another path. But I can't work like that. When I realize my logic is off base, I have to go back and begin again at the point where the interior logic took the wrong turn."

Sometimes, he says, the point of departure is a couple or three hundred pages back.

"And as I go along again, things shape up and I'm on the right route. There are times when I'm amazed. Sometimes I think it's luck."

Percy says he starts a novel with a concrete situation and lets the action proceed through a combination of circumstances and people. "The trick is to preserve the spontaneity and freshness, while keeping unity and coherence."

While watching his 12-year-old daughter, Ann, as she took art instructions near the edge of the woods surrounding the family home (his other daughter, Mary Pratt, is a freshman at Trinity College in Washington, D.C.), Percy explained his concept of novels and his approach to a successful rapport with readers.

"As I see it, the function of fiction is to tell someone something about himself he already knows, but doesn't know he knows. It gives a reader a sensation of recognition.

"If the subject or situation is all too strange, then the message goes unrecognized and loses its point.

"If the reader finds the matter too familiar, then it automatically becomes redundant and trite; there's no fascination.

"The 'in-between' area is the target and must be successfully hit for fictional accomplishment."

Although much of Percy's fiction has Southern overtones, he denies that he should be considered a student of the "Southern School," and asserts that he has no intention of trying short stories because of their limitations.

"I think of myself as being more in the European group than the American or Southern. I use the fiction form as a vehicle for incarnating ideas, as did Jean Paul Sartre and Gabriel Marcel. I long ago decided that my philosophy is in the vein of the existentialist, as theirs were. Both said that fiction is not just recreation. In my case, it is the embodiment of ideas of both philosophy and psychiatry into a form through which the reader can see a concept which otherwise might not be recognized. I would hope it is an authentic attempt at art."

Walker Percy slapped at the wall with a rolled-up magazine. "It looks like this summer will be a bad one for mosquitoes," he said.—DON L. KEITH, "Walker Percy Talks of Many Things," *DelR*, May–June 1966, pp. 38–39

Works

I missed *The Moviegoer* by Walker Percy when it came out last spring. It was Percy's first published novel, although he was 45 and had written two earlier novels, unpublished and, he says, "very bad." I was not the only person who missed it, since Knopf did not push the book very hard, reportedly because the head of the firm was "baffled and somewhat irritated" by it. When *The Moviegoer* received the National Book Award as the "most distinguished" work of fiction published in 1961, there were howls of rage, as though the umpire had made a bum call against the home team.

⟨. . .⟩ in calling *The Moviegoer* to the attention of a wider public, the National Book Award has performed a service. Like George P. Elliott's *David Knudsen*, Percy's book is a detailed pathology of modern neurosis, but unlike Elliott's it embodies its pathology in a realized fictional form. The book's narrator-protagonist, Jack Bolling, is a young Louisiana stockbroker of good family, undergoing very considerable emotional difficulties. Although he has a wallet full of identity cards, he has no sense of identity, and much of the time he has no sense of inhabiting a real place at a real time. Only four activities give him any illusion of meaningfulness, and he has reduced his life to them: "I spend my entire time working, making money, going to movies and seeking the company of women." "What do you think is the purpose of life—to go to the movies and dally with every girl that comes along?" his aunt asks him. "No," Jack answers, but only because he doesn't think that there is any purpose of life.

Women stir him, particularly their beautiful bottoms or "splendid butts," and he spends quite a lot of time chasing them, but he does not appear anxious to catch any. When, after an elaborate campaign, a girl fends him off, he seems more relieved than not. "The truth is that nowadays one is hardly up to it," he concludes unhappily at another point. In an experience that Percy has said is autobiographical, Jack spent his college years "propped on the front porch of the fraternity house, bemused and dreaming." He suffers from what he calls "invincible apathy," combined with periodic severe depression. He is obsessed with death, not the fear of death, but the sense "that everyone is dead," himself particularly. It is visibly the wish for death, and Jack thinks of "the grandest coup of all: to die."

On this neurotic disturbance Jack erects a sizable mystique. One of its features is the concept of "the search," which transforms his aimless and apathetic rambling into a quest for identity and value. Another is a concept of "repetition," a deliberate "re-enactment of past experience toward the end of isolating the time segment which has lapsed." The third is a concept of "rotation," defined as "the experiencing of the new beyond the expectation of the experiencing of the new."

All of these heady ideas result in moviegoing. "The movies are onto the search," Jack says, "but they screw it up." Seeing a western film in the same seat in the same theater in which one saw a western film 14 years before, in the same season, is "a successful repetition." Seeing a western film in the company of the invalid half-brother one loves *and* a girl one is pursuing, a "fine big sweet piece," is "a good rotation." Once Jack drove into a Louisiana village to see a movie in which the characters drive into a Louisiana village to see a movie, a triumphant "repetition within a rotation."

Jack sees all experience, even the death of his brother, in terms of remembered movies, and he acts in the stances of movie heroes. Movies "certify" the reality of places they show. Jack goes to see them alone, or if he goes with anyone, "it is understood that we do not speak during the movie." In his mind, Jack explains and justifies his behavior in dialogues with movie actors. He sometimes identifies a person he meets as "a moviegoer, though of course he does not go to the movies."

Pleased to learn "that a significantly large percentage of solitary moviegoers are Jews," Jack becomes a metaphoric Jew: "Anyhow it is true that I am Jewish by instinct. We share the same exile. The fact is, however, I am more Jewish than the Jews I know. They are more at home than I am. I accept my exile." Jack insists that his life is so unreal that he goes to the movies to find reality, but his descriptions of the experience make it clear what special reality he is searching for, what major event requires repetition—it is the uterine state, and the book's title translates as *The Womb-Returner*.

The heroine of *The Moviegoer* is Jack's cousin Kate Cutrer, a thin girl with a "marvelously ample" behind. She is more desperately neurotic than he, although she repeatedly denies it, insisting "You're like me, but worse. Much worse," or "You're nuttier than I am." After an automobile accident in which she was unhurt and her fiancé was killed, Kate had a breakdown. Now she is a secret wino and an addict of barbiturates. Where Jack is sunk in apathy, Kate has periods of despair and terror; where he longs dreamily for death, she has true suicidal impulses, and makes a try at it once in the book.

The Moviegoer is more than pathology because Jack and Kate are not only case histories but complex human beings. Percy's talent for the creation of character brings the minor characters just as vividly alive: gentle Uncle Jules, "whose victory in the world is total and unqualified"; bluestocking Aunt Emily, who expects more of Jack because he and she used to read the *Crito* together; Jack's formidable, beautiful secretary Sharon Kinkaid, a comic masterpiece; half-brother Lonnie in his wheelchair, like Jack "a moviegoer."

The book's language is sometimes quite fancy, as when Jack's neck manifests "eschatological prickling," or a train corridor has a "gelid hush" and "the peculiar gnosis of trains." Some sentences are elaborately Jamesian. For the most part, however, the language is spare and effective, and Percy has a superb ear for speech. He hears a Negro servant turn the word "is" into a diphthong "Harlem-style," or Alabama-raised Sharon protest "Ho no, you son," report "I said nayo indeed," and euphemize "God damn" as "Got dog."

Percy's use of symbolism shows a sure touch. The symbol that dominates the book is New Orleans Carnival Week culminating in the Mardi Gras parade, and its monstrous and mechanical gaiety is the background against which the drama of neurotic quest is peformed. Some lesser symbols are subtler yet equally powerful: the elderly married authors of a *Technique*

in Marriage manual, imagined "at their researches, solemn as a pair of brontosauruses, their heavy old freckled limbs twined about one another"—a vision of the enlightened joylessness of our world; Aunt Emily lecturing Jack with a paperknife in her hand, its tip bent by him as a child—an image of the inclined tree in the bent twig; a deserted ocean wave in a playground, on which Jack often sits, that is recognizably some life rhythm that has been stilled in him; Kate's nervous habit of tearing at the flesh around her thumbnail, which might as readily be her heart.

More than character, language or symbol, the strength of *The Moviegoer* is its clear strong line of action. Jack's Aunt Emily, Kate's stepmother, puts him in the essentially false and crippling role of Kate's keeper. He breaks out of it by taking her to Chicago and going to bed with her on the train, the two of them just barely managing it under "the cold and fishy eye of the malaise," both terrified, both shaking like leaves. On their return, Jack stands up to his aunt and answers her question, "Were you intimate with Kate?" with the marvelous phrase, "Not very." He is then free to create a valid relationship with her, a marriage in which they pool their neuroses democratically. At the end of the book, with Jules and Lonnie sacrificially dead, there is some hope that each, with the help of the other, will be better able to function in the world. At least they have no illusions about how hard the world really is.

There are flaws in *The Moviegoer*, certainly. One character, Sam Yerger, a figure of superhuman wisdom who imitates Amos 'n' Andy, is preposterous from start to finish, and a mistake. Sometimes Jack's philosophy, as when he meditates on "the genie-soul," is just blather. There are occasional pretentious attempts to make Jack's search seem not neurotic but deeply spiritual, along the lines of Percy's unfortunate statement on receiving the National Book Award that his novel shows Judaeo-Christian man as "a wayfarer and a pilgrim." These are minor failings in a considerable success. I think that *The Moviegoer* is a better novel than the work it most readily brings to mind, Albert Camus' *The Stranger*. It is patronizing and ridiculous to say of a 46-year-old man who has been late publishing his excellent first novel that he shows "promise." Walker Percy shows performance.—STANLEY EDGAR HYMAN, "Moviegoer and Other Intimacies," *NL*, April 30, 1962, pp. 23–24

Walker Percy's second novel, *The Last Gentleman*, is altogether richer and more intriguing than his first, *The Moviegoer*, which won him the National Book Award in 1962. It is a highly whimsical kind of picaresque tale that puts one in mind of both Faulkner and Camus, though only peripherally: the Faulknerian concern for the South, the "problem" of the South, the land, the engaging domesticity of a past tradition however past, and above all the traumatic suicide of a philosophically inclined father; and the floating, detached, "Existential" world of Camus that is rendered to us through the amnesia-plagued hero who cannot quite connect but who advances no titanic anguish because of his condition.

Percy's moviegoer was a man of a modern sort, addicted to public, commercial fantasies, and trying however numbly to break through to "reality"; his "last gentleman" is clearly kin, represented as he is by his telescope and his attachment to both love and death in an attempt to find his destiny, a man in whom something is mysteriously missing. The dissociated hero, subject to distressing attacks of *déjà vu* that render all reality suspect, taken up by an upper-middle-class Southern family of a comic-page type, in love with a pretty cipher of a girl, is a recognizable fictional type: a man without a soul, without an essence because he is without a sensible environment or past.

The young hero encounters a dying boy and his family, and the bulk of the novel concerns his being companion to and rendering up to the dying boy the attention that the dignity of death demands. The death of Jamie, which finally occurs in the concluding pages of the novel, is the central event of the work but it is not a very important event, strangely enough, because it works so obviously as a symbol, as theme. Percy's use of the naturalistically approached and staged death is out of keeping with his lovely and brilliant whimsy. This novel is one no critic should want to snipe at, for it is rare to encounter a work engaging in nearly every line; but Percy's strength simply does not extend to the naturalistic. Or perhaps it is beyond the naturalistic. His success with the country-club golfers, the pseudo-Negro who is really a white man working on a behind-the-scenes Negro piece, the Southern ladies who outlive their men by fifty years and 35,000 hearty meals, the Negro boy butler who falls "sappily" between Negro and white styles of living, are triumphs that suggest that Percy's power is in the reaction against the naturalistic, the half-comic half-horrified reflection of the naturalistic through a whimsical temperament.

But, how are we to take the apparently sincere love the hero feels for his brainless Chi Omega, and how are we to reconcile it with other graver, deeper pronouncements of his? The phrase "holding her charms in his arms" recurs enough to evoke in us the faintly sickish sensation we hope Percy intends, but we cannot believe that Normal Love and Life are exclusively Kitty Vaught. And how are we to reconcile the unforgettable and deeply moving death of Jamie with the ease with which he gets into college a few months before, apparently in one day, without medical examination, without the usual clutter of transcripts, applications, etc.? Trivial criticism indeed, but this inconsistency of vision mars the novel's dreamlike (though never nightmarish) logic.

Percy's writing is strangely similar to the highly gifted but rather hallucinatory pieces of Janet Frame: the more closely one looks at each sentence, each glimpse of a detail or image, the more hypnotic is the spell; but when one stands back for a larger view something has failed. Between Percy's main character and his excellent walk-on people there is an unhappy wasteland of secondary characters who just do not work. Percy can handle language as sheer language in a way strictly his own, though at times parodied-Faulkner, but as one starts moving out to larger units like the paragraph and the chapter, something is missing. The crankish and quackish journal of a discredited doctor ("We are doomed to the transcendence of abstraction and I choose the only reentry into the world which remains to us. What is better than the beauty and exaltation of the practice of transcendence . . . and of the delectation of immanence . . . lewd love?") becomes quite important near the end of the novel, but it is to be hoped that Percy is not advancing Dr. Vaught's verbose Lawrentian theology with any more seriousness than he is advancing the novel's other fragmentary concerns.—JOYCE CAROL OATES, "Gentleman without a Past," *Nation*, Aug. 8, 1966, pp. 129–30

Let's christen this thing right, with a quote from the panjandrum, Edmund Wilson: "The Northerner is apt to underestimate the degree to which the Southern writer—however intuitive, intelligent, imaginative, well-travelled, well-read—may fail to accept our assumptions or to sympathize with our aims. We do not realize that he lives in a world in which planning, reform, progress, making the world safe for democracy, laying the foundations of a classless society, promoting the American way of life do not really mean anything at all."

This lack of concern is not necessarily villainous. Mr. Percy, for one, is not the kind of Southerner who sets his face against the great Yankee abstractions (you might as well battle the wind), any more than he minds their overgrown children—psychiatry, sociology, high-level ecumenism. What puzzles him is a world in which the abstraction comes first: the conceptualized Yankee world where plans are always proceeding for this and that but where nobody asks the serious questions such as what does the neighborhood feel like, how does it sound in the afternoons, can you get a decent nap, how do the children look, etc.—the questions that the poet puts to the schoolman concerning the texture of life.

Mr. Percy is above all a student of textures (even his lovers "rub dorsal surfaces") and *The Last Gentleman* is a fantastically intuitive report on how America feels to the touch. He uses for probe a Southern Gulliver named Williston Bibb Barrett, who for some years has been trying to suck nourishment out of the thin Northern air. Barrett has no objection to joining groups and interrelating with his peers, if those are the things one does (this is the sense of the word "gentleman"); but he regards them mainly as cultural pastimes, like attending games or sitting on the porch with his aunts. To worry first about their intellectual validity would be to approach life backwards.

Unfortunately, Barrett's psyche tends to collapse on this diet. He learns group-therapy like a young gentleman learning to dance, but he might as well be chewing on air. It does nothing for the sense of emptiness and obliteration in New York, the awareness that the Great Disaster has already occurred. The important landmarks of the imagination, i.e., the sense of time and place, have become so pale in the North that at moments they wash away completely, and Barrett forgets who he is and wanders off arbitrarily to Ohio or Virginia. (In Mississippi you can tell a Tuesday afternoon from a Thursday; here he is always forgetting what month it is.) Other times he finds himself being bombarded by "ravening particles" of collective anxiety which obstruct vision, and which Barrett can only fend off by straining everything through a giant telescope.

The answer would seem to be to return to the South, and this in a roundabout way he does. But all is not well here either. For he finds that in some ways he now prefers the sad self-consciousness of the North to the pointless good cheer of the South. He catches himself saying "hi" to people before they are in earshot. His trick knee jumps so often that he has to hold it down and hobble like a spastic. When he discovers his uncle and colored servant cackling over Cap'n Kangaroo he realizes that time and place are being washed away here too, that the Madison Avenue bulldozer has already begun to work. And beyond all this, the unsolved question of race has left the South a blank, a fixed grin at an old joke. So Barrett lights out West where the air is empty of both memory *and* ravening particles.

Mr. Percy looks at Barrett through both ends of Barrett's own telescope. Through the small, comic end he is the last of a line of Southern gentlemen who have passed from bravery through irony to ironic helplessness—culminating, in Barrett's case, in a sensibility so fine that you can't use it any more: a perfect instrument that snaps in your fingers. Through the other end, he looks rather different. There he becomes the robust American naif, a little like George Brush in *Heaven's My Destination*—the gypsy-missionary on pilgrimage through America. Oddly enough, the two halves match: one of several truths that Mr. Percy is on to. It is all a question of context.

Mr. Percy in fact does so many things so well that he managed to accordion several types of novel into one. There are semiparodies of the hectic on-the-road novel (where the hero keeps waking with mysterious bumps on the back of his neck), of the mysterious-gothic-family novel (this he has more trouble with, and small wonder) and of the novel of galloping-disaster (models: *Candide, A Cool Million*). He even manages to pull off a deathbed baptism scene exactly the way Evelyn Waugh should have done it in *Brideshead Revisited*.

This fiendish dexterity has annoyed a critic or two, who feel that too much cleverness can be a formal defect. But on the whole the book is seamlessly designed. The set-pieces are knitted from the same material as the others, and come in the right places. The only jarring note is a casebook kept by one of the characters in which ideas are discussed explicitly. This offends against one's Northern taste for smoothness and technical efficiency; worse, it substitutes for the rendering of an important character, and this hurts.

But it is gentlemanly to make at least one mistake, and Mr. Percy doesn't make many others. Page-for-page and line-for-line this is certainly one of the best-written books in recent memory. As a Southern writer, Percy inherits the remains of a sonorous musical language. But beyond that, his unique point of view forms beautiful sentences like a diamond cutting glass.

Most writers nowadays are like the advertisers who have to stress marginal differences to conceal basic similarities. But with Percy, the problem would seem to be the reverse. He must make concessions in order to sound even a little like the others. As a Southern Catholic and as a comparatively late-blooming novelist, he sees everything his own way. Like his hero, who feels at his best in thunderstorms, his reactions are bizarre and effortlessly unexpected. By a constant play of metaphor and acute literalness—seeing the thing as something else, seeing it as precisely itself, a whipsaw arrangement—he recreates the world, and gives the readers the run of a brand-new sensibility. His humor, which is considerable, consists largely of this breaking-down of received categories. (E.g. The old Chestertonian question: If you saw a man eating and didn't know what eating was, what would you suppose he was up to? Percy sees things that way all the time.)

⟨. . .⟩ On top of its other distinctions, *The Last Gentleman* is one of the few serious religious novels of recent years. The question, among others, that concerns Mr. Percy is the one that fretted Albert Camus—why do we not commit suicide? But Percy, characteristically, does not answer the question with a formula. Like a good Christian, he writes a novel instead.—WILFRID SHEED, "Ravening Particles of Anxiety," *Critic*, Oct.–Nov. 1966, pp. 92–93

The two books that have most engaged me in the past few months are Walker Percy's novel *The Last Gentleman* and J. H. Baker's book *The Peregrine*. As poetry, both of these are better than almost all the recent poetry I have read. I consider Mr. Percy the most original novelist now writing in English. His power of phrase is breathtaking, and is the more so because it is quiet. There is no sentence of his that does not reflect the mysterious quality of amazement that is characteristic of the poetic view of the world. Mr. Percy's fiction makes one glad that the English language is what it is, and that certain writers use it for purposes beyond any that the rest of us could ever have imagined.—JAMES DICKEY, AS, Summer 1968, p. 524

The title of Walker Percy's fine new novel pertinently recalls the Browning poem "Love among the Ruins," which, through the device of a girl's awaiting her lover in the crumbling turret that alone remains of a vast and vanished empire, asserts the superiority of enduring human love to man's always ephemeral monuments to himself. At the beginning of *Love in the Ruins* not one girl but three await their common lover in the rooms of

a gutted Howard Johnson Motor Inn. The backdrop of Mr. Percy's story is thus the shards of our own civilization, rather than those of a lost heroic age, and these shards are moral before they are physical.

In 1983 Louisiana is an armed camp: fortunate professional men—bitterly divided between the conservative Knotheads and the liberal Left—live and work together restively in Paradise Estates and the nearby technocratic complex of Fedville. In the surrounding Honey Island Swamp live the disenchanted: the blacks—both American Negros and fierce Bantu guerrillas—and the young—draft-dodgers, dropouts and love children. The blacks, trumpeting the failures of white Christendom and desiring the Paradise Golf Course for themselves, plan all-out war; in a preliminary incursion five years earlier, they had sacked the Paradise Plaza, looting a bowling alley and a Sears store as well as the motel.

All hope for survival in this apocalyptic age rests with narrator-protagonist Dr. Thomas More, a clear-eyed diagnostician, and a victim, of social malaise. Alternatively a clinician and a patient in the Fedville Behavioral Center, Dr. More is a believing, non-practicing Catholic who loves "women best, music and science next, whiskey next, God fourth, and my fellowman hardly at all." He is the lyrical and exuberant lover of the three women in the motel, but his bouts of lovemaking nevertheless produce hives and respiratory difficulties, depression, possibly a suicide attempt, and guilt because he feels no guilt. He is the occasionally grief-stricken father of a dead daughter, whose death drove him to gin fizzes and (symbolically) Early Times bourbon, while it was driving his wealthy wife, now dead also, to transcendental meditation, to Herman Hesse, and specifically to two fortune-hunting English homosexuals with whom she decamped.

The divergent escape routes pursued by More and his wife serve as a model of what is wrong with the world. It is More's discovery that the problems of society evolve from a modern, intransigent dualism, a separation of materialists from idealists with both denying the human soul where body and mind meet and form whole human beings. Consequently, individuals have become politically divided between the Knotheads and the Left. The former invariably suffer constipation, uncontrollable rages and persecution complexes, while the latter are victims of sexual impotence, excessive abstraction and identity crises. The Knotheads practice proctology and worship Spiro Agnew; the men of the Left work in the behavioral sciences and choose as heroes Hesse, B. F. Skinner and William O. Douglas. These symptoms are the fruits, More tells us, of "the modern Black Death, the current hermaphroditism of the spirit, namely More's syndrome."

The antidote for this syndrome, as it is for the ruins in Browning's poem, is the acceptance of a universal love that exposes the real triviality of human ambition and bickering. "Dear God," More says in an uncharacteristic moment of moral lucidity, "I can see it now, why can't I see it other times, that it is you I love in the beauty of the world and in all the lovely girls and dear good friends, and it is pilgrims we are, wayfarers on a journey, and not pigs, nor angels." To eliminate practically the paralyzing dualism of his world, More invents a lapsometer, a kind of wireless electroencephalograph, that can pinpoint the exact area of psychic malfunction in a man's brain. But the word "lapsometer" also has obviously theological implications: Dr. More applies his "first caliper of the soul" and measures the extent of a man's fall, a finding unacceptable to the scientific community of the novel.

The threat of revolution demands more than a diagnosis of man's ills, however; Thomas More needs a cure to have his

Utopia. Enter the novel's strange antagonist, Art Immelmann, who plays Mephistopheles to More's Faust, and does as much as the black insurrection to precipitate the major crisis of the story (which I shall not reveal). Immelmann invents an attachment for the lapsometer that can temper cerebral excesses; but in the wrong hands into which it falls, it can exacerbate these same excesses. Or perhaps people will always be themselves despite a coupling of technology and visions of love. "We never never 'do' anything to anybody," Immelmann tells More. "We only help people do what they want to do."

Love in the Ruins is an exhaustive catalogue, serious and comical, of the things that men and women want and then proceed to do—to each other and to themselves—in an irrationally polarized society. Through Thomas More, Mr. Percy observes their behavior with perfect accuracy and then records it with the vigor and delight of the accomplished satirist.

The lampoons occasionally come too easily and attain ends too predictable: for example, America's military support of South Ecuador in an endless civil war against the Maoist North scarcely makes the reader sit up and take notice. Also, the Bantu presence in the United States seems largely gratuitous. And though many pages of description are given to two of More's girl friends, Lola and Moira, I can differentiate between them mainly by their respective musical preferences for Dvořák and Mantovani.

But these are petty complaints about a book whose triumphs are so numerous and so impressive: I think especially of a parody of that self-parodying fragment of modern Americana, the Masters and Johnson Clinic; of a debate, mostly on euthanasia, between Dr. More and a colleague in front of hundreds of howling medical students; and of Dr. More himself, a richly complex man struggling to be honest and sane in a world he understands too well, a man who tells us about himself and in the process lets his book supplant *Portnoy's Complaint* as the modern fictional descendant of Augustine's *Confessions*. *Love in the Ruins* is a remarkable anatomy of our times, and one that may offer a possibility, if not quite a promise, of deliverance.—MARK TAYLOR, *Com*, Oct. 29, 1971, pp. 118–19

Walker Percy has an intellectual range and rigor few American novelists can match. Barth and Pynchon play with a profusion of information and ideas. But only Bellow and Gass have Percy's learning, precision and passion for concepts both in and out of fiction. Years before *The Moviegoer* won the National Book Award for fiction in 1962, Percy was writing on language, philosophy, psychiatry and science for high-powered intellectual quarterlies. His importance as a novelist established by *The Last Gentleman* and *Love in the Ruins*, Percy now offers these early essays and some recent ones as tentative sketches of a "theory of man for a new age."

He asks no less than the following question: "Where does one start with a theory of man if the theory of man as an organism in an environment doesn't work and all the attributes of man which were accepted in the old modern age are now called into question: his soul, mind, freedom, will, God-likeness?" His answer is the singularity of language. This doesn't sound like news until Percy shows how behaviorists dispose of our popular assumptions about man as noble language-user. Because he's an amateur-outsider, a "visitor from Mars" in his term, Percy believes he can put a strict empirical footing under old assumptions and can restore singularity to people who never even knew they'd lost it.

His aim is to demonstrate that the naming act—the assigning of meaning—is a queer, open place in language that makes man qualitatively different from other animals. The consequences are not just academic. If we could understand the strange nature of language, Percy suggests, we might understand "man's peculiar upside-down and perverse behavior"—feeling anxious without knowing why, feeling homeless while at home, longing for catastrophe—that plagues the best of times.

The Message in the Bottle is ambitious, dense and difficult. Percy says most readers won't want to read all of it and admits that he can't imagine any audience for the last chapter, "A Theory of Language." Who, then, is the book for? Admirers of Percy's novels (and I am one) will find interesting his amplifying of ideas dramatized in the fiction. The individual's loss of his sovereignty to scientific formulation, language as an intersubjective process, the strangeness of alienation, Christianity as news, the role of the Christian novelists, Percy's debt to existential writers from Kierkegaard to Marcel—these are some of the themes developed in the more accessible essays: "The Loss of the Creature," "The Man on the Train," "The Message in the Bottle," "Notes for a Novel about the End of the World" and others.

Psycholinguists, transformationalists, semioticists, structuralists, phenomenologists, behaviorists, and those in the interstices should read *The Message in the Bottle* for the differences Percy has with them. Half of the 15 essays are primarily for these specialists.

Still, the book can be read with interest by people who, with Percy, wonder about strange facts: why men speak and animals don't, why man feels so sad in the 20th century, why war is man's greatest pleasure. Percy worries the problems of language and inverted values through many levels of understanding and a college catalogue of disciplines, but his purpose—a new working definition of man—carries the reader through more of the thickets of specialization.

In "The Delta Factor" Percy describes the experience that generated his persistent inquiry. Reading Helen Keller's account of her childhood learning, Percy realized that the naming process—water run on one palm, the word water written in the other palm, Helen's coupling of the two—was a symbolic transformation that could not be explained in behavioral terms. Naming "could not be set forth as a series of energy exchanges or causal relations. It was something new under the sun." Its nature is triadic rather than linear (the behaviorists' model). In visual terms, word and water converge on Helen the coupler at the apex of a triangle, the delta of meaning. She unites them with the word "is."

While denying the behaviorists' analysis, Percy avoids the idealists' notion of preexisting symbolic forms. What he finds and savors in naming is the empirical necessity of "is." Some language analysts say that existence (or "is") cannot logically be an attribute. Percy sees the assertion of being as the base of language—and as an empirical rationale for an existential philosophy.

Who or what pronounces the "is" Percy does not specify: "The apex of the triangle, the coupler, is a complete mystery. What it is, an 'I,' a 'self,' or some neurophysiological correlate thereof, I could not begin to say." Sufficient for Percy is the mystery, the tear in the behaviorists' grid, and, although he doesn't directly say so, the regained possibility of divine intervention in the circuitry.

Much of the book deals with the implications of the "*minimal* concept of man" that Percy derives from naming. He discusses the deprivation man suffers when he gives up naming to scientists and other packagers of experience, the workings of metaphor and literary naming, and how language mistakenly defined pervades psychiatry, anthropology, sociology, religion and the epistemological disciplines. The need, Percy maintains throughout, is to restore the category of being as protection from the tyranny of function.

Because Percy's intent is to salvage mystery from accepted but inadequate scientific explanation, his method is not so much assertion of new truths as disproving old ones. Percy's is a holding action—a "not yet you haven't" to the experts—so the ultimate validity of his ideas about naming is difficult to judge. He holds that the coupler has not yet been explained and offers persuasive evidence, some simple, some very technical, for his position. Linguists and psychologists will surely have their arguments. After thousands of pages of illustration, we will again need Percy to explain what was resolved.

What can be judged is Percy's suggestion that modern psychic complaints—boredom, rage, free-floating sadness and anxiety in the midst of the good life—are closely connected with the nature of language. Some of the specialized essays make the connection. More often, though, the link between the queerness of language and the queerness of man's behavior is only the common queerness. One finishes the book with a sense of incompletion. Despite their unity of focus and repetition, the essays remain discrete probes into what Percy calls the "terra incognita" of language use. There is no map—just an open place for being.

In the light of these essays, Percy's fiction is also a promise unfulfilled or, more accurately, a promise not quite made yet still somehow unkept. The novels are important—thoughtful, observant, skillfully ironic and written with laconic precision. Yet only *The Moviegoer* comes close to achieving a style that registers Percy's profound thinking about language. Binx Bolling in that novel is the man among persons and things for whom naming and its wonder constitute existence. The other novels have a meditative, alienated stranger-in-a-mad-land hero, but much of *The Last Gentleman* is about sixties doings in the New South and *Love in the Ruins* engages in scenario-like action and some trivial socio-political naming.

Despite knowing more about language than other novelists, many of whom make it their subject, Percy chose to go on telling stories with ideas in them. They are good stories, yet one comes to wish Percy had imagined a form that would have transmuted his enormous intelligence into some supreme verbal fiction. There are plenty of reasons—esthetic, social and religious—why Percy continues in the realistic mode. Perhaps one shouldn't complain about what he doesn't do. It's just that these essays create after-the-fact expectations about his fiction that are not met, a sense of possibilities described rather than created.

In "The Man on the Dump" Wallace Stevens calls truth "The the." With different esthetic choices, Percy could have written—could still write—a fiction of the is.—THOMAS LECLAIR, NYTBR, June 8, 1975, pp. 6–7

Mention "the Jewish novel," and everyone knows that you refer to a substantial body of fiction—books that probably represent the most vital force in American letters in the postwar years. Speak of "the Christian novel," and you will be met by blank stares. No such genre. The term suggests, if anything at all, something you might buy in a forlorn religious bookshop. And yet there are a few writers, though certainly not enough to be called a movement, who do dwell on the increasing strangeness of Christian experience in the United States. One of the most interesting is Walker Percy.

Percy's new novel, *Lancelot*, is about the problem of faith. I think that is an accurate description, but it may also be an utterly misleading one, since it doesn't go far toward suggesting

the book's tone or its events. Here is some of what happens. Its hero, Lancelot Lamar, discovers himself to be a cuckold. (He confirms his initial suspicions by spying with the help of a videotape machine.) One night he leaps upon the coupled bodies of wife and lover and attempts to bear-hug them to death. He fails, but he does manage to slit the lover's throat with a Bowie knife. The New Orleans mansion in which this action takes place has a wing conveniently built atop a capped natural gas well. Lance—as he's known—uses the residual methane to blow up the mansion. Others perish, but he is thrown clear by the blast, and survives to tell his tale from his madhouse cell, where he harangues inventively about the depravity of modern life. It's obvious that comedy removes the curse of implausibility from these occurrences. But how they lend themselves to Percy's theological impulses takes a bit of explaining.

"The specific character of despair is precisely this: it is unaware of being despair." The quotation is from Kierkegaard, and it serves as the epigraph to Walker Percy's first novel, *The Moviegoer* (1961). It also describes the condition of the hero of *Lancelot*.

Lance Lamar is a southerner of aristocratic descent, a former football star and frat man who grows up to preside over a depleted fortune, a perfunctory law practice, and the mansion "Belle Isle," which he opens to tourists in the style of an impoverished duke. His life is not without its solace. He dabbles in the "happy strife" of sixties liberalism, but liberalism sours. He marries a beautiful Texas heiress who keeps him in style and (for a while) in a state of exalted nuptial lust. But their appetites sour. He drinks a great deal of bourbon. It is in fact his most durable pleasure. He thinks of himself as "moderately happy," though it occurs to him to wonder why there are days when he can bear his life only by simultaneously drinking, reading Raymond Chandler, and listening to Beethoven.

Enter Adversity. His apprehension that his wife is unfaithful has an odd effect. It changes his life, and not entirely for the worse. He stops drinking—not out of willpower; he discovers it is unnecessary. No more whiskey, no more Chandler. He looks into the mirror and realizes he has not actually done so for years, he has been avoiding his own glance. "I had lived in a state of comfort and abstraction, waiting for the ten o'clock news, and had not allowed myself to feel anything," he remarks.

Lance is awakening from the sleep that Walker Percy believes to be endemic in the modern world. "Abstraction" is one of the novelist's favorite words: by it, he means the dissociation of thought from feeling, of body from soul (a term that causes him little embarrassment), the false shelter that keeps out discomfort but into which despair creeps like a chill.

Lance is reborn by trial, and like his legendary namesake he sets off on a quest of sorts—an "anti-quest" might be a more accurate description. Jealousy leads him steadily into a demented vengefulness, but he thinks of it as a spiritual search. "Can good come from evil? Have you ever considered the possibility that one might undertake a search not for God but for evil?" It's Lance's notion that proving the existence of evil—of a single sin—would go further toward demonstrating the existence of God than would any number of perceptions of heavenly order, which can be accounted for by science. He reasons that the diabolical is an even more forgotten concept than the divine. Evil, he points out, has been diluted into craziness. "Everything and everyone's either wonderful or sick and nothing is evil. . . . The mark of the age is that terrible things happen but there is no 'evil' involved."

So Lance sets out to encounter, in fact to participate in,

evil. But he quests in vain. Even at the moment of murder, he feels nothing. "What I remember better than the cutting was the sense I had of casting about for an appropriate feeling to match the deed. Weren't we raised to believe that 'great deeds' were performed with great feelings, anger, joy, revenge, and so on. I remember casting about for the feeling and not finding one."

Thus to the madhouse. It is one of the devices of this novel that its hero's tale is given us in the form of a long monologue delivered to a silent interlocutor—not a doctor but an old friend who is a priest. He acts as a mute witness to Lance's fulminations. Lance rants against the "Sodom" of contemporary society, the "great whoredom and fagdom of America," revels in misogyny, yearns for a return of chivalry and moral certainty and the Church Militant. His refrain is "I cannot tolerate this age," and he imagines himself as a one-man crusade for a new one. "There will be honorable men and there will be thieves, just as now, but the difference is one will know which is which, and there will be no confusion, no nice thieves, no honorable Mafia. . . . The New Woman will have perfect freedom. She will be free to be a lady or a whore."

These tirades are in their way quite glorious, but the burden of the novel lies elsewhere. It ends not in vituperation but in gentle enigma—an enigma wrapped in affirmation. Lance's voice softens, mellows, grows hesitant. And the priest who has been hearing this 250-page confession at last speaks. He admits that he shares the narrator's sense of hopelessness about the modern age. The priest nevertheless is going to carry on his own work. "One of us is wrong," Lancelot exclaims. "It will be your way or it will be my way. All we can agree on is that it will not be their way. Out there." And the priest assents. Lancelot asks his confessor finally if there is anything *he* wants to tell *him*. And the priest responds with the novel's last word, *Yes.*—RICHARD TODD, "Lead Us into Temptation, Deliver Us Evil," *At*, March 1977, pp. 113–15

There are what appear to be repetitions here: some lines, even passages, are paraphrases from Percy's earlier novels. And the metaphor of the hurricane which worked so well in *The Last Gentleman* (people are happier, and better to each other, during a hurricane) is expanded in *Lancelot*: the climactic action of the novel occurs during a hurricane.

I believe there are good reasons for this, and that finally what we are seeing is not repetition at all. Walker Percy was forty-five years old when he published his first novel, *The Moviegoer*. So what we don't see in Percy's novels is the changing vision of the world that we often get from a writer who publishes while he is young, and then continues to write. With *The Moviegoer* we were in the hands of a mature writer whose theme had already chosen him. He has been possessed by it ever since, and that is why he is not truly repetitious. A repetitious writer is a tired writer, perhaps filling the blank page because there is nothing else to do. Percy is not tired; he is growing stronger; so that when parts of *Lancelot* sound like parts of the earlier novels, it's not repetition we're hearing, but the resonant sound of a writer grappling with his theme. He could not have known, when he discovered the hurricane metaphor in *The Last Gentleman*, that years later *Lancelot* would demand it again. And for Percy to find different metaphors, different words, would be little more than vanity, a surface concern subordinate to his real struggle with the question that will not leave him alone.

The question is simple and profound: What is one supposed to do on an ordinary afternoon? Therefore, what is time for? What is a human being for? To ask the questions and to find no answers causes despair (Sutter Vaught in *The Last Gentleman*). Not to ask the questions causes a despair that doesn't know it is despair; this is what troubles most of the secondary characters in Percy's novels, which is why they feel better during hurricanes (from *Lancelot*: "Hurricanes, which are very bad things, somehow neutralize the other bad thing, which has no name"). Percy's heroes are assaulted by both: they ask the questions and find no absolute answers, and they are surrounded by friends and relatives who don't ask the questions who are dead while they yet breathe, talk, make plans, carry them out. From *The Moviegoer*: "'I don't feel a bit gloomy!' she cries. 'Now that Mark and Lance have grown up and flown the coop, I am having the time of my life. I'm taking philosophy courses in the morning and working nights at Le Petit Théâtre. Eddie and I have reexamined our values and found them pretty darn enduring. . . .' Very good. And then I can't help wondering to myself: why does she talk as if she were dead?"

Love will disappear from the face of the public world, but the more precious will be that love which flows from one lonely person to another. . . . The world to come will be filled with animosity and danger, but it will be a world open and clean. That's a portion of one of the epigraphs of *The Last Gentleman*, a quotation from Romano Guardini's *The End of the Modern World*. It could serve as an epigraph for Percy's four novels. In each of them the hero is searching; he is searching because he has to, because if he does not search he will join the active dead who move about Percy's joyless landscape, making sounds, making money, making children. The search remains the same from novel to novel, as it must—for how can Percy ever find the answer? And how can he quit without the answer? ⟨. . .⟩

In *Lancelot*, Percy is again confronting the forces which make it so difficult for us to make moral choices and live by them. And his hero, Lancelot Lamar, is angry. Because of this, the novel goes further, more deeply, than the three before it. Lancelot cannot be content with amused tolerance of others, while he takes his lady to bed. In a land where so many are devoting their energy to coping, to being like everyone else and surviving it, Lancelot cries out no. It is a different kind of no. It is not the no of dope or booze or television or what we call recreation. It is the no of Jean Anouilh's Antigone, who finally tells Creon that she simply refuses to live in the world as it is; and that no causes her death. Lancelot's no causes death too, and a new world. It is a small world: the world of the soul, of moral choice and action, is always limited to the few who choose it.

I am avoiding giving details of the novel's action because this is the only Percy novel in which suspense is an essential part of the reader's pleasure. The suspense is created by Lancelot; he cannot, like the earlier Percy heroes, find a peaceful bemused niche within the world he sees: he must act, and his action is the center of the novel. He struggles against loss of personal worth and values, a history that haunts him, the infidelity of his wife, his own lust and its purpose, the loss of two of his children to the nonvalues of the age, the invasion of his empty life by even emptier Hollywood directors and actors (for a while their emptiness is active enough to make his emptiness even more passive), with women whose liberation, he believes, has further enslaved them to their unique condition of being the only female creatures who are always in heat, and with God.

In all of Percy's novels Catholicism is essential as an alternative. In this one Lancelot recognizes (as Suttter Vaught did in *The Last Gentleman*) the failure of the church: what Percy calls world-weary Catholic tolerance, which no longer makes a stand, for it has befriended the wrong people, become too much like them. Lancelot says to Percival, his boyhood friend, now a priest: "I won't have it your way with your God-bless-everything-because-it's-good-only-don't-but-if-you-do-it's-not-so-bad." And later he says: "So you plan to take a little church in Alabama, Father, preach the gospel, turn bread into flesh, forgive the sins of Buick dealers, administer communion to suburban housewives?" If Catholicism demanded a stoic life in the desert, no doubt Lancelot would happily do it. But, looking at the flabbiness of the modern church, Lancelot decides there is only one way to leave the present world and enter the new one which all Percy's heroes have yearned for. Lancelot, through his own will and action, destroys the present world, and after that cleansing destruction, he starts over. This novel is Percy's strongest counterattack against those forces which I suspect are still shrieking at his door.—ANDRÉ DUBUS, "Paths to Redemption," *Harper's*, April 1977, pp. 86–88

Williston Bibb Barrett, hero of Walker Percy's fifth novel, *The Second Coming*, makes it big as a New York lawyer, marries a handsome fortune, heads home with his wife to the Southland for early retirement—and is at once overwhelmed with problems. His mate dies. Her religious adviser commences hounding him to underwrite a "total love-and-faith" retirement village as a monument to the departed. By accident a neighbor nearly shoots him dead. His daughter, Leslie, a granny-beglassed Kahlil Gibran fan who's soft on creative relationships ("Jason and I level") and the expression "You better believe it," tells him he's never been honest in his life. Mysterious forces knock him off his feet into *petit mal* trances. An old girlfriend, appearing from nowhere, bends herself to the enterprise of seducing him. He contracts an obsession with the circumstances of his father's suicide. He contracts a determination to prove or disprove—by a "rational" experiment that combines a retreat to a cave, the use of advanced pharmaceutical technology, and a suicidal gamble—the existence of God. He contracts a golf slice. Yet despite these and other troubles, frustrations, misconceived projects, and flat-out disasters, *The Second Coming* is miles removed from tragedy. At the end of the book Will Barrett isn't a mere survivor, he's flourishing.

The reason is that, in a central although only gradually emerging dimension, *The Second Coming* is a love story. At the height of his anguish Will Barrett chances upon a young female, Allison Hunnicutt Huger by name—a lieder-singing escapee from a sanitarium for the mentally ill. Allison is less God-haunted than he, but she shares his hunger for true knowledge of the nature of our situation on earth, and of how best to endure it. And this shared longing draws them close, ultimately transforming their responses to the world's contradictions, perplexities, trials. By falling in love they save—or at least freshen—their souls.

It's not quite that simple, of course. For a considerable while after first meeting Allie Huger, the hero remains in thrall to raddling religious uncertainties—and to the experiment he dreams will end them. Seething in alienation, despising the complacencies of liberated skeptics on the one hand and the hypocrisies of the unfaithful on the other—people oblivious to the difference between Christendom and Christianity—he has lost his gift for connection. "I am surrounded by two classes of maniacs," he insists:

> The first are the believers, who think they know the reason why we find ourselves in this ludicrous predicament yet act for all the world as if they don't. The second are the unbelievers, who don't know the reason and don't care if they don't.

The only refuge he can imagine is "a search for the third alternative, a tertium quid—if there is one." And the notion of Allie Huger as belonging to that search—opening his secret, self-immured, God-tormented inner life to new possibilities—is slow in coming. Through pride of mind he hangs back.

As for Allie Huger: while eager from the start for lyrical union, she too has distracting preoccupations. By the time she encounters Will Barrett she has suffered years of institutional infantilization. Chapters interleaved with those detailing the hero's troubles show us Allie Huger's parents and analyst conniving to cheat her out of her inheritance. We watch the young woman struggling to plan an escape—writing extended instructions to her "disturbed" self about how to function on the outside, as a free being, while still partially crippled by electroshock treatment. (Only in the period just after her "buzzing" does sanitarium security ease sufficiently to permit an escape attempt.) Warily, painfully, at length exhilaratingly, in pages as delicately imagined as anything we're likely to have for some seasons from an American fictionist, Allie conceives ambitions of her own—projects infinitely more concrete than Barrett's, but to her not a whit less bemusing. She's engaged in constructing a language, a home (in an abandoned greenhouse), and a personal life. She's learning to see and hear for herself again, to hunt for clues to the insides of the human creatures with whom she's obliged to deal, to begin once more to appreciate:

> ". . . Have a nice day."
> "What?" She was puzzled by the way [the policeman] said it, in a perfunctory way like good-bye. But what a nice thing to say.
> But he only repeated it—"Have a nice day"—and raised a finger to the place where the brim of his hat would have been. He returned to his street corner.

Her experience in supermarkets and hardware stores echoes the joys of provisioning as they exist in *Robinson Crusoe*; her awakening by the tinkle of a sliced golf ball through her greenhouse roof (Barrett the slicer arrives soon after) shapes a cute meet reminiscent of that between Shakespeare's Ferdinand and Miranda. But everywhere the fascination of her own second coming edges her back from the obvious answer to the brave new longings nascent within her.

And because the elements of her recovered nature—kindness, courage, resourcefulness, candor, sweet sensuality—emerge unselfconsciously, utterly unpolluted by self-promotion, we're impatient with the hesitations and reluctancies. How can the golfing metaphysician hang back? Granted, Will Barrett is a thoughtful chap with a splendidly savage eye for the deceitfulness round about. Granted, his spiritual aspirations deserve respect. Granted, Allie Huger has the whole of the "sane" world to master. But where are these people's eyes? Why can't they recognize their best hope for salvation? How much longer will he go on in her company without junking embitterment and convolution and taking her into his arms?

We're in the presence, in short, of that surest-fire of literary things: deliciously dramatic—deliciously romantic—obtuseness.—BENJAMIN DEMOTT, "A Thinking Man's Kurt Vonnegut," *At*, July 1980, pp. 81–82

Though Walker Percy has always been a critic of how twentieth-century Americans live, and though *The Second Coming*, his fifth novel, continues this critique, this new work attempts in much greater detail than before to accentuate the positive: to explore, with great imaginative joy, states in which human beings may live together with authenticity. *The Second Coming* especially harkens back to and develops those scenes in

Percy's previous work where authentic, human community occurs: a few conversations between Binx Bolling and Kate Cutrer in *The Moviegoer* (1961); the fleeting gesture of solidarity between Will Barrett and Sutter Vaught at the end of *The Last Gentleman* (1966); the epilogue to *Love in the Ruins* (1971), in which Tom More enjoys a family Christmas; and the mad-house visions of a peaceful life in the Shenandoah Valley of Lance Lamar in *Lancelot* (1977). *The Second Coming* continues the troubled life of Will Barrett; it explores and defines a "tertium quid," as Will calls it, between the extremes of suicide and mindless living which American society habitually offers in Percy's novels.

Will Barrett is now in his mid-fifties, a retired widower living in North Carolina, very wealthy, and still falling into the psychic gaps which had plagued his early years. He meets Allison Hunnicutt Huger, the daughter of his old girlfriend, Kitty Vaught. Allie has just escaped from the mental home in which her parents have placed her. Will and Allie found their relationship on simplicity. Because of Allie's mental illness and the shock treatments forced upon her, she must relearn basic language skills; Will alone appreciates that in her careful naming of things she makes more sense than the rest of the world. They build up a language together; they court each other and make love. To create a shelter Allie and the artisans Will later recruits use only the simplest tools and materials. Will and Allie are building up human society over again, from scratch. In the eyes of the world, represented by Allie's mother, this is all shocking. It would appear from the end of the novel, though much is left unresolved, that Will, Allie, and the community they found will survive.

Percy's heroes invariably have to come to terms with the memory of their fathers; generally social misfits, like their sons, these fathers are often depressed individuals and sometimes suicidal. In *The Second Coming*, Will manages to remember what was hidden from us in *The Last Gentleman*: that his father attempted to kill his twelve-year-old son and himself several years before a second attempt on his own life was successful. Will often speaks with his dead father in this novel; in these imaginary conversations, his father tempts him, almost successfully, to suicide. Percy's use of psychiatric models of behavior is always interesting. Will's act of remembering recall the structure of psychoanalysis; it is only when he recovers the memory of what his father had tried to do that he is free to act. Yet Percy's principals must always pass beyond the various clinical helps offered to them—in this novel, therapy, shock treatments, and pills—for living in the future. This is so even when the hero himself, as in *Love in the Ruins*, insists on a fully scientific, empirical view of the psyche. In Percy, salvation only occurs with the advent of the other, the right person, the friend or lover, whose subjectivity is eternally and irreducibly hostile to empirical analysis. However clinically ill the subjects who relate to one another may be, intersubjectivity is the purpose of their existence. An unabashed, tendentious romantic, Percy also has the great ability to construct scenes, especially in this novel, where intersubjectivity becomes so real it hurts.

From the notebooks of Sutter Vaught in *The Last Gentleman* on into the present work, Walker Percy has been reluctant to understand his action and characters in anything less than a fully theological background. Will and Allie recapitulate, in their choice of words and tools, the history of culture; in his religious development, Will progresses from the mentality of a cranky Old Testament prophet, who rejects the world, to a hesitant awareness, given to him only on the last page of the novel, of God's incarnational presence in the world.

Will initially seeks his "tertium quid" by retreating to a cave to await a "sign" from God; if God exists, he will appear to save him from death by starvation. This demand for empirical proof parallels, on the religious level, the scientific reductionism that recurs in the novels and that is a major theme of Percy's collected essays, *The Message in the Bottle* (1975). A toothache eventually drives Will from the cave and into Allie's arms. God gives his "sign" in and through the comedy of the human body; he will not give it in response to abstract demands placed upon him—a human strategy called "angelism" in *Love in the Ruins*—and Will, in spite of himself, is saved. "Is she a gift and therefore a sign of a giver?," Will asks himself, about Allie, at the end. "Could it be that the Lord is here, masquerading himself behind this simple silly holy face?" Read as a whole, the five novels present their own sign of contradiction; the reader who does not believe in the "simple silly holy" body—"holy" because God has been there—must be puzzled indeed by the way Percy rescues a few characters from the nonsense going on around them.

The reader of *The Second Coming* who expects rowdy social criticism will not be disappointed. Percy's satirical targets here include: old-age homes, overeating, makers of pornographic films, born-again Christians, belief in reincarnation, a priest in a jump suit who feels "uneasy" talking about religion, ecumenism, astrology, and California, where "everyone believed everything," and which has apparently replaced Ohio as the object of Percy's special disfavor. No redemption is offered to these many social and religious realities, as it is to Will and Allie. At the end of *The Moviegoer*, Binx Bolling has an inkling that God just might have something to do with organized religion; no such intuition bothers Will Barrett here. Percy cannot do everything in every novel: *The Second Coming* is complex enough as it stands and it is right for the author tacitly to let his novels comment on one another. Sometimes Will's thoughts make for difficult reading; for most of us, it is the interspersed social satire, thematically integrated or not, which relieves the strain of the ongoing personal drama.

Much has already been written about the relative merits of *The Second Coming* in the Percy canon. For me, the novel lacks the purity and simplicity of *The Moviegoer* and the richly theological development of *Love in the Ruins*. Some of the structural difficulties of *The Last Gentleman* recur: Will's trip down and across the country there and his car and bus trip to Atlanta here—however much they symbolize the lot of *homo viator*—interfere with the forward progress of the book. Percy feels compelled at times to comment on current events like integration and Southern real estate dealing, as in these travel narratives, that do not fire his imagination. On the other hand, Percy integrates his philosophical interest in language more successfully here than he has been able to do before; Allie's recreation of the world through language is stunning in conception and execution. Certain residual ambiguities in the characters of Will and Kitty and Sutter Vaught are nicely cleared up; also, we get a humane explanation at last why so many Percy heroes prefer war to peace ("thinking of peace during war is better than peace"). Like all of Percy's novels, *The Second Coming* is a challenging work; like other Percy heroes, Will is slightly mad, and, once again, it is occasionally difficult to see where the author's irony begins and ends. The major change *The Second Coming* rings on the previous novels lies in its greater exploration of the peaceful, romantic images that have always been present in Percy's work and are here amplified to challenge, if not drown out, the discord of twentieth-century America.—GERARD REEDY, "Gestures of Solidarity," *Com*, Aug. 29, 1980, pp. 471–72

Walker Percy insists that the serious writer is a prophetic figure who descends into the world like the canary into the mineshaft to test the spiritual atmosphere of the times and report back. *Lost in the Cosmos* is Percy's latest report—a witty, elliptical, nonfiction work which both examines the state of the beleaguered contemporary soul and offers "help" in understanding its predicament.

However, Percy's approach is wholly unconventional. Parodying the popular Carl Sagan television series *Comos*, Percy undermines the glib scientific-humanistic assumptions of modern culture by inverting the usual format of self-help books (follow these simple steps and you will achieve *x*). Instead of clear answers, he presents a series of thought problems that probe aspects of the modern riven self—lonely, demonic, gnostic, depressed, bored, promiscuous and essentially misplaced. The reader is then challenged by a series of questions to identify himself amid this baffling maze of behavior analysis. Percy offers no solutions, no pat directions or advice. He does give persistent clues, "help" in the form of a clever, satiric unveiling of false notions of selfhood and self-discovery and clues to man's being as a semiotic creature.

Devotees may regard this as Percy's attempt to popularize ideas treated earlier in straightforward philosophical essays (there is considerable repetition). Other readers may regard it as a piece of Percyan irony, a wry "antibook." Both are mistaken. The oblique approach of *Lost in the Cosmos*, while tongue-in-cheek, is deadly serious; it derives from Percy's belief in the "unspeakableness" of the self indicated in the Nietzschean epigraph, "Each is the farthest away from himself—as far as ourselves are concerned we are not knowers." In short, Percy presents the mystery of self as mystery, a provocation to the reader to explore this inner cosmos himself.

If the reader finds Percy's deliberate frustration of his expectations exasperating, he might wonder what assumptions underlie his expectations. Then the real thinking which the book demands can begin.—JOHN F. DESMOND, *WLT*, Spring 1984, p. 275

ALFRED KAZIN

"The Pilgrimage of Walker Percy"

Harper's, June 1971, pp. 81–86

. . . goofy as he was, he knew two things not many people know. He knew how to listen and he knew how to get at that most secret and aggrieved enterprise upon which almost everyone is embarked. (Walker Percy, *The Last Gentleman*)

Don't think . . . *look!* (Ludwig Wittgenstein)

In 1962 the National Book Award for fiction was awarded to a first novel, *The Moviegoer*, by an unknown writer in Louisiana, Walker Percy, who was a doctor of medicine but had never practiced. The book's publisher, Alfred A. Knopf, was not elated by the news—he had been rooting for another novel on his list, William Maxwell's *The Château*—and more than one editor in his employ heard him exclaim, "They're running the prize into the ground!" "They" could have been that year's fiction jury for the National Book Awards—Jean Stafford, Lewis Gannett, Herbert Gold. But it was no secret that Jean Stafford's husband, the *New Yorker* writer A. J. Liebling, had discovered *The Moviegoer* while in Louisiana doing the series of pieces on Huey Long's brother that became *The Earl of Louisiana*.

The book had not been launched with any great expectations. *The Moviegoer* was indeed published only because one editor at Knopf's had stuck with it. In its first draft this editor had found only forty good pages and a rather evangelical Catholic ending, and under his patient counseling the book was twice rewritten from start to finish. The final draft was the fourth.

Mr. Knopf's open lack of enthusiasm for the prizewinning novel suddenly gave *The Moviegoer* rather more notice than the National Book Award necessarily creates. Mr. Knopf is as famous for the crusty independence of his ways as he is for being the last great individual entrepreneur and tastemaker in American publishing who can afford to please only himself. Mr. A. J. Liebling, in his turn, was a man of equally formidable temperament, and a writer who at the moment, already irritated with his old publisher Alfred A. Knopf for not having done at all well by a book of his called *Chicago: The Second City*, became further irritated over what he felt to be Mr. Knopf's failure to cheer a National Book Award-winning novel that he, A. J. Liebling, had initially brought to influential attention. (*The Moviegoer* had had good reviews in *The National Observer* and *The New Leader*, but had been indifferently reviewed in the unencouraging "Other Fiction" columns of the principal Sunday book supplements.) Mr. Liebling's irritation with Mr. Knopf even led him to make some comments about Mr. Knopf at a Columbia seminar held in conjunction with the Book Awards. While Liebling's remarks were reported in the city edition of the *Times* that night, they disappeared from further editions, supposedly because Mr. Knopf called Mr. Arthur Hays Sulzberger on the subject.

Meanwhile, the astonished and grateful author of *The Moviegoer* quietly accepted the award in New York, expressed his thanks to Mr. Knopf for appearing at the ceremony, and returned to his house, wife, and two daughters in Covington, in the parish of St. Tammany, a small town on the other side of Lake Pontchartrain from New Orleans, where he lived a most comfortable and studious existence and wrote in the bedroom. The ladies in their set—the best in Covington—often asked Mrs. Percy how she could bear having her husband around the house all day.

The agitation over the prize in New York was in sharp contrast with Walker Percy himself and with *The Moviegoer*—a sardonic, essentially philosophical novel about the spiritual solitude of a young stockbroker in the New Orleans suburb of Gentilly who eventually marries a tragically vulnerable young woman to whom he is distantly related. *The Moviegoer* was certainly not a book to arouse the usually tired reviewers of "Other Fiction," or even those editors of Sunday book supplements to whom any book on public affairs nowadays seems more immediately newsworthy than any novel not left by Hemingway in a bank vault. Novels these days get written off with dismaying ease, and *The Moviegoer* was in any event a book difficult to place. It was a lean, tartly written, subtle, not very dramatic attack on the wholly bourgeois way of life and thinking in a "gracious" and "historic" part of the South. But instead of becoming another satire on the South's retreat from its traditions, it was, for all the narrator's bantering light tone, an altogether tragic and curiously noble study in the loneliness of necessary human perceptions.

The narrator and protagonist—John Bickerson Bolling, "Binx"—cleverly increases his income every year and carries on in a mechanical way with one of his secretaries after another. But he has become obsessed with the meaninglessness of everything he is just beginning to *see*, with the despair whose specific character, said Kierkegaard, is precisely that it is unaware of being despair. His father, a doctor, perished during the war; Binx has a distinct sense of fatherlessness, of traditions he is supposed to carry on that he cannot locate or justify in the cozy ways around him. In the secrecy of his own mind he is excited by the possibility of newly looking at life with the special, hallucinated feeling of discovery that he gives to the movies where he spends many evenings. He has become an enraptured observer of the human face, a man who is training himself to look steadily at the most commonplace things in his path. He has found some tiny chink in the wall of his despair—the act of looking, of seeing and discovering. He is a man who can look and listen, in a world where most people don't. His real life, you might say, is dominated by the excitement of conversion. There is a newness in his life. He is a spiritual voyeur, a seeker after the nearest but most unfathomable places of the human heart. He can listen to the tortured girl Kate, who has a powerful attraction to death and belabors him—his ability to give her all his attention constitutes the love between them. He has become the one man around him who seems to want nothing for himself but to look, to be a spectator in the dark. This clinician and diagnostician of the soul trains himself in the movies. The enlarged, brilliantly lighted and concentrated figures upon the screen have taught him how to focus on the secret human places.

The Moviegoer, essentially a sophisticated search of the search for faith in a world that seems almost bent on destroying it, was not calculated to win great popularity. It was not exactly about going to the movies. It was a brilliant novel about our abandonment, our *Geworfenheit*, as the existentialists used to say—our cast-off state. Yet Binx the narrator and presiding figure was so tart and intractable in tone that one had to be sympathetic to the mind behind it, not impatient with the lack of action, in order to respond. It was, in fact, a book about an outsider for outsiders. Southerners used to call themselves outsiders because they came from the rural, underdeveloped, old-fashioned, defeated South. But as Binx shows, in every passage of his involvement with the sophisticated upper-middle class in New Orleans, it is the South itself that today makes outsiders of its people, breeds a despair that will never know it is despair.

The Moviegoer was, in fact, an odd, haunting, unseizable sort of book. It was not "eccentric," did not overplay tone and incident in the current style—it was as decorous as an old-fashioned comedy of manners. But it was evidently and deeply the expression of some inner struggle. The author himself seemed in some fundamentals to feel himself in the wrong, to be an outsider in relation to his society. Southern novelists have made their fame in the twentieth century by proving just how different the South is from the rest of country. The point of *The Moviegoer* was precisely that Gentilly, New Orleans, the South, had become the representative examples of an America in which people no longer know how to *look* at anything, did not know how or what to look for. They lived with only the most distant intimations of their own pain. One man would have to learn to *see* (as if for the first time) with only the minimum chance of saving himself at all. His bride-to-be, Kate, they both know he cannot save.

The author of *The Moviegoer* was, in every respect, far off the beaten track of the contemporary writing business in New York. He was a Percy, and the Percys of the Deep South—Walker was born in Birmingham, Alabama, and grew up in Greenville, Mississippi—if not ascertainably descended from Hotspur, were definitely descended from a British naval lieutenant, Charles Percy, who by all accounts was an ancestor with some go to him. In 1776 he removed himself from the Dutch West Indies to Wilkinson County in Mississippi where, as one history of the Percy family puts it, "He acquired quite a

fortune in lands and slaves." Charles Percy became Don Carlos Percy, something of a Spanish grandee, during the period when Spain controlled the West Florida territory that included the lower third of what is now Mississippi. But, as the Percy family history does not state, he was bedeviled by too many wives—he had had one in England, acquired one in Mississippi—and when the first wife appeared in Mississippi with his son, a full-grown captain in the English Navy, Don Carlos was thoroughly provoked, everybody immediately began suing everybody else, and during the commotion Don Carlos walked down to the creek with a sugar kettle, tied it around his neck, and hopped in. The creek is called Percy's Creek to this day. This ancestor's marital problems are related without sympathy in *Lanterns on the Levee* by the poet-lawyer William Alexander Percy, a lifelong bachelor, a painfully dutiful man and generally full of the most immense regard and concern for the Percy family. William Alexander Percy, "Uncle Will,"—*The Moviegoer* is dedicated "in gratitude to W.A.P."—a first cousin of Walker's father LeRoy, became Walker's foster father. His own father died when he was eleven, his mother died two years later, and Walker and his younger brothers LeRoy and Phinizy were brought up by "Uncle Will" in Greenville—in the old Percy house on Percy Street.

W.A.P. was a minor poet (his books were published by Alfred A. Knopf) in the still romantic style of so many minor poets in the Twenties; a graduate of Sewanee and Harvard Law School; a planter without much interest in the family's great cotton plantation, Trail Lake, a noticeable adornment of Greenville; a strong foe of the K.K.K.; sensitive and chivalrous and hot-tempered. By his admission in *Lanterns on the Levee*, the only fun in his life, the only time he broke clear of the Percy family and Greenville, was in the A.E.F. during World War I. Greenville produced some notable literary talents—Shelby Foote, David Cohn, Hodding Carter, Charles Bell—and writers from Mississippi liked to remind the world that Mississippi had produced Faulkner, Eudora Welty, and Tennessee Williams. "Uncle Will" seems to have been proud of Mississippi writers even when his literary tastes were counter to theirs—Faulkner used to play tennis on the Percy court (retiring into the house at regular intervals for the libations that spaced the slow collapse of his game). In some ways William Alexander Percy must have been like Faulkner's lawyer-savant, Gavin Stevens. He was a man almost too sensitive to his family. His father (still another LeRoy Percy) was the last great "aristocratic" figure in Mississippi politics—he was a United States Senator but was replaced by the poor whites' favorite, James Vardaman. Will was so much under the influence of his strict, pure, and burdeningly impressive father that he had the sculptress Malvina Hoffman create over Senator Percy's grave the heroic figure of a medieval knight pensively leaning on his sword. The inscription reads PATRIOT and does not seem to stop the citizenry from leaving empty beer cans around it.

One way to Walker Percy is by way of William Alexander Percy. *Lanterns on the Levee* came out in 1941 (the year W. J. Cash brought out *The Mind of the South*) and is as testily defensive about the South and its traditions as Cash was sardonic. From *Lanterns on the Levee* one gets the impression of a much-harried man, brave, all too responsible to his family and regional heritage, rarely happy, chafing under restrictions that he did not always understand. Since he owned a cotton plantation in the Delta but was bored by business, was a lawyer whose greatest interest was literature, and a man of obviously deep emotions that he could not always find employment for in Greenville, one way out of his many conflicts and dilemmas was to romanticize the South in a way that his cousin Walker has never been tempted to do. In *Lanterns on the Levee* W.A.P. says of the old slaveholders, the landed gentry, the governing class: "Though they have gone, they were not sterile; they have their descendants, whose evaluation of life approximates theirs." In 1965, writing in *Harper's* on "Mississippi: The Fallen Paradise," Walker Percy wrote:

> The bravest Mississippians in recent years have not been Confederates or the sons of Confederates but rather two Negroes, James Meredith and Medgar Evers. . . . No ex-Mississippian is entitled to write of the tragedy with which has overtaken his former state with any sense of moral superiority. . . . He strongly suspects that he would not have been counted among the handful . . . who not only did not keep silent but fought hard . . . The Gavin Stevenses have disappeared and the Snopeses have won. . . . Not even Faulkner foresaw the ironic denouement of the tragedy: that the Compsons and Sartorises should not only be defeated by the Snopeses but that in the end they should join them.

William Alexander Percy was perhaps like Gavin Stevens in his love of both the law and literature, but his book shows how completely he lacked the philosophic temper even as he praised it. Everything he says about the struggle between the classes and the races in the South reveals a taste for sentimental abstractions rather than for the facts in social evidence. He of course detested the poor whites who eliminated his father from the United States Senate, and he says proudly of the Delta: "It was not settled by these people; its pioneers were slave-owners and slaves." But as he admits about the descendants of the slaves, "the sober fact is that we understand one another not at all." Despite the usual condescending praise of their "good manners," it is obvious from his book that his black retainers were a constant trial to him, exceeded in their power to annoy him only by the liberals during the New Deal period who were prodding him to expressions of concern for blacks and sharecroppers that he obstinately refused to make. He says of the blacks: "This failure on their part to hold and to pass on their own history is due, I think, not so much to their failure to master any written form of communication as to their obliterating genius for living in the present . . . [The Negro] neither remembers nor plans. The white man does little else; to him the present is the one great unreality."

William Alexander Percy was a romantic agnostic who turned away from his mother's Catholicism; Walker Percy is a Catholic convert—who is by no means romantic about that or about the Church. W.A.P. liked to compare Southerners to Russian aristocrats. Defending the sharecropping system on the Percy cotton plantation, he wrote: "Sharecropping is one of the best systems ever devised to give security and a chance to profit to the simple and the unskilled. It has but one drawback—it must be administered by human beings to whom it offers an unusual opportunity to rob without detection or punishment. The failure is not in the system itself . . . the failure is in human nature. The Negro is no more on an equality with the white man in plantation matters than in any other dealings between the two." Both *The Moviegoer* and *The Last Gentleman* say some concrete things about money-getting in the South, about the coarsening and thickening of upper-class Southerners, that W.A.P. would surely have found too shocking to swallow.

Yet there is one striking link between these two Percys, quite apart from the fact that one brought the other up, made him financially independent, and that both are Southern gentlemen for whom literature has been an avocation. Will Percy could never feel that he was living up to his father, "The

Patriot," whose monument is so out of keeping with the modest gravestones in the Greenville cemetery. Will obviously felt himself to be an inadequate son of the Southern Tradition which finally enclosed him, the small-town litterateur, in wistful gestures of regret, lyric flight, and a nostalgia for a South that perhaps never was. But it has been the genius of Southern writing in our time to keep tradition alive. It has been the South's writers, not its politicians, who have maintained our interest in the South as another country. The Southern writers have in fact perpetuated the idea of the South by personalizing its history, by their obstinate moralism, their scorn for corruption, their belief in a true country of the spirit—and their compassion for the Negro.

So Walker Percy seems to me very much a Southern son who believes in the existence of a spiritual tradition, another Southerner orphaned by modern history who still believes in the great cause of Christian truth, not the "lost" cause of the Confederacy. He is a subtle mind and in many respects a hidden one, distinctly different from most American novelists today; Walker Percy becomes clear only when you realize how much he is a pilgrim of faith who believes that there is a true way, a lost tradition, that he will yet discover.

In our time it has been the Southern writer who has been the conscience of the South, who has restored its legends, who has taken on the terror as well as the romance of its history. When Percy was asked at the National Book Awards why the South produced so many good writers, he replied in his usual offhand style, "Because we got beat." But the Byrds as well as the Wallaces rose from "defeat" a long time ago. The Southern writer feels that *he* is still in a state of defeat, of exile, of classic outsidedness and apartness. It is the Southern writer who remains "unreconciled" at a time when dominant elements in the South have become the voice of our spurious Americanism.

Walker Percy belongs with the "defeated" and the "exiled"—one might say that he knows exile and defeat in their purest American state. The story of how he became a writer at all is an important part of it. Percy graduated from the University of North Carolina in 1937 and Columbia's College of Physicians and Surgeons in 1941. He did not particularly like medical school, thought many of his classmates childish—one of their recreations was to fill balloons with water and drop them onto 168th Street—and he still remembers with distaste a box of bones he had to learn to identify. "P and S" emphasized the mechanics of disease, and it was in some revolt against this, and because of his interest in psychiatry, that he had himself psychoanalyzed while a medical student. The study of pathology, with its marvelously colored slides, fascinated him. Then, as an intern at Bellevue, he caught pulmonary tuberculosis from one of the many bodies on which he performed autopsies, caught it from "the same scarlet tubercle bacillus I used to see lying crisscrossed like Chinese characters in the sputum and lymphoid tissue of the patients at Bellevue. Now I was one of them."

Two years of physical inactivity followed. America was in the full tide of World War II. His brother LeRoy was a captain in the Air Force, and would get the Bronze Star; his brother Phinizy, an Annapolis graduate, would be on a PT boat in the Pacific with Jack Kennedy. Dr. Walker Percy was in Saranac Lake. But there wasn't any room for him in the famous Trudeau sanitarium, and while waiting to be admitted, Percy lived in a boardinghouse, all alone, reading and beginning to write. He says now, "TB liberated me." His illness, the enforced absence from his family, the solitariness—all seem to have brought out in him one of those religious personalities whom William James, in *The Varieties of Religious Experience*, called the "twice-born." His real life, his spiritual and intellectual life, his vocation as a writer, his growing concern with symbolism, the philosophy of language, and those whom James had called "sick souls"—all this began when he found himself cut off from the career he had planned, from the war that was to be decisive for his generation, from the South that on Percy Street in Greenville he had taken for granted. Typically, it was the religious existentialists Kierkegaard and Dostoevsky, not Faulkner the Southern genius, who influenced him; with his wife Mary, a Mississippi girl who had been a medical technician, he became a Catholic. This was only one of his many actual "conversions." In becoming a writer, as in his professing Catholicism, he declared himself born again, born to a new understanding.

Chekhov, William James, Maugham were also doctors who became writers. But although Percy has in fact never practiced, one feels about him that in becoming a writer he underwent an unusually significant personal change, a change of faith within his change of profession. Although he is a natural writer, downright, subtle, mischievous, his novels seem to me essentially the self-determination of a religious personality, of a seeker who after being ejected from the expected and conventional order of things has come to himself as a stranger in the world.

A disposition to look at things, at oneself, in a radically new way is very much what happens in both *The Moviegoer* and *The Last Gentleman*. The violence of Southern history— the violence you can feel in the streets of Greenville today, where stores advertise "Guns and Ammo," where every truck driver seems to have a rifle with him—is not in Percy's books. In each case the protagonist is someone who feels himself in the grip of a profound disorder, and who as a result cultivates the art of looking, examining, taking things in, with an intellectual intensity that clearly has personal significance. Binx, in *The Moviegoer*, is only subtly, secretly estranged from the life around him. "Whenever I approach a Jew, the Geiger counter in my head starts rattling away like a machine gun . . . I am more Jewish than the Jews I know. They are more at home than I am. I accept my exile." Making money is a game at which he is very good, but living has also become a kind of game with which he must appear outwardly unconcerned. This pose makes him seem frivolous and immoral to his great-aunt (whose opinions, romantic and traditionalist, bear a marked resemblance to those of William Alexander Percy). But Binx is not really in the world he seems to be thriving in. In his usual mock-correct way he says:

> My uncle and aunt live in a gracious house in the Garden District and are very kind to me . . . It is a pleasure to carry on the duties of a citizen and to receive in return a receipt or a neat styrene card with one's name on it certifying, so to speak, one's right to exist. . . . But things have suddenly changed. My peaceful existence in Gentilly has become complicated. This morning, for the first time in years, there occurred to me the possibility of a search. What are generally considered to be the best of times are for me the worst of times, and that worst of times was one of the best. . . .

The mental refusal, the silent spiritual opposition, the effort to make some countervailing gesture are those of a man who seems to be *here*, with us, but is really out *there*, all by himself. One day he puts the contents of his wallet out on the dresser and suddenly looks at the stuff.

> I stood in the center of the room and gazed at the little pile, sighting through a hole made by

thumb and forefinger. What was unfamiliar about them was that I could see them. . . .

Binx complains of Harry Stern, a dedicated biologist he had worked with in the lab, that "he is no more aware of the mystery which surrounds him than a fish is aware of the water it swims in." In the office Binx reads a copy of Doughty's *Arabia Deserta* enclosed in a *Standard & Poor's* binder; in hotel rooms he reads science.

> There I lay in my hotel room with my search over yet still obliged to draw one breath and then the next. But now I have undertaken a different kind of search, a horizontal search. . . .
>
> Today is my thirtieth birthday . . . and knowing less than I ever knew before, having learned only to recognize merde when I see it, having inherited no more from my father than a good nose for merde, for every species of shit that flies. . . .

This contrast of the here and the there, of the "regular" American world that can never understand the panic it breeds and the self training itself to face despair, to become a microscopist of salvation, gives *The Moviegoer* its special wry charm. Binx does see things in a special light—not God's light, perhaps, but, like the light on a movie screen, the light of hallucination, excessive concentration, obsession, that is given to those who at least turn their faces in the right direction. There emerges, to use a favorite word of Percy's, a hypertrophy of detail. Things become oddly distinct, enlarged on the movie screen we carry in our heads when we make the supreme effort to see the world in a new relation—by this alone may we lift ourselves out of our sickness.

In *The Last Gentleman* the hero—always called "the engineer"—is more obviously sick than Binx in *The Moviegoer*, more publicly in exile, for he is a Southerner who works at night as a maintenance engineer at Macy's in New York so he can spend his days looking through the high-powered telescope on which he has spent his savings. He needs above all to make himself new organs of sight, and from his room at the YMCA he discovers two women sitting on a bench in Central Park who come to have the greatest possible influence on his life.

The point of *The Last Gentleman* is hardly that the hero is a "gentleman"; the point of *The Moviegoer* is hardly the movies. Percy has trouble with his titles; a new novel I have seen in manuscript about the "end of the world" is tentatively entitled *How to Make Love in the Ruins*.[1] These are all stories of the effort at cognition, in a mad world, by men who on the surface seem mad but really aren't. Both the "moviegoer" and the "engineer" are the only knights of faith left among people who have given up all knowledge of a "search." Both have taken on the burden of being declared "sick." As in the classical Russian novels that Percy loves, it is the sick man, the outsider, the "idiot" in Dostoevsky's beautiful sense of the word, who by the sacrifice of his good name may yet teach the others charity. "I'm not well," reflects the engineer, "and therefore it is fitting that I should sit still, like an Englishman in his burrow, and see what can be seen." Even as a college student he saw that the young men around him were "very much with themselves, set, that is, for the next fifty years in the actuality of themselves and their own good names. They knew what they were, how things were and how things should be. As for the engineer, he didn't know. I'm from the Delta too, thought he . . . and I'm Episcopal; why ain't I like them, easy and actual?" With his girl (he discovered her through his telescope) he reflects: ". . . goofy as he was, he knew two things not many people know. He knew how to listen and he knew how to get at that most secret and aggrieved enterprise upon which almost everyone is embarked. He'd give her the use of his radar."

Wilfrid Sheed, an admirer of his, interestingly lists Percy among the "dandys" of contemporary fiction. Certainly the lean, subtle Percy style, the unmistakable breeding behind the style, do put Percy among the "dandys" now writing fiction when there are so many real and would-be roughnecks. A. J. Liebling, a great connoisseur of style in boxing, journalism, and food, must have been delighted by this aspect of *The Moviegoer*. And with his spare, economical, utterly quiet personal style, Walker Percy is himself so impressive an example of the cultivated upper-class Southerner that after going around the French Quarter with him in New Orleans, spending a weekend with him and his family at their house in Covington, accompanying him to Mass, one could easily leave it at that: the upper-class sense of style, fitness, leanness. Percy lives what seems on the surface a wholly typical suburban life in the beautiful house in Covington with his wife Mary and younger daughter Ann—the other daughter, Mary Pratt, is married, has a son, and lives near enough for Walker and Mary Percy to baby-sit frequently with their first grandchild. He is easy to talk to, a great listener but no very enthusiastic talker himself—it was from his brother LeRoy that I learned of threats to Walker from the local K.K.K. after he objected to the Confederate flag's hanging in a school, and when the issue was brought into court in New Orleans, he testified there. It is somehow typical of a certain shyness, reserve, a charming gift in his nature for not bearing down too hard in personal conversation, that he likes to keep the television picture on without the sound. He has cultivated the art of restful sitting and lounging, of looking easy, in a way that keeps conversation with him as casual as drifting through a summer afternoon. He seems a most domesticated creature, intensely devoted to his family, but also at home with himself.

But to one admirer of his novels, it seems clear that Walker Percy, a philosopher among novelists, is just as atypical a Southerner and Catholic. There is a singularity to his life, to his manifest search for a new religious humanism, there is a closeness to pain and extreme situations, that makes him extraordinarily "sensitive"—to the existentialist theme of life as shipwreck—without suggesting weakness. Percy in his novels touches the rim of so many human mysteries and despairs that one criticism I have is that he remains equidistant from many *different* problems—psychological, social, Godly—without his getting near enough to use them. After I left him in Covington and was shown around Greenville and the Percy cotton plantation in the Delta by Walker's brother LeRoy, I wondered why so little of the town and the Delta itself has as yet appeared in his fiction. Walker Percy seems far away from what is near to many Southerners, and he sees the "near" in the light of a symbolism that is almost too speculative. Faith for him seems to express a search rather than something found, a *way* of seeing, not an end. Though Walker Percy of Covington (Dr. Percy in the society page) seems solidly there, one knows from his novels, his history, from the extraordinary *philosophical* poignance of the man, that he remains betwixt and between many things. The madness (very real) of the women in his books signifies their never having attempted the "search." The "madness" of his heroes is a figure of speech for the immense loneliness of looking for a God who, in Nietzsche's phrase, is the great unknown and so cannot be found.

That a *novelist* should make one think of such things says much about Walker Percy. Unlike the United States of America, unlike the bustling bourgeois South of today, Walker Percy does not feel that he is a success. He is still looking. "Looking" as a way of life reminds me of a sentence by Simone Weil: Attentiveness without a "goal" is a supreme form of prayer.

Notes

1. Published as *Love in the Ruins*.

S. J. PERELMAN

1904–1979

Sidney Joseph Perelman was born in Brooklyn, New York, on February 1, 1904. He was educated at Brown University, where he was a pre-medical student between 1921 and 1925. While at Brown he became a cartoonist for the campus humor magazine, the *Brown Jug*, to which he then began to submit humorous articles, the first of his to appear in print. Eventually he became the magazine's editor. Upon leaving the university he joined the staff of *Judge*, for which he supplied cartoons and humorous pieces. In 1930 he moved on to the magazine *College Humor*, where he began developing his own distinctive writing style.

In 1929, after his marriage to Laura West, Perelman's first collection of humorous pieces was published under the title *Dawn Ginsbergh's Revenge*. This was so successful that the Marx Brothers invited him to write screenplays in Hollywood, where over the next ten years he worked on eight movies for Paramount and MGM, including the Marx Brothers' own *Monkey Business* (1931) and *Horse Feathers* (1932). Perelman also started writing for the *New Yorker* in 1934, and contributed to the scripts of various Broadway shows, most notably *One Touch of Venus* (1943), written with Ogden Nash, with music by Kurt Weill.

Perelman's many collections of humorous pieces include *Strictly from Hunger* (1937); *Look Who's Talking* (1940); *Dream Department* (1943); *Crazy Like a Fox* (1944); and *Acres and Pains* (1947). He died on October 17, 1979.

It is a strange force that compels a writer to be a humorist. It is a strange force, if you care to go back farther, that compels anyone to be a writer at all, but this is neither the time nor the place to bring up that matter. The writer's way is rough and lonely, and who would choose it while there are vacancies in more gracious professions, such as, say, cleaning out ferryboats? In all understatement, the author's lot is a hard one, and yet there are those who deliberately set out to make it harder for themselves. There are those who, in their pride and their innocence, dedicate their careers to writing humorous pieces. Poor dears, the world is stacked against them from the start, for everybody in it has the right to look at their work and say, "I don't think that's funny."

It is not a pleasant thought, though, I am afraid, an unavoidable one, that there cannot be much demand for written humor in this our country today. For the supply is—with one exception—scanty and shopworn. There are quantities of those who, no doubt, if filling out a questionnaire, put, "Occupation, humorist," but their pieces are thin and tidy and timid. They find a little formula and milk it until it moos with pain. They stay with the good old comic symbols so that you won't be upset—the tyrannical offspring, the illiterate business associate, the whooping, devil-may-care old spinster (always reliable), the pitiable inadequacies of a man trying to do a bit of carpentry, the victorious criticisms of the little wife.

Over and over and on and on, they write these pieces, in the rears of magazines, in glossy Sunday supplements of newspapers, over and over and on and on, like a needle stuck in a phonograph record. I could name names, if I could remember them. But that would mean nothing. You have seen those pieces, and they were dead before the sun went down on the day on which they were published.

I had thought, on starting this composition, that I should define what humor means to me. However, every time I tried to, I had to go and lie down with a cold wet cloth on my head. Still, here I go. (For the British I had great reverence, until now, when it is so much about how charming Lady Cicely looked when she fell out of the punt.) Humor to me, Heaven help me, takes in many things. There must be courage; there must be no awe. There must be criticism, for humor, to my mind, is encapsulated in criticism. There must be a disciplined eye and a wild mind. There must be a magnificent disregard of your reader, for if he cannot follow you, there is nothing you can do about it. There must be some lagniappe in the fact that the humorist has read something written before 1918. There must be, in short, S. J. Perelman.

Mr. Perelman stands alone in this day of humorists. Mr. Perelman—there he is. Robert Benchley, who was probably nearest to Perelman, and Ring Lardner, who was nearest to nobody, are gone, and so Mr. Perelman stands by himself. Lonely he may be—but there he is.

And here he is in his own words:

> Button-cute, rapier-keen, wafer-thin and pauper-poor is S. J. Perelman, whose tall, stooping figure is better known to the twilit half-world of five continents than to Publishers' Row. That he possesses the power to become invisible to finance companies; that his laboratory is tooled up to manufacture Frankenstein-type monsters on an incredible scale; and that he owns one of the rare mouths in which butter has never melted are legends treasured by every schoolboy.

> Retired today to peaceful Erwinna, Pennsylvania, Perelman raises turkeys which he occasionally displays on Broadway, stirs little from his alembics and retorts. Those who know hint that the light burning late in his laboratory may result in a

breathtaking electric bill. Queried, he shrugs with the fatalism of your true Oriental. "*Mektoub*," he observes curtly. "It is written."

His latest book, *The Road to Miltown, or Under the Spreading Atrophy*, seems to me by far his best; but that is what everybody says about a Perelman latest book. The only snide thing I can find to say about this one—and I had to strain to dig that up—is that I find the subtitle unnecessary, and in no way up to the title proper. I have been told often, and I know and have known that one should not read through at a sitting a book of short pieces. Well, it turns out that those who told me were fools and so was I, for you can go right through *The Road to Miltown*. There is in this compilation a variety that knocks you dizzy.

Mr. Perelman has bounded over continents and seas, and come back to put it all before you—not quietly, not sweetly, nothing about the messes of nations, but just right there. Mr. Perelman every time he writes takes a leap that causes you to say, "Now wait a minute," but it is so well worth waiting for. Mr. Perelman went around the world, of course, but he took the world by the tail and slung it casually over his shoulder.

These pieces in *The Road to Miltown* have been in *The New Yorker* and, I think, *Holiday*, but you never have a feeling of having read any of it before. The remarkable bits called "Cloudland Revisited" are spaced through his book. They are his bloodcurdling experiences with old-time movies. For six months after seeing Erich von Stroheim in *Foolish Wives*, confesses Mr. Perelman, "I exhibited a maddening tendency to click my heels and murmur 'Bitte?' along with a twitch as though a monocle were screwed into my eye. The mannerisms finally abated, but not until the dean of Brown University had taken me aside and confided that if I wanted to transfer to Heidelberg, the faculty would not stand in my way."

There are his days as a young rapier-keen cartoonist for a comic weekly whose editors, he complains, were inexplicably unmoved by such masterpieces from his drawing board as one showing "a distraught gentleman careening into a doctor's office clutching a friend by the wrist and whimpering, 'I've got Bright's disease and he has mine.'"

But Mr. Perelman does not tilt at windmills (Dear, dear—is it National Cliché Week already—so early in the year?); he goes after the big nasty ones, the cruel, the ignorant, the mean. He is not frightened by the rich and the idiotic. As he says, "I don't know anything about medicine, but I know what I like."

Well, I think that Mr. Perelman's book, *The Road to Miltown*, is fine. That's all I meant to say.

A week or two ago Mr. Perelman had pressed on his humid brow a wreath of laurels for being the best screen writer of the year (for *Around the World in 80 Days*). I think I may say that Mr. Perelman never wanted to be a great screen writer, never saw screen writing as a goal. Still, if you're going to be a screen writer, it must be a satisfaction to be the best. And that is also true of a humorist writer.—DOROTHY PARKER, "Humor Takes In Many Things," *NYTBR*, Jan. 20, 1957, pp. 1, 36

There are at least two distinct types of laughter that the writing of S. J. Perelman produces in the reader, the Honk and the Yurble. Of these, the Honk is the more frequent. It might be the effect of a line of dialogue ("He opened a vein in his bath." "I never knew baths had veins.") or one of his intricately bizarre openings ("Every so often, when business slackens up in the bowling alley and the other pin boys are hunched over their game of bezique, I like to exchange my sweatshirt for a crisp white surgical tunic, polish up my optical mirror, and examine the corset advertisements in *The New York Herald Tribune*. . . .") or one of his all-purpose endings ("We bashed in his conk and left him to the vultures."). The Yurble is caused by Perelman's linguistic cobbling, as for example when "a panoply of porn" becomes "a pornoply" or he asserts "I hold no buff for the briefalo" or he gathers a cast that includes Gonifson, Hornbostel and Groin, and the atmosphere begins to resemble that of Nighttown with Leopold Bloom cruising through its surreal precincts.

In a sense, the humorist is like the man who hijacks a jumbo jet and its 300 passengers by threatening the pilot with a 10-cent water pistol. The arsenal is simple—technique matters, manner is everything, and fury helps. Mr. Perelman is good on the grotesque, because he is great at his tetchiest and best when he is angry. A movie such as *I Loved You Wednesday* or *The Texas Chainsaw Massacre*, a magazine like *House and Garden*, the book *Oh, Doctor! My Feet!* by Dr. Dudley J. Morton, or practically any inedible sandwich is enough to set him off. But he is never more furiously comic as when dealing with a specific geographical location, whether it is a house in eastern Pennsylvania (about which he wrote an entire book, *Acres and Pains*) or a back street in Kowloon.

We are still waiting for his autobiography, *The Hindsight Saga*, although many of the facts are known. Having made a substantial reputation in the 30's taking apart monthlies like *The Jitterbug* and *The Cleaning and Dyeing World*, Mr. Perelman set sail in the 40's, and I can think of nowhere (McMurdo Sound might be an exception) he has not traveled. The Island of Lamu, the remote city of Pagan, the bars on Suriwongse Road, the Cameron Highlands of Malaysia—all have been visited and satirized by this tireless jokester whose 20 books have over the years not shown the slightest diminution in inventiveness. His new book is all travel, beginning 33,000 feet over Cape Ann, heading east, and after sojourns in Scotland, Turkey, Iran, Israel, Southeast Asia and the Pacific, winding up in Hollywood. One can only conclude, after such an ambitious itinerary, that Mr. Perelman swallowed enough Kaopectate to turn him into a vase, but in the event his "peregrination of the planet" (as he neatly puts it) seems to have resulted in his becoming a vessel of wrath, though not the less readable for all that.

"From bar mitzvah on," Mr. Perelman writes at the start of *Eastward Ha!*, "I had longed to qualify as a Jewish Robert Louis Stevenson." It is one of Mr. Perelman's more modest claims, but after reading "Unshorn Locks and Bogus Bagels," an account of his stay in Israel, one tends to think that he is in grave danger of being read out of the tribe for his having brought such ill tidings to Zion. "What magic, what ingenuity and manpower it had taken to re-create Grossinger's, the Miami Fountainebleau and the Concord Hotel on a barren strand in the Near East!" In Tel Aviv he came across a brand of perfume called Chutzpah. He describes this as a breakthrough even Dr. Chaim Weizmann ("himself a chemist") would have applauded: "Not a soul in history, from Helen of Troy to Helena Rubinstein, had ever thought of pure, unadulterated gall as a cosmetic." He notes in passing that the best hotel in Jerusalem—if not in the whole country—is run "by a family of Baptists." But Perelman is nothing if not fair-minded, and I cannot think of anyone better equipped to describe the troglodyte face of Yassir Arafat—indeed, I believe he has already done so, with devastating results.

Typically, because he hated the place so thoroughly, the Israel piece is one of his funniest. Discomfort, pomposity, bad service, importuning natives, hideous weather—anything vile makes Mr. Perelman's prose sing with mockery. Years ago, miffed in this present book's companion volume, *Westward Ha!* he was forced to leave "enough baksheesh in Santa Sophia

to gild the transept"; and who but Perelman would have tilted a comedy *The Rising Gorge?* In his disgust resides his eloquence. His experience of the Soviet Union in "The Millennium, and What They Can Do with It" is pure acid. Nothing went right, yet the result is not a tantrum but a glorious backhander in which everything he saw from Moscow to Yalta is dismissed. "Yalta contains sanitariums that ignite more hypochondria in the onlooker than the Magic Mountain . . . that Chekhov managed to glean any literary nuggets from Yalta is merely added proof of his stature." In Iran, which is (in spite of the protestations of the diabolical regime's former apologist, Mrs. Javits) one of the earth's nightmares of unspeakable modernity and uncompromising barbarism, Mr. Perelman lets fly, but always with grace: "the demented thoroughfares" in Teheran are terrifying, "as a result, there are only two kinds of pedestrians . . . the quick and the dead."

It is only when Mr. Perelman is describing a dear friend or a well-loved place that his voice drops and one hears his so-rarely-used tone of gratitude or good will. In Penang, the colonial buildings and warehouses and dockside life "typified for me the magic of Kipling's Far East." It sounds like sarcasm; one waits for his swift deflation, but none comes—it is, almost incredibly, nostalgia. This is unexpected, but perhaps not all that odd, for like the references to Daddy Browning and Peaches, Joshua Slocum, Tazio Nuvolari, the Three Stooges, the reminiscences of Rhode Island and Hollywood, the exact price of brooms in Tzmir and words like "mazuma," "chicken-flicker" and "simoleon," there is room in Perelman's prose style for nearly everything. It is not so strange that in her introduction to a Perelman collection some years ago, ⟨Dorothy⟩ Parker was at a loss for words. Perelman is incomparable.—PAUL THEROUX, "No Buff for the Briefalo," *NYTBR*, Oct. 2, 1977, p. 9

Like Benchley, Perelman—especially in his earlier writings—exploited the antics of a persona gone mad in a world that also had gone mad. But the Perelman character had some significant differences from Benchley's Little Man. Benchley's Little Man looked in the mirror and saw Wimpy; Perelman's creation saw "a man who looks like Ronald Colman and dances like Fred Astaire." On another occasion, he describes himself: "I am a fairly typical Yankee who looks like Gary Cooper, sings like Frank Sinatra and dances like Fred Astaire." His delusions tended as often to be those of grandeur as of persecution.

"Benchley" pretended to have wisdom he didn't have in lectures; "Perelman" sprinkles his daily conversation with exotic foreign words and obscure allusions, as when he tells his maid, who has observed that "You mus' be crazy":

> "But aren't we all?" I reminded her with a charming smile. "*C'est la maladie du temps*—the sickness of the times—don't you think? *Fin-de-siècle* and lost generation, in a way. 'I should have been a pair of ragged claws scuttling across the floors of silent seas.' How well Eliot puts it! D'ye ever see any of the old *transition* crowd?"

All this to impress a maid!

Or perhaps the comic "Perelman" has been brainwashed. Many of his fantasies, it seems clear, come from taking literally the make-believe world of commercial advertising or Hollywood. He reads, for instance, in *Harper's Bazaar* the suggestion, "Why don't you try the effect of diamond roses and ribbons flat on your head, as Garbo wears them when she says good-bye to Armand in their country retreat?" Obeying the advice when he goes to collect the day's mail at the post office,

> Piling my head high with diamond roses and ribbons, I pulled on a pair of my stoutest *espadrilles* and

set off, my cat frisking ahead of me with many a warning cry of "Here comes my master, the Marquis of Carabas!" We reached the post office without incident, except for the elderly Amish woman hoeing cabbages in her garden. As I threw her a cheery greeting, Goody Two-shoe looked up, gave a rapid exhibition of Cheyne-Stokes breathing, and immediately turned to stone. In case you ever get down that way, she is still standing there, slightly chipped but otherwise in very good condition, which is more than I can say for the postmaster. When I walked in, he was in process of spitting into the top drawer, where he keeps the money-order blanks. One look at Boxholder 14 and he went out the window without bothering to raise the sash. A second later I heard a frightened voice directing a small boy to run for the hex doctor next door to the Riegels'. I spent the night behind some willows, . . . but it was a matter of months before I was able to convince the countryside that I had a twin brother, enormously wealthy but quite mad, who had eluded his guards and paid me a visit.

Even more often, reading advertising, unusual books, and newspaper stories sends the Perelman character into a daydream during which, using a cast of frenzied and surreal characters, he dramatizes the exaggerations. Again like Benchley, he makes associations that lead him to wrench words into puns and feckless combinations:

The color drained slowly from my face, entered the auricle, shot up the escalator, and issued from the ladies' and misses' section into the housewares department.

"Have a bit of the wing, darling?" queried Diana solicitously, indicating the roast Long Island aeroplane with apple-sauce. . . . Soon we were exchanging gay bantam over the mellow Vouvray, laughing as we dipped fastidious fingers into the Crisco parfait for which Diana was famous. Our meal finished, we sauntered into the rumpus room and Diana turned on the radio. With a savage snarl the radio turned on her. . . .

The conductor . . . told me he had been riding on trains for so long that he had begun to smell like one, and sure enough, two brakemen waved their lanterns at him that night and tried to tempt him down a siding in Kansas City.

Living almost entirely on cameo brooches and the few ptarmigan which fell to the ptrigger of his pfowling piece. . . .

Among lesser triumphs: "every nook and granny," "as far as the ground could see the eye was white," and "with a blow I sent him grovelling. In ten minutes he was back with a basket of appetising fresh-picked grovels."

Where the Benchley Little Man doggedly fights the real world in spite of unrelieved failure, the Perelman character is actually propelled into his world of fantasy. Though "Perelman" attempts a bravado much like that of Benchley's lecturer, neither Joe Doakes nor Perelman's cultivated *bon vivant* controls his future or his fate.

In their use of a central character—mostly in first-person narratives—who resembles his creator, who finds the hysteria of his world reflected in the hysteria of his language, and who bumbles his way through a universe conspiring against him, Benchley and Perelman to some extent resemble earlier comics, such as Artemus Ward, Charles Heber Clark, George Horatio Derby and others. (The performance of the typical American humorist, Harry Levin claimed in 1972, "is that of an *eiron*, a self-ironist who dissembles his wit—like Socrates himself, or like Will Rogers . . . or like the accident-prone anecdotists of the *New Yorker*.")

But in the later humor there are some important innovations.

For one thing, clinical psychiatry gave effective names and descriptions for the mad behaviors they describe—neurosis, dementia praecox, manic depressive. For another, neither common sense nor erudition helped them to get along in the world; there was no choice but to suffer humiliation, defeat, and failure. Most significantly of all, the world itself had become so chaotic and unreasonable that instead of feeling comfortably superior, a large segment of readers could identify with these comic types. Their problems, their futile attempts to solve them, and their defense mechanisms for surviving among them seemed all too universal.—WALTER BLAIR, HAMLIN HILL, "Benchley and Perelman," *America's Humor: From Poor Richard to Doonesbury*, 1978, pp. 434–36

I doubt if there is a reader anywhere prepared to read 650 consecutive pages of Perelman at a sitting; Perelman's brew is far too heavily seasoned to swallow at a single meal, but an essay a night for three months and the trick is done.

There is a sense in which he is the most negative writer of his era. When I first read 'A Farewell to Omsk', nearly thirty years ago, and laughed over the passage describing a Russian who 'dislodged a piece of horse-radish from his tie and shied it at a passing Nihilist', it escaped me at the time that the Nihilist was Perelman himself, a lampoonist who all his life has clutched gratefully at any wisps of literary horse-radish that might come his way, with a view to analysing it in the minutest detail. Advertisements, Show-Biz handouts, ghosted memoirs, the captions to photographs, reported speeches, nothing is too inconsequential for his attention. Were there no bad writing in the world, there would have been no Perelman with his odd gift for disclosing the nature of its rankness. Sometimes, indeed, the target is so idiotic that no satirist's hand is required at all, witness the Louella Parsons pastiche, 'Nirvana Small by a Waterfall'; it must have been people like Miss Parsons that Dickens had in mind when he complained that he went to America to lampoon the inhabitants, only to discover on arrival that God had anticipated him. Perelman's best targets are those with a kind of daft integrity of their own, Fu Manchu, Tarzan, Cecil B. de Mille, Elinor Glyn, Valentino, where he can work safe in the assumption that his reader is perfectly well acquainted with the unconscious humour of the originals.

His favourite method is to quote the original in all its pristine lunacy, and then construct a short story or playlet developing the idea, often throwing in for good measure a cast-line that reads like something which has been translated through several languages; when it comes to christening his creatures, Perelman is not far behind the master Beachcomber, a point of which I was reminded on meeting once again Milo Usufruct, Manuel Dexterides, Punkins Janeway and Tom Pulsifer. There are even a few specimens of nomenclature requiring a passing knowledge of Yiddish, for example Ivy Nudnick, and that bilingual pearl, Olaf Hasholem. A schoolmaster in summing it all up would conclude, quite rightly, that Perelman had devoured rubbish all his life, with a kind of instinctive knowledge that it was the rubbish that oiled the engines of his literary endeavour. In *Eastward Ha!*, the latest in a long line of collected essays, the gift for coining a cliché remains undimmed, although he is very careful to place himself in his own era so that there can be no possible misunderstandings—'a smile more saccharine than Don Ameche in a kiddie pageant'.

As to where other people's clichés end and his own begin, Perelman is a slippery customer indeed. He seems to have read everything and forgotten nothing, so that when in writing of sobbing saxophones he tiptoes to the brink of *The Great Gatsby* with its 'all night long the saxophones wailed', I assume he is testing us out, seeing how acute our sense is of the thin line between inspiration and perspiration. An annotated Perelman would be at least three times as long as the original works, for allusion springs, many-headed, from the thickets of his every adjectival clause; in any case, there is only one man qualified to undertake such a work, and that man is Perelman himself. One question I would like to ask him: in an essay called 'Second-Class Matter', he develops the idea of running a magazine's ads into its fiction. The essay in question appeared at about the time the novel I love so much, Tomlinson's *The Day Before*, was published. Here is Tomlinson:

> Nonconformist summoned for refusing to pay the Education rate. Are you bald? Japanese blockade Port Arthur. Mother Seigal's Syrup. Garden Party for War Cripples. Constipation Eradicated Gratis.

And here is Perelman:

> We have scoured the fiction market to set before you Three Million Tiny Sweat Glands Functioning in that vibrant panorama of tomorrow so that Your Sensitive Bowel Muscles can React.

As I say, it is a reasonable assumption that Perelman has read everything.—BENNY GREEN, "Indigestible," *Spec*, May 27, 1978, p. 24

S. J. Perelman, it turns out, left behind four chapters of an autobiography when he died in 1979. He planned to call it *The Hindsight Saga*, a perelmaniacal spin off *The Forsythe Saga*. These bits of memoir, published for the first time in *The Last Laugh*, are the tailpiece to a collection of seventeen of Perelman's comic sketches for *The New Yorker*. Even in its fragmentary state, *The Hindsight Saga* strikes me as the best thing Perelman ever wrote. So much so, in fact, I can't help but wonder why some editor, somewhere along the way, didn't take El Sid, as admirers sometimes called Sidney Joseph Perelman, by the back of his custom-collared neck and push his nose and round-rimmed spectacles on the bridge above and the Cold Stream Guards thatch on the lip below into this sort of material long ago.

Perelman wrote steadily until the day he died at the age of 75, and from the beginning of his career to the end he was capable of being the funniest writer in America—over the quarter-horse distance of 1,500 words. Reading his little sketches, I grew used to hearing myself laugh out loud during the opening romp. Then, before I knew it, I would find my fingers rustling through the pages ahead to see how long it was going to be before he finished.

And why? For a start, the typical Perelman story is pure farce. He seldom pauses to develop his characters. For that matter, he doesn't even expect the reader to care about them. They, like the stories themselves, are but the stage for the big show: S. J. Perelman's virtuosity as a stylist. And a virtuoso he was. Yet his stylistic devices were neither wide-ranging nor profound.

His peculiar tone was a parody of the grandiloquence of the late 19th-century prose that high school and college students were steeped in during his youth. Even the best writers of the late Victorian era, such as Thomas Hardy and Henry James, seemed to regard circumlocution as a necessary mark of cultivation. Hardy would never set a scene in a straightforward way if he could work in a little paraphrasis instead: "The village of Marlott lay amid the north-eastern undulations of the

beautiful vale of Blakemore on Blackmoor, aforesaid, an engirdled and secluded region for the most part untrodden as yet by tourist or landscape-painter . . ." Not only S. J. Perelman, but also H. L. Mencken, Westbrook Pegler, James Branch Cabell, Malcolm Muggeridge, Joseph Hergesheimer, John P. Marquand and A. J. Liebling enjoyed sending up this antique style by inflating the circumlocutions until they burst with silliness and irony or else puncturing them with sudden insertions of slang. But only S. J. Perelman carried the joke to sucn extremes—or so far forward into the second half of the 20th century.

In *The Hindsight Saga* he describes the arrival of a private plane in Palm Springs, California. "In two shakes of a lamb's tail—the official signal for aircraft to land in Palm Springs—the plane had landed and a flourish of trumpets greeted its three passengers, two of whom were familiar to any bystander. They were the renowned *vedette* Elizabeth Taylor and her producer husband, Mike Todd. The third, who bore more than a passing resemblance to the *Apollo Belvedere* but could not be said, in all justice, to rank with him in intellect, was the present writer. His chief distinction—if one may borrow G. K. Chesterton's facility with paradox for a moment—was that he possessed no distinction whatsoever. What startling conjunction of the planets, what mysterious and inexplicable forces of the *I Ching* had mingled the destiny of this utter cipher with that of these eminent face cards?"

In these five sentences, we have a fairly good sample of the Perelman devices: the parody of 19th-century circumlocution, the puncturing slang ("face cards," which he used often), the subverted cliché ("two shakes of a lamb's tail"), the ironically elegant or perelmannered foreign word ("vedette," for star). A full set would have also included the brazen Perelman pun ("My choler wilted," for "My anger subsided"), the extruded Perelman simile ("like walking through a room full of absorbent cotton," for "feeling woozy"), the Perelman micro-metonymy ("Hanna listened to the veins throbbing in my temple," for "I was speechless with anger at Hanna"), and the Perelman extrapolation of cliché into metaphor ("The whole aviary in my head burst into song," for "I was bird-brained").

In *The Hindsight Saga* these often astonishing stunts are, at last, put in the service of real situations and real characters. True, most of the characters are idiots, but they are genuine idiots, nonetheless. We see Mike Todd, on the visit to Palm Springs, trying to put on a blockbuster flurry of fatherhood for two of Elizabeth Taylor's young sons. From the trunk of his limousine he produces a huge aluminum model of a naval destroyer: "A jewel of craftsmanship such as a retired admiral would treasure in his den, it must have cost at least nineteen thousand dollars at F. A. O. Schwartz.

"'Look what Daddy's brought you!' Todd shouted at the boys. 'Boom, boom! Come watch it work!'

"The effect on the lads was hardly that intended: the younger fell to the ground howling in fright; the elder stared paralyzed at Mike, torn between curiosity and dread." Next we see Todd in the swimming pool with a cigar in his teeth, "tugging furiously on a string designed to operate the toy, his face contorted like a Japanese print." Eventually the huge toy explodes into action and goes amok, and a servant has "to beat it with sticks till it subsides."

We see Dorothy Parker in Hollywood working as a scriptwriter for Hunt Stromberg and trying to keep her dignity and the money at the same time. At story conferences she sits with her head down, "knitting a gray artifact seven feet long that looked like a staircase runner" and looking up only when asked directly for comments on the progress of the story, whereupon she says, "Oh, I *do* think it's altogether marvelous, don't you?"

The theme of much of *The Hindsight Saga* is a familiar one in Hollywood memoirs: the sophisticated but needy artist from the East at the mercy of golden boors of the West such as Todd and Herman Mankiewicz.

Mankiewicz produced *Horse Feathers*, one of the movies S. J. Perelmann helped write for the Marx Brothers. We see Mankiewicz having lunch at a restaurant called Eddie Brand-stetter's, "where he treated his palate to two whiskey sours and a Gargantuan lunch consisting of lentil soup with frankfurters, rinderbrust with spaetzle, red cabbage and roast potatoes, and noodle pudding, irrigating the mixture with three or four flagons of Pilsener. Then, eyeballs protruding, he lumbered painfully to his car and drove to his office at Paramount." At the office he tells his secretary he will be incommunicado for the next two or three hours and goes to sleep on a sofa. Ten minutes later he is awakened by "a timid, repeated knocking at the door." It's S. J. Perelman and a co-writer.

"What the devil do you want!" says Mankiewicz. "Well, it's like this," says Perelman. "In this sequence we're working on, we're kind of perplexed about the identity of the Marx Brothers—the psychology of the characters they're supposed to represent, so to speak. I mean, who *are* they? We—we wondered if you could analyze or define them for us."

"Oh, you did, did you?" says Mankiewicz. "O.K., I'll tell you in a word. One of them is a [expletive for Italian], another a mute who picks up spit, and the third an old [expletive for Jew] with a cigar. Is that all clear, Beaumont and Fletcher? Fine." Putting on "a poisonous smile," he adds: "Now get back to your hutch, and at teatime I'll send over a lettuce leaf for the two of you to chew on. Beat it!"

Throughout, we learn next to nothing about S. J. Perelman himself. His "preoccupation with clichés, baroque language, and elegant variation," as he characterized it, like his preoccupation with English clothes and English manners, from Mayfair to Belgravia, created a screen through which neither readers nor casual acquaintances could get a very clear picture of the soul of S. J. Perelman. That screen remains intact in *The Hindsight Saga*. Yet his picture of the world begins to take on definite edges and long shadows. For the first time, in my opinion, he truly becomes a satirist—a label that Paul Theroux, in his excellent introduction to *The Last Laugh*, places upon Perelman as a matter of course but which I have always felt never suited him terribly well.

As I read the fragments of *The Hindsight Saga*, I was reminded of the career of the French artist Paul Gustave Doré. Doré was a tremendously successful illustrator of the classics, *Don Quixote, Paradise Lost*, Rabelais, Poe. Only once did he undertake a book of drawings from life. This was *London*—drawings of London life high and low—which came to be recognized as the glory of his career and one of the most powerful achievements in the history of French graphic art. There are those who regard Perelman as one of American literature's perfect but limited talents. A corollary notion is that if you tamper with the limits, you also tamper with the perfection. All the same I, for one, would have liked to have seen El Sid make a warrior's heedless charge into realism. In these few pages of *The Hindsight Saga* we get some idea of the greater El Dorado he might have led us to.—TOM WOLFE, "The Exploits of El Sid," *NYTBR*, July 19, 1981, pp. 1, 16

EUDORA WELTY

"The Most of S. J. Perelman;
Baby, It's Cold Inside" (1958/1970)
The Eye of the Story
1978, pp. 235-40

I

Give him a cliché and he takes a mile. "The color drained slowly from my face, entered the auricle, shot up the escalator, and issued from the ladies' and misses' section into the housewares department." "I sent him groveling. In ten minutes he was back with a basket of appetizing fresh-picked grovels. We squeezed them and drank the piquant juice thirstily." Spring returns to Washington Square: "It lacked only Nelson Eddy to appear on a penthouse terrace and loose a chorus of deep-throated song, and, as if by magic, Nelson Eddy suddenly appeared on a penthouse terrace and . . . launched into an aria. A moment later, Jeanette MacDonald, in creamy negligee, joined the dashing rascal, making sixty-four teeth, and the lovers began a lilting duet."

Our garden of prose has no more been the same since a certain silky party put in an appearance than the Garden of Eden after the Serpent called. S. J. Perelman—for it was indeed he—has this to say by way of a concluding note to this collection of thirty years' work:

> If I were to apply for a library card in Paris, I would subscribe myself as a *feuilletoniste*, that is to say, a writer of little leaves. I may be in error, but the word seems to me to carry a hint of endearment rather than patronage. In whatever case . . . I should like to affirm my loyalty to it as a medium. The handful of chumps who still practice it are as lonely as the survivors of Fort Zinderneuf; a few more assaults by television and picture journalism and we might as well post their bodies on the ramparts, pray for togetherness, and kneel for the final annihilation. Until then, so long and don't take any wooden rhetoric.

"There has never been a year like this for the giant double-flowering fatuity and gorgeous variegated drivel," Mr. Perelman said in "Caution—Soft Prose Ahead" and that was back in the thirties. If the only trouble is that all he's lampooned has now caught up with its parody, it's anybody's fault but S. J. Perelman's.

The book is put together chronologically, which is as good a way as any to see what was going on, prosewise, from 1930 and the Odets parody "Waiting for Santy" to 1958 when Louella Parsons, whose syntax Mr. P. recommends for its narcotic value ("You don't even need a prescription") sets him the scene for "Nirvana Small by a Waterfall." Each reader will make a leap for his own favorites. Here's "Strictly from Hunger," the masterpiece on Hollywood (" 'Have a bit of the wing, darling?' queried Diana solicitously, indicating the roast Long Island airplane with applesauce.") Here's "Farewell, My Lovely Appetizer," the one that gets Raymond Chandler right between the private eyes, both of a dusty lapis lazuli; and "Genuflection in the Sun," in which a gourmet journeys to pay his respects to the author of a piece of fountain-menu prose—"the finest thing since Baudelaire's *The Flowers of Evil*." (" 'Did you ever get any figures from Liggett's? Were there many conversions?' ") Here's "Nesselrode to Jeopardy," an intrigue—Eric Amblerish, almost Tom Swiftian—of the Macy's food taster aboard the S.S. *Dyspepsia*. ("The real

Colonel Firdausi is reposing at this instant in the Bosporus, in a burlap sack weighted with stale nougat.")

Shall I not simply list some of the old friends you will find again here? The Schrafft hostess "well over nine feet tall, with ice mantling her summit." Mrs. Lafcadio Mifflin—of "Kitchenware, Notions, Lights, Action, Camera!"—"seated at the console of her Wurlitzer, softly wurlitzing to herself." And Mr. Mifflin, "in a porous-knit union suit from Franklin Simon's street floor, stretched out by the fire like a great, tawny cat. Inasmuch as there is a great, tawny cat stretched out alongside him, also wearing a porous-knit union suit, it is not immediately apparent which is Mifflin." And, as a matter of fact, Gisele Mifflin, who delivers that indelible speech about the shades her wedding *tailleur* comes in at Altman's—"among them wine, russet, beige, peach, grackle, stone, liver, lover, blubber, blabber and clabber."

There is "my escort, a Miss Chicken-Licken"; "Pandemonium, the upstairs girl" (she entered on a signal); "my hostess, Violet Hush" (of Los Angeles, of course); "my brokers, Whitelipped and Trembling"; "kindly old Professor Gompers, whose grizzled chin and chiseled grin had made his name a byword at Tunafish College for Women." "John J. Antennae, spiritual father to millions, . . . fox-nosed, sallow, closely related to God on his mother's side." Manual Dexterides, who knows a lot about Tommy Manville; Hyacinth Beddoes Laffoon, "queen-pin of the pulp oligarchy embracing Gory Story, Sanguinary Love, Popular Dissolution, and Spicy Mortician." There is Rosy Fahrleit (she plays over your face), and old man Huysmans, owner of a delicatessen. ("In slicing Huysman's brisket," it comes to be asked, "does one go with or against the grain?")

These also have I loved: the Vulturine and Serpentine National Bank; the San Culotte, "a rather dusty family hotel in the West Forties"; *The Skin around Us*, a popular medical book; and that rollicking song they sing in Asia Minor, "Sohran and Rustum Were Lovers."

Here are the well-known biopsies of the fashion magazines—a certain June issue of *Vogue* "was certainly a serious contender for the ecstasy sweepstakes." "Cloudland Revisited" is here, those vignettes of the twenties—Dr. Fu Manchu and victims to the left, Theda Bara and victims to the right. Here are the plays about (I mean, anent) the advertising world. "You mean that the finger of suspicion points to Loose-Wiles, the Thousand Window Bakeries, whose agents have recently been skulking about in dirty gray caps and gooseneck sweaters?" Here is *Westward, Ha!* and *Acres and Pains*. Here in the Hollywood pieces we find him among colleagues "listening to the purr of their ulcers," or noting how the movie *Stanley and Livingstone* "by an almost unbelievable coincidence was released the very same day luminal was first synthesized." Groucho Marx, for whom, of course, Mr. Perelman has done his share of writing, seems imminent here and once appears in person; we get an intimate glimpse of him indulging "his passionate avocation, the collecting and cross-fertilization of various kinds of money." As always, Mr. Perelman's sources are allowed to play about upon each other. When he, "together with five hundred other bats, hung from the rafters at Loew's Strabismus to see Joan Crawford's latest vehicle," we are shot from there into a parody of a Ventura column on a Barbara Hutton story.

In my dictionary is an engraving of most intricate design, labeled "Human Ear." When I consulted it recently, in connection with this review, I was forced to exclaim, "But this must be the ear of S. J. Perelman!" When I looked up the ear also in my *Nouveau Petit Larousse* (under "*feuilletoniste*") and

found the very same picture of the very same ear, I think I may quietly say it can hardly be laid any longer to mere coincidence. Mr. Perelman misses no mad word we write or say, and its image and essence he translates back to us with an artistry acute, brilliant, devastating, and, heaven keep preserving him, funny.

Now for the sequel.

II

It can do no harm to tell it now. At the age of fifteen, this reviewer fell hopelessly in love with S. J. Perelman. It was from afar, for I was sitting in Jackson (Mississippi) High School in Cicero class. While the others were studying "How long, O Catiline, must we endure your orations?" I was taking in "'Gad, Lucy, You're Magnificent!' Breathed the Great Painter," drawing and caption by S. J. Perelman, from a copy of *Judge* on my lap. S. J. Perelman filled the whole copy of that now-forgotten magazine every week—drawings (in the style of a woodcut), sketches, playlets. I didn't guess he was just a jump ahead of me in school himself at the time. I only knew what any child with a grain of prophecy would know—that here was one of the extraordinary wits of our time, who would come to be known, loved and feared by all. Well, it happened in less than a minute.

. . . *Baby, It's Cold Inside* has the brilliance we expect. If the insouciance of the early Perelman—"I had gone into a Corn Exchange bank to exchange some corn"; "I have Bright's disease and he has mine"—is not as evident here, nobody could keep up *that* effervescence. (And if he could, he'd run into trouble today, with, at least, the Bright's disease people.) In its place is a mood very much of its times, and all the more telling in its effects.

Folly is perennial, but something has happened to parody. Life has caught up with it. When Mr. Perelman wrote the superbly hilarious pieces of the thirties and forties, our misuse of the language was in its own vintage years, or so it seems in retrospect. The misuse had its natural place in the movie dialogue, the advertising pages and the sentimental fiction of the day.

Now the misuse has proliferated and spread everywhere, and, to make it more menacing, it is taken seriously. Promoters of products, promoters of causes, promoters of self have a common language, though one with a small vocabulary.

. . . The value of the word has declined. Parody is one of the early casualties of this disaster, for it comes to be no longer recognizable apart from its subject. Parody makes its point by its precision and strictness in use of the word, probing to expose the distinction between the true and the false, the real and the synthetic. It's a demanding and exacting art, and there are few with the gift of penetration, and the temerity, let alone the wit and the style, to practice it. Right now it's in danger of becoming a lost cause. The only writer I know who can save it is the author of this book. He stands alone. We already owe him a great deal for years of delight, but we owe him even more now.

Not for nothing is the new book called *Baby, It's Cold Inside*. Back of some of these pieces, and not very far, lies deep sadness, lies outrage. What an achievement Mr. S. J. Perelman makes today, that out of our own sadness and outrage we are brought, in these pieces, to laugh at ourselves once more.

PHILIP FRENCH ET AL.
"Perelman's Revenge; or,
The Gift of Providence, Rhode Island"
Listener, November 15, 1979, pp. 667–69

*T*his is an edited version of the programme, written and produced by Philip French, which was originally broadcast on Radio 3 at the time of S. J. Perelman's 75th birthday. Perelman died last month, and the programme was repeated on Radio 3 last Saturday.

Groucho: Ah, this is the only way to travel, boys . . . the only way. I was gonna bring along the wife and kiddies but the grocer couldn't spare another barrel.
Chico: I was goin' to bring my grandfather, but there's no room for his beard.
Groucho: Why don't you send for the old swine and let his beard come later?
Chico: I sent for his beard.
Groucho: You did?
Chico: Yeah, it's coming by hairmail.
Zeppo: Sssh! Say, fellas, I think I hear someone.
Groucho: Well, if it's the captain, I'm gonna have a few words with him. My hot water's been cold for three days and I haven't got room enough in here to swing a cat. In fact I haven't even got a cat.

Philip French: Those lines, exchanged between stowaways on a luxury ship in mid-Atlantic, are the first words spoken in Hollywood by the Marx Brothers. The film was *Monkey Business* in 1931, and the man who wrote them S. J. Perelman, the 26-year-old author of two books, one of which had gone to press leaving his name off the title-page, while the other had sunk without trace during a publishers' price-war. He wrote only one more Marx Brothers script, and he was to collaborate with Kurt Weill and Ogden Nash on a successful Broadway musical, and produce more than a dozen books. Yet for many, possibly most people, his name has remained permanently associated with the Marx Brothers, particularly with Groucho.

In later life, their carefully clipped moustaches, metal-rimmed glasses, trim figures and slightly professorial appearances, made Groucho and Sid Perelman look rather alike. However, Perelman's sternest critic, Sidney Namlerep, took a rather different view in his introduction to *Crazy Like a Fox* back in the mid-Forties.

Under a forehead roughly comparable to that of the Javanese or Piltdown Man are visible a pair of tiny pig eyes, lit up alternately by greed and concupiscence. His nose, broken in childhood by a self-inflicted blow with a hockey stick, has a prehensile tip, ever quick to smell out an insult; at the least suspicion of an affront, Perelman, who has the pride of a Spanish grandee, has been known to whip out his sword-cane and hide in the closet . . . In motion, the man's body may best be likened to a New Bedford whaler in the teeth of an equinoctial gale; in repose it is strongly reminiscent of a giant sloth.

French: Perelman responded with rare frankness when I asked him what was the impetus behind his writing.
Perelman: Chiefly, it's commercial, to be very frank about it. And secondly it's the desire to get one's own back. George Orwell listed four principal reasons why people write, the fourth of which was 'revenge'. Otherwise, the general reason is an escape from boredom. I wait, just as most people do, I wait

to a point when I'm so fed up with doing nothing that I reluctantly go to the typewriter.
French: He first went to the typewriter in the late 1920s, and the first people he wanted to revenge himself on, outside of relatives, were smug shop-assistants, floor-walkers and the petty functionaries of department stores who got on his back when he was taking vacation jobs as a student in Providence, Rhode Island. They recur throughout his work. What may have begun as revenge has been transmuted into art by a comic vision. Perelman attacked the vulgar, the pretentious, the overbearing, bullies who abuse power, privilege and the English language. And he did it on behalf of us all. He was a man hopelessly trying to make sense of an essentially absurd universe; and it is a world he found increasingly difficult to satirise. For, like other humorous writers, he saw reality itself pass beyond the wildest fantasies of the satirist.

From the time he started writing in the late twenties, Perelman's style has been pervasive. His own acknowledged mentors are George Ade, Robert Benchley, Ring Lardner, Stephen Leacock and James Joyce, whom he called '*the* great comic writer of our time'. Before I ever read Perelman, his form of humour was mediated to me through Marx Brothers' films, and through Muir and Norden's *Take It from Here* radio scripts of the 1940s. Many young people today come across it first in the night-club routines, essays and films of Woody Allen. I asked Woody Allen when he first came across Perelman.

Woody Allen: I discovered him when I was in high school. I came across certain pieces that he had written and I immediately was stunned by them. I thought they were just the best and the funniest things that I had ever read, and not at all heavy-handed, which most humour writers are. There have just been a few that weren't. Benchley was one that wasn't, and Perelman, of course, is just as light as a soufflé. What happens to you when you read Perelman and you're a young writer is fatal because his style seeps into you. He's got such a pronounced, overwhelming comic style that it's very hard not to be influenced by him.
French: Allen's private-eye parodies 'Mr Big' and 'The Whore of Mensa' are indebted to Perelman. His film *Love and Death* reflects the influence of 'A Farewell to Omsk', the parody of the Constance Garnett translations of Dostoevsky, that concludes with the immortal lines:

'Don't take any flannel kopecks,' said Afya gloomily. He dislodged a piece of horseradish from his tie, shied it at a passing nihilist, and slid forward into the fresh loam.

French: A writer of a rather different kind who acknowledges the influence of Perelman is the poet, critic and Professor of English at Yale, John Hollander.
John Hollander: He was part of my very basic literary education, part of my education as someone who is aware of language. I suppose that reading those Perelman pieces in the *New Yorker*, and then later in collections like *Crazy Like a Fox* which I read when I was in high school, made me aware that there was such a thing as linguistic sensibility, that there was such a thing as a sense of style, made me far more aware than anything my parents might have said to me that one doesn't say certain things. Not defined on a class basis but defined with respect to a sense of style, a sense of elegance. His devastating attacks on American vulgarity were, of course, frequently aimed as much from below as from above. One of the things that I began to realise early on reading him was that he would combine in the same sentence, and sometimes in the same phrase, absolute gutter Yiddish and high elegant 18th-century

prose; put these together and they would combine to drive out the middle level of vulgarity. When he would home in on the language and the various conceptual *données* of advertising, for example, it would always be in that way.

French: It was as an avant-garde artist and comic illustrator that Perelman had started out, not as a writer. And giving up art was to be his second major change of direction—he had entered Brown University in 1922 as a pre-medical student before turning to English literature. Al Hirschfeld, now America's most celebrated caricaturist, knew Perelman and his work back in those days, over 40 years ago, when Perelman was primarily a cartoonist.

Al Hirschfeld: He was drawing and writing, but mostly he was interested in graphic drawing and he did things for the old *Judge* magazine, and he used to do these one-line jokes and then they became two lines and then they became six lines and finally the editors said to him: 'Listen, Sid. Why are you bothering with the drawing? Why don't you just extend the caption?' Which is what he did and that's how he started writing.

French: Sid Perelman himself spoke to me about this particular crossroads in his work around 1930.

Perelman: I had progressed through a number of stages in my drawing and I was rapidly approaching a point when I felt I was getting into design. I had been doing collages and things of that sort. I was influenced by what was happening in Europe and I could see myself drifting into something that was getting away from sheer comic art. But I think the thing that really stopped my drawing altogether was the fact that I encountered the Marx Brothers and drifted into working in film; so that I could keep on with my writing for the printed page. But drawing seemed to be a little remote from that, and it just naturally faded away.

French: The experience of Hollywood was profound. From his earliest years, he was steeped in the movies; now he confronted the industry itself and it became for him an obsession, a perennial source of material, the objective correlative of his love-hate relationship with American popular culture, American vulgarity. Yet Perelman was never part of the Hollywood world. Perelman found little satisfaction in screenwriting; indeed, he tends to view it with something approaching contempt.

Perelman: Writing for the movies was, and is, a technique. I believe it's a technique that can be learned by a semi-intelligent person in not more than, at the outside, three weeks. It depends chiefly upon surprise. The object all sublime is to jar the movie audience every so often with an unexpected turn of events, and he who learns this art and works at it can, I believe, become a very successful movie writer. There's not a great deal more to it. Writing for the theatre is much more complex because the boundaries are more severe.

French: After the first year-long sojourn at Paramount, Perelman bought a farm in Bucks County, Pennsylvania, 60-odd miles from New York, the one he describes in *Acres and Pains*, and he severed his connection with the Marx Brothers, though he always wrote of them warmly, which is more than the ageing Groucho was to do of Perelman. Perelman learnt a lot from Groucho, but his own influence on Groucho was strong and permanent. Perelman did, of course, make frequent forays to California, for co-writing assignments with his wife, and to report on his unfavourite city. On his last visit there, he found the scene around Hollywood Boulevard much as it used to be.

> Curiously enough the human tide flowing sluggishly by was unchanged. If many were Hare Krishnas, a

sect of loafers undreamt of in the Thirties, most of the pedestrians were the same old screwballs and screwboxes—losers of beauty contests, Texas gigolos, nature fakers, shoe salesmen and similar voyeurs, absconding bank cashiers, unemployed flagellants, religious messiahs, and jail bait. Did there exist anywhere, I wondered, a Hogarth or a Hieronymus Bosch who could do justice to these satanic troglodyte faces preoccupied with unimaginable larcenies and *Schweinerei?*

French: The sources of Perelman's humorous style are various, and one potent element is his Jewish background. He wasn't, however, reared in the densely textured Jewish immigrant world of New York, though he was born there, in 1904. His parents, who had come from Eastern Europe, moved when he was a small child to the solid New England city of Providence, Rhode Island, where he attended Classical High School, and the local Ivy League University, Brown. His upbringing then was markedly different from, say, the Marx Brothers', or indeed from Malamud's or Bellow's, for that matter. He wasn't a child of the ghetto. Israel Shenker, who interviews authors and keeps a watchful eye on the state of the English language for the *New York Times*, had this to say about the sources of Perelman's comic style.

Israel Shenker: I think it goes back to biblical culture because a great deal of his wit is the wit that you can find emitted in the Bible, and I think that a great deal of his writing stems from the exaggerations and the technique of Mark Twain completely mingled with what he described as sludge—that is the kind of precipitate from the elements that were poured in when he was a child—the slang that he heard in the streets, the nonsense that he was hearing from his teachers, the boasts that he accumulated from his companions at school, and the Yiddish that he never got quite right, but never entirely wrong. He has enough of a Jewish accent to be understandable to me and to be totally incomprehensible to one or two others. But in New York and in America generally, I think he is fairly well understood. I think his most perfect use of Yiddish was in a piece he did about a visit to Scotland when he used the Yiddish expressions as though they were Scottish. For example, Auchund-vay became one of the place-names that he used in this story about Scotland.

French: Sidney Namlerep, however, wrote less flatteringly of Perelman's style.

> In his pages proliferate all the weird grammatical flora tabulated by H. W. Fowler in his *Modern English Usage*—the Elegant Variation, the Facetious Zeugma, the Cast-Iron Idiom, the Battered Ornament, the Bower's-Bird Phrase, the Sturdy Indefensible, the Side-Slip and the Unequal Yokefellow. His work is a museum of mediocrity, a monument to the truly banal. What Flaubert did to the French bourgeois in *Bouvard et Pécuchet*, what Pizarro did to the Incas, what Jack Dempsey did to Paolino Uzcudun, S. J. Perelman has done to American belles-lettres.

French: There are plenty of Perelman phrases that can amuse out of context, and he is one of the great punsters of our time. But the quotable Dorothy Parker one-liners don't pepper his conversation. One remembers things more for their style. I recall for instance some years ago arriving at a party, just as Perelman alighted from a taxi. He needed half-a-crown to tip the driver, and he borrowed it from me. With a raised finger like the hero in a Victorian melodrama, he said: 'Philip, in the immortal words of Edmond Dantès, I shall repay.' He never did give me the half-crown back, but he let me keep the joke. I once asked him who was the most detestable Hollywood producer he'd worked for. He paused, and then said: 'You would need a pair of jeweller's scales to make such a fine calculation.'

It was as a contributor to the *New Yorker* that Perelman developed his comic style, and he was associated with the paper from 1931. The current editor William Shawn saw him as the last of the great full-time comic writers, a humorist who found his chosen form early and stuck to it, and he views him as an innovative literary stylist comparable with Eliot, Pound and Céline.

The typical Perelman piece takes off from a crazy item in a newspaper or one of the trade journals he regularly peruses, or a personal experience, and becomes a play, an investigation, a wild disquisition. On the shape of a characteristic article, Caskie Stinnett, former editor of *Holiday* magazine.

Caskie Stinnett: There is a certain uniformity in the Perelman pieces—in the craftsmanship, in the construction. They invariably start off with a highly challenging introduction, a ludicrous statement or something that is made in the very first sentence, that so intrigues the reader that you have to follow through to find out just how this nonsense could possibly end up. It's my conviction that Perelman must labour very hard on his introductions because they must be difficult to do, but they're superb and in many cases flawless. I really don't believe that an editor could improve in any way on a Perelman introduction.

French: How about the opening of 'Impresario on the Lam'?

The voice that came over the wire last Thursday was full of gravel and Hollywood subjunctives.

Or the start of his 'Eat, Drink and Be Wary'?

Had anyone pressed his nose against the windows of our brownstone late yesterday afternoon—a feat requiring no more than a 19-foot ladder and the agility of a Blondin—he might have beheld a scene that, while it lacked a haywain and browsing cattle, rivalled in tranquillity anything Constable ever painted.

These pieces are carefully wrought, highly polished, and have a poise and a precision—in, for instance, the use of names and movie references.

A particularly influential aspect of Perelman's writing is the way unusual words, expressions and names are mixed with the slang. 'Button Button, Who's Got the Button,' opens:

About eight o'clock last night, I was lounging at the corner of Hollywood Boulevard and Vine Street, an intersection celebrated in the eclogues of Louella Parsons and Ed Sullivan, waiting for a pert baggage to accompany me to a double feature.

French: The word hovering around my mind at this point, one often used of Perelman, is 'surrealism'. But John Hollander took me to task for what he considered a somewhat unrevealing use of the term.

Hollander: A very easy move of a certain kind of middle-brow criticism for the past 40 years has been to call anything you don't understand surrealist, and I dare say there are people who would call him surreal. I don't think so in the least. I think that his metamorphic vision, that is his ability to take some idiotic phrase, some idiotic situation and suddenly let it happen in the full garishness of its ramification, does all come in one sense from the 'Circe' episode of *Ulysses*. I think that this is a very important text for him, and that one of the things that he did was to make that element of instant externalisation, instant metamorphosis, available to a great deal of post-World War

Two American fiction. I would think that he and Henry Miller were both tremendously important influences on all kinds of novelists, not only karmic ones but, of course, on comic ones as well.

French: There is no lack of recognition now for Perelman's writing. Last year, he was given a special National Book Award, not for any particular book, but for his contribution to American letters. And the *New York Times* humorous columnist Russell Baker, in a celebrated essay called 'Why Being Serious is Hard', wrote this about the difference between 'Serious' and 'Solemn':

Shakespeare is serious, David Susskind is solemn. Chicago is serious, California is solemn. *Playboy* is solemn, *The New Yorker* is serious. S. J. Perelman is serious, Norman Mailer is solemn. The Roman Empire was solemn. Periclean Athens was serious.

I make no apologies for being solemn rather than serious. Nor should anyone else. It is the national attitude. It is perfectly understandable. It is hard to be Periclean Athens. It is hard to be Shakespeare. It is hard to be S. J. Perelman. It is hard to be serious.

PAUL THEROUX
From "Introduction"
The Last Laugh
1981, pp. 9–15

Humorists are often unhappy men and satirists downright miserable, but S. J. Perelman was a cheery soul who, when he flew into one of his exalted rages, seemed to have the gift of tongues. He gave his mockery a bewitching style. In his stories, or feuilletons as he liked to call them, he represented himself as a victimized clown. He was "button-cute, wafer-thin" and reared turkeys ("which he occasionally exhibits on Broadway"); or Dr. Perelman, "small bore in Africa"; or a mixture of Sad Sack and Pierre Loti, haplessly sampling the pleasures of out-of-the-way places; or finally as a sort of boulevardier and roué who, at the moment of sexual conquest, is defeated by a wayward bedspring.

When I first began reading him in the 1950s—I was in junior high school—I was excited by his malicious humor, his huge vocabulary and what I took to be his lunatic fantasy. I sensed a spirit of rebellion in him that stirred the anarchy in my schoolboy soul. After I started to travel, it struck me that much of what he wrote was true: Perelman's Africa was the Africa no one else had noticed. His stories were bizarre because he sought out the bizarre. He cherished oddity and, being truly adventurous, was willing to put himself to a lot of trouble to find it (he strolled around Shanghai in 1947 looking for it). Then I met him. He *was* button-cute, and also a bit of a roué, and accident-prone. If he had been writing fantasies, we would think of him as a humorist, a writer of gags, whose object was merely to entertain. But he wrote about the world, and his intensity and his anger made him into a satirist.

A satirist seems a sour and forbidding figure—a mocker, a pessimist, a grudge-bearer, a smirker, something of a curmudgeon, perhaps with a streak of cruelty, who, in inviting the reader to jeer at his victim, never misses a trick or withholds a nudge. How does one suggest that such a man may also have a great deal of charm? Perelman's friends liked him very much. He was generous, he was funny, he was enormously social, he didn't boast. Travel has the effect of turning most people into monologuists; it made Perelman an accomplished watcher and an appreciative listener. When he talked in his croaky drawl he did so in the elaborate way he wrote, with unlikely locutions and slang and precise descriptions diverted into strings of subordinate clauses. He was small and neatly made; he wore very handsome clothes, usually of an English cut; and in his pockets he carried clippings he tore from the newspapers—one he showed me was about the movie *The Texas Chainsaw Massacre*, which he eventually worked into a story. He read the London *Times* every day (he had an airmail subscription), more, I think, for the unusual names than for anything else. In today's *Times*, Sir Ranulph Twisleton-Wykeham-Fiennes has just reached the South Pole; Captain Sir Weldon Dalrymple-Champneys has just died; and both Miss C. Inch and Miss E. L. F. I. Lunkenheimer have just got married. Perelman welcomed news of this kind.

In his way, he was a man of the world. A man of the world, almost by definition, is never content anywhere. Perelman was a bit like that. He had a great capacity for pleasure, but he was restless, always active, game for anything; he fed himself on change. He began writing at Brown University, where a fellow classmate was Nathanael West (Perelman married West's sister Laura in 1929), and at the age of 25, with the success of his first book, *Dawn Ginsbergh's Revenge*, he was invited to Hollywood to write jokes for the Marx Brothers. He went, and he liked to say that Hollywood reminded him of a novel he had read in Providence as a boy, *In the Sargasso Sea*, by Thomas Janvier (anyone who has the luck to find this 1899 story of marooning and murder in the nightmare swamp will immediately see the connection). From time to time throughout his life, Perelman returned to Hollywood, struggled with scripts and then fought free. At the age of 74, fresh from the travels he recounted in *Eastward Ha!*, he tried to drive his vintage 1949 MG from Paris to Peking, commemorating the trip of Count Something-or-other. It was not such a crazy scheme. He had been around the world a dozen times. He was in good health, his car had recently had a tune-up, he had a generous sponsor and many well-wishers, and he liked to say (though joshing himself with his chain-smoker's chuckle) that he knew Malaysia and Hong Kong like the back of his hand.

In a Thai restaurant, in London, on Christmas Eve, he told me about his drive to Peking. He had just flown in from China. The trip, he said, was a total disaster. The glamour girl he had chosen for navigator had been fired at the outset for selling her story to a magazine. He had quarreled with his fellow drivers all the way through India. There had been kerfuffles with customs men in Turkey. The car was not allowed through Burma and, as there was no room on a ship to Malaysia, the car had been air-freighted to Hong Kong. There were more scenes in Hong Kong. "The others freaked out," Perelman said, but with the old car now parked in Kowloon, he flew to Peking and spent two weeks in a Chinese hospital with a severe case of bronchitis, aggravated by double pneumonia.

"Now I have to write about it," he said. "It'll be horrible."

Frankly, I thought the subject was made for him. Nothing is more Perelmanesque than a marathon drive across the world interlarded with setbacks, blown gaskets, howling Turks and long delays in flea-ridden Indian hotels. And pneumonia in Peking was the perfect ending for someone who always racked his brain for grand finales. (His editor at *The New Yorker*, William Shawn, told me recently, "He always had trouble with endings.") But this last collection of Perelman pieces contains nothing about that Paris to Peking trip. This is odd, because he had made his reputation by describing the complicated orchestration of fiascos.

A month before he died, he wrote me a letter in which he said, "I myself have spent altogether too much time this year breaking my nails on the account of the Paris-Peking trip I made . . . and after a lot of bleeding cuticle, I decided to abandon it. I guess there are certain subjects—or maybe one's subjective reactions to them—that in spite of the most manful attempts are totally unproductive. The one I picked certainly was, and it took a lot of Sturm und Drang to make me realize that my Sisyphean labors were getting me nowhere."

This was the only gloomy paragraph in an otherwise chirpy letter. His letters were long, frequent, and sensationally funny—indeed, so funny that, after receiving a few, Raymond Chandler (always a hoarder and procrastinator where writing was concerned) replied worriedly, warning Perelman against squandering his wit: "You shouldn't give the stuff away like that when you can sell it, unless of course your letters are just rough notes for articles."

But they weren't "just rough notes for articles." They were generous and intelligent expressions of friendship and most of them far too scandalous to be retailed. Here is the opening paragraph of a letter Perelman wrote me on Christmas Eve, 1976:

> Between the constant repetition of "White Christmas" and "Jingle Bells" on station WPAT and the increasing frenzy of the Saks and Gimbels newspaper ads as these fucking holidays draw near, I have been in a zombie-like state for weeks, totally incapable of rational thought or action. I must have arrived at near-paralysis yesterday afternoon when I was in the 4th-floor lingerie section ("Intimate Apparel") in Saks 5th Avenue. I had just purchased two such intimate garments for gifties to a couple of ladies of my acquaintance, a tall blonde and a somewhat shorter brunette. For the former, I had chosen a black lace chemise in the style known as a teddy back in the twenties (familiar to you as the scanty garment worn by Rita Hayworth in the wartime pinup). For the shorter brunette, a similar peach-colored job. Both of these real silk, parenthetically, and as I signed the charge slip, I knew that when the bill came in after January 1st, I would kick myself for my prodigality. Anyway, while the hard-featured saleslady was wrapping them up with appropriate mash notes to each bimbo, I went upstairs to the men's dept. to buy myself a cheap tie-tack. When I returned for the feminine frillies, I found (a) that the saleslady had forgotten to identify which box was which, and (b) that she had switched the notes. In other words, the blonde Amazon would find herself with the brunette's undershirt and some steamy sentiment addressed to the latter, and vice versa. I broke out into a perspiration—it's tropically hot in those department stores anyway—and insisted on the saleslady clawing open the boxes, which meant destroying all the fake holly berries, silver cord, and mishmash they were entwined in. This of course put her in a foul temper, and meanwhile a waiting queue of customers became incensed. The upshot was a group shot of seven or eight people leering and cackling obscenely as I stood there holding the two chemises and the notes appropriate to the recipients. Given the savoire faire of Cary Grant I might have risen above it, but the only savoir faire I possess is Oliver Hardy's, and little enough of that. . . .

When Perelman's letters are collected, as they surely deserve to be, they will comprise the autobiography he promised and began, but never get around to finishing. The three chapters printed here are all we have of *The Hindsight Saga*. Anyway, with a title that good you hardly need a book; or did its promise of disclosures intimidate him? He was always more personal and ruminative and risqué in his letters than he was in his stories, and he heartily disliked people who boasted by reminiscing about the past. "I see Scott Fitzgerald's gossip-columnist mistress has been cleaning out the contents of a thimble," he wrote me when Sheilah Graham's *The Real Scott Fitzgerald* appeared.

Perelman knew Fitzgerald as a sober, hard-working script-writer, who had gone to Hollywood for the money, much as today's writers accept tenure at universities. Fitzgerald believed himself a failure, but Perelman was one man (Faulkner was another) who used Hollywood to fuel his other projects; his script-writing career coincided with his first appearance in the pages of *The New Yorker*. It seems extraordinary that he was able to keep his enthusiasms separate, but to California and New York he added the world. From the thirties onward he traveled widely, first in the Pacific and then in Africa, Europe and Asia. I cannot think of another writer who was so adept as Perelman in prevailing over such vast cultural incongruities and whose appreciations included B-movies, pulp magazines, Joyce's *Ulysses*, Hollywood dives, the societal norms in Bucks County, Manhattan and Nairobi, detective fiction, English country-house weekends, vintage cars, dogs (he once, on a whim, bought a bloodhound), cantankerous producers and pretty women. He talked with passionate energy about Fellini's *Satyricon* and Alfred Russel Wallace's *The Malay Archipelago*. He knew Dorothy Parker well and had a close friendship with Eric Ambler. He was the only person I have ever known who dropped in on J. D. Salinger, whom he called "Jerry."

His greatest passion was language. In "Listen to the Mockingbird" he wrote, "As recently as 1918, it was possible for a housewife in Providence, where I grew up, to march into a store with a five-cent piece, purchase a firkin of cocoa butter,

a good second-hand copy of Bowditch, a hundredweight of quahogs, a shagreen spectacle case and sufficient nainsook for a corset cover and emerge with enough left over to buy a balcony admission to *The Masquerader* with Guy Bates Post, and a box of maxixe cherries." He was parodying inflation, but it is impossible to read "cocoa butter," "Bowditch," "quahogs," "shagreen," "nainsook," and the rest without a sense of mounting hilarity. He worked hard for a kind of insane exactitude in his prose and would not settle for "sad" if he could use "chopfallen." I think his travels were bound up with his quest to find odd words or possible puns. They were more than mere souvenirs of travel: they were the object of his arduous jaunts. The uniqueness of his writing depends for its effects on linguistic virtuosity, finding room for "oppidan" or the verb "swan" or the weirder lingo he abstracted in India and Africa. E. B. White once wrote about how Perelman, after crashing his car in Florida, savored the phrase "We totaled it!" and how his pleasure in being able to use it took the sting out of the accident.

His interests and his travels swelled his vocabulary and gave him his style. But none of this would have been accessible without his memory, which was faultless. That too is a distinguishing feature in his fiction. A good memory is one of the most valuable assets a writer has, and Perelman's memory amounted to genius. One day, years ago, he was passing through Shropshire, and a glimpse of that green countryside stayed with him. He plotted to return to Shropshire and rent a house and live there like a squire; but though he visited England often, he always became restive. Apart from the precincts of *Punch*, where he was feted, he found England tight and dry and a little dull. And the house rents in Shropshire were too high. He was too much of an Anglophile to like England greatly.

He died on October 17, 1979, in New York City, where he was born. ⟨. . .⟩ His writing did not flag in fifty years, and this, his twentieth book, is as funny as anything he ever wrote.

JULIA PETERKIN

1880–1961

Julia Mood Peterkin was born October 31, 1880, in Laurens County, South Carolina. After graduating from Converse College in Spartenburg at the age of sixteen, Peterkin went to Fort Motte as a schoolteacher. In 1903 she was married to William George Peterkin and became the new mistress of Lang Syne, a thriving, decades-old cotton plantation whose hundreds of black workers lived in the "Quarter" much as they had before the Civil War.

After years of running the plantation and raising a family, Peterkin undertook a serious study of music. It was her piano instructor who encouraged her to write and then introduced her to Carl Sandburg in 1921. On Sandburg's recommendation Peterkin sent some of her writing to H. L. Mencken. While he did not accept her work for his magazine, *Smart Set*, he did refer her efforts to Emily Clark, publisher of the *Reviewer*.

Peterkin's first piece, "From Lang Syne Plantation," appeared in the December 1921 issue of Clark's magazine. A collection of short stories was published in 1924 under the title *Green Thursday*. Peterkin went on to write three novels, *Black April* (1927), *Scarlet Sister Mary* (1928), and *Bright Skin* (1932), as well as a book of essays, *Roll, Jordan, Roll* (1933). *Scarlet Sister Mary* won the Pulitzer Prize in 1929.

After her last novel Peterkin went back to writing short stories and was for many years an unofficial writer-in-residence for the state of South Carolina. She participated in the Bread Loaf Inn Writers Conference and taught at Bennington College in Vermont in 1936.

Peterkin died in August 1961 in Orangeburg, South Carolina.

I soon discovered that the ability to see is an acquirement. It takes skill to mark differences between things that look just alike, and to make out distinctions between forms that are very close kin. To learn how to do it requires time and patience, and not only a keen wish to know about things themselves but also to know how all things are bound together into one common whole.

Our individual worlds are made up of the things we perceive, and no two of us ever see things alike. The impressions given us by our senses may be accurate or false; they may be a record of absolute truth, or a jumbled confusion of mistakes; yet, whatever they are, the sum of them constitutes for us the only information we can ever have concerning the particular world we live in. No two of us live in the same world. We must each make our own environment and mold our individual universe, and the only material we have to use for this purpose is what our senses have gathered for us. There is no way out of it. All well-being depends on seeing things. The more things we see clearly, the more interesting is the exclusive world that we must make for ourselves.

It has taken time for me to become aware of the great tide of life that flows around me, for its stealth and silence are deceiving to the untrained. But I find that its current is filled with things that not only excite pity and terror, but that also stir devout admiration and wonder.

The plantation is somewhat removed from the beaten track of civilization, and changes take place here slowly, quietly, almost too quietly to be noticed when they come. Few things appear to happen except what the seasons bring or what the sky sends of cloud and sunshine and wind and rain. But here, the same as in the world outside, change is the only permanent thing.

Forms of life here are ceaselessly varied and shifted and interchanged. Nothing abides. Not even beauty is spared. Not a flower or fruit or sunset cloud can escape the ever-moving circle. Men, beasts, crops, trees, rise up, grow strong, then weaken, give way, and pass on into the multitude of things that have been, to be melted, changed, merged into something else, something young and new and strong.

To the Negroes, this bit of earth has a definite entity. It is the center of the whole universe, with Heaven, the home of the Great-I-Am, in the sky, straight overhead. There on His throne, which is higher and brighter than the sun, He not only directs the clouds and stars and sun and moon as they patiently mark out the patterns He sets for them but He also listens to the plantation prayers and watches the plantation happenings.

For His children, the rain falls and the sun shines. His voice speaks to them when the thunder rolls and the wind howls and sings. Every inanimate thing is endowed with intelligence and intention. Some are kind and helpful, others malicious and envious. Things have sense, like people, and are sometimes good, sometimes evil; but all things forever keep warning men to prepare to meet the Hereafter. When the sun heat burns them and the rain drops wet them and the strong winds whip then, they are all saying, "Pray! Do try to escape Hell if you can."

Hell, the terror of all the plantation people, lies dark and deep and terrible straight down underneath the plantation woods and fields, its hot fires swarming with the poor, pitiful souls of the dead who have passed into eternity without making peace with the Great Creator.

The present must be endured patiently, no matter what hardships come; troubles are to be borne without resentment, because true life does not begin until after Death. Then the blessed join the angels in Heaven and are happy forevermore.

Feet that walk along the plantation paths and roads, with soles toughened and cracked with dust and mud, will wear silver slippers and walk on golden streets. Weary bodies accustomed to patched, faded garments, will don shining white robes and wings. Tattered old hats will be replaced with golden crowns. Hands grown callous from jerking hoes in the fight with grass or with holding plows straight to the row will pluck out tunes on harps of gold.

But every spring, as a tide of green rises and spreads through the forest and fields, and life multiplies the birds and beasts and insects and people, it is easy to see how the trees in the graveyard raise rich bold heads above their fellows, as if they boasted that proud plantation masters and mistresses lie still, under their feet. On all sides, with no effort at concealment, youth and strength can be seen rising out of decay.

The game in the woods is carefully hued to match the autumn leaves, and wild bodies are fashioned to be nimble and swift to keep out of harm's way, yet these are ruthlessly crammed into hunters' bags, limp, blood-stained, the warmth of fur and feather chilled, in order that black pots on open hearths may steam with savory stew which may add pigment to dusky skins or light to eyes already bright.

Riddles are here to be answered, paradoxes, to confuse and perplex. Clues to answers appear, then are shrouded in mystery. Thoughts that flit through human foreheads seem to matter no more than the tunes hummed by the wind through the trees. The lagging steps of a tired man or mule seems to be of no more importance than the traipsing up and down of the beetles that creep under the bark of mighty pines and kill them. I reach conclusions, then discard them for new ones, as I learn a little more about seeing things.—JULIA PETERKIN, "Seeing Things," *Collected Short Stories*, ed. Frank Durham, 1970, pp. 67–69.

In April 1928 I went to Lang Syne for the first time, but only for a day. I was staying with Josephine Pinckney in Charleston, and at that time I knew only Charleston and its most immediate surroundings. I had never seen the "up-country." On the Sunday before I left, a day so cold and rainy that all the glory of Magnolia Gardens and Middleton Place and Summerville, an iridescent glory of azaleas, wisteria, and roses, at its dazzling climax only a few days before, must have been effectively laid waste, Josephine and I decided to motor the hundred miles from Charleston to Lang Syne Plantation at Fort Motte, only forty miles from Columbia, under the care of a very gentle, perfect Southern gentleman whose rôle at the moment was not to reason why and to hold firmly to the wheel through menacingly slippery roads. We arrived at Lang Syne chilled through our very bones, to be presently warmed and cheered by Julia's glowing voice and hair and fire and corn whisky. With Julia and her husband were Carl Sandburg, whom Josephine knew well and whom I had met in Richmond as a friend of *The Reviewer*, and a young man whose name I have now forgotton and whose passion for the folk-songs and folk-lore of America is unexcelled in my experience. So passionate was this young man in his love and his single-minded pursuit of it that when Josephine and I expressed anxiety for him that dark night on our way back to Charleston over a sliding, tricky road—for he had told us that he was motoring in quite unfamiliar country—our Charleston escort murmured: "He won't mind, wherever he's overturned, because he can always sing himself to sleep with folk-songs." And we dismissed the matter from our minds. The rain continued throughout the day, so that we visited none of the cabins, invisible in the background of the wide white frame house, except Julia's own private cabin, used by her as a study. She was finishing *Scarlet Sister Mary*, which, as all the reading world now knows, was published in the autumn of 1928 and won, the next spring, a Pulitzer prize. It is, unlike many Pulitzer prizewinners, its author's best work, a character study so tremendous in its strength, so true in its appeal, that Ethel Barrymore has disconcerted both her own following and the following of the new Negro theatre by selecting it as her current play. The local library at Gaffney, South Carolina, by the way, has barred *Scarlet Sister Mary* from its shelves. In spite of this amusing exclusion South Carolina now recognizes Julia Peterkin as the indisputable celebrity which she has become. Indeed, a prophecy concerning her made by Henry Mencken in a letter to me in October 1924 is now in process of fulfillment: "Mrs. Peterkin's book appears to have shocked the South Carolina Junker," he wrote. "She tells me that they are powerfully silent about it. I am advising her to be patient. Some day they will take visiting delegations of Elks and Rotarians to see her."

In my recent reading of the correspondence between Julia Peterkin and me, of less than a decade ago, the swiftness and the extraordinary dramatic values of her career are sharply impressed upon me. An urge to write more dynamic, more compulsive, than the urge which drives many writers must have impelled Julia towards the career now so triumphantly her own. During her girlhood in a small town and her married life on the plantation, there was no direct incentive, no influent contact responsible for this desire. It was absolute, inherent in herself. In her constant visits to the cabins she heard, comprehended, and remembered many stories of primitive passion and horror and pity. When Carl Sandburg went to Charleston to lecture there to the new Poetry Society of South Carolina in 1921, Henry Bellamann took him to Lang Syne to see Julia, who told him some of the stories she had learned. He immediately begged her to write them down. She did, and the first results, too appalling in their nature for any established magazine, even the old Mencken and Nathan *Smart Set*, found their way into *The Reviewer*. For we, realizing that a little magazine, like a little theatre, must be experimental in order to justify its existence, were a laboratory, where chemical explosions, occasionally astonishing even to ourselves, occurred almost monthly. After the publication of her first book Julia left the plantation for several interludes at the MacDowell Colony and in France.

Julia Peterkin's story is one of the brilliant chapters of our magazine's history. It is also one of the brilliant chapers of Southern literary history, for in spite of the strict limits of her own special field her name has become almost universal. She has given to a modern public the half-barbaric plantation Negro in a form quite new; a creature far removed from low comedy or from conventional romance; a courageous, inarticulate, heart-tearing creature to whom propaganda or race conflict is yet unknown; a creature in conflict, as she herself has said, single-handedly and rather majestically with Fate itself, more inescapable, uncompromising, and pitiless than any superior race or individual.—EMILY CLARK, "Julia Peterkin," *Innocence Abroad*, 1931, pp. 228–31

There are several reasons for the success of Mrs. Peterkin's new novel *Scarlet Sister Mary*. The reason that is perhaps first apparent may be called a sociological one, though it may be only a matter of good manners. It is that, writing exclusively of negroes, Mrs. Peterkin thinks of them with an engaging directness and does not allow any adumbrations of kindly condescension, of sentimentality, of the hysterical resentment of injustices to cloud her clear perception of a simple object. Books about negroes have been praised, one remembers,

because the writer so much "enjoyed" the subject and used such gusto in treating of it. The implication was that the subject was much such a one as wine or food or old books, something quaint and extraneous to the importances of life and to be treated with an assumedly naive delight. This tempting mistake Mrs. Peterkin does not make, and she gets, consequently, a lovely, simple dignity.

Partly to avoid, one suspects, the possibility of allowing her characters to assume the childish imitativeness to which we have referred and which has become incorporated in the popular notion of the negro, Mrs. Peterkin chooses for her scene a completely isolated settlement.

The greatest critical danger that this book can suffer is over-admiration of its heroine, Sister Mary. We have had so much literary adoration of the mother—woman, the brave, clear-sighted, wise woman, so constantly procreating that she is no longer a woman, but a comic principle, and the thing has been so done out of its reality that, to give such a figure as Mary what she best deserves, we must temper our admiration with indifference. Mary is a strong, handsome Gullah negro girl of a race very proud of itself. Passionate and daring, she is not therefore the less well-bred and gently mannered, for this seemingly simple community has a strict and complicated formality for life and her moral sense is constantly with her, as it is with almost all the villagers; the prevailing sentiment is not for the rollicking and roaring happy-go-lucky, but for the sedate church member. She loves and marries July, the most attractive young man in the community, a singer and dancer, a fickle and successful lover. Six months after marriage, Mary, walking alone down the road, is delivered of a child.

For a while the family is comfortable and happy, but soon July takes up with the sinful Cinders and eventually disappears with her. Mary is smashed by the blow, but in time rallies and has a child, Seraphina, by July's twin brother, the attractive but staid June.

The charm which Daddy Cudjoe, the conjurer, had given her for July, upon whom she did not use it, she now uses often. Man after man succumbs to it and each leaves her with a child which she bears indifferently. Many years after his departure, July, of whom she had said that if he were to come home stiff and cold in a box she would look upon him as a stranger "an' not a water wouldn' dream out of her eye," returns with wealth. Riven by desire for him, she nevertheless sends him away.

But it is not in the story that the crisp, limited beauty of the book lies. It is rather in the atmosphere of strength and dignity which is around Maum Hannah, the crippled, cursing Budda Ben, the righteous Deacon Andrew. Mary herself, as one remembers her, is likely to become an abstract principle, and July is almost completely the type of the romantic, faithless one on whom the heroine of every story by a woman bruises herself. The gentle simplicity of these minor characters, the mass of the townsfolk with their generous decency and the author's delicate perception of their country and their way of life give complete validity to a story which is in itself not entirely weak.—LIONEL TRILLING, *NYEP*, Nov. 3, 1928, p. 8

FRANK DURHAM
From "Introduction: The Stories"
Collected Short Stories
1970, pp. 8–17

The formal stories, which comprise the major portion of her short fiction, may be loosely divided into three groups on the basis of their content and tone. Naturally, no one of these divisions is air-tight, for there is considerable overlapping. The greatest number deal with the daily life and domestic experiences of the plantation Negro, including work, family relationships, love, birth, death, aspirations, disappointments, religion, folklore, and superstitions. The first of these, which I have entitled "Mose," was included in "From Lang Syne Plantation," her initial work in *The Reviewer*, October, 1921. It sets both the tone and the point of view she was to use throughout her career. The tone is one of understatement, a detachment and austerity implying respect and compassion for her characters and their problems and, through its economy, intensifying the dramatic effect of the narrative. She rarely dramatizes overtly, letting the facts stand without authorial comment.

Her point of view is almost always that of her Negro characters. It is this immersion of her own personality in that of the Negro which lends her work its unique authority and which gave rise to the local complaint that she did not write like a Southern lady. One "Southern conservative" declared in horror that she "'would be writing romances about mules.'" Julia retorted, "'I should love to . . . but I don't think I know enough about mules.'"[1] A Negro woman at Lang Syne said, "'Miss got a white skin fo-true, but I believe his heart is black as my-own,'"[2] Almost always she writes from *inside* her Negro characters, avoiding the paternalistic amusement and tolerant affection typical of the work of most Southerners, notably Thomas Nelson Page. Only occasionally, as in "The Right Thing" and "Green Walnuts," does she introduce white characters, and when she does, there is a suggestion of the old master-slave paternalistic stereotypes. But, for the most part, her world is a totally black one, presenting the Negro in isolation from the white and in strictly Negro terms. It is this view of the world through the Negro's eyes and mind which differentiates her work from that of her predecessors and most of her contemporaries and gives it its lasting stature.

As a result of this point of view, her style is often bare, sometimes staccato. Some critics denigrated her style for these reasons, though most were aware of her intentions and praised her realization of them as one of the marks of her artistry.

At first, she keeps scenic description to a minimum, selecting a few vivid, concrete details: the cook comes to the door, her hands white with flour. Gradually the setting grows more important and serves not only as setting but as a means of suggesting the flow of time, the endless cycle of the seasons, and symbolizing or reflecting the emotions of the characters. In "Over the River," for example, the sinister vegetation and swampy undergrowth mirror the fears and uncertainties of the deaf-mute girl seeking the father of her unborn child, and then the vine struggling upward over insuperable obstacles parallels the girl's growing determination to go onward to her goal. Every object, every creature in the natural environment is alive, has a personality. The cabin fire is a prominent feature in several stories, symbolizing both beneficence and malicious destructiveness. In others animals and fowls are intensely personalized. In "The Red Rooster" Julia even projects herself into the rooster's consciousness, seeing and feeling from the point of view of the bird. Killdee's mule Mike and his dog Son are empathetic characters and at the same time present allegorically the human struggle against fate and the elements. This attitude, approaching a kind of primitive animism, is derived from her close study of the minds and the beliefs of the Negroes on Lang Syne, to whom all nature, all objects, were alive.

Among the short stories, all those in *Green Thursday*, with the exception of "Ashes" and "The Red Rooster," belong in the group of narratives of daily life and domestic experiences. Of the separately published stories, "A Sketch," "Maum Lou," "Manners," "'Whose Children?'," "A Proudful Fellow," "The Greasy Spoon," "Santy Claw," and "The Diamond Ring" fall into the same category. Reading the *Green Thursday* stories in this group, one finds almost the unity of a novel, for they trace the lives of Killdee, his wife Rose, their children, and young Missie, the waif they take in to be raised by them. In these we see Killdee's love of his work, his skepticism about religion, his affection for Rose and his children, his sorrow at death and disappointment, his growing love for Missie, and his guilt at this love. The daily lives of this family and their neighbors on the plantation, their religion and their superstitions, their problems and their hopes, are played out against the lush background of nature and the eternal round of the seasons. Similar to these *Green Thursday* stories and sometimes dealing with the same family group are the domestic stories published separately. They, too, treat of the world of Blue Brook Plantation and its people, with the exception of "The Greasy Spoon," the only one of Julia's pieces to be set in a town. In "A Sketch" there is the hunger of a baby while its mother works in the fields; in "Maum Lou," the pathos of old age; in "Manners," a child's learning of death; in "'Whose Children?'," a girl's realization that all human beings, sinners and saints, are God's children; in "A Proudful Fellow," a tragic love-triangle culminating in murder and the husband's fatalistic acceptance of his own death; in "The Diamond Ring," the bittersweet comedy of a young boy tempted beyond his strength. In all these, the range of emotions is wide, going through comedy, drama, pathos, and tragedy. Taken together, these domestic tales present a detailed and complex tapestry of the life of the plantation Negro, done with beauty and sensitivity and dignity.

⟨. . . "The Greasy Spoon" and "Santy Claw"⟩ were published in *The Ladies' Home Journal* in 1929 and, in my opinion, are not among the author's best. Set in a Negro cafe in town, "The Greasy Spoon" deals a little sentimentally with young Seraphina's dancing and singing at Big Sue's place and being courted by Joe and by Big Jim, her accompanist. She refuses Joe's offer of a diamond ring and is reunited with her legal husband, who promises not to be "mean" to her again. The plot is tenuous, and the atmosphere seems less authentic than that of the plantation stories.

"Santy Claw" is overburdened with atmospheric details of the plans for the white folks' Christmas dinner at the Big House, anticipating the more factual *A Plantation Christmas*. The plot is both contrived and sentimental. The grandson of old Daddy Champagne and Dicey brings home a town girl who disapproves of oyster stew, stone crabs, shrimp, and collard greens, and the old couple fear that the boy will marry this "foreigner." Returning from meeting, they are greeted in their cabin by a costumed "Santy Claw." When they ask him to give them for Christmas a granddaughter-in-law of whom they approve, "Santy Claw" agrees and unmasks, revealing himself to be the boy who now sees things properly and will marry his local girl. Of all of Julia's stories, this is perhaps the least successful.

The second group of domestic stories is the smallest. These deal more or less directly with the relationship between the plantation Negroes and white people, and, as I have said, in them Julia sometimes reverts to the Thomas Nelson Page type of paternalism. Undoubtedly she is reflecting faithfully and factually the attitude of the white toward the Negro and that of the Negro toward the white on Lang Syne and on most other Southern plantations and farms in the 1920's and 1930's.

From my own knowledge of my uncle's farm near Orangeburg in this period I can vouch for the authenticity of Julia's pictures. Right or wrong, paternalism and at least the outward semblance of loyalty and respect and affection were the order of the day. And Julia wrote of them as they were. But this was a subject not new to fiction. It had been done to death by the purveyors of the plantation tradition, and hence her stories in this vein lack the originality and strength of her strictly Negro pieces.

In this group I place "The Merry-Go-Round," "The Right Thing," "Green Walnuts," and, from *Green Thursday,* "Ashes." Her one play, a short one called *Boy-Chillen,* also reflects this somewhat outworn, though truthful, facet of Negro-white paternalism.[3] But even in these narratives dealing with threadbare materials she sometimes deviated from the traditional norm. Certainly, "The Merry-Go-Round," though it does show the white "gentlemen" of a rural community rallying to save a white interloper from Negro vengeance, also presents a white-Negro relationship untypical of the plantation stereotype. Here a white man from outside the South (he rolls his r's in an unfamiliar way) sets up a merry-go-round in a Negro community, wants to stay at a Negro woman's house and take his meals there (the woman refuses—it's not fitting), and makes advances to a Negro girl. Outraged, the Negroes recognize him as no "white gentleman," and the girl's fiancé strikes him to protect the girl. When the man shoots and wounds the Negro boy, the gentlemen of the area gather and see him safely off on the next train. This situation in which a white man makes amorous suggestions to a Negro girl was indeed not typical of the Southern tradition—at least, in fiction, and Julia's presenting it was daring for 1921.

In "Ashes" there are the customary relationships between the Negro and the "po' buckra," or lower-caste white, and the Negro and the upper-caste white. When the "po' buckra" callously tells Maum Hannah she must move from her home, she acts, as she believes, on a sign from the Lord and burns down the "po' buckra's" newly-built house. Then her conscience and her knowledge of the kindness of the upper-caste white lead her to confess her act to the sheriff. Paternalistically and conventionally, he sides with the loyal old Negro against the "po' buckra," and she goes free of punishment and is able to keep her home. This alignment of the traditional Negro and the aristocratic white against the poor white is true to the older plantation literature—as it was to actual plantation life.

"The Right Thing" ⟨. . .⟩ and the play *Boy-Chillen* rather sentimentally show the mistress of the plantation shielding a Negro from the sterner white master and the toils of the law. In each case the Negro is guilty of a crime. In *Boy-Chillen* the crime is that of murder; but the white mistress plays the role of the indulgent mother protecting the naughty but not morally responsible child from the too-harsh penalty for his misdeeds.

"Green Walnuts" ⟨. . .⟩ is a rather archly comic sketch of a young Negro boy suffering from a bad stomachache but staunchly denying that he has eaten anything unusual. Not until "Miss" comes from the Big House and gently interrogates him does he sheepishly list the vast catalogue of his gastronomic excesses, culminating with green walnuts. Only to "Miss," that beloved and respect-inspiring figure, will he yield up the truth.

With the exception of "The Merry-Go-Round," and possibly "Ashes," these stories with white characters are among Julia's weakest. It is not that they are unskillfully written or untruthful which mitigates against them today. It is merely that they resemble hundreds of other stories and lack the mark of her individual talent. She was wise to confine herself usually to Negro characters alone. Like DuBose Heyward and many other Southern writers, when she attempts to depict Southern whites she falls back on the romantic plantation stereotypes—in large part, I think, because that is the way the aristocratic Southerner is inclined to see himself and his peers.

The third and last group of domestic stories includes pieces which show Julia Peterkin at her best. These are grim, sometimes horrifying narratives of death, cruelty, and austere tragedy. Their power is heightened by her refusal to dramatize for the sake of drama and the often unspoken but always understood compassion and respect she has for her characters in their confrontations with an inexplicable, often malignant, and always inescapable fate. Even as these people go down in defeat, their courage, their stoicism, and their strength emphasize what Bellamann calls her constant theme—the affirmation of life.

Julia Peterkin said, "Among the Negros . . . I saw sickness and death and superstition and frenzy and desire. My eyes looked on horror and misery. These things stayed with me and I had to get rid of them."[4] And later, "I mean to present these people in a patient struggle with fate. . . ."[5] These stories of cutting a mouth for a baby born without one, of a rooster mistaking an infant's eyes for berries, of a man's toes coming off and floating gaily in the water, of dogs digging up and eating the bodies of newborn babies—these were the products, not of a diseased imagination nor of a desire to shock for the sake of shocking. These things Julia Peterkin saw with her own eyes, and she saw, too, the manner in which the Negroes met these disasters and went on living.

From the beginning she has an almost instinctive gift for the structure of the short story, and it is in these stories dealing with the macabre and the tragic and the grim that this gift manifests itself most effectively. Each is a tight little drama in which no word is wasted, no motion made without purpose.

A consideration of only one of them, "A Baby's Mouth," will serve to suggest the penetrating vision, the adeptness in style and characterization, and the structural proficiency typical of the entire group.

"A Baby's Mouth" commences with passages of the sort of description she was increasingly employing—exact, concrete, and often symbolically relevant to the emotions and the action:

> Day had come at last. The sun rose red and clear in a purple sky. The frost that whitened the roof of a little square weather-stained cabin glistened, then melted to dew. Wide frost-browned cotton fields in front of the cabin turned to bronze in the sunshine and the tall pines growing thick in the woods behind it seemed touched with gold. Crisp leaves still clung to the oak trees and they fluttered and crackled in the light wind that murmured musically through the pines and curling down carried some of their fresh fragance through the cabin's door.

Thus she establishes the peace, the beauty, the apparent beneficence of nature.

In the cabin old Maum Hannah, the midwife, dozes, waiting for Doll's baby to come. At last the baby is born, and all seems well until Doll tries to nurse it. Something is wrong. The puzzled mother calls to Maum Hannah, who takes the baby into the firelight so that she can see.

"'Gawd hab mussy on us!' she prayed." Then, gently, she tells Doll, "'You mus' hol' up. Dis chile ain' got no mout'.'"

Something must be done. "'Somebody got to cut a mout' fo' dat chile. . . . Ef dey don't, he gwine dead.'"

But who? John Green, who does barbering, has sharp scissors. Gip Ragin, the butcher, has a sharp knife. Dunk

Bruce is good at pulling teeth. Maum Hannah leaves and returns with Gip Ragin, the butcher, "a big square-shouldered man." But when the moment comes to cut the baby, Gip freezes. He shivers. He grows sick. So, with Doll holding the child, Maum Hannah will try. "'I dunno des how big fo' cut 'em,' she reflected. . . . 'But den, ef I don' git 'em big 'nough fus' time, I kin cut 'em mo', enty?'" She works in silence. Doll faints, but Maum Hannah succeeds. The baby is placed on the bed beside its mother. Maum Hannah says, "'Po' t'ing. Trouble sta't soon wid 'em, enty, Gip? Po' lil *creeter*.'" She reassures the mother, and then, with the tact born of consideration for others, she thanks Gip for coming, tells him that nobody will learn of his weakness, and politely asks him to pay another visit.

All is peace again. Gip is gone, the baby is fed, Maum Hannah seats herself once more in the rocker. Midwife, mother, and child sleep before the fire.

This is all. It is, of course, the material of melodrama, but Julia Peterkin has treated it quietly, directly, simply. Still, through the objective surface comes the compassion of Maum Hannah's words: "Po' t'ing. Trouble sta't soon wid 'em, enty, Gip? Po' lil *creeter*.'" And once again the deceptive serenity of nature engulfs the tiny figures, deceptive because for all its beauty it is detached, indifferent. The tragedy having been faced and overcome, the sleepers rest, ready for a new day, a new life.

In "Over the River" the deaf-mute girl's pilgrimage in search of the father of her unborn child anticipates a similar journey by the pregnant girl in Faulkner's *Light in August*, though the ending in "Over the River" is grimmer, more

artistically complete with the death of the child and the mother's return to her home. The scene in "The Foreman" in which the man laughs hysterically at the sight of his gangrenous toes chasing each other in the milky water is without parallel for horror in American literature, even as it is psychologically and esthetically unimpeachable. The sharp contrast in "Missy's Twins" between the babies eaten by the hounds and the safe and protected sleeping white child implies more than could a volume of polemics on suffering and injustice. The futile struggle of the root doctor in "The Sorcerer" who mistakenly drinks lye instead of one of his potions has all the irony of Thomas Hardy's malignant tricks of nature.

If Julia Peterkin had written nothing but these few stories, she would rank as one of the early and still viable practitioners of the realistic short story in the genre of the Southern Gothic, so much admired in the works of William Faulkner, Eudora Welty, the early Truman Capote, Carson McCullers, Flannery O'Connor, and others.

Notes

1. Julian R. Meade, "Julia Peterkin," *New York Herald Tribune*, January 17, 1933. A clipping in The South Caroliniana Library.
2. Julia Peterkin, autobiographical sketch in *On Parade*, edited by Erich Posselt (New York: Coward-McCann, 1929), p. 118.
3. *Boy-Chillen*, A Play in One Act, in *One-Act Plays for Stage and Study, Seventh Series* (New York: Samuel French, 1932), pp. 2–15.
4. Julian R. Meade, "Julia Peterkin," loc. cit.
5. Emily Clark, *Innocence Abroad* (New York: Alfred A. Knopf, 1931), p. 219.

ANN PETRY

1912–

Ann (Lane) Petry was born on October 12, 1912, in Old Saybrook, Connecticut. She attended the College of Pharmacy of the University of Connecticut and worked for seven years at pharmacies in Old Saybrook and Lyme, Connecticut. In 1938 she married George D. Petry; they have one daughter. Petry moved to Harlem, working on newspapers there and writing short stories. In 1943 she enrolled in a writing course at Columbia University, and shortly thereafter published her first short story in the *Crisis*.

In 1946 Petry published *The Street*, a highly acclaimed novel about Black women in Harlem; it won the Houghton Mifflin Literary Fellowship. The next year she published *Country Place*, and in 1953 her third novel, *The Narrows*, appeared.

In the late 1940s Petry began to turn her attention to children's works, and she has produced *The Drugstore Cat* (1949), *Harriet Tubman: Conductor of the Underground Railroad* (1955), *Tituba of Salem Village* (1964), and *Legends of the Saints* (1970). The collection *Miss Muriel and Other Stories* appeared in 1971.

Ann Petry continues to reside in Old Saybrook.

General

Mrs. Petry has—this first must be granted—an uncomfortable tendency to contrive sordid plots (as opposed to merely writing of sordid events). She seems to require a "shocking" chain of scandalous doings, secret affairs, family skeletons revealed, brutal crimes, whispered evil, adulterous intrigue on which to cast her creative imagination, in the manner of the great Victorians or the tawdry moderns. So wise is her writing, though, so real are her characters, so total is her sympathy, that

one can often accept the faintly cheap horrors and contrivances. Even if not, though, he can dispense with them. It may seem odd to suggest reading a novel while skipping the plot; but it can be done. And if one allows himself to be overexcited by these intrigues (it *is* hard to escape their clutches, but one should), he misses, I think, the real treasures of Ann Petry's fiction.

There is, first, more intelligence in her novels, paragraph for paragraph, than in those of any other writer I have mentioned; solid, earned, tested intelligence. This woman is sharp. Her wisdom is more useful, even, more durable, than the brilliant, diamond-edged acuteness of Gwendolyn Brooks.

This wisdom, secondly, reveals itself in a prose that is rich and crisp, and suavely shot with the metallic threads of irony. It is a style of constant surprise and delight, alive and alight on the page. It is so charged with sense and pleasure you can taste it—and yet never (almost never) is it mere "display."

And out of the female wisdom, the chewy style, grow characters of shape and dimension, people made out of love, with whole histories evoked in a page. There is not one writer in a thousand who owns so genuine and generous and undiscriminating a creative sympathy. Ann Petry *becomes* each character she mentions, grants each one a full, felt intensity of being, the mean and the loving, the white and the black, even when they come and go in only fifty words. Rich sick old ladies, lecherous toads, toddlers, half-animal brutes, the belligerently independent, the loved and unloved, the passion- and obsession-maddened, those who scarcely exist: each one, difficult as it may seem, she enters to become, becomes to create, with a universality of creative sympathy that is honestly Shakespearean. (Or at least Faulknerian; he does it too.)

This, to me, the intelligence, the style, and above all the creative sympathy, is what sets Ann Petry apart among this second rank of American Negro novelists, sets her, in fact, into a place almost as prominent and promising as that of the bigger three. She is not, of course, writing "about" the race war, any more than most of the last eight or ten novelists mentioned are. This is a delusion fostered either by publishers, playing up a profitable approach, or by the fake guilty egocentricity of white readers, who presume that all books by Negroes must somehow be about them. But if an American Negro can, despite all, develop such an understanding of other people as Ann Petry's—and more prodigious still, *convey* that understanding—then let her write what *Peyton Place*–plots she will, she is working toward a genuine truce in the war.—DAVID LITTLE-JOHN, "Negro Writers Today: The Novelists II," *Black on White*, 1966, pp. 154–56

Works

The Street tells the story of Lutie Johnson, who tried unsuccessfully to make a normal life for herself and her young son Bub after she moved into a grubby little apartment on Harlem's 116th Street. Lutie, light-brown and luscious, had been a maid during the depression when Joe, her husband, had been without work; but taking a job in Connecticut while he remained in Harlem had meant that she lost him to another woman. Now, after a business course and a crack at the civil-service examinations, she has a precarious position as a white-collar worker while awaiting the security of a city job. After living with Pop, who had a succession of women after his wife died, and Granny, who was steeped in bitterness, this grimy little apartment seemed the key to a new and better life; yet at the same time the street outside seemed a menace. First there was Jones, the super, who wanted her, and the one bulwark against that ever present danger, Mrs. Hedges, the madam on the ground floor who ran a nice, quiet little house, and said the trouble with Jones was that he was "cellar-crazy." Then there was the neighborhood and its relationship to Bub, who was in school until three, but then on the street until she returned from her job at night. Later there was Boots Smith, an orchestra leader who heard her singing to herself in Mr. Junto's Bar and Grill and asked her to join his band, though she knew there were strings attached to his proposition. And finally there was Mr. Junto, the white man who controlled everything in the neighborhood and had a fixation about the color of a woman's skin.

With these elements Mrs. Petry has woven the rich tapestry of life on a Harlem street. She has done so with insight and courage, with the basic honesty toward Negro life that Richard Wright, and more recently Chester Himes, have projected into their novels, yet with something added to the sociological realism of a bitter pen. She can show the "cellar-crazed" super, Jones, who is sexually dangerous and a menace to society, not as a black brute who must be trampled to death by a mob, but as a product of what Roi Ottley calls "slum shock," the inevitable result of a wrong system, as a human being rather than a symbol. Or she can paint a picture of a Harlem madam, a great, gaunt amazon who has been badly burned in a fire and refuses to show her body to any man, badly as she wants one, because of a fierce inner pride. For Mrs. Petry knows what it is to live as a Negro in New York City and she also knows how to put it down on paper so that it is as scathing an indictment of our society as has ever appeared, notwithstanding the sugar-coating. Yet with all this—and to this reviewer Mrs. Petry is the most exciting new Negro writer of the last decade—still, there is a serious limitation in both the author and this book.

It is difficult to detract from something that seems so nearly perfect, and from a writer with such genuine talent, yet the truth of the matter is that there is a bad sag in the last third of the book which is almost fatal. In the midst of my real excitement (and an opening chapter which is as good writing as I have encountered almost anywhere), I was suddenly dumped into a bog of hopelessness that made me, as a reader, flounder rather badly. It seemed almost as though two people had collaborated on the book, one of them a sincere and honest writer, the other a slick-magazine technician with a completely mechanical heart and mind. The whole sequence of plot built around Lutie and her aspirations to sing in Boots Smith's band in order to get herself and Bub away from the street, and the relationship of them both toward Mr. Junto and its inevitable conclusion, are as banal and contrived as anything that ever appeared in the slicks. And even though Mrs. Petry has partially saved things by not going soft in the ending, one is left with a bad taste in the mouth that persists.

Normally, perhaps, one would not mention this, for certainly Mrs. Petry's batting average is high enough to stand one poop-out. Yet it seems to this reviewer that there is something basic here, something that not only concerns Mrs. Petry but all of us who are deeply interested in seeing the novel as an important factor in the fight against racial intolerance and for the logical integration of the Negro into the American life stream. Ann Petry has it within her power to be a vital force in that protest movement, or she can, almost as easily, become a popular writer who, within the taboos of marketability, will find success almost too easy. That she can be either is shown clearly in this book, but to be both, as also seems proved in these pages, makes her a writer whose work exhibits the flaws that may eventually alienate her from both audiences. That she is a real writer few, I think, will deny, but so long as she remains a paradox, the road before her may well be as menacing as 116th Street. Either fork will probably assure her a wide audience; which will bring her the greater inner satisfaction is for her to decide.—BUCKLIN MOON, "Both Sides of the Street," *NR*, Feb. 11, 1946, pp. 193–94

The heart of Miss Petry's story ⟨*The Narrows*⟩ is a love affair that various forces of evil bring to a tragic conclusion. The girl is Camilla Treadway, the beautiful daughter of a wealthy white family; the man is Link Williams, an educated Negro who has accepted the lowbrow life of The Narrows, a Negro community about two hours' drive from New York. Link is the adopted son of Abbie Crunch, who is a symbol of the old-fashioned virtues and discredited attitudes that Link has carefully examined and rejected. He chooses the more realistic world of Bill Hod and Creepy Williams at The Last Chance Saloon.

The girl meets Link Williams on the foggy night she drives into The Narrows to do a bit of slumming, and finds herself pursued by the Cat Jimmie, a human monster. Link rescues her—and, in the fog, she does not recognize him as a Negro until they enter a local night club.

Later they go for a drive in her red convertible. The high implausibility of this scene is symbolic of their subsequent love affair and the dilemma that Miss Petry is not able to resolve. The dramatic center of her story is never credible. The lovers meet many times, they have their troubles, quarrel. Finally, the girl, in a fit of temper, accuses Link of attacking her. This leads to his arrest, to scandal in the tabloids and to murder.

The other half of the story, the past, as it is revealed in a series of flashbacks, is always credible, and sometimes extremely good. But the reader is caught between an unreal present and a convincing past. Mamie Powther, a café-au-lait Molly Bloom, is real enough, whenever the author gets around to her, and so, at times, is her husband, the Treadway butler. The canvas has depth and complexity, but the surface drama central to the tragedy is like a tissue of tabloid daydreams, projected by the characters. The living past overwhelms the lifeless present, but the present is obliged to give the past its meaning.

It is hard to see why Miss Petry did not realize this herself. Her first novel, *The Street*, published several years ago, attracted well-deserved praise—and, though it dealt with the familiar elements of the Negro-problem novel, it seemed to point the way to a brilliant creative future. But *The Narrows* reads like the first draft of an ambitious conception that has not been labored into imaginative life. It indicates what the author might have done but did not do. The forces that have lowered the craft of fiction have made it more difficult, not less, to write the book that will cry havoc and be heard. Miss Petry can do it, but it will take more brooding labor—and less space. —WRIGHT MORRIS, "The Complexity of Evil," *NYTBR*, Aug. 16, 1953, p. 4

By contrast with Mr. ⟨Henry⟩ Van Dyke and/or the majority of black novelists, Ann Petry seems old-fashioned, so surprisingly "slow" in her narrative rhythm that you wonder if the title story in *Miss Muriel and Other Stories* took place in another century. Mrs. Petry's timing is as different from most contemporary black writing as is her locale, which in the best of these leisurely paced stories is a small upstate New York town where a pharmacist and his family are the only Negroes. Their life centers entirely around the drugstore itself. The longest and most successful of these stories, "Miss Muriel," tells of an eccentric elderly white shoemaker in the town, Mr. Bemish, who, to the astonishment and terror of the Negro family, falls in love with Aunt Sophronia. There is no "Muriel" in the story; the title is a sad joke about an old Negro who asked for "Muriel" cigars and was sternly told that *he* would have to ask for them as "Miss Muriel." But the feeling behind the "joke" is so strong in the small, isolated black family that poor Mr. Bemish not only doesn't get Aunt Sophronia, but is driven out of town for falling in love with a black lady.

This reversal of roles is typical of Mrs. Petry's quiet, always underplayed but deeply felt sense of situation. The other stories aren't as lovingly worked out as "Miss Muriel"—which is an artful period piece that brings back a now legendary age of

innocence in white-black relationships. Several stories are just tragic situations that are meant to touch you by that quality alone. A famous black drummer loses his adored wife to a pianist in his band, but the drumming must go on; a Harlem old-clothes man falls in love with the oversized statue of a dark woman he calls "Mother Africa"; a Negro teacher is unable to stand up to a gang of young students and flees town, ashamed of not having played a more heroic part; a Negro woman at a convention is insulted by a white woman, and realizes in the morning, on learning that the other woman died of a heart attack during the night, that she might have saved her. These delicate points are characteristic of Mrs. Petry's quietly firm interest in fiction as moral dilemma. Clearly, her sense of the Negro situation is still "tragic." Her stories are very far from contemporary black nationalist writing, and by no means necessarily more interesting. But they are certainly different. —ALFRED KAZIN, "Brothers Crying Out for More Access to Life," *SR*, Oct. 2, 1971, pp. 34–35

ROBERT BONE
From "The Contemporary Negro Novel"
The Negro Novel in America (1958)
1965, pp. 180–85

*T*he Street is a *roman à thèse* whose aim, in the words of the author, is "to show how simply and easily the environment can change the course of a person's life." The heroine is a declassed *bourgeoise* who is driven to murder by the corrupting influence of "the street." As in Wright and Motley, a whole bookful of sociological data is adduced to validate the murder. Of an environmentalist who chooses to focus on society we can demand more than a superficial social analysis. The trouble with *The Street* is that it tries to make racial discrimination responsible for slums. It is an attempt to interpret slum life in terms of *Negro* experience, when a larger frame of reference is required. As Alain Locke has observed, "*Knock on Any Door* is superior to *The Street* because it designates class and environment, rather than mere race and environment, as its antagonist."

Country Place is a novel of another magnitude, large enough to justify a better acquaintance with its author. Ann Petry was born and raised in Old Saybrook, Conn., where her father was the local druggist. After graduating from the College of Pharmacy at the University of Connecticut, she disappointed family plans by abandoning small-town life for the big city. In New York she tried her hand at advertising, social work, and newspaper reporting. Evenings were occupied with courses in creative writing and planned readings in psychology. Her first short stories were published in *Crisis* and *Phylon*. One was reprinted in Foley's *Best American Short Stories of 1946;* another, which attracted the attention of talent scouts, led to a Houghton Mifflin Literary Fellowship. A novella, "In Dark Confusion," based on the Harlem riot of August 1943, completes her literary apprenticeship.

One senses in Mrs. Petry's life and art a tension between metropolis and small town, between New York and Old Saybrook. In *The Street* she explores New York from an Old Saybrook point of view; in *Country Place* she reverses the process. Reminiscent of *Winesburg, Ohio* and *Spoon River*, the novel treats small-town life from the perspective of a refugee. Like the writers of the Chicago Renaissance who fled from Main Street to Fifty-Seventh Street, it was necessary for Mrs. Petry to renounce the village before she could realize its literary potential. A record of this experience, *Country Place* embodies both the struggle for emancipation and the desire, once liberated, to re-establish one's ties with the past through art.

Conceived in the spirit of revolt from the village, the novel probes beneath the quiet surface of a country town to the inquisitiveness, bigotry, and malice which are typical of its inner life. On the theory that village life revolves around the drugstore, Mrs. Petry introduces Doc, the druggist-narrator, who serves to "place" the action of the novel. To encompass the collective personality of the town, she employs a shifting point of view which rotates among the chief participants. The burden of conflict, however, is borne by Johnnie Roane, a returning veteran who has outgrown the town. His sole remaining tie is his young wife, Glory; when he discovers her infidelity with Ed, the town bull, he renounces his father's contracting business and embarks upon an apprenticeship as an artist in New York.

A second center of dramatic interest is provided by Mrs. Gramby, whose inner struggle parallels that of Johnnie Roane. Like Johnnie, she fights her way free of the town and achieves a kind of affirmation. With her old-fashioned virtues of dignity and formality, she represents the best of the town's traditions, about to be inundated by the cheap and brassy vulgarity of the modern age. Confronted with the obnoxious "pushing" of her son's wife, Lil, she wonders what can be done to stem the tide, to affirm the values of the past in the context of the present. In the end, she revises her will, passing judgment on the younger generation from beyond the grave. The will thus becomes an effective device for resolving the central value-conflict of the novel.

The fundamental clash of values occurs between those who exemplify the village mores and those who transcend them. Among the former are several minor characters with well-defined symbolic roles. The village cab driver, known locally as "the Weasel," typifies the town's spirit of petty vindictiveness. Glory, pretty but empty-headed, suggests the frustrated romantic yearnings of the townswomen. Ed Barrell—"good old Ed"—is a symbol of the town's pride in its own lechery. Glory's mother, Lil, with her hawklike appearance, suggests vulgar materialism and acquisitiveness. Her middle-aged husband, Mearns Gramby, represents wasted talent and sexual repression. The town is of course xenophobic: anti-Catholic, anti-Semitic, anti-Negro. As counterweights, Mrs. Petry provides Neola, Mrs. Gramby's colored maid; the Portegee, her gardener; and Rosenberg, the Jewish laywer. The village outcasts are in touch with fundamental reality; they offer some hope of redemption to a declining Yankee tradition.

The most notable feature of village life is its resistance to change, its tendency toward stagnation. Smugness and complacency are the outer signs, but they are symptomatic of a stubborn commitment to live in the past, by the light of some outmoded ideal. Doc, who is cast in the role of village philosopher, makes the diagnosis and prescribes the remedy: "I remember when electric lights were first installed in the town of Lennox. My father, whose reaction was fairly typical of the period, objected to them as being a wicked invention of the devil, expressly designed to ruin man's eyesight—the light being too harsh—and to soften his moral fiber." Personally, Doc goes on, he prefers to have his moral fiber softened by using electricity. Doc's drugstore contains an old-fashioned ice-cream parlor where he still mixes his own fountain sirups, but he dispenses penicillin and the sulfa drugs as well. Striving for a balance between change and tradition, Doc combines the best of the old with the best of the new.

Individuals, like communities, may fasten their lives to the past, but then, like barnacles, they pay the price of stagnation. Consider the case of Johnnie Roane, who has lived through four years of war with only the memory of his young wife to sustain him. Returning from overseas, he clings desperately to that memory, even though it means the death of his ambitions: "You want Glory . . . but having her means Lennox. So you forget you ever heard of a paintbrush or a drawing pencil or a place known in some circles as Manhattan Island." Only when his image of the past is irrevocably shattered by the knowledge of his wife's infidelity does he revise his attitudes toward permanence and change. Losing Glory, he has gained New York; he has learned to weigh the pain against the possibility of growth. If change is not always desirable, he concludes, it is in any case inevitable, and it brings in its wake an admixture, if often an imbalance, of good and evil.

Mrs. Gramby, as a living embodiment of the New England tradition, is particularly prone to idealize the past. She has watched the town change under the impact of two world wars, and in her opinion largely for the worse: "As I get older, I keep going back to the past, comparing it with the present, making myself unhappy by remembering it as a more gracious time in which to have lived." In her personal life, moreover, she has sacrificed her son to the past, keeping him in Lennox against his will for the sake of family tradition. Through a crisis in her son's marriage, however, she is forced to revise her values. Her new-found wisdom consists in recognizing the inevitability of change and attempting to influence its direction. In a conscious effort to alter certain of the town's established ways, she revises her will, underwriting an interracial marriage and financing Johnnie Roane's apprenticeship in New York.

On its deepest level, the novel suggests that resistance to change is not a parochial trait but a universal human tendency. Seeking for certainty in a world of flux, man creates images or dreams which he tries to invest with timelessness. Each of the characters in *Country Place* pursues a "soapbubble dream"; each seeks to protect his heart's desire from the ravages of time. Glory and Lil defy time in the shallow fashion of the Hollywood glamor-merchant: Glory, by her restless search for romance and adventure; Lil, by her pathetic efforts to stave off middle age. Mrs. Gramby's defiance takes the form of a refusal to allow her son to grow up, to live his own life. Mearns Gramby tries to arrest time by making a middle-age marriage; Johnnie Roane expects time to have stood still during his absence overseas. All, in the end, are stripped of their illusions, but the positive characters are able to transform their loss into a source of growth.

It is from the theme of lost illusion that the narrative structure of the novel flows. *Country Place* develops a strong narrative drive, paced by a storm whose intensity is reminiscent of the New England hurricane of 1938. The action of the novel takes place in a single week (one cycle of weather), reaching a climax along with the storm. Through a kind of Lear motif the storm reduces each character to moral (or literal) nakedness. Faced with the death of their dreams, they are forced to re-evaluate the past, balancing achievement with desire. The storm thus becomes considerably more than a narrative device; it suggests first of all the widespread uprootedness caused by the war. Ultimately it emerges as a symbol of time and flux, relentless killers of the dream.

Mrs. Petry's style, like her narrative strategy, supports her main intent. In the Wright School manner, she will describe a cat, mangled by an auto accident, without flinching. Her realism, however, expresses more than a conventional tough-mindedness; it is well suited to a novel so largely concerned with deflating the romantic attitude. Beyond this, she achieves a metaphorical depth virtually unknown among Wright's disciples. Concrete, poetic, her style persistently seeks an "objective correlative" to human emotion. In the following passage she captures Glory's restless frustration through a vivid description of a marshy cove: "It was black, sullen, bordered by a ripple of white foam that gnawed restlessly at the edges of the marsh. The foam retreated and returned, retreated and then returned; and as she watched it she got the feeling that she could hear it snarl because it could not get free of the marsh that confined it."

From individual descriptive passages, image patterns and symbols emerge as part of a total design. The stifling atmosphere of small-town life is evoked, for example, by a recurrent image of confinement and restraint: "the grated window made the ticket-seller look as though he were in a cage." Each character, in fact, has his personal "cage," and through this symbol the essential village psychology is revealed. The townsfolk strive for an equal distribution of frustration; it is this that accounts for their vindictiveness. If the cage symbol is closed and static, the tree symbol is open and expansive. Initially the trees are used to dramatize the destructiveness of the storm, but later on they acquire another significance. Concern or indifference to their fate divides the positive from the negative characters. "Trees will grow," Mrs. Gramby insists, "people will live here." The town recovers from the storm, and life goes on. In a subtle movement which parallels the main direction of the novel, what has been a symbol of uprootedness becomes a symbol of growth.

Because of Mrs. Petry's technical proficiency it is especially difficult to account for the incredible lapse of taste which mars the closing pages of the novel. Somehow she can never manage (it is equally true of *The Street*) to remove her villains gracefully from the stage. Glory is handled throughout with unexceptionable irony, but in the final scene, during the reading of the will, Lil becomes an object of the author's unrestrained invective. The root of the trouble lies, one suspects, in Mrs. Petry's New England heritage. She understands evil, motivates her villains well, but fails to achieve distance in the end. Evil cannot go unpunished, even if the author has to administer the lash in person. This momentary loss of poise is unfortunate, but it cannot seriously detract from Mrs. Petry's distinguished achievement in *Country Place*.

ARTHUR P. DAVIS
From "Ann Petry"
From the Dark Tower:
Afro-American Writers 1900–1960
1974, pp. 193–97

Ann Lane Petry came to national attention with the publication of *The Street* (1946), a first novel which won the Houghton Mifflin Literary Award. In this work Miss Petry follows the tradition of hard-hitting social commentary which characterized the Richard Wright school of naturalistic protest writing. *The Street* is perhaps the best novel to come from the followers of Wright. Her last full-length adult novel, *The Narrows* (1953), depicts Negro life in a small New England city, a subject not often treated in black writing. 〈. . .〉

A depressing work, *The Street* follows the thesis implied by this type of naturalistic writing: namely, that the black poor in the ghetto do not have much of a chance to live decent and meaningful lives, to say nothing of happy lives. The main character in the work is Lutie Johnson, a hard-working, intelligent, and ambitious young Nergo mother who has come

to New York to seek a better chance for herself and for her son. Because they are poor and black, they become victims of 116th Street, a symbol for all that is bad in ghetto living. The rest of the novel spells out in bleak detail the specific forces that bring about their undoing.

Since her husband cannot find work, Lutie has to leave home to get a job in order to support their son. In her absence the husband turns to another woman. On 116th Street in Harlem, where Lutie finally secures an apartment within her means, she and her son become the victims of an assorted group of big-city vicious characters: the depraved janitor in the building, a "madam" who lives in one of the apartments, the lustful white landlord, and a musician (a so-called friend) whom she finally kills. As the novel ends, we find Lutie buying a one-way ticket to Chicago, leaving her son, who has been tricked by the janitor into robbing mail boxes, in the hands of the police.

In an article that appeared in *The Crisis* Miss Petry tells us her objectives in this work:

. . . my aim is to show how simply and easily the environment can change the course of a person's life. . . .

I try to show why the Negro has a high crime rate, a high death rate, and little or no chance of keeping his family unit intact in large northern cities. . . .[1]

There is a suggestion of inevitability in the above statement *and* in the novel itself. The trouble is that the environment alone does not "easily" change the course of a ghetto person's life. There are other factors involved. The main thrust of her position is valid: ghetto Negroes do have formidable odds against them, but the simple, realistic truth is that many, perhaps the majority, do survive, do rise above the 116th Streets of America.

The second novel, *Country Place* (1947), is set in a small New England town, the kind of place in which Miss Petry was born and reared. The work follows in the tradition of small-town realistic fiction that goes back to *Main Street* (perhaps to George Crabbe in the eighteenth century). In this novel Ann Petry wrote about a life that in all probability she knew better than the life she wrote about in *The Street*. The action is narrated by the town druggist. Miss Petry's family, as noted earlier, have been druggists in Old Saybrook for several generations. In short, Ann Petry knew at first hand the background on which she placed her second novel and the characters that appeared in it.

Country Place deals with the class lines between aristocrats and nobodies, the antiforeign, anti-Roman Catholic prejudices, and the sexual looseness and the ugliness and viciousness found behind the innocent-appearing life in a small town like "Lennox, Connecticut." One of the main characters is Mrs. Gramby, a domineering Yankee aristocrat who eventually overcomes some of her inherited prejudices. The two central characters are Johnnie Roane and Gloria, his wife. A returned veteran, Johnnie finds out that his wife has become the mistress of the town "stud." At the end of the work the good are rewarded and the bad are punished or killed off. Johnnie, aided by Mrs. Gramby, is able to free himself from his straying wife and go to New York to study art, an ambition he had long held. The best drawn character in the work is Weasel, who knew all of the town's skeletons and took joy in telling them. *Country Place* is an entertaining work. It is difficult to say more.

In *The Narrows* (1953) Miss Petry has depicted Negro life in a small New England city. As has been suggested above, this is virtually an untried field for the black writer. Miss Petry seems to be saying in many different ways that these ghettos in small New England cities are for more isolated and cut off from the mainstreams of American life and are far more sterile than the black districts of border and Southern communities. The blacks in these Northern cities are rootless. Having severed, for the most part, their connections with the Southland from which many come, they live on the periphery of these Northern towns and cities, far more cut off than even the most recent European immigrants. Miss Petry naturally does not *say* these things in so many words. She does not have to. Her depiction of life in fictional Monmouth, Connecticut, gives us the message.

In *The Narrows* the author incorporates many of the racial myths well known to Northern-born Negroes and to those who have gone North for an education, especially a New England education. Among them are the examples of the anti-Negro high school teacher who subtly discourages and ridicules young blacks; the different versions of the question often asked by deans and presidents: "Wouldn't you be happier in a Negro school?"; and always the sting of being called *nigger* by immigrants who haven't even learned to speak English.

The major plot of *The Narrows* deals with a theme that was to become fairly popular among Negro writers in the 1960's: that of the relationship between the black man and the white mistress/wife. Through the soul-searching of her principal character, Ann Petry analyzes this relationship in considerable depth. In this novel Link Williams, a handsome, talented black boy, meets quite by accident a patrician white girl, the daughter of the town's richest family and the wife of a socialite. The two fall hopelessly and helplessly in love. Link at first does not know that Camilo is married or that she belongs to the famous Treadway family of Monmouth. When he does find out and does half-heartedly try to break off the affair, it is far too late. Link in the end pays for his innocence and indiscretion in what amounts to an Ivy League type of lynching.

The reader gets the impression that Link, though admirable in many respects, is basically a weak, vacillating character. Miss Petry accounts for this, it seems to us, in two ways. Link was an orphan reared by two very different persons: by puritannical Miss Abbie, who had adopted him, but who in her grief over the loss of her husband temporarily forgot the eight-year-old boy, and by Bill Hod, the worldly town racketeer. The divided loyalties which Link held in all probability helped shape his character. But there was another influence, the author implies. Here is a strikingly handsome star athlete and Phi Beta Kappa graduate of Dartmouth College who returns home and takes a job as bartender in Bill Hod's place. This is all that a New England ghetto has to offer to a trained black youth.

Though it certainly holds the reader's interest, *The Narrows* has serious weaknesses as a novel. First, the author leans too heavily on flashbacks to tell her story. There are too many of them, and after the first few they begin to irritate. Second, Miss Petry puts a heavy strain on our "suspension of disbelief" when she asks us to believe that it would take an intelligent boy like Link Williams two or three months to find out who his girl friend actually was. And third, Ann Petry tries too often to create suspense by having her characters in moments of crisis think back, sometimes for as long as three pages, over past incidents in their lives. Although it may have its aesthetic value, this kind of interior monologue as used by Ann Petry somehow fails to impress.

The Narrows is an exciting work, and it does give us a fresh background, which is sorely needed in Afro-American fiction, but it is not a strong novel. Strangely enough, Miss Petry's delineation of white small-town New England life in *Country Place* is more convincing than her depiction of black life in *The Narrows*. *The Street* is Ann Petry's most impressive novel.

With *The Drugstore Cat* (1949) Ann Petry left adult writing and turned to writing for children and young adults. This first work is for six-to-ten-year-olds. The second work, *Harriet Tubman* (1955), and the third, *Tituba of Salem Village* (1963), are for young adults. On the dust jacket of *Harriet Tubman* Mrs. Petry gives her reason for writing on the famous Underground Railroad worker:

> It is my belief that the majority of textbooks used in high school do not give an adequate or accurate picture of the history of slavery in the United States. . . . It is to answer this need that *Harriet Tubman* . . . was written.

There is nothing unusual about her approach in either type. Both of the young adult works, however, do give sympathetic and idealized portrayals of two historic black women, and both give a lot of entertaining and informative background material, excellent material to fill in "gaps" which white American history tends to leave.

The short stories of Ann Petry show a great sensitivity. They tend to deal with those subtle aspects of racial hurt which are not always understood by nonblacks. For example, in "Like a Winding Sheet" she shows a Negro, confronted downtown by what he thinks is prejudice, coming home and beating his wife when she playfully calls him "nigger." "In Darkness and Confusion" depicts the action of two respectable, hard-working Harlemites who, thinking about the injustice meted out to their son in an army camp in Georgia, express their anger and frustrations in the Harlem Riot of 1943. Miss Petry's voice is low when she speaks of the tragedy of ghetto living in these stories—the broken homes, the deserted children, the faithless wives, the young girls going on the street—and it is more effective than shouting. These stories show a genuine concern for the unfortunate victims of American racism, and the sincerity of her feelings comes through in the stories. They also show an artist's concern for structure and effect.

Ann Petry's best story, however, differs slightly from the type described above. Entitled "The Bones of Louella Jones," it uses a rich blend of humor, satire, and superstition to poke fun at several things—the way the news is manipulated by journals, at racial science (the physician who was an authority on white and black physical differences), and at racial segregation. The story concerns the dilemma a certain town gets into when it wants to separate the bones (white) of Elizabeth Countess of Castro and the bones (black) of Louella Jones, her servant, after both have been long buried in the same cemetery. After the ghost of Louella has exerted a little pressure, an "either-or" slab has to be placed over the graves in Bedford Abbey.

The word *competent* best describes Ann Petry as a writer. She does several things well, but none superlatively. Her short stories will probably stand up best after the critical years have passed judgment.

Notes

1. James W. Ivy, "Ann Petry Talks about First Novel." *The Crisis* (February, 1946), pp. 48–49.

SYLVIA PLATH

JULIA PETERKIN

MARGE PIERCY

CHAIM POTOK

KATHERINE ANNE PORTER

EZRA POUND

MARGE PIERCY

1936–

Marge Piercy was born March 31, 1936, in a predominantly black section of Detroit. The first in her family to go to college, she attended the University of Michigan on an undergraduate scholarship and Northwestern University as a graduate student. Between 1958 and 1969 Piercy supported herself with odd jobs while trying to publish her writing. During that time she joined the civil rights movement and became an organizer for Students for a Democratic Society (SDS). In 1969 she shifted her political allegiance to the budding women's movement. An openly feminist novelist and poet, Piercy has acknowledged her wish to be "useful" to women: "that the poems may give voice to something in the experience of a life has been my intention. To find ourselves spoken for in art gives dignity to our pain, our anger, our lust, our losses."

Piercy's first published works were a volume of poetry (*Breaking Camp*) and a novel (*Going Down Fast*), both of which came out in 1969. Included among her nine volumes of poetry are *Living in the Open* (1976), *The Moon Is Always Female* (1980), and *Stone, Paper, Knife* (1983). She is perhaps better known for her eight novels which include *Small Changes* (1973), *Woman on the Edge of Time* (1976), *Vida* (1980), and *Fly Away Home* (1984). She lives in Wellfleet, Massachusetts.

The first thing you notice in *Small Changes* ⟨. . .⟩ is the extraordinary confidence that suffuses the prose. It is written with a moralistic insistence that recalls nineteenth-century novels. Beyond questions of individual sensibilities, I'd say there is a cultural explanation for the difference: Marge Piercy is writing about womanhood—about nascent, not waning, attitudes. She writes from an evident feminist perspective, and the book rides a wave of contemporary feeling that seems to free her from self-consciousness. It's a mixed blessing.

Small Changes recounts the tortured young adulthood of two women who come from quite different pasts to Cambridge, where their lives touch. (It's one of the difficulties of the novel that in fact the connection doesn't go very deep. The women serve as symbolic Sisters, demonstrating the essential solidarity of female experience.) Beth: a lower-middle-class Wasp from Syracuse, whom we meet as a timid bride. Denied the college education she wants, she marries her high school sweetheart, who proves to be a lout, and in sudden bold desperation she flees to Boston, where, following an unsatisfying affair, she moves into a woman's commune, and ultimately to lesbianism. Miriam: a Jew from Brooklyn, who spends a long while in the grip of an affair with the man who is her first lover (he had picked her up in the courtyard of the Museum of Modern Art), an affair that ultimately turns into a *ménage à trois*, the third being his best friend. They are louts of a sort, too. A talented and well-educated mathematician, Miriam gets a job with a computer outfit, shakes free of her lovers, and marries her gentle, intellectual boss—only to discover his capacity for loutishness. She ends up where Beth began, institutionalized in marriage.

The vision of marriage in this novel is no cheerier than you'd expect to find by raising the topic in a Los Angeles divorce court. Oppression. Entrapment. Amputated lives. Despair and desperation. That that contract holds some chance of communion is not an allowable idea. Miriam, awash in high hopes, says early in her marriage, "I can enjoy being a woman," explaining that she's learned to like cooking. It is an ironic prelude to the misery ahead. Not that woe is limited to marriage. Wherever they go in this novel's world, women have two roles open to them: they may be prisoners or fugitives.

All the newly classic scenes of womanly suffering that we have read in memoirs of the past half-decade are anthologized here. The anesthetic wedding night. ("They had made love finally, but where was the love they had made?") The wife as unpaid servant. The secretary as sexual object. Dirty socks. Sexist rock lyrics. False moans of sexual pleasure. The discovery by the small-breasted that large breasts are no fun either.

If much of this material is programmatic, though, Marge Piercy's voice has its strengths. What father, for instance, can emerge unshaken from this contemptuous passage: "He was what people called good with his children. He did try hard to teach them things, but he got annoyed if they were not interested. He grew more involved in the course of his exposition than in their reactions. His disappointment was crushing. Ariane was already learning to pretend to understand." There is much else to praise in *Small Changes*. The energy of the book doesn't all go toward polemic; events move along compellingly and the social reportage is acute. Piercy is at ease in the trendy computer company (where the air is full of lingo such as "LISP," "compilers," the "Fall Joint"), as well as in communal apartments.

The book begins with a set-piece description of Beth's wedding, for which, her mother says, "We haven't cut any corners. This is no hole in the wall at the courthouse or in the front room. . . ." Even as you accede to the accuracy of the scene, you wonder at the chilliness of the author's portraits of those who perpetrate this awful show. What is absent in this novel is an adequate sense of the oppressor (and his allies), for one thing; and beyond that a recognition that there are limits to a world view that is organized around sexual warfare. It's hard not to think that Piercy feels this, knows that much of the multiplicity and mystery of life is getting squeezed out of her prose, but her polemical urge wins out.

The book ends with the appearance of a new character, to whom Miriam is about to lose her husband. The younger woman, herself divorced, reflects that Miriam hasn't tried hard enough, and she resolves: "Her first marriage had been a disaster, but she thought her second had to be better, with her so willing to work and work at it, unlike some women." How that irony is savored! Marge Piercy gazes down at these hapless characters with the finger-wagging authority of George Eliot. The novel doesn't justify that gusto, though I imagine it's an agreeable feeling.—RICHARD TODD, *At*, Sept. 1973, pp. 105–6

Because of Marge Piercy's strong views on social reform, from the very beginning her work has almost automatically divided people into two groups: those opposed to wide-sweeping social reform, and those in favor of it. Nevertheless she finds herself in the rather ambiguous position of being recognized, even embraced, by both the Movement, loosely-bound groups dedicated to radical change in American life, and the Establishment. She writes about radical living styles, communes, war protests, and women's liberation; yet her books are published by such institutions as Pocket Books and Doubleday. The standard technique of propaganda, over-simplification, separates "them" from "us" in her work; yet once this distinction has been made, her best work, while retaining elements of propaganda, notes similarities between the two groups as well as differences. While it focuses on the social problems of America, it focuses also on her own personal problems, so that tension exists not only between "us" and "them," but between "us" and "me."

Not content to wait for happiness and prosperity in some other life, she is driven to find a social and personal happiness on this earth, and the driving force behind her poetry is a stubborn utopian vision. At the same time she remains aware—almost too aware—of the obstacles, social and personal, confronting her. In "The Peaceable Kingdom" *(Breaking Camp)*, she comments on the famous American painting by Edward Hicks wherein all animals live side by side in idyllic harmony.

> Creamcheese babies square and downy as bolsters
> in nursery clothing nestle among curly lions and
>   lowing cattle,
> a wolf of scythe and ashes, a bear smiling in sleep.
> The paw of a leopard with spots and eyes of
>   headlights
> rest near calf and vanilla child.

She knows the nature of beasts, how animal life exists by eating other animal life. Such adjectives as "creamcheese" and "vanilla" give the poem what the painting lacks, bite. And the poet too has teeth and an appetite: "I have eaten five of those animals."

The poem contrasts Hicks's fantasy with the actual history of the United States.

> We glitter and spark righteousness.
> We are blinding as a new car in the sunshine.
> Gasoline rains form our fluffy clouds.
> Everywhere our evil froths polluting the waters—
> in what stream on what mountain do you miss
> the telltale redbrown sludge and rim of suds?
> Peace: the word lies like a smooth turd
> on the tongues of politicians ordering
> the sweet flesh seared on the staring bone.
> Guilt is added to the municipal water,
> guilt is deposited in the marrow and teeth.
> In my name they are stealing from people with
>   nothing
> their slim bodies. When did I hire these assassins?

She broods on the possibilities of her own indirect guilt, outraged that her country has acted thus in the name of democracy. The poem ends with a return to the American dream, which has now become ironic.

> This nation is founded on blood like a city on
>   swamps
> yet its dream has been beautiful and sometimes just
> that now grows brutal and heavy as a burned out star.

The image is strikingly apt—present coldness and darkness on earth contrasting with past heat and light in the heavens. This contrast between American dream and American reality motivates Marge Piercy's poetry. ⟨. . .⟩

Her first book, *Breaking Camp*, presents a rather strange mixture of styles. "Last Scene in the First Act," a clever, ironic meditation on a pair of lovers, shows the slick poetic technique of the academic poets of the 1950's: "Which the lamb and which the tiger / neither knows just yet. / Each lies down in a different bed / to incur a private debt." In "A Cold and Married War" she complains of her lover's indifference: "His cock crowed / I know you not." There is even a sonnet. But in spite of such superficial cleverness, a breathing person moves behind the poetry. We know her life, her concerns.

The first poem in the book, "Visiting a Dead Man on a Summer Day" shows the poet in Graceland cemetery in Chicago where she has gone to visit the tomb of Louis Sullivan. She compares his grave with the Getty tomb and sees the contrast as symbolic of American life.

> All poets are unemployed nowadays.
> My country marches in its sleep.
> The past structures a heavy mausoleum
> hiding its iron frame in masonry.
> Men burn like grass
> while armies grow.
> Thirty years in the vast rumbling gut
> of this society you stormed
> to be used, screamed
> no louder than any other breaking voice.
> The waste of a good man
> bleeds the future that's come
> in Chicago, in flat America,
> where the poor still bleed from the teeth,
> housed in sewers and filing cabinets,
> where prophets may spit into the wind
> till anger sleets their eyes shut,
> where this house that dances the seasons
> and the braid of all living
> and the joy of a man making his new good thing
> is strange, irrelevant as a meteor,
> in Chicago, in flat America
> in this year of our burning.

Such poetry has much in common with propaganda. Its subjects, the country, the past, the poor, are so vast that the poet cannot hope to develop completely her thoughts about them. Instead she relies on a common interpretation of history which she assumes she shares with the reader. The image of the poor housed in sewers and filing cabinets is a startling exaggeration which serves both poetry and propaganda. And the extreme imagery reinforces the basic divisions of the poem. On the one hand we have the heavy, the cold, the mechanical, and the closed-in darkness (mausoleum, iron, sewers, filing cabinets, and Chicago itself); on the other we have the light, the heat, and the organic (men, grass, meteor). Yet much of the impact of the poem comes from imagery that unexpectedly applies to both sides. People burn their body heat naturally, but they are also burned to death by mechanical means in Southeast Asia. And the state, which throughout the poem is associated with the cold and the mechanical, has a "vast rumbling gut" which digests its members—and we are shocked by the natural imagery in its unnatural context.

The basic imagery of "Visiting a Dead Man on a Summer Day"—even the title contains the basic contrast between cold and heat—is expanded throughout the rest of *Breaking Camp*, which itself progresses through summer and winter and ends with the approach of spring. "S. Dead," "Hallow Eve with Spaces for Ghosts," and "Landed Fish" (which concerns the death of her Uncle Danny) are other poems which treat the relationship between the living and the dead. Body heat between lovers is reflected in the stars of the cosmos, and the image of the meteor, so seemingly casual in the last parts of "Visiting a Dead Man" and "The Peaceable Kingdom" underlies the entire book, indeed her entire utopian vision. Everything and everybody loses heat. People burn—literally in Vietnam, figuratively in love, and even mythologically when the sun god visits a sunbather and burns her to ashes. In "A Few Ashes for Sunday Morning" she laments the loss of her own body heat.

> I'm telling you, this body could bake bread,
> heat a house, cure rheumatic pains,
> warm at least a bed.

But nobody profits from such energy.

> Reek of charred hair clotting in my lungs.
> My teeth are cinders,
> cured my lecherous tongue.
> Only me burnt, and warmed:
> no one.

In contrast "The Simplification" presents a capitalist, who like the poet, burns—but with coldness instead of heat. And his "burning" moves the business world.

> His face is burnished and dark, eclipsed sun
> whose eerie silver mane of corona shimmers.
> He is perhaps fatter. His cold touch burns,
> and he is reluctant to touch and gentle with words.
> Rooms revolve around him into silence.

Rooms *revolve* (beautiful word) around him like planets around a sun, and suddenly we move from the specific to the general. The basic opposition of the two systems results not only from their differences in America in the 1960's but from their elemental opposition throughout the galaxies of our universe.

But, as the title "The Simplification" suggests, the poet is not content to rest with such broad division between the good and the bad. In "The 184th Demonstration" she notes uneasily similarities between the two.

> we are well behaved like the police
> we march along the allotted route
> we sit down where we are supposed to
> to hear speakers approved by the committee
> when the speakers finish we disperse.

The ending, heroic and whimsical, stubborn and sad, leaves us with mixed feelings.

> Tomorrow is the 185th Demonstration
> will you be there?
> of course.

In the final poem of the book, "Breaking Camp," spring begins, but it brings no corresponding regeneration to the human spirit. "Peace," the poet confesses, "was a winter hope." Civilization appears to be breaking up; an atomic holocaust threatens.

> Soon we will be setting up camp on a
>   plain of nails.
> Soon we will be drinking blood out of
>   shattered bone.
> The dead will be stacked like bricks.
> The suns of power will dance on the
>   black sky
> and scorch us to dust.

The poet and her lover, isolated from the rest of the world, follow their star, though significantly it is a *private* star, an inward light, "the north star of your magnetic conscience." The community seems to have vanished.—VICTOR CONTOSKI, "Marge Piercy: A Vision of the Peacable Kingdom," *MPS*, Winter 1977, pp. 205–10

Almost alone among her American contemporaries, Marge Piercy is radical and writer simultaneously, her literary identity so indivisible that it is difficult to say where one leaves off and the other begins. The author of five previous novels and five books of poetry, ⟨. . .⟩ she has used her prose, particularly, to chronicle the lives of those society considers marginal—the young, the mad, the different—or those caught up in the forefront of movements for social change. Her new novel, *Vida*, which follows the life of a young woman radical from her emergence in the antiwar movement of the 1960's through her life in the underground network of the 1970's, evokes life in the radical movement so realistically that it seems at times more literal than imagined. Yet it is also a fully controlled, tightly structured dramatic narrative of such artful intensity that it leads the reader on at almost every page. As is often the case with radical fiction, it is the content rather than the formal characteristics that hold the mind, for it is not "simply" a novel but a political brief. I have my differences with *Vida*, but I think they are substantive rather than literary. It is an interesting—and challenging—book.

When the novel opens, the time is the present and Vida Asch is returning East from the West Coast to prepare for a gathering of the underground "network" leaders and to pick up some of the threads of her past. She does not surface—indeed, a large part of the book's action takes place "underground"— but she does see some of the people she had been close to before, members of that loose community of former comrades to which even those in the underground still belong. Her reunions, inevitably, are full of comparisons. Her husband has a new lover and is becoming less political. Her sister has her family and a full life in the women's movement. Intelligent, introspective, relatively free of illusions about the role of the underground in the politics of the 1970's, Vida "felt . . . as if she had outlived her own times, a creature produced by an earlier conglomeration of demands, judgments, necessities, passions, crises." But somewhere in her, the old political spirit still burns brightly, and she rarely has another thought for her future than to continue. It is a time of severe threat to the underground. Kevin, a comrade of long standing, has been picked up in New York. Two others are considering turning themselves in. To protect herself from their possible lapses, Vida shelters herself in a safe house by the sea that is also sheltering Joel, a lesser fugitive, wanted by the Army for desertion. It is in the context of their unfolding confidences that the story of the past, with all its tentacles in the present, is revealed.

1967: Optimism. Hope. A huge, spontaneous, democratic antiwar movement that believes all things are possible. 1970: Frustration as the war continues. The formation of secret collectives within the mass movement that undertake actions of their own. Infiltration. Violence. 1974: The wages of violence in a constricting, largely irrelevant, underground life. Vida's biography is a kind of microcosm of the period. 1967: Steering committee, Students Against the War. 1970: Membership in the Little Red Wagon, which specializes in bombing capitalist targets after the workers have gone home. One of the other members is an agent; there is a raid on their apartment, which harbors the bombs; Vida and two comrades carry out their last successful action and disappear. 1974: The penalties of history in the privations, dangers and—yes—satisfactions of a life lived almost wholly underground.

What is most remarkable about Miss Piercy's representations of each of these periods is the density and complexity with which they are drawn. Events change, organizations change, beliefs change, relationships change, all with a miscroscopic fidelity to actuality that is almost astounding. How, precisely, was this year different from that year? When, exactly, did one "line" succeed the next? Miss Piercy recalls it all. Demonstrations, political meetings, conversations in movement settings ranging from an apartment in Brooklyn to a hideout in Vermont—these, too, she reproduces with a passion to get it all straight that is the mark of a true calling. With such a mass of characters pulling and hauling in so many directions, it is a wonder that none of them gets away from her, but they do not. Vida, in particular, is completely credible throughout.

Nor does Miss Piercy stop at the past. The present, too, is thoroughly and richly detailed. Life is subtle in the underground, but it is far from over. There are meetings, there are arguments, there are decisions, there are even actions. There are families, there are friends, there are love affairs. For Vida there is, especially, Joel. Their direction may be lost as they flounder in the new realities of the 1970's, but in the rising tide of public awareness of new issues the underground will get its bearings again, and, meanwhile, there are old comrades all over the country still willing to lend a hand. "What swept through us and cast us forward is a force that will gather and rise again," thinks Vida, as she is flung back on her own resources for the last time. Marge Piercy has written about movement people before but never, I think, as lovingly as here. If you are looking to recommend to your students one book that would convey to them how it was in the movement of the 1960's and where it led, you might well want to consider *Vida*.

And yet, in a sense, that is exactly the problem. If a characteristic flaw of the radical literature of the 1930's, taken from the movement that inspired it, was pomposity, a characteristic flaw of the literature stemming from the 1960's may be juvenility. In the "present" sequences the characters are 10 years older than they were, but all their years and experiences have somehow failed to put weight on their bones. Throughout the novel, there is scarcely a significant character who holds views substantially departing from the opinions of the majority—or holds them strongly—and the ones who do are more or less figurine "enemies." In both language and thought, *Vida* is bound by the limitations of its period. The characters are far from stationary—indeed, they remake themselves constantly—but the re-examinations are superficial, taking place only within the framework of the movement. There is no perspective, there are not even any explanations. Why we are against the war, who the enemy is, what measures are justified against the state—all these are simply taken for granted. This hermetic quality is precisely the complaint outsiders had against the movement in life, and now here it is exacerbated in art, for if the movement itself was hermetic, the underground is inevitably more so. To read *Vida* is to be back in the atmosphere of the 1960's movement once again. Suffocating. But righteous.

This insular presentation of life in the movement is a political more than a literary matter, a deliberate decision, a product of the subordination of the novelist's detachment to the radical's allegiance. If the underground metaphor means that the necessities of survival will always dominate the possibilities of reappraisal, she will accept the limitation rather than alter the point of view. In Miss Piercy's view, it appears, there is nothing more to be said. The movement is dead. Long live the movement. Above all, she is loyal to her constituency. This is not only the way we were, but the way we are now, and not only the way we will but the way we ought to be. I do not happen to agree, yet it is a tribute to Miss Piercy's skill as a writer that it is as much the past as it is the book that I wish were otherwise. So far as the novel itself is concerned, I believe she has accomplished what she intended. In a recent poem,

"Sage and Rue," occasioned by the preparation of herbs from her garden, Miss Piercy concluded: "I praise things that remain themselves / Though cut off from what fed them, through transformations." She is praising the same thing in *Vida*.
—ELINOR LANGER, "After the Movement," *NYTBR*, Feb. 24, 1980, pp. 1, 36

MARGARET ATWOOD
"An Unfashionable Sensibility"
Nation, December 4, 1976, pp. 601–2

Marge Piercy now has eight books to her credit, four novels and four books of poetry. Her work has always had the courage both of her convictions and of its own (the difference between the two has occasionally been one of her problems), and the present books are no exception. She is a serious writer who deserves the sort of considered attention which, too often, she does not get.

For instance, none of the reviews of *Women on the Edge of Time* I've read to date even seems to have acknowledged its genre. Most have assumed that the book is intended as a realistic novel for that is certainly how it starts out. It appears to be the slice-of-life story of a 37-year-old Chicana welfare recipient named Consuelo, whose past history we are given in the first few pages of the book. Consuelo had a child, was deserted by her husband, and subsequently took up with a black, blind pickpocket whose death drove her into a depression in which she accidentally broke her daughter's wrist. For this offense she was committed to a mental institution and has had her child taken away from her. The only person left for her to love is her doped-up prostitute niece Dolly, but in defending Dolly she breaks the nose of Dolly's pimp and is recommitted by him. The rest of the book takes place "inside" (with one escape and one visit to the outside) and the descriptions of institutional life are enough to make the reader believe that Connie will be driven mad by sadistic doctors and indifferent attendants. This part of the book is rendered in excruciating, grotty, Zolaesque detail, pill by deadening pill, meal by cardboard meal, ordeal by ordeal, and as a rendition of what life in a New York bin is like for those without money or influence it is totally convincing and depressing.

However, even before Connie is recommitted she has been having visits from a strange creature named Luciente. Luciente turns out to be a visitor from the future; Connie thinks the visitor is a young man and is surprised when she is revealed as a woman. By making contact with Connie's mind, Luciente can help Connie project herself into the world of the future, Luciente's world. Connie travels there extensively, and needless to say the reader goes with her.

Some reviewers treated this part of the book as a regrettable daydream or even a hallucination caused by Connie's madness. Such an interpretation undercuts the entire book. If Connie is insane, her struggles to escape from the institution must be viewed in an entirely different light from that in which the author puts them, and the doctors, the pimp and the indifferent family are somewhat justified in their callous treatment. Other reviewers did not see Connie as insane but took Luciente and her troupe to be a pointless exercise in "science fiction," an exercise which should have no place in a piece of social realism. But Piercy is not that stupid. If she had intended a realistic novel she would have written one. *Woman on the Edge of Time* is a utopia, with all the virtues and shortcomings of the form, and many of the things reviewers found irksome are indigenous to the genre rather than the author.

By *utopia*, I mean books such as Morris's *News from Nowhere*, Bellamy's *Looking Backward*, Hudson's *A Crystal Age*, or even Wyndham's *Consider Her Ways*. These differ greatly from plot-centered otherworld fantasies such as Tolkien's, and though they may share some elements with "science fiction," this category is too broad for them. The books I've mentioned all send an emissary from an oppressive contemporary society into the future as a sort of tourist-journalist, to check out improved conditions and report back. Such books are not really about the hero's adventures, though a love affair of some sort is usually thrown in to sweeten the didactic pill. The real hero is the future society; the reader is intended to comparison-shop in company with the time-traveler, questioning the invariably polite inhabitants and grumbling over disconcerting details. The moral intent of such fables is to point out to us that our own undesirable conditions are not necessary: if things can be imagined differently, they can be done differently.

Hence, the inevitable long-winded conversations in which traveler and tour guide, in this case, Connie and Luciente, plod through the day-to-day workings of their societies. What about sewage disposal? birth control? ecology? education? Books of this sort *always* contain conversations like this, and it is to Piercy's credit that she has given us a very human and rather grouchy traveler and a guide who sometimes loses her temper. The world of the future depicted here is closest in spirit perhaps to Morris's. It's a village economy, with each village preserving the ethnic flavor of some worthy present-day minority: American Indian, American black, European Jewish (suburban WASP is not represented). It is, however, racially mixed, sexually equal, and ecologically balanced. Woman have "given up" childbirth in order that men won't regret having given up power, and children are educated more or less communally, with a modified apprentice system. There's quite a lot of advanced biofeedback, and instant communication through "kenners," which is uncomfortably reminiscent of silliness such as Dick Tracy's two-way wristwatch radios. But they do have communal "fooders," and, I'm happy to note, dishwashers.

Reading utopias is addictive—I found myself skipping through some perfectly acceptable passages about electric shock treatments and visiting hours at the asylum to find out what the inhabitants of Mattapoisett do about breast-feeding (both sexes indulge; men get hormone shots), about motherhood (bottle babies, elective "mothers," production in balance with nature's capacity to support it, adolescent separation rituals), about criminals (if incorrigible they're executed, because no one wants to be a prison guard), even about what they use to mulch the cabbages. Writing utopias is addictive too, and Piercy expends a good deal of energy trying to get every last detail *in*, to get it *right*, and to make rather too sure we get the point.

Numerous dangers await the author of a utopia. For one thing, inhabitants of utopias somehow cannot help coming across as slightly sanctimonious and preachy; they've been like that since More. And in addition all utopias suffer from the reader's secret conviction that a perfect world would be dull, so Piercy is careful to liven things up with festivals, ceremonies, nice clothes, and a hopeful description of untrammeled sexual interchange. There are problems, of course, but we are allowed to see the inhabitants working them out through council meetings and "wormings," a wonderful name for a session at which you accuse and complain. Some of these projections are a bit much: it's especially hard to write about communication between cats and humans in any way that isn't whimsical; and utopian children have difficulty being anything but cute or

bratty. But the language Piercy has devised for her utopians has unexpected felicities as well as its leaden moments; some of the utopian passages even manage to be oddly moving. The poignancy comes in part from Connie's hunger for human contact and love, some from the resemblances she sees between the utopians and her lost child, lover, and friends. The outer virtues of Mattapoisett are overshadowed by an inner one: it is the only place where Connie is loved.

However, several issues are dodged. The utopians refuse to fill Connie in on history, so we never find out much about how it all happened. They're engaged in a war with an enemy, but we don't learn much about this, either. And they tell Connie they are not "the" future, but only a possible future, and that they need her help in the present to avoid "winking out." (I wish this didn't sound so much like the resuscitation of Tinker Bell into *Peter Pan*.) At one point Connie stumbles into *another* future—presumably what will happen if we don't all put our shoulders to the wheel—in which women are termitelike objects, and the air is so polluted you can't see the sky. The Mattapoisett call to action only bewilders poor Connie, whose scope is of necessity limited. She ends by bumping off a few of the evil asylum shrinks, and because of the ambiguity of the last sections we're left with the uneasy feeling that Mattapoisett may have been a paranoid fantasy after all. The only evidence against this interpretation is that Connie isn't educated enough to have such a utopian vision.

This is a genre more at home in 19th-century England than in the America of the 1970s, where moral earnestness seems to have gone out of fashion. It's a daring thing for Piercy to have attempted, and it's entirely in keeping with her previous literary production that she should have done so. *Woman on the Edge of Time* is like a long inner dialogue in which Piercy answers her own questions about how a revised American society would work. The curious thing about serious utopias, as opposed to the satirical or entertainment variety, is that their authors never seem to write more than one of them; perhaps because they are products, finally, of the moral rather than the literary sense.

To turn from Piercy's utopia to her poetry is to turn from an imagined world to an imagination, from a sense to a sensibility. The poetry investigates the values which Mattapoisett assumes as axioms, and for this reason—although utopias intrigue me—I find the poetry more convincing. Piercy is committed to the search for honesty, however painful; to action, however futile; to getting it said and getting it done, however awkward the results may be. She's a feminist and a radical, but her poetry fleshes out these concepts in complex and sometimes startling ways, and she's no simpleminded sloganeer. "I ram on," she says of herself and her poetry; "I must make from this soft body some useful thing." And, most succinctly,

> Like the common blackbird I sit in the wind
> scrapping for my food, my place, my kind
> sometimes shrieking and sometimes singing.

Her poetry is "unfashionable," in that it is not flattish, understated, careful or bled. It reads as if she's never been in a creative writing class. The words crowd, lavish and lush, metaphors logjam, polemic rages, similes breed similes and sometimes unconscious puns, and it's all part of Piercy's earthy aesthetic:

> Better, I thought, for me in my rough being
> to force makeshift connections,
> patches, encounters, rows,
> better to swim in trouble like a muddy river rising
> than to become at last all thesis

correct, consistent but hollow
the finished ghost
of my own struggle.

And it *is* better, because out of all the surge and flux, the sometimes dutiful rhetoric, Piercy can build moments and sometimes whole poems that she would not have achieved with careful elegance. "People of the Shell," for instance, is superb, and it is not alone. Lines and aphorisms surface, flash and sink, poems transform themselves, words swirl. The literary ancestor here is not Dickinson but Whitman, and the vision is finally, despite the small ironies, a romantic one.

Like Whitman, Piercy must be read in chunks, not sips, and appreciated for her courage, gut energy and verbal fecundity, not for laconic polish. Dancing is hard and you may fall down, her poetry implies, but she is going to dance anyway. She rams on, and the reader can only applaud.

CELIA BETSKY
From "Talk with Marge Piercy"

New York Times Book Review, February 24, 1980, pp. 36–37

In the late 1960's, Marge Piercy was an organizer in the New York regional office of Students for a Democratic Society—one of those people who believed in taking their protests to the streets. It was a time, she recalls, of "rich alternatives, of possibility. I remember walking around with other organizers and fantasizing about what we would do after the revolution with all the buildings, what human uses they could be put to. What marvelous daycare centers and hospices they would become, what beautiful public places you could have and in what beautiful places people could finally live, when you didn't have the best part of Manhattan occupied by corporate headquarters and the houses of the wealthy."

Since then Miss Piercy has retreated to a more placid landscape. Wellfleet, on Cape Cod, where she now lives, seems empty in winter; the air is clear, the summer cottages are shuttered. "This is my area; I've walked every inch of it," she says. "I've been here since 1971, longer than anywhere else I've ever lived—though to the locals I'm still just a 'washashore.' I feel very attached to this piece of land, I have a very intimate relationship with it." It is also the source of her abundant nature poetry, which Miss Piercy, never one to shrink from assessing her own strengths and weaknesses, calls "some of the best being written." ⟨. . .⟩

Miss Piercy has never, as she puts it, "opted out of the struggle." "I am political as thoroughly as I am alive or female," she once wrote. "The two issues I'm hottest about at the moment are nukes and saving abortion rights, especially for women without a lot of money. It's an issue I've cared about since I was 17. And I live right across from the Pilgrim Pond reactor: It turns out there's no way to evacuate the Cape. It's also one of the worst industries for not protecting its workers."

In 1969, when she realized that women in the movement were being treated "with very little equality" by their male comrades, Miss Piercy decided to leave the antiwar movement and devote herself to the feminist cause. Among the rights that women have yet to win, she argues, is "control over our own bodies." The novel Miss Piercy is working on at the moment, set in the 1950's, is concerned in part with "how the illegality and fear of abortion shaped women's lives. It's about trying, in the situation of the 50's, to establish oneself as a woman, to discover what one is." Her work addresses itself to "many buried lives, especially the lives of women who have never heard what they must hear said."

Vida, the eponymous heroine of her new novel, is the quintessential activist. "One of the things that has struck me is that women have been tremendously important politically in the United States from the beginning. When you look at the Abolitionists, the feminists who came out of the Abolitionists, at labor organizing, women have been workhorses of every movement as well as charismatic figures—writers, speakers, extremists, from Elizabeth Cady Stanton to Mother Jones. But except in very recent fiction by women, American literature uses women usually as love objects—Thurber's housewife, or the sort of figure Huckleberry Finn runs away from. In Henry James, they're viewed as neurasthenic and neurotic. There's a real lack of portraits of political women."

Miss Piercy's politics are inseparable from her literary convictions: "The notion that politics have nothing to do with art is a very modern heresy. Alexander Pope wouldn't have known what we were talking about, nor would Catullus. Nor would Homer, for that matter. For most of the world's history, poets have thought of themselves as human beings in a social web, with the same duties in the public sphere as anyone else, with the same set of human interests. My art is political, but no more political than a lot of art not so labeled, which also contains strong notions about what's immoral, moral, what's good and bad, having and getting, who's smart and who's stupid."

In *Vida* Miss Piercy tried "to make real how the war felt to those of us who were living then, how dirty, how compromised—that if you didn't end the war, you didn't deserve to live." For Vida, political responsibility has implications in one's private life. "More things go wrong because of people's inability to deal with each other, with their own feelings about each other or their own reactions, than from any kind of ideological conflict—even though differences may be fought out in the ideological realm."

In the novel, being a fugitive reflects more general conflicts: "The fugitive seemed to be an interesting and rather rich metaphor for an extreme type of woman's experience, but nonetheless one which connected up with all women's experiences. It seems to be one very common dream of women to dream about being hunted, chased, pursued, harried."

Miss Piercy's recent work celebrates the special bond that she feels exists between women. Her own brief and unhappy marriage to a French physicist left her so bitter that she won't talk about it, though she jokes that "what I really regret is that I was so hostile afterward I lost most of my French." She has no children and intends never to have any; she considers her books her offspring, freely offered to the world. "I cut the umbilical cord very cleanly. I know that once something is published it belongs to other people and not to me."

Not surprisingly, most of the writers Miss Piercy admires are women. "I have a heroine: Simone de Beauvoir. I can't imagine anyone else in the world I would absolutely fall on my face in front of. Sartre was important also." She enjoys reading Margaret Atwood and Audre Lorde, June Jordan, Toni Morrison, Alice Walker, Adrienne Rich, Philip Levine, Elizabeth Fisher *(Woman's Creation)*, Dorothy Dinnerstein *(The Mermaid and the Minotaur)*. She calls such books "useful"—a compliment in Miss Piercy's vocabulary. One of her own books is entitled *To Be of Use.*

Vida is only the most recent in a long line of lesbian or bisexual characters in her work—a reflection of her own involvement with women. "To me it is political for women to be free to choose to have relationships with other women; it's an important option." In *The High Cost of Living* (1978), the novel that preceded *Vida*, she "wanted to write about a lesbian protagonist, and that would just be a given. But the book was much more about class, about how hard it is for working-class kids growing up, kids who could expect to move up in class but find they can't without paying an extravagant price."

Growing up white in a predominantly black community, Miss Piercy thought of herself as "somewhere between black and white." During the 70's, Miss Piercy avoided using minority-group characters in her work. "But I finally decided that I was a writer and that I had to write responsibly, and I couldn't write without writing about racism in the United States. And you can't write about racism if you only write about white people."

Detroit, with its "high energy, good music and its contradictions," was a significant influence on her work. "You see class so clearly there: the indifference of the rich, racism, the strength of different groups, the working-class pitted against itself." Miss Piercy's central characters tend to come from this background, and she ascribes her fascination with "class fate" to her own origins: "My father repaired and installed heavy industrial machinery all over Detroit. My mother was a housewife, she never even finished the 10th grade. My mother made me: she taught me how to look at things, to observe, to notice."

Miss Piercy contends that her mother is a psychic, and she herself is drawn to Tarot cards, the lunar calendar and witchcraft. "I have a strong sense of the power of the nonrational," a sense evident in her poetry: "It is utterance shaped into artifact. It has a healing function. It combines all the different ways of knowing that we have, analytically, synthetically—the sort of gestalt grasping of images. We know through dream images, in many of the same ways that other mammals know, that reptiles know: by senses, sense memory, rhythms. I feel that when I write poems I can speak directly out of my own life, or through masks, when I choose. Other people's lives can speak through me. Art dignifies and validates experience. You can recite poetry to people. A momentary community is created, a ritual."

Poetry can also be the source of what Miss Piercy calls "a new consciousness": "We would be more fully social, more responsible to each other, aware, gentle, open, respectful of our differences. People would be free to concentrate on more creative problems." Best of all, the world would not be run by those who run it now, "nutty and greedy old men."

No matter what the successes and failures of the past few decades, however, there is revolution and revolution. "You know, nothing ever stays the same. The great gift of the 60's was the sense that everybody could change, anything could be done. I still have it, but not with the same euphoria. The other great gift was the sense of community. I learned a lot about other people in that time, how they change in struggle, how extraordinarily people change. The 60's have been caricatured and merchandised. In *Vida*, I wanted to restore them as they were."

SYLVIA PLATH

1932–1963

Sylvia Plath, poet and novelist, was born in Boston in 1932. Her father, who died when she was eight, was a German immigrant professor and entomologist. She attended Smith College in Massachusetts on a scholarship endowed by Olive Higgins Prority, who later befriended her. In 1953 she had a nervous breakdown and left school; she was eventually able to return, however, and graduated in 1955. A Fulbright Fellowship allowed her to continue her studies in England, at Newnham College. In February 1956 she met her future husband, the English poet Ted Hughes, and in April of that year they were married. She received her M.A. from Cambridge in 1957 and moved with her husband to the United States, where she took a teaching position at Smith College. By 1958 she had stopped teaching, and in the following year she worked briefly as a secretary in the office for records of mental patients in the Massachusetts General Hospital in Boston; she and her husband then returned to England, where they lived in London. Sylvia Plath's daughter Frieda was born in April 1960, and later that year Plath's poem *A Winter Ship*, was published. Before moving to Devon in the fall of 1961 she wrote her autobiographical novel *The Bell Jar*, based on her breakdown in college. In January 1962 her second child, Nicholas, was born, and then in October she and her husband separated and she moved back to London with her two children. In January 1963 *The Bell Jar*, published under the pseudonym "Victoria Lucas," came out in London, after having been rejected by two U.S. publishers. On February 11, 1963, Sylvia Plath committed suicide.

Ariel, Sylvia Plath's best-known book, was published in 1965; it is a collection of poems written in 1962 and 1963, and was edited by Ted Hughes. *Crossing the Water* (1971), also edited by Hughes, contains most of the poems written during the two-and-a-half years between the completion of *The Colossus* and July 1962. Also in 1971 appeared *Winter Trees*, consisting of eighteen uncollected late poems together with Plath's verse play for radio, *Three Women*, which was written in early 1962. *Johnny Panic and the Bible of Dreams* (1977) is a collection of prose, the title story of which reflects her experiences at the Massachusetts General Hospital. *Letters Home* (1975) is a selection of correspondence edited by her mother, A. S. Plath. The *Collected Poems*, edited by Ted Hughes and published in 1981, were awarded a Pulitzer Prize. Her *Journals* were published in 1982.

Personal

As I was reading the poem 'Daddy' for the first time, I suddenly recalled my earliest impression of Sylvia Plath, before I knew who she was. It was at the opening lecture of my course on Henry James, at the beginning of the Michaelmas term 1955, Sylvia's first year at Cambridge. I had walked into the Mill Lane lecture-room a few minutes early, and was gazing idly at my new audience, observing that it was small and probably wondering whether it was also choice. As I gazed, I noticed a conspicuously tall girl standing in one of the aisles, facing towards me, and staring at me intently. I was struck by the concentrated intensity of her scrutiny, which gave her face an ugly, almost coarse, expression, accentuated by the extreme redness of her heavily painted mouth and its downward turn at the corners. I distinctly remember wondering whether she was Jewish. This was a thought that could not have occurred to me more than half a dozen times in all my thirteen years at Cambridge; one somehow never wondered whether people were or were not Jewish, unless presumably the Jewish marks were especially prominent. The tall girl with the face distorted by the intensity of her interest, curiosity, whatever it was, must have seemed to me to show the marks in this way, or I cannot imagine why the thought should have crossed my mind. I have remembered it often since, with the strangest emotions, as more and more has come to be known about her passionate feeling for Jews and her sense of belonging with them.

I never again, literally never, saw that expression on Sylvia's face in all the time I knew her at Cambridge. Only when at the time of her death the London *Observer* published a picture of her, along with Alvarez's moving notice, I seemed to catch a glimpse of it again, in the wildly feverishly staring eyes of that dreadful unfamiliar face, the desperate-defiant look in the eye somehow intensified by the distaff of unkempt hair hanging about her shoulders.

There was nothing wild, feverish or defiant, and nothing unkempt, about the Sylvia Plath who came to me for supervision on the English Moralists from the second or third term of that year 1955–6. I see her clearly at this moment before my mind's eye, sitting on the sofa in my small sitting-room at 111 Grantchester Meadows: always neat and fresh, wearing charming, girlish clothes, the kind of clothes that made you look at the girl, not the garments; hair down to the shoulders still, but ever so neatly brushed and combed, and held back in place by a broad bandeau on the crown. I remember the bandeau because I think I never saw her without it; my first irrelevant thought as I stared, stupefied, at the picture in the *Observer* was 'Where is the bandeau? It *can't* be her—she's not wearing her bandeau.' This charming American neatness and freshness is what I chiefly recall about her physical person, even more than her beauty; though she was of course beautiful, as Wendy Campbell says, as we must have said to each other often enough. She seemed also, I remember, less tall than she was, because she did not hold herself in a tall girl's way: always straight and graceful, but somehow humble at the same time, which had the effect of diminishing her physical height.

This effect was produced even more by the typical expression of her face. Eager and mobile, tranquil and serene, all at once: I never saw her face express anything else in the many long supervision hours we spent together. I did not think of her as one of my most 'brilliant' pupils (I shall return to this point); I thought of her rather as one of the most deeply, movingly, responsive pupils I had ever had. I felt the things I said, we said, her authors said, mattered to her in an intimate way, answering to intense personal needs, reaching to depths of her spirit to which I had no direct access (and didn't mind not having, being satisfied with the visible effects). ⟨. . .⟩

⟨Our⟩ relationship, it will already be clear, was mainly impersonal, or non-personal: the teacher-pupil relationship, full of the warmth, affection, appreciation that its blessed communications so often breed, particularly in the Cambridge setting and atmosphere with its magical power of encouraging the growth of intellectual intimacies. Ours were indeed almost exclusively intellectual; and though the mutual impact of personalities was an inseparable part of them, and the teacher's upon the pupil's was bound to be stronger than the other way about (the teacher having always the unfair advantage of a more developed personality to make the impact), I was never conscious of its intruding upon the sacred ground on which our minds met. Sylvia was extraordinarily modest, self-effacing, unassuming, unspoilt; never inviting attention to herself, seeming to want only the selfless intellectual relationship. I remember noting and appreciating it at the time; I think of it now—now that I know the full extent of the personality that refused to claim attention—with the utmost tenderness and admiration.

The more personal side of our friendship developed, I seem to recall, from the time of her marriage to Ted Hughes. I became involved in this for reasons serious enough for Sylvia at the start, though in the end amusing as well. At the beginning of the Michaelmas term 1956, her second year at Cambridge, Sylvia appeared, extremely agitated, to tell me that she had 'secretly' married Ted during the long vacation, that they had had a marvellous summer in Spain, ecstatically happy, wonderfully productive—happy, obviously, because they adored each other, productive because (she said) they had both managed to write a great deal. But now the hour of reckoning had come: she had got married without tutorial permission, and had up to now kept it from tutorial knowledge (this is what she meant by saying she had done it 'secretly', which I had at first not understood), she was afraid now that her outraged college would recommend that her Fulbright scholarship be taken away, in which case she would have to leave Cambridge and come away without a degree, and please *what* was she to do?

I was a little taken aback, I remember, by the intensity of her fear and agitation, and, even more perhaps, by what I sensed to be a strong suppressed resentment: presumably, at Cambridge rules and practices, Cambridge dons and their demands, the Cambridge set-up as a whole perhaps. It was the first and the only time I glimpsed in Sylvia (without, of course, at the time knowing it for what it was) a small touch of the passionate *rage* which has since come to be recognised as a dominating emotion of her poetry, especially her last poems.

The problem of the illicit marriage was soon resolved. To mollify her resentment, I said some soothing things about the idiocy of Cambridge rules, and that the only way to live with them was not to take their idiocy too much to heart. I suggested that she go to her tutor, make a full confession of her crime, express a decent (though not abject) regret about not having asked permission, and plead love, passion, the marriage of true minds, and so on, as the irresistible cause. She was not however (I urged) to 'criticise' the immortal rules or moralise about their iniquity. I knew her tutor to be a warm-hearted, rather romantic person, who I felt was likely to take a kindly view of Sylvia's lapse. And so in the event it turned out. Within a day or two Sylvia came back, happy and beaming. Her tutor had been completely charming, kind, understanding; she would not have her Fulbright award taken away; and she could now go and live with her legally recognised husband in any convenient place in Cambridge.

Soon after this, she and Ted moved into a small flat in Eltisley Avenue, just round the corner from my own place in Grantchester Meadows. She was passionately, brilliantly, happy: incandescent with happiness, as Wendy Campbell has beautifully said. She spoke about it from time to time; and I remember at least once experiencing a thrill of fear at the idyllic pitch and intensity of her happiness. What would happen (I said, or half-said, to myself) if something should ever *go wrong* with this marriage of true minds? Nothing of course would, nothing *could*, go wrong: I was sublimely sure of this. Yet if, inconceivably, it should, she would suffer terribly; I held my breath to think how she would suffer. That was as far as my momentary fear carried my imagination; nor was it possible it should go further, in the face of her serenity, her tranquility, her confidence, and (most of all) her marvellous vitality, which seemed a guarantee of limitless powers of resistance. ⟨. . .⟩

By a strange poignant coincidence, she chose to die on my birthday, 11 February. It could not have been anything but coincidence, and I am not a superstitious person; but it has haunted and oppressed me ever since I have known. Following a traditional Jewish custom, I have each year since her death burnt a candle in her memory on that day: the tallest, handsomest I could find, of a brilliant jewel colour if possible. The custom is simple and beautiful, and would I think have appealed to her imagination. You light the candle in the morning, and it burns quietly all day, letting you forget it most of the time as you go about your usual tasks; but each time you notice it, it meets your eyes, steadily, silently, a true *memento mori*. Though I hate and fear death, I am glad I am prevented from forgetting hers. My birthday, her deathday, a last sad, precious bond.—DOROTHEA KROOK, "Recollections of Sylvia Plath," *CQ*, Winter 1976, pp. 5–14

I knew her for a while in Boston. We did grow up in the same suburban town, Wellesley, Massachusetts, but she was about four years behind me and we never met. Even if we had, I wonder if we would have become close friends, back then— she was so bright, so precocious and determined to be special while I was only a pimply boy-crazy thing, flunking most subjects, thinking I was never special. We didn't meet, at any rate, until she was married to Ted Hughes and living in Boston. We met because we were poets. Met, not for protocol, but for truth. She heard, and George Starbuck heard, that I was auditing a class at Boston University given by Robert Lowell. They kind of followed me in, joined me there and so we orbited around the class silently. If we talked at all then we were fools. We knew too much about it to talk. Silence was wiser, when we could command it. We tried, each one in his own manner; sometimes letting our own poems come up, as for a butcher, as for a lover. Both went on. We kept as quiet as possible in view of the father.

Then, after the class, we would pile into the front seat of my old Ford and I would drive quickly through the traffic to, or near, The Ritz. I would always park illegally in a LOADING ONLY ZONE, telling them gayly, "It's okay, because we are only going to get loaded!" Off we'd go, each on George's arm, into The Ritz to drink three or four or two martinis. George even has a line about this in his first book of poems, *Bone Thoughts*. He wrote, *I weave with two sweet ladies out of The Ritz.* Sylvia and I, such sleep mongers, such death mongers, were those two sweet ladies.

In the lounge-bar of The Ritz, not a typical bar at all, but very plush, deep dark red carpeting, red leather chairs around polite little tables and with waiters, white coated and awfully hushed where one knew upon stepping down the five velvet red steps that he was entering *something*, we entered. The waiters knew their job. They waited on the best of Boston, or at least, celebrities. We always hoped they'd make a mistake in our case and think us some strange Hollywood types. There had to be something to explain all our books, our snowboots, our clutter of poems, our oddness, our quick and fiery conversations—and always the weekly threesome hunched around their small but fashionable table.

Often, very often, Sylvia and I would talk at length about our first suicides; at length, in detail and in depth between the free potato chips. Suicide is, after all, the opposite of the poem. Sylvia and I often talked opposites. We talked death with burned-up intensity, both of us drawn to it like moths to an electric light bulb. Sucking on it! She told the story of her first suicide in sweet and loving detail and her description in *The Bell Jar* is just the same story. It is a wonder that we didn't depress George with our egocentricity. Instead, I think, we three were stimulated by it, even George, as if death made each of us a little more real at the moment. Thus we went on, in our fashion, ignoring Lowell and the poems left behind. Poems left behind were technique—lasting but, actually, over. We talked death and this was life for us, lasting in spite of us, or better, because of us, our intent eyes, our fingers clutching the glass, three pairs of eyes fixed on someone's—each one's gossip. I know that such fascination with death sounds strange (one does not argue that it isn't sick—one knows it *is*—there's no excuse), and that people cannot understand. They keep, every year, each year, asking me "why, why?" ⟨. . .⟩

After this we would weave out of The Ritz to spend our last pennies at The Waldorf Cafeteria—a dinner for 70 cents. George was in no hurry. He was separating from his wife. Sylvia's Ted was either able to wait or was busy enough with his own work and I had to stay in the city (I live outside of it) for a 7 p.m. appointment with my psychiatrist. A funny three.

I have heard since that Sylvia was determined from childhood to be great, a great writer at the least of it. I tell you, at the time I did not notice this in her. Something told me to bet on her but I never asked it why. I was too determined to bet on myself to actually notice where she was headed in her work. Lowell said, at the time, that he liked her work and that he felt her poems got right to the point. I didn't agree. I felt they really missed the whole point. (These were early poems of hers— poems on the way, on the working toward way.) I told Mr. Lowell that I felt she dodged the point and did so perhaps because of her preoccupation with form. Form was important for Sylvia and each really good poet has one of his own. No matter what he calls it—free verse or what. Still, it belongs to you or it doesn't. Sylvia hadn't then found a form that belonged to her. Those early poems were all in a cage (and not even her own cage at that). I felt she hadn't found a voice of her own, wasn't, in truth, free to be herself. Yet, of course, I knew she was skilled—intense, skilled, perceptive, strange, blonde, lovely, Sylvia.

From England to America we exchanged a few letters. I have them now, of course. She mentions my poems and perhaps I sent her new ones as I wrote—I'm not sure. The time of the LOADING ZONE ONLY was gone as now we sent aerograms back and forth, now and then. George was in Rome. He never wrote. He divorced and remarried over there. Sylvia wrote of one child, keeping bees, another child, my poems— happy, gossip-letters, and then, with silence between us, she died.

After her death, with the printing of her last poems, I read that she gave me credit on a BBC program, credit as an influence upon her work. Certainly she never told me anything about it. But then, maybe she wouldn't have—nothing that ordinary, nothing that direct. She gave me and Robert Lowell (both is a rather casual lump, Sylvia!) credit for our breakthrough into the personal in poetry. I suppose we might have shown her something about daring—daring to tell it true. W. D. Snodgrass showed me in the first place. Perhaps he influenced Robert Lowell too—I can't speak for him. But let's get down to facts. I'm sure Sylvia's influences are hidden, as with most of us, and if one feels compelled to name an influence then let us begin with Theodore Roethke. I remember writing to Sylvia in England after *The Colossus* came out and saying something like . . . "if you're not careful, Sylvia, you will out-Roethke Roethke", and she replied that I had guessed accurately and that he had been a strong influence on her work. Believe me, no one ever tells one's real influences—and certainly not on the radio or the TV or in interviews, if he can help it. As a matter of fact, I probably guessed wrong and she was lying to me. She ought to. I'd never tell anyone and she was smarter than I am about such hidden things. Poets will not only hide influences. They will bury them! And not that her lines reminded me of Roethke—but the openness to mataphor, the way they both have (and Sylvia even more so in her last work) of jumping straight into their own image and then believing it. No doubt of it—at the end, Sylvia burst from her cage and came riding straight out with the image-ridden-darer, Roethke. But maybe she buried her so called influence deeper than that, deeper than any one of us would think to look, and if she did I say good luck to her. Her poems do their own work. I don't need to sniff them for distant relatives of some sort. I'm against it. Maybe I did give her a sort of daring, but that's all she should have said. That's all that's similar about our work. Except for death—yes, we have that in common (and there must be enough other poets with that theme to fill an entire library). Never mind last diggings. They don't matter. What matters is her poems. These last poems stun me. They eat time.—ANNE SEXTON, "The Barfly Ought to Sing," *TriQ*, Fall 1966, pp. 89–93

I first met Sylvia Plath in February 1962, almost exactly a year before her death; her daughter Frieda was nearly three and Nick was a month old. She and Ted had bought Court Green, a beautiful seventeenth-century thatched house in North Tawton, a tiny mill town in mid-Devon.

My first impression of Sylvia was of a tall, slim, vividly alive young woman, with waist-length brown hair. She wore a long skirt and dark stockings, which was unusual for those days, and I admit to being enchanted by her and Ted and the beautiful house.

As they were in the process of furnishing Court Green we sat and had tea in the playroom on deckchairs by a long trestle table which Sylvia had painted white and decorated with little enamelled flowers. The room had a black and white tiled floor like a Flemish painting and looked out onto a lawn with a laburnum tree, and beyond was the orchard and village church and graveyard. One wall of the room was shelves full of children's books, many of which Sylvia had reviewed for the American press, and there was a piano in the room which Sylvia admitted to 'trying to play, but I have no ear'.

Ted and my (then) husband David, who was also a writer, at once began writers' talk of agents and publishers, and our small son James set up the watchful parallel-play of the three-year-old with Frieda.

Sylvia's approach to me was all questions—children, home, interests and politics. When I admitted to being a

member of the Liberal Party she jumped up and almost shouted 'Thank God, a committed woman' which made me smile as it wasn't totally true, but pleasing. We discussed national policies on armaments, and she told me with bitter anger of the involvement of American big business with weaponry. She obviously cared deeply about her country, and felt its imperfections personally.

The baby was asleep in his pram under the laburnum tree, and Sylvia kept running out to see if he was warm and sleeping well. She told me of her bees and the vegetables she was growing and the plans they had for the house—'We shall have five children, the boys will sleep here and the girls there. This is Ted's writing room, here is where Nick was born.'

She had painted brilliant little hearts and flowers on her sewing machine, a doll's cradle and even the door sills; later she told me she had decorated her beehives too. 'Now bees land on *my* flowers.' So much energy, such intensity of experience and expression. I felt then a sense of urgency in her to do everything and to do it now, a pressure on her and in her towards excellence which was both stimulating and daunting, but made me afraid for her.

I told her of our remote North Devon mill house, with no electricity and well water, which delighted the purist in her. She hated smoking and phoney packet food. Frieda had dates and nuts instead of sweets, and Sylvia made delicious banana bread with whole flour which we ate for tea.

At this stage I didn't know of her literary talent; I knew that she was a writer, but of what and with what success I had no idea. Neither she nor Ted gave any indication of this; all Sylvia's literary talk with me was of Ted's brilliance and successes, and her grave pride in him was most moving.

When we were leaving we made plans for them to visit us, and she spoke of Devon as the first place she had really felt at home, the ancient roots which she so desperately desired and had never found in America. Her 'wall of old corpses' which she 'loved like history'—from the poem 'Letter in November'—has been construed by some critics as morbid schizophrenic imagery, but in fact the boundary of her orchard was formed by the bank below the churchyard, topped by ranks of ancient gravestones. She valued their quiet presence.

I was the wife of a poor and hard-working author with very little time for discovering myself or my own potential. Bringing up three children in a primitive remote cottage on a tiny and fluctuating income took all my energy and mental strength; therefore Sylvia conceived a picture of me which was very incomplete and in some ways unreal. I think one of her faults was a tendency to see what she wanted in people, rather than what was there.

We did talk a great deal about books—I was perfect for market research, having read avidly from the age of four but entirely without academic training or critical analysis. My pleasure in poetry and prose must have been refreshing to a writer, I suppose.

My concentration on homemaking and child-rearing in such an out-of-date and rural setting made me something of an Earth Mother figure for Sylvia, and she had a need to see me as such. She once said: 'You must never leave here, I see you with your little twinkly lights always round you.' (She meant our smoky oil lamps.) Later she said that we were to appear as saints in the novel she was writing about North Tawton. 'For God's sake don't let my pseudonym get around or I shall be sued.'

When they came to visit us I felt the impact of their stature, and their unassailable closeness, a 'keep out' sign which one respected totally, the reactions to life which needed no words between them. I have a picture of them together leaning over an ancient stone bridge gazing down into the peat-brown Devon trout stream below our house, entranced and silent with a quality of utter concentration usual only in children.

I first learnt of Sylvia's work from Ted some weeks later when I asked 'Does Sylvia write poetry too?' Ted answered 'No, she *is* a poet'. ⟨. . .⟩

Over these months I got to know Sylvia, I recognised a timidity and fearfulness which she often cloaked with defensive acerbity. I saw her being extremely entertaining and humorous with our Devon friends from whom she felt no threat, I learnt of her love of riding and the pleasure she got from gathering wood and lighting incense-smelling fires. She was very greedy but never put on any weight. I remember her gleeful face at lunch one day telling me how much she loved food. Little Nick's face peered over the edge of our farmhouse table, as he sat on her knee, with brilliant dark eyes watching everything and I swear he looked gleeful and greedy too. We laughed about that so much. I once asked her if she had made one particularly light and beautiful sponge cake from a packet; she turned on me in a fury and said 'I separated and whipped those eggs for twenty minutes.' I hastily apologised.

This same intensity and joy showed itself also in her wish to share in any vivid experience or special knowledge one had. We spent hours talking about music and plants. Her real delight was to discover that someone knew something that she did not; she would turn and stare piercingly into one's face. 'I didn't know you knew about *that*. How marvelous. Tell me all about it.' I was told a story, after her death, of how Sylvia had met a girl on a bus in London, and finding she was a potter insisted on accompanying the girl back to her flat to be shown and told 'all about it'. This is so typical of her that I'm sure it's true.

On my thirty-fourth birthday (in July) she and Ted arrived unexpectedly in the evening. He was bringing a bottle of wine and she carried a glorious iced cake wrapped in her beautiful shawl. She had baked and iced the cake and put thirty-five candles on it—'One for you to grow on', she said.

No one gave Sylvia one candle to grow on. Seven months later she was dead.

We talked so much and planned trips to the sea; the children had grown fond of each other and the assumption was that we should know each other for years. There was no hint of any trouble to come, no mention of any worries about Ted, and only some slight anxiety she felt about her mother's visit, but I could only assume later that it was pride and also fear of admitting her worries that kept her from talking to me before the actual break occurred.

It was a terrible shock when it happened with no warning. Sylvia arrived one evening not long after my birthday with Nick in his carry cot. The change in her was appalling. She kept saying 'My milk has dried up, I can't feed Nick. My milk has gone.' At last she told me that Ted was in love with another woman, Assia Wevill, who was the wife of a Canadian poet and had stayed with Ted and Sylvia at Court Green soon after Nick's birth. She wept and wept and held onto my hands saying 'Help me'. What could I do? I have never felt so inadequate in my life. She said 'Ted lies to me, he lies all the time, he has become a little man'. The most frightening thing she said was: 'When you give someone your whole heart and he doesn't want it, you cannot take it back. It's gone forever.'

I knew that this was the truth, I had seen it in her. Having seen them together so often and sensed the minute and powerful filaments of perception and understanding between them, I knew that to break these would be for Sylvia the greatest agony imaginable.

Brought up, as she was, in a male orientated society, conditioned to develop all the competitive striving intellectual side of her nature, this life with Ted here in Devon, with all its sane roots in history and the natural cycles of planting and harvesting, birth and death, had allowed her to begin to recognise and feel her female self. With this flowering came the terrible vulnerability of all dependent creatures.

She stayed that night with us, refusing to take our bed and sleeping on the sofa. First thing next morning I came down to find her bending over a box containing a cat and her new kittens. I see her now, wearing a pink woolly dressing gown with a long brown plait of hair falling into the box, turning her head and saying 'I never saw anything so small and new and vulnerable. They are blind.' ⟨. . .⟩

Her last letter to me was all plans, dated February 7, 1963. She was coming back to Devon ('Thank God you are there'), she was to be on 'The Critics' and was to compere a poetry reading. *Punch* had asked for some articles and she had got Frieda into a nursery school for a while. She said 'I shall miss all my daffodils' (the orchard of Court Green was full of them). She had considered letting it but couldn't. 'Court Green. The thought of other people living there hurts me.' She wrote to Nancy by the same post, saying much the same things, and asking her to have the two cats, Tiger and Skunky, doctored: 'I don't want to come home to a house full of kittens.' She wrote: 'I long to see my home, and will be back soon.' Four days later she was dead.—ELIZABETH SIGMUND, "Sylvia, 1962: A Memoir," *NeR*, May 1976, pp. 63–65

Why ⟨. . .⟩ did she kill herself? In part, I suppose, it was "a cry for help" which fatally misfired. But it was also a last desperate attempt to exorcise the death she had summed up in her poems. I have already suggested that perhaps she had begun to write obsessively about death for two reasons. First, when she and her husband separated, however mutual the arrangement, she again went through the same piercing grief and bereavement she had felt as a child when her father, by his death, seemed to abandon her. Second, I believe she thought her car crash the previous summer had set her free; she had paid her dues, qualified as a survivor and could now write about it. But as I have written elsewhere, for the artist himself art is not necessarily therapeutic; he is not automatically relieved of his fantasies by expressing them. Instead, by some perverse logic of creation, the act of formal expression may simply make the dredged-up material more readily available to him. The result of handling it in his work may well be that he finds himself living it out. For the artist, in short, nature often imitates art. Or, to change the cliché, when an artist holds up a mirror to nature he finds out who and what he is; but the knowledge may change him irredeemably so that he becomes that image.

I think Sylvia, in one way or another, sensed this. In an introductory note she wrote to "Daddy" for the BBC, she said of the poem's narrator, "She has to act out the awful little allegory once over before she is free of it." The allegory in question was, as she saw it, the struggle in her between a fantasy Nazi father and a Jewish mother. But perhaps it was also a fantasy of containing in herself her own dead father, like a woman possessed by a demon (in the poem she actually calls him a vampire). In order for her to be free of him, he had to be released like a genie from a bottle. And this is precisely what the poems did: they bodied forth the death within her. But they also did so in an intensely living and creative way. The more she wrote about death, the stronger and more fertile her imaginative world became. And this gave her everything to live for.

I suspect that in the end she wanted to have done with the theme once and for all. But the only way she could find was "to act out the awful little allegory once over." She had always been a bit of a gambler, used to taking risks. The authority of her poetry was in part due to her brave persistence in following the thread of her inspiration right down to the Minotaur's lair. And this psychic courage had its parallel in her physical arrogance and carelessness. Risks didn't frighten her; on the contrary, she found them stimulating. Freud has written: "Life loses in interest, when the highest stake in the game of living, life itself, may not be risked." Finally, Sylvia took that risk. She gambled for the last time, having worked out that the odds were in her favor, but perhaps, in her depression, not much caring whether she won or lost. Her calculations went wrong and she lost.

It was a mistake, then, and out of it a whole myth has grown. I don't think she would have found it much to her taste, since it is a myth of the poet as a sacrificial victim, offering herself up for the sake of her art, having been dragged by the Muses to that final altar through every kind of distress. In these terms, her suicide becomes the whole point of the story, the act which validates her poems, gives them their interest and proves her seriousness. So people are drawn to her work in much the same spirit as *Time* magazine featured her at length: not for the poetry but for the gossipy, extraliterary "human interest." Yet just as the suicide adds nothing at all to the poetry, so the myth of Sylvia as a passive victim is a total perversion of the woman she was. It misses altogether her liveliness, her intellectual appetite and harsh wit, her great imaginative resourcefulness and vehemence of feeling, her control. Above all, it misses the courage with which she was able to turn disaster into art. The pity is not that there is a myth of Sylvia Plath, but that the myth is not simply that of an enormously gifted poet whose death came carelessly, by mistake and too soon.

I used to think of her brightness as a façade, as though she were able, in a rather schizoid way, to turn her back on her suffering for the sake of appearance, and pretend it didn't exist. But maybe she was also able to keep her unhappiness in check because she could write about it, because she knew she was salvaging from all those horrors something rather marvelous. The end came when she felt she could stand the subject no longer. She had written it out and was ready for something new.

> The blood jet is poetry,
> There is no stopping it.

The only method of stopping it she could see, her vision by then blinkered by depression and illness, was that last gamble. So having, as she thought, arranged to be saved, she lay down in front of the gas oven almost hopefully, almost with relief, as though she were saying, "Perhaps this will set me free."

On Friday, February 15, there was an inquest in the drab, damp coroner's court behind Camden Town: muttered evidence, long silences, the Australian girl in tears. Earlier that morning I had gone with Ted to the undertaker's in Mornington Crescent. The coffin was at the far end of a bare, draped room. She lay stiffly, a ludicrous ruff at her neck. Only her face showed. It was gray and slightly transparent, like wax. I had never before seen a dead person and I hardly recognized her; her features seemed too thin and sharp. The room smelled of apples, faint, sweet but somehow unclean, as though the apples were beginning to rot. I was glad to get out into the cold and noise of the dingy streets. It seemed impossible that she was dead.

Even now I find it hard to believe. There was too much life in her long, flat, strongly boned body, and her longish face

with its fine brown eyes, shrewd and full of feeling. She was practical and candid, passionate and compassionate. I believe she was a genius. I sometimes catch myself childishly thinking I'll run into her walking on Primrose Hill or the Heath, and we'll pick up the converstion where we left off. But perhaps that is because her poems still speak so distinctly in her accents: quick, sardonic, unpredictable, effortlessly inventive, a bit angry, and always utterly her own.—A. ALVAREZ, "Prologue: Sylvia Plath," *The Savage God: A Study of Suicide* (1971), 1972, pp. 38–41

General

How I envy the novelist!

I imagine him—better say her, for it is the women I look to for a parallel—I imagine her, then, pruning a rosebush with a large pair of shears, adjusting her spectacles, shuffling about among the teacups, humming, arranging ashtrays or babies, absorbing a slant of light, a fresh edge to the weather, and piercing, with a kind of modest, beautiful X-ray vision, the psychic interiors of her neighbours—her neighbours on trains, in the dentist's waiting room, in the corner teashop. To her, this fortunate one, what is there that *isn't* relevant! Old shoes can be used, doorknobs, airletters, flannel nightgowns, cathedrals, nail varnish, jet planes, rose arbours and budgerigars; little mannerisms—the sucking at a tooth, the tugging at a hemline—any weird or warty or fine or despicable thing. Not to mention emotions, motivations—those rumbling, thunderous shapes. Her business is Time, the way it shoots forward, shunts back, blooms, decays and double exposes itself. Her business is people in Time. And she, it seems to me, has all the time in the world. She can take a century if she likes, a generation, a whole summer.

I can take about a minute.

I'm not talking about epic poems. We all know how long *they* can take. I'm talking about the smallish, unofficial garden-variety poem. How shall I describe it?—a door opens, a door shuts. In between you have had a glimpse: a garden, a person, a rainstorm, a dragonfly, a heart, a city. I think of those round glass Victorian paperweights which I remember, yet can never find—a far cry from the plastic mass-productions which stud the toy counters in Woolworths. This sort of paperweight is a clear globe, self-complete, very pure, with a forest or village or family group within it. You turn it upside down, then back. It snows. Everything is changed in a minute. It will never be the same in there—not the fir trees, nor the gables, nor the faces.

So a poem takes place.

And there is really so little room! So little time! The poet becomes an expert packer of suitcases:

> The apparition of these faces in the crowd;
> Petals on a wet black bough.

There it is: the beginning and the end in one breath. How would the novelist manage that? In a paragraph? In a page? Mixing it, perhaps, like paint, with a little water, thinning it, spreading it out.

Now I am being smug, I am finding advantages.

If a poem is concentrated, a closed fist, then a novel is relaxed and expanisve, an open hand: it has roads, detours, destinations; a heart line, a head line; morals and money come into it. Where the fist excludes and stuns, the open hand can touch and encompass a great deal in its travels.

I have never put a toothbrush in a poem.

I do not like to think of all the things, familiar, useful and worthy things, I have never put into a poem. I did, once, put a yew tree in. And that yew tree began, with astounding egotism, to manage and order the whole affair. It was not a yew tree by a church on a road past a house in a town where a certain woman lived . . . and so on, as it might have been, in a novel. Oh no. It stood squarely in the middle of my poem, manipulating its dark shades, the voices in the churchyard, the clouds, the birds, the tender melancholy with which I contemplated it—everything! I couldn't subdue it. And, in the end, my poem was a poem about a yew tree. That yew tree was just too proud to be a passing black mark in a novel.

Perhaps I shall anger some poets by implying that the *poem* is proud. The poem, too, can include everything, they will tell me. And with far more precision and power than those baggy, dishevelled and undiscriminate creatures we call novels. Well, I concede these poets their steamshovels and old trousers. I really *don't* think poems should be all that chaste. I would, I think, even concede a toothbrush, if the poem was a real one. But these apparitions, these poetical toothbrushes, are rare. And when they do arrive, they are inclined, like my obstreperous yew tree, to think themselves singled out and rather special.

Not so in novels.

There the toothbrush returns to its rack with beautiful promptitude and is forgot. Time flows, eddies, meanders, and people have leisure to grow and alter before our eyes. The rich junk of life bobs all about us: bureaus, thimbles, cats, the whole much-loved, well-thumbed catalogue of the miscellaneous which the novelist wishes us to share. I do not mean that there is no pattern, no discernment, no rigorous ordering here.

I am only suggesting that perhaps the pattern does not insist so much.

The door of the novel, like the door of the poem, also shuts.

But not so fast, nor with such manic, unanswerable finality.—SYLVIA PLATH, "The Novelist and the Poet" (1962), *LT*, July 7, 1977, p. 26

Sylvia Plath died on February 11, aged 30. An American, Miss Plath lived in England for a number of years and her book of poems, *The Colossus*, was published here in 1960. It is a clever, remarkably sophisticated first volume, displaying a real gift for the exotically arresting single phrase or image without in the end carrying more than a few wholly impressive poems. Its debts—to Wallace Stevens, Theodore Roethke and, most pervasively, to Marianne Moore—seem somewhat too obtrusive and there are times when her pursuit of the odd word, the glittering simile that resonates, or throws its sparks, into areas that have too marginal a bearing on the poem's subject, seems too deliberate, too whimsical even. The subjects themselves—and they are always, at bottom, the perennial important ones—often seem bricked up with a tasteful hand, or glanced at from too many directions too quaintly; the assured, leisured accent that is so attractive in a *tour de force* like 'Mushrooms' seems to diminish the seriousness of, say, 'The Ghost's Leavetaking', a poem that is dense with disturbances of an important kind, all demanding to be followed through differently, more tentatively perhaps; certainly with less literary gusto.

Several of her poems—'Night Shift', for example, and 'Sows'—remind one of Valéry's comment on the confident realist, the confronter of things as they are: 'the universe cannot for one instance endure to be only what it is . . . the mistakes, the appearances, the play of the dioprics of the mind deepen and quicken the world's miserable mass . . . the idea introduces into what is, the leaven of what is not.' Frank Kermode has very appropriately quoted this statement in his book on Stevens and it has relevance to Sylvia Plath in a similar way. It is a peculiar perception because it can encourage poetry to ends that are quite antithetical; it can make poetry into a

high-class game or it can see it as a vitally necessary instrument for controlling and bodying into consciousness a whole puzzled quality of experiencing. The danger, maybe, is in systematizing it too narrowly in the way that Valéry seems to; he implies that everyone really knows what the universe is and that poetry is a way of telling lively fictions about it, of pretending that it is something else, something more entertaining. It could be that this is, in effect, what poetry does with our experience but one ought not to feel that sure about it. In Sylvia Plath's 'Sows', for instance, the experience is approached in terms of the appearances that it might conceivably assume; it assumes a number of these, one by one, and they form the bulk of the poem, acting as an appetizing prelude to the appearance of the 'real'. This is a dangerous method, it seems to me, because it sets up no available scheme for discriminating between the various illusions, nor is there any way of limiting their number; the 'real' is known to the poet from the beginning and the spirit in which it is withheld from the reader is the spirit of fun-and-games; the strategy can easily come to seem like a way of using up powers of invention for which no more serious function can, meantime, be found.

This feeling that Miss Plath has great gifts but that she is marking time with them runs through *The Colossus*; there are notable exceptions, such as the excellent 'A Winter Ship', in which the experience absorbs and vitalizes the range of her curiosity, but these are largely successes of an orthodox, descriptive kind; they are concentrated and very accurately detailed, but there is a minimum of personal involvement in them.

In her poems published since *The Colossus*, and particularly in those that have been appearing very recently, Miss Plath has certainly developed. I hesitate before welcoming the achievement of these last poems as enthusiastically as A. Alevarez has in *The Observer*; I am not at all sure that in them 'the peculiar intensity of her genius found its perfect expression', nor that they represent a 'totally new breakthrough for modern verse'. There has certainly been an enormous gain in intensity and, one suspects, in seriousness of purpose. But it is as if she has taken that Valéry quotation and re-written it as the subject that her skills have been in search of; that is to say it is the impossibility of 'seeing things as they are', and the blank horror this provokes, that preoccupies her in these poems. There is a kind of nightmarish panic beneath their tough, enigmatic surfaces; the concrete world fragments into emblems of menace that are denoted in a tone of flat surrender:

> This man makes a pseudonym
> And crawls behind it like a worm
> This woman on the telephone
> Says she is a man, not a woman
> The mask increases, eats the worm,
> Stripes for mouth and eyes and nose.

Now and then the tone is one of barely controlled malevolence, as if experience has in some way cheated by seeming to be coherent; this is her most powerful note mainly because it does set up a relation between the world of organized human endeavour and her own terribly disorganized subjective world. It is a peculiar, slightly arid relation, perhaps, but it can breed the powerfully chilling hostilities of a poem like 'Kindness':

> Kindness glides about my house.
> Dame Kindness, she is so nice!
> The blue and red jewels of her rings smoke
> In the windows, the mirrors
> Are filling with smiles.
> What is so real as the cry of a child?
> A rabbit's cry may be wilder

But it has no soul.
Sugar can cure everything, so Kindness says.
Sugar is a necessary fluid.

The danger facing a poetry that commits itself to the recreation of nightmare experience is that it will be no less fragmentary and arbitrary than the experience that occasions it. That is to say, there must be some kind of coherent reflection upon experience, some effort of understanding it in terms of the urban, civilized world that its readers inhabit; this need not narrow nor constrict what it re-creates—on the contrary, it should simply extend its relevance. When Alvarez, in his *Observer* tribute to Miss Plath, says that 'in these last poems she was systematically probing that narrow, violent area between the viable and the impossible, between experience that can be transmuted into poetry and that which is overwhelming' I think he must surely be pointing out a danger rather than a legitimate mode. If we are to finally settle that there is experience which is too overwhelming to be transmuted into poetry then it is the poets who must assume the blame. In the best of her work Miss Plath has demonstrated, with formidable assurance, that she is aware of this; the less successful poems, those in which 'the world buckles and warps like a flame in mad draft', in which 'there is no sure objective ground—stillness and motion, near and far, telescope upsettingly, and become one'—they testify to the appalling difficulties she faced.—IAN HAMILTON, *Lon*, July 1963, pp. 54–56

Works

POETRY

Their power, their decisiveness, the positiveness and starkness of their outline, are decided not by an identifiable poetic personality expressing herself, but by the poet, a woman finding herself in a situation, out of which she produces these disconcerting, terrifying poems. The guarantees of the authenticity of the situation are insanity (or near-insanity) and death. All the way through we feel that the last thing the poet cares about is her book, her name, whether she will get a critical accolade, a Book Award, a Pulitzer, a Guggenheim, or whatever. She is writing out of a pure need of expression, certified, as I say, by death. The miracle is an effect of controlled uncontrolledness. As one reads on, one begins to seek the dark outlines of a mythology of people and places which provide the structure of the control, the landmarks among which the poetry is moving. There is the German and Austrian background (Sylvia Plath was born in Boston in 1932 of German and Austrian parents), feelings about her German father (which correspond rather to those of Theodore Roethke about his), concentration camps, her daughter, and her son, her husband (the English poet, Ted Hughes), the Cornish landscape, villagers, the sea. Probably at some later stage, critics will chart this autobiographic territory. One will be grateful when they do this, but one can be grateful also that they have not done so already. Part of the impressiveness of these poems is the feeling they give the reader of finding his way darkly through a dark and ominous landscape.

The landscape is an entirely interior, mental one in which external objects have become converted into symbols of hysterical vision:

This is my property.
Two times a day
I pace it, sniffing
The barbarous holly with its viridian
Scallops, pure iron,
And the wall of old corpses.

I love them.
I love them like history.
The apples are golden,
Imagine it—
My seventy trees
Holding their gold-ruddy balls
In a thick grey death-soup,
Their million
Gold leaves metal and breathless.

One can enjoy the "description" in this, the autumn-golden apples in the grey-soup mist. All the same, this nature is not in the least alleviating, it is not outside the poet, it is not the great furniture of the continuity of the seasonal earth, on which the distraught mind can rest. Or if there are some externals in these poems (they do give one a strong panicky feeling of kitchens, utensils, babies, gardens) they exist in an atmosphere where the external is in immediate process of becoming the internal, opposites identical with one another.

The same fusion of opposites applies to the feelings expressed. Sylvia Plath's imagination does not, like D. H. Lawrence's, merely oscillate between feelings of love and of hatred. With her the two attitudes seem completely fused. How else can one take lines like these?

Darling, all night
I have been flickering, on, off, on.
The sheets grow heavy as a lecher's kiss.
Three days. Three nights.
Lemon water, chicken
Water, water make me retch.
I am too pure for you or anyone.
You body hurts me as the world hurts God.

Considered simply as art, these poems have line to line power and rhythm which, though repetitive, is too dynamic to be monotonous. Beyond this, they don't have "form." From poem to poem they have little principle of beginning or ending, but seem fragments, not so much of one long poem, as of an outpouring which could only stop with the lapsing of the poet's hysteria. In this respect they have to be considered emotional-mystical poetry, like the poems of St. John of the Cross, in which the length of the poem is decided by the duration of the poet's vision, which is far more serious to the poet than formal considerations.

They are like nothing more than poems of prophecy, written by some priestess cultivating her hysteria, come out of Nazi and war-torn Europe, gone to America, and then situated on the rocky Cornish Atlantic coast. One does not think of Clytemnestra as *a hysteric*: one thinks of her as hysterical for very good reasons, against which she *warns*. Sylvia Plath would have agreed with Wilfred Owen that "all a poet can do today is to warn." But being a woman, her warning is more shrill, penetrating, visionary than Owen's. Owen's came out of the particular circumstances of the trenches, and there is nothing to make us think that if he had not been on the Western Front—the mud and blood into which his nose was rubbed—he would not have warned anyone about anything at all. He would have been a nice chap and a quiet poet. With Sylvia Plath, her femininity is that her hysteria comes completely out of herself, and yet seems about all of us. And she has turned out horrors and our achievements into the same witches' brew. In the following lines one feels that a space man promenading in space is not too distant a relation from a man in a concentration camp, and that everything is a symptom of the same holocaust:

The same fire
Melting the tallow heretics,
Ousting the Jews

Their thick palls float
Over the cicatrix of Poland, burnt-out
Germany
They do not die.

Grey birds obsess my heart,
Mouth-ash, ash of eye.
They settle. On the high

Precipice
That emptied one man into space
The ovens glowed like heavens incandescent.

It is a heart,
This holocaust I walk in,
O golden child the world will kill and eat.

As with all visionary poetry, one can sup here on horror even with enjoyment.—STEPHEN SPENDER, "Warnings from the Grave," *NR*, June 18, 1966, pp. 23–26

Being somebody always eluded Sylvia Plath, and to her as a poet it seems to have mattered. To achieve poetic being in this way may be a matter of talent, or come of itself, but it must not be seen to be attempted. Now, at this distance in time and after the ballyhoo has died down, we can see with what determination, what saving absence of tact, she tried to achieve it. Indeed it seems part of her skill and intention to invite the reader to cast a cold eye, to involve her or him with the same displays that a patient makes up for an analyst. Patients make them as effective as possible not because they are malingering but for the opposite reason: their efficiency in creating the story of themselves both conceals and reveals the desperation of nothingness, the sense of not being anyone.

I do it so it feels like hell.
I do it so it feels real.
I guess you could say I've a call.

As Lady Lazarus she achieves her individuality by the power to die and revive. The reader, the doctor, can see that the vocation to neurosis is wholly genuine, but also that its tales and acts are made up in order that the vocation, and the personality that goes with it, can be seen to exist.

Another way of putting it would be to say that Sylvia Plath's poems are verbal games of attention and observation, beautifully controlled, and not—as Lowell's and Berryman's are—the history and projection of a self. Her poetic gifts are more like those of Marianne Moore, or even Elizabeth Bishop, for although one can say that Marianne Moore's patterns and animals are really perceptive acts of vengeance on the way she has to live and the people she has to meet, it is none the less true that the game of close attention is what counts. This sort of talent has an increasingly weightless role in Sylvia Plath's poetry, because its powers are seeking to establish a situation which would give them a true natural history, an interior both personal and inevitable. The new woman's cliché of discovering 'who I really am', exploited today in a hundred mostly bad novels, gives a pervasive anxiety to her poems and yet seems irrelevant to their true qualities.

How much do they need it? In one sense the only subject of her poetry is its own anxiety to become poetry. Paradoxically it would have been much easier for her if she had been a neurotic of the comfortably self-absorbed, self-communing kind, like Stevie Smith. As pretty girl, bright student and teacher, wife and mother, and then as poet, professional author and trauma-maker as well, she had an impossible task in adding herself up to an incontestable personality. The poetry is in the gallantry of the process, and its failure.

⟨. . .⟩ Two points may strike us particularly, already foreshadowed in what I have been saying. First the posthumous

Ariel poems no longer seem the 'revelation' they seemed to many after the poet's death, when they were at once assimilated into the mushrooming legend about her. Second, and relatedly, her 'development' is really a sort of hallucination, produced by our sense of the ending. Hughes, in an appropriate metaphor, puts the matter in a significantly negative way. She went 'through successive moults of style . . . at each move we made, she seemed to shed a style'.

What then was new grown? Sentences become shorter, more elliptic—here she has influenced a new generation of poets today—and their isolate meanings more rigorously workmanlike. This is especially notable in 'Berck-Plage', of which every couplet is a succulent and separate pleasure. But it is not, except in striving and intention, an integrated poem. Hughes's note is again of interest, if only theoretically. We learn that there was a hospital for war veterans at this coast resort in Normandy, and that the patients took their exercise on the beach; also that the funeral in the poem is that of the poet's friend Peter Key, an old countryman 'who died in June 1962, exactly a year after her visit to Berck-Plage'.

The poem's virtues are really much the same as those of the neat and composed 'Cut', which almost uncannily anticipates the small 'metaphysical' domestic poems fashionable today.

What a thrill—
My thumb instead of an onion.
The top quite gone
Except for a sort of hinge . . .
Little pilgrim,
The Indian's axed your scalp . . .
Out of a gap
A million soldiers run,
Redcoats, every one.
Whose side are they on?

And so on. Like a good many other poems of the same sort 'Cut' has a rather disturbing air of being exactly fitted to Sylvia Plath's practice and techniques as is the equally successful 'Balloon', the penultimate poem she ever wrote, date 5 February 1963 (she died on the 11th).

Since Christmas they have lived with us,
Guileless and clear,
Oval soul-animals . . .

The balloons and her children's reaction to them provide just the right set-up for her intentness, and as in 'Cut' the subject lends itself naturally to something unstable and sinister just outside the focus of the poem but a vital part of its total effect. Hughes observes that 'her attitude to her verse was artisan-like: if she couldn't get a table out of the material, she was quite happy to get a chair, or even a toy . . . something that temporarily exhausted her ingenuity'. Certainly the image that fits these poems—'Blackberrying', 'Mushrooms', 'Stars over the Dordogne', 'Mussel Hunter at Rock Harbour' are other such of the many successful ones—is of a delicate carver using a keen tool that may suddenly enter her own body. It is this that gives an impression of dangerous games with words, what Hughes calls 'her unique excitement', an excitement symbolised in the very striking early poem 'Aerialist' ⟨. . .⟩ 'This adroit young lady' 'serenely plummets down' from the most hazardous trapeze act, but 'as penalty for her skill' must walk in dread of the day, the traffic, the normality of things.

Lest, out of spite, the whole
Elaborate scaffold of sky overhead
Fall racketing finale on the luck.

'Aerialist' recalls the later 'Ariel', which, we learn, was also the name of a horse which the poet used to ride in Devon.

It is in such poems that Sylvia Plath spoke with what has to be called her most natural voice. But she must also do 'the big bow-wow', ad the poems that helped to launch her cult— 'Lesbos', 'Lady Lazarus', and particularly 'Daddy'—make embarrassing reading today. The willed violence, the sturm and drang of Auschwitz lampshade skins and 'the man in black with a Meinkampf look', now seem merely factitious. Strange that Robert Lowell, in almost equally frenetic terms, praised this farrago as if it triumphantly equated and surmounted the sufferings of death camps and of personal madness. Sylvia Plath herself, one feels, would have come to dislike it and would have made no claims for it. Indeed there is something slightly embarrassed about the glosses on the poems she prepared for BBC radio. 'Daddy' is a poem 'spoken by a girl with an Electra complex. Her father died while she thought he was God. Her case is complicated by the fact that her father was also a Nazi and her mother very possibly part Jewish . . . the two strains marry and she has to act out the awful little allegory before she is free of it'. Certainly it is an awful little allegory, but one must remember that the poet needed the publicity that went with such things. Her amibition was fighting indifference and publishers who turned her down. The same reasons must be behind the almost equally disastrous 'public' poem set in a maternity ward, *Three Women*.

These poems sink under a weight of willed significance, and her explications both are outside them and occlude them. The exception is 'Death and Co.', a poem about death as a quiet man, as a smiling insinuating man, in which the true Plath humour appears in the poem if not in the explication ('the poem is about the double or schizophrenic nature of death—the marmoreal coldness of Blake's death mask, say, hand in glove with the fearful softness of worms, water, and other katabolists . . .'). The reason may be that the actual occasion, as Hughes records in his deadpan way, was 'a visit by two well-meaning men who invited me to live abroad at a tempting salary, and whom she therefore resented'.

Sylvia Plath wrote that 'The blood jet is poetry/There is no stopping it', but that is not the impression that her poetry as a whole gives. Rather it seems a particular triumph of hard work and artifice, attempting more than it can do in the same spirit in which the poet attempts more than she can be, a natural and involuntary spirit instead of 'the voice of nothing, that was your madness'.

> Love is a shadow.
> How you lie and cry after it
> Listen: these are its hooves: it has gone off, like a
>   horse.

But the lack of identity is also a strength, as is the rare sense of a poetry succeeding by doing more than it can. Schizophrenia brings its own rewards; death, like the horse Ariel, must somehow be caught up with. 'The only trouble is', as Sylvia Plath wrote of Lady Lazarus, 'she has to die first. She is the Phoenix, the libertarian spirit, what you will. She is also just a good, plain, very resourceful woman'.—JOHN BAYLEY, "Games with Death and Co.," NS, Oct. 2, 1981, pp. 19–20

In *The Colossus* ⟨. . .⟩ her options still seem relatively open as to the eventual direction of her writing. After its publication, the year 1960 is something of a watershed; only eleven poems are written, and only one of them, the happy, lyrical "You're", about the child she was carrying, was chosen from them for a new volume (to be *Ariel*). But thereafter, beginning early in 1961 (the year in which she also wrote *The Bell Jar*), came an astonishing acceleration into the themes and manner of her final poems. Some of the new poems still bear the stamp of exercises or excursions ("Zoo Keeper's Wife" is a particularly scary little *tour de force*); but with "Tulips" the style has become both more profoundly frightening and more fluent, the cadences beginning to shorten towards the brief, violent lines of "The Other" or "Daddy":

> The tulips are too red in the first place, they hurt me.
> Even through the gift paper I could hear them
>   breathe
> Lightly, through their light swaddlings, like an awful
>   baby.
> Their redness talks to my wound, it corresponds.
> They are subtle, they seem to float. . . .

Increasingly the poems seem to be made (she felt this to be an essential element in their composition) to be said aloud, the voice angry, insistent, eloquent. The sickening maze of both crude and moving effects she achieves in "The Surgeon at 2 a.m.", anticipates the prevailing mood of many of the *Ariel* poems (where the imagery is harsh, clear and almost unbearably poignant): "It is a statue the orderlies are wheeling off. / I have prefected it. / I am left with an arm or a leg, / A set of teeth, or stones / To rattle in a bottle . . .".

In the verse Sylvia Plath wrote in the last year of her life, a particular way of handling images constituted her most original contribution to poetry, although it is only part of her wider achievement. On to a natural world alertly observed and reanimated in her words, she imposes frightening images from the world of man to produce an extra dimension of terror or pathos. Almost automatically, the natural phenomena with which she contended and concluded an uneasy truce in her earlier poems, acquire an inescapable, stifling menace. There is a continual, agonized, brilliant conflation of the external world and the inner world of an anguish wholly characteristic of our age. In "Apprenhensions" she asks:

> Is there no way out of the mind?
> Steps at my back spiral into a well.
> There are no trees or birds in this world,
> There is only a sourness.

The "sourness" comes in a profusion of uneasy images: "This is the sea, then, this great abeyance. / How the sun's poultice draws on my inflammation." ("Berck-Plage"), "But my god, the clouds are like cotton. / Armies of them. They are carbon monoxide." ("A Birthday Present"); "Hothouse baby in its crib. / The ghastly orchid / Hanging its hanging garden in the air" ("Fever 103°"). And in "Edge", her last poem of all:

> Each dead child coiled, a white serpent,
> One at each little
> Pitcher of milk, now empty.
> She has folded
> Them back into her body as petals
> Of a rose close when the garden
> Stiffens and odors bleed
> From the sweet deep throats of the night flower.

She speaks in such images, if not for all mankind, or even for its creatives artists, then at least for those many whose imagination extends personal suffering to include a sensitivity to the peculiar cruelties of our world. No poet has spoken this suffering more beautifully and pitifully, in a more brutally candid way, or registered it (in "Cut", or "Contusion") with more physical immediacy. Yet she insisted on the element of control:

> I believe that one should be able to control and
>   manipulate experiences, even the most terrifying—
>   like madness, being tortured, this kind of experi-
>   ence—and one should be able to manipulate these
>   experiences with an informed and intelligent mind.

She was in earnest, hot commiting an evasion, when she spoke of "Daddy" and "Lady Lazarus" almost as if they were impersonal dramatic monologues: "a poem spoken by a girl with an Electra complex", "the speaker is a woman who has the great and terrible gift of being reborn."

Certainly, as her teacher Dorothea Krook wrote, there occurred "a great, perhaps even a titanic, struggle for 'normalcy' against the forces of disintegration within her." But in early October 1962, among the most harrowing and frank of her late poems come the five poems about bees and beekeeping. Sinister hints and parallels abound in them; yet there is a kind of exuberant fascination at being able to escape into a science, an activity, which drew her temporarily from personal distress, a dark joyousness in spinning out elaborate metaphors that recalls some much earlier poems:

> The bees have got so far. Seventy feet high!
> Russia, Poland and Germany!
> The mild hills, the same old magenta
> Fields shrunk to a penny
> Spun into a river, the river crossed.
> The bees argued, in their black ball,
> A flying hedgehog, all prickles.
>
> ("The Swarm")

And in "Wintering", the final one of this five, "The bees are flying. They taste the spring." The beekeeping was to be her last thorough—even happy—absorption in the world outside her own febrile, questing imagination, and her own pain.
—ALAN BROWNJOHN, "A Way Out of the Mind," *TLS*, Feb. 12, 1982, p. 166

THE BELL JAR

The Bell Jar is a novel about the events of Sylvia Plath's 20th year: about how she tried to die, and how they stuck her together with glue. It is a fine novel, as bitter and remorseless as her last poems—the kind of book Salinger's Franny might have written about herself 10 years later, if she had spent those 10 years in Hell. It is very much a story of the fifties, but written in the early sixties, and now, after being effectively suppressed in this country for eight years, published in the seventies.

F. Scott Fitzgerald used to claim that he wrote with "the authority of failure," and he did. It was a source of power in his later work. But the authority of failure is but a pale shadow of the authority of suicide, as we feel it in *Ariel* and in *The Bell Jar*. This is not so much because Sylvia Plath, in taking her own life, gave her readers a certain ghoulish interest they could not bring to most poems and novels, though this is no doubt partly true. It is because she knew that she was "Lady Lazarus." Her works do not only come to us posthumously. They were written posthumously. Between suicides. She wrote her novel and her *Ariel* poems feverishly, like a person "stuck together with glue" and aware that the glue was melting. Should we be grateful for such things? Can we accept the price she paid for what she has given us? Is dying really an art?

There are no easy answers for such questions, maybe no answers at all. We are all dying, of course, banker and bum alike, spending our limited allotment of days, hours and minutes at the same rate. But we don't like to think about it. And those men and women who take the matter into their own hands, and spend all at once with prodigal disdain, seem frighteningly different from you and me. Sylvia Plath is one of those others, and to them our gratitude and our dismay are equally impertinent. When an oracle speaks it is not for us to say thanks but to attend to the message.

The Bell Jar is about the way this country was in the nineteen-fifties and about the way it is to lose one's grip on sanity and recover it again. It is easy to say (and it is said too often) that insanity is the only sane reaction to the America of the past two decades. And it is also said frequently (especially by R. D. Laing and his followers) that the only thing to do about madness is relax and enjoy it. But neither of these "clever" responses to her situation occur to Esther Greenwood, who is the narrator and central character in this novel.

To Esther, madness is the descent of a stifling bell jar over her head. In this state, she says, "wherever I sat . . . I would be sitting under the same glass bell jar, stewing in my sour air." And she adds, "To the person in the bell jar, blank and stopped as a dead baby, the world itself is the bad dream." Which is not to say that Esther believes the world outside the asylum is full of people living an authentic existence. She asks, "What was there about us, in Belsize, so different from the girls playing bridge and gossiping and studying in the college to which I would return? Those girls, too, sat under bell jars of a sort."

The world in which the events of this novel take place is a world bounded by the cold war on one side and the sexual war on the other. We follow Esther Greenwood's personal life from her summer job in New York with *Ladies' Day* magazine, back through her days at New England's largest school for women, and forward through her attempted suicide, her bad treatment at one aslyum and her good treatment at another, to her final re-entry into the world like a used tire: "patched, retreaded, and approved for the road."

But this personal life is delicately related to larger events—especially the execution of the Rosenbergs, whose impending death by electrocution is introduced in the stunning first paragraph of the book. Ironically, that same electrical power which destroys the Rosenbergs, restores Esther to life. It is shock therapy which finally lifts the bell jar and enables Esther to breathe freely once again. Passing through death she is reborn. This novel is not political or historical in any narrow sense, but in looking at the madness of the world and the world of madness it forces us to consider the great question posed by all truly realistic fiction: What is reality and how can it be confronted?

In *The Bell Jar*, Sylvia Plath has used superbly the most important technical device of realism—what the Russian critic Shklovsky called "defamiliarization." True realism defamiliarizes our world so that it emerges from the dust of habitual acceptance and becomes visible once again. This is quite the opposite of that comforting false realism that presents the world in terms of clichés that we are all too ready to accept.

Sylvia Plath's technique of defamiliarization ranges from tiny verbal witticisms that bite, to images that are deeply troubling. When she calls the hotel for women that Esther inhabits in New York the "Amazon," she is not merely enjoying the closeness of the sound of that word to "Barbizon," she is forcing us to rethink the entire concept of a hotel for women: "mostly girls of my age with wealthy parents who wanted to be sure that their daughters would be living where men couldn't get at them and deceive them." And she is announcing a major theme in her work, the hostility between men and women.

With Esther Greenwood this hostility takes the form of obsessive attempts to get herself liberated from a virginity she finds oppressive, by a masculinity she finds hideous. When her medical-student boy friend suggests that they play a round of the traditional children's game—I'll show you mine if you show me yours—she looks at his naked maleness and reacts this way: "The only thing I could think of was a turkey neck and turkey gizzards and I felt very depressed." This is defamiliarization with a vengeance. The image catches up all cocky masculine pride of flesh and reduces it to the level of giblets. It sees the inexorable link between generation and death and makes us see it too, because the image is so fitting. All flesh comes from this—and comes to this.

In the face of such cosmic disgust, psychological explanations like "penis-envy" seem pitifully inadequate. Esther Greenwood is not a woman who wants to be a man but a human being who cannot avoid seeing that the price we pay for life is death. Sexual differentiation itself is only a metaphor for human incompletion. The battle of the sexes is, after all, a civil war.

Esther Greenwood's account of her year in the bell jar is as clear and readable as it is witty and disturbing. It makes for a novel such as Dorothy Parker might have written if she had not belonged to a generation infected with the relentless frivolity of the college-humor magazine. The brittle humor of that earlier generation is reincarnated in *The Bell Jar*, but raised to a more serious level because it is recognized as a resource of hysteria. Why, then, has this extraordinary work not appeared in the United States until eight years after its appearance in England?

This story is partly told in the useful biographical note that has been written for the American edition by Lois Ames. The novel was initially rejected by its American publisher and when, after its success in England, Harper & Row sought to publish it, they were refused permission by the family. Sylvia Plath's mother has insisted that her daughter thought of the book as a "pot-boiler" and did not want it published in the United States. And Mrs. Plath herself felt that the book presented ungrateful caricatures of people who had tried to help her daughter. These sentiments are understandable. But a book published in England cannot be kept away from the United States. Already, the student underground has been smuggling copies from abroad into the country. Literature will out. And *The Bell Jar* is not a pot-boiler, nor a series of ungrateful caricatures; it is literature. It is finding its audience, and will hold it.—ROBERT SCHOLES, *NYTBR*, April 11, 1971, p. 7

The Bell Jar is fiction that cannot escape being read in part as autobiography. It begins in New York with an ominous lightness, grows darker as it moves to Massachusetts, then slips slowly into madness. Esther Greenwood, one of a dozen girls in and on the town for a month as "guest editors" of a teen-age fashion magazine, is the product of a German immigrant family and a New England suburb. With "fifteen years of straight A's" behind her, a depressing attachment to a dreary but handsome medical student, Buddy Willard, still unresolved, and a yearning to be a poet, she is the kind of girl who doesn't know what drink to order or how much to tip a taxi driver but is doing her thesis on the "twin images" in *Finnegans Wake*, a book she has never managed to finish. Her imagination is at war with the small-town tenets of New England and the bigtime sham of New York. She finds it impossible to be one of the army of college girls whose education is a forced stop on the short march to marriage. The crises of identity, sexuality, and survival are grim, and often funny. Wit, irony, and intelligence as well as an inexplicable, withdrawn sadness separate Esther from her companions. Being an involuntary truth-seeker, she uses irony as a weapon of judgment, and she is its chief victim. Unable to experience or mime emotions, she feels defective as a person. The gap between her and the world widens: "I couldn't get myself to react. I felt very still and very empty." . . . "The silence depressed me. It wasn't the silence of silence. It was my own silence." . . . "That morning I had tried to hang myself."

Camouflage and illness go together in *The Bell Jar*; moreover, illness is often used to lift or tear down a façade. Doreen, a golden girl of certainty admired by Esther, begins the process by getting drunk. The glimpse of her lying with her head in a pool of her own vomit in a hotel hallway is repellent but crucial. Her illness is followed by a mass ptomaine poisoning at a "fashion" lunch. Buddy gets tuberculosis and goes off to a sanatorium. Esther, visiting him, breaks her leg skiing. When she has her first sexual experience, with a young math professor she has picked up, she hemorrhages. Taken in by a lesbian friend, she winds up in a hospital. Later, she learns that the friend has hanged herself. A plain recital of the events in *The Bell Jar* would be ludicrous if they were not balanced by genuine desperation at one side of the scale and a sure sense of black comedy at the other. Sickness and disclosure are the keys to *The Bell Jar*. On her last night in New York, Esther climbs to the roof of her hotel and throws her city wardrobe over the parapet, piece by piece. By the end of the novel, she has tried to get rid of her very life, which is given back to her by another process of divestment—psychiatry. Pain and gore are endemic to *The Bell Jar*, and they are described objectively, self-mockingly, almost humorously to begin with. Taken in by the tone (the first third of *The Bell Jar* might be a mordant, sick-joke version of *Breakfast at Tiffany's*), the reader is being lured into the lion's den—that sterile cement room in the basement of a mental hospital where the electric-shock-therapy machine waits for its frightened clients.

The casualness with which physical suffering is treated suggests that Esther is cut off from the instinct for sympathy right from the beginning—for herself as well as for others. Though she is enormously aware of the impingements of sensation, her sensations remain impingements. She lives close to the nerve, but the nerve has become detached from the general network. A thin layer of glass separates her from everyone, and the novel's title, itself made of glass, is evolved from her notion of disconnection: the head of each mentally ill person is enclosed in a bell jar, choking on his own foul air.

Torn between conflicting roles—the sweetheart-*Hausfrau*-mother and "the life of the poet," neither very real to her—Esther finds life itself inimical. Afraid of distorting the person she is yet to become, she becomes the ultimate distortion—nothing. As she descends into the pit of depression, the world is a series of wrong reverberations: her mother's face is a perpetual accusation, the wheeling of a baby carriage underneath her window a grinding irritation. She becomes obsessed by the idea of suicide, and one of the great achievements of *The Bell Jar* is that it makes real the subtle distinctions between a distorted viewpoint and the distortions inherent in what it sees. Conventions may contribute to Esther's insanity, but she never loses her awareness of the irrationality of convention. Moved to Belsize, a part of the mental hospital reserved for patients about to go back to the world, she makes the connection explicit:

> What was there about us, in Belsize, so different from the girls playing bridge and gossiping and studying in the college to which I would return? Those girls, too, sat under bell jars of a sort.

Terms like "mad" and "sane" grow increasingly inadequate as the action develops. Esther is "psychotic" by definition, but the definition is merely a descriptive tag: by the time we learn how she got to be "psychotic" the word has ceased to be relevant. (As a work of fiction, *The Bell Jar* seems to complement the clinical theories of the Scottish analyst R. D. Laing.) Because it is written from the distraught observer's point of view rather than from the viewpoint of someone observing her, there is continuity to her madness; it is not one state suddenly supplanting another but the most gradual of processes.

Suicide, a grimly compulsive game of fear and guilt, as addictive as alcohol or drugs, is experimental at first—a little blood here, a bit of choking there, just to see what it will be like. It quickly grows into an overwhelming desire for annihilation. By the time Esther climbs into the crawl space of a cellar and swallows a bottle of sleeping pills—by this time we are faced by the real thing—the event, instead of seeming grotesque, seems like a natural consequence. When she is about to leave the hospital, after a long series of treatments, her psychiatrist tells her to consider her breakdown "a bad dream." Esther, "patched, retreaded, and approved for the road," thinks, "To the person in the bell jar, blank and stopped as a dead baby, the world itself is the bad dream."

That baby is only one of many in *The Bell Jar*. They smile up from the pages of magazines, they sit like little freaks pickled in glass jars on display in the pediatric ward of Buddy's hospital. A "sweet baby cradled in its mother's belly" seems to wait for Esther at the end of the ski run when she has her accident. And in the course of the novel she witnesses a birth. In place of her never-to-be-finished thesis on the "twin images" in *Finnegans Wake*, one might be written on the number and kinds of babies that crop up in *The Bell Jar*. In a gynecologist's office, watching a mother fondling her baby, Esther wonders why she is so separated from this easy happiness, this carrying out of the prescribed biological and social roles. She does not want a baby; she is a baby herself. But she is also a potential writer. She wants to fulfill herself, not to *be* fulfilled. To her, babies are The Trap, and sex is the bait. But she is too intelligent not to realize that babies don't represent life, they *are* life, though not necessarily the kind Esther wants to live; that is, if she wants to live at all. She is caught between the monstrous fetuses on display in Buddy's ward and the monstrous slavery of the seemingly permanent pregnancy of her neighbor Dodo Conway, who constantly wheels a baby carriage under Esther's window, like a demented figure in a Greek chorus. Babies lure Esther toward suicide by luring her toward a life she cannot—literally—bear. There seem to be only two solutions, and both involve the invisible: to pledge faith to the unborn or fealty to the dead. Life, so painfully visible and present, defeats her, and she takes it, finally, into her own hands. With the exception of the psychiatrist's disinterested affection for her, love is either missing or unrecognized in *The Bell Jar*. Its overwhelming emotion is disgust—disgust that has not yet become contempt and is therefore more damaging.—HOWARD MOSS, "Dying: An Introduction," *NY*, July 10, 1971, pp. 73–74

BARBARA HARDY
From "The Poetry of Sylvia Plath"
The Advantage of Lyric
1977, pp. 121–40

I

Passions of hate and horror prevail in the poetry of Sylvia Plath, running strongly counter to the affirmative and life-enhancing quality of most great English poetry, even in this century. We cannot reconcile her despairing and painful protest with the usual ideological demands of Christian, Marxist, and humanist writers, whether nobly and sympathetically eloquent, like Wordsworth, breezily simplified, like Dylan Thomas, or cunning in ethical and psychological argument, like W. H. Auden or F. R. Leavis. Her poetry rejects instead of accepting, despairs instead of glorying, turns its face with steady consistency towards death, not life. But these hating and horrified passions are rooted in love, are rational as well as irrational, lucid as well as bewildered, so humane and honourable that they are constantly enlarged and expanded. We are never enclosed in a private sickness here, and if derangement is a feature of the poetry, it works to enlarge and generalise, not to create an enclosure. Moreover, its enlargment works through passionate reasoning, argument and wit. Its judgment is equal to its genius.

The personal presence in the poetry, though dynamic and shifting, makes itself felt in a full and large sense, in feeling, thinking and language. In view of certain tendencies to admire or reject her so-called derangement as a revelatory or an enclosed self-exploration, I want to stress this breadth and completeness. The poetry constantly breaks beyond its own personal cries of pain and horror, in ways more sane than mad, enlarging and generalising the particulars, attaching its maladies to a profoundly moved and moving sense of human ills. Working through a number of individual poems, I should like to describe this poetry as a poetry of enlargement, not derangement. In much of the poetry the derangement is scarcely present, but where it is, it is out-turned, working though reason and love.

I want to disagree with David Holbrook's view that hers is a schizophrenic poetry which 'involves us in false solutions and even the *huis clos* circuits of death', while indeed agreeing with much that he has to say about the cult of schizophrenia in his essay 'The 200-inch distorting mirror' (*New Society*, 11 July 1968).

> Sylvia Plath's poetry demands a selfless mirror-role from us; we feel that it would be worse than inhuman of us not to give it. If this involves us in entering into her own distorted view of existence, never mind. We will bravely become the schizoid's 200-inch astronomical reflector.

An excessive love for the cult of pain and dying, in such tributes as those of Anne Sexton[1] and Robert Lowell,[2] seems to divert our attention from the breadth and rationality of Sylvia Plath's art. Lowell is strongly drawn to that very quality which David Holbrook finds repulsive or pathetic, the invitation to a deadly closure:

> There is a peculiar, haunting challenge to these poems. Probably many, after reading *Ariel*, will recoil from their first over-awed shock, and painfully wonder why so much of it leaves them feeling empty, evasive and inarticulate. In her lines, I often hear the serpent whisper, 'Come, if only you had the courage, you too could have my rightness, audacity and ease of inspiration.' But most of us will turn back. These poems are playing Russian roulette with six cartridges in the cylinder, a game of 'chicken', the wheels of both cars locked and unable to swerve.

It seems worth recording a different reaction.

I want to begin by looking at a poem from *Ariel* which shows how dangerous it is to talk, as Holbrook clearly does, and as Lowell seems to, about the 'typical' Sylvia Plath poem, or even the 'typical' late poem. I must make it clear that I do not want to rest my case on the occasional presence of life-enhancing poems, but to use one to explain what I mean by imaginative enlargement. 'Nick and the Candlestick' (from *Ariel*, 1965; written October/November 1962) is not only a remarkable poem of love, but that much rarer thing—are there any others?—a fine poem of maternal love. It is a poem which moves towards two high points of feeling, strongly personal and particular, deeply eloquent of maternal feeling, and lucidly open to a Christian mythical enlargement. The first peak comes in the tenth stanza, and can perhaps be identified at its highest point in one word, the endearment 'ruby', which is novel, surprising, resonant, and beautiful:

> Remembering, even in sleep,
> Your crossed position.
> The blood blooms clean
>
> In you, ruby.
> The pain
> You wake to is not yours.

The second peak comes at the end, in a strongly transforming conclusion, a climax in the very last line. It comes right out of all that has been happening in the poem but transforms what has gone before, carrying a great weight and responsibility, powerfully charged and completing a process, like an explosion or a blossoming:

> You are the one
> Solid the spaces lean on, envious.
> You are the baby in the barn.

The final enlargement is daring, both in the shock of expansion and in the actual claim it makes. She dares to call her baby Christ and in doing so makes the utmost claim of her personal love, but so that the enlargement does not take us away from this mother, this child, this feeling. This most personally present mother-love moves from the customary hyperbole of endearment in 'ruby' to the vast claim. When we look back, when we read again, the whole poem is pushing towards that last line. 'You are the baby in the barn'. The symbol holds good, though at first invisibly, for the cold, the exposure, the dark, the child, the mother, the protection, and the redemption from a share of pain. Each sensuous and emotional step holds for the mother in the poem and for Mary: this is the warmth of the mother nursing her child in the cold night; this is a proud claim for the child's beauty and the mother's tenderness; this is love and praise qualified by pain. Any mother loving her child in a full awareness of the world's horror—especially seeing it and feeling it vulnerable and momentarily safe in sleep—is re-enacting the feeling in the Nativity, has a right to call the child the baby in the barn.

'Ruby' is a flash of strong feeling. It treasures, values, praises, admires, measures, contemplates, compares, rewards. Its full stretch of passion is only apparent when the whole poem is read, but even on first encounter it makes a powerful moment, and strikes us as thoroughly formed and justified at that stage. Like every part of the poem, even the less-urgent-sounding ones, it refers back and forwards, and has also continuity not only within the poem but with large traditions of amorous and religious language, in medieval poetry (especially *The Pearl*), in the Bible, in Hopkins. The fusion of the new and the old is moving. This baby has to be newly named, like every baby, and has its christening in a poem, which bestows a unique name, in creative energy, as ordinary christenings cannot, but with something too of the ritual sense of an old and common feeling. Sylvia Plath is a master of timing and placing, and the naming endearment comes after the physically live sense of the sleeping child, in the cold air, in the candlelight, in its healthy colour. The mildly touched Christian reference in 'crossed position' prepares for the poem's future. Its gentleness contrasts strongly, by the way, with the violence of very similar puns in Dylan Thomas, and confirms my general feeling that Sylvia Plath is one of the very few poets to assimilate Thomas without injury, in an entirely benign influence. Her sensuous precision is miles away from Thomas: 'ruby' is established by the observation, 'The blood blooms clean/In you', and the comparison works absolutely, within the

poem, though it has an especially poignant interest when we think of the usual aggressiveness and disturbance of redness in her other poems, where the blooming red of tulips or poppies are exhausting life-demands, associated with the pain of red wounds, or the heavy urgency of a surviving beating heart. Here it is a beloved colour, because it is the child's, so in fact there is a constancy of symbolism, if we are interested. 'Clean', like 'crossed' and 'ruby', has the same perfectly balanced attachment to the particularity of the situation—this mother, this baby—and to the Christian extension. 'The pain/You wake to is not yours' works in the same way, pointing out and in, though the words 'out' and 'in' do less than justice to the fusion here.

The perfected fusion is the more remarkable for being worked out in a complex tone, which includes joking. Like the medieval church, or the Nativity play, it can be irreverent, can make jokes about what it holds sacred, is sufficiently inclusive and sufficiently certain. So we are carried from the fanciful rueful joke about 'A piranha/Religion, drinking/Its first communion out of my live toes' to the final awe. Or from the casual profane protest, 'Christ! they are panes of ice' to the crossed position, the pain not his, the baby in the barn. An ancient and audacious range.

If this is a love-poem, it is one which exists in the context of the other *Ariel* poems, keeping a sense of terrors as well as glories, in imagery which is vast and vague: the stars 'plummet to their dark address'; and topically precise and scientific: 'the mercuric/Atoms that cripple drip/Into the terrible well'. It is a poisoned world that nourishes and threatens that clean blood. Perhaps only a child can present an image of the uncontaminated body, as well as soul, and there is also present the sense of a mother's fear of physical contamination. The mercuric atoms are presumably a reference to the organo-mercury compounds used in agriculture, and the well seems to be a real well. There may also, I suppose, be a reference to radioactive fall-out. Ted Hughes has a note about the poet's horror of 'the chemical poisonings of nature, the pile-up of atomic waste', in his article 'The Chronological Order of Sylvia Plath's Poems' (*Triquarterly*, no. 7, Fall 1966).

The poet loves and praises, but in no innocent or ideal glorying. This is a cold air in which the candle burns blue before yellow, nearly goes out, reminds us of the radiance in so many paintings of Mother and Child, but also of a real cold night, and of the miner's cold, his dark, his cave, his nightwork, his poisoned breathing. The intimacies and protections and colours are particular too: 'roses', 'the last of Victoriana', 'soft rugs'. The expansion moves firmly into and out of a twentieth-century world, a medieval poetry, ritual, and painting, and the earliest Christ-story, and this holds for its pains and its loving. It moves from light to dark, from love to fear. It moves beyond the images of mother-love, indeed begins outside in the first line's serious wit, 'I am a miner'. It uses—or, better, feels for—the myth of Redemption not in order to idealise the particulars but rather to revise and qualify the myth, to transplant it again cheerfully, to praise only after a long hard look at the worst. The love and faith and praise are there, wrung out and achieved against the grain, against the odds. David Holbrook is sorry that Sylvia Plath, judged from *The Bell Jar*, shows no experience of togetherness. This poem seems to embarrass his case, and it strikes me at being beyond the reach of such diagnosis or compassion. She said of the poem, in a BBC broadcast quoted by Lois Ames:[3] 'a mother nurses her baby son by candlelight and finds in him a beauty which, while it may not ward off the world's ills, does redeem her share of it'.

True, it is not typical. There are two other very loving poems of maternal feeling, 'Riddle' and 'You're', happy peals of conceits, but nothing else moves so, between these two extremities of love and pain, striking spark from such poles. 'Nick and the Candlestick' is not proffered as an instance of togetherness, but as a lucid model of the enlargement I want to discuss.

At the heart of her poetry lies the comment that she herself made about this enlargement:

> I think my poems come immediately out of the sensuous and emotional experiences I have, but I must say I cannot sympathize with these cries from the heart that are informed by nothing except a needle or a knife or whatever it is. I believe that one should be able to control and manipulate experiences, even the most terrifying—like madness, being tortured, this kind of experience—and one should be able to manipulate these experiences with an informed and intelligent mind. I think that personal experience shouldn't be a kind of shut box and mirror-looking narcissistic experience. I believe it should be generally relevant, to such things as Hiroshima and Dachau, and so on. (*Triquarterly*, no. 7, Fall 1966, p. 71)

It is interesting that Sylvia Plath uses the image of the mirror which David Holbrook also uses in that *New Society* article, called 'The 200-inch distorting mirror', in order to reject the kind of poetry he also rejects (to my mind, rightly) and which he finds (to my mind, wrongly) in Sylvia Plath.

A mere explicit statement that the poet believes personal experience of pain should not be a mirror or a shut box but should be relevant to Hiroshima and Dachau, is plainly not an answer to Holbrook. Nor would a mere listing of such references do much: the intelligent poet can after all attempt but fail to break open the shut box, may impose intellectually schematic associations with the larger world. Resnais in *Hiroshima mon amour* seems to be open to the charge of using the larger pain of atomic war to illuminate his personal centre, so that the movement is not that of enlargement but of diminution. Something similar seems to happen in a good many Victorian attempts to enlarge the personal problem, to combine the personal and social pain, and we may well object that the endings of *Bleak House* and *Crime and Punishment* are unsuccessful attempts to solve the large pain by the smaller reconciliation. I have spent what may seem an excessive time on 'Nick and the Candlestick' in order to establish not so much a typical feeling, but a form: the particularity and the generalisation run together in equal balance, asking questions of each other, eroding each other, unifying in true imaginative modification. I want to suggest that this is the mode of Sylvia Plath's major poetry, and that it succeeds exactly where Resnais failed. But it should be said, perhaps, that this problem of combination or enlargement works in a special way, involving artists working from experience of personal pain, depression, despair. The optimist, like Dickens and Dostoevsky, may well find it easy to join his larger pain and his smaller triumph. For the tragic artist like Sylvia Plath it is more the problem of competitive pains: how to dwell in and on the knives and needles of the personal life without shutting off the knives and needles in Biafra, Vietnam, Dachau, and Hiroshima. It is almost a problem of competing sensibilities, and the tragic artist's temptation in our time is probably to combine indecorously, like Resnais, to make the Hiroshima a metaphor for an adultery, to move from outer to inner and confirm an especially terrible shut box. ⟨. . .⟩

III

Moving to *Ariel*, the later volume, is to recognise that ⟨her⟩ inventiveness has become more powerful, and sometimes less lucid. In a poem of pain and delirium, 'Fever 103°', the wildness and fast movement of the conceits are excused by the feverishness they dramatise. They cover a wide range. They jerk from Isadora's scarves to Hiroshima ash to lemon water and chicken water; from the bizarre conceit to the simple groping, 'whatever these pink things are'; glimpses of horrors to lucidity, self-description, affectionateness, childishness: the range and the confusion establish the state of sickness. There are the other well-known poems of sickness, "Tulips', 'In Plaster' and 'Paralytic' which dramatise individual, and different, sick states, all of them appropriately formed, in process and style. Each of these four poems is personal (which is not to say that the *persona* is not imaginary: in 'In Plaster' and 'Paralytic' it seems to be so, judging from external and internal evidence) but each is a complete and controlled drama of sick mind and body. Because it is sickness that is overtly dramatised there is no sense of an improperly won competition with the world's ills. They are brought in, by a species of decorous hallucinations. But the plainness of the act of hullucination, the lucid proffering of a febrile, convalescent, enclosed or paralysed state, allows the larger world to makes its presence properly felt. The burning in 'Fever 103°' reminds us of atomic ash, while keeping the separation clear. The plaster cast in 'In Plaster' reminds us of the other imprisonments and near-successful relationships: 'I used to think we might make a go of it together/ After all, it was a kind of marriage, being so close.' I think Alun Jones is wrong to see this as an allegory about marriage:[4] these poems of sickness allow her to suggest a whole number of identifications which move towards and back from allegory. David Holbrook seems to make a different though related error in his discussion of 'Tulips': this is not a sick poem but a poem about being sick. Quite different. Of course it is a sick person who is drawn to poems about sickness, but the physical sickness makes up actual chunks of her existence, and sometimes the poems are about chilblains, cuts, influenza and appendicitis. She is drawn to sickness, multilation, attacks, and dying, but each poem is a controlled and dynamic image with windows, not a lining of mirrors. In 'Fever' and 'In Plaster' the dramatised act of hallucination holds the personal and the social in stable and substantial mutual relationships, neither absorbing the other.

In 'Tulips' there is a slow, reluctant acceptance of the tulips, which means a slow, reluctant acceptance of a return to life. The poem dramatises a sick state, making it clear that it is sickness. The flowers are hateful, as emblems of cruel spring, as presents from the healthy world that wants her back, as suspect, like all presents. They are also emblems of irrational fear: science is brilliantly misued (as it can be in feeble and deranged states of many kinds) and phototropism and photosynthesis are used to argue the fear: the flowers really do move towards the light, do open out, do take up oxygen. The tulips are also ihabitants of the bizarre world of private irrational fantasy, even beyond the bridge of distorted science: they contrast with the whiteness of nullity and death, are like a baby, an African cat, are like her wound (a real red physical wound, stitched so as to heal, not to gape like opened tulips) and, finally, like her heart. David Holbrook's analysis of this poem seems to stop short of the transforming end, which opens up the poem. The poem, like the tulips, has really been opening from the beginning, but all is not plain until the end, as in 'Nick'. Holbrook says, 'The tulips, as emissaries of love, seem to threaten her with emptying of the identity: "the vivid tulips eat my oxygen"', but the tulips win, and that is the point. It is a painful victory for life. We move from the verge of hallucination, which can hear them as noisy, or see them as like dangerous animals, to a proper rationality, which accepts recovery. The poem hinges on this paradox: while most scientific, it is most deranged; while most surreal, it is most healthy:

> And I am aware of my heart: it opens and closes
> Its bowl of red blooms out of sheer love of me.
> The water I taste is warm and salt, like the sea,
> And comes from a country far away as health.

It is the country she has to return to, reluctant though she is: the identification of the breathing, opened, red, springlike tulips with her heart makes this plain. She wanted death, certainly, as one may want it in illness or, moving back from the poem to the other poems and to her real death, as she wanted it in life. But the poem enacts the movement from the peace and purity of anaesthesia and feebleness to the calls of life. Once more, the controlled conceits and the movement from one state to another create expansion. The poem opens out to our experience of sickness and health, to the overwhelming demands of love, which we sometimes have to meet. The symbolism of present-giving and spring-flowers makes a bridge from a personal death-longing to common experience: something very similar can be found in the short poem 'Poppies in October' which uses a similar symbolism and situation for a different conclusion and feeling; and in the magnificent Bee poems, where the solid facts and documentations of beekeeping act as a symbolic base for irrational and frightening fantasy *and* as a bridge into the everyday and ordinary explanations and existences.

The concept of explicit hallucination seems useful. In the Bee poems we move away from the poetry of sickness to another kind of rejected allegory. These poems stress technical mysteries. The craft and ritual of bee-keeping are described with a Kafkaesque suggestiveness, and can take off into a larger terror and come back after all into the common and solid world. In 'The Bee Meeting', her lack of protective clothing, her feeling of being an outsider, then an initiate, the account of the disguised villagers and the final removal of disguise, the queenbee, the spiky gorse, the box—all are literal facts which suggest paranoic images but remain literal facts. The poem constantly moves between the two poles of actuality and symbolic dimension, right up to and including the end. A related poem, 'The Arrival of the Bee Box', works in the same way, but instead of suggesting paranoiac fear and victimisation, puts the beekeeper into an unstable allegorical God-position. The casual slangy 'but my god' unobtrusively works towards the religious enlargement:

> I am no source of honey
> So why should they turn on me?
> Tomorrow I will be sweet God, I will set them free.
> The box is only temporary.

After the suggestiveness comes the last line, belonging more to the literal beekeeping facts, but pulled at least briefly into the symbolic orbit. These are poems of fear, a fear which seems mysterious, too large for its occasion. They allow for a sinister question to raise itself, between the interpretation and the substance. The enlargement which is inseparable from this derangement is morally vital and viable: these poems are about power and fear, killing and living, and the ordinariness and the factual detail work both to reassure us and to establish that most sinister of fears, the fear of the familiar world. Perhaps the most powerful Bee poem comes in the New Year edition of *Ariel*, 'The Swarm' (also printed in *Winter Trees*). Here the enlarge-

ment is total and constant, for the poem equates the destruction of the swarm with a Napoleonic attack, and presents a familiar argument for offensive action: 'They would have killed *me*'. It presents two objective correlatives, the bees and Napoleon, in an unfailing grim humour:

> Stings big as drawing pins!
> It seems bees have a notion of honour,
> A black, intractable mind.
> Napoleon is pleased, he is pleased with everything.
> O Europe! O ton of honey!

The humour comes out of the very act of derangement: imagine comparing this with that, just imagine. It depends on the same kind of rationally alert intelligence that controls 'Fever 103°'.

It is present in the great *Ariel* poems: 'Lady Lazarus', 'Daddy',[5] 'Death & Co.', 'A Birthday Present' and 'The Applicant', which are very outgoing, very deranged, very enlarged. In 'Lady Lazarus' the *persona* is split, and deranged. The split allows the poem to peel off the personal, to impersonate suicidal feeling and generalise it. It is a skill, it is a show, something to look at. The poem seems to be admitting the exhibitionism of suicide (and death-poetry?) as well as the voyeurism of spectators (and readers?). It is also a foul resurrection, stinking of death. This image allows her to horrify us, to complain of being revived, to attack God and confuse him with a doctor, any doctor (bringing round a suicide) and a Doktor in a concentration camp, experimenting in life and death. It moves from Herr Doktor to Herr Enemy and to miraclemakers, scientists, the torturer who may be a scientist, to Christ, Herr God, and Herr Lucifer (the last two after all collaborated in experiments on Adam, Eve, and Job). They poke and nose around in the ashes, and this is the last indignity, forcing the final threat: 'I eat men like air'. It is a threat that can intelligibly be made by martyred victims (she has red hair, is Jewish), by phoenixes, by fire, by women. The fusion and dispersal, once more rational and irrational, makes the pattern of controlled derangement, creating not one mirror but a hall of mirrors, all differently distorting, and revealing many horrors. Such complexity of reference, such enactment of desperation, hysteria and hate, permits at times the utterly bare cry, like the endearment in 'Nick': 'I turn and burn'. Again, the range of tone is considerable. There is the dry irony, only capable of life in such surroundings of hysteria: 'Do not think I underestimate your great concern', and the slangy humour, 'I guess you could say I've a call', which, like the communion tablet in 'Tulips' is an anti-religious joke, not a solemn allusion, though you do not see the joke unless you feel the solemnity. There is the sensuous particularity, extremely unpleasant. It is tactual, visual and olfactory: 'Picks the worms off me like sticky pearls', 'full set of teeth' and 'sour breath'. The sheer active hostility of the poem works through the constant shift from one mode to another, one tone to another, one *persona* to another. It races violently and spasmodically towards the climax.

This kind of structural derangement of structure, which allows for collision, a complex expansion, and a turn in several directions, sometimes becomes very surrealist in dislocation. It fragments into opaque parts, as in that most baffling poem, 'The Couriers', and in 'The Applicant'. We might be tempted to see the enlargement in 'The Applicant' as an allegory of marriage, relationship, dependence, were if not for the violent twist with which the poem shuffles off such suggestions:

> First, are you our sort of a person?
> Do you wear
> A glass eye, false teeth or a crutch,

A brace or a hook,
Rubber breasts or a rubber crotch,
Stitches to show something's missing? No, no? Then
How can we give you a thing?
Stop crying.
Open your hand.
Empty? Empty. Here is a hand
To fill it and willing
To bring teacups and roll away headaches
And do whatever you tell it.
Will you marry it?
It is guaranteed
To thumb shut your eyes at the end
And dissolve of sorrow.
We make new stock from the salt.
I notice you are stark naked.
How about this suit—
Black and stiff, but not a bad fit.
Will you marry it?
It is waterproof, shatterproof, proof
Against fire and bombs through the roof.
Believe me, they'll bury you in it.

The hand to fill the empty hand and shut the eyes, or (later) the naked doll that can sew, cook, talk, move towards this allegory, but the black stiff suit 'waterproof, shatterproof' in which 'they'll bury you' moves away towards any kind of panacea or protection. What holds the poem together, controlling such opacities of derangement, is the violent statement of deficiency hurled out in the first stanza, and the whole violent imitation of the language of salesmanship, the brisk patter of question, observation, suggestion and recommendation. The enlargement works not just through the ill-assembled fragments—hand, suit, and in the later stanzas, doll—but through the satirised speech, which relates needs, deficiencies, dependence and stupid panaceas to the larger world. Life (or love) speaks in the cheap-jack voice, as well it may, considering what it may seem to have to offer. This is an applicant not just for relationship, for marriage, for love, for healing, but for life and death.

This brilliant linguistic impersonation works more generally in these poems, as a source of black humour, as satiric enlargement, as a link with ordinariness, as unselfpitying speech. It is present in small doses but with large effect in the massive, rushing, terrible poem, 'Getting there'. Here the death train is also the painful dying, the dragging life, also wars, machines, labour. The poem questions, and the questions stagger: 'How far is it? How far is it now?' It dwells painfully and slowly in the present tense: 'I am dragging my body . . . And now detonations . . . The train is dragging itself'. Its derangements present animals and machines in a mangling confusion: the interior of the wheels is 'a gorilla interior', the wheels eat, the machines are brains and muzzles, the train breathes, has teeth, drags and screams like an animal. There is a painful sense of the body's involvement in the machine, the body made to be a wheel. The image creates an entanglement, involves what Sartre calls the 'dilapidation' of surrealism. There is the horror of a hybrid monster, a surrealist crossing of animal with machine. The rational arguments and logical connections are frightening in their precision. The wheel and the gorilla's face can be confused into one image, big, round, dark, powerful. Krupp's 'brains' is almost literally correct. The train noise can sound like a human scream, the front of a train can look like a face.

The method of combination as well as the content, as in all good poetry, generates the passions. The sense of strain, of hallucination, of doing violence to the human imagery is a consequence of the derangements. The rational excuses simply play into the hands of such sense of strain, by making it work visually, bringing it close, giving it substance and connection with the real European world. The movement is a double one, it creates a trope and a form for unbearable pain, and intolerable need for release. It enlarges the personal horror and suggests a social context and interpretation, in Krupp, in the train, in Russia, in the marvellously true and fatigued 'some war or other', in the nurses, men, hospital, in Adam's side and the woman's body 'Mourned by religious figures, by garlanded children'. And finally, in Lethe. Its end and climax is as good as that in 'Nick':

And I, stepping from this skin
Of old bandages, boredoms, old faces
Step to you from the black car of Lethe,
Pure as a baby.

There is the naked appearance of the myth new-made, the feeling that Lethe has had to wait till now to be truly explained, as the Nativity had to wait for 'Nick'. After such pain of living and dying, after so many bewildered identifications, after such pressure and grotesque confusion, we must step right out of the skin. And when we do, the action reflects back, and the body seems to have been the train. This adds another extension of the derangement of human, animal, and mechanical. After this, only Lethe. The poem then begins to look like a nightmare of dying, the beginning of forgetting, the lurching derangements working as they do in dreams.

Once more, the expansion permits the naked cry. This happens more quietly and sadly in 'The Moon and the Yew Tree' where the movement outward is against the Christian myth, but works so as to generalise, to show the active seeking mind in the exercise of knowledge and comparison. This movement explains, permits, and holds up the bare dreadful admission, 'I simply cannot see where there is to get to'. The feeling throughout is one of deep and tried depression. The moon is no light, no door:

It is a face in its own right,
White as a knuckle and terribly upset.

The oddity and childishness of the funny little analogy, and the simple bare statement, 'terribly upset' all contribute to the tiredness. So does the science of 'drags the sea after it like a dark crime' and the conceit 'the O-gape of complete despair', which have a slight archness and flickering humour, like someone very tired and wretched who tries a smile. Nature is all too simply interpreted, coloured by 'the light of the mind', is cold, planetary, black, blue. The moon is quite separate from the consolations of religion, though there are echoes of other myths which emphasise this, of Hecate and witchcraft, as in 'The Disquieting Muses'. Such sinister suggestions, like the remote and decorative images of the saints, 'all blue,/Floating on their delicate feet over the cold pews,/Their hands and faces stiff with holiness' are made in a matter-of-fact, slightly arch way. These are Stanley Spencer–like visions, made in a childish, tired voice: 'The moon is my mother. She is not sweet like Mary./Her blue garments unloose small bats and owls'. The very quietness, compared with her more violent poems of fear, has its own stamp of acceptance. The several bald statements in the poem belong to the quiet tired prevailing tone: 'How I would like to believe in tenderness' and 'the message of the yew tree is blackness—blackness and silence'.

This poem of deep depression still enlarges, still knows about the larger world, still tries a tired but personal humour:

Eight great tongues affirming the Resurrection.
At the end, they soberly bong out their names.

The poem's empathy is powerful, but it is perhaps most

powerful when it is dropped. The end returns to the explicit act of interpretation—what do the moon and the yew tree mean?—of the beginning. The poem moves heavily into the meditation, then out of it. There has been an an attempt at enlargement, but the colours here are the colours of the mind, and the attempts at mythical explanation or extension all fail. It seems like a poem about making the effort to write out of depression, where the act of enlargement is difficult, the distance that can be covered is short.

In 'A Birthday Present' the same process shapes a different passion. The enlargement in this poem is again a movement towards Christian myth, this time a perverted annunciation. The poem longs for release, like so many others, but in its individual mood. This time she pleads and reasons carefully, patiently, with humility, is willing to take a long time over it. The pace of her poems varies tremendously, and while 'Daddy', 'Lady Lazarus' and 'Getting There' move with sickening speed, 'A Birthday Present' is appallingly slow. Its slowness is right for its patience and its feeling of painful burden. It is created by the pleas, 'Let it not . . . Let it not', and the repetitions which here put the brakes on, though in other poems they can act as accelerators. Its questioning slows up, and so does its vagueness, and its unwillingness to argue endlessly—or almost endlessly. The humilities are piteously dramatised: 'I would not mind . . . I do not want much of a present . . . Can you not . . . If you only knew . . . only you can give it to me . . . Let it not'. There is the childishness, horrifying in the solemn pleasure of 'there would be a birthday'. From time to time there is the full, adult, knowing, reasoning voice, that can diagnose, 'I know why you will not'; reassure, 'Do not be afraid'; and be ironic, 'O adding machine/Is it impossible for you to let something go and have it whole?/Must you stamp each piece in purple . . .'

It is not surprising that Sylvia Plath felt constrained to speak these late poems: they are dramatised, voiced, often opaque but always personalised. Their enlargements are made within the personal voice: groping for the resemblance to some war, some annunciation, some relationship, some institution, some Gothic shape, some prayer, some faith. Even where there is a movement towards the larger world, as in 'The Moon and the Yew Tree' or 'A Birthday Present', it has a self-consciousness, a deployment of knowledge, a reasoning, a sense of human justice, that keeps it from being sick or private. The woman who measures the flour and cuts off the surplus, adhering 'to rules, to rules, to rules', and the mind that sees the shortcomings of adding-machines is a *persona* resisting narcissism and closure, right to the death.

Ronald Laing is involved in that cult of schizophrenia which has encouraged both an excessive admiration and an excessive rejection of a clinically limited poetry of derangement. I believe that Sylvia Plath's poetry is not so limited, but I should nevertheless like to remember Laing's comment that few books in our time are forgiveable, and to suggest that *The Colossus* and *Ariel* are amongst those few.

Notes

1. 'The Barfly Ought to Sing', *Triquarterly*, no. 7, Fall 1966. Reproduced in *The Art of Sylvia Plath*, ed. Charles Newman (London, 1970).
2. Introduction to *Ariel* (New York, 1966). Republished in *New York Review of Books*, vol. 6, no. 8, 12 March 1966.
3. 'Notes towards a Biography', *The Art of Sylvia Plath*, ed. Charles Newman (London, 1970).
4. 'Necessity and Freedom: The Poetry of Robert Lowell, Sylvia Plath, and Anne Sexton', *Critical Quarterly*, vol. vii, no. 1, Spring 1965.

5. A. Alvarez is particularly good on this poem, 'Sylvia Plath', *Triquarterly*, no. 7, Fall 1966, reproduced in *Beyond All This Fiddle* (London, 1968).

ANTHONY LIBBY
From "Sylvia Plath, God's Lioness and the Priest of Sycorax"
Mythologies of Nothing:
Mystical Death in American Poetry 1940–70
1984, pp. 126–52

Poets deep and mysterious can too easily become mirrors, their central obscurities burnished to reflect our cultural preoccupations. So popular categories falsify. We are invited to understand Sylvia Plath as feminist, despite the rather strong animosity to women in *The Bell Jar* which led Harriet Rothstein (writing in *Ms.*) to question "her falsely assigned role as feminist heroine."[1] And in a culture fascinated by the spectacle of its own gradual self-destruction, there is perhaps even more preoccupation with Plath as suicide, despite various brave but questionable critical assertions that suicides have little of general importance to say to us.[2] Clearly it is impossible to deny that the feminist and suicidal categories touch on Plath's vision of sexual destruction, but those classifications fail to take us deeply enough into her poetry; even taken together they suggest too simple a direction for the violence she evokes, too reductive a preoccupation with Plath as victim. Victimizer as well, she achieves a strange mythic power. Even more clearly than Lowell's, her poetry illuminates the anti-human side of the negative mysticisms.

The problem of interpretation is compounded by the extreme and unevenly obscure nature of her poetry, which invites extreme critical responses. The most basic judgments about the significance and value of her central poems vary enormously according to the preoccupations of her critics. The difficulty is nicely exemplified by two critical books about the poet in which David Holbrook and Judith Kroll describe two radically opposed Sylvia Plaths. In fact these critics agree that the poems dramatize a basic duality in the poet, but their accounts of the fruits of that duality have little to do with each other. Holbrook, who has nothing but heartfelt scorn for the "Women's Liberation fanatics" who glorify Plath,[3] orchestrates a Freudian case study which concludes that almost all of Plath's poetry is the record of "paranoid-schizoid" delusions, worthwhile primarily as a documentation of the nature of madness. With a very different sort of ingenuity, which I find more sympathetic but equally extreme, Kroll makes the poet a priestess in search of absolute transcendence. Her Plath dies (not before seeing God) because of a "religious crisis," after producing poetry which seems morbid only to a culture inordinately afraid of death and suspicious of mysticism.[4]

The radical contrast between these critical approaches inevitably appears in their reactions to the very late poem "Edge," which is fortunately only in part prophetic in its depiction of a woman accompanied to death by her two children. Holbrook finds the poem "beautiful but psychotic" and argues that it "idolizes infanticide."[5] Kroll, who sees Plath's actual suicide as an attempt to liberate her true self and to achieve some (undefined) immortality, seems to invite Holbrook's accusation, precisely by justifying (poetic) infanticide. "The dead woman . . . has reabsorbed her world and her children, an act which emphasizes the perfectedness of her life." This is done "in a way that goes beyond judgement or blame."[6] Neither critic entertains the possibility that Plath may present the whole tableau, including the initial line "The woman is perfected," with some irony, that she is not necessarily idolizing anything here. Surely that irony is suggested by the description of each child as "a white serpent," and especially by the reference to "the *illusion* of a Greek necessity" (*Ariel*, 84, my emphasis), which—instead of genuine fate—seems to govern the action.[7] The discussion of Plath's attitudes toward death, and even more of Plath herself as a mystic—a term which appears not only in Kroll but repeatedly in the critical collection *The Art of Sylvia Plath*[8]— must never lose sight of her pervasive irony. She does, finally, write visionary poetry, and it will be essential to determine what myth informs her mysticism. But first it is important to define the limits of that mysticism. The problem is not the degree of her morbidity, or fascination with death for its own simple sake, but her cynicism; mystics are often fascinated by death, but seldom so given to callous jokes about transcendence.

Like Roethke, Plath is at times a mystic of immanent union. But like Wallace Stevens she is quite capable of using religious terminology for her own sometimes devious purposes. Like Stevens she rejects the traditional mysticism of transcendence; "I am not mystical" (*Winter*, 28), one poem says in reference to belief in spirits. In "Love Letter" Plath, like Lowell, uses the vocabulary of transcendence to describe romantic love, but she does it more playfully than he. The lover has resurrected the "dead" speaker:

> I started to bud like a March twig:
> An arm and a leg, an arm, a leg.
> From stone to cloud, so I ascended.
> Now I resemble a sort of god
> Floating through the air in my soul-shift
> Pure as a pane of ice. It's a gift.
>
> (*Crossing*, 27)

Less playful and more mocking is the imagery of rising in "Fever 103°," which deflates both transcendent mysticism and its source, orthodox Christianity, by using them to describe a sickness. Plath becomes the central figure in a tawdry holy picture of the Assumption defaced by images of modern mechanical flame:

> I think I am going up,
> I think I may rise—
> The beads of hot metal fly, and I, love, I
> Am a pure acetylene
> Virgin
> Attended by roses,
> By kisses, by cherubim,
> By whatever these pink things mean.
>
> (*Ariel*, 54)[9]

Amused by her own rising, she is flippant about the myth of Christ's Ascension; "Years" describes him as "Christus . . . Dying to fly and be done with it" (*Ariel*, 72).

Even the specific images of the *via negativa* are irreverently manipulated, though here Plath's frequent irony fails to conceal a terminal longing. She imagines not the cloud of unknowing but a sky of forgetting: "the black amnesias of heaven" (*Ariel*, 17). But such blankness draws her. The temptation is explicitly dramatized in some of her poems of sickness, among her most humanly appealing because they show her resisting the powerful pull. How sweet, as well as saintly, to turn from the complexities of ordinary existence to the simple blankness at the end of her version of the negative way. Plath will ultimately confront a divinity that offers little peace, but in "Tulips" she allows herself a wistful parodic use of mystical terminology to describe a confrontation with nothingness uncomplicated by savage deities. "I am nobody," Plath writes:

> I didn't want any flowers, I only wanted
> To lie with my hands turned up and be utterly empty.
> How free it is, you have no idea how free—
> The peacefulness is so big it dazes you,
> And it asks nothing, a name tag, a few trinkets.
> It is what the dead close on, finally; I imagine them
> Shutting their mouths on it, like a Communion tablet.
>
> (*Ariel*, 11)

The loss of self, the hands posed to fit the traditional inconography of mysticism, the evocation of death, the reference to the union with God in Communion—all these signs of ecstasy accompany a mental state presented as a dead end and finally resisted. Similarly in "Paralytic" the speaker achieves an enforced and empty transcendence, like a "buddha," asking "nothing of life" (*Ariel*, 78). In both poems the equation between sickness and mystic peace suggests how easily the negative way can turn perverse, the deadly self-involvement of the suicide only one step beyond the ecstatic death to the world of the mystic. As W. S. Merwin will at times demonstrate, mysticism may reveal a psychological deficiency as well as psychic power, inability to accept ordinary human life and death.

Some of Plath's mocking references to the way of unknowing imply that the deficiency is an attribute of "the big god," who meets the mystic's emptiness of self with his own: "The white gape of his mind was the real Tabula Rasa" (*Winter*, 32). When Plath does allow herself to write straight descriptions of peaceful loss of self in unknowing, she tends to leave the transcendent God out. In fact these poems allow very little of man, either; the context is nature. In "Two Campers in Cloud Country" the purity of the landscape is defined, as it will be in Merwin's poetry of icy mysticism, by its distance from the human: "It is comfortable, for a change, to mean so little, / These rocks offer no purchase to herbage or people: / They are conceiving a dynasty of perfect cold" (*Crossing*, 32). Under the spell of these clouds unknowing ("No gesture of yours or mine could catch their attention,") the campers drift into an ancient union:

> Around our tent the old simplicities sough
> Sleepily as Lethe, trying to get in.
> We'll wake blank-brained as water in the dawn.

This occasional poem is not fully typical of Plath. In her later work "the old simplicities" will be defined by a strange and far less peaceful combination of ancient myth and new magic, but the early poems of mystical contact are frequently dominated by a simple loss of self in landscape or animals, Lowell's "dark downward kingdom." As Robert Phillips puts it, "Always in these first poems one observes Plath's identification with the lower forms of existence—mushrooms and moles, snakes and insects, stones and bones."[10] Sometimes the imagined union comes, as in "Blue Moles," in the depths of sleep, more dream vision than mystical vision in any exact sense.

Whether the result of dream or meditation, the evocations of natural union in the early landscape poetry are marked by an uncharacteristic gentleness, even when they describe that ultimate union, death. In Plath's more mature poetry, mystical contact is usually characterized by a mysterious violence. Here the connection between Plath and Lowell may supplement the comparison between Roethke and Plath. Because her mysticism is ultimately dominated by a violent anthropomorphic deity, it is directly comparable to the mythology of the younger Lowell. His influence on her has less to do with confession than communion with a savage god. Initially, she internalized the violence of his world by copying the violence of his imagery. In direct imitation of him she wrote shore poems marked by what he called, in introducing her later poetry, "Massachusetts' low-tide dolor" (*Ariel*, ix). "Point Shirley" is more characteristically a Lowell poem than many of Lowell's own, if only because of an image like "The sun sinks under Boston, bloody red," or the rhythms of "Against both bar and tower the black sea runs" (*Colossus*, 25, 26). Specifically reminiscent of "The Quaker Graveyard at Nantucket" is imagery that describes "a dog-faced sea" as an animal in mortal combat with the shore. (Similar imagery appeared in T. S. Eliot's Massachusetts North Shore poem "The Dry Salvages"; like Lowell, Eliot concentrates on the sea's voices when the sea is caught in "the granite teeth" of the shore.)

As the sea, which both "Quaker Graveyard" and Plath's "Finisterre" describe as "exploding," becomes a source of savage violence, the consolations of traditional belief recede. In "Finisterre" the ocean expands to infinite "nothing": "With no bottom, or anything on the other side of it, / Whitened by the faces of the drowned" (*Crossing*, 3). At land's end Plath describes a statue of "Our Lady of the Shipwrecked," as intent on eternity and ignorant of human concerns as Lowell's Lady of Walsingham. Supplicants sculpted and real pray to her, but "She does not hear what the sailor or the peasant is saying— / She is in love with the beautiful formlessness of the sea." Sometimes in Plath, as in "Quaker Graveyard," the way to union with that beautiful formlessness is a literal drowning; under the coldly maternal "full moon" of "Lorelei," the speaker is tempted to join the "great goddess of peace" who call to her from "the great depths" (*Colossus*, 23). But in the later poems to the great goddess, peace is far away, a forgotten and boring condition.

Even more than the early Lowell, the late Plath scorns the peace that passes understanding, or presents peace as sterile though tempting passivity. Only occasionally does she celebrate the type of revelation that happens to the traditionally passive recipient, and the revelation is presented as a relief from passivity. The epiphany poem "Black Rook in Rainy Weather" describes her jolted out of "neutrality" by a miracle of ordinary vision ("If you care to call those spasmodic / Tricks of radiance miracles"). But the revelation received passively leads nowhere; afterwards she can only wait for recurrence, "for the angel, / For that rare, random descent" (*Crossing*, 42). Like "The Moon and the Yew Tree," "Years" rejects peaceful mysticism and the transcendent theology that advocates it.

> O God, I am not like you
> In your vacuous black,
> Stars stuck all over, bright stupid confetti,
> Eternity bores me,
> I never wanted it.

(Ariel, 72).

To this transcendent God, "great Stasis," is opposed the worldly ecstasy of motion and violent flow:

> What I love is
> The piston in motion—
> My soul dies before it,
> And the hooves of the horses,
> Their merciless churn.

The hint of sexual movement, as well as the horse in flight and the soul dying of excitement, also appear in Plath's ultimate hymn to the mystical flow, "Ariel." The basic reality for her is not peace but the storm, sometimes Roethke's "steady storm of correspondences," often "a wind of such violence" that "I break up in pieces that fly about like clubs" (*Ariel*, 15). Like "Years," "Getting There," a strangely hallucinatory poem also driven by "these pistons," gives up on an Eliot-like transcen-

dence ("Is there no still place / Turning and turning in the middle air"). Instead, there is the earthy drive of "these wheels / Fixed to their arcs like gods" (*Ariel*, 36). Whether with reluctance or excitement, Plath must seek her true mystic perceptions not in the stasis of traditional faith, or eternity, or even death, but in a myth of ecstatic and violent kinesis, in a transforming progression of which death is only a part.

II

The deity involved in her myth is seldom clearly described by Plath. To understand her final secret we must look to a more intimate influence than Lowell or Roethke, to the poet who inhabited her life and participated in her mystic search as well as her poetry. But to mention Ted Hughes with Sylvia Plath is to risk a long and ultimately tedious descent into biographical and sexual controversy. "Ted" and "Sylvia" threaten to become the Scott and Zelda of our time, though Ted has fewer defenders than Scott, despite feminist poet Robin Morgan's tritely phrased assertion that "the entire British and American / literary and critical establishment / has been at great lengths to deny" that Hughes is responsible for "the murder of Sylvia plath."[11]

Somehow the denial seems more reasonable than Morgan's glib accusation, but who knows? Hughes's psychological influence on Plath must inevitably remain partly hidden; if her poetry is "confessional" it is often the most abstract and evasive of confessions. More obvious and interesting is the great stylistic and philosophical influence each exerted on the other. From the beginning they shared a vision of elemental mythic conflict, which should not be oversimplified by too rigid a concentration on their biographies. Plath's death and Hughes's emergence as a survivor and, in A. Alvarez's term, a "survivor-poet," tempt us to see them in simple opposition. As Phyllis Chesler writes, "traditionally, the ideal female is trained to 'lose,' and the ideal male is trained to 'win' (i.e., psychologically females are trained to die, males to survive)."[12] Sometimes their poetry about each other seems to reinforce this dichotomy. Most conspicuously, "Daddy" has popularized the image of Hughes as "A man in black with a Meinkampf look," the "vampire" who "drank my blood for . . . / Seven years" (*Ariel*, 51), presumably the same ambiguously destructive honeymoon Hughes gives his account of in "Crow Improvises" (*Crow*, 53). But even in "Daddy" the female speaker is as much manipulator as victim; she creates the man in black—"I made a model of you"—and she finally destroys him—"If I've killed one man, I've killed two." Of course this murder is metaphorical; except herself, Plath never actually killed anyone. But neither, as far as we know, did Hughes.

They did shape each other's work. We can easily discover characteristic Plath images in Hughes's later poetry, and his images in hers. Even more striking is the probability that each anticipated imagery characteristic of the other. Although we have Hughes's precise dating of the composition of much of Plath's poetry, and therefore it seems safe to assume that *Lupercal* (1960) influenced the imagery of *Ariel* (composed 1961–1963) more than *Ariel* influenced *Lupercal*, that assumption is open to question. For instance Hughes's "Cleopatra to the Asp" in subject (a woman's vengeful suicide), imagery (a mirror, waters, the moon), and even tone ("the devil in it / Loved me like my soul, my soul," *Lupercal*, 60) sounds so characteristic of the later Plath that Hughes seems here to be influenced by her unwritten poetry, to be working in her vein before she herself has fully discovered it. They lived and worked together, probably choosing to do so partly because they shared the same vision from the start; neither created the other, each constantly influenced the other. That influence probably began—through publications—before they met, and it continues after they have parted; if Sylvia Plath is still somehow fully alive in *Ariel*, she is at least a presiding spirit in *Wodwo* and *Crow*. If we are to discover the final resonances of her mythology, we must look not only to the posthumous publication Hughes the editor gives us in her name, but also to the poetry he wrote in the years after her death.

Despite the pervasive similarities between the two poets, there are clearly certain areas which one seems to occupy more fully than the other, and in those areas the direction of influence is obvious. When Plath ends "Watercolor of Grantchester Meadows" with the sudden and rather arbitrary suggestion that "The owl shall stoop from his turret, the rat cry out" (*Colossus*, 41), she has projected herself with some effort into Hughes's territory. When, with more success, she envisions a gull with "The whole flat harbor anchored in / The round of his yellow eye-button" ("A Winter Ship," *Colossus*, 44), she seems directly influenced by Hughes's hawk, who "hangs his still eye. / His wings hold all creation in a weightless quiet" (*Hawk*, 11). So in "Zoo Keeper's Wife" the cold eel immersed in the dark "like a dead lake" with a belly "Where the heads and tails of my sisters decompose" (*Crossing*, 38) specifically suggests his "Pike," though here as in "Elm" Hughes's projection becomes her internalization.

While Hughes's explicit influence shows more clearly in Plath's early work, her clear influences on him, his excursions into her territory, are more evident in his later collections. In at least one of the poems in *Wodwo*, Plath as presiding spirit is perhaps more than metaphorically present. "Cadenza," according to M. L. Rosenthal, "has precisely the type of dynamics that Sylvia Plath at her best achieved, especially in her poem 'Ariel.'"[13] Remarkably like a Plath poem, it echoes not only "I am the arrow" from "Ariel" but these lines from "Fever 103°":

> . . . I
> Am a pure acetylene
> Virgin
> Attended by roses.
> (*Ariel*, 54)
> . . . I am the cargo
> of a coffin attended by swallows.
> (*Wodwo*, 20)

Presumably this is what Robin Morgan refers to when she accuses Hughes of "malappropriating" Plath's imagery, but perhaps there is something more here than stylistic imitation. Rosenthal describes "Cadenza" as a "lament" for Plath; in fact it seems an attempt to conjure her up, and to reexperience some basic union with her, to join with her spirit and to see with her eyes. The attempt leads to a dream of descent into a realm of elemental force. The poem begins its impressionistic fantasy by connecting the coffin with "a woman walking water," the act of a god; the coffin returns to violate the silence of "The loaded estuary of the dead" with some message or accusation. The one who dreams or speaks the poem identifies himself not only with the coffin's cargo but with the dark rising water that carries it: "And I am the water / Bearing the coffin that will not be silent." Given water and the presence of death, the will toward dark union in these lines suggest Roethkean immersion mysticism, but the poem is more magic spell than mystic meditation and it ends not in peace but in hallucinations of apocalyptic violence. As the coffin rises, the sky falls, "dives shut like a burned land"; the woman who walks the estuary of the dead brings visions not of peaceful death but of cosmic turbulence. What Hughes makes clear about Plath is that despite her popular reputation death is not so much the

center of her poetry as violence. She herself says of her poetic terrain (showing a casual blunt humor usually ignored) "It isn't England, It isn't France, It isn't Ireland. / It's violent" (*Winter*, 17). If there is mystical revelation to follow the magic more or less seriously practiced by Plath and Hughes, in general that revelation will come, like the early Lowell's, out of the heart of violence.

That "Cadenza" is in fact intended as a sort of magical spell seems probable; it would not be Hughes's first attempt to invoke a violent spirit. Responding in an interview to the charge that his poems about jaguars are "celebrations of violence," Hughes replies that he considers them "invocations of a jaguarlike body of elemental force, demonic force." Lest we interpret this talk of "real summoning force" as metaphor he continues, "Lots of people might consider I'm overrating the powers of these two poems, but I'm speaking from my own evidence."[14] The "evidence" is not described, but according to Hughes the role he plays as poet must be understood literally in terms of the activity of the shaman. He uses the same term to describe Plath's poetic activity: "Her poetry escapes ordinary analysis in the way that clairvoyance and mediumship do: her psychic gifts, at almost any time, were strong enough to make her frequently wish to be rid of them. In her poetry, in other words, she had free and controlled acces to depths formerly reserved to the primitive ecstatic priests, shamans and holy men, and more recently flung open to tourists with the passport of such hallucinogens as LSD."[15] Whether or not we can fully assent to the implications of the analysis Hughes offers here, we have a certain amount of evidence that Plath did. For instance A. Alvarez, who tends to dismiss Hughes's "black magic" as "a metaphor for . . . creative powers," writes that in describing to him her final rapidly productive period Plath made it sound like "demonic possession."[16] Later Hughes would speak of the poems of *Crow* in similar terms. "Most of them appeared as I wrote them. They were usually something of a shock to write. Mostly they wrote themselves quite rapidly . . . arrived with a sense of having done something . . . tabu."[17]

But where, really, did they come from? It is difficult to imagine that this "demonic possession" depends on a literal belief in devils, especially in view of various early poems on the subject by both authors. In the late fifties both wrote on the contemporary failure of myth. In "Fourth of July" Hughes says "The right maps have no monsters" (*Lupercal*, 20), and in "The Death of Myth-Making," Plath writes that "lantern-jawed Reason, squat Common Sense" have "minced the muddling devil."[18] The undertone of complaint here would become more explicit a decade later, when Hughes would lash out at "rational skepticism"; his response is not to revive the devil, but to find "completely new Holy Ground, a new divinity, one that won't be under the rubble when the churches collapse."[19] The argument here is more developed, but something of the underlying vision is already there in 1959, in Plath's "On the Decline of Oracles."

> In the Temple of Broken Stones, above
> A worn curtain, rears the white head
> Of a god or madman.[20]

But here the god only communicates trivia, "tomorrow's gossip," and the poem carries little force.

The connection with Yeats is evident. At this time Hughes and Plath, perhaps simply searching for a framework for their poetic powers, felt the need of, and apparently genuine intimations of, a mystical theology both ancient and new. Though it seems unlikely that either of them anticipated how extreme, or how literal, it would eventhually become, there emerge early suggestions of their ultimate myth. In "I Want, I

Want," Plath imagines "a baby god / Immense, bald, though baby-headed" (*Colossus*, 39), whose suffering creates the world's suffering; he will be reborn, more clearly understood because linked to the Mother, in Hughes's "Logos." Another savage god appears—or almost appears—in Hughes's "Crag Jack's Apostasy," where he comes in a constantly elusive dream of "a wolf's head, of eagles' feet" (*Lupercal*, 55); similarly in "The Hermit at Outermost House" Plath evokes "The great gods, Stone-Head, Claw-Foot" (*Colossus*, 56). Very early "The Manor Garden" describes "a difficult borning" which is somehow the end of an evolutionary movement toward something ambiguously destructive.

> Incense of death. Your day approaches
> . . .
> You move through the era of fishes,
> The smug centuries of the pig—
> Head, toe, and finger
> Come clear of the shadow. . . .
>
> (*Colossus*, 3)

Still it remains unclear what is being born, whether man, or god, or something between.

Clearly the conditions of its birth are appropriate to the savage god. Plath's pleasure in its very alieness is first seductive, then chilling. Again her mysticism of extreme negation casts a strange light on all the mystic patterns that begin by rejecting the world. Often she turns Roethkean lines celebrating earth contact into evocations of something alien in the most innocent landscapes. In "Sheep and Fog" she speaks with Roethke's voice to the extent of an apparently unknowing anticipation of the title of his final collection of poems: "the far / Fields melt my heart" (*Ariel*, 3). The line cannot actually refer to Roethke's "The Far Field," which had probably (in 1961) not been written, and would not for three years give its title to the posthumous collection. Still the phrase seems to promise, in Roethke's own words, a Roethkean merging of internal and external. But since Plath feels more than Roethke the terrors of immersion in the flow of being, the following stanza gives "melt my heart" a dark coloration, suggesting not the enriching flow into the world that often lifts Roethke's heart, but a terrible dissolution of self in watery emptiness.

> My bones hold a stillness, the far
> Fields melt my heart.
> They threaten
> To let me through to a heaven
> Starless and fatherless, a dark water.
>
> (*Ariel*, 3)

"Poem for a Birthday," which contains more of Roethke's spirit as well as his style, moves beyond dissolution toward some alien affirmation despite the fact that the experience behind the poetry—mental collapse and shock treatment—seems on the face of it far more terrifying than the experience of casual observation that produced "Sheep and Fog." The electric revelations of this sequence predict the final nature and direction of Plath's transformation mythology, still in images inherited from Roethke. In "Birthday" she operates partly in the potting shed world she had just seen Roethke describe as she studied his greenhouse poems for the first time. This is a world of immersion in a damp vegetable kingdom, "in the bowel of the root," among "little humble loves" (*Crossing*, 50). Not only do Roethke's words echo but the poems recall his excursions into loss of self and self-discovery. Further, "The Beast," about Plath's father, suggests Roethke's poetic versions of his father, and "Who" takes place in a potting shed. But again the correspondences will not go all the way. Plath's intimations of vegetable rebirth are deeply opposed to Roeth-

ke's, not so much because the creature that may emerge from her dark cocooned gestation would be radically different from his enlightened man—that creature is never really presented—but because of the alien force that presides over the gestation. Constantly there is the sense of a threatening, illuminating, and apparently conscious power which is described in most of these poems in similar terms, "Mother of otherness," "mother of mouths, "Mother of beetles," "mother of pestles." Plath's interaction with this "Mother" will become a dominant theme in *Ariel*, and finally the same being will emerge at the center of Hughes's mythic vision.

Who is she? Of the poems in the sequence "Who" most clearly describes the Mother, but as its title predicts it offers primarily suggestive ambiguity. It recalls the memory of an event partially blotted out by shock treatment, an event which involves experiencing the inertness of "a root, a stone, an owl pellet" in a shed which Plath describes as "fusty as a mummy's stomach." The suggestions are double; she had been devoured, or she is gestating in some ancient womb. To add complexity, she says "I am all mouth," which may present "I" as baby, like the "foetus" who sucks "the paps of darkness" in "The Stones," or it may imply that "I" devours, participates in the being of the savage devouring Mother. Finally it seems the speaker wants to be both eater and eaten.

> Mother, you are the one mouth
> I would be tongue to. Mother of otherness
> Eat me. Wastebasket gaper, shadow of doorways.
>
> (*Crossing*, 49)

"Shadows of doorways," this Mother is "nothing," but she is also a spirit of transformation into otherness, not simply death.

Never simply death. "Maenad" describes another movement into darkness, into the Mother's womb, "the moon's vat," a more frightening movement this time because it is more strenuously resisted at first. The speaker wants to remain "ordinary," existing in the realm of "my father," "eating the fingers of wisdom," but the time of a deeper wisdom is on her.

> A red tongue is among us.
> Mother, keep out of my barnyard,
> I am becoming another.
>
> (*Crossing*, 51)

The plea to this "mother of mouths," "devourer," is futile; time and change unwind, and Plath writes "I must swallow it all." The poem ends in mystery, with a question to the "Lady" that we must consider repeatedly as we read Plath's poetry of madness and vision: "Tell me my name." For Plath is herself united with the Mother, an eater, a tongue, another. In her poetry, as in her life, her name was becoming "Mother" too.

III

We think of "Daddy" as typical of her—far from her best poem, but surely her most sensationally memorable one. In a time when no one memorizes poetry, most of us could probably quote at least some of "Daddy." But like her suicide its dominance in our imagination may oversimplify our sense of what was dominant in her imagination; the poetry of the *Ariel* period is more often concerned with mothers and babies than with fathers and daughters. The birth of her children released in Plath not simply a generalized creative urge, but an urge to construct images which would allow her to explore herself as mother, her relation to her own mother, and her relation to some underlying elemental force which with Hughes she came more and more to understand in mythic terms as a terrifying but compelling female, not God but the Great Mother, her antagonist and her ally, an enemy and a self. Her ambivalence toward this figure, which often accounts for the real confusion at the base of some of her poetry, will never reach any resolution. The extremity of this ambivalence seems schizophrenic, or at least understandable in terms of what R. D. Laing calls "ontological insecurity."[21] One of the forms of this is the fear of "engulfment," the sense that one's own reality is so tenuous that a more vital other may swallow one up, creating a psychic parody of mystical immersion. Paradoxically, the insecure self may desire as well as fear this engulfment, because it allows the security of participation in the vitality of the other.

Another aspect of ontological insecurity Laing mentions is the fear of "petrification," of being turned to stone. Plath dramatizes this fear in "Medusa," a companion piece to "Daddy" which begins by evoking an apparently real person but rapidly expands into the mythic territory suggested by its title. Like "Daddy" it depicts a parent looming from the ocean like a massive head, still umbilically connected to the poet, still oppressive as a womb, still constricting. But the "Bottle in which I live" of "Medusa" carries more present force than the "black shoe / In which I have lived like a foot" of "Daddy" (*Ariel*, 39, 49). "Daddy, daddy, you bastard, I'm through" may work as exorcism, but the end of "Medusa," "Off, off, eely tentacle! / There is nothing between us," has more the sound of a futile plea; the tentacle is the maternal umbilicus, which unlike the black telephone to daddy remains "in a state of miraculous repair." The connection is sustained by "Your stooges," the speaker's children, described in foetal terms. The children are so identified with the speaker's mother that "you" in the poem often suggests them more than her. "You steamed to me over the sea, / Fat and red, a placenta" seems to imply both, since the placenta, associated with the baby, remains a part of the mother. Caught up in a cycle of generation which "paralyzes" her, Plath the mother feels the oppression of babies as an aspect of some larger maternal force which winds into her own maternal mind along some ancient umbilicus.

This maternal force cannot be described simply as the poet's own mother, if only because of the mystic or divine context introduced by: "Who do you think you are? / A Communion wafer? Blubbery Mary?" As *The Bell Jar* and various poems suggest, Plath may have felt oppressed by her own mother, and in general by dominant older women interested in influencing her,[22] but the personal obsession only leads to something more fundamental. In "Medusa" as in other poems the Mother turns Plath to stone, in the "Birthday" sequence she devours the poet, in "The Moon and the Yew Tree" she is a terrible deity, "bald and wild," and again opposed to the orthodox goddess: "The moon is my mother. She is not sweet like Mary" (*Ariel*, 41). But the destructive or oppressive aspects of the devouring Mother seldom prevent Plath's willing or unwilling impulse to union with her. Even in "Ocean 1212-W," her short prose piece about her early childhood, the dangerously enticing sea is described not only as "maternal," but as a mirror. "I often wondered what would have happened if I had managed to pierce that looking glass. Would my infant gills have taken over, the salt in by blood?"[23] As we will see, this suggests the dominant pattern; in this terrible and oppressive Mother Plath sees possible self, and from immersion in the Mother she hopes for transformation into a purer existence, a terrible rebirth. ⟨. . .⟩

IV

Plath herself never made such explicit statements about her "visions" as Hughes has, but given the extent to which they shared a general poetic vision, we may hypothetically assume that he speaks for her. This hypothesis is supported by the dominant imagery of her poems, imagery historically as-

sociated, according to Neumann, with the dark side of the Mother: the moon, the sea, poppies, stones ("among the oldest symbols of the Great Mother Goddess"),[24] even the lioness and bees that appear in *Ariel*. From the beginning, in *Colossus*, she often evokes the fundamental Mother image of women rising out of darkness to invite her into a deadly sisterhood. The mythic creatures of "Lorelei," whom Neumann associates with Medusa as "figures of fatal enchantment,"[25] sing to her not from their traditional rocks but from the watery depths: "these shapes float / Up toward me, troubling the face / Of quiet" (*Colossus*, 22). Though they rise, they seem living stone, "ponderous," "hair heavier / Than sculpted marble."

As these dark forces rise from mystic water and the unconscious, the poet often descends to ultimate union. In "All the Dead Dears," which begins with the image of a woman "with a granite grin,"

> Mother, grandmother, greatgrandmother
> Reach hag hands to haul me in,
> And an image looms under the fishpond surface.
> (*Colossus*, 30)

"Nick and the Candlestick" employs the image of descent into the earth to enact a darkly sacramental movement into the unconscious, now the realm of the savage Goddess. In the blue light which often illuminates visionary experience in Plath and Hughes, the poet sinks into the realm of the Mother, to immersion in "the earthen womb," "Old cave of calcium." There she finds "A piranha / Religion, drinking / Its first Communion out of my live toes" (*Ariel*, 33), as the distinction between human communicant and sacrificed deity grows dim. Awakening from her long fall she discovers her child ("O embryo") sleeping as if in a womb himself. She looks to him for human relief from her apocalyptic vision, but we know the comfort he provides cannot last, though it makes her bold in the teeth of doom:

> Let the stars
> Plummet to their dark address,
>
> Let the mercuric
> Atoms that cripple drip
> Into the terrible well.

Here as in "Medusa" the devouring Mother evokes from Plath not the desire for union but fear of engulfment, finally of annihilation. As Neumann explains, the contemporary woman existing in a rationalist patriarchy also has "a symbolically male consciousness and may experience the unconscious as 'negatively feminine.'"[26]

But this fear only dramatizes a characteristic of mystical union, with any sort of god, that has always existed. Plath only takes the stock imagery of death and immersion to an extreme. The *via negativa* has always implied the destruction of self in the service of ultimate otherness, ultimate power. As the opposition between the child and the ritual immersion in "Nick" indicates, the pull of otherness can move the mystic away from human concerns, away from the love of men into the primal whirl of power. Even Christian mystics seem often to regard the love of humanity as a distracting duty. What tends to emerge in visionary writing, despite the rhetoric of love, is a God of power. (Even in St. Theresa's description of the dart of love and spiritual marriage, the conspicuously sexual metaphors depict power more than love. Her intense pleasure in her "delicious wound" and "delightful" pain reveal a masochism closer to Plath's than most mystics'.)[27] So in the poetry of dark union, from Stevens and Eliot through Plath and Merwin, few avowals of love for humanity balance the desire for immersion in otherness. When Williams allowed people realistically imagined (not simply metaphors for the Mother) into *Paterson*, they tended to distract him and finally turn him away from the mystic quest.

Ultimately Plath, seldom distracted by love for humanity, finds something like transcendence within immanence, within the physical world. Her descent into darkness ends in a rising under the sign of the ascendant Terrible Mother. Her poetry is unusual not for its preoccupation with death, but in its references to a mysterious rebirth, ascension not to redemption but to vengeance. "It is inherent in the mysteries of the Great Goddess and in her spiritual character that she grants life only through death"; as in "Nick and the Candlestick," "rebirth can occur through sleep in the nocturnal cave, [or] through a descent to the underworld realm of the spirits."[28] More literal suggestions of rebirth and ascendance come in "Lady Lazarus," the ending of which is inexplicable except in terms of the devouring Mother, who is out to get not only "Herr Doktor," but also "Herr God."

> Out of the ash
> I rise with my red hair
> And I eat men like air.
> (*Ariel*, 9)

Plath's war against God the Father is not always so potentially successful, especially in those poems which apparently refer to her shock treatments, the most dramatic imaginable imposition of a mechanical otherness on the unconscious. But shock treatment, as in the "Poem for a Birthday" sequence, almost invariably assumes mystical resonance, as a metaphor for intimately violent contact between the boldest searchers and a god perceived as totally alien. If the mystic is not destroyed (as in Lowell) by contact with such otherness, union can bring painful revelation. By referring to Prometheus ("vulturous boredom") as well as the hanged man of the Tarot, punished for spiritual presumption, "The Hanging Man" suggests the arrogance of those who would put on the fiery knowledge of gods. For such mystical overreachers, revelation comes as punishment: "I sizzled in his blue volts like a desert prophet" (*Ariel*, 69), and later imagery describes eyes fixed open in a terrible excess of vision. But paradoxically, in a line as full of blunt authority as anything Plath wrote, the drive to know forbidden truth is described as something divine, though destructive, in man; the hanging mystic says of the god, "If he were I, he would do what I did."

This experience of elemental conflict is far from the peaceful orthodox mysticism it reflects and parodies. But the loving beatitude imagined by Eliot, or before him Juliana of Norwich, was itself a radical departure from an earlier way of knowing, reflected in Judaeo-Christian mythology (the Old Testament) as well as pagan. Unconvinced by the Christian story, Plath feels the need to confront the god who dwells in the whirlwind, who may put out reason's eyes, but who knows truths deeper than the pallid evasions of Christianity. "Mystic" suggests that this confrontation, as much as violent identification with Mother or land, constitutes Plath's most intense mystical experience, which nothing can top:

> Once one has seen God, what is the remedy?
> Once one has been seized up
>
> . . .
>
> Used utterly, in the sun's conflagrations, the stains
> That lengthen from ancient cathedrals
> What is the remedy?
> (*Winter*, 7)

The only remedy is further conflict. In words reminiscent of Hughes, the "Second Voice" of Plath's "Three Women" explains the reason for rebellion against the Father. She says of "the Father" and "the Son," "They are jealous gods / That

would have the whole world flat because they are" (*Winter*, 51), and she goes on to describe the response of her Mother the earth as "now the world conceives / Its end and runs toward it."

> She is the vampire of us all. So she supports us,
> Fattens us, is kind. Her mouth is red.
>
> . . .
>
> Men have used her meanly. She will eat them.
> Eat them, eat them, eat them in the end.
> (*Winter*, 53–54)

Many of Plath's bee poems turn on this idea that oppressed female nature will escape and rise to destroy the constrictions of a masculine and mechanical civilization. In "The Swarm," escape fails, but "the man with grey hands / . . . a man of business, intensely practical" remarks as he shoots the swarm down, "They would have killed *me*" (*Ariel*, 65). Mythically he speaks the truth; the matriarchal bees, who kill males after mating, are "a favorite with the Great Mother."[29] In the strange poem "Stings," the poet leaves the company of drudging women to find an earlier identity as queen bee, elsewhere described as "murderess." "I / Have a self to recover, a queen." As usual the matriarch ascends from death, red and threatening:

> Now she is flying
> More terrible than she ever was, red
> Scar in the sky, red comet
> Over the engine that killed her—
> (*Ariel*, 63)

The queen's "lion-red" body connects her with the woman in "Purdah" who will "unloose / . . . The Lioness" against "the bridegroom" who owns her (*Winter*, 42).

But the most striking lion image celebrates mystic motion but not mythic violence: in "Ariel" "God's Lioness" reconciles male and female in a phrase. If Hughes's "Cadenza" is an evocation not so much of the personal spirit of Plath as of the underlying terrible Goddess, "Ariel" is an attempt to imagine sexual and mystical interaction in a context so ecstatic that underlying sexual conflict is resolved in cosmic union. Like Roethke's more still but no less ecstatic "A Field of Light" the poem begins in dark motionlessness, a condition dramatized by the perfect balance of syllables and accents in the brief end-stopped first line. As in "Field" the initial stasis gives way to liquid flow before any subject, any "I" is defined or even mentioned. Undefined stasis gives way to undefined motion, both subject and verb withheld until the second stanza.

> Stasis in darkness.
> Then the substanceless blue
> Pour of tor and distances.
> God's lioness,
> How one we grow,
> Pivot of heels and knees!—The furrow
> Splits and passes, sister to
> The brown arc
> Of the neck I cannot catch.
> (*Ariel*, 26)

Even as they begin to emerge the actors remain vague, looming out of the darkness, defined in small detail by Plath's resonant monosyllables; but the larger shapes continue to be ambiguous. "God's lioness" seems both above and below the human, both divine and animal, perhaps a shape with lion body and the head of a woman, perhaps simply brown horse, white rider. But the sexual resonances become so conspicious that they do more than simply color the image of horse and rider; they cause the superimposition of another image, of human lovers. The powerful monosyllables "How one we grow" can be explained in terms of riding as well as loving, but the specifically sexual interpretation seems necessary to explain a later image. "The child's cry / Melts in the wall" can only happen in a bedroom, as the imagery of lovemaking mixes with and then overcomes the fragmented image of horse and rider.

Finally both sex and riding are overcome by a stronger force, as the landscape/bedscape recedes and the passive rider is "hauled through the air" like Yeats's Leda, caught up by "something else," some force of otherness that takes her beyond ordinary self and landscape in orgasmic rising. After the suspenseful line "And now I," pausing before the final rush of action, everything passes into unity as the poet internalizes the landscape and wheat and seas exchange characteristics in another beautifully balanced line. The interlocking images shimmer with light both still and moving in the heart of flow:

> And now I
> Foam to wheat, a glitter of sea.
> The child's cry
> Melts in the wall.
> And I
> Am the arrow.

"And now I . . . And I. . . ." In the moment of loss of self, the moment of orgasm/merging that extinguishes such ordinary sensation as the child's cry, the "I" is still conspicuous, separate and indomitable. As in Roethke, loss of self becomes the only complete self-assertion, here a self-assertion which joins male (the arrow) and female (wheat, seas, dew) imagery not in violent conflict but in a bold leap to ecstatic energy.

> Am the arrow,
> The dew that flies
> Suicidal, at one with the drive
> Into the red
> Eye, the cauldron of morning.

In such a poem of sexual fulfillment, the devouring Mother cannot appear, so "Ariel" is Plath's most ecstatic dream of merging with various others. But without murderous violence, the Mother's patterns are fulfilled: the female ascent from darkness and stasis into light and motion, the sense of transformation and purification, and finally the death that is also a rebirth in the cauldron of the Mother, a fall into cosmic rising. Throughout the poem, the perimeters of union expand; first Plath is "one" with horse or lover, both in the "pour" of landscape turned liquid, "substanceless"; the horse is "sister" to the road; and then Plath begins to become everything, wheat, seas, and finally the dew which carries her into the sun as the horse carried her into the world. Despite its emphasis on air and fire the poem abounds with liquid, even to the "cauldron" of the sun. Images of transcendence and immersion alternate as motion submerges violence in Plath's most fully realized poem of union. Only in one word does the pervasive violence of her mythology remain; under the circumstances we cannot simply read "suicidal" as ecstatic metaphor.

So even in a poem which rather beautifully suggests the white magic of Ariel, Hughes's Sycorax, mother of Caliban, looms behind the ascent to triumphant union. For Plath's identification with the destructive Mother dominates her mystical imagination. At war with the archetypal Father, and not finally able to remain in the world, much less to sustain mystical immersion in the flow of being that is also an aspect of the Mother, she followed the way of violence to the end. She was psychologically more vulnerable than Hughes to the Great Mother because she was a mother, and imaged herself as prey, but also because she identified with the vengeful aspect of the archetype. For the vengeance was all inside, and from her death there was no rising. There the identification broke down, with inexorable logic. The female can no more survive

destruction of the male principle than men can survive the ongoing destruction of the mythically feminine, whether imagined as mother earth, women, or their own unconscious. As Hughes projected his sense of cosmic violence onto the animal landscape, Plath internalized the apocalypse, became both avenger and victim. Out of the tension between these two roles came much of her most obsessive poetry, poetry often obscure or ambiguous, marked by flashes of genius but also by a certain amount of that oracular confusion that always attends struggle with mystery.

But her poetry is as deep as it is dark and narrow, and it goes to the heart of our time, not only in its psychodrama of sexual conflict but in its exploration of the darker reaches of mysticism. Though not aimed so conspicuously beyond the concerns of ordinary humanity as the mysticism of transcendence, immersion mysticism can be characterized by a coldness toward men and women which lives at the heart of visionary ecstasy. In the frame of eternity, in the poetry of death, the love and suffering of other humans can fade into exemplary abstraction. If humanity considered as a combination of self and others is elided from poetry and meditation, the mystical poet can become as lost in inwardness and morally insensitive as any of the mystics of the past who turned away from men to total concentration on a divinity hallucinated as an image of self in absolute otherness. The familiar otherness, immanent or transcendent, provides endless fascination, but even if it actually is some ultimate ground of goodness as well as power, the claims of human morality lead away from it, back to the world of men. Such claims are explicitly confronted by Robert Bly, like Hughes a poet not only of the Great Mother but of imminent apocalypse; they will have a curious effect on the poetry of W. S. Merwin, who discovers for himself a mystical territory even colder and more remote than Plath's, a place somehow full of that otherness never fully described by Stevens.

Notes

1. Harriet Rothstein, "Reconsidering Sylvia Plath," in *Ms.*, Sept. 1972, p. 99.
2. For instance Irving Howe, "Sylvia Plath: A Partial Disagreement," in *Harper's*, Jan. 1972, pp. 88–91. Interestingly, Howe makes much the same judgment about the Quentin Compson section of *The Sound and the Fury* in his *William Faulkner* (1952; rpt., New York: Vintage, 1962), p. 167.
3. David Holbrook, *Sylvia Plath, Poetry and Existence* (London: Univ. of London Press, 1976), p. 184. Later he says of feminists, "what they want to be liberated from is being female and being human" (p. 200).
4. Judith Kroll, *Chapters in a Mythology, the Poetry of Sylvia Plath* (New York: Harper & Row, 1976), p. 210. Kroll's ideas about Plath's use of the "Moon-muse" or White Goddess have, for me, the distinct advantage of making my own very similar ideas about Plath, Hughes, and the Great Mother sound considerably less eccentric than they did when I first published them, in an early version of this chapter printed as a 1974 *Contemporary Literature* article. Inevitably I find her account of Plath attractive, but in defending Plath (and probably in writing a book acceptable to Ted Hughes) she relentlessly discovers mystical affirmation in the poems, sometimes turning the bitterly ironic ones upside down to do so.

   In the still more recent study *Sylvia Plath and Ted Hughes* (Urbana: Univ. of Illinois Press, 1979), Margaret Uroff correctly argues that "Kroll's discussion of the death in this poem as an intermediate step toward rebirth suggests the limitations of her effort to fit all of Plath's poetry into *The White Goddess* mythology" (p. 170n). Still, Kroll sees depths not adequately fathomed in Uroff's analysis of Plath.
5. Holbrook, *Sylvia Plath*, pp. 271, 272.
6. Kroll, *Chapters in a Mythology*, p. 147.

7. Primary sources will be identified by their first word in the text. Plath collections cited are *The Colossus and Other Poems* (New York: Knopf, 1962), *Ariel* (New York: Harper & Row, 1966), *Crossing the Water* (Harper, 1971), and *Winter Trees* (Harper, 1972). Hughes collections cited include *Lupercal* (London: Faber & Faber, 1960), *Wodwo* (Faber, 1967), *Crow* (Faber, 1970), and *Cave Birds* (New York: Viking, 1978), p. 42.

8. *The Art of Sylvia Plath*, ed. Charles Newman (Bloomington: Indiana Univ. Press, 1970).

9. Typically, Judith Kroll argues that these lines should be taken seriously: "The farce in a sense rises by its own levity above itself" (*Chapters in a Mythology*, p. 179). Worse, Uroff, (*Sylvia Plath and Ted Hughes*, pp. 167–168) seems unaware of the possibility of farce.

10. Robert Phillips, "The Dark Funnel: A Reading of Sylvia Plath," in *Sylvia Plath, the Woman and the Work*, ed. Edward Butscher (New York: Dodd, Mead, 1977), p. 191.

11. Robin Morgan, "Arraignment," *Monster* (New York: Vintage, 1972), p. 76. Plath herself suggests a response to this accusation when in *The Bell Jar* she has Esther Greenwood laugh at Buddy Willard's assumption of responsibility for her suicide attempt and the successful suicide of another of his girls. After all, as *The Bell Jar* also indicates, Plath's first attempts occurred long before she met Hughes.

12. Phyllis Chesler, *Women and Madness* (New York: Doubleday, 1972), p. 294.

13. M. L. Rosenthal, *The New Poets: American and British Poetry since World War II* (New York: Oxford Univ. Press, 1967), p. 233.

14. Ekbert Faas, "Ted Hughes and *Crow*," Interview in *London Magazine*, Jan. 1971, pp. 8–9.

15. Ted Hughes, "Notes on the Chronological Order of Sylvia Plath's Poems," *Triquarterly*, 7 (Fall 1966), 82. When this essay was reprinted in *The Art of Sylvia Plath*, the sentence about shamans and LSD was discreetly omitted.

16. A. Alvarez, *The Savage God* (London: Weidenfeld & Nicholson, 1971), pp. 24, 14.

17. Faas, "Ted Hughes," p. 18.

18. Sylvia Plath, "The Death of Myth-Making," *Triquarterly*, 7 (Fall 1966), 11.

19. Faas, "Ted Hughes," p. 19.

20. Sylvia Plath, "On the Decline of Oracles," *Poetry*, Sept. 1959, p. 368.

21. R. D. Laing, *The Divided Self* (1960; rpt., Baltimore: Pelican, 1965), pp. 39ff. Marjorie Perloff also notes the connection between Laing's "engulfment" and a Plath poem ("Parliament Hill Fields") in "On the Road to *Ariel*: The Transitional Poetry of Sylvia Plath," *Iowa Review*, 4 (Spring 1973), 96–97.

22. In "reconsidering Sylvia Plath," Rothstein contends that Esther Greenwood's complaint that she is manipulated by "weird old women" is a rather "malicious" distortion of her actual situation (p. 49). About Plath's feelings for her own mother we can only speculate, drawing on a range of descriptions from Holbrook's "the poet had a happy relationship with her mother" (*Sylvia Plath*, p. 9) to biographer Butscher's "she was a monster, this sincere Aurelia Plath of Wellsley, a vampire of the unconscious" (*Sylvia Plath, Woman and Work*, p. 8). If the second opinion sounds extreme, the first seems almost willfully naive. Similar disagreements exist about everyone in the Plath cosmos, including Ted and (especially) Olwyn Hughes.

23. Sylvia Plath, "Ocean 1212-W," appearing in *Art of Sylvia Plath*, p. 266.

24. Erich Neumann, *The Great Mother* (New York: Pantheon, 1955), p. 260.

25. Neumann, *Great Mother*, pp. 80–81.

26. Neumann, *Great Mother*, p. 148.

27. St. Theresa, *The Interior Castle*, trans. "A Benedictine of Stanbrook," rev. Prior Benedict Zimmerman (London: Thomas Baker, 1930), p. 132. Theresa also compares her God to "a burning furnace," as Lowell does in "Where the Rainbow Ends." Finally her desire for total union with this fiery Love leads her to an "ardent" longing for death: "life becomes a painful though delicious torture" (p. 172).

28. Neumann, *Great Mother*, pp. 279, 292.

29. Neumann, *Great Mother*, p. 265. An example of the lion-bee-Mother connection is Cybele, whom Graves calls "the Mother of All Living" (*The White Goddess* [New York: Creative Age Press, 1948], p. 259). He initially identifies her as "the Lion and Bee Goddess of Phrygia in whose honor young men castrated themselves" (p. 45).

ALAN WILLIAMSON
From "Real and Numinous Selves: A Reading of Sylvia Plath"
Introspection and Contemporary Poetry
1984, pp. 47–64

Very near the core of Plath's strictly poetic genius is her ability to create in the reader a trance-like, floating sensation—at once vividly attuned to, and alienated from, the outside—which must have played a very important role in her own experience of the world. In my case, at least, this was the strongest initial appeal of the poetry: it was exhilarating, no matter how often the reviewers told me that it should be "depressing," "pessimistic," or "tortured." It now seems to me that a great deal of the power I felt lay in metrics and sound-patterns, and in a peculiarly subtle mastery of pacing. Let me illustrate first, therefore, with a passage which produced this trance-like effect in me, despite the fact that it contains no particularly striking *trouvailles* of diction:

> Over your body the clouds go
> High, high and icily
> And a little flat, as if they
> Floated on a glass that was invisible.
> ("Gulliver")

The first line, ringed with *o*'s; the second, with three accented long *i*'s in the first four syllables, trailing off, as the sound itself does, to long *e*: the element of incantation is clear enough. (Nor is the still greater visual predominance of the letters *o* and *i* insignificant. These letters are, I think, symbolic for Plath: zero and one; female and male; the full/void and the utterly separated, purified "I.") But it is in the third line that the genius for pacing appears. With the qualification "And a little flat," the state of dissociated freedom comes to seem slightly dangerous, or, at least, unreachable. The vowel sounds themselves flatten; and the peculiarity of the rhyme with the preceding line (assonance on the first syllable; eye-rhyme on the second; and the particular bizarreness of a spondee rhymed with a pyrrhic) gives a sense of straining to get past an obstacle. Then, the very word that poses the threat ("flat") is occupied from within by the tonic *o*, and we and the poem "float" into the freedom of a new stanza.

Often such musical analogies seem the most adequate to describe Plath's use of imitative pacing. (Interestingly enough, Plath was indifferent to music until she began writing the poems in *Ariel*, when she became fascinated with Mozart and, especially, Beethoven.) Consider the beginning of a much finer poem, "Ariel" itself:

> Stasis in darkness.
> Then the substanceless blue
> Pour of tor and distances.

The two near-spondees, rhyming, balanced around the insignificant pivot "in": a line could hardly contrive to have more "stasis," less forward movement to it. Moving ahead another five syllables, a hypothetical second line completes itself with the third occurrence of the rhyme—falling, yet again, on an abstract word denoting a privation of quality or presence. Thus, "blue" enters like the declaration of a second theme: because it is a quality; because it is formally unexpected; because it is only the second long vowel in the poem. The theme expands instantaneously, in a "pour" of long-vowel assonance and rhyme, then curiously sinks back under the first theme, as the velocity of the bolting horse melts concrete objects to an abstract blue of "distances."

This little sonata already contains the essential action of the poem. The second theme, of velocity, intensified quality, intensified selfhood, will be developed around the symbolic long *i* and the related long *e*, in what must be one of the most aurally spectacular passages in English poetry since Dylan Thomas:

> And now I
> Foam to wheat, a glitter of seas.
> The child's cry
> Melts in the wall.
> And I
> Am the arrow,
> The dew that flies
> Suicidal, at one with the drive
> Into the red
> Eye, the cauldron of morning.

As in the mountain vision in *The Bell Jar*, the "I" is "honed" against the sun until it is "saintly and thin and essential." It is thrust to the end of the line, against unconditioned space; underscored with ideas of purification, expansion, intensity, and above all speed and daring ("White / Godiva," "unpeel," "seas," "child's cry," "flies," "suicidal," "drive"). But finally, at the crisis, "I" metamorphoses into "Eye," fuses with the cosmic, impersonal awareness, or sheer Being, of the sun itself.[1] Specific identity—like specific perception in the opening stanza—"melts" in the "cauldron" of its own acceleration, back to a formless monism.[2]

I have dwelt on this poem not only because it is a tour de force, but because its melding opposites reveal a side of Plath's ontological vision peculiarly relevant to her stylistic development. In a certain sense, as we shall see, the opening stanza we examined so laboriously contains the plot not only of "Ariel" the poem but of *Ariel* the book.

The philosophical vacillation between motion and stasis runs through all of Plath's late writing. Where one poem yearns for a "still place . . . Untouched and untouchable," another insists: "Perfection is terrible, it cannot have children." "Years" scornfully dismisses the attractions of a "great Stasis"—

> O God, I am not like you
> In your vacuous black,
> Stars stuck all over, bright stupid confetti.
> Eternity bores me,
> I never wanted it.

—and asserts a contrary preference:

> What I love is
> The piston in motion—
> My soul dies before it.

But surely, in the reader's mind, this piston is uncomfortably close to the "engine / Chuffing me off like a Jew" in "Daddy"; while in "Getting There," "The gigantic gorilla interiors / Of the wheels" are themselves "The terrible brains / Of Krupp," "The silver leash of the will"—the power-obsessed, reductively scientific late-capitalist (and masculine) culture frequently under attack in *Ariel*. But they are also the element of indomitable will in the poet herself. In a less well-known poem, "The Courage of Shutting-Up," the "black disks" that (echoing a phrase in "Getting There") "revolve, like the muzzles of cannon" are the recording disks of the poet's brain, driven by vindictiveness against her husband, "Loaded . . .

with accounts of . . . Bastardies, usages, desertions and doubleness." By the end of "Getting There," the train has become indistinguishable from the speaker's "skin / Of . . . old faces," the false self; and the image of an "engine" has this resonance in a number of other poems ("Stings," "Totem").

Finally, one also notes in "Getting There" that the wheels are thought of as divine precisely because they are not free: "Fixed to their arcs like gods." And this brings us to the really important point: that the most crucial ideas, death and divinity, freedom and law, will not stay relegated to one side of the division. When Plath says of the piston, "My soul dies before it," one might sense that the Elizabethan meaning of "die" is in play, and thus the familiar theme of sexual masochism, submission to the dark father. But later in "Years" the feeling is grounded more deeply, in a realization that the wish for an absolutely unchecked, exhaustive expression of energy is a hurtling toward death, like the ominous wish "to do everything once and for all" in *The Bell Jar*. It is also a wish that goes beyond human capacity, so that it brings back the idea of divinity; and the new year becomes

> a Christus,
> The awful
> God-bit in him
> Dying to fly and be done with it

In other words, the initial premise in "Years" that the choice of motion is a choice in favor of life, and against the supernatural, is no sooner set forth than it must be inverted. Motion itself is deathly and divine. As in the first stanza of "Ariel," the two extremes inexorably converge.

What this system of unsatisfactory—and, finally, equally nihilistic—opposites implies, on a psychological level, is an inability to conceive of an even interchange between the self and the world, neither side overbalancing the other. For Plath—as a great deal of evidence, poetic and biographical, suggests—there were only two possible stances toward life. I have called them "will" and "convention," but that does not really state the matter adequately. Like the secretary, the most depressive of her alter egos in "Three Women," Plath draws into close conjunction the idea of merely responding to life's demands, the idea of spatial and temporal fixity, and the sense of underlying meaninglessness:

> I shall not be accused by isolate buttons,
> Holes in the heels of socks, the white mute faces
> Of unanswered letters, coffined in a letter case.
> I shall not be accused, I shall not be accused.
> The clock shall not find me wanting, nor these stars
> That rivet in place abyss after abyss.

One can, then, be held in place by reality—"reality" meaning the world of objects *and* the social mask *and* poetic convention *and* the laws of one's fate, the "fixed stars"—and so threatened with slowing to a depressive standstill. Or one can continuously, consciously keep ahead of all these things, by a hurtling pace of living and writing, by the imposition of fantasy on reality, by violence acted or suffered—"death hurdle after death hurdle topped," in Lowell's melodramatic but suggestive phrase. But this too is a kind of unfreedom, and brings its own horror of the "engine"-self. Perhaps this is why having children was so terribly important to Plath: it and perhaps art are the only ways of keeping ahead of oneself in time that confirm, rather than fragment, one's integral humanity.

For the stylistic equivalent of being held in place by reality, we have only to look at Plath's early development. Plath often concedes obliquely that it was as difficult for her to be born as a poet as a person. Her practical mother and her hired teachers could not teach her a sense of rhythm; only the mother's evil double, the Disquieting Muse, did. I do not, in fact, believe that Plath was ever truly indifferent to sound values; but she was capable of rendering them unfluid to a degree that amounts to a kind of negative genius. What gives the poems in *The Colossus* a claustrophobic feeling is not the fact that they are set pieces, almost all visual description; or that the morals are tidy (they aren't always); but that one moves forward in the poems so slowly and effortfully. Many of the shorter lines seem to aspire to the condition of having no unstressed syllables at all—

> Goat-horns. Marked how god rose
> ("Faun")

> Tablets of blank blue, couldn't,
> Clapped shut, flatten this man out.
> ("The Hermit at Outermost House")

—while in more elaborated forms the spondaic quality tends to undermine the governing cadence, producing rather torpid and glutinous lines like "Bellied on a nimbus of sun-glazed buttercup" ("Watercolour of Grantchester Meadows"), or the choppy quality that mars the complicated stanzas of "All the Dead Dears." This style does, of course, have compensating advantages. It bears a distant relation to Pound's revival of alliterative verse forms; and, as in Pound, the reward is often a sense of the gritty obtrusiveness of the object—the wonderful dead snake, for instance, whose belly is "Sunset looked at through milk glass." This is, in short, no "academic poetry," correct and mild-spirited. It is the expression of a mind so obsessed with issues of will and stubbornness, with the obstructiveness of the material world, that it could call a hurricane a "collusion of mulish elements"; the only mind, perhaps, that could have invented such a combination of the vivid and the inert.

It is not, however, insignificant that Plath did very readily adopt the "academic" genre conventions of her time: or that those conventions called for the externalization of emotion in a landscape or spectacle, a spatial location; or that she wrote the poems, as Ted Hughes has described it, "very slowly, Thesaurus open on her knee . . . as if she were working out a mathematical problem," in a handwriting "like a mosaic, where every letter stands separate."[3] All of these facts, even the handwriting, have a common element psychologically: a submission to the given, a refusal of forward or self-generated motion.

It is hardly news at this point (but nonetheless true) that the poems in *The Colossus* that do show marked forward movement and fluidity of pacing, an unforced conversational voice, deal most commonly with familial anger ("The Colossus," "The Disquieting Muses") or a mesmeric fascination with suffering ("The Thin People," "The Stones"). It is generally these situations—violence acted or suffered—that break the deadlock with reality, and empower the second phase, the manic keeping-ahead-of-experience characteristic of *Ariel*. The hurtling momentum of the most famous of the later poems has often been remarked on, as have some of the technical qualities that contribute to it: the incisive, exclamatory conversational voice; the run-on, comma-spliced sentences broken over short lines; the irregular but richly overused rhymes, culminating in the nursery-rhyme repetitions of "Daddy."[4] In quieter poems, too, the reader is kept tautly aware of quickenings and slackenings of pace. The characteristic two- and three-line stanzas—cultivated, in *The Colossus*, as exercises in difficult rhyming—now function as a kind of musical measure, a fixed unit against which an often subtle drama of long and short lines, long and short sentences, may take shape. (A simple instance would be the end of "Berck-Plage," where it takes the

children one sentence and four stanzas really to see the funeral; then takes the author one two-sentence stanza to draw her grim conclusions.) We have already seen the virtuosity Plath could rise to when these resources were blended with her strongly developed sense for onomatopoeia and sound-pattern. Her destructive Muse had only to teach Plath a sense of rhythm—to teach her, that is, her own need to control the tempo of experience—and she was, almost overnight, one of the masters of pacing in modern poetry.

But it is not only pacing that makes us aware of a tense contest between mind and reality in *Ariel*. It is also a matter of rhetoric, of how the poems attack the subject. The poems in *The Colossus* generally do not. The subject is there, and the speaker is located in relation to it, by loaded description or else by plain statement. The poems in *Ariel* have a method at once more active and more tentative. They proceed by explicit acts of definition ("This is the sea, then, this great abeyance"; "This is the light of the mind, cold and planetary"). They proceed by questions, questions which tend, slightly paranoiacally, to generate other questions without the pretense, even in punctuation, of waiting for an answer ("Why is it so quiet, what are they hiding?"). They proceed, too, by an offer of alternatives, sometimes made explicit in a question ("It is shimmering, has it breasts, has it edges?"), sometimes merely implicit in the doubling of images ("These lamps, these planets / Falling like blessings, like flakes"). Doubling can also take the inverse form of a simple repetition of crucial words or phrases ("Love, love"; "things, things,"; "I let her go. I let her go"). Sometimes this expands into a litany-like repetition-with-variation, dramatizing at once the ceaseless activity and the obsessive sameness of the thought:

> What is the name of that colour?—
> Old blood of caked walls the sun heals,
> Old blood of limb stumps, burnt hearts.
> ("Berck-Plage")

All these techniques keep us aware of language as a reaction to, an absorption of, the shocks of reality (and thus of a mind imposing itself, but aware of its self-revealing isolation). In this sense, the poems enact their own making; they are what is called "poetry of process," but without the loss of tension, of external precision, which that concept can imply in less anxiety-ridden poets.

The extended image-chains, the surrealist cadenzas, which are one of *Ariel*'s defining features, present the same paradox: they are obsessive and helpless from an intrapsychic point of view; yet aggressive, multiplicative, centrifugal—a kind of escape velocity—where the givenness of outside reality is concerned. They can certainly be bewildering. One may be reading about a sleeping baby—"the drenched grass / Smell of your sleeps, lilies, lilies"—then cross a stanza-break to

> Their flesh bears no relation.
> Cold folds of ego, the calla,
> And the tiger, embellishing itself—
> Spots, and a spread of hot petals.
> The comets
> Have such a space to cross,
> Such coldness, forgetfulness.
> ("The Night Dances")

One learns to read these image-chains as one grasps how—far more than with most surrealist poets—they are fueled by characteristic ambivalences, unresolvable contradictions of feeling. Here, for instance, the thought of "lilies" (the repeated word, I think, a sign of an effort of self-persuasion, as in "With excessive love I enamelled it / Thinking 'Sweetness, sweetness'") brings out an underlying uneasiness at the fact that the child's flesh has become wholly separate from her own. This theme is elaborated in moral terms as "cold" egotism and then as narcissistic sexual flaunting (always a sensitive topic in the late poems). In this poem, there is a resolution, or at least a surcease: with the "comets" (linked, by sound, to the "hot petals"), the absolute separateness of our beings and desires, grasped as a universal condition, moves the poet to empathy rather than fear; and the current of "normal" maternal feeling is restored.

Whether, beyond their psychological verisimilitude, these improvisations help or hurt the structure of the poems has to be a matter for delicate *ad hoc* judgments. For me, this one—by the very unpredictableness of the movement of revulsion—deepens the sense of isolation in the poem. The longer, more confused series of transvaluations in "Fever 103°," however, seems to me uneconomical, and a defect.

As Edward Butscher and others have seen, the momentum of this phase of Plath's writing—and especially of the famous poems of anger—represents, on the whole, a will to life and health. By pressing back against the pressure of reality—vengefully externalizing the sources of evil, but also, as A. Alvarez has said, insisting on willing her own suffering—Plath defended herself against the dangers of engulfment and dependency, and experienced herself as active and autonomous.[5] (This is not to mention the simpler proof of solidity inherent in creative energy itself.) But if this were all Plath had done, the poems might be less interesting than they are, being essentially misrepresentations clung to in desperation. But this was not all; Plath was very conscious of creating fictions or dramas, and thereby of externalizing (and, we must assume, hoping to exorcise) her own motives as well. For me, the most remarkable thing about the angry poems is that while they are, as Alvarez says, "unforgiving," they are not unfair, in that they make the ambivalent feelings behind them, and the need to manipulate an unacceptable reality, so plain that we accept the statements about others as emotionally inescapable but not, therefore, as true. In this, the poems perfectly exemplify what I have tried to define as a "reflexive" mode.

Earlier I suggested how "Daddy" seems to me to undermine its own fictions, to rule out a clear allocation of blame. Let us look now at the emotional dynamics of a somewhat more complicated, many-leveled poem, "A Birthday Present." On the surface or "unfair" level, the poem seems to argue that suicide is the only way not to "kill" life, but to have it (in two senses) "go whole." The "you" of the poem, presumably Ted Hughes, is an "adding machine," lacking in "nobility" or true compassion, because he wants to prevent the speaker from taking her life.

Beyond the obvious paradoxes, there are two difficulties with this argument. The first is that the "present" only becomes death in the course of the poem. It is the Angel of the Annunciation before it is the Passion of Christ. At the beginning, as the characteristic jabbing questions circle around it—"It is shimmering, has it breasts, has it edges?"—it is something far more indefinite. It has the "shimmer" we associate with unfixity, but also with living substance. It may be round or sharply delimited, nourishing or cutting, female or male. It is as if we were thrown back to a child's first tentative movements—of recognition, distinction, reliance—toward the outside world. (Perhaps, incidentally, it is only the contrast with "breasts" that makes me take "edges" as male; but later aggressive phallic images accrue—"a tusk," "a ghost-column"—and the annunciatory angel is, after all, an impregnator as well as a messenger from God.) There is also a

vacillation between megalomania and self-deprecation in the speaker's attitude toward herself. If the gift may be "enormity," a sign of divine favor vouchsafed to a suffering saint, it may also be "small," suited to the chastened status of someone who has nearly given up on her own life. (And so the idea of suicide enters the poem, somewhat insidiously, as a danger safely past, which leaves the speaker grateful for life on the humblest terms.) In sum, we know that the present will somehow give, or define, the meaning of the speaker's life; but it seems to do so in quite contradictory ways.

The second difficulty perhaps arises only if one knows—as admittedly one does not, directly, from the poem—that Plath and her husband were separated when the poem was written, and that she entertained definite, but diminishing, hopes for a reconciliation. In this light, her desire for him to give her a birthday present however "small," and her vision of the two of them eating dinner beside it, have a poignantly simpler meaning. And her reproach to him—"Is it impossible for you to let something go and have it go whole?"—becomes an ironic projection, since it is she who cannot let him go, cannot affirm her life on self-sufficient terms. To put the matter a little differently, his reasonable anxiety that she not commit suicide stands in, becomes a scapegoat, for his truly intolerable refusal to give himself, his love. This, after all, is the one gift that "only you can give . . . to me"; death can come from herself, or from a million accidental causes. (But, of course, she does want death to come "only" from him, in the sense that she wants him to bear the blame:

I know why you will not give it to me,
You are terrified
The world will go up in a shriek, and your head with
   it,
Bossed, brazen, an antique shield,
A marvel to your great-grandchildren.

If the surface sense here is that he cannot share her passion for the subsuming moment, the under-sense is that—as both of them understand—one of the goals of her suicide is to petrify the meaning of his life, turning him into a medieval monster out of one of his own poems.)

By the same token, death becomes a way of never losing contact with him. In this context, to choose a knife as the means of suicide is at once an act of poetic justice—identifying the criminal—and an expression of sexual longing. (The choice of stabbing is unique to this poem, and would seem to go against the distaste for messy deaths expressed in *The Bell Jar*.) At the end of the poem, the knife does "not carve, but enter" (a word rarely used for stabbing, frequently used for sexual penetration), and its entry leads to immediate parturition, the birth-separation of the universe. To notice these things is not to deny the mystical dimension—the subsuming moment, in which the self realizes the universe by purging it of subjectivity, of selfhood—which has been so ably charted by Richard Howard, among others.[6] It is, however, to double these meanings with darker psychic ones, in which death at once symbolically recovers the loss—of a lover, and of future children—and takes vengeance for it.[7] It is also to leave the "present" finally mysterious (as the syntax itself does: "If it were death . . ."), with the mystery of what is truly satisfying in life; or perhaps one should say the mystery of what—which of the great experiences, love or death or the pride of parenthood or the initial fluidity of the infant's landscape—places one in an ultimately significant relation to the world beyond one.

It is the inability not to register the convergence of contradictory motives, combined with the sense of the final mysteriousness of desire, that gives this poem, and some others from the same period, the quality of tragic action rather than special pleading. Is it this same lack, or subversion, of the useful defenses of the closed mind that made the poems finally of little therapeutic use to their author? Or does the problem—as an existential analyst might see it—lie deeper, in the very splitting of ontological tempi which helped rush Plath's clarity ahead of any natural rate of emotional growth? (I myself find Alvarez's comparison of the stance of the poems to "manic defense" solider than his attack on the idea of catharsis per se.)[8] Whatever the reason, I think every reader must have felt that at a certain point in *Ariel* the hurtling anger, impatience, and energy in the voice begin to flag. Perhaps the turning-point is "Years"—written in mid-November 1962—in which the preference for motion over stasis is argued and yet, as we have seen, subtly undermined. After that, the tempo slows. Oracular statements replace the questions, the probings, the alternatives. Images are lingered over longer and more tenderly; but the spaces between them—syntactic and conceptual—widen. There are ambiguities of perception, and ambiguities of emotional tone. Instead of the earlier sharp tension between mind and world, there are moments when everything seems to blur into everything else. There are other moments when the concern is rather with a total loss of contact with reality: the sheeted mirror, the paralytic lying like a "Dead egg . . . Whole / On a whole world I cannot touch," the "riderless" words that run "Off from the center like horses." This is a poetry of the dissolution of the ego—perhaps one of the most accurate and interesting such poetries we have; in it, the principle of stillness again triumphs, though in a wholly new way.[9]

"Totem" may serve to illustrate both the difficulties and the fascination of the very late work. The title concedes the difficulty, for Plath intended it—according to the note in the new *Collected Poems*—to suggest a totem pole, "a pile of interconnected images"—but with the interconnections, as the word "pile" implies, left largely to the reader's imagination.[10] But I cannot help suspecting that Plath was also thinking of Freud's *Totem and Taboo*, in which totemism is connected to the killing and eating of a primal father. For the poem is perhaps best summarized as an extremely depressed meditation on the idea that all life lives at the expense of other life—an idea carried to an absurd extreme in the opening lines: "The engine is killing the track, the track is silver, / It stretches into the distance. It will be eaten nevertheless." As the poem develops, this paradigm is applied to questions of religious and intellectual sustenance:

Let us eat it like Plato's afterbirth,

Let us eat it like Christ.

These are the people that were important—

Their round eyes, their teeth, their grimaces

On a stick that rattles and clicks, a counterfeit snake.

The uncertainties of emotional stance are, I think, evident. Is it a reverent act to eat Plato, or does the brutal double sense of "afterbirth" convey scorn for his notions of immortality and preexistence? Is the tone of "the people that were important" wistful (*if only anyone were*) or satiric (*it all boils down to ego*)? Is it the living who devour the dead, or is it the dead, with their conspicuous "teeth," who gain immortality by preying on the living? Or is the last image really an image of death itself, the grinning skull that devours everything? In the image that follows, the horrifying apartness of the predator is identified with what should be its opposite, the apartness of mystical vision, which sees through the particular to eternity or nothingness:

Shall the hood of the cobra appal me—

The loneliness of its eye, the eye of the mountains

Through which the sky eternally threads itself?

Dimly, one senses that both of these things are part of the speaker's vision of herself, perhaps because of the association of "madness" with another universally feared animal a few lines later: "I am mad, calls the spider, waving its many arms." It is, again, very hard to specify the meaning of this strangely jocular line. Is it that madness is a theatrical gesture; that it is a breaking apart into multiple selves; or that it is merely a beholder's misunderstanding of the all-too-natural horribleness of the one self? Whatever it is in itself, "in truth it is terrible, / Multiplied in the eyes of the flies." The flies ("like blue children") are perhaps Plath's own threatened children, doomed to see her distorted but ubiquitous, as she has seen her own mother and father.[11] But the ending of the poem seems to dismiss the question of accurate or inaccurate perception, personal or cosmic reference; for the "infinite" itself has only one meaning, "the one / Death with its many sticks."

A poem with so fluid a sense of outside and inside, truth and fiction—with so many "short circuits and folding mirrors"—poses obvious and large-scale problems for the reader. Still, for me at least, the poems of this period have a dramatic power comparable to that of the more aggressive, more externally articulated poems earlier. Perhaps this power lies in the baleful unarguableness of depressed perceptions; or perhaps, conversely, in the fact that such perceptions are sometimes more transparent to the world than expectant or angry ones. There is, in these poems, a new—or newly intense—tone of wistfulness, a leaping out of context to hold on to evanescent beauties: the "beauty of drowned fields" in "Totem," or the balloons "we live with / Instead of dead furniture,"

Guileless and clear,

Oval soul-animals,

Taking up half the space,

Moving and rubbing on the silk

Invisible air drifts,

Giving a shriek and pop

When attacked, then scooting to rest, barely trembling.

The insolidity, the nonresistance to shock, of this beauty may well trouble the reader. It suggests that within the psyche, too, there is no holding center, and the gentler feeling-states may simply vanish when the angry or suicidal ones come forward. Still, the tender appreciativeness is genuine; there is no paranoiac sense of beauty as a deceit, or an assault on the psyche. The anthropomorphisms in these poems ("Dawn," "Kindness," and "the spider" speaking) have a childlike conspicuousness that conveys mainly the poet's yearning—yet her inability—to believe in and draw sustenance from a common symbolic language. Almost the greatest sadness in the poems lies in the fact that objects can produce in us a sense of positive negation just by their unimaginable inactivity, like the wonderful telephone "digesting / Voicelessness" in "The Munich Mannequins."

Nevertheless, the tendency toward a complete severance of relations with the outside is clear from one of the poems from the last week of Plath's life, "Contusion." The "dead egg" is now tangent to the world at only one point, a point of response to injury. Elsewhere there is a pervasive numbness—a numbness associated, by "The color of pearl," with the idea of death as an aesthetic "perfection." The next two stanzas recast the same idea in different imagistic terms. The vaguely vaginal imagery of the second (the "pit of rock" where "The sea sucks obsessively") suggests that the injury is still sexual loneliness, but at the same time subsumes that longing under earlier, less appeasable oceanic ones. With its next reshaping, the image passes beyond any object that clearly exists in the world—

> The size of a fly,
> The doom mark
> Crawls down the wall

—though the feeling of helpless fascination before "doom" is clear enough; and we see a little further thanks to the allusion to Emily Dickinson's "I heard a fly buzz when I died," and the (possible) suggestion of a countdown before a missile is fired. The last stanza tells us what really we already know: that all search for connection or correspondence on the outside—including metaphor itself—is on the point of ceasing.

> The heart shuts,
> The sea slides back,
> The mirrors are sheeted.

Here our own consideration might cease, if the last poems, "Edge" and "Words," did not bring us to a further meaning of stasis too little emphasized hitherto: that of pattern, aesthetic "perfection," psychic determinism, law and the "fixed stars." Law is always, as we have seen, an ambivalent concept in Plath's writing. In science, it is repellent; as ritual, archetype, "Greek necessity," it is hypnotically attractive. It, rather than freedom, is the privilege of the gods. And as the Nazi becomes the truly desirable love-object, the professor of high mathematics becomes the ritually obligatory seducer. And—in the physics class, or in Irwin's apartment, or in "Edge"—law is always, in some sense, "death." From this vantage point, Plath's surface hatred of the impersonality of process and scientific law seems in part a reaction formation not only against her own potential manipulativeness, but against the impulse to suicide.

The later Freud might not have found any of these equations particularly surprising. In *Beyond the Pleasure Principle*, the existence of a compulsion to repeat even unpleasurable experiences is the principal evidence for the conservative character of the instincts, and thence for the hypothesis of a death-instinct. But needless to say, when the equation of pattern and death appears in an individual as an emotional given, not as a theoretical conclusion, the possibility of its abstract validity does not lessen the need to look for personal determinants—the most important of these, surely, being the father's death, which seals up in itself the usual goal of repetition, the world of early childhood. Perhaps the most tragic equation is the one, evident in "Edge," between death and the completion of an aesthetic pattern, artistic "perfection" or "accomplishment." It is the more tragic because it helps explain the lack of normal defenses against the intolerable coalescence of contrary feelings which is the chief merit, precisely, of Plath's most dynamic poems. As in the first stanza of "Ariel," the extreme of motion becomes a stillness.

Are we to conclude, then, that poetry itself, for Plath, belongs finally to the realm of law, the inhuman, and death? A number of elements in our experience of the poetry rightly prejudice us to reject this conclusion as over-simple. One is the real and exhilarating momentum of the poems; another, the vivid presence of particular things and—as Robert Pinsky has pointed out in a brief but brilliant discussion of "Poppies in July"—the peculiar independence allowed them.[12] From a biographical point of view—since Plath was always ambivalent about law—her statement that she felt "absolutely fulfilled" while writing, and the occasional comparisons of writing to childbirth, the paradigmatic positive action, reinforce this impression.[13]

It seems more accurate to compare poetry not to death but to the moment of courting death, which, so often in Plath's work, does bring a kind of absolute fulfillment. Stéphane Mallarmé—another poet whose dissatisfaction with materiality and the present moment has been judiciously and persuasively connected with the early death of a parent[14]—spoke somewhere of the pleasure of poetry as the "vibratory near-disappearance" of the world of things. Plath's masterly concentration on tempo, on the dynamics of her mind's absorption of reality, accomplishes this difficult balance; and makes us—like Esther on the ski-run—feel the "inrush," the implosive pressure of reality, momentarily as a joyful increase of vividness. Which is to say that for Plath, as for many poets, poetry is a kind of sacred space, not quite in real experience, where contradictions elsewhere felt to be irreconcilable—vitality and perfection, ecstatic self-assertion and the otherness of the world—coexist, and the psyche feels momentarily whole.

A final word is perhaps needed on the kind of universality Plath laid claim to directly, by incorporating World War II and the death camps (and the atomic bomb) into her own story. Irving Howe and others have felt this incorporation to be unjustified, hysterical, even immoral.[15] The first point to be made is that the public dimension is in fact part of the self-portrait, and not a separate issue. It is a psychological fact that melancholic temperaments, once they hear of certain kinds of terrible events, cannot stop thinking of them, or cannot separate them from themselves—as one's skin will freeze instantaneously to a cold enough piece of metal. (We see this in *The Bell Jar*, in Esther's obsession with the execution of the Rosenbergs.) All of the confessional poets have been particularly interested in the events that elicited this reaction in them: in Lowell's case, the subtle cruelties of tyrants who were artists *manqués*; in Berryman's, theatrical mass murders. Their implicit premise has been that if the hidden element of attraction in the obsession is once unearthed, it will teach us something about why it occurs to human beings actually to do atrocious things. The neurotic artist makes his own personality a bridge between the surface innocence of social life and the eruption of horror. (The gap between the two evidently troubles most of the confessional poets—Lowell speaking of "the chafe and jar / of nuclear war" considered as a conversation piece; Berryman contrasting his own sense of diffuse, unverifiable guilt with the clear framework that an age of afflictions and dogmas gave Mistress Bradstreet.) The connections arrived at may, of course, be more or less successful, more or less melodramatic. But Howe's article shows no awareness of this more general confessional ambition, an ambition which creates its own standards of proportion, and makes Howe's more literal ones somewhat beside the point.

It is true that some of Plath's psychopolitical formulations are simplistically superior: for instance, the passage in *Three Women* which attributes all cruelty to the will to "flatten" in masculinity and in abstract thought, ignoring her own ambivalence about these things. It is also true that one must sometimes read very carefully to disentangle her from that peculiarly contemporary sentimentality that imposes a paradigm of "victimization"—hence a black and white morality—on the trickier, grayer modalities of common psychological pain. But finally Plath's stance is more guilty, more involved, than this. Her psychically weak life was lived under the aegis of humanly narrow ideals of being "good" and "successful" which are often thought of as characteristically German (and American). Out of this life, she drew a nexus of themes—sacrifice; purity; scapegoating; depersonalization and counter-depersonalization; the grandiose archetypalization of the self, and of heroes, and its implicit underside, the wise for a surcease from individuality—which have a great deal to do with the appeal of totalitarian ideas. These connections are drawn quite firmly in some of the better, quieter poems touching on the Nazi theme—for instance, "Mary's Song," where the "same fire" of purification in which the "Sunday lamb . . . Sacrifices its opacity" and becomes "A window, holy gold" also consumes "the tallow heretics" and "the Jews." It is unclear how far Plath consciously connected these mechanisms to her own specific personality, how far she saw them as necessary consequences of the condition of having or being a self at all, as it is set forth in "Totem" or "The Applicant." But there are times when the personal connection flashes out weirdly and wonderfully in her imagery—as in the prose statement where she speaks of "big business and the military in America" as if they were herself and Ted Hughes, a "terrifying, mad, omnipotent marriage."[16] (In a different way, Plath's sense of psychic invasion by negative numina is positively sublimated in her sane fear of nuclear fallout, "mercuric atoms," thalidomide.) Thus, as with Lowell, though less consciously, confession is the basis and measure for the understanding of public motives; the things that terrify Plath outwardly are the same things that terrify her in herself; and for the reader, the two converge in a coherent, if narrow, insight into the psychic appeal of evil.

Notes

1. Judith Kroll, *Chapters in a Mythology* (New York: Harper & Row, 1976), pp. 185–86, also discusses this sound-pattern, and the significance of its last metamorphosis.
2. David Holbrook, *Sylvia Plath: Poetry and Existence* (London: University of London, Athlone Press, 1976), p. 160, finds it "strange" to call the dew "suicidal," but he forgets how Marvell used the same image to describe the soul "careless of its Mansion new"—the body—and yearning, instead, to "run / Into the Glories of th' Almighty Sun" ("On a Drop of Dew").
3. Charles Newman, ed., *The Art of Sylvia Plath* (Bloomington: Indiana University Press, 1981), p. 188.
4. John Frederick Nims, "The Poetry of Sylvia Plath: A Technical Analysis," ibid., pp. 136–52, draws the distinctions between the two books very nicely, and does muh more justice than I have done to the achievements of *The Colossus*.
5. For Alvarez's view, see Newman, ed., *The Art of Sylvia Plath*, pp. 56–68, esp. p. 66. See also Edward Butscher, *Sylvia Plath: Method and Madness* (New York: Seabury, 1976), esp. pp. 326, 341–42.
6. See Newman, ed., *The Art of Sylvia Plath*, pp. 77–88.
7. According to Butscher, Plath was obsessively preoccupied with the idea of having more children—and with her rival's supposed sterility. The lines "my sheets, the cold dead centre / where spilt lives congeal and stiffen to history" draw an emotionally clear—if not altogether logical—connection between the failure to procreate and the negative vision of "history," of merely sequential time.
8. See Newman, ed., *The Art of Sylvia Plath*, pp. 66–68.
9. Gilbert Bettman, "Some Continuities in Sylvia Plath's Poetry" (honors thesis, Harvard University, 1970), describes the increasing staticness of the late poems very well, though from different initial premises.
10. *The Collected Poems of Sylvia Plath* (New York: Harper & Row, 1981), p. 295.
11. The idea of an evil mother is probably in play, unconsciously, earlier, since the "counterfeit snake" image closely echoes a savage description of the protagonist's mother in Robert Lowell's "Between the Porch and the Altar."
12. Robert Pinsky, *The Situation of Poetry* (Princeton: Princeton University Press, 1976), pp. 129–133.
13. Peter Orr, ed., *The Poet Speaks* (New York: Barnes & Noble, 1966), p. 172.
14. See Charles Mauron, *Introduction to the Psychoanalysis of Mallarmé*, tr. Archibald Henderson, Jr., and Will L. McLendon (Berkeley: University of California Press, 1963).
15. Irving Howe, "The Plath Celebration: A Partial Dissent," in Howe, *The Critical Point* (New York: Horizon, 1973).
16. Quoted in Newman, ed., *The Art of Sylvia Plath*, p. 32.

KATHERINE ANNE PORTER

1890–1980

Katherine Anne Porter, short-story writer and novelist, was born on May 15, 1890, at Indian Creek, Texas, and was educated at a Southern convent and other private schools. For many years she lived abroad—in Mexico, Paris, and Berlin—and these experiences, as well as those of her childhood in the South, are reflected in her fiction.

Porter has been praised as a stylist of subtlety and refinement, who at the same time produces penetrating psychological portraits and stories of great emotional power. Her first collection of stories, *Flowering Judas*, did not appear until 1930, although she had already been writing for many years; on its release she won immediate critical acclaim. This was followed by *Hacienda* (1934), about the filming of Eisenstein's *Que Viva Mexico!*; *Pale Horse, Pale Rider: Three Short Novels* (1939), consisting of "Noon Wine" (published separately in 1937), "Old Mortality," and the title piece; and two short-story collections, *The Leaning Tower* (1944) and *Collected Stories* (1965). Her only novel, *Ship of Fools* (1962), is an allegory about passengers on board a ship sailing from Mexico to Nazi Germany. *The Days Before* (1952) is a collection of her essays, articles, and book reviews, and a brief journalistic memoir, *The Never Ending Wrong* (1977), records her impressions of the trial of Sacco and Vanzetti. Porter died on September 18, 1980.

EDMUND WILSON
"Katherine Anne Porter" (1944)
Classics and Commericals
1950, pp. 219–23

Miss Katherine Anne Porter has published a new book of stories, her third: *The Leaning Tower and Other Stories*. To the reviewer, Miss Porter is baffling because one cannot take hold of her work in any of the obvious ways. She makes none of the melodramatic or ironic points that are the stock in trade of the ordinary short story writers; she falls into none of the usual patterns and she does not show anyone's influence. She does not exploit her personality either inside or outside her work, and her writing itself makes a surface so smooth that the critic has little opportunity to point out peculiarities of color or weave. If he is tempted to say that the effect is pale, he is prevented by the realization that Miss Porter writes English of a purity and precision almost unique in contemporary American fiction. If he tries to demur that some given piece fails to mount with the accelerating pace or arrive at the final intensity that he is in the habit of expecting in short stories, he is deterred by a nibbling suspicion that he may not have grasped its meaning and have it hit him with a sudden impact some minutes after he has closed his book.

Not that this meaning is simple to formulate even after one has felt its emotional force. The limpidity of the sentence, the exactitude of the phrase, are deceptive in that the thing they convey continues to seem elusive even after it has been communicated. These stories are not illustrations of anything that is reducible to a moral law or political or social analysis or even a principle of human behavior. What they show us are human relations in their constantly shifting phases and in the moments of which their existence is made. There is no place for general reflections; you are to live through the experience as the characters do. And yet the writer has managed to say something about the values involved in the experience. But what is it? I shall try to suggest, though I am afraid I shall land in ineptitude.

Miss Porter's short stories lend themselves to being sorted into three fairly distinct groups. There are the studies of family life in working-class or middle-class households (there are two of these in *The Leaning Tower*), which, in spite of the fact that the author is technically sympathetic with her people, tend to be rather bitter and bleak, and, remarkable though they are, seem to me less satisfactory than the best of her other stories. The impression we get from these pieces is that the qualities that are most amiable in human life are being gradually done to death in the milieux she is presenting; but Miss Porter does not really much like these people or feel comfortable in their dismal homes, and so we, in turn, don't really much care. Another section of her work, however, contains what may be called pictures of foreign parts, and here Miss Porter is much more successful. The story which gives its name to her new collection and which takes up two-fifths of the volume belongs to this category. It is a study of Germany between the two wars in terms of a travelling American and his landlady and fellow-lodgers in a Berlin rooming house. By its material and its point of view, it rather recalls Christopher Isherwood's *Goodbye to Berlin*, but it is more poetic in treatment and more general in implication. The little plaster leaning tower of Pisa which has been cherished by the Viennese landlady but gets broken by her American tenant stands for something in the destruction of which not merely the Germans but also the Americans have somehow a criminal part (though the American is himself an artist, he finds that he can mean nothing to the Germans but the power of American money). So, in a fine earlier story, "Hacienda," a Mexican peon is somehow destroyed—with no direct responsibility on the part of any of the elements concerned—by a combination of Soviet Russians intent on making a Communist movie, their American business manager, and a family of Mexican landowners.

In both cases, we are left with the feeling that, caught in the meshes of interwoven forces, some important human value has been crushed. These stories especially, one gathers, are examples of what Miss Porter means when she says, in her foreword to *Flowering Judas* in the Modern Library edition, that most of her "energies of mind and spirit have been spent in the effort to grasp the meaning" of the threats of world catastrophe in her time, "to trace them to their sources and to understand the logic of this majestic and terrible failure of the life of man in the Western world."

But perhaps that most interesting section of Katherine Anne Porter's work is composed of her stories about women—particularly her heroine Miranda, who figured in two of the three novelettes that made up her previous volume, *Pale Horse, Pale Rider*. The first six pieces of *The Leaning Tower* deal with Miranda's childhood and her family background of Louisianians living in southern Texas. This is the setting in which Miss Porter is most at home, and one finds in it the origins of that spirit of which the starvation and violation elsewhere make the subjects of her other stories. One recognizes it in the firm little sketches that show the relations between Miranda's grandmother and her lifelong colored companion, the relations between the members of the family, and the relations between the family and the Negro servants in general. Somewhere behind Miss Porter's stories there is a conception of a natural human spirit in terms of their bearing on which all the other forces of society are appraised. This spirit is never really idealized, it is not even sentimentalized; it can be generous and loving and charming, but it can also be indifferent and careless, inconsequent, irresponsible, and silly. If the meaning of these stories is elusive, it is because this essential spirit is so hard to isolate or pin down. It is peculiar to Louisianians in Texas, yet one misses it in a boarding house in Berlin. It is the special personality of a woman, yet it is involved with international issues. It evades all the most admirable moralities, it escapes through the social net, and it resists the tremendous oppressions of national bankruptcies and national wars. It is outlawed, driven underground, exiled; it becomes rather unsure of itself and may be able, as in "Pale Horse, Pale Rider," to assert itself only in the delirium that lights up at the edge of death to save Miranda from extinction by war flu. It suffers often from a guilty conscience, knowing too well its moral weakness; but it can also rally bravely if vaguely in vindication of some instinct of its being which seems to point toward justice and truth.

But I said that this review would be clumsy. I am spoiling Miss Porter's stories by attempting to find a formula for them when I ought simply to be telling you to read them (and not merely the last volume but also its two predecessors). She is absolutely a first-rate artist, and what she wants other people to know she imparts to them by creating an object, the self-developing organism of a work of prose. The only general opinion on anything which, in her books, she has put on record has been a statement about her craft of prose fiction, and I may quote it—from the foreword to which I have referred—as more to the purpose than anything that the present critic could say. Here is the manifesto of the builder of this solid little sanctuary, so beautifully proportioned and finished, for the queer uncontrollable spirit that it seems to her important to save:

In the face of such shape and weight of present misfortune, the voice of the individual artist may seem perhaps of no more consequence than the whirring of a cricket in the grass, but the arts do live continuously, and they live literally by faith; their names and their shapes and their uses and their basic meanings survive unchanged in all that matters through times of interruption, diminishment, neglect; they outlive governments and creeds and the societies, even the very civilizations that produced them. They cannot be destroyed altogether because they represent the substance of faith and the only reality. They are what we find again when the ruins are cleared away. And even the smallest and most incomplete offering at this time can be a proud act in defense of that faith.

V. S. PRITCHETT
From "Stones and Stories"
New Statesman, January 10, 1964, pp. 47–48

Katherine Anne Porter's stories have rightly had the highest reputation in America since they first appeared in the early Thirties. Her scene changes often, a good sign. Her subjects bear out O'Connor's theory: Mexico, but in revolution; life in the decaying American South, in rootless New York, in hysterical post-1914 Berlin. Where she settles she writes from the inside. Her singularity is truthfulness: it comes out in the portrait of Laura, the virginal but reckless American schoolteacher in 'Flowering Judas' who has ventured her political and personal chastity among the vanities and squalors of the Mexican revolution, perhaps as a religious exercise. She is a good old Calvinist-Catholic:

> But she cannot help feeling that she has been betrayed irresponsibly by the disunion between her way of living and her feeling of what life should be, and at times she is almost contented to rest in this sense of grievance as a private consolation. Sometimes she wishes to run away but she stays.

Laura wishes to live near enough to violent passion to be singed by it and is willing to pay for the experience in terrifying dreams. The Mexicans appeal to her because of their boundless vanity, their violence, their ability to forget and their indifference: Miss Porter austerely tests her characters against things that are elemental or ineluctable—a classical writer. There is a point at which life or circumstance does not give: when human beings come to this point she is ready for them. Braggioni, the Stalin-like Mexican revolutionary leader, is at this point: he is identified in a frightening, yet slightly fatuous and amicable way with the shady needs of revolution.

In the tale 'Maria Concepcion' it is the respectable churchwoman, with her classical Christian sense of the rights of jealously and vengeance, who murders and who is backed up by the villagers. Her husband will punish her: she accepts that. In 'Noon Wine' we have an incompetent poor white farmer whose fortunes are saved by a Swedish hired hand down from Dakota. The hand speaks to no one, slaves night and day and consoles himself only by playing the harmonica. Years pass and then a blackmailer comes down from Dakota to reveal that the Swede is a murderous escaped lunatic. The farmer, faced with losing his saviour, kills the blackmailer. The Swede runs away, consoled by his harmonica. The poor farmer has nothing but a sense of social injustice. He kills himself out of self-pity.

Katherine Anne Porter does not find her tests only in these Verga-like subjects. The girl reporter and the soldier-boy in

New York 'dig in' in spiritual self-defence against the hysteria of the 1914 war. The choice is between reality and illusion and the reality is harder to bear. It is no reward. It is the same in the comic tale of the Depression: the domestic war between the out-of-work Irishman turned windbag and drunk and his avaricious and scornful wife who keeps him and ends by beating him up with a knotted towel. Violent: these classical heroes and heroines are always that. Again, in the comical sad history of the old Southern aunts and cousins one sees that Aunt Amy was wild, amusing, cruel and destructive because she knew she would soon die; she had inner knowledge of Fate. Killed, she could be a killer. Old Granny Weatherall fights to the last drop of consciousness on her death-bed because her pride will not really accept, even now, that she was once jilted as a girl. And that is not funny, it is terrifying. To every human being there eventually comes—Miss Porter seems to say—the shock of perception of something violent or rock-like in themselves, in others, or in circumstance. We awaken to primitive knowledge and become impersonal in our tragedies. There will arise a terrible moment of crisis, a kind of illness, when, for Laura, there will be *no* disunion between her way of living and her feeling for what life should be. She will discover what life is. It is something out of one's control, scarcely belonging to one, and that has to be borne as if one were a stone.

Miss Porter's singularity as a writer is in her truthful explorations of a complete consciousness of life. Her prose is severe and exact; here ironies are subtle but hard. If she is arbitrary it is because she identifies as a conservative with a classical view of human nature. Laura listens to Braggioni with 'pitiless courtesy' because she dare not smile at his bad performance on the guitar:

> He is so vain of his talents and so sensitive to slights that it would require a cruelty and vanity greater than his own to lay a finger on the vast careless world of his self-esteem.

Miss Porter has a fine power of nervous observation. Her picture of Berlin in the Isherwood period is eerie and searching. She sees everything that disturbs. She notices peculiar local things that one realises afterwards are true: how often, for example, the Berliners' eyes filled with tears when they were suddenly faced with small dilemmas. Hysteria is near to the surface. Yet the tears were a kind of mannerism. Her power to make a landscape, a room, a group of people, thinkingly alive is not the vague, brutal talent of the post-Hemingway reporter but belongs to the explicit Jamesian period and suggests the whole rather than the surface of a life. Her stories are thoroughly planted. It is true that she is chastely on the edge of her subjects, that one catches the wild look of the runaway in her eye; but if her manner is astringent it is not precious. She is an important writer in the genre because she solves the essential problem: how to satisfy exhaustively in writing briefly.

EUDORA WELTY
From "Katherine Anne Porter:
The Eye of the Story" (1965)
The Eye of the Story
1978, pp. 30–39

In "Old Mortality" how stirring the horse race is! At the finish the crowd breaks into its long roar "like the falling walls of Jericho." This we hear, and it is almost like seeing, and we know Miss Lucy has won. But beyond a fleeting glimpse—the "mahogany streak" of Miss Lucy on the track—we never get much sight of the race with our eyes. What we see comes afterward. Then we have it up close: Miss Lucy bleeding at the nose. For Miranda has got to say "That's winning too." The race would never have got into the story except that Miranda's heart is being prepared to reject victory, to reject the glamour of the race and the cheering grandstand; to distrust from now on all evidence except what she, out of her own experience, can testify to. By the time we *see* Miss Lucy, she is a sight for Miranda's eyes alone: as much symbol as horse.

Most good stories are about the interior of our lives, but Katherine Anne Porter's stories (in *The Collected Stories of Katherine Anne Porter*) take place there; they show surface only at her choosing. Her use of the physical world is enough to meet her needs and no more; she is not wasteful with anything. This artist, writing her stories with a power that stamps them to their last detail on the memory, does so to an extraordinary degree without sensory imagery.

I have the most common type of mind, the visual, and when first I began to read her stories it stood in the way of my trust in my own certainty of what was there that, for all my being bowled over by them, I couldn't see them happening. This was a very good thing for me. As her work has done in many other respects, it has shown me a thing or two about the eye of fiction, about fiction's visibility and invisibility, about its clarity, its radiance.

Heaven knows she can see. Katherine Anne Porter has seen all her life, sees today, most intimately, most specifically, and down to the bones, and she could date the bones. There is, above all, "Noon Wine" to establish it forever that when she wants a story to be visible, it is. "Noon Wine" is visible all the way through, full of scenes charged with dramatic energy; everything is brought forth into movement, dialogue; the title itself is Mr. Helton's tune on the harmonica. "Noon Wine" is the most beautifully objective work she has done. And nothing has been sacrificed to its being so (or she wouldn't have done it); to the contrary, I find Mr. Hatch the scariest character she ever made, and he's just set down there in Texas like a chair. There he stands, part of the everyday furniture of living. He's opaque, and he's the devil. Walking in at Mr. Thompson's gate—the same gate by which his tracked-down victim walked in first—he is that much more horrifying, almost too solid to the eyes to be countenanced. (So much for the visual mind.)

Katherine Anne Porter has not in general chosen to cast her stories in scenes. Her sense of human encounter is profound, is fundamental to her work, I believe, but she has not often allowed it the dramatic character it takes in "Noon Wine." We may not see the significant moment happen within the story's present; we may not watch it occur between the two characters it joins. Instead, a silent blow falls while one character is alone—the most alone in his life, perhaps. (And this is the case in "Noon Wine" too.) Often the revelation that pierces a character's mind and heart and shows him his life or his death comes in a dream, in retrospect, in illness or in utter defeat, the moment of vanishing hope, the moment of dying. What Miss Porter makes us see are those subjective worlds of hallucination, obsession, fever, guilt. The presence of death hovering about Granny Weatherall she makes as real and brings as near as Granny's own familiar room that stands about her bed—realer, nearer, for we recognize not only death's presence but the character death has come in for Granny Weatherall.

The flash of revelation is revelation but is unshared. But how unsuspecting we are to imagine so for a moment—it *is*

shared, and by ourselves, her readers, who must share it feeling the doubled anguish of knowing this fact, doubled still again when it is borne in upon us how close to life this is, to *our* lives.

It is to be remembered that the world of fiction is not of itself visible. A story may or may not be born in sensory images in a given writer's mind. Experience itself is stored in no telling how many ways in a writer's memory. (It was "the sound of the sea, and Beryl fanning her hair at the window" that years later and thousands of miles away brought Katherine Mansfield to writing "At the Bay.") But if the physical world *is* visible or audible in the story, it has to be made so. Its materialization is as much a created thing as are the story's characters and what they think or do or say.

Katherine Anne Porter shows us that we do not have to see a story happen to know what is taking place. For all we are to know, she is not looking at it happen herself when she writes it; for her eyes are always looking through the gauze of the passing scene, not distracted by the immediate and transitory; her vision is reflective.

Her imagery is as likely as not to belong to a time other than the story's present, and beyond that it always differs from it in nature; it is *memory* imagery, coming into the story from memory's remove. It is a distilled, re-formed imagery, for it is part of a language made to speak directly of premonition, warning, surmise, anger, despair.

It was soon borne in upon me that Katherine Anne Porter's moral convictions have given her readers another way to see. Surely these convictions represent the fixed points about which her work has turned, and not only that, but they govern her stories down to the smallest detail. Her work has formed a constellation, with its own North Star.

Is the writer who does not give us the pictures and bring us the sounds of a story as it unfolds shutting out part of life? In Katherine Anne Porter's stories the effect has surely been never to diminish life but always to intensify life in the part significant to her story. It is a darkening of the house as the curtain goes up on this stage of her own.

Her stories of Mexico, Germany, Texas all happen there: where love and hate, trust and betrayal happen. And so their author's gaze is turned not outward but inward, and has confronted the mysterious dark from her work's beginning.

Since her subject is what lies beneath the surface, her way—quite direct—is to penetrate, brush the stuff away. It is the writer like Chekhov whose way of working is indirect. He moved indeed toward the same heart and core but by building up some corresponding illusion of life. Writers of Chekhov's side of the family are themselves illusionists and have necessarily a certain fondness for, lenience toward, the whole shimmering fabric as such. Here we have the professional scientist, the good doctor, working with illusion and the born romantic artist—is she not?—working without it. Perhaps it is always the lyrical spirit that takes on instantaneous color, shape, pattern of motion in work, while the meditative spirit must fly as quickly as possible out of the shell.

All the stories she has written are moral stories about love and the hate that is love's twin, love's impostor and enemy and death. Rejection, betrayal, desertion, theft roam the pages of her stories as they roam the world. The madam kicking the girl in "Magic" and the rest of the brutality in the characters' treatment of one another; the thieving that in one form or another infects their relationships; the protests they make, from the weakness of false dreams or of lying down with a cold cloth over the eyes, on up to towering rages—all this is a way of showing to the inward eye: Look at what you are doing to human love.

We hear in how many more stories than the one the litany of the little boy at the end of "The Downward Path to Wisdom," his "comfortable, sleeping song": "I hate Papa, I hate Mama, I hate Grandma, I hate Uncle David, I hate Old Janet, I hate Marjory, I hate Papa, I hate Mama . . ." It is like the long list of remembered losses in the story "Theft" made vocal, and we remember how that loser's decision to go on and let herself be robbed coincides with the rising "in her blood" of a "deep almost murderous anger."

"If one is afraid of looking into a face, one hits the face," remarked W. B. Yeats, and I think we must conclude that to Katherine Anne Porter's characters this face is the challenging face of love itself. And I think it is the faces—the inner, secret faces—of her characters, in their self-delusion, their venom and pain, that their author herself is contemplating. More than either looking at the face or hitting it, she has made a story out of her anger.

If outrage is the emotion she has most strongly expressed, she is using outrage as her cool instrument. She uses it with precision to show what monstrosities of feeling come about not from the lack of the existence of love but from love's repudiation, betrayal. From which there is no safety anywhere. Granny Weatherall, eighty, wise, affectionate and good, and now after a full life dying in her bed with the priest beside her, "knew hell when she saw it."

The anger that speaks everywhere in the stories would trouble the heart for their author whom we love except that her anger is pure, the reason for it evident and clear, and the effect exhilarating. She has made it the tool of her work; what we do is rejoice in it. We are aware of the compassion that guides it, as well. Only compassion could have looked where she looks, could have seen and probed what she sees. Real compassion is perhaps always in the end unsparing; it must make itself a part of knowing. Self-pity does not exist here; these stories come out trenchant, bold, defying; they are tough as sanity, unrelinquished sanity, is tough.

Despair is here, as well described as if it were Mexico. It is a despair, however, that is robust and sane, open to negotiation by the light of day. Life seen as a savage ordeal has been investigated by a straightforward courage, unshaken nerve, a rescuing wit, and above all, with the searching intelligence that is quite plainly not to be daunted. In the end the stories move us not to despair ourselves but to an emotion quite opposite because they are so seriously and clear-sightedly pointing out what they have been formed to show: that which is true under the skin, that which will remain a fact of the spirit.

Miranda, by the end of "Old Mortality" rebelling against the ties of the blood, resenting their very existence, planning to run away now from these and as soon as she can from her own escape into marriage, Miranda saying "I hate loving and being loved," is hating what destroys loving and what prevents being loved. She is, in her own particular and her own right, fighting back at the cheat she has discovered in all that's been handed down to her as gospel truth.

Seeing what is not there, putting trust in a false picture of life, has been one of the worst nightmares that assail her characters. "My dreams never renege on me, Mr. Richards. They're all I have to go by," says Rosaleen. (The Irish are no better than the Southerners in this respect.) Not only in the comic and touching Rosaleen, the lovely and sentient and tragic Miranda, but in many other characters throughout the stories we watch the romantic and the anti-romantic pulling each other to pieces. Is the romantic ever scotched? I believe not. Even if there rises a new refrain, even if the most ecstatic

words ever spoken turn out to be "I hate you," the battle is not over for good. That battle is in itself a romance.

Nothing is so naturally subject to false interpretation as the romantic, and in furnishing that interpretation the Old South can beat all the rest. Yet some romantic things happen also to be true. Miss Porter's stories are not so much a stand against the romantic as such, as a repudiation of the false. What alone can instruct the heart is the experience of living, experience which can be vile; but what can never do it any good, what harms it more than vileness, are those tales, those legends of more than any South, those universal false dreams, the hopes sentimental and ubiquitous, which are not on any account to be gone by.

For there comes a confrontation. It is then that Miss Porter's characters, behaving so entirely like ourselves, make the fatally wrong choice. Enter betrayal. Again and again, enter betrayal. We meet the betrayal that lies in rejection, in saying No to others or No to the self, or that lies with still more cunning in saying Yes when this time it should have been No.

And though we are all but sure what will happen, we are possessed by suspense.

It appears to me irrelevant whether or not the story is conceived and put down in sensory images, whether or not it is dramatic in construction, so long as its hold is a death-grip. In my own belief, the suspense—so acute and so real—in Katherine Anne Porter's work never did depend for its life on disclosure of the happenings of the narrative (nothing is going to turn out very well) but in the writing of the story, which becomes one single long sustained moment for the reader. Its suspense is one with its meaning. It must arise, then, from the mind, heart, spirit by which it moves and breathes.

It is a current like a strand of quicksilver through the serenity of her prose. In fiction of any substance, serenity can only be an achievement of the work itself, for any sentence that is alive with meaning is speaking out of passion. Serenity never belonged to the *now* of writing; it belongs to the later *now* offered its readers. In Katherine Anne Porter's work the forces of passion and self-possession seem equal, holding each other in balance from one moment to the next. The suspense born of the writing abides there in its own character, using the story for its realm, a quiet and well-commanded suspense, but a genie.

There was an instinct I had, trustworthy or not, that the matter of visibility in her stories had something to do with time. Time permeates them. It is a grave and formidable force.

Ask what time it is in her stories and you are certain to get the answer: the hour is fateful. It is not necessary to see the hands of the clock in her work. It is a time of racing urgency, and it is already too late. And then recall how many of her characters are surviving today only for the sake of tomorrow, are living on tomorrow's coming; think how we see them clearest in reference to tomorrow. Granny Weatherall, up to the last—when God gives her no sign acceptable to her and jilts her Himself—is thinking: "There was always so much to be done, let me see: tomorrow." Laura in "Flowering Judas" is "waiting for tomorrow with a bitter anxiety as if tomorrow may not come." Ordinary, self-respecting and—up to a certain August day—fairly well blessed Mr. Thompson, because he has been the one to kill the abominable Mr. Hatch, is self-tried, self-pleaded for, and self-condemned to no tomorrow; neither does he leave his sons much of a tomorrow, and certainly he leaves still less of one to poor, red-eyed Mrs. Thompson, who had "so wanted to believe that tomorrow, or at least the day after, life, such a battle at best, was going to be better." In "Old Mortality" time takes Miranda by the hand and leads her into promising herself "in her hopefulness, her ignorance": "At least I can know the truth about what happens to me." In "Pale Horse, Pale Rider" the older Miranda asks Adam, out of her suffering, "Why can we not save each other?" and the straight answer is that there is no time. The story ends with the unforgettable words "Now there would be time for everything" because tomorrow has turned into oblivion, the ultimate betrayer is death itself.

But time, one of the main actors in her stories—teacher, fake healer, conspirator in betrayal, ally of death—is also, within the complete control of Miss Porter, with his inimical powers made use of, one of the movers of her writing, a friend to her work. It occurred to me that what is *seeing* the story is the dispassionate eye of time. Her passionate mind has asked itself, schooled itself, to use time's eye. Perhaps Time is the genie's name.

Laura is stuck in time, we are told in "Flowering Judas"— and told in the timeless present tense of dreaming, a brilliant working upon our very nerves to let us know precisely Laura's dilemma. There is in all Katherine Anne Porter's work the strongest sense of unity in all the parts; and if it is in any degree a sound guess that an important dramatic element in the story has another role, a working role, in the writing of the story, might this not be one source of a unity so deeply felt? Such a thing in the practice of an art is unsurprising. Who can separate a story from the story's writing?

And there is too, in all the stories, a sense of long, learning life, the life that is the story's own, beginning from very far back, extending somewhere into the future. As we read, the initial spark is not being struck before our eyes; the fire we see has already purified its nature and burns steadied by purpose, unwavering in meaning. It is no longer impulse, it is a signal, a beacon.

To me, it is the image of the eye of time that remains the longest in the mind at her story's end. There is a judgment to be passed. A moral judgment has to be, in all reason, what she has been getting at. But in a still further act of judiciousness, I feel, she lets Time pass that judgment.

Above all, I feel that what we are responding to in Katherine Anne Porter's work is the intensity of its life, which is more powerful and more profound than even its cry for justice.

They are excoriating stories. Does she have any hope for us at all? Well, do we not feel its implication everywhere—a desperate hope for the understanding that may come, if we use great effort, out of tomorrow, or if not then, maybe the day after? Clearly it has to become at some point an act of faith. It is toward this that her stories all point: here, it seems to me, is the North Star.

And how calm is the surface, the invisible surface of it all! In a style as invisible as the rhythm of a voice, and as much her own as her own voice, she tells her stories of horror and humiliation and in the doing fills her readers with a rising joy. The exemplary prose that is without waste or extravagance or self-indulgence or display, without any claim for its triumph, is full of pride. And her reader shares in that pride, as well he might: it is pride in the language, pride in using the language to search out human meanings, pride in the making of a good piece of work. A personal spell is about the stories, the something of her own that we refer to most often, perhaps, when we mention its beauty, and I think this comes from the *making* of the stories.

M. M. LIBERMAN
"The Responsibility of the Novelist"
Criticism, Fall 1966, pp. 377–88

The title of this essay is, I suppose, somewhat misleading, in the way that a title can be, when it seems to promise a discourse on an arguable concept. In this instance it suggests a certain premise: namely, that the question, "What does the author owe society?" is one which still lives and breathes. In fact, I think it does not. I suspect, rather, that its grave can be located somewhere between two contentions: André Gide's that the artist is under no moral obligation to present a useful idea, but that he is under a moral obligation to present an idea well; and Henry James's, that we are being arbitrary if we demand, to begin with, more of a novel than that it be interesting. As James uses the word *novel* here, I take it to mean any extended, largely realistic, narrative fiction, but his view is applicable as well to fiction in other forms and modes.

If a literary work is more than immediately engaging, if, for example, it stimulates the moral imagination, it is doing more than is fairly required of it as art.

Why, then, if I think it is in most respects dead, do I choose to raise the question of the writer's responsibility? The answer is that I do not choose to raise the question. The question is continually being raised for me, and because literature is my profession, it haunts my house. Thus, I am moved to invoke certain commonplaces, as above, of a sort I had supposed to be news only to sophomore undergraduates. This was the case markedly on the occasion of the publication of Katherine Anne Porter's *Ship of Fools* in 1962. Twenty years in the making, a book club selection even before it was set up in type, restlessly awaited by a faithful coterie, reviewed widely and discussed broadly almost simultaneously with its appearance on the store shelves, this book caused and still causes consternation in the world of contemporary letters to a degree which I find interesting, curious, and suspect. The focus of this paper will be on the critical reception of this book and I hope that the relevance of what remains of the responsibility question will issue naturally from it. Finally, I must quote at awkward length, in two instances, in order to be fair to other commentators.

The first brief waves of reviews were almost unanimous in their praise of *Ship of Fools* and then very shortly the many dissenting opinions began to appear, usually in the most respectable intellectual journals where reviewers claim to be, and often are, critics. These reviews were characterized by one of two dominant feelings: bitter resentment or acute disappointment. A remarkable instance of the former appeared in the very prestigious journal, *Commentary* (October, 1962) as its featured article of the month, under the byline of one of its associate editors. That Miss Porter's book should have been originally well-received so rankled *Commentary*'s staff that a lengthy rebuttal was composed, taking priority over other articles on ordinarily more-pressing subjects, such as nuclear destruction and race violence. The article progresses to a frothing vehemence in its later pages. I will quote from the opening of the piece which begins relatively calmy, as follows:

> Whatever the problems were that kept Katherine Anne Porter's *Ship of Fools* from appearing during the past twenty years, it has been leading a charmed life ever since it was published last March. In virtually a single voice, a little cracked and breathless with excitement, the reviewers announced that Miss Porter's long-awaited first novel was a "triumph," a "masterpiece," a "work of genius . . . a moment-

ous work of fiction," "a phenomenal, rich, and delectable book," a "literary event of the highest magnitude. . . ."

Riding the crest of this wave of acclaim, *Ship of Fools* made its way to the top of the best-seller lists in record time and it is still there as I write in mid-September. During these four months, it has encountered virtually as little opposition in taking its place among the classics of literature as it did in taking and holding its place on the best-seller lists. A few critics . . . wound up by saying that *Ship of Fools* fell somewhat short of greatness, but only after taking the book's claim to greatness with respectful seriousness. Some of the solid citizens among the reviewers, like John K. Hutchens, found the novel to be dull and said so. Here and there, mainly in the hinterlands, a handful of independent spirits . . . suspected that the book was a failure. But who was listening?

Prominent among the circumstances which have helped to make a run-away best-seller and a *succès d'estime* out of this massive, unexciting, and saturnine novel was the aura of interest, partly sentimental and partly deserved, that Miss Porter's long struggle with it had produced. Most of the reviews begin in the same way: a distinguished American short-story writer at the age of seventy-one has finally finished her first novel after twenty years of working on it. As this point was developed, it tended to establish the dominant tone of many reviews—that of an elated witness to a unique personal triumph, almost as though this indomitable septuagenarian had not written a book, but had done something even more remarkable—like swimming the English Channel.

The *Commentary* critic goes on to charge Miss Porter with having written a novel contemptible in two decisive ways: (1) badly executed in every conceivable technical sense, particularly characterization and (2) unacceptable on moral grounds, being pessimistic and misanthropic. "But the soul of humanity is lacking," he says, quoting still another reviewer sympathetic to his own position. Why Dostoevsky, for example, is permitted to be both massive and saturnine and Miss Porter not is a question spoken to later only by implication. The critic's charge that her writing is "unexciting" is curious considering his own high emotional state in responding to the work. The charge of misanthropy is, of course, directly related to the alleged technical failure of the characterization, which he says "borders on caricature" in the way it portrays nearly every human type as loathesome and grotesque, with hardly a single redeeming feature. In considering the charge of misanthropy we are, perforce, confronted with the question of the writer's social responsibility in the moral sphere, for the attribution of misanthropy to a writer by a critic is typically a censure and is seldom merely a description of the writer's stance. The writer is usually, as in this case, denied the right to be misanthropic on the ground that it is immoral to hate and, given the writer's influential function, it is deemed irresponsible of him to clothe such a negative sentiment as hate in intellectually attractive garb. In my efforts at synthesis, I will get back to these questions. But for the moment I should like to point out that *Commentary*'s view of *Ship of Fools* as depicting mankind in a hatefully distorted, therefore, untruthful, therefore, immoral way, is in fact the view of the book commonly held by the normally intelligent and reasonably well-educated reader of fiction, if my impressions are accurate.

I turn now to the other mode of reception: acute disappointment. One of the most clearly and intelligently presented of this group was Professor Wayne Booth's critique in the *Yale Review* (Summer, 1962) from which I quote, in part, as follows:

> Katherine Anne Porter's long-awaited novel is more likely to fall afoul of one's bias for finely-constructed, concentrated plots. In this respect her own earlier fiction works against her; part of the strength of those classics, "Pale Horse, Pale Rider" and "Noon Wine," lies in their concision, their economy, their simplicity. *There* is *my* Katherine Anne Porter, I am tempted to protest, as she offers me, now, something so different as to be almost unrecognizable—a 225,000-word novel (more words, I suppose, than in all of the rest of her works put together) with nearly fifty characters. What is worse, the manner of narration is fragmented, diluted. Her plan is to create a shipload of lost souls and to follow them, isolated moment by isolated moment, in their alienated selfishness, through the nasty, exasperating events of a twenty-seven day voyage, in 1931, from Veracruz to Bremerhaven. She deliberately avoids concentrating strongly on any one character; even the four or five that are granted some sympathy are kept firmly, almost allegorically, subordinated to the portrayal of the ship of fools ("I am a passenger on that ship," she reminds us in an opening note).
>
> Her method is sporadic, almost desultory, and her unity is based on theme and idea rather than coherence of action. We flash from group to group, scene to scene, mind to mind, seldom remaining with any group or observer for longer than three or four pages together. While the book is as a result full of crosslights and ironic juxtapositions, it has, for me, no steady center of interest except the progressively more intense exemplification of its central truth: men are pitifully, foolishly self-alienated. At the heart of man lies a radical corruption that can only occasionally, fitfully, be overcome by love. . . .
>
> Once the various groupings are established— the four isolated, self-torturing Americans, two of them lovers who hate and fear each other when they are not loving; the sixteen Germans, most of them in self-destructive family groups, and all but two of them repugnant almost beyond comedy; the depraved swarm of Spanish dancers with their two demon-children; the carefree and viciously irresponsible Cuban students; the half-mad, lost Spanish countess; the morose Swede; and so on—each group or lone traveler is taken to some sort of climactic moment, most often in the form of a bungled chance for genuine human contact. These little anti-climaxes are scattered throughout the latter fourth of the book, but for most of the characters the nadir is reached during the long "gala" evening, almost at the end of the journey. . . .
>
> Such a work, lacking, by design, a grand causal, temporal sequence, depends for complete success on the radiance of each part; the reader must feel that every fragment as it comes provides proof of its own relevance in its illustrative power, or at least in its comic or pathetic or satiric intensity. For me only about half of the characters provide this kind of self-justification. There are many great things: moments of introspection, including some masterful dreams, from the advanced young woman and the faded beauty; moments of clear and effective observation of

viciousness and folly. But too often one finds, when the tour of the passenger list is undertaken again and again, that it is too much altogether. Why, why did Miss Porter feel that she should try to get everything in?

Since a useful version of Aristotle's *Poetics* has been available to us, there have been critics who have been engaged in what has been called criticism proper, the task of determining what literature in general is, and what a given work of literature in particular is. One fundamental assumption of criticism proper is that by a more and more refined classification, according to a work's properties, all literature can be first divided into kinds and sub-kinds. Ideally, and as such a process becomes more and more discriminating and precise, and as the subdivisions become small and smaller, criticism will approach the individual work. Accordingly the proper critic assumes that all questions of evaluation, including, of course, moral evaluation, are secondary to and issue from questions of definition. Or to put yet otherwise, the proper critic asks: How can we tell what a work means, let alone whether it's good or bad, if we don't know what it is to begin with?

At this turn, I call attention to the fact that in none of my own references to *Ship of Fools* have I spoken of it as a novel. The *Commentary* editor calls it a novel and Mr. Booth calls it a novel, and in the very process of describing what it is about this alleged novel that displeases them, they go a long way toward unintentionally defining the work as something else altogether. But instead of evaluating *Ship of Fools* on the grounds of their own description of its properties, both insist on ignoring this analytical data, making two substitutions in its stead: (1) the publisher's word for it that *Ship of Fools* is a novel and (2) their own bias as to how the work would have to be written to have been acceptable as a novel. Mr. Booth is both candid and disarming in making explicit his bias for finely-constructed, concentrated plots. To entertain a preference for *Pride and Prejudice* or *The Great Gatsby* over, say, *Moby-Dick* or *Finnegans Wake* is one thing and legitimate enough in its way. To insist, however, that the latter two works are inferior because their integrity does not depend on traditional plot structure would be to risk downgrading two admittedly monumental works in a very arbitrary and dubious way. Finally, to insist that every long work of prose fiction should be as much like *Pride and Prejudice* as possible is to insist that every such work be not only a novel, but a nineteenth-century one at that.

The *Commentary* critique has its own bias which is not, however, stated explicitly. It is the bias of the journal itself as much as of the critic, and is one it shares with many another respectable publication whose voice is directed at an audience it understands to have a highly developed, independent, post-Freudian, post-Marxist, humanitarian social consciousness. Neither especially visionary, nor especially doctrinaire, such a publication has, typically, nevertheless, a low tolerance for anything that smacks of the concept of original sin, having, as this concept does, a way of discouraging speculation about decisively improving the human lot. Miss Porter's book appears to take a dim view of the behavior of the race and that is enough for the intellectual journal, despite its implied claim to broad views and cultivated interests, including an interest in fiction. The aggrieved critic cannot come down from high dudgeon long enough to see that a view of literature as merely an ideological weapon is in the first place a strangely puritanical one and wildly out of place in his pages. Secondly, there are a few more commonplaces about literature which are usually lost sight of in the urgency to claim that people are not all bad and therefore can and must be portrayed in fiction as likely candidates for salvation. Most works of fiction, *as anyone should know*, are not written to accomplish anything but themselves, but some works of fiction are written to demonstrate to the innocent that there is much evil in the world. And others are written to demonstrate to the initiated, but phlegmatic, that there is more evil than even they had supposed and that, moreover, this evil is closer to home than they can comfortably imagine. In any case, since fiction is by definition artificial, the author is within his rights in appearing to overstate the case for the desired results. It is nowhere everlastingly written that literature must have a sanguine, optimistic, and uplifting effect. Is there not sometimes something salutary in a work which has the effect of inducing disgust and functioning therefore as a kind of emetic? Had the critic given Miss Porter her due as an artist he might have seen that *Ship of Fools* condemns human folly, but it never once confuses good and evil. It is one thing to be a writer who smirks at human decency and argues for human destruction (Marquis de Sade)—it is another to be a writer who winces at human limitations and pleads by her tone, her attitude towards her readers, for a pained nod of agreement.

Said Dr. Johnson to the Honourable Thomas Erskine some 200 years ago: "Why, sir, if you were to read Richardson for the story, your impatience would be so much fretted that you would hang yourself. But you must read him for the sentiment." In the case of *Ship of Fools*, this sentiment is so consistent and so pervasive as to make us wonder how anyone could have scanted or mistaken it. It is the very opposite of misanthropy in that far from taking delight in exposing human foibles, in "getting" her characters' "number," Miss Porter's narrative voice has the quality of personal suffering even as it gives testimony. It seems to say: "This is the way with the human soul, as I knew it, at its worst, in the years just prior to the Second World War. And alas for all of us that it should have been so." By way of illustration, recall the characters Ric and Rac. I select them because Miss Porter's readers of all stripes agree that these two children, scarcely out of their swaddling clothes, are probably as thoroughly objectionable as any two fictional characters in all literature in English. Twin offspring of a pimp and a prostitute, they lie, steal, torture, attempt to murder a dumb animal, cause the death of an innocent man and fornicate incestuously; they are not very convincing as ordinary real children and for a very good reason. They are not meant to be. I cite a passage from that section where, having made a fiasco of their parents' larcenous schemes, they are punished by those parents:

> Tito let go of Rac and turned his fatherly discipline upon Ric. He seized his right arm by the wrist and twisted it very slowly and steadily until the shoulder was nearly turned in its socket and Ric went to his knees with a long howl that died away in a puppy-like whimper when the terrible hold was loosed. Rac, huddled on the divan nursing her bruises, cried again with him. Then Manolo and Pepe and Tito and Pancho, and Lola and Concha and Pastora and Amparo, every face masking badly a sullen fright, went away together to go over every step of this dismaying turn of affairs; with a few words and nods, they decided it would be best to drink coffee in the bar, to appear as usual at dinner, and to hold a rehearsal on deck afterwards. They were all on edge and ready to fly at each other's throats. On her way out, Lola paused long enough to seize Rac by the hair and shake her head until she was silenced, afraid to cry. When they were gone, Ric and Rac crawled into the upper berth looking for safety; they lay there half naked, entangled like some afflicted, misbegot-

ten little monster in a cave, exhausted, mindless,
soon asleep.

For 357 pages a case has been carefully built for the twins' monstrous natures. The reader has been induced to loathe the very sound of their names. Suddenly the same reader finds himself an eye witness to the degree of punishment he has privately imagined their deserving. But even as they are being terribly chastised they demonstrate an admirable recalcitrance and suddenly it is the adult world which appears villainous, monstrous and cruel. Finally, in the imagery of our last view of them, they are not demons altogether, or even primarily, but in their nakedness, which we see first, they are also merely infants and this is what does—or should—break the reader's heart. The reader is meant to sympathize, finally, with these hideous children, but more than that, his moral responses have been directed to himself. He has been led to ask himself: Who am I that I should have for so long despised these children, however demonic they are. Am I, then, any better than their parents?

When I contend that Ric and Rac are not meant to be taken as real children, I am agreeing for the moment with the *Commentary* critic who spoke of Miss Porter's method of characterization as caricature, as if to speak of this method so, were, *ipso facto*, to condemn it, as if realism were the only possible fictional mode and the only category into which a long fiction can be cast. But if *Ship of Fools* is not a novel, what would a novel be? I rely on the recent study by Sheldon Sacks, *Fiction and the Shape of Belief*, to define it as follows: a novel would be an action organized so that it introduces characters about whose fates the reader is made to care, in unstable relationships, which are then further complicated, until the complication is finally resolved, by the removal of the represented instability. This plainly is not *Ship of Fools*. Our most human feelings go out to Ric and Rac, but we cannot care further about them precisely *not* because we are made to hate them, but because they are clearly doomed to perpetual dehumanization by the adult world which spawned and nurtured them. In the same image in which Miss Porter represents them as helpless infants, she also declares them "mindless." The generally unstable relationships which define the roles of most of the other characters in the book remain unstable to the very end and are not so much resolved as they are revealed. The resolution of the manifold conflicts in the work is part of the encompassing action of the work, that which the reader can logically suppose will happen after the story closes. The Germans will march against Poland and turn Europe into a concentration camp. The others will, until it is too late, look the other way. This is a fact of history which overrides in importance the fact that no one on the ship can possibly come to good.

Nor is *Ship of Fools* a satire which is organized so that it ridicules objects external to the fictional world created in it. Rather, it is, I believe, a kind of modern apologue, a work organized as a fictional example of the truth of a formulable statement or a series of such statements. As such it owes more than its title to the didactic Christian verses of Sebastian Brant, whose *Das Narrenschiff, The Ship of Fools*, was published sometime between 1497 and 1548. Brant's work was very influential and no one thinks of it as misanthropic when he reads:

> The whole world lives in darksome night,
> In blinded sinfulness persisting,
> While every street sees fools existing
> Who know but folly, to their shame,
> Yet will not own to folly's name.
> Hence I have pondered how a ship

> Of fools I'd suitably equip—
> A galley, brig, bark, skiff, or float,
> A carack, scow, dredge, racing-boat,
> A sled, cart, barrow, carryall—
> One vessel would be far too small
> To carry all the fools I know.
> Some persons have no way to go
> And like the bees they come a-skimming,
> While many to the ship are swimming,
> Each one wants to be the first.
> A mighty throng with folly curst,
> Whose pictures I have given here.
> They who at writings like a sneer
> Or are with reading not afflicted
> May see themselves herewith depicted
> And thus discover who they are.
> Their faults, to whom they're similar.
> For fools a mirror shall it be,
> Where each his counterfeit may see.

As an apologue Miss Porter's work has more in common with Johnson's *Rasselas* than with *Gone with the Wind*. As an apologue it not only has the right, it has the function by its nature to "caricature" its actors, to be "saturnine," to have a large cast, to be "fragmented" in its narration and above all, to quote Mr. Booth again, to achieve "unity based on theme and idea rather than coherence of action . . . [to have] no steady center of interest except the progressively more intense exemplification of its central truth. . . ."

In addition to calling attention to its formal properties for evaluating Miss Porter's book not as a novel but as something else, one ought to stand back a bit to see how the work fits a reasonable definition of the novel historically, that is, according to traditional and conventional themes and types of action. Recall that though the English word novel, to designate a kind of fiction, is derived from the Italian *novella*, meaning "a little new thing," this is not the word used in most European countries. That word is, significantly, *roman*. One forgets that a work of fiction, set in our own time, and thus bringing us knowledge of our own time, that is, news, is not, however a novel by that fact alone, but may be a literary form as yet undefined and, therefore, unnamed. For, in addition to bringing us news, the novel, if it is such on historical principles, must pay its respects to its forebears in more than a nominal way. It must do more than bear tales and look like the *Brothers Karamazov*. It must, I suspect, as a *roman*, be in some specific ways romantic.

We understand that the novel is the modern counterpart of various earlier forms of extended narrative. The first of these, the epic, was succeeded in the middle ages by the *romance* written at first like the epic, in verse, and later in prose as well. The romance told of the adventures of royalty and the nobility, introduced a heroine and made love a central theme. It relocated the supernatural realm from the court of Zeus to fairyland. The gods were replaced by magical spells and enchantments. When magical spells and enchantments were replaced, in the precursors of contemporary fiction, by the happy accident, the writer took unto himself a traditional given and the romantic tradition continued in the novel. When Henry James arranged for his heroine, Isabel Archer, to inherit a substantial sum of money from a relative who didn't know her, this was very Olympian of him; at any rate it was a piece of modern magic, legitimately granted to the novelist. Realist though he was, James recognized that the romantic element gets the novel going, frees the hero or heroine from those confinements of everyday life which make moral adventure undramatic. When in the most arbitrary way James makes

Isabel an heiress he launches her on a quest for self-realization. He gives her her chance. Now in this connection, I quote again from *Ship of Fools*:

> While he [Freytag] shaved he riffled through his ties and selected one, thinking that people on voyage mostly went on behaving as if they were on dry land, and there is simply not room for it on a ship. Every smallest act shows up more clearly and looks worse, because it has lost its background. The train of events leading up to and explaining it is not there; you can't refer it back and set it in its proper size and place.

When Miss Porter, who could have put her cast of characters anywhere she wanted, elected to put them aboard ship, she made as if to free them, in the manner of a romance, for a moral quest; that is, they are ostensibly liberated, as if by magic, precisely because they *are* aboard ship—liberated from the conventions of family background, domestic responsibility, national custom, and race consciousness. Theoretically, they can now emerge triumphant at the end of the journey, over duplicity, cruelty, selfishness and bigotry. But they do not.

Freedom they are incapable of utilizing for humane ends. Freedom Miss Porter can grant them, but since they are men of our time, they cannot, in her view, accept it responsibly. That is, they cannot make good use of their lucky accident because their freedom is only nominal. On the one hand, history has caught up with them; on the other hand, psychology has stripped their spiritual and emotional lives of all mystery. In Miss Porter's world the past is merely the genesis of neurosis (there is no point in pretending we've never heard of Freud) and the future, quite simply, is the destruction of Isabel Archer's Europe of infinite possibilities (there is no point in pretending we've never heard of Neville Chamberlain). *Ship of Fools* argues that romantic literary conventions do not work in the modern world, and emerges as even more remote from the idea of the novel than a study of its formal properties alone would suggest. One can see it finally as anti-novel.

In her 1940 introduction to *Flowering Judas*, Miss Porter says that she spent most of her "energies" and "spirit" in an effort to understand "the logic of this majestic and terrible failure of man in the Western world." This is the dominant theme of *Ship of Fools* as it is of all her writing. Nearly every character in the work is a staggering example of an aspect of this failure. And here is the only passage in the work emphasized by italics:

> What they were saying to each other was only, *Love me, love me in spite of all! Whether or not I love you, whether I am fit to love, whether you are able to love, even if there is no such thing as love, love me!*

CLEANTH BROOKS
"On 'The Grave'"

Yale Review, Winter 1966, pp. 275–79

If I had to choose a particular short story of Katherine Anne Porter's to illustrate her genius as a writer—the choice is not an easy one—I think that I should choose "The Grave." I did choose it some months ago for a lecture in Athens, where the special nature of the audience, whose English ranged from excellent to moderately competent, provided a severe test. The ability of such an audience to understand and appreciate this story underlines some of Miss Porter's special virtues as a writer. Hers is an art of apparent simplicity, with nothing forced or mannered, and yet the simplicity is rich, not thin, full of

subtleties and sensitive insights. Her work is compact and almost unbelievably economical.

The story has to do with a young brother and sister on a Texas farm in the year 1903. Their grandmother, who in some sense had dominated the family, had survived her husband for many years. He had died in the neighboring state of Louisiana, but she had removed his body to Texas. Later, when her Texas farm was sold and with it the small family cemetery, she had once more moved her husband's body, and those of the other members of her family, to a plot in the big new public cemetery. One day the two grandchildren, out rabbit hunting with their small rifles, find themselves in the old abandoned family cemetery.

> Miranda leaped into the pit that had held her grandfather's bones. Scratching round aimlessly and pleasurably as any young animal, she scooped up a lump of earth and weighed it in her palm. It has a pleasantly sweet, corrupt smell, being mixed with cedar needles and small leaves, and as the crumbs fell apart, she saw a silver dove no larger than a hazel nut, with spread wings and a neat fan-shaped tail.

Miranda's brother recognizes what the curious little ornament is—the screw-head for a coffin. Paul has found something too—a small gold ring—and the children soon make an exchange of their treasures, Miranda fitting the gold ring onto her thumb.

Paul soon becomes interested in hunting again, and looks about for rabbits, but the ring,

> shining with the serene purity of fine gold on [the little girl's] rather grubby thumb, turned her feelings against her overalls and sockless feet. . . . She wanted to go back to the farm house, take a good cold bath, dust herself with plenty of Maria's violet talcum powder . . . put on the thinnest, most becoming dress she ever owned, with a big sash, and sit in the wicker chair under the trees.

The little girl is thoroughly feminine, and though she has enjoyed knocking about with her brother, wearing her summer roughing outfit, the world of boys and sports and hunting and all that goes with it is beginning to pall.

Then something happens. Paul starts up a rabbit, kills it with one shot, and skins it expertly as Miranda watches admiringly. "Brother lifted the oddly bloated belly. 'Look,' he said, in a low amazed voice. 'It was going to have young ones.'" Seeing the baby rabbits in all their perfection, "their sleek wet down lying in minute even ripples like a baby's head just washed, their unbelievably small delicate ears folded close," Miranda is "excited but not frightened." Then she touches one of them, and exclaims, "Ah, there's blood running over them!" and begins to tremble. "She had wanted most deeply to see and to know. Having seen, she felt at once as if she had known all along."

The meaning of life and fertility and of her own body begin to take shape in the little girl's mind as she sees the tiny creatures just taken from their mother's womb. The little boy says to her "cautiously, as if he were talking about something forbidden: 'They were just about ready to be born.' 'I know,' said Miranda, 'like kittens. I know, like babies.' She was quietly and terribly agitated, standing again with her rifle under her arm, looking down at the bloody heap." Paul buries the rabbits and cautions his sister "with an eager friendliness, a confidential tone quite unusual in him, as if he were taking her into an important secret on equal terms: Listen now. . . . Don't tell a soul."

The story ends with one more paragraph, and because the

ending is told with such beautiful economy and such care for the disposition of incidents and even the choice of words, one dares not paraphrase it.

> Miranda never told, she did not even wish to tell anybody. She thought about the whole worrisome affair with confused unhappiness for a few days. Then it sank quietly into her mind and was heaped over by accumulated thousands of impressions, for nearly twenty years. One day she was picking her path among the puddles and crushed refuse of a market street in a strange city of a strange country, when without warning, plain and clear in its true colors as if she looked through a frame upon a scene that had not stirred nor changed since the moment it happened, the episode of that far-off day leaped from its burial place before her mind's eye. She was so reasonlessly horrified she halted suddenly staring, the scene before her eyes dimmed by the vision back of them. An Indian vendor had held up before her a tray of dyed sugar sweets, in the shapes of all kinds of small creatures: birds, baby chicks, baby rabbits, lambs, baby pigs. They were in gay colors and smelled of vanilla, maybe. . . . It was a very hot day and the smell in the market, with its piles of raw flesh and wilting flowers, was like the mingled sweetness and corruption she had smelled that other day in the empty cemetery at home: the day she had remembered always until now vaguely as the time she and her brother had found treasure in the opened graves. Instantly upon this thought the dreadful vision faded, and she saw clearly her brother, whose childhood face she had forgotten, standing again in the blazing sunshine, again twelve years old, a pleased sober smile in his eyes, turning the silver dove over and over in his hands.

The story is so rich, it has so many meanings that bear close and subtle relations to each other, that a brief summary of what the story means will oversimplify it and fail to do justice to its depth, but I shall venture a few comments.

Obviously the story is about growing up and going through a kind of initiation into the mysteries of adult life. It is thus the story of the discovery of truth. Miranda learns about birth and her own destiny as a woman; she learns these things suddenly, unexpectedly, in circumstances that connect birth with death. Extending this comment a little further, one might say that the story is about the paradoxical nature of truth: truth wears a double face—it is not simple but complex. The secret of birth is revealed in the place of death and through a kind of bloody sacrifice. If there is beauty in the discovery, there is also awe and even terror.

These meanings are dramatized by their presentation through a particular action, which takes place in a particular setting. Something more than illustration of a statement is involved—something more than mere vividness or the presentation of a generalization in a form to catch the reader's eye. One notices, for example, how important is the fact of the grandmother's anxiety to keep the family together, even the bodies of the family dead. And the grandmother's solicitude is not mentioned merely to account for the physical fact of the abandoned cemetery in which Miranda makes her discovery about life and death. Throughout this story, birth and death are seen through a family perspective.

Miranda is, for example, thoroughly conscious of how her family is regarded in the community. We are told that her father had been criticized for letting his girls dress like boys and career "around astride barebacked horses." Miranda herself had encountered such criticism from old women whom she

met on the road—women who smoked corncob pipes. They had always "treated her grandmother with most sincere respect," but they ask her "What yo Pappy thinkin about?" This matter of clothes, and the social sense, and the role of women in the society are brought into the story unobtrusively, but they powerfully influence its meaning. For if the story is about a rite of initiation, an initiation into the meaning of sex, the subject is not treated in a doctrinaire polemical way. In this story sex is considered in a much larger context, in a social and even a philosophical context.

How important the special context is will become apparent if we ask ourselves why the story ends as it does. Years later, in the hot tropical sunlight of a Mexican city, Miranda sees a tray of dyed sugar sweets, moulded in the form of baby pigs and baby rabbits. They smell of vanilla, but this smell mingles with the other odors of the marketplace, including that of raw flesh, and Miranda is suddenly reminded of the "sweetness and corruption" that she had smelled long before as she stood in the empty grave in the family burial plot. What is it that makes the experience not finally horrifying or nauseating? What steadies Miranda and redeems the experience for her? I quote again the concluding sentence:

> Instantly upon this thought the dreadful vision faded, and she saw clearly her brother, whose childhood face she had forgotten, standing again in the blazing sunshine, again twelve years old, a pleased sober smile in his eyes, turning the silver dove over and over in his hands.

I mentioned earlier the richness and subtlety of this beautiful story. It needs no further illustration; yet one can hardly forbear reminding oneself how skilfully, and apparently almost effortlessly, the author has rendered the physical and social context that gives point to Miranda's discovery of truth and has effected the modulation of her shifting attitudes—toward the grave, the buried ring, her hunting clothes, the dead rabbit—reconciling these various and conflicting attitudes and, in the closing sentences, bringing into precise focus the underlying theme.

JOAN GIVNER
From "Katherine Anne Porter, Journalist"
Southwest Review, Autumn 1979, pp. 316–21

The shift of Porter's attention from the villian to the saintly heroine (in the early 20s) was not a temporary change of focus but a permanent one, and her attitude toward the virtuous heroine eventually formed the cornerstone of her moral philosophy. The main tenet of this philosophy is that the evildoers are not the most reprehensible people in the world, because they at least have the courage of their convictions. Nor are they the most dangerous people, since they can be easily recognized. The people who really need to be watched are the so-called innocents who stand by and allow others to perpetrate evil. Porter was to express repeatedly the opinion that the innocent bystanders allow the activity of evildoers, not merely because of fear and indifference, but because they gain vicarious pleasure from seeing others perform the wicked deeds which they themselves wish but fear to perform. She came eventually to see the passive virtuous people as guilty of promoting evil even when they do not consciously do so.

This theory about the relationship between saints and evildoers and their collusion in evil became her lifelong gospel, the subject of numerous informal talks, the message she preached from political platforms, and the basis of her interpretation of current events. After the publication of *Ship of Fools* she gave this account of some of the events of the twentieth century:

> . . . . the collusion in evil that allows creatures like Mussolini, or Hitler, or Huey Long or McCarthy— you can make your own list, petty and great,—to gain hold of things, who permits it? Oh, we're convinced we're not evil. We don't believe in that sort of thing, do we? And the strange thing is that if these agents of evil are all clowns, why do we put up with them? God knows, such men are evil, without sense—forces of pure ambition and will—but they enjoy our tacit consent.[1]

Her judgments in literary criticism were influenced by the same point of view. She praised Eudora Welty's stories because she depicted villains pure and unmitigated and with none of the sympathy and understanding which Porter believed amounted to criminal collusion in evil between author and character. Consistently, when Robert Penn Warren published *All the King's Men* she wrote to various friends of her shock and horror that he should have explored carefully the motivation of the character based on Huey Long. She felt that he should have portrayed the character as a villain, and she condemned the book as a sentimental apology for the worst kind of fascist demogogue.

The same theory informed all her fiction. An early spare version of her theme appears in the short story "Magic." Here a maid, hoping to relax her mistress as she brushes her hair, tells a story of a villainous madam who cheats and bullies the prostitutes in a New Orleans brothel. The point of the story is that the madam's activity is made possible by those around her—the male clients, the police, and the cook—who do nothing. Not only are these people as guilty as the one who perpetrates the violence, but so too are the woman and the maid who relish the story. The woman sniffs scent (a detail which suggests her desire to hide the unpleasant realities), stares at her blameless reflection in the mirror, and urges the storyteller to continue whenever she pauses. Lest there be any doubt about the equation of guilt between both madams and both maids, they resemble each other so closely as to invite confusion. When the storyteller describes the cook of the brothel she might be describing herself: "she was a woman, colored like myself with much French blood all the same, like myself always among people who worked spells. But she had a very hard heart, she helped the madam in everything, she liked to watch all that happen."[2] The theme of the story echoes Porter's words that the evil of our time is not an accident but a total consent.

A fuller version of the theme appears in "Flowering Judas," which, like many of Porter's stories, has a triangular arrangement of characters, consisting of villain, victim, and "heroine." Braggioni, like all Porter's villains, is pure caricature and looms in the story like a grotesque Easter egg in shades of mauve and purple and yellow. A hideous creature with the eyes of a cat and the paunch of a pig, he embodies each of the seven deadly sins.

The implication of the story is that if Braggioni is a self-serving, self-indulgent villain, he has not always been so. Once he was a young idealist in both politics and love. It is Laura and people like her who have caused him to change from idealist to opportunist, and the main focus of the story is upon her and upon her motivation. She neither loves nor opposes Braggioni, because she is basically indifferent to him as she is to most people. She has trained herself to remain uncommitted in her relationships with others and has developed a principle of rejection: ". . . . the very cells of her flesh reject knowledge

and kinship in one monotonous word. No. No. No. She draws her strength from this one holy talismanic word which does not suffer her to be led into evil. Denying everything she may walk anywhere in safety, she looks at everything without amazement."[3] It is the death of Eugenio in which she has conspired with Braggioni that causes her finally to become aware of her guilt, and then only in a dream. As she falls asleep she receives a message from her own depths which warns her of motives and the meaning of her acts.

Porter's longest treatment of her theme is, of course, *Ship of Fools*. She described her intentions in the novel in a 1946 letter to Josephine Herbst. She said that her book was about the constant endless collusion between good and evil. She said that she believed human beings to be capable of total evil but thought that no one had ever been totally good, and that gave the edge to evil. She intended not to present any solution, but simply to show the principle at work and why none of us had an alibi in the world. She said that her plan and conclusion had been worked out ten years before and that nothing had happened since to change her mind—indeed, everything confirmed her old opinion.

Again in the novel the villains are depicted in caricature. Herr Rieber is piglike and the Zarzuela Company, a group of thieves, pimps, and prostitutes who stop at nothing, is described as a flock of crows or other quarreling, thieving birds.

The pivotal character who corresponds with Laura of "Flowering Judas" is Dr. Schumann. He is well qualified by his superior intelligence and by his professional training to be influential, but he has developed a detachment which distances him from the others. He is introduced in the novel standing above the other characters to watch them come aboard. As he looks down from his elevated position his interest is clinical, aloof. The hunchback stirs his interest as a case of extreme malformation; Jenny excites his disapproval as an immodest woman; and Mrs. Treadwell with her bruise arouses his worst, and as it turns out, totally unfounded suspicions. Typically, he soon loses interest, and it is apparent that his physical weakness of the heart is symptomatic of a corresponding spiritual weakness. He is a professional helper of mankind who gives help automatically but is incapable of love or involvement. When the Captain asks his advice on what to do about the Zarzuela Company his reply, "Do nothing at all," marks his kinship with Laura. Like her, he eventually experiences a moment when the implications of his acts become apparent, even to himself: "The Doctor suffered the psychic equivalent of a lightning stroke, which cleared away there and then his emotional fogs and vapors, and he faced his truth, nearly intolerable but the kind of pain he could deal with, something he recognized and accepted unconditionally."[4]

Within the novel the theme is stated in a crucial discussion which takes place at the Captain's table of the *Vera*. The guests are discussing the activities of the Spanish dancers, and Frau Rittersdorf expresses the opinion that they are "dangerous criminals." The Captain disagrees because "it requires a certain force of character to be really evil." (His remark has the special interest of being almost word for word what Katherine Anne Porter wrote in 1919 in an editorial on the villains of the Denver stage.) Dr. Schumann elaborates on the Captain's statement:

> I agree with the Captain it takes a strong character to be really evil. Most of us are too slack, half-hearted or cowardly—luckily, I suppose. Our collusion with evil is only negative, consent by default you might say. I suppose in our hearts our sympathies are with the criminal because he really commits the deed we only dream of doing.[5]

Katherine Anne Porter was not embarrassed by her changelessness and indeed often congratulated herself on it. After the publication of her novel she said: "It's astonishing how little I've changed: nothing in my point of view or way of feeling. I'm going back now to finish some of the great many short stories that I have begun and not been able to finish for one reason or another."[6]

In the last years of her life she did complete a number of stories and essays which she had started earlier, among them an account of her participation in the movement protesting the execution of Sacco and Vanzetti in Boston in 1927. Her publication of her essay, *The Never Ending Wrong*, fifty years later made it the work with the longest gestation period, twenty years longer than that of *Ship of Fools*.

Reactions to the book were mixed. Others who were involved in the Sacco-Vanzetti case felt that the writers who flocked to Boston did so seeking grist for conversations in such gathering places of the literati as the round table of the Algonquin. One reviewer felt that the essay was an inconsequential work which told too little about the case and too much about how Porter felt on every occasion of human betrayal. Only Porter's friend Eudora Welty pointed out the close thematic link between the essay and the fiction. In fact, the theme of the essay is exactly that of the stories and the novel, the arrangement of characters in a triangle of villain, victim, and not-so-innocent hero/heroine, the same that appears in all her work.

The villains have all the recognizable porcine, complacent traits of such other villains as Braggioni and Herr Rieber. They are Governor Fuller, Judge Thayer (who is reported to have said while playing golf, "Did you see what I did to those anarchistic bastards?"), and the Judges who preside over the trial of the picketers and who are described as follows:

. . . . three entirely correct old gentlemen looking much alike in their sleekness, pinkness, baldness, glossiness of grooming, such stereotypes as no proletarian novelist would have dared to use as the example of a capitalist monster in his novel. . . .

The gentlemen regarded us glossily, then turned to each other. As we descended the many floors in silence, one of them said to the others in a cream-cheese voice, "It is very pleasant to know that we may expect things to settle down properly again," and the others nodded with wise, smug, complacent faces.[7]

Arrayed against these representatives of corrupt authority are all those who wish to help the victims and protest their unfair trial. On close inspection, however, they turn out like other of Porter's blameless people to be secretly in collusion with the villains and conspiring toward the same end. Chief among these are the Communists, represented by Rosa Baron. When Porter expressed the wish that the victims might be saved, she was astonished to hear Rosa Baron reply, "Why, what on earth good would they be to us alive?" And there are other protesters of dubious intention, notably the journalists who profit from the scenes of high emotion when the members of the victim's family appear. One gloats that he arranged the whole show. The victims, of course, are not saved and they die, like Eugenio of "Flowering Judas" and Echegaray of *Ship of Fools*, with dignity and resignation gazing steadfastly at death. Their families are dazed and filled with horror, as are many of Porter's characters when they recognize the presence of Evil, "its power and its bestial imbecility."

Notes

1. James Ruoff and Del Smith, "Katherine Anne Porter on *Ship of Fools*," *College English* 24 (February 1963), pp. 396–97.
2. Katherine Anne Porter, *The Collected Stories of Katherine Anne Porter* (New York: Harcourt Brace & World, 1965), p. 41.
3. Ibid., p. 97.
4. Katherine Anne Porter, *Ship of Fools* (Boston: Little, Brown & Co., 1962), p. 373.
5. Ibid., p. 294.
6. Barbara Thompson, "Katherine Anne Porter: An Interview," *Paris Review* 24 (Winter-Spring, 1963), pp. 87–114; reprinted in Lodwich Hartley and George Core, eds., *Katherine Anne Porter: A Critical Symposium* (University of Georgia Press, 1970).
7. Katherine Anne Porter, *The Never Ending Wrong* (Boston: Little, Brown & Co., 1977), p. 49.

CHAIM POTOK

1929–

Chaim Potok was born in New York City on February 17, 1929, to a family of Polish-Jewish immigrants. Raised in a traditionally observant Jewish home, educated at Jewish parochial schools, the young Potok displayed a lively intellectual curiosity. While still in his early teens he read Evelyn Waugh's *Brideshead Revisited*, and was tremendously influenced by it; by his account, Waugh's novel brought him forcefully to the realization of fiction's power to convey readers into cultural milieux utterly different from their own. Armed with this insight, Potok decided to write fiction that would help integrate traditional Jewish civilization into American life and letters, and toward this end he took a B.A. *summa cum laude* at Yeshiva University in 1950, an M.H.L. and ordination as a rabbi at the Jewish Theological Seminary in 1954, and a Ph.D. in philosophy at the University of Pennsylvania in 1965.

Potok's novels, all of which emphasize cross-cultural encounters of one form or another, include *The Chosen* (1967), *My Name Is Asher Lev* (1972), *In the Beginning* (1975), *The Book of Lights* (1981), and *Davita's Harp* (1985). In addition, Potok has also written many essays for both secular and Jewish periodicals, taught extensively at universities on both coasts of the United States, and served as an editor for the magazine *Conservative Judaism* and for the Jewish Publication Society, where he has been involved with overseeing various aspects of a new translation of the

Torah. In 1978 Potok published a popular nonfiction work, *Wanderings: Chaim Potok's History of the Jews.*

In 1958, soon after leaving a two-year stint as a U.S. Army chaplain in Korea, Potok married Adena Sarah Mosevitsky; they live in Philadelphia and have three children.

SAM BLUEFARB
From "The Head, the Heart, and the Conflict of Generations in Chaim Potok's *The Chosen*"
CLA Journal, June 1971, pp. 402–9

The locale of ⟨*The Chosen*⟩ is the Crown Heights section of Williamsburg in Brooklyn from the Depression years to the founding of the State of Israel. Although much of the story's direction is determined by the conflict between Hassidic and Misnagdic traditions of Judaism (as respectively represented by the Saunders and Malter families), it is the conflict between two generations and the Hawthornesque split between the obsessions of the head and the impulses of the heart that carry the major thrust of *The Chosen*.

The Hassidic view originated as a revolt against the arid intellectual concerns of 18th century scholastic (i.e., Misnagdic) Judaism with its tortuous explications in Talmudic *pilpul* and its aristocratic disdain for the poor and illiterate Jew. This resulted in the Hassidic heresy (according to the Vilna Gaon) toward the stress on joy and the intuitions. Yet in its turn (especially as portrayed in *The Chosen*) Hassidism itself evolved into the very thing it had attacked. The distance between the *Ba'al Shem Tov* (or the *Besht*, as he was affectionately called by his followers) and his latter-day followers is relatively short, as history goes: a mere two hundred years or so; but the distance between the gentle piety of the founder of Hassidism and the fanaticism of his later followers qualitatively spans a greater distance than time alone can account for. Indeed, Reb Saunders, the Hassidic leader in *The Chosen*, has really reverted to the earlier arid scholasticism which Hassidism in its own beginnings had set itself up in opposition to.

However, in *The Chosen*, the quarrel between the Hassidim and the Misnagdim (these days, roughly those practicing Jews who are not Hassidim) though decreasing in intensity and bitterness after the slaughter of six million in the Nazi Holocaust, still makes up a substantial aspect of this novel. It is to this group—the Misnagdim (or, to acknowledge Potok's Sephardic dialectal usage, Mitnagdim)—to which Reuven Malter, the young protagonist, belongs. We must of course remember that many Hassidim consider most Jews beyond their own circle *apikorsim* (heretics). While it is true that the Misnagdim in *The Chosen* did not actively oppose the Hassidim, the baseball game between the Misnagdic and the Hassidic schools on which the novel opens, not only triggers the conflict but determines the direction the novel will take. In a sense, *The Chosen* is a kind of exercise in the "Hegelian" dialectic which the Hassidim and the Misnagdim have engaged in for the last two and a half centuries; however, in doing so, they have articulated their respective visions toward life and God, and, in a sense, have managed to exert some beneficial influence on each other.

One of the central problems in *The Chosen* is communication—or lack of it. Part of this is deliberate and "chosen." Reb Saunders, in his oddly "Talmudic" way, believes that he can best teach his son the language and wisdom of the heart by forbidding, or discouraging, what he considers "frivolous" discourse—what most of us might think of as the minimal conversational civilities. Thus Reb Saunders denies Danny what Mr. Malter the yeshiva teacher freely gives to his son

Reuven: warmth, communication, and understanding. On those rare occasions when Reb Saunders permits himself to address Danny, these exchanges take place during the periodic quizzes on Talmud which the *rebbe* subject Danny to—or when he blows up in exasperation at his son's passivity in the face of his own religious (near violent) commitments.

On the other hand, the relationship between Reuven and *his* father is a tender one, made all the more trusting by the easy and affectionate exchange of confidences that go on between them. They, at least, can do what Danny and his father seem unable to do: communicate. In the instance of Reb Saunders it is an admixture of pride and fanatic pietism that prevents any intimacy between himself and his son (rationalized by the elder Saunders' commitment to the Talmudic *A word is worth one coin; silence is worth two*). In Danny's case it is simply fear of his father that prevents any viable relationship between the two. Conceivably, Mr. Malter, the yeshiva teacher, and Reb Saunders, the Hassidic Talmudist, are of a common generation, if not of a common age; yet it is Reb Saunders' rigidity, and his stiff-necked pride, that give the illusion that he is much older than Mr. Malter—even as Hassidism itself *appears* to be rooted in an older tradition than its Misnagdic counterpart.

The difference between Mr. Malter and Reb Saunders expresses itself most forcefully in their respective visions toward the Holocaust: Reb Saunders can do little more than shed (very real) tears for the martyred Jews of Europe. "'How the world drinks our blood. . . . [But] It is the will of God. We must accept the will of God.'"[1] Reuven's more Westernized father, on the other hand, attempts to counter the existential nullity of the "world" by becoming ever more active in a resuscitated Zionist movement. Reb Saunders, to the contrary, in conformance with orthodox Hassidism, is bound by the Messianic belief—that only with the coming of the Messiah will Jews achieve the millennial dream, the ingathering of the exiles, the return to Eretz Yisroel.

What we find in *The Chosen* is a kind of *doppelgänger* effect—minus the *doppelgänger* itself. For Reuven and Danny are symbolically two halves of a single (perhaps ideal? Jewish?) personality, each half searching for its complement, which we already know can never be found in an imperfect world (*Siz a falsher velt!*—It's a hypocritical world! says a Yiddish Koheleth.). In short, no perfection is to be attained, except in unity. But that is precisely the problem of the characters in *The Chosen*: theirs is a search for that elusive (or illusory) goal. For neither of these two boys growing into manhood can really be said to exist at their fullest potential unless they retain some sort of relationship with each other, which on one occasion is suspended when Reb Saunders forbids Danny any association with Reuven for an interval of about a year, making the two boys doubly miserable.

Reuven, whose father allows his sons forays into symbolic logic, the mathematics of Bertrand Russell, ends up a rabbi! Danny, who throughout the novel is coerced into following Hassidic tradition, and is expected to succeed Reb to the leadership of the sect on his father's death, ultimately breaks away. Danny, for want of a better word—the word has been overly used and abused, though it applies here—has been alienated—from his father, from Hassidism, and finally from the Hassidic community itself. In a sense Danny is recapitulating (suffering through) the transitions and adjustments so traumatically demanded by the exodus from the Old World to the New, adjustments required of his father and his followers, "pilgrims" who came to America from the East European *shtetle* on step ahead of Hitler's kill-squads.

The American Diaspora has also given Danny, Freud and Behaviorist psychology (though initially he has mixed feelings about the latter); but after reading Graetz's *History of the Jews*, he has found that "Freud had clearly upset him in a fundamental way—had thrown him off-balance" (p. 148). 〈. . .〉

As the novel progresses, Danny the intellectual wizard, *Wunderkind*, finds himself increasingly boxed in by the restrictive ghetto mentality of the Hassidim. He sees that his father "'Intellectually . . . was born trapped. I don't ever want to be trapped the way he's trapped'" (p. 191).

Ultimately, though, *The Chosen* is a paradigm of two visions that have not only sundered Judaism but have affected other areas of life—the split between head and heart. The Saunderses seem to have an excess of head in their (paradoxical streak of zealousness and emotional) makeup; but the Malters have heart *and* head: they are in balance. For Reuven is not only an outstanding student of Talmud but he "has a head" for mathematics and symbolic logic. Like his father, he also has a spark of tolerance which illuminates his own knowledge of human essences as opposed to ritualistic forms.

Reuven's studies are "brain" disciplines—logic, mathematics, philosophy—yet it is he who finally turns out to have more "heart" than the brilliant son of a Hassid. Danny, on the other hand, having been raised in the tradition of the *Ba'al Shem*, should have been a "heart-and-joy specialist." Yet it is he who is all brain. And this produces a keen irony, since Hassidism, a movement that was originally a revolt against arid scholasticism became (as portrayed in *The Chosen*) transformed into its opposite. Piety, joy, even learning (a latecomer to Hassidism) becomes pietism, rote learning, memorization. 〈. . .〉

Reb Saunders' "conversion"—his resignation to Danny's break with Hassidism—doesn't convince. The novel is too mechanical in this sense—with Danny, who was to have inherited his father's leadership going off to become a clinical or behavioral psychologist, while Reuven turns to the rabbinate.[2]

The climax of the novel is illustrated by the following exchange the two young men engage in: Danny tells Reuven: "'I can't get over you becoming a rabbi.'" Whereupon Reuven answers: "'I can't get over your becoming a psychologist'" (p. 247). Even the dialogue is weak here, betraying the Procrustean ending; it is virtually the antithesis to the brilliant verbal fencing—stychomythia—that the great dramatists from Shakespeare to Shaw were such virtuosos at. In this instance, the dialogue verges on the cliché.

Thus, as Reuven moves closer to Misnagdic—non-Hassidic—Judaism, so Danny moves away from its Hassidic counterpart, giving the novel this mechanical symmetry. The saving feature in spite of the contrived ending is that the choices of the two young men are as much determined by motive and character (or lack of it) as by superimposed plot strictures.

The almost explicit theme of *The Chosen*, then, is that the more repression one is forced to knuckle under to (no matter the noble intentions), the greater will be the rebellion against the source of that repression; it's the old postulate of an opposite and equal reaction for every action. In other words, the contrivance of the rebellious son against the father and the father's resignation to the son's rebellion—"'You will remain

an observer of the Commandments?'" he pathetically asks Danny (p. 268)—are developments which make it all the more difficult to believe in Reb Saunders as a strong, if stubborn, man.[3]

Still—and this I mean to stress—the "contrivance of symmetry" with which the novel ends is a minor flaw in a larger pattern: that of tolerance against intolerance, empty ritual against the vital deed, rote learning against eager wonder. In any effective fiction it is the process rather than the outcome that is more important. This is especially true in *The Chosen*. For in this novel Chaim Potok gives us as keen an insight into the split between head and heart, tolerance and fanaticism, the strictures of tradition against the impulses of *rachmonis* (pity) as has appeared in the Jewish-American novel in a long time.

Notes

1. Chaim Potok, *The Chosen*, Fawcett Crest edition, p. 181. All further quotations are cited by page number within parentheses following them.
2. In Danny's escape from the Hassidic milieu, he is acting out the time-honored impulse that fills the pages of American literature generally—from Mark Twain's Huck Finn to Joseph Heller's Orr.
3. In the writing of this article, I wish to acknowledge the helpful suggestions of my brother-in-law, Aaron Guterman, who revolted against his own (Misnagdic) father in the Poland of some sixty years ago.

DAVID STERN
"Two Worlds"

Commentary, October 1972, pp. 102–4

The protagonists of Chaim Potok's novels—*The Chosen*, *The Promise*, and now *My Name Is Asher Lev*—follow a common career; in the course of the narrative they are seen moving slowly and with agonizing reluctance out of, and away from, the religious community in which they were born and brought up (a highly sentimentalized version of Brooklyn's Williamsburg or Crown Heights section twenty years ago) and into secular society. Yet for all the suffering they undergo in this process, and despite the relentless psychological motion through which Potok pushes and pulls them, his characters display no real understanding of the dilemma which they have been chosen to exemplify, which is nothing short of the dilemma of modern religious Judaism itself.

Historically, the Orthodox-Jewish community, insular by choice and by dint of outside pressure, has gone to extreme lengths in its rejection of the secular, and those Jews who have attempted to lead both religious and secular lives have often fallen prey to a real confusion of identity, a kind of metaphorical schizophrenia. Potok's heroes, however, move from the religious to the secular under the spell of an aimless, even a gratuitous, inevitability. In fact his novels *assume* the impossibility of existing in both the religious and the secular spheres—an assumption whose net effect amounts in the end to a kind of apology for assimilationism. The schizophrenic trap of living a double life and of speaking in two, often exclusive, languages—the subject of all of Potok's novels—is precisely what he has been most unsuccessful either in depicting or in attempting to resolve.

In *My Name Is Asher Lev*, Potok deals with one very special aspect of this dilemma. Asher Lev is a uniquely talented artist, born to a Hasidic family otherwise distinguished not only for its piety and scholarship but for service to the *rebbe* and to the community. As a child, dabbling in crayons and watercolors, Asher Lev is treated with condescension and indulgence; he is considered a mild curiosity. When, however, he commits himself unequivocally as a young adult to the traditions of Western art and begins to paint nudes and crucifixions (as though nudes and crucifixions were the only subject matter of Western art), his family and community turn upon him with the violence and hatred reserved only for representatives of the *sitra achra*, literally *the other side*, a kabbalistic euphemism for the satanic and the diabolic.

The specific issue that Potok raises here—the status of art and artists within the traditional Jewish community—is symptomatic of the larger problem raised by Judaism's attitude toward the creative arts in general. While the Orthodox-Jewish community has given birth to great painters, musicians, and writers, it has not encouraged, nurtured, or sustained them in their achievements, and, in the case of representational art especially, it has been downright hostile to their calling. The biblical prohibition against the fashioning of idols ("Ye shall not make with me gods of silver, neither shall ye make unto you gods of gold") was traditionally interpreted to forbid all three-demensional, sculptured representations of the human body; as for painting, although not explicitly forbidden, it came to be viewed, because of its origins, as essentially the heritage and property of pagan (Greek and Roman) and Christian culture—unsuitable by definition for the Jew.

Behind such an attitude lies a basic philosophical antagonism between *halacha* (Jewish law) and art. Whereas the one, the legal embodiment of revealed truth, forms the very basis of social and religious order, the other, as the expression *par excellence* of the individual voice and the private vision, represents an actual or potential threat to all communal values. On this point, oddly enough, Orthodox Judaism sees eye to eye with Plato, and whenever the community has seen fit, or been compelled, to permit artistic expression in its midst, it has proceeded more or less along the lines suggested in the *Republic*: tolerating and indulging that which clearly lies within the boundaries of the Law or, at the least, does not subvert the religious interests of the community, rigorously forbidding everything that refuses to yield to the needs of didacticism. The case has never been one of overt or official censorship, but of a subtle and persistent pressure which has discouraged the pursuit of artistic talent and attempted to channel that energy into more conventional disciplines. Yet whatever form it has taken, the hostility fostered by *halacha* has contributed to a common view of the artist as heretical or, at the least, immoral.

Children are, of course, most susceptible to prejudices of this kind. In the baseball game with which his first novel, *The Chosen*, begins, Potok captured very well the zeal and inventiveness with which children turn play into a ritualization of their parents' animosities. Similarly, the most successful passages in *Asher Lev* occur when the child artist is caught in class drawing the face of the *rebbe* on the page of a Bible. He is taunted by his classmates as "the destroyer of Torah," and "goy Lev"; then one day he discovers a mildly scatological poem inserted between the pages of his Talmud text. In revenge, Asher copies a detail from Michelangelo's *Last Judgment* that depicts "a man being pulled headlong into hell by serpentine demons"; substituting the face of an expecially obnoxious classmate for that of the man, he inserts the copy into the classmate's Talmud:

> He said nothing to me about the drawings. But he began to avoid me. His thin face would fill with dread whenever he caught me looking at him. I had the feeling he regarded me now as evil and malevolent, as a demonic and contaminating spawn of the Other Side.

Even should he wish to remain within his community, Asher

Lev stands beyond its circle if not outside God's Creation as well.

Exactly what there is for him on the "other side," however, is hard to say. As a portrait of the artist and a study of his growth and maturing, *Asher Lev* is without distinction. We are constantly told of Asher Lev's prodigious talent, and of the extent to which he suffers for his art, but from Potok's banal and sentimental descriptions of his painting, Asher Lev sounds dreadfully untalented. Moreover, his conflict with his father, which provides the impetus to his creative energies and is the dramatic focus of the novel, is treated in a heavy-handed and even careless way. Thus, when Asher Lev finally cuts off his side-curls, a gesture rich in psychological suggestiveness precisely because it is at once an assertion of self and an act of self-castration, Potok treats the incident merely as an indication of Asher Lev's movement from one social ambience to another.

My Name is Asher Lev concludes with the description of a rather horrendous painting, *The Brooklyn Crucifixion*—a portrait of the artist's mother tied to the Venetian blinds of her front window as she waits for her husband and son to return—which nevertheless poses an overwhelming question: the possibility, or viability, of an art authentically Jewish. The artist committed to remaining within Judaism in a more than peripheral way, who makes his concern the creation of a work that will stand firmly within Jewish tradition, faces the necessity of working in genres whose origins and structures are all secular. The paradox implicit here may itself begin to suggest an aesthetics rooted in the same "schizophrenia" characteristic of Jewish existence within secular society. Chaim Potok no doubt would wish to be understood as working in the direction of such an aesthetic, but he has yet to write a novel whose imaginative richness and narrative strength would begin to approach the standard to which he aspires.

DAPHNE MERKIN
From "Why Potok Is Popular"
Commentary, February 1976, pp. 73–75

"The readiness is all": after the countless portrayals in American fiction of wandering and assimilated Jews—from Malamud's S. Levin to Bellow's Moses Herzog to Roth's Alexander Portnoy—the literary public, at least a large and enthusiastic segment of it, would seem to be ready for Chaim Potok's version of the American Jew—one who has never left the traditional religious community. Potok's latest exploration of the world of Orthodox Judaism is *In the Beginning*; his fourth novel and an all-but-negligible variation on the theme of his first three (*The Chosen*, *The Promise*, and *My Name Is Asher Lev*), it is also his fourth best-seller, and it, too, like the first three, has been treated with respect, if not acclaim, by the critics.

What Potok's main theme consists of exactly is difficult to say. All his books center on the conflict between the religious life and the life of the imagination, but it is certain that his books are not bought—much less remembered—for the quality of their author's metaphysical speculations. A better clue to his popularity lies perhaps in the fortuitous coinciding of timing and a talent, howsoever meager, that is capable of rising to an occasion it has suddenly come upon. That occasion is the rediscovery, in the culture at large and among Jews in particular, of "ethnic consciousness," and Potok has put this rising awareness to profitable use, spinning out tales of unassimilated "people of the book" to the delight of the many assimilated Jews who read him.

It is understandable enough: after Portnoy and his alarming fantasies, who would not be ready to gather Potok's resuscitated ghetto Jews, with their delicate feelings and righteous habits, into his arms? In each successive novel, Potok has imparted freshness to an image of Jews as otherworldly wraiths, innocent, devoutly principled, without so much as a touch of the cosmopolitan *angst* that afflicts so many of their fictional (and real-life) brothers. Potok's figures still live in exclusively Jewish worlds; their energy is spent on issues most contemporary Jews have abandoned, together with separate dishes for meat and dairy foods. And this perhaps suggests yet another reason for Potok's popularity: laden as his works are with the colorful details of Orthodox ritual and with gobbets of Jewish history and folklore, they perform a pedagogical function in a relatively painless way, informing Jews about their heritage and making them feel nostalgically good about it at the same time.

That Potok's books are badly written seems to bother no one. *In the Beginning* was reviewed glowingly in the New York *Times Book Review*, and was treated in what can only be called a kindly fashion by the *New Yorker*: clearly Potok's work is not accorded the normal critical reception, but is handled in the way matters of faith are handled by the non-religious in a carefully tolerant age, with kid gloves (or the way ethnic theater, for example, is reviewed in the daily press, with critical judgment suspended). Aesthetically damning as this slackened attitude may be, it is in its own way just, for Potok writes more as a rabbi (which in fact he is) than as a novelist, inspired by the responsibilities of the pulpit rather than the license of the muse. Potok seems to conceive of his novels as instruction or even initiation into such perplexing issues as the conditions for religious belief in a faithless time—issues rarely if ever dealt with in contemporary fiction. Unlike more consequential Jewish writers whose heritage colors but does not dictate to their material, Potok writes both *as* a Jew and *because* he is a Jew: one aspect validates the other. So Potok feels himself duty bound to present Orthodox Judaism in the best possible light: not as a mere moral code or a set of historical imperatives tacked on to the everyday business of life, which goes on elsewhere, but as a magically powered and all-pervasive essence that somehow affects the very character of that life at its core.

As a novelist then, Potok has consciously forgone the attempt to write about situations or characters that might stand in for the situations of humanity in general, and has concentrated instead on the particular, writing from an insularly Jewish perspective that denies broader implications. Yet by keeping to his own side of town, to the restricted but fertile Jewish territory of high-toned wrestlings with God and self, he has hit upon both a formula for success and a comfortable frame in which the only limits to artistic achievement are the limits of his own imagination. Unfortunately, as *In the Beginning* demonstrates once again, those limits are rather quickly reached. ⟨. . .⟩

Potok's strength, here as in his earlier books, is his storytelling skill. His panoramic plots feature something for everyone, and the narrative thread weaves in and out of locales and periods with enviable effortlessness. There is no denying that *In the Beginning*, in its own plodding way, is a good read, and this in itself goes far toward excusing the black-and-white moral scheme, the pseudo-profundities, and the spurious bits of homely wisdom in which it abounds.

It does not, however, excuse Potok's misleading and sentimentalized version of Orthodox Judaism, which functions in all of Potok's novels less as a reality than as a symbol. For all

its intricately wrought scenes and its wealth of detail, *In the Beginning* does not succeed in capturing the quixotic spirit of observant Judaism; its conception is at once too hallowed and too facile. Thus, emotions in the novel all take place on a spiritual level; no one experiences any primitive appetitive urges. ⟨. . .⟩ Judaism in Potok's world is never simply lived; it is, rather, an intellectual curiosity that is always being examined, questioned, held up to the light, displayed.

In an astute essay originally published in these pages,[1] Philip Roth once maintained that the real question lurking behind the attacks on him by the rabbinical "establishment" was the defensive one: "What will the *goyim* think?" With Potok, this question would never appear to arise. Yet the attitude toward Judaism in his novels does turn out to be defensive after all, one that implicitly acknowledges the insufficiency of all those quaint rituals and historical ideas to stand on their own and compel the mind. Writing from within a world whose sympathetic spokesman he has become, Potok might have risen to the chance to see that world steadily and whole. That he has failed to do so, that his portrait of Orthodoxy is as carefully selective as it is, may in part be a failure of talent, but it may also be attributable to an unspoken fear of what the *goyim* will think—even though in this case the "*goyim*" happen to be the assimilated Jews who are the majority of his readers. Potok's rendition of Orthodox life is entertaining and informative, but his work does not expand to the dimensions it reaches for, and he has so far not exhibited enough confidence in the viability of his own materials to accord them the rounded and unapologetic treatment they are still waiting to receive.

Notes

1. "Writing about Jews," *Commentary*, December 1963.

ERICH ISAAC
From "Among the Nations"
Commentary, April 1979, pp. 84–86

The novelist's hand is evident in the flow of the narrative and the often felicitous turns of phrase ⟨in *Wanderings: Chaim Potok's History of the Jews*⟩. Despite the fact that it is not the work of a historian, it is sophisticated and judicious in its use of professional sources. Yet as the title makes clear, this is meant as a personal history, and its personal character is emphasized through the deliberate intrusion of the author into the narrative. Here, for example, is Potok on Rome: "I see her through my Jewish eyes; I have no love for Rome. Of all the peoples of her vast empire she understood the Jews least." On Islam:

> When I was very young I was told by a white bearded man I revered that Muslims were desert barbarians who had somehow stumbled upon the God of our fathers and had taken Him for themselves, distorting His worship to suit their whims. This man, gentle and very old, was deeply pious and sealed within the world of Torah. Beyond that world lay the poison fruit of alien civilizations. How easily we label unknown worlds barbaric. Everyone is a barbarian to someone.

This sort of thing has a purpose: to help Potok formulate a perspective on Jewish history, and especially—as the two quotations above suggest—on the Jewish confrontation with other cultures and civilizations. Yet considered as history, the volume never makes its thesis clear. And considered as personal history, it never makes clear how Potok's own faith has been reshaped, as he says it has been, by his encounter with non-Jewish, particularly Eastern, cultures.

The title, *Wanderings*, is suggestive of a perspective. Wanderings normally lack direction; they are not pilgrimages but random movements, perhaps searches for something whose exact location is elusive. The Church Fathers saw Jewish wandering as a punishment; the same notion was widespread among Jews, though they had a different notion of what they were being punished for. But despite the title and the frequent repetition of the idea in the book, I do not think that Potok's central thesis is that the Jews are a wandering people. Indeed, the book reveals the extent to which Jews in the last two thousand years have been at home in various civilizations and made efforts to remain where they have settled, often long beyond the time when it would have been wise for them to move.

There is another problem with finding this book's perspective. It is possible to come away from Potok's narrative with a clear impression of the fabulous achievements of Sumer and Akkad, Egypt and Persia, Greece and Rome, Christendom and Islam, and also of what Potok calls "modern paganism"—all the civilizations through which the Jews have passed—but without any real understanding of what the Jewish role in these civilizations has been. Potok's volume leaves one with the sense that even Christianity and Islam, in all but their earliest stages, show little or no trace of Jewish influence.

Why should this be so? According to Potok: "The central idea of biblical civilization was the covenant . . . the central idea of rabbinic civilization was the Messiah." In his book, the covenantal idea is fully discussed; its roots in the pre-Hebrew world are analyzed in detail, and the transformation of the covenant idea in Judaism is lucidly described. No such treatment, however, is accorded to the messianic strain in Judaism—precisely that element in Jewish thought and life which perhaps has made the greatest impact on others, and whose influence continues to be felt to this day.

While one can only speculate as to why Potok should have devoted so much less attention to messianism than to the covenant idea, one reason may be that there exists a large specialist literature on Middle Eastern covenants while the origins of the messianic idea in Israel are shrouded in fog. In general, historical information about the Second Temple period has many gaps. We know next to nothing about the Persian period after Ezra and Nehemiah, practically nothing about the transition to Greek rule and the Greek period itself. With the Maccabees the documentation is better but still not good. Yet it is this period that saw the beginnings of an apocalyptic and messianic literature. Like the Pharisees and Sadducees, who suddenly appear as fully defined groups, messianic doctrines at the time of their first known literary expressions are well developed.

But whatever their antecedents, these ideas were a factor of first importance, both in national resistance to the declining cultural paganism of the Greco-Roman world and in the attraction Judaism exerted upon Gentiles in this period. It was, of course, Christianity that ultimately capitalized on the enormous power of the messianic idea. Although Potok might have found it difficult to discuss the roots of the concept, he might well have described the subsequent transmutation of Jewish messianic and apocalyptic expectations into their Christian and Muslim versions and their continuation in chiliastic, millenarian, and modern secular garb.

For this reader there are also difficulties with Potok's division of Jewish history into two chronological civilizations, separated by the destruction of the Second Temple. Potok never defines what he means by a Jewish civilization. He says only that the central idea of the first is the covenant; of the second, messianism. But this is to say both too much and too little. It is too much because messianism predates rabbinic Judaism and because the covenant remained a central idea even after the maturation of the messianic concept. It is too little because a definition of Jewish civilization in terms of these two themes alone is oversimplified. The true distinctiveness of Jewish civilization both before and after the destruction of sovereignty lay in Jewish religious law and in the life that it shaped—biblical law in the first instance, rabbinic law in the second. Yet about this element of key importance Potok has relatively little to say. Furthermore, if one is talking about civilizations, perhaps a distinction of another kind should be made between the Jewish culture that grew up under Islam and the Jewish culture that grew up under Christianity. May not these be different enough to be considered separate Jewish civilizations?

At the end we are told that a third civilization of the Jews may be at hand. In Potok's diagnosis, today "everything seems to be in fragments: Judaism, Christendom, socialism, the secular dream . . . it is all in pieces around us." But there is also renewal, "a troubled springtime for the Jewish people in the United States and Israel. . . ." American Jews, together with Israel, will succeed in creating a third civilization: "We will renew our people." The reader may be forgiven a certain skepticism on this point. Jews historically have been able to create for themselves images of their host societies which accord with their own specific identities and expectations. They did it in France, in Germany, in Italy, to name but a few places. At this time, toward the end of a terrible century, it appears a specifically American Jewish habit to glide from an appreciation of the distinctive and receptive elements of American society and culture to an implicit foreclosure of negative developments which despite all due vigilance may prove impossible to arrest.

RUTH R. WISSE
From "Jewish Dreams"
Commentary, March 1982, pp. 45–48

Modern Jewish literature, one of the major by-products of Jewish secularization during the past two centuries, has long been obsessed with the rebellion against tradition that brought it into being. The autobiographies of such 18th- and 19th-century Enlighteners as Solomon Maimon, Moshe Leib Lilienblum, and I.L. Peretz, written in German, Hebrew, and Yiddish respectively, are still remarkably absorbing accounts of the struggle that was waged by these men against their traditional Jewish families and communities, and of their own intellectual transformations as they confronted Western thought.

By the turn of the 20th century, with the development of European literary genres, dramatists and novelists ferreted out figures from the past with whom to identify the rebellious posture of the Enlightener—figures like Uriel da Costa, the early 17th-century freethinker whose challenge to rabbinic authority was said to have prefigured Spinoza, or one of the false messiahs, inspired visionaries in a world not yet prepared for their coming. These became the true heroes of modern Jewish literature, representing the courage of personal conviction in the face of a stolid or reactionary society, and credited by their modern interpreters with a dedication to their people's cause that was all the more valuable for having been rejected or ignored.

⟨. . .⟩ Chaim Potok in *The Book of Lights* has adapted his by now standard structure to the story of yet another mild Jewish insubordinate. In each of Potok's previous novels, a representative of Jewish tradition comes into conflict with some incursion of modernity—psychology, comparative philology, art—and makes the perilous move to the other side. His present hero moves from the accepted province of talmudic law to the Kabbalah, the source of a more mysterious, and currently more fashionable, light.

Gershon Loran, the central character in *The Book of Lights*, is a troubled rabbinical student at the Riverside Hebrew Institute—a thinly-veiled fictional version of the Jewish Theological Seminary—in the early 1950's. He is torn between the required study of Talmud and an attraction to Jewish mysticism. The book includes certain staples of Potok's fiction: a friendship between the hero and a young man from a different sociopolitical stratum, in this case the son of a prominent physicist who has been involved in the development of the atom bomb; and the guiding presence of a mentor, modeled on a recognizable Jewish authority, in this case Gershom Scholem, whose pioneering studies of Jewish mysticism from the early 1920's onward have forced upon Jewish historiography and consciousness a serious reconsideration of the mystical component in Judaism. In a subsidiary role there is also a girlfriend with a Ph.D. who (this is circa 1950!) chooses to go to Chicago to teach rather than get married. The historicity of the novel is selective, with current attitudes and cultural trends superimposed on events of three decades ago.

The rabbinical students are required to serve in the chaplaincy overseas—the book takes place during and immediately after the Korean war—and though Loran's academic performance wins him the alternative of graduate work, he decides after all to serve. The greater part of the novel, no doubt based on the author's own experiences as a chaplain in Korea, is set in that country after the war's conclusion. There the sheltered Judaism of the young rabbi is put to the test of alien surroundings, physical hardship, and personal confrontations with unsympathetic superiors. A more serious problem is faced by Loran's friend, who bears the guilt of his father's "complicity" in the bombing of Hiroshima and comes to East Asia to do penance. Drawn compulsively back to Japan, he is killed in a plane crash which leaves his parents childless.

His experiences in Korea and the death of his friend force upon the hero a spiritual crisis, from which he emerges with professional resolve. Without explaining precisely how this is so, the book suggests that the light of the Kabbalah is more effective than the Talmud when it comes to coping with such natural and human mysteries as physics and war. At the end of the book Loran is in the Jerusalem home of his mentor, about to enter graduate work in the spiritually more satisfying area of Jewish mysticism. ⟨. . .⟩

More interesting than the book itself is its place in the author's development. Potok once seemed to be the writer for whom the American Jewish community had been waiting—an educated Jew who knew Jewish life from the inside and could give it authentic representation. As against the second-generation sons and daughters who inhabited most American Jewish fiction, figures estranged from the culture of their parents, with attitudes ranging from indifference to contempt, he presented a generation still raised in traditional homes and only tentatively facing the challenges of the Enlightenment. At the start of each of his early books, Potok's characters feel as if they are emerging out of the pre-modern period, and are only beginning to make an adjustment.

By now, however, the author himself has made an adjustment, one that is apparent in this novel in various ways. During his stay in Korea, for example, the hero tries to prove himself a good chaplain and a good Jew. As a demonstration of his honesty he gives preference to a hard-working Mormon over a Jewish boy from Brooklyn who tries to invoke "tribal familiarity" as the key to a cushy job. The scene bears an unmistakable similarity to Philip Roth's early story, "Defender of the Faith," but at least in the Roth story both Jews are seen to be suspect, the one for trying to use the Jewish connection for personal gain, the other for his discomfort in acknowledging it. Potok is less complex: he differentiates between the good Jew, his hero, who serves the army selflessly, and the bad Jew, who puts his comfort above the common weal. He puffs up his hero at the cost of employing a classical anti-Semitic stereotype, with none of the mitigating irony or sympathy that marks Philip Roth's treatment of the same moral dilemma.

Potok's oddest innovation is his attempt to Judaize the development of the atom bomb, one of the few modern events with which the Jews, as Jews, have happily not heretofore been associated. In one episode in the first part of the book, the seminary grants an honorary degree to Albert Einstein, in the presence of many who have been responsible for the bomb's creation; in the denouement, the son of one of them is sacrificed by the author in a symbolic atonement. Not only the boy's father, but his mother too is shown to have been implicated; as a noted art scholar, she had dissuaded the Secretary of War from bombing the beautiful city of Kyoto. "You helped save Kyoto and helped destroy Hiroshima," says her husband, trying to establish their common share in the deed. Of course their involvement was inadvertent, but "it was [their] part in all the inadvertence that [their son] had found unendurable."

We did not need Chaim Potok to tell us that Jews have an uncommon talent for cultivating guilt, but he is more than the bearer of the tale here. The book, in fact, takes a peculiar relish in this drama of Jewish self-accusation and expiation. The insensitivity this shows to the Jews may actually endear the novel to a kind of self-lacerating Jewish reader, but at least its trivialization of Hiroshima should not pass unnoticed.

The nature of the dilemma in this novel is the clearest indication of the author's present concerns. To have chosen the Kabbalah over the Halakhah might have been noteworthy within the rabbinate in 1950, but in a novel of the 1980's—after Harold Bloom and all America have approved Jewish mysticism—it is no more than what the publisher ordered. All the learned discussions and quotations from Jewish sources that run through the book, as they do through the author's work generally, do not add up to any perceptible interest in Judaism, the scholarship under discussion, or the Jews. A writer who began by validating traditional Judaism now takes his cues from the culture at large.

EZRA POUND

1885–1972

Ezra Weston Loomis Pound, poet, critic, and translator, was born to Quaker parents in Mailey, Idaho, on October 30, 1885. He received an education in Romance philology at the University of Pennsylvania (B.A., 1905) and at Hamilton College (M.A., 1906). He taught briefly at Wabash College, Indiana, but was fired after only four months, in January 1908. In February of that year he sailed for Europe and, while in Venice somewhat later, published his first volume of poetry, *A Lume Spento* (1908). He then moved to London, where he quickly established a literary reputation, and joined Wyndham Lewis and others in the short-lived Vorticist movement. Along with F. S. Flint, Richard Aldington, and Hilda Doolittle (H.D.), Pound also involved himself in the Imagist movement, which, inspired in part by the aesthetic theories of T. E. Hulme, produced poetry characterized by free rhythms, concreteness, and concision of language and imagery. *Des Imagistes*, an anthology of Imagist poems edited by Pound, appeared in 1914. Pound also championed the work of such Modernist writers as James Joyce and T. S. Eliot, and later edited Eliot's *Waste Land* (1922). During this period he published several volumes of his own verse, including *Personae* (1909), *Canzoni* (1911), *Ripostes* (1912), and *Lustra* (1916). In addition, Pound's wide interests led him to a series of translations which foreshadowed the pan-cultural diversity of his *Cantos*; early volumes contained translations from Provençal and archaic Italian, as well as a loose translation of the Old English poem *The Seafarer*. In 1915 he published *Cathay*, translations of Chinese poems by Li Bai (Li Po). Further volumes of original poetry appeared, including *Quia Pauper Amavi* (1919), containing *Homage to Sextus Propertius*, and *Hugh Selwyn Mauberley* (1920).

By the 1920s Pound began to move away from the principles of Imagism, which had become too restrictive for him. Pound left London for Paris in 1920 with his English wife, Dorothy Shakespear, whom he had married in 1914; in Paris he became part of a literary circle which included Gertrude Stein and Ernest Hemingway. In 1925 he settled in Rapallo, Italy, where he remained for the next twenty years; here he continued work on the *Cantos*, the first three of which had been published in 1917. These appeared intermittently over several decades until his death.

In Italy Pound's support for Mussolini's Fascism led him during the war years to give a series of talks on Italian radio; these were on a variety of subjects ranging from Confucianism to Social Credit theories to allegations of Jewish control of the American Government. In 1945 he was arrested at Genoa, and sent to a U.S. Army Disciplinary Training Center near Pisa. While in internment Pound produced *The Pisan Cantos* (1948), which was selected by the Fellows of the Library of Congress to receive the Bollingen Prize for 1948. This caused major political repercussions in the United States and led to a demand for the investigation of the Fellows themselves. In 1946 Pound was moved to Washington to stand trial for treason, but was found incompetent to do so by reason of insanity. Until 1958 he was confined in a mental institution, where he continued to write, and from which he issued various unsigned or pseudonymous articles. On his release he returned to Italy, where he continued to work on his *Cantos*. He died there in 1972.

Despite the controversy still surrounding him, Ezra Pound has been widely recognized as one of the central figures in modern poetry.

Personal

C. DAVID HEYMANN
From *Ezra Pound: The Last Rower*
1976, pp. 272–75, 309–14

Paradise
II
Li Sao, Li Sao, for sorrow . . .
(Canto CXIII)
M'amour, m'amour
what do I love and
where are you?
That I lost my center
fighting the world.
The dreams clash
and are shattered—

and that I tried to make a paradiso
terrestre.
(Notes from Canto CXVII et seq.)

The great silence descended the summer of 1961. Aphasia, abulia, cut off the flow. Pound simply stopped communicating with the world. It was an awesome silence, transcendent, "deep as the grave." It seemed to spring from the flesh, as though he had numbed the flesh. It was mystifying. A man who had once spilled words had succeeded in stilling his voice. Rumors circulated and crisscrossed. Had he discovered in silence a new language? A fulfillment?

When he did venture a remark, it was apt to cause a stir. At a gathering of scholars in Rimini in celebration of the d'Annunzio Centennial (1963), which he was attending with the Nobel laureate Salvatore Quasimodo, he was recognized and applauded until he rose. "Tempus loquendi, tempus tacendi," murmured the broken voice, quoting Ecclesiasticus, Jefferson, and the opening lines of Canto 31.[1] This dark and brooding silence at the end of his life was a reversal for Pound, but curiously it rhymed with the structure of his own major works. *The Cantos* drift into fragments, terminate pianissimo with the stillness of nature, the quiet of mountains and fields; *The Confucian Odes* close to the beat of soft drums and the description of a castle "high in the air and quiet"; *Mauberley* ends with a glazed, gazing face, *Propertius* on the Waters of the Damned.[2]

With the silence came a retreat from the written word as well. First *The Cantos* ground to a halt, then his correspondence. "I dodder and don't get the letters written,"[3] he wrote to Harry Meacham. "The plain fact," he added in another note, "is that my head just doesn't work."[4] That was while he was at Martinsbrunn late in 1960. But gradually he had regained enough strength to travel, and by the early spring of 1961 he was a guest in the Eternal City again and was staying with Ugo Dadone.

A brief revival accompanied his return to Rome. He began to come alive, to re-enact a scenario long since played out. In the glittering hours of the evening—supper at Crispi's, a tour among the byways of former days, ice cream at a café—Pound bounded along with the energetic gait of a much younger man. As before, he was champion of the proverbial Latin Quarter, monarch of his own fictional kingdom. He allowed himself to be courted by the pretentious *haut-monde*, the heralded literary set which he had denounced for most of his life, attending their roustabout galas and affairs, taking himself from one social gathering to another, from one sorrowful soirée to the next. He was made the fulcrum of a personality cult organized around him by those closest to him. With his floppy hat and coat, which he trailed like a cape, he was up and down the Via Veneto, turning up simply everywhere, like a bad penny, and always accompanied by his campy entourage.

On the other side of the fence stood the well-established and ostensibly well-intentioned Italian literati, the Ungarettis, Montales, and Pasolinis, who generally had a romantic affection for Pound and were glad to have him back in Italy. Their attempts to welcome him and make him feel at home, however, were often stymied by the poet's egregious followers and by some of his own unflattering remarks to the press. He was starting to rave again, preparing himself for the final outcry, which in turn must accompany the ultimate collapse and fall.

It was in the center of Rome, in the middle of the day. He was photographed at the head of a neo-Fascist, May Day parade, five hundred strong, a writhing column of *Missini* (MSI) goose-stepping their way up the Via del Corso from the Piazza di San Lorenzo in Lucina to the Piazza Venezia and the Vittoriana. They wore jack boots and black arm bands. They flaunted banners and shouted anti-Semitic slogans. They gave the Roman salute and displayed the swastika. They heaved rocks and bottles at the crowd, overturned cars, attacked bystanders. *Sinceritas? Chêng Ming? Decency in his conduct? Persistent awareness?*

The mind that had purified the language of the tribe and the body that had withstood the trials of the "gorilla cage" at Pisa and the snake pit in Washington now declined steadily.[5] The poet entered a clinic in Rome. From Rome he was transferred to the Villa Chiara, a rest home outside Rapallo, and in June 1961, he was taken to Merano and redeposited at Martinsbrunn. Discouragement was mingled with disdain for illness and all its dreadful apparatus. Pound was an aging relic, an old-fashioned agrarian populist who had outlived himself and the bulk of his generation.

Silence fell, and the pattern of his life underwent still another change. Summers were spent with Olga Rudge in the tiny hillside village of Sant' Ambrogio, with its vertiginous view of Rapallo on one side and Zoagli on the other. They lived in the same Casa 60, repainted and refurbished, where the Pounds and Miss Rudge had spent the last year of the war. The other months—January to June and September through December—they resided in Venice in the Hidden Nest. The proto-Odyssey had taken him back, out of Martinsbrunn *circa* May 1962, to where he began. Martinsbrunn specialized in general afflictions; his main trouble had been desiccation and refusal to eat food. And he wanted sea, sky, and sun and needed far more care than Dorothy Pound, at her age—nearly his—could give.

So he had allowed Olga Rudge to cart him off. But now the poet endured further vagaries of health. In the summer of 1962 he underwent surgery for prostate infection and less than a year later a second operation in the clinic at Rapallo. Afterward, he appeared to grow stronger, although he rarely spoke and seemed to have given up writing altogether. "Too much terrible anxiety loaded onto such a sensitivity," the Committee for Ezra Pound explained after his departure. For all his downheartedness, he nevertheless had made a full physical recovery. He could climb the long and steep *salita*, recently paved, from Rapallo on up to Sant' Ambrogio without a break in stride. And he could take the flats of Venice with ease. His peregrinations about the languorous city island took him from the Bridge of Sighs to the Accademia, from the Campo San Polo to the Doge's Palace. And quite often he still enjoyed a refreshing swim, periodically at the Lido, and in Rapallo off the sand-and-pebble Ligurian beaches.

In Venice there were other diversions as well: the opera, concerts, public lectures, art exhibits (notably the Biennale), and friends. The Ivanciches, Peter Russell, Joan Fitzgerald, Ugo Fasolo, Liselotte Höhs, Lotte Frumi, Giuseppe Santomaso, Count Vittorio Cini comprised the hub of the Venetian Vortex. It pleased the poet to take his friends on the rounds of local sites: the Giardini Publicanni (where on a plinth sits the stone bust of Richard Wagner); the Scuola degli Schiavone with its *quattrocento* Carpaccios; Peggy Guggenheim's walled-in loggia and treasure-laden museum. And at those times when he and Olga visited the San Marco area or the Fenice Theatre they took the opportunity to walk the maze past Santa Maria della Salute (the "Jewel Box") to the customs house and there took a *traghetto* across the Grand Canal. This chosen route reminded the poet of another compass-course age: Venice, 1908. In six decades he had, so to speak, come full circle.

He sometimes read or was read to: Confucius, Chaucer, Shakespeare, Sartre, Auden, Burroughs. He spent long hours in the Faustian dark at his desk in the third-story studio, sitting and staring into the dark, brooding on his past and how he might have altered it. More often than not, flames crackled in the fireplace; the Dolmetsch clavichord, a duplicate of the original which had been restrung for his grandson, leaned against a wall. From time to time, when the mood struck him, he read, and quite spiritedly, into a Grundig tape recorder: Shakespeare's "They that have power to hurt and will do none" and Christopher Smart's "I will remember my cat . . ."[6] Early one November morning, following his seventy-ninth birthday, he woke up the house with a startling outburst of

Winter is icumen in,
Lhude sing GOD-DAMN!!!

—and on that occasion, "with ferocious emphasis," there followed a long taping session of other pre-epic bits and pieces.[7]
⟨. . .⟩

Coda: To the End

September 1972: my second visit with Ezra Pound. A year and a summer have passed since our first encounter. And in the interim another controversy has flared up around the poet. This time the in-fighting was over the Emerson-Thoreau Medal awarded annually by the American Academy of Arts and Sciences "for outstanding contributions to the broad field of literature over the recipient's entire lifetime." A nominating committee—Leon Edel, Chairman; John Cheever; Lillian Hellman; James Laughlin; Harry Levin; Louis Martz; and Lewis Mumford[8]—had recommended that the octogenarian poet's towering influence on modern letters be recognized, that it was time to set aside his wartime activities, which they attributed wholly to mental illness. But nothing, with the exception of the writing of verse, had ever come easily to Pound; within a few weeks the opposition, led by Daniel Bell, the Harvard sociologist, contended that while Pound's literary contributions could not be challenged, his broadcasts for Mussolini during the war and the strident anti-Semitic texture of some of his Cantos made him a poor candidate for a humanistic award. It was the Bollingen Prize controversy all over again, a rekindling of that irresoluble debate: can a man's artistic achievement be separated from his morality and ideology? And if a moral yardstick is applied, whose morality is to be used?

The poet on trial again: it is as Leslie Fiedler describes it in *Waiting for the End:* "Each age must have its own, brand-new defendants, and the mass audience sitting in judgment in the middle of the twentieth century has tried and sentenced the poet once more, yet as if for the first time, in the person of Ezra Pound." Sitting in judgment, the *Staatsrat* or High Commission,[9] by a tally of 13 to 9, with two abstentions and two absentees, had voted against the committee's recommendation and against Pound. The verdict was official: Ezra Pound was not to join the ranks of the select—Robert Frost, T. S. Eliot, Katherine Anne Porter, Mark Van Doren, John Crowe Ransom, Hannah Arendt, and the other poets, novelists, and critics who had been chosen for the prize in the past; instead he was to remain forever outside the Kingdom of Art, a literary outcast, a permanent exile.

Then came the predictable aftermath—the approbations, accusations, denunciations, and denials, the same shower of pro-and-anti pronouncements that had followed the 1948 Bollingen Prize announcement:

Daniel Bell: "We have to distinguish between those who explore hate and those who approve hate. In short, one may appreciate the painful work of a man who has, at great personal cost, spent a season in hell; but it does not follow that one honors a man who advocates a way of life that makes the world hellish. Necessarily, one has to draw a distinction between the work and the man."

Irving Howe: "Pound wished none of us personal harm; his rantings against the Jews were utterly *abstract*, a phantasm of ideology that is a major dimension of their terribleness. . . . But the question of whether to honor Pound involves neither the granting nor the refusal of forgiveness. It involves something else: I do not believe that we can yet close the books of twentieth-century history, certainly not as long as any of us remains alive who can remember the days of the mass murder."

Martin Kilson: "As a Negro I am as outraged about anti-Negro intellectuals as a Jew about anti-Semitic ones but such outrage is not a matter of intellect but of politics, and in evaluating an intellectual's works I believe that short of the intellectual himself committing criminal or atrocious acts against humanity under the influence of his politics, his intellectual works should stand on their own."

Harry Levin: "The majority of the council, in overriding the recommendation, has attempted to rationalize its decision by repeated assertions that art cannot be isolated from morality. This is misleading, if not disingenuous, in its implication that Pound and his proponents were irresponsible aesthetes. There was never any disagreement over the principle involved. Members of the committee never questioned the assumption that aesthetics is grounded in ethics. Pound, like his master, Dante, is not only an artist but an impassioned moralist."

The Bollingen Prize committee, in 1949, resolved the Pound dilemma by separating the man from his work and giving the work the prize; the Council of the American Academy of Arts and Sciences, deciding twenty-three years later not to give the academy's Emerson-Thoreau Medal to Pound, did just the opposite. The endless philosophical debate seemed too remote, too abstract, for a poet of Pound's stature. It had nothing to do with him now as he lay on his back, lifeless, the classic Grecian head buoyed up by pillows, blue pajamas draped over his emaciated body. The haunting sapphirine eyes had clouded over. Hands were clenched to the bone. He chipped away with them at dead, eczematous skin. Like his adopted Venezia, he was wasting away.

An Arno Breker bust of Pound, which I had failed to notice before, stood at one end of the room atop a shelf. Breker had frozen the subject in old age, a robust old age, a distinct counterpoise to the man stretched out this day before me. The expression the sculptor had captured re-created the portrait of the persona who had been spotted mid-April 1971 inside the church of San Zanipolo at the funeral of Igor Stravinsky. He sat that morning at the rear of the large Gothic cathedral, attentive, poised, staring vibrantly at the black coffin, his ear trained on the strains of the composer's *Requiem Canticles.*

Absorbed in his own universe, the Great Bass seemed now not aware of anyone else's presence in the room. Then, slowly, his focus shifted. He studied me. After a short while he said: "You're from New York aren't you?" The conversation was resumed by him as if, indeed, it had never ceased, as if sixteen months hadn't actually passed, as if time itself had stood still.

He pulled himself, with some difficulty, to a half-sitting position. He stared at me openly and candidly. He moved his mouth as though to speak. And then he did speak, his emotion tearing loose in clots: "I hold no delusions. . . . What's done cannot be undone. . . . The error is all in the not done. . . . I was wrong. . . . Ninety-per-cent wrong. . . . I lost my head in a storm."

Olga Rudge, standing next to me, responded to his lament: "It's always because we love that we are rebellious; it takes a great deal of love to care what happens."

"Or hatred," Pound whispered.

Looking at him, seeing him before me like this, I felt strangly out of sync. I felt I had somehow traveled backward in time. I remembered reading some place a quotation by Jean Cocteau. He had called Pound "a rower on the river of the dead"—"un rameur sur le fleuve des morts." The Last Rower: it is the Ulysses image in its peculiarly American form—"that non-Homeric, romanticized figure out of Dante by way of Tennyson which so spectacularly haunts the imagination of Ezra Pound."[10]

Early-morning jaunts with Olga Rudge were still part of his day. He liked to walk along the Zattere, the promenade that runs parallel to the very blue Canale della Giudecca. Across the canal, shimmering dreamlike in the rippling water, the majestic churches and palaces of the Giudecca. Italians on their way to work often stopped and stared, or sometimes tipped their hats as the old gentleman moved along. But American tourists recognized one of their best-known poets.

Once in the public eye—whether a restaurant, a café or simply a long, leisurely stroll—he would inevitably hide behind his veil of silence. It was at such moments that Miss Rudge took over, guiding the conversation, exercising charm, putting at ease whoever happened to be in their presence. If Pound resented his companion's overprotective demeanor he did not show it. When they entertained, they generally took their guests to Harry's Bar, Hemingway's old haunt, or Montin's, a *trattoria* in San Trovaso, frequented by artists and writers since the 1930's, when d'Annunzio made it his eating place. The young waiter at the San Trovaso restaurant was well acquainted with much of Pound's verse and seemed to know the old man's way. *"Volto sciolto, pensiero stretto,"* were the words he used to describe it—"An open countenance and closed thoughts."

Return to the occasion at hand, to the silence richer than almost any talk. I posed a question or two for the poet. Pound blinked: no response. But soon his parched lips began to move, sounds followed:

"It's very difficult for me to answer your questions. . . ."
One final exchange:
"Will you ever return to the United States?"
A quizzical smile, a long pause before answering:
"Anything is possible."

* * *

He passed away in Venice in November 1, 1972, two days after his eighty-seventh birthday, a few hours after being taken to Saints John and Paul Hospital, opposite the Colleoni Statue. He died peacefully in sleep.

In the last week of his life he saw a noh play and the Peter Brook production of *A Midsummer Night's Dream.* His last birthday party was full of joy: cake, champagne, neighboring children, friends. His conversation that day touched briefly on Jules Laforgue, Henri Michaux, and Marianne Moore. A number of months before his own death, he had lamented the passing of Miss Moore by reading her very beautiful and apt poem "What Are Years?" at a memorial service in Venice's Protestant Church. That was his last public reading. He read from his own work for a small gathering of friends inside the Hidden Nest two weeks before the end. And his last written words were very likely the few thoughts he had strung together as foreword to the Cookson-edited anthology published posthumously (Pound, *Selected Prose, 1909–1965*). The poet's statement ends:

> In sentences referring to groups or races 'they'
> should be used with great care.
> re USURY:
> I was out of focus, taking a symptom for a cause.
> The cause is AVARICE.

The funeral, on November 3, was more formality than rite. A simple and brief service, in the Palladium Basilica on the isle of San Gregorio, was without the customary black drapes, and there were none of the flowers for which Venetian funerals are known. The plain chestnut coffin stood before the altar in a shroud of Gregorian chant and Monteverdi; absolution was performed by a charcoal-robed Benedictine with aspergillum and censer (*te supplices exoramus pro anima famuli tui Ezra*).[11] No tributes came from either the Italian or American government. There were relatively few mourners.

Neither Dorothy Pound nor Omar was present. Olga Rudge and Mary and Patrizia de Rachewiltz accompanied him on his last voyage.[12]

A poster printed by the "Gruppo di studio Ezra Pound" appeared the day after his death on what had become the neo-Fascist billboards of Milan—the granite and marble columns of Piazzo San Biblia—loudly proclaiming in bold black print "Ezra Pound is dead," followed by several paragraphs in small print extolling the man found "guilty of having taken the Fascist side against the old, materialistic, usura-ridden world," and concluding with "Ezra Pound is born" in the same oversized black letters.[13] The controversy surrounding Pound had obviously not been resolved; he could not escape it even in death.

Following the service, four Venetian friends shouldered the coffin down the aisle, and then it was placed in a black-and-gold gondola and covered with wreaths. Chrysanthemums spilled yellow and white along the gondola's side, backed by long fronds of emerald palm. A bronze crucifix was affixed to the casket. The gondoliers pushed off from the landing stage and four of them, clad in black, guided the vessel out across the azure *laguna*, under bright sun, to the *campo santo* on the burial island of San Michele, not far from the plots of Sergei Diaghilev and Igor Stravinsky. Here, among exiles, surrounded by grass and trees, he was laid to rest. *In paradisum deducant te Angeli*, the priest sang, *in tuo adventu suscipiant te Martyres, et perducant te in civitatem sanctam Jerusalem.*[14]

Some weeks later a stone, designed by the American sculptress Joan Fitzgerald, was set in place at the head of the grave; in a delicate and solemn script it read simply:

EZRA POUND

Notes

1. Hugh Kenner, "The Magic of Place: Ezra Pound," *Italian Quarterly*, vol. 16, 64 (Spring 1973), p. 9, addresses itself to "hallowed shades," Italian cities and their ghosts, *virtù*, as well as divine visions. Dante's tomb and Pietro Lombardo's mermaids are dealt with by Kenner in *The Pound Era* (Berkeley and Los Angeles: University of California Press, 1971), p. 342.
2. Kenner, *The Pound Era*, p. 536.
3. Kenner, "The Magic of Place: Ezra Pound," p. 5.
4. Ibid.
5. Letter to John Sullivan (June 18, 1959), Humanities Research Center, University of Texas, Austin.
6. Noel Stock, *The Life of Ezra Pound* (New York: Pantheon, 1970), p. 450.
7. Charles Norman, *The Case of Ezra Pound* (New York: Funk & Wagnalls, 1968), p. 462.
8. Of these members, Lillian Hellman did not vote, and Lewis Mumford was opposed to Pound's nomination, writing Edel: "Why not give it to Henry Miller?"
9. The Emerson-Thoreau committee meeting at which Pound was nominated was held on January 18, 1972. The council meeting at which the nomination was rejected took place April 19, 1972. The members present at the second and decisive meeting were: Thomas Adams, David Apter, Daniel Bell, Konrad Bloch, Nicolaas Bloembergen, Morton Bloomfield, Harvey Brooks, Bernard Davis, Richard Douglas, Jacob Fine, Paul Freund, Eli Goldston, Stephen Graubard, William Jencks, Wassily Leontief, Jean Mayer, Agnes Mongan, Talcott Parsons, Alexander Rich, Walter O. Roberts, Cyril Smith, Krister Stendahl, Arthur Sutherland, and Walter Whitehill. Of the approximately 2100 Fellows of the Academy, the following members resigned as a result of the controversy: Jerome Lettvin, O. B. Hardison, Brooks Atkinson, Malcolm Cowley, and Allen Tate; Hugh Kenner refused to accept election.
10. Leslie Fiedler, "Caliban or Hamlet: A Study in Literary Anthropology," published in *Unfinished Business* (New York: Stein & Day, 1972), pp. 93–103.

11. Guy Davenport, "Ezra Pound: 1885–1972," *Arion* [new series], vol. I, 1 (1973), p. 188.

12. Omar Pound, accompanied by Peter de Sautoy, took the first available flight from London to Venice but was unable to arrive in time for the ceremonies, which were held during the morning hours; Ezra Pound's son-in-law and grandson also arrived too late from the United States; and Dorothy Pound was too old and frail to undertake the long journey from her home in England.

13. Aldo Tagliaferri, "Ezra Pound's *Jefferson and/or Mussolini*," *Italian Quarterly*, vol. 16, 64 (Spring 1973): 115.

14. Davenport, "Ezra Pound: 1885–1972," p. 188.

General

LOUIS ZUKOFSKY
From "Ezra Pound" (1929)
Prepositions: The Collected Critical Essays of Louis Zukofsky (1967)
1981, pp. 67–71

I

T A H I O

Thus, if her colour
Came against his gaze,
Tempered as if
It were through a perfect glaze

He made no immediate application
Of this to the relation of the state
To the individual, the month was more temperate
Because this beauty had been.

('The Age Demanded,' *Hugh Selwyn Mauberley*)

This classifying of values shows Pound sufficiently moral. For a quarter of a century he has been engaged in 'the expression of an idea of beauty (or order)' and his results are one aspect of a further personal comprehension.

out of key with his time
He strove to resuscitate the dead art
Of poetry; to maintain 'the sublime'
In the old sense.

—intent upon 'language not petrifying on his hands, preparing for new advances along the lines of true metaphor, that is, interpretative metaphor, or image, as opposed to the ornamental.' 'Artists are the antennae of the race,' words to him are principals of a line of action, a store, a purpose, a retaining of speech and manner, a constant reinterpreting of processes becoming in himself one continuous process, essentially simplification.

He has treated the arts as a science so that their morality and immorality become a matter of accuracy and inaccuracy.

The arts give us a great percentage of the lasting and unassailable data regarding the nature of man, of immaterial man, of man considered as a thinking and sentient creature. They begin where the science of medicine leaves off or rather they overlap that science. The borders of the two arts overcross.

From medicine we learn that man thrives best when duly washed, aired and sunned. From the arts we learn that man is whimsical, that one man differs from another.

As there are in medicine the art of diagnosis and the art of cure, so in the arts, so in the particular arts of poetry and of literature, there is the art of diagnosis and there is the art of cure. They call one the cult of ugliness and the other the cult of beauty. Villon, . . . Corbière, . . . Flaubert, . . . diagnosis. Satire, if we are to ride this metaphor to staggers, satire is surgery, insertions and amputations.

In the beginning simple words were enough: Food; water; fire. Both prose and poetry are but an extension of language. Man desires an ever increasingly complicated communication. Gesture serves up to a point. Symbols may serve. When you desire something not present to the eye or when you desire to communicate ideas, you must have recourse to speech. Gradually you wish to communicate something less bare and ambiguous than ideas. You wish to communicate an idea and its modifications, an idea and a crowd of its effects, atmospheres, contradictions. You wish to question whether a certain formula works in every case, or in what percent of cases, etc., etc., etc., you get the Henry James novel.

So that Pound's poetry of music, image and logopoeia, his humanity always the sieve through which the three commute to organic perception, is the same as his personal morality which harbors the clarity of words as well as all beautiful objects, and the peoples who have caused them. And while it harbors their permanence steers through, and around, and is aware of, their temporal situations.

The literary make-up which notices:

The old swimming hole
And the boys flopping off the planks
Or sitting in the underbrush playing mandolins
(Canto 13)

is inwrapped with the philosophy of Kung, who said:

Without character you will
be unable to play on that instrument
Or to execute the music fit for the Odes.
The blossoms of the apricot
blow from the east to the west,
And I have tried to keep them from falling.
(Canto 13)

'Character' implies enough order to be radiated outward. Order allows that Kung may permit himself to raise his cane against Yuan Jang,

Yuan Jang being his elder,
For Yuan Jang sat by the roadside pretending to
be receiving wisdom.
(Canto 13)

And Kung may also note:

Wang ruled with moderation,
In his day the State was well kept,
And even I can remember
A day when historians left blanks in their writings,
I mean for things they didn't know,
But that time seems to be passing.
(Canto 13)

Concern with 'the bright principle of our reason,' with the use of Ta Hio or The Great Learning as a gauge of action, involves: recognition of the beauty of everytime in which alone we have being; interest in the present, so that life, as Pound has said, may not make mock of motion and humans not move as ossifications.

It follows that Pound has been both the isolated creator and the worldly pamphleteer. To put the defences of his own being in order, he has drafted himself into the defence of innovation clarifying and making sincere the intelligence. Contrasted with the leavings of transcendentalism and belated

scholasticism around him, he has said that 'Lenin invented
. . . a new medium, something between speech and action
which is worth . . . study'; (*Exile* 4, 1928)

That the Soviet Idea is as old as the Ta Hio's 'Private gain
is not prosperity';

That 'a new language is always said to be obscure
. . . After a few years the difficult passage appears to be a
simple lucidity';

That 'perhaps art is healthiest when anonymous . . . in
the Grosstadt Symphony we have at last a film that will take
serious aesthetic criticism: one that is in the movement, and
that should flatten out the opposition (to Joyce, to [Pound], to
Rodker's *Adolphe*) with steam-rolling ease and commodity, not
of course that the authors intended it';

And has implied that Sovkino's *The End of St Petersburg*
had an inertia of mass power behind it impossible of attainment
in a single Chekov.

Pound anticipated *The End of St Petersburg* as poetry
some years before the production of the film:

> There was a man there talking,
> To a thousand, just a short speech, and
> Then move 'em on. And he said:
> Yes, these people, they are all right, they
> Can do everything, everything except act;
> And go an' hear 'em, but when they are through
> Come to the bolsheviki . . .
> And when it broke, there was the crowd there,
> And the cossacks, just as always before,
> But one thing, the cossacks said:
>   'Pojalouista.'
> And that got round in the crowd,
> And then a lieutenant of infantry
> Ordered 'em to fire into the crowd,
>   in the square at the end of the Nevsky,
> In front of the Moscow station,
> And they wouldn't,
> And he pulled his sword on a student for laughing,
> And killed him,
> And a cossack rode out of his squad
> On the other side of the square,
> And cut down the lieutenant of infantry
> And that was the revolution . . .
>   as soon as they named it.
> And you can't make 'em,
> Nobody knew it was coming. They were all
>   ready, the old gang,
> Guns on the top of the post-office and the palace,
> But none of the leaders knew it was coming.
> And there were some killed at the barracks,
> But that was between the troops.
>   (Canto 16)

That Pound, previous to this presentation, chose to
benefit by the clarity and intelligence of Chinese written
character and Confucius is an indication of the scale he has
constructed to measure his values.

Good humor has a great deal to do with this measure. The
Cantos say 'nothing of the life after death.'

>   Anyone can run to excesses.
>   (Canto 13)

Good humor, which is not ashamed to set down fact, has
also to do with Pound's transcriptions of the spoken tongue—
his colloquial spelling, and with exploring music.

T. S. ELIOT
From "Ezra Pound"
Poetry, September 1946, pp. 335–38

Half of the work that Pound did as a critic can be known
only from the testimony of those who have benefited
from his conversation or correspondence. At a certain moment, my debt to him was for his advice to read Gautier's
Emaux et Camées, to which I had not before paid any close
attention. I have already spoken of his operation upon *The
Waste Land*. I have sometimes tried to perform the same sort of
maieutic task; and I know that one of the temptations against
which I have to be on guard, is trying to re-write somebody's
poem in the way in which I should have written it myself if I
had wanted to write that poem. Pound never did that: he tried
first to understand what one was attempting to do, and then
tried to help one do it in one's own way. There did come a
point, of course, at which difference of outlook and belief
became too wide; or it may have been distance and different
environment; or it may have been both.

I have already said that Pound's criticism would not have
the great value it has, without his poetry; and in his poetry there
is, for the analytical reader, a great deal of criticism exemplified. I find nothing to abate in my introduction to a volume
of Pound's *Selected Poems*, published in London in 1928,
except that I should now speak more respectfully of Whitman—a matter irrelevant to my present theme. In that
introduction I said nothing about the *Propertius*, which I rate
very high indeed. (I am aware of the censure of those who have
treated it as a translation; and if it is treated as a translation,
they are of course right.) If I am doubtful about some of the
Cantos, it is not that I find any poetic decline in them. I am
doubtful on somewhat the same ground as that on which I
once complained to him about an article on the monetary
theory of Gesell, which he had written at my suggestion for *The
Criterion*. I said (as nearly as I can remember): "I asked you to
write an article which would explain this subject to people who
had never heard of it; yet you write as if your readers knew
about it already, but had failed to understand it." In the *Cantos*
there is an increasing defect of communication, not apparent
when he is concerned with Sigismondo Malatesta, or with
Chinese dynasties, but, for instance, whenever he mentions
Martin Van Buren. Such passages are very opaque: they read as
if the author was so irritated with his readers for not knowing all
about anybody so important as Van Buren, that he refused to
enlighten them. I am incidentally annoyed, myself, by
occasional use of the peculiar orthography which characterizes
Pound's correspondence, and by lines written in what he
supposes to be a Yankee dialect. But the craftsman up to this
moment—and I have in mind certain recent and unpublished
cantos—has never failed. There is nobody living who can write
like this: how many can be named, who can write half so well?

I have before now expressed the opinion, that the
"greatness" of a poet is not a question for critics of his own age
to raise: it is only after he has been dead for a couple of
generations that the term begins to have meaning. "Greatness," when the term means anything at all, is an attribute
conferred by time. The question of "genuineness" is the first
question for contemporary criticism to raise. But there is a third
aspect, under which it is proper to consider a poet, a third kind
of judgment which may be passed upon him in his later years,
the material for which is not only his poetry, but the principle
of writing which he has exemplified and defended. I avoid the
word *influence*, for there are dangers in estimating a poet by his
influence. It takes at least two to make an influence: the man

who exerts it and the man who experiences it. The latter may be a writer whose verse would have been bad, whatever influences had gone to form it; or he may have been influenced in the wrong way, or by the wrong things in the work of the poet under whose influence he has come; or he may be born into a period less favorable to the creation of art—though this is a subject we cannot know very much about. So I am not speaking of influence, but of the things for which a man like Pound has stood, in his own time. To appreciate these, we need first, as I suggested at the beginning, some understanding of the state of poetry when the poet began writing. And that is soon forgotten, for each generation tends to accept the situation it finds, as if that situation had always prevailed. I think that Pound was original in insisting that poetry is an art, an art which demands the most arduous application and study; and in seeing that in our time it had to be a highly conscious art. He also saw that a poet who knows only the poetry of his own language is as poorly equipped as the painter or musician who knows only the painting or the music of his own country. The business of the poet is to be more conscious of his own language than other men, to be more sensitive to the feeling, more aware of the meaning of every word he uses, more aware of the history of the language and of every word he uses, than other men. He needs, however, to know as much as he can of several other languages: because one advantage of a knowledge of other languages is that it makes us understand our own language better. Pound's "erudition" has been both exaggerated and irrelevantly under-estimated: for it has been judged chiefly by scholars who did not understand poetry, and by poets who have had little scholarship. Pound's great contribution to the work of other poets (if they choose to accept what he offers) is his insistence upon the immensity of the amount of *conscious* labor to be performed by the poet; and his invaluable suggestions for the kind of training the poet should give himself—study of form, metric and vocabulary in the poetry of divers literature, and study of good prose. Poets should continue to study—and if poetry survives they no doubt will—Pound's poetry, which bridges the gap separating Browning and Swinburne from the present day, and his writings about poetry. He also provides an example of devotion to "the art of poetry" which I can only parallel in our time by the example of Valéry, and to some extent that of Yeats: and to mention these names is to give some impression of Pound's importance as an exponent of the art of poetry in a time when

> The "age demanded" chiefly a mould in plaster
> Made with no loss of time,
> A prose kinema, not, not assuredly, alabaster
> Or the "sculpture" of rhyme.

MARIANNE MOORE
"Teach, Stir the Mind, Afford Enjoyment" (1952)
Predilections
1955, pp. 75–83

Our debt to Ezra Pound is prodigious for the effort he has made to share what he knows about writing and, in particular, about rhythm and melody; most of all, for his insistence on liveness as opposed to deadness. "Make it new," he says. "Art is a joyous thing." He recalls "that sense of sudden growth we experience in the presence of the greatest works of art." The ode to *Hugh Selwyn Mauberley* applies of course to himself:

> For three years, out of key with his time,
> He strove to resuscitate the dead art

> Of poetry; to maintain "the sublime"
> In the old sense. . . .

And, above all, it is the art of letters in America that he has wished to resuscitate. He says in "Cantico del Sole":

> The thought of what America would be like
> If the classics had a wide circulation
>   Troubles my sleep. . . .

America's imperviousness to culture irks him; but he is never as indignant as he is elated.

Instruction should be painless, he says, and his precept for writers is an epitome of himself: teach, stir the mind, afford enjoyment. (Cicero's *Ut doceat, ut moveat, ut delectet.*[1]) Hugh Kenner grants him his wish and says: "The Pound letters are weirdly written; they are nevertheless a treatise on creative writing, treasure-trove, *corpus aureum, mina de oro.* . . . The vivacity of these letters is enchanting." Mr. Kenner also says, "The whole key to Pound, the basis of his Cantos, his music, his economics and everything else, is the concern for exact definition"—a passion shared by T. S. Eliot, Mr. Kenner adds—"a quality which neither has defined." What is it? a neatening or cleancutness, to begin with, as caesura is cutting at the end (*caedo,* cut off). For Dante, it was making you see the thing that he sees, Mr. Pound says; and, speaking of Rimbaud, says there is "such firmness of coloring and such certitude." Pound admires Chinese codifyings and for many a year has been ordering, epitomizing, and urging explicitness, as when he listed "A Few Don'ts" for Imagists:

> Direct treatment, ecomony of words; compose in the sequence of the musical phrase rather than that of the metronome.
> The true poet is most easily distinguished from the false when he trusts himself to the simplest expression and writes without adjectives.
> No dead words or phrases.
> A thought should be expressed in verse at least as well as it could be expressed in prose. Great literature is language charged with meaning to the utmost possible degree. There is no easy way out.

Mr. Pound differentiates poetry as

> logopoeia (music of words),
> melopoeia (music of sound)—the music of rhymes, he says, depends upon their arrangement, not only on their multiplicity—and
> phanopoeia (casting images on the imagination).

Under the last head, one recalls the statement by Dante that Beatrice walked above herself—*come una crana.* Confucius says the fish moves on winglike foot; and Prior, in his life of Edmund Burke, says Burke "had a peculiarity in his gait that made him look as if he had two left legs." Affirming Coleridge's statement that "Our admiration of a great poet is for a continuous undercurrent of feeling everywhere present, but seldom anywhere a separate excitement," Mr. Pound says Dante "has gone living through Hell and the words of his lament sob as branches beaten by the wind."

What is poetry? Dante said, "a song is a composition of words set to music." As for free verse, "it is *not* prose," Mr. Pound says. It is what we have "when the thing builds up a rhythm more beautiful than that of set metres"—as here:

> The birds flutter to rest in my tree,
>   and I think I have heard them saying,
> "It is not that there are no other men—,
> But we like this fellow the best. . . ."

In Dante, "we have blending and lengthening of the sounds, heavy beats, running and light beats," Mr. Pound says. "Don't make each line stop dead at the end. Let the beginning of the next line catch the rise of the rhythm wave, unless you want a longish definite pause." For example, the lines from "Envoi" in *Mauberley*, when he speaks of "her graces":

> I would bid them live
> As roses might, in magic amber laid,
> Red overwrought with orange and all made
> One substance and one colour
> Braving time.

This is the way in which to cement sound and thought. In *Mauberley*, also note the identical rhymes in close sequence without conspicuousness, of "Medallion":

> The face-oval beneath the glaze,
> Bright in its suave bounding-line, as,
> Beneath half-watt rays,
> The eyes turn topaz.

"Words," T. S. Eliot says, "are perhaps the hardest medium of all material of art. One must simultaneously express visual beauty, beauty of sound, and communicate a grammatical statement." We have in "her" a mundane word, but note the use made of it in Portrait, from "La Mère Inconnue" *(Exultations)*:

> Nay! For I have seen the purplest shadows stand
> Always with reverent chere that looked on her,
> Silence himself is grown her worshipper
> And ever doth attend her in that land
> Wherein she reigneth, wherefore let there stir
> Naught but the softest voices, praising her.

Again, from Ezra Pound's translation of Guido Cavalcanti: "A Bernardo da Bologna,"

> And in that Court where Love himself fableth
> Telling of beauties he hath seen, he saith:
> This pagan and lovely woman hath in her
> All strange adornments that ever were.

William Carlos Williams is right. "Pound is not 'all poetry.' . . . But he has an ear that is unsurpassable." "Some poems," Mr. Pound himself says, "have form as a tree has form and some as water poured into a vase." He also says, quoting Arnold Dolmetsch and Mace: "Mark not the beat too much"— a precept essential to light rhyme and surprises within the line; but inapplicable to satire, as in W. S. Gilbert's *Pirates of Penzance*—the policemen:

> And yet when someone's near
> We manage to appear
> As unsusceptible to fear
> As anybody here.

"The churn, the loom, the spinning-wheel, the oars," Mr. Pound says, "are bases for distinctive rhythm which can never degenerate into the monotony of mere iambs and trochees"; and one notices in "Nel Biancheggiar" the accenting of "dies," in "but dies not quite":

> I feel the dusky softness whirr
> Of colour, as upon a dulcimer
>
> . . .
>
> As when the living music swoons
> But dies not quite. . . .

One notes in "Guido Invites You Thus" *(Exultations)* the placing of the pauses and quickened "flames of an altar fire":

> Lo, I have known thy heart and its desire;
> Life, all of it, my sea, and all men's streams
> Are fused in it as flames of an altar fire!

And "A Prologue" *(Canzoni)* has the same exactitude in variety:

> Shepherds and kings, with lambs and frankincense
> Go and atone for mankind's ignorance:

> Make ye soft savour from your ruddy myrrh.
> Lo, how God's son is turned God's almoner.

Unending emphasis is laid by Ezra Pound on honesty— on voicing one's own opinion. He is indignant that "trout should be submerged by eels." The function of literature, he says, is "to incite humanity to continue living; to ease the mind of strain; to feed it" (Canto XXV):

> What we thought had been thought for too long;
>
> . . .
>
> We have gathered a sieve full of water.

> The dead words, keeping form.
> We suffer from
>   Noble forms lacking life,
>
> . . .
>
>   The dead concepts, never the solid;

As for comprehension of what is set forth, the poet has a right to expect the reader, at least in a measure, to be able to complete poetic statement; and Ezra Pound never spoils his effects by over-exposition. He alludes as follows to the drowning of a Borgia:

> The bust outlasts the shrine;
> The coin, Tiberius.
>
> . . .
>
> John Borgia is bathed
> at last. And the cloak floated.

"As for *Cathay*, it must be pointed out," T. S. Eliot says, "that Pound is the inventor of Chinese poetry of our time"; and seeing a connection between the following incident and "the upper-middlebrow press," Hugh Kenner recalls that when Charles Münch offered Bach to the regiment, the commandant said, "Here, none of that mathematical music." One ventures, commits one's self, and if readers are not pleased, one can perhaps please one's self and earn that slender right to persevere.

"A poet's work," Mr. Eliot says, "may proceed along two lines of an imaginary graph; one of the lines being his conscious and continuous effort in technical excellence," and the other "his normal human course of development. Now and then the two lines may converge at a high peak, so that we get a masterpiece. That is to say, an accumulation of experience has crystallized to form material of art, and years of work in technique have prepared an adequate medium; and something results in which medium and material, form and content, are indistinguishable."

In *The Great Digest and Unwobbling Pivot* of Confucius, as in his *Analects*, Ezra Pound has had a theme of major import. *The Great Digest* makes emphatic this lesson: He who can rule himself can govern others; he who can govern others can rule the kingdom and families of the Empire.

> The men of old disciplined themselves.
> Having attained self-discipline they set their houses
>   in order.
> Having order in their own homes, they brought good
>   government to their own state.
> When their states were well governed, the empire
>   was brought into equilibrium.

We have in the *Digest*, content that is energetic, novel, and deep: "If there be a knife of resentment in the heart or enduring rancor, the mind will not attain precision; under suspicion and fear it will not form sound judgment, nor will it, dazzled by love's delight nor in sorrow and anxiety, come to precision." As for money, "Ill got, ill go." When others have ability, if a man "shoves them aside, he can be called a real pest." "The archer when he misses the bullseye, turns and seeks the cause of error in himself." There must be no rationalizing. "Abandon every clandestine egoism to realize the true root." Of the golden rule, there are many variants in the *Analects*: "Tze-kung asked if there was a single principle that you could practise through life to the end. He said sympathy; what you don't want, don't inflict on another" (Book Fifteen, XXIII). "Require the solid of yourself, the trifle of others" (Book Fifteen, XIV). "The proper man brings men's excellence to focus, not their evil qualities" (Book Twelve, XVI). "I am not worried that others do not know me; I am worried by my incapacity" (Book Fourteen, XXXII). Tze-chang asked Kung-tze about maturity. Kung-tze said: To be able to practise five things would humanize the whole empire—sobriety (*serenitas*), magnanimity, sticking by one's word, promptitude (in attention to detail), kindliness (*caritas*). As for "the problem of style. Effect your meaning. Then stop" (Book Fifteen, XL).

In "Salvationists," Mr. Pound says:

> Come, my songs, let us speak of perfection—
> We shall get ourselves rather disliked.

We shall get ourselves disliked and very much liked, because the zest for perfection communicates its excitement to others.

Notes

1. See Kenneth Burke's "The Language of Poetry, 'Dramatistically' Considered," paper written for a symbolism seminar conducted in 1952–53 by the Institute for Religious and Social Studies, New York (*Chicago Review*, Fall 1954): "We would spin this discussion from Cicero's terms for the 'three offices of the orator.' (See *Orator, De Oratore*, and St. Augustine's use of this analysis of Christian persuasion in his *De Doctrina Christiana*.) First office: to teach or inform (*docere*). Second office: to please (*delectare*). Third office: to move or 'bend' (*movere, flectare*)."

HUGH KENNER
From "The Muse in Tatters"
The Pound Era
1971. pp. 54–55, 68–75

The Sapphic fragment concerning Gongyla, which in 1916 yielded Pound his "Papyrus," is actually parchment, one of three such parchment scraps torn by good fortune from a book destroyed centuries ago, the kind of book into which especially precious things were transcribed because papyrus disintegrates. They were salvaged from among masses of illegible papyrus scraps that came to Berlin from Egypt in 1896. Professor Schubart six years later published in a German journal[1] the letters he could then make out, bits of three poems of Sappho's, and in 1907 a reconsidered deciphering[2] which by two years later (*Classical Review*, July 1909) J. M. Edmonds had reconsidered yet more fully. There we may find

ἦρ ἀ[. . . . .
δῆρα τό[. . . . .
Γογγύλα τ[. . . . .

. . . plus parts of a dozen more lines, nine of which, the parchment scrap growing suddenly wider, contained enough more words and bits of words to tempt Prof. Edmonds' skill as an ancient Greek poet. He diligently "restored" them, and offered a confident translation into Wardour Street. ("I would fain have thee set me in the dewy meadow whither aforetime. . . .") Half the Greek words he was rendering were his own. In subsequent versions he grew still more confident, and the incautious user of his Loeb Classical Library Sappho (*Lyra Graeca*, Vol. 1, 245) has been likely to suppose the poem substantially intact. It is not; and a half-century later Pound's

dry rendering of three words in the upper left corner Edmonds left untinkered with still displaces in the memory Edmonds' tushery. Which was part of what Pound meant. ⟨ . . .⟩

Pound's attention ⟨ . . .⟩ tended to fix on the constellated words in ancient texts, not on their syntactic connections. He has even suggested that preoccupation with reproducing syntax may get in the translator's way, that Aeschylus' Greek is nearly agglutinative.[3] In 1912 he conjectured that Arnaut Daniel might have evolved Moncli and Audierna,[4] two lovers of whom nothing else is known, from two passages misread in Vergil's ninth eclogue, Moncil being Menalcas glimpsed through scribes' contractions, and Audierna a form of the verb *audio* mistaken for a name, and the whole translated "without too much regard for Latin syntax, with which Arnaut would have been much less familiar than he was with the Latin vocabulary." Pound has gone through such processes himself, not always unconsciously.

It is tenable that he saw diction rather than syntax because not having learned declensions accurately he could not follow the syntax. This is very likely often true, but does not itself explain why a man who was never lazy, and had an appetite for old poems, did not feel an incentive to perfect his grammatical knowledge. That he was impatient with people who possessed such knowledge is not an explanation but something else to explain. What did he know that they didn't? Which means, since a man will not willingly pore over what is opaque to him, what was he responding to when he read Greek? To rhythms and dictions, nutriment for his purposes. Especially in Greek lyrics he is sensitive to the boundaries of individual words, and apt to discern a talismanic virtue in relevant English words of his discovery. In the rare plural "satieties" he found a Sapphic quality concentrated. It appears in " Ἰμέρρω," it is cherished and carefully laminated into the fifth Canto, and we learn nothing of its virtue from knowing that it was prompted by Aldington's misreading of ἄσαι. It suffices that Pound came upon it in the rich field of his English vocabulary, and cherished it as affording a mysterious glimpse into intensities important to Sappho. ⟨ . . .⟩

Pound was most deeply entangled in the aesthetic of glimpses in the *Lustra-Mauberley* period, the years when the elements of his mature method were being worked out. It is a period of looking back a little wistfully, a period of laments for departed experience, the period inaugurated by *Cathay*. Sappho, her fragments, her crystalline single words, remained bound up in his mind with this time, and with its end she drops out of his zone of preoccupation. By 1920 the fifth canto was in print, and the aesthetic of Paterian elegy which its first page recalls, the aesthetic he had exorcised in *Mauberley*, was replaced by the studied aesthetic of "hard squares" worked out under the sign of Fenollosa. In the 1920's, making reading lists for young students, he cited "of the Greeks, Homer, Sappho," and in the 1930's he set Mary Barnard to writing Sapphics ("have a care against spondee too often for second foot"[5]), but the explicit use of Sappho in his work remained confined to those last London years and their cultivated regrets: *Lustra*, Canto 5, *Mauberley*.

Then suddenly after a quarter-century circumstances changed the tone of the *Cantos* once more to elegy, and Sappho returned.

Irreparable death hung over the poet's head, and there were no books but Legge's Confucius and a Bible, and no sights but guards and prisoners and a sky and mountains and dust, and the *Pisan Cantos* invoked memory, seizing moments from the past "for those moments' sake." It was then that, reaching back to the time when Pound had pored over Greek fragments, memory yielded up, strangely, the splendid word of Sappho's that Canto 5 had skirted: *brododaktylos*. The word presented itself amid a sense that his own personality was dissolving into recollections. "To such a tremulous wisp constantly reforming itself on the stream, to a single sharp impression, with a sense in it, a relic more or less fleeting, of such moments gone by, what is real in our life fines itself down": so Pater had written in 1868, and so Pound felt in the summer of 1945. His mind ran on devouring Time, on the dead Ignez da Castro who brought the phrase "time is the evil" into the *Cantos*, on a woman's face remembered as though "dead the long year," on Mauberley's effort to memorialize such glimpses, working as Pisanello had worked on medallions in the Greek manner "to forge Achaia"; on new-made Aphrodite blown upon by winds; and on Aubrey Beardsley, doomed. And did he remember that Beardsley had designed the cover for the third printing of Wharton's *Sappho?*

> Time is not, Time is the evil, beloved
> Beloved the hours βροδοδάκτυλος
>   as against the half-light of the window
>   with the sea beyond making horizon
> le contre-jour the line of the cameo
> profile "to carve Achaia"
>   a dream passing over the face in the half-light
>   Venere, Cytherea "aut Rhodon"
>   vento ligure, veni
> "beauty is difficult sd/ Mr Beardsley . . .
>   (74/444:472)

So Canto 74; and though the lament for a lost woman in a lost time accords with Sappho's theme, and the vocation of Beardsley and H. S. Mauberley with the sensibility of a time when fragments had seemed especially radiant, though Sappho's word thus bridges the two motifs of this passage, the fact should be recorded that in 1949 Pound could not say why he had used the Aeolic rather than the Homeric form of the word "rosy-fingered."[6] No matter: memory at the time of writing had supplied what was appropriate, and supplied it again in Canto 80 when amid memories of those London days Aubrey Beardsley's saying again drew up with it the Greek polysyllable:

> La beauté, "Beauty is difficult, Yeats" said Aubrey
>   Beardsley
>   when Yeats asked why he drew horrors
>   or at least not Burne-Jones
>   and Beardsley knew he was dying and had to
>   make his hit quickly
> hence no more B-J in his product.
>   So very difficult, Yeats, beauty so difficult.
>   "I am the torch" wrote Arthur "she saith"
> in the moon barge βροδοδάκτυλος Ἠώς
> with the veil of faint cloud before her
>   Κύθηρα δεινά as a leaf borne in the current
> pale eyes as if without fire.
>   (80/511:546)

It is a poignant cluster: Beardsley; Arthur Symons, whose "Modern Beauty" began,

> I am the torch, she saith, and what to me
> If the moth die of me?

Κύθηρα δεινά, remembering perhaps Yeats' "terrible beauty"; her as-if-fireless pale eyes those of the moon (and perhaps of Agostino di Duccio's triumphant Diana in the Tempio at Rimini); the moon like Sappho's moon rosy-fingered, and rosy fingers specifying Homer's dawn.

The writer of those lines was living like Beardsley in the shadow of death, like Symons and Pater in the consciousness of a transience whose term is death, and as never before in his life

was building with precious fragments, conserved by memory as the letters of parchments were conserved by chance: conserved for imaginations quickened by transience to scrutinize and irradiate. When he used Sappho's fragment on Atthis in 1916 it was as a means of writing elegiac poems, the elegy being the poetic genre his time gave him, a gift that corresponded to one of the moods of youth in that decade. When she returned to him in 1945, as it were anonymously, so that later he did not know that it was she and not Homer who had brought him a magical word, she re-enacted a rite celebrated by Symons and Yeats, assuming the guise of eternal Aphrodite who visits poets and whose gaze confers a sad ecstasy. Aphrodite comes in mean vestments, the myth runs: in the rags of the girl who posed for Burne-Jones's beggar-maid, or in a scrap of parchment.

Notes

1. Professor Schubart published in a German journal: *Sitzungsberichte der Akademie de Wissenschaften*, 1902, 195–206.
2. A reconsidered deciphering: *Berliner Klassikertexte*, V–2.
3. Aeschylus nearly agglutinative: *The Literary Essays of Ezra Pound* (1954), 273.
4. Moncli and Audierna: *The Translations of Ezra Pound* (enlarged edition, 1963), 424.
5. "Have a care against spondee": *The Letters of Ezra Pound*, ed. D. D. Paige, #281.
6. In 1949 Pound could not say: conversation with Hugh Kenner.

DONALD DAVIE
"Romance Languages"
Ezra Pound
1975, pp. 11–26

Nothing could be more genteel, or less iconoclastic in its tone and implications, than Pound's subtitle to his first prose book, *The Spirit of Romance* (1910): *An Attempt to Define Somewhat the Charm of the Pre-Renaissance Literature of Latin Europe* ("by Ezra Pound, M.A., Author of *Personae* and *Exultations*"). "Somewhat" and "charm" are such worlds away from the brutally emphatic language of Pound's later prose that we are tempted to think this title page was composed tongue-in-cheek. But there is no evidence of that. On the contrary, if we're to pick up Pound at the start of his career we have to transport ourselves into a climate where "somewhat" and "charm" and indeed "romance" are part of the vocabulary with which serious and accomplished people address themselves to serious questions about culture.

Moreover, the ground that Pound covers in this book, as he had in public lectures in London in 1908–09 and again in 1909–10—Bion and Moschus from ancient Sicily, the Provençal troubadours, *The Song of Roland* and *Poema del Cid*, the *dolce stil nuovo* and Dante, Villon, Lope de Vega, Camoëns, Latin poets of the Renaissance—is thoroughly in line with such a monument of Edwardian literary culture as George Saintsbury's *Periods of European Literature*. As epigraph to the twelve volumes of this encyclopedic work stands a quotation from Matthew Arnold:

> The criticism which alone can help us for the future
> is a criticism which regards Europe as being, for
> intellectual and spiritual purposes, one great confed-
> eration, bound to a joint action and working to a
> common result.

But when Saintsbury in 1907 gets to his twelfth volume, and is compelled to notice some Russian and Polish and Scandinavian authors, he does so with marked impatience and distaste, and we see that "Europe," as conceived by Saintsbury following Arnold's directive, is not the same as the geographical entity thus named, but something much smaller, centered on the Mediterranean and in effect comprising only the area of the Romance languages, though English and German are allowed in as special cases. And this seems to be true also of Pound—not only of the young scholar who published *The Spirit of Romance*, and in 1906 had been a graduate fellow of the University of Pennsylvania, his field the Romance languages; but also of the Pound who in the 1920s confessed to Ernest Hemingway, "To tell the truth, Hem, I've never read the Rooshians"; and even of the Pound who, after two world wars had broken over Europe, was to write from a prison camp (Canto 76):

As a lone ant from a broken ant-hill
from the wreckage of Europe, ego scriptor.

The European "confederation" that Pound thought he spoke for throughout his life was effectively a Europe that spoke Latin and its Romance derivatives, including English as the most remote and partial of those derivatives, and making special provision for classical Greek as in important ways the orginal source of them all, even of Latin. And the sanities and wisdoms that Pound conceived of himself as promoting against the ever-more impudent barbarians were carried—so he thought, and was to think—pre-eminently in Latin and the Romance languages: Italian, Spanish, French (and, when he remembered, Portuguese). What looks like a glaring exception to this rule—Pound's enthusiasm for Chinese language and culture—is far more apparent than real, as we shall see. Such a prejudice or predisposition was more common in Saintsbury's generation than it has been since, when Dostoevski and Nietzsche, Freud and Ibsen and Frantz Fanon have increasingly jostled Arnaud Daniel and François Villon for the attention of people who aspire to be well-read. And coming at it from this point of view, we see it was no accident that when the time came for Pound like most of his contemporaries to swerve into political aberrations, it should have been Italian fascism that trapped him, not German National Socialism or Russian communism.

But if the language trusted by the young Pound is Romance language in this respectable, technical, and well-defined sense, what's to be said of language like this:

Aye, I am wistful for my kin of the spirit
And I have none about me save in the shadows
When come they, surging of power, 'DAEMON'
'Quasi KALOUN'. S.T. says Beauty is most that, a
    'calling of the soul.'
Well then, so call they, the swirlers out of the mist of
    my soul,
They that come mewards, bearing old magic.

Here we have "Romance language" in an altogether less reputable sense, which has more to do with romanticism (and with Victorian late-romanticism) than with the harshly direct language of a genuine "Romance" poet like Villon. The lines above are from "In Durance" (1907), which appeared in Pound's third collection, *Personae* (London 1909); and what they are struggling to say is after a fashion in keeping with the language that Pound tries to say it in. "S.T." is Coleridge, and the Coleridge text appealed to is the essay "On the Principles of Genial Criticism," which advances a Platonic or neo-Platonic idea of the nature and function of poetry, as Pound's poem does also. Moreover, the neo-Platonic matter of these lines is something that persisted in Pound's thought. And if, as historians of ideas, we were to concentrate on the paraphrasable content of Pound's poetry, we could see such an early poem as saying things which he will still be saying at the end of

his life. But it is precisely the radical difference in the manner of saying, early and late, which is crucial. For the experience of reading Pound's *Cantos* isn't remotely like the experience of reading neo-Platonic romantic poets like Shelley or D. G. Rossetti. So what is the point of establishing that if Pound had written differently he might have sounded like the Shelley who wrote *Epipsychidion*? The historian of ideas may be interested but the reader of poetry is not, nor should he be. What he needs to attend to is the Foreword that Pound supplied in 1964 when he allowed his very first collection, *A Lume Spento* (originally Venice, 1908), to be reprinted:

As to why a reprint? No lessons to be learned save the depth of ignorance, or rather the superficiality of non-perception—neither eye nor ear. Ignorance that didn't know the meaning of "Wardour Street."

Who knows that meaning now? The expression was more current in 1908 than in 1964. In 1976 we need a dictionary:

The name of a street in London, mainly occupied by dealers in antique and imitation-antique furniture . . . applied to the pseudo-archaic diction affected by some writers, esp. of historical novels, 1888.

"Pseudo-archaic" is exact for "Aye, I am wistful," and "They that come mewards." Whole books were written in this excruciating idiom, notably by Pound's English friend Maurice Hewlett, who shared his enthusiasm for medieval Aquitaine of the troubadours. This is romance language in the sense that it is the language of historical romances written in late-Victorian and Edwardian England; it is not a medium in which anything can be communicated forcefully or crisply.

This is, however, only one component in the language of these lines. "Surging of power" belongs in some different idiom altogether, which is impossible to name; the notetaker's telegraphese of "S.T." belongs in another idiom again; and the Greek expressions, "DAEMON" and "Quasi KALOUN," belong in yet another. These last are syntactically quite without anchorage in what offers itself as a normal English sentence. And this abandonment of grammar mirrors accurately the desperation of the poet, who can manage no more than to have these disparate idioms jostle helplessly one against another, though he is possessed of a conviction that they could be articulated one with another, if only he could find the key. At this stage he cannot; and so all that is conveyed is the desperation of the effort and the need. The language is a chronically unstable mix of linguistic elements from the European past, held together by will, by nothing more than the urgency of the poet's need. Their coherence is something wished for and vehemently gestured at, certainly not demonstrated or achieved. The vehemence of the need is quite without parallel among poets writing and publishing in London in the first decade of this century, and it is what at least one London reviewer of the time recognized and responded to. This was Edward Thomas, himself still several years short of working out the idiom which he commanded under the stress of World War I for long enough to make his own achievement in poetry irreplaceable. In Pound's *Personae*, Thomas saw, as he said, a "battlefield"; certainly not achievement, on the contrary the debris of a defeat, but a defeat in which stronger forces had been engaged than in any other engagement of a living poet with the resources of the English tongue. Pound's desperation, the ambitiousness or enormity of what he was attempting, the scope of the conflict he provoked, the range of linguistic resources he challenged to battle—this was what Edwardian London, in the admittedly unrepresentative figure of Edward Thomas, responded to and recognized.[1] It is (to put it mildly) unlikely that London of the 1960s or 1970s would have responded with that generosity and percipience to a poet whose claim was, when all is said, almost wholly in promise rather than in achievement. Pound was lucky to secure a firm reputation with the London elite on the score of *A Quinzaine for This Yule* (1908), and of *Personae* and *Exultations* (both 1909). Pound deserved the reputation; but in other periods reputations no less deserved have been withheld.

What Edward Thomas seems not to have recognized was that the peculiar rashness and impetuosity of the Edwardian poet he was responding to had everything to do with the fact that *this* Edwardian was American; that is to say, a poet of the English tongue to whom it came naturally to regard English as just one of the princely dialects of Europe.[2] An American like Pound came to *Europe*; and if he came to England, it was to one of the provinces of that larger cultural entity. No Edwardian Englishman thought of England that way; even if he was so intensely a Europeanist as Saintsbury, he defined himself in his national identity as that which Continental Europe was not. But to a devoted American Europeanist like the young Pound, what was precious about England was not what marked her off from the Continent but what bound her to the Mediterranean heartlands. Hence the unconvincing impetuosity with which the poet of "In Durance" moves from mock-archaic English to Greek. Whitman before Pound had interlarded his American English with tags of Spanish, just as, after Pound, Wallace Stevens was to trick out his American English with bits of French. But Pound's endeavor was more serious altogether: he wanted to create or re-create a *lingua franca* of Greco-Roman Christendom in which English would operate as a sister language with French and Spanish and Italian. The mere *mix* of "In Durance" was to become the compound language of *The Cantos*—a compound still perhaps unstable, but not so easily dissoluble.

The author of "In Durance" and of *The Spirit of Romance* was the author also of *Patria Mia* (1912), in which he wrote consciously and explicitly as a citizen of the United States, addressing himself specifically to the state of culture, and the prospects for culture, in his native land. This curious brief work by Pound has had an odd history, and was not published in book form until more than thirty years after it was written, and first appeared in A. R. Orage's London periodical, *The New Age*. What is striking about it is that Pound the American patriot is defeated almost before he starts; he is trying to persuade himself that his native land is ripe for a Renascence or a Risorgimento (he uses both terms, as if they meant the same thing), and yet the evidence belies him even as he assembles it. For he cannot bring himself to acknowledge the implications of a paragraph on his second page:

> . . . the non-constructive idealist, the person who is content with his own thoughts, the person whom it is the fashion to call "sentimentalist," does not emigrate [Pound means, from Europe to the United States]. I mean the person who has "the finer feelings," love of home, love of land, love of place, of atmosphere, be he peasant or no. He may come as an act of heroism, but he returns to his land. He is almost negligible in our calculations.

Faced with the consequences of the Open Door policy on immigration, many relatively long-established American families, especially if they had come down in the world (and Pound's grandfather had been conspicuously richer and more notable than Pound's father was), shared, sixty years ago, this suspicion or conviction that Europe in the nineteenth century had unloaded on the United States only her more feckless and rootless and shallow-minded citizens. Because a significant proportion of those immigrants had been Jews from Eastern

Europe, one product of his state of feeling was a distinctively American sort of anti-Semitism; and sure enough, anti-Jewish animus crops up in the original version of *Patria Mia*. In *Patria Mia*, Pound, sorting out his memories of going home for a long visit in 1910, oscillates between this annoyed snobbishness toward the recent immigrants and, on the other hand, a resentment as British condescension; he wants to believe that the United States is due to become a great cultural force in the world, and he tires to persuade himself of this, but in the end he fails. One must sympathize: it is hard for a man to acknowledge to himself at twenty-seven that he is always going to be happier outside his own country than in it. But the consequences were to be calamitous thirty years later, when Pound, still conceiving of himself as an American patriot, broadcast from Rome radio to the advancing American armies. And a particularly poignant twist emerges when Pound lists the things that the United States needed to do to bring her Renascence nearer: his recommendations are thoroughly American in that they are quite specific, and organizational, and practical. Most of them—for instance, massive endowments to the arts as well as to learning through charitable foundations, and the calculated provision for exchanges between scholars and practicing artists on university campuses— have, in fact, been implemented. Few Americans would want to assert, however, that these changes have brought about an artistic and cultural flowering in America, such as Pound tried to persuade himself was imminent in 1912.

It is in any case highly significant that this, Pound's most obviously and explicitly American book, should have a Latin title. He attempts to foresee a future for America according to paradigms he had learned about in Europe. Neither at this time nor afterward does Pound share the conviction and the hope which as a matter of historical record have fired the cultural achievements of the white man in North America ever since Plymouth Plantation—the hope and belief that the new continent offered a new start, a new Eden for a new Adam, liberated from the corruptions and errors of Europe and forewarned by European history of how to avoid European mistakes. On the contrary, Pound takes it for granted that if America is ever to produce or become a noble civilization, it can do so only by modeling itself on European precedents, precedents that are ultimately or originally Greek and Roman. In 1976 not many professors of Greek or Latin would make such sweeping claims for the worth of their studies. To one of them, Charles Doria, "trying to find the genesis and 'genius' of Western civilization through the classics" was the characteristic bent of classical studies for only a brief period—"from the 18th century until around the end of the first world war"; and throughout that period classical studies conducted in this style was serving some ugly ideological ends:

> Greece and Italy become the discoverers and true cradles of our civilization. Classical writers, when read correctly, provided explanations for why Europe (and by extension America) grew to dominate the rest of the world. Democracy and Technology, the "gifts" of Athens and Rome respectively, can be traced back to the institutions and attitudes of the Ancients. Without them such modern touch-stones as progress, liberalism, individualism and "liberty under the law"—but above all the enlightened use of political and economic power for the good of the state (as taught in the Melian Dialogue of Thucydides) would have been philosophically impossible.

This relatively modern attitude of cultural autarky for Europe, of demonstrating her cultural and racial supremacy at the expense of everyone else, can best be described as the conversion of Classical Studies into Aryan Studies. It is no accident that throughout this period—. . . "from Winckelmann to Wilamowitz"—Germany was the acknowledged leader in the scholarship of Antiquity.[3]

Obviously this account is as sweeping and schematic as the set of assumptions it sets out to discredit. But it is certainly instructive to see what Pound looks like from this standpoint. According to Doria, Pound, schooled in this way of thinking, "never got to the point . . . of seeing that Europe was not necessarily the daughter of Antiquity. . . . Pound made himself into a self-confident European who sums up in his poetry and criticism the contradictions and scattered beauties of that brutal civilization—possibly because he grew up at a time when that brutality was neither displayed openly nor recognized internally."[4] This is to see Pound as a desperate rear guard with a set of preconceptions that were superannuated almost as soon as he came to hold them. Thus it is near to the sense we have of him when we call him "Edwardian." And yet why on this showing is it always the professional classicists who assail him most brutally? There is a puzzle here, which we must grapple with in due course.

Yet this is far from being the view of Pound that prevails at the present day. One prevalent alternative view we have encountered already. It merges him, implausibly, with William Blake. But this too is a late-come image: one need not have lived to any advanced age to remember when Americans furiously denounced Pound as not American at all. Had he not lived all his adult years outside America? Was he not a notorious Fascist and anti-Semite? Had he not escaped conviction for treason on the trumped-up pretext of being unfit to plead? Memories are short; and now it is as if this climate of opinion had never been. In the interim the American literary intellectual, relieved of the embarrassment of Pound's incarceration in a Washington mental hospital, has found it possible to extol him as a great American poet—in contexts where "American" means emphatically "non-European." In these contexts the name that matters is not Blake but (inevitably) Whitman:

> . . . our sense of the vital relationship between Whitman and Pound . . . is indispensable to an understanding of the theory and history of American poetry. . . .[5]

Or again:

> The line from Whitman to Pound is the radical tradition of American poetry: the connection between them is quite as firm and unassailable as the *traditio* from Chaucer to Spenser to Milton. . . .[6]

"Firm and unassailable"—if this sounds like someone shouting down objections before they are raised, there is reason for it. For in *Patria Mia* what Pound wrote was:

> America of today is the sort of country that loses Henry James and retains to its appreciative bosom a certain Henry Van Dyke.
>
> The statement is a little drastic, but it has the facts behind it.
>
> America's position in the world of art and letters is, relatively, about that which Spain held in the time of the Senecas. So far as civilization is concerned America is the great rich, Western province which has sent one or two notable artists to the Eastern capital. And that capital is, needless to say, not Rome, but the double city of London and Paris.
>
> From our purely colonial conditions came Irving and Hawthorne. There [? Their] tradition was

English unalloyed, and we had to ourselves Whitman, "The Reflex," who left us a human document, for you cannot call a man an artist until he shows himself capable of reticence and restraint, until he shows himself in some degree master of the forces which beat upon him.

> And in our own time the country has given to the world two men, Whistler, of the school of master-work, of the world of Dürer, and of Hokusai, and of Velazquez, and Mr. Henry James, in the school of Flaubert and Turgenev.

This passage has to mean that Whistler and James are superior to Whitman; that they are artists whereas Whitman is only "a reflex." Edwin Fussell quotes another passage of *Patria Mia* where Whitman is called "not an artist, but a reflex, the first honest reflex in an age of papier-mâché letters," and he comments: "Pound calls Whitman a 'reflex' and himself, by implication, another. . . ." But the inference is unwarranted: on the contrary, all the evidence suggests that Pound was vowing himself to be, not a "reflex" like Whitman, but an "artist" like James or Whistler. It was not thus that Milton looked back on Spenser, nor Spenser on Chaucer.

And at a time when a defaulting President of the United States has lately been forced from office by procedures laid down in the Constitution, the least one can say is that the question is still open whether the United States—its polity (in this case vindicated) framed on neoclassical models by assiduous Grecians like Jefferson and Adams—is not indeed, as Pound supposed, a last colony of the Greco-Roman world.

Meanwhile, though Pound's verse style is still radically insecure—in due course Allen Upward shall explain this for us, defining it as, in all its varieties, "Babu English"—Pound nonetheless had begun mapping what was to be his imaginative universe. And "mapping" is not altogether a metaphor: the most straightforward, and not the least reliable, way of apprehending Pound's universe is by recognizing the half-dozen geographical areas that are for him, and are to remain, "sacred places."[7] One of these, one of the most important, is already fixed upon and celebrated in the early poems. It is Lake Garda, haunt of Catullus and the scene, years later in Pound's life, of his momentous meeting with Joyce:

> What hast thou, O my soul, with paradise?
> Will we not rather, when our freedom's won,
> Get us to some clear place wherein the sun
> Let's drift in on us through the olive leaves
> A liquid glory? If at Sirmio,
> My soul, I meet thee, when this life's outrun,
> Will we not find some headland consecrated
> By aery apostles of terrene delight,
> Will not our cult be founded on the waves,
> Clear sapphire, cobalt, cyanine,
> On triune azures, the impalpable
> Mirrors unstill of the eternal change?
>
> Soul, if She meet us there, will any rumour
> Of havens more high and courts desirable
> Lure us beyond the cloudy peak of Riva?
>
> (*Canzoni*, 1911)

This is far from being the only place in the early collections where Pound's style achieves a temporary and trembling synthesis, and a sort of limpid eagerness that is very attractive indeed. In another early poem, for instance, "The Flame," he used the Latin name for Lake Garda, "Benacus," to come up with the astonishing lines:

> Sapphire Benacus, in thy mists and thee
> Nature herself's turned metaphysical.
> Who can look on that blue and not believe?

It will be noted that these verses have none of the characteristics that we are likely to think of as "modern," any more than the verses which Thomas Hardy, because of the same Catullan associations, had devoted to the same spot only a few years before.[8]

Notes

1. Edward Thomas, "Two Poets," *English Review*, Vol. 3 (1909), valuably excerpted in J. P. Sullivan, ed., *Ezra Pound*, Penguin Critical Anthology (1970). The full involvement of Thomas with early Pound is more extensive than had been realized, and it has yet to be studied; see items listed by Robert A. Corrigan, *Paideuma*, Vol. 1, no. 2 (1972), and Vol. 2, no. 1 (1973).
2. I borrow this splendid phrase, without permission, from Donald Carne-Ross.
3. Charles Doria, "Pound, Olson, and the Classical Tradition," in *Charles Olson: Essays, Reminiscences, Reviews*, Matthew Corrigan, ed., *Boundary*, Vol. 2, nos. 1 and 2 (State University of New York at Binghamton, 1973–74).
4. Ibid.
5. Edwin Fussell, *Lucifer in Harness: American Meter, Metaphor, and Diction* (Princeton, 1973), pp. 20–21.
6. Ibid. Even "What I Feel about Walt Whitman" (1909) *American Literature*, xxvii, 1955, the one place where Pound is enthusiastic about Whitman, is much more ambiguous about him than Fussell's quotation from it would suggest.
7. For another of the "sacred places" see Davie, "*The Cantos*: Towards a Pedestrian Reading," *Paideuma*, Vol. 1, no. 1 (1972).
8. See "Catullus: XXXI. (After passing Sirmione, April 1887)," *The Collected Poems of Thomas Hardy* (London, 1952), p. 166.

WILLIAM HARMON
From "Pound's Poetics of Time and Timelessness"
Time in Ezra Pound's Work
1977, pp. 44–62

Ezra Pound's ideas about space and time are realized in subordinate ideas about culture; his ideas about culture are, in turn, realized in practical criticism of political and poetic structures; and finally, his practical literary criticism is actively carried over into poems. (However shaky his political thinking, there is nothing uncertain about his critical ideas,) although a degree of subtlety is necessary for the reader to separate Pound's critical maxims from what actually takes place in his poems.

Pound's poetics cannot be found in a single volume. The principal outlines can be discerned in *ABC of Reading*, but that book is little more than a dilation of the long essay "How to Read." Details and examples can be found in miscellaneous essays and reviews, most of which were written between 1910 and 1931. ⟨. . .⟩

When writing about novels or plays, Pound often dwells on issues of biography, audience, and working conditions; when dealing with poetry, however, he becomes emphatically formal and technical, and it is in the detailed criticism of poetry that his aesthetic writing has been most abundant and most durable. *ABC of Reading* and "How to Read" could be called *ABC of Reading Poetry* and "How to Read Poetry." For these reasons, the essence of Pound's criticism of novels—since it deals mainly with problems of social thought—has already been discussed above, especially in the passages that concern Henry James and James Joyce.

Pound's criticism, which remained much more consistent than his cultural and political thought, treats two major aspects of poetry: mimesis and expression. Poetry imitates certain objects (actions, characters, states of mind) by means of the power of words to cast images, make music, and appeal to the imagination. By the quality of imitation, furthermore, a poem is "polysemous," to use Dante's term; a poem can imitate several objects at once because the objects themselves bear mimetic and analogical linkages one to another. Words, let us say, represent an action (for example, a journey); and this action, in turn, represents a more general action (for example, the course of a life). By further extensions, the "curriculum" of one man's life can represent the course of all human life; and that course, subsumed under a general metaphor of organic change, can represent the fate of all things under the aspects of time and eternity. Taken as a whole, the concentric aesthetic act of polysemous mimesis suggests a second universe of representation as well, because the work of art, in addition to imitating objects, expresses the individual maker at a particular time, his total character up to the time of the making, the specific character of his circumstances (zeitgeist or *paideuma*), and again, as *this* circle widens, the whole human condition.

Pound's aesthetic of mimesis and expression was crystallized around a set of terms—luminous detail, image, persona, vortex, ideogram—that all suggest an objective correlative that the poet uses to externalize certain internal states. The poet ought to articulate his own set of correlatives in such a way that the reader can experience similar states of mind. To this extent Pound's aesthetic is merely technical. It takes on a moral dimension, however, as soon as it is recognized that the medium of poetic imitation is also the medium of social communication and that a language thrives or suffers in proportion to the nourishment or abuse it receives in the work of its poets. The relation between the imitating work and the particular zeitgeist that it expresses is another factor in the moral dimension of the work of art—a factor that embodies the social and political values of a culture. If the character of the artist is in harmony with the character of his surroundings and if these respective characters are virtuous, the works of art will receive support from their cultures. On the other hand, if the artist's character is radically out of key with his surroundings, the work may still be the culmination of one man's individual civilization, like Sigismundo Malatesta's Tempio in Rimini, but, fragmentary and incomplete, it will lack logical consistency and aesthetic integrity.

Such, in outline, is my conception of Pound's aesthetics. Space and time are obviously important considerations in this kind of thinking, because the aesthetic act is concentrated precisely on transcending its own physical limits and on removing the object and the audience from their conditions of spatiality and temporality by putting them into a refreshing and illuminating connection with free, timeless values.

But how? Poetry exists in time and therefore best imitates objects that are arranged sequentially. For objects that are arranged in a timeless pattern of simultaneous relations, the spatial media provide the best expression. In Pound's aesthetic there is a search for means by which the immediate impact of spatial arts can be achieved by words in time. Pound accepts the assumption that time and space are properties of the real world and its aesthetic counterpart, but he rejects the conclusion that poetry is limited by its own temporality to the imitation of temporal objects; he seeks a form of art that combines all the virtues of painting and poetry.

In criticism as in social thought, Pound is seldom systematic or thorough. He first gathered technical observations, some dating back to 1911, in an essay called "A Retrospect" that appeared in his *Pavannes and Divisions* (1918). Here he justifies his immethodical approach: "Criticism is not a circumscription or a set of prohibitions. It provides fixed points of departure. It may startle a dull reader into alertness. That little of it which is good is mostly in stray phrases; or if it be an older artist helping a younger it is in great measure but rules of thumb, cautions gained by experience."[1] (A few years later T. S. Eliot said that there is no critical method "except to be very intelligent."[2]). In "A Retrospect" Pound reproduces the imagist principles supposedly agreed on in 1912 by Hilda Doolittle, Richard Aldington, and himself. Even construed as temporary rules of thumb, these three laws governing treatment, vocabulary, and rhythm are so vaguely stated that their terms can be adjusted to praise or condemn almost any work of art. The first principle—"Direct treatment of the 'thing' whether subjective or objective" (*LE*, p. 3)— contains only one term ("direct") to which any definite meaning can be attached; and immediately one can imagine any number of circumstances in which the poet may properly be allowed the indirect treatment of a thing, especially a subjective thing. Similar reservations apply to the second principle—"To use absolutely no word that does not contribute to the presentation" (*LE*, p. 3). It is easy to feel that a word in a certain poem is inert—possessing nothing but metrical value, if indeed any value at all; but again one can imagine any number of instances in which the "presentation" of an objective or subjective thing requires the use of lexical or syntactic devices that under different circumstances might seem quite worthless. Dramatic verse is full of "bad" poetry that is perfectly suited to its purpose because its very obscurity, clumsiness, or inertness serves to reveal a character. The third imagist principle—"As regarding rhythm: to compose in the sequence of the musical phrase, not in the sequence of the metronome" (*LE*, p. 3)—is the least objectionable because its proscription of monotonous rhythms, even though *they* may occasionally be appropriate, accords with most readers' feelings about sing-song verse. As appealing as the negative half of this third principle may be, its positive endorsement of the "musical phrase" as the unit of poetic sequence is as vague as the arguments of the first two principles. A musical phrase is infinitely variable: within the limits of one "measure" of a given time signature, an endless series of endlessly subdivided units of both sound and silence is possible. Such unlimited variety is probably more attractive than monotony, but since the "musical phrase" is so variable, not much value can be derived from the use of its sequence—its sequence can be anything. This kind of license is as monotonous as monotony.

The celebrated imagist principles are too weak to have much value either as practical advice or as aesthetic doctrine. What remains interesting about them today is their opposition to limitations of time. They are against the "time," in the historical sense, that imposes conventions of excessive obliquity and elaboration on the treatment of the subject of poetry; they are against the "time," in what can be called the "chronometronomic" sense, that imposes mechanical patterns on the musically flexible contours of poetry.

Time is also an important factor in "A Few Don'ts" (originally in *Poetry* for March 1913), another of the emphatic documents collected in "A Retrospect." Here Pound defines an image as "that which presents an intellectual and emotional complex in an instant of time." He describes this presentation, not in terms of its structure, but in terms of its effect on the reader: "It is the presentation of such a 'complex' instantaneously which gives that sense of sudden liberation; that sense of freedom from time limits and space limits; that sense of sudden growth, which we experience in the presence of the greatest works of art" (*LE*, p. 4). Here, with such complex notions as "instant of time" and "sudden growth," Pound is far beyond

the kind of technical rules of thumb that one would pass along to apprentices.

Since the means for achieving these effects of sudden liberation and growth still need to be clarified, it may help to look at one of Pound's imagist poems and his comments on it. In April 1913, one month after the appearance of his "A Few Don'ts," *Poetry* printed "In a Station of the Metro":

> The apparition of these faces in the crowd;
> Petals on a wet, black bough.[3]

The poem clearly demonstrates the imagist principles of economy and variable phrasing; the problem of the directness of treatment is handled by Pound in an article called "How I Began" that was published soon after the poem appeared:

> For well over a year I have been trying to make a poem of a very beautiful thing that befell me in the Paris Underground. I got out of a train at, I think, La Concorde and in the jostle I saw a beautiful face, and then, turning suddenly, another and another, and then a beautiful child's face, and then another beautiful face. All that day I tried to find words for what this made me feel. That night as I went home along the rue Raynouard I was still trying. I could get nothing but spots of colour. I remember thinking that if I had been a painter I might have started a wholly new school of painting. I tried to write the poem weeks afterwards in Italy, but found it useless. Then only the other night, wondering how I should tell the adventure, it struck me that in Japan, where a work of art is not estimated by its acreage and where sixteen syllables are counted enough for a poem if you arrange and punctuate them properly, one might make a very little poem which would be translated about as follows:—
>
> > The apparition of these faces in the crowd;
> > Petals on a wet, black bough.
>
> And there, or in some very old, very quiet civilisation, some one else might understand the significance.[4]

The same anecdote is elaborated in "Vorticism," an essay that was printed in the *Fortnightly Review* for 1 September 1914 and was later included in *Gaudier-Brzeska* (1916). Here Pound describes his tactic for escaping the sequential presentation inherent in the verbal medium, and he uses many of the same terms—notably "sudden" and "instant"—that occur in his earlier definition of *image*:

> The "one image poem" is a form of super-position, that is to say, it is one idea set on top of another. I found it useful in getting out of the impasse in which I had been left by my metro emotion. I wrote a thirty-line poem, and destroyed it because it was what we call a work "of second intensity." Six months later I made a poem half that length; a year later I made the following hokku-like sentence:—
>
> > The apparition of these faces in the crowd;
> > Petals on a wet, black bough.
>
> I dare say it is meaningless unless one has drifted into a certain vein of thought. In a poem of this sort one is trying to record the precise instant when a thing outward and objective transforms itself, or darts into a thing inward and subjective.[5]

Pound's definition of *image*, as displayed in the two-line poem and his comments on its development, is an early step in his journey to discover aesthetic devices that make it possible for the ostensibly time-bound verbal medium to escape time and to express, instantaneously, moments or complexes of sudden illumination.

In "Vorticism" Pound cites a Japanese poem that is so concentrated it seems to need parenthetical enlargement to make its meaning clear:

> Victor Plarr tells me that once, when he was walking over snow with a Japanese naval officer, they came to a place where a cat had crossed the path, and the officer said, "Stop, I am making a poem." Which poem was, roughly, as follows:—
>
> *"The footsteps of the cat upon the snow:*
> *(are like) plum-blossoms."*
>
> The words "are like" would not occur in the original, but I add them for clarity.[6]

Pound is repeating a gesture that he employed in *The Spirit of Romance*. There, explanatory phrases are inserted in translations of difficult lines. Pound says in a footnote, "I have thought it necessary to insert in brackets the subjects of some of the relative pronouns."[7] Such explanations are usually not necessary and may even seem intrusive, but Pound apparently feels constrained to make the meaning of other people's poetry as clear as possible. At any rate, in his own "hokku-like" poem that is similar to the Japanese officer's, there is no explicit verbal indication of likeness between the two juxtaposed—or superposed—images. Indeed, there is no verb at all.

The Japanese officer's poem, which seems rather trifling, capitalizes on the simple fact that paw prints and blossoms look alike. As in Housman's lyric about the cherry trees hung with snow, the harmony between the visual patterns of footprints (seen) and petals (recalled) accents the irony in the fact that a winter scene can suggest an image of spring. To be sure, this procedure is one way of collapsing temporal and discursive sequences by means of a compressed comparison, but it hardly seems to be powerful or versatile enough to sustain a whole aesthetic doctrine. Fortunately, Pound's Metro poem, although it too uses an image of petals and suppresses the verbal expression of the simile, seems quite a bit more complex than the footprint-blossom poem. Pound's poem enjoys the additional quality of mystery. Instead of a pat equation of visual images already laden with accepted meanings, it offers two parallel patterns of mysterious vision. (Without his testimony in "How I Began" and "Vorticism," we would have no way of being sure that he thought the faces in the station were uniformly beautiful, nor would we know how intensely the personal experience had affected him.) Two senses of "apparition"—both "appearance" in the simplest sense as well as "spirit"—seem to be at work in the poem; using a word with two meanings at once is another device for avoiding temporal sequence. The faces are seen in a way that suggests disembodiment, and their apparitional quality, whether beautiful or not, is emphasized by the setting of an underground station that, even sixty years ago and even with art nouveau metal flowers for entrance decoration, must have been dismal. The mysterious vision by which Pound was so challenged and disturbed generates an antithetical vision, a pastoral image of petals, but it too is mysterious. The flesh-colored, face-shaped petals seem to have fallen during a spring shower and come to rest on a lower branch. The rapid succession of the image of faces and the "afterimage" of petals produces a composite image—"spots of colour"—that gives virtually instantaneous expression to an emotional and intellectual complex. It is not possible to paraphrase this complex faithfully in any words other than those of the poem, but its components, very crudely stated, seem to include love for the life and beauty of the faces and petals along with grief for their attachment to some dark, nearly infernal tubular structure, whether an underground tunnel or a wet, black bough.[8] (A polyglot may be aware that the root of

"Metro" means "mother" and also yields the name "Demeter.") ⟨. . .⟩

The imagist documents of the period between 1912 and 1920 contain most of Pound's early technical criticism. The central problem there ⟨. . .⟩ is discovering the means for subverting the temporal sequence of language so that images can present the essence or effect of sudden illuminations that transcend space and time. "How to Read," written when he was in his early forties, is his first sustained attempt to give his aesthetic of technique a semblance of organization. "Great literature," he says here, "is simply language charged with meaning to the utmost possible degree" (*LE*, p. 23).[9] This maximal charge of meaning presumably makes of a linguistic construct the highly efficient concentration—image, vortex, ideogram—that presents an emotional and intellectual complex so directly and so powerfully that its operation *seems*, at any rate, to take but an instant of time.

This instant of sudden illumination that collapses time and space is invoked in a letter from Pound to his father in 1927, not long before "How to Read." Giving an "outline of main scheme" of *The Cantos*, he lists three chief subjects, among them "the 'magic moment' or moment of metamorphosis, bust thru from quotidien into 'divine or permanent world.'"[10] The power of words to record the moment of transcendence when an objective thing is metamorphosed into either an inward subjective experience or an ideal entity—called respectively the "darting into" and the "bust thru"—is the mysterious force that Pound's criticism works to elucidate.[11]

To explain the charging of language, Pound uses in "How to Read" a set of terms—*melopoeia, phanopoeia,* and *logopoeia*—that first appeared in his writings around 1918.[12] Melopoeia, which covers the musical qualities of poetry, projects "a force tending often to lull, or to distract the reader from the exact sense of the language." Here he makes a claim for melopoeia that relates it to his preoccupation with metamorphosis: "It is poetry on the borders of music and music is perhaps the bridge between consciousness and the unthinking sentient or even insentient universe" (*LE*, p. 26).

Aside from this power to link consciousness with its surroundings, melopoeia is the simplest of the means of charging language, and it is the one that Pound dealt with most in his earlier technical criticism. In "A Few Don'ts" (1913) he suggested that "the candidate fill his mind with the finest cadences he can discover, preferably in a foreign language, so that the meaning of the words may be less likely to divert his attention from the movement" (*LE*, p. 5). According to "How to Read," the three functional categories of melopoeia—speech, chant, and song—cut across the two structural categories, melody and rhythm (*LE*, p. 28). Melody comprises such arrangements of sounds as alliteration, assonance, and rhyme; and since syllables vary in length and stress, rhythmic patterns can be built up of various clusters of "feet" arranged by meter or by number of syllables.

As early as the introduction to his first translations of the poems of Guido Cavalcanti (1910), Pound entered a very strong claim for the powers of rhythm: "I believe in an ultimate and absolute rhythm as I believe in an absolute symbol or metaphor. The perception of the intellect is given in the word, that of the emotions in the cadence. It is only, then, in the perfect rhythm joined to the perfect word that the two-fold vision can be recorded."[13] This line of speculation is continued in a way that explains Pound's later handling of melopoeia:

> Rhythm is perhaps the most primal of all things known to us. It is basic in poetry and music mutually, their melodies depending on a variation on

tone quality and of pitch respectively, as is commonly said, but if we look more closely we will see that music is, by further analysis, pure rhythm; rhythm and nothing else, for the variation of pitch is the variation in rhythms of the individual notes, and the harmony the blending of these varied rhythms. When we know more of overtones we will see that the tempo of every masterpiece is absolute, and is exactly set by some further law of rhythmic accord. Whence it should be possible to show that any given rhythm implies about it a complete musical form— fugue, sonata, I cannot say what form, but a form, perfect, complete. Ergo, the rhythm set in a line of poetry connotes its symphony, which, had we a little more skill, we could score for orchestra. *Sequitur*, or rather *inest*: the rhythm of any poetic line corresponds to emotion.

     It is the poet's business that this correspondence be exact, i.e., that it be the emotion which surrounds the thought expressed.[14]

The complex relation between absolute rhythm and poetic emotion can hardly be expressed by a simple *sequitur* or *inest*, and Pound does not explain the connection. He evidently feels it strongly, however, for he repeats the point in "Prolegomena" (1912): "I believe in an 'absolute rhythm,' a rhythm, that is, in poetry which corresponds exactly to the emotion or shade of emotion to be expressed. A man's rhythm must be interpretative, it will be, therefore, in the end, his own, uncounterfeitable" (*LE*, p. 9). Clearly, the operation of rhythm *takes time*, so that its effect cannot present a complex object in an instant. On the other hand, the "two-fold" effect of melopoeia, by furnishing a bridge between consciousness and the universe and by reminding the reader of "the most primal of all things known to us," may release the poet and reader alike from the world of ordinary time and space.

Of phanopoeia, defined as "a casting of images upon the visual imagination" (*LE*, p. 25), Pound says little that has not already been said in his imagist statements. Image casting is a power of words that relates more to their intellectual content than to their charge of emotion, and in "How to Read" Pound pays less attention to phanopoeia than he does to melopoeia (one of his most enduring concerns) and to logopoeia. The "visual imagination" in his aesthetic is chiefly a matter of apprehending the shapes and colors of objects, and as such it is the faculty that is appealed to by the "clarity and directness" (*LE*, p. 33) that holds such a high place among imagist ideals.

"How to Read" does not mention the visionary possibilities of phanopoeia; the concentration there is strictly on the visual. But in Pound's handling of the term ten years earlier, the vision-seeing dimension is as prominent as the perception of physical shapes and colors. The three Cantos of 1917, subsequently rejected, are full of visions,[15] and they are parts of the poem that Pound thought of calling "Phanopoeia." In 1918, between definitions of "melopoeia" and "logopoeia" that sound much like the definitions in "How to Read," Pound offered the element that was to become phanopoeia: "Imagism, or poetry wherein the feelings of painting and sculpture are predominant (certain men move in phantasmagoria; the images of their gods, whole countrysides, stretches of hill land and forest, travel with them).[16] And, in the set of poems that have kept the name "Phanopoeia," shapes and colors are used to evoke a mysterious experience of transfiguration:

    The wire-like bands of colour involute mount from
       my fingers;
    I have wrapped the wind round your shoulders
    And the molten metal of your shoulders

    bends into the turn of the wind,
AOI!
    The whirling tissue of light
       is woven and grows solid beneath us;
    The sea-clear sapphire of air, the sea-dark clarity,
       stretches both sea-cliff and ocean.[17]

Just as melopoeia is not simply a matter of pleasing musical effects, phanopoeia is much more than the use of shapes and colors to describe physical objects. In both of these elements of poetry, as Pound defines and uses them, it is possible to register timeless moments of metamorphosis from the objective to the subjective and from the casual to the permanent.

Logopoeia, Pound says, "employs words not only for their direct meaning, but it takes count in a special way of habits of usage, of the context we *expect* to find with the word, its usual concomitants, of its known acceptances, and of ironical play. It holds the aesthetic content which is peculiarly the domain of verbal manifestation, and cannot possibly be contained in plastic or in music. It is the latest come, and perhaps most tricky and undependable mode" (*LE*, p. 25). The *logo* in Pound's term means "idea" as well as "word," so that "logopoeia" means "thought making" or "the poetry of thoughts." This aspect of poetry is most conspicuous in texts that are deliberately ambiguous for purposes of irony or humor. Elizabethan puns of the *color-collar-choler* variety, for example, depend on the audience's knowledge of many meanings of all three words; a composite total meaning is generated by the complex of references and connotations attached to each word. This is one more device that permits the expression of intellectual and emotional complexes in an instant; the richness of logopoeia makes it possible for a poet to say several different things, some of which may even be contradictory, at once.

"How to Read" is, I think, Pound's best critical work. With the triad of melopoeia, phanopoeia, and logopoeia, Pound illuminates the abundance and complexity of the devices by which language can be so highly charged that it effects an instantaneous presentation and seems thereby to transcend the limits and conditions of time.[18]

Pound continues, "All writing is built up of these three elements, plus 'architectonics' or 'the form of the whole'" (*LE*, p. 26). Regrettably, he does not pursue the problem of form, and such failure to talk much about anything but language is a serious flaw in Pound's formal and technical criticism. Another flaw is the omission of any thoroughgoing examination of the problem of genres. Prose is distinguished from poetry only because the language of prose is "much less highly charged"; and drama too is dismissed in terms of the charging of language: "The drama is a mixed art; it does not rely on the charge that can be put into the word, but calls on gesture and mimicry and 'impersonation' for assistance" (*LE*, pp. 26, 29). We have seen already that Pound's criticism of the novel tends to get away from technical and formal questions and to concentrate instead on social circumstances. For him, as for many other modern critics, literature is a problem of language and not much else. Since there are things besides words in drama, he must categorize it as a mixed art; a more comprehensive critic, like Aristotle, is able to consider drama as an organized whole of which language is one part. It is to such comprehensive critics that one must go for discussion of the "architectonics," for Pound stops far short of that question.

An undated note at the end of "How to Read" in *Literary Essays* says that the "argument of this essay is elaborated in the author's *ABC of Reading*" (*LE*, p. 40), but in that book there is very little that is not already adequately presented in "How to Read." At the same time, *ABC of Reading* does nothing to correct the deficiencies of "How to Read"—such failures as the lack of consideration given to important elements of poetry other than the language. For this "textbook" Pound adopts a rather pompous epigrammatic style, often with paragraphs only one sentence long separated by portentous-looking extra spaces. The style, to be sure, produces some memorable slogans—"Artists are the antennae of the race" or "More writers fail from lack of character than from lack of intelligence"[19]—but this approach does not facilitate the systematic development of the author's argument. As in "How to Read," the emphasis is all on the language of poetry. In his consideration of drama, Pound simply repeats the idea that it contains elements that are extraneous to the operation of language; and he modestly grants that he cannot say much about novels because he has never written one (*ABC*, pp. 76, 89). He says that "an epic is a poem containing history" and that Shakespeare's historical plays "form the true English EPOS" (*ABC*, pp. 46, 59); but that is all he has to say about the subject, perhaps because he thinks that criticism, like poetry, should consist only of "gists and piths" (*ABC*, p. 92).

Earlier, in connection with "In a Station of the Metro," it was seen that the suppression of verbs in a poem contributes to the effect of instantaneous presentation. Without the causal and chronological process of predication and without the explicit indication of time inherent in verbs by virtue of tense inflections,[20] the linguistic pattern, as experienced and as remembered, seems to take on a kind of timelessness, even though the apprehension of the pattern still takes time. (The shorter the poem, of course, the closer will the apprehension approach timelessness.)

Pound's grasp of the use of such grammatical effects seems to be chiefly intuitive, for there is no reference to them in either "How to Read" or *ABC of Reading*. In scattered places, however, he does suggest a conscious manipulation of grammatical distinctions. At one point in *Jefferson and/or Mussolini*, for example, he says:

> Again a little grammar or a little mediaeval scholarship would be useful. Albertus Magnus or Aquinas or some fusty old scribbler passed on an age-old distinction between the verb and the noun.
>
> The verb implies a time, a relation to time. Be Christian, go back to the newer part of your Bible. Be Catholic (not Anglo-Catholic), consider the "mystery of the incarnation."[21]

In his essay on Guido Cavalcanti, he displays the same sense of grammatical subtleties (and uses almost the same language and examples) when justifying his choice of certain readings in the corrupt text of the canzone "Donna mi priegha":

> I guessed right in stressing the difference between *Amore* (noun) and *Amare* (verb) in the first strophe. The philosophical difference is that a noun is a significant sound which makes no discrimination as to time. "Nomen est vox significativa, ad placitum, sine tempore, cuius nulla pars est significativa separate." The verb locates in time. "Verbum logice consideratum est quod consignificat tempus" (Albertus Magnus).
>
> The reader will see that the English version of St. John loses this philosophical or metaphysical shade in reading: "the word became flesh," for "verbum caro," etc. [*LE*, pp. 174–75][22]

Pound does take up again the question of rhythm and time in a "Treatise on Metrics" appended to *ABC of Reading*. Here he says, "Rhythm is a form cut into TIME, as a design is determined SPACE" (*ABC*, p. 198). Conventional prosodic measurements, depending on a misconception of the basic unit of rhythm, simply do not apply to poetic language as it is spoken, chanted, or sung. Pound says that the "articulate sounds" of the language, with variable weights and duration that vary even more according to context, are "the medium wherewith the poem cuts his design in TIME." He accounts for failure in this department of poetry:

> If the poet hasn't a sense of time and of the different qualities of sound, this design will be clumsy and uninteresting just as a bad draughtsman's drawing will be without distinction.
>
> The bad draughtsman is bad because he does not perceive space and spatial relations, and cannot therefore deal with them.
>
> The writer of bad verse is a bore because he does not perceive time and time relations, and cannot therefore delimit them in an interesting manner, by means of longer and shorter, heavier and lighter syllables, and the varying qualities of sound inseparable from the words of his speech. [*ABC*, pp. 198–99]

But in a ten-page treatise Pound cannot give anything like a full examination of the complexities of prosody, which must include procedures for the measurement of quantity and quality of syllables, number of syllables or feet, and the interaction of syntactic articulations, prosodic patterns, and the arrangements of lines on a page.

ABC of Reading is Pound's last full book devoted to criticism, but it would be unjust to end an examination of his aesthetic ideas without looking briefly at some of the work he did after 1934. In the anthology *Confucius to Cummings* (1964), it is evident that he has modified some earlier judgments; Sophocles, for example, is elevated to a new position in the gallery of masters.[23] But it is also evident that the general principles of Pound's thoughts have changed hardly at all since *ABC of Reading*. He still thinks that "England's great, true, uneven epic is the series of Shakespeare's 'Histories,' as distinct from literary imitations,"[24] and his rough differentiation of genres remains what it has been for thirty years: "Some distinction among the various kinds of poetry may eliminate gross miscomprehension. Lyric and epic have their own rights. If you define an epic as a 'poem including history' you admit elements improper to brief emotional utterance. Drama differs from poetry made to be sung or spoken by one person in that it is a text to be used in combination with human beings or puppets in action, gesticulating or quiet. The verbal manifest is not the whole show but can be or usually needs to be completed by movement and interplay."[25]

As with his social thought, then, Pound's technical and formal criticism can be seen as a complex of dialectical relations between kinds of time and timelessness. In his early imagist writings he controverted a traditional principle—that the verbal medium is necessarily subjugated by the temporal dimension—by trying to show that certain ways of handling the medium enable it to give at least the impression of timelessness. Thereafter he refined the general idea of imagist concentration and impact by analyzing poetry into three components—each of which, by charging language to the utmost degree, is capable of transcending temporal and spatial limits. But if poetry of a certain sort contains history, then it must bear some conditional relation to its own times and move with or against the zeitgeist. Such poetry may be said to express its time, just as all poetry expresses the character of its maker at a given time. It remains now for us to see how in his own poems Pound has realized his cultural and critical thought, which moves back and forth between temporal circumstances and timeless values.

Notes

1. In Ezra Pound, *Literary Essays* (1954), p. 4.
2. T. S. Eliot, "The Perfect Critic," in *The Sacred Wood* (1920), p. 11.
3. In Ezra Pound, *Collected Shorter Poems* (1949), p. 119.
4. Ezra Pound, "How I Began," *T. P.'s Weekly*, 6 June 1913, p. 707; reproduced in Noel Stock, ed., *Ezra Pound* (1965), p. 1.
5. Ezra Pound, *Gaudier-Brzeska* (1916), p. 87. The punctuation at the end of the first line of the Metro poem appears as a colon in some places and a semicolon in others. For remarks on the idiosyncratic spacings in the original publication of the poem in *Poetry*, see Hugh Kenner, *The Pound Era* (1971), p. 197.
6. Pound, *Gaudier-Brzeska*, p. 87.
7. Ezra Pound, *The Spirit of Romance* (1910), p. 108.
8. For another examination of "In a Station of the Metro" as an example of Pound's aesthetic in action, see Hugh Witemeyer, *The Poetry of Ezra Pound* (1969), pp. 35–53.
9. William Carlos Williams echoes Pound: "I would say that poetry is language charged with emotion." William Carlos Williams, *Paterson* (1950), p. 261.
10. Pound, *Ltrs*, p. 210.
11. See above, p. 81. The metamorphosis can move from the objective thing in two possible directions: toward the inward subjective world or toward the divine permanent world. At times Pound seems to consider these two modes of metamorphosis—internalization and deification—as essentially a single phenomenon. His catechism, "Religio, or The Child's Guide to Knowledge," begins: "What is a god? A god is an eternal state of mind." Ezra Pound, *Pavannes and Divisions* (1918), p. 23. I return to this point when I discuss Pound's poetry.
12. "Phanopoeia" and "logopoeia" seem to be Pound's coinages, on analogy with "melopoeia," which is not his invention. In a letter of 17 March 1917 from Pound to Joyce, "Phanopoeia" is mentioned as the possible title of a long poem (clearly *The Cantos*); a suite of poems so titled (not *The Cantos*) appeared in the *Little Review* in November 1918. See Forrest Read, ed., *Pound/Joyce* (1965), p. 102. Pound uses "melopoeia" in the review "Swinburne versus Biographers," *Poetry* 11 (March 1918): 328; in the same month the triad "melopoeia," "imagism," and "logopoeia" appears in Ezra Pound, "A List of Books," *Little Review* 4 (March 1918): 57.
13. Ezra Pound, *Translations* (1953), p. 23. The Introduction to *Cavalcanti Poems* is dated November 1910. The association of word with intellect and rhythm with emotion contains the germ of two later ideas: the "intellectual and emotional complex" in the definition of "image" and the operations of melopoeia and logopoeia. Another early idea that is important here is what Pound called the "method of Luminous Detail," according to which "certain facts give one a sudden insight into circumjacent conditions." "I Gather the Limbs of Osiris, Part 2," *New Age* 10 (7 December 1911): 130.
14. Pound, *Translations*, pp. 23–24.
15. "Ghosts move about me / Patched with histories"; "And the place is full of spirits"; "Gods float in the azure air." Ezra Pound, "Three Cantos, 1," *Poetry* 10 (June 1917: 114, 116, 118.
16. Pound, "List of Books," p. 57.
17. Pound, "Concava Vallis," part 3 of "Phanopoeia," in *CSP*, p. 188. The poem first appeared, with its title in Greek script, in *Little Review* 5 (November 1918).
18. An attempt to align melopoeia, phanopoeia, and logopoeia with Aristotle's *melos, opsis,* and *lexis* is made by Northrop Frye in his *Anatomy of Criticism* (1957), p. 244. This is an engaging and suggestive comparison, but it does not do full justice to the subtleties of Pound's thought. *Melos* and *opsis*—musical accompaniment and scenery (spectacle)—are for Aristotle relatively unimportant formal elements of dramatic poetry, inferior to *lexis* (diction), which, in turn, is subordinate to thought, character, and plot. Pound's theory of the poetic charging of language, concerned almost exclusively with *lexis*, shows the working of words to be somewhat more complicated than the one-to-one relation between words and things assumed by Aristotle. Pound elucidates forms of poetry in which the musical-emotional or visual-

visionary impact of language—far from being simply an added attraction to fortify the intellectual content of a given word—is of paramount importance.
19. Ezra Pound, *ABC of Reading* (1934), pp. 73, 193.
20. Verbs are called *Zeitwörter* in German.
21. Ezra Pound, *Jefferson and/or Mussolini* (1935), p. 22. The distinction between noun and verb in terms of time is at least as old as Aristotle, *Poetics* 20. 1457ª 10–19. Evidently, Pound is suggesting that "verbum caro factum est" equals "*verb* made flesh."
22. The essay first appeared in Ezra Pound, *Make It New* (1934), but Pound says it should be dated 1910–31 (Pound, *LE*, p. 149). The crux under discussion is the phrase "E 'l piacimento / che 'l fa dire amare" (Pound, *LE*, p. 164), which Pound ultimately translated "or delight whereby 'tis called 'to love'" (Ezra Pound, *The Cantos* 1970, p. 177). But in an earlier version, which is the subject of the paragraphs quoted from the essay, he had produced a fantastic line: "What his placation; why he is in verb" (Pound, *LE*, p. 155; Pound, *CSP*, p. 265).
23. Ezra Pound and Marcella Spann, eds., *Confucius to Cummings: An Anthology of Poetry* (1964), p. xi.
24. Ibid., p. 171. (Pound's remarks are clearly indicated as his and not the other editor's.)
25. Ibid., p. 322.

LEWIS HYDE

From "Ezra Pound and the Fate of Vegetable Money"
The Gift:
Imagination and the Erotic Life of Property
1983, pp. 216–72

I. Scattered Light

"The images of the gods," wrote Ezra Pound, ". . . move the soul to contemplation and preserve the tradition of the undivided light." But those who turn to face either the poetry or the political economy of Ezra Pound will find no such light to guide them there. Something has scattered it in all directions, and it is this scattering to which we shall have to address ourselves if we are to speak of Pound.

Born in 1885, seven years before Whitman died, Pound grew up in the vicinity of Philadelphia, where his father was an assayer at the U.S. Mint. He attended the University of Pennsylvania and, briefly, Hamilton College in upstate New York. After graduation, Pound taught at Wabash College in Indiana, but not for long: his landlady one morning discovered an "actress" in his rooms and reported the discovery to the college authorities. They suggested that he marry the girl or leave. He left. He left the country, in fact, and but for two brief visits did not return until the end of the Second World War, when the U.S. government flew him home to charge him with treason for having taken the side, vocally, of the Axis powers during the war.

During the course of his long career (he did not die until 1972) Ezra Pound came to promulgate an elaborate economic theory and to write, among many other things, an 800-page sequence of poems, the *Cantos*. In order to describe the work and fate of this poet we could tell either of these stories, the one about art or the one about politics. It is the politics that will receive most of our attention here, but by that emphasis we shall not be slighting the poetry entirely, for in telling one story we will be giving at least an outline of the other. They have the same plot, it seems to me: the playing out of an opposition in Pound's own temperament between forces of fertility and forces of order, or, to use slightly different terms, between two powers of the soul, imagination and will. Several people have made this point, but I think Clark Emery was the first, putting it in the language that Pound himself might have used: "One of the tensions [in the *Cantos*] . . . is the effort to bring together the Eleusinian (or Dionysian) concept of natural fecundity and the Confucian concept of human order. . . . Without Eleusinian energy civilizations would not rise, without Kungian order they dissipate themselves. Civilization occurs and maintains itself when the two forces—the striving and the ordering—approach equipoise."

"Before sewing one must cut," the proverb says, and to begin our tale we must cut the pattern of these two forces, beginning with Eleusinian fecundity.

Pound referred broadly to all polytheistic religions as "pagan," and when he speaks of them he tends to speak of mystery, fertility, and procreation. His 1939 statement, "Religio," reads:

> Paganism included a certain attitude toward, a certain understanding of, coitus, which is the mysterium.
>
> The other rites are the festivals of fecundity of the grain and the sun festivals, without revival of which religion can not return to the hearts of the people.

A decade earlier he had written that "at the root of any mystery" lies what we now call "consciousness of the unity of nature." The point is simple: nature's fecundity depends upon its unity, and we shall not long enjoy the fruits of that fecundity if we cannot perceive the unity. The rituals of ancient mysteries were directed toward the apprehension (and therefore the preservation) of this unity.

Pound is after something even broader than the fertility of the crops when he speaks of mystery, however. In a prose text he once described how a man can become "suddenly conscious of the reality of the *nous*, of mind, apart from any man's individual mind, of the sea crystalline and enduring, of the bright . . . molten glass that envelops us, full of light." When Pound speaks of Eleusinian mysteries, he is speaking not only of the wheat whose recurrence bespeaks the fecundity of nature but also of this light that bespeaks the fecundity of the mind. Twitted once by Eliot to reveal his religious beliefs, Pound (after sending us to Confucius and Ovid) wrote: "I believe that a light from Eleusis persisted throughout the middle ages and set beauty in the song of Provence and of Italy." This "undivided light" occasions beauty in art, and vice versa—that is, beauty in art sets, or awakens, the knowledge of this light in the mind of man.

Over and over in essays and in the *Cantos*, Pound tries to make it clear that fecundity can be destroyed by any dividing or splitting of the unity; in art and spiritual life the destructive force is a certain kind of abstraction.

> We find two forces in history: one that divides . . . and one that contemplates the unity of the mystery. . . . There is the force that destroys every clearly delineated symbol, dragging man into a maze of abstract arguments, destroying not one but every religion.

Before we go any further, I want to point out that this line of thought is of a piece with the central tenets of Imagism, that literary movement to which Pound's name will be forever linked. "Go in fear of abstractions" was the cardinal Imagist injunction according to Pound's own 1913 manifesto. "Don't use such an expression as 'dim lands of peace.' It dulls the image. It mixes an abstraction with the concrete." Pound was drawn to the study of Chinese written characters partly because they are image-writing, concrete speech. Pictograms "[have] to stay poetic," he says, because their form itself prohibits the

"maze" of abstractions that destroy the unity. He explains in the *ABC of Reading*:

> In Europe, if you ask a man to define anything, his definition always moves away from the simple things that he knows perfectly well, it recedes into an unknown region, that is a region of remoter and progressively remoter abstractions.
>
> Thus if you ask him what red is, he says it is a 'colour.'
>
> If you ask him what a colour is, he tells you it is a vibration or a refraction of light, or a division of the spectrum.
>
> And if you ask him what vibration is, he tells you it is a mode of energy, or something of that sort, until you arrive at a modality of being, or non-being, or at any rate you get in beyond your depth, and beyond his depth. . . .
>
> But when the Chinaman wanted to make a picture of . . . a general idea, how did he go about it? He is to define red. How can he do it in a picture that isn't painted in red paint?
>
> He puts . . . together the abbreviated pictures of
>
> | ROSE | CHERRY |
> |------|--------|
> | IRON RUST | FLAMINGO |

Ezra Pound was essentially a religious poet. His cautions against abstraction in art serve the spiritual ends of the work; they are not merely advice on style. An Italian country priest once turned a corner of the temple of St. Francis in Rimini—the temple erected by that hero of the *Cantos*, Sigismondo Malatesta—to find the poet bowing to the stone elephants carved in the side of the building rather than to the "altar furniture." Pound was an idolater in the old sense: he put himself in the service of images. One of the most remarkable things about the *Cantos* is Pound's ability to convey a sense of the undivided light in concrete speech:

> rain beat as with colour of feldspar
> in the gloom, the gold gathers the light against it
> with a sky wet as ocean / flowing with liquid slate
>   Such light is in sea-caves
> e la bella Ciprigna
>   where copper throws back the flame
> from pinned eyes, the flames rise to fade
>   in green air.

And in old age:

> When one's friends hate each other
>   how can there be peace in the world?
> Their asperities diverted me in my green time.
> A blown husk that is finished
>   but the light sings eternal
> a pale flare over marshes
>   where the salt hay whispers to tide's change. . . .

While teaching in Indiana, long before he had discovered Chinese written characters, Pound wrote to William Carlos Williams: "I am interested in art and ecstasy, ecstasy which I would define as the sensation of the soul in ascent, art as the expression and sole means . . . of passing on that ecstasy to others." In an essay on the art of fiction Flannery O'Connor once wrote that "the world of the fiction writer is full of matter"; fiction is an "incarnational art," she says, full of "those concrete details of life that make actual the mystery of our position on earth." I imagine Pound would have broadened the stroke: all art is incarnational, full of matter, and for the same reason, to make actual the mystery. Pound is right: some knowledge cannot survive abstraction, and to preserve this knowledge we must have art. The liquid light, the *nous*, the fecundity of nature, the feeling of the soul in ascent—only the imagination can articulate our apprehension of these things, and the imagination speaks to us in images.

Confucius (or Kung Fu Tseu, as Pound usually has it) first appears in Canto 13. For the question of "Kungian order" the important lines are these:

> And Kung said, and wrote on the bo leaves:
>   If a man have not order within him
> He can not spread order about him;
> And if a man have not order within him
> His family will not act with due order;
>   And if the prince have not order within him
> He can not put order in his dominions.

"The principle of good is enunciated by Confucius," Pound had explained in his magazine, *The Exile*. "It consists in establishing order within oneself. This order or harmony spreads by a sort of contagion without specific effort. The principle of evil consists in messing into other people's affairs."

Clark Emery speaks of a "tension" in the *Cantos* between Eleusinian fecundity and Confucian order, but I am not sure it is immediately apparent why any such tension should exist. Fecundity is not without order. Order inheres in all that is fertile in nature, and the liquid light of the *nous*, Pound tells us, induces order in those who perceive it.

> This liquid is certainly a
>   property of the mind
> nec accidens est   but an element
>   in the mind's make-up . . .
>   Hast 'ou seen the rose in the steel dust
>   (or swansdown ever?)
> so light is the urging, so ordered the dark petals of
>   iron
> we who have passed over Lethe.

In art and in human affairs there is a force corresponding to that which has given swansdown its beauty, and that force is *virtù* ("in the light of light is the *virtù*," says the same Canto). Just as electromagnetism induces order in a pile of iron filings, so *virtù* induces order in the works of man. And like the magnet, or so the image leads us to believe, this *virtù* creates order by its presence alone, "by a sort of contagion without specific effort."

At this point, however, we come to a slight disparity in Pound's idea of order. There is a strange phrase in his prose writings—strange, at least, if we set it beside this other one about "contagion"—and that phrase is "the will toward order." *Virtù* is not the same thing as willpower, but for Pound it is the will that directs the force of *virtù* and in the last analysis, therefore, it is the will that is the agent of order. In the context from which I have taken the phrase, "the will toward order" refers to social order and to the men through whose will societies have developed and maintained their structures. But willpower plays a role in Pound's aesthetic as well: "The greater the artist the more permanent his creation, and this is a matter of WILL," he writes, a sentence that belongs beside Clark Emery's explication: "Without Eleusinian energy civilizations would not rise, without Kungian order they dissipate themselves." I am not, at this point, trying to address the validity of these ideas. I am only trying to point out that, for Pound, Confucian order is associated with two things, willpower and durability. The will is the agent of the forces of order, and durability is the consequence of its agency.

We shall have more to say of political will in a later section of this chapter; at this point I want to offer a few remarks on the role of will power in art. There are at least two phases in the completion of a work of art, one in which the will is suspended and another in which it is active. The suspension is primary. It is when the will is slack that we feel moved or we are struck by an event, intuition, or image. The *materia* must begin to flow before it can be worked, and not only is the will powerless to initiate that flow, but it actually seems to interfere, for artists have traditionally used devices—drugs, fasting, trances, sleep deprivation, dancing—to suspend the will so that something "other" will come forward. When the material finally appears, it is usually in a jumble, personally moving, perhaps, but not much use to someone else—not, at any rate, a work of art. There are exceptions, but the initial formulation of a work is rarely satisfactory—satisfactory, I mean, to the imagination itself, for, like a person who must struggle to say what he means, the imagination stutters toward the clear articulation of its feeling. The will has the power to carry the material back to the imagination and contain it there while it is re-formed. The will does not create the "germinating image" of a work, nor does it give the work its form, but it does provide the energy and the directed attention called for by a dialogue with the imagination.

Artists might be classified by the different weight given to these two phases of the work. Whitman or a prose writer like Jack Kerouac fall on the suspend-the-will side of the spectrum. Whitman begins to work by lolling on the grass. Kerouac's "Belief & Technique for Modern Prose"—a list of thirty aphorisms—includes the following:

· Submissive to everything, open listening
· Something that you feel will find its own form
· Be crazy dumbsaint of the mind
· No time for poetry by exactly what is
· In tranced fixation dreaming upon object before you
· Composing wild, undisciplined, pure, coming in from under, crazier the better.

All these and one more—"Don't think of words when you stop but to see picture better"—amount to an aesthetic of the imagination without the will, the "spontaneous bop prosody" of accepting the image as it comes. (Yeats's trance writing would be another example, the one, in fact, that Kerouac credits as his model.) "Never revise" was Kerouac's rule; he used to claim that he wrote the first draft of *On the Road* on a roll of teletype paper in a single two-week sitting, sniffing Benzedrine inhalers as he typed. Such writing is both more original and more chaotic than writing with a larger admixture of will. It is more personal and more of the moment. At its best it strengthens the imagination through trusting its primary speech and conveys that trust to the reader, along with the "crazy" energy that comes from unqualified transcription of image and experience, that is, from taking everything bestowed upon perception as holy.

A writer with greater trust in the will works the text, turning the plasm of the moment into more durable gems. Such work has the virtues that come of revision—precision, restraint, intellectual consistency, density of images, coherence, and so forth. For a certain kind of author, Pound is correct, I think, to connect the presence of the will to the durability of the creation. Yeats, for example, may have cultivated his "spooks" and written in trances, but unlike Kerouac, he educated the will. He worked at his craft; he refined what the imagination gave him.

I have gone into the issue of willpower a little because it is through this particular element in Pound's Confucian side that we can come to understand the tension between fecundity and order. Pound's work displays a curious incongruity: it is framed by clear declarations of erotic and spiritual ends which it does not achieve. There are moments of remarkable light in the *Cantos*, yes, but taken as a whole the poem scatters the very unity it set out to preserve (and the last lines of the last Canto read: "Let those I love try to forgive / what I have made"). Pound's work is acerbic, impatient, argumentative, obsessed, and disappointed. The young man had written that he was "interested in art and ecstasy," but the poem he came to write does not convey "the feeling of a soul in ascent"; it conveys the feeling of a soul in torment.

Pound's tone of voice in his prose writings offers a way to approach this incongruity. His shortness with something called "stupidity" seems particularly telling. The tone of voice of the man who wrote the *ABC of Reading*, for example, is that of a schoolmaster irritated by the ignorance of his pupils. The reader who approaches the book with sympathy begins to feel either like the dunce receiving the lecture or like the peeved schoolmaster set above the class. Either way, the sympathy is betrayed, the self divided. Eliot once asked Pound to write an explanation of Silvio Gesell's economic ideas for *The Criterion*. Pound handed in his usual complaint about the thickheadedness of his audience. Said Eliot to Pound, "I asked you to write an article which would explain this subject to people who had never heard it; yet you write as if your readers knew about it already, but had failed to understand it."

If we ⟨examine⟩ Whitman for a moment, we may be able to triangulate the irritability these examples reveal. We have seen Pound's "Religio"; Whitman's is found in the original preface to *Leaves of Grass*:

> This is what you shall do: Love the earth and sun and the animals, despise riches, give alms to every one that asks, stand up for the stupid and crazy . . . , argue not concerning God, have patience and indulgence toward the people . . . , go freely with powerful uneducated persons and with the young and with the mothers of families . . . , dismiss whatever insults your own soul, and your very flesh shall be a great poem and have the richest fluency not only in its words but in the silent lines of its lips and face and between the lashes of your eyes and in every motion and joint of your body. . . .

Contrast this passage with lines from the opening paragraph of Pound's *Guide to Kulchur*: "In attacking a doctrine, a doxy, a form of stupidity, it might be remembered that one isn't of necessity attacking the man . . . to whom the doctrine is attributed or on whom it is blamed. One may quite well be fighting the same idiocy that he fought and where into his followers have reslumped from laziness, from idiocy. . . ." The point may be well taken, but mark the underlying assumption, to wit, that culture will only stand up if we fight stupidity, idiocy and laziness, as if culture were a slouching adolescent being sent to a military academy in Pennsylvania.

I do not pretend that I can unravel the mare's nest of Pound's psychology in this one chapter, but I can proffer at least one intuition: what Pound is calling "stupidity" and "idiocy" and "laziness" should be associated with the erotic and, therefore, with the Eleusinian side of his temperament. As Whitman understood (and Pound, too, at times), one of the wellsprings of the creative spirit lies with "the stupid . . . crazy . . . uneducated" and idle. Fertility itself is dumb and lazy. Put it this way: unity—the unity of nature, or of "coitus . . . the mysterium," or of the *nous*—is unwilled and unreflective. If we assume, therefore, that the only smart thought is reflective thought and the only active person is the willful person, fecundity itself will soon seem tinged with idiocy and laziness.

It may seem odd, I realize, to speak of Pound's irritation—

or better, his frustration—with the erotic. But there it is. He has a clear sense of the value and power of that side of creative life, but he is also exasperated by its nature.

In seeking to reconcile this disparity, I found myself led into imagining a fable about Pound as a young poet. Was there a time, I wondered, when Pound himself has this experience of "the soul in ascent"? Was there a Poundian epiphany, like Whitman's or Ginsberg's or like the moment when the young Eliot, walking in Boston, saw the street and all its objects turn to light? Such moments are rare, given only once or twice in a lifetime, and yet they serve as a fountain for a life's work. Did Pound have one, and if he did, what happened afterwards?

In *Pavannes and Divagations* Pound paused to imagine how a myth might have come about, saying:

> The first myths when a man walked sheer into the "nonsense," that is to say, when some very vivid and undeniable adventure befell him, and he told someone else who called him a liar. Thereupon, after bitter experience, perceiving that no one could understand what he meant when he said that he "turned into a tree," he made a myth—a work of art that is,—an impersonal or objective story woven out of his own emotion, as the nearest equation that he was capable of putting into words. The story, perhaps, then gave rise to a weaker copy of his emotion in others, until there arose a cult, a company of people who could understand each other's nonsense about the gods.

Let us set this rumination beside the first poem in Pound's *Personae*:

THE TREE

I stood still and was a tree amid the wood,
Knowing the truth of things unseen before;
Of Daphne and the laurel bow
And that god-feasting couple old
That grew elm-oak amid the wold.
'Twas not until the gods had been
Kindly entreated, and been brought within
Unto the hearth of their heart's home
That they might do this wonder thing;
Nathless I have been a tree amid the wood
And many a new thing understood
That was rank folly to my head before.

Certainly, it does no violence to the spirit of the work for us to imagine that there was a time Pound felt himself "turned into a tree" (or more simply, when he felt moved to the core of his being by the mosaics in Santa Maria in Trastevere, or became suddenly conscious of the reality of the *nous*). Nor does it seem unlikely that, on feeling with his whole being the worth of his experience, he set out to labor in the service of that metamorphosis or that image or that light.

Then: some "bitter experience." They think he's a liar. He discovers, in some way not hard to imagine, that what moves him the most has no currency in his age and homeland. Worse, it is under attack from all sides, ignored, belittled, and devalued. Ginsberg tells of such a reaction to his Blake vision:

> I tried to evoke the sensations of the experience myself, artificially, by dancing around my apartment chanting a sort of homemade mantra: "Come, spirit. O spirit, spirit, come. Come spirit. O spirit, spirit, come." Something like that. There I was, in the dark, in an apartment in the middle of Harlem, whirling like a dervish and invoking powers.
>
> And everybody I tried to talk to about it thought I was crazy. Not just [my] psychiatrist. The two girls who lived next door. My father. My teachers. Even most of my friends.

Now in a society which was open and dedicated to spirit, like in India, my actions and my address would have been considered quite normal. Had I been transported to a street-corner potato-curry shop in Benares and begun acting that way, I would have been seen as in some special, holy sort of state and sent on my way to the burning grounds, to sit and meditate. And when I got home, I would have been like gently encouraged to express myself, to work it out, and then left alone.

That was 1948. Imagine Pound a half a century earlier! His moment of light would have come sometime before 1908. The turn of the century was hardly a time of great spiritual awakening in America. American mercantile expansion was at its height, running from China, where the Boxer Rebellion had just been put down, to a South America newly "freed" from Spain. A Rough Rider sat in the White House, and hardly a single great poet was alive and read on the American continent with the exception, I suppose, of Teddy Roosevelt's preferred bard, Edwin Arlington Robinson. I do not mean to ascribe all of Pound's bitterness to exterior sources, but even if his struggles are more aptly described as interior, we cannot say his countrymen offered him much solace.

In any event, I was led to imagine a Poundian epiphany such as this in order to fill the gap, to make sense of the odd combination of erotic intent and divisive tone that we find in the work. The little story in *Pavannes and Divagations* caught my eye because it speaks of the bitterness of lost worth and of a spiritual knowledge that could *not* be passed along. And although the faith in fertility can be seen in flashes, it is bitterness and disappointment that live on the surface of Ezra Pound's poetry.

Like Whitman, Pound knew very well that he had not been born into a world receptive to the spirit of his art.

> In meiner Heimat
>   where the dead walked
>   and the living were made of cardboard.

He never accepted the barrenness of his age, and there is no reason that he should have. But he never accepted, either, the limits of his ability to do anything about that barrenness. There is only so much that can be done to create fertile ground where none exists. Harmony may emanate from the unity of nature or the *nous* or the prince, but harmony cannot be imposed on those who are not ready to receive it. Electromagnetism may trace a rose in iron filings, but it is powerless to induce order into sawdust. The forces of fertility have no power in certain situations, and it is in Pound's response to that powerlessness, it seems to me, that we shall find the true roots of the tension between fecundity and order, imagination and will. Pound's notion that we slump into "stupidity" from "laziness" implies its opposite, that we shall overcome it through hard work. Where Whitman senses that the ends of art call for long periods of idleness, Pound imagines that they might be accomplished through discipline and exertion. He is like a man who, unable to grieve upon discovering that his wife no longer loves him, becomes more and more aggressive in the dumb belief that love could be forced back into existence. Pound's Confucian side is marked not only by willfulness, but by a willfulness exaggerated in direct proportion to his frustration with the powerlessness of the erotic.

We can see some of this in Pound's reading of history. In its barest formulation the idea of "Kungian order" seems like an anarchist ideal, order spread not by coercion but "by a sort of contagion." In practice, however, those who are drawn to Confucius usually end up working for the state government (or running it). The proverbial advice in China is that during the years when a man is a civil servant he should study Confucius; later, when he retires, he should study Buddhism. Why? It seems that when Confucius turned inward he discovered the "right order" of a state bureaucrat (or maybe it was the bureaucrats who discovered him; either way, there is a connection). When the anarchist speaks of an inner, natural, noncoercive order, he does not suddenly leap to: "If the prince has order within him he can put his dominions in order." He finds no prince at all, or at least not one with dominions to worry about. But Confucius did, and so did Ezra Pound.

The prince that Pound found within, we must note, was one who loved poetry. "And Kung said . . . ," a Canto tells us, " 'When the prince has gathered about him / All the savants and artists, his riches will be fully employed.' " There was nothing in either history or politics that attracted Pound more than a ruler who liked art. He loved a "boss" who'd been to the mysteries, from Odysseus down to the Renaissance rulers (Malatesta, the Estes, the Medicis), from Jefferson—who first appears in Canto 21 with a letter asking a friend to find him a gardener who plays the French horn—to Napoleon, who gets a bow in Canto 43 for supposedly having said:

> "Artists high rank, in fact sole social summits
> which the tempest of politics can not reach."

And from Napoleon to Mussolini: "The Duce and Kung Fu Tseu equally perceive that their people need poetry. . . ."

But these are not just strong men. With the exception of Jefferson, they are also bullies. One cannot talk of these "princes" without talking of their overweening will. In the *Odyssey* Odysseus is plagued not by Trojans, after all, but by sleep, forgetfulness, animals, reveries, and women. He deals with these through violence, power, cunning, lies, seduction, and bravado. He whips his men who want to stay with the lotus-eaters; he takes Circe to bed at the point of a sword. When he gets home, he begins to pull his affairs in order by murdering all the servant girls who've been sleeping with the suitors. He's the Mussolini of the ancient world.

To give Pound his due, we must add that although his heroes are men of the developed will, he goes to some lengths to distinguish good will from bad. When he tells us that "the greater the artist the more permanent his creations, and this is a matter of WILL," he does add that "it is also a matter of the DIRECTION OF THE WILL. . . ." Good will lifts us up and bad will pulls us down. And Pound took his heroes to be men of good will. "Perhaps," remarks Emery, "it does not oversimplify to say that [in the *Cantos*] good and evil are a matter of *directio voluntatis*, with money-power . . . representing the most powerful leverage for evil will."

The problem with this dichotomy is that it omits another form of evil: the use of the will when the will is of no use. Such evil is usually invisible to a willful man. Good will can fight bad will, but only in those cases where will is called for in the first place. At times when the will should be suspended, whether it is good or bad is irrelevant. Or to put it more strongly: at such times all will, no matter its direction, is bad will. For when the will dominates, there is no gap through which grace may enter, no break in the ordered stride for error to escape, no way by which a barren prince may receive the *virtù* of his people, and for an artist, no moment of receptiveness when the engendering images may come forward.

Any artist who develops the will risks its hegemony. If he is at all wary of that sympathy by which we become receptive to things beyond the self, he may not encourage the will to abandon its position when its powers are exhausted. Willpower has a tendency to usurp the functions of imagination, particularly in a man in a patriarchy. Yeats's shopworn formula—

that "rhetoric is the will doing the work of the imagination"—refers to such a state, for when the will works in isolation, it turns of necessity to dictionary studies, syntactical tricks, intellectual formulae, memory, history, and convention—any source of material, that is, which can imitate the fruits of imagination without actually allowing them to emerge. Just as there are limits to the power of the erotic, so there are limits to the power of the will. The will knows about survival and endurance; it can direct attention and energy; it can finish things. But we cannot remember a tune or a dream on willpower. We cannot stay awake on willpower. Will may direct *virtù* but it cannot bring it into the world. The will by itself cannot heal the soul. And it cannot create.

Pound seems to have felt deeply the limits of the erotic, but I'm not so sure he felt the limits of willpower. Long portions of the *Cantos*—particularly those written in the decade 1935–45—are rhetorical in Yeats's sense. The voice is full of opinion without erotic heat, like an old pensioner chewing his disappointed politics in a barbershop. The history cantos, in particular—all the material about China and the long portrait of John Adams—are deadly dull, never informed with the fire, complexity, or surprise that are the mark of living images. They are 2 percent poetry and 98 percent complaint, obsession, and cant theory, what Whitman called "talk." Working out of "good will" alone, the poem becomes mired in time, argument, and explanation, forgetting the atemporal mystery it set out to protect.

> I don't receive a shilling a month, wrote Mr Adams
>   to Abigail
>   in seventeen 74
> June 7th. approve of committee from the several
>   colonies
> Bowdoin, Cushing, Sam Adams, John A. and Paine
>   (Robert)
> 'mope, I muse, I ruminate' *le*
> *personnel manque* we have not men for the times
> Cut the overhead my dear wife and keep yr / eye on
>   the dairy
> non importation, non eating, non export, all bug-
>   wash
> but until they have proved it
>   in experiment
> no use in telling 'em.
> Local legislation / that is basic /
>   we wd. consent in matters of empire trade, It
>   is
> by no means essential to trade with foreign nations at
>   all
>   as sez Chas Francis, China and Japan have
>   proved it. . . .

Etcetera, etcetera. The talk goes on for two hundred pages before we come to real poetry again in the "Pisan Cantos."

And where were the "Pisan Cantos" written? Pound stayed in Italy during the Second World War, making radio broadcasts denouncing the Allies; when the war was over, the U.S. Army captured him and locked him up in an army jail near Pisa. They treated him horribly: they kept him outdoors in a wire-mesh cage with the lights on; they allowed no one to speak with him. He had a breakdown. In short, they broke his will. He was forced to walk backwards, out of pride into sympathy. "The ant's a centaur in his dragon world. / Pull down thy vanity. . . ." He was shoved toward an inner life again, out of his mechanical opinions, and the poems return to poetry for a while.

II. Durable Treasure

Pound once wrote to Louis Zukofsky: "My poetry and my econ are NOT separate or opposed. Essential unity." To illustrate the connection and by so doing to move into the economics, I want to retell some old anecdotes about Pound and his fellow modernists. No one seems to deny that Ezra Pound could be arrogant and autocratic at times, but we have several remarkable testimonies to a gentler side of his personality as well. All of them bespeak a connection between art and generosity.

T. S. Eliot took a boat to London shortly before the First World War. He was working on a doctoral thesis. He had written some poems, most of which had been lying in a drawer for several years. Pound read them. "It is such a comfort," he wrote to Harriet Monroe, "to meet a man and not have to tell him to wash his face, wipe his feet, and remember the date (1914) on the calendar." He sent "Prufrock" to *Poetry* magazine and midwifed it into print, refusing to let Monroe change it, refusing even to give her Eliot's address so she might, as he put it, "insult" him through the mails with suggested alterations.

In 1921 Eliot left the manuscript of *The Waste Land* with Pound, and Pound went through it with his red pencil. He thought it was a masterpiece. And why should its author not go on writing such masterpieces? Well, he was working as a clerk in Lloyd's Bank in London and didn't have time. Pound decided to free him. He organized a subscription plan called "Bel Esprit." The idea was to find thirty people who could chip in fifty dollars each to help support Eliot. Pound chipped in, as did Hemingway, Richard Aldington, and others. Pound threw himself into it, hammering the typewriter, printing up a circular, sending out a stream of letters. (In the end, not enough subscribers were found and Eliot was embarrassed by the show. The publicity may have helped to draw the $2,000 *Dial* prize to him in 1922, however.)

A quarter of a century later Eliot wrote a portrait of his sponsor:

> No one could have been kinder to younger men, or to writers who . . . seemed to him worthy and unrecognized. No poet, furthermore, was, without self-depreciation, more unassuming about his own achievement in poetry. The arrogance which some people have found in him, is really something else; and whatever it is, it has not expressed itself in an undue emphasis or the value of his own poems.
>
> He liked to be the impresario for younger men, as well as the animator of artistic activity in any milieu in which he found himself. In this role he would go to any lengths to generosity and kindness; from inviting constantly to dinner a struggling author whom he suspected of being under-fed, or giving away clothing (though his shoes and underwear were almost the only garments which resembled those of other men sufficiently to be worn by them), to trying to find jobs, collect subsidies, get work published and then get it criticised and praised.

When W. B. Yeats showed Pound one of James Joyce's poems, Pound wrote to Joyce, then living in Italy, and before long he'd reviewed *Dubliners* and arranged for *The Egoist* to print *A Portrait of the Artist*, both serially and in book form. Joyce had earned his keep in Italy by teaching English, and he tried to do the same when he later moved to Zurich with his wife and children. By then he was writing *Ulysses*. Pound's efforts to place the art at the center of Joyce's labors were unflagging. He prevailed upon Yeats to squeeze £75 out of the Royal Literary Fund for Joyce, and he mailed him £25 of his own money as well, saying it came from an anonymous donor. He got the Society of Authors to send Joyce £2 a week for three months.

When the two men finally met in Paris, Joyce arrived thin as a rail, wearing a long overcoat and tennis shoes. Pound, on his return to London, sent a package back across the Channel which, when Joyce finally untangled its string cocoon, revealed a collection of used clothes and a pair of old brown shoes.

Finally, as Wyndham Lewis tells it,

Ezra Pound "sold" the idea of Joyce to Miss Harriet Weaver. Subsequently that lady set aside a capital sum, variously computed but enough to change him overnight from a penniless Berlitz teacher into a modest rentier; sufficiently for him to live comfortably in Paris, write *Ulysses*, have his eyes regularly treated and so forth. These *rentes* were his—I know nothing beyond that—until he had become a very famous person: and the magician in this Arabian Nights' Tale was undoubtedly Ezra.

There are other stories with similar plots—Hemingway, Frost, Blunt, Cummings, Zukofsky, and others. In 1927 the $2,000 *Dial* award went to Pound himself. He invested the money (or put it in the bank) at 5 percent and gave away the interest. He sent some of the money to John Cournos, writing: "Investment of Dial prize is due to yield about one hundred bucks per annum. The first 100 has already gone, discounted in three lots, one ten guinea s.o.s. earlier this week. . . . I think you better regard the enclosed as advance payment for something to be written for *Exile*, when the skies are clearer." Pound's magazine, *The Exile*, was itself a fruit of this award.

Wealth that came to Pound left him in the service of art. As Hemingway wrote in a little "Homage to Ezra":

We have Pound . . . devoting, say, one fifth of his time to poetry. With the rest of his time he tries to advance the fortunes, both material and artistic, of his friends. He defends them when they are attacked, he gets them into magazines and out of jail. He loans them money. He sells their pictures. He arranges concerts for them. He writes articles about them. He introduces them to wealthy women. He gets publishers to take their books. He sits up all night with them when they claim to be dying and he witnesses their wills. He advances them hospital expenses and dissuades them from suicide.

No one failed to mention this part of Pound's spirit. It is a cornerstone of his way of being. Each anecdote has a simple structure: from the "Bel Esprit" to the old brown shoes we have a man who responds with generosity when he is moved by art. True worth, for such a person, inheres in the creative spirit, and the objects of the world should move accordingly, not to some other, illusory value. Pound's essay "What Is Money For?" begins with its own answer: money is "for getting the country's food and goods justly distributed." The title could as well have been "Why Have No Proper Shoes Been Distributed to James Joyce?" In approaching Pound's economic theories, it seems to me that our work will be most fruitful if we use these anecdotes as a backdrop, if we see his work as an attempt to find a political economy that would embody the spirit they reveal. Pound sought a "money system" that might replicate, or at least support, the form of value that emanates from creative life. He cared for neither Marxism nor bourgeois materialism because, he felt, neither held a place for the artist. He was attracted to the theories of an Englishman—Major C. H. Douglas—because Douglas was one of the first, according to Pound, "to postulate a place for the arts, literature, and the amenities in a system of economics." During the 1930s Pound printed his economic ideas in a series of "Money Pamphlets"; in one of them he describes two different kinds of bank—one in Siena and one in Genoa—the first built "for beneficence"

and the second "to prey on the people." The last line of his analysis reads: "The arts did not flourish in Genoa, she took almost no part in the intellectual activity of the renaissance. Cities a tenth her size have left more durable treasure."

The point for the moment is not that Pound was either right or wrong about the Bank of Siena or about Major Douglas, but simply that Pound's money theories, at least at the start, were addressed to the situation of the artist and the liveliness of culture. Something had happened after the Renaissance, he felt, that ate away at art and made it less likely that an artist would have a decent pair of shoes. ⟨. . .⟩

We may address ourselves to Imagism in slightly different terms now. If, in turning toward the imagination, you begin with Pound's demand for concrete speech (and with the spiritual ends of that demand), or if you begin with William Carlos Williams's "no ideas but in things," or with T. S. Eliot's "objective correlative," and if the date on the calendar is 1914, you are in a fix. For when all exterior objects can be sold at will, when usury has found a home even in the family food and clothing, then the objects of the outer world can no longer carry the full range of emotional and spiritual life. Feeling and spirit mysteriously drain away when the imagination tries to embody them in commodities. Certainly this is part of the melancholy in those poems of Eliot's in which men and women are surrounded by coffee spoons and cigarettes but cannot speak to one another. *The Waste Land* could be a gloss on Marx's declaration that "the only comprehensible language which we can speak to each other . . . is not that of ourselves, but only that of our commodities and their mutual relations." The imagination senses that packs of cigarettes or cafeteria trays are not emanation of *eros*. Some spirit other than the creative spirit attended to their manufacture. There is a line of modern poets who have continued to work with such materials, accepting (or not feeling) the limited amount of emotional and spiritual life in the poem. But another group of modern poets—and Eliot and Pound belong here—admitted the tension of lost life to their writing, allowing the missing vitality to disturb the surface of the poem. And some of these artists turned outward, drawn toward those ideologies that promised to limit the domain of the commodity. They undertook, in short, the redemption of the imagination, and their task led them, willy-nilly, into politics. Poets as disparate in temperament as Pound, Neruda and Vallejo all began with a strong pull toward "thinking in images"; all found themselves brought up short, and all turned toward politics. ⟨. . .⟩

III. The Jew in the Hedge

Don't shoot him, don't shoot him, don't shoot the President. Assassins deserve worse, but don't shoot him. Assassination only makes more murderers. . . . Don't shoot him, diagnose him, diagnose him. (Ezra Pound, in a radio broadcast from Rome, February 18, 1943)

It is difficult to speak directly of Ezra Pound's economic ideas. He was a man who rarely uttered a simple "2 + 2 = 4." He would say, instead, "2 + 2 = 4, as anyone can see who isn't a ninny completely ballyhooed by the gombeen-men and hyper-kikes who CHOKE UP the maze of Jew-governed radio transmissions." The specifics of his argument emerge with a tag line, a challenge or a baiting remark, and we must speak of both—both the substance and the style—if we are to speak at all. ⟨. . .⟩

To approach the crazy side of Pound's economics, we may begin by looking for those places in his presentation where the tone suddenly slips, where his voice becomes unaccountably shrill. Pound constantly addresses himself to money, for example, but it is the Jew as moneylender who comes in for the strange twists of phrase and affect. Pound could write an entire Money Pamphlet with sufficient cogent ideas to make his argument discussable, but then on the last page suddenly say that "the Jewspapers and worse than Jewspapers" have been hiding the facts from the public.

If we list the topics that come to us with this fishy smell we find the following: stupid and ignorant people, lazy people, the Americans and the English, the Allied leaders (Roosevelt and Churchill in particular, American presidents in general), usurers, monetary criminals, the Jews, and, to a lesser extent, the Protestants. The elements in this list are all connected to one another in Pound's cosmology: the lazy are ignorant; the ignorant are usually Americans; the Americans elect "their sewage" (the best example being Roosevelt, whom Pound thought of as a Jew, calling him "Jews-feldt," "stinkie Roosen-stein," etc.); England hasn't been the same since they let in the Jew, who, of course, is the best example of the usurer and the monetary criminal. We are not dealing with discrete elements here, we're dealing with a lump. If we speak of any part of the lump, we will be well on our way to describing the whole. The part I shall focus on is the Jew as he appears in Pound's writing.

"Pound's Jew," as I would call this image, seems to me to be a version of the classical god Hermes. One of Pound's early poems invokes Mercury, the Roman counterpart to Hermes:

O God, O Venus, O Mercury, patron of thieves,
Give me in due time, I beseech you, a little tobacco-
    shop,
With the little bright boxes
        piled up neatly upon the shelves
And the loose fragrant cavendish
        and the shag,
And the bright Virginia
        loose under the bright glass cases,
And a pair of scales not too greasy,
And the whores dropping in for a word or two in
        passing,
For a flip word, and to tidy their hair a bit.
O God, O Venus, O Mercury, patron of thieves,
Lend me a little tobacco-shop,
        or install me in any profession
Save this damn'd profession of writing,
        where one needs one's brains all the time.

Hermes is a god of trade—of money and merchandise and the open road. I shall say more about him in a moment; for now we need only note that the poem says this deity could free the poet from some confinement. If Hermes were to answer the call—with a little shop, some dirty money, and cheap sex— Pound might be released from the troublesome burden of his profession. My position here is that Hermes did in fact respond to Pound's invocation, but that Pound backed off, refused his approach, and consigned the god to his own shadow.

In psychoanalytic terms, the "shadow" is the personifica-tion of those parts of the self that *could* be integrated into the ego but for one reason or another are not. Many people leave their feelings about death in the shadow, for example. They *could* be carried in the daylight self but are left unspoken. Random sexual desire remains in the shadow for most people. It could be acted upon openly or it could be acknowledged and dismissed (which still removes it from the shadow), but it isn't. What the ego needs but cannot accept the psyche will personify and either present in dreams or project onto someone in the outer world. These shadow figures then become objects of simultaneous fascination and disgust—a recurrent and trou-bling figure in dreams or someone in the neighborhood we don't like but can't stop talking about.

Pound began to become obsessed with the money ques-tion around 1915, so I take that to be the approximate date when Hermes answered his invocation. But, as I say, Pound backed off. Then, like any spurned deity, Hermes began to increase in power, taking on a more and more threatening aspect, until, by 1935, he had enough power to pull the ego from its pivot. By then Pound had projected this "destructive" figure from his own darker side onto the Jew. His image of the Jew has in fact little to do with Jews; it is, as we shall see, an almost verbatim description of the classical Hermes. ⟨. . .⟩

Hermes can't be trusted, of course. They say "he either guides the way or leads astray." If you are stuck, Hermes will get you into bed or sell you something or push you down the path, but after that there's no guarantee. In this way he is identified with intellect and invention. In a Hermetic mood we will make a hundred intellectual connections only to find, when we check them with a less restless god, that ninety-nine of them are useless.

Homer tells us that Zeus gave Hermes "an office . . . to establish deeds of barter amongst men throughout the fruitful earth," and he has done his job well. He may be the twentieth century's healthiest Greek god. He is present wherever things move quickly without regard to specific moral content, in all electronic communication, for example, or in the mails, in computers and in the stock exchange (especially in internation-al money markets).

Hermes will exchange gifts, but he is quite different from any god of the gift because his connections are made without concern for lasting affection. He isn't opposed to durable bonds, he just doesn't care. In a *strict* gift-consciousness, then, or in any consciousness with a high moral tone, Hermes will be forced into the background. If your god says, "Thou shalt not steal," Hermes will not leave (he's too tricky), but he will have to disguise himself. He'll turn his collar around and sell Bibles over the radio.

There are obvious connections between the mythology of Hermes and the European myth of the Jew. When the double law of Moses fell into disrepute, Christians identified them-selves with the first half of the law, the call to brotherhood, and remembered the Jews primarily for the second half, the permission to usure. When a "limit to generosity" was dropped from the collective attitude, it reappeared in the collective shadow as a tricky Jew, skilled in trade and not part of the group. Furthermore, ever since the Diaspora the Jew has been seen as the uprooted one, the wanderer and the stranger. Jews in Europe were taken to be a-local, able to live in a place without becoming identified with it. Jews have always been attacked, therefore, in times of local nationalism.[1]

Ezra Pound's image of the Jew is basically an elaboration of this mythology. First of all, for Pound the Jew was an international force, bearing allegiance to no particular country and therefore destructive to all. Pound tells the English, for example, that they used to have a fine empire, "but you let in the Jew and the Jew rotted your Empire, and you yourselves outjewed the Jew. Your allies in your victimized holdings are the *bunya*, that is, the money lender."

Second, as this quote already makes clear, for Pound the Jew is the usurer, not simply skilled in finance but a sneak thief who bleeds the nation. The "kike god" is monopoly, and "the first great HOAX" of these evil people "was substitution of kike god . . . for universal god." The main trick of Jewish bankers is to secretly steal the banking powers away from local governments. "After Lincoln's death the real power in the United states passed from the hands of the official government into those of the Rothschilds and others of their evil combine."

Third, for Pound the Jew is in charge of communication. Not only are the newspapers actually "Jewspapers," but "the Morgenthau-Lehman gang control 99% of all means of communication inside the United States and . . . they can drown out and buy out nearly all opposition. . . ." Jews fill the press and the radio waves with lies for their own selfish gain: "An artificial ignorance is diffused, artificially created by the usurocratic press . . .," and so on.

Finally, as you can see, Pound's Jew has remarkable powers. He secretly controls huge nations, he controls ideas and intellectual life, he controls the money and he controls "99% of all means of communication." Surely we are in the presence of a god! And though Hermes himself is not marked by the greed that Pound finds in this character, all the rest is pure Hermes—the Protector of Thieves and God of Commerce, the Messenger of the Gods and the Lord of the Roads.

The character Pound seeks to describe has one final trait: he is diseased (or disease-transmitting). Pound once wrote a newspaper article with the simple title "The Jew: Disease Incarnate." The sickness is sexual: "Jewish control is the syphilis of any gentile nation"; Jews are the "gonorrhoeal elements" of international finance. "Usury and sodomy the Church condemned as a pair, to one hell, the same for one reason, namely that they are both against natural increase." The image here is an extension of the natural metaphor out of which Pound works (as natural increase is sexual, so its enemy is a sexual disease), but I don't think we will get very far trying to connect this part of Pound's Jew to Pound's ideas. Nor does it have much to do with Hermes. It has to do with psychological repression. An aspect of the self forced to remain in the shadow invariably takes on a negative cast not at all inherent in it. It becomes dirty or violent, trivial or huge, diseased or evil. To integrate the shadow with the ego involves holding a sort of dialogue with it in which these negative aspects fall away and the repressed element comes forward in a simplified form, accepted as "no big thing" into the daylight self. So long as the ego refuses commerce with the shadow, however, the shadow will always seem repulsive.

IV. *Imagist Money*

⟨. . .⟩ In a book by Christopher Hollis called *The Two Nations* Pound came across a quote attributed to (the Bank of England's) founder, William Paterson. A prospectus written in 1694 for potential investors included this sentence: "The bank hath benefit of the interest on all moneys which it creates out of nothing." Pound repeats the sentence over and over in the *Cantos* and in his prose. Here value is detached from its root in the natural world; here lies the seed of the dissociation between real and financial credit. Money "created out of nothing" cannot have real value or real increase, but the "hell banks," through abstraction or mystification, make it appear to have both. Once such false money is at large, it secretly gnaws away at the true value that rests on the growing grass and the living sheep. ⟨. . .⟩

The point of Pound's economics—we mentioned it long ago—is to "get the country's food and goods justly distributed." That, at any rate, is the point if we put it positively. But it often seems more accurate to state it as a negative: Pound wants to *prevent* unjust distribution—he wants, that is, to keep the swindlers from bleeding the public, to catch the crooks and wipe out trickery. No picture of Pound's political economy would be complete without a description of the crimes it is intended to prevent. We have already seen the first example, the Bank of England creating money out of nothing. Three more specific cases will cover the field:

Aristotle . . . relates how Thales . . ., forseeing a bumper crop of olives, hired by paying a small deposit, all the olive presses on the islands. . . . When the abundant harvest arrived, everybody went to see Thales. . . . The Exchange frauds are . . . [all] variants on this theme—artificial scarcity of grain and of merchandise, artificial scarcity of money. . . .

The imperfections of the American electoral system were . . . demonstrated by the scandal of the Congressmen who speculated in the "certificates of owed pay" that had been issued . . . to the soldiers of the Revolution. It was an old trick, and a simple one: a question of altering the value of the monetary unit. Twenty-nine Congressmen . . . bought up the certificates from veterans and others at twenty per cent of their face value. The nation . . . then "*assumed*" responsibility for redeeming the certificates at their full face value. [This was the "Scandal of the Assumption."]

Only God knows how much gold the people have bought during the war, from 1939 to the present time. The trick is simple. Whenever the Rothschild and other gents in the gold business have gold to sell, they raise the price. The public is fooled by propagandising the devaluation of the dollar, or other monetary unit according to the country chosen to be victimized.

For a general description of these crimes we need first to distinguish between embodied value and abstract value. When you exchange a commodity for cash, the object—the body of the thing—is abandoned, and you are left with the symbol of its market value, the dollar bills in your pocket. In one of the phases of market exchange, value is detached from the object and carried symbolically. The symbols of market value are supposed to bear some relation to the commodity, of course—you don't pay $12 for a hacksaw unless you think it's a $12 hacksaw—but there is always a little slack in the line. The symbol is alienable. There is a gap between it and the body. In a famous essay on "Geometry and Experience," Albert Einstein wrote: "As far as the laws of mathematics refer to reality, they are not certain; and as far as they are certain, they do not refer to reality." Symbolization in either exchange or cognition requires that the symbol be detached from the particular thing.[2] We could not think mathematically if we always used real oranges and apples the way children do in the first grade; in a market economy, without money we would have to lug the table and chair to the store when we needed beefsteak and wine. In a symbolic commerce we hope, of course, that our currency or our mathematics will bear some relation to reality when we come back down to earth, but for the duration we sever the link.

In these terms, the arch-criminal for Pound is the man who makes sure that value is detached from its concrete embodiment and then "plays the gap" between symbol and object, between abstract money and embodied wealth. Either the swindler fools the public into using a phantom currency and then grows rich on its increase, or else he gets a monopoly (either on a particular commodity or, better, on the actual symbol of value) and stirs up the market, inducing fluctuations in the relationship between embodied and symbolic value and getting rich playing the one against the other. All the crimes that Pound warns us against come down to one: to profit on the alienation of the symbol from the real. "The finance of financiers is largely the juggling of general tickets against specific tickets." In a corrupt economy the real worth of the creations of man falls every time some crook makes money by a mere manipulation of the market, or worse, makes money out of nothing. "An increasingly large proportion of goods never gets its certificate [of value] . . . ," says Pound. "We artists have known this for a long time, and laughed. We took it as our punishment for being artists, we expected nothing else, but now it occurs to the artisan. . . ."

The difference between an image and a symbol is simple: an image has a body and a symbol does not. And when an image changes, it undergoes metamorphosis: body changes into body without any intervening abstraction—without, that is, the gap which is both the freedom and the alienation of symbol-thought and symbol-change. To connect Pound's economics to his aesthetics, we need simply say that the crime he would prevent is one in which the enemies of the imagination enrich themselves through the trick of symbolic thought. The economist who connects credit to sheep or who writes that "the Navy depended on iron, timber and tar, and not on the manoeuvers of a false finance," is the same as the Imagist who preferred to define "red" with "ROSE CHERRY IRON RUST FLAMINGO" rather than resort to successive layers of generality.

In his sober moments Pound does not oppose abstraction or symbolic thought, but behind his argument lies the longing—and it is a poet's longing—to pull the whole world into the imagination. Money itself is a crime against that desire.

> The nineteenth century, the infamous century of usury . . . creat[ed] a species of monetary Black Mass. Marx and Mill, in spite of their superficial differences, agreed in endowing money with properties of a quasi-religious nature. There was even the concept of energy being 'concentrated in money,' as if one were speaking of the divine quality of consecrated bread.

We are back with Müntzer condemning Luther. When a writer declares that "money alone is capable of being transmuted immediately into any form of activity," Pound exclaims: "This is the idiom of the black myth! . . . Money does not contain energy. The half-lira piece cannot *create* the platform ticket . . . or piece of chocolate that issues from the slot-machine." To speak as if it does is "the falsification of the word" and portrays a "satanic transubstantiation."

Pound's remarks on the image are typically cited in explications of his aesthetic ideas, but their meaning cannot be accurately conveyed if they have been removed from their original context, an ongoing argument for a spiritual economy of the imagination:

> The power of putrefaction . . . seeks to destroy not one but every religion . . . by leading off into theoretical argument. Theological disputes take the place of contemplation. Disputation destroys faith. . . . Suspect anyone who destroys an image. . . .

And in the same line:

> The theologians who put reason (logic) in the place of faith began the slithering process which has ended up with theologians who take no interest in theology whatsoever.

> Tradition inheres . . . in the images of the gods, and gets lost in dogmatic definitions.

When Pound asks, "Who destroyed the mystery of fecundity, bringing in the cult of sterility?" he himself might have answered, "The Protestants and the Jews," but let us say, rather: the rise of market-value as *the* form of value. Karl Marx

once wrote that "Logic is the money of mind . . . ; logic is alienated thinking and therefore thinking which abstracts from nature and from real man." Both men discern this constellation: logical thinking, detachment from the real, and cash exchange. It is one and the same country where the form of commerce allows financiers to enrich themselves by juggling the general against the specific, where faith is replaced by logic, and where images have lost their life to layers of abstraction. ⟨. . .⟩

V. *Bathed in Alkali*

One way to tell Pound's story is as a history of the world, saying that his mind wakes at the time of Homer and moves forward, through Aristotle, through Saint Ambrose, through the Middle Ages and the song of Provence, on into the Renaissance—where it stops. Or rather, sensing something in the Reformation antithetical to the creative spirit, it stops its organic maturation and leaps four hundred years to graft a medieval economics onto the modern state.

Pound's assumptions are tribal and ancient, connecting art, erotic life, natural fertility, and abundance. "The opposing systems of European morality go back to the opposed temperaments of those who thought copulation was good for the crops, and the opposed faction who thought it was bad for the crops (the scarcity economists of pre-history)." Accepting Aristotle's distinction between "natural" wealth-getting (farming and so forth) and "unnatural" foreign trade, Pound proceeds to imagine "a natural economic order" (as Gesell called it) in which credit is founded on the pastures, and money imitates the clover. The imagination would be at ease with such an order, for it senses that it is somehow kin to the plants and the animals, and that its products will increase abundantly if only they may be given away, like grain, like clover, like love.

From such tribal (or classic, or agrarian) assumptions, Pound moves easily into the Middle Ages. He is completely at home with canon law, which sought to codify the structure of a Brotherhood of Man: "My efforts during the last ten years . . . ," he wrote in 1944, "have been toward establishing a correlation between Fascist economics and the economics of canon law (i.e. Catholic & medieval economics). . . ."

But this modernist did not live in the Middle Ages and his economy cannot stop there. In the development of his thought he now must face the same problems that Luther and Calvin faced: how to reconcile the emerging forms of exchange (commodities, cash, the "little usury" of interest) with a spiritual commonwealth. Pound refuses the solution offered by the Reformation, a separation of spiritual and secular life through a new "double law." It didn't work, he declares—"Thereafter design went to hell. . . . Azure hath a canker by usura"; spiritual and aesthetic life were destroyed by unbridled market exchange and logic let in to feed in the house of faith.

Rather than separate spirit and empire, Pound combines them to arrive at an ideology of the state which has in it elements of both tribalism and the medieval Church.[3] But here his troubles begin. Canon law could rest on the assumption of a common and lively faith in the Lord. But the modernist, in assuming the structures of medieval law, must allow the state to stand in for the deity. In the community of faith the Lord gave us our daily bread, but in "the perfect Fascist State" the state distributes purchasing power. Where "Apollus watered and God gave the increase," the workers work and the state pays national dividends. And where does stamp scrip ⟨i.e., self-devaluing currency, advocated by Social Credit theoreticians as a medium for exchanges involving perishable goods⟩ go when it dies? Not to heaven. In ancient times the first fruits were returned to the Lord in smoke, but now a hundredth part goes to the state in stamps on the first of the month. Under the natural economic order the gift circles into neither nature nor mystery; it circles into bureaucracy.

In Pound's favor we should remember that the character of state power was not as obvious in 1930 as it is now; nor was he the only writer in that decade who felt moved to combine commonwealth and state. But the course of this century has revealed a strange equation: state power + good will = state power. The reason is simple: at the level of the state the ties of affection through which the will becomes good can no longer be felt. ⟨. . .⟩ There are definite limits to the size of the feeling community. Gift exchange, as an economy of feeling life, is also the economy of the small group. When the commonwealth is too large to be based on emotional ties, the gift-feeling must be abandoned as a structuring element. For gift-feeling is not impartial. It will always seek to suppress its opposite. Small groups can absorb such antagonism because they can also support affection, but the antagonism of large groups is organized and cold. All commonwealths are wary of the stranger, but the huge ones—especially when threatened—put him to death.

One of the issues in the Peasants' War of 1524–26 was the introduction into Germany of Roman law, Roman property rights, and Roman cash purchase. Taken as a whole, these represent the forms of alienated thought, property, and exchange which are necessary in the organization and operation of a state that is *not* a commonwealth or brotherhood. Hermes, now the Roman Mercury, springs to life in such empires, for it is Hermes who will make connections when the scale is too large for affective bonds. In separating Church and state, Luther and Calvin gave some space to this god.[4] If you accept the large rationalized institutions that emerged after the Reformation, *if* you accept in particular the idea of the state, you must also accept amoral stranger economics.

In terms of intellectual history, the transition from the Middle Ages to the modern world marked a new emphasis on (or need for) symbol-thought and symbol-exchange. Modern logic and the rise of the scientific method quickly followed the Reformation. Less than a hundred years separates Descartes and Newton from Luther and Calvin. But as I suggested two chapters ago, just as "logic is the money of mind," so is the imagination its gift, and Pound was correct, I think, to mark this as the moment in which the imagination was wounded by abstraction. And he was also correct in connecting that wound with the rise of market exchange and its servants—usury, foreign trade, monopoly, and "detached" units of value. The peasants of the Peasants' War were fighting the same battle Ezra Pound fought, the same hopeless battle.

Ezra Pound schooled himself "to write an epic poem which begins 'In the Dark Forest,' crosses the Purgatory of human error, and ends in the light. . . ." In his version of the form of the *Cantos*, there was to be a descent into hell followed by an ascent with error burned away, "bathed in alkali, and in acid." But Pound did not return from the underworld.

In Virgil's story of the founding of Rome, Aeneas, too, makes a descent into hell. After the war with the Greeks, Aeneas is buffeted about the Mediterranean until he beaches at Carthage, where Dido, the queen, falls in love with him. They spend one happy season together, but in the spring Aeneas grows restless and sets sail for Italy, abandoning his love. Dido is brokenhearted. She kills herself for grief. The Trojans can see the light of her funeral pyre as they slip over the horizon.

Once he has returned to Italy, a sibyl offers to guide Aeneas into Hades so that he may speak with his dead father. As they cross the river Styx, he sees Dido's ghost. But she won't look at him; she turns her head away, still resentful over his betrayal. Aeneas pushes on to find his father, whose prophecy tells him how he will establish the city of Rome.

The *Aeneid* is the myth of the founding of a patriarchal urban culture. In the background lies an erotic connection cut off by politics. The love affair is destroyed for the sake of empire, and the feminine figure is left as a suicidal, unredeemed, and restless ghost. Aeneas' descent into hell is meant not to heal that wound but to seek out the father and his advice about government.

Ezra Pound's father was an assayer at the U.S. Mint in Philadelphia. If a man wanted to know if his gold was *real* or just fool's gold, Homer Pound would weigh it and drill it and tell him the truth. The most luminous memory from Pound's childhood concerns a time his father took him to visit the mint. In the enormous basement vaults, four million silver dollars lay where their sacks had rotted. "They were heaving it into the counting machines with shovels bigger than coal shovels. This spectacle of coin being shovelled around like it was litter— these fellows naked to the waist shovelling it around in the gas flares—things like that strike your imagination."

Like Aeneas, Pound descended into hell on the side of the father. A memory of *eros* lingers in the background. There had been a desire to live with those "who thought copulation was good for the crops." There was a man who had once turned into a tree. There was a gifted man, moved by the undivided light of Eleusis, who brought his consciousness forward to the Renaissance and who, wary of the centuries of usury that followed, descended into the underworld to try to bring that gift out again in its clarity. But this was a modern man, living at the height of the patriarchies, wary of his own emotions, classic by temperament, and given to willfulness. He chose the *via voluntatis*. Rather than revalue the gift through affirmation, he undertook the hopeless task of changing the nature of money itself. And so he met no Tiresias in hell. He met no boy lover, nor did he see the face of the beloved. He met, instead, his own devil, a Hermes/Jew whom he chose to fight man to man: he fought bad money with good money, bad will with good will, politics with politics, and avarice with power, all in the name of generosity and the imagination.

In 1961 Pound fell into silence. For the last eleven years of his life he rarely spoke. When visitors would come to his apartment, he would shake hands and then, while the others chatted, sit in silence or disappear upstairs. Toward the beginning of these years a newspaper reporter came to see him. "Where are you living now?" the man asked. "In hell," replied Pound. He never came up. He lost his voice.

In October of 1967 Allen Ginsberg visited Pound in Italy. Pound was eighty-two; he had been in his silence for six years. Ginsberg spent several days with him during which Pound hardly spoke at all and Ginsberg told him stories—told him about his Blake vision and drug experiences and Buddhism and what was happening in America. He chanted sutras for Pound and played him phonograph records of Bob Dylan, Donovan, the Beatles, and Ali Akbar Khan. On the third of these days, in a small Venetian restaurant with a few friends, Ginsberg having been told that Pound would respond to specific textual questions about the *Cantos*, they finally began to talk. Ginsberg later recalled part of the exchange:

> [I explained] how his attention to specific perceptions . . . had been great help to me in finding language and balancing my mind—and to many young poets—and asked "am I making sense to you?"
>
> "Yes," he replied finally, and then mumbled "but my own work does not make sense." . . . "A mess," he said.

"What, you or the *Cantos* or me?"

"My writing—stupidity and ignorance all the way through," he said. "Stupidity and igorance."

[Ginsberg and the others objected, Ginsberg concluding:] "Williams told me . . . in 1961—we were talking about prosody . . . anyway Williams said, 'Pound has a mystical ear'—did he ever tell you that?"

"No," said Pound, "he never said that to me"—smiling almost shyly and pleased—eyes averted, but smiling, almost curious and childlike.

"Well I'm reporting it to you now seven years later—the judgment of the tender-eyed Doctor that you had a 'mystical ear'—not gaseous mystical he meant—but a natural ear for rhythm and tone."

I continued explaining the concrete value of his perceptions. I added that as humor—HUMOR—the ancient humours—his irritations, . . . against Buddhists, Taoists and Jews—fitted into place, despite his intentions, as part of the drama. . . . "The Paradise is in the desire, not in the imperfection of accomplishment—it was the intention of Desire we all respond to—Bhakti—the Paradise is in the magnanimity of the *desire* to manifest coherent perceptions in language."

"The intention was bad—that's the trouble—anything I've done has been an accident—any good has been spoiled by my intentions—the preoccupation with irrelevant and stupid things—" Pound said this quietly, rusty voiced like an old child, looked directly in my eye while pronouncing "intention."

"Ah well, what I'm trying to tell you—what I came here for all this time—was to give you my blessing then, because despite your disillusion . . . , [my] perceptions have been strengthened by the series of practical exact language models which are scattered thruout the *Cantos* like stepping stones—ground for *me* to occupy, walk on—so that despite your intentions, the practical effect has been to clarify my perceptions—and, anyway, now, do you accept my blessing?"

He hesitated, opening his mouth, like an old turtle.

"I do," he said—"but my worst mistake was the stupid suburban prejudice of antisemitism, all along, that spoiled everything—" . . .

"Ah, that's lovely to hear you say that. . . ."[5]

Later, Ginsberg and the others walked Pound back to his apartment. At the door, Ginsberg took him by the shoulders and said, "I also came here for your blessing. And now may I have it, sir?"

"Yes," nodded Pound, "for whatever it's worth."

In the history of the creative spirit in America, this encounter seems as significant as the day, thirty-five years before, when Pound handed the *Cantos* to Mussolini. For here

the Jew—or rather, the Buddhist Jew (for he has left the judge behind)—came to exchange a blessing with the bitter servant. There were Jews who thought that Pound should have been put to death for his broadcasts during the war. But that would have been no more of a solution than the killing of the Jew in the fairy tale. Rather than fighting devils with devils, Ginsberg managed to change the form of the drama itself, and a light suddenly fell from a window no one had noticed. The story of our poetry need not be finished in one man's life. Ginsberg calls the light out of Pound's labor; the forces of decay will strip away the "stupidity and ignorance." The servant of the gift may yet regain his voice and feel, with each word that leaves his body, his own worth return to him as undivided light.

Notes

1. All cultures seem to find a slightly alien local population to carry the Hermes projection. For the Vietnamese it is the Chinese, and for the Chinese it is the Japanese. For the Hindu it is the Moslem; for the North Pacific tribes it was the Chinook; in Latin America and in the American South it is the Yankee. In Uganda it is the East Indians and Pakistanis. In French Quebec it is the English. In Spain the Catalans are "the Jews of Spain." On Crete it is the Turks, and in Turkey it is the Armenians. Lawrence Durrell says that when he lived in Crete he was friends with the Greeks, but that when he wanted to buy some land they sent him to a Turk, saying that a Turk was what you needed for trade, though of course he couldn't be trusted.

   This figure who is good with money but a little tricky is always treated as a foreigner even if his family has been around for centuries. Often he actually is a foreigner, of course. He is invited in when the nation needs trade and he is driven out—or murdered—when nationalism begins to flourish: the Chinese out of Vietnam in 1978, the Japanese out of China in 1949, the Yankees out of South America and Iran, the East Indians out of Uganda under Idi Amin, and the Armenians out of Turkey in 1915–16. The "outsider" is always used as a catalyst to arouse nationalism, and when times are hard he will always be its victim as well.

2. Here we have another reason why Hermes is both the god of trade and of thieves. A commerce in commodities involves the trick of symbolic exchange.

3. His repeated call for state sovereignty and his prohibition on foreign money in the homeland both seem tribal to me. (If you begin with such tribal nationalism, however, you soon must have either complete isolation *or* a double standard for dealing with strangers. With what can only be called the wisdom of Moses, Pound arrives at the latter solution: "A country CAN have one currency for internal use, and another for home and foreign use.")

4. In formulating a modified permission to practice usury, the reformers revived the Mosaic law, and in that sense they brought the Jew into the Church. That, at any rate, was how Pound saw it; he was of the opinion, for example, that Calvin was really a Jew: "that heretical scoundrel Calvin (the alias of Cauein, or Cohen, philo-usurer)."

5. One of Pound's last pieces of writing was a clarification: "Re USURY. I was out of focus, taking a symptom for a cause. The cause is AVARICE."

Early Works

JOHN ESPEY
"Physique de l'Amour"
Ezra Pound's Mauberley: A *Study in Composition*
1955, pp. 62–83

If *Mauberley* is, as Pound has said, "a mere surface," it is a surface of considerable complexity, a surface, even, of some depth. But a surface must rest upon a foundation, and though it would be foolish to insist upon any single source other than

Pound's own mind as ultimate base, it is still possible, I think, to push a little farther into the process of the poem's composition.

Hugh Kenner, certainly *Mauberley's* most sensitive and sympathetic interpreter, asserts in a note in *The Poetry of Ezra Pound* that "the primary echo is as a matter of fact with Corbière," and writes in a later note:

At the time when *Mauberley* was written, Eliot was getting rid of Laforgue and in collaboration with Pound assimilating Corbière and Gautier. The Corbière reverberations are functional in Pound's poem, relating it to still more complex modes of self-knowledge than we have opportunity to go into here. At its deepest levels the poem is still virtually unread.

Pound himself, in ⟨a⟩ letter to René Taupin ⟨. . .⟩ remarks (and in his own French): "Ce que vous prenez pour influence de Corbière est probablement influence direct de Villon." To support this Villon-Corbière echo as *Mauberley's* primary one, it would, I think, be necessary to insist that somewhere in the second section the ironic voice of the opening *Ode* speaks again, that Mauberley himself offers an obliquely personal commentary on Pound. But as I shall try to demonstrate shortly, the contrast here is so complete a one and of such a nature that it is ultimately a total dissociation. I believe that whatever there is of Villon or Corbière here is contained in the *Ode* and that what Kenner calls Pound's "impersonality" appears only in the "Mauberley" section, and even there, as I shall also try to show, merely on the surface. That the account of Mauberley himself "cannot be taken as an account of the poet of the *Cantos*" is certainly true, but only, I think, because the voice of the first section *is* the voice of the author of *The Cantos*. And though there is surely no need to accept at face value a poet's own statement of his sources and influences, Pound so automatically picks up and reproduces rhythm, theme, and vocabulary that it is difficult to believe without considerable evidence of this sort that the work of Corbière stands in more intimate relation to *Mauberley* than that of most of the poets discussed in "A Study in French Poets."

Another of these poets, however, Jules Laforgue, whose work Pound claimed, in writing to Taupin, he had used and understood even more thoroughly than Eliot had, has left important marks upon *Mauberley*. Warren Ramsey, in his excellent study *Jules Laforgue and the Ironic Inheritance*, notes how insistently Pound was concerned with Laforgue in various magazines at this time, expounding, translating, and para-phrasing, and points out the probability of Pound's deriving his use of dramatic contrast from Laforgue. Of *Mauberley* he writes:

> One of Laforgue's favorite images, that of the foetus, turns up. The cliché, 'march of events,' is pressed into ironic service, according to characteristic Lafor-guian procedure. The verse depends on the literary reference as Laforgue's does, with 'l'an trentiesme de son eage' woven in. Here too are the long 'interna-tional' words out of Latin, the sort of polysyllables to which Laforgue resorted on slight pretext. At the end of the [fifth] quatrain, 'No adjunct to the Muses' diadem' furnishes a familiar ironic sparkle of gran-deur. Taken singly, no one of these traits would justify the term 'Laforguian.' Occurring all together, sustained by the ironically learned tone which was Laforgue's contribution to nineteenth-century verse, they send us back to the Pierrot poems.

To this one might add that the shift from "sieve" to "seismo-graph" and the use of "the half-watt rays" in the "Mauberley" section probably derive from Laforgue's fascination with the "new" vocabulary of his century. They are exact illustrations of what Pound, writing on Laforgue in *Poetry* for November, 1917 ("Irony, Laforgue, and Some Satire"), calls his "verbal-ism," adding: "He has dipped his wings in the dye of scientific terminology."

At the same time, it may be instructive to look for a moment at Pound's use of "foetus." When Eliot wrote

> In the palace of Mrs. Phlaccus, at Professor
> Channing-Cheetah's
> He laughed like an irresponsible foetus,
> (Mr. Apollinax)

he was certainly using "one of Laforgue's favorite images." But when Pound wrote

> Among the pickled foetuses and bottled bones,
> Engaged in perfecting the catalogue,
> I found the last scion of the
> Senatorial families of Strasbourg, Monsieur Verog,

he may have been pressing into service a word he was led to by Laforgue's repeated use of it, but he was using it primarily on an altogether literal level. Monsieur Verog is Pound's *nom de guerre* for Victor Gustave Plarr (1863–1929), friend of Lionel Johnson and Ernest Dowson, and author, among other works, of *In the Dorian Mood*. Plarr was Librarian of the Royal College of Surgeons when Pound knew him and he was indeed "among the pickled foetuses and bottled bones," busy with the Library's catalogue, one half of which he completed in manuscript during his tenure of the office. If the word is Laforguian, its use is not, for it is precisely the use Gautier makes of it twice in descriptive passages of *Albertus*, first in the ninth stanza,

> Fœtus mal conservés saisissant d'une lieue
> L'odorat, et collant leur face jaune et bleue
> Contre le verre du bocal!

and again in the one hundred and twelfth stanza,

> Squelettes conservés dans les amphithéâtres,
> Animaux empaillés, monstres, fœtus verdâtres,
> Tout humides encor de leur bain d'alcool,
> Culs-de-jatte, pieds-bots, montés sur les limaces,
> Pendus tirant la langue et faisant des grimaces.

One should also point out that the first two lines of the stanza

> Conduct, on the other hand, the soul
> "Which the highest cultures have nourished"
> To Fleet St. where
> Dr. Johnson flourished,

are a translation of the first line of Laforgue's *Complainte des pianos qu'on entend dans les quartiers aisés*:

> Menez l'âme que les Lettres ont bien nourrie,
> Les pianos, les pianos, dans les quartiers aisés!

The lines reflect Pound's brilliance of tone as translator, rejecting the obvious "Letters" and hitting upon the freshly precise "highest cultures." They probably reflect even more than this, for the piano of the "Medallion" shares with Laforgue's pianos the voice, never answered, of invitation and love.

Pound included in *Instigations* a translation of one of the Pierrot poems, and just as Laforgue's Pierrots advance and withdraw in their sophistication, viewing the human scene with a double sense of desire and detachment, so Mauberley, disarmed by his own sensibility, gelded by his own perceptions, withdraws altogether. *Instigations* contains another work of Laforgue's, Pound's rehandling of *Salomé* from *Moralités légendaires* in which "mousseline" and "enmousselined" are used with almost metronomic regularity in announcing Salomé's arrivals and in describing her costumes. The presence of Pound's "divagation" from Laforgue serves as reminder of the heroes of *Moralités légendaires*, most specifically of Lohengrin, whom Elsa woos on their wedding night with the first refrain of *Complainte des pianos*, and who, in the transports of nuptial rapture, embraces his pillow rather than his bride, escaping from a marriage he is incapable of completing when the pillow transforms itself into the beloved Swan and lifts him "vers les altitudes de la Métaphysique de l'Amour, aux glaciers miroirs que nulle haleine de jeune fille ne saurait ternir de buée pour y tracer du doigt son nom avec la date! . . ."

Another relationship between *Mauberley* and *Moralités légendaires* is that between a descriptive passage in *Le Miracle des roses* and the sequence's "Medallion," which, though undoubtedly based on a Luini portrait also echoes the details of

> . . . cheveux d'ambre roux massés sur le front et minutieusement tressés en doux chignon plat à la Julia Mammea sur la nuque pure. . . .

Laforgue's essential tone occurs rarely in *Mauberley* after the *Ode*, however. Pound's white remains Gautier's "blanc d'albâtre" rather than Laforgue's "blanc de cold-cream," but the contrasts, the musical pattern of development and variation, do stand in close relation to Laforgue and are early evidence of Pound's application of the Laforguian techniques.

Nevertheless, there is a remaining influence to be investigated. In some ways its neglect parallels the neglect of Gautier; for just as the lack of any primary influence upon Eliot's 1920 poems by Gautier may have obscured the influence of *Émaux et Camées* upon *Mauberley*, so may Eliot's use of Remy de Gourmont in *The Sacred Wood* have placed an emphasis for today's reader on only one part of Gourmont's work.

In both *Instigations* and *Make It New*, the study *Remy de Gourmont: A Distinction Followed by Notes* follows immediately the survey of Henry James. In *Make It New* the two are placed together under the joint title "Henry James and Remy de Gourmont," logically enough, for the first sentences of the Gourmont study read:

> The mind of Remy de Gourmont was less like the mind of Henry James than any contemporary mind I can think of. James's drawing of *mœurs contemporaines* was so circumstantial, so concerned with the setting, with detail, nuance, social aroma, that his transcripts were 'out of date' almost before his books had gone into a second edition. . . .

The similarity between the range of Gourmont's work and Pound's is striking. An interest in Provençal poetry, in the later Latin poets, in a studied eroticism, and a willingness to generalize from sometimes slender evidence or even from a single fixed point characterize both men. The Gourmont used by Eliot is a somewhat different Gourmont from the author of the *Épilogues* and *Promenades littéraires*, from the Gourmont of *Physique de l'amour* with its vivid account of the virgin mole's flight before her inflamed pursuer, from the Gourmont of the cheerfully erotic collection of stories, *Couleurs*, in which Gourmont, carrying on the vowel-color symbolism of Rimbaud and René Ghil, equates colors with feminine types, each of whom finds her own shade of amorous fulfillment.

It is this second Gourmont who attracted Pound. In his first tribute to him, published in *The Fortnightly Review* (December 1, 1915) and reprinted in *Pavannes and Divisions*, Pound was already celebrating him as one in touch with the younger generation of writers: "He had not lost touch with *les jeunes*." Pound writes enthusiastically of Gourmont's sonnets in prose and praises what Gourmont called "la géometrie subordonnée du corps humain." For *Mauberley* the most important links here are Pound's extractions from Gourmont on this theme:

> J'ai plus aimé les yeux que toutes les autres manifestations corporelles de la beauté. . . .
> Les yeux sont le manomètre de la machine animale. . . .

and again

> Je parlerais des yeux, je chanterais les yeux toute ma vie. Je sais toutes leurs couleurs et toutes leurs volontés, leur destinée. . . .

In a note for *Poetry* (January, 1916) that Pound must have written at about the same time, he again comments on Gourmont's connection with the younger generation and remarks that "Nietzsche has done no harm in France because France has understood that thought can exist apart from action. . . ."

Pound's full study of Gourmont (*Little Review*, February–March, 1919) repeats these points and expands them. The high regard in which Pound held the book that he was to publish a translation of in 1921 under the title *The Natural Philosophy of Love*[1] is shown when he writes:

> *Physique de l'amour* (1903) should be used as a textbook of biology. Between the biological basis in instinct, and the "Sequaire of Goddeschalk" in *Le Latin mystique* (1892) stretch Gourmont's studies of amour and aesthetics.

It is these studies that form one of Pound's chief preoccupations with Gourmont, as an extensive quotation will show:

> The emotions are equal before the aesthetic judgment. He does not grant the duality of body and soul, or at least suggests that this mediaeval duality is unsatisfactory; there is an inter-penetration, an osmosis of body and soul, at least for hypothesis.
> My words are the unspoken words of my body.
> And in all his exquisite treatment of all emotion he will satisfy many whom August Strindberg, for egregious example, will not. From the studies of insects to Christine evoked from the thoughts of Diomede, sex is not a monstrosity or an exclusively German study.[2] And the entire race is not bound to the habits of the *mantis* or of other insects equally melodramatic. Sex, in so far as it is not a purely physiological reproductive mechanism, lies in the domain of aesthetics, the junction of tactile and magnetic senses; as some people have accurate ears both for rhythm and for pitch, and as some are tone deaf, some impervious to rhythmic subtlety and variety, so in this other field of the senses some desire the trivial, some the processional, the stately, the master-work.
> As some people are good judges of music, and insensible to painting and sculpture, so the fineness of one sense may entail no corresponding fineness in another, or at least no corresponding critical perception of differences.
> Emotions to Henry James were more or less things that other people had and that one didn't go into; at any rate not in drawing rooms. The gods had not visited James, and the Muse, whom he so frequently mentions, appeared doubtless in corsage, the narrow waist, the sleeves puffed at the shoulders, *à la mode* 1890-2.

Here, then, in the contrast drawn between Gourmont and James we see Mauberley as a Jamesian figure, sensitive indeed to painting and sculpture, perceptive of physical detail, but victim of another, and quite basic, kind of "anaesthesis." In a note on one of Gourmont's statements about aesthetics, Pound says: "Each of the senses has its own particular eunuchs." And to make the dissociation of James and Gourmont quite explicit, Pound writes in a single sentence: "In contradiction to, in wholly antipodal distinction from, Henry James, Gourmont was an artist of the nude." It is in such passages, I think, that one begins to sense the fundamental importance of Gourmont to *Mauberley*.

At the same time, one would expect to find in *Mauberley* the sort of immediate trace for Gourmont that has already been pointed out for Gautier, Bion, James, and Laforgue. It is contained in the portrait of the modern woman:

"Conservatrix of Milésien"
Habits of mind and feeling,
Possibly. But in Ealing
With the most bank-clerkly of Englishmen?

Pound provides his own note in the essay, during the course of a survey of Gourmont's books similar to the survey of James's:

In *Histoires magiques* (1894): *La Robe blanche, Yeux d'eau, Marguerite Rouge, soeur de Sylvie, Danaette*, are all of them special cases, already showing his perception of neurosis, of hyperaesthesia. His mind is still running on tonal variations in *Les Litanies de la rose*.
"Pourtant il y a des yeux aux bout des doigts."
"Femmes, conservatrices des traditions milésiennes."

Both quotations come from the last story in *Histoires magiques, Stratagèmes*,[3] and for Mauberley the context of the second is important. The narrator of *Stratagèmes* reviews his successive conquests among women, and after recounting a few early and more or less normal, adventures, he pauses:

. . . Mettre de l'esprit dans la saveur, de l'âme dans le parfum, du sentiment dans le toucher . . .
Désirs, grenades pleines de rubis prisonniers dont un coup de dent fait ruisseler l'éblouissance,— un coup de dent de femme.
Des femmes, au bon endroit, savent mordre. Elles ne doivent pas être méprisées, ces conservatrices des traditions milésiennes,—mais c'est bien monotone et les artistes sont rares.

It is necessary to stress the sexual connotation here, for Pound early began to use the phrase in a more general sense. Writing to John Quinn about Maud Gonne on November 15, 1918, he said:

The other point M.G. omits from her case is that she went to Ireland without permit and in disguise, in the first place, during war time. "Conservatrices des traditions Milesiennes," as de Gourmont calls them. There are people who have no sense of the value of "civilization" or public order.

And in his own note to the translation of *Physique de l'amour*, Pound rephrases the tag in a way that includes both the original sexual sense and his own generalization: "Woman, the conservator, the inheritor of past gestures . . ." That for *Mauberley* the "gestures" are close to Gourmont's original intention is made clear by the remainder of the stanza, the "conservatrix" living with the most bank-clerkly of Englishmen and the "bon endroit" the suburb of Ealing. Certainly she is no "artiste," no stimulus to even the mildest Milesian Tale.

To return, then—Gourmont's immediate presence established—to the passage already quoted in which the music-love theme is sounded. The crucial poem in *Mauberley* to be examined here is the second of the "Mauberley" section, which derives its entire meaning from a music-flower-love symbolism. I have already noted the sexual level of this poem, specifically in connection with the "orchid." On the flower level, the irides wait with opened petals for the "botticellian sprays" of *The Birth of Venus*, in which the entwined male and female zephyrs direct their jets through a curtain of falling flowers. For the detail of this passage, Pound turned to the painting and also to Botticelli's own literary source, Poliziano's *La Giostra*, deriving his "diastasis" of the eyes from two lines describing Cyparissus, however, instead of the Cyprian:

Bagna Cipresso ancor pel cervio gli occhi
Con chiome or aspre a già distese e bionde,
(82: 5, 6)

In this picture of Cyparissus' metamorphosis into the cypress, the pair of adjectives "distese e bionde" modify "chiome," as the young man's crown of hair ("chiome" is used here both as "head of hair" and "crown of a tree") is already "divided and yellowish." Pound, seizing on the two words and linking them with "gli occhi" immediately above, translated something like "the wide-spaced and light-colored eyes," which is accurate enough for the painting itself. "La dea Ciprigna" a few stanzas beyond these lines, together with "distesi" used twice in nearby passages, and the "zefiri lascivi" from the actual description of Venus' birth, apparently contributed to this accidental confusion. (It may, on the other hand, be a completely conscious distortion, though this seems doubtful to me.) This indication of the source of Pound's "diastasis" would be highly speculative if he had not with fine economy used the other of the two adjectives in Canto VII, applying it to the eye (as if the complete phrase were "occhio biondo") and precisely to the iris of the eye:

Eyes floating in dry, dark air,
E biondo, with glass-grey iris, with an even side-fall
of hair
The stiff, still features.

There is every reason to hesitate, however; for despite the emphasis on eyes, there may be an intermediate echo here from Dante:

. . . e quell' altro ch'è biondo
È Opizzo da Esti . . .
(*Inf.* XII, 110, 111)

But even if, ignoring the absence of the accent, one decides to read the phrase in Canto VII as "He is fair," the ultimate source still seems to be Poliziano when one finds in Canto LXXXI, one of *The Pisan Cantos*, the full phrase used at last:

Saw but the eyes and stance between the eyes,
colour, diastasis. . . .

So far as *Mauberley* is concerned, this is simply evidence of the way in which this particular poem is dominated by the image of Venus.

Pound's memory was probably ranging back over a number of years, for the only other indication in his work that he had read *La Giostra*, beyond a passing reference to Poliziano in *The Spirit of Romance*, occurs in the first version of *Canto I*, published in *Poetry* for April, 1917. Here, as in *Mauberley*, he is writing specifically of *The Birth of Venus* and Botticelli's use of Simonetta de Vespucci, whose favor Giuliano de Medici had won as victor of the tournament the poem celebrated:

How many worlds we have! If Botticelli
Brings her ashore on that great cockle-shell—
His Venus (Simonetta?),
And Spring and Aufidus fill all the air
With their clear-outlined blossoms?
World enough.

To return once more to Gourmont, the one poem of his that Pound quoted in "A Study in French Poets" was *Litanies de la rose*, of which Pound wrote: "The procession of all beautiful women moves before one in the 'Litanies de la Rose'; and the rhythm is incomparable." For *Mauberley*, two of Gourmont's roses are of particular importance, the first for the "tea-rose tea-gown . . . mousseline of Cos" passage, the second for the poem under immediate discussion:

Rose rose, pucelle au cœur désordonné, rose rose, robe de mousseline, entr'ouvre tes ailes fausses, ange, fleur hypocrite, fleur du silence.

Rose bleue, rose iridine, monstre couleur des yeux de la Chimère, rose bleue, lève un peu tes paupières: as-tu peur qu'on te regarde, les yeux dans les yeux, Chimère, fleur hypocrite, fleur du silence!

Here, and in many other passages from Gourmont appears his insistence on flower symbolism, and in "rose iridine" lies the probable clue to Pound's use of the "irides" as a double flower-eye image. One would expect to find somewhere in Gourmont's work the conjunction of orchid and iris with a sexual connotation to complete the pattern, but Pound picked up this hint from another source. *Instigations* includes what Pound identifies no more specifically than a translation "from an eighteenth-century author," entitled *Genesis, or the First Book in the Bible.* This translation, which originally appeared in the *Little Review* (November, 1918), is a translation of the entry *Genèse* in Voltaire's *Dictionnaire philosophique*, and in the course of it Voltaire, discussing the sons of the gods who found the daughters of earth fair, comments: "There is no race, except perhaps the Chinese, which has not recorded gods getting young girls with child." Pound adds his own note to this:

In Fenellosa's notes on Kutsugen's[4] ode to "Sir in the Clouds," I am unable to make out whether the girl is more than a priestess. She bathes in hot water made fragrant by boiling orchids in it, she washes her hair and binds iris into it, she puts on the dress of flowery colors, and the god illimitable in his brilliance descends; she continues her attention to her toilet, in very reverent manner.

Pound has used flowers as sexual symbols long before this, specifically in the poem *Coitus* (entitled *Pervigilium* in *Lustra*), which opens:

The gilded phaloi of the crocuses
are thrusting at the spring air.

And later, in *Moeurs Contemporaines*:

You enter and pass hall after hall,
Conservatory follows conservatory,
Lilies lift their white symbolical cups,
Whence their symbolical pollen has been excerpted.

With this flower-music-sex theme in mind, one should turn to examine the separate epigraph of the second "Mauberley" poem:

"Qu'est ce qu'ils savent de l'amour, et qu'est ce qu'ils peuvent comprendre?

S'ils ne comprennent pas la poésie, s'ils ne sentent pas la musique, qu'est ce qu'ils peuvent comprendre de cette passion en comparaison avec laquelle la rose est grossière et le parfum des violettes un tonnerre?" CAID ALI

As I have already noted, Pound has written to Kimon Friar that "Caid Ali" is his own pseudonym. I assume it was chosen in salute to the part played by floral figures in the elaborate erotic symbolism of Persian poetry, with, perhaps, a bow in the direction of the *Rubaiyat*. At the same time, one recognizes immediately the reflection of Gourmont, in tone, in the flowers, in the rhetorical questions,[5] and one suspects that somewhere in this aesthetic bouquet must lurk a specifically sexual reference beyond the mention of "amour." The "grossness" of the rose suggests it, and the reader of *Physique de l'amour* in Pound's translation recognizes its full statement instantly in "un tonnerre." Twice in *The Natural Philosophy of Love* Pound uses "thunder-clap" to describe the sexual climax (of the bull!), once to translate Gourmont's "éclair" and again to translate "foudre." The full irony of the epigraph in relation

to Mauberley's "fundamental passion" and his "anæsthesis" is not revealed without this clue.

With it, the underlying theme and the underlying musical structure of *Mauberley* are apparent. The musical development takes the form of what might be called a double counterpoint, or a major and minor counterpoint. In the "eye" passages from Gourmont and his "unspoken words of my body" one sees Pound's source of the minor counterpoint, and simply to trace the series of eye-images reveals much of the method: *inward gaze—quick eyes gone under earth's lid—all of Yeux Glauques —skylike limpid eyes—eye-lid and cheek-bone—irides—diastasis—if her colour came against his gaze—the eyes turn topaz.* The fullest series, however, and the one that displays the method at its most effective level of variation is made up of mouth-images: *trout for factitious bait—accelerated grimace—an old bitch gone in the teeth—charm, smiling at the good mouth*—all the references in *Envoi*, particularly *some other mouth—firmness, not the full smile—mouths biting empty air* (*Vacuos exercet [in] aera morsus*)—*unfit as the red-beaked steeds of the Cytheræan for a chain bit—the faint susurrus of his subjective hosannah—the grand piano utters a profane protest with her clear soprano.* The same method produces the balance between "the elegance of Circe's hair" in the *Ode* and the "basket-work of braids" in the "Medallion," the latter an echo of the "Minoan undulation" that strengthened Mauberley's hopes for a time.

This minor counterpoint is implicit in the major counterpoint: the severe and exact balance maintained between the poems in the first section dominated by Pound and the poems in the second section dominated by Mauberley. The first statement of the suite sounds this with

For three years, out of key with his time
He strove

answered in the "Mauberley" section by

For three years, diabolus in the scale,[6]
He drank ambrosia.

Whereas Pound's reaction to what the age demands is a scathing and agile denunciation of the modern world leading him to his first attack on usury, Mauberley lacks agility and at the sight of beauty he makes "no immediate application / Of this to relation of the state." Pound's subjective and active crowning of himself with Daphne's laurel is set against "the faint susurrus" of Mauberley's "subjective hosannah."

The most telling contrast in this major counterpoint is a sexual one, with the "phallic and ambrosial" of the first section diminished to the purely "ambrosial circumstances" of the second. Even the intermediate poems, the "contacts" of the two men, share this theme. Both the pre-Raphaelite and the Nineties sections echo it in terms of sexual frustration. The stylist can enjoy only an "uneducated mistress" as against the "conservatrix of Milésien" and the final sterility of the Lady Valentine's and the Lady Jane's circles. The inadequacy of the age is embodied in the eunuch who rules over it; its victims do not know the faun's flesh; they have the vote instead of the religio-sexual rite of circumcision.

It is with this contrast in mind that one must examine the portrait of Mauberley as it is revealed beneath the surface gravity, the mild objectivity and sympathy of the Jamesian observer. The most obvious contrast here is the balancing of the *Envoi* against the "Medallion." The two poems handle the same scene, but whereas the poet of the *Envoi*, working from Waller's "Go, Lovely Rose," writes a poem that echoes down the entire line of the English poets, most specifically Shakespeare with

One substance and one colour
Braving time,

and implies throughout an invitation to active passion, the poet of the "Medallion" scrupulously notes each detail of the scene, not recognizing the invitation of the song beyond the grand piano's "profane protest," not seeing in "the gold-yellow frock" the color of Hymen, not finding a living Venus but a reminder of Reinach's *Apollo*, and closing with a careful "scientific" record of the inviting eyes as they turn topaz beneath the half-watt rays of the final star-lit night. To emphasize this quality of the "Medallion" one can turn to Canto V, where the same nexus of music, topaz, the Hymeneal color, and the star Hesperus (νυκτὸς ἄγαλμα is used with the full implication of active passion, "The bride awaiting the god's touch":

> Topaz I manage, and three sorts of blue;
>   but on the barb of time.
> The fire? always, and the vision always,
> Ear dull, perhaps, with the vision, flitting
> And fading at will. Weaving with points of gold,
> Gold-yellow, saffron . . . The roman shoe,
>   Aurunculeia's
> And come shuffling feet, and cries "Da nuces!
> "Nuces!" praise, and Hymenaeus "brings the girl to
>   her man"
> Or "here Sextus had seen her."
> Titter of sound about me, always.
>   and from "Hesperus . . ."
> Hush of the older song: "Fades light from sea-crest,
> "And in Lydia walks with pair'd women
> "Peerless among the pairs, that once in Sardis
> "In satieties . . ."[7]

With this ironic revelation of Mauberley's inadequacy in mind, and remembering the implications of "un tonnerre" in the Caid Ali epigraph, one can turn back to the first "Mauberley" poem and see that it announces with ribald frankness this entire theme, but announces it so blatantly that it is almost automatically overlooked. The first stanza of the poem suggests it, with Mauberley turning from the etching to the severe head of the insatiable empress, and the bald announcement follows with

> "His true Penelope
> Was Flaubert,"
> And his tool
> The engraver's.

It is particularly bald when one recalls Gautier's reference to "la roue du graveur."

Here one must turn to Pound's own note appended to his translation of *Physique de l'amour*. Gourmont advances his personal theories of intellectual fecundation, saying, as translated by Pound:

> Virgin-birth might establish itself. Certain males could be born in each century, as happens in the intellectual order, and they could fecundate the generation of lions, as genius fecundates the generation of minds.

From this passage in Gourmont and from some of Gourmont's remarks on the sexual mechanism of vertebrates Pound developed his note, in which he elaborates on his own intuitive theory of the human brain as "a clot of genital fluid":

> There are traces of it [this theory] in the symbolism of phallic religions, man really the phallus or spermatozoid charging, head-on, the female chaos; integration of the male in the male organ. Even oneself has felt it, driving any new idea into the great passive vulva of London, a sensation analagous to the male feeling in copulation.

Not only is *Mauberley* Pound's farewell to London; it contains in itself a definition of the "female chaos" that now rejected or ignored the pressure of his advances. For Pound characterizes the ultimate dissolution of the age after the War as "hysterias, trench confessions, laughter out of dead bellies," in which "hysteria," like Mauberley's "orchid," uses the full power of its Greek root, ὑστέρα (womb) to reveal the new, "female" formlessness.

Yet if the second stanza of the first "Mauberley" poem is actually the ribald declaration that it now appears to be, one would expect to find some balance for it in the first section, preferably in the *Ode*, just as the first two lines of the stanza come from the *Ode*. The balancing line is there, with a sort of sixth-form wild sexual humor about it, in a statement far more ribald than its "Mauberley" echo. The line is "Bent resolutely on wringing lilies from the acorn," and to read it fully one must remember that just as "orchid" is ὄρχις, and just as "hysteria" is ὑστέρα, so is "acorn" *glans* in Latin and *gland* in French. Thus what appears to be a proverbial, almost a Biblical expression—*Do men gather figs of thistles? Can the fig tree bear olive berries?*—is actually a raucous echo of the sort of humor that had always delighted Pound in Catullus and Ovid and had led him to write lines like those that open *Fratres Minores*:

> With minds still hovering above their testicles
> Certain poets here and in France
> Still sigh over established and natural fact
> Long since fully discussed by Ovid.

Through the glandular implications of the line from the *Ode* seem clear enough, it is possible to go farther and indicate where Pound picked up the suggestion for it in *Physique de l'amour*. The sentence reads, and again in his own translation:

> The gland, which takes all intermediate forms between ball and point, has in the rhinocerus the shape of a gross fleur-de-lis.[8]

Only after an exploration of all these images can one place beside the eye and mouth images—the musical series itself, from the sirens' song to the song of the "Medallion" is worth equal attention—the final, sexual series on which *Mauberley* rests.

But if this is the final level on which *Mauberley* is to be read, one is struck by the disparity between the astonishing complexity of its surface and the apparent simplicity of its base, a disparity that comes close to being disconcerting. R. P. Blackmur is, I think, treating this problem when he writes of *Mauberley* in *The Double Agent*:

> What we see is Mr. Pound fitting his substance with a surface; he is a craftsman, and we are meant to appreciate his workmanship. When we try to discern the substance, we find that the emphasis on craft has produced a curious result. Instead of the poem being, as with most poets of similar dimensions, a particularised instance of a plot, myth, attitude, or convention, with Mr. Pound movement is in the opposite direction; the poem flows into the medium and is lost in it, like water in sand.

I find it difficult to believe that the "substance" of *Mauberley* even at this level, once discerned, is altogether swallowed up by the medium, but that the relationship between substance and surface here presents difficulties is, I think, undeniable.

Actually, however, Pound is trying to do far more than simply exercise what Marianne Moore was later to call his over-emphasis on "unprudery" or merely assert the great completeness of the complete man over the incomplete. Once again, the study of Gourmont gives the key, not only to *Mauberley* but also to Pound's *Propertius*:

> If in Diomède we find an Epicurean receptivity, a certain aloofness, an observation of contacts and auditions, in contrast to the Propertian attitude:

Ingenium nobis ipsa puella facit,
this is perhaps balanced by

"Sans vous, je crois bien que je n'aimerais
plus beaucoup et que je n'aurais plus une
extrême confiance ni dans la vie ni moi-
même." (In "Lettres à l'Amazone.")

But there is nothing more unsatisfactory than
saying that de Gourmont "had such and such ideas"
or held "such and such views," the thing is that he
held ideas, intuitions, perceptions in a certain personal exquisite manner. In a criticism of him,
"criticism" being an over-violent word, in, let us say,
an indication of him, one wants merely to show that
one has oneself made certain dissociations; as here,
between the æsthetic receptivity of tactile and magnetic values, of the perception of beauty in these
relationships, and the conception of love, passion,
emotion as an intellectual instigation; such as Propertius claims it; such as we find it declared in the
King of Navarre's

"De fine amor vient science et beauté";
and constantly in the troubadours.

Here, then, is *Mauberley*'s base, expressed through Pound's
own dissociation of ideas in Gourmont's work. The dissociation
is precisely the dissociation Pound makes between the Muses of
Gourmont and James; it is the structural dissociation made
between the two parts of *Hugh Selwyn Mauberley* as a
composition; it is the dissociation made between Pound, the
poet of "love, passion, emotion as an intellectual instigation,"
and Mauberley, the poet of "aesthetic receptivity of tactile and
magnetic values, of the perception of beauty in these relationships."

Perhaps it is anticlimactic to insist that a problem still
remains, the problem of what one might call the "exterior"
relationship between Hugh Selwyn Mauberley and Ezra
Pound. For *Mauberley* taken entirely on its own terms, the
relation is, I think, clear enough: the passive aesthete played off
against the active instigator. But perhaps even those who feel
that a poet's biography has no part in a reading of his works will
admit that the presence of E. P. in the title of the *Ode* may
excuse brief consideration of issues outside the strict limits of
the poem.

In the "Autobiography" prefixed to the New Directions
Selected Poems Pound writes: "1918 began investigation of
causes of war, to oppose same." The importance of this to
Mauberley is its indication that at the close of the war Pound
was moving toward what he was eventually to call his
"renunciation of poetry for politics." That the Pound of *The
Oxford Book of Victorian Verse* was already a figure of the past
seems clear, but it is hardly satisfactory to follow custom and
look upon Mauberley as a mask of Pound's own early aesthetic
focus; for Pound's allegiances here were always with those who,
however hampered by the age and their own limitations, did,
in Pound's judgment, play their roles as instigators: Swinburne
and Rossetti, Dowson and Johnson. What is, perhaps, useful
and pertinent is to suggest that in the person of Mauberley
Pound was rejecting—though it is always necessary to insist
that this is altogether outside the limits of the poem and in no
sense on a personal level—a mask of what he feared to become
as an artist by remaining in England.

Notes

1. That Pound was already translating the book, or at least considering
   the problems of translating it, at the time he wrote the *Little Review*
   article is indicated by his reference to it as Gourmont's "Physiologie
   de l'Amour" in a note he wrote concerning Frederic Manning's
   article "M. de Gourmont and the Problem of Beauty."
2. "A German study, Hobson, A German study!" *Tarr.* [Pound's note.]

3. "Pourtant, il y a des yeux au bout des doigts, des yeux de chat faits
   pour les ténèbres . . ." *Stratagèmes* also provided the "nevrosis" of
   the entry, which Pound apparently insisted upon in both *Instigations* and *Make It New* as against what I take to be the *Little Review*
   proofreaders's "neurosis." ". . . la contagieuse névrose me
   gagne . . ."
4. Kutsugen is the Japanese form of Ch'ü Yüan. Pound's *Cathay*,
   founded on Fenollosa's notes, has produced a rash of reference to
   "the Chinese poet Rihaku," or "Omakitsu," or "Kakuhaku." There
   is surely no reason to retain these Japanese forms instead of using
   the standard romanized spelling of the poets' actual Chinese names:
   Li Po, Wang Wei, and Kuo P'u in these three instances.
5. For comparison, one might cite an example from Gourmont's
   notice of Octave Uzanne's *Le Célibat et l'amour*: "C'est une
   philosophie colorée par le rêve, car où mettrait-on du rêve, si on
   n'en mettrait dans l'amour?"
6. "The devil in music" is the augmented fourth, which gave the
   medieval musicians great difficulty and gave rise to the tag:

   > Mi contra Fa
   > Diabolus in musica.

   I take it to be pure coincidence that Hugh Selwyn Mauberley's
   initials are the same as His Satanic Majesty's, but considering the
   association of Joyce and Pound at this time, it is a point worth
   passing mention. In the same doubtful area is the possibility of
   "Mauberley," the name, apparently a lavender extension of
   "Moberly," being derived from Brigadier Hugh Stephenson Moberly (1873–1947) and even connected with the folk-saying "Always
   too late like Mobberly clock."
7. The principal bases here are Catullus and Sappho.
8. The original may be of interest here for its use of "grossière," which
   occurs also in the Caid Ali passage. "Le gland, qui affecte toutes les
   formes intermédiaires entre la boule et la pointe, prend, chez le
   rhinocéros, celle d'une grossière fleur de lys."

DONALD DAVIE

From "*Hugh Selwyn Mauberley* and *Homage to Sextus Propertius*" *Ezra Pound*

1975, pp. 54–61

In Allen Upward's *The New Word*, the word in question is
"idealist," as used by Alfred Nobel when prescribing that
his prize for literature should go to "the most distinguished
work of an idealist tendency." Quite early in his investigation
(in chapter three), Upward decides that "idealist" as thus used
is a Babu word. And he explains:

> The English in India . . . have set up schools to
> train the natives in our ways, and, to begin with, in
> our speech. There is a very large class of natives
> called Babus who learn very readily up to a certain
> point, that is to say, they spell our words correctly,
> and they have some notion of what the words mean;
> but English has not replaced their native speech, and
> hence it fits them like a borrowed garment, and they
> are betrayed into awkward and laughable mistakes in
> using it, which have given rise to the term Babu
> English.

I cannot be held responsible for the unworried arrogance with
which Upward, in the age of Kipling, speaks of "the natives."
The linguistic phenomenon which he describes and names is
nonetheless familiar to anyone who has had dealings in ex-
colonial territories; presumably there is Babu French and Babu
Dutch as well as Babu English. And this is the language that
much of *Homage to Sextus Propertius* is written in. How this
can be, comes clear if we allow Upward to continue:

> Now that is just the process from which a great part of
> Europe, and especially England itself, has been
> suffering for many hundreds of years. Our speech

betrays us to be the freedmen of Rome. Our schools are Roman schools set up by missionaries from the Mediterranean in whose minds it was the very aim and end of education to tame the young barbarian of the North into an obedient provincial of the great Roman Raj. . . . Our schools are still called grammar schools, which means Latin-grammar schools, and Latin is the chief thing taught in them. Latin is the official language of our universities, and by an educated man we mean a man who has been taught Latin. The whole theory of our education still is that the young Englishman should make-believe to be an ancient Roman. . . .

Upward, it will be realized, is no Mediterranean-centered man, such as Pound was. Yet he does not, any more than Pound, fly off the handle into the easy and wrong assumptions which since his day have changed Anglophone education beyond recognition, and mostly for the worse: the assumption, for instance, that the Babu can be "true to himself" only by forgetting his Babu English and reverting to, say, Tamil; or the assumption that, because the paradigms of Latin grammar are foreign to the nature of spoken English, therefore those paradigms have no relevance and no usefulness to us as we try to communicate clearly in our language. Upward does not conclude that, because Nobel's "idealist" is a word foreign to both Swedish and English, it has no meaning in either language. Quite to the contrary. And Pound's practice is quite to the contrary also; that is what is meant by "Make It New." We *do* have access to the Mediterranean wisdoms, and our Babu Latin goes halfway to making the most of that access. It is for asserting that the rest of the way is left to travel, and for traveling that distance on our behalf, that Pound has been, and is, reviled.

Accordingly, it should be clear why Pound's most virulent revilers have been professional classicists, and why *Homage to Sextus Propertius*, along with his translation decades later of the *Women of Trachis* of Sophocles, has been the text of his that has given most offense.[1] For the professor of classics is preeminently the Babu, the beneficiary and hence the custodian of a mandarin language acquired in just the way Upward describes. To the professional classicist it seems a matter of life and death to maintain that he has gone, not halfway, but *all* the way. What is involved is social and economic status, precisely as in Anglo-India—hence the way that such critics harp upon "dignity."[2] What Pound renders from Propertius as "Death has its tooth in the lot" had years before been translated by him into acceptable Babu English, thoroughly dignified and thoroughly bland—as he pointed out good-naturedly, when replying to a genial but sharp reviewer.[3] In all seriousness it can be said that when, even leaving aside the professional classicists, we confront Robert Nichols' review of 1920 or, decades later, attacks on *Homage to Sextus Propertius* by Robert Graves and Robert Conquest,[4] what we have to deal with is the entire snarled complex of feelings that we encounter in Frantz Fanon or in the timid and inconclusive suggestions of the young (Algerian) Camus. Every white-skinned English-speaker, however used he may be to regarding himself as a *colon* (colonist), has also been *colonisé* (colonized). The evidence is in our language, as soon as we set it beside Latin; and just that, I suggest, explains the passion with which we contemplate such tricks with our language as Pound played in *Homage to Sextus Propertius*.

I have said before that the language of *Homage to Sextus Propertius*, or of much of it, is "translatorese."[5] The term from Upward, "Babu English," makes the same point, and makes it better:

The twisted rhombs ceased their clamour of accompaniment;
The scorched laurel lay in the fire-dust;
The moon still declined to descend out of heaven,
But the black ominous owl hoot was audible.

The absurdly misplaced formality of "declined to" and the ludicrously stilted passive "was audible" exemplify the English of the bored schoolboy lazily construing his Latin homework but, equally, the proudly pompous clerk (Pakistani, Cypriot, or whatever) using the language of those who were lately his imperial masters. The point is a crucial one, for *Homage to Sextus Propertius* is often presented as a model of how to translate, whereas much of the time it is a deliberate model of how not to![6] So far from being a model for translators to follow, it deliberately and consistently incorporates *mis*translation— the "awkward and laughable mistakes" that the Babu inevitably makes:

These are your images, and from you *the sorcerizing of shut-in young ladies.* . . .
No barbarism would *go to the extent of* doing him harm. . . .
Who so indecorous as to *shed the pure gore of a suitor.* . . .
'Death why tardily come?! . .
Have you *contempted* Juno's Pelasgian temples . . .?
Zeus' clever rapes, in the old days, *combusted* Semele's, of Io strayed. . . .

In each of these lines I have italicized the words which seem unmistakably Babu English or "translatorese," examples of "how not to do it." It is most often a case of unsuitably heightened diction; and this accounts for hilarious passages in an idiom which we have learned to call, since Pound's day, "camp." But sometimes, as in the fourth example above, the comical oddity is not in the vocabulary so much as in word order and syntax, as in:

Sailor, of winds; a plowman, concerning his oxen;
Soldier, the enumeration of wounds; the sheep-feeder, of ewes;
We, in our narrow bed, turning aside from battles:
Each man where he can, wearing out the day in his manner.

(Here the deliberate incongruity of reproducing in a relatively uninflected language the word order and syntax of a highly inflected one produces a comic effect which, with a mastery that is the peculiar glory of this poem, modulates into profound and plangent feeling. And this is a way of saying that the Babu is a hopeful and suffering human creature, no less than the rest of us.)

Every one of these examples of mistranslation can be detected as such by an attentive and halfway sophisticated reader of the English. There is no need to check back to the Latin text of Propertius. But Pound, for good measure, deliberately planted ludicrous howlers, to amuse those who knew the Latin or chose to consult it. This was a miscalculation, given the pompousness and prickliness of the Babu mentality. ("Propertius Soliloquizes" might have saved Pound some of the storm that broke over his head, but not much.) The Babus were *not* amused, and they remain unreconciled to the present day; we've already seen why they would. Wyndham Lewis in 1920, writing to *The Observer* to protest at Robert Nichols' review, made the essential point: "Mr Pound . . . may conceivably know that Chaucer, Landor, Ben Jonson, and many contemporaries of Rowlandson found other uses for classic texts than that of making literal English versions of them." And Lewis points out that Pound's poem parodies Yeats at one point, and names Wordsworth at another.[7] But he cannot nail what is insupportable about Nichols, because what is insupportable is Nichols' *tone*. Nichols is well informed, and some of his information deserves more consideration than Poundians have given it—the fact, for instance, that Propertius was Thomas Campion's favorite Latin poet, that Campion or some other described him as a poet of "melancholy remembrance and vesperal," which is not altogether the impression Pound gives of him. But Nichols' information goes for nothing because it is offered sneeringly, in a tone of vindictive insolence which thinly papers over a wounded sense of personal and professional affront. It is the very tone of Gifford in the *Quarterly* reviewing Keats's *Endymion*. It is the tone of the Babu. And in a sense it proves that the poem has struck home. For all the manifold ironies of *Homage to Sextus Propertius* are directed ultimately at the reader, who is convicted, line by line, of having only pompously imperial, Babu English, into which to render a poem that derides and deflates imperial pretensions. Thus it appears that by wholly transposing "imperialism" into language, into the texture of style, by forgetting his own existence "for the sake of the lines," Pound has effected a far more wounding and penetrating critique of imperialism in general than he could have done by fabricating consciously a schematic correspondence between himself and Propertius, the British Empire and the Roman.

Notes

1. The most immediately damaging attack on *Homage to Sextus Propertius* by a classicist was launched by William Gardner Hale, whose censures on part of the poem that had appeared in *Poetry* in March 1919 were partly reproduced in the Chicago *Tribune*. This was damaging because Hale was a friend of Harriet Monroe, who in Chicago, as editor of *Poetry*, had been bullied by Pound into publishing "the new poetry"—an arrangement which now foundered. Pound's version of the *Trachiniae* (in *Hudson Review*, 1954; in book form as *Women of Trachis*, 1956) was discussed by classicists and others in *The Pound Newsletter*, 5 (Berkeley, 1955). Their views are discussed in my *Ezra Pound: Poet as Sculptor* (New York, 1964), pp. 233–39.
2. See Frederic Peachy and Richmond Lattimore in *The Pound Newsletter*, 5; and *The New Age*, November 27, 1919: "Unfortunately, Propertius' dignity and passion have also to be forced into this jaunty mould. . . ."
3. *The New Age*, Vol. 26 (1919): 82–83. Both this reply and the review to which Pound replies are usefully reproduced in J. P. Sullivan, *Ezra Pound and Sextus Propertius: A Study in Creative Translation* (Austin, 1964), pp. 6–10. The earlier version of some crucial Propertius lines appeared in *Canzoni* (1911) as "Prayer for His Lady's Life." Pound calls it, accurately, "a perfectly literal and, by the same token, perfectly lying and . . . mendacious translation."
4. Robert Nichols, "Poetry and Mr Pound," *The Observer* (Sunday, January 11, 1920); Robert Graves, "These Be Your Gods," in *The Crowning Privilege* (New York, 1956); Robert Conquest, in *The London Magazine* (April 1963).
5. *Ezra Pound: Poet as Sculptor*, p. 87. John Espey has traced in poems in *Lustra* Pound's discovery and gradual mastery of "the technique of the deliberate howler." *Paideuma*, Vol. 1, no. 1 (1972).
6. J. P. Sullivan's *Ezra Pound and Sextus Propertius*, though valuable, is vitiated by this assumption that Pound's dealings with Propertius are a model of what the translator's should be with his original; a doubtless more dangerously influential statement of the same error is in George Steiner's Introduction to his *Penguin Book of Modern Translated Verse* (London, 1966). Pound has indeed renovated the art of verse translation in our time, but this is not one of the works by which he did so!
7. *The Observer* (January 18, 1920).

The Cantos

ALLEN TATE
"Ezra Pound" (1931)
Essays of Four Decades
1968, pp. 364–71

. . . and as for text we have taken it
from that of Messire Laurentius
and from a codex once of the Lords Malatesta. . . .

I

One is not certain who Messire Laurentius was; one is not very certain that it makes no difference. Yet one takes comfort in the vast range of Mr. Pound's obscure learning, which no one man could be expected to know much about. In his great work ⟨*A Draft of XXX Cantos* (New York, 1930)⟩ one is continually uncertain, as to space, time, history. The codex of the Lords Malatesta is less disconcerting than Laurentius; for more than half of the first thirty cantos contain long paraphrases or garbled quotations from the correspondence, public and private, of the Renaissance Italians, chiefly Florentine and Venetian. About a third of the lines are versified documents. Another third are classical allusions, esoteric quotations from the ancients, fragments of the Greek poets with bits of the Romans thrown in; all magnificently written into Mr. Pound's own text. The rest is contemporary—anecdotes, satirical pictures of vulgar Americans, obscene stories, evenings in low Mediterranean dives, and gossip about intrigants behind the scenes of European power. The three kinds of material in the *Cantos* are antiquity, the Renaissance, and the modern world. They are combined on no principle that seems in the least consistent to a first glance. They appear to be mixed in an incoherent jumble, or to stand up in puzzling contrasts.

This is the poetry which, in early and incomplete editions, has had more influence on us that any other of our time; it has had an immense "underground" reputation. And deservedly. For even the early reader of Mr. Pound could not fail to detect the presence of a new poetic form in the individual cantos, though the full value and intention of this form appears for the first time in the complete work. It is not that there is any explicit feature of the whole design that is not contained in each canto; it is simply that Mr. Pound must be read in bulk. It is only then that the great variety of his style and the apparent incoherence turn into implicit order and form. There is no other poetry like the *Cantos* in English. And there is none quite so simple in form. The form is in fact so simple that almost no one has guessed it, and I suppose it will continue to puzzle, perhaps to enrage, our more academic critics for a generation to come. But this form by virtue of its simplicity remains inviolable to critical terms: even now it cannot be technically described.

I begin to talk like Mr. Pound, or rather in the way in which most readers think Mr. Pound writes. The secret of his form is this: conversation. The *Cantos* are talk, talk, talk; not by anyone in particular to anyone else in particular; they are just rambling talk. At least each canto is a cunningly devised imitation of a casual conversation in which no one presses any subject very far. The length of breath, the span of conversational energy, is the length of a canto. The conversationalist pauses; there is just enough unfinished business left hanging in the air to give him a new start; so that the transitions between the cantos are natural and easy.

Each canto has the broken flow and the somewhat elusive climax of a good monologue: because there is no single speaker, it is a many-voiced monologue. That is the method of the poems—though there is another quality of the form that I must postpone for a moment—*and that is what the poems are about*.

There are, as I have said, three subjects of conversation—ancient times, Renaissance Italy, and the present—but these are not what the *Cantos* are about. They are not about Italy, nor about Greece, nor are they about us. They are not about anything. But they are distinguished verse. Mr. Pound himself tells us:

And they want to know what we talked about? *"de
      litteris et de armis, praestantibus ingeniis,*
Both of ancient times and our own; books, arms,
And men of unusual genius
Both of ancient times and our own, in short the usual
      subjects
Of conversation between intelligent men."

II

There is nothing in the *Cantos* more difficult than that. There is nothing inherently obscure; nothing too profound for any reader who has enough information to get to the background of the allusions in a learned conversation. But there is something that no reader, short of some years of hard textual study, will understand. This is the very heart of the *Cantos*, the secret of Mr. Pound's poetic character, which will only gradually emerge from a detailed analysis of every passage. And this is no more than our friends are constantly demanding of us. We hear them talk, and we return to hear them talk, we return to hear them again, but we never know what they talk about; we return for the mysterious quality of charm that has no rational meaning that we can define. It is only after a long time that the order, the direction, the rhythm of the talker's mind, the logic of his character as distinguished from anything logical he may say—it is a long time before this begins to take on form for us. So with Mr. Pound's *Cantos*. It is doubtless easier for us (who are trained in the more historic brands of poetry) when the poems are about God, Freedom, and Immortality, but there is no reason why poetry should not be so perplexingly simple as Mr. Pound's, and be about nothing at all.

The ostensible subjects of the *Cantos*—ancient, middle, and modern times—are only the materials round which Mr. Pound's mind plays constantly; they are the screen upon which he throws a flowing quality of poetic thought. Now in conversation the memorable quality is a sheer accident of character, and is not designed; but in the *Cantos* the effect is deliberate, and from the first canto to the thirtieth the set tone is maintained without a lapse.

It is this tone, it is this quality quite simply which is the meaning of the *Cantos*, and although, as I have said, it is simple and direct, it is just as hard to pin down, it is as hidden in its shifting details, as a running, ever-changing conversation. It cannot be taken out of the text; and yet the special way that Mr. Pound has of weaving his three materials together, of emphasizing them, of comparing and contrasting them, gives us a clue to the leading intention of the poems. I come to that quality of the form which I postponed.

The easiest interpretation of all poetry is the allegorical: there are few poems that cannot be paraphrased into a kind of symbolism, which is usually false, being by no means the chief intention of the poet. It is very probable, therefore, that I am about to falsify the true simplicity of the *Cantos* into a simplicity that is merely convenient and spurious. The reader must bear this in mind, and view the slender symbolism that I am going to read into the *Cantos* as a critical shorthand, useful perhaps, but which when used must be dropped.

One of the finest *Cantos* is properly the first. It describes a voyage:

And then went down to the ship,
Set keel to breakers, forth on the godly sea, and
We set up mast and sail on that swart ship,
Bore sheep aboard her, and our bodies also
Heavy with weeping, and winds from sternward
Bore us out onward with bellying canvas,
Circe's this craft, the trim-coifed goddess.

They land, having come "to the place aforesaid by Circe"—whatever place it may be—and Tiresias appears, who says:

                              "Odysseus
Shall return through spiteful Neptune, over dark
      seas,
Lose all companions." And then Anticlea came.
Lie quiet Divus. I mean, that is, Andreas Divus,
In officina Wecheli, 1538, out of Homer.
And he sailed, by Sirens and thence outward and
      away
And unto Circe.

Mr. Pound's world is the scene of a great Odyssey, and everywhere he lands it is the shore of Circe, where men "lose all companions" and are turned into swine. It would not do at all to push this hint too far, but I will risk one further point: Mr. Pound is a typically modern, rootless, and internationalized intelligence. In the place of the traditional supernaturalism of the older and local cultures, he has a cosmopolitan curiosity that seeks out marvels, which are all equally marvelous, whether it be a Greek myth or the antics in Europe of a lady from Kansas. He has the bright, cosmopolitan *savoir faire* which refuses to be "taken in": he will not believe, being a traditionalist at bottom, that the "perverts, who have set money-lust before the pleasures of the senses," are better than swine. And ironically, being modern and a hater of modernity, he sees all history as deformed by the trim-coifed goddess.

The *Cantos* are a book of marvels—marvels that he has read about, or heard of, or seen; there are Greek myths, tales of Italian feuds, meetings with strange people, rumors of intrigues of state, memories of remarkable dead friends like T. E. Hulme, comments on philosophical problems, harangues on abuses of the age; the "usual subjects of conversation between intelligent men."

It is all fragmentary. Now nearly every canto begins with a bit of heroic antiquity, some myth, or classical quotation, or a lovely piece of lyrical description in a grand style. It invariably breaks down. It trails off into a piece of contemporary satire, or a flat narrative of the rascality of some Italian prince. This is the special quality of Mr. Pound's form, the essence of his talk, the direction of these magnificent conversations.

For not once does Mr. Pound give himself up to any single story or myth. The thin symbolism from the Circe myth is hardly more than a leading tone, an unconscious prejudice about men which he is not willing to indicate beyond the barest outline. He cannot believe in myths, much less in his own power of imagining them out to a conclusion. None of his myths is compelling enough to draw out his total intellectual resources; none goes far enough to become a belief or even a momentary fiction. They remain marvels to be looked at, but they are meaningless, the wrecks of civilization. His powerful juxtapositions of the ancient, the Renaissance, and the modern worlds reduce all three elements to an unhistorical miscellany, timeless and without origin, and no longer a force in the lives of men.

III

And that is the peculiarly modern quality of Mr. Pound. There is a certain likeness in this to another book of marvels, stories of antiquity known to us as *The Golden Ass. The Cantos* are a sort of *Golden Ass.* There is a likeness, but there is no parallel beyond the mere historical one: both books are the productions of worlds without convictions and given over to a hard pragmatism. Here the similarity ends. For Mr. Pound is a powerful reactionary, a faithful mind devoted to those ages when the myths were not merely pretty, but true. And there is a cloud of melancholy irony hanging over the *Cantos.* He is persuaded that the myths are only beautiful, and he drops them after a glimpse, but he is not reconciled to this aestheticism: he ironically puts the myths against the ugly specimens of modern life that have defeated them. But neither are the specimens of modernity worthy of the dignity of belief:

> She held that a sonnet was a sonnet
> And ought never to be destroyed
> And had taken a number of courses
> And continued with hope of degrees and
> Ended in a Baptist learnery
>   Somewhere near the Rio Grande.

I am not certain that Mr. Pound will agree with me that he is a traditionalist; nor am I convinced that Mr. Pound, for his part, is certain of anything but his genius for poetry. He is probably one of two or three living Americans who will be remembered as poets of the first order. Yet there is no reason to infer from that that Mr. Pound, outside his craft (or outside his written conversation) knows in the least what he is doing or saying. He is and always has been in a muddle of revolution; and for some appalling reason he identifies his crusade with liberty—liberty of speech, liberty of press, liberty of conduct—in short, liberty. I do not mean to say that either Mr. Pound or his critic knows what liberty is. Nevertheless, Mr. Pound identifies it with civilization and intelligence of the modern and scientific variety. And yet the ancient cultures, which he so much admires, were, from any modern viewpoint, hatched in barbarism and superstition. One is entitled to the suspicion that Mr. Pound prefers barbarism, and that by taking up the role of revolution against it he has bitten off his nose to spite his face. He is the confirmed enemy of provincialism, never suspecting that his favorite, Lorenzo the Magnificent, for example, was provincial to the roots of his hair.

The confusion runs through the *Cantos.* It makes the irony that I have spoken of partly unconscious. For as the apostle of humane culture, he constantly discredits it by crying up a rationalistic enlightenment. It would appear from this that his philosophical tact is somewhat feminine, and that, as intelligence, it does not exist. His poetic intelligence is of the finest: and if he doesn't know what liberty is, he understands poetry, and how to write it. This is enough for one man to know. And the first thirty *Cantos* are enough to occupy a loving and ceaseless study—say a canto a year for thirty years, all thirty to be read every few weeks just for the tone.

DELMORE SCHWARTZ
"Ezra Pound and History"

New Republic, February 8, 1960, pp. 17–19

As one reads these thirteen new cantos ⟨*Thrones de los Cantares* (Cantos 96–109)⟩ of Ezra Pound's long poem and then rereads the ninety-five which have preceded it, one's first strong impression is that little change or genuine development of these and attitude have occurred throughout the entire work. Through the years Pound has remembered a great deal, but he has learned nothing—nothing that could be called a new insight into the attitudes with which he began to write. Thus Canto 100 begins with

> "Has packed the Supreme Court
>   so they declare anything he does constitutional."
>   —Senator Wheeler, 1936

Here, in this denunciatory reference to Franklin D. Roosevelt and the New Deal, as elsewhere in these cantos, it is clear that Pound's view of the New Deal and the Second World War have not been altered since the lamentable attempt to pack the Supreme Court. And this is but one instance of the fact that Pound has not reviewed, in the light of recent experience and recent knowledge, his attitude toward the Second World War: he has not asked himself what would have happened to Western civilization, American, modern literature and his own poetry, if Germany had won the Second World War. And yet Pound must know—in some sense—that to the Nazis his own kind of work and the creative work he admired and helped to bring into being was regarded as an intolerable and barbaric manifestation of *Kulturbolscheivismus* and decadent cosmo-politanism.

Since the Cantos as a whole aspire to be a kind of philosophy of history, it is necessary to point out how, despite their frequent passages of great beauty, learning, metrical invention and prophetic significance, they are often no more than Pound's discursive monologue about his own *personal* experience of history, particularly 20th Century history, and particularly in relation to his own understandable obsession with the relationship of the creative artist and the statesman. This is perhaps the chief reason that he writes so often about economics and politics.

As a poet whose theme is the nature of history, Pound is inadequate in two important ways: he has an intense tendency to overinterpret and overgeneralize experience from a purely personal point of view or from the point of view very often of the assumed supremacy of the creative artist (as if other human beings were not necessary to the existence of creativity); and this inadequacy is made worse, time and again, by Pound's undisciplined and very often uninformed abstractions.

Here is a somewhat elaborate example: if the Cantos had been concerned with the fall of the Roman Empire as they are concerned again and again with the rise and fall of other great civilizations, Pound clearly would have blamed the fall of Rome upon the weakness and stupidity of a Caesar, or the personal strength of a Barbarian general, or perhaps upon the rise of debt and usury in Rome and the corruption of the aristocracy. What actually happened to cause the fall of Rome, according to J. B. Bury, was something seemingly trivial and implausable: the extraordinary advent of historical *coincidence* or historical *luck.* For centuries, the Barbarians had attacked Rome in great strength: it was only when the unique moment of Barbarian attack and Roman weakness occurred *at the same time* that the huge event of Rome's fall occurred and a great civilization perished. It can be argued that sooner or later this unique historical coincidence was bound to occur unless a great and wise Caesar extirpated the deeply-rooted causes of Roman weakness, and thus that political leadership is very important. But nowhere in this long poem about the nature of history is a sustained effort made to rise to the level of generality necessary to the extreme ambition of the poem; nor is there very much evidence of the intellectual awareness necessary to deal with the questions Pound raises about the nature of history.

The new cantos have many interesting passages, some

passages of unique lyrical beauty, and too many passages when inspiration and excited self-indulgence have been confused with one another.

Thus, at one point, in a passage dealing, I think, with the Byzantine Empire, Pound writes

> Some sort of embargo, Theodora died in the 19th
>   Justinian.
> And the money sellers Ablavius and Marcellus
> Thought they would just bump off Justinian.
> A flood of fads swelled over Europe.
>
> But there could have been two Abduls
> And it would not have annoyed one.
> That is something to note. I mean as personality,
>   when one says "oriental." The third bahai
> Said nothing remarkable. Edgar Wallace had his
>   kind of modesty.

Here Edgar Wallace, a detective story writer once as well-known as Agatha Christie and Erle Stanley Gardner, suddenly emerges, and as suddenly departs from the 20th Century and appears in Byzantium as part of a discussion of the virtues and defects of an obscure historical regime's political luminaries. The relevance of a popular mystery story writer to a political discussion of a distant and for the most part very obscure historical period is, I think, tenuous but real. Edgar Wallace, of whose mystery fiction Pound avowed himself to be very fond in a book published more than twenty years ago, probably was *modest*, and it is probably true that Pound believes in and likes modesty—in other human beings. But the entire passage which is fairly characteristic of Pound's political discourses in the cantos, is a good example of how easy it is to confuse inspiration and self-indulgence, and childishness.

The reference to Edgar Wallace's personal modesty in a passage dealing with Byzantine politicos is not bad in itself, but it is, in addition, quite self-indulgent and personal in the worst way. It does not matter that Pound takes a childish pride in being fond of Wallace and knowing him and bringing his character into an epic poem; and the passage is not bad because of the sudden transition to Wallace's modesty or because of the obscurity of Byzantine history. It is bad because some other and better embodiment or touchstone of modesty would have made the poetic point less tangential and lessened the strain upon the reader who not only has to find out or know who the third bahai and the two Abduls are, and in what way Edgar Wallace possessed the same kind of modesty as his predecessors. To be self-indulgent myself for a moment, I am willing to entertain the possibility that the third bahai was a really important personage, but I don't see what Wallace had to be modest *about*, although I am sure he did the best he could and received adequate compensation.

Nevertheless it must immediately be added that what is bad and self-indulgent in this passage is inseparable from Pound's poetic genius at its best: in other passages, the suddenness of transition and apparent randomness of historical juxtaposition and range are necessary to create the historical perspective of the cantos, the sense that all history is relevant to any moment of history, and the profound belief that the entire past, at any moment and in any place, is capable of illuminating the present and the whole nature of historical experience.

The prose of the book jacket of *Thrones de los Cantares* can serve as a summary of what is good and what is bad in this new section of the cantos. As a description of the new cantos, it is neither better nor worse than most book jacket prose. This is how the preceding section of the cantos, *Rock Drill*, is described:

'The human soul is not love, but love flows from it . . . it cannot, ergo, delight in itself, but only in the love flowing from it'. This is the major theme as the Cantos move into their final phase: 'The domination of benevolence'. Now the great poem has progressed into the realms of the 'permanent'; the poet has passed through 'the casual' and 'the recurrent' and come to values that endure like the sea.

The *Cantos* are a poem containing history; it is their purpose to give the true meaning of history as one man has found it: in the annals of China, in the Italian Renaissance, in the letters and diaries of Jefferson, the Adamses and Van Buren, in the personalities and currents of his own time. The truth must be hammered home by reiteration, with the insistence of a rock drill 'Drilling it into their heads . . . much in the way that a composer does in music'.

As a description of Cantos 85–95 and the new Cantos this is not only adequate, it has a good deal of the obscurity of unavoidable truth and the immense confusion of reality. And it participates in the barbarous contempt for most human beings—unless they are creative artists or patrons of the arts—which recurs throughout Pound's great poem. For it should be clear, by inspection, that the domination of benevolence, is a bad and impractical description of both love and statesmanship. It was, I think, Tallyrand who said to Napoleon, pointlessly enough: "Sire, you cannot sit on bayonets." And it should not be necessary to say, at this late date, that power which is maintained through domination of any kind—benevolent paternalism, for example—is worthless because it is temporary and must be sustained by tyranny. It should be a truism by now that genuine power depends upon consent, just as genuine love requires requited love. Finally to say that the truth must be hammered home by reiteration, with the insistence of a rock drill is revealing in ways which the author of the jacket did not intend: revealing and novel. This must be the first time that the acetylene torch has been advocated as a method of teaching the truth to human beings or writing poetry. One might just as well try out the surgeon's scalpel, psychoacoustical bombing, brainwashing and all the other forms of psychological warfare. And to compare the insistence of a rock drill with the repetition of musical phrases is to reveal a complete ignorance of music and to show how metaphor may be a means of justifying anything, if one is also eager to deceive oneself. If the insistence of a rock drill and the repetition of musical phrases resembled each other in any whatever, the interest in good music, which is small enough as it is, would not exist at all.

I have dwelt at length on the book jacket for several reasons. One is that it is a good summary of Pound's intention and what is wrong with it. But there is a more important reason. In recent years, for extra-literary reasons of all sorts, Pound's work has been praised too often and for the wrong reasons, without qualification or reservation, by ardent admirers and friends, in such a way as to antagonize readers who are not very well acquainted with his work. Indeed, Pound has been praised by his friends—sometimes, perhaps, out of sympathy for his personal plight, rather than his poetry—in so lavish and uncritical a way as to have exactly the reverse of the effect which was intended. The mixed feelings of the reading public toward complicated new poetry are such that uncritical praise is at best merely bewildering. Indeed, the effort and ardor of most of Pound's friends is unfortunate enough to make one think, again: any human being who has friends of this kind has no need of enemies.

There is also an unfortunate and unnecessary antagonism to Pound's work which takes a variety of forms and which, whatever its form, is unjustified. Sometimes the antagonism is purely personal; sometimes the antagonism is political; sometimes it is literary; sometimes it is literary and asserts itself as political liberalism and sometimes it is political and literary; as in the critics who dislike modern poetry and Pound's kind of modern poetry and his political views which Pound makes explicit, from time to time in his poetry. The reference to Roosevelt and the New Deal which I have already quoted is but one of a good many in the present volume. Here is another explicit passage concerning Hitler:

> Adolf furious from perception.
>   But there is a blindness comes from inside—
>   they try to explain themselves out of nullity.

This is enough to make the uninformed reader—or the reader who has been told that Pound is a Fascist and an Anti-Semite—dismiss Pound as a bad poet, or dismiss that which is valuable and beautiful in Pound's writing as trivial when the basic attitude of his work is anti-human. But here is another passage from an early Canto which should illustrate, among other things, the way in which Pound became a great poet:

> The boughs are not more fresh
> where the almond shoots
> take their March green.
>   And that year I went up to Freiburg,
> And Rennert had said: "Nobody, no, nobody
> Knows anything about Provençal, or if there is
>   anybody
> It's old Levy."
> And so I went up to Freiburg,
> And the vacation was just beginning,
> The students getting off for the summer,
> Freiburg im Breisgau
> And everything clean, seeming clean, after Italy.

There is a great deal more to be said about Pound's work and about the passages which disfigure it. For example there are several other passages—the description of a synagogue in Italy and its religious ceremonies and cantos which contain the passionate denunciations of modern war which show that if Pound is, at times, anti-Semitic, he is also, at other times, philo-Semitic; and if he is anti-human, it is, at least, in part, partly through a disappointed and embittered love of mankind. Certainly no one who was wholly misanthropic could be so avidly interested in what happens to human beings and to so many forms of human art and culture. But this is a complicated subject which cannot be discussed with brevity. The first and most important thing to say about Pound's Cantos is that they ought to be read again and again by anyone interested in any form of literature.

DANIEL D. PEARLMAN
"Canto I as Microcosm"
The Barb of Time:
On the Unity of Ezra Pound's Cantos
1969, pp. 37–45

Through the symbolic use of Greek myth, the first canto suggests not only the major themes to be elaborated in the poem, but foreshadows, like a microcosm, the total structural development of the *Cantos*. Except for the last seven lines, Canto 1 consists of Pound's abbreviated English translation of Andreas Divus's Renaissance Latin translation of the opening lines of the eleventh book of the *Odyssey*. Book XI is called the

"Book of the Dead" or "Nekuia," because it concerns Odysseus' visit to Hades.[1] The blood-sacrifice Odysseus makes to Tiresias, who gives the voyager prophetic counsel on how to return to Ithaca, announces the *Cantos'* all-embracing theme of the need for cultural renewal—man's need to re-establish contact with whatever has been vital in his cultural heritage so that he may know what meaningful course to pursue in the future.

Pound begins his epic in the midst of chronological or narrative time, *in medias res*. But in another and deeper sense he begins outside this "profane" flow of time, for the Nekuia and the ritual act of sacrifice abolish chronological time and place Odysseus in the timeless realm of unchanging myth. The historical chain of events, the concatenation of cause and effect, is broken and will no longer determine the fate of Pound's Odysseus until such time as he disregards Tiresias' wisdom and deviates from the pattern of behavior prescribed by the myth. Just as Odysseus' act of blood-sacrifice puts him in touch with the living past and contradicts the irreversible flow of historical time, so too Pound's reverent act of *translation* denies meaning to historical time by showing Homer still to be alive in the so-called present. This translation of a translation of Homer collapses time and makes co-eval not three, but actually five different layers of civilization. Not only is there a continuity of creative impulse between Homeric Greece, Renaissance Italy, and the present, but the Anglo-Saxon rhythms of Pound's English suggest another period whose vital spark has been recaptured; and the Renaissance Latin of Andreas Divus evidences the living continuity of the classical Latin tongue as a literary vehicle.

In the original version of the present canto, then entitled "Canto III," Divus's translation is introduced by the following comment, which quotes Burckhardt: " 'More than the Roman city, the Roman speech' /(Holds fast its part among the ever-living)." Pound wants us to understand especially that Divus has dealt fittingly with Homer, has "Caught up his cadence, word and syllable."[2] When Pound, in line 68 of Canto 1 as it now stands, says, "Lie quiet Divus," this is indeed a critical moment in the canto, but the command is not as cryptic as *The Analyst* would suppose. It is simply that Pound has propitiated Divus's ghost by the sacrificial offering of vital translation, just as Odysseus has satisfied Tiresias' ghost by giving it new life through a blood transfusion. In the same way, Divus might have said, "Lie quiet Homer," after successfully translating him into Latin. Whatever was truly alive in the past, Pound is saying through all this, is always capable of rebirth; and the dead weight of historical time can always be abolished.

There is no conscious intimation here of the theme of organic time, which Pound will set in opposition to mechanical time in the middle phase of the *Cantos*. And yet the Nekuia of Canto 1, which suggests the need to renew vital contact with the cultural tradition, stands as prototype for the later Nekuia passage of Canto 47, which mythically represents man's need for vital contact with chthonic nature and the cosmic and seasonal cycles, a contact which must serve as the basis of cultural renewal. The myths, symbols, and structure of Canto 1 foreshadow the major developments of theme and structure in the poem as a whole.

Time in the first canto is Odysseus' antagonist. It is broadly symbolized by the rough, inimical sea, "spiteful Neptune," as Tiresias calls it, which Odysseus will overcome but at the loss of "all companions." It is historical time which Pound's Odysseus must conquer, and the souls of its victims rise up "out of Erebus"—"souls stained with recent tears," men "mauled with bronze lance heads"—crowding about

Odysseus and crying out to him and to Pound for more blood sacrifices, which I read as a symbolic cry for vindication against the brutality of history. The sea symbolizes not only history, but even more obviously nature, both of which the will must learn to cope with if it is creatively to transform the environment. And Odysseus *polumetis*, the man of many counsels or wiles, dramatizes the creative will capable of effective resistance to the destructive countercurrents of historical time.

The Odyssean voyager-poet of the *Cantos* stands in marked contrast to the Odyssean poet-hero of the *Hugh Selwyn Mauberley* sequences, which Pound wrote while putting the finishing touches on the early cantos. Mauberley is a type of the ineffectual aesthete of the 'nineties. In the first poem of the sequence, which sums up his failure to make an impression on his environment, Mauberley is presented as an Odysseus "out of key with his time" who has "Observed the elegance of Circe's hair" without having gained the wisdom needed to bridge the gap between his poetic self and the world. The result, in the second sequence, is Pound's vision of a Mauberley seen passively *drifting*, not actively steering, in the suspiciously calm waters of an utterly psychotic withdrawal from reality. Announcing his end, he writes on an oar "Here drifted / an hedonist,"[3] and the suggestion is of the fate of drunken Elpenor in the *Odyssey* and in Pound's first canto. *Mauberley* depicts the downhill journey of a comparatively narrow, will-less aesthete, quite unlike the Odysseus of Canto 1, who is heroically many-minded and active in gaining wisdom for the effective exertion of his will upon the environment.

If *Mauberley* presents Pound's conception of the poet as decadant, the *Cantos* presents Pound's conception of the poet as hero, whose ideal role is actively to exert a determining influence on the social environment. Odysseus is the archetype for all those later "heroes" of active, creative will who crop up in the *Cantos*: Malatesta, Confucius, Thomas Jefferson, Mussolini, and others. Odysseus against the sea, the initial image of the poem, establishes in symbolic form the basic polarity or conflict of forces which will reappear in many guises throughout the *Cantos* but can always be reduced to the formulation of will versus nature or will versus history. The polarity which I have suggested earlier to be all-encompassing remains that of *spirit* and *time* (for the concept of time ultimately includes both nature and history).

The second part of Canto 1, consisting of the last seven lines only, is a flash preview of the spiritual adventures in store for the poet-hero of the *Cantos*. As opposed to the rational narrative style of the Nekuia passage, the method here is elliptical, discontinuous, and the tone is oracular or *prophetic*, for reasons which I will soon make clear. The brevity of the passage makes it worth quoting in full:

> And he sailed, by Sirens and thence outward and
> away
> And unto Circe.
> Venerandam,
> In the Cretan's phrase, with the golden crown,
> Aphrodite,
> Cypri munimenta sortita est, mirthful, oricalchi,
> with golden
> Girdles and breast bands, thou with dark eyelids
> Bearing the golden bough of Argicida. So that:

The first two lines reverse the actual sequence of events in Book XII of the *Odyssey*, where, after leaving the underworld, Odysseus first rejoins Circe and later encounters the Sirens. The apparent justification for the reversal is that Pound is presenting images of the feminine in ascending order of desirability. We shall meet the Sirens, Circe, and Aphrodite later on, always in significant contexts, throughout the *Cantos*.

First mentioned in the passage quoted are the Sirens, whose beauty promises only disaster. The ambiguous Circe is next, the goddess who can turn men to swine or, if dominated by an Odysseus, provide physical love and practical guidance. Aphrodite is the "crown" of feminine beauty, and because she is "venerandam," worthy of reverence, she symbolizes equally the spiritual dimensions of such beauty.

The same sea of nature, the same life-force, throws up these three possibilities of experience for Odysseus, which range from physical danger to the most exalted vision of beauty. It is worth noting that Pound, unlike T. S. Eliot, rejects dualism and does not regard material and spiritual reality as essentially at odds. In an early essay he speaks favorably of Remy de Gourmont, who "does not grant the duality of body and soul, or at least suggests that this medieval duality is unsatisfactory; there is an interpenetration, an osmosis of body and soul, at least for hypothesis."[4] Pound goes on to praise Gourmont's "conception of love, passion, emotion as an intellectual instigation," and throughout the *Cantos* we shall see that Aphrodite, goddess of love, stands for both physical passion and for the highest and most enduring kind of beauty that the spirit of man motivated by love can create. In one way or another all the villains of the poem attempt to deny, repress, or abuse sex, nature, the life-force in any and all of its forms; the heroes try to enter into creative harmony with nature.

Pound's non-dualistic view of nature as a physical-spiritual continuum is so important to the *Cantos* that it is worth giving it a name. I find the term *holism*, as defined by Jan Smuts in *Holism and Evolution*, the most fitting one available. Holism, says Smuts,

> represents the organic order as arising from and inside the inorganic or physical order without in any way derogating from it. If in the end it erects on the physical a superstructure which is more and more ideal and spiritual, that does not mean a denial of the physical. The idealism of Holism does not deny matter, but affirms and welcomes and affectionately embraces it.[5]

The pagan, and the archaic man in general, have tended to regard the world holistically, at least in the sense of a physical-spiritual continuum. Odysseus' communication with Tiresias through the blood of a sacrificed sheep symbolizes, in Canto 1, Pound's belief that the world of spirit and the world of nature are interdependent aspects of the same underlying *Ding an sich* that manifests itself temporally in the form of polarity. One of the most important metaphysical principles of Confucianism, the philosophy which informs the *Cantos* from beginning to end (as we shall see), is just this holistic principle expressed by the sage and rendered thus in Pound's translation:

> The celestial and earthly process can be defined in a single phrase, its actions and its creations have no duality.[6]

When the last seven lines of Canto 1 are examined in the light of the holistic principle, Aphrodite and the Sirens are seen as the two polar extremes of the *Ding an sich* which is nature. Circe, as a mediating center between the destructive and creative extremes, will come to represent that harmony with nature which Odysseus-Pound must attain before he can be vouchsafed the vision of Aphrodite. The point is that nature will be for man no more than what he wills it to be, its creative or destructive effects on him depending entirely on the quality of his will—or, better, the direction of his will. This concept of the direction of the will is the foundation of Pound's ethical world-view. Whether it be the creation of an enduring work of art or of a lasting social order, neither comes about by chance.

It is "a matter of WILL," says Pound. "It is also a matter of the DIRECTION OF THE WILL," and "this phrase," he says, "brings us ultimately both to Confucius and Dante."[7] It was in Dante's *De vulgari eloquentia* "that Pound . . . discovered the term *directio voluntatis*, link between Confucius and the best of medieval Europe."[8] Pound takes the Confucian ideogram 志 as "The will, the direction of the will, . . . the officer standing over the heart."[9] The ideogram can thus represent the harmonious conjunction of Odysseus and the sea, the will and nature, or Kung (Confucius) and Eleusis. In the *Cantos* Kung stands for the principle of order, the force of reason, intelligence, and human-heartedness, whereas Eleusis stands for Dionysian energy, the life-force itself. Civilizations rise because of Eleusinian energy, but they are maintained in health and stability by Kung, the principle of order.

If the proper direction of the will is the result of an educative process, then it seems to me clear that the three necessary stages in the development of the will are appropriately represented in the sequence Sirens-Circe-Aphrodite. Lacking knowledge of the self and knowledge of the world, the will is incapable of proper direction and acts destructively. The Sirens symbolize the danger of self-annihilation encountered not only by individuals but by entire civilizations whose wills are misdirected. Circe represents that crucial middle stage of development, the attainment of self-knowledge and harmony with nature which individuals must have if they are to create enduring works, and which societies must possess if they are to maintain themselves for long against the forces of chaos and dissolution. In Canto 39 Odysseus achieves harmony with Circe, whose power bestializes the other members of his crew, because Odysseus alone is capable of a balanced reaction to the lure of sex and can assign it a proper place in his psychic economy. The third stage of the development of the will, the vision of Aphrodite, is the fruitful result of the achievement of inner harmony: cultural rebirth in general, enduring creations in art and the kind of social order that promotes the fullest realization of human potential. For Pound, the Highest Good is based upon the balanced functioning of *all* the human faculties *in due proportion*. He quotes with favor a translator of Aristotle who criticizes that philosopher's

> tendency to think of the End not as the sum of the Goods, but as one Good which is the Best. Man's welfare thus is ultimately found to consist not in the employment of all his faculties in due proportion, but only in the activity of the highest faculty, the "theoretic" intellect,[10]

and Pound adds, "That leads you plumb bang down to the 'split man.'" For Pound, as a Confucian, the proper direction of the will hinges as much upon "the sense of proportion"[11] as upon the sense of "timeliness" which I dwelt upon in the introduction.

Earlier I expressed the feeling that these last lines of Canto 1 were "prophetic." The evidence seems unequivocal that Pound had no clear, conscious conception when beginning the *Cantos* of the over-all design the apparent fragments would fall into; yet I find in the sequence Sirens-Circe-Aphrodite an extraordinarily accurate outline of what I conceive to be the ultimate major form. The Sirens seem to represent what I describe as the first phase of the poem, the spirit's encounter with time: Nature and history will overwhelmingly come to mean chaos and destruction for the embattled spirit of Odysseus-Pound in this phase of the poem. (For Pound's villains and life-deniers, nature appears unqualifiedly destructive.) Circe, literally the major female figure in the second phase of the poem, could very well symbolize nature as

order. In this phase of the poem, hope is seen for man if he adjusts the rhythms of his life to those of organic time. Aphrodite seems to represent the final phase of the poem, the attainment of the earthly paradise, "*Paradiso:* Time as Love."[12]

If my conception of the major form of the *Cantos* is defensible, then Canto 1 foreshadows in microcosm not only the major themes to be developed, but the over-all design of the poem as well. A profound intuition, I believe, gave Pound a sense of the whole from the very start. His use of myth rather than abstract statement enabled him to express much more than he could have "known." "The mythological exposition," Pound says, ". . . permits an expression of intuition without denting the edges or shaving off the nose and ears of a verity."[13]

Notes

1. E. M. Glenn, *The Analyst*, No. VIII (Department of English, Northwestern University, n.d.), p. 3. (*The Analyst*, in mimeographed form, appears irregularly under the general editorship of Robert Mayo. The intention of the publication with regard to the *Cantos* has been mainly to provide scholarly background rather than critical interpretation.) My own debt to *The Analyst* is considerable, for it is one of the chief scholarly sources for the first eleven cantos.
2. Ezra Pound, "Canto III," *Poetry* X (August 1917), p.250.
3. *Personae* (New York, 1950), p. 203.
4. Ezra Pound, "*Rémy de Gourmont*," in *Literary Essays*, ed. T. S. Eliot (Norfolk, 1954), p. 341.
5. Jan Christiaan Smuts, *Holism and Evolution* (New York, 1961), p. 329. (Originally published in 1926.) I might mention here that Pound has told me he did not read Smuts.
6. Ezra Pound, trans., *Confucius: The Great Digest & Unwobbling Pivot* (New York, 1951), p. 183.
7. Ezra Pound, *Jefferson and/or Mussolini: L'idea statale: Fascism as I Have Seen It* (New York, 1935), p. 16.
8. Noel Stock, "Introduction," *Impact*, p. xiii.
9. *Confucius*, p. 22.
10. Ezra Pound, *Guide to Kulchur* (Norfolk, 1952), pp. 342–43.
11. Ezra Pound, *Impact*, p. 134.
12. A partial parallel to the Sirens-Circe-Aphrodite trio is afforded in Canto 1 of the *Commedia*, where Dante encounters three mysterious beasts, leopard, lion, and she-wolf, which critics variously interpret as representative of the three major regions of the damned which the poet is to pass through in the *Inferno*.
13. *Guide to Kulchur*, p. 127.

JAMES J. WILHELM
"The Three Changing Phases of Woman and Gold"
The Later Cantos of Ezra Pound
1977, pp. 20–34

One of the greatest barriers to a full appreciation of Pound's *Cantos* is an unwillingness on the part of many readers to accept the fact that the work is built upon a dynamic principle of change. The concept of Ovid's *Metamorphoses* that the world is constantly in a state of mutation is central to the epic, and this concept of constant change is in turn linked to the triadic division that underlies the poem: the ephemeral (hell), the recurrent (purgatory), and the eternal (paradise). The continual development of forms can be seen clearly if one fixes one's attention on two basic thematic archetypal images of the poem: woman and gold. Why these two subjects in particular? Aside from their eternal fascination for men—both objects of avarice, the dominant vice of mankind—they are inextricably linked together, even though, for purposes of analysis, it is necessary to speak of them separately.

The first of the Early Cantos (1–30) offers three women who fit the triadic organization outlined in the previous chapter: Circe, a hellish temptress who is herself benevolent when she sends Odysseus to the Underworld to gain the knowledge that will lead to his salvation; Anticleia, Odysseus' mother, a representative of the home and order; and Aphrodite, the goddess of love who is a dominant figure in the heavenly constellation of the Poundian poem. From the start, then, the reader sees the range of womanliness from an ambivalent type, who can change a man into a swine, to types who can redeem socially, such as the mother, or metaphysically, such as the goddess.

Gold is also mentioned conspicuously in the first canto:

> with the golden crown, Aphrodite,
> Cypri munimenta sortita est,[1] mirthful, orichalchi,
> with golden
> Girdles and breast bands, thou with dark eyelids
> Bearing the golden bough of Argicida . . .
>
> (1/5)

The canto thus rises steadily from the dark deprivation in Circe's house to knowledge gained from the dead (the prophet Tiresias carries a "golden wand"). It ends with the promise of the "golden bough," the traditional symbol of entrance into an Underworld for purposes of enlightenment. The gold in Canto 1 is primarily that of illumination and regal splendor, both things that are paradisal in their effect, and both are clearly linked to the divine; but in the mentions of Aphrodite's golden raiment, there is also the clear suggestion of the baubles of the temptress, like the Circe who opens the work. So in this single canto occur three manifestations of woman, with the suggestion that all three are variations of the one.

The notion of the female force as something ungodly and even destructive recurs in Canto 2, with a brief portrayal of that archetypal destroyer, Helen of Troy. Pound uses various Greek words to describe her, punning on her name: *helenaus* (destroyer of ships) and *heleptolis* (destroyer of cities). Then, instead of the name Helen, he uses Eleanor. One might guess Eleanor of Aquitaine, and this identification is confirmed in Cantos 6 and 7.[2] Pound is forcing the reader to see the Greek and the south French woman as one. They are both seductive forces with "naked beauty" and "tropic skin" (7/26), objects which may lure men to their destruction. Helen of Troy caused the Trojan War, and Eleanor's marriage to Henry II of England after her divorce from Louis VII of France led to that interminable series of wars that plagued the two countries. The Greek verb *helein* (destroy) is a part of their names and also one side of their characters, although just one side.

The reader can see three levels of womanhood established in Canto 3. Near the start one finds oneself in the house of a fertility goddess, Kore or Proserpina, and then outside among the bright Tuscan gods in nature. But this heavenly calm does not last, for in the second strophe emerges that adventuresome rascal, The Cid, riding the Burgos, where he is greeted and warned by a nine-year-old girl. This charming picture, dear to the readers of romantic epic, changes swiftly as The Cid deceives two pawnbrokers and is found "Breaking his way to Valencia." This violent action culminates with the mention of "Ignez da Castro murdered." Without pressing very deeply, one can see that the rhythm falls from the heavenly order of nature into man-made chaos, and that three females pinpoint the descent: the goddess, the little girl, and the murdered Portuguese lady—a range that extends from religion to romanticism to brutal realism.

The destructive potential of women occurs again in Canto 6, in which Pound emphasizes the sexual excesses of the troubadours ⟨. . .⟩. Here one finds swashbuckling men and potentially dangerous women in an atmsophere of wildness.

Yet ⟨. . .⟩ the hellish note does not dominate, for the lines of the poets linger in the mind of the reader and have a redemptive value. The troubadours here are more the makers of poems than the seducers of women, and the ladies are raised up a step by being the sources of much of their inspiration.

Women, in fact, fare rather well in the distinctly hellish passages of the Early Cantos. Pound exempts them largely from the "real" Hell of Cantos 12 and 14–16, where men are the worst perpetrators of social injustice. Pound's famous tirades against usury obviously are not going to be directed to women, since women, even today, are usually not powerful in the ranks of financiers, bankers, munitions-makers, and industrialists— although time may change that situation. Pound's obsession with money crimes as the worst sins against man and nature spares him from any suspicion of antifeminism.

Furthermore, as made clear in the Introduction, Pound was never a Puritan. He himself had been the victim of "bluenose" moralty at Wabash College, and he was not about to point a finger at other people's sexual activities. In Canto 39, he presents a convincing case for sexuality as natural and necessary, and, even though the canto contains at least one passage that may remind one of Henry Miller, it is written with much more taste:

> When I lay in the ingle of Circe
> I heard a song of that kind.
> Fat panther lay by me
> Girls talked there of fucking, beasts talked there of eating,
> All heavy with sleep, fucked girls and fat leopards,
> Lions loggy with Circe's tisane,
> Girls leery with Circe's tisane
>
> (193)

Pound runs the risk of downgrading woman only in the sense that he is an heir to Christian Neoplatonism, and thinkers in this tradition sometimes equate woman with matter, as in Canto 20/91:

> Jungle:
> Glaze green and red feathers, jungle,
> Basis of renewal, renewals;
> Rising over the soul, green virid, of the jungle,
> Lozenge of the pavement, clear shapes,
> Broken, disrupted, body eternal . . .
> Glazed grape, and the crimson,
> HO BIOS, [life]
> cosi Elena vedi [so see Helen]

There is no doubt here that the destructive Helen (Elena in Pound's adaptation of Dante's Italian phrase from *Inferno* 5.64) blurs into a confused, chaotic world that is distinctly feminine at base. Yet, what redeems the scene are the words "body eternal" and "renewals." Mother Earth in her archetypal role restores as much as she devours.

A similar passage occurs in Canto 29/144:

> Wein, Weib, TAN AOIDAN [wine, woman, song]
> Chiefest of these the second, the female
> Is an element, the female
> Is a chaos
> An octopus
> A biological process

Here the woman-matter parallel is fully spelled out, but the lines go on to mention two verses of Sordello's poetry and speak of "Our mulberry leaf, woman, TAN AOIDAN." It would be difficult to say that Pound is doing anything worse here than what Joyce did with Molly Bloom: that is, he is making archetypal woman the basis upon which all else grows, just as the finest Neoplatonics, such as Scotus Erigena, delighted in matter as the base of the universe, and did not run to condemn it.

If Pound tends to see woman as a "biological process," he also notes that "Matter is the lightest of all things" (143). Perhaps he uses this idea of Plotinus to make his definition of matter coincide with Richard of St. Victor's notion of cogitation (the lowest form of thought) as a whirring, moving, chafing activity that is disruptive and chaotic. This concept is in keeping with his notion of the infernal, and it may also explain why he likes to concentrate on drifters like Cunizza da Romano or women with hellfire in them—Parisina d'Este and Lucrezia Borgia. But for every incestuous destroyer like Parisina, Pound balances with an Isotta, the wife of Sigismundo Malatesta, for whom the Italian nobleman built the beautiful Temple of Rimini. And although Cunizza was a hellcat in her youth, one learns in Canto 29/142 that she redeemed herself with a great act of kindness when she freed her slaves in the house of the Cavalcantis in Florence in 1265:

> Free go they all as by full manumission
> All serfs of Eccelin my father da Romano
> Save those who were with Alberic at Castra San Zeno
> And let them go also
> The devils of hell in their body.

Cunizza is depicted first as a loose woman who runs away with the troubadour Sordello, but later Pound stresses her purgatorial activities and qualities, her kindness and compassion, which enable her to change from slut to saint. Dante finally put her in his third heaven; but in Dante's *Paradiso*, she is *just* a saint because Christian judgment sees the soul as a fixed entity. In Pound's *Cantos*, her being ranges over the three degrees of human conduct from the lowest to the highest. In the *Pisan Cantos*, Pound sees Cunizza's face with the faces of other beautiful women and with goddesses. Her apotheosis is thus completed.

If Pound sees woman as truly infernal in any lasting sense, it is only woman as whore. Most women, Pound believes, are victims of the game of men, political pawns such as Helen and Eleanor. The worst females are the prostitutes mentioned obliquely in Cantos 19/88 and 22/105–6, or perhaps those stiff, wooden, unsensual American-Puritan women in Canto 28/135, women who have a "ligneous solidity" that is not a part of the easy, flowing activity that Pound most admires. The prostitute, who lives and loves for gold, is cursed by Pound, although the woman who lives for love is not. In general, the Early Cantos are typified by a lack of solidity, of something to hold onto. Everything fades away, as the light does around the brilliant gold mosaics in the tomb of the Roman empress Galla Placidia in Ravenna: "In the gloom, the gold gathers the light against it" (11/51).

Human beings and objects become much more solid and identifiable in the Middle Cantos (31–84), which serve as Pound's intellectual Purgatory. Here people are engaged in tasks: Jefferson and Adams in the building of America, the Tuscan people in the founding of the Bank of Siena, the Chinese emperors in the ruling of China. The central cantos continue the work of Sigismundo and the Medicis and the Estes in the first thirty cantos, and in them woman is placed next to man, as in the famous gold mosaics in San Vitale, Ravenna, where Theodora faces her husband, Justinian. Thus, Abigail Adams is mentioned quite undramatically with John (62/344 ff.), the mother of Emperor Yong Tching is given her due (61/339 ff.), and faithful Chinese wives abound in Canto 54. The most important woman is Maria Maddalena, the mother of Duke Ferdinand II of Tuscany, one of the prime movers in the establishment of the Bank at Siena that was based on the distribution of nature's bounty for all, rather than upon the personal greed of a select few. Pound emphasizes her femininity in this great act, calling her "M. Magdalene the She Guardian" of her young son (42/214), with the last word from Latin "tutrices" (43/215). In several cases where Maria's name occurs, the Virgin Mary is also mentioned, for Pound wants to create the distinct impression that a great act of social love has a divine aura about it.

Of course, there are bad women, too: Peggy Eaton, who scandalized Washington at the time of President Jackson (34/169), the Chinese empresses who hired their relatives (56/302), the women who tried to gain control of their men ("brat was run by his missus," 55/299), and the prostitutes (71/420). Pound stresses the fact that the Bank of Siena (Monte dei Paschi) made it possible for the town whores to reform and to strike their names off the city rolls as streetwalkers: 43/219. In the main, he emphasizes the dignity of women when he repeats the mullings of John Adams: "why exclude women from franchise?" (70/411).

But if the general status of women improves in the Middle Cantos, with just a few relinkings of the feminine with the material forces of life (largely in Cantos 39 and 47), the role of gold assumes much greater importance. In these cantos, economics begins to emerge more clearly as one of the organizing principles of Pound's view of history. People who misuse gold become more obviously the villains of the epic. In their direst form, the misusers include the usurers, the great international frauds who tamper with the value of money or monopolize it, as in the famous Usury Canto, 45, or even more clearly in 46/234:

> Aurum est commune sepulchrum. Usura,
>   commune sepulchrum.
> helandros   kai heleptolis   kai helarxe.
> Hic Geryon est. Hic hyperusura.

These words, like an epitaph written in mixed Latin and Greek, can be translated as follows:

> Gold is a common sepulchre. Usury, a common sepulchre. / Man-destroying / and city-destroying / and rule-destroying / Here is Geryon. Here is hyperusury.

The *hel-* words, which were earlier applied to Helen and Eleanor, are now applied to the real culprits: the men who manipulate woman and gold for their own private ends.

Pound hit hard on a selfish handling of coin in 52/257:

> Thus we lived on through sanctions, through Stalin
>   Litvinof, gold brokers made profit
> rocked the exchange against gold

In fact, he clearly contrasts this ill-gotten gold with the brilliant gold of the Church of La Daurade (the Gilded) in Toulouse, where the Italian poet Guido Cavalcanti met the beautiful girl Mandetta:

> Between KUNG and ELEUSIS
> Under the Golden Roof, la Dorata

In this canto occur two seminal lines: "Life and death are now equal/Strife is between light and darkness." Here, at what might have been the midpoint of the poem (Pound was never sure about the exact length), one begins to leave the pits of darkness behind and to enter the corridors of light. Even though the image is not underlined, the gold of the sun emerges as an obvious metaphor. Canto 51 opens with the Neoplatonic analogy of God with the sun, using Guido Guinizelli's famous *Al cor gentil repara sempre amore* (Love always repairs to the noble heart) as its source. Perhaps the most beautiful occurrence comes in Canto 55/292:

In the city of Tching-tcheou are women like
   clouds
                                       of heaven,
   Silk, gold, piled mountain high.

With lines like these, the reader knows that he is on the road to
Heaven.

But Pound does not want to rush there, in the manner of
T. S. Eliot. He wants to examine history carefully, showing
that those who steeped themselves in gold, such as the debased
heirs of the Estes in Ferrara, who used gold forks (aureis
furculis: 26/122), did not create anything lasting. Pound
stresses the fact that "gold is inedible" (56/303), and that the
benevolent ruler provides bread. He is anticipating what he
later emphasized from the work of the statistician Alexander del
Mar: that gold is merely a measure of value, not necessarily a
valuable commodity per se.[3] Similarly, Pound rails out against
the alchemists, who tried to pervert nature by converting
perfectly good minerals into magic elixirs, as if the very
possession of gold were a salvation in itself. The hoarding
tendency Pound views as the basest drive in the human animal.
Gold-vultures, or gold-lice as he calls them, cannot exist
without a host to feed on (one can't forever create money *ex
nihilo,* the way banks do, without clients to loan it to), and yet
they almost unconsciously destroy the organism upon which
their survival depends.

The *Pisan Cantos* form an important interlude in Pound's
poem. As the poet was placed in the detention camp at Pisa, he
realized that he would have to align himself with nature in
order to survive. In so doing, he directed his appeal largely to
the feminine forces: the pagan goddesses (Venus-Aphrodite,
Demeter, Proserpina), the Chinese figure of mercy Kuanon
(Kuan-Yin), Christian saints (Perpetua, Agatha, Anastasia),
beautiful women from Renaissance and nineteenth-century
painting, and women from actual life (H.D. or Hilda Doolittle, Anne Blunt, and others). Naturally, men also appear
here, but in the main it was the soft, compassionate spirit of
women nurtured in memory that helped the poet to survive.

In expressing this attitude toward the feminine, Pound
had to reshape his earlier words about matter, the Madame
Hyle of Canto 30. Instead of presenting woman as a biological
process or the mansion of darkness that man's reason must
penetrate and illuminate, Pound sees her as an integral part of
the beautiful natural landscape around him. He calls the
nameless hills around Pisa the breasts of Tellus or Helen, or he
uses a composite name:[4]

   Mist covers the breasts of Tellus-Helena and drifts up
      the Arno
   came night and with night the tempest
                                              (77/473)

This redemption of the feminine is completed in the poet's
"marriage with Earth" ⟨. . .⟩:

   How drawn, O GEA TERRA,   [Mother Earth]
      what draws as thou drawest
         till one sink into thee by an arm's width
      embracing thee. Drawest,
         truly thou drawest.
   Wisdom lies next thee,
      simply, past metaphor.
                                              (82/526)

Another transformation of the feminine occurs with relationship to the moon. Pound frequently sees his women in triads,
and in one of the most common groups, he links Cunizza with
a barefoot girl (la scalza), who says, "Io son' la Luna" (74/438),
"I am the moon"; there is also a little sister who danced on a

six-pence ("sorella, / che ballava sobr'un zecchin'": 77/475).
This grouping brings the little girl and the historic woman into
conjunction with the lunar force. Thus, the range of femininity extends from the mythic to the physical to the cosmic.
When one reads the seminal line "Cythera, in the moon's
barge whither?" (80/510) and soon after learns that the rosy-
fingered Dawn is "in the moon barge," one sees all these forces
coalescing. Woman is love, is the moon, is universal compassion. Her darkness is that of the night, but this can be soothing,
especially after the brutal glare of the lights of the detention
camp.

As noted in Chapter One, Pound effects some even
stranger mythic transformations in these Later Cantos.[5] First,
he clearly shows that his idea of Paradise is, at its base, social
and earthly by titling his two major sections *Rock-Drill* and
Thrones. Canto 85 begins with the mention of two queens,
Elizabeth I and Cleopatra. They are cited not for their beauty,
but for their devotion to work and thought:

   That Queen Bess translated Ovid,
         Cleopatra wrote of the currency.

Cleopatra is mentioned again in 86/565 with the Hapsburg
empress Maria Theresa. From the start, then, women are
presented equally with men as excellent rulers. Theodora is
mentioned side by side with Justinian I in 91/611, and the
Mémoires of Madame de Rémusat dominate Canto 101.
Pound voices a slight antifeminism only in Cantos 98 and 99,
where he is following the words of the *Sacred Edict* of the
Chinese emperor, K'ang Hsi; but these passages are muted, and
he emphasizes that "there be no slovenly sloppiness / between
goodman & wife" (99/705).

The equality theme is stated even more strongly in terms
of the gods who hover over the kingly thrones. The hero of
justice is Athena (*Athana*), the asexual goddess (87/571):

   Was not unanimous
         Athana broke tie,
   That is 6 jurors against 6 jurors
                  needed *Athana.*

She is cited again in Canto 89/601. Other feminine spirits
appear frequently in the Later Cantos, and they continue to
merge together: Isis and Kuanon in 90/606, St. Ursula with
Ysolt and Piccarda Donati (of Dante's *Paradiso* 3) in 93/628,
and Fortuna or Fortune with Luna (86/566)—all with the
suggestion of the moon somewhere in the design.

Then, a further transformation takes place as the women
begin to merge with their male counterparts:

   Beatific spirits welding together
         as in one ash-tree in Ygdrasail.
            Baucis, Philemon.
                  (90/605)

Sometimes the assimilation brings the solar force in touch with
the lunar, as when Kuanon is mentioned as wearing "the sun
and moon on her shoulders" (101/726). The earlier linking of
the female with the moon is taken a step further as the Egyptian
male sun god, Ra, is fused with the male god of evil, Set, and
the composite figure is spoken of as if it were feminine:[6]

   The Princess Ra-Set has climbed
         to the great knees of stone . . .
                  (91/611)

This figure is then linked to Helen of Troy and Queen
Elizabeth (through Francis Drake) as riders in the moon-barge
that is pictured as a hieroglyph on page 612:

   Helenaus That Drake saw the armada
         & sea caves
   Ra-Set over crystal
                  moving

In fact, Pound is effecting poetically here what he knew, years before, that Scotus Erigena had done philosophically in Book 5 of his *On the Division of Nature:* he is abolishing sexual differences.[7] Even in Canto 91, which can be called the Queen's Canto, in part because of the strange name Reina (variant of Regina or "Queen") with which it opens, this marriage of male and female in a chaste, mystical world of light and shadow is beautifully hymned:

> Merlin's fader may no man know
> Merlin's moder is made a nun . . .
>   all that she knew was a spirit bright,
> A movement that moved in cloth of gold
>   into her chamber.
> "By the white dragon, under a stone
>   Merlin's fader is known to none."
> Lay me by Aurelie, at the east end of Stonehenge[8]
>   where lie my kindred
> Over harm
> Over hate
>   overflooding, light over light . . .
> the light flowing, whelming the stars.
>   In the barge of Ra-Set
> On river of crystal
>
>   (613)

On the highest mystical plane, as Scotus Erigena had affirmed, woman is not differentiated from man. There is no sexuality in the upper spheres of contemplation, just as there is no temporal difference between night and day. Both sun and moon have their purposes: "Our science is from the watching of shadows" (85/543). Even the Underworld entered in Canto 1 is redeemed in the Later Cantos as two members fly upward in a shower of light: "out of Erebus, the delivered, / Tyro, Alcmene, free now, ascending" (90/608). As Scotus had written and prayed, Hell has finally been abolished by being understood, and Heaven has become universal.

In Canto 106/755, Pound remarks that Selena, an alternate name for Moon in Greek, has risen as a queen to Heaven. This statement alone is somewhat extraordinary, but it is eclipsed in the previous canto, when reason, which is frequently thought of as male, is aligned with the moon: Ratio . . . luna (105/747). This is then followed by the strongest statement of the purity of woman in *The Cantos*, and it is attributed to one of Pound's favorite medieval philosophers, St. Anselm, who will be discussed further in Chapter Twelve:

> "Ugly? a bore,
>   Pretty, a whore!"
>   brother Anselm is pessimistic,
> digestion weak,
>   but had a clear line on the Trinity, and
> By sheer grammar: Essentia
>   feminine
>   Immaculata
>   (750)

Essence is immaculate! No matter how much Pound may be reading into Anselm—he merely implies that the feminine gender of the word "Essentia" determines the femininity—this is surely one of the strongest cases for redeemed femininity from the pen of a man.[9] These lines show the heritage of years of devotion to the finest elements of Christian thought.

Perhaps the whole vindication of woman can be seen best in the Chinese character that opens and acts as a presiding emblem for the Later Cantos, *ling* (Canto 85/543). This character is analyzed in Canto 104/740 as "The small breasts snow-soft over tripod." *Ling* means "sensibility, tradition" or "ghost, soul." It has been analyzed in descending fashion as the rain radical over three mouths which are in turn propped up by

two feet.[10] But Pound, instead, sees the mouths as breasts, like the hills in the *Pisan Cantos*, which in turn are supported by tripods (accoutrements both of monarchs and of wizards). Then he immediately shifts his interpretation and takes a more accepted one: "under the cloud / the three voices." Pound is telling us that sensibility or a knowledge of the traditions of the past is, in Confucian terms, an absolute essential for good government or the ideal life; it is a sentient, feminine force, and is observable all around us in the beating heart of nature (some people see the two bottom elements in the *ling* character as dancing feet).

If woman is aptheosized in the Later Cantos, gold also finds its way to Heaven. For gold is presented primarily in two ways: as material, in the form of money, and as a color or symbol with a hieratic value. In those cantos where economics predominates, the first point of view prevails. Thus, Canto 96, which treats the history of the Lombards and gives the rules for governing Byzantium, abounds with mentions of gold objects or the work of goldsmiths. Pound's point here, lifted in part from the work of Alexander del Mar, is that it is a government's job to superintend the minting and proper distribution of gold.[11] This duty cannot be allowed to fall into the hands of private enterprise, as it did under Charles II of England and thereafter. Even when talking about money, Del Mar titles his chapter "The Sacred Character of Gold."

Canto 97 opens with a consideration of the just ratio between silver and gold in coining, but as the poetry progresses, it leaves behind the marvelous names of coins that Pound the nominalist-at-base adores—the dinars and scats and mithcals and tussujs and baugs and vadmals—and rises on the wings of Pound-the-idealist's vision into the "russet-gold" lacquer of the sunlight (675). For Pound is both a realist and an idealist, dreaming of perfection but concerned with the here and now. Similarly, his vision of woman embraces both her mysterious capacity to destroy as well as her power to redeem: "And in every woman, somewhere in the snarl is a tenderness" (113/789).

Pound's encompassing vision is nowhere better exemplified than in Canto 109, where, after considering one of the kind acts from the Statues of the 31st year of the great Elizabeth I of England, he ties in his economic idea that justice is achieved only by a control of the gold of the realm.[12] The gold, the love (amor), and the Great Queen are like a resplendent mosaic in verse:

> For every new cottage   4 acres
>   Stat de 31 Eliz.
>
>   Angliae amor
> And false stone not to be set in true gold
> to the king onely to put value
>   and to make price of the quantity

On this note of acceptance—of England, which he had formerly despised, and woman, whom he had occasionally denigrated—the elderly Pound wrote a close to the formally ordered *Cantos*, demonstrating a vision and a balance that point to a world outside of time.

Notes

1. "She has won by lot the monuments of Cyprus"; the *orichalchi* is translated in the phrase that follows.
2. For identifications, see *Annotated Index to the* Cantos, ed. J.H. Edwards and W.W. Vasse (Berkeley: Univ. California, 1971).
3. *The Science of Money*, 2nd ed. rev. (New York: 1896; rpt. Burt Franklin, 1968), p. 3.
4. Cf. Cantos 77/468; 79/487. See Hugh Kenner, *The Pound Era* (Berkeley: Univ. California, 1971), p. 473, for picture, and p. 471.

5. See John Peck, "Pound's Lexical Mythography: King's Journey and Queen's Eye," *Paideuma*, vol. 1, no. 1 (1972), 3–36; also, Guy Davenport, "Persephone's Ezra," *New Approaches to Ezra Pound*, ed. Eva Hesse (Berkeley: Univ. California, 1969), pp. 145–73.

6. For Pound's uses of Egyptian material, see Boris de Rachewiltz, "Pagan and Magic Elements in Ezra Pound's Works," *New Approaches*, ed. Hesse, pp. 174–97.

7. Scotus, *De Divisione Naturae*, chaps. 20–23, in vol. 122 of *Patrologia Latina*, cols. 893–905; trans. in part by Myra L. Uhlfelder as *Periphyseon* (Indianapolis: Bobbs-Merrill, 1976).

8. Christine Brooke-Rose, *A ZBC of Ezra Pound* (Berkeley: California, 1971), pp. 183–207, has a masterly analysis.

9. Most professional philosophers will resent Pound's suggestion of pantheism here, as with Scotus, but the point is grammatical; alternate title of *Monologion* is *De Divinitatis Essentia* (On the Essence of Divinity) and that essence is rational *and* amatory: *Patrologia Latina*, vol. 158, esp. cols. 200 ff. Despite Anselm's disclaimer that he is talking about essences and not substances, the Highest Nature is "through all and in all": *per omnia, et in omnibus* (chap. 14, col. 161).

10. Analyzed by Kenner, *Pound Era*, p. 544; Thomas Grieve, *Paideuma*, vol. 4, nos. 2–3 (1975), 390.

11. *History of Monetary Systems* (London, 1895; rpt. New York: Kelley, 1969), pp. 463–69 for Charles; 107–32 on gold.

12. Excellent treatment of this difficult part of poem by David Gordon, "The Azalea Is Grown," *Paideuma*, vol. 4, nos. 2–3 (1975), 223–99, esp. 291–92.

M. L. ROSENTHAL

"Pound at His Best: Canto 47 as a Model of Poetic Thought"

Paideuma, Winter 1977, pp. 309–21

A poet's thought counts—as it works poetically. By traditional standards, Longinian or whatever, *The Cantos* are superb in their copiousness, their breadth of concrete realization, and their ability to ride and control the emotional and lyrical dynamics of a turbulent associative process. True, they are uneven. But their successive groupings should be read as one reads successive volumes in the usual poetic career; naturally, some volumes are better than others and one finds the most supremely accomplished poems scattered here and there. At the same time, Pound was our great adventurer in the formation of the modern poetic sequence, that largely unrecognized genre which is the crowning formal discovery of modern poetry, revealing the underlying motives and heroic purposes of a century of artistic labors. Pound can be tiresome. He has his rancid fascist dimension, and his wantonly allusive surfaces have summoned up an army of annotators from the vasty deep. Yet we cannot ignore the way that, at his best, he makes his thought count as poetic energy. Even his defects that so heavy upon him lie project tones and drives of the age that cannot be ignored.

What does it mean for a poet to be this sort of living presence? In Book X of the *Odyssey* Circe tells Odysseus he must seek out the prophet Tiresias, "who even dead, yet hath his mind entire!" (The translation is of course Pound's, in the opening line of Canto 47.) Odysseus, since he existed in that realm of myth where no flesh has trod, sailed forth, performed the necessary ritual, fed sacrificial blood to Tiresias, and held converse with the amazed, momentarily reincarnated sage.

But we, since we no longer hold with ritual sacrifice or bed with tutelary goddesses, must do with Pound as Pound did with Homer. We must open ourselves to possession by his "mind entire." A poem of decisive energy insists upon its own linguistic priority. It replaces the system of language we ordinarily inhabit with its own system, which is perforce alien to us because it is at once the discovery and the creation of an original mind engaged with reality in its own way. I have just recalled how, at the start of Canto 47 (as in earlier cantos as well), Pound recovers the world the *Odyssey* for himself. In the act of so doing, he stamps his poem—in this momentarily confusing opening line—with his own obsessions and his own methods of poetic realization.

> Who even dead, yet hath his mind entire!
> This sound came in the dark
> First must thou go the road
>   to hell
> And to the bower of Ceres' daughter Proserpine,
> Through overhanging dark, to see Tiresias,
> Eyeless that was, a shade, that is in hell
> So full of knowing that the beefy men know less than he,
> Ere thou come to thy road's end.

I choose Canto 47 as a primary touchstone for several reasons. The very embodiment of Pound's genius, it acts directly out of that communion of past and present which, felt at the pitch of experience, is nothing less than our human meaning in process. Even more than Browning, from whom he learned so much, Pound is our keenest exemplar of such communion. What is involved is the linguisitic mobilization of memory and knowledge as energy acting in the immediate present, not as dead "information" about an inert past.

How does this happen? The attentive reader will surely be struck by the subtleties of Pound's recasting the Homeric text into modern poetic idiom. The opening lines of Canto 47 that I have quoted still present Odysseus speaking, but we no longer have a completely straightforward narrative. The very first line jolts our understanding deliberately. Unless we recognize the quotation at once, it looks at first like a riddle, one unaccountably couched in an exclamation rather than a question. Pound has lifted it out of its proper context, the description of Tiresias a few lines further along. And so this paradoxical outcry stays floating there at the start of the canto, portentous and waiting for its relevance to be made clear. Even the mysterious second line—"This sound came in the dark"—floats in place a little ambiguously and ominously, perhaps a reference to the opening line, perhaps to the lines that follow, perhaps to both. Plainer than the first line, it is nevertheless almost as ringing and riddling.

So the two initial musical phrases seem to enter arbitrarily and disconcertingly. But they settle into context as the succeeding lines emerge with perfect clarity. These lines project the primitive awe of Homer's text. The third and fourth lines drop us, with a lurch, into a vision of hell, and the deepened tone is sustained by occasional archaic diction and by a stock epithet ("beefy men") suggestive of traditional epic as well as by the long, prophetically incantatory sentence.

The passage as a whole is as much an experimental use of traditional materials as it is a reminder of their continuing magnetism and mystery. It is serious verbal play, or syntactic play. We have seen how it plucks a paradoxical note from its original context and gains extraordinary emphasis by the displacement. Read as a series of tonal notes, the passage begins with its riddling exclamation and then sustains the ominousness and mystification by the reverberating second line, "This sound came in the dark." In the echoing associations of these two lines a sort of equivalence exists between communication with the dead in Homer's mythic world and the invasion of dark psychic recesses by the repossessed mentality of a past age. Heightened alertness to the encroachments of death and darkness is a necessary condition of the sensitized awareness of this speaker, whose voice is a fusion of that of Odysseus and of a modern intelligence close to Pound's own.

What is the point of this reimprovisation of Homer? The whole glow of its movement comes from its entranced companionship with the older text, yet that companionship merely sets the poem on a further journey of awareness.

> Knowledge the shade of a shade,
> Yet must thou sail after knowledge
> Knowing less than the drugged beasts. *phthego-*
>   *metha thasson*
>   φθεγγώμεθα θᾶσσον
>   The small lamps drift in the bay
> And the sea's claw gathers them.
> Neptunus drinks after neap-tide.

The opening displacements were a clue to the method further revealed here, where Homer is decisively subordinated to a modern sensibility. Homer's Odysseus was not a subjective man; Pound's isolation of the one paradoxical thought about Tiresias begins to make him so. It is this reconceived Odysseus who defines for himself a task at once virtually hopeless and yet irrevocable. Nor would Homer's Odysseus ever have called knowledge "the shade of a shade." Dante's and Tennyson's Odysseus (i.e., "Ulysses") might have pondered the matter, but not Homer's man. Such modern skepticism, and the Platonic sophistication underlying it, would have been thoroughly alien to him for all his wiliness. Nor would he have entertained the notion of a doomed voyage to seek out knowledge for its own sake—not that archaic pragmatist whose world was a perfect balance between absolute certainty and absolute terror! Similarly, what was for the Homeric Greeks a calculated risk under pressure—Polites' rallying cry at Circe's gate (*"phtheggometha thasson"*—"Let's give a shout right now!") becomes for Pound an image of leaping into the unkown for the sake of knowledge. Living dangerously on principle is the only alternative to remaining forever ignorant out of timidity, more ignorant even than Odysseus's companions after they were drugged by Circe and turned into beasts.

Like Odysseus, Pound guards against hubris. In the next three lines, beginning "The small lamps drift," he wards off any impression of it. We have the gentlest suggestion here that the small lamps in the bay are like men who "sail after knowledge." They are vulnerable to "the sea's claw" just as Odysseus was, and like him they are enduring and resistant despite their exposure as they are drawn, smoothly at first, out into potentially violent seas. Traditionally they symbolize the souls of the dead setting out into the unkown chaos beyond life, and in the West they are often associated with All Souls' Night. Pound converts the symbolism into a suggestion of his own poetic enterprise as well as of Odysseus's perilous adventure: associations of vulnerability and courage rather than power.

Canto 47, then, reenacts Homer's Book X but does so by planting Odyssean moments amid disjunct passages of varying tones and intensities. It thus shifts attention from the tradition-al, myth-based epic to the workings of an alert, subjective modern sensibility completely at home with the older work and to an important degree obsessed by it. The *Odyssey* becomes a set of points of reference for that sensibility, one end of a scale that, at the other end, extends to the intimate psyche of the modern speaker. The canto moves through phases of feeling and awareness that depend on the Homeric narrative in that they *occupy* it. At the same time, they dismantle its structure and redistribute the components according to the needs of the speaking sensibility that plays the role of Odysseus *redivivus*. We could hardly have a more beautiful instance of poetic repossession and reawakening of the significant past.

The process began, as we have seen, with the two opening lines, whose mysterious and ominous resonance holds sway even after the immediately succeeding lines firmly anchor them in their proper original context. Then, in the passage last quoted, more non-Homeric notes are introduced. In the next stage, even the clearly Odyssean associations grow unexpect-edly intense and centrifugal.

> Neptunus drinks after neap-tide.
> Tamuz! Tamuz!!
> The red flame going seaward.
>   By this gate art thou measured,
> From the long boats they have set lights in the water,
> The sea's claw gathers them outward.
> Scilla's dogs snarl at the cliff's base,
> The white teeth gnaw in under the crag,
> But in the pale night the small lamps float seaward
>   Τυ Διώνα
>   TU DIONA
>
> Καὶ Μοῖραι᾽ ῎Αδονιν
> Kai MOIRAI' ADONIN
> The sea is streaked red with Adonis,
> The lights flicker red in small jars.
> Wheat shoots rise new by the altar,
>   flower from the swift seed.
> Two span, two span to a woman,
> Beyond that she believes not. Nothing is of any importance.
> To that is she bent, her intention
> To that art thou called ever turning intention . . .

The rapidly accumulating associations and images here are only tangentially relevant to the *Odyssey*. Once the presence of the older work had been established (something that happened at the very start of *The Cantos*), it became a subordinate if highly important aspect of the speaker's con-sciousness. Sometimes the speaker adds images of his own even when the immediate context is Homeric, as in the alliterative line "Neptunus drinks after neap-tide." Pound's addition suggests hyperanimality as one attribute of the god, who awaits the optimum time to drink deep of the sea. Moreover, Homer did not of course use the Latin name of Poseidon, Odysseus's great enemy. Pound *uses* Homer rather than merely rendering him. The echoing sounds of "Neptunus" and "neap-tide" were reasons enough for the shift; but in addition Pound casts a wide net of multiple cultural and mythological association, and "Neptunus" gives us a Roman dimension. Similarly, Homer does not speak of Tammuz, the Babylonian equivalent of Adonis. Yet Pound introduces him and, for good measure, follows his name with double exclamation-points to stress the extended association.

In short, the speaker has occupied his symbol: Odysseus in the context of Homeric consciousness and of mythical con-sciousness generally. He has grafted the persona of Odysseus onto himself. Thus Pound brings his interest in comparative religion directly into the poem. The archaic image of Odysseus becomes a living mask of the sophisticated Pound in such a way that the original Homeric context merges with a twentieth-century awareness of myth and ritual. Hence the whole body of lore concerning phallic vegetation gods and their earth-mother counterparts—Adonis and Tammuz, Dione and Aphrodite—enters the poem. (Canto 47 was published in 1937, twenty-two years after the final volume appeared of Sir James Frazer's *The Golden Bough*.) Odysseus's sexual knowledge of Circe and other goddesses, and of Penelope in their bed carved out of the living tree, becomes part of that lore. So does the speaker himself. At the center of the poem's consciousness, the poet is an Odysseus of the modern imagination and the ultimate embodiment of the male creative principle. He cannot help penetrating the female principle of responsive, malleable reality that actively compels the direction of his power.

The poem itself is nevertheless something other than all this explanation. Its immediacies of image, tone, and rhythm simply present realization in action, in a world simultaneously empirical and mythical but never abstract. The speaker is at once Pound himself and Odysseus and Tammuz-Adonis. He is lying with a real woman who is also the fertility goddess (Circe-Dione-Aphrodite) imperiously intent on being impregnated. "The stars are not in her counting, / To her they are but wandering holes. / Begin thy plowing." The darkness in which they are lying is the breeding-place of the unknown. The depths of Erebus and of inescapable sexuality, and the mythical figures with which the speaker's mind teems, are all aspects of his own human situation, his range of awareness that is the poem's given reality.

The thou who is addressed (and who becomes "I" in the closing stanza) is summoned by "she"—the female darkness. He must embark on the self-obliterating, sacrificial voyage into death of his old self and toward rebirth: "By this gate art thou measured." In visualizing this destiny, the poem elaborates on the images of terror always present in the *Odyssey* (Scylla and Charybdis, for example) but also introduces multiple associations from the Adonis-Aphrodite mythology. The line "The sea is streaked red with Adonis" is a perfect instance. Its clear evocation is of bloody death associated with the very nature of the hero who "sails after knowledge." Earlier images—"the small lamps drift in the bay," "the sea's claw," "the red flame going seaward"—have built into this one. I have mentioned only a few elements in an intricate lacework of suggestion that culminates, in the passage beginning "Neptunus drinks after neap-tide," in the elegiac words from Bion's "Lament for Adonis"—"Kai MOIRAI' ADONIN'" ("And the fates [weep for] Adonis")—and in the line that refers explicitly to the blood of Adonis.

It is interesting that the first line in the poem ("Who even dead, yet hath his mind entire!") refers to Tiresias, yet carries over to the slain hero-god who will be reborn and to the modern speaker in whom the "dead" experience of the past reawakens. An analogy with musical structure will help show how the poem works. Each effect is self-contained but flows into and is picked up by other effects, and each is clear in itself even while it builds into a larger pattern of tonal exploration. The poem begins in dark, death-involved mystery and terror, strong with the sense of personal doom; it quickly introduces a mood of desolate resolution, sustained by the strangeness and hardness of a new set of images constructed around Tammuz-Adonis and the "small lamps" and the hostile sea. Then, with "Wheat shoots rise new by the altar," a second large tonal movement, in a new key, enters the poem brilliantly.

The shift of key in the new movement is modulated by the persistence of a fatalistic tone despite the emphasis now on the fructifying sexual act. To plunge into the charged, fecund darkness is the hero's dangerous, unavoidable task, an engagement with impersonal destiny in an impossible if irresistible private struggle. The result is the triumph of the life principle at the expense of individuality—the most delightful of disasters, no doubt, but something very different from sheer voluptuous joy. In the mythology the hero dies in the process—"Wheat shoots rise new by the altar," but the price is that "the sea is streaked red with Adonis." And as we have seen in lines already quoted, the female principle is not so much seductive as magnetically controlling—

Two span, two span to a woman,
Beyond that she believes not. Nothing is of any
    importance.

To that is she bent, her intention
To that art thou called ever turning intention . . .

These lines give one example among many of Pound's extraordinary craftsmanship. His compulsive repetitions (like D. H. Lawrence's in comparable moments of realization) and sound-echoings act out the experience of impassioned subjection of one's will. The internal rhymes and half-rhymes and consonance are enormously effective in this emotional context: "span," "woman," "beyond," "any," "importance," "bent," "intention"—particularly the last two. Nor is it fanciful to note that the passage creates a special implied stress (though not in the actual pronunciation) on the prefix *in-* in "intention" as if a coined word, "*in-*tension," were also present. As with "bent," there is a play here on the ideas of "purpose" and of "tension." Further along, this absorption with the ceaseless sexuality of nature and our helpless participation in it evolves a culminating passage that is one of the triumphs of modern lyric poetry.

And the small stars now fall from the olive branch,
Forked shadow falls dark on the terrace
More black than the floating martin
        that has no care for your presence,
His wing-print is black on the roof tiles
And the print is gone with his cry.
So light is thy weight on Tellus
Thy notch no deeper indented
Thy weight less than the shadow
Yet hast thou gnawed through the mountain,
        Scylla's white teeth less sharp.
Hast thou found a nest softer than cunnus
Or hast thou found better rest
Hast'ou a deeper planting, doth thy death year
Bring swifter shoot?
Hast thou entered more deeply the mountain?

These lovely images sustain much of the earlier paradoxical melancholy, the sense of being carried into oblivion by one's fatal potency. But the delicacy of the opening lines and the erotic fullness of the five closing ones, as well as the godlike conception of being Tellus's lover, change the proportions of feeling. The rhetorical question "Hast thou found a nest softer than cunnus?" is exultant, even if asked of Dionysus himself in the full knowledge that he must die in the service of cosmic procreation. The passage finds a perfect metaphor, precise and sympathetic, for the insignificance of all individual achievement—"So light is thy weight on Tellus / Thy notch no deeper indented / Thy weight less than the shadow." At the same time it insists that male creative power does nevertheless prevail. Two sides of heroic experience are balanced here. Part of that experience is to learn how minimal is the effect of one's efforts. The other part is to see that the effort must nevertheless be made and that it will have its successes after all: "Yet hast thou gnawed through the mountain, / Scylla's white teeth less sharp."

The movement from lightly falling or floating sense-impressions, at once disappearing and incisive, to utterly rich possession by the softness of "cunnus" and then to imagery of deep-thrusting sexual power condenses and epitomizes the consciousness of the canto in all its aspects. The remainder of the canto takes its falling energy from this curve of movement. That is, it mingles notes of ripe flourishing with death-notes. "Adonis falleth. / Fruit cometh after. The small lights drift out with the tide." The curve is plotted, almost, along points of imagery that are at once independent of literal sexual reference and sexually suggestive—"Forked shadow fall," for instance, or "Thy notch no deeper indented," or "a deeper planting." It is not a matter of haranguing us but of carrying us along a complex network of awareness that is in effect a system of sensitized encompassment.

This last consideration brings me to one final observation among the many that fuller attention to the canto would demand. It is the use of the word "Molü" (usually spelled "Moly" in transliteration from the Greek). The word occurs at the end of the "two span, two span to a woman" passage whose beginning I have quoted and discussed. The longer passage reads:

Two span, two span to a woman,
Beyond that she believes not. Nothing is of any
    importance.
To that is she bent, her intention
To that art thou called ever turning intention,
Whether by night the owl-call, whether by sap in
    shoot,
Never idle, by no means by no wiles intermittent
Moth is called over mountain
The bull runs blind on the sword, *naturans*
To the cave art thou called, Odysseus,
By Molü hast thou respite for a little,
By Molü art thou freed from the one bed
            that thou may'st return to another

Literally, we remember, Molü was the magical herb that Hermes gave Odysseus to keep him from being turned into a beast by Circe's magic. Simple symbolic conversion, such as we normally avoid unless the text itself pushes us into it, would translate Molü into a gift of spiritual and intellectual power over our grosser tendencies. This interpretation would provide a "rational" explanation to nonpuritanical readers of how the hero became the goddess's lover without being reduced by her to abject bestiality. I mention all this because Pound, after referring to Molü in the sense of its literal use by Odyssesus in the foregoing passage, alludes to it again, differently, in the two lines that close the canto:

            that hath the gift of healing,
    that hath the power over wild beasts.

Here the spiritual meaning of Molü is obviously intended, and also a further meaning: the power of the remembering and transcendent imagination. It is the artistic equivalent of the heroic and sexual mission of Odysseus, and it puts in unsentimental yet emotionally reassuring perspective the relation of human genius to the irresistible nonhuman force of natural process. This is the "knowledge" spoken of earlier, toward which the entire canto has "sailed." It is the key to the program of the *Cantos* through the Pisan group—harshly intelligent, with a fatalism that cuts sharply against its own insistence on the redeeming power—however shortlived—of courageous humanistic imagination. The open associative form gives an impression of rigor rather than looseness, of an inner coherence in the highly charged dynamics.

Yeats seems to me the greatest poet in English of the century, and yet the spell of Canto 47 is such that for the moment I find it impossible to think of a poem of his that quite matches it. I know I have only to launch myself Yeats-wards, into a poem like "Sailing to Byzantium" or "News for the Delphic Oracle" (both of which have preoccupations in common with Canto 47), and soon enough I will be caught up in its orbit. But the hold of a superb poem one has just been giving oneself to is negative as well as positive; that is, it tends to detach us from other works toward which we have felt an affinity.

The authority of Canto 47 is related to its fused traditionalism and modernity. Despite the archaic diction with which it conjures up the vitality of myth and incantation in the past, the poem is harshly intelligent and unsentimental. Its fatalism cuts sharply against its own insistence on the redeem-

ing power, however shortlived, of courageous imaginative awareness. The open, associative form gives an impression of rigor rather than looseness, of an inner coherence in the highly charged dynamics. The poem's complex volatility would certainly have bogged it down had Pound tried more conventional modes to poetic exposition and narration, or even of stanza-form. Ideas in this poem are not superimposed but are an aspect of its conceptual energy. In a poem like this one, the speaker's initial positioning is very different from that in a characteristic poem by Yeats. The process is already fully underway at the start. It is up to us—we are given clues aplenty in the successive units of phrasing—to let it draw us into its developing context. Vibrant nodules mark the way as the process tentatively completes itself.

Now Yeats, too, often begins a poem in the middle of things, but very much more in the manner of one of Browning's dramatic monologues or one of Keats's odes. He presents a speaker looking at a scene or situation, so that we have as it were a static moment of placement, a setting of the stage or focusing of the relationship between the speaker and the object of his attention. "That is no country for old men," says the old man who speaks in "Sailing to Byzantium." And then we are off into the speaker's predicament of exclusion from "that country," the country of youth and procreation, and the way in which he will deal with the predicament (for even the aged poet-hero needs his appropriate kind of Molü). Thus begins the volume called *The Tower*, in which Yeats reached his full maturity. "Sailing to Byzantium" is followed by the title-poem, which again starts out by posing an issue—in fact the same issue, introduced this time with an almost embarrassing outcry:

    What shall I do with this absurdity—
    O heart, O troubled heart—this caricature,
    Decrepit age that has been tied to me
    As to a dog's tail?

Compare these lines with the opening of Canto 47—"Who even dead, yet hath his mind entire!" One can see Pound's appeal to the schools of "post-modernism" that have tried to get out from under what they consider the burden of subjectivity. Their avowed aim is to subordinate the poem's movement to objective process—that is, to have the thinking mind of the poem take its cues from wherever it is at a given moment in the midst of swirling or stagnant reality. The connection with Pound's method is that Pound expects the reader to locate the specific context from the process of the poem itself. There is, though, an important difference in the two positions. Although they are challenging and suggestive, the "post-modernist" writers—Charles Olson, for example—actually indulge in subjectivity far more than do the older masters who are sometimes called "ego-centered." The explorations of a Pound or a Yeats are after all serious efforts to place their objectified awareness in a purview beyond the merely personal. On the other hand, submitting one's art to undifferentiated process is a kind of random videotaping. What other aim can it have than to confirm one's presence, mainly as a con plaisant recorder, in the indifferent universe? It is voting for entropy with a vengeance. But that is a subject to be dealt with elsewhere. Meanwhile, there is an important sense in which none of this sort of thinking matters a bit. That sense takes charge once one turns from literary "positions" to actual poems. Somehow the "positions" do have a relationship to the way poets write and readers read and critics criticize, but it all seems far away from the place where the real poem, of any school, lives. How can we do anything else but attend when the authentic voice and music catch our attention? What they bring us is like

the floating martin
that has no care for your presence,
His wing-print is black on the roof tiles
And the print is gone with his cry.

That was Pound in 1937: the mature poet in a poem blessedly free, in this instance, of political tendentiousness or any sterile didacticism. It is interesting to see the obvious parallels to this poem in a canto published 18 years later—Canto 90. By that point the entire set or method of Canto 47 was, as it were, an organic condition of reference. The transforming power of Molü in the earlier canto had evolved into a volatile context whose specific terms were open to changes, substitutions, of all sorts. From the beginning Pound's tendency to spiritualize the Dionysian was present, but it was originally held in check (probably as a tendency toward "macerations"—*vide Mauberley*) by the powerful sexual and pagan emphasis in Canto 47 and other earlier work. Now that emphasis, though still referred to savingly, is replaced by a modulation toward Christian transcendence by way of Eleusinian and other pre-Christian mysteries. The shift is underlined by the epigraph from Richard of St. Victor, repeated in translation just before the canto's end:

Animus humanus amor non est,
sed ab ipso amor procedit, et
ideo seipse non diligit, sed amore
qui seipso procedit

and (in the context of a nostalgically visionary turn of imagery):

Trees die & the dream remains
Not love but that love flows from it
ex animo
& cannot ergo delight in itself
but only in the love flowing from it
UBI AMOR IBI OCULUS EST.

It is not Pound's fault that the quotation resembled some of Eliot's soggier phrasing and rhythms in *Four Quartets*. His translation has more bounce than the Latin original and makes him sound like a merry member of some teaching order, though at the expense of his poem's harder possibilities.

In Canto 90, too, as in Canto 47, the poem proper begins with a delphic quotation—rather abstract, however, and ultimately not as familiar in its context or as disturbing in its effect as "Who even dead, yet hath his mind entire!" The speaker as Odyssean voyager has, despite certain traces, all but disappeared now. Instead, he has become a sort of intercultural prophet. The epigraph, with its Pythagorean fumes of entranced profundity, is followed by another utterance expressing the spiritual convergence of varied mythical traditions:

"From the colour the nature
& by the nature the sign!"
Beatific spirits welding together
as in one ash-tree in Ygdrasail.
Baucis, Philemon.

A third utterance follows quickly on this one—a lovely triad, elegantly Classical. It beautifully completes the restrained musical celebration of universal order that is the poem's opening movement:

Castalia is the name of that fount in the hill's fold,
the sea below,
narrow beach.

The series of riddling utterances in an as yet unfocused, developing context parallels the method of Canto 47 and at first seems to promise a similar gathering of emotional strength. Instead, we are favored with more such effects, suggestive in themselves but still isolated from any central affective drive. When the more powerful movements do arrive, they consist of an incantation to a somewhat Christianized Kuthera and a wonderful moment presenting the "furry assemblage" of Dionysus. The invoked state of transport is handled with typical Poundian virtuosity—no one else could conceiveably match him at this sort of thing—although one can see the almost mechanical mobilization of elements and effects present in so many of the cantos. That is, one sees the interweaving of disparate images and melodic notes with intellectual pronouncements that are themselves disparate as well but that, like the images and the incantatory passages, create a relatively familiar complex—the inevitable redundancy and tautology of so prolonged an enterprise. As in Canto 47, again, assertion is maintained against all the odds of fatality. Faint allusions appear to Pound's prison-camp experience and to other notes introduced in *The Pisan Cantos*; and one line— "Evita, beer-halls, semina motuum"—ambiguously evokes the world of fascist agitation and terror that Pound curiously identified with his humanist idealism. It seems to be a preparation, a moment of foreshadowing, for the italicized outburst against democracy, Jews, and Western thinkers like Maritain and Hutchins that begrimes Canto 91. But even that outburst lacks the baleful power of, say, the vituperation in Canto 74, whose painful outcry of defeated idealism in a bad cause is nevertheless wrenching in itself.

The ear, the gift of phrasing, the rhythmic improvisation are as fine as ever in Canto 90. Yet it is a work of declining genius, a thinning of the rich passion of Canto 47 and a merely nostalgic exploitation of the tragic private drama that gave such special life to the Pisan group: all in all, a triumph of what might be called complacently repeated method. Even so, just compare Canto 90 with the very late work of almost any other modern poet except Yeats. So much of it remains fresh and intense, the instinct to project present states of the thinking mind in action is so compelling, and the sense of that mind's control of the relationship among its whirling fragments is so glowingly clear, that it is only by comparison with his own best work that Pound seems to be lacking here. Whatever our quarrels with him, and they are deeply serious ones, they are not with the fact but with the nature of his greatness.

ADDITIONAL READING

JAMES MERRILL

Donoghue, Denis. "Waiting for the End." *New York Review of Books*, 6 May 1971, pp. 27–31.

Eaves, Maurice. "Decision and Revision in James Merrill's *(Diblos) Notebook.*" *Contemporary Literature* 12 (1971): 156–65.

Ettin, Andrew V. "On James Merrill's *Nights and Days.*" *Perspective* 15 (1967): 33–51.

Hallberg, Robert von. "James Merrill: 'Revealing by Obscuring.'" *Contemporary Literature* 21 (1980): 549–71.

Howard, Richard. "James Merrill." In *Alone with America*. New York: Atheneum, 1969, pp. 532–35.

Kennedy, X. J. "Translations from the American." *Atlantic* 231 (March 1973): 101–3.

McClatchy, J. D. "The Art of Poetry XXXI: James Merrill." *Paris Review* No. 84 (Summer 1982): 184–219.

Nemerov, Howard. "The Careful Poets and the Reckless Ones." In *Poetry and Fiction: Essays*. New Brunswick, NJ: Rutgers University Press, 1963, pp. 195–96.

Park, Clara Claiborne. "Where *The Wasteland* Ends." *Nation*, 3 May 1980, pp. 532–35.

Sloss, Henry. "James Merrill's 'The Book of Ephraim.'" *Shenandoah* 27 (Fall 1976): 63–91; 28 (Winter 1977): 83–110.

Spender, Stephen. "Can Poetry Be Reviewed?" *New York Review of Books*, 20 September 1973, pp. 8–14.

———. "Heaven Can't Wait." *New York Review of Books*, 21 December 1978, pp. 34–36.

Yenser, Stephen. "Feux d'Artifice." *Poetry* 122 (1973): 163–68.

———. "The Fullness of Time: James Merrill's 'Book of Ephraim.'" *Canto* 3 (1980): 130–59.

THOMAS MERTON

Labrie, Ross. *The Art of Thomas Merton*. Fort Worth: Texas Christian University Press, 1979.

Lentfoehr, Sister Thérèse. *Words and Silence: On the Poetry of Thomas Merton*. New York: New Directions, 1979.

Woodcock, George. *Thomas Merton: Monk and Poet*. New York: Farrar, Straus & Giroux, 1978.

W. S. MERWIN

Byers, Thomas P. "The Peace in the Middle of the Floor: W. S. Merwin's Prose." *Modern Language Quarterly* 44 (1983): 65–79.

Carroll, Paul. "The Spirit with Long Ears and Paws." In *The Poem In Its Skin*. Chicago: Follett, 1968, pp. 142–52.

Davis, Cheri. *W. S. Merwin*. Boston: Twayne, 1981.

Donoghue, Denis. "Objects Solitary and Terrible." *New York Review of Books*, 6 June 1968, pp. 22–23.

Stiffler, Randall. "'The Annunciation' of W. S. Merwin." *Concerning Poetrey* 16 (1983): 55–63.

Young, Vernon. "Same Sea, Same Dangers: W. S. Merwin." *American Poetry Review* 7 (January–February 1978): 4–5.

LEONARD MICHAELS

H., A. Review of *I Would Have Saved Them If I Could*. *Atlantic* 236 (October 1975): 108.

Howard, Maureen. "Seize the Day." *Partisan Review* 37 (1970): 134–35.

Maloff, Saul. Review of *The Men's Club*. *Commonweal*, 4 December 1981, p. 696.

Segal, Lore. "Captivating Horrors." *New Republic*, 19 July 1969, pp. 31–33.

Woiwode, Larry. "Out of the Fifties." *Partisan Review* 44 (1977): 125–30.

JOSEPHINE MILES

Davie, Donald. "The Twain Not Meeting." *Parnassus: Poetry in Review* 8 (Fall-Winter 1979): 84–91.

Hammond, Karla M. "An Interview with Josephine Miles." *Southern Review* 19 (1983): 606–31.

Leibowitz, Herbert. "Questions of a Reality." *Hudson Review* 21 (1968): 557–59.

Lieberman, Laurence. *Yale Review* 57 (1968): 608–11.

Shapiro, David. "Into the Gloom." *Poetry* 127 (1976); 230–32.

Smith, Lawrence R. "Josephine Miles: Metaphysician of the Irrational." In *A Book of Rereadings*, ed. Greg Kuzma. Lincoln, NE: Pebble Press, 1979, pp. 22–35.

EDNA ST. VINCENT MILLAY

Brittin, Norman A. *Edna St. Vincent Millay*. Boston: Twayne, 1982.

Ciardi, John. "Edna St. Vincent Millay, a Figure of Passionate Living" (1950). In *Dialogue with an Audience*. Philadelphia: Lippincott, 1963, pp. 61–67.

Gregory, Horace. Review of *Wine from These Grapes*. *New York Herald Tribune Books*, 11 November 1934, p. 3.

Nierman, Judith. *Edna St. Vincent Millay: A Reference Guide*. Boston: G. K. Hall, 1977.

Ransom, John Crowe. "The Poet as Woman." In *The World's Body*. New York: Scribner's, 1938, pp. 76–110.

Stanborough, Jane. "Edna St. Vincent Millay and the Language of Vulnerability." In *Shakespeare's Sisters*, eds. Sandra Gilbert and Susan Gubar. Bloomington: Indiana University Press, 1979, pp. 183–99.

ARTHUR MILLER

Bigsby, C. W. E. "The Fall and After—Arthur Miller's Confession." *Modern Drama* 10 (1967): 124–36.

Clark, Eleanor. "Old Glamour, New Gloom." *Partisan Review* 16 (1949): 631–35.

Ganz, Arthur. "The Silence of Arthur Miller." *Drama Survey* 3 (1963): 224–37.

———. "Arthur Miller: After the Silence." *Drama Survey* 3 (1964): 520–30.

Hansen, Chadwick. "The Metamorphosis of Tituba, or Why American Intellectuals Can't Tell a Witch from a Negro." *New England Quarterly* 47 (1974): 3–12.

Hayashi, Tetsumaro. *An Index to Arthur Miller Criticism* Metuchen, NJ: Scarecrow Press, 1976.

Huftel, Sheila. *Arthur Miller: The Burning Glass*. New York: Citadel, 1965.

Hynes, Joseph A. "Arthur Miller and the Impasse of Naturalism." *South Atlantic Quarterly* 62 (1963): 327–34.

McAnany, Emile G. "The Tragic Commitment: Some Notes on Arthur Miller." *Modern Drama* 5 (1962): 11–20.

Popkin, Henry. "Arthur Miller Out West." *Commentary* 31 (May 1961): 433–36.

Reno, Raymond H. "Arthur Miller and the Death of God." *Texas Studies in Literature and Language* 11 (1969): 1069–87.

Steinbeck, John. "The Trial of Arthur Miller." *Esquire* 47 (June 1957): 86.

Steinberg, M. W. "Arthur Miller and the Idea of Modern Tragedy." *Dalhousie Review* 40 (1961): 329–40.

Welland, Dennis. *Arthur Miller.* Edinburgh: Oliver & Boyd, 1961.

HENRY MILLER

Brady, Mildred Edie. "The New Cult of Sex and Anarchy." *Harper's* 194 (April 1947): 312–22.

Clark, Eleanor. "Images of Revolt." *Partisan Review* 7 (1940): 160–63.

Durrell, Lawrence. "Studies in Genius: Henry Miller." *Horizon,* July 1949, pp. 45–61.

Jones, Roger. "Henry Miller at Eight-four: An Interview." *Queen's Quarterly* 84 (1977): 351–64.

Krim, Seymour. "The Netherworld of Henry Miller." *Commonweal,* 24 October 1952, pp. 68–71.

Mailer, Norman. *Genius and Lust.* New York: Grove Press, 1976.

Martin, Jay. *Always Merry and Bright.* Santa Barbara: Capra Press, 1978.

Mathieu, Bertrand. "Henry Miller and the *Symboliste* Theory of 'Correspondences.'" *Texas Quarterly,* Autumn 1977, pp. 33–40.

Mitchell, Edward, ed. *Henry Miller: Three Decades of Criticism.* New York: New York University Press, 1971.

Moravia, Alberto. "Two American Writers." *Sewanee Review* 68 (1960): 473–77.

Nin, Anaïs. "Preface" to *Tropic of Cancer.* New York: Grove Press, 1961, pp. xxix–xxxi.

Parkinson, Thomas. "The Hilarity of Henry Miller." *Listener,* 19 June 1958, pp. 1021–22.

Powell, Lawrence Clark. "The Miller of Big Sur." In *Books in My Baggage.* Cleveland: World Publishing Co., 1960, pp. 148–53.

———. "Remembering Henry Miller." *Southwest Review* 66 (1981): 117–28.

Read, Herbert. "Henry Miller." In *The Tenth Muse.* London: Routledge & Kegan Paul, 1957, pp. 250–55.

Shapiro, Karl. "The Greatest Living Author." In *In Defense of Ignorance.* New York: Random House, 1959, pp. 313–38.

Traschen, Isadore. "Henry Miller: The Ego and I." *South Atlantic Quarterly* 65 (1966): 345–54.

Wickes, George, ed. *Henry Miller and the Critics.* Carbondale: Southern Illinois Press, 1963.

JOAQUIN MILLER

Allen, Merritt Parmlee. *Joaquin Miller: Frontier Poet.* New York: Harper, 1932.

Frost, O. W. *Joaquin Miller.* New York: Twayne, 1967.

Lawson, Benjamin S. *Joaquin Miller.* Boise: Boise State University, 1980.

Longtin, Ray C. *Three Writers of the Far West: A Reference Guide.* Boston: G. K. Hall, 1980.

Marberry, M. M. *Splendid Poseur: Joaquin Miller—American Poet.* New York: Crowell, 1953.

Rosenus, A. H. "Joaquin Miller and His 'Shadow.'" *Western American Literature* 11 (1976): 51–59.

Sherman, Stuart P. "Joaquin Miller: Poetical Conquistador of the West." In *Americans.* New York: Scribner's, 1923, pp. 186–238.

Sterling, George. "Joaquin Miller." *American Mercury* 7 (1926): 220–29.

Talbot, Norma. "Joaquin Miller's Reception in English Periodicals." *Review of English Literature* 4 (1963): 63–79.

Wagner, Harr. *Joaquin Miller and His Other Self.* San Francisco: Harr Wagner, 1929.

STEVEN MILLHAUSER

Bell, Pearl. "It's a Wise Child." *New Leader,* 16 October 1972, p. 15.

Dunn, Robert. "First Love and the Last Automatons." *New York Times Book Review,* 19 January 1986, p. 9.

Frank, Sheldon. Review of *Portrait of a Romantic. Saturday Review,* 1 October 1977, p. 28.

Hjortsberg, William. Review of *Edwin Mullhouse. New York Times Book Review,* 17 September 1972, p. 2.

Klein, T. E. D. "The Great Cartoon Mystery." *Twilight Zone,* August 1984, p. 6.

Unsigned. Review of *Edwin Mullhouse. New Republic,* 16 September 1972, pp. 30–31.

N. SCOTT MOMADAY

Brumble, H. David, III. "Anthropologists, Novelists and Indian Sacred Material." *Canadian Review of American Studies* 11 (1980): 31–48.

Dickinson-Brown, Roger. "The Art and Importance of N. Scott Momaday." *Southern Review* 14 (1978): 30–45.

Evers, Lawrence J. "Words and Place: A Reading of *House Made of Dawn.*" *Western American Literature* 11 (1977): 297–320.

Hirsch, Bernard A. "Self-Hatred and Spiritual Corruption in *House Made of Dawn.*" *Western American Literature* 17 (1983): 307–320.

Hogan, Linda. "Who Puts Together." *Denver Quarterly* 14, No. 4 (1980): 103–12.

Hylton, Marion Willard. "On a Trail of Pollen: Momaday's *House Made of Dawn.*" *Critique* 14, No. 2 (1972): 60–69.

Lincoln, Kenneth. "Word Senders: Black Elk and N. Scott Momaday." In *Native American Renaissance.* Berkeley: University of California Press, 1983, pp. 82–121.

McAllister, H. S. "Be a Man, Be a Woman: Androgyny in *House Made of Dawn.*" *American Indian Quarterly* 2 (1975): 14–22.

Oleson, Carole. "The Remembered Earth: Momaday's *House Made of Dawn.*" *South Dakota Review* 11, No. 1 (1973): 59–78.

Rosen, Kenneth. "American Indian Literature: Current Condition and Suggested Research." *American Indian Culture and Research Journal* 3 (1979): 57–66.

Trimble, Martha Scott. *N. Scott Momaday.* Boise: Boise State College Western Writers Series, No. 9, 1973.

Velie, Alan R. "The Search for Identity: N. Scott Momaday's Autobiographical Works." In *Four American Indian Literary Masters.* Norman: University of Oklahoma Press, 1982.

MARIANNE MOORE

Auden, W. H. Review of *Nevertheless. New York Times Book Review,* 15 October 1944, pp. 7, 20.

Borroff, Marie. "Marianne Moore's Promotional Prose." In *Language and the Poet.* Chicago: University of Chicago Press, 1979, pp. 80–135.

Burke, Kenneth. "Likings of an Observationist." *Poetry* 87 (1956): 239–47.

Costello, Bonnie. *Marianne Moore: Imaginary Possessions.* Cambridge, MA: Harvard University Press, 1981.

Donoghue, Denis. "The Proper Plenitude of Fact." In *The Ordinary Universe.* New York: Macmillan, 1968, pp. 42–50.

Hadas, Pamela White. *Marianne Moore, Poet of Affection.* Syracuse: Syracuse University Press, 1977.

Hall, Donald. "An Interview with Marianne Moore." *Paris Review* No. 26 (Winter 1961): 41–66.

Quarterly Review of Literature 4, No. 2 (1948). Special Marianne Moore issue.

Sheehy, Eugene P., and Kenneth A. Lohf. *The Achievement of Marianne Moore: A Bibliography 1907–1957.* New York: New York Public Library, 1958.

Snodgrass, W. D. "Elegance in Marianne Moore." *Western Review* 19 (1954): 57–64.

Stevens, Wallace. "About One of Marianne Moore's Poems" (1948). In *The Necessary Angel.* New York: Knopf, 1951, pp. 91–103.

CHRISTOPHER MORLEY

Altick, Richard D. "Average Citizen in Grub Street: Christopher Morley after Twenty-five Years." *South Atlantic Quarterly* 41 (1942): 18–31.

Canby, Henry Seidel. "Persons and Personalities: Christopher Morley." In *American Estimates.* New York: Harcourt, Brace, 1929, pp. 61–70.

Wallach, Mark I., and Jon Bracker. *Christopher Morley.* Boston: Twayne, 1976.

WRIGHT MORRIS

Baumbach, Jonathan. "Wake before Bomb: *Ceremony in Lone Tree* by Wright Morris." In *The Landscape of Nightmare.* New York: New York University Press, 1965, pp. 152–70.

Booth, Wayne C. "The Two Worlds in the Fiction of Wright Morris." *Sewanee Review* 65 (1957): 375–99.

Crump, G. B. *The Novels of Wright Morris.* Lincoln: University of Nebraska Press, 1978.

Eisinger, Chester E. "Wright Morris: The Artist in Search of America." In *Fiction of the Forties.* Chicago: University of Chicago Press, 1963, pp. 328–41.

Howard, Leon. *Wright Morris.* Minneapolis: University of Minnesota Press, 1968.

Klein, Marcus. "Wright Morris: The American Territory." In *After Alienation: American Novels at Mid-Century.* Cleveland: World Publishing Co., 1962, pp. 196–246.

Knoll, Robert E., ed. *Conversations with Wright Morris.* Lincoln: University of Nebraska Press, 1977.

Linden, Stanton J., and David Madden. "A Wright Morris Bibliography." *Critique* 4, No. 3 (Winter 1961–62): 77–87.

Madden, David. *Wright Morris.* New York: Twayne, 1964.

Morris, Wright. *Will's Boy: A Memoir.* New York: Harper & Row, 1981.

TONI MORRISON

Blackburn, Sara. "You Still Can't Go Home Again." *New York Times Book Review,* 30 December 1973, p. 3.

Davis, Cynthia. "Self, Society and Myth in Toni Morrison's Fiction." *Contemporary Literature* 23 (1982): 323–42.

Fikes, Robert Jr. "Echoes from Small Town Ohio: A Toni Morrison Bibliography." *Obsidian* 5 (Spring-Summer 1979): 142–48.

Howard, Maureen. "A Novel of Exile and Home." *New Republic,* 21 March 1981, pp. 29–30, 32.

Lange, Bonnie Shipman. "Toni Morrison's Rainbow Code." *Critique* 24, No. 3 (1983): 173–81.

Lounsberry, Barbara and Hovet, Grace Anne. "Principles of Perception in Toni Morrison's *Sula*." *Black American Literature Forum* 8 (1979): 126–29.

McKay, Nellie. "An Interview with Toni Morrison." *Contemporary Literature* 24 (1983): 413–29.

Miller, Adam David. "Breedlove, Peace, and the Dead: Some Observations on the World of Toni Morrison." *Black Scholar* 9 (March 1978): 47–50.

Ogunyemi, Chikwenye Okonjo. "*Sula*: 'A Nigger Joke.'" *Black American Literature Forum* 8 (1979): 130–33.

Tate, Claudia. "Toni Morrison." In *Black Women Writers at Work,* ed. Claudia Tate. New York: Continuum, 1983, pp. 117–31.

Willis, Susan. "Eruptions of Funk: Historicizing Toni Morrison." *Black American Literature Forum* 16 (1982): 34–42.

WILLARD MOTLEY

Bontemps, Arna. Review of *Knock on Any Door. New York Herald Tribune,* 18 May 1947, p. 8.

Ellison, Bob. "Three Best-Selling Authors: Conversations." *Rogue* 8 (December 1963): 20, 22, 24, 75.

Fleming, Robert E. *Willard Motley.* Boston: Twayne, 1978.

Klinkowitz, Jerome, ed. *The Diaries of Willard Motley.* Ames: Iowa State University Press, 1979.

LEWIS MUMFORD

Adams, Robert M. "A Cosmic and Practical Man." *New York Review of Books,* 22 January 1976, pp. 41–42.

Buchanan, Scott. "Mumford Tilts at Windmills." *Virginia Quarterly Review* 10 (1934): 447–51.

Dow, Eddy. "Van Wyck Brooks and Lewis Mumford: A Confluence in the 'Twenties." *American Literature* 45 (1973): 407–22.

Glicksburg, Charles I. "Lewis Mumford and the Organic Synthesis." *Sewanee Review* 45 (1937): 55–73.

Newman, Elmer S. *Lewis Mumford: A Bibliography, 1914–1970.* New York: Harcourt Brace Jovanovich, 1971.

VLADIMIR NABOKOV

Appel, Alfred, Jr. *Nabokov's Dark Cinema.* New York: Oxford University Press, 1974.

De Jonge, Alex. "Nabokov's Use of Pattern." In *Vladimir Nabokov: A Tribute,* ed. Peter Quennell. New York: William Morrow, 1980, pp. 59–62.

Dembo, L. S., ed. *Nabokov: The Man and His Work.* Madison: University of Wisconsin Press, 1967.

Field, Andrew. *Nabokov: A Bibliography.* New York: McGraw-Hill, 1973.

———. *Vladimir Nabokov: His Life in Part.* New York: Viking Press, 1977.

Grayson, Jane. *Nabokov Translated: A Comparison of Nabokov's Russian and English Prose.* Oxford: Oxford University Press, 1977.

Hogart, Matthew. "Happy Families." *New York Review of Books,* 22 May 1969, pp. 3–4.

Karlinsky, Simon. "Introduction" to *The Nabokov-Wilson Letters, 1940–1971,* ed. Simon Karlinsky. New York: Harper & Row, 1979, p. 1–25.

McCarthy, Mary. "Vladimir Nabokov's Pale Fire." *Encounter* 19 (1962): 71–84.

McDonald, Dwight. "Virtuosity Rewarded or Dr. Kinbote's Revenge." *Partisan Review* 24 (1962): 436–42.

Merrill, Robert. "Nabokov and Fictional Artifice." *Modern Fiction Studies* 25 (1979): 439–62.

Packman, David. *Vladimir Nabokov: The Structure of Literary Desire.* Columbia: Universitey of Missouri Press, 1982.

Pifer, Ellen. *Nabokov and the Novel.* Cambridge, MA: Harvard University Press, 1980.

Proffer, Carl R., ed. *A Book of Things about Vladimir Nabokov.* Ann Arbor: Ardis, 1974.

Schuman, Samuel. *Vladimir Nabokov: A Reference Guide.* Boston: G. K. Hall, 1979.

Stuart, Dabney. *Nabokov: The Dimensions of Parody.* Baton Rouge: Louisiana State University Press, 1978.

OGDEN NASH

Axford, Lavonne. *An Index to the Poems of Ogden Nash.* Metuchen, NJ: Scarecrow Press, 1972.

Benét, William Rose. "The Funniest Yet." *Saturday Review of Literature,* 17 January 1931, p. 530.

Gibson, Walker. "Some Rhymes with Reason." *New York Times Book Review,* 8 November 1959, p. 12.

Unsigned. "The Monument Ogdenational." *Time,* 31 May 1971, p. 23.

GEORGE JEAN NATHAN

Angoff, Charles. "George Jean Nathan." In *The Tune of the Twenties and Other Essays.* South Brunswick, NJ: A. S. Barnes, 1966, pp. 47–61.

Boyd, Ernest. "George Jean Nathan." In *Portraits: Real and Imaginary.* London: Jonathan Cape, 1924, pp. 197–207.

Frick, Constance. *The Dramatic Criticism of George Jean Nathan.* Ithaca, NY: Cornell University Press, 1943.

Goldberg, Isaac. *The Theatre of George Jean Nathan.* New York: Simon & Schuster, 1926.

Jack, Peter Monro. "Mr. Nathan Holds Forth on the Theatre's Shortcomings." *New York Times Book Review,* 6 January 1935, p. 4.

Kozlenko, Vladimir. *The Quintessence of Nathanism.* New York: Vrest Orton, 1930.

Lewisohn, Ludwig. "The Critic and the Theatre." In *The Drama and the Stage.* New York: Harcourt, Brace, 1922, pp. 12–18.

ROBERT NATHAN

Hatcher, Harlan. "Fantasy as a Way of Escape." In *Creating the Modern Novel.* New York: Farrar & Rinehart, 1935.

Redman, Ben Ray. "Expert in Depressions: A Portrait of Robert Nathan." *Saturday Review of Literature,* 13 October 1934, p. 206.

Sandelin, Clarence. *Robert Nathan.* New York: Twayne, 1968.

Tapley, Roberts. "Robert Nathan: Poet and Ironist." *Bookman* (New York) 75 (1932): 607–14.

Trachtenberg, Stanley. "Robert Nathan's Fiction." Ph.D. diss.: New York University, 1963.

HOWARD NEMEROV

Bartholomay, Julia. *The Shield of Perseus: The Vision and Imagination of Howard Nemerov.* Gainesville: University of Florida Press, 1972.

Harvey, R. D. "A Prophet Armed: An Introduction to the Poetry of Howard Nemerov." In *Poets in Progress,* ed. H. B. Hungerford. Evanston, IL: Northwestern University Press, 1967, pp. 116–33.

Labrie, Ross. *Howard Nemerov.* Boston: Twayne, 1980.

Mills, William. *The Stillness in Moving Things: The World of Howard Nemerov.* Memphis: Memphis State University Press, 1975.

Wood, Susan. "A Poet Collected in Tranquility." *Washington Post Book World,* 25 December 1977, p. 3.

ANAÏS NIN

Hinz, Evelyn J., ed. "The World of Anaïs Nin." Special Anaïs Nin issue of *Mosaic* 11 (Winter 1978).

Killoh, Ellen Peck. "The Woman Writer and the Element of Destruction." *College English* 34 (1972): 31–38.

Schneider, Duane, and Benjamin Franklin V. *Anaïs Nin: An Introduction.* Athens: Ohio University Press, 1979.

Scholar, Nancy. *Anaïs Nin.* Boston: Twayne, 1984.

Spencer, Sharon. *Collage of Dreams: The Writings of Anaïs Nin.* Chicago: Swallow Press, 1977.

Zaller, Robert. *A Casebook on Anaïs Nin.* New American Library, 1974.

JOYCE CAROL OATES

Creighton, Joanne V. *Joyce Carol Oates.* Boston: Twayne, 1979.

Friedman, Ellen. "The Journey from the 'I' to the 'Eye': Joyce Carol Oates's *Wonderland.*" *Studies in American Fiction* 8 (1980): 37–50.

Harter, Carol. "America as 'Consumer Garden': The Nightmare Vision of Joyce Carol Oates." *Revue des Langues Vivantes,* Bicentennial issue (1976); 171–87.

Phillips, Robert. "Joyce Carol Oates: The Art of Fiction." *Paris Review* No. 74 (Fall-Winter 1978): 199–226.

Pickering, S. F., Jr. "The Short Stories of Joyce Carol Oates." *Georgia Review* 28 (1974): 218–26.

Ricks, Christopher. "The Unignorable Real." *New York Review of Books,* 12 February 1970, pp. 22–24.

Waller, G. F. *Dreaming America: Obsession and Transcendence in the Fiction of Joyce Carol Oates.* Baton Rouge: Louisiana State University Press, 1979.

EDWIN O'CONNOR

Blotner, Joseph. "The Boss." In *The Modern American Political Novel 1900–1960.* Austin: University of Texas Press, 1966, pp. 55–92.

Dunlavey, Ronald J. "Last Year's Hurrah." *New Republic,* 25 March 1957, pp. 16–17.

Dunne, John Gregory. "Steerage to Suburbia." *National Review,* 7 October 1961, pp. 239–40.

Milne, Gordon. "Professionals: Warren, O'Connor, and Drury." In *The American Political Novel.* Norman: University of Oklahoma Press, 1966, pp. 163–71.

Rank, Hugh. "O'Connor's Image of the Priest." *New England Quarterly* 41 (1968): 3–29.

———. *Edwin O'Connor.* New York: Twayne, 1974.

West, Anthony. "When in Rome . . ." *New Yorker,* 11 February 1956, pp. 121–24.

FLANNERY O'CONNOR

Baumbach, Jonathan. "The Acid of God's Grace: The Fiction of Flannery O'Connor." *Georgia Review* 17 (1963): 334–46.

Detweiler, Robert. "The Curse of Christ in Flannery O'Connor's Fiction." *Comparative Literature Studies* 3 (1966): 235–45.

Howe, Irving. "On Flannery O'Connor." *New York Review of Books,* 30 September 1965, pp. 22–26.

Hyman, Stanley Edgar. "Flannery O'Connor's Tattooed Christ." *New Leader,* 10 May 1965, pp. 9–10.

Lindroth, James R. "A Consistency of Voice and Vision: O'Connor as Self-Critic." *Religion and Literature* 16 (Summer 1984): 43–58.

Napier, James J. "Flannery O'Connor's Last Three: 'The Sense of an Ending.'" *Southern Literary Journal* 14 (Spring 1982): 19–27.

Orvell, Miles. *Invisible Parade: The Fiction of Flannery O'Connor.* Philadelphia: Temple University Press, 1972.

Smith, J. Oates. "Ritual and Violence in Flannery O'Connor." *Thought* 41 (1966): 545–60.

Wynne, Judith F. "The Sacramental Irony of Flannery O'Connor." *Southern Literary Journal* 7 (Spring 1975): 33–49.

CLIFFORD ODETS

Brenman-Gibson, Margaret. *Clifford Odets, American Playwright*. New York: Atheneum, 1981.

Dozier, Richard J. "Recovering Odets's *Paradise Lost*." *Essays in Literature* 5 (1978): 209–21.

Goldstein, Malcolm. "The Group Theatre." In *The Political Stage: American Drama and Theatre of the Great Depression*. New York: Oxford University Press, 1974, pp. 92–100, 300–337.

McCarten, John. "Revolution's Number One Boy." *New Yorker*, 22 January 1938, pp. 21–27.

McCarthy, Mary. "Odets Deplored" (1938). In *Sights and Spectacles: 1937–1956*. New York: Farrar, Straus & Giroux, 1956.

Weales, Gerald. *Clifford Odets, Playwright*. New York: Pegasus, 1971.

FRANK O'HARA

Berkson, Bill, and LeSueur, Joe, Eds. *Homage to Frank O'Hara*. (Special issue of *Big Sky* 11/12 (1978).

Carroll, Paul. "Frank O'Hara." In *The Poem in Its Skin*. Chicago: Follet, 1968, pp. 157–68.

Feldman, Alan. *Frank O'Hara*. Boston: Twayne, 1979.

Myer, Thomas. "Glistening Torsos, Sandwiches, Coca Cola." *Parnassus: Poetry in Review* (1977): 241–57.

Perloff, Marjorie. *Frank O'Hara: Poet among Painters*. New York: George Braziller, 1977.

Smith, Alexander. *Frank O'Hara: A Comprehensive Bibliography*. New York: Garland, 1979.

JOHN O'HARA

Bassett, Charles W. "Naturalism Revisited: The Case of John O'Hara." *Colby Library Quarterly* 11 (1975): 198–218.

Bruccoli, Matthew J. *The O'Hara Concern: A Biography of John O'Hara*. New York: Random House, 1975.

Farr, Finis. *O'Hara: A Biography*. Boston: Little, Brown, 1973.

Grebstein, Sheldon Norman. *John O'Hara*. New York: Twayne, 1966.

Long, Robert Emmet. *John O'Hara*. New York: Ungar, 1983.

McCormick, Bernard. "A John O'Hara Geography." *Journal of Modern Literature* 1 (1970–1971): 151–58.

MacShane, Frank. *The Life of John O'Hara*. New York: Dutton, 1980.

Tuttleton, James W. "John O'Hara: Class Hatred and Sexuality." In *The Novel of Manners in America*. Chapel Hill: University of North Carolina Press, 1972, pp. 184–206.

TILLIE OLSEN

Burkom, Selma, and Williams, Margaret. "De-Riddling Tillie Olsen's Writing." *San Jose Studies* 2 (1976): 65–83.

Gottlieb, Annie. Review of *Yonnondio. New York Times Book Review*, 31 March 1974, p. 5.

O'Connor, William Van, "The Short Stories of Tillie Olson." *Studies in Short Fiction* 1 (1963): 21–25.

Paden, William. "Dilemmas of Day-to-Day Living." *New York Times Book Review*, 12 November 1961, p. 54.

Stimpson, Catherine R. "Tillie Olsen: Witness as Servant." *Polit: A Journal for Literature and Politics*. 1 (1977): 1–12.

CHARLES OLSON

Butterick, George F. *A Guide to the Maximus Poems of Charles Olson*. Berkeley: University of California Press, 1978.

————, and Albert G. Glover. *A Bibliography of Works by Charles Olson*. New York: Phoenix Book Shop, 1967.

Charters, Ann. *Olson/Melville: a Study in Affinity*. Berkeley: Oyez, 1968.

Christensen, Paul, *Charles Olson: Call Him Ishmael*. Austin: University of Texas Press, 1975.

Creeley, Robert. "Some Notes on Olson's *Maximus*." *Yugen* 8 (1962): 51–55.

Davey, Frank. "Six Readings of Olson's *Maximus*." *Boundary 2* 2 (1973–74): 291–322.

Ford, O. J. "Charles Olson and Carl Sauer: Towards a Methodology of Knowing." *Boundary 2* 2 (1973–74): 145–50.

Lieberman, Marsha, and Philip Lieberman. "Olson's Projective Verse and the Use of Breath Control as a Structural Element." *Language and Style* 5 (1972): 287–98.

Merrill, Thomas F. *The Poetry of Charles Olson: A Primer*. Newark: University of Delaware Press, 1982.

Paul, Sherman. *Olson's Push: Origin, Black Mountain, and Recent American Poetry*. Baton Rouge: Louisiana State University Press, 1978.

Perloff, Marjorie J. "Charles Olson and the 'Inferior Predecessors': 'Projective Verse' Revisited." *ELH* 40 (1973): 285–306.

EUGENE O'NEILL

Atkinson, Jennifer McCabe. *Eugene O'Neill: A Descriptive Bibliography*. Pittsburgh: University of Pittsburgh Press, 1974.

Barlow, Judith E. *Final Acts: The Creation of Three Late O'Neill Plays*. Athens: University of Georgia Press, 1985.

Bogard, Travis. *Contour in Time: The Plays of Eugene O'Neill*. New York: Oxford University Press, 1972.

Brustein, Robert. *The Theatre of Revolt*. Boston: Little, Brown, 1964.

Carpenter, Frederick I. *Eugene O'Neill*. Rev. ed. Boston: Twayne, 1979.

Chabrowe, Leonard. *Ritual and Pathos: The Theater of Eugene O'Neill*. Lewisburg, PA: Bucknell University Press, 1976.

Chothia, Jean. *Forging a Language: A Study of the Plays of Eugene O'Neill*. Cambridge: Cambridge University Press, 1979.

Gassner, John. *Eugene O'Neill*. Minneapolis: University of Minnesota Press, 1965.

Leech, Clifford. *Eugene O'Neill*. New York: Grove Press, 1963.

Long, Chester Clayton. *The Role of Nemesis in the Structure of Selected Plays by Eugene O'Neill*. The Hague: Mouton, 1968.

Mickle, Alan D. *Six Plays of Eugene O'Neill*. New York: Liveright, 1929.

Miller, Jordan Y. *Eugene O'Neill and the American Critic: A Bibliographical Checklist*. Rev. ed. Hamden, CT: Archon Books, 1973.

Sheaffer, Louis. *O'Neill, Son and Playwright*. Boston: Little, Brown, 1968.

————. *O'Neill, Son and Artist*. Boston: Little, Brown, 1973.

Sinha, C. P. *Eugene O'Neill's Tragic Vision*. New Delhi: New Statesman, 1981.

Tönqvist, Egil. *A Drama of Souls: Studies in O'Neill's Super-*

naturalistic Technique. Uppsala: Acta Universitatis Up-saliensis, 1968.

Winther, Sophus Keith. *Eugene O'Neill: A Critical Study.* New York: Random House, 1934.

GEORGE OPPEN

Dembo, L. S. "The Existential World of George Oppen." *Iowa Review* 3 (1972): 64–91.

DuPlessis, Rachel Blau. "George Oppen: 'What Do We Believe to Live With?'" *Ironwood* 5 (1975): 62–77.

Heller, Michael. "The Mind of George Oppen: Convistion's Net of Branches." In *Convistion's Net of Braches: Essays on the Objectivist Poets and Poetry.* Carbondale: Southern Illinois University Press, 1985, pp. 73–97.

Kenner, Hugh. "Classroom Accuracies." In *A Homemade World: The American Modernist Writers.* New York: Knopf, 1975, pp. 163–88.

McAleavey, David. "A Bibliography of the Works of George Oppen." *Paideuma* 10 (1981): 155–72.

———. "A Bibliography of Discussion of George Oppen's Work." In *George Oppen: Man and Poet,* ed. Burton Hatlen. Orono, Me: National Poetry Foundation, 1981, pp. 451–62.

CYNTHIA OZICK

Bell, Pearl K. "Idylls of the Tribe." *New Leader,* 12 April 1976, pp. 18–19.

Goodheart, Eugene. "Cynthia Ozick's *Trust.*" *Critique* 9, No. 2 (1967): 99–102.

Knapp, Josephine Z. "The Jewish Stories of Cynthia Ozick." *Studies in American Jewish Literature* 1 (1975): 31–38.

Ottenberg, Eve. "The Rich Visions of Cynthia Ozick." *New York Times Magazine,* 10 April 1983, pp. 46–47, 62–66.

Rainwater, Cynthia, and Scheick, William J. "An Interview with Cynthia Ozick (Summer 1982)." *Texas Studies in Literature and Language* 25 (1983): 255–65.

Rosenberg, Ruth. "Covenanted to the Law: Cynthia Ozick." *MELUS* 9, No. 3 (1982): 29–38.

Rovit, Earl. "The Bloodletting." *The Nation,* 20 February 1982, pp. 207–8.

Strandberg, Victor. "The Art of Cynthia Ozick." *Texas Studies in Literature and Language* 25 (1983): 266–312.

THOMAS NELSON PAGE

Gordon, Armistead C. "Thomas Nelson Page." *Scribner's Magazine* 73 (1923): 75–80.

Gross, Theodore L. *Thomas Nelson Page.* New York: Twayne, 1967.

Holman, Harriet R. "Attempt and Failure: Thomas Nelson Page as Playwright." *Southern Literary Journal* 3 (1970): 72–82.

Hubbell, Jay B. *The South in American Literature 1607–1900.* Durham, NC: Duke University Press, 1954.

Longest, George C. *Three Virginia Writers; Mary Johnston, Thomas Nelson Page and Amelie Rives Troubetzkoy: A Reference Guide.* Boston: G. K. Hall, 1978.

Page, Rosewell. *Thomas Nelson Page: A Memoir of a Virginia Gentleman.* New York: Scribner's, 1923.

Wilson, Edmund. *Patriotic Gore.* New York: Oxford University Press, 1962.

GRACE PALEY

Davis, Hope Hale. "A Memoir: On Writers and Politics." *New Leader,* 19 December 1981, pp. 22–24.

Gelfant, Blanche. "Grace Paley: Fragments for a Portrait in Collage." *New England Review* 3 (1980): 276–93.

Harris, Lis. Review of *Enormous Changes at the Last Minute.* *New York Times Book Review,* 17 March 1974, p. 3.

Hulley, Kathleen, ed. *Grace Paley.* Montpellier: Université Paul Valéry, 1982.

Mickelson, Anne Z. "Grace Paley." In *Reaching Out: Sensitivity and Order in Recent American Fiction by Women.* Metuchen, NJ: Scarecrow Press, 1979, pp. 221–34.

Sorkin, Adam J. "'What Are We, Animals?': Grace Paley's World of Talk and Laughter." *Studies in American Jewish Literature* 2 (1982): 144–57.

DOROTHY PARKER

Cooper, Wyatt. "Whatever You Think Dorothy Parker Was Like, She Wasn't." *Esquire* 70 (July 1967): 57–114.

Maugham, W. Somerset. "Introduction" to *The Portable Dorothy Parker.* New York: Viking Press, 1944, pp. ix–xiv.

Plomer, William. Review of *Here Lies. Spectator,* 17 November 1939, p. 708.

KENNETH PATCHEN

Ciardi, John. "Kenneth Patchen: Poetry, and Poetry with Jazz." *Saturday Review,* 14 May 1960, p. 57.

Morgan, Richard G., ed. *Kenneth Patchen: A Collection of Essays.* New York: AMS Press, 1977.

Rexroth, Kenneth. "Kenneth Patchen: Naturalist of the Public Nightmare." In *Bird in the Bush: Obvious Essays.* New York: New Directions, 1959, pp. 94–105.

See, Carolyn. "The Jazz Musician as Patchen's Hero." *Arizona Quarterly* 17 (1961): 136–46.

Smith, Larry R. *Kenneth Patchen.* Boston: Twayne, 1978.

Wilder, Amos N. "Revolutionary and Proletarian Poetry." In *The Spiritual Aspects of the New Poetry.* New York: Harper, 1940, pp. 178–95.

WALKER PERCY

Allen, William Rodney. "All the Names of Death: Walker Percy and Hemingway." *Mississippi Quarterly* 36 (1982–83): 3–19.

Atkins, Anselm. "Walker Percy and Post-Christian Search." *Centennial Review* 12 (1968): 73–95.

Brooks, Cleanth. "The Southernness of Walker Percy." *South Carolina Review* 13 (Spring 1981): 34–38.

Broughton, Panthea Reid, ed. *The Art of Walker Percy.* Baton Rouge: Louisiana State University Press, 1979.

Cheney, Brainard. "To Restore a Fragmented Image." *Sewanee Review* 69 (1961): 691–700.

Coles, Robert. *Walker Percy: An American Search.* Boston: Little, Brown, 1978.

Daniel, Robert D. "Walker Percy's *Lancelot*: Secular Ravings and Religious Silence." *Southern Review* 14 (1978): 186–94.

Douglas, Ellen. *Walker Percy's The Last Gentleman.* New York: Seabury Press, 1969.

Dowie, William, S.J. "Walker Percy: Sensualist-Thinker." *Novel* 6 (1972): 52–65.

Hoggard, James. "Death of the Vicarious." *Southwest Review* 49 (1964): 366–74.

Johnson, Mark. "*Lancelot*: Percy's Romance." *Southern Literary Journal* 15 (Spring 1983): 19–30.

Lawson, Lewis A. "Walker Percy as Martian Visitor." *Southern Literary Journal* 8 (Spring 1976): 102–13.

———. "Walker Percy: The Physician as Novelist." *South Atlantic Bulletin* 37 (May 1972): 58–63.

———. "Walker Percy's Indirect Communications." *Texas Studies in Language and Literature* 11 (1969): 867–900.

Lawson, Lewis A., and Victor A. Kramer, eds. *Conversations with Walker Percy.* Jackson: University Press of Mississippi, 1985.

Lehan, Richard. "The Way Back: Redemption in the Novels of Walker Percy." *Southern Review* 4 (1968): 306–19.

Luschei, Martin. *Sovereign Wayfarer*. Baton Rouge: Louisiana State University Press, 1972.

Stevenson, John W. "Walker Percy: The Novelist as Poet." *Southern Review* 17 (1981): 164–74.

Telotte, J. P. "Walker Percy's Language of Creation." *Southern Quarterly* 16 (1978): 105–16.

Thale, Mary. "The Moviegoer of the 1950's." *Twentieth Century Literature* 14 (1968): 84–89.

Tharpe, Jac, ed. *Walker Percy: Art and Ethics*. Jackson: University of Mississippi Press, 1980.

Wood, Ralph C. "Walker Percy as Satirist: Christian and Humanist Still in Conflict." *Christian Century*, 19 November 1980, pp. 1122–27.

S. J. PERELMAN

Davies, Russell. "S. J. Perelman: 1904–1979." *New Statesman*, 26 October 1979, pp. 646–47.

Fowler, Douglas. *S. J. Perelman*. Boston: G. K. Hall, 1983.

French, Philip. "The Comedy of Calamity." *Times Literary Supplement*, 25 December 1981, p. 1500.

Hasley, Louis. "The Kangaroo Mind of S. J. Perelman." *South Atlantic Quarterly* 72 (1973): 115–21.

Lamport, Felicia. "The Perils of Perelman." *New Republic*, 29 March 1975, p. 23.

Martin, Jay. *Nathanael West: The Art of His Life*. New York: Farrar, Straus & Giroux, 1970.

Rosen, R. D. "Literate Wit." *New Republic*, 4 November 1981, pp. 37–38.

Sheed, Wilfred. "No Need for Names." *New York Review of Books*, 5 November 1981, pp. 35–37.

Theroux, Paul. "Marxist." *New Statesman*, 9 April 1976, p. 476.

Ward, J. A. "The Hollywood Metaphor: The Marx Brothers, S. J. Perelman, and Nathanael West." *Southern Review* 12 (1976): 659–72.

Yates, Norris W. "The Sane Psychoses of S. J. Perelman." In *The American Humorist: Conscience of the Twentieth Century*. Ames: Iowa State University Press, 1964, pp. 331–50.

Zinsser, William. "The Perelman of Great Price is 65." *New York Times Magazine*, 26 January 1969, pp. 25–26, 72–74, 76.

JULIA PETERKIN

Cheney, Brainard. "Can Julia Peterkin's 'Genius' Be Revived for Today's Black Myth-Making?" *Sewanee Review* 80 (1972): 173–79.

Landless, Thomas. *Julia Peterkin*. Boston: Twayne, 1976.

Shealy Ann. "Julia Peterkin, A Souvenir." In *The Passionate Mind: Four Studies*. Philadelphia: Dorrance, 1977.

ANN PETRY

Bontemps, Arna. "The Line." *Saturday Review*, 22 August 1953, p. 11.

Downing, Francis. Review of *Country Place*. *Commonweal*, 2 January 1948, pp. 306–7.

O'Brien, John, ed. *Interviews with Black Writers*. New York: Liveright, 1973.

Purdy, Theodore M. "The Ghetto That Is Harlem." *Saturday Review*, 2 March 1946, p. 30.

Shinn, Thelma J. "Women in the Novels of Ann Petry." *Critique* 16, No. 1 (1974): 110–20.

Smith, Bradford. "Glandular Imbalance." *Saturday Review*, 18 October 1947, pp. 17, 21.

Trilling, Diana. "Class and Color." *Nation*, 9 March 1946, pp. 290–91.

MARGE PIERCY

Atwood, Margaret. Review of *Circles on the Water*, *New York Times Book Review*, 8 Aug. 1982, pp. 10–11, 22.

Piercy, Marge. "Mirror Images." In *Women's Culture: The Women's Renaissance of the Seventies*, ed. Gayle Kimball. Metuchen, NJ: Scarecrow Press, 1981, pp. 187–94.

Rosenbaum, Jean. "You Are Your Own Magician: A Vision of Integrity in the Poetry of Marge Piercy." *Modern Poetry Studies* 8 (1977): 193–205.

SYLVIA PLATH

Aird, Eileen M. *Sylvia Plath*. Edinburgh: Oliver & Boyd, 1973.

Alexander, Paul, ed. *Ariel Ascending: Writings about Sylvia Plath*. New York: Harper & Row, 1985.

Barnard, Caroline King. *Sylvia Plath*. Boston: Twayne, 1978.

Broe, Mary Lynn. *Protean Poetic: The Poetry of Sylvia Plath*. Columbia: University of Missouri Press, 1980.

Bundtzen, Lynda K. *Plath's Incarnations: Woman and the Creative Process*. Ann Arbor: University of Michigan Press, 1983.

Butscher, Edward. *Sylvia Plath, Method and Madness*. New York: Seabury Press, 1976.

Holbrook, David. *Sylvia Plath: Poetry and Existence*. London: Athlone Press, 1976.

Kroll, Judith. *Chapters in a Mythology: The Poetry of Sylvia Plath*. New York: Harper & Row, 1976.

Lane, Gary, ed. *Sylvia Plath: New Views on the Poetry*. Baltimore: Johns Hopkins University Press, 1979.

———, and Maria Stevens. *Sylvia Plath: A Bibliography*. Metuchen, NJ: Scarecrow Press, 1978.

Melander, Ingrid. *The Poetry of Sylvia Plath: A Study in Themes*. Stockholm: Almqvist & Wicksell, 1972.

Northouse, Cameron, and Thomas P. Walsh. *Sylvia Plath and Anne Sexton: A Reference Guide*. Boston: G. K. Hall, 1974.

Rosenblatt, Jon. *Sylvia Plath: The Poetry of Initiation*. Chapel Hill: University of North Carolina Press, 1979.

Steiner, Nancy Hunter. *A Closer Look at Ariel: A Memory of Sylvia Plath*. New York: Harper's Bazaar Press, 1973.

Uroff, Margaret Dickie. *Sylvia Plath and Ted Hughes*. Urbana: University of Ilinois Press, 1979.

KATHERINE ANNE PORTER

Curley, Daniel. "Treasure in 'The Grave.'" *Modern Fiction Studies* 9 (1963–64): 377–84.

Moss, Howard. "No Safe Harbor." *New Yorker*, 28 April 1962, pp. 165–73.

Schwartz, Edward Greenfield. "The Fictions of Memory." *Southwest Review* 55 (1960): 204–15.

Solotaroff, Theodore. "*Ship of Fools* and the Critics." *Commentary* 4 (October 1962): 277–86.

Warren, Robert Penn. "Uncorrupted Consciousness: The Stories of Katherine Anne Porter." *Yale Review* 55 (1966): 280–90.

Wiesenfarth, Joseph. "Internal Opposition in Porter's 'Granny Weatherall.'" *Critique* 11, No. 2 (1969): 47–55.

CHAIM POTOK

Barnes, Julian. "Zion Tamers." *New Statesman*, 9 April 1976, p. 478.

Kaplan, Johanna. "Two Ways of Life." *New York Times Book Review*, 11 October 1981, pp. 14–15.

Nissenson, Hugh. Review of *The Promise. New York Times Book Review*, 14 September 1969, pp. 5, 21.

———. "The Spark and the Shell." *New York Times Book Review*, 7 May 1967, pp. 4–5, 34.

Reynolds, Stanley. "Quipped the Raven." *New Statesman*, 27 February 1970, p. 300.

Riemer, Jack. "Emerging Histories, Promising Pasts: *Wanderings*: Chaim Potok's History of the Jews." *America*, 17 February 1969, pp. 116–17.

EZRA POUND

Bagicalupo, Massimo. *The Forméd Trace: The Later Poetry of Ezra Pound*. New York: Columbia University Press, 1980.

Bell, Ian F. A., ed. *Ezra Pound: Tactics for Reading*. London: Vision, 1982.

Brooke-Rose, Christine. *A ZBC of Ezra Pound*. Berkeley: University of California Press, 1971.

Davie, Donald. *Ezra Pound: Poet as Sculptor*. New York: Oxford University Press, 1964.

Davis, Earle. *Vision Fugitive: Ezra Pound and Economics*. Lawrence: University Press of Kansas, 1968.

Davis, Kay. *Fugue and Fresco: Structures in Pound's* Cantos. Orono, ME: National Poetry Foundation, 1984.

Emery, Clark M. *Ideas into Actions: A Study of Pound's* Cantos. Coral Gables: University of Miami Press, 1959.

Flory, Wendy Stallard. *Ezra Pound and* The Cantos: *A Record of Struggle*. New Haven: Yale University Press, 1980.

Ginsberg, Allen. "Encounters with Ezra Pound: Journal Notes" (1967). In *Composed on the Tongue*. Bolinas, CA: Grey Fox Press, 1980, pp. 1–17.

Kazin, Alfred. "The Fascination and Terror of Ezra Pound." *New York Review of Books*, 13 March 1986, pp. 16–24.

Kenner, Hugh. *The Poetry of Ezra Pound*. New York: New Directions, 1951.

Makin, Peter. *Provence and Pound*. Berkeley: University of California Press, 1978.

Nassar, Eugene Paul. The Cantos *of Ezra Pound: The Lyric Mode*. Baltimore: Johns Hopkins University Press, 1975.

Nicholls, Peter. *Ezra Pound: Politics, Economics and Writing*. London: Macmillan, 1984.

Read, Forrest. *'76: One World and* The Cantos *of Ezra Pound*. Chapel Hill: University of North Carolina Press, 1981.

Schneidau, Herbert N. *Ezra Pound: The Image and the Real*. Baton Rouge: Louisiana State University Press, 1969.

Stock, Noel. *The Life of Ezra Pound*. Expanded edition. San Francisco: North Point Press, 1982.

Surette, Leon. *A Light from Eleusis: A Study of Ezra Pound's* Cantos. Oxford: Clarendon Press, 1979.

Wilhelm, James J. *Dante and Pound: The Epic of Judgement*. Orono: University of Maine Press, 1974.

Woodward, Anthony. *Ezra Pound and* The Pisan Cantos. London: Routledge & Kegan Paul, 1980.

ACKNOWLEDGMENTS

Peter Ackroyd. "The Living Image," *Spectator*, December 14, 1974, copyright © 1974 by *Spectator*. Reprinted with permission of The Spectator, Ltd.

Timothy Dow Adams. " The Mock-Biography of Edwin Mullhouse," *Biography*, Summer 1972, copyright © 1982 by The Biographical Research Center.

John W. Aldridge. "Wright Morris's Reputation," *The Devil in the Fire*, copyright © 1972 by John W. Aldridge. Reprinted with permission of the author.

Mary Allen. "Henry Miller: Yea-Sayer," *Tennessee Studies in Literature*, copyright © 1978 by The University of Tennessee Press.

Robert Allen. "Nabokov's Ardor," *Commentary*, August 1969, copyright © 1969 by The American Jewish Committee.

A. Alvarez. "Prologue: Sylvia Plath," *The Savage God: A Study of Suicide*, copyright © 1972 by A. Alvarez.

Kingsley Amis. "Russian Salad," *Spectator*, September 27, 1957, copyright © 1957. Reprinted with permission of The Spectator, Ltd.

Charles Angoff. "Introduction" to *The World of George Jean Nathan*, copyright © 1952 by George Jean Nathan.

Alfred Appel, Jr. "Remembering Nabokov," *Vladimir Nabokov*, ed. Peter Quennell, copyright © 1979 by George Weidenfeld & Nicolson, Ltd. By permission of William Morrow & Company and Weidenfeld Publishers, Ltd.

John Ashbery. "Introduction" to *The Collected Poems of Frank O'Hara*, copyright © 1971 by Alfred A. Knopf, Inc. Reprinted with permission of the publisher.

Roger Asselineau. "Eugene O'Neill's Transcendental Phase," *The Transcendental Constant in American Literature*, copyright © 1980 by New York University. Reprinted with permission of New York University.

Brooks Atkinson. "*The Iceman Cometh*," *Broadway Scrapbook*, copyright © 1947 by Brooks Atkinson. *New York Times*, December 29, 1954, copyright © 1954 by The New York Times Company. Reprinted with permission. *New York Times*, September 3, 1963, copyright © 1963 by The New York Times Company. Reprinted with permission.

James Atlas. "Dininishing Returns: The Writings of W. S. Merwin," *American Poetry since 1960: Some Critical Perspectives*, ed. Robert B. Shaw, copyright © 1973 by James Atlas. Reprinted with permission of James Atlas.

Margaret Atwood. "Obstacle Course," *New York Times Book Review*, July 30, 1978, copyright © 1978 by The New York Times Company. Reprinted with permission. "An Unfashionable Sensibility," *Nation*, December 4, 1976, copyright © 1976 by The Nation Associates. Reprinted with permission of *The Nation*.

Louis Auchincloss. "The Novel of Manners Today: Marquand and O'Hara," *Reflections of a Jacobite*, copyright © 1951, 1960, 1961 by Louis Auchincloss. Reprinted by permission of Houghton Mifflin Company and Curtis Brown, Ltd.

Paul Auster. "A Few Words in Praise of George Oppen," *Paideuma*, Vol. 10, No. 1, Spring 1981, copyright © 1981 by the National Poetry Foundation. Reprinted with permission of the National Poetry Foundation, University of Maine, Orono, Maine.

Jonathan Baumbach. "Life-Size," *Partisan Review*, Spring 1975, copyright © 1975 by *Partisan Review*. Reprinted with permission.

John Bayley. "Games with Death and Co.," *New Statesman*, October 2, 1981, copyright © 1981 by Statesman and Nation Publishing Co.

Joe David Bellamy. "The Dark Lady of American Letters," *Atlantic*, February 1972, copyright © 1972 by the Atlantic Monthly Co.

Helen Benedict. "A Talk with Leonard Michaels," *New York Times Book Review*, April 12, 1981, copyright © 1981 by The New York Times Company. Reprinted with permission.

Stephen Vincent Benét. "The World of Robert Nathan," *The Barly Fields*, copyright © 1938 by Alfred A. Knopf, Inc. Reprinted with permission of the publisher.

Peter Berek. "Bills Past Due," *Nation*, April 8, 1968, copyright © 1968 by The Nation Associates. Reprinted with permission of *The Nation*.

Normand Berlin. "The Early Twenties," *Eugene O'Neill*, copyright © 1982 by Normand Berlin. Reprinted with permission of Grove Press, Inc., and Macmillan, London and Basingstoke.

Michael André Bernstein. "Resicence and Rhethoric: The Poetry of George Oppen," *George Oppen: Man and Poet*, copyright © 1981 by the National Poetry Foundation. Reprinted with permission of the National Poetry Foundation, University of Maine, Orono, Maine.

Celia Betsky. "Talk with Marge Piercy," *New York Times Book Review*, February 24, 1980, copyright © 1980 by The New York Times Company. Reprinted with permission.

R. P. Blackmur. "A Morality of Pointlessness," *Nation*, August 22, 1934, copyright © 1934 by The Nation Associates. Reprinted with permission of *The Nation*.

Walter Blair and Hamlin Hill. "Benchley and Perelman," *America's Humor: From Poor Richard to Doonesbury*, copyright © 1968 by Oxford University Press.

Andre Bleikasten. "Writing on the Flesh: Tattoos and Taboos in 'Parker's Back,'" *Southern Literary Journal*, Spring 1982, copyright © 1982 by Department of English, University of North Carolina at Chapel Hill.

William Bloodworth. "Neihardt, Momaday, and the Art of Indian Autobiography," *Where the West Begins*, copyright © 1978 by East Carolina University Publications. Reprinted with permission of *Teaching English in the Two-Year College*.

Sam Bluefarb. "The Head, The Heart, and the Conflict of Generations in Chaim Potok's *The Chosen*," *CLA Journal*, June 1971, copyright © 1971, by The College Language Association. Reprinted with permission.

Louise Bogan. "Unofficial Feminine Laureate," *Selected Criticism*, copyright © 1955 by Louise Bogan.

Robert Bone. "The Contemporary Negro Novel," *The Negro Novel in America*, copyright © 1958, 1965 by Yale University Press.

Paul A. Bové. "The Particularities of Tradition: History and Locale in *The Maximus Poems*," *Destructive Poetics: Heidegger and Modern American Poetry*, copyright © 1975, 1980 by Columbia University Press. Reprinted with permission of Columbia University Press.

William Boyd. "Adolescent Agonies," *Times Literary Supplement*, July 28, 1978, copyright © 1978. Reprinted with permission of Times Literary Supplement, London.

Kay Boyle. "The New Novels," *New Republic*, January 26, 1942, copyright © 1942 by The New Republic, Inc. Reprinted with permission of *The New Republic*.

Jon Bracker. "Introduction" to *Bright Cages*, copyright © 1965 by The Trustees of the University of Pennsylvania.

Robert Bridges. "Marse Tom at Co'te," *Bookman* (New York), August 1913, copyright © 1913.

Cleanth Brooks. "Miss Marianne Moore's Zoo," *Quarterly Review of Literature*, 1948, copyright © 1948 by T. Weiss. "On 'The Grave,'" *Yale Review*, Winter 1966, copyright © 1966.

Van Wyck Brooks. "The Byron of the Sierras," *Sketches in Criticism*, copyright © 1932 by E. P. Dutton & Co. Reprinted with permission of E. P. Dutton & Co. "The South," *The Confident Years: 1885–1915*, copyright © 1952 by Van Wyck Brooks. Reprinted with permission of J. M. Dent & Sons, Ltd.

John Mason Brown. "George Jean Nathan," *Upstage: The American Theatre in Performance*, copyright © 1930 by W. W. Norton & Co., Inc. "The Man Who Came Back," *Saturday Review of Literature*, December 9, 1950, copyright © 1950 by Saturday Review.

Alan Brownjohn. "A Way out of the Mind," *Times Literary Supplement*, February 12, 1982, copyright © 1982. Reprinted with permission of Times Literary Supplement, London.

Jerry Bryant. "Something Ominous Here," *Nation*, July 6, 1974, copyright © 1974 The Nation Associates. Reprinted with permission of *The Nation*.

Jackson R. Bryer. "'Hell Is Other People': *Long Day's Journey into Night*," *The Fifties: Fiction, Poetry, Drama*, copyright © 1970 by Warren French.

David Burnham. *Commonweal*, January 16, 1942, copyright © 1942 by *Commonweal*. Reprinted with permission of *Commonweal*.

Alan Burns and Charles Signet. "Grace Paley," *The Imagination on Trial: British and American Writers Discuss Their Working Methods*, copyright © 1981 by Alan Burns and Charles Signet.

Rebecca R. Butler. "What's So Funny about Flannery O'Connor?", *Flannery O'Connor Bulletin*, Autumn 1980, copyright © *Flannery O'Connor Bulletin*. Reprinted with permission of *Flannery O'Connor Bulletin*.

Don Byrd. "The New Democracy," *Charles Olson's Maximus*, copyright © 1980 by the Board of Trustees of the University of Illinois. Reprinted with permission of the University of Illionis Press.

Hortense Calisher. *New York Times Book Review*, January 9, 1972, copyright © 1972 by The New York Times Company. Reprinted with permission.

J. M. Cameron. "High Spirits," *New York Review of Books*, September 27, 1979, copyright © 1979 by The New York Review of Books.

Henry Seidel Canby. "Scarlet Becomes Crimson," *Seven Years' Harvest*, copyright © 1936 by Henry Seidel Canby.

Nicola Chiaromonte. "Eugene O'Neill," *Sewanee Review*, Summer 1960, copyright © 1960 by the University of the South. Reprinted with permission of the editor of *Sewanee Review*.

Barbara Christian. "The Concept of Class in the Novels of Toni Morrison," *Black Feminist Criticism: Perspectives of Black Woman Writers*, copyright © 1985 Pergamon Press, Inc. Reprinted with permission of Pergamon Press.

Emily Clark. "Julia Peterkin," *Innocence Abroad*, copyright © 1931 by Alfred A. Knopf, Inc.

William M. Clements. "Review of *House Made of Dawn*," *Explicator*, Winter 1983, copyright © 1983 by Helen Dwight Reid Foundation. Reprinted by permission of Heldref Publications.

Harold Clurman. "*Awake and Sing*," "The Winter of Our Discontent," *The Fervent Years*, copyright © 1945 by Harold Clurman. Reprinted with permission of Random House, Inc. "*The Great God Brown*, 1959," *The Naked Image*, copyright © 1959, 1966 by Harold Clurman. Reprinted with permission of Macmillan Publishing Company. "Will They *Awake and Sing* in 1970?," *The Divine Pastime*, copyright © 1970, 1974 by Harold Clurman. Reprinted with permission of Macmillan Publishing Company.

Arthur A. Cohen. *Commonweal*, September 3, 1971, copyright © 1971 by Commonweal Publishing Co., Inc. Reprinted with permission of *Commonweal*.

Sarah Blacker Cohen. "The Jewish Literary Comediennes," *Comic Relief: Humor in Contemporary American Literature*, copyright © 1978 by the Board of Trustees of the University of Illinois. Reprinted with permission of the University of Illinois Press.

Ruby Cohn. "The Wet Sponge of Eugene O'Neill," *Dialogue in American Drama*, copyright © 1971 by Indiana University Press. Reprinted with permission by Indiana University Press.

Robert Coles. "Reconsideration," *New Republic*, December 6, 1975, copyright © 1975 by The New Republic, Inc. Reprinted with permission of *The New Republic*.

Robert Conquest. "Nabokov's *Eugene Onegin*," *Poetry*, June 1965, copyright © 1965.

Victor Contoski. "Marge Piercy: A Vision of the Peaceable Kingdom," *Modern Poetry Studies*, copyright © 1977 by Jerome Mazzaro. Reprinted with permission of *Modern Poetry Studies*.

Alfred Corn. "The Lenore Marshall Prize," *Nation*, October 20, 1984, copyright © 1984 by The Nation Associates. Reprinted with permission of *The Nation*.

Joanne V. Creighton. "Joyce Carol Oates's Craftsmanship in *The Wheel of Love*," *Studies in Short Fiction*, Fall 1978, copyright © 1979 by Newberry College.

Sally Cunneen. "Tillie Olsen: Storyteller of Working America," *Christian Century*, May 21, 1980, copyright © 1980 by The Christian Century Foundation. Reprinted with permission of the publisher.

Elizabeth Dalton. "Violence in the Head," *Commentary*, June 1970, copyright © 1970 by The American Jewish Committee.

Michael Davidson. "Languages of Post-Modernism," *Chicago Review*, Summer 1975, copyright © 1975 by Chicago Review.

Donald Davie. "*Hugh Selwyn Manberley* and *Homage to Sextus Propertius*" and "Romantic Languages," *Ezra Pound*, copyright © 1975 by Donald Davie. Reprinted with permission of the author and publisher.

Arthur P. Davis. "Ann Petry," *From the Dark Tower: Afro-American Writers 1900–1960*, copyright © 1974 by Arthur P. Davis. Reprinted with permission of Howard University Press, Washington, D.C.

Barnabas Davis. "Flannery O'Connor: Christian Belief in Recent Fiction," *Listening*, August 1965, copyright © 1965.

Fielding Dawson. "A Letter from Black Mountain (July 12, 1949)," *Olson*, Fall 1974, copyright © 1974 by University of Connecticut Library.

Anthony DeCurtis. "Self under Siege: The Stories of Leonard Michaels," *Critique*, Volume 21, Number 2 (1979), copyright © 1979 by James Dean Young. Reprinted with permission of Heldref Publications.

Marianne DeKoven. "Mrs. Hegel-Stein's Tears," *Partisan Review*, Vol. 48, No. 2 (1981), copyright © 1981 by *Partisan Review*. Reprinted with permission of the author.

L. S. Dembo. "Charles Olson and the Moral History of Cape Ann," *Criticism*, Spring 1972, copyright © 1972 by Wayne State University Press.

Benjamin DeMott. "A Thinking Man's Kurt Vonnegut," *Atlantic*, July 1980, copyright © 1980 by The Atlantic Monthly Co.

James Dickey. "Kenneth Patchen," *Babel to Byzantium*, copyright © 1958, 1968 by James Dickey.

Bonamy Dobrée. "The Plays of Eugene O'Neill," *Southern Review*, Winter 1973, copyright © 1936–37 by the Louisiana State University.

Scott Donaldson. "Appointment with the Dentist: O'Hara's Naturalistic Novel," *Modern Fiction Studies*, Winter 1968–69, copyright © 1968 by Purdue Research Foundation, West Lafayette, Indiana 47907. Reprinted with permission.

Denis Donoghue. "The Habits of the Past," *Times Literary Supplement*, April 25, 1975, copyright © 1975. Reprinted with permission of Times Literary Supplement, London. *Listener*, October 10, 1968, copyright © 1968 by The British Broadcasting Corporation. "The Old Drama and the New," *The Ordinary Universe*, copyright © 1968 by Denis Donoghue. Reprinted with permission of Macmillan Publishing Company and Faber & Faber.

Edith McEwen Dorian. "While a Little Dog Dances—Robert Nathan: Novelist of Simplicity," *Sewannee Review*, April–June 1933, copyright © 1933. Reprinted with permission of the editor.

Edward Dorn. "Some Questions of Precision," *Poetry*, June 1964, copyright © 1964 by Poetry.

Louise Doyle. "The Myth of Eugene O'Neill," *Renascence*, Winter 1964, copyright © 1964 by Catholic Renascence Society. Reprinted with permission of Marquette University Press.

Robert Drake. "'The Bleeding Stinking Mad Shadow of Jesus' in the Fiction of Flannery O'Connor," *Comparative Literature Studies*, 1966, copyright © 1966. Reprinted by permission of the University of Illinois Press.

Andre Dubus. "Paths of Redemption," *Harper's*, April 1977, copyright © 1977 by *Harper's Magazine*. All rights reserved; reprinted by special permission.

Erika Duncan. "Coming of Age in the Thirties: A Portrait of Tillie Olsen," *Book Forum*, 1982, copyright © 1982 by The Hudson River Press. Reprinted by permission of The Hudson River Press.

Robert Duncan. "Notes on Poetics Regarding Olson's *Maximus*," *Black Mountain Review*, Spring 1956, copyright © 1956 by The Trustees of Black Mountain College.

F. W. Dupee. "Nabokov: The Prose and Poetry of It All," *New York Review of Books*, December 12, 1963, copyright © 1963 by NYREV, Inc.

Frank Durham. "Introduction: The Stories," *Collected Short Stories*, copyright © 1970 by University of South Carolina Press. Reprinted with permission of the publisher.

Lawrence Durrell. "Introduction" to *The Henry Miller Reader*, copyright © 1959 by New Directions Publishing Corporation. Reprinted by permission of the publisher.

Max Eastman. "My Friendship with Edna Millay," *Great Companions*, copyright © 1942, 1959 by Max Eastman.

Frederick Eckman. "The Comic Apocalypse of Kenneth Patchen," *Poetry*, September 1958, copyright © 1958 by Frederick Eckman. Reprinted with permission of the author.

Leon Edel. "Eugene O'Neill: The Face and the Mask," *University of Toronto Quarterly*, October 1937, copyright © 1937 by The University of Toronto Press. "Life without Father," *Saturday Review*, May 7, 1966, copyright © 1966 by Saturday Review.

Thomas H. Eliot. "Robin Hood in Boston," *New Republic*, March 12, 1956, copyright © 1956 by The New Republic, Inc. Reprinted with permission of *The New Republic*.

T. S. Eliot. "Ezra Pound," *Poetry*, September 1946, copyright © 1946 by Poetry. "Introduction" to *Selected Poems*, copyright © 1935 by Marianne Moore, renewed 1963 by Marianne Moore and T. S. Eliot. Reprinted with permission of Macmillan Publishing Company and Faber & Faber, London.

Edwin A. Engel. "Conclusion," *The Haunted Heroes of Eugene O'Neill*, copyright © 1953 by The President and Fellows of Harvard College; copyright © 1981 by Edwin A. Engel. Reprinted with permission of Harvard University Press.

Leslie Epstein. "The Unhappiness of Arthur Miller," *TriQuarterly*, Spring 1965, copyright © 1965 by Northwestern University Press. Reprinted with permission of the author and *TriQuarterly*, a publication of Northwestern University.

John Espey. "Physique de l'Amour," *Ezra Pound's* Mauberley: A *Study in Composition*, copyright © 1955 by John Espey. Reprinted with permission of the University of California Press.

Clifton Fadiman. "Kit Morley and His Philadelphians," *New Yorker*, October 28, 1939, copyright © 1939, 1967 by The New Yorker Magazine, Inc.

James T. Farrell. "The Faith of Lewis Mumford," *The League of Frightened Philistines*, copyright © 1945 by The Vanguard Press.

Herbert Feis. "Speaking of Books: Robert Nathan, Storyteller," *New York Times Book Review*, December 19, 1965, copyright © 1965 by The New York Times Company. Reprinted with permission.

Stephen Fender. "Precision and Pseudo-Precision in *The Crucible*," *Journal of American Studies*, 1967, copyright © 1967 by Cambridge University Press.

Leslie A. Fiedler. "The Beginning of the Thirties," *Waiting for the End*, copyright © 1964 by Leslie A. Fiedler. Reprinted with permission of Stein & Day Publishers.

John Finch. "Dancer and Clerk," *Massachusetts Review*, Winter 1971, copyright © 1971 by The Massachusetts Review, Inc. Reprinted with permission.

Robert H. Fossum. "Only Control: The Novels of Joyce Carol Oates," *Studies in the Novel*, Summer 1975, copyright © 1975 by North Texas State University. Reprinted with permission.

Steven Foster. "A Critical Appraisal of Henry Miller's *Tropic of Cancer*," *Twentieth Century Literature*, January 1964, copyright © 1964. Reprinted with permission.

Waldo Frank. "Dusk and Dawn," *In the American Jungle*, copyright © 1937 by Waldo Frank.

Haskel Frankel, "The Bluest Eye," *New York Times Book Review*, November 1, 1970, copyright © 1970 by The New York Times Company. Reprinted with permission.

Horst French. "Conclusion," *Eugene O'Neill*, copyright © 1971 by Frederick Ungar Publishing Co.

Philip French et al. "Perelman's Revenge; or, The Gift of Providence, Rhode Island," *Listener*, November 15, 1979, copyright © 1979 by The British Broadcasting Corporation.

Joanne S. Frye. "I Stand Here Ironing: Motherhood as Experience and Metaphor," *Studies in Short Fiction*, Summer 1981, copyright © 1981 by Newberry College. Reprinted with permission.

John Gardner. "The Strange Real World," *New York Times Book Review*, July 20, 1980, copyright © 1980 by The New York Times Company. Reprinted with permission.

George Garrett. "Morris the Magician: A Look at *In Orbit*," *Hollins Critic*, June 1967, copyright © 1967 by Hollins College.

John Gassner. "O'Neill in Our Time," *The Theatre in Our Time*, copyright © 1954 by John Gassner. Used by permission of Crown Publishers, Inc.

Blanche Housman Gelfant. "'What of the Back Yard, and the Alley?,'" *The American City Novel*, copyright © 1954 by University of Oklahoma Press.

Elliot L. Gilbert. "Reviews," *Kenyon Review*, Summer 1969, copyright © 1969 by Kenyon College.

Brendan Gill. "Introduction" to *The Portable Dorothy Parker*, copyright © 1973 by Brendall Gill.

Robert Giroux. "Merton the Writer," *Merton By Those Who Knew Him Best*, copyright © 1984 by Paul Wilkes.

Joan Givner. "Katherine Anne Porter, Journalist," *Southwest Review*, Autumn 1979, copyright © 1979 by Southern Methodist University Press. Reprinted with permission of the author and of *Southwest Review*.

Ivan Gold. "On Having Grace Paley Once More among Us," *Commonweal*, October 25, 1968, copyright © 1968 by Commonweal Publishing Co., Inc. Reprinted with permission of *Commonweal*.

F. C. Golffing. "Question of Strategy," *Poetry*, September 1947, copyright © Francis Golffing. Reprinted with permission of the author.

Mary Kathryn Grant. "The Tragic Vision," *The Tragic Vision of Joyce Carol Oates*, copyright © 1974, 1978 by Duke University Press. Reprinted with permission of Duke University Press.

Benny Green. "Indigestible," *Spectator*, May 1978, copyright © 1978. Reprinted with permission of The Spectator, Ltd.

Theodore L. Grose. "Thomas Nelson Page: Creator of a Virginia Classic," *Georgia Review*, Fall 1966, copyright © 1966 by The University of Georgia. Reprinted with permission of the author.

Thom Gunn. "Outside Faction," *Yale Review*, Summer 1961, copyright © 1961 by Yale Review. Reprinted with permission of the publisher.

Ian Hamilton. "Subject: Sylvia Plath," *London Magazine*, July 1963, copyright © 1963 by *London Magazine*. Reprinted by permission of *London Magazine*.

Elizabeth Hardwick. *Partisan Review*, June 1948, copyright © 1948 by *Partisan Review*. Reprinted with permission.

Barbara Hardy. "The Poetry of Sylvia Plath," *The Advantage of Lyric*, copyright © 1977 by Barbara Hardy. Reprinted with permission of the Athlone Press.

Joseph H. Harkley. "Foreshadowing in 'The Monkey's Paw,'" *Studies in Short Fiction*, Fall 1969, copyright © 1969 by Newberry College. Reprinted with permission.

William Harmon. "Pound's Poetics of Time and Timelessness," *Time in Ezra Pound's Work*, copyright © 1977 by The University of North Carolina Press. Reprinted with permission.

Louis Hasley. "The Golden Trashery of Ogden Nashery," *Arizona Quarterly*, Autumn 1971, copyright © 1971. Used by permission of the publishers and the author.

Peter L. Hays. "The Danger of Henry Miller," *Arizona Quarterly*, Autumn 1971, copyright © 1971. Used by permission of the publishers and author.

John L. Hess. "A Mumford Chronicle," *Hudson Review*, copyright © 1980 by The Hudson Review, Inc. Reprinted with permission.

C. David Heymann. *Ezra Pound: The Last Rower*, copyright © 1976 by C. David Heymann.

Granville Hicks. "All about Vladimir," *Saturday Review*, January 7, 1967, copyright © 1967 by The Southern Review. "Wright Morris as Critic," *Saturday Review*, October 25, 1958, copyright © 1958 by Saturday Review.

John Hollander. *Yale Review*, September 1960, copyright © 1960 by Yale University Press.

Richard Howard. "A Poetry of Darkness," *Nation*, December 14, 1970, copyright © 1970 by The Nation Associates. Reprinted with permission of *The Nation*. "W. S. Merwin: 'We Survived the Selves That We Remembered,'" *Alone with America*, copyright © 1969 by Richard Howard.

Irving Howe. "Vectors," *New York Review of Books*, November 13, 1975, copyright © 1975.

Lewis Hyde. "Ezra Pound and the Fate of Vegetable Money," *The Gift: Imagination and the Erotic Life of Property*, copyright © 1983 by W. Lewis Hyde.

Stanley Edgar Hyman. "Moviegoing and Other Intimacies," *New Leader*, April 30, 1962, copyright © the American Labor Conference on International Affairs, Inc. Reprinted with permission of *The New Leader*.

John Irving. "Morrison's Black Fable," *New York Times Book Review*,

March 29, 1981, copyright © 1981 by The New York Times Company. Reprinted with permission.

Erich Isaac. "Among the Nations," *Commentary*, April 1979, copyright © 1979 by The American Jewish Committee.

Madison Jones. "A Good Man's Predicament," *Southern Review*, October 1984, copyright © 1984 by Louisiana State University. Reprinted with permission of Madison Jones, who is Writer-in-Residence at Auburn University.

David Kalstone. "James Merrill: Transparent Things," *Five Temperaments*, copyright © 1977 by David Kalstone. Reprinted with permission.

Joseph Kanon. "Satire and Sensibility," *Saturday Review*, September 30, 1972, copyright © 1972 by Saturday Review.

Brina Kaplan. "A Fierce Conflict of Colors," *Nation*, May 2, 1981, copyright © 1981 by The Nation Associates. Reprinted with permission of *The Nation*.

Simon Karlinsky. "Illusion, Reality, and Parody in Nabokov's Plays," *Wisconsin Studies in Contemporary Literature*, Spring 1967, copyright © 1967 by The Regents of the University of Wisconsin. Reprinted with permission of the publisher.

Alfred Kazin. "The Great American Bore," *Contemporaries*, copyright © 1958, 1962 by Alfred Knopf, Inc. "Professional Observors: Cozzens to Updike," "Cassandras," *Bright Book of Life*, copyright © 1971, 1973 by Alfred Kazin. "The Pilgrimage of Walker Percy," *Harper's*, June 1971, copyright © 1971 by *Harper's Magazine*. All rights reserved. Reprinted by special permission. *Triquarterly*, Winter 1970, copyright © 1970 by Northwestern University Press.

Don L. Keith. "Walker Percy Talks of Many Things," *Delta Review*, May–June 1966, copyright © 1966.

John V. Kelleher. "Edwin O'Connor and the Irish-American Process," *Atlantic*, July 1968, copyright © 1968 by The Atlantic Monthly Co.

Hugh Kenner. "Disliking It," *A Homemade World*, copyright © 1975 by Hugh Kenner. Reprinted with permission of Random House, Inc. "The Muse in Tatters," *The Pound Era*, copyright © 1971 by Hugh Kenner. Reprinted with permission of the University of California Press. *New York Times Review*, October 19, 1975, copyright © 1975 by The New York Times Company. Reprinted with permission. "Supreme in Her Abnormality," *Poetry*, September 1954, copyright © 1954 by Modern Poetry Association.

Frank Kermode. "Aesthetic Bliss," *Encounter*, June 1960, copyright © 1960 by Encounter Ltd.

Baine Kerr. "The Novel as a Sacred Text: N. Scott Momaday's Myth-Making Ethic," *Southwest Review*, Spring 1978, copyright © 1978 by Southern Methodist University Press.

Vladislar Khodasevich. "On Sirin," *Triquarterly*, Winter 1970, copyright © 1970 by Northwestern University Press.

Robin King. "Potted Miller," *New Statesman*, February 1, 1947, copyright © 1947.

Mary Kinzie. "The Judge Is Rue," *Poetry*, September 1981, copyright © 1981 by Mark Kinzie. Reprinted with permission of the author and the editor of *Poetry*.

Dorothea Krook. "Recollections of Sylvia Plath," *Critical Quarterly*, Winter 1976, copyright © 1976 by Manchester University Press. Reproduced by permission of Manchester University Press.

Joseph Wood Krutch. *Nation*, March 19, 1949, copyright © 1949 by The Nation Associates. Reprinted with permission of *The Nation*. "Mr. Odets Speaks His Mind," *Nation*, April 10, 1935, copyright © 1935 by The Nation Associates. Reprinted with permission of *The Nation*.

David Kubal. "Fiction Chronicle," *Hudson Review*, Autumn 1981, copyright © 1981 by The Hudson Review, Inc. Reprinted with permission.

Elinor Langer. "After the Movement," *New York Times Book Review*, February 24, 1980, copyright © 1980 by The New York Times Company. Reprinted with permission.

Lawrence Langner. "O'Neill and *Strange Interlude*," *The Magic Curtain*, copyright © 1951 by Lawrence Langner.

Lillie Langtry. *The Days I Knew*, copyright © 1925. Reprinted with permission of the author and Doubleday & Company, Inc.

James Laughlin. "Merton the Writer," *Merton By Those Who Knew Him Best*, copyright © 1984 by Paul Wilkes.

David Leavitt. "The Unsung Voices," *Esquire*, February 1986, copyright © 1986 by David Leavitt. Reprinted with permission of *Esquire* and Wylie, Aitken & Stone, Inc.

Thomas LeClair. "'The Language Must Not Sweat': A Conversation with Toni Morrison," *New Republic*, March 21, 1981, copyright © 1981 by The New Republic, Inc. Reprinted with permission of *The New Republic*. *New York Times Book Review*, June 8, 1975, copyright © 1975 by The New York Times Company. Reprinted with permission.

Charles Lee. "Disciple of Dreiser," *New York Times Book Review*, May 4, 1947, copyright © 1947 by The New York Times Company. Reprinted with permission.

David Levin. "Salem Witchcraft in Recent Fiction and Drama," *New England Quarterly*, December 1955, copyright © 1955 by New England Quarterly.

Ludwig Lewisohn. "Eugene O'Neill," *Nation*, November 30, 1921, copyright © 1921 by The Nation Associates. Reprinted with permission of *The Nation*.

Anthony Libby. "O'Hara on the Silver Range," *Contemporary Literature*, Spring 1976, copyright © 1976 by The Board of Regents of the University of Wisconsin. Reprinted with permission of the publisher. "Sylvia Plath, God's Lioness and the Priest of Sycorax," *Mythologies of Nothing: Mystical Death in American Poetry 1940–1970*, copyright © 1984 by the Board of Trustees of the University of Illinois. Reprinted with permission of the University of Illinois Press.

M. M. Liberman. "The Responsibility of the Novelist," *Criticism*, Fall 1966, copyright © 1966 by Wayne State University Press.

Laurence Lieberman. "W. S. Merwin and Anthony Hecht: Risks and Faiths," *Unassigned Frequencies*, copyright © 1977 by Laurence Lieberman. Reprinted with permission of University of Illinois Press. "Words into Skin," *Atlantic*, April 1969, copyright © 1969 by The Atlantic Monthly Co.

Robert Lowell. "The Verses of Thomas Merton," *Commonweal*, June 22, 1945, copyright © 1945 by Commonweal Foundation. Reprinted with permission of *Commonweal*.

Mary McCarthy. "Naming Names: the Arthur Miller Case," *Encounter*, May 1957, copyright © 1957 by Enounter Ltd.

David McCord. "Christopher Morley," *English Journal*, January 1930, copyright © by Wilbur Hatfield.

Lucinda H. Mackethan. "Thomas Nelson Page: The Plantation as Arcady," *Virginia Quarterly Review*, Spring 1978, copyright © 1978 by the *Virginia Quarterly Review*, the University of Virginia. Reprinted with permission.

Patricia MacManus. "Laughter from Tears," *New York Times Book Review*, April 19, 1959, copyright © 1959 by the New York Times Company. Reprinted with permission.

David Madden. "The Violent World of Joyce Carol Oates," *The Poetic Image in 6 Genres*, copyright © 1969 by Southern Illinois University Press.

Norman Mailer. "Henry Miller: Genius and Lust, Narcissism," *American Review*, April 1976, copyright © 1976 by Bantam Books, Inc.

Clarence Major. "Willard Motley: Vague Ghost after the Father," *The Dark and Feeling*, copyright © 1974 by Clarence Major.

Russell Maloney. "Ogden Nash Nosegay," *New York Times Book Review*, October 14, 1945, copyright © 1945 by The New York Times Company. Reprinted with permission.

Michael Mannheim. "*Desire under the Elms*," *Eugene O'Neill's Language of Kinship*, copyright © 1982 by Michael Mannheim.

H. L. Mencken. "George Jean Nathan," *Prejudices: First Series*, copyright © 1919 by Alfred A. Knopf, Inc. Reprinted with permission of the publisher.

Michael J. Mendelsohn. "the Dramatist in Hollywood," *Clifford Odets: Humane Dramatist*, copyright © 1969 by Michael J. Mendelsohn.

Vivian Mercier. "A Talking Poet," *Commonweal*, February 10, 1961, copyright © 1961 by Commonweal Publishing Co., Inc. Reprinted with permission of *Commonweal*.

Daphne Merkin. "Why Potok Is Popular," *Commentary*, February 1976, copyright © 1976 by The American Jewish Committee.

James Merrill. "Condemned to Write about Real Things," *New York Times Book Review*, February 12, 1982, copyright © 1982 by The New York Times Company. Reprinted with permission.

Julia Randall. "Genius of the Shore: The Poetry of Howard Nemerov," *Hollins Critic*, June 1969, copyright © 1969 by Hollins College.

Gerard Reedy. "Gestures of Solidarity," *Commonweal*, August 29, 1980, copyright © 1980 by Commonweal Publishing Co. Reprinted with permission of *Commonweal*.

Kenneth Rexroth. "The Neglected Henry Miller," *Nation*, November 5, 1955, copyright © 1955 by the Nation Associates. Reprinted with permission of *The Nation*.

M. L. Rosenthal. "Pound at His Best: Canto 47 as a Model of Poetic Thought," *Paideuma*, 6:3 (Winter 1977), copyright © 1982 by the National Poetry Foundation. Reprinted with permission of the National Poetry Foundation, University of Maine, Orono, Maine. "Olson/His Poetry," *Massachusetts Review*, Winter 1973, copyright © 1971 The Massachusetts Review, Inc. Reprinted with permission.

Richard Rovere. "Arthur Miller's Conscience," *The New Republic*, June 17, 1957, copyright © 1957 by The New Republic, Inc. Reprinted with permission of *The New Republic*.

Peter Sacks. "The Divine Translation: Elegiac Aspects of *The Changing Light at Sandover*," *James Merrill: Essays in Criticism*, copyright © 1983 by Cornell University Press. Reprinted with permission of Cornell University Press.

Arthur Schlesinger Jr. "Introduction" to *The Best and the Last of Edwin O'Connor*, copyright © 1951, 1966 by Edwin O'Connor, copyright © 1969, 1970 by Little Brown & Co.

Robert Scholes. *New York Times Book Review*, Aprill 11, 1971, copyright © 1971 by The New York Times Company. Reprinted with permission.

James Schuyler. "Frank O'Hara: Poet among Painters," *ARTnews*, May 1974, copyright © 1974 by ARTnews Associates. Reprinted with permission of the publisher.

Delmore Schwartz. "Ezra Pound and History," *New Republic*, February 8, 1960, copyright © 1960 by The New Republic, Inc. Reprinted with permission of *The New Republic*.

Winfield Townley Scott. "Millay Collected," *Poetry*, March 1944, copyright © 1944 by W. S. Monroe and E. S. Fetcher, Executors. "Ring around a Hero," *Saturday Review*, October 6, 1956, copyright © 1956 by Saturday Review.

Anne Sexton. "The Barfly Ought to Sing," *TriQuarterly*, Fall 1966, copyright © 1966 by Northwestern University Press. Reprinted with permission of the Sterling Lord Agency, Inc.

Wilfred Sheed. "Ravening Particles of Anxiety," *Critic*, October–November 1966, copyright © 1966 by The Thomas More Association.

Alix Kates Shulman. "The Children's Hour," *Voice Literary Supplement*, June 1985, copyright © 1985 by the News Group Publications, Inc. Reprinted with permission of the author and the *Village Voice* © 1986.

Elizabeth Sigmund. "Sylvia, 1962: A Memoir," *New Review*, May 1976, copyright © 1976 by TNR Publications, Inc.

Upton Sinclair. "The Springs of Pessimism," *Money Writes!*, copyright © 1927 by Upton Sinclair.

Raymond Smith. "Nemerov and Nature: 'The Stillness in Moving Things,'" *Southern Review*, January 1974, copyright © 1974 by The Southern Review.

William James Smith. *Commonweal*, September 20, 1968, copyright © 1968 by Commonweal Publishing Co. Reprinted with permission of *Commonweal*.

Susan Sontag. "Going to Theater, etc.," *Against Interpretation*, 1966, copyright © 1966 by Susan Sontag.

Gilbert Sorrentino. "Black Mountaineering," *Poetry*, May 1970, copyright © 1970 by *Poetry*. Reprinted with permission of the William Morris Agency, Inc., on behalf of the author.

Stephen Spender. "Warnings from the Grave," *New Republic*, June 18, 1966, copyright © 1966 by The New Republic, Inc. Reprinted with permission of *The New Republic*.

Marshall Sprague. "Anglos and Indians," *New York Times Book Review*, June 9, 1968, copyright © 1968 by The New York Times Company. Reprinted with permission.

Roger Starr. "Mumford's Utopia," *Commentary*, June 1976, copyright © 1976 by *Commentary*.

David Stern. "Two Worlds," *Commentary*, October 1972, copyright © 1972 by The American Jewish Committee.

George Stevens. "Ogden Nash: A Memoir," *Saturday Review*, June 19, 1971, copyright © 1971 by Saturday Review.

David L. Stevenson. "Daughter's Reprieve," *New York Times Book Review*, July 17, 1966, copyright © 1966 by The New York Times Company. Reprinted with permission.

Catherine Stimpson. "Three Women Work It Out," *Nation*, November 30, 1974, copyright © 1974 by The Nation Associates. Reprinted with permission of *The Nation*.

Jean Strouse. "Toni Morrison's Black Magic," *Newsweek*, March 30, 1981, copyright © 1981.

Lynn Suckenick. "The Diaries of Anaïs Nin," *Shenandoah*, Spring 1976, copyright © 1976 by Washington and Lee University. Reprinted with permission from the editor of *Shenandoah: The Washington and Lee Review*.

Richard Suez. "James Merrill's Oedipal Fire," *Parnassus: Poetry in Review*, Fall–Winter 1974, copyright © 1974 by *Parnassus: Poetry in Review*. Reprinted with permission of *Parnassus: Poetry in Review* (Poetry in Review Foundation).

Walter Sullivan. "Flannery O'Connor, Sin, and Grace: *Everything That Rises Must Converge*," *Hollins Critic*, September 1965, copyright © 1965 by Hollins College.

Allan Tate. "Ezra Pound," *Essays of Four Decades*, copyright © 1968 by Allan Tate. Reprinted with permission of The Ohio University Press, Athens.

Robert Taubman. "Allegra's Daughter," *New Statesman*, January 20, 1967, copyright © 1967 by Statesman and Nation Publishing Co.

Mark Taylor. *Commonweal*, October 29, 1971, copyright © 1971 by Commonweal Publishing Co., Inc. Reprinted with permission of *Commonweal*.

Paul Theroux. "Henry Miller 1891–1980," *Sunrise with Seamonsters*, copyright © 1985 by Cape Cod Scriveners Company. Reprinted with permission of Houghton Mifflin Company. "Introduction" to *The Last Laugh*, copyright © 1981 by the Cape Cod Scrivners Company. "No Buff for the Briefalo," *New York Times Book Review*, October 2, 1977, copyright © 1977 by the New York Times Company. Reprinted with permission. "Miseries and Splendours of the Short Story," *Encounter*, September 1972, copyright © 1962 by Encounter Ltd.

Timo Tiusanen. "Conclusion: O'Neill's Scenic Images," *O'Neill's Scenic Images*, copyright © 1968 by Princeton University Press.

Richard Todd. *Atlantic*, September 1973, copyright © 1973 by The Atlantic Monthly Co. "Lend Us into Temptation, Deliver Us Evil," *Atlantic*, March 1977, copyright © 1977 by The Atlantic Monthly Co.

Charles Tomlinson. "Objectivists: Zukofsky and Oppen, a Memoir," *Paideuma*, Winter 1973, copyright © 1978 by the National Poetry Foundation. Reprinted with permission of the National Poetry Foundation, University of Maine, Orono, Maine. "Abundance, Not Too Much: The Poetry of Marianne Moore," *Sewanee Review*, Autumn 1957, copyright © 1957 (renewed 1985) by the University of the South. Reprinted with permission of the editor of the *Sewanee Review*.

Robert Towers. "Men Talking about Women," *New York Times Book Review*, April 12, 1981, copyright © 1981 by The New York Times Company. Reprinted with permission.

Alan Trachtenberg. "The Craft of Vision," *Critique*, Volume 4, Number 3 (Winter 1961–62), copyright © 1962 by *Critique*. Reprinted by permission of Heldref Publications.

Lionel Trilling. "Introduction" to *Selected Short Stories of John O'Hara*, copyright © 1956 by Random House, Inc. *New York Evening Post*, November 3, 1928, copyright © 1928 by The New York Evening Post.

Louis Untermeyer. "Inventory of Nash: 1938," *Saturday Review*, June 4, 1938, copyright © 1938 by Saturday Review.

John Updike. "Notes and Comments," *New Yorker*, July 18, 1977, copyright © 1977 by The New Yorker Magazine, Inc. Reprinted with permission.

Miklos Vajda. "Arthur Miller—Moralist as Playwright," *New Hungarian Quarterly*, Summer 1975, copyright © 1975 The New Hungarian Quarterly.

Alan Velve. "Cain and Abel in N. Scott Momaday's *House Made of Dawn*," *Journal of the West*, April 1978, copyright © 1978 by *The Journal of the West*, Inc. Reprinted by permission of the publisher and author.

Helen Vendler. "James Merrill: *Divine Comedies: Mirabell:* Books of Number," *Part of Nature, Part of Us: Modern American Poets,* copyright © 1980 by The President and Fellows of Harvard College. Reprinted with permission of Harvard University Press. "James Merrill's Myth: An Interview," *New York Review of Books,* May 3, 1979, copyright © 1979 by The New York Review of Books. "A Quarter of Poetry," *New York Times Book Review,* April 6, 1975, copyright © 1975 by The New York Times Company. Reprinted with permission. "The Virtue of the Unalterable," *Parnassus: Poetry in Review,* Fall–Winter 1972, copyright © 1972.

Gore Vidal. "John O'Hara," *Homage to Daniel Shays,* copyright © 1964, 1972 by Gore Vidal. *Two Sisters: A Memoir in the Form of a Novel,* copyright © 1970 by Gore Vidal.

Eugene M. Waith. "Eugene O'Neill: An Exercise in Unmasking," *Educational Theatre Journal,* October 1961, copyright © by the American Educational Theatre Association, Inc. Reprinted by permission of Johns Hopkins University Press.

Eudora Welty. "Katherine Anne Porter: The Eye of the Story," *The Eye of the Story,* copyright © 1965, 1978 by Eudora Welty. "The Most of S. J. Perelman: Baby, It's Cold Inside," *The Eye of the Story,* copyright © 1958, 1978 by Eudora Welty.

Paul West. "Arthur Miller and the Human Mice," *Hibbert Journal,* January 1963, copyright © 1963. Reprinted with permission of The Hibbert Trust.

N. Jill Weyant. "Willard Motley's Pivotal Novel: *Let No Man Write My Epitaph,*" *Black American Literature Forum,* Summer 1977, copyright © 1977 Indiana State University. Reprinted with permission.

Edmund White. "The Aesthetics of Bliss," *Saturday Review of the Arts,* January 6, 1973, copyright © 1973 by Saturday Review.

James J. Wilhelm. "The Three Changing Phases of Woman and Gold," *The Later Cantos of Ezra Pound,* copyright © 1977 by James J. Wilhelm.

Carol T. Williams. "Nabokov's Dozen Short Stories: His World in Microcosm," *Studies in Short Fiction,* Summer 1975, copyright © 1974 by Newberry College. Reprinted with permission.

John Williams. "Henry Miller: The Success of Failure," *Virginia Quarterly Review,* Spring 1966, copyright © 1968 by The Virginia Quarterly Review.

William Carlos Williams. "A Counsel of Madness," *Counsel of Madness,* copyright © 1942 by William Carlos Williams. Reprinted with permission of New Directions Publishing Corporation. "Marianne Moore," *Selected Essays of William Carlos Williams,* copyright © 1925, 1954 by William Carlos Williams. "The New Poetical Economy," *Poetry,* June 1934, copyright © 1934 by William Carlos Williams. Reprinted with permission of New Directions Publishing Corporation.

Alan Williamson. "Real and Numinous Selves: A Reading of Sylvia Plath," *Introspection and Contemporary Poetry,* copyright © 1984 by The President and Fellows of Harvard College. Reprinted with permission of Harvard University Press.

Garry Wills. "The Devil and Lolita," *New York Review of Books,* February 21, 1974, copyright © 1974 by NYREV, Inc.

Edmund Wilson. "The Boys in the Back Room," "A Toast and a Tear for Dorothy Parker," "Katherine Anne Porter," *Classics and Commercials,* copyright © 1950 by Edmund Wilson. "Edna St. Vincent Millay," "Twilight of the Expatriates," *Shore of Light,* copyright © 1952 by Edmund Wilson. *New Yorker,* April 1, 1944, copyright © 1944 by The New Yorker Magazine, Inc.

Ruth R. Wisse. "American Jewish Writing, Act II," *Commentary,* June 1976, copyright © by The American Jewish Committee. "Jewish Dreams, *Commentary,* March 1982, copyright © 1982 by The American Jewish Committee.

Tom Wolfe. "The Exploits of El Sid," *New York Times Book Review,* July 19, 1981, copyright © 1981 by The New York Times Company. Reprinted with permission.

Charles L. Woodward. "Review of *House Made of Dawn,*" *Explicator,* Winter 1978, copyright © 1978 by Helen Dwight Reid Foundation. Reprinted by permission of Heldref Publications.

Alexander Woollcott. "Mr. Nathan's Criticism of Dramatic Criticism," *New York Times Book Review,* October 26, 1919, copyright © 1919 by The New York Times Company. Reprinted with permission. "Our Mrs. Parker," *While Rome Burns,* copyright © 1934 by Alexander Woollcott.

Stark Young. "Eugene O'Neill: Notes from a Critics Diary," *Harper's,* June 1957, copyright © 1957 by *Harper's Magazine.* All rights reserved; reprinted by special permission. *New Republic,* November 17, 1937, copyright © 1937 by The New Republic, Inc. Reprinted with permission of The New Republic.

Maurice Zolotow. "Re-enter Mr. Miller," *Marilyn Monroe,* copyright © 1960 by Maurice Zolotow.

Louis Zukofsky. "Ezra Pound," *Prepositions: The Collected Critical Essays of Louis Zukofsky,* copyright © 1981 by the Regents of the University of California. Reprinted with permission of the University of California Press.

Paul Zweig. "Delicate Intentions," *Harper's,* September 1975, copyright © 1975 by *Harper's Magazine.* All rights reserved; reprinted by special permission.